APPLICATION

LETTER OF THE LAW

ON THE WEB

These margin features give specific Uniform Resource Locators (URLs), or Internet addresses, concerning topics discussed in the text. You will find over one hundred such references throughout this text. Two examples are shown here.

ON THE WEB

Toli ndstatecom pila-tions (codes) of statutory laws, goto **http://www.findlaw.com/casecode/state.html.**

ONTH E WEB

Cyberjury has a Web site at which visitors are invitedtoactas jurorsdecidin g realcases . Goto **http://www.cyberjury.com.**

For the Student

This printed textbook is not all you have to use to make learning the law easier. Check out the rest.

The *Business Law Today*, Sixth Edition, Web Site

Explore the text's companion Web site at **http://blt.westbuslaw.com**. You will find the following:

- **Internet exercises for every chapter**—You can perform these exercises (access them through the "Interactive Study Center" on the text's Web site) to become familiar with important legal sources on the Web!
- **Interactive quizzes for every chapter**—Don't forget to try these quizzes to test your knowledge of topics covered in each chapter, especially before an exam!
- **Answers to the "Test Your Knowledge" questions**—Check out these answers (in the "Interactive Study Center" section of the Web site) to learn how the authors have answered the problems!
- **Court case updates.** Find out about recent court decisions in an area that you are studying by going to this section of the text's Web site!

Student CD-ROM

The CD-ROM that came with your new textbook can enhance your learning experience. This CD-ROM includes the following elements:

- **Video clips from the *Drama of the Law* video series.**
- **Handbook on Critical Thinking and Writing.**
- **A Guide to Personal Law.**
- **Handbook of Landmark Cases and Statutes in Business Law.**
- **The full text of each case that was presented in briefed form in the text.**
- **Supreme Court audio clips.**
- **Links to the *Business Law Today* Web site.**

Business Law Today 6TH EDITION

STANDARD EDITION
Text & Summarized Cases
E-Commerce, Legal, Ethical, and International Environment
SIXTH EDITION

Roger LeRoy Miller
Institute for University Studies
Arlington, Texas

Gaylord A. Jentz
Herbert D. Kelleher
Emeritus Professor in Business Law
MSIS Department
University of Texas at Austin

THOMSON
SOUTH-WESTERN
WEST

Australia · Canada · Mexico · Singapore · Spain · United Kingdom · United States

Business Law Today. STANDARD EDITION

Text & Summarized Cases

E-Commerce, Legal, Ethical, and International Environment

SIXTH EDITION

Roger LeRoy Miller
Institute for University Studies
Arlington, Texas

Gaylord A. Jentz
Herbert D. Kelleher Emeritus Professor in Business Law
MSIS Department
University of Texas at Austin

Vice President and Team Director:
Michael P. Roche

Sr. Acquisitions Editor:
Rob Dewey

Sr Developmental Editor:
Jan Lamar

Marketing Manager:
Nicole C. Moore

Production Manager:
Bill Stryker

Manufacturing Coordinator:
Rhonda Utley

Compositor:
Parkwood Composition
New Richmond, WI

Printer:
Quebecor World
Versailles, KY

Design Project Manager:
Michelle Kunkler

Internal Designer:
Bill Stryker

Cover Designer:
Grannan Graphic Design, Cincinnati

Cover Image:
© Getty Images, Andrew Parish

Printed in the United States of America
1 2 3 4 5 04 03 02

For more information contact South-Western, 5191 Natorp Boulevard, Mason, Ohio 45040.
Or you can visit our Internet site at:
http://www.westbuslaw.com

Library of Congress Cataloging-in-Publication Data
Miller, Roger LeRoy.
Business law today: standard edition: text & summarized cases; e-commerce, legal, ethical, and international environment / Roger LeRoy Miller, Gaylord A. Jentz.
—6th ed.
p. cm.
Includes bibliographical references and index.
ISBN 0–324–12097–4
1. Commercial law—United States—Cases. 2. Business law—United States. I. Jentz, Gaylord A. II. Title.
KF888.M5543 2003
346.7307—dc21
99–21224

CIP

Contents in Brief

UNIT SEVEN

UNIT EIGHT

UNIT NINE

APPENDICES

Contents

UNIT ONE

THE LEGAL ENVIRONMENT OF BUSINESS 1

APPENDICES

PREFACE To the Instructor . . .

We have always felt that business law and the legal environment should be an exciting, contemporary, and interesting course. We believe that *Business Law Today,* Sixth Edition, imparts this excitement to your students. We have spent a great deal of effort in giving this book a visual appeal that will encourage students to learn the law. We have also worked hard to make sure that *Business Law Today* continues in the established tradition of being the most up-to-date text on the market. The law presented in the Sixth Edition of *Business Law Today* includes new statutes, regulations, and cases, as well as the most recent developments in cyberlaw.

You will find that coverage of traditional business law has not been sacrificed in the process of creating this text. Additionally, *Business Law Today* explicitly addresses the American Assembly of Collegiate Schools of Business's (AACSB's) broad array of curriculum requirements. As you will see, many of the features and special pedagogical devices in this text focus on the global, political, ethical, social, environmental, technological, and cultural contexts of business law.

Student CD-ROM

Included with every new copy of *Business Law Today,* Sixth Edition, is a CD-ROM entitled *Student CD-ROM to Accompany Business Law Today, Sixth Edition.* This CD-ROM includes the following elements:

- Video clips from the *Drama of the Law* video series.
- *Handbook on Critical Thinking and Writing.*
- *A Guide to Personal Law.*
- *Handbook of Landmark Cases and Statutes in Business Law.*
- The full text of each case that was presented in briefed form in *Business Law Today,* Sixth Edition.
- Supreme Court audio clips.
- Links to the *Business Law Today* Web site at **http://blt.westbuslaw.com**.

Revised Article 9

To ensure that *Business Law Today,* Sixth Edition, offers the most up-to-date coverage possible, we have virtually rewritten the chapter covering secured transactions to base it on the requirements of the revised Article 9 of the Uniform Commercial Code. Because all of the states have now adopted the revised version, we do not make references to the unrevised Article 9 within this text, nor do we include it in the most current version of the Uniform Commercial Code that is presented at the end of this text as Appendix C.

Emphasis on Internet Law

Business Law Today, Sixth Edition, is truly up to date and reflects current law to the fullest extent possible. We have included throughout the text, whenever relevant, sections discussing the most recent developments in the law as it is being applied to Internet transactions and e-commerce. For example, in Chapter 5, which focuses on intellectual property, we point out how traditional laws—and some newly enacted laws—are being applied to online issues relating to *copyrights, trademarks, patents*, and *trade secrets*. Other chapters in the text include sections on *privacy rights* in the online world, *jurisdictional issues* as they arise in cyberspace, *cyber torts* and *cyber crimes, online securities offerings*, and a number of other topics relating to the online legal environment. We have also added an entirely new chapter (Chapter 17) devoted solely to the topic of *electronic contracts*, or e-contracts.

The Internet Connection

In addition to incorporating cyberlaw throughout the basic text of the book, the Sixth Edition offers several other components focusing on technology.

Business Law Today on the Web

When your students visit our Web site at **http://blt.westbuslaw.com**, they will find, at a minimum, the following:

- Interactive quizzes for every chapter in *Business Law Today*, Sixth Edition.
- Internet exercises for each chapter in this text as well as selected Web sources of information relevant to each chapter. (These are included in the Interactive Study Center.)
- Answers to the end-of-chapter "Test Your Knowledge" case problems. (These can be accessed through the Interactive Study Center.).
- Court case updates, which present summaries of new cases from various West legal publications, all linked to this text.
- Links to legal resources available for free on the Web.
- A "Talk to the Authors" feature that allows you and your students to e-mail your questions about *Business Law Today* to the authors.

Online Legal Research Guide

With every new book, your students will receive a free copy of the *Online Legal Research Guide*. This is the most complete brief guide to using the Internet that exists today. Text co-author Roger LeRoy Miller developed and wrote this supplement, which has been updated for the Sixth Edition, especially to accompany *Business Law Today* There is even an appendix on how to evaluate information obtained from the Internet.

Special Technology Online Features and Pedagogy

The following special features and pedagogy in the Sixth Edition of *Business Law Today* are designed to acquaint your students with online trends in business law, as well as with the broad array of legal resources available on the Web.

- *Business Law in the Online World*—Nearly every chapter in the Sixth Edition contains one of these special features. Each feature explores how a court has applied a traditional legal concept (or a newly enacted statute) to a specific real-world dispute relating to an online transaction.
- *Test Your Knowledge—Answer on the Web*—At the end of each chapter, we include one case problem, titled *Test Your Knowledge—Answer on the Web,* for which students can find the answer by going to the text's companion Web site at **http://blt.westbuslaw.com**. This problem-answer set, which is new to this edition, is designed to help your students learn how to answer case problems by acquainting them with model answers to selected problems.
- *On the Web*—These margin features direct students to online articles, statutes, or other legal or information sources concerning a topic being discussed in the text. The features include specific Uniform Resource Locators (URLs), or Internet addresses, as well as navigational instructions when necessary.
- *URLs for Cases*—Whenever possible, we have included URLs that can be used to access the cases presented in the text of *Business Law Today.* When a URL is available, it appears just below the case citation.
- *Online Activities*—To familiarize your students with online legal resources and help them learn to navigate the Internet, we have included at the end of every chapter one or more Internet exercises. The exercises refer students to Internet activities presented on the *Business Law Today* Web site at **http://blt.westbuslaw.com**.
- *Before the Test*—At the end of every chapter, just following the Internet exercises in the *Online Activities* section, students are again directed to the *Business Law Today* Web site to access interactive questions relating to the topics covered in the chapter. There are at least twenty of these questions for each chapter.

Other Special Features and Pedagogy

In addition to the components of *Business Law Today,* Sixth Edition, described above, the text offers a number of other special features and pedagogy.

FEATURES

Virtually all of the chapters in this text have one or more of the following special features, which are designed both to instruct and to pique the interest of the student of business law and legal environment. To emphasize critical thinking, many of these features conclude with a question section titled *For Critical Analysis.* **Suggested answers for these questions are included in the *Answers Manual* that accompanies this text.**

- *Landmark in the Law*—This feature, which appears in most of the chapters in this edition, discusses a landmark case, statute, or other law that has had a significant effect on business law. Each of these features concludes with a section titled *Application to Today's World,* which indicates how the law discussed in the feature affects the legal landscape of today's world.
- *Application*—Almost all of the chapters have an *Application* feature, which presents the student with some practical advice on how to apply the law discussed in the chapter to real-world business problems. Each *Application* ends with a "Checklist" for the future businessperson on how to avoid legal problems.

- *Letter of the Law*—This feature provides students with a glimpse at sometimes humorous, sometimes serious illustrations of how the letter of the law has been phrased, interpreted, or applied. Each feature concludes with a section called *The Bottom Line,* which consists of a statement summarizing the implications of the illustrated topic for businesspersons.
- *Ethical Issues*—In addition to a chapter on ethics, chapter-ending ethical questions, and the *Ethical Considerations* following many of the cases presented in this text, we have included special features called *Ethical Issues.* These features, which are closely integrated with the text, open with a question addressing an ethical dimension of the topic being discussed. Each *Ethical Issue* has been given a number so that it can be easily located for review or discussion.
- *International Perspectives*—These features give students an awareness of the global legal environment by indicating how international laws or the laws of other nations deal with a specific legal concept or topic being discussed in the chapter.

Cases

In each chapter, we present cases that have been selected to illustrate the principles of law discussed in the text. The cases are numbered sequentially for easy referencing in class discussions, homework assignments, and examinations. In choosing the cases to be included in this edition, our goal has been to include the most recent cases from the late 1990s and early 2000s, as well as some of the landmark and classic cases in business law.

For the Sixth Edition of *Business Law Today,* we have given special emphasis to landmark and classic cases by setting these off with a special heading and logo. Additionally, a *Comment* section at the end of each landmark or classic case stresses the importance of the court's decision in the case to the evolution of the law concerning the issue

Other Pedagogical Devices within Each Chapter

- *Learning Objectives* (a series of brief questions at the beginning of each chapter designed to provide a framework for the student as he or she reads through the chapter).
- *Chapter Contents* (an outline of the chapter's first-level and second-level headings).
- *Margin definitions.*
- Margin *On the Web* features directing students to relevant Web sites.
- *Highlighted and numbered examples illustrating legal principles.*
- *Quotations.*
- *Exhibits and forms* (about one hundred).
- *Photographs (with critical-thinking questions).*

Chapter-Ending Pedagogy

- *Key Terms* (with appropriate page references).
- *Chapter Summary* (in graphic format with page references).
- *For Review* (the questions set forth in the chapter-opening *Learning Objectives* section are again presented to aid the student in reviewing the chapter).

- *Questions and Case Problems* (including hypotheticals and case problems; many of the case problems are based on cases from the late 1990s and early 2000s).
- *Test Your Knowledge—Answer on the Web* (each chapter contains one of these case problems, for which the answer has been provided on the text's Web site at **http://blt.westbuslaw.com**).
- *A Question of Ethics and Social Responsibility.*
- *For Critical Analysis.*
- *Online Activities* (including online Internet exercises and chapter-by-chapter interactive quizzes).

Unit-Ending Pedagogy—Cumulative Business Hypotheticals

Each unit in *Business Law Today,* Sixth Edition, concludes with a section titled ***Cumulative Business Hypothetical.*** The section introduces a hypothetical business firm and then asks a series of questions about how the law applies to various actions taken by the firm. To answer the questions, the student must apply the laws discussed throughout the unit. **Suggested answers to the unit-ending cumulative questions are included in the *Answers Manual.***

Unit-Ending Pedagogy—Extended Case Studies

At the end of each unit, is a two-page feature entitled ***Extended Case Study.*** This feature focuses on a specific court case relating to a topic covered in the unit. Each feature opens with an introductory section, which discusses the background and significance of the case being presented. Then we present excerpts from the court's majority opinion and, at times, from a dissenting opinion in the case as well. The feature concludes with a series of questions, under the heading *Questions for Analysis,* that prompt the student to think critically about the legal, ethical, economic, international, or general business implications of the case. **Suggested answers to these questions are included in the *Answers Manual.***

Appendices

To help students learn how to find and analyze case law, we have included a special appendix at the end of Chapter 1. There your students will find information, including an exhibit, on how to read case citations, how to locate cases in case reporters, and what the different components of URLs (Internet addresses) mean. *The appendix to Chapter 1 also presents an annotated sample court case to help your students understand how to read and understand the cases presented within this text.*

Because the majority of students keep their business law text as a reference source, we have included at the end of the book the following full set of appendices (Appendices A, N, O, P, and Q are new to the Sixth Edition):

A. How to Brief Cases and Analyze Case Problems.
B. The Constitution of the United States.
C. Uniform Commercial Code (including the revised Article 9).
D. Uniform Partnership Act.
E. Revised Model Business Corporation Act (Excerpts).
F. Uniform Limited Liability Company Act (Excerpts).
G. Restatement (Second) of Torts (Excerpts).
H. Restatement (Third) of Torts (Excerpts).

I. Sherman Antitrust Act of 1890 (Excerpts).
J. Securities Act of 1933 (Excerpts).
K. Securities Exchange Act of 1934 (Excerpts).
L. Americans with Disabilities Act of 1990 (Excerpts).
M. United Nations Convention on Contracts for the International Sale of Goods (Excerpts).
N. Digital Millennium Copyright Act of 1998 (Excerpts).
O. Uniform Electronic Transactions Act (Excerpts).
P. Uniform Computer Information Transactions Act (Excerpts).
Q. Electronic Signatures in Global and National Commerce Act of 2000 (Excerpts).
R. Spanish Equivalents for Important Legal Terms in English.

A Flexible Teaching/Learning Package

We realize that different people have different teaching philosophies and learning goals. We believe that the Sixth Edition of *Business Law Today* and its extensive supplements offer business law instructors a flexible teaching/learning package. For example, although we have attempted to make the materials flow from chapter to chapter, most of the chapters are self-contained. In other words, you can use the chapters in any order you wish.

Additionally, the extensive number of supplements accompanying *Business Law Today* allows instructors to choose those supplements that will most effectively complement classroom instruction.

Suggestions on how you can adapt the *Business Law Today* teaching/learning package to fit your particular teaching and learning goals are given in the *Instructor's Course Planning Guide*. Furthermore, each chapter of the *Instructor's Manual* contains teaching suggestions, possible discussion questions, and additional information on key statutes or other legal sources that you may wish to use in your classroom. These and numerous other supplementary materials (including printed and multimedia supplements) all contribute to the goal of making *Business Law Today* the most flexible teaching/learning package on the market today.

Supplemental Teaching Materials

This edition of *Business Law Today* is accompanied by an expansive number of teaching and learning supplements. Individually and in conjunction with a number of our colleagues, we have developed supplementary teaching materials that we believe are the best available today. Each component of the supplements package is listed below.

Printed Supplements

- ***Online Legal Research Guide*** (free with every new copy of the text; updated for the Sixth Edition).
- ***Instructor's Course Planning Guide*** (also available on the *Instructor's Resource CD-ROM*, or IRCD).
- ***Instructor's Manual*** (also available on the IRCD).
- ***Study Guide.***
- A comprehensive ***Test Bank*** (also available on the IRCD).

- *Case Printouts,* including printouts of cases referred to in selected features (also available on the IRCD).
- *Answers Manual* (also available on the IRCD).
- *Instructor's Manual for the Drama of the Law* video series (also available on the IRCD).
- *Handbook on Critical Thinking and Writing.*
- *Handbook of Landmark Cases and Statutes in Business Law.*
- *A Guide to Personal Law.*

SOFTWARE, VIDEO, AND MULTIMEDIA SUPPLEMENTS

- **Student CD-ROM**—Allows students to have access to relevant video and audio clips, selected supplements, and other learning enhancements; included with every new copy of the text.
- *Instructor's Resource CD-ROM*—Includes the following supplements: Instructor's Course Planning Guide, Instructor's Manual, Answers Manual, Case-Problem Cases, ExamView, PowerPoint slides, Instructor's Manual for the *Drama of the Law* video series, Lecture Outline System, Test Bank, and Case Printouts.
- **ExamView Testing Software.**
- **Web Tutor** (on WebCT or Blackboard)—Features chat, discussion groups, testing, student progress tracking, and business law course materials.
- **Lecture Outline System** (also available on the IRCD).
- **PowerPoint slides.**
- **Transparency Acetates.**
- **Westlaw®**—to qualified adopters.
- **Video Library**—Including Court TV® and the *Drama of the Law* videos. (For further information on video supplements, go to **http://www.westbuslaw.com**.)
- **InfoTrac® College Edition.**

For Users of the Fifth Edition

We thought that those of you who have been using *Business Law Today* would like to know some of the major changes that have been made for the Sixth Edition. We think that we have improved the book and its supplements package greatly, thanks in part to the many letters, telephone calls, and reviews that we have received.

NEW CD-ROMS

As mentioned earlier, every new copy of the Sixth Edition is accompanied by a Student CD-ROM containing video clips and other resources. Additionally, as already noted, many of the supplements are now available on the *Instructor's Resource CD-ROM*.

EXPANDED COVERAGE OF CYBERLAW

In the last several years, cyberspace has become a normal part of the business environment. For that reason, instead of treating cyberlaw in a separate chapter, we have integrated coverage of Internet law throughout the text. We indicate below, in the subsection describing significantly revised chapters, those chapters that now include substantial coverage of cyberlaw. Additionally, as mentioned earlier, an entirely new chapter titled E-Contracts (Chapter 17) has been added for the Sixth Edition. Finally, most chapters in the book include a *Business Law in the Online World* feature that focuses on a specific court case involving a dispute arising in the online environment.

Incorporation of Revised Article 9 Provisions

As mentioned earlier, the chapter on secured transactions has been updated and, in many sections, completely rewritten to base the coverage of this topic on the revised Article 9 of the Uniform Commercial Code.

New Features and Special Pedagogy

All of the features that have been retained from the Fifth Edition of *Business Law Today* have been updated or modified as necessary. A great number of them have been replaced with newly written features. In addition, we have added the following entirely new elements for the Sixth Edition:

- *Business Law in the Online World.*
- An *Application to Today's World* section concluding each *Landmark in the Law* feature.
- A *Comment* section concluding each landmark and classic case.
- *Test Your Knowledge—Answer on the Web* (in the *Questions and Case Problems* section).

Significantly Revised Chapters

Every chapter of the Sixth Edition has been revised as necessary to incorporate new developments in the law or to streamline the presentations. A number of new trends in business law are also addressed in the cases and special features of the Sixth Edition. Other major changes and additions made for this edition include the following:

- Chapter 1 (The Legal Environment)—The section entitled "The Nature of Law" has been revised and now includes discussions of the historical school and the sociological school.
- Chapter 2 (Constitutional Law)—The section on federalism has been expanded, and the section on the commerce clause now includes a subsection (and a feature) discussing the dormant commerce clause. Cyberlaw issues, including online speech and privacy rights, are now covered in this chapter.
- Chapter 3 (Traditional and Online Dispute Resolution)—Several sections were added to this chapter, including sections covering electronic filing, the courts' use of Web sites, cyber courts, online dispute resolution, and the difficulty parties sometimes face in enforcing court judgments.
- Chapter 4 (Torts and Cyber Torts)—This chapter now includes a discussion of cyber torts, including online defamation and spamming.
- Chapter 5 (Intellectual Property and Internet Law)—Cyberlaw has been integrated into this chapter throughout. New sections cover cyber marks, business process patents and patent databases, copyrights in digital information, MP3/file sharing (and the case against Napster), the No Electronic Theft Act of 1997, the Digital Millennium Copyright Act of 1998, and trade secrets in cyberspace.

- Chapter 6 (Criminal Law and Cyber Crimes)—The section on crimes affecting business has been reorganized and rewritten to streamline the presentation. New to the chapter is a discussion of cyber crimes, including cyber theft, cyber stalking, hacking, cyber terrorism, prosecuting cyber crime, and the Computer Fraud and Abuse Act.
- Chapter 7 (Ethics and Social Responsibility)—The section on duty-based ethics was expanded to include a discussion of the principle of rights. A new section on ethical decision making was added to the chapter, and the section on corporate social responsibility was rewritten to focus on three views on social responsibility—profit maximization, stakeholders, and corporate citizenship.
- Chapter 17 (E-Contracts)—As mentioned earlier, this chapter is entirely new to the text. Sections in the chapter cover online contract formation, linking and framing, e-signatures, partnering agreements, the Uniform Computer Information Transactions Act, and the Uniform Electronic Transactions Act.
- Chapter 21 (Checks, the Banking System, and E-Money)—This chapter now includes sections covering e-money, online banking, and the Uniform Money Services Act.
- Chapter 22 (Secured Transactions)—This chapter was virtually rewritten to base it on the revised version of Article 9 of the Uniform Commercial Code. Existing exhibits were replaced as necessary to reflect concepts and requirements set forth in the revised Article 9.
- Chapter 23 (Creditors' Rights and Bankruptcy)—This chapter now includes the updated dollar amounts of various provisions of the Bankruptcy Code.
- Chapter 29 (Investor Protection and Online Securities Offerings)—This chapter now includes sections covering online securities offerings and disclosures, as well as online securities fraud.
- Chapter 30 (Limited Liability Companies and Partnerships)—The coverage of limited liability companies was revised and expanded for the Sixth Edition.
- Chapter 31 (Special Business Forms and Private Franchises)—The section on cooperatives was revised and expanded to present a more substantial description of this business form.
- Chapter 34 (Labor and Employment Law) and Chapter 35 (Employment Discrimination)—These two chapters covering employment law now include references to the latest developments in the areas of labor and employment law, including an expanded discussion of electronic performance monitoring and a new section covering online sexual harassment.

What Else Is New?

In addition to the changes noted above, you will find a number of other new items or features in *Business Law Today,* Sixth Edition, as listed below.

New Cases and Case Problems Nearly 60 percent of the cases in this text are new to the Sixth Edition, including forty-three cases decided in 2000 or 2001. Additionally, each unit-ending *Extended Case Study* is based on a 2000 or 2001 case. We have also added nearly one hundred new case problems, and virtually every chapter now has at least one problem based on a case decided in the early 2000s.

New Exhibits We have modified exhibits retained from the Fifth Edition whenever necessary to achieve greater clarity or accuracy. In addition, we have added ten new exhibits for the Sixth Edition, including a two-page exhibit summarizing the various forms of intellectual property (in Chapter 5), a sample "click-on" contractual agreement (in Chapter 17), an exhibit illustrating the process of digital encryption (in Chapter 21), new exhibits showing requirements relating to secured transactions under the revised Article 9 of the Uniform Commercial Code (in Chapter 22), and a table showing the extent of electronic monitoring in the workplace (in Chapter 34).

New Supplements

- A greatly enhanced and streamlined Web site at **http://blt.westbuslaw.com**.
- A Student CD-ROM (included with every new copy of the text).
- *Instructor's Resource CD-ROM.*
- Web Tutor (on WebCT or Blackboard).

Acknowledgments

Numerous careful and conscientious users of *Business Law Today* were kind enough to help us revise the book. In addition, the staff at West went out of its way to make sure that this edition came out early and in accurate form. In particular, we wish to thank Rob Dewey for his countless new ideas, many of which have been incorporated into the Sixth Edition. Our production manager and designer, Bill Stryker, made sure that we came out with an error-free, visually attractive edition. We will always be in his debt. We also extend special thanks to Jan Lamar, our long-time developmental editor, for her many useful suggestions and for her efforts in coordinating reviews and ensuring the timely and accurate publication of all supplemental materials. We are particularly indebted to Nicole Moore for her support and excellent marketing advice, and to Peggy Buskey for her help in managing the Web site and working on the CD-ROMs. We are also grateful to Tim Butz for his technological help on the computerized elements of some of the supplements, particularly the *Test Bank*.

We must especially thank William Eric Hollowell, coauthor of the *Instructor's Manual, Study Guide, Test Bank,* and *Online Legal Research Guide* for his excellent research efforts. We also wish to thank Lavina Leed Miller, who provided expert research, editing, and proofing services for this project. The copyediting and proofreading services of Pat Lewis and Suzie Franklin DeFazio, respectively, will not go unnoticed. We also thank Roxie Lee for her proofreading and other assistance, which helped us meet our ambitious publishing schedule, and the proofreading skills of Erin Wait helped to ensure an error-free text. Finally, our appreciation goes to Suzanne Jasin for her many special efforts on the projects.

Acknowledgments for Previous Editions

John J. Balek
Morton College, Illinois

Lorraine K. Bannai
Western Washington University

Marlene E. Barken
Ithaca College, New York

Daryl Barton
Eastern Michigan University

Merlin Bauer
Mid State Technical College, Wisconsin

Donna E. Becker
Frederick Community College, Maryland

Brad Botz
Garden City Community College, Kansas

Teresa Brady
Holy Family College, Philadelphia

Lee B. Burgunder
California Polytechnic University—San Luis Obispo

Dale Clark
Corning Community College, New York

Sandra J. Defebaugh
Eastern Michigan University

Patricia L. DeFrain
Glendale College, California

Julia G. Derrick
Brevard Community College, Florida

Joe D. Dillsaver
Northeastern State University, Oklahoma

Claude W. Dotson
Northwest College, Wyoming

Larry R. Edwards
Tarrant County Junior College, South Campus, Texas

Jacolin Eichelberger
Hillsborough Community College, Florida

George E. Eigsti
Kansas City, Kansas, Community College

Tony Enerva
Lakeland Community College, Ohio

Benjamin C. Fassberg
Prince George's Community College, Maryland

Jerry Furniss
University of Montana

Elizabeth J. Guerriero
Northeast Louisiana University

Phil Harmeson
University of South Dakota

Nancy L. Hart
Midland College, Texas

Janine S. Hiller
Virginia Polytechnic Institute & State University

Florence E. Elliott-Howard
Stephen F. Austin State University, Texas

Fred Ittner
College of Alameda, California

Susan S. Jarvis
University of Texas, Pan American, Texas

Jack E. Karns
East Carolina University, North Carolina

Sarah Weiner Keidan
Oakland Community College, Michigan

Richard N. Kleeberg
Solano Community College, California

Bradley T. Lutz
Hillsborough Community College, Florida

Darlene Mallick
Anne Arundel Community College, Maryland

John D. Mallonee
Manatee Community College, Florida

Joseph D. Marcus
Prince George's Community College, Maryland

Woodrow J. Maxwell
Hudson Valley Community College, New York

Beverly McCormick
Morehead State University, Kentucky

William J. McDevitt
Saint Joseph's University, Pennsylvania

John W. McGee
Aims Community College, Colorado

James K. Miersma
Milwaukee Area Technical Institute, Wisconsin

Susan J. Mitchell
Des Moines Area Community College, Iowa

Jim Lee Morgan
West Los Angeles College

Jack K. Morton
University of Montana

Solange North
Fox Valley Technical Institute, Wisconsin

Robert H. Orr
Florida Community College at Jacksonville

George Otto
Truman College, Illinois

Thomas L. Palmer
Northern Arizona University

Donald L. Petote
Genessee Community College, New York

Francis D. Polk
Ocean County College, New Jersey

Gregory Rabb
Jamestown Community College, New York

Hugh Rode
Utah Valley State College

William M. Rutledge
Macomb Community College, Michigan

Martha Wright Sartoris
North Hennepin Community College, Minnesota

Anne W. Schacherl
Madison Area Technical College, Wisconsin

Edward F. Shafer
Rochester Community College, Minnesota

Lou Ann Simpson
Drake University, Iowa

Denise Smith
Missouri Western State College

Hugh M. Spall
Central Washington University

James D. Van Tassel
Mission College, California

Frederick J. Walsh
Franklin Pierce College, New Hampshire

James E. Walsh, Jr.
Tidewater Community College, Virginia

Edward L. Welsh, Jr.
Phoenix College

Clark W. Wheeler
Santa Fe Community College, Florida

Kay O. Wilburn
The University of Alabama at Birmingham

James L. Wittenbach
University of Notre Dame

Joseph Zavaglia, Jr.
Brookdale Community College, New Jersey

ACKNOWLEDGMENTS FOR THE SIXTH EDITION

Daryl L. Barton
Eastern Michigan University

Gretchen Carroll
Owens Community College, Ohio

Jere Crago
Delgado Community College, Louisiana

Robert Diotalevi
The College of West Virginia

Cheryl Gracie
Washtenaw Community College, Michigan

Dan Hall
East Central College, Missouri

Susan J. Mitchell
Des Moines Area Community College

Pamela Moore
Riverside City College, California

James G. Rittenbaum
St. Louis University

Anne W. Schacherl
Madison Area Technical College, Wisconsin

John Thomas
Northampton County Area Community College, Pennsylvania

Maurice Tonissi
Quinsigamond Community College, Massachusetts

Robert Wm. Young
University of Nebraska at Kearney

We know that we are not perfect. If you or your students find something you don't like or want us to change, write to us or let us know via e-mail, using the "Talk to the Author" feature on this text's Web site. That is how we can make *Business Law Today* an even better book in the future.

Roger LeRoy Miller
Gaylord A. Jentz

Inviting on Every Page

With this new edition of their exciting text, Miller and Jentz invite your students to explore everything that is *CONTEMPORARY*, *INTERESTING*, and *EXCITING* in business law today.

CONTEMPORARY

CONTEMPORARY COVERAGE OF E-COMMERCE, THE LATEST STATUTES, REGULATIONS, AND CASES.

INTERESTING

INTERESTING, STUDENT-FRIENDLY FEATURES THAT PIQUE INTEREST AND ENHANCE UNDERSTANDING.

EXCITING

EXCITING USE OF THE LATEST INTERACTIVE TECHNOLOGY—FROM A STUDENT CD-ROM TO A TEXT-SPECIFIC WEB SITE.

Business Law Today has an established tradition of being both up to date and comprehensive. To that end, this sixth edition features a heavily revised chapter that covers secured transactions based on the requirements of the revised Article 9, as well as numerous sections discussing the most recent developments in Internet law.

Explore this special preview and discover why *Business Law Today*, Sixth Edition, is the most inviting text you'll find for the course!

CONTEMPORARY coverage of

Build student understanding with Business Law Today's **outstanding coverage of cyberlaw.** Instead of treating it in a separate chapter, the authors integrate coverage of Internet law throughout the text. Several chapters include sections on privacy rights in the online world, jurisdictional issues as they arise in cyberspace, cyber torts and cyber crimes, online securities offerings, and a number of other topics relating to the online legal environment.

UPDATED!

Each chapter presents cases that illustrate Internet law and other principles discussed in the text. Nearly 60 percent of the cases are new to the sixth edition, including 43 decided in 2000 or 2001.

CASE 32.3 United States v. Microsoft Corp.

United States Court of Appeals, District of Columbia Circuit, 2001.
253 F.3d 34.
http://www.cadc.uscourts.gov[a]

HISTORICAL AND TECHNOLOGICAL SETTING *In 1981, Microsoft Corporation released the first version of its Microsoft Disk Operating System (MS-DOS). When International Business Machines Corporation (IBM) selected MS-DOS for pre-installation on its first generation of personal computers (PCs), Microsoft's product became the dominant operating system for Intel-compatible PCs.*[b] *In 1985, Microsoft began shipping a software package called Windows. Although originally a user-interface on top of MS-DOS, Windows took on more operating-system functionality over time. Throughout the 1990s, Microsoft's share of the market for Intel-compatible operating systems was more than 90 percent.*

FACTS In 1994, Netscape Communications Corporation began marketing Navigator, the first popular graphical Internet browser. Navigator worked with Sun Micro... ...va technology. Java technol...

ware sellers into believing that this code would help in designing cross-platform applications when, in fact, it would run only on Windows. The U.S. Department of Justice and a number of state attorneys general filed a suit in a federal district court against Microsoft, alleging, in part, monopolization in violation of Section 2 of the Sherman Act. The court ruled against Microsoft.[c] Microsoft appealed to the U.S. Court of Appeals for the District of Columbia Circuit.

ISSUE Did Microsoft possess and maintain monopoly power in the market for Intel-compatible operating systems?

DECISION Yes. The U.S. Court of Appeals for the District of Columbia Circuit affirmed this part of the lower court's opinion. The appellate court reversed other holdings of the lower court, however, and remanded the case for a reconsideration of the appropriate remedy.

REASON The U.S. Court of Appeals for the District of Columbia Circuit ...

LAW:// in the Online World

Internet Wine Sales and the Constitution

In the past decade, the Internet has come to be widely used for direct sales to consumers, including direct sales of wine. Yet a number of state statutes effectively prohibit consumers from purchasing and receiving wine directly from out-of-state sellers. In a series of recent cases, plaintiffs have alleged that such statutes violate the commerce clause of the Constitution. As mentioned elsewhere, the commerce clause implies a negative, or "dormant," aspect: the states do *not* have the authority to regulate interstate commerce. Here we look at how the dormant commerce clause applies to state regulations affecting the sale and purchase of wine via the Internet.

For example, in *Dickerson v. Bailey*,[a] the plaintiffs—Texas residents who wanted to receive wine shipments directly from out-of-state suppliers—claimed that a Texas statute prohibiting such purchases violated the dormant commerce clause. The statute prohibited Texans from ...

Does the Twenty-First Amendment Trump the Dormant Commerce Clause?

Does the Twenty-first Amendment create an exception to the normal operation of the commerce clause? The courts are giving different answers to this question. In the Texas case, for example, the court held that the amendment did not create such an exception. The court did note that substantial deference is given to a state's power to regulate the sale and distribution of liquor within its boundaries when the goal of the regulation is "to combat the perceived evils of an unrestricted traffic in liquor." The court concluded, however, that no temperance (abstinence from alcohol) goal was served by the Texas statute because residents of that state could "become as drunk on local wines" as they could on wines that were effectively "kept out of the state by the statute." Because the goal of the Texas law was primarily to protect the economic interests of in-state wine producers and distributors, the law was not entitled to ... and violated the com...

NEW!

Law:// in the Online World sections focus on a specific court case involving a dispute arising in the online environment.

e-Commerce and cyberlaw

NEW!

Chapter 17, E-Contracts, covers online contract formation, linking and framing, e-signatures, partnering agreements, the Uniform Computer Information Transactions Act, the Uniform Electronic Transactions Act, and more.

CHAPTER 17

E-Contracts

"The law of toasters, televisions, and chain saws is not appropriate for contracts involving online databases, artificial intelligence systems, software, multimedia, and Internet trade in information."

Prefatory Note, Uniform Computer Information Transactions Act

CHAPTER CONTENTS

FORMING CONTRACTS ONLINE
Online Offers
Online Acceptances

LINKING AND FRAMING
Linking to Others' Web Pages
Framing Others' Web Pages

E-SIGNATURES
E-Signature Technologies
State Laws Governing E-Signatures
Federal Law on E-Signatures and

LEARNING OBJECTIVES

After reading this chapter, you should be able to answer the following questions:

① What are some important clauses that offerors should include when making offers to form electronic contracts, or e-contracts?

② What are shrink-wrap agreements? What traditional laws have been applied to such agreements? Do click-on acceptances in electronic contracts present problems that are not covered by traditional laws governing contracts, including the Uniform Commercial Code (UCC)? Explain.

③ What is an electronic signature? Are electronic signatures valid?

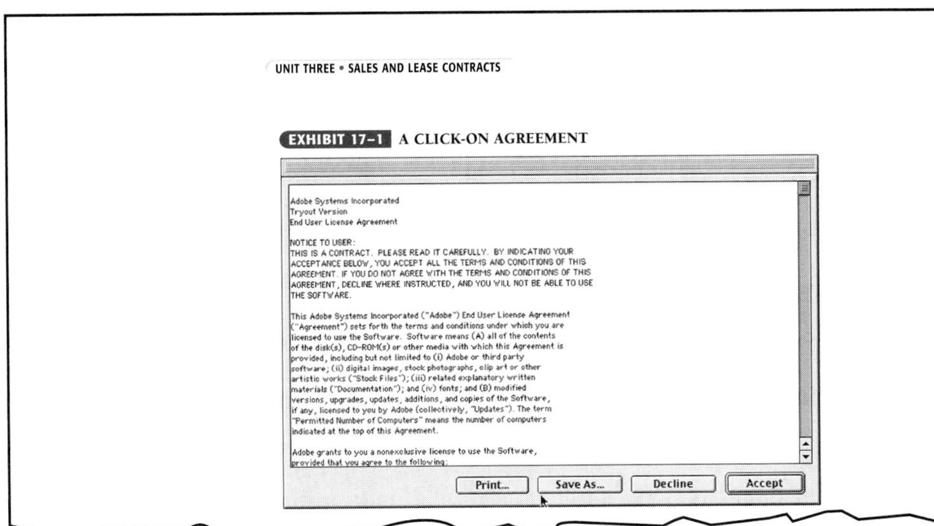

UNIT THREE • SALES AND LEASE CONTRACTS

EXHIBIT 17–1 A CLICK-ON AGREEMENT

NEW!

This edition features ten new exhibits, including a sample "click-on" contractual agreement and an illustration of the process of digital encryption.

INTERESTING pedagogy that

Invite your students to think about the law through engaging features that keep them interested and ready to learn more. Many of the text's features conclude with a **For Critical Analysis** section of questions that emphasize critical thinking.

Internet exercises at the end of every chapter familiarize students with online legal resources and help them navigate the Internet. The exercises refer students to activities posted on the ***Business Law Today*** Web site. Through this site students can also access interactive questions relating to topics covered in each chapter. In addition, ***On the Web*** directs students to online articles, statutes, or other legal or informational sources concerning a topic being discussed in the text.

Internet Exercises

Go to the *Business Law Today* home page at **http://blt.westbuslaw.com**. Select "Internet Applications" and then click on "Chapter 35." There you will find the following Internet research exercises ... ing employment discrimination

Activity 35–1: Americans with ...
Activity 35–2: Equal Employm...

Before the Test

Go to the *Business Law Toda*...
"Interactive Quizzes." You will ...

TEST YOUR KNOWLEDGE—ANSWER ON THE WEB

35–10 PGA Tour, Inc., sponsors professional golf tournaments. A player may enter in several ways, but the most common method is to successfully compete in a three-stage qualifying tournament known as the "Q-School." Anyone may enter the Q-School by submitting two letters of recommendation and paying $3,000 to cover greens fees and the cost of a golf cart, which is permitted during the first two stages, but is prohibited during the third stage. The rules governing the events include the "Rules of Golf," which apply at all levels of amateur and professional golf and do not prohibit the use of golf carts, and the "hard card," which applies specifically to the PGA tour and requires the players to walk the course during most of a tournament. Casey Martin is a talented golfer with a degenerative circulatory disorder that prevents him from walking golf courses. Martin entered the Q-School and asked for permission to use a cart during the third stage. PGA refused. Martin filed a suit in a federal district court against PGA, alleging a violation of the Americans with Disabilities Act. Is a golf cart in these circumstances a "reasonable accommodation" under the ADA? Why or why not? [*PGA Tour, Inc. v. Martin*, 531 U.S. 1049, 121 S.Ct. 1879, 149 L.Ed.2d 904

ON THE WEB

You can find the complete text of Title VII and information about the activities of the EEOC at that agency's Web site. Go to **http://www.eeoc.gov**.

CHAPTER 5 • INTELLECTUAL PROPERTY AND INTERNET LAW

LANDMARK IN THE LAW
The Digital Millennium Copyright Act of 1998

The United States leads the world in the production of creative products, including books, films, videos, recordings, and software. In fact, as indicated earlier in this chapter, the creative industries are more important to the U.S. economy than the traditional product industries are. Exports of U.S. creative products, for example, surpass those of every other U.S. industry in value. Creative industries are growing at nearly three times the rate of the economy as a whole.

Steps have been taken, both nationally and internationally, to protect ownership rights in intellectual property, including copyrights. As you will read later in this chapter, to curb unauthorized copying of copyrighted materials, the World Intellectual Property Organization (WIPO) enacted a treaty in 1996 to upgrade global standards of copyright protection, particularly for the Internet.

Implementing the WIPO Treaty In 1998, Congress implemented the provisions of the WIPO treaty by updating U.S. copyright law. The new law—the Digital Millennium Copyright Act of 1998—is a landmark step in the protection of copyright owners and, because of the leading position of the United States in the creative indus- ...

Pivotal cases and statutes come to light through ***Landmark in the Law*** sections found throughout the text. Concluding ***Application to Today's World*** sections demonstrate how the law discussed affects the legal landscape of today's world.

enhances understanding

Students can explore the sometimes humorous and sometimes serious illustrations of how the law has been phrased, interpreted, or applied in ***Letter of the Law***. Each ***Letter of the Law*** concludes with ***The Bottom Line***, which summarizes the implications of the topic.

UNIT SEVEN • GOVERNMENT REGULATION

LETTER OF THE LAW

"Equal Opportunity" Harassment

The prohibition against sexual harassment in the workplace is an extension of Title VII's prohibition against gender-based discrimination. This means that there can be no sexual harassment if there is no gender-based discrimination involved. It also means, among other things, that Title VII does not protect employees from "equal opportunity" harassers—those who harass both sexes equally—because such persons are not discriminating on the basis they sued their employer for sexual harassment. The Holmans alleged that their supervisor had sexually harassed each of them individually on separate occasions and that the supervisor retaliated against them—by denying them certain privileges and pay—when they rejected his advances. In evaluating their claim, the court looked at the letter of Title VII, which states, "It shall be an unlawful employment practice for an employer to . . . discriminate there was no discrimination "because of . . . sex" because the supervisor harassed both of them. Thus, concluded the court, the Holmans could not maintain a Title VII action against their employer.[a]

THE BOTTOM LINE

Harassment in the workplace takes many forms, including harassment based on gender, race, national origin, religion, age, and disability. In cases alleging sexual harassment, however

CHAPTER 35 • EMPLOYMENT DISCRIMINATION

ETHICAL ISSUE 35.1

Are English-only policies in the workplace a form of national-origin discrimination?

As the U.S. population becomes more multilingual, so does the work force. In response to this development, many employers have instituted English-only policies in their workplaces, particularly in states with large immigrant populations, such as Texas and California. Are English-only policies fair to workers who do not speak English? Do they violate Title VII's prohibition against discrimination on the basis of race or national origin, as workers in a number of lawsuits have alleged? Generally, the courts have shown a fair degree of tolerance with respect to English-only rules, especially when an employer can show that there is a legitimate business reason for the rules, such as improved communication among employees or worker safety. Yet the courts tend to regard with suspicion "blanket" English-only policies—policies that require that only English be spoken not only during work time but also on breaks, lunch hours, and the like. For example, a federal district court held that a Texas firm had engaged in disparate-treatment discrimination based on national origin by requiring that

Ethical Issues open with a question addressing an ethical dimension of the topic being discussed. Ethics are also covered in chapter-ending ethical questions, the ***Ethical Considerations*** following many of the cases, and in a separate chapter.

International Perspectives give students an awareness of the global legal environment by showing how international laws and laws of other nations deal with specific legal concepts or topics being discussed.

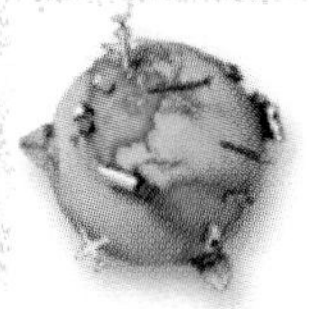

INTERNATONAL PERSPECTIVE

Resolving International Jurisdictional Problems

Given the global nature of e-commerce, jurisdictional problems understandably arise. To address these problems, more than fifty nations, including the United States, have been negotiating an agreement referred to as the Hague Convention on International Jurisdiction and Foreign Judgments in Civil and Commercial Matters. The agreement is intended to create uniform rules governing jurisdiction and enforcement of judgments in cross-border disputes. A draft of the agreement approved in June 2001 would make more predictable the rules governing jurisdiction in disputes between parties located in different countries. Among other things, nations that are signatory to the convention would be required to recognize judgments rendered in the courts of other signatory countries. Special rules would apply to disputes involving consumers. The final draft was expected to be completed in 2002.

FOR CRITICAL ANALYSIS

Some Internet-based activities—such as posting critical comments or hate speech on Web sites—may be legal in the United States but illegal in some other nations. What might result if, because the United States is a signatory to the Hague Convention, U.S.

EXCITING interactive technology

We invite you to take your course to a new level with these unparalleled teaching and learning tools. *Business Law Today* is accompanied by a host of cutting-edge resources that expand course topics, clarify concepts, and give you and your students access to up-to-the-minute information.

The text's accompanying ***Student Resource CD-ROM*** gives students instant access to helpful supplements and materials that allow them to explore business law in greater detail. This CD-ROM includes clips from *West's Drama of the Law* video as well as the *Introduction to Critical Thinking and Writing, Guide to Personal Law,* and *Handbook of Landmark Cases and Statutes* supplements.

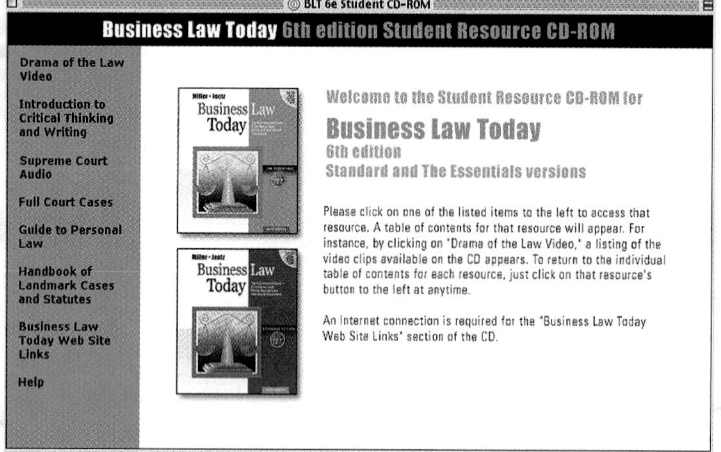

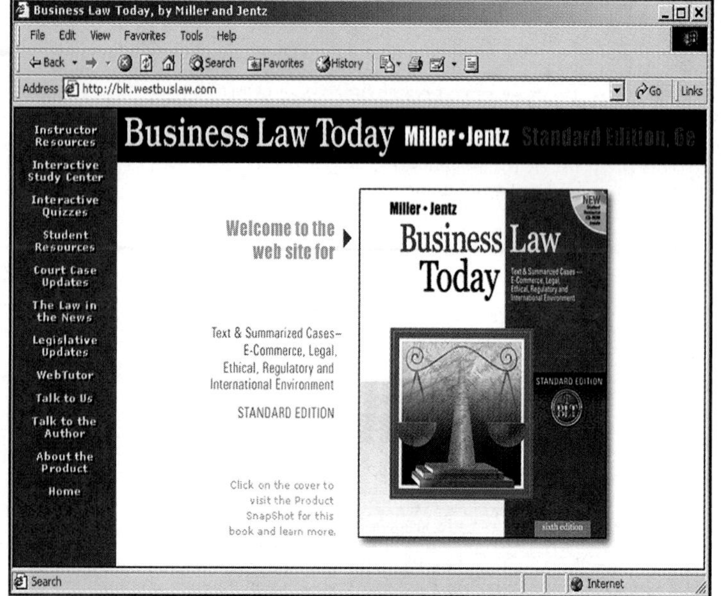

Interactive quizzes, Internet exercises, court case updates — all this and more are available online at the ***Business Law Today*** Web site **(http://blt.westbuslaw.com)**. This dynamic site also provides links to important legal resources, answers to end-of-chapter *Test Your Knowledge* case problems, and a *Talk to the Authors* feature that puts students in direct contact with Miller and Jentz.

Take the business law course beyond classroom boundaries to an anywhere, anytime environment with **WebTutor™ on WebCT and Blackboard**. Students have access to study tools that correspond chapter-by-chapter and topic-by-topic with the book, including flashcards, practice quizzes, and online tutorials. Instructors can use **WebTutor** to provide virtual office hours, post syllabi, set up threaded discussions, and track student progress on the practice quizzes.

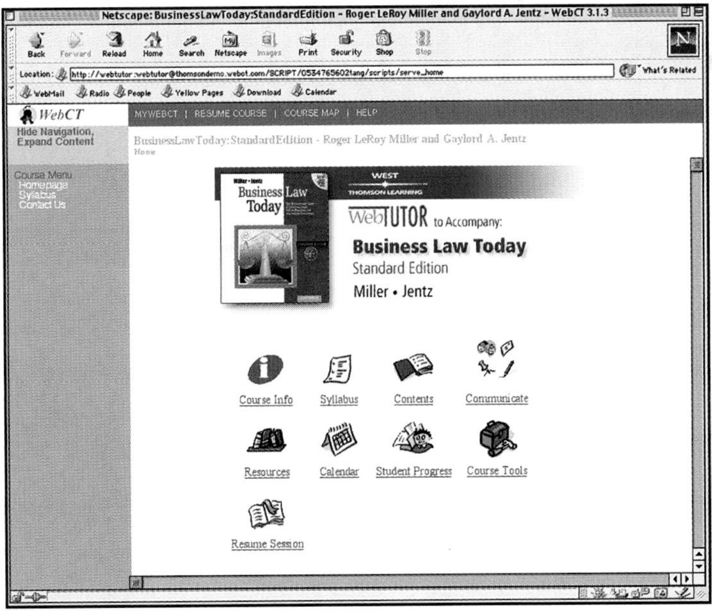

With more and more technology choices for the legal environment course, **BESTech** makes it easy to find out how to integrate various levels of technology into your course. Learn more at **http://besttech.westbuslaw.com**.

Dedication

We dedicate this edition to
the victims of the terrorist
attacks of September 11, 2001,
and to their families and loved ones.

R.L.M.
G.A.J.

The Legal Environment of Business

UNIT 1

UNIT CONTENTS

CHAPTER 1

The Legal Environment

"The law is of as much interest to the layman as it is to the lawyer."
Lord Balfour, 1848–1930
(British prime minister, 1902–1905)

CHAPTER CONTENTS

LEARNING OBJECTIVES

After reading this chapter, you should be able to answer the following questions:

① What is the common law tradition?

② What is a precedent? When might a court depart from precedent?

③ What is the difference between remedies at law and remedies in equity?

④ What is the Uniform Commercial Code?

⑤ What are some important differences between civil law and criminal law?

Lord Balfour's assertion in the quotation above emphasizes the underlying theme of every page in this book—that law is of interest to all persons, not just to lawyers. Those entering the world of business will find themselves subject to numerous laws and government regulations. A basic knowledge of these laws and regulations is beneficial—if not essential—to anyone contemplating a successful career in the business world of today.

In this introductory chapter, we first look at the nature of law and at some concepts that have significantly influenced how jurists (those skilled in the law, including judges, lawyers, and legal scholars) view the nature and function of law. We then examine the common law tradition of the United States, as well as some of the major sources and classifications of American law. The chapter concludes with a discussion of the global legal environment, which frames many of today's business transactions.

The Nature of Law

LAW
A body of enforceable rules governing relationships among individuals and between individuals and their society.

There have been and will continue to be different definitions of law. Although the definitions vary in their particulars, they all are based on the general observation that, at a minimum, **law** consists of *enforceable rules governing relationships among individuals and between individuals and their society.* These "enforceable rules" may consist of unwritten principles of behavior established by a nomadic tribe. They may be set forth in an ancient or a modern law code. They may consist of written laws and court decisions created by modern legislative and judicial bodies, as in the United States. Regardless of how such rules are created, they all have one thing in common: they establish rights, duties, and privileges that are consistent with the values and beliefs of their society or its ruling group.

JURISPRUDENCE
The science or philosophy of law.

Those who embark on a study of law will find that these broad statements leave unanswered some important questions concerning the nature of law. Part of the study of law, often referred to as **jurisprudence**, involves learning about different schools of jurisprudential thought and discovering how each school's approach to law can affect judicial decision making.

You may think that legal philosophy is far removed from the practical study of business law and the legal environment. In fact, it is not. As you will learn in the chapters of this text, how judges apply the law to specific disputes, including disputes relating to the business world, depends in part on their philosophical approaches to law. We look now at some of the significant schools of legal, or jurisprudential, thought that have evolved over time.

The Natural Law Tradition

"An individual who breaks a law that his conscience tells him is unjust, . . . in order to arouse the conscience of the community over its injustices, is in reality expressing the highest respect for the law."

Martin Luther King, Jr., 1929–1968 (American civil rights leader)

An age-old question about the nature of law has to do with the finality of a nation's laws, such as the laws of the United States at the present time. For example, what if a particular law is deemed to be a "bad" law by a substantial number of that nation's citizens? Must a citizen obey the law if it goes against his or her conscience to do so? Is there a higher or universal law to which individuals can appeal? One who adheres to the natural law tradition would answer this question in the affirmative. **Natural law** denotes a system of moral and ethical principles that are inherent in human nature and that people can discover through the use of their natural intelligence.

NATURAL LAW
The belief that government and the legal system should reflect universal moral and ethical principles that are inherent in human nature. The natural law school is the oldest and one of the most significant schools of legal thought.

The natural law tradition is one of the oldest and most significant schools of jurisprudence. It dates back to the days of the Greek philosopher Aristotle (384–322 B.C.E.), who distinguished between natural law and the laws governing a particular nation. According to Aristotle, natural law applies universally to all humankind.

The notion that people have "natural rights" stems from the natural law tradition. Those who claim that a specific foreign government is depriving certain citizens of their human rights are implicitly appealing to a higher law that has universal applicability. The question of the universality of basic human rights also comes into play in the context of international business operations. For example, U.S. companies that have operations abroad often hire foreign workers as employees. Should the same laws protecting U.S. employees apply to these foreign employees? This question is rooted implicitly in a concept of universal rights that has its origins in the natural law tradition.

Legal Positivism

POSITIVE LAW
The body of conventional, or written, law of a particular society at a particular point in time.

In contrast, **positive law**, or national law (the written law of a given society at a particular point in time), applies only to the citizens of that nation or society. Those who

LEGAL POSITIVISM
A school of legal thought centered on the assumption that there is no law higher than the laws created by the government. Laws must be obeyed, even if they are unjust, to prevent anarchy.

adhere to **legal positivism** believe that there can be no higher law than a nation's positive law. According to the positivist school, there is no such thing as "natural rights." Rather, human rights exist solely because of laws. If the laws are not enforced, anarchy will result. Thus, whether a law is "bad" or "good" is irrelevant. The law is the law and must be obeyed until it is changed—in an orderly manner through a legitimate law-making process. A judge with positivist leanings probably would be more inclined to defer to an existing law than would a judge who adheres to the natural law tradition.

THE HISTORICAL SCHOOL

HISTORICAL SCHOOL
A school of legal thought that emphasizes the evolutionary process of law and that looks to the past to discover what the principles of contemporary law should be.

The **historical school** of legal thought emphasizes the evolutionary process of law by concentrating on the origin and history of the legal system. Thus, this school looks to the past to discover what the principles of contemporary law should be. The legal doctrines that have withstood the passage of time—those that have worked in the past—are deemed best suited for shaping present laws. Hence, law derives its legitimacy and authority from adhering to the standards that historical development has shown to be workable. Adherents of the historical school are more likely than those of other schools to strictly follow decisions made in past cases.

LEGAL REALISM

LEGAL REALISM
A school of legal thought of the 1920s and 1930s that generally advocated a less abstract and more realistic approach to the law, an approach that takes into account customary practices and the circumstances in which transactions take place. The school left a lasting imprint on American jurisprudence.

SOCIOLOGICAL SCHOOL
A school of legal thought that views the law as a tool for promoting justice in society.

In the 1920s and 1930s, a number of jurists and scholars, known as legal realists, rebelled against the historical approach to law. **Legal realism** is based on the idea that law is just one of many institutions in society and that it is shaped by social forces and needs. The law is a human enterprise, and judges should take social and economic realities into account when deciding cases. Legal realists also believe that the law can never be applied with total uniformity. Given that judges are human beings with unique personalities, value systems, and intellects, obviously different judges will bring different reasoning processes to the same case.

Legal realism strongly influenced the growth of what is sometimes called the **sociological school** of jurisprudence. This school views law as a tool for promoting justice in society. In the 1960s, for example, the justices of the United States Supreme Court played a leading role in the civil rights movement by upholding long-neglected laws calling for equal treatment for all Americans, including African Americans and other minorities. Generally, jurists who adhere to the sociological school are more likely to depart from past decisions than are those jurists who adhere to the other schools of legal thought.

"Law cannot stand aside from the social changes around it."

WILLIAM J. BRENNAN, JR.,
1906–1997
(Associate justice of the United States Supreme Court, 1956–1990)

The Common Law Tradition

How jurists view the law is particularly important in a legal system in which judges play a paramount role, as they do in the American legal system. Because of our colonial heritage, much of American law is based on the English legal system. A knowledge of this tradition is necessary to an understanding of the nature of our legal system today.

EARLY ENGLISH COURTS OF LAW

After the Normans conquered England in 1066, William the Conqueror and his successors began the process of unifying the country under their rule. One of the means they used to this end was the establishment of the king's courts, or *curiae regis*. Before the Norman Conquest, disputes had been settled according to the local legal customs and traditions in various regions of the country. The king's courts sought to establish a uniform set of rules for the country as a whole. What evolved in these courts was the beginning of the **common law**—a body of general legal principles that eventually was applied throughout the entire English realm.

COMMON LAW
That body of law developed from custom or judicial decisions in English and U.S. courts, not attributable to a legislature.

PRECEDENT
A court decision that furnishes an example or authority for deciding subsequent cases involving identical or similar facts.

STARE DECISIS
A common law doctrine under which judges are obligated to follow the precedents established in prior decisions.

BINDING AUTHORITY
Any source of law that a court must follow when deciding a case. Binding authorities include constitutions, statutes, and regulations that govern the issue being decided, as well as court decisions that are controlling precedents within the jurisdiction.

Courts developed the common law rules from the principles underlying judges' decisions in actual legal controversies. Judges attempted to be consistent, and whenever possible, they based their decisions on the principles suggested by earlier cases. They sought to decide similar cases in a similar way and considered new cases with care, because they knew that their decisions would make new law. Each interpretation became part of the law on the subject and served as a legal **precedent**—that is, a decision that furnished an example or authority for deciding subsequent cases involving similar legal principles or facts.

In the early years of the common law, there was no single place or publication where court opinions, or written decisions, could be found. Beginning in the late thirteenth and early fourteenth centuries, however, each year portions of significant decisions of that year were gathered together and recorded in *Year Books*. The *Year Books* were useful references for lawyers and judges. In the sixteenth century, the *Year Books* were discontinued, and other reports of cases became available. (See the appendix to this chapter for a discussion of how cases are reported, or published, in the United States today.)

STARE DECISIS

The practice of deciding new cases with reference to former decisions, or precedents, eventually became a cornerstone of the English and American judicial systems. The practice forms a doctrine called ***stare decisis***[1] ("to stand on decided cases").

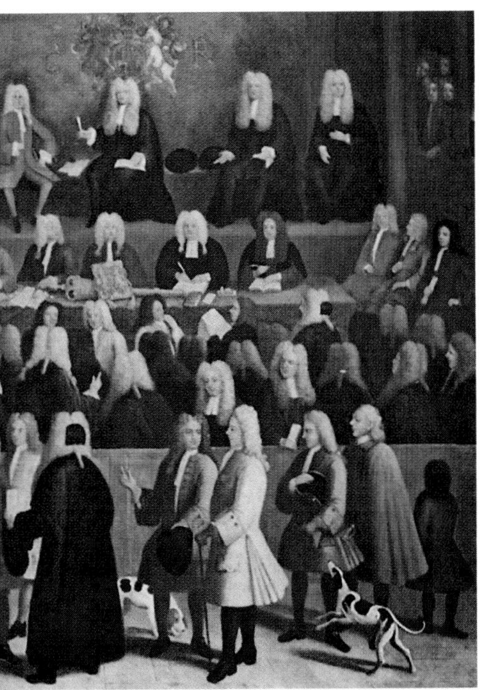

The court of chancery in the reign of George I. Early English court decisions formed the basis of what type of law?

The Importance of Precedents in Judicial Decision Making The doctrine of *stare decisis* means that once a court has set forth a principle of law as being applicable to a certain set of facts, that court and courts of lower rank must adhere to that principle and apply it in future cases involving similar fact patterns.

• **EXAMPLE 1.1** Suppose that the lower state courts in California have reached conflicting conclusions on whether drivers are liable for accidents they cause while merging into freeway traffic, even though the drivers looked and did not see any oncoming traffic and even though witnesses (passengers in their cars) testified to that effect. To settle the law on this issue, the California Supreme Court decides to review a case involving this fact pattern. The court rules that in such a situation, the driver who is merging into traffic is liable for any accidents caused by the driver's failure to yield to freeway traffic, regardless of whether the driver looked carefully and did not see an approaching vehicle. The California Supreme Court's decision on the matter will influence the outcome of all future cases on this issue brought before the California state courts. •

Similarly, a decision on a given issue by the United States Supreme Court (the nation's highest court) is binding on all inferior courts. Controlling precedents in a jurisdiction (an area in which a court or courts have the power to apply the law—see Chapter 3) are referred to as binding authorities. A **binding authority** is any source

1. Pronounced *ster*-ay dih-*si*-ses.

LETTER OF THE LAW
Is an 1875 Case Precedent Still Binding?

In a suit against the U.S. government for breach of contract, Boris Korczak sought compensation for services that he had allegedly performed for the Central Intelligence Agency (CIA) from 1973 to 1980. Korczak claimed that the government had failed to pay him an annuity and other compensation required by a secret *oral* agreement with the CIA. The federal trial court dismissed Korczak's claim, and Korczak appealed the decision to the U.S. Court of Appeals for the Federal Circuit.

At issue on appeal was whether a Supreme Court case decided in 1875, *Totten v. United States*,[a] remained the controlling precedent in this area. In *Totten*, the plaintiff alleged that he had formed a secret contract with President Lincoln to collect information on the Confederate army during the Civil War. When the plaintiff sued the government for compensation for his services, the Supreme Court held that the agreement was unenforceable. According to the Court, to enforce such agreements could result in the disclosure of information that "might compromise or embarrass our government" or cause other "serious detriment" to the public. In Korczak's case, the federal appellate court held that the *Totten* case precedent was still "good law," and therefore Korczak, like the plaintiff in *Totten*, could not recover compensation for his services. Said the court, "*Totten*, despite its age, is the last pronouncement on this issue by the Supreme Court. . . . We are duty bound to follow the law given us by the Supreme Court unless and until it is changed."[b]

THE BOTTOM LINE

Supreme Court precedents, no matter how old, remain controlling until they are overruled by a subsequent decision of the Supreme Court, by a constitutional amendment, or by congressional legislation.

a. 92 U.S. 105 (1875).

b. *Korczak v. United States*, 124 F.3d 227 (Fed.Cir. 1997).

of law that a court must follow when deciding a case. Binding authorities include constitutions, statutes, and regulations that govern the issue being decided, as well as court decisions that are controlling precedents within the jurisdiction.

***Stare Decisis* and Legal Stability** The doctrine of *stare decisis* helps the courts to be more efficient, because if other courts have carefully reasoned through a similar case, their legal reasoning and opinions can serve as guides. *Stare decisis* also makes the law more stable and predictable. If the law on a given subject is well settled, someone bringing a case to court can usually rely on the court to make a decision based on what the law has been.

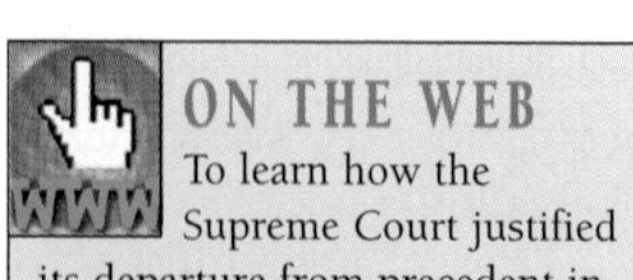

ON THE WEB To learn how the Supreme Court justified its departure from precedent in the 1954 *Brown* decision, you can access the Court's opinion online by going to **http://guide.lp.findlaw.com/casecode/supreme.html** and entering "347 U.S. 483" in the "Citation Search" box.

Departures from Precedent Sometimes a court will depart from the rule of precedent if it decides that a given precedent should no longer be followed. If a court decides that a precedent is simply incorrect or that technological or social changes have rendered the precedent inapplicable, the court might rule contrary to the precedent. Cases that overturn precedent often receive a great deal of publicity.

• **EXAMPLE 1.2** In *Brown v. Board of Education of Topeka*,[2] the United States Supreme Court expressly overturned precedent when it concluded that separate educational facilities for whites and blacks, which had been upheld as constitutional in numerous previous cases,[3] were inherently unequal. The Supreme Court's departure from prece-

2. 347 U.S. 483, 74 S.Ct. 686, 98 L.Ed. 873 (1954). (See the appendix at the end of this chapter for an explanation of how to read legal citations.)

3. See *Plessy v. Ferguson*, 163 U.S. 537, 16 S.Ct. 1138, 41 L.Ed. 256 (1896).

dent in *Brown* received a tremendous amount of publicity as people began to realize the ramifications of this change in the law.●

When There Is No Precedent At times, courts hear cases for which there are no precedents within their jurisdictions on which to base their decisions. When hearing such cases, called "cases of first impression," courts often look to precedents set in other jurisdictions for guidance. Precedents from other jurisdictions, because they are not binding on the court, are referred to as **persuasive authorities.** A court may also consider a number of factors, including legal principles and policies underlying previous court decisions or existing statutes, fairness, social values and customs, public policy, and data and concepts drawn from the social sciences.

PERSUASIVE AUTHORITY
Any legal authority or source of law that a court may look to for guidance but on which it need not rely in making its decision. Persuasive authorities include cases from other jurisdictions and secondary sources of law.

EQUITABLE REMEDIES AND COURTS OF EQUITY

REMEDY
The relief given to an innocent party to enforce a right or compensate for the violation of a right.

A **remedy** is the means given to a party to enforce a right or to compensate for the violation of a right. ● **EXAMPLE 1.3** Suppose that Shem is injured because of Rowan's wrongdoing. A court may order Rowan to compensate Shem for the harm by paying Shem a certain amount of money.●

In the early king's courts of England, the kinds of remedies that could be granted were severely restricted. If one person wronged another, the king's courts could award as compensation either money or property, including land. These courts became known as *courts of law,* and the remedies were called *remedies at law.* Even though this system introduced uniformity in the settling of disputes, when plaintiffs wanted a remedy other than economic compensation, the courts of law could do nothing, so "no remedy, no right."

Remedies in Equity *Equity* refers to a branch of the law, founded in justice and fair dealing, that seeks to supply a fairer and more adequate remedy when no remedy is available at law. In medieval England, when individuals could not obtain an adequate remedy in a court of law, they petitioned the king for relief. Most of these petitions were decided by an adviser to the king called the *chancellor.* The chancellor was said to be the "keeper of the king's conscience." When the chancellor thought that the claim was a fair one, new and unique remedies were granted. In this way, a new body of rules and remedies came into being, and eventually formal *chancery courts,* or *courts of equity,* were established. The remedies granted by these courts were called *remedies in equity.* Thus, two distinct court systems were created, each having a different set of judges and a different set of remedies.

PLAINTIFF
One who initiates a lawsuit.

DEFENDANT
One against whom a lawsuit is brought; the accused person in a criminal proceeding.

Plaintiffs (those bringing lawsuits) had to specify whether they were bringing an "action at law" or an "action in equity," and they chose their courts accordingly. ● **EXAMPLE 1.4** A plaintiff might ask a court of equity to order a **defendant** (a person against whom a lawsuit is brought) to perform within the terms of a contract. A court of law could not issue such an order, because its remedies were limited to payment of money or property as compensation for damages. A court of equity, however, could issue a decree for *specific performance*—an order to perform what was promised. A court of equity could also issue an *injunction,* directing a party to do or refrain from doing a particular act. In certain cases, a court of equity could allow for the *rescission* (cancellation) of the contract so that the parties would be returned to the positions that they held prior to the contract's formation.● Equitable remedies will be discussed in greater detail in Chapter 13.

REMEMBER Even though, in most states, courts of law and equity have merged, the principles of equity still apply.

The Merging of Law and Equity Today, in most states, the courts of law and equity are merged, and thus the distinction between the two courts has largely disappeared. A plaintiff may now request both legal and equitable remedies in the same action, and the trial court judge may grant either form—or both forms—of relief. The merging of law and equity, however, does not diminish the importance of distinguishing legal remedies from equitable remedies. To request the proper remedy, a businessperson (or his or her attorney) must know what remedies are available for the specific kinds of harms suffered. Today, as a rule, courts will grant an equitable remedy only when the remedy at law (money damages) is inadequate. Exhibit 1–1 summarizes the procedural differences (applicable in most states) between an action at law and an action in equity.

EQUITABLE PRINCIPLES AND MAXIMS General propositions or principles of law that have to do with fairness (equity).

Equitable Principles and Maxims Over time, a number of **equitable principles and maxims** evolved that have since guided the courts in deciding whether plaintiffs should be granted equitable relief. Because of their importance, both historically and in our judicial system today, these principles and maxims are set forth in this chapter's *Landmark in the Law.*

Sources of American Law

PRIMARY SOURCE OF LAW A document that establishes the law on a particular issue, such as a constitution, a statute, an administrative rule, or a court decision.

There are numerous sources of American law. **Primary sources of law**, or sources that establish the law, include the following:

- The U.S. Constitution and the constitutions of the various states.
- Statutes, or laws, passed by Congress and by state legislatures.
- Regulations created by administrative agencies, such as the federal Food and Drug Administration.
- Case law (court decisions).

We describe each of these important primary sources of law in the following pages. (See the appendix at the end of this chapter for a discussion of how to find statutes, regulations, and case law.)

SECONDARY SOURCE OF LAW A publication that summarizes or interprets the law, such as a legal encyclopedia, a legal treatise, or an article in a law review.

Secondary sources of law are books and articles that summarize and clarify the primary sources of law. Legal encyclopedias, compilations (such as *Restatements of the Law*—to be discussed later in this chapter), official comments to statutes, treatises, articles in law reviews published by law schools, and articles in other legal journals are examples of secondary sources of law. Courts often refer to secondary sources of law for guidance in interpreting and applying the primary sources of law discussed here.

EXHIBIT 1–1 PROCEDURAL DIFFERENCES BETWEEN AN ACTION AT LAW AND AN ACTION IN EQUITY

PROCEDURE	ACTION AT LAW	ACTION IN EQUITY
Initiation of lawsuit	By filing a complaint	By filing a petition
Decision	By jury or judge	By judge (no jury)
Result	Judgment	Decree
Remedy	Monetary damages	Injunction, specific performance, or rescission

LANDMARK IN THE LAW

Equitable Principles and Maxims

In medieval England, courts of equity had the responsibility of using discretion in supplementing the common law. Even today, when the same court can award both legal and equitable remedies, such discretion is exercised. Courts often invoke equitable principles and maxims when making their decisions. Here are some of the more significant equitable principles and maxims:

1. *Whoever seeks equity must do equity.* (Anyone who wishes to be treated fairly must treat others fairly.)
2. *Where there is equal equity, the law must prevail.* (The law will determine the outcome of a controversy in which the merits of both sides are equal.)
3. *One seeking the aid of an equity court must come to the court with clean hands.* (Plaintiffs must have acted fairly and honestly.)
4. *Equity will not suffer a wrong to be without a remedy.* (Equitable relief will be awarded when there is a right to relief and there is no adequate remedy at law.)
5. *Equity regards substance rather than form.* (Equity is more concerned with fairness and justice than with legal technicalities.)
6. *Equity aids the vigilant, not those who rest on their rights.* (Equity will not help those who neglect their rights for an unreasonable period of time.)

STATUTE OF LIMITATIONS
A federal or state statute setting the maximum time period during which a certain action can be brought or certain rights enforced.

The last maxim has become known as the *equitable doctrine of laches.* The doctrine arose to encourage people to bring lawsuits while the evidence was fresh; if they failed to do so, they would not be allowed to bring a lawsuit. What constitutes a reasonable time, of course, varies according to the circumstances of the case. Time periods for different types of cases are now usually fixed by **statutes of limitations.** After the time allowed under a statute of limitations has expired, no action can be brought, no matter how strong the case was originally.

APPLICATION TO TODAY'S WORLD

The equitable maxims listed above underlie many of the legal rules and principles that are commonly applied by the courts today—and that you will read about in this book. For example, in Chapter 9 you will read about the doctrine of promissory estoppel. *Under this doctrine, a person who has reasonably and substantially relied on the promise of another may be able to obtain some measure of recovery, even though no enforceable contract, or agreement, exists. The court will* estop *(bar, or impede) the one making the promise from asserting the lack of a valid contract as a defense. The rationale underlying the doctrine of promissory estoppel is similar to that expressed in the fourth and fifth maxims above.*

CONSTITUTIONAL LAW

CONSTITUTIONAL LAW
Law based on the U.S. Constitution and the constitutions of the various states.

The federal government and the states have separate written constitutions that set forth the general organization, powers, and limits of their respective governments. **Constitutional law** is the law as expressed in these constitutions.

Young students view the U.S. Constitution on display in Washington, D.C. Can a law be in violation of the Constitution and still be enforced? Why or why not?

The U.S. Constitution is the supreme law of the land. As such, it is the basis of all law in the United States. A law in violation of the Constitution, no matter what its source, will be declared unconstitutional and will not be enforced. Because of its paramount importance in the American legal system, we discuss the U.S. Constitution at length in Chapter 2 and present the complete text of the Constitution in Appendix B.

The Tenth Amendment to the U.S. Constitution, which defines the powers of and limitations on the federal government, reserves all powers not granted to the federal government to the states. Each state in the union has its own constitution. Unless they conflict with the U.S. Constitution or a federal law, state constitutions are supreme within their respective borders.

ON THE WEB To learn more about the federal Constitution, visit the Web site of the National Constitution Center in Philadelphia at **http://www.constitutioncenter.org**. The constitutions of almost all of the states are now also online. You can find them at **http://www.findlaw.com/11stategov**.

STATUTORY LAW

Statutes enacted by legislative bodies at any level of government make up another source of law, which is generally referred to as **statutory law.**

STATUTORY LAW
The body of law enacted by legislative bodies (as opposed to constitutional law, administrative law, or case law).

Federal Statutes Federal statutes are laws that are enacted by the U.S. Congress. As mentioned, any law—including a federal statute—that violates the U.S. Constitution will be held unconstitutional.

Federal statutes that affect business operations include laws regulating the purchase and sale of securities (corporate stocks and bonds—discussed in Chapter 29), consumer protection statutes (discussed in Chapter 33), and statutes prohibiting employment discrimination (discussed in Chapter 35). Whenever a particular statute is

CITATION
A reference to a publication in which a legal authority--such as a statute or a court decision--or other source can be found.

mentioned in this text, we usually provide a footnote showing its **citation** (a reference to a publication in which a legal authority—such as a statute or a court decision—or other source can be found). In the appendix following this chapter, we explain how you can use these citations to find statutory law.

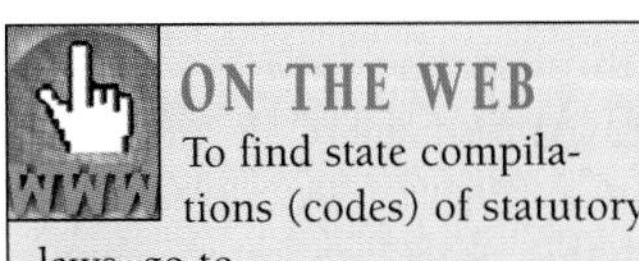

To find state compilations (codes) of statutory laws, go to

http://www.findlaw.com/casecode/state.html.

State and Local Statutes and Ordinances State statutes are laws enacted by state legislatures. Any state law that is found to conflict with the U.S. Constitution, with federal laws enacted by Congress, or with the state's constitution will be deemed unconstitutional. Statutory law also includes the ordinances passed by cities and counties, none of which can violate the U.S. Constitution, the relevant state constitution, or federal or state laws.

State statutes include state criminal statutes (discussed in Chapter 6), state corporation statutes (discussed in Chapters 26 through 29), state deceptive trade practices acts (referred to in Chapter 33), state laws governing wills and trusts (discussed in Chapter 38), and state versions of the Uniform Commercial Code (to be discussed shortly). Local ordinances include zoning ordinances and local laws regulating housing construction and such things as the overall appearance of a community.

A federal statute, of course, applies to all states. A state statute, in contrast, applies only within the state's borders. State laws thus vary from state to state.

Uniform Laws The differences among state laws were particularly notable in the 1800s, when conflicting state statutes frequently created problems for the rapidly developing trade and commerce among the states. To counter these problems, a group of legal scholars and lawyers formed the National Conference of Commissioners on Uniform State Laws (NCCUSL) in 1892 to draft uniform ("model") statutes for adoption by the states. The NCCUSL still exists today and continues to issue uniform statutes.

BE CAREFUL Even though uniform laws are intended to be adopted without changes, states often modify them to suit their particular needs.

Adoption of a uniform law is a state matter, and a state may reject all or part of the statute or rewrite it as the state legislature wishes. Hence, even when a uniform law is said to have been adopted in many states, those states' laws may not be entirely "uniform." Once adopted by a state legislature, a uniform act becomes a part of the statutory law of that state.

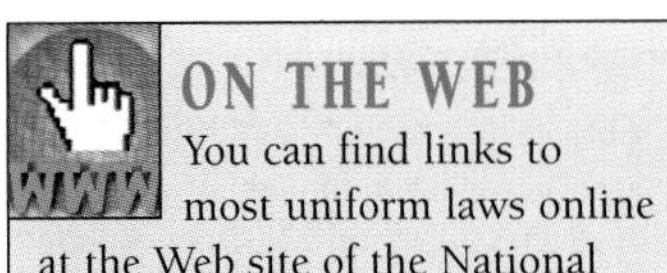

You can find links to most uniform laws online at the Web site of the National Conference of Commissioners on Uniform State Laws. Go to

http://www.nccusl.org.

The earliest uniform law, the Uniform Negotiable Instruments Law, was completed by 1896 and was adopted in every state by the early 1920s (although not all states used exactly the same wording). Over the following decades, other acts were drawn up in a similar manner. In all, over two hundred uniform acts have been issued by the NCCUSL since its inception. Recent uniform acts issued by the NCCUSL include the Uniform Computer Information Transactions Act and the Uniform Electronic Transactions Act. These acts, which address some of the specific legal needs created by e-commerce, will be discussed at length in Chapter 17, in the context of electronic contracts. The most ambitious uniform act of all, however, was the Uniform Commercial Code.

The Uniform Commercial Code (UCC) The Uniform Commercial Code (UCC), which was created through the joint efforts of the NCCUSL and the American Law Institute,[4] was first issued in 1952. The UCC has been adopted in all fifty states,[5] the District of Columbia, and the Virgin Islands. The UCC facilitates commerce among the states by providing a uniform, yet flexible, set of rules governing commercial transactions. The UCC assures businesspersons that their contracts, if validly entered into, normally will be enforced.

4. This institute was formed in the 1920s and consists of practicing attorneys, legal scholars, and judges.
5. Louisiana has adopted only Articles 1, 3, 4, 5, 7, 8, and 9.

Because of its importance in the area of commercial law, we cite the UCC frequently in this text. We also present the latest version of the UCC in its entirety in Appendix C. (For a discussion of the creation of the UCC, see the *Landmark in the Law* in Chapter 14.)

ADMINISTRATIVE LAW

ADMINISTRATIVE LAW
The body of law created by administrative agencies (in the form of rules, regulations, orders, and decisions) in order to carry out their duties and responsibilities.

ADMINISTRATIVE AGENCY
A federal or state government agency established to perform a specific function. Administrative agencies are authorized by legislative acts to make and enforce rules to administer and enforce the acts.

EXECUTIVE AGENCY
An administrative agency within the executive branch of government. At the federal level, executive agencies are those within the cabinet departments.

INDEPENDENT REGULATORY AGENCY
An administrative agency that is not considered part of the government's executive branch and is not subject to the authority of the president. Independent agency officials cannot be removed without cause.

Another important source of American law consists of **administrative law**—the rules, orders, and decisions of administrative agencies. An **administrative agency** is a federal, state, or local government agency established to perform a specific function. Rules issued by various administrative agencies now affect virtually every aspect of a business's operations, including the firm's capital structure and financing, its hiring and firing procedures, its relations with employees and unions, and the way it manufactures and markets its products.

At the national level, numerous **executive agencies** exist within the cabinet departments of the executive branch. For example, the Food and Drug Administration is within the Department of Health and Human Services. Executive agencies are subject to the authority of the president, who has the power to appoint and remove officers of federal agencies. There are also major **independent regulatory agencies** at the federal level, including the Federal Trade Commission, the Securities and Exchange Commission, and the Federal Communications Commission. The president's power is less pronounced in regard to independent agencies, whose officers serve for fixed terms and cannot be removed without just cause.

There are administrative agencies at the state and local levels as well. Commonly, a state agency (such as a state pollution-control agency) is created as a parallel to a federal agency (such as the Environmental Protection Agency). Just as federal statutes take precedence over conflicting state statutes, so do federal agency regulations take precedence over conflicting state regulations. Because the rules of state and local agencies vary widely, we focus here exclusively on federal administrative law.

Agency Creation Because Congress cannot possibly oversee the actual implementation of all the laws it enacts, it must delegate such tasks to others, particularly when

Buyers check the quality of tobacco being auctioned at a Kentucky warehouse in July 1996. The sign refers to the Food and Drug Administration (FDA), a federal administrative agency, which, in 1996, issued a rule that placed restrictions on the marketing and sale of tobacco products to younger Americans. The United States Supreme Court, however, invalidated the rule in 2000, concluding that tobacco is not a "drug" subject to regulation by the FDA. Generally, why has the federal government found it so difficult to regulate—or ban outright—the sale of tobacco products?

the issues relate to highly technical areas, such as air and water pollution. Congress creates an administrative agency by enacting **enabling legislation**, which specifies the name, composition, purpose, and powers of the agency being created.

ENABLING LEGISLATION
A statute enacted by Congress that authorizes the creation of an administrative agency and specifies the name, composition, purpose, and powers of the agency being created.

• **EXAMPLE 1.5** The Federal Trade Commission (FTC) was created in 1914 by the Federal Trade Commission Act.[6] This act prohibits unfair and deceptive trade practices. It also describes the procedures the agency must follow to charge persons or organizations with violations of the act, and it provides for judicial review (review by the courts) of agency orders. Other portions of the act grant the agency powers to "make rules and regulations for the purpose of carrying out the Act," to conduct investigations of business practices, to obtain reports from interstate corporations concerning their business practices, to investigate possible violations of the act, to publish findings of its investigations, and to recommend new legislation. The act also empowers the FTC to hold trial-like hearings and to **adjudicate** (resolve judicially) certain kinds of trade disputes that involve FTC regulations. •

ADJUDICATE
To render a judicial decision. In the administrative process, the proceeding in which an administrative law judge hears and decides on issues that arise when an administrative agency charges a person or a firm with violating a law or regulation enforced by the agency.

Note that the FTC's grant of power incorporates functions associated with the legislative branch of government (rulemaking), the executive branch (investigation and enforcement), and the judicial branch (adjudication). Taken together, these functions constitute what has been termed **administrative process**, which is the administration of law by administrative agencies.

ADMINISTRATIVE PROCESS
The procedure used by administrative agencies in the administration of law.

Rulemaking One of the major functions of an administrative agency is **rulemaking**—creating or modifying rules, or regulations, pursuant to its enabling legislation. The Administrative Procedure Act[7] of 1946 imposes strict procedural requirements that agencies must follow in their rulemaking and other functions.

RULEMAKING
The process undertaken by an administrative agency when formally adopting a new regulation or amending an old one. Rulemaking involves notifying the public of a proposed rule or change and receiving and considering the public's comments.

The most common rulemaking procedure involves three steps. First, the agency must give public notice of the proposed rulemaking proceedings, where and when the proceedings will be held, the agency's legal authority for the proceedings, and the terms or subject matter of the proposed rule. The notice must be published in the *Federal Register*, a daily publication of the U.S. government. Second, following this notice, the agency must allow ample time for interested parties to comment in writing on the proposed rule. After the comments have been received and reviewed, the agency takes them into consideration when drafting the final version of the regulation. The third and final step is the drafting of the final version of the rule and its publication in the *Federal Register*. (See the appendix at the end of this chapter for an explanation of how to find agency regulations.)

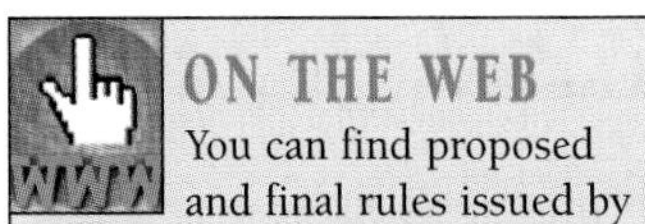

ON THE WEB
You can find proposed and final rules issued by administrative agencies by accessing the *Federal Register* online at **http://www.access.gpo.gov/su_docs/aces/aces140.html**.

Investigation and Enforcement Agencies have both investigatory and prosecutorial powers. An agency can request that individuals or organizations hand over specified books, papers, records, or other documents. In addition, agencies may conduct on-site inspections, although a search warrant is normally required for such inspections. Sometimes the search of a home, an office, or a factory is the only means of obtaining evidence needed to prove a regulatory violation. Agencies investigate a wide range of activities, including coal mining, automobile manufacturing, and the industrial discharge of pollutants into the environment.

Adjudication After conducting its own investigation of a suspected rule violation, an agency may decide to take action against a specific party. The action may involve a trial-like hearing before an **administrative law judge (ALJ)**. The ALJ may compel the charged party to pay fines or may forbid the party to carry on some specified activity.

ADMINISTRATIVE LAW JUDGE (ALJ)
One who presides over an administrative agency hearing and has the power to administer oaths, take testimony, rule on questions of evidence, and make determinations of fact.

6. 15 U.S.C. Sections 45–58.
7. 5 U.S.C. Sections 551–706.

ON THE WEB
The *United States Government Manual* describes the origins, purposes, and administrators of every federal department and agency. You can access this publication online at

http://www.access.gpo.gov/nara/browse-gm.html.

Either side may appeal the ALJ's decision to the commission or board that governs the agency. If the party fails to get relief there, appeal can be made to a federal court.

ETHICAL ISSUE 1.1

Do administrative agencies exercise too much authority?
Administrative agencies, such as the FTC, combine functions normally divided among the three branches of government in a single governmental entity. The broad range of authority that agencies exercise sometimes poses questions of fairness. After all, agencies create rules that are as legally binding as the laws passed by Congress—the only federal government institution authorized by the Constitution to make laws. To be sure, arbitrary rulemaking by agencies is checked by the procedural requirements set forth in the Administrative Procedure Act (APA), as well as by the courts, to which agency decisions may be appealed. Yet some people claim that these checks are not enough.

Consider that in addition to *legislative rules,* which are subject to the procedural requirements of the APA, agencies also create *interpretive rules*—rules that specify how the agency will interpret and apply its regulations. The APA does not apply to interpretative rulemaking. Additionally, although a firm that challenges an agency's rule may be able to appeal the agency's decision in the matter to a court, the policy of the courts is generally to defer to agency rules, including interpretative rules, and to agency decisions.

CASE LAW AND COMMON LAW DOCTRINES

The body of law that was first developed in England and that is still used today in the United States consists of the rules of law announced in court decisions. These rules of law include interpretations of constitutional provisions, of statutes enacted by legislatures, and of regulations created by administrative agencies. Today, this body of law is referred to variously as the common law, judge-made law, or **case law**.

CASE LAW
The rules of law announced in court decisions. Case law includes the aggregate of reported cases that interpret judicial precedents, statutes, regulations, and constitutional provisions.

The common law—the doctrines and principles embodied in case law—governs all areas not covered by statutory law (or agency regulations issued to implement various statutes). • **EXAMPLE 1.6** In disputes concerning contracts for the sale of goods, the Uniform Commercial Code (statutory law) applies when one of its provisions supersedes the common law of contracts. Similarly, in a dispute concerning a particular employment practice, a statute regulating that practice will apply rather than the common law doctrine governing employment relationships that applied prior to the enactment of the statute.•

The Relationship between the Common Law and Statutory Law The body of statutory law has expanded greatly since the beginning of this nation, and this expansion has resulted in a proportionate reduction in the applicability of common law doctrines. Nonetheless, there is a significant overlap between statutory law and the common law, and thus common law doctrines remain a significant source of legal authority.

Many statutes essentially codify existing common law rules, so the courts, in interpreting the statutes, often rely on the common law as a guide to what the legislators intended. Additionally, how the courts interpret a particular statute determines how that statute will be applied. Thus, if you wanted to learn about the coverage and applicability of a particular statute, for example, you would, of course, need to locate the statute and study it. You would also need to see how the courts in your jurisdiction have interpreted the statute—in other words, what precedents have been established in regard to that statute. Often, the applicability of a newly enacted statute does not become clear until a body of case law develops to clarify how, when, and to whom the statute applies.

BE AWARE *Restatements of the Law* are authoritative sources, but they do not have the force of law.

Restatements of the Law The American Law Institute (ALI) drafted and published compilations of the common law called *Restatements of the Law,* which generally summarize the common law rules followed by most states. There are *Restatements of the Law* in many areas of the law, including contracts, torts, agency, trusts, property, restitution, security, judgments, and conflict of laws. Although the *Restatements,* like other secondary sources of law, do not in themselves have the force of law, they are an important source of legal analysis and opinion on which judges often rely in making their decisions.

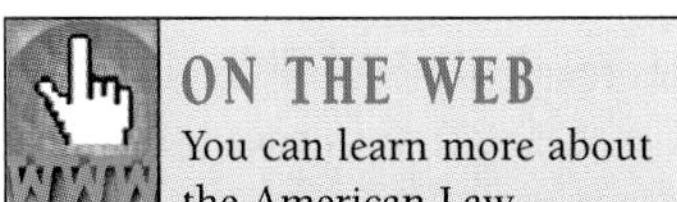

ON THE WEB You can learn more about the American Law Institute and its projects and publications by accessing its Web site at **http://www.ali.org**.

The ALI periodically revises the *Restatements,* and many of them are now in their second or third editions. For instance, as you will read in Chapter 18, the ALI has recently published the first volume of the third edition of the *Restatement of the Law of Torts.*

We refer to the *Restatements* frequently in subsequent chapters of this text, indicating in parentheses the edition to which we are referring. For example, we refer to the second edition of the *Restatement of the Law of Contracts* simply as the *Restatement (Second) of Contracts.*

Classifications of Law

SUBSTANTIVE LAW Law that defines, describes, regulates, and creates legal rights and obligations.

PROCEDURAL LAW Law that establishes the methods of enforcing the rights established by substantive law.

The huge body of the law may be broken down according to several classification systems. For example, one classification system divides law into **substantive law** (all laws that define, describe, regulate, and create legal rights and obligations) and **procedural law** (all laws that establish the methods of enforcing the rights established by substantive law). Other classification systems divide law into federal law and state law, private law (dealing with relationships between persons) and public law (addressing the relationship between persons and their government), and so on.

We look below at two broad classifications. One divides the law into criminal and civil law; the other divides the law into national law and international law. Following that, we mention an emerging body of law regulating transactions in cyberspace, informally characterized as "cyberlaw."

Civil Law and Criminal Law

CIVIL LAW The branch of law dealing with the definition and enforcement of all private or public rights, as opposed to criminal matters.

Civil law spells out the rights and duties that exist between persons and between persons and their governments, and the relief available when a person's rights are violated. Typically, in a civil case, a private party sues another private party (although the government can also sue a party for a civil law violation) to make that other party comply with a duty or pay for the damage caused by the failure to comply with a duty. • **Example 1.7** If a seller fails to perform a contract with a buyer, the buyer may bring a lawsuit against the seller. The purpose of the lawsuit will be either to compel the seller to perform as promised or, more commonly, to obtain money damages for the seller's failure to perform. •

Much of the law that we discuss in this text is civil law. Contract law, for example, which we discuss in Chapters 8 through 13, is civil law. The whole body of tort law (see Chapter 4), is civil law. Note that *civil law* is not the same as a *civil law system.* As you will read shortly, in the subsection discussing international law, a civil law system is a legal system based on a written code of laws.

CRIMINAL LAW
Law that defines and governs actions that constitute crimes. Generally, criminal law has to do with wrongful actions committed against society for which society demands redress.

Criminal law has to do with wrongs committed against society for which society demands redress (see Chapter 6). Criminal acts are proscribed by local, state, or federal government statutes. Criminal defendants are thus prosecuted by public officials, such as a district attorney (D.A.), on behalf of the state, not by their victims or other private parties. Whereas in a civil case the object is to obtain remedies (such as money damages) to compensate the injured party, in a criminal case the object is to punish the wrongdoer in an attempt to deter others from similar actions. Penalties for violations of criminal statutes consist of fines and/or imprisonment—and, in some cases, death. We will discuss the differences between civil and criminal law in greater detail in Chapter 6.

ON THE WEB
The Library of Congress offers extensive information on national and international law at
http://www.loc.gov.

NATIONAL AND INTERNATIONAL LAW

Although the focus of this book is U.S. business law, increasingly businesspersons in this country engage in transactions that extend beyond our national borders. In these situations, the laws of other nations or the laws governing relationships among nations may come into play. For this reason, those who pursue a career in business today should have an understanding of the global legal environment.

NATIONAL LAW
Law that pertains to a particular nation (as opposed to international law).

National Law The law of a particular nation, such as the United States or Sweden, is **national law.** National law, of course, varies from country to country, because each country's law reflects the interests, customs, activities, and values that are unique to that nation's culture. Even though the laws and legal systems of various countries differ substantially, broad similarities do exist.

Basically, there are two legal systems in today's world. One of these systems is the common law system of England and the United States, which we have already discussed. The other system is based on Roman civil law, or "code law." The term *civil law,* as used here, refers not to civil as opposed to criminal law but to codified law—an ordered grouping of legal principles enacted into law by a legislature or governing body. In a **civil law system,** the primary source of law is a statutory code, and case precedents are not judicially binding, as they normally are in a common law system. Although judges in a civil law system commonly refer to previous decisions as sources of legal guidance, they are not bound by precedent; in other words, the doctrine of *stare decisis* does not apply.

CIVIL LAW SYSTEM
A system of law derived from that of the Roman Empire and based on a code rather than case law; the predominant system of law in the nations of continental Europe and the nations that were once their colonies. In the United States, Louisiana, because of its historical ties to France, has in part a civil law system.

Exhibit 1–2 lists the countries that today follow either the common law system or the civil law system. Generally, those countries that were once colonies of Great Britain retained their English common law heritage after they achieved their independence. Similarly, the civil law system, which is followed in most of the continental European countries, was retained in the Latin American, African, and Asian countries that were once colonies of those nations. Japan and South Africa also have civil law systems, and ingredients of the civil law system are found in the Islamic courts of predominantly Muslim countries. In the United States, the state of Louisiana, because of its historical ties to France, has in part a civil law system. The legal systems of Puerto Rico, Québec, and Scotland are similarly characterized as having elements of the civil law system.

INTERNATIONAL LAW
The law that governs relations among nations. National laws, customs, treaties, and international conferences and organizations are generally considered to be the most important sources of international law.

International Law In contrast to national law, international law applies to more than one nation. **International law** can be defined as a body of written and unwritten laws observed by independent nations and governing the acts of individuals as well as governments. International law is an intermingling of rules and constraints derived from

EXHIBIT 1–2 THE LEGAL SYSTEMS OF NATIONS

CIVIL LAW		COMMON LAW	
Argentina	Indonesia	Australia	Nigeria
Austria	Iran	Bangladesh	Singapore
Brazil	Italy	Canada	United Kingdom
Chile	Japan	Ghana	United States
China	Mexico	India	Zambia
Egypt	Poland	Israel	
Finland	South Korea	Jamaica	
France	Sweden	Kenya	
Germany	Tunisia	Malaysia	
Greece	Venezuela	New Zealand	

a variety of sources, including the laws of individual nations, the customs that have evolved among nations in their relations with one another, and treaties and international organizations. In essence, international law is the result of centuries-old attempts to reconcile the traditional need of each nation to be the final authority over its own affairs with the desire of nations to benefit economically from trade and harmonious relations with one another.

The key difference between national law and international law is that national law can be enforced by government authorities. If a nation violates an international law, however, the most that other countries or international organizations can do (if persuasive tactics fail) is to resort to coercive actions against the violating nation. Coercive actions range from the severance of diplomatic relations and boycotts to, at the last resort, war. We examine the laws governing international business transactions in later chapters (including parts of Chapters 14 through 18, which cover contracts for the sale of goods, and all of Chapter 39).

CYBERLAW

CYBERLAW
An informal term used to refer to all laws governing electronic communications and transactions, particularly those conducted via the Internet.

"Science and technology revolutionize our lives, but memory, tradition, and myth frame our response."
ARTHUR SCHLESINGER, JR., 1917–
(American historian)

Increasingly, traditional laws are being applied to new legal issues stemming from the use of the Internet to conduct business transactions. Additionally, new laws are being created to deal specifically with such issues. Frequently, people use the term **cyberlaw** to refer to the emerging body of law (consisting of court decisions, newly enacted or amended statutes, and so on) that governs cyberspace transactions. Note that cyberlaw is not really a classification of law; rather, it is an informal term used to describe how traditional classifications of law, such as civil law and criminal law, are being applied to online activities.

Realize, too, that cyberlaw is not a new *type* of law. For the most part, it consists of traditional legal principles that have been modified and adapted to fit situations that are unique to the online world. Of course, in some areas new statutes have been enacted, at both the federal and state levels, to cover specific types of problems stemming from online communications.

Anyone preparing to enter today's business world will find it useful to know how old and new laws are being applied to activities conducted online, such as advertising, contracting, banking, filing documents with the courts or government agencies, employment relations, and a variety of other transactions. For that reason, many sections in this text are devoted to this topic. Special features throughout the book also focus on how the law is evolving to govern specific legal issues that continue to emerge in the online environment.

APPLICATION Law and the Businessperson . . .

How to Choose and Use a Lawyer*

If you are contemplating a career in the business world, sooner or later you will probably face the question, "Do I need a lawyer?" The answer to this question will likely be "Yes," at least at some time during your career. Even individuals who have gone to law school and later entered a business often hire an outside lawyer to help them with their legal problems. Today, it is virtually impossible for nonexperts to keep up with the myriad rules and regulations that govern the conduct of business in the United States. It is also increasingly possible for businesspersons to incur penalties for violating laws or regulations of which they are totally unaware.

Although lawyers may seem expensive—anywhere from $75 to $500 per hour—the cautious businessperson will make sure that she or he is not "penny wise and pound foolish." The consultation fee paid to an attorney may be a drop in the bucket compared with the potential liability facing a businessperson.

SELECTING AN ATTORNEY

In selecting an attorney, you can ask friends, relatives, or business associates to recommend someone. Alternatively, you can call the local or state bar association to obtain the names of several lawyers. West Group has an online database containing biographies of attorneys throughout the country, listed by area of specialty and by state. You can find attorneys in your area by accessing West's Legal Directory online at **http://directory.findlaw.com**. Some legal aid programs have staff attorneys, and others may refer you to volunteers. You might also investigate legal clinics and prepaid legal service plans.

At your initial meeting with the attorney you have selected, you should have a written list of your questions in hand, and perhaps a summary of the problem for which you need legal advice. Attach to your list copies of any relevant documents that you can leave with the lawyer. While at the meeting, ask about legal fees, discuss the legal problem you are facing (remember that virtually everything you say to your attorney is protected by the attorney-client privilege of confidentiality), and clarify the scope of what you want the lawyer to do for you.

EVALUATING YOUR ATTORNEY

Ask yourself the following questions after your first meeting: Did the attorney seem knowledgeable about what is needed to address your concerns? Did he or she seem willing to investigate the law and the facts further to ensure an accurate understanding of your legal situation? Did you communicate well with each other? Did the attorney perceive what issues were of foremost concern to you and address those issues to your satisfaction? Did the attorney "speak your language" when explaining the legal implications of those issues?

Continue to evaluate the relationship over time. For many businesspersons, relationships with attorneys last for decades. Make sure that your relationship with your attorney will be a fruitful one.

CHECKLIST FOR CHOOSING AND USING A LAWYER

1. If you ever think that you need legal advice, you probably do.
2. When choosing an attorney, try to get recommendations from friends, relatives, or business associates who have had long-standing relationships with their attorneys. If that fails, check with your local or state bar association or check West Group's online directory.
3. When you initially consult with an attorney, bring a written list of questions to which you want answers, perhaps a summary of your problem, and copies of relevant documents.
4. Do not hesitate to ask about the legal fees that your attorney will charge, and be sure to clarify the scope of the work to be undertaken by the attorney. Ask whatever questions are necessary to ensure that you understand what your legal options are. Do not worry about appearing stupid.

*With appreciation to James D. Van Tassel at Mission College, California, for his helpful suggestions on this topic.

Key Terms

adjudicate 13
administrative agency 12
administrative law 12
administrative law judge (ALJ) 13
administrative process 13
binding authority 5
case law 14
citation 11
civil law 15
civil law system 16
common law 5
constitutional law 9
criminal law 16
cyberlaw 17
defendant 7
enabling legislation 13
equitable principles and maxims 8
executive agency 12
historical school 4
independent regulatory agency 12
international law 16
jurisprudence 3
law 3
legal positivism 4
legal realism 4
national law 16
natural law 3
persuasive authority 7
plaintiff 7
positive law 3
precedent 5
primary source of law 8
procedural law 15
remedy 7
rulemaking 13
secondary source of law 8
sociological school 4
stare decisis 5
statute of limitations 9
statutory law 10
substantive law 15

Chapter Summary The Legal Environment

The Nature of Law (See pages 3–4.)	Law can be defined as a body of rules of conduct with legal force and effect, prescribed by the controlling authority (the government) of a society. Important schools of legal thought, or legal philosophies, include the following: 1. *Natural law tradition*—One of the oldest and most significant schools of legal thought. Those who believe in natural law hold that there is a universal law applicable to all human beings and that this law is of a higher order than positive, or conventional, law. 2. *Legal positivism*—A school of legal thought centered on the assumption that there is no law higher than the laws created by the government. Laws must be obeyed, even if they are unjust, to prevent anarchy. 3. *The historical school*—A school of legal thought that stresses the evolutionary nature of law and that looks to doctrines that have withstood the passage of time for guidance in shaping present laws. 4. *Legal realism*—A school of legal thought, popular during the 1920s and 1930s, that left a lasting imprint on American jurisprudence. Legal realists generally advocated a less abstract and more realistic approach to the law, an approach that would take into account customary practices and the circumstances in which transactions take place. Legal realism strongly influenced the growth of the *sociological school* of jurisprudence, which views law as a tool for promoting social justice.
The Common Law Tradition (See pages 4–8.)	1. *Common law*—Law that originated in medieval England with the creation of the king's courts, or *curiae regis,* and the development of a body of rules that were common to (or applied throughout) the land. 2. *Stare decisis*—A doctrine under which judges "stand on decided cases"—or follow the rule of precedent—in deciding cases. *Stare decisis* is the cornerstone of the common law tradition. 3. *Remedies*— a. Remedies at law—Money or something else of value.

(continued)

Chapter Summary The Legal Environment—continued

The Common Law Tradition—continued	b. Remedies in equity—Remedies that are granted when the remedies at law are unavailable or inadequate. Equitable remedies include specific performance, an injunction, and contract rescission (cancellation).
Sources of American Law (See pages 8–15.)	1. *Constitutional law*—The law as expressed in the U.S. Constitution and the various state constitutions. The U.S. Constitution is the supreme law of the land. State constitutions are supreme within state borders to the extent that they do not violate the U.S. Constitution or a federal law. 2. *Statutory law*—Laws or ordinances created by federal, state, and local legislatures and governing bodies. None of these laws can violate the U.S. Constitution or the relevant state constitutions. Uniform laws, when adopted by a state legislature, become statutory law in that state. 3. *Administrative law*—The rules, orders, and decisions of federal or state government administrative agencies. Federal administrative agencies are created by enabling legislation enacted by the U.S. Congress. Agency functions include rulemaking, investigation and enforcement, and adjudication. 4. *Case law and common law doctrines*—Judge-made law, including interpretations of constitutional provisions, of statutes enacted by legislatures, and of regulations created by administrative agencies. The common law—the doctrines and principles embodied in case law—governs all areas not covered by statutory law (or agency regulations issued to implement various statutes).
Classifications of Law (See pages 15–17.)	The law may be broken down according to several classification systems, such as substantive or procedural law, federal or state law, and private or public law. Two broad classifications are civil and criminal law, and national and international law. Cyberlaw is not really a classification of law but a term that is applied to the growing body of case law and statutory law that applies to Internet transactions.

For Review

① What is the common law tradition?

② What is a precedent? When might a court depart from precedent?

③ What is the difference between remedies at law and remedies in equity?

④ What is the Uniform Commercial Code?

⑤ What are some important differences between civil law and criminal law?

Questions and Case Problems

1–1. Philosophy of Law. After World War II ended in 1945, an international tribunal of judges convened at Nuremberg, Germany. The judges convicted several Nazi war criminals of "crimes against humanity." Assuming that the Nazis who were convicted had not disobeyed any law of their country and had merely been following their government's (Hitler's) orders, what law had they violated? Explain.

1–2. Legal Systems. What are the key differences between a common law system and a civil law system? Why do some countries have common law systems and others have civil law systems?

1–3. Reading Citations. Assume that you want to read the entire court opinion in the case of *Thompson v. Altheimer & Gray,* 248 F.3d 621 (7th Cir. 2001). The case deals with whether an attorney may dismiss "for cause" a prospective juror in a case involving racial discrimination. Read the section entitled "Finding Case Law" in the appendix that follows this chapter, and then explain specifically where you would find the court's opinion.

1–4. Sources of American Law. This chapter discussed a number of sources of American law. Which source of law takes priority in the following situations, and why?

(a) A federal statute conflicts with the U.S. Constitution.
(b) A federal statute conflicts with a state constitution.
(c) A state statute conflicts with the common law of that state.
(d) A state constitutional amendment conflicts with the U.S. Constitution.
(e) A federal administrative regulation conflicts with a state constitution.

1–5. *Stare Decisis.* In the text of this chapter, we stated that the doctrine of *stare decisis* "became a cornerstone of the English and American judicial systems." What does *stare decisis* mean, and why has this doctrine been so fundamental to the development of our legal tradition?

1–6. Court Opinions. Read through the subsection entitled "Case Titles and Terminology" in the appendix following this chapter. What is the difference between a concurring opinion and a majority opinion? Between a concurring opinion and a dissenting opinion? Why do judges and justices write concurring and dissenting opinions, given that these opinions will not affect the outcome of the case at hand, which has already been decided by majority vote?

1–7. Statute of Limitations. The equitable principle "Equity aids the vigilant, not those who rest on their rights" means that courts will not aid those who do not pursue a cause of action while the evidence is fresh and the true facts surrounding the issue can be discovered. State statutes of limitations are based on this principle. Under Article 2 of the Uniform Commercial Code, which has been adopted by virtually all of the states, the statute of limitations governing sales contracts states that parties must bring an action for the breach of a sales contract within four years, although the parties (the seller and the buyer) can reduce this period by agreement to only one year. Which party (the seller or the buyer) would benefit more by a one-year period, and which would benefit more by a four-year period? Discuss.

1–8. Binding versus Persuasive Authority. A county court in Illinois is deciding a case involving an issue that has never been addressed before in that state's courts. The Iowa Supreme Court, however, recently decided a case involving a very similar fact pattern. Is the Illinois court obligated to follow the Iowa Supreme Court's decision on the issue? If the United States Supreme Court had decided a similar case, would that decision be binding on the Illinois court? Explain.

TEST YOUR KNOWLEDGE—ANSWER ON THE WEB*

1–9. Arthur Rabe is suing Xavier Sanchez for breaching a contract in which Sanchez promised to sell Rabe a Van Gogh painting for $150,000.

(a) In this lawsuit, who is the plaintiff and who is the defendant?
(b) If Rabe wants Sanchez to perform the contract as promised, what remedy should Rabe seek?
(c) Suppose that Rabe wants to cancel the contract because Sanchez fraudulently misrepresented the painting as an original Van Gogh when in fact it is a copy. In this situation, what remedy should Rabe seek?
(d) Will the remedy Rabe seeks in either situation be a remedy at law or a remedy in equity?
(e) Suppose that the court finds in Rabe's favor and grants one of these remedies. Sanchez then appeals the decision to a higher court. Read through the subsection entitled "Appellants and Appellees" in the appendix following this chapter. On appeal, which party in the Rabe-Sanchez case will be the appellant (or petitioner), and which party will be the appellee (or respondent)?

*To find the answer to this problem and the remaining "Test Your Knowledge" problems in this book, go to this text's Web site at **http://blt.westbuslaw.com** and select "Interactive Study Center."

A QUESTION OF ETHICS AND SOCIAL RESPONSIBILITY

1–10. On July 5, 1884, Dudley, Stephens, and Brooks—"all able-bodied English seamen"—and an English teen-age boy were cast adrift in a lifeboat following a storm at sea. They had no water with them in the boat, and all they had for sustenance were two one-pound tins of turnips. On July 24, Dudley proposed that one of the four in the lifeboat be sacrificed to save the others. Stephens agreed with Dudley, but Brooks refused to consent—and the boy was never asked for his opinion. On July 25, Dudley killed the boy, and the three men then fed on the boy's body and blood. Four days later, the men were rescued by a passing vessel. They were taken to England and tried for the murder of the boy. If the men had not fed on the boy's body, they would probably have died of starvation within the four-day period. The boy, who was in a much weaker condition, would likely have died before the rest. [*Regina v. Dudley and Stephens,* 14 Q.B.D. (Queen's Bench Division, England) 273 (1884)]

1. The basic question in this case is whether the survivors should be subject to penalties under English criminal law, given the men's unusual circumstances. You be the judge, and decide the issue. Give the reasons for your decisions.
2. Should judges ever have the power to look beyond the written "letter of the law" in making their decisions? Why or why not?

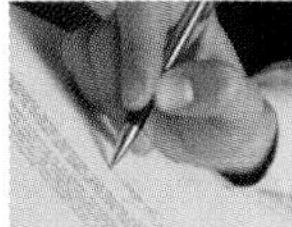

FOR CRITICAL ANALYSIS

1–11. Courts of equity tend to follow general rules or maxims rather than common law precedents, as courts of law do. Some of these maxims were listed in this chapter's *Landmark in the Law* on page 9. Why would equity courts give credence to such general maxims rather than to a hard-and-fast body of law?

Internet Exercises

Go to the *Business Law Today* home page at **http://blt.westbuslaw.com**. Select "Interactive Study Center" and then click on "Chapter 1." There you will find the following Internet research exercise that you can perform to learn more about legal sources on the Internet:

Activity 1–1: Internet Sources of Law

Before the Test

Go to the *Business Law Today* home page at **http://blt.westbuslaw.com**. Click on "Interactive Quizzes." You will find at least twenty interactive questions relating to this chapter.

CHAPTER 1

Appendix

Finding and Analyzing the Law

ON THE WEB
The Bluebook: A Uniform System of Citation offers detailed information on the format for citations to legal sources. The "Bluebook" is now online at **http://www.legalbluebook.com**.

The statutes, agency regulations, and case law referred to in this text establish the rights and duties of businesspersons engaged in various types of activities. The cases presented in the following chapters provide you with concise, real-life illustrations of how the courts interpret and apply these laws. Because of the importance of knowing how to find statutory, administrative, and case law, this appendix offers a brief introduction to how these laws are published and to the legal "shorthand" employed in referencing these legal sources.

Finding Statutory and Administrative Law

When Congress passes laws, they are collected in a publication titled *United States Statutes at Large*. When state legislatures pass laws, they are collected in similar state publications. Most frequently, however, laws are referred to in their codified form—that is, the form in which they appear in the federal and state codes.

ON THE WEB
You can search the *United States Code* online at **http://www4.law.cornell.edu/uscode**.

In these codes, laws are compiled by subject. The *United States Code* (U.S.C.) arranges all existing federal laws of a public and permanent nature by subject. Each of the fifty subjects into which the U.S.C. arranges the laws is given a title and a title number. For example, laws relating to commerce and trade are collected in Title 15, which is titled "Commerce and Trade." Titles are subdivided by sections. A citation to the U.S.C. includes title and section numbers. Thus, a reference to "15 U.S.C. Section 1" means that the statute can be found in Section 1 of Title 15. ("Section" may also be designated by the symbol §, and "Sections" by §§.)

Sometimes a citation includes the abbreviation *et seq.*—as in "15 U.S.C. Sections 1 *et seq.*" The term is an abbreviated form of *et sequitur*, which in Latin means "and the following"; when used in a citation, it refers to sections that concern the same subject as the numbered section and follow it in sequence.

State codes follow the U.S.C. pattern of arranging law by subject. The state codes may be called codes, revisions, compilations, consolidations, general statutes, or statutes, depending on the preference of the states. In some codes, subjects are designated by number. In others, they are designated by name. For example, "13 Pennsylvania Consolidated Statutes Section 1101" means that the statute can be found in Title 13, Section 1101, of the Pennsylvania code. "California Commercial Code Section 1101" means that the statute can be found under the subject heading "Commercial Code" of the California code in Section 1101. Abbreviations may be used. For example, "13 Pennsylvania Consolidated Statutes Section 1101" may be abbreviated "13 Pa. C.S. § 1101," and "California Commercial Code Section 1101" may be abbreviated "Cal. Com. Code § 1101."

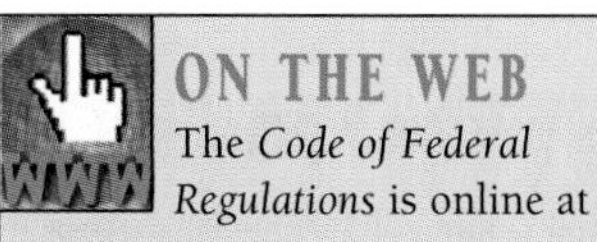

ON THE WEB The *Code of Federal Regulations* is online at **http://www.access.gpo.gov/nara/cfrindex.html**.

Rules and regulations adopted by federal administrative agencies are compiled in the *Code of Federal Regulations* (C.F.R.). Like the U.S.C., the C.F.R. is divided into fifty titles. Rules within each title are assigned section numbers. A full citation to the C.F.R. includes title and section numbers. For example, a reference to "17 C.F.R. Section 230.504" means that the rule can be found in Section 230.504 of Title 17.

Commercial publications of these laws and regulations are available and are widely used. For example, West Group publishes the *United States Code Annotated* (U.S.C.A.). The U.S.C.A. contains the complete text of laws included in the U.S.C., as well as notes of court decisions that interpret and apply specific sections of the statutes, plus the text of presidential proclamations and executive orders. The U.S.C.A. also includes research aids, such as cross-references to related statutes, historical notes, and library references. A citation to the U.S.C.A. is similar to a citation to the U.S.C.: "15 U.S.C.A. Section 1."

Finding Case Law

Before discussing the case reporting system, we need to look briefly at the court system (which will be discussed in detail in Chapter 3). There are two types of courts in the United States, federal courts and state courts. Both the federal and state court systems consist of several levels, or tiers, of courts. *Trial courts,* in which evidence is presented and testimony given, are on the bottom tier (which also includes lower courts handling specialized issues). Decisions from a trial court can be appealed to a higher court, which commonly would be an intermediate *court of appeals,* or an *appellate court.* Decisions from these intermediate courts of appeals may be appealed to an even higher court, such as a state supreme court or the United States Supreme Court.

STATE COURT DECISIONS

ON THE WEB You can find information on state courts, including whether they publish any of their decisions online, at Villanova Law School's State Court Locator. Go to **http://vls.law.vill.edu/Locator/statecourt**.

Most state trial court decisions are not published. Except in New York and a few other states that publish selected opinions of their trial courts, decisions from state trial courts are merely filed in the office of the clerk of the court, where the decisions are available for public inspection. Written decisions of the appellate, or reviewing, courts, however, are published and distributed. As you will note, most of the state court cases presented in this book are from state appellate courts. The reported appellate decisions are published in volumes called *reports* or *reporters,* which are numbered consecutively. State appellate court decisions are found in the state reporters of that particular state.

Additionally, state court opinions appear in regional units of the *National Reporter System,* published by West Group. Most lawyers and libraries have the West reporters because they report cases more quickly and are distributed more widely than the state-published reports. In fact, many states have eliminated their own reporters in favor of West's National Reporter System. The National Reporter System divides the states into the following geographic areas: *Atlantic* (A. or A.2d), *South Eastern* (S.E. or S.E.2d), *South Western* (S.W., S.W.2d, or S.W.3d), *North Western* (N.W. or N.W.2d), *North Eastern* (N.E. or N.E.2d), *Southern* (So. or So.2d), and *Pacific* (P., P.2d, or P.3d). (The *2d* and *3d* in the abbreviations refer to *Second Series* and *Third Series,* respectively.) The states included in each of these regional divisions are indicated in Exhibit 1A–1, which illustrates West's National Reporter System.

EXHIBIT 1A–1 NATIONAL REPORTER SYSTEM—REGIONAL/FEDERAL

Regional Reporters	Coverage Beginning	Coverage
Atlantic Reporter (A. or A.2d)	1885	Connecticut, Delaware, Maine, Maryland, New Hampshire, New Jersey, Pennsylvania, Rhode Island, Vermont, and District of Columbia.
North Eastern Reporter (N.E. or N.E.2d)	1885	Illinois, Indiana, Massachusetts, New York, and Ohio.
North Western Reporter (N.W. or N.W.2d)	1879	Iowa, Michigan, Minnesota, Nebraska, North Dakota, South Dakota, and Wisconsin.
Pacific Reporter (P., P.2d, or P.3d)	1883	Alaska, Arizona, California, Colorado, Hawaii, Idaho, Kansas, Montana, Nevada, New Mexico, Oklahoma, Oregon, Utah, Washington, and Wyoming.
South Eastern Reporter (S.E. or S.E.2d)	1887	Georgia, North Carolina, South Carolina, Virginia, and West Virginia.
South Western Reporter (S.W., S.W.2d, or S.W.3d)	1886	Arkansas, Kentucky, Missouri, Tennessee, and Texas.
Southern Reporter (So. or So.2d)	1887	Alabama, Florida, Louisiana, and Mississippi.
Federal Reporters		
Federal Reporter (F., F.2d, or F.3d)	1880	U.S. Circuit Courts from 1880 to 1912; U.S. Commerce Court from 1911 to 1913; U.S. District Courts from 1880 to 1932; U.S. Court of Claims (now called U.S. Court of Federal Claims) from 1929 to 1932 and since 1960; U.S. Courts of Appeals since 1891; U.S. Court of Customs and Patent Appeals since 1929; U.S. Emergency Court of Appeals since 1943.
Federal Supplement (F.Supp. or F.Supp.2d)	1932	U.S. Court of Claims from 1932 to 1960; U.S. District Courts since 1932; and U.S. Customs Court since 1956.
Federal Rules Decisions (F.R.D.)	1939	U.S. District Courts involving the Federal Rules of Civil Procedure since 1939 and Federal Rules of Criminal Procedure since 1946.
Supreme Court Reporter (S.Ct.)	1882	U.S. Supreme Court since the October term of 1882.
Bankruptcy Reporter (Bankr.)	1980	Bankruptcy decisions of U.S. Bankruptcy Courts, U.S. District Courts, U.S. Courts of Appeals, and U.S. Supreme Court.
Military Justice Reporter (M.J.)	1978	U.S. Court of Military Appeals and Courts of Military Review for the Army, Navy, Air Force, and Coast Guard.

After appellate decisions have been published, they are normally referred to (cited) by the name of the case; the volume, name, and page number of the state's official reporter (if different from West's National Reporter System); the volume, unit, and page number of the *National Reporter;* and the volume, name, and page number of any other selected reporter. This information is included in the *citation.* (Citing a reporter by volume number, name, and page number, in that order, is common to all citations.) When more than one reporter is cited for the same case, each reference is called a *parallel citation.* For example, consider the following case: *Tiberino v. Spokane County,* 103 Wash.App. 680, 13 P.3d 1104 (2001). We see that the opinion in this case may be found in Volume 103 of the official *Washington Appellate Reports,* on page 680. The parallel citation is to Volume 13 of the *Pacific Reporter, Third Series,* page 1104. In presenting appellate opinions in this text, in addition to the reporter, we give the name of the court hearing the case and the year of the court's decision.

A few states—including those with intermediate appellate courts, such as California, Illinois, and New York—have more than one reporter for opinions issued by their courts. Sample citations from these courts, as well as others, are listed and explained in Exhibit 1A–2 beginning on the next page.

FEDERAL COURT DECISIONS

ON THE WEB
To find links to Supreme Court opinions and opinions issued by the federal appellate courts, a good starting point is FindLaw's guide at
http://guide.lp.findlaw.com/10fedgov/judicial.

Federal district court decisions are published unofficially in West's *Federal Supplement* (F.Supp. or F.Supp.2d), and opinions from the circuit courts of appeals (federal reviewing courts) are reported unofficially in West's *Federal Reporter* (F., F.2d, or F.3d). Cases concerning federal bankruptcy law are published unofficially in West's *Bankruptcy Reporter* (Bankr.). The official edition of United States Supreme Court decisions is the *United States Reports* (U.S.), which is published by the federal government. Unofficial editions of Supreme Court cases include West's *Supreme Court Reporter* (S.Ct.) and the *Lawyers' Edition of the Supreme Court Reports* (L.Ed. or L.Ed.2d). Sample citations for federal court decisions are also listed and explained in Exhibit 1A–2.

UNPUBLISHED OPINIONS

Many court opinions that are not yet published or that are not intended for publication can be accessed through Westlaw® (abbreviated in citations as "WL"), an online legal database maintained by West Group. When no citation to a published reporter is available for cases cited in this text, we give the WL citation (see Exhibit 1A–2 for an example).

OLD CASE LAW

On a few occasions, this text cites opinions from old, classic cases dating to the nineteenth century or earlier; some of these are from the English courts. The citations to these cases appear not to conform to the descriptions given above, because the reporters in which they were published have since been replaced.

Reading and Understanding Case Law

The cases in this text have been condensed from the full text of the courts' opinions and paraphrased by the authors. For those wishing to review court cases for future

EXHIBIT 1A–2 HOW TO READ CITATIONS

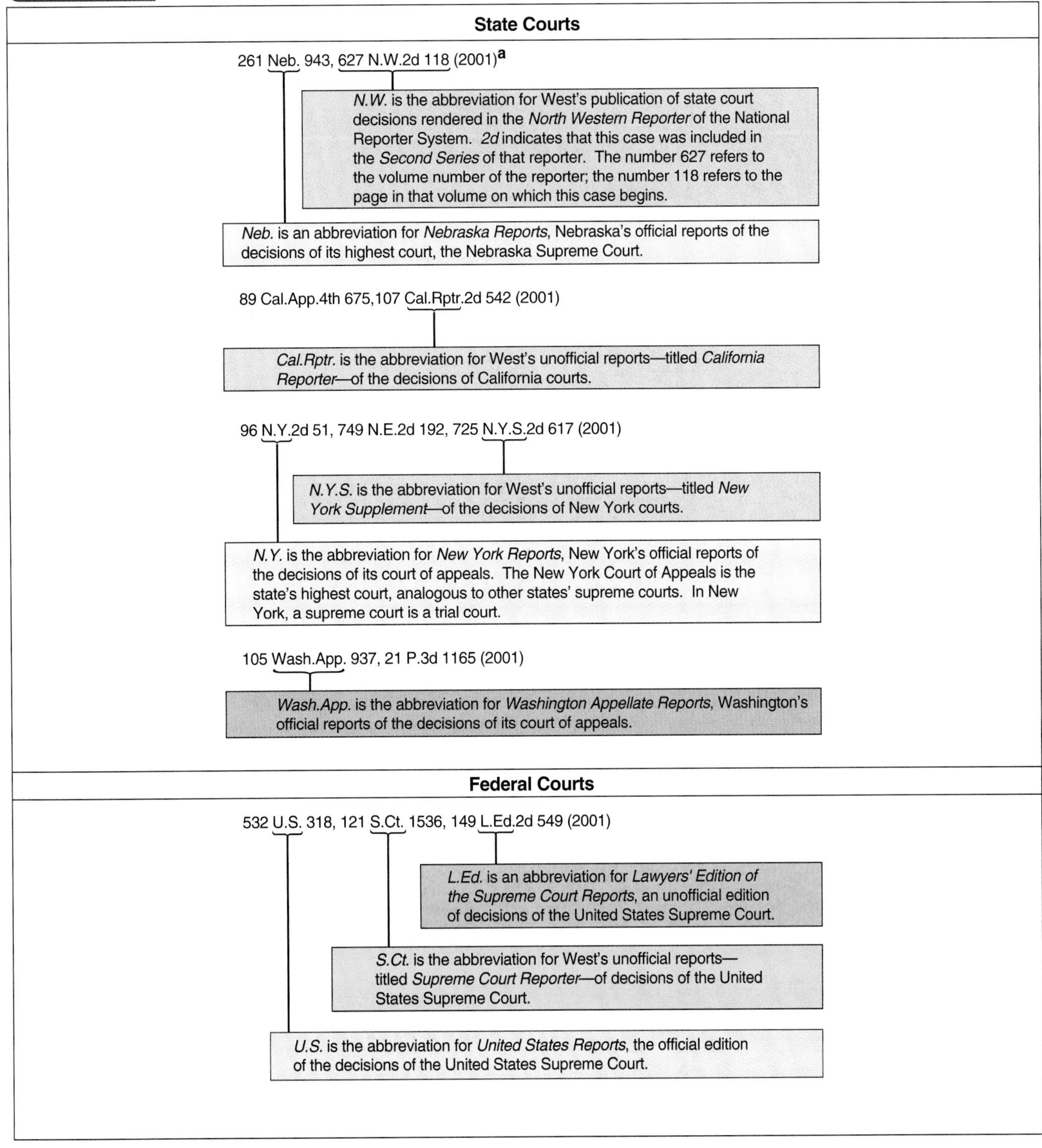

a. The case names have been deleted from these citations to emphasize the publications. It should be kept in mind, however, that the name of a case is as important as the specific page numbers in the volumes in which it is found. If a citation is incorrect, the correct citation may be found in a publication's index of case names. In addition to providing a check on error in citations, the date of a case is important because the value of a recent case as an authority is likely to be greater than that of earlier cases.

EXHIBIT 1A–2 HOW TO READ CITATIONS—CONTINUED

Federal Courts (continued)

252 F.3d 712 (5th Cir. 2001)

5th Cir. is an abbreviation denoting that this case was decided in the United States Court of Appeals for the Fifth Circuit.

990 F.Supp. 657 (E.D.Ark. 1998)

E.D.Ark. is an abbreviation indicating that the United States District Court for the Eastern District of Arkansas decided this case.

English Courts

9 Exch. 341, 156 Eng.Rep. 145 (1854)

Eng.Rep. is an abbreviation for *English Reports, Full Reprint,* a series of reports containing selected decisions made in English courts between 1378 and 1865.

Exch. is an abbreviation for *English Exchequer Reports*, which included the original reports of cases decided in England's Court of Exchequer.

Statutory and Other Citations

18 U.S.C. Section 1961(1)(A)

U.S.C. denotes *United States Code*, the codification of *United States Statutes at Large*. The number 18 refers to the statute's U.S.C. title number and 1961 to its section number within that title. The number 1 refers to a subsection within the section and the letter A to a subdivision within the subsection.

UCC 2–206(1)(b)

UCC is an abbreviation for *Uniform Commercial Code*. The first number 2 is a reference to an article of the UCC and 206 to a section within that article. The number 1 refers to a subsection within the section and the letter b to a subdivision within the subsection.

Restatement (Second) of Torts, Section 568

Restatement (Second) of Torts refers to the second edition of the American Law Institute's *Restatement of the Law of Torts.* The number 568 refers to a specific section.

17 C.F.R. Section 230.505

C.F.R. is an abbreviation for *Code of Federal Regulations*, a compilation of federal administrative regulations. The number 17 designates the regulation's title number, and 230.505 designates a specific section within that title.

EXHIBIT 1A–2 HOW TO READ CITATIONS—CONTINUED

Westlaw® Citations

2001 WL 12345

WL is an abbreviation for Westlaw®. The number 2001 is the year of the document that can be found with this citation in the Westlaw® database. The number 12345 is a number assigned to a specific document. A higher number indicates that a document was added to the Westlaw® database later in the year.

Uniform Resource Locators[b]

www.westlaw.com

The suffix *com* is the top-level domain (TLD) for this Web site. The TLD *com* is an abbreviation for "commercial," which usually means that a for-profit entity hosts (maintains) this Web site.

westlaw is the host name—the part of the domain name selected by the organization that registered the name. In this case, West Group registered the name. This Internet site is the Westlaw database on the Web.

www is an abbreviation for "World Wide Web." The Web is a system of Internet servers[c] that support documents formatted in *HTML* (hypertext markup language). HTML supports links to text, graphics, and audio and video files.

www.uscourts.gov

This is "The Federal Judiciary Home Page." The host is the Administrative Office of the U.S. Courts. The TLD *gov* is an abbreviation for "government." This Web site includes information and links from, and about, the federal courts.

www.law.cornell.edu/index.html

This part of an URL points to a Web page or file at a specific location within the host's domain. This page, at this Web site, is a menu with links to documents within the domain and to other Internet resources.

This is the host name for a Web site that contains the Internet publications of the Legal Information Institute (LII), which is a part of Cornell Law School. The LII site includes a variety of legal materials and links to other legal resources on the Internet. The TLD *edu* is an abbreviation for "educational institution" (a school or a university).

www.ipl.org.ref/RR

RR is an abbreviation for this Web site's "Ready Reference Collection," which contains links to a variety of Internet resources.

ref is an abbreviation for "Internet Public Library Reference Center," which is a map of the topics into which the links at this Web site have been categorized.

ipl is an abbreviation for Internet Public Library, which is an online service that provides reference resources and links to other information services on the Web. The IPL is supported chiefly by the School of Information at the University of Michigan. The TLD *org* is an abbreviation for "organization (usually nonprofit)."

b. The basic form for a URL is "service://hostname/path." The Internet service for all of the URLs in this text is *http* (hypertext transfer protocol). Most Web browsers will add this prefix automatically when a user enters a host name or a hostname/path.

c. A *server* is hardware that manages the resources on a network. For example, a network server is a computer that manages the traffic on the network, and a print server is a computer that manages one or more printers.

research projects or to gain additional legal information, the following sections will provide useful insights into how to read and understand case law.

CASE TITLES AND TERMINOLOGY

The title of a case, such as *Adams v. Jones,* indicates the names of the parties to the lawsuit. The *v.* in the case title stands for *versus,* which means "against." In the trial court, Adams was the plaintiff—the person who filed the suit. Jones was the defendant. If the case is appealed, however, the appellate court will sometimes place the name of the party appealing the decision first, so the case may be called *Jones v. Adams.* Because some reviewing courts retain the trial court order of names, it is often impossible to distinguish the plaintiff from the defendant in the title of a reported appellate court decision. You must carefully read the facts of each case to identify the parties.

The following terms and phrases are frequently encountered in court opinions and legal publications. Because it is important to understand what these terms and phrases mean, we define and discuss them here.

Plaintiffs and Defendants As mentioned in Chapter 1, the plaintiff in a lawsuit is the party that initiates the action. The defendant is the party against which a lawsuit is brought. Lawsuits frequently involve more than one plaintiff and/or defendant.

Appellants and Appellees The *appellant* is the party that appeals a case to another court or jurisdiction from the court or jurisdiction in which the case was originally brought. Sometimes, an appellant that appeals a judgment is referred to as the *petitioner.* The *appellee* is the party against which the appeal is taken. Sometimes, the appellee is referred to as the *respondent.*

Judges and Justices The terms *judge* and *justice* are usually synonymous and represent two designations given to judges in various courts. All members of the United States Supreme Court, for example, are referred to as justices. And justice is the formal title usually given to judges of appellate courts, although this is not always the case. In New York, a justice is a judge of the trial court (which is called the Supreme Court), and a member of the Court of Appeals (the state's highest court) is called a judge. The term *justice* is commonly abbreviated to J., and *justices* to JJ. A Supreme Court case might refer to Justice O'Connor as O'Connor, J., or to Chief Justice Rehnquist as Rehnquist, C.J.

Decisions and Opinions Most decisions reached by reviewing, or appellate, courts are explained in written *opinions.* The opinion contains the court's reasons for its decision, the rules of law that apply, and the judgment. When all judges or justices unanimously agree on an opinion, the opinion is written for the entire court and can be deemed a *unanimous opinion.* When there is not a unanimous opinion, a *majority opinion* is written, outlining the views of the majority of the judges or justices deciding the case.

Often, a judge or justice who feels strongly about making or emphasizing a point that was not made or emphasized in the unanimous or majority opinion will write a *concurring opinion.* That means the judge or justice agrees (concurs) with the judgment given in the unanimous or majority opinion but for different reasons. In other than unanimous opinions, a *dissenting opinion* is usually written by a judge or justice who does not agree with the majority. (See the *Extended Case Study* following Chapter 7 for an example of a dissenting opinion.) The dissenting opinion is important because it may form the basis of the arguments used years later in overruling the precedential majority opinion. Occasionally, a court issues a *per curiam* (Latin for "of the court") opinion, which does not indicate which judge or justice authored the opinion.

A Sample Court Case

Knowing how to read and analyze a court opinion is an essential step in undertaking accurate legal research. A further step involves "briefing" the case. Legal researchers routinely brief cases by summarizing and reducing the texts of the opinions to their essential elements. (For instructions on how to brief a case, go to Appendix A at the end of this text.) The cases contained within the chapters of this text have already been analyzed and briefed by the authors, and the essential aspects of each case are presented in a convenient format consisting of four basic sections: *Facts, Issue, Decision,* and *Reason,* as shown on the next page in Exhibit 1A–3, which has also been annotated to illustrate the kind of information that is contained in each section.

As you can see in Exhibit 1A–3, in addition to this basic format, we have included a special introductory section entitled *Historical and Social Setting.* We include introductory settings in many of the cases presented in this text. In these settings, the word *Social* in the title of the section may be replaced by *Economic* or *Political* or some other term, depending on the nature of the case and its background. In some instances, a *Company Profile* is included in place of the *Historical and Social Setting.* These profiles provide a background on one of the parties to the lawsuit. Each case is followed by a brief section entitled *For Critical Analysis,* which, as in Exhibit 1A–3, presents a question regarding some issue raised by the case.

The Supreme Court building in Washington, D.C. In what reporters are Supreme Court opinions published?

EXHIBIT 1A–3 A SAMPLE COURT CASE

1 **CLARK COUNTY SCHOOL DISTRICT V. BREEDEN**
2 Supreme Court of the United States, 2001.
3 532 U.S. 268,
121 S.Ct. 1508,
4 149 L.Ed.2d 509.
5 http://supct.law.cornell.edu/supct[a]

6 **HISTORICAL AND SOCIAL SETTING** *Title VII of the Civil Rights Act of 1964 forbids actions taken on the basis of gender that "discriminate against any individual with respect to his compensation, terms, conditions, or privileges of employment." This federal statute protects employees from sexual harassment in the workplace. The courts differ on what circumstances are sufficient to constitute sexual harassment, and the issue is a frequent subject of lawsuits.*

7 **FACTS** Ms. Breeden was an employee of Clark County School District, Nevada. As part of her job, she met with her male supervisor and another male employee to review the psychological evaluation reports of job applicants. The report for one of the applicants disclosed that the applicant had once commented to a co-worker, "I hear making love to you is like making love to the Grand Canyon." Breeden's supervisor read the comment aloud, looked at her, and said, "I don't know what that means." The other employee said, "Well, I'll tell you later," and both men chuckled. Breeden later complained about the comment to the employee, the employee's supervisor, and others. Breeden filed a suit in a federal district court against the school district, alleging sexual harassment. The court granted a summary judgment in favor of the school district. When the U.S. Court of Appeals for the Ninth Circuit reversed this ruling, the school district appealed to the United States Supreme Court.

8 **ISSUE** Does a single incident of offhand comments constitute sexual harassment?

9 **DECISION** No. The United States Supreme Court held that "no one could reasonably believe that [this] incident" constituted sexual harassment. The Court reversed the decision of the U.S. Court of Appeals for the Ninth Circuit and reinstated the summary judgment in the school district's favor.

10 **REASON** The Supreme Court explained that alleged harassment is actionable "only if it is so severe or pervasive as to alter the conditions of the victim's employment and create an abusive working environment." A court looks at all of the circumstances, including the "frequency of the discriminatory conduct; its severity; whether it is physically threatening or humiliating, or a mere offensive utterance; and whether it unreasonably interferes with an employee's work performance. * * * [S]imple teasing, offhand comments, and isolated incidents (unless extremely serious)" are not enough. In this case, "[t]he ordinary terms and conditions of respondent's job required her to review the sexually explicit statement in the course of screening job applicants. Her co-workers who participated in the hiring process were subject to the same requirement * * * . Her supervisor's comment, made at a meeting to review the application, that he did not know what the statement meant; her co-worker's responding comment; and the chuckling of both are at worst an isolated incident that cannot remotely be considered extremely serious."

11 **FOR CRITICAL ANALYSIS—Social Consideration** *What should employers do to prevent sexual harassment in the workplace?*

a. This URL will take you to a Web site maintained by the Legal Information Institute of Cornell Law School in Ithaca, New York. In the right-hand column, in the "For the 2000–2001 term:" section, click on "Decisions arrayed by date." When that page opens, click on "April 2001." In the result, scroll to the name of the case and click on it. On that page, click the appropriate link to access the opinion.

Review of Sample Court Case

① The name of the case is *Clark County School District v. Breeden*. The school district is the petitioner on appeal; Ms. Breeden is the respondent.

② The court deciding this case is the United States Supreme Court. The case was decided in 2001.

③ The first case citation is to Volume 532 of the official *United States Reports*, page 268.

④ The case citation includes parallel citations to Volume 121 of the *Supreme Court Reporter*, page 1508, and Volume 149 of the *Lawyers' Edition of the Supreme Court Reports, Second Series*, page 509.

⑤ The case citation includes a citation to a page on the Web where the case can be found. This page is among the online collection of documents of the Legal Information Institute, which is part of Cornell Law School in Ithaca, New York.

⑥ The *Historical and Social Setting* section outlines the background of the federal statute on which Breeden based her suit against the school district. In other cases, this section examines other aspects of the cultural, economic, environmental, ethical, international, political, social, or technological background.

⑦ The *Facts* section identifies the parties and describes the events leading up to this suit, the allegations made by Breeden in the initial suit, and (because this case is an appellate court decision) the lower courts' rulings and the party appealing those rulings. The appellant's contention on appeal is also sometimes included here.

⑧ The *Issue* section presents the central issue (or issues) to be decided by the court. In this case, the United States Supreme Court faced an issue raised by the school district on appeal. Cases frequently involve more than one issue.

⑨ The *Decision* section, as the term indicates, contains the court's decision on the issue or issues before the court. The decision reflects the opinion of the majority of the judges or justices hearing the case. Decisions by appellate courts are frequently phrased in reference to the lower court's decision. That is, the appellate court may "affirm" the lower court's ruling or "reverse" it. In this particular case, the United States Supreme Court reversed the judgment of the U.S. Court of Appeals for the Ninth Circuit and remanded the case (sent it back to the lower court) for the reinstatement of the federal district court's decision.

⑩ The *Reason* section indicates what relevant laws and judicial principles were applied in forming the particular conclusion arrived at in the case at bar ("before the court"). In this case, the relevant statute was Title VII of the Civil Rights Act of 1964, which prohibits employment discrimination on the basis of gender. The Court determined that alleged sexual harassment, to violate the statute, must consist of more than a single, isolated incident involving an offhand comment.

⑪ The *For Critical Analysis—Social Consideration* section raises a question to be considered in relation to the case just presented. Here the question involves a "social" consideration. In other cases presented in this text, the "consideration" may involve a cultural, economic, environmental, ethical, international, political, or technological consideration.

CHAPTER 2

Constitutional Law

"The United States Constitution has proved itself the most marvelously elastic compilation of rules of government ever written."

Franklin D. Roosevelt, 1882–1945
(Thirty-second president of the United States, 1933–1945)

CHAPTER CONTENTS

LEARNING OBJECTIVES

After reading this chapter, you should be able to answer the following questions:

① What is the basic structure of the U.S. government?

② What constitutional clause gives the federal government the power to regulate commercial activities among the various states?

③ What constitutional clause allows laws enacted by the federal government to take priority over conflicting state laws?

④ What is the Bill of Rights? What freedoms are guaranteed by the First Amendment?

⑤ Where in the Constitution can the due process clause be found?

The U.S. Constitution is brief.[1] It consists of only about seven thousand words, which is less than one-third of the number of words in the average state constitution. Perhaps its brevity explains why it has proved to be so "marvelously elastic," as Franklin Roosevelt pointed out in the above quotation, and why it has survived for over two hundred years—longer than any other written constitution in the world.

Laws that govern business have their origin in the lawmaking authority granted by this document, which is the supreme law in this country. As mentioned in Chapter 1, neither Congress nor any state may pass a law that conflicts with the Constitution.

In this chapter, we first look at some basic constitutional concepts and clauses and their significance for business. Then we examine how certain fundamental freedoms guaranteed by the Constitution affect businesspersons and the workplace.

1. See Appendix B for the full text of the U.S. Constitution.

ON THE WEB You can find a copy of the U.S. Constitution online, as well as information about the document, including its history, at **http://www.constitutioncenter.org**.

The Constitutional Powers of Government

Following the Revolutionary War, the states created a *confederal* form of government. The Articles of Confederation, which went into effect in 1781, established a confederation of independent states and a central (national) government that could exercise only very limited powers. The sovereign power, or supreme authority to govern, rested largely with the states. The limitation on the central government's powers reflected a basic tenet of the American Revolution—that a national government should not have unlimited power that could be used to tyrannize over the states.

The confederation, however, faced serious problems. For one thing, laws passed by the various states hampered national commerce and foreign trade by preventing the free movement of goods and services. By 1784, the nation faced a serious economic depression. Many who could not afford to pay their debts were thrown into "debtors' prisons." By 1786, a series of uprisings by farmer debtors were proving difficult to control because the national government did not have the authority to demand revenues (by levying taxes, for example) to support a militia.

Because of these problems, a national convention was called to amend the Articles of Confederation. Instead of amending the articles, however, the delegates to the convention, now called the Constitutional Convention, wrote the U.S. Constitution. This document, after its ratification by the states in 1789, became the basis for an entirely new form of government. Many of the provisions of the Constitution, including those discussed in the following pages, were shaped by the delegates' experiences during the confederal era (1781–1789).

A Federal Form of Government

The new government created by the Constitution reflected a series of compromises made by the convention delegates on various issues. Some delegates wanted sovereign power to remain with the states; others wanted the national government alone to exercise sovereign power. The end result was a compromise—a **federal form of government** in which the national government and the states *share* sovereign power.

FEDERAL FORM OF GOVERNMENT A system of government in which the states form a union and the sovereign power is divided between a central government and the member states.

The Constitution sets forth specific powers that can be exercised by the national government and provides that the national government has the implied power to undertake actions necessary to carry out its expressly designated powers. All other powers are "reserved" to the states. The broad language of the Constitution, though, has left much room for debate over the specific nature and scope of these powers. Generally, it has been the task of the courts to determine where the boundary line between state and national powers should lie—and that line changes over time. For most of the twentieth century, for example, the national government met little resistance from the courts when extending its regulatory authority over broad areas of social and economic life. Today, in contrast, the courts, and particularly the United States Supreme Court, are more willing to interpret the Constitution in such a way as to curb the national government's regulatory powers.

ON THE WEB To learn the founders' views on federalism, a good source is *The Federalist Papers*, a series of essays authored by Alexander Hamilton, James Madison, and John Jay. You can access these essays online at **http://www.law.emory.edu/FEDERAL**.

The Separation of Powers

To make it difficult for the national government to use its power arbitrarily, the Constitution divided the national government's powers among the three branches of government. The legislative branch makes the laws, the executive branch enforces the laws, and the judicial branch interprets the laws. Each branch performs a separate function, and no branch may exercise the authority of another branch.

INTERNATIONAL PERSPECTIVE

Should the EU Create a Federal Form of Government?

Today, the European Union (EU) consists of fifteen nations. Numerous other countries have applied for membership in the union. In 2000, the European University Institute in Florence, Italy, at the request of the European Commission, drafted a model constitution for the EU that essentially would establish a federal form of government. The preamble of the model constitution states, among other things, that "[t]his Constitution shall prevail over other European and national law, including Treaties of the Union, should conflict arise."[a] This is similar to the U.S. constitutional provision that if a state or local law conflicts with a national law, the national law will take precedence.

Just as delegates to the Constitutional Convention in the United States were reluctant to forfeit state sovereign powers, so are European nations. In the United States in the 1780s, at the time of the Constitutional Convention, the independent status of the states was relatively new. In contrast, most European nations have been in existence for centuries, making it even more difficult for them to part with any sovereign powers. Many other controversial issues remain. Some believe that signatory member states should have the right to leave the EU at any time. In the United States, we fought a civil war over that issue.

a. As cited in "Our Constitution for Europe," *The Economist,* October 28, 2000, p. 18.

FOR CRITICAL ANALYSIS
Why should an existing EU member nation agree to give up any of its sovereignty?

CHECKS AND BALANCES
The national government is composed of three separate branches: the executive, the legislative, and the judicial branches. Each branch of the government exercises a check on the actions of the others.

Additionally, a system of **checks and balances** allows each branch to limit the actions of the other two branches, thus preventing any one branch from exercising too much power. Some examples of these checks and balances are the following:

1. The legislative branch (Congress) can enact a law, but the executive branch (the president) has the constitutional authority to veto that law.
2. The executive branch is responsible for foreign affairs, but treaties with foreign governments require the advice and consent of the Senate.
3. Congress determines the jurisdiction of the federal courts and the president appoints federal judges, with the advice and consent of the Senate, but the judicial branch has the power to hold actions of the other two branches unconstitutional.[2]

THE COMMERCE CLAUSE

COMMERCE CLAUSE
The provision in Article I, Section 8, of the U.S. Constitution that gives Congress the power to regulate interstate commerce.

To prevent states from establishing laws and regulations that would interfere with trade and commerce among the states, the Constitution expressly delegated to the national government the power to regulate interstate commerce. Article I, Section 8, of the U.S. Constitution expressly permits Congress "[t]o regulate Commerce with foreign Nations, and among the several States, and with the Indian Tribes." This clause, referred to as the **commerce clause**, has had a greater impact on business than any other provision in the Constitution.

2. See the *Landmark in the Law* in Chapter 3 on *Marbury v. Madison,* 5 U.S. (1 Cranch) 137, 2 L.Ed. 60 (1803), a case in which the doctrine of judicial review was clearly enunciated by Chief Justice John Marshall.

LANDMARK IN THE LAW
Gibbons v. Ogden (1824)

The commerce clause, which is found in Article I, Section 8, of the U.S. Constitution, gives Congress the power "[t]o regulate Commerce with foreign Nations, and among the several States, and with the Indian Tribes." What exactly does "to regulate commerce" mean? What does "commerce" entail? These questions came before the United States Supreme Court in 1824 in the case of *Gibbons v. Ogden.*[a]

Background In 1803, Robert Fulton, inventor of the steamboat, and Robert Livingston, who was then American minister to France, secured a monopoly on steam navigation on the waters in the state of New York from the New York legislature. Fulton and Livingston licensed Aaron Ogden, a former governor of New Jersey and a U.S. senator, to operate steam-powered ferryboats between New York and New Jersey. Thomas Gibbons, who had obtained a license from the U.S. government to operate boats in interstate waters, competed with Ogden without New York's permission. Ogden sued Gibbons. The New York state courts granted Ogden's request for an injunction—an order prohibiting Gibbons from operating in New York waters. Gibbons appealed the decision to the United States Supreme Court.

Marshall's Decision Sitting as chief justice on the Supreme Court was John Marshall, an advocate of a strong national government. In his decision, Marshall defined the word *commerce* as used in the commerce clause to mean all commercial intercourse—that is, all business dealings that affect more than one state. The Court ruled against Ogden's monopoly, reversing the injunction against Gibbons. Marshall used this opportunity not only to expand the definition of commerce but also to validate and increase the power of the national legislature to regulate commerce. Said Marshall, "What is this power? It is the power . . . to prescribe the rule by which commerce is to be governed." Marshall held that the power to regulate interstate commerce was an exclusive power of the national government and that this power included the power to regulate any intrastate commerce that substantially affects interstate commerce.

APPLICATION TO TODAY'S WORLD

Marshall's broad definition of the commerce power established the foundation for the expansion of national powers in the years to come. Today, the national government continues to rely on the commerce clause for its constitutional authority to regulate business activities. Marshall's conclusion that the power to regulate interstate commerce was an exclusive power of the national government has also had significant consequences. By implication, this means that a state cannot regulate activities that extend beyond its borders, such as out-of-state online gambling operations that affect the welfare of in-state citizens. It also means that state regulations over in-state activities normally will be invalidated if the regulations substantially burden interstate commerce.

a. 22 U.S. (9 Wheat.) 1, 6 L.Ed. 23 (1824).

For some time, the commerce power was interpreted as being limited to *interstate* commerce (commerce among the states) and not applicable to *intrastate* commerce (commerce within the states). In 1824, however, in *Gibbons v. Ogden* (see this chapter's *Landmark in the Law* on the previous page), the United States Supreme Court held that commerce within states could also be regulated by the national government as long as the commerce *substantially affected* commerce involving more than one state.

"We are under a Constitution, but the Constitution is what judges say it is."

CHARLES EVANS HUGHES, 1862–1948 (Chief justice of the United States Supreme Court, 1930–1941)

The Commerce Clause and the Expansion of National Powers In *Gibbons v. Ogden,* the commerce clause was expanded to regulate activities that "substantially affect interstate commerce." As the nation grew and faced new kinds of problems, the commerce clause became a vehicle for the additional expansion of the national government's regulatory powers. Even activities that seemed purely local came under the regulatory reach of the national government if those activities were deemed to substantially affect interstate commerce. • **EXAMPLE 2.1** In 1942, in *Wickard v. Filburn,*[3] the Supreme Court held that wheat production by an individual farmer intended wholly for consumption on his own farm was subject to federal regulation. The Court reasoned that the home consumption of wheat reduced the demand for wheat and thus could have a substantial effect on interstate commerce.•

The following landmark case involved a challenge to the scope of the national government's constitutional authority to regulate local activities.

3. 317 U.S. 111, 63 S.Ct. 82, 87 L.Ed. 122 (1942).

Landmark and Classic Cases

CASE 2.1 Heart of Atlanta Motel v. United States

Supreme Court of the United States, 1964.
379 U.S. 241,
85 S.Ct. 348,
13 L.Ed.2d 258.
http://supct.law.cornell.edu/supct/cases/name.htm[a]

HISTORICAL AND SOCIAL SETTING *In the first half of the twentieth century, state governments sanctioned segregation on the basis of race. In 1954, the United States Supreme Court decided that racially segregated school systems violated the Constitution. In the following decade, the Court ordered an end to racial segregation imposed by the states in other public facilities, such as beaches, golf courses, buses, parks, auditoriums, and courtroom seating. Privately owned facilities that excluded or segregated African Americans and others on the basis of race were not subject to the same constitutional restrictions, however. Congress passed the Civil Rights Act of 1964 to prohibit racial discrimination in "establishments affecting interstate commerce." These facilities included "places of public accommodation."*

a. This is the "Historic Supreme Court Decisions—by Party Name" page within the "Caselists" collection of the Legal Information Institute available at its site on the Web. Click on the "H" link or scroll down the list of cases to the entry for the *Heart of Atlanta* case. Click on the case name. When the link opens, click on one of the choices to read the "Syllabus," the "Full Decision," or the "Edited Decision."

FACTS The owner of the Heart of Atlanta Motel, in violation of the Civil Rights Act of 1964, refused to rent rooms to African Americans. The motel owner brought an action in a federal district court to have the Civil Rights Act declared unconstitutional, alleging that Congress had exceeded its constitutional authority to regulate commerce by enacting the act. The owner argued that his motel was not engaged in interstate commerce but was "of a purely local character." The motel, however, was accessible to state and interstate highways. The owner advertised nationally, maintained billboards throughout

CASE 2.1—Continued

the state, and accepted convention trade from outside the state (75 percent of the guests were residents of other states). The court sustained the constitutionality of the act and enjoined (prohibited) the owner from discriminating on the basis of race. The owner appealed. The case ultimately went to the United States Supreme Court.

ISSUE Did Congress exceed its constitutional power to regulate interstate commerce by enacting the Civil Rights Act of 1964?

DECISION No. The United States Supreme Court upheld the constitutionality of the act.

REASON The Court noted that the act was passed to correct "the deprivation of personal dignity" accompanying the denial of equal access to "public establishments." Testimony before Congress leading to the passage of the act indicated that African Americans in particular experienced substantial discrimination in attempting to secure lodging while traveling. This discrimination impeded interstate travel and thus impeded interstate commerce. As for the owner's argument that his motel was "of a purely local character," the Court said that even if this was true, "if it is interstate commerce that feels the pinch, it does not matter how local the operation that applies the squeeze." Therefore, under the commerce clause, "the power of Congress to promote interstate commerce also includes the power to regulate the local incidents thereof, including local activities."

COMMENTS *If the Supreme Court had invalidated the Civil Rights Act of 1964, the legal landscape of the United States would be much different today. The act prohibited discrimination based on race, color, national origin, religion, or gender in all "public accommodations" and discrimination in employment based on these criteria. Although state laws now prohibit many of these forms of discrimination as well, the protections available vary from state to state–and it is not certain when (and if) such laws would have been passed had the 1964 federal Civil Rights Act been deemed unconstitutional.*

ON THE WEB
An ongoing debate in our federal system is whether the national government exercises too much regulatory control over intrastate affairs. To find current articles on this topic, go to **http://www.vote-smart.org/issues/FEDERALISM_STATES_RIGHTS.**

The Commerce Power Today Today, at least theoretically, the power over commerce authorizes the national government to regulate every commercial enterprise in the United States. Federal (national) legislation governs virtually every major activity conducted by businesses—from hiring and firing decisions, to workplace safety, competitive practices, and financing.

In the last decade, however, the Supreme Court has begun to curb somewhat the national government's regulatory authority under the commerce clause. In 1995, the Court held—for the first time in sixty years—that Congress had exceeded its regulatory authority under the commerce clause. The Court stated that the Gun-Free School Zones Act of 1990, which banned the possession of guns within one thousand feet of any school, was unconstitutional because it attempted to regulate an area that had "nothing to do with commerce."[4]

Two years later, in 1997, the Court struck down portions of the Brady Handgun Violence Prevention Act of 1993, which obligated state and local law enforcement officers to do background checks on prospective handgun buyers until a national instant check system could be implemented. The Court stated that Congress lacked the power to "dragoon" state employees into federal service through an unfunded mandate of this kind.[5] In 2000, the Court invalidated key portions of the federal Violence Against Women Act of 1994, which allowed women to sue in federal court when they were victims of gender-motivated violence, such as rape. According to the Court, the commerce clause did not justify national regulation of noneconomic, criminal conduct.[6]

4. *United States v. Lopez,* 514 U.S. 549, 115 S.Ct. 1624, 131 L.Ed.2d 626 (1995).
5. *Printz v. United States,* 521 U.S. 898, 117 S.Ct. 2365, 138 L.Ed.2d 914 (1997).
6. *United States v. Morrison,* 529 U.S. 598, 120 S.Ct. 1740, 146 L.Ed.2d 658 (2000).

State and local governments, as part of their police powers, have the power to condemn unsafe buildings. What other powers can be exercised by state and local governments as part of their constitutional powers?

Nonetheless, the commerce clause continues to serve as the constitutional backbone for national laws regulating a broad number of activities. (See, for example, Case 2.4 later in this chapter.)

POLICE POWERS
Powers possessed by states as part of their inherent sovereignty. These powers may be exercised to protect or promote the public order, health, safety, morals, and general welfare.

The Regulatory Powers of the States As part of their inherent sovereignty, state governments have the authority to regulate affairs within their borders. This authority stems in part from the Tenth Amendment to the Constitution, which reserves all powers not delegated to the national government to the states. State regulatory powers are often referred to as **police powers**. The term encompasses not only criminal law enforcement but also the right of state governments to regulate private activities to protect or promote the public order, health, safety, morals, and general welfare. Fire and building codes, antidiscrimination laws, parking regulations, zoning restrictions, licensing requirements, and thousands of other state statutes covering virtually every aspect of life have been enacted pursuant to a state's police powers. Local governments, including cities, also exercise police powers.[7]

The "Dormant" Commerce Clause The United States Supreme Court has interpreted the commerce clause to mean that the national government has the *exclusive* authority

7. Local governments derive their authority to regulate their communities from the state, because they are creatures of the state. In other words, they cannot come into existence unless authorized by the state to do so.

to regulate commerce that substantially affects trade and commerce among the states. This express grant of authority to the national government, which is often referred to as the "positive" aspect of the commerce clause, implies a negative aspect—that the states do *not* have the authority to regulate interstate commerce. This negative aspect of the commerce clause is often referred to as the "dormant" (implied) commerce clause.

RECALL Any law in violation of the U.S. Constitution will not be enforced.

The dormant commerce clause comes into play when state regulations impinge on interstate commerce. In this situation, the courts normally weigh the state's interest in regulating a certain matter against the burden that the state's regulation places on interstate commerce. • **EXAMPLE 2.2** In one case, the United States Supreme Court invalidated state regulations that, in the interest of promoting traffic safety, limited the length of trucks traveling on the state's highways. The Court invalidated the regulations, concluding that although they imposed a "substantial burden on interstate commerce," they failed to "make more than the most speculative contribution to highway safety."[8] • Because courts balance the interests involved, it is extremely difficult to predict the outcome in a particular case.

An emerging issue related to state laws that impinge on interstate commerce involves the Internet. For some examples of how commerce clause principles are being applied in cases involving the sale of wine via the Internet, see this chapter's *Business Law in the Online World* feature on the next page.

THE SUPREMACY CLAUSE

Article VI of the Constitution provides that the Constitution, laws, and treaties of the United States are "the supreme Law of the Land." This article, commonly referred to as the **supremacy clause**, is important in the ordering of state and federal relationships. When there is a direct conflict between a federal law and a state law, the state law is rendered invalid. Because some powers are *concurrent* (shared by the federal government and the states), however, it is necessary to determine which law governs in a particular circumstance.

SUPREMACY CLAUSE
The provision in Article VI of the Constitution that provides that the Constitution, laws, and treaties of the United States are "the supreme Law of the Land." Under this clause, state and local laws that directly conflict with federal law will be rendered invalid.

PREEMPTION
A doctrine under which certain federal laws preempt, or take precedence over, conflicting state or local laws.

Preemption occurs when Congress chooses to act exclusively in a concurrent area. In this circumstance, a valid federal statute or regulation will take precedence over a conflicting state or local law or regulation on the same general subject. • **EXAMPLE 2.3** The federal Controlled Substances Act[9] of 1970 strictly prohibits the manufacture and distribution of marijuana. When California legalized the use of marijuana for medical purposes, by a ballot initiative in 1996, the law was challenged as unconstitutional because it conflicted with the federal law. Ultimately, the United States Supreme Court ruled that the law was preempted by the 1970 federal act. The defendant in the case (an Oakland cooperative producing and distributing marijuana for medical purposes) had argued that the 1970 act provided for a "medical necessity" exception. The Supreme Court, however, held that there was no such exception, and thus the California law was preempted by the federal act.[10] •

Often, it is not clear whether Congress, in passing a law, intended to preempt an entire subject area against state regulation. In these situations, it is left to the courts to determine whether Congress intended to exercise exclusive power over a given area. No single factor is decisive as to whether a court will find preemption. Generally, congressional intent to preempt will be found if a federal law regulating an activity is so pervasive, comprehensive, or detailed that the states have no room to regulate in that area. Also, when

8. *Raymond Motor Transportation, Inc. v. Rice,* 434 U.S. 429, 98 S.Ct. 787, 54 L.Ed.2d 664 (1978).

9. This is the popular name for the Comprehensive Drug Abuse Prevention and Control Act of 1970, 21 U.S.C. Sections 801 *et seq.*

10. *United States v. Oakland Cannabis Buyers' Co-op,* ___U.S.___, 121 S.Ct. 1711, 149 L.Ed.2d 722 (2001).

BUSINESS LAW: //in the Online World

Internet Wine Sales and the Constitution

In the past decade, the Internet has come to be widely used for direct sales to consumers, including direct sales of wine. Yet a number of state statutes effectively prohibit consumers from purchasing and receiving wine directly from out-of-state sellers. In a series of recent cases, plaintiffs have alleged that such statutes violate the commerce clause of the Constitution. As mentioned elsewhere, the commerce clause implies a negative, or "dormant," aspect: the states do *not* have the authority to regulate interstate commerce. Here we look at how the dormant commerce clause applies to state regulations affecting the sale and purchase of wine via the Internet.

For example, in *Dickerson v. Bailey,*[a] the plaintiffs—Texas residents who wanted to receive wine shipments directly from out-of-state suppliers—claimed that a Texas statute prohibiting such purchases violated the dormant commerce clause. The statute prohibited Texans from importing for their personal use more than three gallons of wine without a permit unless the resident "personally accompan[ies] the wine or liquor as it enters the state." A federal court held that the statute violated the dormant commerce clause. In effect, the law discriminated against interstate commerce by prohibiting out-of-state wineries from shipping wines to Texas residents while allowing local Texas wineries or retailers to do so.

Enter the Twenty-First Amendment

In the Texas case, and in other recent cases involving the same issue, one of the arguments made by state authorities is that their liquor regulations are justified by Section 2 of the Twenty-first Amendment.[b] That section reads, "The transportation or importation into any State, Territory, or possession of the United States for delivery or use therein of intoxicating liquors, *in violation of the laws thereof,* is hereby prohibited." [Emphasis added.]

a. 87 F.Supp.2d 691 (S.D.Tex. 2000).

b. Section 1 of the Twenty-first Amendment (ratified in 1933) repealed the Eighteenth Amendment (ratified in 1919), which had made the manufacture, sale, or transportation of alcoholic beverages illegal. Section 2 of the Twenty-first Amendment effectively left the regulation of such activity up to the states.

Does the Twenty-First Amendment Trump the Dormant Commerce Clause?

Does the Twenty-first Amendment create an exception to the normal operation of the commerce clause? The courts are giving different answers to this question. In the Texas case, for example, the court held that the amendment did not create such an exception. The court did note that substantial deference is given to a state's power to regulate the sale and distribution of liquor within its boundaries when the goal of the regulation is "to combat the perceived evils of an unrestricted traffic in liquor." The court concluded, however, that no temperance (abstinence from alcohol) goal was served by the Texas statute because residents of that state could "become as drunk on local wines" as they could on wines that were effectively "kept out of the state by the statute." Because the goal of the Texas law was primarily to protect the economic interests of in-state wine producers and distributors, the law was not entitled to such deference and violated the commerce clause.

The first federal appellate court to rule on this issue reached a different conclusion. In *Bridenbaugh v. Freeman-Wilson,*[c] Indiana residents challenged the constitutionality of a state statute making it unlawful for persons in another state or country to ship alcoholic beverages directly to Indiana residents. The court concluded that the primary purpose of the Twenty-first Amendment was not necessarily to promote temperance; rather, it was designed to close a "loophole" created by the dormant commerce clause. This loophole allowed direct shipments from out-of-state sellers to consumers to "bypass state regulatory (and tax) systems." The Indiana statute did not involve any substantial discrimination against interstate commerce; it merely enabled the state "to collect its excise tax equally from in-state and out-of-state sellers."

FOR CRITICAL ANALYSIS

Suppose that a state passed a law prohibiting direct sales of tobacco products via the Internet to in-state consumers. Would such a law necessarily violate the commerce clause? Why or why not?

c. 227 F.3d 848 (7th Cir. 2000).

a federal statute creates an agency—such as the National Labor Relations Board—to enforce the law, matters that may come within the agency's jurisdiction will likely preempt state laws.

THE TAXING AND SPENDING POWERS

Article I, Section 8, provides that Congress has the "Power to lay and collect Taxes, Duties, Imposts, and Excises." Section 8 further provides that "all Duties, Imposts and Excises shall be uniform throughout the United States." The requirement of uniformity refers to uniformity among the states, and thus Congress may not tax some states while exempting others.

Traditionally, if Congress attempted to regulate indirectly, by taxation, an area over which it had no authority, the tax would be invalidated by the courts. Today, however, if a tax measure bears some reasonable relationship to revenue production, it is generally held to be within the national taxing power. Moreover, the expansive interpretation of the commerce clause almost always provides a basis for sustaining a federal tax.

Under Article I, Section 8, Congress has the power "to pay the Debts and provide for the common Defence and general welfare of the United States." Through the spending power, Congress disposes of the revenues accumulated from the taxing power. Congress can spend revenues not only to carry out its enumerated powers but also to promote any objective it deems worthwhile, so long as it does not violate the Constitution or its amendments. For example, Congress could not condition welfare payments on the recipients' political views. The spending power necessarily involves policy choices, with which taxpayers may disagree.

Business and the Bill of Rights

BILL OF RIGHTS
The first ten amendments to the U.S. Constitution.

The importance of a written declaration of the rights of individuals eventually caused the first Congress of the United States to submit twelve amendments to the Constitution to the states for approval. The first ten of these amendments, commonly known as the **Bill of Rights**, were adopted in 1791 and embody a series of protections for the individual against various types of interference by the federal government.[11] Some constitutional protections apply to business entities as well. For example, corporations exist as separate legal entities, or legal persons, and enjoy many of the same rights and privileges as natural persons do. Summarized here are the protections guaranteed by these ten amendments (see the Constitution in Appendix B for the complete text of each amendment):

BE CAREFUL Although most of these rights apply to actions of the states, some of them apply only to actions of the federal government.

① The First Amendment guarantees the freedoms of religion, speech, and the press and the rights to assemble peaceably and to petition the government.

② The Second Amendment guarantees the right to keep and bear arms.

③ The Third Amendment prohibits, in peacetime, the lodging of soldiers in any house without the owner's consent.

④ The Fourth Amendment prohibits unreasonable searches and seizures of persons or property.

⑤ The Fifth Amendment guarantees the rights to indictment by grand jury, to due process of law, and to fair payment when private property is taken for public use.

11. One of these proposed amendments was ratified 203 years later (in 1992) and became the Twenty-seventh Amendment to the Constitution. See Appendix B.

"The Constitution is not neutral. It was designed to take the government off the backs of people."
WILLIAM O. DOUGLAS, 1898–1980
(Associate justice of the United States Supreme Court, 1939–1975)

The Fifth Amendment also prohibits compulsory self-incrimination and double jeopardy (trial for the same crime twice).

⑥ The Sixth Amendment guarantees the accused in a criminal case the right to a speedy and public trial by an impartial jury and with counsel. The accused has the right to cross-examine witnesses against him or her and to solicit testimony from witnesses in his or her favor.

⑦ The Seventh Amendment guarantees the right to a trial by jury in a civil case involving at least twenty dollars.[12]

⑧ The Eighth Amendment prohibits excessive bail and fines, as well as cruel and unusual punishment.

⑨ The Ninth Amendment establishes that the people have rights in addition to those specified in the Constitution.

⑩ The Tenth Amendment establishes that those powers neither delegated to the federal government nor denied to the states are reserved for the states.

As originally intended, the Bill of Rights limited only the powers of the national government. Over time, however, the Supreme Court "incorporated" most of these rights into the protections against state actions afforded by the Fourteenth Amendment to the Constitution. That amendment, passed in 1868 after the Civil War, provides in part that "[n]o State shall . . . deprive any person of life, liberty, or property, without due process of law." Starting in 1925, the Supreme Court began to define various rights and liberties guaranteed in the national Constitution as constituting "due process of law," which was required of state governments under the Fourteenth Amendment. Today, most of the rights and liberties set forth in the Bill of Rights apply to state governments as well as the national government.

We will look closely at several of the amendments in the above list in Chapter 6, in the context of criminal law and procedures. Here we examine two important guarantees of the First Amendment—freedom of speech and freedom of religion. These and other First Amendment freedoms (of the press, assembly, and petition) have all been

12. Twenty dollars was forty days' pay for the average person when the Bill of Rights was written.

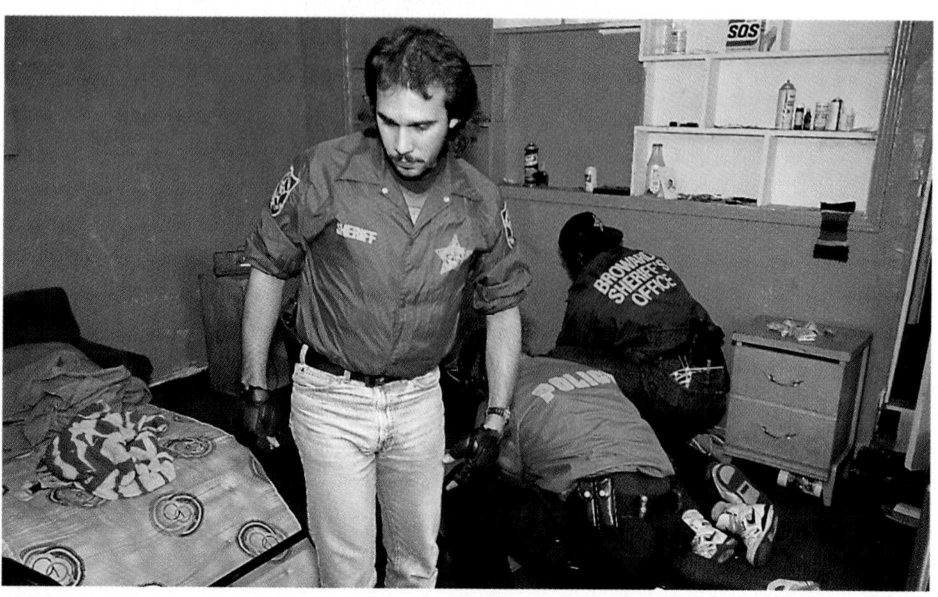

Police search a crack house in Florida. Do the owners and occupants of such houses receive protection from unreasonable searches and seizures under the U.S. Constitution? Should they?

applied to the states through the due process clause of the Fourteenth Amendment. As you read through the following pages, keep in mind that none of these (or other) constitutional freedoms confers an absolute right. Ultimately, it is the United States Supreme Court, as the final interpreter of the Constitution, that gives meaning to these rights and determines their boundaries.

THE FIRST AMENDMENT—FREEDOM OF SPEECH

Freedom of speech is the most prized freedom that Americans have. Indeed, it forms the basis for our democratic form of government, which could not exist if people could not express their political opinions freely and criticize government actions or policies. Because of its importance, the courts traditionally have protected this right to the fullest extent possible.

SYMBOLIC SPEECH Nonverbal expressions of beliefs. Symbolic speech, which includes gestures, movements, and articles of clothing, is given substantial protection by the courts.

The courts also protect **symbolic speech**—gestures, movements, articles of clothing, and other forms of nonverbal expressive conduct. • **EXAMPLE 2.4** In 1989, the Supreme Court held that the burning of the American flag to protest government policies is a constitutionally protected form of expression.[13] In a subsequent case, the Supreme Court ruled that a city statute banning bias-motivated disorderly conduct (including, in this case, the placing of a burning cross in another's front yard as a gesture of hate) was an unconstitutional restriction of speech.[14] •

REMEMBER The First Amendment guarantee of freedom of speech applies only to *government* restrictions on speech.

Corporate Political Speech Political speech by corporations also falls within the protection of the First Amendment. • **EXAMPLE 2.5** In *First National Bank of Boston v. Bellotti*,[15] national banking associations and business corporations sought United States Supreme Court review of a Massachusetts statute that prohibited corporations from making political contributions or expenditures that individuals were permitted to make. The Court ruled that the Massachusetts law was unconstitutional because it violated the right of corporations to freedom of speech. • Similarly, the Court has held that a law prohibiting a corporation from using bill inserts to express its views on controversial issues violates the First Amendment.[16] Although a more conservative Supreme Court subsequently reversed this trend somewhat,[17] corporate political speech continues to be given significant protection under the First Amendment.

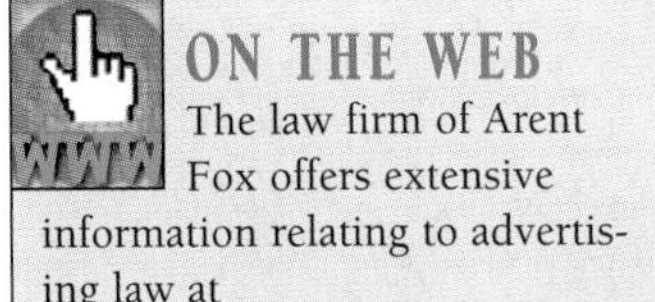

ON THE WEB The law firm of Arent Fox offers extensive information relating to advertising law at **http://www.advertisinglaw.com**.

Commercial Speech—Advertising The courts also give substantial protection to "commercial" speech, which consists of speech and communications—primarily advertising—made by business firms. The protection given to commercial speech under the First Amendment is not as extensive as that afforded to noncommercial speech, however. A state may restrict certain kinds of advertising, for example, in the interest of protecting consumers from being misled by the advertising practices. States also have a legitimate interest in the beautification of roadsides, and this interest allows states to place restraints on billboard advertising.

Generally, a restriction on commercial speech will be considered valid as long as it meets the following three criteria: (1) it must seek to implement a substantial govern-

13. See *Texas v. Johnson*, 491 U.S. 397, 109 S.Ct. 2533, 105 L.Ed.2d 342 (1989).
14. *R.A.V. v. City of St. Paul, Minnesota*, 505 U.S. 377, 112 S.Ct. 2538, 120 L.Ed.2d 305 (1992).
15. 435 U.S. 765, 98 S.Ct. 1407, 55 L.Ed.2d 707 (1978).
16. *Consolidated Edison Co. v. Public Service Commission*, 447 U.S. 530, 100 S.Ct. 2326, 65 L.Ed.2d 319 (1980).
17. See *Austin v. Michigan Chamber of Commerce*, 494 U.S. 652, 110 S.Ct. 1391, 108 L.Ed.2d 652 (1990), in which the Court upheld a state law prohibiting corporations from using general corporate funds for independent expenditures in state political campaigns.

ment interest, (2) it must directly advance that interest, and (3) it must go no further than necessary to accomplish its objective. • **EXAMPLE 2.6** The South Carolina Supreme Court recently held that a state statute banning ads for video gambling violated the First Amendment because the statute did not directly advance a substantial government interest. Although the court acknowledged that the state had a substantial interest in minimizing gambling, there was no evidence that a reduction in video gambling ads would result in a reduction in gambling.[18] •

At issue in the following case was whether a government agency's decision to prohibit the inclusion of a certain illustration on beer labels unconstitutionally restricted commercial speech.

18. *Evans v. State,* 344 S.C. 60, 543 S.E.2d 547 (2001).

CASE 2.2 Bad Frog Brewery, Inc v. New York State Liquor Authority

United States Court of Appeals,
Second Circuit, 1998.
134 F.3d 87.
http://www.tourolaw.edu/2ndCircuit/January98/97-79490.html[a]

HISTORICAL AND CULTURAL SETTING *Hand gestures signifying insults have been in use throughout the world for centuries. Hand gestures regarded as insults in some countries include an extended right thumb, an extended little finger, raised index and middle fingers, and gestures effected with two hands. A gesture using the extended middle finger of either hand (sometimes referred to as "giving the finger" or "flipping the bird") is generally acknowledged to convey an obscene, offensive message: a suggestion to have intercourse with one's self. This gesture is said to have been used by Diogenes (a Greek philosopher in the fourth century* B.C.E. *who was known for his disregard of social niceties) to insult Demosthenes (a Greek statesman and contemporary of Diogenes).*[b]

FACTS Bad Frog Brewery, Inc., makes and sells alcoholic beverages. Some of the beverages feature labels that display a drawing of a frog making the gesture generally known as "giving the finger." Bad Frog's authorized New York distributor, Renaissance Beer Company, applied to the New York State Liquor Authority (NYSLA) for brand label approval, as required by state law before the beer could be sold in New York. The NYSLA denied the application, in part because "the label could appear in grocery and convenience stores, with obvious exposure on the shelf to children of tender age." Bad Frog filed a suit in a federal district court against the NYSLA, asking for, among other things, an injunction against the denial of Bad Frog's application. The court granted a summary judgment in favor of the NYSLA. Bad Frog appealed to the U.S. Court of Appeals for the Second Circuit.

a. This page is part of a Web site maintained by the Touro College Jacob D. Fuchsberg Law Center in Huntington, New York.

b. Betty J. Bauml and Franz H. Bauml, *Dictionary of Worldwide Gestures,* 2d ed. (Lanham, Md.: Scarecrow Press, 1997), p. 159.

Different labels on these bottles suggest different things about the beer inside them. Can a brewery use any type of label on its beer? If not, what are the constraints?

CASE 2.2—Continued

ISSUE Did the NYSLA's denial of Bad Frog's application violate the First Amendment?

DECISION Yes. The U.S. Court of Appeals for the Second Circuit reversed the judgment of the district court and remanded the case for the entry of a judgment in favor of Bad Frog. The NYSLA's ban on the use of the labels lacked a "reasonable fit" with the state's interest in shielding minors from vulgarity, and the NYSLA did not adequately consider alternatives to the ban.

REASON The U.S. Court of Appeals for the Second Circuit acknowledged that the NYSLA's interest "in protecting children from vulgar and profane advertising" was "substantial." The question was whether banning Bad Frog's labels "directly advanced" that interest. "In view of the wide currency of vulgar displays throughout contemporary society, including comic books targeted directly at children, barring such displays from labels for alcoholic beverages cannot realistically be expected to reduce children's exposure to such displays to any significant degree." The court concluded that a "commercial speech limitation" must be "part of a substantial effort to advance a valid state interest, not merely the removal of a few grains of offensive sand from a beach of vulgarity." Finally, as to whether the ban on the labels was more extensive than necessary to serve this interest, the court pointed out that there were "numerous less intrusive alternatives." For example, the NYSLA's "concern could be less intrusively dealt with by placing restrictions on the permissible locations where the appellant's products may be displayed within * * * stores."

FOR CRITICAL ANALYSIS—Political Consideration *Whose interests are advanced by the banning of certain types of advertising?*

Unprotected Speech The United States Supreme Court has made it clear that certain types of speech will not be given any protection under the First Amendment. Speech that harms the good reputation of another, or defamatory speech (see Chapter 4), will not be protected. Speech that violates criminal laws (such as threatening speech) is not constitutionally protected. Other unprotected speech includes "fighting words," or words that are likely to incite others to respond violently.

The Supreme Court has also held that obscene speech is not protected by the First Amendment. The Court has grappled from time to time with the problem of trying to establish an objective definition of obscene speech. In a 1973 case, *Miller v. California,*[19] the Supreme Court created a test for legal obscenity, which involved a set of requirements that must be met for material to be legally obscene. Under this test, material is obscene if (1) the average person finds that it violates contemporary community standards; (2) the work taken as a whole appeals to a prurient interest in sex; (3) the work shows patently offensive sexual conduct; and (4) the work lacks serious redeeming literary, artistic, political, or scientific merit.

Because community standards vary widely, the *Miller* test has had inconsistent applications, and obscenity remains a constitutionally unsettled issue. Numerous state and federal statutes make it a crime to disseminate obscene materials, however, and such laws have often been upheld by the Supreme Court, including laws prohibiting the sale and possession of child pornography.[20]

Online Obscenity A significant problem facing the courts and lawmakers today is how to control obscenity and child pornography that are disseminated via the Internet.

19. 413 U.S. 15, 93 S.Ct. 2607, 37 L.Ed.2d 419 (1973).

20. For example, see *Osborne v. Ohio,* 495 U.S. 103, 110 S.Ct. 1691, 109 L.Ed.2d 98 (1990).

ON THE WEB
To learn about issues involving free speech and cyberspace, go to the Web site of the American Civil Liberties Union at **http://www.aclu.org**. Click on one of the issues listed on the right side of the screen for links to ACLU articles on that issue.

Congress first attempted to protect minors from pornographic materials on the Internet by passing the Communications Decency Act (CDA) of 1996. The CDA made it a crime to make available to minors online any "obscene or indecent" message that "depicts or describes, in terms patently offensive as measured by contemporary community standards, sexual or excretory activities or organs."[21]

The act was immediately challenged by civil rights groups as an unconstitutional restraint on speech, and ultimately the United States Supreme Court ruled that portions of the act were unconstitutional. The Court held that the terms *indecent* and *patently offensive* covered large amounts of nonpornographic material with serious educational or other value. Moreover, said the Court, "the 'community standards' criterion as applied to the Internet means that any communication available to a nationwide audience will be judged by the standards of the community most likely to be offended by the message."[22]

Later attempts by Congress to curb pornography on the Internet have also encountered constitutional stumbling blocks. For example, the Children's Online Privacy Protection Act (COPPA)[23] of 1998 imposed criminal penalties on those who distribute material that is "harmful to minors" without using some kind of age-verification system to separate adult and minor users. The act has been tied up in the courts since its passage, and in 2001 the Supreme Court agreed to review the case. In 2000, Congress enacted the Children's Internet Protection Act,[24] which requires public schools and libraries to block adult content from access by children by installing **filtering software.** Such software is designed to prevent persons from viewing certain Web sites at certain times by responding to a site's uniform resource locator (URL), or Internet address, or its **meta tags**, or key words. The 2000 act has also been challenged in court as unconstitutional, on the ground that it blocks access to too much information, including information of educational value.

FILTERING SOFTWARE
A computer program that includes a pattern through which data are passed. When designed to block access to certain Web sites, the pattern blocks the retrieval of a site whose URL or key words are on a list within the program.

META TAG
A key word in a document that can serve as an index reference to the document. On the Web, search engines return results based, in part, on the tags in Web documents.

ETHICAL ISSUE 2.1

Should "virtual" pornography be deemed a crime?

Recently, the Supreme Court agreed to review a case challenging the constitutionality of another federal act attempting to protect minors in the online environment—the Child Pornography Prevention Act (CPPA) of 1996. This act made it illegal to distribute or possess computer-generated images that appear to depict minors engaging in lewd and lascivious behavior. At issue in the case before the Court is a question with significant ethical and legal implications: Should digital child pornography be considered a crime? Clearly, child pornography laws are meant to protect children, in particular those who are involved in actual child pornography. Yet no actual children are involved in digital child pornography. In the case pending before the Supreme Court, the U.S. Court of Appeals for the Ninth Circuit held that the CPPA was unconstitutional. The court emphasized that the government can place significant restraints on free speech rights only if the restraints are necessary to promote a com-

21. 47 U.S.C. Section 223(a)(1)(B)(ii).
22. *Reno v. American Civil Liberties Union,* 521 U.S. 844, 117 S.Ct. 2329, 138 L.Ed.2d 874 (1997).
23. 15 U.S.C. Sections 6501–6506.
24. 17 U.S.C. Sections 1701–1741.

ON THE WEB According to a page within the Web site of Lehigh University, "citizens of the electronic community of learners" have fundamental rights that include a right of access to information resources. These rights are declared in the "Bill of Rights for Electronic Learners" at

http://www.lehigh.edu/www/www-data/bill-of-rights/top.html.

pelling government interest. In the court's eyes, the government has a compelling interest only in protecting children from actual, not "fake," child pornography.[25] Other courts, however, have held that there is little difference, in effect, between digital and real pornography.

Other Forms of Online Speech On the Internet, extreme hate speech is known as *cyber hate speech.* Racist materials and Holocaust denials on the Web, for example, are cyber hate speech. Can the federal government restrict this type of speech? Should it? Are there other forms of speech that the government should restrict?[26] Content restrictions generally amount to censorship and can be difficult to enforce. Even if it were possible to enforce content restrictions online, U.S. federal law is only "local" law in cyberspace—less than half of the users of the Internet are in the United States. Speech that may be legal in one country may not be legal in another, thus making it extremely difficult for any one nation to regulate Internet speech.

THE FIRST AMENDMENT—FREEDOM OF RELIGION

ESTABLISHMENT CLAUSE
The provision in the First Amendment to the Constitution that prohibits Congress from creating any law "respecting an establishment of religion."

FREE EXERCISE CLAUSE
The provision in the First Amendment to the Constitution that prohibits Congress from making any law "prohibiting the free exercise" of religion.

The First Amendment states that the government may neither establish any religion nor prohibit the free exercise of religious practices. The first part of this constitutional provision is referred to as the **establishment clause**, and the second part is known as the **free exercise clause.** Government action, both federal and state, must be consistent with this constitutional mandate.

The Establishment Clause The establishment clause prohibits the government from establishing a state-sponsored religion, as well as from passing laws that promote (aid or endorse) religion or that show a preference for one religion over another. The establishment clause does not require a complete separation of church and state, however. On the contrary, it requires the government to accommodate religions.[27]

The establishment clause covers all conflicts about such matters as the legality of state and local government support for a particular religion, government aid to religious organizations and schools, the government's allowing or requiring school prayers, and the teaching of evolution versus fundamentalist theories of creation. The Supreme Court has held that for a government law or policy to be constitutional, it must be secular in aim, must not have the primary effect of advancing or inhibiting religions, and must not create "an excessive government entanglement with religion."[28] Generally, federal or state regulation that does not promote religion or place a significant burden on religion is constitutional even if it has some impact on religion.

● **EXAMPLE 2.7** "Sunday closing laws" make the performance of some commercial activities on Sunday illegal. These statutes, also known as "blue laws" (from the color of the paper on which an early Sunday law was written), have been upheld on the ground that it is a legitimate function of government to provide a day of rest. The

25. *Free Speech Coalition v. Reno,* 198 F.3d 1083 (9th Cir. 1999); rehearing denied, 220 F.3d 1113 (2000).

26. The content of some speech is regulated to a certain extent by tort law, copyright law, trademark law, and other laws. See Chapter 5 for a discussion of these topics.

27. *Zorach v. Clauson,* 343 U.S. 306, 72 S.Ct. 679, 96 L.Ed. 954 (1952).

28. *Lemon v. Kurtzman,* 403 U.S. 602, 91 S.Ct. 2105, 29 L.Ed.2d 745 (1971).

United States Supreme Court has held that the closing laws, although originally of a religious character, have taken on the secular purpose of promoting the health and welfare of workers.[29] Even though Sunday closing laws admittedly make it easier for Christians to attend religious services, the Court has viewed this effect as an incidental, not a primary, purpose of Sunday closing laws. ●

ETHICAL ISSUE 2.2

Do religious displays on public property violate the establishment clause?

The thorny issue of whether religious displays on public property violate the establishment clause often arises during the holiday season. Time and again, the courts have wrestled with this issue, but it has never been resolved in a way that satisfies everyone. In a 1984 case, the United States Supreme Court decided that a city's official Christmas display, which included a crèche (Nativity scene), did not violate the establishment clause because it was just one part of a larger holiday display that featured secular symbols, such as reindeer and candy canes.[30] In a later case, the Court held that the presence of a crèche within a county courthouse violated the establishment clause because it was not in close proximity to nonreligious symbols, including a Christmas tree, which were located outside, on the building's steps. The presence of a menorah (a nine-branched candelabrum used in celebrating Chanukah) on the building's steps, however, did not violate the establishment clause because the menorah was situated in close proximity to the Christmas tree.[31] The courts continue to apply this reasoning in cases involving similar issues.

The Free Exercise Clause The free exercise clause guarantees that a person can hold any religious belief that she or he wants; or a person can have no religious belief. When religious *practices* work against public policy and the public welfare, however, the government can act. For example, regardless of a child's or parent's religious beliefs, the government can require certain types of vaccinations. Similarly, although children of Jehovah's Witnesses are not required to say the Pledge of Allegiance at school, their parents cannot prevent them from accepting medical treatment (such as blood transfusions) if in fact their lives are in danger. Additionally, public school students can be required to study from textbooks chosen by school authorities.

For business firms, an important issue involves the accommodation that businesses must make for the religious beliefs of their employees. For example, if an employee's religion prohibits him or her from working on a certain day of the week or at a certain type of job, the employer must make a reasonable attempt to accommodate these religious requirements. Employers must reasonably accommodate an employee's religious beliefs even if the beliefs are not based on the tenets or dogma of a particular church, sect, or denomination. The only requirement is that the belief be religious in nature and sincerely held by the employee. (We will look further at this issue in Chapter 35, in the context of employment discrimination.)

---

29. *McGowan v. Maryland,* 366 U.S. 420, 81 S.Ct. 1101, 6 L.Ed.2d 393 (1961).
30. *Lynch v. Donnelly,* 465 U.S. 668, 104 S.Ct. 1355, 79 L.Ed.2d 604 (1984).
31. See, for example, *County of Allegheny v. American Civil Liberties Union,* 492 U.S. 573, 109 S.Ct. 3086, 106 L.Ed.2d 472 (1989).

"What is due process of law depends on circumstances. It varies with the subject-matter and necessities of the situation."

OLIVER WENDELL HOLMES, JR., 1841–1935
(Associate justice of the United States Supreme Court, 1902–1932)

Due Process and Equal Protection

Two other constitutional guarantees of great significance to Americans are mandated by the due process clauses of the Fifth and Fourteenth Amendments and the equal protection clause of the Fourteenth Amendment.

DUE PROCESS

Both the Fifth and the Fourteenth Amendments provide that no person shall be deprived "of life, liberty, or property, without due process of law." The **due process clause** of each of these constitutional amendments has two aspects—procedural and substantive.

DUE PROCESS CLAUSE
The provisions of the Fifth and Fourteenth Amendments to the Constitution that guarantee that no person shall be deprived of life, liberty, or property without due process of law. Similar clauses are found in most state constitutions.

Procedural Due Process Procedural due process requires that any government decision to take life, liberty, or property must be made fairly. For example, fair procedures must be used in determining whether a person will be subjected to punishment or have some burden imposed on him or her. Fair procedure has been interpreted as requiring that the person have at least an opportunity to object to a proposed action before a fair, neutral decision maker (which need not be a judge). Thus, for example, if a driver's license is construed as a property interest, some sort of opportunity to object to its suspension or termination by the state must be provided.

Substantive Due Process Substantive due process focuses on the content, or substance, of legislation. If a law or other governmental action limits a *fundamental right*, it will be held to violate substantive due process unless it promotes a compelling or overriding state interest. Fundamental rights include interstate travel, privacy, voting, and all First Amendment rights. Compelling state interests could include, for example, the public's safety. • **EXAMPLE 2.8** Laws designating speed limits may be upheld even though they affect interstate travel, if they are shown to reduce highway fatalities, because the state has a compelling interest in protecting the lives of its citizens.•

In situations not involving fundamental rights, a law or action does not violate substantive due process if it rationally relates to any legitimate governmental end. It is almost impossible for a law or action to fail the "rationality" test. Under this test, virtually any business regulation will be upheld as reasonable—the United States Supreme Court has sustained insurance regulations, price and wage controls, banking controls, and controls of unfair competition and trade practices against substantive due process challenges.

• **EXAMPLE 2.9** If a state legislature enacted a law imposing a fifteen-year term of imprisonment without a trial on all businesspersons who appeared in their own television commercials, the law would be unconstitutional on both substantive and procedural grounds. Substantive review would invalidate the legislation because it abridges freedom of speech. Procedurally, the law is unfair because it imposes the penalty without giving the accused a chance to defend her or his actions.• The lack of procedural due process will cause a court to invalidate any statute or prior court decision. Similarly, a denial of substantive due process requires courts to overrule any state or federal law that violates the Constitution.

EQUAL PROTECTION

Under the Fourteenth Amendment, a state may not "deny to any person within its jurisdiction the equal protection of the laws." The United States Supreme Court has

EQUAL PROTECTION CLAUSE
The provision in the Fourteenth Amendment to the Constitution that guarantees that no state will "deny to any person within its jurisdiction the equal protection of the laws." This clause mandates that the state governments treat similarly situated individuals in a similar manner.

used the due process clause of the Fifth Amendment to make the **equal protection clause** applicable to the federal government as well. Equal protection means that the government must treat similarly situated individuals in a similar manner.

Both substantive due process and equal protection require review of the substance of the law or other governmental action rather than review of the procedures used. When a law or action limits the liberty of all persons to do something, it may violate substantive due process; when a law or action limits the liberty of some persons but not others, it may violate the equal protection clause. ● **EXAMPLE 2.10** If a law prohibits all persons from buying contraceptive devices, it raises a substantive due process question; if it prohibits only unmarried persons from buying the same devices, it raises an equal protection issue.●

"When one undertakes to administer justice, . . . what is done for one, must be done for everyone in equal degree."

THOMAS JEFFERSON, 1743–1826 (Third president of the United States, 1801–1809)

Basically, in determining whether a law or action violates the equal protection clause, a court will consider questions similar to those previously noted as applicable in a substantive due process review. Under an equal protection inquiry, when a law or action distinguishes between or among individuals, the basis for the distinction—that is, the classification—is examined. Depending on the classification, the courts apply different levels of scrutiny, or "tests," to determine whether the law or action violates the equal protection clause.

Minimal Scrutiny—The "Rational Basis" Test Generally, laws regulating economic and social matters are presumed to be valid and are subject to only minimal scrutiny. A classification will be considered valid if there is any conceivable "rational basis" on which the classification might relate to any *legitimate government interest*. It is almost impossible for a law or action to fail the rational basis test.

● **EXAMPLE 2.11** A city ordinance that in effect prohibits all pushcart vendors except a specific few from operating in a particular area of the city will be upheld if the city proffers a rational basis—perhaps regulation and reduction of traffic in the particular area—for the ordinance. In contrast, a law that provides unemployment benefits only to people over six feet tall would violate the guarantee of equal protection. There is no rational basis for determining the distribution of unemployment compensation on the basis of height. Such a distinction could not further any legitimate government objective.●

In the following case, the court applied the rational basis test to consider the constitutionality of a government-imposed dress code for cab drivers.

CASE 2.3 Bah v. City of Atlanta

United States Court of Appeals, Eleventh Circuit, 1997.
103 F.3d 964.
http://www.law.emory.edu/11circuit/jan97/96-8095.opa.html[a]

FACTS The Atlanta City Council adopted a dress code for cab drivers that required them, while driving a cab, to wear "shoes which entirely cover the foot (no sandals) and dark pants to ankle length or dark skirt or dress and solid white or light blue shirt or solid white or light blue blouse with sleeves and folded collar. * * * If a hat is worn, it shall be a baseball-style cap with an Atlanta or taxicab theme."[b] Mohamed Bah, a cab driver, was cited for violating the code and filed a suit in a federal district court against the city. Bah contended in part that the code violated the equal protection clause and asked the court to enjoin its enforcement. The city offered several reasons for the code, including "public safety," "identification of gypsy taxicab drivers," and "promoting a safe image." The court issued the injunc-

a. This is a page within an online library of court decisions maintained by the Hugh F. Macmillan Law Library at Emory University School of Law in Atlanta, Georgia.

b. Atlanta Code of Ordinances Section 14–8005(d)(2). The Atlanta Code of Ordinances was renumbered in 1996. This is the prior number for this section, which is the number that the court cited in this case.

CASE 2.3—Continued

tion. The city appealed to the U.S. Court of Appeals for the Eleventh Circuit.

ISSUE Is the dress code rationally related to a legitimate government objective?

DECISION Yes. The U.S. Court of Appeals for the Eleventh Circuit reversed the decision of the lower court and remanded the case.

REASON The U.S. Court of Appeals for the Eleventh Circuit held that the dress code did not violate the equal protection clause. The court applied the rational basis test and concluded that the dress code was rationally related to a legitimate government interest. The court determined that "even if the district court was correct in rejecting the two reasons it discussed–public safety and identification of gypsy taxicab drivers," there was a third reason for the code. The code was related to the city's interest in promoting a safe image. The court pointed out that cab drivers are often among the first people that out-of-town visitors encounter. "It is in the City's interest to promote a safe appearance and image, and a rational way to do that is by prescribing that its self-styled 'ambassadors' wear innocuous, conventional, relatively uniform clothing."

FOR CRITICAL ANALYSIS—Social Consideration *Would it be constitutional to impose a dress code on others who are licensed by the city and who deal with out-of-town visitors–food servers, bellhops, and outdoor vendors, for example?*

Intermediate Scrutiny A harder standard to meet, that of "intermediate scrutiny," is applied in cases involving discrimination based on gender or legitimacy. Laws using these classifications must be substantially related to *important government objectives.* • **EXAMPLE 2.12** An important government objective is preventing illegitimate teen-age pregnancies. Because males and females are not similarly situated in this circumstance—only females can become pregnant—a law that punishes men but not women for statutory rape will be upheld. A state law requiring illegitimate children to bring paternity suits within six years of their births, however, will be struck down if legitimate children are allowed to seek support from their parents at any time. •

Strict Scrutiny The most difficult standard to meet is that of "strict scrutiny." Very few cases survive strict-scrutiny analysis. Strict scrutiny is applied when a law or action inhibits some persons' exercise of a fundamental right or is based on a suspect trait (such as race, national origin, or citizenship status). Strict scrutiny means that the court will examine the law or action involved very closely, and the law or action will be allowed to stand only if it is necessary to promote a *compelling government interest.*

• **EXAMPLE 2.13** Suppose that a city gives preference to minority applicants in awarding construction contracts. Because the policy is based on suspect traits (race and national origin), it will violate the equal protection clause *unless* it is necessary to promote a compelling state interest. Courts have often held that states have a compelling interest in remedying past unconstitutional or illegal discrimination. The Supreme Court has declared, however, that such programs must be narrowly tailored. In other words, the city must identify the past unconstitutional or illegal discrimination against minority construction firms that it is attempting to correct, go no further than necessary to correct the problem, and change or drop its program once it has succeeded in correcting the problem.[32] •

32. *Adarand Constructors, Inc. v. Peña,* 515 U.S. 200, 115 S.Ct. 2097, 132 L.Ed.2d 158 (1995).

Privacy Rights

Until relatively recently, most privacy issues concerned the public's belief that personal information collected by government agencies posed a threat to individual privacy. In other words, typical privacy issues in the past related to personal information that government agencies, including the Federal Bureau of Investigation (FBI), might obtain and keep about an individual. Later, concerns about what banks and insurance companies might know and transmit to others about individuals became an issue. One of the major concerns of individuals in recent years has been the increasing value of personal information for online marketers—who are willing to pay a high price to those who collect and sell them such information—and how to protect privacy rights in cyberspace.

"I think there is a world market for maybe five computers."
THOMAS WATSON,
1874–1956
(President of IBM Corporation, 1924–1952)

Indeed, some people believe that privacy rights are quickly becoming a thing of the past in today's online world. "Cookies" on their hard drives allow Internet users' Web movements to be tracked. Technology is now available that makes it possible to connect previously anonymous Internet users to actual geographic locations. Furthermore, any person who wants to purchase goods from online merchants or auctions inevitably must reveal some personal information, which may include the purchaser's name, address, and credit-card number.

Clearly, an area of pressing concern today is how to secure privacy rights in an online world. In this section, we look at the protection of privacy rights under the U.S. Constitution and various federal statutes. Note that state constitutions and statutes also protect individuals' privacy rights, often to a significant degree. Privacy rights are also protected under tort law (see Chapter 4). Additionally, the Federal Trade Commission has played an active role in protecting the privacy rights of online consumers (see Chapter 33). The protection of employees' privacy rights, particularly with respect to electronic monitoring practices, is another area of growing concern (see Chapter 34).

CONSTITUTIONAL PROTECTION OF PRIVACY RIGHTS

The U.S. Constitution does not explicitly mention a general right to privacy, and only relatively recently have the courts regarded the right to privacy as a constitutional right. In a 1928 Supreme Court case, *Olmstead v. United States*,[33] Justice Louis Brandeis stated in his dissent that the right to privacy is "the most comprehensive of rights and the right most valued by civilized men." The majority of the justices at that time did not agree, and it was not until the 1960s that a majority on the Supreme Court endorsed the view that the Constitution protects individual privacy rights.

In a landmark 1965 case, *Griswold v. Connecticut*,[34] the Supreme Court invalidated a Connecticut law that effectively prohibited the use of contraceptives. The Court held that the law violated the right to privacy. Justice William O. Douglas formulated a unique way of reading this right into the Bill of Rights. He claimed that "emanations" from the rights guaranteed by the First, Third, Fourth, Fifth, and Ninth Amendments formed and gave "life and substance" to "penumbras" (partial shadows) around these guaranteed rights. These penumbras included an implied constitutional right to privacy.

When we read these amendments, we can see the foundation for Justice Douglas's reasoning. Consider the Fourth Amendment. By prohibiting unreasonable searches and seizures, the amendment effectively protects individuals' privacy. Consider also the words of the Ninth Amendment: "The enumeration in the Constitution of certain rights, shall not be construed to deny or disparage others retained by the people." In

33. 277 U.S. 438, 48 S.Ct. 564, 72 L.Ed. 944 (1928).
34. 381 U.S. 479, 85 S.Ct. 1678, 14 L.Ed.2d 510 (1965).

other words, just because the Constitution, including its amendments, does not specifically mention the right to privacy does not mean that this right is denied to the people. Indeed, in a recent survey of America Online subscribers, respondents ranked privacy second behind freedom of speech and ahead of freedom of religion as the most important rights guaranteed by the Constitution. A recent Harris poll showed that almost 80 percent of those questioned believed that if the framers were writing the Constitution today, they would add privacy as an important right.[35]

FEDERAL STATUTES PROTECTING PRIVACY RIGHTS

In the last several decades, Congress has enacted a number of statutes that protect the privacy of individuals in various areas of concern. In the 1960s, Americans were sufficiently alarmed by the accumulation of personal information in government files that they pressured Congress to pass laws permitting individuals to access their files. Congress responded in 1966 with the Freedom of Information Act, which allows any person to request copies of any information on him or her contained in federal government files. In 1974, Congress passed the Privacy Act, which also gives persons the right to access such information. These and other major federal laws protecting privacy rights are listed and described in Exhibit 2–1 starting on the following page.

As mentioned earlier, the federal government's constitutional authority to regulate activities on a national level, including activities that may jeopardize privacy rights, is rooted primarily in the commerce clause. At issue in the following case was whether Congress had exceeded its constitutional authority when it passed the Driver's Privacy Protection Act (DPPA) of 1994.

35. *Public Perspective,* November/December 2000, p. 9.

CASE 2.4 Reno v. Condon

Supreme Court of the United States, 2000.
528 U.S. 141,
120 S.Ct. 666,
145 L.Ed.2d 587.
http://supct.cornell.law.edu/supct[a]

HISTORICAL AND TECHNOLOGICAL SETTING *In 1994, Congress passed the Driver's Privacy Protection Act (DPPA) when it learned that states were selling information obtained by state motor vehicle departments to commercial database suppliers. As a result, personal information given by those who applied for driver's licenses or vehicle registrations was finding its way to Web sites that anyone could access. This information included people's names, addresses, telephone numbers, vehicle descriptions, Social Security numbers, medical information, and photographs. Congress was pressured to take action after an actress, Rebecca Schaeffer, was killed by a stalker who obtained her address—which was not published in any phone book—from state driver's license records. Subsequent congressional investigation unearthed many similar incidents in which motor vehicle files were used to locate women trying to escape domestic abuse, as well as other victims, who were subsequently threatened or harmed. The 1994 act prevents states from disclosing or selling a driver's personal information without the driver's consent.*

FACTS Each state's Department of Motor Vehicles (DMV) requires drivers and automobile owners to provide per-

(continued)

a. In the right-hand column, in the "For the 1999–2000 term:" section, click on "Decisions arrayed by date." On that page, click on "January 2000." When the result appears, scroll to the name of the case and click on it. On that page, click on the appropriate link to access the opinion.

CASE 2.4—Continued

sonal information, including a name, address, telephone number, and Social Security number, as a condition of obtaining a driver's license or registering an automobile. Many states sell this information to individuals and businesses.[b] Before a state can sell the information, under the DPPA a driver must consent to its release, or, in other words, choose to "opt in." In contrast to the federal DPPA, under South Carolina state law, information in DMV records is available to anyone who promises not to use it for telemarketing. The state can sell the data unless a South Carolina driver affirmatively "opts out." Charles Condon, the attorney general of South Carolina, filed a suit in a federal district court against Janet Reno, the attorney general of the United States, alleging that the DPPA violated the Constitution. The court granted an injunction to prevent the DPPA's enforcement, and the U.S. Court of Appeals for the Fourth Circuit upheld the order. Reno appealed to the United States Supreme Court.

ISSUE Is the DPPA a proper exercise of Congress's power under the commerce clause?

b. Wisconsin's DMV, for example, receives approximately $8 million each year from the sale of this information.

DECISION Yes. The United States Supreme Court reversed the judgment of the U.S. Court of Appeals for the Fourth Circuit. The Supreme Court held that the DPPA did not violate constitutional provisions.

REASON The United States Supreme Court explained that "[t]he motor vehicle information which the States have historically sold is used by insurers, manufacturers, direct marketers, and others engaged in interstate commerce to contact drivers with customized solicitations. * * * Because drivers' information is, in this context, an article of commerce, its sale or release into the interstate stream of business is sufficient to support congressional regulation." Condon also argued that the DPPA violated the Tenth Amendment. On this point, the Court acknowledged that the federal government may not require the states to administer or enforce a federal regulatory program. However, the DPPA "does not require the South Carolina Legislature to enact any laws or regulations, and it does not require state officials to assist in the enforcement of federal statutes regulating private individuals."

FOR CRITICAL ANALYSIS—Ethical Consideration *Are there ethical reasons for a state to keep private its drivers' personal information?*

EXHIBIT 2–1 FEDERAL LEGISLATION RELATING TO PRIVACY

TITLE	PROVISIONS CONCERNING PRIVACY
Freedom of Information Act (1966)	Provides that individuals have a right to obtain access to information about them collected in government files.
Fair Credit Reporting Act (1970)	Provides that consumers have the right to be informed of the nature and scope of a credit investigation, the kind of information that is being compiled, and the names of the firms or individuals who will be receiving the report.
Crime Control Act (1973)	Safeguards the confidentiality of information amassed for certain state criminal systems.
Family and Educational Rights and Privacy Act (1974)	Limits access to computer-stored records of education-related evaluations and grades in private and public colleges and universities.
Privacy Act (1974)	Protects the privacy of individuals about whom the federal government has information. Specifically, the act provides as follows: 1. Agencies originating, using, disclosing, or otherwise manipulating personal information must ensure the reliability of the information and provide safeguards against its misuse. 2. Information compiled for one purpose cannot be used for another without the concerned individual's permission.

EXHIBIT 2–1 FEDERAL LEGISLATION RELATING TO PRIVACY—CONTINUED

TITLE	PROVISIONS CONCERNING PRIVACY
Privacy Act (1974)—continued	3. Individuals must be able to find out what data concerning them are being compiled and how the data will be used. 4. Individuals must be given a means by which to correct inaccurate data.
Tax Reform Act (1976)	Preserves the privacy of personal financial information.
Right to Financial Privacy Act (1978)	Prohibits financial institutions from providing the federal government with access to customers' records unless a customer authorizes the disclosure.
Electronic Fund Transfer Act (1978)	Prohibits the use of a computer without authorization to retrieve data in a financial institution's or consumer reporting agency's files.
Cable Communications Policy Act (1984)	Regulates access to information collected by cable service operators on subscribers to cable services.
Electronic Communications Privacy Act (1986)	Prohibits the interception of information communicated by electronic means.
Driver's Privacy Protection Act (1994)	Prevents states from disclosing or selling a driver's personal information without the driver's consent.
Health Insurance Portability and Accountability Act (1996)	Prohibits the use of a consumer's medical information for any purpose other than that for which such information was provided, unless the consumer expressly consents to the use. Final rules under the act, issued by the Department of Health and Human Services, became effective on April 14, 2001.
Children's Online Privacy Protection Act (1998)	Requires operators of Web sites aimed at children under the age of thirteen to clearly provide notice about the information being collected and how it will be used; requires verifiable parental consent for certain types of information about children.
Financial Services Modernization Act (Gramm-Leach-Bliley Act) (1999)	Requires all financial institutions to provide customers with information on their privacy policies and practices; prohibits the disclosure of nonpublic personal information about a consumer to an unaffiliated third party unless strict disclosure and opt-out requirements are met. Final rules under the act, issued by the Federal Trade Commission, became mandatory on July 1, 2001.

APPLICATION Law and the Businessperson . . .

Creating a Web Site Privacy Policy*

Firms with online business operations realize that to do business effectively with their customers, they need to have some information about those customers. Yet online consumers are often reluctant to part with personal information because they do not know how that information may be used. To allay consumer fears about the privacy of their personal data, as well as to avoid liability under exist-

*This *Application* is not meant to substitute for the services of an attorney who is licensed to practice law in your state.

(continued)

APPLICATION Law and the Businessperson . . .

Creating a Web Site Privacy Policy—continued

ing laws, most online businesses today are taking steps to create and implement Web site privacy policies.

Privacy Policy Guidelines

In the last several years, a number of independent, nonprofit organizations have developed model Web site privacy policies and guidelines for online businesses to use. Web site privacy guidelines are now available from a number of online privacy groups and other organizations, including the Online Privacy Alliance, the Internet Alliance, and the Direct Marketing Association. Some organizations, including the Better Business Bureau, have even developed a "seal of approval" that Web-based businesses can display at their sites if they follow the organization's privacy guidelines.

One of the best known of these organizations is TRUSTe. Web site owners that agree to TRUSTe's privacy standards are allowed to post the TRUSTe "seal of approval" on their Web sites. The idea behind the seal, which many describe as the online equivalent of the "Good Housekeeping Seal of Approval," is to allay users' fears about privacy problems.

Drafting a Privacy Policy

Online privacy guidelines generally recommend that businesses post notices on their Web sites about the type of information being collected, how it will be used, and the parties to whom it will be disclosed. Other recommendations include allowing Web site visitors to access and correct or remove personal information and giving visitors an "opt-in" or "opt-out" choice. For example, if a user selects an "opt-out" policy, the personal data collected from that user would be kept private.

In the last several years, the Federal Trade Commission (FTC) has developed privacy standards that can serve as guidelines. An online business that includes these standards in its Web site privacy policies—and makes sure that they are enforced—will be in a better position to defend its policy should consumers complain about the site's practices to the FTC. The FTC standards are incorporated in the following checklist.

Checklist for a Web Site Privacy Policy

1. Include on your Web site a notice of your privacy policy.
2. Give consumers a choice (such as opt-in or opt-out) with respect to any information collected.
3. Outline the safeguards that you will employ to secure all consumer data.
4. Let consumers know that they can correct and update any personal information collected by your business.
5. State that parental consent is required if a child is involved.
6. Create a mechanism to enforce the policy.

Key Terms

Bill of Rights 43
checks and balances 36
commerce clause 36
due process clause 51
equal protection clause 52
establishment clause 49
federal form of government 35
filtering software 48
free exercise clause 49
meta tag 48
police powers 40
preemption 40
supremacy clause 40
symbolic speech 45

Chapter Summary Constitutional Law

The Constitutional Powers of Government (See pages 35–36.)	The U.S. Constitution established a federal form of government, in which government powers are shared by the national government and the state governments. At the national level, government powers are divided among the legislative, executive, and judicial branches.
The Commerce Clause (See pages 36–41.)	1. *The expansion of national powers*—The commerce clause expressly permits Congress to regulate commerce. Over time, courts expansively interpreted this clause, thereby enabling the national government to wield extensive powers over the economic life of the nation. 2. *The commerce power today*—Today, the commerce power authorizes the national government, at least theoretically, to regulate every commercial enterprise in the United States. In recent years, the Supreme Court has reined in somewhat the national government's regulatory powers under the commerce clause. 3. *The regulatory powers of the states*—The Tenth Amendment reserves all powers not expressly delegated to the national government to the states. Under their police powers, state governments may regulate private activities to protect or promote the public order, health, safety, morals, and general welfare. 4. *The "dormant" commerce clause*—If state regulations substantially interfere with interstate commerce, they will be held to violate the "dormant" commerce clause of the U.S. Constitution. The commerce clause, which gives the national government the exclusive authority to regulate interstate commerce, implies a "dormant" aspect of the clause—that the states do *not* have this power.
The Supremacy Clause (See pages 41–43.)	The U.S. Constitution provides that the Constitution, laws, and treaties of the United States are "the supreme Law of the Land." Whenever a state law directly conflicts with a federal law, the state law is rendered invalid.
The Taxing and Spending Powers (See page 43.)	The U.S. Constitution gives Congress the power to impose uniform taxes throughout the United States and to spend revenues accumulated from the taxing power. Congress can spend revenues to promote any objective it deems worthwhile, so long as it does not violate the Bill of Rights.
Business and the Bill of Rights (See pages 43–50.)	The Bill of Rights, which consists of the first ten amendments to the U.S. Constitution, was adopted in 1791 and embodies a series of protections for individuals—and, in some cases, business entities—against various types of interference by the federal government. Freedoms guaranteed by the First Amendment that affect businesses include the following: 1. *Freedom of speech*—Speech, including symbolic speech, is given the fullest possible protection by the courts. Corporate political speech and commercial speech also receive substantial protection under the First Amendment. Certain types of speech, such as defamatory speech and lewd or obscene speech, are not protected under the First Amendment. Government attempts to regulate unprotected forms of speech in the online environment have, to date, met with little success. 2. *Freedom of religion*—Under the First Amendment, the government may neither establish any religion (the establishment clause) nor prohibit the free exercise of religion (the free exercise clause).
Due Process and Equal Protection (See pages 51–53.)	1. *Due process*—Both the Fifth and the Fourteenth Amendments provide that no person shall be deprived of "life, liberty, or property, without due process of law." Procedural due process requires that any government decision to take life, liberty, or property must be made fairly, using fair procedures. Substantive due process focuses on the content of legislation. Generally, a law that is not compatible with the Constitution violates substantive due process unless the law promotes a compelling state interest, such as public safety.

(continued)

Chapter Summary Constitutional Law—continued

Due Process and Equal Protection—continued	2. *Equal protection*—Under the Fourteenth Amendment, a state may not "deny to any person within its jurisdiction the equal protection of the laws." A law or action that limits the liberty of some persons but not others may violate the equal protection clause. Such a law may be deemed valid, however, if there is a rational basis for the discriminatory treatment of a given group or if the law substantially relates to an important government objective.
Privacy Rights (See pages 54–57.)	Americans are increasingly becoming concerned over privacy issues raised by Internet-related technology. The Constitution does not contain a specific guarantee of a right to privacy, but such a right has been derived from guarantees found in several constitutional amendments. A number of federal statutes protect privacy rights. Privacy rights are also protected by many state constitutions and statutes, as well as under tort law.

For Review

① What is the basic structure of the U.S. government?

② What constitutional clause gives the federal government the power to regulate commercial activities among the various states?

③ What constitutional clause allows laws enacted by the federal government to take priority over conflicting state laws?

④ What is the Bill of Rights? What freedoms are guaranteed by the First Amendment?

⑤ Where in the Constitution can the due process clause be found?

Questions and Case Problems

2–1. Government Powers. The framers of the Constitution feared the twin evils of tyranny and anarchy. Discuss how specific provisions of the Constitution and the Bill of Rights reflect these fears and protect against both of these extremes.

2–2. Commercial Speech. A mayoral election is about to be held in a large U.S. city. One of the candidates is Luis Delgado, and his campaign supporters wish to post campaign signs on lampposts and utility posts throughout the city. A city ordinance, however, prohibits the posting of any signs on public property. Delgado's supporters contend that the city ordinance is unconstitutional, because it violates their rights to free speech. What factors might a court consider in determining the constitutionality of this ordinance?

2–3. Commerce Clause. Suppose that Georgia enacts a law requiring the use of contoured rear-fender mudguards on trucks and trailers operating within its state lines. The statute further makes it illegal for trucks and trailers to use straight mudguards. In thirty-five other states, straight mudguards are legal. Moreover, in the neighboring state of Florida, straight mudguards are explicitly required by law. There is some evidence suggesting that contoured mudguards might be a little safer than straight mudguards. Discuss whether this Georgia statute would violate the commerce clause of the U.S. Constitution.

2–4. Freedom of Religion. A business has a backlog of orders, and to meet its deadlines, management decides to run the firm seven days a week, eight hours a day. One of the employees, Marjorie Tollens, refuses to work on Saturday on religious grounds. Her refusal to work means that the firm may not meet its production deadlines and may therefore suffer a loss of future business. The firm fires Tollens and replaces her with an employee who is willing to work seven days a week. Tollens claims that her employer, in terminating her employment, violated her constitutional right to the free exercise of her religion. Do you agree? Why or why not?

2–5. Equal Protection. In 1988, the Nebraska legislature enacted a statute that required any motorcycle operator or passenger on Nebraska's highways to wear a protective helmet. Eugene Robotham, a licensed motorcycle operator, sued the state of Nebraska to block enforcement of the law. Robotham asserted, among other things, that the statute violated the equal protection clause, because it placed requirements on motorcyclists that were not imposed on other motorists. Will the court agree with Robotham that the law violates the equal protection clause? Why or why not? [*Robotham v. State,* 241 Neb. 379, 488 N.W.2d 533 (1992)]

2–6. Freedom of Religion. Isaiah Brown was the director of the information services department for Polk County, Iowa. During department meetings in his office, he allowed occasional prayers and, in addressing one meeting, referred to Bible passages related to sloth and "work ethics." There was no apparent disruption of the work routine, but the county administrator reprimanded Brown. Later, the administrator ordered Brown to remove from his office all items with a religious connotation. Brown sued the county, alleging that the reprimand and the order violated, among other things, the free exercise clause of the First Amendment. Could the county be held liable for violating Brown's constitutional rights? Discuss. [*Brown v. Polk County, Iowa,* 61 F.3d 650 (8th Cir. 1995)]

2–7. Equal Protection. With the objectives of preventing crime, maintaining property values, and preserving the quality of urban life, New York City enacted an ordinance to regulate the locations of commercial establishments that featured adult entertainment. The ordinance expressly applied to female, but not male, topless entertainment. Adele Buzzetti owned the Cozy Cabin, a New York City cabaret that featured female topless dancers. Buzzetti and an anonymous dancer filed a suit in a federal district court against the city, asking the court to block the enforcement of the ordinance. The plaintiffs argued in part that the ordinance violated the equal protection clause. Under the equal protection clause, what standard applies to the court's consideration of this ordinance? Under this test, how should the court rule? Why? [*Buzzetti v. City of New York,* 140 F.3d 134 (2d Cir. 1998)]

2–8. Free Speech. The city of Tacoma, Washington, enacted an ordinance that prohibited the playing of car sound systems at a volume that would be "audible" at a distance greater than fifty feet. Dwight Holland was arrested and convicted for violating the ordinance. The conviction was later dismissed, but Holland filed a civil suit in a Washington state court against the city. He claimed in part that the ordinance violated his freedom of speech under the First Amendment. On what basis might the court conclude that this ordinance is constitutional? (Hint: In playing a sound system, was Holland actually expressing himself?) [*Holland v. City of Tacoma,* 90 Wash.App. 533, 954 P.2d 290 (1998)]

TEST YOUR KNOWLEDGE—ANSWER ON THE WEB

2–9. In February 1999, Carl Adler mailed a driver's license renewal application form and a check for $28 to the New York Department of Motor Vehicles (DMV). The form required Adler's Social Security number, which he intentionally omitted. The DMV returned the application and check and told Adler to supply his Social Security number or send proof that the Social Security Administration could not give him a number. Claiming a right to privacy, Adler refused to comply. The DMV responded that federal law authorizes the states to obtain Social Security numbers from individuals in the context of administering certain state programs, including driver's license programs, and that Adler's application would not be processed until he supplied the number. Adler filed a suit in a New York state court against the DMV, asserting in part that it was in violation of the federal Privacy Act of 1974. Adler asked the court to, among other things, order the DMV to renew his license. Should the court grant Adler's request? Why or why not? [*Adler v. Jackson,* 712 N.Y.S.2d 240 (Sup. 2000)]

A QUESTION OF ETHICS AND SOCIAL RESPONSIBILITY

2–10. In 1999, in an effort to reduce smoking by children, the attorney general of Massachusetts issued comprehensive regulations governing the advertising and sale of tobacco products. Among other things, the regulations banned cigarette advertisements within one thousand feet of any elementary school, secondary school, or public playground and required retailers to post any advertising in their stores at least five feet off the floor, out of the immediate sight of young children. A group of tobacco manufacturers and retailers filed suit against the state, claiming that the regulations were preempted by the federal Cigarette Labeling and Advertising Act (FCLAA) of 1965, as amended. That act sets uniform labeling requirements and bans broadcast advertising for cigarettes. Ultimately, the case reached the United States Supreme Court, which held that the federal law on cigarette ads preempted the cigarette advertising restrictions adopted by Massachusetts. The only portion of the Massachusetts regulatory package to survive was the requirement that retailers had to place tobacco products in an area accessible only by the sales staff. In view of these facts, consider the following questions. [*Lorillard Tobacco Co. v. Reilly,* 533 U.S. 525, 121 S.Ct. 2404, 69 L.Ed.2d 532 (2001)]

1. Some argue that having a national standard for tobacco regulation is more important than allowing states to set their own standards for tobacco regulation. Do you agree? Why or why not?
2. According to the Court in this case, the federal law does not restrict the ability of state and local governments to adopt general zoning restrictions that apply to cigarettes, as long as those restrictions are "on equal terms with other products." How would you argue in support of this reasoning? How would you argue against it?

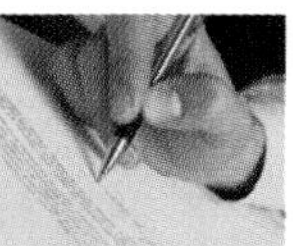

FOR CRITICAL ANALYSIS

2–11. In recent years, many people have criticized the film and entertainment industries for promoting violence by exposing the American public, and particularly American youth, to extremely violent films and song lyrics. Do you think that the right to free speech can (or should) be traded off to reduce violence in America? Generally, in the wake of the September 11, 2001, terrorist attack on the World Trade Center towers and the Pentagon, do you think that Americans should trade off some of their civil liberties for more protection against violence and terrorism?

Internet Exercises

Go to the *Business Law Today* home page at **http://blt.westbuslaw.com**. Select "Interactive Study Center" and then click on "Chapter 2." There you will find the following Internet research exercises that you can perform to learn more about free speech issues:

Activity 2–1: Flag Burning
Activity 2–2: Begging and the First Amendment

Before the Test

Go to the *Business Law Today* home page at **http://blt.westbuslaw.com**. Click on "Interactive Quizzes." You will find at least twenty interactive questions relating to this chapter.

CHAPTER 3

Traditional and Online Dispute Resolution

"The Judicial Department comes home in its effects to every man's fireside: it passes on his property, his reputation, his life, his all."

John Marshall, 1755–1835
(Chief justice of the United States Supreme Court, 1801–1835)

CHAPTER CONTENTS

LEARNING OBJECTIVES

After reading this chapter, you should be able to answer the following questions:

① What is judicial review? How and when was the power of judicial review established?

② Before a court can hear a case, it must have jurisdiction. Over what must it have jurisdiction? How are the courts applying traditional jurisdictional concepts to cases involving Internet transactions?

③ What is the difference between a trial court and an appellate court?

④ In a lawsuit, what are the pleadings? What is discovery? What is electronic filing?

⑤ How are online forums being used to resolve disputes?

As Chief Justice John Marshall remarked in the above quotation, ultimately, we are all affected by what the courts say and do. This is particularly true in the business world—nearly every businessperson faces either a potential or an actual lawsuit at some time or another in her or his career. For this reason, anyone contemplating a career in business will benefit from an understanding of American court systems, including the mechanics of lawsuits.

In this chapter, after examining the judiciary's overall role in the American governmental scheme, we discuss some basic requirements that must be met before a party may bring a lawsuit before a particular court. We then look at the court systems of the United States in some detail and, to clarify judicial procedures, follow a hypothetical case through a state court system. Even

"I am unaware that any nation of the globe has hitherto organized a judicial power in the same manner as the Americans . . . . A more imposing judicial power was never constituted by any people."

ALEXIS DE TOCQUEVILLE, 1805–1859
(French historian and statesman)

though there are fifty-two court systems—one for each of the fifty states, one for the District of Columbia, plus a federal system—similarities abound. Keep in mind that the federal courts are not superior to the state courts; they are simply an independent system of courts, which derives its authority from Article III, Section 2, of the U.S. Constitution. The chapter concludes with an overview of some alternative methods of settling disputes, including methods for settling disputes in online forums.

Note that technological developments are affecting court procedures just as they are affecting all other areas of the law. In this chapter, we will also indicate how court doctrines and procedures, as well as alternative methods of dispute settlement, are being adapted to the needs of a cyber age.

The Judiciary's Role in American Government

As you learned in Chapter 1, the body of American law includes the federal and state constitutions, statutes passed by legislative bodies, administrative law, and the case decisions and legal principles that form the common law. These laws would be meaningless, however, without the courts to interpret and apply them. This is the essential role of the judiciary—the courts—in the American governmental system: to interpret and apply the law.

JUDICIAL REVIEW

JUDICIAL REVIEW
The process by which a court decides on the constitutionality of legislative enactments and actions of the executive branch.

As the branch of government entrusted with interpreting the laws, the judiciary can decide, among other things, whether the laws or actions of the other two branches are constitutional. The process for making such a determination is known as **judicial review**. The power of judicial review enables the judicial branch to act as a check on the other two branches of government, in line with the checks-and-balances system established by the U.S. Constitution.

INTERNATIONAL PERSPECTIVE

Judicial Review in Other Nations

The concept of judicial review was pioneered by the United States. Some maintain that one of the reasons the doctrine was readily accepted in this country was that it fit well with the checks and balances designed by the founders. Today, all established constitutional democracies have some form of judicial review—the power to rule on the constitutionality of laws—but its form varies from country to country.

For example, Canada's Supreme Court can exercise judicial review but is barred from doing so if a law includes a provision explicitly prohibiting such review. France has a Constitutional Council that rules on the constitutionality of laws *before* the laws take effect. Laws can be referred to the council for prior review by the president, prime minister, and the heads of the two chambers of parliament. Prior review is also an option in Germany and Italy, if requested by the national or a regional government. In contrast, the United States Supreme Court does not give advisory opinions; there must be an actual dispute concerning an issue before the Supreme Court will render a decision on the matter.

FOR CRITICAL ANALYSIS
In any country in which a constitution sets forth the basic powers and structure of government, some government body has to decide whether laws enacted by government are consistent with that constitution. Is this task best handled by the courts? Can you think of a better alternative?

James Madison. If Madison had delivered the commissions of the Federalist judges, would the U.S. Supreme Court today have the power of judicial review?

THE ORIGINS OF JUDICIAL REVIEW IN THE UNITED STATES

The power of judicial review was not mentioned in the Constitution, but the concept was not new at the time the nation was founded. Indeed, prior to 1789 state courts had already overturned state legislative acts that conflicted with state constitutions. Additionally, many of the founders expected the United States Supreme Court to assume a similar role with respect to the federal Constitution. Alexander Hamilton and James Madison both emphasized the importance of judicial review in their essays urging the adoption of the new Constitution. The doctrine of judicial review was not legally established, however, until 1803, when the United States Supreme Court rendered its decision in *Marbury v. Madison*.[1] Details of this case are offered in the *Landmark in the Law* that follows.

1. 5 U.S. (1 Cranch) 137, 2 L.Ed. 60 (1803).

LANDMARK IN THE LAW
Marbury v. Madison (1803)

In the edifice of American law, the *Marbury v. Madison* decision in 1803 can be viewed as the keystone of the constitutional arch. The facts of the case were as follows. John Adams, who had lost his bid for reelection to Thomas Jefferson in 1800, feared the Jeffersonians' antipathy toward business and toward a strong central government. Adams thus worked feverishly to "pack" the judiciary with loyal Federalists (those who believed in a strong national government) by appointing what came to be called "midnight judges" just before Jefferson took office. All of the fifty-nine judicial appointment letters had to be certified and delivered, but Adams's secretary of state (John Marshall) had succeeded in delivering only forty-two of them by the time Jefferson took over as president. Jefferson, of course, refused to order his secretary of state, James Madison, to deliver the remaining commissions.

Marshall's Dilemma William Marbury and three others to whom the commissions had not been delivered sought a writ of *mandamus* (an order directing a government official to fulfill a duty) from the United States Supreme Court, as authorized by Section 13 of the Judiciary Act of 1789. As fate would have it, John Marshall had stepped down as Adams's secretary of state only to become chief justice of the Supreme Court. Marshall faced a dilemma: If he ordered the commissions delivered, the new secretary of state (Madison) could simply refuse to deliver them—and the Court had no way to compel action, because it had no police force. At the same time, if Marshall simply allowed the new administration to do as it wished, the Court's power would be severely eroded.

Marshall's Decision Marshall masterfully fashioned his decision. On the one hand, he enlarged the power of the Supreme Court by affirming the Court's power of judicial review. He stated, "It is emphatically the province and duty of the Judicial

(continued)

LANDMARK IN THE LAW—Continued

Department to say what the law is. . . . If two laws conflict with each other, the courts must decide on the operation of each. . . . So if the law be in opposition to the Constitution . . . [t]he Court must determine which of these conflicting rules governs the case. This is the very essence of judicial duty."

On the other hand, his decision did not require anyone to do anything. He stated that the highest court did not have the power to issue a writ of *mandamus* in this particular case. Marshall pointed out that although the Judiciary Act of 1789 specified that the Supreme Court could issue writs of *mandamus* as part of its original jurisdiction, Article III of the Constitution, which spelled out the Court's original jurisdiction, did not mention writs of *mandamus*. Because Congress did not have the right to expand the Supreme Court's jurisdiction, this section of the Judiciary Act of 1789 was unconstitutional—and thus void. The decision still stands today as a judicial and political masterpiece.

APPLICATION TO TODAY'S WORLD

Since the Marbury v. Madison *decision, the power of judicial review has remained unchallenged. Today, this power is exercised by both federal and state courts. This power clearly acts as a restraint on Congress today. For example, as you read in Chapter 2, Congress has recently passed a number of laws in an attempt to protect minors from pornographic materials on the Internet. Several of these laws have been held unconstitutional by the courts—in some cases, by the United States Supreme Court—on the ground that they violate constitutional provisions, such as freedom of speech. If the courts did not have the power of judicial review, the constitutionality of these acts of Congress could not be challenged in court—a congressional statute would remain law until changed by Congress.*

Basic Judicial Requirements

Before a court can hear a lawsuit, certain requirements must first be met. These requirements relate to jurisdiction, venue, and standing to sue. We examine each of these important concepts here.

JURISDICTION

In Latin, *juris* means "law," and *diction* means "to speak." Thus, "the power to speak the law" is the literal meaning of the term **jurisdiction.** Before any court can hear a case, it must have jurisdiction over the person against whom the suit is brought or over the property involved in the suit. The court must also have jurisdiction over the subject matter.

JURISDICTION
The authority of a court to hear and decide a specific action.

Jurisdiction over Persons Generally, a court can exercise personal jurisdiction (*in personam* jurisdiction) over residents of a certain geographic area. A state trial court, for example, normally has jurisdictional authority over residents of a particular area of the state, such as a county or district. A state's highest court (often called the state supreme court)[2] has jurisdictional authority over all residents within the state.

LONG ARM STATUTE
A state statute that permits a state to obtain personal jurisdiction over nonresident defendants. A defendant must have certain "minimum contacts" with that state for the statute to apply.

In some cases, under the authority of a state **long arm statute**, a court can exercise personal jurisdiction over nonresident defendants as well. Before a court can exercise jurisdiction over a nonresident under a long arm statute, though, it must be demonstrated that the nonresident had sufficient contacts, or *minimum contacts*, with the state to justify the jurisdiction.[3] • **EXAMPLE 3.1** If an individual has committed a wrong within the state, such as causing an automobile injury or selling defective goods, a court can usually exercise jurisdiction even if the person causing the harm is located in another state. Similarly, a state may exercise personal jurisdiction over a nonresident defendant who is sued for breaching a contract that was formed within the state.•

In regard to corporations,[4] the minimum-contacts requirement is usually met if the corporation does business within the state. • **EXAMPLE 3.2** Suppose that a corporation incorporated under the laws of Maine and headquartered in that state has a branch office or manufacturing plant in Georgia. Does this corporation have sufficient minimum contacts with the state of Georgia to allow a Georgia court to exercise jurisdiction over the Maine corporation? Yes, it does. If the Maine corporation advertises and sells its products in Georgia, those activities may suffice to meet the minimum-contacts requirement.•

In the following case, the issue was whether phone calls and letters constituted sufficient minimum contacts to give a court jurisdiction over a nonresident defendant.

2. As will be discussed shortly, a state's highest court is often referred to as the state supreme court, but there are exceptions. For example, in New York, the supreme court is a trial court.

3. The minimum-contacts standard was established in *International Shoe Co. v. State of Washington,* 326 U.S. 310, 66 S.Ct. 154, 90 L.Ed. 95 (1945).

4. In the eyes of the law, corporations are "legal persons"—entities that can sue and be sued. See Chapter 26.

CASE 3.1 Cole v. Mileti

United States Court of Appeals,
Sixth Circuit, 1998.
133 F.3d 433.
http://www.law.emory.edu/6circuit/jan98/index.html[a]

HISTORICAL AND ECONOMIC SETTING *A movie production company is expensive to operate. Over the several years it can take to produce a film, there are many expenses, including maintaining an office and hiring professionals of all kinds. Newcomers to the industry make many of the same wrong moves that are the pitfalls of all businesses. Novice producers or investors risk being outnegotiated by those who prey on a novice's ignorance or inexperience. Finally, once the film is made, the public may choose not to see it.*

a. This is a page, at the Web site of the Emory University School of Law, that lists the published opinions of the U.S. Court of Appeals for the Sixth Circuit for January 1998. Scroll down the list of cases to the *Cole* case. To access the opinion, click on the case name.

FACTS Nick Mileti, a resident of California, co-produced a movie called *Streamers* and organized a corporation, Streamers International Distributors, Inc., to distribute the film. Joseph Cole, a resident of Ohio, bought two hundred shares of Streamers stock. Cole also lent the firm $475,000, which he borrowed from Equitable Bank of Baltimore. The film was unsuccessful. Mileti agreed to repay Cole's loan in a contract arranged through phone calls and correspondence between California and Ohio. When Mileti did not repay the loan, the bank sued Cole, who in turn filed a suit against Mileti in a federal district court in Ohio. The court entered a judgment against Mileti. He appealed to the U.S. Court of Appeals for the

(continued)

CASE 3.1—Continued

Sixth Circuit, arguing in part that the district court's exercise of jurisdiction over him was unfair.

ISSUE Can a federal district court in Ohio[b] exercise personal jurisdiction over a resident of California who does business in Ohio via phone calls and letters?

DECISION Yes. The U.S. Court of Appeals for the Sixth Circuit held that the district court could exercise personal jurisdiction over Mileti.

b. As will be discussed shortly, federal district courts can exercise jurisdiction over disputes between parties living in different states. This is called *diversity-of-citizenship* jurisdiction. When a federal district court exercises diversity jurisdiction, the court normally applies the law of the state in which the court sits—in this case, the law of Ohio.

REASON The appellate court set out a three-part test to determine whether a court has jurisdiction over a nonresident defendant. A defendant must conduct activities in the state in which the suit is filed, the cause of action must arise from those activities, and those activities or their consequences must have a substantial connection to the state. The court reasoned that a nonresident who does business by "negotiating and executing a contract via telephone calls and letters to an Ohio resident" has conducted sufficient activities in the state. A cause of action arises from those activities if it is for breach of that contract. Finally, under those circumstances, the activities have a substantial connection to the state, and "the assertion of personal jurisdiction was proper."

FOR CRITICAL ANALYSIS—Economic Consideration *Why might a defendant prefer to be sued in one state rather than in another?*

Jurisdiction over Property A court can also exercise jurisdiction over property that is located within its boundaries. This kind of jurisdiction is known as *in rem* jurisdiction, or "jurisdiction over the thing." • **EXAMPLE 3.3** Suppose that a dispute arises over the ownership of a boat in dry dock in Fort Lauderdale, Florida. The boat is owned by an Ohio resident, over whom a Florida court normally cannot exercise personal jurisdiction. The other party to the dispute is a resident of Nebraska. In this situation, a lawsuit concerning the boat could be brought in a Florida state court on the basis of the court's *in rem* jurisdiction. •

Jurisdiction over Subject Matter Jurisdiction over subject matter is a limitation on the types of cases a court can hear. In both the federal and state court systems, there are courts of *general* (unlimited) *jurisdiction* and courts of *limited jurisdiction*. An example of a court of general jurisdiction is a state trial court or a federal district court. An example of a state court of limited jurisdiction is a probate court. **Probate courts** are state courts that handle only matters relating to the transfer of a person's assets and obligations after that person's death, including matters relating to the custody and guardianship of children. An example of a federal court of limited subject-matter jurisdiction is a bankruptcy court. **Bankruptcy courts** handle only bankruptcy proceedings, which are governed by federal bankruptcy law (discussed in Chapter 23). In contrast, a court of general jurisdiction can decide a broad array of cases.

PROBATE COURT A state court of limited jurisdiction that conducts proceedings relating to the settlement of a deceased person's estate.

BANKRUPTCY COURT A federal court of limited jurisdiction that handles only bankruptcy proceedings. Bankruptcy proceedings are governed by federal bankruptcy law.

A court's jurisdiction over subject matter is usually defined in the statute or constitution creating the court. In both the federal and state court systems, a court's subject-matter jurisdiction can be limited not only by the subject of the lawsuit but also by the amount of money in controversy, by whether a case is a felony (a more serious type of crime) or a misdemeanor (a less serious type of crime), or by whether the proceeding is a trial or an appeal.

Original and Appellate Jurisdiction The distinction between courts of original jurisdiction and courts of appellate jurisdiction normally lies in whether the case is being heard for the first time. Courts having original jurisdiction are courts of the first

LETTER OF THE LAW
The (Poetic) Language of the Law

Not all judges couch their legal reasoning in lengthy, ponderous, complicated opinions filled with Latin phrases and terms that only lawyers can understand. In fact, several judges over the years have peppered their opinions with humor and flights of fancy that entertain their readers. Some judges enjoy puns; others indulge in picturesque speech; still others wax poetic.

For example, in one case,[a] a bankruptcy judge, A. Jay Cristol, wrote his entire opinion in the form of a poem. In the poem, the judge first decided to dismiss the case, based on the conclusion that it would constitute an abuse of bankruptcy law (see Chapter 23) to let the debtor avoid his debts. During his poetic travels, however, he considered the debtor's plight and decided to allow the debtor to obtain bankruptcy relief.

a. *In re Robin E. Love,* 61 Bankr. 558 (S.D.Fla. 1986). (*In re* is one of the terms used in cases that typically involve only one party, as in bankruptcy cases.)

THE BOTTOM LINE

Increasingly, judges are being encouraged to use "plain language" and "simple English" in their opinions so that laypersons (and even other lawyers) can understand them. Notably, Judge Cristol's opinion clearly indicated his thoughts on the options available to him, as well as his decision in the matter.

instance, or trial courts—that is, courts in which lawsuits begin, trials take place, and evidence is presented. In the federal court system, the *district courts* are trial courts. In the various state court systems, the trial courts are known by various names, as will be discussed shortly.

The key point here is that, normally, any court having original jurisdiction is known as a trial court. Courts having appellate jurisdiction act as reviewing courts, or appellate courts. In general, cases can be brought before appellate courts only on appeal from an order or a judgment of a trial court or other lower court.

Jurisdiction of the Federal Courts Because the federal government is a government of limited powers, the jurisdiction of the federal courts is limited. Article III of the U.S. Constitution establishes the boundaries of federal judicial power. Section 2 of Article III states that "[t]he judicial Power shall extend to all Cases, in Law and Equity, arising under this Constitution, the Laws of the United States, and Treaties made, or which shall be made, under their Authority."

FEDERAL QUESTION
A question that pertains to the U.S. Constitution, acts of Congress, or treaties. A federal question provides a basis for federal jurisdiction.

Whenever a plaintiff's cause of action is based, at least in part, on the U.S. Constitution, a treaty, or a federal law, then a **federal question** arises, and the case comes under the judicial power of the federal courts. Any lawsuit involving a federal question can originate in a federal court. People who claim that their rights under the U.S. Constitution have been violated can begin their suits in a federal court.

DIVERSITY OF CITIZENSHIP
Under Article III, Section 2, of the Constitution, a basis for federal district court jurisdiction over a lawsuit between (1) citizens of different states, (2) a foreign country and citizens of a state or of different states, or (3) citizens of a state and citizens or subjects of a foreign country. The amount in controversy must be more than $75,000 before a federal district court can take jurisdiction in such cases.

Federal district courts can also exercise original jurisdiction over cases involving **diversity of citizenship.** Such cases may arise between (1) citizens of different states, (2) a foreign country and citizens of a state or of different states, or (3) citizens of a state and citizens or subjects of a foreign country. The amount in controversy must be more than $75,000 before a federal court can take jurisdiction in such cases. For purposes of diversity jurisdiction, a corporation is a citizen of both the state in which it is incorporated and the state in which its principal place of business is located. A case involving diversity of citizenship can be filed in the appropriate federal district court, or, if the case starts in a state court, it can sometimes be transferred to a federal court. A large percentage of the cases filed in federal courts each year are based on diversity of citizenship.

Note that in a case based on a federal question, a federal court will apply federal law. In a case based on diversity of citizenship, however, a federal court will apply the relevant state law (which is often the law of the state in which the court sits).

CONCURRENT JURISDICTION Jurisdiction that exists when two different courts have the power to hear a case. For example, some cases can be heard in a federal or a state court.

EXCLUSIVE JURISDICTION Jurisdiction that exists when a case can be heard only in a particular court or type of court.

Exclusive versus Concurrent Jurisdiction When both federal and state courts have the power to hear a case, as is true in suits involving diversity of citizenship, **concurrent jurisdiction** exists. When cases can be tried only in federal courts or only in state courts, exclusive jurisdiction exists. Federal courts have **exclusive jurisdiction** in cases involving federal crimes, bankruptcy, patents, and copyrights; in suits against the United States; and in some areas of admiralty law (law governing transportation on the seas and ocean waters). States also have exclusive jurisdiction in certain subject matters—for example, in divorce and adoption. The concepts of exclusive and concurrent jurisdiction are illustrated in Exhibit 3–1.

When concurrent jurisdiction exists, a party has a choice of whether to bring a suit in, for example, a federal or a state court. The party's lawyer will consider several factors in counseling the party as to which choice is preferable. The lawyer may prefer to litigate the case in a state court because he or she is more familiar with the state court's procedures, or perhaps the attorney believes that the state's judge or jury would be more sympathetic to the client and the case. Alternatively, the lawyer may advise the client to sue in federal court. Perhaps the state court's **docket** (the court's schedule listing the cases to be heard) is crowded, and the case could be brought to trial sooner in a federal court. Perhaps some feature of federal practice or procedure could offer an advantage in the client's case. Other important considerations include the law in an available jurisdiction, how that law has been applied in the jurisdiction's courts, and what the results in similar cases have been in that jurisdiction.

DOCKET The list of cases entered on a court's calendar and thus scheduled to be heard by the court.

JURISDICTION IN CYBERSPACE

The Internet's capacity to bypass political and geographic boundaries undercuts the traditional basic limitations on a court's authority to exercise jurisdiction. These limits include a party's contacts with a court's geographic jurisdiction. As already discussed,

EXHIBIT 3–1 EXCLUSIVE AND CONCURRENT JURISDICTION

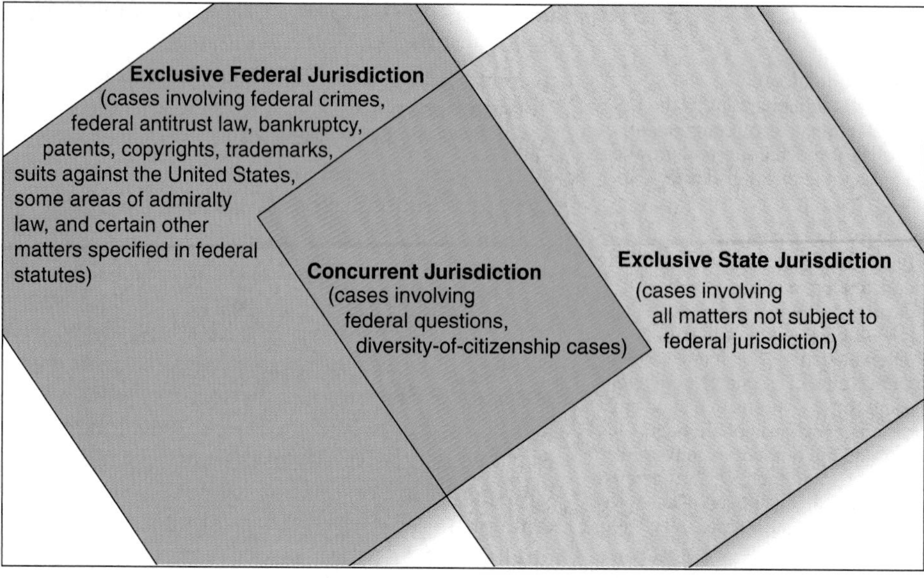

for a court to compel a defendant to come before it, there must be at least minimum contacts—the presence of a salesperson within the state, for example. Are there sufficient minimum contacts if the only connection to a jurisdiction is an ad on the Web originating from a remote location?

The "Sliding-Scale" Standard Gradually, the courts are developing a standard—called a "sliding-scale" standard—for determining when the exercise of jurisdiction over an out-of-state defendant is proper. In developing this standard, the courts have identified three types of Internet business contacts: (1) substantial business conducted over the Internet (with contracts, sales, and so on); (2) some interactivity through a Web site; and (3) passive advertising. Jurisdiction is proper for the first category, improper for the third, and may or may not be appropriate for the second.[5] (For a discussion of whether a single e-mail can constitute "minimum contacts," see this chapter's *Business Law in the Online World* feature.)

5. For a leading case on this issue, see *Zippo Manufacturing Co. v. Zippo Dot Com, Inc.,* 952 F.Supp. 1119 (W.D.Pa. 1997).

BUSINESS LAW: //in the Online World

Web Contacts and Jurisdiction

In virtually every area of the law, the use of the Internet to conduct business activities has raised new legal questions—or, more often, new variations on old questions. This is certainly true with respect to jurisdiction. To be sure, the courts are coming to some consensus as to when jurisdiction over a Web site owner or operator in another state is proper. Yet cases continue to come before the courts that do not readily "fit" into the categories and rules being developed by case law.

Consider a case that recently came before a federal court sitting in Mississippi. The case involved a lawsuit brought by Internet Doorway, Inc., an Internet service provider based in Mississippi, against Connie Davis, a Texas resident. Internet Doorway alleged that Davis had sent an unsolicited e-mail message, advertising a pornographic Web site, to persons all over the world, including Mississippi residents. The problem for Internet Doorway was that Davis had falsified the "from" header to make the e-mail appear to have been sent from an Internet Doorway account. In its suit, Internet Doorway claimed that Davis had committed the tort (civil wrong—see Chapter 4) of trespass to chattels, or personal property—the property in this case consisting of Internet Doorway's name and Internet accounts. Internet Doorway claimed that its reputation and goodwill in the community had been harmed as a result of Davis's action. Davis asked the court to dismiss the case for lack of personal jurisdiction.

The Minimum-Contacts Requirement

Years ago, in *International Shoe Co. v. State of Washington,*[a] the United States Supreme Court made it clear that before a state can exercise jurisdiction over a nonresident, the nonresident must have some minimum contacts with the state. If there were no minimum-contacts requirement, the exercise of personal jurisdiction "would offend traditional notions of fair play and substantial justice" mandated by the due process clause of the Fourteenth Amendment (see Chapter 2). Generally, the courts have concluded that a defendant's conduct in connection with the forum state (the state in which a lawsuit is initiated) must be such that she or he should reasonably anticipate "being haled into court" in that state.

Does One E-Mail Constitute "Minimum Contacts"?

In determining whether jurisdiction over Davis was proper, the federal court in Mississippi had to decide, among other things, whether Davis's single e-mail to Mississippi residents satisfied the minimum-contacts requirement for jurisdiction

a. 326 U.S. 310, 66 S.Ct. 154, 90 L.Ed. 95 (1945).

(continued)

BUSINESS LAW: //in the Online World

Web Contacts and Jurisdiction

over an out-of-state defendant. The court held that "even a single contact" could satisfy the minimum-contacts requirement in certain situations, including this one.

In its reasoning, the court distinguished between "active" and "passive" Internet communications. In this case, the message was not posted on a "passive" Web site, which people would have to voluntarily access in order to read the message. Rather, the message was sent via "active" e-mail to specific recipients. The court further noted that exercising jurisdiction over Davis did not offend any notions of fair play and substantial justice. The court concluded that Davis, by sending her e-mail solicitation "to the far reaches of the earth," had done so "at her own peril." She should reasonably have expected that she could be "haled into court in a distant jurisdiction to answer for the ramifications of that [e-mail]."[b]

FOR CRITICAL ANALYSIS

What if Internet Doorway had never become aware of Davis's action? Davis would still have committed a tort, but who would file a suit?

b. *Internet Doorway, Inc. v. Parks,* 138 F.Supp.2d 773 (S.D.Miss. 2001).

International Jurisdictional Issues Because the Internet is international in scope, international jurisdictional issues understandably have come to the fore. What seems to be emerging in the world's courts is a standard that echoes the requirement of "minimum contacts" applied by the U.S. courts. Most courts are indicating that minimum contacts—doing business within the jurisdiction, for example—are enough to compel a defendant to appear and that a physical presence is not necessary.[6] The effect of this standard is that a business firm has to comply with the laws in any jurisdiction in which it targets customers for its products.

The question then arises as to whether, in light of current technology, it is possible to do business over the Internet in one jurisdiction but not in another. If a company provides a link on its Web site through which a person in one country can do business with the firm, is it technically possible for that company to block access to persons in other countries? This question was one of the issues in the following widely publicized case.

6. Currently under negotiation is the Hague Convention on Jurisdiction, an international treaty that is intended to make civil judgments enforceable across national borders. One issue in the negotiations is whether to require that all disputes be settled in the country of the seller or the country of the buyer. It has also been suggested that mandatory jurisdiction provisions be left out of the treaty.

CASE 3.2 International League Against Racism and Antisemitism v. Yahoo! Inc.

Tribunal de Grande Instance de Paris, 2000.

HISTORICAL AND TECHNOLOGICAL SETTING
The Internet is a combination of several hundred million computer networks and associated sites that are interconnected throughout the world. Between 1973 and 1980, the U.S. Department of Defense defined a set of procedures by which the networks connected to the Internet could communicate. These procedures are known as Transmission Control Protocol/Internet Protocol, or TCP/IP. Each unit connected to the Internet must have what is known as an IP address, which is a series of numbers. For convenience, the numbers are associated with names, which are referred to as domain names (see Chapter 6).

FACTS Yahoo! Inc., operates a "Yahoo Auctions" Web site (at **http://auctions.yahoo.com**) that is directed principally at customers in the United States. Items offered for sale have included objects representing symbols of Nazi ideology. In France, the act of displaying such objects is a crime and is also subject to civil liability. The International

CASE 3.2—Continued

League Against Racism and Antisemitism and others filed a suit in the Tribunal de Grande Instance de Paris (a French court) against Yahoo and others, seeking an injunction and damages. The court ordered Yahoo to, among other things, "take all necessary measures to dissuade and make impossible any access [by persons in France or French territory] via yahoo.com to the auction service for Nazi merchandise as well as to any other site or service that may be construed as an apology for Nazism or contesting the reality of Nazi crimes." Two months later, Yahoo returned to the court, arguing in part that the court did not have jurisdiction and that even if it did, Yahoo could not do technically what the court ordered.

ISSUE Does a business firm have to comply with the laws of a jurisdiction in which it targets business?

DECISION Yes. The court affirmed the injunction, reasoning that the "combination of [the] technical measures at [Yahoo's] disposal" rendered compliance possible. The court gave Yahoo three months to comply, after which it would be fined 100,000 francs (approximately $14,000) for each day that it failed to do so. The court also ordered Yahoo to pay each plaintiff 10,000 francs.

REASON First, the court reasoned that because "YAHOO is aware that it is addressing French parties," as evidenced by the Web site's advertising banners in French, "a sufficient basis is thus established in this case for a connecting link with France, which renders our jurisdiction perfectly competent to rule in this matter." Next, on the technical questions, the court found that "it is possible to determine the physical location of a surfer from the IP address" and that Yahoo "already carries out geographical identification of French surfers or surfers operating out of French territory and visiting its auctions site." Surfers "whose IP address is ambiguous" can be asked "to provide a declaration of nationality, * * * when the home page is reached, or when a search is initiated for Nazi objects * * * before the request is processed by the search engine." These techniques "would enable a filtering success rate approaching 90%." Also, Yahoo "would know the place of delivery, and would be in a position to prevent the delivery from taking place if the delivery address was located in France."

FOR CRITICAL ANALYSIS—Technological Consideration *With this case in mind, how is the technology that underlies the Internet likely to change?*

COMMENT *Subsequent to this decision, Yahoo filed a suit in a U.S. federal court, arguing that the French court's order was not enforceable in the United States on the ground that the order presented a "real and immediate threat" to Yahoo's constitutional right to free speech. The federal court agreed and refused to recognize the French court's order. See* Yahoo!, Inc. v. La Ligue Contre le Racisme et L'Antisemitisme, *169 F.Supp.2d 1181 (N.D.Cal. 2001).*

VENUE

VENUE
The geographic district in which an action is tried and from which the jury is selected.

Jurisdiction has to do with whether a court has authority to hear a case involving specific persons, property, or subject matter. **Venue**[7] is concerned with the most appropriate location for a trial. Two state courts (or two federal courts) may have the authority to exercise jurisdiction over a case, but it may be more appropriate or convenient to hear the case in one court than in the other.

Basically, the concept of venue reflects the policy that a court trying a suit should be in the geographic neighborhood (usually the county) where the incident leading to the lawsuit occurred or where the parties involved in the lawsuit reside. Pretrial publicity or other factors, though, may require a change of venue to another community, especially in criminal cases in which the defendant's right to a fair and impartial jury has been impaired. ● **EXAMPLE 3.4** A change of venue from Oklahoma City to Denver, Colorado, was ordered for the trials of Timothy McVeigh and Terry Nichols, who had been indicted in connection with the 1995 bombing of the Alfred P. Murrah Federal Building in Oklahoma City. (At trial, both McVeigh and Nichols were convicted. McVeigh received the death penalty and was put to death by lethal injection in early 2001. Nichols was sentenced to life imprisonment.)●

7. Pronounced *ven*-yoo.

STANDING TO SUE

STANDING TO SUE
The requirement that an individual must have a sufficient stake in a controversy before he or she can bring a lawsuit. The plaintiff must demonstrate that he or she either has been injured or threatened with injury.

Before a person can bring a lawsuit before a court, the party must have **standing to sue**, or a sufficient "stake" in a matter to justify seeking relief through the court system. In other words, a party must have a legally protected and tangible interest at stake in the litigation in order to have standing. The party bringing the lawsuit must have suffered a harm, or have been threatened by a harm, as a result of the action about which she or he complained. At times, a person will have standing to sue on behalf of another person. • **EXAMPLE 3.5** Suppose that a child suffered serious injuries as a result of a defectively manufactured toy. Because the child is a minor, a lawsuit could be brought on his or her behalf by another person, such as the child's parent or legal guardian. •

JUSTICIABLE CONTROVERSY
A controversy that is not hypothetical or academic but real and substantial; a requirement that must be satisfied before a court will hear a case.

Standing to sue also requires that the controversy at issue be a **justiciable**[8] **controversy**—a controversy that is real and substantial, as opposed to hypothetical or academic. • **EXAMPLE 3.6** In the above example, the child's parent could not sue the toy manufacturer merely on the ground that the toy was defective. The issue would become justiciable only if the child had actually been injured due to the defect in the toy as marketed. In other words, the parent normally could not ask the court to determine, for example, what damages might be obtained if the child had been injured, because this would be merely a hypothetical question. •

The State and Federal Court Systems

"The perfect judge fears nothing—he could go front to front before God."
WALT WHITMAN, 1819–1892 (American poet)

As mentioned earlier in this chapter, each state has its own court system. Additionally, there is a system of federal courts. Although state court systems differ, Exhibit 3–2 illustrates the basic organizational structure characteristic of the court systems in many states. The exhibit also shows how the federal court system is structured. We turn now to an examination of these court systems, beginning with the state courts.

8. Pronounced jus-*tish*-uh-bul.

EXHIBIT 3–2 FEDERAL COURTS AND STATE COURT SYSTEMS

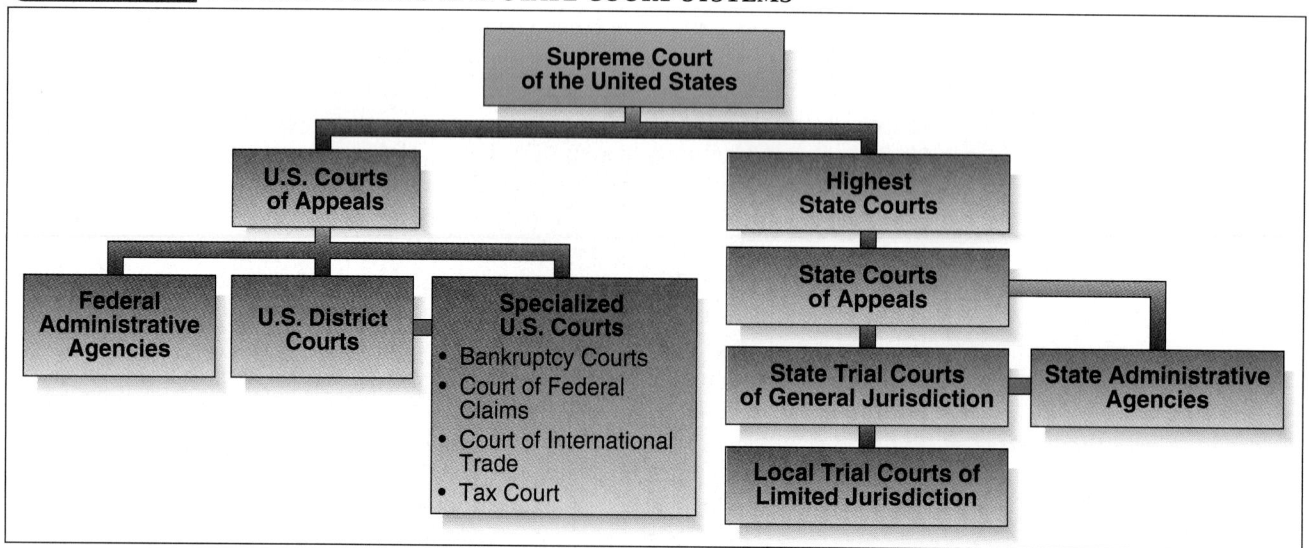

ON THE WEB If you want to find information on state court systems, the National Center for State Courts (NCSC) offers links to the Web pages of all state courts at **http://www.ncsconline.org**.

State Court Systems

Typically, a state court system will include several levels, or tiers, of courts. As indicated in Exhibit 3–2, state courts may include (1) trial courts of limited jurisdiction, (2) trial courts of general jurisdiction, (3) appellate courts, and (4) the state's highest court (often called the state supreme court). Generally, any person who is a party to a lawsuit has the opportunity to plead the case before a trial court and then, if he or she loses, before at least one level of appellate court. Finally, if a federal statute or federal constitutional issue is involved in the decision of the state supreme court, that decision may be further appealed to the United States Supreme Court.

Judges in the state court system are usually elected by the voters for a specified term. In contrast, as you will read shortly, judges in the federal court system are appointed by the president of the United States and, if they are confirmed by the Senate, hold office for life—unless they engage in blatantly illegal conduct.

ETHICAL ISSUE 3.1

Are state court systems too political?

Judges in the federal court system, because they are appointed, do not have to worry about reelection and, consequently, can make rulings on specific issues without having to take public opinion into account. Although some state judges are appointed (the procedures vary widely from state to state), in most states at least some judges are elected. To gain (or retain) their seats, those judges typically must conduct political campaigns—and obtain funds to pay for those campaigns. In some judicial races, campaign contributions have exceeded $5 million. Typically, a substantial portion of those funds has come from trial lawyers, many of whom argue cases before the very judges whose campaigns they help to finance. In 2000, affiliates of the U.S. Chamber of Commerce spent close to $10 million on ads in state judicial races in support of or against specific judges. Because of increasing influence of campaign contributions on state judicial elections, some have advocated legal reforms that include placing caps on contributions to state judicial candidates.[9]

Trial Courts Trial courts are exactly what their name implies—courts in which trials are held and testimony taken. State trial courts have either general or limited jurisdiction. Trial courts that have general jurisdiction as to subject matter may be called county, district, superior, or circuit courts.[10] The jurisdiction of these courts is often determined by the size of the county in which the court sits. State trial courts of general jurisdiction have jurisdiction over a wide variety of subjects, including both civil disputes and criminal prosecutions. In some states, trial courts of general jurisdiction may hear appeals from courts of limited jurisdiction.

SMALL CLAIMS COURT
A special court in which parties may litigate small claims (such as $5,000 or less). Attorneys are not required in small claims courts and, in some states, are not allowed to represent the parties.

Some courts of limited jurisdiction are called special inferior trial courts or minor judiciary courts. **Small claims courts** are inferior trial courts that hear only civil cases involving claims of less than a certain amount, such as $5,000 (the amount varies from

9. For further information on this issue, see Emily Heller and Mark Ballard, "Hard-Fought, Big-Money Judicial Races," *The National Law Journal,* November 6, 2000, pp. A1 and A8.
10. The name in Ohio is court of common pleas; the name in New York is supreme court.

A mother talks with a social worker after a court awarded the mother custody of her child. Are child-custody matters decided by federal or state courts?

state to state). Suits brought in small claims courts are generally conducted informally, and lawyers are not required. In a minority of states, lawyers are not even allowed to represent people in small claims courts for most purposes. Another example of an inferior trial court is a local municipal court that hears mainly traffic cases. Decisions of small claims courts and municipal courts may be appealed to a state trial court of general jurisdiction.

Other courts of limited jurisdiction as to subject matter include domestic relations courts, which handle only divorce actions and child-custody cases, and probate courts, as mentioned earlier.

Courts of Appeals Every state has at least one court of appeals (appellate court, or reviewing court), which may be an intermediate appellate court or the state's highest court. About three-fourths of the states have intermediate appellate courts. Generally, courts of appeals do not conduct new trials, in which evidence is submitted to the court and witnesses are examined. Rather, an appellate court panel of three or more judges reviews the record of the case on appeal, which includes a transcript of the trial proceedings, and determines whether the trial court committed an error.

Usually, appellate courts do not look at questions of *fact* (such as whether a party did, in fact, commit a certain action, such as burning a flag) but at questions of *law* (such as whether the act of flag-burning is a form of speech protected by the First Amendment to the Constitution). Only a judge, not a jury, can rule on questions of law. Appellate courts normally defer to a trial court's findings on questions of fact because the trial court judge and jury were in a better position to evaluate testimony—by directly observing witnesses' gestures, demeanor, and nonverbal behavior during the trial. At the appellate level, the judges review the written transcript of the trial, which does not include these nonverbal elements.

An appellate court will challenge a trial court's finding of fact only when the finding is clearly erroneous (that is, when it is contrary to the evidence presented at trial) or when there is no evidence to support the finding. • **EXAMPLE 3.7** If a jury concluded that a manufacturer's product harmed the plaintiff but no evidence was submitted to the court to support that conclusion, the appellate court would hold that the trial court's decision was erroneous. The options exercised by appellate courts will be further discussed later in this chapter. •

BE CAREFUL The decisions of a state's highest court are final on questions of state law.

State Supreme (Highest) Courts The highest appellate court in a state is usually called the supreme court but may be called by some other name. For example, in both New York and Maryland, the highest state court is called the court of appeals. The decisions of each state's highest court on all questions of state law are final. Only when issues of federal law are involved can a decision made by a state's highest court be overruled by the United States Supreme Court.

THE FEDERAL COURT SYSTEM

ON THE WEB To find information about the federal court system and links to all federal courts, go to the home page of the federal judiciary at **http://www.uscourts.gov**.

The federal court system is basically a three-tiered model consisting of (1) U.S. district courts (trial courts of general jurisdiction) and various courts of limited jurisdiction, (2) U.S. courts of appeals (intermediate courts of appeals), and (3) the United States Supreme Court.

Unlike state court judges, who are usually elected, federal court judges—including the justices of the Supreme Court—are appointed by the president of the United States and confirmed by the U.S. Senate. All federal judges receive lifetime appointments (because under Article III they "hold their offices during Good Behavior").

U.S. District Courts At the federal level, the equivalent of a state trial court of general jurisdiction is the district court. There is at least one federal district court in every state. The number of judicial districts can vary over time, primarily owing to population changes and corresponding caseloads. Currently, there are ninety-four federal judicial districts.

U.S. district courts have original jurisdiction in federal matters. Federal cases typically originate in district courts. There are other courts with original, but special (or limited), jurisdiction, such as the federal bankruptcy courts and others shown in Exhibit 3–2.

ON THE WEB

The decisions of all of the U.S. courts of appeals, as well as those of the United States Supreme Court, are now published online shortly after the decisions are rendered. You can find these decisions and obtain information about the federal court system by accessing the Federal Court Locator at **http://vls.law.vill.edu/Locator/fedcourt.html**.

U.S. Courts of Appeals In the federal court system, there are thirteen U.S. courts of appeals—also referred to as U.S. circuit courts of appeals. The federal courts of appeals for twelve of the circuits, including the U.S. Court of Appeals for the District of Columbia Circuit, hear appeals from the federal district courts located within their respective judicial circuits. The Court of Appeals for the Thirteenth Circuit, called the Federal Circuit, has national appellate jurisdiction over certain types of cases, such as cases involving patent law and cases in which the U.S. government is a defendant.

The decisions of the circuit courts of appeals are final in most cases, but appeal to the United States Supreme Court is possible. Exhibit 3–3 shows the geographic boundaries

EXHIBIT 3–3 U.S. COURTS OF APPEALS AND U.S. DISTRICT COURTS

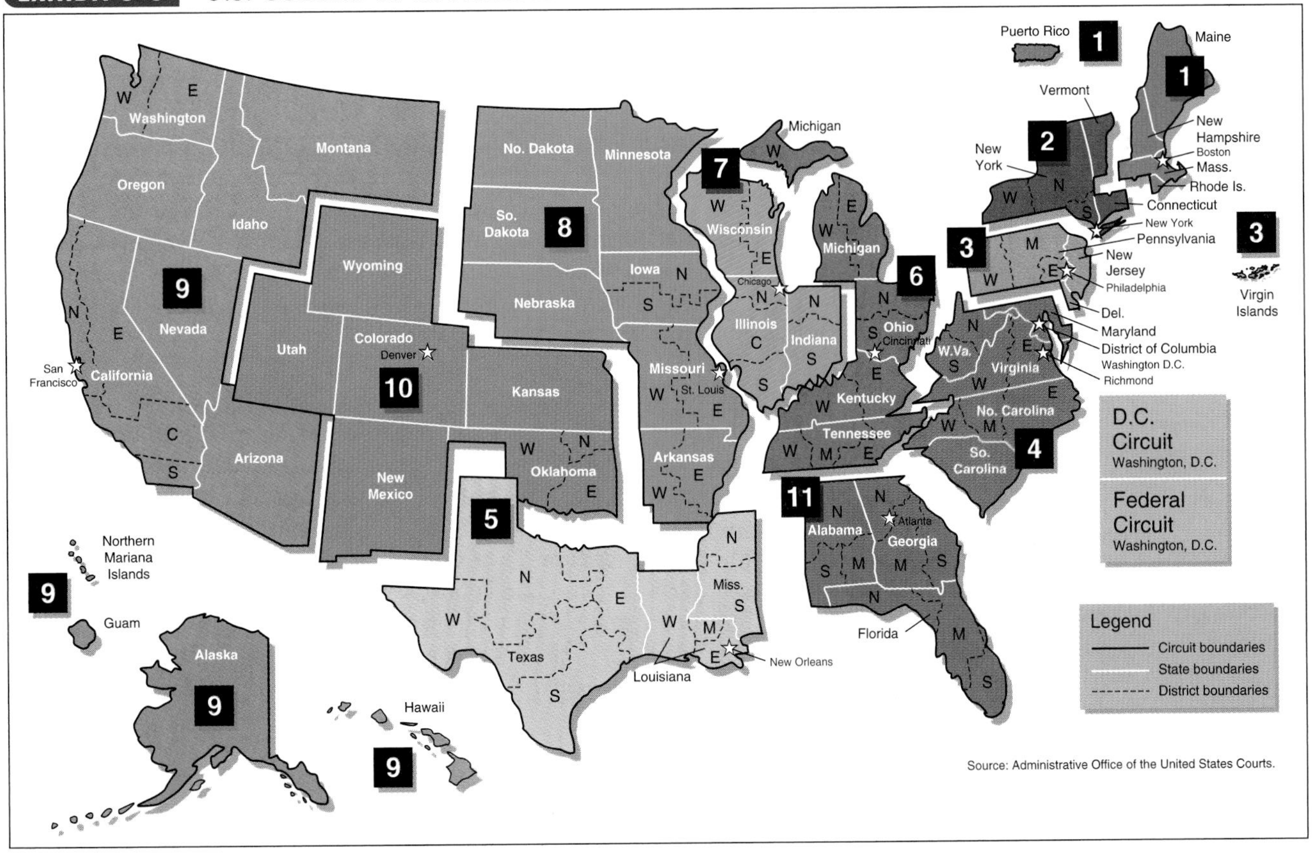

Source: Administrative Office of the United States Courts.

The justices of the U.S. Supreme Court are, seated left to right, Antonin Scalia, John Paul Stevens, Chief Justice William H. Rehnquist, Sandra Day O'Connor, and Anthony M. Kennedy; and standing left to right, Ruth Bader Ginsgurg, David H. Souter, Clarence Thomas, and Stephen Breyer. Does the fact that these justices are appointed for life have any effect on the decisions they reach in the cases they hear?

of the U.S. circuit courts of appeals and the boundaries of the U.S. district courts within each circuit.

"We are not final because we are infallible, but we are infallible only because we are final."

ROBERT H. JACKSON, 1892–1954
(Associate justice of the United States Supreme Court, 1941–1954)

The United States Supreme Court The highest level of the three-tiered model of the federal court system is the United States Supreme Court. According to the language of Article III of the U.S. Constitution, there is only one national Supreme Court. All other courts in the federal system are considered "inferior." Congress is empowered to create other inferior courts as it deems necessary. The inferior courts that Congress has created include the second tier in our model—the U.S. courts of appeals—as well as the district courts and any other courts of limited, or specialized, jurisdiction.

The United States Supreme Court consists of nine justices. Although the Supreme Court has original, or trial, jurisdiction in rare instances (set forth in Article III, Section 2), most of its work is as an appeals court. The Supreme Court can review any case decided by any of the federal courts of appeals, and it also has appellate authority over some cases decided in the state courts.

WRIT OF *CERTIORARI*
A writ from a higher court asking the lower court for the record of a case.

RULE OF FOUR
A rule of the United States Supreme Court under which the Court will not issue a writ of *certiorari* unless at least four justices approve of the decision to issue the writ.

Appeals to the Supreme Court. To bring a case before the Supreme Court, a party requests the Court to issue a writ of *certiorari*. A **writ of *certiorari***[11] is an order issued by the Supreme Court to a lower court requiring the latter to send it the record of the case for review. The Court will not issue a writ unless at least four of the nine justices approve of it. This is called the **rule of four.** Whether the Court will issue a writ of *certiorari* is entirely within its discretion. The Court is not required to issue one, and most petitions for writs are denied. (Thousands of cases are filed with the Supreme Court each year, yet it hears, on average, fewer than one hundred of these cases.)[12] A denial is not a decision on the merits of a case, nor does it indicate agreement with the lower court's opinion. Furthermore, a denial of the writ has no value as a precedent.

11. Pronounced sur-shee-uh-*rah*-ree.

12. From the mid-1950s through the early 1990s, the Supreme Court reviewed more cases per year than it has in the last few years. In the Court's 1982–1983 term, for example, the Court issued opinions in 151 cases. In contrast, in its 2000–2001 term, the Court issued opinions in only 79 cases.

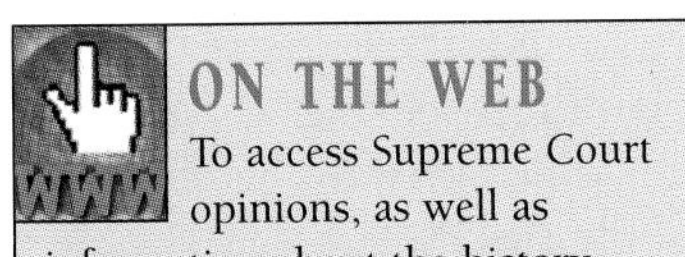

To access Supreme Court opinions, as well as information about the history and function of the Court, go to the Court's official Web site at **http://supremecourtus.gov**.

Petitions Granted by the Court. Typically, the petitions granted by the Court involve cases that raise important constitutional questions or cases that conflict with other state or federal court decisions. Similarly, if federal appellate courts are rendering inconsistent opinions on an important issue, the Supreme Court may review the case and issue a decision to define the law on the matter. The justices, however, never explain their reasons for hearing certain cases and not others, so it is difficult to predict which type of case the Court might select.

Certainly, many legal scholars were surprised when the Court, in the confusing aftermath of the 2000 elections, decided to review the Florida Supreme Court's decision that the votes in selected Florida counties could be manually recounted. Many observers had predicted that, given the Court's tendency to support states' rights and its traditional reluctance to get involved in "political questions," it would deny *certiorari* in that case. The Court, however, concluded that the case raised an important constitutional question—whether manually counting votes in some counties but not others violated the equal protection clause—and thus reviewed (and overturned) the Florida court's decision.[13]

Following a State Court Case

To illustrate the procedures that would be followed in a civil lawsuit brought in a state court, we present a hypothetical case and follow it through the state court system. The case involves an automobile accident in which Kevin Anderson, driving a Mercedes, struck Lisa Marconi, driving a Ford Taurus. The accident occurred at the intersection of Wilshire Boulevard and Rodeo Drive in Beverly Hills, California. Marconi suffered personal injuries, incurring medical and hospital expenses as well as lost wages for four months. Anderson and Marconi are unable to agree on a settlement, and Marconi sues Anderson. Marconi is the plaintiff, and Anderson is the defendant. Both are represented by lawyers.

LITIGATION
The process of resolving a dispute through the court system.

During each phase of the **litigation** (the process of working a lawsuit through the court system), Marconi and Anderson will be required to observe strict procedural requirements. A large body of law—procedural law—establishes the rules and standards for determining disputes in courts. Procedural rules are very complex, and they vary from court to court. There is a set of federal rules of procedure as well as various sets of rules for state courts. Additionally, the applicable procedures will depend on whether the case is a civil or criminal proceeding. Generally, the Marconi-Anderson civil lawsuit will involve the procedures discussed in the following subsections. Keep in mind that attempts to settle the case may be ongoing throughout the trial.

PLEADINGS
Statements made by the plaintiff and the defendant in a lawsuit that detail the facts, charges, and defenses involved in the litigation; the complaint and answer are part of the pleadings.

COMPLAINT
The pleading made by a plaintiff alleging wrongdoing on the part of the defendant; the document that, when filed with a court, initiates a lawsuit.

THE PLEADINGS

The complaint and answer (and the counterclaim and reply)—all of which are discussed below—taken together are called the **pleadings**. The pleadings inform each party of the other's claims and specify the issues (disputed questions) involved in the case.

The Plaintiff's Complaint Marconi's suit against Anderson commences when her lawyer files a **complaint** with the appropriate court. The complaint contains a statement alleging (asserting to the court, in a pleading) the facts necessary for the court to

13. *Bush v. Gore,* 531 U.S. 98, 121 S.Ct. 525, 148 L.Ed.2d 388 (2000).

SUMMONS
A document informing a defendant that a legal action has been commenced against him or her and that the defendant must appear in court on a certain date to answer the plaintiff's complaint. The document is delivered by a sheriff or any other person so authorized.

take jurisdiction, a brief summary of the facts necessary to show that the plaintiff is entitled to a remedy, and a statement of the remedy the plaintiff is seeking. Exhibit 3–4 illustrates how the complaint might read in the Marconi-Anderson case. Complaints may be lengthy or brief, depending on the complexity of the case.

After the complaint has been filed, the sheriff, a deputy of the county, or another *process server* (one who delivers a complaint and summons) serves a **summons** and a

EXHIBIT 3–4 EXAMPLE OF A TYPICAL COMPLAINT

IN THE LOS ANGELES MUNICIPAL COURT
FOR THE LOS ANGELES JUDICIAL DISTRICT

CIVIL NO. 8–1026

Lisa Marconi
Plaintiff

v.

COMPLAINT

Kevin Anderson
Defendant

Comes now the plaintiff and for her cause of action against the defendant alleges and states as follows:

1. The jurisdiction of this court is based on Section 86 of the California Civil Code.
2. This action is between plaintiff, a California resident living at 1434 Palm Drive, Anaheim, California, and defendant, a California resident living at 6950 Garrison Avenue, Los Angeles, California.
3. On September 10, 2001, plaintiff, Lisa Marconi, was exercising good driving habits and reasonable care in driving her car through the intersection of Rodeo Drive and Wilshire Boulevard when defendant, Kevin Anderson, negligently drove his vehicle through a red light at the intersection and collided with plaintiff's vehicle. Defendant was negligent in the operation of the vehicle as to:
    a. Speed,
    b. Lookout,
    c. Management and control.
4. As a result of the collision plaintiff suffered severe physical injury that prevented her from working and property damage to her car. The costs she incurred included $10,000 in medical bills, $9,000 in lost wages, and $5,000 for automobile repairs.

WHEREFORE, plaintiff demands judgment against the defendant for the sum of $24,000 plus interest at the maximum legal rate and the costs of this action.

By *Roger Harrington*
Roger Harrington
Attorney for the Plaintiff
800 Orange Avenue
Anaheim, CA 91426

copy of the complaint on defendant Anderson. The summons notifies Anderson that he must file an answer to the complaint with both the court and the plaintiff's attorney within a specified time period (usually twenty to thirty days). The summons also informs Anderson that failure to answer may result in a **default judgment** for the plaintiff, meaning the plaintiff will be awarded the damages alleged in her complaint.

DEFAULT JUDGMENT
A judgment entered by a court against a defendant who has failed to appear in court to answer or defend against the plaintiff's claim.

ANSWER
Procedurally, a defendant's response to the plaintiff's complaint.

The Defendant's Answer The defendant's **answer** either admits the statements or allegations set forth in the complaint or denies them and outlines any defenses that the defendant may have. If Anderson admits to all of Marconi's allegations in his answer, the court will enter a judgment for Marconi. If Anderson denies any of Marconi's allegations, the litigation will go forward.

Anderson can deny Marconi's allegations and set forth his own claim that Marconi was in fact negligent and therefore owes him money for damages to his Mercedes. This is appropriately called a **counterclaim**. If Anderson files a counterclaim, Marconi will have to answer it with a pleading, normally called a **reply**, which has the same characteristics as an answer.

COUNTERCLAIM
A claim made by a defendant in a civil lawsuit against the plaintiff. In effect, the defendant is suing the plaintiff.

REPLY
Procedurally, a plaintiff's response to a defendant's answer.

Anderson can also admit the truth of Marconi's complaint but raise new facts that may result in dismissal of the action. This is called raising an affirmative defense. For example, Anderson could assert the expiration of the time period under the relevant statute of limitations (a state or federal statute that sets the maximum time period during which a certain action can be brought or rights enforced) as an affirmative defense.

MOTION TO DISMISS
A pleading in which a defendant asserts that the plaintiff's claim fails to state a cause of action (that is, has no basis in law) or that there are other grounds on which a suit should be dismissed.

Motion to Dismiss A **motion to dismiss** requests the court to dismiss the case for stated reasons. A defendant often makes a motion to dismiss before filing an answer to the plaintiff's complaint. Grounds for dismissal of a case include improper delivery of the complaint and summons, improper venue, and the plaintiff's failure to state a claim for which a court could grant relief (a remedy). For example, if Marconi had suffered no injuries or losses as a result of Anderson's negligence, Anderson could move to have the case dismissed because Marconi had not stated a claim for which relief could be granted.

If the judge grants the motion to dismiss, the plaintiff generally is given time to file an amended complaint. If the judge denies the motion, the suit will go forward, and the defendant must then file an answer. Note that if Marconi wishes to discontinue the suit because, for example, an out-of-court settlement has been reached, she can likewise move for dismissal. The court can also dismiss the case on its own motion.

PRETRIAL MOTIONS

Either party may attempt to get the case dismissed before trial through the use of various pretrial motions. We have already mentioned the motion to dismiss. Two other important pretrial motions are the motion for judgment on the pleadings and the motion for summary judgment.

MOTION FOR JUDGMENT ON THE PLEADINGS
A motion by either party to a lawsuit at the close of the pleadings requesting the court to decide the issue solely on the pleadings without proceeding to trial. The motion will be granted only if no facts are in dispute.

MOTION FOR SUMMARY JUDGMENT
A motion requesting the court to enter a judgment without proceeding to trial. The motion can be based on evidence outside the pleadings and will be granted only if no facts are in dispute.

At the close of the pleadings, either party may make a **motion for judgment on the pleadings**, or on the merits of the case. The judge will grant the motion only when there is no dispute over the facts of the case and the only issue to be resolved is a question of law. In deciding on the motion, the judge may consider only the evidence contained in the pleadings.

In contrast, in a **motion for summary judgment** the court may consider evidence outside the pleadings, such as sworn statements (affidavits) by parties or witnesses or other documents relating to the case. A motion for summary judgment can be made by either party. As with the motion for judgment on the pleadings, a motion for summary judgment will be granted only if there are no genuine questions of fact and the only question is a question of law.

DISCOVERY

Before a trial begins, each party can use a number of procedural devices to obtain information and gather evidence about the case from the other party or from third parties. The process of obtaining such information is known as **discovery.** Discovery includes gaining access to witnesses, documents, records, and other types of evidence.

DISCOVERY
A phase in the litigation process during which the opposing parties may obtain information from each other and from third parties prior to trial.

The Federal Rules of Civil Procedure and similar rules in the states set forth the guidelines for discovery activity. The rules governing discovery are designed to make sure that a witness or a party is not unduly harassed, that privileged material (communications that need not be presented in court) is safeguarded, and that only matters relevant to the case at hand are discoverable.

Discovery prevents surprises at trial by giving parties access to evidence that might otherwise be hidden. This allows both parties to learn as much as they can about what to expect at a trial before they reach the courtroom.[14] It also serves to narrow the issues so that trial time is spent on the main questions in the case.

Depositions and Interrogatories Discovery can involve the use of depositions or interrogatories, or both. **Depositions** are sworn testimony by a party to the lawsuit or any witness. The person being deposed (the deponent) answers questions asked by the attorneys, and the questions and answers are recorded by an authorized court official and sworn to and signed by the deponent. (Occasionally, written depositions are taken when witnesses are unable to appear in person.) The answers given to depositions will, of course, help the attorneys prepare their cases. They can also be used in court to impeach (challenge the credibility of) a party or a witness who changes testimony at the trial. In addition, the answers given in a deposition can be used as testimony if the witness is not available at trial.

DEPOSITION
The testimony of a party to a lawsuit or a witness taken under oath before a trial.

Interrogatories are written questions for which written answers are prepared and then signed under oath. The main difference between interrogatories and written depositions is that interrogatories are directed to a party to the lawsuit (the plaintiff or the defendant), not to a witness, and the party can prepare answers with the aid of an attorney. The scope of interrogatories is broader, because parties are obligated to answer questions, even if it means disclosing information from their records and files.

INTERROGATORIES
A series of written questions for which written answers are prepared, usually with the assistance of the party's attorney, and then signed under oath by a party to a lawsuit.

Other Information A party can serve a written request to the other party for an admission of the truth of matters relating to the trial. Any matter admitted under such a request is conclusively established for the trial. For example, Marconi can ask Anderson to admit that he was driving at a speed of forty-five miles an hour. A request for admission saves time at trial, because the parties will not have to spend time proving facts on which they already agree.

A party can also gain access to documents and other items not in her or his possession in order to inspect and examine them. Likewise, a party can gain "entry upon land" to inspect the premises. Anderson's attorney, for example, normally can gain permission to inspect and duplicate Marconi's car repair bills.

14. This is particularly evident in the 1993 revision of the Federal Rules of Civil Procedure. The revised rules provide that each party must disclose to the other, on an ongoing basis, the types of evidence that will be presented at trial, the names of witnesses that may or will be called, and so on.

When the physical or mental condition of one party is in question, the opposing party can ask the court to order a physical or mental examination. If the court is willing to make the order, which it will do only if the need for the information outweighs the right to privacy of the person to be examined, the opposing party can obtain the results of the examination.

PRETRIAL CONFERENCE

Either party or the court can request a pretrial conference, or hearing. Usually, the hearing consists of an informal discussion between the judge and the opposing attorneys after discovery has taken place. The purpose of the hearing is to explore the possibility of a settlement without trial and, if this is not possible, to identify the matters that are in dispute and to plan the course of the trial.

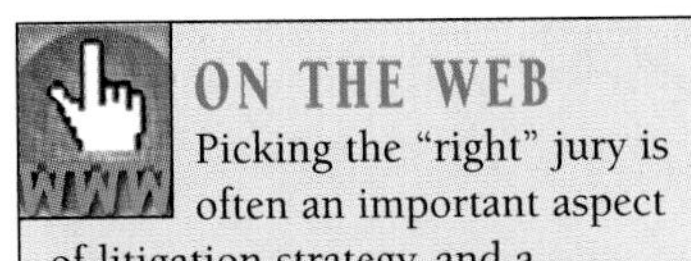

ON THE WEB Picking the "right" jury is often an important aspect of litigation strategy, and a number of firms now specialize in jury consulting services. You can learn more about these services by going to the Web site of the Jury Research Institute at **http://www.jri-inc.com**.

VOIR DIRE
French verbs that mean, literally, "to see" and "to speak." In jury trials, the phrase refers to the process in which the attorneys question prospective jurors to determine whether they are biased or have any connection with a party to the action or with a prospective witness.

TAKE NOTE A prospective juror cannot be excluded solely on the basis of his or her race or gender.

JURY SELECTION

A trial can be held with or without a jury. The Seventh Amendment to the U.S. Constitution guarantees the right to a jury trial for cases in federal courts when the amount in controversy exceeds $20. Most states have similar guarantees in their own constitutions (although the threshold dollar amount is higher than $20). The right to a trial by jury does not have to be exercised, and many cases are tried without a jury. In most states and in federal courts, one of the parties must request a jury, or the right is presumed to be waived.

Before a jury trial commences, a jury must be selected. The jury-selection process is known as ***voir dire***.[15] In most jurisdictions, *voir dire* consists of oral questions that attorneys for the plaintiff and the defendant ask prospective jurors to determine whether a potential jury member is biased or has any connection with a party to the action or with a prospective witness.

During *voir dire*, a party may challenge a certain number of prospective jurors *peremptorily*—that is, ask that an individual not be sworn in as a juror without providing any reason. Alternatively, a party may challenge a prospective juror *for cause*—that is, provide a reason why an individual should not be sworn in as a juror. If the judge grants the challenge, the individual is asked to step down. A prospective juror may not be excluded from the jury by the use of discriminatory challenges, however, such as those based on racial criteria[16] or gender.[17]

AT THE TRIAL

At the beginning of the trial, the attorneys present their opening arguments, setting forth the facts that they expect to provide during the trial. Then the plaintiff's case is presented. In our hypothetical case, Marconi's lawyer would introduce evidence (relevant documents, exhibits, and the testimony of witnesses) to support Marconi's position. The defendant has the opportunity to challenge any evidence introduced and to cross-examine any of the plaintiff's witnesses.

---

15. Pronounced vwahr *deehr.* Literally, these French verbs mean "to see, to speak." During the *voir dire* phase of litigation, attorneys do in fact see the prospective jurors speak. In legal language, however, the phrase refers to the process of interrogating prospective jurors to learn about their backgrounds, attitudes, and so on.

16. *Batson v. Kentucky,* 476 U.S. 79, 106 S.Ct. 1712, 90 L.Ed.2d 69 (1986).

17. *J.E.B. v. Alabama ex rel. T.B.,* 511 U.S. 127, 114 S.Ct. 1419, 128 L.Ed.2d 89 (1994). (*Ex rel.* is Latin for *ex relatione.* The phrase refers to an action brought on behalf of the state, by the attorney general, at the instigation of an individual who has a private interest in the matter.)

At the end of the plaintiff's case, the defendant's attorney has the opportunity to ask the judge to direct a verdict for the defendant on the ground that the plaintiff has presented no evidence that would justify the granting of the plaintiff's remedy. This is called a **motion for a directed verdict** (known in federal courts as a *motion for judgment as a matter of law*). If the motion is not granted (it seldom is), the defendant's attorney then presents the evidence and witnesses for the defendant's case. At the conclusion of the defendant's case, the defendant's attorney has another opportunity to make a motion for a directed verdict. The plaintiff's attorney can challenge any evidence introduced and cross-examine the defendant's witnesses.

MOTION FOR A DIRECTED VERDICT
In a jury trial, a motion for the judge to take the decision out of the hands of the jury and direct a verdict for the party who filed the motion on the ground that the other party has not produced sufficient evidence to support her or his claim.

After the defense concludes its presentation, the attorneys present their closing arguments, each urging a verdict in favor of her or his client. The judge instructs the jury in the law that applies to the case (these instructions are often called *charges*), and the jury retires to the jury room to deliberate a verdict. In the Marconi-Anderson case, the jury will not only decide for the plaintiff or for the defendant but, if it finds for the plaintiff, will also decide on the amount of the **award** (the money to be paid to her).

AWARD
The amount of money awarded to a plaintiff in a civil lawsuit as damages.

Posttrial Motions

After the jury has rendered its verdict, either party may make a posttrial motion. If Marconi wins, and Anderson's attorney has previously moved for a directed verdict, Anderson's attorney may make a **motion for judgment** ***n.o.v.*** (from the Latin *non obstante veredicto,* which means "notwithstanding the verdict"—called a *motion for judgment as a matter of law* in the federal courts) in Anderson's favor on the ground that the jury verdict in favor of Marconi was unreasonable and erroneous. If the judge decides that the jury's verdict was reasonable in light of the evidence presented at trial, the motion will be denied. If the judge agrees with Anderson's attorney, then he or she will set the jury's verdict aside and enter a judgment in favor of Anderson.

MOTION FOR JUDGMENT *N.O.V.*
A motion requesting the court to grant judgment in favor of the party making the motion on the ground that the jury verdict against him or her was unreasonable and erroneous.

Alternatively, Anderson could make a **motion for a new trial**, requesting the judge to set aside the adverse verdict and to hold a new trial. The motion will be granted if the judge is convinced, after looking at all the evidence, that the jury was in error but does not feel it is appropriate to grant judgment for the other side. A new trial may also be granted on the ground of newly discovered evidence, misconduct by the participants or the jury during the trial, or error by the judge.

MOTION FOR A NEW TRIAL
A motion asserting that the trial was so fundamentally flawed (because of error, newly discovered evidence, prejudice, or other reason) that a new trial is necessary to prevent a miscarriage of justice.

The Appeal

Assume here that any posttrial motion is denied and that Anderson appeals the case. (If Marconi wins but receives a smaller money award than she sought, she can appeal also.) A notice of appeal must be filed with the clerk of the trial court within a prescribed time. Anderson now becomes the appellant, or petitioner, and Marconi becomes the appellee, or respondent.

Filing the Appeal Anderson's attorney files with the appellate court the record on appeal, which includes the pleadings, the trial transcript, the judge's rulings on motions made by the parties, and other trial-related documents. Anderson's attorney will also provide a condensation of the record, known as an abstract, which is filed with the reviewing court along with the brief. The **brief** is a formal legal document outlining the facts and issues of the case, the judge's rulings or jury's findings that should be reversed or modified, the applicable law, and arguments on Anderson's behalf (citing applicable statutes and relevant cases as precedents).

BRIEF
A formal legal document submitted by the attorney for the appellant or the appellee (in answer to the appellant's brief) to an appellate court when a case is appealed. The appellant's brief outlines the facts and issues of the case, the judge's rulings or jury's findings that should be reversed or modified, the applicable law, and the arguments on the client's behalf.

Marconi's attorney will file an answering brief. Anderson's attorney can file a reply to Marconi's brief, although it is not required. The reviewing court then considers the case.

Appellate Review As mentioned earlier, a court of appeals does not hear evidence. Rather, it reviews the record for errors of law. Its decision concerning a case is based on the record on appeal, the abstracts, and the attorneys' briefs. The attorneys can present oral arguments, after which the case is taken under advisement. In general, appellate courts do not reverse findings of fact unless the findings are unsupported or contradicted by the evidence.

If the reviewing court believes that an error was committed during the trial or that the jury was improperly instructed, the judgment will be *reversed*. Sometimes the case will be *remanded* (sent back to the court that originally heard the case) for a new trial. ● **EXAMPLE 3.8** A case may be remanded for several reasons. For instance, if the appellate court decides that a judge improperly granted summary judgment, the case will be remanded for trial. If the appellate court decides that the trial judge erroneously applied the law, the case will be remanded for a new trial, with instructions to the trial court to apply the law as clarified by the appellate court. If the appellate court decides that the trial jury's award of damages was too high, the case will be remanded with instructions to reduce the damages award.● In most cases, the judgment of the lower court is *affirmed*, resulting in the enforcement of the court's judgment or decree.

As noted earlier in this text, in the appendix following Chapter 1, most of the state court opinions presented in this book are from state appellate courts. In part, this is because most state trial court decisions are not published in reporters and are thus not readily available. Also important, however, is the fact that appellate courts decide questions of law, and all trial courts within that jurisdiction will be obligated to follow the appellate court's opinion with respect to a particular issue. Thus, appellate court decisions have a broader reach and more final authority than decisions rendered by trial courts. Even when a case is remanded to a trial court for further proceedings, the appellate court normally spells out how the relevant law should be interpreted and applied to the case. Thus, you may not learn about the ultimate disposition of a case after it has been remanded, but you will discover the relevant legal principles and laws that apply to the case.

Appeal to a Higher Appellate Court If the reviewing court is an intermediate appellate court, the losing party normally may appeal to the state supreme court (the highest state court). Such a petition corresponds to a petition for a writ of *certiorari* from the United States Supreme Court. If the petition is granted (in some states, a petition is automatically granted), new briefs must be filed before the state supreme court, and the attorneys may be allowed or requested to present oral arguments. Like the intermediate appellate courts, the supreme court may reverse or affirm the appellate court's decision or remand the case. At this point, unless a federal question is at issue, the case has reached its end.

ENFORCING THE JUDGMENT

The uncertainties of the litigation process are compounded by the lack of guarantees that any judgment will be enforceable. Even if a plaintiff wins an award of damages in court, the defendant may not have sufficient assets or insurance to cover that amount. Usually, one of the factors considered before a lawsuit is initiated is whether the defendant has sufficient assets to cover the amount of damages sought, should the plaintiff win the case. Other factors to be considered when deciding whether to initiate a lawsuit will be discussed in the *Application* at the end of this chapter.

The Courts Adapt to the Online World

We have already mentioned how the courts have attempted to adapt traditional jurisdictional concepts to the online world. Not surprisingly, the Internet has also brought about changes in court procedures and practices, including new methods for filing pleadings and other documents and issuing decisions and opinions. Several courts are experimenting with electronic delivery, such as via the Internet or CD-ROM. Some jurisdictions are exploring the possibility of cyber courts, in which legal proceedings could be conducted totally online.

Electronic Filing

The federal court system first experimented with an electronic filing system in January 1996, in an asbestos case heard by the U.S. District Court for the Northern District of Ohio. Currently, a number of federal courts permit attorneys to file documents electronically in certain types of cases. At last count, more than 130,000 documents in approximately 10,000 cases had been filed electronically in federal courts. The Administrative Office of the U.S. Courts has recently announced that it is considering permitting electronic filing in all U.S. district courts on a nationwide basis.

State and local courts are also setting up electronic court filing systems. Since the late 1990s, the court system in Pima County, Arizona, has been accepting pleadings via e-mail. The supreme court of the state of Washington also now accepts online filings of litigation documents. In addition, electronic filing projects are being developed in other states, including Kansas, Virginia, Utah, and Michigan. Notably, the judicial branch of the state of Colorado recently implemented the first statewide court e-filing system in the United States. E-filing is now an option in over sixty courts in that state. In California, Florida, and a few other states, some court clerks offer docket information and other searchable databases online.

Typically, when electronic filing is made available, it is optional. In early 2001, however, a trial court judge in the District of Columbia launched a pilot project that *required* attorneys to file electronically all documents relating to certain types of civil cases.

ETHICAL ISSUE 3.2

How will electronic filing affect privacy?

From a practical perspective, trial court records, although normally available to the public, remain obscure. Because the decisions of most state trial courts (and some federal courts) are not published, someone must be strongly motivated to go to the trouble of traveling to the relevant courthouse in person to access the documents. If electronic filing becomes the norm, however, this "practical obscurity," as lawyers call it, may soon disappear. Electronic filing on a nationwide basis would open up all federal trial court documents to anyone with an Internet connection and a Web browser. Utilizing special "data-mining" software, anyone could go online and within just a few minutes access information—ranging from personal health records to financial reports to criminal violations—from dozens of courts. This means that serious privacy issues are at stake if courts nationwide adopt electronic filing. Should the courts restrict public access to certain types of documents, such as bankruptcy records or documents containing personal information that is not directly related to the legal issue being decided? Clearly, finding solutions to the privacy issues raised by electronic filing will not be easy.

"[C]ompanies looking to profit from this growing marketplace need to learn to avoid the pitfalls of protracted court battles that can last years and cost billions."

WILLIAM SLATE II, 1946–
(President, American Arbitration Association, 1994–)

COURTS ONLINE

Most courts today have sites on the Web. Of course, it is up to each court to decide what to make available at its site. Some courts display only the names of court personnel and office phone numbers. Others add court rules and forms. Some include judicial decisions, although generally the sites do not feature archives of old decisions. Instead, decisions are available online for only a limited time. For example, California keeps opinions online for only sixty days.

Appellate court decisions are often posted online immediately after they are rendered. Recent decisions of the U.S. courts of appeals, for example, are available online at their Web sites. The United States Supreme Court has also launched an official Web site and publishes its opinions there immediately after they are announced to the public. (These Web sites are listed elsewhere in this chapter in the *On the Web* features.)

CYBER COURTS AND PROCEEDINGS

Someday, litigants may be able to use cyber courts, in which judicial proceedings take place only on the Internet. The parties to a case could meet online to make their arguments and present their evidence. This might be done with e-mail submissions, through video cameras, in designated "chat" rooms, at closed sites, or through the use of other Internet facilities. These courtrooms could be efficient and economical. We might also see the use of virtual lawyers, judges, and juries—and possibly the replacement of court personnel with computers or software.

ON THE WEB Smith & Johnson, P.C., a Michigan law firm, offers a summary of Michigan's proposed cyber court legislation on its Web page at **http://www.smith-johnson.com/businesslaw/cybercourt.htm**.

The governor of Michigan recently proposed that separate cyber courts be created for cases involving technology and high-tech businesses. In these courts, everything would be done via computer and the Internet, rather than in a courtroom. The state of Maryland is also planning a separate judicial division for cases involving high-tech businesses. Many lawyers predict that other states will do likewise.

The courts may also use the Internet in other ways. In a ground-breaking decision in early 2001, for example, a Florida county court granted "virtual" visitation rights in a couple's divorce proceeding. Although the court granted custody rights to the father of the couple's ten-year-old daughter, the court also ordered each parent to buy a computer and a videoconferencing system so that the mother could "visit" with her child via the Internet at any time.[18]

Alternative Dispute Resolution

Litigation is expensive. It is also time consuming. Because of the backlog of cases pending in many courts, several years may pass before a case is actually tried. For these and other reasons, more and more businesspersons are turning to **alternative dispute resolution** (ADR) as a means of settling their disputes.

ALTERNATIVE DISPUTE RESOLUTION (ADR)
The resolution of disputes in ways other than those involved in the traditional judicial process. Negotiation, mediation, and arbitration are examples of ADR methods.

Methods of ADR range from neighbors sitting down over a cup of coffee in an attempt to work out their differences to huge multinational corporations agreeing to resolve a dispute through a formal hearing before a panel of experts. The great advantage of ADR is its flexibility. Normally, the parties themselves can control how the dispute will be settled, what procedures will be used, and whether the decision reached (either by themselves or by a neutral third party) will be legally binding or nonbinding.

18. For a discussion of this case, see Shelley Emling, "After the Divorce, Internet Visits?" *Austin American-Statesman,* January 30, 2001, pp. A1 and A10.

Today, approximately 95 percent of cases are settled before trial through some form of ADR. Indeed, the majority of the states either require or encourage parties to undertake ADR prior to trial. Several federal courts have instituted ADR programs as well. In the following pages, we examine various forms of ADR. Keep in mind, though, that ADR is an ongoing experiment. In other words, new methods of ADR—or new combinations of existing methods—are continuously being devised and employed. In recent years, several organizations have been offering dispute-resolution services via the Internet. After looking at traditional forms of ADR, we examine some of the ways in which disputes are being resolved in various online forums.

NEGOTIATION

NEGOTIATION
A process in which parties attempt to settle their dispute informally, with or without attorneys to represent them.

One of the simplest forms of ADR is **negotiation,** a process in which the parties attempt to settle their dispute informally, with or without attorneys to represent them. Attorneys frequently advise their clients to negotiate a settlement voluntarily before they proceed to trial.

Negotiation traditionally involves just the parties themselves and (typically) their attorneys. The attorneys, though, are advocates—they are obligated to put their clients' interests first. Often, parties find it helpful to have the opinion and guidance of a neutral (unbiased) third party when deciding whether or how to negotiate a settlement of their dispute. The methods of ADR discussed next all involve neutral third parties.

MEDIATION

MEDIATION
A method of settling disputes outside of court by using the services of a neutral third party, who acts as a communicating agent between the parties and assists them in negotiating a settlement.

In the **mediation** process, the parties themselves attempt to negotiate an agreement, but with the assistance of a neutral third party, a mediator. In mediation, the mediator talks with the parties separately as well as jointly. The mediator emphasizes points of agreement, helps the parties evaluate their positions, and proposes solutions. The mediator, however, does not make a decision on the matter being disputed. The mediator, who need not be a lawyer, usually charges a fee for his or her services (which can be split between the parties). States that require parties to undergo ADR before trial often offer mediation as one of the ADR options or (as in Florida) the only option.

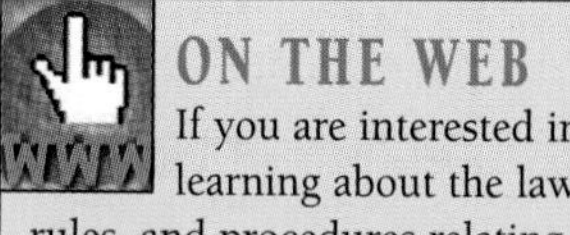

ON THE WEB If you are interested in learning about the laws, rules, and procedures relating to mediation and arbitration, as well as about providers of these services, go to the following Web site, which is operated by an agency of the federal government:

http://www.legal.gsa.gov/legal89.htm.

Mediation is not adversarial in nature, as lawsuits are. In litigation, the parties "do battle" with each other in the courtroom, while the judge is the neutral party. Because of its nonadversarial nature, the mediation process tends to reduce the antagonism between the disputants and to allow them to resume their former relationship. For this reason, mediation is often the preferred form of ADR for disputes involving business partners, employers and employees, or other parties involved in long-term relationships. • **EXAMPLE 3.9** Suppose that two business partners have a dispute over how the profits of their firm should be distributed. If the dispute is litigated, the parties will be adversaries, and their respective attorneys will emphasize how the parties' positions differ, not what they have in common. In contrast, when a dispute is mediated, the mediator emphasizes the common ground shared by the parties and helps them work toward agreement.•

In a recent development in ADR, characteristics of mediation are being combined with those of arbitration (to be discussed next). In *binding mediation,* for example, the parties agree that if they cannot resolve the dispute, the mediator can make a legally binding decision on the issue. In *mediation-arbitration,* or "med-arb," the parties agree to first attempt to settle their dispute through mediation. If no settlement is reached, the dispute will be arbitrated.

ARBITRATION

ARBITRATION
The settling of a dispute by submitting it to a disinterested third party (other than a court), who renders a decision that is (most often) legally binding.

A more formal method of ADR is **arbitration**, in which an arbitrator (a neutral third party or a panel of experts) hears a dispute and renders a decision. The key difference between arbitration and the forms of ADR just discussed is that in arbitration, the parties typically agree that the third party's decision will be *legally binding*. Parties can also agree to *nonbinding* arbitration, however. Additionally, when a court refers a case for arbitration, the arbitrator's decision is not binding on the parties. If the parties do not agree with the arbitrator's decision, they can go forward with the lawsuit.

In some respects, formal arbitration resembles a trial, although usually the procedural rules are much less restrictive than those governing litigation. In the typical hearing format, the parties present opening arguments to the arbitrator and state what remedies should or should not be granted. Evidence is then presented, and witnesses may be called and examined by both sides. The arbitrator then renders a decision, which is called an *award*.

KEEP IN MIND Litigation—even of a dispute over whether a particular matter should be submitted to arbitration—can be time consuming and expensive.

An arbitrator's award is usually the final word on the matter. Although the parties may appeal an arbitrator's decision, a court's review of the decision will be much more restricted in scope than an appellate court's review of a trial court's decision. The general view is that because the parties were free to frame the issues and set the powers of the arbitrator at the outset, they cannot complain about the results. The award will be set aside only if the arbitrator's conduct or "bad faith" substantially prejudiced the rights of one of the parties, if the award violates an established public policy, or if the arbitrator exceeded her or his powers (arbitrated issues that the parties did not agree to submit to arbitration).

ARBITRATION CLAUSE
A clause in a contract that provides that, in case of a dispute, the parties will submit the dispute to arbitration rather than litigate the dispute in court.

Arbitration Clauses and Statutes Virtually any commercial matter can be submitted to arbitration. Frequently, parties include an **arbitration clause** in a contract (a written agreement—see Chapter 8); the clause provides that any dispute that arises under the contract will be resolved through arbitration rather than through the court system. Parties can also agree to arbitrate a dispute after a dispute arises.

Most states have statutes (often based in part on the Uniform Arbitration Act of 1955) under which arbitration clauses will be enforced, and some state statutes compel arbitration of certain types of disputes, such as those involving public employees. At the federal level, the Federal Arbitration Act (FAA), enacted in 1925, enforces arbitration clauses in contracts involving maritime activity and interstate commerce. Because of the breadth of the commerce clause (see Chapter 2), arbitration agreements involving transactions only slightly connected to the flow of interstate commerce may fall under the FAA.

The Issue of Arbitrability When a dispute arises as to whether the parties have agreed in an arbitration clause to submit a particular matter to arbitration, one party may file suit to compel arbitration. The court before which the suit is brought will decide not the basic controversy but rather the issue of arbitrability—that is, whether the matter is one that must be resolved through arbitration. If the court finds that the subject matter in controversy is covered by the agreement to arbitrate, then a party may be compelled to arbitrate the dispute. Even when a claim involves a violation of a statute passed to protect a certain class of people, such as employees, a court may determine that the parties must nonetheless abide by their agreement to arbitrate the dispute. Usually, a court will allow the claim to be arbitrated if the court, in interpreting the statute, can find no legislative intent to the contrary.

No party, however, will be ordered to submit a particular dispute to arbitration unless the court is convinced that the party has consented to do so.[19] Additionally, the courts will not compel arbitration if it is clear that the prescribed arbitration rules and procedures are inherently unfair to one of the parties. • **EXAMPLE 3.10** In one case, an employer asked a court to issue an order compelling a former employee to submit to arbitration in accordance with an arbitration agreement that the parties had signed. Under that agreement, it was the employer's responsibility to establish the procedure and the rules for the arbitration. The court held that the employee did not have to submit her claim to arbitration because "the rules were so one-sided that their only possible purpose is to undermine the neutrality of the proceeding." According to the court, the biased rules created "a sham system unworthy even of the name of arbitration" in violation of the parties' contract to arbitrate.[20] •

Mandatory Arbitration in the Employment Context A significant question in the last several years has concerned mandatory arbitration clauses in employment contracts. Many claim that employees' rights are not sufficiently protected when they are forced, in order to be hired, to agree to arbitrate all disputes and thus to waive their rights under statutes specifically designed to protect employees. The Supreme Court, however, has generally held that mandatory arbitration clauses in employment contracts are enforceable.

• **EXAMPLE 3.11** In a landmark 1991 decision, *Gilmer v. Interstate/Johnson Lane Corp.*,[21] the Supreme Court held that a claim brought under a federal statute prohibiting age discrimination (see Chapter 35) could be subject to arbitration. The Court concluded that the employee had waived his right to sue when he agreed, as part of a required registration application to be a securities representative with the New York Stock Exchange, to arbitrate "any dispute, claim, or controversy" relating to his employment. •

The *Gilmer* decision was—and remains—controversial. By the early 2000s, at issue was whether the Federal Arbitration Act even applied to employment contracts. Some lower courts claimed that Congress, when passing the FAA, intended to exempt such contracts from coverage. In the following case, the Supreme Court addressed this issue.

19. See, for example, *Wright v. Universal Maritime Service Corp.*, 525 U.S. 70, 119 S.Ct. 391, 142 L.Ed.2d 361 (1998).
20. *Hooters of America, Inc. v. Phillips*, 173 F.3d 933 (4th Cir. 1999).
21. 500 U.S. 20, 111 S.Ct. 1647, 114 L.Ed.2d 26 (1991).

CASE 3.3 Circuit City Stores, Inc. v. Adams

Supreme Court of the United States, 2001.
532 U.S. 105,
121 S.Ct. 1302,
149 L.Ed.2d 234.
http://supct.law.cornell.edu/8080/supct[a]

a. In the "For the 2000–2001 term:" section, click on "Decisions arrayed by date." When that page opens, click on "March 2001." In the result, click on the name of the case to access the opinion. The Legal Information Institute of Cornell Law School in Ithaca, New York, maintains this Web site.

FACTS Saint Clair Adams applied for a job at Circuit City Stores, Inc. Adams signed an employment application that contained a clause requiring the arbitration of any employment-related disputes, including claims under federal and state law. Adams was hired as a sales counselor in a Circuit City store in Santa Rosa, California. Two years later, Adams filed a suit in a California state court against Circuit City, alleging employment discrimination in violation of state law. Circuit City immediately filed a suit

CASE 3.3—Continued

against Adams in a federal district court, asking the court to compel arbitration of Adams's claim. Adams argued that Section 1 of the Federal Arbitration Act (FAA), which excludes from coverage "contracts of employment of seamen, railroad employees, or any other class of workers engaged in foreign or interstate commerce," excluded all employment contracts. The court entered an order in favor of Circuit City. Adams appealed to the U.S. Court of Appeals for the Ninth Circuit, which held that the arbitration agreement between Adams and Circuit City was contained in a "contract of employment" and thus was not subject to the FAA. The court interpreted the language in Section 1 to exclude all employment contracts. Circuit City appealed to the United States Supreme Court.

ISSUE Are all employment contracts excluded from coverage under the FAA?

DECISION No. The United States Supreme Court reversed the judgment of the lower court and remanded the case, holding that the FAA applies to most employment contracts (excluding only those involving interstate transportation workers).

REASON The Supreme Court found that the federal appellate court's decision to exclude all employment contracts was inconsistent with the Court's previous decisions. The Court also reasoned that interpreting "the residual phrase to exclude all employment contracts fails to give independent effect to the statute's enumeration of the specific categories of workers which precedes it; there would be no need for Congress to use the phrases 'seamen' and 'railroad employees' if those same classes of workers were subsumed within the meaning of the 'engaged in * * * commerce' residual clause. * * * [W]here general words follow specific words in a statutory enumeration, the general words are construed to embrace only objects similar in nature to those objects enumerated by the preceding specific words. Under this rule of construction the residual clause should be read to give effect to the terms 'seamen' and 'railroad employees,' and should itself be controlled and defined by reference to the enumerated categories of workers which are recited just before it."

FOR CRITICAL ANALYSIS—Cultural Consideration *What does the decision in this case indicate about the courts' interpretation of the phrases used in statutes?*

Other Types of ADR

EARLY NEUTRAL CASE EVALUATION A form of alternative dispute resolution in which a neutral third party evaluates the strengths and weaknesses of the disputing parties' positions; the evaluator's opinion forms the basis for negotiating a settlement.

MINI-TRIAL A private proceeding in which each party to a dispute argues its position before the other side and vice versa. A neutral third party may be present as an adviser and may render an opinion if the parties fail to reach an agreement.

SUMMARY JURY TRIAL (SJT) A method of settling disputes, used in many federal courts, in which a trial is held, but the jury's verdict is not binding. The verdict acts only as a guide to both sides in reaching an agreement during the mandatory negotiations that immediately follow the summary jury trial.

The three forms of ADR just discussed are the oldest and traditionally the most commonly used forms. In recent years, a variety of new types of ADR have emerged, some of which were mentioned earlier in the discussion of mediation. Other ADR forms that are used today are sometimes referred to as "assisted negotiation" because they involve a third party in what is essentially a negotiation process. For example, in **early neutral case evaluation**, the parties select a neutral third party (generally an expert in the subject matter of the dispute) to evaluate their respective positions. The parties explain their positions to the case evaluator in any manner they choose. The case evaluator then assesses the strengths and weaknesses of the parties' positions, and this evaluation forms the basis for negotiating a settlement.

Another form of assisted negotiation that is often used by business parties is the **mini-trial**, in which each party's attorney briefly argues the party's case before representatives of each firm who have the authority to settle the dispute. Typically, a neutral third party (usually an expert in the area being disputed) acts as an adviser. If the parties fail to reach an agreement, the adviser renders an opinion as to how a court would likely decide the issue. The proceeding assists the parties in determining whether they should negotiate a settlement of the dispute or take it to court.

Today's courts are also experimenting with a variety of ADR alternatives to speed up (and reduce the cost of) justice. Numerous federal courts now hold **summary jury trials (SJTs)**, in which the parties present their arguments and evidence and the jury renders a verdict. The jury's verdict is not binding, but it does act as a guide to both sides in reaching an agreement during the mandatory negotiations that immediately follow the trial. Other alternatives being employed by the courts include summary procedures for commercial litigation and the appointment of special masters to assist judges in deciding complex issues.

PROVIDERS OF ADR SERVICES

> **ON THE WEB**
> To obtain information on the services offered by the American Arbitration Association (AAA), as well as forms that are used to submit a case for arbitration, go to the AAA's Web site at
> **http://www.adr.org**.

ADR services are provided by both government agencies and private organizations. A major provider of ADR services is the American Arbitration Association (AAA), which was founded in 1926. Currently, about 150,000 disputes are submitted to the AAA for resolution each year in its numerous offices in the United States and other countries. Most of the largest U.S. law firms are members of this nonprofit association.

Cases brought before the AAA are heard by an expert or a panel of experts in the area relating to the dispute and are usually settled quickly. Generally, about half of the panel members are lawyers. To cover its costs, the AAA charges a fee, paid by the party filing the claim. In addition, each party to the dispute pays a specified amount for each hearing day, as well as a special additional fee for cases involving personal injuries or property loss.

Hundreds of for-profit firms around the country also provide various forms of dispute-resolution services. Typically, these firms hire retired judges to conduct arbitration hearings or otherwise assist parties in settling their disputes. The judges follow procedures similar to those of the federal courts and use similar rules. Usually, each party to the dispute pays a filing fee and a designated fee for a hearing session or conference.

Online Dispute Resolution

ONLINE DISPUTE RESOLUTION (ODR) The resolution of disputes with the assistance of organizations that offer dispute-resolution services via the Internet.

An increasing number of companies and organizations offer dispute-resolution services using the Internet. The settlement of disputes in these online forums is known as **online dispute resolution (ODR)**. To date, the disputes resolved in these forums have most commonly involved disagreements over the rights to domain names (Web site addresses—see Chapter 5) and disagreements over the quality of goods sold via the Internet, including goods sold through Internet auction sites.

Currently, ODR may be best for resolving small- to medium-sized business liability claims, which may not be worth the expense of litigation or traditional methods of alternative dispute resolution. Rules being developed in online forums, however, may ultimately become a code of conduct for all of those who do business in cyberspace. Most online forums do not automatically apply the law of any specific jurisdiction. Instead, results are often based on general, universal legal principles. As with offline methods of dispute resolution, any party may appeal to a court at any time.

NEGOTIATION AND MEDIATION SERVICES

The online negotiation of a dispute is generally simpler and more practical than litigation. Typically, one party files a complaint, and the other party is notified by e-mail. Password-protected access is possible twenty-four hours a day, seven days a week. Fees

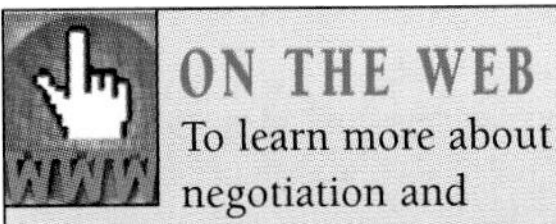

ON THE WEB To learn more about negotiation and mediation services available on the Web, go to **http://clicknsettle.com**, **http://cybersettle.com**, and **http://SquareTrade.com**.

are sometimes nominal and otherwise low (often 2 to 4 percent, or less, of the disputed amount).

CyberSettle.com. Inc., clickNsettle.com, U.S. Settlement Corporation (ussettle.com), and other Web-based firms offer online forums for negotiating monetary settlements. The parties to a dispute may agree to submit offers; if the offers fall within a previously agreed-on range, they will end the dispute, and the parties will split the difference. Special software keeps secret any offers that are not within the range. If there is no agreed-on range, typically an offer includes a deadline within which the other party must respond before the offer expires. The parties can drop the negotiations at any time.

Mediation providers have also tried resolving disputes online. SquareTrade, one of the mediation providers that has been used by eBay, the online auction site, mediates disputes involving $100 or more among eBay customers, currently for no charge. SquareTrade, which also resolves disputes among other parties, uses Web-based software that walks participants through a five-step e-resolution process. Negotiation between the parties occurs on a secure page within SquareTrade's Web site. The parties may consult a mediator. The entire process takes as little as ten to fourteen days, and there is no fee unless the parties use a mediator.

Arbitration Programs

A number of organizations and companies offer online arbitration programs. The Internet Corporation for Assigned Names and Numbers (ICANN), a nonprofit corporation that the federal government set up to oversee the distribution of domain names, has issued special rules for the resolution of domain name disputes.[22] ICANN has also authorized several organizations to arbitrate domain name disputes in accordance with ICANN's rules. Recently, the American Arbitration Association announced that it will soon be launching technology-based arbitration services as well.

Resolution Forum, Inc. (RFI), a nonprofit organization associated with the Center for Legal Responsibility at South Texas College of Law, offers arbitration services through its CAN-WIN conferencing system. Using standard browser software and an RFI password, the parties to a dispute access an online conference room. When multiple parties are involved, private communications and break-out sessions are possible via private messaging facilities. RFI also offers mediation services.

The Virtual Magistrate Project (VMAG) is affiliated with the American Arbitration Association, Chicago-Kent College of Law, Cyberspace Law Institute, National Center for Automated Information Research, and other organizations. VMAG offers arbitration for disputes involving users of online systems; victims of wrongful messages, postings, and files; and system operators subject to complaints or similar demands. VMAG also arbitrates intellectual property, personal property, real property, and tort disputes related to online contracts. VMAG attempts to resolve a dispute within seventy-two hours. The proceedings occur in a password-protected online newsgroup setting, and private e-mail among the participants is possible. A VMAG arbitrator's decision is issued in a written opinion. A party may appeal the outcome to a court.

22. ICANN's Rules for Uniform Domain Name Dispute Resolution Policy are online at **http://www.icann.org/udrp/udrp-rules-24oct99.htm**. Domain names will be discussed in more detail in Chapter 5, in the context of trademark law.

APPLICATION **Law and the Businessperson . . .**

To Sue or Not to Sue*

Wrongs are committed every minute of every day in the United States. These wrongs may be committed inadvertently or intentionally. Sometimes, businesspersons believe that wrongs have been committed against them by other businesspersons, by consumers, or by the local, state, or federal government. If you are deciding whether or not to sue for a wrong that has been committed against you or your business, you must consider many issues.

The Question of Cost

Competent legal advice is not inexpensive. Good commercial business law attorneys charge $75 to $500 an hour, plus expenses. It is almost always worthwhile to make an initial visit to an attorney who has skills in the area in which you are going to sue to get an estimate of the expected costs of pursuing a redress for your grievance. You may be charged for the initial visit as well.

Note that less than 10 percent of all corporate lawsuits end up in trial—the rest are settled beforehand. You may end up settling for far less than you thought you were "owed" simply because of the length of time it takes your attorney to bring your case to trial and to finish the trial. And then you might not win, anyway!

Basically, then, you must do a cost-benefit analysis to determine whether you should sue. Your attorney can give you an estimate of the dollar costs involved in litigating the dispute. Realize, though, that litigation also involves nondollar costs: time away from your business, stress, and so on. You need to weigh all of these costs against the benefits. You can "guesstimate" the benefits by multiplying the probable size of the award by the probability of obtaining that award.

The Alternatives before You

Another method of settling your grievance is by alternative dispute resolution (ADR). Negotiation, mediation, arbitration, and other ADR forms are becoming increasingly attractive alternatives to court litigation, because they usually yield quick results at a comparatively low cost. Most disputes relating to business can be mediated or arbitrated through the American Arbitration Association (AAA), which can be accessed online at **http://www.adr.org**.

There are numerous other ADR centers as well. You can obtain information on ADR from the AAA, courthouses, chambers of commerce, law firms, state bar associations, or the American Bar Association. The latter's Web site can be accessed at **http://www.abanet.org**. The Yellow Pages in large metropolitan areas usually list agencies and firms that could help you settle your dispute out of court; look under "Mediation" or "Social Service Agencies."

Depending on the nature of the dispute and the amount of damages you seek, you might wish to contact one of the organizations that offer online dispute-resolution services. To contact these services, go to the Web sites given in the *On the Web* features in this chapter.

*This *Application* is not meant to substitute for the services of an attorney who is licensed to practice law in your state.

Checklist for Deciding Whether to Sue

1. Are you prepared to pay for going to court? Make this decision only after you have consulted an attorney to get an estimate of the costs of litigating the dispute.
2. Do you have the patience to follow a court case through the judicial system, even if it takes several years?
3. Is there a way for you to settle your grievance without going to court? Even if the settlement is less than you think you are owed—in net terms corrected for future expenses, lost time, and frustration—you may be better off settling now for the smaller figure.
4. Can you use some form of alternative dispute resolution? Before you say no, investigate these alternatives—they are usually cheaper and quicker to use than the standard judicial process.

Key Terms

alternative dispute resolution (ADR) 87
answer 81
arbitration 89
arbitration clause 89
award 84
bankruptcy court 68
brief 84
complaint 79
concurrent jurisdiction 70
counterclaim 81
default judgment 81
deposition 82
discovery 82
diversity of citizenship 69
docket 70
early neutral case evaluation 91
exclusive jurisdiction 70
federal question 69
interrogatories 82
judicial review 64
jurisdiction 66
justiciable controversy 74
litigation 79
long arm statute 67
mediation 88
mini-trial 91
motion for a directed verdict 84
motion for a new trial 84
motion for judgment *n.o.v.* 84
motion for judgment on the pleadings 81
motion for summary judgment 81
motion to dismiss 81
negotiation 88
online dispute resolution 92
pleadings 79
probate court 68
reply 81
rule of four 78
small claims court 75
standing to sue 74
summary jury trial (SJT) 91
summons 80
venue 73
voir dire 83
writ of *certiorari* 78

Chapter Summary Traditional and Online Dispute Resolution

The Judiciary's Role in American Government (See pages 64–65.)	The role of the judiciary—the courts—in the American governmental system is to interpret and apply the law. Through the process of judicial review—determining the constitutionality of laws—the judicial branch acts as a check on the executive and legislative branches of government.
Basic Judicial Requirements (See pages 66–74.)	1. *Jurisdiction*—Before a court can hear a case, it must have jurisdiction over the person against whom the suit is brought or the property involved in the suit, as well as jurisdiction over the subject matter. a. Limited versus general jurisdiction—Limited jurisdiction exists when a court is limited to a specific subject matter, such as probate or divorce. General jurisdiction exists when a court can hear any kind of case. b. Original versus appellate jurisdiction—Original jurisdiction exists with courts that have authority to hear a case for the first time (trial courts). Appellate jurisdiction exists with courts of appeals, or reviewing courts; generally, appellate courts do not have original jurisdiction. c. Federal jurisdiction—Arises (1) when a federal question is involved (when the plaintiff's cause of action is based, at least in part, on the U.S. Constitution, a treaty, or a federal law) or (2) when a case involves diversity of citizenship (citizens of different states, for example) and the amount in controversy exceeds $75,000. d. Concurrent versus exclusive jurisdiction—Concurrent jurisdiction exists when two different courts have authority to hear the same case. Exclusive jurisdiction exists when only state courts or only federal courts have authority to hear a case. 2. *Jurisdiction in cyberspace*—Because the Internet does not have physical boundaries, traditional jurisdictional concepts have been difficult to apply in cases involving activities conducted via the Web. Gradually, the courts are developing standards to use in determining when jurisdiction over a Web owner or operator in another state is proper.

(continued)

Chapter Summary Traditional and Online Dispute Resolution—continued

Basic Judicial Requirements—continued	3. *Venue*—Venue has to do with the most appropriate location for a trial, which is usually the geographic area where the event leading to the dispute took place or where the parties reside. 4. *Standing to sue*—A requirement that a party must have a legally protected and tangible interest at stake sufficient to justify seeking relief through the court system. The controversy at issue must also be a justiciable controversy—one that is real and substantial, as opposed to hypothetical or academic.
The State and Federal Court Systems (See pages 74–79.)	1. *Trial courts*—Courts of original jurisdiction, in which legal actions are initiated. a. State—Courts of general jurisdiction can hear any case; courts of limited jurisdiction include divorce courts, probate courts, traffic courts, small claims courts, and so on. b. Federal—The federal district court is the equivalent of the state trial court. Federal courts of limited jurisdiction include the U.S. Tax Court, the U.S. Bankruptcy Court, and the U.S. Court of Federal Claims. 2. *Intermediate appellate courts*—Courts of appeals, or reviewing courts; generally without original jurisdiction. Many states have an intermediate appellate court; in the federal court system, the U.S. circuit courts of appeals are the intermediate appellate courts. 3. *Supreme (highest) courts*—Each state has a supreme court, although it may be called by some other name, from which appeal to the United States Supreme Court is possible only if a federal question is involved. The United States Supreme Court is the highest court in the federal court system and the final arbiter of the Constitution and federal law.
Following a State Court Case (See pages 79–85.)	Rules of procedure prescribe the way in which disputes are handled in the courts. Rules differ from court to court, and separate sets of rules exist for federal and state courts, as well as for criminal and civil cases. A sample civil court case in a state court would involve the following procedures: 1. *The pleadings*— a. Complaint—Filed by the plaintiff with the court to initiate the lawsuit; served with a summons on the defendant. b. Answer—Admits or denies allegations made by the plaintiff; may assert a counterclaim or an affirmative defense. c. Motion to dismiss—A request to the court to dismiss the case for stated reasons, such as the plaintiff's failure to state a claim for which relief can be granted. 2. *Pretrial motions (in addition to the motion to dismiss)*— a. Motion for judgment on the pleadings—May be made by either party; will be granted if the parties agree on the facts and the only question is how the law applies to the facts. The judge bases the decision solely on the pleadings. b. Motion for summary judgment—May be made by either party; will be granted if the parties agree on the facts. The judge applies the law in rendering a judgment. The judge can consider evidence outside the pleadings when evaluating the motion. 3. *Discovery*—The process of gathering evidence concerning the case. Discovery involves depositions (sworn testimony by a party to the lawsuit or any witness), interrogatories (written questions and answers to these questions made by parties to the action with the aid of their attorneys), and various requests (for admissions, documents, medical examination, and so on). 4. *Pretrial conference*—Either party or the court can request a pretrial conference to identify the matters in dispute after discovery has taken place and to plan the course of the trial. 5. *Trial*—Following jury selection *(voir dire)*, the trial begins with opening statements from both parties' attorneys. The following events then occur:

Chapter Summary Traditional and Online Dispute Resolution—continued

Following a State Court Case—continued	a. The plaintiff's introduction of evidence (including the testimony of witnesses) supporting the plaintiff's position. The defendant's attorney can challenge evidence and cross-examine witnesses. b. The defendant's introduction of evidence (including the testimony of witnesses) supporting the defendant's position. The plaintiff's attorney can challenge evidence and cross-examine witnesses. c. Closing arguments by attorneys in favor of their respective clients, the judge's instructions to the jury, and the jury's verdict. 6. *Posttrial motions*— a. Motion for judgment *n.o.v.* ("notwithstanding the verdict")—Will be granted if the judge is convinced that the jury was in error. b. Motion for a new trial—Will be granted if the judge is convinced that the jury was in error; can also be granted on the grounds of newly discovered evidence, misconduct by the participants during the trial, or error by the judge. 7. *Appeal*—Either party can appeal the trial court's judgment to an appropriate court of appeals. After reviewing the record on appeal, the abstracts, and the attorneys' briefs, the appellate court holds a hearing and renders its opinion.
The Courts Adapt to the Online World (See pages 86–87.)	A number of state and federal courts now allow parties to file litigation-related documents with their courts via the Internet or other electronic means. The federal courts are considering the implementation of electronic filing systems in all federal district courts. Virtually every court now has a Web page offering information about the court and its procedures, and an increasing number of courts publish their opinions online. In the future, we may see "cyber courts," in which all trial proceedings are conducted online.
Alternative Dispute Resolution (See pages 87–92.)	1. *Negotiation*—The parties come together, with or without attorneys to represent them, and try to reach a settlement without the involvement of a third party. 2. *Mediation*—The parties themselves reach an agreement with the help of a neutral third party, called a mediator, who proposes solutions. At the parties' request, a mediator may make a legally binding decision. 3. *Arbitration*—A more formal method of ADR in which the parties submit their dispute to a neutral third party, the arbitrator, who renders a decision. The decision may or may not be legally binding, depending on the circumstances. 4. *Other types of ADR*—These include early neutral case evaluation, mini-trials, and summary jury trials (SJTs); generally, these are forms of "assisted negotiation." 5. *Providers of ADR services*—The leading nonprofit provider of ADR services is the American Arbitration Association. Hundreds of for-profit firms also provide ADR services.
Online Dispute Resolution (See pages 92–93.)	A number of organizations and firms are now offering negotiation, mediation, and arbitration services through online forums. To date, these forums have been a practical alternative for the resolution of domain name disputes and e-commerce disputes in which the amount in controversy is relatively small.

For Review

① What is judicial review? How and when was the power of judicial review established?

② Before a court can hear a case, it must have jurisdiction. Over what must it have jurisdiction? How are the courts applying traditional jurisdictional concepts to cases involving Internet transactions?

③ What is the difference between a trial court and an appellate court?

④ In a lawsuit, what are the pleadings? What is discovery? What is electronic filing?

⑤ How are online forums being used to resolve disputes?

Questions and Case Problems

3–1. Appellate Process. If a judge enters a judgment on the pleadings, the losing party can usually appeal but cannot present evidence to the appellate court. Does this seem fair? Explain.

3–2. Arbitration. In an arbitration proceeding, the arbitrator need not be a judge or even a lawyer. How, then, can the arbitrator's decision have the force of law and be binding on the parties involved?

3–3. Appellate Process. Sometimes on appeal there are questions concerning whether the facts presented in the trial court support the conclusion reached by the judge or the jury. An appellate court, however, normally defers to the trial court's decision with regard to the facts. Can you see any reason for this?

3–4. Jurisdiction. Marya Callais, a citizen of Florida, was walking near a busy street in Tallahassee one day when a large crate flew off a passing truck and hit her, resulting in numerous injuries to Callais. She incurred a great deal of pain and suffering plus numerous medical expenses, and she could not work for six months. She wishes to sue the trucking firm for $300,000 in damages. The firm's headquarters are in Georgia, although the company does business in Florida. In what court may Callais bring suit—a Florida state court, a Georgia state court, or a federal court? What factors might influence her decision?

3–5. Jurisdiction. Shem and Nadine Maslov, who live in Massachusetts, saw a national hotel chain's advertisement for vacationers in the *Boston Globe:* "Stay in Maximum Inns' beachfront hotel in Puerto Rico for one week for only $800; continental breakfast included." The Maslovs decided to accept the offer and spent a week at the hotel. On the last day, Nadine fell on a wet floor in the hotel lobby and sustained multiple fractures to her left ankle and hip. Because of her injuries, which were subsequently complicated by infections, she was unable to work at her job as an airline flight attendant for ten months. The hotel chain does not do business in Massachusetts. If Nadine sues Maximum Inns in a Massachusetts state court, can the court exercise jurisdiction over Maximum Inns? What factors should the court consider in deciding this jurisdictional issue?

3–6. Arbitration. Randall Fris worked as a seaman on an Exxon Shipping Co. oil tanker for eight years without incident. One night, he boarded the ship for duty while intoxicated, in violation of company policy. This policy also allowed Exxon to discharge employees who were intoxicated and thus unfit for work. Exxon discharged Fris. Under a contract with Fris's union, the discharge was submitted to arbitration. The arbitrators ordered Exxon to reinstate Fris on an oil tanker. Exxon filed a suit against the union, challenging the award as contrary to public policy, which opposes having intoxicated persons operate seagoing vessels. Can a court set aside an arbitration award on the ground that the award violates public policy? Should the court set aside the award in this case? Explain. [*Exxon Shipping Co. v. Exxon Seamen's Union,* 11 F.3d 1189 (3d Cir. 1993)]

3–7. Jurisdiction. George Noonan, a Boston police detective and a devoted nonsmoker, has spent most of his career educating Bostonians about the health risks of tobacco use. In 1992, an ad for Winston cigarettes featuring Noonan's image appeared in several French magazines. Some of the magazines were on sale at newsstands in Boston. Noonan filed a suit in a federal district court against The Winston Co., Lintas:Paris (the French ad agency that created the ads), and others. Lintas:Paris and the other French defendants claimed that they did not know the magazines would be sold in Boston and filed a motion to dismiss the suit for lack of personal jurisdiction. Does the court have jurisdiction? Why or why not? [*Noonan v. The Winston Co.,* 135 F.3d 85 (1st Cir. 1998)]

3–8. Standing. Blue Cross and Blue Shield insurance companies (the Blues) provide 68 million Americans with health-care financing. The Blues have paid billions of dollars for care attributable to illnesses related to tobacco use. In an attempt to recover some of this amount, the Blues filed a suit in a federal district court against tobacco companies and others, alleging fraud, among other things. The Blues claimed that beginning in 1953, the defendants conspired to addict millions of Americans, including members of Blue Cross plans, to cigarettes and other tobacco products. The conspiracy involved misrepresentation about the safety of nicotine and its addictive properties, marketing efforts targeting children, and agreements not to produce or market safer cigarettes. Their success caused lung, throat, and other cancers, as well as heart disease, stroke, emphysema, and other illnesses. The defendants asked the court to dismiss the case on the ground that the plaintiffs did not have standing to sue. Do the Blues have standing in this case? Why or why not? [*Blue Cross and Blue Shield of New Jersey, Inc. v. Philip Morris, Inc.,* 36 F.Supp.2d 560 (E.D.N.Y. 1999)]

3–9. Discovery. Advance Technology Consultants, Inc. (ATC), contracted with RoadTrac, L.L.C., to provide software and client software systems for products utilizing global positioning satellite (GPS) technology being developed by RoadTrac. RoadTrac agreed to provide ATC with hardware with which ATC's software would interface. Problems soon arose, however. ATC claimed that RoadTrac's hardware was defective, making it difficult to develop the software. RoadTrac contended that its hardware was fully functional and that ATC simply failed to provide supporting software. ATC told RoadTrac that it considered their contract terminated. RoadTrac filed a suit in a Georgia state court against ATC, charging, among other things, breach of contract. During discovery, RoadTrac requested ATC's customer lists and marketing procedures. Before producing this material, ATC asked the court to limit RoadTrac's use of the information. Meanwhile, RoadTrac and ATC had become competitors in the GPS industry. How should the court rule regarding RoadTrac's discovery request? [*Advance Technology Consultants, Inc. v. RoadTrac, L.L.C.,* 236 Ga.App. 582, 512 S.E.2d 27 (1999)]

TEST YOUR KNOWLEDGE—ANSWER ON THE WEB

3–10. Ms. Thompson filed a suit in a federal district court against her employer, Altheimer & Gray, seeking damages for alleged racial discrimination in violation of federal law. During *voir dire,* the judge asked the prospective jurors whether "there is something about this kind of lawsuit for money damages that would start any of you leaning for or against a particular party?" Ms. Leiter, one of the prospective jurors, raised her hand and explained that she had "been an owner of a couple of businesses and am currently an owner of a business, and I feel that as an employer and owner of a business that will definitely sway my judgment in this case." She explained, "I am constantly faced with people that want various benefits or different positions in the company or better contacts or, you know, a myriad of issues that employers face on a regular basis, and I have to decide whether or not that person should get them." Asked by Thompson's lawyer whether "you believe that people file lawsuits just because they don't get something they want," Leiter answered, "I believe there are some people that do." In answer to another question, she said, "I think I bring a lot of background to this case, and I can't say that it's not going to cloud my judgment. I can try to be as fair as I can, as I do every day." Thompson filed a motion to strike Leiter for cause. Should the judge grant the motion? Explain. [*Thompson v. Altheimer & Gray,* 248 F.3d 621 (7th Cir. 2001)]

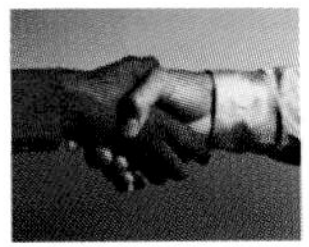

A QUESTION OF ETHICS AND SOCIAL RESPONSIBILITY

3–11. Linda Bender brought an action in a federal court against her supervisor at A. G. Edwards & Sons, Inc., a stockbrokerage firm (the defendants). Bender alleged sexual harassment in violation of Title VII of the Civil Rights Act of 1964, which prohibits, among other things, employment discrimination based on gender. In her application for registration as a stockbroker, Bender had agreed to arbitrate any disputes with her employer. The defendants moved to compel arbitration. The district court judge denied the motion, holding that Bender could not be forced to waive her right to adjudicate Title VII claims in federal court. The appellate court reversed, ruling that Title VII claims are arbitrable. The court held that compelling Bender to submit her claim for arbitration did not deprive her of the right to a judicial forum, because if the arbitration proceedings were somehow legally deficient, she could still take her case to a federal court for review. [*Bender v. A. G. Edwards & Sons, Inc.,* 971 F.2d 698 (11th Cir. 1992)]

1. Does the right to a postarbitration judicial forum equate to the right to initial access to a judicial forum in employment disputes?
2. Should the fact that reviewing courts rarely set aside arbitrators' awards have any bearing on the arbitrability of certain types of claims, such as those brought under Title VII?

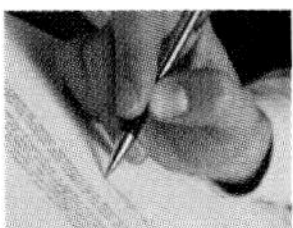

FOR CRITICAL ANALYSIS

3–12. American courts are forums for adversarial justice, in which attorneys defend the interests of their respective clients before the court. This means that an attorney may end up claiming before a court that his or her client is innocent, even though the attorney knows that the client acted wrongfully. Is it ethical for attorneys to try to "deceive" the court in these situations? Can the adversarial system of justice really lead to "truth"?

Internet Exercises

Go to the *Business Law Today* home page at **http://blt.westbuslaw.com**. Select "Interactive Study Center" and then click on "Chapter 3." There you will find the following Internet research exercises that you can perform to learn more about traditional and online dispute resolution:

Activity 3–1: Civil Procedure
Activity 3–2: Small Claims Court
Activity 3–3: Online Dispute Resolution

Before the Test

Go to the *Business Law Today* home page at **http://blt.westbuslaw.com**. Click on "Interactive Quizzes." You will find at least twenty interactive questions relating to this chapter.

CHAPTER 4

Torts and Cyber Torts

"'Tort' more or less means 'wrong'.... One of my friends [in law school] said that Torts is the course which proves that your mother was right."

Scott Turow, 1949–
(American lawyer and author)

CHAPTER CONTENTS

LEARNING OBJECTIVES

After reading this chapter, you should be able to answer the following questions:

① What is a tort?

② What is the purpose of tort law? What are two basic categories of torts?

③ What are the four elements of negligence?

④ What is meant by strict liability? In what circumstances is strict liability applied?

⑤ What is a cyber tort, and how are tort theories being applied in cyberspace?

As Scott Turow's statement in the above quotation indicates, **torts** are wrongful actions.[1] Through tort law, society compensates those who have suffered injuries as a result of the wrongful conduct of others. Although some torts, such as assault and trespass, originated in the English common law, the field of tort law continues to expand. As new ways to commit wrongs are discovered, such as the use of the Internet to commit wrongful acts, the courts are extending tort law to cover these wrongs.

As you will see in later chapters of this book, many of the lawsuits brought by or against business firms are based on the tort theories discussed in this chapter. Some of the torts examined here can occur in any context, including the business environment. Others traditionally have been referred to as **business torts**, which are defined as wrongful interferences with the business rights of others. Included in business torts are such vaguely worded concepts

TORT
A civil wrong not arising from a breach of contract. A breach of a legal duty that proximately causes harm or injury to another.

BUSINESS TORT
The wrongful interference with another's business rights.

1. The word *tort* is French for "wrong."

CYBER TORT
A tort committed in cyberspace.

as *unfair competition* and *wrongfully interfering with the business relations of others.* Torts committed via the Internet are sometimes referred to as **cyber torts.** We look at how the courts have applied traditional tort law to wrongful actions in the online environment in the concluding pages of this chapter.

The Basis of Tort Law

DAMAGES
Money sought as a remedy for a breach of contract or a tortious action.

Two notions serve as the basis of all torts: wrongs and compensation. Tort law recognizes that some acts are wrong because they cause injuries to others. In a tort action, one person or group brings a personal suit against another person or group to obtain compensation (money **damages**) or other relief for the harm suffered.

Generally, the purpose of tort law is to provide remedies for the invasion of various *protected interests.* Society recognizes an interest in personal physical safety, and tort law provides remedies for acts that cause physical injury or that interfere with physical security and freedom of movement. Society recognizes an interest in protecting real and personal property, and tort law provides remedies for acts that cause destruction or damage to property. Society also recognizes an interest in protecting certain intangible interests, such as personal privacy, family relations, reputation, and dignity, and tort law provides remedies for invasion of these protected interests.

There are two broad classifications of torts: *intentional torts* and *unintentional torts* (torts involving negligence). The classification of a particular tort depends largely on how the tort occurs (intentionally or negligently) and the surrounding circumstances.

Intentional Torts against Persons

INTENTIONAL TORT
A wrongful act knowingly committed.

TORTFEASOR
One who commits a tort.

ON THE WEB
You can find cases and articles on torts in the tort law library at the Internet Law Library's Web site. Go to **http://www.lawguru.com/ilawlib.**

An **intentional tort,** as the term implies, requires *intent.* The **tortfeasor** (the one committing the tort) must intend to commit an act, the consequences of which interfere with the personal or business interests of another in a way not permitted by law. An evil or harmful motive is not required—in fact, the actor may even have a beneficial motive for committing what turns out to be a tortious act. In tort law, intent means only that the actor intended the consequences of his or her act or knew with substantial certainty that certain consequences would result from the act. The law generally assumes that individuals intend the *normal* consequences of their actions. Thus, forcefully pushing another—even if done in jest and without any evil motive—is an intentional tort (if injury results), because the object of a strong push can ordinarily be expected to go flying.

This section discusses intentional torts against persons, which include assault and battery, false imprisonment, infliction of emotional distress, defamation, invasion of the right to privacy, appropriation, misrepresentation, and wrongful interference.

Assault and Battery

ASSAULT
Any word or action intended to make another person fearful of immediate physical harm; a reasonably believable threat.

Any intentional, unexcused act that creates in another person a reasonable apprehension or fear of immediate harmful or offensive contact is an **assault.** Apprehension is not the same as fear. If a contact is such that a reasonable person would want to avoid it, and if there is a reasonable basis for believing that the contact will occur, then the plaintiff suffers apprehension whether or not he or she is afraid. The interest protected by tort law concerning assault is the freedom from having to expect harmful or offensive contact. The occurrence of apprehension is enough to justify compensation.

BATTERY The unprivileged, intentional touching of another.

The *completion* of the act that caused the apprehension, if it results in harm to the plaintiff, is a **battery**, which is defined as an unexcused and harmful or offensive physical contact *intentionally* performed. For example, suppose that Ivan threatens Jean with a gun, then shoots her. The pointing of the gun at Jean is an assault; the firing of the gun (if the bullet hits Jean) is a battery. The interest protected by tort law concerning battery is the right to personal security and safety. The contact can be harmful, or it can be merely offensive (such as an unwelcome kiss). Physical injury need not occur. The contact can involve any part of the body or anything attached to it—for example, a hat or other item of clothing, a purse, or a chair or an automobile in which one is sitting. Whether the contact is offensive or not is determined by the *reasonable person standard.*[2] The contact can be made by the defendant or by some force the defendant sets in motion—for example, a rock thrown, food poisoned, or a stick swung.

Compensation If the plaintiff shows that there was contact, and the jury agrees that the contact was offensive, the plaintiff has a right to compensation. There is no need to show that the defendant acted out of malice; the person could have just been joking or playing around. The underlying motive does not matter, only the intent to bring about the harmful or offensive contact to the plaintiff. In fact, proving a motive is never necessary (but is sometimes relevant). A plaintiff may be compensated for the emotional harm or loss of reputation resulting from a battery, as well as for physical harm.

DEFENSE That which a defendant offers and alleges in an action or suit as a reason why the plaintiff should not recover or establish what she or he seeks.

BE AWARE Some of these same four defenses can be raised by a defendant who is sued for other torts.

Defenses to Assault and Battery A number of legally recognized **defenses** (reasons why plaintiffs should not obtain what they are seeking) can be raised by a defendant who is sued for assault or battery, or both:

① *Consent.* When a person consents to the act that damages her or him, there is generally no liability (legal responsibility) for the damage done.

② *Self-defense.* An individual who is defending his or her life or physical well-being can claim self-defense. In situations of both *real* and *apparent* danger, a person may use whatever force is *reasonably* necessary to prevent harmful contact.

③ *Defense of others.* An individual can act in a reasonable manner to protect others who are in real or apparent danger.

④ *Defense of property.* Reasonable force may be used in attempting to remove intruders from one's home, although force that is likely to cause death or great bodily injury can never be used just to protect property.

FALSE IMPRISONMENT

False imprisonment is defined as the intentional confinement or restraint of another person's activities without justification. False imprisonment interferes with the freedom to move without restraint. The confinement can be accomplished through the use of physical barriers, physical restraint, or threats of physical force. Moral pressure or threats of future harm do not constitute false imprisonment. It is essential that the person being restrained not comply with the restraint willingly.

Businesspersons are often confronted with suits for false imprisonment after they have attempted to confine a suspected shoplifter for questioning. Under the "privilege

2. The reasonable person standard is an objective test of how a reasonable person would have acted under the same circumstances. See "The Duty of Care and Its Breach" later in this chapter.

to detain" granted to merchants in some states, a merchant can use the defense of *probable cause* to justify delaying a suspected shoplifter. Probable cause exists when the evidence to support the belief that a person is guilty outweighs the evidence against that belief. Although laws governing false imprisonment vary from state to state, generally they require that any detention be conducted in a *reasonable* manner and for only a *reasonable* length of time.

INFLICTION OF EMOTIONAL DISTRESS

The tort of *infliction of emotional distress* can be defined as an intentional act that amounts to extreme and outrageous conduct resulting in severe emotional distress to another. • **EXAMPLE 4.1** A prankster telephones an individual and says that the individual's spouse has just been in a horrible accident. As a result, the individual suffers intense mental pain or anxiety. The caller's behavior is deemed to be extreme and outrageous conduct that exceeds the bounds of decency accepted by society and is therefore **actionable** (capable of serving as the ground for a lawsuit). •

ACTIONABLE
Capable of serving as the basis of a lawsuit. An actionable claim can be pursued in a lawsuit or other court action.

The tort of infliction of emotional distress poses several problems for the courts. One problem is the difficulty of proving the existence of emotional suffering. For this reason, courts in some jurisdictions require that the emotional distress be evidenced by some physical symptom or illness or some emotional disturbance that can be documented by a psychiatric consultant or other medical professional.

Another problem is that emotional distress claims must be subject to some limitation, or they could flood the courts with lawsuits. A society in which individuals are rewarded if they are unable to endure the normal emotional stresses of day-to-day living is obviously undesirable. Therefore, the law usually holds that indignity or annoyance alone is not enough to support a lawsuit based on infliction of emotional distress. Repeated annoyances (such as those experienced by a person who is being stalked), however, coupled with threats, are enough. In the business context, the repeated use of extreme methods to collect a delinquent account may be actionable.

In the following case, the court looks at one of the requirements that plaintiffs must meet to establish an emotional distress claim.

CASE 4.1 Roach v. Stern

Supreme Court of New York,
Appellate Division, Second Department, 1998.
675 N.Y.S.2d 133.

HISTORICAL AND SOCIAL SETTING *What some persons may consider extreme and outrageous, others may consider humorous or insightful. Never has this been truer than in the case of Howard Stern. Stern is a talk-show host whose style is to ask irreverent questions and make off-color jokes. The subjects of his interviews—and the objects of his comments—include celebrities and less well-known personalities with offbeat interests.* The Howard Stern Show *is broadcast on radio and on television. The show is popular—the radio broadcasts alone have more than 16 million weekly listeners. Stern's style can be controversial, however. Over the years, the Federal Communications Commission has fined his employer, Infinity Broadcasting, Inc., more than $2 million for indecency.*

FACTS Deborah Roach—known as "Debbie Tay"—was a perennial guest on *The Howard Stern Show,* on which she discussed her purported sexual encounters with female aliens. Tay used the notoriety to launch her own cable television show. After her death from a drug overdose at the age of twenty-seven, her sister Melissa Driscol had the body cremated and gave a portion of the remains to Tay's friend Chaunce Hayden. Shortly afterward, Tay's brother Jeff Roach learned that Hayden was to appear on Stern's show

(continued)

CASE 4.1—Continued

and asked the producer to cancel the appearance. Hayden went on as planned, and during his appearance, the participants in the program handled and joked about Tay's remains. For example, Stern held up bone fragments while he guessed whether they came from Tay's skull or ribs. Tay's brother and sister filed a suit in a New York state court against Stern and others, seeking $8 million in damages for, among other things, intentional infliction of emotional distress. The defendants filed a motion to dismiss, contending that the conduct at issue was not particularly shocking, in light of Stern's reputation for vulgar humor and Tay's actions during her guest appearances on his show. The court granted the motion, and the plaintiffs appealed.

ISSUE Could a jury reasonably conclude that the manner in which Tay's remains were handled supported a claim for intentional infliction of emotional distress?

DECISION Yes. The state intermediate appellate court reversed the decision of the lower court and remanded the case for trial.

REASON The appellate court recognized that "to impose liability for the tort of intentional infliction of emotional distress, the conduct complained of must be so outrageous in character, and so extreme in degree, as to go beyond all possible bounds of decency, and to be regarded as atrocious, and utterly intolerable in a civilized community." The court stated that the purpose of this element is to "filter out trivial complaints and assure that the claim of severe emotional distress is genuine." The court concluded that in this case, the plaintiffs sufficiently pleaded a cause of action—including the element of outrageous conduct—to recover damages for the intentional infliction of emotional distress.

FOR CRITICAL ANALYSIS—Social Consideration *What would be the result for society if broadcasters such as Howard Stern were never held liable for any distress caused by their broadcasts?*

DEFAMATION

DEFAMATION
Anything published or publicly spoken that causes injury to another's good name, reputation, or character.

SLANDER
Defamation in oral form.

LIBEL
Defamation in writing or other form (such as in a videotape) having the quality of permanence.

Defamation of character involves wrongfully hurting a person's good reputation. The law has imposed a general duty on all persons to refrain from making false, defamatory statements about others. Breaching this duty orally involves the tort of **slander**; breaching it in writing involves the tort of **libel**. The tort of defamation also arises when a false statement is made about a person's product, business, or title to property. We deal with these torts later in the chapter.

The common law defines four types of false utterances that are considered slander *per se* (meaning that no proof of injury or harm is required for these false utterances to be actionable):

① A statement that another has a loathsome communicable disease.

② A statement that another has committed improprieties while engaging in a profession or trade.

③ A statement that another has committed or has been imprisoned for a serious crime.

④ A statement that an unmarried woman is unchaste.

"Reputation, reputation, reputation! Oh, I have lost my reputation! I have lost the immortal part of myself, and what remains is bestial."

WILLIAM SHAKESPEARE, 1564–1616 (English dramatist and poet)

The Publication Requirement The basis of the tort of defamation is the publication of a statement or statements that hold an individual up to contempt, ridicule, or hatred. *Publication* here means that the defamatory statements are communicated to persons other than the defamed party. • **EXAMPLE 4.2** If Thompson writes Andrews a private letter accusing him of embezzling funds, the action does not constitute libel. If Peters calls Gordon dishonest, unattractive, and incompetent when no one else is around, the action does not constitute slander. In neither case was the message communicated to a third party.•

"Truth is generally the best vindication against slander."

ABRAHAM LINCOLN, 1809–1865 (Sixteenth president of the United States, 1861–1865)

The courts have generally held that even dictating a letter to a secretary constitutes publication, although the publication may be privileged (privileged communications will be discussed shortly). Moreover, if a third party overhears defamatory statements by chance, the courts usually hold that this also constitutes publication. Defamatory statements made via the Internet are also actionable. Note further that any individual who republishes or repeats defamatory statements is liable even if that person reveals the source of such statements.

Defenses against Defamation Truth is normally an absolute defense against a defamation charge. In other words, if the defendant in a defamation suit can prove that his or her allegedly defamatory statements were true, the defendant will not be liable.

PRIVILEGE
In tort law, the ability to act contrary to another person's right without that person's having legal redress for such acts. Privilege may be raised as a defense to defamation.

Another defense that is sometimes raised is that the statements were **privileged** communications, and thus the defendant is immune from liability. Privileged communications are of two types: absolute and qualified. Only in judicial proceedings and certain legislative proceedings is *absolute* privilege granted. For example, statements made in the courtroom by attorneys and judges during a trial are absolutely privileged. So are statements made by legislators during congressional floor debate, even if the legislators make such statements maliciously—that is, knowing them to be untrue. An absolute privilege is granted in these situations because judicial and legislative personnel deal with matters that are so much in the public interest that the parties involved should be able to speak out fully and freely without restriction.

ACTUAL MALICE
Real and demonstrable evil intent. In a defamation suit, a statement made about a public figure normally must be made with actual malice (with either knowledge of its falsity or a reckless disregard of the truth) for liability to be incurred.

In general, false and defamatory statements that are made about *public figures* (public officials who exercise substantial governmental power and any persons in the public limelight) and that are published in the press are privileged if they are made without **actual malice.**[3] To be made with actual malice, a statement must be made *with either knowledge of falsity or a reckless disregard of the truth.* Statements made about public figures, especially when they are made via a public medium, are usually related to matters of general public interest; they are made about people who substantially affect all of us. Furthermore, public figures generally have some access to a public medium for answering disparaging (belittling, discrediting) falsehoods about themselves; private individuals do not. For these reasons, public figures have a greater burden of proof in defamation cases (they must prove actual malice) than do private individuals.

INVASION OF THE RIGHT TO PRIVACY

ON THE WEB
The Cyberspace Law Center of FindLaw, which is now a part of West Group, offers numerous links to privacy laws and cases at
http://cyber.lp.findlaw.com/privacy.

A person has a right to solitude and freedom from prying public eyes—in other words, to privacy. As discussed in Chapter 2, the Supreme Court has held that a fundamental right to privacy is also implied by various amendments to the U.S. Constitution. Some state constitutions explicitly provide for privacy rights. In addition, a number of federal and state statutes have been enacted to protect individual rights in specific areas. Tort law also safeguards these rights through the tort of *invasion of privacy.* Four acts qualify as an invasion of privacy:

① *The use of a person's name, picture, or other likeness for commercial purposes without permission.* This tort, which is usually referred to as the tort of *appropriation,* will be examined shortly.

② *Intrusion in an individual's affairs or seclusion.* For example, invading someone's home or illegally searching someone's briefcase is an invasion of privacy. The tort

3. *New York Times Co. v. Sullivan,* 376 U.S. 254, 84 S.Ct. 710, 11 L.Ed.2d 686 (1964).

has been held to extend to eavesdropping by wiretap, the unauthorized scanning of a bank account, compulsory blood testing, and window peeping.

③ *Publication of information that places a person in a false light.* This could be a story attributing to the person ideas not held or actions not taken by the person. (Publishing such a story could involve the tort of defamation as well.)

④ *Public disclosure of private facts about an individual that an ordinary person would find objectionable.* A newspaper account of a private citizen's sex life or financial affairs could be an actionable invasion of privacy.

ON THE WEB You can find information and cases relating to employee privacy rights with respect to electronic monitoring at the Web site of the American Civil Liberties Union (ACLU). Go to **http://www.aclu.org/library/pbr2.html**.

A pressing issue in today's online world has to do with the privacy rights of Internet users. As noted in Chapter 2, this is particularly true with respect to personal information collected not only by government agencies but by online merchants. Internet users also face significant privacy issues in the employment context. In the following case, for example, a state government agency threatened to disclose to the media the personal e-mail messages that an employee had sent or received over the Internet from her work computer. The same rules concerning public disclosure do not apply in the context of private employment. The case illustrates, however, the problems associated with sending and receiving personal e-mail in any workplace where it is prohibited. (See Chapter 34 for a more detailed examination of privacy rights in the employment context.)

CASE 4.2 Tiberino v. Spokane County

Court of Appeals of Washington,
Division 3, 2000.
13 P.3d 1104.

FACTS In August 1998, Gina Tiberino was hired as a secretary in the Prosecuting Attorney's Office in Spokane County, Washington. The county provided her with a personal computer with an e-mail application. According to county policy, Tiberino was told that her employer could monitor all e-mail, that she was not to put anything into an e-mail message that she would not want on the front page of a newspaper, and that county equipment was not for personal use. In October, Tiberino's co-workers complained that she was using her computer to send personal e-mail over the Internet. Her supervisor reminded her that county computers were not to be used for personal business. In November, she was discharged for unsatisfactory work performance related to her use of e-mail for personal matters. When she threatened to sue the county, her ex-employer printed out all of her e-mail. Of 551 items, 467 were personal messages. When the media asked the prosecutor's office to release copies of the e-mail (more than 3,700 pages), Tiberino filed a suit in a Washington state court against the county to stop the release. The court concluded that the messages were "public records" and refused to grant her request. On Tiberino's appeal, the state intermediate appellate court agreed that the messages were public records and then considered whether, under a state statutory exception, their disclosure would violate her right to privacy.

ISSUE Does public disclosure of private e-mail violate a person's right to privacy if that disclosure would be highly offensive to a reasonable person and is not of legitimate concern to the public?

DECISION Yes. The state intermediate appellate court reversed the judgment of the lower court. The appellate court concluded that Tiberino's e-mail messages were "public records," but that they were exempt from public disclosure as personal information.

REASON The court explained that "Ms. Tiberino's e-mails contain intimate details about her personal and private life and do not discuss specific instances of misconduct. * * * Any reasonable person would find disclosure of Ms. Tiberino's e-mails to be highly offensive." The court acknowledged that "records of governmental

CASE 4.2—Continued

agency expenditures * * * are of legitimate public interest and therefore not exempt from disclosure," because of the concern that "government conduct itself fairly and use public funds responsibly." In this case, however, "[t]he content of Ms. Tiberino's e-mails is personal and is unrelated to governmental operations. Certainly, the public has an interest in seeing that public employees are not spending their time on the public payroll pursuing personal interests. But it is the amount of time spent on personal matters, not the content of personal e-mails or phone calls or conversations, that is of public interest. The fact that Ms. Tiberino sent 467 e-mails over a 40 working-day time frame is of significance in her termination action and the public has a legitimate interest in having that information. But what she said in those e-mails is of no public significance."

FOR CRITICAL ANALYSIS—Social Consideration *Instead of serving as a flash point for a lawsuit, as in the Tiberino case, how might an employer's monitoring of employees' e-mail* prevent *litigation?*

APPROPRIATION

APPROPRIATION In tort law, the use by one person of another person's name, likeness, or other identifying characteristic without permission and for the benefit of the user.

The use by one person of another person's name, likeness, or other identifying characteristic, without permission and for the benefit of the user, constitutes the tort of **appropriation**. Under the law, an individual's right to privacy normally includes the right to the exclusive use of her or his identity.

• **EXAMPLE 4.3** Vanna White, the hostess of the popular television game show *Wheel of Fortune*, brought a case against Samsung Electronics America, Inc. Without White's permission, Samsung included in an advertisement for its videocassette recorders (VCRs) a depiction of a robot dressed in a wig, gown, and jewelry, posed in a scene that resembled the *Wheel of Fortune* set, in a stance for which White is famous. The court held in White's favor, holding that the tort of appropriation does not require the use of a celebrity's name or likeness. The court stated that Samsung's robot ad left "little doubt" as to the identity of the celebrity whom the ad was meant to depict.[4] •

Cases of wrongful appropriation, or misappropriation, may also involve the rights of those who invest time and money in the creation of a special system, such as a method of broadcasting sports events. Commercial misappropriation may also occur when a person takes and uses the property of another for the sole purpose of capitalizing unfairly on the goodwill or reputation of the property owner.

MISREPRESENTATION (FRAUD)

FRAUDULENT MISREPRESENTATION Any misrepresentation, either by misstatement or omission of a material fact, knowingly made with the intention of deceiving another and on which a reasonable person would and does rely to his or her detriment.

A misrepresentation leads another to believe in a condition that is different from the condition that actually exists. This is often accomplished through a false or an incorrect statement. Misrepresentations may be innocently made by someone who is unaware of the existing facts, but the tort of **fraudulent misrepresentation**, or fraud, involves intentional deceit for personal gain. The tort includes several elements:

① Misrepresentation of facts or conditions with knowledge that they are false or with reckless disregard for the truth.

② Intent to induce another to rely on the misrepresentation.

③ Justifiable reliance by the deceived party.

④ Damages suffered as a result of the reliance.

⑤ Causal connection between the misrepresentation and the injury suffered.

---

4. *White v. Samsung Electronics America, Inc.*, 971 F.2d 1395 (9th Cir. 1992).

PUFFERY
A salesperson's often exaggerated claims concerning the quality of property offered for sale. Such claims involve opinions rather than facts and are not considered to be legally binding promises or warranties.

ON THE WEB The 'Lectric Law Library's Legal Lexicon includes an informative discussion of the elements of fraud as well as different types of fraud. To access this page, go to **http://www.lectlaw.com/def/1079.htm**.

For fraud to occur, more than mere **puffery**, or *seller's talk,* must be involved. Fraud exists only when a person represents as a fact something he or she knows is untrue. For example, it is fraud to claim that a building does not leak when one knows it does. Facts are objectively ascertainable, whereas seller's talk is not. "I am the best accountant in town" is seller's talk. The speaker is not trying to represent something as fact, because the term *best* is a subjective, not an objective, term.[5]

Normally, the tort of misrepresentation or fraud occurs only when there is reliance on a *statement of fact.* Sometimes, however, reliance on a *statement of opinion* may involve the tort of misrepresentation if the individual making the statement of opinion has a superior knowledge of the subject matter. For example, when a lawyer makes a statement of opinion about the law in a state in which the lawyer is licensed to practice, a court would construe reliance on such a statement to be equivalent to reliance on a statement of fact. We examine fraudulent misrepresentation in further detail in Chapter 11, in the context of contract law.

Wrongful Interference

Business torts involving wrongful interference are generally divided into two categories: wrongful interference with a contractual relationship and wrongful interference with a business relationship.

Wrongful Interference with a Contractual Relationship The body of tort law relating to *intentional interference with a contractual relationship* has expanded greatly in recent years. A landmark case involved an opera singer, Joanna Wagner, who was under contract to sing for a man named Lumley for a specified period of years. A man named Gye, who knew of this contract, nonetheless "enticed" Wagner to refuse to carry out the agreement, and Wagner began to sing for Gye. Gye's action constituted a tort because it wrongfully interfered with the contractual relationship between Wagner and Lumley.[6] (Of course, Wagner's refusal to carry out the agreement also entitled Lumley to sue Wagner for breach of contract.)

REMEMBER It is the intent to do an act that is important in tort law, not the motive behind the intent.

Three elements are necessary for wrongful interference with a contractual relationship to occur:

① A valid, enforceable contract must exist between two parties.

② A third party must know that this contract exists.

③ The third party must *intentionally* cause either of the two parties to breach the contract.

The contract may be between a firm and its employees or a firm and its customers. Sometimes a competitor of a firm draws away one of the firm's key employees. If the original employer can show that the competitor induced the breach—that is, that the former employee would not otherwise have broken the contract—damages can be recovered from the competitor.

The following case illustrates the elements of the tort of wrongful interference with a contractual relationship in the context of an agreement not to compete (see Chapter 10).

5. In contracts for the sale of goods, Article 2 of the Uniform Commercial Code distinguishes, for warranty purposes, between statements of opinion ("puffery") and statements of fact. See Chapter 18 for a further discussion of this issue.

6. *Lumley v. Gye,* 118 Eng.Rep. 749 (1853).

CASE 4.3 Kallok v. Medtronic, Inc.

Supreme Court of Minnesota, 1998.
573 N.W.2d 356.
http://www.lawlibrary.state.mn.us/archive/sctjl.html[a]

COMPANY PROFILE *Medtronic, Inc., is the world's leading manufacturer of implantable biomedical devices. The company was started in 1949 by Earl Bakken, who was then a graduate student at the University of Minnesota, and Palmer Hermundslie, who worked in a lumberyard. The company's initial focus was the repair of hospital laboratory equipment. Today, Medtronic's most important products relate to cardiovascular and neurological health. It makes the most-often-prescribed heart pacemakers, as well as heart valves, implantable neurostimulation and drug-delivery systems, catheters used in angioplasties, and other products. Medtronic sells these products in more than 120 countries.*

FACTS Michael Kallok signed a series of noncompete agreements when he worked for Medtronic, Inc., a medical device manufacturer. The agreements restricted his ability to work for Medtronic's competitors, including Angeion Corporation. When Kallok later approached Angeion for a job, he told it about the agreements. Angeion consulted with its attorneys, who advised that Kallok would not breach the agreements by accepting a job with Angeion. Angeion did not tell the attorneys all of the details of the agreements, however. After Kallok resigned to work for Angeion, he and Angeion filed a suit in a Minnesota state court against Medtronic, asserting that the noncompete agreements were unenforceable. Medtronic counterclaimed, alleging wrongful interference by Angeion. Angeion argued that its hiring of Kallok was justified because it consulted attorneys first. The court held Angeion liable and, among other things, awarded Medtronic damages. The plaintiffs appealed. The state intermediate appellate court took away the award. Medtronic appealed to the Minnesota Supreme Court.

ISSUE Can Medtronic recover damages for Angeion's interference with the noncompete agreements between Medtronic and Kallok?

DECISION Yes. The Minnesota Supreme Court reversed the decision of the lower court.

REASON First, the state supreme court pointed out that Medtronic "easily" established the elements for wrongful interference with a contractual relationship. Medtronic and Kallok signed valid noncompete agreements, Angeion knew of the agreements before it hired Kallok, and Angeion caused Kallok to breach the agreements by offering him the job that he accepted. Second, as for Angeion's argument that its actions were justified, the court emphasized that Angeion did not tell its attorneys "all relevant information." If it had, "Angeion would have understood that hiring Kallok would cause him to breach his noncompete agreements with Medtronic." Finally, as for Medtronic's damages, the court explained that Angeion's tortious actions forced Medtronic into court to protect its interest in the noncompete agreements. Therefore, Medtronic was entitled to recover those expenses.

FOR CRITICAL ANALYSIS—Social Consideration *What might be the result for society if there were no cause of action for wrongful interference with a contractual relationship?*

a. This page lists, in alphabetical order, Minnesota Supreme Court opinions and orders that have been issued since May 2, 1996, with first party names beginning with the letter J, K, or L. Scroll down the list to the *Kallok* case and click on the docket number to access the opinion. This page is part of the Web site for the "Minnesota State Court System" maintained by the Minnesota state government.

PREDATORY BEHAVIOR
Business behavior that is undertaken with the intention of unlawfully driving competitors out of the market.

Wrongful Interference with a Business Relationship Businesspersons devise countless schemes to attract customers, but they are forbidden by the courts to interfere unreasonably with another's business in their attempts to gain a share of the market. There is a difference between competitive methods and **predatory behavior**—actions undertaken with the intention of unlawfully driving competitors completely out of the market.

The distinction usually depends on whether a business is attempting to attract customers in general or to solicit only those customers who have shown an interest in a

"Anyone can win unless there happens to be a second entry."

GEORGE ADE, 1866–1944 (American humorist)

similar product or service of a specific competitor. If a shopping center contains two shoe stores, an employee of Store A cannot be positioned at the entrance of Store B for the purpose of diverting customers to Store A. This type of activity constitutes the tort of wrongful interference with a business relationship, which is commonly considered to be an unfair trade practice. If this type of activity were permitted, Store A would reap the benefits of Store B's advertising.

REMEMBER What society and the law consider permissible often depends on the circumstances.

Defenses to Wrongful Interference A person will not be liable for the tort of wrongful interference with a contractual or business relationship if it can be shown that the interference was justified, or permissible. Bona fide competitive behavior is a permissible interference even if it results in the breaking of a contract. • **EXAMPLE 4.4** If Antonio's Meats advertises so effectively that it induces Beverly's Restaurant Chain to break its contract with Otis Meat Company, Otis Meat Company will be unable to recover against Antonio's Meats on a wrongful interference theory. After all, the public policy that favors free competition in advertising outweighs any possible instability that such competitive activity might cause in contractual relations. •

Intentional Torts against Property

Intentional torts against property include trespass to land, trespass to personal property, conversion, and disparagement of property. These torts are wrongful actions that interfere with individuals' legally recognized rights with regard to their land or personal property. The law distinguishes real property from personal property (see Chapters 36 and 37). *Real property* is land and things "permanently" attached to the land. Personal property consists of all other items, which are basically movable. Thus, a house and lot are real property, whereas the furniture inside a house is personal property. Money and stocks and bonds are also personal property.

TRESPASS TO LAND

TRESPASS TO LAND The entry onto, above, or below the surface of land owned by another without the owner's permission or legal authorization.

A **trespass to land** occurs whenever a person, without permission, enters onto, above, or below the surface of land that is owned by another; causes anything to enter onto the land; remains on the land; or permits anything to remain on it. Actual harm to the land is not an essential element of this tort because the tort is designed to protect the right of an owner to exclusive possession of his or her property. Common types of trespass to land include walking or driving on the land, shooting a gun over the land, throwing rocks at a building that belongs to someone else, building a dam across a river and thus causing water to back up on someone else's land, and placing part of one's building on an adjoining landowner's property.

A sign warns trespassers. Should a trespasser be allowed to recover from a landowner for injuries sustained on the premises?

Trespass Criteria, Rights, and Duties Before a person can be a trespasser, the owner of the real property (or other person in actual and exclusive possession of the property) must establish that person as a trespasser. For example, "posted" trespass signs expressly establish as a trespasser a person who ignores these signs and enters onto the property. A guest in your home is not a trespasser—unless she or he has been asked to leave but refuses. Any person who enters onto your property to commit an illegal act (such as a thief entering a lumberyard at night to steal lumber) is established impliedly as a trespasser, without posted signs.

At common law, a trespasser is liable for damages caused to the property and generally cannot hold the owner liable for injuries sustained on the premises. This common law rule is being abandoned in many jurisdictions in favor of a "reasonable duty of care" rule that varies depending on the status of the parties; for example, a landowner may have a duty to post a notice that the property is patrolled by guard dogs. Furthermore, under the "attractive nuisance" doctrine, children do not assume the risks of the premises if they are attracted to the premises by some object, such as a swimming pool, an abandoned building, or a sand pile. Trespassers normally can be removed from the premises through the use of reasonable force without the owner's being liable for assault and battery.

Defenses against Trespass to Land Trespass to land involves wrongful interference with another person's real property rights. If it can be shown that the trespass was warranted, however, as when a trespasser enters to assist someone in danger, a defense exists. Another defense exists when the trespasser can show that he or she had a license to come onto the land. A *licensee* is one who is invited (or allowed to enter) onto the property of another for the licensee's benefit. A person who enters another's property to read an electric meter, for example, is a licensee. When you purchase a ticket to attend a movie or sporting event, you are licensed to go onto the property of another to view that movie or event. Note that licenses to enter onto another's property are *revocable* by the property owner. If a property owner asks a meter reader to leave and the meter reader refuses to do so, the meter reader at that point becomes a trespasser.

TRESPASS TO PERSONAL PROPERTY

TRESPASS TO PERSONAL PROPERTY
The unlawful taking or harming of another's personal property; interference with another's right to the exclusive possession of his or her personal property.

Whenever any individual unlawfully harms the personal property of another or otherwise interferes with the personal property owner's right to exclusive possession and enjoyment of that property, **trespass to personal property**—also called *trespass to personalty*[7]—occurs. If a student takes another student's business law book as a practical joke and hides it so that the owner is unable to find it for several days prior to a final examination, the student has engaged in a trespass to personal property.

If it can be shown that trespass to personal property was warranted, then a complete defense exists. Most states, for example, allow automobile repair shops to hold a customer's car (under what is called an *artisan's lien,* discussed in Chapter 23) when the customer refuses to pay for repairs already completed.

CONVERSION

CONVERSION
The wrongful taking or retaining possession of a person's personal property and placing it in the service of another.

KEEP IN MIND In tort law, the underlying motive for an act does not matter. What matters is the intent to do the act that results in the tort.

Whenever personal property is wrongfully taken from its rightful owner or possessor and placed in the service of another, the act of **conversion** occurs. Conversion is defined as any act depriving an owner of personal property without that owner's permission and without just cause. When conversion occurs, the lesser offense of trespass to personal property usually occurs as well. If the initial taking of the property was unlawful, there is trespass; retention of that property is conversion. If the initial taking of the property was permitted by the owner or for some other reason is not a trespass, failure to return it may still be conversion. Conversion is the civil side of crimes related to theft. A store clerk who steals merchandise from the store commits a crime and engages in the tort of conversion at the same time.

Even if a person mistakenly believed that she or he was entitled to the goods, a tort of conversion may occur. In other words, good intentions are not a defense against conversion; in fact, conversion can be an entirely innocent act. Someone who buys stolen goods, for example, is guilty of conversion even if he or she did not know that the goods were stolen. If the true owner brings a tort action against the buyer, the buyer must either return the property to the owner or pay the owner the full value of the property, despite having already paid money to the thief.

7. Pronounced *per*-sun-ul-tee.

A successful defense against the charge of conversion is that the purported owner does not in fact own the property or does not have a right to possess it that is superior to the right of the holder. Necessity is another possible defense against conversion. • **EXAMPLE 4.5** If Abrams takes Mendoza's cat, Abrams is guilty of conversion. If Mendoza sues Abrams, Abrams must return the cat or pay damages. If, however, the cat has rabies and Abrams took the cat to protect the public, Abrams has a valid defense—necessity (and perhaps even self-defense, if he can prove that he was in danger because of the cat). •

DISPARAGEMENT OF PROPERTY

DISPARAGEMENT OF PROPERTY
An economically injurious falsehood made about another's product or property. A general term for torts that are more specifically referred to as slander of quality or slander of title.

Disparagement of property occurs when economically injurious falsehoods are made not about another's reputation but about another's product or property. Disparagement of property is a general term for torts that can be more specifically referred to as *slander of quality* or *slander of title*.

SLANDER OF QUALITY (TRADE LIBEL)
The publication of false information about another's product, alleging that it is not what its seller claims.

Slander of Quality Publication of false information about another's product, alleging that it is not what its seller claims, constitutes the tort of **slander of quality**, or **trade libel.** The plaintiff must prove that actual damages proximately resulted from the slander of quality. In other words, the plaintiff must show not only that a third person refrained from dealing with the plaintiff because of the improper publication but also that there were associated damages. The economic calculation of such damages—they are, after all, conjectural—is often extremely difficult.

An improper publication may be both a slander of quality and a defamation. For example, a statement that disparages the quality of a product may also, by implication, disparage the character of the person who would sell such a product. In one case, for instance, the claim that a product that was marketed as a sleeping aid contained "habit-forming drugs" was held to constitute defamation.[8]

During the 1990s, at least thirteen states enacted special statutes to protect against disparagement of perishable food products. Food producers began to push for such laws in 1991 after Washington state apple growers, using traditional libel and product-disparagement laws, failed to win a lawsuit against CBS News for a *60 Minutes* broadcast on the growth regulator Alar. Food-disparagement laws received national media attention when a group of Texas cattle ranchers sued talk-show host Oprah Winfrey for saying on one of her shows that the fear of "mad cow" disease "stopped her cold from eating a hamburger." The ranchers claimed that Winfrey had defamed their product, beef, in violation of the Texas food-disparagement statute. In 1998, the federal judge hearing the case held that the cattle ranchers had failed to make a case under the Texas statute.

SLANDER OF TITLE
The publication of a statement that denies or casts doubt on another's legal ownership of any property, causing financial loss to that property's owner.

Slander of Title When a publication denies or casts doubt on another's legal ownership of any property, and when this results in financial loss to that property's owner, the tort of **slander of title** may exist. Usually, this is an intentional tort in which someone knowingly publishes an untrue statement about property with the intent of discouraging a third person from dealing with the person slandered. For example, it would be difficult for a car dealer to attract customers after competitors published a notice that the dealer's stock consisted of stolen autos.

8. *Harwood Pharmacal Co. v. National Broadcasting Co.*, 9 N.Y.2d 460, 174 N.E.2d 602, 214 N.Y.S.2d 725 (1961).

Unintentional Torts (Negligence)

NEGLIGENCE
The failure to exercise the standard of care that a reasonable person would exercise in similar circumstances.

The tort of **negligence** occurs when someone suffers injury because of another's failure to live up to a required *duty of care*. In contrast to intentional torts, in torts involving negligence, the tortfeasor neither wishes to bring about the consequences of the act nor believes that they will occur. The actor's conduct merely creates a *risk* of such consequences. If no risk is created, there is no negligence.

Many of the actions discussed in the section on intentional torts constitute negligence if the element of intent is missing. • **EXAMPLE 4.6** If Juarez intentionally shoves Natsuyo, who falls and breaks an arm as a result, Juarez will have committed the intentional tort of assault and battery. If Juarez carelessly bumps into Natsuyo, however, and she falls and breaks an arm as a result, Juarez's action will constitute negligence. In either situation, Juarez has committed a tort.•

In examining a question of negligence, one should ask four questions:

1. Did the defendant owe a duty of care to the plaintiff?
2. Did the defendant breach that duty?
3. Did the plaintiff suffer a legally recognizable injury as a result of the defendant's breach of the duty of care?
4. Did the defendant's breach cause the plaintiff's injury?

Each of these elements of negligence is discussed in this section.

"To answer your question. Yes, if you shoot an arrow into the air and it falls to earth you should know not where, you could be liable for any damage it may cause."

THE DUTY OF CARE AND ITS BREACH

DUTY OF CARE
The duty of all persons, as established by tort law, to exercise a reasonable amount of care in their dealings with others. Failure to exercise due care, which is normally determined by the "reasonable person standard," constitutes the tort of negligence.

The concept of a **duty of care** arises from the notion that if we are to live in society with other people, some actions can be tolerated and some cannot; some actions are right and some are wrong; and some actions are reasonable and some are not. The basic principle underlying the duty of care is that people are free to act as they please so long as their actions do not infringe on the interests of others.

When someone fails to comply with the duty of exercising reasonable care, a potentially tortious act may have been committed. Failure to live up to a standard of care may be an act (setting fire to a building) or an omission (neglecting to put out a campfire). It may be a careless act or a carefully performed but nevertheless dangerous act that results in injury. Courts consider the nature of the act (whether it is outrageous or commonplace), the manner in which the act is performed (cautiously versus heedlessly), and the nature of the injury (whether it is serious or slight) in determining whether the duty of care has been breached.

REASONABLE PERSON STANDARD
The standard of behavior expected of a hypothetical "reasonable person." The standard against which negligence is measured and that must be observed to avoid liability for negligence.

The Reasonable Person Standard Tort law measures duty by the **reasonable person standard.** In determining whether a duty of care has been breached, the courts ask how a reasonable person would have acted in the same circumstances. The reasonable person standard is said to be (though in an absolute sense it cannot be) objective. It is not necessarily how a particular person would act. It is society's judgment on how people *should* act. If the so-called reasonable person existed, he or she would be careful, conscientious, even tempered, and honest. This hypothetical reasonable person is frequently used by the courts in decisions relating to other areas of law as well.

That individuals are required to exercise a reasonable standard of care in their activities is a pervasive concept in business law, and many of the issues dealt with in subsequent chapters of this text have to do with this duty. What constitutes reasonable care varies, of course, with the circumstances.

ETHICAL ISSUE 4.1

Does a person's duty of care include a duty to come to the aid of a stranger in peril?

Suppose that you are walking down a city street and notice that a pedestrian is about to step directly in front of an oncoming bus. Do you have a legal duty to warn that individual? No. Although most people would probably concede that in this situation, the observer has an *ethical* or moral duty to warn the other, tort law does not impose a general duty to rescue others in peril. People involved in special relationships, however, have been held to have a duty to rescue other parties within the relationship. A person has a duty to rescue his or her child or spouse if either is in danger, for example. Other special relationships, such as those between teachers and students or hiking and hunting partners, may also give rise to a duty to rescue. In addition, if a person who has no duty to rescue undertakes to rescue another, then the rescuer is charged with a duty to follow through with due care on the rescue attempt.

The Duty of Landowners Landowners are expected to exercise reasonable care to protect persons coming onto their property from harm. As mentioned earlier, in some jurisdictions, landowners are held to owe a duty to protect even trespassers against certain risks. Landowners who rent or lease premises to tenants (see Chapter 37) are expected to exercise reasonable care to ensure that the tenants and their guests are not harmed in common areas, such as stairways, entryways, laundry rooms, and the like.

BUSINESS INVITEE
A person, such as a customer or a client, who is invited onto business premises by the owner of those premises for business purposes.

Retailers and other firms that explicitly or implicitly invite persons to come onto their premises are usually charged with a duty to exercise reasonable care to protect those persons, who are considered **business invitees.** For example, if you entered a supermarket, slipped on a wet floor, and sustained injuries as a result, the owner of the supermarket would be liable for damages if when you slipped there was no sign warning that the floor was wet. A court would hold that the business owner was negligent because the owner failed to exercise a reasonable degree of care in protecting the store's customers against foreseeable risks about which the owner knew or *should have known.* That a patron might slip on the wet floor and be injured as a result was a foreseeable risk, and the owner should have taken care to avoid this risk or to warn the customer of it. The landowner also has a duty to discover and remove any hidden dangers that might injure a customer or other invitee.

Some risks, of course, are so obvious that the owner need not warn of them. For instance, a business owner does not need to warn customers to open a door before attempting to walk through it. Other risks, however, even though they may seem obvious to a business owner, may not be so in the eyes of another, such as a child. For example, a hardware store owner may not think it is necessary to warn customers that a stepladder leaning against the back wall of the store could fall down and harm them. It is possible, though, that a child could tip the ladder over and be hurt as a result and that the store could be held liable.

In the following case, the court had to decide whether a store owner should be held liable for a customer's injury on the premises. The question was whether the owner had notice of the condition that led to the customer's injury.

CASE 4.4 Martin v. Wal-Mart Stores, Inc.

United States Court of Appeals,
Eighth Circuit, 1999.
183 F.3d 770.
http://guide.lp.findlaw.com/casecode/courts/8th.html[a]

FACTS Harold Martin was shopping in the sporting goods department of a Wal-Mart store. There was one employee in the department at that time. In front of the sporting goods section, in the store's main aisle (which the employees referred to as "action alley"), there was a large display of stacked cases of shotgun shells. On top of the cases were individual boxes of shells. Shortly after the sporting goods employee walked past the display, Martin did so, but Martin slipped on some loose shotgun shell pellets and fell to the floor. He immediately lost feeling in, and control of, his legs. Sensation and control returned, but during the next week, he lost the use of his legs several times for periods of ten to fifteen minutes. Eventually, sensation and control did not return to the front half of his left foot. Doctors diagnosed the condition as permanent. Martin filed a suit against Wal-Mart in a federal district court, seeking damages for his injury. The jury found in his favor, and the court denied Wal-Mart's motion for a directed verdict. Wal-Mart appealed to the U.S. Court of Appeals for the Eighth Circuit.

ISSUE Should Wal-Mart be held liable for Martin's injury?

DECISION Yes. The U.S. Court of Appeals for the Eighth Circuit affirmed the judgment of the lower court.

REASON The appellate court stated, "The traditional rule * * * required a plaintiff in a slip and fall case to establish that the defendant store had either actual or constructive notice[b] of the dangerous condition." The court, however, explained that this case involved the self-

a. This URL will take you to a Web site maintained by FindLaw, which is now a part of West Group. When you access the site, enter "Wal-Mart" in the "Party Name Search" box and then click on "Search." Scroll down the list on the page that opens and select the link to "Harold Martin v. Wal-Mart Stores."

b. *Constructive notice* is notice that is implied by law, in view of the circumstances.

(continued)

CASE 4.4—Continued

service store exception to the traditional slip-and-fall rule. A self-service store has notice that certain dangers arising through customer involvement are likely to occur and has a duty to anticipate them. Part of this duty is to "warn customers or protect them from the danger." Here, Wal-Mart had constructive notice of the pellets on the floor in the main aisle. "Martin slipped on pellets next to a large display of shotgun shells immediately abutting the sporting goods department. The chance that merchandise will wind up on the floor (or merchandise will be spilled on the floor) in the department in which that merchandise is sold or displayed is exactly the type of foreseeable risk" that is part of the self-service store exception.

FOR CRITICAL ANALYSIS—Ethical Consideration *Why do the courts impose constructive notice requirements on owners of self-service stores but not on owners of other stores?*

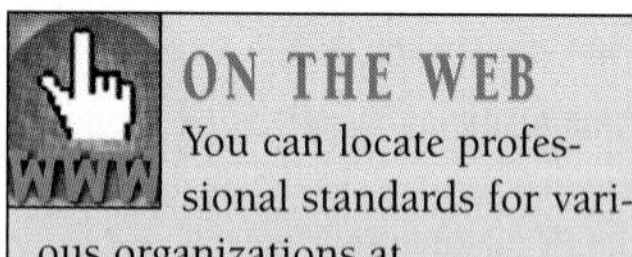

ON THE WEB You can locate professional standards for various organizations at **http://www.lib.uwaterloo.ca/society/standards.html**.

The Duty of Professionals If an individual has knowledge, skill, or intelligence superior to that of an ordinary person, the individual's conduct must be consistent with that status. Professionals—including physicians, dentists, psychiatrists, architects, engineers, accountants, lawyers, and others—are required to have a standard minimum level of special knowledge and ability. Therefore, in determining what constitutes reasonable care in the case of professionals, their training and expertise are taken into account. In other words, an accountant cannot defend against a lawsuit for negligence by stating, "But I was not familiar with that principle of accounting."

If a professional violates her or his duty of care toward a client, the professional may be sued for **malpractice**. For example, a patient might sue a physician for *medical malpractice*. A client might sue an attorney for *legal malpractice*.

MALPRACTICE
Professional misconduct or the lack of the requisite degree of skill as a professional. Negligence—the failure to exercise due care—on the part of a professional, such as a physician, is commonly referred to as malpractice.

THE INJURY REQUIREMENT AND DAMAGES

For a tort to have been committed, the plaintiff must have suffered a *legally recognizable* injury. To recover damages (receive compensation), the plaintiff must have suffered some loss, harm, wrong, or invasion of a protected interest. Essentially, the purpose of tort law is to compensate for legally recognized injuries resulting from wrongful acts. If no harm or injury results from a given negligent action, there is nothing to compensate—and no tort exists.

• **EXAMPLE 4.7** If you carelessly bump into a passerby, who stumbles and falls as a result, you may be liable in tort if the passerby is injured in the fall. If the person is unharmed, however, there normally could be no suit for damages, because no injury was suffered. Although the passerby might be angry and suffer emotional distress, few courts recognize negligently inflicted emotional distress as a tort unless it results in some physical disturbance or dysfunction. •

As already mentioned, the purpose of tort law is not to punish people for tortious acts but to compensate the injured parties for damages suffered. Occasionally, however, damages awarded in tort lawsuits include both **compensatory damages** (which are intended to reimburse a plaintiff for actual losses—to make the plaintiff whole) and **punitive damages** (which are intended to punish the wrongdoer and deter others from similar wrongdoing).

COMPENSATORY DAMAGES
A money award equivalent to the actual value of injuries or damages sustained by the aggrieved party.

PUNITIVE DAMAGES
Money damages that may be awarded to a plaintiff to punish the defendant and deter future similar conduct.

CAUSATION

Another element necessary to a tort is *causation*. If a person fails in a duty of care and someone suffers injury, the wrongful activity must have caused the harm for a tort to

INTERNATIONAL PERSPECTIVE

Tort Liability and Damages in Other Nations

In contrast to U.S. courts, courts in Europe generally limit damages to compensatory damages; punitive damages are virtually unheard of in European countries. Even when plaintiffs do win compensatory damages, they generally receive much less than would be awarded in a similar case brought in the United States. In part, this is because governments in Europe usually provide for health care and have relatively generous Social Security payments. Yet it is also because European courts tend to view the duty of care and the concept of risk differently than U.S. courts do. In the United States, if a swimmer is injured while falling off a high diving board, a court may decide that the pool owner should be held liable, given that such a fall is a foreseeable risk. If punitive damages are awarded, they could total millions of dollars. In a similar situation in Europe, a court might hold that the plaintiff, not the pool owner, was responsible for the injury.

Tort laws in other nations also differ in the way damages are calculated. For example, under Swiss law and Turkish law, a court is permitted to reduce damages if an award of full damages would cause undue hardship for a party who was found negligent. In some nations of northern Africa, different amounts of damages are awarded depending on the type of tortious action committed and the degree of intent involved. In the United States, in contrast, the calculation of compensatory damages does not depend on whether the tort was negligent or intentional—although they are most often awarded in cases involving intentional torts.

FOR CRITICAL ANALYSIS
Punitive damages are an important element in American tort litigation. Why is this? What do awards of punitive damages achieve?

have been committed. In deciding whether there is causation, the court must address two questions:

① *Is there causation in fact?* Did the injury occur because of the defendant's act, or would it have occurred anyway? If an injury would not have occurred without the defendant's act, then there is causation in fact. **Causation in fact** can usually be determined by the use of the *but for* test: "but for" the wrongful act, the injury would not have occurred. Theoretically, causation in fact is limitless. One could claim, for example, that "but for" the creation of the world, a particular injury would not have occurred. Thus, as a practical matter, the law has to establish limits, and it does so through the concept of proximate cause.

CAUSATION IN FACT
An act or omission without which an event would not have occurred.

② *Was the act the proximate cause of the injury?* **Proximate cause**, or legal cause, exists when the connection between an act and an injury is strong enough to justify imposing liability. • **EXAMPLE 4.8** Ackerman carelessly leaves a campfire burning. The fire not only burns down the forest but also sets off an explosion in a nearby chemical plant that spills chemicals into a river, killing all the fish for a hundred miles downstream and ruining the economy of a tourist resort. Should Ackerman be liable to the resort owners? To the tourists whose vacations were ruined? These are questions of proximate cause that a court must decide.•

PROXIMATE CAUSE
Legal cause; exists when the connection between an act and an injury is strong enough to justify imposing liability.

NOTE Proximate cause can be thought of as a question of social policy. Should the defendant be made to bear the loss instead of the plaintiff?

Probably the most cited case on proximate cause is the *Palsgraf* case discussed in this chapter's *Landmark in the Law* feature on the next page. In determining the issue of proximate cause, the court addressed the following question: Does a defendant's duty of care extend only to those who may be injured as a result of a foreseeable risk, or does it extend also to a person whose injury could not reasonably be foreseen?

LANDMARK IN THE LAW
Palsgraf v. Long Island Railroad Co. (1928)

In 1928, the New York Court of Appeals (that state's highest court) issued its decision in *Palsgraf v. Long Island Railroad Co.*,[a] a case that has become a landmark in negligence law with respect to proximate cause.

The Facts of the Case The plaintiff, Palsgraf, was waiting for a train on a station platform. A man carrying a small package wrapped in newspaper was rushing to catch a train that had begun to move away from the platform. As the man attempted to jump aboard the moving train, he seemed unsteady and about to fall. A railroad guard on the train car reached forward to grab him, and another guard on the platform pushed him from behind to help him board the train. In the process, the man's package fell on the railroad tracks and exploded, because it contained fireworks. The repercussions of the explosion caused scales at the other end of the train platform to fall on Palsgraf, who was injured as a result. She sued the railroad company for damages in a New York state court.

The Question of Proximate Cause At the trial, the jury found that the railroad guards were negligent in their conduct. On appeal, the question before the New York Court of Appeals was whether the conduct of the railroad guards was the proximate cause of Palsgraf's injuries. In other words, did the guards' duty of care extend to Palsgraf, who was outside the zone of danger and whose injury could not reasonably have been foreseen?

The court stated that the question of whether the guards were negligent *with respect to Palsgraf* depended on whether her injury was *reasonably foreseeable* to the railroad guards. Although the guards may have acted negligently with respect to the man boarding the train, this has no bearing on the question of their negligence with respect to Palsgraf. This is not a situation in which a person commits an act so potentially harmful (for example, firing a gun at a building) that he or she would be held responsible for any harm that resulted. The court stated that here, "there was nothing in the situation to suggest to the most cautious mind that the parcel wrapped in newspaper would spread wreckage through the station." The court thus concluded that the railroad guards were not negligent with respect to Palsgraf because her injury was not reasonably foreseeable.

APPLICATION TO TODAY'S WORLD

The Palsgraf *case established* foreseeability *as the test for proximate cause. Today, the courts continue to apply this test in determining proximate cause—and thus tort liability for injuries. Generally, if the victim of a harm or the consequences of a harm done are unforeseeable, there is no proximate cause. Note, though, that in the online environment, distinctions based on physical proximity, such as the "zone of danger" cited by the court in this case, are largely inapplicable.*

a. 248 N.Y. 339, 162 N.E. 99 (1928).

Defenses to Negligence

Defendants often defend against negligence claims by asserting that the plaintiffs failed to prove the existence of one or more of the required elements for negligence. Additionally, there are three basic *affirmative* defenses in negligence cases (defenses that defendants can use to avoid liability even if the facts are as the plaintiffs state): (1) assumption of risk, (2) superseding cause, and (3) contributory negligence.

ASSUMPTION OF RISK
A doctrine whereby a plaintiff may not recover for injuries or damages suffered from risks he or she knows of and has voluntarily assumed. A defense against negligence that can be used when the plaintiff has knowledge of and appreciates a danger and voluntarily exposes himself or herself to the danger.

CONTRIBUTORY NEGLIGENCE
A theory in tort law under which a complaining party's own negligence contributed to or caused his or her injuries. Contributory negligence is an absolute bar to recovery in a minority of jurisdictions.

NOTE The concept of superseding cause is not a question of physics but is, like proximate cause, a question of responsibility.

Assumption of Risk A plaintiff who voluntarily enters into a risky situation, knowing the risk involved, will not be allowed to recover. This is the defense of **assumption of risk.** The requirements of this defense are (1) knowledge of the risk and (2) voluntary assumption of the risk.

The risk can be assumed by express agreement, or the assumption of risk can be implied by the plaintiff's knowledge of the risk and subsequent conduct. For example, a driver entering a race knows that there is a risk of being killed or injured in a crash. Of course, the plaintiff does not assume a risk different from or greater than the risk normally carried by the activity. In our example, the race driver would not assume the risk that the banking in the curves of the racetrack will give way during the race because of a construction defect.

Risks are not deemed to be assumed in situations involving emergencies. Neither are they assumed when a statute protects a class of people from harm and a member of the class is injured by the harm. For example, employees are protected by statute from harmful working conditions and therefore do not assume the risks associated with the workplace. If an employee is injured, he or she will generally be compensated regardless of fault under state workers' compensation statutes (discussed in Chapter 34).

A bungee jumper leaps from a platform. If the jumper is injured and sues the operator of the jump for negligence, what defenses might the operator use to avoid liability?

Superseding Cause An unforeseeable intervening event may break the connection between a wrongful act and an injury to another. If so, it acts as a *superseding cause*—that is, it relieves a defendant of liability for injuries caused by the intervening event. • **EXAMPLE 4.9** Suppose that Derrick keeps a can of gasoline in the trunk of his car. The presence of the gasoline creates a foreseeable risk and is thus a negligent act. If Derrick's car skids and crashes into a tree, causing the gasoline can to explode, Derrick would be liable for injuries sustained by passing pedestrians because of his negligence. If the explosion had been caused by lightning striking the car, however, the lightning would supersede Derrick's original negligence as a cause of the damage, because the lightning was not foreseeable. •

Contributory Negligence All individuals are expected to exercise a reasonable degree of care in looking out for themselves. In a few jurisdictions, recovery for injury resulting from negligence is prevented if the plaintiff was also negligent (failed to exercise a reasonable degree of care). This is the defense of **contributory negligence.** Under the common law doctrine of contributory negligence, no matter how insignificant the plaintiff's negligence is relative to the defendant's negligence, the plaintiff will be precluded from recovering any damages.

An exception to the doctrine of contributory negligence may apply if the defendant failed to take advantage of an opportunity to avoid causing the damage. Under the "last clear chance" rule, the plaintiff may recover full damages despite her or his own negligence. (Note that in those states that have adopted the comparative negligence rule, discussed next, the last clear chance doctrine does not apply.) • **EXAMPLE 4.10** Murphy is walking across the street against the light, and Lewis, a motorist, sees her in time to avoid hitting her but hits her anyway. In this situation, Lewis (the defendant) is not permitted to use Murphy's (the plaintiff's) prior negligence as a defense. The defendant negligently missed the opportunity to avoid injuring the plaintiff.●

COMPARATIVE NEGLIGENCE
A theory in tort law under which the liability for injuries resulting from negligent acts is shared by all persons who were guilty of negligence (including the injured party), on the basis of each person's proportionate carelessness.

The majority of states now allow recovery based on the doctrine of **comparative negligence**. This doctrine enables both the plaintiff's and the defendant's negligence to be computed and the liability for damages distributed accordingly. Some jurisdictions have adopted a "pure" form of comparative negligence that allows the plaintiff to recover, even if the extent of his or her fault is greater than that of the defendant. For example, if the plaintiff was 80 percent at fault and the defendant 20 percent at fault, the plaintiff may recover 20 percent of his or her damages. Many states' comparative negligence statutes, however, contain a "50 percent" rule by which the plaintiff recovers nothing if she or he was more than 50 percent at fault.

SPECIAL NEGLIGENCE DOCTRINES AND STATUTES

There are a number of special doctrines and statutes relating to negligence. We examine a few of them here.

Res Ipsa Loquitur Generally, in lawsuits involving negligence, the plaintiff has the burden of proving that the defendant was negligent. In certain situations, however, when negligence is very difficult or impossible to prove, the courts may infer that negligence has occurred; then, the burden of proof rests on the defendant—to prove he or she was *not* negligent. The inference of the defendant's negligence is known as the doctrine of ***res ipsa loquitur***,[9] which translates as "the facts speak for themselves."

RES IPSA LOQUITUR
A doctrine under which negligence may be inferred simply because an event occurred, if it is the type of event that would not occur in the absence of negligence. Literally, the term means "the facts speak for themselves."

This doctrine is applied only when the event creating the damage or injury is one that ordinarily would occur only as a result of negligence. ● **EXAMPLE 4.11** If a person undergoes knee surgery and following the surgery has a severed nerve in the knee area, that person can sue the surgeon under a theory of *res ipsa loquitur.* In this case, the injury would not have occurred but for the surgeon's negligence.[10]● For the doctrine of *res ipsa loquitur* to apply, the event must have been within the defendant's power to control, and it must not have been due to any voluntary action or contribution on the part of the plaintiff.

Negligence *Per Se* Certain conduct, whether it consists of an action or a failure to act, may be treated as **negligence *per se*** (*per se* means "in or of itself"). Negligence *per se* may occur if an individual violates a statute or an ordinance providing for a criminal penalty and that violation causes another to be injured. The injured person must prove (1) that the statute clearly sets out what standard of conduct is expected, when and where it is expected, and of whom it is expected; (2) that he or she is in the class intended to be protected by the statute; and (3) that the statute was designed to prevent the type of injury that he or she suffered. The standard of conduct required by the statute is the duty that the defendant owes to the plaintiff, and a violation of the statute is the breach of that duty.

NEGLIGENCE *PER SE*
An action or failure to act in violation of a statutory requirement.

● **EXAMPLE 4.12** A statute may require a landowner to keep a building in safe condition and may also subject the landowner to a criminal penalty, such as a fine, if the building is not kept safe. The statute is meant to protect those who are rightfully in the building. Thus, if the owner, without a sufficient excuse, violates the statute and a tenant is thereby injured, then a majority of courts will hold that the owner's unexcused violation of the statute conclusively establishes a breach of a duty of care—that is, that the owner's violation is negligence *per se.*●

9. Pronounced *rihz ihp*-suh *low*-kwuh-duhr.

10. *Edwards v. Boland,* 41 Mass.App.Ct. 375, 670 N.E.2d 404 (1996).

"No one would remember the Good Samaritan if he'd only had good intentions—he had money, too."

MARGARET THATCHER, 1925–
(British prime minister, 1979–1990)

"Danger Invites Rescue" Doctrine Typically, in cases in which an individual takes a defensive action, such as swerving to avoid an oncoming car, the original wrongdoer will not be relieved of liability even if the injury actually resulted from the attempt to escape harm. The same is true under the "danger invites rescue" doctrine. Under this doctrine, if Lemming commits an act that endangers Salter, and Yokem sustains an injury trying to protect Salter, then Lemming will be liable for Yokem's injury, as well as for any injuries Salter may sustain. Rescuers can injure themselves, or the person rescued, or even a stranger, but the original wrongdoer will still be liable.

Special Negligence Statutes A number of states have enacted statutes prescribing duties and responsibilities in certain circumstances. For example, most states now have what are called **Good Samaritan statutes.** Under these statutes, persons who are aided voluntarily by others cannot turn around and sue the "Good Samaritans" for negligence. These laws were passed largely to protect physicians and medical personnel who voluntarily render their services in emergency situations to those in need, such as individuals hurt in car accidents.

GOOD SAMARITAN STATUTE
A state statute stipulating that persons who provide emergency services to, or rescue, others in peril—unless they do so recklessly, thus causing further harm—cannot be sued for negligence.

DRAM SHOP ACT
A state statute that imposes liability on the owners of bars and taverns, as well as those who serve alcoholic drinks to the public, for injuries resulting from accidents caused by intoxicated persons when the sellers or servers of alcoholic drinks contributed to the intoxication.

Many states have also passed **dram shop acts**, under which a tavern owner or bartender may be held liable for injuries caused by a person who became intoxicated while drinking at the bar or who was already intoxicated when served by the bartender. In some states, statutes impose liability on *social hosts* (persons hosting parties) for injuries caused by guests who became intoxicated at the hosts' homes. Under these statutes, it is unnecessary to prove that the tavern owner, bartender, or social host was negligent.

Strict Liability

STRICT LIABILITY
Liability regardless of fault. In tort law, strict liability is imposed on a merchant who introduces into commerce a good that is unreasonably dangerous when in a defective condition.

Another category of torts is called **strict liability**, or *liability without fault*. Intentional torts and torts of negligence involve acts that depart from a reasonable standard of care and cause injuries. Under the doctrine of strict liability, liability for injury is imposed for reasons other than fault. Strict liability for damages proximately caused by an abnormally dangerous or exceptional activity is one application of this doctrine. Courts apply the doctrine of strict liability in such cases because of the extreme risk of the activity. Even if blasting with dynamite is performed with all reasonable care, there is still a risk of injury. Balancing that risk against the potential for harm, it seems reasonable to ask the person engaged in the activity to pay for injuries caused by that activity. Although there is no fault, there is still responsibility because of the dangerous nature of the undertaking.

There are other applications of the strict liability principle. Persons who keep dangerous animals, for example, are strictly liable for any harm inflicted by the animals. A significant application of strict liability is in the area of *product liability*—liability of manufacturers and sellers for harmful or defective products. Liability here is a matter of social policy and is based on two factors: (1) the manufacturing company can better bear the cost of injury, because it can spread the cost throughout society by increasing prices of goods and services, and (2) the manufacturing company is making a profit from its activities and therefore should bear the cost of injury as an operating expense. We will discuss product liability in greater detail in Chapter 18.

Cyber Torts

A significant issue that has come before the courts in recent years relates to the question of who should be held liable for *cyber torts*, or torts committed in cyberspace. For example, who should be held liable when someone posts a defamatory message online? Should an Internet service provider (ISP), such as Yahoo! or America Online (AOL), be liable for the remark if the ISP was unaware that it was being made?

Other questions involve issues of proof. How, for example, can it be proved that an online defamatory remark was "published" (which requires that a third party see or hear it)? How can the identity of the person who made the remark be discovered? Can an ISP be forced to reveal the source of an anonymous comment? We explore some of these questions in this section, as well as some of the legal questions that have arisen with respect to bulk e-mail advertising. In the *Ethical Issue* that follows, we look at yet another topic: the legal questions raised by computer viruses.

ETHICAL ISSUE 4.2

Who should be held liable for computer viruses?

As everybody knows, viruses sent into cyberspace can cause significant damage to the computer systems they "infect." To date, adapting tort law to virus-caused damages has been difficult because it is not all that clear who should be held liable for these damages. For example, who should be held liable for damages caused by the "ILOVEYOU" virus that spread around the globe in 2000 and caused an estimated $10 billion in damage? Of course, the person who wrote the virus is responsible. But what about the producer of the e-mail software that the virus accessed to spread itself so rapidly? What about the antivirus software companies? Were they negligent in failing to market products that were capable of identifying and disabling the virus before damage occurred? Should the users themselves share part of the blame? After all, even after the virus had received widespread publicity, users continued to open e-mail attachments containing the virus.

Generally, determining what tort duties apply in cyberspace and the point at which one of those duties is breached is not an easy task for the courts.

ON THE WEB To avoid liability for online defamation, you need to know the difference between "safe speech" and defamatory speech. Some guidelines that may be helpful are set forth in an article by attorney Guylyn Cummins at **http://www.gcwf.com/arttoc/cyber/index.html**.

DEFAMATION ONLINE

Online forums allow anyone—customers, employees, or crackpots—to complain about a business firm's personnel, policies, practices, or products. Regardless of whether the complaint is justified or whether it is true, it might have an impact on the business of the firm. One of the early questions in the online legal arena was whether the providers of such forums could be held liable for defamatory statements made in those forums.

Liability of Internet Service Providers Newspapers, magazines, and television and radio stations may be held liable for defamatory remarks that they disseminate, even if those remarks are prepared or created by others. Under the Communications Decency Act of 1996, however, Internet service providers (ISPs), or "interactive computer service providers," are not liable for such material.[11] An ISP typically provides access to the Internet through a local phone number and may provide other services, including access to databases available only to the ISP's subscribers. (See this chapter's *Business Law in the Online World* feature for a further discussion of the immunity of interactive service providers.)

Piercing the Veil of Anonymity A threshold barrier to anyone who seeks to bring an action for online defamation is discovering the identity of the person who posted the defamatory

11. 47 U.S.C. Section 230.

BUSINESS LAW: //in the Online World

Interactive Service Providers and Tort Liability

Recall from the discussion of defamation earlier in this chapter that one who repeats or otherwise republishes a defamatory statement is subject to liability as if he or she had originally published it. Thus, publishers generally can be held liable for defamatory contents in the books and periodicals that they publish.

Prior to the passage of the Communications Decency Act (CDA) of 1996, the courts grappled on several occasions with the question of whether Internet service providers (ISPs) should be regarded as publishers and thus held liable for defamatory messages made by users of their services. The CDA resolved the issue by stating that "[n]o provider or user of an interactive computer service shall be treated as the publisher or speaker of any information provided by another information content provider." Although portions of the CDA were held unconstitutional by the United States Supreme Court (the provisions prohibiting the transmission of materials harmful to minors—see Chapter 2), the provision regarding the liability of ISPs was not.

The CDA Shields ISPs from Liability

In a number of key cases, the ISP provisions of the CDA have been invoked to shield ISPs from liability for defamatory postings on their bulletin boards. In a leading case, decided the year after the CDA was enacted, America Online, Inc. (AOL), was not held liable even though it did not promptly remove defamatory messages of which it had been made aware. In upholding a district court's ruling in AOL's favor, a federal appellate court stated that the CDA "plainly immunizes computer service providers like AOL from liability for information that originates with third parties." The court explained that the purpose of the statute is "to maintain the robust nature of Internet communication and, accordingly, to keep government interference in the medium to a minimum." The court added, "None of this means, of course, that the original culpable party who posts defamatory messages would escape accountability."[a]

Extending CDA Immunity to Online Auction Services

Most of the cases concerning ISP immunity under the CDA have involved bulletin boards and other forums provided by ISPs. In 2000, however, a California state court extended the CDA further into the realm of e-commerce when it ruled that eBay, the online auction house, could not be held liable for the sale of pirated sound recordings on its Web site. In *Stoner v. eBay, Inc.*,[b] the plaintiff alleged that eBay had knowingly reaped "massive profits" from the sale of pirated sound recordings in violation of a California statute prohibiting unfair business practices. A California state court however, concluded that there was nothing to indicate that eBay's function should be transformed from that of an interactive service provider to that of a seller responsible for items sold on the site. The court noted that "a principal objective of the immunity provision [of the CDA] is to encourage commerce over the Internet by ensuring that interactive computer service providers are not held responsible for how third parties use their services."

FOR CRITICAL ANALYSIS

Although publishers traditionally have been held liable for defamatory contents in the books and periodicals that they publish, distributors (libraries, bookstores, newsstands, and the like) have not—unless it can be shown that a distributor was aware of the defamatory nature of a particular work and distributed it anyway. Can you think of any reason why the drafters of the CDA decided to grant virtually total immunity to ISPs instead of treating them as "distributors"? Explain.

a. *Zeran v. America Online, Inc.*, 129 F.3d 327 (4th Cir. 1997); *cert. denied*, 524 U.S. 934, 141 L.Ed.2d 712, 118 S.Ct. 2341 (1998).
b. Cal.Super.Ct. 2000. For further details on this unpublished decision, see "California Judge Finds eBay Immune under CDA," *e-commerce Law & Strategy*, November 2000, p. 9.

message online. ISPs can disclose personal information about their customers only when ordered to do so by a court. Because of this, businesses and individuals are increasingly resorting to lawsuits against "John Does." Then, using the authority of the courts, they can obtain from the ISPs the identities of the persons responsible for the messages.

In one case, for example, Eric Hvide, a former chief executive of a company called Hvide Marine, sued a number of "John Does" who had posted allegedly defamatory statements about his company on various online message boards. Hvide, who eventually lost his job, sued the John Does for libel in a Florida court. The court ruled that Yahoo! and AOL had to reveal the identities of the defendant Does.[12]

In another case, however, discovering the identity of the person who had posted an online defamatory message was more difficult. The case involved a physician, Dr. Sam D. Graham, Jr., who at the time was the chair of the Urology Department at Emory University's School of Medicine. A posting on a Yahoo! message board suggested that Graham had taken kickbacks from a urology company after giving his department's pathology business to the company. Graham resigned from his position and sued the anonymous poster for libel. Because the person posting the message was not actually a Yahoo! customer, an extensive investigation and, according to Graham's attorney, a lot of "dumb luck" were required to learn the person's identity. The case went to trial, and a federal district court awarded Graham $675,000 in damages.[13]

SPAM

SPAM
Bulk, unsolicited ("junk") e-mail.

Bulk, unsolicited e-mail ("junk" e-mail) sent to all of the users on a particular e-mailing list is often called **spam.**[14] Typical spam consists of a product ad sent to all of the users on an e-mailing list or all of the members of a newsgroup.

Spam can waste user time and network bandwidth (the amount of data that can be transmitted within a certain time). It can also impose a burden on an ISP's equipment. • **EXAMPLE 4.13** In one case, Cyber Promotions, Inc., sent bulk e-mail to subscribers of CompuServe, Inc., an ISP. CompuServe subscribers complained to the service about ads, and many canceled their subscriptions. Handling the ads also placed a tremendous burden on CompuServe's equipment. CompuServe told Cyber Promotions to stop using CompuServe's equipment to process and store the ads—in effect, to stop sending the ads to CompuServe subscribers. Ignoring the demand, Cyber Promotions stepped up the volume of its ads. After CompuServe attempted unsuccessfully to block the flow with screening software, it filed a suit against Cyber Promotions in a federal district court, seeking an injunction on the ground that the ads constituted trespass to personal property. The court agreed and ordered Cyber Promotions to stop sending its ads to e-mail addresses maintained by CompuServe.[15] •

Because of the problems associated with spam, some states have taken steps to prohibit or regulate its use. For example, a few states, such as Washington, prohibit unsolicited e-mail that is promoting goods, services, or real estate for sale or lease. In California, an unsolicited e-mail ad must state in its subject line that it is an ad ("ADV:"). The ad must also include a toll-free phone number or return e-mail address through which the recipient can contact the sender to request that no more ads be e-mailed.[16] An ISP can bring a successful suit in a California state court against a spammer who violates the ISP's policy prohibiting or restricting unsolicited e-mail ads. The court can award damages of up to $25,000 per day.[17] The Internet is a public forum, however. Thus, free speech issues may be involved—see Chapter 2.

12. *Does v. Hvide,* 770 So.2d 1237 (Fla.App.3d 2000).
13. *Graham v. Oppenheimer* (E.D.Va. 2000). For details on this unpublished decision, see "Net Libel Verdict Is Upheld," *The National Law Journal,* December 25, 2000, p. A19.
14. The term *spam* is said to come from a Monty Python song with the lyrics, "Spam spam spam spam, spam spam spam spam, lovely spam, wonderful spam." Like these lyrics, spam online is often considered to be a repetition of worthless text.
15. *CompuServe, Inc. v. Cyber Promotions, Inc.,* 962 F.Supp.2d 1015 (S.D.Ohio 1997).
16. Ca. Bus. & Prof. Code Section 17538.4.
17. Ca. Bus. & Prof. Code Section 17538.45.

APPLICATION Law and the E-tailer . . .

Online Advertising*

Traditionally, merchants have marketed their wares through direct (bulk) mail to potential customers. The online equivalent of direct mail is *direct e-mail.* Increasingly, online businesses are finding that direct e-mail is less expensive and results in more responses than "click-through" banner ads on Web sites. E-mail can be sent to customers only, as most of it is, or to a wider group of Internet users to advertise new or upgraded products. Generally, though, direct e-mailers should be careful not to cross the line between permissible and impermissible e-mailings. As you learned in this chapter, "spamming" may result in liability under tort law or under a state statute regulating or prohibiting certain forms of direct e-mail.

There are also several Web groups, such as SpamCop, that are dedicated to eliminating spam from the Internet. On numerous occasions, complaints of alleged spam have been completely inaccurate. Nonetheless, the supposedly offending "spammer" may face unpleasant consequences, including harm to its reputation and goodwill in the cyber community. So far, there have been no lawsuits for such incidents, but there may be in the future.

A Counter to Spam—Opt-In E-Mail Advertising

To avoid spamming complaints, some online marketers have created alliances with online communities, such as iVillage.com and Hotmail.com. These communities consist of subscribers who have agreed to the terms and conditions of the communities. Normally, one condition is that the subscriber or member opts in to receive a limited number of direct e-mail advertisements. This is called opt-in advertising. Thus, those who are members of, say, iVillage.com or Hotmail.com have explicitly agreed to receive targeted e-mail ads.

The owners of such communities, either through their own sales representatives or through advertising intermediaries, essentially rent their members' e-mail addresses so that advertisers, such as Hewlett Packard, Microsoft, and General Motors, can "mail" their ads. This is no different than so-called junk mail advertising using paper and envelopes. The owners of the addresses—the online communities—receive, on net, from 2¢ to 25¢ each time an e-mail ad is sent to a particular address. As online communities find their advertising revenues from standard banner ads dropping, they are aggressively seeking this relatively new source of revenue.

Double Opt In—Reducing the Risk Even More

Online community owners sometimes go one step further to assure that they are not accused of spamming. In addition to requiring their subscribers to sign a general terms and conditions agreement, which gives the community owners permission to allow direct e-mail ads, the owners also send out a separate explicit agreement to each member of the community. This agreement states again that the members who click on an acceptance to the agreement are consenting to receive targeted e-mail ads; hence, the appellation *double opt in.* Some online advertisers will rent e-mail addresses only from communities that have double opt-in agreements for each member.

Checklist for the E-tailer

1. Before sending direct e-mail, become familiar with the laws governing direct e-mail in your jurisdiction.
2. To avoid spamming complaints, consider using "opt-in" e-mail advertising, in which members of an online community have explicitly agreed to receive e-mail ads.
3. An online merchant can reduce the risk of spamming liability even further by providing for "double opt-in" e-mail advertising.

*This *Application* is not meant to substitute for the services of an attorney who is licensed to practice law in your state.

Key Terms

Chapter Summary Torts and Cyber Torts

Intentional Torts against Persons (See pages 101–110.)	1. *Assault and battery*—An assault is an unexcused and intentional act that causes another person to be apprehensive of immediate harm. A battery is an assault that results in physical contact. 2. *False imprisonment*—The intentional confinement or restraint of another person's movement without justification. 3. *Infliction of emotional distress*—An intentional act that amounts to extreme and outrageous conduct resulting in severe emotional distress to another. 4. *Defamation (libel or slander)*—A false statement of fact, not made under privilege, that is communicated to a third person and that causes damage to a person's reputation. For public figures, the plaintiff must also prove actual malice. 5. *Invasion of the right to privacy*—The use of a person's name or likeness for commercial purposes without permission, wrongful intrusion into a person's private activities, publication of information that places a person in a false light, or disclosure of private facts that an ordinary person would find objectionable. 6. *Appropriation*—The use of another person's name, likeness, or other identifying characteristic, without permission and for the benefit of the user. 7. *Misrepresentation (fraud)*—A false representation made by one party, through misstatement of facts or through conduct, with the intention of deceiving another and on which the other reasonably relies to his or her detriment. 8. *Wrongful interference*—The knowing, intentional interference by a third party with an enforceable contractual relationship or an established business relationship between other parties for the purpose of advancing the economic interests of the third party.

Chapter Summary Torts and Cyber Torts—continued

Intentional Torts against Property (See pages 110–112.)	1. *Trespass to land*—The invasion of another's real property without consent or privilege. Specific rights and duties apply once a person is expressly or impliedly established as a trespasser. 2. *Trespass to personal property*—Unlawfully damaging or interfering with the owner's right to use, possess, or enjoy his or her personal property. 3. *Conversion*—A wrongful act in which personal property is taken from its rightful owner or possessor and placed in the service of another. 4. *Disparagement of property*—Any economically injurious falsehood that is made about another's product or property; an inclusive term for the torts of *slander of quality* and *slander of title.*
Unintentional Torts—Negligence (See pages 113–121.)	1. *Negligence*—The careless performance of a legally required duty or the failure to perform a legally required act. Elements that must be proved are that a legal duty of care exists, that the defendant breached that duty, and that the breach caused damage or injury to another. 2. *Defenses to negligence*—The basic affirmative defenses in negligence cases are (a) assumption of risk, (b) superseding cause, and (c) contributory negligence. 3. *Special negligence doctrines and statutes*— a. *Res ipsa loquitur*—A doctrine under which a plaintiff need not prove negligence on the part of the defendant because "the facts speak for themselves." b. Negligence *per se*—A type of negligence that may occur if a person violates a statute or an ordinance providing for a criminal penalty and the violation causes another to be injured. c. Special negligence statutes—State statutes that prescribe duties and responsibilities in certain circumstances, the violation of which will impose civil liability. Dram shop acts and Good Samaritan statutes are examples of special negligence statutes.
Strict Liability (See page 121.)	Under the doctrine of strict liability, a person may be held liable, regardless of the degree of care exercised, for damages or injuries caused by her or his product or activity. Strict liability includes liability for harms caused by abnormally dangerous activities, by dangerous animals, and by defective products (product liability).
Cyber Torts (See pages 121–124.)	General tort principles are being extended to cover cyber torts, or torts that occur in cyberspace, such as online defamation or spamming (which may constitute trespass to personal property). Federal and state statutes may also apply to certain forms of cyber torts. For example, under the federal Communications Decency Act of 1996, Internet service providers (ISPs) are not liable for defamatory messages posted by their subscribers. Some states restrict the use of direct e-mail, or spam. Certain types of online wrongs, such as the transmission of computer viruses, pose unique legal challenges.

For Review

① What is a tort?

② What is the purpose of tort law? What are two basic categories of torts?

③ What are the four elements of negligence?

④ What is meant by strict liability? In what circumstances is strict liability applied?

⑤ What is a cyber tort, and how are tort theories being applied in cyberspace?

Questions and Case Problems

4–1. Defenses to Negligence. Corinna was riding her bike on a city street. While she was riding, she frequently looked back to verify that the books that she had fastened to the rear part of her bike were still attached. On one occasion while she was looking behind her, she failed to notice a car that was entering an intersection just as she was crossing it. The car hit her, causing her to sustain numerous injuries. Three eyewitnesses stated that the driver of the car had failed to stop at the stop sign before entering the intersection. Corinna sued the driver of the car for negligence. What defenses might the defendant driver raise in this lawsuit? Discuss fully.

4–2. Liability to Business Invitees. Kim went to Ling's Market to pick up a few items for dinner. It was a rainy, windy day, and the wind had blown water through the door of Ling's Market each time the door opened. As Kim entered through the door, she slipped and fell in the approximately one-half inch of rainwater that had accumulated on the floor. The manager knew of the weather conditions but had not posted any sign to warn customers of the water hazard. Kim injured her back as a result of the fall and sued Ling's for damages. Can Ling's be held liable for negligence in this situation? Discuss.

4–3. Negligence. In which of the following situations will the acting party be liable for the tort of negligence? Explain fully.

(a) Mary goes to the golf course on Sunday morning, eager to try out a new set of golf clubs she has just purchased. As she tees off on the first hole, the head of her club flies off and injures a nearby golfer.

(b) Mary's doctor gives her some pain medication and tells her not to drive after she takes it, as the medication induces drowsiness. In spite of the doctor's warning, Mary decides to drive to the store while on the medication. Owing to her lack of alertness, she fails to stop at a traffic light and crashes into another vehicle, injuring a passenger.

4–4. Causation. Ruth carelessly parks her car on a steep hill, leaving the car in neutral and failing to engage the parking brake. The car rolls down the hill, knocking down an electric line. The sparks from the broken line ignite a grass fire. The fire spreads until it reaches a barn one mile away. The barn houses dynamite, and the burning barn explodes, causing part of the roof to fall on and injure a passing motorist, Jim. Can Jim recover from Ruth? Why or why not?

4–5. Wrongful Interference. Jennings owns a bakery shop. He has been trying to obtain a long-term contract with the owner of Julie's Tea Salon for some time. Jennings starts a local advertising campaign on radio and television and in the newspaper. The campaign is so persuasive that Julie decides to break the contract she has had for several years with Orley's Bakery so that she can patronize Jennings's bakery. Is Jennings liable to Orley's Bakery for the tort of wrongful interference with a contractual relationship? Is Julie liable for this tort? For anything?

4–6. Negligence *Per Se*. A North Carolina Department of Transportation regulation prohibits the placement of telephone booths within public rights-of-way. Despite this regulation, GTE South, Inc., placed a booth in the right-of-way near the intersection of Hillsborough and Sparger Roads in Durham County. Laura Baldwin was using the booth when an accident at the intersection caused a dump truck to cross the right-of-way and smash into the booth. To recover for her injuries, Baldwin filed a suit in a North Carolina state court against GTE and others. Was Baldwin within the class of persons protected by the regulation? If so, did GTE's placement of the booth constitute negligence *per se*? [*Baldwin v. GTE South, Inc.*, 335 N.C. 544, 439 S.E.2d 108 (1995)]

4–7. Duty of Care. As pedestrians exited at the close of an arts and crafts show, Jason Davis, an employee of the show's producer, stood near the exit. Suddenly and without warning, Davis turned around and collided with Yvonne Esposito, an eighty-year-old woman. Esposito was knocked to the ground, fracturing her hip. After hip-replacement surgery, she was left with a permanent physical impairment. Esposito filed a suit in a federal district court against Davis and others, alleging negligence. What are the factors that indicate whether Davis owed Esposito a duty of care? What do those factors indicate in these circumstances? [*Esposito v. Davis*, 47 F.3d 164 (5th Cir. 1995)]

4–8. Duty to Business Invitees. Flora Gonzalez visited a Wal-Mart store. While walking in a busy aisle from the store's cafeteria toward a refrigerator, Gonzalez stepped on some macaroni that came from the cafeteria. She slipped and fell, sustaining injuries to her back, shoulder, and knee. She filed a suit in a Texas state court against Wal-Mart, alleging that the store was negligent. She presented evidence that the macaroni had "a lot of dirt" and tracks through it and testified that the macaroni "seemed like it had been there awhile." What duty does a business have to protect its patrons from dangerous conditions? In Gonzalez's case, should Wal-Mart be held liable for a breach of that duty? Why or why not? [*Wal-Mart Stores, Inc. v. Gonzalez*, 968 S.W.2d 934 (Tex.Sup. 1998)]

4–9. Misappropriation. The United States Golf Association (USGA) was founded in 1894. In 1911, the USGA developed the Handicap System, which was designed to enable individual golfers of different abilities to compete fairly with one another. The USGA revised the system and implemented new handicap formulas between 1987 and 1993. The USGA permits any entity to use the system free of charge as long as it complies with the USGA's procedure for peer review through authorized golf associations of the handicaps issued to individual golfers. In 1991, Arroyo Software Corp. began marketing software known as EagleTrak, which incorporated the USGA's system, and used the USGA's name in the software's ads without permission. Arroyo's EagleTrak did not incorporate any means for obtaining peer review of handicap computations. The USGA filed a suit in a California state court against Arroyo, alleging, among other things, misappropriation. The USGA asked the court to stop Arroyo's use of its system. Should the court grant the injunction? Why or why not? [*United States Golf Association v. Arroyo Software Corp.*, 69 Cal.App.4th 607, 81 Cal.Rptr.2d 708 (1999)]

TEST YOUR KNOWLEDGE—ANSWER ON THE WEB

4–10. America Online, Inc. (AOL), provides services to its customers (members), including the transmission of e-mail to and from other members and across the Internet. To become a member, a person must agree not to use AOL's computers to send bulk, unsolicited, commercial e-mail (spam). AOL uses filters to block spam, but bulk e-mailers sometimes use other software to thwart the filters. National Health Care Discount, Inc. (NHCD), sells discount optical and dental service plans. To generate leads for NHCD's products, sales representatives, who included AOL members, sent more than 300 million pieces of spam through AOL's computer system. Each item cost AOL an estimated $.00078 in equipment expenses. Some of the spam used false headers and other methods to hide the source. After receiving more than 150,000 complaints, AOL asked NHCD to stop. When the spam continued, AOL filed a suit in a federal district court against NHCD, alleging in part trespass to chattels—an unlawful interference with another's rights to possess personal property. AOL asked the court for a summary judgment on this claim. Did the spamming constitute trespass to chattels? Explain. [*America Online, Inc. v. National Health Care Discount, Inc.*, 121 F.Supp.2d 1255 (N.D.Iowa 2000)]

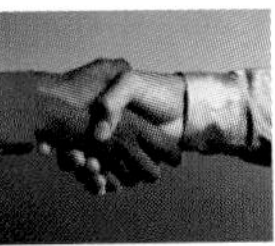

A QUESTION OF ETHICS AND SOCIAL RESPONSIBILITY

4–11. Patsy Slone, while a guest at the Dollar Inn, a hotel, was stabbed in the thumb by a hypodermic needle concealed in the tube of a roll of toilet paper. Slone, fearing that she might have been exposed to the virus that causes acquired immune deficiency syndrome (AIDS), sued the hotel for damages to compensate her for the emotional distress she suffered after the needle stab. An Indiana trial court held for Slone and awarded her $250,000 in damages. The hotel appealed, and one of the issues before the court was whether Slone had to prove that she was actually exposed to AIDS to recover for emotional distress. The appellate court held that she did not and that her fear of getting AIDS was reasonable in these circumstances. [*Slone v. Dollar Inn, Inc.*, 395 N.E.2d 185 (Ind.App. 1998)]

1. Should the plaintiff in this case have been required to show that she was actually exposed to the AIDS virus in order to recover for emotional distress? Should she have been required to show that she actually acquired the AIDS virus as a result of the needle stab?
2. In some states, plaintiffs are barred from recovery in emotional distress cases unless the distress is evidenced by some kind of physical symptoms. Is this fair?

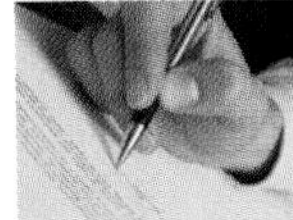

FOR CRITICAL ANALYSIS

4–12. What general principle underlies the common law doctrine that business owners have a duty of care toward their customers? Does the duty of care unfairly burden business owners? Why or why not?

Internet Activities

Go to the *Business Law Today* home page at **http://blt.westbuslaw.com**. Select "Interactive Study Center" and then click on "Chapter 4." There you will find the following Internet research exercises that you can perform to learn more about privacy rights in the online world and the elements of negligence:

Activity 4–1: Privacy Rights in Cyberspace
Activity 4–2: Negligence and the *Titanic*

Before the Test

Go to the *Business Law Today* home page at **http://blt.westbuslaw.com**. Click on "Interactive Quizzes." You will find at least twenty interactive questions relating to this chapter.

CHAPTER 5

Intellectual Property and Internet Law

"The Internet, by virtue of its ability to mesh what will be hundreds of millions of people together, . . . is . . . a profoundly different capability that by and large human beings have not had before."

Tony Rutkowski, 1943–
(Executive director of the Internet Society, 1994–1996)

CHAPTER CONTENTS

LEARNING OBJECTIVES

After reading this chapter, you should be able to answer the following questions:

① What is intellectual property?

② Why are trademarks and patents protected by the law?

③ What laws protect authors' rights in the works they generate?

④ What are trade secrets, and what laws offer protection for this form of intellectual property?

⑤ What steps have been taken to protect intellectual property rights in today's digital age?

Of significant concern to businesspersons today is the need to protect their rights in intellectual property. **Intellectual property** is any property resulting from intellectual, creative processes—the products of an individual's mind. Although it is an abstract term for an abstract concept, intellectual property is nonetheless wholly familiar to virtually everyone. The information contained in books and computer files is intellectual property. The software you use, the movies you see, and the music you listen to are all forms of intellectual property. In fact, in today's information age, it should come as no surprise that the value of the world's intellectual property now exceeds the value of physical property, such as machines and houses.

The need to protect creative works was voiced by the framers of the U.S. Constitution over two hundred years ago: Article I, Section 8, of the Constitution authorized Congress "[t]o promote the Progress of Science and useful Arts, by securing for limited Times to Authors and Inventors the

INTELLECTUAL PROPERTY
Property resulting from intellectual, creative processes.

exclusive Right to their respective Writings and Discoveries." Laws protecting patents, trademarks, and copyrights are explicitly designed to protect and reward inventive and artistic creativity. Exhibit 5–1 beginning on page 133 offers a comprehensive summary of these forms of intellectual property, as well as intellectual property that consists of *trade secrets*.

"The protection of trademarks is the law's recognition of the psychological function of symbols. If it is true that we live by symbols, it is no less true that we purchase goods by them."

FELIX FRANKFURTER, 1882–1965
(Associate justice of the United States Supreme Court, 1939–1962)

An understanding of intellectual property law is important because intellectual property has taken on increasing significance, not only in the United States but globally as well. Today, ownership rights in intangible intellectual property are more important to the prosperity of many U.S. companies than are their tangible assets. As you will read in this chapter, protecting these assets in today's online world has proved particularly challenging. This is because, as indicated in the chapter-opening quotation, the Internet's capability is "profoundly different" from anything we have had in the past.

Trademarks and Related Property

TRADEMARK
A distinctive mark, motto, device, or emblem that a manufacturer stamps, prints, or otherwise affixes to the goods it produces so that they may be identified on the market and their origins made known. Once a trademark is established (under the common law or through registration), the owner is entitled to its exclusive use.

A **trademark** is a distinctive mark, motto, device, or emblem that a manufacturer stamps, prints, or otherwise affixes to the goods it produces so that they may be identified on the market and their origin vouched for. At common law, the person who used a symbol or mark to identify a business or product was protected in the use of that trademark. Clearly, by using another's trademark, a business could lead consumers to believe that its goods were made by the other business. The law seeks to avoid this kind of confusion. In the following famous case concerning Coca-Cola, the defendants argued that the Coca-Cola trademark was entitled to no protection under the law, because the term did not accurately represent the product.

Landmark and Classic Cases

CASE 5.1 The Coca-Cola Co. v. Koke Co. of America

Supreme Court of the United States, 1920.
254 U.S. 143,
41 S.Ct. 113,
65 L.Ed. 189.
http://www.findlaw.com/casecode/supreme.html[a]

COMPANY PROFILE *John Pemberton, an Atlanta pharmacist, invented a caramel-colored, carbonated soft drink in 1886. His bookkeeper, Frank Robinson, named the beverage Coca-Cola after two of the ingredients, coca leaves and kola nuts. Asa Candler bought the Coca-Cola Company in 1891, and within seven years, he made the soft drink available in all of the United States, as well as in parts of Canada and Mexico. Candler continued to sell Coke aggressively and to open up new markets, reaching Europe before 1910. In doing so, however, he attracted numerous competitors, some of whom tried to capitalize directly on the Coke name.*

FACTS The Coca-Cola Company brought an action in a federal district court to enjoin other beverage companies from using the words "Koke" and "Dope" for the defendants' products. The defendants contended that the Coca-Cola trademark was a fraudulent representation and that Coca-Cola was therefore not entitled to any help from the courts. By use of the Coca-Cola name, the

(continued)

a. This is the "U.S. Supreme Court Opinions" page within the Web site of the "Findlaw Internet Legal Resources" database. This page provides several options for accessing an opinion. Because you know the citation for this case, you can go to the "Citation Search" box, type in the appropriate volume and page numbers for the *United States Reports* ("254" and "143," respectively, for the *Coca-Cola* case), and click on "Get It."

CASE 5.1—Continued

defendants alleged, the Coca-Cola Company represented that the beverage contained cocaine (from coca leaves). The district court granted the injunction, but the federal appellate court reversed. The Coca-Cola Company appealed to the United States Supreme Court.

ISSUE Did the marketing of products called Koke and Dope by the Koke Company of America and other firms constitute an infringement on Coca-Cola's trademark?

DECISION Yes for Koke, but no for Dope. The Supreme Court enjoined the competing beverage companies from calling their products Koke, but did not prevent them from calling their products Dope.

REASON The Court noted that, to be sure, prior to 1900 the Coca-Cola beverage had contained a small amount of cocaine, but this ingredient had been deleted from the formula by 1906 at the latest, and the Coca-Cola Company had advertised to the public that no cocaine was present in its drink. Coca-Cola was a widely popular drink "to be had at almost any soda fountain." Because of the public's widespread familiarity with Coca-Cola, the retention of the name of the beverage (referring to coca leaves and kola nuts) was not misleading: "Coca-Cola probably means to most persons the plaintiff's familiar product to be had everywhere rather than a compound of particular substances." The name Coke was found to be so common a term for the trademarked product Coca-Cola that the defendants' use of the similar-sounding Koke as a name for their beverages was disallowed. The Court could find no reason to restrain the defendants from using the name Dope, however.

COMMENT *In this classic case, the United States Supreme Court made it clear that trademarks and trade names (and nicknames for those marks and names, such as the nickname "Coke" for "Coca-Cola") that are in common use receive protection under the common law. This holding is significant historically because the federal statute later passed to protect trademark rights (the Lanham Trade-Mark Act of 1946, to be discussed shortly) in many ways represented a codification of common law principles governing trademarks.*

ON THE WEB You can find answers to frequently asked questions (FAQs) about trademark and patent law, as well as a host of other information, at the Web site of the U.S. Patent and Trademark Office. Go to **http://www.uspto.gov**.

STATUTORY PROTECTION OF TRADEMARKS

Statutory protection of trademarks and related property is provided at the federal level by the Lanham Trade-Mark Act of 1946.[1] The Lanham Act was enacted in part to protect manufacturers from losing business to rival companies that used confusingly similar trademarks. The Lanham Act incorporates the common law of trademarks and provides remedies for owners of trademarks who wish to enforce their claims in federal court. Many states also have trademark statutes.

In 1995, Congress amended the Lanham Act by passing the Federal Trademark Dilution Act,[2] which extended the protection available to trademark owners by creating a federal cause of action for trademark *dilution.* Until the passage of this amendment, federal trademark law only prohibited the unauthorized use of the same mark on competing—or on noncompeting but "related"—goods or services when such use would likely confuse consumers as to the origin of those goods and services. Trademark dilution laws, which about half of the states have also enacted, protect "distinctive" or "famous" trademarks (such as Jergens, McDonald's, RCA, and Macintosh) from certain unauthorized uses of the marks *regardless* of a showing of competition or a likelihood of confusion.

A famous mark may be diluted not only by the use of an *identical* mark but also by the use of a *similar* mark. ● **EXAMPLE 5.1** Ringling Bros.–Barnum & Bailey, Combined Shows, Inc., brought a suit against the state of Utah, claiming that Utah's use of the slogan "The Greatest Snow on Earth"—to attract visitors to the state's recreational and

1. 15 U.S.C. Sections 1051–1128.
2. 15 U.S.C. Section 1125.

EXHIBIT 5–1 FORMS OF INTELLECTUAL PROPERTY

	PATENT	COPYRIGHT	TRADEMARKS (SERVICE MARKS AND TRADE DRESS)	TRADE SECRETS
Definition	A grant from the government that gives an inventor exclusive rights to an invention.	An intangible property right granted to authors and originators of a literary work or artistic production that falls within specified categories.	Any distinctive word, name, symbol, or device (image or appearance), or combination thereof, that an entity uses to identify and distinguish its goods or services from those of others.	Any information (including formulas, patterns, programs, devices, techniques, and processes) that a business possesses and that gives the business an advantage over competitors who do not know the information or processes.
Requirements	An invention must be: 1. Novel. 2. Not obvious. 3. Useful.	Literary or artistic works must be: 1. Original. 2. Fixed in a durable medium that can be perceived, reproduced, or communicated. 3. Within a copyrightable category.	Trademarks, service marks, and trade dresses must be sufficiently distinctive (or must have acquired a secondary meaning) to enable consumers and others to distinguish the manufacturer's, seller's, or business user's products or services from those of competitors.	Information and processes that have commercial value, that are not known or easily ascertainable by the general public or others, and that are reasonably protected from disclosure.
Types or Categories	1. Utility (general). 2. Design. 3. Plant (flowers, vegetables, and so on).	1. Literary works (including computer programs). 2. Musical works. 3. Dramatic works. 4. Pantomime and choreographic works. 5. Pictorial, graphic, and sculptural works. 6. Films and audiovisual works. 7. Sound recordings.	1. Strong, distinctive marks (such as fanciful, arbitrary, or suggestive marks). 2. Marks that have acquired a secondary meaning by use. 3. Other types of marks, including certification marks and collective marks. 4. Trade dress (such as a distinctive decor, menu, or style or type of service).	1. Customer lists. 2. Research and development. 3. Plans and programs. 4. Pricing information. 5. Production techniques. 6. Marketing techniques. 7. Formulas. 8. Compilations.
How Acquired	By filing a patent application with the U.S. Patent and Trademark Office and receiving that office's approval.	Automatic (once in tangible form).	1. At common law, ownership is created by use of mark. 2. Registration (either with the U.S. Patent and Trademark Office or with the appropriate state office)	Through the originality and development of information and processes that are unique to a business, that are unknown by others, and that would

(continued)

EXHIBIT 5–1 FORMS OF INTELLECTUAL PROPERTY—CONTINUED

	PATENT	COPYRIGHT	TRADEMARKS (SERVICE MARKS AND TRADE DRESS)	TRADE SECRETS
How Acquired–continued			gives constructive notice of date of use. 3. Federal registration is permitted if the mark is currently in use *or* if the applicant intends use within six months (period can be extended to three years). 4. Federal registration can be renewed between the fifth and sixth years and, thereafter, every ten years.	be valuable to competitors if they knew of the information and processes.
Rights	An inventor has the right to make, use, sell, assign, or license the invention during the duration of the patent's term. The first to invent has patent rights.	The author or originator has the exlusive right to reproduce, distribute, display, license, or transfer a copyrighted work.	The owner has the right to use the mark or trade dress and to exclude others from using it. The right of use can be licensed or sold (assigned) to another.	The owner has the right to sole and exclusive use of the trade secrets and the right to use legal means to protect against misappropriation of the trade secrets by others. The owner can license or assign a trade secret.
Duration	Twenty years from the date of application; for design patents, fourteen years.	1. For authors: the life of the author, plus 70 years. 2. For publishers: 95 years after the date of publication or 120 years after creation.	Unlimited, as long as it is in use. To continue notice by registration, the registration must be renewed by filing.	Unlimited, as long as not revealed to others. (Once revealed to others, they are no longer trade secrets.)
Civil Remedies for Infringement	Monetary damages, which include reasonable royalties and lost profits, *plus* attorneys' fees. (Treble damages are available for intentional infringement.)	Actual damages, plus profits received by the infringer; *or* statutory damages of not less than \$500 and not more than \$20,000 (\$100,000, if infringement is willful); *plus* costs and attorneys' fees.	1. Injunction prohibiting future use of mark. 2. Actual damages, plus profits received by the infringer (can be increased to three times the actual damages under the Lanham Act). 3. Impoundment and destruction of infringing articles. 4. *Plus* costs and attorneys' fees.	Monetary damages for misappropriation (the Uniform Trade Secrets Act permits punitive damages up to twice the amount of actual damages for willful and malicious misappropriation); *plus* costs and attorneys' fees.

scenic resorts—diluted the distinctiveness of the circus's famous trademark, "The Greatest Show on Earth." Utah moved to dismiss the suit, arguing that the 1995 provisions protect owners of famous trademarks only against the unauthorized use of identical marks. A federal court disagreed and refused to grant Utah's motion to dismiss the case.[3] •

TRADEMARK REGISTRATION

ON THE WEB To access the federal database of registered trademarks, go to **http://www.uspto.gov/web/menu/tm.html**.

Trademarks may be registered with the state or with the federal government. To register for protection under federal trademark law, a person must file an application with the U.S. Patent and Trademark Office in Washington, D.C. Under current law, a mark can be registered (1) if it is currently in commerce or (2) if the applicant intends to put the mark into commerce within six months.

Under extenuating circumstances, the six-month period can be extended by thirty months, giving the applicant a total of three years from the date of notice of trademark approval to make use of the mark and file the required use statement. Registration is postponed until the mark is actually used. Nonetheless, during this waiting period, any applicant can legally protect his or her trademark against a third party who previously has neither used the mark nor filed an application for it. Registration is renewable between the fifth and sixth years after the initial registration and every ten years thereafter (every twenty years for trademarks registered before 1990).

TRADEMARK INFRINGEMENT

Registration of a trademark with the U.S. Patent and Trademark Office gives notice on a nationwide basis that the trademark belongs exclusively to the registrant. The registrant is also allowed to use the symbol ® to indicate that the mark has been registered. Whenever that trademark is copied to a substantial degree or used in its entirety by another, intentionally or unintentionally, the trademark has been *infringed* (used without authorization). When a trademark has been infringed, the owner of the mark has a cause of action against the infringer. A person need not have registered a trademark in order to sue for trademark infringement, but registration does furnish proof of the date of inception of the trademark's use.

Only those trademarks that are deemed sufficiently distinctive from all competing trademarks will be protected, however. The trademarks must be sufficiently distinct to enable consumers to identify the manufacturer of the goods easily and to differentiate among competing products.

A billboard and theater marquee in New York City. Why are trademarks protected by the law?

Strong Marks Fanciful, arbitrary, or suggestive trademarks are generally considered to be the most distinctive (strongest) trademarks, because they are normally taken from outside the context of the particular product and thus provide the best means of distinguishing one product from another.

• **EXAMPLE 5.2** Fanciful trademarks include invented words, such as "Xerox" for one manufacturer's copiers and "Kodak" for another company's photographic products. Arbitrary trademarks include actual words that have no literal connection to the product such as "English Leather" used as a name for an after-shave lotion (and not for leather processed in England). Suggestive trademarks are those that suggest something about a product without describing the product directly. For example, "Dairy Queen" suggests an association between its products and milk, but it does not directly describe ice cream. •

3. *Ringling Bros.–Barnum & Bailey, Combined Shows, Inc. v. Utah Division of Travel Development,* 935 F.Supp. 736 (E.D.Va. 1996).

Secondary Meaning Descriptive terms, geographic terms, and personal names are not inherently distinctive and do not receive protection under the law until they acquire a secondary meaning. A secondary meaning may arise when customers begin to associate a specific term or phrase, such as "London Fog," with specific trademarked items (coats with "London Fog" labels). Whether a secondary meaning becomes attached to a term or name usually depends on how extensively the product is advertised, the market for the product, the number of sales, and other factors. The United States Supreme Court has held that even a color can qualify for trademark protection.[4] Once a secondary meaning is attached to a term or name, a trademark is considered distinctive and is protected.

Generic Terms Generic terms (general, commonly used terms that refer to an entire class of products, such as *bicycle* or *computer*) receive no protection, even if they acquire secondary meanings. A particularly thorny problem arises when a trademark acquires generic use. For example, *aspirin* and *thermos* were originally trademarked products, but today the words are used generically. Other examples are *escalator, trampoline, raisin bran, dry ice, lanolin, linoleum, nylon,* and *corn flakes*. Even so, the courts will not allow another firm to use those marks in such a way as to deceive a potential consumer.

Note that a generic term will not be protected under trademark law even if the term has acquired a secondary meaning. • **EXAMPLE 5.3** In one case, America Online, Inc. (AOL), sued AT&T Corporation, claiming that AT&T's use of "You Have Mail" on its WorldNet Service infringed AOL's trademark rights in the same phrase. The court ruled, however, that because each of the three words in the phrase was a generic term, the phrase as a whole was generic. Although the phrase had become widely associated with AOL's e-mail notification service, and thus may have acquired a secondary mean-

4. *Qualitex Co. v. Jacobson Products Co.,* 514 U.S. 159, 115 S.Ct. 1300, 131 L.Ed.2d 248 (1995).

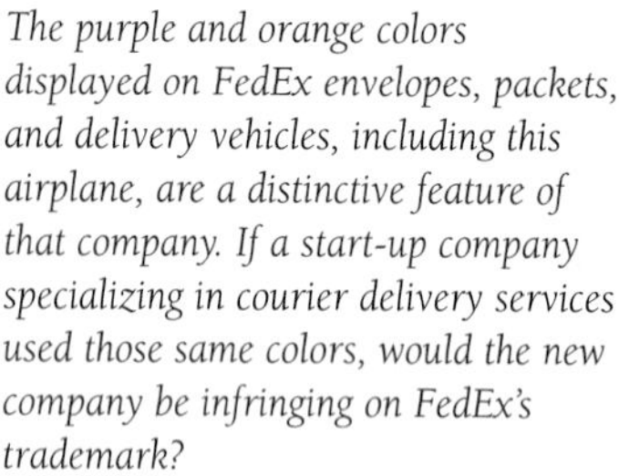

The purple and orange colors displayed on FedEx envelopes, packets, and delivery vehicles, including this airplane, are a distinctive feature of that company. If a start-up company specializing in courier delivery services used those same colors, would the new company be infringing on FedEx's trademark?

A "UL" certification mark. How does a certification mark differ from a trademark?

ing, this issue was of no significance in the case. The court stated that it would not consider whether the mark had acquired any secondary meaning because "generic marks with secondary meaning are still not entitled to protection."[5] •

SERVICE, CERTIFICATION, AND COLLECTIVE MARKS

SERVICE MARK
A mark used in the sale or the advertising of services to distinguish the services of one person from those of others. Titles, character names, and other distinctive features of radio and television programs may be registered as service marks.

A **service mark** is similar to a trademark but is used to distinguish the services of one person or company from those of another. For example, each airline has a particular mark or symbol associated with its name. Titles and character names used in radio and television are frequently registered as service marks.

Other marks protected by law include certification marks and collective marks. A *certification mark* is used by one or more persons other than the owner to certify the region, materials, mode of manufacture, quality, or accuracy of the owner's goods or services. When used by members of a cooperative, association, or other organization, it is referred to as a *collective mark.* • **EXAMPLE 5.4** Certification marks include such marks as "Good Housekeeping Seal of Approval" and "UL Tested." Collective marks appear at the ends of the credits of movies to indicate the various associations and organizations that participated in making the movie. The union marks found on the tags of certain products are also collective marks. •

TRADE NAMES

TRADE NAME
A term that is used to indicate part or all of a business's name and that is directly related to the business's reputation and goodwill. Trade names are protected under the common law (and under trademark law, if the name is the same as the firm's trademarked property).

Trademarks apply to *products*. The term **trade name** is used to indicate part or all of a business's name, whether the business is a sole proprietorship, a partnership, or a corporation. Generally, a trade name is directly related to a business and its goodwill. Trade names may be protected as trademarks if the trade name is the same as the company's trademarked product—for example, Coca-Cola. Unless also used as a trademark or service mark, a trade name cannot be registered with the federal government. Trade names are protected under the common law, however. As with trademarks, words must be unusual or fancifully used if they are to be protected as trade names. The word *Safeway,* for example, was held by the courts to be sufficiently fanciful to obtain protection as a trade name for a food-store chain.[6]

TRADE DRESS

TRADE DRESS
The image and overall appearance of a product—for example, the distinctive decor, menu, layout, and style of service of a particular restaurant. Basically, trade dress is subject to the same protection as trademarks.

The term **trade dress** refers to the image and overall appearance of a product. Basically, trade dress is subject to the same protection as trademarks. • **EXAMPLE 5.5** The distinctive decor, menu, layout, and style of service of a particular restaurant may be regarded as the restaurant's trade dress. Similarly, if a golf course is distinguished from other golf courses by prominent features, those features may be considered the golf course's trade dress. • In cases involving trade dress infringement, as in trademark infringement cases, a major consideration is whether consumers are likely to be confused by the allegedly infringing use.

Cyber Marks

CYBER MARK
A trademark in cyberspace.

In cyberspace, trademarks are sometimes referred to as **cyber marks.** We turn now to a discussion of trademark-related issues in cyberspace and how new laws and the courts are addressing these issues. One concern relates to the rights of a trademark's

5. *America Online, Inc. v. AT&T Corp.,* 243 F.3d 812 (4th Cir. 2001).
6. *Safeway Stores v. Suburban Foods,* 130 F.Supp. 249 (E.D.Va. 1955).

owner to use the mark as part of a domain name (Internet address). Other issues have to do with cybersquatting, meta tags, and trademark dilution on the Web. The use of licensing as a way to avoid liability for infringing on another's intellectual property rights in cyberspace will be discussed later in this chapter.

DOMAIN NAMES

In the real world, one business can often use the same name as another without causing any conflict, particularly if the businesses are small, their goods or services are different, and the areas where they do business are separate. In the online world, however, there is only one area of business—cyberspace. Thus, disputes between parties over which one has the right to use a particular domain name have become common. A **domain name** is part of an Internet address, such as "westlaw.com." The top-level domain (TLD) is the part of the name to the right of the period and represents the type of entity that operates the site (for example, "com" is an abbreviation for "commercial"). The second level (the part of the name to the left of the period) is chosen by the business entity or individual registering the domain name.

DOMAIN NAME
The last part of an Internet address, such as "westlaw.com." The top level (the part of the name to the right of the period) represents the type of entity that operates the site ("com" is an abbreviation for "commercial"). The second level (the part of the name to the left of the period) is chosen by the entity.

Conflicts over rights to domain names emerged during the 1990s as e-commerce expanded on a worldwide scale. Of the TLDs then available (*.com, .org, .net, .edu, .int, .mil,* and *.gov*), only one—*.com*—was typically used by commercial enterprises. As e-commerce expanded, the *.com* TLD came to be widely used by businesses on the Web. Competition among firms with similar names and products for the names preceding the *.com* TLD led, understandably, to numerous disputes over domain name rights. By using the same, or a similar, domain name, parties have attempted to profit from the goodwill of a competitor, to sell pornography, to offer for sale another party's domain name, and to otherwise infringe on others' trademarks.

"It was not so very long ago that people thought semiconductors were part-time orchestra leaders and microchips were very small snack foods."

GERALDINE FERRARO, 1935–
(American politician; Democratic candidate for vice president in 1984)

As noted in Chapter 3, the Internet Corporation for Assigned Names and Numbers (ICANN), a nonprofit corporation that the federal government set up to oversee the distribution of domain names, has played a leading role in facilitating the settlement of domain name disputes worldwide. ICANN has also attempted to reduce domain name conflicts by approving seven additional TLDs for use in domain names. The new TLDs, which were approved by ICANN in November 2000, are *.biz, .info, .name, .pro, .museums, .coop,* and *.aero*.

ETHICAL ISSUE 5.1

Are additional top-level domain options a blessing or a curse?

ICANN's decision to approve seven new top-level domain names (TLDs) was surrounded by a significant amount of controversy. Among other things, some contend that having additional choices for TLDs will complicate the process of protecting corporate trademarks. To protect their trademarks, businesses often buy up all available domain names associated with a particular word or set of words. With additional TLDs, this becomes more difficult. For example, if a business markets a product called XYZ, the firm would want to own the domain name XYZ.com, as well as XYZ.biz and possibly, depending on the nature of its product, XYZ.coop, XYZ.aero, or XYZ.info. There is also a cost factor, because registering domain names is not free. In fact, the Gartner Group, Inc., in Stamford, Connecticut, estimates that companies now have to spend an average of about $70,000 a year to maintain a domain name strategy to protect their trademarks.

ANTICYBERSQUATTING LEGISLATION

CYBERSQUATTING
An act that occurs when a person registers a domain name that is the same as, or confusingly similar to, the trademark of another and offers to sell the domain name back to the trademark owner.

In the late 1990s, Congress passed legislation prohibiting another practice that had given rise to numerous disputes over domain names: cybersquatting. **Cybersquatting** occurs when a person registers a domain name that is the same as, or confusingly similar to, the trademark of another and then offers to sell the domain name back to the trademark owner. During the 1990s, cybersquatting became a contentious issue and led to much litigation. Often in dispute in these cases was whether cybersquatting constituted a commercial use of the mark so as to violate federal trademark law. Additionally, it was not always easy to separate cybersquatting from legitimate business activity. Although no clear rules emerged from this litigation, many courts held that cybersquatting violated trademark law.[7]

In 1999, Congress addressed this issue by passing the Anticybersquatting Consumer Protection Act (ACPA), which amended the Lanham Act—the federal law protecting trademarks, discussed earlier in this chapter. The ACPA makes it illegal for a person to "register, traffic in, or use" a domain name (1) if the name is identical or confusingly similar to the trademark of another and (2) if the one registering, trafficking in, or using the domain name has a "bad faith intent" to profit from that trademark. The act does not define what constitutes bad faith. Instead, it lists several factors that courts can consider in deciding whether bad faith exists. Some of these factors are the trademark rights of the other person, whether there is an intent to divert consumers in a way that could harm the goodwill represented by the trademark, whether there is an offer to transfer or sell the domain name to the trademark owner, and whether there is an intent to use the domain name to offer goods and services.

The ACPA applies to all domain name registrations, even domain names registered before the passage of the act. Successful plaintiffs in suits brought under the act can collect actual damages and profits, or elect to receive statutory damages of from $1,000 to $100,000.

META TAGS

Search engines compile their results by looking through a Web site's key words field. Meta tags, or key words, may be inserted into this field to increase the frequency of a site's appearance in search engine results, even though the site has nothing to do with the inserted words. Using this same technique, one site may appropriate the key words of other sites with more frequent hits, so that the appropriating site appears in the same search engine results as the more popular sites. Using another's trademark in a meta tag without the owner's permission, however, constitutes trademark infringement.

● **EXAMPLE 5.6** An early case concerning meta tags involved Calvin Designer Label's use of "Playboy," "Playboy magazine," and "Playmate"—marks that were all owned by Playboy Enterprises, Inc. (PEI)—as meta tags for its Web sites on the Internet. As tags, the terms were invisible to viewers (in black type on a black background), but they caused the Web sites to be returned at the top of the list of a search engine query for "Playboy" or "Playmate." PEI sued Calvin Designer Label, alleging, among other things, trademark infringement. The court granted PEI's motion for summary judgment and ordered Calvin Designer Label to stop using PEI's trademarks.[8] ●

---

7. See, for example, *Panavision International, L.P. v. Toeppen,* 141 F.3d 1316 (9th Cir. 1998).
8. *Playboy Enterprises, Inc. v. Calvin Designer Label,* 985 F.Supp.2d 1220 (N.D.Cal. 1997).

DILUTION IN THE ONLINE WORLD

As discussed earlier, trademark *dilution* occurs when a trademark is used, without authorization, in a way that diminishes the distinctive quality of the mark. Unlike trademark infringement, a dilution cause of action does not require proof that consumers are likely to be confused by a connection between the unauthorized use and the mark. For this reason, the products involved do not have to be similar. In the first case alleging dilution on the Web, a court precluded the use of "candyland.com" as the URL for an adult site. The suit was brought by the maker of the "Candyland" children's game and owner of the "Candyland" mark.[9]

In one case, a court issued an injunction on the ground that spamming under another's logo is trademark dilution. In that case, Hotmail, Inc., provided e-mail services and worked to dissociate itself from spam. Van$ Money Pie, Inc., and others spammed thousands of e-mail customers, using the free e-mail Hotmail as a return address. The court ordered the defendants to stop.[10]

Patents

PATENT
A government grant that gives an inventor the exclusive right or privilege to make, use, or sell his or her invention for a limited time period.

A **patent** is a grant from the government that gives an inventor the exclusive right to make, use, and sell an invention for a period of twenty years from the date of filing the application for a patent. Patents for designs, as opposed to inventions, are given for a fourteen-year period. For either a regular patent or a design patent, the applicant must demonstrate to the satisfaction of the U.S. Patent and Trademark Office that the invention, discovery, process, or design is genuine, novel, useful, and not obvious in light of current technology. A patent holder gives notice to all that an article or design is patented by placing on it the word *Patent* or *Pat.* plus the patent number. In contrast to patent law in other countries, in the United States patent protection is given to the first person to invent a product or process, even though someone else may have been the first to file for a patent on that product or process.

At one time, it was difficult for developers and manufacturers of software to obtain patent protection because many software products simply automate procedures that can be performed manually. In other words, the computer programs do not meet the "novel" and "not obvious" requirements previously mentioned. Also, the basis for software is often a mathematical equation or formula, which is not patentable. In 1981, however, the United States Supreme Court held that it is possible, to obtain a patent for a *process* that incorporates a computer program—providing, of course, that the process itself is patentable.[11] Subsequently, many patents have been issued for software-related inventions.

ON THE WEB
A good online source for information on patents can be found at
http://www.patents.com.

A significant development relating to patents is the availability online of the world's patent databases. The Web site of the U.S. Patent and Trademark Office provides searchable databases covering U.S. patents granted since 1976. The Web site of the European Patent Office maintains databases covering all patent documents in sixty-five nations and the legal status of patents in twenty-two of those countries.

9. *Hasbro, Inc. v. Internet Entertainment Group, Ltd.,* 1996 WL 84853 (W.D.Wash. 1996).
10. *Hotmail Corp. v. Van$ Money Pie, Inc.,* 47 U.S.P.Q.2d 1020 (N.D.Cal. 1998). For a further discussion of this case, see the *Business Law in the Online World* feature in Chapter 11.
11. *Diamond v. Diehr,* 450 U.S. 175, 101 S.Ct. 1048, 67 L.Ed.2d 155 (1981).

"The patent system . . . added the fuel of interest to the fire of genius."

ABRAHAM LINCOLN, 1809–1865 (Sixteenth president of the United States, 1861–1865)

PATENT INFRINGEMENT

If a firm makes, uses, or sells another's patented design, product, or process without the patent owner's permission, it commits the tort of patent infringement. Patent infringement may exist even though the patent owner has not put the patented product in commerce. Patent infringement may also occur even though not all features or parts of an invention are copied. (With respect to a patented process, however, all steps or their equivalent must be copied for infringement to exist.)

Often, litigation for patent infringement is so costly that the patent holder will instead offer to sell to the infringer a license to use the patented design, product, or process—licensing is discussed later in this chapter. Indeed, in many cases the costs of detection, prosecution, and monitoring are so high that patents are valueless to their owners; the owners cannot afford to protect them.

BUSINESS PROCESS PATENTS

Traditionally, patents have been granted to inventions that are "new and useful processes, machines, manufactures, or compositions of matter, or any new and useful improvements thereof." The U.S. Patent and Trademark Office routinely rejected computer systems and software applications because they were deemed not to be useful processes, machines, articles of manufacture, or compositions of matter. They were simply considered to be mathematical algorithms, abstract ideas, or "methods of doing business." In a landmark 1998 case, however, *State Street Bank & Trust Co. v. Signature Financial Group, Inc.*,[12] the U.S. Court of Appeals for the Federal Circuit ruled that only three categories of subject matter will always remain unpatentable: (1) the laws of nature, (2) natural phenomena, and (3) abstract ideas. This decision meant, among other things, that business processes were patentable.

After this decision, numerous technology firms applied for business process patents. Walker Digital applied for a business process patent for its "Dutch auction" system, which allowed consumers to make offers for airline tickets on the Internet and led to the creation of Priceline.com. About.com obtained a patent for its "Elaborative Internet Data Mining System," which creates and pulls together the Web content of a large range of topics onto a single Web site. Amazon.com obtained a business process patent for its "one-click" ordering system, a method of processing credit-card orders securely without asking for the customer's card number or other personal information, such as the customer's name and address, more than once. Indeed, since the *State Street* decision, the number of Internet-related patents issued by the U.S. Patent and Trademark Office has increased more than 800 percent.

ETHICAL ISSUE 5.2

Will business process patents have a chilling effect on e-commerce?

Business process patents have raised some troublesome legal (and ethical) questions with respect to Internet commerce. Some argue that venture capitalists are more inclined to invest in Internet and high-tech companies if they believe that such start-ups can obtain patents for their business processes. Others believe that business process patents will have a chilling effect on Internet businesses. This group points out that Internet firms have

12. 149 F.3d 1368 (Fed. Cir. 1998).

obtained business process patents for processes that are neither new nor nonobvious. For example, the Dutch auction system, which was patented for use by Priceline.com, is simply the electronic version of a system that has been around for centuries. So are other business processes that have received patent protection, such as Internet incentive systems that involve paying people to look at Web ads. Essentially, such an incentive system is no different from enclosing a dollar bill with a survey and asking people to fill out the survey and send it in. Some argue that the more patents are granted for some of the building blocks of e-commerce, the more those involved in e-commerce will have to pay licensing fees to use those building blocks. Consider an analogy: had a business process patent been obtained for the granting of frequent flyer miles, then all airlines would have to pay a license fee for such programs.

Copyrights

COPYRIGHT
The exclusive right of "authors" to publish, print, or sell an intellectual production for a statutory period of time. A copyright has the same monopolistic nature as a patent or trademark, but it differs in that it applies exclusively to works of art, literature, and other works of authorship (including computer programs).

A **copyright** is an intangible property right granted by federal statute to the author or originator of certain literary or artistic productions. Currently, copyrights are governed by the Copyright Act of 1976,[13] as amended. Works created after January 1, 1978, are automatically given statutory copyright protection for the life of the author plus 70 years. For copyrights owned by publishing houses, the copyright expires 95 years from the date of publication or 120 years from the date of creation, whichever is first. For works by more than one author, the copyright expires 70 years after the death of the last surviving author.[14]

Copyrights can be registered with the U.S. Copyright Office in Washington, D.C. A copyright owner no longer needs to place a © or *Copr.* or *Copyright* on the work, however, to have the work protected against infringement. Chances are that if somebody created it, somebody owns it.

What Is Protected Expression?

BE CAREFUL If a creative work does not fall into a certain category, it may not be copyrighted, but it may be protected by other intellectual property law.

Works that are copyrightable include books, records, films, artworks, architectural plans, menus, music videos, product packaging, and computer software. To obtain protection under the Copyright Act, a work must be original and fall into one of the following categories: (1) literary works; (2) musical works; (3) dramatic works; (4) pantomimes and choreographic works; (5) pictorial, graphic, and sculptural works; (6) films and other audiovisual works; and (7) sound recordings. To be protected, a work must be "fixed in a durable medium" from which it can be perceived, reproduced, or communicated. Protection is automatic. Registration is not required.

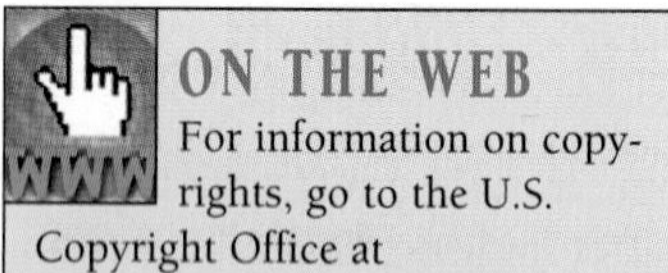

ON THE WEB For information on copyrights, go to the U.S. Copyright Office at **http://lcweb.loc.gov/copyright**.

Section 102 of the Copyright Act specifically excludes copyright protection for any "idea, procedure, process, system, method of operation, concept, principle, or discovery, regardless of the form in which it is described, explained, illustrated, or embodied." Note that it is not possible to copyright an *idea*. The underlying ideas embodied in a work may be freely used by others. What is copyrightable is the particular way in which an idea is *expressed*. Whenever an idea and an expression are inseparable, the expression cannot be copyrighted. Generally, anything that is not an original expres-

13. 17 U.S.C. Sections 101 *et seq.*

14. These time periods reflect the extensions set forth in the Sonny Bono Copyright Term Extension Act of 1998.

sion will not qualify for copyright protection. Facts widely known to the public are not copyrightable. Page numbers are not copyrightable, because they follow a sequence known to everyone. Mathematical calculations are not copyrightable.

Compilations of facts, however, are copyrightable. Section 103 of the Copyright Act defines a compilation as "a work formed by the collection and assembling of preexisting materials of data that are selected, coordinated, or arranged in such a way that the resulting work as a whole constitutes an original work of authorship." The key requirement for the copyrightability of a compilation is originality. ● **EXAMPLE 5.7** The White Pages of a telephone directory do not qualify for copyright protection when the information that makes up the directory (names, addresses, and telephone numbers) is not selected, coordinated, or arranged in an original way.[15] In one case, even the Yellow Pages of a telephone directory did not qualify for copyright protection.[16] ●

COPYRIGHT INFRINGEMENT

ON THE WEB You can find a host of information on copyright law, including the Copyright Act and significant United States Supreme Court cases in the area of copyright law, at

http://supct.law.cornell.edu/supct/cases/copyrt.htm.

Whenever the form or expression of an idea is copied, an infringement of copyright occurs. The reproduction does not have to be exactly the same as the original, nor does it have to reproduce the original in its entirety.

Penalties or remedies can be imposed on those who infringe copyrights. These range from actual damages (damages based on the actual harm caused to the copyright holder by the infringement) or statutory damages (damages provided for under the Copyright Act, not to exceed $100,000) to criminal proceedings for willful violations (which may result in fines and/or imprisonment).

An exception to liability for copyright infringement is made under the "fair use" doctrine. In certain circumstances, a person or organization can reproduce copyrighted material without paying royalties (fees paid to the copyright holder for the privilege of reproducing the copyrighted material). Section 107 of the Copyright Act provides as follows:

> [T]he fair use of a copyrighted work, including such use by reproduction in copies or phonorecords or by any other means specified by [Section 106 of the Copyright Act,] for purposes such as criticism, comment, news reporting, teaching (including multiple copies for classroom use), scholarship, or research, is not an infringement of copyright. In determining whether the use made of a work in any particular case is a fair use the factors to be considered shall include—
>
> (1) the purpose and character of the use, including whether such use is of a commercial nature or is for nonprofit educational purposes;
> (2) the nature of the copyrighted work;
> (3) the amount and substantiality of the portion used in relation to the copyrighted work as a whole; and
> (4) the effect of the use upon the potential market for or value of the copyrighted work.

Because these guidelines are very broad, the courts determine whether a particular use is fair on a case-by-case basis. Thus, anyone reproducing copyrighted material may be subject to a violation.

COPYRIGHT PROTECTION FOR SOFTWARE

In 1980, Congress passed the Computer Software Copyright Act, which amended the Copyright Act of 1976 to include computer programs in the list of creative works

15. *Feist Publications, Inc. v. Rural Telephone Service Co.,* 499 U.S. 340, 111 S.Ct. 1282, 113 L.Ed.2d 358 (1991).
16. *Bellsouth Advertising & Publishing Corp. v. Donnelley Information Publishing, Inc.,* 999 F.2d 1436 (11th Cir. 1993).

protected by federal copyright law. The 1980 statute, which classifies computer programs as "literary works," defines a computer program as a "set of statements or instructions to be used directly or indirectly in a computer in order to bring about a certain result."

Because of the unique nature of computer programs, the courts had many problems applying and interpreting the 1980 act. Generally, though, the courts have held that copyright protection extends not only to those parts of a computer program that can be read by humans, such as the high-level language of a source code, but also to the binary-language object code of a computer program, which is readable only by the computer.[17] Additionally, such elements as the overall structure, sequence, and organization of a program were deemed copyrightable.[18] The courts have disagreed on the issue of whether the "look and feel"—the general appearance, command structure, video images, menus, windows, and other screen displays—of computer programs should also be protected by copyright. The courts have tended, however, not to extend copyright protection to look-and-feel aspects of computer programs.

Copyrights in Digital Information

Copyright law is probably the most important form of intellectual property protection on the Internet. This is because much of the material on the Internet consists of works of authorship (including multimedia presentations, software, and database information), which are the traditional focus of copyright law. Copyright law is also important because the nature of the Internet requires that data be "copied" to be transferred online. Copies are a significant part of the traditional controversies arising in this area of the law. (For an example of one controversy concerning unauthorized copies of copyrighted materials, see this chapter's *Business Law in the Online World* feature.)

The Copyright Act of 1976 When Congress drafted the principal U.S. law governing copyrights, the Copyright Act of 1976, cyberspace did not exist for most of us. The threat to copyright owners was posed not by computer technology but by unauthorized *tangible* copies of works and the sale of rights to movies, television, and other media.

Some of the issues that were unimagined when the Copyright Act was drafted have posed thorny questions for the courts. For example, to sell a copy of a work, permission of the copyright holder is necessary. Because of the nature of cyberspace, however, one of the early controversies was determining at what point an intangible, electronic "copy" of a work has been made. The courts have held that loading a file or program into a computer's random access memory, or RAM, constitutes the making of a "copy" for purposes of copyright law.[19] RAM is a portion of a computer's memory into which a file, for example, is loaded so that it can be accessed (read or written over). Thus, a copyright is infringed when a party downloads software into RAM without owning the software or otherwise having a right to download it.[20]

---

17. See *Stern Electronics, Inc. v. Kaufman*, 669 F.2d 852 (2d Cir. 1982); and *Apple Computer, Inc. v. Franklin Computer Corp.*, 714 F.2d 1240 (3d Cir. 1983).
18. *Whelan Associates, Inc. v. Jaslow Dental Laboratory, Inc.*, 797 F.2d 1222 (3d Cir. 1986).
19. *MAI Systems Corp. v. Peak Computer, Inc.*, 991 F.2d 511 (9th Cir. 1993).
20. *DSC Communications Corp. v. Pulse Communications, Inc.*, 170 F.3d 1354 (Fed. Cir. 1999).

BUSINESS LAW: //in the Online World

DVD "Piracy"—The Courts Speak

Digital versatile disks (DVDs) provide numerous advantages over traditional videocassettes. For one thing, they are more compact. They also offer superior audio and video quality. Additionally, they provide for numerous enhancements, such as directors' commentaries, separate foreign language audio tracks, and various foreign language subtitles. Not surprisingly, the owners of motion picture copyrights have a vested interest in preventing renters and owners of DVDs from making the contents of those DVDs available on the Internet. All DVDs include an encryption system created to protect against the unauthorized copying of the contents.

Almost as soon as encryption technology was used to safeguard the contents of DVDs, however, the code was cracked by a group of hackers, including nineteen-year-old Norwegian Jon Johansen. His decryption program, called DeCCS, was quickly made available at various sites on the Internet including 2600.com, owned by Ed Corly. Almost immediately after DeCCS was posted, a group of movie companies, including Disney and Twentieth Century-Fox, filed suit.

Violation of the Digital Millennium Copyright Act

In what was seen as a victory for the motion picture industry, a federal district court ruled, in *Universal City Studios, Inc. v. Reimerdes,*[a] that DeCCS violated the Digital Millennium Copyright Act of 1998. As you will read elsewhere in this chapter, this act essentially prohibits individuals from breaking encryption programs put in place to protect digital versions of intellectual property such as movies, music, and the like. After all, reasoned the court, since the posting of DeCCS, along with a separate video-compression program known as Divx, the pirating of movies had become increasingly common on the Internet.

The defendants argued that software programs designed to break encryption schemes were simply a form of constitutionally protected speech. The court, however, rejected the free speech argument. "Computer code is not purely expressive any more than the assassination of a political figure is purely a political statement. . . . The Constitution, after all, is a framework for building a just and democratic society. It is not a suicide pact," stated the court.

New Forms of Encryption May Curb DVD Piracy

New forms of encryption and copyright protection now being developed may at least slow down the amount of piracy on the Internet. New DVD-Audio discs contain a digital "watermark" that can be tracked. In this way, if pirated copies of the watermarked DVD-Audio disc are found, record labels can better pursue the originator of the pirated copies. Additionally, DVD-Audio discs that are copied have much poorer sound quality than the originals do.

New versions of Microsoft's Media Player software allow digital restrictions dictated by copyright holders. The software then scrambles the digital output so that it cannot be recorded. Finally, IBM is developing an encryption system designed to prevent DVD piracy.

If the past is any predictor of the future, however, no matter how well a copyrighted work is encrypted, the technically skilled will be able to "crack" the encryption code, thereby allowing pirated copies to resurface.

FOR CRITICAL ANALYSIS

Will the decision in the Universal City Studios *case have any practical effect, given that literally thousands of copies of DeCCS already existed on the Internet before the decision was issued?*

a. 111 F.Supp.2d 294 (S.D.N.Y. 2000).

Other rights, including those relating to the revision of "collective works" such as magazines, were acknowledged thirty years ago but were considered to have only limited economic value. Today, technology has made some of those rights vastly more significant. How does the old law apply to these rights? That was one of the questions in the following case.

CASE 5.2 New York Times Co. v. Tasini

Supreme Court of the United States, 2001.
533 U.S. 483,
121 S.Ct. 2381,
120 L.Ed.2d 500.
http://supct.law.cornell.edu:8080/supct[a]

FACTS Magazines and newspapers, including the *New York Times,* buy and publish articles written by freelance writers. Besides circulating hard copies of their periodicals, these publishers sell the contents to e-publishers for inclusion in online, and other electronic, databases. Jonathan Tasini and other freelance writers filed a suit in a federal district court against The New York Times Company and other publishers, including the e-publishers, contending that the e-publication of the articles violated the Copyright Act. The publishers responded, among other things, that the Copyright Act gave them a right to produce "revisions" of their publications. The writers argued that the Copyright Act did not cover electronic "revisions." The court granted a summary judgment in the publishers' favor, which was reversed on the writers' appeal to the U.S. Court of Appeals for the Second Circuit. The publishers appealed to the United States Supreme Court.

ISSUE To put the contents of periodicals into e-databases and onto CD-ROMs, do publishers need to obtain the permission of the writers whose contributions are included in the periodicals?

DECISION Yes. The United States Supreme Court affirmed the lower court's judgment. The Supreme Court remanded the case for a determination as to how the writers should be compensated.

REASON The Court pointed out that databases are "vast domain[s] of diverse texts," consisting of "thousands or millions of files containing individual articles from thousands of collective works." The Court found that these databases have little relationship to the articles' original publication. The databases are not "revisions," as the publishers argued, because the databases reproduce and distribute articles "clear of the context provided by the original periodical editions"—not "as part of that particular collective work" to which the author contributed, not "as part of * * * any revision," and not "as part of * * * any later collective work in the same series," as the Copyright Act provides. The Court reasoned that a database composed of such articles was no more a revision of an original work than "a 400-page novel quoting a sonnet in passing would represent a 'revision' of that poem."

FOR CRITICAL ANALYSIS—Economic Consideration *When technology creates a situation in which rights such as those in this case become more valuable, should the law be changed to redistribute the economic benefit of those rights?*

a. In the right-hand column, in the "For the 2000–2001 term:" section, click on "Decisions by date." When that page opens, click on "June 2001." In the result, scroll to the name of the case and click on it. On that page, click the appropriate link to access the opinion.

Further Developments in Copyright Law In the last several years, Congress has enacted legislation designed specifically to protect copyright holders in a digital age. For example, prior to 1997 criminal penalties under copyright law could be imposed only if unauthorized copies were exchanged for financial gain. Yet much piracy of copyrighted materials was "altruistic" in nature; that is, unauthorized copies were made and distributed not for financial gain but simply for reasons of generosity—to share the copies with others.

To combat altruistic piracy and for other reasons, Congress passed the No Electronic Theft (NET) Act of 1997. This act extends criminal liability for the piracy of copyrighted materials to persons who exchange unauthorized copies of copyrighted works, such as software, even though they realize no profit from the exchange. The act also imposes penalties on those who make unauthorized electronic copies of books, magazines, movies, or music for *personal* use, thus altering the traditional "fair use" doctrine. The criminal penalties for violating the act are steep; they include fines as high as $250,000 and incarceration for up to five years.

More recently, Congress passed further legislation to protect copyright holders—the Digital Millennium Copyright Act of 1998. Because of its significance in protecting against the piracy of copyrighted materials in the online environment, this act is presented as this chapter's *Landmark in the Law* on page 149.

MP3 and File-Sharing Technology At one time, music fans swapped compact disks (CDs) and recorded the songs that they liked from others' CDs onto their own cassettes. This type of "file sharing" was awkward at best. Soon after the Internet became popular, a few enterprising programmers created software to compress large data files, particularly those associated with music. The reduced file sizes make transmitting music over the Internet feasible. The most widely known compression and decompression system is MP3, which enables music fans to download songs or entire CDs onto their computers or onto a portable listening device, such as Rio. The MP3 system also made it possible for music fans to access other music fans' files by engaging in file sharing via the Internet.

PEER-TO-PEER (P2P) NETWORKING A technology that allows Internet users to access files on other users' computers.

DISTRIBUTED NETWORK A network that can be used by persons located (distributed) around the country or the globe to share computer files.

File sharing via the Internet is accomplished through what is called **peer-to-peer (P2P) networking.** The concept is simple. Rather than going through a central Web server, P2P involves numerous personal computers (PCs) that are connected to the Internet. Files stored on one PC can be accessed by others who are members of the same network. Sometimes this is called a **distributed network.** In other words, parts of the network are distributed all over the country or the world. File sharing offers an unlimited number of uses for distributed networks. Currently, for example, many researchers allow their home computers' computing power to be accessed through file-sharing software so that very large mathematical problems can be solved quickly. Additionally, persons scattered throughout the country or the world can work together on the same project by using file-sharing programs.

"People will continue to share files over the Internet, and we cannot escape facts."

ANDREAS SCHMIDT, 1961–
(Bertelsmann e-Commerce Group president and chief executive officer, 2000–)

When file sharing is used to download others' stored music files, however, copyright issues arise. Recording artists and their labels stand to lose large amounts of royalties and revenues if relatively few CDs are purchased and then made available on distributed networks, from which everyone can get them for free. In the following widely publicized case, several firms in the recording industry sued Napster, Inc., the owner of the then popular Napster Web site. The firms alleged that Napster was contributing to copyright infringement by those who downloaded CDs from other computers in the Napster file-sharing system. At issue was whether Napster could be held vicariously liable for the infringement.[21]

21. Vicarious (indirect) liability exists when one person is subject to liability for another's actions. A common example occurs in the employment context, when an employer is held vicariously liable by third parties for torts committed by employees in the course of their employment.

CASE 5.3 A&M Records, Inc. v. Napster, Inc.

United States Court of Appeals,
Ninth Circuit, 2001.
239 F.3d 1004.
http://guide.lp.findlaw.com/casecode/courts/9th.html[a]

a. This URL will take you to a Web site maintained by FindLaw, which is now a part of West Group. When you access the site, enter "Napster" in the "Party Name Search" box and then click on "Search." Select the second *Napster* case in the the list (dated "02/12/2001") on the page that opens.

HISTORICAL AND TECHNOLOGICAL SETTING

In 1987, the Moving Picture Experts Group set a standard file format for the storage of audio recordings in a digital format called MPEG-3, abbreviated as "MP3." Digital MP3 files are created through a process called "ripping." Ripping software allows a computer owner to copy an audio compact disk (CD) directly onto a computer's hard

(continued)

CASE 5.3—Continued

drive by compressing the audio information on the CD into the MP3 format. The MP3's compressed format allows for rapid transmission of digital audio files from one computer to another by e-mail or any other file transfer protocol.

FACTS Napster, Inc. (**http://www.napster.com**), facilitated the transmission of MP3 files among the users of its Web site through a process called "peer-to-peer" file sharing. Napster allowed users to transfer exact copies of the contents of MP3 files from one computer to another via the Internet. This was made possible by Napster's MusicShare software, available free of charge from Napster's site, and Napster's network servers and server-side software. Napster also provided technical support. A&M Records, Inc., and others engaged in the commercial recording, distribution, and sale of copyrighted musical compositions and sound recordings, filed a suit in a federal district court against Napster, alleging copyright infringement. The court issued a preliminary injunction ordering Napster to stop "facilitating others in copying, downloading, uploading, transmitting, or distributing plaintiffs' copyrighted musical compositions and sound recordings, * * * without express permission of the rights owner." Napster appealed to the U.S. Court of Appeals for the Ninth Circuit.

ISSUE Did Napster's failure to obtain permission before facilitating the transmission of copyrighted material via its Web site constitute copyright infringement?

DECISION Yes. The U.S. Court of Appeals for the Ninth Circuit affirmed the lower court's decision that Napster was obligated to police its own system and had likely infringed the plaintiffs' copyrights. Holding that the injunction was "overbroad," however, the appellate court remanded the case for a clarification of Napster's responsibility to determine whether music on its Web site was copyrighted.

REASON The U.S. Court of Appeals for the Ninth Circuit pointed out that "[i]n the context of copyright law, vicarious liability extends * * * to cases in which a defendant has the right and ability to supervise the infringing activity and also has a direct financial interest in such activities." The court found that "plaintiffs have demonstrated that Napster retains the right to control access to its system." To avoid liability, "the reserved right to police must be exercised to its fullest extent." Napster "failed to exercise that right to prevent the exchange of copyrighted material." The court explained that Napster "has the ability to locate infringing material listed on its search indices, and the right to terminate users' access to the system," even though the file names "may not match copyrighted material exactly (for example, the artist or song could be spelled wrong)." Napster's failure to police its system, "combined with a showing that Napster financially benefits from the continuing availability of infringing files on its system, leads to the imposition of vicarious liability."

FOR CRITICAL ANALYSIS—Technological Consideration *How might the Napster system be put to commercially significant but noninfringing uses?*

COMMENT *The court's ruling in this case essentially put Napster out of business with respect to the free downloading of music. Napster is currently in the process of reorganizing its business into a for-fee arrangement.*

Trade Secrets

TRADE SECRETS
Information or processes that give a business an advantage over competitors who do not know the information or processes.

Some business processes and information that are not or cannot be patented, copyrighted, or trademarked are nevertheless protected against appropriation by a competitor as trade secrets. **Trade secrets** consist of customer lists, plans, research and development, pricing information, marketing techniques, production techniques, and generally anything that makes an individual company unique and that would have value to a competitor.

Unlike copyright and trademark protection, protection of trade secrets extends both to ideas and to their expression. (For this reason, and because a trade secret involves no registration or filing requirements, trade secret protection may be well suited for software.) Of course, the secret formula, method, or other information must be disclosed to some persons, particularly to key employees. Businesses generally attempt to

LANDMARK IN THE LAW
The Digital Millennium Copyright Act of 1998

The United States leads the world in the production of creative products, including books, films, videos, recordings, and software. In fact, as indicated earlier in this chapter, the creative industries are more important to the U.S. economy than the traditional product industries are. Exports of U.S. creative products, for example, surpass those of every other U.S. industry in value. Creative industries are growing at nearly three times the rate of the economy as a whole.

Steps have been taken, both nationally and internationally, to protect ownership rights in intellectual property, including copyrights. As you will read later in this chapter, to curb unauthorized copying of copyrighted materials, the World Intellectual Property Organization (WIPO) enacted a treaty in 1996 to upgrade global standards of copyright protection, particularly for the Internet.

Implementing the WIPO Treaty In 1998, Congress implemented the provisions of the WIPO treaty by updating U.S. copyright law. The new law—the Digital Millennium Copyright Act of 1998—is a landmark step in the protection of copyright owners and, because of the leading position of the United States in the creative industries, serves as a model for other nations. Among other things, the act created civil and criminal penalties for anyone who circumvents (bypasses, or gets around—through clever maneuvering, for example) encryption software or other technological antipiracy protection. Also prohibited are the manufacture, import, sale, and distribution of devices or services for circumvention.

The act provides for exceptions to fit the needs of libraries, scientists, universities, and others. In general, the law does not restrict the "fair use" of circumvention methods for educational and other noncommercial purposes. For example, circumvention is allowed to test computer security, to conduct encryption research, to protect personal privacy, and to enable parents to monitor their children's use of the Internet. The exceptions are to be reconsidered every three years.

Limiting the Liability of Internet Service Providers The 1998 act also limited the liability of Internet service providers (ISPs). Under the act, an ISP is not liable for any copyright infringement by its customer *unless* the ISP is aware of the subscriber's violation. An ISP may be held liable only if it fails to take action to shut the subscriber down after learning of the violation. A copyright holder has to act promptly, however, by pursuing a claim in court, or the subscriber has the right to be restored to online access.

APPLICATION TO TODAY'S WORLD

The application of the Digital Millennium Copyright Act of 1998 to today's world is fairly self-evident. If Congress had not enacted this legislation, copyright owners would have a far more difficult time obtaining legal redress against those who, without authorization, decrypt and/or copy copyrighted materials. Of course, problems remain, particularly because of the global nature of the Internet. From a practical standpoint, the degree of protection afforded to copyright holders depends on the extent to which other nations that have signed the WIPO treaty actually implement its provisions.

protect their trade secrets by having all employees who use the process or information agree in their contracts, or in confidentiality agreements, never to divulge it.

State and Federal Law on Trade Secrets

Under Section 757 of the *Restatement of Torts,* "One who discloses or uses another's trade secret, without a privilege to do so, is liable to the other if (1) he discovered the secret by improper means, or (2) his disclosure or use constitutes a breach of confidence reposed in him by the other in disclosing the secret to him." The theft of confidential business data by industrial espionage, as when a business taps into a competitor's computer, is a theft of trade secrets without any contractual violation and is actionable in itself.

Until recently, virtually all law with respect to trade secrets was common law. In an effort to reduce the unpredictability of the common law in this area, a model act, the Uniform Trade Secrets Act, was presented to the states for adoption in 1979. Parts of the act have been adopted in more than twenty states. Typically, a state that has adopted parts of the act has adopted only those parts that encompass its own existing common law. Additionally, in 1996 Congress passed the Economic Espionage Act, which made the theft of trade secrets a federal crime. We will examine the provisions and significance of this act in Chapter 6, in the context of crimes related to business.

Does a trade secret lose its protection under the Uniform Trade Secrets Act when an employee commits it to memory rather than taking it in written form? That was the question in the following case.

CASE 5.4 Ed Nowogroski Insurance, Inc. v. Rucker

Supreme Court of Washington, 1999.
137 Wash.2d 427,
971 P.2d 936.

FACTS Jerry Kiser, Darwin Rieck, and Michael Rucker worked for Ed Nowogroski Insurance, Inc., an insurance agency, as sales and service representatives. When friction developed between the agency and Kiser, Rieck, and Rucker, the three quit to go to work for Potter, Leonard and Cahan, Inc., a competing insurance firm. During their employment with Potter, the former Nowogroski employees used Nowogroski customer lists to attract business. Kiser and Rucker used written client information that they had copied from their ex-employer's files. Rieck worked chiefly from memory. The Nowogroski agency filed a suit in a Washington state court against its former employees and their new employer, alleging misappropriation of trade secrets. The court concluded that the client information fit the definition of a trade secret under the Uniform Trade Secrets Act and issued a judgment in the plaintiff's favor. The court decided, however, that only the written information was protected and did not award damages for the use of the memorized data. Nowogroski appealed to an intermediate state appellate court, which held that there is no distinction between written and memorized information and ordered a recalculation of the damages. The defendants appealed to the Washington Supreme Court.

ISSUE Does the Uniform Trade Secrets Act distinguish between written and memorized information?

DECISION No. The state supreme court affirmed the state appellate court's decision that the Uniform Trade Secrets Act made no distinction between written and memorized information.

REASON The court pointed out that the act "defines a 'trade secret' to include compilations of information which have certain characteristics without regard to the form that such information might take." According to the court, "Whether the information is on a CD, a blueprint, a film, a recording, a hard paper copy or memorized by the employee, the inquiry is whether it meets the definition of a trade secret under the Act and whether it was misappropriated." The court also emphasized that "a former employee may use general knowledge, skills, and experi-

CASE 5.4—Continued

ence acquired during * * * prior employment" but may not "actively solicit customers from [the former employer's] confidential customer list."

FOR CRITICAL ANALYSIS—Economic Consideration *Suppose that you own a firm whose success has been due to a formula or process that you have kept secret from your competitors. What steps might you take to ensure that your employees will not pass on this trade secret to your competitors or use it to set up a competing business?*

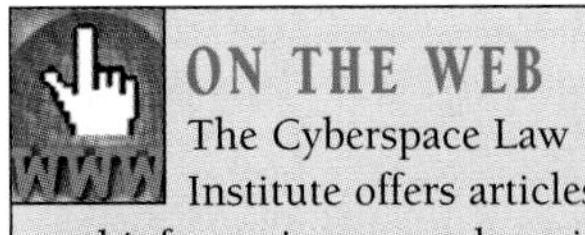

ON THE WEB The Cyberspace Law Institute offers articles and information on such topics as trade secrets at **http://www.cli.org.**

TRADE SECRETS IN CYBERSPACE

The nature of new computer technology undercuts a business firm's ability to protect its confidential information, including trade secrets.[22] For example, a dishonest employee could e-mail trade secrets in a company's computer to a competitor or a future employer. If e-mail is not an option, the employee might walk out with the information on a computer disk. Dissatisfied former employees have resorted to other options as well. • **EXAMPLE 5.8** In one case, a former employee of Intel Corporation, Ken Hamidi, became a thorn in Intel's side when he criticized the company's policies in e-mail sent to current employees. Hamidi, an engineer who had operated an Intel employee Web site, e-mailed from 25,000 to 35,000 messages at a time to Intel employees. Intel eventually took Hamidi to court, and the court ordered him to cease sending e-mails to Intel employees.[23] •

Licensing

One of the ways to make use of another's trademark, copyright, patent, or trade secret, while avoiding litigation, is to obtain a license to do so. A license in this context is essentially an agreement to permit the use of a trademark, copyright, patent, or trade secret for certain purposes. For example, a licensee (the party obtaining the license) might be allowed to use the trademark of the licensor (the party issuing the license) as part of the name of its company, or as part of its domain name, without otherwise using the mark on any products or services. (As with all contracts, contracts granting licenses must be carefully drafted—see, for example, the problems faced by the parties in the case discussed in this chapter's *Letter of the Law* feature on the next page.)

In 1999, the National Conference of Commissioners on Uniform State Laws approved the Uniform Computer Information Transactions Act (UCITA) and submitted it to the states for adoption. The act was drafted to address problems unique to electronic contracting and to the purchase and sale (licensing) of computer information, such as software. We will look at some of the key provisions of this act in Chapter 17, in the context of electronic contracts.

International Protection for Intellectual Property

For many years, the United States has been a party to various international agreements relating to intellectual property rights. For example, the Paris Convention of 1883, to

22. Note that in a recent case, the court indicated that customers' e-mail addresses may constitute trade secrets. See *T-N-T Motorsports, Inc. v. Hennessey Motorsports, Inc.*, 965 S.W.2d 18 (Tex.App.–Hous. [1 Dist.] 1998), rehearing overruled (1998), petition dismissed (1998).

23. *Intel Corp. v. Hamidi,* 1999 WL 450944 (Cal.Super. 1999).

LETTER OF THE LAW

A Book Is a Book Is a Book—But Is It an "E-Book"?

One of the significant issues raised by the cyber age has to do with whether copyrights in printed materials extend to the same materials presented in digital form over the Internet. Recall that this question was at issue in *New York Times Co. v. Tasini*, which was presented as Case 5.2 earlier in this chapter. Recently, a related issue involving licensing agreements came before a federal district court sitting in New York. The case was brought by the well-known publishing firm Random House, Inc., against Rosetta Books, LLC,[a] with which several authors had arranged to publish works electronically. At issue in the case was the following question: Did contracts in which the authors had licensed Random House to "print, publish and sell" their works in "book form" include the right to publish their works in electronic formats (as "e-books") as well?

In evaluating the issue, the court looked to the letter of the law, as decided by other court cases, but found little guidance. Hence, it looked to the words of the contract and to the definition of the term *book* given by the *Random House Webster's Unabridged Dictionary.* That dictionary defines a "book" as "a written or printed work of fiction or nonfiction, usually on sheets of paper fastened or bound together within covers." The court ultimately concluded that a book is not an e-book and therefore refused to grant Random House's motion to enjoin (prohibit) Rosetta Books from publishing the authors' works as e-books.[b]

THE BOTTOM LINE

To avoid litigation, anyone signing a licensing contract should make sure that the specific wording in the contract makes very clear what rights are or are not being conveyed.

a. *LLC* stands for "Limited Liability Company," a form of business organization that will be discussed in Chapter 30.

b. *Random House, Inc. v. Rosetta Books, LLC,* 150 F.Supp.2d 613 (S.D.N.Y. 2001).

which about ninety countries are signatory, allows parties in one country to file for patent and trademark protection in any of the other member countries. Other international agreements include the Berne Convention and the TRIPS agreement.

THE BERNE CONVENTION

ON THE WEB

The Web site of Cornell University's Legal Information Institute includes the texts of the Berne Convention and other international treaties on copyright issues at **http://www.law.cornell.edu/topics/copyright.html**.

Under the Berne Convention of 1886, an international copyright agreement, if an American writes a book, her or his copyright in the book must be recognized by every country that has signed the convention. Also, if a citizen of a country that has not signed the convention first publishes a book in a country that has signed, all other countries that have signed the convention must recognize that author's copyright. Copyright notice is not needed to gain protection under the Berne Convention for works published after March 1, 1989.

This convention and other international agreements have given some protection to intellectual property on a worldwide level. None of them, however, has been as significant and far-reaching in scope as the agreement on Trade-Related Aspects of Intellectual Property Rights, or, more simply, TRIPS.

THE TRIPS AGREEMENT

The TRIPS agreement was signed by representatives from over one hundred nations in 1994. The agreement established, for the first time, standards for the international pro-

INTERNATIONAL PERSPECTIVE

Setting Global Standards for Copyright Protection

Technology, particularly the Internet, offers new outlets for creative products. It also makes them easier to steal—copyrighted works can be pirated and distributed around the world quickly and efficiently. To curb this crime, in 1996 the World Intellectual Property Organization (WIPO) enacted the WIPO Copyright Treaty, a special agreement under the Berne Convention. The purpose was to upgrade global standards of copyright protection, particularly for the Internet.

Special provisions of the WIPO treaty relate to rights in digital data. The treaty strengthens some rights for copyright owners, in terms of their application in cyberspace, but leaves other questions unresolved. For example, the treaty does not make clear what constitutes the making of a "copy" in electronic form for purposes of international law. The United States signed the WIPO treaty in 1996 and, as mentioned earlier in this chapter's *Landmark in the Law,* implemented its terms in the Digital Millennium Copyright Act of 1998.

FOR CRITICAL ANALYSIS
Is there any practical way to prevent the piracy of digital data via the Internet?

tection of intellectual property rights, including patents, trademarks, and copyrights for movies, computer programs, books, and music.

Prior to the agreement, U.S. sellers of intellectual property in the international market faced difficulties because many other countries had no laws protecting intellectual property rights or failed to enforce existing laws. To address this problem, the TRIPS agreement provides that each member country must include in its domestic laws broad intellectual property rights and effective remedies (including civil and criminal penalties) for violations of those rights.

Generally, the TRIPS agreement provides that each member nation must not discriminate (in the administration, regulation, or adjudication of intellectual property rights) against foreign owners of such rights. In other words, a member nation cannot give its own nationals (citizens) favorable treatment without offering the same treatment to nationals of all member countries. For example, if a U.S. software manufacturer brings a suit for the infringement of intellectual property rights under a member nation's national laws, the U.S. manufacturer is entitled to receive the same treatment as a domestic manufacturer. Each member nation must also ensure that legal procedures are available for parties who wish to bring actions for infringement of intellectual property rights. Additionally, in a related document, a mechanism was established for settling disputes among member nations.

Particular provisions of the TRIPS agreement refer to patent, trademark, and copyright protection for intellectual property. The agreement specifically provides copyright protection for computer programs by stating that compilations of data, databases, or other materials are "intellectual creations" and that they are to be protected as copyrightable works. Other provisions relate to trade secrets and the rental of computer programs and cinematographic works.

APPLICATION Law and the Businessperson . . .

Law and the Intellectual Property Owner*

Most intellectual property is sold at a price that reflects heavy research costs for ingenious ideas. Any property that involves high development costs and low production costs is vulnerable to "piracy"—the unauthorized copying and use of the property.

The Business Software Alliance estimates that half of the global market for software is supplied today by pirated products. The International Federation of the Phonographic Industry believes that 20 percent of recorded music is pirated. There is also a problem with the distinction made under copyright law between reproduction for public use (which requires the copyright holder's permission) and reproduction for private use (which, within limits, does not require such permission). The difficulty here is distinguishing between private and public use.

Additionally, current copyright law is based on national boundaries. The Internet, however, knows no such limits. Despite attempts to increase protection for intellectual property on a global level (discussed in this chapter), countries vary widely in their implementation and enforcement of international agreements.

Finding Solutions

There is no complete solution to the growing problem of the piracy of intellectual property via the Internet. Efforts to find partial solutions are being made, nonetheless. One such attempt is the development of pirate-proof ways of transmitting materials. For example, IBM has developed so-called secure packaging for sending digital information over the Internet.

New technologies are also simplifying the task of searching online databases for pirated copies of copyrighted materials. Providers of online "business intelligence," such as Cyveillance, Ewatch, and Cybercheck, help companies detect and combat infringing uses of their software, text, music, or other copyrighted works. These "digital detectives" use special search tools, called "spiders" or "robots," to monitor the Web for sites containing copyrighted works, such as music files. By using these programs or similar software, you can search the Web to detect infringing uses of your copyrighted materials.

Taking Action

Once you have detected an infringing use, you have several options. You can send a cease-and-desist (warning) letter to the infringer, take the infringer to court, or issue a license to the infringer. Often, the last option is preferable, simply because the other two may be impractical. For one thing, efforts to shut down infringing Web sites have had only limited success. In part, this is because of the ease with which a "mirror" site can be created—at a new location. Initiating a lawsuit against a Web site or user may also be difficult because of jurisdictional problems (see Chapter 3).

*This *Application* is not meant to substitute for the services of an attorney who is licensed to practice law in your state.

Checklist for the Intellectual Property Owner

1. Anybody who has ownership rights in intellectual property should be aware that it is increasingly possible for the property to be pirated via the Internet.
2. When detecting an infringing use of trademarked, patented, or copyrighted material, a businessperson should consider the merits of selling the infringer a license to use the property rather than resorting to costly litigation.
3. Generally, businesspersons must weigh potential benefits against potential costs when deciding how many resources to devote to combating the online piracy of their copyrighted works.

Key Terms

copyright 142
cyber mark 137
cybersquatting 139
distributed network 147
domain name 138
intellectual property 130
patent 140
peer-to-peer (P2P) networking 147
service mark 136
trade dress 137
trade name 136
trade secret 148
trademark 131

Chapter Summary Intellectual Property and Internet Law

Trademarks and Related Property (See pages 131–137.)	1. A *trademark* is a distinctive mark, motto, device, or emblem that a manufacturer stamps, prints, or otherwise affixes to the goods it produces so that they may be identified on the market and their origin vouched for. 2. The major federal statutes protecting trademarks and related property are the Lanham Trade-Mark Act of 1946 and the Federal Trademark Dilution Act of 1995. Generally, to be protected, a trademark must be sufficiently distinctive from all competing trademarks. 3. *Trademark infringement* occurs when one uses a mark that is the same as, or confusingly similar to, the protected trademark, service mark, trade name, or trade dress of another without permission when marketing goods or services.
Cyber Marks (See pages 137–140.)	A *cyber mark* is a trademark in cyberspace. Trademark infringement in cyberspace occurs when one person uses a name that is the same as, or confusingly similar to, the protected mark of another in a domain name or in meta tags.
Patents (See pages 140–142.)	1. A *patent* is a grant from the government that gives an inventor the exclusive right to make, use, and sell an invention for a period of twenty years from the date of filing the application for a patent. To be patentable, an invention (or a discovery, process, or design) must be genuine, novel, useful, and not obvious in light of current technology. Computer software may be patented. 2. *Patent infringement* occurs when one uses or sells another's patented design, product, or process without the patent owner's permission.
Copyrights (See pages 142–148.)	1. A *copyright* is an intangible property right granted by federal statute to the author or originator of certain literary or artistic productions. Computer software may be copyrighted. 2. *Copyright infringement* occurs whenever the form or expression of an idea is copied without the permission of the copyright holder. An exception applies if the copying is deemed a "fair use." 3. Copyrights are governed by the Copyright Act of 1976, as amended. To protect copyrights in digital information, Congress passed the No Electronic Theft Act of 1997 and the Digital Millennium Copyright Act of 1998.
Trade Secrets (See pages 148–151.)	*Trade secrets* include customer lists, plans, research and development, pricing information, and so on. Trade secrets are protected under the common law and, in some states, under statutory law against misappropriation by competitors. The Economic Espionage Act of 1996 made the theft of trade secrets a federal crime (see Chapter 6).
Licensing (See page 151.)	In the context of intellectual property rights, a *license* is an agreement in which the owner of a trademark, copyright, patent, or trade secret permits another person or entity to use that property for certain purposes.
International Protection (See pages 151–153.)	International protection for intellectual property exists under various international agreements. A landmark agreement is the 1994 agreement on Trade-Related Aspects of Intellectual Property Rights (TRIPS), which provides for enforcement procedures in all countries signatory to the agreement.

For Review

① What is intellectual property?
② Why are trademarks and patents protected by the law?
③ What laws protect authors' rights in the works they generate?
④ What are trade secrets, and what laws offer protection for this form of intellectual property?
⑤ What steps have been taken to protect intellectual property rights in today's digital age?

Questions and Case Problems

5–1. Copyright Infringement. In which of the following situations would a court likely hold Maruta liable for copyright infringement?

(a) At the library, Maruta photocopies ten pages from a scholarly journal relating to a topic on which she is writing a term paper.
(b) Maruta makes leather handbags and sells them in her small leather shop. She advertises her handbags as "Vutton handbags," hoping that customers might mistakenly assume that they were made by Vuitton, the well-known maker of high-quality luggage and handbags.
(c) Maruta owns a video store. She purchases one copy of all the latest videos from various video manufacturers. Then, using blank videotapes, she makes copies to rent or sell to her customers.
(d) Maruta teaches Latin American history at a small university. She has a videocassette recorder (VCR) and frequently tapes television programs relating to Latin America. She then takes the videos to her classroom so that her students can watch them.

5–2. Trademark Infringement. Alpha Software, Inc., announced a new computer operating system to be marketed under the name McSoftware. McDonald's Corp. wrote Alpha a letter stating that the use of this name infringed on McDonald's family of trademarks characterized by the prefix "Mc" attached to a generic term. Alpha claimed that "Mc" had come into generic use as a prefix and therefore McDonald's had no trademark rights to the prefix itself. Alpha filed an action seeking a declaratory judgment from the court that the mark McSoftware did not infringe on McDonald's federally registered trademarks or common law rights to its marks and would not constitute an unfair trade practice. What factors must the court consider in deciding this issue? What will be the probable outcome of the case? Explain.

5–3. Patent Infringement. John and Andrew Doney invented a hard-bearing device for balancing rotors. Although they registered their invention with the U.S. Patent and Trademark Office, it was never used as an automobile wheel balancer. Some time later, Exetron Corp. produced an automobile wheel balancer that used a hard-bearing device with a support plate similar to that of the Doneys. Given the fact that the Doneys had not used their device for automobile wheel balancing, does Exetron's use of a similar hard-bearing device infringe on the Doneys' patent?

5–4. Copyright Infringement. Max plots a new Batman adventure and carefully and skillfully imitates the art of DC Comics to create an authentic-looking Batman comic. Max is not affiliated with the owners of the copyright to Batman. Can Max publish the comic without infringing on the owners' copyright?

5–5. Copyright Infringement. James Smith, the owner of Michigan Document Services, Inc. (MDS), a commercial copyshop, concluded that it was unnecessary to obtain the copyright owners' permission to reproduce copyrighted materials in course packs. Smith publicized his conclusion, claiming that professors would not have to worry about any delay in production at his shop. MDS then compiled, bound, and sold course packs to students at the University of Michigan without obtaining the permission of the copyright owners. Princeton University Press and two other publishers filed a suit in a federal district court against MDS, alleging copyright infringement. MDS claimed that its course packs were covered under the fair use doctrine. Were they? Explain. [*Princeton University Press v. Michigan Document Services, Inc.*, 99 F.3d 1381 (6th Cir. 1996)]

5–6. Trademark Infringement. Elvis Presley Enterprises, Inc. (EPE), owns all of the trademarks of the Elvis Presley estate. None of these marks is registered for use in the restaurant business. Barry Capece registered "The Velvet Elvis" as a service mark for a restaurant and tavern with the U.S. Patent and Trademark Office. Capece opened a nightclub called "The Velvet Elvis" with a menu, décor, advertising, and promotional events that evoked Elvis Presley and his music. EPE filed a suit in a federal district court against Capece and others, claiming, among other things, that "The Velvet Elvis" service mark infringed on EPE's trademarks. During the trial, witnesses testified that they thought the bar was associated with Elvis Presley. Should Capece be ordered to stop using "The Velvet Elvis" mark? Why or why not? [*Elvis Presley Enterprises, Inc. v. Capece*, 141 F.3d 188 (5th Cir. 1998)]

5–7. Copyrights. Webbworld operates a Web site called Neptics, Inc. The site accepts downloads of certain images from third parties and makes these images available to any user who accesses the site. Before being allowed to view the images, however, the user must pay a subscription fee of $11.95 per month. Over a period of several months, images were available that were originally created by or for Playboy Enterprises, Inc. (PEI). The images were displayed at Neptics's site without PEI's permission. PEI filed a suit in a federal district court against Webbworld, alleging copyright infringement. Webbworld argued in part that it should not be held liable because, like an Internet service provider that furnishes access to the Internet, it did not create or control the content of the information available to its subscribers. Do you agree with Webbworld? Why or why not? [*Playboy Enterprises, Inc. v. Webbworld*, 968 F.Supp. 1171 (N.D.Tex. 1997)]

5–8. Trademark Infringement. A&H Sportswear, Inc., a swimsuit maker, obtained a trademark for its MIRACLESUIT in 1992. The MIRACLESUIT design makes the wearer appear slimmer. The MIRACLESUIT was widely advertised and discussed in the media. The MIRACLESUIT was also sold for a brief time in the Victoria's Secret (VS) catalogue, which is published by Victoria's Secret Catalogue, Inc. In 1993, Victoria's Secret Stores, Inc., began selling a cleavage-enhancing bra, which was named THE MIRACLE BRA and for which a trademark was obtained. The next year, THE MIRACLE BRA swimwear debuted in the VS catalogue and stores. A&H filed a suit in a federal district court against VS Stores and VS Catalogue, alleging in part that THE MIRACLE BRA mark, when applied to swimwear, infringed on the MIRACLESUIT mark. A&H argued that there was a "possibility of confusion" between the marks. The VS entities contended that the appropriate standard was "likelihood of confusion" and that, in this case, there was no likelihood of confusion. In whose favor will the court rule, and why? [*A&H Sportswear, Inc. v. Victoria's Secret Stores, Inc.*, 166 F.3d 197 (3d Cir. 1999)]

TEST YOUR KNOWLEDGE—ANSWER ON THE WEB

5–9. In 1999, Steve and Pierce Thumann and their father, Fred, created Spider Webs, Ltd., a partnership, to, according to Steve, "develop Internet address names." Spider Webs registered nearly two thousand Internet domain names for an average of $70 each, including the names of cities, the names of buildings, names related to a business or trade (such as air conditioning or plumbing), and the names of famous companies. It offered many of the names for sale on its Web site and through eBay.com. Spider Webs registered the domain name "ERNESTANDJULIOGALLO.COM" in Spider Webs's name. E. and J. Gallo Winery filed a suit against Spider Webs, alleging, in part, violations of the Anticybersquatting Consumer Protection Act (ACPA). Gallo asked the court for, among other things, statutory damages. Gallo also sought to have the domain name at issue transferred to Gallo. During the suit, Spider Webs published anti-corporate articles and opinions, and discussions of the suit, at the URL "ERNESTANDJULIOGALLO.COM." Should the court rule in Gallo's favor? Why or why not? [*E. & J. Gallo Winery v. Spider Webs, Ltd.*, 129 F.Supp.2d 1033 (S.D.Tex. 2001)]

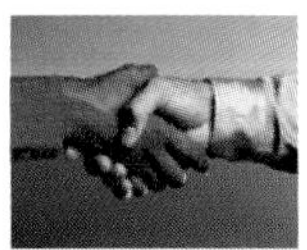

A QUESTION OF ETHICS AND SOCIAL RESPONSIBILITY

5–10. Texaco, Inc., conducts research to develop new products and technology in the petroleum industry. As part of the research, Texaco employees routinely photocopy articles from scientific and medical journals without the permission of the copyright holders. The publishers of the journals brought a copyright infringement action against Texaco in a federal district court. The court ruled that the copying was not a fair use. The U.S. Court of Appeals for the Second Circuit affirmed this ruling "primarily because the dominant purpose of the use is 'archival'—to assemble a set of papers for future reference, thereby serving the same purpose for which additional subscriptions are normally sold, or . . . for which photocopying licenses may be obtained." [*American Geophysical Union v. Texaco, Inc.*, 37 F.3d 881 (2d Cir. 1994)]

1. Do you agree with the court's decision that the copying was not a fair use? Why or why not?
2. Do you think that the law should impose a duty on every person to obtain permission to photocopy or reproduce any article under any circumstance? What would be some of the implications of such a duty for society? Discuss fully.

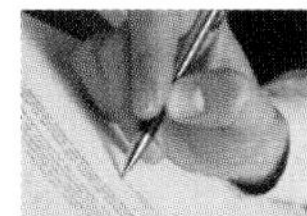

FOR CRITICAL ANALYSIS

5–11. Patent protection in the United States is granted to the first person to invent a given product or process, even though another person may be the first to file for a patent on the same product or process. What are the advantages of this patenting procedure? Can you think of any disadvantages? Explain.

Internet Exercises

Go to the *Business Law Today* home page at **http://blt.westbuslaw.com**. Select "Interactive Study Center" and then click on "Chapter 5." There you will find the following Internet research exercise that you can perform to learn more about intellectual property rights:

Activity 5–1: The Price of Free Speech

Before the Test

Go to the *Business Law Today* home page at **http://blt.westbuslaw.com**. Click on "Interactive Quizzes." You will find at least twenty interactive questions relating to this chapter.

CHAPTER 6

Criminal Law and Cyber Crimes

"No State shall . . . deprive any person of life, liberty, or property without due process of law, nor deny to any person within its jurisdiction the equal protection of the laws."

Fourteenth Amendment to the U.S. Constitution, July 28, 1868

CHAPTER CONTENTS

LEARNING OBJECTIVES

After reading this chapter, you should be able to answer the following questions:

① What two elements must exist before a person can be held liable for a crime? Can a corporation be liable for crimes?

② What are five broad categories of crimes? What is white-collar crime?

③ What defenses might be raised by criminal defendants to avoid liability for criminal acts?

④ What constitutional safeguards exist to protect persons accused of crimes? What are the basic steps in the criminal process?

⑤ What is cyber crime? What laws apply to crimes committed in cyberspace?

Various sanctions are used to bring about a society in which individuals engaging in business can compete and flourish. These sanctions include damages for various types of tortious conduct (as discussed in Chapter 4), damages for breach of contract (to be discussed in Chapter 13), and the equitable remedies discussed in Chapter 1. Additional sanctions are imposed under criminal law. Many statutes regulating business provide for criminal as well as civil sanctions. Therefore, criminal law joins civil law as an important element in the legal environment of business.

In this chapter, following a brief summary of the major differences between criminal and civil law, we look at how crimes are classified and what elements must be present for criminal liability to exist. We then examine various categories of crime, the defenses that can be raised to avoid liability for criminal actions, and criminal procedural law. Criminal procedural law attempts to ensure that a criminal defendant's right to the Fourteenth Amendment's guarantee of "due process of law" (see the chapter-opening quotation) is enforced.

Since the advent of computer networks and, more recently, the Internet, new types of crimes or new variations of traditional crimes have been committed in cyberspace. For that reason, they are often referred to as **cyber crime**. Generally, cyber crime refers more to the way particular crimes are committed than to a new category of crimes. We devote the concluding pages of this chapter to a discussion of this increasingly significant area of criminal activity.

CYBER CRIME
A crime that occurs online, in the virtual community of the Internet, as opposed to the physical world.

Civil Law and Criminal Law

Remember from Chapter 1 that *civil law* spells out the duties that exist between persons or between persons and their governments, excluding the duty not to commit crimes. Contract law, for example, is part of civil law. The whole body of tort law, which deals with the infringement by one person on the legally recognized rights of another, is also an area of civil law.

Criminal law, in contrast, has to do with crime. A **crime** can be defined as a wrong against society proclaimed in a statute and, if committed, punishable by society through fines and/or imprisonment—and, in some cases, death. As mentioned in Chapter 1, because crimes are *offenses against society as a whole*, they are prosecuted by a public official, such as a district attorney (D.A.), not by victims.

CRIME
A wrong against society proclaimed in a statute and, if committed, punishable by society through fines, removal from public office, and/or imprisonment—and, in some cases, death.

KEY DIFFERENCES BETWEEN CIVIL LAW AND CRIMINAL LAW

Because the state has extensive resources at its disposal when prosecuting criminal cases, there are numerous procedural safeguards to protect the rights of defendants. One of these safeguards is the higher standard of proof that applies in a criminal case. As you can see in Exhibit 6–1 on the next page, which summarizes some of the key differences between civil law and criminal law, in a civil case the plaintiff usually must prove his or her case by a *preponderance of the evidence*. Under this standard, the plaintiff must convince the court that, based on the evidence presented by both parties, it is more likely than not that the plaintiff's allegation is true.

In a criminal case, in contrast, the state must prove its case **beyond a reasonable doubt**. Every juror in a criminal case must be convinced, beyond a reasonable doubt, of the defendant's guilt. The higher standard of proof in criminal cases reflects a fundamental social value—a belief that it is worse to convict an innocent individual than to let a guilty person go free. We will look at other safeguards later in the chapter, in the context of criminal procedure.

BEYOND A REASONABLE DOUBT
The standard of proof used in criminal cases. If there is any reasonable doubt that a criminal defendant did not commit the crime with which she or he has been charged, then the verdict must be "not guilty."

CIVIL LIABILTY FOR CRIMINAL ACTS

Those who commit crimes may be subject to both civil and criminal liability. • **EXAMPLE 6.1** Joe is walking down the street, minding his own business, when suddenly a person attacks him. In the ensuing struggle, the attacker stabs Joe several times, seriously injuring him. A police officer restrains and arrests the wrongdoer. In this situation, the attacker may be subject both to criminal prosecution by the state and to a tort lawsuit brought by Joe. • Exhibit 6–2 on page 161 illustrates how the same act can result in both a tort action and a criminal action against the wrongdoer.

EXHIBIT 6–1 CIVIL AND CRIMINAL LAW COMPARED

ISSUE	CIVIL LAW	CRIMINAL LAW
Area of concern	Rights and duties between individuals and between persons and their government	Offenses against society as a whole
Wrongful act	Harm to a person or to a person's property	Violation of a statute that prohibits some type of activity
Party who brings suit	Person who suffered harm	The state
Standard of proof	Preponderance of the evidence	Beyond a reasonable doubt
Remedy	Damages to compensate for the harm, or a decree to achieve an equitable result	Punishment (fine, removal from public office, imprisonment, or death)

Classification of Crimes

FELONY
A crime—such as arson, murder, rape, or robbery—that carries the most severe sanctions, which range from one year in a state or federal prison to the death penalty.

Depending on their degree of seriousness, crimes are classified as felonies or misdemeanors. **Felonies** are serious crimes punishable by death or by imprisonment in a federal or state penitentiary for more than a year. The Model Penal Code[1] provides for four degrees of felony: (1) capital offenses, for which the maximum penalty is death; (2) first degree felonies, punishable by a maximum penalty of life imprisonment; (3) second degree felonies, punishable by a maximum of ten years' imprisonment; and (4) third degree felonies, punishable by a maximum of five years' imprisonment.

MISDEMEANOR
A lesser crime than a felony, punishable by a fine or incarceration in jail for up to one year.

Under federal law and in most states, any crime that is not a felony is considered a **misdemeanor.** Misdemeanors are crimes punishable by a fine or by confinement for up to a year. If incarcerated (imprisoned), the guilty party goes to a local jail instead of a prison. Disorderly conduct and trespass are common misdemeanors. Some states have different classes of misdemeanors. For example, in Illinois misdemeanors are either Class A (confinement for up to a year), Class B (not more than six months), or Class C (not more than thirty days). Whether a crime is a felony or a misdemeanor can also determine whether the case is tried in a magistrate's court (for example, by a justice of the peace) or in a general trial court.

PETTY OFFENSE
In criminal law, the least serious kind of criminal offense, such as a traffic or building-code violation.

In most jurisdictions, **petty offenses** are considered to be a subset of misdemeanors. Petty offenses are minor violations, such as driving under the influence of alcohol or violations of building codes. Even for petty offenses, however, a guilty party can be put in jail for a few days, fined, or both, depending on state or local law.

1. The American Law Institute issued the Official Draft of the Model Penal Code in 1962. The Model Penal Code is not a uniform code. Uniformity of criminal law among the states is not as important as uniformity in other areas of the law. Types of crimes vary with local circumstances, and it is appropriate that punishments vary accordingly. The Model Penal Code contains four parts: (1) general provisions, (2) definitions of special crimes, (3) provisions concerning treatment and corrections, and (4) provisions on the organization of corrections.

EXHIBIT 6–2 TORT LAWSUIT AND CRIMINAL PROSECUTION FOR THE SAME ACT

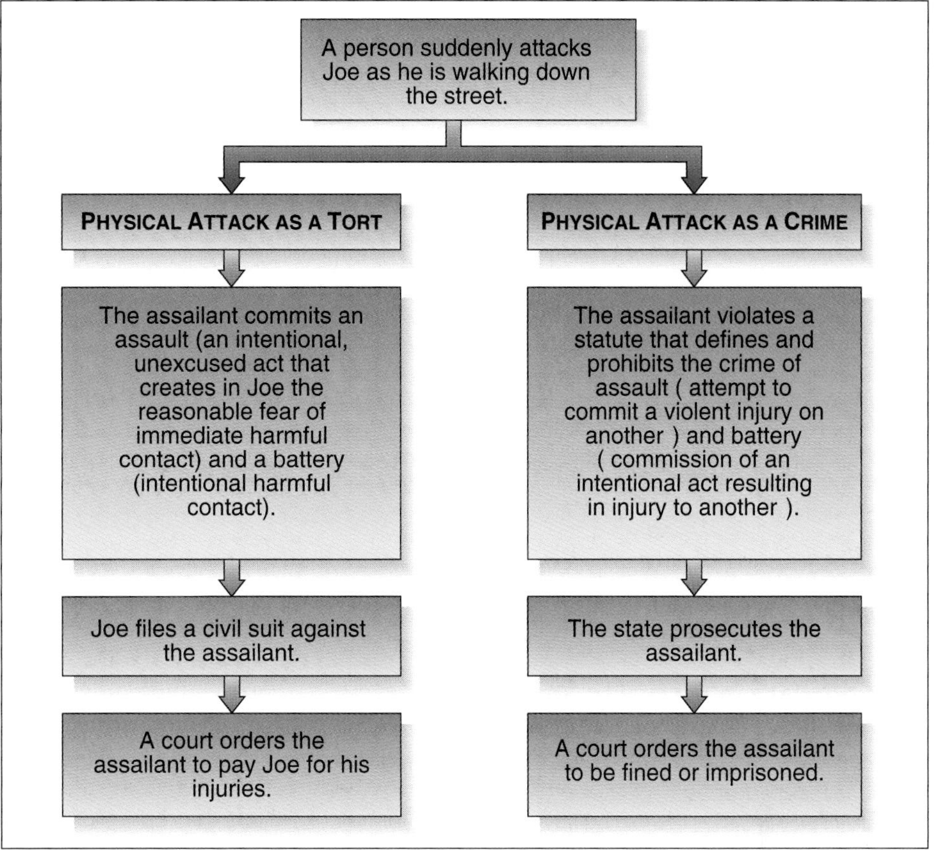

Criminal Liability

Two elements must exist simultaneously for a person to be convicted of a crime: (1) the performance of a prohibited act and (2) a specified state of mind or intent on the part of the actor. Every criminal statute prohibits certain behavior. Most crimes require an act of *commission;* that is, a person must *do* something in order to be accused of a crime.[2] In some cases, an act of *omission* can be a crime, but only when a person has a legal duty to perform the omitted act. Failure to file a tax return is an example of an omission that is a crime.

"I haven't committed a crime. What I did was fail to comply with the law."

DAVID DINKINS, 1927–
(Mayor of New York City, 1990–1994)

The *guilty act* requirement is based on one of the premises of criminal law—that a person is punished for harm done to society. Thinking about killing someone or about stealing a car may be wrong, but the thoughts do no harm until they are translated into action. Of course, a person can be punished for attempting murder or robbery, but normally only if he or she took substantial steps toward the criminal objective.

A *wrongful mental state*[3] is as necessary as a wrongful act in establishing criminal liability. What constitutes such a mental state varies according to the wrongful action. For murder, the act is the taking of a life, and the mental state is the intent to take life.

2. Called the *actus reus* (pronounced *ak*-tuhs *ray*-uhs), or "guilty act."
3. Called the *mens rea* (pronounced mehns *ray*-uh), or "evil intent."

For theft, the guilty act is the taking of another person's property, and the mental state involves both the knowledge that the property belongs to another and the intent to deprive the owner of it.

Criminal liability typically arises for actions that violate state criminal statutes. Federal criminal jurisdiction is limited to crimes that occur outside the jurisdiction of any state, crimes involving interstate commerce or communications, crimes that interfere with the operation of the federal government or its agents, and crimes directed at citizens or property located outside the United States. Federal jurisdiction also exists if a federal law or a federal government agency (such as the U.S. Department of Justice or the federal Environmental Protection Agency) defines a certain type of action as a crime. Today, businesspersons are subject to criminal penalties under numerous federal laws and regulations. We will examine many of these laws in later chapters of this text.

Regardless of the type of criminal activity involved, generally the rule is that without the intent required by law for a particular crime, there is no crime. At issue in the following case was whether the required intent for a crime was present.

ON THE WEB Many state criminal codes are now online. To find your state's code, go to **http://www.findlaw.com** and select "State" under the link to "Laws: Cases and Codes."

CASE 6.1 In re Gavin T.

California Court of Appeal,
First District, Division 5, 1998.
66 Cal.App.4th 238,
77 Cal.Rptr.2d 701.

HISTORICAL AND SOCIAL SETTING *Many observers believe that public education deteriorated between the 1950s and the 1990s. Some commentators blame this deterioration on changing achievement standards. Others fault a societal mistrust of institutional authority in general. Suggestions for improving education and the educational environment also range across a wide spectrum. Despite these differences, however, a safe environment is generally considered a necessity for a quality education. A safe environment might be defined as one in which there is little crime or unruly behavior. Discipline is seen as a key to creating a safe environment.*

FACTS On the grounds of a school, Gavin T., a fifteen-year-old student, was eating lunch. He threw a half-eaten apple toward the outside wall of a classroom some distance away. The apple sailed through a slowly closing door and struck a teacher who was in the room. The teacher was knocked to the floor and lost consciousness for a few minutes. Gavin was charged, in a California state court, with assault by "any means of force likely to produce great bodily injury." The court found that he did not intend to hit the teacher but intended only to see the apple splatter against the outside wall. To send a "message" to his classmates that his actions were wrong, however, the court convicted him of the charge. Gavin appealed.

ISSUE Can a defendant be convicted of assault without having had the intent to commit the crime?

DECISION No. The state intermediate appellate court vacated the order of the lower court and remanded the case with instructions to dismiss it.

REASON The state intermediate appellate court pointed out that under California law, "to be found guilty of a criminal assault, one must have either the intent to batter, hit, strike, or wrongfully touch a victim; or one must have a general criminal intent to do an act which is inherently dangerous to human life—such as firing a cannon at an inhabited castle, or driving an elephant into a crowded judicial conference." The court emphasized that in this case, there was no evidence that Gavin intended to strike the teacher with the apple and that "all the evidence and circumstances showed the contrary." Gavin's "urge" to see the apple splatter against the wall "may have been juvenile and, therefore, rather appropriate to appellant's age; but it did not constitute a criminal intent to batter the victim or a general criminal intent to act in a manner inherently dangerous to human life."

FOR CRITICAL ANALYSIS—Ethical Consideration *If the lower court's "message" to Gavin and his classmates was that reckless behavior would not be condoned, what was the appellate court's message to the lower court?*

Corporate Criminal Liability

At one time, it was thought that a corporation could not incur criminal liability because, although a corporation is a legal person, it can act only through its agents (corporate directors, officers, and employees). Therefore, the corporate entity itself could not "intend" to commit a crime. Under modern criminal law, however, a corporation may be held liable for crimes. Obviously, corporations cannot be imprisoned, but they can be fined or denied certain legal privileges (such as a license). Today, corporations are normally liable for the crimes committed by their agents and employees within the course and scope of their employment.

Corporate directors and officers are personally liable for the crimes they commit, regardless of whether the crimes were committed for their personal benefit or on the corporation's behalf. Additionally, corporate directors and officers may be held liable for the actions of employees under their supervision. Under what has become known as the "responsible corporate officer" doctrine, a court may impose criminal liability on a corporate officer regardless of whether she or he participated in, directed, or even knew about a given criminal violation.

• **EXAMPLE 6.2** In *United States v. Park*,[4] the chief executive officer of a national supermarket chain was held personally liable for sanitation violations in corporate warehouses, in which the food was exposed to contamination by rodents. The court imposed personal liability on the corporate officer not because he intended the crime or even knew about it but because he was in a "responsible relationship" to the corporation and had the power to prevent the violation.• Since the *Park* decision, courts have applied this "responsible corporate officer" doctrine on a number of occasions to hold corporate officers liable for their employees' statutory violations. The following case illustrates that corporate officers and supervisors who oversee operations causing environmental harm may be held liable under the criminal provisions of environmental statutes.

4. 421 U.S. 658, 95 S.Ct. 1903, 44 L.Ed.2d 489 (1975).

CASE 6.2 United States v. Hanousek

United States Court of Appeals,
Ninth Circuit, 1999.
176 F.3d 1116.
http://www.ca9.uscourts.gov[a]

FACTS Edward Hanousek worked for Pacific & Arctic Railway and Navigation Company (P&A) as a roadmaster of the White Pass & Yukon Railroad in Alaska. Hanousek was responsible "for every detail of the safe and efficient maintenance and construction of track, structures and marine facilities of the entire railroad," including special projects. One project was a rock quarry, known as "6-mile," above the Skagway River. Next to the quarry, and just beneath the surface, ran a high-pressure oil pipeline owned by Pacific & Arctic Pipeline, Inc., P&A's sister company. When the quarry's backhoe operator punctured the pipeline, an estimated 1,000 to 5,000 gallons of oil were discharged into the river. Hanousek was charged with, among other things, negligently discharging a harmful quantity of oil into a navigable water of the United States in violation of the criminal provisions of the Clean Water Act (CWA). After a trial in a federal district court, a jury convicted Hanousek, and the court imposed a sentence of six months' imprisonment, six months in a halfway house, six months' supervised release, and a fine of $5,000. Hanousek appealed to the U.S. Court of Appeals for the Ninth Circuit, arguing in part that the

(continued)

a. The U.S. Court of Appeals for the Ninth Circuit maintains this Web site. Click on the "OPINIONS" oval. From that page, click on the "1999" icon, and when the menu opens, click on "March." Scroll down to "USA V HANOUSEK" and click on the case name to access the case.

CASE 6.2—Continued

statute under which he was convicted violated his right to due process because he was not aware of what the CWA required.

ISSUE Were Hanousek's due process rights violated?

DECISION No. The U.S. Court of Appeals for the Ninth Circuit affirmed Hanousek's conviction.

REASON A corporate manager who has responsibility for operations with the potential to cause harm can be held criminally liable for harm that results even if he or she does not actually know of the specific statute under which liability may be imposed. The CWA is public welfare legislation, which "is designed to protect the public from potentially harmful or injurious items and may render criminal a type of conduct that a reasonable person should know is subject to stringent public regulation." The court stated, "[I]t is well established that a public welfare statute may subject a person to criminal liability for his or her ordinary negligence without violating due process." When "dangerous or deleterious [harmful] devices or products or obnoxious waste materials are involved, the probability of regulation is so great that anyone who is aware that he is in possession of them or dealing with them must be presumed to be aware of the regulation." Hanousek knew about the pipeline and the danger that a puncture would pose. "Therefore, Hanousek should have been alerted to the probability of strict regulation."

FOR CRITICAL ANALYSIS—Environmental Consideration *If corporate actors were able to avoid responsibility for violations of environmental statutes of which they were unaware, what might result?*

Types of Crimes

The number of acts that are defined as criminal is nearly endless. Federal, state, and local laws provide for the classification and punishment of hundreds of thousands of different criminal acts. Traditionally, though, crimes have been grouped into five broad categories, or types: violent crime (crimes against persons), property crime, public order crime, white-collar crime, and organized crime. Cyber crime—which consists of crimes committed in cyberspace with the use of computers—is, as mentioned earlier in this chapter, less a category of crime than a new way to commit crime. We will examine cyber crime later in this chapter.

Violent Crime

Crimes against persons, because they cause others to suffer harm or death, are referred to as *violent crimes*. Murder is a violent crime. So is sexual assault, or rape. Assault and battery, which were discussed in Chapter 4 in the context of tort law, are also classified as violent crimes. **Robbery**—defined as the taking of money, personal property, or any other article of value from a person by means of force or fear—is also a violent crime. Typically, states have more severe penalties for *aggravated robbery*—robbery with the use of a deadly weapon.

ROBBERY
The act of forcefully and unlawfully taking personal property of any value from another; force or intimidation is usually necessary for an act of theft to be considered a robbery.

Each of these violent crimes is further classified by degree, depending on the circumstances surrounding the criminal act. These circumstances include the intent of the person committing the crime, whether a weapon was used, and (in cases other than murder) the level of pain and suffering experienced by the victim.

Property Crime

The most common type of criminal activity is property crime—crimes in which the goal of the offender is some form of economic gain or the damaging of property.

Robbery is a form of property crime, as well as a violent crime, because the offender seeks to gain the property of another. We look here at a number of other crimes that fall within the general category of property crime.

BURGLARY
The unlawful entry or breaking into a building with the intent to commit a felony. (Some state statutes expand this to include the intent to commit any crime.)

Burglary Traditionally, **burglary** was defined under the common law as breaking and entering the dwelling of another at night with the intent to commit a felony. Originally, the definition was aimed at protecting an individual's home and its occupants. Most state statutes have eliminated some of the requirements found in the common law definition. The time at which the breaking and entering occurs, for example, is usually immaterial. State statutes frequently omit the element of breaking, and some states do not require that the building be a dwelling. Aggravated burglary, which is defined as burglary with the use of a deadly weapon, burglary of a dwelling, or both, incurs a greater penalty.

LARCENY
The wrongful taking and carrying away of another person's personal property with the intent to permanently deprive the owner of the property. Some states classify larceny as either grand or petit, depending on the property's value.

Larceny Any person who wrongfully or fraudulently takes and carries away another person's personal property is guilty of **larceny.** Larceny includes the fraudulent intent to deprive an owner permanently of property. Many business-related larcenies entail fraudulent conduct. Whereas robbery involves force or fear, larceny does not. Therefore, picking pockets is larceny. Similarly, taking company products and supplies home for personal use, if one is not authorized to do so, is larceny.

In most states, the definition of property that is subject to larceny statutes has expanded. Stealing computer programs may constitute larceny even though the "property" consists of magnetic impulses. Stealing computer time can also constitute larceny. So, too, can the theft of natural gas. Trade secrets can be subject to larceny statutes. Obtaining another's phone-card number and then using that number, without authorization, to place long-distance calls is a form of property theft. These types of larceny are covered by "theft of services" statutes in many jurisdictions.

The common law distinguishes between grand and petit larceny depending on the value of the property taken. Many states have abolished this distinction, but in those that have not, grand larceny is a felony and petit larceny, a misdemeanor.

Obtaining Goods by False Pretenses It is a criminal act to obtain goods by means of false pretenses—for example, buying groceries with a check, knowing that one has insufficient funds to cover it. Statutes dealing with such illegal activities vary widely from state to state.

"A large number of houses deserve to be burnt."

H. G. WELLS,
1866–1946
(English author)

Receiving Stolen Goods It is a crime to receive stolen goods. The recipient of such goods need not know the true identity of the owner or the thief. All that is necessary is that the recipient knows or should have known that the goods are stolen, which implies an intent to deprive the owner of those goods.

ARSON
The intentional burning of another's dwelling. Some statutes have expanded this to include any real property regardless of ownership and the destruction of property by other means—for example, by explosion.

Arson The willful and malicious burning of a building (and in some states, personal property) owned by another is the crime of **arson.** At common law, arson traditionally applied only to burning down another person's house. The law was designed to protect human life. Today, arson statutes have been extended to cover the destruction of any building, regardless of ownership, by fire or explosion.

Every state has a special statute that covers a person's burning a building for the purpose of collecting insurance. • **EXAMPLE 6.3** If Smith owns an insured apartment building that is falling apart and sets fire to it himself or pays someone else to do so, he is guilty not only of arson but also of defrauding insurers, which is an attempted larceny. • Of course, the insurer need not pay the claim when insurance fraud is proved.

FORGERY
The fraudulent making or altering of any writing in a way that changes the legal rights and liabilities of another.

Forgery The fraudulent making or altering of any writing in a way that changes the legal rights and liabilities of another is **forgery.** If, without authorization, Severson signs Bennett's name to the back of a check made out to Bennett, Severson is committing forgery. Forgery also includes changing trademarks, falsifying public records, counterfeiting, and altering a legal document.

PUBLIC ORDER CRIME

Historically, societies have always outlawed activities that are considered to be contrary to public values and morals. Today, the most common public order crimes include public drunkenness, prostitution, gambling, and illegal drug use. These crimes are sometimes referred to as victimless crimes because they often harm only the offender. From a broader perspective, however, they are deemed detrimental to society as a whole because they often create an environment that may give rise to property and violent crimes.

WHITE-COLLAR CRIME

WHITE-COLLAR CRIME
Nonviolent crime committed by individuals or corporations to obtain a personal or business advantage.

Crimes that typically occur only in the business context are commonly referred to as **white-collar crimes.** Although there is no official definition of white-collar crime, the term is popularly used to mean an illegal act or series of acts committed by an individual or business entity using some nonviolent means. Usually, this kind of crime is committed in the course of a legitimate occupation. Corporate crimes fall into this category.

EMBEZZLEMENT
The fraudulent appropriation of funds or other property by a person to whom the funds or property has been entrusted.

Embezzlement When a person entrusted with another person's property or money fraudulently appropriates it, **embezzlement** occurs. Typically, embezzlement involves an employee who steals funds. Banks face this problem, and so do a number of businesses in which corporate officers or accountants "jimmy" the books to cover up the fraudulent conversion of funds for their own benefit. Embezzlement is not larceny, because the wrongdoer does not physically take the property from the possession of another, and it is not robbery, because force or fear is not used.

It does not matter whether the accused takes the funds from the victim or from a third person. If, as the financial officer of a large corporation, Saunders pockets a certain number of checks from third parties that were given to her to deposit into the corporate account, she is embezzling.

Ordinarily, an embezzler who returns what has been taken will not be prosecuted, because the owner usually will not take the time to make a complaint, give depositions, and appear in court. That the accused intended eventually to return the embezzled property, however, does not constitute a sufficient defense to the crime of embezzlement.

Mail and Wire Fraud One of the most potent weapons against white-collar criminals is the Mail Fraud Act of 1990.[5] Under this act, it is a federal crime (mail fraud) to use the mails to defraud the public. Illegal use of the mails must involve (1) mailing or causing someone else to mail a writing—something written, printed, or photocopied—for the purpose of executing a scheme to defraud and (2) a contemplated or an organized scheme to defraud by false pretenses. If, for example, Johnson advertises by mail the sale of a cure for cancer that he knows to be fraudulent because it has no medical validity, he can be prosecuted for fraudulent use of the mails.

5. 18 U.S.C. Sections 1341–1342.

Federal law also makes it a crime (wire fraud) to use wire (for example, the telephone), radio, or television transmissions to defraud.[6] Violators may be fined up to $1,000, imprisoned for up to five years, or both. If the violation affects a financial institution, the violator may be fined up to $1 million, imprisoned for up to thirty years, or both.

"[It is] very much better to bribe a person than kill him."
SIR WINSTON CHURCHILL, 1874–1965 (British prime minister, 1940–1945, 1951–1955)

Bribery Basically, three types of bribery are considered crimes: bribery of public officials, commercial bribery, and bribery of foreign officials. The attempt to influence a public official to act in a way that serves a private interest is a crime. As an element of this crime, intent must be present and proved. The bribe can be anything the recipient considers to be valuable. Realize that *the crime of bribery occurs when the bribe is offered.* It does not matter whether the person to whom the bribe is offered accepts the bribe or agrees to perform whatever action is desired by the person offering the bribe. *Accepting a bribe* is a separate crime.

Typically, people make commercial bribes to obtain proprietary information, cover up an inferior product, or secure new business. Industrial espionage sometimes involves commercial bribes. For example, a person in one firm may offer an employee in a competing firm some type of payoff in exchange for trade secrets or pricing schedules. So-called kickbacks, or payoffs for special favors or services, are a form of commercial bribery in some situations.

Bribing foreign officials to obtain favorable business contracts is a crime. The Foreign Corrupt Practices Act of 1977, which is presented as the *Landmark in the Law* in Chapter 7, was passed to curb the use of bribery by American businesspersons in securing foreign contracts.

Bankruptcy Fraud Today, federal bankruptcy law (see Chapter 23) allows individuals and businesses to be relieved of oppressive debt through bankruptcy proceedings. Numerous white-collar crimes may be committed during the many phases of a bankruptcy proceeding. A creditor, for example, may file a false claim against the debtor, which is a crime. Also, a debtor may fraudulently transfer assets to favored parties before or after the petition for bankruptcy is filed. For example, a company-owned automobile may be "sold" at a bargain price to a trusted friend or relative. Closely related to the crime of fraudulent transfer of property is the crime of fraudulent concealment of property, such as hiding gold coins.

The Theft of Trade Secrets As discussed in Chapter 5, trade secrets constitute a form of intellectual property that for many businesses can be extremely valuable. The Economic Espionage Act of 1996[7] made the theft of trade secrets a federal crime. The act also made it a federal crime to buy or possess trade secrets of another person, knowing that the trade secrets were stolen or otherwise acquired without the owner's authorization.

Violations of the act can result in steep penalties. An individual who violates the act can be imprisoned for up to ten years and fined up to $500,000. If a corporation or other organization violates the act, it can be fined up to $5 million. Additionally, the law provides that any property acquired as a result of the violation and any property used in the commission of the violation are subject to criminal *forfeiture*—meaning that the government can take the property. A theft of trade secrets conducted via the Internet, for example, could result in the forfeiture of every computer, printer, or other device used to commit or facilitate the violation.

---

6. 18 U.S.C. Section 1343.
7. 18 U.S.C. Sections 1831–1839.

Insider Trading An individual who obtains "inside information" about the plans of a publicly listed corporation can often make stock-trading profits by using the information to guide decisions relating to the purchase or sale of corporate securities. **Insider trading** is a violation of securities law and will be considered more fully in Chapter 29. At this point, it may be said that one who possesses inside information and who has a duty not to disclose it to outsiders may not profit from the purchase or sale of securities based on that information until the information is available to the public.

INSIDER TRADING
The purchase or sale of securities on the basis of "inside information" (information that has not been made available to the public).

ORGANIZED CRIME

As mentioned, white-collar crime takes place within the confines of the legitimate business world. *Organized crime,* in contrast, operates *illegitimately* by, among other things, providing illegal goods and services. For organized crime, the traditional preferred markets are gambling, prostitution, illegal narcotics, pornography, and loan sharking (lending money at higher than legal interest rates), along with more recent ventures into counterfeiting and credit-card scams.

Money Laundering The profits from illegal activities amount to billions of dollars a year, particularly the profits from illegal drug transactions and, to a lesser extent, from racketeering, prostitution, and gambling. Under federal law, banks, savings and loan associations, and other financial institutions are required to report currency transactions involving more than $10,000. Consequently, those who engage in illegal activities face difficulties in depositing their cash profits from illegal transactions.

As an alternative to simply storing cash from illegal transactions in a safe-deposit box, wrongdoers and racketeers have invented ways to launder "dirty" money to make it "clean." This **money laundering** is done through legitimate businesses.

MONEY LAUNDERING
Falsely reporting income that has been obtained through criminal activity as income obtained through a legitimate business enterprise—in effect, "laundering" the "dirty money."

● **EXAMPLE 6.4** Matt, a successful drug dealer, becomes a partner with a restaurateur. Little by little, the restaurant shows an increasing profit. As partner in the restaurant, Matt is able to report the "profits" of the restaurant as legitimate income on which he pays federal and state taxes. He can then spend those monies without worrying that his lifestyle may exceed the level possible with his reported income. ●

The Federal Bureau of Investigation estimates that organized crime has invested tens of billions of dollars in as many as a hundred thousand business establishments in the United States for the purpose of money laundering. Globally, it is estimated that more than $500 billion in illegal money moves through the world banking system every year.

The Racketeer Influenced and Corrupt Organizations Act In 1970, in an effort to curb the apparently increasing entry of organized crime into the legitimate business world, Congress passed the Racketeer Influenced and Corrupt Organizations Act (RICO).[8] The act, which was enacted as part of the Organized Crime Control Act, makes it a federal crime to (1) use income obtained from racketeering activity to purchase any interest in an enterprise, (2) acquire or maintain an interest in an enterprise through racketeering activity, (3) conduct or participate in the affairs of an enterprise through racketeering activity, or (4) conspire to do any of the preceding activities.

Racketeering activity is not a new type of substantive crime created by RICO; rather, RICO incorporates by reference twenty-six separate types of federal crimes and nine types of state felonies[9] and declares that if a person commits two of these offenses, he or she is guilty of "racketeering activity." Additionally, RICO is more often used today as an effective tool in attacking white-collar crimes rather than organized crime.

8. 18 U.S.C. Sections 1961–1968.
9. See 18 U.S.C. Section 1961(1)(A).

ON THE WEB You can gain insights into criminal law and procedures, including a number of the defenses that can be raised to avoid criminal liability, by looking at some of the famous criminal law cases included on Court TV's Web site. Go to **http://www.courttv.com/index.html**.

In the event of a violation, the statute permits the government to seek civil penalties, including the divestiture of a defendant's interest in a business (called forfeiture) or the dissolution of the business. Perhaps the most controversial aspect of RICO is that, in some cases, private individuals are allowed to recover three times their actual losses (treble damages), plus attorneys' fees, for business injuries caused by a violation of the statute. Under criminal provisions of RICO, any individual found guilty of a violation is subject to a fine of up to $25,000 per violation, imprisonment for up to twenty years, or both. Additionally, the statute provides that those who violate RICO may be required to forfeit (give up) any assets, in the form of property or cash, that were acquired as a result of the illegal activity or that were "involved in" or an "instrumentality of" the activity.

Defenses to Criminal Liability

Among the most important defenses to criminal liability are infancy, intoxication, insanity, mistake, consent, duress, justifiable use of force, entrapment, and the statute of limitations. Many of these defenses involve assertions that the intent requirement for criminal liability is lacking. Also, in some cases, defendants are given immunity and thus relieved, at least in part, of criminal liability for crimes they committed. We look at each of these defenses here.

Note that procedural violations, such as obtaining evidence without a valid search warrant, may operate as defenses also. As you will read later in this chapter, evidence obtained in violation of a defendant's constitutional rights normally may not be admitted in court. If the evidence is suppressed, then there may be no basis for prosecuting the defendant.

Fourteen-year-old Lionel Tate walks into the courtroom for a hearing at a courthouse in Fort Lauderdale, Florida, in March 2001. Tate, who was convicted for murdering his playmate when he was only thirteen years old, is now serving a life sentence. Should a juvenile who commits a criminal act be tried in a regular court, or should a juvenile be entitled to the protections associated with juvenile courts?

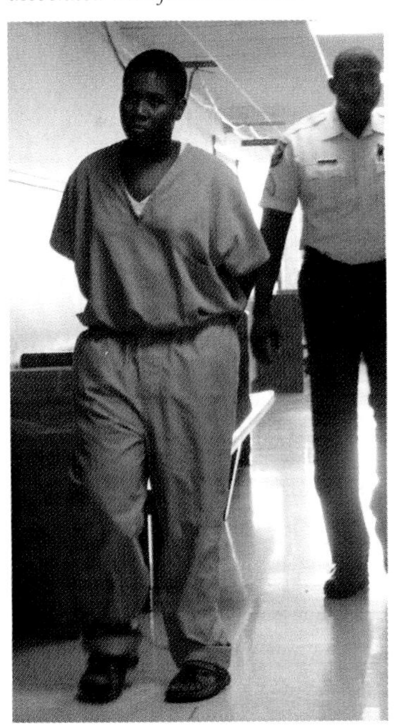

INFANCY

The term *infant,* as used in the law, refers to any person who has not yet reached the age of majority (see Chapter 10). In all states, certain courts handle cases involving children who are alleged to have violated the law. In some states, juvenile courts handle children's cases exclusively. In other states, however, courts that handle children's cases may also have jurisdiction over other matters.

Originally, juvenile court hearings were informal, and lawyers were rarely present. Since 1967, however, when the United States Supreme Court ordered that a child charged with delinquency must be allowed to consult with an attorney before being committed to a state institution,[10] juvenile court hearings have become more formal. In some states, a child may be treated as an adult and tried in a regular court if she or he is above a certain age (usually fourteen) and is guilty of a felony, such as rape or murder.

INTOXICATION

The law recognizes two types of intoxication, whether from drugs or from alcohol: *involuntary* and *voluntary.* Involuntary intoxication occurs when a person either is physically forced to ingest or inject an intoxicating substance or is unaware that a substance contains drugs or alcohol. Involuntary intoxication is a defense to a crime if its effect was to make a person incapable of obeying the law or incapable of understanding that

10. *In re Gault,* 387 U.S. 1, 87 S.Ct. 1428, 18 L.Ed.2d 527 (1967).

"Insanity is often the logic of an accurate mind overtaxed."

OLIVER WENDELL HOLMES, JR., 1841–1935 (Associate justice of the United States Supreme Court, 1902–1932)

the act committed was wrong. Voluntary intoxication is rarely a defense, but it may be effective in cases in which the defendant was *extremely* intoxicated when committing the wrong.

INSANITY

Just as a child is often judged incapable of the state of mind required to commit a crime, so also may be someone suffering from a mental illness. Thus, insanity may be a defense to a criminal charge. The courts have had difficulty deciding what the test for legal insanity should be, however, and psychiatrists as well as lawyers are critical of the tests used. Almost all federal courts and some states use the relatively liberal standard set forth in the Model Penal Code:

> A person is not responsible for criminal conduct if at the time of such conduct as a result of mental disease or defect he lacks substantial capacity either to appreciate the wrongfulness of his conduct or to conform his conduct to the requirements of the law.

Andrea Yates, who allegedly drowned her five children, pleaded not guilty to the crime by reason of insanity. How will the court decide whether she was insane when she committed the crime?

Some states use the *M'Naghten* test,[11] under which a criminal defendant is not responsible if, at the time of the offense, he or she did not know the nature and quality of the act or did not know that the act was wrong. Other states use the irresistible-impulse test. A person operating under an irresistible impulse may know an act is wrong but cannot refrain from doing it.

MISTAKE

Everyone has heard the saying, "Ignorance of the law is no excuse." Ordinarily, ignorance of the law or a mistaken idea about what the law requires is not a valid defense. In some states, however, that rule has been modified. Criminal defendants who claim that they honestly did not know that they were breaking a law may have a valid defense if (1) the law was not published or reasonably made known to the public or (2) the defendant relied on an official statement of the law that was erroneous.

A *mistake of fact,* as opposed to a *mistake of law,* operates as a defense if it negates the mental state necessary to commit a crime. • **EXAMPLE 6.5** If Oliver Wheaton mistakenly walks off with Julie Tyson's briefcase because he thinks it is his, there is no theft. Theft requires knowledge that the property belongs to another. (If Wheaton's act causes Tyson to incur damages, however, Wheaton may be subject to liability for trespass to personal property or conversion, torts that were discussed in Chapter 4.) •

CONSENT

CONSENT
The voluntary agreement to a proposition or an act of another; a concurrence of wills.

COMPARE "Ignorance" is a lack of information. "Mistake" is a confusion of information.

What if a victim consents to a crime or even encourages the person intending a criminal act to commit it? The law allows **consent** as a defense if the consent cancels the harm that the law is designed to prevent. In each case, the question is whether the law forbids an act that was committed against the victim's will or forbids the act without regard to the victim's wish. The law forbids murder, prostitution, and drug use regardless of whether the victim consents to it. Also, if the act causes harm to a third person who has not consented, there is no escape from criminal liability. Consent or forgiveness given after a crime has been committed is not really a defense, though it can affect the likelihood of prosecution. Consent operates most successfully as a defense in crimes against property.

11. A rule derived from *M'Naghten's Case,* 8 Eng.Rep. 718 (1843).

DURESS

DURESS
Unlawful pressure brought to bear on a person, causing the person to perform an act that she or he would not otherwise perform.

Duress exists when the *wrongful threat* of one person induces another person to perform an act that she or he would not otherwise perform. In such a situation, duress is said to negate the mental state necessary to commit a crime. For duress to qualify as a defense, the following requirements must be met:

① The threat must be of serious bodily harm or death.
② The harm threatened must be greater than the harm caused by the crime.
③ The threat must be immediate and inescapable.
④ The defendant must have been involved in the situation through no fault of his or her own.

JUSTIFIABLE USE OF FORCE

SELF-DEFENSE
The legally recognized privilege to protect oneself or one's property against injury by another. The privilege of self-defense protects only acts that are reasonably necessary to protect oneself, one's property, or another person.

Probably the most well-known defense to criminal liability is **self-defense.** Other situations, however, also justify the use of force: the defense of one's dwelling, the defense of other property, and the prevention of a crime. In all of these situations, it is important to distinguish between the use of deadly and nondeadly force. *Deadly force* is likely to result in death or serious bodily harm. *Nondeadly force* is force that reasonably appears necessary to prevent the imminent use of criminal force.

Generally speaking, people can use the amount of nondeadly force that seems necessary to protect themselves, their dwellings, or other property or to prevent the commission of a crime. Deadly force can be used in self-defense if there is a *reasonable belief* that imminent death or grievous bodily harm will otherwise result, if the attacker is using unlawful force (an example of lawful force is that exerted by a police officer), and if the defender has not initiated or provoked the attack. Deadly force normally can be used to defend a dwelling only if the unlawful entry is violent and the person believes deadly force is necessary to prevent imminent death or great bodily harm or—in some jurisdictions—if the person believes deadly force is necessary to prevent the commission of a felony (such as arson) in the dwelling.

ENTRAPMENT

ENTRAPMENT
In criminal law, a defense in which the defendant claims that he or she was induced by a public official—usually an undercover agent or police officer—to commit a crime that he or she would otherwise not have committed.

Entrapment is a defense designed to prevent police officers or other government agents from encouraging crimes in order to apprehend persons wanted for criminal acts. In the typical entrapment case, an undercover agent *suggests* that a crime be committed and somehow pressures or induces an individual to commit it. The agent then arrests the individual for the crime.

For entrapment to be considered a defense, both the suggestion and the inducement must take place. The defense is intended not to prevent law enforcement agents from setting a trap for an unwary criminal but rather to prevent them from pushing the individual into it. The crucial issue is whether a person who committed a crime was predisposed to commit the crime or did so because the agent induced it.

STATUTE OF LIMITATIONS

With some exceptions, such as for the crime of murder, statutes of limitations apply to crimes just as they do to civil wrongs. In other words, criminal cases must be prosecuted within a certain number of years. If a criminal action is brought after the statutory time period has expired, the accused person can raise the statute of limitations as a defense.

IMMUNITY

At times, the state may wish to obtain information from a person accused of a crime. Accused persons are understandably reluctant to give information if it will be used to prosecute them, and they cannot be forced to do so. The privilege against self-incrimination is granted by the Fifth Amendment to the Constitution, which reads, in part, "nor shall [any person] be compelled in any criminal case to be a witness against himself." In cases in which the state wishes to obtain information from a person accused of a crime, the state can grant *immunity* from prosecution or agree to prosecute for a less serious offense in exchange for the information. Once immunity is given, the person can no longer refuse to testify on Fifth Amendment grounds because he or she now has an absolute privilege against self-incrimination.

PLEA BARGAINING The process by which a criminal defendant and the prosecutor in a criminal case work out a mutually satisfactory disposition of the case, subject to court approval; usually involves the defendant's pleading guilty to a lesser offense in return for a lighter sentence.

Often, a grant of immunity from prosecution for a serious crime is part of the **plea bargaining** between the defendant and the prosecuting attorney. The defendant may be convicted of a lesser offense, while the state uses the defendant's testimony to prosecute accomplices for serious crimes carrying heavy penalties.

Constitutional Safeguards and Criminal Procedures

Criminal law brings the power of the state, with all its resources, to bear against the individual. Criminal procedures are designed to protect the constitutional rights of individuals and to prevent the arbitrary use of power on the part of the government.

The U.S. Constitution provides specific safeguards for those accused of crimes. Most of these safeguards protect individuals against state government actions, as well as federal government actions, by virtue of the due process clause of the Fourteenth Amendment. These safeguards are set forth in the Fourth, Fifth, Sixth, and Eighth Amendments.

FOURTH AMENDMENT PROTECTIONS

SEARCH WARRANT An order granted by a public authority, such as a judge, that authorizes law enforcement personnel to search particular premises or property.

PROBABLE CAUSE Reasonable grounds for believing that a person should be arrested or searched.

The Fourth Amendment protects the "right of the people to be secure in their persons, houses, papers, and effects." Before searching or seizing private property, law enforcement officers must obtain a **search warrant**—an order from a judge or other public official authorizing the search or seizure.

Search Warrants and Probable Cause To obtain a search warrant, the officers must convince a judge that they have reasonable grounds, or **probable cause**, to believe a search will reveal a specific illegality. Probable cause requires law enforcement officials to have trustworthy evidence that would convince a reasonable person that the proposed search or seizure is more likely justified than not. Furthermore, the Fourth Amendment prohibits general warrants. It requires a particular description of that which is to be searched or seized. General searches through a person's belongings are impermissible. The search cannot extend beyond what is described in the warrant.

There are exceptions to the requirement of a search warrant, as when it is likely that the items sought will be removed before a warrant can be obtained. For example, if a police officer has probable cause to believe an automobile contains evidence of a crime and it is likely that the vehicle will be unavailable by the time a warrant is obtained, the officer can search the vehicle without a warrant.

Searches and Seizures in the Business Context Constitutional protection against unreasonable searches and seizures is important to businesses and professionals. As

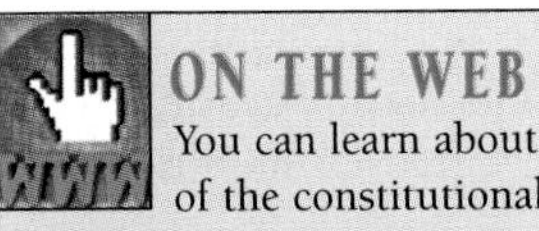

ON THE WEB You can learn about some of the constitutional questions raised by various criminal laws and procedures by going to the Web site of the American Civil Liberties Union at **http://www.aclu.org**.

federal and state regulation of commercial activities increased, frequent and unannounced government inspections were conducted to ensure compliance with the regulations. Such inspections were extremely disruptive at times. In *Marshall v. Barlow's, Inc.*,[12] the United States Supreme Court held that government inspectors do not have the right to enter business premises without a warrant, although the standard of probable cause is not the same as that required in nonbusiness contexts. The existence of a general and neutral enforcement plan will justify issuance of the warrant.

Lawyers and accountants frequently possess the business records of their clients, and inspecting these documents while they are out of the hands of their true owners also requires a warrant. No warrant is required, however, for seizures of spoiled or contaminated food. Nor are warrants required for searches of businesses in such highly regulated industries as liquor, guns, and strip mining. General manufacturing is not considered to be one of these highly regulated industries, however.

Of increasing concern to many employers is how to maintain a safe and efficient workplace without jeopardizing the Fourth Amendment rights of employees "to be secure in their persons." Requiring employees to undergo random drug tests, for example, may be held to violate the Fourth Amendment. In Chapter 34, we discuss Fourth Amendment issues in the employment context, as well as the privacy rights of employees in general, in detail.

FIFTH AMENDMENT PROTECTIONS

The Fifth Amendment offers significant protections for accused persons. One is the guarantee that no one can be deprived of "life, liberty, or property without due process of law." Two other important Fifth Amendment provisions protect persons against double jeopardy and self-incrimination.

Due Process of Law Remember from Chapter 2 that *due process of law* has both procedural and substantive aspects. Procedural due process requirements underlie criminal procedures. Basically, the law must be carried out in a fair and orderly way. In criminal cases, due process means that defendants should have an opportunity to object to the charges against them before a fair, neutral decision maker, such as a judge. Defendants must also be given the opportunity to confront and cross-examine witnesses and accusers and to present their own witnesses.

DOUBLE JEOPARDY
A situation occurring when a person is tried twice for the same criminal offense; prohibited by the Fifth Amendment to the Constitution.

Double Jeopardy The Fifth Amendment also protects persons from **double jeopardy** (being tried twice for the same criminal offense). The prohibition against double jeopardy means that once a criminal defendant is acquitted (found "not guilty") of a particular crime, the government may not reindict the person and retry him or her for the same crime.

The prohibition against double jeopardy does not preclude the crime victim from bringing a civil suit against the same person to recover damages, however. Additionally, a state's prosecution of a crime will not prevent a separate federal prosecution relating to the same activity, and vice versa. ● **EXAMPLE 6.6** A person found "not guilty" of assault and battery in a criminal case may be sued by the victim in a civil tort case for damages. A person who is prosecuted for assault and battery in a state court may be prosecuted in a federal court for civil rights violations resulting from the same action.●

12. 436 U.S. 307, 98 S.Ct. 1816, 56 L.Ed.2d 305 (1978).

SELF-INCRIMINATION The giving of testimony that may subject the testifier to criminal prosecution. The Fifth Amendment to the Constitution protects against self-incrimination by providing that no person "shall be compelled in any criminal case to be a witness against himself."

BE AWARE The Fifth Amendment protection against self-incrimination does not cover partnerships or corporations.

Self-Incrimination The Fifth Amendment guarantees that no person "shall be compelled in any criminal case to be a witness against himself." Thus, in any criminal proceeding, an accused person cannot be compelled to give testimony that might subject her or him to any criminal prosecution.

The Fifth Amendment's guarantee against **self-incrimination** extends only to natural persons. Because a corporation is a legal entity and not a natural person, the privilege against self-incrimination does not apply to it. Similarly, the business records of a partnership do not receive Fifth Amendment protection.[13] When a partnership is required to produce these records, it must do so even if the information incriminates the persons who constitute the business entity. Sole proprietors and sole practitioners (those who fully own their businesses) who have not incorporated cannot be compelled to produce their business records. These individuals have full protection against self-incrimination, because they function in only one capacity; there is no separate business entity (see Chapter 25).

PROTECTIONS UNDER THE SIXTH AND EIGHTH AMENDMENTS

The Sixth Amendment guarantees several important rights for criminal defendants: the right to a speedy trial, the right to a jury trial, the right to a public trial, the right to confront witnesses, and the right to counsel. The Eighth Amendment prohibits excessive bail and fines, and cruel and unusual punishment.

13. The privilege has been applied to some small family partnerships. See *United States v. Slutsky,* 352 F.Supp. 1005 (S.D.N.Y. 1972).

INTERNATIONAL PERSPECTIVE
The Death Penalty

The United States is now the only Western democracy that uses the death penalty. All fifteen countries of the European Union have banned its use and are actively promoting its abolition elsewhere. The United Nations Commission on Human Rights has called for its restriction and eventual abolition on a global level. When President George W. Bush visited Pope John Paul II in July 2001, the Pope urged him to put an end to this practice in the United States. Nonetheless, in the United States, thirty-eight states and the federal government continue to allow for the death penalty. During the year 2000, eighty-five inmates in the nation's prisons were put to death. Although polls indicate that public support for the death penalty has started to decline, it still remains high—about two-thirds of Americans support the death penalty.

Some supporters of capital punishment believe that it functions as a deterrent to crime. In their view, it prevents future violence by showing how serious the consequences of violent criminal behavior can be. Critics of capital punishment maintain that it violates the Eighth Amendment's prohibition against cruel and unusual punishment. They also point out that despite the use of the death penalty, the United States has the highest murder rates in the industrialized world, and those rates are highest in the southern states, such as Texas, where the most executions occur. In contrast, in the European countries that have abolished the death penalty, murder rates are far lower than in the United States.

FOR CRITICAL ANALYSIS
The objectives of our criminal justice system include both punishment and rehabilitation. How can the concept of rehabilitation of wrongdoers be reconciled with the death penalty?

The Exclusionary Rule and the *Miranda* Rule

Two other procedural protections for criminal defendants are the exclusionary rule and the *Miranda* rule.

EXCLUSIONARY RULE
In criminal procedure, a rule under which any evidence that is obtained in violation of the accused's constitutional rights guaranteed by the Fourth, Fifth, and Sixth Amendments, as well as any evidence derived from illegally obtained evidence, will not be admissible in court.

The Exclusionary Rule Under what is known as the **exclusionary rule**, all evidence obtained in violation of the constitutional rights spelled out in the Fourth, Fifth, and Sixth Amendments normally must be excluded from the trial, as well as all evidence derived from the illegally obtained evidence. Evidence derived from illegally obtained evidence is known as the "fruit of the poisonous tree." For example, if a confession is obtained after an illegal arrest, the arrest is "the poisonous tree," and the confession, if "tainted" by the arrest, is the "fruit."

The purpose of the exclusionary rule is to deter police from conducting warrantless searches and from engaging in other misconduct. The rule is sometimes criticized because it can lead to injustice. Many a defendant has "gotten off on a technicality" because law enforcement personnel failed to observe procedural requirements. Even though a defendant may be obviously guilty, if the evidence of that guilt was obtained improperly (without a valid search warrant, for example), it normally cannot be used against the defendant in court.

"A search is not to be made legal by what it turns up."
ROBERT H. JACKSON,
1892–1954
(Associate justice of the United States Supreme Court, 1941–1954)

The *Miranda* Rule In *Miranda v. Arizona*, a case decided in 1966, the United States Supreme Court established the rule that individuals who are arrested must be informed of certain constitutional rights, including their Fifth Amendment right to remain silent and their Sixth Amendment right to counsel. If the arresting officers fail to inform a criminal suspect of these constitutional rights, any statements the suspect makes normally will not be admissible in court. Because of its importance in criminal procedure, the *Miranda* case is presented as this chapter's *Landmark in the Law* on the next page.

REMEMBER Once a suspect has been informed of his or her rights, anything that person says can be used as evidence in a trial.

The Supreme Court's *Miranda* decision was controversial, and in 1968 Congress attempted to overrule the decision when it enacted Section 3501 of the Omnibus Crime Control Act of that year. Essentially, Section 3501 reinstated the rule that had

Police officers take a suspect into custody. Why must a criminal suspect be informed of his or her legal rights?

LANDMARK IN THE LAW
Miranda v. Arizona (1966)

The United States Supreme Court's decision in *Miranda v. Arizona*[a] has been cited in more court decisions than any other case in the history of American law. Through television shows and other media, the case has also become familiar to most of America's adult population.

The case arose after Ernesto Miranda was arrested in his home, on March 13, 1963, for the kidnapping and rape of an eighteen-year-old woman. Miranda was taken to a Phoenix, Arizona, police station and questioned by two police officers. Two hours later, the officers emerged from the interrogation room with a written confession signed by Miranda.

Rulings by the Lower Courts The confession was admitted into evidence at the trial, and Miranda was convicted and sentenced to prison for twenty to thirty years. Miranda appealed the decision, claiming that he had not been informed of his constitutional rights. He did not claim that he was innocent of the crime or that his confession was false or made under duress. He only claimed that he would not have confessed to the crime if he had been advised of his right to remain silent and to have an attorney. The Supreme Court of Arizona held that Miranda's constitutional rights had not been violated and affirmed his conviction. In forming its decision, the court emphasized the fact that Miranda had not specifically requested an attorney.

The Supreme Court's Decision The *Miranda* case was subsequently consolidated with three other cases involving similar issues and reviewed by the United States Supreme Court. In its decision, the Supreme Court stated that whenever an individual is taken into custody, "the following measures are required: He must be warned prior to any questioning that he has the right to remain silent, that anything he says can be used against him in a court of law, that he has the right to the presence of an attorney, and that if he cannot afford an attorney one will be appointed for him prior to any questioning if he so desires." If the accused waives his or her rights to remain silent and to have counsel present, the government must be able to demonstrate that the waiver was made knowingly, intelligently, and voluntarily.

APPLICATION TO TODAY'S WORLD

Today, both on television and in the real world, police officers routinely advise suspects of their "Miranda *rights" on arrest. When Ernesto Miranda himself was later murdered, the suspected murderer was "read his* Miranda *rights." Despite Congress's attempt to overrule the* Miranda *decision through legislation in 1968, the requirements continue to exist and, as noted below, were recently affirmed by the Supreme Court as constitutional.*

a. 384 U.S. 436, 86 S.Ct. 1602, 16 L.Ed.2d 694 (1966).

been in effect for 180 years before *Miranda*—namely, that statements by defendants can be used against them as long as the statements are made voluntarily. The U.S. Justice Department immediately disavowed Section 3501 as unconstitutional, however, and the section has never been enforced. Although the U.S. Court of Appeals for the Fourth Circuit attempted to enforce the provision in 1999, the court's decision was reversed by the United States Supreme Court in 2000. The Supreme Court held that the *Miranda*

ON THE WEB If you are interested in reading the Supreme Court's opinion in *Miranda v. Arizona,* go to

http://supct.law.cornell.edu:8080/supct/cases/name.htm.

Select "M" from the menu at the top of the page, and scroll down the page that opens to the *Miranda v. Arizona* case.

rights enunciated by the Court in the 1966 case were constitutionally based and thus could not be overruled by a legislative act.[14]

Exceptions to the *Miranda* Rule Over time, as part of a continuing attempt to balance the rights of accused persons against the rights of society, the United States Supreme Court has carved out numerous exceptions to the *Miranda* rule. In 1984, for example, the Court recognized a "public safety" exception to the *Miranda* rule. The need to protect the public warranted the admissibility of statements made by the defendant (in this case, indicating where he placed the gun) as evidence at trial, even though the defendant had not been informed of his *Miranda* rights.[15]

In 1985, the Supreme Court further held that a confession need not be excluded even though the police failed to inform a suspect in custody that his attorney had tried to reach him by telephone.[16] In an important 1991 decision, the Court stated that a suspect's conviction will not be automatically overturned if the suspect was coerced into making a confession. If other, legally obtained evidence admitted at trial is strong enough to justify the conviction without the confession, then the fact that the confession was obtained illegally can be, in effect, ignored.[17]

In yet another case, in 1994, the Supreme Court ruled that a suspect must unequivocally and assertively request to exercise his or her right to counsel in order to stop police questioning. Saying, "Maybe I should talk to a lawyer" during an interrogation after being taken into custody is not enough. The Court held that police officers are not required to decipher the suspect's intentions in such situations.[18]

ETHICAL ISSUE 6.1

Are there too many exceptions to the Miranda *rule?*

As mentioned, the Supreme Court's decision in *Miranda* has always been controversial. Initially, many were concerned that the *Miranda* requirements would hamper efforts by law enforcement officials to bring criminals to justice. After all, even obviously guilty persons could "get off on a technicality" if their *Miranda* rights were violated. Over time, these criticisms lessened as the courts carved out various exceptions to the *Miranda* rule. As a result of these decisions, some legal scholars now contend that there are too many exceptions to the rule. David Steinberg, the director of the Thomas Jefferson School of Law's Center for Law and Social Justice in San Diego, argues that "the current patchwork of exceptions to *Miranda* is confusing and costly." Steinberg believes that the Supreme Court should either create a "standard rule," under which the *Miranda* rule would be strictly applied in all cases, or "deregulate confessions." Under the latter approach, it would be left to the courts to decide whether a confession was coerced by the police and should be excluded.[19] Others have suggested abandoning *Miranda* entirely and requiring instead that all custodial interrogations be videotaped.

14. *Dickerson v. United States,* 530 U.S. 428, 120 S.Ct. 2326, 147 L.Ed.2d 405 (2000).
15. *New York v. Quarles,* 467 U.S. 649, 104 S.Ct. 2626, 81 L.Ed.2d 550 (1984).
16. *Moran v. Burbine,* 475 U.S. 412, 106 S.Ct. 1135, 89 L.Ed.2d 410 (1985).
17. *Arizona v. Fulminante,* 499 U.S. 279, 111 S.Ct. 1246, 113 L.Ed.2d 302 (1991).
18. *Davis v. United States,* 512 U.S. 452, 114 S.Ct. 2350, 129 L.Ed.2d 362 (1994).
19. David Steinberg, "*Miranda* No Longer Works," *The National Law Journal,* August 14, 2000, p. A18.

Criminal Process

As mentioned, a criminal prosecution differs significantly from a civil case in several respects. These differences reflect the desire to safeguard the rights of the individual against the state. Exhibit 6–3 summarizes the major steps in processing a criminal case.

EXHIBIT 6–3 MAJOR STEPS IN PROCESSING A CRIMINAL CASE

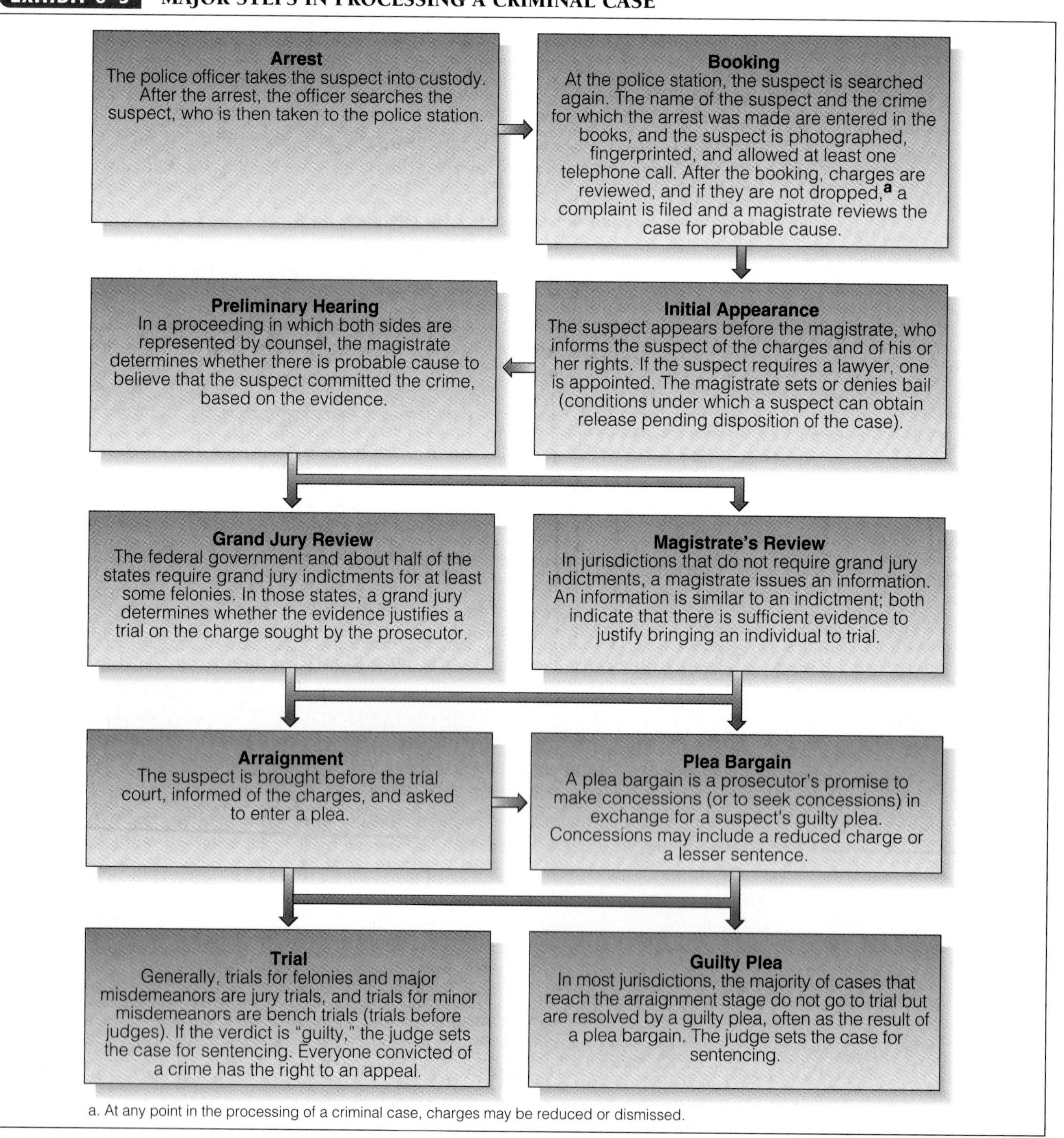

a. At any point in the processing of a criminal case, charges may be reduced or dismissed.

ON THE WEB To learn more about criminal procedures, access the following site and select "Anatomy of a Murder: A Trip through Our Nation's Legal Justice System":

http://library.thinkquest.org/2760/homep.htm.

We discuss three phases of the criminal process—arrest, indictment or information, and trial—in more detail below.

ARREST

Before a warrant for arrest can be issued, there must be probable cause for believing that the individual in question has committed a crime. As discussed earlier, *probable cause* can be defined as a substantial likelihood that the person has committed or is about to commit a crime. Note that probable cause involves a likelihood, not just a possibility. Arrests may sometimes be made without a warrant if there is no time to get one, as when a police officer observes a crime taking place, but the action of the arresting officer is still judged by the standard of probable cause.

INDICTMENT OR INFORMATION

INDICTMENT
A charge by a grand jury that a named person has committed a crime.

GRAND JURY
A group of citizens called to decide, after hearing the state's evidence, whether a reasonable basis (probable cause) exists for believing that a crime has been committed and whether a trial ought to be held.

INFORMATION
A formal accusation or complaint (without an indictment) issued in certain types of actions (usually criminal actions involving lesser crimes) by a law officer, such as a magistrate.

Individuals must be formally charged with having committed specific crimes before they can be brought to trial. If issued by a grand jury, this charge is called an **indictment.**[20] A **grand jury** usually consists of more jurors than the ordinary trial jury. A grand jury does not determine the guilt or innocence of an accused party; rather, its function is to determine, after hearing the state's evidence, whether a reasonable basis (probable cause) exists for believing that a crime has been committed and whether a trial ought to be held.

Usually, grand juries are called in cases involving serious crimes, such as murder. For lesser crimes, an individual may be formally charged with a crime by what is called an **information**, or criminal complaint. An information will be issued by a magistrate (a public official vested with judicial authority) if the magistrate determines that there is sufficient evidence to justify bringing the individual to trial.

TRIAL

At a criminal trial, the accused person does not have to prove anything; the entire burden of proof is on the prosecutor (the state). As mentioned earlier, the prosecution must show that, based on all the evidence presented, the defendant's guilt is established *beyond a reasonable doubt*. If there is any reasonable doubt as to whether a criminal defendant did, in fact, commit the crime with which she or he has been charged, then the verdict must be "not guilty." Note that giving a verdict of "not guilty" is not the same as stating that the defendant is innocent; it merely means that not enough evidence was properly presented to the court to prove guilt beyond all reasonable doubt.

Courts have complex rules about what types of evidence may be presented and how the evidence may be brought out in criminal cases, especially in jury trials. These rules are designed to ensure that evidence in trials is relevant, reliable, and not prejudicial against the defendant.

SENTENCING GUIDELINES

Traditionally, persons who had committed the same crime might have received very different sentences, depending on the judge hearing the case, the jurisdiction in which it was heard, and many other factors. Today, however, court judges typically must follow state or federal guidelines when sentencing convicted persons.

At the federal level, the Sentencing Reform Act created the U.S. Sentencing Commission, which was charged with the task of standardizing sentences for federal crimes. The commission fulfilled its task, and since 1987 its sentencing guidelines for all federal crimes have been applied by federal court judges. The guidelines establish a range

20. Pronounced in-*dyte*-ment.

LETTER OF THE LAW

The Case of the Sleeping Lawyer

Suppose that a criminal defendant is being tried in a death-penalty case and his lawyer sleeps during significant portions of the trial. Does a "sleeping lawyer" satisfy the right to counsel guaranteed by the Sixth Amendment to the U.S. Constitution? This was the question in *Burdine v. Johnson.*[a] Calvin Burdine had been sentenced to death for killing his former lover. At the trial, which was conducted in a Texas state court, Burdine's court-appointed lawyer repeatedly fell asleep while the prosecutor presented the case against Burdine. Burdine claimed on appeal that he had been denied effective counsel during his trial and therefore the trial proceedings were prejudiced against him. After looking at the letter of the law as enunciated in several previous cases, however, the U.S. Court of Appeals for the Fifth Circuit concluded in 2000 that a sleeping lawyer did not violate Burdine's constitutional rights.[b] After all, as the Texas attorney general argued on appeal, a sleeping lawyer is no different from one who is intoxicated, psychotic, or suffering from Alzheimer's disease—and death sentences have been upheld in such cases. When the case was heard *en banc* (by the full panel of judges sitting on the Fifth Circuit Court of Appeals), however, the full court concluded that a sleeping lawyer did violate a criminal defendant's right to counsel. Burdine was thus entitled to a new trial.

a. 231 F.3d 950 (5th Cir. 2000); rehearing *en banc*, 262 F.3d 336 (5th Cir. 2001).

b. According to the United States Supreme Court, a defendant must prove that his or her counsel's conduct, even if shown to be "unreasonable," in fact altered the outcome of the trial before a sentence or verdict will be set aside. See *Strickland v. Washington*, 466 U.S. 668, 104 S.Ct. 2052, 80 L.Ed.2d 674 (1984).

THE BOTTOM LINE

The letter of the law can be convoluted indeed—and unnecessarily so, according to a dissenting opinion in the Fifth Circuit's initial decision. The dissenting judge argued that there was little need to delve into precedents or any other legal sources. The fact that the lawyer slept during much of the trial was well documented, and the appropriate ruling was obvious: a capital trial in which the defendant's lawyer sleeps "shocks the conscience" and clearly constitutes prejudice against the defendant. When the case was reheard en banc *in 2001, the Fifth Circuit judges agreed.*

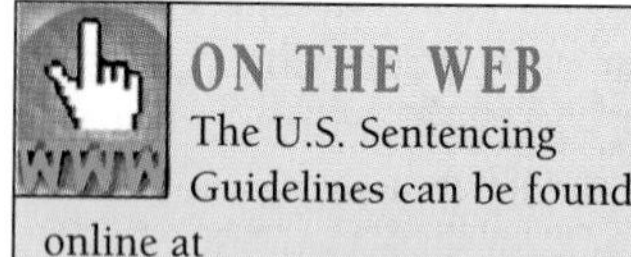

ON THE WEB The U.S. Sentencing Guidelines can be found online at **http://www.ussc.gov.**

of possible penalties for each federal crime. Depending on the defendant's criminal record, the seriousness of the offense, and other factors specified in the guidelines (see this chapter's *Business Law in the Online World* on page 182 for a factor considered in one case), federal judges must select a sentence from within this range.

The commission also created specific guidelines for the punishment of crimes committed by corporate employees (white-collar crimes). These guidelines established stiffer penalties for criminal violations of securities laws (see Chapter 29), antitrust laws (see Chapter 32), employment laws (see Chapters 34 and 35), mail and wire fraud, commercial bribery, and kickbacks and money laundering. The guidelines allow federal judges to take into consideration a number of factors when selecting from the range of possible penalties for a specified crime. These factors include the defendant company's history of past violations, the extent of management's cooperation with federal investigators, and the extent to which the firm has undertaken specific programs and procedures to prevent criminal activities by its employees.

"Three Strikes" Laws Many states have enacted "three strikes and you're out" legislation. Typically, this legislation states that any "career" criminal who already has two violent felony convictions on his or her record will go to prison for a longer period (in some states, for life and without parole) if convicted of a third similar felony. A federal crime bill enacted in 1994 adopted this provision as well. A California law, enacted in

Probably the most famous case under a "three strikes" law was the case against Jerry Dewayne Williams. In 1995, Williams was sentenced by a California court to twenty-five years in prison for stealing a slice of pepperoni pizza (he was released two years later as a result of a California Supreme Court decision). Are "three strikes" laws too harsh? Should judges have more freedom in sentencing criminal defendants?

1994, requires longer prison sentences for felons who have had at least one prior conviction for a serious or violent felony.

Cyber Crime

COMPUTER CRIME Any act that is directed against computers and computer parts, that uses computers as instruments of crime, or that involves computers and constitutes abuse.

Some years ago, the American Bar Association defined **computer crime** as any act that is directed against computers and computer parts, that uses computers as instruments of crime, or that involves computers and constitutes abuse. Today, because much of the crime committed with the use of computers occurs in cyberspace, many computer crimes fall under the broad label of cyber crime.

BE AWARE Technological change is one of the primary factors that lead to new types of crime.

As we mentioned earlier, most cyber crimes are not "new" crimes. Rather, they are existing crimes in which the Internet is the instrument of wrongdoing. The challenge for law enforcement is to apply traditional laws—which were designed to protect persons from physical harm or to safeguard their physical property—to crimes committed in cyberspace. Here we look at several types of activity that constitute cyber crimes against persons or property. Other cyber crimes will be discussed in later chapters of this text as they relate to particular topics, such as banking or consumer law.

Cyber Theft

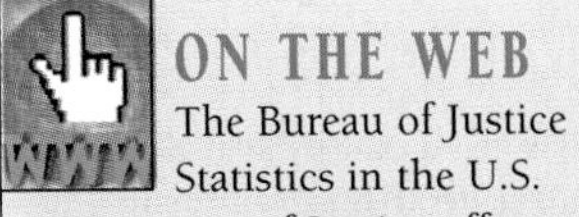

ON THE WEB The Bureau of Justice Statistics in the U.S. Department of Justice offers an impressive collection of statistics on crime, including cyber crime, at the following Web site: **http://www.ojp.usdoj.gov/bjs**.

In cyberspace, thieves are not subject to the physical limitations of the "real" world. A thief can steal data stored in a networked computer with dial-in access from anywhere on the globe. Only the speed of the connection and the thief's computer equipment limit the quantity of data that can be stolen.

Financial Crimes Computer networks also provide opportunities for employees to commit crimes that can involve serious economic losses. For example, employees of a company's accounting department can transfer funds among accounts with little effort and often with less risk than that involved in transactions evidenced by paperwork.

Generally, the dependence of businesses on computer operations has left firms vulnerable to sabotage, fraud, embezzlement, and the theft of proprietary data, such as

BUSINESS LAW: //in the Online World

Web Site Ads and the Sentencing Guidelines

The Internet is a boon for advertisers. Ads offering goods for sale can be disseminated quickly and inexpensively to hundreds of millions of people throughout the world. Yet the same characteristics that make the Internet a valuable tool in today's commerce also allow unscrupulous individuals to reap profits by defrauding innocent victims. As you will read shortly, attempts to prosecute cyber crimes have raised new types of questions—including questions related to sentencing offenders convicted of cyber fraud.

A Case of Wire Fraud

Consider, for example, a case that recently came before the U.S. Court of Appeals for the Ninth Circuit. Michael Pirello posted a series of ads on a Web site known as *Excite Classifieds* (at **http://classifieds.excite.com**) offering computers for sale. In the ads, Pirello described the computers at great length, including details about their operating systems, monitors, memory capacities, modems, weights, processors, and the like. In fact, the ads were part of a fraudulent scheme whereby Pirello would induce prospective buyers to send him money for computers that he never intended to deliver. Over the course of three months, Pirello received checks totaling more than $4,000 for the nonexistent computers.

Ultimately, Pirello was convicted of, among other things, three counts of wire fraud. For this crime, the U.S. Sentencing Guidelines instruct district courts to enhance a defendant's sentence by two levels if the offense was committed through "mass-marketing." The guidelines define mass-marketing as "a plan, program, promotion, or campaign that is conducted through *solicitation by* telephone, mail, *the Internet,* or other means to induce a large number of persons to . . . purchase goods or services." (Emphasis added.) The judge concluded that Pirello's fraud was committed through mass-marketing and applied the enhanced penalty.

Does Advertising on a Web Site Constitute "Mass-Marketing"?

One of Pirello's arguments on appeal was that his actions could not have constituted mass-marketing because his ads did not amount to "solicitation by . . . the Internet." Mass-marketing in the Internet context, claimed Pirello, occurs only where the seller actively solicits a large number of purchasers by circulating mass e-mail to a purchased list of e-mail addresses. The appellate court did not agree. The court noted that Pirello's use of a classified ad arguably enabled him to solicit even more people than would have been possible with a mass e-mail. While mass e-mail is sent to a finite number of people, there is no similar limitation on the number of people who can be exposed to an ad on a Web site accessible by the public.

One of the appellate court judges dissented from this reasoning. According to the dissenting judge, solicitation involves more than simply advertising goods for sale and suggests "some sort of one-on-one importuning [requesting or demanding]." Pirello's passive placement of an ad on a Web site did not, in this judge's mind, constitute the "solicitation by . . . the Internet" required by the sentencing guidelines for the enhanced penalty.[a]

FOR CRITICAL ANALYSIS

The outcome of this case clearly hinged on how the court interpreted the phrase "solicitation by . . . the Internet." Do you agree with the majority's interpretation of the phrase or with the dissenting judge's interpretation? Explain.

a. *United States v. Pirello,* 255 F.3d 728 (9th Cir. 2001).

trade secrets or other intellectual property. As noted in Chapter 5, the piracy of intellectual property via the Internet is one of the most serious legal challenges facing lawmakers and the courts today.

IDENTITY THEFT
Occurs when a person steals another's identifying information—such as a name, date of birth, or Social Security number—and uses the information to access the victim's financial resources.

Identity Theft A form of cyber theft that has become particularly troublesome in recent years is **identity theft.** Identity theft occurs when the wrongdoer steals a form of identification—such as a name, date of birth, or Social Security number—and uses the information to access the victim's financial resources. This crime existed to a certain extent before the widespread use of the Internet. Thieves would "steal" calling-card numbers

Abraham Abdullah, shown here in a 2001 police photo, allegedly used a library computer and Forbes *magazine's list of America's richest people to steal the Social Security numbers, home addresses, birth dates, and credit-card numbers of more than two hundred executives and celebrities. What can police and individuals do to make identity theft more difficult for criminals?*

by watching people using public telephones, or they would rifle through garbage to find bank account or credit-card numbers. The identity thieves would then use the calling-card or credit-card numbers or would withdraw funds from the victims' accounts.

The Internet, however, has turned identity theft into perhaps the fastest growing financial crime in the United States. From the identity thief's perspective, the Internet provides those who steal information offline with an easy medium for using items such as stolen credit-card numbers or e-mail addresses while protected by anonymity. An estimated 500,000 Americans are victims of identity theft each year.

CYBER STALKING

California enacted the first stalking law in 1990, in response to the murders of six women—including Rebecca Schaeffer, a television star—by men who had harassed them. The law made it a crime to harass or follow a person while making a "credible threat" that puts that person in reasonable fear for his or her safety or the safety of the person's immediate family.[21] Most other states have also enacted stalking laws, yet in about half of the states these laws require a physical act (following the victim). **Cyber stalkers** (stalkers who commit their crimes in cyberspace), however, find their victims through Internet chat rooms, Usenet newsgroups or other bulletin boards, or e-mail. To close this "loophole" in existing stalking laws, more than three-fourths of the states now have laws specifically designed to combat cyber stalking and other forms of online harassment.

Note that cyber stalking can be even more threatening than physical stalking in some respects. While it takes a great deal of effort to physically stalk someone, it is relatively easy to harass a victim with electronic messages. Furthermore, the possibility of personal confrontation may discourage a stalker from actually following a victim. This disincentive is removed in cyberspace. Finally, there is always the possibility that a cyber stalker will eventually pose a physical threat to her or his target.

CYBER STALKER
A person who commits the crime of stalking in cyberspace. Generally, stalking consists of harassing a person and putting that person in reasonable fear for his or her safety or the safety of the person's immediate family.

HACKER
A person who uses one computer to break into another. Professional computer programmers refer to such persons as "crackers."

HACKING

Persons who use one computer to break into another are sometimes referred to as **hackers.** Hackers who break into computers without authorization often commit cyber theft. Sometimes, however, their principal aim is to prove how smart they are by gaining access to others' password-protected computers and causing random data errors or making unpaid-for telephone calls.[22]

The Computer Crime and Security Survey polled 538 companies and large government institutions and found that 85 percent had experienced security breaches through computer-based means in 2000. It is difficult to know, however, just how frequently hackers succeed in breaking into databases across the United States. The Federal Bureau of Investigation (FBI) estimates that only 25 percent of all corporations that suffer such security breaches report the incident to a law enforcement agency. For one thing, corporations do not want it to become publicly known that the security of their data has been breached. For another, admitting to a breach would be admitting to a certain degree of incompetence, which could damage their reputations.

CYBER TERRORISM

CYBER TERRORIST
A hacker whose purpose is to exploit a target computer for a serious impact, such as corrupting a program to sabotage a business.

Cyber terrorists are hackers who, rather than trying to gain attention, strive to remain undetected so that they can exploit computers for a serious impact. Just as "real"

21. Cal. Penal Code Section 646.9.
22. The total cost of crime on the Internet is estimated to be several billion dollars annually, but two-thirds of that total is said to consist of unpaid-for toll calls.

terrorists destroyed the World Trade Center towers and a portion of the Pentagon in September 2001, cyber terrorists might explode "logic bombs" to shut down central computers. Such activities can pose a danger to national security. After an American surveillance airplane collided with a Chinese military jet in 2001, hackers from China bombarded American Web sites with messages such as "Hack the USA" and "For our pilot Wang." Over a period of several weeks, these hackers were able to destroy or deface hundreds of Web sites, including some from the White House, the FBI, and NASA.

Businesses may also be targeted by cyber terrorists. The goals of a hacking operation might include a wholesale theft of data, such as a merchant's customer files, or the monitoring of a computer to discover a business firm's plans and transactions. A cyber terrorist might also want to insert false codes or data. For example, the processing control system of a food manufacturer could be changed to alter the levels of ingredients so that consumers of the food would become ill. A cyber terrorist attack on a major financial institution such as the New York Stock Exchange or a large bank could leave securities or money markets in flux and seriously affect the daily lives of millions of citizens. Similarly, any prolonged disruption of computer, cable, satellite, or telecommunications systems due to the actions of expert hackers would have serious repercussions on business operations—and national security—on a global level. Computer viruses (see Chapter 4) are another tool that can be used by cyber terrorists to cripple communications networks.

ETHICAL ISSUE 6.2

Is it possible to control cyber crime without sacrificing some civil liberties?

Governments in some countries, such as Russia, have succeeded in controlling Internet crime to a certain extent by monitoring the e-mail and other electronic transmissions of users of specific Internet service providers. In the United States, however, any government attempt to monitor Internet use to detect criminal conspiracies or terrorist activities was likely to be challenged as violating the constitutional rights of Americans. This traditional attitude that civil liberties must be safeguarded at any cost may now be changing, however. The terrorist attacks on the World Trade Center towers and the Pentagon in September 2001 made terrorism—and the threat of future terrorist attacks—real and immediate for U.S. citizens. In the future, Americans may be less reluctant to trade off some of their civil liberties for greater national security.

Prosecuting Cyber Crimes

The "location" of cyber crime (cyberspace) has raised new issues in the investigation of crimes and the prosecution of offenders. A threshold issue is, of course, jurisdiction. A person who commits an act against a business in California, where the act is a cyber crime, might never have set foot in California but might instead reside in New York, or even in Canada, where the act may not be a crime. If the crime was committed via e-mail, the question arises as to whether the e-mail would constitute sufficient "minimum contacts" (see Chapter 3) for the victim's state to exercise jurisdiction over the perpetrator.

Identifying the wrongdoers can also be difficult. Cyber criminals do not leave physical traces, such as fingerprints or DNA samples, as evidence of their crimes. Even electronic "footprints" can be hard to find and follow. For example, e-mail may be sent through a remailer, an online service that guarantees that a message cannot be traced to its source.

For these reasons, laws written to protect physical property are difficult to apply in cyberspace. Nonetheless, governments at both the state and federal levels have taken significant steps toward controlling cyber crime, both by applying existing criminal statutes and by enacting new laws that specifically address wrongs committed in cyberspace.

The Computer Fraud and Abuse Act Perhaps the most significant federal statute specifically addressing cyber crime is the Counterfeit Access Device and Computer Fraud and Abuse Act of 1984 (commonly known as the Computer Fraud and Abuse Act, or CFAA). This act, as amended by the National Information Infrastructure Protection Act of 1996,[23] provides, among other things, that a person who accesses a computer online, without authority, to obtain classified, restricted, or protected data, or attempts to do so, is subject to criminal prosecution. Such data could include financial and credit records, medical records, legal files, military and national security files, and other confidential information in government or private computers. The crime has two elements: accessing a computer without authority and taking the data.

This theft is a felony if it is committed for a commercial purpose or for private financial gain, or if the value of the stolen data (or computer time) exceeds $5,000. Penalties include fines and imprisonment for up to twenty years. A victim of computer theft can also bring a civil suit against the violator to obtain damages, an injunction, and other relief.

The CFAA defines *damage* as a "loss aggregating at least $5,000 in value during any one-year period to one or more individuals." At issue in the following case was whether the term *individuals* in this definition included a corporation.

23. 18 U.S.C. Section 1030.

CASE 6.3 United States v. Middleton

United States Court of Appeals,
Ninth Circuit, 2000.
231 F.3d 1207.

FACTS Nicholas Middleton worked as the personal computer administrator for Slip.net, an Internet service provider. His responsibilities included installing software and hardware on the company's computers and providing technical support to its employees. He had extensive knowledge of Slip.net's internal computer system. Dissatisfied with his job, Middleton quit. Through various subterfuges, he obtained access to a computer that the company had named "Lemming." Slip.net used Lemming to perform internal administrative functions and to host customers' Web sites. Lemming also contained the software for a new billing system. Middleton changed all the administrative passwords, altered the computer's registry, and deleted the entire billing system and two internal databases. To correct the damage cost Slip.net more than 150 worker-hours, in addition to the expense of an outside consultant and new software. Middleton was convicted of intentionally causing damage to a "protected computer" without authorization, in violation of the CFAA. He appealed to the U.S. Court of Appeals for the Ninth Circuit, arguing that the term *individuals,* as used in the statute, did not include a corporation.

ISSUE Does the CFAA's use of the term *individuals* include a corporation?

DECISION Yes. The U.S. Court of Appeals for the Ninth Circuit affirmed Middleton's conviction. He was

(continued)

CASE 6.3—Continued

sentenced to three years' probation, subject to a condition of 180 days in community confinement, and ordered to pay $9,147 in restitution.

REASON The U.S. Court of Appeals for the Ninth Circuit noted that Congress amended the CFAA in 1996, altering the definition of damage to read, "loss aggregating at least $5,000 in value during any one-year period to one or more individuals." Although the court found no explanation for this change, "[w]e do not believe * * * that this change evidences an intent to limit the statute's reach. To the contrary, Congress has consciously broadened the statute consistently since its original enactment." The court pointed out, for example, that a Senate report on the 1996 amendments noted that "the interaction between the provision that prohibits conduct causing damage and the provision that defines damage will prohibit a hacker from stealing passwords from an existing log-on program, when this conduct requires 'all system users to change their passwords, and requires the system administrator to devote resources to resecuring the system.'" The court reasoned that "if Congress intended to limit the definition of the crime to conduct causing financial damage to a natural person only, its report would not use the example of a 'system administrator' devoting resources to fix a computer problem as illustrative of the 'damage' to be prevented and criminalized."

FOR CRITICAL ANALYSIS—Technological Consideration *How might Middleton's employer have avoided the damage to its computer systems?*

Other Federal Statutes The federal wire fraud statute, the Economic Espionage Act of 1996, and RICO, all of which were discussed earlier in this chapter, extend to crimes committed in cyberspace as well. Other federal statutes that may apply include the Electronic Fund Transfer Act of 1978, which makes the unauthorized access to an electronic fund transfer system a crime; the Anticounterfeiting Consumer Protection Act of 1996, which increased penalties for stealing copyrighted or trademarked property; and the National Stolen Property Act of 1988, which concerns the interstate transport of stolen property. Recall from Chapter 2 that the federal government has also enacted laws (many of which have been challenged on constitutional grounds) to protect minors from online pornographic materials. In later chapters of this text, you will read about other federal statutes and regulations that are designed to address wrongs committed in cyberspace in specific areas of the law.

APPLICATION **Law and the Businessperson . . .**

Protecting against Cyber Crime*

In addition to protecting their physical property, businesspersons today also are concerned about protecting their intangible property–such as computer data or files–from unauthorized access. U.S. business firms lose millions of dollars to industrial espionage and sabotage every year. Once a computer system has been corrupted, it can be difficult to recover. To prevent losses through computer systems, some firms hire experts to improve the security of the systems.

*This *Application* is not meant to substitute for the services of an attorney who is licensed to practice law in your state.

COMPUTER SYSTEM SAFEGUARDS

Many sources of software offer security programs that can be easily used to protect computers that are connected to an internal network or to the Internet. For

APPLICATION Law and the Businessperson . . .

Protecting against Cyber Crime—continued

example, most word processing programs include a "password" function. To gain access to information within the program, a user must know the password. A document that can be unlocked only with the password can be e-mailed as an attachment, providing some security.

Cryptography also provides increased protection for computer data and files. Encryption hardware is available in the form of computer chips and is commonly used in automatic teller machines (ATMs). These chips quickly encrypt, or decrypt, information. The same results can be achieved using encryption software.

Additionally, effective "firewalls" can be installed at the interface between computers and the Internet to protect against unwanted intruders. Firewall software can also be used to keep internal network segments secure.

EMPLOYMENT POLICIES

Although outside hackers are a threat, employees, former employees, and other "insiders" are responsible for most computer abuse, including breaches of information security. Generally, employees should be given access only to information that they need to know. Additionally, employees and other insiders should be instructed in what constitutes proper and improper use of your company's computer systems. They should also be told that any form of computer abuse is against company policy, is illegal, and will be the basis for termination of employement.

Another safeguard is to have employees agree, in a written confidentiality agreement, not to disclose confidential information during or after employment without the employer's consent. Monitoring certain computer-related employee activities may be appropriate, but if monitoring is to take place, employees should be informed (see Chapter 34). Still other security measures include the use of digital signatures (see Chapter 17), facility lockups, visitor screenings, and announced briefcase checks.

CHECKLIST FOR THE BUSINESSPERSON

1. Consider protecting your computer security and documents through the use of passwords, encryption, and firewalls.
2. Instruct your employees in how computers and computer information are to be used and not used.
3. Consider using confidentiality agreements, monitoring, and digital signatures to protect your computer system and data against unauthorized use.

Key Terms

arson 165
beyond a reasonable doubt 159
burglary 165
computer crime 181
consent 170
crime 159
cyber crime 159
cyber stalker 183
cyber terrorist 183
double jeopardy 173
duress 171
embezzlement 166
entrapment 171
exclusionary rule 175
felony 160
forgery 166
grand jury 179
hacker 183
identity theft 182
indictment 179
information 179
insider trading 168
larceny 165
misdemeanor 160
money laundering 168
petty offense 160
plea bargaining 172

Chapter Summary Criminal Law and Cyber Crimes

Civil Law and Criminal Law (See pages 159–160.)	1. *Civil law*—Spells out the duties that exist between persons or between citizens and their governments, excluding the duty not to commit crimes. 2. *Criminal law*—Has to do with crimes, which are defined as wrongs against society proclaimed in statutes and, if committed, punishable by society through fines, removal from public office, and/or imprisonment—and, in some cases, death. Because crimes are *offenses against society as a whole,* they are prosecuted by a public official, not by victims. 3. *Key differences*—An important difference between civil and criminal law is that the standard of proof is higher in criminal cases (see Exhibit 6–1 for other differences between criminal and civil laws). 4. *Civil liability for criminal acts*—A criminal act may give rise to both criminal liability and tort liability (see Exhibit 6–2 for an example of criminal and tort liability for the same act).
Classification of Crimes (See page 160.)	1. *Felonies*—Serious crimes punishable by death or by imprisonment in a penitentiary for more than one year. 2. *Misdemeanors*—Under federal law and in most states, any crimes that are not felonies.
Criminal Liability (See pages 161–162.)	1. *Guilty act*—In general, some form of harmful act must be committed for a crime to exist. 2. *Intent*—An intent to commit a crime, or a wrongful mental state, is required for a crime to exist.
Corporate Criminal Liability (See pages 163–164.)	1. *Liability of corporations*—Corporations normally are liable for the crimes committed by their agents and employees within the course and scope of their employment. Corporations cannot be imprisoned, but they can be fined or denied certain legal privileges. 2. *Liability of corporate officers and directors*—Corporate directors and officers are personally liable for the crimes they commit and may be held liable for the actions of employees under their supervision.
Types of Crimes (See pages 164–169.)	1. *Violent crime*—Crimes that cause others to suffer harm or death. Examples include murder, assault and battery, rape, and robbery. 2. *Property crime*—Crimes in which the goal of the offender is some form of economic gain or the damaging of property. Examples include burglary, larceny, arson, receiving stolen goods, forgery, and obtaining goods by false pretenses. 3. *Public order crime*—Crimes contrary to public values and morals. Examples include public drunkenness, prostitution, gambling, and illegal drug use. 4. *White-collar crime*—Nonviolent crimes committed in the course of a legitimate occupation to obtain a personal or business advantage. Examples include embezzlement, mail and wire fraud, bribery, bankruptcy fraud, insider trading, and the theft of trade secrets. 5. *Organized crime*—Crime committed by groups operating illegitimately to satisfy the public's demand for illegal goods and services (such as narcotics or pornography). Often, organized crime involves *money laundering*—the establishment of legitimate enterprises through which "dirty" money obtained through criminal activities can be "laundered" and made to appear as legitimate income. The Racketeer Influenced and Corrupt Organizations Act (RICO) of 1970, which prohibits racketeering activity, was passed, in part, to control organized crime.

Chapter Summary Criminal Law and Cyber Crimes—continued

Defenses to Criminal Liability (See pages 169–172.)	1. *Infancy.* 2. *Intoxication.* 3. *Insanity.* 4. *Mistake.* 5. *Consent.* 6. *Duress.* 7. *Justifiable use of force.* 8. *Entrapment.* 9. *Statute of limitations.* 10. *Immunity.*
Constitutional Safeguards and Criminal Procedures (See pages 172–177.)	1. *Fourth Amendment*—Provides protection against unreasonable searches and seizures and requires that probable cause exist before a warrant for a search or an arrest can be issued. 2. *Fifth Amendment*—Requires due process of law, prohibits double jeopardy, and protects against self-incrimination. 3. *Sixth Amendment*—Provides guarantees of a speedy trial, a trial by jury, a public trial, the right to confront witnesses, and the right to counsel. 4. *Eighth Amendment*—Prohibits excessive bail and fines, and cruel and unusual punishment. 5. *Exclusionary rule*—A criminal procedural rule that prohibits the introduction at trial of all evidence obtained in violation of constitutional rights, as well as any evidence derived from the illegally obtained evidence. 6. Miranda *rule*—A rule set forth by the Supreme Court in *Miranda v. Arizona* that individuals who are arrested must be informed of certain constitutional rights, including their right to counsel.
Criminal Process (See pages 178–181.)	1. *Arrest, indictment, and trial*—Procedures governing arrest, indictment, and trial for a crime are designed to safeguard the rights of the individual against the state. See Exhibit 6–3 for the steps involved in prosecuting a criminal case. 2. *Sentencing guidelines*—Both the federal government and the states have established sentencing laws or guidelines. The federal sentencing guidelines indicate a range of penalties for each federal crime; federal judges must abide by these guidelines when imposing sentences on those convicted of federal crimes.
Cyber Crime (See pages 181–186.)	Cyber crime is any crime that occurs in cyberspace. Examples include cyber theft (financial crimes committed with the aid of computers, as well as identity theft), cyber stalking, hacking, and cyber terrorism. Significant federal statutes addressing cyber crimes include the Electronic Fund Transfer Act of 1978 and the Counterfeit Access Device and Computer Fraud and Abuse Act of 1984, as amended by the National Information Infrastructure Protection Act of 1996.

For Review

① What two elements must exist before a person can be held liable for a crime? Can a corporation be liable for crimes?

② What are five broad categories of crimes? What is white-collar crime?

③ What defenses might be raised by criminal defendants to avoid liability for criminal acts?

④ What constitutional safeguards exist to protect persons accused of crimes? What are the basic steps in the criminal process?

⑤ What is cyber crime? What laws apply to crimes committed in cyberspace?

Questions and Case Problems

6–1. Criminal versus Civil Trials. In criminal trials, the defendant must be proved guilty beyond a reasonable doubt, whereas in civil trials, the defendant need only be proved guilty by a preponderance of the evidence. Discuss why a higher standard of proof is required in criminal trials.

6–2. Types of Crimes. The following situations are similar (all involve the theft of Makoto's television set), yet they represent three different crimes. Identify the three crimes, noting the differences among them.

(a) While passing Makoto's house one night, Sarah sees a portable television set left unattended on Makoto's lawn. Sarah takes the television set, carries it home, and tells everyone she owns it.

(b) While passing Makoto's house one night, Sarah sees Makoto outside with a portable television set. Holding Makoto at gunpoint, Sarah forces him to give up the set. Then Sarah runs away with it.

(c) While passing Makoto's house one night, Sarah sees a portable television set in a window. Sarah breaks the front-door lock, enters, and leaves with the set.

6–3. Types of Crimes. Which, if any, of the following crimes necessarily involve illegal activity on the part of more than one person?

(a) Bribery.
(b) Forgery.
(c) Embezzlement.
(d) Larceny.
(e) Receiving stolen property.

6–4. Double Jeopardy. Armington, while robbing a drugstore, shot and seriously injured Jennings, a drugstore clerk. Armington was subsequently convicted in a criminal trial of armed robbery and assault and battery. Jennings later brought a civil tort suit against Armington for damages. Armington contended that he could not be tried again for the same crime, as that would constitute double jeopardy, which is prohibited by the Fifth Amendment to the Constitution. Is Armington correct? Explain.

6–5. Receiving Stolen Property. Rafael stops Laura on a busy street and offers to sell her an expensive wristwatch for a fraction of its value. After some questioning by Laura, Rafael admits that the watch is stolen property, although he says he was not the thief. Laura pays for and receives the wristwatch. Has Laura committed any crime? Has Rafael? Explain.

6–6. Criminal Liability. In January 1988, David Ludvigson was hired as chief executive officer of Leopard Enterprises, a group of companies that owned funeral homes and cemeteries in Iowa and sold "pre-need" funeral contracts. Under Iowa law, 80 percent of monies obtained under such a contract must be set aside in trust until the death of the person for whose benefit the funds were paid. Shortly after Ludvigson was hired, the firm began having financial difficulties. Ludvigson used money from these contracts to pay operating expenses until the company went bankrupt and was placed in receivership. Ludvigson was charged and found guilty on five counts of second degree theft stemming from the misappropriation of these funds. He appealed, alleging, among other things, that because none of the victims whose trust funds were used to cover operating expenses was denied services, no injury was done and thus no crime was committed. Will the court agree with Ludvigson? Explain. [*State v. Ludvigson*, 482 N.W.2d 419 (Iowa 1992)]

6–7. Defenses to Criminal Liability. The Child Protection Act of 1984 makes it a crime to receive knowingly through the mails sexually explicit depictions of children. After this act was passed, government agents found Keith Jacobson's name on a bookstore's mailing list. (Jacobson previously had ordered and received from a bookstore two *Bare Boys* magazines containing photographs of nude preteen and teen-age boys.) To test Jacobson's willingness to break the law, government agencies sent mail to him, through five fictitious organizations and a bogus pen pal, over a period of two and a half years. Many of these "organizations" claimed that they had been founded to protect sexual freedom, freedom of choice, and so on. Jacobson eventually ordered a magazine. He testified at trial that he ordered the magazine because he was curious about "all the trouble and the hysteria over pornography and I wanted to see what the material was." When the magazine was delivered, he was arrested for violating the 1984 act. What defense discussed in this chapter might Jacobson raise to avoid criminal liability under the act? Explain fully. [*Jacobson v. United States*, 503 U.S. 540, 112 S.Ct. 1535, 118 L.Ed.2d 174 (1992)]

6–8. Searches and Seizures. The city of Ferndale enacted an ordinance regulating massage parlors. Among other things, the ordinance provided for periodic inspections of the establishments by "[t]he chief of police or other authorized inspectors from the City." Operators and employees of massage parlors in Ferndale filed a suit in a Michigan state court against the city. The plaintiffs pointed out that the ordinance did not require a warrant to conduct a search and argued in part that this was a violation of the Fourth Amendment. On what ground might the court uphold the ordinance? Do massage parlors qualify on this ground? Why or why not? [*Gora v. City of Ferndale*, 456 Mich. 704, 576 N.W.2d 141 (1998)]

6–9. Fifth Amendment. The federal government was investigating a corporation and its employees. The alleged criminal wrongdoing, which included the falsification of corporate books and records, occurred between 1993 and 1996 in one division of the corporation. In 1999, the corporation pleaded guilty and agreed to cooperate in an investigation of the individuals who might have been involved in the improper corporate activities. "Doe I," "Doe II," and "Doe III" were officers of the corporation during the period when the illegal activities occurred and worked in the division where the wrongdoing took place. They were no longer working for the corporation, however, when, as part of the subsequent investigation, the government asked them to provide specific corporate documents in their possession. All three asserted the Fifth

Amendment privilege against self-incrimination. The government asked a federal district court to order the three to produce the records. Corporate employees can be compelled to produce corporate records in a criminal proceeding because they hold the records as representatives of the corporation, to which the Fifth Amendment privilege against self-incrimination does not apply. Should *former employees* also be compelled to produce corporate records in their possession? Why or why not? [*In re Three Grand Jury Subpoenas* Duces Tecum *Dated January 29, 1999,* 191 F.3d 173 (2d Cir. 1999)]

TEST YOUR KNOWLEDGE—ANSWER ON THE WEB

6–10. The District of Columbia Lottery Board licensed Soo Young Bae, a Washington, D.C., merchant, to operate a terminal that prints and dispenses lottery tickets for sale. Bae used the terminal to generate tickets with a face value of $525,586, for which he did not pay. The winning tickets among these had a total redemption value of $296,153, of which Bae successfully obtained all but $72,000. Bae pleaded guilty to computer fraud, and the court sentenced him to eighteen months in prison. In sentencing a defendant for fraud, a federal court must make a reasonable estimate of the victim's loss. The court determined that the value of the loss due to the fraud was $503,650—the market value of the tickets less the commission Bae would have received from the lottery board had he sold those tickets. Bae appealed, arguing that "[a]t the instant any lottery ticket is printed," it is worth whatever value the lottery drawing later assigns to it; that is, losing tickets have no value. Bae thus calculated the loss at $296,153, the value of his winning tickets. Should the U.S. Court of Appeals for the District of Columbia Circuit affirm or reverse Bae's sentence? Why? [*United States v. Bae,* 250 F.3d 774 (C.A.D.C. 2001)]

A QUESTION OF ETHICS AND SOCIAL RESPONSIBILITY

6–11. A troublesome issue concerning the constitutional privilege against self-incrimination has to do with "jail plants"—that is, undercover police officers placed in cells with criminal suspects to gain information from the suspects. For example, in one case the police placed an undercover agent, Parisi, in a jail cell block with Lloyd Perkins, who had been imprisoned on charges unrelated to the murder that Parisi was investigating. When Parisi asked Perkins if he had ever killed anyone, Perkins made statements implicating himself in the murder. Perkins was then charged with the murder. [*Illinois v. Perkins,* 496 U.S. 914, 110 S.Ct. 2394, 110 L.Ed.2d 243 (1990)]

1. Review the discussion of *Miranda v. Arizona* in this chapter's *Landmark in the Law.* Should Perkins's statements be suppressed—that is, not be treated as admissible evidence at trial—because he was not "read his rights," as required by the *Miranda* decision, prior to making his self-incriminating statements? Does *Miranda* apply to Perkins's situation?
2. Do you think that it is fair for the police to resort to trickery and deception to bring those who have committed crimes to justice? Why or why not? What rights or public policies must be balanced in deciding this issue?

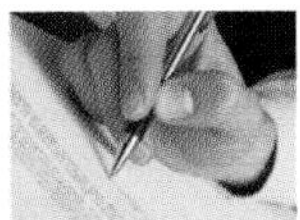

FOR CRITICAL ANALYSIS

6–12. Do you think that criminal procedure in this country is weighted too heavily in favor of accused persons? Can you think of a fairer way to balance the constitutional rights of accused persons against the right of society to be protected against criminal behavior? Should different criminal procedures be used when terrorism is involved? Explain.

Internet Exercises

Go to the *Business Law Today* home page at **http://blt.westbuslaw.com**. Select "Interactive Study Center" and then click on "Chapter 6." There you will find the following Internet research exercises that you can perform to learn more about the *Miranda* decision and the elements of cyber crime:

Activity 6–1: Revisiting *Miranda*
Activity 6–2: Cyber Crime

Before the Test

Go to the *Business Law Today* home page at **http://blt.westbuslaw.com**. Click on "Interactive Quizzes." You will find at least twenty interactive questions relating to this chapter.

CHAPTER 7

Ethics and Social Responsibility

"New occasions teach new duties."

James Russell Lowell, 1819–1891
(American editor, poet, and diplomat)

CHAPTER CONTENTS

LEARNING OBJECTIVES

After reading this chapter, you should be able to answer the following questions:

① What is ethics? What is business ethics? What is the relationship between business ethics and the law?

② How do duty-based ethical standards differ from outcome-based ethical standards?

③ When engaging in ethical decision making, what questions do businesspersons typically consider?

④ What is corporate social responsibility? What are some different theories of social responsibility?

⑤ What is the difference between maximum profits and optimum profits?

Business owners and managers traditionally have had to ensure that their profit-making activities do not exceed the ethical boundaries established by society. In the past, though, these boundaries were often regarded as being coterminous with the law—that is, if something was legal, it was ethical. Shady business dealings were regarded as "just business" more often than not.

In the last few decades, however, the ethical boundaries within which business firms must operate have narrowed significantly. As indicated in the chapter-opening quotation, "New occasions teach new duties," and in the rights-conscious world of today, a business firm that decides it has no duties other than those prescribed by law may find it difficult to survive. If a firm's behavior is perceived as unethical—even though it may be legal—that firm may suffer adverse consequences, including negative publicity and lost profits.

In preparing for a career in business, you will find that a background in business ethics and a commitment to ethical behavior are just as important as a knowledge of the specific laws that you will read about in this text. In this chapter, we first examine the nature of business ethics and some of the sources of ethical standards that have guided others in their business decision making. We then look at the ethical component of business decision making in some detail. In the concluding pages of the chapter, we explore various theories relating to the social responsibility of corporations.

The Nature of Business Ethics

ETHICS
Moral principles and values applied to social behavior.

To understand the nature of business ethics, we need to define what is meant by ethics generally. **Ethics** can be defined as the study of what constitutes right or wrong behavior. It is the branch of philosophy that focuses on morality and the way in which moral principles are applied to daily life. Ethics has to do with questions relating to the fairness, justness, rightness, or wrongness of an action. What is fair? What is just? What is the right thing to do in this situation? These are essentially ethical questions.

Often, moral principles serve as the guiding force in an individual's personal ethical system. Although the terms *ethical* and *moral* are often used interchangeably, the terms refer to slightly different concepts. Whereas ethics has to do with the philosophical, rational basis for morality, morals are often defined as universal rules or guidelines (such as those rooted in religious precepts) that determine our actions and character.

Business Ethics

BUSINESS ETHICS
Ethics in a business context; a consensus of what constitutes right or wrong behavior in the world of business and the application of moral principles to situations that arise in a business setting.

Business ethics focuses on what constitutes ethical behavior in the world of business. Personal ethical standards, of course, play an important role in determining what is or is not ethical, or appropriate, business behavior. Business activities are just one part of the human enterprise, and the ethical standards that guide our behavior as, say, mothers, fathers, or students apply equally well to our activities as businesspersons. Businesspersons, though, must often address more complex ethical issues and conflicts in the workplace than they do in their personal lives—as you will learn in this chapter and throughout this book.

Conflicting Duties

BE CAREFUL Ethical concepts about what is right and what is wrong can change.

One of the reasons that ethical decision making is more complex in the business context than in our personal lives is that business firms are perceived to owe duties to a number of groups. Generally, these groups include the firm's owners (in a corporation, the shareholders), its employees, its suppliers, those who use its products or services (consumers), the community in which it operates, and, according to many, society at large. When these duties come into conflict, difficult choices must be made. These choices may concern the welfare of shareholders versus consumers, shareholders versus employees, and so on.

● **Example 7.1** Suppose that the Farris Company, a paint manufacturer, decides to reduce its costs by downsizing and restructuring its operations. Among other things, this would allow the company to cut back on its overhead by consolidating various supervisory and managerial positions. Yet which employees should be retained and which should be let go? Should the firm retain highly paid employees who have worked for—and received annual raises from—the firm for years? Alternatively, in the interests of cutting costs, should it retain (or hire) younger, less experienced persons at lower salaries?

The Farris Company would not necessarily be acting illegally if it pursued the second option. Unless a fired employee can prove that the employer has breached an employment contract or violated the Age Discrimination in Employment Act (ADEA) of 1967, he or she will not have a cause of action against the employer. As you will learn in Chapter 35, the ADEA prohibits discrimination against workers forty years of age and older on the basis of their age.

In deciding this issue, remember that the company must keep its eye on its profit margin. If it does not, the firm may fail, and the shareholders will lose their investments. Furthermore, why should the firm retain highly paid employees if it can obtain essentially the same work output for a lower cost from less highly paid employees? Does Farris owe an ethical duty to employees who have served the firm loyally over a long period of time? Most people would say yes. Should this duty take precedence over Farris's duty to the firm's owners to maintain or increase the profitability of the firm? What if the firm faces imminent bankruptcy if it cannot lower its operational costs? What if longtime employees are willing to take a slight reduction in pay to help the firm through its financial difficulties? What if they are not? •

In the following case, an employer was confronted with a dwindling market and decreasing sales. The employer decided to reduce its costs of doing business by eliminating some of its obligations to its employees.

CASE 7.1 Varity Corp. v. Howe

Supreme Court of the United States, 1996.
516 U.S. 489,
116 S.Ct. 1065,
134 L.Ed.2d 130.
http://laws.findlaw.com/US/000/U10206.html[a]

HISTORICAL AND ECONOMIC SETTING *Since 1950, the number of U.S. farms has declined as small farms have been driven out of business by corporate agribusinesses with assets that small farmers cannot match. Between 1980 and 1996, the number of farms decreased by more than 14 percent, to fewer than 2 million, even as the average acreage per farm increased by 10 percent, to nearly 470 acres. Agribusinesses require fewer workers than do small farms, and thus, the total farm population also decreased by 24 percent in the 1980s. Fewer farmers means a smaller market for those who cater to it.*

FACTS Varity Corporation manufactures and sells farm implements. In 1986, Varity set up a subsidiary, Massey Combines Corporation (MCC), to market its self-propelled combines and four-wheel-drive tractors. The sales of both products were at an all-time low. Varity convinced current and former employees who were, or had been, involved with the products to accept a transfer of their jobs and retirement benefit plans to MCC. Varity did not tell those employees that it expected MCC to fail. Within two years, MCC failed. Among other consequences, some retirees stopped receiving benefits. The retirees and other ex-employees sued Varity in a federal district court under the Employee Retirement Income Security Act of 1974 (ERISA).[b] They claimed that Varity owed them a fiduciary duty, which it had breached.[c] The court ruled in their favor, and the U.S. Court of Appeals for the Eighth Circuit affirmed the deci-

a. This is a page within the Web site of FindLaw. In addition to its own databases, FindLaw provides links to other legal resources on the Internet.

b. 29 U.S.C. Sections 1001–1461. See Chapter 34.

c. A fiduciary is a party who, because of something that he or she has undertaken to do, has a duty to act primarily for another's benefit.

CASE 7.1—Continued

sion. Varity then appealed to the United States Supreme Court.

ISSUE Did Varity owe a fiduciary duty to its employees with respect to their retirement benefits? If so, did it violate that duty?

DECISION Yes, to both questions. The United States Supreme Court affirmed the decision of the lower court.

REASON The Supreme Court pointed out that under ERISA, a fiduciary is required to "discharge his [or her] duties with respect to a [retirement] plan solely in the interest of the participants and beneficiaries." It was on this statute that the Varity retirees based their suit. To participate knowingly and significantly in deceiving a plan's beneficiaries in order to save the employer money at the beneficiaries' expense is not to act "solely in the interest of the participants and beneficiaries." The Court stated that "[l]ying is inconsistent with the duty of loyalty owed by all fiduciaries."

FOR CRITICAL ANALYSIS—Ethical Consideration *Should a company continue to market a slow-selling line of products for the sole purpose of employing those who work on the products?*

BUSINESS ETHICS AND THE LAW

Because the law reflects and codifies a society's ethical values, many of our ethical decisions are made for us—by our laws. Nevertheless, simply obeying the law does not fulfill all ethical obligations. In the interest of preserving personal freedom, as well as for practical reasons, the law does not—and cannot—codify all ethical requirements. No law says, for example, that it is *illegal* to lie to one's family, but it may be *unethical* to do so.

Likewise, in the business world, numerous actions may be unethical but not necessarily illegal. Even though it may be convenient for businesspersons merely to comply with the law, such an approach may not always yield ethical outcomes. • **EXAMPLE 7.2** A pharmaceutical company may be banned from marketing a particular drug in the United States because of the drug's possible adverse side effects. Yet no law prohibits the company from selling the drug in foreign markets—even though some consumers in those markets may suffer serious health problems as a result of using the drug. At issue here is not whether it would be legal to market the drug in other countries but whether it would be *ethical* to do so.•

In short, the law has its limits—it cannot make all ethical decisions for us. When it does not, ethical standards must guide the decision-making process.

Sources of Ethical Standards

How do business decision makers decide whether a given action is the "right" one for their firms? What ethical standards should be applied? Broadly speaking, ethical reasoning relating to business traditionally has been characterized by two fundamental approaches. One approach defines ethical behavior in terms of *duty.* The other approach determines what is ethical in terms of the *consequences*, or outcome, of any given action. We examine each of these approaches here.

DUTY-BASED ETHICS

Duty-based ethical standards often are derived from revealed truths, such as religious precepts. They can also be derived through philosophical reasoning.

Religion Duty-based ethical standards are often derived from moral principles rooted in religious sources. In the Judeo-Christian tradition, the Ten Commandments of the Old Testament establish rules for moral action. Other religions have their own sources of revealed truth—such as the Koran (Qur'an) in the Muslim world. Within the confines of their influence, moral principles are universal and *absolute*—they are not to be questioned. • **EXAMPLE 7.3** Consider one of the Ten Commandments: "Thou shalt not steal." This is an absolute mandate. Even a benevolent motive for stealing (such as Robin Hood's) cannot justify the act, because the act itself is inherently immoral and thus wrong. When an act is prohibited by religious teachings that serve as the foundation of a person's moral or ethical standards, the act is unethical for that person and should not be undertaken, regardless of its consequences. •

Ethical standards based on religious teachings may also involve an element of compassion. Therefore, even though it might be profitable for a firm to lay off a less productive employee, the decision makers would give substantial weight to potential suffering that might result, such as the effect on the employee's family if she or he could not readily find employment elsewhere. Compassionate treatment of others is also mandated—to a certain extent, at least—by the Golden Rule of the ancients ("Do unto others as you would have them do unto you"), which has been adopted by most religions.

Kantian Philosophy Ethical standards based on a concept of duty may also be derived solely from philosophical principles. The German philosopher Immanuel Kant (1724–1804), for example, identified some general guiding principles for moral behavior based on what he believed to be the fundamental nature of human beings. Kant held that it is rational to assume that human beings are qualitatively different from other physical objects occupying space. Humans are endowed with moral integrity and the capacity to reason and conduct their affairs rationally. Therefore, their thoughts and actions should be respected. When human beings are treated merely as a means to an end, they are being treated as the equivalent of objects and are being denied their basic humanity.

A central postulate in Kantian ethics is that individuals should evaluate their actions in light of the consequences that would follow if everyone in society acted in the same way. This **categorical imperative** can be applied to any action. • **EXAMPLE 7.4** Say that you are deciding whether to cheat on an examination. If you have adopted Kant's categorical imperative, you will decide not to cheat because if everyone cheated, the examination would be meaningless. •

CATEGORICAL IMPERATIVE
A concept developed by the philosopher Immanuel Kant as an ethical guideline for behavior. In deciding whether an action is right or wrong, or desirable or undesirable, a person should evaluate the action in terms of what would happen if everybody else in the same situation, or category, acted the same way.

The Principle of Rights Duty-based ethical standards imply that human beings have basic rights because a duty cannot exist without a corresponding right. For example, the commandment "Thou shalt not kill" implies that individuals have a right to live. Additionally, religious ethics may involve a rights component because of the belief—characteristic of many religions—that an individual is "made in the image of God" or "Allah." This belief confers on the individual great dignity as a person. For one who holds this belief, not to respect that dignity—and the rights and status that flow from it—would be morally wrong. Kantian ethics also implies fundamental rights based on the personal dignity of each individual. Just as individuals have a duty not to treat others as means to an end, so individuals have a right to have their status and moral integrity as human beings treated with respect.

The principle that human beings have certain fundamental rights (to life, freedom, and the pursuit of happiness, for example) is deeply embedded in Western culture. As discussed in Chapter 1, the natural law tradition embraces the concept that certain actions (such as killing another person) are morally wrong because they are contrary to nature (the natural desire to continue living). Those who adhere to this **principle of rights**, or "rights theory," believe that a key factor in determining whether a business decision is ethical is how that decision affects the rights of various groups. These groups include the firm's owners, its employees, the consumers of its products or services, its suppliers, the community in which it does business, and society as a whole.

PRINCIPLE OF RIGHTS
The principle that human beings have certain fundamental rights (to life, freedom, and the pursuit of happiness, for example). Those who adhere to this "rights theory" believe that a key factor in determining whether a business decision is ethical is how that decision affects the rights of various groups. These groups include the firm's owners, its employees, the consumers of its products or services, its suppliers, the community in which it does business, and society as a whole.

OUTCOME-BASED ETHICS

"Thou shalt act so as to generate the greatest good for the greatest number." This is a paraphrase of the major premise of the utilitarian approach to ethics. **Utilitarianism** is a philosophical theory first developed by Jeremy Bentham (1748–1832) and then advanced, with some modifications, by John Stuart Mill (1806–1873)—both British philosophers. In contrast to duty-based ethics, utilitarianism is outcome oriented. It focuses on the consequences of an action, not on the nature of the action itself or on any set of preestablished moral values or religious beliefs.

UTILITARIANISM
An approach to ethical reasoning that evaluates behavior not on the basis of any absolute ethical or moral values but on the consequences of that behavior for those who will be affected by it. In utilitarian reasoning, a "good" decision is one that results in the greatest good for the greatest number of people affected by the decision.

Under a utilitarian model of ethics, an action is morally correct, or "right," when, among the people it affects, it produces the greatest amount of good for the greatest number. When an action affects the majority adversely, it is morally wrong. Applying the utilitarian theory thus requires (1) a determination of which individuals will be affected by the action in question; (2) a **cost-benefit analysis**—an assessment of the negative and positive effects of alternative actions on these individuals; and (3) a choice as to which alternative action will produce maximum societal utility (the greatest positive benefits for the greatest number of individuals).

COST-BENEFIT ANALYSIS
A decision-making technique that involves weighing the costs of a given action against the benefits of that action.

Utilitarianism is often criticized because it tends to focus on society as a whole rather than on individual human rights. • **EXAMPLE 7.5** From a utilitarian standpoint, it might be ethically acceptable to test drugs or medicines on human beings, even if one of those human subjects might suffer or die, because a majority of the population

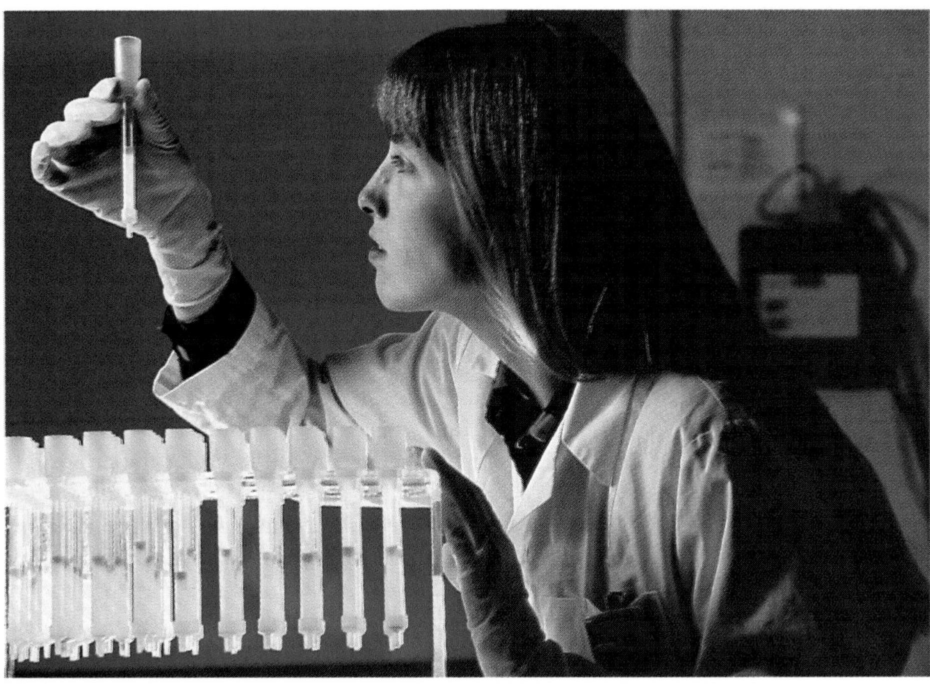

A lab worker conducts research for the development of a drug. If the drug proves beneficial to most people but adverse to a few, would it, under a utilitarian model of ethics, be marketed?

would presumably benefit from the experiments. If, however, one accepts the principle that each individual has basic human rights (to life, freedom, and the pursuit of happiness), then an action that deprives an individual or group of individuals of these rights—even for the greater good of society—is ethically unacceptable. No amount of cost-benefit analysis can justify the action.●

Business Decisions and Ethics

Most major companies today ask three questions about any action before it is undertaken: Is the action profitable? Is it legal? Is it ethical? The first prong of this test for business decision making—determining whether a given course of action will be profitable—is foremost. After all, for-profit firms remain in business only if they make a profit. If the action will not be profitable, it probably will not be undertaken. If the action will be profitable, then the decision makers need to evaluate whether it will also be legal and ethical.

Is the Contemplated Action Legal?

MORAL MINIMUM
The minimum degree of ethical behavior expected of a business firm, which is usually defined as compliance with the law.

In today's business world, legal compliance usually is regarded as the **moral minimum**—the minimal acceptable standard for ethical business behavior. It might seem that determining the legality of a given action should be simple. Either something is legal or it is not. In fact, one of the major challenges businesspersons face is that the legality of a particular action is not always clear. In part, this is because there are so many laws regulating business that it is possible to violate one of them without realizing it. There are also numerous "gray areas" in the law, making it difficult to predict with certainty how a court may apply a given law to a particular action.

Laws Regulating Business Today's business firms are subject to extensive government regulation. As mentioned in Chapter 1, virtually every action a firm undertakes—from the initial act of going into business to hiring and firing personnel to selling products in the marketplace—is subject to statutory law and to numerous rules and regulations issued by administrative agencies. Furthermore, these rules and regulations are changed or supplemented frequently.

Determining whether a planned action is legal thus requires the decision makers to keep abreast of the law. Normally, large business firms have attorneys on their staffs to assist them in making key decisions. Small firms must also seek legal advice before making important business decisions—because the consequences of just one violation of a regulatory rule may be costly.

Ignorance of the law will not excuse a business owner or manager from liability for violating a statute or regulation. Recall from Chapter 6 that in one case, the court imposed criminal fines, as well as imprisonment, on a company's supervisory employee for violating a federal environmental act—even though the employee was totally unaware of what was required under the provisions of that act.[1]

In the following case, a company was alleged to have infringed on another's service mark "willfully or in bad faith." (Service marks, which are used in the sale or advertising of services, were discussed in Chapter 5.) In its defense, the company offered what it called a "credible, innocent explanation" for its continued use of the mark.

1. *United States v. Hanousek*, 176 F.3d 1116 (9th Cir. 1999). This case was presented as Case 6.2 in Chapter 6.

CASE 7.2 New York State Society of Certified Public Accountants v. Eric Louis Associates, Inc.

United States District Court,
Southern District of New York, 1999.
79 F.Supp.2d 331.

FACTS The New York State Society of Certified Public Accountants (the Society) has more than 30,000 members. The Society sets standards for certified public accountants (CPAs) and protects the interests of its members and the public with respect to the practice of accounting. Since 1984, the Society has used the service mark "NYSSCPA" on its business cards and other promotional material. In 1994, the Society registered the domain name "nysscpa.org" and, since 1997, has operated a Web site at this Internet address. Eric Louis Associates, Inc. (ELA), is a small firm engaged in the job placement of accountants and other professionals. Brian Elias was ELA's founder and president. In January 1999, ELA registered the domain name "nysscpa.com" and began operating a Web site at that address, using "NYSSCPA" as a meta tag.[a] ELA's home page stated that it was "not affiliated with" the Society, but clicking on a hyperlink from that page to the Society's site framed that site within ELA's site. On March 25, 1999, the Society wrote a letter to ELA, demanding that ELA stop using the "nysscpa.com" domain name and stop framing the Society's Web site. ELA agreed to do so if the Society would pay it $20,000 or provide, free of charge, an exhibitor's booth at the annual NYSSCPA conference for the next five years. On April 6, the Society sent a second letter, refusing ELA's offer and repeating its demands. When ELA did nothing, the Society filed a suit against ELA in a federal district court, which held that ELA had infringed the Society's mark. The next question was whether the infringement was willful or in bad faith, which would entitle the Society to collect its attorneys' fees from ELA.

a. A *meta tag* is a key word in the source code of a Web page. A meta tag prompts a search engine to include that Web site in the search engine's results. The acceptability of the use of meta tags was discussed in Chapter 5.

ISSUE Was ELA's infringement willful or in bad faith?

DECISION Yes. The court held that the Society was entitled to collect from ELA the attorneys' fees the Society owed for work done after April 6. ELA's conduct was willful and in bad faith after that date because, on learning that it might not have any rights to the Society's service mark, ELA did not stop its use of the mark or seek the advice of counsel.

REASON The court explained that the Society's demand on March 25 put ELA "on notice that ELA's use of the 'nysscpa.com' domain name and the 'NYSSCPA' meta-tag was potentially illegal," and despite the notice, ELA attempted only to sell the domain name to the Society. "Defendant responded to [the] second cease and desist demand by continuing its two-pronged strategy of neither ceasing and desisting nor seeking the advice of counsel. On this date, therefore—at the latest—Mr. Elias's belief that ELA's actions were not violative of Plaintiff's trademark rights ceased being reasonable. As such, on this date—at the latest—Defendant's conduct commenced being willful and tinged with bad faith."

FOR CRITICAL ANALYSIS—Ethical Consideration *The concept of good faith permeates the law. Why should good faith, which is essentially a subjective quality, determine whether an act is legal or illegal?*

"Gray Areas" in the Law In many situations, business firms face another problem. Even though they are aware of what laws govern a particular activity, how the law will be applied may not be clear. • **EXAMPLE 7.6** Suppose that a firm decides to launch a new advertising campaign. How far can the firm go in making claims for its product or services? Federal and state laws prohibit firms from engaging in "deceptive advertising." At the federal level, the test for deceptive advertising normally used by the Federal Trade Commission is whether an advertising claim would deceive a "reasonable consumer."[2] At what point, though, would a reasonable consumer be deceived by a particular ad? •

2. See Chapter 33 for a discussion of the Federal Trade Commission's role in regulating deceptive trade practices, including misleading advertising.

Business decision makers thus need to proceed with caution and evaluate planned actions and their consequences from an ethical perspective. Generally, if a company can demonstrate that it acted in good faith and responsibly in the circumstances, it has a better chance of successfully defending its action in court.

ETHICAL ISSUE 7.1

How can a business decide whether a warning is "adequate"?

One of the "gray areas" in the law has to do with product misuse. As you will read in Chapter 18, product liability laws require manufacturers and sellers to warn consumers of the kind of injuries that might result from the foreseeable misuse of their products. An exception to this rule is made when a risk associated with a product is "open and obvious." Sharp knives, for example, can obviously injure their users. Sometimes, however, a business has no way of predicting how a court might rule in deciding whether a particular risk is open and obvious or whether consumers should be warned of the risk. If consumers should be warned, a further question arises: What constitutes an adequate warning? Even the courts often disagree on such matters.

In one case, for example, a company sold small aerosol cans of butane, a fuel for cigarette lighters. On each can was the warning "DO NOT BREATHE SPRAY." Nonetheless, twenty-year-old Stephen Pavlik died from intentionally inhaling the contents of one of the cans. In the lawsuit that followed, brought by Pavlik's father, the trial court and the appellate court came to different conclusions. The trial court reasoned that Pavlik must have been aware of the dangers of inhaling butane and that a more specific warning would not have affected his conduct. The appellate court, though, concluded that the warning gave Pavlik "no notice of the serious nature of the danger posed by inhalation, intentional or otherwise."[3] Cases such as this send a clear message to businesspersons: never assume that a risk that may seem open and obvious to you will necessarily be open and obvious to a court.

Technological Developments and Legal Uncertainties Uncertainties concerning how particular laws may apply to specific factual situations have been compounded in the cyber age. As noted in earlier chapters, the widespread use of the Internet has given rise to situations never before faced by the courts.

The following case is illustrative. The case involved an airline pilot who claimed that defamatory, gender-based messages made by her co-workers in an online forum created a hostile working environment. Federal law prohibits harassment in the workplace, including "hostile-environment harassment," which occurs when an employee is subjected to sexual conduct or comments that he or she perceives as offensive. Generally, employers are expected to take immediate and appropriate corrective action in response to an employee's complaints of sexual harassment or abuse. Otherwise, they may be held liable for the harassing actions of the employee's co-workers or supervisors (see Chapter 35). At issue in the case was whether the online forum could be considered part of the "workplace" over which the employer had control.

3. *Pavlik v. Lane Ltd./Tobacco Exporters International,* 135 F.3d 876 (3d Cir. 1998).

CASE 7.3 Blakey v. Continental Airlines, Inc.

New Jersey Supreme Court, 2000.
751 A.2d 538.
http://lawlibrary.rutgers.edu/search.shtml[a]

HISTORICAL AND TECHNOLOGICAL SETTING *CompuServe, Inc., a subsidiary of America Online, Inc., is the Internet service provider for Continental Airlines, Inc. CompuServe provides Continental's pilots and other crew members with online access to their flight schedules. As part of the service, CompuServe makes a "Crew Members Forum" available for the exchange of ideas and information via messages and threads.*[b] *Through customized software, any individual with a Continental pilot or crew member identification number can access the Forum. This includes chief pilots and assistant chief pilots, who are considered management at Continental. Technical assistance is provided by system operators (SYSOPS), who are volunteer crew members.*

FACTS Tammy Blakey, a pilot for Continental Airlines since 1984, was the airline's first female captain—and one of only five Continental pilots—to fly an Airbus, or A300, aircraft. Shortly after qualifying to be a captain on the A300, Blakey complained about pornographic photos and vulgar gender-based comments directed at her in her plane's cockpit and other work areas by her male co-employees. Blakey pursued claims against Continental with the Equal Employment Opportunity Commission, the federal agency that administers federal laws prohibiting employment discrimination, and in a federal district court.[c] Meanwhile, Continental pilots published a series of harassing, gender-based, defamatory messages about Blakey on the Forum. When the court refused to consider these messages, Blakey filed a complaint against Continental and others in a New Jersey state court. She alleged, in part, gender-based harassment arising from a hostile work environment. Continental filed a motion for summary judgment on this claim, which the court granted. A state intermediate appellate court upheld the summary judgment, and Blakey appealed to the New Jersey Supreme Court.

ISSUE Can an employees' online forum be such an integral part of the workplace that harassment on it may be regarded as an extension of a pattern of harassment in the workplace?

DECISION Yes. The New Jersey Supreme Court reversed the judgment of the lower court and remanded the case for further proceedings. The state supreme court indicated that the trial court was to determine, among other things, which messages were harassing, whether Continental had notice of those messages, and the severity or pervasiveness of the harassing conduct.

REASON The state supreme court explained that "[o]ur common experience tells us how important are the extensions of the workplace where the relations among employees are cemented or sometimes sundered. If an 'old boys' network' continued, in an after-hours setting, the belittling conduct that edges over into harassment, what exactly is the outsider (whether black, Latino, or woman) to do? Keep swallowing the abuse or give up the chance to make the team? We believe that severe or pervasive harassment in a work-related setting that continues a pattern of harassment on the job is sufficiently related to the workplace that an informed employer who takes no effective measures to stop it, sends the harassed employee the message that the harassment is acceptable and that the management supports the harasser." The court compared CompuServe's role to "that of a company that builds an old-fashioned bulletin board. If the maker of an old-fashioned bulletin board provided a better bulletin board by setting aside space on it for employees to post messages, we would have little doubt that messages on the company bulletin board would be part of the workplace setting."

FOR CRITICAL ANALYSIS—Social Consideration *Does the holding in the* Blakey *case mean that employers have a duty to monitor their employees' e-mail and other online communications?*

a. This page includes a search box for a database of the recent opinions of the New Jersey state courts. In the box, type "Blakey" and click on the "Search" link. When the results appear, scroll down the list and click on the *Blakey* case name to access the opinion. This Web site is maintained by Rutgers School of Law in Camden, New Jersey.

b. A *thread* is a sequence of responses to an initial message posting. This enables a user to follow or join an individual discussion.

c. In 1997, the federal court ruled in favor of Blakey on a claim of gender-based harassment, awarding her $480,000 in back pay, $15,000 in front pay, and $250,000 for emotional distress, pain, and suffering. The court also found that Blakey had failed to mitigate damages (reduce her damages—by finding other work, for example) and subtracted $120,000 from her back pay award.

IS THE CONTEMPLATED ACTION ETHICAL?

Even if a company is certain of the legality of a particular action, that does not necessarily mean that the action is ethical. • **EXAMPLE 7.7** Suppose that a corporation that markets baby formula in developing countries has learned that mothers in those countries often mix the formula with impure water to make the formula go further. As a result, babies there are suffering from malnutrition, diarrhea, and even death. Although the corporation is not violating any law, many would contend that it should suspend sales of the formula in those countries.[4] •

Typically, in deciding whether a given action would be ethical, a firm's decision makers are guided not only by their own ethical principles and reasoning processes but also by their company's ethical policies and code of conduct. At times, public opinion on an issue may guide a corporation's decision.

Ethical Codes Virtually all large corporations today have established ethical policies or codes of conduct to help guide their executives and managers (and all company personnel) in making decisions. Typically, an ethical code, or code of conduct, will indicate the company's commitment to legal compliance, as well as to the welfare of its employees, suppliers, consumers, and others who may be affected by the company's decisions and practices.

For example, look at the fold-out exhibit in this chapter showing Costco's Code of Ethics. This code clearly indicates Costco's commitment to legal compliance, as well as to the welfare of its members (those who belong to its wholesale clubs and purchase its products), its employees, and its vendors (suppliers). The code also details some specific ways in which the interests and welfare of these groups will be protected. If you look closely at the exhibit, you will also see that Costco acknowledges that by protecting these groups' interests, it will realize its "ultimate goal"—which is to reward its shareholders (those who own the company). Costco's code can guide management and supervisory personnel as they make decisions involving the ethical rights and obligations of each group.

Corporate Compliance Programs In a large corporation, an ethical code usually is just one part of a comprehensive corporate compliance program. Other components of such a program may include a corporate ethics committee, ethical training programs, and internal audits (to monitor compliance with applicable laws and the company's standards of conduct). Some companies also have a special office to which employees can report—in person or perhaps anonymously via an 800 number—suspected improper conduct, including any legal, ethical, or policy violations that may occur.

Generally, to be effective, ethical policies must be clearly communicated to employees and must bear on the real ethical issues confronting business decision makers. Additionally, a compliance program should be integrated throughout the firm so that unethical behavior in one corporate department does not escape the attention of those in control of the corporation or the corporate officials responsible for implementing and monitoring the company's program. Finally, corporate management, by its own conduct, should indicate that ethical considerations take priority.

"What you do speaks so loudly that I cannot hear what you say."
RALPH WALDO EMERSON, 1803–1882
(American poet and essayist)

• **EXAMPLE 7.8** If management makes no attempt to deter unethical behavior—by reprimanding or firing employees, for example—it will be clear to employees that management is not all that serious about ethics. Likewise, if a company awards promotions or salary increases to those who obviously engage in unethical tactics to increase the

4. This situation faced the Nestlé Company in the 1970s. That company had concluded, on the basis of a cost-benefit analysis, that it was ethically justified in continuing to market its baby formula in developing countries. Nestlé was severely criticized for its behavior.

firm's profits, then employees who do not resort to such tactics will be at a disadvantage. An employee in this situation may decide that because "everyone else does it," he or she might as well do so also.●

ON THE WEB For an example of an online group that focuses on corporate activities from the perspective of corporate social responsibility, go to **http://www.corpwatch.org**.

The Role of Public Opinion Complicating business ethical decision making is the increasingly important role played by public opinion in determining whether business behavior is ethical. In the last two decades, and particularly since the advent of the Internet, the actions of business firms have been much more closely scrutinized by the media and various interest groups (groups supporting human rights, animal rights, the environment, consumers, employees, and so on) than they ever were in the past. "Corporate watch" groups routinely report on their Web sites any corporate activities that the groups deem unethical. Usually, the groups also urge those who access the site to take action—by printing out and sending a prepared letter to the offending firm, for example. Numerous Web sites today have been set up to protest against specific companies' products or services. (For a further discussion of this issue, see this chapter's *Business Law in the Online World* feature on the next page.)

"Never doubt that a small group of committed citizens can change the world; indeed, it is the only thing that ever has."

MARGARET MEAD, 1901–1978 (American anthropologist)

Generally, if a corporation undertakes or continues an action deemed to be unethical by one or more interest groups, the firm's "unethical" behavior will probably become widely known. In the interests of maintaining their good reputations and their profitability, business firms therefore pay attention to public opinion.

Business ethics thus has a practical element. As a manager, you might personally be convinced that there is nothing unethical about a certain business action. If a highly vocal interest group believes otherwise, though, you might want to reassess your decision with a view toward preserving the firm's goodwill and reputation in the community. If you decide to pursue the action regardless of public opinion, you may violate your ethical (and legal) duty to act in the firm's best interests.

Corporate Social Responsibility

As mentioned earlier in this chapter, at one time businesses had few ethical requirements other than complying with the law. Generally, if an action was legal, it was regarded as ethical—no more, no less. By the 1960s, however, this attitude had begun to change significantly. Groups concerned with civil rights, employee safety and welfare, consumer protection, environmental preservation, and other causes began to pressure corporate America to behave in a more responsible manner with respect to these causes. Thus was born the concept of **corporate social responsibility**—the idea that corporations can and should act ethically and be accountable to society for their actions.

CORPORATE SOCIAL RESPONSIBILITY The concept that corporations can and should act ethically and be accountable to society for their actions.

VIEWS ON CORPORATE SOCIAL RESPONSIBILITY

Just what constitutes corporate social responsibility has been debated for some time. No one contests the claim that corporations have duties to their shareholders, employees, and product or service users (consumers). Many of these duties are written into law—that is, they are legal duties. The nature of a corporation's duties to other groups and to society at large, however, is not so clear. Today, there are a number of views on this issue, including those discussed in the following subsections.

Profit Maximization Corporate directors and officers have a duty to act in the shareholders' interest. Because of the nature of the relationship between corporate directors

BUSINESS LAW: //in the Online World

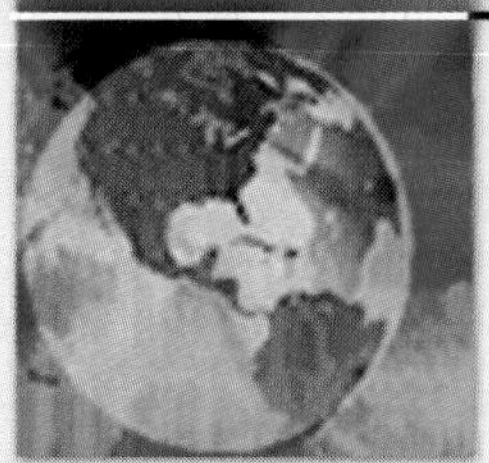

Cybergriping

In today's online world, a recurring challenge for businesses is how to deal with cybergripers—those who complain in cyberspace about corporate products, services, or activities. For trademark owners, the issue becomes particularly thorny when cybergriping sites add the word "sucks" or "stinks" or some other disparaging term to the domain name of particular companies. These sites, sometimes referred to collectively as "sucks" sites, are established solely for the purpose of criticizing the products or services sold by the companies that own the marks. Can businesses do anything to ward off these cyber attacks on their reputations and goodwill?

Trademark Protection versus Free Speech Rights

A number of companies have sued the owners of "sucks" sites for trademark infringement in the hope that a court or an arbitrating panel will order the owner of that site to cease using the domain name. To date, however, companies have had little success pursuing this alternative. In one case, for example, Bally Total Fitness Holding Corporation sued Andrew Faber, who had established a "Bally sucks" site for the purpose of criticizing Bally's health clubs and business practices. Bally claimed that Faber had infringed on its trademark. The court did not agree, holding that the "speech"—consumer commentary—on Faber's Web site was protected by the First Amendment. According to the court, "The explosion of the Internet is not without its growing pains. It is an efficient means for business to disseminate information, but it also affords critics of those businesses an equally efficient means of disseminating commentary." In short, Bally could not look to trademark law for a remedy against cyber critics.[a]

Generally, the courts have been reluctant to hold that the use of a business's domain name for a "sucks" site infringes on the trademark owner's rights. After all, one of the primary reasons trademarks are protected under U.S. law is to prevent customers from becoming confused over the origins of the goods for sale—and a cybergriping site would certainly not create such confusion. Furthermore, American courts give extensive protection to free speech rights, including the right to express opinions about companies and their products.

Preventive Tactics

Many businesses have concluded that while they cannot control what people say about them, they can make it more difficult for it to be said—by buying up insulting domain names before the cybergripers can register them. For example, United Parcel Service (UPS) recently bought UPSstinks.com, IHateUPS.com, UPSBites.com, and a number of similar names. This has now become standard procedure for many firms. Indeed, a study by Company Sleuth of domain name registrations revealed that in just one month (August 2000), nearly 250 companies had registered domain names containing "stinks," "bites," "sucks," or similarly disparaging words. Wal-Mart alone registered more than two hundred anti–Wal-Mart names.[b]

FOR CRITICAL ANALYSIS

Do you believe that cybergriping sites help to improve the ethical performance of the businesses they criticize?

a. *Bally Total Fitness Holding Corp. v. Faber,* 29 F.Supp.2d 1161 (C.D.Cal. 1998).

b. David Stretfield, "Making Bad Names for Themselves: Firms Preempt Critics with Nasty Domains," *The Washington Post,* September 8, 2000, p. A1.

and officers and the shareholder-owners, the law holds directors and officers to a high standard of care in business decision making (see Chapter 27).

In the traditional view, this duty to shareholders takes precedence over all other corporate duties, and the primary goal of corporations should be profit maximization. Milton Friedman, the Nobel Prize–winning economist and a proponent of the profit-maximization view, sees "one and only one" social responsibility of a corporation: "to use its resources and engage in activities designed to increase its profits, so long as it

Ben and Jerry, of Ben and Jerry's Ice Cream, at the One World, One Heart Festival in New York City. According to Ben, "Business has a responsibility to give back to the community." Does giving back to the community conflict with other corporate purposes? If so, can a balance be struck? How?

stays within the rules of the game, which is to say, engages in open and free competition without deception and fraud."[5]

Those who accept this position argue that a firm can best contribute to society by generating profits. Society benefits because a firm realizes profits only when it markets products or services that are desired by society. These products and services enhance the standard of living, and the profits accumulated by successful business firms generate national wealth. Our laws and court decisions promoting trade and commerce reflect the public policy that the fruits of commerce (income and wealth) are desirable and good. Because our society regards income and wealth as ethical goals, corporations, by contributing to income and wealth, automatically are acting ethically.

ON THE WEB You can find articles on issues relating to shareholders and corporate accountability at the Corporate Governance Web site. Go to **http://www.corpgov.net**.

The Stakeholder Approach Another view of corporate social responsibility stresses that a corporation's duty to its shareholders should be weighed against its duties to other groups affected by corporate decisions. Corporate decision makers should consider not only the welfare of shareholders but also the welfare of other *stakeholders*—employees, customers, creditors, suppliers, and the community in which the corporation operates. The reasoning behind this "stakeholder view" of corporate social responsibility is that in some circumstances, one or more of these other groups may have a greater stake in company decisions than the shareholders do.

• **Example 7.9** A heavily indebted corporation is facing imminent bankruptcy. The shareholder-investors have little to lose in this situation because their stock is already next to worthless. The corporation's creditors will be first in line for any corporate assets remaining. Thus, in this situation the creditors have the greatest "stake" in the corporation. Therefore, under the stakeholder view, corporate directors and officers should give greater weight to the creditors' interests than to those of the shareholders. •

Corporate Citizenship Another theory of social responsibility argues that corporations should actively promote goals that society deems worthwhile and take positive

5. Milton Friedman, "Does Business Have Social Responsibility?" *Bank Administration,* April 1971, pp. 13–14.

"Next to doing the right thing, the most important thing is to let people know you are doing the right thing."

JOHN D. ROCKEFELLER, 1839–1897 (American industrialist and philanthropist)

steps toward solving social problems. Because so much of the wealth and power of this country is controlled by business, business in turn has a responsibility to society to use that wealth and power in socially beneficial ways. To be sure, since the nineteenth century and the emergence of large business enterprises in America, corporations have generally contributed some of their shareholders' wealth to meet social needs. Indeed, virtually all large corporations today have established nonprofit foundations for this purpose. Yet corporate citizenship requires more than just making donations to worthwhile causes. Under a corporate citizenship view of social responsibility, companies are also judged on how they conduct their affairs with respect to employment discrimination, human rights, environmental concerns, and so on.

Critics of this view believe that it is inappropriate to use the power of the corporate business world to fashion society's goals by promoting social causes. Determinations as to what exactly is in society's best interest involve questions that are essentially political; therefore, the public, through the political process, should have a say in making those determinations. The legislature—not the corporate board room—is thus the appropriate forum for such decisions.

MAXIMUM VERSUS OPTIMUM PROFITS

Today's corporate decision makers are, in a sense, poised on a fulcrum between profitability and ethical responsibility. If they emphasize profits at the expense of perceived ethical responsibilities to other groups, they may become the target of negative media exposure and even lawsuits. If they go too far in the other direction (keep an unprofitable plant open so that the employees do not lose their jobs, invest too heavily in charitable works or social causes, and so on), their profits will suffer, and they may have to go out of business.

Striking the right balance on this fulcrum is difficult, and usually some profits must be sacrificed in the process. Instead of maximum profits, many firms today aim for **optimum profits**—the maximum profits a firm can realize while staying within legal *and* ethical limits.

OPTIMUM PROFITS
The amount of profits that a business can make and still act ethically, as opposed to maximum profits, defined as the amount of profits a firm can make if it is willing to disregard ethical concerns.

Ethics in the Global Context

Given the varied cultures and religions of the world's nations, one should not be surprised that frequent conflicts in ethics arise between foreign and U.S. businesspersons. • **EXAMPLE 7.10** In Islamic (Muslim) countries, the consumption of alcohol and certain foods is forbidden by the Koran (the sayings of the prophet Muhammad, which lie at the heart of Islam and Islamic law). It would be thoughtless and imprudent to invite a Saudi Arabian business contact out for a drink. •

The role played by women in other countries may also present some difficult ethical problems for firms doing business internationally. Equal employment opportunity is a fundamental public policy in the United States, and Title VII of the Civil Rights Act of 1964 prohibits discrimination against women in the employment context (see Chapter 35). Some other countries, however, offer little protection for women against gender discrimination in the workplace, including sexual harassment.

We look here at how laws governing workers in other countries, particularly in the developing countries, have created some especially difficult ethical problems for U.S. sellers of goods manufactured in foreign countries. We also examine some of the ethical ramifications of a U.S. law that prohibits American businesspersons from bribing foreign officials to obtain favorable business contracts.

Global Exchange offers information on global business activities, including some of the ethical issues stemming from such activities, at **http://www.globalexchange.org**.

INTERNATIONAL PERSPECTIVE

International Guidelines for Business Conduct

In today's global marketplace, conflicts and misunderstandings often arise due to different languages, business customs, national policies, and legal requirements. In 1976, the Organization for Economic Cooperation and Development (OECD), to which twenty-six of the world's leading industrialized nations belong, issued its Guidelines for Multinational Enterprises. The guidelines set forth international standards of business conduct that governments, businesses, and other groups can voluntarily implement to prevent misunderstandings and build an atmosphere of predictability. Over time, the guidelines have been updated to address new concerns. For example, the 2000 revision of the guidelines included recommendations relating to the elimination of child and forced labor, environmental performance, human rights, combating corruption, and protecting consumer interests. Although many public codes of business conduct are now available, the guidelines constitute the only multilaterally endorsed and comprehensive code that governments are committed to promoting.

FOR CRITICAL ANALYSIS
Why might an American corporation comply with the guidelines, which are recommendations only, if compliance would be more costly to the corporation than noncompliance?

THE FOREIGN CORRUPT PRACTICES ACT

Another ethical problem in international business dealings has to do with the legitimacy of certain side payments to government officials. In the United States, the majority of contracts are formed within the private sector. In many foreign countries, however, decisions on most major construction and manufacturing contracts are made by government officials because of extensive government regulation and control over trade and industry. Side payments to government officials in exchange for favorable business contracts are not unusual in such countries; nor are such payments considered to be unethical—although this is now changing, as you will read shortly.

In the 1970s, the U.S. press, and government officials as well, uncovered a number of business scandals involving large side payments by American corporations to foreign representatives for the purpose of securing advantageous international trade contracts. In response to this unethical behavior, Congress passed the Foreign Corrupt Practices Act (FCPA) in 1977, which prohibits American businesspersons from bribing foreign officials to secure advantageous contracts. The act, which is the subject of this chapter's *Landmark in the Law* on the following page, made it difficult for American companies to compete as effectively as they otherwise might have in the global marketplace.

REMEMBER Changing ethical notions about social responsibility often motivate lawmakers to enact or repeal laws.

MONITORING THE EMPLOYMENT PRACTICES OF FOREIGN SUPPLIERS

Suppose that the Farris Company, to save costs, contracts with companies in developing nations to manufacture some of its products because the wage rates in those nations are significantly lower than in the United States. Further suppose that one of the foreign companies exploits its workers—it hires women and children at below-minimum-wage rates and requires its employees to work long hours in a workplace full of health hazards. Additionally, the company's supervisors routinely engage in workplace conduct that is offensive to women.

LANDMARK IN THE LAW
The Foreign Corrupt Practices Act of 1977

The Foreign Corrupt Practices Act (FCPA) of 1977 is divided into two major parts. The first part applies to all U.S. companies and their directors, officers, shareholders, employees, and agents. This part of the FCPA prohibits the bribery of most officials of foreign governments if the purpose of the payment is to get the official to act in his or her official capacity to provide business opportunities.

Permissible Payments The FCPA does not prohibit payment of substantial sums to minor officials whose duties are ministerial. These payments are often referred to as "grease," or facilitating payments. They are meant to ensure that administrative services that might otherwise be performed at a slow pace are sped up. Thus, for example, if a firm makes a payment to a minor official to speed up an import licensing process, the firm has not violated the FCPA. Generally, the act, as amended, permits payments to foreign officials if such payments are lawful in the foreign country. The act also does not prohibit payments to private foreign companies or other third parties unless the American firm knows that the payments will be passed on to a foreign government in violation of the FCPA.

Accounting Duties The second part of the FCPA is directed toward accountants because in the past bribes were often concealed in corporate financial records. All companies must keep detailed records that "accurately and fairly" reflect the company's financial activities. In addition, all companies must have an accounting system that provides "reasonable assurance" that all transactions entered into by the company are accounted for and legal. These requirements assist in detecting illegal bribes. The FCPA further prohibits any person from making false statements to accountants or false entries in any record or account.

In 1988, the FCPA was amended to provide that business firms that violate the act may be fined up to $2 million. Individual officers or directors who violate the FCPA may be fined up to $100,000 (the fine cannot be paid by the company) and may be imprisoned for up to five years.

APPLICATION TO TODAY'S WORLD

The FCPA did not change international trade practices in other countries, but it effectively tied the hands of American firms trying to secure foreign contracts. For twenty years, the FCPA remained the only law of its kind in the world, despite attempts by U.S. political leaders to convince other nations to pass similar legislation. The international ethical landscape has changed significantly, however, and today other nations besides the United States regard payments to public officials in return for favorable contracts as unethical. Indeed, in 1997 the twenty-six member nations of the Organization for Economic Cooperation and Development signed a convention (treaty) that made the bribery of foreign public officials a serious crime. Each signatory was obligated to enact domestic legislation in accordance with the treaty.

REMEMBER There is a constant tension among ethics, social forces, profits, and the law.

What is the Farris Company's ethical responsibility in this situation? Should it refuse to deal with this supplier (and sacrifice profits)? Should it use the supplier's services but only on the condition that Farris employees are allowed to monitor the supplier's workplace to make sure that the workers are not being mistreated?

At one time, society's concept of ethical business behavior did not include concerns over other nations' employment laws and practices. Today, the situation has changed. Few activities of business firms go unnoticed by interest groups supporting human rights on a worldwide level, often in easily accessed online forums. If a firm such as Farris fails to take steps to protect foreign workers' rights, its reputation as an ethically responsible firm may be damaged—and its profits significantly affected—by the adverse publicity sponsored by such interest groups.

APPLICATION **Law and the Businessperson . . .**

Law and the Manager: How to Create an Ethical Workplace*

The most important factor in creating and maintaining an ethical workplace is the attitude of top management. If you are a manager, rest assured that unless you are totally committed to this goal, you will not succeed in achieving it. In addition to your conduct, two other factors help to create an ethical workplace environment: a written code of ethics, or policy statement, and the effective communication of the firm's ethical policies to employees.

THE ROLE OF MANAGEMENT

Surveys of business executives indicate that management's behavior, more than anything else, sets the ethical tone of a firm. If an employee persists in unethical behavior, you should consider discharging the employee as a clear example to other employees that you will not tolerate unethical behavior. Although this may seem harsh, business managers have found that discharging even one employee for ethical reasons has a tremendous impact as a deterrent to unethical behavior in the workplace. Additionally, you should ensure that your firm's production or marketing goals are realistic. If a sales quota, for example, can be met only through high-pressure, unethical sales tactics, employees trying to act "in the interest of the firm" may think that management is implicitly asking them to behave unethically.

INSTRUCT EMPLOYEES IN ETHICAL STANDARDS

A written ethics code or policy statement helps to make clear to employees how they are expected to relate to their supervisors or managers, to consumers, to suppliers, and to other employees. Above all, it is important to state explicitly what your firm's ethical priorities are.

For an ethical code to be effective, its provisions must be clearly communicated to employees. A good way to do this is by implementing an ethics training program, in which management discusses with employees–face to face–the firm's policies and the importance of ethical conduct. Some firms hold periodic ethics seminars where employees can openly

*This *Application* is not meant to substitute for the services of an attorney who is licensed to practice law in your state.

(continued)

APPLICATION Law and the Businessperson . . .

Law and the Manager: How to Create an Ethical Workplace—continued

discuss any ethical problems that they may be experiencing and how the firm's ethical policies apply to those specific problems. Generally, the smaller the group, the more effective these discussions are. It is important that employees know that the ethical program is a "two-way street." That is, management must make it clear that feedback from employees and their ethical concerns are a top priority.

Another effective technique is to evaluate periodically the ethical performance of each individual employee. One company, for example, asks its employees to fill out an ethical checklist each week and return it to their supervisors. This practice serves two purposes: first, it demonstrates to employees that ethics matters; and second, employees have an opportunity to reflect on how well they have measured up in terms of ethical performance.

Checklist for Creating an Ethical Workplace

1. Make sure that management is committed to ethical behavior and sets an ethical example.
2. Create, print, and distribute an ethical code clearly stating your firm's ethical goals and priorities, as well as what behavior is expected of employees in their areas of responsibility.
3. Implement an ethics training program to communicate your firm's ethical policies to employees.
4. Hold seminars or small group meetings where ethical policies and performance can be discussed on an ongoing basis.
5. Devise a method, such as an ethical checklist, for evaluating the ethical performance of each individual employee.

Key Terms

Chapter Summary Ethics and Social Responsibility

The Nature of Business Ethics (See pages 193–195.)	Ethics can be defined as the study of what constitutes right or wrong behavior. Business ethics focuses on how moral and ethical principles are applied in the business context. Business ethics is complicated by the fact that corporations owe ethical (and legal) duties to a number of groups; when these duties come into conflict, difficult choices must be made. The law reflects society's convictions on what constitutes right or wrong behavior. The law has its limits, though, and some actions may be legal yet not be ethical.
Sources of Ethical Standards (See pages 195–197.)	1. *Duty-based ethics*—Ethics based on religious beliefs; philosophical reasoning, such as that of Immanuel Kant; and the basic rights of human beings (the principle of rights). 2. *Outcome-based ethics (utilitarianism)*—Ethics based on philosophical reasoning, such as that of John Stuart Mill.

Chapter Summary Ethics and Social Responsibility—continued

Business Decisions and Ethics (See pages 197–203.)	When deciding whether to undertake a given action, an ethical business firm will typically consider the following questions (if the answer to any question is no, the action should not be undertaken): 1. *Is it profitable?*—If it is not, the action likely will not be undertaken. 2. *Is it legal?*—This may be difficult to predict with certainty given the numerous and frequently changing laws regulating business and the "gray areas" in the law. 3. *Is it ethical?*—Most large firms have ethical codes or policies and corporate compliance programs that guide their determinations of whether certain actions are ethical. Public opinion may also play a role in making such determinations.
Corporate Social Responsibility (See pages 203–206.)	Corporate social responsibility means that corporations can and should act ethically and be accountable to society for their actions. Different views on what constitutes social responsibility include the following: 1. *Profit maximization*—The view that the only concern of corporations should be to maximize profits while operating within legal limits so that the shareholders and society in general benefit from increased wealth. 2. *Stakeholder view*—The view that a corporation has other stakeholders besides shareholders (including employees, consumers of the corporation's product, suppliers, creditors, and so on) and that the interests of shareholders should be balanced against the interests of these other stakeholders in corporate decision making. 3. *Corporate citizenship*—The view that corporations, through philanthropy and their own conduct, should promote social goals (promote equal opportunity for women, minority groups, and persons with disabilities; protect the human rights of employees; and so on).
Ethics in the Global Context (See pages 206–209.)	There are many cultural, religious, and legal differences among nations. Notable differences relate to the role of women in society, employment laws governing workplace conditions, and the practice of giving side payments to foreign officials to secure favorable contracts.

For Review

① What is ethics? What is business ethics? What is the relationship between business ethics and the law?

② How do duty-based ethical standards differ from outcome-based ethical standards?

③ When engaging in ethical decision making, what questions do businesspersons typically consider?

④ What is corporate social responsibility? What are some different theories of social responsibility?

⑤ What is the difference between maximum profits and optimum profits?

Questions and Case Problems

7–1. Business Ethics. Some business ethicists maintain that whereas personal ethics has to do with right or wrong behavior, business ethics is concerned with appropriate behavior. In other words, ethical behavior in business has less to do with moral principles than with what society deems to be appropriate behavior in the business context. Do you agree with this distinction? Do personal and business ethics ever overlap? Should personal ethics play any role in business ethical decision making?

7–2. Business Ethics and Public Opinion. Assume that you are a high-level manager for a shoe manufacturer. You know that your firm could increase its profit margin by producing shoes in

Indonesia, where you could hire women for $100 a month to assemble them. You also know, however, that a competing shoe manufacturer recently was accused by human rights advocates of engaging in exploitative labor practices because the manufacturer sold shoes made by Indonesian women for similarly low wages. You personally do not believe that paying $100 a month to Indonesian women is unethical, because you know that in their country, $100 a month is a better-than-average wage rate. Assuming that the decision is yours to make, should you have the shoes manufactured in Indonesia and make higher profits for your company? Should you instead avoid the risk of negative publicity and the consequences of that publicity for the firm's reputation and subsequent profits? Are there other alternatives? Discuss fully.

7–3. Business Ethics and Public Opinion. In recent years, human rights groups, environmental activists, and other interest groups concerned with unethical business practices have conducted publicity campaigns against various corporations that those groups feel have engaged in unethical practices. Do you believe that a small group of well-organized activists should dictate how a major corporation conducts its affairs? Discuss fully.

7–4. Ethical Decision Making. Shokun Steel Co. owns many steel plants. One of its plants is much older than the others. Equipment at that plant is outdated and inefficient, and the costs of production are twice as high as at any of Shokun's other plants. The company cannot raise the price of steel because of competition, both domestic and international. The plant is located in Twin Firs, Pennsylvania, which has a population of about 45,000, and currently employs over a thousand workers. Shokun is contemplating whether to close the plant. What factors should the firm consider in making its decision? Will the firm violate any ethical duties if it closes the plant? Analyze these questions from the two basic perspectives on ethical reasoning discussed in this chapter.

7–5. Product Warnings. Isuzu Motors America, Inc., does not warn its customers of the danger of riding unrestrained in the cargo beds of its pickup trucks. Seventeen-year-old Donald Josue was riding unrestrained in the bed of an Isuzu truck driven by Iaone Frias. When Frias lost control of the truck, it struck a concrete center divider. Josue was ejected and his consequent injuries rendered him a paraplegic. Josue filed a suit in a Hawaii state court against Isuzu, asserting a variety of legal claims based on its failure to warn of the danger of riding in the bed of the truck. Should Isuzu be held liable for Josue's injuries? Why or why not? [*Josue v. Isuzu Motors America, Inc.*, 87 Haw. 413, 958 P.2d 535 (1998)]

7–6. Ethical Conduct. Richard and Suzanne Weinstein owned Elm City Cheese Co. Elm City sold its products to three major customers that used the cheese as a "filler" to blend into their cheeses. In 1982, Mark Federico, a certified public accountant, became Elm City's accountant and the Weinsteins' personal accountant. The Weinsteins had known Federico since he was seven years old, and even before he became their accountant, he knew the details of Elm City's business. Federico's duties went beyond typical accounting work, and when the Weinsteins were absent, Federico was put in charge of operations. In 1992, Federico was made a vice president of the company, and a year later he was placed in charge of day-to-day operations. He also continued to serve as Elm City's accountant. The relationship between Federico and the Weinsteins deteriorated, and in 1995, he resigned as Elm City's employee and as its accountant. Less than two years later, Federico opened Lomar Foods, Inc., to make the same products as Elm City by the same process and to sell the products to the same customers. Federico located Lomar closer to Elm City's suppliers. Elm City filed a suit in a Connecticut state court against Federico and Lomar, alleging, among other things, misappropriation of trade secrets. Elm City argued that it was entitled to punitive damages because Federico's conduct was "willful and malicious." Federico responded in part that he did not act willfully and maliciously because he did not know that Elm City's business details were trade secrets. Were Federico's actions "willful and malicious"? Were they ethical? Explain. [*Elm City Cheese Co. v. Federico*, 251 Conn. 59, 752 A.2d 1037 (1999)]

7–7. Cybergriping. Lockheed Corp. has used the name "Lockheed" since the 1930s. In 1995, Lockheed merged with Martin Marietta Corp., another large company with an international reputation, to form Lockheed Martin Corp. Lockheed Martin, one of the world's largest and best-known aerospace, electronics, and advanced materials manufacturers, continued to use the Lockheed name. In 1998, Dan Parisi registered the domain names "lockheedsucks.com" and "lockheedmartinsucks.com." Parisi used the names to point to a Web site that offered visitors an opportunity to vent their views on Lockheed and other companies. Lockheed demanded that Parisi transfer the names to it. Parisi refused. Lockheed filed a complaint with a provider of arbitration services—the World Intellectual Property Organization Arbitration and Mediation Center (WIPO Center)—asking it to transfer the names. Lockheed contended in part that the names were "confusingly similar" to Lockheed's trademarks. Parisi responded that "no one would reasonably believe [Lockheed] operates a website that appends the word 'sucks' to its name and then uses it to criticize corporate America." In whose favor should the WIPO Center rule, and why? [*Lockheed Martin Corp. v. Parisi*, WIPO Case No. D2000-1015 (2000)]

TEST YOUR KNOWLEDGE—ANSWER ON THE WEB

7–8. Richard Fraser was an "exclusive career insurance agent" under a contract with Nationwide Mutual Insurance Co. Fraser leased computer hardware and software from Nationwide for his business. During a dispute between Nationwide and the Nationwide Insurance Independent Contractors Association, an organization representing Fraser and other exclusive career agents, Fraser prepared a letter to Nationwide's competitors asking whether they were interested in acquiring the represented agents' policyholders. Nationwide obtained a copy of the letter and searched its electronic file server for e-mail indicating that the letter had been sent. It found a stored e-mail that Fraser had sent to a co-worker indicating that the letter had been sent to at least one competitor. The e-mail was retrieved from the co-worker's file of already received and discarded messages stored on the receiver. When Nationwide canceled its contract with Fraser, he filed a suit in a federal district court against the firm, alleging, among other things, violations of various federal laws that prohibit the interception of electronic communications during transmission. In whose favor should the court rule, and why? In any case, did Nationwide act ethically in retrieving the e-mail? [*Fraser v. Nationwide Mutual Insurance Co.*, 135 F.Supp.2d 623 (E.D.Pa. 2001)]

A QUESTION OF ETHICS AND SOCIAL RESPONSIBILITY

7–9. Hazen Paper Co. manufactured paper and paperboard for use in such products as cosmetic wrap, lottery tickets, and pressure-sensitive items. Walter Biggins, a chemist hired by Hazen in 1977, developed a water-based paper coating that was both environmentally safe and of superior quality. By the mid-1980s, the company's sales had increased dramatically as a result of its extensive use of "Biggins Acrylic." Because of this, Biggins thought he deserved a substantial raise in salary, and from 1984 to 1986, Biggins's persistent requests for a raise became a bone of contention between him and his employers. Biggins ran a business on the side, which involved cleaning up hazardous wastes for various companies. Hazen told Biggins that unless he signed a "confidentiality agreement" promising to restrict his outside activities during the time he was employed by Hazen and for a limited time afterward, he would be fired. Biggins said he would sign the agreement only if Hazen raised his salary to $100,000. Hazen refused to do so, fired Biggins, and hired a younger man to replace him. At the time of his discharge in 1986, Biggins was sixty-two years old, had worked for the company nearly ten years, and was just a few weeks away from being entitled to pension rights worth about $93,000. In view of these circumstances, evaluate and answer the following questions. [*Hazen Paper Co. v. Biggins*, 507 U.S. 604, 113 S.Ct. 1701, 123 L.Ed.2d 338 (1993)]

1. Did the company owe an ethical duty to Biggins to increase his salary, given that its sales increased dramatically as a result of Biggins's efforts and ingenuity in developing the coating? If you were one of the company's executives, would you have raised Biggins's salary? Why or why not?
2. Generally, what public policies come into conflict in cases involving employers who, for reasons of cost and efficiency of operations, fire older, higher-paid workers and replace them with younger, lower-paid workers? If you were an employer facing the need to cut back on personnel to save costs, what would you do, and on what ethical premises would you justify your decision?

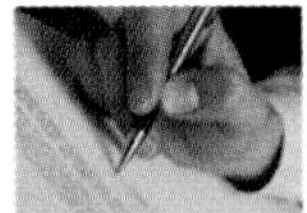

FOR CRITICAL ANALYSIS

7–10. If a firm engages in "ethically responsible" behavior solely for the purpose of gaining profits from the goodwill it generates, the "ethical" behavior is essentially a means toward a self-serving end (profits and the accumulation of wealth). In this situation, is the firm acting unethically in any way? Should motive or conduct carry greater weight on the ethical scales in this situation?

Internet Activities

Go to the *Business Law Today* home page at **http://blt.westbuslaw.com**. Select "Interactive Study Center" and then click on "Chapter 7." There you will find the following Internet research exercise that you can perform to learn more about ethics and social responsibility in business:

Activity 7–1: Environmental Self-Audits

Before the Test

Go to the *Business Law Today* home page at **http://blt.westbuslaw.com**. Click on "Interactive Quizzes." You will find at least twenty interactive questions relating to this chapter.

UNIT ONE Cumulative Business Hypothetical

CompTac, Inc., which is headquartered in San Francisco, California, is one of the leading software manufacturers in the United States. The company invests millions of dollars in researching and developing new software applications and computer games that are sold worldwide. It also has a large service department and has taken great pains to offer its customers excellent support services.

① CompTac routinely purchases some of the materials necessary to produce its computer games from a New York firm, Electrotex, Inc. A dispute arises between the two firms, and CompTac wants to sue Electrotex for breach of contract. Can CompTac bring the suit in a California state court? Can CompTac bring the suit in a federal court? Explain.

② A customer at one of CompTac's retail stores stumbles over a crate in the parking lot and breaks her leg. The crate had just moments before fallen off a CompTac truck that was delivering goods from a CompTac warehouse to the store. The customer sues CompTac, alleging negligence. Will she succeed in her suit? Why or why not?

③ Roban Electronics, a software manufacturer and one of CompTac's major competitors, has been trying to convince one of CompTac's key employees, Jim Baxter, to come to work for Roban. Roban knows that Baxter has a written employment contract with CompTac, which Baxter would breach if he left CompTac before the contract expired. Baxter goes to work for Roban, and the departure of its key employee causes CompTac to suffer substantial losses due to delays in completing new software. Can CompTac sue Roban to recoup some of these losses? If so, on what ground?

④ One of CompTac's employees in its accounting division, Alan Green, has a gambling problem. To repay a gambling debt of $10,000, Green decides to "borrow" some money from CompTac to cover the debt. Using his "hacking" skills and his knowledge of CompTac account numbers, Green electronically transfers CompTac funds into his personal checking account. A week later, he is luckier at gambling and uses the same electronic procedures to transfer funds from his personal checking account to the relevant CompTac account. Has Green committed any crimes? If so, what are they?

⑤ One of CompTac's best-selling products is a computer game that involves some extremely violent actions. Groups of parents, educators, and consumer activists have bombarded CompTac with letters and e-mail messages requesting the company to discontinue its sales of the product. CompTac executives are concerned about the public outcry, but at the same time they realize that the game is CompTac's major source of profits. If it ceased marketing the game, the company could go bankrupt. If you were a CompTac decision maker, what would your decision be in this situation? How would you justify your decision from an ethical perspective?

UNIT ONE Extended Case Study

Kyllo v. United States

We explained, in Chapter 6, that the Fourth Amendment protects the "right of the people to be secure in their persons, houses, papers, and effects." In this extended case study, we examine Kyllo v. United States,[1] *a decision that considered the requirement that law enforcement officers obtain a search warrant before searching private property. The question was whether police officers are required to obtain a warrant before using sense-enhancing technology that reveals information about the inside of a home that the officers would otherwise be able to learn only if they physically entered the house.*

CASE BACKGROUND

Suspicious that marijuana was being grown in Danny Lee Kyllo's home in a triplex in Florence, Oregon, federal agents used an Agema Thermovision 210, a thermal imaging device, to scan the building to determine if the amount of heat emanating from it was consistent with the high-intensity lamps often used to grow marijuana indoors. The scan showed that Kyllo's garage roof and a side wall were relatively hot compared to the rest of his home and substantially warmer than the neighboring units. Based in part on the thermal imaging, a judge issued a warrant to search Kyllo's home, where the agents found marijuana growing. Kyllo was indicted for violations of federal law. He filed a motion to suppress the evidence seized from his home. The court denied the motion. Kyllo pleaded guilty and appealed the court's ruling to the U.S. Court of Appeals for the Ninth Circuit.

The appellate court affirmed the trial court's decision. The appellate court upheld the thermal imaging on the ground that Kyllo had no subjective expectation of privacy because he made no attempt to conceal the heat escaping from his home. The court ruled that even if he had made such an attempt, there was no objectively reasonable expectation of privacy because the thermal imager did not expose any intimate details of Kyllo's life, only hot spots on the outside of his home. Kyllo appealed to the United States Supreme Court.

1. 533 U.S. 27, 121 S.Ct. 2038, 150 L.Ed.2d 94 (2001). To access this case online, go to **http://supct.cornell.law.edu/supct**. In the right-hand column of the page that opens, in the "For the 2000–2001 term:" section, click on "Decisions arrayed by date." When that page opens, click on "June 2001." In the result, scroll to the name of the case and click on it. On that page, click on the appropriate link to access the opinion.

MAJORITY OPINION

Justice *SCALIA* delivered the opinion of the Court.

* * * *

* * * [A] Fourth Amendment search occurs when the government violates a subjective expectation of privacy that society recognizes as reasonable. * * *

* * * The question we confront today is what limits there are upon [the] power of technology to shrink the realm of guaranteed privacy.

* * * While it may be difficult to [set limits] when the search of areas such as telephone booths, automobiles, or even the curtilage [the enclosed land surrounding a house or dwelling] and uncovered portions of residences are at issue, *in the case of the search of the interior of homes—the prototypical and hence most commonly litigated area of protected privacy—there is a ready criterion, with roots deep in the common law, of the minimal expectation of privacy that exists, and that is acknowledged to be reasonable.* To withdraw protection of this minimum expectation would be to permit police technology to erode the privacy guaranteed by the Fourth Amendment. We think that obtaining by sense-enhancing technology any information regarding the interior of the home that could not otherwise have been obtained without physical intrusion into a constitutionally protected area, constitutes a search—at least where (as here) the technology in question is not in general public use. This assures preservation of that degree of privacy against government that existed when the Fourth Amendment was adopted. On the basis of this criterion, the information obtained by the thermal imager in this case was the product of a search. [Emphasis added.]

The Government maintains, however, that the thermal imaging must be upheld because it detected "only heat radiating from the external surface of the house." * * * But just as a thermal imager captures only heat emanating from a house, so also a powerful directional microphone picks up only sound emanating from a house—and a satellite capable of scanning from many miles away would pick up only visible light emanating from a house. * * * [Adopting the government's argument] would leave the homeowner at the mercy of advancing technology—including imaging technology that could discern all human activity in the home. While the technology used in the present case was relatively crude, the rule we adopt must take account of more sophisticated systems that are already in use or in development. * * *

The Government also contends that the thermal imaging was constitutional because it did not "detect private activities occurring in private areas." * * * The Fourth Amendment's protection of the home has never been tied to measurement of the quality or quantity of information obtained. * * * *In the home,* * * * *all details are intimate details, because the entire area is held safe from prying government eyes.* * * * [Emphasis added.]

* * * *

Where, as here, the Government uses a device that is not in general public use, to explore details of the home that would previously have been unknowable without physical intrusion, the surveillance is a "search" and is presumptively unreasonable without a warrant.

Since we hold the Thermovision imaging to have been an unlawful search, it will remain for the [trial court] to determine whether, without the evidence it provided, the search warrant issued in this case was supported by probable cause—and if not, whether there is any other basis for supporting admission of the evidence that the search pursuant to the warrant produced.

DISSENTING OPINION

Justice *STEVENS,* with whom the Chief Justice [*REHNQUIST*], Justice *O'CONNOR,* and Justice *KENNEDY* join, dissenting.

There is, in my judgment, a distinction of constitutional magnitude between "through-the-wall surveillance" that gives the observer or listener direct access to information in a private area, on the one hand, and the thought processes used to draw inferences from information in the public domain, on the other hand. The Court has crafted a rule that purports to deal with direct observations of the inside of the home, but the case before us merely involves indirect deductions from "off-the-wall" surveillance, that is, observations of the exterior of the home. Those observations were made with a fairly primitive thermal imager that gathered data exposed on the outside of petitioner's home but did not invade any constitutionally protected interest in privacy. Moreover, I believe that the supposedly "bright-line" rule the Court has created in response to its concerns about future technological developments is unnecessary, unwise, and inconsistent with the Fourth Amendment.

There is no need for the Court to craft a new rule to decide this case, as it is controlled by established principles from our Fourth Amendment jurisprudence. One of those core principles, of course, is that searches and seizures inside a home without a warrant are presumptively unreasonable. But it is equally well settled that searches and seizures of property in plain view are presumptively reasonable. Whether that property is residential or commercial, the basic principle is the same: What a person knowingly exposes to the public, even in his own home or office, is not a subject of Fourth Amendment protection. That is the principle implicated here.

While the Court "take[s] the long view" and decides this case based largely on the potential of yet-to-be-developed technology that might allow "through-the-wall surveillance," this case involves nothing more than off-the-wall surveillance by law enforcement officers to gather information exposed to the general public from the outside of petitioner's home. All that the infrared camera did in this case was passively measure heat emitted from the exterior surfaces of petitioner's home; all that those measurements showed were relative differences in emission levels, vaguely indicating that some areas of the roof and outside walls were warmer than others.

QUESTIONS FOR ANALYSIS

① **Law.** Considering the decision in this case, can law enforcement officers ever use a thermal imaging device without obtaining a warrant? If so, when?

② **Law.** What effect might the decision in this case have on the government's use of the DCS-1000 system (popularly known as Carnivore)?[2]

③ **Ethics.** What is the ethical basis for the warrant requirement of the Fourth Amendment?

④ **International Dimensions.** To what extent should U.S. law regarding search and seizure be applied to foreign persons who reside, visit, or do business in the United States?

⑤ **Implications for the Business Manager.** Is there a sufficient difference between the expectation of privacy in a person's place of business and his or her home that could allow the police to use technology to search the business, but not the home, without a warrant?

2. DCS-1000 is a modified version of software known as a packet sniffer that Internet service providers (ISPs) use to maintain their networks. DCS-1000 taps the traffic coming through an ISP's networks in search of data from the target of an investigation.

Contracts

UNIT 2

UNIT CONTENTS

CHAPTER 8

Nature and Classification

"The social order rests upon the stability and predictability of conduct, of which keeping promises is a large item."

Roscoe Pound, 1870–1964
(American jurist)

CHAPTER CONTENTS

LEARNING OBJECTIVES

After reading this chapter, you should be able to answer the following questions:

① What is a contract? What is the objective theory of contracts?

② What are the four basic elements necessary to the formation of a valid contract?

③ What is the difference between an implied-in-fact contract and an implied-in-law contract (quasi contract)?

④ What is a void contract? How does it differ from a voidable contract? What is an unenforceable contract?

⑤ What rules guide the courts in interpreting contracts?

As Roscoe Pound—an eminent jurist—observed in the above quotation, "keeping promises" is important to a stable social order. Contract law deals with, among other things, the formation and keeping of promises. A **promise** is a declaration that something either will or will not happen in the future.

PROMISE
A declaration that something either will or will not happen in the future.

Like other types of law, contract law reflects our social values, interests, and expectations at a given point in time. It shows, for example, what kinds of promises our society thinks should be legally binding. It shows what excuses our society accepts for breaking such promises. Additionally, it shows what promises are considered to be contrary to public policy, or against the interests of society, and therefore legally void. If a promise goes against the interests of society as a whole, it will be invalid. Also, if it was made by a child or a mentally incompetent person, or on the basis of false information, a question will arise as to whether the promise should be enforced. Resolving such questions is the essence of contract law.

ON THE WEB You can keep abreast of recent and planned revisions of the *Restatements of the Law* by accessing the American Law Institute's Web site at **http://www.ali.org**.

In the business world, questions and disputes concerning contracts arise daily. Although aspects of contract law vary from state to state, much of it is based on the common law. In 1932, the American Law Institute compiled the *Restatement of the Law of Contracts*. This work is a nonstatutory, authoritative exposition of the present law on the subject of contracts and is currently in its second edition (although a third edition is in the process of being drafted). Throughout the following chapters on contracts, we will refer to the second edition of the *Restatement of the Law of Contracts* as simply the *Restatement (Second) of Contracts*.

The Uniform Commercial Code (UCC), which governs contracts and other transactions relating to the sale and lease of goods, occasionally departs from common law contract rules. Generally, the different treatment of contracts falling under the UCC stems from the general policy of encouraging commerce. The ways in which the UCC changes common law contract rules will be discussed extensively in later chapters. In this unit covering the common law of contracts (Chapters 8 through 13), we only indicate briefly or in footnotes those common law rules that have been altered significantly by the UCC for sales and lease contracts.

The Function of Contracts

No aspect of modern life is entirely free of contractual relationships. You acquire rights and obligations, for example, when you borrow funds, when you buy or lease a house, when you procure insurance, when you form a business, when you purchase goods or services—the list goes on. Contract law is designed to provide stability and predictability for both buyers and sellers in the marketplace.

Contract law assures the parties to private agreements that the promises they make will be enforceable. Clearly, many promises are kept because the parties involved feel a moral obligation to do so or because keeping a promise is in their mutual self-interest, not because the **promisor** (the person making the promise) or the **promisee** (the person to whom the promise is made) is conscious of the rules of contract law. Nevertheless, the rules of contract law are often followed in business agreements to avoid potential problems.

PROMISOR A person who makes a promise.

PROMISEE A person to whom a promise is made.

By supplying procedures for enforcing private agreements, contract law provides an essential condition for the existence of a market economy. Without a legal framework of reasonably assured expectations within which to plan and venture, businesspersons would be able to rely only on the good faith of others. Duty and good faith are usually sufficient, but when dramatic price changes or adverse economic conditions make it costly to comply with a promise, these elements may not be enough. Contract law is necessary to ensure compliance with a promise or to entitle the innocent party to some form of relief.

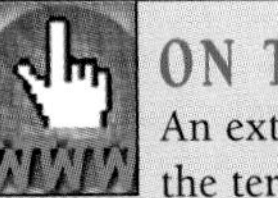

ON THE WEB An extensive definition of the term *contract* is offered by the 'Lectric Law Library at **http://www.lectlaw.com/def/c123.htm**.

Definition of a Contract

A **contract** is an agreement that can be enforced in court. It is formed by two or more parties who agree to perform or to refrain from performing some act now or in the future. Generally, contract disputes arise when there is a promise of future performance. If the contractual promise is not fulfilled, the party who made it is subject to the sanctions of a court (see Chapter 13). That party may be required to pay money damages for failing to perform the contractual promise; in limited instances, the party may be required to perform the promised act.

CONTRACT An agreement that can be enforced in court; formed by two or more competent parties who agree, for consideration, to perform or to refrain from performing some legal act now or in the future.

OBJECTIVE THEORY OF CONTRACTS
A theory under which the intent to form a contract will be judged by outward, objective facts (what the party said when entering into the contract, how the party acted or appeared, and the circumstances surrounding the transaction) as interpreted by a reasonable person, rather than by the party's own secret, subjective intentions.

In determining whether a contract has been formed, the element of intent is of prime importance. In contract law, intent is determined by what is referred to as the **objective theory of contracts**, not by the personal or subjective intent, or belief, of a party. The theory is that a party's intention to enter into a contract is judged by outward, objective facts as interpreted by a reasonable person, rather than by the party's own secret, subjective intentions. Objective facts include (1) what the party said when entering into the contract, (2) how the party acted or appeared, and (3) the circumstances surrounding the transaction. As will be discussed later in this chapter, in the section on express versus implied contracts, intent to form a contract may be manifested not only in words, oral or written, but also by conduct.

INTERNATIONAL PERSPECTIVE

How Intent to Form a Contract Is Measured in Other Countries

Courts in the United States routinely adhere to the objective theory of contracts. Courts in some other nations, however, give more weight to subjective intentions. Under French law, for example, when the objective and subjective interpretations of a contract conflict, the French civil law code prefers the subjective construction. Other nations that have civil law codes take this same approach. French courts, nonetheless, will look to writings and other objective evidence to determine a party's subjective intent. Thus, in operation, the difference between the French and U.S. approaches is perhaps not as significant as it may seem at first blush.

FOR CRITICAL ANALYSIS
What problems may arise when a court attempts to look at the subjective basis of a contract?

Requirements of a Contract

The following list describes the four requirements that must be met before a valid contract exists. Each item will be explained more fully in the chapter indicated. Although we pair these requirements in subsequent chapters (for example, agreement and consideration are treated in Chapter 9), it is important to stress that each requirement is separate and independent. They are paired merely for reasons of space.

① *Agreement.* An agreement includes an offer and an acceptance. One party must offer to enter into a legal agreement, and another party must accept the terms of the offer (Chapter 9).

② *Consideration.* Any promises made by parties must be supported by legally sufficient and bargained-for consideration (something of value received or promised, to convince a person to make a deal) (Chapter 9).

③ *Contractual capacity.* Both parties entering into the contract must have the contractual capacity to do so; the law must recognize them as possessing characteristics that qualify them as competent parties (Chapter 10).

④ *Legality.* The contract's purpose must be to accomplish some goal that is legal and not against public policy (Chapter 10).

If any of these four elements is lacking, no contract will have been formed. Even if all of these elements exist, however, a contract may be unenforceable if the following

ON THE WEB
For easy-to-understand definitions of legal terms and concepts, including terms and concepts relating to contract law, go to

http://dictionary.law.com

and key in a term, such as "contract" or "consideration."

requirements are not met. These requirements typically are raised as *defenses* to the enforceability of an otherwise valid contract.

① ***Genuineness of assent.*** The apparent consent of both parties must be genuine (Chapter 11).

② ***Form.*** The contract must be in whatever form the law requires; for example, some contracts must be in writing to be enforceable (Chapter 11).

Freedom of Contract and Freedom from Contract

As a general rule, the law recognizes everyone's ability to enter freely into contractual arrangements. This recognition is called *freedom of contract,* a freedom protected by the U.S. Constitution in Article I, Section 10. Because freedom of contract is a fundamental public policy of the United States, courts rarely interfere with contracts that have been voluntarily made.

Of course, as in other areas of the law, there are many exceptions to the general rule that contracts voluntarily negotiated will be enforced. For example, illegal bargains, agreements that unreasonably restrain trade, and certain unfair contracts made between one party with a great amount of bargaining power and another with little power are generally not enforced. In addition, as you will read in Chapter 10, certain contracts and clauses may not be enforceable if they are contrary to public policy, fairness, and justice. (For an example of a clause that was held to be contrary to public policy, see this chapter's *Business Law in the Online World* feature on the following page.) These exceptions provide freedom from contract for persons who may have been forced into making contracts unfavorable to themselves.

Types of Contracts

There are numerous types of contracts. They are categorized based on legal distinctions as to formation, enforceability, or performance. The best way to explain each type of contract is to compare one type with another.

BILATERAL VERSUS UNILATERAL CONTRACTS

OFFEROR
A person who makes an offer.

OFFEREE
A person to whom an offer is made.

Every contract involves at least two parties. The **offeror** is the party making the offer. The **offeree** is the party to whom the offer is made. The offeror always promises to do or not to do something and thus is also a promisor. Whether the contract is classified as *unilateral* or *bilateral* depends on what the offeree must do to accept the offer and bind the offeror to a contract.

BILATERAL CONTRACT
A type of contract that arises when a promise is given in exchange for a return promise.

Bilateral Contracts If to accept the offer the offeree must only promise to perform, the contract is a **bilateral contract.** Hence, a bilateral contract is a "promise for a promise." An example of a bilateral contract is a contract in which one person agrees to buy another person's automobile for a specified price. No performance, such as the payment of money or delivery of goods, need take place for a bilateral contract to be formed. The contract comes into existence at the moment the promises are exchanged.

BUSINESS LAW: //in the Online World

Forum-Selection Clauses and Public Policy

Parties to contracts frequently include clauses in their contracts relating to how any disputes that arise may be resolved. For example, as you read in Chapter 3, parties often include arbitration clauses in contracts, stipulating that any dispute will be resolved through arbitration proceedings rather than litigation. A contract may also include a *forum-selection clause,* specifying the forum (such as the court or jurisdiction) in which the dispute will be resolved.

Forum Selection and Online Contracts

Because parties to contracts formed online may be located in physically distant sites, online sellers of goods and services often include forum-selection clauses in their contracts. This helps to prevent problems for the online sellers, who might otherwise end up being haled into court in many distant jurisdictions. Recall from Chapter 3 that under a state long arm statute, a state may exercise jurisdiction over an out-of-state defendant if the defendant had "minimum contacts" with the state.

As mentioned elsewhere in this chapter, the courts rarely refuse to enforce clauses or contracts to which parties have voluntarily agreed, and this principle extends to online contracts as well. Exceptions to this rule are made, however, as America Online, Inc. (AOL), the Internet service provider, recently learned.

The Case against AOL

In a case against AOL, the plaintiffs—Al Mendoza and other former AOL subscribers living in California—sought compensatory and punitive damages. They claimed that AOL had continued to debit their credit cards for monthly service fees, without authorization, for some time after they had terminated their subscriptions. AOL moved to dismiss the action on the basis of the forum-selection clause in its "Terms of Service" agreement with subscribers. That clause required all lawsuits under the agreement to be brought in Virginia, AOL's home state. At issue in the case was whether the clause was enforceable.

A California trial court held that it was not. The court based its conclusion on the finding that the clause, among other things, was contained in a standard form and was not readily identifiable by subscribers because of its small type and location at the end of the agreement. According to the court, the clause was "unfair and unreasonable," and public policy was best served by denying enforceability to the clause. A California appellate court affirmed the lower court's ruling and also gave another reason why the clause should not be enforced. The appellate court noted that Virginia law provides "significantly less" consumer protection than California law, and therefore enforcing the forum-selection clause would violate the "strong California public policy" expressed in the state's consumer protection statutes.[a]

Be aware that this case may mark an exception to the rule that forum-selection clauses in online contracts are generally enforceable. Yet, different courts have reached different conclusions on this issue, so businesspersons forming online contracts would be wise to take special care in drafting such clauses. As one court held (in a case challenging the enforceability of the forum-selection clause in Microsoft Network's online agreement), "If a forum-selection clause is clear in its purport and has been presented to the party to be bound in a fair and forthright fashion, no consumer fraud policies or principles have been violated."[b]

FOR CRITICAL ANALYSIS

Do you believe that the outcome in the case against AOL would have been different if the forum-selection clause had been conspicuous and easily identifiable by those agreeing to AOL's Terms of Service? Why or why not?

a. *America Online, Inc. v. Superior Court,* 90 Cal.App.4th 1, 108 Cal.Rptr.2d 699 (2001).

b. *Caspi v. Microsoft Network, LLC,* 323 N.J.Super. 118, 732 A.2d 528 (1999). This case is presented in Chapter 17 as Case 17.2.

UNILATERAL CONTRACT
A contract that results when an offer can be accepted only by the offeree's performance.

Unilateral Contracts If the offer is phrased so that the offeree can accept only by completing the contract performance, the contract is a **unilateral contract.** Hence, a unilateral contract is a "promise for an act." • **EXAMPLE 8.1** Joe says to Celia, "If you drive my car from New York to Los Angeles, I'll give you $1,000." Only on Celia's completion of the act—bringing the car to Los Angeles—does she fully accept Joe's offer to pay $1,000. If she chooses not to accept the offer to bring the car to Los Angeles, there are no legal consequences. •

Contests, lotteries, and other competitions offering prizes are also examples of offers for unilateral contracts. If a person complies with the rules of the contest—such as by submitting the right lottery number at the right place and time—a unilateral contract is formed, binding the organization offering the prize to a contract to perform as promised in the offer.

Revocation of Offers for Unilateral Contracts A problem arises in unilateral contracts when the promisor attempts to *revoke* (cancel) the offer after the promisee has begun performance but before the act has been completed. • **EXAMPLE 8.2** Suppose that Roberta offers to buy Ed's sailboat, moored in San Francisco, on delivery of the boat to Roberta's dock in Newport Beach, three hundred miles south of San Francisco. Ed rigs the boat and sets sail. Shortly before his arrival at Newport Beach, Ed receives a radio message from Roberta withdrawing her offer. Roberta's offer is an offer for a unilateral contract, and only Ed's delivery of the sailboat at her dock is an acceptance. •

In contract law, offers are normally *revocable* (capable of being taken back, or canceled) until accepted. Under the traditional view of unilateral contracts, Roberta's revocation would terminate the offer. Because of the harsh effect on the offeree of the revocation of an offer to form a unilateral contract, the modern-day view is that once performance has been *substantially* undertaken, the offeror cannot revoke the offer. Thus, in our example, even though Ed has not yet accepted the offer by complete performance, Roberta is prohibited from revoking it. Ed can deliver the boat and bind Roberta to the contract.

EXPRESS VERSUS IMPLIED CONTRACTS

EXPRESS CONTRACT
A contract in which the terms of the agreement are stated in words, oral or written.

An **express contract** is one in which the terms of the agreement are fully and explicitly stated in words, oral or written. A signed lease for an apartment or a house is an

What determines whether a contract for accounting, tax preparation, or any other service is an express contract or an implied-in-fact contract?

express written contract. If a classmate accepts your offer to sell your textbooks from last semester for $50, an express oral contract has been made.

IMPLIED-IN-FACT CONTRACT
A contract formed in whole or in part from the conduct of the parties (as opposed to an express contract).

"Outward actions are a clue to hidden secrets."
LEGAL MAXIM

A contract that is implied from the conduct of the parties is called an **implied-in-fact contract**, or an implied contract. This type of contract differs from an express contract in that the *conduct* of the parties, rather than their words, creates and defines at least some of the terms of the contract. • **EXAMPLE 8.3** Suppose that you need an accountant to fill out your tax return this year. You look through the Yellow Pages and find an accounting firm located in your neighborhood. You drop by the firm's office, explain your problem to an accountant, and learn what fees will be charged. The next day you return and give the receptionist all of the necessary information and documents, such as canceled checks, W-2 forms, and so on. Then you walk out the door without saying anything expressly to the receptionist. In this situation, you have entered into an implied-in-fact contract to pay the accountant the usual and reasonable fees for the accounting services. The contract is implied by your conduct. The accountant expects to be paid for completing your tax return. By bringing in the records the accountant will need to do the work, you have implied an intent to pay for the services. •

The following three steps establish an implied-in-fact contract:

① The plaintiff furnished some service or property.

② The plaintiff expected to be paid for that service or property, and the defendant knew or should have known that payment was expected (by using the objective-theory-of-contracts test, discussed previously).

③ The defendant had a chance to reject the services or property and did not.

In the following case, the question before the court was whether a contract for electrical work had come into existence, given the absence of any written agreement.

CASE 8.1 Homer v. Burman

Indiana Court of Appeals, 2001.
743 N.E.2d 1144.

FACTS Dave and Annette Homer owned a rental house in Marion, Indiana. When their tenant, Stephanie Clevenger, complained of malfunctioning lights, the Homers paid Burman Electric Service $2,650 to rewire the house. The parties did not sign a written contract. After the work was supposedly done, the Homers discovered, among other things, holes in the ceiling, plaster damage around electrical outlets, and exposed wires along aluminum siding on the outside of the house. When the power was reconnected, Clevenger's television, VCR, satellite receiver, and Playstation were destroyed. Over the next two months, her hair dryers, clocks, and lamps repeatedly burned out. The Homers filed a suit against Burman in an Indiana state court, alleging breach of contract. The court ruled against the Homers, who appealed to a state intermediate appellate court.

ISSUE Despite the absence of a written agreement, did the parties have a contract?

DECISION Yes. The state intermediate appellate court reversed the decision of the lower court and remanded the case to determine the amount of damages and attorneys' fees to be awarded to the Homers.

REASON The appellate court stated, "An offer, acceptance, plus consideration make up the basis for a contract. A mutual assent or a meeting of the minds on all essential elements or terms must exist in order to form a binding contract. Assent to the terms of a contract may be expressed by acts which manifest acceptance." The court concluded that the parties had a contract even though they did not put anything in writing. The court explained that "the Homers paid Burman Electric $2,650.00 to rewire their home. Burman Electric accepted the payment and began work. Therefore, because we have an offer, acceptance, consideration, and a manifestation of mutual assent, an implied-in-fact contract was in existence."

FOR CRITICAL ANALYSIS—Social Consideration
What might be the most important term of an implied contract to perform work?

QUASI CONTRACTS—CONTRACTS IMPLIED IN LAW

QUASI CONTRACT
A fictional contract imposed on parties by a court in the interests of fairness and justice; usually imposed to avoid the unjust enrichment of one party at the expense of another.

"A legal fiction is always consistent with equity."
LEGAL MAXIM

Quasi contracts, or contracts *implied in law*, are wholly different from actual contracts. Express contracts and implied-in-fact contracts are actual, or true, contracts. The word *quasi* is Latin for "as if" or "analogous to." Quasi contracts are thus not true contracts. They do not arise from any agreement, express or implied, between the parties themselves. Rather, quasi contracts are fictional contracts imposed on parties by courts "as if" the parties had entered into an actual contract. Usually, quasi contracts are imposed to avoid the *unjust enrichment* of one party at the expense of another. The doctrine of unjust enrichment is based on the theory that individuals should not be allowed to profit or enrich themselves inequitably at the expense of others.

● **EXAMPLE 8.4** Suppose that a vacationing physician is driving down the highway and comes upon Emerson, who is lying unconscious on the side of the road. The physician renders medical aid that saves Emerson's life. Although the injured, unconscious Emerson did not solicit the medical aid and was not aware that the aid had been rendered, Emerson received a valuable benefit, and the requirements for a quasi contract were fulfilled. In such a situation, the law normally will impose a quasi contract, and Emerson will have to pay the physician for the reasonable value of the medical services rendered. ●

ETHICAL ISSUE 8.1

When does enrichment qualify as "unjust enrichment"?

There are times when a party is enriched by (benefits from) the actions of another, yet such benefits do not necessarily constitute unjust enrichment. For example, in one case the owner of a building (the lessor) leased the building to a commercial tenant (the lessee) for five years. The lessee, which assumed all responsibility for repairs, maintenance, and alterations to the premises, hired DCB Construction Company to make alterations to the premises that cost about $300,000. The lessor told DCB that it would not be responsible for any of the costs. Nonetheless, when the lessee quit paying rent, was evicted, and failed to pay DCB for the completed work, DCB sued the lessor for the amount still owing ($280,000). In this case, clearly the lessor had benefited from DCB's work. Yet did this benefit amount to unjust enrichment under the law? No, stated the court. The court pointed out that DCB did the work for the lessee and was notified by the lessor that it would not be held liable for the costs of the work. Further, there was no fraud or mistake involved. The court noted that unjust enrichment claims such as this one are almost always rejected by the courts.[1]

ON THE WEB
For an excellent overview of the basic principles of contract law, go to
http://profs.lp.findlaw.com/contracts/index.html.

Limitations on Quasi-Contractual Recovery Although quasi contracts exist to prevent unjust enrichment, in some situations the party who obtains a benefit will not be deemed to have been unjustly enriched. Basically, the quasi-contractual principle cannot be invoked by a party who has conferred a benefit on someone else unnecessarily or as a result of misconduct or negligence.

● **EXAMPLE 8.5** You take your car to the local car wash and ask to have it run through the washer and to have the gas tank filled. While your car is being washed, you go to a nearby shopping center for two hours. In the meantime, one of the workers at the car

1. *DCB Construction Co. v. Central City Development Co.*, 940 P.2d 958 (Colo.App. 1997).

wash mistakenly assumes that your car is the one that he is supposed to hand wax. When you come back, you are presented with a bill for a full tank of gas, a wash job, and a hand wax. Clearly, you have received a benefit, but this benefit was conferred because of a mistake by the car wash employee. You have not been *unjustly* enriched under these circumstances. People normally cannot be forced to pay for benefits "thrust" on them. •

When a Contract Already Exists The doctrine of quasi contract generally cannot be used when an actual contract covers the area in controversy.[2] This is because a remedy already exists if a party is unjustly enriched as a result of a breach of contract: the nonbreaching party can sue the breaching party for breach of contract. No quasi contract need be imposed by the court in this instance to achieve justice.

A worker takes apart machinery. If the worker makes a design modification that the manufacturer incorporates into later models of the machine, without a contract, should the worker be compensated?

Formal versus Informal Contracts

Formal contracts require a special form or method of creation (formation) to be enforceable. They include (1) contracts under seal, (2) recognizances, (3) negotiable instruments, and (4) letters of credit.[3] *Contracts under seal* are formalized writings with a special seal attached.[4] The significance of the seal has lessened, although about ten states require no consideration when a contract is under seal. A *recognizance* is an acknowledgment in court by a person that he or she will perform some specified obligation or pay a certain sum if he or she fails to perform. One form of recognizance is the surety bond.[5] Another is the personal recognizance bond used as bail in a criminal matter. As will be discussed at length in subsequent chapters, *negotiable instruments* include checks, notes, drafts, and certificates of deposit; letters of credit are agreements to pay contingent on the purchaser's receipt of invoices and bills of lading (documents evidencing receipt of, and title to, goods shipped).

Informal contracts (also called *simple contracts*) include all other contracts. No special form is required (except for certain types of contracts that must be in writing), as the contracts are usually based on their substance rather than their form. Typically, businesspersons put their contracts in writing to ensure that there is some proof of a contract's existence should problems arise.

FORMAL CONTRACT
A contract that by law requires a specific form, such as being executed under seal, for its validity.

INFORMAL CONTRACT
A contract that does not require a specified form or formality to be valid.

EXECUTED CONTRACT
A contract that has been completely performed by both parties.

EXECUTORY CONTRACT
A contract that has not as yet been fully performed.

Executed versus Executory Contracts

Contracts are also classified according to their state of performance. A contract that has been fully performed on both sides is called an **executed contract.** A contract that has not been fully performed on either side is called an **executory contract.** If one party has fully performed but the other has not, the contract is said to be executed on the one side and executory on the other, but the contract is still classified as executory.

• **Example 8.6** Assume that you agree to buy ten tons of coal from Western Coal Company. Further assume that Western has delivered the coal to your steel mill, where it is now being burned. At this point, the contract is an executory contract—it is exe-

KEEP IN MIND Not every contract is a document with "Contract" printed in block letters at the top. A contract can be expressed in a letter, a memo, or another document.

2. See, for example, *Industrial Lift Truck Service Corp. v. Mitsubishi International Corp.,* 104 Ill.App.3d 357, 432 N.E.2d 999, 60 Ill.Dec. 100 (1982).

3. *Restatement (Second) of Contracts,* Section 6.

4. A seal may be actual (made of wax or some other durable substance), impressed on the paper, or indicated simply by the word *seal* or the letters *L.S.* at the end of the document. L.S. stands for *locus sigilli* and means "the place for the seal."

5. An obligation of a party who guarantees that he or she will pay a second party if a third party does not perform.

cuted on the part of Western and executory on your part. After you pay Western for the coal, the contract will be executed on both sides.●

VALID, VOID, VOIDABLE, AND UNENFORCEABLE CONTRACTS

VALID CONTRACT
A contract that results when the elements necessary for contract formation (agreement, consideration, legal purpose, and contractual capacity) are present.

VOID CONTRACT
A contract having no legal force or binding effect.

VOIDABLE CONTRACT
A contract that may be legally avoided (canceled, or annulled) at the option of one or both of the parties.

UNENFORCEABLE CONTRACT
A valid contract rendered unenforceable by some statute or law.

A **valid contract** has the four elements necessary for contract formation: (1) an agreement (offer and acceptance) (2) supported by legally sufficient consideration (3) for a legal purpose and (4) made by parties who have the legal capacity to enter into the contract. As mentioned, we will discuss each of these elements in the following chapters.

A **void contract** is no contract at all. The terms *void* and *contract* are contradictory. None of the parties has any legal obligations if a contract is void. A contract can be void because, for example, one of the parties was adjudged by a court to be legally insane (and thus lacked the legal capacity to enter into a contract) or because the purpose of the contract was illegal.

A **voidable contract** is a *valid* contract but one that can be avoided at the option of one or both of the parties. The party having the option can elect either to avoid any duty to perform or to *ratify* (make valid) the contract. If the contract is avoided, both parties are released from it. If it is ratified, both parties must fully perform their respective legal obligations.

As you will read in Chapter 10, contracts made by minors, insane persons, and intoxicated persons may be voidable. As a general rule, for example, contracts made by minors are voidable at the option of the minor. Additionally, contracts entered into under fraudulent conditions are voidable at the option of the defrauded party. Contracts entered into under legally defined duress or undue influence are voidable (see Chapter 11).

An **unenforceable contract** is one that cannot be enforced because of certain legal defenses against it. It is not unenforceable because a party failed to satisfy a legal requirement of the contract; rather, it is a valid contract rendered unenforceable by some statute or law. For example, some contracts must be in writing (see Chapter 11), and if they are not, they will not be enforceable except in certain exceptional circumstances.

Interpretation of Contracts

Common law rules of contract interpretation have evolved over time to provide the courts with guidelines for determining the meaning of contracts.

THE PLAIN MEANING RULE

NOTE No one can avoid a contract by claiming that she or he did not read it. A contract is interpreted as if each party read every word carefully.

When the writing is clear and unequivocal, a court will enforce the contract according to its plain terms (what is clearly stated in the contract), and there is no need for the court to interpret the language of the contract. The meaning of the terms must be determined from *the face of the instrument*—from the written document alone. This is sometimes referred to as the *plain meaning rule*. Under this rule, if a contract's words appear to be clear and unambiguous, a court cannot consider *extrinsic evidence*, which is any evidence not contained in the document itself. Admissibility of extrinsic evidence can significantly affect how a court interprets ambiguous contractual provisions and thus can affect the outcome of litigation.

The court in the following case applied these principles to a contract's "no-cause termination clause."

CASE 8.2 United Airlines, Inc. v. Good Taste, Inc.

Supreme Court of Alaska, 1999.
982 P.2d 1259.
http://www.touchngo.com/sp/spslip99.htm[a]

FACTS Good Taste, Inc., a food service company in Anchorage, Alaska, does business under the name Saucy Sisters Catering. Saucy Sisters contracted with United Airlines, Inc., to handle its in-flight catering. The parties' "Catering Agreement" stated that it would run for a period of three years, "provided, however, either party may terminate this Agreement upon ninety (90) days' prior written notice." To fulfill the contract, Saucy Sisters expanded its operation at a cost of nearly $1 million. Just over a year later, United gave Saucy Sisters ninety days' notice, after which their agreement terminated. Saucy Sisters filed a suit against United in an Alaska state court, asserting, among other things, that it had breached their contract.

Saucy Sisters argued that the termination clause was ambiguous and alleged that before signing the contract, United had said it had never used the clause and included it only as an "out" in the event that United discontinued its flights to Anchorage. Saucy Sisters filed a motion for summary judgment. The judge denied the motion, ruling that the clause was not ambiguous and that United had not breached the contract. The jury returned a verdict in favor of the plaintiff on its other claims, however, and the court entered a judgment for more than $3.6 million in favor of Saucy Sisters. Both parties appealed to the Alaska Supreme Court. Saucy Sisters continued to argue that the termination clause was ambiguous and that the trial court should have ruled in its favor on that claim.

a. On this page, scroll down to the name of the case to access the opinion, which was issued on July 9, 1999. This Web site is made available by Touch N' Go Systems, Inc., and the Law Offices of James B. Gottstein, in Anchorage, Alaska.

ISSUE Was the termination clause ambiguous?

DECISION No. The Alaska Supreme Court held that the termination clause was clear and unambiguous and that the contract could be terminated with proper notice by either party. The court also ruled in favor of United on all of the other claims and remanded the case for the entry of a judgment for the airline.

REASON The court explained, "A disagreement as to contract terms does not in itself create an ambiguity. * * * [W]hen the language of a contract is unambiguous, the express provision governs and there is no need for construction or inquiry as to the intention of the parties. Here, the meaning of the disputed termination clause is clear and unambiguous on its face when its words are given their plain, ordinary, popular, and natural meaning. * * * Anyone familiar with real world business practices would instantly recognize this provision as a no-cause termination provision that is often used to limit an otherwise definite term. No-cause termination clauses like the one considered here are widely used, and this one in particular would not cause anyone to second-guess its clear and unambiguous terms."

FOR CRITICAL ANALYSIS—Social Consideration *When forming a contract, should a party ever give more weight to the other party's oral promises than to the terms expressed clearly in the written contract?*

OTHER RULES OF INTERPRETATION

"How many a dispute could have been deflated into a single paragraph if the disputants had dared define their terms."

ARISTOTLE,
384–322 B.C.E.
(Greek philosopher)

When the writing contains ambiguous or unclear terms, a court will interpret the language to give effect to the parties' intent *as expressed in their contract.* This is the primary purpose of the rules of interpretation—to determine the parties' intent from the language used in their agreement and to give effect to that intent. A court normally will not make or remake a contract, nor will it normally interpret the language according to what the parties *claim* their intent was when they made it. The courts use the following rules in interpreting ambiguous contractual terms:

① Insofar as possible, a reasonable, lawful, and effective meaning will be given to all of a contract's terms.

② A contract will be interpreted as a whole; individual, specific clauses will be considered subordinate to the contract's general intent. All writings that are a part of the same transaction will be interpreted together.

③ Terms that were the subject of separate negotiation will be given greater consideration than standardized terms and terms that were not negotiated separately.

④ A word will be given its ordinary, commonly accepted meaning, and a technical word or term will be given its technical meaning, unless the parties clearly intended something else.

⑤ Specific and exact wording will be given greater consideration than general language.

⑥ Written or typewritten terms prevail over preprinted terms.

⑦ Because a contract should be drafted in clear and unambiguous language, a party that uses ambiguous expressions is held to be responsible for the ambiguities. Thus, when the language has more than one meaning, it will be interpreted against the party that drafted the contract.

⑧ Evidence of trade usage, prior dealing, and course of performance may be admitted to clarify the meaning of an ambiguously worded contract. (We define and discuss these terms in Chapter 14.) What each of the parties does pursuant to the contract will be interpreted as consistent with what the other does and with any relevant usage of trade and course of dealing or performance. Express terms (terms expressly stated in the contract) are given the greatest weight, followed by course of performance, course of dealing, and custom and usage of trade—in that order. When considering custom and usage, a court will look at the trade customs and usage common to the particular business or industry and to the locale in which the contract was made or is to be performed.

ETHICAL ISSUE 8.2

Why do courts interpret vague or ambiguous contract terms against the party that drafted the contract?

Point number 7 in the above list—a party that uses ambiguous language will be held responsible for the ambiguities—expresses the ethical conviction that those who draft contracts should not be allowed to reap benefits from vague language. Often, the party responsible for drafting a contract has superior bargaining power relative to the other party. For example, a person who wants to obtain life or health insurance must either accept the terms of the insurance company's policy, as drafted, or not obtain insurance coverage from that company. (Of course, the person can shop around for a policy with terms that are acceptable.) Insurance contracts are essentially adhesion contracts. An adhesion contract is a contract drafted by the dominant party and then presented to the other (adhering) party on a "take it or leave it" basis (see Chapter 10). If an insurance policy contains an ambiguous clause, the insurance company could, by interpreting the clause in its favor, deny coverage to the policyholder in the event of a claim. To prevent such unfairness, the courts interpret vague or ambiguous statements against the party that drafted the contract.

LANDMARK IN THE LAW

Plain Language Laws

Plain language is increasingly being required in contracts, and for a good reason: parties to contracts cannot genuinely assent to contractual terms that they do not understand.

Plain Language Requirements Today, a majority of the states regulate legal writing through "plain language laws." The New York law, which has strongly influenced the plain language laws adopted by other states, illustrates how state statutes address the language problem. In New York, an agreement must be (1) "written in a clear and coherent manner using words with common and everyday meanings" and (2) "appropriately divided and captioned by its various sections."[a]

If a party to a contract, such as an insurance company, violates a plain language statute, the contract may be void—unless the party can show that it made a good faith effort to comply with the statute. Some state statutes even allow proposed contracts to be submitted to the state attorney general, whose approval then eliminates any liability for damages because of a supposed violation of the plain language statute.

Difficult-to-read federal government forms have also come under attack. In one case, for example, a court found that a government form giving immigrants notice of possible deportation was so difficult to read that it violated due process requirements.[b] In 1998, the federal government addressed this problem. In that year, President Bill Clinton issued a presidential executive memorandum to all federal agencies ordering them to use plain language in most of their forms and written communications. The memorandum stated that to be in "plain language," documents had to be organized logically, be easy to read, and use the following: common, everyday words, except when the use of technical terms was necessary; "you" and other pronouns; the active voice; and short sentences. By 1999, plain language requirements had been extended to agency rulemaking as well.

a. N.Y. Gen. Oblig. Law, Section 5-702.

b. *Walters v. Reno*, 145 F.3d 1032 (9th Cir. 1998).

PLAIN LANGUAGE LAWS

DON'T FORGET Most law, like most contracts, can be expressed in ordinary English.

To avoid disputes over contract interpretation, business managers should make sure that their intentions are clearly expressed in their contracts. Careful drafting of contracts not only helps prevent potential disputes over the meaning of certain terms but may also be crucial if the firm brings or needs to defend against a lawsuit for breach of contract.

In the interests of helping consumers, as well as easing the work of the courts, the federal and state governments have been actively pushing for more clearly written legal contracts by enacting "plain language laws." These laws, which are the subject of this chapter's *Landmark in the Law,* deal with private contracts in their entirety. Plain language laws attempt to reach a broad variety of consumer agreements relating to personal, family, and household matters, including residential leases.

LANDMARK IN THE LAW—Continued

You can learn about these and other requirements by going to **http://www.plainlanguage.gov**. For a discussion of what plain language is and tips on how to write clearly, see the Small Business Administration's article on "Plain Language" at **http://www.sbaonline.sba.gov/plain/whatis.html**. For more detailed guidelines on how to write in plain English, see the Securities and Exchange Commission's "Plain English Handbook"—a guide for businesspersons and their attorneys who create documents to be filed with the commission—at **http://www.sec.gov/pdf/handbook.pdf**.

Legal Professionals Move toward Plain English In response to plain language laws, the legal profession has attempted to abandon the traditional preference for often turgid and verbose language in favor of clear and easily understandable legal writing. Judges and clients are also pressuring lawyers to make legal concepts and documents more comprehensible. In some cases, they have refused to accept motions that are incoherent due to the legal language. In some areas, judges themselves are being asked to write their opinions more clearly. For example, the chief judge of New York's highest court has encouraged judges in the New York court system to hand down clearly written rulings so that other judges, lawyers, lawmakers, and the taxpayers who pay judicial salaries know what the decisions mean.

APPLICATION TO TODAY'S WORLD

Consumers who form contracts to purchase goods or services can easily be confused or misled by "legalese" in contracts. Plain English requirements are helping to reduce this confusion and are thus an effective complement to laws designed to protect consumers. The use of plain English is particularly notable in Internet communications, such as e-mail among lawyers and their clients, contract parties, and others. Typically, online communications tend to use less formal and more direct language than is used in hard-copy letters and memoranda.

APPLICATION Law and the Employer. . .

Avoiding Unintended Employment Contracts*

Employers have learned many lessons from court decisions. In recent years, for example, the message has been clear that employers should be cautious about what they say in their employment manuals.

EMPLOYMENT MANUALS AND IMPLIED-IN-FACT CONTRACTS

Promises made in an employment manual may create an implied-in-fact employment contract. If an employment handbook states that employees will be fired only for specific causes, the employer may be held to that "promise." Even if, by state law, employment is "at will"—that is, the employer is allowed to hire and fire employees at will, with or without cause—the at-will doctrine will not apply if the terms of employment are subject to a contract between the employer and employee. If a court holds that an implied employment contract exists—on the basis of promises made in an employment manual—the employment is no longer at will. The employer will be bound by the contract and liable for damages for breaching the contract.

TAKING PRECAUTIONS

Employers who wish to avoid potential liability for breaching unintended employment contracts should therefore make it clear to employees that the policies expressed in an employment manual are not to be interpreted as contractual promises. An effective way to do this is to inform employees, when initially giving them the handbook or discussing its contents with them, that the handbook is not intended as a contract and to include a disclaimer to that effect in the employment manual. The disclaimer might read as follows: "This policy manual describes the basic personnel policies and practices of our Company. You should understand that the manual does not modify our Company's 'at will' employment doctrine or provide employees with any kind of contractual rights."

The employer should make the disclaimer clear and prominent so that the applicant cannot later claim that it was the employer's fault that the employee did not see the disclaimer. A disclaimer will be clear and prominent if it is set off from the surrounding text by the use of larger type, a different color, all capital letters, or some other device that calls the reader's attention to it.

In the handbook, the employer should also avoid making definite promises that employees will be fired only for cause, that they will not be fired after they have worked for a certain length of time except for certain reasons, or the like. The handbook itself should include a clear and prominent disclaimer of contractual liability for its contents.

CHECKLIST FOR THE EMPLOYER

1. Inform new employees that statements in an employment handbook are not intended as contractual terms.
2. Include a clear and prominent disclaimer to this effect in employment applications.
3. Avoid including in the handbook any definite promises relating to job security, and include a clear and prominent disclaimer of contractual liability for any statements made within the handbook.

*This *Application* is not meant to substitute for the services of an attorney who is licensed to practice law in your state.

Key Terms

Chapter Summary Nature and Classification

The Function of Contracts (See page 219.)	Contract law establishes what kinds of promises will be legally binding and supplies procedures for enforcing legally binding promises, or agreements.
The Definition of a Contract (See pages 219–220.)	A contract is an agreement that can be enforced in court. It is formed by two or more competent parties who agree to perform or to refrain from performing some act now or in the future.
Requirements of a Contract (See pages 220–221.)	1. *Elements of a valid contract*—Agreement, consideration, contractual capacity, and legality. 2. *Possible defenses to the enforcement of a contract*—Genuineness of assent and form.
Types of Contracts (See pages 221–227.)	1. *Bilateral*—A promise for a promise. 2. *Unilateral*—A promise for an act (acceptance is the completed—or substantial—performance of the contract by the offeree). 3. *Express*—Formed by words (oral, written, or a combination). 4. *Implied in fact*—Formed at least in part by the conduct of the parties. 5. *Quasi contract (contract implied in law)*—Imposed by law to prevent unjust enrichment. 6. *Formal*—Requires a special form for creation. 7. *Informal*—Requires no special form for creation. 8. *Executed*—A fully performed contract. 9. *Executory*—A contract not yet fully performed. 10. *Valid*—A contract that has the necessary contractual elements of offer and acceptance, consideration, parties with legal capacity, and having been made for a legal purpose. 11. *Void*—No contract exists, or there is a contract without legal obligations. 12. *Voidable*—A contract in which a party has the option of avoiding or enforcing the contractual obligation. 13. *Unenforceable*—A valid contract that cannot be enforced because of a legal defense.
Interpretation of Contracts (See pages 227–231.)	When the terms of a contract are unambiguous, a court will enforce the contract according to its plain terms, the meaning of which must be determined from the written document alone. (Plain language laws enacted by the federal government and the majority of the states require contracts to be clearly written and easily understandable.) When the terms of a contract are ambiguous, the courts use the following rules in interpreting the terms: 1. A reasonable, lawful, and effective meaning will be given to all contract terms. 2. A contract will be interpreted as a whole, specific clauses will be considered subordinate to the contract's general intent, and all writings that are a part of the same transaction will be interpreted together. 3. Terms that were negotiated separately will be given greater consideration than standardized terms and terms not negotiated separately. 4. Words will be given their commonly accepted meanings and technical words their technical meanings, unless the parties clearly intended otherwise. 5. Specific wording will be given greater consideration than general language.

(continued)

Chapter Summary Nature and Classification—continued

Interpretation of Contracts—continued	6. Written or typewritten terms prevail over preprinted terms. 7. A party that uses ambiguous expressions is held to be responsible for the ambiguities. 8. Evidence of prior dealing, course of performance, or usage of trade is admissible to clarify an ambiguously worded contract. In these circumstances, express terms are given the greatest weight, followed by course of performance, course of dealing, and custom and usage of trade—in that order.

For Review

① What is a contract? What is the objective theory of contracts?
② What are the four basic elements necessary to the formation of a valid contract?
③ What is the difference between an implied-in-fact contract and an implied-in-law contract (quasi contract)?
④ What is a void contract? How does it differ from a voidable contract? What is an unenforceable contract?
⑤ What rules guide the courts in interpreting contracts?

Questions and Case Problems

8–1. Express versus Implied Contracts. Suppose that a local businessperson, McDougal, is a good friend of Krunch, the owner of a local candy store. Every day on his lunch hour McDougal goes into Krunch's candy store and spends about five minutes looking at the candy. After examining Krunch's candy and talking with Krunch, McDougal usually buys one or two candy bars. One afternoon, McDougal goes into Krunch's candy shop, looks at the candy, and picks up a $1 candy bar. Seeing that Krunch is very busy, he waves the candy bar at Krunch without saying a word and walks out. Is there a contract? If so, classify it within the categories presented in this chapter.

8–2. Contractual Promises. Rosalie, a wealthy widow, invited an acquaintance, Jonathan, to her home for dinner. Jonathan accepted the offer and, eager to please her, spent lavishly in preparing for the evening. His purchases included a new blazer, new shoes, an expensive floral arrangement, and champagne. At the appointed time, Jonathan arrived at Rosalie's house only to find that she had left for the evening. Jonathan wants to sue Rosalie to recover some of his expenses. Can he? Why or why not?

8–3. Contract Classification. Jennifer says to her neighbor, Gordon, "On your completion of mowing my lawn, I'll pay you $25." Gordon orally accepts her offer. Is there a contract? Is Jennifer's offer intended to create a bilateral or a unilateral contract? What is the legal significance of the distinction?

8–4. Contract Classification. High-Flying Advertising, Inc., contracted with Big Burger Restaurants to fly an advertisement above the Connecticut beaches. The advertisement offered $5,000 to any person who could swim from the Connecticut beaches to Long Island across the Long Island Sound in less than a day. McElfresh saw the streamer and accepted the challenge. He started his marathon swim that same day at 10 A.M. After he had been swimming for four hours and was about halfway across the sound, McElfresh saw another plane pulling a streamer that read, "Big Burger revokes." Is there a contract between McElfresh and Big Burger? If there is a contract, what type(s) of contract is (are) formed?

8–5. Equitable Doctrines. Ashton Co., which was engaged in a construction project, leased a crane from Artukovich & Sons, Inc., and hired the Reliance Truck Co. to deliver the crane to the construction site. Reliance, while the crane was in its possession and without permission from either Ashton or Artukovich, used the crane to install a transformer for a utility company, which paid Reliance for the job. Reliance then delivered the crane to the Ashton construction site at the appointed time of delivery. When Artukovich learned of the unauthorized use of the crane by Reliance, it sued Reliance for damages. What equitable doctrine could be used as a basis for awarding damages to Artukovich? [*Artukovich & Sons, Inc. v. Reliance Truck Co.,* 126 Ariz. 246, 614 P.2d 327 (1980)]

8–6. Bilateral versus Unilateral Contracts. Nichols is the principal owner of Samuel Nichols, Inc., a real estate firm. Nichols signed an exclusive brokerage agreement with Molway to find a purchaser for Molway's property within ninety days. This type of agreement entitles the broker to a commission if the property is sold to any purchaser to whom the property is shown during the ninety-day period. Molway tried to cancel the brokerage agreement before the ninety-day term had expired. Nichols had already advertised the property, put up a "for sale" sign, and shown the property to prospective buyers. Molway claimed that the brokerage contract was unilateral and that she could cancel the contract at any time before Nichols found a buyer. Nichols claimed the contract was bilateral and that Molway's cancellation breached the contract. Discuss who should prevail at trial. [*Samuel Nichols, Inc. v. Molway,* 25 Mass.App. 913, 515 N.E.2d 598 (1987)]

8–7. Recovery for Services Rendered. After Walter Washut had suffered a heart attack and could no longer take care of himself, he asked Eleanor Adkins, a friend who had previously refused Washut's proposal to marry him, to move to his ranch. For the next twelve years, Adkins lived with Washut, although she retained ownership of her own house and continued to work full-time at her job. Adkins took care of Washut's personal needs, cooked his meals, cleaned and maintained his house, cared for the livestock, and handled other matters for Washut. According to Adkins, Washut told her on numerous occasions that "everything would be taken care of" and that she would never have to leave the ranch. After Washut's death, Adkins sought to recover in quasi contract for the value of the services she had rendered to Washut. Adkins stated in her deposition that she performed the services because she loved Washut, not because she expected to be paid for them. What will the court decide, and why? [*Adkins v. Lawson,* 892 P.2d 128 (Wyo. 1995)]

8–8. Interpretation of Contracts. Jerilyn Dawson hired Michael Shaw of the law firm of Jones, Waldo, Holbrook & McDonough to represent her in her divorce. Dawson signed an agreement to pay the attorneys' fees. The agreement did not include an estimate of how much the divorce would cost. When Dawson failed to pay, the firm filed a suit in a Utah state court to collect, asking for an award of more than $43,000. During the trial, Shaw testified that he had told Dawson the divorce would cost "something in the nature of $15,000 to $18,000." The court awarded the firm most—but not all—of what it sought. Both parties appealed: Dawson contended that the award was too high, and the firm complained that it was too low. What rule of interpretation discussed in this chapter might the appellate court apply in deciding the appropriate amount of damages in this case? If this rule is applied, what will the court likely decide? Explain. [*Jones, Waldo, Holbrook & McDonough v. Dawson,* 923 P.2d 1366 (Utah 1996)]

8–9. Implied Contract. Thomas Rinks and Joseph Shields developed Psycho Chihuahua, a caricature of a Chihuahua dog with a "do-not-back-down" attitude. They promoted and marketed the character through their company, Wrench, L.L.C. Ed Alfaro and Rudy Pollak, representatives of Taco Bell Corp., learned of Psycho Chihuahua and met with Rinks and Shields to talk about using the character as a Taco Bell "icon." Wrench sent artwork, merchandise, and marketing ideas to Alfaro, who promoted the character within Taco Bell. Alfaro asked Wrench to propose terms for Taco Bell's use of Psycho Chihuahua. Taco Bell did not accept Wrench's terms, but Alfaro continued to promote the character within the company. Meanwhile, Taco Bell hired a new advertising agency, which proposed an advertising campaign involving a Chihuahua. When Alfaro learned of this proposal, he sent the Psycho Chihuahua materials to the agency. Taco Bell made a Chihuahua the focus of its marketing but paid nothing to Wrench. Wrench filed a suit against Taco Bell in a federal district court, claiming in part that it had an implied contract with Taco Bell, which the latter breached. Do these facts satisfy the requirements for an implied contract? Why or why not? [*Wrench L.L.C. v. Taco Bell Corp.,* 51 F.Supp.2d 840 (W.D.Mich. 1999)]

TEST YOUR KNOWLEDGE—ANSWER ON THE WEB

8–10. Professor Dixon was an adjunct professor at Tulsa Community College (TCC) in Tulsa, Oklahoma. Each semester, near the beginning of the term, the parties executed a written contract that always included the following provision: "It is agreed that this agreement may be cancelled by the Administration or the instructor at anytime before the first class session." In the spring semester of Dixon's seventh year, he filed a complaint with TCC alleging that one of his students, Meredith Bhuiyan, had engaged in disruptive classroom conduct. He gave her an incomplete grade and asked TCC to require her to apologize as a condition of receiving a final grade. TCC later claimed, and Dixon denied, that he was told to assign Bhuiyan a grade if he wanted to teach in the fall. Toward the end of the semester, Dixon was told which classes he would teach in the fall, but the parties did not sign a written contract. The Friday before classes began, TCC terminated him. Dixon filed a suit in an Oklahoma state court against TCC and others, alleging breach of contract. Did the parties have a contract? If so, did TCC breach it? Explain. [*Dixon v. Bhuiyan,* 10 P.3d 888 (Okla. 2000)]

A QUESTION OF ETHICS AND SOCIAL RESPONSIBILITY

8–11. When LeRoy McIlravy began working for Kerr-McGee Corp., he was given an employee handbook that listed examples of misconduct that could result in discipline or discharge and spelled out specific procedures that would be used in those instances. When McIlravy was later laid off, he and other former employees filed a suit against Kerr-McGee, contending, among other things, that the handbook constituted an implied contract that Kerr-McGee had breached, because the handbook implied that employees would not be dismissed without "cause." In view of these facts, consider the following questions. [*McIlravy v. Kerr-McGee Corp.,* 119 F.3d 876 (10th Cir. 1997)]

1. Would it be fair to the employer for the court to hold that an implied contract had been created in this case, given that the employer did not *intend* to create a contract? Would it be fair to the employees to hold that no contract was created? If the decision were up to you, how would you decide this issue?

2. Suppose that the handbook contained a disclaimer stating that the handbook was not to be construed as a contract. How would this affect your answers to the above questions? From an ethical perspective, would it ever be fair to hold that an implied contract exists *notwithstanding* such a disclaimer?

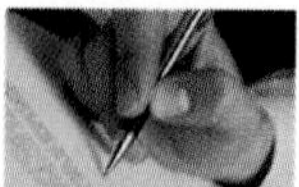

FOR CRITICAL ANALYSIS

8–12. Review the list of basic requirements for contract formation given at the beginning of this chapter. In view of those requirements, analyze the relationship entered into when a student enrolls in a college or university. Has a contract been formed? If so, is it a bilateral contract or a unilateral contract? Discuss.

Internet Exercises

Go to the *Business Law Today* home page at **http://blt.westbuslaw.com**. Select "Interactive Study Center" and then click on "Chapter 8." There you will find the following Internet research exercises that you can perform to learn more about contract law:

Activity 8–1: Contracts and Contract Provisions
Activity 8–2: Contracts in Ancient Mesopotamia

Before the Test

Go to the *Business Law Today* home page at **http://blt.westbuslaw.com**. Click on "Interactive Quizzes." You will find at least twenty interactive questions relating to this chapter.

CHAPTER 9

Agreement and Consideration

"It is necessity that makes laws."

Voltaire, 1749–1832
(French philosopher and writer)

CHAPTER CONTENTS

LEARNING OBJECTIVES

After reading this chapter, you should be able to answer the following questions:

① What elements are necessary for an effective offer? What are some examples of nonoffers?

② In what circumstances will an offer be irrevocable?

③ What are the elements that are necessary for an effective acceptance?

④ What is consideration? What is required for consideration to be legally sufficient?

⑤ In what circumstances might a promise be enforced despite a lack of consideration?

Voltaire's statement that it is "necessity that makes laws" is certainly true in regard to contracts. In Chapter 8, we pointed out that promises and agreements, and the knowledge that certain of those promises and agreements will be legally enforced, are essential to civilized society. The homes we live in, the food we eat, the clothes we wear, the cars we drive, the books we read, the videos and recordings we watch and listen to—all of these have been purchased through contractual agreements. Contract law developed over time, through the common law tradition, to meet society's need to know with certainty what kinds of promises, or contracts, will be enforced and the point at which a valid and binding contract is formed.

For a contract to be considered valid and enforceable, the requirements listed in Chapter 8 must be met. In this chapter, we look closely at two of these requirements, *agreement* and *consideration*. As you read through this chapter, keep in mind that the requirements of agreement and consideration apply to all contracts, regardless of how they are formed. Many contracts continue to be formed in the traditional way—through the exchange of paper documents. Increasingly, contracts are also being formed online—through the exchange of electronic messages or documents. Although we discuss online contracts to a limited extent in this chapter, we will look at them more closely in Chapter 17.

Agreement

AGREEMENT A meeting of two or more minds in regard to the terms of a contract; usually broken down into two events—an offer by one party to form a contract, and an acceptance of the offer by the person to whom the offer is made.

An essential element for contract formation is **agreement—**the parties must agree on the terms of the contract. Ordinarily, agreement is evidenced by two events: an *offer* and an *acceptance.* One party offers a certain bargain to another party, who then accepts that bargain.

Because words often fail to convey the precise meaning intended, the law of contracts generally adheres to the *objective theory of contracts,* as discussed in Chapter 8. Under this theory, a party's words and conduct are held to mean whatever a reasonable person in the offeree's position would think they meant. The court will give words their usual meanings even if "it were proved by twenty bishops that [the] party . . . intended something else."[1]

Requirements of the Offer

OFFER A promise or commitment to perform or refrain from performing some specified act in the future.

An **offer** is a promise or commitment to perform or refrain from performing some specified act in the future. As discussed in Chapter 8, the party making an offer is called the *offeror,* and the party to whom the offer is made is called the *offeree.*

Three elements are necessary for an offer to be effective:

① There must be a serious, objective intention by the offeror.

② The terms of the offer must be reasonably certain, or definite, so that the parties and the court can ascertain the terms of the contract.

③ The offer must be communicated to the offeree.

Once an effective offer has been made, the offeree's acceptance of that offer creates a legally binding contract (providing the other essential elements for a valid and enforceable contract are present).

In today's e-commerce world, offers are frequently made online. Essentially, the requirements for traditional offers apply to online offers as well, as you will read in Chapter 17.

ON THE WEB For information on and examples illustrating the common law requirements governing offers and acceptance, go to FindLaw's Web site at **http://profs.lp.findlaw.com/contracts/index.html**.

Intention The first requirement for an effective offer to exist is a serious, objective intention on the part of the offeror. Intent is not determined by the *subjective* intentions, beliefs, or assumptions of the offeror. Rather, it is determined by what a reasonable person in the offeree's position would conclude the offeror's words and actions meant. Offers made in obvious anger, jest, or undue excitement do not meet the serious-and-objective-intent test. Because these offers are not effective, an offeree's acceptance does not create an agreement.

1. Judge Learned Hand in *Hotchkiss v. National City Bank of New York,* 200 F. 287 (2d Cir. 1911), aff'd 231 U.S. 50, 34 S.Ct. 20, 58 L.Ed. 115 (1913). (The term *aff'd* is an abbreviation for *affirmed;* an appellate court can affirm a lower court's judgment, decree, or order, thereby declaring that it is valid and must stand as rendered.)

"[Contracts] must not be the sports of an idle hour, mere matters of pleasantry and badinage, never intended by the parties to have any serious effect whatever."

WILLIAM STOWELL,
1745–1836
(English jurist)

● **EXAMPLE 9.1** You and three classmates ride to school each day in Julio's new automobile, which has a market value of $18,000. One cold morning the four of you get into the car, but Julio cannot get it started. He yells in anger, "I'll sell this car to anyone for $500!" You drop $500 in his lap. A reasonable person, taking into consideration Julio's frustration and the obvious difference in value between the car's market price and the purchase price, would declare that Julio's offer was not made with serious and objective intent and that you do not have an agreement.● In the subsections that follow, we examine the concept of intention further as we look at the distinctions between offers and nonoffers.

Lucy v. Zehmer, presented below, is a classic case in the area of contractual agreement. The case involved a business transaction in which boasts, brags, and dares "after a few drinks" resulted in a contract to sell certain property. The sellers claimed that the offer had been made in jest and that, in any event, the contract was voidable at their option because they were intoxicated when the offer was made and thus lacked contractual capacity (see Chapter 10). The court, however, looked to the words and actions of the parties—not their secret intentions—to determine whether a contract had been formed.

Landmark and Classic Cases

CASE 9.1 Lucy v. Zehmer

Supreme Court of Appeals of Virginia, 1954.
196 Va. 493,
84 S.E.2d 516.

FACTS Lucy and Zehmer had known each other for fifteen or twenty years. For some time, Lucy had been wanting to buy Zehmer's farm. Zehmer had always told Lucy that he was not interested in selling. One night, Lucy stopped in to visit with the Zehmers at a restaurant they operated. Lucy said to Zehmer, "I bet you wouldn't take $50,000 for that place." Zehmer replied, "Yes, I would, too; you wouldn't give fifty." Throughout the evening, the conversation returned to the sale of the farm. At the same time, the parties were drinking whiskey. Eventually, Zehmer wrote up an agreement, on the back of a restaurant check, for the sale of the farm, and he asked his wife to sign it—which she did. When Lucy brought an action in a Virginia state court to enforce the agreement, Zehmer argued that he had been "high as a Georgia pine" at the time and that the offer had been made in jest: "two doggoned drunks bluffing to see who could talk the biggest and say the most." Lucy claimed that he had not been intoxicated and did not think Zehmer had been, either, given the way Zehmer handled the transaction. The trial court ruled in favor of the Zehmers, and Lucy appealed.

ISSUE Can the agreement be avoided on the basis of intoxication?

DECISION No. The agreement to sell the farm was binding.

REASON The opinion of the court was that the evidence given about the nature of the conversation, the appearance and completeness of the agreement, and the signing all tended to show that a serious business transaction, not a casual jest, was intended. The court had to look into the objective meaning of the words and acts of the Zehmers: "An agreement or mutual assent is of course essential to a valid contract, but the law imputes to a person an intention corresponding to the reasonable meaning of his words and acts. If his words and acts, judged by a reasonable standard, manifest an intention to agree, it is immaterial what may be the real but unexpressed state of mind."

COMMENT *This is a classic case in contract law because it illustrates so clearly the objective theory of contracts with respect to determining whether an offer was intended. Today, the objective theory of contracts*

(continued)

CASE 9.1—Continued

continues to be applied by the courts, and Lucy v. Zehmer *is routinely cited as a significant precedent in this area. Note that in cases involving contracts formed online, the issue of contractual intent rarely arises. Perhaps this is because an online offer is, by definition, "objective" in the sense that it consists of words only—the offeror's physical actions and behavior are not evidenced.*

BE CAREFUL An opinion is not an offer and not a contract term. Goods or services can be "perfect" in one party's opinion and "poor" in another's.

Expressions of Opinion. An expression of opinion is not an offer. It does not evidence an intention to enter into a binding agreement. • **EXAMPLE 9.2** In *Hawkins v. McGee,*[2] Hawkins took his son to McGee, a doctor, and asked McGee to operate on the son's hand. McGee said that the boy would be in the hospital three or four days and that the hand would *probably* heal a few days later. The son's hand did not heal for a month, but nonetheless the father did not win a suit for breach of contract. The court held that McGee did not make an offer to heal the son's hand in three or four days. He merely expressed an opinion as to when the hand would heal.•

Statements of Intention. A statement of an *intention* to do something in the future is not an offer. • **EXAMPLE 9.3** If Ari says "I *plan* to sell my stock in Novation, Inc., for $150 per share," a contract is not created if John "accepts" and tenders the $150 per share for the stock. Ari has merely expressed his intention to enter into a future contract for the sale of the stock. If John accepts and tenders the $150 per share, no contract is formed, because a reasonable person would conclude that Ari was only *thinking about* selling his stock, not promising to sell it.•

Preliminary Negotiations. A request or invitation to negotiate is not an offer; it only expresses a willingness to discuss the possibility of entering into a contract. Examples are statements such as "Will you sell Forest Acres?" and "I wouldn't sell my car for less than $1,000." A reasonable person in the offeree's position would not conclude that such a statement evidenced an intention to enter into a binding obligation. Likewise, when the government and private firms need to have construction work done, contractors are invited to submit bids. The *invitation* to submit bids is not an offer, and a contractor does not bind the government or private firm by submitting a bid. (The bids that the contractors submit are offers, however, and the government or private firm can bind the contractor by accepting the bid.)

KEEP IN MIND Advertisements are not binding, but they cannot be deceptive.

Advertisements, Catalogues, and Circulars. In general, advertisements, mail-order catalogues, price lists, and circular letters (meant for the general public) are treated as invitations to negotiate, not as offers to form a contract.[3] • **EXAMPLE 9.4** Suppose that you put an ad in the classified section of your local newspaper offering to sell your guitar for $75. Seven people call and "accept" your "offer" before you can remove the ad from the newspaper. If the ad were truly an offer, you would be bound by seven contracts to sell your guitar. Because *initial* advertisements are treated as *invitations* to make offers rather than offers, however, you will have seven offers to choose from, and you can accept the best one without incurring any liability for the six you reject.• On some occasions, though, courts have construed advertisements to be offers because the

---

2. 84 N.H. 114, 146 A. 641 (1929).

3. *Restatement (Second) of Contracts,* Section 26, Comment b.

ads contained definite terms that invited acceptance (such as an ad offering a reward for the return of a lost dog).[4]

Price lists are another form of invitation to negotiate or trade. A seller's price list is not an offer to sell at that price; it merely invites the buyer to offer to buy at that price. In fact, the seller usually puts "prices subject to change" on the price list. Only in rare circumstances will a price quotation be construed as an offer.[5]

ETHICAL ISSUE 9.1

Should promises of prizes made in ads and circulars always be enforced?

Businesses and other organizations commonly promote their products or services by offering prizes, rewards, and the like for certain performance. Often, these ads for prizes present few problems. At times, though, people perform whatever is necessary to win advertised prizes only to learn that the offers were made in jest—that is, the ads' sponsors had no real intention of giving anyone the prizes. Consider an example. PepsiCo launched an ad campaign in which consumers could use "Pepsi Points"—which could be found on specially marked packages of Pepsi or purchased for ten cents each—to obtain T-shirts and other merchandise with the Pepsi logo. One of the ads featured a Harrier Fighter Jet, which was listed at 7,000,000 Pepsi Points. When a consumer, John Leonard, raised $700,000, purchased 7,000,000 Pepsi Points, and laid claim to the prize, however, PepsiCo contended that the Harrier Jet in the commercial was "fanciful" and that the offer was made in jest. In the lawsuit that followed, the court agreed, stating that "no objective person could reasonably have concluded that the commercial actually offered consumers a Harrier Jet."[6] Yet Leonard obviously did draw that conclusion, and in a number of other cases, individuals have undertaken serious efforts to win nonexistent prizes. Some claim that not enforcing such promises is unfair to individuals who rely on the promises, as John Leonard did in the *PepsiCo* case.

Auctions. In an auction, a seller "offers" goods for sale through an auctioneer. This is not, however, an offer for purposes of contract. The seller is really expressing only a willingness to sell. Unless the terms of the auction are explicitly stated to be *without reserve,* the seller (through the auctioneer) may withdraw the goods at any time before the auctioneer closes the sale by announcement or by fall of the hammer. The seller's right to withdraw the goods characterizes an auction with reserve; all auctions are assumed to be of this type unless a clear statement to the contrary is made.[7] At auctions without reserve, the goods cannot be withdrawn and must be sold to the highest bidder.

In an auction with reserve, there is no obligation to sell, and the seller may refuse the highest bid. The bidder is actually the offeror. Before the auctioneer strikes the hammer, which constitutes acceptance of the bid, a bidder may revoke her or his bid, or the auctioneer may reject that bid or all bids. Typically, an auctioneer will reject a bid that is below the price the seller is willing to accept. When the auctioneer accepts

4. See, for example, *Lefkowitz v. Great Minneapolis Surplus Store, Inc.,* 251 Minn. 188, 86 N.W.2d 689 (1957).
5. See, for example, *Fairmount Glass Works v. Grunden-Martin Woodenware Co.,* 106 Ky. 659, 51 S.W. 196 (1899).
6. *Leonard v. PepsiCo,* 88 F.Supp.2d 116 (S.D.N.Y. 1999); aff'd 210 F.3d 88 (2d Cir. 2000).
7. See UCC 2–328.

An auction in progress at Christie's in London. When a seller puts up goods for a bid in an auction with reserve, has the seller made an offer for purposes of contract law? Why or why not?

a higher bid, he or she rejects all previous bids. Because rejection terminates an offer (as will be pointed out later), those bids represent offers that have been terminated. Thus, if the highest bidder withdraws his or her bid before the hammer falls, none of the previous bids is reinstated. If the bid is not withdrawn or rejected, the contract is formed when the auctioneer announces, "Going once, going twice, sold!" (or something similar) and lets the hammer fall.

In auctions with reserve, the seller may reserve the right to confirm or reject the sale even after "the hammer has fallen." In this situation, the seller is obligated to notify those attending the auction that sales of goods made during the auction are not final until confirmed by the seller.

Agreements to Agree. Traditionally, agreements to agree—that is, agreements to agree to the material terms of a contract at some future date—were not considered to be binding contracts. The modern view, however, is that agreements to agree may be enforceable agreements (contracts) if it is clear that the parties intend to be bound by the agreements. In other words, under the modern view the emphasis is on the parties' intent rather than on form.

● **EXAMPLE 9.5** When the Pennzoil Company discussed with the Getty Oil Company the possible purchase of Getty's stock, a memorandum of agreement was drafted to reflect the terms of the conversations. After more negotiations over the price, both companies issued press releases announcing an agreement in principle on the terms of the memorandum. The next day, Texaco, Inc., offered to buy all of Getty's stock at a higher price. The day after that, Getty's board of directors voted to accept Texaco's offer, and Texaco and Getty signed a merger agreement. When Pennzoil sued Texaco for tortious interference with its "contractual" relationship with Getty, a jury concluded that Getty and Pennzoil had intended to form a binding contract, with only the details left to be worked out, before Texaco made its offer. Texaco was held liable for wrongfully interfering with this contract.[8] ●

8. *Texaco, Inc. v. Pennzoil Co.*, 729 S.W.2d 768 (Tex.App—Houston [1st Dist.] 1987, writ ref'd n.r.e.). (Generally, a complete Texas Court of Appeals citation includes the writ-of-error history showing the Texas Supreme Court's disposition of the case. In this case, *writ ref'd n.r.e.* is an abbreviation for "writ refused, no reversible error," which means that Texas's highest court refused to grant the appellant's request to review the case, because the court did not think there was any reversible error.)

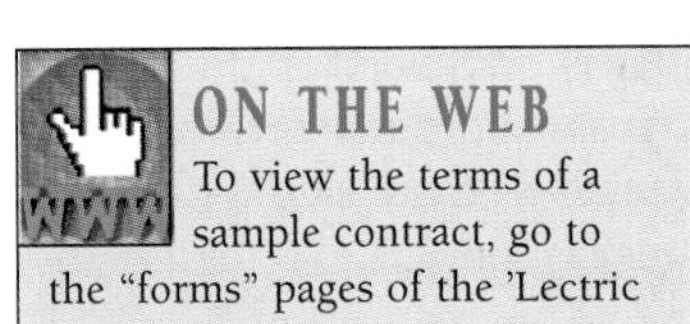

ON THE WEB To view the terms of a sample contract, go to the "forms" pages of the 'Lectric Law Library at

http://www.lectlaw.com/formb.htm

and select one of the types of contracts listed on this page to review.

Definiteness The second requirement for an effective offer involves the definiteness of its terms. An offer must have reasonably definite terms so that a court can determine if a breach has occurred and give an appropriate remedy.[9]

An offer may invite an acceptance to be worded in such specific terms that the contract is made definite. ● **EXAMPLE 9.6** Suppose that Marcus Business Machines contacts your corporation and offers to sell "from one to ten MacCool copying machines for $1,600 each; state number desired in acceptance." Your corporation agrees to buy two copiers. Because the quantity is specified in the acceptance, the terms are definite, and the contract is enforceable. ●

Communication A third requirement for an effective offer is communication—the offer must be communicated to the offeree. ● **EXAMPLE 9.7** Suppose that Tolson advertises a reward for the return of her lost cat. Dirlik, not knowing of the reward, finds the cat and returns it to Tolson. Ordinarily, Dirlik cannot recover the reward because an essential element of a reward contract is that the one who claims the reward must have known it was offered. A few states would allow recovery of the reward, but not on contract principles—Dirlik would be allowed to recover on the basis that it would be unfair to deny him the reward just because he did not know about it. ●

TERMINATION OF THE OFFER

The communication of an effective offer to an offeree gives the offeree the power to transform the offer into a binding, legal obligation (a contract) by an acceptance. This power of acceptance, however, does not continue forever. It can be terminated by action of the parties or by operation of law.

REVOCATION
In contract law, the withdrawal of an offer by an offeror; unless the offer is irrevocable, it can be revoked at any time prior to acceptance without liability.

Termination by Action of the Parties An offer can be terminated by the action of the parties in any of three ways: by revocation, by rejection, or by counteroffer.

Revocation of the Offer. The offeror's act of withdrawing an offer is referred to as **revocation.** Unless an offer is irrevocable, the offeror usually can revoke the offer (even if he or she has promised to keep the offer open), as long as the revocation is communicated to the offeree before the offeree accepts. Revocation may be accomplished by an express repudiation of the offer (for example, with a statement such as "I withdraw my previous offer of October 17") or by the performance of acts that are inconsistent with the existence of the offer and that are made known to the offeree.

A poster offers a reward. How can this offer be revoked?

● **EXAMPLE 9.8** Geraldine offers to sell some land to Gary. A week passes, and Gary, who has not yet accepted the offer, learns from his friend Konstantine that Geraldine has in the meantime sold the property to Nunan. Gary's knowledge of Geraldine's sale of the land to Nunan, even though he learned of it through a third party, effectively revokes Geraldine's offer to sell the land to Gary. Geraldine's sale of the land to Nunan is inconsistent with the continued existence of the offer to Gary, and thus the offer to Gary is revoked. ●

The general rule followed by most states is that a revocation becomes effective when the offeree or offeree's agent (a person who acts on behalf of another) actually receives it. Therefore, a letter of revocation mailed on April 1 and delivered at the offeree's residence or place of business on April 3 becomes effective on April 3.

An offer made to the general public can be revoked in the same manner in which the offer was originally communicated. ● **EXAMPLE 9.9** Suppose that a department store offers a $10,000 reward to anyone giving information leading to the apprehension of

9. *Restatement (Second) of Contracts,* Section 33. The UCC has relaxed the requirements regarding the definiteness of terms in contracts for the sale of goods. See UCC 2–204(3).

the persons who burglarized its downtown store. The offer is published in three local papers and in four papers in neighboring communities. To revoke the offer, the store must publish the revocation in all seven papers for the same number of days it published the offer. The revocation is then accessible to the general public, and the offer is revoked even if some particular offeree does not know about the revocation.●

Irrevocable Offers. Although most offers are revocable, some can be made irrevocable. Increasingly, courts refuse to allow an offeror to revoke an offer when the offeree has changed position because of justifiable reliance on the offer (under the doctrine of detrimental reliance, or promissory estoppel, discussed later in the chapter). In some circumstances, "firm offers" made by merchants may also be considered irrevocable. We discuss these offers in Chapter 14.

OPTION CONTRACT
A contract under which the offeror cannot revoke his or her offer for a stipulated time period, and the offeree can accept or reject the offer during this period without fear that the offer will be made to another person. The offeree must give consideration for the option (the irrevocable offer) to be enforceable.

Another form of irrevocable offer is an option contract. An **option contract** is created when an offeror promises to hold an offer open for a specified period of time in return for a payment (consideration) given by the offeree. An option contract takes away the offeror's power to revoke an offer for the period of time specified in the option. If no time is specified, then a reasonable period of time is implied. ● **EXAMPLE 9.10** Suppose that you are in the business of writing movie scripts. Your agent contacts the head of development at New Line Cinema and offers to sell New Line your new movie script. New Line likes your script and agrees to pay you $5,000 for a six-month option. In this situation, you (through your agent) are the offeror, and New Line is the offeree. You cannot revoke your offer to sell New Line your script for the next six months. If after six months no contract has been formed, however, New Line loses the $5,000, and you are free to sell the script to another firm.●

Option contracts are also frequently used in conjunction with the sale of real estate. ● **EXAMPLE 9.11** You might agree with a landowner to lease a home and include in the lease contract a clause stating that you will pay $2,000 for an option to purchase the home within a specified period of time. If you decide not to purchase the home after the specified period has lapsed, you lose the $2,000, and the landlord is free to sell the property to another buyer.●

BE CAREFUL The way a response to an offer is phrased can determine whether the offer is accepted or rejected.

Rejection of the Offer by the Offeree. An offer may be rejected by the offeree, in which case the offer is terminated. Any subsequent attempt by the offeree to accept will be construed as a new offer, giving the original offeror (now the offeree) the power of acceptance. A rejection is ordinarily accomplished by words or by conduct evidencing an intent not to accept the offer.

As with revocation, rejection of an offer is effective only when it is actually received by the offeror or the offeror's agent. ● **EXAMPLE 9.12** Suppose that Growgood Farms mails a letter to Campbell Soup Company offering to sell carrots at ten cents a pound. Campbell Soup Company could reject the offer by sending or faxing a letter to Growgood Farms expressly rejecting the offer, or by mailing the offer back to Growgood, evidencing an intent to reject it. Alternatively, Campbell could offer to buy the carrots at eight cents per pound (a counteroffer), necessarily rejecting the original offer.●

Merely inquiring about the offer does not constitute rejection. ● **EXAMPLE 9.13** A friend offers to buy your CD-ROM library for $300. You respond, "Is this your best offer?" or "Will you pay me $375 for it?" A reasonable person would conclude that you did not reject the offer but merely made an inquiry for further consideration of the offer. You can still accept and bind your friend to the $300 purchase price. When the offeree merely inquires as to the firmness of the offer, there is no reason to presume that she or he intends to reject it. ●

COUNTEROFFER
An offeree's response to an offer in which the offeree rejects the original offer and at the same time makes a new offer.

Counteroffer by the Offeree. A **counteroffer** is a rejection of the original offer and the simultaneous making of a new offer. ● **EXAMPLE 9.14** Suppose that Burke offers to sell his home to Lang for $170,000. Lang responds, "Your price is too high. I'll offer to purchase your house for $165,000." Lang's response is called a counteroffer because it rejects Burke's offer to sell at $170,000 and creates a new offer by Lang to purchase the home at a price of $165,000. ●

MIRROR IMAGE RULE
A common law rule that requires that the terms of the offeree's acceptance adhere exactly to the terms of the offeror's offer for a valid contract to be formed.

At common law, the **mirror image rule** requires that the offeree's acceptance match the offeror's offer exactly. In other words, the terms of the acceptance must "mirror" those of the offer. If the acceptance materially changes or adds to the terms of the original offer, it will be considered not an acceptance but a counteroffer—which, of course, need not be accepted. The original offeror can, however, accept the terms of the counteroffer and create a valid contract.[10]

Termination by Operation of Law The offeree's power to transform an offer into a binding, legal obligation can be terminated by operation of law if any of four conditions occur: lapse of time, destruction of the specific subject matter, death or incompetence of the offeror or offeree, or supervening illegality of the proposed contract.

Lapse of Time. An offer terminates automatically by law when the period of time *specified in the offer* has passed. If the offer states that it will be left open until a particular date, then the offer will terminate at midnight on that day. If the offer states that it will be left open for a number of days, such as ten days, this time period normally begins to run when the offer is actually received by the offeree, not when it is formed or sent. When the offer is delayed (through the misdelivery of mail, for example), the period begins to run from the date the offeree would have received the offer, but only if the offeree knows or should know that the offer is delayed.[11]

● **EXAMPLE 9.15** Suppose that Beth offers to sell her boat to Jonah, stating that the offer will remain open until May 20. Unless Jonah accepts the offer by midnight on May 20, the offer will lapse (terminate). Now suppose that Beth writes a letter to Jonah, offering to sell him her boat if Jonah accepts the offer within twenty days of the letter's date, which is May 1. Jonah must accept within twenty days after May 1, or the offer will terminate. The same rule would apply even if Beth had used improper postage when mailing the offer, and Jonah received the letter ten days after May 1, not knowing of the improper mailing. If, however, Jonah knew about the improper mailing, the offer would lapse twenty days after the day Jonah ordinarily would have received the offer had Beth used proper postage. ●

If no time for acceptance is specified in the offer, the offer terminates at the end of a *reasonable* period of time. A reasonable period of time is determined by the subject matter of the contract, business and market conditions, and other relevant circumstances. An offer to sell farm produce, for example, will terminate sooner than an offer to sell farm equipment, because farm produce is perishable and subject to greater fluctuations in market value.

---

10. The mirror image rule has been greatly modified in regard to sales contracts. Section 2–207 of the UCC provides that a contract is formed if the offeree makes a definite expression of acceptance (such as signing the form in the appropriate location), even though the terms of the acceptance modify or add to the terms of the original offer (see Chapter 14).

11. *Restatement (Second) of Contracts,* Section 49.

Destruction of the Subject Matter. An offer is automatically terminated if the specific subject matter of the offer is destroyed before the offer is accepted. For example, if Bekins offers to sell his prize cow to Yatsen, but the cow is struck by lightning and dies before Yatsen can accept, the offer is automatically terminated. (Note that if Yatsen accepted the offer just before lightning struck the cow, a contract would have been formed, but, because of the cow's death, a court would likely excuse Bekins's obligation to perform the contract on the basis of impossibility of performance—see Chapter 12.)

Death or Incompetence of the Offeror or Offeree. An offeree's power of acceptance is terminated when the offeror or offeree dies or is deprived of legal capacity to enter into the proposed contract, *unless the offer is irrevocable.*[12] An offer is personal to both parties and normally cannot pass to the decedent's heirs, guardian, or estate. This rule applies whether or not one party had notice of the death or incompetence of the other party.

Supervening Illegality of the Proposed Contract. A statute or court decision that makes an offer illegal will automatically terminate the offer. • **EXAMPLE 9.16** If Acme Finance Corporation offers to lend Jack $20,000 at 15 percent annually, and the state legislature enacts a statute prohibiting loans at interest rates greater than 12 percent before Jack can accept, the offer is automatically terminated. (If the statute is enacted after Jack accepts the offer, a valid contract is formed, but the contract may still be unenforceable—see Chapter 10.) •

ACCEPTANCE

ACCEPTANCE
A voluntary act by the offeree that shows assent, or agreement, to the terms of an offer; may consist of words or conduct.

An **acceptance** is a voluntary act by the offeree that shows assent, or agreement, to the terms of an offer. The offeree's act may consist of words or conduct. The acceptance must be unequivocal and must be communicated to the offeror.

Who Can Accept? Generally, a third person cannot substitute for the offeree and effectively accept the offer. After all, the identity of the offeree is as much a condition of a bargaining offer as any other term contained therein. Thus, except in special circumstances, only the person to whom the offer is made or that person's agent can accept the offer and create a binding contract. For example, Lottie makes an offer to Paul. Paul is not interested, but Paul's friend José accepts the offer. No contract is formed.

Unequivocal Acceptance To exercise the power of acceptance effectively, the offeree must accept unequivocally. This is the *mirror image rule* previously discussed. If the acceptance is subject to new conditions or if the terms of the acceptance materially change the original offer, the acceptance may be deemed a counteroffer that implicitly rejects the original offer.

DON'T FORGET When an offer is rejected, it is terminated.

Certain terms, when added to an acceptance, will not qualify the acceptance sufficiently to constitute rejection of the offer. • **EXAMPLE 9.17** Suppose that in response to a person offering to sell a painting by a well-known artist, the offeree replies, "I accept; please send a written contract." The offeree is requesting a written contract but is not making it a condition for acceptance. Therefore, the acceptance is effective without the written contract. If the offeree replies, "I accept *if* you send a written con-

12. *Restatement (Second) of Contracts,* Section 48. If the offer is irrevocable, it is not terminated when the offeror dies. Also, if the offer is such that it can be accepted by the performance of a series of acts, and those acts began before the offeror died, the offeree's power of acceptance is not terminated.

"It's a deal, but just to be on the safe side let's have our lawyers look at this handshake.

tract," however, the acceptance is expressly conditioned on the request for a writing, and the statement is not an acceptance but a counteroffer. (Notice how important each word is!)[13] ●

Silence as Acceptance Ordinarily, silence cannot constitute acceptance, even if the offeror states, "By your silence and inaction, you will be deemed to have accepted this offer." This general rule applies because an offeree should not be put under a burden of liability to act affirmatively in order to reject an offer. No consideration—that is, nothing of value—has passed to the offeree to impose such a liability.

In some instances, however, the offeree does have a duty to speak, in which case his or her silence or inaction will operate as an acceptance. Silence may be an acceptance when an offeree takes the benefit of offered services even though he or she had an opportunity to reject them and knew that they were offered with the expectation of compensation. ● **EXAMPLE 9.18** Suppose that John, a college student who earns extra income by washing store windows, taps on the window of a store and catches the attention of the store's manager. John points to the window and raises his cleaner, signaling that he will be washing the window. The manager does nothing to stop him. Here, the store manager's silence constitutes an acceptance, and an implied-in-fact contract is created. The store is bound to pay a reasonable value for John's work. ●

Silence can also operate as acceptance when the offeree has had prior dealings with the offeror. If a merchant, for example, routinely receives shipments from a supplier

13. As noted in footnote 10, in regard to sales contracts, the UCC provides that an acceptance may still be effective even if some terms are added. The new terms are simply treated as proposals for additions to the contract, unless both parties are merchants—in which case the additional terms (with some exceptions) become part of the contract [UCC 2–207(2)].

and in the past has always notified the supplier of rejection of defective goods, then silence constitutes acceptance. Also, if a person solicits an offer specifying that certain terms and conditions are acceptable, and the offeror makes the offer in response to the solicitation, the offeree has a duty to reject—that is, a duty to tell the offeror that the offer is not acceptable. Failure to reject (silence) would operate as an acceptance.

REMEMBER A bilateral contract is a promise for a promise, and a unilateral contract is performance for a promise.

Communication of Acceptance Whether the offeror must be notified of the acceptance depends on the nature of the contract. In a bilateral contract, communication of acceptance is necessary, because acceptance is in the form of a promise (not performance), and the contract is formed when the promise is made (rather than when the act is performed). Communication of acceptance is not necessary, however, if the offer dispenses with the requirement. Also, if the offer can be accepted by silence, no communication is necessary.[14]

In a unilateral contract, the full performance of some act is called for; therefore, acceptance is usually evident, and notification is unnecessary. Exceptions do exist, however. When the offeror requests notice of acceptance or has no adequate means of determining whether the requested act has been performed, or when the law requires such notice of acceptance, then notice is necessary.[15]

MAILBOX RULE
A rule providing that an acceptance of an offer becomes effective on dispatch (on being placed in an official mailbox), if mail is, expressly or impliedly, an authorized means of communication of acceptance to the offeror.

Mode and Timeliness of Acceptance The general rule is that acceptance in a bilateral contract is timely if it is effected within the duration of the offer. Problems arise, however, when the parties involved are not dealing face to face. In such situations, the offeree may use an authorized mode of communication.

The Mailbox Rule. Acceptance takes effect, thus completing formation of the contract, at the time the offeree sends or delivers the communication via the mode expressly or impliedly authorized by the offeror. This is the so-called **mailbox rule**, also called the "deposited acceptance rule," which the majority of courts uphold. Under this rule, if the authorized mode of communication is the mail, then an acceptance becomes valid when it is dispatched (placed in the control of the U.S. Postal Service)—*not* when it is received by the offeror.

If an offeror expressly authorizes acceptance of his or her offer by first-class mail or express delivery, can the offeree accept by a faster means, such as by fax or e-mail?

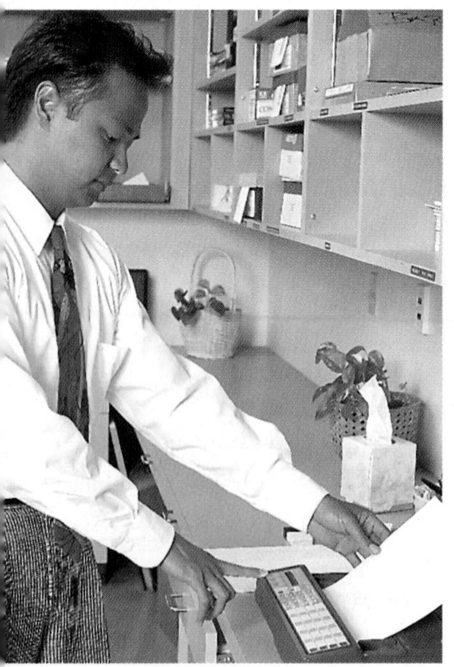

The mailbox rule was formed to prevent the confusion that arises when an offeror sends a letter of revocation but, before it arrives, the offeree sends a letter of acceptance. Thus, whereas a revocation becomes effective only when it is *received* by the offeree, an acceptance becomes effective on *dispatch* (even if it is never received), provided that an *authorized* means of communication is used.

Authorized Means of Communication. Authorized means of communicating an acceptance can be either expressly authorized—that is, expressly stipulated in the offer—or impliedly authorized by facts or law.[16] An acceptance sent by means not expressly or impliedly authorized is normally not effective until it is received by the offeror.

14. Under the UCC, an order or other offer to buy goods that are to be promptly shipped may be treated as either a bilateral or a unilateral offer and can be accepted by a promise to ship or by actual shipment. See UCC 2–206(1)(b).

15. UCC 2–206(2).

16. *Restatement (Second) of Contracts,* Section 30, provides that an offer invites acceptance "by any medium reasonable in the circumstances," unless the offer is specific about the means of acceptance. Under Section 65, a medium is reasonable if it is one used by the offeror or one customary in similar transactions, unless the offeree knows of circumstances that would argue against the reasonableness of a particular medium (the need for speed because of rapid price changes, for example).

When an offeror specifies how acceptance should be made (for example, by first-class mail or express delivery), *express authorization* is said to exist. Moreover, both the offeror and the offeree are bound in contract the moment that such means of acceptance are employed. Most offerors do not expressly specify the means by which the offeree is to accept. Thus, the common law recognizes the following implied authorized means of acceptance:[17]

① The choice of a particular means by the offeror in making the offer implies that the offeree is authorized to use the same or a faster means for acceptance.

② When two parties are at a distance, mailing is impliedly authorized.

At issue in the following case was whether a notice of intent to renew a lease contract was sent by authorized means.

17. Note that UCC 2–206(1)(a) states specifically that an acceptance of an offer for the sale of goods can be made by any medium that is *reasonable* under the circumstances.

CASE 9.2 Osprey L.L.C. v. Kelly-Moore Paint Co.

Supreme Court of Oklahoma, 1999.
984 P.2d 194.
http://www.oscn.net[a]

FACTS Kelly-Moore Paint Company leased a store in Edmond, Oklahoma, from Osprey L.L.C. The parties signed a fifteen-year lease with two five-year renewal options. The lease required Kelly-Moore to give Osprey written notice of the lessee's intent to renew at least six months before the lease expired. The notice "may be delivered either personally or by depositing the same in United States mail, first class postage prepaid, registered or certified mail, return receipt requested." Six months before the end of the fifteen-year term, Kelly-Moore sent the required notice by certified mail. Five years later, however, at the end of the first five-year term, on the last day of the six-month notification deadline, at 5:28 P.M., Kelly-Moore sent the notice by fax. Phone company records indicated that the fax was transmitted correctly, but Osprey denied receiving it. Osprey filed a suit in an Oklahoma state court to evict Kelly-Moore. Osprey argued that the lease specifically prescribed delivery of the notice personally or by mail. Kelly-Moore countered that the lease's use of the word "may" permitted other means of delivery. The court granted a judgment in favor of Kelly-Moore, and Osprey appealed. The state intermediate appellate court reversed this judgment, and Kelly-Moore appealed to the Oklahoma Supreme Court.

ISSUE Was Kelly-Moore's notice by fax defective?

DECISION No. The Oklahoma Supreme Court vacated the decision of the state intermediate appellate court. The state supreme court held that the use of an alternative method to exercise a lease option does not render the notice defective if the alternative method accomplishes the same objective as the authorized method.

REASON The court pointed out that "[t]he provision for delivery * * * uses the permissive 'may' and it does not bar other modes of transmission which are just as effective." The court also explained that "[t]he purpose of providing notice by personal delivery or registered mail is to insure the delivery of the notice, and to settle any dispute which might arise between the parties concerning whether the notice was received. A substituted method of notice which performs the same function and serves the same purpose as an authorized method of notice is not defective." In this case, "[t]he fax provided immediate written communication similar to personal delivery and, like a telegram, would be timely if it were properly transmitted before the expiration of the deadline to renew."

FOR CRITICAL ANALYSIS—Social Consideration *How would you have drafted the lease term regarding renewal notice in order to prevent this lawsuit (and the costs associated with it for both parties)?*

a. This is the Oklahoma Supreme Court Network Web site, which is part of the Oklahoma Supreme Court Information System. In the box near the top of this page, type "1999 OK 50" and, in the pull-down menu beneath it, select "Retrieve Document." Click "Go" to access the opinion.

Exceptions. There are three basic exceptions to the rule that a contract is formed when acceptance is sent by authorized means:

① If the acceptance is not properly dispatched (if a letter is incorrectly addressed, for example, or is without the proper postage), in most states it will not be effective until it is received by the offeror.

② The offeror can specifically condition her or his offer on the receipt of an acceptance by a certain time; in this case, to be effective, the acceptance must be received prior to the end of the specified time period.

③ Sometimes an offeree sends a rejection first, then later changes his or her mind and sends an acceptance. Obviously, this chain of events could cause confusion and even detriment to the offeror, depending on whether the rejection or the acceptance arrived first. In such situations, the law cancels the rule of acceptance on dispatch, and the first communication received by the offeror determines whether a contract is formed. If the rejection arrives first, there is no contract.[18]

Technology and Acceptances Technology, and particularly the Internet, has all but eliminated the need for the mailbox rule because online acceptances typically are communicated instantaneously to the offeror. As you will learn in Chapter 17, while online offers are not significantly different from traditional offers contained in paper documents, online acceptances have posed some unusual problems. (For an example of one such problem, see this chapter's *Business Law in the Online World* feature.)

Consideration and Its Requirements

In every legal system, some promises will be enforced, and some promises will not be enforced. The simple fact that a party has made a promise, then, does not mean the promise is enforceable. Under the common law, a primary basis for the enforcement of promises is consideration. **Consideration** is usually defined as the value given in return for a promise. We look here at the basic elements of consideration and then at some other contract doctrines relating to consideration.

CONSIDERATION
Generally, the value given in return for a promise. The consideration must result in a detriment to the promisee (something of legally sufficient value and bargained for) or a benefit to the promisor.

Elements of Consideration

Often, consideration is broken down into two parts: (1) something of *legally sufficient value* must be given in exchange for the promise, and (2) there must be a *bargained-for exchange*.

Legal Value The "something of legally sufficient value" may consist of (1) a promise to do something that one has no prior legal duty to do (to pay money on receipt of certain goods, for example), (2) the performance of an action that one is otherwise not obligated to undertake (such as providing accounting services), or (3) the refraining from an action that one has a legal right to undertake. Generally, to be legally sufficient, consideration must be either *detrimental to the promisee* (the one receiving the promise) or *beneficial to the promisor* (the one making the promise).

● **Example 9.19** Jerry says to his son, "When you finish painting the garage, I will pay you $100." Jerry's son paints the garage. The act of painting the garage is the con-

18. *Restatement (Second) of Contracts,* Section 40.

BUSINESS LAW: //in the Online World

Click-On Acceptances Must Be Reasonable

Online offers normally invite offerees to indicate their acceptance of the terms of the offer by clicking on an "I agree" or "I accept" box on the computer screen. For example, suppose that you wish to download software from a Web site. Typically, you will be presented with a "Terms of Service" agreement, or offer, by the licensor (the party licensing, or permitting, you to use the software under certain conditions) and asked to indicate your assent by clicking on an "I agree" box or icon (or something similar). Suppose, however, that you are not presented with any such agreement until *after* you have downloaded the software. Further suppose that the software damages your computer system and files. If you click "I agree" after having downloaded the software, are you bound by the terms of the contract (license)?

Is There a Contract?

Whether a contract had been formed in such a situation was essentially the question at issue in a case brought by Mark Williams and other Massachusetts residents against America Online, Inc. (AOL). Williams and the other plaintiffs sought damages for the harms caused to their computer systems after they downloaded AOL's Version 5.0 software. The plaintiffs claimed that the installation of the software caused unauthorized changes to the configuration of their computers. Because of these changes, they could no longer access other Internet service providers, run e-mail programs other than AOL's program, or access personal information and files.

When Williams and the others sued AOL in a Massachusetts state court, AOL moved for dismissal. AOL argued that the contract to which the plaintiffs had agreed contained a forum-selection clause[a] specifying that any disputes under the contract would have to be brought in Virginia courts. Therefore, contended AOL, the plaintiffs could not bring their suit against AOL in a Massachusetts court.

The court, however, concluded that the damage complained of occurred before the plaintiffs were given the opportunity to accept or reject the agreement's terms. The plaintiffs' injuries were thus precontractual in nature, and they could obtain redress for their injuries in a Massachusetts court. In other words, they were not bound by the contract's forum-selection clause.

An Unreasonable Process

The court also took issue with the way AOL invited acceptance of its terms. Once the installation was complete, the user had the option of choosing between "I agree" or "Read now," with the default being set to "I agree." If a user chose to "Read now," a second choice between the default "I agree" and "Read now" was presented. In other words, to read the text of the agreement, the user had to overcome two defaults. Even then, if a user declined to accept the agreement, it was too late to reverse the harm already caused to his or her computer system. The court refused to accept this process as reasonable.[b]

FOR CRITICAL ANALYSIS

Do you agree with the court that AOL's method of acceptance was unreasonable? Why or why not?

a. As noted in Chapter 8, a forum-selection clause specifies the forum (court or jurisdiction) in which any contract dispute will be resolved. Forum-selection clauses are commonly included in contracts, particularly when the parties are at a distance from one another.

b. *Williams v. America Online, Inc.*, 2001 WL 135825 (Mass.Super. 2001).

sideration that creates Jerry's contractual obligation to pay his son $100. In this situation, the consideration is both detrimental to the promisee (the son) and beneficial to the promisor (Jerry). Jerry's garage was painted, and his son undertook an action that he was not otherwise legally obligated to undertake. •

What if, in return for a promise to pay, a person forbears to pursue harmful habits, such as the use of tobacco and alcohol? Does such forbearance represent a legal detriment to the promisee and thus create consideration for the contract, or does it in fact benefit the promisee and thus not create consideration for the contract? This was the issue before the court in *Hamer v. Sidway*, a classic case concerning consideration that we present as this chapter's *Landmark in the Law* feature on the next page.

LANDMARK IN THE LAW
Hamer v. Sidway (1891)

In *Hamer v. Sidway,*[a] the issue before the court arose from a contract created in 1869 between William Story, Sr., and his nephew, William Story II. The uncle promised his nephew that if the nephew refrained from drinking alcohol, using tobacco, and playing billiards and cards for money until he reached the age of twenty-one, the uncle would pay him $5,000. The nephew, who indulged occasionally in all of these "vices," agreed to refrain from them and did so for the next six years. Following his twenty-first birthday in 1875, the nephew wrote to his uncle that he had performed his part of the bargain and was thus entitled to the promised $5,000. A few days later, the uncle wrote the nephew a letter stating, "[Y]ou shall have the five thousand dollars, as I promised you." The uncle said that the money was in the bank and that the nephew could "consider this money on interest."

The Issue of Consideration The nephew left the money in the care of his uncle, who held it for the next twelve years. When the uncle died in 1887, however, the executor of the uncle's estate refused to pay the $5,000 claim brought by Hamer, a third party to whom the promise had been *assigned.* (The law allows parties to assign, or transfer, rights in contracts to third parties; see Chapter 12.) The executor, Sidway, contended that the contract was invalid because there was insufficient consideration to support it. He argued that neither a benefit to the promisor (the uncle) nor a detriment to the promisee (the nephew) existed in this case. The uncle had received nothing, and the nephew had actually benefited by fulfilling the uncle's wishes. Therefore, no contract existed.

The Court's Conclusion Although a lower court upheld Sidway's position, the New York Court of Appeals reversed and ruled in favor of the plaintiff, Hamer. "The promisee used tobacco, occasionally drank liquor, and he had a legal right to do so," the court stated. "That right he abandoned for a period of years upon the strength of the promise of the testator [one who makes a will] that for such forbearance he would give him $5,000. We need not speculate on the effort which may have been required to give up the use of those stimulants. It is sufficient that he restricted his lawful freedom of action within certain prescribed limits upon the faith of his uncle's agreement."

APPLICATION TO TODAY'S WORLD

Although this case was decided over a century ago, the principles enunciated in the case remain applicable to contracts formed today, including online contracts. For a contract to be valid and binding, consideration must be given, and that consideration must be either beneficial to the promisor or detrimental to the promisee.

a. 124 N.Y. 538, 27 N.E. 256 (1891).

Bargained-for Exchange The second element of consideration is that it must provide the basis for the bargain struck between the contracting parties. The promise given by the promisor must induce the promisee to incur a legal detriment either now or in the future, and the detriment incurred must induce the promisor to make the promise. This element of bargained-for exchange distinguishes contracts from gifts.

FOR CRITICAL ANALYSIS
Do you think that promises to make gifts should be enforceable in the United States? Why or why not?

INTERNATIONAL PERSPECTIVE

Consideration in Germany

Many of the principles of contract law are common around the globe. There are some differences, however, including differences in what constitutes consideration for contractual purposes. In the United States, as just discussed, consideration is a required element for a valid contract. Something of legally sufficient value must be given in exchange for a promise, and there must be a bargained-for exchange. Promises to make gifts normally are not enforceable because the donee does not give consideration for the gift. In Germany, in contrast, the exchange of consideration is not required for a contract to be legally binding.

"Man is an animal that makes bargains; no other animal does this—one dog does not change a bone with another."

ADAM SMITH,
1723–1790
(Scottish political economist and philosopher)

• **EXAMPLE 9.20** Suppose that Jerry says to his son, "In consideration of the fact that you are not as wealthy as your brothers, I will pay you $500." This promise is not enforceable because Jerry's son has not given any return consideration for the $500 promised.[19] The son (the promisee) incurs no legal detriment; he does not have to promise anything or undertake (or refrain from undertaking) any action to receive the $500. Here, Jerry has simply stated his motive for giving his son a gift. The fact that the word *consideration* is used does not, by itself, mean that consideration has been given.•

LEGAL SUFFICIENCY AND ADEQUACY OF CONSIDERATION

ON THE WEB The Web site of the New Hampshire Consumer's Sourcebook provides information on contract law from a consumer's perspective. You can access this site at **http://www.state.nh.us/nhdoj/Consumer/cpb.html.**

Legal sufficiency of consideration involves the requirement that consideration be something of value in the eyes of the law. Adequacy of consideration involves "how much" consideration is given. Essentially, adequacy of consideration concerns the fairness of the bargain. On the surface, fairness would appear to be an issue when the items exchanged are of unequal value. In general, however, courts do not question the adequacy of consideration if the consideration is legally sufficient. Under the doctrine of freedom of contract, parties are usually free to bargain as they wish. If people could sue merely because they had entered into an unwise contract, the courts would be overloaded with frivolous suits.

In extreme cases, however, a court of law may look to the amount or value (the adequacy) of the consideration because apparently inadequate consideration can indicate that fraud, duress, or undue influence was involved or that a gift was made (if a father "sells" a $100,000 house to his daughter for only $1, for example). Additionally, in cases in which the consideration is grossly inadequate, the courts may declare the contract unenforceable on the ground that it is unconscionable[20]—that is, generally speaking, it is so one-sided under the circumstances as to be clearly unfair. (Unconscionability will be discussed further in Chapter 10.)

BE AWARE A consumer's signature on a contract does not always guarantee that the contract will be enforced. Ultimately, the terms must be fair.

At issue in the following case was whether an agreement between company executives was void for lack of consideration.

19. See *Fink v. Cox,* 18 Johns. 145, 9 Am.Dec. 191 (N.Y. 1820).
20. Pronounced un-*kon*-shun-uh-bul.

CASE 9.3 Powell v. MVE Holdings, Inc.

Minnesota Court of Appeals, 2001.
626 N.W.2d 451.
http://www.lawlibrary.state.mn.us/archive[a]

FACTS CAIRE, Inc., in Burnsville, Minnesota, is a subsidiary of MVE Holdings, Inc., and manufactures home health-care products. R. Edwin Powell worked for CAIRE for thirteen years before becoming its chief executive officer (CEO) and president. In 1996, a group of investors became the primary owners of MVE by buying a majority of its stock for $125.456 per share. In January 1997, David O'Halloran, MVE's CEO and president, met with Powell. O'Halloran asked Powell to resign as CAIRE's CEO and president, but to continue to attend trade-association board meetings and lobby Congress on MVE's behalf. O'Halloran also asked Powell to tell CAIRE's key customers and industry contacts that his resignation was voluntary. Powell later claimed that, in return, O'Halloran offered that MVE would pay Powell $125.456 per share for his MVE stock. Powell did as O'Halloran asked until April, when O'Halloran asked him to stop. When MVE refused to pay Powell $125.456 per share for his stock, he filed a suit in a Minnesota state court against MVE, alleging breach of contract. The court ruled in Powell's favor. MVE appealed to a state intermediate appellate court, arguing in part that any alleged agreement between O'Halloran and Powell was void for lack of consideration.

a. In the "Court of Appeals Opinions" box, click on "Index by Case Name (First Party)." When the page opens, in the "Published" section, click on "P–R." On that page, scroll to the case name and click on the docket number to access the opinion. The Minnesota State Law Library in St. Paul, Minnesota, maintains this database.

ISSUE Was there consideration for an agreement between O'Halloran and Powell?

DECISION Yes. The state intermediate appellate court affirmed the decision of the lower court, upholding the award to Powell of nearly $3.5 million for his MVE stock.

REASON The state intermediate appellate court acknowledged that "[w]hen a contract is not supported by consideration, no valid contract is formed." Consideration is "something of value given in return for a performance or promise of performance," and "requires that a contractual promise be the product of a bargain." The court emphasized that Powell performed lobbying efforts and "other tasks" on MVE's behalf at O'Halloran's request. MVE argued that many of these tasks "were of no value." The court pointed out, however, that it "will not examine the adequacy of consideration so long as something of value has passed between the parties. Although the consideration that Powell furnished may not have been as significant as the benefits that [MVE] promised to confer, Powell provided adequate consideration, and the agreement between Powell and [MVE] is not void for lack of consideration."

FOR CRITICAL ANALYSIS—Economic Consideration *Why might a corporation refuse to honor an agreement entered into by its president?*

CONTRACTS THAT LACK CONSIDERATION

Sometimes, one of the parties (or both parties) to a contract may think that they have exchanged consideration when in fact they have not. Here we look at some situations in which the parties' promises or actions do not qualify as contractual consideration.

Preexisting Duty Under most circumstances, a promise to do what one already has a legal duty to do does not constitute legally sufficient consideration because no legal detriment is incurred.[21] The preexisting legal duty may be imposed by law or may arise out of a previous contract. A sheriff, for example, cannot collect a reward for information leading to the capture of a criminal if the sheriff already has a legal duty to capture the criminal. Likewise, if a party is already bound by contract to perform a certain duty, that duty cannot serve as consideration for a second contract.

21. See *Foakes v. Beer,* 9 App.Cas. 605 (1884).

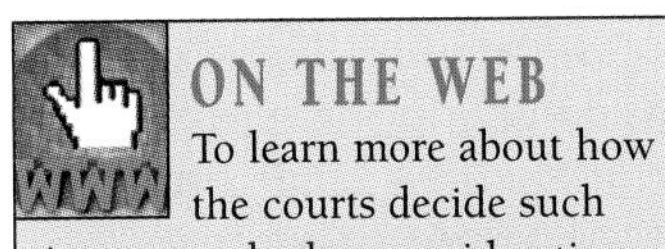

To learn more about how the courts decide such issues as whether consideration was lacking for a particular contract, look at relevant case law, which can be accessed through Cornell University's School of Law site at

http://www.law.cornell.edu/topics/contracts.html.

• **EXAMPLE 9.21** Suppose that Bauman-Bache, Inc., begins construction on a seven-story office building and after three months demands an extra $75,000 on its contract. If the extra $75,000 is not paid, it will stop working. The owner of the land, having no one else to complete construction, agrees to pay the extra $75,000. The agreement is not enforceable because it is not supported by legally sufficient consideration; Bauman-Bache had a preexisting contractual duty to complete the building.•

Unforeseen Difficulties. The rule regarding preexisting duty is meant to prevent extortion and the so-called holdup game. What happens, though, when an honest contractor, who has contracted with a landowner to build a house, runs into extraordinary difficulties that were totally unforeseen at the time the contract was formed? In the interests of fairness and equity, the courts sometimes allow exceptions to the preexisting duty rule. In the example just mentioned, if the landowner agrees to pay extra compensation to the contractor for overcoming the unforeseen difficulties (such as having to use dynamite and special equipment to remove an unexpected rock formation to excavate for a basement), the court may refrain from applying the preexisting duty rule and enforce the agreement. When the "unforeseen difficulties" that give rise to a contract modification are the types of risks ordinarily assumed in business, however, the courts will usually assert the preexisting duty rule.[22]

Rescission and New Contract. The law recognizes that two parties can mutually agree to rescind their contract, at least to the extent that it is executory (still to be carried out). **Rescission**[23] is defined as the unmaking of a contract so as to return the parties to the positions they occupied before the contract was made. When rescission and the making of a new contract take place at the same time, the courts frequently are given a choice of applying the preexisting duty rule or allowing rescission and letting the new contract stand.

RESCISSION
A remedy whereby a contract is canceled and the parties are returned to the positions they occupied before the contract was made; may be effected through the mutual consent of the parties, by their conduct, or by court decree.

Past Consideration Promises made in return for actions or events that have already taken place are unenforceable. These promises lack consideration in that the element of bargained-for exchange is missing. In short, you can bargain for something to take place now or in the future but not for something that has already taken place. Therefore, **past consideration** is no consideration.

PAST CONSIDERATION
An act done before the contract is made, which ordinarily, by itself, cannot be consideration for a later promise to pay for the act.

• **EXAMPLE 9.22** Suppose that Elsie, a real estate agent, does her friend Judy a favor by selling Judy's house and not charging any commission. Later, Judy says to Elsie, "In return for your generous act, I will pay you $3,000." This promise is made in return for past consideration and is thus unenforceable; in effect, Judy is stating her intention to give Elsie a gift.•

Illusory Promises If the terms of the contract express such uncertainty of performance that the promisor has not definitely promised to do anything, the promise is said to be *illusory*—without consideration and unenforceable. • **EXAMPLE 9.23** The president of Tuscan Corporation says to his employees, "All of you have worked hard, and if profits continue to remain high, a 10 percent bonus at the end of the year will be given—if management thinks it is warranted." This is an *illusory promise,* or no promise at all, because performance depends solely on the discretion of the

22. Note that under the UCC, any agreement modifying a contract within Article 2 on Sales needs no consideration to be binding. See UCC 2–209(1).
23. Pronounced reh-*sih*-zhen.

president (the management). There is no bargained-for consideration. The statement declares merely that management may or may not do something in the future.●

Option-to-cancel clauses in contracts for specified time periods sometimes present problems in regard to consideration. ● **EXAMPLE 9.24** Abe contracts to hire Chris for one year at $5,000 per month, reserving the right to cancel the contract at any time. On close examination of these words, you can see that Abe has not actually agreed to hire Chris, as Abe could cancel without liability before Chris started performance. Abe has not given up the opportunity of hiring someone else. This contract is therefore illusory. Now suppose that Abe contracts to hire Chris for a one-year period at $5,000 per month, reserving the right to cancel the contract at any time after Chris has begun performance by giving Chris thirty days' notice. Abe, by saying that he will give Chris thirty days' notice, is relinquishing the opportunity (legal right) to hire someone else instead of Chris for a thirty-day period. If Chris works for one month, at the end of which Abe gives him thirty days' notice, Chris has a valid and enforceable contractual claim for $10,000 in salary.●

SETTLEMENT OF CLAIMS

REMEMBER Businesspersons should consider settling potential legal disputes to save both their own time and resources and those of the courts.

Businesspersons or others can settle legal claims in several ways. It is important to understand the nature of consideration given in these kinds of settlement agreements, or contracts. A common means of settling a claim is through an *accord and satisfaction,* in which a debtor offers to pay a lesser amount than the creditor purports to be owed. Two other methods that are commonly used to settle claims are the *release* and the *covenant not to sue.*

ACCORD AND SATISFACTION
A common means of settling a disputed claim, in which a debtor offers to pay a lesser amount than the creditor purports to be owed. The creditor's acceptance of the offer creates an accord (agreement), and when the accord is executed, satisfaction occurs.

Accord and Satisfaction In an **accord and satisfaction**, a debtor offers to pay, and a creditor accepts, a lesser amount than the creditor originally purported to be owed. Thus, in an accord and satisfaction, the obligor attempts to extinguish an obligation. The *accord* is the agreement under which one of the parties undertakes to give or perform, and the other to accept, in satisfaction of a claim, something other than that on which the parties originally agreed. *Satisfaction* may take place when the accord is executed. A basic rule is that there can be no satisfaction unless there is first an accord.

For accord and satisfaction to occur, the amount of the debt *must be in dispute.* If a debt is *liquidated,* accord and satisfaction cannot take place. A liquidated debt is one whose amount has been ascertained, fixed, agreed on, settled, or exactly determined. An example of a liquidated debt would be a loan contract in which the borrower agrees to pay a stipulated amount every month until the amount of the loan is paid. In the majority of states, acceptance of (an accord for) a lesser sum than the entire amount of a liquidated debt is not satisfaction, and the balance of the debt is still legally owed. The rationale for this rule is that the debtor has given no consideration to satisfy the obligation of paying the balance to the creditor—because the debtor has a preexisting legal obligation to pay the entire debt.

ON THE WEB You can find a copy of a release form and the information that should be included in a release by going to **http://www.nolo.com/category/cm_home.html** and clicking on "Release from Legal Claims" in the right-hand column of the page.

An *unliquidated debt* is the opposite of a liquidated debt. Here, reasonable persons may differ over the amount owed. It is not settled, fixed, agreed on, ascertained, or determined. In these circumstances, acceptance of payment of the lesser sum operates as a satisfaction, or discharge, of the debt. One argument to support this rule is that the parties give up a legal right to contest the amount in dispute, and thus consideration is given.

RELEASE
A contract in which one party forfeits the right to pursue a legal claim against the other party.

Release A **release** is a contract in which one party forfeits the right to pursue a legal claim against the other party. Releases will generally be binding if they are (1) given in good faith, (2) stated in a signed writing (required by many states), and (3) accompanied by consideration.[24] Clearly, persons are better off if they know the extent of their injuries or damages before signing releases.

● **EXAMPLE 9.25** Suppose that you are involved in an automobile accident caused by Raoul's negligence. Raoul offers to give you $1,000 if you will release him from further liability resulting from the accident. You believe that this amount will cover your damages, so you agree to and sign the release. Later you discover that it will cost $1,200 to repair your car. Can you collect the balance from Raoul? The answer is normally no; you are limited to the $1,000 in the release. Why? The reason is that a valid contract existed. You and Raoul both assented to the bargain (hence, agreement existed), and sufficient consideration was present. Your consideration for the contract was the legal detriment you suffered (by releasing Raoul from liability, you forfeited your right to sue to recover damages, should they be more than $1,000). This legal detriment was induced by Raoul's promise to give you the $1,000. Raoul's promise was, in turn, induced by your promise not to pursue your legal right to sue him for damages. ●

COVENANT NOT TO SUE
An agreement to substitute a contractual obligation for some other type of legal action based on a valid claim.

Covenant Not to Sue A **covenant not to sue**, unlike a release, does not always bar further recovery. The parties simply substitute a contractual obligation for some other type of legal action based on a valid claim. Suppose (following the earlier example) that you agree with Raoul not to sue for damages in a tort action if he will pay for the damage to your car. If Raoul fails to pay, you can bring an action for breach of contract.

PROMISES ENFORCEABLE WITHOUT CONSIDERATION—PROMISSORY ESTOPPEL

PROMISSORY ESTOPPEL
A doctrine that applies when a promisor makes a clear and definite promise on which the promisee justifiably relies; such a promise is binding if justice will be better served by the enforcement of the promise.

ESTOPPED
Barred, impeded, or precluded.

Sometimes, individuals rely on promises, and such reliance may form a basis for contract rights and duties. Under the doctrine of **promissory estoppel** (also called *detrimental reliance*), a person who has reasonably relied on the promise of another can often hope to obtain some measure of recovery. When the doctrine of promissory estoppel is applied, the promisor (the offeror) is **estopped** (barred, or impeded) from revoking the promise. For the doctrine of promissory estoppel to be applied, the following elements are required:

① There must be a clear and definite promise.

② The promisee must justifiably rely on the promise.

③ The reliance normally must be of a substantial and definite character.

④ Justice will be better served by the enforcement of the promise.

"To break an oral agreement which is not legally binding is morally wrong."

THE TALMUD, Bava Metzi'a

● **EXAMPLE 9.26** Your uncle tells you, "I'll pay you $150 a week so you won't have to work anymore." In reliance on your uncle's promise, you quit your job, but your uncle refuses to pay you. Under the doctrine of promissory estoppel, you may be able to enforce his promise.[25] Now your uncle makes a promise to give you $10,000 with which to buy a car. If you buy the car with your own funds and he does not pay you, you may once again be able to enforce the promise under this doctrine. ●

24. Under the UCC, a written, signed waiver or renunciation by an aggrieved party discharges any further liability for a breach, even without consideration [UCC 1–107].

25. *Ricketts v. Scothorn,* 57 Neb. 51, 77 N.W. 365 (1898).

ETHICAL ISSUE 9.2

Should the doctrine of promissory estoppel be applied to promises of employment?

A number of cases have come before the courts in which the story is strikingly similar: in reliance on an offer of employment, a person has left a job, sold her or his home, and moved to another location—only to learn that the offer has been revoked. In those jurisdictions that are governed by the common law doctrine of employment at will,[26] these persons often have little recourse. Courts in these jurisdictions often hold that even though an employer has made an offer of employment to a particular job candidate, under the at-will doctrine the employer need not hire that person.

Occasionally, however, a court will apply the doctrine of promissory estoppel in such circumstances. For example, in one case, Julie Goff-Hamel, who had worked for a family planning clinic for eleven years and who enjoyed an excellent benefits package, left her job in reliance on a job offer from a group of obstetricians and gynecologists. The day before she was to begin her new job, one of the obstetricians told her that they were hiring someone else for the position. Goff-Hamel sued the group for damages on the basis of detrimental reliance (promissory estoppel). Although the trial court granted summary judgment in favor of the group, concluding that the doctrine of promissory estoppel did not apply because the employment was at will, the appellate court reversed. The case was remanded to the trial court for a determination of the amount of damages that should be awarded to Goff-Hamel.[27]

26. *Employment at will* is an employment relationship that either party may terminate at any time for any reason—see Chapter 34 for a further discussion of this doctrine.

27. *Goff-Hamel v. Obstetricians & Gynecologists, P.C.,* 256 Neb. 19, 588 N.W.2d 798 (1999).

APPLICATION Law and the Offeror . . .

Controlling the Terms of the Offer*

The courts normally attempt to "save" contracts whenever possible, but sometimes it is simply impossible to do so. Two common reasons why contracts fail are that (1) the terms of the offer were too unclear or indefinite to constitute a binding contract on the offer's acceptance and (2) the acceptance was not timely. If you are an offeror, you can control both of these factors: you can determine what the terms of the future contract will be, as well as the time and mode of acceptance.

*This *Application* is not meant to substitute for the services of an attorney who is licensed to practice law in your state.

INCLUDE CLEAR AND DEFINITE TERMS

If a contract's terms are too unclear or indefinite, the contract will fail. Unless a court can ascertain exactly what the rights and duties of the parties are under a particular contract, the court cannot enforce those rights and duties. Therefore, as an offeror, make sure that the terms of your

APPLICATION Law and the Offeror . . .

Controlling the Terms of the Offer—continued

offer are sufficiently definite to constitute a binding contract if the offer is accepted. A statement such as "Quantity to be determined later" may allow the offeree, after acceptance, to claim that a contract was never formed because the quantity term was not specified.

Another reason why an offeror should make sure that the offer's terms are clear and definite is that if a contract results, any ambiguous provision may be interpreted against the party that drafted the contract (see Chapter 8).

SPECIFY THE TIME AND MODE OF ACCEPTANCE

Problems concerning contract formation also arise when it is unclear whether an acceptance is effective. To avoid such problems, you should take some precautions when phrasing the offer. Whether your offer is made via the Internet, fax, express delivery, or mail, you can specify that the offer must be accepted (or even that the acceptance must be received by you) by a certain time, and if it is not, the offer will terminate. Similarly, you can specify the mode of acceptance. In online offers, you can indicate that to accept the offer, the user must click on a certain box on the screen. If you make an offer and want the acceptance to be faxed to you, make sure that you clearly indicate that the acceptance must be faxed to you at a given fax number by a specific time or it will not be effective.

CHECKLIST FOR THE OFFEROR

1. Make sure that the terms of the offer are sufficiently clear and definite to allow both the parties and a court to determine the specific rights and obligations of the parties. Otherwise, the contract may fail for indefiniteness.
2. Specify in the offer the date on which the offer will terminate and the authorized mode of acceptance. For example, you can indicate that an acceptance, to be effective, must be faxed to you at a specific fax number by a specific time or date.

Key Terms

acceptance 246
accord and satisfaction 256
agreement 238
consideration 250
counteroffer 245
covenant not to sue 257
estopped 257
mailbox rule 248
mirror image rule 245
offer 238
option contract 244
past consideration 255
promissory estoppel 257
release 257
rescission 255
revocation 243

Chapter Summary Agreement and Consideration

AGREEMENT	
Requirements of the Offer (See pages 238–243.)	1. *Intent*—There must be a serious, objective intention by the offeror to become bound by the offer. Nonoffer situations include (a) expressions of opinion; (b) statements of intention; (c) preliminary negotiations; (d) generally, advertisements, catalogues, price lists, and circulars; (e) solicitations for bids made by an auctioneer; and (f) traditionally, agreements to agree in the future.

(continued)

Chapter Summary Agreement and Consideration—continued

Requirements of the Offer—continued	2. *Definiteness*—The terms of the offer must be sufficiently definite to be ascertainable by the parties or by a court. 3. *Communication*—The offer must be communicated to the offeree.
Termination of the Offer (See pages 243–246.)	1. *By action of the parties*— a. Revocation—Unless the offer is irrevocable, it can be revoked at any time before acceptance without liability. Revocation is not effective until received by the offeree or the offeree's agent. Some offers, such as the merchant's firm offer and option contracts, are irrevocable. b. Rejection—Accomplished by words or actions that demonstrate a clear intent not to accept the offer; not effective until received by the offeror or the offeror's agent. c. Counteroffer—A rejection of the original offer and the making of a new offer. 2. *By operation of law*— a. Lapse of time—The offer terminates (1) at the end of the time period specified in the offer or (2) if no time period is stated in the offer, at the end of a reasonable time period. b. Destruction of the specific subject matter of the offer—Automatically terminates the offer. c. Death or incompetence—Terminates the offer unless the offer is irrevocable. d. Illegality—Supervening illegality terminates the offer.
Acceptance (See pages 246–250.)	1. Can be made only by the offeree or the offeree's agent. 2. Must be unequivocal. Under the common law (mirror image rule), if new terms or conditions are added to the acceptance, it will be considered a counteroffer. 3. Acceptance of a unilateral offer is effective on full performance of the requested act. Generally, no communication is necessary. 4. Acceptance of a bilateral offer can be communicated by the offeree by any authorized mode of communication and is effective on dispatch. Unless the mode of communication is expressly specified by the offeror, the following methods are impliedly authorized: a. The same mode used by the offeror or a faster mode. b. Mail, when the two parties are at a distance. c. In sales contracts, by any reasonable medium.
	CONSIDERATION
Elements of Consideration (See pages 250–253.)	Consideration is broken down into two parts: (1) something of *legally sufficient value* must be given in exchange for the promise, and (2) there must be a *bargained-for exchange.* To be legally sufficient, consideration must involve a legal detriment to the promisee, a legal benefit to the promisor, or both. One incurs a legal detriment by doing (or refraining from doing) something that one had no prior legal duty to do (or to refrain from doing).
Adequacy of Consideration (See pages 253–254.)	Legal sufficiency of consideration relates to the first element of consideration just mentioned—something of legal value must be given in exchange for a promise. Adequacy of consideration relates to "how much" consideration is given and whether a fair bargain was reached. Courts will inquire into the adequacy of consideration (if the consideration is legally sufficient) only when fraud, undue influence, duress, or unconscionability may be involved.
Contracts That Lack Consideration (See pages 254–256.)	Consideration is lacking in the following situations: 1. *Preexisting duty*—Consideration is not legally sufficient if one is either by law or by contract under a *preexisting duty* to perform the action being offered as consideration for a new contract.

Chapter Summary Agreement and Consideration—continued

Contracts That Lack Consideration—continued	2. *Past consideration*—Actions or events that have already taken place do not constitute legally sufficient consideration. 3. *Illusory promises*—When the nature or extent of performance is too uncertain, the promise is rendered illusory (without consideration and unenforceable).
Settlement of Claims (See pages 256–257.)	1. *Accord and satisfaction*—An *accord* is an agreement in which a debtor offers to pay a lesser amount than the creditor purports to be owed. *Satisfaction* may take place when the accord is executed. 2. *Release*—An agreement by which, for consideration, a party is barred from further recovery beyond the terms specified in the release. 3. *Covenant not to sue*—An agreement not to sue on a present, valid claim.
Promises Enforceable without Consideration—Promissory Estoppel (See pages 257–258.)	The equitable doctrine of promissory estoppel applies when a promisor reasonably expects a promise to induce definite and substantial action or forbearance by the promisee, and the promisee does act in reliance on the promise. Such a promise is binding if injustice can be avoided only by enforcement of the promise. Also known as the doctrine of detrimental reliance.

For Review

① What elements are necessary for an effective offer? What are some examples of nonoffers?

② In what circumstances will an offer be irrevocable?

③ What are the elements that are necessary for an effective acceptance?

④ What is consideration? What is required for consideration to be legally sufficient?

⑤ In what circumstances might a promise be enforced despite a lack of consideration?

Questions and Case Problems

9–1. Offer. Chernek, the sole owner of a small business, has a large piece of used farm equipment for sale. He offers to sell the equipment to Bollow for $10,000. Discuss the legal effects of the following events on the offer:

(a) Chernek dies prior to Bollow's acceptance, and at the time she accepts, Bollow is unaware of Chernek's death.

(b) The night before Bollow accepts, a fire destroys the equipment.

(c) Bollow pays $100 for a thirty-day option to purchase the equipment. During this period Chernek dies, and Bollow accepts the offer, knowing of Chernek's death.

(d) Bollow pays $100 for a thirty-day option to purchase the equipment. During this period Bollow dies, and Bollow's estate accepts Chernek's offer within the stipulated time period.

9–2. Offers versus Nonoffers. On June 1, Jason placed an ad in a local newspaper, to be run on the following Sunday, June 5, offering a reward of $100 to anyone who found his wallet. When his wallet had not been returned by June 12, he purchased another wallet and took steps to obtain duplicates of his driver's license, credit cards, and other items that he had lost. On June 15, Sharith, who had seen Jason's ad in the paper, found Jason's wallet, returned it to Jason, and asked for the $100. Is Jason obligated to pay Sharith the $100? Why or why not?

9–3. Offer and Acceptance. Carrie offered to sell a set of legal encyclopedias to Antonio for $300. Antonio said that he would think about her offer and let her know his decision the next day. Norvel, who had overheard the conversation between Carrie and Antonio, said to Carrie, "I accept your offer" and gave her $300. Carrie gave Norvel the books. The next day, Antonio, who had no idea that Carrie had already sold the books to Norvel, told Carrie that he accepted her offer. Has Carrie breached a valid contract with Antonio? Explain.

9–4. Consideration. Ben hired Lewis to drive his racing car in a race. Tuan, a friend of Lewis, promised to pay Lewis $3,000 if he won the race. Lewis won the race, but Tuan refused to pay the $3,000. Tuan contended that no legally binding contract had been formed because he had received no consideration from Lewis for his promise to pay the $3,000. Lewis sued Tuan for breach of contract, arguing that winning the race was the consideration given in exchange for Tuan's promise to pay the $3,000. What rule of law discussed in this chapter supports Tuan's claim? Explain.

9–5. Acceptance. On Saturday, Arthur mailed Tanya an offer to sell his car to her for $2,000. On Monday, having changed his mind and not having heard from Tanya, Arthur sent her a letter revoking his offer. On Wednesday, before she had received Arthur's letter of revocation, Tanya mailed a letter of acceptance to Arthur. When Tanya demanded that Arthur sell his car to her as promised, Arthur claimed that no contract existed because he had revoked his offer prior to Tanya's acceptance. Is Arthur correct? Explain.

9–6. Accord and Satisfaction. John and Alan Padgett sold their business, Econotax, Inc., to Taxpro, Inc. The terms of the sale required Taxpro to take over the Padgetts' payments to Wanda Austin under a promissory note as part of the price. When Wanda Austin died, James Austin inherited the right to payment. A dispute arose over the exact amount owed. Taxpro sent Austin three checks and a new promissory note as a proposed settlement, asking Austin to sign and return the note to accept the settlement. Austin cashed the checks but did not return the note. Instead, he filed a suit against the Padgetts in a Mississippi state court. The Padgetts sued Taxpro. Did Austin's cashing the checks and keeping the note constitute an accord and satisfaction? Why or why not? [*Austin v. Padgett,* 678 So.2d 1002 (Miss. 1996)]

9–7. Intention. For an employee convention, Nationwide Mutual Insurance Co. created a committee, whose members included Mary Peterson, to select a theme. The committee announced a contest for theme suggestions: "Here's what you could win: His and Hers Mercedes. An all-expense-paid trip for two around the world. Additional prizes to be announced. (All prizes subject to availability.)" David Mears submitted the theme "At the Top and Still Climbing." At a dinner of Nationwide employees, Peterson told Mears that he had won two Mercedes. Mears and others who heard this believed that he had won the cars. Nationwide never gave him the cars, however, and he filed a suit in a federal district court, alleging breach of contract. At the trial, Peterson claimed that she spoke with a facetious tone and, in reality, had no intention of awarding the cars. Is Mears entitled to the cars? Why or why not? [*Mears v. Nationwide Mutual Insurance Co.,* 91 F.3d 1118 (8th Cir. 1996)]

9–8. Preexisting Duty. New England Rock Services, Inc., agreed to work as a subcontractor on a sewer project on which Empire Paving, Inc., was the general contractor. For drilling and blasting a certain amount of rock, Rock Services was to be paid $29 per cubic yard or on a time-and-materials basis, whichever was less. From the beginning, Rock Services experienced problems. The primary obstacle was a heavy concentration of water, which, according to the custom in the industry, Empire should have controlled but did not. Rock Services was compelled to use more costly and time-consuming methods than anticipated, and it was unable to complete the work on time. The subcontractor asked Empire to pay for the rest of the project on a time-and-materials basis. Empire signed a modification of the original agreement. On completion of the work, Empire refused to pay Rock Services the balance due under the modification. Rock Services filed a suit in a Connecticut state court against Empire. Empire claimed that the modification lacked consideration and was thus not valid and enforceable. Is Empire right? Why or why not? [*New England Rock Services, Inc. v. Empire Paving, Inc.,* 53 Conn.App. 771, 731 A.2d 784 (1999)]

TEST YOUR KNOWLEDGE—ANSWER ON THE WEB

9–9. In 1995, Helikon Furniture Co. appointed Gaede as its independent sales agent for the sale of its products in parts of Texas. The parties signed a one-year contract that specified, among other things, the commissions that Gaede would receive. Over a year later, although the parties had not signed a new contract, Gaede was still representing Helikon when it was acquired by a third party. Helikon's new management allowed Gaede to continue to perform for the same commissions and sent him a letter stating that it would make no changes in its sales representatives "for at least the next year." Three months later, in December 1997, the new managers sent Gaede a letter proposing new terms for a contract. Gaede continued to sell Helikon products until May 1997 when he received a letter effectively reducing the amount of his commissions. Gaede filed a suit in a Texas state court against Helikon, alleging breach of contract. Helikon argued in part that there was no contract because there was no consideration. In whose favor should the court rule, and why? [*Gaede v. SK Investments, Inc.,* 38 S.W.3d 753 (Tex.App.—Houston [14 Dist.] 2001)]

A QUESTION OF ETHICS AND SOCIAL RESPONSIBILITY

9–10. E. S. Herrick Co. grows and sells blueberries. Maine Wild Blueberry Co. agreed to buy all of Herrick's 1990 crop under a contract that left the price unliquidated. Herrick delivered the berries, but a dispute arose over the price. Maine Wild sent Herrick a check with a letter stating that the check was the "final settlement." Herrick cashed the check but filed a suit in a Maine state court against Maine Wild, on the ground of breach of contract, alleging that the buyer owed more. Given these facts, consider the following questions. [*E. S. Herrick Co. v. Maine Wild Blueberry Co.,* 670 A.2d 944 (Me. 1996)]

1. What will the court likely decide in this case? Why?
2. Generally, what are the ethical underpinnings of the legal concept of accord and satisfaction? Why does this concept apply to only unliquidated debts?

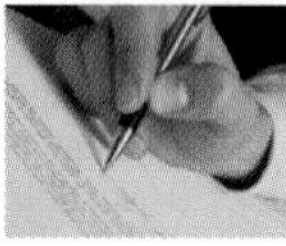

FOR CRITICAL ANALYSIS

9–11. Under what circumstances should courts examine the adequacy of consideration?

Internet Exercises

Go to the *Business Law Today* home page at **http://blt.westbuslaw.com**. Select "Interactive Study Center" and then click on "Chapter 9." There you will find the following Internet research exercise that you can perform to learn more about contract terms.

Activity 9–1: Contract Terms

Before the Test

Go to the *Business Law Today* home page at **http://blt.westbuslaw.com**. Click on "Interactive Quizzes." You will find at least twenty interactive questions relating to this chapter.

CHAPTER 10

Capacity and Legality

"Liberty of contract is not an absolute concept. It is relative to many conditions of time and place and circumstance."

Benjamin Cardozo, 1870–1938
(Associate justice of the United States Supreme Court, 1932–1938)

CHAPTER CONTENTS

LEARNING OBJECTIVES

After reading this chapter, you should be able to answer the following questions:

① What are some exceptions to the rule that a minor can disaffirm any contract?

② Under what circumstances does intoxication make a contract voidable?

③ Does mental incompetence necessarily render a contract void?

④ Under what circumstances will a covenant not to compete be enforceable? When will such covenants not be enforced?

⑤ What is an exculpatory clause? In what circumstances might exculpatory clauses be enforced? When will they not be enforced?

Courts generally want contracts to be enforceable, and much of the law is devoted to aiding the enforceability of contracts. Nonetheless, as indicated in the opening quotation, "liberty of contract" is not absolute. In other words, not all people can make legally binding contracts at all times. Contracts entered into by persons lacking the capacity to do so may be unenforceable. Similarly, contracts calling for the performance of an illegal act are illegal and thus void—they are not contracts at all.

In this chapter, we examine contractual capacity and some aspects of illegal bargains. As you read through the chapter, keep in mind that contractual capacity and legality are not inherently related other than that they are both contract requirements. We treat these topics in one chapter merely for convenience and reasons of space.

Contractual Capacity

CONTRACTUAL CAPACITY
The threshold mental capacity required by law for a party who enters into a contract to be bound by that contract.

Contractual capacity is the legal ability to enter into a contractual relationship. Courts generally presume the existence of contractual capacity, but in some situations, capacity is lacking or may be questionable. A person *adjudged by a court* to be mentally incompetent, for example, cannot form a legally binding contract with another party. In other situations, a party may have the capacity to enter into a valid contract but also have the right to avoid liability under it. For example, minors—or *infants,* as they are commonly referred to legally—usually are not legally bound by contracts. In this section, we look at the effect of youth, intoxication, and mental incompetence on contractual capacity.

MINORS

Today, in virtually all states, the *age of majority* (when a person is no longer a minor) for contractual purposes is eighteen years for both sexes. (The age of majority may still be twenty-one for other purposes, however, such as the purchase and consumption of alcohol.) In addition, some states provide for the termination of minority on marriage. Subject to certain exceptions, the contracts entered into by a minor are voidable at the option of that minor.

The general rule is that a minor can enter into any contract an adult can, provided that the contract is not one prohibited by law for minors (for example, the sale of alcoholic beverages or tobacco). Although minors have the right to avoid their contracts, there are exceptions (to be discussed shortly).

DISAFFIRMANCE
The legal avoidance, or setting aside, of a contractual obligation.

Disaffirmance To exercise the option to avoid a contract, a minor need only manifest an intention not to be bound by it. The minor "avoids" the contract by disaffirming it. **Disaffirmance** is the legal avoidance, or setting aside, of a contractual obligation. Words or conduct may serve to express this intent. The contract can ordinarily be disaffirmed at any time during minority or for a reasonable time after the minor comes of age. In some states, however, a minor who enters into a contract for the sale of land cannot disaffirm the contract until she or he reaches the age of majority. When a minor disaffirms a contract, all property that he or she has transferred to the adult as consideration can be recovered, even if it is then in the possession of a third party.[1]

Disaffirmance must be timely. If, for example, an individual wishes to disaffirm an executed contract made as a minor but fails to do so until two years after reaching the age of majority, a court will likely hold that the contract has been ratified (see the discussion of ratification below). Additionally, if a minor disaffirms a contract, the *entire* contract must be disaffirmed. The minor cannot decide to keep part of the goods contracted for and return the remainder.

Note that an adult who enters into a contract with a minor cannot avoid his or her contractual duties on the ground that the minor can do so. Unless the minor exercises the option to disaffirm the contract, the adult party normally is bound by it.

A Minor's Obligations on Disaffirmance. All state laws permit minors to disaffirm contracts (with certain exceptions—as mentioned), including executed contracts. States differ, however, on the extent of a minor's obligations on disaffirmance. Courts

1. The Uniform Commercial Code, in Section 2–403(1), allows an exception if the third party is a "good faith purchaser for value." See Chapter 15.

INTERNATIONAL PERSPECTIVE
Minors and Legal Capacity in Britain

As mentioned elsewhere, in the United States the age of majority, for contractual purposes, is eighteen years. Persons under the age of eighteen (minors) are allowed to avoid their contracts, with some exceptions, because they lack full contractual capacity.

Like courts in the United States, courts in Great Britain may also permit minors' contracts to be avoided on the ground that minors lack contractual capacity. Great Britain, however, has no single, fixed age limit for lack of capacity. British courts deal with contracts on a case-by-case basis. In deciding whether a minor can avoid a particular contract, a British court will consider a number of factors, including the specific circumstances of the case, the nature of the item contracted for, and the psychological maturity of the minor.

FOR CRITICAL ANALYSIS
What benefit is there to the U.S. system, which lacks flexibility with respect to the contractual capacity of minors?

in a majority of states hold that the minor need only return the goods (or other consideration) subject to the contract, provided the goods are in the minor's possession or control. • **EXAMPLE 10.1** Jim Garrison, a seventeen-year-old, purchases a computer from Radio Shack. While transporting the computer to his home, Garrison, through no fault of his own, is involved in a car accident. As a result of the accident, the plastic casing of the computer is broken. The next day, he returns the computer to Radio Shack and disaffirms the contract. Under the majority view, this return fulfills Garrison's duty even though the computer is now damaged. Garrison is entitled to receive a refund of the purchase price (if paid in cash) or to be relieved of any further obligations under an agreement to purchase the computer on credit.•

A growing number of states, either by statute or by court decision, place an additional duty on the minor—the duty to restore the adult party to the position he or she held before the contract was made. In the example just given, Garrison would be required not only to return the computer but also to pay Radio Shack for the damage to the computer.

In the following case, the Tennessee Supreme Court faced the issue of whether a minor should be held responsible for damage, ordinary wear and tear, and depreciation of goods used by the minor prior to his disaffirmance of the contract. The case illustrates the trend among today's courts in regard to this issue.

CASE 10.1 Dodson v. Shrader

Supreme Court of Tennessee, 1992.
824 S.W.2d 545.

FACTS When Joseph Dodson was sixteen years old, he bought a used pickup truck for $4,900 from Shrader's Auto, which was owned by Burns and Mary Shrader. Nine months later, the truck developed mechanical problems. A mechanic informed Dodson that the problem might be a burnt valve. Without having the truck repaired, Dodson continued to drive it. One month later, the truck's engine "blew up," and the truck was rendered inoperable. Dodson disaffirmed the contract and sought to return the truck to the Shraders and obtain a full refund of the purchase price. The Shraders refused to refund the purchase price and would not accept possession of the truck. Later, while parked in Dodson's front yard, the pickup was hit by an unknown driver. Dodson filed suit against the Shraders to compel a refund of the purchase price. Although the Shraders claimed that the truck's value

CASE 10.1—Continued

had been reduced to $500, the trial court granted rescission and ordered the Shraders to refund the full $4,900 purchase price to Dodson on Dodson's delivery of the truck to them. The Shraders appealed.

ISSUE Are the Shraders legally obligated to refund the full purchase price of the truck to Dodson?

DECISION No. The Supreme Court of Tennessee adopted a rule that required the seller to be compensated for the depreciated value—not the purchase price—of the pickup and remanded the case for a determination of the fairness of the contract and the fair market value of the vehicle.

REASON The court concluded that if the minor "has not been overreached in any way, and there has been no undue influence, and the contract is a fair and reasonable one, and the minor has actually paid money on the purchase price, and taken and used the article purchased, [then] he ought not to be permitted to recover the amount actually paid, without allowing the vendor of the goods reasonable compensation for the use of, depreciation, and willful or negligent damage to the article purchased, while in his hands." The court recognized "modern conditions under which minors * * * transact a great deal of business for themselves, long before they have reached the age of legal majority." To rule otherwise, explained the court, "can only lead to the corruption of principles and encourage young people in habits of trickery and dishonesty."

FOR CRITICAL ANALYSIS—Ethical Consideration *Do you believe that the goal of protecting minors from the consequences of unwise contracts should ever outweigh the goal of encouraging minors to behave in a responsible manner?*

Disaffirmance and Misrepresentation of Age. Suppose that a minor tells a seller she is twenty-one years old when she is really seventeen. Ordinarily, the minor can disaffirm the contract even though she has misrepresented her age. Moreover, in certain jurisdictions the minor is not liable for the tort of fraud for such misrepresentation, the rationale being that such a tort judgment might indirectly force the minor to perform the contract.

Many jurisdictions, however, do find circumstances under which a minor can be bound by a contract when the minor has misrepresented his or her age. First, several

Two young men discuss the sale of a car. When a minor disaffirms a contract, such as contract to buy a car, most states require the minor to return whatever he or she purchased, if it is within his or her control. Why do some states require more?

states have enacted statutes for precisely this purpose. In these states, misrepresentation of age is enough to prohibit disaffirmance. Other statutes prohibit disaffirmance by a minor who has engaged in business as an adult. Second, some courts refuse to allow minors to disaffirm executed (fully performed) contracts unless they can return the consideration received. The combination of the minors' misrepresentations and their unjust enrichment has persuaded these courts to *estop* (prevent) the minors from asserting contractual incapacity.

Third, some courts allow a misrepresenting minor to disaffirm the contract, but they hold the minor liable for damages in tort. Here, the defrauded party may sue the minor for misrepresentation or fraud. Authority is split on this point because some courts, as previously noted, have recognized that allowing a suit in tort is equivalent to indirectly enforcing the minor's contract.

Liability for Necessaries, Insurance, and Loans. A minor who enters into a contract for necessaries may disaffirm the contract but remains liable for the reasonable value of the goods used. **Necessaries** are basic needs, such as food, clothing, shelter, and medical services, at a level of value required to maintain the minor's standard of living or financial and social status. Thus, what will be considered a necessary for one person may be a luxury for another. Additionally, what is considered a necessary depends on whether the minor is under the care or control of his or her parents, who are required by law to provide necessaries for the minor. If a minor's parents provide the minor with shelter, for example, then a contract to lease shelter (such as an apartment) normally will not be classified as a contract for necessaries.

NECESSARIES
Necessities required for life, such as food, shelter, clothing, and medical attention; may include whatever is believed to be necessary to maintain a person's standard of living or financial and social status.

BE AWARE A minor's station in life (financial and social status, lifestyle, and so on) is important in determining whether an item is a necessary or a luxury. For example, clothing is a necessary, but if a minor from a low-income family contracts for the purchase of a $2,000 coat, a court may deem the coat a luxury. In this situation, the contract would not be for "necessaries."

Generally, then, to qualify as a contract for necessaries, (1) the item contracted for must be necessary to the minor's existence, (2) the value of the necessary item may be up to a level required to maintain the minor's standard of living or financial and social status, and (3) the minor must not be under the care of a parent or guardian who is required to supply this item. Unless these three criteria are met, the minor can disaffirm the contract *without* being liable for the reasonable value of the goods used.

Traditionally, insurance has not been viewed as a necessary, so minors can ordinarily disaffirm their insurance contracts and recover all premiums paid. Some jurisdictions, however, prohibit the right to disaffirm insurance contracts—for example, when minors contract for life insurance on their own lives. Financial loans are seldom considered to be necessaries, even if the minor spends the money borrowed on necessaries. If, however, a lender makes a loan to a minor for the express purpose of enabling the minor to purchase necessaries, and the lender personally makes sure the money is so spent, the minor normally is obligated to repay the loan.

Ratification In contract law, **ratification** is the act of accepting and giving legal force to an obligation that previously was not enforceable. A minor who has reached the age of majority can ratify a contract expressly or impliedly.

RATIFICATION
The act of accepting and giving legal force to an obligation that previously was not enforceable.

Express ratification occurs when the minor expressly states, orally or in writing, that she or he intends to be bound by the contract. Implied ratification exists when the conduct of the minor is inconsistent with disaffirmance (as when the minor enjoys the benefits of the contract) or when the minor fails to disaffirm an executed (fully performed) contract within a reasonable time after reaching the age of majority. If the contract is still executory (not yet performed or only partially performed), however, failure to disaffirm the contract will not necessarily imply ratification.

Generally, the courts base their determination on whether the minor, after reaching the age of majority, has had ample opportunity to consider the nature of the contractual obligations he or she entered into as a minor and the extent to which the adult party to the contract has performed.

Parents' Liability As a general rule, parents are not liable for the contracts made by minor children acting on their own, except contracts for necessaries, which the parents are legally required to provide. This is why businesses ordinarily require parents to cosign any contract made with a minor. The parents then become personally obligated under the contract to perform the conditions of the contract, even if their child avoids liability.

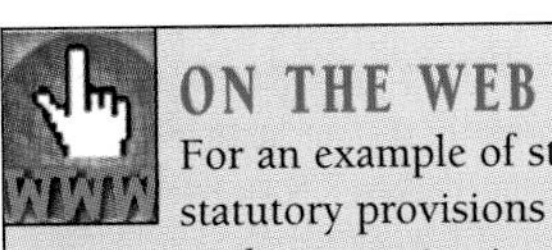

ON THE WEB For an example of state statutory provisions governing the emancipation of minors, you can view Wyoming's statutory provisions on this topic at **http://legisweb.state.wy.us/statutes/sub14.htm**.

Generally, a minor is held personally liable for the torts he or she commits. Therefore, minors cannot disaffirm their liability for their tortious conduct. The parents of the minor can *also* be held liable under certain circumstances. For example, if the minor commits a tort under the direction of a parent or while performing an act requested by a parent, the injured party can hold the parent liable. In addition, in many states parents are liable up to a statutory amount for malicious torts committed by a minor child living in their home.

EMANCIPATION
In regard to minors, the act of being freed from parental control; occurs when a child's parent or legal guardian relinquishes the legal right to exercise control over the child. Normally, a minor who leaves home to support himself or herself is considered emancipated.

Emancipation The release of a minor by his or her parents is known as emancipation. **Emancipation** occurs when a child's parent or legal guardian relinquishes the legal right to exercise control over the child. Normally, a minor who leaves home to support himself or herself is considered emancipated. Several jurisdictions permit minors to petition a court for emancipation themselves. For business purposes, a minor may petition a court to be treated as an adult. If the court grants the minor's request, it removes the minor's lack of contractual capacity and right of disaffirmance for those contracts entered into in conducting the business.

INTOXICATED PERSONS

Contractual capacity also becomes an issue when a contract is formed by a person who claims to have been intoxicated at the time the contract was made. The general rule is that if a person who is sufficiently intoxicated to lack mental capacity enters into a contract, the contract is voidable at the option of that person. This is true even if the intoxication was purely voluntary. For the contract to be voidable, it must be proved that the intoxicated person's reason and judgment were impaired to the extent that she or he did not comprehend the legal consequences of entering into the contract. In addition, to avoid the contract in the majority of states, the person claiming intoxication must be able to return all consideration received. If the person was intoxicated but understood the legal consequences, the contract is enforceable.

Simply because the terms of the contract are foolish or are obviously favorable to the other party does not mean the contract is voidable (unless the other party fraudulently induced the person to become intoxicated). Problems often arise in determining whether a party was sufficiently intoxicated to avoid legal duties. Generally, courts rarely permit contracts to be avoided on the ground of intoxication.

MENTALLY INCOMPETENT PERSONS

If a person has been adjudged mentally incompetent by a court of law and a guardian has been appointed, any contract made by the mentally incompetent person is *void*—no contract exists. Only the guardian can enter into a binding contract on behalf of the mentally incompetent person.

If a mentally incompetent person not previously so adjudged by a court enters into a contract, the contract may be *voidable* if the person does not know he or she is entering into the contract or lacks the mental capacity to comprehend its nature, purpose, and consequences. In such situations, the contract is voidable at the option of the mentally incompetent person but not the other party. The contract may then be disaffirmed or ratified. To disaffirm the contract, the person claiming mental incompetence must return any consideration received. Ratification must occur after the person has regained mental competence or after a guardian is appointed and ratifies the contract. Like minors and intoxicated persons, mentally incompetent persons are liable for the reasonable value of any necessaries they receive.

A contract entered into by a mentally incompetent person (but not previously so adjudged by a court) may also be deemed valid and enforceable if the contract was formed during a lucid interval. For such a contract to be valid, it must be shown that the person was able to comprehend the nature, purpose, and consequences of the contract *at the time the contract was formed.*

Legality

To this point, we have discussed three of the requirements for a valid contract to exist—agreement, consideration, and contractual capacity. Now we examine a fourth—legality. For a contract to be valid and enforceable, it must be formed for a legal purpose. A contract to do something that is prohibited by federal or state statutory law is illegal and, as such, void from the outset and thus unenforceable. Additionally, a contract to commit a tortious act or to commit an action that is contrary to public policy is illegal and unenforceable.

Contracts Contrary to Statute

Statutes sometimes prescribe the terms of contracts. In some instances, the laws are specific, even providing for the inclusion of certain clauses and their wording. Other statutes prohibit certain contracts on the basis of their subject matter or the status of the contracting parties, or for other reasons. We examine here several ways in which contracts may be contrary to a statute and thus illegal.

USURY
Charging an illegal rate of interest.

Usury Virtually every state has a statute that sets the maximum rate of interest that can be charged for different types of transactions, including ordinary loans. A lender who makes a loan at an interest rate above the lawful maximum commits **usury**. The maximum rate of interest varies from state to state.

Although usury statutes place a ceiling on allowable rates of interest, exceptions have been made to facilitate business transactions. For example, many states exempt corporate loans from the usury laws. In addition, almost all states have adopted special statutes allowing much higher interest rates on small loans to help those borrowers who need funds and who could not otherwise obtain loans.

The effects of a usurious loan differ from state to state. A number of states allow the lender to recover only the principal of a loan along with interest up to the legal maximum. In effect, the lender is denied recovery of the excess interest. In other states, the lender can recover the principal amount of the loan but not the interest. In a few states, a usurious loan is a void transaction, and the lender cannot recover either the principal or the interest.

Gambling In general, gambling contracts are illegal and thus void. All states have statutes that regulate gambling—defined as any scheme that involves the distribution

Adults gamble at a casino. Would this same activity be illegal if it were conducted online? If so, could it be prevented? How?

of property by chance among persons who have paid valuable consideration for the opportunity (chance) to receive the property.[2] Gambling is the creation of risk for the purpose of assuming it.

In some states, such as Nevada, New Jersey, and Louisiana, casino gambling is legal. In other states, certain other forms of gambling are legal. California, for example, has not defined draw poker as a crime, although criminal statutes prohibit numerous other types of gambling games. Several states allow horse racing, and many states have legalized state-operated lotteries, as well as lotteries (such as bingo) conducted for charitable purposes. Many states also allow gambling on Indian reservations.

Sometimes it is difficult to distinguish a gambling contract from the risk sharing inherent in almost all contracts. • **EXAMPLE 10.2** In one case, each of five co-workers received a free lottery ticket from a customer and agreed to split the winnings if one of the tickets turned out to be the winning one. At first glance, this may seem entirely legal. The court, however, noted that the oral contract in this case "was an exchange of promises to share winnings from the parties' individually owned lottery tickets upon the happening of the uncertain event" that one of the tickets would win. Consequently, concluded the court, the agreement at issue was "founded on a gambling consideration" and therefore void.[3] •

ETHICAL ISSUE 10.1

How can states enforce gambling laws in the age of the Internet?

One of the threshold issues in regulating online gambling is jurisdictional in nature. For example, in those states that do not allow casino gambling or off-track betting, what can a state government do if res-

2. See *Wishing Well Club v. Akron,* 66 Ohio Law Abs. 406, 112 N.E.2d 41 (1951).
3. *Dickerson v. Deno,* 770 So.2d 63 (Ala. 2000).

idents of the state place bets online? After all, as you read in Chapter 2, states have no constitutional authority to regulate activities that occur in other states. Another threshold issue in regulating online gambling involves determining where the physical act of placing a bet on the Internet occurs. Is it where the gambler is located or where the gambling site is based? For example, suppose that a resident of New York places bets via the Internet at a gambling site located in Antigua. Is the actual act of "gambling" taking place in New York or in Antigua?

When this exact question came before a New York court, the court, in a precedent-setting decision, concluded that the act of gambling occurred in New York, because under New York law a bet had to be legal in both the jurisdiction where the bet was placed and the jurisdiction where it was received. According to the court, "if the person engaged in gambling is located in New York, then New York is the location where the gambling occurred." Significantly, the U.S. Court of Appeals for the Second Circuit upheld the New York court's decision.[4]

ON THE WEB If you are interested in reading the earliest legislation regulating activities on the Sabbath in colonial America (and about some of the punishments meted out for failing to obey these regulations), go to **http://www.natreformassn.org/statesman/99/charactr.html.**

BLUE LAWS
State or local laws that prohibit the performance of certain types of commercial activities on Sunday.

Sabbath (Sunday) Laws Statutes called Sabbath (Sunday) laws prohibit the formation or performance of certain contracts on a Sunday. Under the common law, such contracts are legal in the absence of this statutory prohibition. Under some state and local laws, all contracts entered into on a Sunday are illegal. Laws in other states or municipalities prohibit only the sale of certain types of merchandise, such as alcoholic beverages, on a Sunday.

As noted in Chapter 2, these laws, which date back to colonial times, are often called **blue laws.** Blue laws get their name from the blue paper on which New Haven, Connecticut, printed its new town ordinance in 1781. The ordinance prohibited all work on Sunday and required all shops to close on the "Lord's Day." A number of states and municipalities enacted laws forbidding the carrying on of "all secular labor and business on the Lord's Day." Exceptions to Sunday laws permit contracts for necessities (such as food) and works of charity. Additionally, a fully performed (executed) contract that was entered into on a Sunday normally cannot be rescinded (canceled).

Sunday laws are often not enforced, and some of these laws have been held to be unconstitutional on the ground that they are contrary to the freedom of religion. Nonetheless, as a precaution, business owners contemplating doing business in a particular locality should check to see if any Sunday statutes or ordinances will affect their business activities.

Licensing Statutes All states require that members of certain professions obtain licenses allowing them to practice. Physicians, lawyers, real estate brokers, architects, electricians, and stockbrokers are but a few of the people who must be licensed. Some licenses are obtained only after extensive schooling and examinations, which indicate to the public that a special skill has been acquired. Others require only that the particular person be of good moral character.

Generally, business licenses provide a means of regulating and taxing certain businesses and protecting the public against actions that could threaten the general welfare. For example, in nearly all states, a stockbroker must be licensed and must file a bond with the state to protect the public from fraudulent transactions in stock. Similarly, a plumber must be licensed and bonded to protect the public against incompetent plumbers and to protect the public health. Only persons or businesses possessing the qualifications and complying with the conditions required by statute are entitled to licenses. Typically, for example, an owner of a saloon or tavern is required

4. *United States v. Cohen,* 260 F.3d. 68 (2d Cir. 2001).

to sell food as a condition of obtaining a license to sell liquor for consumption on the premises.

When a person enters into a contract with an unlicensed individual, the contract may still be enforceable, depending on the nature of the licensing statute. Some states expressly provide that the lack of a license in certain occupations bars the enforcement of work-related contracts. If the statute does not expressly state this, one must look to the underlying purpose of the licensing requirements for a particular occupation. If the purpose is to protect the public from unauthorized practitioners, a contract involving an unlicensed individual is illegal and unenforceable. If, however, the underlying purpose of the statute is to raise government revenues, a contract with an unlicensed practitioner is enforceable—although the unlicensed person is usually fined.

At issue in the following case was whether a contract entered into with an unlicensed contractor could serve as the basis for an action for wrongful interference with a contractual relationship.

CASE 10.2 RCDI Construction, Inc. v. Spaceplan/Architecture, Planning & Interiors, P.A.[a]

United States District Court,
Western District of North Carolina, 2001.
148 F.Supp.2d 607.

FACTS RCDI Construction Management, Inc. (RCDI-CM), signed a contract with Dr. Anjil Patel for the construction of a hotel in North Carolina. At the time, RCDI-CM was a licensed contractor in West Virginia but not in North Carolina. The contract was assigned to RCDI Construction, Inc. (RCDI), a wholly owned subsidiary of RCDI-CM that did have a North Carolina contractor's license. RCDI began to build the hotel. When construction was nearly complete, a discharge of water damaged the hotel. On behalf of Patel, Spaceplan/Architecture, Planning & Interiors, P.A. (SAPI), assessed the condition of the building. SAPI recommended that Patel terminate the contract with RCDI, gut the building, and reconstruct the hotel. Following its termination, RCDI agreed to forfeit to Patel $421,000 owed under the construction contract and to pay Patel $6.7 million. RCDI then filed a suit in a federal district court against SAPI, alleging, among other things, wrongful interference with a contractual relationship (see Chapter 4). SAPI filed a motion for a judgment on the pleadings.[b]

a. "P.A." is an abbreviation for "Professional Association," a form of business organization.

b. Recall from Chapter 3 that in a motion for judgment on the pleadings, a party asks the court to decide the issue based only on the pleadings (complaint, answer, and so on). The motion will be granted only if there are no facts in dispute and the only issue is how the law applies to the facts.

ISSUE Is a contract with an unlicensed contractor valid for the purpose of maintaining a suit for wrongful interference with the contract?

DECISION No. The court granted SAPI's motion and dismissed RCDI's complaint.

REASON The court stated that the first element of wrongful interference with a contractual relationship is "that a valid contract existed between the plaintiff and a third person. * * * Here, Plaintiffs' claim fails because they cannot satisfy the first element." The court acknowledged that "[w]hile there is no question that a contract for the construction of a hotel was signed by RCDI-CM and Dr. Patel, it is equally uncontested that Plaintiff RCDI-CM was not a contractor licensed by the State of North Carolina at the time * * * . [C]ontracts entered into by unlicensed construction contractors, in violation of a statute passed for the protection of the public, are unenforceable by the contractor." The court explained that "[t]he authorities from the earliest time to the present unanimously hold that no court will lend its assistance in any way towards carrying out the terms of an illegal contract. In case any action is brought in which it is necessary to prove the illegal contract in order to maintain the action, courts will not enforce it."

FOR CRITICAL ANALYSIS—Social Consideration *Considering the amount of money involved, does it seem harsh to apply the illegality doctrine to contracts such as the one in the* RCDI *case?*

> "Public policy is in its nature so uncertain and fluctuating, varying with the habits of the day, . . . that it is difficult to determine its limits with any degree of exactness."
>
> JOSEPH STORY, 1779–1845 (Associate justice of the United States Supreme Court, 1811–1844)

CONTRACTS CONTRARY TO PUBLIC POLICY

Although contracts involve private parties, some are not enforceable because of the negative impact they would have on society. These contracts are said to be *contrary to public policy.* Examples include a contract to commit an immoral act (such as a surrogate-parenting contract, which several courts and state statutes equate with "baby selling") and a contract that prohibits marriage. ● **EXAMPLE 10.3** Everett offers a young man $10,000 if he refrains from marrying Everett's daughter. If the young man accepts, no contract is formed (the contract is void) because it is contrary to public policy. Thus, if the man marries Everett's daughter, Everett cannot sue him for breach of contract.● Business contracts that may be contrary to public policy include contracts in restraint of trade and unconscionable contracts or clauses.

Contracts in Restraint of Trade Contracts in restraint of trade (anticompetitive agreements) usually adversely affect the public policy that favors competition in the economy. Typically, such contracts also violate one or more federal or state statutes.[5] An exception is recognized when the restraint is reasonable and is *ancillary* to (is a subsidiary part of) a contract, such as a contract for the sale of a business or an employment contract. Many such exceptions involve a type of restraint called a *covenant not to compete,* or a restrictive covenant.

5. Federal statutes prohibiting anticompetitive agreements include the Sherman Antitrust Act, the Clayton Act, and the Federal Trade Commission Act (see Chapter 32).

LETTER OF THE LAW

For Sale: "The Most Beautiful Baby in the World"

Lawrence Schaub, a former windshield repairman in Detroit, Michigan, was facing financial problems. He was out of work. He was behind in his mobile home payments. He had three children to feed. Desperate to obtain funds, he decided to sell the youngest of his three children. To that end, he created a videotape titled "The Most Beautiful Baby in the World" to show to prospective buyers. Unfortunately for Mr. Schaub, his baby-sitter informed the police of his plan, and he was caught in a "sting" operation in which undercover police officers posed as a would-be adoptive family. Schaub accepted a $10,000 payment from the officers as a down payment on the $60,000 contract price.

If a case involving a similar contract came before a civil court, the court would likely deem the contract void as against public policy. Schaub's was a criminal case, however, and a significant question immediately arose: What statute had Schaub violated? Until September 1, 2000, Michigan was one of about twenty-five states that did not explicitly outlaw the sale of children. Shortly after Schaub's arrest drew attention to this "oversight" in state law, the Michigan legislature passed a bill making trafficking in humans punishable by up to twenty years in prison and a $100,000 fine. At the time Schaub tried to sell his daughter, however, the law did not exist. At worst, the only state crime that Schaub committed was attempting to profit from an adoption, which is subject to a penalty of ninety days in jail.[a]

THE BOTTOM LINE

Occasionally, bizarre cases such as this one alert state legislatures to loopholes in their laws. Note, though, that the prosecutors in Schaub's case found other ways to keep Schaub in jail for a while—at least until his former wife claimed custody of the children. The prosecutors charged Schaub with child abandonment, driving with a suspended license, and violating his probation stemming from an earlier drug case.

a. For a summary of Schaub's actions and the prosecution's case against him, see M. L. Elrick, "Baby for Sale," *The National Law Journal,* September 11, 2000, pp. A1–A2.

Covenants Not to Compete and the Sale of an Ongoing Business. Covenants not to compete are often contained in contracts concerning the sale of an ongoing business. A covenant not to compete is created when a seller agrees not to open a new store in a certain geographic area surrounding the old store. Such an agreement, when it is ancillary to a sales contract and reasonable in terms of time and geographic area, enables the seller to sell, and the purchaser to buy, the "goodwill" and "reputation" of an ongoing business. If, for example, a well-known merchant sells his or her store and opens a competing business a block away, many of the merchant's customers will likely do business at the new store. This renders valueless the good name and reputation sold to the other merchant for a price. If a covenant not to compete is not ancillary to a sales agreement, however, it will be void, because it unreasonably restrains trade and is contrary to public policy.

Covenants Not to Compete in Employment Contracts. Agreements not to compete can also be contained in employment contracts. People in middle-level and upper-level management positions commonly agree not to work for competitors or not to start a competing business for a specified period of time after terminating employment. Such agreements are generally legal so long as the specified period of time is not excessive in duration and the geographic restriction is reasonable. Basically, the restriction on competition must be reasonable—that is, not any greater than necessary to protect a legitimate business interest.

What time and geographic restrictions are "reasonable" in the online environment? For a discussion of this issue, see this chapter's *Business Law in the Online World* feature on page 277.

Enforcement Problems. The laws governing the enforceability of covenants not to compete vary significantly from state to state. In some states, such as Texas, such a covenant will not be enforced unless the employee has received some benefit in return for signing the noncompete agreement. This is true even if the covenant is reasonable as to time and area. If the employee receives no benefit, the covenant will be deemed void. California prohibits the enforcement of covenants not to compete altogether.

Occasionally, depending on the jurisdiction, courts will *reform* covenants not to compete. If a covenant is found to be unreasonable in time or geographic area, the court may convert the terms into reasonable ones and then enforce the reformed covenant. This presents a problem, however, in that the judge, implicitly, has become a party to the contract. Consequently, contract **reformation** is usually carried out by a court only when necessary to prevent undue burdens or hardships.

REFORMATION
A court-ordered correction of a written contract so that it reflects the true intentions of the parties.

ETHICAL ISSUE 10.2

Do covenants not to compete stifle innovation?

One of the reasons that the courts usually look closely at covenants not to compete and evaluate them on a case-by-case basis is the strong public policy favoring competition in this country. If a court finds that a restraint is not reasonable in light of the circumstances, it will either not enforce the covenant or reform the unreasonable provision and then enforce it. Even so, claim some scholars, covenants not to compete, regardless of their "reasonability," may stifle competition and innovation.

Consider, for example, the argument put forth by Ronald Gilson, a Stanford University professor of law and business. He contends that California's prohibition on covenants not to compete may help to explain why technological innovation and economic growth have skyrocketed in California's Silicon Valley, while the technological area along Massachusetts's Route 128 has languished. According to Gilson, "The different legal rules governing postemployment covenants not to compete in California and Massachusetts help explain the difference in employee job mobility and therefore the knowledge transfer that [is] a critical factor in explaining the differential performance of Silicon Valley and Route 128."[6] For this and other reasons, some scholars contend that covenants not to compete may not survive the cyber age.[7] Certainly, in an era of rapid technological change, such covenants are presenting new types of challenges for the courts.

Unconscionable Contracts or Clauses Ordinarily, a court does not look at the fairness or equity of a contract; for example, a court normally will not inquire into the adequacy of consideration. Persons are assumed to be reasonably intelligent, and the court does not come to their aid just because they have made unwise or foolish bargains. In certain circumstances, however, bargains are so oppressive that the courts relieve innocent parties of part or all of their duties. Such a bargain is called an **unconscionable contract** (or **unconscionable clause**). Both the Uniform Commercial Code (UCC) and the Uniform Consumer Credit Code (UCCC) embody the unconscionability concept—the former with regard to the sale of goods and the latter with regard to consumer loans and the waiver of rights.[8]

UNCONSCIONABLE CONTRACT OR CLAUSE
A contract or clause that is void on the basis of public policy because one party, as a result of disproportionate bargaining power, is forced to accept terms that are unfairly burdensome and that unfairly benefit the dominating party.

Procedural Unconscionability. Procedural unconscionability has to do with how a term becomes part of a contract and relates to factors bearing on a party's lack of knowledge or understanding of the contract terms because of inconspicuous print, unintelligible language ("legalese"), lack of opportunity to read the contract, lack of opportunity to ask questions about its meaning, and other factors. Procedural unconscionability sometimes relates to purported lack of voluntariness because of a disparity in bargaining power between the two parties. Contracts entered into because of one party's vastly superior bargaining power may be deemed unconscionable. These situations usually involve an **adhesion contract**, which is a contract drafted by the dominant party and then presented to the other—the adhering party—on a "take it or leave it" basis.[9]

ADHESION CONTRACT
A "standard-form" contract, such as that between a large retailer and a consumer, in which the stronger party dictates the terms.

Substantive Unconscionability. Substantive unconscionability characterizes those contracts, or portions of contracts, that are oppressive or overly harsh. Courts generally focus on provisions that deprive one party of the benefits of the agreement or leave that party without remedy for nonperformance by the other. For example, suppose that a welfare recipient with a fourth-grade education agrees to purchase a refrigerator for $2,000 and signs a two-year installment contract. The same type of refrigerator usually sells for $400 on the market. Some courts have held this type of contract to be unconscionable, despite the general rule that the courts will not inquire into the adequacy of the consideration, because the contract terms are so oppressive as to "shock the conscience" of the court.[10]

6. Ronald J. Gilson, "The Legal Infrastructure of High Technology Industrial Districts: Silicon Valley, Route 128, and Covenants Not to Compete," 575 *New York University Law Review* 579 (June 1999).

7. See, for example, Robert C. Welsh, Larry C. Drapkin, and Samantha C. Grant, "Are Noncompete Clauses Kaput?" *The National Law Journal*, August 14, 2000, pp. B13–B14.

8. See, for example, UCC Sections 2–302 and 2–719 (discussed in Chapters 14 and 16, respectively) and UCCC Sections 5.108 and 1.107 (see Chapter 33).

9. See, for example, *Henningsen v. Bloomfield Motors, Inc.*, 32 N.J. 358, 161 A.2d 69 (1960).

10. See, for example, *Jones v. Star Credit Corp.*, 59 Misc.2d 189, 298 N.Y.S.2d 264 (1969). This case is presented in Chapter 14 as Case 14.3.

BUSINESS LAW: //in the Online World

Covenants Not to Compete in the Internet Context

For some companies today, particularly those in the high-tech industry, trade secrets are their most valuable assets. Often, to prevent departing employees from disclosing trade secrets to competing employers, business owners and managers have their key employees sign covenants not to compete. A question of growing significance to employers—and the courts—today is how to adapt traditional requirements relating to such covenants to a cyber age.

Restrictions Must Be Reasonable

As mentioned elsewhere in this chapter, in a covenant not to compete the employee typically agrees not to set up a competing business, or work for a competitor, in a specified geographic area for a certain period of time. Generally, the time and geographic restrictions must be "reasonable." For example, while a time restriction of one year may be upheld by a court as reasonable, a time restriction of two, three, or five years may not be. For some time, attorneys typically have advised their business clients to restrict the noncompete period to one year for this reason.

Yet can time and space restrictions that have been deemed reasonable in the past serve as a guide to what might constitute reasonable restrictions in today's changing legal landscape? After all, in the Internet environment there are no physical borders, so geographic restrictions are no longer relevant. Similarly, given the rapid pace of development within the information technology industry, restricting an employee from working in the area for one year could seriously affect the employee's career.

Defining "Reasonability" in the Internet Context

In view of the dynamic nature and the global reach of the Internet, some courts have begun to redefine what constitute "reasonable" restrictions in covenants not to compete. A case decided by a federal district court in New York is instructive in this respect. The case involved Mark Schlack, who worked as a Web site manager and vice president for EarthWeb, Inc. EarthWeb provides products and services to business professionals in the information technology industry. When he was hired by EarthWeb, Schlack signed a covenant not to compete stating that, on termination of his employment, he would not work for any competing company for one year. When Schlack later accepted an offer from another company to design a Web site, EarthWeb sued to enforce the covenant not to compete.

The court refused to enforce the covenant, in part because there was no evidence that Schlack had misappropriated any of EarthWeb's trade secrets or solicited EarthWeb's clients, as EarthWeb had claimed. The court also stated, "When measured against the information technology industry in the Internet environment, a one-year hiatus [break] from the work force is several generations, if not an eternity." In effect, concluded the court, the covenant prohibited Schlack from working for a competing company located anywhere in the world for one year—because the Internet lacks physical borders.[a]

Implications for High-Tech Industries

What are the implications of this case—and some similar cases[b]—for employers in high-tech industries? The consensus among legal specialists in this area is that employees who sign covenants not to compete should be given some counterbalancing benefits—such as a continuation of salary and/or other benefits during the specified period of noncompetition. Generally, a court will be much more likely to enforce a noncompete agreement if it contains fair and reasonable counterbalancing provisions. Additionally, because for Web-based work the geographic restriction can be worldwide in scope, the time restriction should be narrowed considerably to compensate for the extensive geographic restriction.[c]

FOR CRITICAL ANALYSIS

Other than having their employees sign covenants not to compete, what actions might companies in the high-tech industry take to encourage their employees to keep trade secrets confidential?

a. *EarthWeb, Inc. v. Schlack,* 71 F.Supp.2d 299 (S.D.N.Y. 1999).
b. See, for example, *National Business Services, Inc. v. Wright,* 2 F.Supp.2d 701 (E.D.Pa. 1998).
c. For other guidelines for high-tech companies to consider when forming noncompete covenants, see Beverly Garofalo and Mitchell L. Fishberg, "Trade Secrets: Noncompete Agreements," *The National Law Journal,* January 17, 2000.

EXCULPATORY CLAUSE
A clause that releases a contractual party from liability in the event of monetary or physical injury, no matter who is at fault.

REMEMBER Virtually everyone is liable for his or her own torts, and this responsibility cannot be contracted away.

Exculpatory Clauses Often closely related to the concept of unconscionability are **exculpatory clauses**, defined as clauses that release a party from liability in the event of monetary or physical injury, *no matter who is at fault*. Indeed, some courts refer to such clauses in terms of unconscionability. • **EXAMPLE 10.4** Suppose, for example, that Madison Manufacturing Company hires a laborer and has him sign a contract containing the following clause:

> Said employee hereby agrees with employer, in consideration of such employment, that he will take upon himself all risks incident to his position and will in no case hold the company liable for any injury or damage he may sustain, in his person or otherwise, by accidents or injuries in the factory, or which may result from defective machinery or carelessness or misconduct of himself or any other employee in service of the employer.

This contract provision attempts to remove Madison's potential liability for injuries occurring to the employee, and it would usually be held contrary to public policy.[11] • Additionally, exculpatory clauses found in agreements to lease commercial property are also, in the majority of cases, held to be contrary to public policy, and such clauses are almost universally held to be illegal and unenforceable when they are included in residential property leases.

Generally, an exculpatory clause will not be enforced if the party seeking its enforcement is involved in a business that is important to the public interest. These businesses include public utilities, common carriers, and banks. Because of the essential nature of these services, the companies offering them have an advantage in bargaining strength and could insist that anyone contracting for their services agree not to hold them liable. With no potential liability, the companies might be less careful, and the number of injuries could increase.

Exculpatory clauses may be enforced, however, when the parties seeking their enforcement are not involved in businesses considered important to the public interest. These businesses have included health clubs, amusement parks, horse-rental concessions, golf-cart concessions, and skydiving organizations. Because these services are not essential, the firms offering them are sometimes considered to have no relative advantage in bargaining strength, and anyone contracting for their services is considered to do so voluntarily. In the following case, the question was whether an exculpatory clause could be enforced against a racer who, although she was likely aware of the organizers' requirement that she sign the clause, somehow participated in the race without signing it.

11. For a case with similar facts, see *Little Rock & Fort Smith Railway Co. v. Eubanks,* 48 Ark. 460, 3 S.W. 808 (1887). In such a case, the exculpatory clause may also be illegal because it violates a state workers' compensation law.

CASE 10.3 Beaver v. Grand Prix Karting Association, Inc.

United States Court of Appeals,
Seventh Circuit, 2001.
246 F.3d 905.
http://www.ca7.uscourts.gov[a]

a. In the left-hand column, click on "Judicial Opinions." On that page, in the "Last Name or Corporation" section, click on "Begins," enter "Beaver" in the box, and click on "Search for Person." When the result appears, click on the docket number to access the opinion. The U.S. Court of Appeals for the Seventh Circuit maintains this Web site.

FACTS Dorothy Beaver began racing go karts in 1985. Many of the races required her to sign an exculpatory clause to participate. In 1993, she signed a clause to participate in the annual Elkhart Grand Prix, a series of races in Elkhart, Indiana, organized by Grand Prix Karting Association, Inc., and others. The next year, she returned for another Grand Prix. During the event in which she drove, a piece of foam padding used as a course barrier was torn from its base and ended up on the track. A por-

CASE 10.3—Continued

tion of the padding struck Beaver in the head, and another portion was thrown into oncoming traffic, causing a multikart collision during which she sustained severe injuries. She and her husband, Stacy, filed a suit in federal district court against the organizers and others on various tort grounds. The organizers could not find an exculpatory clause signed by Beaver for the 1994 race, but argued in part that even if she had not signed one, her actions showed her intent to be bound by its terms. When the court entered a judgment in favor of the organizers, Beaver appealed to the U.S. Court of Appeals for the Seventh Circuit.

ISSUE Can an individual, by participating in an event that requires the execution of an exculpatory clause, be bound to its terms even if she or he has not signed it?

DECISION Yes. The U.S. Court of Appeals for the Seventh Circuit affirmed the decision of the lower court, binding Beaver to the terms of the clause.

REASON The U.S. Court of Appeals for the Seventh Circuit pointed out that "courts repeatedly have held that assent to a contract—and that, in essence, is what [an exculpatory clause] is—may be established by acts which manifest acceptance." A "manifestation or expression of assent necessary to form a contract may be by work, act, or conduct which evinces the intention of the parties to contract." In other words, exculpatory clauses "are governed by the same rules as other contracts." Thus, assent "may be assumed where a knowledgeable party enters into the contract, aware of the limitation and its legal effect, without indicating non-acquiescence to those terms." The court noted that "[b]ased on the evidence presented, the jury reasonably concluded that it is the custom and practice of the go kart industry, as well as the Elkhart Grand Prix, to require race participants to execute releases. The jury further reasonably concluded that Beaver was well aware of this requirement and chose to participate in the 1994 race anyway. * * * [T]hese facts sufficiently establish Beaver's assent to the release."

FOR CRITICAL ANALYSIS—Economic Consideration *Why would the organizers of a race require that all participants sign exculpatory clauses?*

The Effect of Illegality

As a general rule, a court will not enforce or rescind (cancel) an illegal contract. In other words, a court will not aid either party. In most illegal contracts, both parties are considered to be equally at fault—*in pari delicto.* If the contract is executory (not yet fulfilled), neither party can enforce it. If it is executed, there can be neither contractual nor quasi-contractual recovery.

That one wrongdoer in an illegal contract is unjustly enriched at the expense of the other is of no concern to the law—except under certain circumstances (to be discussed shortly). The major justification for this hands-off attitude is that it is improper to place the machinery of justice at the disposal of a plaintiff who has broken the law by entering into an illegal bargain. Another justification is the hoped-for deterrent effect of this general rule. A plaintiff who suffers a loss because of an illegal bargain will presumably be deterred from entering into similar illegal bargains in the future.

There are exceptions to the general rule that neither party to an illegal bargain can sue for breach and neither can recover for performance rendered. We look at these exceptions here.

Justifiable Ignorance of the Facts When one of the parties to a contract is relatively innocent (has no knowledge or any reason to know that the contract is illegal), that party can often obtain restitution or recovery of benefits conferred in a partially executed contract. The courts do not enforce the contract but do allow the parties to return to their original positions.

It is also possible for an innocent party who has fully performed under the contract to enforce the contract against the guilty party. For example, if a party engages in an illegal act by selling certain goods in violation of the law and contracts with a trucking firm to deliver the goods for $1,000, the trucking firm, as an innocent party, will be entitled to collect the $1,000 once the delivery is made.

Members of Protected Classes When a statute protects a certain class of people, a member of that class can enforce an illegal contract even though the other party cannot. For example, statutes prohibit certain employees (such as flight attendants) from working more than a specified number of hours per month. These employees thus constitute a class protected by statute. An employee who is required to work more than the maximum can recover for those extra hours of service.

BLUE SKY LAWS
State laws that regulate the offer and sale of securities.

Another example of statutes designed to protect a particular class of people are **blue sky laws**, which are state laws that regulate and supervise investment companies for the protection of the public. (The phrase *blue sky laws* dates to a 1917 decision by the United States Supreme Court in which the Court declared that the purpose of such laws was to prevent "speculative schemes which have no more basis than so many feet of 'blue sky.'")[12] These laws are intended to stop the sale of stock in fly-by-night concerns, such as visionary oil wells and distant and perhaps nonexistent gold mines. Investors are protected as a class and can sue to recover the purchase price of stock issued in violation of such laws.

Most states also have statutes regulating the sale of insurance. If an insurance company violates a statute when selling insurance, the purchaser can nevertheless enforce the policy and recover from the insurer.

Withdrawal from an Illegal Agreement If the illegal part of a bargain has not yet been performed, the party tendering performance can withdraw from the bargain and recover the performance or its value. • **EXAMPLE 10.5** Suppose that Martha and Andy decide to wager (illegally) on the outcome of a boxing match. Each deposits money with a stakeholder, who agrees to pay the winner of the bet. At this point, each party has performed part of the agreement, but the illegal part of the agreement will not occur until the money is paid to the winner. Before such payment occurs, either party is entitled to withdraw from the agreement by giving notice to the stakeholder of his or her withdrawal. •

Fraud, Duress, or Undue Influence Whenever a plaintiff has been induced to enter into an illegal bargain as a result of fraud, duress, or undue influence, she or he can either enforce the contract or recover for its value.

Severable, or Divisible, Contracts A contract that is *severable,* or divisible, consists of distinct parts that can be performed separately, with separate consideration provided for each part. If a contract is divisible into legal and illegal portions, a court may enforce the legal portion but not the illegal one, so long as the illegal portion does not affect the essence of the bargain. This approach of the courts is consistent with the basic policy of enforcing the legal intentions of the contracting parties whenever possible. • **EXAMPLE 10.6** If an overly broad and thus illegal covenant not to compete was drafted into an employment contract, the court could declare the covenant illegal (and thus void) and enforce the remaining employment terms. •

12. *Hall v. Geiger-Jones Co.,* 242 U.S. 539, 37 S.Ct. 217, 61 L.Ed. 480 (1917).

APPLICATION Law and the Retailer . . .

Contracts with Minors and Intoxicated Persons*

Sales personnel, particularly those who are paid on a commission basis, are often eager to make contracts. Sometimes, however, these salespersons must deal with minors and intoxicated persons, both of whom have limited contractual capacity. Therefore, if you are a retailer, you should make sure that your employees are acquainted with the law governing minors and intoxicated persons.

Contracts with Minors

If your business involves selling consumer durables, such as furniture or automobiles, your sales personnel must be careful in forming contracts with minors and should heed the adage, "When in doubt, check." Remember that a contract signed by a minor (unless it is for necessaries) normally is voidable, and the minor may exercise the option to disaffirm the contract. Employees should demand proof of legal age when they have any doubt about whether a customer is a minor.

In addition, because the law governing minors' rights varies substantially from state to state, you should check with your attorney concerning the laws governing disaffirmance in your state. You and those you hire to sell your products should know, for example, what the consequences will be if a minor has misrepresented his or her age when forming a sales contract. Similarly, you need to find out whether and in what circumstances a minor, on disaffirming a contract, can be required to pay for damage to goods sold under the contract.

Dealing with Intoxicated Persons

Little need be said about a salesperson's dealings with obviously intoxicated persons. If the customer, despite intoxication, understands the legal consequences of the contract being signed, the contract is enforceable. Nonetheless, it may be extremely difficult to establish that the intoxicated customer understood the consequences of entering into the contract if the customer claims that she or he did not understand those consequences. Therefore, the best advice is, "When in doubt, don't." In other words, if you suspect a customer may be intoxicated, do not sign a contract with that customer.

Checklist for the Salesperson

1. When in doubt about the age of a customer to whom you are about to sell major consumer durable goods or anything other than necessaries, require proof of legal age.
2. If such proof is not forthcoming, require that a parent or guardian sign the contract.
3. Check with an attorney about the laws governing minors' contracts in your state.
4. Do not sign contracts with intoxicated customers.

*This *Application* is not meant to substitute for the services of an attorney who is licensed to practice law in your state.

Key Terms

adhesion contract 276
blue laws 272
blue sky laws 280
contractual capacity 265
disaffirmance 265
emancipation 269
exculpatory clause 278
necessaries 268
ratification 268
reformation 275
unconscionable contract or clause 276
usury 270

Chapter Summary Capacity and Legality

CONTRACTUAL CAPACITY	
Minors (See pages 265–269.)	A minor is a person who has not yet reached the age of majority. In most states, the age of majority is eighteen for contract purposes. Contracts with minors are voidable at the option of the minor. 1. *Disaffirmance*—Defined as the legal avoidance of a contractual obligation. a. Disaffirmance can take place (in most states) at any time during minority and within a reasonable time after the minor has reached the age of majority. b. If a minor disaffirms part of a contract, the entire contract must be disaffirmed. c. When disaffirming executed contracts, the minor has a duty to return received goods if they are still in the minor's control or (in some states) to pay their reasonable value. d. A minor who has committed an act of fraud (such as misrepresentation of age) will be denied the right to disaffirm by some courts. e. A minor may disaffirm a contract for necessaries but remains liable for the reasonable value of the goods. 2. *Ratification*—Defined as the acceptance, or affirmation, of a legal obligation; may be express or implied. a. Express ratification—Exists when the minor, through a writing or an oral agreement, explicitly assumes the obligations imposed by the contract. b. Implied ratification—Exists when the conduct of the minor is inconsistent with disaffirmance or when the minor fails to disaffirm an executed contract within a reasonable time after reaching the age of majority. 3. *Parents' liability*—Generally, except for contracts for necessaries, parents are not liable for the contracts made by minor children acting on their own, nor are parents liable for minors' torts except in certain circumstances. 4. *Emancipation*—Occurs when a child's parent or legal guardian relinquishes the legal right to exercise control over the child. Normally, a minor who leaves home to support himself or herself is considered emancipated. In some jurisdictions, minors themselves are permitted to petition for emancipation for limited purposes.
Intoxicated Persons (See page 269.)	1. A contract entered into by an intoxicated person is voidable at the option of the intoxicated person if the person was sufficiently intoxicated to lack mental capacity, even if the intoxication was voluntary. 2. A contract with an intoxicated person is enforceable if, despite being intoxicated, the person understood the legal consequences of entering into the contract.
Mentally Incompetent Persons (See pages 269–270.)	1. A contract made by a person adjudged by a court to be mentally incompetent is void. 2. A contract made by a mentally incompetent person not adjudged by a court to be mentally incompetent is voidable at the option of the mentally incompetent person.
LEGALITY	
Contracts Contrary to Statute (See pages 270–273.)	1. *Usury*—Usury occurs when a lender makes a loan at an interest rate above the lawful maximum. The maximum rate of interest varies from state to state. 2. *Gambling*—Gambling contracts that contravene (go against) state statutes are deemed illegal and thus void. 3. *Sabbath (Sunday) laws*—These laws prohibit the formation or the performance of certain contracts on Sunday. Such laws vary widely from state to state, and many states do not enforce them.

Chapter Summary Capacity and Legality—continued

Contracts Contrary to Statute—continued	4. *Licensing statutes*—Contracts entered into by persons who do not have a license, when one is required by statute, will not be enforceable *unless* the underlying purpose of the statute is to raise government revenues (and not to protect the public from unauthorized practitioners).
Contracts Contrary to Public Policy (See pages 274–279.)	1. *Contracts in restraint of trade*—Contracts to reduce or restrain free competition are illegal. Most such contracts are now prohibited by statutes. An exception is a *covenant not to compete.* It is usually enforced by the courts if the terms are ancillary to a contract (such as a contract for the sale of a business or an employment contract) and are reasonable as to time and area of restraint. Courts tend to scrutinize covenants not to compete closely. If a covenant is overbroad, a court may either reform the covenant to fall within reasonable constraints and then enforce the reformed contract or declare the covenant void and thus unenforceable. 2. *Unconscionable contracts and clauses*—When a contract or contract clause is so unfair that it is oppressive to one party, it can be deemed unconscionable; as such, it is illegal and cannot be enforced. 3. *Exculpatory clauses*—An exculpatory clause is a clause that releases a party from liability in the event of monetary or physical injury, no matter who is at fault. In certain situations, exculpatory clauses may be contrary to public policy and thus unenforceable.
Effect of Illegality (See pages 279–280.)	In general, an illegal contract is void, and the courts will not aid either party when both parties are considered to be equally at fault *(in pari delicto).* If the contract is executory, neither party can enforce it. If the contract is executed, there can be neither contractual nor quasi-contractual recovery. Exceptions (situations in which recovery is allowed): 1. When one party to the contract is relatively innocent. 2. When one party to the contract is a member of a group of persons protected by statute. 3. When either party seeks to recover consideration given for an illegal contract before the illegal act is performed. 4. When one party was induced to enter into an illegal bargain through fraud, duress, or undue influence.

For Review

① What are some exceptions to the rule that a minor can disaffirm any contract?

② Under what circumstances does intoxication make a contract voidable?

③ Does mental incompetence necessarily render a contract void?

④ Under what circumstances will a covenant not to compete be enforceable? When will such covenants not be enforced?

⑤ What is an exculpatory clause? In what circumstances might exculpatory clauses be enforced? When will they not be enforced?

Questions and Case Problems

10–1. Contracts by Minors. Kalen is a seventeen-year-old minor who has just graduated from high school. He is attending a university two hundred miles from home and has contracted to rent an apartment near the university for one year at $500 per month. He is working at a convenience store to earn enough income to be self-supporting. After living in the apartment and paying monthly rent for four months, he becomes involved in a dispute with his landlord. Kalen, still a minor, moves out and returns the key to the landlord. The landlord wants to hold Kalen liable for the balance of the payments due under the lease. Discuss fully Kalen's liability in this situation.

10–2. Covenants Not to Compete. Joseph, who owns the only pizza parlor in Middletown, learns that Giovanni is about to open a competing pizza parlor in the same small town, just a few blocks from Joseph's restaurant. Joseph offers Giovanni $10,000 in return for Giovanni's promise not to open a pizza parlor in the Middletown area. Giovanni accepts the $10,000 but goes ahead with his plans, in spite of the agreement. When Giovanni opens his restaurant for business, Joseph sues to enjoin (prevent) Giovanni's continued operation of his restaurant or to recover the $10,000. The court denies recovery. On what basis?

10–3. Intoxication. After Katie has several drinks one night, she sells Emily a valuable fur stole for $10. The next day, Katie offers the $10 to Emily and requests the return of her stole. Emily refuses, claiming that they had a valid contract of sale. Katie explains that she was intoxicated at the time the bargain was made, and thus the contract is voidable at her option. Who is right? Explain.

10–4. Mental Incompetence. Jermal has been the owner of a car dealership for a number of years. One day, Jermal sold one of his most expensive cars to Kessler. At the time of the sale, Jermal thought Kessler acted in a peculiar manner, but he gave the matter no further thought until four months later, when Kessler's court-appointed guardian appeared at Jermal's office, tendered back the car, and demanded Kessler's money back. The guardian informed Jermal that Kessler had been adjudicated mentally incompetent two months earlier by a proper court.

(a) Discuss the rights of the parties in this situation.
(b) If Kessler had been adjudicated mentally incompetent before the contract was formed, what would be the legal effect of the contract?

10–5. Licensing Statutes. State X requires that persons who prepare and serve liquor in the form of drinks at commercial establishments be licensed by the state to do so. The only requirement for obtaining a yearly license is that the person be at least twenty-one years old. Mickey, aged thirty-five, is hired as a bartender for the Southtown Restaurant. Gerald, a staunch alumnus of a nearby university, brings twenty of his friends to the restaurant to celebrate a football victory one afternoon. Gerald orders four rounds of drinks, and the bill is nearly $200. On learning that Mickey has failed to renew his bartender's license, Gerald refuses to pay, claiming that the contract is unenforceable. Discuss whether Gerald is correct.

10–6. Usury. Tony's Tortilla Factory, Inc., had two checking accounts with First Bank. Due to financial difficulties, Tony's wrote a total of 2,165 checks (totaling $88,000) for which there were insufficient funds in the accounts. First Bank paid the overdrawn checks but imposed an "NSF" (nonsufficient funds) fee of $20 for each check paid. The owners of Tony's sued First Bank and one of its officers, alleging, among other things, that the $20-per-check fee was essentially "interest" charged by the bank for Tony's use of the bank's funds (the funds the bank advanced to cover the bad checks); because the rate of "interest" charged by the bank ($20 per check) exceeded the rate allowed by law, it was usurious. First Bank claimed that its NSF fees were not interest but fees charged to cover its costs in processing checks drawn on accounts with insufficient funds. How should the court decide this issue? Discuss fully. [*First Bank v. Tony's Tortilla Factory, Inc.*, 877 S.W.2d 285 (Tex. 1994)]

10–7. Minority. Sergei Samsonov is a Russian and one of the top hockey players in the world. When Samsonov was seventeen years old, he signed a contract to play hockey for two seasons with the Central Sports Army Club, a Russian club known by the abbreviation CSKA. Before the start of the second season, Samsonov learned that because of a dispute between CSKA coaches, he would not be playing in Russia's premier hockey league. Samsonov hired Athletes and Artists, Inc. (A&A), an American sports agency, to make a deal with a U.S. hockey team. Samsonov signed a contract to play for the Detroit Vipers (whose corporate name was, at the time, Arena Associates, Inc.). Neither A&A nor Arena knew about the CSKA contract. CSKA filed a suit in a federal district court against Arena and others, alleging, among other things, wrongful interference with a contractual relationship. What effect will Samsonov's age have on the outcome of this suit? [*Central Sports Army Club v. Arena Associates, Inc.*, 952 F.Supp. 181 (S.D.N.Y. 1997)]

10–8. Exculpatory Clause. Norbert Eelbode applied for a job with Travelers Inn in the state of Washington. As part of the application process, Eelbode was sent to Laura Grothe, a physical therapist at Chec Medical Centers, Inc., for a preemployment physical exam. Before the exam, Eelbode signed a document that stated in part, "I hereby release Chec and the Washington Readicare Medical Group and its physicians from all liability arising from any injury to me resulting from my participation in the exam." During the exam, Grothe asked Eelbode to lift an item while bending from the waist using only his back with his knees locked. Eelbode experienced immediate sharp and burning pain in his lower back and down the back of his right leg. Eelbode filed a suit in a Washington state court against Grothe and Chec, claiming that he was injured because of an improperly administered back torso strength test. Citing the document that Eelbode signed, Grothe and Chec filed a motion for summary judgment. Should the court grant the motion? Why or why not? [*Eelbode v. Chec Medical Centers, Inc.*, 984 P.2d 436 (Wash.App. 1999)]

TEST YOUR KNOWLEDGE—ANSWER ON THE WEB

10–9. In 1993, Mutual Service Casualty Insurance Co. and its affiliates (collectively, MSI) hired Thomas Brass as an insurance agent. Three years later, Brass entered into a career agent's contract with MSI. This contract contained provisions regarding Brass's activities after termination. These provisions stated that, for a period of not less than one year, Brass could not solicit any MSI customers to "lapse, cancel, or replace" any insurance contract in force with MSI in an effort to take that business to a competitor. If he did, MSI could at any time refuse to pay the commissions that it otherwise owed him. The contract also restricted Brass from working for American National Insurance Co. for three years after termination. In 1998, Brass quit MSI and immediately went to work for American National, soliciting MSI customers. MSI filed a suit in a Wisconsin state court against Brass, claiming that he had violated the noncompete terms of his MSI contract. Should the court enforce the covenant not to compete? Why or why not? [*Mutual Service Casualty Insurance Co. v. Brass*, 625 N.W.2d 648 (Wis.App. 2001)]

A QUESTION OF ETHICS AND SOCIAL RESPONSIBILITY

10–10. Nancy Levy worked for Health Care Financial Enterprises, Inc., and signed a noncompete agreement in June 1992. When Levy left Health Care and opened her own similar business in 1993, Health Care brought a court action in a Florida state court to enforce the covenant not to compete. The trial court concluded that the noncompete agreement prevented Levy from working in too broad a geographic area and thus refused to enforce the agreement. A Florida appellate court, however, reversed the trial court's ruling and remanded the case with instructions that the trial court modify the geographic area to make it reasonable and then enforce the covenant. [*Health Care Financial Enterprises, Inc. v. Levy*, 715 So.2d 341 (Fla.App.4th 1998)]

1. At one time in Florida, under the common law, noncompete covenants were illegal, although modern Florida statutory law now allows such covenants to be enforced. Generally, what interests are served by refusing to enforce covenants not to compete? What interests are served by allowing them to be enforced?
2. What argument could be made in support of reforming (and then enforcing) illegal covenants not to compete? What argument could be made against this practice?

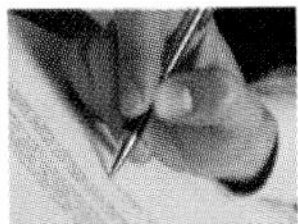

FOR CRITICAL ANALYSIS

10–11. Do you think that the advent of legalized forms of gambling, such as state-operated lotteries, is consistent with a continued public policy against the enforcement of gambling contracts? Why or why not?

Internet Exercises

Go to the *Business Law Today* home page at **http://blt.westbuslaw.com**. Select "Interactive Study Center" and then click on "Chapter 10." There you will find the following Internet research exercise that you can perform to learn more about the law governing contracts with minors:

Activity 10–1: Minors and the Law

Before the Test

Go to the *Business Law Today* home page at **http://blt.westbuslaw.com**. Click on "Interactive Quizzes." You will find at least twenty interactive questions relating to this chapter.

CHAPTER 11

Defenses to Contract Enforceability

"Law is a pledge that the citizens of a state will do justice to one another."

Aristotle, 384–322 B.C.E.
(Greek philosopher)

CHAPTER CONTENTS

LEARNING OBJECTIVES

After reading this chapter, you should be able to answer the following questions:

① In what types of situations might genuineness of assent to a contract's terms be lacking?

② What is the difference between a mistake of value or quality and a mistake of fact?

③ What elements must exist for fraudulent misrepresentation to occur?

④ What contracts must be in writing to be enforceable?

⑤ What is parol evidence? When is it admissible to clarify the terms of a written contract?

An otherwise valid contract may still be unenforceable if the parties have not genuinely assented to its terms. As mentioned in Chapter 8, lack of genuine assent is a *defense* to the enforcement of a contract. As Aristotle stated in the above quotation, the law seeks to ensure that "the citizens of a state will do justice to one another." If the law were to enforce contracts not genuinely assented to by the contracting parties, injustice would result. The first part of this chapter focuses on the kinds of factors that indicate that genuineness of assent to a contract may be lacking.

A contract that is otherwise valid may also be unenforceable if it is not in the proper form. For example, if a contract is required by law to be in writing and there is no written evidence of the contract, it may not be enforceable. In the second part of this chapter, we examine the kinds of contracts that require a writing under what is called the *Statute of Frauds*. The chapter concludes with a discussion of the parol evidence rule, under which courts determine the admissibility at trial of evidence extraneous (external) to written contracts.

Genuineness of Assent

Genuineness of assent may be lacking because of mistake, fraudulent misrepresentation, undue influence, or duress. Generally, a party who demonstrates that he or she did not genuinely assent to the terms of a contract can choose either to carry out the contract or to rescind (cancel) it and thus avoid the entire transaction.

MISTAKES

"Mistakes are the inevitable lot of mankind."

SIR GEORGE JESSEL, 1824–1883 (English jurist)

We all make mistakes, so it is not surprising that mistakes are made when contracts are created. In certain circumstances, contract law allows a contract to be avoided on the basis of mistake. Realize, though, that the concept of mistake in contract law has to do with mistaken assumptions relating to contract formation. For example, the error you make when you send your monthly bank loan payment to your plumber "by mistake" is totally different from the kind of mistake that we are discussing here. In contract law, a mistake may be a defense to the enforcement of a contract if it can be proved that the parties entered into the contract under different assumptions relating to the subject matter of the contract.

Courts have considerable difficulty in specifying the circumstances that justify allowing a mistake to invalidate a contract. Generally, though, courts distinguish between *mistakes as to judgment of market value or conditions* and *mistakes as to fact*. Only the latter normally have legal significance.

• **EXAMPLE 11.1** Jud Wheeler contracts to buy ten acres of land because he believes that he can resell the land at a profit to Bart. Can Jud escape his contractual obligations if it later turns out that he was mistaken? Not likely. Jud's overestimation of the value of the land or of Bart's interest in it is an ordinary risk of business for which a court normally will not provide relief. Now suppose that Jud purchases a painting of a landscape from Roth's Gallery. Both Jud and Roth believe that the painting is by the artist Van Gogh. Jud later discovers that the painting is a very clever fake. Because neither Jud nor Roth was aware of this fact when they made their deal, Jud can normally rescind the contract and recover the purchase price of the painting. •

Mistakes occur in two forms—*unilateral* and *bilateral (mutual)*. A unilateral mistake is made by only one of the contracting parties; a mutual mistake is made by both.

Unilateral Mistakes A unilateral mistake occurs when only one party is mistaken as to a *material fact*—that is, a fact important to the subject matter of the contract. Generally, a unilateral mistake does not afford the mistaken party any right to relief from the contract. In other words, the contract normally is enforceable against the mistaken party. • **EXAMPLE 11.2** Ellen intends to sell her motor home for $17,500. When she learns that Chin is interested in buying a used motor home, she types a letter offering to sell her vehicle to him. When typing the letter, however, she mistakenly keys in the price of $15,700. Chin writes back, accepting Ellen's offer. Even though Ellen intended to sell her motor home for $17,500, she has made a unilateral mistake and is bound by contract to sell the vehicle to Chin for $15,700. •

BE CAREFUL What a party to a contract knows or should know can determine whether the contract is enforceable.

There are at least two exceptions to this rule.[1] First, if the *other* party to the contract knows or should have known that a mistake of fact was made, the contract may not be enforceable. In the above example, if Chin knew that Ellen intended to sell her motor home for $17,500, then Ellen's unilateral mistake (stating $15,700 in her offer) may

1. The *Restatement (Second) of Contracts,* Section 153, liberalizes the general rule to take into account the modern trend of allowing avoidance in some circumstances even though only one party has been mistaken.

render the resulting contract unenforceable. The second exception arises when a unilateral mistake of fact was due to a mathematical mistake in addition, subtraction, division, or multiplication and was made inadvertently and without gross (extreme) negligence. If a contractor's bid was low because he or she made a mistake in addition when totaling the estimated costs, any contract resulting from the bid normally may be rescinded. Of course, in both situations, the mistake must still involve some *material fact.*

Bilateral (Mutual) Mistakes When both parties are mistaken about the same material fact, the contract can be rescinded by either party.[2] Note that, as with unilateral mistakes, the mistake must be about a *material fact* (one that is important and central to the contract—as was the "Van Gogh" painting in Example 11.1). If, instead, a mutual mistake concerns the later market value or quality of the object of the contract, the contract normally can be enforced by either party. This rule is based on the theory that both parties assume certain risks when they enter into a contract. Without this rule, almost any party who did not receive what she or he considered a fair bargain could argue bilateral mistake.

A word or term in a contract may be subject to more than one reasonable interpretation. In that situation, if the parties to the contract attach materially different meanings to the term, their mutual misunderstanding may allow the contract to be rescinded.

• **EXAMPLE 11.3** In *Raffles v. Wichelhaus,*[3] a classic case involving a mutual mistake, Wichelhaus purchased a shipment of cotton from Raffles to arrive on a ship called the *Peerless* from Bombay, India. Wichelhaus meant a ship called the *Peerless* sailing from Bombay in October; Raffles meant another ship called the *Peerless* sailing from Bombay in December. When the goods arrived on the December *Peerless,* Raffles delivered them to Wichelhaus. By that time, however, Wichelhaus was no longer willing to accept them. The British court hearing the case stated, "There is nothing on the face of the contract to show that any particular ship called the 'Peerless' was meant; but the moment it appears that two ships called the 'Peerless' were about to sail from Bombay there is a latent ambiguity. . . . That being so, there was no consensus . . . and therefore no binding contract." •

FRAUDULENT MISREPRESENTATION

"It was beautiful and simple as all truly great swindles are."
O. HENRY, 1862–1910 (American author)

Although fraud is a tort, the presence of fraud also affects the genuineness of the innocent party's consent to a contract. When an innocent party consents to a contract with fraudulent terms, the contract usually can be avoided because he or she has not *voluntarily* consented to the terms.[4] Normally, the innocent party can either rescind (cancel) the contract and be restored to his or her original position or enforce the contract and seek damages for injuries resulting from the fraud.

Typically, fraud involves three elements:

REMEMBER To collect damages in almost any lawsuit, there must be some sort of injury.

① A misrepresentation of a material fact must occur.

② There must be an intent to deceive.

③ The innocent party must justifiably rely on the misrepresentation.

2. *Restatement (Second) of Contracts,* Section 152.
3. 159 Eng.Rep. 375 (1864).
4. *Restatement (Second) of Contracts,* Sections 163 and 164.

Additionally, to collect damages, a party must have been injured as a result of the misrepresentation.

Fraudulent misrepresentation can also occur in the online environment—see, for example, the case discussed in this chapter's *Business Law in the Online World* feature. Indeed, a major challenge today is how to curb Internet fraud—a topic that will be explored further in Chapter 33, in the context of consumer law.

Misrepresentation Must Occur The first element of proving fraud is to show that misrepresentation of a material fact has occurred. This misrepresentation can take the form of words or actions. For example, an art gallery owner's statement "This painting is a Picasso" is a misrepresentation of fact if the painting was done by another artist.

BUSINESS LAW: //in the Online World

Hotmail versus the Spammers

Hotmail Corporation provides free e-mail service to more than eighty million subscribers. To obtain the service, a prospective subscriber goes to Hotmail's Web site and clicks on an "I accept" button to indicate agreement to Hotmail's "Terms of Service." These terms prohibit a subscriber from using the service to send spam—unsolicited bulk e-mail similar to junk mail sent through the U.S. Postal Service. What if a subscriber, after agreeing to the Terms of Service, uses Hotmail's service to send spam? Does Hotmail have a cause of action against the subscriber?

This issue came before the court in a case brought by Hotmail against Van$ Money Pie, Inc., and others (the defendants) after they began using Hotmail's service to send spam offering to sell pornography, "get-rich-quick" schemes, and other items. Hotmail was soon inundated with hundreds of thousands of misdirected responses to the spam, including complaints from subscribers and returned e-mail that had been sent to nonexistent or incorrect addresses. The flood of responses took up a substantial amount of Hotmail's computer capacity, threatened to adversely affect subscribers' ability to send and receive e-mail, and resulted in significant costs to Hotmail for increased personnel to sort and respond to the complaints. Hotmail sued the defendants for, among other things, fraud and breach of contract and asked the court to enjoin (prohibit) the defendants from using Hotmail's service.

The Fraud Issue

The court concluded that Hotmail had presented enough evidence of fraud to warrant the granting of a preliminary injunction against the defendants' further use of Hotmail's service. The evidence indicated that the defendants had promised to abide by the Terms of Service without any intention of doing so and had suppressed the fact that such accounts were created for the purpose of facilitating a spamming operation. Furthermore, Hotmail had relied on the misrepresentations to allow e-mails to be transmitted over its services and to take up storage space on its computers.

Breach of Contract

A threshold issue in this case was whether Hotmail's online service agreement, with its click-on acceptance button, was an enforceable contract. Significantly, the court held that it was (for an examination of the evolution of the law regarding click-on acceptances, see Chapter 17). The court also held that the evidence indicated that the defendants had breached this contract by using their Hotmail accounts to send spam. The court concluded that "if defendants are not enjoined they will continue to create such accounts in violation of the Terms of Service."[a]

FOR CRITICAL ANALYSIS

What if the defendants claimed that they had not read the Terms of Service before they clicked on the "I accept" button? Would this claim affect the enforceability of the contract?

a. *Hotmail Corp. v. Van$ Money Pie, Inc.*, 1998 WL 388389 (N.D.Cal. 1998).

A statement of opinion is generally not subject to a claim of fraud. For example, claims such as "This computer will never break down" and "This car will last for years and years" are statements of opinion, not fact, and contracting parties should recognize them as such and not rely on them. A fact is objective and verifiable; an opinion is usually subject to debate. Therefore, a seller is allowed to "huff and puff his wares" without being liable for fraud. In certain cases, however, particularly when a naïve purchaser relies on an expert's opinion, the innocent party may be entitled to rescission or reformation (an equitable remedy granted by a court in which the terms of a contract are altered to reflect the true intentions of the parties).

In the following classic case, the court addressed the issue of whether statements made by instructors at a dancing school to one of the school's dance students qualified as statements of opinion or statements of fact.

Landmark and Classic Cases

CASE 11.1 Vokes v. Arthur Murray, Inc.

District Court of Appeal of Florida, Second District, 1968.
212 So.2d 906.

FACTS Audrey Vokes was a fifty-one-year-old widow. While she was attending a dance party at Davenport's School of Dancing, an Arthur Murray dancing school, an instructor sold her eight half-hour dance lessons for the sum of $14.50. Thereafter, over a period of less than sixteen months, she was sold a total of fourteen dance courses, which amounted to 2,302 hours of dancing lessons for a total cash outlay of $31,090.45 (in 2002, this would amount to more than $120,000). All of these lessons were sold to her by salespersons who continually assured her that she was very talented, that she was progressing in her lessons, that she had great dance potential, and that they were "developing her into a beautiful dancer." Vokes contended that, in fact, she was not progressing in her dancing ability, had no "dance aptitude," and had difficulty even "hearing the musical beat." She filed suit against the school in a Florida state court, seeking rescission of her contract on the ground of fraudulent misrepresentation. When the trial court dismissed her complaint, she appealed.

ISSUE Could Vokes's contract be rescinded because the salespersons misrepresented her dancing ability?

DECISION Yes. The Florida appellate court reinstated Vokes's complaint and remanded the case to the trial court for further proceedings consistent with the appellate court's opinion.

REASON The court held that Vokes could avoid the contract because it was procured by false representations that she had a promising career in dancing. The court acknowledged that ordinarily, to be grounds for rescission, a misrepresentation must be one of fact rather than of opinion. The court concluded that "[a] statement of a party having * * * superior knowledge may be regarded as a statement of fact although it would be considered as opinion if the parties were dealing on equal terms. It could be reasonably supposed here that defendants [the dance studio] had 'superior knowledge' as to whether plaintiff had 'dance potential.' "

COMMENT *This case has become a classic in contract law because it so clearly illustrates an important principle. The general rule (that a misrepresentation must be one of fact rather than one of opinion to be actionable) does not apply when the parties do not deal at arm's length or when the person to whom representations are made (such as Vokes, in this case) does not have an equal opportunity to become aware of the truth or falsity of the fact represented.*

Misrepresentation by Conduct. Misrepresentation can occur by conduct, as well as through express oral or written statements. For example, if a seller, by her or his actions, prevents a buyer from learning of some fact that is material to the contract, such an action constitutes misrepresentation by conduct.[5] • **EXAMPLE 11.4** Cummings contracts to purchase a racehorse from Garner. The horse is blind in one eye, but when Garner shows the horse, he skillfully conceals this fact by keeping the horse's head turned so that Cummings does not see the defect. The concealment constitutes fraud. • Another example of misrepresentation by conduct is the false denial of knowledge or information concerning facts that are material to the contract when such knowledge or information is requested.

"Ignorance of the law is no excuse in any country. If it were, the laws would lose their effect, because ignorance can always be pretended."

THOMAS JEFFERSON, 1743–1826 (Third president of the United States, 1801–1809)

Misrepresentation of Law. Misrepresentation of law does not *ordinarily* entitle a party to be relieved of a contract. • **EXAMPLE 11.5** Debbie has a parcel of property that she is trying to sell to Barry. Debbie knows that a local ordinance prohibits building anything higher than three stories on the property. Nonetheless, she tells Barry, "You can build a condominium fifty stories high if you want to." Barry buys the land and later discovers that Debbie's statement is false. Normally, Barry cannot avoid the contract because under the common law, people are assumed to know state and local laws. • Exceptions to this rule occur, however, when the misrepresenting party is in a profession known to require greater knowledge of the law than the average citizen possesses.

Misrepresentation by Silence. Ordinarily, neither party to a contract has a duty to come forward and disclose facts, and a contract normally will not be set aside because certain pertinent information has not been volunteered. • **EXAMPLE 11.6** Suppose that you are selling a car that has been in an accident and has been repaired. You do not need to volunteer this information to a potential buyer. If, however, the purchaser asks

5. *Restatement (Second) of Contracts,* Section 160.

Workers excavate a site and bury a sewer line. Would the party who contracted for this work be liable for fraud if the party knew, or should have known, that subsoil conditions could increase the expense of the work and failed to disclose this to the bidders?

you if the car has had extensive body work and you lie, you have committed a fraudulent misrepresentation.●

Generally, if a serious defect or a serious potential problem is known to the seller but cannot reasonably be suspected to be known by the buyer, the seller may have a duty to speak. ● **EXAMPLE 11.7** Suppose that a city fails to disclose to bidders for sewer-construction contracts the fact that subsoil conditions will cause great expense in constructing the sewer. In this situation, the city has committed fraud.[6]● Also, when the parties are in a *fiduciary relationship* (one of trust, such as partners, physician and patient, or attorney and client), there is a duty to disclose material facts; failure to do so may constitute fraud.

SCIENTER
Knowledge by the misrepresenting party that material facts have been falsely represented or omitted with an intent to deceive.

Intent to Deceive The second element of fraud is knowledge on the part of the misrepresenting party that facts have been misrepresented. This element, normally called ***scienter,***[7] or "guilty knowledge," generally signifies that there was an intent to deceive. *Scienter* clearly exists if a party knows that a fact is not as stated. *Scienter* also exists if a party makes a statement that he or she believes not to be true or makes a statement recklessly, without regard to whether it is true or false. Finally, this element is met if a party says or implies that a statement is made on some basis, such as personal knowledge or personal investigation, when it is not.

● **EXAMPLE 11.8** Suppose that Rolando, when selling a house to Cariton, tells Cariton that the plumbing pipe is of a certain quality. Rolando knows nothing about the quality of the pipe but does not believe it to be what she is representing it to be (and in fact it is not what she says it is). Rolando's statement induces Cariton to buy the house. Rolando's statement is a fraudulent misrepresentation because she does not believe that what she says is true and because she knows that she does not have any basis for making the statement. Cariton can avoid the contract.●

Can an employer avoid liability for the breach of a contract that was induced by an employee's fraud during the hiring process? That was the question in the following case.

6. *City of Salinas v. Souza & McCue Construction Co.,* 66 Cal.2d 217, 424 P.2d 921, 57 Cal.Rptr. 337 (1967). Normally, the seller must disclose only "latent" defects—that is, defects that would not readily be discovered. Thus, termites in a house would not be a latent defect, because a buyer could normally discover their presence.
7. Pronounced sy-*en*-ter.

CASE 11.2 Sarvis v. Vermont State Colleges

Supreme Court of Vermont, 2001.
772 A.2d 494.
http://dol.state.vt.us [a]

FACTS In 1995, Robert Sarvis was convicted of bank fraud, ordered to pay more than $12 million in restitution, and sentenced to forty-six months in prison. While incarcerated, he worked in the prison's electrical department. Two weeks after his release in 1998, he applied for an adjunct professor position at Community College of Vermont (CCV). On his résumé, he stated that during "1984–1998" he was "President and Chairman of the Board" of "CMI International Inc., Boston, Massachusetts," where he was "[r]esponsible for all operations and financial matters." For a position as CCV's Coordinator of Academic Services, he submitted a second résumé, on which he added, "1998–present. Semi-retired. Adjunct Instructor of Business at Colby-Sawyer College and Franklin Pierce College." He stated that he was "well

a. In the "Vermont Government and Library Information" section, click on "Legal Decisions." On that page, click on "Supreme Court Opinions." In the result, click on "VT Supreme Court Opinions—Current List," then scroll to the case name and click on it to access the opinion. The Vermont Department of Libraries maintains this Web site.

CASE 11.2—Continued

equipped to teach" business law and business ethics, that he had "a great interest and knowledge of business law," and that he believed he would do "an excellent job" teaching a business ethics class because this subject was "of particular concern" to him. CCV hired him as academic coordinator, teacher, and independent studies instructor. After he began work, his probation officer alerted CCV to Sarvis's criminal history, and CCV terminated his employment. Sarvis filed a suit in a Vermont state court against CCV, alleging, among other things, breach of contract. CCV filed a motion for summary judgment, in part on the ground of fraud, seeking rescission. The court granted CCV's motion, and Sarvis appealed to the Vermont Supreme Court.

ISSUE Can a partial disclosure during the preemployment process, with an intent to deceive, support the termination of an employment contract?

DECISION Yes. The Vermont Supreme Court affirmed the lower court's judgment and rescinded the contract between Sarvis and CCV.

REASON The state supreme court explained that "[t]he misrepresentation in this case occurred through plaintiff's partial disclosure of his past work history and references and his effort to limit defendant's inquiry into his past." The court emphasized that Sarvis "was not silent; he carefully drafted his résumés and supplemental materials to lead defendant to believe he had made a full disclosure about his past and his qualifications. He listed classes in business ethics and law in which he claimed he had the highest level of capability and knowledge but failed to mention his felony bank fraud conviction. Plaintiff assured defendant that making additional inquiries into his background would have revealed 'more of the same' type of information * * *. This was not true. Contact with plaintiff's probation officer or supervisor at the * * * prison would have notified defendant of plaintiff's fraud convictions, period of incarceration, and work history at the prison."

FOR CRITICAL ANALYSIS—Ethical Consideration *Is honesty an implicit duty of every employee?*

Reliance on the Misrepresentation The third element of fraud is *justifiable reliance* on the misrepresentation of fact. The deceived party must have a justifiable reason for relying on the misrepresentation, and the misrepresentation must be an important factor (but not necessarily the sole factor) in inducing the party to enter into the contract.

REMEMBER An opinion is not a contract offer, not a contract term, and not fraud.

Reliance is not justified if the innocent party knows the true facts or relies on obviously extravagant statements. • **EXAMPLE 11.9** If a used-car dealer tells you, "This old Cadillac will get over sixty miles to the gallon," you normally would not be justified in relying on this statement. Suppose, however, that Merkel, a bank director, induces O'Connell, a co-director, to sign a statement that the bank's assets will satisfy its liabilities by telling O'Connell, "We have plenty of assets to satisfy our creditors." This statement is false. If O'Connell knows the true facts or, as a bank director, should know the true facts, he is not justified in relying on Merkel's statement. If O'Connell does not know the true facts, however, *and has no way of finding them out,* he may be justified in relying on the statement.•

ETHICAL ISSUE 11.1

How much information must employers disclose to prospective employees?

One of the problems employers face is that it is not always clear what information they should disclose to prospective employees. To lure qualified employees, employers are often tempted to "promise the moon" to prospective employees and paint their companies' prospects as bright. Employers must be careful, though, to avoid any conduct that could be interpreted by a court as intentionally deceptive. In particular, they must avoid making any statements about their companies' future prospects or financial health that they know to be false. If they do make a false statement on which a prospective employee relies to his or her detriment, they may be sued for fraudulent misrepresentation. In one case, for example, an employee accepted a job with a brokerage firm, relying on assurances that the firm was not about to be sold. In fact, as the employee was able to prove in his later lawsuit against the firm for fraud, negotiations to sell the firm were under way at the time he was hired.[8] Generally, employers must be truthful in their hiring to avoid possible lawsuits for fraudulent misrepresentation.

Injury to the Innocent Party Most courts do not require a showing of injury when the action is to *rescind* (cancel) the contract—these courts hold that because rescission returns the parties to the positions they held before the contract was made, a showing of injury to the innocent party is unnecessary.[9]

For a person to recover damages caused by fraud, however, proof of an injury is universally required. The measure of damages is ordinarily equal to the property's value had it been delivered as represented, less the actual price paid for the property. In actions based on fraud, courts often award *punitive,* or *exemplary, damages,* which are granted to a plaintiff over and above the proved, actual compensation for the loss. As pointed out in Chapter 4, punitive damages are based on the public-policy consideration of punishing the defendant or setting an example to deter similar wrongdoing by others.

UNDUE INFLUENCE

Undue influence arises from relationships in which one party can greatly influence another party, thus overcoming that party's free will. Minors and elderly people, for example, are often under the influence of guardians. If a guardian induces a young or elderly ward (a person placed by a court under the care of a guardian) to enter into a contract that benefits the guardian, the guardian may have exerted undue influence.

Undue influence can arise from a number of confidential or fiduciary relationships, including attorney-client, physician-patient, guardian-ward, parent-child, husband-wife, and trustee-beneficiary relationships. The essential feature of undue influence is that the party being taken advantage of does not, in reality, exercise free will in entering into a contract. A contract entered into under excessive or undue influence lacks genuine assent and is therefore voidable.[10]

DURESS

Assent to the terms of a contract is not genuine if one of the parties is forced into the agreement. Forcing a party to enter into a contract because of the fear created by threats is referred to as *duress.*[11] In addition, inducing consent to a contract through blackmail or extortion constitutes duress. Duress is both a defense to the enforcement of a contract and a ground for rescission, or cancellation, of a contract. Therefore, a party who signs a contract under duress can choose to carry out the contract or to

8. *McConkey v. Zarb,* No. 845797 (Super.Ct. Essex Co., N.J. 2000). For a discussion of this unpublished case, see "Employment Fraud," *The National Law Journal,* November 27, 2000, p. A10.
9. See, for example, *Kaufman v. Jaffe,* 244 App.Div. 344, 279 N.Y.S. 392 (1935).
10. *Restatement (Second) of Contracts,* Section 177.
11. *Restatement (Second) of Contracts,* Sections 174 and 175.

avoid the entire transaction. (The wronged party usually has this choice in cases in which assent is not real or genuine.)

Economic need is generally not sufficient to constitute duress, even when one party exacts a very high price for an item the other party needs. If the party exacting the price also creates the need, however, economic duress may be found. • **EXAMPLE 11.10** The Internal Revenue Service (IRS) assessed a large tax and penalty against Weller. Weller retained Eyman to resist the assessment. Two days before the deadline for filing a reply with the IRS, Eyman declined to represent Weller unless he agreed to pay a very high fee for Eyman's services. The agreement was held to be unenforceable.[12] Although Eyman had threatened only to withdraw his services, something that he was legally entitled to do, he was responsible for delaying his withdrawal until the last two days. Because Weller was forced into either signing the contract or losing his right to challenge the IRS assessment, the agreement was secured under duress. •

The Statute of Frauds—Requirement of a Writing

STATUTE OF FRAUDS
A state statute under which certain types of contracts must be in writing to be enforceable.

Today, every state has a statute that stipulates what types of contracts must be in writing. In this text, we refer to such statutes as the **Statute of Frauds.** The primary purpose of the statute is to ensure that, for certain types of contracts, there is reliable evidence of the contracts and their terms. These types of contracts are those deemed historically to be important or complex. Although the statutes vary slightly from state to state, the following types of contracts are normally required to be in writing or evidenced by a written memorandum:

① Contracts involving interests in land.

② Contracts that cannot by their terms be performed within one year from the date of formation.

③ Collateral contracts, such as promises to answer for the debt or duty of another.

④ Promises made in consideration of marriage.

⑤ Contracts for the sale of goods priced at $500 or more.

KEEP IN MIND Although only certain types of contracts must be in writing to be enforceable, it is good practice to put other contracts in writing as well to prevent disputes over contract terms.

Agreements or promises that fit into one or more of these categories are said to "fall under" or "fall within" the Statute of Frauds. (Certain exceptions are made to the applicability of the Statute of Frauds in some circumstances, however, as you will read later in this section.)

The actual name of the Statute of Frauds is misleading because it does not apply to fraud. Rather, the statute denies enforceability to certain contracts that do not comply with its requirements. The name derives from an English act passed in 1677, which is presented as this chapter's *Landmark in the Law* feature on the next page.

CONTRACTS INVOLVING INTERESTS IN LAND

Land is a form of *real property,* or real estate, which includes not only land but all physical objects that are permanently attached to the soil, such as buildings, plants, trees, and the soil itself. Under the Statute of Frauds, a contract involving an interest in land, to be enforceable, must be evidenced by a writing.[13] If Carol, for example, contracts

12. *Thompson Crane & Trucking Co. v. Eyman,* 123 Cal.App.2d 904, 267 P.2d 1043 (1954).

13. In some states, the contract will be enforced, however, if each party admits to the existence of the oral contract in court or admits to its existence during discovery before trial (see Chapter 3).

LANDMARK IN THE LAW

The Statute of Frauds

On April 12, 1677, the English Parliament passed "An Act for the Prevention of Frauds and Perjuries." Four days later, the act was signed by King Charles II and became the law of the land. The act contained twenty-five sections and stipulated that if certain types of contracts were to be enforceable by the courts, they would henceforth have to be in writing or evidenced by a written memorandum.[a]

Enforcement of Oral Promises The English act was enacted specifically to prevent the further perpetration of the many frauds that had been brought about through the perjured testimony of witnesses in cases involving breached oral agreements, for which no written evidence existed. During the early history of the common law in England, oral contracts were generally not enforced by the courts, but in the fourteenth century, they began to be enforced in certain *assumpsit* actions.[b] These actions, to which the origins of modern contract law are traced, allowed a party to sue and obtain relief in cases in which a promise or contract had been breached. Enforcement of oral promises in actions in *assumpsit* became a common practice in the king's courts during the next two centuries.

King Charles II, under whose reign parliament enacted the Statute of Frauds. What reasons support the application of the statute today?

Problems with Oral Contracts Because courts enforced oral contracts on the strength of oral testimony by witnesses, it was not too difficult to evade justice by alleging that a contract had been breached and then procuring "convincing" witnesses to support the claim. The possibility of fraud in such actions was enhanced by the fact that in seventeenth-century England, courts did not allow oral testimony to be given by the parties to a lawsuit—or by any parties with an interest in the litigation, such as husbands or wives. Defense against actions for breach of contract was thus limited to written evidence and the testimony given by third parties. The Statute of Frauds was enacted to minimize the possibility of fraud in oral contracts relating to certain types of transactions.

APPLICATION TO TODAY'S WORLD

Essentially, the Statute of Frauds offers a defense against contracts that fall under the statute. Indeed, the statute has been criticized by some because, although it was created to protect the innocent, it can also be used as a technical defense by a party who has breached a genuine, mutually agreed-on oral contract—if the contract falls within the Statute of Frauds. For this reason, some legal scholars believe the act has caused more fraud than it has prevented. Nonetheless, U.S. courts continue to apply the Statute of Frauds to disputes involving oral contracts. The definitions of such terms as writing *and* signature, *however, are changing as we move further into an electronic age—as you will read in Chapter 17, which covers e-contracts.*

a. These contracts are discussed in the text of this chapter.

b. *Assumpsit* is Latin for "he undertook" or "he promised." The emergence of remedies given on the basis of breached promises and duties dates to these actions. One of the earliest occurred in 1370, when the court allowed an individual to sue a person who, in trying to cure the plaintiff's horse, had acted so negligently that the horse died. Another such action was permitted in 1375, when a plaintiff obtained relief for having been maimed by a surgeon hired to cure him.

ON THE WEB
Professor Eric Talley of the University of Southern California provides an interesting discussion of the history and current applicability of the Statute of Frauds, both internationally and in the United States, at
http://www-bcf.usc.edu/~etalley/frauds.html.

orally to sell Seaside Shelter to Axel but later decides not to sell, Axel cannot enforce the contract. Similarly, if Axel refuses to close the deal, Carol cannot force Axel to pay for the land by bringing a lawsuit. The Statute of Frauds is a *defense* to the enforcement of this type of oral contract.

A contract for the sale of land ordinarily involves the entire interest in the real property, including buildings, growing crops, vegetation, minerals, timber, and anything else affixed to the land. Therefore, a *fixture* (personal property so affixed or so used as to become a part of the realty—see Chapter 37) is treated as real property.

The Statute of Frauds requires written contracts not just for the sale of land but also for the transfer of other interests in land, such as mortgages and leases. We describe these other interests in Chapter 37.

THE ONE-YEAR RULE

Contracts that cannot, *by their own terms,* be performed within one year from the day after the contract is formed must be in writing to be enforceable. Because disputes over such contracts are unlikely to occur until some time after the contracts are made, resolution of these disputes is difficult unless the contract terms have been put in writing. The one-year period begins to run *the day after the contract is made.* Exhibit 11–1 illustrates the one-year rule.

Normally, the test for determining whether an oral contract is enforceable under the one-year rule of the Statute of Frauds is not whether the agreement is *likely* to be performed within one year from the date of contract formation but whether performance within a year is *possible.* When performance of a contract is objectively impossible during the one-year period, the oral contract will be unenforceable.

COLLATERAL PROMISES

COLLATERAL PROMISE
A secondary promise that is ancillary (subsidiary) to a principal transaction or primary contractual relationship, such as a promise made by one person to pay the debts of another if the latter fails to perform. A collateral promise normally must be in writing to be enforceable.

A **collateral promise**, or secondary promise, is one that is ancillary (subsidiary) to a principal transaction or primary contractual relationship. In other words, a collateral promise is one made by a third party to assume the debts or obligations of a primary party to a contract if that party does not perform. Any collateral promise of this nature falls under the Statute of Frauds and therefore must be in writing to be enforceable. To understand this concept, it is important to distinguish between primary and secondary promises and obligations.

Primary versus Secondary Obligations As a general rule, a contract in which a party assumes a primary obligation does not need to be in writing to be enforceable.

EXHIBIT 11–1 THE ONE-YEAR RULE

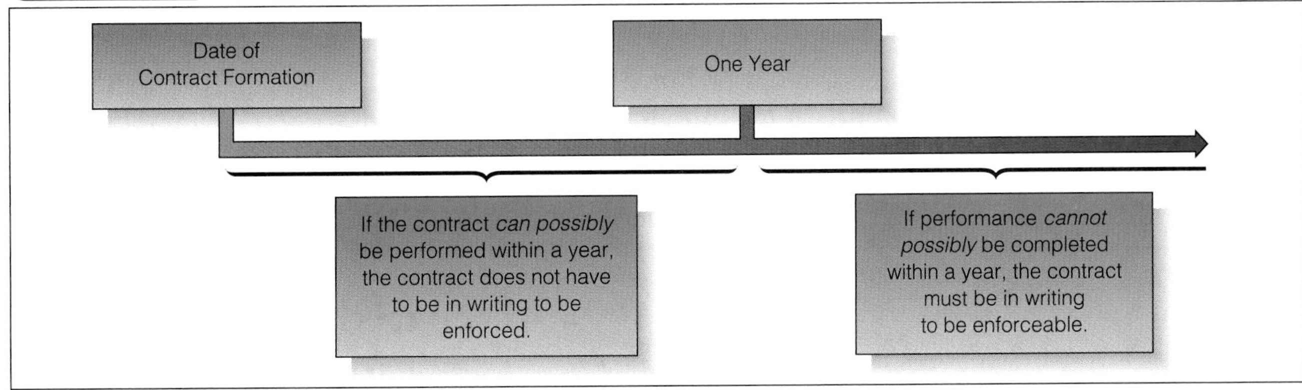

• **EXAMPLE 11.11** Suppose that Kenneth orally contracts with Joanne's Floral Boutique to send his mother a dozen roses for Mother's Day. Kenneth promises to pay the boutique when he receives the bill for the flowers. Kenneth is a direct party to this contract and has incurred a *primary* obligation under the contract. Because he is a party to the contract and has a primary obligation to Joanne's Floral Boutique, this contract does not fall under the Statute of Frauds and does not have to be in writing to be enforceable. If Kenneth fails to pay the florist and the florist sues him for payment, Kenneth cannot raise the Statute of Frauds as a defense. He cannot claim that the contract is unenforceable because it was not in writing.•

In contrast, a contract in which a party assumes a secondary obligation does have to be in writing to be enforceable. • **EXAMPLE 11.12** Suppose that Kenneth's mother borrows $1,000 from the Medford Trust Company on a promissory note payable six months later. Kenneth promises the bank officer handling the loan that he will pay the $1,000 *if his mother does not pay the loan on time.* Kenneth, in this situation, becomes what is known as a *guarantor* on the loan. That is, he is guaranteeing to the bank (the creditor) that he will pay the loan if his mother fails to do so. This kind of collateral promise, in which the guarantor states that he or she will become responsible only if the primary party does not perform, must be in writing to be enforceable.• We return to the concept of guaranty and the distinction between primary and secondary obligations in Chapter 23, in the context of creditors' rights.

An Exception—The "Main Purpose" Rule An oral promise to answer for the debt of another is covered by the Statute of Frauds *unless* the guarantor's purpose in accepting secondary liability is to secure a personal benefit. Under the "main purpose" rule, this type of contract need not be in writing.[14] The assumption is that a court can infer from the circumstances of a case whether a "leading objective" of the promisor was to secure a personal benefit.

• **EXAMPLE 11.13** Oswald contracts with Machine Manufacturing Company to have some machines custom-made for Oswald's factory. She promises Allrite Materials Supply Company, Machine Manufacturing's supplier, that if Allrite continues to deliver materials to Machine Manufacturing, she will guarantee payment. This promise need not be in writing, even though the effect may be to pay the debt of another, because Oswald's main purpose is to secure a benefit for herself.[15]•

Another typical application of the so-called main purpose doctrine is the situation in which one creditor guarantees the debtor's debt to another creditor to forestall litigation. This allows the debtor to remain in business long enough to generate profits sufficient to pay *both* creditors. In this situation, the guaranty does not need to be in writing to be enforceable.

PROMISES MADE IN CONSIDERATION OF MARRIAGE

PRENUPTIAL AGREEMENT
An agreement made before marriage that defines each partner's ownership rights in the other partner's property. Prenuptial agreements must be in writing to be enforceable.

A unilateral promise to pay a sum of money or to give property in consideration of marriage must be in writing. If Mr. Baumann promises to pay Joe Villard $10,000 if Villard marries Baumann's daughter, the promise must be in writing to be enforceable. The same rule applies to **prenuptial agreements**—agreements made before marriage (also called *antenuptial agreements*) that define each partner's ownership rights in the other partner's property. For example, a prospective wife or husband may wish to limit the amount the prospective spouse can obtain if the marriage ends in divorce. Prenuptial agreements made in consideration of marriage must be in writing to be enforceable.

14. *Restatement (Second) of Contracts,* Section 116.

15. See *Kampman v. Pittsburgh Contracting and Engineering Co.,* 316 Pa. 502, 175 A. 396 (1934).

"And do you, Bob, agree to the wording of Alice's pre-nuptial agreements, and do you, Alice, agree to the wording of Bob's?"

Generally, courts tend to give more credence to prenuptial agreements that are accompanied by consideration. • **EXAMPLE 11.14** Maureen, who has little money, marries Kaiser, who has a net worth of $300 million. Kaiser has several children, and he wants them to receive most of his wealth on his death. Prior to their marriage, Maureen and Kaiser draft and sign a prenuptial agreement in which Kaiser promises to give Maureen $100,000 per year for the rest of her life should they divorce. As consideration for consenting to this amount, Kaiser offers Maureen $500,000. If Maureen consents to the agreement and accepts the $500,000, very likely a court would hold this to be a valid prenuptial agreement should the agreement ever be contested. •

ETHICAL ISSUE 11.2

Should prenuptial agreements be enforced if one party did not have advice of counsel?

Cases occasionally come before the courts in which a party to a prenuptial agreement claims that the agreement should not be enforced because he or she was not advised to consult an attorney before signing the agreement. In one case, for example, a woman challenged the enforceability of a prenuptial agreement on the ground that her husband's lawyer, who was hired to draft the agreement, did not advise her to have it reviewed by her own attorney. The Supreme Court of North Dakota held that the agreement may be unenforceable. The court joined a number of other jurisdictions in concluding that advice of independent counsel is a significant factor in determining whether a party signed a prenuptial agreement voluntarily.[16]

It is not the only factor, however. In a California case, a wife alleged that she had not signed a prenuptial agreement knowingly or voluntarily on the ground that her

16. *Estate of Lutz,* 563 N.W.2d 90 (N.Dak. 1997).

husband's attorney, who drafted the agreement, did not advise her to obtain independent counsel and did not inform her that by signing the agreement she would forfeit certain property rights. Nevertheless, the court held that the agreement was enforceable because the evidence indicated that the woman agreed to the terms of the contract and had an opportunity to obtain counsel but failed to do so.[17]

CONTRACTS FOR THE SALE OF GOODS

ON THE WEB The online version of UCC Section 2–201 on the Statute of Frauds includes links to definitions of certain terms used in the section. To access this site, go to **http://www.law.cornell.edu/ucc/2/2-201.html**.

The Uniform Commercial Code (UCC) contains Statute of Frauds provisions that require written evidence of a contract. Section 2–201 contains the major provision, which generally requires a writing or memorandum for the sale of goods priced at $500 or more. A writing that will satisfy the UCC requirement need only state the quantity term; other terms agreed on need not be stated "accurately" in the writing, as long as they adequately reflect both parties' intentions. The contract will not be enforceable, however, for any quantity greater than that set forth in the writing. In addition, the writing must be signed by the person against whom enforcement is sought. Beyond these two requirements, the writing need not designate the buyer or the seller, the terms of payment, or the price.

EXCEPTIONS TO THE STATUTE OF FRAUDS

Exceptions to the applicability of the Statute of Frauds are made in certain situations. We describe those situations here.

Partial Performance In cases involving contracts relating to the transfer of interests in land, if the purchaser has paid part of the price, taken possession, and made valuable improvements to the property, and if the parties cannot be returned to their status quo prior to the contract, a court may grant *specific performance* (performance of the contract according to its precise terms). Whether a court will enforce an oral contract for an interest in land when partial performance has taken place is usually determined by the degree of injury that would be suffered if the court chose *not* to enforce the oral contract. In some states, mere reliance on certain types of oral contracts is enough to remove them from the Statute of Frauds.

Under the UCC, an oral contract for goods priced at $500 or more is enforceable to the extent that a seller accepts payment or a buyer accepts delivery of the goods.[18] For example, if Ajax Corporation orders by telephone twenty crates of bleach from Cloney, Inc., and repudiates the contract after ten crates have been delivered and accepted, Cloney can enforce the contract to the extent of the ten crates accepted by Ajax.

Admissions In some states, if a party against whom enforcement of an oral contract is sought admits in pleadings, testimony, or otherwise in court proceedings that a contract for sale was made, the contract will be enforceable.[19] A contract subject to the UCC will be enforceable, but only to the extent of the quantity admitted.[20] Thus, if the president of Ajax Corporation admits under oath that an oral agreement was made with Cloney, Inc., for the twenty crates of bleach, the agreement will be enforceable to that extent.

17. See, for example, *In re Marriage of Bonds,* 24 Cal.4th 1, 5 P.3d 815, 99 Cal.Rptr.2d 252 (2000).
18. UCC 2–201(3)(c). See Chapter 14.
19. *Restatement (Second) of Contracts,* Section 133.
20. UCC 2–201(3)(b). See Chapter 14.

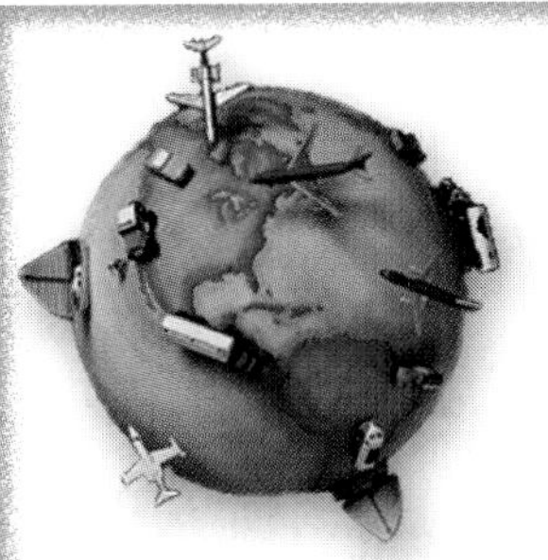

INTERNATIONAL PERSPECTIVE

The Statute of Frauds and International Sales Contracts

As you will read in Chapter 14, the Convention on Contracts for the International Sale of Goods (CISG) provides rules that govern international sales contracts between citizens of countries that have ratified the convention (agreement). Article 11 of the CISG does not incorporate any Statute of Frauds provisions. Rather, it states that a "contract for sale need not be concluded in or evidenced by writing and is not subject to any other requirements as to form."

Article 11 accords with the legal customs of most nations, which no longer require contracts to meet certain formal or writing requirements to be enforceable. Ironically, even England, the nation that created the original Statute of Frauds in 1677, has repealed all of it except the provisions relating to collateral promises and to transfers of interests in land. Many other countries that once had such statutes have also repealed all or parts of them. Civil law countries, such as France, have never required certain types of contracts to be in writing.

FOR CRITICAL ANALYSIS
If there were no Statute of Frauds and a dispute arose concerning an oral agreement, how would the parties substantiate their respective positions?

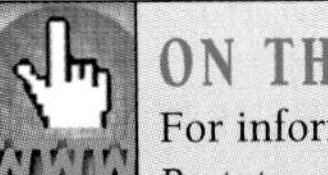

ON THE WEB
For information on the *Restatements of the Law*, including the *Restatement (Second) of Contracts*, go to the American Law Institute's Web site at
http://www.ali.com.

Promissory Estoppel In some states, an oral contract that would otherwise be unenforceable under the Statute of Frauds may be enforced under the doctrine of promissory estoppel, or detrimental reliance. Recall from Chapter 9 that if a promisor makes a promise on which the promisee justifiably relies to her or his detriment, a court may *estop* (prevent) the promisor from denying that a contract exists. Section 139 of the *Restatement (Second) of Contracts* provides that in these circumstances, an oral promise can be enforceable notwithstanding the Statute of Frauds if the reliance was foreseeable to the person making the promise and if injustice can be avoided only by enforcing the promise.

Special Exceptions under the UCC Special exceptions to the applicability of the Statute of Frauds exist for sales contracts. Oral contracts for customized goods may be enforced in certain circumstances. Another exception has to do with oral contracts between merchants that have been confirmed in writing. We will examine these exceptions in Chapter 14.

The Statute of Frauds—Sufficiency of the Writing

A written contract will satisfy the writing requirement of the Statute of Frauds. A *written memorandum* (written evidence of the oral contract) signed by the party against whom enforcement is sought will also satisfy the writing requirement.[21] The signature need not be placed at the end of the document but can be anywhere in the writing; it can even be initials rather than the full name.

A significant issue in today's business world has to do with how "signatures" can be created and verified on electronic contracts and other documents. We will examine electronic signatures in Chapter 17.

21. As mentioned earlier, under the UCC Statute of Frauds, a writing is required only for contracts for the sale of goods priced at $500 or more. See Chapter 14.

WHAT CONSTITUTES A WRITING?

A writing can consist of any confirmation, invoice, sales slip, check, or fax—or such items in combination. The written contract need not consist of a single document to constitute an enforceable contract. One document may incorporate another document by expressly referring to it. Several documents may form a single contract if they are physically attached such as by staple, paper clip, or glue. Several documents may form a single contract even if they are only placed in the same envelope.

● **EXAMPLE 11.15** Sam orally agrees to sell to Terry some land next to a shopping mall. Sam gives Terry an unsigned memo that contains a legal description of the property, and Terry gives Sam an unsigned first draft of their contract. Sam sends Terry a signed letter that refers to the memo and to the first and final drafts of the contract. Terry sends Sam an unsigned copy of the final draft of the contract with a signed check stapled to it. Together, the documents can constitute a writing sufficient to satisfy the Statute of Frauds and bind both parties to the terms of the contract as evidenced by the writings. ●

WHAT MUST BE CONTAINED IN THE WRITING?

A memorandum evidencing the oral contract need only contain the essential terms of the contract. Under most provisions of the Statute of Frauds, the writing must name the parties, subject matter, consideration, and quantity. With respect to contracts for the sale of land, some states require that the memorandum also set forth the essential terms of the contract, such as location and price, with sufficient clarity to allow the terms to be determined from the memo itself, without reference to any outside sources.[22] Under the UCC, in regard to the sale of goods, the writing need only name the quantity term and be signed by the party against whom enforcement is sought.

Because only the party against whom enforcement is sought need have signed the writing, a contract may be enforceable by one of its parties but not by the other. ● **EXAMPLE 11.16** Rock orally agrees to buy Devlin's lake house and lot for $150,000. Devlin writes Rock a letter confirming the sale by identifying the parties and the essential terms of the sales contract—price, method of payment, and legal address—and signs the letter. Devlin has made a written memorandum of the oral land contract. Because she signed the letter, she normally can be held to the oral contract by Rock. Rock, however, because he has not signed or entered into a written contract or memorandum, can plead the Statute of Frauds as a defense, and Devlin cannot enforce the contract against him. ●

The Parol Evidence Rule

PAROL EVIDENCE RULE
A substantive rule of contracts, as well as a procedural rule of evidence, under which a court will not receive into evidence the parties' prior negotiations, prior agreements, or contemporaneous oral agreements if that evidence contradicts or varies the terms of the parties' written contract.

The **parol evidence rule** prohibits the introduction at trial of evidence of the parties' prior negotiations, prior agreements, or contemporaneous oral agreements if that evidence contradicts or varies the terms of the parties' written contract. The written contract is ordinarily assumed to be the complete embodiment of the parties' agreement. Because of the rigidity of the parol evidence rule, however, courts make several exceptions:

22. *Rhodes v. Wilkins,* 83 N.M. 782, 498 P.2d 311 (1972).

NOTE The parol evidence rule and its exceptions relate to the rules concerning the *interpretation* of contracts.

① Evidence of a *subsequent modification* of a written contract can be introduced in court. Keep in mind that the oral modifications may not be enforceable if they come under the Statute of Frauds—for example, if they increase the price of the goods for sale to $500 or more or increase the term for performance to more than one year. Also, oral modifications will not be enforceable if the original contract provides that any modification must be in writing.[23]

② Oral evidence can be introduced in all cases to show that the contract was voidable or void (for example, induced by mistake, fraud, or misrepresentation). In this situation, if deception led one of the parties to agree to the terms of a written contract, oral evidence indicating fraud should not be excluded. Courts frown on bad faith and are quick to allow the introduction at trial of parol evidence when it establishes fraud.

③ When the terms of a written contract are ambiguous, evidence is admissible to show the meaning of the terms.

④ Evidence is admissible when the written contract is incomplete in that it lacks one or more of the essential terms. The courts allow evidence to "fill in the gaps" in the contract.

⑤ Under the UCC, evidence can be introduced to explain or supplement a written contract by showing a prior dealing, course of performance, or usage of trade.[24] We discuss these terms in further detail in Chapter 14, in the context of sales contracts. Here, it is sufficient to say that when buyers and sellers deal with each other over extended periods of time, certain customary practices develop. These practices are often overlooked in the writing of the contract, so courts allow the introduction of evidence to show how the parties have acted in the past. Usage of trade—practices and customs generally followed in a particular industry—can also shed light on the meaning of certain contract provisions, and thus evidence of trade usage may be admissible.

⑥ The parol evidence rule does not apply if the existence of the entire written contract is subject to an orally agreed-on condition. Proof of the condition does not alter or modify the written terms but affects the *enforceability* of the written contract. ● **EXAMPLE 11.17** Jelek agrees to purchase Armand's car for $4,000, but only if Jelek's mechanic, Frank, inspects the car and approves of the purchase. Armand agrees to this condition, but because he is leaving town for the weekend and Jelek wants to use the car (if he buys it) before Armand returns, Jelek drafts a contract of sale, and they both sign it. Frank, the mechanic, does not approve of the purchase, and when Jelek does not buy the car, Armand sues him, alleging that he breached the contract. In this case, Jelek's oral agreement did not alter or modify the terms of the written agreement but concerned whether the contract existed at all. Therefore, the parol evidence rule does not apply. ●

⑦ When an *obvious* or *gross* clerical (or typographic) error exists that clearly would not represent the agreement of the parties, parol evidence is admissible to correct the error. ● **EXAMPLE 11.18** Sharon agrees to lease 1,000 square feet of office space at the current monthly rate of $3 per square foot from Stone Enterprises. The signed written lease provides for a monthly lease payment of $300 rather than

23. UCC 2–209(2), (3). See Chapter 14.
24. UCC 1–205, 2–202. See Chapter 14.

the $3,000 agreed to by the parties. Because the error is obvious, Stone Enterprises would be allowed to admit parol evidence to correct the mistake. •

INTEGRATED CONTRACT
A written contract that constitutes the final expression of the parties' agreement. If a contract is integrated, evidence extraneous to the contract that contradicts or alters the meaning of the contract in any way is inadmissible.

The determination of whether evidence will be allowed basically depends on whether the written contract is intended to be a complete and final embodiment of the terms of the agreement. If it is so intended, it is referred to as an **integrated contract**, and extraneous evidence is excluded. If the contract is only partially integrated, evidence of consistent additional terms is admissible to supplement the written agreement.[25]

In the following case, the court applied the parol evidence rule, among other legal principles, in the context of a franchise agreement. (A *franchise* is an arrangement by which the owner of a trademark, trade name, or copyright licenses another to use it, under certain conditions. Franchises are discussed in detail in Chapter 31.)

25. *Restatement (Second) of Contracts,* Section 216.

CASE 11.3 Cousins Subs Systems, Inc. v. McKinney

United States District Court,
Eastern District of Wisconsin, 1999.
59 F.Supp.2d 816.

FACTS Michael McKinney owns Best Oil Company, which operates a chain of gas station/convenience stores known as The Little Stores in northern Minnesota and Wisconsin. McKinney contracted with Cousins Subs Systems, Inc., to operate Cousins submarine sandwich shops in The Little Stores. McKinney signed an "Area Development Agreement" and a "Franchise Agreement." Each document stated that it constituted the parties' entire agreement, that there were no other "understandings or agreements," and that McKinney had not been promised any particular level of profits. Within two years, McKinney became disillusioned with the arrangement and told Cousins that he was ending it. Cousins filed a suit in a federal district court against McKinney, charging, among other things, that he had wrongfully terminated their agreement. McKinney filed a counterclaim against Cousins and others, alleging, in part, breach of contract. McKinney claimed that Daniel Sobiech, a Cousins representative, orally guaranteed, among other things, annual sales of "$250,000 to $500,000 per franchise" at each of McKinney's franchises. Cousins filed a motion to dismiss McKinney's counterclaim.

ISSUE Should the court grant Cousins's motion and dismiss McKinney's counterclaim?

DECISION Yes. The court granted Cousins's motion and dismissed McKinney's counterclaim.

REASON The court recognized that "[t]he parol evidence rule prohibits the use of oral agreements of the type McKinney relies on to contradict written contracts if the written contract is intended by the parties to be the final expression of their agreement." The court held that "the oral promises allegedly made by Cousins are directly contradicted by the written terms of the agreement signed by McKinney." The court pointed out that "[t]he presence of the integration clauses in the written agreements makes clear that the contracts were intended to embody all of the agreed-on terms." The court saw McKinney as "an experienced businessman who made a deal which turned out to be less favorable than he anticipated." The court concluded that the parol evidence rule barred McKinney's allegation that oral promises contradicted the terms of his written contract with Cousins.

FOR CRITICAL ANALYSIS—Ethical Consideration
What general ethical precept underlies the parol evidence rule?

APPLICATION Law and the Businessperson . . .

The Problem with Oral Contracts*

As a general rule, most business contracts should be in writing even when they fall outside the Statute of Frauds. Businesspersons frequently make oral contracts over the telephone, however, particularly when the parties have done business with each other in the past.

Preventing Problems with Oral Contracts

Any time an oral contract is made, it is advisable for one of the parties to send either a written memorandum or a confirmation of the oral agreement by fax or e-mail to the other party. This accomplishes two purposes: (1) it demonstrates the party's clear intention to form a contract, and (2) it provides the terms of the contract as that party understood them. If the party receiving the memorandum or confirmation then disagrees with the terms as described, the issue can be addressed before performance begins.

Special Rules for Contracts between Merchants

What about the sale of goods between merchants? Under the UCC, written confirmation received by one merchant removes the Statute of Frauds requirement of a writing unless the merchant receiving the confirmation objects in writing within ten days of its receipt. This law (discussed in Chapter 14) clearly points out the need for the merchant receiving the confirmation to review it carefully to ascertain that the confirmation conforms to the oral contract. If the writing does not so conform, the merchant can object in writing (the Statute of Frauds still applies), and the parties can resolve misunderstandings without legal liability. If the merchant fails to object, the written confirmation can be used as evidence to prove the terms of the oral contract. Note, however, that this ten-day rule does not apply to contracts for interests in realty or for services, to which the UCC does not apply.

*This *Application* is not meant to substitute for the services of an attorney who is licensed to practice law in your state.

Checklist for Oral Contracts

1. When feasible, use written contracts.
2. If you enter into an oral contract over the telephone, fax or e-mail a written confirmation outlining your understanding of the oral contract.
3. If you receive the other party's written or faxed confirmation, read it carefully to make sure that its terms agree with what you believed was already agreed on in the oral contract.
4. If you have any objections, notify the other party of these objections, in writing, within ten days.

Key Terms

collateral promise 297
integrated contract 304
parol evidence rule 302
prenuptial agreement 298
scienter 292
Statute of Frauds 295

Chapter Summary Defenses to Contract Enforceability

GENUINENESS OF ASSENT	
Mistakes (See pages 287–288.)	1. *Unilateral*—Generally, the mistaken party is bound by the contract *unless* (a) the other party knows or should have known of the mistake or (b) the mistake is an inadvertent mathematical error—such as an error in addition or subtraction—committed without gross negligence. 2. *Bilateral (mutual)*—When both parties are mistaken about the same material fact, such as identity, either party can avoid the contract. If the mistake concerns value or quality, either party can enforce the contract.
Fraudulent Misrepresentation (See pages 288–294.)	When fraud occurs, usually the innocent party can enforce or avoid the contract. The elements necessary to establish fraud are as follows: 1. A misrepresentation of a material fact must occur. 2. There must be an intent to deceive. 3. The innocent party must justifiably rely on the misrepresentation.
Undue Influence (See page 294.)	Undue influence arises from special relationships, such as fiduciary or confidential relationships, in which one party's free will has been overcome by the undue influence exerted by the other party. Usually, the contract is voidable.
Duress (See pages 294–295.)	Duress is defined as the tactic of forcing a party to enter a contract under the fear of a threat—for example, the threat of violence or serious economic loss. The party forced to enter the contract can rescind the contract.
FORM	
The Statute of Frauds—Requirement of a Writing (See pages 295–301.)	*Applicability*—The following types of contracts fall under the Statute of Frauds and must be in writing to be enforceable: 1. *Contracts involving interests in land*—The statute applies to any contract for an interest in realty, such as a sale, a lease, or a mortgage. 2. *Contracts whose terms cannot be performed within one year*—The statute applies only to contracts objectively impossible to perform fully within one year from (the day after) the contract's formation. 3. *Collateral promises*—The statute applies only to express contracts made between the guarantor and the creditor whose terms make the guarantor secondarily liable. *Exception:* the "main purpose" rule. 4. *Promises made in consideration of marriage*—The statute applies to promises to pay money or give property in consideration of a promise to marry and to prenuptial agreements made in consideration of marriage. 5. *Contracts for the sale of goods priced at $500 or more*—Under the UCC Statute of Frauds provision in UCC 2–201. *Exceptions*—Partial performance, admissions, and promissory estoppel.
The Statute of Frauds—Sufficiency of the Writing (See pages 301–302.)	To constitute an enforceable contract under the Statute of Frauds, a writing must be signed by the party against whom enforcement is sought, must name the parties, must identify the subject matter, and must state with reasonable certainty the essential terms of the contract. In a sale of land, the price and a description of the property may need to be stated with sufficient clarity to allow them to be determined without reference to outside sources. Under the UCC, a contract for a sale of goods is not enforceable beyond the quantity of goods shown in the contract.

Chapter Summary Defenses to Contract Enforceability—continued

The Parol Evidence Rule (See pages 302–304.)	The parol evidence rule prohibits the introduction at trial of evidence of the parties' prior negotiations, prior agreements, or contemporaneous oral agreements that contradicts or varies the terms of the parties' written contract. The written contract is assumed to be the complete embodiment of the parties' agreement. Exceptions are made in the following circumstances: 1. To show that the contract was subsequently modified. 2. To show that the contract was voidable or void. 3. To clarify the meaning of ambiguous terms. 4. To clarify the terms of the contract when the written contract lacks one or more of its essential terms. 5. Under the UCC, to explain the meaning of contract terms in light of a prior dealing, course of performance, or usage of trade. 6. To show that the entire contract is subject to an orally agreed-on condition. 7. When an obvious clerical or typographic error was made.

For Review

① In what types of situations might genuineness of assent to a contract's terms be lacking?

② What is the difference between a mistake of value or quality and a mistake of fact?

③ What elements must exist for fraudulent misrepresentation to occur?

④ What contracts must be in writing to be enforceable?

⑤ What is parol evidence? When is it admissible to clarify the terms of a written contract?

Questions and Case Problems

11–1. Genuineness of Assent. Jerome is an elderly man who lives with his nephew, Philip. Jerome is totally dependent on Philip's support. Philip tells Jerome that unless Jerome transfers a tract of land he owns to Philip for a price 30 percent below market value, Philip will no longer support and take care of him. Jerome enters into the contract. Discuss fully whether Jerome can set aside this contract.

11–2. Collateral Promises. Gemma promises a local hardware store that she will pay for a lawn mower that her brother is purchasing on credit if the brother fails to pay the debt. Must this promise be in writing to be enforceable? Why or why not?

11–3. Fraudulent Misrepresentation. Larry offered to sell Stanley his car and told Stanley that the car had been driven only 25,000 miles and had never been in an accident. Stanley hired Cohen, a mechanic, to appraise the condition of the car, and Cohen said that the car probably had at least 50,000 miles on it and probably had been in an accident. In spite of this information, Stanley still thought the car would be a good buy for the price, so he purchased it. Later, when the car developed numerous mechanical problems, Stanley sought to rescind the contract on the basis of Larry's fraudulent misrepresentation of the auto's condition. Will Stanley be able to rescind his contract? Discuss.

11–4. Collateral Promises. Jeffrey took his mother on a special holiday to Mountain Air Resort. Jeffrey was a frequent patron of the resort and was well known by its manager. The resort required each of its patrons to make a large deposit to ensure payment for the room. Jeffrey asked the manager to waive the requirement for his mother and told the manager that if his mother for any reason failed to pay the resort for her stay there, he would cover the bill. Relying on Jeffrey's promise, the manager waived the deposit requirement for Jeffrey's mother. After she returned home from her holiday, Jeffrey's mother refused to pay the resort bill. The resort manager tried to collect the sum from Jeffrey, but Jeffrey also refused to pay, stating that his promise was not enforceable under the Statute of Frauds. Is Jeffrey correct? Explain.

11–5. Genuineness of Assent. Linda Lorenzo purchased Lurlene Noel's home in 1988 without having it inspected. The basement started leaking in 1989. In 1991, Lorenzo had the paneling removed from the basement walls and discovered that the walls were bowed inward and cracked. Lorenzo then had a civil engineer inspect the basement walls, and he found that the cracks had been caulked and painted over before the paneling was installed. He concluded that the "wall failure" had existed "for at least thirty years" and that the basement walls were "structurally unsound." Does Lorenzo have a cause of action against Noel? If so, on what ground? Discuss. [*Lorenzo v. Noel,* 206 Mich.App. 682, 522 N.W.2d 724 (1994)]

11–6. Misrepresentation. W. B. McConkey owned commercial property, including a building that, as McConkey knew, had experienced flooding problems for years. McConkey painted the building, replaced damaged carpeting, and sold the property to M&D, Inc., on an "as is" basis. M&D did not ask whether there were flooding problems, and McConkey said nothing about them. M&D leased the property to Donmar, Inc., to operate a pet supplies store. Two months after the store opened, the building flooded following heavy rain. M&D and Donmar filed a suit in a Michigan state court against McConkey and others, claiming in part that McConkey had committed misrepresentation by silence. Based on this claim, will the court hold McConkey liable? Why or why not? [*M&D, Inc. v. McConkey,* 585 N.W.2d 33 (Mich.App. 1998)]

11–7. The Parol Evidence Rule. Vision Graphics, Inc., provides printing services to customers such as Milton Bradley Co. To perform its services, Vision agreed to buy or lease parts of a computer software system from E. I. du Pont de Nemours & Co. Vision needed the system to accept files written in "PostScript," a computer language used in the printing industry. Du Pont orally represented to Vision that with three upgrades, its system would be completely "postscriptable." None of the parties' written contracts included any promises regarding postscriptability. Each contract, however, included an integration clause stating that the contract contained the entire agreement of the parties. Before the three upgrades were complete, du Pont determined that for financial reasons, it could no longer support its system and told Vision that the software would not be made postscriptable. Vision lost customers and could not attract new accounts, and its reputation in the industry was damaged. Vision filed a suit in a federal district court against du Pont, alleging, among other things, breach of contract on the basis of the oral promises. Du Pont filed a motion for summary judgment, arguing that whether it breached any oral agreement was "immaterial." Will the court agree? Why or why not? [*Vision Graphics, Inc. v. E. I. du Pont de Nemours & Co.,* 41 F.Supp.2d 93 (D.Mass. 1999)]

11–8. Fraudulent Misrepresentation. In 1987, United Parcel Service Co. and United Parcel Service of America, Inc. (together known as "UPS"), decided to change its parcel delivery business from relying on contract carriers to establishing its own airline. During the transition, which took sixteen months, UPS hired 811 pilots. At the time, UPS expressed a desire to hire pilots who remained throughout that period with its contract carriers, which included Orion Air. A UPS representative met with more than fifty Orion pilots and made promises of future employment. John Rickert, a captain with Orion, was one of the pilots. Orion ceased operation after the UPS transition, and UPS did not hire Rickert, who obtained employment about six months later as a second officer with American Airlines, but at a lower salary. Rickert filed a suit in a Kentucky state court against UPS, claiming, in part, fraud based on the promises made by the UPS representative. UPS filed a motion for a directed verdict. What are the elements for a cause of action based on fraudulent misrepresentation? In whose favor should the court rule in this case, and why? [*United Parcel Service, Inc. v. Rickert,* 996 S.W.2d 464 (Ky. 1999)]

11–9. Fraudulent Misrepresentation. William Meade, Leland Stewart, Doug Vierkant, and David Girard applied for, and were offered, jobs at the El-Jay Division of Cedarapids, Inc., in Eugene, Oregon. During the interviews, each applicant asked about El-Jay's future. They were told, among other things, that El-Jay was a stable company with few downsizings and layoffs, sales were up and were expected to increase, and production was expanding. Cedarapids management had already planned to close El-Jay, however. Each applicant signed an at-will employment agreement. To take the job at El-Jay, each new employee either quit the job he was doing or passed up other employment opportunities. Each employee and his family then moved to Eugene. When El-Jay closed soon after they started their new jobs, Meade and the others filed a suit in a federal district court against Cedarapids, alleging, in part, fraudulent misrepresentation. Were the plaintiffs justified in relying on the statements made to them during their job interviews? Explain. [*Meade v. Cedarapids, Inc.,* 164 F.3d 1218 (9th Cir. 1999)]

TEST YOUR KNOWLEDGE—ANSWER ON THE WEB

11–10. Robert Pinto, doing business as Pinto Associates, hired Richard MacDonald as an independent contractor in March 1992. The parties orally agreed on the terms of employment, including payment to MacDonald of a share of the company's income, but they did not put anything in writing. In March 1995, MacDonald quit. Pinto then told MacDonald that he was entitled to $9,602.17—25 percent of the difference between the accounts receivable and the accounts payable as of MacDonald's last day. MacDonald disagreed and demanded more than $83,500—25 percent of the revenue from all invoices, less the cost of materials and outside processing, for each of the years that he worked for Pinto. Pinto refused. MacDonald filed a suit in a Connecticut state court against Pinto, alleging breach of contract. In Pinto's response and at the trial, he testified that the parties had an oral contract under which MacDonald was entitled to 25 percent of the difference between accounts receivable and payable as of the date of MacDonald's termination. Did the parties have an enforceable contract? How should the court rule, and why? [*MacDonald v. Pinto,* 62 Conn.App. 317, 771 A.2d 156 (2001)]

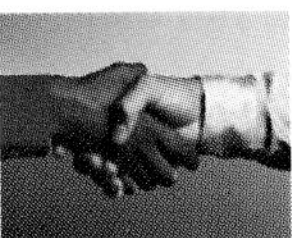

A QUESTION OF ETHICS AND SOCIAL RESPONSIBILITY

11–11. Mark Van Wagoner, an attorney experienced in real estate transactions, and his wife, Kathryn, were interested in buying certain property being sold by Carol Klas for her former husband, John Klas. When the Van Wagoners asked Carol Klas if there had been any appraisals of the property, she replied that there had been several appraisals, ranging from $175,000 to $192,000. (At trial, Carol claimed that she understood the term *appraisal* to mean any opinion as to the market value of the house.) The Van Wagoners did not request a written appraisal of the property until after signing an agreement to purchase the property for $175,000. Carol Klas then provided them with a written appraisal that listed the house's value as $165,000. When the Van Wagoners refused to go through with the deal, John Klas brought suit to recover the difference between the agreement price and the price for which the house was later sold. In view of these facts, answer the following questions. [*Klas v. Van Wagoner,* 829 P.2d 135 (Utah App. 1992)]

1. The Van Wagoners claimed that the contract should be rescinded on the basis of their mistaken assumption as to the value of the house. What kind of mistake was made in this situation (mutual or unilateral, mistake of value or mistake of fact)? How should the court rule on this issue?
2. Mark Van Wagoner was an attorney experienced in real estate transactions. Should the court take this fact into consideration when making its decision?
3. Generally, what ethical principles, as expressed in public policies, are in conflict here and in similar situations in which parties enter into a contract with mistaken assumptions?

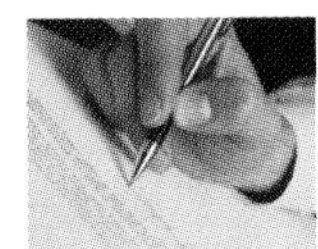

FOR CRITICAL ANALYSIS

11–12. Describe the types of individuals who might be capable of exerting undue influence on others.

Internet Exercises

Go to the *Business Law Today* home page at **http://blt.westbuslaw.com**. Select "Interactive Study Center" and then click on "Chapter 11." There you will find the following Internet research exercises that you can perform to learn more about the requirements of assent and form in contracts:

Activity 11–1: Fraudulent Misrepresentation
Activity 11–2: The Statute of Frauds

Before the Test

Go to the *Business Law Today* home page at **http://blt.westbuslaw.com**. Click on "Interactive Quizzes." You will find at least twenty interactive questions relating to this chapter.

CHAPTER 12

Third Party Rights and Discharge

"The laws of a state change with the changing times."

Aeschylus, 525–456 B.C.E. (Greek dramatist)

CHAPTER CONTENTS

LEARNING OBJECTIVES

After reading this chapter, you should be able to answer the following questions:

① What is the difference between an assignment and a delegation?

② What rights can be assigned despite a contract clause expressly prohibiting assignment?

③ What factors indicate that a third party beneficiary is an intended beneficiary?

④ How are most contracts discharged?

⑤ What is a contractual condition, and how might a condition affect contractual obligations?

PRIVITY OF CONTRACT
The relationship that exists between the promisor and the promisee of a contract.

Because a contract is a private agreement between the parties who have entered into it, it is fitting that these parties alone should have rights and liabilities under the contract. This concept is referred to as **privity of contract**, and it establishes the basic principle that third parties have no rights in contracts to which they are not parties.

You are probably convinced by now that for every rule of contract law there seems to be an exception. As times change, so must the laws, as indicated in the opening quotation. When justice cannot be served by adherence to a rule of law, exceptions to the rule must be made. In this chapter, we look at some exceptions to the rule of privity of contract. We also examine how a contract is *discharged*. Normally, contract discharge is accomplished when both parties have performed the acts promised in the contract. In the latter part of this chapter, we look at the degree of performance required to discharge a contractual obligation, as well as at some other ways in which contract discharge can occur.

Assignments and Delegations

When third parties acquire rights or assume duties arising from contracts to which they were not parties, the rights are transferred to them by *assignment*, and the duties are transferred by *delegation*.

ASSIGNMENTS

ASSIGNMENT
The act of transferring to another all or part of one's rights arising under a contract.

ASSIGNOR
A party who transfers (assigns) his or her rights under a contract to another party (called the assignee).

ASSIGNEE
A party to whom the rights under a contract are transferred, or assigned.

In a bilateral contract, normally one party has a right to require the other to perform some task, and the other has a duty to perform it. The transfer of *rights* to a third person is known as an **assignment**. When rights under a contract are assigned unconditionally, the rights of the **assignor** (the party making the assignment) are extinguished.[1] The third party (the **assignee**, or party receiving the assignment) has a right to demand performance from the other original party to the contract (the *obligor*). • **EXAMPLE 12.1** Brent owes Alex $1,000, and Alex assigns to Carmen the right to receive the $1,000. Here, a valid assignment of a debt exists. Carmen, the assignee, can enforce the contract against Brent if Brent fails to perform.• Exhibit 12–1 illustrates assignment relationships.

The assignee takes only those rights that the assignor originally had. Furthermore, the assignee's rights are subject to the defenses that the obligor has against the assignor. • **EXAMPLE 12.2** Brent owes Alex $1,000 under a contract in which Brent agreed to buy Alex's computer work station. Alex assigns his right to receive the $1,000 to Carmen. Brent, in deciding to purchase the work station, relied on Alex's fraudulent misrepresentation that the computer's hard drive had a storage capacity of forty gigabytes.

1. *Restatement (Second) of Contracts,* Section 317.

EXHIBIT 12–1 ASSIGNMENT RELATIONSHIPS

In the assignment relationship illustrated here, Alex assigns his *rights* under a contract that he made with Brent to a third party, Carmen. Alex thus becomes the *assignor* and Carmen the *assignee* of the contractual rights. Brent, the *obligor* (the party owing performance under the contract), now owes performance to Carmen instead of Alex. Alex's original contract rights are extinguished after assignment.

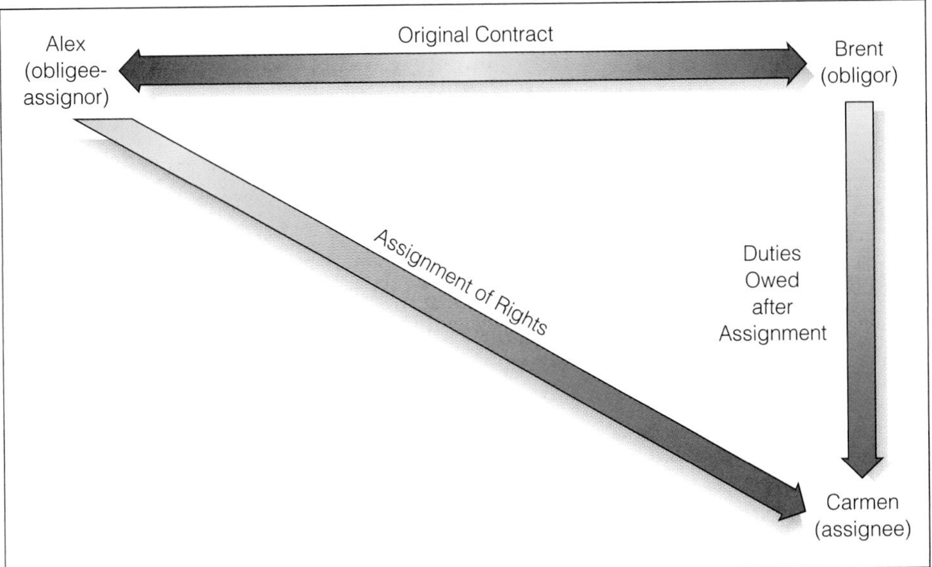

When Brent discovers that the computer can store only ten megabytes, he tells Alex that he is going to return the work station to him and cancel the contract. Even though Alex has assigned his "right" to receive the $1,000 to Carmen, Brent need not pay Carmen the $1,000—Brent can raise the defense of Alex's fraudulent misrepresentation to avoid payment. •

ON THE WEB You can find a summary of the law governing assignments, as well as "SmartAgreement" forms that you can use for various types of contracts, at **http://www.smartagreements.com.** Click on "All agreements" in the menu on the right-hand side of the screen, and when that page opens, click on "Assignment of Contract."

The Importance of Assignments in the Business Context Assignments are important because they are utilized in much business financing. Lending institutions, for example, such as banks, frequently assign the rights to receive payments under their loan contracts to other firms, which pay for those rights. If you obtain a loan from your local bank to purchase a car, you might later receive in the mail a notice stating that your bank has transferred (assigned) its rights to receive payments on the loan to another firm and that, when the time comes to repay your loan, you must make the payments to that other firm.

Lenders that make *mortgage loans* (loans to allow prospective home buyers to purchase land or a home) often assign their rights to collect the mortgage payments to a third party, such as GMAC Mortgage Corporation. Following an assignment, the home buyer is notified that future payments must be made not to the lender that loaned the funds but to the third party. Millions of dollars change hands daily in the business world in the form of assignments of rights in contracts. If it were not possible to transfer (assign) contractual rights, many businesses could not continue to operate.

Rights That Cannot Be Assigned As a general rule, all rights can be assigned. Exceptions are made, however, in the following special circumstances:

1. If a statute expressly prohibits assignment, the particular right in question cannot be assigned. • **EXAMPLE 12.3** Marn is a new employee of CompuFuture, Inc. CompuFuture is an employer under workers' compensation statutes (see Chapter 34) in this state, and thus Marn is a covered employee. Marn has a relatively high-risk job. In need of a loan, Marn borrows some money from Stark, assigning to Stark all workers' compensation benefits due her should she be injured on the job. The assignment of *future* workers' compensation benefits is prohibited by state statute, and thus such rights cannot be assigned. •
2. When a contract is for personal services, the rights under the contract normally cannot be assigned unless all that remains is a money payment.[2] • **EXAMPLE 12.4** Brent signs a contract to be a tutor for Alex's children. Alex then attempts to assign to Carmen his right to Brent's services. Carmen cannot enforce the contract against Brent. Brent may not like Carmen's children or may for some other reason not want to tutor them. Because personal services are unique to the person rendering them, rights to receive personal services cannot be assigned. •
3. A right cannot be assigned if assignment will materially increase or alter the risk or duties of the obligor.[3] • **EXAMPLE 12.5** Alex has a hotel, and to insure it, he takes out a policy with Northwest Insurance Company. The policy insures against fire, theft, floods, and vandalism. Alex attempts to assign the insurance policy to Carmen, who also owns a hotel. The assignment is ineffective because it may substantially alter the insurance company's duty of performance and the risk that the company undertakes. An insurance company evaluates the particular risk of a cer-

2. *Restatement (Second) of Contracts,* Sections 317 and 318.
3. See UCC 2–210(2).

An adult tutors children. Can personal services such as tutoring children be assigned? Why or why not?

tain party and tailors its policy to fit that risk. If the policy is assigned to a third party, the insurance risk is materially altered. ●

④ If a contract stipulates that the right cannot be assigned, then *ordinarily* it cannot be assigned. ● **EXAMPLE 12.6** Brent agrees to build a house for Alex. The contract between Brent and Alex states, "This contract cannot be assigned by Alex without Brent's consent. Any assignment without such consent renders this contract void, and all rights hereunder will thereupon terminate." Alex then assigns his rights to Carmen, without first obtaining Brent's consent. Carmen cannot enforce the contract against Brent. ●

The fourth rule has several exceptions:

① A contract cannot prevent an assignment of the right to receive money. This exception exists to encourage the free flow of money and credit in modern business settings.

② The assignment of ownership rights in real estate often cannot be prohibited because such a prohibition is contrary to public policy in most states. Prohibitions of this kind are called restraints against **alienation** (the voluntary transfer of land ownership).

ALIENATION
The process of transferring land out of one's possession (thus "alienating" the land from oneself).

③ The assignment of negotiable instruments (see Chapter 19) cannot be prohibited.

④ In a contract for the sale of goods, the right to receive damages for breach of contract or for payment of an account owed may be assigned even though the sales contract prohibits such assignment.[4]

4. UCC 2–210(2).

Notice of Assignment Once a valid assignment of rights has been made to a third party, the third party should notify the obligor of the assignment (for example, in Exhibit 12–1, Carmen should notify Brent). Giving notice is not legally necessary to establish the validity of the assignment, because an assignment is effective immediately, whether or not notice is given. Two major problems arise, however, when notice of the assignment is *not* given to the obligor:

① If the assignor assigns the same right to two different persons, the question arises as to which one has priority—that is, which one has the right to the performance by the obligor. Although the rule most often observed in the United States is that the first assignment in time is the first in right, some states follow the English rule, which basically gives priority to the first assignee who gives notice. • **EXAMPLE 12.7** Brent owes Alex $5,000 on a contractual obligation. On May 1, Alex assigns this monetary claim to Carmen. Carmen gives no notice of the assignment to Brent. On June 1, for services Dorman has rendered to Alex, Alex assigns the same monetary claim (to collect $5,000 from Brent) to Dorman. Dorman immediately notifies Brent of the assignment. In the majority of states, Carmen would have priority because the assignment to her was first in time. In some states, however, Dorman would have priority, because he gave first notice.•

② Until the obligor has notice of assignment, the obligor can discharge his or her obligation by performance to the assignor, and performance by the obligor to the assignor constitutes a discharge to the assignee. Once the obligor receives proper notice, only performance to the assignee can discharge the obligor's obligations. • **EXAMPLE 12.8** In the above example, Alex assigns to Carmen his right to collect $5,000 from Brent. Carmen does not give notice to Brent. Brent subsequently pays Alex the $5,000. Although the assignment was valid, Brent's payment to Alex was a discharge of the debt, and Carmen's failure to notify Brent of the assignment caused her to lose the right to collect the money from Brent. If Carmen had given Brent notice of the assignment, however, Brent's payment to Alex would not have discharged the debt.•

In the following case, the issue was whether the right to buy advertising space in certain publications at a steep discount was validly assigned from the original owner to companies that he later formed.

CASE 12.1 Gold v. Ziff Communications Co.

Appellate Court of Illinois, First District, 2001.
322 Ill.App.3d 32,
748 N.E.2d 198,
254 Ill.Dec. 752.
http://state.il.us/court/default.htm[a]

FACTS In 1982, Ziff Communications Company, a publisher of specialty magazines, bought *PC Magazine* from its founder, Anthony Gold, for more than $10 million. As part of the deal, Ziff gave Gold, or a company that he "controlled," "ad/list rights"—rights to advertise at an 80 percent discount on a limited number of pages in Ziff publications and free use of Ziff's subscriber lists. In 1983, Gold formed Software Communications, Inc. (SCI), a mail-order software business that he wholly owned, to use the ad/list rights. In 1987 and 1988, he formed two new mail-order companies, Hanson & Connors, Inc., and PC Brand, Inc. Gold told Ziff that he was allocating his ad/list rights to Hanson & Connors, which took over most of SCI's business, and to PC Brand, of which Gold owned 90 percent. Ziff's other advertisers complained about this "allocation." Ziff refused to run large ads for Hanson & Connors or to release its subscriber lists to the company.

a. On this page, click on "Appellate Court of Illinois." On the next page, in the "Appellate Court Documents" section, click on "Appellate Court opinions." In the result, in the "Appellate Court" section, click on "2001." On the next page, in the "First District" section, click on "March." Finally, scroll to the bottom of the chart and click on the case name to access the opinion. The state of Illinois maintains this Web site.

CASE 12.1—Continued

Ziff also declared PC Brand ineligible for the ad discount because it "was not controlled by Gold." Gold and his companies filed a suit in an Illinois state court against Ziff, alleging breach of contract. The court ordered Ziff to pay the plaintiffs more than $88 million in damages and interest. Ziff appealed to an intermediate state appellate court, arguing in part that Gold had not properly assigned the ad/list rights to Hanson & Connors and PC Brand.

ISSUE Was there a valid assignment of rights from Gold and SCI to Hanson & Connors and PC Brand?

DECISION Yes. The state intermediate appellate court affirmed the lower court's decision on this issue. The appellate court remanded the case, however, for a new trial on the amount of the damages, reasoning that some parts of the award "were not within the reasonable contemplation of the parties."

REASON The court explained, "We agree with plaintiffs that assignments can be implied from circumstances. No particular mode or form * * * is necessary to effect a valid assignment, and any acts or words are sufficient which show an intention of transferring or appropriating the owner's interest. In the instant case, it is undisputed that Gold owned 100 [percent] of SCI. In a letter dated May 13, 1988, Gold, as president of SCI, instructed Ziff that he was allocating the ad/list rights to Hanson and PC Brand. Additionally, SCI stopped using the ad/list rights when PC Brand and Hanson were formed. * * * Gold's behavior toward his companies and his conduct toward the obligor, Ziff, implied that the ad/list rights were assigned to PC Brand and Hanson."

FOR CRITICAL ANALYSIS—Social Consideration *Would the assignments in this case have been valid if Gold had not notified Ziff?*

DELEGATIONS

DELEGATION OF DUTIES
The act of transferring to another all or part of one's duties arising under a contract.

DELEGATOR
A party who transfers (delegates) her or his obligations under a contract to another party (called the delegatee).

DELEGATEE
A party to whom contractual obligations are transferred, or delegated.

Just as a party can transfer rights to a third party through an assignment, a party can also transfer duties. Duties are not assigned, however; they are *delegated.* Normally, a **delegation of duties** does not relieve the party making the delegation (the **delegator**) of the obligation to perform in the event that the party to whom the duty has been delegated (the **delegatee**) fails to perform. No special form is required to create a valid delegation of duties. As long as the delegator expresses an intention to make the delegation, it is effective; the delegator need not even use the word *delegate.* Exhibit 12–2 on the next page graphically illustrates delegation relationships.

Duties That Cannot Be Delegated As a general rule, any duty can be delegated. This rule has some exceptions, however. Delegation is prohibited in the following circumstances:

① When performance depends on the personal skill or talents of the obligor.

② When special trust has been placed in the obligor.

③ When performance by a third party will vary materially from that expected by the obligee (the one to whom performance is owed) under the contract.

④ When the contract expressly prohibits delegation.

The following examples will help to clarify the kinds of duties that can and cannot be delegated:

① Brent contracts with Alex to tutor Alex in various aspects of financial underwriting and investment banking. Brent, an experienced businessperson known for his expertise in finance, delegates his duties to a third party, Carmen. This delegation is ineffective because Brent contracted to render a service that is founded on Brent's *expertise,* and the delegation changes Alex's expectancy under the contract.

EXHIBIT 12–2 **DELEGATION RELATIONSHIPS**

In the delegation relationship illustrated here, Brent delegates his *duties* under a contract that he made with Alex to a third party, Carmen. Brent thus becomes the *delegator* and Carmen the *delegatee* of the contractual duties. Carmen now owes performance of the contractual duties to Alex. Note that a delegation of duties normally does not relieve the delegator (Brent) of liability if the delegatee (Carmen) fails to perform the contractual duties.

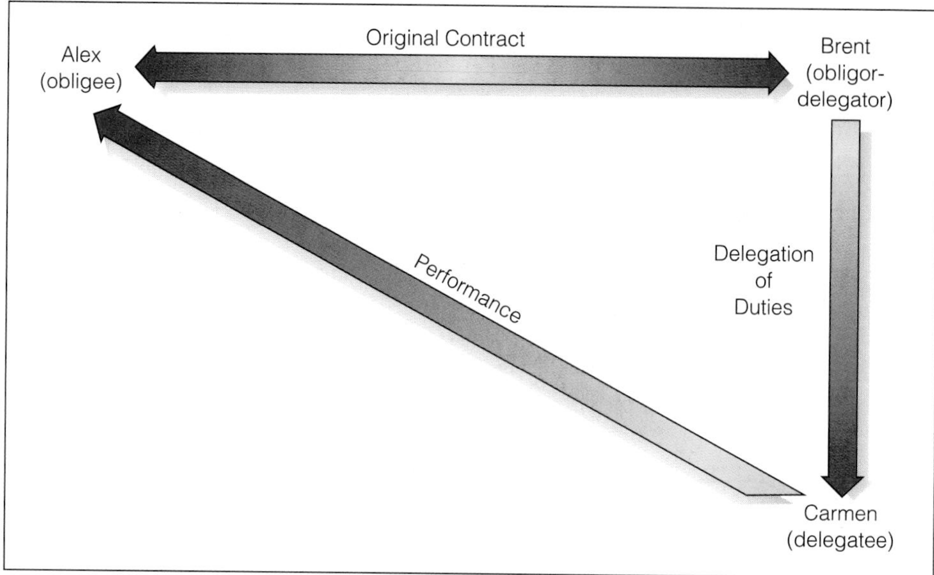

② Brent contracts with Alex to *personally* mow Alex's lawn during June, July, and August. Then Brent decides that he would rather spend the summer at the beach. Brent delegates his lawn-mowing duties to Carmen, who is in the business of mowing lawns and doing other landscaping work to earn income to pay for college. No matter how competent Carmen is, the delegation is not effective without Alex's consent. The contract was for *personal* performance.

③ Brent contracts with Alex to pick up and deliver heavy construction machinery to Alex's property. Brent delegates this duty to Carmen, who is in the business of delivering heavy machinery. This delegation is effective. The performance required is of a routine and nonpersonal nature, and the delegation does not change Alex's expectations under the contract.

Effect of a Delegation If a delegation of duties is enforceable, the *obligee* (the one to whom performance is owed) must accept performance from the delegatee (the one to whom the duties are delegated). ● **EXAMPLE 12.9** In the third example in the above list, Brent delegates his duty (to pick up and deliver heavy construction machinery to Alex's property) to Carmen. In that situation, Alex (the obligee) must accept performance from Carmen (the delegatee), because the delegation was effective. The obligee can legally refuse performance from the delegatee only if the duty is one that cannot be delegated. ●

COMPARE In an assignment, the assignor's original contract rights are extinguished after assignment. In a delegation, the delegator remains liable for performance under the contract if the delegatee fails to perform.

A valid delegation of duties does not relieve the delegator of obligations under the contract.[5] In the above example, if Carmen (the delegatee) fails to perform, Brent (the delegator) is still liable to Alex (the obligee). The obligee can also hold the del-

5. *Crane Ice Cream Co. v. Terminal Freezing & Heating Co.*, 147 Md. 588, 128 A. 280 (1925).

egatee liable if the delegatee made a promise of performance that will directly benefit the obligee. In this situation, there is an "assumption of duty" on the part of the delegatee, and breach of this duty makes the delegatee liable to the obligee. For example, if Carmen (the delegatee) promises Brent (the delegator), in a contract, to pick up and deliver the construction equipment to Alex's property but fails to do so, Alex (the obligee) can sue Brent, Carmen, or both. Although there are many exceptions, the general rule today is that the obligee can sue both the delegatee and the delegator.

"Assignment of All Rights"

Sometimes, a contract provides for an "assignment of all rights." The traditional view was that under this type of assignment, the assignee did not assume any duties. This view was based on the theory that the assignee's agreement to accept the benefits of the contract was not sufficient to imply a promise to assume the duties of the contract.

Modern authorities, however, take the view that the probable intent in using such general words is to create both an assignment of rights and an assumption of duties.[6] Therefore, when general words are used (for example, "I assign the contract" or "all my rights under the contract"), the contract is construed as implying both an assignment of rights and an assumption of duties.

Third Party Beneficiaries

THIRD PARTY BENEFICIARY
One for whose benefit a promise is made in a contract but who is not a party to the contract.

INTENDED BENEFICIARY
A third party for whose benefit a contract is formed; an intended beneficiary can sue the promisor if such a contract is breached.

As mentioned earlier in this chapter, to have contractual rights, a person normally must be a party to the contract. In other words, privity of contract must exist. An exception to the doctrine of privity exists when the original parties to the contract intend, at the time of contracting, that the contract performance directly benefit a third person. In this situation, the third person becomes a **third party beneficiary** of the contract. As an **intended beneficiary** of the contract, the third party has legal rights and can sue the promisor directly for breach of the contract.

Who, though, is the promisor? In bilateral contracts, both parties to the contract are promisors because they both make promises that can be enforced. In third party beneficiary contracts, courts determine the identity of the promisor by asking which party made the promise that benefits the third party—the answer indicates which person is the promisor. Allowing the third party to sue the promisor directly in effect circumvents the "middle person" (the promisee) and thus reduces the burden on the courts. Otherwise, the third party would sue the promisee, who would then sue the promisor.

ON THE WEB
A *New York Law Journal* article discussing *Lawrence v. Fox* and other leading decisions from the New York Court of Appeals is online at
http://www6.law.com/ny/links/150sterk.html.

A classic case in the area of third party beneficiary contracts is *Lawrence v. Fox*—a case decided in 1859. In *Lawrence,* which is presented as this chapter's *Landmark in the Law* on the following page, the court set aside the traditional requirement of privity and allowed a third party to bring a suit directly against the promisor.

Types of Intended Beneficiaries

The law distinguishes between *intended* beneficiaries and *incidental* beneficiaries. Only intended beneficiaries acquire legal rights in a contract. One type of intended

6. See UCC 2–210(1), (4); *Restatement (Second) of Contracts,* Section 328.

LANDMARK IN THE LAW
Lawrence v. Fox (1859)

In 1859, the New York Court of Appeals (that state's highest court) decided a case, *Lawrence v. Fox,*[a] in which the court departed from the doctrine of privity of contract and allowed a third party to sue the promisor directly. Prior to that time, contractual liability had always been limited to the parties to the contract.

Case Background The case involved three parties—Holly, Lawrence, and Fox. Holly had borrowed $300 from Lawrence. Shortly thereafter, Holly loaned $300 to Fox, who in return promised Holly that he would pay Holly's debt to Lawrence on the following day. When Lawrence failed in his attempts to obtain the $300 from Fox, he sued Fox to recover the money.

Why didn't Lawrence sue Holly directly, rather than pursue the unusual route of suing Fox, which meant that his chances at recovery were much slimmer? According to one scholar, the answer to this question is that the "Holly" in this case was probably Merwin Spencer Hawley. Both Hawley and the defendant, Arthur Wellesley Fox, were prominent members of the business community in Buffalo, New York. Evidence at trial suggested that the debt Hawley owed Lawrence was a gambling debt. Because gambling was illegal under New York law, Lawrence could not recover directly from Hawley in court, as the contract would have been deemed illegal.[b]

The Issue before the Court and the Court's Ruling In any event, the issue before the court was whether Lawrence, who was not a party to the Holly-Fox contract, could sue Fox directly to recover the $300. The court held that Lawrence could do so. It was manifestly "just," declared the court, to allow Lawrence to recover the money from Fox. The principle of law enunciated was that "[in the case of] a promise made for the benefit of another, he for whose benefit it is made may bring an action for its breach."

APPLICATION TO TODAY'S WORLD

At the time this decision was rendered, allowing a third party to sue a promisor directly was a novel idea and represented a radical departure from contract law. Although privity of contract remained the guiding principle until after the turn of the century, in two leading cases decided in 1916[c] *and 1918,*[d] *the New York Court of Appeals cited* Lawrence v. Fox *in justifying its departure from the principle of privity of contract. Since then, the third party beneficiary rule has been continuously expanded in scope.*

a. 20 N.Y. 268 (1859).

b. See Antony Jon Waters, "The Property in the Promise: A Study of the Third Party Beneficiary Rule," 98 *Harvard Law Review* 1109, 1168 (1985).

c. *MacPherson v. Buick Motor Co.,* 217 N.Y. 382, 111 N.E. 1050 (1916).

d. *Seaver v. Ransom,* 224 N.Y. 233, 120 N.E. 639 (1918).

beneficiary is a *creditor beneficiary.* A creditor beneficiary is one who, like the plaintiff in *Lawrence v. Fox,* benefits from a contract in which one party (the promisor) promises another party (the promisee) to pay a debt that the promisee owes to a third party (the creditor beneficiary). As an intended beneficiary, the creditor beneficiary can sue the promisor directly to enforce the contract.

Another type of intended beneficiary is a *donee* beneficiary. When a contract is made for the express purpose of giving a *gift* to a third party, the third party (the donee beneficiary) can sue the promisor directly to enforce the promise.[7] The most common donee beneficiary contract is a life insurance contract. ● **EXAMPLE 12.10** Akins (the promisee) pays premiums to Standard Life, a life insurance company, and Standard Life (the promisor) promises to pay a certain amount of money on Akins's death to anyone Akins designates as a beneficiary. The designated beneficiary is a donee beneficiary under the life insurance policy and can enforce the promise made by the insurance company to pay him or her on Akins's death. ●

As the law concerning third party beneficiaries evolved, numerous cases arose in which the third party beneficiary did not fit readily into either category—creditor beneficiary or donee beneficiary. Thus, the modern view, and the one adopted by the *Restatement (Second) of Contracts,* does not draw such clear lines and distinguishes only between intended beneficiaries (who can sue to enforce contracts made for their benefit) and incidental beneficiaries (who cannot sue, as will be discussed shortly).

ETHICAL ISSUE 12.1

Should third party beneficiaries be able to recover from attorneys on the basis of negligence?

One of the questions that periodically comes before the courts is whether a designated beneficiary under a legal document, such as a deed, can sue the attorney who handled the land transfer to recover for benefits that were lost as a result of the attorney's negligence. This is a significant issue for the beneficiaries when the party signing the deed is no longer living and thus cannot rectify the problem. The same problem arises occasionally when intended beneficiaries under a will do not receive what the will's maker intended them to because of the attorney's negligence. Traditionally, the rule was that third party beneficiaries could not sue the attorney in these situations because they were not in privity of contract with the attorney. That is, an attorney's duty of care extends only to his or her client, and thus third parties do not have standing to sue the attorney for negligence.

Clearly, restricting suits against attorneys in these situations can have harsh results for intended beneficiaries. Although some courts continue to adhere to the traditional rule, increasingly courts are allowing third party beneficiaries to sue attorneys in these circumstances.[8]

WHEN THE RIGHTS OF AN INTENDED BENEFICIARY VEST

An intended third party beneficiary cannot enforce a contract against the original parties until the rights of the third party have *vested,* which means the rights have taken effect and cannot be taken away. Until these rights have vested, the original parties to the contract—the promisor and the promisee—can modify or rescind the contract without the consent of the third party. When do the rights of third parties vest? Generally, the rights vest when one of the following occurs:

① When the third party demonstrates manifest assent to the contract, such as sending a letter or note acknowledging awareness of and consent to a contract formed for her or his benefit.

7. *Seaver v. Ransom,* 224 N.Y. 233, 120 N.E. 639 (1918).
8. See, for example, *Passell v. Watts,* 794 So.2d 651 (Fla.App. 2 Dist. 2001).

② When the third party materially alters his or her position in detrimental reliance on the contract, such as when a donee beneficiary contracts to have a home built in reliance on the receipt of funds promised to him or her in a donee beneficiary contract.

③ When the conditions for vesting mature. For example, the rights of a beneficiary under a life insurance policy vest when the insured person dies.

If the contract expressly reserves to the contracting parties the right to cancel, rescind, or modify the contract, the rights of the third party beneficiary are subject to any changes that result. In such a situation, the vesting of the third party's rights does not terminate the power of the original contracting parties to alter their legal relationships.[9]

INCIDENTAL BENEFICIARIES

INCIDENTAL BENEFICIARY A third party who incidentally benefits from a contract but whose benefit was not the reason the contract was formed; an incidental beneficiary has no rights in a contract and cannot sue to have the contract enforced.

The benefit that an **incidental beneficiary** receives from a contract between two parties is unintentional. Therefore, an incidental beneficiary cannot enforce a contract to which he or she is not a party. • **EXAMPLE 12.11** In one case, spectators of a Mike Tyson boxing fight in which Tyson was disqualified for biting his opponent's ear sued Tyson and the fight's promoters for a refund of their money on the basis of breach of contract. The spectators claimed that they had standing to sue the defendants as third party beneficiaries of the contract between Tyson and the fight's promoters. The court, however, held that the spectators did not have standing to sue because they were not in contractual privity with any of the defendants. Furthermore, any benefits they received from the contract were incidental to the contract. The court noted that the spectators got what they paid for: "the right to view whatever event transpired."[10] • (For another illustration of the rule that incidental beneficiaries cannot enforce contracts to which they are not parties, see this chapter's *Business Law in the Online World* feature on page 322.)

INTENDED VERSUS INCIDENTAL BENEFICIARIES

In determining whether a third party beneficiary is an intended or an incidental beneficiary, the courts generally use the *reasonable person* test. That is, a beneficiary will be considered an intended beneficiary if a reasonable person in the position of the beneficiary would believe that the promisee *intended* to confer on the beneficiary the right to bring suit to enforce the contract. In determining whether a party is an intended or an incidental beneficiary, the courts also look at a number of other factors. The presence of one or more of the following factors strongly indicates that the third party is an intended (rather than an incidental) beneficiary to the contract:

① Performance is rendered directly to the third party.

② The third party has the right to control the details of performance.

③ The third party is expressly designated as a beneficiary in the contract.

Is a party who borrows money to build a house an intended beneficiary of a contract between the lender and a party whom the lender hires to monitor the progress of the home's construction? That was the question in the following case.

9. Defenses raised against third party beneficiaries are given in *Restatement (Second) of Contracts*, Section 309.

10. *Castillo v. Tyson*, 268 A.D.2d 336, 701 N.Y.S.2d 423 (Sup.Ct.App.Div. 2000).

CASE 12.2 Vogan v. Hayes Appraisal Associates, Inc.

Supreme Court of Iowa, 1999.
588 N.W.2d 420.
http://www.judicial.state.ia.us/decisions[a]

FACTS Susan and Rollin Vogan wanted to build a home in West Des Moines, Iowa. They met with builder Gary Markley of Char Enterprises, Inc., who agreed to build the home for $169,633.59. The Vogans obtained a $170,000 construction loan from MidAmerica Savings Bank, which hired Hayes Appraisal Associates, Inc., to monitor the progress of the construction. MidAmerica was to disburse payments to Markley based on Hayes's reports. There were cost overruns on the job, and after three months, less than $2,000 of the initial loan remained. Markley said that it would take another $70,000 to finish the house. The Vogans borrowed $42,050 more, added some of their own money, and gave it to the bank to continue payments to Markley based on Hayes's reports. A few weeks later, Hayes reported that the house was 90 percent complete. Seven months later, with the house still unfinished, Markley ceased working on the job. Another contractor estimated that completion would cost an additional $60,000. The Vogans filed a suit in an Iowa state court against Hayes, based in part on Hayes's contract with MidAmerica. Hayes answered in part that the Vogans were not third party beneficiaries of that contract. The court issued a judgment in favor of the Vogans. Hayes appealed to a state intermediate appellate court, which reversed the judgment. The Vogans then appealed to the Iowa Supreme Court.

a. This Web site is maintained by the state of Iowa. In the left column, click on "Supreme Court." On that page, again in the left column, click on "Opinions Archive." When the archive opens, click on "1999," and in that list, next to "January 21, 1999," click on "Index." Scroll down the list of cases to the *Vogan* case and click on the case name to access the opinion.

ISSUE Were the Vogans intended third party beneficiaries of the contract between Hayes and MidAmerica?

DECISION Yes. The Iowa Supreme Court held that the Vogans were intended third party beneficiaries of the contract between Hayes and MidAmerica, as evidenced by the statements in the contract. The state supreme court vacated the decision of the state intermediate appellate court and affirmed the judgment of the trial court.

REASON The court stated that "the primary question in a third-party beneficiary case is whether the contract manifests an intent to benefit a third party. However, this intent need not be to benefit a third party directly." The court reasoned that in this case, "[t]he promised performance of Hayes Appraisal to MidAmerica will be of pecuniary benefit to the Vogans, and the contract is so expressed as to give Hayes reason to know that such benefit is contemplated by MidAmerica as one of the motivating causes of making the contract. * * * [In] these circumstances, the Vogans qualify as [intended] third-party beneficiaries of the agreement between MidAmerica and Hayes Appraisal."

FOR CRITICAL ANALYSIS—Social Consideration *If the Vogans could not recover as third party beneficiaries of the Hayes-MidAmerica contract, would they have any legal recourse? If so, against whom?*

Contract Discharge

DISCHARGE
The termination of an obligation. In contract law, discharge occurs when the parties have fully performed their contractual obligations or when events, conduct of the parties, or operation of the law releases the parties from performance.

PERFORMANCE
In contract law, the fulfillment of one's duties arising under a contract with another; the normal way of discharging one's contractual obligations.

The most common way to **discharge**, or terminate, one's contractual duties is by the **performance** of those duties. The duty to perform under a contract may be *conditioned* on the occurrence or nonoccurrence of a certain event, or the duty may be *absolute*. In addition to performance, a contract can be discharged in numerous other ways, including discharge by agreement of the parties and discharge by operation of law.

Conditions of Performance

In most contracts, promises of performance are not expressly conditioned or qualified. Instead, they are *absolute promises*. They must be performed, or the party promising the

BUSINESS LAW: //in the Online World

Beneficiaries of Contracts for Internet Services

As you will read elsewhere in this chapter, the courts generally consider several factors when deciding whether a party is an *intended* third party beneficiary of a contract or only an *incidental* third party beneficiary of the contract. One of these factors is whether the third party is expressly designated as a beneficiary in the contract.

How Specific Must the Designation of a Third Party Beneficiary Be?

Suppose that a contract between an Internet service provider (ISP) and a subscriber states that the subscriber will not use the services of the ISP to, among other things, "infringe on the rights of others." If, in violation of this contract, a subscriber does infringe on the rights of others, do "others" have the right, as intended third party beneficiaries, to sue the ISP? Do the "others" referred to in this contract constitute incidental or intended beneficiaries of the contract?

This question came before a court in a case that arose when subscribers of two ISPs offered for sale over the Internet videotapes of intercollegiate athletes in various states of undress. The athletes were videotaped, without their knowledge or consent, by hidden cameras in rest rooms, locker rooms, and showers. Among other things, the athletes contended that they were intended third party beneficiaries of the contracts between the ISPs and the subscribers. The contracts provided that the subscribers would not use the services of the ISPs "to violate federal or state law, or infringe [on] the rights of others, or distribute child pornography or obscenity over the Internet." The athletes argued that they qualified as "others" and thus were intended third party beneficiaries.

"Others" Is Not Specific Enough

The court held that the athletes did not acquire the status of third party beneficiaries merely because they qualified as "others." Said the court, "This is insufficient to state a claim as an intended third party beneficiary. Plaintiffs [the athletes] must allege express language in the contract identifying the third party beneficiary or imply a showing where the implication that the contract applies to third parties is so strong as to be practically an express declaration." Because the plaintiffs failed to accomplish this, they failed to state a claim as third party beneficiaries.[a]

FOR CRITICAL ANALYSIS

Why did the athletes sue the ISPs as third party beneficiaries under contract law? Did they have recourse against the subscribers' actions under any other legal theory?

a. *Doe v. Franco Productions,* 2000 WL 816779 (N.D.Ill. 2000).

act will be in breach of contract. • **EXAMPLE 12.12** JoAnne contracts to sell Alfonso a painting for $10,000. The parties' promises are unconditional: JoAnne's transfer of the painting to Alfonso and Alfonso's payment of $10,000 to JoAnne. The payment does not have to be made if the painting is not transferred. •

CONDITION
A qualification, provision, or clause in a contractual agreement, the occurrence or nonoccurrence of which creates, suspends, or terminates the obligations of the contracting parties.

In some situations, however, contractual promises are conditioned. A **condition** is a possible future event, the occurrence or nonoccurrence of which will trigger the performance of a legal obligation or terminate an existing obligation under a contract. If the condition is not satisfied, the obligations of the parties are discharged. • **EXAMPLE 12.13** Suppose that Alfonso, in the above example, offers to purchase JoAnne's painting only if an independent appraisal indicates that it is worth at least $10,000. JoAnne accepts Alfonso's offer. Their obligations (promises) are conditioned on the outcome of the appraisal. Should this condition not be satisfied (for example, if the appraiser deems the value of the painting to be only $5,000), their obligations to each other are discharged and cannot be enforced. •

An appraiser examines a painting by the artist Henri Matisse. If a party agrees to buy a painting on the condition that the work's value be a certain minimum as determined by an independent appraisal and the appraisal sets the value at less than the minimum, what happens to the agreement to buy the work?

We look here at three types of conditions that can be present in any given contract: conditions precedent, conditions subsequent, and concurrent conditions.

CONDITION PRECEDENT
In a contractual agreement, a condition that must be met before a party's promise becomes absolute.

Conditions Precedent A condition that must be fulfilled before a party's promise becomes absolute is called a **condition precedent**. The condition precedes the absolute duty to perform. ● **EXAMPLE 12.14** In the JoAnne-Alfonso example just given, Alfonso's promise is subject to the condition precedent that the appraised value of the painting be at least $10,000. Until the condition is fulfilled, Alfonso's promise is not absolute. Insurance contracts frequently specify that certain conditions, such as passing a physical examination, must be met before the insurance company will be obligated to perform under the contract.●

CONDITION SUBSEQUENT
A condition in a contract that, if not fulfilled, operates to terminate a party's absolute promise to perform.

Conditions Subsequent When a condition operates to terminate a party's absolute promise to perform, it is called a **condition subsequent**. The condition follows, or is subsequent to, the absolute duty to perform. If the condition occurs, the party need not perform any further. ● **EXAMPLE 12.15** A law firm hires Julia Darby, a recent law school graduate and a newly licensed attorney. Their contract provides that the firm's obligation to continue employing Darby is discharged if Darby fails to maintain her license to practice law. This is a condition subsequent because a failure to maintain the license will discharge a duty that has already arisen.[11]●

Generally, conditions precedent are common, while conditions subsequent are rare. The *Restatement (Second) of Contracts* deletes the terms *condition subsequent* and *condition precedent* and refers to both simply as "conditions."[12]

---

11. The difference between conditions precedent and conditions subsequent is relatively unimportant from a substantive point of view but very important procedurally. Usually, the plaintiff must prove conditions precedent because typically it is the plaintiff who claims that there is a duty to be performed. Similarly, the defendant must normally prove conditions subsequent because typically it is the defendant who claims that a duty no longer exists.

12. *Restatement (Second) of Contracts,* Section 224.

CONCURRENT CONDITIONS
Conditions that must occur or be performed at the same time; they are mutually dependent. No obligations arise until these conditions are simultaneously performed.

Concurrent Conditions When each party's absolute duty to perform is conditioned on the other party's absolute duty to perform, **concurrent conditions** are present. These conditions exist only when the parties expressly or impliedly are to perform their respective duties *simultaneously.* • **EXAMPLE 12.16** If a buyer promises to pay for goods when they are delivered by the seller, each party's absolute duty to perform is conditioned on the other party's absolute duty to perform. The buyer's duty to pay for the goods does not become absolute until the seller either delivers or attempts to deliver the goods. Likewise, the seller's duty to deliver the goods does not become absolute until the buyer pays or attempts to pay for the goods. Therefore, neither can recover from the other for breach without first tendering performance. •

DISCHARGE BY PERFORMANCE

TENDER
An unconditional offer to perform an obligation by a person who is ready, willing, and able to do so.

BREACH OF CONTRACT
The failure, without legal excuse, of a promisor to perform the obligations of a contract.

The contract comes to an end when both parties fulfill their respective duties by performance of the acts they have promised. Performance can also be accomplished by tender. **Tender** is an unconditional offer to perform by a person who is ready, willing, and able to do so. Therefore, a seller who places goods at the disposal of a buyer has tendered delivery and can demand payment according to the terms of the agreement. A buyer who offers to pay for goods has tendered payment and can demand delivery of the goods.

Once performance has been tendered, the party making the tender has done everything possible to carry out the terms of the contract. If the other party then refuses to perform, the party making the tender can consider the duty discharged and sue for **breach of contract.**

Complete versus Substantial Performance Normally, conditions expressly stated in the contract must fully occur in all aspects for *complete performance* (strict performance) of the contract to occur. Any deviation breaches the contract and discharges the other party's obligations to perform. Although in most contracts the parties fully discharge their obligations by complete performance, sometimes a party fails to fulfill all of the duties or completes the duties in a manner contrary to the terms of the contract. The issue then arises as to whether the performance was nonetheless sufficiently substantial to discharge the contractual obligations.

To qualify as *substantial performance,* the performance must not vary greatly from the performance promised in the contract, and it must create substantially the same benefits as those promised in the contract. If performance is substantial, the other party's duty to perform remains absolute (less damages, if any, for the minor deviations).

• **EXAMPLE 12.17** A couple contracts with a construction company to build a house. The contract specifies that Brand X plasterboard be used for the walls. The builder cannot obtain Brand X plasterboard, and the buyers are on holiday in the mountains of Peru and virtually unreachable. The builder decides to install Brand Y instead, which he knows is identical in quality and durability to Brand X plasterboard. All other aspects of construction conform to the contract. Does this deviation constitute a breach of contract? Can the buyers avoid their contractual obligation to pay the builder because Brand Y plasterboard was used instead of Brand X? Very likely, a court would hold that the builder had substantially performed his end of the bargain, and therefore the couple will be obligated to pay the builder. •

Different brands of construction supplies displayed at a site. If a contract for the construction of a building or house specifies a particular brand, can a product of a different brand of comparable quality be substituted?

What if the plasterboard substituted for Brand X was not of the same quality as Brand X, and the value of the house was reduced by $10,000? Again, a court would likely hold that the contract was substantially performed and that the contractor should be paid the price agreed on in the contract, less that $10,000.

ON THE WEB For a summary of how contracts may be discharged and other principles of contract law, go to **http://www.lawyers.com/lawyers-com/content/aboutlaw/about_contr.html**.

"Men do less than they ought, unless they do all that they can."

THOMAS CARLYLE, 1795–1881 (Scottish historian and essayist)

Performance to the Satisfaction of Another Contracts often state that completed work must personally satisfy one of the parties or a third person. The question is whether this satisfaction becomes a condition precedent, requiring actual personal satisfaction or approval for discharge, or whether the test of satisfaction is performance that would satisfy a *reasonable person* (substantial performance).

When the subject matter of the contract is personal, a contract to be performed to the satisfaction of one of the parties is conditioned, and performance must actually satisfy that party. For example, contracts for portraits, works of art, and tailoring are considered personal. Therefore, only the personal satisfaction of the party fulfills the condition—unless a jury finds the party is expressing dissatisfaction only to avoid payment or otherwise is not acting in good faith.

Contracts that involve mechanical fitness, utility, or marketability need be performed only to the satisfaction of a reasonable person unless they *expressly state otherwise*. When such contracts require performance to the satisfaction of a third party (for example, "to the satisfaction of Robert Ames, the supervising engineer"), the courts are divided. A majority of courts require the work to be satisfactory to a reasonable person, but some courts hold that the personal satisfaction of the third party designated in the contract (Robert Ames, in this example) must be met. Again, the personal judgment must be made honestly, or the condition will be excused.

Material Breach of Contract When a breach of contract is *material*[13]—that is, when performance is not deemed substantial—the nonbreaching party is excused from the performance of contractual duties and has a cause of action to sue for damages caused by the breach. If the breach is *minor* (not material), the nonbreaching party's duty to perform may sometimes be suspended until the breach is remedied, but the duty is not entirely excused. Once the minor breach is cured, the nonbreaching party must resume performance of the contractual obligations that had been undertaken.

A breach entitles the nonbreaching party to sue for damages, but only a material breach discharges the nonbreaching party from the contract. The policy underlying these rules is that contracts should go forward when only minor problems occur, but contracts should be terminated if major problems arise.[14]

Does preventing an employee from working constitute a breach of contract if the employer continues to pay her salary? That was the issue in the following case.

13. *Restatement (Second) of Contracts,* Section 241.
14. See UCC 2–612, which deals with installment contracts for the sale of goods.

CASE 12.3 Van Steenhouse v. Jacor Broadcasting of Colorado, Inc.

Supreme Court of Colorado, 1998.
958 P.2d 464.

FACTS Jacor Broadcasting of Colorado, Inc., owns and operates Newsradio 85 KOA. In June 1991, Andrea Van Steenhouse signed a three-year agreement to perform as a radio talk-show host for KOA. She was to receive a base salary and a performance bonus, depending on how many people tuned into her show. In January 1994, Jacor replaced her show with Rush Limbaugh's program. Jacor paid Van Steenhouse her base salary for the rest of the term of their agreement but did not employ her as a talk-show host. Van Steenhouse filed a suit in a Colorado state court against Jacor and others, claiming, among other things, breach of contract. The court ruled that Jacor had materially breached the contract and awarded Van Steenhouse an amount representing the bonus she could have received

(continued)

CASE 12.3—Continued

if she had not been taken off the air. The state intermediate appellate court affirmed the judgment. Jacor appealed to the Supreme Court of Colorado.

ISSUE Can an employee's claim for breach of contract be based solely on an employer's failure to provide an opportunity to work?

DECISION Yes. The Supreme Court of Colorado affirmed this part of the lower court's decision.

REASON The state supreme court acknowledged that, ordinarily, an employment agreement does not obligate an employer to furnish work for an employee. The court reasoned, however, that an obligation to furnish work arises "if the employee materially benefits from performing the duties described in the agreement." In such a situation, if the employer fails to furnish the kind of work specified in an employment agreement, the employee has a cause of action for breach of contract. The court explained that in this case "Van Steenhouse lost the opportunity to build and maintain her professional marketability. In addition, Van Steenhouse lost the opportunity to earn a 1994 performance bonus. Jacor deprived Van Steenhouse of these benefits by refusing to broadcast her show" as specified by their agreement.

FOR CRITICAL ANALYSIS—Social Consideration *If courts routinely held that only performance could discharge employment contracts, how would this affect employment relations?*

ANTICIPATORY REPUDIATION An assertion or action by a party indicating that he or she will not perform an obligation that the party is contractually obligated to perform at a future time.

"There are two ways of meeting difficulties. You alter the difficulties or you alter yourself to meet them."

PHYLLIS BOTTOME, 1882–1963 (British author)

REMEMBER The risks that prices will fluctuate and values will change are ordinary business risks for which the law does not provide relief.

Anticipatory Repudiation of a Contract Before either party to a contract has a duty to perform, one of the parties may refuse to perform her or his contractual obligations. This is called **anticipatory repudiation.**[15] When anticipatory repudiation occurs, it is treated as a material breach of contract, and the nonbreaching party is permitted to bring an action for damages immediately, even though the scheduled time for performance under the contract may still be in the future.[16] Until the nonbreaching party treats this early repudiation as a breach, however, the breaching party can retract the anticipatory repudiation by proper notice and restore the parties to their original obligations.[17]

An anticipatory repudiation is treated as a present, material breach for two reasons. First, the nonbreaching party should not be required to remain ready and willing to perform when the other party has already repudiated the contract. Second, the nonbreaching party should have the opportunity to seek a similar contract elsewhere and may have the duty to do so to minimize his or her loss.

Quite often, an anticipatory repudiation occurs when a sharp fluctuation in market prices creates a situation in which performance of the contract would be extremely unfavorable to one of the parties. • **EXAMPLE 12.18** Shasta Manufacturing Company contracts to manufacture and sell 100,000 personal computers to New Age, Inc., a computer retailer with 500 outlet stores. Delivery is to be made two months from the date of the contract. One month later, three suppliers of computer parts raise their prices to Shasta. Because of these higher prices, Shasta stands to lose $500,000 if it sells the computers to New Age at the contract price. Shasta writes to New Age, informing New Age that it cannot deliver the 100,000 computers at the agreed-on contract price. Even though you might sympathize with Shasta, its letter is an anticipatory repudiation of the contract, allowing New Age the option of treating the repudiation as a material breach and proceeding immediately to pursue remedies, even though the contract delivery date is still a month away.[18] •

15. *Restatement (Second) of Contracts,* Section 253, and UCC 2–610.

16. The doctrine of anticipatory repudiation first arose in the landmark case of *Hochster v. De La Tour,* 2 Ellis and Blackburn Reports 678 (1853), when the English court recognized the delay and expense inherent in a rule requiring a nonbreaching party to wait until the time of performance before suing on an anticipatory repudiation.

17. See UCC 2–611.

18. Another illustration can be found in *Reliance Cooperage Corp. v. Treat,* 195 F.2d 977 (8th Cir. 1952).

DISCHARGE BY AGREEMENT

Any contract can be discharged by the agreement of the parties. The agreement can be contained in the original contract, or the parties can form a new contract for the express purpose of discharging the original contract.

Discharge by Rescission As discussed in an earlier chapter, rescission is the process in which the parties cancel the contract and are returned to the positions they occupied prior to the contract's formation. For *mutual rescission* to take place, the parties must make another agreement that also satisfies the legal requirements for a contract—there must be an *offer,* an *acceptance,* and *consideration.* Ordinarily, if the parties agree to rescind the original contract, their promises not to perform those acts promised in the original contract will be legal consideration for the second contract.

Mutual rescission can occur in this manner when the original contract is executory on both sides (that is, neither party has completed performance). The agreement to rescind an executory contract is generally enforceable, even if it is made orally and even if the original agreement was in writing.[19] When one party has fully performed, however, an agreement to rescind the original contract usually is not enforceable unless additional consideration or restitution is made.[20]

NOVATION
The substitution, by agreement, of a new contract for an old one, with the rights under the old one being terminated. Typically, novation involves the substitution of a new person who is responsible for the contract and the removal of the original party's rights and duties under the contract.

Discharge by Novation The process of **novation** substitutes a third party for one of the original parties. Essentially, the parties to the original contract and one or more new parties all get together and agree to the substitution. The requirements of a novation are as follows:

① The existence of a previous, valid obligation.

② Agreement by all of the parties to a new contract.

③ The extinguishing of the old obligation (discharge of the prior party).

④ A new, valid contract.

An important distinction between an assignment or delegation and a novation is that a novation involves a new contract, and an assignment or delegation involves the old contract.

● **EXAMPLE 12.19** Suppose that you contract with A. Logan Enterprises to sell it your office-equipment business. Logan later learns that it should not expand at this time but knows of another party, MBI Corporation, that is interested in purchasing your business. All three of you get together and agree to a novation. As long as the new contract is supported by consideration, the novation discharges the original contract between you and Logan and replaces it with the new contract between you and MBI Corporation. Logan prefers the novation to an assignment because the novation discharges all the contract liabilities stemming from Logan's contract with you. If the original contract had been an installment sales contract requiring twelve monthly payments, and Logan had merely assigned the contract (assigned its rights and delegated its duties under the contract) to MBI Corporation, Logan would have remained liable to you for the payments if MBI Corporation defaulted.●

---

19. Agreements to rescind contracts involving transfers of realty, however, must be evidenced by a writing. Another exception has to do with the sale of goods under the UCC, when the sales contract requires written rescission.

20. Under UCC 2–209(1), however, no consideration is needed to modify a contract for a sale of goods. See Chapter 14. Also see UCC 1–107.

Discharge by Accord and Satisfaction As discussed in Chapter 9, in an *accord and satisfaction,* the parties agree to accept performance different from the performance originally promised. An *accord* is an executory contract (one that has not yet been performed) to perform some act in order to satisfy an existing contractual duty that is not yet discharged.[21] A *satisfaction* is the performance of the accord agreement. An *accord* and its *satisfaction* discharge the original contractual obligation.

Once the accord has been made, the original obligation is merely suspended until the accord agreement is fully performed. If it is not performed, the party to whom performance is owed can bring an action on the original obligation or for breach of the accord. • **EXAMPLE 12.20** Shea obtains a judgment against Marla for $4,000. Later, both parties agree that the judgment can be satisfied by Marla's transfer of her automobile to Shea. This agreement to accept the auto in lieu of $4,000 in cash is the accord. If Marla transfers her automobile to Shea, the accord agreement is fully performed, and the $4,000 debt is discharged. If Marla refuses to transfer her car, the accord is breached. Because the original obligation is merely suspended, Shea can bring an action to enforce the judgment for $4,000 in cash or bring an action for breach of the accord. •

DISCHARGE BY OPERATION OF LAW

"Law is a practical matter."
ROSCOE POUND, 1870–1964 (American jurist)

Under some circumstances, contractual duties may be discharged by operation of law. These circumstances include material alteration of the contract, the running of the relevant statute of limitations, bankruptcy, and impossibility of performance.

Contract Alteration To discourage parties from altering written contracts, the law operates to allow an innocent party to be discharged when one party has materially altered a written contract without the knowledge or consent of the other party. For example, if a party alters a material term of the contract—such as the quantity term or the price term—without the knowledge or consent of the other party, the party who was unaware of the alteration can treat the contract as discharged or terminated.

Statutes of Limitations As mentioned earlier in this text, statutes of limitations limit the period during which a party can sue on a particular cause of action. After the applicable limitations period has passed, a suit can no longer be brought. For example, the limitations period for bringing suits for breach of oral contracts is usually two to three years; for written contracts, four to five years; and for recovery of amounts awarded in judgment, ten to twenty years, depending on state law. Suits for breach of a contract for the sale of goods must be brought within four years after the cause of action has accrued. By original agreement, the parties can reduce this four-year period to a one-year period. They cannot, however, extend it beyond the four-year limitations period.

Bankruptcy A proceeding in bankruptcy attempts to allocate the assets the debtor owns to the creditors in a fair and equitable fashion. Once the assets have been allocated, the debtor receives a *discharge in bankruptcy*—see Chapter 23. A discharge in bankruptcy will ordinarily bar enforcement of most of a debtor's contracts by the creditors.

IMPOSSIBILITY OF PERFORMANCE
A doctrine under which a party to a contract is relieved of his or her duty to perform when performance becomes objectively impossible or totally impracticable (through no fault of either party).

When Performance Is Impossible After a contract has been made, performance may become impossible in an objective sense. This is known as **impossibility of performance** and may discharge the contract.[22]

21. *Restatement (Second) of Contracts,* Section 281.
22. *Restatement (Second) of Contracts,* Section 261.

Objective Impossibility. *Objective impossibility* ("It can't be done") must be distinguished from subjective impossibility ("I'm sorry, I simply can't do it"). An example of subjective impossibility is a contract in which funds cannot be paid on time because the bank is closed.[23] In effect, the nonperforming party is saying, "It is impossible for *me* to perform," rather than "It is impossible for *anyone* to perform." Accordingly, such excuses do not discharge a contract, and the nonperforming party is normally held in breach of contract. Four basic types of situations will generally qualify as grounds for the discharge of contractual obligations based on impossibility of performance:[24]

1. *When a party whose personal performance is essential to the completion of the contract dies or becomes incapacitated prior to performance.* • **EXAMPLE 12.21** Fred, a famous dancer, contracts with Ethereal Dancing Guild to play a leading role in its new ballet. Before the ballet can be performed, Fred becomes ill and dies. His personal performance was essential to the completion of the contract. Thus, his death discharges the contract and his estate's liability for his nonperformance.•
2. *When the specific subject matter of the contract is destroyed.* • **EXAMPLE 12.22** A-1 Farm Equipment agrees to sell Gudgel the green tractor on its lot and promises to have it ready for Gudgel to pick up on Saturday. On Friday night, however, a truck veers off the nearby highway and smashes into the tractor, destroying it beyond repair. Because the contract was for this specific tractor, A-1's performance is rendered impossible owing to the accident.•
3. *When a change in the law renders performance illegal.* An example is a contract to build an apartment building, when the zoning laws are changed to prohibit the construction of residential rental property at this location. This change renders the contract impossible to perform.
4. *When performance becomes commercially impracticable.* The inclusion of this type of "impossibility" as a basis for contract discharge results from a growing trend to allow parties to discharge contracts in which the originally contemplated performance turns out to be much more difficult or expensive than anticipated. In such situations, courts may excuse parties from their performance obligations under the doctrine of *commercial impracticability.* For example, in one case, a court held that a contract could be discharged because a party would have to pay ten times more than the original estimate to excavate a certain amount of gravel.[25]

NOTE The doctrine of commercial impracticability does not provide relief from such events as ordinary price increases or easily predictable changes in the weather.

A production line in a commercial bakery. If a fire incapacitated the bakery's oven, would the bakery be excused from performing its contracts until the oven was fixed? If a contract involved a special holiday order and the oven could not be fixed until after the holiday, would the contract be discharged?

ETHICAL ISSUE 12.2

Should the courts allow the defense of impossibility of performance to be used more often?

The doctrine of impossibility is applied only when the parties could not have reasonably foreseen, at the time the contract was formed, the event or events that rendered performance impossible. In some cases, the courts may seem to go too far in holding that certain events or conditions should have been foreseen by the parties, thus precluding parties from avoiding contractual obligations under the doctrine of impossibility of performance. Yet even though the courts rarely excuse parties from performance under the doctrine of impossibility, they allow parties to raise this defense more often than they

23. *Ingham Lumber Co. v. Ingersoll & Co.,* 93 Ark. 447, 125 S.W. 139 (1910).
24. *Restatement (Second) of Contracts,* Sections 262–266, and UCC 2–615.
25. *Mineral Park Land Co. v. Howard,* 172 Cal. 289, 156 P. 458 (1916).

once did. Indeed, until the latter part of the nineteenth century, courts were reluctant to discharge a contract even when it appeared that performance was literally impossible. Generally, the courts must balance the freedom of parties to contract as they will (and assume the risks involved) against the injustice that may result when certain contractual obligations are enforced. If the courts allowed parties to raise impossibility of performance as a defense to contractual obligations more often, freedom of contract would suffer.

Temporary Impossibility. An occurrence or event that makes performance temporarily impossible operates to suspend performance until the impossibility ceases. Then, ordinarily, the parties must perform the contract as originally planned. If, however, the lapse of time and the change in circumstances surrounding the contract make it substantially more burdensome for the parties to perform the promised acts, the contract is discharged.

• **EXAMPLE 12.23** The leading case on the subject, *Autry v. Republic Productions*,[26] involved an actor who was drafted into the army in 1942. Being drafted rendered the actor's contract temporarily impossible to perform, and it was suspended until the end of the war. When the actor got out of the army, the purchasing power of the dollar had so changed that performance of the contract would have been substantially burdensome to him. Therefore, the contract was discharged. •

26. 30 Cal.2d 144, 180 P.2d 888 (1947).

Key Terms

Chapter Summary Third Party Rights and Discharge

THIRD PARTY RIGHTS

Assignments (See pages 311–315.)

1. An assignment is the transfer of rights under a contract to a third party. The person assigning the rights is the *assignor,* and the party to whom the rights are assigned is the *assignee.* The assignee has a right to demand performance from the other original party to the contract.
2. Generally, all rights can be assigned, except in the following circumstances:
   a. When assignment is expressly prohibited by statute (for example, workers' compensation benefits).
   b. When a contract calls for the performance of personal services.

Chapter Summary Third Party Rights and Discharge—continued

Assignments—continued	c. When the assignment will materially increase or alter the risks or duties of the obligor (the party that is obligated to perform). d. When the contract itself stipulates that the rights cannot be assigned (with some exceptions). 3. The assignee should give notice of the assignment to the obligor. a. If the assignor assigns the same right to two different persons, generally the first assignment in time is the first in right, although in some states the first assignee to give notice takes priority. b. Until the obligor is notified of the assignment, the obligor can tender performance to the assignor; and if performance is accepted by the assignor, the obligor's duties under the contract are discharged without benefit to the assignee.
Delegations (See pages 315–317.)	1. A delegation is the transfer of duties under a contract to a third party (the *delegatee*), who then assumes the obligation of performing the contractual duties previously held by the one making the delegation (the *delegator*). 2. As a general rule, any duty can be delegated, except in the following circumstances: a. When performance depends on the personal skill or talents of the obligor. b. When special trust has been placed in the obligor. c. When performance by a third party will vary materially from that expected by the obligee (the one to whom the duty is owed) under the contract. d. When the contract expressly prohibits delegation. 3. A valid delegation of duties does not relieve the delegator of obligations under the contract. If the delegatee fails to perform, the delegator is still liable to the obligee. 4. An "assignment of all rights" or an "assignment of contract" is often construed to mean that both the rights and the duties arising under the contract are transferred to a third party.
Third Party Beneficiaries (See pages 317–321.)	A third party beneficiary contract is one made for the purpose of benefiting a third party. 1. *Intended beneficiary*—One for whose benefit a contract is created. When the promisor (the one making the contractual promise that benefits a third party) fails to perform as promised, the third party can sue the promisor directly. Examples of third party beneficiaries are creditor and donee beneficiaries. 2. *Incidental beneficiary*—A third party who indirectly (incidentally) benefits from a contract but for whose benefit the contract was not specifically intended. Incidental beneficiaries have no rights to the benefits received and cannot sue to have the contract enforced.
	CONTRACT DISCHARGE
Conditions of Performance (See pages 321–324.)	Contract obligations may be subject to the following types of conditions: 1. *Condition precedent*—A condition that must be fulfilled before a party's promise becomes absolute. 2. *Condition subsequent*—A condition that operates to terminate a party's absolute promise to perform. 3. *Concurrent conditions*—In this case, each party's absolute duty to perform is conditioned on the other party's absolute duty to perform.

(continued)

Chapter Summary Third Party Rights and Discharge—continued

Discharge by Performance (See pages 324–326.)	A contract may be discharged by complete (strict) performance or by substantial performance. In some cases, performance must be to the satisfaction of another. Totally inadequate performance constitutes a material breach of contract. An anticipatory repudiation of a contract allows the other party to sue immediately for breach of contract.
Discharge by Agreement (See pages 327–328.)	Parties may agree to discharge their contractual obligations in several ways: 1. *By rescission*—The parties mutually agree to rescind (cancel) the contract. 2. *By novation*—A new party is substituted for one of the primary parties to a contract. 3. *By accord and satisfaction*—The parties agree to render and accept performance different from that on which they originally agreed.
Discharge by Operation of Law (See pages 328–330.)	Parties' obligations under contracts may be discharged by operation of law owing to one of the following: 1. Contract alteration. 2. Statutes of limitations. 3. Bankruptcy. 4. Impossibility of performance.

For Review

① What is the difference between an assignment and a delegation?
② What rights can be assigned despite a contract clause expressly prohibiting assignment?
③ What factors indicate that a third party beneficiary is an intended beneficiary?
④ How are most contracts discharged?
⑤ What is a contractual condition, and how might a condition affect contractual obligations?

Questions and Case Problems

12–1. Substantial Performance. Complete performance is full performance according to the terms of a contract. Discuss the effect on the parties if there is less than full performance.

12–2. Third Party Beneficiaries. Wilken owes Rivera $2,000. Howie promises Wilken that he will pay Rivera the $2,000 in return for Wilken's promise to give Howie's children guitar lessons. Is Rivera an intended beneficiary of the Howie-Wilken contract? Explain.

12–3. Assignments. Aron, a college student, signs a one-year lease agreement that runs from September 1 to August 31. The lease agreement specifies that the lease cannot be assigned without the landlord's consent. In late May, Aron decides not to go to summer school and assigns the balance of the lease (three months) to a close friend, Erica. The landlord objects to the assignment and denies Erica access to the apartment. Aron claims that Erica is financially sound and should be allowed the full rights and privileges of an assignee. Discuss fully whether the landlord or Aron is correct.

12–4. Novation versus Accord and Satisfaction. Doug owes creditor Cartwright $1,000, which is due and payable on June 1. Doug has a car accident, misses several months of work, and consequently does not have the funds to pay Cartwright on June 1. Doug's father, Bert, offers to pay Cartwright $1,100 in four equal installments if Cartwright will discharge Doug from any further liability on the debt. Cartwright accepts. Is the transaction a novation or an accord and satisfaction? Explain.

12–5. Impossibility of Performance. Millie contracted to sell Frank 1,000 bushels of corn to be grown on Millie's farm. Owing to a drought during the growing season, Millie's yield was much less than anticipated, and she could deliver only 250 bushels to

Frank. Frank accepted the lesser amount but sued Millie for breach of contract. Can Millie defend successfully on the basis of objective impossibility of performance? Explain.

12–6. Assignments. Joseph LeMieux, of Maine, won $373,000 in a lottery operated by the Tri-State Lotto Commission. The lottery is sponsored by the three northern New England states and is administered in Vermont. Under its usual payment plan, Tri-State was to pay the $373,000 to LeMieux in equal annual installments over a twenty-year period. LeMieux assigned his rights to the lottery installment payments for the years 1996 through 2006 to Singer Freidlander Corp. for the sum of $80,000. LeMieux and Singer Freidlander (the plaintiffs) sought a declaratory judgment from a court authorizing the assignment agreement between them despite Tri-State's regulation barring the assignment of lottery proceeds. The trial court granted Tri-State's motion for summary judgment. On appeal, the plaintiffs argued that Tri-State's regulation was invalid. Is it? Discuss. [*LeMieux v. Tri-State Lotto Commission*, 666 A.2d 1170 (Vt. 1995)]

12–7. Conditions. Heublein, Inc., manufactures wines and distilled spirits. Tarrant Distributors, Inc., agreed to distribute Heublein brands. When problems arose, the parties entered mediation. Under a settlement agreement, Heublein agreed to pay Tarrant the amount of its "net loss" as determined by Coopers & Lybrand, an accounting firm, according to a specified formula. The parties agreed that Coopers & Lybrand's calculation would be "final and binding." Heublein disagreed with Coopers & Lybrand's calculation, however, and refused to pay. The parties asked a federal district court to rule on the dispute. Heublein argued that the settlement agreement included an implied condition precedent that Coopers & Lybrand would correctly apply the specified formula before Heublein was obligated to pay. Tarrant pointed to the clause that the calculation would be "final and binding." With whom will the court agree, and why? [*Tarrant Distributors, Inc. v. Heublein, Inc.*, 127 F.3d 375 (5th Cir. 1997)]

12–8. Third Party Beneficiary. John Castle and Leonard Harlan, who headed Castle Harlan, Inc., an investment firm, entered into an agreement with the federal government to buy Western Empire Federal Savings and Loan. Under the agreement, Castle Harlan was to invest a nominal amount in the bank and arrange for others to invest much more, in exchange for, among other things, a promise that for two years, Western Empire would not be subject to certain restrictions in federal regulations. The government's enforcement of other regulations against Western Empire, however, caused the bank to go out of business. Castle, Harlan, and the other investors filed a suit in the U.S. Court of Federal Claims against the government, alleging breach of contract. The government filed a motion to dismiss all of the plaintiffs except Castle and Harlan, on the ground that the others did not sign the contract between the government and Castle and Harlan. Is the government correct? Should the court dismiss the claims brought by the other investors? Why or why not? [*Castle v. United States*, 42 Fed.Cl. 859 (1999)]

12–9. Performance. Steven McPheters, a house builder and developer, hired Terry Tentinger, who did business as New Horizon Construction, to do some touching up and repainting on one of McPheters's new houses. Tentinger worked two days, billed McPheters $420 (a three-man crew for fourteen hours at $30 per hour), and offered to return to the house to remedy any defects in his work at no cost. McPheters objected to the number of hours on the bill—although he did not express dissatisfaction with the work—and offered Tentinger $250. Tentinger refused to accept this amount and filed a suit in an Idaho state court to collect the full amount. McPheters filed a counterclaim, alleging that Tentinger failed to perform the job in a skilled manner, resulting in $2,500 in damages, which it would cost $500 to repair. Tentinger's witnesses testified that although some touch-up work needed to be done, the job had been performed in a skilled manner. McPheters presented testimony indicating that the work was so defective as to render it commercially unreasonable. On what basis could the court rule in Tentinger's favor? Explain fully. [*Tentinger v. McPheters*, 132 Idaho 620, 977 P.2d 234 (Idaho App. 1999)]

TEST YOUR KNOWLEDGE—ANSWER ON THE WEB

12–10. In May 1996, O'Brien-Shiepe Funeral Home, Inc., in Hempstead, New York, hired Teramo & Co. to build an addition to O'Brien's funeral home. The parties' contract did not specify a date for the completion of the work. The city of Hempstead issued a building permit for the project on June 14, and Teramo began work about two weeks later. There was some delay in construction because O'Brien asked that no work be done during funeral services, but by the end of March 1997, the work was substantially complete. The city of Hempstead issued a "Certificate of Completion" on April 15. During the construction, O'Brien made periodic payments to Teramo, but there was a balance due of $17,950, which O'Brien did not pay. To recover this amount, Teramo filed a suit in a New York state court against O'Brien. O'Brien filed a counterclaim to recover lost profits for business allegedly lost due to the time Teramo took to build the addition, and for $6,180 spent to correct problems caused by poor work. Which, if any, party is entitled to an award in this case? Explain. [*Teramo & Co. v. O'Brien-Shiepe Funeral Home, Inc.*, 725 N.Y.S.2d 87 (A.D. 2 Dept. 2001)]

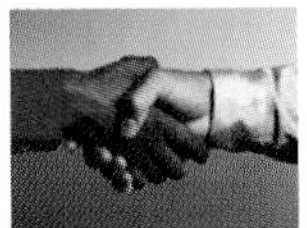

A QUESTION OF ETHICS AND SOCIAL RESPONSIBILITY

12–11. Bath Iron Works (BIW) offered a job to Thomas Devine, contingent on Devine's passing a drug test. The testing was conducted by NorDx, a subcontractor of Roche Biomedical Laboratories. When NorDx found that Devine's urinalysis showed the presence of opiates, a result confirmed by Roche, BIW refused to offer Devine permanent employment. Devine claimed that the ingestion of poppy seeds can lead to a positive result and that he tested positive for opiates only because of his daily consumption of poppy seed muffins. In Devine's suit against Roche, Devine argued, among other things, that he was a third party beneficiary of the contract between his employer (BIW) and NorDx (Roche). Given this factual background, consider the following questions. [*Devine v. Roche Biomedical Laboratories,* 659 A.2d 868 (Me. 1995)]

1. Is Devine an intended third party beneficiary of the BIW–NorDx contract? In deciding this issue, should the court focus on the nature of the promises made in the contract itself or on the consequences of the contract for Devine, a third party?
2. Should employees whose job security and reputation have suffered as a result of false test results be allowed to sue the drug-testing labs for the tort of negligence? In such situations, do drug-testing labs have a duty to the employees to exercise reasonable care in conducting the tests?

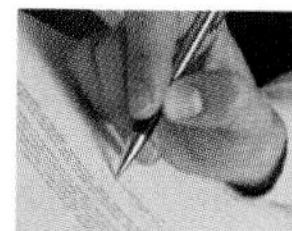

FOR CRITICAL ANALYSIS

12–12. The concept of substantial performance permits a party to be discharged from a contract even though the party has not fully performed his or her obligations according to the contract's terms. Is this fair? What policy interests are at issue here?

Internet Exercises

Go to the *Business Law Today* home page at **http://blt.westbuslaw.com**. Select "Interactive Study Center" and then click on "Chapter 12." There you will find the following Internet research exercises that you can perform to learn more about the requirements of third party beneficiaries and anticipatory repudiation:

Activity 12–1: **Third Party Beneficiaries**
Activity 12–2: **Anticipatory Repudiation**

Before the Test

Go to the *Business Law Today* home page at **http://blt.westbuslaw.com**. Click on "Interactive Quizzes." You will find at least twenty interactive questions relating to this chapter.

CHAPTER 13

Breach and Remedies

"Men keep their engagements when it is to the advantage of both not to break them."

Solon, sixth century B.C.E.
(Athenian legal reformer)

CHAPTER CONTENTS

LEARNING OBJECTIVES

After reading this chapter, you should be able to answer the following questions:

1. What is the difference between compensatory damages and consequential damages? What are nominal damages, and when might they be awarded by a court?
2. What is the usual measure of damages on a breach of contract for a sale of goods?
3. Under what circumstances will the remedy of rescission and restitution be available?
4. When might specific performance be granted as a remedy?
5. What is the rationale underlying the doctrine of election of remedies?

As the Athenian political leader Solon instructed centuries ago, a contract will not be broken so long as "it is to the advantage of both" parties to fulfill their contractual obligations. Normally, a person enters into a contract with another to secure an advantage. When it is no longer advantageous for a party to fulfill his or her contractual obligations, breach of contract may result. As discussed in Chapter 12, a *breach of contract* occurs when a party fails to perform part or all of the required duties under a contract.[1] Once a party fails to perform or performs inadequately, the other party—the nonbreaching party—can choose one or more of several remedies.

The most common remedies available to a nonbreaching party under contract law include damages, rescission and restitution, specific performance,

1. *Restatement (Second) of Contracts,* Section 235(2).

and reformation. As discussed in Chapter 1, courts distinguish between *remedies at law* and *remedies in equity.* Today, the remedy at law is normally money damages. We discuss this remedy in the first part of this chapter. Equitable remedies include rescission and restitution, specific performance, and reformation, all of which we examine later in the chapter. Usually, a court will not award an equitable remedy unless the remedy at law is inadequate. In the final pages of this chapter, we look at some special legal doctrines and concepts relating to remedies.

Damages

REMEMBER The terms of a contract must be sufficiently definite for a court to determine the amount of damages to award.

A breach of contract entitles the nonbreaching party to sue for money damages. As you read in Chapter 4, damages are designed to compensate a party for harm suffered as a result of another's wrongful act. In the context of contract law, damages are designed to compensate the nonbreaching party for the loss of the bargain. Often, courts say that innocent parties are to be placed in the position they would have occupied had the contract been fully performed.[2]

TYPES OF DAMAGES

There are basically four kinds of damages: compensatory, consequential, punitive, and nominal damages.

Compensatory Damages As discussed in Chapter 4, *compensatory damages* compensate an injured party for injuries or damages actually sustained by that party. The nonbreaching party must prove that the actual damages arose directly from the loss of the bargain caused by the breach of contract. The amount of compensatory damages is the difference between the value of the breaching party's promised performance under the contract and the value of her or his actual performance. This amount is reduced by any loss that the injured party has avoided, however.

"The duty to keep a contract at common law means a prediction that you must pay damages if you do not keep it—and nothing else."

OLIVER WENDELL HOLMES, JR., 1841–1935 (Associate justice of the United States Supreme Court, 1902–1932)

● **EXAMPLE 13.1** You contract with Marinot Industries to perform certain personal services exclusively for Marinot during August for a payment of $3,500. Marinot cancels the contract and is in breach. You are able to find another job during August but can earn only $1,000. You normally can sue Marinot for breach and recover $2,500 as compensatory damages. You may also recover from Marinot the amount that you spent to find the other job.● Expenses that are directly incurred because of a breach of contract—such as those incurred to obtain performance from another source—are called *incidental damages.*

The measurement of compensatory damages varies by type of contract. Certain types of contracts deserve special mention—contracts for the sale of goods, contracts for the sale of land, and construction contracts.

ON THE WEB For a summary of how contracts may be breached and other information on contract law, go to **http://www.lawyers.com/lawyers-com/content/aboutlaw/about_contr.html.**

Sale of Goods. In a contract for the sale of goods, the usual measure of compensatory damages is an amount equal to the difference between the contract price and the market price.[3] ● **EXAMPLE 13.2** MediQuick Laboratories contracts with Cal Computer Industries to purchase ten Model X-15 computer work stations for $8,000 each. If Cal Computer fails to deliver the ten work stations, and the current market price of the

2. *Restatement (Second) of Contracts,* Section 347; and UCC 1–106(1).

3. That is, the difference between the contract price and the market price at the time and place at which the goods were to be delivered or tendered. See UCC 2–708, 2–713, and 2–715(1) (discussed in Chapter 16).

work stations is $8,150, MediQuick's measure of damages is $1,500 (10 × $150).● When the buyer breaches and the seller has not yet produced the goods, compensatory damages normally equal the lost profits on the sale rather than the difference between the contract price and the market price.

Sale of Land. The measure of damages in a contract for the sale of land is ordinarily the same as it is for contracts involving the sale of goods—that is, the difference between the contract price and the market price of the land. The majority of states follow this rule regardless of whether the buyer or the seller breaches the contract.

Construction Contracts. With construction contracts, the measure of damages often varies depending on which party breaches and at what stage the breach occurs. See Exhibit 13–1 for illustrations.

EXHIBIT 13–1 MEASUREMENT OF DAMAGES—BREACH OF CONSTRUCTION CONTRACTS

PARTY IN BREACH	TIME OF BREACH	MEASUREMENT OF DAMAGES
Owner	Before construction begins	Profits (contract price less cost of materials and labor)
Owner	After construction begins	Profits plus costs incurred up to time of breach
Owner	After construction is completed	Contract price
Contractor	Before construction is completed	Generally, all costs incurred by owner to complete construction

CONSEQUENTIAL DAMAGES
Special damages that compensate for a loss that does not directly or immediately result from the breach (for example, lost profits). For the plaintiff to collect special damages, they must have been reasonably foreseeable at the time the breach or injury occurred.

NOTE A seller who does not wish to take on the risk of having to pay consequential damages can limit the buyer's remedies.

Consequential Damages Foreseeable damages that result from a party's breach of contract are referred to as **consequential damages**, or *special damages*. Consequential damages differ from compensatory damages in that they are caused by special circumstances beyond the contract itself. When a seller does not deliver goods, knowing that a buyer is planning to use or resell those goods immediately, consequential damages are awarded for the loss of profits from the planned resale.

● EXAMPLE **13.3** Gilmore contracts to have a specific item shipped to her—one that she desperately needs to repair her printing press. In her contract with the shipper, Gilmore states that she must receive the item by Monday or she will not be able to print her paper and will lose $950. If the shipper is late, Gilmore normally can recover the consequential damages caused by the delay (that is, the $950 in losses).●

For a nonbreaching party to recover consequential damages, the breaching party must know (or have reason to know) that special circumstances will cause the nonbreaching party to suffer an additional loss.[4] This rule was enunciated in *Hadley v. Baxendale*, the case presented as this chapter's *Landmark in the Law* on the next page.

Punitive Damages Recall from Chapter 4 that punitive damages are designed to punish a wrongdoer and set an example to deter similar conduct in the future. Punitive

4. UCC 2–715(2). See Chapter 16.

LANDMARK IN THE LAW
Hadley v. Baxendale (1854)

A landmark case in establishing the rule that notice of special ("consequential") circumstances must be given if consequential damages are to be recovered is *Hadley v. Baxendale,*[a] decided in 1854.

Case Background This case involved a broken crankshaft used in a flour mill run by the Hadley family in Gloucester, England. The crankshaft attached to the steam engine in the mill broke, and the shaft had to be sent to a foundry located in Greenwich so that a new shaft could be made to fit the other parts of the engine.

The Hadleys hired Baxendale, a common carrier, to transport the shaft from Gloucester to Greenwich. Baxendale received payment in advance and promised to deliver the shaft the following day. It was not delivered for several days, however. As a consequence, the mill was closed during those days because the Hadleys had no extra crankshaft on hand to use. The Hadleys sued Baxendale to recover the profits they lost during that time. Baxendale contended that the loss of profits was "too remote."

In the mid-1800s, it was common knowledge that large mills, such as that run by the Hadleys, normally had more than one crankshaft in case the main one broke and had to be repaired, as happened in this case. It is against this background that the parties argued their respective positions on whether the damages resulting from loss of profits while the crankshaft was out for repair were "too remote" to be recoverable.

The Issue before the Court and the Court's Ruling The crucial issue before the court was whether the Hadleys had informed the carrier, Baxendale, of the special circumstances surrounding the crankshaft's repair, particularly that the mill would have to shut down while the crankshaft was being repaired. If Baxendale had been notified of this circumstance at the time the contract was formed, then the remedy for breaching the contract would have been the amount of damages that would reasonably follow from the breach—including the Hadleys' lost profits.

In the court's opinion, however, the only circumstances communicated by the Hadleys to Baxendale at the time the contract was made were that the item to be transported was a broken crankshaft of a mill and that the Hadleys were the owners and operators of that mill. The court concluded that these circumstances did not reasonably indicate that the mill would have to stop operations if the delivery of the crankshaft was delayed.

APPLICATION TO TODAY'S WORLD

Today, the rule enunciated by the court in this case still applies. When damages are awarded, compensation is given only for those injuries that the defendant could reasonably have foreseen as a probable result of the usual course of events following a breach. If the injury complained of is outside the usual and foreseeable course of events, the plaintiff must show specifically that the defendant had reason to know the facts and foresee the injury. This is true with respect to contracts in the online environment as well. For example, suppose that a Web merchant loses business (and profits) due to a computer system's failure. If the failure was caused by malfunctioning software, the merchant may recover the lost profits from the software maker if these consequential damages were foreseeable.

a. 9 Exch. 341, 156 Eng.Rep. 145 (1854).

damages, which are also referred to as *exemplary damages,* are generally not recoverable in an action for breach of contract. Such damages have no legitimate place in contract law because they are, in essence, penalties, and a breach of contract is not unlawful in a criminal sense. A contract is simply a civil relationship between the parties. The law may compensate one party for the loss of the bargain—no more and no less.

In a few situations, a person's actions can cause both a breach of contract and a tort. For example, the parties can establish by contract a certain reasonable standard or duty of care. Failure to live up to that standard is a breach of contract, and the act itself may constitute negligence. An intentional tort (such as fraud) may also be tied to a breach of contract. In such a situation, it is possible for the nonbreaching party to recover punitive damages for the tort in addition to compensatory and consequential damages for the breach of contract.

NOMINAL DAMAGES
A small monetary award (often one dollar) granted to a plaintiff when no actual damage was suffered.

"Nominal damages are, in effect, only a peg to hang costs on."
SIR WILLIAM HENRY MAULE, 1788–1858 (British jurist)

Nominal Damages Damages that are awarded to an innocent party when only a technical injury is involved and no actual damage (no financial loss) has been suffered are called **nominal damages.** Nominal damage awards are often small, such as one dollar, but they do establish that the defendant acted wrongfully. Most lawsuits for nominal damages are brought as a matter of principle under the theory that a breach has occurred and some damages must be imposed regardless of actual loss.

● **EXAMPLE 13.4** Parrott contracts to buy potatoes at fifty cents a pound from Lentz. Lentz breaches the contract and does not deliver the potatoes. Meanwhile, the price of potatoes falls. Parrott is able to buy them in the open market at half the price he agreed to pay Lentz. Parrott is clearly better off because of Lentz's breach. Thus, in a suit for breach of contract, Parrott may be awarded only nominal damages for the technical injury he sustained, as no monetary loss was involved.●

(Note that nominal damages may take on greater significance in tort cases involving defamation or trade libel. If a false statement made by a competing firm calls into question a business's integrity or good reputation, the business may find it desirable to establish the falsity of the statement in public court proceedings. If the business wins in court, the court may award nominal damages because actual damages in such cases are difficult to estimate.)

MITIGATION OF DAMAGES

MITIGATION OF DAMAGES
A rule requiring a plaintiff to have done whatever was reasonable to minimize the damages caused by the defendant.

In most situations, when a breach of contract occurs, the injured party is held to a duty to mitigate, or reduce, the damages that he or she suffers. Under this doctrine of **mitigation of damages**, the required action depends on the nature of the situation. For example, some states require a landlord to use reasonable means to find a new tenant if a tenant abandons the premises and fails to pay rent. If an acceptable tenant becomes available, the landlord is required to lease the premises to the tenant to mitigate the damages recoverable from the former tenant. The former tenant is still liable for the difference between the amount of the rent under the original lease and the rent received from the new tenant. If the landlord has not used the reasonable means necessary to find a new tenant, presumably a court can reduce any award by the amount of rent the landlord could have received had such reasonable means been used.

In the majority of states, wrongfully terminated employees have a duty to mitigate damages suffered by their employers' breach. The damages they will be awarded are their salaries less the incomes they would have received in similar jobs obtained by reasonable means. The employer has the burden of proving that such jobs existed and that the employee could have been hired. An employee is, of course, under no duty to take a job that is not of the same type and rank.

Whether a business firm failed to mitigate its damages was at issue in the following case.

CASE 13.1 Fujitsu Ltd. v. Federal Express Corp.

United States Court of Appeals,
Second Circuit, 2001.
247 F.3d 423.
http://www.tourolaw.edu/2ndCircuit/index.htm[a]

FACTS On May 30, 1996, Fujitsu, Ltd., shipped a container of silicon wafers (computer chips) from Narita, Japan, to Ross Technologies, Inc., in Austin, Texas, using Federal Express (FedEx) as the carrier. The next day, the container arrived in Austin and was held for clearance by the U.S. Customs Service. (FedEx cannot release imported goods until the Customs Service has approved delivery and all applicable taxes have been paid.) Meanwhile, Ross told FedEx that it was rejecting the shipment and that FedEx should return the goods to Fujitsu at Ross's expense. The goods left Austin in good condition, but when they arrived in Japan, Fujitsu found the outer container broken and covered with an oily substance that had permeated some of the interior boxes and coated the sealed aluminum bags containing the wafers. Fujitsu reported the damage, which FedEx acknowledged, and on the instructions of Fujitsu's insurance company, disposed of the container and the wafers without opening any of the bags. Fujitsu filed a suit in a federal district court against FedEx, alleging, in part, breach of contract. The court found FedEx liable for damages in the amount of $726,640. FedEx appealed to the U.S. Court of Appeals for the Second Circuit, arguing that Fujitsu failed to mitigate its damages.

a. In the left-hand column, click on "Reported Decisions." From the menu, click on "2001." From the list, click on "April." Scroll to the name of the case and click on it to access the opinion. Touro College Jacob D. Fuchsberg Law Center in Huntington, New York, maintains this Web site.

ISSUE Did Fujitsu fail to mitigate its damages by not opening the bags and attempting to salvage at least some of the wafers?

DECISION No. The U.S. Court of Appeals for the Second Circuit affirmed the judgment of the lower court.

REASON The appellate court acknowledged, "FedEx is correct that the record contains no evidence that the wafers themselves were damaged," but found that "the shipment was a total loss because the residue on the outer packaging made it impossible to access the wafers." The court explained that "the bags containing the wafers could only be opened in a specially designed and maintained 'clean room' so as to prevent dust contamination. However, because the bags themselves were coated with the oily residue, they could not be brought into a clean room for inspection, as the residue itself would contaminate the clean room." Consequently, even if the wafers had been undamaged, "Fujitsu was unable to extract them from the bags in an operable condition." The court concluded that there is "no difference between damage rendering the wafers inoperable and damage that prevents otherwise operable wafers from being used or salvaged." The court added that "efforts to salvage the wafers would have been prohibitively expensive."

FOR CRITICAL ANALYSIS—Ethical Consideration *Should Fujitsu have been sanctioned for its "spoliation of the evidence" (its disposal of the container and wafers on the instructions of its insurance company)?*

LIQUIDATED DAMAGES
An amount, stipulated in the contract, that the parties to a contract believe to be a reasonable estimation of the damages that will occur in the event of a breach.

PENALTY
A contractual clause that states that a certain amount of money damages will be paid in the event of a future default or breach of contract. The damages are not a measure of compensation for the contract's breach but rather a punishment for a default. The agreement as to the amount will not be enforced, and recovery will be limited to actual damages.

LIQUIDATED DAMAGES VERSUS PENALTIES

A **liquidated damages** provision in a contract specifies that a certain dollar amount is to be paid in the event of a future default or breach of contract. (*Liquidated* means determined, settled, or fixed.) Liquidated damages differ from penalties. A **penalty** specifies a certain amount to be paid in the event of a default or breach of contract and is designed to penalize the breaching party. Liquidated damages provisions normally are enforceable. In contrast, if a court finds that a provision is a penalty provision, the agreement as to the amount will not be enforced, and recovery will be limited to actual damages.[5]

To determine whether a particular provision is for liquidated damages or for a penalty, the court must answer two questions: First, at the time the contract was formed, was it difficult to estimate the potential damages that would be incurred if the

5. This is also the rule under the Uniform Commercial Code. See UCC 2–718(1).

contract was not performed on time? Second, was the amount set as damages a reasonable estimate of those potential damages and not excessive?[6] If the answers to both questions are yes, the provision normally will be enforced. If either answer is no, the provision will normally not be enforced. In a construction contract, it is difficult to estimate the amount of damages that might be caused by a delay in completing construction, so liquidated damages clauses are often used.

ETHICAL ISSUE 13.1

Should liquidated damages clauses be enforced when no actual damages are incurred?

One of the questions that occasionally comes before the courts has to do with deposits on the purchase price of a home or other real estate. For example, in one case a couple signed a contract to buy a home and paid a nonrefundable deposit of $18,000 toward the purchase price. The full agreement was contingent on the buyers' sale of their current home. Because the couple was unable to sell their existing home, they had to back out of the agreement. Shortly thereafter, another buyer agreed to purchase the home for a higher price than the initial buyers had agreed to pay. Thus, the seller incurred no actual damages and in fact reaped higher profits as a result of the buyers' inability to perform. In such situations, does a clause requiring the buyers to forgo their deposit constitute a penalty clause rather than a liquidated damages clause?

No, say the courts. The courts routinely hold that such clauses are enforceable liquidated damages clauses. While this may seem unfair to home buyers who cannot perform due to events beyond their control, consider the alternative: if the courts refused to enforce liquidated damages clauses in these circumstances, it would, in the words of one court, undermine "the peace of mind and certainty of result the parties sought when they contracted for liquidated damages."[7]

Rescission and Restitution

As discussed in Chapter 12, *rescission* is essentially an action to undo, or cancel, a contract—to return nonbreaching parties to the positions that they occupied prior to the transaction. When fraud, mistake, duress, or failure of consideration is present, rescission is available. The failure of one party to perform under a contract entitles the other party to rescind the contract.[8] The rescinding party must give prompt notice to the breaching party. Furthermore, both parties must make **restitution** to each other by returning goods, property, or funds previously conveyed.[9] If the physical property or goods can be returned, they must be. If the property or goods have been consumed, restitution must be made in an equivalent dollar amount.

RESTITUTION
An equitable remedy under which a person is restored to his or her original position prior to loss or injury, or placed in the position he or she would have been in had the breach not occurred.

Essentially, restitution involves the recapture of a benefit conferred on the defendant that has unjustly enriched her or him. • **EXAMPLE 13.5** Andrea pays $12,000 to Myles

6. *Restatement (Second) of Contracts,* Section 356(1).
7. *Kelly v. Marx,* 705 N.E.2d 1114 (Mass. 1999).
8. The rescission discussed here refers to *unilateral* rescission, in which only one party wants to undo the contract. In *mutual* rescission, both parties agree to undo the contract. Mutual rescission discharges the contract; unilateral rescission is generally available as a remedy for breach of contract.
9. *Restatement (Second) of Contracts,* Section 370.

CONTRAST The advantages of obtaining restitution instead of damages include the possibility of recovering specific property, the possibility of making a recovery when damages cannot be proved, and the possibility of obtaining a greater award.

in return for his promise to design a house for her. The next day, Myles calls Andrea and tells her that he has taken a position with a large architectural firm in another state and cannot design the house. Andrea decides to hire another architect that afternoon. Andrea can require restitution of $12,000 because Myles has received an unjust benefit of $12,000. •

Specific Performance

SPECIFIC PERFORMANCE
An equitable remedy requiring exactly the performance that was specified in a contract; usually granted only when money damages would be an inadequate remedy and the subject matter of the contract is unique (for example, real property).

The equitable remedy of **specific performance** calls for the performance of the act promised in the contract. This remedy is often attractive to a nonbreaching party because it provides the exact bargain promised in the contract. It also avoids some of the problems inherent in a suit for money damages. First, the nonbreaching party need not worry about collecting the judgment.[10] Second, the nonbreaching party need not look around for another contract. Third, the actual performance may be more valuable than the money damages. Although the equitable remedy of specific performance is often preferable to other remedies, normally it is not granted unless the party's legal remedy (money damages) is inadequate and the subject matter of the contract is unique.[11]

Contracts for the sale of goods that are readily available in the market, for instance, rarely qualify for specific performance. Money damages ordinarily are adequate in such situations because substantially identical goods can be bought or sold in the market. If the goods are unique, however, a court of equity will decree specific performance. For example, paintings, sculptures, and rare books and coins are often unique, and money damages will not enable a buyer to obtain substantially identical substitutes in the mar-

10. Courts dispose of cases, after trials, by entering judgments. A judgment may order the losing party to pay money damages to the winning party. Collecting a judgment, however, can pose problems—such as when the judgment debtor is insolvent (cannot pay his or her bills when they become due) or has only a small net worth, or when the debtor's assets cannot be seized, under exemption laws, by a creditor to satisfy a debt (see Chapter 23).

11. *Restatement (Second) of Contracts,* Section 359.

Suppose that a seller contracts to sell some valuable coins to a buyer. If the seller breaches the contract, would specific performance be an appropriate remedy for the buyer to seek?

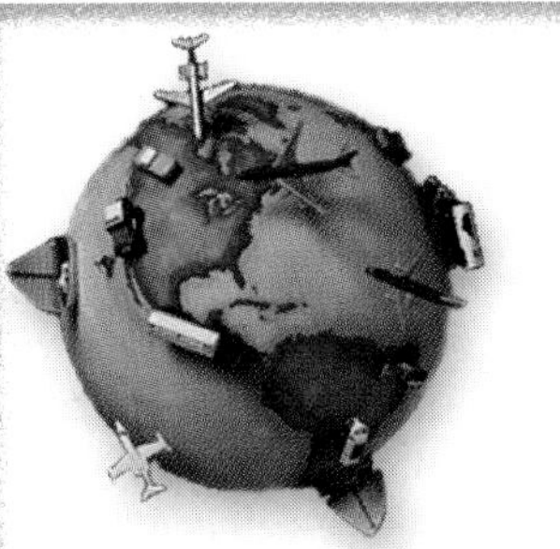

INTERNATIONAL PERSPECTIVE

Specific Performance in Germany

In the United States, the general rule is that the equitable remedy of specific performance will be granted only if the remedy at law (money damages) is inadequate and the subject matter of the contract is unique. For example, the remedy may be granted when a seller breaches a land-sales contract, because each parcel of land is unique. In Germany, in contrast, the typical remedy for a breach of contract is specific performance. In other words, a German court normally will order a breaching party to go forward and perform the contract as promised. German courts will award damages for breach of contract in some circumstances, but damages are available only after notice and other procedures have been employed to seek performance.

FOR CRITICAL ANALYSIS
If U.S. courts commonly granted the remedy of specific performance, as German courts do, would parties be less likely to breach their contracts?

"Specific performance is a remedy of grace and not a matter of right, and the test of whether or not it should be granted depends on the particular circumstances of each case."
GEORGE BUSHNELL, 1887–1965 (American jurist)

ket. The same principle applies to contracts relating to sales of land or interests in land because each parcel of land is unique by legal description.

Courts refuse to grant specific performance of contracts for personal services. This is because to order a party to perform personal services against his or her will amounts to a type of involuntary servitude, which is contrary to the public policy expressed in the Thirteenth Amendment to the Constitution. Moreover, the courts do not want to monitor personal-services contracts. • **EXAMPLE 13.6** If you contract with a brain surgeon to perform brain surgery on you and the surgeon refuses to perform, the court will not compel (and you certainly would not want) the surgeon to perform under these circumstances. There is no way the court can assure meaningful performance in such a situation.[12] •

Reformation

When the parties have imperfectly expressed their agreement in writing, the equitable remedy of *reformation* allows the contract to be rewritten to reflect the parties' true intentions. This remedy applies most often when fraud or mutual mistake has occurred. • **EXAMPLE 13.7** If Keshan contracts to buy a fork lift from Shelley but the written contract refers to a crane, a mutual mistake has occurred. Accordingly, a court could reform the contract so that the writing conforms to the parties' original intention as to which piece of equipment is being sold. •

Two other examples deserve mention. The first involves two parties who have made a binding oral contract. They further agree to reduce the oral contract to a writing, but in doing so, they make an error in stating the terms. Universally, the courts allow into evidence the correct terms of the oral contract, thereby reforming the written contract.

The second example has to do with written covenants not to compete. As discussed in Chapter 10, if a covenant not to compete is for a valid and legitimate purpose (such as the sale of a business) but the area or time restraints of the covenant are unreasonable, some courts reform the restraints by making them reasonable and enforce the entire contract as reformed. Other courts throw the entire restrictive covenant out as illegal.

12. Similarly, courts often refuse to order specific performance of construction contracts because courts are not set up to operate as construction supervisors or engineers.

Recovery Based on Quasi Contract

DON'T FORGET The function of a quasi contract is to impose a legal obligation on a party who made no actual promise.

Recall from Chapter 8 that a quasi contract is not a true contract but a fictional contract that is imposed on the parties to obtain justice and prevent unjust enrichment. Hence, a quasi contract becomes an equitable basis for relief. Generally, when one party confers a benefit on another, equity requires that the party receiving the benefit pay a reasonable value for it so as not to be unjustly enriched at the other party's expense.

Quasi-contractual recovery is useful when one party has partially performed under a contract that is unenforceable. It can be an alternative to suing for damages, and it allows the party to recover the reasonable value of the partial performance. For quasi-contractual recovery to occur, the party seeking recovery must show the following:

① A benefit was conferred on the other party.

② The party conferring the benefit did so with the expectation of being paid.

③ The party seeking recovery did not act as a volunteer in conferring the benefit.

④ Retaining the benefit without paying for it would result in an unjust enrichment of the party receiving the benefit.

ON THE WEB Cornell University's Legal Information Institute offers a menu of sources on contract law at **http://www.law.cornell.edu/topics/contracts.html**.

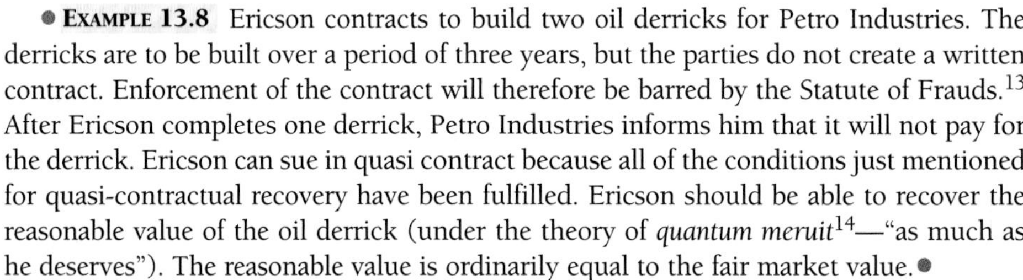

• **EXAMPLE 13.8** Ericson contracts to build two oil derricks for Petro Industries. The derricks are to be built over a period of three years, but the parties do not create a written contract. Enforcement of the contract will therefore be barred by the Statute of Frauds.[13] After Ericson completes one derrick, Petro Industries informs him that it will not pay for the derrick. Ericson can sue in quasi contract because all of the conditions just mentioned for quasi-contractual recovery have been fulfilled. Ericson should be able to recover the reasonable value of the oil derrick (under the theory of *quantum meruit*[14]—"as much as he deserves"). The reasonable value is ordinarily equal to the fair market value. •

In the following case, the court considered how the amount of a recovery under the theory of *quantum meruit* should be calculated.

13. Contracts that by their terms cannot be performed within one year must be in writing to be enforceable. See Chapter 11.

14. Pronounced *kwahn*-tuhm *mehr*-oo-wuht.

CASE 13.2 Maglica v. Maglica

California Court of Appeal, Fourth District, Division 3, 1998.
66 Cal.App.4th 442,
66 Cal.App.4th 1367C,
78 Cal.Rptr.2d 101.

HISTORICAL AND SOCIAL SETTING *The absence of a contract does not preclude recovery in* quantum meruit. *"The measure of recovery in* quantum meruit *is the reasonable value of the services rendered provided they were of direct benefit to the defendant."*[a] *The underlying idea behind* quantum meruit *is the law's distaste for unjust enrichment. If a person receives a benefit that he or she may not justly retain, the person should return whatever was received or pay for it. The idea that one must be benefited by the goods or services bestowed is thus an essential element to recovery in* quantum meruit. *Courts have always required that a plaintiff must have bestowed a benefit on the defendant in order to recover in* quantum meruit.

a. *Palmer v. Gregg,* 65 Cal.2d 657, 422 P.2d 985, 56 Cal.Rptr. 97 (1967).

FACTS Anthony Maglica founded a machine shop business called Mag Instrument in 1955. In 1971, he and Claire Halasz began to live together, holding themselves out as husband and wife, but they never actually married. Claire worked with Anthony to build Mag Instrument, although when it was incorporated in 1974, all shares were issued to Anthony. Anthony, as president, and Claire, as secretary, were paid equal salaries. In 1978, the business began manufacturing flashlights, and thanks to

CASE 13.2—Continued

ideas and hard work on Claire's part, the business boomed. The couple separated in 1992, and Claire filed a suit in a California state court against Anthony, seeking a recovery in *quantum meruit,* among other grounds. The jury awarded Claire $84 million, based on the business's benefit from her services. Anthony appealed.

ISSUE Can a plaintiff's recovery in *quantum meruit* be based on the benefit conferred on the defendant?

DECISION No. The state intermediate appellate court reversed the lower court's decision and remanded the case for a recalculation of the award. The appellate court held that Claire could recover for the value of her services, but she could not recover for the benefit conferred on the business.

REASON The court recognized that the requirement, under *quantum meruit,* that there be a benefit from services "can lead to confusion." The court explained that "[i]t is one thing to require that the defendant be benefited by services, it is quite another to measure the reasonable value of those services by the value by which the defendant was 'benefited' as a result of them." Allowing a plaintiff to recover based on the benefit received by the business would mean that "the law imposes an exchange of equity for services, and that can result in a windfall–as in the present case." In this case, that would also mean imposing "a highly generous and extraordinary contract that the parties did not make."

FOR CRITICAL ANALYSIS—Economic Consideration *Should the result be the same in a case involving a business firm such as the Walt Disney Company and an idea such as Mickey Mouse?*

Provisions Limiting Remedies

RECALL Exculpatory clauses may be held unconscionable, depending on the relative bargaining positions of the parties and the importance to the public interest of the business seeking to enforce the clause.

A contract may include provisions stating that no damages can be recovered for certain types of breaches or that damages must be limited to a maximum amount. The contract may also provide that the only remedy for breach is replacement, repair, or refund of the purchase price. Provisions stating that no damages can be recovered are called *exculpatory clauses* (see Chapter 10). Provisions that affect the availability of certain remedies are called *limitation-of-liability clauses.*

Whether these contract provisions and clauses will be enforced depends on the type of breach that is excused by the provision. For example, a clause excluding liability for negligence may be enforced in some cases. When an exculpatory clause for negligence is contained in a contract made between parties who have roughly equal bargaining positions, the clause usually will be enforced. A provision excluding liability for fraudulent or intentional injury will not be enforced. Likewise, a clause excluding liability for illegal acts or violations of law will not be enforced.

The UCC provides that in a contract for the sale of goods, remedies can be limited.[15] (See this chapter's *Business Law in the Online World* feature on the next page for a discussion of a limitation-of-liability clause in a licensing agreement accompanying the sale of a software program.) We will examine the UCC's provisions on limited remedies in more detail in Chapter 16.

Election of Remedies

BE AWARE Which remedy a plaintiff elects depends on the subject of the contract, the defenses of the breaching party, the advantages that might be gained in terms of tactics against the defendant, and what the plaintiff can prove with respect to the remedy sought.

In many cases, a nonbreaching party has several remedies available. Because the remedies may be inconsistent with one another, the common law of contracts requires the party to choose which remedy to pursue. This is called *election of remedies.* The purpose of the doctrine of election of remedies is to prevent double recovery. • **EXAMPLE 13.9**

15. UCC 2–719.

BUSINESS LAW: //in the Online World

Limitation-of-Liability Clauses in Software Licenses

Businesses today rely to a significant extent on computer hardware and software to conduct their operations. While this technology simplifies and streamlines business operations, it also poses some hazards. For example, suppose that, due to a software glitch, a construction company's bid for a construction project is $2 million less than it should have been. Clearly, if the company is awarded the project due to the inaccurate bid, the firm stands to incur a significant loss. This was essentially the problem facing the M. A. Mortenson Company, a nationwide construction contractor, when a bug in a software program that it used to submit bids for construction work caused the bid to be significantly lower than it should have been.

The Problem Facing the M. A. Mortenson Company

The M. A. Mortenson Company purchased software from Timberline Software Corporation. The software analyzed construction project requirements and bid information from subcontractors and found the lowest-cost combination of subcontractors to do the work. The software was distributed subject to a license set forth on the outside of each disk's pouch and on the inside cover of the instruction manuals. The first screen that appeared each time the program was used also referred to the license, which included a limitation on Timberline's liability arising from use of the software. After using the software to prepare a bid, Mortenson discovered that the bid was $1.95 million less than it should have been. The software clearly had a bug, and Timberline was aware of this problem. In fact, Timberline had already provided a newer version of the software to some of its other customers.

Was the Limitation-of-Liability Clause a Part of the Contract?

Mortenson sued Timberline, alleging that the limitation on Timberline's liability was not a part of the parties' contract. Timberline filed a motion for summary judgment, which the court granted. Mortenson fared no better in its appeal—ultimately, to the Washington state supreme court. That court held that the terms of the license were part of the contract between Mortenson and Timberline, and that Mortenson's use of the software constituted its assent to the agreement, including the limitation-of-liability clause in the license. The court stated that "as the license was part of the contract between Mortenson and Timberline, its terms are enforceable."

The court noted that the parties had dealt with each other for years, and that the terms of the license, which were similar to those used throughout the software industry, were set forth in several locations. In other words, Mortenson had to accept that it had no legal recourse against Timberline because of the limitation-of-liability clause in the licensing agreement.[a]

FOR CRITICAL ANALYSIS

Is it fair to hold that a business firm is bound by an agreement to limit liability when the firm did not intend to be bound by such an agreement? Why or why not?

a. *M. A. Mortenson Co. v. Timberline Software Corp.,* 140 Wash.2d 568, 998 P.2d 305 (2000).

Suppose that Jefferson agrees to sell his land to Adams. Then Jefferson changes his mind and repudiates the contract. Adams can sue for compensatory damages or for specific performance. If Adams receives damages as a result of the breach, she should not also be granted specific performance of the sales contract because that would mean she would unfairly end up with both the land and the damages. The doctrine of election of remedies requires Adams to choose the remedy she wants, and it eliminates any possibility of double recovery.●

In contrast, remedies under the UCC are cumulative. They include all of the remedies available under the UCC for breach of a sales or lease contract.[16]

16. See UCC 2–703 and 2–711.

In the following case, the frustrated sellers of a house were apparently attempting to avoid the doctrine of election of remedies in order to, as the old saying goes, "have their cake and eat it, too."

CASE 13.3 Palmer v. Hayes

Court of Appeals of Utah, 1995.
892 P.2d 1059.

FACTS Kenneth and Rebecca Palmer wanted to sell their house. Edward and Stephanie Hayes signed a proposed contract of sale, under which they agreed to give the Palmers' real estate agent, Maple Hills Realty, $2,000 as a deposit on the house. The agreement provided that in the event of default, the Palmers could either keep the deposit or sue to enforce their rights. The Palmers accepted the Hayeses' offer and signed the contract. Before the property changed hands, however, the Hayeses changed their minds and asked for the return of their deposit. The Palmers refused and filed a suit against the Hayeses in a Utah state court, seeking damages. The Hayeses filed a motion for summary judgment on the ground that, by not releasing the deposit, the Palmers had elected their remedy. The court ruled in favor of the Hayeses on this point, and the Palmers appealed.

ISSUE Did the Palmers' failure to release the deposit money before filing their suit for damages constitute an election of remedies?

DECISION Yes. The Court of Appeals of Utah, concluding that the Palmers had elected the remedy of retaining the deposit, affirmed the lower court's ruling.

REASON The state appellate court held that "a seller's failure to offer to return * * * deposits precludes the seller from pursuing other remedies." The court explained that the Palmers "needed only to indicate to Maple Hills Realty, in writing, that they released the deposit money to the Hayeses. Then they could have proceeded with their suit for damages." The court concluded that "by failing to release the deposit money, the Palmers elected to retain it as liquidated damages."

FOR CRITICAL ANALYSIS—Economic Consideration *What are the reasons for applying the doctrine of election of remedies to preclude sellers who keep deposits from suing for damages?*

APPLICATION Law and the Contractor . . .

When You Cannot Perform*

Not every contract can be performed. If you are a contractor, you may take on a job that, for one reason or another, you cannot or do not wish to perform. Simply walking away from the job and hoping for the best normally is not the most effective way to avoid litigation—which can be costly, time consuming, and emotionally draining. Instead, you should consider different options that may reduce the likelihood of litigation.

For example, suppose that you are a building contractor and you sign a contract to build a home for the Andersons. Performance is to begin on June 15. On June 1, Central Enterprises offers you a position that will yield you two and a half times the amount of net income you

*This *Application* is not meant to substitute for the services of an attorney who is licensed to practice law in your state.

(continued)

APPLICATION Law and the Contractor . . .

When You Cannot Perform—continued

could earn as an independent builder. To take the job, you have to start on June 15. You cannot be in two places at the same time, so to accept the new position you must breach the contract with the Andersons.

Consider Your Options

What can you do in this situation? One option is to subcontract the work to another builder and oversee the work yourself to make sure it conforms to the contract. Another option is to negotiate with the Andersons for a release. You can offer to find another qualified builder who will build a house of the same quality at the same price. Alternatively, you can offer to pay any additional costs if another builder takes the job and is more expensive. In any event, this additional cost would be the measure of damages that a court would impose on you if the Andersons prevailed in a suit for breach of contract. Thus, by making the offer, you might be able to avoid the expense of litigation—if the Andersons accept your offer.

Settlement Offers

Often, parties are reluctant to propose compromise settlements because they fear that what they say will be used against them in court if litigation ensues. The general rule, however, is that offers for settlement cannot be used in court to prove that you are liable for a breach of contract.

Checklist for the Contractor Who Cannot Perform

1. Consider a compromise.
2. Subcontract out the work and oversee it.
3. Offer to find an alternative contractor to fulfill your obligation.
4. Make a cash offer to "buy" a release from your contract. If anything other than an insignificant amount of money is involved, however, work with an attorney in making the offer.

Key Terms

Chapter Summary Breach and Remedies

COMMON REMEDIES AVAILABLE TO NONBREACHING PARTY	
Damages (See pages 336–341.)	The legal remedy designed to compensate the nonbreaching party for the loss of the bargain. By awarding money damages, the court tries to place the parties in the positions that they would have occupied had the contract been fully performed. The nonbreaching party frequently has a duty to *mitigate* (lessen or reduce) the damages incurred as a result of the contract's breach. There are five broad categories of damages: 1. *Compensatory damages*—Damages that compensate the nonbreaching party for injuries actually sustained and proved to have arisen directly from the loss of the bargain resulting from the breach of contract.

Chapter Summary Breach and Remedies—continued

Damages—continued	a. In breached contracts for the sale of goods, the usual measure of compensatory damages is an amount equal to the difference between the contract price and the market price. b. In breached contracts for the sale of land, the measure of damages is ordinarily the same as in contracts for the sale of goods. c. In breached construction contracts, the measure of damages depends on which party breaches and at what stage of construction the breach occurs. 2. *Consequential damages*—Damages resulting from special circumstances beyond the contract itself; the damages flow only from the consequences of a breach. For a party to recover consequential damages, the damages must be the foreseeable result of a breach of contract, and the breaching party must have known at the time the contract was formed that special circumstances existed that would cause the nonbreaching party to incur additional loss on breach of the contract. Also called *special damages.* 3. *Punitive damages*—Damages awarded to punish the breaching party. Usually not awarded in an action for breach of contract unless a tort is involved. 4. *Nominal damages*—Damages small in amount (such as one dollar) that are awarded when a breach has occurred but no actual damages have been suffered. Awarded only to establish that the defendant acted wrongfully. 5. *Liquidated damages*—Damages that may be specified in a contract as the amount to be paid to the nonbreaching party in the event the contract is breached in the future. Clauses providing for liquidated damages are enforced if the damages were difficult to estimate at the time the contract was formed and if the amount stipulated is reasonable. If construed to be a penalty, the clause will not be enforced.
Rescission and Restitution (See pages 341–342.)	1. *Rescission*—A remedy whereby a contract is canceled and the parties are restored to the original positions that they occupied prior to the transaction. Available when fraud, a mistake, duress, or failure of consideration is present. The rescinding party must give prompt notice of the rescission to the breaching party. 2. *Restitution*—When a contract is rescinded, both parties must make restitution to each other by returning the goods, property, or funds previously conveyed. Restitution prevents the unjust enrichment of parties.
Specific Performance (See pages 342–343.)	An equitable remedy calling for the performance of the act promised in the contract. This remedy is available only in special situations—such as those involving contracts for the sale of unique goods or land—and when monetary damages would be an inadequate remedy. Specific performance is not available as a remedy in breached contracts for personal services.
Reformation (See page 343.)	An equitable remedy allowing a contract to be "reformed," or rewritten, to reflect the parties' true intentions. Available when an agreement is imperfectly expressed in writing.
Recovery Based on Quasi Contract (See pages 344–345.)	An equitable theory imposed by the courts to obtain justice and prevent unjust enrichment in a situation in which no enforceable contract exists. The party seeking recovery must show the following: 1. A benefit was conferred on the other party. 2. The party conferring the benefit did so with the expectation of being paid. 3. The benefit was not volunteered. 4. Retaining the benefit without paying for it would result in the unjust enrichment of the party receiving the benefit.

(continued)

Chapter Summary Breach and Remedies—continued

CONTRACT DOCTRINES RELATING TO REMEDIES	
Provisions Limiting Remedies (See page 345.)	A contract may provide that no damages (or only a limited amount of damages) can be recovered in the event the contract is breached. Clauses excluding liability for fraudulent or intentional injury or for illegal acts cannot be enforced. Clauses excluding liability for negligence may be enforced if both parties hold roughly equal bargaining power. Under the UCC, in contracts for the sale of goods, remedies may be limited.
Election of Remedies (See pages 345–347.)	A common law doctrine under which a nonbreaching party must choose one remedy from those available. This doctrine prevents double recovery. Under the UCC, in contracts for the sale of goods, remedies are cumulative.

For Review

① What is the difference between compensatory damages and consequential damages? What are nominal damages, and when might they be awarded by a court?
② What is the usual measure of damages on a breach of contract for a sale of goods?
③ Under what circumstances will the remedy of rescission and restitution be available?
④ When might specific performance be granted as a remedy?
⑤ What is the rationale underlying the doctrine of election of remedies?

Questions and Case Problems

13–1. Liquidated Damages. Carnack contracts to sell his house and lot to Willard for $100,000. The terms of the contract call for Willard to pay 10 percent of the purchase price as a deposit toward the purchase price, or as a down payment. The terms further stipulate that should the buyer breach the contract, the deposit will be retained by Carnack as liquidated damages. Willard pays the deposit, but because her expected financing of the $90,000 balance falls through, she breaches the contract. Two weeks later, Carnack sells the house and lot to Balkova for $105,000. Willard demands her $10,000 back, but Carnack refuses, claiming that Willard's breach and the contract terms entitle him to keep the deposit. Discuss who is correct.

13–2. Election of Remedies. Perez contracts to buy a new Oldsmobile from Central City Motors, paying $2,000 down and agreeing to make twenty-four monthly payments of $350 each. He takes the car home and, after making one payment, learns that his Oldsmobile has a Chevrolet engine in it rather than the famous Olds Super V-8 engine. Central City never informed Perez of this fact. Perez immediately notifies Central City of his dissatisfaction and returns the car to Central City. Central City accepts the car and returns to Perez the $2,000 down payment plus the one $350 payment. Two weeks later Perez, without a car and feeling angry, files a suit against Central City, seeking damages for breach of warranty and fraud. Discuss the effect of Perez's actions.

13–3. Specific Performance. In which of the following situations might a court grant specific performance as a remedy for the breach of the contract?

(a) Tarrington contracts to sell her house and lot to Rainier. Then, on finding another buyer willing to pay a higher purchase price, she refuses to deed the property to Rainier.
(b) Marita contracts to sing and dance in Horace's nightclub for one month, beginning June 1. She then refuses to perform.
(c) Juan contracts to purchase a rare coin from Edmund, who is breaking up his coin collection. At the last minute, Edmund decides to keep his coin collection intact and refuses to deliver the coin to Juan.
(d) Astro Computer Corp. has three shareholders: Coase, who owns 48 percent of the stock; De Valle, who owns 48 percent; and Cary, who owns 4 percent. Cary contracts to sell his 4 percent to De Valle but later refuses to transfer the shares to him.

13–4. Measure of Damages. Johnson contracted to lease a house to Fox for $700 a month, beginning October 1. Fox stipulated in the contract that before he moved in, the interior of the house had to be completely repainted. On September 9, Johnson hired Keever to do the required painting for $1,000. He told Keever that the painting had to be finished by October 1 but did not explain why. On September 28, Keever quit for no reason, having completed approximately 80 percent of the work. Johnson then paid Sam $300 to finish the painting, but Sam did not finish until October 4. Fox, when the painting had not been completed as stipulated in his contract with Johnson, leased another home. Johnson found another tenant who would lease the property at $700 a month, beginning October 15. Johnson then sued Keever for breach of contract, claiming damages of $650. This amount included the $300 Johnson paid Sam to finish the painting and $350 for rent for the first half of October, which Johnson had lost as a result of Keever's breach. Johnson had not yet paid Keever anything for Keever's work. Can Johnson collect the $650 from Keever? Explain.

13–5. Measure of Damages. Ben owns and operates a famous candy store. He makes most of the candy sold in the store, and business is particularly heavy during the Christmas season. Ben contracts with Sweet, Inc., to purchase ten thousand pounds of sugar, to be delivered on or before November 15. Ben informs Sweet that this particular order is to be used for the Christmas season business. Because of production problems, the sugar is not tendered to Ben until December 10, at which time Ben refuses the order because it is so late. Ben has been unable to purchase the quantity of sugar needed to meet the Christmas orders and has had to turn down numerous regular customers, some of whom have indicated that they will purchase candy elsewhere in the future. The sugar that Ben has been able to purchase has cost him ten cents per pound above Sweet's price. Ben sues Sweet for breach of contract, claiming as damages the higher price paid for the sugar from others, lost profits from this year's lost Christmas sales, future lost profits from customers who have indicated that they will discontinue doing business with him, and punitive damages for failure to meet the contracted-for delivery date. Sweet claims Ben is limited to compensatory damages only. Discuss who is correct and why.

13–6. Liquidated Damages versus Penalties. The Ivanovs, who were of Russian origin, agreed to purchase the Sobels' home for $300,000. A $30,000 earnest money deposit was placed in the trust account of Kotler Realty, Inc., the broker facilitating the transaction. Tiasia Buliak, one of Kotler's salespersons, negotiated the sale because she spoke fluent Russian. To facilitate the closing without the Ivanovs having to be present, Buliak suggested they form a Florida corporation, place the balance of the cash necessary to close the sale in a corporate account, and give her authority to draw checks against it. The Ivanovs did as Buliak had suggested. Before the closing date of the sale, Buliak absconded with all of the closing money, which caused the transaction to collapse. Subsequently, because the Ivanovs had defaulted, Kotler Realty delivered the $30,000 earnest money deposit in its trust account to the Sobels. The Ivanovs then sued the Sobels, seeking to recover the $30,000. Was the clause providing that the seller could retain the earnest money if the buyer defaulted an enforceable liquidated damages clause or an unenforceable penalty clause? Discuss. [*Ivanov v. Sobel*, 654 So.2d 991 (Fla.App.3d 1995)]

13–7. Mitigation of Damages. Charles Kloss had worked for Honeywell, Inc., for over fifteen years when Honeywell decided to transfer the employees at its Ballard facility to its Harbour Pointe facility. Honeywell planned to hire a medical person at the Harbour Pointe facility and promised Kloss that if he completed a nursing program and became a registered nurse (RN), the company would hire him for the medical position. When Kloss graduated from his RN program, however, Honeywell did not assign him to a nursing or medical position. Instead, the company gave Kloss a job in its maintenance department. Shortly thereafter, Kloss left the company and eventually sued Honeywell for damages (lost wages) resulting from Honeywell's breach of the employment contract. One of the issues facing the court was whether Kloss, by voluntarily leaving the maintenance job at Honeywell, had failed to mitigate his damages. How should the court rule on this issue? Discuss. [*Kloss v. Honeywell, Inc.*, 77 Wash.App. 294, 890 P.2d 480 (1995)]

13–8. Mitigation of Damages. Patricia Fair worked in a Red Lion restaurant. The employee manual provided that "[d]uring a medical leave of absence, every effort will be made to keep a position available for the employee's return." After sustaining an injury that was unrelated to her work, Fair was given a month's medical leave. On her return, she asked for, and was granted, additional time to submit a physician's release to return to work. She provided the release within the extra time, but before she went back to work, she was terminated, effective as of her original return date. When she attempted to resolve the matter, Red Lion offered to reinstate her in her old job. Her response was to set several conditions for a return, including a different job. Red Lion said no, and Fair did not return. Fair filed a suit in a Colorado state court against Red Lion, alleging in part breach of contract. Red Lion argued that by rejecting its offer of reinstatement, Fair failed to mitigate her damages. Assuming that Red Lion was in breach of contract, did Fair fail to mitigate her damages? Explain. [*Fair v. Red Lion Inn, L.P.*, 943 P.2d 431 (Colo. 1997)]

13–9. Damages. In December 1992, Beys Specialty Contracting, Inc., contracted with New York City's Metropolitan Transportation Authority (MTA) for construction work. Beys subcontracted with Hudson Iron Works, Inc., to perform some of the work for $175,000. Under the terms of the subcontract, within seven days after the MTA approved Hudson's work and paid Beys, Beys would pay Hudson. The MTA had not yet approved any of Hudson's work when Beys submitted to the MTA invoices dated May 20 and June 21, 1993. Without proof that the MTA had paid Beys on those invoices, Hudson submitted to Beys an invoice dated September 10, claiming that the May 20 and June 21 invoices incorporated its work. Beys refused to pay, Hudson stopped working, and Beys paid another contractor $25,083 more to complete the job than if Hudson had completed its subcontract. Hudson filed a suit in a New York state court to collect on its invoice. Beys filed a counterclaim for the additional money spent to complete Hudson's job. In whose favor should the court rule, and why? What might be the measure of damages, if any? [*Hudson Iron Works, Inc. v. Beys Specialty Contracting, Inc.*, 691 N.Y.S.2d 132 (N.Y.A.D., 2 Dept. 1999)]

TEST YOUR KNOWLEDGE—ANSWER ON THE WEB

13–10. Ms. Vuylsteke, a single mother with three children, lived in Portland, Oregon. Cynthia Broan also lived in Oregon until she moved to New York City to open and operate an art gallery. Broan contacted Vuylsteke to manage the gallery under a one-year contract for an annual salary of $72,000. To begin work, Vuylsteke relocated to New York. As part of the move, Vuylsteke transferred custody of her children to her husband, who lived in London, England. In accepting the job, Vuylsteke also forfeited her husband's alimony and child support payments, including unpaid amounts of nearly $30,000. Before Vuylsteke started work, Broan repudiated the contract. Unable to find employment for more than an annual salary of $25,000, Vuylsteke moved to London to be near her children. Vuylsteke filed a suit in an Oregon state court against Broan, seeking damages for breach of contract. Should the court hold, as Broan argued, that Vuylsteke did not take reasonable steps to mitigate her damages? Why or why not? [*Vuylsteke v. Broan,* 172 Or.App. 74, 17 P.3d 1072 (2001)]

A QUESTION OF ETHICS AND SOCIAL RESPONSIBILITY

13–11. Julio Garza was employed by the Texas Animal Health Commission (TAHC) as a health inspector in 1981. His responsibilities included bleeding and tagging cattle, vaccinating and tattooing calves, and working livestock markets. Garza was injured on the job in 1988 and underwent surgery in January 1989. When his paid leave was exhausted, he asked TAHC for light-duty work, specifically the job of tick inspector, but his supervisor refused the request. In September, TAHC notified Garza that he was fired. Garza sued TAHC and others, alleging in part wrongful termination, and an important issue before the court was whether Garza had mitigated his damages. The court found that in the seven years between his termination and his trial date, Garza had held only one job—an unpaid job on his parents' ranch. When asked how often he looked for work during that time, Garza responded that he did not know, but he had looked in "several" places. The last time he looked for work was three or four months before the trial. That effort was merely an informal inquiry to his neighbors about working on their ranch. In view of these facts, consider the following questions. [*Texas Animal Health Commission v. Garza,* 27 S.W.3d 54 (Tex.App.—San Antonio 2000)]

1. The court in this case stated that the "general rule as to mitigation of damages in breach of employment suits is that the discharged employee must use reasonable diligence to mitigate damages by seeking other employment." In your opinion, did Garza fulfill this requirement? If you were the judge, how would you rule in this case?
2. Assume for the moment that Garza had indeed been wrongfully terminated. In this situation, would it be fair to Garza to require him to mitigate his damages? Why or why not?
3. Generally, what are the ethical underpinnings of the rule that employees seeking damages for breach of employment contracts must mitigate their damages?

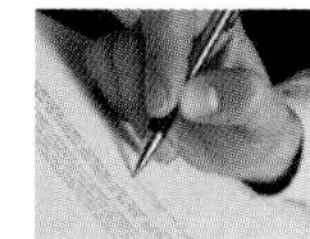

FOR CRITICAL ANALYSIS

13–12. Review the discussion of the doctrine of election of remedies in this chapter. What are some of the advantages and disadvantages of this doctrine?

Internet Exercises

Go to the *Business Law Today* home page at **http://blt.westbuslaw.com**. Select "Interactive Study Center" and then click on "Chapter 13." There you will find the following Internet research exercise that you can perform to learn more about damages for breach of contract:

Activity 13–1: Contract Damages and Contract Theory

Before the Test

Go to the *Business Law Today* home page at **http://blt.westbuslaw.com**. Click on "Interactive Quizzes." You will find at least twenty interactive questions relating to this chapter.

UNIT TWO Cumulative Business Hypothetical

Alberto Corelli offers to purchase for $2,500 a painting titled Moonrise *from Tara Shelley, an artist whose works have been causing a stir in the art world. Shelley accepts Corelli's offer. Assuming that the contract has met all of the requirements for a valid contract, answer the following questions:*

① Corelli was a minor when he purchased the painting. Is the contract void? Is it voidable? What is the difference between these two concepts? A month after his eighteenth birthday, Corelli decides that he would rather have the $2,500 than the painting. He informs Shelley that he is disaffirming the contract and requests that Shelley return the $2,500 to him. When Shelley refuses to do so, Corelli brings a court action to recover the $2,500. What will the court likely decide in this situation? Why?

② Both parties are adults, the contract is oral, and the painting is still in progress. Corelli pays Shelley the $2,500 in return for her promise to deliver the painting to his home when it is finished. A week or so later, after Shelley finishes the painting, a visitor to her gallery offers her $3,500 for it. Shelley sells the painting to the visitor and sends Corelli a signed letter explaining that she is "canceling" their contract for the *Moonrise* painting. Corelli sues Shelley to enforce the contract. Is the contract enforceable? Explain.

③ Both parties are adults, and the contract, which is in writing, states that Corelli will pay Shelley the $2,500 the following day. In the meantime, Shelley allows Corelli to take the painting home with him. The next day, Corelli's son returns the painting to Shelley, stating that he is canceling the contract. He explains that his father has been acting strangely lately, that he seems to be mentally incompetent at times, and that he clearly was not acting rationally when he bought the painting, which he could not afford. Is the contract enforceable? Discuss fully.

④ Both parties are adults, and the contract is in writing. The contract calls for Shelley to deliver the painting to Corelli's gallery in two weeks. Corelli has already arranged to sell the painting to a third party for $4,000, for a $1,500 profit, but it must be available for the third party in two weeks or the sale will not go through. Shelley knows this but does not deliver the painting at the time promised. Corelli sues Shelley for $1,500 in damages. Shelley claims that performance was impossible because her mother fell seriously ill and required Shelley's care. Who will win this lawsuit, and why?

⑤ After Shelley has agreed to sell Corelli the painting, he takes it home, promising to pay her the $2,500 the following day. That night, he has second thoughts about the value of the painting. The next day, he writes a letter to Shelley, stating that she overpriced the painting and that he is enclosing a check for $1,500 as "payment in full" for it. He delivers the letter to Shelley. Later that day, Shelley indorses the check and deposits it into her account. The day after that, she writes to Corelli stating that if he refuses to pay her the additional $1,000, she will sue him. Would Shelley succeed in a suit against Corelli for the remainder of the purchase price? Explain.

Kline v. Turner

In Chapter 11, we discussed fraudulent misrepresentation in the context of entering into contracts. As with other causes of action, suits based on fraud are subject to statutes of limitations, which are covered in Chapter 12. In this extended case study, we examine Kline v. Turner,[1] *a decision that concerned the application of a statute of limitations to a suit involving allegations of fraud.*

CASE BACKGROUND

Thomas Kline, a talent agent, entered into an oral contract through Bryan Turner with Priority Records, Inc., for the services of a musical group, "Miss Allen and Nem." Priority agreed to immediately issue a check payable to Kline for $50,000, with an additional $50,000 to be paid after the completion of a master recording. On August 31, 1990, Kline sent a business associate, Marion Knight, to pick up the first check. When Knight did not soon return, Kline called Priority and learned that at Knight's insistence the check was made payable to Knight. When Kline objected, Priority assured Kline that it would stop payment on the check.[2] On Monday, Priority told Kline that the check was cashed before payment was stopped. Later, Knight confronted Kline, showed Kline a gun, and told him to "back off." Fearful of Knight and believing that Priority had either been intimidated or thought it appropriate to make the check payable to Knight, Kline did nothing.

In 1996, Kline learned that Priority and Knight had entered into a contract on August 31, 1990, for the services of "Miss Allen and Nem." Kline also saw a copy of the $50,000 check given to Knight on that date. A stamp on the check indicated that it was cashed on September 4, not on August 31. In 1999, Kline filed a suit in a California state court against Priority and Turner, alleging fraud. The defendants filed a motion for summary judgment, arguing that the suit was barred by a three-year state statute of limitations. Kline asserted that his suit was within the limitations period because he was not on notice of the fraud until 1996. The trial court granted the motion for summary judgment. Kline appealed to a state intermediate appellate court.

1. 87 Cal.App.4th 1369, 105 Cal.Rptr.2d 699 (4th Dist. 2001). This opinion is available online through FindLaw's Web site at **http://California.lp.findlaw.com/CA02_caselaw/3_2001ca.html**. When this page opens, scroll down the list to the category "Fourth Appellate District." Then click on "Kline v. Turner," which follows the date "March 27, 2001."

2. Stop-payment orders on checks are discussed in detail in Chapter 21.

MAJORITY OPINION

BENKE, Acting P.J.

* * * *

An action for relief on the grounds of fraud or mistake must be commenced within three years. However, such action is not deemed accrued until the discovery, by the aggrieved party, of the facts constituting the fraud or mistake. The courts interpret discovery in this context to mean not when the plaintiff became aware of the specific wrong alleged, but when the plaintiff suspected or should have suspected that an injury was caused by wrongdoing. *The statute of limitations begins to run when the plaintiff has information which would put a reasonable person on inquiry. A plaintiff need not be aware of the specific facts necessary to establish a claim since they can be developed in pretrial discovery.* Wrong and wrongdoing in this context are understood in their lay and not legal senses. [Emphasis added.]

* * * *

The trial court correctly found Kline's lawsuit was time barred. The only legitimate inference based on the uncontroverted facts is that in September 1990 a reasonable person in Kline's position would conclude he was injured as the result not only of Knight's wrongdoing but Priority's as well. Priority had agreed to pay Kline $50,000 in the form of a check made payable to him. On the representation of Knight, who was acting merely as Kline's courier, Priority's staff, without clearing the change with Kline, gave Knight Kline's $50,000. Doing so was wrong and injurious in both a lay and legal sense. Kline was thus on inquiry. Discovery and/or investigation concerning the events would have revealed the fraud and the statute of limitations had begun to run.

* * * *

* * * We conclude as a matter of law that Kline was reasonably on inquiry that Priority was engaged in fraud. Priority had done an inexplicable act. With an agreement that Priority would pay him $50,000, it instead made the check out to Kline's courier. It told Kline it did so based on the courier's representation such a change was with Kline's approval. It did this without attempting to notify Kline there had been a change in plan. * * * Kline's contract with Priority involved a continuing relationship

between Kline, Priority and Miss Allen and Nem. A change in the representation of Miss Allen and Nem could not have been lost on Kline. Kline was on inquiry notice. Thus, the fraud cause of action accrued in 1990 and the fraud cause of action was time barred.

We also note Kline's claimed fear of Knight is of no legal consequence. The present case deals with a suit against Turner and Priority. * * * Kline asserts that until he discovered he had been defrauded by Turner and Priority, he believed they were also victims of Knight. However, this assertion does not advance his position. That Knight may have fooled Turner and Priority does not mean they had not, in both a lay and legal sense, also wronged Kline. Kline was on inquiry in 1990 concerning the actions of Turner and Priority. His suit for fraud filed against them in 1999 was time barred.

The judgment is affirmed.

DISSENTING OPINION

McINTYRE, J., dissenting.

* * * *

The principal case cited by the majority * * * does indeed state that the statute of limitations begins to run when the plaintiff has information that would put a reasonable person on inquiry and that a party need not be aware of the specific facts necessary to establish a claim since they can be developed in pretrial discovery. However, the context in which this language appears is quite different than the facts in this case. In [the cited case], the question was whether the plaintiff had sufficient information about whether the ingestion of a particular drug might have caused her medical conditions and injuries of which she was clearly aware. Here, that language is being used to support the holding that *as a matter of law* the statute of limitations for fraud commences to run even though it is arguable whether Kline had reason to know or suspect that Priority had defrauded him. * * *

* * * *

Kline's opposition to the motion for summary judgment was that in 1990, Priority told him that Knight persuaded it to issue the check to Knight rather than Kline, and further stated that although it had tried a stop payment on the check, its efforts were ineffective because Knight cashed the check immediately. Neither Priority nor Knight told Kline in 1990 that at the same time the check was given to Knight, Priority signed a record contract with Knight to represent the same group which Kline already represented and that had contracted with Priority to provide certain recordings. Kline contends that this piece of information was learned only in 1996, within three years of the filing of the lawsuit. There is [an] issue of fact as to whether Kline was on * * * notice of a potential fraud claim against Priority in 1990 or only when he obtained the additional information in 1996. Accordingly, I would reverse the grant of the summary judgment in this case.

QUESTIONS FOR ANALYSIS

① **Law.** What was the plaintiff's major argument? Why did the court conclude that this argument was invalid?

② **Law.** Would the result in this case have been different if the parties to the original contract had put their agreement in writing?

③ **Ethics.** What is an ethical basis for the majority's holding in this case? What is an ethical basis for the dissent's position?

④ **International Dimensions.** How might the decision in this case affect the manner in which foreign parties do business in the United States?

⑤ **Implications for the Business Manager.** How are the circumstances in this case of interest to those who do business in a less formal manner?

UNIT 3

Sales and Lease Contracts

UNIT CONTENTS

CHAPTER 14

The Formation of Sales and Lease Contracts

"The great object of the law is to encourage commerce."

J. Chambre, 1739–1823
(British jurist)

CHAPTER CONTENTS

LEARNING OBJECTIVES

After reading this chapter, you should be able to answer the following questions:

① How do Article 2 and Article 2A of the UCC differ? What types of transactions does each article cover?

② What is a merchant's firm offer?

③ If an offeree includes additional or different terms in an acceptance, will a contract result? If so, what happens to these terms?

④ Article 2 and Article 2A of the UCC both define three exceptions to the writing requirements of the Statute of Frauds. What are these three exceptions?

⑤ What law governs contracts for the international sale of goods?

The opening quotation states that the object of the law is to encourage commerce. This is particularly true with respect to the Uniform Commercial Code (UCC). The UCC facilitates commercial transactions by making the laws governing sales and lease contracts uniform, clearer, simpler, and more readily applicable to the numerous difficulties that can arise during such transactions. Recall from Chapter 1 that the UCC is one of many uniform (model) acts drafted by the National Conference of Commissioners on Uniform State Laws and submitted to the states for adoption. Once a state legislature has adopted a uniform act, the act becomes statutory law in that state. Thus, when we turn to sales and lease contracts, we move away from common law principles and into the area of statutory law.

We open this chapter with a discussion of the general coverage of the UCC and its significance as a legal landmark. We then look at the scope of the UCC's

Article 2 (on sales) and Article 2A (on leases) as a background to the focus of this chapter, which is the formation of contracts for the sale and lease of goods. Because international sales transactions are increasingly commonplace in the business world, we conclude this chapter with an examination of the United Nations Convention on Contracts for the International Sale of Goods (CISG), which governs international sales contracts.

As you read through this chapter, keep in mind that UCC requirements relating to the formation of sales and lease contracts also apply to contracts formed online. Of course, online contracts have created legal issues not addressed by the UCC, and new uniform laws have been drafted specifically to address those issues. You will read about these laws in Chapter 17, in the context of electronic contracts.

The Scope of the UCC

ON THE WEB To view the text of the UCC—and keep up to date on its various revisions—go to the Web site of the National Conference of Commissioners on Uniform State Laws (NCCUSL) at **http://www.nccusl.org**. Cornell University's Legal Information Institute also offers the full text of the UCC at **http://www.law.cornell.edu/uniform/ucc.html**.

The UCC attempts to provide a consistent and integrated framework of rules to deal with all phases ordinarily arising in a commercial sales transaction from start to finish. For example, consider the following events, all of which occur during a single sales transaction:

1. *A contract for the sale or lease of goods is formed and executed.* Article 2 and Article 2A of the UCC provide rules governing all the facets of this transaction.
2. *The transaction may involve a payment—by check, electronic fund transfer, or other means.* Article 3 (on negotiable instruments), Article 4 (on bank deposits and collections), Article 4A (on fund transfers), and Article 5 (on letters of credit) cover this part of the transaction.
3. *If the goods purchased are shipped or stored, they may be covered by a bill of lading or a warehouse receipt.* Article 7 (on documents of title) deals with this subject.
4. *The transaction may involve the demand by a seller or lender for some form of security for a remaining balance owed.* Article 9 (on secured transactions) covers this part of the transaction.

Two articles of the UCC seemingly do not address the "ordinary" commercial sales transaction. Article 6, on bulk transfers, has to do with merchants who sell off the major part of their inventory. Such bulk sales are not part of the ordinary course of business. Article 8, which covers investment securities, deals with transactions involving negotiable securities (stocks and bonds)—transactions that do not involve the sale of goods. The UCC's drafters, however, considered the subject matter of Articles 6 and 8 to be *sufficiently* related to commercial transactions to warrant its inclusion in the UCC. The most recent version of the UCC is included as Appendix C in this text.

The UCC has been adopted in whole or in part by all of the states. Because of its importance in the area of commercial transactions, we present the UCC as this chapter's *Landmark in the Law* on the following page.

BE CAREFUL Although the UCC has been widely adopted without many changes, states have modified some of the details to suit their particular needs.

The Scope of Article 2—Sales

SALES CONTRACT
A contract for the sale of goods under which the ownership of goods is transferred from a seller to a buyer for a price.

Article 2 of the UCC governs **sales contracts**, or contracts for the sale of goods. To facilitate commercial transactions, Article 2 modifies some of the common law contract requirements that were summarized in Chapter 8 and discussed in detail in Chapters 9 through 13. To the extent that it has not been modified by the UCC, however, the

LANDMARK IN THE LAW
The Uniform Commercial Code

Of all the attempts in the United States to produce a uniform body of laws relating to commercial transactions, none has been as comprehensive or successful as the Uniform Commercial Code (UCC).

The Origins of the UCC The UCC was the brainchild of William A. Schnader, president of the National Conference of Commissioners on Uniform State Laws (NCCUSL). The drafting of the UCC began in 1945. The most significant individual involved in the project was its chief editor, Karl N. Llewellyn of the Columbia University Law School. Llewellyn's intellect, continuous efforts, and ability to compromise made the first version of the UCC (1949) a legal landmark. Over the next several years, the UCC was substantially accepted by virtually every state in the nation.

Periodic Changes and Updates Various articles and sections of the UCC are periodically changed or supplemented to clarify certain rules or to establish new rules when changes in business customs render the existing UCC provisions inapplicable. For example, because of the increasing importance of leases of goods in the commercial context, Article 2A, governing leases, was added to the UCC. To clarify the rights of parties to commercial fund transfers, particularly electronic fund transfers, Article 4A was issued. Articles 3 and 4, on negotiable instruments and banking relationships, underwent a significant revision in the 1990s. Because of other changes in business and in the law, the NCCUSL has recommended the repeal of Article 6 (on bulk transfers), offering a revised Article 6 to those states that prefer not to repeal it. More recently, the NCCUSL revised Article 9, covering secured transactions. The revised Article 9, which has been adopted by all of the states, will be discussed at length in Chapter 22. Currently, the NCCUSL is in the process of creating amendments to Article 2.

APPLICATION TO TODAY'S WORLD

By periodically revising UCC articles, the NCCUSL has been able to adapt its provisions to changing business customs and practices. UCC provisions governing sales and lease contracts have also been extended to contracts formed in the online environment. Note, though, that in addition to updating UCC provisions, the NCCUSL has also issued other significant uniform laws relating to electronic contracts. We will discuss these laws in detail in Chapter 17.

common law of contracts also applies to sales contracts. In general, the rule is that when a UCC provision addresses a certain issue, the UCC governs; when the UCC is silent, the common law governs.

In regard to Article 2, you should keep in mind two things. First, Article 2 deals with the sale of *goods*; it does not deal with real property (real estate), services, or intangible property such as stocks and bonds. Thus, if the subject matter of a dispute is goods, the UCC governs. If it is real estate or services, the common law applies. The relationship between general contract law and the law governing sales of goods is illustrated in Exhibit 14–1. Second, in some cases, the rules may vary quite a bit, depending on whether the buyer or the seller is a merchant. We look now at how the UCC defines three important terms: *sale, goods,* and *merchant status.*

WHAT IS A SALE?

SALE
The passing of title to property from the seller to the buyer for a price.

The UCC defines a **sale** as "the passing of title from the seller to the buyer for a price" [UCC 2–106(1)]. The price may be payable in money or in other goods, services, or realty (real estate).

WHAT ARE GOODS?

TANGIBLE PROPERTY
Property that has physical existence and can be distinguished by the senses of touch, sight, and so on. A car is tangible property; a patent right is intangible property.

To be characterized as a *good*, the item of property must be *tangible*, and it must be *movable*. **Tangible property** has physical existence—it can be touched or seen. Intangible property—such as corporate stocks and bonds, patents and copyrights, and ordinary contract rights—has only conceptual existence and thus does not come under Article 2. A movable item can be carried from place to place. Hence, real estate is excluded from Article 2.

Two areas of dispute arise in determining whether the object of a contract is goods and thus whether Article 2 is applicable. One problem has to do with *goods associated with real estate*, such as crops or timber, and the other concerns contracts involving a combination of *goods and services*.

Goods Associated with Real Estate Goods associated with real estate often fall within the scope of Article 2. Section 2–107 provides the following rules:

① A contract for the sale of minerals or the like (including oil and gas) or a structure (such as a building) is a contract for the sale of goods if *severance*, or *separation*, is to be made by the *seller*. If the *buyer* is to sever (separate) the minerals or structure from the land, the contract is considered to be a sale of real estate governed by the principles of real property law, not the UCC.

EXHIBIT 14–1 LAW GOVERNING CONTRACTS

This exhibit graphically illustrates the relationship between general contract law and the law governing contracts for the sale of goods. Contracts for the sale of goods are not governed exclusively by Article 2 of the Uniform Commercial Code but are also governed by general contract law whenever it is relevant and has not been modified by the UCC.

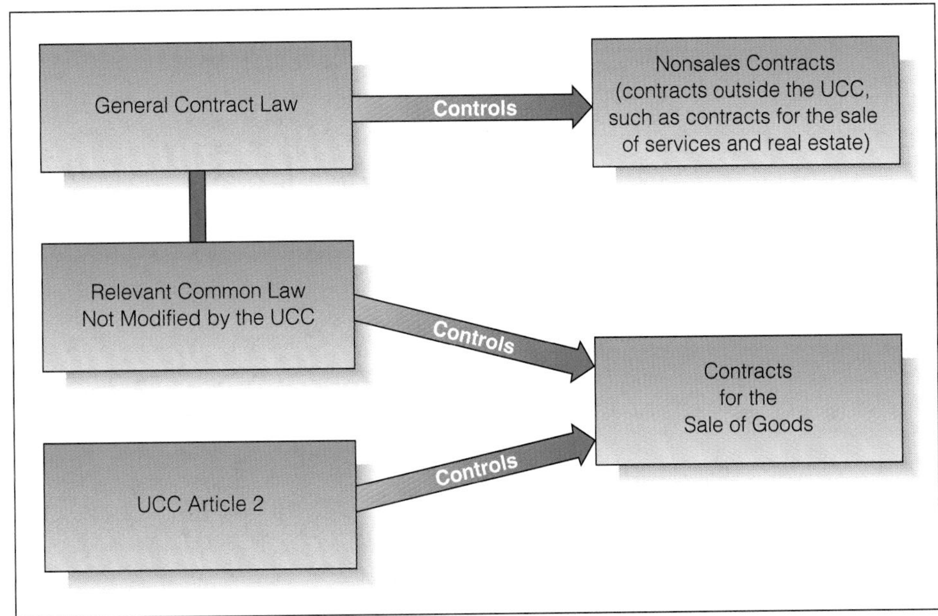

② A sale of growing crops (such as potatoes, carrots, wheat, and the like) or timber to be cut is considered to be a contract for the sale of goods *regardless of who severs them.*

③ Other "things attached" to realty but capable of severance without material harm to the land are considered goods *regardless of who severs them.*[1] "Things attached" that are severable without harm to realty could include such items as a heater, a window air conditioner in a house, and stools in a restaurant. Thus, removal of one of these things would be considered a sale of goods. The test is whether removal will cause substantial harm to the real property to which the item is attached.

ON THE WEB Cornell University's Legal Information Institute offers online access to the UCC as enacted in several of the states at **http://www.law.cornell.edu/statutes.html#state**.

Goods and Services Combined In cases in which goods and services are combined, courts disagree. For example, is the blood furnished to a patient during an operation a "sale of goods" or the "performance of a medical service"? Some courts say it is a good; others say it is a service. Similarly, contracts to sell and install software have posed the question of whether such contracts are primarily contracts for the sale of goods or contracts for the sale of services.[2] Because the UCC does not provide the answers to such questions, the courts try to determine which factor is predominant—the good or the service.

The UCC does stipulate, however, that serving food or drink to be consumed either on or off restaurant premises is a "sale of goods," at least for the purpose of an implied warranty of merchantability (to be explained in Chapter 18) [UCC 2–314(1)]. Other special transactions are also explicitly characterized as sales of goods by the UCC, including sales of unborn animals and rare coins. Whether the transaction in question

1. The UCC avoids the term *fixtures* here because of the numerous definitions of the word. A fixture is anything so firmly or permanently attached to land or to a building as to become a part of it. Once personal property becomes a fixture, it is governed by real estate law. See Chapter 37.

2. See, for example, *Richard Haney Ford v. Ford Dealer Computer Services,* 218 Ga.App. 315, 461 S.E.2d 282 (1995).

Sunflowers in bloom. Does Article 2 apply to the sale of sunflower seeds to a snack foods company?

involves the sale of goods or services is important because the majority of courts treat services as being excluded by the UCC. If the transaction is not covered by the UCC, then UCC provisions, including those relating to implied warranties, would not apply.

WHO IS A MERCHANT?

Article 2 governs the sale of goods in general. It applies to sales transactions between all buyers and sellers. In a limited number of instances, however, the UCC presumes that in certain phases of sales transactions involving merchants, special business standards ought to be imposed because of the merchants' relatively high degree of commercial expertise.[3] Such standards do not apply to the casual or inexperienced seller or buyer ("consumer"). Section 2–104 defines three ways in which merchant status can arise:

① A merchant is a person who *deals in goods of the kind* involved in the sales contract. Thus, a retailer, a wholesaler, or a manufacturer is a merchant of those goods sold in the business. A merchant for one type of goods is not necessarily a merchant for another type. For example, a sporting-equipment retailer is a merchant when selling tennis equipment but not when selling a used computer.

② A merchant is a person who, by occupation, holds himself or herself out as having knowledge and skill unique to the practices or goods involved in the transaction. Note that this broad definition may include banks or universities as merchants.

③ A person who *employs a merchant as a broker, agent, or other intermediary* has the status of merchant in that transaction. Hence, if a "gentleman farmer" who ordinarily does not run the farm hires a broker to purchase or sell livestock, the farmer is considered a merchant in the transaction.

MERCHANT
A person who is engaged in the purchase and sale of goods. Under the UCC, a person who deals in goods of the kind involved in the sales contract or who holds himself or herself out as having skill or knowledge peculiar to the practices or use of the goods being purchased or sold. For definitions, see UCC 2–104.

In summary, a person is a **merchant** when he or she, acting in a mercantile capacity, possesses or uses an expertise specifically related to the goods being sold. This basic distinction is not always clear-cut. For example, courts in most states have determined that farmers may be merchants if they sell products or livestock on a regular basis, but courts in other states have held that the drafters of the UCC did not intend to include farmers as merchants.

The court in the following case considered whether a trucking company, buying diesel fuel for its trucks, was a merchant under those circumstances for purposes of the UCC.

3. The provisions that apply only to merchants deal principally with the Statute of Frauds, firm offers, confirmatory memoranda, warranties, and contract modification. These special rules reflect expedient business practices commonly known to merchants in the commercial setting. They will be discussed later in this chapter.

CASE 14.1 Ready Trucking, Inc. v. BP Exploration & Oil Co.

Georgia Court of Appeals, 2001.
248 Ga.App. 701,
548 S.E.2d 420.

FACTS Ready Trucking, Inc., is an interstate common carrier. At its terminal in Ellenwood, Georgia, Ready maintains two 10,000-gallon storage tanks for diesel fuel for its truck fleet. To facilitate regular purchases of the fuel, Ready opened an account with BP Exploration & Oil Company. Ready sent BP a Georgia state "ST-5 Sales and Use Tax Certificate," which provided that Ready was exempt from state taxes on the purchase of certain goods. Based on this certificate, BP mistakenly believed that Ready was exempt from state and local sales taxes on diesel fuel purchases. Consequently, on Ready's 149 separate purchases of fuel from BP, the seller did not collect these taxes, as was otherwise required by law. For each sale, BP sent Ready an invoice showing the price,

(continued)

CASE 14.1—Continued

the amount of fuel, and the unpaid taxes. The Georgia Department of Revenue discovered the error and billed Ready $37,801.46, including $25,560.55 in back taxes and $12,240.91 in penalties and interest. Ready filed a suit in a Georgia state court against BP, alleging breach of contract. BP responded that by accepting the fuel after seeing the invoices, Ready, as a merchant, had agreed that it would pay the taxes. The court granted BP's motion for summary judgment. Ready appealed to a state intermediate appellate court.

ISSUE Was Ready a merchant for purposes of the UCC?

DECISION Yes. The state intermediate appellate court affirmed the decision of the lower court. Thus, BP's invoices governed the fuel sales, and there was no breach of contract. Ready alone was liable for the payment of the taxes.

REASON The court pointed out that between *merchants,* under UCC 2–201(2), "if within a reasonable time a writing in confirmation of the contract and sufficient against the sender is received and the party receiving it has reason to know its contents, it [constitutes a writing enforceable] against such party unless written notice of objection to its contents is given within ten days after it is received." The writing then becomes the "final expression of their agreement." (This rule is discussed in detail later in this chapter.) A buyer may be considered a merchant when it is a "business professional as opposed to a casual or inexperienced seller or buyer, and the purchase involves a type of goods related and necessary to the business or occupation of the purchaser." Here "Ready is an interstate motor carrier and it made nearly 150 purchases from BP * * *. Ready was familiar with the purchase of diesel fuel and the taxation issues, and it had the knowledge necessary to discover BP's initial error. We therefore hold that Ready is a merchant for the purposes of [UCC 2–201(2)] when buying diesel fuel for its business." The invoices sent to Ready confirmed that BP was not withholding certain taxes, to which Ready did not object within ten days. Thus, the invoices constituted an agreement between the parties that the taxes would not be collected and remitted by BP.

FOR CRITICAL ANALYSIS—Social Consideration
How might these parties have avoided this situation?

The Scope of Article 2A—Leases

In the past few decades, leases of personal property (goods) have become increasingly common. Article 2A of the UCC was created to fill the need for uniform guidelines in this area. Article 2A covers any transaction that creates a lease of goods, as well as subleases of goods [UCC 2A–102, 2A–103(k)]. Except that it applies to leases of goods, rather than sales of goods, Article 2A is essentially a repetition of Article 2 and varies only to reflect differences between sale and lease transactions. (Note that Article 2A is not concerned with leases of real property, such as land or buildings. The laws governing these types of transactions will be examined in Chapter 37.)

LEASE AGREEMENT
In regard to the lease of goods, an agreement in which one person (the lessor) agrees to transfer the right to the possession and use of property to another person (the lessee) in exchange for rental payments.

LESSOR
A person who sells the right to the possession and use of goods to another in exchange for rental payments.

LESSEE
A person who acquires the right to the possession and use of another's goods in exchange for rental payments.

DEFINITION OF A LEASE

Article 2A defines a **lease agreement** as a lessor and lessee's bargain with respect to the lease of goods, as found in their language and as implied by other circumstances, including course of dealing and usage of trade or course of performance [UCC 2A–103(k)]. A **lessor** is one who sells the right to the possession and use of goods under a lease [UCC 2A–103(p)]. A **lessee** is one who acquires the right to the possession and use of goods under a lease [UCC 2A–103(o)]. Article 2A applies to all types of leases of goods, including commercial leases and consumer leases. Special rules apply to certain types of leases, however, including consumer leases and finance leases.

"When there's no law, there's no bread."

BENJAMIN FRANKLIN, 1706–1790 (American diplomat, author, and scientist)

CONSUMER LEASES

A *consumer lease* involves three elements: (1) a lessor who regularly engages in the business of leasing or selling, (2) a lessee (except an organization) who leases the goods "primarily for a personal, family, or household purpose," and (3) total lease payments that are less than a dollar amount set by state statute [UCC 2A–103(1)(e)]. In the interest of providing special protection for consumers, certain provisions of Article 2A apply only to consumer leases. For example, one provision states that a consumer may recover attorneys' fees if a court finds that a term in a consumer lease contract is unconscionable [UCC 2A–108(4)(a)].

FINANCE LEASES

A *finance lease* involves a lessor, a lessee, and a supplier. The lessor buys or leases goods from a supplier and leases or subleases them to the lessee [UCC 2A–103(g)]. Typically, in a finance lease, the lessor is simply financing the transaction. ● **EXAMPLE 14.1** Suppose that Marlin Corporation wants to lease a crane for use in its construction business. Marlin's bank agrees to purchase the equipment from Jennco, Inc., and lease the equipment to Marlin. In this situation, the bank is the lessor-financer, Marlin is the lessee, and Jennco is the supplier. ●

Article 2A, unlike ordinary contract law, makes the lessee's obligations under a commercial finance lease irrevocable and independent from the financer's obligations [UCC

LETTER OF THE LAW

Finance Leases and the "Hell or High Water" Payment Term

As mentioned, in a finance lease, the lessee is obligated to pay the lessor, or financer, no matter what, or—as some say—come hell or high water. Typically, this "hell or high water" payment obligation is specified in the lease agreement. For example, in one finance lease, a provision stated that the lessee could not "withhold, set off, or reduce such payments for any reason." Yet what if a lessee arranges to lease equipment under a finance lease and the equipment turns out to be defective? Must the lessee still make the payments? Yes. Even if the obligation to pay the lease had not been expressly stated in the lease contract, the lessee would be obligated to pay—because Article 2A makes it clear that the lessee is obligated to pay the financer/lessor regardless of problems with the goods being leased.

To illustrate: In one case, American Transit Insurance Company (ATIC) arranged to lease telephone equipment through a finance lease. The manufacturer of the equipment transferred the equipment to Siemens Credit Corporation, which then leased the equipment to ATIC for a five-year term at $2,314 per month. When the equipment turned out to be defective, ATIC stopped making the lease payments. Siemens subsequently sued ATIC for the lease payments due. ATIC alleged, among other things, that it was unconscionable to require it to make payments on defective equipment. The court, though, viewed the matter differently. The lease clearly qualified as a finance lease under Article 2A, and the letter of the law was clear: the insurance company was obligated to "make all payments due under the lease regardless of the condition or performance of the leased equipment."[a]

THE BOTTOM LINE

The fact that ATIC was obligated to make the lease payments regardless of the condition of the equipment does not mean that ATIC was without a remedy. As the court noted in this case, "ATIC has raised triable issues of fact [issues that could go to trial] as to its equipment problems, but . . . they are properly brought only against the manufacturer," not against the lessor (Siemens).

a. *Siemens Credit Corp. v. American Transit Insurance Co.*, 2001 WL 40775 (S.D.N.Y. 2001).

2A–407]. That is, the lessee must perform whether or not the financer performs. The lessee also must look almost entirely to the supplier for warranties.

The Formation of Sales and Lease Contracts

In regard to the formation of sales and lease contracts, the UCC modifies the common law in several ways. We look here at how Article 2 and Article 2A of the UCC modify common law contract rules. Remember, though, that parties to sales contracts are free to establish whatever terms they wish. The UCC comes into play only when the parties have failed to provide in their contract for a contingency that later gives rise to a dispute. The UCC makes this clear time and again by its use of such phrases as "unless the parties otherwise agree" or "absent a contrary agreement by the parties."

NOTE Under the UCC, it is the actions of the parties that determine whether they intended to form a contract.

OFFER

In general contract law, the moment a definite offer is met by an unqualified acceptance, a binding contract is formed. In commercial sales transactions, the verbal exchanges, the correspondence, and the actions of the parties may not reveal exactly when a binding contractual obligation arises. The UCC states that an agreement sufficient to constitute a contract can exist even if the moment of its making is undetermined [UCC 2–204(2), 2A–204(2)].

Open Terms Remember from Chapter 9 that under the common law of contracts, an offer must be definite enough for the parties (and the courts) to ascertain its essential terms when it is accepted. In contrast to the common law, the UCC states that a sales or lease contract will not fail for indefiniteness even if one or more terms are left open as long as (1) the parties intended to make a contract and (2) there is a reasonably certain basis for the court to grant an appropriate remedy [UCC 2–204(3), 2A–204(3)].

● **EXAMPLE 14.2** Mike agrees to lease from CompuQuik a highly specialized computer work station. Mike and one of CompuQuik's sales representatives sign a lease agreement that leaves some of the details blank, to be "worked out" the following week, when the leasing manager will be back from her vacation. In the meantime, CompuQuik obtains the necessary equipment from one of its suppliers and spends several days modifying the equipment to suit Mike's needs. When the leasing manager returns, she calls Mike and tells him that his work station is ready. Mike says he is no longer interested in the work station, as he has arranged to lease the same type of equipment for a lower price from another firm. CompuQuik sues Mike to recover its costs in obtaining and modifying the equipment, and one of the issues before the court is whether the parties had an enforceable contract. The court will likely hold that they did, based on their intent and conduct, despite the "blanks" in their written agreement.●

Although the UCC has radically lessened the requirement of definiteness of terms, keep in mind that the more terms left open, the less likely it is that a court will find that the parties intended to form a contract. (This is also true with respect to online contracts—see Chapter 17.)

Open Price Term. If the parties have not agreed on a price, the court will determine a "reasonable price at the time for delivery" [UCC 2–305(1)]. If either the buyer or the seller is to determine the price, the price is to be fixed (set) in good faith [UCC 2–305(2)].

Sometimes the price fails to be fixed through the fault of one of the parties. In that situation, the other party can treat the contract as canceled or fix a reasonable price. ● **EXAMPLE 14.3** Johnson and Merrick enter into a contract for the sale of unfinished doors and agree that Johnson will determine the price. Johnson refuses to fix the price. Merrick can either treat the contract as canceled or set a reasonable price [UCC 2–305(3)].●

ETHICAL ISSUE 14.1

Should merchants be required to act in good faith?

This question was one of many facing the drafters of the UCC. Their answer was a resounding "Yes." UCC 1–203 states, "Every contract or duty within this act imposes an obligation of good faith in its performance or enforcement." The difficulty, of course, was in defining good faith in a meaningful way. The UCC resolved the problem by stating that good faith in the case of a merchant means honesty in fact and the observance of reasonable commercial standards of fair dealing in the trade [UCC 2–103(1)(b)]. Thus, the concepts of *good faith* and *commercial reasonableness* permeate the UCC. As you just read, if the buyer or the seller is to determine the price, the UCC requires that the price be determined in good faith. This is but one of many UCC provisions requiring good faith in the formation and performance of sales contracts. The concept of commercial reasonableness also underlies numerous UCC provisions. A merchant is expected to act in a reasonable manner according to reasonable commercial customs. The importance of commercial reasonableness as a component of good faith is underscored by the fact that the word *reasonable* appears about ninety times in Article 2.

CONTRAST The common law requires that the parties make their terms definite before they have a contract. The UCC applies general commercial standards to make the terms of a contract definite.

Open Payment Term. When parties do not specify payment terms, payment is due at the time and place at which the buyer is to receive the goods [UCC 2–310(a)]. The buyer can tender payment using any commercially normal or acceptable means, such as a check or credit card. If the seller demands payment in cash, however, the buyer must be given a reasonable time to obtain it [UCC 2–511(2)]. This is especially important when the contract states a definite and final time for performance.

Open Delivery Term. When no delivery terms are specified, the buyer normally takes delivery at the seller's place of business [UCC 2–308(a)]. If the seller has no place of business, the seller's residence is used. When goods are located in some other place and both parties know it, delivery is made there. If the time for shipment or delivery is not clearly specified in the sales contract, the court will infer a "reasonable" time for performance [UCC 2–309(1)].

Duration of an Ongoing Contract. A single contract might specify successive performances but not indicate how long the parties are required to deal with each other. Although either party may terminate the ongoing contractual relationship, principles of good faith and sound commercial practice call for reasonable notification before termination so as to give the other party reasonable time to seek a substitute arrangement [UCC 2–309(2), (3)].

Options and Cooperation regarding Performance. When specific shipping arrangements have not been made but the contract contemplates shipment of the goods, the seller has the right to make these arrangements in good faith, using commercial reasonableness in the situation [UCC 2–311].

When terms relating to the assortment of goods are omitted from a sales contract, the *buyer* can specify the assortment. • **EXAMPLE 14.4** Petry Drugs, Inc., agrees to purchase one thousand toothbrushes from Marconi's Dental Supply. The toothbrushes come in a variety of colors, but the contract does not specify color. Petry, the buyer, has the right to take six hundred blue toothbrushes and four hundred green ones if it wishes. Petry, however, must exercise good faith and commercial reasonableness in making its selection [UCC 2–311]. •

Open Quantity Term. Normally, if the parties do not specify a quantity, a court will have no basis for determining a remedy. The UCC recognizes two exceptions in requirements and output contracts [UCC 2–306(1)]. In a **requirements contract**, the buyer agrees to purchase and the seller agrees to sell all or up to a stated amount of what the buyer *needs* or *requires*. • **EXAMPLE 14.5** Southern State Cannery forms a contract with Al Cupp. The cannery agrees to purchase from Cupp, and Cupp agrees to sell to the cannery, all of the green beans that the cannery needs or requires during the summer of 2002. • There is implicit consideration in a requirements contract, for the buyer (the cannery, in this situation) gives up the right to buy green beans from any other seller, and this forfeited right creates a legal detriment.

REQUIREMENTS CONTRACT
An agreement in which a buyer agrees to purchase and the seller agrees to sell all or up to a stated amount of what the buyer needs or requires.

Requirements contracts are common in the business world and are normally enforceable. If, however, the buyer promises to purchase only if the buyer *wishes* to do so, or if the buyer reserves the right to buy the goods from someone other than the seller, the promise is illusory (without consideration) and unenforceable by either party.

In an **output contract**, the seller agrees to sell and the buyer agrees to buy all or up to a stated amount of what the seller *produces*. • **EXAMPLE 14.6** Al Cupp forms a contract with Southern State Cannery. Cupp agrees to sell to the cannery, and the cannery agrees to purchase from Cupp, all of the beans that Cupp produces on his farm during the summer of 2002. • Again, because the seller essentially forfeits the right to sell goods to another buyer, there is implicit consideration in an output contract.

OUTPUT CONTRACT
An agreement in which a seller agrees to sell and a buyer agrees to buy all or up to a stated amount of what the seller produces.

The UCC imposes a *good faith limitation* on requirements and output contracts. The quantity under such contracts is the amount of requirements or the amount of output that occurs during a *normal* production year. The actual quantity purchased or sold cannot be unreasonably disproportionate to normal or comparable prior requirements or output [UCC 2–306].

Merchant's Firm Offer Under regular contract principles, an offer can be revoked at any time before acceptance. The major common law exception is an *option contract* (discussed in Chapter 9), in which the offeree pays consideration for the offeror's irrevocable promise to keep the offer open for a stated period. The UCC creates a second exception for firm offers made by a merchant to sell, buy, or lease goods. A **firm offer** arises when a merchant-offeror gives *assurances* in a *signed writing* that the offer will remain open. The merchant's firm offer is irrevocable without the necessity of consideration[4] for the stated period or, if no definite period is stated, a reasonable period (neither period to exceed three months) [UCC 2–205, 2A–205].

FIRM OFFER
An offer (by a merchant) that is irrevocable without consideration for a stated period of time or, if no definite period is stated, for a reasonable time (neither period to exceed three months). A firm offer by a merchant must be in writing and must be signed by the offeror.

It is necessary that the offer be both *written* and *signed* by the offeror.[5] When a firm offer is contained in a form contract prepared by the offeree, the offeror must also sign

4. If the offeree pays consideration, then an option contract (not a merchant's firm offer) is formed.
5. "Signed" includes any symbol executed or adopted by a party with a present intention to authenticate a writing [UCC 1–201(39)]. A complete signature is not required. Therefore, initials, a thumbprint, a trade name, or any mark used in lieu of a written signature will suffice, regardless of its location on the document.

FOR CRITICAL ANALYSIS
What are the advantages and disadvantages of the CISG's provisions on firm offers relative to the UCC's provisions?

INTERNATIONAL PERSPECTIVE

Firm Offers under the CISG

As mentioned elsewhere, under the UCC a merchant's firm offer is irrevocable, even without consideration, if the offeror gives assurances in a signed writing that the offer will remain open. The United Nations Convention on Contracts for the International Sale of Goods (CISG), which will be discussed later in this chapter, takes a different approach in regard to international sales contracts. Article 16(2) of the CISG provides that an offer will be irrevocable if the merchant-offeror simply states orally that the offer is irrevocable or if the offeree reasonably relies on the offer as being irrevocable. In either of these situations, the offer will be irrevocable even without a writing and without consideration.

a separate firm offer assurance. This requirement ensures that the offeror will be made aware of the offer. If the firm offer is buried amid copious language in one of the pages of the offeree's form contract, the offeror may inadvertently sign the contract without realizing that it contains a firm offer, thus defeating the purpose of the rule—which is to give effect to a merchant's deliberate intent to be bound to a firm offer.

ACCEPTANCE

BE AWARE The UCC's rules on means of acceptance illustrate the UCC's flexibility. The rules have been adapted to new forms of communication, such as faxes and online communications.

The following sections examine the UCC's provisions governing acceptance. As you will see, acceptance of an offer to buy, sell, or lease goods generally may be made in any reasonable manner and by any reasonable means.

Methods of Acceptance The general common law rule is that an offeror can specify, or authorize, a particular means of acceptance, making that means the only one effective for contract formation. As you will read in Chapter 17, online sellers typically specify, or authorize, acceptance through "click-on" boxes. In other words, to accept an online offer, the offeree merely clicks on a box stating "I agree" or "I accept."

Even an unauthorized means of communication is effective, however, as long as the acceptance is received by the specified deadline. • **EXAMPLE 14.7** Suppose that an offer states, "Answer by fax within five days." If the offeree sends a letter, and the offeror receives it within five days, a valid contract is still formed. •

Any Reasonable Means. When the offeror does not specify a means of acceptance, the UCC provides that acceptance can be made by any means of communication reasonable under the circumstances [UCC 2–206(1), 2A–206(1)]. This broadens the common law rules concerning authorized means of acceptance. (For a review of the requirements relating to mode and timeliness of acceptance, see Chapter 9.)

• **EXAMPLE 14.8** Anodyne Corporation writes Bethlehem Industries a letter offering to lease $1,000 worth of postage meters. The offer states that Anodyne will keep the offer open for only ten days from the date of the letter. Before the ten days have lapsed, Bethlehem sends Anodyne an acceptance by fax. Is a valid contract formed? The answer is yes, because acceptance by fax is a commercially reasonable medium of acceptance under the circumstances. Acceptance would be effective on Bethlehem's transmission of the fax, which occurred before the offer lapsed. •

This is the agreement for subscribing to EarthLink Network online. By clicking on the "I agree" button, the subscriber indicates his or her acceptance of the terms of the offer.

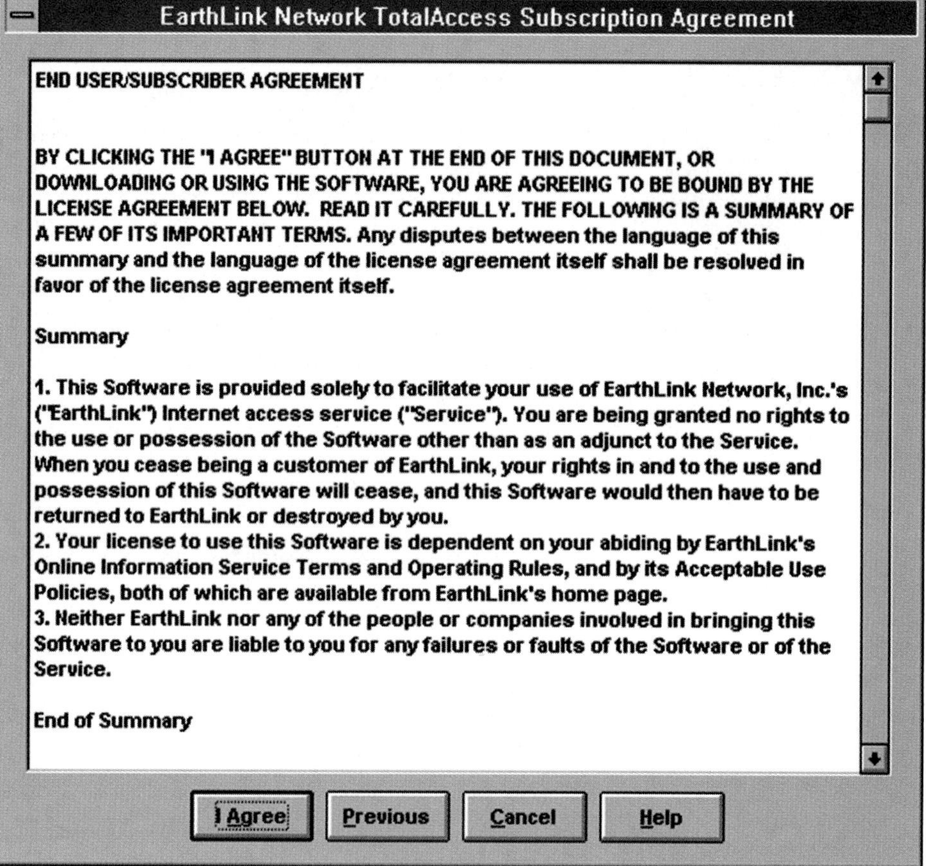

Promise to Ship or Prompt Shipment. The UCC permits a seller to accept an offer to buy goods for current or prompt shipment by either a prompt *promise* to ship the goods to the buyer or the *prompt shipment* of conforming goods (that is, goods that accord with the contract's terms) to the buyer [UCC 2–206(1)(b)]. The seller's prompt shipment of *nonconforming goods* in response to the offer constitutes both an acceptance (a contract) and a *breach* of that contract.

SEASONABLY
Within a specified time period, or, if no period is specified, within a reasonable time.

This rule does not apply if the seller **seasonably** (within a reasonable amount of time) notifies the buyer that the nonconforming shipment is offered only as an *accommodation*, or as a favor. The notice of accommodation must clearly indicate to the buyer that the shipment does not constitute an acceptance and that, therefore, no contract has been formed.

● **EXAMPLE 14.9** McFarrell Pharmacy orders five cases of Johnson & Johnson 3-by-5-inch gauze pads from Halderson Medical Supply, Inc. If Halderson ships five cases of Xeroform 3-by-5-inch gauze pads instead, the shipment acts as both an acceptance of McFarrell's offer and a *breach* of the resulting contract. McFarrell may sue Halderson for any appropriate damages. If, however, Halderson notifies McFarrell that the Xeroform gauze pads are being shipped *as an accommodation*—because Halderson has only Xeroform pads in stock—the shipment will constitute a counteroffer, not an acceptance. A contract will be formed only if McFarrell accepts the Xeroform gauze pads. ●

Notice of Acceptance As noted in Chapter 9, notice of acceptance is not an issue in *bilateral* contracts because such contracts are formed by an exchange of promises. In other words, a bilateral contract is formed when the promise is made. In contrast, unilateral contracts invite acceptance by performance. Under the common law, because acceptance (performance) of a unilateral contract was usually evident, the offeree normally was not required to notify the offeror of the acceptance. The UCC changes this common law rule. According to the UCC, when "the beginning of requested performance is a reasonable mode of acceptance[,] an offeror who is not notified of acceptance within a reasonable time may treat the offer as having lapsed before acceptance" [UCC 2–206(2), 2A–206(2)].

Additional Terms Under the common law, if Alderman makes an offer to Beale, and Beale in turn accepts but in the acceptance makes some slight modification to the terms of the offer, there is no contract. The so-called *mirror image rule*, which requires that the terms of the acceptance exactly match those of the offer (see Chapter 9), makes Beale's action a rejection of—and a counteroffer to—Alderman's offer. This rule often results in the so-called *battle of the forms*.

● **EXAMPLE 14.10** A buyer negotiates with a seller over the phone to purchase digital videodisc (DVD) players. The parties agree to all of the specific terms of the sale—price, quantity, delivery date, and so on. The buyer then offers to buy the DVD players, using its standard purchase order form, and sends the form to the seller. At the same time, the seller accepts the offer, using its standard sales form. Because the parties presume that they have reached an agreement, discrepancies in the terms and conditions contained in their respective forms may go unnoticed. If a dispute arises, however, the discrepancies become significant, and a "battle of the forms" begins, in which each party claims that its form represents the true terms of the agreement.●

DON'T FORGET The UCC recognizes that a proposed deal is a contract if, in commercial understanding, the deal has been closed.

Under the common law, the courts tended to resolve this difficulty by holding that no contract was formed, because the last form to be sent was not an acceptance but a counteroffer. To avoid the battle of the forms, the UCC dispenses with the mirror image rule. The UCC generally takes the position that if the offeree's response indicates a *definite* acceptance of the offer, a contract is formed even if the acceptance includes additional or different terms from those contained in the offer [UCC 2–207(1)]. What happens to these additional terms? The answer to this question depends, in part, on whether the parties are nonmerchants or merchants.

One Party or Both Parties Are Nonmerchants. If one (or both) of the parties is a *nonmerchant*, the contract is formed according to the terms of the original offer submitted by the original offeror and not according to the additional terms of the acceptance [UCC 2–207(2)]. ● **EXAMPLE 14.11** Tolsen offers in writing to sell his personal computer and color printer and scanner to Valdez for $1,500. Valdez faxes a reply to Tolsen in which Valdez states, "I accept your offer to purchase your computer, color printer, and scanner for $1,500. I *would like* two extra sets of color toner for the printer to be included in the purchase price." Valdez has given Tolsen a definite expression of acceptance (creating a contract), even though the acceptance also suggests an added term for the offer. Because Tolsen is not a merchant, the additional term is merely a proposal (suggestion), and Tolsen is not legally obligated to comply with that term.●

Both Parties Are Merchants. In contracts *between merchants* (that is, when both parties to the contract are merchants), the additional terms automatically become part of the contract unless (1) the original offer expressly limits acceptance to the terms of the offer, (2) the new or changed terms *materially* alter the contract, or (3) the offeror objects to the new or changed terms within a reasonable period of time [UCC 2–207(2)].

What constitutes a material alteration is frequently a question of fact that only a court can decide. Generally, if the modification involves no unreasonable element of surprise or hardship for the offeror, the court will hold that the modification did not materially alter the contract. The issue in the following case was whether a party was bound to conditions of sale included in a confirmation form sent after a phone order.

CASE 14.2 Tupman Thurlow Co. v. Woolf International Corp.

Appeals Court of Massachusetts, 1997.
43 Mass.App. 334,
682 N.E.2d 1378.

HISTORICAL AND SOCIAL SETTING *When the first cases arose under the UCC, some merchant-litigants contended that UCC 2–207 gave them the freedom to ignore, for example, a confirmation form if its terms did not match the original order. They argued that if they (the offerors) did not expressly agree to the terms, the terms were not part of their agreements. In the leading case on this issue, the court concluded that if this were the result, "the statute would lead to an absurdity," because there would be no reason for an offeror to agree to the new terms. Instead, the court held that if an offeror receives a response that includes new terms and the offeror goes ahead with the deal, the new terms are part of the contract.*[a] *This rule applies, however, only if the new terms are presented before the goods are accepted.*

FACTS Woolf International Corporation and Tupman Thurlow Company are meat wholesalers. Over a two-year period, Woolf bought meat from Tupman sixty-four times. Woolf ordered the meat by phone, and Tupman mailed a confirmation form. After delivery, Tupman sent an invoice, which Woolf paid. The confirmation form and the invoice set out the same conditions of sale, including a clause requiring arbitration, in New York, of any dispute. On Woolf's sixty-fifth order, Tupman delivered $45,792 worth of meat, but Woolf did not pay. Tupman initiated arbitration proceedings. Woolf refused to participate, claiming that there was no agreement to arbitrate. The arbitrator ruled otherwise and awarded Tupman damages. A New York state court affirmed the award, and Tupman filed a petition in a Massachusetts state court to enforce the judgment. The Massachusetts court concluded that Woolf was bound by the New York judgment. Woolf appealed.

a. *Roto-Lith, Ltd. v. F. P. Bartlett & Co.*, 297 F.2d 497 (1st Cir. 1962).

ISSUE Can a buyer be held to an arbitration clause contained in a confirmation form sent by the seller following a phone order?

DECISION Yes. The Appeals Court of Massachusetts affirmed the lower court's decision. Woolf was bound by the conditions of sale on the confirmation form.

REASON The state intermediate appellate court acknowledged that under UCC 2–207(2), as between merchants, additional terms that are included in a written confirmation do not become part of the parties' contract if the terms materially alter the contract. The court pointed out, however, that Massachusetts law required the arbitration provision to be enforced because it was included in the order confirmation forms that were received prior to the delivery of the goods. The court emphasized that "Woolf never refuted that the arbitration provision was set out on Tupman's order confirmation forms which preceded delivery of the order, that the conditions of sale were set out on the confirmation forms as well as the invoices, that Tupman followed this procedure in every transaction with Woolf, and that Woolf had a long history of dealings with Tupman."

FOR CRITICAL ANALYSIS—Social Consideration *Woolf argued in part that it had never read the invoices. Why didn't the court rule in Woolf's favor on this basis?*

Conditioned on Offeror's Assent. Regardless of merchant status, the UCC provides that the offeree's expression cannot be construed as an acceptance if additional or different terms in the acceptance are expressly conditioned on the offeror's assent to the additional or different terms [UCC 2–207(1)]. • **EXAMPLE 14.12** Philips offers to sell Hundert 650 pounds of turkey thighs at a specified price and with specified delivery terms. Hundert responds, "I accept your offer for 650 pounds of turkey thighs *on the condition that you give me ninety days to pay for them.*" Hundert's response will be construed not as an acceptance but as a counteroffer, which Philips may or may not accept.●

Additional Terms May Be Stricken. The UCC provides yet another option for dealing with conflicting terms in the parties' writings. Section 2–207(3) states that conduct by both parties that recognizes the existence of a contract is sufficient to establish a contract for the sale of goods even though the writings of the parties do not otherwise establish a contract. In this situation, "the terms of the particular contract will consist of those terms on which the writings of the parties agree, together with any supplementary terms incorporated under any other provisions of this Act." In a dispute over contract terms, this provision allows a court simply to strike from the contract those terms on which the parties do not agree.

ETHICAL ISSUE 14.2

How can the "battle of the forms" be avoided?

The drafters of UCC Section 2–207 attempted to eliminate the "battle of the forms" by providing that a contract can be formed even though the acceptance includes additional terms. Nonetheless, the battle continues in earnest. Indeed, one of the results of Section 2–207 is that buyers and sellers go to great lengths to draft their acceptances as "offers" or "counteroffers" (instead of acceptances) so that their terms will control the resulting contracts. This is because under UCC 2–207(2), additional terms in an acceptance that materially alter the contract do not become part of the contract—the terms of the offer control. Whether a form is defined as an acceptance or an offer can thus have significant legal consequences for the parties.

One of the goals in the proposed revision of Article 2 of the UCC is to redesign UCC 2–207 so that the battle of the forms can be avoided. Some have suggested that this section should be revised to focus less on contract formation (offer and acceptance) and more on the approach currently provided under UCC 2–207(3)—that the terms of a contract are only those on which the parties have agreed. To be sure, this could mean that parties may end up with a contract containing a UCC gap-filling term to which neither party agrees. Yet, as one court noted, "the offeror and the offeree both have the power to protect any term they deem critical by expressly making acceptance conditional on assent to that term."[6]

CONSIDERATION

The common law rule that a contract requires consideration also applies to sales and lease contracts. Unlike the common law, however, the UCC does not require a contract modification to be supported by new consideration. An agreement modifying a contract for the sale or lease of goods "needs no consideration to be binding" [UCC 2–209(1), 2A–208(1)].

Modifications Must Be Made in Good Faith Of course, contract modification must be sought in good faith [UCC 1–203]. ● **EXAMPLE 14.13** Allied, Inc., agrees to lease a new

6. *Superior Boiler Works, Inc. v. R. J. Sanders, Inc.,* 711 A.2d 628 (R.I. 1998).

recreational vehicle (RV) to Louise for a stated monthly payment. Subsequently, a sudden shift in the market makes it difficult for Allied to lease the new RV to Louise at the contract price without suffering a loss. Allied tells Louise of the situation, and she agrees to pay an additional sum for the lease of the RV. Later Louise reconsiders and refuses to pay more than the original price. Under the UCC, Louise's promise to modify the contract needs no consideration to be binding. Hence, she is bound by the modified contract.●

In this example, a shift in the market is a *good faith* reason for contract modification. What if there really was no shift in the market, however, and Allied knew that Louise needed to lease the new RV immediately but refused to deliver it unless she agreed to pay an additional sum of money? This attempt at extortion through modification without a legitimate commercial reason would be ineffective because it would violate the duty of good faith. Allied would not be permitted to enforce the higher price.

When Modification without Consideration Requires a Writing In some situations, modification of a sales or lease contract without consideration must be in writing to be enforceable. If the contract itself prohibits any changes to the contract unless they are in a signed writing, for example, then only those changes agreed to in a signed writing are enforceable. If a consumer (nonmerchant buyer) is dealing with a merchant and the merchant supplies the form that contains a prohibition against oral modification, the consumer must sign a separate acknowledgment of such a clause [UCC 2–209(2), 2A–208(2)].

Additionally, any modification that brings a sales contract under the Statute of Frauds must usually be in writing to be enforceable. Thus, if an oral contract for the sale of goods priced at $400 is modified so that the contract goods are now priced at $600, the modification must be in writing to be enforceable [UCC 2–209(3)]. If, however, the buyer accepts delivery of the goods after the modification, he or she is bound to the $600 price [UCC 2–201(3)(c)]. (Unlike Article 2, Article 2A does not say whether a lease as modified needs to satisfy the Statute of Frauds.)

STATUTE OF FRAUDS

BE AWARE It has been proposed that the UCC be revised to eliminate the Statute of Frauds.

The UCC contains Statute of Frauds provisions covering sales and lease contracts. Under these provisions, sales contracts for goods priced at $500 or more and lease contracts requiring payments of $1,000 or more must be in writing to be enforceable [UCC 2–201(1), 2A–201(1)].

Sufficiency of the Writing The UCC has greatly relaxed the requirements for the sufficiency of a writing to satisfy the Statute of Frauds. A writing or a memorandum will be sufficient as long as it indicates that the parties intended to form a contract and as long as it is signed by the party (or agent of the party) against whom enforcement is sought. The contract normally will not be enforceable beyond the quantity of goods shown in the writing, however. All other terms can be proved in court by oral testimony. For leases, the writing must reasonably identify and describe the goods leased and the lease term.

(Note that other laws may require certain clauses in sales and lease contracts to be in writing. For an example of one such law as it applies to arbitration clauses, see this chapter's *Business Law in the Online World* feature.)

Written Confirmation between Merchants Once again, the UCC provides a special rule for merchants. Merchants can satisfy the requirements of a writing for the Statute of Frauds if, after the parties have agreed orally, one of the merchants sends a signed

BUSINESS LAW: //in the Online World

Writing Requirements for Arbitration Clauses

As you learned in Chapter 3, parties frequently include arbitration clauses in their contracts. These clauses reflect the parties' agreement to submit any dispute that may arise under the contract to arbitration. Generally, public policy has long favored arbitration as a dispute-settlement method, as reflected in state statutes and the Federal Arbitration Act (FAA) of 1925, which provide for the enforcement of arbitration clauses. Yet the FAA also states that arbitration clauses must be in writing to be enforceable. Does that mean that arbitration clauses in electronic contracts are not enforceable? Does an electronic contract constitute a "writing" for FAA purposes?

The Case against RealNetworks, Inc.

This question came before a federal district court in 2000 in a case brought by a group of plaintiffs against RealNetworks, Inc. The plaintiffs complained that RealNetworks' software products secretly allowed RealNetworks to access and intercept users' electronic communications and stored information without their knowledge or consent and thus violated their privacy rights. RealNetworks asked the court to stay the proceedings and enforce the arbitration clause in the licensing agreement accepted by the plaintiffs when they downloaded the software. These agreements were "click-on" agreements, which will be discussed in more detail in Chapter 17. Before the plaintiffs could install RealNetworks' software, they had to accept RealNetworks' licensing agreement, which appeared in a pop-up window on their computer screens. A provision at the end of the agreement stated that any disputes would be submitted to arbitration.

Does an Electronic Contract Constitute a "Writing" under the FAA?

The question before the court was whether the click-on licensing agreement constituted a writing, as required by the FAA. The plaintiffs asserted that it did not, because the agreement could not be printed or saved. RealNetworks argued that it did and that it could be printed and saved.

The court, after delving into a series of dictionary definitions to determine the plain meaning of the word *writing*, decided that the agreement did constitute a writing. Contrary to the plaintiffs' assertions, the agreement could be rather easily printed and automatically stored on the user's hard drive despite the absence of "print" and "save" buttons. In fact, noted the court, there was more than one way to print the agreement. While Congress did not specifically mention electronic communications when it enacted the FAA in 1925, it also did not specifically *exclude* electronic communications from the category of written communications. In short, the plaintiffs were bound by the "written" agreement, including its arbitration clause.[a]

FOR CRITICAL ANALYSIS

If an Internet user does not print out a document temporarily displayed on her or his computer screen, should that document still qualify as a "writing"?

a. *In re RealNetworks, Inc., Privacy Litigation,* 2000 WL 631341 (N.D.Ill. 2000).

written confirmation to the other merchant within a reasonable time after the oral agreement was reached. The communication must indicate the terms of the agreement, and the merchant receiving the confirmation must have reason to know of its contents. Unless the merchant who receives the confirmation gives written notice of objection to its contents within ten days after receipt, the writing is sufficient against the receiving merchant, even though he or she has not signed anything [UCC 2–201(2)].[7]

● **EXAMPLE 14.14** Alfonso is a merchant buyer in Cleveland. He contracts over the telephone to purchase $4,000 worth of spare aircraft parts from Goldster, a New York City merchant seller. Two days later, Goldster sends a written confirmation detailing

7. According to the Comments accompanying UCC 2A–201 (Article 2A's Statute of Frauds), the "between merchants" provision was not included because the number of such transactions involving leases, as opposed to sales, was thought to be modest.

the terms of the oral contract, and Alfonso subsequently receives it. If Alfonso does not give Goldster written notice of objection to the contents of the written confirmation within ten days of receipt, Alfonso cannot raise the Statute of Frauds as a defense against the enforcement of the oral contract.●

Exceptions The UCC defines three exceptions to the writing requirements of the Statute of Frauds. An oral contract for the sale of goods priced at $500 or more or the lease of goods involving total payments of $1,000 or more will be enforceable despite the absence of a writing in the circumstances discussed in the following subsections [UCC 2–201(3), 2A–201(4)]. These exceptions and other ways in which sales law differs from general contract law are summarized in Exhibit 14–2.

EXHIBIT 14–2 MAJOR DIFFERENCES BETWEEN CONTRACT LAW AND SALES LAW

	CONTRACT LAW	SALES LAW
Contract Terms	Contract must contain all material terms.	Open terms are acceptable if parties intended to form a contract, but contract not enforceable beyond quantity term.
Acceptance	Mirror image rule applies. If additional terms are added in acceptance, counteroffer is created.	Additional terms will not negate acceptance unless acceptance is made expressly conditional on assent to the additional terms.
Contract Modification	Requires consideration.	Does not require consideration.
Irrevocable Offers	Option contracts (with consideration).	Merchants' firm offers (without consideration).
Statute of Frauds Requirements	All material terms must be included in the writing.	Writing required only in sale of goods priced at $500 or more but not enforceable beyond quantity specified. *Exceptions:* 1. Contracts for specially manufactured goods. 2. Contracts admitted to by party against whom enforcement is sought. 3. Contracts will be enforced to extent goods delivered or paid for. 4. A contract between merchants is enforceable if a merchant fails to object in writing to a confirming memorandum within ten days of its receipt.

An artisan creates a specially designed "bowl within a bowl" out of one piece of clay. If a restaurant orally contracted with the artisan to create twenty of the specially designed bowls for use in its business, at a price of $500, would the contract have to be in writing to be enforceable?

REMEMBER An admission can be made in documents, including internal memos and employee reports, that may be obtained during discovery prior to trial.

Specially Manufactured Goods. An oral contract is enforceable if it is for (1) goods that are specially manufactured for a particular buyer or specially manufactured or obtained for a particular lessee, (2) these goods are not suitable for resale or lease to others in the ordinary course of the seller's or lessor's business, and (3) the seller or lessor has substantially started to manufacture the goods or has made commitments for the manufacture or procurement of the goods. In this situation, once the seller or lessor has taken action, the buyer or lessee cannot repudiate the agreement claiming the Statute of Frauds as a defense.

● **EXAMPLE 14.15** Womach orders custom-made draperies for her new boutique. The price is $1,000, and the contract is oral. When the merchant seller manufactures the draperies and tenders delivery to Womach, Womach refuses to accept them even though the quality of the work is satisfactory and the job has been completed on time. Womach claims that she is not liable because the contract was oral. Clearly, if the unique style and color of the draperies make it improbable that the seller can find another buyer, Womach is liable to the seller. Note that the seller must have made a substantial beginning in manufacturing the specialized item prior to the buyer's repudiation. (Here, the manufacture was completed.) Of course, the court must still be convinced by evidence of the terms of the oral contract. ●

Admissions. An oral contract for the sale or lease of goods is enforceable if the party against whom enforcement of a contract is sought admits in pleadings, testimony, or other court proceedings that a contract for sale was made. In this situation, the contract will be enforceable even though it was oral, but enforceability will be limited to the quantity of goods admitted.

● **EXAMPLE 14.16** Lane and Pyron negotiate an agreement over the telephone. During the negotiations, Lane requests a delivery price for five hundred gallons of gasoline and a separate price for seven hundred gallons of gasoline. Pyron replies that the price would be the same, $1.10 per gallon. Lane orally orders five hundred gallons. Pyron honestly believes that Lane ordered seven hundred gallons and tenders that amount. Lane refuses the shipment of seven hundred gallons, and Pyron sues for breach. In his pleadings and testimony, Lane admits that an oral contract was made, but only for five hundred gallons. Because Lane admits the existence of the oral contract, Lane cannot plead the Statute of Frauds as a defense. The contract is enforceable, however, only to the extent of the quantity admitted (five hundred gallons). ●

Partial Performance. An oral contract for the sale or lease of goods is enforceable if payment has been made and accepted or goods have been received and accepted. This is the "partial performance" exception. The oral contract will be enforced at least to the extent that performance *actually* took place.

● **EXAMPLE 14.17** Suppose that Jeffrey Allan orally contracts to lease to Opus Enterprises a thousand chairs at $2 each to be used during a one-day concert. Before delivery, Opus sends Allan a check for $1,000, which Allan cashes. Later, when Allan attempts to deliver the chairs, Opus refuses delivery, claiming the Statute of Frauds as a defense, and demands the return of its $1,000. Under the UCC's partial performance rule, Allan can enforce the oral contract by tender of delivery of five hundred chairs for the $1,000 accepted. Similarly, if Opus had made no payment but had accepted the delivery of five hundred chairs from Allan, the oral contract would have been enforceable against Opus for $1,000, the lease payment due for the five hundred chairs delivered. ●

Parol Evidence

If the parties to a contract set forth its terms in a confirmatory memorandum (a writing expressing offer and acceptance of the deal) or in a writing intended as their final expression, the terms of the contract cannot be contradicted by evidence of any prior agreements or contemporaneous oral agreements. The terms of the contract may, however, be explained or supplemented by *consistent additional terms* or by *course of dealing, usage of trade,* or *course of performance* [UCC 2–202, 2A–202].

Consistent Additional Terms If the court finds an ambiguity in a writing that is supposed to be a complete and exclusive statement of the agreement between the parties, it may accept evidence of consistent additional terms to clarify or remove the ambiguity. The court will not, however, accept evidence of contradictory terms. This is the rule under both the UCC and the common law of contracts.

"No written law has ever been more binding than unwritten custom."

CARRIE CHAPMAN CATT, 1859–1947 (American suffragist)

Course of Dealing and Usage of Trade Under the UCC, the meaning of any agreement, evidenced by the language of the parties and by their actions, must be interpreted in light of commercial practices and other surrounding circumstances. In interpreting a commercial agreement, the court will assume that the course of prior dealing between the parties and the usage of trade were taken into account when the agreement was phrased.

COURSE OF DEALING
Prior conduct between parties to a contract that establishes a common basis for their understanding.

A **course of dealing** is a sequence of previous actions and communications between the parties to a particular transaction that establishes a common basis for their understanding [UCC 1–205(1)]. A course of dealing is restricted to the sequence of actions and communications between the parties that has occurred prior to the agreement in question. The UCC states, "A course of dealing between the parties and any usage of trade in the vocation or trade in which they are engaged or of which they are or should be aware give particular meaning to [the terms of the agreement] and supplement or qualify the terms of [the] agreement" [UCC 1–205(3)].

USAGE OF TRADE
Any practice or method of dealing having such regularity of observance in a place, vocation, or trade as to justify an expectation that it will be observed with respect to the transaction in question.

Usage of trade is defined as any practice or method of dealing having such regularity of observance in a place, vocation, or trade as to justify an expectation that it will be observed with respect to the transaction in question [UCC 1–205(2)]. Further, the express terms of an agreement and an applicable course of dealing or usage of trade will be construed to be consistent with each other whenever reasonable. When such a construction is *unreasonable,* however, the express terms in the agreement will prevail [UCC 1–205(4)].

COURSE OF PERFORMANCE
The conduct that occurs under the terms of a particular agreement; such conduct indicates what the parties to an agreement intended it to mean.

Course of Performance A **course of performance** is the conduct that occurs under the terms of a particular agreement. Presumably, the parties themselves know best what they meant by their words, and the course of performance actually undertaken under their agreement is the best indication of what they meant [UCC 2–208(1), 2A–207(1)].

● **EXAMPLE 14.18** Janson's Lumber Company contracts with Barrymore to sell Barrymore a specified number of "two-by-fours." The lumber in fact does not measure 2 inches by 4 inches but rather 1⅞ inches by 3¾ inches. Janson's agrees to deliver the lumber in five deliveries, and Barrymore, without objection, accepts the lumber in the first three deliveries. On the fourth delivery, however, Barrymore objects that the two-by-fours do not measure 2 inches by 4 inches. The course of performance in this transaction—that is, the fact that Barrymore accepted three deliveries without objection under the agreement—is relevant in determining that here the term "two-by-four" actually means "1⅞ by 3¾." Janson's can also prove that two-by-fours need not be exactly 2 inches by 4 inches by applying usage of trade, course of prior dealing, or

"Merchants know perfectly well what they mean when they express themselves, not in the language of lawyers, but in the language of courteous mercantile communication."

LORD CAIRNS, 1819–1885 (British jurist)

both. Janson's can, for example, show that in previous transactions, Barrymore took 1⅞-by-3¾-inch lumber without objection. In addition, Janson's can show that in the lumber trade, two-by-fours are commonly 1⅞ inches by 3¾ inches. ●

Rules of Construction The UCC provides *rules of construction* for interpreting contracts. Express terms, course of performance, course of dealing, and usage of trade are to be construed together when they do not contradict one another. When such a construction is unreasonable, however, the following order of priority controls: (1) express terms, (2) course of performance, (3) course of dealing, and (4) usage of trade [UCC 1–205(4), 2–208(2), 2A–207(2)].

UNCONSCIONABILITY

As discussed in Chapter 10, an unconscionable contract is one that is so unfair and one sided that it would be unreasonable to enforce it. The UCC allows the court to evaluate a contract or any clause in a contract, and if the court deems it to have been unconscionable at the time it was made, the court can (1) refuse to enforce the contract, (2) enforce the remainder of the contract without the unconscionable clause, or (3) limit the application of any unconscionable clauses to avoid an unconscionable result [UCC 2–302, 2A–108]. The following landmark case illustrates an early application of the UCC's unconscionability provisions.

Landmark and Classic Cases

CASE 14.3 Jones v. Star Credit Corp.

Supreme Court of New York, Nassau County, 1969.
59 Misc.2d 189,
298 N.Y.S.2d 264.

HISTORICAL AND ECONOMIC SETTING *In the sixth century, Roman civil law allowed the rescission of a contract when the court determined that the market value of the goods that were the subject of the contract equaled less than half the contract price. This same ratio has appeared over the last thirty years in many cases in which courts have found contract clauses to be unconscionable under UCC 2–302 on the ground that the price was excessive. In a Connecticut case, for example, the court held that a contract requiring a welfare recipient to make payments totaling $1,248 for a television set that retailed for $499 was unconscionable.*[a] *The seller had not told the buyer the full purchase price. Most of the litigants who have used UCC 2–302 successfully have been consumers who are poor or otherwise at a disadvantage. In one New York case, for example, the court held that a contract requiring a Spanish-speaking consumer to make payments totaling nearly $1,150 for a freezer that wholesaled for less than $350 was unconscionable.*[b] *The contract was in English, and the salesperson did not translate or explain it.*

FACTS The Joneses, the plaintiffs, agreed to purchase a freezer for $900 as the result of a salesperson's visit to their home. Tax and financing charges raised the total price to $1,234.80. At trial, the freezer was found to have a maximum retail value of approximately $300. The plaintiffs, who had made payments totaling $619.88, brought a suit in a New York state court to have the purchase contract declared unconscionable under the UCC.

ISSUE Can this contract be denied enforcement on the ground of unconscionability?

DECISION Yes. The court held that the contract was not enforceable as it stood, and the contract was reformed so that no further payments were required.

a. *Murphy v. McNamara*, 36 Conn.Supp. 183, 416 A.2d 170 (1979).

b. *Frostifresh Corp. v. Reynoso*, 52 Misc.2d 26, 274 N.Y.S.2d 757 (Dist. 1966); rev'd on issue of relief, 54 Misc.2d 119, 281 N.Y.S.2d 946 (Sup. 1967).

(continued)

CASE 14.3—Continued

REASON The court relied on UCC 2–302(1), which states that if "the court as a matter of law finds the contract or any clause of the contract to have been unconscionable at the time it was made the court may * * * so limit the application of any unconscionable clause as to avoid any unconscionable result." The court then examined the disparity between the $900 purchase price and the $300 retail value, as well as the fact that the credit charges alone exceeded the retail value. These excessive charges were exacted despite the seller's knowledge of the plaintiffs' limited resources. The court reformed the contract so that the plaintiffs' payments, amounting to more than $600, were regarded as payment in full.

COMMENT *Classical contract theory holds that a contract is a bargain in which the terms have been worked out freely between the parties. In many modern commercial transactions, this may not be the case. For example, standard-form contracts and leases are often signed by consumer-buyers who understand few of the terms used and who often do not even read them. The inclusion of Sections 2–302 and 2A–108 in the UCC gave the courts a powerful weapon for policing such transactions, and the courts continue to use this weapon to prevent injustice.*

Contracts for the International Sale of Goods

International sales contracts between firms or individuals located in different countries are governed by the 1980 United Nations Convention on Contracts for the International Sale of Goods (CISG)—if the countries of the parties to the contract have ratified the CISG (and if the parties have not agreed that some other law will govern their contract). As of 2002, fifty-seven countries had ratified or acceded to the CISG, including the United States, Canada, Mexico, some Central and South American countries, and most European nations.

Applicability of the CISG

Essentially, the CISG is to international sales contracts what Article 2 of the UCC is to domestic sales contracts. As discussed in this chapter, in domestic transactions the UCC applies when the parties to a contract for a sale of goods have failed to specify in writing

A production line in a globe factory. If, in the United States, a contract for a sale of globes is not in writing, is it enforceable? Is a contract for an international sale of the globes enforceable if it is not in writing?

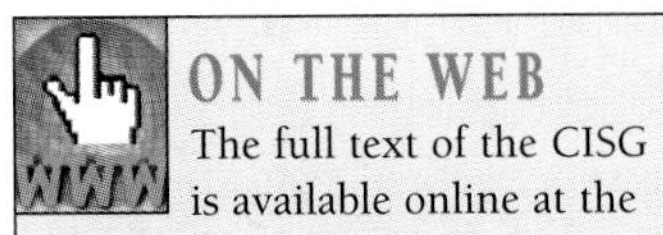

ON THE WEB The full text of the CISG is available online at the Pace University School of Law's Institute of International Commercial Law. Go to

http://cisgw3.law.pace.edu/cisg/text/treaty.html.

some important term concerning price, delivery, or the like. Similarly, whenever the parties subject to the CISG have failed to specify in writing the precise terms of a contract for the international sale of goods, the CISG will be applied. Although the UCC applies to consumer sales, the CISG does not, and neither applies to contracts for services.

Businesspersons must take special care when drafting international sales contracts to avoid problems caused by distance, including language differences and varying national laws. The fold-out exhibit contained within this chapter, which shows an actual international sales contract used by Starbucks Coffee Company, illustrates many of the special terms and clauses that are typically contained in international contracts for the sale of goods. Annotations in the exhibit explain the meaning and significance of specific clauses in the contract. (See Chapter 39 for a discussion of other laws that frame global business transactions.)

A Comparison of CISG and UCC Provisions

The provisions of the CISG, although similar for the most part to those of the UCC, differ from them in certain respects. We have already mentioned some of these differences. In the *International Perspective* in Chapter 11, for example, we pointed out that the CISG does not include the requirements imposed by the UCC's Statute of Frauds. Rather, Article 11 of the CISG states that an international sales contract "need not be concluded in or evidenced by writing and is not subject to any other requirements as to form."

We look here at some differences between the UCC and the CISG with respect to contract formation. In the following chapters, we will continue to point out differences between the CISG and the UCC as they relate to the topics covered. These topics include risk of loss, performance, remedies, and warranties.

Offers Some differences between the UCC and the CISG have to do with offers. A number of these differences were indicated in this chapter's *International Perspective* discussing firm offers. Another difference is that, under the UCC, if the price term is left open, the court will determine "a reasonable price at the time for delivery" [UCC 2–305(1)]. Under the CISG, however, the price term must be specified, or at least provisions for its specification must be included in the agreement; otherwise, normally no contract will exist.

Acceptances Like UCC 2–207, the CISG provides that a contract can be formed even though the acceptance contains additional terms, unless the additional terms materially alter the contract. Virtually any difference in terms is regarded as a "material alteration" under the CISG, however. In effect, then, the CISG requires that the terms of the acceptance mirror those of the offer.

Additionally, under the UCC, an acceptance is effective on dispatch. Under the CISG, however, a contract is created not at the time the acceptance is transmitted but only on its receipt by the offeror. (The offer becomes irrevocable, however, when the acceptance is sent.) Additionally, in contrast to the UCC, the CISG provides that acceptance by performance does not require that the offeror be notified of the performance.

Key Terms

Chapter Summary The Formation of Sales and Lease Contracts

The Scope of the UCC (See page 359.)	The UCC attempts to provide a consistent, uniform, and integrated framework of rules to deal with all phases *ordinarily arising* in a commercial sales or lease transaction, including contract formation, passage of title and risk of loss, performance, remedies, payment for goods, warehoused goods, and secured transactions. If there is a conflict between a common law rule and the UCC, the UCC controls.
The Scope of Article 2—Sales (See pages 359–364.)	Article 2 governs contracts for the sale of goods (tangible, movable personal property). The common law of contracts also applies to sales contracts to the extent that the common law has not been modified by the UCC.
The Scope of Article 2A—Leases (See pages 364–366.)	Article 2A governs contracts for the lease of goods. Except that it applies to leases, instead of sales, of goods, Article 2A is essentially a repetition of Article 2, and varies only to reflect differences between sale and lease transactions.
Offer and Acceptance (See pages 366–373.)	1. *Offer*— a. Not all terms have to be included for a contract to be formed (only the subject matter and quantity term must be specified). b. The price does not have to be included for a contract to be formed. c. Particulars of performance can be left open. d. A written and signed offer by a *merchant,* covering a period of three months or less, is irrevocable without payment of consideration. 2. *Acceptance*— a. Acceptance may be made by any reasonable means of communication; it is effective when dispatched. b. The acceptance of a unilateral offer can be made by a promise to ship or by prompt shipment of conforming goods, or by prompt shipment of nonconforming goods if not accompanied by a notice of accommodation. c. Acceptance by performance requires notice within a reasonable time; otherwise, the offer can be treated as lapsed. d. A definite expression of acceptance creates a contract even if the terms of the acceptance vary from those of the offer unless the varied terms in the acceptance are expressly conditioned on the offeror's assent to the varied terms.
Consideration (See pages 373–374.)	A modification of a contract for the sale of goods does not require consideration.
Requirements under the Statute of Frauds (See pages 374–377.)	1. All contracts for the sale of goods priced at $500 or more must be in writing. A writing is sufficient as long as it indicates a contract between the parties and is signed by the party against whom enforcement is sought. A contract is not enforceable beyond the quantity shown in the writing. 2. When written confirmation of an oral contract *between merchants* is not objected to in writing by the receiver within ten days, the contract is enforceable. 3. Exceptions to the requirement of a writing exist in the following situations: a. When the oral contract is for specially manufactured goods not suitable for resale to others, and the seller has substantially started to manufacture the goods. b. When the defendant admits in pleadings, testimony, or other court proceedings that an oral contract for the sale of goods was made. In this case, the contract will be enforceable to the extent of the quantity of goods admitted.

Chapter Summary The Formation of Sales and Lease Contracts—continued

Requirements under the Statute of Frauds—continued	c. The oral agreement will be enforceable to the extent that payment has been received and accepted by the seller or to the extent that the goods have been received and accepted by the buyer.
Parol Evidence Rule (See pages 378–379.)	1. The terms of a clearly and completely worded written contract cannot be contradicted by evidence of prior agreements or contemporaneous oral agreements. 2. Evidence is admissible to clarify the terms of a writing in the following situations: a. If the contract terms are ambiguous. b. If evidence of course of dealing, usage of trade, or course of performance is necessary to learn or to clarify the intentions of the parties to the contract.
Unconscionability (See pages 379–380.)	An unconscionable contract is one that is so unfair and one sided that it would be unreasonable to enforce it. If the court deems a contract to have been unconscionable at the time it was made, the court can (1) refuse to enforce the contract, (2) refuse to enforce the unconscionable clause of the contract, or (3) limit the application of any unconscionable clauses to avoid an unconscionable result.
Contracts for the International Sale of Goods (See pages 380–381.)	International sales contracts are governed by the United Nations Convention on Contracts for the International Sale of Goods (CISG)—if the countries of the parties to the contract have ratified the CISG (and if the parties have not agreed that some other law will govern their contract). Essentially, the CISG is to international sales contracts what Article 2 of the UCC is to domestic sales contracts. Whenever parties who are subject to the CISG have failed to specify in writing the precise terms of a contract for the international sale of goods, the CISG will be applied.

For Review

① How do Article 2 and Article 2A of the UCC differ? What types of transactions does each article cover?

② What is a merchant's firm offer?

③ If an offeree includes additional or different terms in an acceptance, will a contract result? If so, what happens to these terms?

④ Article 2 and Article 2A of the UCC both define three exceptions to the writing requirements of the Statute of Frauds. What are these three exceptions?

⑤ What law governs contracts for the international sale of goods?

Questions and Case Problems

14–1. Terms of the Offer. The UCC changes the effect of the common law of contracts in several ways. For instance, at common law, an offer must be definite enough for the parties to ascertain its essential terms when it is accepted. What happens under the UCC if some of an offer's terms—the price term, for example—are left open? What if the quantity term is left open?

14–2. Statute of Frauds. Fresher Foods, Inc., orally agreed to purchase from Dale Vernon, a farmer, one thousand bushels of corn for $1.25 per bushel. Fresher Foods paid $125 down and agreed to pay the remainder of the purchase price on delivery, which was scheduled for one week later. When Fresher Foods tendered the balance of $1,125 on the scheduled day of delivery and requested the corn, Vernon refused to deliver it. Fresher Foods sued Vernon for damages, claiming that Vernon had breached their oral contract. Can Fresher Foods recover? If so, to what extent?

14–3. Merchant's Firm Offer. On September 1, Jennings, a used-car dealer, wrote a letter to Wheeler in which he stated, "I have a 1955 Thunderbird convertible in mint condition that I will sell you for $13,500 at any time before October 9. [signed] Peter Jennings." By September 15, having heard nothing from Wheeler, Jennings sold the Thunderbird to another party. On September 29, Wheeler accepted Jennings's offer and tendered the $13,500. When Jennings told Wheeler he had sold the car to another party, Wheeler claimed Jennings had breached their contract. Is Jennings in breach? Explain.

14–4. Accommodation Shipments. M. M. Salinger, Inc., a retailer of television sets, orders one hundred Model Color-X sets from manufacturer Fulsom. The order specifies the price and that the television sets are to be shipped via Interamerican Freightways on or before October 30. Fulsom receives the order on October 5. On October 8, Fulsom writes Salinger a letter indicating that it has received the order and that it will ship the sets as directed, at the specified price. Salinger receives this letter on October 10. On October 28, Fulsom, in preparing the shipment, discovers it has only ninety Color-X sets in stock. Fulsom ships the ninety Color-X sets and ten television sets of a different model, stating clearly on the invoice that the ten sets are being shipped only as an accommodation. Salinger claims that Fulsom is in breach of contract. Fulsom claims that there was not an acceptance, and therefore no contract was formed. Explain who is correct, and why.

14–5. Merchant Status. Albert Reifschneider was raised on a farm and had been in the business of selling corn and other crops under futures contracts (contracts for goods to be harvested in the future) for twenty years. In April 1988, Reifschneider orally agreed to sell Colorado-Kansas Grain Co. 12,500 bushels of corn after the harvest in the fall. The company sent Reifschneider a written confirmation of the agreement with instructions to sign and return it. In June, Reifschneider told the company that he would not sign the confirmation and that no contract existed between the parties. The company demanded that Reifschneider deliver the corn, but the demand was to no avail. The company sued Reifschneider for breach of contract, and the issue turned on whether Reifschneider was a "merchant" within the meaning of the UCC. How should the court rule? Discuss fully. [*Colorado-Kansas Grain Co. v. Reifschneider,* 817 P.2d 637 (Colo.App. 1991)]

14–6. Goods and Services Combined. Jane Pittsley contracted with Donald Houser, who was doing business as the Hilton Contract Carpet Co., for the installation of carpet in her home. Following installation, Pittsley complained to Hilton that some seams were visible, gaps appeared, the carpet did not lie flat in all areas, and the carpet failed to reach the wall in certain locations. Although Hilton made various attempts to fix the installation by stretching the carpet and other methods, Pittsley was not satisfied with the work and eventually sued Hilton to recover the $3,500 she had paid toward the $4,319.50 contract price for the carpet and its installation. Hilton paid the installers $700 for the work done in laying Pittsley's carpet. One of the issues before the court was whether the contract was a contract for the sale of goods or a contract for the sale of services. How should the court decide this issue? Discuss fully. [*Pittsley v. Houser,* 125 Idaho 820, 875 P.2d 232 (1994)]

14–7. Statute of Frauds. GPL Treatment, Ltd., orally agreed to sell a large quantity of cedar shakes to Louisiana-Pacific Corp. (L-P). GPL sent L-P order confirmation forms that stated the prices and quantities of shakes ordered. Each form also contained a "sign and return" clause, asking L-P to sign and return one copy. L-P did not sign or return any of the forms, but it also did not object to any of the terms. When L-P accepted only about 15 percent of the orders, GPL filed a suit in an Oregon state court against the buyer for breach of contract. Do GPL's confirmation forms satisfy the requirement of a writing under the Statute of Frauds? Are they enforceable against L-P? Discuss fully. [*GPL Treatment, Ltd. v. Louisiana-Pacific Corp.,* 323 Or. 116, 914 P.2d 682 (1996)]

14–8. Statute of Frauds. SNK, Inc., makes video arcade games and sells them to distributors, including Entertainment Sales, Inc. (ESI). Most sales between SNK and ESI were phone orders. Over one four-month period, ESI phoned in several orders for "Samurai Showdown" games. SNK did not fill the orders. ESI filed a suit against SNK and others, alleging, among other things, breach of contract. There was no written contract covering the orders. ESI claimed that it had faxed purchase orders for the games to SNK but did not offer proof that the faxes had been sent or received. SNK filed a motion for summary judgment. In whose favor will the court rule, and why? [*Entertainment Sales Co. v. SNK, Inc.,* 232 Ga.App. 669, 502 S.E.2d 263 (1998)]

14–9. Goods and Services Combined. Dennis Dahlmann and Dahlmann Apartments, Ltd., entered into contracts with Sulchus Hospitality Technologies Corp. and Hospitality Management Systems, Inc. (HMS), to buy property management systems. The systems included computer hardware and software, as well as installation, training, and support services, for the Bell Tower Hotel and the Campus Inn in Ann Arbor, Michigan. The software controlled the central reservations systems at both hotels. When Dahlmann learned that the software was not Y2K compliant—that it could not be used to post reservations beyond December 31, 1999—he filed a suit against Sulchus and HMS, alleging in part breach of contract. The defendants filed a motion for summary judgment. One of the issues was whether the contracts were subject to Article 2 of the UCC. Are they? Why or why not? Explain fully. [*Dahlmann v. Sulchus Hospitality Technologies Corp.,* 63 F.Supp.2d 772 (E.D.Mich. 1999)]

TEST YOUR KNOWLEDGE—ANSWER ON THE WEB

14–10. In 1988, International Business Machines Corp. (IBM) and American Shizuki Corp. (ASC) signed an agreement for "future purchase by IBM" of plastic film capacitors made by ASC to be used in IBM computers. The agreement stated that IBM was not obligated to buy from ASC and that future purchase orders "shall be [ASC]'s only authorization to manufacture Items." In February 1989, IBM wrote to ASC about "the possibility of IBM purchasing 15,000,000 Plastic Capacitors per two consecutive twelve (12) month periods. * * * This quantity is a forecast only, and represents no commitment by IBM to purchase these quantities during or after this time period." ASC said that it wanted greater assurances. In a second letter, IBM re-expressed its "intent to order" from ASC 30 million capacitors over a minimum period of two years, contingent on the condition "[t]hat IBM's requirements for these capacitors continue." ASC spent about $2.6 million on equipment to make the capacitors. By 1997, the need for plastic capacitors had dissipated with the advent of new technology, and IBM told ASC that it would no longer buy them. ASC filed a suit in a federal district court against IBM, seeking $8.5 million in damages. On what basis might the court rule in favor of IBM? Explain fully. [*American Shizuki Corp. v. International Business Machines Corp.*, 251 F.3d 1206 (8th Cir. 2001)]

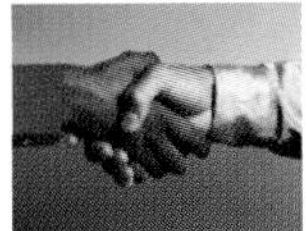

A QUESTION OF ETHICS AND SOCIAL RESPONSIBILITY

14–11. John Schwanbeck entered into negotiations with Federal-Mogul Corp. to purchase Federal-Mogul's Vellumoid Division. The two parties drew up a letter of intent stating that "[n]o further obligation will arise until a definitive agreement is reduced to writing" and that it was the parties' intention "to proceed in good faith in the negotiation of such binding definitive agreement." At another place in the letter of intent were the following words: "Of course, this letter is not intended to create, nor do you or we presently have any binding legal obligation whatever in any way relating to such sale and purchase." Federal-Mogul eventually sold the Vellumoid Division to another party. Schwanbeck sued Federal-Mogul, alleging, among other things, that Federal-Mogul had breached an agreement to negotiate in good faith the proposed contract with Schwanbeck. Given these facts, consider the following questions. [*Schwanbeck v. Federal-Mogul Corp.*, 412 Mass. 703, 592 N.E.2d 1289 (1992)]

1. Did the letter of intent create a legally binding obligation, or was the letter merely an "agreement to agree" in the future? (You may wish to review the section on "Agreements to Agree" in Chapter 9 before you answer this question.)
2. Regardless of its legal duties, did Federal-Mogul have an ethical duty to proceed in negotiating a contract with Schwanbeck? Discuss.

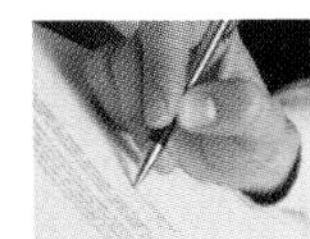

FOR CRITICAL ANALYSIS

14–12. Why is the designation "merchant" or "nonmerchant" important?

Internet Exercises

Go to the *Business Law Today* home page at **http://blt.westbuslaw.com**. Select "Interactive Study Center" and then click on "Chapter 14." There you will find the following Internet research exercise that you can perform to learn more about sales contract formation:

Activity 14–1: Is It a Contract?

Before the Test

Go to the *Business Law Today* home page at **http://blt.westbuslaw.com**. Click on "Interactive Quizzes." You will find at least twenty interactive questions relating to this chapter.

CHAPTER 15

Title and Risk of Loss

"Now, it is of great moment that well-drawn laws should themselves define all the points they possibly can and leave as few as may be to the decision of the judges."

Aristotle, 384–322 B.C.E. (Greek philosopher)

CHAPTER CONTENTS

LEARNING OBJECTIVES

After reading this chapter, you should be able to answer the following questions:

① What is the significance of identifying goods to a contract?

② If the parties to a contract do not expressly agree on when title to goods passes, what determines when title passes?

③ Risk of loss does not necessarily pass with title. If the parties to a contract do not expressly agree when risk passes and the goods are to be delivered without movement by the seller, when does risk pass?

④ Under what circumstances will the seller's title to goods being sold be void? Under what circumstances will a seller have voidable title? What is the legal effect on a good faith purchaser of the goods of the seller's having a void title versus a voidable title?

⑤ At what point does the buyer acquire an insurable interest in goods subject to a sales contract? Can both the buyer and the seller have an insurable interest in the goods simultaneously?

A sale of goods transfers ownership rights in (title to) the goods from the seller to the buyer. Often, a sales contract is signed before the actual goods are available. For example, a sales contract for oranges might be signed in May, but the oranges may not be ready for picking and shipment until October. Any number of things can happen between the time the sales contract is signed and the time the goods are actually transferred into the buyer's possession. Fire, flood, or frost may destroy the orange groves, or the oranges may be lost or damaged in transit. The same problems may occur under a lease contract. Because of these possibilities, it is important to know the rights and liabilities of the parties between the time the contract is formed and the time the goods are actually received by the buyer or lessee.

Before the creation of the Uniform Commercial Code (UCC), *title*—the right of ownership—was the central concept in sales law, controlling all issues of rights and remedies of the parties to a sales contract. In some situations, title is still relevant under the UCC, and the UCC has special rules for determining who has title. These rules will be discussed in the sections that follow. In most situations, however, the UCC has replaced the concept of title with three other concepts: (1) identification, (2) risk of loss, and (3) insurable interest. By breaking down the transfer of ownership into these three components, the drafters of the UCC have essentially followed Aristotle's advice in the chapter-opening quotation and created greater precision in the law governing sales—leaving as few points of law as possible "to the decision of the judges."

In lease contracts, of course, title to the goods is retained by the lessor-owner of the goods. Hence, the UCC's provisions relating to passage of title do not apply to leased goods. Other concepts discussed in this chapter, though, including identification, risk of loss, and insurable interest, relate to lease contracts as well as to sales contracts.

Identification

IDENTIFICATION
In a sale of goods, the express designation of the goods provided for in the contract.

Before any interest in specific goods can pass from the seller or lessor to the buyer or lessee, two conditions must prevail: (1) the goods must be in existence, and (2) they must be identified as the specific goods designated in the contract. **Identification** takes place when specific goods are designated as the subject matter of a sales or lease contract. Title and risk of loss cannot pass from seller to buyer unless the goods are identified to the contract. (As mentioned, title to leased goods remains with the lessor—or, if the owner is a third party, with that party. The lessee does not acquire title to leased goods.) Identification is significant because it gives the buyer or lessee the right to insure (or to have an insurable interest in) the goods and the right to recover from third parties who damage the goods.

In their contract, the parties can agree on when identification will take place, but identification is effective to pass title and risk of loss to the buyer only after the goods are considered to be in existence. If the parties do not so specify, however, the UCC provisions discussed here determine when identification takes place [UCC 2–501(1), 2A–217].

Existing Goods

If the contract calls for the sale or lease of specific and ascertained goods that are already in existence, identification takes place at the time the contract is made. For example, you contract to purchase or lease a fleet of five cars by the serial numbers listed for the cars.

Future Goods

ON THE WEB You can obtain information on current commercial law topics from the law firm of Hale and Dorr at **http://www.haledorr.com**.

If a sale involves unborn animals to be born within twelve months after contracting, identification takes place when the animals are conceived. If a lease involves any unborn animals, identification occurs when the animals are conceived. If a sale involves crops that are to be harvested within twelve months (or the next harvest season occurring after contracting, whichever is longer), identification takes place when the crops are planted or begin to grow. In a sale or lease of any other future goods, identification occurs when the goods are shipped, marked, or otherwise designated by the seller or lessor as the goods to which the contract refers.

A freeze can destroy an orange grove. If a contract for a sale of the oranges had already been signed, who would suffer the loss?

GOODS THAT ARE PART OF A LARGER MASS

As a general rule, goods that are part of a larger mass are identified when the goods are marked, shipped, or somehow designated by the seller or lessor as the particular goods to pass under the contract. • **EXAMPLE 15.1** A buyer orders 1,000 cases of beans from a 10,000-case lot. Until the seller separates the 1,000 cases of beans from the 10,000-case lot, title and risk of loss remain with the seller. •

FUNGIBLE GOODS
Goods that are alike by physical nature, by agreement, or by trade usage. Examples of fungible goods are wheat, oil, and wine that are identical in type and quality. When owners of fungible goods hold the goods as tenants in common, title and risk can pass without actually separating the goods being sold from the mass of fungible goods.

A common exception to this rule involves fungible goods. **Fungible goods** are goods that are alike by physical nature, by agreement, or by trade usage. Typical examples are specific grades or types of wheat, oil, and wine, usually stored in large containers. If these goods are held or intended to be held by owners as tenants in common (owners having shares undivided from the entire mass), a seller-owner can pass title and risk of loss to the buyer without an actual separation. The buyer replaces the seller as an owner in common [UCC 2–105(4)].

• **EXAMPLE 15.2** Anselm, Braudel, and Carpenter are farmers. They deposit, respectively, 5,000 bushels, 3,000 bushels, and 2,000 bushels of grain of the same grade and quality in a bin. The three become owners in common, with Anselm owning 50 percent of the 10,000 bushels, Braudel 30 percent, and Carpenter 20 percent. Anselm contracts to sell her 5,000 bushels of grain to Tareyton; because the goods are fungible, she can pass title and risk of loss to Tareyton without physically separating the 5,000 bushels. Tareyton now becomes an owner in common with Braudel and Carpenter. •

Passage of Title

Once goods exist and are identified, the provisions of UCC 2–401 apply to the passage of title. In virtually all subsections of UCC 2–401, the words "unless otherwise explicitly agreed" appear, meaning that any explicit understanding between the buyer and the seller determines when title passes. Unless an agreement is explicitly made, title passes to the buyer at the time and the place the seller performs the *physical* delivery of the goods [UCC 2–401(2)].

SHIPMENT AND DESTINATION CONTRACTS

SHIPMENT CONTRACT
A contract for the sale of goods in which the seller is required or authorized to ship the goods by carrier. The seller assumes liability for any losses or damage to the goods until they are delivered to the carrier.

DESTINATION CONTRACT
A contract for the sale of goods in which the seller is required or authorized to ship the goods by carrier and tender delivery of the goods at a particular destination. The seller assumes liability for any losses or damage to the goods until they are tendered at the destination specified in the contract.

Unless otherwise agreed, delivery arrangements can determine when title passes from the seller to the buyer. In a **shipment contract**, the seller is required or authorized to ship goods by carrier, such as a trucking company. Under a shipment contract, the seller is required only to deliver conforming goods into the hands of a carrier, and title passes to the buyer at the time and place of shipment [UCC 2–401(2)(a)]. Generally, *all contracts are assumed to be shipment contracts if nothing to the contrary is stated in the contract.*

In a **destination contract**, the seller is required to deliver the goods to a particular destination, usually directly to the buyer, but sometimes the buyer designates that the goods should be delivered to another party. Title passes to the buyer when the goods are *tendered* at that destination [UCC 2–401(2)(b)]. A tender of delivery is the seller's placing or holding of conforming goods at the buyer's disposition (with any necessary notice), enabling the buyer to take delivery [UCC 2–503(1)].

DELIVERY WITHOUT MOVEMENT OF THE GOODS

DOCUMENT OF TITLE
Paper exchanged in the regular course of business that evidences the right to possession of goods (for example, a bill of lading or a warehouse receipt).

When the sales contract does not call for the seller to ship or deliver the goods (when the buyer is to pick up the goods), the passage of title depends on whether the seller must deliver a **document of title**, such as a bill of lading or a warehouse receipt, to the buyer. A *bill of lading* is a receipt for goods that is signed by a carrier and that serves as a contract for the transportation of the goods. A *warehouse receipt* is a receipt issued by a warehouser for goods stored in a warehouse.

When a document of title is required, title passes to the buyer *when and where the document is delivered.* Thus, if the goods are stored in a warehouse, title passes to

Goods may be destroyed while they are being shipped to the buyer. How would a court decide who held title to the goods at the time they were destroyed?

ON THE WEB To review bills of lading, access the following Web site:

http://www.showtrans.com/bl.htm.

the buyer when the appropriate documents are delivered to the buyer. The goods never move. In fact, the buyer can choose to leave the goods at the same warehouse for a period of time, and the buyer's title to those goods will be unaffected.

When no documents of title are required and delivery is made without moving the goods, title passes at the time and place the sales contract is made, if the goods have already been identified. If the goods have not been identified, title does not pass until identification occurs. • **EXAMPLE 15.3** Rogers sells lumber to Bodan. They agree that Bodan will pick up the lumber at the lumberyard. If the lumber has been identified (segregated, marked, or in any other way distinguished from all other lumber), title passes to Bodan when the contract is signed. If the lumber is still in storage bins at the lumberyard, title does not pass to Bodan until the particular pieces of lumber to be sold under this contract are identified [UCC 2–401(3)]. •

SALES OR LEASES BY NONOWNERS

Problems occur when persons who acquire goods with imperfect titles attempt to sell or lease them. Sections 2–402 and 2–403 of the UCC deal with the rights of two parties who lay claim to the same goods, sold with imperfect titles. Generally, a buyer acquires at least whatever title the seller has to the goods sold.

The UCC also protects a person who leases such goods from the buyer. Of course, a lessee does not acquire whatever title the lessor has to the goods. A lessee acquires a right to possess and use the goods—that is, a *leasehold interest*. A lessee acquires whatever leasehold interest the lessor has or has the power to transfer, subject to the lease contract [UCC 2A–303, 2A–304, 2A–305].

REMEMBER Theft is a crime (larceny, embezzlement, and so on) and a tort (conversion). Receiving goods that the recipient knows were stolen is both a crime and a tort.

Void Title A buyer may unknowingly purchase goods from a seller who is not the owner of the goods. If the seller is a thief, the seller's title is *void*—legally, no title exists. Thus, the buyer acquires no title, and the real owner can reclaim the goods from the buyer. If the goods were only leased, the same result would occur because the lessor has no leasehold interest to transfer.

• **EXAMPLE 15.4** If Jim steals diamonds owned by Maren, Jim has a *void title* to those diamonds. If Jim sells the diamonds to Shannon, Maren can reclaim them from Shannon even though Shannon acted in good faith and honestly was not aware that the goods were stolen. • (Article 2A contains similar provisions for leases.)

Voidable Title A seller has a *voidable title* if the goods that he or she is selling were obtained by fraud, paid for with a check that is later dishonored, purchased from a minor, or purchased on credit when the seller was insolvent. (Under the UCC, a person is **insolvent** when that person ceases to "pay his debts in the ordinary course of business or cannot pay his debts as they become due or is insolvent within the meaning of federal bankruptcy law" [UCC 1–201(23)].)

INSOLVENT
Under the UCC, a term describing a person who ceases to pay "his debts in the ordinary course of business or cannot pay his debts as they become due or is insolvent within the meaning of federal bankruptcy law" [UCC 1–201(23)].

GOOD FAITH PURCHASER
A purchaser who buys without notice of any circumstance that would put a person of ordinary prudence on inquiry as to whether the seller has valid title to the goods being sold.

In contrast to a seller with *void title*, a seller with *voidable title* has the power to transfer a good title to a good faith purchaser for value. A **good faith purchaser** is one who buys without knowledge of circumstances that would make a person of ordinary prudence inquire about the validity of the seller's title to the goods. One who purchases *for value* gives legally sufficient consideration (value) for the goods purchased. The real, or original, owner cannot recover goods from a good faith purchaser for value [UCC 2–403(1)].[1] If the buyer of the goods is not a good faith purchaser for value, then the actual owner of the goods can reclaim them from the buyer (or from the seller, if the goods are still in the seller's possession).

1. The real owner could, of course, sue the person who initially obtained voidable title to the goods.

The same rules apply in circumstances involving leases. A lessor with voidable title has the power to transfer a valid leasehold interest to a good faith lessee for value. The real owner cannot recover the goods, except as permitted by the terms of the lease. The real owner can, however, receive all proceeds arising from the lease, as well as a transfer of all rights, title, and interest as lessor under the lease, including the lessor's interest in the return of the goods when the lease expires [UCC 2 A–305 (1)].

The question in the following case was whether a third party buyer was a good faith purchaser in the context of a sale of timber.

CASE 15.1 Memphis Hardwood Flooring Co. v. Daniel

Mississippi Supreme Court, 2000.
771 So.2d 924.
http://www.mssc.state.ms.us[a]

FACTS Jamie Swann Daniel, a retired teacher, owned approximately 800 acres of land in Union County, Mississippi. After an ice storm, Lucky Easley and William Heppler, officers of Northern Hardwood, Inc., convinced Daniel to allow some cutting of the storm-damaged timber on the land. Daniel contracted with Northern to cut from the southern half of the property the "disaster hardwood timber" that was twenty inches or more in diameter.[b] More than a year later, in a second contract, Daniel agreed to the cutting of the timber down to sixteen inches, for which Easley would pay her $150,000. The same day, Easley told Robert Luther, a timber buyer for Memphis Hardwood Flooring Company, that he had an agreement to cut all of the timber on all of Daniel's land. Luther and Easley agreed that Easley, acting for both Northern and Memphis, would buy Daniel's timber for Northern while concealing from Daniel that Northern was actually buying for Memphis. Luther agreed to pay $410,000 to Easley. At Easley's request, Luther had Memphis's lawyer draft the agreements ("timber deeds") between Daniel and Northern and between Northern and Memphis. When Memphis proceeded to cut the timber, Daniel filed a suit in a Mississippi state court against Memphis and the others, alleging fraud. Among other things, the court canceled the agreement between Northern and Memphis.[c] Memphis appealed to the Mississippi Supreme Court, asserting that it was a good faith purchaser.

ISSUE Was Memphis a good faith purchaser?

DECISION No. The Mississippi Supreme Court affirmed the decision of the lower court.

REASON The state supreme court noted that to establish the status of a good faith purchaser "[t]he elements the innocent purchaser must prove are a valuable consideration, the presence of good faith, and the absence of notice." In this case, "[t]he first element is established in favor of Memphis. The record reveals that Memphis paid $410,000 to Northern for the timber. * * * The second element, the presence of good faith, was not adequately shown by Memphis. * * * Easley made the deal with Daniel on behalf of both Northern and Memphis and * * * Memphis was a knowing participant in this scheme * * * . Such actions reveal the absence of good faith. Even the circumstances surrounding the drafting of the deeds indicate the joint nature of the scheme and Memphis' lack of good faith." As for the third element, "Memphis was not only on actual notice, it was a knowing and willing participant in the defrauding of Daniel. Thus, Memphis fails to establish the third

a. In the top row, click on the "Decisions" box. On that page, in the list, click on "Supreme Court & Court of Appeals Opinions." In the left-hand frame, in the "Year" menu select "2000," in the "Alphabetical" menu choose the letter "M," and click "Search." In the result, scroll to the case name and click on it to access the opinion. The state of Mississippi maintains this Web site.

b. For the sale of this timber, Northern received $498,905, of which Daniel's share under their contract was $299,343. Daniel was paid only $134,000, however. Ultimately, she reached a settlement with Northern, Easley, and Heppler as to their liability on this contract.

c. The court also awarded Daniel more than $800,000 in damages, including reforestation costs, and issued an injunction against Memphis's further cutting. In a separate case, Northern, Easley, and Heppler pleaded guilty to charges of embezzlement and agreed to make restitution to Daniel in the amount of $250,000.

(continued)

CASE 15.1—Continued

element. The record supports the [lower court's] finding that Memphis was not" a good faith purchaser.

FOR CRITICAL ANALYSIS—Social Consideration *Would Memphis have been considered a participant in the fraud against Daniel if Memphis had not agreed specifically that Easley would act in its behalf?*

BE AWARE The purpose of most goods held in inventory is to turn those goods into cash by selling them. That is one of the reasons for the entrustment rule.

The Entrustment Rule According to Section 2–403(2), entrusting goods to a merchant *who deals in goods of that kind* gives the merchant the power to transfer all rights to *a buyer in the ordinary course of business.* Entrusting includes both turning over the goods to the merchant and leaving the purchased goods with the merchant for later delivery or pickup [UCC 2–403(3)]. A buyer in the ordinary course of business is a person who, in good faith and without knowledge that the sale violates the ownership rights or security interest of a third party, buys in ordinary course from a person (other than a pawnbroker) in the business of selling goods of that kind [UCC 1–201(9)]. (A *security interest* is any interest in personal property that secures payment or the performance of an obligation—see Chapter 22.)

● **EXAMPLE 15.5** Jan leaves her watch with a jeweler to be repaired. The jeweler sells used watches. The jeweler sells Jan's watch to Kim, a customer, who does not know that the jeweler has no right to sell it. Kim, as a good faith buyer, gets good title against Jan's claim of ownership.[2] Kim, however, obtains only those rights held by the person entrusting the goods (here, Jan). Suppose that in fact Jan had stolen the watch from Greg and then left it with the jeweler to be repaired. The jeweler then sells it to Kim. In this situation, Kim gets good title against Jan, who entrusted the watch to the jeweler, but not against Greg (the real owner), who neither entrusted the watch to Jan nor authorized Jan to entrust it. ●

Article 2A provides a similar rule for leased goods. If a lessor entrusts goods to a lessee-merchant who deals in goods of that kind, the lessee-merchant has the power to transfer all of the rights the lessor had in the goods to a buyer or sublessee in the ordinary course of business [UCC 2A–305(2)]. The following case involves an application of the entrustment doctrine.

2. Jan, of course, can sue the jeweler for the tort of trespass to personalty or conversion (see Chapter 4) for the equivalent money value of the watch.

CASE 15.2 DeWeldon, Ltd. v. McKean

United States Court of Appeals, First Circuit, 1997.
125 F.3d 24.
http://www.law.emory.edu/1circuit/2nd-idx.html[a]

HISTORICAL AND SOCIAL SETTING *During World War II, after more than three years of fighting, U.S. forces invaded the island of Iwo Jima in February 1945. In the midst of the costly, month-long battle, five Marines and a Navy corpsman raised a U.S. flag on the peak of Mount Suribachi. A photograph of the flag raising epitomized the valor of the U.S. forces. Within days, work began on a statue to commemorate this courage. The United States Marine Corps Memorial took more than eight years to complete. Today, it is the world's tallest bronze statue. The sculptor was Felix DeWeldon.*

a. This is a page, within the Web site of the Emory University School of Law, that lists the published opinions of the U.S. Court of Appeals for the First Circuit since November 1995. Scroll down the list of cases to the *DeWeldon* case (included with the cases under the letter "M" for "McKean"). Click on the case name to access the opinion.

FACTS Felix DeWeldon, a sculptor and an art collector, owned three paintings valued at $26,000 that were displayed in his home in Rhode Island. When he declared

CASE 15.2—Continued

bankruptcy, DeWeldon, Ltd.,[b] bought all of his personal property from the bankruptcy trustee (a person appointed by the bankruptcy court to collect and distribute the debtor's assets—see Chapter 23) and entrusted the paintings to Felix. DeWeldon, Ltd., did not put signs on the premises or tags on the paintings to indicate that Felix no longer owned the paintings. Later, Felix paid for an option to repurchase the paintings and the right to retain their possession until the option expired. Within a year, Felix sold the paintings to Robert McKean for $50,000. DeWeldon, Ltd., claiming that Felix DeWeldon had no right to sell the paintings, sued in a federal district court to recover them. McKean argued that the entrustment doctrine applied, and therefore, as a buyer in the ordinary course of business, McKean acquired good title to the paintings. The court held that the entrustment doctrine applied and ruled in favor of McKean. DeWeldon, Ltd., appealed.

ISSUE Did the entrustment doctrine apply to Felix DeWeldon's sale of the paintings to McKean?

DECISION Yes. The U.S. Court of Appeals for the First Circuit affirmed the judgment of the lower court.

b. The abbreviation *Ltd.* stands for *Limited,* which is another word that can be used to designate a corporation.

REASON The U.S. Court of Appeals for the First Circuit applied the Uniform Commercial Code (UCC) as adopted by Rhode Island, which provides that "an owner who entrusts items to a merchant who deals in goods of that kind gives him or her power to transfer all rights of the entruster to a buyer in the ordinary course of business." The court concluded that (1) DeWeldon, Ltd., had entrusted the paintings to Felix DeWeldon; (2) McKean was a buyer in the ordinary course of business because McKean gave value for the paintings without notice that Felix DeWeldon was no longer the true owner of the paintings, and DeWeldon, Ltd., "did nothing to shield the paintings in the cloak of its ownership"; and (3) Felix DeWeldon acted as a merchant within the meaning of the [UCC]—he was a "well-known" artist whose work was for sale commercially and a "collector." The court pointed out that there was "artwork all over [his] home. He had recently sold paintings to a European buyer. By his occupation he held himself out as having knowledge and skill peculiar to art and the art trade."

FOR CRITICAL ANALYSIS—Ethical Consideration *Under the entrustment doctrine, when a person gives possession of her or his property to a merchant dealing in goods of that kind, that person assumes the risk that the merchant may sell the property to an innocent good faith purchaser for value. Is this fair?*

Risk of Loss

"This doing of something about disputes, this doing of it reasonably, is the business of law."

KARL N. LLEWELLYN, 1893–1962 (American legal scholar)

Under the UCC, risk of loss does not necessarily pass with title. When risk of loss passes from a seller or lessor to a buyer or lessee is generally determined by the contract between the parties. Sometimes, the contract states expressly when the risk of loss passes. At other times, it does not, and a court must interpret the performance and delivery terms of the contract to determine whether the risk has passed.

Delivery with Movement of the Goods—Carrier Cases

When there is no specification in the agreement, the following rules apply to cases involving movement of the goods (carrier cases).

Shipment Contracts In a shipment contract, if the seller or lessor is required or authorized to ship goods by carrier (but not required to deliver them to a particular final destination), risk of loss passes to the buyer or lessee when the goods are duly delivered to the carrier [UCC 2–319(1)(a), 2–509(1)(a), 2A–219(2)(a)].

● **EXAMPLE 15.6** A seller in Texas sells five hundred cases of grapefruit to a buyer in New York, F.O.B. Houston (free on board in Houston—that is, the buyer pays the transportation charges from Houston). The contract authorizes shipment by carrier; it does not require that the seller tender the grapefruit in New York. Risk passes to the buyer when conforming goods are properly placed in the possession of the carrier. If the goods are damaged in transit, the loss is the buyer's. (Actually, buyers have recourse against carriers, subject to certain limitations, and buyers usually insure the goods from the time the goods leave the seller.) ● The following case illustrates these principles.

CASE 15.3 Windows, Inc. v. Jordan Panel System Corp.

United States Court of Appeals,
Second Circuit, 1999.
177 F.3d 114.
http://csmail.law.pace.edu/lawlib/legal/us-legal/judiciary/second-circuit.html[a]

FACTS Jordan Panel System Corporation, Inc., a construction subcontractor, contracted to install window wall panels at an air cargo facility at John F. Kennedy Airport in New York City. Jordan ordered custom-made windows from Windows, Inc., a fabricator and seller of windows, based in South Dakota. The contract specified that the windows were to be shipped properly packaged for cross-country motor freight transit and "delivered to New York City." Windows built the windows and arranged to ship them to Jordan by Consolidated Freightways Corporation. During the shipment, much of the glass was broken, and many of the frames were gouged and twisted. Jordan employees disassembled the window frames to salvage as much of the shipment as possible. Jordan made a claim with Consolidated for the damages, including labor costs from the salvage efforts and other costs from Jordan's inability to perform its contracts on schedule. Jordan also ordered a new shipment from Windows, which was delivered without incident. Jordan did not pay Windows for either shipment. As part of the ensuing litigation, a federal district court heard Jordan's claim against Windows for incidental and consequential damages resulting from the damaged shipment. When the court granted Windows's motion for summary judgment, concluding that the contract was a shipment contract. Thus, when the seller (Windows) put conforming goods into the hands of the carrier (Consolidated), the risk of loss passed to the buyer (Jordan). Jordan appealed to the U.S. Court of Appeals for the Second Circuit.

a. This Web site is a joint project of Touro and Pace University School of Law with the cooperation of the U.S. Court of Appeals for the Second Circuit. In the "1999" column, click on "April." When that page opens, scroll down the list of cases to the case name and click on "Opinion" to access the case.

ISSUE Was the contract in this case a shipment contract?

DECISION Yes. The U.S. Court of Appeals for the Second Circuit affirmed the lower court's decision.

REASON The appellate court pointed out that "[w]here the terms of an agreement are ambiguous, there is a strong presumption under the U.C.C. favoring shipment contracts. Unless the parties 'expressly specify' that the contract requires the seller to deliver to a particular destination, the contract is generally construed as one for shipment." Thus, because the parties did not "expressly specify" that Windows was to deliver the goods to a particular destination, "the contract should be deemed a shipment contract. Under the terms of its contract, Windows thus satisfied its obligations to Jordan when it put the goods, properly packaged, into the possession of the carrier for shipment." Therefore, in a shipment contract under UCC 2– 509(1)(a), "the risk of loss passes to the buyer when the goods are duly delivered to the carrier."

FOR CRITICAL ANALYSIS—Ethical Consideration *Why do the courts assume that a contract is a shipment contract unless the contract expressly specifies that the goods are to be delivered to a particular destination? Is this fair? Why or why not?*

Destination Contracts In a destination contract, the risk of loss passes to the buyer or lessee when the goods are tendered to the buyer or lessee at the specified destination [UCC 2–319(1)(b), 2–509(1)(b), 2A–219(2)(b)]. In Example 15.6, if the contract had been F.O.B. New York, the risk of loss during transit to New York would have been the seller's.

Contract Terms Specific terms in the contract help determine when risk of loss passes to the buyer. These terms, which are listed and defined in Exhibit 15–1, relate generally to the determination of which party will bear the costs of delivery. Unless otherwise agreed, these terms also determine who has the risk of loss.

Delivery without Movement of the Goods

The UCC also addresses situations in which the seller or lessor is required neither to ship nor to deliver the goods. Frequently, the buyer or lessee is to pick up the goods from the seller or lessor, or the goods are held by a bailee. Under the UCC, a **bailee** is a party who, by a bill of lading, warehouse receipt, or other document of title, acknowledges possession of goods and/or contracts to deliver them. A warehousing company, for example, or a trucking company that normally issues documents of title for the goods it receives is a bailee.[3]

BAILEE
Under the UCC, a party who, by a bill of lading, warehouse receipt, or other document of title, acknowledges possession of goods and/or contracts to deliver them.

COMPARE A business that is to make delivery at its own place has control of the goods and can be expected to insure its interest in them. The buyer has no control of the goods and will likely not carry insurance on goods that he or she does not possess or control.

Goods Held by the Seller If the goods are held by the seller, a document of title is usually not used. If the seller is a merchant, risk of loss to goods held by the seller passes to the buyer when the buyer *actually takes physical possession of the goods* [UCC 2–509(3)]. If the seller is not a merchant, the risk of loss to goods held by the seller passes to the buyer on *tender of delivery* [UCC 2–509(3)]. (As you will read in Chapter 16, tender of delivery occurs when the seller places conforming goods at the disposal of the buyer and gives the buyer whatever notification is reasonably necessary to enable the buyer to take possession.) With respect to leases, the risk of loss passes to the lessee on the lessee's receipt of the goods if the lessor—or supplier, in a finance lease (see Chapter 14)—is a merchant. Otherwise, the risk passes to the lessee on tender of delivery [UCC 2A–219(c)].

Goods Held by a Bailee When a bailee is holding goods for a person who has contracted to sell them and the goods are to be delivered without being moved, the goods are usually represented by a negotiable or nonnegotiable document of title (a bill of

3. Bailments will be discussed in detail in Chapter 36.

EXHIBIT 15–1 CONTRACT TERMS—DEFINITIONS

F.O.B. (free on board)—Indicates that the selling price of goods includes transportation costs (and that the seller carries the risk of loss) to the specific F.O.B. place named in the contract. The place can be either the place of initial shipment (for example, the seller's city or place of business) or the place of destination (for example, the buyer's city or place of business) [UCC 2–319(1)].
F.A.S. (free alongside)—Requires that the seller, at his or her own expense and risk, deliver the goods alongside the ship before risk passes to the buyer [UCC 2–319(2)].
C.I.F. or **C.&F.** (cost, insurance, and freight, or just cost and freight)—Requires, among other things, that the seller "put the goods in possession of a carrier" before risk passes to the buyer [UCC 2–320(2)]. (These are basically pricing terms, and the contracts remain shipment contracts, not destination contracts.)
Delivery ex-ship (delivery from the carrying ship)—Means that risk of loss does not pass to the buyer until the goods leave the ship or are otherwise properly unloaded [UCC 2–322].

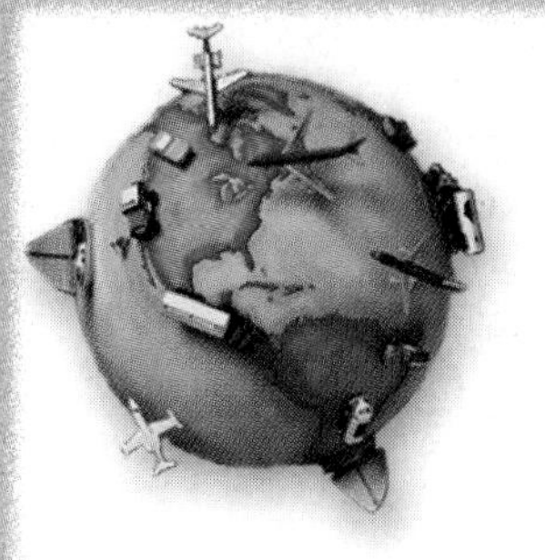

INTERNATIONAL PERSPECTIVE

Risk of Loss in International Sales Contracts

The possibility that goods will be lost or damaged in transit or at some time before the buyer takes possession of the goods is enhanced when goods are shipped great distances, as is normally the situation with international sales contracts. Therefore, those who form international sales contracts should safeguard their interests by indicating in the contract the point at which risk of loss passes from the seller to the buyer. Note that the international sales contract between Starbucks Coffee Company and one of its coffee suppliers, shown in the fold-out exhibit included in Chapter 14, includes a specific (insurance) clause indicating when risk of loss will pass to the buyer (see annotation 18 to that exhibit).

The United Nations Convention on Contracts for the International Sale of Goods (CISG), which governs international sales contracts (see Chapter 14), contains provisions relating to risk of loss. Article 67 of the CISG provides that unless the contract requires the seller to hand the goods over at a particular place, the risk passes to the buyer when the goods identified to the contract "are handed over to the first carrier for transmission to the buyer in accordance with the contract of sale." In regard to goods sold in transit, Article 68 provides that risk of loss "passes to the buyer from the time of the conclusion of the contract." If the seller knew or should have known that the contract goods were lost or damaged, however, and failed to disclose this to the buyer, then the seller bears the risk.

FOR CRITICAL ANALYSIS
Why would buyers of goods that are to be shipped internationally ever agree to shipment contracts—which subject them to liability for any loss or damage to the goods while they are in transit?

lading or a warehouse receipt). Risk of loss passes to the buyer when (1) the buyer receives a negotiable document of title for the goods, (2) the bailee acknowledges the buyer's right to possess the goods, or (3) the buyer receives a nonnegotiable document of title *and* has had a *reasonable time* to present the document to the bailee and demand the goods. Obviously, if the bailee refuses to honor the document, the risk of loss remains with the seller [UCC 2–503(4)(b), 2–509(2)].

In respect to leases, if goods held by a bailee are to be delivered without being moved, the risk of loss passes to the lessee on acknowledgment by the bailee of the lessee's right to possession of the goods [UCC 2A–219(2)(b)].

CONDITIONAL SALES

Buyers and sellers sometimes form sales contracts that are conditioned either on the buyer's approval of the goods or on the buyer's resale of the goods. Under such contracts, the buyer is in possession of the goods. Sometimes, however, problems arise as to whether the buyer or seller should bear the loss if, for example, the goods are damaged or stolen while in the possession of the buyer.

SALE OR RETURN
A type of conditional sale in which title and possession pass from the seller to the buyer; however, the buyer retains the option to return the goods during a specified period even though the goods conform to the contract.

Sale or Return A **sale or return** (sometimes called a *sale and return*) is a type of contract by which the seller sells a quantity of goods to the buyer with the understanding that the buyer can set aside the sale by returning the goods or any portion of the goods. The buyer is required to pay for any goods *not* returned. When the buyer receives possession of the goods under a sale-or-return contract, the title and risk of loss pass to the buyer. Title and risk of loss remain with the buyer until the buyer returns the goods to the seller within the time period specified. If the buyer fails to return the goods within this time period, the sale is finalized. The return of the goods is made at the buyer's risk and expense. Goods held under a sale-or-return contract are subject to the claims of the buyer's creditors while they are in the buyer's possession (even if the buyer has not paid for the goods) [UCC 2–326, 2–327].

CONSIGNMENT
A transaction in which an owner of goods (the consignor) delivers the goods to another (the consignee) for the consignee to sell. The consignee pays the consignor only for the goods that are sold by the consignee.

The UCC treats a **consignment** as a sale or return. Under a consignment, the owner of goods (the *consignor*) delivers them to another (the *consignee*) for the consignee to sell. If the consignee sells the goods, the consignee must pay the consignor for them. If the consignee does not sell the goods, they may simply be returned to the consignor. While the goods are in the possession of the consignee, the consignee holds title to them, and creditors of the consignee will prevail over the consignor in any action to repossess the goods [UCC 2–326(3)].[4]

ETHICAL ISSUE 15.1

What happens to consigned goods when the consignee declares bankruptcy?

As just noted, under UCC 2–326(3) consignees hold title to goods in their possession. Thus, if the consignee enters bankruptcy proceedings, the consignor is left out in the cold, so to speak. Creditors of the consignee will lay claim to the goods, and their claims will prevail over those of any consignors. Consider an example. Samuel Schick, Inc., a jewelry supplier, consigned jewelry to Wedlo Holdings, Inc., one of the largest jewelry retailers in the southeastern United States. When Wedlo filed for bankruptcy, Schick wanted the jewelry back but had no recourse under the UCC.[5] Is there anything a consignor can do to avoid the prospect of facing such a seemingly unfair result? Yes. As noted in footnote 4 at the bottom of this page, there are several exceptions to the rule stated in UCC 2–326(3). A consignor, for example, can arrange to have a sign placed by the consigned goods indicating that the goods are on consignment (the specific requirements for such signs vary from state to state). Another option is for the consignor to perfect a security interest in the consigned goods (see Chapter 22). This will give the consignor priority over other creditors' claims to the same goods and is usually the safest course to take if a consignor wishes to fully protect his or her interest in the goods.

SALE ON APPROVAL
A type of conditional sale in which the buyer may take the goods on a trial basis. The sale becomes absolute only when the buyer approves of (or is satisfied with) the goods being sold.

Sale on Approval When a seller offers to sell goods to a buyer and permits the buyer to take the goods on a trial basis, a **sale on approval** is usually made. The term *sale* here is a misnomer, as only an *offer* to sell has been made, along with a *bailment* created by the buyer's possession. (A bailment is a temporary delivery of personal property into the care of another—see Chapter 36.)

Therefore, title and risk of loss (from causes beyond the buyer's control) remain with the seller until the buyer accepts (approves) the offer. Acceptance can be made expressly, by any act inconsistent with the *trial* purpose or the seller's ownership, or by the buyer's election not to return the goods within the trial period. If the buyer

4. UCC 2–326(3) states that this rule does not apply in certain circumstances. For example, if the consignor establishes that the consignee is generally known by his or her creditors to be "substantially engaged in selling the goods of others," then the consignor will prevail over the consignee's creditors in any action brought by those creditors to repossess the goods. The consignor will also prevail in such actions if she or he has a perfected security interest in the goods (see Chapter 22) or complies with an applicable law providing for a consignor's interest in the goods to be evidenced by a sign indicating that the goods are on consignment.
5. *In re Wedlo Holdings, Inc.*, 248 Bankr. 336 (N.D.Ill. 2000).

does not wish to accept, the buyer may notify the seller of that fact within the trial period, and the return is made at the seller's expense and risk [UCC 2–327(1)]. Goods held on approval are not subject to the claims of the buyer's creditors until acceptance.

It is often difficult to determine what type of contract a particular transaction involves—a contract for a sale on approval, a contract for a sale or return, or a contract for sale. The UCC states that (unless otherwise agreed) "if the goods are delivered primarily for use," the transaction is a sale on approval; "if the goods are delivered primarily for resale," the transaction is a sale or return [UCC 2–326(1)].

RISK OF LOSS WHEN A SALES OR LEASE CONTRACT IS BREACHED

There are many ways to breach a sales or lease contract, and the transfer of risk operates differently depending on which party breaches. Generally, the party in breach bears the risk of loss.

CURE The right of a party who tenders nonconforming performance to correct that performance within the contract period [UCC 2–508(1)].

When the Seller or Lessor Breaches If the goods are so nonconforming that the buyer has the right to reject them, the risk of loss does not pass to the buyer until the defects are **cured** (that is, until the goods are repaired, replaced, or discounted in price by the seller) or until the buyer accepts the goods in spite of their defects (thus waiving the right to reject). • **EXAMPLE 15.7** A buyer orders ten white refrigerators from a seller, F.O.B. the seller's plant. The seller ships amber refrigerators instead. The amber refrigerators (nonconforming goods) are damaged in transit. The risk of loss falls on the seller. Had the seller shipped white refrigerators (conforming goods) instead, the risk would have fallen on the buyer [UCC 2–510(2)]. •

If a buyer accepts a shipment of goods and later discovers a defect, acceptance can be revoked. Revocation allows the buyer to pass the risk of loss back to the seller, at least to the extent that the buyer's insurance does not cover the loss [UCC 2–510(2)].

In regard to leases, Article 2A states a similar rule. If the lessor or supplier tenders goods that are so nonconforming that the lessee has the right to reject them, the risk of loss remains with the lessor or the supplier until cure or acceptance [UCC 2A–220(1)(a)]. If the lessee, after acceptance, revokes his or her acceptance of nonconforming goods, the revocation passes the risk of loss back to the seller or supplier, to the extent that the lessee's insurance does not cover the loss [UCC 2A–220(1)(b)].

When the Buyer or Lessee Breaches The general rule is that when a buyer or lessee breaches a contract, the risk of loss immediately shifts to the buyer or lessee. This rule has three important limitations:

1. The seller or lessor must already have identified the contract goods.
2. The buyer or lessee bears the risk for only a commercially reasonable time after the seller has learned of the breach.
3. The buyer or lessee is liable only to the extent of any deficiency in the seller's insurance coverage [UCC 2–510(3), 2A–220(2)].

Insurable Interest

"When the praying does no good, insurance does help."
BERTOLT BRECHT, 1898–1956 (German playwright and poet)

Parties to sales and lease contracts often obtain insurance coverage to protect against damage, loss, or destruction of goods. Any party purchasing insurance, however, must have a sufficient interest in the insured item to obtain a valid policy. Insurance laws—not the UCC—determine sufficiency. The UCC is helpful, however, because it contains certain rules regarding insurable interests in goods.

INSURABLE INTEREST OF THE BUYER OR LESSEE

INSURABLE INTEREST
In regard to the sale or lease of goods, a property interest in the goods that is sufficiently substantial to permit a party to insure against damage to the goods.

A buyer or lessee has an **insurable interest** in identified goods. The moment the contract goods are identified by the seller or lessor, the buyer or lessee has a special property interest that allows the buyer or lessee to obtain necessary insurance coverage for those goods even before the risk of loss has passed [UCC 2–501(1), 2A–218(1)].

The rule stated in UCC 2–501(1)(c) is that such buyers obtain an insurable interest in crops by identification, which occurs when the crops are planted or otherwise become growing crops, provided that the contract is for "the sale of crops to be harvested within twelve months or the next normal harvest season after contracting, whichever is longer." • **EXAMPLE 15.8** In March, a farmer sells a cotton crop he hopes to harvest in October. The buyer acquires an insurable interest in the crop when it is planted, because those goods (the cotton crop) are identified to the sales contract between the seller and the buyer. •

INSURABLE INTEREST OF THE SELLER OR LESSOR

A seller has an insurable interest in goods if she or he retains title to the goods. Even after title passes to a buyer, a seller who has a security interest in the goods (a right to secure payment—see Chapter 22) still has an insurable interest and can insure the goods [UCC 2–501(2)]. Hence, both a buyer and a seller can have an insurable interest in identical goods at the same time. Of course, the buyer or seller must sustain an actual loss to have the right to recover from an insurance company. In regard to leases, the lessor retains an insurable interest in leased goods until an option to buy has been exercised by the lessee and the risk of loss has passed to the lessee [UCC 2A–218(3)].

Bulk Transfers

Bulk transfers are the subject of UCC Article 6. A *bulk transfer* is defined as any transfer of a major part of the transferor's material, supplies, merchandise, or other inventory *not made in the ordinary course of the transferor's business* [UCC 6–102(1)]. Difficulties sometimes occur with bulk transfers. For example, when a business that owes debts to numerous creditors sells a substantial part of its equipment and inventories to a buyer, the business should use the proceeds to pay off the debts. What happens, though, if the merchant instead spends the funds on a vacation trip, leaving the creditors without payment? Can the creditors lay any claim to the goods that were transferred in bulk to the buyer?

REQUIREMENTS OF ARTICLE 6

WATCH OUT The notice provisions of Article 6 can sometimes interfere with and delay normal business transactions.

The purpose of Article 6 is to protect creditors in transactions involving bulk transfers. UCC 6–104 and 6–105 provide that the following requirements must be met when a bulk transfer is undertaken:

① The seller must provide the buyer with a sworn list of his or her existing creditors. The list must include those whose claims are disputed and must state names, business addresses, and amounts due.

② The buyer and the seller must prepare a schedule of the property that is to be transferred.

③ The buyer must preserve the list of creditors and the schedule of property for six months and permit inspection of the list by any creditor of the seller or must file the list and the schedule of property in a designated public office.

④ The buyer must give notice of the proposed bulk transfer to each of the seller's creditors at least ten days before the buyer takes possession of the goods or makes payments for them, whichever happens first.

If these requirements are met, the buyer acquires title to the goods free of all claims by the seller's creditors. If the requirements are not met, goods in the possession of the buyer continue to be subject to the claims of the seller's unpaid creditors for six months [UCC 6–111].

THE MAJORITY OF STATES HAVE REPEALED ARTICLE 6

In 1988, the National Conference of Commissioners on Uniform State Laws recommended that those states that have adopted Article 6 repeal it because changes in the business and legal contexts in which bulk sales are conducted have made their regulation unnecessary. For states disinclined to do so, Article 6 has been revised to provide creditors with better protection while reducing the burden imposed on good faith purchasers. To date, at least thirty-five states have repealed Article 6, and four states have opted for the revised version. The remainder of the states have retained Article 6 in its original form.

The revised Article 6 limits its application to bulk sales by sellers whose principal business is the sale of inventory from bulk stock. It does not apply to transactions involving property valued at less than $10,000 or more than $25 million. If a seller has more than two hundred creditors, a buyer, rather than having to send individual notice to each creditor, can give notice by public filing (for example, in the office of a state's secretary of state). The notice period is increased from ten to forty-five days, and the statute of limitations is extended from six months to one year.

APPLICATION Law and the Seller or Buyer . . .

Who Bears the Risk of Loss?*

The shipment of goods is a major aspect of commercial transactions. Many issues arise when the unforeseen occurs, such as fire, theft, or other forms of damage to goods in transit. At the time of contract negotiation, both the seller and the buyer should determine the importance of risk of loss. In some circumstances, risk is relatively unimportant (such as when ten boxes of copier paper are being sold), and the delivery terms should simply reflect costs and price. In other circumstances, risk is extremely important (such as when a fragile piece of pharmaceutical testing equipment is being sold), and the parties will need an express agreement as to the moment risk is to pass so that they can

*This *Application* is not meant to substitute for the services of an attorney who is licensed to practice law in your state.

APPLICATION Law and the Seller or Buyer . . .

Who Bears the Risk of Loss?—continued

insure the goods accordingly. The point is that risk should be considered before the loss occurs, not after.

A major consideration relating to risk is when to insure goods against possible losses. Buyers and sellers should determine the point at which they have an insurable interest in the goods and obtain insurance coverage to protect them against loss from that point.

Checklist to Determine Risk of Loss

The UCC uses a three-part checklist to determine risk of loss:

1. If the contract includes terms allocating risk of loss, those terms are binding and must be applied.
2. If the contract is silent as to risk, and either party breaches the contract, the breaching party is liable for risk of loss.
3. When a contract makes no reference to risk, and neither party breaches, risk of loss is borne by the party having control over the goods (delivery terms).

If You Are the Seller

If you are a seller of goods to be shipped, realize that as long as you have control over the goods, you are liable for any loss unless the buyer is in breach or the contract contains an explicit agreement to the contrary. When there is no explicit agreement, the UCC uses the delivery terms in your contract as a basis for determining control. Thus, "F.O.B. buyer's business" is a destination-delivery term, and risk of loss for goods shipped under these terms does not pass to the buyer until there is a tender of delivery at the point of destination. Any loss or damage in transit falls on the seller because the seller has control until proper tender has been made.

If You Are the Buyer

From the buyer's point of view, it is important to remember that most sellers prefer "F.O.B. seller's business" as a delivery term. Under these terms, once the goods are delivered to the carrier, the buyer bears the risk of loss. Thus, if conforming goods are completely destroyed or lost in transit, the buyer not only suffers the loss but is obligated to pay the seller the contract price.

Checklist for the Shipment of Goods

1. Prior to entering a contract, determine the importance of risk of loss for a given sale.
2. If risk is extremely important, the contract should expressly state the moment risk of loss will pass from the seller to the buyer. This clause could even provide that risk will not pass until the goods are "delivered, installed, inspected, and tested (or in running order for a period of time)."
3. If an express clause is not agreed on, delivery terms determine passage of risk of loss.
4. When appropriate, either party or both parties should consider procuring insurance.

Key Terms

bailee 395
consignment 397
cure 398
destination contract 389
document of title 389
fungible goods 388
good faith purchaser 390
identification 387
insolvent 390
insurable interest 399
sale on approval 397
sale or return 396
shipment contract 389

Chapter Summary Title and Risk of Loss

Shipment Contracts (See page 389.)	In the absence of an agreement, title and risk pass on the seller's or lessor's delivery of conforming goods to the carrier [UCC 2–319(1)(a), 2–401(2)(a), 2–509(1)(a), 2A–219(2)(a)].
Destination Contracts (See page 389.)	In the absence of an agreement, title and risk pass on the seller's or lessor's *tender* of delivery of conforming goods to the buyer or lessee at the point of destination [UCC 2–401(2)(b), 2–319(1)(b), 2–509(1)(b), 2A–219(2)(b)].
Delivery without Movement of the Goods (See pages 389–390.)	1. In the absence of an agreement, if the goods are not represented by a document of title: a. Title passes on the formation of the contract [UCC 2–401(3)(b)]. b. Risk passes to the buyer or lessee, if the seller or lessor (or supplier, in a finance lease) is a merchant, on the buyer's or lessee's receipt of the goods or, if the seller or lessor is a nonmerchant, on the seller's or lessor's *tender* of delivery of the goods [UCC 2–509(3), 2A–219(c)]. 2. In the absence of an agreement, if the goods are represented by a document of title: a. If the document is negotiable and the goods are held by a bailee, title and risk pass on the buyer's *receipt* of the document [UCC 2–401(3)(a), 2–509(2)(a)]. b. If the document is nonnegotiable and the goods are held by a bailee, title passes on the buyer's receipt of the document, but risk does *not* pass until the buyer, after receipt of the document, has had a reasonable time to present the document to demand the goods [UCC 2–401(3)(a), 2–509(2)(c), 2–503(4)(b)]. 3. In the absence of an agreement, if the goods are held by a bailee and no document of title is transferred, risk passes to the buyer when the bailee acknowledges the buyer's right to the possession of the goods [UCC 2–509(2)(b)]. 4. In respect to leases, if goods held by a bailee are to be delivered without being moved, the risk of loss passes to the lessee on acknowledgment by the bailee of the lessee's right to possession of the goods [UCC 2A–219(2)(b)].
Sales or Leases by Nonowners (See pages 390–392.)	Between the owner and a good faith purchaser or sublessee: 1. *Void title*—Owner prevails [UCC 2–403(1)]. 2. *Voidable title*—Buyer prevails [UCC 2–403(1)]. 3. *Entrusting to a merchant*—Buyer or sublessee prevails [UCC 2–403(2), (3); 2A–305(2)].
Sale-or-Return Contracts (See pages 396–397.)	When the buyer receives possession of the goods, title and risk of loss pass to the buyer, with the buyer's option to return the goods to the seller. If the buyer returns the goods to the seller, title and risk of loss pass back to the seller [UCC 2–327(2)].
Sale-on-Approval Contracts (See pages 397–398.)	Title and risk of loss (from causes beyond the buyer's control) remain with the seller until the buyer approves (accepts) the offer [UCC 2–327(1)].
Risk of Loss When a Sales or Lease Contract Is Breached (See page 398.)	1. If the seller or lessor breaches by tendering nonconforming goods that are rejected by the buyer or lessee, the risk of loss does not pass to the buyer or lessee until the defects are cured (unless the buyer or lessee accepts the goods in spite of their defects, thus waiving the right to reject) [UCC 2–510(1), 2A–220(1)]. 2. If the buyer or lessee breaches the contract, the risk of loss immediately shifts to the buyer or lessee. Limitations to this rule are as follows [UCC 2–510(3), 2A–220(2)]: a. The seller or lessor must already have identified the contract goods. b. The buyer or lessee bears the risk for only a commercially reasonable time after the seller or lessor has learned of the breach. c. The buyer or lessee is liable only to the extent of any deficiency in the seller's or lessor's insurance coverage.

Chapter Summary Title and Risk of Loss—continued

Insurable Interest (See pages 398–399.)	1. Buyers and lessees have an insurable interest in goods the moment the goods are identified to the contract by the seller or the lessor [UCC 2–501(1), 2A–218(1)]. 2. Sellers have an insurable interest in goods as long as they have (1) title to the goods or (2) a security interest in the goods [UCC 2–501(2)]. Lessors have an insurable interest in leased goods until an option to buy has been exercised by the lessee and the risk of loss has passed to the lessee [UCC 2A–218(3)].
Bulk Transfers (See pages 399–400.)	1. In a bulk transfer of assets, in those states that have not repealed Article 6 of the UCC or replaced it with the revised Article 6, the buyer acquires title to the goods free of all claims of the seller's creditors if the following requirements are met: a. The transferor (seller) provides the transferee (buyer) with a sworn list of existing creditors, stating their names, business addresses, amounts due, and any disputed claims [UCC 6–104(1)(a)]. b. The buyer and seller prepare a schedule of the property to be transferred [UCC 6–104(1)(b)]. c. The buyer preserves the list of creditors and the schedule of property for six months, allowing any creditors of the seller to inspect it, or files the list and schedule of property in a designated public office [UCC 6–104(1)(c)]. d. Notice of the proposed bulk transfer is given by the buyer to each creditor of the seller at least ten days before the buyer takes possession of the goods or pays for them, whichever happens first [UCC 6–105]. 2. If these requirements are not met, goods in the possession of the buyer continue to be subject to the claims of the seller's unpaid creditors for six months.

For Review

① What is the significance of identifying goods to a contract?
② If the parties to a contract do not expressly agree on when title to goods passes, what determines when title passes?
③ Risk of loss does not necessarily pass with title. If the parties to a contract do not expressly agree when risk passes and the goods are to be delivered without movement by the seller, when does risk pass?
④ Under what circumstances will the seller's title to goods being sold be void? Under what circumstances will a seller have voidable title? What is the legal effect on a good faith purchaser of the goods of the seller's having a void title versus a voidable title?
⑤ At what point does the buyer acquire an insurable interest in goods subject to a sales contract? Can both the buyer and the seller have an insurable interest in the goods simultaneously?

Questions and Case Problems

15–1. Sales by Nonowners. In the following situations, two parties lay claim to the same goods sold. Discuss which party would prevail in each situation.

(a) Terry steals Dom's television set and sells the set to Blake, an innocent purchaser, for value. Dom learns that Blake has the set and demands its return.
(b) Karlin takes her television set for repair to Orken, a merchant who sells new and used television sets. By accident, one of Orken's employees sells the set to Grady, an innocent purchaser-customer, who takes possession. Karlin wants her set back from Grady.

15–2. Risk of Loss. When will risk of loss pass from the seller to the buyer under each of the following contracts, assuming the parties have not expressly agreed on when risk of loss would pass?

(a) A New York seller contracts with a San Francisco buyer to ship goods to the buyer F.O.B. San Francisco.
(b) A New York seller contracts with a San Francisco buyer to ship goods to the buyer in San Francisco. There is no indi-

cation as to whether the shipment will be F.O.B. New York or F.O.B. San Francisco.

(c) A seller contracts with a buyer to sell goods located on the seller's premises. The buyer pays for the goods and makes arrangements to pick them up the next week at the seller's place of business.

(d) A seller contracts with a buyer to sell goods located in a warehouse.

15–3. Sales by Nonowners. Julian Makepeace, who had been declared mentally incompetent by a court, sold his diamond ring to Golding for value. Golding later sold the ring to Carmichael for value. Neither Golding nor Carmichael knew that Makepeace had been adjudged mentally incompetent by a court. Farrel, who had been appointed as Makepeace's guardian, subsequently learned that the diamond ring was in Carmichael's possession and demanded its return from Carmichael. Who has legal ownership of the ring? Why?

15–4. Risk of Loss. Alberto's Food Stores contracts to purchase from Giant Food Distributors, Inc., one hundred cases of Golden Rod corn to be shipped F.O.B. seller's warehouse by Janson Truck Lines. Giant Food Distributors, by mistake, delivers one hundred cases of Gold Giant corn to Janson Truck Lines. While in transit, the Gold Giant corn is stolen. Between Alberto's and Giant Food Distributors, who suffers the loss? Explain.

15–5. Sale on Approval. Chi Moy, a student, contracts to buy a television set from Ted's Electronics. Under the terms of the contract, Moy is to try out the set for thirty days, and if he likes it, he is to pay for the set at the end of the thirty-day period. If he does not want to purchase the set after thirty days, he can return the TV to Ted's Electronics with no obligation. Ten days after Moy takes the set home, it is stolen from his apartment, although he was not negligent in his care of the set in any way. Ted's Electronics claims that Moy must pay for the stolen set. Moy argues that the risk of loss falls on Ted's Electronics. Which party will prevail?

15–6. Entrustment Rule. Bobby Locke, the principal stockholder and chief executive officer (CEO) of Worthco Farm Center, Inc., hired Mr. Hobby as the company's manager. Subsequently, it was discovered that during the approximately thirteen months of Locke's tenure as CEO, Hobby had sold corn stored with Worthco to Arabi Grain & Elevator Co. and pocketed the proceeds. When Locke brought an action against Arabi to recover the corn, Arabi alleged, among other things, that Locke had entrusted the corn to Hobby and that because Arabi was a purchaser in the ordinary course of business, Hobby had transferred ownership rights in the corn to Arabi. Assuming that Arabi was a buyer in the ordinary course of business, how should the court rule? Discuss. [*Locke v. Arabi Grain & Elevator Co.,* 197 Ga.App. 854, 399 S.E.2d 705 (1991)]

15–7. Risk of Loss. Marilyn Thomas contracted with Sunkissed Pools for an "installed pool heater" for her home. One afternoon, Thomas noticed that a heating unit had been left in her driveway. When Sunkissed returned to install the heater, it had been stolen. Thomas subsequently filed for personal bankruptcy. Sunkissed filed a claim for the price of the heater. Thomas objected. She argued that when she had noticed the heater in her driveway, she had called Sunkissed and told it that it needed to move the unit because the neighborhood was not safe. She said that the unit sat in her driveway for four days before it disappeared, after which she again called Sunkissed and was told "not to worry." Sunkissed's president testified that the firm did not receive any calls from Thomas and that he had gone to her home the day after the unit was left in her driveway and found that it was gone. In this situation, had the risk of loss of the pool heater passed from the seller to the buyer? Explain. [*In re Thomas,* 182 Bankr. 347 (S.D.Fla. 1995)]

15–8. Shipment and Destination Contracts. Roderick Cardwell owns Ticketworld, which sells tickets to entertainment and sporting events to be held at locations throughout the United States. Ticketworld's Massachusetts office sold tickets to an event in Connecticut to Mary Lou Lupovitch, a Connecticut resident, for \$125 per ticket, although each ticket had a fixed price of \$32.50. There was no agreement that Ticketworld would bear the risk of loss until the tickets were delivered to a specific location. Ticketworld gave the tickets to a carrier in Massachusetts who delivered the tickets to Lupovitch in Connecticut. The state of Connecticut brought an action against Cardwell in a Connecticut state court, charging in part a violation of a state statute that prohibited the sale of a ticket for more than \$3 over its fixed price. Cardwell contended in part that the statute did not apply because the sale to Lupovitch involved a shipment contract that was formed outside the state. Is Cardwell correct? How will the court rule? Why? [*State v. Cardwell,* 246 Conn. 721, 718 A.2d 954 (1998)]

15–9. Risk of Loss. Mark Olmstead sells trailers, doing business as World Cargo in St. Croix Falls, Wisconsin. In 1997, he also sold trailers from a site in Elk River, Minnesota. Gerald McKenzie ordered a custom-made trailer from Olmstead and mailed him a check for \$3,620. McKenzie said that he would pick up the trailer at the Elk River site. After the trailer was made, Olmstead shipped it to Elk River and kept it in a locked, fenced area. He told McKenzie that the trailer could be picked up any Tuesday or Thursday before 6:00 P.M. Over Olmstead's protest, McKenzie asked that the trailer be left outside the fenced area. Olmstead told McKenzie that the area was not secure and that the trailer could not be locked, except to chain the tires. McKenzie insisted, however, and Olmstead complied. When McKenzie arrived to pick up the trailer, it was gone—apparently stolen. McKenzie filed a suit in a Minnesota state court against Olmstead to recover the amount of the check. Who bore the risk of loss in these circumstances? Why? [*McKenzie v. Olmstead,* 587 N.W.2d 863 (Minn.App. 1999)]

TEST YOUR KNOWLEDGE—ANSWER ON THE WEB

15–10. Phillip and Genevieve Carboy owned and operated Gold Hill Service Station in Fairbanks, Alaska. Gold Hill maintained underground storage tanks on its property to hold gasoline. When Gold Hill needed more fuel, Phillip placed an order with Petroleum Sales, Inc., which delivered the gasoline by filling the tanks. Gold Hill and Petroleum Sales were separately owned companies. Petroleum Sales did not oversee or operate Gold Hill and did not construct, install, or maintain the station's tanks, and Gold Hill did not tell Petroleum Sales's personnel how to fill the tanks. Parks Hiway Enterprises, LLC, owned the land next to Gold Hill. The Alaska Department of Environmental Conservation determined that benzene had contaminated the groundwater under Parks Hiway's property and identified the gasoline in Gold Hill's tanks as the probable source. Gold Hill promptly removed the tanks, but because of the contamination, Parks Hiway stopped drawing drinking water from its well. Parks Hiway filed a suit in an Alaska state court against Petroleum Sales, among others. Should the court hold the defendant liable for the pollution? Who had title to the gasoline when it contaminated the water? Explain. [*Parks Hiway Enterprises, LLC v. CEM Leasing, Inc.*, 995 P.2d 657 (Alaska 2000)]

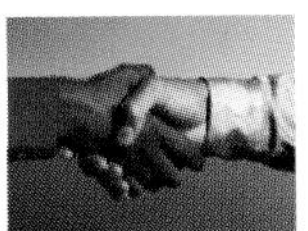

A QUESTION OF ETHICS AND SOCIAL RESPONSIBILITY

15–11. Toby and Rita Kahr accidentally included a small bag containing their sterling silver in a bag of used clothing that they donated to Goodwill Industries, Inc. The silverware, which was valued at over $3,500, had been given to them twenty-seven years earlier by Rita's father as a wedding present and had great sentimental value for them. The Kahrs realized what had happened shortly after Toby returned from Goodwill, but when Toby called Goodwill, he was told that the silver had immediately been sold to a customer, Karon Markland, for $15. Although Goodwill called Markland and asked her to return the silver, Markland refused to return it. The Kahrs then brought an action against Markland to regain the silver, claiming that Markland did not have good title to it. In view of these circumstances, discuss the following issues. [*Kahr v. Markland*, 187 Ill.App.3d 603, 543 N.E.2d 579, 135 Ill.Dec. 196 (1989)]

1. Did Karon Markland act wrongfully in any way by not returning the silver to Goodwill Industries when requested to do so? What would you have done in her position?
2. Goodwill argued that the entrustment rule should apply. Why would Goodwill want the rule to be applied? How might Goodwill justify its argument from an ethical point of view?

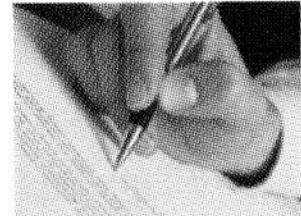

FOR CRITICAL ANALYSIS

15–12. Under the UCC, passage of title does not always occur simultaneously with passage of risk of loss. Why is this? Give some examples of what might result if risk of loss and title always passed from the buyer to the seller at the same time.

Internet Exercises

Go to the *Business Law Today* home page at **http://blt.westbuslaw.com**. Select "Interactive Study Center" and then click on "Chapter 15." There you will find the following Internet research exercise that you can perform to learn more about passage of title when goods are sold:

Activity 15–1: Passage of Title

Before the Test

Go to the *Business Law Today* home page at **http://blt.westbuslaw.com**. Click on "Interactive Quizzes." You will find at least twenty interactive questions relating to this chapter.

CHAPTER 16

Performance and Breach of Sales and Lease Contracts

"It has been uniformly laid down . . . , as far back as we can remember, that good faith is the basis of all mercantile transactions."

J. Buller, 1746–1800
(British jurist)

CHAPTER CONTENTS

LEARNING OBJECTIVES

After reading this chapter, you should be able to answer the following questions:

① What are the respective obligations of the parties under a contract for the sale or lease of goods?

② What is the perfect tender rule? What are some important exceptions to this rule that apply to sales and lease contracts?

③ What options are available to the nonbreaching party when the other party to a sales or lease contract repudiates the contract prior to the time for performance?

④ What remedies are available to a seller or lessor when the buyer or lessee breaches the contract? What remedies are available to a buyer or lessee if the seller or lessor breaches the contract?

⑤ In contracts subject to the UCC, are parties free to limit the remedies available to the nonbreaching party on a breach of contract? If so, in what ways?

The performance that is required of the parties under a sales or lease contract consists of the duties and obligations each party has under the terms of the contract. Keep in mind that "duties and obligations" under the terms of the contract include those specified by the agreement, by custom, and by the Uniform Commercial Code (UCC). In this chapter, we examine the basic performance obligations of the parties under a sales or lease contract.

Sometimes, circumstances make it difficult for a person to carry out the promised performance, in which case the contract may be breached. When breach occurs, the aggrieved party looks for remedies—which we deal with in the second half of the chapter.

Performance Obligations

As discussed in previous chapters and stressed in the opening quotation to this chapter, the standards of good faith and commercial reasonableness are read into every contract. These standards provide a framework in which the parties can specify particulars of performance. Thus, when one party delays specifying particulars of performance for an unreasonable period of time or fails to cooperate with the other party, the innocent party is excused from any resulting delay in performance. The innocent party can proceed to perform in any reasonable manner, and the other party's failure to specify particulars or to cooperate can be treated as a breach of contract. Good faith is a question of fact for the jury.

In the performance of a sales or lease contract, the basic obligation of the seller or lessor is to *transfer and deliver conforming goods*. The basic obligation of the buyer or lessee is to *accept and pay for conforming goods* in accordance with the contract [UCC 2–301, 2A–516(1)]. Overall performance of a sales or lease contract is controlled by the agreement between the parties. When the contract is unclear and disputes arise, the courts look to the UCC.

Obligations of the Seller or Lessor

"It is only when merchants dispute about their own rules that they invoke the law."

J. BRETT,
1815–1899
(British jurist)

The major obligation of the seller or lessor under a sales or lease contract is to tender conforming goods to the buyer or lessee.

TENDER OF DELIVERY

Tender of delivery requires that the seller or lessor have and hold *conforming goods* at the disposal of the buyer or lessee and give the buyer or lessee whatever notification is reasonably necessary to enable the buyer or lessee to take delivery [UCC 2–503(1), 2A–508(1)].

Tender must occur at a *reasonable hour* and in a *reasonable manner.* In other words, a seller cannot call the buyer at 2:00 A.M. and say, "The goods are ready. I'll give you twenty minutes to get them." Unless the parties have agreed otherwise, the goods must be tendered for delivery at a reasonable time and kept available for a reasonable period of time to enable the buyer to take possession of them [UCC 2–503(1)(a)].

All goods called for by a contract must be tendered in a single delivery unless the parties agree otherwise or the circumstances are such that either party can rightfully request delivery in lots [UCC 2–307, 2–612, 2A–510]. Hence, an order for 1,000 shirts cannot be delivered 2 shirts at a time. If, however, the seller and the buyer contemplate that the shirts will be delivered in four orders of 250 each, as they are produced (for summer, fall, winter, and spring stock), and the price can be apportioned accordingly, it may be commercially reasonable to deliver the shirts in this way.

PLACE OF DELIVERY

The UCC provides for the place of delivery pursuant to a contract if the contract does not. Of course, the parties may agree on a particular destination, or their contract's terms or the circumstances may indicate the place of delivery.

Noncarrier Cases If the contract does not designate the place of delivery for the goods, and the buyer is expected to pick them up, the place of delivery is the *seller's* *place of business* or, if the seller has none, the seller's residence [UCC 2–308]. If the contract involves the sale of *identified goods,* and the parties know when they enter into the contract that these goods are located somewhere other than at the seller's place of business (such as at a warehouse), then the *location of the goods* is the place for their delivery [UCC 2–308].

DON'T FORGET Documents of title include bills of lading, warehouse receipts, and any other documents that, in the regular course of business, entitle a person holding these documents to obtain possession of, and title to, the goods covered.

• **EXAMPLE 16.1** Rogers and Aguirre live in San Francisco. In San Francisco, Rogers contracts to sell Aguirre five used trucks, which both parties know are located in a Chicago warehouse. If nothing more is specified in the contract, the place of delivery for the trucks is Chicago. • The seller may tender delivery by either giving the buyer a *negotiable or nonnegotiable document of title* or obtaining the *bailee's (warehouser's) acknowledgment* that the buyer is entitled to possession.[1]

Carrier Cases In many instances, attendant circumstances or delivery terms in the contract make it apparent that the parties intend that a carrier be used to move the goods. In carrier cases, a seller can complete performance of the obligation to deliver the goods in two ways—through a shipment contract and through a destination contract.

Shipment Contracts. Recall from Chapter 15 that a shipment contract requires or authorizes the seller to ship goods by a carrier. The contract does not require that the seller deliver the goods at a particular destination [UCC 2–319, 2–509]. Under a shipment contract, unless otherwise agreed, the seller must do the following:

KEEP IN MIND If goods never arrive, the buyer or seller usually has at least some recourse against the carrier. Also, a buyer normally insures the goods from the time they leave the seller's possession.

① Put the goods into the hands of the carrier.

② Make a contract for their transportation that is reasonable according to the nature of the goods and their value. (For example, certain types of goods need refrigeration in transit.)

③ Obtain and promptly deliver or tender to the buyer any documents necessary to enable the buyer to obtain possession of the goods from the carrier.

④ Promptly notify the buyer that shipment has been made [UCC 2–504].

If the seller fails to notify the buyer that shipment has been made or fails to make a proper contract for transportation, the buyer can treat the contract as breached and reject the goods, but only if a *material loss* of the goods or a significant *delay* results.

Destination Contracts. Under a *destination contract,* the seller agrees to see that conforming goods will be duly tendered to the buyer at a particular destination. The goods must be tendered at a reasonable hour and held at the buyer's disposal for a reasonable length of time. The seller must also give the buyer any appropriate notice that is necessary to enable the buyer to take delivery. In addition, the seller must provide the buyer with any documents of title necessary to enable the buyer to obtain delivery from the carrier [UCC 2–503].

THE PERFECT TENDER RULE

As previously noted, the seller or lessor has an obligation to ship or tender *conforming goods,* and the buyer or lessee is required to accept and pay for the goods according to

1. If the seller delivers a nonnegotiable document of title or merely writes instructions to the bailee to release the goods to the buyer without the bailee's *acknowledgment* of the buyer's rights, this is also a sufficient tender, unless the buyer objects [UCC 2–503(4)]. Risk of loss, however, does not pass until the buyer has a reasonable amount of time in which to present the document or to give the bailee instructions for delivery.

the terms of the contract. Under the common law, the seller was obligated to deliver goods in conformity with the terms of the contract in every detail. This was called the *perfect tender* doctrine. The UCC preserves the perfect tender doctrine by stating that if goods or tender of delivery fail *in any respect* to conform to the contract, the buyer or lessee has the right to accept the goods, reject the entire shipment, or accept part and reject part [UCC 2–601, 2A–509].

● **EXAMPLE 16.2** A lessor contracts to lease fifty Vericlear monitors to be delivered at the lessee's place of business on or before October 1. On September 28, the lessor discovers that it has only thirty Vericlear monitors in inventory, but that it will have another forty Vericlear monitors within the next two weeks. The lessor tenders delivery of the thirty Vericlear monitors on October 1, with the promise that the other monitors will be delivered within three weeks. Because the lessor failed to make a perfect tender of fifty Vericlear monitors, the lessee has the right to reject the entire shipment and hold the lessor in breach.●

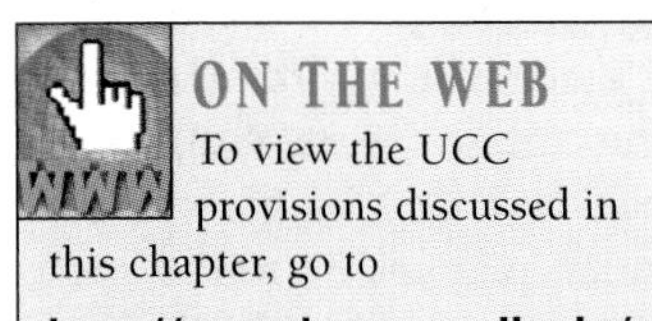

ON THE WEB
To view the UCC provisions discussed in this chapter, go to
http://www.law.cornell.edu/ucc/ucc.table.html.

EXCEPTIONS TO PERFECT TENDER

Because of the rigidity of the perfect tender rule, several exceptions to the rule have been created, some of which are discussed here.

Agreement of the Parties Exceptions to the perfect tender rule may be established by agreement. If the parties have agreed, for example, that defective goods or parts will not be rejected if the seller or lessor is able to repair or replace them within a reasonable period of time, the perfect tender rule does not apply.

Cure The UCC does not specifically define the term *cure*, but it refers to the right of the seller or lessor to repair, adjust, or replace defective or nonconforming goods [UCC 2–508, 2A–513]. When any tender of delivery is rejected because of nonconforming goods and the time for performance has not yet expired, the seller or lessor can notify the buyer or lessee promptly of the intention to cure and can then do so *within the contract time for performance* [UCC 2–508(1), 2A–513(1)]. Once the time for performance has expired, the seller or lessor can still, for a reasonable time, exercise the right to cure with respect to the rejected goods if he or she had, at the time of delivery, *reasonable grounds to believe that the nonconforming tender would be acceptable to the buyer or lessee* [UCC 2–508(2), 2A–513(2)].

Sometimes, a seller or lessor will tender nonconforming goods with some type of price allowance. The allowance serves as the "reasonable grounds" for the seller or lessor to believe that the nonconforming tender will be acceptable to the buyer or lessee. Other reasons might also serve as the basis for the assumption that a buyer or lessee will accept a nonconforming tender. ● **EXAMPLE 16.3** Suppose that in the past a buyer, an office-supply store, frequently accepted blue pens when the seller did not have black pens in stock. In this context, the seller has reasonable grounds to believe the store will again accept such a substitute. If the store rejects the substituted goods (blue pens) on a particular occasion, the seller nonetheless had reasonable grounds to believe that the blue pens would be acceptable. Therefore, the seller can cure within a reasonable time, even though the delivery of black pens will occur after the time limit for performance allowed under the contract.●

"It is the duty of a judge to inquire not only into the matter but into the circumstances of the matter."

OVID,
43 B.C.E.–17 C.E.
(Roman poet)

The right to cure means that, in order to reject goods, the buyer or lessee must give notice to the seller or lessor of a particular defect. For example, if a lessee refuses a tender of goods as nonconforming but does not disclose the nature of the defect to the lessor, the lessee cannot later assert the defect as a defense if the defect is one that

Competitors' trucks travel the same route. When is it acceptable to substitute one carrier for another specified in a contract?

INSTALLMENT CONTRACT
Under the UCC, a contract that requires or authorizes delivery in two or more separate lots to be accepted and paid for separately.

the lessor could have cured. Generally, buyers and lessees must act in good faith and state specific reasons for refusing to accept goods [UCC 2–605, 2A–514].

Substitution of Carriers When an agreed-on manner of delivery (such as which carrier will be used to transport the goods) becomes impracticable or unavailable through no fault of either party, but a commercially reasonable substitute is available, the seller must use this substitute performance, which is sufficient tender to the buyer [UCC 2–614(1)]. • **EXAMPLE 16.4** A sales contract calls for the delivery of a large generator to be shipped by Roadway Trucking Corporation on or before June 1. The contract terms clearly state the importance of the delivery date. The employees of Roadway Trucking go on strike. The seller is required to make a reasonable substitute tender, perhaps by rail if one is available. Note that the seller here will normally be held responsible for any additional shipping costs, unless contrary arrangements have been made in the sales contract. •

Installment Contracts An **installment contract** is a single contract that requires or authorizes delivery in two or more separate lots to be accepted and paid for separately. In an installment contract, a buyer or lessee can reject an installment *only if the nonconformity substantially impairs the value* of the installment and cannot be cured [UCC 2–612(2), 2–307, 2A–510(1)].

Unless the contract provides otherwise, the entire installment contract is breached only when one or more nonconforming installments *substantially* impair the value of the *whole contract*. If the buyer or lessee subsequently accepts a nonconforming installment and fails to notify the seller or lessor of cancellation, however, the contract is reinstated [UCC 2–612(3), 2A–510(2)].

A major issue to be determined is what constitutes substantial impairment of the "value of the whole contract." • **EXAMPLE 16.5** Consider an installment contract for the sale of twenty carloads of plywood. The first carload does not conform to the contract because 9 percent of the plywood deviates from the thickness specifications. The buyer cancels the contract, and immediately thereafter the second and third carloads of conforming plywood arrive at the buyer's place of business. If a lawsuit ensues, the court will have to grapple with the question of whether the 9 percent of nonconforming plywood substantially impaired the value of the whole.[2] •

The point to remember is that the UCC significantly alters the right of the buyer or lessee to reject the entire contract if the contract requires delivery to be made in several installments. The UCC strictly limits rejection to cases of *substantial* nonconformity.

"Inability suspends the law."
LEGAL MAXIM

Commercial Impracticability As mentioned in Chapter 12, occurrences unforeseen by either party when a contract was made may make performance commercially impracticable. When this occurs, the rule of perfect tender no longer holds. According to UCC 2–615(a) and 2A–405(a), delay in delivery or nondelivery in whole or in part is not a breach when performance has been made impracticable "by the occurrence of a contingency the nonoccurrence of which was a basic assumption on which the contract was made." The seller or lessor must, however, notify the buyer or lessee as soon as practicable that there will be a delay or nondelivery.

Foreseeable versus Unforeseeable Contingencies. An increase in cost resulting from inflation does not in and of itself excuse performance, as this kind of risk is ordinar-

2. *Continental Forest Products, Inc. v. White Lumber Sales, Inc.,* 256 Or. 466, 474 P.2d 1 (1970). The court held that the deviation did not substantially impair the value of the whole contract. Additionally, the court stated that the nonconformity could be cured by an adjustment in the price.

ily assumed by a seller or lessor conducting business. The unforeseen contingency must be one that would have been impossible to contemplate in a given business situation. • **EXAMPLE 16.6** A major oil company that receives its supplies from the Middle East has a contract to supply a buyer with 100,000 gallons of oil. Because of an oil embargo by the Organization of Petroleum Exporting Countries (OPEC), the seller is prevented from securing oil supplies to meet the terms of the contract. Because of the same embargo, the seller cannot secure oil from any other source. This situation comes fully under the commercial impracticability exception to the perfect tender doctrine. •

Can unanticipated increases in a seller's costs, which make performance "impracticable," constitute a valid defense to performance on the basis of commercial impracticability? The court dealt with this question in the following case.

Landmark and Classic Cases

CASE 16.1 Maple Farms, Inc. v. City School District of Elmira

Supreme Court of New York, 1974.
76 Misc.2d 1080,
352 N.Y.S.2d 784.

FACTS On June 15, 1973, Maple Farms, Inc., formed an agreement with the city school district of Elmira, New York, to supply the school district with milk for the 1973–1974 school year. The agreement was in the form of a requirements contract, under which Maple Farms would sell to the school district all the milk the district required at a fixed price—which was the June market price of milk. By December 1973, the price of raw milk had increased by 23 percent over the price specified in the contract. This meant that if the terms of the contract were fulfilled, Maple Farms would lose $7,350. Because it had similar contracts with other school districts, Maple Farms stood to lose a great deal if it was held to the price stated in the contracts. When the school district would not agree to release Maple Farms from its contract, Maple Farms brought an action in a New York state court for a declaratory judgment (a determination of the parties' rights under a contract). Maple Farms contended that the substantial increase in the price of raw milk was an event not contemplated by the parties when the contract was formed and that, given the increased price, performance of the contract was commercially impracticable.

ISSUE Can Maple Farms be released from the contract on the ground of commercial impracticability?

DECISION No. the court ruled that performance in this case was not impracticable.

REASON The court reasoned that commercial impracticability arises when an event occurs that is totally unexpected and unforeseeable by the parties. The increased price of raw milk was not totally unexpected, given that in the previous year the price of milk had risen 10 percent and that the price of milk had traditionally varied. Additionally, the general inflation of prices in the United States should have been anticipated. Maple Farms had reason to know these facts and could have included a clause in its contract with the school district to protect itself from its present situation. The court also noted that the primary purpose of the contract, on the part of the school district, was to protect itself (for budgeting purposes) against price fluctuations.

COMMENT *This case is a classic illustration of the UCC's commercial impracticability doctrine. Under this doctrine, parties who freely enter into contracts normally will not be excused from their contractual obligations simply because changed circumstances make performance difficult or very costly. Rather, to be excused from performance, a party must show that the changed circumstances were impossible to foresee at the time the contract was formed. This principle continues to be applied today.*

Partial Performance. Sometimes, an unforeseen event only *partially* affects the capacity of the seller or lessor to perform, and the seller or lessor is thus able to fulfill the contract *partially* but cannot tender total performance. In this event, the seller or lessor is required to allocate in a fair and reasonable manner any remaining production and deliveries among those to whom it is contractually obligated to deliver the goods, and this allocation may take into account its regular customers [UCC 2–615(b), 2A–405(b)]. The buyer or lessee must receive notice of the allocation and has the right to accept or reject the allocation [UCC 2–615(c), 2A–405(c)].

• **EXAMPLE 16.7** A Florida orange grower, Best Citrus, Inc., contracts to sell this season's production to a number of customers, including Martin's grocery chain. Martin's contracts to purchase two thousand crates of oranges. Best Citrus has sprayed some of its orange groves with a chemical called Karmoxin. The Department of Agriculture discovers that persons who eat products sprayed with Karmoxin may develop cancer. The department issues an order prohibiting the sale of these products. Best Citrus picks all of the oranges not sprayed with Karmoxin, but the quantity does not fully meet all the contracted-for deliveries. In this situation, Best Citrus is required to allocate its production, and it notifies Martin's that it cannot deliver the full quantity agreed on in the contract and specifies the amount it will be able to deliver under the circumstances. Martin's can either accept or reject the allocation, but Best Citrus has no further contractual liability.•

Destruction of Identified Goods The UCC provides that when an unexpected event, such as a fire, totally destroys *goods identified at the time the contract is formed* through no fault of either party and *before risk passes to the buyer or lessee,* the parties are excused from performance [UCC 2–613, 2A–221]. If the goods are only partially destroyed, however, the buyer or lessee can inspect them and either treat the contract as void or accept the goods with a reduction of the contract price.

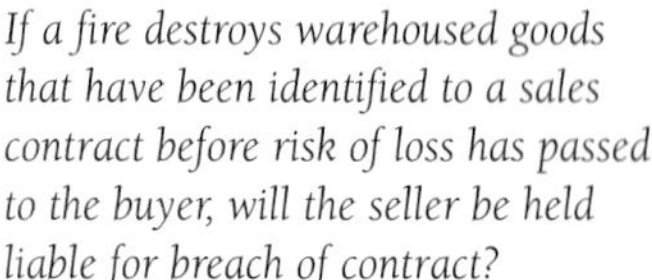
If a fire destroys warehoused goods that have been identified to a sales contract before risk of loss has passed to the buyer, will the seller be held liable for breach of contract?

• **EXAMPLE 16.8** Atlas Sporting Equipment agrees to lease to River Bicycles sixty bicycles of a particular model that has been discontinued. No other bicycles of that model are available. River specifies that it needs the bicycles to rent to tourists. Before Atlas can deliver the bikes, they are destroyed by a fire. In this situation, Atlas is not liable to River for failing to deliver the bikes. The goods were destroyed through no fault of either party, before the risk of loss passed to the lessee. The loss was total, so the contract is avoided. Clearly, Atlas has no obligation to tender the bicycles, and River has no obligation to pay for them.•

Assurance and Cooperation Two other exceptions to the perfect tender doctrine apply equally to parties to sales and lease contracts: the right of assurance and the duty of cooperation. The UCC provides that if one of the parties to a contract has "reasonable grounds" to believe that the other party will not perform as contracted, he or she may *in writing* "demand adequate assurance of due performance" from the other party. Until such assurance is received, he or she may "suspend" further performance (such as payments due under the contract) without liability. What constitutes "reasonable grounds" is determined by commercial standards. If such assurances are not forthcoming within a reasonable time (not to exceed thirty days), the failure to respond may be treated as a *repudiation* of the contract [UCC 2–609, 2A–401].

Sometimes, the performance of one party depends on the cooperation of the other. The UCC provides that when such cooperation is not forthcoming, the other party can suspend her or his own performance without liability and hold the uncooperative party in breach or proceed to perform the contract in any reasonable manner [UCC 2–311(3)(b)].

Obligations of the Buyer or Lessee

Once the seller or lessor has adequately tendered delivery, the buyer or lessee is obligated to accept the goods and pay for them according to the terms of the contract. In

LETTER OF THE LAW

When "in Writing" Does Not Mean "in Writing"

By now, you are probably aware that how the letter of the law is applied depends to a significant extent on how particular courts interpret the law. Yet it would seem that if a law requires that something be "in writing," it means just that. For example, as noted elsewhere, the UCC requires that if a party to a contract demands adequate assurance of performance from the other party, the demand must be in writing. If such a demand is made orally, you might logically assume that any court would conclude that the demand has not met the requirements of this UCC provision. Yet if you made this assumption, you would be wrong.

While some courts apply the requirement quite literally, others do not. When the South Dakota Supreme Court had to decide which was the wiser course, it opted not to apply the requirement literally. The court held that "a demand for adequate assurances may be either written or oral, as long as the demand provides a 'clear understanding' of the insecure party's intent to suspend performance until receipt of adequate assurances from the other party."[a]

THE BOTTOM LINE

Businesspersons should realize that how the courts will rule on a particular issue is never totally predictable.

a. *Atwood-Kellogg, Inc. v. Nickeson Farms*, 602 N.W.2d 749 (S.Dak. 1999).

the absence of any specific agreements, the buyer or lessee must make payment at the time and place the buyer or lessee receives the goods [UCC 2–310(a), 2A–516(1)].

Payment

When a sale is made on credit, the buyer is obliged to pay according to the specified credit terms (for example, 60, 90, or 120 days), not when the goods are received. The credit period usually begins on the *date of shipment* [UCC 2–310(d)]. Under a lease contract, a lessee must pay the lease payment that was specified in the contract [UCC 2A–516(1)].

Payment can be made by any means agreed on by the parties—cash or any other method generally acceptable in the commercial world. If the seller demands cash when the buyer offers a check, credit card, or the like, the seller must permit the buyer reasonable time to obtain legal tender [UCC 2–511].

Right of Inspection

"The buyer needs a hundred eyes, the seller not one."

GEORGE HERBERT, 1593–1633 (English poet)

Unless otherwise agreed, or for C.O.D. (collect on delivery) transactions, the buyer or lessee has an absolute right to inspect the goods. This right allows the buyer or lessee to verify, before making payment, that the goods tendered or delivered are what were contracted for or ordered. If the goods are not what were ordered, the buyer or lessee has no duty to pay. *An opportunity for inspection is therefore a condition precedent to the right of the seller or lessor to enforce payment* [UCC 2–513(1), 2A–515(1)].

Unless otherwise agreed, inspection can take place at any reasonable place and time and in any reasonable manner. Generally, what is reasonable is determined by custom of the trade, past practices of the parties, and the like. Costs of inspecting conforming goods are borne by the buyer unless otherwise agreed [UCC 2–513(2)].

C.O.D. Shipments If a seller ships goods to a buyer C.O.D. (or under similar terms) and the buyer has not agreed to a C.O.D. shipment in the contract, the buyer can rightfully *reject* the goods. This is because a C.O.D. shipment does not permit inspection before payment, which is a denial of the buyer's right of inspection. When the buyer has agreed to a C.O.D. shipment in the contract, however, or has agreed to pay for the goods on the presentation of a bill of lading, no right of inspection exists because it was negated by the agreement [UCC 2–513(3)].

Payment Due—Documents of Title Under certain contracts, payment is due on the receipt of the required documents of title even though the goods themselves may not have arrived at their destination. With C.I.F. and C.&F. contracts (see Exhibit 15–1 in Chapter 15), payment is required on receipt of the documents unless the parties have agreed otherwise. Thus, payment may be required prior to inspection, and payment must be made unless the buyer knows that the goods are nonconforming [UCC 2–310(b), 2–513(3)].

Acceptance

A buyer or lessee can manifest assent to the delivered goods in the following ways, each of which constitutes acceptance:

① The buyer or lessee can expressly accept the shipment by words or conduct. For example, there is an acceptance if the buyer or lessee, after having had a reasonable opportunity to inspect the goods, signifies agreement to the seller or lessor that the goods are either conforming or are acceptable despite their nonconformity [UCC 2–606(1)(a), 2A–515(1)(a)].

② Acceptance is presumed if the buyer or lessee has had a reasonable opportunity to inspect the goods and has failed to reject them within a reasonable period of time [UCC 2–606(1)(b), 2–602(1), 2A–515(1)(b)].

Additionally, in sales contracts, the buyer will be deemed to have accepted the goods if he or she performs any act that would indicate that the seller no longer owns the goods. For example, any use or resale of the goods generally constitutes an acceptance. Limited use for the sole purpose of testing or inspecting the goods is not an acceptance, however [UCC 2–606(1)(c)].

If some of the goods delivered do not conform to the contract and the seller or lessor has failed to cure, the buyer or lessee can make a *partial* acceptance [UCC 2–601(c), 2A–509(1)]. The same is true if the nonconformity was not reasonably discoverable before acceptance. (In the latter situation, the buyer or lessee may be able to revoke the acceptance, as will be discussed later in this chapter.) A buyer or lessee cannot accept less than a single commercial unit, however. A *commercial unit* is defined by the UCC as a unit of goods that, by commercial usage, is viewed as a "single whole" for purposes of sale, division of which would materially impair the character of the unit, its market value, or its use [UCC 2–105(6), 2A–103(1)(c)]. A commercial unit can be a single article (such as a machine), a set of articles (such as a suite of furniture or an assortment of sizes), a quantity (such as a bale, a gross, or a carload), or any other unit treated in the trade as a single whole.

Anticipatory Repudiation

What if, before the time for contract performance, one party clearly communicates to the other the intention not to perform? As discussed in Chapter 12, such an action is a breach of the contract by anticipatory repudiation.[3] When anticipatory repudiation occurs, the nonbreaching party has a choice of two responses: (1) treat the repudiation as a final breach by pursuing a remedy or (2) wait to see if the repudiating party will decide to honor the obligations required by the contract despite the avowed intention to renege [UCC 2–610, 2A–402]. In either situation, the nonbreaching party may suspend performance.

Should the latter course be pursued, the UCC permits the breaching party (subject to some limitations) to "retract" her or his repudiation. This can be done by any method that clearly indicates an intent to perform. Once retraction is made, the rights of the repudiating party under the contract are reinstated [UCC 2–611, 2A–403]. The concept of anticipatory repudiation is further illustrated in the following case.

3. This doctrine was first enunciated in an English case decided in 1853, *Hochster v. De La Tour,* 2 Ellis and Blackburn Reports 678 (1853).

CASE 16.2 Banco International, Inc. v. Goody's Family Clothing

United States District Court,
Eastern District of Tennessee, 1999.
54 F.Supp.2d 765.

FACTS In April 1994, Banco International, Inc., and Goody's Family Clothing contracted for the manufacture of 62,748 custom-made, private-label windsuits (jogging suits) and their delivery in three shipments, for $749,103.60. The first shipment had to be at Goody's distribution center in Knoxville, Tennessee, by September 30

(continued)

CASE 16.2—Continued

in time for holiday season sales, or the order was subject to cancellation. Banco sent to Goody's what Banco claimed were production samples, but Goody's learned that they had been produced by another manufacturer. Goody's also learned that a third party had the fabric and other materials that were needed to make the windsuits and would not release them to Banco without payment of a debt. By August 23, Banco had not started production, despite the representations of Muhammed Akhtar, the president and owner of Banco, to the contrary. On that day, Goody's canceled the contract. Akhtar acknowledged that Banco was behind schedule but said it could meet the delivery dates for the first two shipments if it shipped by air and the deadline for the third shipment by shipping by sea. Had Goody's asked how production could be accomplished so quickly, Akhtar later said he would have responded that it was "none of Goody's business." Goody's did not accept Akhtar's assurances. Banco filed a suit in a federal district court against Goody's, alleging breach of contract. Goody's argued that there was an anticipatory repudiation, or breach, of the contract by Banco.

ISSUE Did Banco's actions constitute an anticipatory repudiation of the contract?

DECISION Yes. The court entered a judgment in Goody's favor, ruling that Goody's was not liable for canceling the purchase orders because of Banco's anticipatory repudiation of their contract.

REASON Banco's repudiation was indicated by Banco's failure to start performance within a reasonable time to meet the contract deadlines and by Banco's misrepresentations concerning the status of its performance. The court explained, "It is not necessary for [anticipatory] repudiation that performance be made literally and utterly impossible. Repudiation can result from action which reasonably indicates a rejection of the continuing obligation." The court found that "Goody's was justified in reasonably concluding that Banco could not deliver the windsuits to it by the date set in the first purchase order between the parties. Additionally, the failure to deliver the goods by that date would have substantially impaired the value of those goods to Goody's." The court stated that "these actions justified Goody's suspension of its own performance and cancellation of the contract."

FOR CRITICAL ANALYSIS—Economic Consideration *Could Goody's have sued Banco to obtain damages for breach of contract in this situation? Why or why not?*

Remedies of the Seller or Lessor

When the buyer or lessee is in breach, the seller or lessor has numerous remedies available under the UCC. Generally, the remedies available to the seller or lessor depend on the circumstances existing at the time of the breach, such as which party has possession of the goods, whether the goods are in transit, whether the buyer or lessee has rejected or accepted the goods, and so on.

NOTE A buyer or lessee breaches a contract by wrongfully rejecting the goods, revoking acceptance, refusing to pay, or repudiating the contract.

When the Goods Are in the Possession of the Seller or Lessor

Under the UCC, if the buyer or lessee breaches the contract before the goods have been delivered to the buyer or lessee, the seller or lessor has the right to pursue the remedies discussed here.

The Right to Cancel the Contract One of the options available to a seller or lessor when the buyer or lessee breaches the contract is simply to cancel (rescind) the contract [UCC 2–703(f), 2A–523(1)(a)]. The seller must notify the buyer or lessee of the cancellation, and at that point all remaining obligations of the seller or lessor are discharged. The buyer or lessee is not discharged from all remaining obligations, however; he or she is in breach, and the seller or lessor can pursue remedies available under the UCC for breach.

"Life is so terrifyingly dependent on the law."

KARL N. LLEWELLYN,
1893–1962
(American legal scholar)

The Right to Withhold Delivery In general, sellers and lessors can withhold or discontinue performance of their obligations under sales or lease contracts when the buyers or lessees are in breach. If a buyer or lessee has wrongfully rejected or revoked acceptance of contract goods (rejection and revocation of acceptance will be discussed later), failed to make proper and timely payment, or repudiated a part of the contract, the seller or lessor can withhold delivery of the goods in question [UCC 2–703(a), 2A–523(1)(c)]. If the breach results from the buyer's or the lessee's insolvency (inability to pay debts as they become due), the seller or lessor can refuse to deliver the goods unless the buyer or lessee pays in cash [UCC 2–702(1), 2A–525(1)].

The Right to Resell or Dispose of the Goods When a buyer or lessee breaches or repudiates a sales contract while the seller or lessor is still in possession of the goods, the seller or lessor can resell or dispose of the goods. The seller can retain any profits made as a result of the sale and can hold the buyer or lessee liable for any loss [UCC 2–703(d), 2–706(1), 2A–523(1)(e), 2A–527(1)].

When the goods contracted for are unfinished at the time of breach, the seller or lessor can do one of two things: (1) cease manufacturing the goods and resell them for scrap or salvage value or (2) complete the manufacture and resell or dispose of them, holding the buyer or lessee liable for any deficiency. In choosing between these two alternatives, the seller or lessor must exercise reasonable commercial judgment to mitigate the loss and obtain maximum value from the unfinished goods [UCC 2–704(2), 2A–524(2)]. Any resale of the goods must be made in good faith and in a commercially reasonable manner.

INCIDENTAL DAMAGES
All costs resulting from a breach of contract, including all reasonable expenses incurred because of the breach.

In sales transactions, the seller can recover any deficiency between the resale price and the contract price, along with **incidental damages**, defined as those costs to the seller resulting from the breach [UCC 2–706(1), 2–710]. The resale can be private or public, and the goods can be sold as a unit or in parcels. The seller must give the original buyer reasonable notice of the resale, unless the goods are perishable or will rapidly decline in value [UCC 2–706(2), (3)]. A good faith purchaser in a resale takes the goods free of any of the rights of the original buyer, even if the seller fails to comply with these requirements of the UCC [UCC 2–706(5)].

In lease transactions, the lessor may lease the goods to another party and recover from the original lessee, as damages, any unpaid lease payments up to the beginning date of the lease term under the new lease. The lessor can also recover any deficiency between the lease payments due under the original lease contract and under the new lease contract, along with incidental damages [UCC 2A–527(2)].

The Right to Recover the Purchase Price or the Lease Payments Due Under the UCC, an unpaid seller or lessor can bring an action to recover the purchase price or payments due under the lease contract, plus incidental damages, if the seller or lessor is unable to resell or dispose of the goods [UCC 2–709(1), 2A–529(1)].

• **EXAMPLE 16.9** Suppose that Southern Realty contracts with Gem Point, Inc., to purchase one thousand pens with Southern Realty's name inscribed on them. Gem Point tenders delivery of the one thousand pens, but Southern Realty wrongfully refuses to accept them. In this situation, Gem Point has, as a proper remedy, an action for the purchase price. Gem Point tendered delivery of conforming goods, and Southern Realty, by failing to accept the goods, is in breach. Gem Point obviously cannot sell to anyone else the pens inscribed with the buyer's business name, so this situation falls under UCC 2–709. •

If a seller or lessor is unable to resell or dispose of goods and sues for the contract price or lease payments due, the goods must be held for the buyer or lessee. The seller

If a seller learns that a buyer is insolvent while the goods being sold are in transit to the buyer, is the seller allowed to stop the carrier from delivering the goods?

or lessor can resell or dispose of the goods at any time prior to collection (of the judgment) from the buyer or lessee, but the net proceeds from the sale must be credited to the buyer or lessee. This is an example of the duty to mitigate damages.

The Right to Recover Damages If a buyer or lessee repudiates a contract or wrongfully refuses to accept the goods, a seller or lessor can maintain an action to recover the damages that were sustained. Ordinarily, the amount of damages equals the difference between the contract price or lease payments and the market price or lease payments (at the time and place of tender of the goods), plus incidental damages [UCC 2–708(1), 2A–528(1)]. The time and place of tender are frequently given by such terms as F.O.B., F.A.S., C.I.F., and the like, which determine whether there is a shipment or destination contract.

When the Goods Are in Transit

If the seller or lessor has delivered the goods to a carrier or a bailee but the buyer or lessee has not as yet received them, the goods are said to be in transit. If, while the goods are in transit, the seller or lessor learns that the buyer or lessee is insolvent, the seller or lessor can stop the carrier or bailee from delivering the goods, regardless of the quantity of goods shipped.

• **Example 16.10** Suppose that Alvin Johnson orders a truckload of lumber from Timber Products, Inc., to be shipped to Johnson six weeks later. Johnson, who owes Timber Products for a past shipment, promises to pay the debt immediately and to pay for the current shipment as soon as it is received. After the lumber has been shipped to Johnson, Timber Products is notified by a bankruptcy court judge that Johnson has filed a petition in bankruptcy and listed Timber Products as one of his creditors (see Chapter 23). If the goods are still in transit, Timber Products can stop the carrier from delivering the lumber to Johnson. • If the buyer or lessee is in breach but is not insolvent, the seller or lessor can stop the goods in transit only if the quantity shipped is at least a carload, a truckload, a planeload, or a larger shipment [UCC 2–705(1), 2A–526(1)].

To stop delivery, the seller or lessor must *timely notify* the carrier or other bailee that the goods are to be returned or held for the seller or lessor. If the carrier has sufficient time to stop delivery, the goods must be held and delivered according to the instructions of the seller or lessor, who is liable to the carrier for any additional costs incurred [UCC 2–705(3), 2A–526(3)].

UCC 2–705(2) and 2A–526(2) provide that the right of the seller or lessor to stop delivery of goods in transit is lost when any of the following events occur:

① The buyer or lessee obtains possession of the goods.

② The carrier acknowledges the rights of the buyer or lessee by reshipping or storing the goods for the buyer or lessee.

③ A bailee of the goods other than a carrier acknowledges that he or she is holding the goods for the buyer or lessee.

Additionally, in sales transactions, the seller loses the right to stop delivery of goods in transit when a negotiable document of title covering the goods has been negotiated (properly transferred, giving the buyer ownership rights in the goods) to the buyer [UCC 2–705(2)].

Once the seller or lessor reclaims the goods in transit, she or he can pursue the remedies allowed to sellers and lessors when the goods are in their possession. In other words, the seller or lessor who has reclaimed goods may do the following:

① Cancel (rescind) the contract.

② Resell the goods and recover any deficiency.

③ Sue for any deficiency between the contract price (or lease payments due) and the market price (or market lease payments), plus incidental damages.

④ Sue to recover the purchase price or lease payments due if the goods cannot be resold, plus incidental damages.

⑤ Sue to recover damages.

WHEN THE GOODS ARE IN THE POSSESSION OF THE BUYER OR LESSEE

When the buyer or lessee breaches a sales or lease contract and the goods are in the buyer's or lessee's possession, the UCC gives the seller or lessor the following limited remedies.

RECALL Incidental damages include all reasonable expenses incurred because of a breach of contract.

The Right to Recover the Purchase Price or Payments Due under the Lease Contract If the buyer or lessee has accepted the goods but refuses to pay for them, the seller or lessor can sue for the purchase price of the goods or for the lease payments due, plus incidental damages [UCC 2–709(1), 2A–529(1)].

The Right to Reclaim the Goods In regard to sales contracts, if a seller discovers that the buyer has received goods on credit and is insolvent, the seller can demand return of the goods, if the demand is made within ten days of the buyer's receipt of the goods. The seller can demand and reclaim the goods at any time if the buyer misrepresented his or her solvency in writing within three months prior to the delivery of the goods [UCC 2–702(2)]. The seller's right to reclaim the goods, however, is subject to the rights of a good faith purchaser or other subsequent buyer in the ordinary course of business who purchases the goods from the buyer before the seller reclaims.

Under the UCC, a seller seeking to exercise the right to reclaim goods receives preferential treatment over the buyer's other creditors—the seller need only demand the return of the goods within ten days after the buyer has received them.[4] Because of this preferential treatment, the UCC provides that reclamation *bars* the seller from pursuing any other remedy as to these goods [UCC 2–702(3)].

In regard to lease contracts, if the lessee is in default (fails to make payments that are due, for example), the lessor may reclaim the leased goods that are in the possession of the lessee [UCC 2A–525(2)].

Remedies of the Buyer or Lessee

NOTE A seller or lessor breaches a contract by wrongfully failing to deliver the goods, delivering nonconforming goods, making an improper tender of the goods, or repudiating the contract.

Under the UCC, numerous remedies are available to the buyer or lessee when the seller or lessor breaches the contract. As with the remedies available to sellers and lessors, the remedies of buyers and lessees depend on the circumstances existing at the time of the breach.

WHEN THE SELLER OR LESSOR REFUSES TO DELIVER THE GOODS

If the seller or lessor refuses to deliver the goods or the buyer or lessee has rejected the goods, the remedies available to the buyer or lessee include those discussed here.

4. A seller who has delivered goods to an insolvent buyer also receives preferential treatment if the buyer enters into bankruptcy proceedings (discussed in Chapter 23).

The Right to Cancel the Contract When a seller or lessor fails to make proper delivery or repudiates the contract, the buyer or lessee can cancel, or rescind, the contract. On notice of cancellation, the buyer or lessee is relieved of any further obligations under the contract but retains all rights to other remedies against the seller [UCC 2–711(1), 2A–508(1)(a)].

The Right to Recover the Goods If a buyer or lessee has made a partial or full payment for goods that remain in the possession of the seller or lessor, the buyer or lessee can recover the goods if the seller or lessor is insolvent or becomes insolvent within ten days after receiving the first payment and if the goods are identified to the contract. To exercise this right, the buyer or lessee must tender to the seller any unpaid balance of the purchase price [UCC 2–502, 2A–522].

The Right to Obtain Specific Performance A buyer or lessee can obtain specific performance when the goods are unique and the remedy at law is inadequate [UCC 2–716(1), 2A–521(1)]. Ordinarily, a successful suit for money damages is sufficient to place a buyer or lessee in the position he or she would have occupied if the seller or lessor had fully performed. When the contract is for the purchase of a particular work of art or a similarly unique item, however, money damages may not be sufficient. Under these circumstances, equity will require that the seller or lessor perform exactly by delivering the particular goods identified to the contract (a remedy of specific performance).

COVER
Under the UCC, a remedy that allows the buyer or lessee, on the seller's or lessor's breach, to purchase the goods, in good faith and within a reasonable time, from another seller or lessor and substitute them for the goods due under the contract. If the cost of cover exceeds the cost of the contract goods, the breaching seller or lessor will be liable to the buyer or lessee for the difference, plus incidental and consequential damages.

The Right of Cover In certain situations, buyers and lessees can protect themselves by obtaining **cover**—that is, by purchasing other goods to substitute for those that were due under the sales contract. This option is available when the seller or lessor repudiates the contract or fails to deliver the goods, or when a buyer or lessee has rightfully rejected goods or revoked acceptance.

In obtaining cover, the buyer or lessee must act in good faith and without unreasonable delay [UCC 2–712, 2A–518]. After purchasing or leasing substitute goods, the buyer or lessee can recover from the seller or lessor the difference between the cost of cover and the contract price (or lease payments), plus incidental and consequential damages, less the expenses (such as delivery costs) that were saved as a result of the breach [UCC 2–712, 2–715, 2A–518]. Consequential damages are any losses suffered by the buyer or lessee that the seller or lessor could have foreseen (had reason to know about) at the time of contract formation and any injury to the buyer's or lessee's person or property proximately resulting from the contract's breach [UCC 2–715(2), 2A–520(2)].

Buyers and lessees are not required to cover, and failure to do so will not bar them from using any other remedies available under the UCC. A buyer or lessee who fails to cover, however, may *not* be able to collect consequential damages that could have been avoided had he or she purchased or leased substitute goods.

REPLEVIN
An action to recover identified goods in the hands of a party who is wrongfully withholding them from the other party. Under the UCC, this remedy is usually available only if the buyer or lessee is unable to cover.

The Right to Replevy Goods Buyers and lessees also have the right to replevy goods. **Replevin**[5] is an action to recover specific goods in the hands of a party who is wrongfully withholding them from the other party. Outside the UCC, the term *replevin* refers to a *prejudgment process* (a proceeding that takes place prior to a court's judgment) that permits the seizure of specific personal property in which a party claims a right or an interest. Under the UCC, the buyer or lessee can replevy goods subject to the contract if the seller or lessor has repudiated or breached the contract. To maintain an action to replevy goods, usually buyers and lessees must show that they are unable to cover for the goods after a reasonable effort [UCC 2–716(3), 2A–521(3)].

5. Pronounced ruh-*pleh*-vun.

RECALL Consequential damages compensate for a loss (such as lost profits) that is not direct but that is reasonably foreseeable at the time of the breach.

The Right to Recover Damages If a seller or lessor repudiates the sales contract or fails to deliver the goods, or the buyer or lessee has rightfully rejected or revoked acceptance of the goods, the buyer or lessee can sue for damages. The measure of recovery is the difference between the contract price (or lease payments) and the market price of (or lease payments that could be obtained for) the goods at the time the buyer (or lessee) *learned* of the breach. The market price or market lease payments are determined at the place where the seller or lessor was supposed to deliver the goods. The buyer or lessee can also recover incidental and consequential damages, less the expenses that were saved as a result of the breach [UCC 2–713, 2A–519].

● **EXAMPLE 16.11** Schilling orders ten thousand bushels of wheat from Valdone for \$5 a bushel, with delivery due on June 14 and payment due on June 20. Valdone does not deliver on June 14. On June 14, the market price of wheat is \$5.50 per bushel. Schilling chooses to do without the wheat. He sues Valdone for damages for nondelivery. Schilling can recover \$0.50 × 10,000, or \$5,000, plus any expenses the breach may have caused him. The measure of damages is the market price less the contract price on the day Schilling was to have received delivery. (Any expenses Schilling saved by the breach would be deducted from the damages.)●

WHEN THE SELLER OR LESSOR DELIVERS NONCONFORMING GOODS

When the seller or lessor delivers nonconforming goods, the buyer or lessee has several remedies available under the UCC.

The Right to Reject the Goods If either the goods or the tender of the goods by the seller or lessor fails to conform to the contract *in any respect,* the buyer or lessee can reject the goods. If some of the goods conform to the contract, the buyer or lessee can keep the conforming goods and reject the rest [UCC 2–601, 2A–509]. If the buyer or lessee rejects the goods, she or he may then obtain cover, cancel the contract, or sue for damages for breach of contract, just as if the seller or lessor had refused to deliver the goods (see the earlier discussion of these remedies).

Whether a buyer's actions constituted a rejection of the goods was at issue in the following case.

CASE 16.3 China National Metal Products Import/Export Co. v. Apex Digital, Inc.

United States District Court,
Central District of California, 2001.
141 F.Supp.2d 1013.

FACTS Apex Digital, Inc., imports consumer electronic goods and distributes them under the "Apex Digital" brand name to national retailers, such as Circuit City Stores, Inc., Best Buy Company, and Kmart Corporation. Apex is based in California. China National Metal Products Import/Export Company is a corporation based in Beijing, China. China National facilitates the import and export of goods between Chinese and foreign companies. Between July and December 2000, Apex imported more than 300,000 Digital Versatile Disk (DVD) players under several contracts with Chinese companies through China National. Soon after selling the first shipment of players in July and August, Apex began receiving customer complaints about the quality, and a flood of returned players began to fill Apex's warehouse. Apex continued to order the players through China National and sell them to retail outlet chains, but Apex refused to pay for them. The parties submitted their dispute to arbitration. Meanwhile, China National filed a suit in a California state court against Apex to obtain a writ of attachment (an order to seize Apex's property to secure payment for the DVD players). Apex claimed in part that it was not liable under the contracts because it had rejected the goods by withholding payment for them.

(continued)

CASE 16.3—Continued

ISSUE Did Apex's withholding of payment for the DVD players constitute rejection of the goods, as allowed under the UCC?

DECISION No. The court granted China National's request for a writ of attachment in an amount of more than $18 million.[a]

REASON The court acknowledged that if Apex had rejected the DVD players, "Apex would have been relieved of its duty to pay for the goods." The court noted that "[t]here can be little doubt in this case that China National failed to deliver conforming goods. Whether it was loader doors falling off or the failure to play DVD movies or the pause function self-activating, many of the DVD players delivered by China National were more useful as doorstops, or as one creative consumer noted, as boat anchors, than as players of multimedia disks and files. These defects provided Apex with the option to reject the contract or contracts affected by the nonconformities or to reject the particular units containing those defects." The court added, however, that buyers can accept nonconforming goods. "Indeed, if the buyer does nothing after receiving goods it learns are nonconforming, the law deems him to have accepted those goods. * * * Once the nonconforming goods are accepted, the buyer is under a duty to pay for them." In this case, "despite knowing of [the players'] defects Apex continued and, in fact, accelerated the number of DVD players it ordered from China National and then sold to its retail distributors."

a. This total represented the amount of the outstanding invoices under the contracts for the delivered DVD players, minus the contract value of the players that Apex returned.

FOR CRITICAL ANALYSIS—Social Consideration *Can a buyer successfully argue that, by continuing to order and sell goods pursuant to a contract, it was only trying to mitigate damages and that it refused to pay for the goods only when selling them proved unsuccessful?*

ON THE WEB The Boeing Company has posted online a summary of the contract rights and duties of parties forming sales contracts with that company. Go to **http://www.boeing.com/companyoffices/doingbiz/tcmdhs/sect7_97.htm#c.**

Timeliness and Reason for Rejection Required. The buyer or lessee must reject the goods within a reasonable amount of time, and the seller or lessor must be notified seasonably—that is, in a timely fashion or at the proper time [UCC 2–602(1), 2A–509(2)]. If the buyer or lessee fails to reject the goods within a reasonable amount of time, acceptance will be presumed. Furthermore, the buyer or lessee must designate defects that would have been apparent to the seller or lessor on reasonable inspection. Failure to do so precludes the buyer or lessee from using such defects to justify rejection or to establish breach when the seller could have cured the defects if they had been stated seasonably [UCC 2–605, 2A–514].

Duties of Merchant Buyers and Lessees When Goods Are Rejected. If a merchant buyer or lessee rightfully rejects goods, and the seller or lessor has no agent or business at the place of rejection, the buyer or lessee is required to follow any reasonable instructions received from the seller or lessor with respect to the goods controlled by the buyer or lessee. The buyer or lessee is entitled to reimbursement for the care and cost entailed in following the instructions [UCC 2–603, 2A–511]. The same requirements hold if the buyer or lessee rightfully revokes his or her acceptance of the goods at some later time [UCC 2–608(3), 2A–517(5)]. (Revocation of acceptance will be discussed shortly.)

If no instructions are forthcoming and the goods are perishable or threaten to decline in value quickly, the buyer can resell the goods in good faith, taking the appropriate reimbursement from the proceeds. In addition, the buyer is entitled to a selling commission (not to exceed 10 percent of the gross proceeds) [UCC 2–603(1), (2); 2A–511(1)]. If the goods are not perishable, the buyer or lessee may store them for the seller or lessor or reship them to the seller or lessor [UCC 2–604, 2A–512].

Buyers who rightfully reject goods that remain in their possession or control have a *security interest* in the goods (basically, a legal claim to the goods to the extent necessary to recover expenses, costs, and the like—see Chapter 22). The security interest encompasses any payments the buyer has made for the goods, as well as any expenses incurred with regard to inspection, receipt, transportation, care, and custody of the goods [UCC 2–711(3)]. A buyer with a security interest in the goods is a "person in the position of a seller." This gives the buyer the same rights as an unpaid seller. Thus, the buyer can resell, withhold delivery of, or stop delivery of the goods. A buyer who chooses to resell must account to the seller for any amounts received in excess of the security interest [UCC 2–706(6), 2–711].

ETHICAL ISSUE 16.1

What if a seller believes that the buyer has wrongfully rejected contract goods?

What happens if the seller suspects that the buyer is wrongfully rejecting contract goods? Does the seller have any recourse? This question becomes important when a seller never sees the goods because they are shipped directly from a third party to the buyer. For example, in one case J. R. Cousin Industries, Inc., a hardware importer, arranged to have sinks and other items shipped from a manufacturer in Mexico directly to Menard, Inc., a seller of home-improvement products. The contract between Cousin and Menard allowed Menard to destroy (and not pay for) any units that were either defective or returned by customers. When the purchaser returns claimed by Menard seemed unusually high, Cousin informed Menard that it wanted to inspect the returned goods before they were destroyed. Menard refused to cooperate, and Cousin sued Menard for $72,000—the amount Menard had deducted from its payment to Cousins for returned (rejected) goods.

Normally, the right of inspection is a concern of the buyer, but does a seller also have such a right? A federal appellate court said yes. The court pointed to UCC 2–515(a), which allows either party to a contract, on reasonable notification to the other "and for the purpose of ascertaining the facts and preserving evidence," to inspect the goods in the possession of the other party. The court concluded that Cousin had a right to inspect the goods and was entitled to be paid for all returned units destroyed by Menard after Menard refused to allow Cousin to inspect the returned items.[6]

Revocation of Acceptance Acceptance of the goods precludes the buyer or lessee from exercising the right of rejection, but it does not necessarily preclude the buyer or lessee from pursuing other remedies. In certain circumstances, a buyer or lessee is permitted to *revoke* his or her acceptance of the goods. Acceptance of a lot or a commercial unit can be revoked if the nonconformity *substantially* impairs the value of the lot or unit and if one of the following factors is present:

① If acceptance was predicated on the reasonable assumption that the nonconformity would be cured, and it has not been cured within a reasonable period of time [UCC 2–608(1)(a), 2A–517(1)(a)].

② If the buyer or lessee did not discover the nonconformity before acceptance, either because it was difficult to discover before acceptance or because assurances made

6. *J. R. Cousin Industries, Inc. v. Menard, Inc.*, 127 F.3d 580 (7th Cir. 1997).

by the seller or lessor that the goods were conforming kept the buyer or lessee from inspecting the goods [UCC 2–608(1)(b), 2A–517(1)(b)].

Revocation of acceptance is not effective until notice is given to the seller or lessor, which must occur within a reasonable time after the buyer or lessee either discovers or *should have discovered* the grounds for revocation. Additionally, revocation must occur before the goods have undergone any substantial change (such as spoilage) not caused by their own defects [UCC 2–608(2), 2A–517(4)].

INTERNATIONAL PERSPECTIVE

The CISG's Approach to Revocation of Acceptance

Under the UCC, a buyer or lessee who has accepted goods may be able to revoke acceptance under the circumstances just mentioned. Provisions of the United Nations Convention on Contracts for the International Sale of Goods (CISG) similarly allow buyers to rescind their contracts after they have accepted the goods. The CISG, however, takes a somewhat different—and more direct—approach to the problem than the UCC does. Circumstances that would permit a buyer to revoke acceptance under the UCC would, under the CISG, allow the buyer simply to declare that the seller has *fundamentally* breached the contract, thus allowing the buyer to sue the seller for breach of contract. Article 25 of the CISG states that a "breach of contract committed by one of the parties is fundamental if it results in such detriment to the other party as substantially to deprive him of what he is entitled to expect under the contract."

FOR CRITICAL ANALYSIS
What is the essential difference between revoking acceptance and bringing a suit for breach of contract?

The Right to Recover Damages for Accepted Goods A buyer or lessee who has accepted nonconforming goods may also keep the goods and recover damages caused by the breach. The buyer or lessee, however, must notify the seller or lessor of the breach within a reasonable time after the defect was or should have been discovered. Failure to give notice of the defects (breach) to the seller or lessor bars the buyer or lessee from pursuing any remedy [UCC 2–607(3), 2A–516(3)]. In addition, the parties to a sales or lease contract can insert a provision requiring that the buyer or lessee give notice of any defects in the goods within a prescribed period.

When the goods delivered and accepted are not as promised, the measure of damages equals the difference between the value of the goods as accepted and their value if they had been delivered as promised [UCC 2–714(2), 2A–519(4)]. For this and other types of breaches in which the buyer or lessee has accepted the goods, the buyer or lessee is entitled to recover for any loss "resulting in the ordinary course of events . . . as determined in any manner which is reasonable" [UCC 2–714(1), 2A–519(3)]. The UCC also permits the buyer or lessee, with proper notice to the seller or lessor, to deduct all or any part of the damages from the price or lease payments still due and payable to the seller or lessor [UCC 2–717, 2A–516(1)].

Who qualifies as a "buyer" under these provisions? Is a party who does not actually purchase a product but who is injured by its alleged defects required to give notice of those defects within a reasonable time in order to recover for those injuries? This was an important question in the following case.

CASE 16.4 Yates v. Pitman Manufacturing, Inc.

Supreme Court of Virginia, 1999.
257 Va. 601,
514 S.E.2d 605.
http://www.courts.state.va.us/opin.html[a]

FACTS In 1982, Pitman Manufacturing, Inc., made and sold a construction crane to Shelton Witt Equipment, a distributor. At the time, Pitman certified that the outrigger on the crane could be seen from its "actuating location"—that is, it could be seen by anyone activating the outrigger. In 1991, Koch Carbon owned the crane and was using it to deliver equipment to Baldwin Coal Corporation. Ira Stiltner, a Koch employee, activated the outrigger from the front of the truck. At the time, he could not see the outrigger or Eddie Yates, a Baldwin employee, who was simultaneously releasing restraining chains from the crane truck's bed. Without warning, the outrigger dropped onto Yates's foot. Yates filed a suit in a Virginia state court against Pitman, seeking $3 million in damages for his injuries on the basis of breach of warranty (see Chapter 18). One of the issues was whether Yates had provided reasonable notice, under UCC 2–607(3), to Pitman of its breach of warranty. Yates argued in part that he did not have to give the notice because he was not the purchaser of the crane. The court entered a judgment in Pitman's favor. Yates appealed to the Virginia Supreme Court.

ISSUE Was Yates required to give notice under UCC 2–607(3) to recover for his injuries?

DECISION No. The Virginia Supreme Court reversed the judgment of the lower court and remanded the case for further proceedings consistent with this decision.

REASON The state supreme court held that "only buyers * * * must give notice of breach of warranty to the seller as a prerequisite to recovery" under UCC 2–607(3). Thus, Yates, because he was not a "buyer," did not have to give the notice to recover for his injuries. The court explained, "It is firmly established that, when a statute is clear and unambiguous, a court must accept its plain meaning and not resort to extrinsic evidence or rules of construction." The statute in this case "is unambiguous and clearly states that 'the buyer must * * * notify the seller of [the] breach.' Thus, accepting the statute's plain meaning, it is apparent that the notice of breach is required from the 'buyer' of the goods. In the present case, Yates was not the buyer of the crane unit."

FOR CRITICAL ANALYSIS—Social Consideration *Suppose that the court had held that Yates was required to give notice to recover for his injuries. Would such a ruling have left Yates entirely without legal recourse? Explain.*

a. In the "Supreme Court of Virginia" section, click on the version in which you want to read this opinion. To view the opinion in text format, click on "Opinions in Text Format." On that page, scroll down the list of cases to the *Yates* case and click on the docket number ("981474") to access the opinion.

Limitation of Remedies

ON THE WEB For an example of a warranty providing for an exclusive remedy, see the "Warranty and Limited Remedy" of 3M Company, which is online at **http://www.mmm.com/promote/warranty.htm.**

The parties to a sales or lease contract can vary their respective rights and obligations by contractual agreement. For example, a seller and buyer can expressly provide for remedies in addition to those provided in the UCC. They can also provide remedies in lieu of those provided in the UCC, or they can change the measure of damages. The seller can provide that the buyer's only remedy on breach of warranty will be repair or replacement of the item, or the seller can limit the buyer's remedy to return of the goods and refund of the purchase price. In sales and lease contracts, an agreed-on remedy is in addition to those provided in the UCC unless the parties expressly agree that the remedy is exclusive of all others [UCC 2–719(1), 2A–503(1)].

If the parties state that a remedy is exclusive, then it is the sole remedy. When circumstances cause an exclusive remedy to fail in its essential purpose, however, it is no longer exclusive [UCC 2–719(2), 2A–503(2)]. For example, a sales contract that limits the buyer's remedy to repair or replacement fails in its essential purpose if the item cannot be repaired and no replacements are available.

A contract can limit or exclude consequential damages, provided the limitation is not unconscionable. When the buyer or lessee is a consumer, the limitation of consequential damages for personal injuries resulting from nonconforming goods is *prima facie* (on its face) unconscionable. The limitation of consequential damages is not necessarily unconscionable, however, when the loss is commercial in nature—for example, if the loss consists of lost profits and property damage [UCC 2–719(3), 2A–503(3)].

ETHICAL ISSUE 16.2

When an exclusive remedy fails in its essential purpose, should the buyer be entitled to sue for damages?

The UCC makes it clear that a contract clause providing for an exclusive remedy is enforceable—*unless* the exclusive remedy fails in its essential purpose. If the exclusive remedy fails in its essential purpose, then the buyer can pursue the full panoply of remedies available to the buyer under the UCC. One of the remedies available to the buyer is to sue for damages, including consequential damages. Yet what if the contract, in addition to providing for an exclusive remedy, also excluded or limited damages? In this situation, does the failure of the exclusive remedy effectively eliminate the limitation-of-damages clause?

The courts have reached different conclusions on this issue, as noted by a federal district court in a case involving just this question. In the court's eyes, however, it was clear that when an exclusive remedy fails, a buyer should be able to pursue all of the remedies available under the UCC, including a suit for consequential damages. The court held that to rule otherwise "ignores a fact the drafters of the UCC certainly contemplated: that exclusive remedy clauses often (if not only) arise in situations where there is also a disclaimer of damages, because without a disclaimer of damages, a remedy is not exclusive."[7]

Statute of Limitations

An action for breach of contract under the UCC must be commenced *within four years after the cause of action accrues*—that is, within four years after the breach occurs. In addition to filing suit within the four-year period, an aggrieved party who has accepted nonconforming goods usually must notify the breaching party of the breach within a reasonable time, or the buyer or lessee is barred from pursuing any remedy [UCC 2–607(3)(a), 2A–516(3)]. By agreement in the contract, the parties can reduce this period to not less than one year but cannot extend it beyond four years [UCC 2–725(1), 2A–506(1)]. A cause of action accrues for breach of warranty when the seller or lessor tenders delivery. This is the rule even if the aggrieved party is unaware that the cause of action has accrued [UCC 2–725(2), 2A–506(2)].

7. *Clandill Seed & Warehouse Co. v. Prophet 21, Inc.*, 123 F.Supp.2d 826 (E.D.Pa. 2000).

APPLICATION Law and the Seller or Buyer . . .

Breach of Contract*

A contract for the sale of goods has been breached. Can such a breach be settled without a trip to court? The answer depends on the willingness of the parties to agree on an appropriate remedy.

Contractual Clauses on Applicable Remedies

Often, the parties to sales and lease contracts agree in advance, in their contracts, on what remedies will be applicable in the event of a breach. This may take the form of a contract provision restricting or expanding remedies available under the Uniform Commercial Code [UCC 2–719]. Such clauses help to reduce uncertainty and the necessity for costly litigation.

When the Contract Is Silent on Applicable Remedies

If there is nothing in your agreement to cover a breach of contract and you are the nonbreaching party, the UCC gives you a variety of alternatives. What you need to do is analyze the remedies that would be available if you were to go to court, put these remedies in order of priority, and then predict how successful you might be in pursuing each remedy. Next, look at the position of the breaching party to determine the basis for negotiating a settlement.

*This *Application* is not meant to substitute for the services of an attorney who is licensed to practice law in your state.

For example, when defective goods are delivered and accepted, usually it is preferable for the buyer and seller to reach an agreement on a reduced purchase price. Practically speaking, the buyer may be unable to obtain a partial refund from the seller. UCC 2–717 allows the buyer in such circumstances to give notice of the intention to deduct the damages from any part of the purchase price not yet paid. If you are a buyer who has accepted defective goods and has not yet paid in full, it may be appropriate for you to exercise your rights under UCC 2–717 and not pay in full when you make your final payment. Remember that most breaches of contract do not end up in court—they are settled beforehand.

Checklist for the Nonbreaching Party to a Contract

1. Ascertain if a remedy is explicitly written into your contract. Use that remedy, if possible, to avoid litigation.
2. If no specific remedy is available, look to the UCC.
3. Assess how successful you might be in pursuing a remedy if you went to court.
4. Analyze the position of the breaching party.
5. Determine whether a negotiated settlement is preferable to a lawsuit, which is best done by consulting your attorney.

Key Terms

cover 420
incidental damages 417
installment contract 410
replevin 420

Chapter Summary Performance and Breach of Sales and Lease Contracts

REQUIREMENTS OF PERFORMANCE	
Obligations of the Seller or Lessor (See pages 407–413.)	1. The seller or lessor must tender *conforming* goods to the buyer. Tender must take place at a *reasonable hour* and in a *reasonable manner.* Under the perfect tender doctrine, the seller or lessor must tender goods that conform exactly to the terms of the contract [UCC 2–503(1), 2A–508(1)]. 2. If the seller or lessor tenders nonconforming goods prior to the performance date and the buyer or lessee rejects them, the seller or lessor may *cure* (repair or replace the goods) within the contract time for performance [UCC 2–508(1), 2A–513(1)]. If the seller or lessor has reasonable grounds to believe the buyer or lessee would accept the tendered goods, on the buyer's or lessee's rejection the seller or lessor has a reasonable time to substitute conforming goods without liability [UCC 2–508(2), 2A–513(2)]. 3. If the agreed-on means of delivery becomes impracticable or unavailable, the seller must substitute an alternative means (such as a different carrier) if one is available [UCC 2–614(1)]. 4. If a seller or lessor tenders nonconforming goods in any one installment under an installment contract, the buyer or lessee may reject the installment only if its value is substantially impaired and cannot be cured. The entire installment contract is breached when one or more nonconforming installments *substantially* impair the value of the *whole* contract [UCC 2–612, 2A–510]. 5. When performance becomes commercially impracticable owing to circumstances unforeseen when the contract was formed, the perfect tender rule no longer holds [UCC 2–615, 2A–405].
Obligations of the Buyer or Lessee (See pages 413–415.)	1. On tender of delivery by the seller or lessor, the buyer or lessee must pay for the goods at the time and place the buyer or lessee *receives* the goods, even if the place of shipment is the place of delivery, unless the sale is made on credit. Payment may be made by any method generally acceptable in the commercial world unless the seller demands cash [UCC 2–310, 2–511]. In lease contracts, the lessee must make lease payments in accordance with the contract [UCC 2A–516(1)]. 2. Unless otherwise agreed, the buyer or lessee has an absolute right to inspect the goods before acceptance [UCC 2–513(1), 2A–515(1)]. 3. The buyer or lessee can manifest acceptance of delivered goods expressly in words or by conduct or by failing to reject the goods after a reasonable period of time following inspection or after having had a reasonable opportunity to inspect them [UCC 2–606(1), 2A–515(1)]. A buyer will be deemed to have accepted goods if he or she performs any act inconsistent with the seller's ownership [UCC 2–606(1)(c)]. 4. Following the acceptance of delivered goods, the buyer or lessee may revoke acceptance only if the nonconformity *substantially* impairs the value of the unit or lot and if one of the following factors is present: a. Acceptance was predicated on the reasonable assumption that the nonconformity would be cured and it was not cured within a reasonable time [UCC 2–608(1)(a), 2A–517(1)(a)]. b. The buyer or lessee did not discover the nonconformity before acceptance, either because it was difficult to discover before acceptance or because the seller's or lessor's assurance that the goods were conforming kept the buyer or lessee from inspecting the goods [UCC 2–608(1)(b), 2A–517(1)(b)].

Chapter Summary Performance and Breach of Sales and Lease Contracts—continued

Anticipatory Repudiation (See page 415.)	If, before the time for performance, either party clearly indicates to the other an intention not to perform, under UCC 2–610 and 2A–402 the aggrieved party may do the following: 1. Await performance by the repudiating party for a commercially reasonable time. 2. Resort to any remedy for breach. 3. In either situation, suspend performance.
REMEDIES FOR BREACH OF CONTRACT	
Remedies of the Seller or Lessor (See pages 416–419.)	1. *When the goods are in the possession of the seller or lessor*—The seller or lessor may do the following: a. Cancel the contract [UCC 2–703(f), 2A–523(1)(a)]. b. Withhold delivery [UCC 2–703(a), 2A–523(1)(c)]. c. Resell or dispose of the goods [UCC 2–703(d), 2–706(1), 2A–523(1)(e), 2A–527(1)]. d. Sue to recover the purchase price or lease payments due [UCC 2–703(e), 2–709(1), 2A–529(1)]. e. Sue to recover damages [UCC 2–703(e), 2–708, 2A–528]. 2. *When the goods are in transit*—The seller may stop the carrier or bailee from delivering the goods [UCC 2–705, 2A–526]. 3. *When the goods are in the possession of the buyer or lessee*—The seller may do the following: a. Sue to recover the purchase price or lease payments due [UCC 2–709(1), 2A–529(1)]. b. Reclaim the goods. A seller may reclaim goods received by an insolvent buyer if the demand is made within ten days of receipt (reclaiming goods excludes all other remedies) [UCC 2–702]; a lessor may repossess goods if the lessee is in default [UCC 2A–525(2)].
Remedies of the Buyer or Lessee (See pages 419–424.)	1. *When the seller or lessor refuses to deliver the goods*—The buyer or lessee may do the following: a. Cancel the contract [UCC 2–711(1), 2A–508(1)(a)]. b. Recover the goods if the seller or lessor becomes insolvent within ten days after receiving the first payment and the goods are identified to the contract [UCC 2–502, 2A–522]. c. Obtain specific performance (when the goods are unique and when the remedy at law is inadequate) [UCC 2–716(1), 2A–521(1)]. d. Obtain cover [UCC 2–712, 2A–518]. e. Replevy the goods (if cover is unavailable) [UCC 2–716(3), 2A–521(3)]. f. Sue to recover damages [UCC 2–713, 2A–519]. 2. *When the seller or lessor delivers or tenders delivery of nonconforming goods*—The buyer or lessee may do the following: a. Reject the goods [UCC 2–601, 2A–509]. b. Revoke acceptance (in certain circumstances) [UCC 2–608, 2A–517]. c. Accept the goods and recover damages [UCC 2–607, 2–714, 2–717, 2A–519].

(continued)

Chapter Summary	Performance and Breach of Sales and Lease Contracts—continued
Limitation of Remedies (See pages 425–426.)	Remedies may be limited in sales or lease contracts by agreement of the parties. If the contract states that a remedy is exclusive, then that is the sole remedy—unless the remedy fails in its essential purpose. Sellers and lessors can also limit the rights of buyers and lessees to consequential damages—unless the limitation is unconscionable [UCC 2–719, 2A–503].
Statute of Limitations (See page 426.)	The UCC has a four-year statute of limitations for actions involving breach of contract. By agreement, the parties to a sales or lease contract can reduce this period to not less than one year, but they cannot extend it beyond four years [UCC 2–725(1), 2A–506(1)].

For Review

① What are the respective obligations of the parties under a contract for the sale or lease of goods?

② What is the perfect tender rule? What are some important exceptions to this rule that apply to sales and lease contracts?

③ What options are available to the nonbreaching party when the other party to a sales or lease contract repudiates the contract prior to the time for performance?

④ What remedies are available to a seller or lessor when the buyer or lessee breaches the contract? What remedies are available to a buyer or lessee if the seller or lessor breaches the contract?

⑤ In contracts subject to the UCC, are parties free to limit the remedies available to the nonbreaching party on a breach of contract? If so, in what ways?

Questions and Case Problems

16–1. Revocation of Acceptance. What events or circumstances must occur before a buyer can rightfully revoke his or her acceptance of a sales contract?

16–2. Remedies. Genix, Inc., has contracted to sell Larson five hundred washing machines of a certain model at list price. Genix is to ship the goods on or before December 1. Genix produces one thousand washing machines of this model but has not yet prepared Larson's shipment. On November 1, Larson repudiates the contract. Discuss the remedies available to Genix in this situation.

16–3. Right of Inspection. Cummings ordered two Model-X Super Fidelity speakers from Jamestown Wholesale Electronics, Inc. Jamestown shipped the speakers via United Parcel Service, C.O.D. (collect on delivery), although Cummings had not requested or agreed to a C.O.D. shipment of the goods. When the speakers were delivered, Cummings refused to accept them because he would not be able to inspect them before payment. Jamestown claimed that it had shipped conforming goods and that Cummings had breached their contract. Had Cummings breached the contract? Explain.

16–4. Anticipatory Repudiation. Moore contracted in writing to sell her 1996 Ford Taurus to Hammer for $8,500. Moore agreed to deliver the car on Wednesday, and Hammer promised to pay the $8,500 on the following Friday. On Tuesday, Hammer informed Moore that he would not be buying the car after all. By Friday, Hammer had changed his mind again and tendered $8,500 to Moore. Moore, although she had not sold the car to another party, refused the tender and refused to deliver. Hammer claimed that Moore had breached their contract. Moore contended that Hammer's repudiation released her from her duty to perform under the contract. Who is correct, and why?

16–5. Remedies. Rodriguez is an antique car collector. He contracts to purchase spare parts for a 1938 engine from Gerrard. These parts are not made anymore and are scarce. To get the contract with Gerrard, Rodriguez has to pay 50 percent of the purchase price in advance. On May 1, Rodriguez sends the required payment, which is received on May 2. On May 3, Gerrard, having found another buyer willing to pay substantially more for the parts, informs Rodriguez that he will not deliver as contracted. That same day, Rodriguez learns that Gerrard is insolvent. Gerrard has the parts, and Rodriguez wants them. Discuss fully any remedies available to Rodriguez.

16–6. Nonconforming Goods. Moore & Moore General Contractors, Inc., contracted to build a Red Lobster restaurant. Basepoint, Inc., agreed to supply and install plywood cabinets for the bar, the food service area, the office, and the rest rooms. Instead of plywood, Basepoint supplied cabinets made of particle board. Moore's on-site supervisors accepted the nonconforming cabinets and had them installed, believing that the restaurant owner would not know the difference. The owner did know the difference, however, and insisted that the cabinets be replaced. Moore replaced the cabinets and refused to pay Basepoint. Basepoint filed a suit in a Virginia state court against Moore to recover its price. Moore counterclaimed for the replacement expense, contending that it had a right to return the nonconforming cabinets. Who should pay whom, and why? [*Moore & Moore General Contractors, Inc. v. Basepoint, Inc.*, 253 Va. 304, 485 S.E.2d 131 (1997)]

16–7. Commercial Impracticability. E+E (US), Inc., Manley-Regan Chemicals Division, agreed to sell to Rockland Industries, Inc., three containers of antimony oxide for $1.80 per pound. At the time, both parties knew that there was a global shortage of the chemical, that prices were rising, and that Manley-Regan would obtain its supply from GFI Chemicals, Inc. When GFI could not deliver, Manley-Regan told Rockland that it could not fulfill the contract. Rockland bought an equivalent amount of the chemical elsewhere at an increased price and filed a suit in a federal district court against Manley-Regan to recover the difference between the cost of the cover and the contract price. Manley-Regan argued that the failure of GFI, its sole source for the oxide, excused its failure to perform on the ground of commercial impracticability. Will the court agree? Why or why not? [*Rockland Industries, Inc. v. E+E (US), Inc., Manley-Regan Chemicals Division*, 991 F.Supp. 468 (D.Md. 1998)]

16–8. Acceptance. OSHI Global Co. designs and sells novelty items, including a small children's plastic toy referred to as the "Number 89 Frog," a realistic replica of a frog that squeaks when it is squeezed. At a trade show in Chicago, Michael Osaraprasop, the owner of OSHI, sold a quantity of the frogs to Jay Gilbert, the president of S.A.M. Electronics, Inc. Gilbert asked Osaraprasop to design, make, and sell to S.A.M. a larger version of the frog with a motion sensor that would activate a "ribbit" sound. Osaraprasop agreed. OSHI delivered fourteen containers of the frogs, a number of which S.A.M. resold to its customers. When some of the buyers complained that the frogs were defective, S.A.M. had them repaired. S.A.M. refused to pay OSHI for any of the frogs and wrote a letter claiming to revoke acceptance of them. S.A.M. filed a suit in a federal district court against OSHI and others, alleging in part breach of contract; OSHI responded with a similar claim against S.A.M. OSHI argued that by reselling some of the frogs from the fourteen containers, S.A.M. had accepted all of them and must pay. In whose favor will the court rule? Discuss fully. [*S.A.M. Electronics, Inc. v. Osaraprasop*, 39 F.Supp.2d 1074 (N.D.Ill. 1999)]

16–9. Limitation of Remedies. Destileria Serralles, Inc., a distributor of rum and other products, operates a rum bottling plant in Puerto Rico. Figgie International, Inc., contracted with Serralles to provide bottle-labeling equipment capable of placing a clear label on a clear bottle of "Cristal" rum within a raised glass oval. The contract stated that Serralles's remedy, in case of a breach of contract, was limited to repair, replacement, or refund. When the equipment was installed in the Serralles plant, problems arose immediately. Figgie attempted to repair the equipment, but when it still did not work properly several months later, Figgie refunded the purchase price and Serralles returned the equipment. Serralles asked Figgie to pay for Serralles's losses caused by the failure of the equipment and by the delay in obtaining alternative machinery. Figgie filed a suit in a federal district court, asserting that it owed nothing to Serralles because the remedy for breach was limited to repair, replacement, or refund. Serralles responded that the limitation had failed in its essential purpose. In whose favor will the court resolve this dispute? Why? [*Figgie International, Inc. v. Destileria Serralles, Inc.*, 190 F.3d 252 (4th Cir. 1999)]

TEST YOUR KNOWLEDGE—ANSWER ON THE WEB

16–10. Metro-North Commuter Railroad Co. decided to install a fall-protection system for elevated walkways, roof areas, and interior catwalks in Grand Central Terminal, in New York City. The system was needed to ensure the safety of Metro-North employees when they worked at great heights on the interior and exterior of the terminal. Sinco, Inc., proposed a system called "Sayfglida," which involved a harness worn by the worker, a network of cables, and metal clips or sleeves called "Sayflinks" that connected the harness to the cables. Metro-North agreed to pay $197,325 for the installation of this system by June 26, 1999. Because the system's reliability was crucial, the contract required certain quality control processes. During a training session for Metro-North employees on June 29, the Sayflink sleeves fell apart. Within two days, Sinco manufactured and delivered two different types of replacement clips without subjecting them to the contract's quality control process, but Metro-North rejected them. Sinco suggested other possible solutions, which Metro-North did not accept. In September, Metro-North terminated its contract with Sinco and awarded the work to Surety, Inc., at a price of about $348,000. Sinco filed a suit in a federal district court, alleging breach of contract. Metro-North counterclaimed for its cost of cover. In whose favor should the court rule, and why? [*Sinco, Inc. v. Metro-North Commuter Railroad Co.*, 133 F.Supp.2d 308 (S.D.N.Y. 2001)]

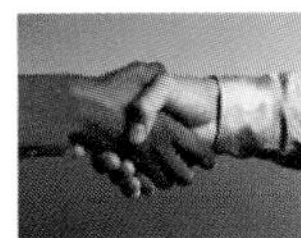

A QUESTION OF ETHICS AND SOCIAL RESPONSIBILITY

16–11. Bobby Murray Chevrolet, Inc., contracted to supply 1,200 school bus chassis to local school boards. The contract stated that "products of any manufacturer may be offered," but Bobby Murray submitted its orders exclusively to General Motors Corp. (GMC). When a shortage in automatic transmissions occurred, GMC informed the dealer that it could not fill the orders. Bobby Murray told the school boards, which then bought the chassis from another dealer. The boards sued Bobby Murray for breach of contract. The dealer responded that its obligation to perform was excused under the doctrine of commercial impracticability, in part because of GMC's failure to fill its orders. Given these facts, answer the following questions. [*Alamance County Board of Education v. Bobby Murray Chevrolet, Inc.*, 121 N.C.App. 222, 465 S.E.2d 306 (1996)]

1. How will the court likely decide this issue? What factors will the court consider in making its decision? Discuss fully.
2. If the decision were yours to make, would you excuse Bobby Murray from its performance obligations in these circumstances? Would your decision be any different if Bobby Murray had specified in its contract that GMC would be the exclusive source of supply instead of stating that "products of any manufacturer may be offered"?
3. Generally, how does the doctrine of commercial impracticability attempt to balance the rights of both parties to a contract?

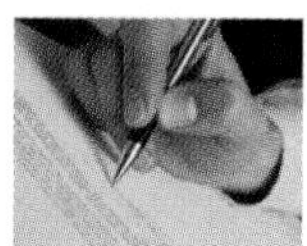

FOR CRITICAL ANALYSIS

16–12. Under what circumstances should courts not allow fully informed contracting parties to agree to limit remedies?

Internet Exercises

Go to the *Business Law Today* home page at **http://blt.westbuslaw.com**. Select "Interactive Study Center" and then click on "Chapter 16." There you will find the following Internet research exercise that you can perform to learn more about performance requirements in international sales transactions:

Activity 16–1: International Performance Requirements

Before the Test

Go to the *Business Law Today* home page at **http://blt.westbuslaw.com**. Click on "Interactive Quizzes." You will find at least twenty interactive questions relating to this chapter.

CHAPTER 17

E-Contracts

"The law of toasters, televisions, and chain saws is not appropriate for contracts involving online databases, artificial intelligence systems, software, multimedia, and Internet trade in information."

Prefatory Note, Uniform Computer Information Transactions Act

CHAPTER CONTENTS

LEARNING OBJECTIVES

After reading this chapter, you should be able to answer the following questions:

① What are some important clauses that offerors should include when making offers to form electronic contracts, or e-contracts?

② What are shrink-wrap agreements? What traditional laws have been applied to such agreements? Do click-on acceptances in electronic contracts present problems that are not covered by traditional laws governing contracts, including the Uniform Commercial Code (UCC)? Explain.

③ What is an electronic signature? Are electronic signatures valid?

④ What problems does the Uniform Computer Information Transactions Act (UCITA) address that were not addressed by the UCC?

⑤ What is the Uniform Electronic Transactions Act (UETA)? What are some similarities and differences between this act and the UCITA?

Many observers argue that the development of cyberspace is revolutionary. Therefore, new legal theories, and new laws, are needed to govern **e-contracts**, or contracts entered into electronically. To date, however, most courts have adapted traditional contract law principles and, when applicable, provisions of the Uniform Commercial Code (UCC) to cases involving e-contract disputes.

E-CONTRACT
A contract that is formed electronically.

In the first part of this chapter, we look at how traditional laws are being applied to contracts formed online. We then examine some new laws that have been created to apply in situations in which traditional laws governing contracts have sometimes been thought inadequate. For example, traditional laws governing signature and writing requirements are not easily adapted to contracts formed in the online environment. Thus, new laws have been created to address these issues. As the chapter-opening quotation indicates, in some ways the law of "toasters, televisions, and chain saws" is simply no longer appropriate to the commercial practices and needs of today.

Forming Contracts Online

B2C TRANSACTION
A business-to-consumer transaction conducted via the Internet; an online sale or lease of goods or services from a business party to a consumer.

B2B TRANSACTION
A business-to-business transaction conducted via the Internet; an online sale or lease of goods or services from one business party to another.

Today, numerous contracts are being formed online. Many of these contracts involve business-to-consumer sales, or **B2C transactions.** Consumers purchase books, CDs, software, airline tickets, clothing, computers, and a host of other goods via the Internet. An increasing number of transactions involve business-to-business sales, or **B2B transactions.** Although the medium through which these sales contracts are generated has changed, the age-old problems attending contract formation have not. Disputes concerning contracts formed online continue to center around contract terms and whether the parties voluntarily assented to those terms.

Online Offers

Sellers doing business via the Internet can protect themselves against contract disputes and legal liability by creating offers that clearly spell out the terms that will govern their transactions if the offers are accepted. All important terms should be conspicuous and easily viewed by potential buyers.

An important rule for a seller to keep in mind is that the offeror controls the offer, and thus the resulting contract. Thus, the seller should anticipate the terms he or she wants to include in a contract and provide for them in the offer. In some instances, a standardized contract form may suffice—the *Application* at the end of this chapter offers suggestions on how to find and use online contract forms.

At a minimum, the following provisions should be included in an online offer:

- A provision specifying the remedies available to the buyer if the goods turn out to be defective or if the contract is otherwise breached, or broken. Any limitation of remedies should be clearly spelled out.
- The statute of limitations governing the transaction (that is, the time period within which a legal action can be brought over a dispute concerning the contract).
- A clause that clearly indicates what constitutes the buyer's agreement to the terms of the offer.
- A provision specifying how payment for the goods and of any applicable taxes must be made.
- A statement of the seller's refund and return policies.
- Disclaimers of liability for certain uses of the goods. For example, an online seller of business forms may add a disclaimer that the seller does not accept responsibility for the buyer's reliance on the forms rather than on an attorney's advice.
- How the information gathered about the buyer will be used by the seller. (See the discussion of privacy rights in Chapter 2 for more information on this topic.)

Dispute-Settlement Provisions In addition to the above provisions, many online offers include provisions relating to dispute settlement. For example, an arbitration clause might be included, specifying that any dispute arising under the contract will be arbitrated in a specified forum.

Many online contracts also contain a forum-selection clause (indicating the forum, or location, for the resolution of any dispute arising under the contract). As discussed in Chapter 3, significant jurisdictional issues may occur when parties are at a great distance, as they often are when they form contracts via the Internet. A forum-selection clause will help to avert future jurisdictional problems and also help to ensure that the seller will not be required to appear in court in a distant state.

FOR CRITICAL ANALYSIS

What might result if, because the United States is a signatory to the Hague Convention, U.S. courts are required to enforce foreign judgments that are contrary to U.S. constitutional law?

INTERNATIONAL PERSPECTIVE

Resolving International Jurisdictional Problems

Given the global nature of e-commerce, jurisdictional problems understandably arise. To address these problems, more than fifty nations, including the United States, have been negotiating an agreement referred to as the Hague Convention on International Jurisdiction and Foreign Judgments in Civil and Commercial Matters. The agreement is intended to create uniform rules governing jurisdiction and enforcement of judgments in cross-border disputes.

A draft of the agreement approved in June 2001 would make more predictable the rules governing jurisdiction in disputes between parties located in different countries. Among other things, nations that are signatory to the convention would be required to recognize judgments rendered in the courts of other countries that had signed the agreement. Special rules would apply to disputes involving consumers. The final draft was expected to be completed in 2002.

Displaying the Offer The seller's Web site should include a hypertext link to a page containing the full contract so that potential buyers are made aware of the terms to which they are assenting. The contract generally must be displayed online in a readable format such as a twelve-point typeface. All provisions should be reasonably clear. • **EXAMPLE 17.1** If a seller is offering certain goods priced according to a complex price schedule, that schedule must be fully provided and explained. •

CLICK-ON AGREEMENT
An agreement that arises when a buyer, engaging in a transaction on a computer, indicates his or her assent to be bound by the terms of an offer by clicking on a button that says, for example, "I agree"; sometimes referred to as a *click-on license* or a *click-wrap agreement.*

SHRINK-WRAP AGREEMENT
An agreement whose terms are expressed in a document located inside a box in which goods (usually software) are packaged; sometimes called a *shrink-wrap license.*

Indicating How the Offer Can Be Accepted An online offer should also include some mechanism by which the customer may accept the offer. Typically, online sellers include boxes containing the words "I agree" or "I accept the terms of the offer" that offerees can click on to indicate acceptance.

ONLINE ACCEPTANCES

In many ways, **click-on agreements** are the Internet equivalents of **shrink-wrap agreements** (or *shrink-wrap licenses,* as they are sometimes called). A *shrink-wrap agreement* is an agreement whose terms are expressed inside a box in which the goods are packaged. (The term *shrink-wrap* refers to the plastic that covers the box.) Usually, the party who opens the box is told that she or he agrees to the terms by keeping whatever is in the box. Similarly, when the purchaser opens a software package, he or she agrees to abide by the terms of the limited license agreement.

• **EXAMPLE 17.2** John orders a new computer from a national company, which ships the computer to John. Along with the computer, the box contains an agreement setting forth the terms of the sale, including what remedies are available. The document also states that John's retention of the computer for longer than thirty days will be construed as an acceptance of the terms. •

In most cases, a shrink-wrap agreement is not between a retailer and a buyer, but between the manufacturer of the hardware or software and the ultimate buyer-user of the product. The terms generally concern warranties, remedies, and other issues associated with the use of the product.

We look next at how the law has been applied to both shrink-wrap and click-on agreements.

> **ON THE WEB** You can access the Uniform Commercial Code (UCC), including Article 2, at the Web site of the University of Pennsylvania Law School. Go to **http://www.law.upenn.edu/bll/ulc/ulc.htm**.

Shrink-Wrap Agreements—Enforceable Contract Terms Section 2–204 of the Uniform Commercial Code (UCC), the law governing sales contracts, provides that any contract for the sale of goods "may be made in any manner sufficient to show agreement, including conduct by both parties which recognizes the existence of a contract." Thus, a buyer's failure to object to terms contained within a shrink-wrapped software package (or an online offer) may constitute an acceptance of the terms by conduct.[1]

In many cases, the courts have enforced the terms of shrink-wrap agreements the same as the terms of other contracts. Some courts have reasoned that by including the terms with the product, the seller proposed a contract that the buyer could accept by using the product after having an opportunity to read the terms.

Also, it seems practical from a business's point of view to enclose a full statement of the legal terms of a sale with the product rather than to read the statement over the phone, for example, when a buyer calls in an order for the product.

Shrink-Wrap Agreements—Proposals for Additional Terms Not all of the terms included in shrink-wrap agreements have been enforced. One important consideration is whether the parties form their contract before or after the seller communicates the terms of the shrink-wrap agreement to the buyer. If a court finds that the buyer learned of the shrink-wrap terms *after* the parties entered into a contract, the court may conclude that those terms were proposals for additional terms and were not part of the contract unless the buyer expressly agreed to them.

In the following case, the court was asked to decide, among other things, whether to enforce an arbitration clause that was part of a set of "Standard Terms and Conditions" included in the box of every computer the defendant sold.

1. See, for example, *ProCD, Inc. v. Zeidenberg,* 86 F.3d 1447 (7th Cir. 1996).

CASE 17.1 Klocek v. Gateway, Inc.

United States District Court,
District of Kansas, 2000.
104 F.Supp.2d 1332.

FACTS Whenever it sells a computer, Gateway, Inc., includes a copy of its "Standard Terms and Conditions Agreement" in the box that contains the power cables and instruction manuals. At the top of the first page, in a printed box and in emphasized type, is the following: "NOTE TO THE CUSTOMER: * * * By keeping your Gateway 2000 computer system beyond five (5) days

CASE 17.1—Continued

after the date of delivery, you accept these Terms and Conditions." This document is four pages long and contains sixteen numbered paragraphs. Paragraph 10 states, "DISPUTE RESOLUTION. Any dispute or controversy arising out of or relating to this Agreement or its interpretation shall be settled exclusively and finally by arbitration." William Klocek bought a Gateway computer. Dissatisfied when it proved to be incompatible with his other computer equipment, he filed a suit in a federal district court against Gateway and others, alleging in part breach of contract. Gateway filed a motion to dismiss, asserting that Klocek was required to submit his claims to arbitration under Gateway's "Standard Terms." Klocek argued that these terms were not part of the contract for the purchase of the computer.

ISSUE Is the arbitration clause, which was a part of the shrink-wrap license in the box with the computer, enforceable against Klocek?

DECISION No. The court denied Gateway's motion to dismiss. The court agreed with Klocek that the arbitration clause was not part of his contract with Gateway.[a]

a. Klocek's complaint was later dismissed on the ground that his claim did not satisfy the court's amount-in-controversy requirement for diversity jurisdiction. See *Klocek v. Gateway, Inc.*, 104 F.Supp.2d 1332 (D.Kan. 2000).

REASON The court first pointed out that under UCC 2–207, an "expression of acceptance * * * operates as an acceptance even though it states terms additional to or different from those offered or agreed upon, unless acceptance is expressly made conditional on assent to the additional or different terms." Those "additional terms are to be construed as proposals for addition to the contract" if the contract is not between merchants. The court concluded that Gateway's "Standard Terms" constituted an acceptance. There was no evidence, however, that "the transaction was conditioned on plaintiff's acceptance of the Standard Terms." Because Klocek was not a merchant, the terms did not become part of the parties' agreement unless he expressly agreed to them. There was no evidence that he had agreed to the terms. "Gateway states only that it enclosed the Standard Terms inside the computer box for plaintiff to read afterwards."

FOR CRITICAL ANALYSIS—Technological Consideration *The court in this case applied UCC provisions to an electronic contract. Can you think of some unique aspects of electronic contracting that would not be covered by traditional laws, such as the UCC?*

Click-On Agreements As described earlier, a click-on agreement (also sometimes called a *click-on license* or *click-wrap agreement*) arises when a buyer, completing a transaction on a computer, indicates his or her assent to be bound by the terms of an offer by clicking on a button that says, for example, "I agree." The terms may be contained on a Web site through which the buyer is obtaining goods or services, or they may appear on a computer screen when software is loaded. Exhibit 17–1 on the following page contains the language of a click-on agreement that accompanies a package of software made and marketed by Adobe Systems, Inc.

As noted, Article 2 of the UCC provides that acceptance can be made by conduct. The *Restatement (Second) of Contracts*, a compilation of common law contract principles, has a similar provision. It states that parties may agree to a contract "by written or spoken words or by other action or by failure to act."[2] The courts have used these provisions to conclude that a binding contract can be created by conduct, including conduct accepting the terms of a shrink-wrap agreement or a click-on agreement.

2. *Restatement (Second) of Contracts*, Section 19.

EXHIBIT 17–1 A CLICK-ON AGREEMENT

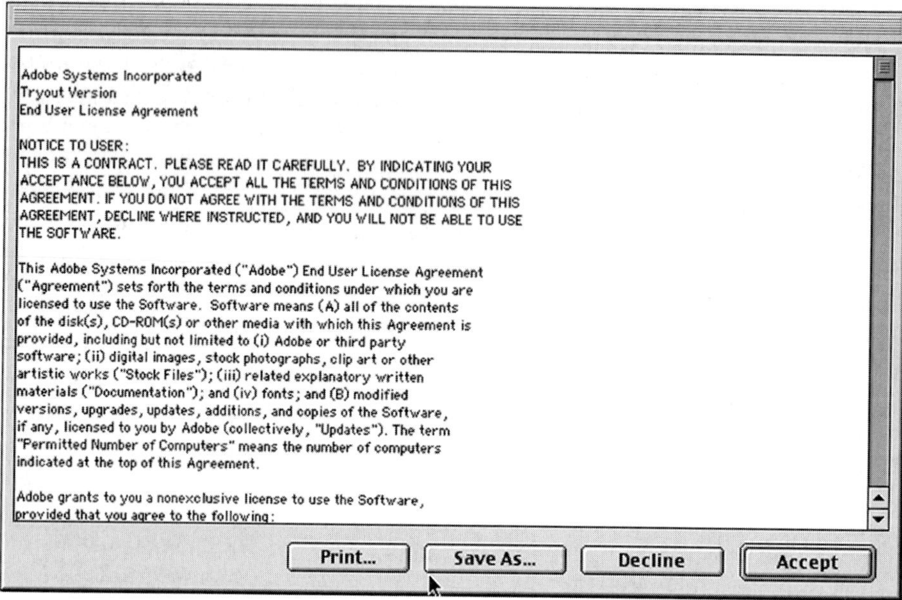

Generally, under the law governing contracts, including sales and lease contracts under the UCC, there is no requirement that all of the terms in a contract must actually have been read by all of the parties to be effective. For example, clicking on a button or box that states "I agree" to certain terms can be enough. The following case illustrates a court's evaluation of the validity of a clause in a click-on agreement.

CASE 17.2 Caspi v. Microsoft Network, LLC[a]

New Jersey Superior Court,
Appellate Division, 1999.
323 N.J.Super. 118,
732 A.2d 528.
http://lawlibrary.Rutgers.edu/search.shtml[b]

FACTS Microsoft Network, LLC (MSN), is an online computer service. Before becoming an MSN member, a prospective subscriber is prompted by MSN software to view multiple computer screens of information, including a membership agreement that contains a forum-selection clause. This clause calls for any claims against MSN to be litigated in the state of Washington. MSN's membership agreement appears on the computer screen in a scrollable window next to blocks providing the choices "I Agree" and "I Don't Agree." Prospective members have the option to click "I Agree" or "I Don't Agree" at any point while scrolling through the agreement. Registration proceeds only after the potential subscriber has the opportunity to view, and assents to, the membership agreement. No charges are incurred until a subscriber clicks on "I Agree." Steven Caspi was a subscriber. Alleging that MSN rolled over his membership into a more expensive plan without notice,[c] Caspi filed a suit in

a. *L.L.C.,* or *LLC,* is an abbreviation for limited liability company, a hybrid form of business enterprise that limits the liability of its members and offers special tax advantages. See Chapter 30.

b. This Web site is maintained by Rutgers University School of Law–Camden. This page contains links to recent opinions of the New Jersey state courts. In the "Additional Information:" row, click on "Search by party name." When that page opens, in the first column, click on the "Appellate Division" box. In the second column, enter "Caspi" in the "First Name" box, and click on "Submit Form." When the results appear, click on the appropriate link to access the opinion.

c. This is known as *unilateral negative option billing,* a practice at one time condemned by the attorneys general of twenty-one states, including New Jersey, with regard to an MSN competitor, America Online, Inc.

CASE 17.2—Continued

a New Jersey state court against MSN. Other subscribers, claiming to represent 1.5 million members, joined the suit. MSN filed a motion to dismiss on the ground that the forum-selection clause called for the suit to be heard in the state of Washington. The court granted the motion. The plaintiffs appealed to a state intermediate appellate court, arguing that they did not have adequate notice of the clause and therefore it was not part of their contracts.

ISSUE Is the forum-selection clause contained in the click-on subscriber agreement part of the parties' contract?

DECISION Yes. The state intermediate appellate court affirmed the decision of the lower court. The forum-selection clause was valid and enforceable.

REASON The court noted first that "[t]he plaintiffs in this case were free to scroll through the various computer screens that presented the terms of their contracts before clicking their agreement." The court pointed out that "the clause was presented in exactly the same format as most other provisions of the contract." In other words, there was "nothing about the style or mode of presentation, or the placement of the provision, that can be taken as a basis for concluding that the forum selection clause was proffered [offered] unfairly, or with a design to conceal or deemphasize its provisions." The court reasoned that "[t]o conclude that plaintiffs are not bound by that clause would be equivalent to holding that they were bound by no other clause either, since all provisions were identically presented."

FOR CRITICAL ANALYSIS—Economic Consideration *Many attorneys advise their business clients that it is especially important to include forum-selection clauses when forming e-contracts. Would including such a clause be more important when forming an e-contract than when forming a traditional, printed contract?*

BROWSE-WRAP TERMS
Terms and conditions of use that are presented to an Internet user at the time certain products, such as software, are being downloaded but that need not be agreed to (by clicking "I agree," for example) before being able to install or use the product.

Browse-Wrap Terms Like the terms of a click-on agreement, **browse-wrap terms** can occur in a transaction conducted over the Internet. Unlike a click-on agreement, however, browse-wrap terms do not require an Internet user to assent to the terms before, say, downloading or using certain software. In other words, a person can install the software without clicking "I agree" to the terms of a license. Offerors of browse-wrap terms generally assert that the terms are binding without the users' active consent.

Critics contend that browse-wrap terms are not enforceable because they do not satisfy the basic elements of contract formation. It has been suggested that to form a valid contract online, a user must at least be presented with the terms before indicating assent.[3] In the case of a browse-wrap term, this would require that a user navigate past it and agree to it before being able to obtain whatever is being granted to the user.

The following case involved the enforceability of a clause in an agreement that the court characterized as a browse-wrap license.

3. American Bar Association Committee on the Law of Cyberspace, "Click-Through Agreements: Strategies for Avoiding Disputes on the Validity of Assent" (document presented at the annual American Bar Association meeting in August 2001).

CASE 17.3 Specht v. Netscape Communications Corp.

United States District Court,
Southern District of New York, 2001.
150 F.Supp.2d 585.

FACTS Netscape Communications Corporation's "SmartDownload" software makes it easier for users to download files from the Internet without losing progress if they pause to do some other task or their Internet connection is interrupted. Netscape offers SmartDownload free of charge on its Web site to those

(continued)

CASE 17.3—Continued

who indicate, by clicking the mouse in a designated box, that they wish to obtain it. John Gibson clicked in the box and downloaded the software. On the Web site's download page is a reference to a license agreement that is visible only by scrolling to the next screen. Affirmatively indicating assent to the agreement is not required to download the software. The agreement provides that any disputes arising from use of the software are to be submitted to arbitration in California. Believing that the use of SmartDownload transmits private information about its users, Gibson and others filed a suit in a federal district court in New York against Netscape, alleging violations of federal law. Netscape asked the court to order the parties to arbitration in California, according to the license agreement.

ISSUE Was the arbitration clause in the license agreement enforceable?

DECISION No. The court denied the motion to compel arbitration.

REASON The court applied UCC Article 2 because, "[a]lthough in this case the product was provided free of charge, the roles are essentially the same as when an individual uses the Internet to purchase software from a company: here, the Plaintiff requested Defendant's product by clicking on an icon marked 'Download,' and Defendant then tendered the product." The court emphasized that "[u]nless the Plaintiffs agreed to the License Agreement, they cannot be bound by the arbitration clause." The court discussed the forms of license agreements that accompany sales of software (shrink-wrap, click-on, and browse-wrap licenses) and their enforceability, and characterized Netscape's license in this case as a browse-wrap license. "Netscape's SmartDownload * * * allows a user to download and use the software without taking any action that plainly manifests assent to the terms of the associated license or indicates an understanding that a contract is being formed." The court pointed out that "the individual obtaining SmartDownload is not made aware that he is entering into a contract * * * [T]he user need not view any license agreement terms or even any reference to a license agreement, and need not do anything to manifest assent." The court reasoned that "the user Plaintiffs did not assent to the license agreement," and thus "they are not subject to the arbitration clause."

FOR CRITICAL ANALYSIS—Social Consideration *What might be the result in other cases if the court in this case had held that the browse-wrap term was enforceable?*

Linking and Framing

Generally, online sellers must be careful to operate within the parameters established by the laws covered in this text. For example, businesses are prohibited from making statements about their products or services that would deceive or mislead consumers. The laws prohibiting deceptive advertising are discussed in Chapter 33, in the context of consumer protection. Privacy laws (see Chapter 2) also place limits on how personal information about consumers who visit an online merchant's Web site can be used. Additionally, the unauthorized use of another's trademark in marketing, for example, could result in extensive liability under trademark law (see Chapter 5). Here we examine how the law applies to two practices commonly used in online marketing—linking to and framing others' Web pages.

Linking to Others' Web Pages

When a user clicks on an icon or on highlighted text that is programmed to be a hypertext link, the user is immediately taken to a new online location. The link may lead to another point within the same site or to a different, unrelated site somewhere else in cyberspace.

Sometimes, a site owner may ask the permission of other owners to link to their sites, but normally no permission is sought. Linking is legal and does not require permission. Linking is a revolutionary aspect of the new technology and is considered a primary reason for the success of Internet commerce. Site owners are less agreeable to *framing*, however.

FRAMING OTHERS' WEB PAGES

If a linking site is a framing site, the pages of the linked site will appear in a window of the original site. With frames, a single site can let users view several sites simultaneously. Using linking and framing technology, any site owner can divert traffic from another site. This may be desired because search engines base their results on the number of hits (visits to a site). More hits can mean more advertising revenue and more sales. An owner may even appropriate a competitor's content and hide it, so that an unsuspecting user is transported to the appropriator's site even though she or he cannot see the appropriated material. This is a violation of trademark law (and copyright law).

Although the law is not settled on this issue, framing has given rise to lawsuits alleging trademark violation. ● **EXAMPLE 17.3** In one case, Ticketmaster Corporation sued Microsoft Corporation in a federal district court, alleging that Microsoft Network's unauthorized links to interior pages of Ticketmaster's site constituted trademark infringement and unfair competition. Ticketmaster argued that its Web site is the same as a trademark and that it should be allowed to control the way others use it. Because the parties settled the dispute in 1999, we do not know how the court might have ruled.●

The issue will likely come up again, however, and to be on the safe side, owners of linking sites should take several precautions. Consent should be obtained if a link falsely implies an affiliation between the sites, if a link uses the linked site's logo or trademark, if the link is "deep" (to internal pages), or if a frame modifies or distorts the linked site. Also, consent should be obtained if the linked site requests or requires

Why is it often said that linking technology is one of the primary reasons for the success of e-commerce?

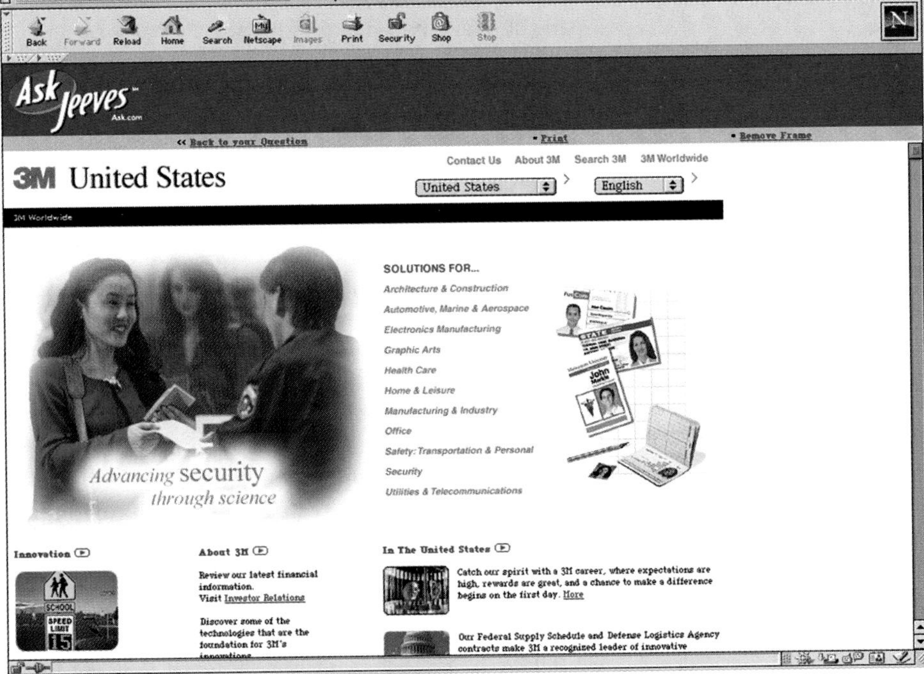

it, or if the link diverts advertising revenue from the linked site. Finally, a linking site should include a disclaimer.

E-Signatures

In many instances, a contract cannot be enforced, unless it is signed by the party against whom enforcement is sought. A significant issue in the context of e-commerce has to do with how electronic signatures, or **e-signatures**, can be created and verified on e-contracts.

E-SIGNATURE
As defined by the Uniform Electronic Transactions Act, "an electronic sound, symbol, or process attached to or logically associated with a record and executed or adopted by a person with the intent to sign the record."

In the days when many people could not write, they signed documents with an "X." Then handwritten signatures became common, followed by typed signatures, printed signatures, and, most recently, digital signatures that are transmitted electronically. Throughout the evolution of signature technology, the question of what constitutes a valid signature has arisen again and again, and with good reason—without some consensus on what constitutes a valid signature, little business or legal work could be accomplished. (Technology has also raised other questions relating to signature requirements—see, for example, the question discussed in this chapter's *Business Law in the Online World.*)

E-Signature Technologies

Today, numerous technologies allow electronic documents to be signed. These include digital signatures and alternative technologies.

Digital Signatures The most prevalent e-signature technology is the *asymmetric cryptosystem,* which creates a digital signature using two different (asymmetric) cryptographic "keys." With this system, a person attaches a digital signature to a document using a private key, or code. The key has a publicly available counterpart. Anyone with the appropriate software can use the public key to verify that the digital signature was made using the private key. A **cybernotary**, or legally recognized certification authority, issues the key pair, identifies the owner of the keys, and certifies the validity of the public key. The cybernotary also serves as a repository for public keys. Cybernotaries already are available.

CYBERNOTARY
A legally recognized authority that can certify the validity of digital signatures.

Signature Dynamics With another type of signature technology, known as *signature dynamics,* a sender's signature is captured using a stylus and an electronic digitizer pad. A computer program takes the signature's measurements, the sender's identity, the time and date of the signature, and the identity of the hardware. This information is then placed in an encrypted *biometric token* attached to the document being transmitted. To verify the authenticity of the signature, the recipient of the document compares the measurements of the signature with the measurements in the token. When this type of e-signature is used, it is not necessary to have a third party verify the signatory's identity.

Other E-Signature Forms Other forms of e-signatures have been—or are now being—developed as well. For example, some e-signatures use "smart cards." A smart card is a credit-card–size device that is embedded with code and other data. Like credit and debit cards, this smart card can be inserted into computers to transfer information. Unlike those other cards, however, a smart card could be used to establish a person's identity as validly as a signature on a piece of paper. In addition, technological innovations now under way will allow an e-signature to be evidenced by an image of a person's retina, fingerprint, or face that is scanned by a computer and then matched to a numeric code. The scanned image and the numeric code are registered with security companies that maintain files on an accessible server that can be used to authenticate a transaction.

BUSINESS LAW: //in the Online World

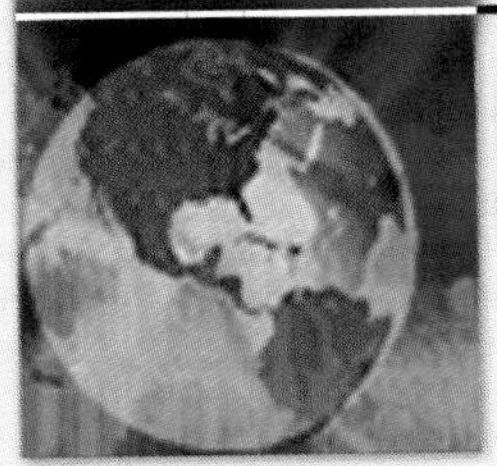

E-Mailed Prescription Orders and Signature Requirements

"It is in the nature of things that statutes must at times be applied to situations unforeseen at the time of their enactment." So said a Wisconsin appellate court when trying to apply a state law governing the requirements of physicians' prescriptions to a program initiated by Walgreen Company. The program enabled physicians to transmit prescription orders to Walgreen pharmacies via e-mail.

The state statute defined a "prescription order" as simply "a written or oral order by a [physician] for a drug or device for a particular patient." If the prescription order was written, it had to be signed. If the order was transmitted to the pharmacist orally—by telephone, for example—it did not, of course, require a signature. The statute, however, said nothing about prescription orders transmitted electronically via e-mail, and therein lay the problem: If e-mailed prescription orders were considered to be "in writing," they violated the statutory requirement for written prescriptions because they were not signed. If such prescriptions were deemed to be oral transmissions, there was no violation.

The Pharmacy Board's Position on the Issue

The Wisconsin Pharmacy Examining Board had little trouble concluding that an e-mailed prescription order was analogous to a writing and that Walgreen's program violated the law. The board voiced a number of concerns to the court. One was that if e-mailed prescription orders were permitted, there would be less control over drugs. While pharmacists can recognize a caller's voice over the telephone and thus verify the caller's identity, a computerized communication is more anonymous, creating a danger that the prescription information "will fall into the wrong hands." The board argued that these security considerations should take priority and that the court should bar the use of e-mailed prescription orders.

The Court's Conclusion

The court was not convinced that it should defer to such security concerns. The court concluded that a computer-transmitted prescription was not analogous to a written prescription. Rather, it was more akin to an order transmitted orally by telephone. This, to the court, seemed to be "a more reasonable interpretation than the board's in light of the simple facts of computer transmission: The prescription is put into a computer as text and the message is then electronically transmitted to the pharmacy's terminal, much as a telephone call—or a facsimile—would be." Thus, concluded the court, the use of e-mailed prescription orders did not violate the statute.

The court justified its rather novel conclusion by perhaps equally novel reasoning. The court stated that when a statute must be applied to a situation unforeseen by its drafters, then the court must try to determine the "manifest intent" of those lawmakers. The court must examine the "pictures actually drawn by the statutory text" and see if they are "sufficient to cover the new type of situation that the course of events has produced." If the legislature has supplied "sufficient specifications to provide a discernible frame of reference within which the situation now presented quite clearly fits, even though it represents in some degree a new condition of affairs unknown to the lawmakers," the statute may be interpreted accordingly.[a]

FOR CRITICAL ANALYSIS

Suppose that two parties form a contract through the exchange of e-mailed messages. Would this court classify the contract as an oral contract?

a. *Walgreen Co. v. Wisconsin Pharmacy Examining Board,* 217 Wis.2d 290, 577 N.W.2d 387 (Wis.App. 1998).

STATE LAWS GOVERNING E-SIGNATURES

Most states have laws governing e-signatures. The problem is that the state e-signature laws are not uniform. Some states—California is a notable example—provide that many types of documents cannot be signed with e-signatures, while other states are more permissive. Additionally, some states recognize only digital signatures as valid, while others permit other types of e-signatures.

In an attempt to create more uniformity among the states, the National Conference of Commissioners on Uniform State Laws promulgated the Uniform Electronic Transactions

RECORD
According to the Uniform Electronic Transactions Act, information that is either inscribed on a tangible medium or stored in an electronic or other medium and that is retrievable. The Uniform Computer Information Transactions Act uses the term *record* instead of *writing*.

Act (UETA) in 1999. The UETA defines an *e-signature* as "an electronic sound, symbol, or process attached to or logically associated with a record and executed or adopted by a person with the intent to sign the record."[4] A **record** is "information that is inscribed on a tangible medium or that is stored in an electronic or other medium and is retrievable in perceivable [visual] form."[5]

This definition of *e-signature* includes encrypted digital signatures, names (intended as signatures) at the ends of e-mail, and a click on a Web page if the click includes the identification of the person. The UETA also states, among other things, that a signature may not be denied legal effect or enforceability solely because it is in electronic form. (Other aspects of the UETA will be discussed later in this chapter.)

FEDERAL LAW ON E-SIGNATURES AND E-DOCUMENTS

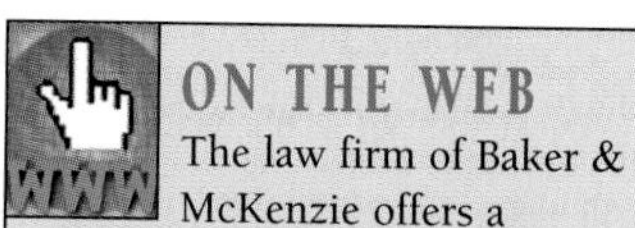

ON THE WEB The law firm of Baker & McKenzie offers a summary of the scope and applicability of the E-SIGN Act of 2000 on its Web site. Go to **http://www.bmck.com/ecommerce/E-SIGN_Act.htm**.

In 2000, Congress enacted the Electronic Signatures in Global and National Commerce Act (E-SIGN Act) to provide that no contract, record, or signature may be "denied legal effect" solely because it is in electronic form. In other words, under this law, an electronic signature is as valid as a signature on paper, and an electronic document can be as enforceable as a paper one.

For an electronic signature to be enforceable, the contracting parties must have agreed to use electronic signatures. For an electronic document to be valid, it must be in a form that can be retained and accurately reproduced.

The E-SIGN Act does not apply to all types of documents, however. Contracts and documents that are exempt include court papers, divorce decrees, evictions, foreclosures, health-insurance terminations, prenuptial agreements, and wills. Also, the only agreements governed by the Uniform Commercial Code (UCC) that fall under this law are those covered by Articles 2 and 2A and UCC 1–107 and 1–206.

Despite these limitations, the E-SIGN Act enormously expands the possibilities for contracting online. • **EXAMPLE 17.4** From a remote location, a businessperson can now open an account with a financial institution, obtain a mortgage or other loan, buy insurance, and purchase real estate over the Internet. Payments and transfers of funds can be done entirely online. Thus, using e-contracts can avoid the time and costs associated with producing, delivering, signing, and returning paper documents. •

Partnering Agreements

PARTNERING AGREEMENT
An agreement between a seller and a buyer who frequently do business with each other on the terms and conditions that will apply to all subsequently formed electronic contracts.

One way that online sellers and buyers can prevent disputes over signatures in their e-contracts, as well as over the terms and conditions of those contracts, is to form partnering agreements. In a **partnering agreement**, a seller and a buyer who frequently do business with each other agree in advance on the terms and conditions that will apply to all transactions subsequently conducted electronically. The partnering agreement can also establish special access and identification codes to be used by the parties when transacting business electronically.

A partnering agreement reduces the likelihood that disputes will arise under the contract because the buyer and the seller have agreed in advance to the terms and conditions that will accompany each sale. Furthermore, if a dispute does arise, a court or arbitration forum will be able to refer to the partnering agreement when determining the parties' intent with respect to subsequent contracts. Of course, even with a part-

4. UETA 102(8).
5. UETA 102(15).

nering agreement fraud remains a possibility. If an unauthorized person uses a purchaser's designated access number and identification code, it may be some time before the problem is discovered.

The Uniform Computer Information Transactions Act

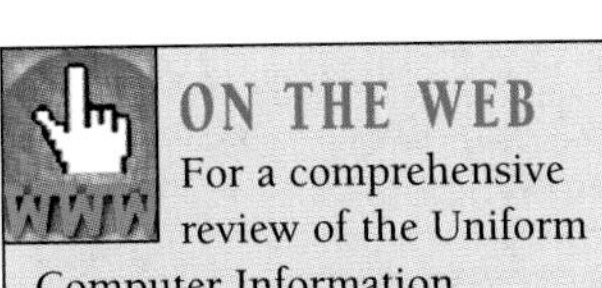

ON THE WEB For a comprehensive review of the Uniform Computer Information Transactions Act, go to **http://www.ucitaonline.com**.

In the early 1990s, as the software industry continued to develop, it became apparent that Article 2 of the UCC, which deals with the sale of goods (tangible property), could not be applied to most transactions involving software for two basic reasons. First, software is not a "good" (tangible property)—it is electronic information (intangible property). Second, the "sale" of software generally involves a license (right to use) rather than a sale (passage of title from the seller to the purchaser). The producer of the software either contracts directly with the licensee (user) or uses a distribution system—for example, authorizing retailers to distribute (sell) copies of the producer's software to customers (end users). Because neither involves the sale of goods, new rules needed to be established.

These new rules were supplied by the Uniform Computer Information Transactions Act (UCITA). The UCITA is a uniform law created by the National Conference of Commissioners on Uniform State Laws and the American Law Institute. As noted earlier in this text, these organizations have initiated many of the most significant laws that apply to traditional commerce, including the UCC. Like other uniform laws, the UCITA, as drafted in 1999 and amended in 2000, has been proposed to the states for adoption as law.

The Scope and Applicability of the UCITA

COMPUTER INFORMATION
As defined by the Uniform Computer Information Transactions Act, "information in an electronic form obtained from or through use of a computer, or that is in digital or an equivalent form capable of being processed by a computer."

The UCITA establishes a comprehensive set of rules covering contracts involving computer information. **Computer information** is "information in electronic form obtained from or through use of a computer, or that is in digital or equivalent form capable of being processed by a computer."[6] Under this definition, the act covers contracts to license or purchase software, contracts to create a computer program, contracts for computer games, contracts for online access to databases, contracts to distribute information on the Internet, contracts for "diskettes" that contain computer programs, contracts for online books, and other similar contracts.

The UCITA consists of nine "parts," covering everything from the formation of a contract to construction rules, warranties available, transfer of interests and financing arrangements, performance rules, breach of contract, and remedies. Its table of contents is shown in Exhibit 17–2 on the next page.

In arrangement and content the UCITA resembles Article 2 of the UCC. Both acts have similar general provisions, including definitions (approximately sixty-six) and formal requirements (such as a Statute of Frauds, which, in the case of the UCITA, requires a written memorandum when a contract involves a payment of $5,000 or more). The UCITA also includes rules for offer and acceptance, as well as other provisions comparable to those found in Article 2.[7] The UCITA is more comprehensive in scope than Article 2, however, with provisions covering the contracting parties' choice of law and choice of forum, the UCITA's relationship to federal law and other state laws, and many others.[8]

6. UCITA 102(10).
7. See, for example, UCITA 111.
8. See, for example, UCITA 109 and 110.

EXHIBIT 17–2 THE UCITA'S TABLE OF CONTENTS

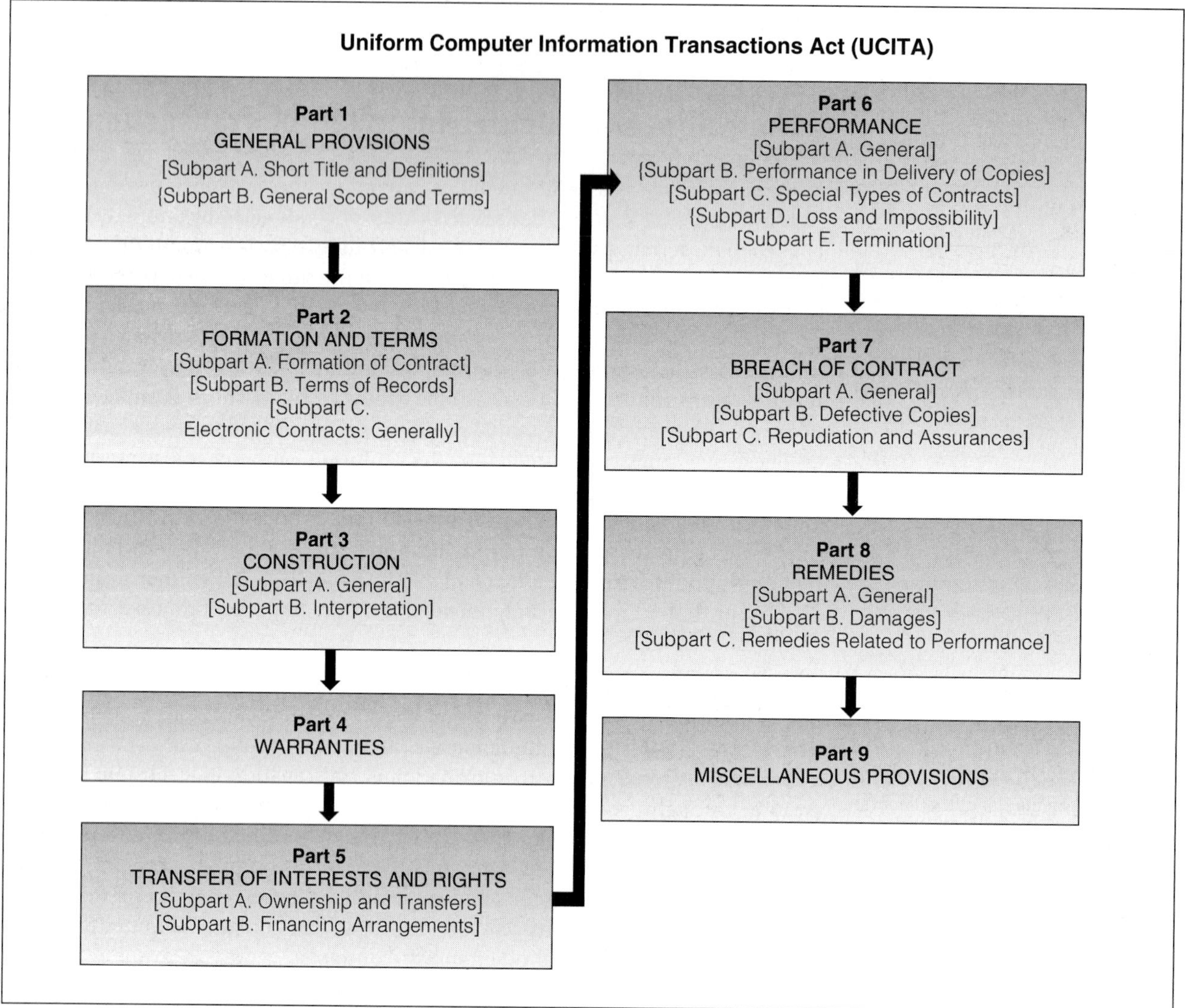

The UCITA May Apply to Only Part of a Transaction The UCITA generally does not apply to the sale of goods even if software is embedded in the goods or used in their production (except computers). For example, it does not apply to television sets, stereos, books, and automobiles. It also does not apply to traditional movies, recordings, or cable television. These industries are specifically excluded for the most part.

When a transaction includes computer information as defined in the act and subject matter other than computer information, the UCITA generally provides that if the primary subject matter deals with computer information rights, the act applies to the entire transaction. If computer information is not the primary subject matter, the act applies only to the part of the transaction "involving computer information, informational rights in it and creation or modification of it."

Parties Can "Opt Out" As with most other uniform acts that apply to business, the UCITA allows the parties to waive or vary its provisions by a contract. The parties may even agree to "opt out" of the act and, for contracts not covered by the act, to "opt in."

In other words, the UCITA expressly recognizes the freedom to contract and supports the idea that this is a basic principle of contract law.

DEFAULT RULES
Rules that apply under the Uniform Computer Information Transactions Act only in the absence of an agreement between contracting parties indicating otherwise.

The UCITA stresses the parties' agreement, but in the absence of an agreement, the act's provisions, called **default rules,** will apply.[9] As with other uniform statutes, rules relating to good faith, diligence, public policy, unconscionability, and related principles cannot be varied or deleted by agreement.

Rights and Restrictions The licensing of information is the primary method used for transferring computer information in business today. A license contract involves a transfer of computer information, such as software, from a seller (the licensor) to a buyer (the licensee). The licensee is given certain rights to use and control the computer information during the license period. Title does not pass, and quite often the license places restrictions on the licensee's use of, and rights to copy and control, the computer information. Many sections of the UCITA deal with the rights and restrictions that can be imposed on the parties in the license.

HIGHLIGHTS OF THE UCITA

In the following subsections, we describe some of the UCITA's highlights. Note that most of them address situations that arise due to the unique nature of licensing computer information.

Mass-Market Licenses Basically, a *mass-market* transaction is either (1) a consumer contract or (2) a transaction in which the computer information is directed to the general public and the end user licensee acquires the information in a retail transaction.

MASS-MARKET LICENSE
An e-contract that is presented with a package of computer information in the form of a *click-on license* or a *shrink-wrap license.*

A **mass-market license** is an electronic form contract that is usually presented along with a package of purchased computer information. The licensee commonly receives the license contract shrink-wrapped or, in the case of an online transaction, click-wrapped with the computer information (when the purchaser clicks on a certain link). Mass-market licenses are different from negotiated licenses in that mass-market licenses are automatically enforceable, as long as the terms are readily available and the licensee has had an opportunity to review the terms.

If the licensee does not want the computer information for any reason, the UCITA allows him or her to return it for a refund and recover any reasonable expenses incurred in removing and returning the information. The UCITA provides that these rights of returning the computer information and recovering reasonable expenses cannot be waived or disclaimed by the licensor.

Warranties Article 2 of the UCC provides for both express warranties and implied warranties. *Express warranties* are affirmations of fact that are made by a seller about a product being sold and that go to the basis of the bargain. Implied warranties can arise in any sale of goods falling under Article 2. The *implied warranty of merchantability* is a warranty that the goods being sold are reasonably fit for the general purpose for which they are sold. The *implied warranty of fitness for a particular purpose* is a warranty that the goods sold are fit for a particular purpose, if the buyer is relying on the seller's skill or judgment in selecting goods that are fit for the buyer's purpose. Article 2 allows sellers to disclaim warranties, provided the disclaimers meet certain requirements set out in the UCC to ensure that the buyer is fully aware of the disclaimers.[10]

---

9. UCITA 113.

10. Article 2's provisions on warranties made in sales contracts are set forth in UCC 2–313, 2–314, 2–315, and 2–316. See Chapter 18.

The UCITA provides for basically the same warranties as Article 2. Thus, a licensor's affirmations of fact or promises concerning computer information (as a basis for the bargain) constitute express warranties.[11] Implied warranties are also provided for by the act (and can be disclaimed, as under UCC Article 2).[12] The UCITA's implied warranties of merchantability and fitness are closely tailored to the information's content and the "compatibility of the computer systems."[13]

Authentication and Attribution Before the emergence of electronic contracting, parties to contracts generally knew each other, and many contracts were signed by the parties. Today, the parties must deal with electronic signatures and need to be able to verify the identity of the "person" sending the electronic message. For this reason, like the revisions of other statutes, the UCITA's rules were revised to provide for the authentication of e-signatures.

AUTHENTICATE
To sign a record, or with the intent to sign a record, to execute or to adopt an electronic sound, symbol, or the like to link with the record. A *record* is retrievable information inscribed on a tangible medium or stored in an electronic or other medium.

Authentication. To **authenticate** means to sign a record, or with the intent to sign a record, to execute or to adopt an electronic sound, symbol, or the like to link with the record. As noted earlier in this chapter, a *record* is retrievable information that is either inscribed on a tangible medium or stored in an electronic or other medium. The UCITA uses the word *record* instead of *writing*.

Attribution Procedure. To ensure that the person sending the electronic computer information is the same person whose e-signature accompanies the information, the UCITA provides an *attribution procedure* that sets forth steps for identifying a person who sends an electronic communication. These steps, which can be specified by the contracting parties, can be simple or complex as long as they are commercially reasonable.

Attribution procedures can also have an effect on liability for errors in the message content. If an attribution procedure is in place to detect errors, the party who conforms to the procedure is not bound by the error. Consumers who make unintended errors are not bound as long as the consumer notifies the other party promptly, returns the computer information received, and has not benefited from its use.

ACCESS CONTRACT
A contract formed for the purpose of obtaining, by electronic means, access to another's database or information processing system.

Access Contracts The UCITA defines an **access contract** as "a contract to obtain by electronic means access to, or information from an information processing system of another person, or the equivalent of such access." Access contracts are important for most of us, if for no other reason than they allow us to use the Internet. Section 611 of the UCITA has special rules governing available times and manner of access.

Support and Service Contracts to Correct Performance Problems The UCITA covers licensor support and service contracts, but no licensor is required to provide such support and service.[14] Computer software support contracts are common, and once made, the licensor is obligated to comply with the express terms of the support contract or, if the contract is silent on an issue, to do what is reasonable in light of ordinary business standards.

Electronic Self-Help The UCITA allows the licensor to cancel, repossess, prevent continued use, and take similar actions on a licensee's breach of a license. The act permits

11. UCITA 402.
12. UCITA 401.
13. UCITA 403 and 405.
14. See UCITA 612.

the licensor to undertake "electronic self-help" to enforce the licensor's rights through electronic means. Outside the UCITA, "self-help" refers to the right of a lessor, for example, under Article 2A of the UCC, to repossess a leased computer if the lessee fails to make payments according to the terms of the lease. A lender may have this same right under UCC Article 9 if a borrower fails to make payments on a loan secured by a computer (for a discussion of the self-help provisions of Article 9, see Chapter 22).

In a transaction governed by the UCITA, electronic self-help includes the right of a software licensor to install a "turn-off" function in the software so that if the licensee violates the terms of the license, the software can be disabled from a distance. This right is most important to a small firm that licenses its software to a much larger company. Electronic self-help may be the licensor's only practical remedy if the license is breached.

Limitations on Electronic Self-Help There are some limitations on the right to electronic self-help, however.[15] For example, the UCITA prohibits electronic self-help in mass-market transactions. In addition, the remedy is not available unless the parties agree to permit electronic self-help. The licensor must give notice of the intent to use the self-help remedy at least fifteen days before doing so, along with full disclosure of the nature of the breach and information to enable the licensee to cure the breach or to communicate with the licensor concerning the situation. Additionally, electronic self-help cannot be used if the licensor "has reason to know that its use will result in substantial injury or harm to the public health or safety or grave harm to the public interest affecting third persons involved in the dispute." These limitations on the use of electronic self-help cannot be waived or varied by contract.

ETHICAL ISSUE 17.1

Does the UCITA favor the software industry over consumers?

Some consumer groups argue that the UCITA favors the software industry and will have harsh effects for consumers. Among other things, they object to the automatic enforceability of licensing agreements formed online, which can easily go unread by consumers. Even with printed documents, consumers often do not take the time to read the "fine print." Consumer groups that object to the enforceability of licensing agreements claim that this problem is even more prevalent with shrink-wrap and click-on agreements. These groups also oppose the limits on the rights of a licensee when a licensor knows that licensed software contains serious defects.

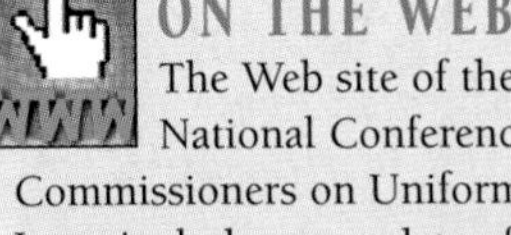

ON THE WEB The Web site of the National Conference of Commissioners on Uniform State Laws includes an update of the list of states that have adopted the UCITA and the UETA or considered them for adoption. The site also contains summaries of the acts and "Question and Answer" sections concerning these laws. Go to

http://www.nccusl.org.

The Uniform Electronic Transactions Act

The National Conference of Commissioners on Uniform State Laws has also proposed another uniform law concerning e-commerce—the Uniform Electronic Transactions Act (UETA). The goal of the UETA is not to create rules for electronic transactions—for example, the act does not require digital signatures—but to support the enforcement of e-contracts.

15. See UCITA 816.

Under the UETA, contracts entered into online, as well as other electronic documents, are presumed valid. In other words, a contract is not unenforceable simply because it is in electronic form. The UETA does not apply to transactions governed by the UCC or the UCITA, or to wills or testamentary trusts.

The UETA and the UCITA are similar in many respects because the drafters of the laws attempted to make them consistent. Both proposals, for example, provide for such items as the following:

① The equivalency of records and writings.

② The validity of e-signatures.

③ The formation of contracts by e-agents.

④ The formation of contracts between an e-agent and a natural person.

⑤ The attribution of an electronic act to a person if it can be proved that the act was done by the person or her or his agent.

⑥ A provision that parties do not need to participate in e-commerce to make binding contracts.

The chief difference between the two uniform acts is that the UCITA addresses e-commerce not covered by the UETA. In particular, the acts differ in the following areas:

① The UETA supports all electronic transactions, but it does not create rules for them. The UCITA concerns only contracts that involve computer information, but it does impose rules for those contracts.

② The UETA does not apply unless contracting parties agree to use e-commerce in their transactions. The UCITA applies to any agreement that falls within its scope.

APPLICATION Law and the Online Seller . . .

Using Online Contract Forms*

Before the printing press, every contract form had to be handwritten. Since the advent of printing, however, most standard contract forms have been readily available at low cost. Now the Internet has made available an even larger variety of contract forms, as well as other legal and business forms.

Where to Obtain Online Contract Forms

The 'Lectric Law Library has a collection of forms at **http://www.lectlaw.com/form.html**. The site includes forms for the assignment of a contract, a contract for the sale of a motor vehicle, and many others. In addition to actual forms, there are comments on how the forms should be used and filled out. Another excellent online resource for various types of forms is FindForms, at **http://www.findforms.com**.

Other online forms collections can be found at LegalWiz.com (go to **http://www.legalwiz.com/forms.htm**), a Web site that provides free legal forms, including a form that can be used to sell personal property. At **http://www.legaldocs.com**, you will find an electronic forms book that offers hundreds of standardized legal forms, some of which are free. Washburn University

*This *Application* is not meant to substitute for the services of an attorney who is licensed to practice law in your state.

APPLICATION **Law and the Online Seller . . .**

Using Online Contract Forms—continued

School of Law has a Web page containing links to an extensive number of forms archives at **http://www.washlaw.edu/legalforms/legalforms.html**.

A special Web site for small-business owners is **http://www.lawvantage.com**. Some documents are free; others require a fee or an annual subscription. Many law firms post legal forms, including contract forms, on their Web sites. For example, see the Web site of Bornstein & Naylor (at **http://lbnlaw.com/Freedownload2.htm**).

Finally, a number of forms are now made available by FindLaw, which is now a part of West Group. Go to **http://forms.lp.findlaw.com** and scroll down the screen to "Other Form Resources."

CHECKLIST FOR THE ONLINE SELLER

1. When looking for a contract form appropriate to your business, "shop around" for a form that most closely meets your needs.
2. Consider customizing any standardized contract form that you use to ensure that it will cover all of the contingencies that you deem important.
3. Make sure when using a standardized contract form that you provide for a means of acceptance—for example, by including a box stating "I accept" or "I agree."
4. Consider posting your own customized contract forms on your Web site for prospective customers or others to use.

Key Terms

access contract 448
authenticate 448
browse-wrap terms 439
B2B transaction 434
B2C transaction 434
click-on agreement 435
computer information 445
cybernotary 442
default rules 447
e-contract 433
e-signature 442
mass-market license 447
partnering agreement 444
record 444
shrink-wrap agreement 435

Chapter Summary E-Contracts

Online Offers (See pages 434–435.)	Businesspersons who present contract offers via the Internet should keep in mind that the terms of the offer should be just as inclusive as the terms in an offer made in a written (paper) document. All possible contingencies should be anticipated and provided for in the offer. Because jurisdictional issues frequently arise with online transactions, it is particularly important to include dispute-settlement provisions in the offer, as well as a forum-selection clause. The offer should be displayed in such a way as to be easily readable and clear. An online offer should also include some mechanism, such as providing an "I agree" or "I accept" box, by which the customer may accept the offer.

(continued)

Chapter Summary E-Contracts—continued

Online Acceptances (See pages 435–440.)	1. *Shrink-wrap agreement*– a. Definition–An agreement whose terms are expressed inside a box in which the goods are packaged. The party who opens the box is informed that, by keeping the goods in the box, he or she agrees to the terms of the shrink-wrap agreement. b. Enforceability–The courts have often enforced shrink-wrap agreements, even if the purchaser-user of the goods did not read the terms of the agreement. A court may deem a shrink-wrap agreement unenforceable, however, if the buyer learns of the shrink-wrap terms *after* the parties entered into the agreement. 2. *Click-on agreement*– a. Definition–An agreement created when a buyer, completing a transaction on a computer, is required to indicate his or her assent to be bound by the terms of an offer by clicking on a button that says, for example, "I agree." The terms of the agreement may appear on the Web site through which the buyer is obtaining goods or services, or they may appear on a computer screen when software is downloaded. b. Enforceability–The courts have enforced click-on agreements, holding that by clicking "I agree," the offeree has indicated acceptance by conduct. Browse-wrap terms, however (terms in a license that an Internet user does not have to read prior to downloading the product, such as software), may not be enforced on the ground that the user is not made aware that he or she is entering into a contract.
E-Signatures (See pages 442–444.)	1. *Definition*–The Uniform Electronic Transactions Act (UETA) defines the term *e-signature* as an electronic sound, symbol, or process attached to or logically associated with a record and executed or adopted by a person with the intent to sign the record. 2. *E-signature technologies*–These include the *asymmetric cryptosystem* (which creates a digital signature using two different cryptographic "keys"); *signature dynamics* (which involves capturing a sender's signature using a stylus and an electronic digitizer pad); a *smart card* (a device the size of a credit card that is embedded with code and other data); and, probably in the near future, scanned images of retinas, fingerprints, or other physical characteristics linked to numeric codes. 3. *State laws governing e-signatures*–Although most states have laws governing e-signatures, these laws are not uniform. Two recently promulgated uniform acts–the UETA and the Uniform Computer Information Transactions Act (UCITA)–provide for the validity of e-signatures and may ultimately create more uniformity among the states in this respect. 4. *Federal law on e-signatures and e-documents*–The Electronic Signatures in Global and National Commerce Act (E-SIGN Act) of 2000 gave validity to e-signatures by providing that no contract, record, or signature may be "denied legal effect" solely because it is in an electronic form.
The Uniform Computer Information Transactions Act (UCITA) (See pages 445–449.)	1. *Definition*–A uniform act submitted to the states for adoption by the National Conference of Commissioners on Uniform State Laws (NCCUSL). 2. *Purpose*–To govern transactions involving the licensing of intangible property, such as computer information, which are not covered by Article 2 of the Uniform Commercial Code (UCC), because Article 2 deals with the sale of goods, defined as the passage of title to tangible goods from a seller to a buyer. 3. *Coverage and content*–The act applies to contracts involving computer information, such as contracts to license or purchase software. *Computer information* is defined as "information in electronic form obtained from or through use of a computer, or that is in digital or equivalent form capable of being processed by a computer." As with most other uniform

Chapter Summary E-Contracts—continued

The Uniform Computer Information Transactions Act (UCITA)—continued	acts that apply to business, the UCITA allows the parties to waive or vary its provisions by contract or even agree to "opt out" or "opt in" to UCITA provisions. The UCITA covers all aspects of e-contracts involving computer information, from contract formation to contract remedies.
The Uniform Electronic Transactions Act (UETA) (See pages 449–450.)	1. *Definition*—A uniform act submitted to the states for adoption by the NCCUSL. 2. *Purpose*—To create rules to support the enforcement of e-contracts. Under the UETA, contracts entered into online, as well as other documents, are presumed valid. The UETA does not apply to transactions governed by the UCC or the UCITA, or to wills or testamentary trusts. 3. *The UETA and the UCITA compared*—The chief difference between the UETA and the UCITA is that the latter addresses e-commerce issues that the UETA does not. For example, the UETA does not apply unless contracting parties agree to use e-commerce in their transactions, while the UCITA applies to any agreement that falls within its scope.

For Review

① What are some important clauses that offerors should include when making offers to form electronic contracts, or e-contracts?

② What are shrink-wrap agreements? What traditional laws have been applied to such agreements? Do click-on acceptances in electronic contracts present problems that are not covered by traditional laws governing contracts, including the Uniform Commercial Code (UCC)? Explain.

③ What is an electronic signature? Are electronic signatures valid?

④ What problems does the Uniform Computer Information Transactions Act (UCITA) address that were not addressed by the UCC?

⑤ What is the Uniform Electronic Transactions Act (UETA)? What are some similarities and differences between this act and the UCITA?

Questions and Case Problems

17–1. Click-On Agreements. Paul is a financial analyst for King Investments, Inc., a brokerage firm. He uses the Internet to investigate the background and activities of companies that might be good investments for King's customers. While visiting the Web site of Business Research, Inc., Paul sees on his screen a message that reads, "Welcome to businessresearch.com. By visiting our site, you have been entered as a subscriber to our e-publication, *Companies Unlimited*. This publication will be sent to you daily at a cost of $7.50 per week. An invoice will be included with *Companies Unlimited* every four weeks. You may cancel your subscription at any time." Has Paul entered into an enforceable contract to pay for *Companies Unlimited?* Why or why not?

17–2. Attribution. Frank, an employee for Lloyd & Wright Architects, orders drafting supplies costing $4,500 from Precision Equipment, Inc., through Precision's Web site at precisionequip.com. On the order page at the site, Frank is asked to type in his name, company name, e-mail address, phone number, a credit-card or Precision account number, and the personal identification number (PIN) issued by the seller. The precisionequip.com site asks Frank to check this information before clicking "SUBMIT," at which time the order will be accepted and the supplies will be shipped. For purposes of the UCITA, what part of this transaction could be considered an attribution procedure? Is there an enforceable contract between Lloyd & Wright and Precision under the UCITA, even though there is nothing in writing? Explain.

17–3. Click-On Agreements. Anne is a reporter for *Daily Business Journal*, a print publication consulted by investors and other businesspersons. She often uses the Internet to perform research for the articles that she writes for the publication. While visiting the Web site of Cyberspace Investments Corp., Anne reads a pop-up window that states, "Our business newsletter, *E-Commerce Weekly*, is available at a one-year subscription rate of $5 per issue. To subscribe, enter your e-mail address below and click 'SUBSCRIBE.' By subscribing, you agree to the terms of the subscriber's agreement. To read this agreement, click 'AGREEMENT.' " Anne enters her e-mail address, but does not click on "AGREEMENT" to read the terms. Has Anne entered into an enforceable contract to pay for *E-Commerce Weekly?* Explain.

17–4. Online Acceptance. Bob, a sales representative for Central Computer Co., occasionally uses the Internet to obtain information about his customers and to look for new sales leads. While visiting the Web site of Marketing World, Inc., Bob is presented with an on-screen message that offers, "To improve your ability to make deals, read our monthly online magazine, *Sales Genius,* available at a subscription rate of $15 a month. To subscribe, fill in your name, company name, and e-mail address below, and click 'YES!' By clicking 'YES!' you agree to the terms of the subscription contract. To read this contract, click 'TERMS.' " Among those terms is a clause that allows Marketing World to charge interest for subscription bills not paid within a certain time. The terms also prohibit subscribers from copying or distributing part or all of *Sales Genius* in any form. Bob subscribes without reading the terms. Marketing World later files a suit against Bob, based on his failure to pay for his subscription. Should the court hold that Bob is obligated to pay interest on the amount? Explain.

17–5. License Agreements. Management Computer Controls, Inc. (known as "MC 2"), is a Tennessee corporation in the business of selling software. Charles Perry Construction, Inc., a Florida corporation, entered into two contracts with MC 2 to buy software designed to perform estimating and accounting functions for construction firms. Each contract was printed on a standard order form containing a paragraph that referred to a license agreement. The license agreement included a choice-of-forum and choice-of-law provision: "Agreement is to be interpreted and construed according to the laws of the State of Tennessee. Any action, either by you or MC 2, arising out of this Agreement shall be initiated and prosecuted in the Court of Shelby County, Tennessee, and nowhere else." Each of the software packages arrived with the license agreement affixed to the outside of the box. Additionally, the boxes were sealed with an orange sticker bearing the following warning: "By opening this packet, you indicate your acceptance of the MC 2 license agreement." Alleging that the software was not suitable for use with Windows NT, Perry filed a suit against MC 2 in a Florida state court. MC 2 filed a motion to dismiss the complaint on the ground that the suit should be heard in Tennessee. How should the court rule? Why? [*Management Computer Controls, Inc. v. Charles Perry Construction, Inc.,* 743 So.2d 627 (Fla.App. 1 Dist. 1999)]

17–6. Browse-Wrap Terms. Ticketmaster Corp. operates a Web site that allows customers to buy tickets to concerts, ball games, and other events. On the site's home page are instructions and an index to internal pages (one page per event). Each event page provides basic information (a short description of the event, with the date, time, place, and price) and a description of how to order tickets over the Internet, by telephone, by mail, or in person. The home page contains—if a customer scrolls to the bottom—"terms and conditions" that proscribe, among other things, linking to Ticketmaster's internal pages. A customer need not view these terms to go to an event page. Tickets.Com, Inc., operates a Web site that also publicizes special events. Tickets.Com's site includes links to the internal events pages of Ticketmaster. These links bypass Ticketmaster's home page. Ticketmaster filed a suit in a federal district court against Tickets.Com, alleging in part breach of contract on the ground that Tickets.Com's linking violated Ticketmaster's "terms and conditions." Tickets.Com filed a motion to dismiss. Should the court grant the motion? Why or why not? [*Ticketmaster Corp. v. Tickets.Com, Inc.,* 54 U.S.P.Q.2d 1344 (C.D.Cal. 2000)]

17–7. Shrink-Wrap/Click-On Agreements. 1-A Equipment Co. signed a sales order to lease Accware 10 User NT software, which is made and marketed by ICode, Inc. Just above the signature line, the order stated: "Thank you for your order. No returns or refunds will be issued for software license and/or services. All sales are final. Please read the End User License and Service Agreement." The software was delivered in a sealed envelope inside a box. On the outside of the envelope, an "End User Agreement" provided in part, "BY OPENING THIS PACKAGING, CLICKING YOUR ACCEPTANCE OF THE AGREEMENT DURING DOWNLOAD OR INSTALLATION OF THIS PRODUCT, OR BY USING ANY PART OF THIS PRODUCT, YOU AGREE TO BE LEGALLY BOUND BY THE TERMS OF THE AGREEMENT. . . . This agreement will be governed by the laws in force in the Commonwealth of Virginia . . . and exclusive venue for any litigation shall be in Virginia." Later, dissatisfied with the software, 1-A filed a suit in a Massachusetts state court against ICode, alleging breach of contract and misrepresentation. ICode asked the court to dismiss the case on the basis of the "End User Agreement." Is the agreement enforceable? Should the court dismiss the suit? Why or why not? [*1-A Equipment Co. v. ICode, Inc.,* 43 UCC Rep.Serv.2d 807 (Mass.Dist. 2000)]

TEST YOUR KNOWLEDGE—ANSWER ON THE WEB

17–8. Peerless Wall & Window Coverings, Inc., is a small business in Pennsylvania. To run the cash registers in its stores, manage inventory, and link the stores electronically, in 1994 Peerless installed Point of Sale V6.5 software produced by Synchronics, Inc., a small corporation in Tennessee that develops and markets business software. Point of Sale V6.5 was written with code that used only a two-digit year field—for example, 1999 was stored as "99." This meant that all dates were interpreted as falling within the twentieth century (2001, stored as "01," would be mistaken for 1901). In other words, Point of Sale V6.5 was not "Year 2000" (Y2K) compliant. The software was licensed under a shrink-wrap agreement printed on the envelopes containing the disks. The agreement included a clause that, among other things, limited remedies to replacement within ninety days if there was a defect in the disks. "The entire risk as to the quality and performance of the Software is with you." In 1995, Synchronics stopped selling and supporting Point of Sale V6.5.

Two years later, Synchronics told Peerless that the software was not Y2K compliant and should be replaced. Peerless sued Synchronics in a federal district court, alleging, in part, breach of contract. Synchronics filed a motion for summary judgment. Who is most likely to bear the cost of replacing the software? Why? [*Peerless Wall & Window Coverings, Inc. v. Synchronics, Inc.*, 85 F.Supp.2d 519 (W.D.Pa. 2000), *aff'd* 234 F.3d 1265 (3d Cir. 2000)]

A QUESTION OF ETHICS AND SOCIAL RESPONSIBILITY

17–9. Over the phone, Rich and Enza Hill ordered a computer from Gateway 2000, Inc. Inside the box were the computer and a list of contract terms, which provided that the terms governed the transaction unless the customers returned the computer within thirty days. Among those terms was a clause that required any claims to be submitted to arbitration. The Hills kept the computer for more than thirty days before complaining to Gateway about the computer's components and its performance. When the matter was not resolved to their satisfaction, the Hills filed a suit in a federal district court against Gateway, arguing, among other things, that the computer was defective. Gateway asked the court to enforce the arbitration clause. The Hills claimed that this term was not part of a contract to buy the computer because the list on which it appeared had been in the box and they did not see the list until after the computer was delivered. In view of these facts, consider the following questions. [*Hill v. Gateway 2000, Inc.*, 105 F.3d 1147 (7th Cir. 1997)]

1. Should the court enforce the arbitration clause in this case? If you were the judge, how would you rule on this issue?
2. In your opinion, do shrink-wrap agreements impose too great a burden on purchasers? Why or why not?

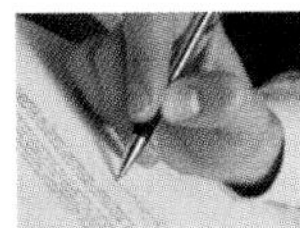

FOR CRITICAL ANALYSIS

17–10. Would you say that most of the legal issues presented by e-commerce are unique to the cyber age or simply old legal issues in a new form?

Internet Exercises

Go to the *Business Law Today* home page at **http://blt.westbuslaw.com**. Select "Interactive Study Center" and then click on "Chapter 17." There you will find the following Internet research exercises that you can perform to learn more about online contracts:

Activity 17–1: E-Contracts
Activity 17–2: The B2B Marketplace

Before the Test

Go to the *Business Law Today* home page at **http://blt.westbuslaw.com**. Click on "Interactive Quizzes." You will find at least twenty interactive questions relating to this chapter.

CHAPTER 18

Warranties and Product Liability

"I'll warrant him heart-whole."

William Shakespeare, 1564–1616
(English dramatist and poet)

CHAPTER CONTENTS

LEARNING OBJECTIVES

After reading this chapter, you should be able to answer the following questions:

① What factors determine whether a seller's or lessor's statement constitutes an express warranty or merely "puffing"?

② What implied warranties arise under the UCC?

③ Can a manufacturer be held liable to any person who suffers an injury proximately caused by the manufacturer's negligently made product?

④ What are the elements of a cause of action in strict product liability?

⑤ What defenses to liability can be raised in a product liability lawsuit?

Warranty is an age-old concept. In sales and lease law, a warranty is an assurance by one party of the existence of a fact on which the other party can rely. Just as William Shakespeare's character warranted his friend "heart-whole" in the play *As You Like It,* so sellers and lessors warrant to those who purchase or lease their goods that the goods are as represented or will be as promised.

The Uniform Commercial Code (UCC) has numerous rules governing the concept of product warranty as it occurs in sales and lease contracts. That will be the subject matter of the first part of this chapter. A natural addition to the discussion is *product liability:* Who is liable to consumers, users, and bystanders for physical harm and property damage caused by a particular good or the use thereof? Product liability encompasses the contract theory of warranty, as well as the tort theories of negligence and strict liability (discussed in Chapter 4).

Warranties

Article 2 (on sales) and Article 2A (on leases) of the UCC designate several types of warranties that can arise in a sales or lease contract, including warranties of title, express warranties, and implied warranties.

WARRANTIES OF TITLE

Title warranty arises automatically in most sales contracts. The UCC imposes three types of warranties of title.

Good Title In most cases, sellers warrant that they have good and valid title to the goods sold and that transfer of the title is rightful [UCC 2–312(1)(a)]. • **EXAMPLE 18.1** Sharon steals goods from Miguel and sells them to Carrie, who does not know that the goods are stolen. If Miguel reclaims the goods from Carrie, which he has a right to do, Carrie can then sue Sharon for breach of warranty. When Sharon sold Carrie the goods, Sharon *automatically* warranted to her that the title conveyed was valid and that its transfer was rightful. Because this was not in fact the case, Sharon breached the warranty of title imposed by UCC 2–312(1)(a) and became liable to the buyer for the appropriate damages. •

LIEN
An encumbrance on a property to satisfy a debt or protect a claim for payment of a debt.

No Liens A second warranty of title provided by the UCC protects buyers who are *unaware* of any encumbrances (claims, charges, or liabilities—usually called **liens**[1]) against goods at the time the contract is made [UCC 2–312(1)(b)]. This warranty protects buyers who, for example, unknowingly purchase goods that are subject to a creditor's security interest (see Chapter 22). If a creditor legally repossesses the goods from a buyer *who had no actual knowledge of the security interest,* the buyer can recover from the seller for breach of warranty.

Article 2A affords similar protection for lessees. Section 2A–211(1) provides that during the term of the lease, no claim of any third party will interfere with the lessee's enjoyment of the leasehold interest.

No Infringements A merchant seller is also deemed to warrant that the goods delivered are free from any copyright, trademark, or patent claims of a third person[2] [UCC 2–312(3), 2A–211(2)]. If this warranty is breached and the buyer is sued by the party holding copyright, trademark, or patent rights in the goods, the buyer must notify the seller of the litigation within a reasonable time to enable the seller to decide whether to defend the lawsuit. If the seller states in writing that she or he has decided to defend and agrees to bear all expenses, including that of an adverse judgment, then the buyer must let the seller undertake litigation; otherwise, the buyer loses all rights against the seller if any infringement liability is established [UCC 2–607(3)(b), 2–607(5)(b)].

Article 2A provides for the same notice of litigation in situations that involve leases rather than sales [UCC 2A–516(3)(b), 2A–516(4)(b)]. There is an exception for leases to individual consumers for personal, family, or household purposes. A consumer who fails to notify the lessor within a reasonable time does not lose his or her remedy against the lessor for any liability established in the litigation [UCC 2A–516(3)(b)].

1. Pronounced *leens.*
2. Recall from Chapter 14 that a *merchant* is defined in UCC 2–104(1) as a person who deals in goods of the kind involved in the sales contract or who, by occupation, presents himself or herself as having knowledge or skill peculiar to the goods involved in the transaction.

Disclaimer of Title Warranty In an ordinary sales transaction, the title warranty can be disclaimed or modified only by *specific language* in the contract [UCC 2–312(2)]. For example, sellers can assert that they are transferring only such rights, title, and interest as they have in the goods. In a lease transaction, the disclaimer must "be specific, be by a writing, and be conspicuous" [UCC 2A–214(4)].

EXPRESS WARRANTIES

EXPRESS WARRANTY
A seller's or lessor's oral or written promise or affirmation of fact ancillary to an underlying sales or lease agreement, as to the quality, description, or performance of the goods being sold or leased.

A seller or lessor can create an **express warranty** by making representations concerning the quality, condition, description, or performance potential of the goods. Under UCC 2–313 and 2A–210, express warranties arise when a seller or lessor indicates any of the following:

① That the goods conform to any affirmation (declaration that something is true) or promise of fact that the seller or lessor makes to the buyer or lessee about the goods. Such affirmations or promises are usually made during the bargaining process. Statements such as "these drill bits will penetrate stainless steel—and without dulling" are express warranties.

② That the goods conform to any description of them. For example, a label that reads "Crate contains one 150-horsepower diesel engine" or a contract that calls for the delivery of a "camel's-hair coat" creates an express warranty.

③ That the goods conform to any sample or model of the goods shown to the buyer or lessee.

"Cheat me in the price, but not in the goods."

THOMAS FULLER, 1608–1661 (English clergyman)

To succeed in a suit against a manufacturer for a breach of express warranty, does a plaintiff have to prove that a specific defect caused the breach? That was the question in the following case.

CASE 18.1 Genetti v. Caterpillar, Inc.

Nebraska Supreme Court, 2001.
261 Neb. 98,
621 N.W.2d 529.

FACTS Robert and Sherrie Genetti are in the business of delivering furniture nationwide. In 1996, they bought a new General Motors Corporation (GMC) truck and trailer for $97,043 from Omaha Truck Center, Inc. The truck was equipped with a Model 3116 medium-duty diesel engine manufactured by Caterpillar, Inc. GMC and Caterpillar expressly warranted the truck for three years or 150,000 miles. Over the next seven months, the truck broke down four times. Each time, the Genettis lost the use of the truck, costing them time and money, including a fourth repair bill of $12,000. They had the truck repaired through GMC and Caterpillar dealerships, whose mechanics stated that the cause of the breakdowns was "engine failure." When GMC and Caterpillar refused to replace the vehicle or refund the price, the Genettis filed a suit in a Nebraska state court against the manufacturers, alleging, in part, breach of express warranty. The court entered separate judgments against GMC and Caterpillar in favor of the Genettis on this claim. The manufacturers appealed to the state supreme court, arguing, in part, that the plaintiffs could not recover for a breach of express warranty simply by asserting "engine failure."

ISSUE To recover for a breach of express warranty, do plaintiffs have to prove that a specific defect caused the breach?

DECISION No. The court affirmed this part of the lower court's judgment and remanded the case for a new trial on other grounds.

CASE 18.1—Continued

REASON The state supreme court reasoned that "a precise or specific defect does not need to be proved" in order to find a product defective under the UCC. The court explained that under many warranties, "a consumer requiring warranty service on a vehicle may take the damaged vehicle only to a service department at an authorized dealer. * * * Placing the burden on the consumer to prove a precise defect is unfair and unconscionable since the dealer and manufacturer could tamper (whether intentionally or inadvertently) with the evidence. * * * To impose an unreasonably heavy burden on consumers is to deny them a meaningful remedy." In this case, the Genettis presented evidence that the actions of their employees were proper. This eliminated abuse or misuse as the cause of the breakdown. "Looking at the evidence," said the court, "a jury using common sense and experience could reasonably arrive at the conclusion that the * * * breakdown[s] [were] caused by a defect in the engine and should have been covered by the warranty."

FOR CRITICAL ANALYSIS—Economic Consideration *In a breach of warranty suit involving more than one defendant and resulting in a verdict in the plaintiff's favor, how should the damages be apportioned?*

Basis of the Bargain To create an express warranty, a seller or lessor does not have to use formal words such as *warrant* or *guarantee* [UCC 2–313(2), 2A–210(2)]. The UCC requires that for an express warranty to be created, the affirmation, promise, description, or sample must become part of the "basis of the bargain" [UCC 2–313(1), 2A–210(1)]. Just what constitutes the basis of the bargain is hard to say. The UCC does not define the concept, and it is a question of fact in each case whether a representation was made at such a time and in such a way that it induced the buyer or lessee to enter into the contract.

Statements of Opinion Statements of fact create express warranties. If the seller or lessor merely makes a statement that relates to the supposed value or worth of the goods, or makes a statement of opinion or recommendation about the goods, however, the seller or lessor is not creating an express warranty [UCC 2–313(2), 2A–210(2)].

• **EXAMPLE 18.2** A seller claims that "this is the best used car to come along in years; it has four new tires and a 350-horsepower engine just rebuilt this year." The seller has made several *affirmations of fact* that can create a warranty: the automobile has an engine; it has a 350-horsepower engine; it was rebuilt this year; there are four tires on the automobile; and the tires are new. The seller's *opinion* that the vehicle is "the best used car to come along in years," however, is known as "puffing" and creates no warranty. (*Puffing* is the expression of opinion by a seller or lessor that is not made as a representation of fact.) •

A statement relating to the value of the goods, such as "it's worth a fortune" or "anywhere else you'd pay $10,000 for it," usually does not create a warranty. If the seller or lessor is an expert and gives an opinion as an expert to a layperson, though, then a warranty may be created.

It is not always easy to determine what constitutes an express warranty and what constitutes puffing. The reasonableness of the buyer's or lessee's reliance appears to be the controlling criterion in many cases. For example, a salesperson's statements that a ladder "will never break" and will "last a lifetime" are so clearly improbable that no reasonable buyer should rely on them. Additionally, the context in which a statement is made might be relevant in determining the reasonableness of the buyer's or lessee's reliance. For example, a reasonable person is more likely to rely on a written statement made in an advertisement than on a statement made orally by a salesperson.

IMPLIED WARRANTIES

IMPLIED WARRANTY
A warranty that arises by law by implication or inference from the nature of the transaction or the relative situation or circumstances of the parties.

An **implied warranty** is one that *the law derives* by implication or inference from the nature of the transaction or the relative situation or circumstances of the parties. In an action based on breach of implied warranty, it is necessary to show that an implied warranty existed and that the breach of the warranty proximately caused[3] the damage sustained. We look here at some of the implied warranties that arise under the UCC.

IMPLIED WARRANTY OF MERCHANTABILITY
A warranty that goods being sold or leased are reasonably fit for the general purpose for which they are sold or leased, are properly packaged and labeled, and are of proper quality. The warranty automatically arises in every sale or lease of goods made by a merchant who deals in goods of the kind sold or leased.

Implied Warranty of Merchantability Every sale or lease of goods made *by a merchant* who deals in goods of the kind sold or leased automatically gives rise to an **implied warranty of merchantability** [UCC 2–314, 2A–212]. Thus, a merchant who is in the business of selling ski equipment makes an implied warranty of merchantability every time the merchant sells a pair of skis, but a neighbor selling his or her skis at a garage sale does not.

Merchantable Goods. Goods that are *merchantable* are "reasonably fit for the ordinary purposes for which such goods are used." They must be of at least average, fair, or medium-grade quality. The quality must be comparable to a level that will pass without objection in the trade or market for goods of the same description. To be merchantable, the goods must also be adequately packaged and labeled as provided by the agreement, and they must conform to the promises or affirmations of fact made on the container or label, if any.

An implied warranty of merchantability also imposes on the merchant liability for the safe performance of the product. It makes no difference whether the merchant knew of or could have discovered a defect that makes the product unsafe—she or he is liable in either situation. Of course, merchants are not absolute insurers against all accidents arising in connection with the goods. For example, a bar of soap is not unmerchantable merely because a user could slip and fall by stepping on it.

Merchantable Food. The UCC recognizes the serving of food or drink to be consumed on or off the premises as a sale of goods subject to the implied warranty of merchantability [UCC 2–314(1)]. "Merchantable" food means food that is fit to eat. Courts generally determine whether food is fit to eat on the basis of consumer expectations. For example, the courts assume that consumers should reasonably expect to find on occasion bones in fish fillets, cherry pits in cherry pie, a nutshell in a package of shelled nuts, and so on—because such substances are natural incidents of the food. In contrast, consumers would not reasonably expect to find an inchworm in a can of peas or a piece of glass in a soft drink—because these substances are not natural to the food product.[4] In the following classic case, the court had to determine whether a fish bone was a substance that one should reasonably expect to find in fish chowder.

---

3. Proximate cause, or legal cause, exists when the connection between an act and an injury is strong enough to justify imposing liability—see Chapter 4.

4. See, for example, *Mexicali Rose v. Superior Court,* 1 Cal.4th 617, 4 Cal.Rptr.2d 145, 822 P.2d 1292 (1992).

Landmark and Classic Cases

CASE 18.2 Webster v. Blue Ship Tea Room, Inc.

Supreme Judicial Court of Massachusetts, 1964.
347 Mass. 421,
198 N.E.2d 309.

HISTORICAL AND CULTURAL SETTING *Chowder, a soup or stew made with fresh fish, possibly originated in the fishing villages of Brittany (a French province located west of Paris) and was probably carried to Canada and New England by Breton fishermen. In the nineteenth century and earlier, recipes for chowder did not call for the removal of the fish bones. Chowder recipes in the first half of the twentieth century remained as they had in previous centuries, sometimes specifying that the fish head, tail, and backbone were to be broken in pieces and boiled, with the "liquor thus produced * * * added to the balance of the chowder."*[a] *By the middle of the twentieth century, there was a considerable body of case law concerning implied warranties and foreign and natural substances in food. It was perhaps inevitable that sooner or later, a consumer injured by a fish bone in chowder would challenge the merchantability of chowder containing fish bones.*

FACTS Blue Ship Tea Room, Inc., was located in Boston in an old building overlooking the ocean. Webster, who had been born and raised in New England, went to the restaurant and ordered fish chowder. The chowder was milky in color. After three or four spoonfuls, she felt something lodged in her throat. As a result, she underwent two esophagoscopies; in the second esophagoscopy, a fish bone was found and removed. Webster filed suit against the restaurant in a Massachusetts state court for breach of the implied warranty of merchantability. The jury rendered a verdict for Webster, and the restaurant appealed to the state's highest court.

a. Fannie Farmer, *The Boston Cooking School Cook Book* (Boston: Little Brown Co., 1937), p. 166.

ISSUE Does serving fish chowder that contains a bone constitute the breach of an implied warranty of merchantability on the part of the restaurant?

DECISION No. The Supreme Judicial Court of Massachusetts held that Webster could not recover against Blue Ship Tea Room because no breach of warranty had occurred.

REASON The court, citing UCC Section 2–314, stated that "a warranty that goods shall be merchantable is implied in a contract for their sale if the seller is a merchant with respect to goods of that kind. Under this section the serving for value of food or drink to be consumed either on the premises or elsewhere is a sale. * * * Goods to be merchantable must at least be * * * fit for the ordinary purposes for which such goods are used." The question here is whether a fish bone made the chowder unfit for eating. In the judge's opinion, "the joys of life in New England include the ready availability of fresh fish chowder. We should be prepared to cope with the hazards of fish bones, the occasional presence of which in chowders is, it seems to us, to be anticipated, and which, in the light of a hallowed tradition, do not impair their fitness or merchantability."

COMMENT *This classic case, phrased in memorable language, was an early application of the UCC's implied warranty of merchantability to food products. The case established the rule that consumers should expect to find, on occasion, elements of food products that are natural to the product (such as fish bones in fish chowder). In such cases, the food preparers or packagers will not be liable. This rule continues to be applied today in cases involving similar issues.*

IMPLIED WARRANTY OF FITNESS FOR A PARTICULAR PURPOSE
A warranty that goods sold or leased are fit for a particular purpose. The warranty arises when any seller or lessor knows the particular purpose for which a buyer or lessee will use the goods and knows that the buyer or lessee is relying on the skill and judgment of the seller or lessor to select suitable goods.

Implied Warranty of Fitness for a Particular Purpose The implied warranty of **fitness for a particular purpose** arises when any seller or lessor (merchant or nonmerchant) knows the particular purpose for which a buyer or lessee will use the goods and knows that the buyer or lessee is relying on the skill and judgment of the seller or lessor to select suitable goods [UCC 2–315, 2A–213].

A "particular purpose" of the buyer or lessee differs from the "ordinary purpose for which goods are used" (merchantability). Goods can be merchantable but unfit for a particular purpose. • **EXAMPLE 18.3** Suppose that you need a gallon of paint to match the color of your living room walls—a light shade somewhere between coral and peach. You take a sample to your local hardware store and request a gallon of paint of that color. Instead, you are given a gallon of bright blue paint. Here, the salesperson has not breached any warranty of implied merchantability—the bright blue paint is of high quality and suitable for interior walls—but he or she has breached an implied warranty of fitness for a particular purpose. •

A seller or lessor does not need to have actual knowledge of the buyer's or lessee's particular purpose. It is sufficient if a seller or lessor "has reason to know" the purpose. The buyer or lessee, however, must have *relied* on the skill or judgment of the seller or lessor in selecting or furnishing suitable goods for an implied warranty to be created.

• **EXAMPLE 18.4** Bloomberg leases a computer from Future Tech, a lessor of technical business equipment. Bloomberg tells the clerk that she wants a computer that will run a complicated new engineering graphics program at a realistic speed. Future Tech leases Bloomberg an Architex One computer with a CPU speed of only 550 megahertz, even though a speed of at least 1200 megahertz would be required to run Bloomberg's graphics program at a "realistic speed." Bloomberg, after discovering that it takes forever to run her program, wants her money back. Here, because Future Tech has breached the implied warranty of fitness for a particular purpose, Bloomberg normally will be able to recover. The clerk knew specifically that Bloomberg wanted a computer with enough speed to run certain software. Furthermore, Bloomberg relied on the clerk to furnish a computer that would fulfill this purpose. Because Future Tech did not do so, the warranty was breached. •

Other Implied Warranties Implied warranties can also arise (or be excluded or modified) as a result of course of dealing, course of performance, or usage of trade [UCC 2–314(3), 2A–212(3)]. In the absence of evidence to the contrary, when both parties to a sales or lease contract have knowledge of a well-recognized trade custom, the courts will infer that both parties intended for that trade custom to apply to their contract. For example, if an industry-wide custom is to lubricate a new car before it is delivered and a dealer fails to do so, the dealer can be held liable to a buyer for damages resulting from the breach of an implied warranty. This, of course, would also be negligence on the part of the dealer.

OVERLAPPING WARRANTIES

BE AWARE Express and implied warranties do not necessarily displace each other. More than one warranty can cover the same goods in the same transaction.

Sometimes, two or more warranties are made in a single transaction. An implied warranty of merchantability, an implied warranty of fitness for a particular purpose, or both can exist in addition to an express warranty. For example, when a sales contract for a new car states that "this car engine is warranted to be free from defects for 36,000 miles or thirty-six months, whichever occurs first," there is an express warranty against all defects and an implied warranty that the car will be fit for normal use.

The rule under the UCC is that express and implied warranties are construed as *cumulative* if they are consistent with one another [UCC 2–317, 2A–215]. If the warranties are inconsistent, the courts usually hold as follows:

① *Express* warranties displace inconsistent *implied* warranties, except for implied warranties of fitness for a particular purpose.

② Samples take precedence over inconsistent general descriptions.

③ Technical specifications displace inconsistent samples or general descriptions.

In the example presented earlier, suppose that when Bloomberg leases the computer from Future Tech, the contract contains an express warranty concerning the speed of the

CPU and the application programs that the computer is capable of running. Bloomberg does not realize that the speed expressly warranted in the contract is insufficient for her needs. Bloomberg later claims that Future Tech has breached the implied warranty of fitness for a particular purpose. Here, although the express warranty would take precedence over any implied warranty of merchantability, it normally would not take precedence over an implied warranty of fitness for a particular purpose. Bloomberg therefore has a good claim for the breach of implied warranty of fitness for a particular purpose, because she made it clear that she was leasing the computer to perform certain tasks.

Third Party Beneficiaries of Warranties

One of the general principles of contract law is that unless you are one of the parties to a contract, you have no rights under the contract. In other words, *privity of contract* must exist between a plaintiff and a defendant before any action based on a contract can be maintained. Two notable exceptions to the rule of privity are assignments and third party beneficiary contracts (these topics were discussed in Chapter 12). Another exception is made under warranty laws so that third parties can recover for harms suffered as a result of breached warranties.

There has been sharp disagreement among state courts as to how far warranty liability should extend, however. In view of this disagreement, the UCC offers three alternatives for liability to third parties [UCC 2–318, 2A–216]. All three alternatives are intended to eliminate the privity requirement with respect to certain enumerated types of injuries (personal versus property) for certain beneficiaries (for example, household members or bystanders).

Warranty Disclaimers

WATCH OUT Courts generally view warranty disclaimers unfavorably, especially when consumers are involved.

Because each type of warranty is created in a special way, the manner in which warranties can be disclaimed or qualified by a seller or lessor varies depending on the type of warranty.

Express Warranties As already stated, any affirmation of fact or promise, description of the goods, or use of samples or models by a seller or lessor creates an express warranty. Obviously, then, express warranties can be excluded if the seller or lessor carefully refrains from making any promise or affirmation of fact relating to the goods, describing the goods, or using a sample or model.

The UCC does permit express warranties to be negated or limited by specific and unambiguous language, provided that this is done in a manner that protects the buyer or lessee from surprise. Therefore, a written disclaimer in language that is clear and conspicuous, and called to a buyer's or lessee's attention, could negate all oral express warranties not included in the written sales contract [UCC 2–316(1), 2A–214(1)]. This allows the seller or lessor to avoid false allegations that oral warranties were made, and it ensures that only representations made by properly authorized individuals are included in the bargain.

Note, however, that a buyer or lessee must be made aware of any warranty disclaimers or modifications *at the time the contract is formed.* In other words, any oral or written warranties—or disclaimers—made during the bargaining process as part of a contract's formation cannot be modified at a later time by the seller or lessor.

Implied Warranties Generally speaking, unless circumstances indicate otherwise, the implied warranties of merchantability and fitness are disclaimed by the expressions "as

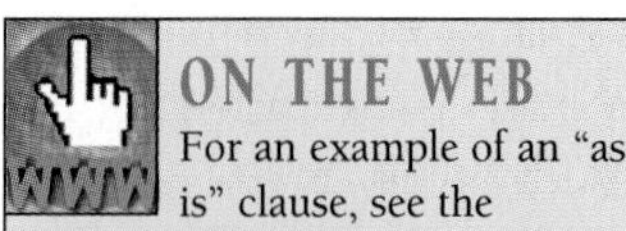

ON THE WEB For an example of an "as is" clause, see the warranty disclaimer provided by the University of Minnesota for one of its research software products at **http://www.cmrr.drad.umn.edu/stimulate/stimUsersGuide/node7.html**.

is," "with all faults," and other similar expressions that in common understanding call the buyer's or lessee's attention to the fact that there are no implied warranties [UCC 2–316(3)(a), 2A–214(3)(a)].

The UCC also permits a seller or lessor to specifically disclaim an implied warranty either of fitness or of merchantability [UCC 2–316(2), 2A–214(2)]. To disclaim an implied warranty of fitness for a particular purpose, the disclaimer *must* be in writing and be conspicuous. The word *fitness* does not have to be mentioned in the writing; it is sufficient if, for example, the disclaimer states, "THERE ARE NO WARRANTIES THAT EXTEND BEYOND THE DESCRIPTION ON THE FACE HEREOF." A merchantability disclaimer must be more specific; it must mention the word *merchantability*. It need not be written, but if it is, the writing must be conspicuous [UCC 2–316(2), 2A–214(4)]. According to UCC 1–201(10),

> [a] term or clause is conspicuous when it is so written that a reasonable person against whom it is to operate ought to have noticed it. A printed heading in capitals . . . is conspicuous. Language in the body of a form is conspicuous if it is in larger or other contrasting type or color.

● **EXAMPLE 18.5** Forbes, a merchant, sells Maves a particular lawn mower selected by Forbes with the characteristics clearly requested by Maves. At the time of the sale, Forbes orally tells Maves that he does not warrant the merchantability of the mower, as it is last year's model and has been used extensively as a demonstrator. If the mower proves to be defective and does not work, Maves can hold Forbes liable for breach of the warranty of fitness for a particular purpose but not for breach of the warranty of merchantability. Forbes's oral disclaimer mentioning the word *merchantability* is a proper disclaimer. For Forbes to have disclaimed the implied warranty of fitness for a particular purpose, however, a conspicuous writing would have been required. Because he made no written disclaimer, Forbes can still be held liable. ●

Disclaimers of warranties, both express and implied, are frequently contained in contracts formed online. For a discussion of one such warranty disclaimer, see this chapter's *Business Law in the Online World* feature.

Buyer's or Lessee's Refusal to Inspect If a buyer or lessee actually examines the goods (or a sample or model) as fully as desired before entering into a contract, or if the buyer or lessee refuses to examine the goods on the seller's or lessor's demand that he or she do so, *there is no implied warranty with respect to defects that a reasonable examination would reveal or defects that are actually found* [UCC 2–316(3)(b), 2A–214(2)(b)].

● **EXAMPLE 18.6** Suppose that Joplin buys an ax at Gershwin's Hardware Store. No express warranties are made. Joplin, even after Gershwin requests that she inspect the ax, refuses to inspect it before buying it. Had she done so, she would have noticed that the handle of the ax was obviously cracked. If Joplin is later injured by the defective ax, she normally will not be able to hold Gershwin liable for breach of the warranty of merchantability, because she would have spotted the defect during an inspection. ●

Warranty Disclaimers and Unconscionability The UCC sections dealing with warranty disclaimers do not refer specifically to unconscionability as a factor. Ultimately, however, the courts will test warranty disclaimers with reference to the UCC's unconscionability standards [UCC 2–302, 2A–108]. Such things as lack of bargaining position, "take-it-or-leave-it" choices, and a buyer's or lessee's failure to understand or know of a warranty disclaimer will become relevant to the issue of unconscionability.

BUSINESS LAW: //in the Online World

Online Warranty Disclaimers

All too often, purchasers of goods or services fail to read the "fine print" of contracts. This is a problem not only with respect to traditional (paper) contracts but also with contracts formed online. Indeed, parties may be more likely to overlook contract provisions when the terms of the contract appear on a computer screen. Consider a case that came before a New York court in 2001.

Web Site Representations

The plaintiffs in the case were a group of subscribers to a DSL (digital subscriber line) service offered by Bell Atlantic Corporation. The subscribers claimed that Bell Atlantic had misrepresented the quality of its DSL service in statements made on its Web site. The representations at issue stated that subscribers would have "high-speed Internet access service up to 126 times faster than your 56K modem" and that the service was dedicated—"You're always connected—no dialing in and no busy signals, ever!" When the subscribers became dissatisfied with the actual connection speed and the fact that they sometimes had difficulty accessing Web sites, they sued Bell Atlantic for, among other things, breach of warranty. Bell Atlantic moved to dismiss the case on the ground that it had disclaimed all warranties in its online "Terms and Conditions" agreement.

It's All in the Contract—Including the Warranty Disclaimer

The court had little difficulty in granting Bell Atlantic's motion to dismiss the case. For one thing, stated the court, the plaintiffs had misunderstood the representations made by Bell Atlantic on its Web site. The representation as to high-speed service set forth a maximum possible speed, not the standard speed at which the service would operate. The representation regarding the dedicated connection referred to the fact that the connection need not be dialed up, not that the connection was infallible and would never be interrupted for any reason. The court also noted that the subscribers were given thirty days to try out the service and, if they were dissatisfied, to cancel it and receive a full refund.

Finally, Bell Atlantic's online "Terms and Conditions" agreement stated, in boldface, large capital letters, that the service was provided on an "as is" or "as available" basis and that "any and all warranties for the services, whether express or implied, including but not limited to the implied warranties of merchantability and fitness for a particular purpose" were disclaimed. In response to the plaintiffs' argument that it was possible to use the service without having read the "Terms and Conditions," the court simply stated that this "does not impair the enforcement of the agreement."[a]

FOR CRITICAL ANALYSIS

If Bell Atlantic had promised on its Web site that DSL subscribers would have maximum-speed Internet access, would the subscribers have had a cause of action for breach of warranty? Why or why not?

a. *Scott v. Bell Atlantic Corp.*, 726 N.Y.S.2d 60 (N.Y.A.D. 1st Dept. 2001).

MAGNUSON-MOSS WARRANTY ACT

The Magnuson-Moss Warranty Act of 1975[5] was designed to prevent deception in warranties by making them easier to understand. The act is mainly enforced by the Federal Trade Commission (FTC). Additionally, the attorney general or a consumer who has been injured can enforce the act if informal procedures for settling disputes prove to be ineffective. The act modifies UCC warranty rules to some extent when consumer transactions are involved. The UCC, however, remains the primary codification of warranty rules for industrial and commercial transactions.

Under the Magnuson-Moss Act, no seller or lessor is required to give an express written warranty for consumer goods sold. If a seller or lessor chooses to make an

5. 15 U.S.C. Sections 2301–2312.

express written warranty, however, and the cost of the consumer goods is more than $10, the warranty must be labeled as "full" or "limited." In addition, if the cost of the goods is more than $15, by FTC regulation, the warrantor must make certain disclosures fully and conspicuously in a single document in "readily understood language." This disclosure must state the names and addresses of the warrantor(s), what specifically is warranted, procedures for enforcement of the warranty, any limitations on warranty relief, and that the buyer has legal rights.

Full Warranty Although a *full warranty* may not cover every aspect of the consumer product sold, what it covers ensures some type of consumer satisfaction in case the product is defective. A full warranty requires free repair or replacement of any defective part; if the product cannot be repaired within a reasonable time, the consumer has the choice of a refund or a replacement without charge. The full warranty frequently does not have a time limit on it. Any limitation on consequential damages must be *conspicuously* stated. Additionally, the warrantor need not perform warranty services if the problem with the product was caused by the consumer's unreasonable use of the product.

REMEMBER When a buyer or lessee is a consumer, a limitation on consequential damages for personal injuries resulting from nonconforming goods is *prima facie* unconscionable.

Limited Warranty A *limited warranty* arises when the written warranty fails to meet one of the minimum requirements of a full warranty. The fact that only a limited warranty is being given must be conspicuously designated. If the only distinction between a limited warranty and a full warranty is a time limitation, the Magnuson-Moss Warranty Act allows the warrantor to identify the warranty as a full warranty by such language as "full twelve-month warranty."

Implied Warranties Implied warranties do not arise under the Magnuson-Moss Warranty Act; they continue to be created according to UCC provisions. Implied warranties may not be disclaimed under the Magnuson-Moss Warranty Act, however. Although a warrantor can impose a time limit on the duration of an implied warranty, it must correspond to the duration of the express warranty.[6]

Lemon Laws

"The biggest corporation, like the humblest private citizen, must be held to strict compliance with the will of the people."

THEODORE ROOSEVELT, 1858–1919 (Twenty-sixth president of the United States, 1901–1909)

Some purchasers of defective automobiles—called "lemons"—found that the remedies provided by the UCC were inadequate due to limitations imposed by the seller. In response to the frustrations of these buyers, all of the states have enacted *lemon laws*. Basically, lemon laws provide that if an automobile under warranty possesses a defect that significantly affects the vehicle's value or use, and the seller fails to remedy the defect within a specified number of opportunities (usually four), the buyer is entitled to a new car, replacement of defective parts, or return of all consideration paid.

In most states, lemon laws require an aggrieved new-car owner to notify the dealer or manufacturer of the problem and to provide the dealer or manufacturer with an opportunity to solve it. If the problem remains, the owner must then submit complaints to the arbitration program specified in the manufacturer's warranty before taking the case to court. Decisions by arbitration panels are binding on the manufacturer (that is, cannot be appealed by the manufacturer to the courts) but usually are not binding on the purchaser.

6. The time limit on an implied warranty occurring by virtue of the warrantor's express warranty must, of course, be reasonable, conscionable, and set forth in clear and conspicuous language on the face of the warranty.

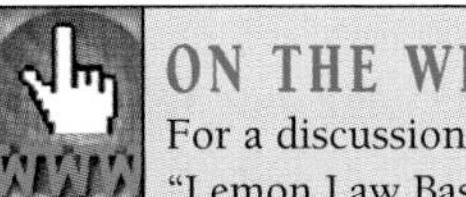

ON THE WEB For a discussion of "Lemon Law Basics," as well as information about other warranty laws, go to Car Talk's Web site at

http://www.cartalk.cars.com/Got-A-Car/Lemon/lemon_general.html.

Most major automobile companies use their own arbitration panels. Some companies, however, subscribe to independent arbitration services, such as those provided by the Better Business Bureau. Although arbitration boards must meet state and/or federal standards of impartiality, industry-sponsored arbitration boards have been criticized for not being truly impartial. In response to this criticism, some states have established mandatory, government-sponsored arbitration programs for lemon-law disputes.

Product Liability

PRODUCT LIABILITY The legal liability of manufacturers, sellers, and lessors of goods to consumers, users, and bystanders for injuries or damages that are caused by the goods.

Manufacturers, sellers, and lessors of goods can be held liable to consumers, users, and bystanders for physical harm or property damage that is caused by the goods. This is called **product liability**. Product liability may be based on the warranty theories just discussed, as well as on the theories of negligence, misrepresentation, and strict liability. We look here at product liability based on negligence and misrepresentation.

NEGLIGENCE

RECALL The elements of negligence include a duty of care, a breach of the duty, and an injury to the plaintiff proximately caused by the breach.

Chapter 4 defined *negligence* as the failure to exercise the degree of care that a reasonable, prudent person would have exercised under the circumstances. If a manufacturer fails to exercise "due care" to make a product safe, a person who is injured by the product may sue the manufacturer for negligence.

Due Care Must Be Exercised Due care must be exercised in designing the product, selecting the materials, using the appropriate production process, assembling the product, and placing adequate warnings on the label informing the user of dangers of which an ordinary person might not be aware. The duty of care also extends to the inspection and testing of any purchased products that are used in the final product sold by the manufacturer.

ETHICAL ISSUE 18.1

Should gun manufacturers be required to warn of the dangers associated with gun use?

Across the nation, numerous plaintiffs have sued gun manufacturers for negligence. One of the allegations in many of these suits is that gun manufacturers have a duty to warn users of the dangers associated with gun use. The gun manufacturers counter that such dangers are "open and obvious" and that under negligence law there is no duty to warn of such dangers (see Chapter 4). In one of the first appellate court decisions addressing this issue, an Ohio appellate court ruled in favor of the gun manufacturer. Said the court, "Knives are sharp, bowling balls are heavy, bullets cause puncture wounds in flesh. The law has long recognized that obvious dangers are an excluded class." "Were we to decide otherwise," concluded the court, "we would open a Pandora's box."[7] Some other appellate courts are helping to make sure that "Pandora's box" stays closed. New York's highest court, for example, has held that a gun manufacturer's duty of care does not extend to those who are injured by the illegal use of handguns.[8]

7. *City of Cincinnati v. Beretta U.S.A. Corp.,* 2000 WL 1133078 (Ohio.App. 1st Dist. 2000).
8. *Hamilton v. Beretta U.S.A. Corp.,* 96 N.Y.2d 222, 750 N.E.2d 1055, 727 N.Y.S.2d 7 (2001).

"The assault upon the citadel of privity [of contract] is proceeding in these days apace."

BENJAMIN CARDOZO, 1870–1938
(Associate justice of the United States Supreme Court, 1932–1938)

Privity of Contract Not Required A product liability action based on negligence does not require privity of contract between the injured plaintiff and the negligent defendant manufacturer. Section 395 of the *Restatement (Second) of Torts* states as follows:

> A manufacturer who fails to exercise reasonable care in the manufacture of a chattel [movable good] which, unless carefully made, he should recognize as involving an unreasonable risk of causing physical harm to those who lawfully use it for a purpose for which the manufacturer should expect it to be used and to those whom he should expect to be endangered by its probable use, is subject to liability for physical harm caused to them by its lawful use in a manner and for a purpose for which it is supplied.

In other words, a manufacturer is liable for its failure to exercise due care to any person who sustained an injury proximately caused by a negligently made (defective) product, regardless of whether the injured person is in privity of contract with the negligent defendant manufacturer or lessor. Relative to the long history of the common law, this exception to the privity requirement is a fairly recent development, dating to the early part of the twentieth century. A leading case in this respect is *MacPherson v. Buick Motor Co.,* which we present as this chapter's *Landmark in the Law* feature.

MISREPRESENTATION

When a fraudulent misrepresentation has been made to a user or consumer, and that misrepresentation ultimately results in an injury, the basis of liability may be the tort of fraud. For example, the intentional mislabeling of packaged cosmetics and the intentional concealment of a product's defects would constitute fraudulent misrepresentation.

LANDMARK IN THE LAW
MacPherson v. Buick Motor Co. (1916)

In the landmark case of *MacPherson v. Buick Motor Co.,*[a] the New York Court of Appeals—New York's highest court—dealt with the liability of a manufacturer that failed to exercise reasonable care in manufacturing a finished product.

Case Background The case was brought by Donald MacPherson, who suffered injuries while riding in a Buick automobile that suddenly collapsed because one of the wheels was made of defective wood. The spokes crumbled into fragments, throwing MacPherson out of the vehicle and injuring him.

MacPherson had purchased the car from a Buick dealer, but he brought suit against the manufacturer, Buick Motor Company. The wheel itself had not been made by Buick; it had been bought from another manufacturer. There was evidence, though, that the defects could have been discovered by reasonable inspection by Buick and that no such inspection had taken place. MacPherson charged Buick with negligence for putting a human life in imminent danger.

The Issue before the Court and the Court's Ruling The major issue before the court was whether Buick owed a duty of care to anyone except the immediate purchaser of the car (that is, the Buick dealer). In deciding the issue, Justice Benjamin Cardozo stated that "[i]f the nature of a thing is such that it is reasonably certain

a. 217 N.Y. 382, 111 N.E. 1050 (1916).

Strict Product Liability

Under the doctrine of strict liability (discussed in Chapter 4), people may be liable for the results of their acts regardless of their intentions or their exercise of reasonable care. Under this doctrine, liability does not depend on privity of contract. The injured party does not have to be the buyer or a third party beneficiary, as required under contract warranty theory. Indeed, this type of liability in law is not governed by the provisions of the UCC because it is a tort doctrine, not a principle of the law relating to sales contracts.

STRICT PRODUCT LIABILITY AND PUBLIC POLICY

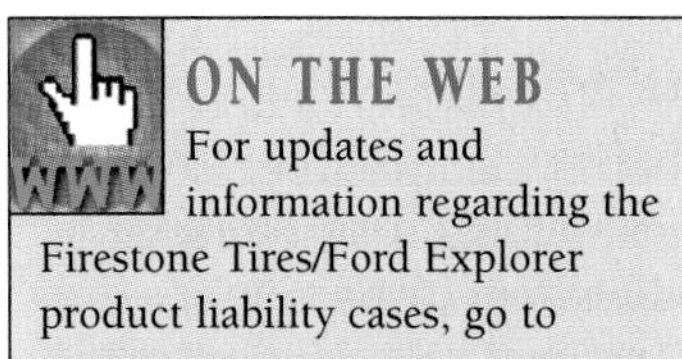

ON THE WEB For updates and information regarding the Firestone Tires/Ford Explorer product liability cases, go to **http://www.safetyforum.com/tires/tires-news.html**.

Strict product liability is imposed by law as a matter of public policy—the general principle of the law that prohibits actions that tend to be injurious to the public. With respect to strict liability, the policy rests on the threefold assumption that (1) consumers should be protected against unsafe products; (2) manufacturers and distributors should not escape liability for faulty products simply because they are not in privity of contract with the ultimate user of those products; and (3) manufacturers, sellers, and lessors of products are generally in a better position than consumers to bear the costs associated with injuries caused by their products—costs that they can ultimately pass on to all consumers in the form of higher prices.

LANDMARK IN THE LAW—Continued

to place life and limb in peril when negligently made, it is then a thing of danger. . . . If to the element of danger there is added knowledge that the thing will be used by persons other than the purchaser, and used without new tests, then, irrespective of contract, the manufacturer of this thing of danger is under a duty to make it carefully."

The court concluded that "[b]eyond all question, the nature of an automobile gives warning of probable danger if its construction is defective. This automobile was designed to go 50 miles an hour. Unless its wheels were sound and strong, injury was almost certain." Although Buick had not manufactured the wheel itself, the court held that Buick had a duty to inspect the wheels and that Buick "was responsible for the finished product." Therefore, Buick was liable to MacPherson for the injuries he sustained when he was thrown from the car.

APPLICATION TO TODAY'S WORLD

This landmark decision was a significant step toward the world we live in today—in which it is common for an automobile manufacturer to be held liable when its negligence causes a product user to be injured. As is often the situation, technological developments had necessitated changes in the law. Had the courts continued to require privity of contract in product liability cases, today's legal landscape would be quite different indeed. Certainly, fewer cases would be pending before the courts; and just as certainly, many purchasers of products, including automobiles, would have little recourse for obtaining legal redress for injuries caused by those products.

California was the first state to impose strict product liability in tort on manufacturers. In the landmark case that follows, the California Supreme Court set out the reason for applying tort law rather than contract law in cases involving consumers injured by defective products.

Landmark and Classic Cases

CASE 18.3 Greenman v. Yuba Power Products, Inc.

Supreme Court of California, 1962.
59 Cal.2d 57,
377 P.2d 897,
27 Cal.Rptr. 697.

FACTS The plaintiff, Greenman, wanted a Shopsmith—a combination power tool that could be used as a saw, drill, and wood lathe—after seeing a Shopsmith demonstrated by a retailer and studying a brochure prepared by the manufacturer. The plaintiff's wife bought and gave him one for Christmas. More than a year later, a piece of wood flew out of the lathe attachment of the Shopsmith while the plaintiff was using it, inflicting serious injuries on him. About ten and a half months later, the plaintiff filed a suit in a California state court against both the retailer and the manufacturer for breach of warranties and negligence. The trial court jury found for the plaintiff. The case was ultimately appealed to the Supreme Court of California.

ISSUE Can the manufacturer and retailer be held liable for the plaintiff's injuries?

DECISION Yes. The Supreme Court of California upheld the verdict for the plaintiff.

REASON The plaintiff had successfully proved that the design and construction of the Shopsmith were defective, that statements in the manufacturer's brochure constituted express warranties and were untrue, and that the plaintiff's injuries were caused by the breach of these express warranties. The manufacturer argued that the plaintiff had waited too long to give notice of the breach of warranty, but the court, in imposing strict liability on the manufacturer, held that it was not necessary for the plaintiff to establish an express warranty or a breach of warranty. The court stated that "a manufacturer is strictly liable in tort when an article he places on the market, knowing that it is to be used without inspection for defects, proves to have a defect that causes injury to a human being." The court stated that the "purpose of such liability is to [e]nsure that the costs of injuries resulting from defective products are borne by the manufacturers * * * rather than by the injured persons who are powerless to protect themselves."

COMMENT *From the earliest days of the common law, English courts applied a doctrine of strict liability. Often, persons whose conduct resulted in injuries to others were held liable for damages, even if they had not intended to injure anyone and had exercised reasonable care. This approach was abandoned around 1800 in favor of a fault-based approach, in which an action was considered tortious only if it was wrongful or blameworthy in some respect. Strict liability began to be reapplied to manufactured goods in several landmark cases in the 1960s, a decade when many traditional assumptions were being challenged. The case just presented is considered a landmark in U.S. law not only because it resuscitated the doctrine of strict liability for defective products but also because it enunciated a compelling reason for doing so—protecting "injured persons who are powerless to protect themselves."*

REQUIREMENTS FOR STRICT LIABILITY

Section 402A of the *Restatement (Second) of Torts* indicates how the drafters envisioned that the doctrine of strict liability should be applied. It was issued in 1964, and during the next decade, it became a widely accepted statement of the liabilities of sellers of goods (including manufacturers, processors, assemblers, packagers, bottlers, wholesalers, distributors, retailers, and lessors). Section 402A states as follows:

(1) One who sells any product in a defective condition unreasonably dangerous to the user or consumer or to his property is subject to liability for physical harm thereby caused to the ultimate user or consumer or to his property, if

(a) the seller is engaged in the business of selling such a product, and

(b) it is expected to and does reach the user or consumer without substantial change in the condition in which it is sold.

(2) The rule stated in Subsection (1) applies although

(a) the seller has exercised all possible care in the preparation and sale of his product, and

(b) the user or consumer has not bought the product from or entered into any contractual relation with the seller.

The Six Requirements for Strict Liability The bases for an action in strict liability as set forth in Section 402A of the *Restatement (Second) of Torts,* and as the doctrine came to be commonly applied, can be summarized as a series of six requirements, which are listed here. Depending on the jurisdiction, if these requirements are met, a manufacturer's liability to an injured party can be virtually unlimited.[9]

① The product must be in a defective condition when the defendant sells it.

② The defendant must normally be engaged in the business of selling (or otherwise distributing) that product.

③ The product must be unreasonably dangerous to the user or consumer because of its defective condition (in most states).

④ The plaintiff must incur physical harm to self or property by use or consumption of the product.

⑤ The defective condition must be the proximate cause of the injury or damage.

9. Some states have enacted what are called *statutes of repose.* Basically, these statutes provide that after a specific statutory period of time from the date of manufacture or sale, a plaintiff is precluded from pursuing a cause of action for injuries or damages sustained from a product, even though the product is defective. The statutes of Illinois, Indiana, Alabama, Tennessee, Florida, Texas, and Nebraska are illustrative.

If a child is injured by a toy, does he or she have a cause of action against the manufacturer?

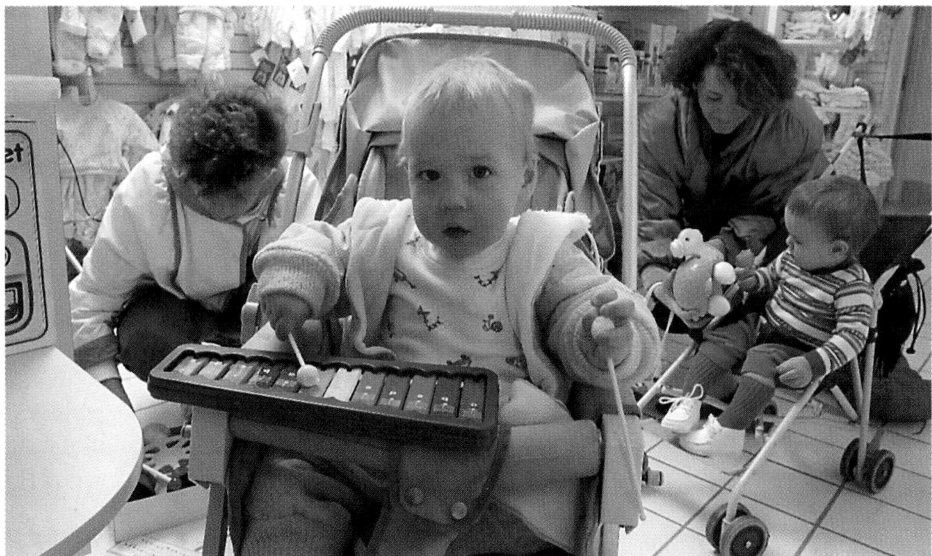

⑥ The goods must not have been substantially changed from the time the product was sold to the time the injury was sustained.

Unreasonably Dangerous Products Under the requirements just listed, in any action against a manufacturer, seller, or lessor, the plaintiff does not have to show why or in what manner the product became defective. To recover damages, however, the plaintiff must show that the product was so "defective" as to be "unreasonably dangerous"; that the product caused the plaintiff's injury; and that at the time the injury was sustained, the product was in essentially the same condition as when it left the hands of the defendant manufacturer, seller, or lessor.

UNREASONABLY DANGEROUS PRODUCT
In product liability, a product that is defective to the point of threatening a consumer's health and safety. A product will be considered unreasonably dangerous if it is dangerous beyond the expectation of the ordinary consumer or if a less dangerous alternative was economically feasible for the manufacturer, but the manufacturer failed to produce it.

A court may consider a product so defective as to be an **unreasonably dangerous product** if either (1) the product is dangerous beyond the expectation of the ordinary consumer or (2) a less dangerous alternative was economically feasible for the manufacturer, but the manufacturer failed to produce it. As will be discussed in the next section, a product may be unreasonably dangerous due to a flaw in the manufacturing process, a design defect, or an inadequate warning.

MARKET-SHARE LIABILITY

Generally, in all cases involving product liability, a plaintiff must prove that the defective product that caused her or his injury was the product of a specific defendant. In the last decade or so, however, some courts have dropped this requirement when plaintiffs could not prove which of many distributors of a harmful product supplied the particular product that caused the injuries.

This has occurred in several cases involving DES (diethylstilbestrol), a drug administered in the past to prevent miscarriages. DES's harmful character was not realized until, a generation later, daughters of the women who had taken DES developed health problems, including vaginal carcinoma, that were linked to the drug. Partly because of the passage of time, a plaintiff daughter often could not prove which pharmaceutical company—out of as many as three hundred—had marketed the DES her mother had ingested. In these cases, some courts applied market-share liability, holding that all firms that manufactured and distributed DES during the period in question were liable for the plaintiffs' injuries in proportion to the firms' respective shares of the market.[10]

Market-share liability has also been applied in other situations. ● **EXAMPLE 18.7** In one case, a plaintiff who was a hemophiliac received injections of a blood protein known as antihemophiliac factor (AHF) concentrate. The plaintiff later tested positive for the AIDS (acquired immune deficiency syndrome) virus. Because it was not known which manufacturer was responsible for the particular AHF received by the plaintiff, the court held that all of the manufacturers of AHF could be held liable under a market-share theory of liability.[11] ●

OTHER APPLICATIONS OF STRICT LIABILITY

Although the drafters of the *Restatement (Second) of Torts,* Section 402A, did not take a position on bystanders, all courts extend the strict liability of manufacturers and other sellers to injured bystanders. ● **EXAMPLE 18.8** In one case, an automobile manufacturer was held liable for injuries caused by the explosion of a car's motor. A cloud of steam that resulted from the explosion caused multiple collisions because other drivers could not see well.[12] ●

10. See, for example, *Martin v. Abbott Laboratories,* 102 Wash.2d 581, 689 P.2d 368 (1984).
11. *Smith v. Cutter Biological, Inc.,* 72 Haw. 416, 823 P.2d 717 (1991).
12. *Giberson v. Ford Motor Co.,* 504 S.W.2d 8 (Mo. 1974).

The rule of strict liability is also applicable to suppliers of component parts. • **EXAMPLE 18.9** General Motors buys brake pads from a subcontractor and puts them in Chevrolets without changing their composition. If those pads are defective, both the supplier of the brake pads and General Motors will be held strictly liable for the damages caused by the defects. •

Restatement (Third) of Torts: Products Liability

Because Section 402A of the *Restatement (Second) of Torts* did not clearly define such terms as "defective" and "unreasonably dangerous," they have been interpreted differently by different courts. Also, over the years, issues that were not even imagined when Section 402A was written became points of contention and debate in the courts. These circumstances led to complex and confusing legal principles in the area of product liability and made it difficult to predict how a court might decide a certain case.

In the early 1990s, the American Law Institute (ALI) began drafting a new restatement of the principles and policies underlying product liability law. In particular, the ALI attempted to respond to questions that had not been part of the legal landscape thirty-five years before. The result was the *Restatement (Third) of Torts: Products Liability.* The final draft of the new *Restatement* was released in 1997, after five years of planning, drafting, and debating. The question now is whether state courts will adopt this new *Restatement* as rapidly as they did the *Restatement (Second) of Torts*, which spread the doctrine of strict liability throughout the United States in the late 1960s and early 1970s.

The law categorizes product defects into three types: manufacturing defects, design defects, and warning defects—each of which will be discussed shortly. The *Restatement (Third) of Torts: Products Liability* defines the three types of defects and integrates the applicable legal principles into the definitions. By defining defects in such a way, the new *Restatement* eliminates some of the hard-to-understand distinctions that developed when different theories of liability were applied to the same defects.

For example, in one case a court upheld a verdict that found a product "not defective" on a theory of strict liability but found its manufacturer liable for harm caused by the product on a theory of breach of warranty.[13] The court based its decision on the different tests that exist under the different legal theories. The new *Restatement* sets out a single test for each type of defect to be applied regardless of the type of legal claim.

MANUFACTURING DEFECTS

According to Section 2(a) of the new *Restatement*, a product "contains a manufacturing defect when the product departs from its intended design even though all possible care was exercised in the preparation and marketing of the product." This statement imposes liability on the manufacturer (and on the wholesaler and retailer) whether or not the manufacturer acted "reasonably." This is strict liability, or liability without fault.

DESIGN DEFECTS

A determination that a product has a design defect (or a warning defect, discussed later in this chapter) can affect all of the units of a product. A product "is defective in design

13. See, for example, *Denny v. Ford Motor Co.*, 87 N.Y.2d 248, 662 N.E.2d 730, 639 N.Y.S.2d 250 (1995). The *Restatement* has not eliminated all of these distinctions, however, because in some cases they may be necessary.

when the foreseeable risks of harm posed by the product could have been reduced or avoided by the adoption of a reasonable alternative design by the seller or other distributor, or a predecessor in the commercial chain of distribution, and the omission of the alternative design renders the product not reasonably safe."[14]

Different states have applied different tests to determine whether a product has a design defect under the *Restatement (Second) of Torts,* Section 402A. There has been much controversy about the different tests, particularly over one that focused on the "consumer expectations" concerning a product. The test prescribed by the *Restatement (Third) of Torts: Products Liability* focuses on a product's actual design and the reasonableness of that design.

To succeed in a product liability suit alleging a design defect, a plaintiff has to show that there is a reasonable alternative design. In other words, a manufacturer or other defendant is liable only when the harm was reasonably preventable. According to the Official Comments accompanying the new *Restatement,* factors that a court may consider on this point include

> the magnitude and probability of the foreseeable risks of harm, the instructions and warnings accompanying the product, and the nature and strength of consumer expectations regarding the product, including expectations arising from product portrayal and marketing. The relative advantages and disadvantages of the product as designed and as it alternatively could have been designed may also be considered. Thus, the likely effects of the alternative design on production costs; the effects of the alternative design on product longevity, maintenance, repair, and esthetics; and the range of consumer choice among products are factors that may be taken into account.

WARNING DEFECTS

Product warnings and instructions alert consumers to the risks of using a product. A "reasonableness" test applies to this material. A product "is defective because of inadequate instructions or warnings when the foreseeable risks of harm posed by the product could have been reduced or avoided by the provision of reasonable instructions or warnings by the seller or other distributor, or a predecessor in the commercial chain of distribution, and the omission of the instructions or warnings renders the product not reasonably safe."[15] Generally, a seller must warn those who purchase its product of the harm that can result from the *foreseeable misuse* of the product as well.

Important factors for a court to consider under the *Restatement (Third) of Torts: Products Liability* include the risks of a product, the "content and comprehensibility" and "intensity of expression" of warnings and instructions, and the "characteristics of expected user groups."[16] For example, children would likely respond more readily to bright, bold, simple warning labels, while educated adults might need more detailed information.

There is no duty to warn about risks that are obvious or commonly known. Warnings about such risks do not add to the safety of a product and could even detract from it by making other warnings seem less significant. The obviousness of a risk and a user's decision to proceed in the face of that risk may be a defense in a product liability suit based on a warning defect. (This defense and other defenses in product liability suits are discussed later in this chapter.)

---

14. *Restatement (Third) of Torts: Products Liability,* Section 2(b).
15. *Restatement (Third) of Torts: Products Liability,* Section 2(c).
16. *Restatement (Third) of Torts: Products Liability,* Section 2, Comment h.

Defenses to Product Liability

Manufacturers, sellers, or lessors can raise several defenses to avoid liability for harms caused by their products. We look at some of these defenses in the following subsections.

ETHICAL ISSUE 18.2

Do pharmacists have a duty to warn customers about the side effects of drugs?

Clearly, manufacturers of pharmaceuticals have a duty to disclose and warn users of any side effects associated with their products. Typically, these disclosures and warnings are given to physicians, and many pharmacies today include a list of possible side effects with the drugs that they dispense. Yet what if a pharmacist does not disclose the potential side effects of a drug being sold? Should the pharmacy be held liable if a purchaser suffers harms from a drug's side effects? This question, which has both legal and ethical implications, has come before several courts in recent years—and the courts have reached different conclusions.

In one case, for example, an Illinois court held that a pharmacist had a duty to warn his customer about a potentially fatal drug interaction with a prescribed medication. The court reasoned that the duty existed because the pharmacist knew of the customer's allergies, knew that the prescribed medication should not be taken by a person with those allergies, and knew that injury or death was substantially certain to result.[17] In another case, however, a Texas appellate court reached the opposite conclusion. The court held that imposing such a duty on pharmacists would necessarily interfere with the physician-patient relationship because pharmacies seeking to avoid liability would "question the propriety of every prescription they fill."[18] Clearly, the arguments put forth in both cases have merit, and as yet the courts have not reached a consensus on the issue.

ASSUMPTION OF RISK

Assumption of risk can sometimes be used as a defense in a product liability action. For example, if a buyer fails to heed a product recall by the seller, a court might conclude that the buyer assumed the risk caused by the defect that led to the recall. To establish such a defense, the defendant must show that (1) the plaintiff knew and appreciated the risk created by the product defect and (2) the plaintiff voluntarily assumed the risk, even though it was unreasonable to do so. (See Chapter 4 for a more detailed discussion of assumption of risk.)

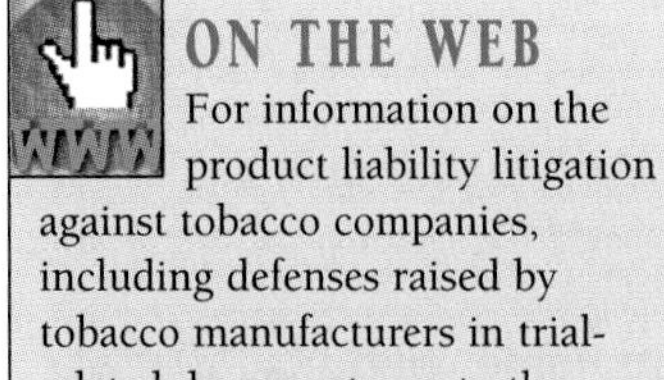

ON THE WEB

For information on the product liability litigation against tobacco companies, including defenses raised by tobacco manufacturers in trial-related documents, go to the State Tobacco Information Center's Web site at **http://stic.neu.edu/index.html**.

PRODUCT MISUSE

Similar to the defense of voluntary assumption of risk is that of misuse of the product. Here, the injured party *does not know that the product is dangerous for a particular use* (contrast this with assumption of risk), but the use is not the one for which the product was designed. The courts have severely limited this defense, however.

17. *Happel v. Wal-Mart Stores, Inc.,* 193 Ill.2d 586, 744 N.E.2d 284, 253 Ill.Dec. 2 (2001).
18. *Morgan v. Wal-Mart Stores, Inc.,* 30 S.W.3d 455 (Tex.App.–Austin 2001).

Even if the injured party does not know about the inherent danger of using the product in a wrong way, if the misuse is foreseeable, the seller must take measures to guard against it.

COMPARATIVE NEGLIGENCE

Developments in the area of comparative negligence (discussed in Chapter 4) have even affected the doctrine of strict liability—the most extreme theory of product liability. Whereas previously the plaintiff's conduct was not a defense to strict liability, today many jurisdictions, when apportioning liability and damages, consider the negligent or intentional actions of both the plaintiff and the defendant. This means that even if the plaintiff misused the product, she or he may nonetheless be able to recover at least some damages for injuries caused by the defendant's defective product.

In the following case, the court was asked whether a plaintiff's "ordinary negligence" could affect the amount of his recovery under a comparative negligence theory.

CASE 18.4 Smith v. Ingersoll-Rand Co.

Alaska Supreme Court, 2000.
14 P.3d 990.
http://www.touchngo.com/sp/spslip.htm[a]

HISTORICAL AND SOCIAL SETTING *In the mid-1980s, believing that judgments in tort suits had become excessive, several states enacted statutes to, among other things, limit the amount of damages recoverable. In 1986, the Alaska state legislature enacted the Tort Reform Act "to create a more equitable distribution of the cost and risk of injury and increase the availability and affordability of insurance." The hope was to reduce the costs of the tort system while still ensuring that "adequate and appropriate compensation for persons injured through the fault of others" was available.*

FACTS Dan Smith was injured at Prudhoe Bay, Alaska, while attempting to start the diesel engine of a portable air compressor manufactured by Ingersoll-Rand Company. Smith, a mechanic, was not wearing a hard hat when he was dispatched to start the compressor's engine. The compressor was an older model that required the door to be opened to start the engine. Because there was no latch on the door, it had to be propped open. While Smith started the engine, the door fell from its open position and hit his head. After the accident, he suffered seizures and was diagnosed with traumatic epilepsy. He lost his job because of the related medical problems and filed a suit against Ingersoll-Rand in an Alaska state court, alleging that the company had designed a defective product. Based on diversity jurisdiction, the case was moved to a federal district court. Ingersoll-Rand argued that Smith's failure to wear a hard hat and his propping the door open in an unsafe manner constituted contributory negligence. The court asked the Alaska Supreme Court to rule whether, under Alaska state law, evidence of Smith's negligence could reduce his recovery.

a. Click on "2000 Chronological Index." On that page, scroll to the name of the case and click on it to access the opinion. This is a Web page within the Alaska Legal Resource Center site, which is maintained by Touch N' Go Systems, Inc., and the Law Offices of James B. Gottstein.

ISSUE Can a plaintiff's recovery in a product liability suit be reduced by proof of the plaintiff's ordinary negligence?

DECISION Yes. The state supreme court held that a defendant in a product liability suit can raise the plaintiff's ordinary negligence in defense.

REASON The court recognized that under a "system of comparative fault * * *, a plaintiff would still be able to recover if he was comparatively at fault for his injuries, but his recovery would be reduced in proportion to his percentage of fault." The court explained that previously, in Alaska, "[o]rdinary negligence [was] generally not sufficient to establish comparative negligence on the part of a

CASE 18.4—Continued

products liability plaintiff," but in the state Tort Reform Act, the state legislature "changed the definition of comparative negligence." The act defined "fault" to include "acts or omissions that are in any measure negligent or reckless." The court added that this "modification of comparative negligence in strict products liability cases reflects a general trend occurring across the nation." The *Restatement (Third) of Torts: Products Liability* "observes that a 'strong majority' of courts now apply comparative negligence principles in strict products liability cases. Moreover, most of these courts * * * allow a plaintiff's ordinary negligence to constitute comparative fault. In addition, legislatures in other states have enacted tort reform statutes similar to the one here," and courts in those states have generally interpreted these statutes to include ordinary negligence.

FOR CRITICAL ANALYSIS—Economic Consideration *What effect does the availability of the theory of comparative negligence in product liability suits have on businesses?*

COMMONLY KNOWN DANGERS

The dangers associated with certain products (such as sharp knives and guns) are so commonly known that manufacturers need not warn users of those dangers. If a defendant succeeds in convincing the court that a plaintiff's injury resulted from a *commonly known danger,* the defendant normally will not be liable.

• **EXAMPLE 18.10** A classic case on this issue involved a plaintiff who was injured when an elastic exercise rope that she had purchased slipped off her foot and struck her in the eye, causing a detachment of the retina. The plaintiff claimed that the manufacturer should be liable because it had failed to warn users that the exerciser might slip off a foot in such a manner. The court stated that to hold the manufacturer liable in these circumstances "would go beyond the reasonable dictates of justice in fixing the liabilities of manufacturers." After all, stated the court, "[a]lmost every physical object can be inherently dangerous or potentially dangerous in a sense. . . . A manufacturer cannot manufacture a knife that will not cut or a hammer that will not mash a thumb or a stove that will not burn a finger. The law does not require [manufacturers] to warn of such common dangers."[19] •

A related defense is the *knowledgeable user* defense. If a particular danger (such as electrical shock) is or should be commonly known by particular users of the product (such as electricians), the manufacturer of electrical equipment need not warn these users of the danger.

OTHER DEFENSES

A defendant can also defend against product liability by showing that there is no basis for the plaintiff's claim. Suppose that a plaintiff alleges that a seller breached an implied warranty. If the seller can prove that he or she effectively disclaimed all implied warranties, the plaintiff cannot recover. Similarly, in a product liability case based on negligence, a defendant who can show that the plaintiff has not met the requirements (such as causation or the breach of a duty of care) for an action in negligence will not be liable. In regard to strict product liability, a defendant could claim that the plaintiff failed to meet one of the requirements for an action in strict liability. If, for example, the defendant establishes that the goods have been subsequently altered after they were sold, the defendant will not be held liable.

19. *Jamieson v. Woodward & Lothrop,* 247 F.2d 23, 101 D.C.App. 32 (1957).

APPLICATION **Law and the Seller . . .**

The Creation of Warranties*

Warranties are important in both commercial and consumer purchase transactions. There are three types of product warranties: express warranties, implied warranties of merchantability, and implied warranties of fitness for a particular purpose. If you are a seller of products, you can make or create any one of these warranties, which are available to both consumers and commercial purchasers.

First and foremost, sellers and buyers need to know whether warranties have been created.

Warranty Creation

Express warranties do not have to be labeled as such, but statements of simple opinion generally do not constitute express warranties. Express warranties can be made by descriptions of the goods. Express warranties can be found in a seller's advertisement, brochure, or promotional materials or can be made orally or in an express writing. A sales representative should use care in describing the merits of a product; otherwise, the seller could be held to an express warranty. If an express warranty is not intended, the sales pitch should not promise too much.

In most sales, because the seller is a merchant, the purchased goods carry the implied warranty of merchantability. If you are a seller, you must also be aware of the importance of the implied warranty of fitness for a particular purpose. Assume that a customer comes to your sales representative, describes the job to be done in detail, and says, "I really need something that can do the job." Your sales representative replies, "This product will do the job." An implied warranty that the product is fit for that particular purpose has been created.

Warranty Disclaimers

Many sellers, particularly in commercial sales, try to limit or disclaim warranties. The Uniform Commercial Code permits all warranties, including express warranties, to be excluded or negated. Conspicuous statements—such as "THERE ARE NO WARRANTIES WHICH EXTEND BEYOND THE DESCRIPTION ON THE FACE HEREOF" or "THERE ARE NO IMPLIED WARRANTIES OF FITNESS FOR A PARTICULAR PURPOSE OR MERCHANTABILITY WHICH ACCOMPANY THIS SALE"—can be used to disclaim the implied warranties of fitness and merchantability. Used goods are sometimes sold "as is" or "with all faults" so that implied warranties of fitness and merchantability are disclaimed. Whenever these warranties are disclaimed, a purchaser should be aware that the product may not be of even average quality.

Checklist for the Salesperson

1. If you wish to limit warranties, do so by means of a carefully worded and prominently placed written or printed provision that a reasonable person would understand and accept.
2. As a seller, you might wish to have the buyer sign a statement certifying that he or she has read all of your warranty disclaimer provisions.
3. If you do not intend to make an express warranty, do not make a promise or an affirmation of fact concerning the performance or quality of a product you are selling.

*This *Application* is not meant to serve as a substitute for the services of an attorney who is licensed to practice law in your state.

Key Terms

express warranty 458
implied warranty 460
implied warranty of fitness for a particular purpose 461
implied warranty of merchantability 460
lien 457
product liability 467
unreasonably dangerous product 472

Chapter Summary Warranties and Product Liability

	WARRANTIES
Warranties of Title (See page 457.)	The UCC provides for the following warranties of title [UCC 2–312, 2A–211]: 1. *Good title*—A seller warrants that he or she has the right to pass good and rightful title to the goods. 2. *No liens*—A seller warrants that the goods sold are free of any encumbrances (claims, charges, or liabilities—usually called *liens*). A lessor warrants that the lessee will not be disturbed in his or her possession of the goods by the claims of a third party. 3. *No infringements*—A merchant seller warrants that the goods are free of infringement claims (claims that a patent, trademark, or copyright has been infringed) by third parties. Lessors make similar warranties.
Express Warranties (See pages 458–460 and 465–466.)	1. *Under the UCC*—An express warranty arises under the UCC when a seller or lessor indicates, as part of the basis of the bargain, any of the following: a. An affirmation or promise of fact. b. A description of the goods. c. A sample shown as conforming to the contract goods [UCC 2–313, 2A–210]. 2. *Under the Magnuson-Moss Warranty Act*—Express written warranties covering consumer goods priced at more than $10, *if made,* must be labeled as one of the following: a. Full warranty—Free repair or replacement of defective parts; refund or replacement for goods if they cannot be repaired in a reasonable time. b. Limited warranty—When less than a full warranty is being offered.
Implied Warranty of Merchantability (See page 460.)	When a seller or lessor is a merchant who deals in goods of the kind sold or leased, the seller or lessor warrants that the goods sold or leased are properly packaged and labeled, are of proper quality, and are reasonably fit for the ordinary purposes for which such goods are used [UCC 2–314, 2A–212].
Implied Warranty of Fitness for a Particular Purpose (See pages 461–462.)	Arises when the buyer's or lessee's purpose or use is expressly or impliedly known by the seller or lessor, and the buyer or lessee purchases or leases the goods in reliance on the seller's or lessor's selection [UCC 2–315, 2A–213].
Other Implied Warranties (See page 462.)	Other implied warranties can arise as a result of course of dealing, course of performance, or usage of trade [UCC 2–314(3), 2A–212(3)].
	PRODUCT LIABILITY
Liability Based on Negligence (See pages 467–468.)	1. Due care must be used by the manufacturer in designing the product, selecting materials, using the appropriate production process, assembling and testing the product, and placing adequate warnings on the label or product. 2. Privity of contract is not required. A manufacturer is liable for failure to exercise due care to any person who sustains an injury proximately caused by a negligently made (defective) product.
Liability Based on Misrepresentation (See page 468.)	Fraudulent misrepresentation of a product may result in product liability based on the tort of fraud.
Strict Liability—Requirements (See pages 470–472.)	1. The defendant must sell the product in a defective condition. 2. The defendant must normally be engaged in the business of selling that product.

(continued)

Chapter Summary Warranties and Product Liability—continued

Strict Liability—Requirements—continued	3. The product must be unreasonably dangerous to the user or consumer because of its defective condition (in most states). 4. The plaintiff must incur physical harm to self or property by use or consumption of the product. (Courts will also extend strict liability to include injured bystanders.) 5. The defective condition must be the proximate cause of the injury or damage. 6. The goods must not have been substantially changed from the time the product was sold to the time the injury was sustained.
Market-Share Liability (See page 472.)	In cases in which plaintiffs cannot prove which of many distributors of a defective product supplied the particular product that caused the plaintiffs' injuries, some courts apply market-share liability. All firms that manufactured and distributed the harmful product during the period in question are then held liable for the plaintiffs' injuries in proportion to the firms' respective shares of the market, as directed by the court.
Other Applications of Strict Liability (See pages 472–473.)	1. Manufacturers and other sellers are liable for harms suffered by bystanders as a result of defective products. 2. Suppliers of component parts are strictly liable for defective parts that, when incorporated into a product, cause injuries to users.
Strict Liability—Product Defects (See pages 473–474.)	A product may be defective in three basic ways: 1. In its manufacture. 2. In its design. 3. In the instructions or warnings that come with it.
Defenses to Product Liability (See pages 475–477.)	1. *Assumption of risk*—The user or consumer knew of the risk of harm and voluntarily assumed it. 2. *Product misuse*—The user or consumer misused the product in a way unforeseeable by the manufacturer. 3. *Comparative negligence and liability*—Liability may be distributed between the plaintiff and the defendant under the doctrine of comparative negligence if the plaintiff's misuse of the product contributed to the risk of injury. 4. *Commonly known dangers*—If a defendant succeeds in convincing the court that a plaintiff's injury resulted from a commonly known danger, such as the danger associated with using a sharp knife, the defendant will not be liable. 5. *Other defenses*—A defendant can also defend against a strict liability claim by showing that there is no basis for the plaintiff's claim (that the plaintiff has not met the requirements for an action in negligence or strict liability, for example).

For Review

① What factors determine whether a seller's or lessor's statement constitutes an express warranty or merely "puffing"?

② What implied warranties arise under the UCC?

③ Can a manufacturer be held liable to any person who suffers an injury proximately caused by the manufacturer's negligently made product?

④ What are the elements of a cause of action in strict product liability?

⑤ What defenses to liability can be raised in a product liability lawsuit?

Questions and Case Problems

18–1. Product Liability. Under what contract theory can a seller be held liable to a consumer for physical harm or property damage that is caused by the goods sold? Under what tort theories can the seller be held liable?

18–2. Product Liability. Carmen buys a television set manufactured by AKI Electronics. She is going on vacation, so she takes the set to her mother's house for her mother to use. Because the set is defective, it explodes, causing considerable damage to her mother's house. Carmen's mother sues AKI for the damages to her house. Discuss the theories under which Carmen's mother can recover from AKI.

18–3. Warranty Disclaimers. Tandy purchased a washing machine from Marshall Appliances. The sales contract included a provision explicitly disclaiming all express or implied warranties, including the implied warranty of merchantability. The disclaimer was printed in the same size and color as the rest of the contract. The machine turned out to be a "lemon" and never functioned properly. Tandy sought a refund of the purchase price, claiming that Marshall had breached the implied warranty of merchantability. Can Tandy recover her money, notwithstanding the warranty disclaimer in the contract? Explain.

18–4. Implied Warranties. Sam, a farmer, needs to install a two-thousand-pound piece of equipment in his barn. The equipment must be lifted thirty feet into a hayloft. Sam goes to Durham Hardware and tells Durham that he needs some heavy-duty rope to be used on his farm. Durham recommends a one-inch-thick nylon rope, and Sam purchases two hundred feet of it. Sam ties the rope around the piece of equipment, puts the rope through a pulley, and with the aid of a tractor lifts the equipment off the ground. Suddenly, the rope breaks. The equipment crashes to the ground and is extensively damaged. Sam files suit against Durham for breach of the implied warranty of fitness for a particular purpose. Discuss how successful Sam will be with his suit.

18–5. Implied Warranty of Merchantability. Marilyn Keaton entered an A.B.C. Drug store to buy a half-gallon bottle of liquid bleach. The bottles were stacked at a height above her eye level. She reached up, grasped the handle of one of the bottles, and began pulling it down from the shelf. The cap was loose, however, causing bleach to splash into her face, injuring her eye. Keaton filed a suit in a Georgia state court against A.B.C., alleging, in part, breach of the implied warranty of merchantability. She claimed that the bleach had not been adequately packaged. A.B.C. argued, in part, that Keaton had failed to exercise care for her own safety. Had A.B.C. breached the implied warranty of merchantability? Discuss. [*Keaton v. A.B.C. Drug Co.*, 266 Ga. 385, 467 S.E.2d 558 (1996)]

18–6. Failure to Warn. When Mary Bresnahan drove her Chrysler LeBaron, she sat very close to the steering wheel—less than a foot away from the steering-wheel enclosure of the driver's side air bag. At the time, Chrysler did not provide any warning that a driver should not sit close to the air bag. In an accident with another car, Bresnahan's air bag deployed. The bag caused her elbow to strike the windshield pillar and fracture in three places, resulting in repeated surgery and physical therapy. Bresnahan filed a suit in a California state court against Chrysler to recover for her injuries, alleging in part that they were caused by Chrysler's failure to warn consumers about sitting near the air bag. At the trial, an expert testified that the air bag was not intended to prevent arm injuries, which were "a predictable, incidental consequence" of the bag's deploying. Should Chrysler pay for Bresnahan's injuries? Why or why not? [*Bresnahan v. Chrysler Corp.*, 76 Cal.Rptr.2d 804, 65 Cal.App.4th 1149 (1998)]

18–7. Product Liability. Among the equipment that Ingersoll-Rand Co. makes is a milling machine. The maintenance manual that accompanies the machine contains warnings that users should stay ten feet away from the rear of the machine when it is operating, verify that the back-up alarm is working, and check the area for the presence of others. There is also a sign on the machine that tells users to stay ten feet away. While using the machine to strip asphalt from a road being repaved, Terrill Wilson backed up. The alarm did not sound, and Cosandra Rogers, who was standing with her back to the machine, was run over and maimed. Rogers filed a suit in a federal district court against Ingersoll-Rand, alleging in part strict liability on the basis of a design defect. The jury awarded Rogers $10.2 million in compensatory damages and $6.5 million in punitive damages. Ingersoll-Rand appealed, emphasizing the adequacy of its warnings. Can an adequate warning immunize a manufacturer from any liability caused by a defectively designed product? Discuss fully. [*Rogers v. Ingersoll-Rand Co.*, 144 F.3d 841 (D.C. Cir. 1998)]

18–8. Express Warranties. Ronald Anderson, Jr., a self-employed construction contractor, went to a Home Depot store to buy lumber for a construction project. It was raining, so Anderson bought a tarp to cover the bed of his pickup truck. To secure the tarp, Anderson bought a bag of cords made by Bungee International Manufacturing Corp. The printed material on the Bungee bag included the words "Made in the U.S.A." and "Premium Quality." To secure the tarp at the rear of the passenger's side, Anderson put one hook into the eyelet of the tarp, stretched the cord over the utility box, and hooked the other end in the drainage hole in the bottom of the box. As Anderson stood up, the upper hook dislodged and hit him in the left eye. Anderson filed a suit in a federal district court against Bungee and others, alleging in part breach of express warranty. Anderson alleged that the labeling on the bag of cords was an express warranty that "played some role in [his] decision to purchase this product." Bungee argued that, in regard to the cords' quality, the statements were puffery. Bungee filed a motion for summary judgment on this issue. Will the court grant the motion? Why or why not? [*Anderson v. Bungee International Manufacturing Corp.*, 44 F.Supp.2d 534 (S.D.N.Y. 1999)]

18–9. Product Liability. New England Ecological Development, Inc. (NEED), a recycling station in Rhode Island, needed a conveyor belt system and gave the specifications to Colmar Belting Co. Colmar did not design or make belts but merely distributed the component parts. For this system, Emerson Power Transmission Corp. (EPT) manufactured the wing pulley, a component of the nip point (the point at which a belt moves over the stationary part of the system). Kenneth Butler, a welder, assembled the system with assistance from Colmar. Neither Colmar nor EPT recommended the use of a protective shield to guard the nip point, and as finally built, NEED's system did not have a shield. Later, as Americo Buonanno, a NEED employee, was clearing debris from the belt, his arm was pulled into the nip point. The arm was severely crushed and later amputated at the elbow. Buonanno filed a suit in a Rhode Island state court against Colmar and EPT, alleging in part strict liability. The defendants filed a motion for summary judgment, arguing that as sellers of component parts, they had no duty to ensure the proper design of the final product. On what grounds might the court deny the motion? [*Buonanno v. Colmar Belting Co.*, 733 A.2d 712 (R.I. 1999)]

TEST YOUR KNOWLEDGE—ANSWER ON THE WEB

18–10. In May 1995, Ms. McCathern and her daughter, together with McCathern's cousin, Ms. Sanders, and her daughter, were riding in Sanders's 1994 Toyota 4Runner. Sanders was driving, McCathern was in the front passenger seat, and the children were in the back seat. Everyone was wearing a seat belt. While the group was traveling south on Oregon State Highway 395 at a speed of approximately 50 miles per hour, an oncoming vehicle veered into Sanders's lane of travel. When Sanders tried to steer clear, the 4Runner rolled over and landed upright on its four wheels. During the rollover, the roof over the front passenger seat collapsed, and as a result, McCathern sustained serious, permanent injuries. McCathern filed a suit in an Oregon state court against Toyota Motor Corp. and others, alleging in part that the 1994 4Runner "was dangerously defective and unreasonably dangerous in that the vehicle, as designed and sold, was unstable and prone to rollover." What is the test for product liability based on a design defect? What would McCathern have to prove to succeed under that test? [*McCathern v. Toyota Motor Corp.*, 332 Or. 59, 23 P.3d 320 (2001)]

A QUESTION OF ETHICS AND SOCIAL RESPONSIBILITY

18–11. On July 1, 1993, Gian Luigi Ferri entered the offices of a law firm against which he had a grudge. Using two semiautomatic assault weapons (TEC-9 and TEC-DC9) manufactured and distributed by Navegar, Inc., he killed eight persons and wounded six others before killing himself. The survivors and the families of some of those who had died sued Navegar, based in part on negligence. They claimed that Navegar had a duty not to create risks to the public beyond those inherent in the lawful use of firearms. They offered evidence that Navegar knew or should have known that the assault guns had "no legitimate sporting or self-defense purpose" and that the guns were "particularly well adapted to military-style assault on large numbers of people." They also claimed that the TEC-DC9 advertising "targets a criminal clientele," further increasing the risk of harm. A California trial court granted summary judgment in Navegar's favor. The appellate court reversed, ruling that the case should go to trial. The court stated that "the likelihood that a third person would make use of the TEC-DC9 in the kind of criminal rampage Ferri perpetrated is precisely the hazard that would support a determination that Navegar's conduct was negligent." Navegar appealed the decision to the California Supreme Court. In view of these facts, consider the following questions. [*Merrill v. Navegar, Inc.*, 26 Cal.4th 465, 28 P.3d 116, 110 Cal.Rptr.2d 370 (2001)]

1. Do you agree with the appellate court that Navegar could be held negligent in marketing the TEC-DC9? What should the California Supreme Court decide? (Before answering this question, you may wish to review the elements of negligence in Chapter 4.)
2. Should gun manufacturers ever be held liable for deaths caused by nondefective guns? Why or why not?
3. Generally, do you believe that policy decisions regarding the liability of gun manufacturers should be made by the courts, whose job is to interpret the law, or by Congress and state legislatures, whose job is to make the law?
4. In your opinion, have Congress and state legislatures gone far enough in regulating the use of firearms, or have they gone too far? Explain.

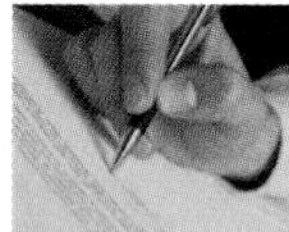

FOR CRITICAL ANALYSIS

18–12. The United States has the strictest product liability laws in the world today. Why do you think many other countries, particularly developing countries, are more lax with respect to holding manufacturers liable for product defects?

Internet Exercises

Go to the *Business Law Today* home page at **http://blt.westbuslaw.com**. Select "Interactive Study Center" and then click on "Chapter 18." There you will find the following Internet research exercises that you can perform to learn more about warranties and product liability:

Activity 18–1: Warranties
Activity 18–2: Product Liability Litigation
Activity 18–3: Lemon Laws

Before the Test

Go to the *Business Law Today* home page at **http://blt.westbuslaw.com**. Click on "Interactive Quizzes." You will find at least twenty interactive questions relating to this chapter.

UNIT THREE Cumulative Business Hypothetical

Sonja owns a bakery in San Francisco. To accommodate the growing demand for her products, she orders two new Model X23 McIntyre ovens from a local company, Western Heating Appliances. The purchase price of the two ovens is $4,000.

① Sonja and Western Heating agreed orally, via the telephone, that Western would deliver the ovens within two weeks and that Sonja would pay for the ovens when they were delivered. Two days later, Sonja receives a fax from Western confirming her order. Shortly thereafter, but before Western delivers the ovens, Sonja learns that she can obtain Model X23 McIntyre ovens from another company at a much lower price. Sonja asks Western if she can cancel her order, but Western states that it intends to enforce the contract. Is the contract enforceable against Sonja? Explain.

② After Western receives Sonja's order, it learns that McIntyre no longer manufactures ovens and that the Model X23 ovens are virtually unobtainable anywhere in the country. Western immediately notifies Sonja that it will not be able to fulfill her order. Sonja, who stands to lose a significant amount in profits if the ovens are not delivered on time, sues Western for breach of contract. Western raises the doctrine of commercial impracticability as a defense. Will Western succeed in this defense? Explain.

③ Assume that Western does have two Model X23 McIntyre ovens in stock. Unbeknownst to the sales representative who formed the contract with Sonja, the two ovens have already been purchased by another customer, Tony Garcia. Western is holding the ovens for Garcia until he returns from a business trip to France. The sales representative who dealt with Sonja has the two ovens delivered to Sonja's bakery. Shortly after the ovens are installed at Sonja's bakery, Western calls Sonja and explains that a mistake was made and that Garcia is demanding the two ovens, which cannot be obtained anywhere else. What are Sonja's legal options in this situation? What are Garcia's rights? What legal consequences might Western face as a result of its "mistake"?

④ One day, Sonja was baking a batch of croissants. When she opened the door to one of the new ovens, part of the door became detached from the oven. As she struggled with the door, Sonja's hands were badly burned, and she was unable to do any baking for several months. Sonja later learned that the hinge mechanism on the door had been improperly installed. Sonja wants to sue the oven's manufacturer to recover damages, including consequential damages for lost profits. In a product liability suit against the manufacturer, under what legal principles and doctrines might Sonja be able to recover damages? Discuss fully.

⑤ Sonja orders Office & Plant software from the Web site of Asset Management, Inc. (AM). AM develops and markets business software. Office & Plant is designed to help small-business owners and operators keep their business records and control their inventories. On AM's Web site is a link to a term that limits AM's liability for defects in its products: "the sole remedy is free replacement of the defective product." The same limitation is printed on the envelopes containing the Office & Plant disks that Sonja receives from AM. The envelopes also state, "By using this product, you agree to this term." In reliance on the software's calculations, Sonja orders too many perishable supplies and bakes too many goods, which must be thrown away, causing her to lose money. Office & Plant is then found to have a defect in its programming, making its calculations inaccurate. Who is most likely to pay for Sonya's losses? Why?

Stecher v. Ford Motor Co.

In Chapter 18, we discussed the common law tort principles of product liability. In this extended case study, we examine Stecher v. Ford Motor Co.,[1] *a decision that follows principles set out in the* Restatement (Third) of Torts: Products Liability. *The specific dispute in this case concerned the plaintiff's burden of proof under the crashworthiness, or enhanced injury, doctrine—see the majority decision below for a definition of this doctrine.*

Enhanced injury cases frequently arise from automobile accidents. For this reason, the courts often discuss enhanced injury issues in terms of impacts and collisions. Enhanced injury situations are not limited to collisions, however.

1. 779 A.2d 491 (Pa.Super. 2001). To find this case online, go to **http://www.courts.state.pa.us/iissamples/issamples/AOPCquery.asp**. Key in the words "Stecher AND Ford" in the query box and click on "Search." In the search results, select "Full" to view the entire case.

CASE BACKGROUND

In February 1992, Sharon Stecher was driving a 1983 Ford LTD on a snow- and ice-covered road when the vehicle spun as she approached a curve. Stecher's vehicle crossed the center line, and its front end struck an embankment on the opposite side of the road. With the driver's side of the vehicle leading, the vehicle spun back onto the roadway into oncoming traffic. The LTD collided with a pickup truck. The point of impact on the LTD was approximately at the "B" pillar, the post that runs vertically from the floor to the roof of the vehicle, behind the driver's left shoulder. Stecher suffered a serious brain injury and a pelvic fracture as a result of the collision.

Stecher and her husband, Joseph, filed a suit in a Pennsylvania state court against Ford Motor Company for product liability based on a manufacturing defect. The plaintiffs claimed that the vehicle's B pillar was unreasonably dangerous because its base welds failed, causing it to detach at the base and strike Stecher's head. A jury found that the Ford LTD was defective, but that the defect was not a substantial factor in causing Stecher's injuries. Both parties appealed to a state intermediate appellate court.

MAJORITY OPINION

Opinion by *TODD, J.* [Justice].

* * * *

*The enhanced injury doctrine is a subset of a products liability action and provides that a manufacturer/seller is liable in situations in which the defect did not cause the accident or initial impact, but rather increased the severity of the injury over that which would have occurred absent the * * * defect.* In this case, the issue is whether a plaintiff in such an action must quantify precisely the extent of the enhanced injuries arising from the defect or whether the plaintiff need only prove that the defect increased the harm. [Emphasis added.]

* * * *

* * * Section 16 of the *Restatement (Third) of Torts* provides:

> [Section] 16. Increased Harm Due to Product Defect
>
> (a) When a product is defective at the time of commercial sale or other distribution and the defect is a substantial factor in increasing the Plaintiff's harm beyond that which would have resulted from other causes, the product seller is subject to liability for the increased harm.
>
> (b) If proof supports a determination of the harm that would have resulted from other causes in the absence of the product defect, the product seller's liability is limited to the increased harm attributable solely to the product defect.
>
> (c) If proof does not support a determination under Subsection (b) of the harm that would have resulted in the absence of the product defect, the product seller is liable for all of the plaintiff's harm attributable to the defect and other causes. * * *

* * * *

After careful consideration, * * * we conclude that [this] approach toward allocation of the burden of proof in enhanced injury cases is * * * consistent with Pennsylvania tort law * * *. This placement of the burden of proof is justified by considerations of fairness. If we were to impose upon an injured party the necessity of proving which impact in a * * * collision did which harm, we would actually be expressing a judicial policy that it is better that a plaintiff, injured through no fault of his [or her] own, take nothing, than that a wrongdoer pay more than his theoretical share of the damages arising out of a situation which his wrong has helped to create. In other words, the rule is a result of a choice made as to where a loss due to failure of proof shall fall—on an innocent plaintiff or on defendants who are clearly proved to have been at fault.

* * * *

* * * *[This] approach does not relieve a plaintiff of his or her burden of proving damages.* Indeed, * * * it is only after a plaintiff has demonstrated that the design defect was a substantial factor in producing damages over and above those that otherwise would have occurred that the burden shifts to the defendant to apportion damages. * * * [Emphasis added.]

* * * *

* * * Accordingly, we vacate the judgment of the Court of Common Pleas of Lancaster County and remand this matter for a new trial.

* * * On retrial, if the Stechers meet their burden of proving by a preponderance of the evidence that a defect in the Ford vehicle was a substantial factor in increasing Mrs. Stecher's injuries, then the burden shifts to Ford to quantify the extent of those injuries caused by the alleged defect.

DISSENTING OPINION

Dissenting Opinion by *TAMILIA, J.*

* * * *

Upon careful examination and evaluation * * * , I find the trial court properly * * * place[d] the burden on the plaintiff to prove the nature and extent of the enhanced injuries, for this approach most accurately reflects the jurisprudence in Pennsylvania with respect to liability and damages. * * * The plaintiff has the duty to establish by evidence such facts as would furnish a basis for the legal assessment of damages according to some definite and legal rule. Our law requires not merely conjecture, but rather sufficient data from which damages can be assessed with reasonable certainty. While we do not require mathematical exactness, we cannot award damages by guess or speculation. There must be before us a reasonably fair basis for calculation.

* * * *

The majority, in adopting [a different] view, rather than that which has clearly been adopted in Pennsylvania, would alter the concept of an even playing field and shift to the defendant the duty of disproving unsubstantiated allegations, the proof of a negative, and in failing to do so, assess full liability on the defendant. In other words, the [majority's] approach shifts the burden of proof to the defendants to establish which injuries were attributable to the defect once the plaintiff proves the defect was a substantial factor in producing the injuries. * * *

* * * The majority is introducing a change in the law of Pennsylvania based on concepts which are not applicable to this case and upon facts which are contrary to those established at trial and as found by the jury. The majority ignores the ancient and time-honored dictum [statement] that allegations must be followed by proof.

QUESTIONS FOR ANALYSIS

① **Law.** What was the majority's holding in this case? What was the rationale for this holding?

② **Law.** What was the dissent's position? On what did the dissent base its principal argument?

③ **Ethics.** What is the ethical basis for requiring that a particular party to a lawsuit prove certain elements of the case?

④ **International Dimensions.** How might the burden of proof, as assigned in this decision, affect foreign manufacturers that do business in the United States?

⑤ **Implications for the Business Manager.** Under the holding in this case, can a manufacturer avoid liability when a plaintiff alleges "enhanced injuries"?

Negotiable Instruments

UNIT 4

UNIT CONTENTS

CHAPTER 19

Negotiability and Transferability

"It took many generations for people to feel comfortable accepting paper in lieu of gold or silver."

Alan Greenspan, 1926–
(Chairman of the Board of Governors of the Federal Reserve System, 1987–)

CHAPTER CONTENTS

LEARNING OBJECTIVES

After reading this chapter, you should be able to answer the following questions:

① What are the four types of negotiable instruments with which Article 3 of the UCC is concerned? Which of these instruments are *orders* to pay, and which are *promises* to pay?

② What requirements must an instrument meet to be negotiable?

③ To whom is a bearer instrument payable?

④ What is the difference between an indorsement in blank and a special indorsement?

⑤ What is a restrictive indorsement? Does a restrictive indorsement prohibit further negotiation of the instrument?

The vast number of commercial transactions that take place daily in the modern business world would be inconceivable without negotiable instruments. A **negotiable instrument** can be defined as a signed writing that contains an unconditional promise or order to pay an exact sum of money on demand or at a specified future time to a specific person or order, or to bearer. The checks you write to pay for groceries and other items are negotiable instruments.

NEGOTIABLE INSTRUMENT
A signed writing that contains an unconditional promise or order to pay an exact sum of money on demand or at an exact future time to a specific person or order, or to bearer.

A negotiable instrument can function in two ways—as a substitute for money or as an extension of credit. When a buyer writes a check to pay for goods, the check serves as a substitute for money. When a buyer gives a seller a promissory note in which the buyer promises to pay the seller the purchase price within sixty days, the seller has essentially extended credit to the buyer for a sixty-day period. For a negotiable instrument to operate *practically* as either a substitute for money or a credit device, or both, it is essential that the instrument be easily transferable without danger of being uncollectible. Each rule described in the following pages can be examined in light of this essential function of negotiable instruments.

As the opening quotation indicates, it took "many generations" before paper became an acceptable substitute for gold or silver. That it did so reflects, in part, the role played by convenience and necessity in the evolution of mercantile law. In the medieval world, merchants engaging in foreign trade used negotiable instruments to finance and conduct their affairs. Problems in transporting and safekeeping gold or coins had prompted this practice. The English king's courts of those times did not recognize the validity of negotiable instruments, however, so the merchants had to develop their own rules governing the use of these instruments. These rules were enforced by "fair" or "borough" courts. Eventually, the decisions of these courts formed a distinct set of laws that became known as the *Lex Mercatoria* (Law Merchant).

The Law Merchant was codified in England in the Bills of Exchange Act of 1882. In 1896, in the United States, the National Conference of Commissioners on Uniform State Laws (NCCUSL) drafted the Uniform Negotiable Instruments Law (UNIL), which was modeled on the British 1882 act and adopted by all of the states over the next three decades. By the 1940s, it was apparent that the UNIL needed to be revised to address then-current business practices. As a part of a movement to create a set of uniform laws to govern commercial business transactions generally, the NCCUSL eventually drafted the Uniform Commercial Code (UCC), Article 3 of which replaced the UNIL.

Article 3 of the UCC

ON THE WEB
To find Article 3 of the UCC as adopted by a particular state, go to the Web site of Cornell University's Law School at
http://www.law.cornell.edu/ucc/ucc.table.html.

Negotiable instruments must meet special requirements relating to form and content. These requirements, which are imposed by Article 3 of the Uniform Commercial Code (UCC), will be discussed at length in this chapter. When an instrument is negotiable, its transfer from one person to another is also governed by Article 3. Indeed, UCC 3–104(b) defines *instrument* as a "negotiable instrument." For that reason, whenever the term *instrument* is used in this book, it refers to a negotiable instrument.

In 1990, a revised version of Article 3 was issued for adoption by the states. Many of the changes to Article 3 simply clarified old sections, but some significantly altered the former provisions. Because almost all of the states have adopted the revised article, references to Article 3 in this chapter and in the following two chapters are to the *revised* Article 3. When the revised Article 3 has made important changes in the law, however, we discuss the previous law in footnotes.

Article 4 of the UCC, which governs bank deposits and collections (discussed in Chapter 21), was also revised in 1990. In part, these changes were necessary to reflect changes in Article 3 that affect Article 4 provisions. The revised Articles 3 and 4 are included in their entirety in Appendix C.

Types of Instruments

The UCC specifies four types of negotiable instruments: *drafts, checks, promissory notes*, and *certificates of deposit (CDs)*. These instruments are frequently divided into the two classifications that we will discuss in the following subsections: *orders to pay* (drafts and checks) and *promises to pay* (promissory notes and CDs).

Negotiable instruments may also be classified as either demand instruments or time instruments. A *demand instrument* is payable on demand; that is, it is payable immediately after it is issued and thereafter for a reasonable period of time. All checks are demand instruments because, by definition, they must be payable on demand. A *time instrument* is payable at a future date.

DRAFTS AND CHECKS (ORDERS TO PAY)

DRAFT
Any instrument drawn on a drawee that orders the drawee to pay a certain sum of money, usually to a third party (the payee), on demand or at a definite future time.

DRAWER
The party that initiates a draft (such as a check), thereby ordering the drawee to pay.

DRAWEE
The party that is ordered to pay a draft or check. With a check, a bank or a financial institution is always the drawee.

PAYEE
A person to whom an instrument is made payable.

TRADE ACCEPTANCE
A draft that is drawn by a seller of goods ordering the buyer to pay a specified sum of money to the seller, usually at a stated time in the future. The buyer accepts the draft by signing the face of the draft, thus creating an enforceable obligation to pay the draft when it comes due. On a trade acceptance, the seller is both the drawer and the payee.

A **draft** (bill of exchange) is an unconditional written order that involves three parties. The party creating the draft (the **drawer**) orders another party (the **drawee**) to pay money, usually to a third party (the **payee**). A *time draft* is payable at a definite future time. A *sight draft* (or demand draft) is payable on sight—that is, when it is presented for payment. A draft can be both a time and a sight draft; such a draft is payable at a stated time after sight.

Exhibit 19–1 shows a typical time draft. For the drawee to be obligated to honor the order, the drawee must be obligated to the drawer either by agreement or through a debtor-creditor relationship. • **EXAMPLE 19.1** On November 16, the Bank of Ourtown orders $1,000 worth of office supplies from Eastman Supply Company, with payment due January 16. On December 16, Eastman borrows $1,000 from the First National Bank of Whiteacre, with payment also due January 16. The First National Bank of Whiteacre will usually accept a draft drawn by Eastman on the Bank of Ourtown as payment for the loan.•

A **trade acceptance** is a type of draft that is frequently used in the sale of goods. The seller is both the drawer and the payee on this draft. Essentially, the draft orders the buyer to pay a specified sum of money to the seller, usually at a stated time in the future. (If the draft orders the buyer's bank to pay, it is called a *banker's acceptance*.) • **EXAMPLE 19.2** Jackson River Fabrics sells fabric priced at $50,000 to Comfort Creations, Inc., each year on terms requiring payment to be made in ninety days. One year Jackson River needs cash, so it draws a *trade acceptance* (see Exhibit 19–2) that orders Comfort Creations to pay $50,000 to the order of Jackson River Fabrics ninety

EXHIBIT 19–1 A TYPICAL TIME DRAFT

EXHIBIT 19–2 A TYPICAL TRADE ACCEPTANCE

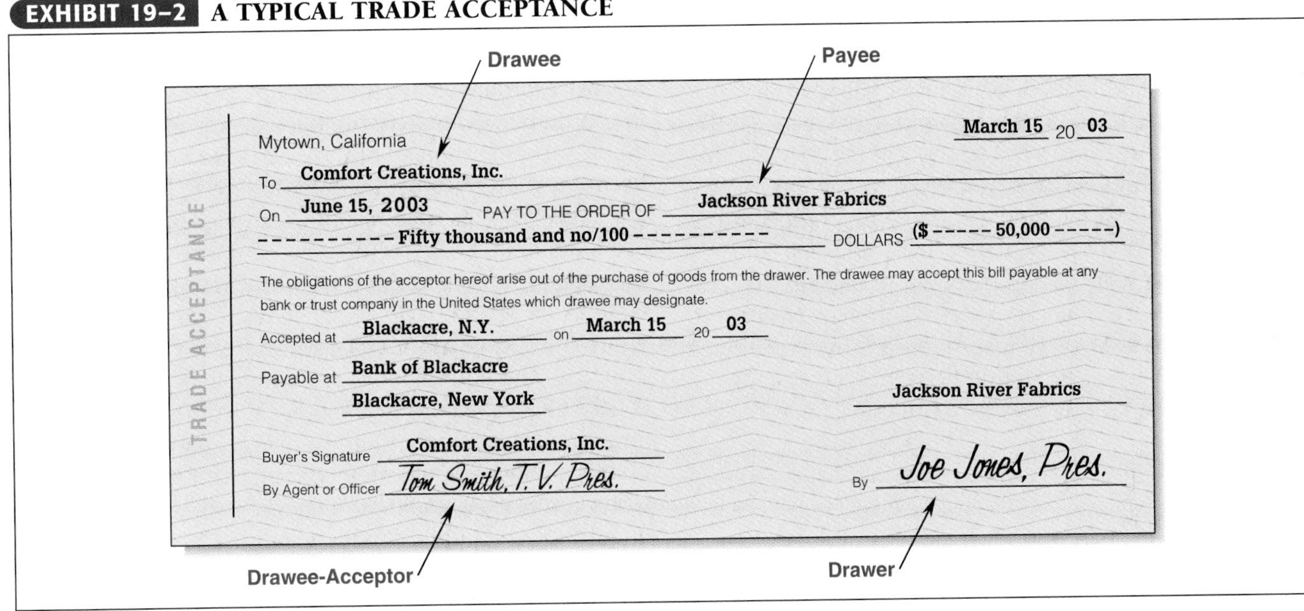

TRADE ACCEPTANCE

Mytown, California March 15 20 03

To Comfort Creations, Inc.

On June 15, 2003 PAY TO THE ORDER OF Jackson River Fabrics

----------Fifty thousand and no/100---------- DOLLARS ($-----50,000-----)

The obligations of the acceptor hereof arise out of the purchase of goods from the drawer. The drawee may accept this bill payable at any bank or trust company in the United States which drawee may designate.

Accepted at Blackacre, N.Y. on March 15 20 03

Payable at Bank of Blackacre
Blackacre, New York

Jackson River Fabrics

Buyer's Signature Comfort Creations, Inc.

By Agent or Officer *Tom Smith, T.V. Pres.*

By *Joe Jones, Pres.*

days hence. Jackson River presents the paper to Comfort Creations. Comfort Creations *accepts* the draft, by signing the face of the draft, and returns it to Jackson River Fabrics. The acceptance by Comfort Creations gives rise to an enforceable obligation to pay the draft when it comes due in ninety days. Jackson River can then immediately sell the trade acceptance in the commercial money market for cash.●

CHECK
A draft drawn by a drawer ordering the drawee bank or financial institution to pay a certain amount of money to the holder on demand.

The most commonly used type of draft is a **check**. The writer of the check is the drawer, the bank on which the check is drawn is the drawee, and the person to whom the check is payable is the payee. As mentioned earlier, checks, because they are payable on demand, are demand instruments.

Checks will be discussed more fully in Chapter 21, but it should be noted here that with certain types of checks, such as *cashier's checks*, the bank is both the drawer and the drawee. The bank customer purchases a cashier's check from the bank—that is, pays the bank the amount of the check—and indicates to whom the check should be made payable. The bank, not the customer, is the drawer of the check—as well as the drawee. The following case illustrates what this means to the payee of a cashier's check.

CASE 19.1 Flatiron Linen, Inc. v. First American State Bank

Colorado Supreme Court, 2001.
23 P.3d 1209.

FACTS Fluffy Reed Foundation, Inc., and one of its officers, Bilgen Reed, promised to secure a $2 million loan for Flatiron Linen, Inc., for which Flatiron paid a fee. Flatiron later accused Fluffy and Reed of fraud in the deal. As a partial refund of the fee, Fluffy issued a check to Flatiron for $4,100, drawn on an account at First American State Bank. When Flatiron attempted to deposit the check, First American returned it due to insufficient

(continued)

CASE 19.1—Continued

funds in the account. Five months later, when the account had sufficient funds, Flatiron took the check to First American and exchanged it for a cashier's check in the amount of $4,100. In the meantime, however, Fluffy had asked First American not to pay the check. When the bank discovered its mistake, it refused to pay the cashier's check. Flatiron filed a suit in a Colorado state court against a number of parties, including First American, from which Flatiron sought to recover the amount of the cashier's check. The court granted a summary judgment in favor of First American. The state intermediate appellate court affirmed this judgment, and Flatiron appealed to the Colorado Supreme Court.

ISSUE Should a cashier's check be treated as the equivalent of cash?

DECISION Yes. The Colorado Supreme Court reversed this part of the lower court's judgment and remanded the case for proceedings consistent with this opinion. Once a cashier's check has been issued, a bank may not legitimately refuse to pay it.

REASON The state supreme court pointed out that it agreed with the majority of courts, which "hold that a cashier's check is the equivalent of cash, accepted when issued." The court explained that UCC 3–104(g) "defines a cashier's check as 'a draft with respect to which the drawer and drawee are the same bank or branches of the same bank.' Because the bank serves as both the drawer and the drawee of the cashier's check, the check becomes a promise by the bank to draw the amount of the check from its own resources and to pay the check upon demand. * * * Once the bank issues and delivers the cashier's check to the payee, the transaction is complete as far as the payee is concerned." The court also noted that "[t]he commercial world treats cashier's checks as the equivalent of cash. People accept cashier's checks as a substitute for cash because the bank, not an individual, stands behind it." To allow a bank not to pay a cashier's check "would be inconsistent with the representation it makes in issuing the check. Such a rule would undermine the public confidence in the bank and its checks and thereby deprive the cashier's check of the essential incident which makes it useful."

FOR CRITICAL ANALYSIS—Economic Consideration *What advantages might cashier's checks have over cash?*

Promissory Notes and Certificates of Deposit (Promises to Pay)

PROMISSORY NOTE
A written promise made by one person (the maker) to pay a fixed amount of money to another person (the payee or a subsequent holder) on demand or on a specified date.

MAKER
One who promises to pay a fixed amount of money to the holder of a promissory note or a certificate of deposit (CD).

CERTIFICATE OF DEPOSIT (CD)
A note of a bank in which the bank acknowledges a receipt of money from a party and promises to repay the money, with interest, to the party on a certain date.

A **promissory note** is a written promise made by one person (the **maker** of the promise to pay) to another (the payee, or the one to whom the promise is made). A promissory note, which is often referred to simply as a *note,* can be made payable at a definite time or on demand. It can name a specific payee or merely be payable to bearer (bearer instruments are discussed later in this chapter). • **EXAMPLE 19.3** On April 30, Laurence and Margaret Roberts sign a writing unconditionally promising to pay "to the order of" the First National Bank of Whiteacre $3,000 (with 8 percent interest) on or before June 29. This writing is a promissory note.• A typical promissory note is shown in Exhibit 19–3.

Notes are used in a variety of credit transactions and often carry the name of the transaction involved. For example, a note that is secured by personal property, such as an automobile, is called a *collateral note,* because the property pledged as security for the satisfaction of the debt is called collateral (see Chapter 22). A note payable in installments, such as for payment for a suite of furniture over a twelve-month period, is called an *installment note.*

A **certificate of deposit (CD)** is a type of note. A CD is issued when a party deposits funds with a bank that the bank promises to repay, with interest, on a certain date

EXHIBIT 19–3 A TYPICAL PROMISSORY NOTE

Payee

☐ SECURITIES ☐ INSURANCE ☐ SAVINGS
☐ OTHER ☐ SEC. AGREEMENT
1. INV. & ACCTS. 2. CONSUMER GOODS
3. EQUIP.

$ 3,000.00 Whiteacre, Minnesota April 30 20 01 Due 6/29/01
On or before sixty days after date.
for value received, the undersigned jointly and severally promise to pay to the order of THE FIRST NATIONAL BANK OF WHITEACRE at its office in Whiteacre, Minnesota, $ Three thousand dollars with interest thereon from date hereof at the rate of - 8 - percent per annum (computed on the basis of actual days and a year of 360 days) indicated in No. 7 below.

7 INTEREST IS PAYABLE AT MATURITY
8 INTEREST IS PAID TO MATURITY
9 INTEREST IS PAYABLE ______ BEGINNING ON ______ 20____

SIGNATURE Laurence E. Roberts SIGNATURE Margaret P. Roberts
SIGNATURE ______ SIGNATURE ______

NO.
OFFICER Clark
BY
ACCRUAL
☐ NEW ☐ REN'L
☐ SECURED
☐ UNSECURED

Co-makers

[UCC 3–104(j)]. The bank is the maker of the note, and the depositor is the payee. • **EXAMPLE 19.4** On February 15, Sara Levin deposits $5,000 with the First National Bank of Whiteacre. The bank issues a CD, in which it promises to repay the $5,000, plus 5 percent interest, on August 15.•

Certificates of deposit in small denominations (for amounts up to $100,000) are often sold by savings and loan associations, savings banks, and commercial banks. Certificates of deposit for amounts over $100,000 are called large (or jumbo) CDs. Exhibit 19–4 shows a typical small CD.

EXHIBIT 19–4 A TYPICAL SMALL CD

Payee (Bearer)

THE FIRST NATIONAL BANK OF WHITEACRE 22-1/960
NEGOTIABLE CERTIFICATE OF DEPOSIT

13992

WHITEACRE, MINN. February 15 20 03
THIS CERTIFIES to the deposit in this Bank the sum of $ 5,000.00

Five thousand and no/100 DOLLARS

which is payable to bearer on the 15th day of August, 20 03 against presentation and surrender of this certificate, and bears interest at the rate of 5 % per annum, to be computed (on the basis of 360 days and actual days elapsed) to, and payable at, maturity. No payment may be made prior to, and no interest runs after, that date. Payable at maturity in federal funds, and if desired, at Manufacturers Hanover Trust Company, New York.

THE FIRST NATIONAL BANK OF WHITEACRE
By John Doe
SIGNATURE

Maker

The following case illustrates how a party can collect on a promissory note—in this case, a note signed by a student to borrow money for his education.

CASE 19.2 United States v. Durbin

United States District Court,
Southern District of Texas,
Houston Division, 1999.
64 F.Supp.2d 635.

FACTS Robert Durbin, a student, borrowed money for his education and issued (signed) a promissory note for its repayment. The bank from which Durbin borrowed the money lent it under a federal program to assist students at postsecondary institutions.[a] Ordinarily, repayment begins nine to twelve months after the student borrower fails to carry at least one-half of the normal full-time course load at his or her school. Under this program, the federal government guarantees that the note will be fully repaid. If the student defaults on the repayment, the lender presents the current balance–principal, interest, and costs–to the government. When the government pays the balance, it becomes the lender, and the borrower owes the government directly. After Durbin defaulted on his note and also failed to pay the government, the government filed a suit in a federal district court against Durbin to collect the amount due. The government showed that it owned the note that Durbin issued and that the note was unpaid.

ISSUE Did the government satisfy the requirements to collect the amount of the note from Durbin?

DECISION Yes. The court issued a judgment in favor of the government, holding Durbin liable for the unpaid balance of the note, plus interest, costs, and fees. Durbin issued the note, the government owned it, and it was unpaid.

REASON The court explained first that "[t]he practice and law of notes developed so that people could lend on the credit of a person with confidence that collecting the debt would not be complicated by side issues." In this case, "[t]he government must show three things to win: (1) the defendant is the person who issued the note; (2) the government owns the note; and (3) the note is unpaid. * * * The note may be enforced against the borrower unless he can show that he did not issue it or that he paid it. Unlike many other kinds of cases, the borrower largely has the responsibility to produce evidence. Evidence is not simply saying that something is true; evidence is specific facts of when, who, where, and how much as well as supporting records like canceled checks and tax returns. Under state law, a note is enforceable unless the borrower can show that he paid the note or that the note was forged." Here, "[t]he government has demonstrated that the defendant issued the promissory note, that the government owns the note, and that the note is in default and unpaid. The law requires that there be a judgment for the government for the principal, interest, costs, and attorney's fees."

FOR CRITICAL ANALYSIS—Social Consideration *Should students have to pay educational loans if they later decide that the education they received is not adequate to allow them to find a "good" job?*

a. Higher Education Act of 1965, 20 U.S.C. Section 1070.

Requirements for Negotiability

"A negotiable bill or note is a courier without luggage."
JOHN B. GIBSON, 1780–1853 (American jurist)

For an instrument to be negotiable, it must meet the following requirements:

① Be in writing.
② Be signed by the maker or the drawer.
③ Be an unconditional promise or order to pay.
④ State a fixed amount of money.

⑤ Be payable on demand or at a definite time.

⑥ Be payable to order or to bearer, unless it is a check.

Written Form

Negotiable instruments must be in written form [UCC 3–103(a)(6)]. This is because negotiable instruments must possess the quality of certainty that only formal, written expression can give. The writing must have the following qualities:

① The writing must be on material that lends itself to permanence. Instruments carved in blocks of ice or recorded on other impermanent surfaces would not qualify as negotiable instruments. Suppose that Suzanne writes in the sand, "I promise to pay $500 to the order of Jack." This cannot be a negotiable instrument because, although it is in writing, it lacks permanence.

② The writing must also have portability. Although this is not a spelled-out legal requirement, if an instrument is not movable, it obviously cannot meet the requirement that it be freely transferable. For example, Charles writes on the side of a cow, "I promise to pay $500 to the order of Jason." Technically, this meets the requirements of a negotiable instrument, but as a cow cannot easily be transferred in the ordinary course of business, the "instrument" is nonnegotiable.

ON THE WEB British author A. P. Herbert has some fun with the "written form" requirement for a negotiable instrument in his humorous (and fictitious) story titled "The Negotiable Cow," which can be found online at **http://www.kmoser.com/herbert/herb04.htm**.

Signatures

For an instrument to be negotiable, it must be signed by (1) the maker, if it is a note or a certificate of deposit, or (2) the drawer, if it is a draft or a check [UCC 3–103(a)(3)]. If a person signs an instrument as an authorized agent of the maker or drawer, the maker or drawer has effectively signed the instrument. (Agents' signatures will be discussed in Chapter 20.)

SIGNATURE Under the UCC, "any symbol executed or adopted by a party with a present intention to authenticate a writing."

The UCC grants extreme latitude in regard to what constitutes a signature. UCC 1–201(39) provides that a **signature** may include "any symbol executed or adopted by a party with a present intention to authenticate a writing." UCC 3–401(b) expands on

LETTER OF THE LAW

What Is a Negotiable Instrument?

The UCC leaves a lot of room for imagination when it comes to negotiable instruments. Bearer instruments, for example, need not always be written to "cash" or to "bearer." They can be written to "Merry Christmas" or "Happy New Year" or just about any nonexistent or inanimate object. Even more extraordinary is the UCC's lack of specificity as to the form of a negotiable instrument. When we think of a check, for example, we normally envision a preprinted form with the "normal" terms and phrases on it, including the bank's name and address, "Pay to the order of," and so on. The UCC, however, says nothing to indicate that negotiable instruments must be typed or printed or placed on any specific kind of material. The UCC stipulates only that a negotiable instrument must be in writing, the writing must lend itself to permanence, and the writing must be portable.

THE BOTTOM LINE

As might be imagined, this lack of specificity has led to some extraordinary negotiable instruments. Checks and notes have been written on napkins, menus, tablecloths, shirts, and a variety of other materials—including a tractor fender, an eggshell, a watermelon, underwear, and a tamale.

this by stating that a "signature may be made (i) manually or by means of a device or machine, and (ii) by the use of any name, including a trade or assumed name, or by a word, mark, or symbol executed or adopted by a person with present intention to authenticate a writing." Thus, initials, an X (if the writing is signed by a witness), or a thumbprint will normally suffice as a signature. A trade name or an assumed name is also sufficient. Signatures that are placed onto instruments by means of rubber stamps are permitted and frequently used in the business world. If necessary, parol evidence (discussed in Chapter 11) is admissible to identify the signer. When the signer is identified, the signature becomes effective.

The location of the signature on the document is unimportant, although the usual place is the lower right-hand corner. A *handwritten* statement on the body of the instrument such as "I, Jerome Cavallo, promise to pay Elaine Grant," is sufficient to act as a signature.

There are virtually no limitations on the manner in which a signature can be made, but one should be careful about receiving an instrument that has been signed in an unusual way. Furthermore, an unusual signature clearly decreases the *marketability* of an instrument because it creates uncertainty.

Unconditional Promise or Order to Pay

REMEMBER Negotiable instruments are classified as promises to pay or orders to pay.

The terms of the promise or order must be included in the writing on the face of a negotiable instrument. The terms must also be *unconditional*—that is, they cannot be conditioned on the occurrence or nonoccurrence of some other event or agreement [UCC 3–104(a)].

Promise or Order For an instrument to be negotiable, it must contain an express order or promise to pay. A mere acknowledgment of the debt, which might logically *imply* a promise, is not sufficient under the UCC, because the promise must be an affirmative (express) undertaking [UCC 3–103(a)(9)]. The traditional I.O.U. is only an acknowledgment of indebtedness. Although the I.O.U. might logically imply a promise, it is not a negotiable instrument, because it does not contain an express promise to repay the debt.

A certificate of deposit is exceptional in this respect. No express promise is required in a CD, because the bank's acknowledgment of the deposit and the other terms of the instrument clearly indicate a promise by the bank to repay the sum of money [UCC 3–104(j)].

An *order* is associated with three-party instruments, such as trade acceptances, checks, and drafts. An order directs a third party to pay the instrument as drawn. In the typical check, for example, the word *pay* (to the order of a payee) is a command to the drawee bank to pay the check when presented, and thus it is an order. The order is mandatory even if it is written in a courteous form with such words as "Please pay" or "Kindly pay." Generally, precise language must be used. An order stating "I wish you would pay" does not fulfill the requirement of precision. The order to the drawee may be addressed to one person or to more than one person, either jointly ("to A *and* B") or alternatively ("to A *or* B") [UCC 3–103(a)(6)].

Unconditionality of Promise or Order A negotiable instrument's utility as a substitute for money or as a credit device would be dramatically reduced if it had conditional promises attached to it. • **Example 19.5** Andrew promises in a note to pay Frances $10,000 only on the condition that a certain ship reaches port. No one could safely purchase the promissory note without first investigating whether the ship had arrived.

Even then, the facts disclosed by the investigation might be incorrect.● To avoid such problems, the UCC provides that only unconditional promises or orders can be negotiable [UCC 3–104(a)].

A promise or order is conditional (and *not* negotiable) if it states (1) an express condition to payment, (2) that the promise or order is subject to or governed by another writing, or (3) that the rights or obligations with respect to the promise or order are stated in another writing. A reference to another writing, however, does not of itself make the promise or order conditional [UCC 3–106(a)]. For example, the words "As per contract" or "This debt arises from the sale of goods X and Y" do not render an instrument nonnegotiable.

Similarly, a statement in the instrument that payment can be made only out of a particular fund or source will not render the instrument nonnegotiable [UCC 3–106(b)(ii)].[1] ● **EXAMPLE 19.6** Suppose that the terms in a note include the statement that payment will be made out of the proceeds of next year's cotton crop. This will not make the note nonnegotiable—although the payee of such a note may find the note commercially unacceptable and refuse to take it.●

Finally, a simple statement in an otherwise negotiable note indicating that the note is secured by a mortgage does not destroy its negotiability. Realize, though, that the statement that a note is secured by a mortgage must not stipulate that the maker's promise to pay is *subject* to the terms and conditions of the mortgage.

A Fixed Amount of Money

Negotiable instruments must state with certainty a fixed amount of money to be paid at any time the instrument is payable [UCC 3–104(a)]. This requirement promises clarity and certainty in determining the value of the instrument.

Fixed Amount The term *fixed amount* means an amount that is ascertainable from the face of the instrument. A demand note payable with 8 percent interest meets the requirement of a fixed amount[2] because its amount can be determined at the time it is payable or at any time thereafter [UCC 3–104(a)]. The rate of interest may also be determined with reference to information that is not contained in the instrument but that is readily ascertainable by reference to a formula or a source described in the instrument [UCC 3–112(b)].[3] For example, when an instrument is payable at the *legal rate of interest* (a rate of interest fixed by statute), the instrument is negotiable. Mortgage notes tied to a variable rate of interest (a rate that fluctuates as a result of market conditions) can also be negotiable. The requirement that to be negotiable a writing must contain a promise or order to pay a fixed amount applies only to the principal [UCC 3–104(a)].

BE AWARE Interest payable on an instrument normally cannot exceed the maximum limit on interest under a state's usury statute.

Payable in Money UCC 3–104(a) provides that a fixed amount is to be *payable in money*. The UCC defines money as "a medium of exchange authorized or adopted by a domestic or foreign government as a part of its currency" [UCC 1–201(24)].

● **EXAMPLE 19.7** Suppose that the maker of a note promises "to pay on demand $1,000 in U.S. gold." Because gold is not a medium of exchange adopted by the U.S.

1. Section 3–105(2)(b) of the unrevised Article 3 provided just the opposite: an instrument with a term providing that payment could be made only out of a particular fund or source rendered the instrument nonnegotiable.
2. Under Section 3–104(1)(b) of the unrevised Article 3, the amount to be paid was called a *sum certain.*
3. This was not possible under the unrevised Article 3, which required that an amount or rate of interest could be determined only from the instrument without reference to any outside source [UCC 3–106].

government, the note is not payable in money. The same result would occur if the maker promises "to pay $1,000 and fifty bottles of 1990 Château Lafite-Rothschild wine," because the instrument is not payable *entirely* in money. An instrument payable in government bonds or in shares of IBM stock is not negotiable, because neither is a medium of exchange recognized by the U.S. government.•

The statement "Payable in $1,000 U.S. currency or an equivalent value in gold" would render the instrument nonnegotiable if the maker reserved the option of paying in money or gold. If the option were left to the payee, some legal scholars argue that the instrument would be negotiable. Any instrument payable in the United States with a face amount stated in a foreign currency is negotiable and can be paid in the foreign money or in the equivalent in U.S. dollars [UCC 3–107].

Payable on Demand or at a Definite Time

ACCEPTOR
A drawee that is legally obligated to pay an instrument when the instrument is presented later for payment.

A negotiable instrument must "be payable on demand or at a definite time" [UCC 3–104(a)(2)]. Clearly, to ascertain the value of a negotiable instrument, it is necessary to know when the maker, drawee, or acceptor (an **acceptor** is a drawee that promises to pay an instrument when it is presented later for payment) is required to pay. It is also necessary to know when the obligations of secondary parties, such as indorsers[4] (to be discussed later in this chapter), will arise. Furthermore, it is necessary to know when an instrument is due in order to calculate when the statute of limitations may apply [UCC 3–118(a)]. Finally, with an interest-bearing instrument, it is necessary to know the exact interval during which the interest will accrue to determine the present value of the instrument.

PRESENTMENT
The act of presenting an instrument to the party liable on the instrument to collect payment; presentment also occurs when a person presents an instrument to a drawee for a required acceptance.

Payable on Demand Instruments that are payable on demand include those that contain the words "Payable at sight" or "Payable upon presentment." **Presentment** occurs when a person presents an instrument to the party liable on the instrument to collect payment; presentment also occurs when a person presents an instrument to a drawee for acceptance (see the discussion of trade acceptances earlier in this chapter).

The very nature of the instrument may indicate that it is payable on demand. For example, a check, by definition, is payable on demand [UCC 3–104(f)]. If no time for payment is specified and the person responsible for payment must pay on the instrument's presentment, the instrument is payable on demand [UCC 3–108(a)].

Payable at a Definite Time If an instrument is not payable on demand, to be negotiable it must be payable at a definite time. An instrument is payable at a definite time if it states that it is payable (1) on a specified date, (2) within a definite period of time (such as thirty days) after sight or acceptance, or (3) on a date or time readily ascertainable at the time the promise or order is issued [UCC 3–108(b)]. The maker or drawee is under no obligation to pay until the specified time.

• **Example 19.8** Suppose that an instrument dated June 1, 2003, states, "One year after the death of my grandfather, Henry Adams, I promise to pay to the order of James Harmon $5,000. [Signed] Jacqueline Wells." This instrument is nonnegotiable. Because the date of the grandfather's death is uncertain, the instrument is not payable at a definite time.•

When an instrument is payable by the maker or drawer on or before a stated date, it is clearly payable at a definite time, although the maker or drawer has the option of

4. We should note here that because the UCC uses the spelling *indorse* (*indorsement,* and so on), rather than *endorse* (*endorsement,* and so on), we adopt that spelling here and in other chapters in the text.

paying before the stated maturity date. If the maker or drawer does not pay early, the holder can still rely on payment being made before the maturity date. Thus, the option to pay early does not violate the definite-time requirement. ● **EXAMPLE 19.9** Suppose that Levine gives Hirsch an instrument dated November 1, 2001, that indicates on its face that it is payable on or before November 1, 2003. This instrument satisfies the requirement.● In contrast, an instrument that is undated and made payable "one month after date" is clearly nonnegotiable. There is no way to determine the maturity date from the face of the instrument.

The issue in the following case was whether a particular promissory note, on which the "date" blanks had not been filled in, was payable at a definite time.

CASE 19.3 Barclays Bank PLC[a] v. Johnson

Court of Appeals of North Carolina, 1998.
129 N.C.App. 370,
499 S.E.2d 768.
http://www.aoc.state.nc.us/www/public/html/opinions.htm[b]

COMPANY PROFILE *Barclays PLC is one of the largest financial services companies in the United Kingdom (UK) and offers banking and investment services in other countries worldwide. Through Barclays Bank PLC and other divisions, the company is involved in consumer and business banking (with nearly two thousand branches in the UK and one thousand branches in seventy-six other countries), credit cards, mortgage lending, factoring, leasing services, and travel agency services. Barclays also sells life insurance, manages pensions, and offers private banking services.*

FACTS Mark Johnson signed a promissory note for $28,979.15 in favor of Healthco International, Inc., as part of Johnson's purchase of supplies from Healthco for his dental practice. The note stated that it was payable as follows:

> Payable in ____ Successive Monthly Installments of $_________ Each, and in 11 Successive Monthly Installments of $2,414.92 Each thereafter, and in a final payment of $2,415.03 thereafter. The first installment being payable on the __ day of ______ 19 __, and the remaining installments on the same date of each month thereafter until paid.

The blanks were never filled in. Barclays Bank PLC bought the note. When Johnson defaulted on the note, Barclays filed a complaint in a North Carolina state court against Johnson. Johnson responded in part that he had not paid off the note because he had not received all of the supplies. Concluding that the note was not negotiable because it was not payable at a definite time, the court issued a summary judgment in Johnson's favor. Barclays appealed.

ISSUE Is a note negotiable if it does not state that it is payable on demand or at a definite time?

DECISION No. The Court of Appeals of North Carolina affirmed the judgment of the lower court. The state intermediate appellate court held that to be negotiable, an instrument must state that it is payable on demand or at a definite time.

REASON The state intermediate appellate court explained that North Carolina state courts "required strict compliance with the requirements set out under the Uniform Commercial Code defining negotiable instruments." The court also noted that the drafters of the UCC encouraged strict interpretations of the requirements for negotiability. In this case, the note did not meet the requirement that it be payable on demand or at a definite time.

FOR CRITICAL ANALYSIS—Economic Consideration *Why are the requirements for negotiability strictly enforced?*

a. *PLC* is an abbreviation for "Public Limited Company," a company in the United Kingdom with more than fifty shareholders that offers its shares for sale to the public but whose shareholders are not liable for company debts beyond the amount of their investments.

b. This page, within the Web site of the North Carolina state courts, contains links to some of the courts' opinions. Click on "1998" under "Court of Appeals Opinions," and on the page that opens, scroll down the list (or use your browser's "Find" function) to locate this case. Click on the link to access the opinion.

ACCELERATION CLAUSE
A clause that allows a payee or other holder of a time instrument to demand payment of the entire amount due, with interest, if a certain event occurs, such as a default in the payment of an installment when due.

HOLDER
Any person in the possession of an instrument drawn, issued, or indorsed to him or her, to his or her order, to bearer, or in blank.

Acceleration Clause An **acceleration clause** allows a payee or other holder of a time instrument to demand payment of the entire amount due, with interest, if a certain event occurs, such as a default in the payment of an installment when due. (A **holder** is any person in the possession of an instrument drawn, issued, or indorsed to him or her, to his or her order, to bearer, or in blank [see UCC 1–201(20)]. The terms *indorse, bearer,* and *in blank* will be explained later in the chapter.) Reasons for acceleration that are stated in the instrument do not affect the instrument's negotiability. For an acceleration clause to be enforced, however, the holder must have a good faith belief that payment will not be made when he or she invokes the acceleration clause.

● **EXAMPLE 19.10** Assume that Martin lends $1,000 to Ruth. Ruth makes a negotiable note promising to pay $100 per month for eleven months. The note contains an acceleration provision that permits Martin or any holder to demand at once all of the remaining payments plus the interest owed to date if Ruth fails to pay an installment in any given month. If, for example, Ruth fails to make the third payment, the note will be due and payable in full. If Martin accelerates the unpaid balance, Ruth will owe Martin the remaining principal plus any unpaid interest. ●

Under the UCC, instruments that include acceleration clauses are negotiable because (1) the exact value of the instrument can be ascertained and (2) the instrument will be payable on a specified date if the event allowing acceleration does not occur [UCC 3–108(b)(ii)]. Thus, the specified date is the outside limit used to determine the value and negotiability of the instrument.

EXTENSION CLAUSE
A clause in a time instrument that allows the instrument's date of maturity to be extended into the future.

Extension Clause The reverse of an acceleration clause is an **extension clause**, which allows the date of maturity to be extended into the future [UCC 3–108(b)(iii), (iv)]. To keep the instrument negotiable, the interval of the extension must be specified if the right to extend is given to the maker of the instrument. If, however, the holder of the instrument can extend it, the extended maturity date does not have to be specified.

● **EXAMPLE 19.11** Suppose that a note reads, "The maker has the right to postpone the time of payment of this note beyond its definite maturity date of January 1, 2003. This extension, however, shall be for no more than a reasonable time." A note with this language is not negotiable because it does not satisfy the definite-time requirement. The right to extend is the maker's, and the maker has not indicated when the note will become due after the extension. In contrast, a note that reads, "The holder of this note at the date of maturity, January 1, 2003, can extend the time of payment until the following June 1 or later, if the holder so wishes," is a negotiable instrument. The length of the extension does not have to be specified because the option to extend is solely that of the holder. After January 1, 2003, the note is, in effect, a demand instrument. ●

PAYABLE TO ORDER OR TO BEARER

Because one of the functions of a negotiable instrument is to serve as a substitute for money, freedom to transfer an instrument to another person is an essential requirement. To assure a proper transfer, the instrument must be "payable to order or to bearer" at the time it is issued or first comes into the possession of the holder [UCC 3–104(a)(1)]. This is no longer required for a check to be negotiable, however [UCC 3104(c)]. Thus, a bank could eliminate the words "the order of" in the familiar phrase "Pay to the order of," and the check would still be negotiable. All other instruments, however, will not be negotiable unless they meet this requirement.

ORDER INSTRUMENT
A negotiable instrument that is payable "to the order of an identified person" or "to an identified person or order."

Order Instruments An **order instrument** is an instrument that is payable (1) "to the order of an identified person" or (2) "to an identified person or order" [UCC 3–109(b)].

An identified person is the person "to whom the instrument is initially payable" as determined by the intent of the maker or drawer [UCC 3–110(a)]. The identified person, in turn, may transfer the instrument to whomever he or she wishes. Thus, the maker or drawer is agreeing to pay either the person specified on the instrument or whomever that person might designate. In this way, the instrument retains its transferability. • **EXAMPLE 19.12** Suppose an instrument states, "Payable to the order of Rocky Reed" or "Pay to Rocky Reed or order." Clearly, the maker or drawer has indicated that a payment will be made to Reed or to whomever Reed designates. The instrument is negotiable. •

INDORSEMENT
A signature placed on an instrument for the purpose of transferring one's ownership rights in the instrument.

Except for bearer instruments (explained in the following paragraph), the person specified must be named with *certainty*, because the transfer of an order instrument requires an indorsement. (An **indorsement** is a signature placed on an instrument, such as on the back of a check, for the purpose of transferring one's ownership rights in the instrument.) • **EXAMPLE 19.13** If an instrument states, "Payable to the order of my kissing cousin," the instrument is nonnegotiable. This is because a holder could not be sure that the person who indorsed the instrument was actually the "kissing cousin" who was supposed to have indorsed it. •

BEARER INSTRUMENT
Any instrument that is not payable to a specific person, including instruments payable to the bearer or to "cash."

BEARER
A person in the possession of an instrument payable to bearer or indorsed in blank.

Bearer Instruments A **bearer instrument** is an instrument that does not designate a specific payee [UCC 3–109(a)]. The term **bearer** refers to a person in the possession of an instrument that is payable to bearer or indorsed in blank (with a signature only, as will be discussed shortly) [UCC 1–201(5), 3–109(a), 3–109(c)]. This means that the maker or drawer agrees to pay anyone who presents the instrument for payment. Any instrument containing the following terms is a bearer instrument:

- "Payable to the order of bearer."
- "Payable to Rocky Reed or bearer."
- "Payable to bearer."
- "Pay cash."
- "Pay to the order of cash."

NOTE An instrument that purports to be payable both to order and bearer is a contradiction in terms. Such an instrument is a bearer instrument.

In addition, an instrument that "indicates that it is not payable to an identified person" is bearer paper [UCC 3–109(a)(3)]. Thus, an instrument "payable to X" or "payable to Batman" can be negotiated as bearer paper, as though it were payable to cash. The UCC does not accept an instrument issued to a nonexistent organization as payable to bearer, however [UCC 3–109, Comment 2]. An instrument "payable to the order of the Camrod Company," if no such company exists, therefore would not be bearer paper.

Factors That Do Not Affect Negotiability

Certain ambiguities or omissions will not affect the negotiability of an instrument. The UCC provides the following rules for clearing up ambiguous terms:

1. Unless the date of an instrument is necessary to determine a definite time for payment, the fact that an instrument is undated does not affect its negotiability. A typical example is an undated check [UCC 3–113(b)].
2. Postdating or antedating an instrument does not affect the instrument's negotiability [UCC 3–113(a)]. For example, on May 1, Beth draws a check on her account with First State Bank made payable to Consumer Credit Corporation. Beth dates

the check "May 15." Consumer Credit can negotiate the check, and, unless Beth tells First State otherwise, the bank can charge the amount of the check to Beth's account before May 15 [UCC 4–401(c)].

③ Handwritten terms outweigh typewritten and printed terms (preprinted terms on forms, for example), and typewritten terms outweigh printed terms [UCC 3–114]. For example, if your check is printed, "Pay to the order of," and in handwriting you insert in the blank, "Anita Delgado or bearer," the check is a bearer instrument.

④ Words outweigh figures unless the words are ambiguous [UCC 3–114]. This rule is important when the numerical amount and the written amount on a check differ. For example, Rob issues a check payable to Standard Appliance Company. For the amount, he fills in the numbers "$100" and writes in the words "One thousand and 00/100" dollars. The check is payable in the amount of $1,000.

⑤ When a particular interest rate is not specified but the instrument simply states "with interest," the interest rate is the *judgment rate of interest* (a rate of interest fixed by statute that is applied to a monetary judgment awarded by a court until the judgment is paid or terminated) [UCC 3–112(b)].

Transfer of Instruments

Once issued, a negotiable instrument can be transferred by *assignment* or by *negotiation*.

TRANSFER BY ASSIGNMENT

Recall from Chapter 12 that an assignment is a transfer of rights under a contract. Under general contract principles, a transfer by assignment to an assignee gives the assignee only those rights that the assignor possessed. Any defenses that can be raised against an assignor can normally be raised against the assignee. This same principle applies when an instrument, such as a promissory note, is transferred by assignment. The transferee is then an *assignee* rather than a *holder.* Sometimes, a transfer fails to qualify as a negotiation because it fails to meet one or more of the requirements of a negotiable instrument, discussed above. When this occurs, the transfer becomes an assignment.

TRANSFER BY NEGOTIATION

NEGOTIATION
The transfer of an instrument in such form that the transferee (the person to whom the instrument is transferred) becomes a holder.

Negotiation is the transfer of an instrument in such form that the transferee (the person to whom the instrument is transferred) becomes a holder [UCC 3–201(a)]. Under UCC principles, a transfer by negotiation creates a holder who, at the very least, receives the rights of the previous possessor [UCC 3–203(b)]. Unlike an assignment, a transfer by negotiation can make it possible for a holder to receive more rights in the instrument than the prior possessor had [UCC 3–202(b), 3–305, 3–306]. A holder who receives greater rights is known as a *holder in due course,* a concept we discuss in Chapter 20.

There are two methods of negotiating an instrument so that the receiver becomes a holder. The method used depends on whether the instrument is order paper or bearer paper.

Negotiating Order Instruments An order instrument contains the name of a payee capable of indorsing it, as in "Pay to the order of Lloyd Sorenson." An order instrument is also an instrument that has as its last or only indorsement a *special* indorsement, as in "Pay to Sorenson. [Signed] Adams." (Special indorsements are discussed in more detail later in this chapter.) If the instrument is an order instrument, it is negotiated by delivery with any necessary indorsements. • **EXAMPLE 19.14** National Express Corporation issues a payroll check "to the order of Lloyd Sorenson." Sorenson takes the check to the supermarket, signs his name on the back (an indorsement), gives it to the cashier (a delivery), and receives cash. Sorenson has *negotiated* the check to the supermarket [UCC 3–201(b)].•

RECALL A person convicted of theft may be sued for conversion. Conversion is the civil side of crimes of theft.

Negotiating Bearer Instruments If an instrument is payable to bearer, it is negotiated by delivery—that is, by transfer into another person's possession. Indorsement is not necessary [UCC 3–201(b)]. The use of bearer instruments thus involves more risk through loss or theft than the use of order instruments.

• **EXAMPLE 19.15** Assume that Richard Kray writes a check "payable to cash" and hands it to Jessie Arnold (a delivery). Kray has issued the check (a bearer instrument) to Arnold. Arnold places the check in her wallet, which is subsequently stolen. The thief has possession of the check. At this point, the thief has no rights to the check. If the thief "delivers" the check to an innocent third person, however, negotiation has occurred. All rights to the check will be passed absolutely to that third person, and Arnold will lose all rights to recover the proceeds of the check from him or her [UCC 3–306]. Of course, Arnold could attempt to recover the money from the thief if the thief can be found.•

Converting Order Instruments to Bearer Instruments and Vice Versa The method used for negotiation depends on the character of the instrument at the time the negotiation takes place. • **EXAMPLE 19.16** Suppose that a check that was originally payable to "cash" is subsequently indorsed with the words "Pay to Arnold." This instrument must be negotiated as an order instrument (by indorsement and delivery), even though it was previously a bearer instrument [UCC 3–205(a)].•

"Money has little value to its possessor unless it also has value to others."

LELAND STANFORD, 1824–1893 (U.S. senator and founder of Stanford University)

An instrument payable to the order of a named payee and indorsed in blank (by the holder's signature only, as will be discussed shortly) becomes a bearer instrument [UCC 3–205(b)]. • **EXAMPLE 19.17** A check made payable to the order of Jessie Arnold is issued to Arnold, and she indorses it by signing her name on the back. The instrument is now a bearer instrument, and Arnold can negotiate the check to whomever she wishes merely by delivery. If Arnold loses the check after she indorses it, then a finder can negotiate it further.• Exhibit 19–5 on the following page illustrates how an indorsement can convert an order instrument into a bearer instrument and vice versa.

Indorsements

ALLONGE
A piece of paper firmly attached to a negotiable instrument, on which transferees can make indorsements if there is no room left on the instrument itself.

Indorsements are required whenever the instrument being negotiated is classified as an order instrument. An *indorsement* is a signature with or without additional words or statements. It is most often written on the back of the instrument itself. If there is no room on the instrument, indorsements can be written on a separate piece of paper, called an **allonge**.[5] The allonge must be "so firmly affixed [to the instrument] as to

5. Pronounced uh-*lohnj.*

EXHIBIT 19–5 CONVERTING AN ORDER INSTRUMENT TO A BEARER INSTRUMENT AND VICE VERSA

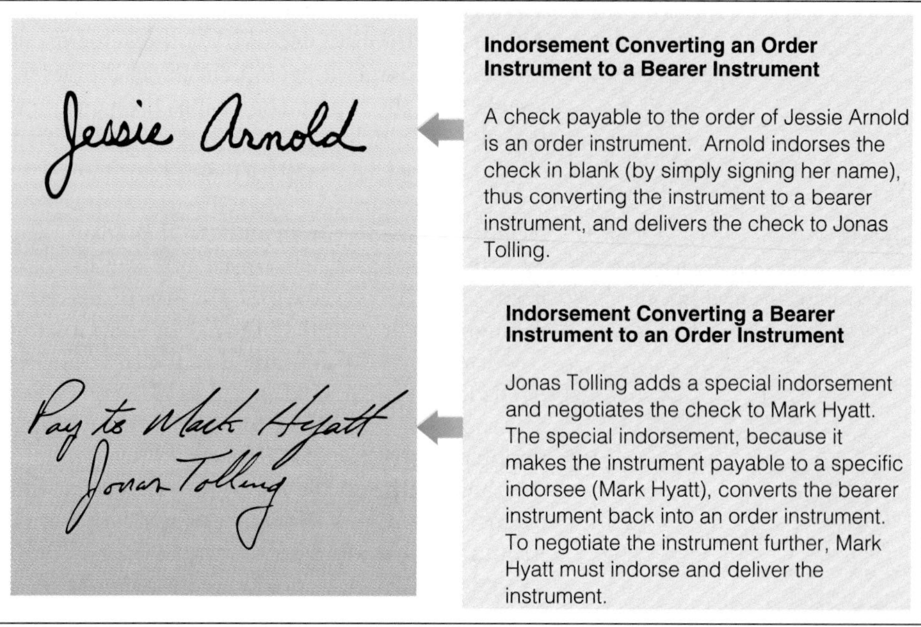

become a part thereof" [UCC 3–204(a)]. Pins or paper clips will not suffice. Most courts hold that staples are sufficient.

INDORSER
A person who transfers an instrument by signing (indorsing) it and delivering it to another person.

INDORSEE
The person to whom a negotiable instrument is transferred by indorsement.

A person who transfers an instrument by signing (indorsing) it and delivering it to another person is an **indorser**. The person to whom the check is indorsed and delivered is the **indorsee**. • **EXAMPLE 19.18** Martha receives a graduation check for $500. She can transfer the check to her mother (or to anyone) by signing it on the back and delivering it. Martha is an indorser. If Martha indorses the check by writing "Pay to Mary Grimes," Mary Grimes is the indorsee. •

One purpose of an indorsement is to effect the negotiation of order paper. Sometimes the transferee of a bearer instrument will request the holder-transferor to indorse the instrument in such a way as to impose liability on the indorser (the liability of indorsers will be discussed in Chapter 20), although the UCC does not require bearer instruments to be indorsed.

We examine here four categories of indorsements: blank indorsements, special indorsements, qualified indorsements, and restrictive indorsements.

BLANK INDORSEMENTS

BLANK INDORSEMENT
An indorsement that specifies no particular indorsee and that can consist of a mere signature. An order instrument that is indorsed in blank becomes a bearer instrument.

A **blank indorsement** specifies no particular indorsee and can consist of a mere signature [UCC 3–205(b)]. Hence, a check payable "to the order of Alan Luberda" can be indorsed in blank simply by having Luberda's signature written on the back of the check. An instrument payable to order and indorsed in blank becomes a bearer instrument and can be negotiated by delivery alone, as already discussed. Exhibit 19–6 shows a blank indorsement.

EXHIBIT 19–6 A BLANK INDORSEMENT

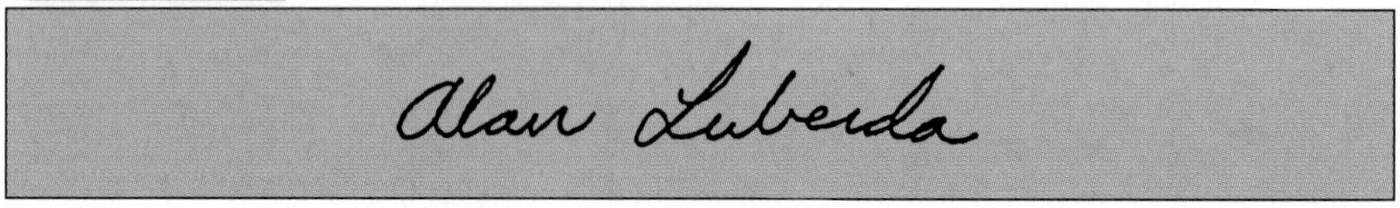

Alan Luberda

SPECIAL INDORSEMENTS

SPECIAL INDORSEMENT
An indorsement on an instrument that indicates the specific person to whom the indorser intends to make the instrument payable; that is, it names the indorsee.

A **special indorsement** indicates the specific person to whom the indorser intends to make the instrument payable; that is, it names the indorsee [UCC 3–205(a)]. For example, words such as "Pay to the order of Storr" or "Pay to Storr," followed by the signature of the indorser, create a special indorsement. When an instrument is indorsed in this way, it is an order instrument.

To avoid the risk of loss from theft, a holder may convert a blank indorsement to a special indorsement. This changes the bearer instrument back to an order instrument. A holder may "convert a blank indorsement that consists only of a signature into a special indorsement by writing, above the signature of the indorser, words identifying the person to whom the instrument is made payable" [UCC 3–205(c)].

• **EXAMPLE 19.19** A check is made payable to Peter Rabe. He indorses his name in blank (signs his name only) on the back of the check and delivers the check to Anthony Bartomo. Anthony is unable to cash the check immediately and wants to avoid any risk should he lose the check. He therefore prints "Pay to Anthony Bartomo" above Peter's blank indorsement (see Exhibit 19–7). In this manner, Anthony has converted Peter's blank indorsement into a special indorsement. Further negotiation now requires Anthony Bartomo's indorsement plus delivery.•

EXHIBIT 19–7 A SPECIAL INDORSEMENT

Pay to Anthony Bartomo

Peter Rabe

QUALIFIED INDORSEMENTS

QUALIFIED INDORSEMENT
An indorsement on a negotiable instrument in which the indorser disclaims any contract liability on the instrument; the notation "without recourse" is commonly used to create a qualified indorsement.

Generally, an indorser, *merely by indorsing*, impliedly promises to pay the holder, or any subsequent indorser, the amount of the instrument in the event that the drawer or maker defaults on the payment [UCC 3–415(b)]. An indorser can use a **qualified indorsement** to disclaim this contract liability on the instrument. The notation "without recourse" is commonly used to create a qualified indorsement, such as the one shown in Exhibit 19–8.

EXHIBIT 19–8 A QUALIFIED INDORSEMENT

Pay to Elvie Ling, without recourse.

Bridgett Cage

Qualified indorsements are often used by persons acting in a representative capacity. • **EXAMPLE 19.20** Insurance agents sometimes receive checks payable to them that are really intended as payment to the insurance company. The agent is merely indorsing the payment through to the insurance company and should not be required to make good on the check if it is later dishonored. The "without recourse" indorsement relieves the agent from any contract liability on a check. If the instrument is dishonored, the holder cannot obtain recovery from the agent who indorsed "without recourse" unless the indorser has breached one of the transfer warranties discussed in Chapter 20, which relate to good title, authorized signature, no material alteration, and so forth. ●

Usually, then, blank and special indorsements are *unqualified indorsements*. That is, the blank or special indorser is guaranteeing payment of the instrument in addition to transferring title to it. The qualified indorser is not guaranteeing payment. Nonetheless, an instrument bearing a qualified indorsement can be negotiated.

A qualified indorsement is accompanied by either a special indorsement or a blank indorsement that determines further negotiation. Accordingly, a special qualified indorsement makes the instrument an order instrument, and it requires an indorsement plus delivery for negotiation. A blank qualified indorsement makes the instrument a bearer instrument, and only delivery is required for negotiation.

● **EXAMPLE 19.21** Assume that a check is made payable to the order of Bridgett Cage and that Bridgett wants to negotiate the check specifically to Elvie Ling with a qualified indorsement. Bridgett would indorse the check as follows: "Pay to Elvie Ling, without recourse. [Signed] Bridgett Cage." For Elvie to negotiate the check further to Joe Nantz, Elvie would have to indorse the check and deliver it to Joe. ● The qualified indorsement shown in Exhibit 19–8, which was referred to earlier, is an example of a special qualified indorsement.

RESTRICTIVE INDORSEMENTS

RESTRICTIVE INDORSEMENT
Any indorsement on a negotiable instrument that requires the indorsee to comply with certain instructions regarding the funds involved. A restrictive indorsement does not prohibit the further negotiation of the instrument.

A **restrictive indorsement** requires the indorsee to comply with certain instructions regarding the funds involved. A restrictive indorsement does not prohibit the further negotiation of an instrument [UCC 3–206(a)]. Restrictive indorsements come in many forms, some of which we discuss here.

Conditional Indorsements When payment depends on the occurrence of some event specified in the indorsement, the instrument has a conditional indorsement [UCC 3–205(a)]. For example, if Ken Barton indorses a check, "Pay to Lars Johansen if he completes the renovation of my kitchen by June 1, 2003. [Signed] Ken Barton," Barton has created a conditional indorsement. Article 3, however, states that an indorsement conditioning the right to receive payment "does not affect the right of the indorsee to enforce the instrument" [UCC 3–206(b)]. A person paying or taking for value an instrument can disregard the condition without liability.[6]

A conditional indorsement does not prevent further negotiation of the instrument. If conditional language appears on the face of an instrument, however, the instrument is not negotiable because it does not meet the requirement that it contain an unconditional promise to pay.

Indorsements Prohibiting Further Indorsement An indorsement such as "Pay to Makoto Chi only. [Signed] Jerome Edelman" does not destroy transfer by negotiation. Chi can negotiate the instrument to a holder just as if it had read "Pay to Makoto Chi. [Signed] Jerome Edelman" [UCC 3–206(a)]. If the holder gives value to Chi, this type of restrictive indorsement has the same legal effect as a special indorsement.

6. Under the unrevised Article 3, neither the indorsee nor any subsequent holder had the right to enforce payment against an indorser who indorsed a check conditionally until the specified condition was met [UCC 3–206(3)].

Indorsements for Deposit or Collection A common type of restrictive indorsement is one that makes the indorsee (almost always a bank) a collecting agent of the indorser [UCC 3–206(c)]. For example, if Stephanie Mallak wants to deposit a check she has received into her checking account at the bank, she could indorse the check "For deposit only. [Signed] Stephanie Mallak." (See Exhibit 19–9.) A "Pay any bank or banker" or "For deposit" indorsement has the effect of locking the instrument into the bank collection process and thus prohibits further negotiation except by a bank. Following this indorsement, only a bank can acquire the rights of a holder.

EXHIBIT 19–9 FOR DEPOSIT/FOR COLLECTION INDORSEMENTS

For deposit
Stephanie Mallak

or

For collection only
Stephanie Mallak

TRUST INDORSEMENT
An indorsement for the benefit of the indorser or a third person; also known as an agency indorsement. The indorsement results in legal title vesting in the original indorsee.

Trust Indorsements An indorsement indicating that the indorsee is to hold or use the funds for the benefit of the indorser or a third party is called a **trust indorsement** (also known as an *agency indorsement*) [UCC 3–206(d)]. • **EXAMPLE 19.22** Assume that Robert Emerson asks his accountant, Ada Johnson, to pay some bills for his invalid wife, Sarah, while he is out of the country. He indorses a check as follows: "Pay to Ada Johnson as Agent for Sarah Emerson." This agency indorsement obligates Johnson to use the funds only for the benefit of Sarah Emerson. • The fiduciary restrictions (restrictions mandated by a relationship involving trust and loyalty) on the instrument do not reach beyond the original indorsee [UCC 3–206(d), (e)]. Exhibit 19–10 shows sample trust indorsements.

EXHIBIT 19–10 TRUST INDORSEMENTS

Pay to Ada Johnson in
trust for Sarah Emerson
Robert Emerson

or

Pay to Ada Johnson as Agent
for Sarah Emerson
Robert Emerson

The result of a trust indorsement is that legal rights in the instrument are transferred to the original indorsee (Ada Johnson, in the example just given). To the extent that the original indorsee pays or applies the proceeds consistently with the indorsement (for example, "in trust for Sarah Emerson"), the indorsee is a holder and can become a holder in due course (described in Chapter 20).

ETHICAL ISSUE 19.1

Why should fiduciary restrictions on an instrument apply only to the original indorsee?

Article 3 gives the force of law to the ethical duties of an indorsee on a trust instrument to use the funds in accordance with the wishes of the indorser. Yet what if the original indorsee disregards the fiduciary restrictions on a trust instrument and then transfers it to another person? In this situation, according to Article 3, the subsequent purchaser has no obligation to verify that the fiduciary requirements were met by the original indorsee. Although this may seem unfair, consider the alternative. If all subsequent holders were obligated to verify that the terms of the trust indorsement were fulfilled, it would impair the ease with which instruments could be transferred—and thus impair their function as substitutes for money. By holding only the original indorsee to the fiduciary restrictions on an instrument with a trust indorsement, the UCC furthers one of its basic goals—to encourage the free flow of commerce by making the laws practical and reasonable. Article 3's provisions relating to trust indorsements provide just one example of the many ways in which the UCC balances this goal against other ethical principles.

Miscellaneous Indorsement Problems

Of course, a significant problem occurs when an indorsement is forged or unauthorized. The UCC's rules concerning unauthorized or forged signatures and indorsements will be discussed in Chapter 20, in the context of signature liability, and again in Chapter 21, in the context of the bank's liability for payment of an instrument over an unauthorized signature. Two other problems that may arise with indorsements concern misspelled names and multiple payees.

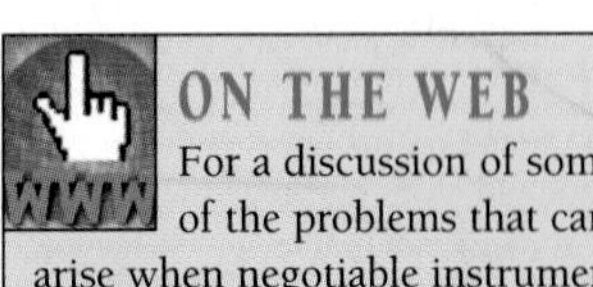

ON THE WEB For a discussion of some of the problems that can arise when negotiable instruments have joint or alternative payees, including hypothetical illustrations of these problems, go to the Web site of the Community Bankers' Advisor at **http://www.minot.com/~obl/news.html.**

An indorsement should be identical to the name that appears on the instrument. A payee or indorsee whose name is misspelled can indorse with the misspelled name, the correct name, or both [UCC 3–204(d)]. For example, if Sheryl Kruger receives a check payable to the order of Sherrill Krooger, she can indorse the check either "Sheryl Kruger" or "Sherrill Krooger," or both. The usual practice is to indorse the name as it appears on the instrument and follow it by the correct name.

An instrument payable to two or more persons *in the alternative* (for example, "Pay to the order of Tuan or Johnson") requires the indorsement of only one of the payees. If, however, an instrument is made payable to two or more persons *jointly* (for example, "Pay to the order of Sharrie and Bob Covington"), all of the payees' indorsements are necessary for negotiation. If an instrument payable to two or more persons does not clearly indicate whether it is payable in the alternative or jointly (for example, "Pay to the order of John and/or Sara Fitzgerald"), then the instrument is payable to the persons alternatively [UCC 3–110(d)]. The same principles apply to special indorsements that indicate more than one identified person to whom the indorser intends to make the instrument payable [UCC 3–205(a)].

APPLICATION Law and the Businessperson . . .

Writing and Indorsing Checks*

As a businessperson (or as a consumer), you will certainly be writing and receiving checks. Both activities can involve pitfalls.

Checks Drawn in Blank

The danger in signing a blank check is clear. Anyone can write in an unauthorized amount and cash the check. Although you may be able to assert lack of authorization against the person who filled in the unauthorized amount, subsequent holders of the properly indorsed check may be able to enforce the check as completed. While you are haggling with the person who inserted the unauthorized figure and who may not be able to repay the amount, you will also have to honor the check for the unauthorized amount to a subsequent holder in due course (see Chapter 20).

Checks Payable to "Cash"

It is equally dangerous to write out and sign a check payable to "cash" until you are actually at the bank. Remember that checks payable to "cash" are bearer instruments. This means that if you lose or misplace the check, anybody who finds it can present it to the bank for payment.

Checks Indorsed in Blank

Just as a check signed in blank or payable to cash may be dangerous, a negotiable instrument with a blank indorsement also has dangers; as a bearer instrument, it is as easily transferred as cash. When you make a bank deposit, therefore, you should sign (indorse) the back of the check in blank only in the presence of a teller. If you choose to sign it ahead of time, make sure you insert the words "For deposit only" before you sign your name. As a precaution, you should consider obtaining an indorsement stamp from your bank. Then, when a check is received payable to your business, you can indorse it immediately. The stamped indorsement will indicate that the check is for deposit only to your business account specified by the number.

Checklist for the Use of Negotiable Instruments

1. A good rule of thumb is never to sign a blank check.
2. Another good rule of thumb is never to write and sign a check payable to "cash" until you are actually at the bank.
3. Be wary of indorsing a check in blank unless a bank teller is simultaneously giving you a receipt for your deposit.
4. Consider obtaining an indorsement stamp from your bank so that when you receive checks you can immediately indorse them "For deposit only" to your account.

* This *Application* is not meant to substitute for the services of an attorney who is licensed to practice law in your state.

Key Terms

acceleration clause 500
acceptor 498
allonge 503
bearer 501
bearer instrument 501
blank indorsement 504
certificate of deposit (CD) 492
check 491
draft 490
drawee 490
drawer 490
extension clause 500
holder 500
indorsee 504
indorsement 501
indorser 504
maker 492
negotiable instrument 488

negotiation 502
order instrument 500
payee 490
presentment 498
promissory note 490
qualified indorsement 505
restrictive indorsement 506
signature 495
special indorsement 505
trade acceptance 490
trust indorsement 507

Chapter Summary Negotiability and Transferability

Article 3 of the UCC (See page 489.)	Article 3 of the Uniform Commercial Code governs the negotiability and transferability of negotiable instruments. Article 3 was significantly revised in 1990. Almost all of the states have adopted the revised article.
Types of Instruments (See pages 489–494.)	The UCC specifies four types of negotiable instruments: drafts, checks, promissory notes, and certificates of deposit (CDs). These instruments fall into two basic classifications: 1. *Demand instruments versus time instruments*—A demand instrument is payable on demand (when the holder presents it to the maker or drawer). A time instrument is payable at a future date. 2. *Orders to pay versus promises to pay*—Checks and drafts are *orders* to pay. Promissory notes and CDs are *promises* to pay.
Requirements for Negotiability (See pages 494–501.)	To be negotiable, an instrument must meet the following requirements: 1. Be in writing. 2. Be signed by the maker or drawer. 3. Be an unconditional promise or order to pay. 4. State a fixed amount of money. 5. Be payable on demand or at a definite time. 6. Be payable to order or bearer.
Factors That Do Not Affect Negotiability (See pages 501–502.)	1. The fact that an instrument is undated does not affect its negotiability unless the date is necessary to determine a definite time for payment. 2. Postdating or antedating an instrument does not affect its negotiability. 3. Handwritten terms take priority over typewritten and printed terms. 4. Words outweigh figures unless the words are ambiguous. 5. An instrument that states "with interest" but does not state the interest rate is payable at the judgment rate of interest.
Transfer of Instruments (See pages 502–503.)	1. *Transfer by assignment*—A transfer by assignment to an assignee gives the assignee only those rights that the assignor possessed. Any defenses against payment that can be raised against an assignor can normally be raised against the assignee. 2. *Transfer by negotiation*—An order instrument is negotiated by indorsement and delivery; a bearer instrument is negotiated by delivery only.
Indorsements (See pages 503–508.)	1. *Blank* (for example, "Alan Luberda"). 2. *Special* (for example, "Pay to Anthony Bartomo. [Signed] Peter Rabe"). 3. *Qualified* (for example, "Without recourse. [Signed] Bridgett Cage"). 4. *Restrictive* (for example, "For deposit only. [Signed] Stephanie Mallak" or "Pay to Ada Johnson in trust for Sarah Emerson. [Signed] Robert Emerson").

Chapter Summary Negotiability and Transferability—continued

Miscellaneous Indorsement Problems (See page 508.)	1. A payee or indorsee whose name is misspelled can indorse with the misspelled name, the correct name, or both. 2. An instrument payable to two or more persons in the alternative requires the indorsement of only one of the payees. 3. An instrument payable to two or more persons jointly requires all of the payees' indorsements for negotiation. 4. If an instrument payable to two or more persons does not clearly indicate whether it is payable in the alternative or jointly, it is payable to the persons alternatively. The same principle applies to special indorsements that contain multiple indorsees.

For Review

① What are the four types of negotiable instruments with which Article 3 of the UCC is concerned? Which of these instruments are *orders* to pay, and which are *promises* to pay?

② What requirements must an instrument meet to be negotiable?

③ To whom is a bearer instrument payable?

④ What is the difference between an indorsement in blank and a special indorsement?

⑤ What is a restrictive indorsement? Does a restrictive indorsement prohibit further negotiation of the instrument?

Questions and Case Problems

19–1. Parties to Negotiable Instruments. A note has two original parties. What are these parties called? A check has three original parties. What are these parties called?

19–2. Indorsements. Bertram writes a check for $200, payable to "cash." He puts the check in his pocket and drives to the bank to cash the check. As he gets out of his car in the bank's parking lot, the check slips out of his pocket and falls to the pavement. Jerrod walks by moments later, picks up the check, and later that day delivers it to Amber, to whom he owes $200. Amber indorses the check "For deposit only. [Signed] Amber Dowel" and deposits it into her checking account. In light of these circumstances, answer the following questions:

(a) Is the check a bearer instrument or an order instrument?
(b) Did Jerrod's delivery of the check to Amber constitute a valid negotiation? Why or why not?
(c) What type of indorsement did Amber make?
(d) Does Bertram have a right to recover the $200 from Amber? Explain.

19–3. Requirements for Negotiability. The following note is written by Muriel Evans on the back of an envelope: "I, Muriel Evans, promise to pay Karen Marvin or bearer $100 on demand." Is this a negotiable instrument? Discuss fully.

19–4. Requirements for Negotiability. The following instrument was written on a sheet of paper by Jeff Nolan: "I, the undersigned, do hereby acknowledge that I owe Stephanie Craig one thousand dollars, with interest, payable out of the proceeds of the sale of my horse, Swiftfoot, next month. Payment is to be made on or before six months from date." Discuss specifically why this instrument is not negotiable.

19–5. Indorsements. A check drawn by David for $500 is made payable to the order of Matthew and issued to Matthew. Matthew owes his landlord $500 in rent and transfers the check to his landlord with the following indorsement: "For rent paid. [Signed] Matthew." Matthew's landlord has contracted to have Juarez do some landscaping on the property. When Juarez insists on immediate payment, the landlord transfers the check to Juarez without indorsement. Later, to pay for some palm trees purchased from Green's Nursery, Juarez transfers the check with the following indorsement: "Pay to Green's Nursery, without recourse. [Signed] Juarez." Green's Nursery sends the check to its bank indorsed "For deposit only. [Signed] Green's Nursery."

(a) Classify each of these indorsements.
(b) Was the transfer from Matthew's landlord to Juarez, without indorsement, an assignment or a negotiation? Explain.

19–6. Fixed Amount of Money. William Bailey and William Vaught, as officers for Bailey, Vaught, Robertson, and Co. (BVR), signed a promissory note to borrow $34,000 from the Forestwood National Bank. The interest rate was variable: "the lender's published prime rate" plus 1 percent. Forestwood National Bank went out of business, and ultimately, the note was acquired by Remington Investments, Inc. When BVR failed to make payments, Remington filed a suit in a Texas state court against BVR. BVR contended in part that the note was not negotiable because after Forestwood closed, there was no "published lender's prime rate" to use to calculate the interest. Did the note provide for payment of a "fixed amount of money"? [*Bailey, Vaught, Robertson, and Co. v. Remington Investments, Inc.*, 888 S.W.2d 860 (Tex.App.—Dallas 1994)]

19–7. Indorsements. Universal Premium Acceptance Corp. issued more than $1 million in drafts, intending the payee to be Great American Insurance Co. When the drafts were issued, they were nonnegotiable instruments. Walter Talbot, an insurance agent, intercepted the drafts, forged Great American's indorsements in blank, and deposited the drafts in a phony account at York Bank & Trust Co. After Talbot was caught and convicted, Universal filed a suit in a federal district court against York to recover some of its losses. One of the issues was whether Talbot's indorsements converted the nonnegotiable drafts into negotiable bearer instruments. Did they? Why or why not? [*Universal Premium Acceptance Corp. v. York Bank & Trust Co.*, 69 F.3d 695 (3d Cir. 1995)]

19–8. Requirements for Negotiability. Walter Peffer loaned $125,000 to the Pefferoni Pizza Co. The note included a clause that allowed the maker (Pefferoni Pizza) to renegotiate the terms of repayment at any time and then extend the time for repayment by up to eighty-four months. Later, Peffer borrowed money from Northern Bank, using the Pefferoni Pizza note as collateral. When Peffer failed to repay his loan, the bank tried to collect on the collateral note, but the pizza company failed to pay. The bank filed a suit in a Nebraska state court against Pefferoni Pizza to recover on the collateral note. Pefferoni Pizza argued in part that its note was not a negotiable instrument because under the renegotiation clause, it was not payable at a definite time. Was the note a negotiable instrument? Explain. [*Northern Bank v. Pefferoni Pizza Co.*, 5 Neb.App. 50, 555 N.W.2d 338 (1996)]

19–9. Negotiability. Regent Corp., U.S.A., an import company in New York, contracted with Azmat Bangladesh, Ltd., a textile company in Bangladesh, for the purchase of bed sheets and pillowcases for import and resale in the United States. An essential condition of the sale was that the goods be manufactured in Bangladesh. The contract required payment by Regent within ninety days of the date on the bill of lading, and Regent issued promissory notes that indicated this term. After the goods were shipped, Azmat's bank presented drafts drawn against Regent to Regent's banks. Like the notes, each draft indicated that payment was to be made "at 90 days deferred from bill of lading date." The drafts were accompanied by dated bills of lading. On delivery of the goods, U.S. Customs refused to allow their entry because they were partially manufactured in Pakistan. Regent filed a suit in a New York state court against its banks, and Azmat, to stop payment on the drafts. One of the issues was whether the notes and drafts were "payable at a definite time." How should the court rule on this issue? Explain fully. [*Regent Corp., U.S.A. v. Azmat Bangladesh, Ltd.*, 253 A.D.2d 134, 686 N.Y.S.2d 24 (1 Dept. 1999)]

TEST YOUR KNOWLEDGE—ANSWER ON THE WEB

19–10. In October 1998, Somerset Valley Bank notified Alfred Hauser, president of Hauser Co., that the bank had begun to receive what appeared to be Hauser Co. payroll checks. None of the payees were Hauser Co. employees, however, and Hauser had not written the checks or authorized anyone to sign them on his behalf. Automatic Data Processing, Inc., provided payroll services for Hauser Co. and used a facsimile signature on all its payroll checks. Hauser told the bank not to cash the checks. In early 1999, Robert Triffin, who deals in negotiable instruments, bought eighteen of the checks, totaling more than $8,800, from various check-cashing agencies. The agencies stated that they had cashed the checks expecting the bank to pay them. Each check was payable to a bearer for a fixed amount, on demand, and did not state any undertaking by the person promising payment other than the payment of money. Each check bore a facsimile drawer's signature stamp identical to Hauser Co.'s authorized stamp. Each check had been returned to an agency marked "stolen check" and stamped "do not present again." When the bank refused to cash the checks, Triffin filed a suit in a New Jersey state court against Hauser Co. Were the checks negotiable instruments? Why or why not? [*Triffin v. Somerset Valley Bank*, 777 A.2d 993 (N.J.Super.App.Div. 2001)]

A QUESTION OF ETHICS AND SOCIAL RESPONSIBILITY

19–11. Richard Caliendo, an accountant, prepared tax returns for various clients. To satisfy their tax liabilities, the clients issued checks payable to various state taxing entities and gave them to Caliendo. Between 1977 and 1979, Caliendo forged indorsements on these checks, deposited them in his own bank account, and subsequently withdrew the proceeds. In 1983, after learning of these events and after Caliendo's death, the state brought an action against Barclays Bank of New York, N.A., the successor to Caliendo's bank, to recover the amount of the checks. Barclays moved for dismissal on the ground that because the checks had never been delivered to the state, the state never acquired the status of holder and therefore never acquired any rights in the instruments. The trial court held for the state, but the appellate court reversed. The state then appealed the case to the state's highest court. That court ruled that the state could not recover the amount of the checks from the bank because, although the state was the named payee on the checks, the checks had never been delivered to the payee. [*State v. Barclays Bank of New York, N.A.*, 561 N.Y.2d 533, 563 N.E.2d 11, 561 N.Y.S.2d 697 (1990)]

1. If you were deciding this case, would you make an exception to the rule and let the state collect the funds from Barclays Bank? Why or why not? What ethical policies must be balanced in this situation?
2. Under agency law, which will be discussed in Chapter 24, delivery to the agent of a given individual or entity constitutes delivery to that person or entity. The court deemed that Caliendo was not an agent of the state but an agent of the taxpayers. Does it matter that the taxpayers may not have known this principle of agency law and might have thought that, by delivering their checks to Caliendo, they were delivering them to the state?

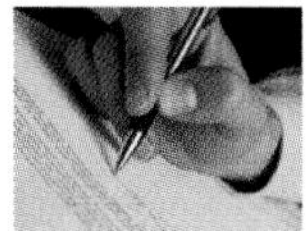

FOR CRITICAL ANALYSIS

19–12. The UCC requirements for negotiable instruments are generally strict. In regard to what constitutes a signature on an instrument, however, the UCC grants extreme latitude—X marks, initials, and rubber-stamped signatures are all permitted. Given the potential for forgery of these kinds of signatures, why does the UCC permit them?

Internet Exercises

Go to the *Business Law Today* home page at **http://blt.westbuslaw.com**. Select "Interactive Study Center" and then click on "Chapter 19." There you will find the following Internet research exercises that you can perform to learn more about negotiable instruments:

Activity 19–1: Overview of Negotiable Instruments
Activity 19–2: Review of Negotiable Instruments

Before the Test

Go to the *Business Law Today* home page at **http://blt.westbuslaw.com**. Click on "Interactive Quizzes." You will find at least twenty interactive questions relating to this chapter.

CHAPTER 20

Rights and Liabilities of Parties

"Wealth, in a commercial age, is made up largely of promises."

Roscoe Pound, 1870–1964
(American jurist)

CHAPTER CONTENTS

LEARNING OBJECTIVES

After reading this chapter, you should be able to answer the following questions:

① What are the requirements for attaining HDC status?

② How can a person who does not qualify as an HDC acquire the rights and privileges of an HDC?

③ What is the key to liability on a negotiable instrument? What is the difference between signature liability and warranty liability?

④ Certain defenses are valid against all holders, including HDCs. What are these defenses called? Name four defenses that fall within this category.

⑤ Certain defenses can be used to avoid payment to an ordinary holder of a negotiable instrument but are not effective against an HDC. What are these defenses called? Name four defenses that fall within this category.

As pointed out in Chapter 19, negotiable instruments function as substitutes for money; they also function as extensions of credit. Any note in which a person promises to pay another a sum of money creates a debtor (the one promising) and a creditor (the one to be paid). As the eminent jurist Roscoe Pound indicated in this chapter's opening quotation, wealth "is made up largely of promises." The extensive exchange of negotiable instruments that takes place daily in the United States is predicated, ultimately, on the existence of law and a government capable of enforcing the promises made by parties to negotiable instruments.

The outcome of litigation concerning negotiable instruments usually turns on whether a holder is entitled to obtain payment on an instrument when it is due. Often, whether a holder is entitled to obtain payment will depend on whether the holder is a *holder in due course (HDC)*, a concept we examine in the opening pages of this chapter. We then discuss the liability of the parties to negotiable instruments. In the remainder of the chapter, we consider the defenses available for avoiding liability and, briefly, the ways in which a person can be discharged from an obligation on a negotiable instrument.

Holder versus Holder in Due Course (HDC)

As pointed out in Chapter 19, the Uniform Commercial Code (UCC) defines a *holder* as a person in the possession of an instrument drawn, issued, or indorsed to him or her, to his or her order, to bearer, or in blank [UCC 1–201(20)]. An ordinary holder obtains only those rights that the transferor had in the instrument. In this respect, a holder has the same status as an assignee (see Chapter 12). Like an assignee, a holder normally is subject to the same defenses that could be asserted against the transferor.

HOLDER IN DUE COURSE (HDC)
A holder who acquires a negotiable instrument for value; in good faith; and without notice that the instrument is overdue, that it has been dishonored, that any person has a defense against it or a claim to it, or that the instrument contains unauthorized signatures, has been altered, or is so irregular or incomplete as to call into question its authenticity.

In contrast, a **holder in due course (HDC)** is a holder who, by meeting certain acquisition requirements (to be discussed shortly), takes the instrument *free* of most of the defenses and claims that could be asserted against the transferor. Stated another way, an HDC can normally acquire a higher level of immunity than can an ordinary holder in regard to defenses against payment on the instrument or ownership claims to the instrument by other parties.

● **EXAMPLE 20.1** Marcia Cambry signs a $1,000 note payable to Alex Jerrod in payment for some ancient Roman coins. Jerrod negotiates the note to Alicia Larson, who promises to pay Jerrod for it in thirty days. During the next month, Larson learns that Jerrod has breached his contract with Cambry by delivering coins that were not from the Roman era, as promised, and that for this reason Cambry will not honor the $1,000 note. Whether Larson can hold Cambry liable on the note depends on whether Larson has met the requirements for HDC status. If Larson has met these requirements and thus has HDC status, Larson is entitled to payment on the note. If Larson has not met these requirements, she has the status of an ordinary holder, and Cambry's defense of breach of contract against payment to Jerrod will also be effective against Larson. ●

Requirements for HDC Status

The basic requirements for attaining HDC status are set forth in UCC 3–302. A holder of a negotiable instrument is an HDC if she or he takes the instrument (1) for value; (2) in good faith; and (3) without notice that it is overdue, that it has been dishonored, that any person has a defense against it or a claim to it, or that the instrument contains unauthorized signatures, contains alterations, or is so irregular or incomplete as to call into question its authenticity. We now examine each of these requirements.

TAKING FOR VALUE

An HDC must have given *value* for the instrument [UCC 3–302(a)(2)(i)]. A person who receives an instrument as a gift or inherits it has not met the requirement of value. In these situations, the person becomes an ordinary holder and does not possess the rights of an HDC.

ON THE WEB To find Article 3 of the UCC as adopted by a particular state, go to the Web site of Cornell University's Law School at

http://www.law.cornell.edu/ucc/ucc.table.html.

The concept of value in the law of negotiable instruments is not the same as the concept of *consideration* in the law of contracts. A promise to give value in the future is clearly sufficient consideration to support a contract [UCC 1–201(44)]. A promise to give value in the future, however, normally does not constitute value sufficient to make one an HDC. A holder takes an instrument for value only to the extent that the promise has been performed [UCC 3–303(a)(1)]. Therefore, if the holder plans to pay for the instrument later or plans to perform the required services at some future date, the holder has not yet given value. In that situation, the holder is not yet an HDC.

In the Larson-Cambry example presented earlier, Larson is not an HDC because she did not take the instrument (Cambry's note) for value—she had not yet paid Jerrod for the note. Thus, Cambry's defense of breach of contract is valid not only against Jerrod but also against Larson. If Larson had paid Jerrod for the note at the time of transfer (which would mean she had given value for the instrument), she would be an HDC. As an HDC, she could hold Cambry liable on the note even though Cambry has a valid defense against Jerrod on the basis of breach of contract. Exhibit 20–1 illustrates these concepts.

Under UCC 3–303(a), a holder can take an instrument for value in one of five ways:

① By performing the promise for which the instrument was issued or transferred.

② By acquiring a security interest or other lien in the instrument, excluding a lien obtained by a judicial proceeding. (Security interests and liens are discussed in Chapters 22 and 23.)

③ By taking an instrument in payment of (or as security for) a preexisting debt.

④ By giving a negotiable instrument as payment.

⑤ By giving an irrevocable commitment as payment.

TAKING IN GOOD FAITH

The second requirement for HDC status is that the holder take the instrument in *good faith* [UCC 3–302(a)(2)(ii)]. This means that the holder must have acted honestly in the process of acquiring the instrument. UCC 3–103(a)(4) defines *good faith* as "honesty in fact and the observance of reasonable commercial standards of fair deal-

EXHIBIT 20–1 TAKING FOR VALUE

By exchanging defective goods for the note, Jerrod breached his contract with Cambry. Cambry could assert this defense if Jerrod presented the note to her for payment. Jerrod exchanged the note for Larson's promise to pay in thirty days, however. Because Larson did not take the note for value, she is not a holder in due course. Thus, Cambry can assert against Larson the defense of Jerrod's breach when Larson submits the note to Cambry for payment. If Larson had taken the note for value, Cambry could not assert that defense and would be liable to pay the note.

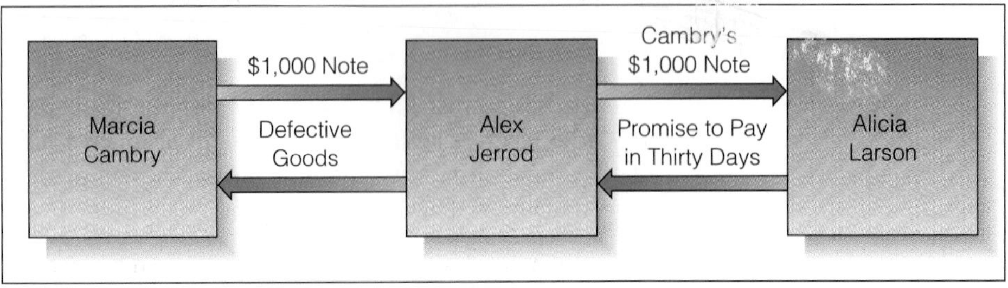

ing." The good faith requirement applies only to the *holder.* It is immaterial whether the transferor acted in good faith. Thus, even a person who takes a negotiable instrument from a thief may become an HDC if the person acquires the instrument in good faith.

Because of the good faith requirement, one must ask whether the purchaser, when acquiring the instrument, honestly believed that the instrument was not defective. If a person purchases a $10,000 note for $300 from a stranger on a street corner, the issue of good faith can be raised on the grounds of both the suspicious circumstances and the grossly inadequate consideration (value). In the following case, the court considered whether a credit union fulfilled the good faith requirement to qualify as an HDC.

CASE 20.1 Maine Family Federal Credit Union v. Sun Life Assurance Co. of Canada

Supreme Judicial Court of Maine, 1999.
727 A.2d 335.
http://www.courts.state.me.us/mescopin.home.html[a]

FACTS On the death of Elden Guerrette, Sun Life Assurance Company of Canada issued three checks, each in the amount of $40,759.35, to each of Elden's three children. The checks were drawn on Sun Life's account at Chase Manhattan Bank in Syracuse, New York, and given to Steven Hall, a Sun Life agent, to give to the Guerrettes. Hall and an associate, Paul Richard, fraudulently induced the Guerrettes to indorse the checks in blank and transfer them to Hall and Richard, purportedly to be invested in "HER, Inc.," a corporation formed by Hall and Richard. Richard deposited the checks in his account at the Maine Family Federal Credit Union, which immediately made the funds available. The next day, the Guerrettes contacted Sun Life, which ordered Chase Manhattan to stop payment on the checks. When the checks were presented for payment, the bank refused to pay them, and they were returned to the Credit Union. By that time, however, Richard had withdrawn from his account all of the funds represented by the checks. The Credit Union recovered almost $80,000 from Richard, but an unpaid balance of $42,366.56 remained. The Credit Union filed a suit in a Maine state court against the Guerrettes and others. When the court entered a judgment against the Credit Union, it appealed to the Supreme Judicial Court of Maine, the state's highest court.

ISSUE Did the Credit Union act in good faith?

DECISION No. The Supreme Judicial Court of Maine, the state's highest court, affirmed the judgment of the lower court, as it related to the Guerrettes. The appellate court held that in relation to the Guerrettes, the Credit Union was not a holder in due course.

REASON The court explained that on the facts in this case, "the jury could rationally have concluded that the reasonable commercial standard of fair dealing would require the placing of a hold on the uncollected funds for a reasonable period of time and that, in giving value under these circumstances, the Credit Union did not act according to commercial standards that were reasonably structured to result in fair dealing." Because of this, the Credit Union had not acted in good faith and could not claim the status of a holder in due course. The court vacated the portion of the judgment entered in favor of Sun Life and against the Credit Union on other grounds, however, and remanded that part of the case for further proceedings.

FOR CRITICAL ANALYSIS—Ethical Consideration
Why is good faith required to attain HDC status?

a. In the "Chronological Lists of Opinions," click on the appropriate link, which, as of this writing, is "Click here for February and March 1999 Opinions." In the "March 1999" section, click on the case name to access the opinion.

TAKING WITHOUT NOTICE

The final requirement for HDC status involves *notice* [UCC 3–302]. A person will not be afforded HDC protection if he or she acquires an instrument and is *on notice* (knows or has reason to know) that it is defective in any one of the following ways [UCC 3–302(a)]:

INTERNATIONAL PERSPECTIVE

"Protected Holder" Status

Good faith is an issue not only in domestic transactions involving negotiable instruments but also internationally. Under the United Nations Convention on International Bills of Exchange and International Promissory Notes (CIBN), the equivalent of a holder in due course is known as a "protected holder." As under the UCC, a protected holder is afforded greater protection than an ordinary holder. The CIBN, however, unlike the UCC, does not provide an objective test by which to measure good faith. Article 3 of the UCC, as revised in 1990, added to the subjective definition of *good faith* (which was defined under the unrevised Article 3 as simply "honesty in fact") the phrase, "and the observance of reasonable commercial standards of fair dealing." Thus, courts applying the UCC have some objective guidelines as to what constitutes good faith. The CIBN, in contrast, simply qualifies someone as a protected holder if she or he was "without knowledge" of a fraud or other defense against the instrument.

FOR CRITICAL ANALYSIS
What might be a reason why the CIBN contains only a very broad and subjective definition of good faith?

① It is overdue.

② It has been previously dishonored.

③ There is an uncured (uncorrected) default with respect to another instrument issued as part of the same series.

④ The instrument contains an unauthorized signature or has been altered.

⑤ There is a defense against the instrument or a claim to the instrument.

⑥ The instrument is so irregular or incomplete as to call into question its authenticity.

What Constitutes Notice? Notice of a defective instrument is given whenever the holder (1) has actual knowledge of the defect; (2) has received a notice of the defect (such as a bank's receipt of a letter listing the serial numbers of stolen bearer instruments); or (3) has reason to know that a defect exists, given all the facts and circumstances known at the time in question [UCC 1–201(25)]. The holder must also have received the notice "at a time and in a manner that gives a reasonable opportunity to act on it" [UCC 3–302(f)]. A purchaser's knowledge of certain facts, such as insolvency proceedings against the maker or drawer of the instrument, does not constitute notice that the instrument is defective [UCC 3–302(b)].

REMEMBER Demand instruments are payable immediately. Time instruments are payable at a future date.

Overdue Instruments What constitutes notice that an instrument is overdue depends on whether it is a demand instrument (payable on demand) or a time instrument (payable at a definite time). For example, a purchaser has notice that a *demand instrument* is overdue if he or she takes the instrument an unreasonable length of time after its issue. A "reasonable time" for the taking of a check is ninety days, but for other demand instruments, what will be considered a reasonable time depends on the circumstances [UCC 3–304(a)].[1]

A holder of a *time instrument* who takes the instrument at any time after its expressed due date is on notice that it is overdue [UCC 3–304(b)(2)]. Nonpayment by

1. Under the unrevised Article 3, a reasonable time for the taking of a domestic check was *presumed* to be thirty days [UCC 3–304(3)(c)].

the due date should indicate to any purchaser that the instrument may be defective. Thus, a promissory note due on May 15 must be acquired before midnight on May 15. If it is purchased on May 16, the purchaser will be an ordinary holder, not an HDC.

Sometimes, an instrument reads, "Payable in thirty days." A promissory note dated December 1 that is payable in thirty days is due by midnight on December 31. If the payment date falls on a Sunday or holiday, the instrument is payable on the next business day. If a debt is to be paid in installments or through a series of notes, the maker's default on any installment of principal (not interest) or on any one note of the series will constitute notice to the purchaser that the instrument is overdue [UCC 3–304(b)(1)].

Dishonored Instruments An instrument is *dishonored* when the party to which the instrument is presented refuses to pay it. If a holder has actual knowledge that an instrument has been dishonored or has knowledge of facts that would lead him or her to suspect that an instrument has been dishonored, the holder is on notice [UCC 3–302(a)(2)].

• **EXAMPLE 20.2** Condor holds a demand note dated September 1 made by JWB Enterprises, Inc., a local business firm. On September 17, Condor demands payment, and JWB refuses to pay (that is, JWB dishonors the instrument). On September 22, Condor negotiates the note to Bream, a purchaser who lives in another state. Bream does not know, and has no reason to know, that the note has been dishonored, so Bream is *not* put on notice and therefore can become an HDC. •

Notice of Claims or Defenses A holder cannot become an HDC if she or he has notice of any claim to the instrument or any defense against it [UCC 3–302(a)]. Knowledge of claims or defenses can be imputed to the purchaser if these claims or defenses are apparent on the face of the instrument or if the purchaser otherwise had reason to know of them from facts surrounding the transaction.

NOTE A difference between the handwriting in the body of a check and the handwriting in the signature does not affect the validity of the check.

A purchaser cannot expect to become an HDC of an instrument so incomplete on its face that an element of negotiability is lacking (for example, the amount is not filled in). Minor omissions (such as the omission of the date—see Chapter 19) are permissible because these do not call into question the validity of the instrument. Similarly, when a person accepts an instrument that has been completed without knowing that it was incomplete when issued, that person can take it as an HDC.

• **EXAMPLE 20.3** Carrie asks Barron to buy a textbook for her at the campus bookstore. Carrie writes a check payable to the bookstore, leaves the amount blank, and tells Barron to fill in the price of the textbook. The cost of the textbook is $85. If Barron fills in the check for $115 before he gets to the bookstore, the bookstore cashier sees only a properly completed instrument. Therefore, because the bookstore had no notice that the check was incomplete when it was issued, the bookstore can take the check for $115 and become an HDC. •

Any irregularity on the face of an instrument (such as an obvious forgery or alteration) that calls into question its validity or terms of ownership, or that creates an ambiguity as to the party to pay, will bar HDC status. A careful forgery of a signature, however, or the careful alteration of an instrument can go undetected by reasonable examination; therefore, the purchaser can qualify as an HDC.

Holder through an HDC

A person who does not qualify as an HDC but who derives his or her title through an HDC can acquire the rights and privileges of an HDC. According to UCC 3–203(b),

> Transfer of an instrument, whether or not the transfer is a negotiation, vests in the transferee any right of the transferor to enforce the instrument, including any right as a holder in due course, but the transferee cannot acquire rights of a holder in due course by a transfer, directly or indirectly, from a holder in due course if the transferee engaged in fraud or illegality affecting the instrument.

SHELTER PRINCIPLE
The principle that the holder of a negotiable instrument who cannot qualify as a holder in due course (HDC), but who derives his or her title through an HDC, acquires the rights of an HDC.

Under this rule, which is sometimes called the **shelter principle**, anyone—no matter how far removed from an HDC—who can trace his or her title ultimately back to an HDC may acquire the rights of an HDC.

There are some limitations on the shelter principle, however. Certain persons who formerly held instruments cannot improve their positions by later reacquiring the instruments from HDCs [UCC 3–203(b)]. Thus, if a holder was a party to fraud or illegality affecting the instrument or if, as a prior holder, she or he had notice of a claim or defense against an instrument, that holder is not allowed to improve her or his status by repurchasing from a later HDC.

Signature Liability

"Most men are admirers of justice—when justice happens to be on their side."

RICHARD WHATELY,
1787–1863
(English theologian and logician)

The key to liability on a negotiable instrument is a *signature*.[2] The general rule is as follows: Every party, except a qualified indorser,[3] who signs a negotiable instrument is either primarily or secondarily liable for payment of that instrument when it comes due. The following subsections discuss these two types of liability, as well as the conditions that must be met before liability can arise.

PRIMARY LIABILITY

A person who is primarily liable on a negotiable instrument is absolutely required to pay the instrument—unless, of course, he or she has a valid defense to payment [UCC 3–305]. Only *makers* and *acceptors* of instruments are primarily liable.

The maker of a promissory note promises to pay the note. It is the maker's promise to pay that makes the note a negotiable instrument. The words "I promise to pay" embody the maker's obligation to pay the instrument according to the terms as written at the time of the signing. If the instrument is incomplete when the maker signs it, then the maker's obligation is to pay it to an HDC according to the terms written when it is completed [UCC 3–115, 3–407(a), 3–412].

A drawee that promises to pay an instrument when it is presented later for payment is called an *acceptor*, as discussed in Chapter 19. A drawee's acceptance of a draft, which is made by signing the draft, guarantees that the drawee will pay the draft when it is presented in the future for payment [UCC 3–409(a)]. A drawee that refuses to accept a draft that *requires* the drawee's acceptance (such as a trade acceptance or a draft payable thirty days after acceptance) has dishonored the instrument. Acceptance of a check is called *certification* (discussed in Chapter 21). Certification is not necessary on checks, and a bank is under no obligation to certify checks. On certification, however, the drawee bank occupies the position of an acceptor and is primarily liable on the check to any holder [UCC 3–409(d)].

---

2. See Chapter 19 for a discussion of how the UCC defines a *signature*.
3. A qualified indorser—one who indorses "without recourse"—undertakes no contractual obligation to pay. A qualified indorser merely assumes warranty liability, which is discussed later in this chapter.

SECONDARY LIABILITY

RECALL A guarantor is liable on a contract to pay the debt of another only if the party who is primarily liable fails to pay.

Drawers and indorsers are secondarily liable. Secondary liability on a negotiable instrument is similar to the liability of a guarantor in a simple contract (described in Chapter 12) in the sense that it is *contingent liability.* In other words, a drawer or an indorser will be liable only if the party that is primarily liable on the instrument dishonors it by nonpayment or, in regard to drafts and checks, the drawee fails to pay or to accept the instrument, whichever is required [UCC 3–412, 3–415].

Dishonor of an instrument thus triggers the liability of parties who are secondarily liable on the instrument—that is, the drawer and *unqualified* indorsers. For example, Nina Lee writes a check on her account at Universal Bank payable to the order of Stephen Miller. Universal Bank refuses to pay the check when Miller presents it for payment, thus dishonoring the check. In this situation, Lee will be liable to Miller on the basis of her secondary liability. Drawers are secondarily liable on drafts unless they disclaim their liability by drawing the instruments "without recourse" (if the draft is a check, however, a drawer cannot disclaim liability) [UCC 3–414(e)].

Parties that are secondarily liable on a negotiable instrument promise to pay on that instrument only if the following events occur:[4]

① The instrument is properly and timely presented.

② The instrument is dishonored.

③ Timely notice of dishonor is given to the secondarily liable party.

Proper and Timely Presentment The UCC requires that presentment by a holder must be made to the proper person, must be made in a proper manner, and must be timely [UCC 3–414(f), 3–415(e), 3–501]. The party to whom the instrument must be presented depends on what type of instrument is involved. A note or certificate of deposit (CD) must be presented to the maker for payment. A draft is presented by the holder to the drawee for acceptance, payment, or both, whichever is required. A check is presented to the drawee for payment [UCC 3–501(a), 3–502(b)].

Presentment can be properly made in any of the following ways, depending on the type of instrument involved [UCC 3–501(b)]:

① By any commercially reasonable means, including oral, written, or electronic communication (but presentment is not effective until the demand for payment or acceptance is received).

② Through a clearinghouse procedure used by banks, such as for deposited checks (see Chapter 21).

③ At the place specified in the instrument for acceptance or payment.

One of the most crucial criteria for proper presentment is timeliness [UCC 3–414(f), 3–415(e), 3–501(b)(4)]. Failure to present on time is the most common reason for improper presentment and results in the complete discharge of unqualified indorsers from secondary liability. For checks, failure to properly present a check discharges the drawer's secondary liability only to the extent that the drawee is deprived of the funds required to pay the check. The time for proper presentment for different types of instruments is shown in Exhibit 20–2 on the following page.

4. These requirements are necessary for a secondarily liable party to have signature liability on a negotiable instrument, but they are not necessary for a secondarily liable party to have warranty liability (to be discussed later in the chapter).

EXHIBIT 20–2 TIME FOR PROPER PRESENTMENT

TYPE OF INSTRUMENT	FOR ACCEPTANCE	FOR PAYMENT
Time	On or before due date.	On due date.
Demand	Within a reasonable time (after date or issue or after secondary party becomes liable on the instrument).	
Check	Not applicable.	Within thirty days of its date, to hold drawer secondarily liable. Within thirty days of indorsement, to hold indorser secondarily liable.[a]

a. Under the unrevised Article 3, these periods are *presumed* to be thirty days to hold the drawer secondarily liable, and seven days to hold the indorser secondarily liable.

Dishonor An instrument is dishonored when the required acceptance or payment is refused or cannot be obtained within the prescribed time, or when required presentment is excused (as it would be, for example, if the maker had died) and the instrument is not properly accepted or paid [UCC 3–502(e), 3–504].

Proper Notice Once an instrument has been dishonored, proper notice must be given to secondary parties for them to be held contractually liable. Notice may be given in any reasonable manner. This includes oral notice, written notice (including notice by fax, e-mail, and the like), and notice written or stamped on the instrument itself. Any necessary notice must be given by a bank before its midnight deadline (midnight of the next banking day after receipt). Notice by any party other than a bank must be given within thirty days following the day of dishonor or the day on which the person who is secondarily liable receives notice of dishonor [UCC 3–503].[5]

Accommodation Parties

ACCOMMODATION PARTY A person who signs an instrument for the purpose of lending his or her name as credit to another party on the instrument.

An **accommodation party** is one who signs an instrument for the purpose of lending his or her name as credit to another party on the instrument [UCC 3–419(a)]. Accommodation parties are one form of security against nonpayment on a negotiable instrument. • **Example 20.4** Frank Huston applies to Northeast Bank for a $1,000 loan. The bank wants some reasonable assurance that if it loans Huston the funds, the debt will be paid. If Huston's financial condition is uncertain, the bank may be reluctant to rely solely on his ability to pay. To reduce the risk of nonpayment, the bank can require that a third person sign Huston's promissory note as an accommodation party. • When one person (such as a parent) cosigns a promissory note with the maker (such as the parent's son or daughter), the cosigner is an accommodation party.

If the accommodation party signs on behalf of the *maker*, he or she becomes an *accommodation maker* and is primarily liable on the instrument. If the accommodation party indorses an instrument on behalf of a *payee or other holder* (usually to make the instrument more marketable), she or he is an *accommodation indorser* and is secondarily liable. If the accommodation party pays the instrument, he or she has a right of recourse against the party accommodated [UCC 3–419(e)].

5. Under the unrevised Article 3, notice by a person other than a bank has to be given "before midnight of the third business day after dishonor or receipt of notice of dishonor" [UCC 3–508(2)].

A family looks at a van on a dealer's lot. If, as prospective borrowers, the family's financial condition were uncertain, how could an accommodation party help the family obtain the funds to pay for the van?

AGENTS' SIGNATURES

AGENT
A person who agrees to represent or act for another, called the principal.

PRINCIPAL
In agency law, a person who agrees to have another, called the agent, act on her or his behalf.

The general law of agency, covered in Chapter 24, applies to negotiable instruments. An **agent** is a person who agrees to represent or act for another, called the **principal.** Agents can sign negotiable instruments and thereby bind their principals [UCC 3–401(a)(ii), 3–402(a)]. Without such a rule, all corporate commercial business would stop—as every corporation can and must act through its agents.

Generally, an *authorized* agent does not bind a principal on an instrument unless the agent's signature *clearly names* the principal. The agent may or may not add his or her own name, but if the signature shows clearly that it is made on behalf of the principal, the agent is not liable on the instrument.

● **EXAMPLE 20.5** Either of the following two signatures by Joan Collingsworth as agent for Brian Peterson will bind Peterson on the instrument, and Collingsworth will not be personally liable for payment on it:

① Peterson, by Collingsworth, agent.

② Peterson.

If Collingsworth (the agent) signs just her own name, however, she will be personally liable to an HDC who has no notice of her agency status. In respect to other holders, an agent can escape liability if the agent proves that the original parties did not intend the agent to be liable on the instrument [UCC 3–402(a), 3–402(b)(2)]. In either situation, the principal is bound if the party entitled to enforce the instrument can prove the agency relationship.[6] ●

In two other situations, an authorized agent can be held personally liable on a negotiable instrument. When the instrument is signed in both the agent's name and the principal's name (for example, "Collingsworth, Peterson"), but nothing on the instrument indicates the agency relationship (so the agent cannot be distinguished from the principal), the agent may be held personally liable. An agent may also be held personally liable

6. Under the unrevised Article 3, a principal is not liable on an instrument unless his or her signature appears on it, even if the parties are aware of the agency relationship [UCC 3–401(1)].

when the agent indicates agency status in signing a negotiable instrument but fails to name the principal (for example, "Joan Collingsworth, agent") [UCC 3–402(b)(2)].

An important exception to these rules is made for checks that are signed by agents. If an agent signs his or her own name on a check that is *payable from the account of the principal,* and the principal is identified on the check, the agent will not be personally liable on the check [UCC 3–402(c)]. • **EXAMPLE 20.6** Suppose that Collingsworth, who is authorized to draw checks on Peterson Company's account, signs a check that is preprinted with Peterson Company's name. The signature reads simply "Joan Collingsworth." In this situation, Collingsworth will not be personally liable on the check. •

The following case involved a question about the liability on a note that a corporate officer claimed to have signed in a representative capacity.

CASE 20.2 Caraway v. Land Design Studio

Texas Court of Appeals—Austin, 2001.
47 S.W.3d 696.

FACTS Hugh Caraway was the president of International Realty, Inc., when Realty hired Land Design Studio to landscape the Deerfield Project, an apartment-complex development. After Land Design completed the work, the parties executed a promissory note. The note stated, "In consideration of design services rendered, I (We) *Hugh Carraway* [sic], *International Realty, Inc.* * * * do hereby promise to pay *Land Design Studio* * * *, the amount of *$42,639.82*." The note was signed by Caraway. Payment in full was to be made in less than seven months, but no payment was received. Land Design filed a suit in a Texas state court against Caraway to collect the amount due. Caraway denied that he was personally liable on the note, arguing in part that he had intended to sign it in a representative capacity. The court granted Land Design's motion for summary judgment. Caraway appealed to a state intermediate appellate court.

ISSUE Was Caraway personally liable on the note?

DECISION Yes. The state intermediate appellate court affirmed the judgment of the lower court. The note did not indicate, and Caraway did not otherwise disclose, that he signed only as an agent of Realty.

REASON The court pointed out that "[w]e have a note bearing the name of the signing party, Caraway, as one of the principals. * * * [T]he language of the instrument reflects that payment was promised from more than one source: * * * Either 'We' refers to both Caraway and Realty, or exclusively to Realty, which leaves 'I' to refer only to Caraway. In either event, Caraway has assumed liability. The note then bears the signature of 'Hugh L. Caraway, Debtor.' Given the language of the instrument, we find that the note, on its face, clearly obligates Caraway as the maker, or debtor." The court also reasoned that under UCC 3–402(b), "Caraway would be in no different a position if the note did not bear his name as a principal," because his "signature on the note bears no indication of his representative capacity." The "assertion of [a] subjective intent alone is not sufficient * * * . The intent must be disclosed or communicated to the other party * * * . The note itself is the best indicator of intent," and the note, which "identifies Caraway as the maker, * * * does not indicate that Caraway signed only in his representative capacity."

FOR CRITICAL ANALYSIS—Ethical Consideration *Why not consider a party's subjective intent when deciding whether to enforce a negotiable instrument?*

UNAUTHORIZED SIGNATURES

People normally are not liable to pay on negotiable instruments unless their signatures appear on the instruments. As already stated, the general rule is that an unauthorized signature is wholly inoperative and will not bind the person whose name is forged. • **EXAMPLE 20.7** Parra finds Dolby's checkbook lying in the street, writes out a check to himself, and forges Dolby's signature. If a bank fails to ascertain that Dolby's signature is not genuine (which banks normally have a duty to do) and cashes the check for

Parra, the bank will generally be liable to Dolby for the amount.● (The liability of banks for paying over forged signatures is discussed further in Chapter 21.) There are two exceptions to this general rule:

① Any unauthorized signature will bind the person whose name is forged if the person whose name is signed ratifies (affirms) it [UCC 3–403(a)]. For example, a mother may ratify her daughter's forgery of the mother's name so that her daughter will not be prosecuted for forgery.

② A person may be precluded from denying the effectiveness of an unauthorized signature if the person's negligence led to the forgery [UCC 3–115, 3–406, 4–401(d)(2)]. ● **EXAMPLE 20.8** Suppose that Jonathan leaves a blank check in a public place. If someone else finds the check, fills it out, and forges Jonathan's signature, Jonathan can be estopped (prevented), on the basis of negligence, from denying liability for payment of the check.●

An unauthorized signature operates as the signature of the unauthorized signer in favor of an HDC. A person who forges a check, for example, can be held personally liable for payment by an HDC [UCC 3–403(a)].

SPECIAL RULES FOR UNAUTHORIZED INDORSEMENTS

"Life is unfair."

MILTON FRIEDMAN, 1912– (American economist)

Generally, when an indorsement is forged or unauthorized, the burden of loss falls on the first party to take the instrument with the forged or unauthorized indorsement. If the indorsement was made by an imposter or by a fictitious payee, however, the loss falls on the maker or drawer. We look at these two situations here.

IMPOSTER
One who, by use of the mails, telephone, or personal appearance, induces a maker or drawer to issue an instrument in the name of an impersonated payee. Indorsements by imposters are treated as authorized indorsements under Article 3 of the UCC.

Imposters An **imposter** is one who, by use of the mails, telephone, or personal appearance, induces a maker or drawer to issue an instrument in the name of an impersonated payee. If the maker or drawer believes the imposter to be the named payee at the time of issue, the indorsement by the imposter is not treated as unauthorized when the instrument is transferred to an innocent party. This is because the maker or drawer intended the imposter to receive the instrument. In this situation, under the UCC's *imposter rule,* the imposter's indorsement will be effective—that is, not considered a forgery—insofar as the drawer or maker is concerned [UCC 3–404(a)]. ● **EXAMPLE 20.9** Carol impersonates Donna and induces Edward to write a check payable to the order of Donna. Carol, continuing to impersonate Donna, negotiates the check to First National Bank. As the drawer of the check, Edward is liable for its amount to First National.●

FICTITIOUS PAYEE
A payee on a negotiable instrument whom the maker or drawer does not intend to have an interest in the instrument. Indorsements by fictitious payees are treated as authorized indorsements under Article 3 of the UCC.

Fictitious Payees An unauthorized indorsement will also be effective when a person causes an instrument to be issued to a payee who will have *no interest* in the instrument [UCC 3–404(b), 3–405]. In this situation, the payee is referred to as a **fictitious payee.** Situations involving fictitious payees most often arise when (1) a dishonest employee deceives the employer into signing an instrument payable to a party with no right to receive payment on the instrument or (2) a dishonest employee or agent has the authority to issue an instrument on behalf of the employer. Under the UCC's *fictitious payee rule,* the payee's indorsement is not treated as a forgery, and the employer can be held liable on the instrument by an innocent holder or a party (such as a bank) that pays the instrument in good faith.

● **EXAMPLE 20.10** Flair Industries, Inc., gives its bookkeeper, Axel Ford, general authority to issue checks in the company name drawn on First State Bank so that Ford can pay employees' wages and other corporate bills. Ford decides to cheat Flair Industries out of $10,000 by issuing a check payable to Erica Nied, an old acquaintance. Neither Flair nor Ford intends Nied to receive any of the money, and Nied is not an employee or creditor of the company. Ford indorses the check in Nied's name, naming himself as indorsee. He then cashes the check at a local bank, which collects payment from the drawee bank, First State Bank. First State Bank charges the Flair Industries account $10,000. Flair Industries discovers the fraud and demands that the account be recredited.

Who bears the loss? UCC 3–404(b)(2) provides the answer. Neither the local bank that first accepted the check nor First State Bank is liable. Because Ford's indorsement in the name of a payee with no interest in the instrument is "effective," there is no "forgery." Hence, the collecting bank is protected in paying on the check, and the drawee bank is protected in charging Flair's account. It is the employer-drawer, Flair Industries, that bears the loss. Of course, Flair Industries has recourse against Axel Ford. ●

Regardless of whether a dishonest employee actually signs the check or merely supplies the employer with names of fictitious creditors (or with true names of creditors having fictitious debts), the UCC makes no distinction in result. ● **EXAMPLE 20.11** Nathan Holtz draws up the payroll list from which employees' salary checks are written. He fraudulently adds the name Sally Slight (a fictitious person) to the payroll, and the employer signs checks to be issued to her. Again, it is the employer-drawer who bears the loss. ●

ETHICAL ISSUE 20.1

Should a bank that acts in "bad faith" be precluded from raising the fictitious payee rule as a defense?

Remember from previous chapters that the requirement of good faith underlies all transactions governed by the UCC. Does this mean that a bank, to avoid liability for paying instruments with forged indorsements involving fictitious payees, must have acted in good faith when accepting the deposits? Yes, according to a number of courts. Recently, a Pennsylvania appellate court held that to assert the rule "the bank must have acted in good faith when paying the instrument." The bank in this case had accepted 882 payroll checks generated and indorsed by Dorothy Heck, a payroll clerk employed by Pavex, Inc. The checks were made payable to various current and former Pavex employees, indorsed by Heck with the payees' names, and deposited into Heck's personal checking account at her bank. In spite of its policy that indorsements on checks must match exactly the names of the payees, the bank never refused any of Heck's deposited checks on which the indorsements did not match the payees' names. Furthermore, even though bank personnel discussed Heck's check-depositing activities on more than one occasion, they never contacted her employer to see if Heck was authorized to deposit third party payroll checks. Given the bank's pattern of ignoring perceived irregularities in Heck's transactions, the trial court jury had concluded that the bank had acted in bad faith and was therefore liable for approximately $170,000 of the $250,000 loss suffered by Pavex. The appellate court affirmed the trial court's decision.[7]

Warranty Liability

In addition to the signature liability discussed in the preceding pages, transferors make certain implied warranties regarding the instruments that they are negotiating. Liability under these warranties is not subject to the conditions of proper presentment, dishonor, or notice of dishonor. These warranties arise even when a trans-

7. *Pavex, Inc. v. York Federal Savings and Loan Association,* 716 A.2d 640 (Pa.Super.Ct. 1998).

feror does not indorse the instrument (as in the delivery of a bearer instrument) [UCC 3–416, 3–417].

Warranties fall into two categories: those that arise on the *transfer* of a negotiable instrument and those that arise on *presentment*. Both transfer and presentment warranties attempt to shift liability back to a wrongdoer or to the person who dealt face to face with the wrongdoer and thus was in the best position to prevent the wrongdoing.

Transfer Warranties

TRANSFER WARRANTIES
Implied warranties, made by any person who transfers an instrument for consideration to subsequent transferees and holders who take the instrument in good faith, that (1) the transferor is entitled to enforce the instrument, (2) all signatures are authentic and authorized, (3) the instrument has not been altered, (4) the instrument is not subject to a defense or claim of any party that can be asserted against the transferor, and (5) the transferor has no knowledge of any insolvency proceedings against the maker, the acceptor, or the drawer of the instrument.

The UCC describes five **transfer warranties** [UCC 3–416]. These warranties provide that any person who transfers an instrument *for consideration* makes the following warranties to all subsequent transferees and holders who take the instrument in good faith (with some exceptions, as will be noted shortly):

① The transferor is entitled to enforce the instrument.

② All signatures are authentic and authorized.

③ The instrument has not been altered.

④ The instrument is not subject to a defense or claim of any party that can be asserted against the transferor.[8]

⑤ The transferor has no knowledge of any insolvency proceedings against the maker, the acceptor, or the drawer of the instrument.

The manner of transfer and the negotiation that is used determine how far and to whom a transfer warranty will run. Transfer of order paper, for consideration, by indorsement and delivery extends warranty liability to any subsequent holder who takes the instrument in good faith. The warranties of a person who transfers *without indorsement* (by the delivery of a bearer instrument), however, will extend the transferor's warranties soley to the immediate transferee [UCC 3–416(a)].

• **Example 20.12** Abraham forges Peter's name as a maker of a promissory note. The note is made payable to Abraham. Abraham indorses the note in blank, negotiates it to Carla, and then leaves the country. Carla, without indorsement, delivers the note to Frank for consideration. Frank in turn, without indorsement, delivers the note to Ricardo for consideration. On Ricardo's presentment of the note to Peter, the forgery is discovered. Ricardo can hold Frank (the immediate transferor) liable for breach of the transfer warranty that all signatures are genuine. Ricardo cannot hold Carla liable because the transfer warranties made by Carla, who negotiated the bearer instrument by delivery only, extend soley to Frank, the immediate transferee. •

Note that if Abraham had added a special indorsement ("Payable to Carla") instead of a blank indorsement, the instrument would have remained an order instrument. In that situation, to negotiate the instrument to Frank, Carla would have had to indorse the instrument, and her transfer warranties would extend to all subsequent holders, including Ricardo. This example shows the importance of the distinction between a transfer by indorsement and delivery (of an order instrument) and a transfer by delivery only, without indorsement (of a bearer instrument).

Presentment Warranties

PRESENTMENT WARRANTIES
Implied warranties, made by any person who presents an instrument for payment or acceptance, that (1) the person obtaining payment or acceptance is entitled to enforce the instrument or is authorized to obtain payment or acceptance on behalf of a person who is entitled to enforce the instrument, (2) the instrument has not been altered, and (3) the person obtaining payment or acceptance has no knowledge that the signature of the drawer of the instrument is unauthorized.

Any person who presents an instrument for payment or acceptance makes the following **presentment warranties** to any other person who in good faith pays or accepts the instrument [UCC 3–417(a), 3–417(d)]:

8. Under the unrevised Article 3, a qualified indorser who indorses an instrument "without recourse" limits this warranty to a warranty that he or she has "no knowledge" of such a defense (rather than that there is no defense). This limitation does not apply under the revised Article 3.

① The person obtaining payment or acceptance is entitled to enforce the instrument or is authorized to obtain payment or acceptance on behalf of a person who is entitled to enforce the instrument. (This is, in effect, a warranty that there are no missing or unauthorized indorsements.)

② The instrument has not been altered.

③ The person obtaining payment or acceptance has no knowledge that the signature of the issuer of the instrument is unauthorized.

These warranties are referred to as presentment warranties because they protect the person to whom the instrument is presented. The second and third warranties do not apply to makers, acceptors, and drawers. It is assumed, for example, that a drawer or a maker will recognize his or her own signature and that a maker or an acceptor will recognize whether an instrument has been materially altered.

An important issue in the following case was whether a bank breached its presentment warranty that there were no unauthorized signatures on an item sent to another bank for payment.

CASE 20.3 First National Bank of Chicago v. MidAmerica Federal Savings Bank

Appellate Court of Illinois,
First District, Sixth Division, 1999.
303 Ill.App.3d 176,
707 N.E.2d 673,
236 Ill.Dec. 546.
http://www.state.il.us/court/Opinions/Search.htm[a]

COMPANY PROFILE *In the mid-1990s, First National Bank of Chicago (First Chicago NBD Corporation) was one of the ten largest banks in the United States in terms of assets. In 1998, the merger of First Chicago and Banc One Corporation resulted in the formation of Bank One Corporation, which then ranked among the top five banks. Bank One operates more than two thousand banking centers and a national network of automated teller machines (ATMs). Bank One is the world's largest issuer of Visa credit cards, the third largest bank lender to small businesses, one of the leading managers of mutual funds, and a major lender to purchasers of automobiles and other motor vehicles.*

FACTS In 1995, First National Bank of Chicago notified Muhamad Mustafa that his certificate of deposit (CD) was coming to maturity. Instructions, apparently signed by Muhamad, were sent to First Chicago to close the CD account. The bank issued a cashier's check in the amount of $157,611.30, payable to Muhamad, and mailed it to his address. A few days later, Michael Mustafa, Muhamad's nephew, deposited the check into his account at MidAmerica Federal Savings Bank. The purported signature of Muhamad and the signature of Michael were both on the check. MidAmerica presented the check for payment, First Chicago paid it, and Michael withdrew the funds. Three weeks later, Michael phoned First Chicago and said that he had forged Muhamad's signature, taken the cash, and lost it gambling at a casino. Muhamad went to First Chicago, stated that he was out of the country when the check was issued, and obtained a replacement check for the full amount of the CD. First Chicago filed a suit in an Illinois state court against MidAmerica, alleging in part breach of warranty. The trial court granted summary judgment in favor of First Chicago. MidAmerica appealed to a state intermediate appellate court.

a. In the "Appellate Court" section, click on "1999." In the "First District" row, click on "February." When that page opens, scroll to the case name to access the opinion.

ISSUE Did MidAmerica breach the presentment warranty that there were no unauthorized indorsements on the check?

DECISION Yes. The state intermediate appellate court affirmed the judgment of the lower court and ordered MidAmerica to pay First Chicago the full amount of the check, plus interest and costs.

REASON The appellate court explained that under UCC 3–417(a), "a bank that accepts and pays a check with an unauthorized or forged indorsement warrants to subsequent transferees the validity of that indorsement and

CASE 20.3—Continued

may be held liable on that warranty. The purpose of the warranty is to place on the bank taking an instrument from a person making an unauthorized indorsement the responsibility of collecting from that person. * * * The rule recognizes that, while none of the parties may have had reason to suspect a fraud, the one who took from the forger was the closest to the person causing the loss and is presumed to have had the best opportunity to have prevented the loss." MidAmerica was liable because it breached the presentment warranty that there were no unauthorized signatures on the check.[b]

FOR CRITICAL ANALYSIS—Economic Consideration *What is the effect on the bank collection process of requiring the first bank taking an item to make sure that the indorsements are valid?*

b. MidAmerica filed a suit against Michael Mustafa and obtained a judgment against him in the amount of $157,611.30, plus $200,000 in punitive damages and $12,000 in attorneys' fees. Michael also pleaded guilty to a federal crime arising out of this incident.

Defenses to Liability

Persons who would otherwise be liable on negotiable instruments may be able to avoid liability by raising certain defenses. There are two general categories of defenses—*universal defenses* and *personal defenses.*

Universal Defenses

UNIVERSAL DEFENSES
Defenses that are valid against all holders of a negotiable instrument, including holders in due course (HDCs) and holders with the rights of HDCs.

Universal defenses (also called *real defenses*) are valid against *all* holders, including HDCs and holders who take through an HDC. Universal defenses include those described here.

Forgery Forgery of a maker's or drawer's signature cannot bind the person whose name is used unless that person ratifies (approves or validates) the signature or is precluded from denying it (because the forgery was made possible by the maker's or drawer's negligence, for example) [UCC 3–403(a)]. Thus, when a person forges an instrument, the person whose name is forged normally has no liability to pay any holder or any HDC the value of the forged instrument.

Fraud in the Execution If a person is deceived into signing a negotiable instrument, believing that she or he is signing something other than a negotiable instrument (such as a receipt), *fraud in the execution,* or fraud in the inception, is committed against the signer [UCC 3–305(a)(1)]. • **EXAMPLE 20.13** A salesperson asks a customer to sign a paper, which the salesperson says is a receipt for the delivery of goods that the customer is picking up from the store. In fact, the paper is a promissory note, but the customer, who is unfamiliar with the English language, does not realize this. In this situation, even if the note is negotiated to an HDC, the customer has a valid defense against payment.•

The defense of fraud in the execution cannot be raised, however, if a reasonable inquiry would have revealed the nature and terms of the instrument.[9] Thus, the signer's age, experience, and intelligence are relevant because they frequently determine whether the signer should have known the nature of the transaction before signing.

Material Alteration An alteration is material if it changes the contract terms between any two parties in any way. Examples of material alterations include completing an

9. *Burchett v. Allied Concord Financial Corp.,* 74 N.M. 575, 396 P.2d 186 (1964).

incomplete instrument, adding words or numbers to an instrument, or making any other change to an instrument in an unauthorized manner that affects the obligation of a party to the instrument [UCC 3–407(a)].

Thus, cutting off part of the paper of a negotiable instrument; adding clauses; or making any change in the amount, the date, or the rate of interest—even if the change is only one penny, one day, or 1 percent—is material. It is not a material alteration, however, to correct the maker's address, for example, or to change the figures on a check so that they agree with the written amount (recall from Chapter 19 that words outweigh figures if there is a conflict between the written amount and the amount given in figures). If the alteration is not material, any holder is entitled to enforce the instrument according to its terms.

Material alteration is a *complete defense* against an ordinary holder. An ordinary holder can recover nothing on an instrument if it has been materially altered [UCC 3–407(b)]. Material alteration, however, may be only a *partial defense* against an HDC. When the holder is an HDC, if an original term, such as the monetary amount payable, has been *altered,* the HDC can enforce the instrument against the maker or drawer according to the original terms but not for the altered amount. If the instrument was originally incomplete and was later completed in an unauthorized manner, however, alteration no longer can be claimed as a defense against an HDC, and the HDC can enforce the instrument as completed [UCC 3–407(b)]. This is because the drawer or maker of the instrument, by issuing an incomplete instrument, will normally be held responsible for the alteration, which could have been avoided by the exercise of greater care. If the alteration is readily apparent, then obviously the holder has notice of some defect or defense and therefore cannot be an HDC [UCC 3–302(a)(1)].

Discharge in Bankruptcy Discharge in bankruptcy is an absolute defense on any instrument, regardless of the status of the holder, because the purpose of bankruptcy is to settle finally all of the insolvent party's debts [UCC 3–305(a)(1)].

BE AWARE Minority, illegality, mental incapacity, and duress can be universal defenses or personal defenses, depending in some cases on state law other than the UCC.

Minority Minority, or infancy, is a universal defense only to the extent that state law recognizes it as a defense to a simple contract (see Chapter 10). Because state laws on minority vary, so do determinations of whether minority is a universal defense against an HDC [UCC 3–305(a)(1)(i)].

Illegality Certain types of illegality constitute universal defenses. Other types constitute personal defenses—that is, defenses that are effective against ordinary holders but not against HDCs. The difference lies in the state statutes or ordinances that make the transactions illegal. If a statute provides that an illegal transaction is void, then the defense is universal—that is, absolute against both an ordinary holder and an HDC. If the law merely makes the instrument voidable, then the illegality is still a defense against an ordinary holder but not against an HDC [UCC 3–305(a)(1)(ii)].

Mental Incapacity If a person is adjudged mentally incompetent by state proceedings, then any instrument issued thereafter by that person is void. The instrument is void *ab initio* (from the beginning) and unenforceable by any holder or HDC [UCC 3–305(a)(1)(ii)]. Mental incapacity in these circumstances is thus a universal defense. If a person has not been adjudged mentally incompetent by state proceedings, mental incapacity operates as a defense against an ordinary holder but not against an HDC.

Extreme Duress When a person signs and issues a negotiable instrument under such extreme duress as an immediate threat of force or violence (for example, at gunpoint), the instrument is void and unenforceable by any holder or HDC [UCC 3–305(a)(1)(ii)]. (Ordinary duress is a defense against ordinary holders but not against HDCs.)

PERSONAL DEFENSES

PERSONAL DEFENSES
Defenses that can be used to avoid payment to an ordinary holder of a negotiable instrument but not a holder in due course (HDC) or a holder with the rights of an HDC.

Personal defenses (sometimes called *limited defenses*), such as those described here, can be used to avoid payment to an ordinary holder of a negotiable instrument, but not an HDC or a holder with the rights of an HDC.

Breach of Contract or Breach of Warranty When there is a breach of the underlying contract for which the negotiable instrument was issued, the maker of a note can refuse to pay it, or the drawer of a check can order his or her bank to stop payment on the check. Breach of warranty can also be claimed as a defense to liability on the instrument.

• **EXAMPLE 20.14** Rhodes agrees to purchase several sets of imported china from Livingston. The china is to be delivered in four weeks. Rhodes gives Livingston a promissory note for $2,000, which is the price of the china. The china arrives, but many of the pieces are broken, and several others are chipped or cracked. Rhodes refuses to pay the note on the basis of breach of contract and breach of warranty. (Under sales law, a seller impliedly promises that the goods are at least merchantable—see Chapter 18.) Livingston cannot enforce payment on the note because of the breach of contract and breach of warranty. If Livingston has negotiated the note to a third party, however, and the third party is an HDC, Rhodes will not be able to use breach of contract or warranty as a defense against liability on the note.•

Lack or Failure of Consideration The absence of consideration (value) may be a successful personal defense in some instances [UCC 3–303(b), 3–305(a)(2)]. • **EXAMPLE 20.15** Tara gives Clem, as a gift, a note that states, "I promise to pay you $100,000." Clem accepts the note. Because there is no consideration for Tara's promise, a court will not enforce the promise.•

Fraud in the Inducement (Ordinary Fraud) A person who issues a negotiable instrument based on false statements by the other party will be able to avoid payment on that instrument, unless the holder is an HDC. • **EXAMPLE 20.16** Jerry agrees to purchase Howard's used tractor for $24,500. Howard, knowing his statements to be false, tells Jerry that the tractor is in good working order, that it has been used for only one harvest, and that he owns the tractor free and clear of all claims. Jerry pays Howard $4,500 in cash and issues a negotiable promissory note for the balance. As it turns out, Howard still owes the original seller $10,000 on the purchase of the tractor. In addition, the tractor is three years old and has been used in three harvests. Jerry can refuse to pay the note if it is held by an ordinary holder. If Howard has negotiated the note to an HDC, however, Jerry must pay the HDC. (Of course, Jerry can then sue Howard to recover the money.)• This chapter's *Business Law in the Online World* feature on page 532 looks at a case involving promissory notes and charges of fraud.

Illegality As mentioned, if a statute provides that an illegal transaction is void, a universal defense exists. If, however, the statute provides that an illegal transaction is voidable, the defense is personal.

Mental Incapacity As mentioned, if a maker or drawer has been declared by a court to be mentally incompetent, any instrument issued by the maker or drawer is void.

BUSINESS LAW: //in the Online World

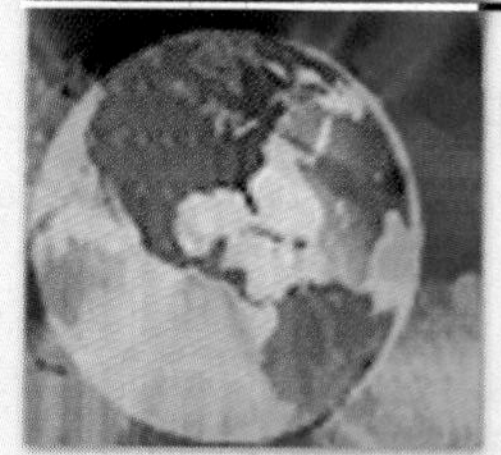

From Start-Up to Finish

When a new business—based on a new idea in a new industry—starts up, the potential for profit may appear unlimited. When the founders of the business include students of computer science and physics, as well as a former vice president of a well-known investment management firm, this expectation may even seem reasonable.

Dreams of wealth can be undercut by reality, however. Day-to-day business operations can be expensive. For this reason, whoever oversees the financial development of a business is as important to the firm as the scientist behind the firm's product or service.

If capital is not forthcoming at the rate that the firm needs it, the founders may resort to desperate measures to keep the business from failing. In the end, the firm may be sold, and relations among the founders may become less than cordial, with each blaming the other. This set of circumstances is not new, but it has been much in the public eye in the twenty-first century, with the collapse of many businesses in the online world.

The Promissory Notes

The founders of the Worldwide Broadcasting Network (WBN) intended to make television programming available over the Internet through customized video channels. Dariush Gholizadeh and Ali Kazeroonian had the technological expertise. Ali Malihi had the financial background, having worked for fourteen years for Paine Webber, where he managed over $100 million in assets.

In January 1996, Malihi agreed to obtain $5 million in financing for WBN by June. In March, however, Malihi lowered the amount to $2 million and extended the date to October. Meanwhile, he used his own money to fund WBN, including $40,910 for which he asked Gholizadeh to sign promissory notes. At Gholizadeh's insistence, each note provided that repayment depended on his WBN salary, which in turn depended on Malihi's obtaining financing.

By March 1997, Malihi had not met the $2 million goal, and WBN faced a financial crisis. Gholizadeh found an investor willing to help in exchange for WBN stock. When WBN fired Malihi as an employee and discharged him as a director, he filed a suit in a Massachusetts state court against Gholizadeh, seeking payment on the notes.

Fraud in the Inducement?

Gholizadeh argued that he should not be held liable on the notes because "Malihi fraudulently misrepresented that his departure from Paine Webber was voluntary." According to Gholizadeh, Malihi's "statement that he left Paine Webber because WBN offered a great start-up opportunity constituted a half truth because he failed to disclose Paine Webber had terminated him."

The court acknowledged that Malihi "may have been less than totally forthcoming about the details of his departure from Paine Webber," but added that he was never asked whether he left voluntarily. Besides, to avoid liability on a negotiable instrument, the alleged fraud must be material to the issuing of the instrument. As the court explained, Gholizadeh and Kazeroonian "brought plaintiff into WBN because of his obvious financial and marketing expertise. There is no credible evidence that plaintiff's involuntary departure from Paine Webber related in any way to his undisputed fund-raising abilities." The court held that Gholizadeh was obligated to repay the notes.[a]

FOR CRITICAL ANALYSIS

In cases involving negotiable instruments issued to support emerging and start-up ventures, should the courts take into special consideration the firms' need for money?

a. *Malihi v. Gholizadeh,* 11 Mass.L.Rptr. 659 (Mass.Super. 2000).

Hence, mental incapacity can serve as a universal defense [UCC 3–305(a)(1)(ii)]. If a maker or drawer issues a negotiable instrument while mentally incompetent but before a formal court hearing has declared him or her to be so, however, the instrument is voidable. In this situation, mental incapacity can serve only as a personal defense.

Other Personal Defenses Other personal defenses can be used to avoid payment to an ordinary holder of a negotiable instrument, including the following:

① Discharge by payment or cancellation [UCC 3–601(b), 3–602(a), 3–603, 3–604].

② Unauthorized completion of an incomplete instrument [UCC 3–115, 3–302, 3–407, 4–401(d)(2)].

③ Nondelivery of the instrument [UCC 1–201(14), 3–105(b), 3–305(a)(2)].

⑤ Ordinary duress or undue influence rendering the contract voidable [UCC 3–305(a)(1)(ii)].

Federal Limitations on the Rights of HDCs

The HDC doctrine can sometimes have harsh effects on consumers. • **EXAMPLE 20.17** A consumer purchases a used car under express warranty from an automobile dealer. The consumer pays $1,000 down and signs a promissory note to the dealer for the remaining $5,000 due on the car. The dealer sells the bank this promissory note, which is a negotiable instrument, and the bank then becomes the creditor, to whom the consumer makes payments. The car does not perform as warranted. The consumer returns the car and asks the dealer to return the down payment and cancel the contract. Even if the dealer refunds the $1,000, however, under the traditional HDC rule, the consumer would normally still owe the remaining $5,000 because the consumer's claim of breach of warranty is a personal defense, and the bank is an HDC. Thus, the traditional HDC rule leaves consumers who have purchased defective products liable to HDCs.•

To protect consumers, the Federal Trade Commission issued a rule in 1976 that effectively abolished the HDC doctrine in consumer transactions. This rule, because of its significance in curbing the rights of HDCs, is presented as this chapter's *Landmark in the Law* on the following page.

Discharge from Liability

Discharge from liability on an instrument can occur in several ways. The liability of all parties to an instrument is discharged when the party primarily liable on it pays to the holder the amount due in full [UCC 3–602, 3–603]. Payment by any other party discharges only the liability of that party and subsequent parties.

Intentional cancellation of an instrument discharges the liability of all parties [UCC 3–604]. Intentionally writing "Paid" across the face of an instrument cancels it. Intentionally tearing up an instrument cancels it. If a holder intentionally crosses out a party's signature, that party's liability and the liability of subsequent indorsers who have already indorsed the instrument are discharged. Materially altering an instrument may discharge the liability of any party affected by the alteration, as previously discussed [UCC 3–407(b)]. (An HDC may be able to enforce a materially altered instrument against its maker or drawer according to the instrument's original terms, however.)

Discharge of liability can also occur when a party's right of recourse is impaired [UCC 3–605]. A *right of recourse* is a right to seek reimbursement. Ordinarily, when a holder collects the amount of an instrument from an indorser, the indorser has a right of recourse against prior indorsers, the maker or drawer, and accommodation parties. If the holder has adversely affected the indorser's right to seek reimbursement from these other parties, however, the indorser is not liable on the instrument. This occurs when, for example, the holder releases or agrees not to sue a party against whom the indorser has a right of recourse.

LANDMARK IN THE LAW
FTC Rule 433

In 1976, the Federal Trade Commission (FTC) issued Rule 433,[a] which severely limited the rights of HDCs that purchase instruments arising out of *consumer credit* transactions. The rule, entitled "Preservation of Consumers' Claims and Defenses," applies to any seller or lessor of goods or services who takes or receives a consumer credit contract. The rule also applies to a seller or lessor who accepts as full or partial payment for a sale or lease the proceeds of any purchase-money loan[b] made in connection with any consumer credit contract. Under the rule, these parties must include the following provision in the consumer credit contract:

> NOTICE
>
> ANY HOLDER OF THIS CONSUMER CREDIT CONTRACT IS SUBJECT TO ALL CLAIMS AND DEFENSES WHICH THE DEBTOR COULD ASSERT AGAINST THE SELLER OF GOODS OR SERVICES OBTAINED PURSUANT HERETO OR WITH THE PROCEEDS HEREOF. RECOVERY HEREUNDER BY THE DEBTOR SHALL NOT EXCEED AMOUNTS PAID BY THE DEBTOR HEREUNDER.

Thus, a consumer who is party to a consumer credit transaction can now bring any defense she or he has against the seller of a product against a subsequent holder as well. In essence, the FTC rule places an HDC of the negotiable instrument in the position of a contract assignee. The rule makes the buyer's duty to pay conditional on the seller's full performance of the contract. Finally, the rule clearly reduces the degree of transferability of negotiable instruments resulting from consumer credit contracts.

What if the seller does not include the notice in a promissory note and then sells the note to a third party, such as a bank? While the seller has violated the rule, the bank has not. Because the FTC rule does not prohibit third parties from purchasing notes or credit contracts that do *not* contain the required provision, the third party does not become subject to the buyer's defenses against the seller. Thus, a few consumers remain unprotected by the FTC rule.

APPLICATION TO TODAY'S WORLD

In the 1990s and 2000s, the FTC rule has been invoked in many cases involving automobiles that turned out to be "lemons," even when the FTC notice is not stated in the consumer credit contract. In these and other actions to collect on notes issued to finance purchases, when the notice has not been included in the accompanying documents, the courts have generally implied its existence as a contract term.

a. 16 C.F.R. Section 433.2. The rule was enacted pursuant to the FTC's authority under the Federal Trade Commission Act, 15 U.S.C. Sections 41–58.

b. A *purchase-money loan* is one in which a seller or lessor advances money to a buyer or lessee, through a credit contract, to purchase or lease goods. See Chapter 22.

APPLICATION Law and the Businessperson . . .

Purchasing Negotiable Instruments*

Negotiable instruments are transferred every business day of the year. Most purchasers of negotiable instruments do not encounter any problems in further negotiating and transferring the instruments or in collecting payment on them if they are time instruments. Potential problems exist, however, and purchasers should take precautions against them.

Overdue Instruments

Suppose that you wish to purchase a demand instrument as a holder in due course (HDC). By definition, such an instrument has no stated time for payment and therefore may be overdue—that is, payment may have been demanded by the payee but not made, or a reasonable amount of time may have passed. (With checks, a reasonable amount of time is presumed to be ninety days from the date on the check.) If you have any doubt about whether a demand instrument is overdue, you should investigate.

*This *Application* is not meant to substitute for the services of an attorney who is licensed to practice law in your state.

Notice of Defects

With any negotiable instrument, as a prospective holder, you cannot afford to ignore a defect in the instrument. A four-month-old date on a check, for example, constitutes notice that the instrument is overdue. Generally, whenever a defect in an instrument exists, you will not qualify as an HDC, and you may be unable to obtain payment. In other words, it is prudent to determine whether the instrument is complete and, in some cases, whether the transfer is such as to qualify you for HDC status.

Checklist for the Purchaser of Negotiable Instruments

1. Make sure that a demand instrument is not overdue before purchasing it.
2. Make sure that the negotiable instrument has no obvious defects—look for signs indicating whether the maker or drawer of the instrument might have a valid reason for refusing to pay.

Key Terms

accommodation party 522
agent 523
fictitious payee 525
holder in due course (HDC) 515
imposter 525
personal defense 531
presentment warranty 527
principal 523
shelter principle 520
transfer warranty 527
universal defense 529

Chapter Summary Rights and Liabilities of Parties

Holder versus Holder in Due Course (HDC) (See page 515.)	1. *Holder*—A person in the possession of an instrument drawn, issued, or indorsed to him or her, to his or her order, to bearer, or in blank. A holder obtains only those rights that the transferor had in the instrument.

(continued)

Chapter Summary Rights and Liabilities of Parties—continued

Holder versus Holder in Due Course (HDC)—continued	2. *Holder in due course (HDC)*—A holder who, by meeting certain acquisition requirements (summarized next), takes the instrument free of most defenses and claims to which the transferor was subject.
Requirements for HDC Status (See pages 515–519.)	To be an HDC, a holder must take the instrument: 1. *For value*—A holder can take an instrument for value in one of five ways [UCC 3–303]: a. By the complete or partial performance of the promise for which the instrument was issued or transferred. b. By acquiring a security interest or other lien in the instrument, excluding a lien obtained by a judicial proceeding. c. By taking an instrument in payment of (or as security for) an antecedent debt. d. By giving a negotiable instrument as payment. e. By giving an irrevocable commitment as payment. 2. *In good faith*—Good faith is defined as "honesty in fact and the observance of reasonable commercial standards of fair dealing" [UCC 3–103(a)(4)]. 3. *Without notice*—To be an HDC, a holder must not be on notice that the instrument is defective in any of the following ways [UCC 3–302, 3–304]: a. It is overdue. b. It has been dishonored. c. There is an uncured (uncorrected) default with respect to another instrument issued as part of the same series. d. The instrument contains an unauthorized signature or has been altered. e. There is a defense against the instrument or a claim to the instrument. f. The instrument is so irregular or incomplete as to call into question its authenticity.
Holder through an HDC (See pages 519–520.)	A holder who cannot qualify as an HDC has the *rights* of an HDC if he or she derives title through an HDC unless the holder engaged in fraud or illegality affecting the instrument [UCC 3–203(b)].
Signature Liability (See pages 520–526.)	Every party (except a qualified indorser) who signs a negotiable instrument is either primarily or secondarily liable for payment of the instrument when it comes due. 1. *Primary liability*—Makers and acceptors are primarily liable (an acceptor is a drawee that promises in writing to pay an instrument when it is presented for payment at a later time) [UCC 3–115, 3–407, 3–409, 3–412]. 2. *Secondary liability*—Drawers and indorsers are secondarily liable [UCC 3–412, 3–414, 3–415, 3–501, 3–502, 3–503]. Parties who are secondarily liable on an instrument promise to pay on that instrument if the following events occur: a. The instrument is properly and timely presented. b. The instrument is dishonored. c. Timely notice of dishonor is given to the secondarily liable party. 3. *Accommodation parties*—An accommodation party is one who signs his or her name as credit to another party on an instrument [UCC 3–419]. Accommodation *makers* are primarily liable; accommodation *indorsers* are secondarily liable. 4. *Agents' signatures*—An *agent* is a person who agrees to represent or act for another, called the *principal.* Agents can sign negotiable instruments and thereby bind their principals.

Chapter Summary Rights and Liabilities of Parties—continued

Signature Liability—continued	Liability on an instrument signed by an agent depends on whether the agent is authorized and on whether the agent's representative capacity and the principal's identity are both indicated on the instrument [UCC 3–401, 3–402, 3–403]. Agents need not indicate their representative capacity on *checks*—provided the checks clearly identify the principal and are drawn on the principal's account. 5. *Unauthorized signatures*—An unauthorized signature is wholly inoperative *unless:* a. The person whose name is signed ratifies (affirms) it or is precluded from denying it [UCC 3–115, 3–401, 3–403, 3–406]. b. The instrument has been negotiated to an HDC [UCC 3–403]. 6. *Special rules for unauthorized indorsements*—An unauthorized indorsement will not bind the maker or drawer except in the following circumstances: a. When an imposter induces the maker or drawer of an instrument to issue it to the imposter (imposter rule) [UCC 3–404(a)]. b. When a person signs as or on behalf of a maker or drawer, intending that the payee will have no interest in the instrument, or when an agent or employee of the maker or drawer has supplied him or her with the name of the payee, also intending the payee to have no such interest (fictitious payee rule) [UCC 3–404(b), 3–405].
Warranty Liability (See pages 526–529.)	1. *Transfer warranties*—Any person who transfers an instrument for consideration makes the following warranties to all subsequent transferees and holders who take the instrument in good faith (but when a bearer instrument is transferred by delivery only, the transferor's warranties extend only to the immediate transferee) [UCC 3–416]: a. The transferor is entitled to enforce the instrument. b. All signatures are authentic and authorized. c. The instrument has not been altered. d. The instrument is not subject to a defense or claim of any party that can be asserted against the transferor. e. The transferor has no knowledge of any insolvency proceedings against the maker, the acceptor, or the drawer of the instrument. 2. *Presentment warranties*—Any person who presents an instrument for payment or acceptance makes the following warranties to any other person who in good faith pays or accepts the instrument [UCC 3–417(a), 3–417(d)]: a. The person obtaining payment or acceptance is entitled to enforce the instrument or is authorized to obtain payment or acceptance on behalf of a person who is entitled to enforce the instrument. (This is, in effect, a warranty that there are no missing or unauthorized indorsements.) b. The instrument has not been altered. c. The person obtaining payment or acceptance has no knowledge that the signature of the drawer of the instrument is unauthorized.
Defenses to Liability (See pages 529–533.)	1. *Universal (real) defenses*—The following defenses are valid against all holders, including HDCs and holders with the rights of HDCs [UCC 3–305, 3–401, 3–403, 3–407]: a. Forgery. b. Fraud in the execution. c. Material alteration. d. Discharge in bankruptcy.

(continued)

Chapter Summary Rights and Liabilities of Parties—continued

Defenses to Liability—continued	e. Minority—if the contract is voidable under state law. f. Illegality, mental incapacity, or extreme duress—if the contract is void under state law. 2. *Personal (limited) defenses*—The following defenses are valid against ordinary holders but not against HDCs or holders with the rights of HDCs [UCC 3–105, 3–115, 3–302, 3–305, 3–306, 3–407, 3–601, 3–602, 3–603, 3–604, 4–401]: a. Breach of contract or breach of warranty. b. Lack or failure of consideration (value). c. Fraud in the inducement. d. Illegality and mental incapacity—if the contract is voidable. e. Previous payment of the instrument. f. Unauthorized completion of the instrument. g. Nondelivery of the instrument. h. Ordinary duress or undue influence that renders the contract voidable.
Federal Limitations on the Rights of HDCs (See page 533.)	Rule 433 of the Federal Trade Commission, issued in 1976, limits the rights of HDCs who purchase instruments arising out of consumer credit transactions. Under the rule, a consumer who is a party to a consumer credit transaction is permitted to bring any defense he or she has against the seller against a subsequent holder as well, even if the subsequent holder is an HDC.
Discharge from Liability (See pages 533–534.)	All parties to a negotiable instrument will be discharged when the party primarily liable on it pays to a holder the amount due in full. Discharge can also occur in other circumstances (if the instrument has been canceled, materially altered, and so on) [UCC 3–601 through 3–606].

For Review

① What are the requirements for attaining HDC status?
② How can a person who does not qualify as an HDC acquire the rights and privileges of an HDC?
③ What is the key to liability on a negotiable instrument? What is the difference between signature liability and warranty liability?
④ Certain defenses are valid against all holders, including HDCs. What are these defenses called? Name four defenses that fall within this category.
⑤ Certain defenses can be used to avoid payment to an ordinary holder of a negotiable instrument but are not effective against an HDC. What are these defenses called? Name four defenses that fall within this category.

Questions and Case Problems

20–1. Unauthorized Indorsements. What are the exceptions to the rule that a bank will be liable for paying a check over an unauthorized indorsement?

20–2. Agents' Signatures. Karen Thorpe is a purchasing agent for GymNast, Inc., a manufacturer of sports equipment. Karen has authority to sign checks in payment for purchases made by GymNast. Karen makes out three checks to suppliers and signs each one differently, as follows:

(a) GymNast, Inc., by Karen Thorpe, purchasing agent.
(b) Karen Thorpe, purchasing agent.
(c) Karen Thorpe.

Discuss briefly whether Karen is personally liable on each signature and whether parol evidence is admissible to hold GymNast, Inc., liable.

20–3. Defenses. Jules sold Alfred a small motorboat for $1,500; Jules maintained to Alfred that the boat was in excellent condition.

Alfred gave Jules a check for $1,500, which Jules indorsed and gave to Sherry for value. When Alfred took the boat for a trial run, he discovered that the boat leaked, needed to be painted, and required a new motor. Alfred stopped payment on his check, which had not yet been cashed. Jules has disappeared. Can Sherry recover from Alfred as a holder in due course? Discuss.

20–4. Defenses. Fox purchased a used car from Emerson for $1,000. Fox paid for the car with a check, written in pencil, payable to Emerson for $1,000. Emerson, through careful erasures and alterations, changed the amount on the check to read $10,000 and negotiated the check to Sanderson. Sanderson took the check for value, in good faith, and without notice of the alteration and thus met the UCC requirements for HDC status. Can Fox successfully raise the universal defense of material alteration to avoid payment on the check? Explain.

20–5. Signature Liability. Marion makes a promissory note payable to the order of Perry. Perry indorses the note by writing "without recourse, Perry" and transfers the note for value to Steven. Steven, in need of cash, negotiates the note to Harriet by indorsing it with the words "Pay to Harriet, [signed] Steven." On the due date, Harriet presents the note to Marion for payment, only to learn that Marion has filed for bankruptcy and will have all debts (including the note) discharged in bankruptcy. Discuss fully whether Harriet can hold Marion, Perry, or Steven liable on the note.

20–6. Unauthorized Indorsements. Nancy Gabbard was the office manager at Golden Years Nursing Home (No. 2), Inc. She was given a signature stamp to issue checks to the nursing home's employees for up to $100 as advances on their pay. The checks were drawn on Golden Years's account at the First National Bank. Over a seven-year period, Gabbard wrote a number of checks to employees exclusively for the purpose of embezzling the money. She forged the employees' indorsements on the checks, signed her name as a second indorser, and deposited the checks in her personal account at Star Bank. First National paid Star Bank for the deposited checks. The employees whose names were on the checks never actually requested them. When the scheme was uncovered, Golden Years filed a suit in an Ohio state court against Gabbard, Star Bank, and others to recover the money. Which party, Golden Years or Star Bank, will bear the loss in this situation? Why? [*Golden Years Nursing Home (No. 2), Inc. v. Gabbard*, 640 N.E.2d 1186 (Ohio App. 1994)]

20–7. Discharge. Mary Ann McClusky and her husband, Curtis, borrowed $75,000 and signed a note payable to Francis and Thomas Gardner. As collateral, Mary Ann gave the Gardners a mortgage on a farm owned in her name only. After the McCluskys divorced, Mary Ann found, in a file in the basement of her house, the note with the word "Paid" written across it. When the Gardners refused to cancel the mortgage, she filed a suit in an Indiana state court against them. During the trial, she testified that she did not know how the note came to be in her basement or who wrote "Paid" across it. The Gardners testified that they had not surrendered it. Should the court presume that the note had been discharged, given that it was in Mary Ann's possession and had the word "Paid" written across it? Discuss. [*Gardner v. McClusky*, 647 N.E.2d 1 (Ind.App. 1995)]

20–8. Good Faith. Stacey Dillabough presented two money orders to Chuckie Enterprise, Inc., a check-cashing operation, for payment. Dillabough was known as a previous customer, the orders were presented within thirty days of the date on them, and there was nothing to indicate they were not valid. Chuckie obtained photo identification from Dillabough, cashed the orders, and submitted them to the issuer, American Express, for payment. American Express recognized the orders as stolen and refused to pay. Chuckie assigned its right to payment to Robert Triffin, who filed a suit against American Express to collect. One of the issues was whether Chuckie was a holder in due course (HDC). One of the requirements of HDC status is good faith. Did Chuckie take the money orders in good faith? Explain. [*Triffin v. Dillabough*, 552 Pa. 550, 716 A.2d 605 (1998)]

20–9. Unauthorized Indorsements. Telemedia Publications, Inc., publishes *Cablecast Magazine*, a weekly guide for the listings of the cable television programming in Baton Rouge, Louisiana. Cablecast hired Jennifer Pennington as a temporary employee. Pennington's duties included indorsing subscription checks received in the mail with the Cablecast deposit stamp, preparing the deposit slip, and taking the checks to be deposited to City National Bank. John McGregor, the manager of Cablecast, soon noticed shortages in revenue coming into Cablecast. When he learned that Pennington had taken checks payable to Cablecast and deposited them in her personal account at Premier Bank, N.A., he confronted her. She admitted to taking $7,913.04 in Cablecast checks. Cablecast filed a suit in a Louisiana state court against Premier Bank. The bank responded in part that Cablecast was solely responsible for losses caused by the fraudulent indorsements of its employees. At trial, Cablecast failed to prove that Premier Bank had not acted in good faith or that it had not exercised ordinary care in its handling of the checks. What rule should the court apply here? Why? [*Cablecast Magazine v. Premier Bank, N.A.*, 729 So.2d 1165 (La.App. 1 Cir. 1999)]

TEST YOUR KNOWLEDGE—ANSWER ON THE WEB

20–10. Robert Helmer and Percy Helmer, Jr., were authorized signatories on the corporate checking account of Event Marketing, Inc. The Helmers signed a check drawn on Event Marketing's account and issued to Rumarson Technologies, Inc. (RTI), in the amount of $24,965. The check was signed on July 13, 1998, but dated August 14. When RTI presented the check for payment, it was dishonored due to insufficient funds. RTI filed a suit in a Georgia state court against the Helmers to collect the amount of the check. Claiming that the Helmers were personally liable on Event Marketing's check, RTI filed a motion for summary judgment. Can an authorized signatory on a corporate account be held personally liable for corporate checks returned for insufficient funds? Are the Helmers liable in this case? Discuss. [*Helmer v. Rumarson Technologies, Inc.*, 538 S.E.2d 504 (Ga.App. 2000)]

A QUESTION OF ETHICS AND SOCIAL RESPONSIBILITY

20–11. One day, while Ort, a farmer, was working alone in his field, a stranger approached him. The stranger said he was the state agent for a manufacturer of iron posts and wire fence. Eventually, the stranger persuaded Ort to accept a townshipwide agency for the same manufacturer. The stranger then asked Ort to sign a document that purportedly was an agency agreement. Because Ort did not have his glasses with him and could read only with great difficulty, he asked the stranger to read what the document said. The stranger then pretended to read the document to Ort, not mentioning that it was a promissory note. Both men signed the note, and Ort assumed that he was signing a document of agency. The stranger later negotiated the note to a good faith purchaser for value. When that person sued Ort, Ort attempted to defend on the basis of fraud in the execution. In view of these facts, consider the following questions. [*Ort v. Fowler*, 31 Kan. 478, 2 P. 580 (1884)]

1. Although this classic case was decided long before the UCC was drafted, the court applied essentially the same rule that would apply under Article 3. What is this rule, and how would it be applied to Ort's attempted defense on the ground of fraud in the execution?
2. This case provides a clear example of a situation in which one of two innocent parties (Ort and the purchaser of the note) must bear the loss caused by a third party (the stranger, who was the perpetrator of the fraud). Under Article 3, which party should bear the loss, and why?

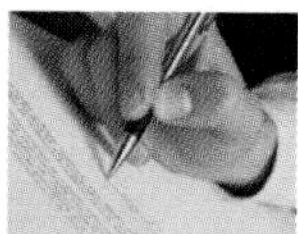

FOR CRITICAL ANALYSIS

20–12. How does the concept of holder in due course further Article 3's general goal of encouraging the negotiability of instruments? How does it further Article 3's goal of balancing the rights of parties to negotiable instruments?

Internet Exercises

Go to the *Business Law Today* home page at **http://blt.westbuslaw.com**. Select "Interactive Study Center" and then click on "Chapter 20." There you will find the following Internet research exercise that you can perform to learn more about fictitious payees:

Activity 20–1: Fictitious Payees

Before the Test

Go to the *Business Law Today* home page at **http://blt.westbuslaw.com**. Click on "Interactive Quizzes." You will find at least twenty interactive questions relating to this chapter.

CHAPTER 21

Checks, the Banking System, and E-Money

"Money is just what we use to keep tally."

Henry Ford, 1863–1947
(American automobile manufacturer)

CHAPTER CONTENTS

LEARNING OBJECTIVES

After reading this chapter, you should be able to answer the following questions:

① Checks are usually three-party instruments. On what type of check, however, does a bank serve as both the drawer and the drawee? What type of check does a bank agree in advance to accept when the check is presented for payment?

② When may a bank properly dishonor a customer's check without liability to the customer?

③ In what circumstances might a bank not be liable for payment of a check containing an unauthorized signature of the drawer?

④ Under the Electronic Fund Transfer Act, under what conditions will a bank be liable for an unauthorized fund transfer? When will the consumer be liable?

⑤ What is e-money? How is e-money stored and used? What are some emerging developments in the area of online banking services?

Checks are the most common type of negotiable instruments regulated by the Uniform Commercial Code (UCC). It is estimated that over sixty-five billion personal and commercial checks are written each year in the United States. Checks are more than a daily convenience; they are an integral part of the American economic system. They serve as substitutes for money and thus, as Henry Ford said in the chapter-opening quotation, help us to "keep tally."

Issues relating to checks are governed by Article 3 and Article 4 of the UCC. Recall from Chapters 19 and 20 that Article 3 establishes the requirements that all negotiable instruments, including checks, must meet. Article 3 also sets forth the rights and liabilities of parties to negotiable instruments. Article 4 of the UCC governs the relationships of banks with one another as they process checks for payment, and it establishes a framework for deposit and checking agreements between a bank and its customers. A check therefore may fall within the scope of Article 3 and yet be subject to the provisions of Article 4 while in the course of collection. If a conflict between Article 3 and Article 4 arises, Article 4 controls [UCC 4–102(a)].

In this chapter, we first identify the legal characteristics of checks and the legal duties and liabilities that arise when a check is issued. Then we examine the collection process—that is, the actual procedure by which the checks deposited into bank accounts move through banking channels, causing the underlying funds to be shifted from one bank account to another. Increasingly, credit cards, debit cards, and other devices and methods to transfer funds electronically are being used to pay for goods and services. In the latter part of this chapter, we look at the law governing electronic fund transfers.

Checks

CHECK
A draft drawn by a drawer ordering the drawee bank or financial institution to pay a fixed amount of money to the holder on demand.

A **check** is a special type of draft that is drawn on a bank, ordering the bank to pay a fixed amount of money on demand [UCC 3–104(f)]. Article 4 defines a bank as "a person engaged in the business of banking, including a savings bank, savings and loan association, credit union or trust company" [UCC 4–105(1)]. If any other institution (such as a brokerage firm) handles a check for payment or for collection, the check is not covered by Article 4.

Recall from the discussion of negotiable instruments in Chapters 19 and 20 that a person who writes a check is called the *drawer*. The drawer is a depositor in the bank on which the check is drawn. The person to whom the check is payable is the *payee*. The bank or financial institution on which the check is drawn is the *drawee*. If Anita Cruzak writes a check from her checking account to pay her college tuition, she is the drawer, her bank is the drawee, and her college is the payee. We now look at some special types of checks.

Cashier's Checks

CASHIER'S CHECK
A check drawn by a bank on itself.

Checks are usually three-party instruments, but on certain types of checks, the bank can serve as both the drawer and the drawee. For example, when a bank draws a check on itself, the check is called a **cashier's check** and is a negotiable instrument on issue (see Exhibit 21–1) [UCC 3–104(g)]. Normally, a cashier's check indicates a specific payee. In effect, with a cashier's check, the bank assumes responsibility for paying the check, thus making the check more readily acceptable as a substitute for cash.

● **Example 21.1** Kramer needs to pay a moving company $8,000 for moving his household goods to a new home in another state. The moving company requests payment in the form of a cashier's check. Kramer goes to a bank (he need not have an account at the bank) and purchases a cashier's check, payable to the moving company, in the amount of $8,000. Kramer has to pay the bank the $8,000 for the check, plus a small service fee. He then gives the check to the moving company.●

Cashier's checks are sometimes used in the business community as nearly the equivalent of cash. Except in very limited circumstances, the issuing bank must honor its cashier's checks when they are presented for payment. If a bank wrongfully dishonors a cashier's check, a holder can recover from the bank all expenses incurred, interest, and consequential damages [UCC 3–411]. This same rule applies

EXHIBIT 21–1 A CASHIER'S CHECK

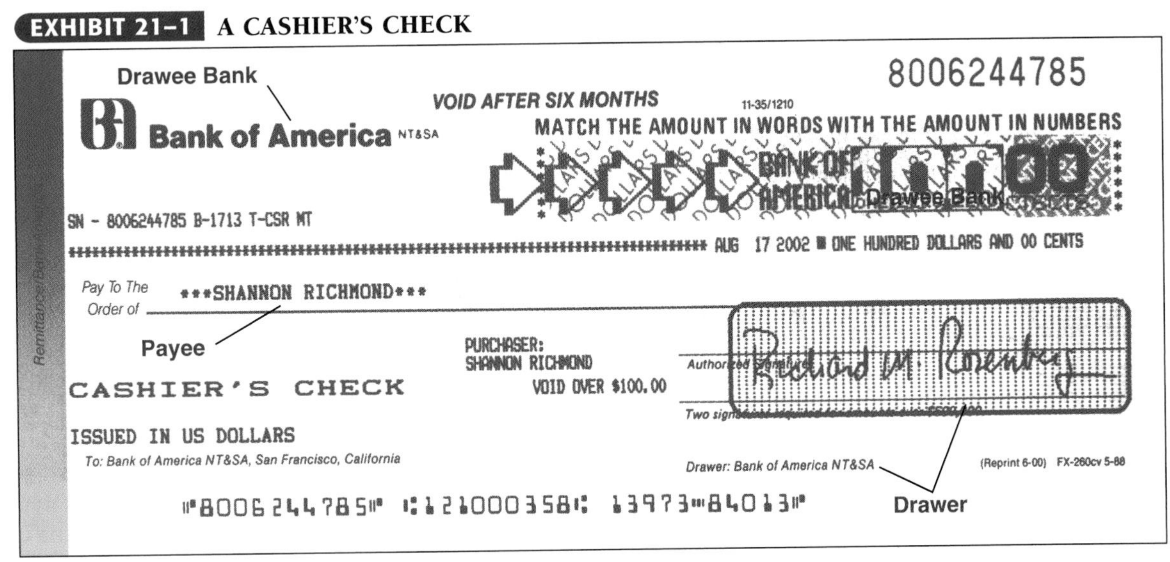

if a bank wrongfully dishonors a certified check (to be discussed shortly) or a teller's check. (A *teller's check* is a check drawn by a bank on another bank or, when drawn on a nonbank, payable at or through a bank [UCC 3–104(h)]). In the following case, the court considered whether a bank could legitimately refuse to honor its own cashier's checks.

CASE 21.1 First Railroad Community Federal Credit Union v. Columbia County Bank

United States District Court,
Middle District of Florida,
Jacksonville Division, 1994.
849 F.Supp. 780.

HISTORICAL AND ECONOMIC SETTING *In the 1980s, the share of the U.S. auto market held by U.S. automakers declined by 10 percent relative to imports. With sales dropping, U.S. manufacturers closed plants, replaced blue-collar workers with robots, substituted computers for white-collar workers, and sometimes used creative bookkeeping to satisfy their shareholders. Domestic auto dealers began to sell foreign models. Instead of selling only Chevrolets, for example, dealers also began to sell Mazdas, Hondas, or BMWs. A few dealers, however, were unable to meet the challenges resulting from declining profits and engaged in criminal schemes to bolster their finances.*

FACTS Clark Crapps operated two automobile dealerships with bank accounts in the First Railroad Community Federal Credit Union and the Columbia County Bank. On one occasion, checks drawn on the account with First Railroad were deposited into the Columbia account. Unaware that the First Railroad account did not have enough funds to pay the checks, Columbia credited the account in its bank and issued two cashier's checks, each for $300,000, based on the credit. Both checks were immediately deposited into the First Railroad account. When Columbia learned of the financial misdealings, it refused to honor the cashier's checks. Seeking payment, First Railroad filed a suit in a federal district court against Columbia. Both parties filed motions for summary judgment.

ISSUE Did Columbia have to pay its cashier's checks?

DECISION Yes. The court held that First Railroad was entitled to payment and granted summary judgment in its favor.

(continued)

CASE 21.1—Continued

REASON The court explained that unlike an ordinary check, a cashier's check "stands on its own foundation as an independent, unconditional, and primary obligation of the bank. People accept a cashier's check as a substitute for cash because the bank stands behind the check, rather than an individual." The court reasoned that "the parties' expectation is that the cashier's check will remove doubt as to whether the instrument will be returned to the holder unpaid due to insufficient funds in the account, a stop payment order, or insolvency." Therefore, "the only inquiry a bank may make upon presentment of a cashier's check is whether or not the payee or [i]ndorsee is in fact a legitimate holder, i.e., whether the cashier's check is being presented by a thief or one who simply found a lost check, or whether the check has been materially altered."

FOR CRITICAL ANALYSIS—Economic Consideration *Why are the grounds on which a bank can refuse to pay a cashier's check so limited?*

Traveler's Checks

TRAVELER'S CHECK
A check that is payable on demand, drawn on or payable through a financial institution (bank), and designated as a traveler's check.

A **traveler's check** has the characteristics of a teller's check. It is an instrument that is payable on demand, drawn on or payable at or through a financial institution (such as a bank), and designated as a traveler's check. The institution is directly obligated to accept and pay its traveler's check according to the check's terms. The purchaser is required to sign the check at the time it is bought and again at the time it is used [UCC 3–104(i)]. Exhibit 21–2 shows an example of a traveler's check.

Certified Checks

CERTIFIED CHECK
A check that has been accepted in writing by the bank on which it is drawn. Essentially, the bank, by certifying (accepting) the check, promises to pay the check at the time the check is presented.

A **certified check** is a check that has been *accepted* in writing by the bank on which it is drawn [UCC 3–409(d)]. When a drawee bank *certifies* (accepts) a check, it immediately charges the drawer's account with the amount of the check and transfers those funds to its own certified check account. In effect, the bank is agreeing in advance to accept that check when it is presented for payment and to make payment from those funds reserved in the certified check account. Essentially, certification prevents the bank from denying liability. It is a promise that sufficient funds are on deposit *and have been set aside* to cover the check. Exhibit 21–3 shows a sample certified check.

A drawee bank is not obligated to certify a check, and failure to do so is not a dishonor of the check [UCC 3–409(d)]. If a bank does certify a check, however, the bank

EXHIBIT 21–2 A TRAVELER'S CHECK

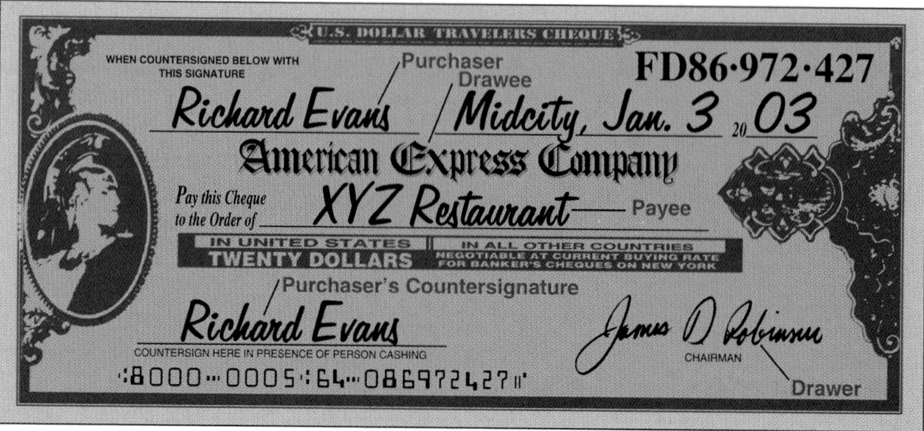

EXHIBIT 21–3 A CERTIFIED CHECK

STEPHANIE ROE
10 PARK AVE.
ST. PAUL, MN 55123

2206

June 8, 20 03

22-1
960

PAY TO THE ORDER OF John Doe $ 5,000.00

Five thousand and no/100 DOLLARS

THE FIRST NATIONAL BANK OF MYTOWN
332 MINNESOTA STREET
MYTOWN, MINNESOTA 55555

Stephanie Roe

NO. 6009 CERTIFIED — THE FIRST NATIONAL BANK OF MYTOWN — Jack Jones — AUTHORIZED

Payee — Drawee — Drawer — Drawee Certification Acceptor

should write on the check the amount that it will pay. If the certification does not state an amount, and the amount is later increased and the instrument negotiated to a holder in due course (HDC), the obligation of the certifying bank is the amount of the instrument when it was taken by the HDC [UCC 3–413(b)].

Certification may be requested by a holder (to ensure that the check will not be dishonored for insufficient funds) or by the drawer. In either circumstance, on certification the drawer and any prior indorsers are completely discharged from liability on the instrument [UCC 3–414(c), 3–415(d)].[1]

The Bank-Customer Relationship

ON THE WEB Cornell University's Legal Information Institute provides an overview of banking, as well as a "menu of sources" of federal and state statutes and court decisions relating to banking transactions. To access this information, go to **http://www.law.cornell.edu/topics/banking.html**.

The bank-customer relationship begins when the customer opens a checking account and deposits funds that the bank will use to pay for checks written by the customer. The rights and duties of the bank and the customer are contractual and depend on the nature of the transaction.

A creditor-debtor relationship is created between a customer and a bank when, for example, the customer makes cash deposits into a checking account. When a customer makes a deposit, the customer becomes a creditor, and the bank a debtor, for the amount deposited.

An agency relationship also arises between the customer and the bank when the customer writes a check on his or her account. In effect, the customer is ordering the bank to pay the amount specified on the check to the holder when the holder presents the check to the bank for payment. In this situation, the bank becomes the customer's agent and is obligated to honor the customer's request. Similarly, if the customer deposits a check into her or his account, the bank, as the customer's agent, is obligated to collect payment on the check from the bank on which the check was drawn. To transfer checkbook funds among different banks, each bank acts as the agent of collection for its customer [UCC 4–201(a)].

1. Under Section 3–411 of the unrevised Article 3, the legal liability of a drawer varies according to whether certification is requested by the drawer or a holder. The drawer who obtains certification remains *secondarily liable* on the instrument if the certifying bank does not honor the check when it is presented for payment. If the check is certified at the request of a holder, the drawer and anyone who indorses the check before certification are completely discharged.

Whenever a bank-customer relationship is established, certain contractual rights and duties arise. The respective rights and duties of banks and their customers are discussed in detail in the following pages.

Bank's Duty to Honor Checks

When a commercial bank provides checking services, it agrees to honor the checks written by its customers with the usual stipulation that there be sufficient funds available in the account to pay each check [UCC 4–401(a)]. The customer is generally obligated to keep sufficient funds on deposit to cover all checks written. The customer is liable to the payee or to the holder of a check in a civil suit if a check is dishonored for insufficient funds. If intent to defraud can be proved, the customer can also be subject to criminal prosecution for writing a bad check.

When the bank properly dishonors a check for insufficient funds, it has no liability to the customer. When a drawee bank *wrongfully* fails to honor a customer's check, however, it is liable to its customer for damages resulting from its refusal to pay [UCC 4–402].

Clearly, the bank's duty to honor its customers' checks is not absolute. As noted, the bank is under no duty to honor a check when there are insufficient funds in the customer's account. In other circumstances, the bank may rightfully make payment or refuse payment on a customer's check. We look here at the rights and duties of both the bank and its customers in relation to specific situations.

OVERDRAFTS

OVERDRAFT
A check that is written on a checking account in which there are insufficient funds to cover the check and that is paid by the bank.

When the bank receives an item properly payable from its customer's checking account but the account contains insufficient funds to cover the amount of the check, the bank has two options. It can either (1) dishonor the item or (2) pay the item and charge the customer's account, thus creating an **overdraft**, providing that the customer has authorized the payment and the payment does not violate any bank-customer agreement [UCC 4–401(a)].[2] The bank can subtract the difference (plus a service charge) from the customer's next deposit or eventually from other deposits made by the customer, because the check carries with it an enforceable implied promise to reimburse the bank.

A bank can expressly agree with a customer to accept overdrafts through what is sometimes called an "overdraft protection agreement." If such an agreement is formed, any failure of the bank to honor a check because it would create an overdraft breaches this agreement and is treated as wrongful dishonor [UCC 4–402(a)].

When a check "bounces," a holder can resubmit the check, hoping that at a later date sufficient funds will be available to pay it. The holder must notify any indorsers on the check of the first dishonor, however; otherwise, they will be discharged from their signature liability.

POSTDATED CHECKS

A bank may also charge a postdated check against a customer's account, unless the customer notifies the bank, in a timely manner, not to pay the check until the stated date. The notice of postdating must be given in time to allow the bank to act on the notice before commiting itself to pay on the check. The UCC states that the bank should treat

2. If there is a joint account, the bank cannot hold any joint-account customer liable for payment of an overdraft unless the customer has signed the check or has benefited from the proceeds of the check [UCC 4–401(b)].

a notice of postdating the same as a stop-payment order—to be discussed shortly. Generally, if the bank receives timely notice from the customer and nonetheless charges the customer's account before the date on the postdated check, the bank may be liable for any damages incurred by the customer as a result [UCC 4–401(c)].[3]

STALE CHECKS

STALE CHECK
A check, other than a certified check, that is presented for payment more than six months after its date.

Commercial banking practice regards a check that is presented for payment more than six months from its date as a **stale check**. A bank is not obligated to pay an uncertified check presented more than six months from its date [UCC 4–404]. When receiving a stale check for payment, the bank has the option of paying or not paying the check. The bank may consult the customer before paying the check. If a bank pays a stale check in good faith without consulting the customer, however, the bank has the right to charge the customer's account for the amount of the check.

STOP-PAYMENT ORDERS

STOP-PAYMENT ORDER
An order by a bank customer to his or her bank not to pay or certify a certain check.

A **stop-payment order** is an order by a customer to his or her bank not to pay or certify a certain check. Only a customer or a person authorized to draw on the account can order the bank not to pay the check when it is presented for payment [UCC 4–403(a)]. For a deceased customer, any person claiming a legitimate interest in the account may issue a stop-payment order [UCC 4–405]. A customer has no right to stop payment on a check that has been certified or accepted by a bank, however. Also, a stop-payment order must be received within a reasonable time and in a reasonable manner to permit the bank to act on it [UCC 4–403(a)]. Although a stop-payment order can be given orally, usually by phone, it is binding on the bank for only fourteen calendar days unless confirmed in writing.[4] A written stop-payment order (see Exhibit 21–4 on the next page) or an oral order confirmed in writing is effective for six months, at which time it must be renewed in writing [UCC 4–403(b)].

If the bank pays the check over the customer's properly instituted stop-payment order, the bank will be obligated to recredit the customer's account—but only for the amount of the actual loss suffered by the drawer because of the wrongful payment [UCC 4–403(c)]. • **EXAMPLE 21.2** Arlene Drury orders six bamboo palms from a local nursery at $50 each and gives the nursery a check for $300. Later that day, the nursery tells Drury that it will not deliver the palms as arranged. Drury immediately calls her bank and stops payment on the check. If the bank nonetheless honors the check, the bank will be liable to Drury for the full $300. The result would be different, however, if the nursery had delivered five palms. In that situation, Drury would owe the nursery $250 for the delivered palms, and her actual losses would be only $50. Consequently, the bank would be liable to Drury for only $50. •

A stop-payment order has its risks for a customer. The customer-drawer must have a *valid legal ground* for issuing such an order; otherwise, the holder can sue the drawer for payment. Moreover, defenses sufficient to refuse payment against a payee may not

3. Under the UCC, postdating does not affect the negotiability of a check. In the past, instead of treating postdated checks as checks payable on demand, some courts treated them as time drafts. Thus, regardless of whether the customer notified the bank of the postdating, a bank could not charge a customer's account for a postdated check without facing potential liability for the payment of later checks. Under the automated check-collection system currently in use, however, a check is usually paid without respect to its date. Thus, today the bank can ignore the postdate on the check (treat it as a demand instrument) unless it has received notice of the postdate.

4. Some states do not recognize oral stop-payment orders; they must be in writing.

EXHIBIT 21–4 A STOP-PAYMENT ORDER

Bank of America

Checking Account Stop Payment Order

To: Bank of America NT&SA
I want to stop payment on the following check(s).

ACCOUNT NUMBER: ______ – ______

SPECIFIC STOP

*ENTER DOLLAR AMOUNT: ______ *CHECK NUMBER: ______

THE CHECK WAS SIGNED BY: ______

THE CHECK IS PAYABLE TO: ______

THE REASON FOR THIS STOP PAYMENT IS: ______

STOP RANGE (Use for lost or stolen check(s) only.)

DOLLAR AMOUNT: 000

*ENTER STARTING CHECK NUMBER: ______ *END CHECK NUMBER: ______

THE REASON FOR THIS STOP PAYMENT IS: ______

I agree that this order (1) is effective only if the above check(s) has (have) not yet been cashed or paid against my account, (2) will end six months from the date it is delivered to you unless I renew it in writing, and (3) is not valid if the check(s) was (were) accepted on the strength of my Bank of America courtesy-check guarantee card by a merchant participating in that program. I also agree (1) to notify you immediately to cancel this order if the reason for the stop payment no longer exists or (2) that closing the account on which the check(s) is (are) drawn automatically cancels this order.

IF ANOTHER BRANCH OF THIS BANK OR ANOTHER PERSON OR ENTITY BECOMES A "HOLDER IN DUE COURSE" OF THE ABOVE CHECK, I UNDERSTAND THAT PAYMENT MAY BE ENFORCED AGINST THE CHECK'S MAKER (SIGNER).

*I CERTIFY THE AMOUNT AND CHECK NUMBER(S) ABOVE ARE CORRECT.

☐ I have written a replacement check (number and date of check).

______

(Optional—please circle one: Mr., Ms., Mrs., Miss) CUSTOMER'S SIGNATURE **X** ______ DATE ______

BANK USE ONLY

TRANCODE:

☐ 21—ENTER STOP PAYMENT (SEE OTHER SIDE TO REMOVE)

NON READS: ______
UNPROC. STMT HIST: ______
PRIOR STMT CYCLE: ______
HOLDS ON COOLS: ______
REJECTED CHKS: ______
LARGE ITEMS: ______
FEE COLLECTED: ______
DATE ACCEPTED: ______
TIME ACCEPTED: ______

be valid grounds to prevent payment against a subsequent holder in due course [UCC 3–305, 3–306]. A person who wrongfully stops payment on a check not only will be liable to the payee for the amount of the check but also may be liable for consequential damages incurred by the payee as a result of the wrongful stop-payment order.

Death or Incompetence of a Customer

A customer's death or incompetence does not affect the bank's authority to honor a check until the bank knows of the situation and has had a reasonable period of time to act on the information. Article 4 provides that if, at the time a check is issued or its collection has been undertaken, a bank does not know of an adjudication of incompetence or of the death of its customer, an item can be paid, and the bank will not incur liability.

Even when a bank knows of the death of its customer, for ten days after the *date of death,* it can pay or certify checks drawn on or before the date of death—unless a person claiming an interest in that account, such as an heir, orders the bank to stop payment [UCC 4–405]. Without this provision, banks would constantly be required to verify the continued life and competence of their drawers.

Forged Drawers' Signatures

When a bank pays a check on which the drawer's signature is forged, generally the bank is liable. A bank, however, may be able to recover at least some of the loss from the customer (if the customer's negligence contributed to the making of the forgery), from the forger of the check (if he or she can be found), or from the holder who presented the check for payment (if the holder knew that the signature was forged).

The General Rule A forged signature on a check has no legal effect as the signature of a drawer [UCC 3–403(a)]. For this reason, banks require signature cards from each customer who opens a checking account. Signature cards allow the bank to verify

FOR CRITICAL ANALYSIS
Who benefits most under the French rule?

INTERNATIONAL PERSPECTIVE

Liability for Forged Instruments

Attempts by the United Nations to form an international law for negotiable instruments have been complicated by the fact that different legal traditions handle liability for forged instruments differently. In the United States, for example, forgery is a universal defense. In other words, the person whose signature is forged normally will not be liable for paying on the note even if the holder is a holder in due course. In civil law systems, however, such as that of France, a good faith taker of a forged instrument is protected by the rule that the person whose signature is forged is liable on the instrument.

whether the signatures on their customers' checks are genuine. The general rule is that the bank must recredit the customer's account when it pays a check with a forged signature.

Customer Negligence When the customer's negligence substantially contributes to the forgery, the bank normally will not be obligated to recredit the customer's account for the amount of the check [UCC 3–406]. The customer's liability may be reduced, however, by the amount of loss caused by negligence on the part of the bank (or other "person") paying the instrument or taking it for value if the negligence substantially contributed to the loss [UCC 3–406(b)].[5]

• **EXAMPLE 21.3** Gemco Corporation uses special check-writing equipment to write its payroll and business checks. Gemco discovers that one of its employees used the equipment to write himself a check for $10,000 and that the bank subsequently honored it. Gemco requests the bank to recredit $10,000 to its account for improperly paying the forged check. If the bank can show that Gemco failed to take reasonable care in controlling access to the check-writing equipment, the bank will not be required to recredit Gemco's account for the amount of the forged check. If Gemco can show that negligence on the part of the bank (or another person) contributed substantially to the loss, however, then Gemco's liability may be reduced proportionately. •

Timely Examination of Bank Statements Required. Banks typically send their customers monthly statements detailing activity in their checking accounts. Banks are not obligated to include the canceled checks themselves with the statement sent to the customer. If the bank does not send the canceled checks (or photocopies of the canceled checks), however, it must provide the customer with information (check number, amount, and date of payment) on the statement that will allow the customer to reasonably identify the checks that the bank has paid [UCC 4–406(a), 4–406(b)]. If the bank retains the canceled checks, it must keep the checks—or legible copies of the checks—for a period of seven years [UCC 4–406(b)]. The customer may obtain a check (or a copy of the check) during this period of time.

The customer has a duty to examine bank statements (and canceled checks or photocopies, if they are included with the statements) promptly and with reasonable care, and to report any alterations or forged signatures promptly [UCC 4–406(c)]. This

5. The unrevised Article 4 does not include a similar provision.

includes forged signatures of indorsers, to be discussed later. If the customer fails to fulfill this duty and the bank suffers a loss as a result, the customer will be liable for the loss [UCC 4–406(d)]. Even if the customer can prove that she or he took reasonable care against forgeries, the UCC provides that the customer must discover the forgeries and notify the bank within a specific time frame in order to require the bank to recredit her or his account.

Consequences of Failing to Detect Forgeries. When a series of forgeries by the same wrongdoer has taken place, the UCC provides that the customer, to recover for all the forged items, must have discovered and reported the first forged check to the bank within thirty calendar days of the receipt of the bank statement (and canceled checks or copies, if they are included) [UCC 4–406(d)(2)].[6] Failure to notify the bank within this period of time discharges the bank's liability for all forged checks that it pays prior to notification. • **EXAMPLE 21.4** Alan forges Beth's signature as the drawer on three checks. Alan presents the first forged check to the bank, and Beth's bank honors the first check on March 15, debits Beth's account, and includes the canceled check with Beth's statement, which Beth receives on April 1 but does not review until May 7. Meanwhile, Alan cashes the second check at Beth's bank on April 10. Beth notifies the bank of the first forgery on May 8. On May 10, Alan cashes the third check. In this situation, the bank is liable only for the amount of the third check, for which it must recredit Beth's account. •

KEEP IN MIND If a bank is forced to recredit a customer's account, the bank may recover from the forger or from the party that cashed the check (usually a different customer or a collecting bank).

When the Bank Is Also Negligent. In one situation, a bank customer can escape liability, at least in part, for failing to notify the bank of forged or altered checks promptly or within the required thirty-day period. If the customer can prove that the bank was also negligent—that is, that the bank failed to exercise ordinary care—then the bank will also be liable, and the loss will be allocated between the bank and the customer on the basis of comparative negligence [UCC 4–406(e)].[7] In other words, even though a customer may have been negligent, the bank may still have to recredit the customer's account for a portion of the loss if the bank failed to exercise ordinary care.

Regardless of the degree of care exercised by the customer or the bank, the UCC places an absolute time limit on the liability of a bank for paying a check with a forged customer signature. A customer who fails to report a forged signature within one year from the date that the statement was made available for inspection loses the legal right to have the bank recredit his or her account [UCC 4–406(f)]. The court in the following case was asked to apply this rule.

6. The unrevised Article 4 limits the period for examining and reporting to *fourteen* days [UCC 4–406(2)(b)].
7. Under the unrevised Article 4, if both parties are negligent, then the bank is wholly liable [UCC 4–406(3)].

CASE 21.2 Halifax Corp. v. First Union National Bank

Supreme Court of Virginia, 2001.
262 Va. 91,
546 S.E.2d 696.

FACTS Between August 1995 and March 1999, Mary Adams served as Halifax Corporation's comptroller. Between August 1995 and January 1997, she wrote at least eighty-eight checks on Halifax's account at First Union National Bank. Adams used facsimile signatures on the checks, made them payable to herself or cash, and deposited them in her personal account at Wachovia

CASE 21.2—Continued

Bank. First Union paid the checks and debited Halifax's account. Most of the checks were drawn in amounts exceeding $10,000, and about twenty were drawn in amounts of between $50,000 and $100,000 each. First Union knew Adams was an employee of Halifax. In January 1999, Halifax discovered accounting irregularities and, during an investigation, learned that Adams had embezzled more than $15 million from its checking account. Halifax filed a suit in a Virginia state court against First Union and others, seeking recovery on the ground of negligence under, in part, UCC 4–406. First Union filed a motion for summary judgment. The court granted the motion. Halifax appealed to the Virginia state supreme court.

ISSUE Were Halifax's claims against First Union barred by the one-year limit of UCC 4–406(f)?

DECISION Yes. The state supreme court affirmed the lower court's judgment.

REASON The state supreme court explained that UCC 4–406(f) "bars a customer, who received a statement or item from a bank but failed to discover or report the customer's unauthorized signature or alteration on the item to the bank within one year after the statement or item is made available to the customer, from asserting a claim against the bank for the unauthorized signature or alteration." UCC 4–406(f) "is devoid of any language which limits the customer's duty to discover and report unauthorized signatures and alterations to items paid in good faith by the bank." The court noted that the UCC includes the phrase "good faith" in other subsections of UCC 4–406. The court concluded that "the exclusion of the good faith requirement in [UCC 4–406(f)] was intentional, and the General Assembly [the Virginia state legislature] did not intend to impose that requirement upon a bank."

FOR CRITICAL ANALYSIS—Ethical Consideration *Why should a customer have to report a forged or unauthorized signature on a paid check within a certain time to recover the amount of the payment?*

FORGED INDORSEMENTS

A bank that pays a customer's check bearing a forged indorsement must recredit the customer's account or be liable to the customer-drawer for breach of contract. • **EXAMPLE 21.5** Suppose that Brian issues a $50 check "to the order of Antonio." Jimmy steals the check, forges Antonio's indorsement, and cashes the check. When the check reaches Brian's bank, the bank pays it and debits Brian's account. The bank must

A bank teller verifies a customer's signature. If a forged indorsement were part of this transaction, why should the bank suffer the loss?

recredit the $50 to Brian's account because it failed to carry out Brian's order to pay "to the order of Antonio" [UCC 4–401(a)]. Of course, Brian's bank can in turn recover—for breach of warranty (see Chapter 20)—from the bank that paid the check when Jimmy presented it [UCC 4–207(a)(2)]. •

Eventually, the loss usually falls on the first party to take the instrument bearing the forged indorsement because, as discussed in Chapter 20, a forged indorsement does not transfer title. Thus, whoever takes an instrument with a forged indorsement cannot become a holder.

COMPARE Three years is also the limit for bringing actions for breach of warranty and to enforce other obligations, duties, and rights under Article 3.

In any event, the customer has a duty to examine the returned checks (or copies of the checks) and statements received from the bank and to report forged indorsements promptly. A customer's failure to report forged indorsements within a three-year period after the forged items have been made available to the customer relieves the bank of liability [UCC 4–111].

ALTERED CHECKS

The customer's instruction to the bank is to pay the exact amount on the face of the check to the holder. The bank has a duty to examine each check before making final payment. If it fails to detect an alteration, it is liable to its customer for the loss because it did not pay as the customer ordered. The loss is the difference between the original amount of the check and the amount actually paid [UCC 4–401(d)(1)]. • **EXAMPLE 21.6** Suppose that a check written for $11 is raised to $111. The customer's account will be charged $11 (the amount the customer ordered the bank to pay). The bank will normally be responsible for the $100. •

The bank is entitled to recover the amount of loss from the transferor, who, by presenting the check for payment, warrants that the check has not been materially altered. If the bank is the drawer (as it is on a cashier's check and a teller's check), however, it cannot recover on this ground from the presenting party if the party is an HDC acting in good faith [UCC 3–417(a)(2), 4–208(a)(2)]. The reason is that an instrument's drawer is in a better position than an HDC to know whether the instrument has been altered.

Similarly, an HDC, acting in good faith in presenting a certified check for payment, will not be held liable under warranty principles if the check was altered before the HDC acquired it [UCC 3–417(a)(2), 4–207(a)(2)]. • **EXAMPLE 21.7** Jordan draws a check for $500 payable to Deffen. Deffen alters the amount to $5,000. The First National Bank of Whiteacre, the drawee bank, certifies the check for $5,000. Deffen negotiates the check to Evans, an HDC. The drawee bank pays Evans $5,000. On discovering the mistake, the bank cannot recover from Evans the $4,500 paid by mistake, even though the bank was not in a superior position to detect the alteration. This is in accord with the purpose of certification, which is to obtain the definite obligation of a bank to honor a definite instrument. •

"Opportunity makes the thief."
THOMAS FULLER, 1608–1661
(English clergyman and writer)

As in a situation involving a forged drawer's signature, when payment is made on an altered check, a customer's negligence can shift the loss (unless the bank was also negligent). A common example occurs when a person carelessly writes a check and leaves large gaps around the numbers and words where additional numbers and words can be inserted (see Exhibit 21–5). Similarly, a person who signs a check and leaves the dollar amount for someone else to fill in is barred from protesting when the bank unknowingly and in good faith pays whatever amount is shown [UCC 4–401(d)(2)]. Finally, if the bank can trace its loss on successive altered checks to the customer's failure to discover the initial alteration, then the bank can reduce its liability for reimbursing the customer's account [UCC 4–406]. The law governing the customer's duty to examine monthly statements and canceled checks (or copies), and to discover and report unauthorized signatures to the drawee bank, applies to altered instruments as well as forgeries.

EXHIBIT 21–5 A POORLY FILLED-OUT CHECK

XYZ CORPORATION
10 INDUSTRIAL PARK
ST. PAUL, MINN.

2206

June 8 20 03

22-1
960

PAY TO THE ORDER OF John Doe $ 100.00

One hundred and no/100 DOLLARS

THE FIRST NATIONAL BANK OF MYTOWN
332 MINNESOTA STREET
MYTOWN, MINNESOTA 55555

Stephanie Roe

⑈94⑈ 77577⑈ 0885

Bank's Duty to Accept Deposits

A bank has a duty to its customer to accept the customer's deposits of cash and checks. When checks are deposited, the bank must make the funds represented by those checks available within certain time frames. A bank also has a duty to collect payment on any checks payable or indorsed to its customers and deposited by them into their accounts. Cash deposits made in U.S. currency are received into customers' accounts without being subject to further collection procedures.

Availability Schedule for Deposited Checks

The Expedited Funds Availability Act of 1987[8] and Regulation CC,[9] which was issued by the Federal Reserve Board of Governors (the Federal Reserve System will be discussed shortly) to implement the act, require that any local check deposited must be available for withdrawal by check or as cash within one business day from the date of deposit. A check is classified as a local check if the first bank to receive the check for payment and the bank on which the check is drawn are located in the same check-processing region (check-processing regions are designated by the Federal Reserve Board of Governors). For nonlocal checks, the funds must be available for withdrawal within not more than five business days.

In addition, the act requires the following:

1. That funds be available on the next business day for cash deposits and wire transfers, government checks, the first $100 of a day's check deposits, cashier's checks, certified checks, and checks for which the depositary and payor banks are branches of the same institution.
2. That the first $100 of any deposit be available for cash withdrawal on the opening of the next business day after deposit. If a local check is deposited, the next $400 is to be available for withdrawal by no later than 5:00 P.M. the next business day. If, for example, you deposit a local check for $500 on Monday, you can withdraw $100 in cash at the opening of the business day on Tuesday, and an additional $400 must be available for withdrawal by no later than 5:00 P.M. on Wednesday.

A different availability schedule applies to deposits made at nonproprietary automated teller machines (ATMs). These are ATMs that are not owned or operated by the

8. 12 U.S.C. Sections 4001–4010.
9. 12 C.F.R. Sections 229.1–229.42.

depositary institution. Basically, a five-day hold is permitted on all deposits, including cash deposits, made at nonproprietary ATMs.

Other exceptions also exist. A depository institution has eight days to make funds available in new accounts (those open less than thirty days). It has an extra four days on deposits over $5,000 (except deposits of government and cashier's checks), on accounts with repeated overdrafts, and on checks of questionable collectibility (if the institution tells the depositor it suspects fraud or insolvency).

The Collection Process

Usually, deposited checks involve parties who do business at different banks, but sometimes checks are written between customers of the same bank. Either situation brings into play the bank collection process as it operates within the statutory framework of Article 4 of the UCC.

DEPOSITARY BANK
The first bank to receive a check for payment.

PAYOR BANK
The bank on which a check is drawn (the drawee bank).

COLLECTING BANK
Any bank handling an item for collection, except the payor bank.

INTERMEDIARY BANK
Any bank to which an item is transferred in the course of collection, except the depositary or payor bank.

Designations of Banks Involved in the Collection Process The first bank to receive a check for payment is the **depositary bank.**[10] For example, when a person deposits an IRS tax-refund check into a personal checking account at the local bank, that bank is the depositary bank. The bank on which a check is drawn (the drawee bank) is called the **payor bank.** Any bank except the payor bank that handles a check during some phase of the collection process is a **collecting bank.** Any bank except the payor bank or the depositary bank to which an item is transferred in the course of this collection process is called an **intermediary bank.**

During the collection process, any bank can take on one or more of the various roles of depositary, payor, collecting, and intermediary bank. • **EXAMPLE 21.8** A buyer in New York writes a check on her New York bank and sends it to a seller in San Francisco. The seller deposits the check in her San Francisco bank account. The seller's bank is both a *depositary bank* and a *collecting bank*. The buyer's bank in New York is the *payor bank*. As the check travels from San Francisco to New York, any collecting bank handling the item in the collection process (other than the ones acting as a depositary bank and a payor bank) is also called an *intermediary bank*. Exhibit 21–6 illustrates how various banks function in the collection process in the context of this example. •

Check Collection between Customers of the Same Bank An item that is payable by the depositary bank (also the payor bank) that receives it is called an "on-us item." If the bank does not dishonor the check by the opening of the second banking day following its receipt, the check is considered paid [UCC 4–215(e)(2)]. • **EXAMPLE 21.9** Williams and Merkowitz both have checking accounts at State Bank. On Monday morning, Merkowitz deposits into his own checking account a $300 check drawn by Williams. That same day, State Bank issues Merkowitz a "provisional credit" for $300. When the bank opens on Wednesday, Williams's check is considered honored, and Merkowitz's provisional credit becomes a final payment. •

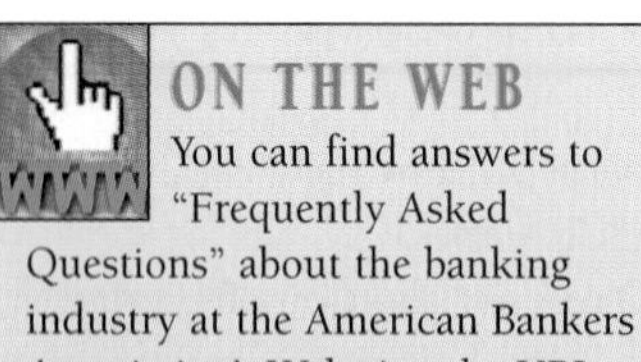

ON THE WEB
You can find answers to "Frequently Asked Questions" about the banking industry at the American Bankers Association's Web site, the URL for which is **http://www.aba.com.**

Check Collection between Customers of Different Banks Once a depositary bank receives a check, it must arrange to present it either directly or through intermediary banks to the appropriate payor bank. Each bank in the collection chain must pass the check on before midnight of the next banking day following its receipt [UCC

10. All definitions in this section are found in UCC 4–105. The terms *depositary* and *depository* have different meanings in the banking context. A depository bank refers to a *physical place* (a bank or other institution) in which deposits or funds are held or stored.

EXHIBIT 21–6 THE CHECK-COLLECTION PROCESS

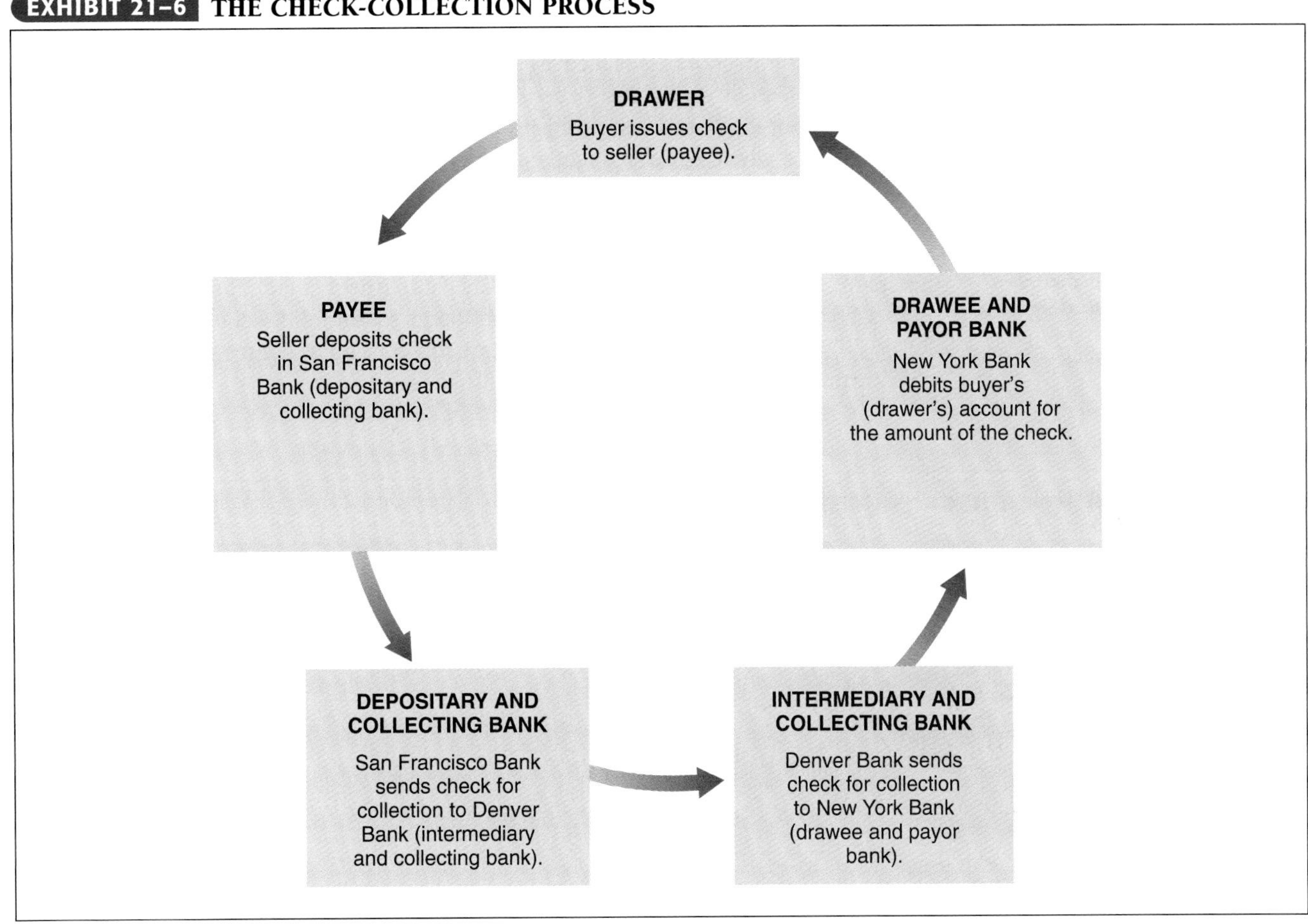

4–202(b)].[11] A "banking day" is any part of a day that the bank is open to carry on substantially all of its banking functions. Thus, if a bank has only its drive-through facilities open, a check deposited on Saturday would not trigger a bank's midnight deadline until the following Monday. When the check reaches the payor bank, unless the payor bank dishonors the check or returns it by midnight on the next banking day following receipt, the payor bank is accountable for the face amount of the check [UCC 4–302].[12]

Because of this deadline and because banks need to maintain an even work flow in the many items they handle daily, the UCC permits what is called *deferred posting*. According to UCC 4–108, "a bank may fix an afternoon hour of 2:00 P.M. or later as a cutoff hour for the handling of money and items and the making of entries on its books." Any checks received after that hour "may be treated as being received at the opening of the next banking day." Thus, if a bank's "cutoff hour" is 3:00 P.M., a check received by a payor bank at 4:00 P.M. on Monday would be deferred for posting until Tuesday. In this situation, the payor bank's deadline would be midnight Wednesday.

11. A bank may take a "reasonably longer time," such as when the bank's computer system is down due to a power failure, but the bank must show that its action is still timely [UCC 4–202(b)].

12. Most checks are cleared by a computerized process, and communication and computer facilities may fail because of weather, equipment malfunction, or other conditions. If such conditions arise and a bank fails to meet its midnight deadline, the bank is "excused" from liability if the bank has exercised "such diligence as the circumstances require" [UCC 4–109(d)].

FEDERAL RESERVE SYSTEM A network of twelve district banks and related branches located around the country and headed by the Federal Reserve Board of Governors. Most banks in the United States have Federal Reserve accounts.

CLEARINGHOUSE A system or place where banks exchange checks and drafts drawn on each other and settle daily balances.

How the Federal Reserve System Clears Checks The **Federal Reserve System** is our nation's central bank. It consists of twelve district banks and related branches located around the country and is headed by the Federal Reserve Board of Governors. Most banks in the United States have Federal Reserve accounts. The Federal Reserve System has greatly simplified the check-collection process by acting as a **clearinghouse**—a system or a place where banks exchange checks and drafts drawn on each other and settle daily balances.

• **Example 21.10** Suppose that Pamela Moy of Philadelphia writes a check to Jeanne Sutton in San Francisco. When Sutton receives the check in the mail, she deposits it in her bank. Her bank then deposits the check in the Federal Reserve Bank of San Francisco, which transfers it to the Federal Reserve Bank of Philadelphia. That Federal Reserve bank then sends the check to Moy's bank, which deducts the amount of the check from Moy's account. Exhibit 21–7 illustrates this process.•

EXHIBIT 21–7 HOW A CHECK IS CLEARED

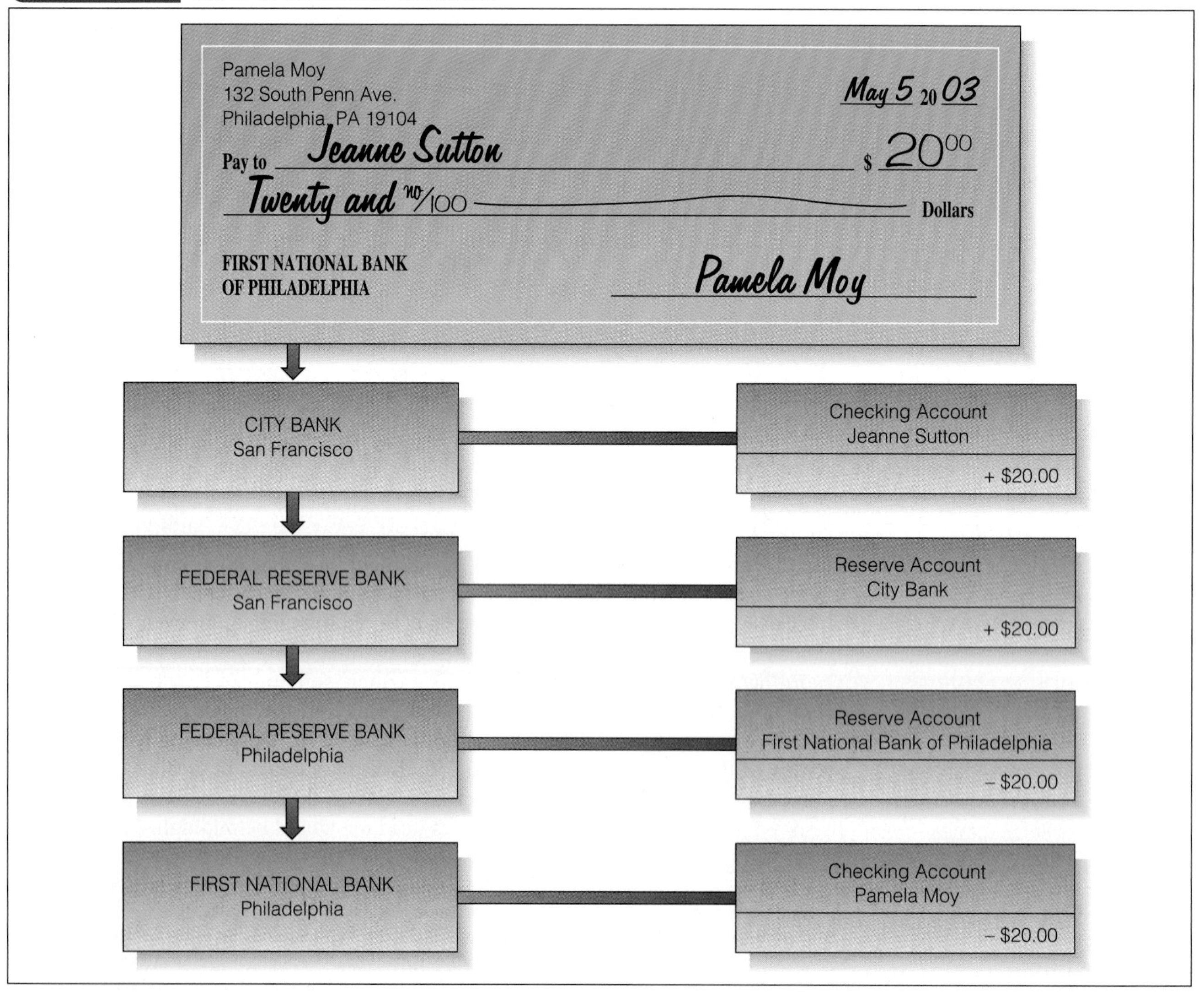

AUTOMATED CLEARINGHOUSE (ACH) An electronic banking system used to transfer payments and settle accounts.

Most electronic payment (e-payment) processing services also use the Federal Reserve's **automated clearinghouse** (ACH). Under ACH rules, a debit from a customer's bank account is reversible for up to forty-eight hours. For this reason, an e-payment service must either hold debited funds for two days and run the risk of displeasing the customer, or immediately send the payment to the intended payee and run the risk that the transaction will be reversed because the customer's account has insufficient funds. To reduce this risk, the service needs to know its customers' creditworthiness. This need led to the following case.

CASE 21.3 Kvalheim v. Checkfree Corp.

United States District Court, Southern District of Alabama, 2000. __ F.Supp.2d __.

COMPANY PROFILE *CheckFree Corporation (**http://www.checkfree.com**) designs, develops, and markets services that allow customers to conduct financial transactions over the Internet. CheckFree processes more than 12 million e-transactions per month on behalf of three million customers at over 350 banks and financial institutions. CheckFree's services are available through several Internet sites, including Yahoo.com, Quicken.com, and WingSpanBank.com. CheckFree is also the exclusive provider of electronic bill payment services to individuals and financial institutions that use Quicken money management software.*

FACTS Following a merger with Intuit Services Corporation (ISC), which was also in the e-payment service business, CheckFree set up procedures to permit customer payments originally initiated through the ISC system to be processed through the CheckFree system. As part of the process, CheckFree needed to assess the credit of the nearly 1.4 million former ISC customers. CheckFree obtained the credit scores of these individuals from Experian Information Solutions, Inc., a credit reporting agency.[a] Meanwhile, Kenneth Kvalheim applied for Compass Bank's online banking service.[b] Because Compass Bank had formerly used ISC's services, CheckFree obtained the credit score of every Compass Bank customer, including Kvalheim. After discovering this credit inquiry, Kvalheim filed a suit in a federal district court against CheckFree, alleging in part that the firm had violated the Fair Credit Reporting Act (FCRA) (see Chapter 33) when it obtained his credit report without permission. CheckFree filed a motion for summary judgment.

a. A *credit score* is a way of assessing the likelihood that a debtor will repay a loan. The score is based on all credit-related data in a credit bureau's report, but it is not a measure of a borrower's income, assets, or bank accounts.

b. Compass Bank's service, CompassPC, allows customers to conduct their banking and pay bills at home through their personal computers.

ISSUE Was CheckFree liable for obtaining Kvalheim's credit report without his permission?

DECISION No. The court granted CheckFree's motion. The court concluded that the FCRA does not impose liability for the actions alleged in the complaint.

REASON The court pointed out that "the FCRA authorizes a party to obtain a consumer report when it 'has a legitimate business need for the information * * * in connection with a business transaction that is initiated by the consumer.' In this case, Kvalheim's credit score was obtained in connection with CheckFree's service of providing electronic payments to third-party creditors, a service which was initiated by Kvalheim when he enrolled in the CompassPC home computer banking service." Because the court concluded that this was a legitimate "business transaction" under the FCRA, "CheckFree is not subject to any liability under the FCRA for obtaining Kvalheim's credit score."

FOR CRITICAL ANALYSIS—Social Consideration *Why would a person in Kvalheim's position object to CheckFree's investigation of his or her credit?*

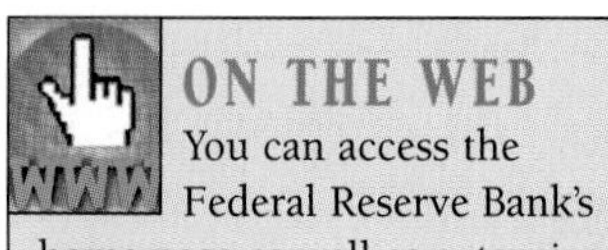

ON THE WEB You can access the Federal Reserve Bank's home page as well as extensive information about "the Fed" at **http://woodrow.mpls.frb.fed.us/info/policy**.

Electronic Check Presentment In the past, most checks were processed manually—the employees of each bank in the collection chain would physically handle each check that passed through the bank for collection or payment. Today, however, most checks are processed electronically. In contrast to manual check processing, which can take days, *electronic check presentment* can be done on the day of the deposit. With electronic check presentment, items may be encoded with information (such as the amount of the check) that is read and processed by other banks' computers. In some situations, a check may be retained at its place of deposit, and only its image or description is presented for payment under a Federal Reserve agreement, clearinghouse rule, or truncation agreement [UCC 4–110]. The term *truncation* refers to presentment by notice rather than by delivery.

Electronic Fund Transfers

ELECTRONIC FUND TRANSFER (EFT) A transfer of funds with the use of an electronic terminal, a telephone, a computer, or magnetic tape.

The application of computer technology to banking, in the form of electronic fund transfer systems, helped to relieve banking institutions of the burden of having to move mountains of paperwork to process fund transfers. An **electronic fund transfer (EFT)** is a transfer of funds through the use of an electronic terminal, a telephone, a computer, or magnetic tape.

The benefits of electronic banking are obvious. Automatic payments, direct deposits, and other fund transfers are now made electronically; no physical transfers of cash, checks, or other negotiable instruments are involved. Not surprisingly, though, electronic banking also poses difficulties on occasion, including the following:

① It is difficult to issue stop-payment orders.

② Fewer records are available to prove or disprove that a transaction took place.

③ The possibilities for tampering (with a resulting decrease in privacy) are increased.

④ The time between the writing of a check and its deduction from an account (float time) is lost.

Types of EFT Systems

Most banks today offer EFT services to their customers. The four most common types of EFT systems used by bank customers are (1) automated teller machines, (2) point-of-sale systems, (3) systems handling direct deposits and withdrawals, and (4) pay-by-telephone systems. We look here at each of these types of EFT systems. Not surprisingly, technology has led to new forms of electronic payment systems. We will look at some emerging forms of online fund transfers later in this chapter. In terms of dollar volume, the most significant fund transfers are those between financial institutions. These commercial transfers of funds will also be discussed later in the chapter.

"Money is human happiness in the abstract."

Arthur Schopenhauer, 1788–1860 (German philosopher)

Automated Teller Machines Automated teller machines (ATMs) are located either on the bank's premises or at convenient locations such as supermarkets, drugstores and other stores, airports, and shopping centers. Automated teller machines receive deposits, dispense funds from checking or savings accounts, make credit-card advances, and receive payments. The devices are connected online to the bank's computers. To access an account through an ATM, the bank customer uses a plastic card (debit card or access card), issued to him or her by the bank, plus a secret *personal identification number (PIN)*. The PIN prevents someone else from using a customer's lost or stolen access card.

The advantages of using an automated teller machine are obvious. Are there any disadvantages?

Point-of-Sale Systems Point-of-sale systems allow consumers to transfer funds to merchants to pay for purchases. Online terminals are located in, for example, grocery stores. When a purchase is made, the customer's **debit card** (issued by the bank to the customer) is inserted into the terminal, which reads the data encoded on it. The computer at the customer's bank verifies that the card and identification code are valid and that there are enough funds in the customer's account to cover the purchase. After the purchase is made, the customer's account is debited for the amount of the purchase.

DEBIT CARD
A plastic card that allows the bearer to transfer funds to a merchant's account, provided that the bearer authorizes the transfer by providing personal identification.

Direct Deposits and Withdrawals A direct deposit may be made to a customer's account through an electronic terminal when the customer has authorized the deposit in advance. The federal government often uses this type of EFT to deposit Social Security payments directly into beneficiaries' accounts. Similarly, an employer may agree to make payroll and pension payments directly into an employee's account at specified intervals.

A customer may also authorize the bank (or other financial institution at which the customer's funds are on deposit) to make automatic payments at regular, recurrent intervals to a third party. For example, insurance premiums, utility bills, and automobile installment loan payments may often be made automatically.

Pay-by-Telephone Systems When it is undesirable to arrange in advance for an automatic payment—as, for example, when the amount of a regular payment varies—some financial institutions permit customers to pay bills through a pay-by-telephone system. This allows the customer to access the institution's computer system by telephone and direct a transfer of funds. Customers frequently pay utility bills directly using pay-by-telephone systems. Customers may also be permitted to transfer funds between accounts—for example, to withdraw funds from a savings account and deposit them in a checking account—in this way.

Consumer Fund Transfers

Consumer fund transfers are governed by the Electronic Fund Transfer Act (EFTA) of 1978. This act provides a basic framework for the rights, liabilities, and responsibilities of users of EFT systems.[13] Additionally, the act gave the Federal Reserve Board authority to issue rules and regulations to help implement the act's provisions. The Federal Reserve Board's implemental regulation is called Regulation E.

The EFTA governs financial institutions that offer electronic fund transfers involving consumer accounts. The types of accounts covered include checking accounts, savings accounts, and any other asset accounts established for personal, family, or household purposes. Note that telephone transfers are covered by the EFTA only if they are made in accordance with a prearranged plan under which periodic or recurring transfers are contemplated.[14]

Because of its importance in establishing the rights of consumers who engage in EFT transactions, the EFTA is presented as this chapter's *Landmark in the Law.* In the subsections that follow, we look more closely at the act's provisions concerning two important issues: unauthorized transfers and error resolution.

BE CAREFUL The EFTA does not provide for the reversal of an electronic transfer of funds once it has occurred.

Unauthorized Electronic Fund Transfers Unauthorized electronic fund transfers are one of the hazards of electronic banking. A paper check leaves visible evidence of a transaction, and a customer can easily detect a forgery or an alteration on a check with ordinary vigilance. Evidence of an electronic transfer, however, is often only an entry in a computer printout of the various debits and credits made to a particular account during a specified time period.

Because of the vulnerability of EFT systems to fraudulent activities, the EFTA of 1978 clearly defined what constitutes an unauthorized transfer. Under the act, a transfer is unauthorized if (1) it is initiated by a person other than the consumer who has no actual authority to initiate the transfer; (2) the consumer receives no benefit from it; and (3) the consumer did not furnish the person "with the card, code, or other means of access" to her or his account.

Error Resolution and Damages Banks must strictly follow the error-resolution procedures prescribed by the EFTA and described briefly in the *Landmark in the Law.* If a bank fails to investigate an error and report its conclusion promptly to the customer, in the specific manner designated by the EFTA, it will be in violation of the act and subject to civil liability. Its liability extends to any actual damages sustained by a customer and to all the costs of a successful action brought against the bank by a customer, including attorneys' fees. In addition, the bank may be liable for punitive damages ranging from $100 to $1,000 for each individual action. Failure to investigate an error in good faith makes the bank liable for treble damages. Even when a customer has sustained no actual damage, the bank may be liable for legal costs and punitive damages if it fails to follow the proper procedures outlined by the EFTA in regard to error resolution.

COMMERCIAL TRANSFERS

NOTE If any part of an electronic fund transfer is covered by the EFTA, the entire transfer is excluded from UCC Article 4A.

The transfer of funds "by wire" between commercial parties is another way in which funds are transferred electronically. In fact, the dollar volume of payments by wire transfer is more than $1 trillion a day—an amount that far exceeds the dollar volume of payments made by other means. The two major wire payment systems are the Federal Reserve wire transfer network (Fedwire) and the New York Clearing House Interbank Payments Systems (CHIPS).

Unauthorized wire transfers are obviously possible and, indeed, have become a problem. If an imposter, for example, succeeds in having funds wired from another's account, the other party will bear the loss (unless he or she can recover from the

13. 15 U.S.C. Sections 1693 *et seq.* The EFTA amended Title IX of the Consumer Credit Protection Act.
14. *Kashanchi v. Texas Commerce Medical Bank, N.A.,* 703 F.2d 936 (5th Cir. 1983).

LANDMARK IN THE LAW
The Electronic Fund Transfer Act (1978)

Congress stated in 1978 that the use of electronic systems to transfer funds promised to provide substantial benefits for consumers. At the same time, Congress acknowledged that existing laws provided inadequate protection for consumers with respect to electronic fund transfers. Thus, Congress passed the Electronic Fund Transfer Act (EFTA).

The Purpose of the EFTA Congress stated that the purpose of the EFTA was "to provide a basic framework establishing the rights, liabilities, and responsibilities of participants in electronic fund transfers." The EFTA is designed to protect consumers. It is not concerned with commercial electronic fund transfers—transfers between businesses or between businesses and financial institutions. (Commercial fund transfers are governed by Article 4A of the UCC.)

Consumer Rights and Responsibilities under the EFTA The EFTA is essentially a disclosure law benefiting consumers. The act requires financial institutions to inform consumers of their rights and responsibilities, including those listed here, with respect to EFT systems.

① If a customer's debit card is lost or stolen and used without his or her permission, the customer may be required to pay no more than $50. The customer, however, must notify the bank of the loss or theft within two days of learning about it. Otherwise, the liability increases to $500. The customer may be liable for more than $500 if he or she does not report the unauthorized use within sixty days after it appears on the customer's statement. (If a customer voluntarily gives her or his debit card to another, who then uses it improperly, the protections just mentioned do not apply.)

② The customer must discover any error on the monthly statement within sixty days and must notify the bank. The bank then has ten days to investigate and must report its conclusions to the customer in writing. If the bank takes longer than ten days, it must return the disputed amount of money to the customer's account until it finds the error. If there is no error, the customer has to give the money back to the bank.

③ The bank must furnish receipts for transactions made through computer terminals, but it is not obligated to do so for telephone transfers.

④ The bank must make a monthly statement for every month in which there is an electronic transfer of funds. Otherwise, the bank must make statements every quarter. The statement must show the amount and date of the transfer, the names of the retailers or other third parties involved, the location or identification of the terminal, and the fees. Additionally, the statement must give an address and a phone number for inquiries and error notices.

⑤ Any authorized prepayment for utility bills and insurance premiums can be stopped three days before the scheduled transfer.

APPLICATION TO TODAY'S WORLD

Many credit-card issuers have voluntarily reduced the customer's liability for unauthorized use of his or her credit-card number to $50, or even to zero, for time periods longer than the EFTA's two days. These extended limits may also apply to transactions completed online. To further assure consumers of the security of e-commerce, some issuers will provide a new card number for each online transaction.

imposter). In the past, any disputes arising as a result of unauthorized or incorrectly made transfers were settled by the courts under the common law principles of tort law or contract law. To clarify the rights and liabilities of parties involved in fund transfers not subject to the EFTA or other federal or state statutes, Article 4A of the UCC was promulgated in 1989. Almost all of the states have adopted this article.

ON THE WEB You can find a series of articles on smart cards at the following Web site:

http://users.aol.com/pjsmart/index.htm.

The type of fund transfer covered by Article 4A is illustrated in the following example. • **EXAMPLE 21.11** Jellux, Inc., owes $5 million to Perot Corporation. Instead of sending Perot a check or some other instrument that would enable Perot to obtain payment, Jellux tells its bank, East Bank, to credit $5 million to Perot's account in West Bank. East Bank forwards this instruction to West Bank via a wire message. In more complex transactions, additional banks would be involved. •

In these and similar circumstances, ordinarily a financial institution's instruction is transmitted electronically. Any means may be used, however, including first-class mail. To reflect this fact, Article 4A uses the term *funds transfer* rather than wire transfer to describe the overall payment transaction. The full text of Article 4A is included in Appendix C, following Article 4 of the Uniform Commercial Code.

E-Money

New forms of electronic payments (e-payments) have the potential to replace *physical* cash—coins and paper currency—with *virtual* cash in the form of electronic impulses. This is the unique promise of **digital cash**, which consists of funds stored on microchips and other computer devices.

DIGITAL CASH Funds contained on computer software, in the form of secure programs stored on microchips and other computer devices.

E-MONEY Prepaid funds recorded on a computer or a card (such as a smart card or a stored-value card).

STORED-VALUE CARD A card bearing magnetic stripes that hold magnetically encoded data, providing access to stored funds.

STORED-VALUE CARDS

The simplest kind of **e-money** system is one that uses **stored-value cards**. These are plastic cards embossed with magnetic stripes containing magnetically encoded data. Using a stored-value card, a person purchases specific goods and services offered by the card issuer. For example, university libraries typically have copy machines that students operate by inserting a stored-value card. Each time a student makes copies, the machine deducts the per-copy fee from the card.

SMART CARDS

SMART CARD A card containing a microprocessor that permits storage of funds via security programming, can communicate with other computers, and does not require online authorization for fund transfers.

Smart cards are plastic cards containing minute computer microchips that can hold far more information than a magnetic stripe. Because of microchip technology, a smart card can do much more than maintain a running cash balance in its memory or authorize the transfer of funds.

A smart card carries and processes security programming. This capability gives smart cards a technical advantage over stored-value cards. The microprocessors on smart cards can also authenticate the validity of transactions. Retailers can program electronic cash registers to confirm the authenticity of a smart card by examining a unique digital signature stored on its microchip. (Digital signatures were discussed in Chapter 17.) Exhibit 21–8 shows how digital encryption helps guarantee the security of e-payments.

Deposit Insurance for Smart-Card Balances Normally, all depository institutions—including commercial banks and savings and loan associations—offer $100,000 of federally backed insurance for deposits. The Federal Deposit Insurance Corporation (FDIC) offers this insurance.

EXHIBIT 21–8 DIGITAL ENCRYPTION AND THE SECURITY OF ELECTRONIC PAYMENTS

An electronic payment instruction starts out in a form readable by a human being, called "plaintext." When this instruction is entered into a computer, it is secured, or encrypted, using an "encryption key," which is a software code. In computer-readable form, the payment instruction is called "ciphertext," which the computer transmits to another location. A computer at that location uses another software code, called a "decryption key," to read the ciphertext and turn it back into a plaintext form that a human operator can read.

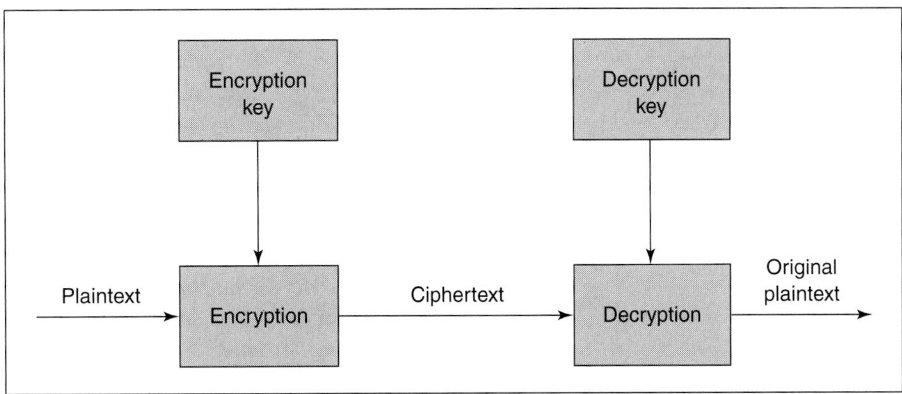

The FDIC has said that most forms of e-money do not qualify as deposits and thus are not covered by deposit insurance. If a bank becomes insolvent, an e-money holder would then be in the position of a general creditor. This means that he or she would be entitled to reimbursement only after nearly everyone else who is owed money is paid. At that point, there may not be any funds left.

Legal Protection for Smart Cards Some laws extend to e-money and e-money transactions. The Federal Trade Commission Act of 1914[15] prohibits unfair or deceptive practices in, or affecting, commerce. Under this law, e-money issuers who misrepresent the value of their products or make other misrepresentations on which e-money consumers rely to their detriment may be liable for engaging in deceptive practices.

General common law principles, discussed in Chapter 1, also apply. For example, the rights and liabilities of e-money issuers and consumers are subject to the common law of contracts. This means that the parties' relationships are affected by the terms of the contracts to which they agree. On the whole, however, it is unclear how existing laws will apply to e-money.

Even without legal protection, e-money payment systems could be safer than cash and checks. Encryption (encoding) may solve some of the problems associated with e-money and with unprotected online exchanges. For example, the theft of encrypted e-money would be a waste of time because without the code a thief could not use the money. The failure of a merchant to give a customer a receipt may not matter if the e-money payment system provides proof of a transaction. Digital signatures could eliminate the problems associated with forged and bounced checks. Digital signatures can also increase the enforceability of contracts entered into online.

15. 15 U.S.C. Sections 41–58.

PRIVACY PROTECTION

Currently, it is not clear which, if any, laws apply to the security of e-money payment information and e-money issuers' financial records. This is partly because it is not clear whether e-money issuers fit within the traditional definition of a financial institution.

REGULATION E
A set of rules issued by the Federal Reserve System's Board of Governors to protect users of elecronic fund transfer systems.

E-Money Payment Information The Federal Reserve has decided not to impose **Regulation E**, which governs certain electronic fund transfers, on e-money transactions. Federal laws prohibiting unauthorized access to electronic communications might apply, however. For example, the Electronic Communications Privacy Act of 1986[16] prohibits any person from knowingly divulging to any other person the contents of an electronic communication while that communication is in transmission or in electronic storage.

E-Money Issuers' Financial Records Under the Right to Financial Privacy Act of 1978,[17] before a financial institution may give financial information about you to a federal agency, you must explicitly consent. If you do not, a federal agency wishing to obtain your financial records must obtain a warrant. A digital cash issuer may be subject to this act if that issuer is deemed to be (1) a bank by virtue of its holding customer funds or (2) any entity that issues a physical card similar to a credit or debit card.

Consumer Financial Data In 1999, Congress passed the Financial Services Modernization Act,[18] also known as the Gramm-Leach-Bliley Act, in an attempt to delineate how financial institutions can treat customer data. In general, the act and its rules[19] place restrictions and obligations on financial institutions to protect consumer data and privacy. All financial institutions must provide their customers with information on their privacy policies and practices. No financial institution can disclose nonpublic personal information about a consumer to an unaffiliated third party unless the act's disclosure and opt-out requirements are met.

Online Banking

Banks have an interest in seeing the widespread use of online banking because of its significant potential for profit. As in other areas of cyberspace, however, it is unclear which laws apply to online banking activities.

ONLINE BANKING SERVICES

Most online bank customers use three kinds of services. One of the most popular is bill consolidation and payment. Another is transferring funds among accounts. These online services are now offered via the Internet as well as by phone. The third is applying for loans, which many banks permit customers to do over the Internet. Customers typically have to appear in person to finalize the terms of a loan.

Two important banking activities generally are not yet available online: depositing and withdrawing funds. With smart cards, people could transfer funds on the Internet,

16. 18 U.S.C. Sections 2510–2521.
17. 12 U.S.C. Sections 3401 *et seq.*
18. 12 U.S.C. Sections 24a, 248b, 1820a, 1828b, 1831v–1831y, 1848a, 2908, 4809; 15 U.S.C. Sections 80b-10a, 6701, 6711–6717, 6731–6735, 6751–6766, 6781, 6801–6809, 6821–6827, 6901–6910; and others.
19. 12 C.F.R. Part 40.

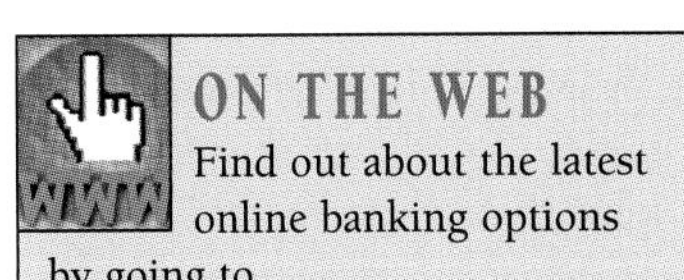

ON THE WEB Find out about the latest online banking options by going to **http://www.onlinebankingreport.com** and clicking on "Finding an Online Bank."

thereby effectively transforming their personal computers into ATMs. Many observers believe that online banking is the way to introduce people to e-money and smart cards.

Since the late 1990s, several banks, such as Bank of Internet (**http://www.bofi.com**), have operated exclusively on the Internet. These "virtual banks" have no physical branch offices. Because few people are equipped to send funds to virtual banks via smart-card technology, the virtual banks have accepted deposits through physical delivery systems, such as the U.S. Postal Service or FedEx.

Regulatory Compliance

A bank is required to define its market area and must also provide information to regulators about its deposits and loans. These compliance efforts are pursuant to the Home Mortgage Disclosure Act (HMDA)[20] and the Community Reinvestment Act (CRA) of 1977.[21]

Under the CRA, banks establish market areas contiguous to their branch offices. The banks map these areas, using boundaries defined by counties or standard metropolitan areas, and annually review the maps. The purpose of these requirements is to prevent discrimination in lending practices.

How does a successful "cyberbank" delineate its community? If Bank of Internet becomes a tremendous success, does it really have any physical communities? Will the Federal Reserve Board simply allow a written description of a cybercommunity for Internet customers? Such regulatory issues are new, challenging, and certain to become more complicated as Internet banking widens its scope internationally.

The Uniform Money Services Act

Over the past few years, many states have enacted various regulations that apply to money services in a rather haphazard fashion. At the same time, e-money services that operate on the Internet—which, of course, cuts across jurisdictional lines—have been asking that these regulations be made more predictable.

In August 2001, the National Conference of Commissioners on Uniform State Laws recommended to state legislatures a new law that would subject traditional money services, as well as online and e-money services, to the same regulations that apply to other, traditional financial service businesses. This new law is known as the Uniform Money Services Act (UMSA).[22]

Traditional Money Services

Before the UMSA, traditional money service businesses were not subject to all of the same regulations that cover other traditional financial services. Unlike banks, money service businesses do not accept deposits. Money service businesses do, however, issue money orders, traveler's checks, and stored-value cards; exchange foreign currency; and cash checks. Immigrants often use these businesses to send money to their relatives in other countries. Because these businesses often do not have continuing relationships with their customers, these customers have sometimes evaded federal law with respect

20. 12 U.S.C. Sections 2801–2810.

21. 12 U.S.C. Sections 2901–2908.

22. Vermont enacted the UMSA in the same month. For a draft of the UMSA, go to the Web site of the National Conference of Commissioners on Uniform State Laws at **http://www.law.upenn.edu** and click on the appropriate links.

to large currency transactions or used the services to launder money (see Chapter 6). This has been particularly true with respect to financing terrorist activities.

The UMSA covers persons engaged in money transmission, check cashing, or currency exchange. The new law requires a money service business involved in these activities to obtain a license from a state, to be examined by state officials, to report on its activities to the state, and to comply with certain record-keeping requirements [UMSA 1–104]. Each of these subjects has its provisions and exceptions.

Under the UMSA, money service businesses would also be covered by rules that govern investments, including restrictions on the types of investments. They would be required to follow what are known as "safety and soundness rules," which concern the posting of bonds as a guaranty of their financial soundness, and the annual auditing of their books [see, for example, UMSA 2–204].

Internet-Based Money Services

Under the UMSA, Internet-based money services, and other types of e-money services, would be treated the same as other money services.[23] The drafters of the UMSA ensured that it would cover these services by referring to *monetary value* instead of simply *money* [UMSA 1–102(c)(11)].

Internet-based monetary value systems subject to the new law may include:

- *E-money and Internet payment mechanisms*—Money, or its substitute, that is stored as data on a chip or a personal computer so that it can be transferred over the Internet or an intranet.
- *Internet scrip*—Monetary value that may be exchanged over the Internet but can also be redeemed for cash.
- *Stored-value products*—Smart cards, prepaid cards, or value-added cards [UMSA 1–102(c)(21)].

23. The UMSA does not apply to state governments, the federal government, securities dealers, banks, businesses that incidentally transport currency and instruments in the normal course of business, payday loan businesses, and others [UMSA 1–103].

APPLICATION Law and the Businessperson . . .

Stop-Payment Orders*

For a variety of reasons, a drawer should not misuse stop-payment orders. We look at some of those reasons here.

Monetary Costs and Risks

One reason is monetary: banks usually charge between $15 and $25 for a stop-payment order, so stopping payment would not be cost-effective for a check written for a small amount. Another reason is the risk attached to the issuing of a stop-payment order for any drawer-customer. The bank is entitled to take a reasonable amount of time to put your stop-payment order into effect before it has liability for improper payment. Hence, the payee or another holder may be able to cash the check despite your stop-payment order if he or she acts quickly. Indeed, you could be writing out a stop-

*This *Application* is not meant to substitute for the services of an attorney who is licensed to practice law in your state.

APPLICATION **Law and the Businessperson . . .**

Stop-Payment Orders—continued

payment order in the bank lobby while the payee or holder cashes the check in the drive-in facility next door. In addition, even if a bank pays over your proper stop-payment order, the bank is only liable to the drawer-customer for the amount of loss the drawer suffers from the improper payment.

When You Can Stop Payment

Remember that a drawer, to avoid liability, must have a legal reason for issuing a stop-payment order. You cannot stop payment on a check simply because you have had a change of heart about the wisdom of your purchase. Generally, you can safely stop payment if you clearly did not get what you paid for or were fraudulently induced to make a purchase. You can also stop payment if a "cooling-off" law governs the transaction—that is, if you legally have a few days in which to change your mind about a purchase. Any wrongful stop order subjects the *drawer* to liability to the payee or a holder, and this liability may include special damages that resulted from the order. When all is considered, it may be unwise to order a stop payment hastily on a check because of a minor dispute with the payee.

Checklist for Stop-Payment Orders

1. Compare the stop-payment fee with the disputed sum to make sure it is worthwhile to issue a stop-payment order.
2. Make sure that your stop-payment order will be honored by your bank prior to the time the payee cashes the check.
3. Make sure that you have a legal reason for issuing the stop-payment order.

Key Terms

automated clearinghouse (ACH) 557
cashier's check 542
certified check 544
check 542
clearinghouse 556
collecting bank 554
debit card 559
depositary bank 554
digital cash 562
electronic fund transfer (EFT) 558
e-money 562
Federal Reserve System 556
intermediary bank 554
overdraft 546
payor bank 554
Regulation E 564
smart card 562
stale check 547
stop-payment order 547
stored-value card 562
traveler's check 544

Chapter Summary Checks, the Banking System, and E-Money

Checks (See pages 542–545.)	1. *Cashier's check*—A check drawn by a bank on itself (the bank is both the drawer and the drawee) and purchased by a customer. In effect, the bank lends its credit to the purchaser of the check, thus making the funds available for immediate use in banking circles. 2. *Traveler's check*—An instrument on which a financial institution is both the drawer and the drawee. The purchaser must provide his or her signature as a countersignature for a traveler's check to become a negotiable instrument.

(continued)

Chapter Summary Checks, the Banking System, and E-Money—continued

Checks—continued	3. *Certified check*—A check for which the drawee bank certifies in writing that it will set aside funds in the drawer's account to ensure payment of the check on presentation. On certification, the drawer and all prior indorsers are completely discharged from liability on the check.
The Bank-Customer Relationship (See pages 545–546.)	1. *Contractual relationship*—The bank's relationship with its customer is contractual; both the bank and the customer assume certain contractual duties when a customer opens a bank account. 2. *Creditor-debtor relationship*—The relationship is also a creditor-debtor relationship (the bank is the debtor because it holds the customer's funds on deposit). 3. *Agency relationship*—Because a bank must act in accordance with the customer's orders in regard to the customer's deposited money, an agency relationship also arises—the bank is the agent for the customer, who is the principal.
Bank's Duty to Honor Checks (See pages 546–553.)	Generally, a bank has a duty to honor its customers' checks, provided that the customers have sufficient funds on deposit to cover the checks [UCC 4–401(a)]. The bank is liable to its customers for actual damages proved to be due to wrongful dishonor. The bank's duty to honor its customers' checks is not absolute. The following list summarizes the rights and liabilities of the bank and the customer in various situations. 1. *Overdrafts*—The bank has the right to charge a customer's account for any item properly payable, even if the charge results in an overdraft [UCC 4–401(a)]. 2. *Postdated checks*—A bank may charge a postdated check against a customer's account as a demand instrument, unless the customer notifies the bank of the postdating in time to allow the bank to act on the notice before the bank commits itself to pay on the check [UCC 4–401(c)]. 3. *Stale checks*—The bank is not obligated to pay an uncertified check presented more than six months after its date, but it may do so in good faith without liability [UCC 4–404]. 4. *Stop-payment orders*—The customer must make a stop-payment order in time for the bank to have a reasonable opportunity to act. Oral orders are binding for only fourteen days unless they are confirmed in writing. Written orders are effective for only six months unless renewed in writing. The bank is liable for wrongful payment over a timely stop-payment order, but only to the extent of the loss suffered by the drawer-customer [UCC 4–403]. 5. *Death or incompetence of a customer*—So long as the bank does not know of the death or incompetence of a customer, the bank can pay an item without liability to the customer's estate. Even with knowledge of a customer's death, a bank can honor or certify checks (in the absence of a stop-payment order) for ten days after the date of the customer's death [UCC 4–405]. 6. *Forged drawers' signatures, forged indorsements, and altered checks*—The customer has a duty to examine account statements with reasonable care on receipt and to notify the bank promptly of any forged signatures, forged or unauthorized indorsements, or alterations. On a series of unauthorized signatures or alterations by the same wrongdoer, examination and report must occur within thirty calendar days of receipt of the statement. Failure to notify the bank releases the bank from any liability unless the bank failed to exercise ordinary care. Regardless of care or lack of care, the customer is estopped from holding the bank liable after one year for unauthorized customer signatures or alterations and after three years for unauthorized indorsements [UCC 3–403, 4–111, 4–401(a), 4–406].
Bank's Duty to Accept Deposits (See pages 553–558.)	A bank has a duty to accept deposits made by its customers into their accounts. Funds represented by checks deposited must be made available to customers according to a schedule mandated by the Expedited Funds Availability Act of 1987 and Regulation CC. A bank

Chapter Summary Checks, the Banking System, and E-Money—continued

Bank's Duty to Accept Deposits—continued	also has a duty to collect payment on any checks deposited by its customers. When checks deposited by customers are drawn on other banks, as they often are, the check-collection process comes into play (summarized next). 1. *Definitions of banks*—UCC 4–105 provides the following definitions of banks involved in the collection process: a. Depositary bank—The first bank to accept a check for payment. b. Payor bank—The bank on which a check is drawn. c. Collecting bank—Any bank except the payor bank that handles a check during the collection process. d. Intermediary bank—Any bank except the payor bank or the depositary bank to which an item is transferred in the course of the collection process. 2. *Check collection between customers of the same bank*—A check payable by the depositary bank that receives it is an "on-us item"; if the bank does not dishonor the check by the opening of the second banking day following its receipt, the check is considered paid [UCC 4–215(e)(2)]. 3. *Check collection between customers of different banks*—Each bank in the collection process must pass the check on to the next appropriate bank before midnight of the next banking day following its receipt [UCC 4–108, 4–202(b), 4–302]. 4. *How the Federal Reserve System clears checks*—The Federal Reserve System facilitates the check-clearing process by serving as a clearinghouse for checks. 5. *Electronic check presentment*—When checks are presented electronically, items may be encoded with information (such as the amount of the check) that is read and processed by other banks' computers. In some situations, a check may be retained at its place of deposit, and only its image or information describing it is presented for payment under a Federal Reserve agreement, clearinghouse rule, or other agreement [UCC 4–110].
Electronic Fund Transfers (See pages 558–562.)	1. *Types of EFT systems*— a. Automated teller machines (ATMs). b. Point-of-sale systems. c. Direct deposits and withdrawals. d. Pay-by-telephone systems. 2. *Consumer fund transfers*—Consumer fund transfers are governed by the Electronic Fund Transfer Act (EFTA) of 1978. The EFTA is basically a disclosure law that sets forth the rights and duties of the bank and the customer in respect to electronic fund transfer systems. Banks must comply strictly with EFTA requirements. 3. *Commercial transfers*—Disputes arising as a result of unauthorized or incorrectly made fund transfers between financial institutions are not covered under the EFTA. Article 4A of the UCC, which has been adopted by almost all of the states, governs fund transfers not subject to the EFTA or other federal or state statutes.
E-Money (See pages 562–564.)	1. *New forms of e-payments*—These include stored-value cards and smart cards. 2. *Deposit insurance*—Most forms of e-money do not qualify as deposits and thus are not covered by federally guaranteed deposit insurance. 3. *Legal protection*—Statutes such as the Federal Trade Commission Act may cover e-money and e-payment transactions. General common law principles also apply.

(continued)

Chapter Summary Checks, the Banking System, and E-Money—continued

E-Money—continued	4. *Privacy protection*—It is not entirely clear which, if any, laws apply to e-payment information and records. The Financial Services Modernization Act (the Gramm-Leach-Bliley Act) outlines how financial institutions can treat consumer data and privacy in general. The Right to Financial Privacy Act may also apply.
Online Banking (See pages 564–565.)	1. *Current online banking services*— a. Bill consolidation and payment. b. Transferring funds among accounts. c. Applying for loans. 2. *Regulatory compliance*—Banks must define their market areas, in communities contiguous to their branch offices, under the Home Mortgage Disclosure Act and the Community Reinvestment Act. It is not clear how an online bank would define its market area.
The Uniform Money Services Act (See pages 565–566.)	In August 2001, the National Conference of Commissioners on Uniform State Laws recommended to state legislatures the Uniform Money Services Act. The purpose of the act is to subject online and e-money services to the same regulations that apply to traditional financial service businesses.

For Review

① Checks are usually three-party instruments. On what type of check, however, does a bank serve as both the drawer and the drawee? What type of check does a bank agree in advance to accept when the check is presented for payment?

② When may a bank properly dishonor a customer's check without liability to the customer?

③ In what circumstances might a bank not be liable for payment of a check containing a forged signature of the drawer?

④ Under the Electronic Fund Transfer Act, under what conditions will a bank be liable for an unauthorized fund transfer? When will the consumer be liable?

⑤ What is e-money? How is e-money stored and used? What are some emerging developments in the area of online banking services?

Questions and Case Problems

21–1. Error Resolution. Sheridan has a checking account at Gulf Bank. She frequently uses her access card to obtain money from the automated teller machines. She always withdraws $50 when she makes a withdrawal, but she never withdraws more than $50 in any one day. When she received the April statement on her account, she noticed that on April 13 two withdrawals for $50 each had been made from the account. Believing this to be a mistake, she went to her bank on May 10 to inform the bank of the error. A bank officer told her that the bank would investigate and inform her of the result. On May 26, the bank officer called her and said that bank personnel were having trouble locating the error but would continue to try to find it. On June 20, the bank sent her a full written report advising her that no error had been made. Sheridan, unhappy with the bank's explanation, filed suit against the bank, alleging that it had violated the Electronic Fund Transfer Act. What was the outcome of the suit? Would it matter if the bank could show that on the day in question it had deducted $50 from Sheridan's account to cover a check that Sheridan had written to a local department store and that had cleared the bank on that day?

21–2. Forged Signatures. Gary goes grocery shopping and carelessly leaves his checkbook in his shopping cart. Dolores steals his checkbook, which has two blank checks remaining. On May 5, Dolores forges Gary's name on a check for $100 and cashes the check at Gary's bank, Citizens Bank of Middletown. Gary has not reported the theft of his blank checks to his bank. On June 1, Gary receives his monthly bank statement and canceled checks from Citizens Bank, including the forged check, but he does not examine the canceled checks. On June 20, Dolores forges Gary's last check. This check is for $1,000 and is cashed at Eastern City Bank, a bank with which Dolores has previously done business. Eastern City Bank puts the check through the collection process, and Citizens Bank honors it. On July 1, Gary receives his bank statement and canceled checks. On July 4, Gary discovers both forgeries and immediately notifies Citizens Bank. Dolores cannot be found. Gary claims that Citizens Bank must recredit his account for both checks, as his signature was forged. Discuss fully Gary's claim.

21–3. Online Banking. First Internet Bank operates exclusively on the Web with no physical branch offices. Although some of First Internet's business is transacted with smart-card technology, most of its business with its customers is conducted through the mail. First Internet offers free checking, no-fee money market accounts, and mortgage refinancing, and other services. With what regulation covering banks might First Internet find it difficult to comply, and what is the difficulty?

21–4. Stale Checks. RPM Pizza, Inc., issued a $96,000 check to Systems Marketing but immediately placed a written stop-payment order on the check. Three weeks after the order expired, Systems cashed the check. Bank One Cambridge, RPM's bank, paid the check with funds from RPM's account. Because the check was more than six months old, it was stale, and thus, according to standard banking procedures as well as Bank One's own procedures, the signature on the check should have been specially verified. RPM filed a suit in a federal district court against Bank One to recover the amount of the check. What should the court consider in deciding whether the bank's payment of the check violated the UCC? [*RPM Pizza, Inc. v. Bank One Cambridge,* 69 F.Supp. 517 (E.D.Mich. 1994)]

21–5. Article 3 versus Article 4. Gary Morgan Chevrolet and Oldsmobile, Inc., issued four checks payable to General Motors Acceptance Corp. (GMAC) on Morgan's account with the Bank of Richmondville. There were insufficient funds in Morgan's account, and the bank gave GMAC oral notice of dishonor. The bank returned the checks two days later. GMAC filed a suit against the bank in a New York state court, claiming that the bank failed to dishonor the checks before its midnight deadline, because notice of dishonor must be in writing under Article 4. The bank countered that notice of dishonor may be made orally under Article 3. Which article controls when there is such a conflict? [*General Motors Acceptance Corp. v. Bank of Richmondville,* 203 A.D.2d 851, 611 N.Y.S.2d 338 (1994)]

21–6. Forged Checks. Roy Supply, Inc., and R.M.R. Drywall, Inc., had checking accounts at Wells Fargo Bank. Both accounts required all checks to carry two signatures—that of Edward Roy and that of Twila June Moore, both of whom were executive officers of both companies. Between January 1989 and March 1991, the bank honored hundreds of checks on which Roy's signature was forged by Moore. On January 31, 1992, Roy and the two corporations notified the bank of the forgeries and then filed a suit in a California state court against the bank, alleging negligence. Who is liable for the amounts of the forged checks? Why? [*Roy Supply, Inc. v. Wells Fargo Bank, N.A.,* 39 Cal.App.4th, 46 Cal.Rptr.2d 309 (1995)]

21–7. Customer Negligence. Clem Macke Bindery hired Vincent Jones without investigating his background. At Clem Macke, blank checks were kept in a safe that was unlocked during working hours. Jones surreptitiously obtained two checks on which he forged Clem Macke's signature. The checks were made payable to a fictitious "Larry Pope," whose name Jones signed on the back. Jones cashed the checks at The Provident Bank, which did not ask for identification. Clem Macke assigned its claim against the bank for the amount of the checks to Atlantic Mutual Insurance Co., which filed a suit in an Ohio state court against the bank, alleging negligence. The bank responded that the employer had been negligent in hiring and failing to monitor Jones. If the court finds that both parties in this case were negligent, which party will bear the loss? Would the result be the same if the *unrevised* Article 3 were applied? Explain. [*Atlantic Mutual Insurance Co. v. The Provident Bank,* 79 Ohio Misc.2d 5, 669 N.E.2d 90 (1996)]

21–8. Stale Checks. On July 15, 1986, IBP, Inc., issued to Meyer Land & Cattle Co. a check for $135,234.18 payable to both Meyer and Sylvan State Bank for the purchase of cattle. IBP wrote the check on its account at Mercantile Bank of Topeka. Someone at the Meyer firm misplaced the check. In the fall of 1995, Meyer's president, Tim Meyer, found the check behind a desk drawer. Jana Huse, Meyer's office manager, presented the check for deposit at Sylvan, which accepted it. After Mercantile received the instrument and its computers noted the absence of any stop-payment order, it paid the check with funds from IBP's checking account. IBP insisted that Mercantile recredit IBP's account. Mercantile refused. IBP filed a suit in a federal district court against Mercantile and others, claiming, among other things, that Mercantile had not acted in good faith because it had processed the check by automated means without examining it manually. Mercantile responded that its check-processing procedures adhered to its own policies, as well as reasonable commercial standards of fair dealing in the banking industry. Mercantile filed a motion for summary judgment. Should the court grant the motion? Why or why not? [*IBP, Inc. v. Mercantile Bank of Topeka,* 6 F.Supp.2d 1258 (D.Kan. 1999)]

21–9. Debit Cards. On April 20, 1999, while visiting her daughter and son-in-law Michael Dowdell, Carol Farrow asked Dowdell to fix her car. She gave him her car keys, attached to which was a small wallet containing her debit card. Dowdell repaired her car and returned the keys. Two days later, Farrow noticed that her debit card was missing and contacted Auburn Bank, which had issued the card. Farrow reviewed her automated-teller-machine (ATM) transaction record and noticed that a large amount of cash had been withdrawn from her checking account on April 22 and April 23. When Farrow reviewed the photos taken by the ATM cameras at the time of the withdrawals, she recognized Dowdell as the person using her debit card. Dowdell was convicted in an Alabama state court of the crime of fraudulent use of a debit card. What procedures are involved in a debit-card transaction? What problems with debit-card transactions are apparent from the facts of this case? How might these problems be prevented? [*Dowdell v. State,* 790 So.2d 359 (Ala.Crim.App. 2000)]

TEST YOUR KNOWLEDGE—ANSWER ON THE WEB

21–10. Robert Santoro was the manager of City Check Cashing, Inc., a check-cashing service in New Jersey, and Peggyann Slansky was the clerk. On July 14, Misir Koci presented Santoro with a $290,000 check signed by Melvin Green and drawn on Manufacturers Hanover Trust Co. (a bank). The check was stamped with a Manufacturers certification stamp. The date on the check had clearly been changed from August 8 to July 7. Slansky called the bank to verify the check and was told that the serial number "did not sound like one belonging to the bank." Slansky faxed the check to the bank with a query about the date, but received no reply. Slansky also called Green, who stated that the date on the check was altered before it was certified. Check Cashing cashed and deposited the check within two hours. The drawee bank found the check to be invalid and timely returned it unpaid. Check Cashing filed a suit in a New Jersey state court against Manufacturers and others, asserting that the bank should have responded to the fax before the midnight deadline in UCC 4–302. Did the bank violate the midnight-deadline rule? Explain. [*City Check Cashing, Inc. v. Manufacturers Hanover Trust Co.,* 166 N.J. 49, 764 A.2d 411 (2001)]

A QUESTION OF ETHICS AND SOCIAL RESPONSIBILITY

21–11. Lorine Daniels worked as a bookkeeper for Wilder Binding Co., which had a checking account with Oak Park Trust and Savings Bank. Among Daniels's responsibilities was the reconciliation of the bank statements with the firm's checkbook each month. Daniels forged signatures on forty-two checks, each for an amount under $1,000, which she made payable to herself. Over a six-month period, she embezzled a total of $25,254.78 in this way. When the forgeries were discovered, Wilder demanded that the bank recredit Wilder's account with the $25,254.78. In the lawsuit that followed, a key issue was whether the bank's custom of manually verifying signatures only on checks drawn for more than $1,000 constituted a breach of its duty of ordinary care. The bank testified that such policies and procedures were customary and routine and that its adherence to the policies and procedures therefore did not violate its duty of care. Given these facts, consider the following questions. [*Wilder Binding Co. v. Oak Park Trust and Savings Bank,* 135 Ill.2d 121, 552 N.E.2d 783, 142 Ill.Dec. 1192 (1990)]

1. This case was decided under Article 3 before it was revised in 1990. The court held that whether the bank had breached its duty of care was a question of fact for the jury. How would a court decide this issue under the revised Article 3?
2. Does the fact that a practice is "customary and routine" in a certain industry, such as the banking industry, mean that it is necessarily ethical?

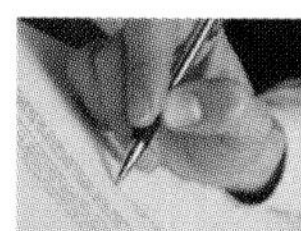

FOR CRITICAL ANALYSIS

21–12. Under the 1990 revision of Article 4, a bank is not required to include the customer's canceled checks when it sends monthly statements to the customers. Banks may simply itemize the checks (by number, date, and amount) or, in addition to this itemization, also provide photocopies of the checks. Often, even when photocopies are included, the photocopies are reduced in size, so they are harder to read than the original canceled checks would be. What implications do the revised rules have for bank customers in terms of liability for unauthorized signatures and indorsements?

Internet Exercises

Go to the *Business Law Today* home page at **http://blt.westbuslaw.com**. Select "Interactive Study Center" and then click on "Chapter 21." There you will find the following Internet research exercises that you can perform to learn more about check fraud and smart cards:

Activity 21–1: Check Fraud

Activity 21–2: Smart Cards

Before the Test

Go to the *Business Law Today* home page at **http://blt.westbuslaw.com**. Click on "Interactive Quizzes." You will find at least twenty interactive questions relating to this chapter.

UNIT FOUR Cumulative Business Hypothetical

Eve Anderson works as an accounts payable clerk for Future Tech, Inc., a software development and marketing firm. Eve, who has worked for the firm for years, is authorized to sign company checks, on which Future Tech's name and address are printed.

① Future Tech pays its employees every two weeks. Eve gets her paycheck from her employer, indorses the back ("Eve Anderson"), and, on her lunch hour, goes to cash it at Future Tech's bank, United First Bank. On the street, in a crowd, she loses the check. Frank Smith finds it. Has the check been negotiated to Frank? Frank signs the back of the check beneath Eve's signature and cashes it. The check goes through the regular bank collection process, and United First Bank debits Future Tech's account for the amount. Future Tech refuses to issue another check to Eve to cover her loss. What might Eve have done to avoid this loss?

② To pay her current bills, Eve asks her employer, Future Tech, to loan her the funds. Future Tech agrees if Eve will sign an instrument regarding the debt. What language do the parties need to include on that instrument to make it negotiable? Future Tech loans Eve the amount that she wants, and she signs a negotiable note to Future Tech due one year from the date signed. Six months later, Future Tech negotiates the note to Commercial Credit Corp. for 75 percent of the face amount in cash and a check for the rest. Is Commercial Credit a holder in due course of the note? To what extent?

③ To pay E-Systems, Inc., a Future Tech supplier, Eve issues a check in the amount due to E-Systems. The check is drawn on United First Bank. An E-Systems employee, with authorization, indorses the check and transfers it to E-Systems's financial institution, Western National Bank. Western National puts the check into the regular bank collection process. If United First refuses to cash the check, who will ultimately suffer the loss? Could Future Tech be subject to criminal prosecution if United First refuses to cash the check?

④ Alice works in Future Tech's accounts payable department with Eve but does not have the authority to sign company checks. Alice steals a blank Future Tech check from Eve's desk, forges Eve's signature, and cashes the check at Friendly Services, Inc., a check-cashing service. Friendly Services, which does not know that Eve's signature was forged, presents the check for payment to United First Bank. United First cashes the check. When the check is returned with Future Tech's bank statement, Eve discovers the forgery. Future Tech tells United First to recredit its account. Can United First legally refuse? If not, can United First recover the amount that it paid to Friendly Services?

Maryott v. First National Bank of Eden

In Chapter 4, we discussed, in the context of negligence, proximate cause. In the same chapter, we covered the infliction of emotional distress. In Chapter 21, we focused on a bank's duty to honor its customers' checks and the bank's liability for wrongful dishonor of those checks. In this extended case study, we examine Maryott v. First National Bank of Eden,[1] *a decision that involved all of these topics.*

CASE BACKGROUND

Ned Maryott owned and operated Maryott Livestock Sales, a cattle-dealing business, near Britton, South Dakota. In July and August 1996, he shipped 887 head of cattle, worth about $480,000, to Oconto Cattle Company. In payment, he received two drafts (see Chapter 19) from Oconto, but during the bank collection process, the drafts were returned unpaid. First National Bank of Eden, Maryott's bank, then froze his checking account, although the account contained nearly $300,000. The bank applied the funds in the account against his outstanding loans and dishonored three of his checks, including one payable to Schaffer Cattle Company. The bank also told Central Livestock Company, which held a fourth Maryott check, that the check would not be honored. Schaffer and Central made claims against the bond that Maryott had filed with the state to obtain his dealer's license. The state took away Maryott's license, and he lost his business, which led him to suffer clinical depression.

Maryott filed a suit in a South Dakota state court against the bank, claiming, among other things, wrongful dishonor and emotional distress. The jury returned a verdict in Maryott's favor and awarded damages of more than $600,000. The bank appealed to the South Dakota Supreme Court.

1. 624 N.W.2d 96 (S.D. 2001). You can find this case online at the FindLaw site by going to **http://guide.lp.findlaw.com/11stategov/sd/sdca.html**. Select "2001" in the list of years, and, when that page opens, scroll down the list to the case (listed after the date "4/4/2001"). Click on "SD 43" just following the case title to access the case.

MAJORITY OPINION

GILBERTSON, Justice.

* * * *

[South Dakota Codified Laws Section 57A-4-402(b), South Dakota's version of UCC 4–402(b)] provides that "[a] payor bank is liable to its customer for damages proximately caused by the wrongful dishonor of an item." * * * Whether the wrongful dishonor proximately caused Maryott's damages is a question of fact for the jury to decide in all but the rarest of cases. Only when legal minds cannot differ as to the failure of proximate cause is judgment as a matter of law [a matter for a judge to decide, not a jury] * * * appropriate. Bank [First National Bank of Eden] claims this is one of those rarest cases. * * *

Bank's argument is based upon its claim that there is no connection between the three dishonored checks and the damage caused to Maryott, namely the loss of his dealer's license and the closing of his business * * *.

* * * *

* * * At trial, the owner of Schaffer testified he would not have filed a claim against Maryott's bond if Bank had honored that check. Bank argues that Schaffer's claim on the bond is irrelevant, as the bond would have been lost because of the actions of Central [Livestock Co.]. * * * If the defendant's conduct was a substantial factor in causing the plaintiff's injury, it follows that he will not be absolved from liability merely because other causes have contributed to the result, *since such causes, innumerable, are always present.* The wrongful dishonor by Bank was clearly a substantial factor causing the actions taken by Schaffer. * * * In addition, [Central's president] testified that but for Bank's actions, Central would not have moved against Maryott's bond. After reviewing the evidence in a light most favorable to the verdict, there is sufficient evidence to support the jury's verdict. * * * [Emphasis added.]

* * * *

Bank [also] argues that the evidence fails to establish the necessary elements for recovery of damages for emotional distress. * * * Maryott argues that his emotional damages are recoverable under [UCC 4–402(b)] which provides that a bank is liable for "actual damages proved and may include * * * other consequential damages." Maryott argues that damages for emotional distress are part of his consequential damages, and he is therefore not required to establish the elements [separately, as an independent tort]. * * *

* * * *

* * * [T]hree principal concerns continue to foster judicial caution and doctrinal limitations on recovery for

emotional distress: (1) the problem of permitting legal redress for harm that is often temporary and relatively trivial; (2) the danger that claims of mental harm will be falsified or imagined; and (3) the perceived unfairness of imposing heavy and disproportionate financial burdens upon a defendant, whose conduct was only negligent * * *. The best way to balance these concerns while still providing adequate relief for injured plaintiffs is to require plaintiffs to meet the standards already established in this state for the recovery of emotional damages. * * * Therefore, while emotional damages may be recoverable under [UCC 4–402(b)] they are not recoverable unless the plaintiff can establish the requirements * * *.

* * * *

* * * [E]motional distress requires manifestation of physical symptoms. Maryott argues that his clinical depression and the symptoms thereof that resulted from Bank's wrongful dishonor are sufficient to establish manifestation of physical symptoms. The physical symptoms of his depression included shame, interruption of sleep, and humiliation. * * *

* * * Maryott's claim that clinical depression satisfies the requirement of physical symptoms is inconsistent with our established law. Nor can shame and humiliation be classified as physical symptoms. Finally, interruption of sleep on its own cannot be considered a physical symptom that would allow for recovery of emotional damages. Because Maryott has failed to establish the elements of * * * emotional distress, his claim for emotional damages under [UCC 4–402(b)] must fail as a matter of law.

* * * *

We affirm the trial court's denial of Bank's motion for judgment notwithstanding the verdict on the issue of proximate cause. The jury's award of emotional damages is reversed as a matter of law. * * *

DISSENTING OPINION

SABERS, Justice (* * * dissenting * * *).

* * * *

* * * [R]ecovery for "actual damages proved" [under UCC 4–402(b)] encompasses the mental suffering caused by a wrongful dishonor. The majority opinion's requirement for an independent tort theory of emotional distress to safeguard against baseless claims is an outdated approach supported only by jury distrust. I submit the juries of this state are capable of discerning when actual damages include mental anguish, as they did here.

* * * In addressing this issue, we are faced with the economic reality that embarrassment and humiliation suffered from the bank's wrongful acts are very real, though sometimes intangible harms. The damage to Maryott's reputation and the ensuing effect on his credit, a lifeline in his type of business, created very real and incredible damage. The jury recognized it * * * and so should we.

QUESTIONS FOR ANALYSIS

① **Law.** What did the majority in this case conclude on the question of proximate cause? What was its holding on emotional distress?
② **Law.** With what part of the majority's holding did the dissent disagree, and why?
③ **Ethics.** What is the ethical basis for requiring that a bank honor the checks written by its customers?
④ **Economic Dimensions.** What does the holding in this case say to small businesses?
⑤ **Implications for the Business Owner.** If a bank recredits its drawer-customer's account on the wrongful dishonor of a check, should the check's payee also be able to recover from the bank?

Debtor-Creditor Relationships

UNIT 5

UNIT CONTENTS

CHAPTER 22

Secured Transactions

"Article 9 is clearly the most novel and probably the most important article of the Code . . . and covers the entire range of transactions in which the debts are secured by personal property."

Walter D. Malcolm, 1904–1979
(President of the National Conference of Commissioners on Uniform State Laws, 1963–1966)

CHAPTER CONTENTS

LEARNING OBJECTIVES

After reading this chapter, you should be able to answer the following questions:

① What is a security interest? Who is a secured party? What is a security agreement? What is a financing statement?

② What three requirements must be met to create an enforceable security interest?

③ What is the most common method of perfecting a security interest under Article 9?

④ If two secured parties have perfected security interests in the collateral of the debtor, which party has priority to the collateral on the debtor's default?

⑤ What rights does a secured creditor have on the debtor's default?

SECURED TRANSACTION
Any transaction in which the payment of a debt is guaranteed, or secured by personal property owned by the debtor or in which the debtor has a legal interest.

Whenever the payment of a debt is guaranteed, or *secured,* by personal property owned by the debtor or in which the debtor has a legal interest, the transaction becomes known as a **secured transaction**. The concept of the secured transaction is as basic to modern business practice as the concept of credit. Logically, sellers and lenders do not want to risk nonpayment, so they usually will not sell goods or lend funds unless the promise of payment is somehow guaranteed. Indeed, business as we know it could not exist without laws permitting and governing secured transactions.

Article 9 of the Uniform Commercial Code (UCC) governs secured transactions as applied to personal property, fixtures by contract, accounts, instruments, commercial assignments of $1,000 or more, *chattel paper* (any writing

ON THE WEB To find Article 9 of the UCC as adopted by a particular state, go to the Web site of Cornell University's Law School at

http://www.law.cornell.edu/ucc/ucc.table.html.

evidencing a debt secured by personal property), agricultural liens, and what are called general intangibles (such as patents and copyrights). Article 9 does not cover other creditor devices, such as landlord's liens, mechanic's liens, real estate mortgages, and the like [UCC 9–109]. The significance of Article 9 is related in this chapter's *Landmark in the Law* feature on the following page. In 1999, the National Conference of Commissioners of Uniform State Laws (NCCUSL) promulgated a revised version of Article 9. Because the revised version, which was later amended, has now been adopted by all of the states, we base this chapter's discussion of secured transactions entirely on the provisions of the revised version.

In this chapter, we first look at the terminology of secured transactions. We then discuss how the rights and duties of creditors and debtors are created and enforced under Article 9. As will become evident, the law of secured transactions tends to favor the rights of creditors; but, to a lesser extent, it offers debtors some protections, too.

SECURED PARTY
A lender, seller, or any other person in whose favor there is a security interest, including a person to whom accounts or chattel paper has been sold.

DEBTOR
Under Article 9 of the UCC, a debtor is any party who owes payment or performance of a secured obligation, whether or not the party actually owns or has rights in the collateral.

SECURITY INTEREST
Any interest "in personal property or fixtures which secures payment or performance of an obligation" [UCC 1–201(37)].

SECURITY AGREEMENT
An agreement that creates or provides for a security interest between the debtor and a secured party.

COLLATERAL
Under Article 9 of the UCC, the property subject to a security interest, including accounts and chattel paper that have been sold.

FINANCING STATEMENT
A document prepared by a secured creditor, and filed with the appropriate state or local official, to give notice to the public that the creditor has a security interest in collateral belonging to the debtor named in the statement. The financing statement must contain the names and addresses of both the debtor and the secured party, and describe the collateral by type or item.

DEFAULT
The failure to observe a promise or discharge an obligation. The term is commonly used to mean the failure to pay a debt when it is due.

The Terminology of Secured Transactions

The UCC's terminology is now uniformly adopted in all documents used in situations involving secured transactions. A brief summary of the UCC's definitions of terms relating to secured transactions follows.

① A **secured party** is any creditor who has a *security interest* in the *debtor's collateral*. This creditor can be a seller, a lender, a cosigner, and even a buyer of accounts or chattel paper [UCC 9–102(a)(72)].

② A **debtor** is the "person" who *owes payment* or other performance of a secured obligation [UCC 9–102(a)(28)].

③ A **security interest** is the *interest* in the collateral (personal property, fixtures, and so on) that *secures payment or performance of an obligation* [UCC 1–201(37)].

④ A **security agreement** is an *agreement* that *creates* or provides for a *security interest* [UCC 9–102(a)(73)].

⑤ **Collateral** is the *subject* of the *security interest* [UCC 9–102(a)(12)].

⑥ A **financing statement**—referred to as the UCC-1 form—is the *instrument normally filed* to give *public notice* to *third parties* of the *secured party's security interest* [UCC 9–102(a)(39)].

These basic definitions form the concept under which a debtor-creditor relationship becomes a secured transaction relationship (see Exhibit 22–1 on page 581).

Creating and Perfecting a Security Interest

A creditor has two main concerns if the debtor **defaults** (fails to pay the debt as promised): (1) satisfaction of the debt through the possession and (usually) sale of the collateral and (2) priority over any other creditors or buyers who may have rights in the same collateral. We look here at how these two concerns are met through the creation and perfection of a security interest.

LANDMARK IN THE LAW
Article 9 Security Interest

Prior to the drafting of Article 9 of the Uniform Commercial Code and its adoption by the states, secured transactions were governed by a patchwork of security devices. The following summary of these devices will help you to understand the significance and landmark status of Article 9.

Security Devices prior to Article 9 The security devices in use prior to the adoption of Article 9 were replete with variations that, according to many, made no logical sense. These devices included chattel mortgages, trust receipts, conditional sales contracts, assignments of accounts, and pledges. Additionally, each device had its own jargon. Depending on the device used, for example, a debtor could be called variously a pledgor, a mortgagor, a conditional vendee, an assignor, or a borrower.

One of the earliest security devices, historically, is the pledge. A *pledge* is a possessory security interest in which the secured party holds or controls possession of the property involved, called the *collateral,* to secure the payment or performance of the secured obligation. The pledge has existed since at least the fourth or fifth century. One security device that developed from the pledge concept involved obtaining a security interest in goods that could not be conveniently moved from the debtor's property. In such a situation, the creditor would have an independent warehouser establish a warehouse on the debtor's premises to obtain possession of the goods. This was called a field warehouse and dates from about 1900.

Article 9 Streamlined the Law Governing Secured Transactions The pledge and many other types of security devices were all designed to protect creditors' interests. Nonetheless, creditors still faced several legal problems. For example, in many states, a security interest could not be taken in inventory or a stock in trade, such as cars for a car dealer or chocolate for a candy manufacturer. Sometimes, highly technical limitations were placed on the use of a particular security device. If a court determined that a particular security device was not appropriate for a given transaction, it might void the security interest.

The drafters of Article 9 concluded that the two elements common to all security devices were (1) the objective of conferring on a creditor or secured party priority in certain property (the collateral) against the risk of the debtor's nonpayment of the debt or the debtor's insolvency or bankruptcy and (2) a means of notifying other creditors of this prior security interest. With these two elements in mind, the drafters created a new, simplified security device with a single set of terms to cover all situations. What is this security device called? It is called, simply, an Article 9 security interest.

APPLICATION TO TODAY'S WORLD

Although the law of secured transactions still remains far from simple, it is now—thanks to the drafters of Article 9—far more rational and uniform than it was in the days prior to the UCC. The revised Article 9, which became totally effective in 2001, further streamlined secured transactions law by, among other things, simplifying the filing process and allowing secured transactions documents to be filed electronically with the appropriate government officials.

EXHIBIT 22–1 SECURED TRANSACTIONS—CONCEPT AND TERMINOLOGY

In a security agreement, a debtor and a creditor agree that the creditor will have a security interest in collateral in which the debtor has rights. In essence, the collateral secures the loan and ensures the creditor of payment should the debtor default.

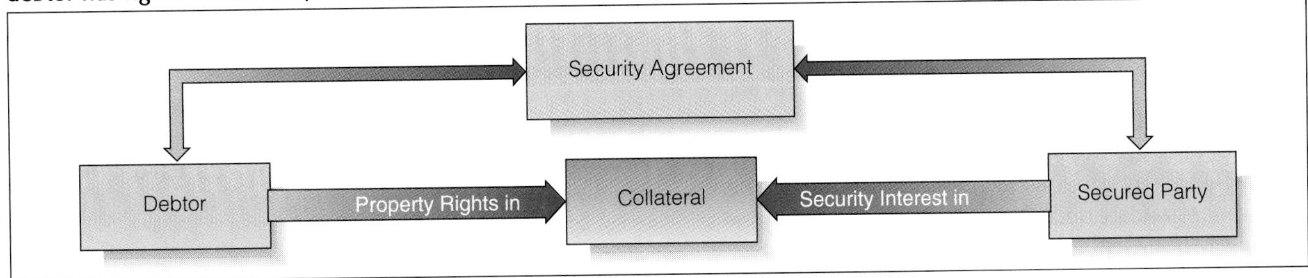

"I will pay you some, and, as most debtors do, promise you infinitely."

WILLIAM SHAKESPEARE, 1564–1616 (English dramatist and poet)

CREATING A SECURITY INTEREST

To become a secured party, the creditor must obtain a security interest in the collateral of the debtor. Three requirements must be met for a creditor to have an enforceable security interest:

1. Either (a) the collateral must be in the possession of the secured party in accordance with an agreement, or (b) there must be a written or authenticated security agreement describing the collateral subject to the security interest and is signed or authenticated by the debtor.
2. The secured party must give to the debtor something of value.
3. The debtor must have "rights" in the collateral.

Once these requirements have been met, the creditor's rights are said to attach to the collateral. **Attachment** gives the creditor an enforceable security interest in the collateral [UCC 9–203].[1]

ATTACHMENT
In a secured transaction, the process by which a secured creditor's interest "attaches" to the property of another (collateral) and the creditor's security interest becomes enforceable.

Written or Authenticated Security Agreement When the collateral is *not* in the possession of the secured party, the security agreement must be either written or authenticated, and it must describe the collateral. Note here that *authentication* includes any agreement or signature inscribed on a tangible medium or stored in an electronic or other medium (called a *record*) that is retrievable [UCC 9–102(a)(7)(69)]. If the security agreement is in writing or authenticated, only the debtor's signature or authentication is required to create the security interest. The reason authentication is acceptable is to provide for electronic filing (the filing process will be discussed later).

A security agreement must contain a description of the collateral that reasonably identifies it. Generally, such words as "all the debtor's personal property" or "all the debtor's assets" would *not* constitute a sufficient description [UCC 9–108(c)]. See Exhibit 22–2 on page 583 for a sample security agreement.

At issue in the following case was whether two documents, when read together, created an enforceable security interest. The debtor signed one of the documents, but the description of the collateral was in the other.

1. Note that in the context of judicial liens, discussed in Chapter 23, the term *attachment* has a different meaning. In that context, it refers to a court-ordered seizure and taking into custody of property prior to the securing of a court judgment for a past-due debt.

CASE 22.1 In re Cantu

United States Bankruptcy Appellate Panel,[a] Eighth Circuit, 1999.
238 Bankr. 796.

FACTS Under the Hormel Employees Credit Union's loan program, an employee who fills out and signs a general loan agreement is eligible to draw funds. The agreement grants a security interest to the credit union but does not describe the property that is to serve as collateral. Instead, the agreement refers to a second document called a "funds advance voucher." This document includes a detailed description of the collateral. The debtor is not required to sign the funds advance voucher. Jesus Cantu bought a truck with financing provided through this program. Cantu signed a loan agreement, and the credit union issued the funds advance voucher, fully describing the collateral by make, model, year, and vehicle identification number. The voucher also provided that all of its terms were incorporated into the loan agreement. Cantu later filed a petition in a federal bankruptcy court to declare bankruptcy. One of the issues was whether the credit union had an enforceable security interest in the truck. Cantu argued that the credit union did not have such an interest because no single document contained his signature, language granting a security interest, and a description of the collateral. The court issued a summary judgment in favor of the credit union. Cantu appealed to the U.S. Bankruptcy Appellate Panel for the Eighth Circuit.

ISSUE Did the general loan agreement and the funds advance voucher, when read together, create an enforceable security interest?

DECISION Yes. The U.S. Bankruptcy Appellate Panel for the Eighth Circuit affirmed the lower court's judgment. The appellate court held that the requirements of UCC 9–203 were satisfied.[b]

REASON The court explained, "The loan agreement grants the Credit Union a security interest in property and expressly states that such property will be described in a separate funds advance voucher. The funds advance voucher, when issued thereafter, contains a full description of the collateral and provides that its terms are made part of the loan agreement. By cross-reference, the description of the collateral in the funds advance voucher is made part and parcel of the loan agreement bearing the debtor's signature." The court added, "The course of conduct of the parties and the purpose of the open-end loan program also support the conclusion that the loan agreement and funds advance voucher are to be read together as comprising the security agreement."

FOR CRITICAL ANALYSIS—Ethical Consideration *Should the court have considered whether the debtor had actually read the loan agreement?*

a. A bankruptcy appellate panel, with the consent of the parties, hears appeals from final judgments, orders, and decrees of bankruptcy judges.

b. This case was decided before the effective date of the revised version of Article 9, but the result would likely have been the same under the revised version.

Secured Party Must Give Value The secured party must give to the debtor something of value. Some examples would be a binding commitment to extend credit, as security for the satisfaction of a preexisting debt, or consideration to support a simple contract [UCC 1–201(44)]. Normally, the value given by a secured party is in the form of a direct loan, or it involves a commitment to sell goods on credit.

Debtor Must Have Rights in the Collateral The debtor must have rights in the collateral; that is, the debtor must have some ownership interest or right to obtain possession of that collateral. The debtor's rights can represent either a current or a future legal interest in the collateral. For example, a retail seller-debtor can give a secured party a security interest not only in existing inventory owned by the retailer but also in *future* inventory to be acquired by the retailer.

One common misconception about having rights in the collateral is that the debtor must have title. This is not a requirement. A beneficial interest in a trust, when title to

EXHIBIT 22–2 AN EXAMPLE OF A SIMPLE SECURITY AGREEMENT

____
Date

____
Name No. and Street City County State

(hereinafter called "Debtor") hereby grants to ________________________
Name

____
No. and Street City County State

(hereinafter called "Secured Party") a security interest in the following property (hereinafter called the "Collateral"): ____

to secure payment and performance of obligations identified or set out as follows (hereinafter called the "Obligations"): ____

Default in payment or performance of any of the Obligations or default under any agreement evidencing any of the Obligations is a default under this agreement. Upon such default Secured Party may declare all Obligations immediately due and payable and shall have the remedies of a secured party under the ________ Uniform Commercial Code.

Signed in (duplicate) triplicate.

____________________	____________________
Debtor	Secured Party
By__________________	By__________________

the trust property is held by the trustee, may be made the subject of a security interest for a loan made to the beneficiary by a secured party (a creditor).

CLASSIFICATIONS AND DEFINITIONS OF COLLATERAL

Where or how to perfect a security interest (perfection will be discussed shortly) sometimes depends on the classification or definition of the collateral. Collateral is generally divided into two classifications: *tangible collateral* (collateral that can be seen, felt, touched, and so on) and *intangible collateral* (collateral that consists of or generates rights).

Exhibit 22–3 on the following pages summarizes the various classifications of collateral and the methods of perfecting a security interest in collateral falling within each of those classifications.[2]

2. There are additional classifications, such as agricultural liens, investment property, and commercial tort claims. For definitions of these types of collateral, see UCC 9–102(a)(5), (a)(13), and (a)(49).

EXHIBIT 22–3 TYPES OF COLLATERAL AND METHODS OF PERFECTION

TYPE OF COLLATERAL	DEFINITION	PERFECTION METHOD	UCC SECTIONS
Tangible	All things that are movable at the time the security interest attaches or that are fixtures. These include timber to be cut, growing crops, and unborn animals.		
1. Consumer Goods	Goods used or bought primarily for personal, family, or household purposes—for example, household furniture [UCC 9–102(a)(23)].	For purchase-money security interest, attachment (that is, the creation of a security interest) is sufficient; for boats, motor vehicles, and trailers, there is a requirement of filing or compliance with a certificate-of-title statute; for other consumer goods, general rules of filing or possession apply.	9–301, 9–303, 9–309(1), 9–310(a), 9–313(a)
2. Equipment	Goods bought for or used primarily in business (and not part of inventory or farm products)—for example, a delivery truck [UCC 9–102(a)(33)].	Filing or (rarely) possession by secured party.	9–301, 9–310(a), 9–313(a)
3. Farm Products	Crops, including aquatic goods, livestock, or supplies produced in a farming operation—for example ginned cotton, milk, eggs, and maple syrup [UCC 9–102(a)(34)].	Filing or (rarely) possession by secured party.	9–301, 9–310(a), 9–313(a)
4. Inventory	Goods held by a person for sale or under a contract of service or lease, or raw materials held for production and work in progress [UCC 9–102(a)(48)].	Filing or (rarely) possession by secured party.	9–301, 9–310(a), 9–313(a)
5. Accessions	Personal property that is so attached, installed, or fixed, to other personal property (goods) that it becomes a part of the goods (the other personal property)—for example, a compact disc player installed in an automobile [UCC 9–102(a)(1)].	Filing or (rarely) possession by secured party (same as personal property being attached).	9–301, 9–310(a), 9–313(a)

EXHIBIT 22–3 TYPES OF COLLATERAL AND METHODS OF PERFECTION (CONTINUED)

TYPE OF COLLATERAL	DEFINITION	PERFECTION METHOD	UCC SECTIONS
Intangible	Nonphysical property that exists only in connection with something else.		
1. Chattel Paper	A writing or writings (records) that evidence both a security interest in goods and software used in goods and a monetary obligation to pay—for example, a security agreement or a security agreement and promissory note. *Note:* If the record or records consist of information stored in an electronic medium, the collateral is called *electronic chattel paper.* If the information is inscribed on a tangible medium, it is called *tangible chattel paper* [UCC 9–102(a)(11), (a)(31), and (a)(78)].	Filing, or possession or control by secured party.	9–301, 9–310(a), 9–312(a), 9–313(a), 9–314(a)
2. Instruments	A negotiable instrument, such as a check, note, certificate of deposit, or draft, or other writing that evidences a right to the payment of money and is not a security agreement or lease, but rather a type that can ordinarily be transferred (after indorsement, if necessary) by delivery [UCC 9–102(a)(47)].	Except for temporary perfected status, filing or possession. For the sale of promissory notes, perfection can be by attachment (automatically on the creation of the security interest).	9–301, 9–309(4), 9–310 (a), 9–312(a) and (e), 9–313(a)
3. Accounts	Any right to receive payment for the following: (a) any property, real or personal, sold, leased, licensed, assigned, or otherwise disposed of, including intellectual licensed property; (b) services rendered or to be rendered, such as contract rights; (c) policies of insurance; (d) secondary obligations incurred; (e) use of a credit card; (f) winnings of a government-sponsored or	Filing required except for certain assignments that can be perfected by attachment (automatically on the creation of the security interest).	9–301, 9–309(2) and (5), 9–310(a)

(continued)

EXHIBIT 22–3 TYPES OF COLLATERAL AND METHODS OF PERFECTION (CONTINUED)

TYPE OF COLLATERAL	DEFINITION	PERFECTION METHOD	UCC SECTIONS
3. Accounts (continued)	government-authorized lottery or other game of chance; and (g) health-care insurance receivables, defined as an interest or claim under a policy of insurance to payment for health-care goods or services provided [UCC 9–102(a)(2) and (a)(46)].		
4. Deposit Accounts	Any demand, time, savings, passbook, or similar account maintained with a bank [UCC 9–102(a)(29)].	Perfection by control.	9–104, 9–304, 9–312(b), 9–314(a)
5. General Intangibles	Any personal property (or debtor's obligation to pay money on such) other than that defined above [UCC 9–102(a)(42)], including software that is independent from a computer or a good [UCC 9–102(a)(44), (a)(61), and (a)(75)].	Filing only (for copyrights, with the U.S. Copyright Office), except a sale of a payment intangible by attachment (automatically on the creation of the security interest).	9–301, 9–309(3), 9–310(a) and (b)(8)

Perfecting a Security Interest

PERFECTION
The legal process by which secured parties protect themselves against the claims of third parties who may wish to have their debts satisfied out of the same collateral; usually accomplished by filing a financing statement with the appropriate government official.

Perfection represents the legal process by which secured parties protect themselves against the claims of third parties who may wish to have their debts satisfied out of the same collateral. Usually, perfection is accomplished by the filing of a financing statement with the office of the appropriate government official. In some circumstances, however, a security interest becomes perfected without the filing of a financing statement.

Perfection by Filing The most common means of perfection is by filing a *financing statement*—a document that gives public notice to third parties of the secured party's security interest—with the office of the appropriate government official. The security agreement itself can also be filed to perfect the security interest. The financing statement must provide the names of the debtor and the secured party and indicate the collateral covered by the financing statement. There is now a uniform financing statement form to be used in all states [see UCC 9–521]. The uniform financing statement is shown in Exhibit 22–4.

Communication of the financing statement to the appropriate filing office, together with the correct filing fee, or the acceptance of the financing statement by the filing officer constitutes a filing [UCC 9–516(a)]. The word *communication* means that the filing can be accomplished electronically [UCC 9–102(a)(18)]. Once completed, filings are indexed in the name of the debtor so that they can be located by subsequent

EXHIBIT 22–4 THE UNIFORM FINANCING STATEMENT

UCC FINANCING STATEMENT

FOLLOW INSTRUCTIONS (front and back) CAREFULLY

A. NAME & PHONE OF CONTACT AT FILER (optional)

B. SEND ACKNOWLEDGEMENT TO: (Name and Address)

THE ABOVE SPACE IS FOR FILING OFFICE USE ONLY

1. DEBTOR'S EXACT FULL LEGAL NAME - Insert only one debtor name (1a or 1b) - do not abbreviate or combine names

1a. ORGANIZATION'S NAME					
OR 1b. INDIVIDUAL'S LAST NAME		FIRST NAME	MIDDLE NAME		SUFFIX
1c. MAILING ADDRESS		CITY	STATE	POSTAL CODE	COUNTRY
1d. TAX ID# SSN OR EIN	ADDL INFO RE ORGANIZATION DEBTOR	1e. TYPE OF ORGANIZATION	1f. JURISDICTION OR ORGANIZATION	1g. ORGANIZATIONAL ID #, if any	NONE

2. ADDITIONAL DEBTOR'S EXACT FULL LEGAL NAME - Insert only one debtor name (2a or 2b) - do not abbreviate or combine names

2a. ORGANIZATION'S NAME					
OR 2b. INDIVIDUAL'S LAST NAME		FIRST NAME	MIDDLE NAME		SUFFIX
2c. MAILING ADDRESS		CITY	STATE	POSTAL CODE	COUNTRY
2d. TAX ID# SSN OR EIN	ADDL INFO RE ORGANIZATION DEBTOR	1e. TYPE OF ORGANIZATION	1f. JURISDICTION OR ORGANIZATION	1g. ORGANIZATIONAL ID #, if any	NONE

3. SECURED PARTY'S NAME - (or NAME of TOTAL ASSIGNOR S/P) Insert only one secured party name (3a or 3b)

3a. ORGANIZATION'S NAME				
OR 3b. INDIVIDUAL'S LAST NAME	FIRST NAME	MIDDLE NAME		SUFFIX
3c. MAILING ADDRESS	CITY	STATE	POSTAL CODE	COUNTRY

4. This FINANCING STATEMENT covers the following collateral:

5. ALTERNATIVE DESIGNATION (if applicable) ☐ LESSEE/LESSOR ☐ CONSIGNEE/CONSIGNOR ☐ BAILEE/BAILOR ☐ SELLER/BUYER ☐ AG. LIEN ☐ NON-UCC FILING

6. ☐ This FINANCING STATEMENT is to be filed [for record] (or recorded) in the REAL ESTATE RECORDS. Attach Addendum (if applicable) 7. Check to REQUEST SEARCH REPORT(S) on Debtor(s) (ADDITIONAL FEE) (optional) ☐ All Debtors ☐ Debtor 1 ☐ Debtor 2

OPTIONAL FILER REFERENCE DATA

NATIONAL UCC FINANCING STATEMENT (FORM UCC1) REV. 07/29/98)

searchers. A financing statement may be filed even before a security agreement is made or a security interest attaches [UCC 9–502(d)].

The Debtor's Name. The UCC requires that a financing statement be filed under the name of the debtor [UCC 9–502(a)(1)]. Because of the use of electronic filing systems in most states, UCC 9–503 sets out some detailed rules for determining when the debtor's name as it appears on a financing statement is sufficient. For corporations, which are part of "registered organizations," the debtor's name on the financing statement must be "the name of the debtor indicated on the public record of the debtor's jurisdiction of organization" [UCC 9–503(a)(1)]. Slight variations in names normally will not be considered misleading if a search of the filing office's records, using a standard computer search engine routinely used by that office, would disclose the filings [UCC 9–506(c)]. Note that if the debtor is identified by the correct name at the time of the filing of a financing statement, the secured party's interest retains its priority even if the debtor later changes his or her name.

If the debtor is a trust, or a trustee with respect to property held in trust, this information must be disclosed on the filed financing statement, and it must provide the trust name as specified in its official documents [UCC 9–503(a)(3)]. In other cases, the filed financing statement must disclose "the individual or organizational name of the debtor" [UCC 9–503(a)(4)(A)]. As used here, the word *organization* includes unincorporated associations, such as clubs and some churches, as well as joint ventures and general partnerships, even when these organizations are created without obtaining any formal certificate of formation.

In general, providing only the debtor's trade name (or a fictitious name) in a financing statement is not sufficient for perfection [UCC 9–503(c)]. • **EXAMPLE 22.1** Assume that a loan is being made to a sole proprietorship owned by Peter Jones. The trade, or fictitious, name is Pete's Plumbing. A financing statement cannot use the trade name Pete's Plumbing; rather, it has to be filed under the name of the actual debtor, who in this instance is Peter Jones.• The reason for this rule is that a sole proprietorship is not a legal entity distinct from the person who owns it. The rule also furthers an important goal of Article 9: to ensure that the debtor's name on a financing statement is one that prospective lenders can locate and recognize in future searches.

Changes in the Debtor's Name. A problem arises when the debtor subject to a filed perfected security interest changes his or her (or its) name. What happens if a subsequent creditor extends credit to the debtor and perfects its security interest under the debtor's new name? Obviously, a search by this subsequent creditor for filed security interests under the debtor's changed name may not disclose the previously filed security interest.

The UCC's revised Article 9 attempts to prevent potential conflicts caused by changes in the debtor's name if the debtor goes into default. First, UCC 9–503 states specifically what constitutes the "sufficiency" of the debtor's name in a financing statement. Second, if the debtor's name is insufficient, the filing is seriously misleading *unless* a search of records using the debtor's correct name by the filing officer's search engine would disclose the security interest [UCC 9–506(b) and (c)]. Third, even if the change of name renders the financing statement misleading, the financing statement is effective as a perfection of a security interest in collateral acquired by the debtor before *or* within four months after the name change. Unless an amendment is filed within this four-month period, collateral acquired by the debtor after the four-month period is unperfected [UCC 9–507(b) and (c)].

Description of the Collateral. The UCC requires that both the security agreement and the financing statement contain a description of the collateral in which the secured party has a security interest. The security agreement must include a description of the collateral because no security interest in goods can exist unless the parties agree on which goods are subject to the security interest. The financing statement must include a description of the collateral because the purpose of filing the statement is to give public notice of the fact that certain goods of the debtor are subject to a security interest. Other parties who might later wish to lend money to the debtor or buy the collateral can thus learn of the security interest by checking with the state or local office in which a financing statement for that type of collateral would be filed. For land-related security interests, a legal description of the realty is also required [UCC 9–502(b)].

Sometimes, the descriptions in the two documents vary, with the description in the security agreement being more precise than the description in the financing statement, which is allowed to be more general. • **EXAMPLE 22.2** A security agreement for a commercial loan to a manufacturer may list all of the manufacturer's equipment subject to the loan by serial number, whereas the financing statement may simply state "all equipment owned or hereafter acquired."• The UCC permits broad, general descriptions in the financing statement, such as "all assets" or "all personal property." Generally, therefore, whenever the description in a financing statement accurately describes the agreement between the secured party and the debtor, the description is sufficient [UCC 9–504].

Where to File. In most states, a financing statement must be filed centrally in the appropriate state office, such as the office of the secretary of state, in the state where

LETTER OF THE LAW

A Walk on the Dark Side

Creditors contemplating a loan to a debtor may change their minds about making the loan if a search through the filing records reveals a filing statement filed under that debtor's name. In other words, debtors listed on filing statements may have difficulty obtaining loans. There is nothing unfair about imposing this burden on debtors—assuming, of course, that the filed financial statement is rooted in an actual credit transaction. But what if the filed statement is phony? Until the "debtor" can arrange to have the filing statement removed (which can be far from easy), his or her creditworthiness may be damaged in the eyes of potential creditors.

The idea of using a phony financing statement as a weapon against one's enemies is a novel one, to be sure, but at least one person has resorted to such a tactic. A prisoner who had been convicted and sentenced to seventeen years in prison for various crimes, including conspiracy to commit murder, decided to "get even" with one of the U.S. attorneys who prosecuted his case. The prisoner filed a phony financing statement against the attorney. The financing statement asserted a claim against the "debtor" for $1 million for violating the prisoner's "commercial, constitutional, and civil rights." Needless to say, the U.S. attorney in question knew exactly what to do: he filed a motion with the court to have the financing statement canceled. The court granted the petition, noting, among other things, that the statement was invalid because it had not been signed by the "debtor."[a]

THE BOTTOM LINE

If one decides to misuse or abuse the law, it is probably not a good idea to target an attorney as one's victim.

a. *United States v. Lopez*, 1997 WL 835419 (N.Y.Sup. 1997). Note that prior to the 1999 revision of Article 9, to be valid, a financing statement had to be signed by the debtor.

the debtor is located. County filings, where the collateral is located, are required only when the collateral consists of timber to be cut, fixtures, and collateral to be extracted—such as oil, coal, gas, and minerals [UCC 9–301(3) and (4), 9–502(b)].

The state office in which a financing statement should be filed depends on the *debtor's location,* not the location of the collateral (as was required under the unrevised Article 9) [UCC 9–301]. The debtor's location is determined as follows [UCC 9–307]:

① For *individual debtors,* it is the state of the debtor's principal residence.

② For a chartered entity created by a filing (such as a corporation), it is in the state of charter or filing. For example, if a debtor is incorporated in Maryland, with its chief executive office in New York, a secured party would file the financing statement in Maryland, which is the state of the debtor's organizational formation.

③ For all other entities, it is the state where the business is located or, if more than one, the state where the chief executive office is located.

Consequences of an Improper Filing. Any improper filing renders the secured party unperfected and reduces a secured party's claim in bankruptcy to that of an unsecured creditor. For example, if the debtor's name on the financing statement is inaccurate or if the collateral is not sufficiently described on the filing statement, the filing may not be effective.

Perfection without Filing In two types of situations, security interests can be perfected without filing a financing statement. First, when the collateral is transferred into the possession of the secured party, the secured party's security interest in the collateral is perfected. Second, there are thirteen different types of security interests that can be perfected on attachment without a filing and without having to possess the goods [UCC 9–309]. The phrase *perfected on attachment* means that these security interests are automatically perfected at the time of their creation. Two of the more common security interests that are perfected on attachment are a *purchase-money security interest* in consumer goods (defined and explained below) and an assignment of a beneficial interest in a decedent's estate [UCC 9–309(1) and (13)].

PLEDGE
A common law security device (retained in Article 9 of the UCC) in which possession of personal property is turned over to the creditor as security for the payment of a debt and retained by the creditor until the debt is paid.

Perfection by Possession. Under the common law, as discussed earlier in this chapter's *Landmark in the Law,* one of the most common means of obtaining financing was to **pledge** certain collateral as security for the debt and transfer the collateral into the creditor's possession. When the debt was paid, the collateral was returned to the debtor. Usually, the transfer of collateral was accompanied by a written security agreement, but the agreement did not have to be in writing. In other words, an oral security agreement was effective as long as the secured party possessed the collateral. Article 9 of the UCC retained the common law pledge and the principle that the security agreement need not be in writing to be enforceable if the collateral is transferred to the secured party [UCC 9–310, 9–312(b), and 9–313].

For most collateral, possession by the secured party is impractical because it denies the debtor the right to use or derive income from the property to pay off the debt. • **EXAMPLE 22.3** Suppose that a farmer takes out a loan to finance the purchase of a piece of heavy farm equipment needed to harvest crops and uses the equipment as collateral. Clearly, the purpose of the purchase would be defeated if the farmer transferred the collateral into the creditor's possession. • Certain items, however, such as stocks, bonds, instruments, and jewelry, are commonly transferred into the creditor's possession when they are used as collateral for loans.

PURCHASE-MONEY SECURITY INTEREST (PMSI) A security interest that arises when a seller or lender extends credit for part or all of the purchase price of goods purchased by a buyer.

Purchase-Money Security Interest. Often, sellers of consumer goods (defined as goods bought or used by the debtor primarily for personal, family, or household purposes [UCC 9–102(a)(23)]) agree to extend credit for part or all of the purchase price of those goods. Additionally, financial institutions that are not in the business of selling such goods often agree to lend consumers much of the purchase price for the goods. The security interest that the seller or the lender obtains when such a transaction occurs is called a **purchase-money security interest (PMSI)** because the lender or seller has essentially provided a buyer with the "purchase money" to buy goods [UCC 9–103(a)(2)].

● **EXAMPLE 22.4** Suppose that Jamie wants to purchase a new large-screen TV from ABC Television, Inc. The purchase price is $2,500. Not being able to pay the entire amount in cash, Jamie signs a purchase agreement to pay $1,000 down and $100 per month until the balance plus interest is fully paid. ABC is to retain a security interest in the purchased goods until full payment has been made. Because the security interest was created as part of the purchase agreement, it is a PMSI. ●

A PMSI in consumer goods is perfected automatically at the time of a credit sale—that is, at the time that the PMSI is created. The seller in this situation need do nothing more to perfect her or his interest.

A PMSI may also exist with respect to goods sold to businesses or entities that are not considered "consumers" for Article 9 purposes. See Example 22.10 later in this chapter for an example of this type of PMSI.

CONTINUATION STATEMENT A statement that, if filed within six months prior to the expiration date of the original financing statement, continues the perfection of the original security interest for another five years. The perfection of a security interest can be continued in the same manner indefinitely.

Effective Time Duration of Perfection A financing statement is effective for five years from the date of filing [UCC 9–515]. If a **continuation statement** is filed within six months *prior to* the expiration date, the effectiveness of the original statement is continued for another five years, starting with the expiration date of the first five-year period [UCC 9–515(d) and (e)]. The effectiveness of the statement can be continued in the same manner indefinitely. Any attempt to file a continuation statement outside the six-month window will render the continuation ineffective, and the perfection will lapse at the end of the five-year period.

If a financing statement lapses, the security interest that had been perfected by the filing now becomes unperfected. It is as if it had never been perfected as against a purchaser for value [UCC 9–515(c)].

The Scope of a Security Interest

In addition to covering collateral already in the debtor's possession, a security agreement can cover various other types of property, including the proceeds of the sale of collateral, after-acquired property, and future advances.

PROCEEDS

PROCEEDS Under Article 9 of the UCC, whatever is received when the collateral is sold or otherwise disposed of, such as by exchange.

Proceeds include whatever is received when collateral is sold or disposed of in some other way [UCC 9–102(a)(64)]. A secured party's security interest in the collateral includes a security interest in the proceeds of the sale of that collateral. ● **EXAMPLE 22.5** Suppose that a bank has a perfected security interest in the inventory of a retail seller of heavy farm machinery. The retailer sells a tractor out of this inventory to a farmer, who is by definition a buyer in the ordinary course of business. The farmer agrees, in a security agreement, to make monthly payments to the retailer for a period of twenty-four months. If the retailer should go into default on the loan from the bank, the bank is entitled to the remaining payments the farmer owes to the retailer as proceeds. ●

A security interest in proceeds perfects automatically on the *perfection* of the secured party's security interest in the original collateral and remains perfected for twenty days after receipt of the proceeds by the debtor. One way to extend the twenty-day automatic perfection period is to provide for such extended coverage in the original security agreement [UCC 9–315(c) and (d)]. This is typically done when the collateral is the type that is likely to be sold, such as a retailer's inventory—for example, of computers or DVD players. The UCC also permits a security interest in identifiable cash proceeds to remain perfected after twenty days [UCC 9–315(d)(2)].

After-Acquired Property

AFTER-ACQUIRED PROPERTY Property that is acquired by the debtor after the execution of a security agreement.

After-acquired property of the debtor is property that the debtor acquired after the execution of the security agreement. The security agreement may provide for a security interest in after-acquired property [UCC 9–204(1)]. This is particularly useful for inventory financing arrangements, because a secured party whose security interest is in existing inventory knows that the debtor will sell that inventory, thereby reducing the collateral subject to the security interest.

Generally, the debtor will purchase new inventory to replace the inventory sold. The secured party wants this newly acquired inventory to be subject to the original security interest. Thus, the after-acquired property clause continues the secured party's claim to any inventory acquired thereafter. This is not to say that the original security interest will be superior to the rights of all other creditors with regard to this after-acquired inventory, as will be discussed later.

● **Example 22.6** Amato buys factory equipment from Bronson on credit, giving as security an interest in all of her equipment—both what she is buying and what she already owns. The security interest with Bronson contains an after-acquired property clause. Six months later, Amato pays cash to another seller of factory equipment for more equipment. Six months after that, Amato goes out of business before she has paid off her debt to Bronson. Bronson has a security interest in all of Amato's equipment, even the equipment bought from the other seller.●

Future Advances

Often, a debtor will arrange with a bank to have a *continuing line of credit* under which the debtor can borrow funds intermittently. Advances against lines of credit can be subject to a properly perfected security interest in certain collateral. The security agreement may provide that any future advances made against that line of credit are also subject to the security interest in the same collateral [UCC 9–204(c)]. Future advances do not have to be of the same type or otherwise related to the original advance to benefit from this type of cross-collateralization.[3]

● **Example 22.7** Stroh is the owner of a small manufacturing plant with equipment valued at $1 million. He has an immediate need for $50,000 of working capital, so he obtains a loan from Midwestern Bank and signs a security agreement, putting up all of his equipment as security. The bank properly perfects its security interest. The security agreement provides that Stroh can borrow up to $500,000 in the future, using the same equipment as collateral for any future advances. In this situation, Midwestern Bank does not have to execute a new security agreement and perfect a security interest in the collateral each time an advance is made up to a cumulative total of $500,000. For priority purposes, each advance is perfected as of the date of the original perfection.●

3. See official Comment 5 to UCC 9–204.

THE FLOATING-LIEN CONCEPT

FLOATING LIEN
A security interest in proceeds, after-acquired property, or collateral subject to future advances by the secured party (or all three); a security interest in collateral that is retained even when the collateral changes in character, classification, or location.

A security agreement that provides for a security interest in proceeds, in after-acquired property, or in collateral subject to future advances by the secured party (or in all three) is often characterized as a **floating lien.** This type of security interest continues in the collateral or proceeds even if the collateral is sold, exchanged, or disposed of in some other way. Floating liens commonly arise in the financing of inventories. A creditor is not interested in specific pieces of inventory, which are constantly changing, so the lien "floats" from one item to another, as the inventory changes.

● **EXAMPLE 22.8** Suppose that Cascade Sports, Inc., a corporation chartered in Oregon that operates as a cross-country ski dealer, has a line of credit with Portland First Bank to finance an inventory of cross-country skis. Cascade and Portland First enter into a security agreement that provides for coverage of proceeds, after-acquired inventory, present inventory, and future advances. This security interest in inventory is perfected by filing centrally (with the office of the secretary of state in Oregon). One day, Cascade sells a new pair of the latest cross-country skis and receives a used pair in trade. That same day, Cascade purchases two new pairs of cross-country skis from a local manufacturer for cash. Later that day, Cascade borrows $2,000 from Portland First Bank under the security agreement to meet its payroll. Portland First gets a perfected security interest in the used pair of skis under the proceeds clause, has a perfected security interest in the two new pairs of skis purchased from the local manufacturer under the after-acquired property clause, and has the new amount of funds advanced to Cascade secured on all of the above collateral by the future-advances clause. All of this is accomplished under the original perfected security interest. The various items in the inventory have changed, but Portland First still has a perfected security interest in Cascade's inventory. Hence, it has a floating lien on the inventory.●

The concept of the floating lien can also apply to a shifting stock of goods. The lien can start with raw materials; follow them as they become finished goods and inventories; and continue as the goods are sold and are turned into accounts receivable, chattel paper, or cash.

Priorities

The importance of being perfected as a secured party cannot be overemphasized, particularly when another party is claiming an interest in the same collateral as covered by the perfected secured party's security interest.

THE GENERAL RULE

The general rule is that a perfected secured party's interest has priority over the interests of the following parties [UCC 9–317, 9–322]:

① An unsecured creditor.

② An unperfected secured party.

③ A subsequent lien creditor, such as a judgment creditor who acquires a lien on the collateral by execution and levy—a process discussed later in this chapter.

④ A trustee in bankruptcy (see Chapter 23)—at least, the perfected secured party has priority to the proceeds from the sale of the collateral by the trustee.

⑤ Most buyers who *do not* purchase the collateral in the ordinary course of a seller's business.

In addition, whether a secured party's security interest is perfected or unperfected may have serious consequences for the secured party if the debtor defaults on the debt or files for bankruptcy. For example, what if the debtor has borrowed money from two different creditors, using the same property as collateral for both loans? If the debtor defaults on both loans, which of the two creditors has first rights to the collateral? In this situation, the creditor with a perfected security interest will prevail.

Buyers of the Collateral

Sometimes, the conflict is between a perfected secured party and a buyer of the collateral. The question then arises as to which party has priority to the collateral.

The UCC recognizes that there are five types of buyers whose interest in purchased goods could conflict with those of a perfected secured party on the debtor's default. These five types are as follows:

1. Buyers in the ordinary course of business—this type of buyer will be discussed in detail shortly.
2. Buyers *not* in the ordinary course of business of consumer goods (see Exhibit 22–5 on page 596 for details).
3. Buyers of chattel paper [UCC 9–330].
4. Buyers of instruments, documents, or securities [UCC 9–330(d), 9–331(a)].
5. Buyers of farm products.[4]

Because buyers should not be required to find out if there is an outstanding security interest in, for example, a merchant's inventory, the UCC also provides that a person who buys "in the ordinary course of business" will take the goods free from any security interest created by the seller in the purchased collateral. This is so even if the security interest is perfected and *even if the buyer knows of its existence* [UCC 9–320(a)].[5] The UCC defines a *buyer in the ordinary course of business* as any person who in good faith, and without knowledge that the sale is in violation of the ownership rights or security interest of a third party in the goods, buys in ordinary course from a person in the business of selling goods of that kind [UCC 1–201(9)].

• **Example 22.9** On August 1, West Bank has a perfected security interest in all of ABC Television's existing inventory and any inventory thereafter acquired. On September 1, Carla, a student at Central University, purchases one of the TVs in ABC's inventory. If on December 1, ABC goes into default, can West Bank repossess the TV set sold to Carla? The answer is no, because Carla is a buyer in the ordinary course of business (ABC is in the business of selling goods of that kind) and takes free and clear of West Bank's perfected security interest. •

Creditors or Secured Parties

KEEP IN MIND Secured creditors—perfected or not—have priority over unsecured creditors.

Generally, the following UCC rules apply when more than one creditor claims rights in the same collateral:

4. Under the Food Security Act of 1985, buyers in the ordinary course of business include buyers of farm products from a farmer. Under this act, these buyers are protected from prior perfected security interests unless the secured parties perfected centrally by a special form called an *effective financing statement* (EFS) or the buyers received proper notice of the secured party's security interest.

5. Remember that, generally, there are three methods of perfection: by filing, by possession, and by attachment.

① *Conflicting perfected security interests.* When two or more secured parties have perfected security interests in the same collateral, generally the first to perfect (file or take possession of the collateral) has priority, unless the state's statute provides otherwise [UCC 9–322(a)(1)].

② *Conflicting unperfected security interests.* When two conflicting security interests are unperfected, the first to attach has priority [UCC 9–322(a)(3)].

③ *Conflicting perfected security interests in commingled or processed goods.* When goods to which two or more perfected security interests attach are so manufactured or commingled that they lose their identities into a product or mass, the perfected parties' security interests attach to the new product or mass "according to the ratio that the cost of goods to which each interest originally attached bears to the cost of the total product or mass" [UCC 9–336].

Under some circumstances, on the debtor's default, the perfection of a security interest will not protect a secured party against certain other third parties having claims to the collateral. For example, the UCC provides that in some instances a PMSI, properly perfected,[6] will prevail over another security interest in after-acquired collateral, even though the other was perfected first (see Exhibit 22–5 on the next page).

An important exception to the first-in-time rule deals with certain types of collateral, such as equipment, in which one of the perfected security parties has a PMSI [UCC 9–324(a)]. • **EXAMPLE 22.10** Suppose that Smith borrows funds from West Bank, signing a security agreement in which she puts up all of her present and after-acquired equipment as security. On May 1, West Bank perfects this security interest (which is not a PMSI). On July 1, Smith purchases a new piece of equipment from XYZ Company on credit, signing a security agreement. XYZ Company thus has a (nonconsumer) PSMI in the new equipment. The delivery date for the new piece of equipment is August 1. If Smith defaults on her payments to both West Bank and XYZ, which party—West Bank or XYZ—has priority to the new piece of equipment? Generally, West Bank would have priority because its interest was perfected first in time. In this situation, however, XYZ has a PMSI, and if it perfects its interest by filing before Smith takes possession on August 1, or within twenty days after that date, XYZ has priority. •

Another important exception to the first-in-time rule has to do with security interests in inventory [UCC 9–324(b)]. • **EXAMPLE 22.11** On May 1, ABC borrows funds from West Bank. ABC signs a security agreement, putting up all of its present inventory and any thereafter acquired as collateral. West Bank perfects its non-PMSI on that date. On June 10, ABC buys new inventory from Martin, Inc., a manufacturer to use for its Fourth of July sale. ABC makes a down payment for the new inventory and signs a security agreement giving Martin a PMSI in the new inventory as collateral for the remaining debt. Martin delivers the inventory to ABC on June 28. Due to a hurricane in the area, ABC's Fourth of July sale is a disaster, and most of ABC's inventory remains unsold. In August, ABC defaults on its payments to both West Bank and Martin. As between West Bank and Martin, who has priority to the new inventory delivered on June 28? If Martin has not perfected its security interest by June 28, West Bank's after-acquired collateral clause has priority because it was the first to be perfected. If, however, Martin has perfected *and* gives proper notice of its security interest to West Bank before ABC takes possession of the goods on June 28, Martin has priority. •

6. Recall that, with some exceptions (such as motor vehicles), a PMSI in consumer goods is automatically perfected—no filing is necessary.

EXHIBIT 22–5 PRIORITY OF CLAIMS TO A DEBTOR'S COLLATERAL

PARTIES	PRIORITY
Unperfected Secured Party	An unperfected secured party prevails over unsecured creditors and creditors who have obtained judgments against the debtor but who have not begun the legal process to collect on those judgments [UCC 9–201(a)].
Purchaser of Debtor's Collateral	1. *Goods purchased in the ordinary course of the seller's business*—Buyer prevails over a secured party's security interest, even if perfected and even if the buyer knows of the security interest [UCC 9–320(a)]. 2. *Consumer goods purchased outside the ordinary course of business*—Buyer prevails over a secured party's interest, even if perfected by attachment, providing buyer purchased as follows: a. For value. b. Without actual knowledge of the security interest. c. For use as a consumer good. d. Prior to secured party's perfection by *filing* [UCC 9–320(b)]. 3. *Buyers of chattel paper*—Buyer prevails if the buyer: a. Gave new value in making the purchase. b. Took possession in the ordinary course of the buyer's business. c. Took without knowledge of the security interest [UCC 9–330]. 4. *Buyers of instruments, documents, or securities*—Buyers who are holders in due course, holders to whom negotiable documents have been duly negotiated, or bona fide purchasers of securities have priority over a previously perfected security interest [UCC 9–330(d), 9–331(a)]. 5. *Buyers of farm products*—Buyers from a farmer take free and clear of perfected security interests unless, where permitted, a secured party files centrally an effective financing statement (EFS) or the buyer receives proper notice of the security interest before the sale.
Perfected Secured Parties to the Same Collateral	1. *The general rule*—Between two perfected secured parties in the same collateral, the general rule is that first in time of perfection is first in right to the collateral [UCC 9–322(a)(1)]. 2. *Exception—Purchase-money security interest (PMSI)*—A PMSI, even if second in time of perfection, has priority providing that the following conditions are met: a. Inventory—PMSI is perfected, and proper written or authenticated notice is given to the other security-interest holder *on* or *before* the time that debtor takes possession [UCC 9–324(b)]. b. Other collateral—PMSI has priority, providing it is perfected within twenty days after debtor receives possession [UCC 9–324(a)]. c. Software—Applies to a PMSI in software only if used in goods subject to a PMSI. Priority is determined the same as if the goods are inventory (if the goods are, in fact, inventory), or if not, as if the goods are other than inventory [UCC 9–103(c) and 9–324(f)].

Rights and Duties of Debtors and Creditors

The security agreement itself determines most of the rights and duties of the debtor and the secured party. The UCC, however, imposes some rights and duties that are applicable in the absence of a valid security agreement that states the contrary.

"Let us live in a small circle as we will, we are either debtors or creditors before we have had time to look round."

JOHANN WOLFGANG VON GOETHE, 1749–1832 (German poet and dramatist)

INFORMATION REQUESTS

Under UCC 9–523(a), a secured party has the option, when making the filing, of furnishing a *copy* of the financing statement being filed to the filing officer and requesting that the filing officer make a note of the file number, the date, and the hour of the original filing on the copy. The filing officer must send this copy to the person designated by the secured party or to the debtor, if the debtor makes the request. Under UCC 9–523(c) and (d), a filing officer must also give information to a person who is contemplating obtaining a security interest from a prospective debtor. The filing officer must issue a certificate that provides information on possible perfected financing statements with respect to the named debtor. The filing officer will charge a fee for the certification and for any information copies provided [UCC 9–525(d)].

RELEASE, ASSIGNMENT, AND AMENDMENT

A secured party can release all or part of any collateral described in the filing, thereby terminating its security interest in that collateral. The release is recorded by filing a uniform amendment form [UCC 9–512 and 9–521(b)]. A secured party can assign all or part of the security interest to a third party (the assignee). The assignee can become the secured party of record if the assignment is filed by use of a uniform amendment form [UCC 9–514 and 9–521(a)].

If the debtor and secured parties so agree, the filing can be amended—by adding new collateral if authorized by the debtor, for example—by filing a uniform amendment form that indicates by file number the initial financing statement [UCC 9–512(a)]. The amendment does not extend the time period of perfection. If, however, the amendment adds collateral, the perfection date (for priority purposes) for the new collateral begins only on the date of the filing of the amendment [UCC 9–512(b) and (c)].

CONFIRMATION OR ACCOUNTING REQUEST BY DEBTOR

The debtor may believe that the unpaid debt amount or the listing of the collateral subject to the security interest is inaccurate. The debtor has the right to request a confirmation of his or her view of the unpaid debt or listing of collateral. The secured party must either approve or correct this confirmation request [UCC 9–210].

The secured party must comply with the debtor's confirmation request by authenticating and sending to the debtor an accounting within fourteen days after the request is received. Otherwise, the secured party will be held liable for any loss suffered by the debtor, plus $500 [UCC 9–210 and 9–625(f)].

The debtor is entitled to one request without charge every six months. For any additional requests, the secured party is entitled to the payment of a statutory fee of up to $25 per request [UCC 9–210(f)].

TERMINATION STATEMENT

When the debtor has fully paid the debt, if the secured party perfected the collateral by filing, the debtor is entitled to have a termination statement filed. Such a statement demonstrates to the public that the filed perfected security interest has been terminated [UCC 9–513].

Whenever consumer goods are involved, a the secured party *must* file a termination statement (or, in the alternative, a release) within one month of the final payment or within twenty days of receipt of the debtor's authenticated demand, whichever is earlier [UCC 9–513(b)].

When the collateral is other than consumer goods, on an authenticated demand by the debtor, the secured party must either send a termination statement to the debtor or file such a statement within twenty days [UCC 9–513(c)]. Otherwise, when the collateral is other than consumer goods, the secured party is not required to file or send a termination statement. Whenever a secured party fails to file or, as required, to send the termination statement as requested, the debtor can recover $500 plus any additional loss suffered [UCC 9–625(e)(4) and (f)].

Default

"If you think nobody cares if you're alive, try missing a couple of car payments."

EARL WILSON, 1907–1987 (American journalist)

Article 9 defines the rights, duties, and remedies of the secured party and of the debtor on the debtor's default. Should the secured party fail to comply with his or her duties, the debtor is afforded particular rights and remedies.

The topic of default is one of great concern to secured lenders and to the lawyers who draft security agreements. What constitutes default is not always clear. In fact, Article 9 does not define the term. Consequently, parties are encouraged in practice—and by the UCC—to include in their security agreements certain standards to be applied in determining when default has actually occurred. In so doing, parties can stipulate the conditions that will constitute a default [UCC 9–601 and 9–603]. Often, these critical terms are shaped by the creditor in an attempt to provide the maximum protection possible. The ultimate terms, however, are not allowed to go beyond the limitations imposed by the good faith requirement and the unconscionability provisions of the UCC. Article 9's definition of good faith includes "honesty in fact and the observance of reasonable commercial standards of fair dealing" [UCC 9–102(a)(43)].

Although any breach of the terms of the security agreement can constitute default, default occurs most commonly when the debtor fails to meet the scheduled payments that the parties have agreed on or when the debtor becomes bankrupt.

BASIC REMEDIES

A secured party's remedies can be divided into two basic categories:

① A secured party can take peaceful or judicial possession of the collateral covered by the security agreement [UCC 9–609(b)]. On taking possession, the secured party may either want to retain the collateral for satisfaction of the debt [UCC 9–620] or resell the goods and apply the proceeds toward the debt [UCC 9–610].

② A secured party can relinquish a security interest and use any judicial remedy available, such as proceeding to judgment on the underlying debt, followed by execution and levy. (**Execution** is the implementation of a court's decree or judgment. **Levy** is the obtaining of funds by legal process through the seizure and sale of noncollateralized property, usually done after a writ of execution has been issued.) Execution and levy are rarely undertaken unless the collateral is no longer in existence or has declined so much in value that it is worth substantially less than the amount of the debt and the debtor has other assets available that may be legally seized to satisfy the debt [UCC 9–601(a)].[7]

EXECUTION
An action to carry into effect the directions in a court decree or judgment.

LEVY
The obtaining of money by legal process through the seizure and sale of property, usually done after a writ of execution has been issued.

The rights and remedies under UCC 9–601(a) are *cumulative* [UCC 9–601(c)]. Therefore, if a creditor is unsuccessful in enforcing rights by one method, he or she can pursue another method.[8]

7. Some assets are exempt from creditors' claims—see Chapter 23.

8. See James J. White and Robert S. Summers, *Uniform Commercial Code,* 4th ed. (St. Paul: West Publishing Co., 1995), pp. 908–909.

When a security agreement covers both real and personal property, the secured party can proceed against the personal property in accordance with the remedies of Article 9. Alternatively, the secured party can proceed against the entire collateral under procedures set down by local real estate law, in which case the UCC does not apply [UCC 9–604(a)]. Determining whether particular collateral is personal or real property at times can prove difficult, especially when dealing with fixtures—things affixed to real property. Under certain circumstances, the UCC allows the removal of fixtures on default; such removal, however, is subject to the provisions of Article 9 [UCC 9–604(c)].

It is clear that a creditor can retain collateral in full satisfaction of a debt. The issue in the following case was whether a creditor could retain the collateral in *partial* satisfaction of the debt.

CASE 22.2 Banks Brothers Corp. v. Donovan Floors, Inc.

Wisconsin Court of Appeals, 2000.
2000 WI App 253,
239 Wis.2d 381,
620 N.W.2d 631.
http://www.wisbar.org/WisCtApp/index.html[a]

FACTS Donovan Floors, Inc., and Breakfall, Inc., two companies controlled by James and Jo-Ann Donovan, borrowed $245,000 from Bank One, Milwaukee, N.A.[b] The companies gave Bank One security interests in their assets, and the Donovans gave the lender a mortgage on their home. When Donovan Floors and Breakfall defaulted on the debt in 1991, Bank One filed a suit in a Wisconsin state court against the debtors. The Donovans agreed to surrender to Bank One some of the firms' assets and agreed to a foreclosure on the home. Bank One promised not to act on the agreement immediately to give the Donovans a chance to revitalize their business. In 1993, Bank One assigned the debt and its security interest to Banks Brothers Corporation. Banks, the Donovans, and the Donovans' firms (Donovan Floors and Breakfall) signed an agreement under which, among other things, Banks was given some of the firms' assets (three cars, a truck, and a van), and Breakfall was released from the debt while the others remained liable. A payment schedule was set up, but none of the payments were made. Six years later, Banks scheduled a sale of the house. The Donovans and Donovan Floors filed a suit in a Wisconsin state court against Banks, arguing that the creditor's retention of assets and release of Breakfall operated as a full satisfaction of the debt. The court denied the request, and the debtors appealed to a state intermediate appellate court.

ISSUE Can a creditor retain collateral that secures a debt in less than full satisfaction of the debt?

DECISION Yes. The state intermediate appellate court affirmed the order of the lower court.

REASON The appellate court acknowledged that "[u]nderstandably, the Donovans and Donovan Floors would love to have their cake (the chance to save their business given to them by Banks's agreement to hold off on its right to claim the assets pledged for the debt) and eat it also (keep those assets). But that is not the way [Article 9] works. Banks had a right * * * to immediate strict foreclosure of all the pledged assets. It gave up that right in consideration for a partial payment on the debt and the concomitant [accompanying] partial satisfaction. The Donovans and Donovan Floors have no legal or moral ground to complain; they agreed to that arrangement, and did so in a statement signed after default." The court noted that although this case involved a provision in effect before the revision of Article 9, under the revised article's UCC 9–620, the result would have been the same.

FOR CRITICAL ANALYSIS—Economic Consideration *What might be the effect on a lender's willingness to loan money if the law allowed the lender to retain collateral only in full satisfaction of the debt?*

a. In the "Court of Appeals Archive" section, click on "Index of 2000 Published Opinions." On that page, scroll to the "November, 2000" section and the name of the case, and click on the docket number to access the opinion. The State Bar of Wisconsin maintains this Web site.

b. The initials *N.A.* stand for National Association.

Repossession of Collateral—The Self-Help Remedy

RECALL A trespass to land occurs when a person, without permission, enters onto another's land and is established as a trespasser.

On the debtor's default, the secured party is entitled to take peaceful possession of the collateral without the use of judicial process [UCC 9–609(b)]. The UCC does not define *peaceful possession,* however. The general rule is that the collateral has been taken peacefully if the secured party can take possession without committing: (1) trespass onto realty, (2) assault and/or battery, or (3) breaking and entering.

ETHICAL ISSUE 22.1

Do the benefits of the "self-help" provision of Article 9 outweigh its potential harm?

The "self-help" provision of Article 9 has generated substantial controversy because of its potential adverse consequences for both creditors and debtors. If a repossession attempt results in a "breach of the peace," the creditor may be barred from recovering the remainder of the debt from the debtor, and the breach may result in tort liability as well. A breach of the peace can, in turn, be emotionally distressful for the debtor. For example, suppose that a creditor (or someone hired by the creditor) appears on the debtor's property in the middle of the night to repossess collateral. A debtor in this situation may logically assume that someone is trying to steal his or her property; thus, violence and a "breach of the peace" may ensue. Additionally, in some cases, creditors (or persons hired by creditors) have engaged in outrageous conduct when repossessing collateral, which again may result in a breach of the peace (see, for example, the *Question of Ethics and Social Responsibility* at the end of this chapter). Finally, the "self-help" provision implicitly gives debtors a motive for resorting to violence and forcing a confrontation when collateral is being repossessed—because if the creditor breaches the peace, the creditor may be barred from recovering the rest of the debt.

Disposition of Collateral

Once default has occurred and the secured party has obtained possession of the collateral, the secured party may attempt to retain the collateral in full satisfaction of the debt or may sell, lease, or otherwise dispose of the collateral in any commercially reasonable manner [UCC 9–602(7), 9–603, 9–610(a), and 9–620]. Any sale is always subject to procedures established by state law.

Retention of Collateral by the Secured Party The UCC acknowledges that parties are sometimes better off if they do not sell the collateral. Therefore, a secured party may retain the collateral unless it consists of consumer goods subject to a PMSI and the debtor has paid 60 percent or more of the purchase price or debt—as will be discussed shortly [UCC 9–620(e)].

This general right, however, is subject to several conditions. The secured party must send notice of the proposal to the debtor if the debtor has not signed a statement renouncing or modifying her or his rights *after default* [UCC 9–620(a) and 9–621]. If the collateral is consumer goods, the secured party does not need to give any other notice. In all other situations, the secured party must also send notice to any other secured party from whom the secured party has received written or authenticated notice of a claim of interest in the collateral in question and any other junior lien claimant (one holding a lien that is subordinate to a prior lien) who has filed a statutory lien (such as a mechanic's lien—see Chapter 23) or a security interest in the collateral ten days before the debtor consented to the retention [UCC 9–621].

If, within twenty days after the notice is sent, the secured party receives an objection sent by a person entitled to receive notification, the secured party must sell or otherwise dispose of the collateral in accordance with the provisions of UCC 9–602, 9–603, 9–610, and 9–613 (disposition procedures will be discussed shortly). If no such written objection is forthcoming, the secured party may retain the collateral in full or partial satisfaction of the debtor's obligation [UCC 9–620(a) and 9–621].

Consumer Goods When the collateral is consumer goods with a PMSI and the debtor has paid 60 percent or more of the debt or the purchase price, the secured party must sell or otherwise dispose of the repossessed collateral within ninety days [UCC 9–620(e) and (f)]. Failure to comply opens the secured party to an action for conversion or other liability under UCC 9–625(b) and (c) unless the consumer-debtor signed a written statement *after default* renouncing or modifying the right to demand the sale of the goods [UCC 9–624].

REMEMBER Conversion is a tort that consists of an act depriving an owner of personal property without the owner's permission.

Disposition Procedures A secured party who does not choose to retain the collateral or who is required to sell it must resort to the disposition procedures prescribed under UCC 9–602(7), 9–603, 9–610(a), and 9–613. The UCC allows a great deal of flexibility with regard to disposition. UCC 9–610(a) states that after default, a secured party may sell, lease, license, or otherwise dispose of any or all of the collateral in its present condition or following any commercially reasonable preparation or processing. While the secured party may purchase the collateral at a public sale, it may not do so at a private sale—unless the collateral is of a kind customarily sold on a recognized market or is the subject of widely distributed standard price quotations [UCC 9–610(c)].

One of the major limitations with respect to the disposition of collateral is that it be accomplished in a commercially reasonable manner. UCC 9–610(b) states as follows:

> Every aspect of a disposition of collateral, including the method, manner, time, place, and other terms, must be commercially reasonable. If commercially reasonable, a secured party may dispose of collateral by public or private proceedings, by one or more contracts, as a unit or in parcels, and at any time and place and on any terms.

Unless the collateral is perishable or will decline rapidly in value or is a type customarily sold on a recognized market, a secured party must send to the debtor and other identified persons "a reasonable authenticated notification of disposition" [UCC 9–611(b) and (c)]. The debtor may waive the right to receive this notice, but only after default [UCC 9–624(a)].

How accurate should such a notice be in terms of informing a debtor of the amount owed, the date of the sale (if the collateral is to be sold), and other details? The court addressed this question in the following case.

CASE 22.3 Fielder v. Credit Acceptance Corp.

United States District Court,
Western District of Missouri, 1998.
19 F.Supp.2d 966.

COMPANY PROFILE *For more than twenty-five years, Credit Acceptance Corporation (CAC) has helped thousands of auto dealers in the United States, Canada, and the United Kingdom obtain funds for used-car loans to people who have difficulty obtaining credit from other lenders. CAC's services include accounts management,*

(continued)

CASE 22.3—Continued

payment collection, and staff training. The firm also provides credit life and disability insurance, vehicle protection insurance, vehicle service contracts, and risk-assessment and fraud-alert services.

FACTS Marvin Fielder and others signed contracts with Northeast Auto Credit, Inc. (NAC), and others to buy used cars. The sellers assigned the contracts to Credit Acceptance Corporation (CAC), which had supplied the contract forms to the sellers. When the buyers defaulted on the loans, CAC repossessed the cars and sent notices that they would be sold. Some of the notices overstated the amounts needed to redeem the vehicles (redemption rights are discussed later in this chapter) without indicating that the figures might be wrong. Others misstated the redemption dates or the dates of the sales. When CAC sold the cars for less than was owed under the contracts, it attempted to collect the difference. Fielder and other buyers filed a suit against CAC and NAC, charging in part that the notices violated Article 9.[a] Both sides filed motions for summary judgment in a federal district court.

a. This case was decided before the effective date of the revised version of Article 9, but the result would likely have been the same. See UCC 9–613 and 9–614.

ISSUE Does a presale notice violate Article 9 if it misstates the amount by which the collateral may be redeemed, without indicating that fact, or if it misstates the date by which the collateral may be redeemed or sold?

DECISION Yes. The court issued a summary judgment in the plaintiffs' favor for notices that contained inflated figures, without indicating that possibility, and for notices that misstated the redemption or sale dates.

REASON The court found that some of the notices violated Article 9 because the figures were "unreasonably misleading" as to the amounts owed and the notices did not tell the debtors that the figures might be inaccurate. The court reasoned that "the debtors did not have reasonable notification of the sale because such notice is designed to ensure the debtors are aware of their rights which include redemption." The court also held that the notices containing defects as to the dates of redemption or the dates of sale violated Article 9.

FOR CRITICAL ANALYSIS—Social Consideration
How could CAC have avoided the result in this case?

Proceeds from Disposition Proceeds from the disposition of collateral after default on the underlying debt are distributed in the following order:

① Expenses incurred by the secured party in repossessing, storing, and reselling the collateral.

② Balance of the debt owed to the secured party.

③ Junior lienholders who have made written or authenticated demands.

④ Unless the collateral consists of accounts, payment intangibles, promissory notes, or chattel paper, any surplus goes to the debtor [UCC 9–608(a) and 9–615(a) and (e)].

Noncash Proceeds Whenever the secured party receives noncash proceeds from the disposition of collateral after default, the secured party must make a value determination and apply this value in a commercially reasonable manner [UCC 9–608(a)(3) and 9–615(c)].

DEFICIENCY JUDGMENT
A judgment against a debtor for the amount of a debt remaining unpaid after collateral has been repossessed and sold.

Deficiency Judgment Often, after proper disposition of the collateral, the secured party has not collected all that the debtor still owes. Unless otherwise agreed, the debtor is liable for any deficiency, and the creditor can obtain a **deficiency judgment** from a court to collect the deficiency. Note, however, that if the underlying transaction was, for example, a sale of accounts or of chattel paper, the debtor is entitled to any surplus or is liable for any deficiency only if the security agreement so provides [UCC 9–615(d) and (e)].

Whenever the secured party fails to conduct a disposition in a commercially reasonable manner or to give proper notice, the deficiency of the debtor is reduced to the extent that such failure affected the price received at the disposition [UCC 9–626(a)(3)].

Redemption Rights At any time before the secured party disposes of the collateral or enters into a contract for its disposition, or before the debtor's obligation has been discharged through the secured party's retention of the collateral, the debtor or any other secured party can exercise the right of *redemption* of the collateral. The debtor or other secured party can do this by tendering performance of all obligations secured by the collateral and by paying the expenses reasonably incurred by the secured party in retaking and maintaining the collateral [UCC 9–623].

APPLICATION **Law and the Creditor . . .**

Perfecting Your Security Interest*

The importance of perfecting your security interest cannot be overemphasized, particularly when the debt is large and you wish to maximize the priority of your security interest in the debtor's collateral. Failure to perfect or to perfect properly may result in your becoming the equivalent of an unsecured creditor.

PERFECTION BY FILING

The filing of a financing statement in the appropriate location, as discussed in this chapter, is the most common method of perfection. Generally, the moment the filing takes place, your priority over the other creditors—as well as over some purchasers of the collateral and a subsequent trustee in bankruptcy—is established.

When you create a security agreement, describe the collateral in terms that are specific enough to put third parties on notice of your security interest in that collateral. If your description is insufficient or misleading, your security interest will not be perfected.

TRANSACTIONS OUTSIDE NORMAL BUSINESS RELATIONSHIPS

Sometimes, credit transactions occur outside normal business relationships. You may be asked, for example, to aid an associate, a relative, or a friend. At that moment, you should reflect on your need for security for any debt that will be owed to you.

If there is a need for security, then you should perfect your security interest, even if you believe this action is unnecessary because the debtor is a friend or a relative. That particular friendship or blood relationship is irrelevant should he or she ever enter into bankruptcy proceedings. Bankruptcy law does not allow friends or relatives to be paid ahead of nonfriends or nonrelatives. You will end up standing in line with the other unsecured creditors if you have not perfected your security interest in the collateral. The best way to protect your security interest by perfection is to have your friend, relative, or associate transfer to your possession the collateral—stocks, bonds, jewelry, or whatever. By possessing such collateral, you can keep the transaction private but still have security for the loan.

*This *Application* is not meant to substitute for the services of an attorney who is licensed to practice law in your state.

CHECKLIST FOR PERFECTING YOUR SECURITY INTEREST

1. File a financing statement promptly.
2. Describe the collateral sufficiently—sometimes, it is better to err by giving too much detail than by giving too little detail.
3. Even with friends, relatives, or associates, be sure to perfect your security interest, perhaps by having the debtor transfer the collateral to your possession.

Key Terms

after-acquired property 592
attachment 581
collateral 579
continuation statement 591
debtor 579
default 579
deficiency judgment 602
execution 598
financing statement 579
floating lien 593
levy 598
perfection 586
pledge 590
proceeds 591
purchase-money security interest (PMSI) 591
secured party 579
secured transaction 578
security agreement 579
security interest 579

Chapter Summary Secured Transactions

Creating a Security Interest (See pages 581–586.)	1. Unless the creditor has possession of the collateral, there must be a written or authenticated security agreement signed or authenticated by the debtor describing the collateral subject to the security interest. 2. The secured party must give value to the debtor. 3. The debtor must have rights in the collateral—some ownership interest or right to obtain possession of the specified collateral.
Perfecting a Security Interest (See pages 586–591.)	1. *Perfection by filing*—The most common method of perfection is by filing a financing statement containing the names of the secured party and the debtor and indicating the collateral covered by the financing statement. a. Communication of the financing statement to the appropriate filing office, together with the correct filing fee, constitutes a filing. b. The financing statement must be filed under the name of the debtor; fictitious (trade) names normally are not accepted. c. The classification of collateral determines whether filing is necessary and where to file (see Exhibit 22–3). 2. *Perfection without filing*— a. By transfer of collateral—The debtor can transfer possession of the collateral to the secured party. For example, a *pledge* is this type of transfer. b. By attachment, such as the attachment of a purchase-money security interest (PMSI) in consumer goods. If the secured party has a PMSI in consumer goods (goods bought or used by the debtor for personal, family, or household purposes), the secured party's security interest is perfected automatically. In all, thirteen types of security interests can be perfected by attachment.
The Scope of a Security Interest (See pages 591–592.)	A security agreement can cover the following types of property: 1. *Collateral in the present possession or control of the debtor.* 2. *Proceeds from a sale, exchange, or disposition of secured collateral.* 3. *After-acquired property*—A security agreement may provide that property acquired after the execution of the security agreement will also be secured by the agreement. This provision often accompanies security agreements covering a debtor's inventory. 4. *Future advances*—A security agreement may provide that any future advances made against a line of credit will be subject to the initial security interest in the same collateral.

Chapter Summary Secured Transactions—continued

<table>
<tr><td>Priority of Claims to a Debtor's Collateral
(See page 596.)</td><td>See Exhibit 22–5.</td></tr>
<tr><td>Rights and Duties of Debtors and Creditors
(See pages 596–598.)</td><td>1. Information request—On request by any person, the filing officer must send a statement listing the file number, the date, and the hour of the filing of financing statements and other documents covering collateral of a particular debtor; a fee is charged.
2. Release, assignment, and amendment—A secured party may (a) release part or all of the collateral described in a filed financing statement, thus ending the creditor's security interest; (b) assign part or all of the security interest to another party; and (c) amend a filed financing statement.
3. Confirmation or accounting request by debtor—If a debtor believes that the unpaid debt amount or the listing of the collateral subject to the security interest is inaccurate, the debtor has the right to request a confirmation of his or her view of the unpaid debt or listing of collateral. The secured party must authenticate and send to the debtor an accounting within fourteen days after the request is received. Only one request without charge is permitted per six-month period.
4. Termination statement—When a debt is paid, the secured party generally must send a termination statement to the debtor or file such a statement with the filing officer to whom the original financing statement was given. Failure to comply results in the secured party's liability to the debtor for $500 plus any loss suffered by the debtor.
a. If the financing statement covers consumer goods, the termination statement must be filed by the secured party within one month after the debt is paid, or if the debtor makes an authenticated demand, it must be filed within twenty days of the demand or one month after the debt is paid—whichever is earlier.
b. In all other cases, the termination statement must be filed or furnished to the debtor within twenty days after an authenticated demand is made by the debtor.</td></tr>
<tr><td>Default
(See pages 598–603.)</td><td>On the debtor's default, the secured party may do either of the following:
1. Take possession (peacefully or by court order) of the collateral covered by the security agreement and then pursue one of two alternatives:
a. Retain the collateral (unless the secured party has a PMSI in consumer goods and the debtor has paid 60 percent or more of the selling price or loan), in which case the secured party must—
(1) Give notice to the debtor if the debtor has not signed a statement renouncing or modifying his or her rights after default. With consumer goods, no other notice is necessary.
(2) Send notice to any other secured party who has given written or authenticated notice of a claim to the same collateral or who has filed a security interest or a statutory lien ten days before the debtor consented to the retention. If an objection is received from the debtor or any other secured party given notice within twenty days, the creditor must dispose of the collateral according to the requirements of UCC 9–602, 9–603, 9–610, and 9–613. Otherwise, the creditor may retain the collateral in full or partial satisfaction of the debt.
b. Dispose of the collateral in accordance with the requirements of UCC 9–602(7), 9–603, 9–610(a), and 9–613, in which case the secured party must—</td></tr>
</table>

(continued)

Chapter Summary Secured Transactions—continued

Default—continued	(1) Dispose of (sell, lease, or license) the goods in a commercially reasonable manner. (2) Notify the debtor and (except in sales of consumer goods) other identified persons, including those who have given notice of claims to the collateral to be sold (unless the collateral is perishable or will decline rapidly in value). (3) Apply the proceeds in the following order: (a) Expenses incurred by the secured party in repossessing, storing, and reselling the collateral. (b) The balance of the debt owed to the secured party. (c) Junior lienholders who have made written or authenticated demands. (d) Surplus to the debtor (unless the collateral consists of accounts, payment intangibles, promissory notes, or chattel paper). 2. Relinquish the security interest and proceed with any judicial remedy available, such as to reduce the claim to judgment on the underlying debt, followed by execution and levy on the nonexempt assets of the debtor.

For Review

① What is a security interest? Who is a secured party? What is a security agreement? What is a financing statement?

② What three requirements must be met to create an enforceable security interest?

③ What is the most common method of perfecting a security interest under Article 9?

④ If two secured parties have perfected security interests in the collateral of the debtor, which party has priority to the collateral on the debtor's default?

⑤ What rights does a secured creditor have on the debtor's default?

Questions and Case Problems

22–1. Priority Disputes. Redford is a seller of electric generators. He purchases a large quantity of generators from a manufacturer, Mallon Corp., by making a down payment and signing an agreement to make the balance of payments over a period of time. The agreement gives Mallon Corp. a security interest in the generators and the proceeds. Mallon Corp. files a financing statement on its security interest properly. Redford receives the generators and immediately sells one of them to Garfield on an installment contract, with payment to be made in twelve equal installments. At the time of sale, Garfield knows of Mallon's security interest. Two months later Redford goes into default on his payments to Mallon. Discuss Mallon's rights against purchaser Garfield in this situation.

22–2. Oral Security Agreements. Marsh has a prize horse named Arabian Knight. Marsh is in need of working capital. She borrows $5,000 from Mendez, who takes possession of Arabian Knight as security for the loan. No written agreement is signed. Discuss whether, in the absence of a written agreement, Mendez has a security interest in Arabian Knight. If Mendez does have a security interest, is it a perfected security interest?

22–3. Default. Delgado is a retail seller of television sets. He sells a color television set to Cummings for $600. Cummings cannot pay cash, so she signs a security agreement, paying $100 down and agreeing to pay the balance in twelve equal installments of $50 each. The security agreement gives Delgado a security interest in the television set sold. Cummings makes six payments on time; then she goes into default because of unexpected financial problems. Delgado repossesses the set and wants to keep it in full satisfaction of the debt. Discuss Delgado's rights and duties in this matter.

22–4. The Scope of a Security Interest. Edward owned a retail sporting goods shop. A new ski resort was being created in his area, and to take advantage of the potential business, Edward decided to expand his operations. He borrowed a large sum of money from his bank, which took a security interest in his present inventory and any after-acquired inventory as collateral for the loan. The bank properly perfected the security interest by filing a financing statement. Edward's business was profitable, so he doubled his inventory. A year later, just a few months after the ski resort had opened, an avalanche destroyed the ski slope and lodge. Edward's business consequently took a turn for the worse, and he defaulted on his debt to the bank. The bank then sought possession of his entire inventory, even though the inventory was now twice as large as it had been when the loan was made. Edward claimed that the bank only had rights to half of his inventory. Is Edward correct? Explain.

22–5. Perfection. Richard E. Walker, Kelly E. Walker, and Kenneth W. Walker were partners in the Walker Brothers Dairy, a general partnership located in Florida. The Walkers purchased a "Model 2955 utility tractor, a round bale saw, and a feed mixer box" from the John Deere Co. John Deere took a security interest in the equipment. The security agreement stated that the debtor was a partnership known as "Walker Brothers Dairy." John Deere filed a financing statement, however, that listed the debtors as "Richard Walker, Kelly Walker, and Kenneth Wendell Walker." Each of the three partners signed the statement. Their signatures were followed by a typewritten declaration indicating that the partners were doing business as "Walker Brothers Dairy." When Walker Brothers Dairy voluntarily filed for bankruptcy, John Deere sought to repossess the equipment. The issue before the court was whether the financing statement, which listed as debtors the partners rather than the partnership, was sufficient to perfect John Deere's security interest in the partnership equipment. What should the court decide? Discuss. [*In re Walker,* 142 Bankr. 482 (M.D.Fla. 1992)]

22–6. Sale of Collateral. To pay for the purchases of several aircraft, Robert Wall borrowed funds from the Cessna Finance Corp., using the aircraft as collateral. Wall defaulted on the loans. Cessna took possession of the collateral (the aircraft) and sold it. Cessna filed a suit in a federal district court against Wall for the difference between the amount due on the loans and the amount received from the sale of the aircraft. Wall claimed that he could have obtained a higher price for the aircraft if he had sold them himself. How does the question of whether a better price could have been obtained affect the issue of whether the sale was commercially reasonable? Discuss. [*Cessna Finance Corp. v. Wall,* 876 F.Supp. 273 (M.D.Ga. 1994)]

22–7. Debtor's Name. Cambria Fuel Oil Co. sold its business to 306 Fuel Oil Corp. As part of the deal, Cambria Fuel took a security interest in 306 Fuel's assets and filed a financing statement that identified 306 Fuel as the debtor. Six weeks later, 306 Fuel changed its name to Cambria Petroleum Co. Cambria Fuel did not file a new financing statement. Fleet Factors Corp. loaned money to Cambria Petroleum and took a security interest in the same assets as those subject to Cambria Fuel's security interest. When Cambria Petroleum failed to repay the loan, Fleet Factors filed suit in a New York state court to foreclose its security interest. Cambria Fuel claimed that its interest had priority. Whose security interest has priority? Why? [*Fleet Factors Corp. v. Bandolene Industries Corp.,* 86 N.Y.2d 519, 658 N.E.2d 202, 634 N.Y.S.2d 425 (1995)]

22–8. Repossession. Leroy Headspeth bought a car under an installment sales contract that expressly permitted the creditor to repossess the car if the debtor defaulted on the payments. The seller assigned the contract to Mercedes-Benz Credit Corp. (MBCC). When Headspeth defaulted on the payments, an agent of Laurel Adjustment Bureau, Inc. (LAB), went onto Headspeth's property and repossessed the car on MBCC's behalf. Headspeth filed a suit against MBCC and LAB, contending in part that LAB trespassed onto his property to retake the car and that therefore the repossession was wrongful. Headspeth admitted that the repossession occurred without confrontation. Can a secured creditor legally retake possession of collateral, on the debtor's default, by entering onto the debtor's land, or would that be an illegal breach of the peace? How will the court rule? Explain. [*Headspeth v. Mercedes-Benz Credit Corp.,* 709 A.2d 717 (D.C.App. 1998)]

22–9. Financing Statement. In 1994, SouthTrust Bank, N.A., loaned money to Environmental Aspecs, Inc. (EAI), and its subsidiary, EAI of NC. SouthTrust perfected its security interest by filing financing statements that listed only EAI as the debtor, described only EAI's assets as collateral, and was signed only on EAI's behalf. SouthTrust believed that both companies were operating as a single business represented by EAI. In 1996, EAI of NC borrowed almost $300,000 from Advanced Analytics Laboratories, Inc. (AAL). AAL filed financing statements that listed the assets of EAI of NC as collateral but identified the debtor as EAI. The statements referred, however, to attached copies of the security agreements, which were signed by the president of EAI of NC and identified the debtor as EAI of NC. One year later, EAI and EAI of NC renegotiated their loan with SouthTrust, and the bank filed financing statements listing both companies as debtors. In 1998, EAI and EAI of NC filed for bankruptcy. One of the issues was the priority of the security interests of SouthTrust and AAL. AAL contended that its failure to identify, on its financing statements, EAI of NC as the debtor did not give SouthTrust priority. Is AAL correct? Why or why not? [*In re Environmental Aspecs, Inc.,* 235 Bankr. 378 (E.D.N.C., Raleigh Div. 1999)]

TEST YOUR KNOWLEDGE—ANSWER ON THE WEB

22–10. When a customer opens a credit-card account with Sears, Roebuck & Co., the customer fills out an application and sends it to Sears for review; if the application is approved, the customer receives a Sears card. The application contains a security agreement, a copy of which is also sent with the card. When a customer buys an item using the card, the customer signs a sales receipt that describes the merchandise and contains language granting Sears a purchase-money security interest (PMSI) in the merchandise. Dayna Conry bought a variety of consumer goods from Sears on her card. When she did not make payments on her account, Sears filed a suit against her in an Illinois state court to repossess the goods. Conry filed for bankruptcy and was granted a discharge. Sears then filed a suit against her to obtain possession of the goods through its PMSI, but it could not find Conry's credit-card application to offer into evidence. Is a signed Sears sales receipt sufficient proof of its security interest? In whose favor should the court rule? Explain. [*Sears, Roebuck & Co. v. Conry,* 321 Ill.App.3d 997, 748 N.E.2d 1248, 255 Ill.Dec. 178 (3 Dist. 2001)]

A QUESTION OF ETHICS AND SOCIAL RESPONSIBILITY

22–11. Raymond and Joan Massengill borrowed money from Indiana National Bank (INB) to purchase a van. Toward the end of the loan period, the Massengills were notified by mail that they were delinquent on their last two loan payments. Joan called INB and said that she and her husband would go to the bank the following Monday morning and take care of the matter. In the meantime, INB had made arrangements for the van to be repossessed. At 1:30 A.M. Sunday morning, two men appeared at the Massengills' driveway and began to hook up the van to a tow truck. Raymond, assuming that the van was being stolen, went outside to intervene and did so vociferously. During the course of events, Massengill became entangled in machinery at the rear of the tow truck and was dragged down the street and then run over by his towed van. The "repo men"—those hired by INB to repossess the van—knew of Raymond's plight but sped away. The trial court granted summary judgment for the bank, ruling that the bank was not liable for the injuries caused by the repossession company. On appeal, however, the court ruled that the bank could be liable for the acts of the repossession company and remanded the case for the determination of damages. [*Massengill v. Indiana National Bank,* 550 N.E.2d 97 (Ind.App.1st Dist. 1990)]

1. Frequently, courts must decide, as in this case, whether the secured party should be held liable for the wrongful acts of persons hired as independent contractors by the secured party to undertake an actual repossession effort. Is it fair to hold the secured party liable for acts that the creditor did not commit? Why or why not?
2. Given the potential for violence during repossession efforts, why do you think Article 9 permits secured parties to resort to "self-help" repossessions?
3. Should repossession companies be prohibited from taking collateral from debtors' property during the middle of the night, when debtors are more likely to conclude that the activity is wrongful?

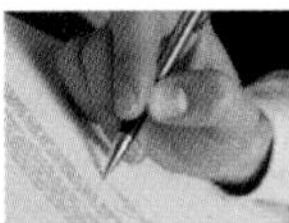

FOR CRITICAL ANALYSIS

22–12. Review the three requirements for an enforceable security interest. Why is each of these requirements necessary?

Internet Exercises

Go to the *Business Law Today* home page at **http://blt.westbuslaw.com**. Select "Interactive Study Center" and then click on "Chapter 22." There you will find the following Internet research exercise that you can perform to learn more about the repossession of collateral under Article 9:

Activity 22–1: Repossession

Before the Test

Go to the *Business Law Today* home page at **http://blt.westbuslaw.com**. Click on "Interactive Quizzes." You will find at least twenty interactive questions relating to this chapter.

CHAPTER 23

Creditors' Rights and Bankruptcy

"Creditors are . . . great observers of set days and times."

Benjamin Franklin, 1706–1790
(American diplomat, author, and scientist)

CHAPTER CONTENTS

LEARNING OBJECTIVES

After reading this chapter, you should be able to answer the following questions:

① What is a prejudgment attachment? What is a writ of execution? How does a creditor use these remedies?

② What is garnishment? When might a creditor undertake a garnishment proceeding?

③ In a bankruptcy proceeding, what constitutes the debtor's estate in property? What property is exempt from the estate under federal bankruptcy law?

④ What is the difference between an exception to discharge and an objection to discharge?

⑤ In a Chapter 11 reorganization, what is the role of the debtor in possession?

America's font of practical wisdom, Benjamin Franklin, observed a truth known to all debtors—that creditors do observe "set days and times" and will expect to recover their money on the agreed-on dates. Historically, debtors and their families have been subjected to punishment, including involuntary servitude and imprisonment, for their inability to pay debts. The modern legal system, however, has moved away from a punishment philosophy in dealing with debtors. In fact, many observers say that it has moved too far in the other direction, to the detriment of creditors.

Normally, creditors have no problem collecting the debts owed to them. When disputes arise over the amount owed, however, or when the debtor simply cannot or will not pay, what happens? What remedies are available to creditors when debtors default? We have already discussed, in Chapter 22, the remedies available to secured creditors under Article 9 of the Uniform Commercial Code (UCC). In the first part of this chapter, we focus on other laws that assist the debtor and creditor in resolving their disputes without the debtor's having to resort to bankruptcy. The second part of this chapter discusses bankruptcy as a last resort in resolving debtor-creditor problems.

"Creditors: One of a tribe of savages dwelling beyond the Financial Straits and dreaded for their desolating incursions."

AMBROSE BIERCE, 1842–1914 (American writer)

Laws Assisting Creditors

Both the common law and statutory laws other than Article 9 of the UCC create various rights and remedies for creditors. We discuss here some of these rights and remedies.

Painters finish the trim on a house. If the homeowner does not pay for the work, what can the painters do to collect what they are owed?

LIENS

As discussed in Chapter 18, a *lien* is an encumbrance on (claim against) property to satisfy a debt or protect a claim for the payment of a debt. Creditors' liens include mechanic's, artisan's, innkeeper's, and judicial liens.

Mechanic's Lien When a person contracts for labor, services, or materials to be furnished for the purpose of making improvements on real property (land and things attached to the land, such as buildings and trees—see Chapter 37) but does not immediately pay for the improvements, the creditor can file a **mechanic's lien** on the property. This creates a special type of debtor-creditor relationship in which the real estate itself becomes security for the debt.

• **EXAMPLE 23.1** A painter agrees to paint a house for a homeowner for an agreed-on price to cover labor and materials. If the homeowner refuses to pay for the work or pays only a portion of the charges, a mechanic's lien against the property can be created. The painter is the lienholder, and the real property is encumbered (burdened) with a mechanic's lien for the amount owed. If the homeowner does not pay the lien, the property can be sold to satisfy the debt. Notice of the foreclosure (the process by which the creditor deprives the debtor of his or her property) and sale must be given to the debtor in advance, however. •

Note that state law governs mechanic's liens. The time period within which a mechanic's lien must be filed is usually 60 to 120 days from the last date labor or materials were provided.

MECHANIC'S LIEN
A statutory lien on the real property of another, created to ensure payment for work performed and materials furnished in the repair or improvement of real property, such as a building.

ARTISAN'S LIEN
A possessory lien given to a person who has made improvements and added value to another person's personal property as security for payment for services performed.

Artisan's Lien An **artisan's lien** is a security device created at common law through which a creditor can recover payment from a debtor for labor and materials furnished in the repair or improvement of personal property. • **EXAMPLE 23.2** Cindy leaves her diamond ring at the jeweler's to be repaired and to have her initials engraved on the band. In the absence of an agreement, the jeweler can keep the ring until Cindy pays for the services. Should Cindy fail to pay, the jeweler has a lien on Cindy's ring for the amount of the bill and normally can sell the ring in satisfaction of the lien. •

In contrast to a mechanic's lien, an artisan's lien is *possessory*. The lienholder ordinarily must have retained possession of the property and have expressly or impliedly agreed to provide the services on a cash, not a credit, basis. Usually, the lienholder retains possession of the property. When this occurs, the lien remains in existence as long as the lienholder maintains possession, and the lien is terminated once possession is voluntarily surrendered—unless the surrender is only temporary. If it is a temporary surrender, there must be an agreement that the property will be returned to the lienholder. Even with such an agreement, if a third party obtains rights in that property while it is out of the possession of the lienholder, the lien is lost. The only way that a lienholder can protect a lien and surrender possession at the same time is to record notice of the lien (if state law so permits) in accordance with state lien and recording statutes.

Modern statutes permit the holder of an artisan's lien to foreclose and sell the property subject to the lien to satisfy payment of the debt. As with the mechanic's lien, the holder of an artisan's lien is required to give notice to the owner of the property prior to foreclosure and sale. The sale proceeds are used to pay the debt and the costs of the legal proceedings, and the surplus, if any, is paid to the former owner.

INNKEEPER'S LIEN
A possessory lien placed on the luggage of hotel guests for hotel charges that remain unpaid.

Innkeeper's Lien An **innkeeper's lien** is another security device created at common law. An innkeeper's lien is placed on the baggage of guests for the agreed-on hotel charges that remain unpaid. If no express agreement has been made concerning the amount of those charges, then the lien will be for the reasonable value of the accommodations furnished. The innkeeper's lien is terminated either by the guest's payment of the hotel charges or by the innkeeper's surrender of the baggage to the guest, unless the surrender is temporary. Additionally, the lien is terminated by the innkeeper's foreclosure and sale of the property.

Judicial Liens When a debt is past due, a creditor can bring a legal action against the debtor to collect the debt. If the creditor is successful in the action, the court awards the creditor a judgment against the debtor (usually for the amount of the debt plus any interest and legal costs incurred in obtaining the judgment). Frequently, however, the creditor is unable to collect the awarded amount.

To ensure that a judgment in the creditor's favor will be collectible, creditors are permitted to request that certain nonexempt property of the debtor be seized to satisfy the debt. (As will be discussed later in this chapter, under state or federal statutes, certain property is exempt from attachment by creditors.) If the court orders the debtor's property to be seized prior to a judgment in the creditor's favor, the court's order is referred to as a *writ of attachment*. If the court orders the debtor's property to be seized following a judgment in the creditor's favor, the court's order is referred to as a *writ of execution*.

Attachment. Recall from Chapter 22 that *attachment*, in the context of secured transactions, refers to the process through which a security interest in a debtor's collateral becomes enforceable. In the context of judicial liens, this word has another meaning: **attachment** is a court-ordered seizure and taking into custody of property prior to the securing of a judgment for a past-due debt. Attachment rights are created by state statutes. Attachment is a *prejudgment* remedy because it occurs either at the time of or immediately after the commencement of a lawsuit and before the entry of a final judgment. By statute, to attach before judgment, a creditor must comply with specific restrictions and requirements. The due process clause of the Fourteenth Amendment to the U.S. Constitution limits the courts' power to authorize seizure of a debtor's property without notice to the debtor or a hearing on the facts.

ATTACHMENT
In the context of judicial liens, a court-ordered seizure and taking into custody of property prior to the securing of a judgment for a past-due debt.

To use attachment as a remedy, the creditor must have an enforceable right to payment of the debt under law and must follow certain procedures. Otherwise, the creditor can be liable for damages for wrongful attachment. She or he must file with the court an *affidavit* (a written or printed statement, made under oath or sworn to) stating that the debtor is in default and stating the statutory grounds under which attachment is sought. The creditor must also post a bond to cover at least court costs, the value of the loss of use of the good suffered by the debtor, and the value of the property attached. When the court is satisfied that all the requirements have been met, it issues a **writ of attachment**, which directs the sheriff or other public officer to seize nonexempt property. If the creditor prevails at trial, the seized property can be sold to satisfy the judgment.

WRIT OF ATTACHMENT
A court's order, prior to a trial to collect a debt, directing the sheriff or other officer to seize nonexempt property of the debtor. If the creditor prevails at trial, the seized property can be sold to satisfy the judgment.

Writ of Execution. If the debtor will not or cannot pay the judgment, the creditor is entitled to go back to the court and obtain a court order directing the sheriff to seize (levy) and sell any of the debtor's nonexempt real or personal property that is within the court's geographic jurisdiction (usually the county in which the courthouse is located). This order is called a **writ of execution.** The proceeds of the sale are used to pay off the judgment, accrued interest, and the costs of the sale. Any excess is paid to the debtor. The debtor can pay the judgment and redeem the nonexempt property any time before the sale takes place. (Because of exemption laws and bankruptcy laws, however, many judgments are virtually uncollectible.)

WRIT OF EXECUTION
A court's order, after a judgment has been entered against the debtor, directing the sheriff to seize (levy) and sell any of the debtor's nonexempt real or personal property. The proceeds of the sale are used to pay off the judgment, accrued interest, and costs of the sale; any surplus is paid to the debtor.

GARNISHMENT

GARNISHMENT
A legal process used by a creditor to collect a debt by seizing property of the debtor (such as wages) that is being held by a third party (such as the debtor's employer).

Garnishment occurs when a creditor is permitted to collect a debt by seizing property of the debtor that is being held by a third party. Typically, a garnishment judgment is served on a debtor's employer so that part of the debtor's usual paycheck will be paid to the creditor. As a result of a garnishment proceeding, the court orders the debtor's employer to turn over a portion of the debtor's wages to pay the debt.

The legal proceeding for a garnishment action is governed by state law, and garnishment operates differently from state to state. According to the laws in some states, the creditor needs to obtain only one order of garnishment, which will then continuously apply to the debtor's weekly wages until the entire debt is paid. In other states, the creditor must go back to court for a separate order of garnishment for each pay period. Garnishment is usually a postjudgment remedy, but it can be a prejudgment remedy with a proper hearing by a court.

Both federal laws and state laws limit the amount of money that can be garnished from a debtor's weekly take-home pay.[1] Federal law provides a framework to protect debtors from suffering unduly when paying judgment debts.[2] State laws also provide dollar exemptions, and these amounts are often larger than those provided by federal law. Under federal law, garnishment of an employee's wages for any one indebtedness cannot be a ground for dismissal of an employee.

CREDITORS' COMPOSITION AGREEMENTS

Creditors may contract with the debtor for discharge of the debtor's liquidated debts (debts that are definite, or fixed, in amount) on payment of a sum less than that owed. These agreements are called **creditors' composition agreements**, or simply *composition agreements,* and are usually held to be enforceable.

CREDITORS' COMPOSITION AGREEMENT
An agreement formed between a debtor and his or her creditors in which the creditors agree to accept a lesser sum than that owed by the debtor in full satisfaction of the debt.

1. Some states (for example, Texas) do not permit garnishment of wages by private parties except under a child-support order.
2. For example, the federal Consumer Credit Protection Act of 1968, 15 U.S.C. Sections 1601–1693r, provides that a debtor can retain either 75 percent of the disposable earnings per week or the sum equivalent to thirty hours of work paid at federal minimum-wage rates, whichever is greater.

MORTGAGE FORECLOSURE

Mortgage holders have the right to foreclose on mortgaged property in the event of a debtor's default. The usual method of foreclosure is by judicial sale of the property, although the statutory methods of foreclosure vary from state to state. If the proceeds of the foreclosure sale are sufficient to cover both the costs of the foreclosure and the mortgaged debt, the debtor receives any surplus. If the sale proceeds are insufficient to cover the foreclosure costs and the mortgaged debt, however, the **mortgagee** (the creditor-lender) can seek to recover the difference from the **mortgagor** (the debtor) by obtaining a deficiency judgment representing the difference between the mortgaged debt and the amount actually received from the proceeds of the foreclosure sale.

MORTGAGEE
Under a mortgage agreement, the creditor who takes a security interest in the debtor's property.

MORTGAGOR
Under a mortgage agreement, the debtor who gives the creditor a security interest in the debtor's property in return for a mortgage loan.

The mortgagee obtains a deficiency judgment in a separate legal action pursued subsequent to the foreclosure action. The deficiency judgment entitles the mortgagee to recover the amount of the deficiency from other property owned by the debtor.

SURETYSHIP AND GUARANTY

When a third person promises to pay a debt owed by another in the event the debtor does not pay, either a *suretyship* or a *guaranty* relationship is created. Suretyship and guaranty have a long history under the common law and provide creditors with the right to seek payment from the third party if the primary debtor defaults on his or her obligations. Exhibit 23–1 illustrates the relationship between a suretyship or guaranty party and the creditor.

EXHIBIT 23–1 SURETYSHIP AND GUARANTY PARTIES

In a suretyship or guaranty arrangement, a third party promises to be responsible for a debtor's obligations. A third party who agrees to be *primarily* liable for the debt (that is, liable even if the principal debtor does not default) is known as a surety; a third party who agrees to be *secondarily* liable for the debt (that is, liable only if the principal debtor defaults) is known as a guarantor. As noted in Chapter 11, normally a promise of guaranty (a collateral, or secondary, promise) must be in writing to be enforceable.

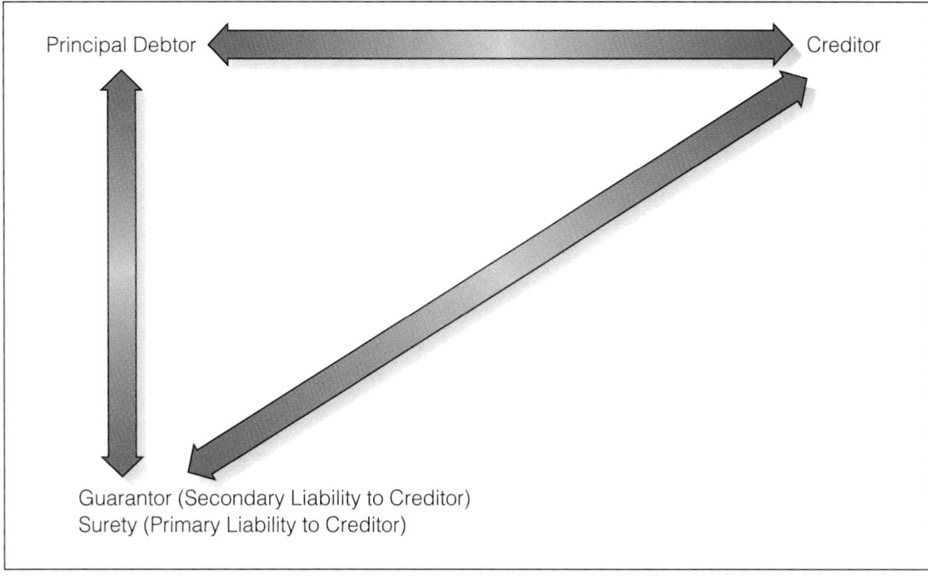

SURETYSHIP
An express contract in which a third party to a debtor-creditor relationship (the surety) promises to be primarily responsible for the debtor's obligation.

SURETY
A person, such as a cosigner on a note, who agrees to be primarily responsible for the debt of another.

Surety A contract of strict **suretyship** is a promise made by a third person to be responsible for the debtor's obligation. It is an express contract between the **surety** (the third party) and the creditor. The surety in the strictest sense is primarily liable for the debt of the principal. The creditor need not exhaust all legal remedies against the principal debtor before holding the surety responsible for payment. The creditor can demand payment from the surety from the moment the debt is due.

• **EXAMPLE 23.3** Robert Delmar wants to borrow money from the bank to buy a used car. Because Robert is still in college, the bank will not lend him the money unless his father, Joseph Delmar, who has dealt with the bank before, will cosign the note (add his signature to the note, thereby becoming a surety and thus jointly liable for payment of the debt). When Joseph Delmar cosigns the note, he becomes primarily liable to the bank. On the note's due date, the bank has the option of seeking payment from either Robert or Joseph Delmar, or both jointly.•

GUARANTOR
A person who agrees to satisfy the debt of another (the debtor) only after the principal debtor defaults; a guarantor's liability is thus secondary.

Guaranty A guaranty contract is similar to a suretyship contract in that it includes a promise to answer for the debt or default of another. With a guaranty arrangement, the **guarantor**—the third person making the guaranty—is *secondarily* liable. The guarantor can be required to pay the obligation *only after the principal debtor defaults,* and default usually takes place only after the creditor has made an attempt to collect from the debtor.

• **EXAMPLE 23.4** A small corporation, BX Enterprises, needs to borrow money to meet its payroll. The bank is skeptical about the creditworthiness of BX and requires Dawson, its president, who is a wealthy businessperson and the owner of 70 percent of BX Enterprises, to sign an agreement making himself personally liable for payment if BX does not pay off the loan. As a guarantor of the loan, Dawson cannot be held liable until BX Enterprises is in default.•

The Statute of Frauds requires that a guaranty contract between the guarantor and the creditor must be in writing to be enforceable unless the *main purpose* exception applies. As discussed in Chapter 11, this exception provides that if the main purpose of the guaranty agreement is to benefit the guarantor, then the contract need not be in writing to be enforceable.

In the following case, the issue was whether a guaranty of a lease signed by the president of a corporation was enforceable against the officer personally, although he claimed to have signed the guaranty only as a representative of the corporation.

CASE 23.1 Wilson Court Limited Partnership v. Tony Maroni's, Inc.

Supreme Court of Washington, 1998.
134 Wash.2d 692,
952 P.2d 590.

COMPANY PROFILE *Tony Riviera founded Tony Maroni's, Inc., to sell Tony Maroni's Famous Gourmet Pizza in Seattle, Washington, in the late 1980s. Tony Maroni's began by offering pizzas, salads, calzones, and lasagna for delivery only. By 1995, the firm had begun franchising (licensing its brand to investors to operate Tony Maroni's outlets—franchising is discussed in Chapter 31). Two years later, with eleven locations in the Seattle area, including six franchise outlets, and ten more stores in development, the company announced plans to open five hundred locations nationwide before 2002. Despite these plans, by the end of 1997, the firm had yet to turn a profit and was nearly $1 million in debt.*

FACTS Tony Maroni's, Inc., agreed to lease retail space owned by Wilson Court Limited Partnership. Tony Riviera, Tony Maroni's president, signed the lease for 1,676 square feet of space for a sixty-month term. The lease provided for improvements, estimated to be worth $45,520. Initially, Tony Maroni's contributed $5,000 toward the improvements and was to pay an additional

CASE 23.1—Continued

$7,000 over the life of the lease, at $148.73 per month. Wilson contributed the balance of $33,520. When he signed the lease, Riviera also signed a guaranty agreement that was incorporated by reference in the lease. On the signature line of the guaranty, Riviera wrote "President" after his name. The guaranty did not specifically identify who was bound, referring only to "the undersigned" or "Guarantor." Riviera also signed the lease in a representative capacity, but the lease clearly indicated that only Tony Maroni's was bound by its terms. When Tony Maroni's defaulted on the lease, Wilson filed a suit in a Washington state court against Tony Maroni's, Riviera, and others. Riviera asserted in part that he was not personally liable on the guaranty because he signed only in his capacity as a corporate officer. The court issued a summary judgment in favor of Wilson. Riviera appealed to the Washington Supreme Court.

ISSUE Was Riviera personally liable on the guaranty?

DECISION Yes. The Washington Supreme Court affirmed the judgment of the lower court.

REASON The state supreme court reasoned that if Riviera, the president, were not personally liable, the corporation would be the guarantor of its own lease, and concluded that this would be commercially unreasonable because, as a matter of law, a party cannot be the guarantor of its own contract. The court pointed out that "any ambiguity in the Guaranty was created by Riviera" and "[s]uch ambiguity will be construed against Riviera as the party who drafted this language." In this case, the "combination of circumstances" made the guaranty ambiguous. "[T]he language of the Guaranty itself compels the view Riviera is personally liable," because it referred to three parties, including the "Guarantor." The court explained that "[i]f Riviera signed the Guaranty only in his representative capacity, Tony Maroni's would be both Tenant and Guarantor, rendering the Guaranty provisions absurd." Thus, "the very nature of a guaranty is such that Riviera created personal liability by his signature."

FOR CRITICAL ANALYSIS—Ethical Consideration *Are there any circumstances in which a collateral document signed by a corporate officer to secure a corporate debt might not create personal liability?*

Defenses of the Surety and the Guarantor The defenses of the surety and the guarantor are basically the same. Therefore, the following discussion applies to both, although it refers only to the surety.

Certain actions will release the surety from the obligation. For example, any binding material modification in the terms of the original contract made between the principal debtor and the creditor—including a binding agreement to extend the time for making payment—without first obtaining the consent of the surety will discharge a gratuitous surety completely and a compensated surety to the extent that the surety suffers a loss. (An example of a gratuitous surety is a father who agrees to assume responsibility for his daughter's obligation; an example of a compensated surety is a venture capitalist who will profit from a loan made to the principal debtor.)

Naturally, if the principal obligation is paid by the debtor or by another person on behalf of the debtor, the surety is discharged from the obligation. Similarly, if valid tender of payment is made, and the creditor rejects it with knowledge of the surety's existence, the surety is released from any obligation on the debt.

Generally, the surety can use any defenses available to a principal debtor to avoid liability on the obligation to the creditor. Defenses available to the principal debtor that the surety *cannot* use include the principal debtor's incapacity or bankruptcy and the statute of limitations. The ability of the surety to assert any defenses the debtor may have against the creditor is the most important concept in suretyship, because most of the defenses available to the surety are also those of the debtor.

Obviously, a surety may also have his or her own defenses—for example, incapacity or bankruptcy. If the creditor fraudulently induced the surety to guarantee the debt of the debtor, the surety can assert fraud as a defense. In most states, the creditor has a legal duty to inform the surety, prior to the formation of the suretyship contract, of material facts known by the creditor that would substantially increase the surety's risk. Failure to do so is fraud and makes the suretyship obligation voidable. In addition, if a creditor surrenders the collateral to the debtor or impairs the collateral while knowing of the surety and without the surety's consent, the surety is released to the extent of any loss suffered from the creditor's actions. The primary reason for this requirement is to protect the surety who agreed to become obligated only because the debtor's collateral was in the possession of the creditor.

Rights of the Surety and the Guarantor The rights of the surety and the guarantor are basically the same. Therefore, again, the following discussion applies to both.

When the surety pays the debt owed to the creditor, the surety is entitled to certain rights. First, the surety has the legal **right of subrogation.** Simply stated, this means that any right the creditor had against the debtor now becomes the right of the surety. Included are creditor rights in bankruptcy, rights to collateral possessed by the creditor, and rights to judgments secured by the creditor. In short, the surety now stands in the shoes of the creditor and may pursue any remedies that were available to the creditor against the debtor.

RIGHT OF SUBROGATION
The right of a person to stand in the place of (be substituted for) another, giving the substituted party the same legal rights that the original party had.

Second, the surety has the **right of reimbursement** from the debtor. Basically, the surety is entitled to receive from the debtor all outlays made on behalf of the suretyship arrangement. Such outlays can include expenses incurred as well as the actual amount of the debt paid to the creditor.

RIGHT OF REIMBURSEMENT
The legal right of a person to be restored, repaid, or indemnified for costs, expenses, or losses incurred or expended on behalf of another.

Third, in the case of **co-sureties** (two or more sureties on the same obligation owed by the debtor), a surety who pays more than her or his proportionate share on a debtor's default is entitled to recover from the co-sureties the amount paid above the surety's obligation. This is the **right of contribution.** Generally, a co-surety's liability either is determined by agreement or, in the absence of agreement between the co-sureties, can be specified in the suretyship contract itself.

CO-SURETY
A joint surety; a person who assumes liability jointly with another surety for the payment of an obligation.

RIGHT OF CONTRIBUTION
The right of a co-surety who pays more than his or her proportionate share on a debtor's default to recover the excess paid from other co-sureties.

● **EXAMPLE 23.5** Assume that two co-sureties are obligated under a suretyship contract to guarantee the debt of a debtor. Together, the sureties' maximum liability is $25,000. As specified in the suretyship contract, surety A's maximum liability is $15,000, and surety B's is $10,000. The debtor owes $10,000 and is in default. Surety A pays the creditor the entire $10,000. In the absence of any agreement between the two co-sureties, surety A can recover $4,000 from surety B ($10,000/$25,000 × $10,000 = $4,000).●

Laws Assisting Debtors

The law protects debtors as well as creditors. Certain property of the debtor, for example, is exempt from creditors' actions. Probably the most familiar of these exemptions is the **homestead exemption.** Each state permits the debtor to retain the family home, either in its entirety or up to a specified dollar amount, free from the claims of unsecured creditors or trustees in bankruptcy. The purpose of the homestead exemption is to ensure that the debtor will retain some form of shelter.

HOMESTEAD EXEMPTION
A law permitting a debtor to retain the family home, either in its entirety or up to a specified dollar amount, free from the claims of unsecured creditors or trustees in bankruptcy.

● **EXAMPLE 23.6** Suppose that Van Cleave owes Acosta $40,000. The debt is the subject of a lawsuit, and the court awards Acosta a judgment of $40,000 against Van Cleave. Van Cleave's home is valued at $50,000, and the state exemption on homesteads is $25,000. There are no outstanding mortgages or other liens. To satisfy the

A notice announces the auction of a house. Under what conditions might a creditor not *receive full payment from the proceeds of the sale?*

judgment debt, Van Cleave's family home is sold at public auction for $45,000. The proceeds of the sale are distributed as follows:

1. Van Cleave is given $25,000 as his homestead exemption.
2. Acosta is paid $20,000 toward the judgment debt, leaving a $20,000 deficiency judgment that can be satisfied from any other nonexempt property (personal or real) that Van Cleave may have, if allowed by state law. ●

State exemption statutes usually include both real and personal property. Personal property that is most often exempt from satisfaction of judgment debts includes the following:

1. Household furniture up to a specified dollar amount.
2. Clothing and certain personal possessions, such as family pictures or a Bible.
3. A vehicle (or vehicles) for transportation (at least up to a specified dollar amount).
4. Certain classified animals, usually livestock but including pets.
5. Equipment that the debtor uses in a business or trade, such as tools or professional instruments, up to a specified dollar amount.

Consumer protection statutes (see Chapter 33) also protect debtors' rights. Of course, bankruptcy laws, which are discussed in the next section, are designed specifically to assist debtors in need of relief from their debts.

"How often have I been able to trace bankruptcies and insolvencies to some lawsuit, . . . the costs of which have mounted up to large sums."

HENRY PETER BROUGHAM, 1778–1868 (English politician)

Bankruptcy and Reorganization

At one time, debtors who could not pay their debts as they came due faced harsh consequences, including imprisonment and involuntary servitude. Today, in contrast, debtors have numerous rights. Some of these rights have already been mentioned. We now look at another significant right of debtors: the right to petition for bankruptcy relief under federal law.

Bankruptcy law in the United States has two goals—to protect a debtor by giving him or her a fresh start, free from creditors' claims, and to ensure equitable treatment to creditors who are competing for a debtor's assets. Bankruptcy law is federal law, but state laws on secured transactions, liens, judgments, and exemptions also play a role in federal bankruptcy proceedings.

Current bankruptcy law is based on the Bankruptcy Reform Act of 1978, as amended. In this chapter, we refer to this act, as amended, as the Bankruptcy Code (or, more simply, the Code). This chapter's *Landmark in the Law* traces the historical evolution of bankruptcy law and explains why the 1978 Bankruptcy Reform Act is so important.

BANKRUPTCY COURTS

RECALL Congress regulates the jursidiction of the federal courts, within the limits set by the Constitution. Congress can expand or reduce the number of federal courts at any time.

Bankruptcy proceedings are held in federal bankruptcy courts. A bankruptcy court's primary function is to hold *core proceedings*[3] dealing with the procedures required to administer the estate of the debtor in bankruptcy. Bankruptcy courts are under the authority of U.S. district courts (see the chart showing the federal court system in Exhibit 3–2 in Chapter 3), and rulings from bankruptcy courts can be appealed to the district courts. Fundamentally, a bankruptcy court fulfills the role of an administrative court for the district court concerning matters in bankruptcy. A bankruptcy court can conduct a jury trial if the appropriate district court has authorized it and if the parties to the bankruptcy consent to a jury trial.

TYPES OF BANKRUPTCY RELIEF

LIQUIDATION
The sale of all of the nonexempt assets of a debtor and the distribution of the proceeds to the debtor's creditors. Chapter 7 of the Bankruptcy Code provides for liquidation bankruptcy proceedings.

The Bankruptcy Code, which is contained in Title 11 of the U.S. Code (U.S.C.), is divided into a series of "chapters." Chapters 1, 3, and 5 of the Code include general definitional provisions and provisions governing case administration and procedures, creditors, the debtor, and the estate. These three chapters of the Code apply generally to all types of bankruptcies. The next five chapters set forth the different types of relief that debtors may seek. Chapter 7 provides for **liquidation** proceedings (the selling of all nonexempt assets and the distribution of the proceeds to the debtor's creditors). Chapter 9 governs the adjustment of the debts of municipalities. Chapter 11 governs reorganizations. Chapter 12 (for family farmers) and Chapter 13 (for individuals) provide for adjustment of the debts of parties with regular income.[4]

In the following pages, we deal first with liquidation proceedings under Chapter 7 of the Code. We then examine the procedures required for Chapter 11 reorganizations and for Chapter 12 and Chapter 13 plans.

Chapter 7—Liquidation

Liquidation is the most familiar type of bankruptcy proceeding and is often referred to as an *ordinary*, or *straight, bankruptcy*. Put simply, debtors in straight bankruptcies state

3. Core proceedings are procedural functions, such as allowance of claims, decisions on preferences, automatic-stay proceedings, confirmation of bankruptcy plans, discharge of debts, and so on. These terms and procedures are defined and discussed in the following sections of this chapter.

4. There are no Chapters 2, 4, 6, 8, or 10 in Title 11. Such "gaps" are not uncommon in the U.S.C. This is because, when a statute is enacted, chapter numbers (or other subdivisional unit numbers) are sometimes reserved for future use. (A gap may also appear if a law has been repealed.)

LANDMARK IN THE LAW
The Bankruptcy Reform Act of 1978

Article I, Section 8, of the U.S. Constitution gives Congress the power to establish "uniform Laws on the subject of Bankruptcies throughout the United States." Congress initially exercised this power in 1800, when the first bankruptcy law was enacted as a result of the business crisis created by restraints imposed on American trade by the British and French. In 1803, the law was repealed, and during the rest of the century—always in response to some crisis—Congress periodically enacted (and later repealed) other bankruptcy legislation. The National Bankruptcy Act of 1898, however, was not repealed, and since that time the United States has had ongoing federal statutory laws concerning bankruptcy. The 1898 act allowed only for *liquidation* in bankruptcy proceedings (which occurs when the debtor's assets are sold and the proceeds distributed to creditors). Some relief through reorganization was first allowed by amendments to the 1898 act in the 1930s.

A Major Overhaul of the Law Modern bankruptcy law is based on the Bankruptcy Reform Act of 1978, which repealed the 1898 act and represented a major overhaul of federal bankruptcy law. The 1978 act attempted to remedy previous abuses of bankruptcy law and introduced more clarity into bankruptcy procedures. A major organizational change in the 1978 act was the establishment of a new system of bankruptcy courts so that each federal judicial district would have an adjunct bankruptcy court with exclusive jurisdiction over bankruptcy cases. The act also specified that, in contrast to the lifetime terms of judges in other federal courts, bankruptcy court judges would have a fourteen-year term.

The 1978 act, referred to now simply as the Bankruptcy Code, has been amended several times since its passage. Amendments to the Code have created additional bankruptcy judgeships, placed bankruptcy court judges under the authority of the U.S. district courts, extended the bankruptcy trustee system nationally, granted more power to bankruptcy trustees in the handling of bankruptcy matters, and added a new chapter to the Bankruptcy Code (Chapter 12) to aid financially troubled farmers. The most significant amendments to the Bankruptcy Code were made by the Bankruptcy Reform Act of 1994. Among the many important changes of the 1994 act was the creation of a "fast-track" procedure for small-business debtors (those not involved in owning or managing real estate and with debts of less than $2 million) under Chapter 11 of the Code.

Criticism of the Act The 1978 act, which generally made it easier for debtors to obtain bankruptcy relief, has been criticized for making it too easy for debtors to discharge their debts in bankruptcy. Since 1980, the number of personal bankruptcy filings per year has climbed from less than 300,000 to over 1.4 million. This steep rise in the number of personal bankruptcy filings, which continued even when the economy was booming during the 1990s, has caused Congress to again consider far-reaching bankruptcy reform measures. Bills currently before Congress would, among other things, make it more difficult to discharge certain debts in bankruptcy.

(continued)

LANDMARK IN THE LAW—Continued

APPLICATION TO TODAY'S WORLD

The bankruptcy reform bill currently being considered in conference by a U.S. House and Senate committee is the most recent attempt to update the Bankruptcy Code. This bill includes provisions that would, among other things, force more debtors to accept a Chapter 13 reorganization rather than a Chapter 7 liquidation, limit the amount of the homestead exemption, make fewer debts dischargeable, and require debtors to participate in financial counseling before filing for bankruptcy.

their debts and turn their assets over to trustees. The trustees sell the assets and distribute the proceeds to creditors. With certain exceptions, the remaining debts are then **discharged** (extinguished), and the debtors are relieved of the obligation to pay the debts.

DISCHARGE
In bankruptcy proceedings, the extinction of the debtor's dischargeable debts.

Any "person"—defined as including individuals, partnerships, and corporations—may be a debtor under Chapter 7. Railroads, insurance companies, banks, savings and loan associations, investment companies licensed by the Small Business Administration, and credit unions *cannot* be Chapter 7 debtors, however. Other chapters of the Code or other federal or state statutes apply to them. A husband and wife may file jointly for bankruptcy under a single petition.

FILING THE PETITION

A straight bankruptcy may be commenced by the filing of either a voluntary or an involuntary **petition in bankruptcy**—the document that is filed with a bankruptcy court to initiate bankruptcy proceedings.

PETITION IN BANKRUPTCY
The document that is filed with a bankruptcy court to initiate bankruptcy proceedings. The official forms required for a petition in bankruptcy must be completed accurately, sworn to under oath, and signed by the debtor.

CONSUMER-DEBTOR
An individual whose debts are primarily consumer debts (debts for purchases made primarily for personal or household use).

Voluntary Bankruptcy A voluntary petition is brought by the debtor, who files official forms designated for that purpose in the bankruptcy court. A **consumer-debtor** (defined as an individual whose debts are primarily consumer debts) who has selected Chapter 7 must state in the petition, at the time of filing, that he or she understands the relief available under other chapters and has chosen to proceed under Chapter 7. If the consumer-debtor is represented by an attorney, the attorney must file an affidavit stating that she or he has informed the debtor of the relief available under each chapter. Any debtor who is liable on a claim held by a creditor can file a voluntary petition. The debtor does not even have to be insolvent to do so.[5] The voluntary petition contains the following schedules:

① A list of both secured and unsecured creditors, their addresses, and the amount of debt owed to each.

② A statement of the financial affairs of the debtor.

5. The inability to pay debts as they become due is known as *equitable* insolvency. A *balance-sheet* insolvency, which exists when a debtor's liabilities exceed assets, is not the test. Thus, it is possible for debtors to petition voluntarily for bankruptcy even though their assets far exceed their liabilities. This situation may occur when a debtor's cash-flow problems become severe.

③ A list of all property owned by the debtor, including property claimed by the debtor to be exempt.

④ A listing of current income and expenses.

The official forms must be completed accurately, sworn to under oath, and signed by the debtor. To conceal assets or knowingly supply false information on these schedules is a crime under the bankruptcy laws. If the voluntary petition for bankruptcy is found to be proper, the filing of the petition will itself constitute an order for relief. An **order for relief** relieves the debtor of the immediate obligation to pay the debts listed in the petition. Once a consumer-debtor's voluntary petition has been filed, the clerk of the court (or person directed) must give the trustee and creditors mailed notice of the order for relief not more than twenty days after the entry of the order.

ORDER FOR RELIEF
A court's grant of assistance to a complainant. In bankruptcy proceedings, the order relieves the debtor of the immediate obligation to pay the debts listed in the bankruptcy petition.

As mentioned previously, debtors do not have to be insolvent to file for voluntary bankruptcy. Debtors do not have unfettered access to Chapter 7 bankruptcy proceedings, however. Section 707(b) of the Bankruptcy Code allows a bankruptcy court to dismiss a petition for relief under Chapter 7 if the granting of relief would constitute "substantial abuse" of Chapter 7.

● **EXAMPLE 23.7** Howard Rock, a consumer-debtor, petitions for Chapter 7 relief. The court might determine, after evaluating Rock's schedule listing current income and expenses, that he would be able to pay his creditors a reasonable amount from future income. In this situation, the court might conclude that it would be a substantial abuse of Chapter 7 to allow Rock to have his debts completely discharged. The court might dismiss Rock's Chapter 7 petition after a hearing and encourage him to file a repayment plan under Chapter 13 of the Code, if that would substantially increase the likelihood that the creditors would receive payment.● In the following case, the court had to decide whether granting a Chapter 7 discharge to the debtor would constitute substantial abuse.

CASE 23.2 In re Lamanna

United States Court of Appeals,
First Circuit, 1998.
153 F.3d 1.
http://www.law.emory.edu/1circuit[a]

FACTS In 1996, Richard Lamanna was living with his parents. For this reason, his monthly expenses were only $580. His monthly income was $1,350.96, leaving a difference of $770.96, the amount of his disposable income.[b] He had no plans to move out of his parents' house. During four weeks in October and November, he charged $9,994.45 on credit cards. In February 1997, when his total unsecured debt was $15,911.96, he filed a voluntary petition in a federal bankruptcy court to declare bankruptcy under Chapter 7. The court noted that Lamanna was capable of paying all of his debts under a Chapter 13 repayment plan and dismissed the case. The U.S. Bankruptcy Appellate Panel for the First Circuit affirmed the dismissal, and Lamanna appealed to the U.S. Court of Appeals for the First Circuit. Lamanna argued in part that if he did not live with his parents, he would not have as much disposable income, and that thus he was being penalized for living with his parents.

ISSUE Would granting Lamanna's petition constitute substantial abuse of Chapter 7?

DECISION Yes. The U.S. Court of Appeals for the First Circuit affirmed the decision of the lower court.

(continued)

a. This Web site is maintained by Emory University School of Law. In the "Listing by Month of Decision" section, click on "1998 Decisions." On that page, in the "1998 Decisions" list, click on "August." When the list of cases appears, click on the case name to access the opinion.

b. *Disposable income* is income "not reasonably necessary to be expended for the maintenance or support of the debtor or a dependent of the debtor," according to 11 U.S.C. Section 1325(b)(2).

CASE 23.2—Continued

REASON The U.S. Court of Appeals for the First Circuit looked at the "totality of the circumstances" to reach its conclusion. Under this test, the court found that Lamanna "has sufficient disposable income to repay his debts under a Chapter 13 repayment plan in three to five years. There is no evidence that Lamanna's living situation was unstable or likely to change in the near future. There is no evidence of other factors that cast doubt on the stability of Lamanna's future income and expenses." The court pointed out that "a consumer debtor's ability to repay his debts out of future disposable income is strong evidence of 'substantial abuse'" of Chapter 7. As for Lamanna's argument that he was penalized for living with his parents, the court said that it "boils down to the notion that Section 707 requires the bankruptcy court to impute a minimum cost of living to a debtor and then measure the debtor's actual income against the higher of the imputed minimum and the debtor's actual expenses. Section 707 does not contain such an implicit requirement."

FOR CRITICAL ANALYSIS—Economic Consideration *A finding of substantial abuse can be based on either a debtor's lack of honesty or his or her ability to pay outstanding debts after satisfying the debtor's living necessities. What are some of the factors that might be considered in deciding whether a debtor is needy?*

A store advertises a court-ordered bankruptcy sale. On what basis might a court enter an order for relief in an involuntary bankruptcy proceeding initiated by the store's creditors?

Involuntary Bankruptcy An involuntary bankruptcy occurs when the debtor's creditors force the debtor into bankruptcy proceedings. An involuntary case cannot be commenced against a farmer[6] or a charitable institution (or those entities not eligible for Chapter 7 relief—mentioned earlier), however. For an involuntary action to be filed against other debtors, the following requirements must be met: If the debtor has twelve or more creditors, three or more of those creditors having unsecured claims totaling at least $11,625 must join in the petition. If a debtor has fewer than twelve creditors, one or more creditors having a claim of $11,625 may file.

If the debtor challenges the involuntary petition, a hearing will be held, and the debtor's challenge will fail if the bankruptcy court finds either of the following:

1. That the debtor is generally not paying debts as they become due.
2. That a general receiver, custodian, or assignee took possession of, or was appointed to take charge of, substantially all of the debtor's property within 120 days before the filing of the petition.

If the court allows the bankruptcy to proceed, the debtor will be required to supply the same information in the bankruptcy schedules as in a voluntary bankruptcy.

An involuntary petition should not be used as an everyday debt-collection device, and the Code provides penalties for the filing of frivolous (unjustified) petitions against debtors. Judgment may be granted against the petitioning creditors for the costs and attorneys' fees incurred by the debtor in defending against an involuntary petition that is dismissed by the court. If the petition is filed in bad faith, damages can be awarded for injury to the debtor's reputation. Punitive damages may also be awarded.

AUTOMATIC STAY

AUTOMATIC STAY
In bankruptcy proceedings, the suspension of virtually all litigation and other action by creditors against the debtor or the debtor's property. The stay is effective the moment the debtor files a petition in bankruptcy.

The filing of a petition, either voluntary or involuntary, operates as an **automatic stay** on (suspension of) virtually all litigation and other action by creditors against the debtor or the debtor's property. In other words, once a petition is filed, creditors cannot

6. *Farmers* are defined as persons who receive more than 80 percent of their gross income from farming operations, such as tilling the soil; dairy farming; ranching; or the production or raising of crops, poultry, or livestock. Corporations and partnerships, as well as individuals, can be farmers.

commence or continue most legal actions against the debtor to recover claims or to repossess property in the hands of the debtor. A secured creditor, however, may petition the bankruptcy court for relief from the automatic stay in certain circumstances. Additionally, the automatic stay does not apply to paternity, alimony, or family maintenance and support debts.

A creditor's failure to abide by an automatic stay imposed by the filing of a petition can be costly. If a creditor *knowingly* violates the automatic-stay provision (a willful violation), any party injured is entitled to recover actual damages, costs, and attorneys' fees and may also be entitled to recover punitive damages.

CREDITORS' MEETING AND CLAIMS

BE AWARE A debtor who lies, commits bribery, conceals assets, uses a false name, or makes false claims at a creditors' meeting is subject to a $5,000 fine and up to five years in prison.

Within a reasonable time after the order of relief is granted (not less than ten days or more than thirty days), the bankruptcy court must call a meeting of the creditors listed in the schedules filed by the debtor. The bankruptcy judge does not attend this meeting. The debtor must attend this meeting (unless excused by the court) and submit to an examination under oath. Failure to appear or the making of false statements under oath may result in the debtor's being denied a discharge of bankruptcy. At the meeting, the trustee ensures that the debtor is advised of the potential consequences of bankruptcy and of his or her ability to file under a different chapter.

In a bankruptcy case in which the debtor has no assets (called a "no-asset" case), creditors are notified of the debtor's petition for bankruptcy but are instructed not to file a claim. In such a situation, the creditors will receive no payment, and most, if not all, of the debtor's debts will be discharged.

If there are sufficient assets to be distributed to creditors, however, each creditor must normally file a *proof of claim* with the bankruptcy court clerk within ninety days of the creditors' meeting to be entitled to receive a portion of the debtor's estate. The proof of claim lists the creditor's name and address, as well as the amount that the creditor asserts is owed to the creditor by the debtor. If a creditor fails to file a proof of claim, the bankruptcy court or trustee may file the proof of claim on the creditor's behalf but is not obligated to do so. If a claim is for a disputed amount, the bankruptcy court will set the value of the claim.

Creditors' claims are automatically allowed unless contested by the trustee, the debtor, or another creditor. The Code, however, does not allow claims for breach of employment contracts or real estate leases for terms longer than one year. These claims are limited to one year's wages or rent, despite the remaining length of either contract in breach.

PROPERTY OF THE ESTATE

ESTATE IN PROPERTY
In bankruptcy proceedings, all of the debtor's legal and equitable interests in property currently held, wherever located, together with certain jointly owned property, property transferred in transactions voidable by the trustee, proceeds and profits from the property of the estate, and certain property interests to which the debtor becomes entitled within 180 days after filing for bankruptcy.

On the commencement of a liquidation proceeding under Chapter 7, an **estate in property** is created. The estate consists of all the debtor's legal and equitable interests in property currently held, wherever located, together with certain jointly owned property, property transferred in transactions voidable by the trustee, proceeds and profits from the property of the estate, and certain after-acquired property. Interests in certain property—such as gifts, inheritances, property settlements (resulting from divorce), or life insurance death proceeds—to which the debtor becomes *entitled within 180 days after filing* may also become part of the estate. Thus, the filing of a bankruptcy petition generally fixes a dividing line: property acquired prior to the filing becomes property of the estate, and property acquired after the filing, except as just noted, remains the debtor's.

EXEMPTED PROPERTY

Any individual debtor is entitled to exempt certain property from the property of the estate. The Bankruptcy Code establishes a federal exemption scheme under which the following property is exempt:[7]

① Up to $17,425 in equity in the debtor's residence and burial plot (the homestead exemption).

② Interest in a motor vehicle up to $2,775.

③ Interest in household goods and furnishings, wearing apparel, appliances, books, animals, crops, and musical instruments up to $450 in a particular item but limited to $9,300 in total.

④ Interest in jewelry up to $1,150.

⑤ Any other property worth up to $925, plus any unused part of the $17,425 homestead exemption up to an amount of $8,725.

⑥ Interest in any tools of the debtor's trade, up to $1,750.

⑦ Certain life insurance contracts owned by the debtor.

⑧ Certain interests in accrued dividends or interests under life insurance contracts owned by the debtor.

⑨ Professionally prescribed health aids.

⑩ The right to receive Social Security and certain welfare benefits, alimony and support payments, and certain pension benefits.

⑪ The right to receive certain personal injury and other awards, up to $17,425.

Individual states have the power to pass legislation precluding debtors in their states from using the federal exemptions. At least thirty-five states have done this. In those states, debtors may use only state (not federal) exemptions. In the rest of the states, an individual debtor (or husband and wife who file jointly) may choose between the exemptions provided under state law and the federal exemptions. State laws may provide significantly greater protection for debtors than federal law. For example, Florida and Texas traditionally have provided for generous exemptions for homeowners. State laws may also define the property coming within an exemption differently than does the federal law.

THE TRUSTEE'S ROLE

U.S. TRUSTEE
A government official who performs certain administrative tasks that a bankruptcy judge would otherwise have to perform.

Promptly after the order for relief has been entered, an interim, or provisional, trustee is appointed by the **U.S. trustee** (a government official who performs certain administrative tasks that a bankruptcy judge would otherwise have to perform). The interim trustee administers the debtor's estate until the first meeting of creditors, at which time either a permanent trustee is elected or the interim trustee becomes the permanent trustee. Trustees are entitled to compensation for services rendered, plus reimbursement for expenses.

The basic duty of the trustee is to collect the debtor's available estate and reduce it to money for distribution, preserving the interests of both the debtor and unsecured creditors. In other words, the trustee is accountable for administering the debtor's estate. To enable the trustee to accomplish this duty, the Code gives her or him certain powers, stated in both general and specific terms.

7. The dollar amounts stated in the Bankruptcy Code were adjusted automatically on April 1, 1998, and will be adjusted every three years thereafter based on changes in the Consumer Price Index. The amounts stated in this chapter are in accordance with those computed on April 1, 2001.

Trustee's Powers The trustee has the power to require persons holding the debtor's property at the time the petition is filed to deliver the property to the trustee. To enable the trustee to implement this power, the Code provides that the trustee occupies a position equivalent in rights to that of certain other parties. For example, in some situations, the trustee has the same rights as creditors and can obtain a judicial lien or levy execution on the debtor's property. This means that a trustee has priority over an unperfected secured party (see Chapter 22) to the debtor's property. The trustee also has rights equivalent to those of the debtor.

In addition, the trustee has the power to avoid (cancel) certain types of transactions, including those transactions that the debtor could rightfully avoid, *preferences*, certain statutory *liens*, and *fraudulent transfers* by the debtor. Avoidance powers must be exercised within two years of the order for relief (the period runs even if a trustee has not been appointed). These powers of the trustee are discussed in more detail in the following subsections.

Voidable Rights A trustee steps into the shoes of the debtor. Thus, any reason that a debtor can use to obtain the return of his or her property can be used by the trustee as well. These grounds for recovery include fraud, duress, incapacity, and mutual mistake.

● **EXAMPLE 23.8** Rob sells his boat to Inga. Inga gives Rob a check, knowing that there are insufficient funds in her bank account to cover the check. Inga has committed fraud. Rob has the right to avoid that transfer and recover the boat from Inga. Thus, if Rob petitions for bankruptcy and the court enters an order for relief, the trustee can exercise the same right to recover the boat from Inga.● If the trustee does not take action to enforce one of his or her rights, the debtor in a Chapter 7 bankruptcy will nevertheless be able to enforce that right.[8]

PREFERENCE
In bankruptcy proceedings, property transfers or payments made by the debtor that favor (give preference to) one creditor over others. The bankruptcy trustee is allowed to recover payments made both voluntarily and involuntarily to one creditor in preference over another.

Preferences A debtor is not permitted to transfer property or to make a payment that favors—or gives a **preference** to—one creditor over others. The trustee is allowed to recover payments made both voluntarily and involuntarily to one creditor in preference over another.

To have made a preferential payment that can be recovered, an *insolvent* debtor generally must have transferred property, for a *preexisting* debt, during the *ninety days* prior to the filing of the petition in bankruptcy. The transfer must give the creditor more than the creditor would have received as a result of the bankruptcy proceedings. The trustee does not have to prove insolvency, as the Code provides that the debtor is presumed to be insolvent during this ninety-day period.

Sometimes, the creditor receiving the preference is an insider—an individual, a partner, a partnership, or an officer or a director of a corporation (or a relative of one of these) who has a close relationship with the debtor. In this situation, the avoidance power of the trustee is extended to transfers made within *one year* before filing; however, the *presumption* of insolvency is confined to the ninety-day period. Therefore, the trustee must prove that the debtor was insolvent at the time of an earlier transfer.

Not all transfers are preferences. To be a preference, the transfer must be made for something other than current consideration. Therefore, most courts generally assume that payment for services rendered within ten to fifteen days prior to the payment of the current consideration is not a preference. If a creditor receives payment in the ordinary course of business, such as payment of last month's telephone bill, the payment

8. In a Chapter 11 reorganization (to be discussed later), for which generally no trustee exists, the debtor has the same avoiding powers as a trustee in a Chapter 7 liquidation. In repayment plans under Chapters 12 and 13 (also to be discussed later), a trustee must be appointed.

cannot be recovered by the trustee in bankruptcy. To be recoverable, a preference must be a transfer for an antecedent (preexisting) debt, such as a year-old printing bill. In addition, the Code permits a consumer-debtor to transfer any property to a creditor up to a total value of $600 without the transfer's constituting a preference. Also, certain other debts, including alimony and child support, are not preferences.

NOTE Usually, when property is recovered as a preference, the trustee sells it and distributes the proceeds to the debtor's creditors.

If a preferred creditor has sold the property to an innocent third party, the trustee cannot recover the property from the innocent party. The creditor, however, generally can be held accountable for the value of the property.

Liens on Debtor's Property The trustee is permitted to avoid the fixing of certain statutory liens, such as a mechanic's lien, on property of the debtor. Liens that first became effective at the time the bankruptcy petition was filed or the debtor became insolvent are voidable by the trustee. Liens that are not perfected or enforceable against a good faith purchaser on the date of the petition are also voidable.

Fraudulent Transfers The trustee may avoid fraudulent transfers or obligations if they were made within one year of the filing of the petition or if they were made with actual intent to hinder, delay, or defraud a creditor. Transfers made for less than reasonably equivalent consideration are also vulnerable if the debtor thereby became insolvent, was left engaged in business with an unreasonably small amount of capital, or intended to incur debts that would be beyond his or her ability to pay. When a fraudulent transfer is made outside the Code's one-year limit, creditors may seek alternative relief under state laws. State laws often allow creditors to recover for transfers made up to three years prior to the filing of a petition.

Property Distribution

Creditors are either secured or unsecured. As discussed in Chapter 22, a *secured* creditor has a security interest in collateral that secures the debt. An *unsecured* creditor does not have any security interest.

Secured Creditors The Code provides that a consumer-debtor, within thirty days of the filing of a Chapter 7 petition or before the date of the first meeting of the creditors (whichever is first), must file with the clerk a statement of intention with respect to the secured collateral. The statement must indicate whether the debtor will retain the collateral or surrender it to the secured party. Additionally, if applicable, the debtor must specify whether the collateral will be claimed as exempt property and whether the debtor intends to redeem the property or reaffirm the debt secured by the collateral. The trustee is obligated to enforce the debtor's statement within forty-five days after the statement is filed.

If the collateral is surrendered to the perfected secured party, the secured creditor can enforce the security interest either by accepting the property in full satisfaction of the debt or by foreclosing on the collateral and using the proceeds to pay off the debt. Thus, the secured party has priority over unsecured parties to the proceeds from the disposition of the secured collateral. Indeed, the Code provides that if the value of the secured collateral exceeds the secured party's claim, the secured party also has priority to the proceeds in an amount that will cover reasonable fees (including attorneys' fees, if provided for in the security agreement) and costs incurred because of the debtor's default. Any excess over this amount is used by the trustee to satisfy the claims of unsecured creditors. Should the secured collateral be insufficient to cover the secured debt owed, the secured creditor becomes an unsecured creditor for the remainder of the debt.

Unsecured Creditors Bankruptcy law establishes an order or priority for classes of debts owed to *unsecured* creditors, and they are paid in the order of their priority. Each class of debt must be fully paid before the next class is entitled to any of the proceeds—if there are sufficient funds to pay the entire class. If not, the proceeds are distributed *proportionately* to each creditor in the class, and all classes lower in priority on the list receive nothing. The order of priority among classes of unsecured creditors is as follows:

① Administrative expenses—including court costs, trustee fees, and bankruptcy attorneys' fees.

② In an involuntary bankruptcy, expenses incurred by the debtor in the ordinary course of business from the date of the filing of the petition up to the appointment of the trustee or the issuance by the court of an order for relief.

③ Unpaid wages, salaries, and commissions earned within ninety days of the filing of the petition, limited to $4,650 per claimant. Any claim in excess of $4,650 is treated as a claim of a general creditor (listed as number 9 below).

④ Unsecured claims for contributions to be made to employee benefit plans, limited to services performed during 180 days prior to the filing of the bankruptcy petition and $4,650 per employee.

⑤ Claims by farmers and fishers, up to $4,650, against debtor operators of grain storage or fish storage or processing facilities.

⑥ Consumer deposits of up to $2,100 given to the debtor before the petition was filed in connection with the purchase, lease, or rental of property or the purchase of services that were not received or provided. Any claim in excess of $2,100 is treated as a claim of a general creditor (listed as number 9 below).

⑦ Paternity, alimony, maintenance, and support debts.

⑧ Certain taxes and penalties due to government units, such as income and property taxes.

⑨ Claims of general creditors.

⑩ Commitments to the Federal Deposit Insurance Corporation, and other organizations, to maintain the capital of an insured depository institution.

If any amount remains after the priority classes of creditors have been satisfied, it is turned over to the debtor.

DISCHARGE

BE AWARE Often, a discharge in bankruptcy—even under Chapter 7—does not free a debtor of *all* of his or her debts.

From the debtor's point of view, the purpose of a liquidation proceeding is to obtain a fresh start through the discharge of debts.[9] Certain debts, however, are not dischargeable in a liquidation proceeding. Also, certain debtors may not qualify—because of their conduct—to have all debts discharged in bankruptcy.

Exceptions to Discharge Claims that are not dischargeable under Chapter 7 include the following:

① Claims for back taxes accruing within three years prior to bankruptcy.

② Claims for amounts borrowed by the debtor to pay federal taxes.

③ Claims against property or money obtained by the debtor under false pretenses or by false representations.

9. Discharges are granted under Chapter 7 only to *individuals,* not to corporations or partnerships. The latter may use Chapter 11, or they may terminate their existence under state law.

LETTER OF THE LAW

A Loan by Any Other Name...

Sometimes, debtors' attempts to get around the student loan exception to discharge in bankruptcy can be quite creative. Consider the argument put forth by LeAnna Johnson, to whom Missouri Baptist College had extended credit in the amount of $5,892.49 for tuition, books, and other expenses. Because Johnson never received any funds from the college, just credit, she asserted that her debt to the college did not qualify as a "loan"; therefore, the debt should be dischargeable. Johnson failed to convince the bankruptcy court (or, on appeal, a bankruptcy appellate panel) of the soundness of her reasoning, however. The appellate panel, after a thorough discussion of case law bearing on the issue of what constitutes a loan and after checking various dictionary definitions of the term, affirmed the bankruptcy court's decision: the college's extension of credit to Johnson was definitely a student loan and, as such, not dischargeable in bankruptcy.[a]

THE BOTTOM LINE

As Johnson learned, a student loan by any other name is still a student loan.

a. *In re Johnson*, 218 Bankr. 449 (B.A.P. [Bankruptcy Appellate Panel] 8th Cir. 1998).

④ Claims by creditors who were not notified of the bankruptcy; these claims did not appear on the schedules the debtor was required to file.

⑤ Claims based on fraud or misuse of funds by the debtor while she or he was acting in a fiduciary capacity or claims involving the debtor's embezzlement or larceny.

⑥ Alimony, child support, and (with certain exceptions) property settlements.

⑦ Claims based on willful or malicious conduct by the debtor toward another or the property of another.

⑧ Certain government fines and penalties.

⑨ Certain student loans, unless payment of the loans imposes an undue hardship on the debtor and the debtor's dependents.

⑩ Consumer debts of more than $1,150 for luxury goods or services owed to a single creditor incurred within sixty days of the order for relief. This denial of discharge is a rebuttable presumption (that is, the denial may be challenged by the debtor), however, and any debts reasonably incurred to support the debtor or dependents are not classified as luxuries.

⑪ Cash advances totaling more than $1,150 that are extensions of open-end consumer credit obtained by the debtor within sixty days of the order for relief. A denial of discharge of these debts is also a rebuttable presumption.

⑫ Judgments or consent decrees against a debtor as a result of the debtor's operation of a motor vehicle while intoxicated.

ETHICAL ISSUE 23.1

Should punitive damages for fraud be dischargeable in bankruptcy?

As stated in item number 5 in the previous list, claims based on fraud are not dischargeable in bankruptcy. Often, a claim based on fraud consists of damages that were awarded to the creditor by a court in a lawsuit against the debtor for fraud. A question that sometimes comes before the courts is whether punitive damages, as well as actual damages, should be nondischargeable. How this question is answered depends on how a court interprets the language of the Bankruptcy Code with respect to fraud-based claims. Section 523(a)(2)(A) of the Code excepts from discharge in bankruptcy "any debt . . . for money, property, services, or an extension, renewal, or refinancing of credit, to the extent obtained by . . . false pretenses, a false representation, or actual fraud." To resolve conflicting interpretations of this provision by the lower courts, the United States Supreme Court addressed the issue. In making its decision, the Court emphasized that the Bankruptcy Code "has long prohibited debtors from discharging liabilities incurred on account of their fraud, embodying a basic policy animating the Code of affording relief only to an 'honest but unfortunate debtor.'" According to the Court, when read in the historical context of bankruptcy law and other provisions of the current Bankruptcy Code, the relevant provision of the Code should be interpreted to mean that punitive damages for fraud are nondischargeable.[10]

In the following case, an employer sought to have a debt to an ex-employee for unpaid commissions discharged in bankruptcy. The question before the court was whether the debt arose from "willful and malicious injury" caused by the debtor's tortious conduct, which would mean that it was not dischargeable.

10. *Cohen v. De La Cruz,* 523 U.S. 213, 118 S.Ct. 1212, 140 L.Ed.2d 341 (1998).

CASE 23.3 In re Jercich

United States Court of Appeals,
Ninth Circuit, 2001.
238 F.3d 1202.

FACTS In June 1981, James Petralia began to work for George Jercich, Inc., a mortgage company wholly owned and operated by George Jercich. Petralia's primary duty was to obtain investors to fund the home loans. Jercich agreed to pay Petralia a salary plus monthly commissions for loans that were funded through his efforts. When Jercich failed to pay the commissions, Petralia quit and filed a suit in a California state court against Jercich. The court found that Jercich had not paid Petralia; that Jercich had the clear ability to make the payments to Petralia, but chose not to do so; that instead of paying Petralia and other employees, Jercich used the money for personal investments, including a horse ranch; and that Jercich's behavior was willful and deliberate and constituted "substantial oppression." The court ruled in Petralia's favor. Jercich appealed this ruling to a state intermediate appellate court and filed for bankruptcy in a federal bankruptcy court. The state court affirmed the judgment against Jercich, but the bankruptcy court held that the debt was dischargeable. A bankruptcy appellate panel affirmed this holding.[a] Petralia appealed to the U.S. Court of Appeals for the Ninth Circuit.

ISSUE Did Jercich's debt to Petralia arise from "willful and malicious injury" caused by the debtor's tortious (wrongful) conduct?

DECISION Yes. The U.S. Court of Appeals for the Ninth Circuit reversed the decision of the bankruptcy appellate panel, holding that Jercich's debt to Petralia was not dischargeable.

REASON The U.S. Court of Appeals for the Ninth Circuit recognized that "an intentional breach of contract *generally* will not give rise to a nondischargeable debt." The court held, however, that "where an intentional breach of contract is accompanied by tortious conduct

a. A bankruptcy appellate panel, with the consent of the parties, has jurisdiction to hear appeals from final judgments, orders, and decrees of bankruptcy judges.

(continued)

CASE 23.3—Continued

which results in willful and malicious injury, the resulting debt is excepted from discharge." Based on the state court's findings, "Jercich's nonpayment of wages * * * constituted tortious conduct." Furthermore, "the injury to Petralia was willful. As the state court found, Jercich knew he owed the wages to Petralia and that injury to Petralia was substantially certain to occur if the wages were not paid; and Jercich had the clear ability to pay Petralia his wages, yet chose not to pay and instead used the money for his own personal benefit. He therefore inflicted willful injury on Petralia. * * * Jercich's deliberate and willful failure to pay was found by the state trial court to constitute substantial oppression, which by definition is 'despicable conduct that subjects a person to cruel and unjust hardship in conscious disregard of that person's rights.' We hold that these * * * findings are sufficient to show that the injury inflicted by Jercich was malicious."

FOR CRITICAL ANALYSIS—Social Consideration *A fundamental policy of bankruptcy law is to give a "fresh start" only to the "honest but unfortunate debtor." What corollary to this policy is the basis for some of the exceptions to discharge listed previously?*

Objections to Discharge In addition to the exceptions to discharge previously listed, the following circumstances (relating to the debtor's conduct and not the debt) will cause a discharge to be denied:

① The debtor's concealment or destruction of property with the intent to hinder, delay, or defraud a creditor.

② The debtor's fraudulent concealment or destruction of financial records.

③ The granting of a discharge to the debtor within six years of the filing of the petition.[11]

When a discharge is denied under these circumstances, the assets of the debtor are still distributed to the creditors, but the debtor remains liable for the unpaid portions of all claims.

Effect of Discharge The primary effect of a discharge is to void, or set aside, any judgment on a discharged debt and prohibit any action to collect a discharged debt. A discharge does not affect the liability of a co-debtor.

Revocation of Discharge The Code provides that a debtor's discharge may be revoked. On petition by the trustee or a creditor, the bankruptcy court may, within one year, revoke the discharge decree if it is discovered that the debtor was fraudulent or dishonest during the bankruptcy proceedings. The revocation renders the discharge void, allowing creditors not satisfied by the distribution of the debtor's estate to proceed with their claims against the debtor.

Reaffirmation of Debt A debtor may voluntarily agree to pay off a debt—for example, a debt owed to a family member, close friend, or some other party—even though the debt could be discharged in bankruptcy. An agreement to pay a debt dischargeable in bankruptcy is referred to as a *reaffirmation agreement.*

To be enforceable, reaffirmation agreements must be made before a debtor is granted a discharge, and they must be filed with the court. If the debtor is represented by an attorney, court approval is not required if the attorney files a declaration or affi-

11. A discharge under Chapter 13 of the Code within six years of the filing of the petition does not bar a subsequent Chapter 7 discharge when a good faith Chapter 13 plan paid at least 70 percent of all allowed unsecured claims and was the debtor's "best effort."

davit stating that (1) the debtor has been fully informed of the consequences of the agreement (and a default under the agreement), (2) the agreement is made voluntarily, and (3) the agreement does not impose undue hardship on the debtor or the debtor's family. If the debtor is not represented by an attorney, court approval is required, and the agreement will be approved only if the court finds that the agreement will result in no undue hardship to the debtor and is in his or her best interest.

The agreement must contain a clear and conspicuous statement advising the debtor that reaffirmation is not required. The debtor can rescind, or cancel, the agreement at any time prior to discharge or within sixty days of filing the agreement, whichever is later. This rescission period must be stated *clearly* and *conspicuously* in the reaffirmation agreement.

"Debt rolls a man over and over, binding him hand and foot, and letting him hang upon the fatal mesh until the long-legged interest devours him."

HENRY WARD BEECHER, 1813–1887 (American clergyman, writer, and abolitionist)

Chapter 11—Reorganization

The type of bankruptcy proceeding used most commonly by a corporate debtor is the Chapter 11 *reorganization*. In a reorganization, the creditors and the debtor formulate a plan under which the debtor pays a portion of his or her debts and the rest of the debts are discharged. The debtor is allowed to continue in business. Although this type of bankruptcy is commonly a corporate reorganization, any debtor (except a stockbroker or a commodities broker) who is eligible for Chapter 7 relief is eligible for relief under Chapter 11.[12] Railroads are also eligible.

The same principles that govern the filing of a liquidation petition apply to reorganization proceedings. The case may be brought either voluntarily or involuntarily. The same principles govern the entry of the order for relief. The automatic-stay provision is also applicable in reorganizations. The *Business Law in the Online World* feature on the next page looks at circumstances involving a failed online business that was petitioned into involuntary bankruptcy under Chapter 11.

WORKOUT
An out-of-court agreement between a debtor and his or her creditors in which the parties work out a payment plan or schedule under which the debtor's debts can be discharged.

In some instances, creditors may prefer private, negotiated debt-adjustment agreements, also known as **workouts**, to bankruptcy proceedings. Often, these out-of-court workouts are much more flexible and thus more conducive to a speedy settlement. Speed is critical because delay is one of the most costly elements in any bankruptcy proceeding. Another advantage of workouts is that they avoid the various administrative costs of bankruptcy proceedings.

A bankruptcy court, after notice and a hearing, may dismiss or suspend all proceedings in a case at any time if dismissal or suspension would better serve the interests of the creditors. The Code also allows a court, after notice and a hearing, to dismiss a case under reorganization "for cause." Cause includes the absence of a reasonable likelihood of rehabilitation, the inability to effect a plan, and an unreasonable delay by the debtor that is prejudicial to (may harm the interests of) creditors.[13] A debtor need not be insolvent to be entitled to Chapter 11 protection.[14]

DEBTOR IN POSSESSION (DIP)
In Chapter 11 bankruptcy proceedings, a debtor who is allowed to continue in possession of the estate in property (the business) and to continue business operations.

Debtor in Possession

On entry of the order for relief, the debtor generally continues to operate her or his business as a **debtor in possession (DIP)**. The court, however, may appoint a trustee

12. *Toibb v. Radloff*, 501 U.S. 157, 111 S.Ct. 2197, 115 L.Ed.2d 145 (1991).
13. See 11 U.S.C. Section 1112(b).
14. *In re Johns-Manville Corp.*, 36 Bankr. 727 (S.D.N.Y. 1984).

BUSINESS LAW: //in the Online World

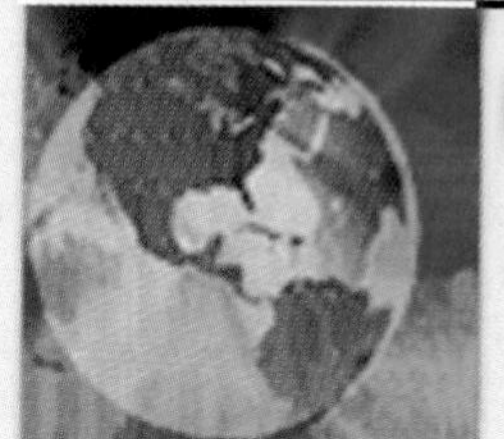

Personal Data on the Auction Block

Businesses on the verge of failure, and businesses that have failed, often find themselves in bankruptcy court. In the spring and summer of 2000, with the sudden drop of investors' interest in online businesses, many of those firms filed for bankruptcy.

One problem facing a failed online business is what to do with its customer list. Offline companies (firms not based on the Web) have commonly bought and sold customer lists, which can attract high prices because they include information about customer buying habits, as well as addresses and other personal data. E-commerce companies, however, generally promise not to sell this information to third parties.

What Am I Bid?

Toysmart.com, LLC, had this policy. Toysmart.com was also a failing dot.com. In June 2000, the company's creditors filed a petition for the firm's involuntary bankruptcy under Chapter 11. As part of the process, Toysmart.com filed a motion seeking court approval for the sale of its assets, including its customer list and customer-profile information. The court put off making a judgment on the propriety of the sale until a prospective purchaser appeared. Toysmart.com then placed an ad in *The Wall Street Journal,* offering to sell its customer data to the highest bidder.

TRUSTe, a nonprofit privacy organization that awards seals of approval to Web sites with strict privacy policies, asked the Federal Trade Commission (FTC) about the legality of this auction. The FTC filed a suit in a federal district court against Toysmart.com, alleging violations of the FTC Act (see Chapter 33) and the Children's Online Privacy Protection Act (see Chapter 2). The controversy swelled because the personal information had been provided, in some instances, by children using the Toysmart.com Web site. More than forty state attorneys general joined the battle against the auction.[a]

Going, Going, Gone

Toysmart.com reached a settlement with the FTC, agreeing, in the event of a sale of substantially all of its assets, to transfer the data to a family-friendly company that would agree to comply with Toysmart.com's privacy policy. When the creditors objected to this proposal, the judge refused to consent to it. Eventually, the creditors agreed to a deal in which Walt Disney Company, one of the owners of Toysmart.com, paid $50,000 to have the data destroyed.

Response to Toysmart.com's case was dramatic. Since the summer of 2000, fewer bankrupt online businesses have tried to sell their customer information. Others have changed their privacy policies to allow such sales. In 2001, TRUSTe issued guidelines on the use of personal information in bankruptcies and other major fundamental changes that occur to Web-based businesses. The guidelines ask that the firms notify customers and offer them the choice to keep their personal data out of a deal (see **http://www.truste.com** for more information).

Finally, one version of the bankruptcy reform bill being considered by a joint committee of the U.S. House and Senate at the time of this writing included an amendment that would prohibit the sale of customer information if that sale would violate a privacy policy.

FOR CRITICAL ANALYSIS

What effect might the privacy policy amendment in the bankruptcy reform bill before Congress have on bankrupt online businesses?

a. For the court's response to a request by the state of Texas regarding the case, see *Federal Trade Commission v. Toysmart.com, LLC,* 2000 WL 1523287 (D.Mass. 2000).

(often referred to as a *receiver*) to operate the debtor's business if gross mismanagement of the business is shown or if appointing a trustee is in the best interests of the estate.

The DIP's role is similar to that of a trustee in a liquidation. The DIP is entitled to avoid preferential payments made to creditors and fraudulent transfers of assets that occurred prior to the filing of the Chapter 11 petition. The DIP has the power to decide whether to cancel or assume obligations under executory contracts (contracts that have not yet been performed) that were made prior to the petition.

ETHICAL ISSUE 23.2

Should those who "bankrupt" a firm be allowed to continue to manage the firm as debtors in possession?

Chapter 11 reorganizations have become the target of substantial criticism. One of the arguments against Chapter 11 is that it allows the very managers who "bankrupted" a firm to continue to manage the firm as debtors in possession while the firm is in Chapter 11 proceedings. According to some critics, the main beneficiaries of Chapter 11 corporate reorganizations are not the shareholder-owners of the corporations but attorneys and current management. Basically, these critics argue that reorganizations do not preserve companies' assets because large firms must pay millions of dollars for attorneys and accountants during the reorganization process, which can take years to complete.

CREDITORS' COMMITTEES

As soon as practicable after the entry of the order for relief, a creditors' committee of unsecured creditors is appointed. The committee may consult with the trustee or the DIP concerning the administration of the case or the formulation of the reorganization plan. Additional creditors' committees may be appointed to represent special interest creditors. Orders affecting the estate generally will not be made without either the consent of the committee or a hearing in which the judge hears the position of the committee.

Certain small businesses that do not own or manage real estate can avoid creditors' committees. In these cases, bankruptcy judges may enter orders without a committee's consent.

THE REORGANIZATION PLAN

A reorganization plan to rehabilitate the debtor is a plan to conserve and administer the debtor's assets in the hope of an eventual return to successful operation and solvency. The plan must be fair and equitable and must do the following:

1. Designate classes of claims and interests.
2. Specify the treatment to be afforded the classes. (The plan must provide the same treatment for each claim in a particular class.)
3. Provide an adequate means for execution.

Filing the Plan Only the debtor may file a plan within the first 120 days after the date of the bankruptcy court's order for relief. If the debtor does not meet the 120-day deadline, however, or if the debtor fails to obtain the required creditor consent (see below) within 180 days, any party may propose a plan. The plan need not provide for full repayment to unsecured creditors. Instead, unsecured creditors receive a percentage of each dollar owed to them by the debtor. If a small-business debtor chooses to avoid creditors' committees, the time for the debtor's filing is shortened to 100 days, and any other party's plan must be filed within 160 days.

Acceptance and Confirmation of the Plan Once the plan has been developed, it is submitted to each class of creditors for acceptance. Each class must accept the plan unless the class is not adversely affected by the plan. A class has accepted the plan when a majority of the creditors, representing two-thirds of the amount of the total claim, vote to approve it. Even when all classes of claims accept the plan, the court may refuse to confirm it if it is not "in the best interests of the creditors." A spouse or child of the debtor can block the plan if it does not provide for payment of his or her claims in cash.

CRAM-DOWN PROVISION A provision of the Bankruptcy Code that allows a court to confirm a debtor's Chapter 11 reorganization plan even though only one class of creditors has accepted it. To exercise the court's right under this provision, the court must demonstrate that the plan does not discriminate unfairly against any creditors and is fair and equitable.

Even if only one class of claims has accepted the plan, the court may still confirm the plan under the Code's so-called **cram-down provision.** In other words, the court may confirm the plan over the objections of a class of creditors. Before the court can exercise this right of cram-down confirmation, it must be demonstrated that the plan "does not discriminate unfairly" against any creditors and that the plan is "fair and equitable."

The plan is binding on confirmation. The debtor is given a reorganization discharge from all claims not protected under the plan. This discharge does not apply to any claims that would be denied discharge under liquidation.

Chapter 13—Repayment Plan

REMEMBER A secured debt is a debt in which a security interest in personal property or fixtures assures payment of the obligation.

Chapter 13 of the Bankruptcy Code provides for the "Adjustment of Debts of an Individual with Regular Income." Individuals (not partnerships or corporations) with regular income who owe fixed unsecured debts of less than \$290,525 or fixed secured debts of less than \$871,550 may take advantage of bankruptcy repayment plans. This includes salaried employees; individual proprietors; and individuals who live on welfare, Social Security, fixed pensions, or investment income. Many small-business debtors have a choice of filing under either Chapter 11 or Chapter 13. Repayment plans offer several advantages. One advantage is that they are less expensive and less complicated than reorganization proceedings or liquidation proceedings.

A Chapter 13 repayment plan can be initiated only by the filing of a voluntary petition by the debtor. Certain liquidation and reorganization cases may be converted to Chapter 13 with the consent of the debtor. A Chapter 13 repayment plan may be converted to a Chapter 7 liquidation at the request of either the debtor or, under certain circumstances, a creditor. A Chapter 13 repayment plan may also be converted to a Chapter 11 reorganization after a hearing. On the filing of a petition under Chapter 13, a trustee must be appointed. The automatic stay previously discussed also takes effect. Although the stay applies to all or part of a consumer debt, it does not apply to any business debt incurred by the debtor.

THE REPAYMENT PLAN

Shortly after the petition is filed, the debtor must file a repayment plan. This plan may provide either for payment of all obligations in full or for payment of a lesser amount. A plan of rehabilitation by repayment provides for the debtor's future earnings or income to be turned over to the trustee as necessary for execution of the plan. The time for payment under the plan may not exceed three years unless the court approves an extension. The term, with extension, may not exceed five years.

The Code requires the debtor to make "timely" payments, and the trustee is required to ensure that the debtor commences these payments. The debtor must begin making payments under the proposed plan within thirty days after the plan has been filed with the court. If the plan has not been confirmed, the trustee is instructed to retain the payments until the plan is confirmed and then distribute them accordingly. If the plan is denied, the trustee will return the payments to the debtor less any costs. If the debtor fails to make timely payments or to begin payments within the thirty-day period, the court may convert the repayment plan to a liquidation bankruptcy or dismiss the petition.

Confirmation of the Plan After the plan is filed, the court holds a confirmation hearing, at which interested parties may object to the plan. The court will confirm a plan with respect to each claim of a secured creditor under any of the following circumstances:

① The secured creditors have accepted the plan.

② The plan provides that creditors retain their claims against the debtor's property, and the value of the property to be distributed to the creditors under the plan is not less than the secured portion of their claims.

③ The debtor surrenders the property securing the claim to the creditors.

Objection to the Plan Unsecured creditors do not have a vote to confirm a repayment plan, but they can object to it. The court can approve a plan over the objection of the trustee or any unsecured creditor only in either of the following situations:

① The value of the property to be distributed under the plan is at least equal to the amount of the claims.

② All the debtor's projected disposable income to be received during the three-year plan period will be applied to making payments. Disposable income is all income received less amounts needed to support the debtor and dependents and/or amounts needed to meet ordinary expenses to continue the operation of a business.

As emphasized by the decision in the following case, the timing of creditors' objections to a Chapter 13 plan is critical.

CASE 23.4 In re Andersen

United States Bankruptcy Appellate Panel, Tenth Circuit, 1998.
215 Bankr. 792.
http://www.utb.uscourts.gov/bap/bap.htm[a]

HISTORICAL AND SOCIAL SETTING *Resolving disputes as to the dischargeability of student loans has been a thorny issue for the courts. The Bankruptcy Code appears to require an all-or-nothing finding—that is, the entire amount of a student loan is either dischargeable or not. Most courts have agreed.*[b] *Frequently, a debtor may be able to pay part, but not all, of a loan, or may be able to pay the loan in full in the future when he or she is gainfully employed. In light of these variables, some courts allow more creative repayment plans, stating that only part of a debt is dischargeable or that repayment terms may be modified by the court. Permitting debtors to use Chapter 13 to resolve a dispute about the dischargeability of a student loan can encourage the parties to find other inventive ways to compromise.*

a. This is the Web site for the U.S. Bankruptcy Court for the District of Utah. When the page opens, click on the "BAP Opinions" link. On that page, scroll down the list to the *Andersen* case (number 39), and click on the link to open it.

b. See, for example, *In re Shankwiler,* 208 Bankr. 701 (Bankr.C.D.Cal. 1997); and *In re Rivers,* 213 Bankr. 616 (Bankr.S.D.Ga. 1997).

FACTS Doreen Andersen had student loan obligations to a number of educational loan guaranty agencies and lending banks. She filed a Chapter 13 plan that contained the following information:

> All timely filed and allowed unsecured claims, including the claims of Higher Education Assistance Foundation [HEAF] and [other] government guaranteed education loans, shall be paid ten percent (10%) of each claim, and the balance of each claim shall be discharged. * * * [E]xcepting the aforementioned education loans from discharge will impose an undue hardship on the debtor and the debtor's dependents. Confirmation of debtor's plan shall constitute a finding to that effect and that said debt is dischargeable.

The lenders filed an objection to the treatment of their claims. Because the objection was untimely, however, the court denied it and confirmed the plan. Three years later, after Andersen fulfilled the plan, the court entered a discharge. When the lenders attempted to collect the balance of the loans, Andersen filed a suit in a bankruptcy court against them. The court held that the debts had not been discharged. Andersen appealed.

ISSUE Did the confirmation of the plan constitute a binding determination that payment of the student loans

(continued)

CASE 23.4—Continued

(beyond what was provided in the plan) would be an undue hardship, making the loans dischargeable?

DECISION Yes. The bankruptcy appellate panel reversed the decision of the lower court and remanded the case for further proceedings, including the entry of a judgment that the unpaid student loans were discharged.

REASON The appellate panel explained that a bankruptcy plan is agreed to "through a bargaining process." There are few requirements, and the Bankruptcy Code allows much flexibility in devising a plan. The court pointed out that "[a] plan that is filed and served is simply an offer to the creditors, one that may be deemed to have been accepted if the creditor does not object." In this case, the lenders received notice of the plan and had an opportunity to object, but failed to object in time. The plan was then confirmed and, once confirmed, "resolved a potential controversy about whether payment of the student [loans] would result in an undue hardship to the debtor." The confirmation rendered the loans dischargeable, and the final order of discharge discharged them.

FOR CRITICAL ANALYSIS—Economic Consideration *How might the lenders have avoided the outcome in this case?*

Modification of the Plan Prior to the completion of payments, the plan may be modified at the request of the debtor, the trustee, or an unsecured creditor. If any interested party has an objection to the modification, the court must hold a hearing to determine approval or disapproval of the modified plan.

DISCHARGE

BE CAREFUL Courts, trustees, and creditors carefully monitor Chapter 13 debtors. If payments are not made, a court can require a debtor to explain why and may allow a creditor to take back her or his property.

After the completion of all payments, the court grants a discharge of all debts provided for by the repayment plan. Except for allowed claims not provided for by the plan, certain long-term debts provided for by the plan, and claims for alimony and child support, all other debts are dischargeable. A discharge of debts under a Chapter 13 repayment plan is sometimes referred to as a "superdischarge." One of the reasons for this is that the law allows a Chapter 13 discharge to include fraudulently incurred debt and claims resulting from malicious or willful injury. Therefore, a discharge under Chapter 13 may be much more beneficial to some debtors than a liquidation discharge under Chapter 7 might be.

Even if the debtor does not complete the plan, a hardship discharge may be granted if failure to complete the plan was due to circumstances beyond the debtor's control and if the value of the property distributed under the plan was greater than creditors would have received in a liquidation proceeding. A discharge can be revoked within one year if it was obtained by fraud.

Chapter 12—Family-Farmer Plan

The Bankruptcy Code defines a *family farmer* as one whose gross income is at least 50 percent farm dependent and whose debts are at least 80 percent farm related. The total debt must not exceed $1.5 million. A partnership or closely held corporation that is at least 50 percent owned by the farm family can also take advantage of Chapter 12.

The procedure for filing a family-farmer bankruptcy plan is very similar to the procedure for filing a repayment plan under Chapter 13. The farmer-debtor must file a plan not later than ninety days after the order for relief. The filing of the petition acts as an automatic stay against creditors' actions against the estate.

The content of a family-farmer plan is basically the same as that of a Chapter 13 repayment plan. The plan can be modified by the farmer-debtor but, except for cause, must be confirmed or denied within forty-five days of the filing of the plan.

Court confirmation of the plan is the same as for a repayment plan. In summary, the plan must provide for payment of secured debts at the value of the collateral. If the secured debt exceeds the value of the collateral, the remaining debt is unsecured. For unsecured debtors, the plan must be confirmed if either the value of the property to be distributed under the plan equals the amount of the claim or the plan provides that all of the farmer-debtor's disposable income to be received in a three-year period (or longer, by court approval) will be applied to making payments. Completion of payments under the plan discharges all debts provided for by the plan.

A farmer who has already filed a reorganization or repayment plan may convert the plan to a family-farmer plan. The farmer-debtor may also convert a family-farmer plan to a liquidation plan.

APPLICATION Law and the Small-Business Owner . . .

Preparing for Bankruptcy*

Chapter 11 of the Bankruptcy Code expresses the broad public policy of encouraging commerce. To this end, Chapter 11 allows financially troubled business firms to petition for reorganization in bankruptcy while they are still solvent so that the firms' business can continue. Small businesses, however, do not fare very well under Chapter 11. Although some corporations that enter Chapter 11 emerge as functioning entities, very few smaller companies survive the process. The reason is that Chapter 11 proceedings are prolonged and extremely costly, and whether a firm survives is largely a matter of size. The greater the firm's assets, the greater the likelihood it will emerge from Chapter 11 intact.

Plan Ahead

If you ever are a small-business owner contemplating Chapter 11 reorganization, you can improve your chances of being among the survivors by planning ahead. You should take action before, not after, entering bankruptcy proceedings to ensure the greatest possibility of success. Your first step, of course, should be to do everything possible to avoid having to resort to Chapter 11. Discuss your financial troubles openly and cooperatively with creditors to see if you can agree on a workout or some other arrangement.

If it appears that you have no choice but to file for Chapter 11 protection, try to interest a lender in loaning you funds to see you through the bankruptcy. If your business is a small corporation, you might try to negotiate a favorable deal with a major investor. For example, you could offer to transfer stock ownership to the investor in return for a loan to pay the costs of the bankruptcy proceedings and an option to repurchase the stock when the firm becomes profitable again.

Consult with Creditors

Most important, you should form a Chapter 11 plan prior to entering bankruptcy proceedings. Consult with creditors in advance to see what kind of a plan would be acceptable to them, and prepare your plan accordingly. Having an acceptable plan prepared before you file will help expedite the proceedings and thus save substantially on costs.

Checklist for the Small-Business Owner

1. Try to negotiate workouts with creditors to avoid costly Chapter 11 proceedings.
2. If your business is a small corporation, see if a major investor will loan you funds to help you pay bankruptcy costs in return for stock ownership.
3. Consult with creditors in advance, and have an acceptable Chapter 11 plan prepared before filing in order to expedite bankruptcy proceedings and save on costs.

*This *Application* is not meant to substitute for the services of an attorney who is licensed to practice law in your state.

Key Terms

Chapter Summary Creditors' Rights and Bankruptcy

REMEDIES AVAILABLE TO CREDITORS	
Liens (See pages 610–612.)	1. *Mechanic's lien*—A nonpossessory, filed lien on an owner's real estate for labor, services, or materials furnished to or made on the realty. 2. *Artisan's lien*—A possessory lien on an owner's personal property for labor performed or value added. 3. *Innkeeper's lien*—A possessory lien on a hotel guest's baggage for hotel charges that remain unpaid. 4. *Judicial liens*— a. *Attachment*—A court-ordered seizure of property prior to a court's final determination of the creditor's rights to the property. Attachment is available only on the creditor's posting of a bond and strict compliance with the applicable state statutes. b. *Writ of execution*—A court order directing the sheriff to seize (levy) and sell a debtor's nonexempt real or personal property to satisfy a court's judgment in the creditor's favor.
Garnishment (See page 612.)	A collection remedy that allows the creditor to attach a debtor's money (such as wages owed or bank accounts) and property that are held by a third person.
Creditors' Composition Agreement (See page 612.)	A contract between a debtor and his or her creditors by which the debtor's debts are discharged by payment of a sum less than the sum that is actually owed.
Mortgage Foreclosure (See page 613.)	On the debtor's default, the entire mortgage debt is due and payable, allowing the creditor to foreclose on the realty by selling it to satisfy the debt.
Suretyship or Guaranty (See pages 613–616.)	Under contract, a third person agrees to be primarily or secondarily liable for the debt owed by the principal debtor. A creditor can turn to this third person for satisfaction of the debt.
LAWS ASSISTING DEBTORS	
Exemptions (See pages 616–617.)	Numerous laws, including consumer protection statutes, assist debtors. Additionally, state laws exempt certain types of real and personal property from levy of execution or attachment.

Chapter Summary Creditors' Rights and Bankruptcy—continued

Exemptions—continued	1. *Real property*—Each state permits a debtor to retain the family home, either in its entirety or up to a specified dollar amount, free from the claims of unsecured creditors or trustees in bankruptcy (homestead exemption). 2. *Personal property*—Personal property that is most often exempt from satisfaction of judgment debts includes the following: a. Household furniture up to a specified dollar amount. b. Clothing and certain personal possessions. c. Transportation vehicles up to a specified dollar amount. d. Certain classified animals, such as livestock and pets. e. Equipment used in a business or trade up to a specified dollar amount.

BANKRUPTCY—A COMPARISON OF CHAPTERS 7, 11, 12, AND 13

ISSUE	CHAPTER 7	CHAPTER 11	CHAPTERS 12 AND 13
Purpose	Liquidation.	Reorganization.	Adjustment.
Who Can Petition	Debtor (voluntary) or creditors (involuntary).	Debtor (voluntary) or creditors (involuntary).	Debtor (voluntary) only.
Who Can Be a Debtor	Any "person" (including partnerships and corporations) except railroads, insurance companies, banks, savings and loan institutions, investment companies licensed by the Small Business Administration, and credit unions. Farmers and charitable institutions cannot be involuntarily petitioned.	Any debtor eligible for Chapter 7 relief; railroads are also eligible.	*Chapter 12*—Any family farmer (one whose gross income is at least 50 percent farm dependent and whose debts are at least 80 percent farm related) or any partnership or closely held corporation at least 50 percent owned by a farm family, when total debt does not exceed $1.5 million. *Chapter 13*—Any individual (not partnerships or corporations) with regular income who owes fixed unsecured debts of less than $290,525 or fixed secured debts of less than $871,550.
Procedure Leading to Discharge	Nonexempt property is sold with proceeds to be distributed (in order) to priority groups. Dischargeable debts are terminated.	Plan is submitted; if it is approved and followed, debts are discharged.	Plan is submitted and must be approved if the debtor turns over disposable income for a three-year period; if the plan is followed, debts are discharged.
Advantages	On liquidation and distribution, most debts are discharged, and the debtor has an opportunity for a fresh start.	Debtor continues in business. Creditors can either accept the plan, or it can be "crammed down" on them. The plan allows for the reorganization and liquidation of debts over the plan period.	Debtor continues in business or possession of assets. If the plan is approved, most debts are discharged after a three-year period.

For Review

① What is a prejudgment attachment? What is a writ of execution? How does a creditor use these remedies?
② What is garnishment? When might a creditor undertake a garnishment proceeding?
③ In a bankruptcy proceeding, what constitutes the debtor's estate in property? What property is exempt from the estate under federal bankruptcy law?
④ What is the difference between an exception to discharge and an objection to discharge?
⑤ In a Chapter 11 reorganization, what is the role of the debtor in possession?

Questions and Case Problems

23–1. Creditors' Remedies. In what circumstances would a creditor resort to each of the following remedies when trying to collect on a debt?

(a) Mechanic's lien.
(b) Artisan's lien.
(c) Innkeeper's lien.
(d) Writ of attachment.
(e) Writ of execution.
(f) Garnishment.

23–2. Rights of the Surety. Meredith, a farmer, borrowed $5,000 from Farmer's Bank and gave the bank $4,000 in bearer bonds to hold as collateral for the loan. Meredith's neighbor, Peterson, who had known Meredith for years, signed as a surety on the note. Because of a drought, Meredith's harvest that year was only a fraction of what it normally was, and he was forced to default on his payments to Farmer's Bank. The bank did not immediately sell the bonds but instead requested $5,000 from Peterson. Peterson paid the $5,000 and then demanded that the bank give him the $4,000 in securities. Can Peterson enforce this demand? Explain.

23–3. Rights of the Guarantor. Sabrina is a student at Sunnyside University. In need of funds to pay for tuition and books, she attempts to secure a short-term loan from University Bank. The bank agrees to make a loan if Sabrina will have someone financially responsible guarantee the loan payments. Abigail, a well-known businessperson and a friend of Sabrina's family, calls the bank and agrees to pay the loan if Sabrina cannot. Because of Abigail's reputation, the bank makes the loan. Sabrina makes several payments on the loan, but because of illness she is not able to work for one month. She requests that University Bank extend the loan for three months. The bank agrees and raises the interest rate for the extended period. Abigail has not been notified of the extension (and therefore has not consented to it). One month later, Sabrina drops out of school. All attempts to collect from Sabrina have failed. University Bank wants to hold Abigail liable. Will the bank succeed? Explain.

23–4. Distribution of Property. Runyan voluntarily petitions for bankruptcy. He has three major claims against his estate. One is by Calvin, a friend who holds Runyan's negotiable promissory note for $2,500; one is by Kohak, an employee who is owed three months' back wages of $4,500; and one is by the First Bank of Sunny Acres on an unsecured loan of $5,000. In addition, Martinez, an accountant retained by the trustee, is owed $500, and property taxes of $1,000 are owed to Micanopa County. Runyan's nonexempt property has been liquidated, with the proceeds totaling $5,000. Discuss fully what amount each party will receive, and why.

23–5. Creditors' Remedies. Orkin owns a relatively old home valued at $45,000. He notices that the bathtubs and fixtures in both bathrooms are leaking and need to be replaced. He contracts with Pike to replace the bathtubs and fixtures. Pike replaces them and submits her bill of $4,000 to Orkin. Because of financial difficulties, Orkin does not pay the bill. Orkin's only asset is his home, which under state law is exempt up to $40,000 as a homestead. Discuss fully Pike's remedies in this situation.

23–6. Artisan's Lien. Air Ruidoso, Ltd., operated a commuter airline and air charter service between Ruidoso, New Mexico, and airports in Albuquerque and El Paso. Executive Aviation Center, Inc., provided services for airlines at the Albuquerque International Airport. When Air Ruidoso failed to pay more than $10,000 that it owed for fuel, oil, and oxygen, Executive Aviation took possession of Air Ruidoso's plane. Executive Aviation claimed that it had a lien on the plane and filed a suit in a New Mexico state court to foreclose. Do supplies such as fuel, oil, and oxygen qualify as "materials" for the purpose of creating an artisan's lien? Why or why not? [*Air Ruidoso, Ltd. v. Executive Aviation Center, Inc.*, 122 N.M. 71, 920 P.2d 1025 (1996)]

23–7. Automatic Stay. David Sisco had about $600 in an account in Tinker Federal Credit Union. Sisco owed DPW Employees Credit Union a little more than $1,100. To collect on the debt, DPW obtained a garnishment judgment and served it on Tinker. The next day, Sisco filed a bankruptcy petition. Tinker then told

DPW that, because of the bankruptcy filing, it could not pay the garnishment. DPW objected, and Tinker asked an Oklahoma state court to resolve the issue. What effect, if any, does Sisco's bankruptcy filing have on DPW's garnishment action? [*DPW Employees Credit Union v. Tinker Federal Credit Union,* 925 P.2d 93 (Okla.App.4th 1996)]

23–8. Guaranty. In 1988, Jamieson-Chippewa Investment Co. entered into a five-year commercial lease with TDM Pharmacy, Inc., for certain premises in Ellisville, Missouri, on which TDM intended to operate a small drugstore. Dennis and Tereasa McClintock ran the pharmacy business. The lease granted TDM three additional five-year options to renew. The lease was signed by TDM and by the McClintocks individually as guarantors. The lease did not state that the guaranty was continuing. In fact, there were no words of guaranty in the lease other than the single word "Guarantors" on the signature page. In 1993, Dennis McClintock, acting as the president of TDM, exercised TDM's option to renew the lease for one term. Three years later, when the pharmacy failed, TDM defaulted on the lease. Jamieson-Chippewa filed a suit in a Missouri state court against the McClintocks for the rent for the rest of the term, based on their guaranty. The McClintocks filed a motion for summary judgment, contending that they had not guaranteed any rent payments beyond the initial five-year term. How should the court rule? Why? [*Jamieson-Chippewa Investment Co. v. McClintock,* 996 S.W.2d 84 (Mo.App.E.D. 1999)]

23–9. Voidable Preference. The Securities and Exchange Commission (SEC) filed a suit in a federal district court against First Jersey Securities, Inc., and others, alleging fraud in First Jersey's sale of securities (stock). The court ordered the defendants to turn over to the SEC $75 million in illegal profits. This order made the SEC the largest unsecured creditor of First Jersey. First Jersey filed a voluntary petition in a federal bankruptcy court to declare bankruptcy under Chapter 11. On the same day, the debtor transferred 200,001 shares of stock to its law firm, Robinson, St. John, & Wayne (RSW), in payment for services in the SEC suit and the bankruptcy petition. The stock represented essentially all of the debtor's assets. RSW did not find a buyer for the stock for more than two months. The SEC objected to the transfer, contending that it was a voidable preference, and asked that RSW be disqualified from representing the debtor. RSW responded that the transfer was made in the ordinary course of business. Also, asserted RSW, the transfer was not in payment of an "antecedent debt," because the firm had not presented First Jersey with a bill for its services and therefore the debt was not yet past due. Was the stock transfer a voidable preference? Should the court disqualify RSW? Why or why not? [*In re First Jersey Securities, Inc.,* 180 F.3d 504 (3d Cir. 1999)]

TEST YOUR KNOWLEDGE—ANSWER ON THE WEB

23–10. Mr. Mallinckrodt received an undergraduate degree from the University of Miami and, in 1995, a graduate degree from Barry University in mental health counseling. To finance this education, Mallinckrodt borrowed from The Education Resources Institute, Inc., and others. Unable to find a job as a counselor, Mallinckrodt worked as a tennis instructor and coach. (At one time, he had played professional tennis and was ranked among the top 800 players in the world.) In 1996, he ruptured his Achilles tendon and was unable to work. After a lengthy rehabilitation, he began work on a part-time, hourly basis at Horizon Psychological Services, but the work was intermittent and low paying. He continued to work as a tennis instructor and was also a licensed real estate broker, but had little income in either field. With monthly income of about $549 after taxes, and expenses of $544, Mallinckrodt filed a bankruptcy petition to discharge his student loan debt, which with interest totaled nearly $73,000. Is this debt dischargeable? Discuss. [*In re Mallinckrodt,* 260 Bankr. 892 (S.D.Fla. 2001)]

A QUESTION OF ETHICS AND SOCIAL RESPONSIBILITY

23–11. In September 1986, Edward and Debora Davenport pleaded guilty in a Pennsylvania court to welfare fraud and were sentenced to probation for one year. As a condition of their probation, the Davenports were ordered to make monthly restitution payments to the county probation department, which would forward the payments to the Pennsylvania Department of Public Welfare, the victim of the Davenports' fraud. In May 1987, the Davenports filed a petition for Chapter 13 relief and listed the restitution payments among their debts. The bankruptcy court held that the restitution obligation was a dischargeable debt. Ultimately, the United States Supreme Court reviewed the case. The Court noted that under the Bankruptcy Code, a debt is defined as a liability on a claim, and a claim is defined as a right to payment. Because the restitution obligations clearly constituted a right to payment, the Court held that the obligations were dischargeable in bankruptcy. [*Pennsylvania Department of Public Welfare v. Davenport,* 495 U.S. 552, 110 S.Ct. 2126, 109 L.Ed.2d 588 (1990)]

1. Critics of this decision contend that the Court adhered to the letter, but not the spirit, of bankruptcy law in arriving at its conclusion. In what way, if any, did the Court not abide by the "spirit" of bankruptcy law?
2. Do you think that Chapter 13 plans, which allow nearly all types of debts to be discharged, tip the scales of justice too far in favor of debtors?

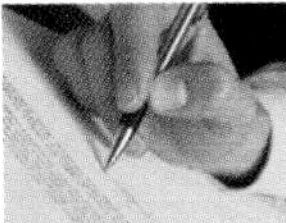

FOR CRITICAL ANALYSIS

23–12. Has the Bankruptcy Code made it too easy for debtors to avoid their obligations by filing for bankruptcy? What are the implications of the increased number of bankruptcy filings for future potential debtors who seek to obtain credit?

Internet Exercises

Go to the *Business Law Today* home page at **http://blt.westbuslaw.com**. Select "Interactive Study Center" and then click on "Chapter 23." There you will find the following Internet research exercises that you can perform to learn more about bankruptcy and bankruptcy alternatives:

Activity 23–1: Bankruptcy
Activity 23–2: Bankruptcy Alternatives

Before the Test

Go to the *Business Law Today* home page at **http://blt.westbuslaw.com**. Click on "Interactive Quizzes." You will find at least twenty interactive questions relating to this chapter.

UNIT FIVE Cumulative Business Hypothetical

Java Jive, Inc., is a small chain of coffee shops. Adam is Java Jive's president.

① Java Jive wants to borrow $40,000 from First National Bank to buy equipment. To secure the loan, First National could accept Java Jive's equipment as collateral. If so, how would First National let other potential creditors know of its interest? If First National secured its loan with the equipment, and Java Jive failed to repay the loan, what would be First National's alternatives with respect to collecting the amount due?

② Java Jive wants to borrow $30,000 from Eagle Credit Corp. to pay Java Jive employees. Java Jive believes that it will be able to repay the loan by the end of the month, which is when Macro Manufacturing Co. has agreed to pay Java Jive for its catering of Macro's facilities. Eagle agrees to make the loan if Adam will sign a promise that if Java Jive defaults on the loan, Adam will be personally liable for the amount. Under these circumstances, is Adam a guarantor, a surety, or neither? If Adam orally promises to assume personal liability if Java Jive defaults, but does not actually sign anything, can Eagle enforce the promise?

③ Java Jive borrows $20,000 from Ace Loan Co. to make physical improvements to the Java Jive stores. Java Jive gives the money to Jones Construction, a contractor, to do the work. The amount represents only half of the cost, but when Jones finishes the work, Java Jive fails to pay the rest. Java Jive also does not repay Ace for the loan. What can Jones do to collect what it is owed? What can Ace do?

④ Ultimately, Java Jive is unable to pay its employees or to repay its creditors. The creditors include First National, whose loan is secured by Java Jive's equipment and fixtures; Eagle, which loaned money to Java Jive to pay its employees without Adam's promise to repay the loan on Java Jive's default; Ace, which was not repaid for its loan to Java Jive to make physical improvements to its stores; and Jones Construction, the contractor that was not fully paid for its work. Java Jive, which also owes unpaid taxes, files a petition to declare bankruptcy. If the court grants the petition, will the creditors be paid? In what order?

UNIT FIVE Extended Case Study

In re Bentz Metal Products Co.

We covered creditor's liens and outlined the parameters of bankruptcy law in Chapter 23. Now, in this extended case study, we examine *In re Bentz Metal Products Co.*,[1] a decision that concerns the priority of a mechanic's lien[2] in the distribution of a debtor's property as part of a Chapter 7 bankruptcy proceeding. The specific dispute in this case concerned employees' vacation pay owed under a collective bargaining agreement. (Collective bargaining agreements are discussed in more detail in Chapter 34.)

CASE BACKGROUND

Twenty employees of Bentz Metal Products Company in Fort Wayne, Indiana, were members of the United Automobile, Aerospace and Agricultural Implement Workers of America, Local 2298. These employees, as union members, were parties to a collective bargaining agreement (CBA) with Bentz.

In 1996, an involuntary bankruptcy petition was filed in a federal bankruptcy court against Bentz. While the proceeding was pending, the employees filed liens under Indiana state law to secure $12,700.38 in unpaid vacation pay owed to them under the CBA. The employees then filed a suit in the same court against Bentz and its secured creditor, Bank One, to determine the validity and priority of their liens.

The court held that Section 301 of the federal Labor Management Relations Act (LMRA) of 1947 preempted the liens, lowering the employees' priority for collection of their vacation pay. (Preemption is explained in Chapter 2, and the LMRA is discussed in more detail in Chapter 34.) On the employees' appeal, a federal district court affirmed this holding. The employees appealed to the U.S. Court of Appeals for the Seventh Circuit.

1. 231 F.3d 1029 (7th Cir. 2001).
2. Note that the type of mechanic's lien discussed in this case differs from the type of mechanic's lien discussed in Chapter 23.

MAJORITY OPINION

TERENCE T. EVANS, Circuit Judge.

Indiana law broadly protects the rights of workers ("mechanics and laborers employed in or about any shop, mill, wareroom, storeroom, * * * bridge, reservoir, * * * drainage ditch * * * or any other earth-moving operation * * * " in the charming, though antiquated, language of the old Hoosier [Indiana] statute) against losing wages due when an employer encounters tough economic times. It does so by moving workers to the front of the company's creditor queue [line] with a mechanic's lien that trumps [takes priority over] the rights of other creditors to the company's assets. Today we consider whether that lien protects unionized workers to the same extent it undoubtedly protects the rights of nonunionized workers. * * *

* * * *

[Section] 301 expresses a policy that the substantive law to apply in [Section] 301 cases is federal law * * *. The guiding principle behind [Section] 301 preemption was that a contract should not have different meanings under federal law and the laws of various states. Today, it is well understood that a claim for breach of a collective bargaining agreement is preempted. But in other cases, not based directly on a CBA [collective bargaining agreement], the scope of preemption continues to cause some bewilderment. * * *

So we must do our best. * * * What has become clear is that preemption can extend beyond contract disputes to other state law claims if resolution of those claims is sufficiently dependent on an interpretation of a CBA. * * *

* * * *

* * * [T]he employees' rights to the monies due, and the precise amount, depend on the collective bargaining agreement. Here, that sum is undisputed. Nevertheless, it remains true that the entitlement to the money due is laid out in the CBA. * * * [W]hether the amount due is resolved, as here, by stipulation, or whether it is resolved through procedures set out in the CBA, the contract issues are separate from the claim the employees presented to the bankruptcy court. Once the contract issues are resolved, the employees can present their separate claim in bankruptcy for priority based on the Indiana mechanic's lien statute. The priority among creditors in a bankruptcy proceeding is not dependent on a CBA. It is not something which a collective bargaining agreement can or does dictate. *No amount of interpretation of a CBA and no arbitrator's decision would, independent of the state law lien, compel a bankruptcy court to let employees jump ahead of a bank in the money line* * * *. [Emphasis added.]

* * * *

To require that for preemption to exist, resolution of a claim must require interpretation of a CBA, not a mere glance at it, is consistent with recent cases in this circuit and in other circuits. * * * Other circuits require the same case-by-case analysis of the state-law claim as it relates to the CBA. As one would expect in case-by-case analysis, in some situations preemption is found and in others it is not. * * *

In summary, the overriding principle is that for preemption to apply, *interpretation* of the CBA and not simply a reference to it is required. If the entitlement to wages (or other employee pay) or the amount due were at issue, the CBA would control; almost certainly, interpretation of the agreement would be necessary and would be subject to the arbitration procedures in the contract. So as to that determination, preemption would apply. The mechanic's lien, however, is a benefit provided to workers based on a state policy protecting workers; it is a separate claim, not dependent on interpretation of the agreement for its existence even though the amount of the pay is dependent on the CBA. In this situation, the claim is not preempted.

Accordingly, the decision of the district court is REVERSED. This case is REMANDED for the entry of judgment in favor of the plaintiffs.

DISSENTING OPINION

BAUER, Circuit Judge, * * * dissenting.

* * * *

* * * [A] claim may be preempted under the LMRA either because it depends on interpretation of the CBA or because the claim is founded on the CBA. So, preemption applies, first, if the right is created by state law and interpretation of the CBA is required or, second, if the claim is founded directly on rights created by the CBA. * * *

I am convinced that preemption applies because the employees' claims are founded on rights created by the CBA. The interpretation prong has been generally applied when independent state rights are implicated, such as tort actions, which require some interpretation of the CBA to resolve. When a cause of action is created by state law, independent of the CBA, a court must determine whether the CBA needs to be interpreted or if a quick look is enough. The employees here seek unpaid vacation pay owing to them only under the CBA, which Bentz failed to pay because it went bankrupt. This means, simply put, that for whatever reason, including lack of funds, Bentz breached its contract with its employees. The employees seek to enforce the CBA, and therefore their claims are wholly founded on rights created by the CBA. This is not a case in which the employees seek enforcement of a state right independent of the CBA. As the majority notes, federal law preempts a claim for breach of a CBA. Since the employees' claims are founded on the CBA, * * * the employees' state mechanic's liens are preempted.

QUESTIONS FOR ANALYSIS

① **Law.** What did the majority conclude in this case? What was the reasoning leading to this conclusion?

② **Law.** What was the dissent's contention? On what did the dissent base its argument?

③ **Ethics.** What is the ethical basis for holding, as the majority does, that the claims of unionized workers should be treated the same as those of nonunionized workers in a bankruptcy proceeding?

④ **Economic Dimensions.** How might the result in this case affect a creditor's decision to lend to an employer with unionized employees?

⑤ **Implications for the Business Lender.** Under the holding in this case, can a lender ever have first priority to an employer's assets in a bankruptcy proceeding?

Business Organizations

UNIT 6

UNIT CONTENTS

CHAPTER 24

Agency Relationships in Business

"[It] is a universal principle in the law of agency, that the powers of the agent are to be exercised for the benefit of the principal only, and not of the agent or of third parties."

Joseph Story, 1779–1845
(Associate justice of the United States Supreme Court, 1811–1844)

CHAPTER CONTENTS

LEARNING OBJECTIVES

After reading this chapter, you should be able to answer the following questions:

1. What is the difference between an employee and an independent contractor, and how do agency relationships arise?
2. What duties do agents and principals owe to each other?
3. When is a principal liable for the agent's actions with respect to third parties? When is the agent liable?
4. What is an e-agent? Does the use of e-agents in commerce pose any special legal issues?
5. What are some of the ways in which an agency relationship can be terminated?

One of the most common, important, and pervasive legal relationships is that of **agency**. As discussed in Chapter 20, in an agency relationship between two parties, one of the parties, called the *agent*, agrees to represent or act for the other, called the *principal*. The principal has the right to control the agent's conduct in matters entrusted to the agent, and the agent must exercise his or her powers "for the benefit of the principal only," as Justice Joseph Story indicated in the above quotation. By using agents, a principal can conduct multiple business operations simultaneously in various locations. Thus, for example, contracts that bind the principal can be made at different places with different persons at the same time.

AGENCY
A relationship between two parties in which one party (the agent) agrees to represent or act for the other (the principal).

Agency relationships permeate the business world. Indeed, agency law is essential to the existence and operation of a corporate entity, because only through its agents can a corporation function and enter into contracts. A familiar example of an agent is a corporate officer who serves in a representative capacity for the owners of the corporation. In this capacity, the officer has the authority to bind the principal (the corporation) to a contract.

Agency Relationships

Section 1(1) of the *Restatement (Second) of Agency*[1] defines agency as "the fiduciary relation which results from the manifestation of consent by one person to another that the other shall act in his behalf and subject to his control, and consent by the other so to act." In other words, in a principal-agent relationship, the parties have agreed that the agent will act *on behalf and instead of* the principal in negotiating and transacting business with third persons.

FIDUCIARY
As a noun, a person having a duty created by his or her undertaking to act primarily for another's benefit in matters connected with the undertaking. As an adjective, a relationship founded on trust and confidence.

The term **fiduciary** is at the heart of agency law. The term can be used both as a noun and as an adjective. When used as a noun, it refers to a person having a duty created by her or his undertaking to act primarily for another's benefit in matters connected with the undertaking. When used as an adjective, as in "fiduciary relationship," it means that the relationship involves trust and confidence.

Agency relationships commonly exist between employers and employees. Agency relationships may sometimes also exist between employers and independent contractors who are hired to perform special tasks or services.

Employer-Employee Relationships

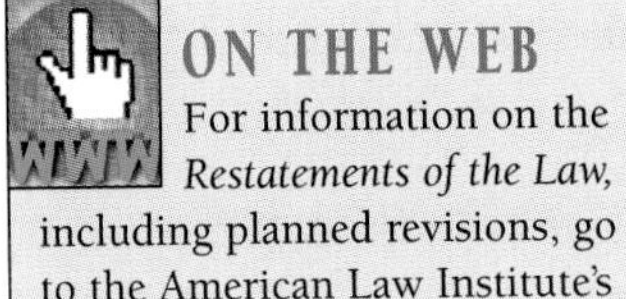

ON THE WEB
For information on the *Restatements of the Law*, including planned revisions, go to the American Law Institute's Web site at
http://www.ali.org.

Normally, all employees who deal with third parties are deemed to be agents. A salesperson in a department store, for example, is an agent of the store's owner (the principal) and acts on the owner's behalf. Any sale of goods made by the salesperson to a customer is binding on the principal. Similarly, most representations of fact made by the salesperson with respect to the goods sold are binding on the principal.

Because employees who deal with third parties are normally deemed to be agents of their employers, agency law and employment law overlap considerably. Agency relationships, though, as will become apparent, can exist outside an employer-employee relationship and thus have a broader reach than employment laws do. Additionally, bear in mind that agency law is based on the common law. In the employment realm, many common law doctrines have been displaced by statutory law and government regulations governing employment relationships.

Employment laws (state and federal) apply only to the employer-employee relationship. Statutes governing Social Security, withholding taxes, workers' compensation, unemployment compensation, workplace safety, employment discrimination, and the like (see Chapters 34 and 35) are applicable only if there is employer-employee status. *These laws do not apply to the independent contractor.*

INDEPENDENT CONTRACTOR
One who works for, and receives payment from, an employer but whose working conditions and methods are not controlled by the employer. An independent contractor is not an employee but may be an agent.

Employer–Independent Contractor Relationships

Independent contractors are not employees because, by definition, those who hire them have no control over the details of their physical performance. Section 2 of the *Restatement (Second) of Agency* defines an **independent contractor** as follows:

1. The *Restatement (Second) of Agency* is an authoritative summary of the law of agency and is often referred to by jurists in their decisions and opinions.

> [An independent contractor is] a person who contracts with another to do something for him but who is not controlled by the other nor subject to the other's right to control with respect to his physical conduct in the performance of the undertaking. *He may or may not be an agent.* [Emphasis added.]

Building contractors and subcontractors are independent contractors, and a property owner does not control the acts of either of these professionals. Truck drivers who own their equipment and hire themselves out on a per-job basis are independent contractors, but truck drivers who drive company trucks on a regular basis are usually employees.

The relationship between a person or firm and an independent contractor may or may not involve an agency relationship. An owner of real estate who hires a real estate broker to negotiate a sale of his or her property not only has contracted with an independent contractor (the real estate broker) but also has established an agency relationship for the specific purpose of assisting in the sale of the property. Similarly, an insurance agent is both an independent contractor and an agent of the insurance company for which he or she sells policies. (Note that an insurance *broker,* in contrast to an insurance agent, normally is an agent of the person obtaining insurance and not of the insurance company.) Typically, in deciding whether an independent contractor is also an agent, the courts look at several factors, including those discussed in this chapter's *Business Law in the Online World* feature.

Determining Employee Status

A question the courts frequently face in determining liability under agency law is whether a person hired by another to do a job is an employee or an independent contractor. Because employers are normally held liable as principals for the actions taken by their employee-agents within the scope of employment (as will be discussed later in this chapter), the court's decision as to employee versus independent-contractor status can be significant for the parties.

Criteria Used by the Courts In determining whether a worker has the status of an employee or an independent contractor, the courts often consider the following questions:

1. How much control can the employer exercise over the details of the work? (If an employer can exercise considerable control over the details of the work, this would indicate employee status.)
2. Is the worker engaged in an occupation or business distinct from that of the employer? (If not, this would indicate employee status.)
3. Is the work usually done under the employer's direction or by a specialist without supervision? (If the work is usually done under the employer's direction, this would indicate employee status.)
4. Does the employer supply the tools at the place of work? (If so, this would indicate employee status.)
5. For how long is the person employed? (If the person is employed for a long period of time, this would indicate employee status.)
6. What is the method of payment—by time period or at the completion of the job? (Payment by time period, such as once every two weeks or once a month, would indicate employee status.)
7. What degree of skill is required of the worker? (If little skill is required, this may indicate employee status.)

Sometimes, it is advantageous to have employee status—to take advantage of laws protecting employees, for example. At other times, it may be advantageous to have

BUSINESS LAW: //in the Online World

Agent or Independent Contractor?

Independent contractors may or may not be agents. That said, how is it determined whether an independent contractor is or is not an agent? This question often comes before the courts, as it did in a recent case involving a company hired to distribute ads via bulk e-mail.

An Unforeseen Consequence

When Modern Computing agreed to advertise online mortgages made available through Greentree Mortgage Company, it had no idea of the problems its advertising would cause for Matthew Seidl. Modern had contracted with Greentree to advertise Greentree's mortgages by bulk e-mail advertising (spamming). The ad contained Greentree's 800 telephone number and its e-mail address. Modern's ad also contained, in its return path fields, the address "nobody@localhost.com." Messages that were sent to incorrect addresses or that were otherwise undelivered would be returned to this address.

Unbeknownst to Modern, Seidl, a graduate student in computer science at a Colorado university, had registered localhost.com as one of his domain names. As a result of Modern's advertising campaign, Seidl received over 7,000 bounced-back ads. He sued Greentree Mortgage, claiming that the messages tied up his computer for three days. He also claimed that because some ads were bounced back by people angry about spamming, his reputation in the Internet community was injured. Greentree countered that Modern was an independent contractor, not an agent, and thus Greentree could not be held liable for Modern's actions.

Can Greentree Be Held Liable?

Seidl asserted that Greentree should be held liable for the damage he suffered because Modern was Greentree's agent. After all, argued Seidl, Modern acted "for or in place of" Greentree when doing the mailing. The court, however, pointed out that an independent contractor ordinarily performs services for others. The court stated, "If this court were to adopt plaintiff's position that such actions make an independent contractor an agent because he or she 'acts for' the other, it would eliminate the distinction between [an] independent contractor and an agent."

The court emphasized that "an agent is one who represents (and may bind) the principal contractually." There was no evidence in this case to show that Modern had the ability to bind Greentree contractually. "This fact alone," stated the court, was enough to show that Modern was an independent contractor and not an agent. Additionally, Greentree exercised no control over the details of Modern's distribution of the spam. Thus, concluded the court, the "undisputed facts" show that Modern was an independent contractor and that Greentree was not responsible for Modern's errors in transmitting the spam.[a]

FOR CRITICAL ANALYSIS

Suppose that Greentree and Modern had formed a written contract in which Modern was designated an independent contractor. Would this contractual designation be sufficient evidence for the court to conclude that Modern was, in fact, an independent contractor?

a. *Seidl v. Greentree Mortgage Co.,* 30 F.Supp.2d 1292 (D.Colo. 1998).

independent-contractor status—for tax purposes, for example, as you will read shortly.

ETHICAL ISSUE 24.1

Why should it be left to the courts to determine who is or who is not an independent contractor?

Not surprisingly, many employers prefer to designate certain workers as independent contractors rather than as employees. As long as an employee agrees to be classified as an independent contractor, why should a court interfere in this decision? The answer is, at least in part, that issues of fairness may be involved, and the common law of agency, as developed and applied by the courts, implicitly recognizes these issues. After all, if a worker is an independent contractor, the worker must pay all Social Security taxes, instead of sharing them with his or her employer. Additionally, the worker will not be entitled to employer-provided benefits—such as pension plans, stock option plans, group insurance coverage, and so on—that are available to employees. Furthermore, the worker will not receive the legal protections afforded to employees under such laws as those regulating safety in the workplace or those protecting employees from discrimination. Finally, workers normally lack "bargaining power." If an employer states that a worker is being hired as an independent contractor, what can the worker do? Generally, in this situation the worker has only two options: he or she must either accept the arrangement or forfeit the job.[2]

Criteria Used by the IRS Often, the criteria for determining employee status are established by a statute or an administrative agency. Businesspersons should be aware that the Internal Revenue Service (IRS) has established its own criteria for determining whether a worker is an independent contractor or an employee. Until 1996 the IRS considered twenty factors in determining a worker's status, but these criteria were abolished in favor of rules that essentially encourage IRS examiners to focus on just one factor—the degree of control the business exercises over the worker.

The IRS tends to scrutinize closely a firm's classification of a worker as an independent contractor rather than an employee because independent contractors can avoid certain tax liabilities by taking advantage of business organizational forms available to small businesses. Even though a firm classifies a worker as an independent contractor, if the IRS decides that the worker should be classified as an employee, the employer will be responsible for paying any applicable Social Security, withholding, and unemployment taxes.

Employee Status and "Works for Hire" Under the Copyright Act of 1976, any copyrighted work created by an employee within the scope of her or his employment at the request of the employer is a "work for hire," and the employer owns the copyright to the work. When an employer hires an independent contractor—a freelance artist, writer, or computer programmer, for example—the independent contractor owns the copyright *unless* the parties agree in writing that the work is a "work for hire" and the work falls into one of nine specific categories, including audiovisual and other works.

The following case involved a dispute over ownership rights in a computer program. The outcome of the case hinged on whether the creator of the program, at the time it was created, was an employee or an independent contractor.

2. See the *Question of Ethics and Social Responsibility* at the end of this chapter for a case brought by Microsoft Corporation's employees who were required to work as independent contractors instead of employees.

CASE 24.1 Graham v. James

United States Court of Appeals,
Second Circuit, 1998.
144 F.3d 229.
http://guide.lp.findlaw.com/casecode/courts/2nd.html[a]

a. This is a page with links to some of the opinions of the U.S. Court of Appeals for the Second Circuit. In the "Party Name Search" Section, key in "Graham" and then click on "Search." When that page opens, scroll down the list of cases to the *Graham* case and click on the link to access it. This is part of the FindLaw Web site.

FACTS Richard Graham marketed CD-ROM discs containing compilations of shareware, freeware, and public domain software.[b] With five to ten thousand programs per disc, Graham needed a file-retrieval program to allow

b. *Shareware* is software released to the public to sample, with the understanding that anyone using it will register with the author and pay a fee. *Freeware* is software available for free use. *Public domain software* is software unprotected by copyright.

CASE 24.1—Continued

users to access the software on the discs. Larry James agreed to create the program in exchange for, among other things, credit on the final product. James built into the final version of the program a notice attributing authorship and copyright to himself. Graham removed the notice, claiming that the program was a work for hire and the copyright was his. Graham used the program on several subsequent releases. When James sold the program to another CD-ROM publisher, Graham filed a suit in a federal district court against James, alleging, among other things, copyright infringement. The court ruled that James was an independent contractor and that he owned the copyright. Graham appealed the ruling.

ISSUE Is a skilled person who controls the manner and method of his work, who is paid no employee benefits and has no payroll taxes withheld, and who is engaged on a project-by-project basis an independent contractor?

DECISION Yes. The U.S. Court of Appeals for the Second Circuit affirmed the lower court's judgment on this issue. The court agreed that James owned the copyright because he was an independent contractor when he developed the program.

REASON The court acknowledged that under the Copyright Act, work done by an employee is work for hire for which the employer owns the copyright. In determining whether a hired party is an employee, the court stated that the important factors are "(i) the hiring party's right to control the manner and means of creation; (ii) the skill required; (iii) the provision of employee benefits; (iv) the tax treatment of the hired party; and (v) whether the hiring party had the right to assign additional projects to the hired party." The court concluded that in this case, these factors favored James.

FOR CRITICAL ANALYSIS—Economic Consideration
What are some other advantages of being an independent contractor? What might be some disadvantages?

Agency Formation

Agency relationships normally are consensual; that is, they come about by voluntary consent and agreement between the parties. Generally, the agreement need not be in writing,[3] and consideration is not required.

A principal must have contractual capacity. A person who cannot legally enter into contracts directly should not be allowed to do so indirectly through an agent. Because an agent derives the authority to enter into contracts from the principal and because a contract made by an agent is legally viewed as a contract of the principal, it is immaterial whether the agent personally has the legal capacity to make that contract. Thus, a minor can be an agent but in some states cannot be a principal appointing an agent.[4] (When a minor is permitted to be a principal, however, any resulting contracts will be voidable by the minor principal but not by the adult third party.) In sum, any person can be an agent, regardless of whether he or she has the capacity to contract. Even a person who is legally incompetent can be appointed an agent.

An agency relationship can be created for any legal purpose. An agency relationship that is created for an illegal purpose or that is contrary to public policy is unenforceable. • **EXAMPLE 24.1** Suppose that Sharp (as principal) contracts with Blesh (as agent) to sell illegal narcotics. This agency relationship is unenforceable because selling illegal

3. There are two main exceptions to the statement that agency agreements need not be in writing: (1) Whenever agency authority empowers the agent to enter into a contract that the Statute of Frauds requires to be in writing, the agent's authority from the principal must likewise be in writing (this is called the *equal dignity rule,* to be discussed later in this chapter). (2) A power of attorney, which confers authority to an agent, must be in writing.

4. Some courts have granted exceptions to allow a minor to appoint an agent for the limited purpose of contracting for the minor's necessities of life. See *Casey v. Kastel,* 237 N.Y. 305, 142 N.E. 671 (1924).

narcotics is a felony and is contrary to public policy.● It is also illegal for medical doctors and other licensed professionals to employ unlicensed agents to perform professional actions.

Generally, an agency relationship can arise in four ways: by agreement of the parties, by ratification, by estoppel, and by operation of law. We look here at each of these possibilities.

ON THE WEB An excellent source for information on agency, including court cases involving agency concepts, is the Legal Information Institute (LII) at Cornell University. You can access the LII's Web page on this topic at **http://www.law.cornell.edu/topics/agency.html**.

Agency by Agreement

Because an agency relationship is, by definition, consensual, normally it must be based on an express or implied agreement that the agent will act for the principal and that the principal agrees to have the agent so act. An agency agreement can take the form of an express written contract. ● **Example 24.2** Renato enters into a written agreement with Troy, a real estate agent, to sell Renato's house. An agency relationship exists between Renato and Troy for the sale of the house and is detailed in a document that both parties sign.●

Many express agency agreements are oral. ● **Example 24.3** Suppose that Renato asks Cary, a gardener, to contract with others for the care of his lawn on a regular basis. Cary agrees. In this situation, an agency relationship exists between Renato and Cary for the lawn care.●

An agency agreement can also be implied by conduct. ● **Example 24.4** A hotel expressly allows only Boris Koontz to park cars, but Boris has no employment contract there. The hotel's manager tells Boris when to work, as well as where and how to park the cars. The hotel's conduct amounts to a manifestation of its willingness to have Boris park its customers' cars, and Boris can infer from the hotel's conduct that he has authority to act as a parking valet. It can be inferred that Boris is an agent-employee for the hotel, his purpose being to provide valet parking services for hotel guests.●

Agency by Ratification

RATIFICATION
The act of accepting and giving legal force to an obligation that previously was not enforceable.

On occasion, a person who is in fact not an agent (or who is an agent acting outside the scope of his or her authority) may make a contract on behalf of another (a principal). If the principal approves or affirms that contract by word or by action, an agency relationship is created by **ratification.** Ratification is a question of intent, and intent can be expressed by either words or conduct. The basic requirements for ratification are discussed later in this chapter.

Agency by Estoppel

When a principal causes a third person to believe that another person is his or her agent, and the third person deals with the supposed agent, the principal is "estopped to deny" the agency relationship. In such a situation, the principal's actions create the *appearance* of an agency that does not in fact exist.

● **Example 24.5** Suppose that Andrew accompanies Charles, a seed sales representative, to call on a customer, Steve, the proprietor of the General Seed Store. Andrew has done independent sales work but has never signed an employment agreement with Charles. Charles boasts to Steve that he wishes he had three more assistants "just like Andrew." Steve has reason to believe from Charles's statements that Andrew is an agent for Charles. Steve then places seed orders with Andrew. If Charles does not correct the impression that Andrew is an agent, Charles will be bound to fill the orders just as if Andrew were really Charles's agent. Charles's representation to Steve created the impression that Andrew was Charles's agent and had authority to solicit orders.●

A proprietor reviews the inventory in her clothing store. Under what circumstances might a clothing importer be considered to act as an agent for the store?

The acts or declarations of a purported *agent* in and of themselves do not create an agency by estoppel. Rather, it is the deeds or statements of the *principal* that create an agency by estoppel. ● **EXAMPLE 24.6** Suppose that Olivia walks into Dru's Dress Boutique and claims to be a sales agent for an exclusive Paris dress designer, Pierre Clinet. Dru has never had business relations with Pierre Clinet. Based on Olivia's claim, however, Dru gives Olivia an order and prepays 15 percent of the sales price. Olivia is not an agent, and the dresses are never delivered. Dru cannot hold Pierre Clinet liable. Olivia's acts and declarations alone do not create an agency by estoppel.●

In addition, to assert the creation of an agency by estoppel, the third person must prove that she or he *reasonably* believed that an agency relationship existed and that the agent had authority. Facts and circumstances must show that an ordinary, prudent person familiar with business practice and custom would have been justified in concluding that the agent had authority.

AGENCY BY OPERATION OF LAW

In certain other situations, the courts will also find an agency relationship in the absence of a formal agreement. This may occur in family relationships. For example, suppose one spouse purchases certain basic necessaries and charges them to the other spouse's charge account. The courts will often rule that the latter is liable for payment for the necessaries, either because of a social policy of promoting the general welfare of the spouse or because of a legal duty to supply necessaries to family members.

Agency by operation of law may also occur in emergency situations, when the agent's failure to act outside the scope of his or her authority would cause the principal substantial loss. If the agent is unable to contact the principal, the courts will often grant this emergency power. For example, a railroad engineer may contract on behalf of her or his employer for medical care for an injured motorist hit by the train.

Duties of Agents and Principals

"I am 'in a fiduciary position'—which is always a[n] . . . uncomfortable position."
FREDERIC W. MAITLAND,
1850–1906
(English jurist and historian)

The principal-agent relationship gives rise to duties that govern both parties' conduct. As discussed previously, an agency relationship is *fiduciary*—one of trust. In a fiduciary relationship, each party owes the other the duty to act with the utmost good faith.

We now examine the various duties of agents and principals. In general, for every duty of the principal, the agent has a corresponding right, and vice versa. When one party to the agency relationship violates his or her duty to the other party, the remedies available to the nonbreaching party arise out of contract and tort law. These remedies include monetary damages, termination of the agency relationship, injunction, and required accountings.

AGENT'S DUTIES TO THE PRINCIPAL

Generally, the agent owes the principal five duties—performance, notification, loyalty, obedience, and accounting.

Performance An implied condition in every agency contract is the agent's agreement to use reasonable diligence and skill in performing the work. When an agent fails to perform her or his duties entirely, liability for breach of contract normally will result. The degree of skill or care required of an agent is usually that expected of a reasonable person under similar circumstances. Generally, this is interpreted to mean ordinary

A real estate agent stands by a "For Sale" sign. If this agent knows a buyer who is willing to pay more than the asking price for this property, what duty would the agent breach if he bought the property from the seller and sold it at a profit to that buyer?

BE AWARE An agent's disclosure of confidential information could constitute the business tort of misappropriation of trade secrets.

care. An agent may, however, have represented himself or herself as possessing special skills (such as those that an accountant or attorney possesses). In these situations, the agent is expected to exercise the skill or skills claimed. Failure to do so constitutes a breach of the agent's duty.

Not all agency relationships are based on contract. In some situations, an agent acts gratuitously—that is, not for money. A gratuitous agent cannot be liable for breach of contract, as there is no contract; he or she is subject only to tort liability. Once a gratuitous agent has begun to act in an agency capacity, he or she has the duty to continue to perform in that capacity in an acceptable manner and is subject to the same standards of care and duty to perform as other agents.

Notification According to a maxim in agency law, notice to the agent is notice to the principal. An agent is thus required to notify the principal of all matters that come to her or his attention concerning the subject matter of the agency. This is the duty of notification. The law assumes that the principal knows of any information acquired by the agent that is relevant to the agency—regardless of whether the agent actually passes on this information to the principal.

Loyalty Loyalty is one of the most fundamental duties in a fiduciary relationship. Basically, the agent has the duty to act solely for the benefit of his or her principal and not in the interest of the agent or a third party. For example, an agent cannot represent two principals in the same transaction unless both know of the dual capacity and consent to it. The duty of loyalty also means that any information or knowledge acquired through the agency relationship is considered confidential. It would be a breach of loyalty to disclose such information either during the agency relationship or after its termination. Typical examples of confidential information are trade secrets and customer lists compiled by the principal.

In short, the agent's loyalty must be undivided. The agent's actions must be strictly for the benefit of the principal and must not result in any secret profit for the agent. • **EXAMPLE 24.7** Suppose that Ryder contracts with Alton, a real estate agent, to sell Ryder's property. Alton knows that he can find a buyer who will pay substantially more for the property than Ryder is asking. If Alton were to secretly purchase Ryder's property, however, and then sell it at a profit to another buyer, Alton would breach his duty of loyalty as Ryder's agent. Alton has a duty to act in Ryder's best interests and can only become the purchaser in this situation with Ryder's knowledge and approval. •

Does an agent breach the duty of loyalty if, while working for a principal, the agent solicits the principal's customers for a new competing business? That was an issue in the following case.

CASE 24.2 American Express Financial Advisors, Inc. v. Topel

United States District Court, District of Colorado, 1999.
38 F.Supp.2d 1233.

FACTS Stephen Topel worked as a financial planner for American Express Financial Advisors, Inc. (AMEX), beginning in April 1992. More than four years later, Topel decided to resign to work for Multi-Financial Securities Corporation, an AMEX competitor. Before resigning, Topel encouraged his customers to liquidate their AMEX holdings and sent them new account forms for Multi-Financial. He ignored the request of customers James and Nancy Hemming to keep their investments with AMEX. In a letter

CASE 24.2—Continued

on AMEX letterhead, Topel told Chris and Teresa Mammel to liquidate their AMEX holdings and invest in Multi-Financial's products. Another couple, Mr. and Ms. Rogers, changed their investments on Topel's advice. Before leaving AMEX, Topel sent a letter to all of his clients telling them that he was ending his relationship with AMEX and that their accounts would be assigned to another AMEX adviser. After Topel resigned in May 1997, he solicited the business of Theodore Benavidez, another AMEX customer. AMEX filed a suit in a federal district court against Topel, alleging, among other things, breach of fiduciary duty (duty of loyalty) and seeking damages. AMEX filed a motion for summary judgment on this issue.

ISSUE Had Topel breached his fiduciary duty of loyalty?

DECISION Yes. The court granted AMEX's motion for summary judgment in its favor with respect to this claim.

REASON The court held that Topel breached his duty of loyalty when, while working for his principal, he solicited his principal's customers for his new competing business. The court cited the principle that an agent has a duty to act solely for the benefit of the principal in all matters connected with an agency. "While an agent is entitled to make some preparations to compete with his principal after the termination of their relationship," the court acknowledged, "an agent violates his duty of loyalty if he engages in pre-termination solicitation of customers for a new competing business." That Topel did not solicit Benavidez's business until after Topel left AMEX "does not negate the testimony of other customers that he solicited their business for Multi-Financial while he was still affiliated with AMEX." As for the letter that Topel sent to all of his clients before resigning, "many customers had already signed new account forms with Multi-Financial by the time this neutral letter was purportedly sent."

FOR CRITICAL ANALYSIS—Ethical Consideration *Can you think of any situations in which the duty of loyalty to one's employer could come into conflict with other duties? Explain.*

Obedience When acting on behalf of a principal, an agent has a duty to follow all lawful and clearly stated instructions of the principal. Any deviation from such instructions is a violation of this duty. During emergency situations, however, when the principal cannot be consulted, the agent may deviate from the instructions without violating this duty. Whenever instructions are not clearly stated, the agent can fulfill the duty of obedience by acting in good faith and in a manner reasonable under the circumstances.

Accounting Unless an agent and a principal agree otherwise, the agent has the duty to keep and make available to the principal an account of all property and money received and paid out on behalf of the principal. This includes gifts from third persons in connection with the agency. For example, a gift from a customer to a salesperson for prompt deliveries made by the salesperson's firm, in the absence of a company policy to the contrary, belongs to the firm. The agent has a duty to maintain separate accounts for the principal's funds and for the agent's personal funds, and no intermingling of these accounts is allowed.

PRINCIPAL'S DUTIES TO THE AGENT

The principal also owes certain duties to the agent. These duties relate to compensation, reimbursement and indemnification, cooperation, and safe working conditions.

Compensation In general, when a principal requests certain services from an agent, the agent reasonably expects payment. The principal therefore has a duty to pay the agent for services rendered. For example, when an accountant or an attorney is asked to act as an agent, an agreement to compensate the agent for such service is implied. The principal also has a duty to pay that compensation in a timely manner. Except in a gratuitous agency relationship, in which an agent does not act for money, the principal must pay the agreed-on value for an agent's services. If no amount has been expressly agreed on, the principal owes the agent the customary compensation for such services.

Reimbursement and Indemnification Whenever an agent disburses sums of money to fulfill the request of the principal or to pay for necessary expenses in the course of a reasonable performance of his or her agency duties, the principal has the duty to reimburse the agent for these payments. Agents cannot recover for expenses incurred by their own misconduct or negligence, however.

REMEMBER An agent who signs a negotiable instrument on behalf of a principal may be personally liable on the instrument. Liability depends in part on whether the identity of the principal is disclosed and whether the parties intend the agent to be bound by his signature.

Subject to the terms of the agency agreement, the principal has the duty to compensate, or *indemnify,* an agent for liabilities incurred because of authorized and lawful acts and transactions. For example, if the principal fails to perform a contract formed by the agent with a third party and the third party then sues the agent, the principal is obligated to compensate the agent for any costs incurred in defending against the lawsuit.

Additionally, the principal must indemnify (pay) the agent for the value of benefits that the agent confers on the principal. The amount of indemnification is usually specified in the agency contract. If it is not, the courts will look to the nature of the business and the type of loss to determine the amount.

Cooperation A principal has a duty to cooperate with the agent and to assist the agent in performing of his or her duties. The principal must do nothing to prevent such performance.

● **EXAMPLE 24.8** Suppose that Akers (the principal) grants Johnson (the agent) an exclusive territory within which Johnson may sell Akers's products, thus creating an exclusive agency. In this situation, Akers cannot compete with Johnson within that territory—or appoint or allow another agent to so compete—because this would violate the exclusive agency. If Akers did so, he would be exposed to liability for Johnson's lost sales or profits.●

Safe Working Conditions The common law requires the principal to provide safe working premises, equipment, and conditions for all agents and employees. The principal has a duty to inspect the working conditions and to warn agents and employees about any unsafe areas. When the agency is one of employment, the employer's liability and the safety standards with which the employer must comply normally are covered by federal and state statutes and regulations (see Chapter 34).

Agent's Authority

An agent's authority to act can be either *actual* (express or implied) or *apparent.* If an agent contracts outside the scope of his or her authority, the principal may still become liable by ratifying the contract.

ACTUAL AUTHORITY

As indicated, an agent's actual authority can be express or implied. We look here at both of these forms of actual authority.

EQUAL DIGNITY RULE
In most states, a rule stating that express authority given to an agent must be in writing if the contract to be made on behalf of the principal is required to be in writing.

Express Authority *Express authority* is authority declared in clear, direct, and definite terms. Express authority can be given orally or in writing. In most states, the **equal dignity rule** requires that if the contract being executed is or must be in writing, then the agent's authority must also be in writing.[5] Failure to comply with the equal dignity rule can make a contract voidable *at the option of the principal.* The law regards the contract at that point as a mere offer. If the principal decides to accept the offer, acceptance must be in writing.

• **EXAMPLE 24.9** Klee (the principal) orally asks Parkinson (the agent) to sell a ranch that Klee owns. Parkinson finds a buyer and signs a sales contract (a contract for an interest in realty must be in writing) on behalf of Klee to sell the ranch. The buyer cannot enforce the contract unless Klee subsequently ratifies Parkinson's agency status *in writing.* Once Parkinson's agency status is ratified, either party can enforce rights under the contract.•

The equal dignity rule does not apply when an agent acts in the presence of a principal or when the agent's act of signing is merely perfunctory. Thus, if Dickens (the principal) negotiates a contract but is called out of town the day it is to be signed and orally authorizes Santini to sign the contract, the oral authorization is sufficient.

POWER OF ATTORNEY
A written document, which is usually notarized, authorizing another to act as one's agent; can be special (permitting the agent to do specified acts only) or general (permitting the agent to transact all business for the principal).

NOTARY PUBLIC
A public official authorized to attest to the authenticity of signatures.

Giving an agent a **power of attorney** confers express authority.[6] The power of attorney normally is a written document and is usually notarized. (A document is notarized when a **notary public**—a public official authorized to attest to the authenticity of signatures—signs and dates the document and imprints it with his or her seal of authority.) A power of attorney can be special (permitting the agent to do specified acts only), or it can be general (permitting the agent to transact all business for the principal). An agent holding a power of attorney for a client is authorized to act *only* on the principal's behalf when exercising that power. An ordinary power of attorney terminates on the incapacity or death of the person giving the power.[7] Exhibit 24–1 shows a sample power of attorney.

Implied Authority *Implied authority* can be (1) conferred by custom, (2) inferred from the position the agent occupies, or (3) inferred as being reasonably necessary to carry out express authority. • **EXAMPLE 24.10** Mueller is employed by Al's Supermarket to manage one of its stores. Al's has not expressly stated that Mueller has authority to contract with third persons. In this situation, however, authority to manage a business implies authority to do what is reasonably required (as is customary or can be inferred from a manager's position) to operate the business. Reasonably required actions include creating contracts to hire employees, to buy merchandise and equipment, and to arrange for advertising the products sold in the store.•

ETHICAL ISSUE 24.2

Does an agent's breach of loyalty terminate the agent's authority?

Suppose that an employee-agent who is authorized to access company trade secrets contained in computer files e-mails those secrets to a competitor for whom the employee is about to begin working. Clearly, in this situation the employee has violated the ethical—and

---

5. An exception to the equal dignity rule exists in modern business practice. An executive officer of a corporation, when acting for the corporation in an ordinary business situation, is not required to obtain written authority from the corporation.

6. An agent who holds the power of attorney is called an *attorney-in-fact* for the principal. The holder does not have to be an attorney-at-law (and often is not).

7. A *durable* power of attorney, however, provides an agent with very broad powers to act and make decisions for the principal and specifies that it is not affected by the principal's incapacity. An elderly person, for example, might grant a durable power of attorney to provide for the handling of property and investments should she or he become incompetent.

EXHIBIT 24–1 A SAMPLE POWER OF ATTORNEY

POWER OF ATTORNEY

GENERAL

Know All Men by These Presents: That I, ______________________________

____

the undersigned (jointly and severally, if more than one) hereby make, constitute and appoint ______________

____

as a true and lawful Attorney for me and in my name, place and stead and for my use and benefit:

(a) To ask, demand, sue for, recover, collect and receive each and every sum of money, debt, account, legacy, bequest, interest, dividend, annuity and demand (which now is or hereafter shall become due, owing or payable) belonging to or claimed by me, and to use and take any lawful means for the recovery thereof by legal process or otherwise, and to execute and deliver a satisfaction or release therefore, together with the right and power to compromise or compound any claim or demand;

(b) To exercise any or all of the following powers as to real property, any interest therein and/or any building thereon: To contract for, purchase, receive and take possession thereof and or evidence of title thereto; to lease the same for any term or purpose, including leases for business, residence, and oil and/or mineral development; to sell, exchange, grant or convey the same with or without warranty; and to mortgage, transfer in trust, or otherwise encumber or hypothecate the same to secure payment of a negotiable or non-negotiable note or performance of any obligation or agreement;

(c) To exercise any or all of the following powers as to all kinds of personal property and goods, wares and merchandise, choses in action and other property in possession or in action: To contract for, buy, sell, exchange, transfer and in any legal manner deal in and with the same; and to mortgage, transfer in trust, or otherwise encumber or hypothecate the same to secure payment of a negotiable or non-negotiable note or performance of any obligation or agreement;

(d) To borrow money and to execute and deliver negotiable or non-negotiable notes therefore with or without security; and to loan money and receive negotiable or non-negotiable notes therefore with such security as he shall deem proper;

(e) To create, amend, supplement and terminate any trust and to instruct and advise the trustee of any trust wherein I am or may be trustor or beneficiary; to represent and vote stock, exercise stock rights, accept and deal with any dividend, distribution or bonus, join in any corporate financing, reorganization, merger, liquidation, consolidation or other action and the extension, compromise, conversion, adjustment, enforcement or foreclosure, singly or in conjunction with others, of any corporate stock, bond, note, debenture or other security; to compound, compromise, adjust, settle and satisfy any obligation, secured or unsecured, owing by or to me and to give or accept any property and/or money whether or not equal to or less in value than the amount owing in payment, settlement or satisfaction thereof;

(f) To transact business of any kind or class and as my act and deed to sign, execute, acknowledge and deliver any deed, lease, assignment of lease, covenant, indenture, indemnity, agreement, mortgage, deed of trust, assignment of mortgage or of the beneficial interest under deed of trust, extension or renewal of any obligation, subordination or waiver of priority, hypothecation, bottomry, charter-party, bill of lading, bill of sale, bill, bond, note, whether negotiable or non-negotiable, receipt, evidence of debt, full or partial release or satisfaction of mortgage, judgment and other debt, request for partial or full reconveyance of deed of trust and such other instruments in writing of any kind or class as may be necessary or proper in the premises.

Giving and Granting unto my said Attorney full power and authority to do so and perform all and every act and thing whatsoever requisite, necessary or appropriate to be done in and about the premises as fully to all intents and purposes as I might or could do if personally present, hereby ratifying all that my said Attorney shall lawfully do or cause to be done by virtue of these presents. The powers and authority hereby conferred upon my said Attorney shall be applicable to all real and personal property or interests therein now owned or hereafter acquired by me and wherever situated.

My said Attorney is empowered hereby to determine in his sole discretion the time when, purpose for and manner in which any power herein conferred upon him shall be exercised, and the conditions, provisions and covenants of any instrument or document which may be executed by him pursuant hereto; and in the acquisition or disposition of real or personal property, my said Attorney shall have exclusive power to fix the terms thereof for cash, credit and/or property, and if on credit with or without security.

The undersigned, if a married woman, hereby further authorizes and empowers my said Attorney, as my duly authorized agent, to join in my behalf, in the execution of any instrument by which any community real property or any interest therein, now owned or hereafter acquired by my spouse and myself, or either of us, is sold, leased, encumbered, or conveyed.

When the context so requires, the masculine gender includes the feminine and/or neuter, and the singular number includes the plural.

WITNESS my hand this __________ day of ________________, 20___

______________________ ______________________

______________________ ______________________

State of California } SS.
County of ______________

On ______________________, before me, the undersigned, a Notary Public in and for said State, personally appeared ______________________

____

known to me to be the person __________ whose name ______________ subscribed to the within instrument and acknowledged that ______________ executed the same.

Witness my hand and official seal. (Seal) ______________________
Notary Public in and for said State.

legal—duty of loyalty to the employer. Does this breach of loyalty mean that the employee's act of accessing the trade secrets was unauthorized? The question has significant implications because if the act was unauthorized, the employee would be subject to state and federal laws prohibiting unauthorized access to computer information and data. If the act was authorized, the employee would not be subject to such laws. When this unusual question came before a federal district court in 2000, the court held that the moment the employee accessed trade secrets for the purpose of divulging them to a competitor, the employee's authority as an agent was terminated. Thus, the employee could be subject to both criminal and civil sanctions under a federal law prohibiting unauthorized access to protected computer information. In reaching its decision, the court cited Section 112 of the *Restatement (Second) of Agency.* That section reads, in part, "Unless otherwise agreed, the authority of an agent terminates if, without knowledge of the principal, he acquires adverse interests or if he is otherwise guilty of a serious breach of loyalty to the principal."[8]

APPARENT AUTHORITY

"The law is not a series of calculating machines where definitions and answers come tumbling out when the right levers are pushed."

WILLIAM O. DOUGLAS, 1898–1980 (Associate justice of the United States Supreme Court, 1939–1975)

Actual authority arises from what the principal manifests *to the agent*. Apparent authority exists when the principal, by either words or actions, causes a *third party* reasonably to believe that an agent has authority to act, even though the agent has no express or implied authority. If the third party changes his or her position in reliance on the principal's representations, the principal may be *estopped* from denying that the agent had authority. Note that here, in contrast to agency formation by estoppel, the issue has to do with the apparent authority of an *agent*, not the apparent authority of a person who is in fact not an agent.

● **EXAMPLE 24.11** Suppose that a traveling salesperson, Anderson (the agent), is authorized to take customers' orders. Anderson, however, does not deliver the ordered goods and is not authorized to collect payments for the goods. A customer, Byron, pays Anderson for a solicited order. Anderson then takes the payment to the principal's accounting department, and an accountant accepts the payment and sends Byron a receipt. This procedure is thereafter followed for other orders solicited from and paid for by Byron. Later, Anderson solicits an order, and Byron pays her as before. This time, however, Anderson absconds with the money. Can Byron claim that the payment to the agent was authorized and was thus, in effect, a payment to the principal?

The answer is normally yes, because the principal's *repeated* acts of accepting Byron's payment led Byron reasonably to expect that Anderson had authority to receive payments for goods solicited. Although Anderson did not have express or implied authority, the principal's conduct gave Anderson *apparent* authority to collect. In this situation, the principal would be estopped from denying that Anderson had authority to collect payments. ●

RATIFICATION

BE AWARE An agent who exceeds his or her authority to enter into a contract that the principal does not ratify may be liable to the third party on the ground of misrepresentation.

As already mentioned, ratification is the affirmation of a previously unauthorized contract. Ratification can be either express or implied. If the principal does not ratify, there is no contract binding on the principal, and the third party's agreement with the agent is viewed merely as an unaccepted offer. The third party can revoke the offer at any time prior to the principal's ratification without liability. Death or incapacity of the third party before ratification will void an unauthorized contract.

8. *Shurgard Storage Centers, Inc. v. Safeguard Self Storage, Inc.*, 119 F.Supp.2d 1121 (W.D.Wash. 2000).

The requirements for ratification can be summarized as follows:

① The purported agent must have acted on behalf of a principal who subsequently ratifies the action.

② The principal must know of all material facts involved in the transaction.

③ The agent's act must be affirmed in its entirety by the principal.

④ The principal must have the legal capacity to authorize the transaction at the time the agent engages in the act and at the time the principal ratifies.

⑤ The principal's affirmance must occur prior to the withdrawal of the third party from the transaction.

⑥ The principal must observe the same formalities when approving the act purportedly done by the agent on the principal's behalf as would have been required to authorize it initially.

Liability in Agency Relationships

Frequently, the issue arises as to which party, the principal or the agent, should be held liable for the contracts formed by the agent or for the torts or crimes committed by the agent. We look here at these aspects of agency law.

LIABILITY FOR CONTRACTS

An important consideration in determining liability for a contract formed by an agent is whether the third party knew the identity of the principal at the time the contract was made. The *Restatement (Second) of Agency,* Section 4, classifies principals as disclosed, partially disclosed, or undisclosed.

DISCLOSED PRINCIPAL
A principal whose identity is known to a third party at the time the agent makes a contract with the third party.

PARTIALLY DISCLOSED PRINCIPAL
A principal whose identity is unknown by a third person, but the third person knows that the agent is or may be acting for a principal at the time the agent and the third person form a contract.

UNDISCLOSED PRINCIPAL
A principal whose identity is unknown by a third person, and the third person has no knowledge that the agent is acting for a principal at the time the agent and the third person form a contract.

Disclosed or Partially Disclosed Principal A principal whose identity is known to the third party at the time the agent makes the contract is a **disclosed principal.** • **EXAMPLE 24.12** Martha Evans, president of Comquant Computing, Inc., purchases ten new copiers for the business from ABC Copiers. She signs the purchase order, "Comquant Computing, Inc., by Martha Evans, President." In this situation, the principal (Comquant Computing, Inc.) is clearly disclosed to the third party (ABC Copiers).•

The identity of a **partially disclosed principal** is not known by the third party, but the third party knows that the agent is or may be acting for a principal at the time the contract is made. • **EXAMPLE 24.13** Sarah has contracted with a real estate agent to sell certain property. She wishes to keep her identity a secret, but the agent can make it perfectly clear to a purchaser of the real estate that the agent is acting in an agency capacity for a principal. In this situation, Sarah is a partially disclosed principal.•

A disclosed or partially disclosed principal is liable to a third party for a contract made by an agent who is acting within the scope of her or his authority. Ordinarily, if the principal is disclosed or partially disclosed, the agent has no contractual liability if the principal or the third party does not perform the contract. If the agent *exceeds* the scope of her or his authority and the principal fails to ratify the contract, however, the third party cannot hold the principal liable for nonperformance. In such situations, the agent is generally liable unless the third party knew of the agent's lack of authority.

Undisclosed Principal The identity of an **undisclosed principal** is totally unknown to the third party. Furthermore, the third party has no knowledge that the agent is acting in an agency capacity at the time the contract is made.

When neither the fact of agency nor the identity of the principal is disclosed, a third party is deemed to be dealing with the agent personally, and the agent is liable as a party to the contract. If an agent has acted within the scope of his or her authority, the undisclosed principal is also liable as a party to the contract, just as if the principal had been fully disclosed at the time the contract was made. Conversely, the undisclosed principal can hold the third party to the contract, unless (1) the undisclosed principal was expressly excluded as a party in the contract, (2) the contract is a negotiable instrument signed by the agent with no indication of signing in a representative capacity, or (3) the performance of the agent is personal to the contract, allowing the third party to refuse the principal's performance.

NOTE An agent-employee going to or from work or meals usually is not considered to be within the scope of employment. An agent-employee whose job requires travel, however, is considered to be within the scope of employment for the entire trip, including the return.

LIABILITY FOR TORTS AND CRIMES

Obviously, any person, including an agent, is liable for her or his own torts and crimes. Whether a principal can also be held liable for an agent's torts and crimes depends on several factors, which we examine here. In some situations, a principal may be held liable not only for the torts of an agent but also for the torts committed by an independent contractor.

RESPONDEAT SUPERIOR
In Latin, "Let the master respond." A doctrine under which a principal or an employer is held liable for the wrongful acts committed by agents or employees while acting within the course and scope of their agency or employment.

Liability for Agent's Torts As mentioned, an agent is liable for her or his own torts. A principal may also be liable for an agent's torts under the doctrine of ***respondeat superior***,[9] a Latin term meaning "let the master respond." This doctrine, which is discussed in this chapter's *Landmark in the Law* feature on the next page, is similar to the theory of strict liability discussed in Chapter 4. The doctrine imposes vicarious (indirect) liability on the employer without regard to the personal fault of the employer for torts committed by an employee in the course or scope of employment.

Scope of Employment. The key to determining whether a principal may be liable for the torts of an agent under the doctrine of *respondeat superior* is whether the torts are committed within the scope of the agency or employment. The *Restatement (Second) of Agency*, Section 229, indicates the factors that today's courts will consider in determining whether a particular act occurred within the course and scope of employment. These factors are as follows:

1. Whether the act was authorized by the employer.
2. The time, place, and purpose of the act.
3. Whether the act was one commonly performed by employees on behalf of their employers.
4. The extent to which the employer's interest was advanced by the act.
5. The extent to which the private interests of the employee were involved.
6. Whether the employer furnished the means or instrumentality (for example, a truck or a machine) by which the injury was inflicted.
7. Whether the employer had reason to know that the employee would do the act in question and whether the employee had ever done it before.
8. Whether the act involved the commission of a serious crime.

A truck lies on its side following an accident. If the driver had stopped at a bar during working hours and become inebriated, and this accident was caused by the driver's inebriated state, who would be held responsible for the damage?

A useful insight into the "scope of employment" concept may be gained from Baron Parke's classic distinction between a "detour" and a "frolic" in the case of *Joel v. Morison* (1834).[10] In this case, the English court held that if a servant merely took a detour from

9. Pronounced ree-*spahn*-dee-uht soo-*peer*-ee-your.
10. 6 Car. & P. 501, 172 Eng. Reprint 1338 (1834).

LANDMARK IN THE LAW
The Doctrine of *Respondeat Superior*

The idea that a master (employer) must respond to third persons for losses negligently caused by the master's servant (employee) first appeared in Lord Holt's opinion in *Jones v. Hart* (1698).[a] By the early nineteenth century, this maxim had been adopted by most courts and was referred to as the doctrine of *respondeat superior.*

Theories of Liability The vicarious (indirect) liability of the master for the acts of the servant has been supported primarily by two theories. The first theory rests on the issue of *control,* or *fault:* the master has control over the acts of the servant and is thus responsible for injuries arising out of such service. The second theory is economic in nature: because the master takes the benefits or profits of the servant's service, he or she should also suffer the losses; moreover, the master is better able than the servant to absorb such losses.

The *control* theory is clearly recognized in the *Restatement (Second) of Agency,* in which the master is defined as "a principal who employs an agent to perform service in his affairs and who controls, or has the right to control, the physical conduct of the other in the performance of the service." Accordingly, a servant is defined as "an agent employed by a master to perform service in his affairs whose physical conduct in his performance of the service is controlled, or is subject to control, by the master."

Limitations on the Employer's Liability There are limitations on the master's liability for the acts of the servant, however. An employer (master) is only responsible for the wrongful conduct of an employee (servant) that occurs in "the scope of employment." The criteria used by the courts in determining whether an employee is acting within the scope of employment are set forth in the *Restatement (Second) of Agency* and will be discussed shortly. Generally, the act must be of a kind the servant was employed to do; must have occurred within "authorized time and space limits"; and must have been "activated, at least in part, by a purpose to serve the master."

APPLICATION TO TODAY'S WORLD

The courts have accepted the doctrine of respondeat superior *for nearly two centuries. This theory of vicarious liability is laden with practical implications in all situations in which a principal-agent (master-servant, employer-employee) relationship exists. Today, the small-town grocer with one clerk and the multinational corporation with thousands of employees are equally subject to the doctrinal demand of "let the master respond." (For a further discussion of employers' liability for wrongs committed by their employees, including such wrongs committed in the online employment environment, see Chapter 35.)*

a. K.B. 642, 90 Eng. Reprint 1255 (1698).

his master's business, the master will be responsible. If, however, the servant was on a "frolic of his own" and not in any way "on his master's business," the master will not be liable.

Misrepresentation. A principal is exposed to tort liability whenever a third person sustains a loss due to the agent's misrepresentation. The principal's liability depends on whether the agent was actually or apparently authorized to make representations and whether such representations were made within the scope of the agency. The principal is always directly responsible for an agent's misrepresentation made within the scope of the agent's authority, whether the misrepresentation was made fraudulently or simply by the agent's mistake or oversight.

INTERNATIONAL PERSPECTIVE

Islamic Law and *Respondeat Superior*

The doctrine of *respondeat superior* is well established in the legal systems of the United States and most Western countries. As you have already read, under this doctrine employers can be held liable for the acts of their agents, including employees.

Middle Eastern countries, in contrast, do not employ the principle. Islamic law, codified in the *Sharia*, holds to a strict principle that responsibility for human actions lies with the individual and cannot be vicariously extended to others. This principle and other concepts of Islamic law are based on the sayings of Muhammad, the seventh-century prophet and founder of Islam.

FOR CRITICAL ANALYSIS
How would American society be affected if employers could not be held vicariously liable for their employees' torts?

Liability for Independent Contractor's Torts Generally, the principal is not liable for physical harm caused to a third person by the negligent act of an independent contractor in the performance of the contract. This is because the employer does not have *the right to control* the details of an independent contractor's performance. Exceptions to this rule are made in certain situations, however, as when exceptionally hazardous activities are involved. Examples of such activities include blasting operations, the transportation of highly volatile chemicals, or the use of poisonous gases. In these situations, a principal cannot be shielded from liability merely by using an independent contractor. Strict liability is imposed on the principal as a matter of law and, in some states, by statute.

In the following case, one of the issues before the court was whether the negligence of an independent contractor, who was acting as an agent, could be imputed to the principal.

CASE 24.3 Haag v. Bongers

Supreme Court of Nebraska, 1999.
256 Neb. 170,
589 N.W.2d 318.
http://www.findlaw.com/11stategov/ne/neca.html[a]

FACTS When Leo Bongers died, his nephew, Alfred Bongers, was appointed one of the personal representatives of his estate, which included more than 120 antique cars, trucks, and motorcycles. The estate hired Bauer-Moravec Auctioneers and Clerks, and Dolan Realty and Auction Company, to jointly conduct an auction of the vehicles. The auctioneers suggested that the auction be held in the summer, with the vehicles lined up outside, but the estate insisted on holding the auction as soon as possible, in the winter. The auction was heavily advertised

(continued)

a. In the "Supreme Court Opinions" section, under "1999," click on "February." On that page, scroll down the list of cases to the name of the case (the decision was issued on "02/12/1999") and click on the docket number to access the opinion.

CASE 24.3—Continued

at the estate's insistence and was held on a farm owned by the estate, in a building open at both ends. With the estate's agreement, tents were set up at either end to enlarge the "bid barn," and each attendee was charged $25. Bongers was there. Assistants paid by the estate moved the vehicles through the members of the crowd, who were standing shoulder to shoulder in the barn. The estate had failed in its responsibility to put all of the vehicles in running order, so many of the vehicles were towed into the building using tractors with hitch balls, which the estate had approved. As the assistants attempted to tow an antique Studebaker truck out of the barn, the hitch ball became detached, flew off the tractor, and hit Joseph Haag, who suffered serious head injuries. Haag filed a suit in a Nebraska state court against the estate and others, alleging, among other things, negligence on the part of the auctioneers. Haag argued that as agents for the estate, the auctioneers' negligence should be imputed to the estate. The estate responded in part that it was not liable for the acts of the auctioneers because they were independent contractors. The court entered a judgment in favor of Haag. The estate appealed to the Nebraska Supreme Court.

ISSUE Should the estate be held liable for the auctioneers' negligence?

DECISION Yes. The Nebraska Supreme Court affirmed the judgment of the trial court.

REASON The negligence of the assistants, who worked for the independent contractors (who acted as the agents of the estate), could be imputed to the estate because of the control exercised by the principal over the independent contractors. Here, "[t]he auction was held on the Estate's property, and the Estate insisted that the auction be conducted in winter rather than in summer in a more expansive setting. The Estate was responsible for putting the vehicles in running order but failed to do so, resulting in the necessity of towing the vehicles at the auction. The Estate approved the use of tractors to tow the vehicles at the auction. The Estate approved the use of assistants. The Estate paid the assistants. The Estate insisted that the auction be heavily advertised, resulting in a shoulder-to-shoulder crowd through which the vehicles were to be towed. The Estate and the auctioneers decided to extend the bid barn and charge a $25 fee. Bongers was present * * *. Although actual performance of the task of towing the vehicles was to be performed by the independent contractor auctioneers, the facts in this case as to the Estate's active and considerable control over the activities that led to the accident are sufficient to subject the Estate to liability."

FOR CRITICAL ANALYSIS—Ethical Consideration *In your opinion, is it ever fair to hold one person liable for the torts of another? Why or why not?*

Liability for Agent's Crimes An agent is liable for his or her own crimes. A principal or employer is not liable for an agent's crime even if the crime was committed within the scope of authority or employment—unless the principal participated by conspiracy or other action. In some jurisdictions, under specific statutes, a principal may be liable for an agent's violation, in the course and scope of employment, of regulations, such as those governing sanitation, prices, weights, and the sale of liquor.

E-Agents

E-AGENT
According to the Uniform Computer Information Transactions Act, "a computer program, electronic or other automated means used to independently initiate an action or to respond to electronic messages or performances without review by an individual."

Gradually, the courts have established fairly clear rules concerning the situations in which an employer may be held liable for an agent's actions. Yet do these rules apply to electronic agents? An electronic agent, or **e-agent**, is not a person but a semiautonomous computer program that is capable of executing specific tasks. Examples of e-agents in e-commerce include software that can search through many databases and retrieve only relevant information for the user.

ON THE WEB There are now at least fifty shopping "bots" that will search the Web to obtain the best prices for specified products. You can obtain the latest reviews on the merits of various shopping bots by going to **http://www.botspot.com**.

Some e-agents are used to make purchases on the Internet. Popular e-agents that search the Web and compare product prices include DealTime.com, mySimon.com, PriceScan.com, and Whenushop.com. An Internet user might employ one of the following e-agents to search the Web for a particular book: BookFinder.com and BestBookBuys.com. These e-agents will scour the Web for the lowest price for that particular book title. Some shopping e-agents actually negotiate product acquisition, as well as delivery.

WHAT AGENCY LAW APPLIES?

Under traditional agency law, contracts formed by an agent normally are legally binding on the principal *if* the principal authorized the agent, either expressly or impliedly, to form the contracts. One of the controversies involving e-agents concerns the extent of an e-agent's authority to act on behalf of its principal. Consider a not-too-uncommon example.

Software that an e-agent might find for its principal will undoubtedly involve a click-on agreement. E-agents searching the Internet may run into a variety of such agreements containing different terms and conditions. If the e-agent ignores the licensing terms and conditions outlined in the click-on agreement, is the principal bound by the agreement? Conversely, a click-on agreement may exempt a third party from liability resulting from an underlying product or service. Is the principal bound by this term? With respect to human agents, the courts occasionally have found that an agent could not agree to such a term without explicit authority.

To avoid problems created by the use of e-agents, some online merchants have blocked e-agents from accessing pricing information. Other online stores are developing click-on agreements that can be understood by a computer and are therefore more conspicuous for e-agents.

In the following case, the court addressed the issue of a principal's liability for the actions of its e-agent.

CASE 24.4 eBay, Inc. v. Bidder's Edge, Inc.

United States District Court,
Northern District of California, 2000.
100 F.Supp.2d 1058.

HISTORICAL AND TECHNOLOGICAL SETTING *A spider (also known as a Web crawler or a software robot, sometimes shortened to "bot") is a computer program that operates, or crawls, across the Internet to perform searching, copying, and retrieving functions. A spider is capable of executing thousands of instructions per minute, far in excess of what a human can accomplish. Spiders consume the processing and storage resources of a system, making that portion of the system's capacity unavailable to the system owner or other users. Consumption of sufficient system resources slows the processing of the system and can overload it, causing a malfunction or crash. A severe malfunction can result in a loss of data and an interruption in services.*

FACTS eBay, Inc. (**http://www.ebay.com**), is an Internet-based, person-to-person trading site that offers sellers the ability to list items for sale and prospective buyers the ability to search those listings and bid on items.[a] Bidder's Edge, Inc. (BE), is the owner and operator of an auction aggregation site designed to offer

a. eBay currently has over 8 million registered users. More than 400,000 new items are added to the site every day. Every minute, 600 bids are placed on almost 3 million items. Users currently perform, on average, 10 million searches per day on eBay's database.

(continued)

CASE 24.4—Continued

online auction buyers the ability to search for items across numerous online auctions without having to search each host site individually. In 1998, eBay gave BE permission to include information regarding some eBay-hosted auctions. In 1999, BE wanted to increase its coverage, and eBay verbally approved BE's crawling the eBay Web site for ninety days. To reduce the load on eBay's system in the future, eBay wanted BE to run a search only in response to a user query. BE wanted to recursively crawl the eBay system to compile its own auction database. Other aggregation sites agreed to eBay's terms, but BE refused. When BE's spider continued to crawl the eBay system, eBay filed a suit in a federal district court against BE, alleging, among other things, trespass to chattels (personal property—see Chapter 4). eBay filed a motion for a preliminary injunction.

ISSUE Is BE liable for the operations of its e-agent?

DECISION Yes. The court concluded that eBay showed at least a possibility of suffering irreparable harm and that BE did not show a balance of hardships in its favor. The court granted eBay's motion for a preliminary injunction, ordering BE to stop accessing eBay's computers with a spider without eBay's written authorization.

REASON The court reasoned that "[i]f BE's activity is allowed to continue unchecked, it would encourage other auction aggregators to engage in similar recursive searching of the eBay system." Comparing eBay to a "brick and mortar auction house with limited seating capacity," the court concluded that "BE's ongoing violation of eBay's fundamental property right to exclude others from its computer system potentially causes * * * irreparable harm." The court explained that although "eBay has carefully chosen to permit crawling by a limited number of aggregation sites that agree to abide by [eBay's] terms," such permission "does not support the inference that carte blanche crawling of the eBay site would pose no threat of irreparable harm." As for BE's claim that it would be harmed by not being allowed to crawl over eBay's site, the court stated, "[A] defendant who builds a business model based upon a clear violation of the property rights of the plaintiff cannot defeat a preliminary injunction by claiming the business will be harmed if the defendant is forced to respect those property rights."

FOR CRITICAL ANALYSIS—Economic Consideration *Why would BE object to complying with eBay's request that it perform the same function as other aggregation sites and search engines in general?*

E-AGENTS AND THE UCITA

As discussed in Chapter 17, in 1999 the National Conference of Commissioners on Uniform State Laws promulgated the Uniform Computer Information Transactions Act (UCITA).[11] The act was drafted to address problems unique to electronic contracting and to the purchase and sale (licensing) of computer information, such as software. Among other things, the act specifically addresses the issue of e-agents. Section 107(d) of the UCITA provides that any individual or company that uses an e-agent "is bound by the operations of the electronic agent, even if no individual was aware of or reviewed the agent's operations or the results of the operations." The liability of individuals and companies for the acts of e-agents, however, is qualified by Section 206(a) of the UCITA, which states that "a court may grant appropriate relief if the operations resulted from fraud, electronic mistake, or the like."

Agency Termination

Agency law is similar to contract law in that both an agency and a contract can be terminated by an act of the parties or by operation of law. Once the relationship between

11. Excerpts from the UCITA are included in Appendix P at the end of this text.

the principal and the agent has ended, the agent no longer has the right to bind the principal. For an agent's apparent authority to be terminated, however, third persons may also need to be notified when the agency has been terminated.

TERMINATION BY ACT OF THE PARTIES

An agency may be terminated by act of the parties in several ways, including those discussed here.

Lapse of Time An agency agreement may specify the time period during which the agency relationship will exist. If so, the agency ends when that time period expires. For example, if the parties agree that the agency will begin on January 1, 2002, and end on December 31, 2003, the agency is automatically terminated on December 31, 2003. If no definite time is stated, the agency continues for a reasonable time and can be terminated at will by either party. What constitutes a "reasonable time" depends, of course, on the circumstances and the nature of the agency relationship.

Purpose Achieved An agent can be employed to accomplish a particular objective, such as the purchase of stock for a cattle rancher. In that situation, the agency automatically ends after the cattle have been purchased. If more than one agent is employed to accomplish the same purpose, such as the sale of real estate, the first agent to complete the sale automatically terminates the agency relationship for all the others.

Occurrence of a Specific Event An agency can be created to terminate on the happening of a certain event. If Posner appoints Rubik to handle his business affairs while he is away, the agency automatically terminates when Posner returns.

Mutual Agreement Recall from the chapters on contract law that parties can cancel (rescind) a contract by mutually agreeing to terminate the contractual relationship. The same holds true under agency law regardless of whether the agency contract is in writing or whether it is for a specific duration.

Termination by One Party As a general rule, either party can terminate the agency relationship. The agent's act is called a *renunciation of authority.* The principal's act is referred to as a *revocation of authority.* Although both parties have the power to terminate the agency, they may not possess the right.

Wrongful termination can subject the canceling party to a suit for damages. • **EXAMPLE 24.14** Rawlins has a one-year employment contract with Munro to act as an agent in return for $35,000. Munro can discharge Rawlins before the contract period expires (Munro has the *power* to breach the contract); however, Munro will be liable to Rawlins for money damages because Munro has no *right* to breach the contract.•

A special rule applies in an *agency coupled with an interest.* This type of agency is not an agency in the usual sense because it is created for the agent's benefit instead of for the principal's benefit. • **EXAMPLE 24.15** Suppose that Julie borrows $5,000 from Rob, giving Rob some of her jewelry and signing a letter giving Rob the power to sell the jewelry as her agent if she fails to repay the loan. After receiving the $5,000 from Rob, Julie attempts to revoke Rob's authority to sell the jewelry as her agent. Julie would not succeed in this attempt because a principal cannot revoke an agency created for the agent's benefit.•

Notice of Termination If the parties themselves have terminated the agency, it is the principal's duty to inform any third parties who know of the existence of the agency that it has been terminated (although notice of the termination may be given by others).

An agent's authority continues until the agent receives some notice of termination. Notice to third parties follows the general rule that an agent's *apparent* authority continues until the third party receives notice (from any source of information) that such authority has been terminated. The principal is expected to notify directly any third person who the principal knows has dealt with the agent. For third persons who have heard about the agency but have not yet dealt with the agent, *constructive notice* is sufficient.[12]

No particular form is required for notice of agency termination to be effective. The principal can actually notify the agent, or the agent can learn of the termination through some other means. • **EXAMPLE 24.16** Manning bids on a shipment of steel, and Stone is hired as an agent to arrange transportation of the shipment. When Stone learns that Manning has lost the bid, Stone's authority to make the transportation arrangement terminates. •

If the agent's authority is written, it must be revoked in writing, and the writing must be shown to all people who saw the original writing that established the agency relationship. Sometimes, a written authorization (such as a power of attorney) contains an expiration date. The passage of the expiration date is sufficient notice of termination for third parties.

TERMINATION BY OPERATION OF LAW

Termination of an agency by operation of law occurs in the circumstances discussed here. Note that when an agency terminates by operation of law, there is no duty to notify third persons.

Death or Insanity The general rule is that the death or mental incompetence of either the principal or the agent automatically and immediately terminates the ordinary agency relationship. Knowledge of the death is not required. • **EXAMPLE 24.17** Suppose that Geer sends Pyron to China to purchase a rare painting. Before Pyron makes the purchase, Geer dies. Pyron's agent status is terminated at the moment of Geer's death, even though Pyron does not know that Geer has died. • Some states, however, have changed this common law rule by statute, and death does not terminate an agency coupled with an interest.

An agent's transactions that occur after the death of the principal are not binding on the principal's estate.[13] • **EXAMPLE 24.18** Assume that Carson is hired by Perry to collect a debt from Thomas (a third party). Perry dies, but Carson, not knowing of Perry's death, still collects the money from Thomas. Thomas's payment to Carson is no longer legally sufficient to discharge Thomas's debt to Perry because Carson's authority to collect the money ended on Perry's death. If Carson absconds with the money, Thomas is still liable for the debt to Perry's estate. •

12. Constructive notice is information or knowledge of a fact imputed by law to a person if he or she could have discovered the fact by proper diligence. Constructive notice is often accomplished by newspaper publication.

13. There is an exception to this rule in banking under which the bank, as the agent of the customer, can continue to exercise specific types of authority even after the customer has died or become mentally incompetent unless it has knowledge of the death or incompetence [UCC 4–405]. Even with knowledge of the customer's death, the bank has authority for ten days following the customer's death to honor checks in the absence of a stop-payment order.

Impossibility When the specific subject matter of an agency is destroyed or lost, the agency terminates. • **EXAMPLE 24.19** Bullard employs Gonzalez to sell Bullard's house. Prior to the sale, the premises are destroyed by fire. In this situation, Gonzalez's agency and authority to sell Bullard's house terminate. • The agency also terminates when it is impossible for the agent to perform the agency lawfully.

Changed Circumstances When an event occurs that has such an unusual effect on the subject matter of the agency that the agent can reasonably infer that the principal will not want the agency to continue, the agency terminates. • **EXAMPLE 24.20** Roberts hires Mullen to sell a tract of land for $20,000. Subsequently, Mullen learns that there is oil under the land and that the land is worth $1 million. The agency and Mullen's authority to sell the land for $20,000 are terminated. •

Bankruptcy and War Bankruptcy of the principal or the agent usually terminates the agency relationship. When the principal's country and the agent's country are at war with each other, the agency is terminated or at least suspended.

APPLICATION Law and the Employer. . .

Using Independent Contractors*

As an employer, you may at some time consider hiring an independent contractor. Hiring workers as independent contractors instead of as employees may help you reduce both your potential tort liability and your tax liability.

Minimizing Potential Tort Liability

One reason for using an independent contractor is that it may reduce your susceptibility to tort liability. If, however, an independent contractor's words or conduct leads another party to believe that the independent contractor is your employee, you may not escape liability for the contractor's tort.

To minimize the possibility of being legally liable for negligence on the part of an independent contractor, you should inquire about the contractor's qualifications before hiring him or her. The degree to which you should investigate depends, of course, on the nature of the work. A more thorough investigation is necessary when there is a potential danger to the public from the contractor's activities (as in delivering explosives).

Generally, it is a good idea to have the independent contractor assume, in a written contract, liability for harms caused to third parties by the contractor's negligence. You should also require the independent contractor to purchase liability insurance to cover the costs of potential lawsuits for harms caused to third persons by the independent contractor's hazardous activities or negligence.

Reducing Tax Liability

Another reason for hiring independent contractors is that you need not pay or deduct Social Security and unemployment taxes on their behalf. The independent contractor is the party responsible for paying these

*This *Application* is not meant to substitute for the services of an attorney who is licensed to practice law in your state.

(continued)

APPLICATION Law and the Employer. . .

Using Independent Contractors—continued

taxes. Additionally, the independent contractor is not eligible for any retirement or medical plans or other fringe benefits that you provide for yourself and your employees, and this is a cost saving to you.

A word of caution, though: simply designating a person as an independent contractor does not make her or him one. Under Internal Revenue Service (IRS) rules, individuals will be treated as employees if they are "in fact" employees, regardless of any classification that you might have made. For example, the IRS will not treat an office assistant as an independent contractor simply because you designate him or her as such. If the IRS determines that you exercise significant control over the assistant, the IRS may decide that the assistant is, in fact, an employee.

If you improperly designate an employee as an independent contractor, the penalty may be high. Usually, you will be liable for back Social Security and unemployment taxes, plus interest and penalties. When in doubt, seek professional assistance in such matters.

Checklist for Using Independent Contractors

1. Check the qualifications of any independent contractor you plan to use to reduce the possibility that you might be legally liable for the contractor's negligence.
2. It is best to require in any contract with an independent contractor that the contractor assume liability for harm to a third person caused by the contractor's negligence.
3. Require that independent contractors working for you carry liability insurance. Examine the policy to make sure that it is current, particularly when the contractor will be undertaking actions that are more than normally hazardous to the public.
4. Make sure that independent contractors do not represent themselves as your employees to the rest of the world.
5. Regularly inspect the work of the independent contractor to make sure that it is being performed in accordance with contract specifications. Such supervision on your part will not change the worker's status as an independent contractor.

Key Terms

agency 646
disclosed principal 660
e-agent 664
equal dignity rule 656
fiduciary 647
independent contractor 647
notary public 657
partially disclosed principal 660
power of attorney 657
ratification 652
respondeat superior 661
undisclosed principal 660

Chapter Summary Agency Relationships in Business

Agency Relationships (See pages 647–651.)	In a *principal-agent* relationship, an agent acts on behalf of and instead of the principal in dealing with third parties. An employee who deals with third parties is normally an agent. An independent contractor is not an employee, and the employer has no control over the details of physical performance. The independent contractor may or may not be an agent.

Chapter Summary Agency Relationships in Business—continued

Agency Formation (See pages 651–653.)	1. *By agreement*—An agency relationship may be formed through express consent (oral or written) or implied by conduct. 2. *By ratification*—The principal, either by act or agreement, ratifies the conduct of an agent who acted outside the scope of authority or the conduct of a person who is in fact not an agent. 3. *By estoppel*—When the principal causes a third person to believe that another person is his or her agent, and the third person deals with the supposed agent in reasonable reliance on the agency's existence, the principal is "estopped to deny" the agency relationship. 4. *By operation of law*—An agency relationship may arise based on a social duty (such as the need to support family members) or be created in emergency situations when the agent is unable to contact the principal.
Duties of Agents and Principals (See pages 653–656.)	1. *Duties of the agent*— a. Performance—The agent must use reasonable diligence and skill in performing her or his duties or use the special skills that the agent has represented to the principal that the agent possesses. b. Notification—The agent is required to notify the principal of all matters that come to his or her attention concerning the subject matter of the agency. c. Loyalty—The agent has a duty to act solely for the benefit of his or her principal and not in the interest of the agent or a third party. d. Obedience—The agent must follow all lawful and clearly stated instructions of the principal. e. Accounting—The agent has a duty to make available to the principal records of all property and money received and paid out on behalf of the principal. 2. *Duties of the principal*— a. Compensation—Except in a gratuitous agency relationship, the principal must pay the agreed-on value (or reasonable value) for an agent's services. b. Reimbursement and indemnification—The principal must reimburse the agent for all sums of money disbursed at the request of the principal and for all sums of money the agent disburses for necessary expenses in the course of reasonable performance of his or her agency duties. c. Cooperation—A principal must cooperate with and assist an agent in performing his or her duties. d. Safe working conditions—A principal must provide safe working conditions for the agent-employee.
Agent's Authority (See pages 656–660.)	1. *Express authority*—Can be oral or in writing. Authorization must be in writing if the agent is to execute a contract that must be in writing. 2. *Implied authority*—Authority customarily associated with the position of the agent or authority that is deemed necessary for the agent to carry out expressly authorized tasks. 3. *Apparent authority*—Exists when the principal, by word or action, causes a third party reasonably to believe that an agent has authority to act, even though the agent has no express or implied authority. 4. *Ratification*—The affirmation by the principal of an agent's unauthorized action or promise. For the ratification to be effective, the principal must be aware of all material facts.

(continued)

Chapter Summary Agency Relationships in Business—continued

Liability in Agency Relationships (See pages 660–664.)	1. *Liability for contracts*—If the principal's identity is disclosed or partially disclosed at the time the agent forms a contract with a third party, the principal is liable to the third party under the contract if the agent acted within the scope of his or her authority. If the principal's identity is undisclosed at the time of contract formation, the agent is personally liable to the third party, but if the agent acted within the scope of authority, the principal is also bound by the contract. 2. *Liability for agent's torts*—Under the doctrine of *respondeat superior,* the principal is liable for any harm caused to another through the agent's torts if the agent was acting within the scope of his or her employment at the time the harmful act occurred. The principal is also liable for an agent's misrepresentation, whether made knowingly or by mistake. 3. *Liability for independent contractor's torts*—A principal is not liable for harm caused by an independent contractor's negligence, unless hazardous activities are involved (in which situation the principal is strictly liable for any resulting harm) or other exceptions apply. 4. *Liability for agent's crimes*—An agent is responsible for his or her own crimes, even if the crimes were committed while the agent was acting within the scope of authority or employment. A principal will be liable for an agent's crime only if the principal participated by conspiracy or other action or (in some jurisdictions) if the agent violated certain government regulations in the course of employment.
E-Agents (See pages 664–666.)	An *electronic agent (e-agent)* is a semiautonomous computer program that is capable of executing specific tasks, such as searching through Internet databases for particular products. Applying traditional agency concepts to these "nonhuman" agents has been difficult. The Uniform Computer Information Transactions Act (UCITA), however, has filled this gap by stating that companies are bound by the operations of their e-agents, although the UCITA also allows the courts to grant relief for operations resulting from mistake.
Agency Termination (See pages 666–669.)	1. *By act of the parties*— a. Lapse of time (when a definite time for the duration of the agency was agreed on when the agency was established). b. Purpose achieved. c. Occurrence of a specific event. d. Mutual rescission (requires mutual consent of principal and agent). e. Termination by act of either the principal (revocation) or the agent (renunciation). (A principal cannot revoke an agency coupled with an interest.) f. When an agency is terminated by act of the parties, all third persons who have previously dealt with the agency must be directly notified; constructive notice will suffice for all other third parties. 2. *By operation of law*— a. Death or mental incompetence of either the principal or the agent (except in an agency coupled with an interest). b. Impossibility (when the purpose of the agency cannot be achieved because of an event beyond the parties' control). c. Changed circumstances (in which it would be inequitable to require that the agency be continued). d. Bankruptcy of the principal or the agent, or war between the principal's and agent's countries. e. When an agency is terminated by operation of law, no notice to third parties is required.

For Review

① What is the difference between an employee and an independent contractor, and how do agency relationships arise?
② What duties do agents and principals owe to each other?
③ When is a principal liable for the agent's actions with respect to third parties? When is the agent liable?
④ What is an e-agent? Does the use of e-agents in commerce pose any special legal issues?
⑤ What are some of the ways in which an agency relationship can be terminated?

Questions and Case Problems

24–1. Agency Formation. Pete Gaffrey is a well-known, wealthy financier living in the city of Takima. Alan Winter, Gaffrey's friend, tells Til Borge that he (Winter) is Gaffrey's agent for the purchase of rare coins. Winter even shows Borge a local newspaper clipping mentioning Gaffrey's interest in coin collecting. Borge, knowing of Winter's friendship with Gaffrey, contracts with Winter to sell to Gaffrey a rare coin valued at $25,000. Winter takes the coin and disappears with it. On the date of contract payment, Borge seeks to collect from Gaffrey, claiming that Winter's agency made Gaffrey liable. Gaffrey does not deny that Winter was a friend, but he claims that Winter was never his agent. Discuss fully whether an agency was in existence at the time the contract for the rare coin was made.

24–2. Ratification by Principal. Springer was a political candidate running for congressional office. He was operating on a tight budget and instructed his campaign staff not to purchase any campaign materials without his explicit authorization. In spite of these instructions, one of his campaign workers ordered Dubychek Printing Co. to print some promotional materials for Springer's campaign. When the printed materials were received, Springer did not return them but instead used them during his campaign. When Dubychek failed to obtain payment from Springer for the materials, he sued for recovery of the price. Springer contended that he was not liable on the sales contract because he had not authorized his agent to purchase the printing services. Dubychek argued that the campaign worker was Springer's agent and that the worker had authority to make the printing contract. Additionally, Dubychek claimed that even if the purchase was unauthorized, Springer's use of the materials constituted ratification of his agent's unauthorized purchase. Is Dubychek correct? Explain.

24–3. Agent's Duties to Principal. Iliana is a traveling sales agent. Iliana not only solicits orders but also delivers the goods and collects payments from her customers. Iliana places all payments in her private checking account and at the end of each month draws sufficient cash from her bank to cover the payments made. Giberson Corp., Iliana's employer, is totally unaware of this procedure. Because of a slowdown in the economy, Giberson tells all its sales personnel to offer 20 percent discounts on orders. Iliana solicits her orders, but she offers only 15 percent discounts, pocketing the extra 5 percent paid by customers. Iliana has not lost any orders by this practice, and she is rated as one of Giberson's top salespersons. Giberson now learns of Iliana's actions. Discuss fully Giberson's rights in this matter.

24–4. Liability for Agent's Contracts. Michael Mosely works as a purchasing agent for Suharto Coal Supply, a partnership. Mosely has authority to purchase the coal needed by Suharto to satisfy the needs of its customers. While Mosely is leaving a coal mine from which he has just purchased a large quantity of coal, his car breaks down. He walks into a small roadside grocery store for help. While there, he runs into Wiley, who owns 360 acres back in the mountains with all mineral rights. Wiley, in need of money, offers to sell Mosely the property at $1,500 per acre. On inspection, Mosely concludes that the subsurface may contain valuable coal deposits. Mosely contracts to purchase the property for Suharto, signing the contract, "Suharto Coal Supply, Michael Mosely, agent." The closing date is set for August 1. Mosely takes the contract to the partnership. The managing partner is furious, as Suharto is not in the property business. Later, just before August 1, both Wiley and the partnership learn that the value of the land is at least $15,000 per acre. Discuss the rights of Suharto and Wiley concerning the land contract.

24–5. Employee versus Independent Contractor. Stephen Hemmerling was a driver for the Happy Cab Co. Hemmerling paid certain fixed expenses and abided by a variety of rules relating to the use of the cab, the hours that could be worked, the solicitation of fares, and so on. Rates were set by the state. Happy Cab did not withhold taxes from Hemmerling's pay. While driving the cab, Hemmerling was injured in an accident and filed a claim against Happy Cab in a Nebraska state court for workers' compensation benefits. Such benefits are not available to independent contractors. On what basis might the court hold that Hemmerling is an employee? Explain. [*Hemmerling v. Happy Cab Co.*, 247 Neb. 919, 530 N.W.2d 916 (1995)]

24–6. Undisclosed Principal. John Dunning was the sole officer of The R. B. Dunning Co. and was responsible for the management and operation of the business. When the company rented a warehouse from Samuel and Ruth Saliba, Dunning did not say that he was acting for the firm. The parties did not have a written lease. Business faltered, and the firm stopped paying rent. Eventually, it went bankrupt and vacated the property. The Salibas filed a suit in a Maine state court against Dunning personally, seeking to recover the unpaid rent.

Dunning claimed the debt belonged to the company because he had been acting only as its agent. Who is liable for the rent, and why? [*Estate of Saliba v. Dunning*, 682 A.2d 224 (Me. 1996)]

24–7. Liability for Employee's Acts. Federated Financial Reserve Corp. leases consumer and business equipment. As part of its credit approval and debt-collection practices, Federated hires credit collectors, whom it authorizes to obtain credit reports on its customers. Janice Caylor, a Federated collector, used this authority to obtain a report on Karen Jones, who was not a Federated customer but who was the ex-wife of Caylor's roommate, Randy Lind. When Jones discovered that Lind had her address and how he had obtained it, she filed a suit in a federal district court against Federated and others. Jones claimed in part that they had violated the Fair Credit Reporting Act, the goal of which is to protect consumers from the improper use of credit reports. Under what theory might an employer be held liable for an agent-employee's violation of a statute? Does that theory apply in this case? Explain. [*Jones v. Federated Financial Reserve Corp.*, 144 F.3d 961 (6th Cir. 1998)]

24–8. Implied Authority. Juanita Miller filed a complaint in an Indiana state court against Red Arrow Ventures, Ltd., Thomas Hayes, and Claudia Langman, alleging that they had breached their promise to make payments on a promissory note issued to Miller. The defendants denied this allegation and asserted a counterclaim against Miller. After a trial, the judge announced that, although he would be ruling against the defendants, he had not yet determined what amount of damages would be awarded to Miller. Over the next three days, the parties' attorneys talked and agreed that the defendants would pay Miller $21,000. The attorneys exchanged correspondence acknowledging this settlement. When the defendants balked at paying this amount, the trial judge issued an order to enforce the settlement agreement. The defendants appealed to a state intermediate appellate court, arguing that they had not consented to the settlement agreement. What is the rule regarding the authority of an agent—in this case, the defendants' attorney—to agree to a settlement? How should the court apply the rule in this case? Why? [*Red Arrow Ventures, Ltd. v. Miller*, 692 N.E.2d 939 (Ind.App. 1998)]

24–9. Agent's Duties to Principal. Ana Barreto and Flavia Gugliuzzi asked Ruth Bennett, a real estate salesperson who worked for Smith Bell Real Estate, to list for sale their house in the Pleasant Valley area of Underhill, Vermont. Diana Carter, a California resident, visited the house as a potential buyer. Bennett worked under the supervision of David Crane, an officer of Smith Bell. Crane knew, but did not disclose to Bennett or Carter, that the house was subject to frequent and severe winds, that a window had blown in years earlier, and that other houses in the area had suffered wind damage. Crane knew of this because he lived in the Pleasant Valley area, had sold a number of nearby properties, and had been Underhill's zoning officer. Many valley residents, including Crane, had wind gauges on their homes to measure and compare wind speeds with their neighbors. Carter bought the house, and several months later, high winds blew in a number of windows and otherwise damaged the property. Carter filed a suit in a Vermont state court against Smith Bell and others, alleging fraud. She argued in part that Crane's knowledge of the winds was imputable to Smith Bell. Smith Bell responded that Crane's knowledge was obtained outside the scope of employment. What is the rule regarding how much of an agent's knowledge a principal is assumed to know? How should the court rule in this case? Why? [*Carter v. Gugliuzzi*, 716 A.2d 17 (Vt. 1998)]

TEST YOUR KNOWLEDGE—ANSWER ON THE WEB

24–10. Register.com is, among other things, a registrar of Internet domain names. Like all registrars, Register.com is required to provide free to the public an online interactive database, called the WHOIS database, containing the names and contact information of its registrants. Verio, Inc., although not a registrar of domain names, is a direct competitor of Register.com in providing other services. Verio used automated software—a spider, or robot (or bot)—to collect the WHOIS data and used the information for mass e-mail solicitations (spam) in a marketing initiative called Project Henhouse. Register.com complained to Verio, which stopped the spam but continued to collect the data with its spider. Register.com filed a suit in a federal district court against Verio, alleging, in part, trespass to chattels (personal property) and asking for an injunction. Verio responded in part that its use of a spider to collect the WHOIS data did not harm Register.com's computers. How should the court rule, and why? [*Register.com v. Verio, Inc.*, 126 F.Supp.2d 238 (S.D.N.Y. 2000)]

A QUESTION OF ETHICS AND SOCIAL RESPONSIBILITY

24–11. In 1990, the Internal Revenue Service (IRS) determined that a number of independent contractors working for Microsoft Corp. were actually employees of the company for tax purposes. The IRS arrived at this conclusion based on the significant control that Microsoft exercised over the independent contractors' work performance. As a result of the IRS's findings, Microsoft was ordered to pay back payroll taxes for hundreds of independent contractors who should have been classified as employees. Rather than contest the ruling, Microsoft required most of the workers in question, as well as a number of its other independent contractors, to become associated with employment agencies and work for Microsoft as temporary workers ("temps") or lose the opportunity to work for Microsoft. Workers who refused to register with employment agencies, as well as some who did register, sued Microsoft. The workers alleged that they were actually employees of the company and, as such, entitled to participate in Microsoft's stock option plan for employees. Microsoft countered that it need not provide such benefits because each of the workers had signed an independent-contractor agreement specifically stating that the worker was responsible for his or her own benefits. In view of these facts, consider the following questions. [*Vizcaino v. Microsoft*, 173 F.3d 713 (9th Cir. 1999)]

1. If the decision were up to you, how would you rule in this case? Why?
2. Normally, when a company hires temporary workers from an employment agency, the agency—not the employer—is responsible for paying Social Security taxes and other withholding taxes. Yet the U.S. Court of Appeals for the Ninth Circuit held that being an employee of a temporary employment agency did not preclude the employee from having the status of a common law employee of Microsoft at the same time. Is this fair to the employer? Why or why not?
3. Generally, do you believe that Microsoft was trying to "skirt the law"—and its ethical responsibilities—by requiring its employees to sign up as "temps"?
4. Each of the employees involved in this case had signed an independent-contractor agreement. In view of this fact, is this decision fair to Microsoft? Why or why not?

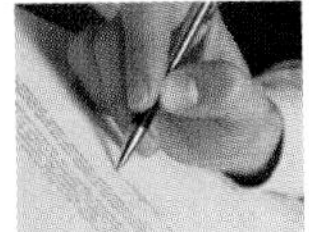

FOR CRITICAL ANALYSIS

24–12. What policy is served by the law that employers do not have copyright ownership in works created by independent contractors (unless there is a written "work for hire" agreement)?

Internet Exercises

Go to the *Business Law Today* home page at **http://blt.westbuslaw.com**. Select "Interactive Study Center" and then click on "Chapter 24." There you will find the following Internet research exercises that you can perform to learn more about agency relationships:

Activity 24–1: Employees or Independent Contractors?
Activity 24–2: Liability in Agency Relationships

Before the Test

Go to the *Business Law Today* home page at **http://blt.westbuslaw.com**. Click on "Interactive Quizzes." You will find at least twenty interactive questions relating to this chapter.

CHAPTER 25

Sole Proprietorships and Partnerships

"[E]veryone thirsteth after gaine."

Sir Edward Coke, 1552–1634
(English jurist and politician)

CHAPTER CONTENTS

LEARNING OBJECTIVES

After reading this chapter, you should be able to answer the following questions:

① What advantages and disadvantages are associated with the sole proprietorship?

② What are the three essential elements of a partnership?

③ What are the rights and duties of partners?

④ What is meant by joint and several liability? Why is this often considered to be a disadvantage of the partnership form of business?

⑥ Can a partner continue the business of a terminated partnership if he or she wishes to do so? How?

Many Americans would agree with Sir Edward Coke that most people, at least, "thirsteth after gaine." Certainly, an entrepreneur's primary motive for undertaking a business enterprise is to make profits. An *entrepreneur* is by definition one who initiates and *assumes the financial risks* of a new enterprise and undertakes to provide or control its management.

One of the questions faced by any entrepreneur who wishes to start up a business is what form of business organization should be chosen for the business endeavor. In making this determination, a number of factors need to be considered. Four important factors are (1) ease of creation, (2) the liability of the owners, (3) tax considerations, and (4) the need for capital. In studying this unit on business organizations, keep these factors in mind as you read about the various business organizational forms available to entrepreneurs.

Traditionally, entrepreneurs have used three major forms to structure their business enterprises—the sole proprietorship, the partnership, and the corporation. In this chapter, we examine the first two of these forms. The third major traditional form—the corporation—is discussed in detail in Chapters 26 through 29. Two relatively new forms of business enterprise—limited liability companies (LLCs) and limited liability partnerships (LLPs)—offer special advantages to businesspersons, particularly with respect to taxation and liability. We look at these business forms, which are coming into widespread use, in Chapter 30. We also include in Chapter 30 an exhibit that summarizes and compares the significant characteristics of each of the major business organizational forms. In Chapter 31, the concluding chapter in this unit on business organizations, we describe a number of other forms of business organization as well as private franchises.

Sole Proprietorships

SOLE PROPRIETORSHIP
The simplest form of business, in which the owner is the business. The owner reports business income on his or her personal income tax return and is legally responsible for all debts and obligations incurred by the business.

The simplest form of business is a **sole proprietorship.** In this form, the owner is the business; thus, anyone who does business without creating a separate business organization has a sole proprietorship.[1] Over two-thirds of all American businesses are sole proprietorships. They are usually small enterprises—about 99 percent of the sole proprietorships existing in the United States have revenues of less than $1 million per year. Sole proprietors can own and manage any type of business, ranging from an informal, home-office undertaking to a large restaurant or construction firm. Today, a number of online businesses that sell goods and services on a nationwide basis are organized as sole proprietorships—see, for example, the business discussed in this chapter's *Business Law in the Online World* feature on the next page.

A major advantage of the sole proprietorship is that the proprietor receives all of the profits (because he or she assumes all of the risk). In addition, it is often easier and less costly to start a sole proprietorship than to start any other kind of business, as few legal forms are involved. This type of business organization also entails more flexibility than does a partnership or a corporation. The sole proprietor is free to make any decision she or he wishes concerning the business—whom to hire, when to take a vacation, what kind of business to pursue, and so on. A sole proprietor pays only personal income taxes on profits, which are reported as personal income on the proprietor's personal income tax return. Sole proprietors are also allowed to establish tax-exempt retirement accounts in the form of Keogh plans.[2]

What are the advantages of doing business as a sole proprietorship?

The major disadvantage of the sole proprietorship is that, as sole owner, the proprietor alone bears the burden of any losses or liabilities incurred by the business enterprise. In other words, the sole proprietor has unlimited liability, or legal responsibility, for all obligations incurred in doing business. This unlimited liability is a major factor to be considered in choosing a business form. The sole proprietorship also has the disadvantage of lacking continuity on the death of the proprietor. When the owner dies, so does the business—it is automatically dissolved. If the business is transferred to family members or other heirs, a new proprietorship is created.

1. Although starting up a sole proprietorship involves relatively few legal formalities compared to other business organizational forms, even small sole proprietorships may need to comply with certain zoning requirements, obtain appropriate licenses, and the like.

2. A *Keogh plan* is a retirement program designed for self-employed persons. The person can contribute a certain percentage of income to the plan, and interest earnings are not taxed until funds are withdrawn from the plan.

BUSINESS LAW: //in the Online World

Online Sole Proprietorships and Venue Requirements

The Internet has expanded the ability of sole proprietorships to market their products nationwide without greatly increasing their costs. As a result, many small sole proprietorships market their goods online on a national basis. Does this mean that sole proprietorships, like unincorporated associations, should now be considered the equivalent of corporations for certain purposes, such as venue requirements?[a] In 2000, a federal district court faced this question in a case brought by a corporation against a competitor that operated as a sole proprietorship.

Background to the Venue Question

The case involved competing sellers of exercise machines. One of the sellers was Hsin Ten Enterprise USA, Inc., a corporation with its principal place of business in Farmingdale, New York. Hsin Ten manufactured and distributed an aerobic exercise product called "The Chi Machine." Hsin Ten also made and sold other products under the "Chi" trademark, which it owned. The other seller was Clark Enterprises, a sole proprietorship owned and operated by Clifford Clark in Salina, Kansas. Clark sold its exercise machines through representatives, trade shows, and its Web sites. One of Clark's Web sites used the name "Chi Exerciser 2000" to promote its exercise machine, and the term *Chi* was frequently used on the Web sites to refer to the product.

Hsin Ten filed a suit in a federal district court in New York against Clark, alleging, among other things, that Clark had infringed on its trademark. Clark filed a motion to dismiss the trademark claim, arguing in part that because it was a sole proprietorship, the court did not have venue under 28 U.S.C. Section 1391(c), the applicable statute. That section provides, "For purposes of venue . . . , a defendant that is a corporation shall be deemed to reside in any judicial district in which it is subject to personal jurisdiction." Hsin Ten asserted that although Clark is an unincorporated sole proprietorship with its principal offices in Kansas, it should be deemed a "corporation" for venue purposes. After all, argued Hsin Ten, Clark is unlike other sole proprietorships because it does business in forty-seven states and resembles a national corporation in all respects except its choice of legal structure.

The Court Says No—A Sole Proprietorship Is Not a Corporation for Venue Purposes

The court noted that although the United States Supreme Court has held that Section 1391(c) extends to unincorporated associations, the courts have been *unwilling* to further extend the definition of "corporation" to include sole proprietorships. First, stated the court, a broad geographic distribution, in itself, does not convert a small sole proprietorship into the functional equivalent of a corporation. Second, continued the court, "Venue is primarily a question of convenience for litigants and witnesses, and venue provisions should be treated in practical terms. In practical terms, expanding the definition of 'corporation' to include sole proprietorships would be overly burdensome and inconvenient to sole proprietors, most of whom would be unable to afford the expense of litigating in distant states."[b] Thus, the court did not have venue under 28 U.S.C. Section 1391(c).

FOR CRITICAL ANALYSIS

If courts could "hear" disputes online, as may occur in the future, how might that have affected the court's reasoning in this case?

a. As explained in Chapter 3, *venue* concerns the most appropriate location for a trial. Venue requirements are often established by statute.

b. *Hsin Ten Enterprise USA, Inc. v. Clark Enterprises*, 138 F.Supp.2d 449 (S.D.N.Y. 2000).

Another disadvantage is that the proprietor's opportunity to raise capital is limited to personal funds and the funds of those who are willing to make loans. If the owner wishes to expand the business significantly, one way to raise more capital to finance the expansion is to join forces with another entrepreneur and establish a partnership or form a corporation.

"Many forms of conduct permissible in a workaday world for those acting at arm's length, are forbidden to those bound by fiduciary ties."

BENJAMIN CARDOZO, 1870–1938
(Associate justice of the United States Supreme Court, 1932–1938)

The Law Governing Partnerships

When two or more persons agree to do business as partners, they enter into a special relationship with one another. To an extent, their relationship is similar to an agency relationship because each partner is deemed to be the agent of the other partners and of the partnership. The common law agency concepts outlined in Chapter 24 thus apply—specifically, the imputation of knowledge of, and responsibility for, acts done within the scope of the partnership relationship. In their relations with one another, partners, like agents, are bound by fiduciary ties.

In one important way, however, partnership law is distinct from agency law. A partnership is based on a voluntary contract between two or more competent persons who agree to place financial capital, labor, and skill in a business with the understanding that profits and losses will be shared. In a nonpartnership agency relationship, the agent usually does not have an ownership interest in the business, nor is he or she obliged to bear a portion of the ordinary business losses.

ON THE WEB You can find summaries, texts, and the legislative history of numerous uniform acts, including the UPA and the RUPA, at the Web site of the National Conference of Commissioners on Uniform State Laws at **http://www.nccusl.org**.

Partnerships are also governed by statutory law. The Uniform Partnership Act (UPA) governs the operation of partnerships *in the absence of express agreement* and has done much to reduce controversies in the law relating to partnerships. Except for Louisiana, all of the states, as well as the District of Columbia, have adopted the UPA. The UPA is presented in Appendix D of this book. A revised version of the UPA, known as the Revised Uniform Partnership Act (RUPA), was formally adopted by the National Conference of Commissioners on Uniform State Laws in 1992 and has already been adopted in several states. The RUPA significantly changes some of the rules governing partnerships.

In the pages that follow, we look at the legal definition of a partnership and at the laws governing the formation, operation, and termination of general partnerships. Whenever relevant, we include bracketed references to specific UPA provisions. Additionally, if the RUPA has significantly changed particular UPA provisions, we indicate these changes in footnotes. (Special types of partnerships, including the limited partnership, or LP, and the limited liability partnership, or LLP, will be examined in Chapter 30.)

Definition of Partnership

PARTNERSHIP
An agreement by two or more persons to carry on, as co-owners, a business for profit.

Conflicts commonly arise over whether a business enterprise is legally a partnership, especially in the absence of a formal, written partnership agreement. The UPA defines a **partnership** as "an association of two or more persons to carry on as co-owners a business for profit" [UPA 6(1)]. The intent to associate is a key element of a partnership, and one cannot join a partnership unless all other partners consent [UPA 18(g)].

PARTNERSHIP STATUS

In resolving disputes over whether partnership status exists, courts will usually look for the following three essential elements, which are implicit in the UPA's definition of a partnership:

① A sharing of profits and losses.

② A joint ownership of the business.

③ An equal right in the management of the business.

KEEP IN MIND Two or more persons are required to form a partnership. Many other forms of business can be organized by a single individual.

If the evidence in a particular case is insufficient to establish all three factors, the UPA provides a set of guidelines to be used. For example, the sharing of profits and losses from a business is considered *prima facie* ("on the face of it") evidence that a partnership has been created. No such inference is made, however, if the profits were received as payment of any of the following [UPA 7(4)]:

① A debt by installments or interest on a loan.

② Wages of an employee.

③ Rent to a landlord.

④ An annuity to a surviving spouse or representative of a deceased partner.

⑤ A sale of goodwill of a business or property.

Joint ownership of property, obviously, does not in and of itself create a partnership. Therefore, if persons own real property as joint tenants or as tenants in common (forms of joint ownership, to be discussed in Chapter 36), this does not mean that they are partners in a partnership. In fact, the sharing of gross returns and even profits from such ownership is usually not enough to create a partnership [UPA 7(2) and (3)]. • **EXAMPLE 25.1** Suppose that Ablat and Burke jointly own a piece of rural property. They lease the land to a farmer, with the understanding that they will receive a share of the profits from the farming operation conducted by the farmer in lieu of set rental payments. This arrangement normally would not make Ablat, Burke, and the farmer partners. Note, though, that although the sharing of profits does not prove the existence of a partnership, sharing *both profits and losses* usually does. •

In the following case, two brothers and their mother bought a ranch that for many years the brothers operated together. After the mother disclaimed her interest and one brother stopped participating in ranch activities, a question arose as to whether the brothers were ever partners.

CASE 25.1 Tarnavsky v. Tarnavsky

United States Court of Appeals,
Eighth Circuit, 1998.
147 F.3d 674.
http://guide.lp.Findlaw.com/casecode/courts/8th.htm[a]

FACTS In 1967, Mary Tarnavsky and her sons Morris and Thomas (who was known as T.R.) bought a ranch known as the Christ place. T.R. and Morris opened a bank account into which they deposited their shares of the ranch's proceeds, which were used to make payments on the property, to pay property taxes, and to buy cattle, equipment, supplies, and services. For the ranch, the brothers took out joint loans and jointly purchased cattle and machinery. They reported their activities on state and federal partnership income tax returns. Morris handled the livestock. T.R. handled the bookkeeping. In 1980, Mary disclaimed her interest in proceeds from the ranch. Eight years later, T.R. stopped doing the bookkeeping and began spending little time on ranch activities. Morris sent T.R. a "Notice of Dissolution of Partnership." After unsuccessful attempts to arrive at a settlement, T.R. filed a suit in a federal district court, requesting payment for his share of the partnership assets. The court ordered a payment of $220,000 to T.R. Morris appealed, arguing in part that there was no partnership.

ISSUE Did a partnership exist between the brothers?

DECISION Yes. The U.S. Court of Appeals for the Eighth Circuit affirmed the lower court's order. Morris and T.R. were partners.

a. From this page, under "Party Name Search," key in "Tarnavsky" and then click on the "Search" box. When that page opens, click on the case name to access the opinion. This database is maintained by FindLaw.

CASE 25.1—Continued

REASON The U.S. Court of Appeals for the Eighth Circuit found that the facts satisfied elements that are critical to the existence of a partnership: "(1) an intention to be partners; (2) co-ownership of the business; and (3) profit motive." The court concluded that the brothers' income tax returns, joint bank account, and joint payments for supplies evidenced their intent to be partners. Co-ownership was shown by their sharing of profits and control. The sharing of profits was clear from the brothers' joint bank account and their tax returns. That both brothers had control of the management of the business was evidenced by their joint handling of some ranch activities and separate handling of other responsibilities. "The final critical element of a partnership is profit motive, and there is no dispute that the farming business was operated with such motive."

FOR CRITICAL ANALYSIS—Economic Consideration *Why would Morris want to argue that there was no partnership between the brothers?*

ENTITY VERSUS AGGREGATE

A partnership is sometimes called a *firm* or a *company*, terms that connote an entity separate and apart from its aggregate members. Sometimes, the law of partnership recognizes a partnership as an independent entity, but for most other purposes, the law treats it as an *aggregate of the individual partners*.

At common law, a partnership was never treated as a separate legal entity. Thus, at common law a suit could never be brought by or against the firm in its own name; each individual partner had to sue or be sued. Today, most states provide specifically that the partnership can be treated as an entity for certain purposes. For example, a partnership usually can sue or be sued, collect judgments, and have all accounting procedures in the name of the partnership entity. In addition, the UPA recognizes that partnership property may be held in the name of the partnership rather than in the names of the individual partners. Finally, federal procedural laws frequently permit the partnership to be treated as an entity in such matters as suits in federal courts, bankruptcy proceedings, and informational federal tax returns.

When the partnership is not regarded as a separate legal entity, it is treated as an aggregate of the individual partners. For example, for federal income tax purposes, a partnership is not a tax-paying entity. The income and losses it incurs are passed through the partnership framework and attributed to the partners on their individual tax returns.

Partnership Formation

"Mr. Morgan buys his partners; I grow my own."

ANDREW CARNEGIE, 1835–1918 (American industrialist and philanthropist)

A partnership is ordinarily formed by an explicit agreement among the parties. The law does recognize another form of partnership, however, called *partnership by estoppel*, which arises when persons who are not partners represent themselves as partners when dealing with third parties. This section will describe the requirements for the creation of a partnership, including references to liability with respect to *alleged* partners.

THE PARTNERSHIP AGREEMENT

Agreements to form a partnership can be oral, written, or implied by conduct. Some partnership agreements, however, must be in writing to be legally enforceable within the Statute of Frauds (discussed in Chapter 11). For example, a partnership agreement

INTERNATIONAL PERSPECTIVE

Doing Business with Foreign Partners

American businesspersons who wish to operate a partnership in another country need to check to see what that country requires in terms of local participation. If a country requires local participation, this means that a specific share of the business must be owned by nationals of the host country. In other words, the American businesspersons would need to admit to the partnership a partner or partners who live in the host country.

Sometimes, Americans seeking to establish partnerships in a country that requires local participation are reluctant to do so. This is because the technology and expertise developed by the partnership business may end up in the hands of a future competitor if the partnership breaks up—and the American parties may have little recourse against their former partners' use of their intellectual property under the host country's law.

FOR CRITICAL ANALYSIS
Do local participation rules benefit countries in the long run?

that, by its terms, is to continue for more than one year must be evidenced by a sufficient writing.

ARTICLES OF PARTNERSHIP
A written agreement that sets forth each partner's rights and obligations with respect to the partnership.

A partnership agreement, called **articles of partnership**, usually specifies the name and location of the business, the duration of the partnership, the purpose of the business, each partner's share of the profits, how the partnership will be managed, how assets will be distributed on dissolution, and other provisions.[3] (Notice that the sample partnership agreement shown in Exhibit 25–1 includes an arbitration clause at the end of the agreement.) As mentioned, the UPA applies only in the absence of the parties' agreement on a particular issue. The partnership agreement is thus binding on the parties, even if certain provisions, such as the distribution of profits, seem to be unfair.

ETHICAL ISSUE 25.1

Why should partnership agreements be in writing?

Time and again, disputes among partners come before the courts because of oral partnership agreements. For example, suppose that Turino and Crowder decide to create a partnership to sell tires. They orally agree that Turino will provide two-thirds of the capital to start up the business and will receive two-thirds of the profits in return. After the business is under way, Crowder claims that he is working harder at the business than Turino is, and thus at least one-half of the profits should be his. The dispute ends up in court, and Turino, because he has no evidence of the oral agreement, ends up with only one-half of the profits. This is because the law assumes that members of a partnership share profits and losses equally unless a partnership agreement provides otherwise, as will be discussed later in this chapter [UPA 18(a)]. Turino and Crowder could have avoided this problem by creating a written partnership agreement that specified how the profits would be shared.

3. The RUPA provides for the voluntary filing of a partnership statement, containing such information as the agency authority of the partners, with the secretary of state. The statement must be executed by at least two partners, a copy must be sent to all of the partners, and a certified copy must be filed in the office for recording transfers of real property (in most states, in the county in which the property is located).

EXHIBIT 25–1 A SAMPLE PARTNERSHIP AGREEMENT

PARTNERSHIP AGREEMENT

This agreement, made and entered into as of the __________, by and among __________ __________________ (hereinafter collectively sometimes referred to as "Partners").

WITNESSETH:

Whereas, the Parties hereto desire to form a General Partnership (hereinafter referred to as the "Partnership"), for the term and upon the conditions hereinafter set forth;

Now, therefore, in consideration of the mutual covenants hereinafter contained, it is agreed by and among the Parties hereto as follows:

Article I
BASIC STRUCTURE

Form. The Parties hereby form a General Partnership pursuant to the Laws of __________ ______________.

Name. The business of the Partnership shall be conducted under the name of __________ ______________.

Place of Business. The principal office and place of business of the Partnership shall be located at ____________________, or such other place as the Partners may from time to time designate.

Term. The Partnership shall commence on __________, and shall continue for _____ years, unless earlier terminated in the following manner: (a) By the completion of the purpose intended, or (b) Pursuant to this Agreement, or (c) By applicable _____________ law, or (d) By death, insanity, bankruptcy, retirement, withdrawal, resignation, expulsion, or disability of all of the then Partners.

Purpose—General. The purpose for which the Partnership is organized is _____________ ____

Article II
FINANCIAL ARRANGEMENTS

Each Partner has contributed to the initial capital of the Partnership property in the amount and form indicated on Schedule A attached hereto and made a part hereof. Capital contributions to the Partnership shall not earn interest. An individual capital account shall be maintained for each Partner. If at any time during the existence of the Partnership it shall become necessary to increase the capital with which the said Partnership is doing business, then (upon the vote of the Managing Partner[s]): each party to this Agreement shall contribute to the capital of this Partnership within ___ days notice of such need in an amount according to his then Percentage Share of Capital as called for by the Managing Partner(s).

The Percentage Share of Profits and Capital of each Partner shall be (unless otherwise modified by the terms of this Agreement) as follows:

Names	Initial Percentage Share of Profits and Capital
________________	____________________
________________	____________________
________________	____________________

No interest shall be paid on any contribution to the capital of the Partnership. No Partner shall have the right to demand the return of his capital contributions except as herein provided. The individual Partners shall have no right to any priority over each other as to the return of capital contributions except as herein provided.

Distributions to the Partners of net operating profits of the Partnership, as hereinafter defined, shall be made at ______________________. Such distributions shall be made to the Partners simultaneously.

For the purpose of this Agreement, net operating profit for any accounting period shall mean the gross receipts of the Partnership for such period, less the sum of all cash expenses of operation of the Partnership, and such sums as may be necessary to establish a reserve for operating expenses. In determining net operating profit, deductions for depreciation, amortization, or other similar charges not requiring actual current expenditures of cash shall *not* be taken into account in accordance with generally accepted accounting principles.

(continued)

EXHIBIT 25–1 A SAMPLE PARTNERSHIP AGREEMENT—CONTINUED

No partner shall be entitled to receive any compensation from the Partnership, nor shall any Partner receive any drawing account from the Partnership.

Article III
MANAGEMENT

The Managing Partner(s) shall be ________________________.

The Managing Partner(s) shall have the right to vote as to the management and conduct of the business of the Partnership as follows:

Names	Vote
________________________	________________________
________________________	________________________
________________________	________________________

Article IV
DISSOLUTION

In the event that the Partnership shall hereafter be dissolved for any reason whatsoever, a full and general account of its assets, liabilities and transactions shall at once be taken. Such assets may be sold and turned into cash as soon as possible and all debts and other amounts due the Partnership collected. The proceeds thereof shall thereupon be applied as follows:

(a) To discharge the debts and liabilities of the Partnership and the expenses of liquidation.

(b) To pay each Partner or his or her legal representative any unpaid salary, drawing account, interest or profits to which he or she shall then be entitled and in addition, to repay to any Partner his capital contributions in excess of his or her original capital contribution.

(c) To divide the surplus, if any, among the Partners or their representatives as follows:

(1) First (to the extent of each Partner's then capital account) in proportion to their then capital accounts. (2) Then according to each Partner's then Percentage Share of [*Capital/Income*].

No Partner shall have the right to demand and receive property in kind for his distribution.

Article V
MISCELLANEOUS

The Partnership's fiscal year shall commence on January 1st of each year and shall end on December 31st of each year. Full and accurate books of account shall be kept at such place as the Managing Partner(s) may from time to time designate, showing the condition of the business and finances of the Partnership; and each Partner shall have access to such books of account and shall be entitled to examine them at any time during ordinary business hours. At the end of each year, the Managing Partner(s) shall cause the Partnership's accountant to prepare a balance sheet setting forth the financial position of the Partnership as of the end of that year and a statement of operations (income and expenses) for that year. A copy of the balance sheet and statement of operations shall be delivered to each Partner as soon as it is available.

Each Partner shall be deemed to have waived all objections to any transaction or other facts about the operation of the Partnership disclosed in such balance sheet and/or statement of operations unless he or she shall have notified the Managing Partner(s) in writing of his or her objectives within thirty (30) days of the date on which such statement is mailed.

The Partnership shall maintain a bank account or bank accounts in the Partnership's name in a national or state bank in the State of ________________. Checks and drafts shall be drawn on the Partnership's bank account for Partnership purposes only and shall be signed by the Managing Partner(s) or their designated agent.

Any controversy or claim arising out of or relating to this Agreement shall only be settled by arbitration in accordance with the rules of the American Arbitration Association, one Arbitrator, and shall be enforceable in any court having competent jurisdiction.

Witnesses	Partners
________________________	________________________
________________________	________________________

Date: ____________

PARTNERSHIP DURATION

The partnership agreement can specify the duration of the partnership in terms of a date or the completion of a particular project. A partnership that is specifically limited in duration is called a *partnership for a term*. A dissolution without the consent of all the partners prior to the expiration of the partnership term constitutes a breach of the agreement, and the responsible partner can be liable for any losses resulting from it. If no fixed duration is specified, the partnership is a *partnership at will*. This type of partnership can be dissolved at any time by any partner without violating the agreement and without incurring liability for losses to other partners resulting from the termination.

ON THE WEB
The Small Business Administration offers an abundance of information for entrepreneurs who wish to start up businesses, including partnerships. For answers to "frequently asked questions" concerning business start-ups and when a partnership may be advantageous, go to

http://www.sba.gov/starting/indexfaqs.html.

THE CORPORATION AS PARTNER

General partners are personally liable for the debts incurred by the partnership. If one of the general partners is a corporation, however, what does personal liability mean? Basically, the capacity of corporations to contract is a question of corporation law. Many states have restrictions on corporations becoming partners, although such restrictions have become less common over the years. The Revised Model Business Corporation Act (discussed in Chapter 26), however, generally allows corporations to make contracts and incur liabilities, and the UPA specifically permits a corporation to be a partner. By definition, "a partnership is an association of two or more persons," and the UPA defines *person* as including corporations [UPA 2].

PARTNERSHIP BY ESTOPPEL

Parties who are not partners sometimes represent themselves as such and cause third persons to rely on their representations. The law of partnership does not confer any partnership rights on these persons, but it may impose liability on them. This is also true when a partner represents, expressly or impliedly, that a nonpartner is a member of the firm. Whenever a third person has reasonably and detrimentally relied on the representation that a nonpartner was part of the partnership, partnership by estoppel is deemed to exist. When this occurs, the nonpartner is regarded as an agent whose acts are binding on the partnership.

Rights among Partners

The rights and duties of partners are governed largely by the specific terms of their partnership agreement. In the absence of provisions to the contrary in the partnership agreement, the law imposes the rights and duties discussed here. The character and nature of the partnership business generally influence the application of these rights and duties.

INTEREST IN THE PARTNERSHIP

A partner's interest in the partnership is a personal asset consisting of a proportionate share of the profits earned [UPA 26] and a return of capital after the partnership is terminated. Each partner is entitled to the proportion of business profits and losses designated in the partnership agreement.

Profits and Losses If the agreement does not apportion profits or losses, the UPA provides that *profits shall be shared equally and losses shall be shared in the same ratio as* *profits* [UPA 18(a)]. ● **EXAMPLE 25.2** The partnership agreement for Ponce and Brent provides for capital contributions of $6,000 from Ponce and $4,000 from Brent, but it is silent as to how Ponce and Brent will share profits or losses. In this situation, Ponce and Brent will share both profits and losses equally. If the partnership agreement provided for profits to be shared in the same ratio as capital contributions, however, 60 percent of the profits would go to Ponce, and 40 percent of the profits would go to Brent. If their partnership agreement was silent as to losses, losses would be shared in the same ratio as profits (60 percent to 40 percent).●

Assignment of Partnership Interest A partner may assign (transfer) her or his interest in the partnership to another party. When a partner's interest is assigned, the assignee (the person to whom the interest was transferred) has the right to receive the partner's share of the profits and, on the partnership's termination, the partner's capital contribution. The assignee, however, does not become a partner in the partnership and thus has no say in the management or administration of the partnership affairs and no right to inspect the partnership books. Rather, the partner who assigned her or his interest remains a partner with the full rights of a partner with respect to those rights that cannot be assigned.

Creditor's Lien on Partnership Interest A partner's interest is also subject to a judgment creditor's lien (described in Chapter 23). A judgment creditor can attach a partner's interest by petitioning the court that entered the judgment to grant the creditor a **charging order.** This order entitles the creditor to the profits of the partner and to any assets available to the partner on the firm's dissolution [UPA 28].

CHARGING ORDER
In partnership law, an order granted by a court to a judgment creditor that entitles the creditor to attach profits or assets of a partner on the dissolution of the partnership.

MANAGEMENT RIGHTS

Under the UPA, all partners have equal rights in managing the partnership [UPA 18(e)]. Each partner has one vote in management matters *regardless of the proportional size of his or her interest in the firm.* Often, in a large partnership, partners will agree to delegate daily management responsibilities to a management committee made up of one or more of the partners.

The majority rule controls decisions in ordinary matters connected with partnership business, unless otherwise specified in the agreement. Decisions that significantly affect the nature of the partnership, however, require the *unanimous* consent of the partners [UPA 9(3), 18(g), and 18(h)]. Unanimous consent is required for a decision to undertake any of the following actions:

① To alter the essential nature of the firm's business as expressed in the partnership agreement or to alter the capital structure of the partnership.

② To admit new partners or to enter a wholly new business.

③ To assign partnership property into a trust for the benefit of creditors.

④ To dispose of the partnership's goodwill.

⑤ To confess judgment against the partnership or to submit partnership claims to arbitration. (A **confession of judgment** is the act of a debtor in permitting a judgment to be entered against him or her by a creditor, for an agreed sum, without the institution of legal proceedings.)

CONFESSION OF JUDGMENT
The act or agreement of a debtor in permitting a judgment to be entered against him or her by a creditor, for an agreed sum, without the institution of legal proceedings.

⑥ To undertake any act that would make further conduct of partnership business impossible.

⑦ To amend the articles of the partnership agreement.

COMPENSATION

A partner has a duty to expend time, skill, and energy on behalf of the partnership business, and such services are generally not compensable in the form of a salary. Rather, as mentioned, a partner's income from the partnership takes the form of a distribution of profits according to the partner's share in the business. Partners can, however, agree otherwise. For example, partners in a law firm often agree that the managing partner of the firm should receive a salary in addition to her or his share of profits for performing special administrative duties in office and personnel management. When a partnership must be terminated because a partner dies, a surviving partner is entitled to reasonable compensation for services relating to the final settlement (winding up) of partnership affairs (and reimbursement for expenses incurred in the process) above and apart from his or her share in the partnership profits [UPA 18(f)].

Each partner impliedly promises to subordinate his or her interests to those of the partnership. • **EXAMPLE 25.3** Assume that Hall, Banks, and Porter enter into a partnership. Porter undertakes independent consulting, in the same area in which the partnership specializes, for an outside firm without the consent of Hall and Banks. Porter's compensation from the outside firm is considered partnership income [UPA 21].• A partner cannot engage in any independent business that involves the partnership's time unless the partnership expressly agrees.

INSPECTION OF BOOKS

Partnership books and records must be kept accessible to all partners. Each partner has the right to receive (and each partner has the corresponding duty to produce) full and complete information concerning the conduct of all aspects of partnership business [UPA 20]. Each firm keeps books for recording and preserving such information. Partners contribute the information, and a bookkeeper or an accountant typically has the duty to preserve it. The books must be kept at the firm's principal business office and cannot be removed without the consent of all of the partners [UPA 19]. Every

Businesspersons examine accounting records. Are there any restrictions on the right of a partner to inspect his or her firm's books and records? Why or why not?

partner, whether active or inactive, is entitled to inspect all books and records on demand and can make copies of the materials. The personal representative of a deceased partner's estate has the same right of access to partnership books and records that the decedent would have had.

Accounting of Assets

An accounting of partnership assets or profits is required to determine the value of each partner's share in the partnership. An accounting can be performed voluntarily, or it can be compelled by a court. Under UPA 22, a partner has the right to a formal accounting in the following situations:

1. When the partnership agreement provides for a formal accounting.
2. When a partner is wrongfully excluded from the business or from the possession of its property, from access to the books, or both.
3. When any partner is withholding profits or benefits belonging to the partnership in breach of his or her fiduciary duty.
4. When circumstances "render it just and reasonable."

A formal accounting also occurs by right in connection with *dissolution* proceedings (discussed later in this chapter). Generally, the principal remedy of a partner against co-partners is a suit for dissolution, an accounting, or both. With minor exceptions, a partner cannot maintain an action against other firm members for damages until partnership affairs are settled and an accounting is done. This rule is necessary because legal disputes between partners invariably involve conflicting claims to shares in the partnership. Logically, the value of each partner's share must first be determined by an accounting.

Property Rights

One of the property rights of partners—the right to a share of the profits made by the partnership—has already been discussed. A partner also has ownership rights in any real or personal property owned by the partnership. Property owned by the partnership, or *partnership property,* is defined by the UPA as "all property originally brought into the partnership's stock or subsequently acquired, by purchase or otherwise, on account of the partnership" [UPA 8(1)].

For example, in the formation of a partnership, a partner may bring into the partnership any property that he or she owns as a part of his or her capital contribution. This property becomes partnership property even though title to it may still be in the name of the contributing partner. The intention that certain assets are to be partnership assets is the heart of the phrase "on account of the partnership." Thus, the more closely an asset is associated with the business operations of the partnership, the more likely it is to be a partnership asset.[4]

UPA 25(1) states that partners are tenants in partnership. This means that every partner is a co-owner with all other partners of specific partnership property, such as

4. Under the RUPA, property that is not acquired in the name of the partnership is nonetheless partnership property if the instrument transferring title (1) refers to the person taking title as a partner or (2) indicates the existence of the partnership [RUPA 204(a)(2)]. Also, the property is still presumed to be partnership property if it is acquired with partnership funds [RUPA 204(c)]. If none of the above occurs, the property is presumed to be the property of individual partners, even if it is used in the partnership business [RUPA 204(d)].

office equipment, paper supplies, and vehicles. Each partner has equal rights to possess partnership property for business purposes or in satisfaction of firm debts, but not for any other purpose without the consent of all the other partners. Tenancy in partnership has several important effects. If a partner dies, the surviving partners, not the heirs of the deceased partner, have the right of survivorship to the specific property. Although surviving partners are entitled to possession, they have a duty to account to the decedent's estate for the value of the deceased partner's interest in the property [UPA 25(2)(d), (e)].

A partner has no right to sell, assign, or in any way deal with a particular item of partnership property as an exclusive owner [UPA 25(2)(a) and (b)]. Therefore, creditors cannot use partnership property to satisfy the personal debts of a partner. Partnership property is available only to satisfy partnership debts, to enhance the firm's credit, or to achieve other business purposes of the partnership.

Duties and Liabilities of Partners

"Of legal knowledge I acquired such a grip, that they took me into the partnership."

WILLIAM S. GILBERT, 1836–1911
(English playwright; Arthur Sullivan's collaborator in comic opera)

The duties and liabilities of partners are basically derived from agency law. Each partner is an agent of every other partner and acts as both a principal and an agent in any business transaction within the scope of the partnership agreement. Each partner is also a general agent of the partnership in carrying out the usual business of the firm.[5] Thus, every act of a partner concerning partnership business and every contract signed in the partnership's name bind the firm [UPA 9(1)]. The UPA affirms general principles of agency law that pertain to the authority of a partner to bind a partnership in contract or tort.

We examine here the fiduciary duties of partners, the authority of partners, the joint and several liability that characterizes partnerships, and the limitations imposed on the liability of incoming partners for preexisting partnership debts.

FIDUCIARY DUTIES

Partners stand in a fiduciary relationship to one another just as principals and agents do. As indicated in Chapter 24, a fiduciary relationship is one of extraordinary trust and loyalty. Each partner has a fiduciary duty to act in good faith and for the benefit of the partnership. Each partner must also subordinate her or his personal interests to those of the partnership if a conflict of interests arises.[6]

This fiduciary duty underlies the entire body of law pertaining to partnership and agency. From it, certain other duties are commonly implied. Thus, a partner must account to the partnership for personal profits or benefits derived from any partnership transaction that is undertaken without the consent of all of the partners.[7]

AUTHORITY OF PARTNERS

Agency concepts relating to actual (express and implied) authority, apparent authority, and ratification are also applicable to partnerships. In an ordinary partnership, firm

5. The RUPA adds "or business of the kind carried on by the partnership" [RUPA 301(1)]. Basically, this addition gives added protection to third persons who deal with an unfamiliar partnership.

6. The RUPA states that partners may pursue their own interests without automatically violating their fiduciary duties [RUPA 404(e)].

7. In this sense, to account to the partnership means not only to divulge the information but also to determine the value of any benefits or profits derived and to hold that money or property in trust on behalf of the partnership.

members can exercise all implied powers reasonably necessary and customary to carry on that particular business. Some customarily implied powers include the authority to make warranties on goods in the sales business, the power to convey real property in the firm's name when such conveyances are part of the ordinary course of partnership business, the power to enter into contracts consistent with the firm's regular course of business, and the power to make admissions and representations concerning partnership affairs [UPA 11].

When a partner acts within the scope of authority, the partnership is bound to third parties by these acts. For example, a partner's authority to sell partnership products carries with it the implied authority to transfer title and to make the usual warranties. Hence, in a partnership that operates a retail tire store, any partner negotiating a contract with a customer for the sale of a set of tires can warrant that "each tire will be warranted for normal wear for 40,000 miles."

This same partner, however, does not have the authority to sell office equipment, fixtures, or the partnership office building without the consent of all of the other partners. In addition, because partnerships are formed to create profits, a partner generally does not have the authority to make charitable contributions without the consent of the other partners. Such actions are not binding on the partnership unless they are ratified by all of the other partners.

As in the law of agency, the law of partnership imputes one partner's knowledge to all other partners because members of a partnership stand in a fiduciary relationship to one another. This relationship implies that each partner will fully disclose to every other partner all information pertaining to the business of the partnership [UPA 12].

The court in the following case was asked to consider whether one partner was liable for another partner's creation of overdrafts in one of the partnership's bank accounts "in the ordinary course of the partnership business."

CASE 25.2 Helpinstill v. Regions Bank

Texas Court of Appeals—Texarkana, 2000.
33 S.W.3d 401.

FACTS Bobby Helpinstill and Mike Brown were partners in MBO Computers. They opened a partnership bank account at Longview National Bank in Longview, Texas, each agreeing in writing that he would be individually liable for any overdrafts created on the account. Brown, who was actively managing the business, regularly wrote overdrafts on the account and covered them later with deposits. In January 1997, to pay creditors of the partnership, Brown began shuffling funds between MBO accounts at the Longview bank and two other banks in a check-kiting scheme.[a] Brown was convicted and sentenced to a term in federal prison. Regions Bank (which had acquired Longview) filed a suit in a Texas state court against Helpinstill to recover $381,011.15, the amount of the overdrafts. When the court ruled in favor of the bank, Helpinstill appealed to a state intermediate appellate court, arguing in part that he was not liable because Brown's check kiting was not within the ordinary course of partnership business.

ISSUE Is Helpinstill liable to the bank for the amount of the overdrafts?

DECISION Yes. The state intermediate appellate court affirmed the judgment of the lower court, concluding that Helpinstill's liability to the bank was established as a matter of law.

REASON The appellate court explained that "Helpinstill's liability was established by virtue of the fact

a. *Check kiting* refers to the practice of moving funds between bank accounts for the purpose of covering account deficiencies. For example, a check drawn on an account in bank A is written to cover a deficiency in an account in bank B. Then a check drawn on an account in bank B is written to cover the deficiency in bank A—and so on.

CASE 25.2—Continued

that the partnership was indebted to the bank for the overdrafts that Brown created in the ordinary course of the partnership's business, and Helpinstill, as a general partner, is responsible for such partnership debts." The court reasoned that "[t]he kiting scheme, rather than creating the overdrafts, was being used to disguise them; and, while not in itself in the ordinary course of the partnership's business, the kiting scheme did not change the fact that the creation of overdrafts was in the ordinary course of the partnership's business."

FOR CRITICAL ANALYSIS—Social Consideration *What is meant by the phrase "in the ordinary course of business"?*

JOINT LIABILITY

JOINT LIABILITY
Shared liability. In partnership law, partners incur joint liability for partnership obligations and debts. For example, if a third party sues a partner on a partnership debt, the partner has the right to insist that the other partners be sued with him or her.

In most states, partners are subject to joint liability on partnership debts and contracts [UPA 15(b)]. **Joint liability** means that if a third party sues a partner on, for example, a partnership debt, the partner has the right to insist that the other partners be sued with him or her. If the third party does not sue all of the partners, the partner sued cannot be required to pay a judgment, and the assets of the partnership cannot be used to satisfy the judgment. (Similarly, a release of one partner releases all partners.) In other words, to bring a successful claim against the partnership on a debt or contract, a plaintiff must name all the partners as defendants.

To simplify this rule, some states, such as California, have enacted statutes providing that a partnership may be sued in its own name and that a judgment will bind the partnership's and the individual partners' property even though not all the partners are named in the complaint. If the third party is successful, she or he may collect on the judgment against the assets of one or more of the partners. Otherwise stated, each partner is liable and may be required to pay the entire amount of the judgment. When one partner pays the entire amount, the partnership is required to indemnify that partner [UPA 18(b)]. If the partnership cannot do so, the obligation falls on the other partners.

JOINT AND SEVERAL LIABILITY

JOINT AND SEVERAL LIABILITY
In partnership law, a doctrine under which a plaintiff may sue, and collect a judgment from, one or more of the partners separately (severally, or individually) or all of the partners together (jointly). This is true even if one of the partners sued did not participate in, ratify, or know about whatever it was that gave rise to the cause of action.

In some states, partners are both jointly liable and severally, or individually, liable for partnership debts and contracts. In all states, partners are jointly and severally liable for torts and breaches of trust [UPA 15(a)].[8] **Joint and several[9] liability** means that a third party may sue any one or more of the partners without suing all of them or the partnership itself. In other words, a third party may sue one or more of the partners separately (severally) or all of the partners together (jointly), at his or her option. This is true even if the partner did not participate in, ratify, or know about whatever it was that gave rise to the cause of action.[10]

A judgment against one partner on her or his several liability does not extinguish the others' liability. (Similarly, a release of one partner discharges the partners' joint but not several liability.) Thus, those not sued in the first action may be sued subsequently. The first action, however, may have been conclusive on the question of liability. If, for

8. Under the RUPA, partners' liability is joint and several for all debts [RUPA 306].

9. The term *several* stems from the medieval English term *severall,* which meant "separately," or "severed from" one another. As used here, *several* liability means *separate* liability, or individual liability.

10. The RUPA prevents creditors from bringing an action to collect debts from the partners of a nonbankrupt partnership without first attempting unsuccessfully to collect from the partnership (or convincing a court that the attempt would be unsuccessful) [RUPA 307(d)].

example, in an action against one partner, the court held that the partnership was in no way liable, the third party cannot bring an action against another partner and succeed on the issue of the partnership's liability.

If the third party is successful in a suit against a partner or partners, he or she may collect on the judgment only against the assets of those partners named as defendants. The partner who committed the tort is required to indemnify the partnership for any damages it pays.

Liability of Incoming Partner

A newly admitted partner to an existing partnership normally has limited liability for whatever debts and obligations the partnership incurred prior to the new partner's admission. The new partner's liability can be satisfied only from partnership assets [UPA 17]. This means that the new partner usually has no personal liability for these debts and obligations, but any capital contribution made by him or her to the partnership is subject to these debts.

Partnership Termination

Any change in the relations of the partners that demonstrates unwillingness or inability to carry on partnership business dissolves the partnership, resulting in termination [UPA 29]. If one of the partners wishes to continue the business, she or he is free to reorganize into a new partnership with the remaining members.

The termination of a partnership has two stages, both of which must take place before termination is complete. The first stage, **dissolution**, occurs when any partner (or partners) indicates an intention to disassociate from the partnership. The second stage, **winding up**,[11] is the actual process of collecting and distributing the partnership assets.

DISSOLUTION
The formal disbanding of a partnership or a corporation. It can take place by (1) acts of the partners or, in a corporation, of the shareholders and board of directors; (2) the death of a partner; (3) the expiration of a time period stated in a partnership agreement or a certificate of incorporation; or (4) judicial decree.

WINDING UP
The second of two stages in the termination of a partnership or corporation. Once the firm is dissolved, it continues to exist legally until the process of winding up all business affairs (collecting and distributing the firm's assets) is complete.

Dissolution

Dissolution of a partnership can be brought about by the acts of the partners, by the operation of law, and by judicial decree. Each of these events will be discussed here.

Dissolution by Acts of the Partners Dissolution of a partnership may come about through the acts of the partners in several ways. First, the partnership can be dissolved by the partners' agreement. For example, when a partnership agreement expresses a fixed term or a particular business objective to be accomplished, the passing of the date or the accomplishment of the objective dissolves the partnership.

Second, because a partnership is a voluntary association, a partner has the power to disassociate himself or herself from the partnership at any time and thus dissolve the partnership. Any change in the partnership, whether by the withdrawal of a partner or by the admission of a new partner, results in dissolution.[12] In practice, this is modified by the provision that the remaining or new partners may continue in the firm's busi-

11. Although "winding down" would seem to describe more accurately the process of settling accounts and liquidating the assets of a partnership, "winding up" has been traditionally used in English and U.S. statutory and case law to denote this final stage of a partnership's existence.

12. The RUPA distinguishes the withdrawal of a partner that causes a breakup of a partnership from a withdrawal that causes only the end of a partner's participation in the business (and results in a buyout of that partner's interest) [RUPA 601, 701, 801]. Dissolution results only if the partnership must be liquidated [RUPA 801].

ness. Nonetheless, a new partnership arises. Creditors of the prior partnership become creditors of the new partnership [UPA 41].

Finally, the UPA provides that neither a voluntary assignment of a partner's interest nor an involuntary sale of a partner's interest for the benefit of creditors [UPA 27 and 28] by itself dissolves the partnership. Either occurrence, however, can ultimately lead to judicial dissolution of the partnership (judicial dissolution will be discussed shortly).

ETHICAL ISSUE 25.2

May departing law partners take their clients with them?

Law firms that are organized as partnerships face the ongoing problem of departing partners who take their clients with them. Nothing in the ethical rules governing attorney conduct expressly prohibits departing attorneys from soliciting business from clients with whom they have had an ongoing relationship. At the same time, partners must take care not to breach their fiduciary duties to the other partners. Thus, as one court noted, departing attorneys are involved in a "delicate venture." On the one hand, common sense dictates that an attorney who is dissatisfied with the existing association should take steps to locate alternative office space and associations—and do so confidentially. The court also noted that it is permissible for departing partners "to inform clients with whom they have a prior professional relationship about their impending withdrawal and new practice, and to remind the client of its freedom to retain counsel of its choice." On the other hand, departing partners must take care not to breach their fiduciary obligations to the other partners. The court stated that "secretly attempting to lure firm clients . . . to the new association . . . and abandoning the firm on short notice (taking clients and files) would not be consistent with a partner's fiduciary duties."[13]

Dissolution by Operation of Law If one of the partners dies, the partnership is dissolved by operation of law, even if the partnership agreement provides for carrying on the business with the executor of the decedent's estate.[14] The bankruptcy of a partner will also dissolve a partnership, and naturally, the bankruptcy of the partnership itself will result in dissolution [UPA 31(4) and (5)].

Additionally, any event that makes it unlawful for the partnership to continue its business or for any partner to carry on in the partnership will result in dissolution [UPA 31(3)]. Note, however, that if the illegality of the partnership business is a cause for dissolution, the partners can decide to change the nature of their business and continue in the partnership. When the illegality applies to an individual partner, dissolution is mandatory. • **EXAMPLE 25.4** Suppose that a state legislature passes a law making it illegal for judges in that state to engage in the practice of law. If Gerald Fowler, an attorney in a law firm, is appointed or elected to a judgeship, then Fowler must leave the law firm, and the partnership must be dissolved. •

Dissolution by Judicial Decree For dissolution of a partnership by judicial decree to occur, an application or petition must be made in an appropriate court. The court then

13. *Dowd & Dowd v. Gleason,* 181 Ill.2d 460, 693 N.E.2d 358, 230 Ill.Dec. 229 (1998).

14. Under the RUPA, the death of a partner represents that partner's "dissociation" from the partnership, but it is not an automatic ground for the partnership's dissolution [RUPA 601].

either denies the petition or grants a decree of dissolution. UPA 32 cites situations in which a court can dissolve a partnership. One situation occurs when a partner is adjudicated mentally incompetent or is shown to be of unsound mind. Another situation arises when a partner appears incapable of performing his or her duties under the partnership agreement. If the incapacity is likely to be permanent and to have substantial effect on the partner's ability to discharge his or her duties to the firm, a court will dissolve the partnership by decree.

A court may also order dissolution when it becomes obviously impractical for the firm to continue—for example, if the business can only be operated at a loss. Additionally, a partner's impropriety involving partnership business (for example, fraud perpetrated on the other partners) or improper behavior reflecting unfavorably on the firm may provide grounds for a judicial decree of dissolution. Finally, if dissension between partners becomes so persistent and harmful as to undermine the confidence and cooperation necessary to carry on the firm's business, dissolution may also be granted.

Notice of Dissolution The intent to dissolve or to withdraw from a firm must be communicated clearly to each partner. A partner can express this notice of intent by either actions or words. All partners will share liability for the acts of any partner who continues conducting business for the firm without knowing that the partnership has been dissolved.

Dissolution of a partnership by the act of a partner requires notice to all affected third persons as well. Any third person who has extended credit to the firm must receive actual notice (notice given to the party directly and personally). For all others, constructive notice (a newspaper announcement or similar public notice) is sufficient [UPA 35]. Dissolution resulting from the operation of law generally requires no notice to third parties.[15]

WINDING UP

DON'T FORGET Secured creditors have priority over unsecured creditors to any assets that serve as collateral for a partnership's debts.

Once dissolution occurs and the partners have been notified, the partners cannot create new obligations on behalf of the partnership. Their only authority is to complete transactions begun but not finished at the time of dissolution and to wind up the business of the partnership [UPA 33 and 37]. *Winding up* includes collecting and preserving partnership assets, discharging liabilities (paying debts), and accounting to each partner for the value of her or his interest in the partnership.

Both creditors of the partnership and creditors of the individual partners can make claims on the partnership's assets. In general, creditors of the partnership have priority over creditors of individual partners in the distribution of partnership assets; the converse priority is usually followed in the distribution of individual partner assets, except under bankruptcy law. A partnership's assets are distributed according to the following priorities [UPA 40]:[16]

① Payment of third party debts.

② Refund of advances (loans) made to or for the firm by a partner.

③ Return of capital contribution to a partner.

15. *Childers v. United States,* 442 F.2d 1299 (5th Cir. 1971).

16. Under the RUPA, partner creditors are included among creditors who take first priority [RUPA 808]. Capital contributions and profits or losses are then calculated together to determine the amounts that the partners receive or the amounts that they must pay.

④ Distribution of the balance, if any, to partners in accordance with their respective shares in the profits.

If the partnership's liabilities are greater than its assets, the partners bear the losses—in the absence of a contrary agreement—in the same proportion in which they shared the profits (rather than, for example, in proportion to their contributions to the partnership's capital). Partners continue in their fiduciary relationship until the winding-up process is completed.

Does winding up require that all of the assets of a partnership be liquidated? Or is it enough if, on the death of a partner, the surviving partners take an inventory, provide an accounting to the dead partner's estate for the value of the business as of the date of dissolution, and pay the estate its proportionate share of the value of the partnership? Can the surviving partners then continue in business as a new partnership? Those were the questions in the following case.

CASE 25.3 Creel v. Lilly

Court of Appeals of Maryland, 1999.
354 Md. 77,
725 A.2d 385.

FACTS Joseph Creel, Arnold Lilly, and Roy Altizer formed a general partnership called "Joe's Racing" to sell NASCAR racing memorabilia. Their written agreement stated, in paragraph 7(a), that "at the termination of this partnership a full and accurate inventory shall be prepared, and the assets, liabilities, and income * * * shall be ascertained." Paragraph 7(d) added, "Upon the death or illness of a partner, his share will go to his estate. If his estate wishes to sell his interest, they must offer it to the remaining partners first." Nine months later, Creel died, and Joe's Racing dissolved. Creel's spouse, Anne Creel, was appointed personal representative of his estate.[a] Lilly and Altizer asked Mrs. Creel to release funds in a partnership account to which only Creel had had access. When she refused, Lilly and Altizer filed a suit in a Maryland state court against her. Meanwhile, Lilly and Altizer took an inventory of the merchandise, had an accountant compute the value of the business, and offered Mrs. Creel payment for Creel's share. Lilly and Altizer then ceased doing business as Joe's Racing and used the assets to begin doing business as "Good Ole Boys Racing." The court held, among other things, that Lilly and Altizer did not breach any fiduciary duty to Creel's estate. Mrs. Creel appealed, arguing in part that they should have liquidated the assets of Joe's Racing. The state intermediate appellate court affirmed the lower court's judgment. Mrs. Creel appealed to the Maryland Court of Appeals, the state's highest court.

a. A *personal representative* administers a deceased person's estate. This administration includes taking an inventory of the deceased's assets and managing them to preserve their value.

ISSUE Does winding up require that all partnership assets be liquidated (sold) to determine the value of the business?

DECISION No. The Maryland Court of Appeals affirmed the decision of the lower court. Winding up does not require a forced sale of all partnership assets to determine the value of the business.

DECISION The court stated that on the death of a partner, it is acceptable to pay the deceased partner's estate its proportionate share of the value of the partnership, derived from an accurate accounting, without having to fully liquidate the business. The court said, "Paragraph 7(a) requires that the assets, liabilities, and income be 'ascertained,' but it in no way mandates that this must be accomplished by a forced sale of the partnership assets. * * * [A] sale of all partnership assets is not required under either UPA or RUPA * * * . We find it is sound public policy to permit a partnership to continue either under the same name or as a successor partnership without all of the assets being liquidated.

(continued)

CASE 25.3—Continued

Liquidation * * * is often unnecessary to determining the true value of the partnership."

FOR CRITICAL ANALYSIS—Economic Consideration *At one point in its opinion, the court stated, "Liquidation can be a harmful and destructive measure, especially to a small business like Joe's Racing." Would the forced liquidation of partnership assets be equally "harmful and destructive" to a large business? Why or why not?*

Partnerships—Advantages and Disadvantages

As with a sole proprietorship, one of the advantages of a partnership is that it can be organized fairly easily and inexpensively. Additionally, the partnership form of business offers important tax advantages. The partnership itself files only an informational tax return with the Internal Revenue Service. In other words, the firm itself pays no taxes. A partner's profit from the partnership (whether distributed or not) is taxed as individual income to the individual partner.

A partnership may also allow for greater capital contributions to the business than is possible in a sole proprietorship. Two or more persons can invest in the business, and lenders may be more willing to make loans to a partnership than they would be to a sole proprietorship.

ON THE WEB For further information on the taxation of partnerships, as compared to other forms of business organizations, see the article by Dennis D'Annunzio in the *Sunbelt Business Journal*, which is online at **http://www.sunbeltnetwork.com/Journal/Current/D970804dsd.html**.

The main disadvantage of the partnership form of business is that the partners are subject to personal liability for partnership obligations. If the partnership cannot pay its debts, the personal assets of the partners are subject to creditors' claims. This disadvantage of the partnership is one of the major reasons that many entrepreneurs choose to form a corporation. As will be discussed in the following chapters, in the corporate form of business the owners' liability is limited to the amount of their investments in the business. The limited liability companies and partnerships discussed in Chapter 30 are additional business forms that allow business owners to limit their personal liability for business debts and obligations.

Key Terms

articles of partnership 682
charging order 686
confession of judgment 686
dissolution 692
joint and several liability 691
joint liability 691
partnership 679
sole proprietorship 677
winding up 692

Chapter Summary Sole Proprietorships and Partnerships

Sole Proprietorship (See pages 677–679.)	The simplest form of business; used by anyone who does business without creating an organization. The owner is the business. The owner pays personal income taxes on all profits and is personally liable for all business debts.
Partnership (See pages 679–696.)	1. Created by agreement of the parties. 2. Not treated as an entity except for limited purposes. 3. Partners have unlimited liability for partnership debts.

Chapter Summary Sole Proprietorships and Partnerships—continued

Partnership—continued	4. Each partner has an equal voice in management unless the partnership agreement provides otherwise. 5. In the absence of an agreement, partners share profits equally and share losses in the same ratio as they share profits. 6. The capital contribution of each partner is determined by agreement. 7. Each partner pays a proportionate share of income taxes on the net profits of the partnership, whether or not they are distributed; the partnership files only an information return with the Internal Revenue Service. 8. Can be terminated by agreement or dissolved by action of the partners (withdrawal), operation of law (death or bankruptcy), or court decree.

For Review

① What advantages and disadvantages are associated with the sole proprietorship?
② What are the three essential elements of a partnership?
③ What are the rights and duties of partners?
④ What is meant by joint and several liability? Why is this often considered to be a disadvantage of the partnership form of business?
⑤ Can a partner continue the business of a terminated partnership if he or she wishes to do so? How?

Questions and Case Problems

25–1. Distribution of Partnership Assets. Shawna and David formed a partnership. At the time of the partnership's formation, Shawna's capital contribution was $10,000, and David's was $15,000. Later, Shawna made a $10,000 loan to the partnership when it needed working capital. The partnership agreement provided that profits were to be shared with 40 percent for Shawna and 60 percent for David. The partnership was dissolved by David's death. At the end of the dissolution and the winding up of the partnership, the partnership's assets were $50,000, and the partnership's debts were $8,000. Discuss fully how the assets should be distributed.

25–2. Partnership Property. Schwartz and Zenov were partners in an accounting firm. Because business was booming and profits were better than ever, they decided to invest some of the firm's profits in Munificent Corp. stock. The investment turned out to be a good one, as the stock continued to increase in value. On Schwartz's death several years later, Zenov assumed full ownership of the business, including the Munificent Corp. stock, a partnership asset. Schwartz's daughter Rosalie, however, claimed a 50 percent ownership interest in the Munificent Corp. stock as Schwartz's sole heir. Can Rosalie enforce her claim? Explain.

25–3. Partner's Property Rights. Maruta, Samms, and Ortega were partners in a business firm. The firm's business equipment included several expensive computers. One day, Maruta borrowed one of the computers for use in his home and never bothered to return it. When the other partners asked him about it, Maruta claimed he had a right to keep the computer because it represented less than one-third of the computers owned by the partnership and he owned one-third of the business. Was he right? Explain.

25–4. Distribution of Assets. Robert Lowther, Fred Riggleman, and Granville Zopp were equal partners in the Four Square Partnership. The partnership was created to acquire and develop real estate for commercial retail use. In the course of the partnership, Riggleman loaned $30,000 to the partnership, and Zopp loaned the partnership $50,000. Donald H. Lowther, Robert's brother and not a partner in the firm, loaned Four Square $80,000 and took a promissory note signed by the three partners. Shortly after the commercial venture began, Four Square encountered financial difficulties and eventually defaulted on payments due on a construction loan it had received from a bank. The bank foreclosed on the property securing the debt. The proceeds of the subsequent foreclosure sale satisfied the bank's interest and left a surplus of $87,783 to be returned to the partnership. In the meantime, the partnership had been dissolved and was in the process of winding up its affairs. Donald H. Lowther maintained that, as a nonpartner creditor, his claim against the firm's assets took priority over those of Riggleman and Zopp. Is Lowther correct? Explain. [*Lowther v. Riggleman,* 189 W.Va. 68, 428 S.E.2d 49 (1993)]

25–5. Rights among Partners. B&R Communications was a general partner in Amarillo CellTelco. Under the partnership agreement, each partner had the right to inspect partnership records "at reasonable times during business hours," so long as the inspection did not "unreasonably interfere with the operation of the partnership." B&R believed that the managers of the firm were using partnership money to engage in lawsuits that were too costly. B&R and other general partners filed a suit in a Texas state court against the managers. B&R wanted to inspect the firm's records to discover information about the lawsuits, but the court denied B&R's request. B&R asked a state appellate court to order the trial judge to grant the request. On what ground did the appellate court issue the order? [*B&R Communications v. Lopez,* 890 S.W.2d 224 (Tex.App.—Amarillo 1994)]

25–6. Liability of Incoming Partner. Conklin Farm sold land to LongView Estates, a general partnership, to build condominiums. LongView gave Conklin a promissory note for $9 million as payment. A few years later, Doris Leibowitz joined LongView as a general partner. Leibowitz left the firm before the note came due, but while she was a partner, interest accrued on the balance. The condominium project failed, and LongView went out of business. Conklin filed a suit in a New Jersey state court against Leibowitz to recover some of the interest on the note. Conklin acknowledged that Leibowitz was not liable for debt incurred before she joined the firm but argued that the interest that accrued while she was a partner was "new" debt for which she was personally liable. To what extent, if any, is Leibowitz liable to Conklin? [*Conklin Farm v. Leibowitz,* 140 N.J. 417, 658 A.2d 1257 (1995)]

25–7. Liability of Partners. Frank Kolk was the manager of Triples American Grill, a sports bar and restaurant. Kolk and John Baines opened bank accounts in the name of the bar, each signing the account signature cards as "owner." Baines was often at the bar and had free access to its office. Baines told others that he was "an owner" and "a partner." Kolk told Steve Mager, the president of Cheesecake Factory, Inc., that Baines was a member of a partnership that owned Triples. On this basis, Cheesecake delivered its goods to Triples on credit. In fact, the bar was owned by a corporation. When the unpaid account totaled more than $20,000, Cheesecake filed a suit in a New Mexico state court against Baines to collect. On what basis might Baines be liable to Cheesecake? What does Cheesecake have to show to win its case? [*Cheesecake Factory, Inc. v. Baines,* 964 P.2d 183 (N.M.App. 1998)]

25–8. Indications of Partnership. Sandra Lerner was one of the original founders of Cisco Systems. When she sold her interest in Cisco, she received a substantial amount of money, which she invested, and she became extremely wealthy. Patricia Holmes met Lerner at Holmes's horse training facility, and they became friends. One evening in Lerner's mansion, while applying nail polish, Holmes layered a raspberry color over black to produce a new color, which Lerner liked. Later, the two created other colors with names like "Bruise," "Smog," and "Oil Slick" and titled their concept "Urban Decay." Lerner and Holmes started a firm to produce and market the polishes but never discussed the sharing of profits and losses. They agreed to build the business and then sell it. Together, they did market research, experimented with colors, worked on a logo and advertising, obtained capital from an investment firm, and hired employees. Then Lerner began working to edge Holmes out of the firm. Several months later, when Holmes was told not to attend meetings of the firm's officers, she filed a suit in a California state court against Lerner, claiming, among other things, a breach of their partnership agreement. Lerner responded in part that there was no partnership agreement because there was no agreement to divide profits. Was Lerner right? Why or why not? How should the court rule? [*Holmes v. Lerner,* 74 Cal.App.4th 442, 88 Cal.Rptr.2d 130 (1 Dist. 1999)]

TEST YOUR KNOWLEDGE—ANSWER ON THE WEB

25–9. In August 1998, Jea Yu contacted Cameron Eppler, president of Design88, Ltd., to discuss developing a Web site that would cater to investors and provide services to its members for a fee. Yu and Patrick Connelly invited Eppler and Ha Tran, another member of Design88, to a meeting to discuss the site. The parties agreed that Design88 would perform certain Web design, implementation, and maintenance functions for 10 percent of the profits from the site, which would be called "The Underground Trader." They signed a "Master Partnership Agreement," which was later amended to include Power Uptik Productions, LLC (PUP). The parties often referred to themselves as partners. From Design88's offices in Virginia, Design88 designed and hosted the site, solicited members through Internet and national print campaigns, processed member applications, provided technical support, monitored access to the site, and negotiated and formed business alliances on the site's behalf. When relations among the parties soured, PUP withdrew. Design88 filed a suit against PUP and the others in a Virginia state court. Did a partnership exist among these parties? Explain. [*Design88 Ltd. v. Power Uptik Productions, LLC,* 133 F.Supp.2d 873 (W.D.Va. 2001)]

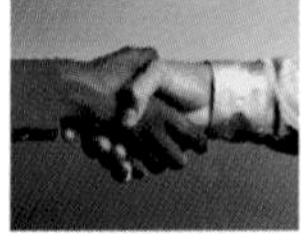

A QUESTION OF ETHICS AND SOCIAL RESPONSIBILITY

25–10. David Murphy and James Canion formed a general partnership to conduct real estate business. Their partnership agreement provided that both partners would devote their full-time efforts to conducting partnership business, that all personal earnings from personal services would be included as partnership income, and that any real estate or other partnership business conducted by either partner during the term of the partnership agreement should be for the joint account of the partnership. Through his business associates and contacts, Canion learned of several profitable real estate opportunities and secretly took advantage of them for his own gain. When Murphy found out about Canion's activities, he told Canion that he was canceling the partnership under a clause in the partnership agreement that allowed termination by a partner with ninety days' notice. In the lawsuit that followed, Murphy alleged that Canion had breached the partnership agreement and his fiduciary duty to the partnership. The trial court agreed with Murphy and awarded him damages, which the court held to be proximately caused by Canion's wrongful appropriation of partnership business opportunities. On appeal, Canion contended, among other things, that his breach of his fiduciary duty did not proximately cause any damages to Murphy because the income generated by Canion's "secret" projects was received after the partnership had terminated. [*Murphy v. Canion*, 797 S.W.2d 944 (Tex.App.—Houston [14th Dist.] 1990)]

1. Should Murphy be entitled, in the form of damages, to a share of the profits made by Canion through his secret dealings even though Canion received the income *after* the partnership had terminated? If you were the judge, how would you decide this issue, and on what legal basis? From an ethical point of view, what solution would be the fairest?
2. What ethical considerations are involved in the rule that partners have a fiduciary duty to subordinate their personal interests to the mutual welfare of all of the partners? Do you think that a partnership would be a viable form of business organization if partners were not held to such a fiduciary duty?

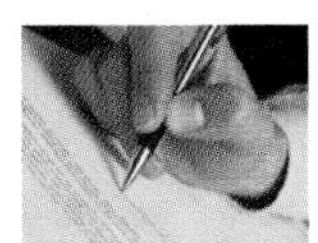

FOR CRITICAL ANALYSIS

25–11. Given the extensive liability of partners, why would any entrepreneur choose to do business with another, or others, as a partnership?

Internet Exercises

Go to the *Business Law Today* home page at **http://blt.westbuslaw.com**. Select "Interactive Study Center" and then click on "Chapter 25." There you will find the following Internet research exercise that you can perform to learn more about partnerships:

Activity 25–1: Partnerships

Before the Test

Go to the *Business Law Today* home page at **http://blt.westbuslaw.com**. Click on "Interactive Quizzes." You will find at least twenty interactive questions relating to this chapter.

CHAPTER 26

Corporate Formation and Financing

"A corporation is an artificial being, invisible, intangible, and existing only in contemplation of law."

John Marshall, 1755–1835
(Chief justice of the United States Supreme Court, 1801–1835)

CHAPTER CONTENTS

LEARNING OBJECTIVES

After reading this chapter, you should be able to answer the following questions:

① What are the express and implied powers of corporations? On what sources are these powers based?

② What steps are involved in bringing a corporation into existence? Who is liable for preincorporation contracts?

③ What is the difference between a *de jure* corporation and a *de facto* corporation?

④ In what circumstances might a court disregard the corporate entity ("pierce the corporate veil") and hold the shareholders personally liable?

⑤ How are corporations financed? What is the difference between stocks and bonds?

The corporation is a creature of statute. As John Marshall indicated in the opening quotation, a corporation is an artificial being, existing only in law and neither tangible nor visible. Its existence generally depends on state law, although some corporations, especially public organizations, can be created under state or federal law.

Each state has its own body of corporate law, and these laws are not entirely uniform. The Model Business Corporation Act (MBCA) is a codification of modern corporation law that has been influential in the drafting and revision of state corporation statutes. Today, the majority of state statutes are guided by the revised version of the MBCA, which is often referred to as the Revised Model Business Corporation Act (RMBCA). You should keep in mind, however, that there is considerable variation among the statutes of the states that have used the MBCA or the RMBCA as a basis for their statutes, and several states do not follow either act. Consequently, individual state corporation laws should be relied on rather than the MBCA or RMBCA.

The Nature of the Corporation

CORPORATION
A legal entity formed in compliance with statutory requirements. The entity is distinct from its shareholder-owners.

A **corporation** is a legal entity created and recognized by state law. It can consist of one or more *natural* persons (as opposed to the artificial "person" of the corporation) identified under a common name. A corporation can be owned by a single person, or it can have hundreds, thousands, or even millions of owners (shareholders). The corporation substitutes itself for its shareholders in conducting corporate business and in incurring liability, yet its authority to act and the liability for its actions are separate and apart from the individuals who own it.

CONTRAST The death of a sole proprietor or a partner can result in the dissolution of a business. The death of a corporate shareholder, however, rarely causes the dissolution of a corporation.

In a corporation, the responsibility for the overall management of the firm is entrusted to a *board of directors*, which is elected by the shareholders. The board of directors hires *corporate officers* and other employees to run the daily business operations of the corporation. When an individual purchases a share of stock in a corporation, that person becomes a *shareholder* and an owner of the corporation. Unlike the members of a partnership, the body of shareholders can change constantly without affecting the continued existence of the corporation. A shareholder can sue the corporation, and the corporation can sue a shareholder. Also, under certain circumstances, a shareholder can sue on behalf of a corporation. The rights and duties of corporate personnel will be examined in detail in Chapter 27.

The shareholder form of business organization emerged in Europe at the end of the seventeenth century. Called *joint stock companies,* these organizations frequently collapsed because their organizers absconded with the funds or proved to be incompetent. Because of this history of fraud and collapse, organizations resembling corporations were regarded with suspicion in the United States during its early years. Although several business corporations were formed after the Revolutionary War, it was not until the nineteenth century that the corporation came into common use for private business. This chapter's *Landmark in the Law* feature on pages 702 and 703 examines a leading case in the early development of private corporations in the United States.

The Constitutional Rights of Corporations

A corporation is recognized under state and federal law as a "person," and it enjoys many of the same rights and privileges that U.S. citizens enjoy. The Bill of Rights guarantees a person, as a citizen, certain protections, and corporations are considered persons in most instances. Accordingly, a corporation has the same right as a natural person to equal protection of the laws under the Fourteenth Amendment. It has the right of access to the courts as an entity that can sue or be sued. It also has the right of due process before denial of life, liberty, or property, as well as freedom from unreasonable searches and seizures (see Chapter 6 for a discussion of searches and seizures in the business context) and from double jeopardy.

Under the First Amendment, corporations are entitled to freedom of speech. As we pointed out in Chapter 2, however, commercial speech (such as advertising) and political speech (such as contributions to political causes or candidates) receive significantly less protection than noncommercial speech.

LANDMARK IN THE LAW
The *Dartmouth College* Case (1819)

In 1819, the United States Supreme Court heard the case of *The Trustees of Dartmouth College v. Woodward.*[a] The decision focused on the continued private existence of the small college in New Hampshire but had a lasting impact on U.S. corporate law.

The Dispute over the Status of Dartmouth College Dartmouth College, named in honor of one of its wealthy patrons, the Earl of Dartmouth, had been founded by the Reverend Eleazar Wheelock, a young Connecticut minister who sought to establish a school to train both missionaries and Native Americans. In 1769, a corporate charter was obtained from the royal governor of New Hampshire. The charter made Wheelock and his English patrons who had donated capital to the college a self-perpetuating board of trustees for the project. When Wheelock died, his son became president of the college. Under the new, less experienced leadership, many disputes arose over the running of the institution, and the participants eventually divided along the prevailing political party lines of New Hampshire.

The Republican group[b] believed that the college ought to be under the control of the state and become a public rather than a sectarian institution. The Republicans persuaded the Republican-controlled New Hampshire Congress to pass legislation that significantly altered the composition of the board of trustees and added a board of overseers that had virtual authority to control the college.

The Federalist[c] board of trustees wanted to preserve the conservative, congregational character of the school and wished to continue to govern the college without interference. They brought suit against William Woodward, the secretary-treasurer of the state-appointed board of overseers, alleging that the legislation violated the college's original charter. The trustees argued that the original grant of the charter, with

a. 17 U.S. (4 Wheaton) 518, 4 L.Ed. 629 (1819).
b. The forerunner of the modern-day Democratic Party.
c. The Federalists were an early political group, or party, that advocated a strong national government.

Only the corporation's individual officers and employees possess the Fifth Amendment right against self-incrimination.[1] Additionally, the privileges and immunities clause of the Constitution (Article IV, Section 2) does not protect corporations, nor does it protect an unincorporated association.[2] This clause requires each state to treat citizens of other states equally with respect to access to courts, travel rights, and so forth.

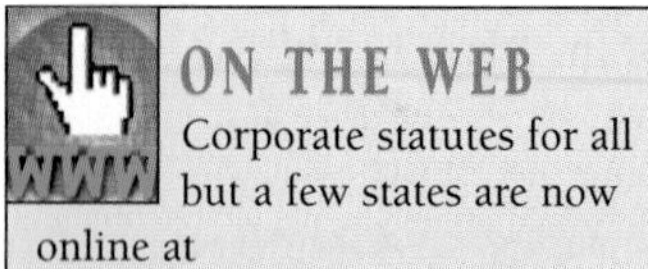

ON THE WEB Corporate statutes for all but a few states are now online at **http://www.law.cornell.edu/topics/state_statutes.html#corporations**.

THE LIMITED LIABILITY OF SHAREHOLDERS

One of the key advantages of the corporate form is the limited liability of its owners (shareholders). Corporate shareholders normally are not personally liable for the obliga-

1. *In re Grand Jury No. 86-3 (Will Roberts Corp.),* 816 F.2d 569 (11th Cir. 1987).
2. *W. C. M. Window Co. v. Bernardi,* 730 F.2d 486 (7th Cir. 1984).

LANDMARK IN THE LAW—Continued

its self-perpetuating board of trustees, was effectively a contract between the king and the board. Thus, the U.S. Constitution, which in Article I, Section 10, forbids states from passing legislation that would impair the obligation of contracts, prohibited the state from legislating changes in the self-governing structure of the board. The New Hampshire legislature was, therefore, without power to add trustees to the board, to create a board of overseers, or to alter the original charter in any manner.

The Supreme Court's Decision Chief Justice John Marshall delivered the opinion of the Court. He stated that the grant of the charter was a contract regarding private property within the meaning of Article I, Section 10, and that the legislative acts of New Hampshire, passed without the trustees' assent, were not binding on them.

Justice Joseph Story, in a separate opinion, distinguished between public and private corporations. He stated that if the shareholders of a corporation were municipal or other public officials, the corporation was a public corporation and therefore subject to continual public regulation. If the shareholders were private individuals, however, quite a contrary situation prevailed. The corporation was private, regardless of whether it consequently was bound only by the terms of its original charter. Had the state reserved regulatory rights in the original grant of the charter, the college would be subject to such control. In the absence of such reservations, the state of New Hampshire's legislative acts clearly impaired the original charter and thus violated the U.S. Constitution.

APPLICATION TO TODAY'S WORLD

This case is a landmark in corporate law because it allowed for the continued existence of private corporations in the United States. Story's opinion opened an avenue for the future regulation of new corporations, while at the same time creating vested rights in private corporations. Marshall and Story both made it clear that the United States Supreme Court would afford the property rights of private corporations the same protection afforded to other forms of property.

"The art of taxation consists in so plucking the goose as to obtain the largest amount of feathers with the smallest possible amount of hissing."

JEAN BAPTISTE COLBERT, 1619–1683
(French politician and financial reformer)

DIVIDEND
A distribution to corporate shareholders of corporate profits or income, disbursed in proportion to the number of shares held.

tions of the corporation beyond the extent of their investments. In certain limited situations, however, the "corporate veil" can be pierced and liability for the corporation's obligations extended to shareholders—a concept that will be explained later in this chapter. Additionally, to enable the firm to obtain credit, shareholders in small companies sometimes voluntarily assume personal liability, as guarantors, for corporate obligations.

CORPORATE TAXATION

Corporate profits are taxed by state and federal governments. Corporations can do one of two things with corporate profits—retain them or pass them on to shareholders in the form of **dividends.** The corporation receives no tax deduction for dividends distributed to shareholders. Dividends are again taxable (except when they represent distributions of capital) as ordinary income to the shareholder receiving them. This double-taxation feature of the corporation is one of its major disadvantages.

RETAINED EARNINGS
The portion of a corporation's profits that has not been paid out as dividends to shareholders.

Profits that are not distributed are retained by the corporation. These **retained earnings**, if invested properly, will yield higher corporate profits in the future and thus cause the price of the company's stock to rise. Individual shareholders can then reap the benefits of these retained earnings in the capital gains they receive when they sell their shares.

The consequences of a failure to pay corporate taxes can be severe. As will be discussed in Chapter 28, the state may dissolve a corporation for this reason. Alternatively, corporate status may be suspended until the taxes are paid.

CORPORATE CHARTER
The document issued by a state agency or authority (usually the secretary of state) that grants a corporation legal existence and the right to function.

In the following case, the state had revoked a corporation's **corporate charter** (the document issued by a state agency or authority—usually the secretary of state—that grants a corporation legal existence and the right to function) because of the corporation's failure to pay certain taxes. The issue before the court was whether a shareholder who had assumed an obligation of the corporation could be held personally liable for the unsatisfactory performance of the contract.

CASE 26.1 Bullington v. Palangio

Arkansas Supreme Court, 2001.
345 Ark. 320,
45 S.W.3d 834.
http://courts.state.ar.us/opinions/opinions.html[a]

FACTS Jerry Bullington, doing business as Bullington Builders, Inc. (BBI), entered into a contract with Helen Palangio for the construction of a new house in Damascus, Arkansas. Bullington signed the contract "Jerry Bullington, d/b/a Bullington Builders, Inc.," but did not indicate any official capacity as a corporate officer. BBI had been incorporated in 1993. Its only shareholders were Bullington, who managed the business, and his wife. About one and a half months before Palangio's house was completed, BBI's charter was revoked for failure to pay Arkansas franchise taxes,[b] and it was not reinstated. Bullington finished the house, but Palangio was not satisfied with the work or with Bullington's attempts to address her complaints. More than a year later, Palangio hired another builder to remedy the alleged defects. Palangio then filed a suit in an Arkansas state court against Bullington, alleging, in part, breach of contract and asserting that the corporate entity did not shield him from personal liability. The court held Bullington liable to Palangio for $19,000. Bullington appealed to the Arkansas Supreme Court.

a. In the "Search Cases by Party Name" box, enter "Bullington." In the page showing search results, scroll down the list to 6/21/2001 and click on the case name to access the opinion. The Arkansas judiciary maintains this Web site.

b. A *franchise tax* is an annual tax imposed for the privilege of doing business in a state.

ISSUE Is a corporate officer who assumes the firm's obligation after its charter has been revoked personally liable for the performance of the obligation?

DECISION Yes. The Arkansas Supreme Court affirmed the lower court's judgment, holding Bullington personally liable for the unsatisfactory performance of the contract with Palangio.

REASON The court stated that "to exempt any association of persons from personal liability for the debts of a proposed corporation, they must comply fully with the [law] under which the corporation is created and that partial compliance with the [law] is not sufficient." The court noted that Arkansas state law required the payment of franchise taxes and provided for the revocation of the charter of a corporation that did not pay them, which occurred in this case. Also, the court explained that "the reasoning behind cases holding officers and stockholders individually liable for obligations that arise during the operation of a corporation when the corporate charter has been revoked for nonpayment of franchise taxes is that they ought not be allowed to avoid personal liability because of their nonfeasance [nonperformance of a duty or a responsibility]."

FOR CRITICAL ANALYSIS—Social Consideration *Would it have made a difference in the outcome of this case if Bullington had not known about the revocation of the corporate charter?*

"Did you expect a corporation to have a conscience, when it has no soul to be damned and no body to be kicked?"

EDWARD THURLOW, 1731–1806 (English jurist)

TORTS AND CRIMINAL ACTS

A corporation is liable for the torts committed by its agents or officers within the course and scope of their employment. This principle applies to a corporation exactly as it applies to the ordinary agency relationships discussed in Chapter 24. It follows the doctrine of *respondeat superior.*

Under modern criminal law, a corporation may be held liable for the criminal acts of its agents and employees, provided the punishment is one that can be applied to the corporation. Although corporations cannot be imprisoned, they can be fined. Of course, corporate directors and officers can be imprisoned, and in recent years, many have faced criminal penalties for their own actions or for the actions of employees under their supervision.

Recall from Chapter 6 that the U.S. Sentencing Commission, which was established by the Sentencing Reform Act of 1984, created standardized sentencing guidelines for federal crimes. These guidelines went into effect in 1987. The commission subsequently created specific sentencing guidelines for crimes committed by corporate employees (white-collar crimes). The net effect of the guidelines has been an increase in criminal penalties for crimes committed by corporate personnel. (For a more detailed discussion of corporate criminal liability, including some examples of when courts have held corporate directors and officers liable under criminal laws, see Chapter 6.)

Corporate Powers

ARTICLES OF INCORPORATION
The document filed with the appropriate governmental agency, usually the secretary of state, when a business is incorporated. State statutes usually prescribe what kind of information must be contained in the articles of incorporation.

BYLAWS
A set of governing rules adopted by a corporation or other association.

When a corporation is created, the express and implied powers necessary to achieve its purpose also come into existence. The express powers of a corporation are found in its **articles of incorporation** (a document containing information about the corporation, including its organization and functions), in the law of the state of incorporation, and in the state and federal constitutions. Corporate **bylaws** (rules of management adopted by the corporation at its first organizational meeting) and the resolutions of the corporation's board of directors also grant or restrict certain powers. The following order of priority is used when conflicts arise among documents involving corporations:

① The U.S. Constitution.
② State constitutions.
③ State statutes.
④ The articles of incorporation.
⑤ Bylaws.
⑥ Resolutions of the board of directors.

Certain implied powers attach when a corporation is created. Barring express constitutional, statutory, or other prohibitions, the corporation has the implied power to perform all acts reasonably appropriate and necessary to accomplish its corporate purposes. For this reason, a corporation has the implied power to borrow funds within certain limits, to lend funds or to extend credit to those with whom it has a legal or contractual relationship, and to make charitable contributions.[3] To borrow money, the corporation acts

3. Early law held that a corporation had no implied authority to make charitable contributions because charitable activities were contrary to the primary purpose of the corporation to make a profit. Modern law, by statutes and court decisions, holds that a corporation has such implied authority.

through its board of directors to authorize the loan. Most often, the president or chief executive officer of the corporation will execute the necessary papers on behalf of the corporation. In so doing, corporate officers have the implied power to bind the corporation in matters directly connected with the *ordinary* business affairs of the enterprise.

ULTRA VIRES
A Latin term meaning "beyond the powers"; in corporate law, acts of a corporation that are beyond its express and implied powers to undertake.

The term ***ultra vires*** means "beyond the powers." In corporate law, acts of a corporation that are beyond its express and implied powers are *ultra vires* acts. Under Section 3.04 of the RMBCA, the following remedies are available for *ultra vires* acts:

① The shareholders may sue on behalf of the corporation to obtain an injunction (to prohibit the corporation from engaging in the *ultra vires* transactions) or to obtain damages for the harm caused by the transactions.

② The corporation itself can sue the officers and directors who were responsible for the *ultra vires* transactions to recover damages.

③ The attorney general of the state may institute a proceeding to obtain an injunction against the *ultra vires* transactions or to institute dissolution proceedings against the corporation for *ultra vires* acts.

Classification of Corporations

The classification of a corporation depends on its purpose, ownership characteristics, and location.

DOMESTIC, FOREIGN, AND ALIEN CORPORATIONS

DOMESTIC CORPORATION
In a given state, a corporation that does business in, and is organized under the law of, that state.

FOREIGN CORPORATION
In a given state, a corporation that does business in the state without being incorporated therein.

ALIEN CORPORATION
A designation in the United States for a corporation formed in another country but doing business in the United States.

A corporation is referred to as a **domestic corporation** by its home state (the state in which it incorporates). A corporation formed in one state but doing business in another is referred to in that other state as a **foreign corporation.** A corporation formed in another country—say, Mexico—but doing business in the United States is referred to in the United States as an **alien corporation.**

A corporation does not have an automatic right to do business in a state other than its state of incorporation. In some instances, it must obtain a *certificate of authority* in any state in which it plans to do business. Once the certificate has been issued, the powers conferred on a corporation by its home state generally can be exercised in the other state.

PUBLIC AND PRIVATE CORPORATIONS

NOTE A private corporation is a voluntary association, but a public corporation is not.

A public corporation is one formed by the government to meet some political or governmental purpose. Cities and towns that incorporate are common examples. In addition, many federal government organizations, such as the U.S. Postal Service, the Tennessee Valley Authority, and AMTRAK, are public corporations. Note that a public corporation is not the same as a *publicly held* corporation. A publicly held corporation is any corporation whose shares are publicly traded in securities markets, such as the New York Stock Exchange or the over-the-counter market.

In contrast to public corporations, private corporations are created either wholly or in part for private benefit. Most corporations are private. Although they may serve a public purpose, as a public electric or gas utility does, they are owned by private persons rather than by the government.[4]

4. For a leading case on the distinction between private and public corporations, see this chapter's *Landmark in the Law* on pages 702 and 703.

INTERNATIONAL PERSPECTIVE

Jurisdiction over Alien Corporations

If a U.S. consumer is injured by a product manufactured by a corporation located in another country, can the consumer sue the corporation in a U.S. state court? In other words, may a U.S. state court exercise personal jurisdiction over an alien corporation? The answer depends on whether the defendant corporation has sufficient "contacts" with the state where the lawsuit is filed. As discussed in Chapter 3, if the defendant corporation meets the "minimum-contacts" requirement, then the state court can exercise jurisdiction over the corporation. Generally, the minimum-contacts requirement is satisfied if a corporation does business in the state, advertises or sells its products in the state, or places its goods into the "stream of commerce" with the intent that the goods be sold in the state.

Alien corporations that are sued in U.S. courts sometimes claim that it is essentially unfair to force them to travel to the United States to defend against the suits—because the transportation of witnesses, documents, and other evidence can be very costly. In response to such arguments, U.S. courts generally hold that alien corporations, by marketing their goods in the United States, should expect to be "haled into court" in this country. As one court stated, any such inconvenience "must be weighed against a public policy which favors providing a forum for an injured resident to bring an action against a non-resident manufacturer."[a]

a. *Loral Fairchild Corp. v. Victor Co. of Japan, Ltd.,* 803 F.Supp. 626 (E.D.N.Y. 1992).

FOR CRITICAL ANALYSIS

Is there any way a foreign manufacturer that sells its products in the United States can avoid being "haled into court" in this country to defend against a product liability action?

NONPROFIT CORPORATIONS

Corporations formed without a profit-making purpose are called *nonprofit* or *not-for-profit* corporations. Private hospitals, educational institutions, charities, and religious organizations, for example, are frequently organized as nonprofit corporations. The nonprofit corporation is a convenient form of organization that allows various groups

BMW automobiles are inspected at a plant in the United States. BMW is classified as an alien corporation. What is the difference between an alien corporation and a foreign corporation?

to own property and to form contracts without the individual members' being personally exposed to liability.

Close Corporations

CLOSE CORPORATION
A corporation whose shareholders are limited to a small group of persons, often including only family members. The rights of shareholders of a close corporation usually are restricted regarding the transfer of shares to others.

Most corporate enterprises in the United States fall into the category of close corporations. A **close corporation** is one whose shares are held by members of a family or by relatively few persons. Close corporations are also referred to as *closely held, family,* or *privately held* corporations. Usually, the members of the small group constituting a close corporation are personally known to each other. Because the number of shareholders is so small, there is no trading market for the shares.

Some states have enacted special statutory provisions that apply to close corporations. These provisions expressly permit close corporations to depart significantly from certain formalities required by traditional corporation law.[5] Additionally, Section 7.32 of the RMBCA, a provision added to the RMBCA in 1991 and adopted in several states, gives close corporations a substantial amount of flexibility in determining the rules by which they will operate. Under Section 7.32, if all of the shareholders of a corporation agree in writing, the corporation can operate without directors, bylaws, annual or special shareholders' or directors' meetings, stock certificates, or formal records of shareholders' or directors' decisions.[6]

Management of Close Corporations The close corporation has a single shareholder or a closely knit group of shareholders, who usually hold the positions of directors and officers. Management of a close corporation resembles that of a sole proprietorship or a partnership.

To prevent a majority shareholder from dominating a close corporation, the corporation may require that more than a simple majority of the directors approve any action taken by the board. Typically, this would not apply to ordinary business decisions but only to extraordinary actions, such as changing the amount of dividends or dismissing an employee-shareholder.

ETHICAL ISSUE 26.1

What if, in a close, family-owned corporation, one family member (shareholder) is treated unfairly by the others?

Close corporations that are owned by family members may face severe problems when relations among the family members deteriorate. For example, suppose that two sisters and their brother are equal shareholders in a close corporation. Each shareholder is both a director and an officer of the corporation. Disagreements over how the corporation should be operated arise, and the two sisters, as the majority on the board of directors, vote to fire the brother from his position as corporate president. Although the brother remains a shareholder and a member of the board, he is deprived of his job (and his salary), which may have important economic consequences. Furthermore, he may be prevented by the corporate articles or by a shareholder agreement (to be discussed shortly) from selling his shares and investing his money elsewhere.

5. For example, in some states (such as Maryland), the close corporation need not have a board of directors.
6. Shareholders cannot agree, however, to eliminate certain rights of shareholders, such as the right to inspect corporate books and records or the right to bring derivative actions (lawsuits on behalf of the corporation—see Chapter 27).

What can the brother do? Often, the only option in this kind of situation is to petition a court to dissolve the corporation or force the majority shareholders to buy the minority shareholder's shares. Although courts generally are reluctant to interfere with corporate decisions, they have held, in several cases, that majority shareholders owe a fiduciary duty to minority shareholders (see Chapter 27). A breach of this duty may cause a court to order the majority shareholders to buy out the minority shareholder's interest in the firm or, as a last resort, to dissolve the corporation.

Transfer of Shares in Close Corporations Because, by definition, a close corporation has a small number of shareholders, the transfer of one shareholder's shares to someone else can cause serious management problems. The other shareholders may find themselves required to share control with someone they do not know or like.

• **EXAMPLE 26.1** Three brothers, Terry, Damon, and Henry Johnson, are the only shareholders of Johnson's Car Wash, Inc. Terry and Damon do not want Henry to sell his shares to an unknown third person. To avoid this situation, the articles of incorporation could restrict the transferability of shares to outside persons by stipulating that shareholders offer their shares to the corporation or the other shareholders before selling them to an outside purchaser. In fact, a few states have statutes that prohibit the transfer of close corporation shares unless certain persons—including shareholders, family members, and the corporation—are first given the opportunity to purchase the shares for the same price •

Another way that control of a close corporation can be stabilized is through the use of a shareholder agreement. A shareholder agreement can provide that when one of the original shareholders dies, her or his shares of stock in the corporation will be divided in such a way that the proportionate holdings of the survivors, and thus their proportionate control, will be maintained. Courts are generally reluctant to interfere with private agreements, including shareholder agreements.

Key employees may be among those who are allowed to buy shares in the close corporation for which they work. A shareholder agreement may provide that if a key employee is discharged, the employee must offer to sell her or his shares to the corporation, which may be required to buy them. In such circumstances, a question may arise as to whether the corporation discharged its employees merely to buy their shares. That was one of the questions raised in the following case.

CASE 26.2 Crowder Construction Co. v. Kiser

Court of Appeals of North Carolina, 1999.
517 S.E.2d 178.
http://www.aoc.state.nc.us/www/public/html/opinions.htm[a]

FACTS Crowder Construction Company allowed only members of the Crowder family and key employees to buy company stock. Under a shareholder agreement, if a key employee was terminated, the employee was obligated to sell his or her shares to the company. Under a "buyout" provision, the company was required to buy the shares at a price based on their book value.[b] If those shares had been held for less than seven years, the price was lower. In 1981, the firm hired Eugene Kiser, a certified public accountant, who became the firm's chief financial officer. As a key employee, he bought Crowder stock at a substantial discount. By the end of 1994, Kiser

a. In the "Court of Appeals Opinions" section, click on the "1999" box. When that page opens, scroll to "20 July 99" and click on the case name to access the opinion. This Web site is maintained by the North Carolina Administrative Office of the Courts.

b. The *book value* of a corporation is generally understood to mean the value of the corporation's total assets less its total liabilities.

(continued)

CASE 26.2—Continued

had begun to openly question the competence of Otis Crowder, the firm's president, to make decisions. In January 1995, Kiser was discharged and told to sell his stock to the company. Had Kiser worked until August, he would have held all of his shares for more than seven years, which would have entitled him to an extra $180,000. When he refused to sell the shares that he had held for less than seven years, the firm filed a suit in a North Carolina state court against him to enforce the shareholder agreement. Kiser argued, among other things, that the shareholder agreement was unconscionable. In support of this argument, he claimed in part that he had been discharged so that the company would not have to pay the full price for his stock. The court granted a summary judgment in favor of Crowder, and Kiser appealed to a state intermediate appellate court.

ISSUE Was the shareholder agreement unconscionable?

DECISION No. The state intermediate appellate court affirmed the judgment of the lower court.

REASON The appellate court noted that in close corporations, shareholder agreements "often contain some version of mandatory 'buy-out' provisions to ensure shareholders a ready market for their shares where there otherwise might not be one." In this case, there was no evidence that Kiser had been discharged so that Crowder could avoid paying him a higher price for his shares in the company. In the absence of such proof, the court concluded that neither the shareholder agreement nor Kiser's termination was unreasonable. "Plaintiff's evidence tends to show that defendant was discharged for openly questioning the ability and competence of Company management to guide the affairs of the Company, resulting in an adversarial relationship between Kiser and other members of management. * * * Other than defendant's argument that an inference of wrongful purpose arises from his termination, defendant does not offer any evidence."

FOR CRITICAL ANALYSIS—Economic Consideration
Lawsuits are costly. Is there anything that the firm might have done—when forming the shareholder agreement, for example—to prevent this lawsuit?

S Corporations

S CORPORATION
A close business corporation that has met certain requirements as set out by the Internal Revenue Code and thus qualifies for special income tax treatment. Essentially, an S corporation is taxed the same as a partnership, but its owners enjoy the privilege of limited liability.

A close corporation that meets the qualifying requirements specified in Subchapter S of the Internal Revenue Code can operate as an S **corporation.** If a corporation has S corporation status, it can avoid the imposition of income taxes at the corporate level while retaining many of the advantages of a corporation, particularly limited liability.

Qualification Requirements for S Corporations Among the numerous requirements for S corporation status, the following are the most important:

① The corporation must be a domestic corporation.

② The corporation must not be a member of an affiliated group of corporations.

③ The shareholders of the corporation must be individuals, estates, or certain trusts. Partnerships and nonqualifying trusts cannot be shareholders. Corporations can be shareholders under certain circumstances.

④ The corporation must have seventy-five or fewer shareholders.

⑤ The corporation must have only one class of stock, although not all shareholders need have the same voting rights.

⑥ No shareholder of the corporation may be a nonresident alien.

Benefits of S Corporations At times, it is beneficial for a regular corporation to elect S corporation status. Benefits include the following:

① When the corporation has losses, the S election allows the shareholders to use the losses to offset other income.

② When the stockholder's tax bracket is lower than the corporation's tax bracket, the S election causes the corporation's pass-through net income to be taxed in the stockholder's bracket (because it is taxed as personal income). This is particularly attractive when the corporation wants to accumulate earnings for some future business purpose.

Because of these tax benefits, many close corporations have opted for S corporation status. Today, however, the S corporation is losing some of its significance—because the limited liability company and the limited liability partnership (discussed in Chapter 30) offer similar advantages plus additional benefits, including more flexibility in forming and operating the business.

PROFESSIONAL CORPORATIONS

CONTRAST Unlike the shareholders of most other corporations, the shareholders of professional corporations must generally be licensed professionals.

Professional persons such as physicians, lawyers, dentists, and accountants can incorporate. Professional corporations are typically identified by the letters *S.C.* (service corporation), *P.C.* (professional corporation), or *P.A.* (professional association). In general, the laws governing professional corporations are similar to those governing ordinary business corporations, but three basic areas of liability deserve special attention.

First, some courts might, for liability purposes, regard the professional corporation as a partnership in which each partner can be held liable for any malpractice liability incurred by the others within the scope of the partnership. Second, a shareholder in a professional corporation is protected from the liability imposed because of any torts (unrelated to malpractice) committed by other members. Third, many professional corporation statutes retain personal liability of professional persons for their acts and the professional acts performed under their supervision.

Corporate Formation

Up to this point, we have discussed some of the general characteristics of corporations. We now examine the process in which corporations come into existence. Generally, this process involves two steps: (1) preliminary organizational and promotional undertakings, particularly obtaining capital for the future corporation; and (2) the legal process of incorporation.

Note that one of the most common reasons for changing from a sole proprietorship or a partnership to a corporation is the need for additional capital to finance expansion. A sole proprietor can seek partners who will bring capital with them. The partnership might be able to secure more funds from potential lenders than could the sole proprietor. When a firm wants to expand greatly, however, simply increasing the number of partners can result in so many partners that it becomes difficult for the firm to operate effectively. Therefore, incorporation might be the best choice for an expanding business organization because a corporation can obtain more capital by issuing shares of stock.

PROMOTER
A person who takes the preliminary steps in organizing a corporation, including (usually) issuing a prospectus, procuring stock subscriptions, making contract purchases, securing a corporate charter, and the like.

PROSPECTUS
A document required by federal or state securities laws that describes the financial operations of the corporation, thus allowing investors to make informed decisions.

PROMOTIONAL ACTIVITIES

Before a corporation becomes a reality, **promoters**—those who, for themselves or others, take the preliminary steps in organizing a corporation—frequently make contracts with investors and others on behalf of the future corporation. One of the tasks of the promoter is to issue a prospectus. A **prospectus** is a document required by federal or state securities laws (discussed in Chapter 29) that describes the financial operations

"A man to carry on a successful business must have imagination. He must see things as in a vision, a dream of the whole thing."
CHARLES M. SCHWAB, 1862–1939 (American industrialist)

of the corporation, thus allowing investors to make informed decisions. The promoter also secures the corporate charter.

In addition, a promoter may purchase or lease property with a view to selling or transferring it to the corporation when the corporation is formed. A promoter may also enter into contracts with attorneys, accountants, architects, or other professionals whose services will be needed in planning for the proposed corporation. Finally, a promoter induces people to purchase stock in the corporation.

Promoter's Liability As a general rule, a promoter is held personally liable on preincorporation contracts. Courts simply hold that promoters are not agents when a corporation has yet to come into existence. If, however, the promoter secures the contracting party's agreement to hold only the corporation (and not the promoter) liable on the contract, the promoter will not be liable in the event of any breach of contract. Basically, the personal liability of the promoter continues even after incorporation unless the third party *releases* the promoter. In most states, this rule is applied whether or not the promoter made the agreement in the name of, or with reference to, the proposed corporation.

Once the corporation is formed (the charter issued), the promoter remains personally liable until the corporation assumes the preincorporation contract by *novation* (discussed in Chapter 12). Novation releases the promoter and makes the corporation liable for performing the contractual obligations. In some situations, the corporation *adopts* the promoter's contract by undertaking to perform it. Most courts hold that adoption in and of itself does not discharge the promoter from contractual liability. Normally, a corporation cannot *ratify* a preincorporation contract, as no principal was in existence at the time the contract was made.

Subscribers and Subscriptions Prior to the actual formation of the corporation, the promoter can contact potential individual investors, and they can agree to purchase capital stock in the future corporation. This agreement is often called a *subscription agreement,* and the potential investor is called a *subscriber.* Depending on state law, subscribers become shareholders as soon as the corporation is formed or as soon as the corporation accepts the agreement.

RECALL Most offers to form a contract can be revoked, without liability, before they are accepted. Exceptions include option contracts, merchants' firm offers, and offers on which the offerees have changed their positions in justifiable reliance.

Most courts view preincorporation subscriptions as continuing offers to purchase corporate stock. On or after its formation, the corporation can choose to accept the offer to purchase stock. Many courts also treat a subscription offer as irrevocable except with the consent of all of the subscribers. A subscription is irrevocable for a period of six months unless the subscription agreement provides otherwise or unless all the subscribers agree to the revocation of the subscription [RMBCA 6.20]. In some courts and jurisdictions, the preincorporation subscriber can revoke the offer to purchase before acceptance without liability, however.

INCORPORATION PROCEDURES

Exact procedures for incorporation differ among states, but the basic requirements are similar.

State Chartering The first step in the incorporation procedure is to select a state in which to incorporate. Because state incorporation laws differ, individuals may look for the states that offer the most advantageous tax or incorporation provisions. Delaware has historically had the least restrictive laws. Consequently, many corporations, including a number of the largest, have incorporated there. Delaware's statutes permit firms to incorporate in that state and conduct business and locate their operating headquarters elsewhere. Most other states now permit this as well. Note, though, that closely held corporations, particularly those of a professional nature, generally incorporate in the state where their principal shareholders live and work.

Articles of Incorporation The primary document needed to begin the incorporation process is called the *articles of incorporation* (see Exhibit 26–1). The articles include basic information about the corporation and serve as a primary source of authority for

EXHIBIT 26–1 ARTICLES OF INCORPORATION

ARTICLE ONE

The name of the corporation is ______________________________.

ARTICLE TWO

The period of its duration is ________ (may be a number of years or until a certain date).

ARTICLE THREE

The purpose (or purposes) for which the corporation is organized is (are) ______________________________ ______________________________.

ARTICLE FOUR

The aggregate number of shares that the corporation shall have authority to issue is ________ of the par value of ________ dollar(s) each (or without par value).

ARTICLE FIVE

The corporation will not commence business until it has received for the issuance of its shares consideration of the value of $1,000 (can be any sum not less than $1,000).

ARTICLE SIX

The address of the corporation s registered office is ______________________________, New Pacum, and the name of its registered agent at such address is ______________________________ ______________________________.

(Use the street or building or rural address of the registered office, not a post office box number.)

ARTICLE SEVEN

The number of initial directors is ____________________, and the names and addresses of the directors are ______________________________ ______________________________.

ARTICLE EIGHT

The name and address of the incorporator is ______________________________ ______________________________.

(signed)______________________________

Incorporator

Sworn to on ____________________ by the above-named incorporator.

(date)

____

Notary Public ________ County, New Pacum

(Notary Seal)

ON THE WEB For answers to "frequently asked questions" on the topic of incorporation, go to **http://www.bizfilings.com/learning/incfaq.htm.**

its future organization and business functions. The person or persons who execute the articles are called *incorporators*. Generally, the articles of incorporation should include the elements discussed in the following subsections.

Corporate Name. The choice of a corporate name is subject to state approval to ensure against duplication or deception. State statutes usually require that the secretary of state run a check on the proposed name in the state of incorporation. Some states require that the incorporators, at their own expense, run a check on the proposed name for the newly formed corporation. Once cleared, a name can be reserved for a short time, for a fee, pending the completion of the articles of incorporation. All corporate statutes require the corporation name to include the word *Corporation, Incorporated, Company,* or *Limited,* or abbreviations of these terms.

A corporate name cannot be the same as (or deceptively similar to) the name of an existing corporation doing business within the state. • **EXAMPLE 26.2** Suppose that there is an existing corporation named General Dynamics, Inc. The state will not allow another corporation to be called General Dynamic, Inc., because that name is deceptively similar to the first and impliedly transfers a part of the goodwill established by the first corporate user to the second corporation.• Note that if a future firm contemplates doing business in other states, the incorporators also need to check on existing corporate names in those states as well. Otherwise, if the firm does business under a name that is the same as or deceptively similar to an existing company's name, it may be liable for trade name infringement.

Duration. A corporation has perpetual existence unless stated otherwise in the articles. The owners may want to prescribe a maximum duration, however, after which the corporation must formally renew its existence.

Nature and Purpose. The articles must specify the intended business activities of the corporation, and naturally, these activities must be lawful. A general statement of corporate purpose is usually sufficient to give rise to all of the powers necessary to carry out the purpose of the organization. The articles of incorporation can state, for example, that the corporation is organized "to engage in the production and sale of agricultural products." There is a trend toward allowing corporate articles to state that the corporation is organized for "any legal business," with no mention of specifics, to avoid the need for future amendments to the corporate articles.

Capital Structure. The articles generally set forth the capital structure of the corporation. A few state statutes require a relatively small capital investment (for example, $1,000) for ordinary business corporations but a larger capital investment for those engaged in insurance or banking. The articles must outline the number of shares of stock authorized for issuance; their valuation; the various types or classes of stock authorized for issuance; and other relevant information concerning equity, capital, and credit.

KEEP IN MIND Unlike the articles of incorporation, bylaws do not need to be filed with a state official.

Internal Organization. The articles should describe the internal management structure of the corporation, although this can be included in bylaws adopted after the corporation is formed. The articles of incorporation commence the corporation; the bylaws are formed after commencement by the board of directors. Bylaws cannot conflict with the incorporation statute or the corporation's charter [RMBCA 2.06].

Under the RMBCA, shareholders may amend or repeal bylaws. The board of directors may also amend or repeal bylaws unless the articles of incorporation or provisions of the incorporation statute reserve this power to shareholders exclusively

[RMBCA 10.20]. Typical bylaw provisions describe such things as voting requirements for shareholders, the election of the board of directors, the methods of replacing directors, and the manner and time of scheduling shareholders' and board meetings (these corporate activities will be discussed in Chapter 27).

Registered Office and Agent. The corporation must indicate the location and address of its registered office within the state. Usually, the registered office is also the principal office of the corporation. The corporation must give the name and address of a specific person who has been designated as an *agent* and who can receive legal documents (such as orders to appear in court) on behalf of the corporation.

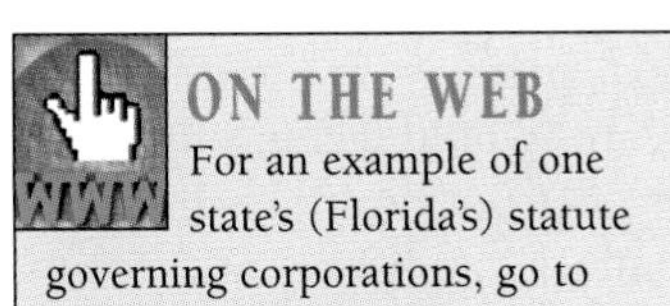

ON THE WEB For an example of one state's (Florida's) statute governing corporations, go to **http://www.ilrg.com/whatsnews/statute.html** and scroll down the page to "Corporations."

Incorporators. Each incorporator must be listed by name and must indicate an address. An incorporator is a person—often, the corporate promoter—who applies to the state on behalf of the corporation to obtain its corporate charter. The incorporator need not be a subscriber and need not have any interest at all in the corporation. Many states do not impose residency or age requirements for incorporators. States vary on the required number of incorporators; it can be as few as one or as many as three. Incorporators are required to sign the articles of incorporation when they are submitted to the state; often, this is their only duty. In some states, they participate at the first organizational meeting of the corporation.

CERTIFICATE OF INCORPORATION The primary document that evidences corporate existence (often referred to as the *corporate charter*).

Certificate of Incorporation Once the articles of incorporation have been prepared, signed, and authenticated by the incorporators, they are sent to the appropriate state official, usually the secretary of state, along with the required filing fee. In many states, the secretary of state then issues a **certificate of incorporation** representing the state's authorization for the corporation to conduct business. (This may be called the *corporate charter.*) The certificate and a copy of the articles are returned to the incorporators.

First Organizational Meeting The first organizational meeting is provided for in the articles of incorporation but is held after the charter has actually been granted. At this meeting, the incorporators elect the first board of directors and complete the routine business of incorporation (pass bylaws and issue stock, for example). Sometimes, the meeting is held after the election of the board, and the business transacted depends on the requirements of the state's incorporation statute, the nature of the business, the provisions made in the articles, and the desires of the promoters. Adoption of bylaws—the internal rules of management for the corporation—is probably the most important function of the meeting. The shareholders, directors, and officers must abide by the bylaws in conducting corporate business.

Corporate Status

The procedures for incorporation are very specific. If they are not followed precisely, others may be able to challenge the existence of the corporation. Errors in the incorporation procedures can become important when, for example, a third person who is attempting to enforce a contract or bring suit for a tort injury learns of them. On the basis of improper incorporation, the plaintiff could seek to make the would-be shareholders personally liable. Additionally, when the corporation seeks to enforce a contract against a defaulting party, that party may be able to avoid liability on the ground of a defect in the incorporation procedure.

To prevent injustice, courts will sometimes attribute corporate status to an improperly formed corporation by holding it to be a *de jure* corporation or a *de facto* corporation. Occasionally, a corporation may be held to exist by estoppel. Additionally, in certain circumstances involving abuse of the corporate form, a court may disregard the corporate entity and hold the shareholders personally liable.

De Jure and *De Facto* Corporations

In the event of substantial compliance with all conditions precedent to incorporation, the corporation is said to have *de jure* (rightful and lawful) existence. In most states and under the RMBCA, the certificate of incorporation is viewed as evidence that all mandatory statutory provisions have been met. This means that the corporation is properly formed, and neither the state nor a third party can attack its existence. If, for example, an incorporator's address was incorrectly listed, this would technically mean that the corporation was improperly formed; but the law does not regard such inconsequential procedural defects as detracting from substantial compliance, and courts will uphold the *de jure* status of the corporate entity.

Sometimes, there is a defect in complying with statutory mandates—for example, the corporation charter may have expired. Under these circumstances, the corporation may have *de facto* (actual) status, meaning that the corporation in fact exists, even if not rightfully or lawfully. A corporation with *de facto* status cannot be challenged by third persons (except for the state). The following elements are required for *de facto* status:

1. There must be a state statute under which the corporation can be validly incorporated.
2. The parties must have made a good faith attempt to comply with the statute.
3. The enterprise must already have undertaken to do business as a corporation.

ETHICAL ISSUE 26.2

Should shareholders be held personally liable for corporate obligations incurred during a temporary corporate dissolution?

One of the major benefits of organizing a business as a corporation is that the corporate owners-shareholders are not subject to personal liability for corporate obligations. Yet suppose that, as a result of failing to pay certain taxes, a corporation is temporarily dissolved by the state and later, after paying the taxes, again acquires *de jure* corporate status. Further suppose that a creditor, after the corporation has reacquired *de jure* corporate status, sues the company *and* its two shareholders for the amount of a debt incurred by the corporation while it was temporarily dissolved. In this situation, is it fair to hold the shareholders personally liable for the debt, given that when the lawsuit was commenced they had paid the taxes due and reacquired *de jure* corporate status? In contrast, would it be fair *not* to allow the creditor to recover the debt from the individual shareholders? After all, the shareholders had obviously violated the law by failing to pay taxes. Should they be rewarded by being shielded from personal liability during the temporary corporate dissolution? While these questions may be significant from an ethical perspective, legally the issue amounts to whether a corporation has *de facto* corporate status during a period of temporary dissolution. When a case involving these facts came before a federal appeals court, the court, applying New York law, concluded that the corporation had *de facto* status during this period of time, and thus the shareholders could not be held personally liable for the corporate debt at issue.[7]

Corporation by Estoppel

If an association that is neither an actual corporation nor a *de facto* or *de jure* corporation holds itself out as being a corporation, it normally will be estopped from denying corporate status in a lawsuit by a third party. This usually occurs when a third party contracts with an association that claims to be a corporation but does not hold a certificate of incorporation. When the third party brings suit naming the so-called corporation as the defendant, the association may not escape liability on the ground that no corporation exists. When justice requires, the courts treat an alleged corporation as if it were an actual corporation for the purpose of determining the rights and liabilities involved in a particular situation. Corporation by estoppel is thus determined by the situation. It does not extend recognition of corporate status beyond the resolution of the problem at hand.

Disregarding the Corporate Entity

PIERCING THE CORPORATE VEIL
An action in which a court disregards the corporate entity and holds the shareholders personally liable for corporate debts and obligations.

Occasionally, the owners use a corporate entity to perpetrate a fraud, circumvent the law, or in some other way accomplish an illegitimate objective. In these situations, the court will ignore the corporate structure by **piercing the corporate veil** and exposing the shareholders to personal liability. Generally, when the corporate privilege is abused for personal benefit or when the corporate business is treated in such a careless manner that the corporation and the shareholder in control are no longer separate entities, the court will require an owner to assume personal liability to creditors for the corporation's debts.

In short, when the facts show that great injustice would result from the use of a corporation to avoid individual responsibility, a court of equity will look behind the corporate structure to the individual stockholder. The following are some of the factors that frequently cause the courts to pierce the corporate veil:

① A party is tricked or misled into dealing with the corporation rather than the individual.

② The corporation is set up never to make a profit or always to be insolvent, or it is too "thinly" capitalized—that is, it has insufficient capital at the time of formation to meet its prospective debts or potential liabilities.

③ Statutory corporate formalities, such as holding required corporation meetings, are not followed.

④ Personal and corporate interests are **commingled** (mixed together) to the extent that the corporation has no separate identity.

COMMINGLE
To mix together. To put funds or goods together into one mass so that the funds or goods are so mixed that they no longer have separate identities. In corporate law, if personal and corporate interests are commingled to the extent that the corporation has no separate identity, a court may "pierce the corporate veil" and expose the shareholders to personal liability.

To elaborate on the fourth factor in the preceding list, consider a close corporation that is formed according to law by a single person or by a few family members. In such a situation, the separate status of the corporate entity and the sole stockholder (or family-member stockholders) must be carefully preserved. Certain practices invite trouble for the one-person or family-owned corporation: the commingling of corporate and personal

7. *L-Tec Electronics Corp. v. Cougar Electronic Organization, Inc.*, 198 F.3d 85 (2d Cir. 1999).

funds, the failure to hold and record minutes of board of directors' meetings, or the shareholders' continuous personal use of corporate property (for example, vehicles).

Corporation laws usually do not specifically prohibit a stockholder from lawfully lending money to her or his corporation. When an officer or director lends the corporation money and takes back security in the form of corporate assets, however, the courts will scrutinize the transaction closely. Any such transaction must be made in good faith and for fair value.

The following case illustrates a situation in which a corporation did business under an assumed name that was not registered with the state. The issue was whether the president of the corporation could be held personally liable for corporate debts incurred under the assumed name.

CASE 26.3 Hoskins Chevrolet, Inc. v. Hochberg

Appellate Court of Illinois,
First District,
First Division, 1998.
294 Ill.App.3d 550,
691 N.E.2d 28,
229 Ill.Dec. 92.
http://www.state.il.us/court/default.htm[a]

FACTS Ronald Hochberg is the president of Diamond Auto Body & Repair, Inc. Under the name "Diamond Auto Construction," Hochberg ordered and received auto parts from Hoskins Chevrolet, Inc. Hoskins Chevrolet sent invoices to "Diamond Auto Construction." Hochberg paid some of the invoices with checks drawn on the bank account of "Diamond Auto Construction." When the unpaid invoices totaled more than $40,000, Hoskins Chevrolet filed a suit in an Illinois state court to collect from Hochberg individually. Hochberg asserted that he did business with Hoskins Chevrolet only as the president of a corporation. Hoskins Chevrolet responded that "Diamond Auto Construction" was not registered with the state as the name of a corporation. The court granted summary judgment in favor of Hoskins Chevrolet. Hochberg appealed.

a. This is a page within a Web site that includes recent opinions of the First District of the Appellate Court of Illinois. Under the "Appellate Court" heading, click on "1998." When that page opens, under the "First District" heading, select "January." Scroll down the list of cases to the *Hoskins* case and click on the link to access the opinion. This site is maintained by the state of Illinois.

ISSUE Does a corporation's use of an unregistered name impose personal liability on a corporate officer who does corporate business under that name?

DECISION Yes. The state intermediate appellate court affirmed the lower court's judgment. A person who incurs corporate debts under an unregistered corporate name is personally liable for those debts.

REASON The state intermediate appellate court explained that state statutes allowed a corporation to use an assumed name if certain procedures were followed. If those procedures were not followed, the corporation was required to do business under its corporate name. In this case, Diamond Auto Body & Repair, Inc., used the name of "Diamond Auto Construction" without following those procedures. Even so, if, while doing business as "Diamond Auto Construction," Hochberg had disclosed Diamond's actual corporate name, he might have avoided liability. He failed to do this, however. "Accordingly, we find no error in the trial court's determination that * * * Diamond Auto Construction was neither a corporation nor the assumed name of a corporation for purposes of establishing contract liability in anyone other than defendant."

FOR CRITICAL ANALYSIS—Social Consideration *Why couldn't "Diamond Auto Construction" qualify as a* de facto *corporation?*

SECURITIES
Generally, stock certificates, bonds, notes, debentures, warrants, or other documents given as evidence of an ownership interest in a corporation or as a promise of repayment by a corporation.

Corporate Financing

Part of the process of corporate formation involves corporate financing. Corporations are financed by the issuance and sale of corporate securities. **Securities** (stocks and bonds) evidence the obligation to pay money or the right to participate in earnings and the distribution of corporate property.

STOCK
An equity (ownership) interest in a corporation, measured in units of shares.

BOND
A certificate that evidences a corporate (or government) debt. It is a security that involves no ownership interest in the issuing entity.

Stocks, or *equity securities*, represent the purchase of ownership in the business firm. **Bonds** (debentures), or *debt securities*, represent the borrowing of money by firms (and governments). Of course, not all debt is in the form of debt securities. For example, some debt is in the form of accounts payable and notes payable. Accounts and notes payable are typically short-term debts. Bonds are simply a way for the corporation to split up its long-term debt so that it can market it more easily.

BONDS

Bonds are issued by business firms and by governments at all levels as evidence of the funds they are borrowing from investors. Bonds normally have a designated *maturity date*—the date when the principal, or face, amount of the bond is returned to the investor. They are sometimes referred to as *fixed-income securities* because their owners (that is, the creditors) receive fixed-dollar interest payments, usually semiannually, during the period of time prior to maturity.

BOND INDENTURE
A contract between the issuer of a bond and the bondholder.

Because debt financing represents a legal obligation on the part of the corporation, various features and terms of a particular bond issue are specified in a lending agreement called a **bond indenture.** A corporate trustee, often a commercial bank trust department, represents the collective well-being of all bondholders in ensuring that the corporation meets the terms of the bond issue. The bond indenture specifies the maturity date of the bond and the pattern of interest payments until maturity. The different types of corporate bonds are described in Exhibit 26–2.

"Equity money [payment for stocks] is dynamic and debt money [payment for bonds] is static."

EDMUND BURKE,
1729–1797
(British political theorist)

STOCKS

Issuing stocks is another way that corporations can obtain financing. The ways in which stocks differ from bonds are summarized in Exhibit 26–3 on the next page. Basically, as mentioned, stocks represent ownership in a business firm, whereas bonds represent borrowing by the firm.

Exhibit 26–4 on page 721 summarizes the types of stocks issued by corporations. We look now at the two major types of stock—*common stock* and *preferred stock*.

EXHIBIT 26–2 TYPES OF CORPORATE BONDS

Debenture Bonds	Bonds for which no specific assets of the corporation are pledged as backing. Rather, they are backed by the general credit rating of the corporation, plus any assets that can be seized if the corporation allows the debentures to go into default.
Mortgage Bonds	Bonds that pledge specific property. If the corporation defaults on the bonds, the bondholders can take the property.
Convertible Bonds	Bonds that can be exchanged for a specified number of shares of common stock under certain conditions.
Callable Bonds	Bonds that may be called in and the principal repaid at specified times or under conditions specified in the bond when it is issued.

EXHIBIT 26–3 HOW DO STOCKS AND BONDS DIFFER?

STOCKS	BONDS
1. Stocks represent ownership.	1. Bonds represent debt.
2. Stocks (common) do not have a fixed dividend rate.	2. Interest on bonds must always be paid, whether or not any profit is earned.
3. Stockholders can elect a board of directors, which controls the corporation.	3. Bondholders usually have no voice in, or control over, management of the corporation.
4. Stocks do not have a maturity date; the corporation usually does not repay the stockholder.	4. Bonds have a maturity date, when the corporation is to repay the bondholder the face value of the bond.
5. All corporations issue or offer to sell stocks. This is the usual definition of a corporation.	5. Corporations do not necessarily issue bonds.
6. Stockholders have a claim against the property and income of a corporation after all creditors' claims have been met.	6. Bondholders have a claim against the property and income of a corporation that must be met before the claims of stockholders.

COMMON STOCK
Shares of ownership in a corporation that give the owner of the stock a proportionate interest in the corporation with regard to control, earnings, and net assets. Shares of common stock are lowest in priority with respect to payment of dividends and distribution of the corporation's assets on dissolution.

Common Stock The true ownership of a corporation is represented by **common stock.** Common stock provides a proportionate interest in the corporation with regard to (1) control, (2) earnings, and (3) net assets. A shareholder's interest is generally in proportion to the number of shares he or she owns out of the total number of shares issued.

Voting rights in a corporation apply to the election of the firm's board of directors and to any proposed changes in the ownership structure of the firm. For example, a holder of common stock generally has the right to vote in a decision on a proposed merger, as mergers can change the proportion of ownership. State corporation law specifies the types of actions for which shareholder approval must be obtained.

"There are two times in a man's life when he should not speculate: when he can't afford it and when he can."

SAMUEL CLEMENS (MARK TWAIN), 1835–1910
(American author and humorist)

Firms are not obligated to return a principal amount per share to each holder of common stock because no firm can ensure that the market price per share of its common stock will not decline over time. The issuing firm also does not have to guarantee a dividend; indeed, some corporations never pay dividends.

Holders of common stock are a group of investors who assume a *residual* position in the overall financial structure of a business. In terms of receiving payment for their investments, they are last in line. They are entitled to the earnings that are left after preferred stockholders, bondholders, suppliers, employees, and other groups have been paid. Once those groups are paid, however, the owners of common stock may be entitled to *all* the remaining earnings as dividends. (The board of directors normally is not under any duty to declare the remaining earnings as dividends, however.)

PREFERRED STOCK
Classes of stock that have priority over common stock as to both payment of dividends and distribution of assets on the corporation's dissolution.

Preferred Stock **Preferred stock** is stock with *preferences.* Usually, this means that holders of preferred stock have priority over holders of common stock as to dividends and as to payment on dissolution of the corporation. Holders of preferred stock may or may not have the right to vote.

EXHIBIT 26–4 TYPES OF STOCKS

Common Stock	Voting shares that represent ownership interest in a corporation. Common stock has the lowest priority with respect to payment of dividends and distribution of assets on the corporation's dissolution.
Preferred Stock	Shares of stock that have priority over common-stock shares as to payment of dividends and distribution of assets on dissolution. Dividend payments are usually a fixed percentage of the face value of the share.
Cumulative Preferred Stock	Required dividends not paid in a given year must be paid in a subsequent year before any common-stock dividends are paid.
Participating Preferred Stock	Stock entitling the owner to receive the preferred-stock dividend and additional dividends if the corporation has paid dividends on common stock.
Convertible Preferred Stock	Stock entitling the owners to convert their shares into a specified number of common shares either in the issuing corporation or, sometimes, in another corporation.
Redeemable, or Callable, Preferred Stock	Preferred shares issued with the express condition that the issuing corporation has the right to repurchase the shares as specified.

Preferred stock is not included among the liabilities of a business because it is equity. Like other equity securities, preferred shares have no fixed maturity date on which the firm must pay them off. Although firms occasionally buy back preferred stock, they are not legally obligated to do so. A sample cumulative convertible preferred-stock certificate is shown in Exhibit 26–5 on the following page.

Holders of preferred stock are investors who have assumed a rather cautious position in their relationship to the corporation. They have a stronger position than common shareholders with respect to dividends and claims on assets, but as a result, they will not share in the full prosperity of the firm if it grows successfully over time. This is because the value of preferred shares will not rise as rapidly as that of common shares during a period of financial success. Preferred stockholders do receive fixed dividends periodically, however, and they may benefit to some extent from changes in the market price of the shares.

The return and the risk for preferred stock lie somewhere between those for bonds and those for common stock. Preferred stock is more similar to bonds than to common stock, even though preferred stock appears in the ownership section of the firm's balance sheet. As a result, preferred stock is often categorized with corporate bonds as a fixed-income security, even though the legal status is not the same.

ON THE WEB

Garage.com provides a list of start-up companies and summaries of their business plans in the "Garage" area of its site and a list of potential investors in the "Heaven" area, at **http://www.garage.com**.

LOCATING POTENTIAL INVESTORS ONLINE

Technology via the Internet has allowed promoters and others to access, easily and inexpensively, a large number of potential investors. Today, there are several online "matching services." These services specialize in matching potential investors with companies or future companies that are seeking investors. A corporate promoter or a small company seeking capital investment can pay a fee to one of these services, which will then include a description of the company in a list that it makes available to investors, also for a fee. Matching services are not new. For decades, several enterprises

EXHIBIT 26–5 CUMULATIVE CONVERTIBLE PREFERRED-STOCK CERTIFICATE

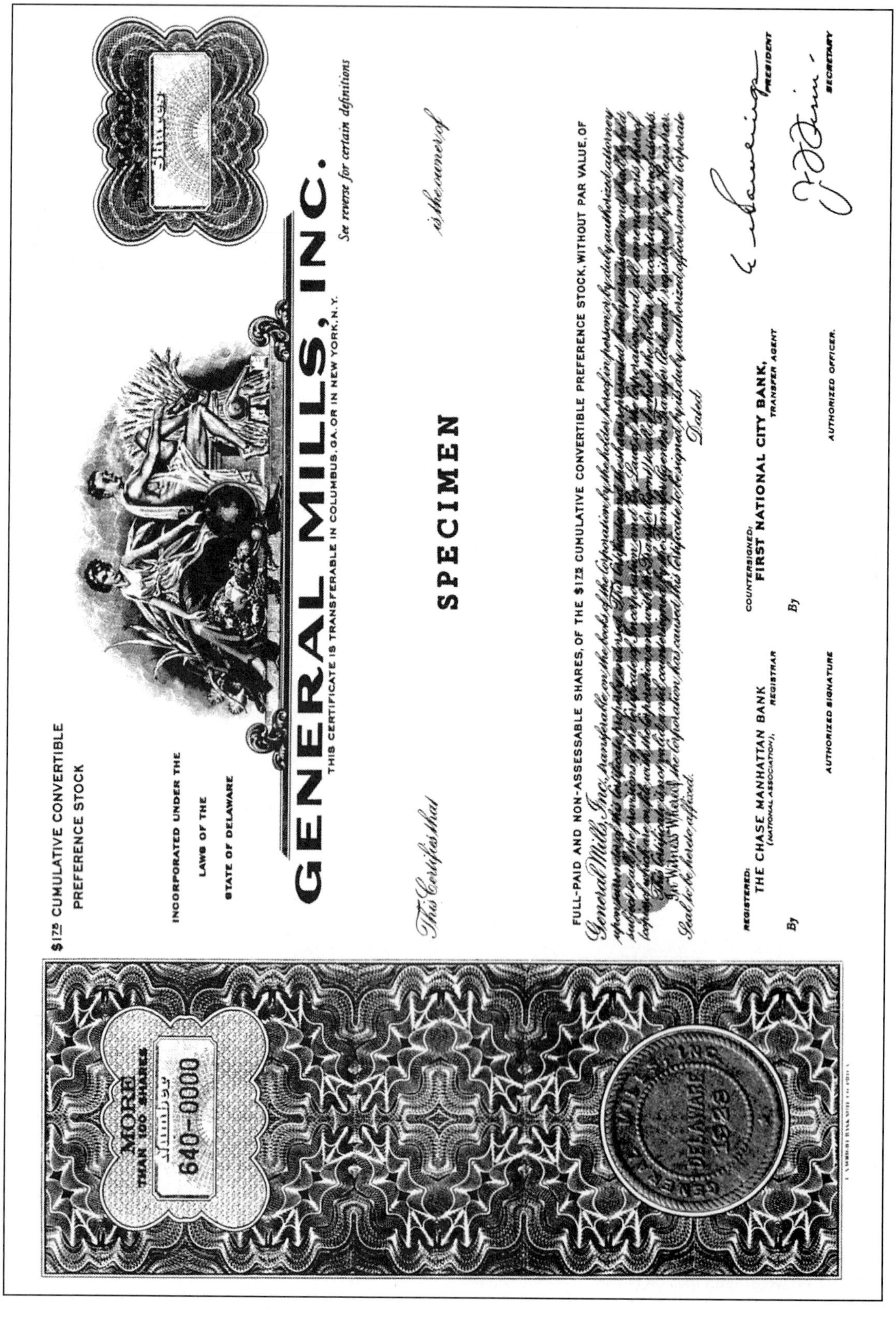

MORE THAN 100 SHARES

Number 640-0000

$1.75 CUMULATIVE CONVERTIBLE PREFERENCE STOCK

INCORPORATED UNDER THE LAWS OF THE STATE OF DELAWARE

Shares

GENERAL MILLS, INC.

THIS CERTIFICATE IS TRANSFERABLE IN COLUMBUS, GA. OR IN NEW YORK, N.Y.

See reverse for certain definitions

This Certifies that **SPECIMEN** *is the owner of*

FULL-PAID AND NON-ASSESSABLE SHARES, OF THE $1.75 CUMULATIVE CONVERTIBLE PREFERENCE STOCK, WITHOUT PAR VALUE, OF *General Mills, Inc., transferable on the books of the Corporation by the holder hereof in person or by duly authorized attorney upon surrender of this Certificate properly endorsed. This Certificate and the shares represented hereby are issued, and shall be held subject to all the provisions of the Certificate of Incorporation and By Laws of the Corporation, and all amendments thereof (copies of which are on file with the Corporation and with the Transfer Agent) to all of which the holder by acceptance hereof assents.*

This Certificate is not valid until countersigned by the Transfer Agent or Transfer Clerk and registered by the Registrar.

In Witness Whereof, the Corporation has caused this Certificate to be signed by its duly authorized officers and its Corporate Seal to be hereto affixed.

Dated

GENERAL MILLS, INC. DELAWARE 1928

REGISTERED: THE CHASE MANHATTAN BANK (NATIONAL ASSOCIATION), REGISTRAR

By

AUTHORIZED SIGNATURE

COUNTERSIGNED: FIRST NATIONAL CITY BANK, TRANSFER AGENT

By

AUTHORIZED OFFICER.

PRESIDENT

SECRETARY

have provided such services by using computerized databases to match business firms' investment needs with potential investors. What is new is that a number of these service providers are now online, and many of them have significantly expanded the geographic scope of their operations.

A number of companies specialize in matching entrepreneurs in specific industries with potential investors. Some companies include listings of companies or start-ups in other countries as well as in the United States. Other enterprises restrict their services to firms within a certain region, such as the Pacific Northwest in the United States.

Online matching services allow entrepreneurs to reach a wide group of potential investors quickly and with relatively little effort. They also make it possible for a new or existing company to locate investors who are interested in the company's specific type of business venture. Several of these online matching services also offer other kinds of assistance, such as help with creating an effective business plan or tips on how to manage financial issues. Businesspersons, and especially entrepreneurs just starting up their businesses, can also benefit from this type of guidance.

APPLICATION Law and the Entrepreneur . . .

Online Incorporation*

Today, just about anybody can form a corporation for any lawful purpose in any state. The requirements differ from state to state. You do not have to form your corporation in the state where you live or the state where you are doing business, however. In fact, many individuals obtain their corporate charters from the state of Delaware because it has the fewest legal restrictions on corporate formation and operation. Traditionally, Delaware has also been the state most often chosen for "mail-order incorporation." Today, instead of incorporating by mail, entrepreneurs have the option of incorporating in the state of their choice via online companies that offer incorporation services.

Finding Information on Incorporation Requirements

Most of the more than one hundred companies that offer incorporation services are now online, and you can obtain information about incorporation at their Web sites. For example, at the Web site of The Company Corporation (TCC) of Delaware (at **http://www.incorporate.com**), you can read about the advantages and disadvantages of incorporating your business, the cost of incorporating in your state (or in any other state), and the pros and cons of the various types of corporate entities that are available.

You can find similar information at other sites, including the Web site of Harvard Business Services, Inc. (at **http://www.delawareinc.com**). Here you can find guidelines that will help you choose the type of corporation that best suits your needs, a list of frequently asked questions about incorporation, telephone numbers for each state's corporations division, the annual legal costs of maintaining a corporation, and so on.

Incorporating Online

If you wish to incorporate via an online incorporation service, all you need to do is fill out a form. For example, if you fill out the incorporation forms at the TCC Web site, TCC will then file the forms with the appropriate state office and obtain a certificate of incorporation (corporate charter) for you. Optional TCC services include making arrangements for a registered agent for your corporation, mail-forwarding services, obtaining a

*This *Application* is not meant to substitute for the services of an attorney who is licensed to practice law in your state.

APPLICATION **Law and the Entrepreneur . . .**

Online Incorporation—continued

tax ID number, and obtaining a domain name registration for your business.

Checklist of Factors to Consider when Incorporating Online or Offline

1. Tax considerations.
2. The initial cost of incorporation and any continuing costs, such as annual fees and possible fees for attorneys and accountants.
3. The formalities that are necessary, and the amount of record keeping that will be required.
4. What should be included in the bylaws.
5. Is "do-it-yourself" online incorporation appropriate? (Depending on the nature and potential growth of your business, you might wish to contact an attorney to take you through the necessary steps in incorporating your business.)

Key Terms

Chapter Summary Corporate Formation and Financing

The Nature of the Corporation (See pages 701–705.)	A corporation is a legal entity distinct from its owners. Formal statutory requirements, which vary somewhat from state to state, must be followed in forming a corporation. The corporation can have perpetual existence or be chartered for a specific period of time. 1. *Corporate parties*—The shareholders own the corporation. They elect a board of directors to govern the corporation. The board of directors hires corporate officers and other employees to run the daily business of the firm. 2. *Corporate taxation*—The corporation pays income tax on net profits; shareholders pay income tax on the disbursed dividends that they receive from the corporation (double-taxation feature). 3. *Torts and criminal acts*—The corporation is liable for the torts committed by its agents or officers within the course and scope of their employment (under the doctrine of *respondeat superior*). In some circumstances, a corporation can be held liable (and be fined) for the criminal acts of its agents and employees. In certain situations, corporate officers may be held personally liable for corporate crimes.

Chapter Summary Corporate Formation and Financing—continued

Corporate Powers (See pages 705–706.)	1. *Express powers*—The express powers of a corporation are granted by the following laws and documents (listed according to their priority): federal constitution, state constitutions, state statutes, articles of incorporation, bylaws, and resolutions of the board of directors. 2. *Implied powers*—Barring express constitutional, statutory, or other prohibitions, the corporation has the implied power to do all acts reasonably appropriate and necessary to accomplish its corporate purposes. 3. Ultra vires *doctrine*—Any act of a corporation that is beyond its express or implied powers to undertake is an *ultra vires* act. The corporation (or shareholders on behalf of the corporation) may sue to enjoin or recover damages for *ultra vires* acts of corporate officers or directors. In addition, the state attorney general may bring an action either to institute an injunction against the transaction or to institute dissolution proceedings against the corporation for *ultra vires* acts.
Classification of Corporations (See pages 706–711.)	1. *Domestic, foreign, and alien corporations*—A corporation is referred to as a *domestic corporation* within its home state (the state in which it incorporates). A corporation is referred to as a *foreign corporation* by any state that is not its home state. A corporation is referred to as an *alien corporation* if it originates in another country but does business in the United States. 2. *Public and private corporations*—A public corporation is one formed by government (for example, cities, towns, and public projects). A private corporation is one formed wholly or in part for private benefit. Most corporations are private corporations. 3. *Nonprofit corporations*—Corporations formed without a profit-making purpose (for example, charitable, educational, and religious organizations and hospitals). 4. *Close corporations*—Corporations owned by a family or a relatively small number of individuals; transfer of shares is usually restricted, and the corporation cannot make a public offering of its securities. 5. *S corporations*—Small domestic corporations (must have seventy-five or fewer shareholders as members) that under Subchapter S of the Internal Revenue Code, are given special tax treatment. These corporations allow shareholders to enjoy the limited legal liability of the corporate form but avoid its double-taxation feature (taxes are paid by shareholders as personal income, and the S corporation is not taxed separately). 6. *Professional corporations*—Corporations formed by professionals (for example, doctors and lawyers) to obtain the benefits of incorporation (such as tax benefits and limited liability). In most situations, the professional corporation is treated as other corporations, but sometimes the courts will disregard the corporate form and treat the shareholders as partners.
Corporate Formation (See pages 711–715.)	1. *Promotional activities*—A corporate promoter is one who takes the preliminary steps in organizing a corporation (issues a prospectus, secures the charter, interests investors in the purchase of corporate stock, forms subscription agreements, makes contracts with third parties so that the corporation can immediately begin doing business, and so on). 2. *Incorporation procedures*— a. A state in which to incorporate is selected. b. The articles of incorporation are prepared and filed. The articles generally should include the corporate name, duration, nature and purpose, capital structure, internal organization, registered office and agent, and incorporators. c. The certificate of incorporation (or charter), which authorizes the corporation to conduct business, is received from the appropriate state office (usually the secretary of state) after the articles of incorporation have been filed.

(continued)

Chapter Summary Corporate Formation and Financing—continued

Corporate Formation—continued	d. The first organizational meeting is held after the charter is granted. The board of directors is elected and other business completed (bylaws passed, stock issued, and so on).
Corporate Status (See pages 715–718.)	1. De jure *or* de facto *corporation*—If a corporation has been improperly incorporated, courts will sometimes impute corporate status to the firm by holding that the firm is a *de jure* corporation (cannot be challenged by the state or third persons) or a *de facto* corporation (can be challenged by the state but not by third persons). 2. *Corporation by estoppel*—If a firm is neither a *de jure* nor a *de facto* corporation but represents itself to be a corporation and is sued as such by a third party, it may be held to be a corporation by estoppel. 3. *Disregarding the corporate entity*—To avoid injustice, courts may "pierce the corporate veil" and hold a shareholder or shareholders personally liable for a judgment against the corporation. This usually occurs only when the corporation was established to circumvent the law, when the corporate form is used for an illegitimate or fraudulent purpose, or when the controlling shareholder commingles his or her own interests with those of the corporation to such an extent that the corporation no longer has a separate identity.
Corporate Financing—Bonds (See page 719.)	Corporate bonds are securities representing *corporate debt*—money borrowed by a corporation. See Exhibit 26–2 for a list describing the various types of corporate bonds.
Corporate Financing—Stocks (See pages 719–721.)	Stocks are equity securities issued by a corporation that represent the purchase of ownership in the business firm. 1. *Important characteristics of stockholders*— a. They need not be paid back. b. The stockholder receives dividends only when so voted by the directors. c. Stockholders are the last investors to be paid on dissolution. d. Stockholders vote for management and on major issues. 2. *Types of stock (see Exhibit 26–4 for details)*— a. Common stock—Represents the true ownership of the firm. Holders of common stock share in the control, earning capacity, and net assets of the corporation. Common stockholders carry more risk than preferred stockholders but, if the corporation is successful, are compensated for this risk by greater returns on their investments. b. Preferred stock—Stock whose holders have a preferred status. Preferred stockholders have a stronger position than common shareholders with respect to dividends and claims on assets, but as a result, they will not share in the full prosperity of the firm if it grows successfully over time. The return and risk for preferred stock lie somewhere between those for bonds and those for common stock.

For Review

① What are the express and implied powers of corporations? On what sources are these powers based?

② What steps are involved in bringing a corporation into existence? Who is liable for preincorporation contracts?

③ What is the difference between a *de jure* corporation and a *de facto* corporation?

④ In what circumstances might a court disregard the corporate entity ("pierce the corporate veil") and hold the shareholders personally liable?

⑤ How are corporations financed? What is the difference between stocks and bonds?

Questions and Case Problems

26–1. Corporate Status. Three brothers inherited a small paper-supply business from their father, who had operated the business as a sole proprietorship. The brothers decided to incorporate under the name of Gomez Corp. and retained an attorney to draw up the necessary documents. The attorney drew up the papers and had the brothers sign them but neglected to send the application for a corporate charter to the secretary of state's office. The brothers assumed that all necessary legal work had been taken care of, and they proceeded to do business as Gomez Corp. One day, a Gomez Corp. employee, while making a delivery to one of Gomez's customers, negligently ran a red light and caused a car accident. Baxter, the driver of the other vehicle, was injured as a result and sued Gomez Corp. for damages. Baxter then learned that no state charter had ever been issued to Gomez Corp., so he sued each of the brothers personally for damages. Can the brothers avoid personal liability for the tort of their employee? Explain.

26–2. Liability for Preincorporation Contracts. Christy, Briggs, and Dobbs are recent college graduates who want to form a corporation to manufacture and sell personal computers. Perez tells them that he will set in motion the formation of their corporation. Perez first makes a contract with Oliver for the purchase of a parcel of land for $25,000. Oliver does not know of the prospective corporate formation at the time the contract is signed. Perez then makes a contract with Kovac to build a small plant on the property being purchased. Kovac's contract is conditional on the corporation's formation. Perez secures all necessary subscription agreements and capitalization, and he files the articles of incorporation. A charter is issued.

(a) Discuss whether the newly formed corporation or Perez (or both) is liable on the contracts with Oliver and Kovac.

(b) Discuss whether the corporation, on coming into legal existence, is automatically liable to Kovac.

26–3. Corporate Powers. Kora Nayenga and two business associates formed a corporation called Nayenga Corp. for the purpose of selling computer services. Kora, who owned 50 percent of the corporate shares, served as the corporation's president. Kora wished to obtain a personal loan from his bank for $250,000, but the bank required the note to be cosigned by a third party. Kora cosigned the note in the name of the corporation. Later, Kora defaulted on the note, and the bank sued the corporation for payment. The corporation asserted, as a defense, that Kora had exceeded his authority when he cosigned the note. Had he? Explain.

26–4. Liability for Preincorporation Contracts. Skandinavia, Inc., manufactured and sold polypropylene underwear. Following two years of poor sales, Skandinavia entered into negotiations to sell the business to Odilon Cormier, an individual who was an experienced textile manufacturer. Skandinavia and Cormier agreed that Cormier would take Skandinavia's underwear inventory and use it in a new corporation, which would be called Polypro, Inc. In return, Skandinavia would receive a commission on future sales from Polypro. Polypro was subsequently established and began selling the underwear. Skandinavia, however, having never received any commissions from the sales, sued Polypro and Cormier to recover its promised commissions. Is Cormier personally liable for the contract he signed in the course of setting up a new corporation? Discuss. [*Skandinavia, Inc. v. Cormier,* 128 N.H. 215, 214 A.2d 1250 (1986)]

26–5. Liability of Shareholders. Moseley Group Management Co. (MGM) provided management services to apartment complexes. MGM's only assets were equipment worth $500 and a bank account with an average balance of $1,500. Richard Moseley ran the company and owned half of the stock. MGM contracted with Property Tax Research Co. (PTR) to obtain a lower property tax assessment on one of its complexes. PTR performed, but MGM refused to pay and transferred its assets and employees to Terrace Management, Inc., a corporation controlled by Moseley. PTR filed a suit in a Missouri state court against Moseley and others to recover the unpaid fees. Should the court pierce the corporate veil and hold Moseley personally liable for the debt? If so, on what basis? [*Sansone v. Moseley,* 912 S.W.2d 666 (Mo.App. W.D. 1995)]

26–6. Corporate Powers. Soda Dispensing Systems, Inc., was owned by two shareholders, each of whom owned half of the stock. One shareholder was the president of the corporation, and the other was vice president. Their shareholder agreement stated that neither shareholder could "encumber any corporate property . . . without the written consent of the other." When Soda Dispensing went out of business, the two shareholders agreed to sell the assets, split the proceeds, and pay $9,900 to their accountants, Cooper, Selvin & Strassberg. Later, the president committed Soda Dispensing to pay Cooper, Selvin more than $24,000, claiming that he had the authority, as president, to make that commitment. When the accountants tried to collect, the vice president objected, asserting that the president had exceeded his authority. Will the court order Soda Dispensing to pay? Explain. [*Cooper, Selvin & Strassberg v. Soda Dispensing Systems, Inc.,* 212 A.D.2d 498, 622 N.Y.S.2d 312 (1995)]

26–7. Corporate Status. Cecil Hill was in the construction trade. He did business as "C&M Builders, Inc.," although there was no such corporation. County Concrete Co. supplied "C&M Builders, Inc." with over $50,000 worth of concrete for which it was not paid. The supplier filed a suit in a Maryland state court against Hill personally. Hill argued that because the supplier thought it was doing business with a corporate entity, C&M was a *de facto* corporation, and thus Hill was not personally liable. Should Hill be allowed to avoid liability on this basis? Why or why not? [*Hill v. County Concrete Co.,* 108 Md.App. 527, 672 A.2d 667 (1996)]

26–8. Disregarding the Corporate Entity. Steven and Janis Gimbert leased a warehouse to a manufacturing business owned by Manzar Zuberi. Zuberi signed the lease as the purported representative of "ATM Manufacturing, Inc.," which was a nonexistent corporation. Zuberi was actually the president of two existing corporations, ATM Enterprises, Inc., and Ameri-Pak International.

Under the Ameri-Pak name, Zuberi manufactured a household cleaning product in the Gimberts' warehouse. The use of hydrochloric acid in the operations severely damaged the premises, and the Gimberts filed a suit in a Georgia state court against Zuberi personally to collect for the damage. On what basis might Zuberi be held personally liable? Discuss fully. [*Zuberi v. Gimbert,* 230 Ga.App. 471, 496 S.E.2d 741 (1998)]

26–9. S Corporations. James, Randolph, and Judith Agley and Michael and Nancy Timmis were shareholders in F & M Distributors, Inc., Venture Packaging, Inc., and Diamond Automations, Inc. James Agley was also a shareholder in Middletown Aerospace. All of the firms were S corporations organized and located in Michigan and doing business in Ohio. None of the shareholders was a resident of Ohio, and none of them personally did business in Ohio. Between 1988 and 1992, the Agleys and the Timmises included their prorated share of the S corporations' income on Ohio personal income tax returns. They believed, however, that an out-of-state shareholder should not be taxed in Ohio on the income that he or she received from an S corporation doing business in Ohio. They contended that the S corporation, not the shareholder, earned the income. They also emphasized that none of them personally did business in the state. Finally, they asked the Ohio Tax Commissioner for refunds for those years. Should the state grant their request? Why or why not? [*Agley v. Tracy,* 87 Ohio St.3d 265, 719 N.E.2d 951 (1999)]

TEST YOUR KNOWLEDGE—ANSWER ON THE WEB

26–10. William Soerries was the sole shareholder of Chickasaw Club, Inc., which operated a popular nightclub of the same name in Columbus, Georgia. Soerries maintained corporate checking accounts, but he paid his employees, suppliers, and entertainers in cash out of the club's proceeds. He owned the property on which the club was located and rented it to the club, but made the mortgage payments out of the club's proceeds. Soerries often paid corporate expenses out of his personal funds. At 11:45 P.M. on July 31, 1996, eighteen-year-old Aubrey Lynn Pursley, who was already intoxicated, entered the Chickasaw Club. A city ordinance prohibited individuals under the age of twenty-one from entering nightclubs, but Chickasaw employees did not check Pursley's identification. Pursley drank more alcohol and was visibly intoxicated when she left the club at 3:00 A.M. with a beer in her hand. Shortly afterward, Pursley was killed when she lost control of her car and struck a tree. Joseph Dancause, Pursley's stepfather, filed a suit in a Georgia state court against Chickasaw Club, Inc., and Soerries for damages. Can Soerries be held personally liable? If so, on what basis? Explain. [*Soerries v. Dancause,* 546 S.E.2d 356 (Ga.App. 2001)]

A QUESTION OF ETHICS AND SOCIAL RESPONSIBILITY

26–11. In 1990, American Design Properties, Inc. (ADP), leased premises at 8604 Olive Blvd. in St. Louis County, Missouri. Under the lease agreement, ADP had the right to terminate the lease on 120 days' written notice, but it did not have the right to sublease the premises without the lessor's (landowner's) consent. ADP had no bank account, no employees, and no money. ADP had never filed an income tax return or held a directors' or shareholders' meeting. In fact, ADP's only business was to collect and pay the exact amount of rent due under the lease. American Design Group, Inc. (ADG), a wholesale distributor of jewelry and other merchandise, actually occupied 8604 Olive Blvd. J. H. Blum owned ADG and was an officer and director of both ADG and ADP. Blum's husband, Marvin, was an officer of ADG and signed the lease as an officer of ADP. Marvin's former son-in-law, Matthew Smith, was a salaried employee of ADG, an officer of ADG, and an officer and director of ADP. In 1995, Nusrala Four, Inc. (later known as Real Estate Investors Four, Inc.), purchased the property at 8604 Olive Blvd. and became the lessor. No one told Nusrala that ADG was the occupant of the premises leased by ADP. ADP continued to pay the rent until November 1998 when Smith paid with a check drawn on ADG's account. No more payments were made. On February 26, 1999, Marvin sent Nusrala a note that read, "We have vacated the property at 8604 Olive," which, Nusrala discovered, had been damaged. Nusrala filed a suit in a Missouri state court against ADG and ADP, seeking money for the damage. In view of these facts, consider the following questions. [*Real Estate Investors Four, Inc. v. American Design Group, Inc.,* 46 S.W.3d 51 (Mo.App. E.D. 2001)]

1. Given that ADG had not signed the lease and was not rightfully a sublessee, could ADG be held liable, at least in part, for the damage to the premises? Under what theory might the court ignore the separate corporate identities of ADG and ADP? If you were the judge, how would you rule in this case?
2. Assuming that ADP had few, if any, corporate assets, would it be fair to preclude Nusrala from recovering money for the damage from ADG?
3. Is it ever appropriate for a court to ignore the corporate structure? Why or why not?

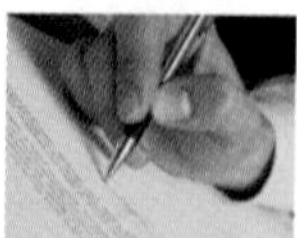

FOR CRITICAL ANALYSIS

26–12. What are some of the ways in which the limited liability of corporate shareholders serves the public interest? Can you think of any ways in which this limited liability is harmful to the public interest? Explain.

Internet Exercises

Go to the *Business Law Today* home page at **http://blt.westbuslaw.com**. Select "Interactive Study Center" and then click on "Chapter 26." There you will find the following Internet research exercises that you can perform to learn more about corporate law and financing:

Activity 26–1: Corporate Law
Activity 26–2: Financing a Business

Before the Test

Go to the *Business Law Today* home page at **http://blt.westbuslaw.com**. Click on "Interactive Quizzes." You will find at least twenty interactive questions relating to this chapter.

CHAPTER 27

Corporate Directors, Officers, and Shareholders

"They [corporations] cannot commit treason, nor be outlawed nor excommunicated, because they have no soul."

Sir Edward Coke, 1552–1634
(English jurist and legal scholar)

CHAPTER CONTENTS

LEARNING OBJECTIVES

After reading this chapter, you should be able to answer the following questions:

① What are the duties of corporate directors and officers?

② Directors are expected to use their best judgment in managing the corporation. What must directors do to avoid liability for honest mistakes of judgment and poor business decisions?

③ What is a voting proxy? What is cumulative voting?

④ If a group of shareholders perceives that the corporation has suffered a wrong and the directors refuse to take action, can the shareholders compel the directors to act? If so, how?

⑤ From what sources may dividends be paid legally? In what circumstances is a dividend illegal? What happens if a dividend is illegally paid?

Sir Edward Coke's observation that a corporation has no "soul" is based on the fact that a corporation is not a "natural" person but a legal fiction. No one individual shareholder or director bears sole responsibility for the corporation and its actions. Rather, a corporation joins the efforts and resources of a large number of individuals for the purpose of producing returns greater than the returns those persons could have obtained individually.

Sometimes, actions that benefit the corporation as a whole do not coincide with the separate interests of the individuals making up the corporation. In such situations, it is important to know the rights and duties of all participants in the corporate enterprise. This chapter focuses on the rights and duties of directors, officers, and shareholders and the ways in which conflicts among them are resolved.

Role of Directors

A corporation typically is governed by a board of directors. A director occupies a position of responsibility unlike that of other corporate personnel. Directors are sometimes inappropriately characterized as *agents* because they act on behalf of the corporation. No *individual* director, however, can act as an agent to bind the corporation; and as a group, directors collectively control the corporation in a way that no agent is able to control a principal. Directors are often incorrectly characterized as *trustees* because they occupy positions of trust and control over the corporation. Unlike trustees, however, they do not own or hold title to property for the use and benefit of others.

ELECTION OF DIRECTORS

ON THE WEB One of the best sources on the Web for information on corporations, including their directors, is the "EDGAR" database of the Securities and Exchange Commission (SEC) at **http://www.sec.gov/edgar.shtml**.

Subject to statutory limitations, the number of directors is set forth in the corporation's articles or bylaws. Historically, the minimum number of directors has been three, but today many states permit fewer. Indeed, the Revised Model Business Corporation Act (RMBCA), in Section 8.01, permits corporations with fewer than fifty shareholders to eliminate the board of directors.

The initial board of directors is normally appointed by the incorporators on the creation of the corporation, or directors are named by the corporation itself in the articles. The first board serves until the first annual shareholders' meeting. Subsequent directors are elected by a majority vote of the shareholders.

The term of office for a director is usually one year—from annual meeting to annual meeting. Longer and staggered terms are permissible under most state statutes. A common practice is to elect one-third of the board members each year for a three-year term. In this way, there is greater management continuity.

BE AWARE The articles of incorporation may provide that a director can be removed only for cause.

A director can be removed *for cause* (that is, for failing to perform a required duty), either as specified in the articles or bylaws or by shareholder action. Even the board of directors itself may be given power to remove a director for cause, subject to shareholder review. In most states, a director cannot be removed without cause unless the shareholders have reserved that right at the time of election.

Vacancies can occur on the board of directors because of death or resignation, or when a new position is created through amendment of the articles or bylaws. In these situations, either the shareholders or the board itself can fill the position, depending on state law or on the provisions of the bylaws.

DIRECTORS' QUALIFICATIONS AND COMPENSATION

Few legal requirements exist concerning directors' qualifications. Only a handful of states impose minimum age and residency requirements. A director is sometimes a shareholder, but this is not a necessary qualification—unless, of course, statutory provisions or corporate articles or bylaws require ownership.

Compensation for directors is ordinarily specified in the corporate articles or bylaws. Because directors have a fiduciary relationship to the shareholders and to the corporation, an express agreement or provision for compensation often is necessary for them to receive money income from the funds that they control and for which they have responsibilities.

BOARD OF DIRECTORS' MEETINGS

The board of directors conducts business by holding formal meetings with recorded minutes. The date on which regular meetings are held is usually established in the articles or bylaws or by board resolution, and no further notice is customarily required. Special meetings can be called, with notice sent to all directors.

QUORUM
The number of members of a decision-making body that must be present before business may be transacted.

Quorum requirements can vary among jurisdictions. (A **quorum** is the minimum number of members of a body of officials or other group that must be present in order for business to be validly transacted.) Many states leave the decision as to quorum requirements to the corporate articles or bylaws. In the absence of specific state statutes, most states provide that a quorum is a majority of the number of directors authorized in the articles or bylaws. Voting is done in person (unlike voting at shareholders' meetings, which can be done by proxy, as discussed later in this chapter).[1] The rule is one vote per director. Ordinary matters generally require a simple majority vote; certain extraordinary issues may require a greater-than-majority vote.

ETHICAL ISSUE 27.1

Should state corporate laws be changed to allow board of directors' meetings to be held in cyberspace?

Today, the corporate laws of most states—including California, Delaware, New York, and Texas—expressly permit telephone conferences for board of directors' meetings as long as the participants can hear one another. Section 8.20 of the RMBCA also allows directors' meetings to be held via telephone conference. Adapting these laws to provide for meetings via the Internet, however, is difficult. California recently attempted to resolve this problem by permitting board of directors' meetings to be held via electronic video screen communication or similar means, as long as three conditions are satisfied: (1) each participant must be able to communicate with all other participants concurrently; (2) each participant must be provided with a means of proposing or objecting to specific corporate actions; and (3) the corporation must have a means of verifying that a person participating in the meeting is a director or other person entitled to participate. Whether other states will follow California's lead is not yet known. Clearly, at the heart of the decision to use cyberspace for corporate board meetings are two basic concerns: confidentiality and effective communication. Ultimately, it will be up to corporate directors to decide if technology can adequately address these concerns.

RIGHTS OF DIRECTORS

A director of a corporation has a number of rights, including the rights of participation, inspection, compensation, and indemnification.

ON THE WEB You can find definitions for terms used in corporate law, as well as court decisions and articles on corporate law topics, at **http://www.law.com**.

Participation and Inspection A corporate director must have certain rights to function properly in that position. The main right is one of participation—meaning that the director must be notified of board of directors' meetings so as to participate in them. As pointed out earlier in this chapter, regular board meetings are usually established by the bylaws or by board resolution, and no notice of these meetings is required. If special meetings are called, however, notice is required unless waived by the director.

A director must have access to all of the corporate books and records to make decisions and to exercise the necessary supervision over corporate officers and employees. This right of inspection is virtually absolute and cannot be restricted.

1. Except in Louisiana, which allows a director to vote by proxy under certain circumstances.

Compensation and Indemnification Historically, directors have had no inherent right to compensation for their services as directors. Nominal sums are often paid as honorariums to directors, however. In many corporations, directors are also chief corporate officers (president or chief executive officer, for example) and receive compensation in their managerial positions. Most directors, however, gain through indirect benefits, such as business contacts, prestige, and other rewards, such as stock options. There is a trend toward providing more than nominal compensation for directors, especially in large corporations where the time, work, effort, and risk involved can impose enormous burdens. Many states permit the corporate articles or bylaws to authorize compensation for directors, and in some cases the board can set its own compensation unless the articles or bylaws provide otherwise.

Corporate directors may become involved in lawsuits by virtue of their positions and their actions as directors. Most states (and RMBCA 8.51) permit a corporation to indemnify (guarantee reimbursement to) a director for legal costs, fees, and judgments involved in defending corporation-related suits. Many states specifically permit a corporation to purchase liability insurance for the directors and officers to cover indemnification. When the statutes are silent on this matter, the power to purchase such insurance is usually considered to be part of the corporation's implied power.

MANAGEMENT RESPONSIBILITIES

Directors have responsibility for all policymaking decisions necessary to the management of corporate affairs. Just as shareholders cannot act individually to bind the corporation, the directors must act as a body in carrying out routine corporate business. The general areas of responsibility of the board of directors include the following:

1. The declaration and payment of corporate dividends to shareholders.
2. The authorization for major corporate policy decisions—for example, the initiation of proceedings for the sale or lease of corporate assets outside the regular course of business, the determination of new product lines, and the overseeing of major contract negotiations and major management-labor negotiations.
3. The appointment, supervision, and removal of corporate officers and other managerial employees and the determination of their compensation.
4. Financial decisions, such as the decision to issue authorized shares and bonds.

The board of directors can delegate some of its functions to an executive committee or to corporate officers. In doing so, the board is not relieved of its overall responsibility for directing the affairs of the corporation, but corporate officers and managerial personnel are empowered to make decisions relating to ordinary, daily corporate affairs within well-defined guidelines.

Role of Corporate Officers and Executives

The officers and other executive employees are hired by the board of directors or, in rare instances, by the shareholders. In addition to carrying out the duties articulated in the bylaws, corporate and managerial officers act as agents of the corporation, and the ordinary rules of agency (discussed in Chapter 24) normally apply to their employment. The qualifications required of officers and executive employees are determined at the discretion of the corporation and are included in the articles or bylaws. In most states, a person can hold more than one office and can be both an officer and a director of the corporation.

CONTRAST Shareholders own a corporation and directors make policy decisions, but officers who run the daily business of the corporation often have significant decision-making power.

The rights of corporate officers and other high-level managers are defined by employment contracts because these persons are employees of the company. Corporate officers normally can be removed by the board of directors at any time with or without cause and regardless of the terms of the employment contracts—although in so doing, the corporation may be liable for breach of contract. The duties of corporate officers are the same as those of directors because both groups are involved in decision making and are in similar positions of control. Hence, officers are viewed as having the same fiduciary duties of care and loyalty in their conduct of corporate affairs as directors have, a subject to which we now turn.

Duties of Directors and Officers

"It is not the crook in modern business that we fear but the honest man who does not know what he is doing."

OWEN D. YOUNG, 1874–1962 (American corporate executive and public official)

Directors and officers are deemed *fiduciaries* of the corporation because their relationship with the corporation and its shareholders is one of trust and confidence. The fiduciary duties of the directors and officers include the duty of care and the duty of loyalty.

DUTY OF CARE

Directors and officers must exercise due care in performing their duties. The standard of *due care* has been variously described in judicial decisions and codified in many corporation codes. Generally, a director or officer is expected to act in good faith, to exercise the care that an ordinarily prudent person would exercise in similar circumstances, and to act in what he or she considers to be the best interests of the corporation.[2] Directors and officers who have not exercised the required duty of care can be held liable for the harms suffered by the corporation as a result of their negligence.

2. RMBCA 8.30.

Corporate executives discuss the business of their firm. How do the rights and duties of corporate officers differ from those of corporate directors?

Duty to Make Informed and Reasonable Decisions Directors and officers are expected to be informed on corporate matters. To be informed, the director or officer must do what is necessary to become informed: attend presentations, ask for information from those who have it, read reports, review other written materials such as contracts—in other words, carefully study a situation and its alternatives. Depending on the nature of the business, directors and officers are often expected to act in accordance with their own knowledge and training. Most states (and Section 8.30 of the RMBCA), however, allow a director to make decisions in reliance on information furnished by competent officers or employees, professionals such as attorneys and accountants, or even an executive committee of the board without being accused of acting in bad faith or failing to exercise due care if such information turns out to be faulty.

Directors are also expected to make reasonable decisions. For example, a director should not accept a **tender offer** (an offer to purchase shares in the company that is made by another company directly to the shareholders, sometimes referred to as a "takeover bid") with only a moment's consideration based solely on the price per share offered by the group making the tender offer.

TENDER OFFER
An offer to purchase shares made by one company directly to the shareholders of another (target) company; often referred to as a "takeover bid."

Duty to Exercise Reasonable Supervision Directors are also expected to exercise a reasonable amount of supervision when they delegate work to corporate officers and employees. ● **EXAMPLE 27.1** Suppose that a corporate bank director fails to attend any board of directors' meetings for five years, never inspects any of the corporate books or records, and generally fails to supervise the efforts of the bank president and the loan committee. Meanwhile, a corporate officer, the bank president, makes various improper loans and permits large overdrafts. In this situation, the corporate director may be held liable to the corporation for losses resulting from the unsupervised actions of the bank president and the loan committee.●

Dissenting Directors Directors are expected to attend board of directors' meetings, and their votes should be entered into the minutes of corporate meetings. Unless a dissent is entered, the director is presumed to have assented. Directors who dissent are rarely held individually liable for mismanagement of the corporation. For this reason, a director who is absent from a given meeting sometimes registers with the secretary of the board a dissent to actions taken at the meeting.

DUTY OF LOYALTY

"It is not within the lawful powers of a board of directors to shape and conduct the affairs of a corporation for the merely incidental benefit of the shareholders."

RUSSELL C. OSTRANDER, 1851–1919 (Michigan jurist)

Loyalty can be defined as faithfulness to one's obligations and duties. In the corporate context, the duty of loyalty requires directors and officers to subordinate their personal interests to the welfare of the corporation. This means, among other things, that directors may not use corporate funds or confidential corporate information for personal advantage. Similarly, they must refrain from self-dealing. For example, a director should not oppose a tender offer that is in the corporation's best interest simply because its acceptance may cost the director her or his position. Cases dealing with fiduciary duty typically involve one or more of the following:

1. Competing with the corporation.
2. Usurping (taking advantage of) a corporate opportunity.
3. Having an interest that conflicts with the interest of the corporation.
4. Engaging in insider trading (using information that is not public to make a profit trading securities, as discussed in Chapter 29).

⑤ Authorizing a corporate transaction that is detrimental to minority shareholders.

⑥ Using corporate facilities for personal business.

An officer or director usurps a corporate opportunity when he or she, for personal gain, takes advantage of a business opportunity that is financially within the corporation's reach, is in line with the firm's business, is to the firm's practical advantage, and is one in which the corporation has an interest.

Whether two directors' violated their fiduciary duties to their corporation by buying certain corporate property was at issue in the following case.

CASE 27.1 Stokes v. Bruno

Court of Appeal of Louisiana,
Third Circuit, 1998.
720 So.2d 388.

HISTORICAL AND SOCIAL SETTING *A nonstock corporation is a corporation whose ownership is not recognized by stock but by a membership charter or agreement. Membership might be created according to a particular attribute, such as the ownership of land within the corporation's geographic reach. A corporation organized for other than a profit-making purpose is a nonprofit corporation. No part of the income of a nonprofit corporation is distributable to the directors, officers, or members. An example of a nonstock, nonprofit corporation might be a homeowner's association that is organized in a corporate form.*

FACTS Point Cotile Parks Association, Inc. (PCPA), is a nonstock, nonprofit corporation whose members are limited to owners of lots or building sites within the Point Cotile Subdivision. The board of directors, including Gerald Bruno and Michael Wright, adopted resolutions that effectively granted Bruno and Wright the authority to sell certain "common ground" on PCPA's behalf. The board designated lots and set prices, based on professional appraisals. Six years later, when some of the lots had not sold for their original prices, Bruno and Wright sold to themselves, and to Bruno's wife, 5.45 acres of the "common ground." The sale included lots with timber that had not been previously offered for sale. On their own appraisal, Bruno and Wright set the price for the acreage lower than the board had set for the individual lots. When the board learned of the sale, Craig Stokes and other PCPA members filed a suit in a Louisiana state court against Bruno and Wright. The court declared the sale *ultra vires* and void. Bruno appealed.

ISSUE Was the sale of PCPA property under these circumstances a breach of Bruno and Wright's fiduciary duties to the corporation?

DECISION Yes. The state intermediate appellate court affirmed the lower court's judgment. The appellate court ordered a rescission of the sale.

REASON The court concluded that this was "a clear case of self-dealing." The court pointed out that Bruno and Wright had a duty to PCPA to maximize its return on the sale of the "common ground." As part of this duty, they should have disclosed to PCPA the size of the sale, the sale of the timber, the price, and that the price was based on their own determination, not an outside source. To fully comply with their duty, Bruno and Wright should have offered the other PCPA members and the public the opportunity they gave themselves—to buy the entire acreage, rather than individual lots, at the reduced price. "[T]he mere fact that a portion of the property had not sold at the original requested prices did not give [them] the unilateral authorization to add more land, reduce the price and then purchase themselves without disclosure."

FOR CRITICAL ANALYSIS—Ethical Consideration *Under what circumstances might a director's sale of corporate property to himself or herself be justified?*

CONFLICTS OF INTEREST

The duty of loyalty also requires officers and directors to disclose fully to the board of directors any possible conflict of interest that might occur in conducting corporate transactions. The various state statutes contain different standards, but a contract will generally *not* be voidable if it was fair and reasonable to the corporation at the time it was made, if there was a full disclosure of the interest of the officers or directors involved in the transaction, and if the contract was approved by a majority of the disinterested directors or shareholders.

● **EXAMPLE 27.2** Southwood Corporation needs office space. Lambert Alden, one of its five directors, owns the building adjoining the corporation's main office building. He negotiates a lease with Southwood for the space, making a full disclosure to Southwood and the other four board directors. The lease arrangement is fair and reasonable, and it is unanimously approved by the corporation's board of directors. In this situation, Alden has not breached his duty of loyalty to the corporation, and the contract is thus valid. If it were otherwise, directors would be prevented from ever giving financial assistance to the corporations they serve.●

ETHICAL ISSUE 27.2

What happens to the duty of loyalty when a director sits on the boards of two corporations?

Corporate directors often have many business affiliations, and they may even sit on the board of more than one corporation. (Of course, directors generally are precluded from sitting on the boards of directors of competing companies.) The duty of loyalty can become cloudy when corporate directors sit on the board of more than one corporation. Because of the potential for abuse in transactions negotiated between corporations whose boards have some members in common, courts tend to scrutinize such actions closely.

For example, suppose that four individuals own a total of 70 percent of the shares of Company A and 100 percent of the shares of Company B. All four of these shareholders sit on the boards of directors of both corporations. Company A decides to purchase all of Company B's stock for $6 million, when in fact it is worth only $3 million. The shareholder-directors of both firms have not breached their duty to Company B because the $6 million price is beneficial to that company. A court would likely hold that the directors breached their duty to the other shareholders of Company A (who owned the remaining 30 percent of Company A's shares), however, because these other shareholders had nothing to gain by the transaction and much to lose by Company A's purchase of Company B at an inflated price.[3]

"All business proceeds on beliefs, or judgments of probabilities, and not on certainties."

CHARLES ELIOT,
1834–1936
(American educator and editor)

Liability of Directors and Officers

Directors and officers are exposed to liability on many fronts. Corporate directors and officers may be held liable for the crimes and torts committed by themselves or by

3. See, for example, *Gries Sports Enterprises, Inc. v. Cleveland Browns Football Co.,* 26 Ohio St.3d 15, 496 N.E.2d 959 (1986).

corporate employees under their supervision, as discussed in Chapter 6 and Chapter 24, respectively. Additionally, shareholders may perceive that the corporate directors are not acting in the best interests of the corporation and may sue the directors, in what is called a *shareholder's derivative suit,* on behalf of the corporation. (This type of action is discussed later in this chapter, in the context of shareholders' rights.) Here, we examine the **business judgment rule**, under which a corporate director or officer may be able to avoid liability to the corporation or to its shareholders for poor business judgments.

BUSINESS JUDGMENT RULE
A rule that immunizes corporate management from liability for actions that result in corporate losses or damages if the actions are undertaken in good faith and are within both the power of the corporation and the authority of management to make.

Directors and officers are expected to exercise due care and to use their best judgment in guiding corporate management, but they are not insurers of business success. Honest mistakes of judgment and poor business decisions on their part do not make them liable to the corporation for resulting damages. The business judgment rule generally immunizes directors and officers from liability for the consequences of a decision that is within managerial authority, as long as the decision complies with management's fiduciary duties and as long as acting on the decision is within the powers of the corporation. Consequently, if there is a reasonable basis for a business decision, it is unlikely that the court will interfere with that decision, even if the corporation suffers as a result.

To benefit from the rule, directors and officers must act in good faith, in what they consider to be the best interests of the corporation, and with the care that an ordinarily prudent person in a similar position would exercise in similar circumstances. This requires an informed decision, with a rational basis, and with no conflict between the decision maker's personal interest and the interest of the corporation.

Role of Shareholders

The acquisition of a share of stock makes a person an owner and shareholder in a corporation. Shareholders thus own the corporation. Although they have no legal title to corporate property, such as buildings and equipment, they do have an equitable (ownership) interest in the firm.

BE AWARE Shareholders normally are not agents of the corporation.

As a general rule, shareholders have no responsibility for the daily management of the corporation, although they are ultimately responsible for choosing the board of directors, which does have such control. Ordinarily, corporate officers and other employees owe no direct duty to individual shareholders. Their duty is to the corporation as a whole. A director, however, is in a fiduciary relationship to the corporation and therefore serves the interests of the shareholders. Generally, there is no legal relationship between shareholders and creditors of the corporation. Shareholders can, in fact, be creditors of the corporation and thus have the same rights of recovery against the corporation as any other creditor.

In this section, we look at the powers and voting rights of shareholders, which are generally established in the articles of incorporation and under the state's general incorporation law.

SHAREHOLDERS' POWERS

The shareholders' approval is needed before any fundamental corporate changes can be effected. Hence, shareholders are empowered to amend the articles of incorporation (charter) and bylaws, approve a merger or the dissolution of the corporation, and approve the sale of all or substantially all of the corporation's assets. Some of these powers are subject to prior board approval.

Shareholders meet to vote on corporate issues. What issues must be put before shareholders for their vote?

Directors are elected to (and removed from) the board of directors by a vote of the shareholders. The first board of directors is either named in the articles of incorporation or chosen by the incorporators to serve until the first shareholders' meeting. From that time on, the selection and retention of directors are exclusively shareholder functions.

Directors usually serve their full terms; if they are unsatisfactory, they are simply not reelected. Shareholders have the inherent power, however, to remove a director from office *for cause* (breach of duty or misconduct) by a majority vote.[4] Some state statutes (and some corporate charters) even permit removal of directors without cause by the vote of a majority of the holders of outstanding shares entitled to vote.

SHAREHOLDERS' MEETINGS

Shareholders' meetings must occur at least annually, and additional, special meetings can be called as needed to take care of urgent matters.

Notice of Meetings Each shareholder must receive written notice of the date, time, and place of a shareholders' meeting.[5] The notice must be received within a reasonable length of time prior to the date of the meeting. Notice of a special meeting must include a statement of the purpose of the meeting, and business transacted at the meeting is limited to that purpose.

PROXY
In corporation law, a written agreement between a stockholder and another under which the stockholder authorizes the other to vote the stockholder's shares in a certain manner.

Proxies and Proxy Materials Because it is usually not practical for owners of only a few shares of stock of publicly traded corporations to attend shareholders' meetings, such shareholders normally give third parties written authorization to vote their shares at the meeting. This authorization is called a **proxy** (from the Latin *procurare*, "to manage, take care of"). Proxies are often solicited by management, but any person can solicit proxies to concentrate voting power. Proxies have been used by a group of shareholders as a device for taking over a corporation (corporate takeovers are discussed in Chapter 28). Proxies are normally revocable (that is, they can be withdrawn), unless they are specifically designated as irrevocable. Under RMBCA 7.22(c), proxies last for eleven months, unless the proxy agreement provides for a longer period.

When shareholders want to change a company policy, they can put their idea up for a shareholder vote. They can do this by submitting a shareholder proposal to the board of directors and asking the board to include the proposal in the proxy materials that are sent to all shareholders before meetings.

The Securities and Exchange Commission (SEC), which regulates the purchase and sale of securities (see Chapter 29), has special provisions relating to proxies and shareholder proposals. SEC Rule 14a-8 requires that when a company sends proxy materials to its shareholders, the company must also include whatever proposals will be considered at the meeting and provide shareholders with the opportunity to vote on the proposals by marking and returning their proxy cards. SEC Rule 14a-8 provides that all shareholders who own stock worth at least $1,000 are eligible to submit proposals for inclusion in corporate proxy material. Only those proposals that relate to significant policy considerations must be included, however. A corporation is not required to include in proxy materials proposals that relate to "ordinary business operations."

ON THE WEB
For information on the SEC's rulings, including rulings on proxy materials, go to **http://www.sec.gov/rules/final.shtml**.

4. A director can often demand court review of removal for cause.

5. The shareholder can waive the requirement of written notice by signing a waiver form. In some states, a shareholder who does not receive written notice, but who learns of the meeting and attends without protesting the lack of notice, is said to have waived notice by such conduct. State statutes and corporate bylaws typically set forth the time within which notice must be sent, what methods can be used, and what the notice must contain.

SHAREHOLDER VOTING

Shareholders exercise ownership control through the power of their votes. Each shareholder is entitled to one vote per share, although the voting techniques that will be discussed shortly all enhance the power of the shareholder's vote. The articles of incorporation can exclude or limit voting rights, particularly for certain classes of shares. For example, owners of preferred shares are usually denied the right to vote.

BE CAREFUL Once a quorum is present, a vote can be taken even if some shareholders leave without casting their votes.

Quorum Requirements For shareholders to act during a meeting, a quorum must be present. Generally, a quorum exists when shareholders holding more than 50 percent of the outstanding shares are present. Corporate business matters are presented in the form of *resolutions,* which shareholders vote to approve or disapprove. Some state statutes have set forth specific voting requirements, and corporations' articles or bylaws must abide by these statutory requirements. Some states provide that the unanimous written consent of shareholders is a permissible alternative to holding a shareholders' meeting. Once a quorum is present, a majority vote of the shares represented at the meeting is usually required to pass resolutions.

"There is no such thing . . . as an innocent stockholder. He may be innocent in fact, but socially he cannot be held innocent. He accepts the benefits of the system. It is his business and his obligation to see that those who represent him carry out a policy which is consistent with the public welfare."

LOUIS BRANDEIS, 1856–1941 (Associate justice of the United States Supreme Court, 1916–1938)

● **EXAMPLE 27.3** Assume that Novo Pictures, Inc., has 10,000 outstanding shares of voting stock. Its articles of incorporation set the quorum at 50 percent of outstanding shares and provide that a majority vote of the shares present is necessary to pass resolutions concerning ordinary matters. Therefore, for this firm, a quorum of shareholders representing 5,000 outstanding shares must be present at a shareholders' meeting to conduct business. If exactly 5,000 shares are represented at the meeting, a vote of at least 2,501 of those shares is needed to pass a resolution. If 6,000 shares are represented, a vote of 3,001 will be required, and so on. ●

At times, a larger-than-majority vote will be required either by a state statute or by the corporate charter. Extraordinary corporate matters, such as a merger, consolidation, or dissolution of the corporation (see Chapter 28), require a higher percentage of the representatives of all corporate shares entitled to vote, not just a majority of those present at that particular meeting.

Voting Lists The corporation prepares voting lists prior to each meeting of the shareholders. Persons whose names appear on the corporation's shareholder records as owners are the ones ordinarily entitled to vote.[6] The voting list contains the name and address of each shareholder as shown on the corporate records on a given cutoff date, or record date. (Under RMBCA 7.07, the record date may be as much as seventy days before the meeting.) The voting list also includes the number of voting shares held by each owner. The list is usually kept at the corporate headquarters and is available for shareholder inspection.

Cumulative Voting Most states permit or even require shareholders to elect directors by *cumulative voting,* a method of voting designed to allow minority shareholders representation on the board of directors.[7] When cumulative voting is allowed or required, the number of members of the board to be elected is multiplied by the number of voting shares a shareholder owns. The result equals the number of votes the shareholder has, and this total can be cast for one or more nominees for director. All nominees

6. When the legal owner is deceased, bankrupt, incompetent, or in some other way under a legal disability, his or her vote can be cast by a person designated by law to control and manage the owner's property.

7. See, for example, California Corporate Code Section 708. Under RMBCA 7.28, however, no cumulative voting rights exist unless the articles of incorporation so provide.

stand for election at the same time. When cumulative voting is not required either by statute or under the articles, the entire board can be elected by a simple majority of shares at a shareholders' meeting.

Cumulative voting can best be understood by an example. • **EXAMPLE 27.4** Suppose that a corporation has 10,000 shares issued and outstanding. One group of shareholders (the minority shareholders) holds only 3,000 shares, and the other group of shareholders (the majority shareholders) holds the other 7,000 shares. Three members of the board are to be elected. The majority shareholders' nominees are Acevedo, Barkley, and Craycik. The minority shareholders' nominee is Drake. Can Drake be elected by the minority shareholders?

If cumulative voting is allowed, the answer is yes. The minority shareholders have 9,000 votes among them (the number of directors to be elected times the number of shares held by the minority shareholders equals 3 times 3,000, which equals 9,000 votes). All of these votes can be cast to elect Drake. The majority shareholders have 21,000 votes (3 times 7,000 equals 21,000 votes), but these votes have to be distributed among their three nominees. Under the principle of cumulative voting, no matter how the majority shareholders cast their 21,000 votes, they will not be able to elect all three directors if the minority shareholders cast all of their 9,000 votes for Drake, as illustrated in Exhibit 27–1. •

Other Voting Techniques Before a shareholders' meeting, a group of shareholders can agree in writing, in a *shareholder voting agreement*, to vote their shares together in a specified manner. Such agreements usually are held to be valid and enforceable. A shareholder can also appoint a voting agent and vote by proxy. As mentioned, a proxy is a written authorization to cast the shareholder's vote, and a person can solicit proxies from a number of shareholders in an attempt to concentrate voting power.

VOTING TRUST
An agreement (trust contract) under which legal title to shares of corporate stock is transferred to a trustee who is authorized by the shareholders to vote the shares on their behalf.

Another technique is for shareholders to enter into a **voting trust**, which is an agreement (a trust contract) under which legal title (record ownership on the corporate books) is transferred to a trustee who is responsible for voting the shares. The agreement can specify how the trustee is to vote, or it can allow the trustee to use his or her discretion. The trustee takes physical possession of the stock certificate and in return gives the shareholder a voting trust certificate. The shareholder retains all of the rights

EXHIBIT 27–1 RESULTS OF CUMULATIVE VOTING

This exhibit illustrates how cumulative voting gives minority shareholders a greater chance of electing a director of their choice. By casting all of their 9,000 votes for one candidate (Drake), the minority shareholders will succeed in electing Drake to the board of directors.

BALLOT	MAJORITY SHAREHOLDERS' VOTES			MINORITY SHAREHOLDERS' VOTES	DIRECTORS ELECTED
	Acevedo	Barkley	Craycik	Drake	
1	10,000	10,000	1,000	9,000	Acevedo/Barkley/Drake
2	9,001	9,000	2,999	9,000	Acevedo/Barkley/Drake
3	6,000	7,000	8,000	9,000	Barkley/Craycik/Drake

of ownership (for example, the right to receive dividend payments) except for the power to vote the shares.

Rights of Shareholders

Shareholders possess numerous rights. A significant right—the right to vote their shares—has already been discussed. We now look at some additional rights of shareholders.

STOCK CERTIFICATES

A **stock certificate** is a certificate issued by a corporation that evidences ownership of a specified number of shares in the corporation. In jurisdictions that require the issuance of stock certificates, shareholders have the right to demand that the corporation issue certificates. In most states and under RMBCA 6.26, boards of directors may provide that shares of stock be uncertificated—that is, that physical stock certificates need not be issued. In that circumstance, the corporation may be required to send the holders of uncertificated shares letters or some other form of notice containing the same information as that included on stock certificates.

Stock is intangible personal property, and the ownership right exists independently of the certificate itself. A stock certificate may be lost or destroyed, but ownership is not destroyed with it. A new certificate can be issued to replace one that has been lost or destroyed.[8] Notice of shareholders' meetings, dividends, and operational and financial reports are all distributed according to the recorded ownership listed in the corporation's books, not on the basis of possession of the certificate.

Stock certificates are displayed. To be a shareholder, is it necessary to have physical possession of a certificate? Why or why not?

STOCK CERTIFICATE
A certificate issued by a corporation evidencing the ownership of a specified number of shares in the corporation.

PREEMPTIVE RIGHTS
Rights held by shareholders that entitle them to purchase newly issued shares of a corporation's stock, equal in percentage to shares currently held, before the stock is offered to any outside buyers. Preemptive rights enable shareholders to maintain their proportionate ownership and voice in the corporation.

PREEMPTIVE RIGHTS

A **preemptive right** is a common law concept under which a preference is given to shareholders over all other purchasers to subscribe to or purchase shares of a new issue of stock in proportion to the percentage of total shares they already hold. This allows each shareholder to maintain her or his portion of control, voting power, or financial interest in the corporation. Most statutes either (1) grant preemptive rights but allow them to be negated in the corporation's articles or (2) deny preemptive rights except to the extent that they are granted in the articles. The result is that the articles of incorporation determine the existence and scope of preemptive rights. Generally, preemptive rights apply only to additional, newly issued stock sold for cash, and the preemptive rights must be exercised within a specified time period, which is usually thirty days.

• **EXAMPLE 27.5** Detering Corporation authorizes and issues 1,000 shares of stock. Lebow purchases 100 shares, making her the owner of 10 percent of the company's stock. Subsequently, Detering, by vote of the shareholders, authorizes the issuance of another 1,000 shares (by amending the articles of incorporation). This increases its capital stock to a total of 2,000 shares. If preemptive rights have been provided, Lebow can purchase one additional share of the new stock being issued for each share she cur-

8. For a lost or destroyed certificate to be reissued, a shareholder normally must furnish an indemnity bond to protect the corporation against potential loss should the original certificate reappear at some future time in the hands of a bona fide purchaser [UCC 8–302, 8–405(2)].

rently owns—or 100 additional shares. Thus, she can own 200 of the 2,000 shares outstanding, and she will maintain her relative position as a shareholder. If preemptive rights are not allowed, her proportionate control and voting power may be diluted from that of a 10 percent shareholder to that of a 5 percent shareholder because of the issuance of the additional 1,000 shares. ●

Preemptive rights can be very important for shareholders in close corporations because each shareholder owns a relatively small number of shares but controls a substantial interest in the corporation. Without preemptive rights, it would be possible for a shareholder to lose his or her proportionate control over the firm.

STOCK WARRANTS

STOCK WARRANT
A certificate that grants the owner the option to buy a given number of shares of stock, usually within a set time period.

Usually, when preemptive rights exist and a corporation is issuing additional shares, each shareholder is given **stock warrants**, which are transferable options to acquire a given number of shares from the corporation at a stated price. Warrants are often publicly traded on securities exchanges. When the option to purchase is in effect for a short period of time, the stock warrants are usually referred to as *rights*.

DIVIDENDS

As mentioned in Chapter 26, a *dividend* is a distribution of corporate profits or income *ordered by the directors* and paid to the shareholders in proportion to their respective shares in the corporation. Dividends can be paid in cash, property, stock of the corporation that is paying the dividends, or stock of other corporations.[9]

State laws vary, but each state determines the general circumstances and legal requirements under which dividends are paid. State laws also control the sources of revenue to be used; only certain funds are legally available for paying dividends. Depending on state law, dividends may be paid from the following sources:

① *Retained earnings*. All state statutes allow dividends to be paid from the undistributed net profits earned by the corporation, including capital gains from the sale of fixed assets. The undistributed net profits are called *retained earnings*.

② *Net profits*. A few state statutes allow dividends to be issued from current net profits without regard to deficits in prior years.

③ *Surplus*. A number of statutes allow dividends to be paid out of any surplus.

Illegal Dividends A dividend paid while the corporation is insolvent is automatically an illegal dividend, and shareholders may be liable for returning the payment to the corporation or its creditors. Furthermore, as just discussed, dividends are generally required by statute to be distributed only from certain authorized corporate accounts. Sometimes, dividends are improperly paid from an unauthorized account, or their payment causes the corporation to become insolvent. Generally, in such cases, shareholders must return illegal dividends only if they knew that the dividends were illegal when they received them. Whenever dividends are illegal or improper, the board of directors can be held personally liable for the amount of the payment. When directors can show that a shareholder knew that a dividend was

9. Technically, dividends paid in stock are not dividends. They maintain each shareholder's proportional interest in the corporation. On one occasion, a distillery declared and paid a "dividend" in bonded whiskey.

illegal when it was received, however, the directors are entitled to reimbursement from the shareholder.

Directors' Failure to Declare a Dividend When directors fail to declare a dividend, shareholders can ask a court to compel the directors to meet and to declare a dividend. For the shareholders to succeed, they must show that the directors have acted so unreasonably in withholding the dividend that the directors' conduct is an abuse of their discretion.

Often, large money reserves are accumulated for a bona fide purpose, such as expansion, research, or other legitimate corporate goals. The mere fact that sufficient corporate earnings or surplus is available to pay a dividend is not enough to compel directors to distribute funds that, in the board's opinion, should not be paid. The courts are reluctant to interfere with corporate operations and will not compel directors to declare dividends unless abuse of discretion is clearly shown. In the following case, the shareholders brought a court action to compel Ford Motor Company to declare a dividend.

CASE 27.2 Dodge v. Ford Motor Co.

Supreme Court of Michigan, 1919.
204 Mich. 459,
170 N.W. 668.

FACTS Henry Ford was the president and major shareholder of Ford Motor Company. In the company's early years, business expanded rapidly, and in addition to regular quarterly dividends, special dividends were often paid. By 1916, surplus above capital was still $111,960,907. That year, however, Henry Ford declared that the company would no longer pay special dividends but would put back into the business all the earnings of the company above the regular dividend of 5 percent. According to the court, Ford stated as follows: "My ambition is to employ still more men, to spread the benefits of this industrial system to the greatest possible number, to help them build up their lives and their homes. To do this, we are putting the greatest share of our profits back into the business." The minority shareholders (who owned 10 percent of the stock) filed a lawsuit in a Michigan state court against Ford and others to force the declaration of a special dividend. The court ordered the Ford directors to declare a dividend, and the case was appealed.

ISSUE Was Ford's refusal to pay a dividend an abuse of managerial discretion?

DECISION Yes. Because of the special circumstances of this case, the court compelled Ford to pay a dividend.

REASON The undisputed facts were that Ford had a surplus of $112 million—approximately $54 million in cash on hand. It had made profits of $59 million in the past year and expected to make $60 million in the coming year. The board of directors gave no reason to justify withholding a dividend. Thus, in doing so, it violated the stated purpose of the corporation's existence. According to the court, "Courts of equity will not interfere in the management of the directors unless it is clearly made to appear that they are guilty of fraud or misappropriation of the corporate funds, or refuse to declare a dividend when the corporation has a surplus of net profits which it can, without detriment to its business, divide among its stockholders, and when a refusal to do so would amount to such an abuse of discretion as would constitute a fraud, or breach of that good faith which they are bound to exercise towards the stockholders."

FOR CRITICAL ANALYSIS—Social Consideration *Generally, how can a court determine when directors should pay dividends?*

INSPECTION RIGHTS

Shareholders in a corporation enjoy both common law and statutory inspection rights.[10] The shareholder's right of inspection is limited, however, to the inspection and copying of corporate books and records for a *proper purpose*, provided the request is made in advance. The shareholder can inspect in person, or an attorney, agent, accountant, or other type of assistant can do so. The RMBCA requires the corporation to maintain an alphabetical voting list of shareholders with addresses and number of shares owned; this list must be kept open at the annual meeting for inspection by any shareholder of record [RMBCA 7.20].

The power of inspection is fraught with potential abuses, and the corporation is allowed to protect itself from them. For example, a shareholder can properly be denied access to corporate records to prevent harassment or to protect trade secrets or other confidential corporate information. Some states require that a shareholder must have held his or her shares for a minimum period of time immediately preceding the demand to inspect or must hold a minimum number of outstanding shares. The RMBCA provides, however, that every shareholder is entitled to examine specified corporate records [RMBCA 16.02].

TRANSFER OF SHARES

Stock certificates generally are negotiable and freely transferable by indorsement and delivery. Transfer of stock in closely held corporations, however, usually is restricted by the bylaws, by a restriction stamped on the stock certificate, or by a shareholder agreement (see Chapter 26). The existence of any restrictions on transferability must always be noted on the face of the stock certificate, and these restrictions must be reasonable.

Sometimes, corporations or their shareholders restrict transferability by reserving the option to purchase any shares offered for resale by a shareholder. This **right of first refusal** remains with the corporation or the shareholders for only a specified time or a reasonable time. Variations on the purchase option are possible. For example, a shareholder might be required to offer the shares to other shareholders first or to the corporation first.

RIGHT OF FIRST REFUSAL
The right to purchase personal or real property—such as corporate shares or real estate—before the property is offered for sale to others.

When shares are transferred, a new entry is made in the corporate stock book to indicate the new owner. Until the corporation is notified and the entry is complete, the current owner of record has the right to be notified of (and attend) shareholders' meetings, the right to vote the shares, the right to receive dividends, and all other shareholder rights.

CORPORATE DISSOLUTION

When a corporation is dissolved and its outstanding debts and the claims of its creditors have been satisfied, the remaining assets are distributed to the shareholders in proportion to the percentage of shares owned by each shareholder. Certain classes of preferred stock can be given priority. If no preferences to distribution of assets on liquidation are given to any class of stock, the shareholders are entitled to the remaining assets.

In some circumstances, shareholders may petition a court to have the corporation dissolved. Suppose, for example, that the minority shareholders know that the board

10. See, for example, *Schwartzman v. Schwartzman Packing Co.*, 99 N.M. 436, 659 P.2d 888 (1983).

RECEIVER
In a corporate dissolution, a court-appointed person who winds up corporate affairs and liquidates corporate assets.

of directors is mishandling corporate assets. The minority shareholders are not powerless to intervene. They can petition a court to appoint a **receiver**, who will wind up corporate affairs and liquidate the business assets of the corporation.

The RMBCA permits any shareholder to initiate such an action in any of the following circumstances [RMBCA 14.30]:

1. The directors are deadlocked in the management of corporate affairs. The shareholders are unable to break that deadlock, and irreparable injury to the corporation is being suffered or threatened.
2. The acts of the directors or those in control of the corporation are illegal, oppressive, or fraudulent.
3. Corporate assets are being misapplied or wasted.
4. The shareholders are deadlocked in voting power and have failed, for a specified period (usually two annual meetings), to elect successors to directors whose terms have expired or would have expired with the election of successors.

The Shareholder's Derivative Suit

SHAREHOLDER'S DERIVATIVE SUIT
A suit brought by a shareholder to enforce a corporate cause of action against a third person.

When those in control of a corporation—the corporate directors—fail to sue in the corporate name to redress a wrong suffered by the corporation, shareholders are permitted to do so "derivatively" in what is known as a **shareholder's derivative suit.** Some wrong must have been done to the corporation, and before a derivative suit can be brought, the shareholders must first state their complaint to the board of directors. Only if the directors fail to solve the problem or take appropriate action can the derivative suit go forward.

The right of shareholders to bring a derivative action is especially important when the wrong suffered by the corporation results from the actions of corporate directors or officers. This is because the directors and officers would probably want to prevent any action against themselves.

The shareholder's derivative suit is unusual in that those suing are not pursuing rights or benefits for themselves personally but are acting as guardians of the corporate entity. Therefore, any damages recovered by the suit normally go into the corporation's treasury, not to the shareholders personally. This is true even if the company is a small, closely held corporation. • **EXAMPLE 27.6** Suppose that a corporation is owned by two shareholders, each holding 50 percent of the corporate shares. If one of the shareholders wants to sue the other for, say, misusing corporate assets or usurping corporate opportunities, the plaintiff-shareholder would have to bring a shareholder's derivative suit (not a suit in his or her own name) because the harm complained of was suffered by the corporation, not the plaintiff personally. Thus, any damages awarded would go to the corporation, not to the plaintiff-shareholder. While this may seem unfair, there are other interests to consider—including the corporation's creditors, whose claims might not be paid if the damages were awarded to the plaintiff-shareholder and not the corporation.•

Liability of Shareholders

One of the hallmarks of the corporate organization is that shareholders are not personally liable for the debts of the corporation. If the corporation fails, shareholders can lose their investments, but that is generally the limit of their liability. As discussed in

INTERNATIONAL PERSPECTIVE

Derivative Actions in Other Nations

Today, most of the claims brought against directors and officers in the United States are those alleged in shareholders' derivative suits. Other nations, however, put more restrictions on the use of such suits. In Germany, for example, there is no provision for derivative litigation, and a corporation's duty to its employees is just as significant as its duty to the shareholder-owners of the company. The United Kingdom has no statute authorizing derivative actions, which are permitted only to challenge directors' actions that the shareholders could not legally ratify. Japan authorizes derivative actions but also permits a company to sue the plaintiff-shareholder for damages if the action is unsuccessful.

FOR CRITICAL ANALYSIS
Do corporations benefit from shareholders' derivative suits? If so, how?

Chapter 26, in certain instances of fraud, undercapitalization, or careless observance of corporate formalities, a court will pierce the corporate veil (disregard the corporate entity) and hold the shareholders individually liable. These situations are the exception, however, not the rule. A shareholder can also be personally liable in certain other rare instances. One relates to illegal dividends, which were discussed previously. Two others relate to stock subscriptions and watered stock, which we discuss here.

Sometimes stock-subscription agreements—written contracts by which one agrees to buy capital stock of a corporation—exist prior to incorporation. Normally, these agreements are treated as continuing offers and are irrevocable (for up to six months under RMBCA 6.20). Once the corporation has been formed, it can sell shares to shareholder investors. In either situation, once the subscription agreement or stock offer is accepted, a binding contract is formed. Any refusal to pay constitutes a breach resulting in the personal liability of the shareholder.

Shares of stock can be paid for by property or by services rendered instead of cash. They cannot be purchased with promissory notes, however. The general rule is that for **par-value shares** (shares that have a specific face value, or formal cash-in value, written on them, such as one penny or one dollar), the corporation must receive a value at least equal to the par-value amount. For **no-par shares** (shares that have no face value—no specific amount printed on their face), the corporation must receive the value of the shares as determined by the board or the shareholders when the stock was issued. When the corporation issues shares for less than these stated values, the shares are referred to as **watered stock.**[11] Usually, the shareholder who receives watered stock must pay the difference to the corporation (the shareholder is personally liable). In some states, the shareholder who receives watered stock may be liable to creditors of the corporation for unpaid corporate debts.

PAR-VALUE SHARES
Corporate shares that have a specific face value, or formal cash-in value, written on them, such as one dollar.

NO-PAR SHARES
Corporate shares that have no face value–that is, no specific dollar amount is printed on their face.

WATERED STOCK
Shares of stock issued by a corporation for which the corporation receives, as payment, less than the stated value of the shares.

• **EXAMPLE 27.7** Suppose that during the formation of a corporation, Gomez, one of the incorporators, transfers his property, Sunset Beach, to the corporation for 10,000 shares of stock. The stock has a par value of $100 per share, and thus the total price of the 10,000 shares is $1 million. After the property is transferred and the shares are issued, Sunset Beach is carried on the corporate books at a value of $1 million. On appraisal, it is discovered that the market value of the property at the time of transfer

11. The phrase *watered stock* was originally used to describe cattle that—kept thirsty during a long drive—were allowed to drink large quantities of water just prior to their sale. The increased weight of the "watered stock" allowed the seller to reap a higher profit.

was only $500,000. The shares issued to Gomez are therefore watered stock, and he is liable to the corporation for the difference.●

Duties of Majority Shareholders

In some cases, a majority shareholder is regarded as having a fiduciary duty to the corporation and to the minority shareholders. This occurs when a single shareholder (or a few shareholders acting in concert) owns a sufficient number of shares to exercise *de facto* control over the corporation. In these situations, when the majority shareholder sells her or his shares, the shareholder owes a fiduciary duty to the minority shareholders because such a sale is, in fact, a transfer of control of the corporation.

A breach of fiduciary duty also occurs when the majority shareholders of a closely held corporation use their control to their own advantage and exclude the minority from the benefits of participating in the firm unless, of course, there is a genuine business purpose for the exercise of control. ● **EXAMPLE 27.8** In one case, a family member who was a minority shareholder in a family-owned corporation was fired after working for the business for forty-five years. The court concluded that the majority shareholders had breached their fiduciary duty to the minority shareholder by firing him, even though state law allowed employees to be hired and fired "at will" (the employment-at-will doctrine will be discussed in Chapter 34).[12]●

Such a breach of fiduciary duties by those who control a closely held corporation normally constitutes what is known as *oppressive conduct.* The court in the following case was asked to examine a pattern of conduct by those in control and determine whether that conduct was oppressive.

12. *Pedro v. Pedro,* 489 N.W.2d 798 (Minn.App. 1992).

CASE 27.3 Hayes v. Olmsted & Associates, Inc.

Oregon Court of Appeals, 2001.
173 Or.App. 259,
21 P.3d 178.
http://www.publications.ojd.state.or.us[a]

FACTS Olmsted & Associates, Inc. (O&A), was a food-brokerage firm in Oregon. Under O&A's bylaws, the board of directors and the shareholders were to hold annual meetings at which the price of O&A stock was to be set. The bylaws also stated that terminated employees were to sell their stock to the firm. The voting shareholders, including David Arbanas, Arthur Olmsted, and Dan Hayes, were also the firm's officers and managers. In 1991, management of the firm was shifted to a "team," which consisted of the voting shareholders and the directors. In 1995, the team implemented a bonus compensation plan. Arbanas took his bonus in cash. During a corporate restructuring, an "Executive Committee," consisting of Arbanas, Olmsted, and two nonshareholders, assumed the functions of the board. The board and the shareholders stopped meeting. Arbanas exchanged his bonus for additional voting shares, and voting control shifted to Olmsted and Arbanas. In 1996, the members of the Executive Committee secretly voted to pay themselves bonuses of more than $100,000 each. Hayes asked about the bonuses, but was denied the information. When he complained, he was fired. O&A offered to buy his stock for $67 per share. Hayes claimed that the price per share was too low. When he was removed from the board, Hayes filed a suit in an Oregon state court against Olmsted, Arbanas, and O&A, alleging, among other things, breach of fiduciary duty and that the court deter-

a. In the left-hand frame, click on "Court of Appeals Opinions." When that page opens, in the "Cases decided in 2001" row, click on "March." In the result, in the "03/28/01" section, click on the name of the case to access the opinion. The Oregon Judicial Department maintains this Web site.

CASE 27.3—Continued

mine whether he should have been offered a higher price for his shares. The court declared the price to be $67 per share. Hayes appealed to a state intermediate appellate court, asserting that the price should be higher, in part because Olmsted and Arbanas had engaged in oppressive conduct.

ISSUE Did the majority shareholders act oppressively toward Hayes?

DECISION Yes. The state intermediate appellate court reversed part of the lower court's judgment and remanded the case for the entry of a modified judgment to reflect a higher price for Hayes's stock.

REASON The appellate court concluded that "minority shareholders were not given the formal and required opportunities to participate in or comment upon major changes in direction of O&A." The court explained that "Olmsted and Arbanas assumed control of O&A by creating a *de facto* Executive Committee in violation of the bylaws. From 1995 to 1997, when plaintiff was fired, the Executive Committee did not observe corporate formalities and failed to hold regular meetings of the corporation's Board of Directors and shareholders. Executive Committee members paid themselves bonuses that were not authorized by or reported to the Board of Directors, also in violation of the bylaws. They kept their bonuses secret from the other shareholders and board members, despite plaintiff's requests for the bonus information, again in violation of the bylaws. . . . When plaintiff complained about his exclusion from corporate decisions and information, the Executive Committee fired him."

FOR CRITICAL ANALYSIS—Economic Consideration *What should be the basis for a "fair and reasonable" price for minority shareholders' stock in a case involving oppressive conduct by majority shareholders?*

APPLICATION Law and the Corporation . . .

Retention Policies for E-Documents*

If a corporation becomes the target of a civil lawsuit or criminal investigation, the company may be required to turn over any documents in its files relating to the matter during the discovery stage of litigation. These documents may include legal documents, contracts, e-mail, faxes, letters, interoffice memorandums, notebooks, diaries, and other materials, even if they are kept in personal files in the homes of directors or officers. Under the current Federal Rules of Civil Procedure, which govern civil litigation procedures (see Chapter 3), a defendant in a lawsuit must disclose all relevant electronic data compilations and documents, as well as all relevant paper documents.

Although certain documents or data might free a company of any liability arising from a claim, others might serve to substantiate a civil claim or criminal charge. It is also possible that information contained in a document–an interoffice e-mail memo, for example (or even a memo referring to that memo)–could be used to convince a jury that the company or its directors or officers condoned a certain action when they denied condoning it.

WHICH E-DOCUMENTS SHOULD BE RETAINED?

How does a company decide which e-documents should be retained and which should be destroyed? By law, corporations are required to keep certain types of documents, such as those specified in the *Code of Federal Regulations* and in regulations issued by government agencies, such as the Occupational Safety and Health Administration. Generally, any records that the company is not legally required to keep or that the

*This *Application* is not meant to substitute for the services of an attorney who is licensed to practice law in your state.

APPLICATION **Law and the Corporation . . .**

Retention Policies for E-Documents—continued

company is sure it will have no legal need for should be removed from the files and destroyed. A partnership agreement, for example, should be kept. A memo about last year's company picnic, however, should be removed from the files and destroyed; obviously, it is just taking up storage space.

Modifications May Be Necessary during an Investigation

If the company becomes the target of an investigation, it usually must modify its document-retention policy until the investigation has been completed. Company officers, after receiving a subpoena to produce specific types of documents, should instruct the appropriate employees not to destroy relevant papers that would otherwise be disposed of as part of the company's normal document-retention program.

Generally, to avoid being charged with obstruction of justice, company officials must always exercise good faith in deciding which documents should or should not be destroyed when attempting to comply with a subpoena. The specter of criminal prosecution would appear to encourage the retention of even those documents that are only remotely related to the dispute–at least until it has been resolved.

Checklist for a Document-Retention Policy

1. Let employees know not only which e-documents should be retained and deleted but also which types of documents should not be created in the first place.
2. Find out which documents must be retained under the *Code of Federal Regulations* and under other government agency regulations to which your corporation is subject.
3. Retain other e-documents only if their retention is in the corporation's interest.
4. If certain corporate documents are subpoenaed, modify your document-retention policy to retain any document that is even remotely related to the dispute until the legal action has been resolved.

Key Terms

business judgment rule 738
no-par share 747
par-value share 747
preemptive right 742
proxy 739
quorum 732
receiver 746
right of first refusal 745
shareholder's derivative suit 746
stock certificate 742
stock warrant 743
tender offer 735
voting trust 741
watered stock 747

Chapter Summary Corporate Directors, Officers, and Shareholders

Role of Directors (See pages 731–733.)	1. *Election of directors*—The first board of directors is usually appointed by the incorporators; thereafter, directors are elected by the shareholders. Directors usually serve a one-year term, although the term can be longer and staggered terms are permitted under most state statutes.

Chapter Summary Corporate Directors, Officers, and Shareholders—continued

Role of Directors—continued	2. *Directors' qualifications and compensation*—Few qualifications are required; a director can be a shareholder but is not required to be. Compensation is usually specified in the corporate articles or bylaws. 3. *Board of directors' meetings*—The board of directors conducts business by holding formal meetings with recorded minutes. The date of regular meetings is usually established in the corporate articles or bylaws; special meetings can be called, with notice sent to all directors. Quorum requirements vary from state to state; usually, a quorum is a majority of the corporate directors. Voting must usually be done in person, and in ordinary matters only a majority vote is required. 4. *Rights of directors*—Directors' rights include the rights of participation, inspection, compensation, and indemnification. 5. *Directors' management responsibilities*—Directors are responsible for declaring and paying corporate dividends to shareholders; authorizing major corporate decisions; appointing, supervising, and removing corporate officers and other managerial employees; determining employees' compensation; making financial decisions necessary to the management of corporate affairs; and issuing authorized shares and bonds. Directors may delegate some of their responsibilities to executive committees and corporate officers and executives.
Role of Corporate Officers and Executives (See pages 733–734.)	Corporate officers and other executive employees are normally hired by the board of directors. In most states, a person can hold more than one office and can be both an officer and a director of a corporation. The rights of corporate officers and executives are defined by employment contracts. The duties of corporate officers are the same as those of directors.
Duties of Directors and Officers (See pages 734–737.)	1. *Duty of care*—Directors are obligated to act in good faith, to use prudent business judgment in the conduct of corporate affairs, and to act in the corporation's best interests. If a director fails to exercise this duty of care, he or she can be answerable to the corporation and to the shareholders for breaching the duty. 2. *Duty of loyalty*—Directors have a fiduciary duty to subordinate their own interests to those of the corporation in matters relating to the corporation. 3. *Conflicts of interest*—To fulfill their duty of loyalty, directors and officers must make a full disclosure of any potential conflicts of interest between their personal interests and those of the corporation.
Liability of Directors and Officers (See pages 737–738.)	Corporate directors and officers are personally liable for their own torts and crimes; additionally, they may be held personally liable for the torts and crimes committed by corporate personnel under their direct supervision (see Chapters 6 and 24). The *business judgment rule* immunizes a director from liability for a corporate decision as long as the decision was within the power of the corporation and the authority of the director to make and was an informed, reasonable, and loyal decision.
Role of Shareholders (See pages 738–742.)	1. *Shareholders' powers*—Shareholders' powers include the approval of all fundamental changes affecting the corporation and the election of the board of directors. 2. *Shareholders' meetings*—Shareholders' meetings must occur at least annually; special meetings can be called when necessary. Notice of the date, time, and place of the meeting (and its purpose, if it is specially called) must be sent to shareholders. Shareholders may vote by proxy (authorizing someone else to vote their shares) and may submit proposals to be included in the company's proxy materials sent to shareholders before meetings. 3. *Shareholder voting*—Shareholder voting requirements and procedures are as follows: a. A minimum number of shareholders (a quorum—generally, more than 50 percent of shares held) must be present at a meeting for business to be conducted; resolutions are passed (usually) by simple majority vote.

(continued)

Chapter Summary Corporate Directors, Officers, and Shareholders—continued

Role of Shareholders—continued	b. The corporation must prepare voting lists of shareholders on record prior to each shareholders' meeting. c. Cumulative voting may or may not be required or permitted. Cumulative voting gives minority shareholders a better chance to be represented on the board of directors. d. A shareholder voting agreement (an agreement of shareholders to vote their shares together) is usually held to be valid and enforceable. e. A shareholder may appoint a proxy (substitute) to vote her or his shares. f. A shareholder may enter into a voting trust agreement by which title (record ownership) of his or her shares is given to a trustee, and the trustee votes the shares in accordance with the trust agreement.
Rights of Shareholders (See page 742–746.)	Shareholders have numerous rights, which may include the following: 1. The right to a stock certificate, preemptive rights, and the right to stock warrants (depending on the corporate charter). 2. The right to obtain a dividend (at the discretion of the directors). 3. Voting rights. 4. The right to inspect the corporate records. 5. The right to transfer shares (this right may be restricted in close corporations). 6. The right to a share of corporate assets when the corporation is dissolved. 7. The right to sue on behalf of the corporation (bring a shareholder's derivative suit) when the directors fail to do so.
Liability of Shareholders (See pages 746–748.)	Shareholders may be liable for the retention of illegal dividends, for breach of a stock-subscription agreement, and for the value of watered stock.
Duties of Majority Shareholders (See pages 748–749.)	In certain situations, majority shareholders may be regarded as having a fiduciary duty to minority shareholders and will be liable if that duty is breached.

For Review

① What are the duties of corporate directors and officers?

② Directors are expected to use their best judgment in managing the corporation. What must directors do to avoid liability for honest mistakes of judgment and poor business decisions?

③ What is a voting proxy? What is cumulative voting?

④ If a group of shareholders perceives that the corporation has suffered a wrong and the directors refuse to take action, can the shareholders compel the directors to act? If so, how?

⑤ From what sources may dividends be paid legally? In what circumstances is a dividend illegal? What happens if a dividend is illegally paid?

Questions and Case Problems

27–1. Rights of Shareholders. Dmitri has acquired one share of common stock of a multimillion-dollar corporation with over 500,000 shareholders. Dmitri's ownership is so small that he is questioning what his rights are as a shareholder. For example, he wants to know whether this one share entitles him to attend and vote at shareholders' meetings, inspect the corporate books, and receive periodic dividends. Discuss Dmitri's rights in these matters.

27–2. Voting Techniques. Algonquin Corp. has issued and has outstanding 100,000 shares of common stock. Four stockholders own 60,000 of these shares, and for the past six years they have nominated a slate of people for membership on the board, all of whom have been elected. Sergio and twenty other shareholders, owning 20,000 shares, are dissatisfied with corporate management and want a representative on the board who shares their views. Explain under what circumstances Sergio and the minority shareholders can elect their representative to the board.

27–3. Duties of Directors. Starboard, Inc., has a board of directors consisting of three members (Ellsworth, Green, and Morino) and approximately five hundred shareholders. At a regular meeting of the board, the board selects Tyson as president of the corporation by a two-to-one vote, with Ellsworth dissenting. The minutes of the meeting do not register Ellsworth's dissenting vote. Later, during an audit, it is discovered that Tyson is a former convict and has openly embezzled $500,000 from Starboard. This loss is not covered by insurance. The corporation wants to hold directors Ellsworth, Green, and Morino liable. Ellsworth claims no liability. Discuss the personal liability of the directors to the corporation.

27–4. Liability of Shareholders. Mallard has made a preincorporation subscription agreement to purchase 500 shares of a newly formed corporation. The shares have a par value of $100 per share. The corporation is formed, and it accepts Mallard's subscription. Mallard transfers a piece of land he owns to the corporation as payment for 250 of the shares, and the corporation issues 250 shares for it. Mallard pays for the other 250 shares with cash. One year later, with the corporation in serious financial difficulty, the board declares and pays a $5-per-share dividend. It is now learned that the land transferred by Mallard had a market value of $18,000. Discuss any liability that shareholder Mallard has to the corporation or to the creditors of the corporation.

27–5. Duties of Directors. Overland Corp. is negotiating with Wharton Construction Co. for the renovation of Overland's corporate headquarters. Wharton, the owner of Wharton Construction, is also one of the five members of the board of directors of Overland. The contract terms are standard for this type of contract. Wharton has previously informed two of the other Overland directors of his interest in the construction company. Overland's board approves the contract on a three-to-two vote, with Wharton voting with the majority. Discuss whether this contract is binding on the corporation.

27–6. Rights of Shareholders. Melissa and Gary Callicoat each owned 50 percent of Callicoat, Inc. They were also Callicoat's only directors. They could not agree on the day-to-day management of the firm. They also could not agree on whether a debt owed to Arthur Baz was a personal or corporate debt. Melissa suggested that they dissolve the corporation. Gary refused and shut her out from the operations of the firm. Melissa filed a petition in an Ohio state court against Gary and Callicoat, asking the court to dissolve the corporation. On what basis might the court order the dissolution? [*Callicoat v. Callicoat,* 73 Ohio Misc.2d 38, 657 N.E.2d 874 (1994)]

27–7. Duty of Loyalty. Mackinac Cellular Corp. offered to sell Robert Broz a license to operate a cellular phone system in Michigan. Broz was a director of Cellular Information Systems, Inc. (CIS). CIS, as a result of bankruptcy proceedings, was in the process of selling its cellular holdings. Broz did not formally present the opportunity to the CIS board, but he told some of the firm's officers and directors, who replied that CIS was not interested. At the time, PriCellular, Inc., a firm that was interested in the Michigan license, was attempting to buy CIS. Without telling PriCellular, Broz bought the license himself. After PriCellular took over CIS, the company filed a suit in a Delaware state court against Broz, alleging that he had usurped a corporate opportunity. For what reasons might a court decide that Broz had done nothing wrong? Discuss. [*Broz v. Cellular Information Systems, Inc.,* 673 A.2d 148 (Del. 1996)]

27–8. Business Judgment Rule. The board of directors of Baltimore Gas and Electric Company (BGE) recommended a merger with Potomac Electric Power Company (PEPCO). After full disclosure, the BGE shareholders approved the merger. On the ground that each BGE director stood a chance of being named to the new company's board, Janice Wittman, a BGE shareholder, filed a suit in a Maryland state court against the directors, alleging, among other things, that they were prohibited from deciding whether to recommend the merger. Did the directors breach their duty of care by voting in favor of the merger? How should the court rule? Discuss. [*Wittman v. Crooke,* 120 Md.App. 369, 707 A.2d 422 (1998)]

27–9. Business Judgment Rule. Charles Pace and Maria Fuentez were shareholders of Houston Industries, Inc. (HII), and employees of Houston Lighting & Power, a subsidiary of HII, when they lost their jobs because of a company-wide reduction in its work force. Pace, as a shareholder, three times wrote to HII, demanding that the board of directors terminate certain HII directors and officers and file a suit to recover damages for breach of fiduciary duty. Three times, the directors referred the charges to board committees and an outside law firm, which found that the facts did not support the charges. The board also received input from federal regulatory authorities about the facts behind some of the charges. The board notified Pace that it was refusing his demands. In response, Pace and Fuentez filed a shareholder's derivative suit in a Texas state court against Don Jordan and the other HII directors, contending that the board's investigation was inadequate. The defendants filed a motion for summary judgment, arguing that the suit was barred by the business judgment rule. Are the defendants right? How should the court rule? Why? [*Pace v. Jordan,* 999 S.W.2d 615 (Tex.App.—Houston [1 Dist.] 1999)]

TEST YOUR KNOWLEDGE—ANSWER ON THE WEB

27–10. Atlas Food Systems & Services, Inc., based in South Carolina, was a food vending service that provided refreshments to factories and other businesses. Atlas was a closely held corporation. John Kiriakides was a minority shareholder of Atlas. Alex Kiriakides was the majority shareholder. Throughout most of Atlas's history, Alex was the chairman of the board, which included John as a director. In 1995, while John was the president of the firm, the board and shareholders decided to convert Atlas to an S corporation. A few months later, however, Alex, without calling a vote, decided that the firm would not convert. In 1996, a dispute arose over Atlas's contract to buy certain property. John and others decided not to buy it. Without consulting anyone, Alex elected to go through with the sale. Within a few days, Alex refused to allow John to stay on as president. Two months later, Atlas offered to buy John's interest in the firm for almost $2 million. John refused, believing the offer was too low. John filed a suit in a South Carolina state court against Atlas and Alex, seeking, among other things, to force a buyout of John's shares. On what basis might the court grant John's request? Discuss. [*Kiriakides v. Atlas Food Systems & Services, Inc.*, 541 S.E.2d 257 (S.C. 2001)]

A QUESTION OF ETHICS AND SOCIAL RESPONSIBILITY

27–11. McQuade was the manager of the New York Giants baseball team. McQuade and John McGraw purchased shares in the National Exhibition Co., the corporation that owned the Giants, from Charles Stoneham, who owned a majority of National Exhibition's stock. As part of the transaction, each of the three agreed to use his best efforts to ensure that the others continued as directors and officers of the organization. Stoneham and McGraw, however, subsequently failed to use their best efforts to ensure that McQuade continued as the treasurer and a director of the corporation, and McQuade sued to compel specific performance of the agreement. A court reviewing the matter noted that McQuade had been "shabbily" treated by the others but refused to grant specific performance on the ground that the agreement was void because it interfered with the duty of the others as directors to do what was best for all the shareholders. Although shareholders may join to elect corporate directors, they may not join to limit the directors' discretion in managing the business affairs of an organization; the directors must retain their independent judgment. Consider the implications of the case, and address the following questions. [*McQuade v. Stoneham*, 263 N.Y. 323, 189 N.E. 234 (1934)]

1. Given that even the court sympathized with McQuade, was it ethical to put the business judgment of the directors ahead of an otherwise valid promise they had made?
2. Are there practical considerations that support the court's decision? How can directors perform their proper tasks if their judgment is constrained by earlier agreements with some of the shareholders?

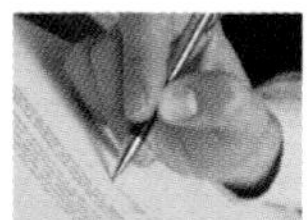

FOR CRITICAL ANALYSIS

27–12. In general, courts are reluctant to grant shareholders' petitions for corporate dissolution in all but the most extreme circumstances, as when corporate directors or shareholders are deadlocked and the corporation suffers as a result. Rather, a court will attempt to "save" the corporate entity whenever possible. Why is this?

Internet Activities

Go to the *Business Law Today* home page at **http://blt.westbuslaw.com**. Select "Interactive Study Center" and then click on "Chapter 27." There you will find the following Internet research exercise that you can perform to learn more about the liability of corporate directors and officers:

Activity 27–1: Liability of Directors and Officers

Before the Test

Go to the *Business Law Today* home page at **http://blt.westbuslaw.com**. Click on "Interactive Quizzes." You will find at least twenty interactive questions relating to this chapter.

CHAPTER 28

Corporate Merger, Consolidation, and Termination

"Business is a combination of war and sport."

André Maurois, 1885–1967
(French author and historian)

CHAPTER CONTENTS

LEARNING OBJECTIVES

After reading this chapter, you should be able to answer the following questions:

① What is the difference between a corporate merger and a corporate consolidation?

② What are the four steps of the merger or consolidation procedure?

③ Under what circumstances is a corporation that purchases the assets of another corporation responsible for the liabilities of the selling corporation?

④ What actions might a target corporation take to resist a takeover attempt?

⑤ What are the two ways in which a corporation can be voluntarily dissolved? Under what circumstances might a corporation be involuntarily dissolved by state action?

Corporations increase the size of their operations for a number of reasons. During the last two decades of the twentieth century, the acquisition of corporations by other corporations became a common phenomenon, and corporate takeovers have continued in the twenty-first century. Observers of the numerous corporate takeovers occurring in the business world today might well conclude, as André Maurois did, that business is indeed a "combination of war and sport."

A corporation typically extends its operations by combining with another corporation through a merger, a consolidation, a purchase of assets, or a purchase of a controlling interest in the other corporation. This chapter will examine these four types of corporate expansion. Dissolution and liquidation are the combined processes by which a corporation terminates its existence. The last part of this chapter will discuss the typical reasons for—and methods used in—terminating a corporation's existence.

Merger and Consolidation

The terms *merger* and *consolidation* often are used interchangeably, but they refer to two legally distinct proceedings. The rights and liabilities of the corporation, its shareholders, and its creditors are the same for both, however.

MERGER

MERGER
A contractual and statutory process in which one corporation (the surviving corporation) acquires all of the assets and liabilities of another corporation (the merged corporation). The shareholders of the merged corporation either are paid for their shares or receive shares in the surviving corporation.

A **merger** involves the legal combination of two or more corporations in such a way that only one of the corporations continues to exist. • **EXAMPLE 28.1** Corporation A and Corporation B decide to merge. It is agreed that A will absorb B, so on merging, B ceases to exist as a separate entity, and A continues as the *surviving corporation.* • Exhibit 28–1 graphically illustrates this process.

After the merger, A is recognized as a single corporation, possessing all the rights, privileges, and powers of itself and B. It automatically acquires all of B's property and assets without the necessity of formal transfer. Additionally, A becomes liable for all of B's debts and obligations. Finally, A's articles of incorporation are deemed amended to include any changes that are stated in the *articles of merger* (a document setting forth the terms and conditions of the merger that is filed with the secretary of state).

In a merger, the surviving corporation inherits the disappearing corporation's preexisting legal rights and obligations. For example, if the disappearing corporation had a right of action against a third party, the surviving corporation can bring suit after the merger to recover the disappearing corporation's damages. The corporation statutes of many states provide that a successor (surviving) corporation inherits a **chose**[1] **in action** (a right to sue for a debt or sum of money) from a merging corporation as a matter of law. The common law similarly recognizes that, following a merger, a chose in action

CHOSE IN ACTION
A right that can be enforced in court to recover a debt or to obtain damages.

1. The word *chose* is French for "thing."

EXHIBIT 28–1 MERGER

In this illustration, Corporation A and Corporation B decide to merge. They agree that A will absorb B, so after the merger, B no longer exists as a separate entity, and A continues as the surviving corporation.

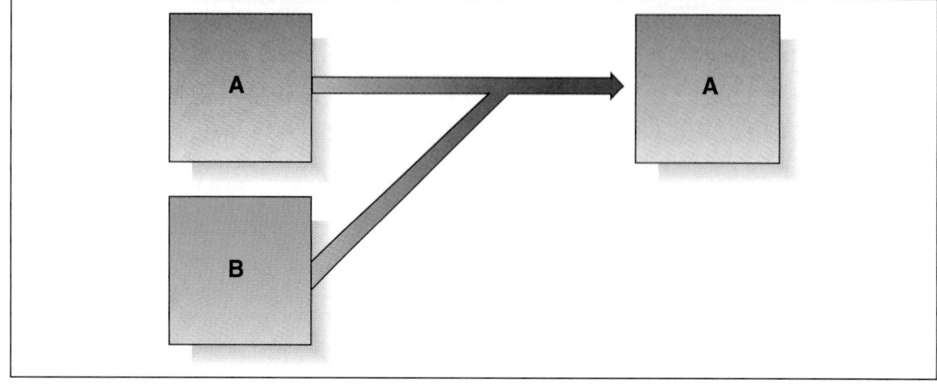

to enforce a property right will vest with the successor (surviving) corporation, and no right of action will remain with the disappearing corporation.

ETHICAL ISSUE 28.1

Should corporate law apply to a merger of labor unions?

Suppose that two labor unions, both of which are unincorporated associations, merge into one union. Does the successor (surviving) union inherit the obligations of the disappearing union, just as a corporate successor inherits the obligations of the disappearing corporation in a corporate merger? This question, which has both legal and ethical implications, arose in a case involving a merger of two Teamsters local unions. When Teamsters Local 513 merged into Teamsters Local 115, an older employee of Local 513 quit and applied for a pension. The pension was denied because Local 513 had not made any contributions to the pension fund on his behalf, as was required by its rules. Local 115, the successor union, denied any liability for Local 513's failure to contribute to the fund. In the lawsuit that followed, the court had to decide whether corporate law governing mergers should apply to the merger of two unincorporated associations. The court ruled that it should, stating that "when two unincorporated local unions merge, the survivor assumes the liabilities of the extinct constituent even if it does not have pre-merger notice of the debt." The court explained that this is a nearly universal principle for corporations, and the same logic applies to unions. Employees of unincorporated associations deserve the same protection as employees of corporations.[2]

CONSOLIDATION

CONSOLIDATION
A contractual and statutory process in which two or more corporations join to become a completely new corporation. The original corporations cease to exist, and the new corporation acquires all their assets and liabilities.

In a **consolidation**, two or more corporations combine in such a way that each corporation ceases to exist and a new one emerges. • **EXAMPLE 28.2** Corporation A and Corporation B consolidate to form an entirely new organization, Corporation C. In the process, A and B both terminate, and C comes into existence as an entirely new entity. Exhibit 28–2 on the next page graphically illustrates this process.

As a result of the consolidation, C is recognized as a new corporation and a single entity; A and B cease to exist. C inherits all of the rights, privileges, and powers that A and B previously held. Title to any property and assets owned by A and B passes to C without formal transfer. C assumes liability for all of the debts and obligations owed by A and B. The terms and conditions of the consolidation are set forth in the *articles of consolidation,* which are filed with the secretary of state. These articles *take the place of* A's and B's original corporate articles and are thereafter regarded as C's corporate articles. •

PROCEDURE FOR MERGER OR CONSOLIDATION

All states have statutes authorizing mergers and consolidations for domestic (in-state) corporations, and most states allow the combination of domestic and foreign (out-of-state) corporations. Although the procedures vary somewhat among jurisdictions, the basic requirements for a merger or a consolidation are as follows:

① The board of directors of each corporation involved must approve a merger or consolidation plan.

2. *Teamsters Pension Trust Fund of Philadelphia & Vicinity v. Littlejohn,* 155 F.3d 206 (3d Cir. 1998).

EXHIBIT 28–2 **CONSOLIDATION**

In this illustration, Corporation A and Corporation B consolidate to form an entirely new organization, Corporation C. In the process, A and B terminate, and C comes into existence as an entirely new entity.

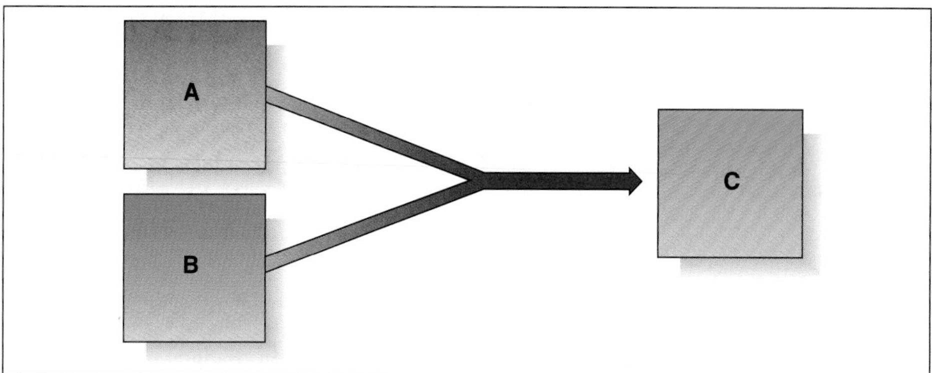

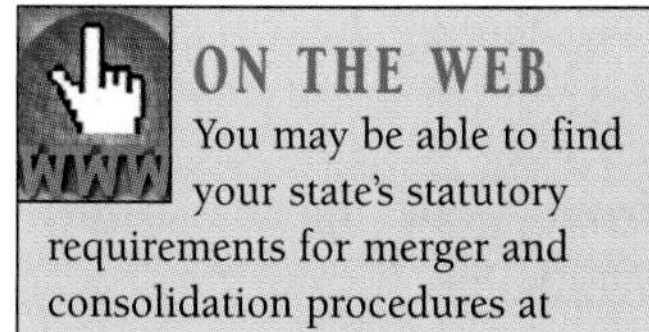

ON THE WEB You may be able to find your state's statutory requirements for merger and consolidation procedures at **http://www.law.cornell.edu/topics/state_statutes.html#corporations.**

② The shareholders of each corporation must approve the plan, by vote, at a shareholders' meeting. Most state statutes require the approval of two-thirds of the outstanding shares of voting stock, although some states require only a simple majority, and others require a four-fifths vote. Frequently, statutes require that each class of stock approve the merger; thus, the holders of nonvoting stock must also approve. A corporation's bylaws can provide for a stricter requirement.

③ Once approved by all of the directors and shareholders, the plan (articles of merger or consolidation) is filed, usually with the secretary of state.

④ When state formalities are satisfied, the state issues a certificate of merger to the surviving corporation or a certificate of consolidation to the newly consolidated corporation.

SHORT-FORM MERGER
A merger between a subsidiary corporation and a parent corporation that owns at least 90 percent of the outstanding shares of each class of stock issued by the subsidiary corporation. Short-form mergers can be accomplished without the approval of the shareholders of either corporation.

Section 11.04 of the Revised Model Business Corporation Act (RMBCA) provides for a simplified procedure for the merger of a substantially owned subsidiary corporation into its parent corporation. Under these provisions, a **short-form merger** can be accomplished *without the approval of the shareholders* of either corporation. The short-form merger can be used only when the parent corporation owns at least 90 percent of the outstanding shares of each class of stock of the subsidiary corporation. The simplified procedure requires that a plan for the merger be approved by the board of directors of the parent corporation before it is filed with the state. A copy of the merger plan must be sent to each shareholder of record of the subsidiary corporation.

Shareholder Approval

REMEMBER State statutes, articles of incorporation, and corporate bylaws can require the approval of more than a majority of shares for some extraordinary matters.

Shareholders invest in a corporate enterprise with the expectation that the board of directors will manage the enterprise and will approve ordinary business matters. Actions taken on extraordinary matters must be authorized by the board of directors and the shareholders. Often, modern statutes require that the shareholders approve certain types of extraordinary matters—such as the sale, lease, or exchange of all or substantially all corporate assets outside of the corporation's regular course of business. Other examples of matters requiring shareholder approval include amendments to the articles of incorporation, transactions concerning merger or consolidation, and dissolution.

Hence, when any extraordinary matter arises, the corporation must proceed as authorized by law to obtain the approval of the shareholders and the board of directors. Sometimes, a transaction can be structured in such a way that shareholder approval is not required, but in that event, a court will use its equity powers to require such approval. To determine the nature of the transaction, the courts will look not only to the details of the transaction but also to its consequences.

ETHICAL ISSUE 28.2

Why should shareholders be required to approve certain types of corporate actions?

The rule requiring shareholder approval for certain types of corporate actions protects the shareholders' interests in the corporate enterprise. Clearly, the shareholder-owners have a stake in the corporation's survival and profitability. Sometimes, corporate directors and officers may take certain actions whose impact is not readily apparent to shareholders; for example, various corporate assets might be sold over a period of time so that the shareholders do not realize how significantly the total number of assets is dwindling. In such a situation, however, a court normally will use its equity powers to require the approval of the shareholders. For example, in one case a corporation was formed for the purpose of engaging in the restaurant business. One of the three shareholders, who was the corporate president, sold off the assets of the company until only one restaurant remained. When the president entered into a contract to sell this remaining asset, the other two shareholders sought to have a court issue an injunction prohibiting the sale. The court did so, in accordance with state law, which prohibited the sale of all or substantially all of a corporation's assets without shareholder approval. The court stated that the purpose of the law was "to protect the shareholders from . . . the destruction of the means to accomplish the purpose or objects for which the corporation was incorporated and actually performs."[3]

APPRAISAL RIGHTS

What if a shareholder disapproves of a merger or a consolidation but is outvoted by the other shareholders? The law recognizes that a dissenting shareholder should not be forced to become an unwilling shareholder in a corporation that is new or different from the one in which the shareholder originally invested. The shareholder has the right to dissent and may be entitled to be paid the fair value for the number of shares held on the date of the merger or consolidation. This right is referred to as the shareholder's **appraisal right**.

APPRAISAL RIGHT
The right of a dissenting shareholder, who objects to an extraordinary transaction of the corporation (such as a merger or a consolidation), to have his or her shares appraised and to be paid the fair value of those shares by the corporation.

Appraisal rights are available only when a state statute specifically provides for them. Appraisal rights normally extend to regular mergers, consolidations, short-form mergers, and sales of substantially all of the corporate assets not in the ordinary course of business.

In a short-form merger, is the exercise of an appraisal right a minority shareholder's only remedy when he or she dissents from the merger? That was the question in the following case.

3. *Schwadel v. Uchitel,* 455 So.2d 401 (Fla.App. 1984).

CASE 28.1 Glassman v. Unocal Exploration Corp.

Delaware Supreme Court, 2001.
777 A.2d 242.

FACTS Unocal Corporation is an earth resources company primarily engaged in the exploration for, and production of, crude oil and natural gas. Unocal owned approximately 96 percent of the stock of Unocal Exploration Corporation (UXC), an oil and gas company operating in the Gulf of Mexico. In 1991, low natural gas prices caused a drop in both companies' revenues and earnings. Unocal decided that by merging with UXC, it could reduce expenses and save money. The boards of directors of the two firms appointed special committees to consider a short-form merger. The UXC committee agreed to a merger exchange ratio of about half a share of Unocal stock for each UXC share. Glassman and other UXC minority shareholders filed a suit in a Delaware state court against Unocal, alleging in part that the firm had breached its fiduciary duty of "entire fairness and full disclosure." The court held that the only remedy in connection with this short-form merger was the minority's appraisal right. The plaintiffs appealed to the Delaware Supreme Court.

ISSUE Is exercising appraisal rights the only recourse for a minority stockholder who is dissatisfied with a short-form merger?

DECISION Yes. The Delaware Supreme Court affirmed the decision of the lower court, holding that in these circumstances appraisal was the exclusive remedy.

REASON The Delaware Supreme Court noted first that the state's short-form merger statute specifically provides for appraisal rights. The court then explained, "In a short-form merger, there is no agreement of merger negotiated by two companies; there is only a unilateral act—a decision by the parent company that its 90% owned subsidiary shall no longer exist as a separate entity. The minority stockholders receive no advance notice of the merger; their directors do not consider or approve it; and there is no vote. Those who object are given the right to obtain fair value for their shares through appraisal. * * * If * * * the corporate fiduciary sets up negotiating committees, hires independent financial and legal experts, etc., then it will have lost the very benefit provided by the statute—a simple, fast and inexpensive process for accomplishing a merger."

FOR CRITICAL ANALYSIS—Ethical Consideration *Does the court's holding in this case mean that a parent corporation does not have a duty of full disclosure in a short-form merger? Explain why or why not.*

Appraisal Rights—Procedures Shareholders may lose their appraisal rights if they do not follow precisely the elaborate statutory procedures. Whenever they lose the right to an appraisal, dissenting shareholders must go along with the transaction despite their objections. One of the usual basic requirements is that the dissenting shareholders must file a written notice of dissent prior to the vote of the shareholders on the proposed transaction. This notice of dissent is also basically a notice to all shareholders of the costs that dissenting shareholders may impose should the merger or consolidation be approved. In addition, after approval, the dissenting shareholders must make a written demand for payment and for the fair value of their shares.

"The greatest of all gifts is the power to estimate things at their true worth."

François La Rochefoucauld, 1613–1680 (French writer and moralist)

Appraisal Rights and Shareholder Status In some jurisdictions, once dissenting shareholders elect appraisal rights under a statute, the shareholders lose their shareholder status. Without that status, the shareholders cannot vote, receive dividends, or sue to enjoin whatever action prompted their dissent. In some of those jurisdictions, statutes provide, or courts have held, that shareholder status may be reinstated during the appraisal process (for example, if a shareholder decides to withdraw from the process and the corporation approves). In other jurisdictions, shareholder status may not be reinstated until the appraisal is concluded. Even if an individual loses his or her shareholder status, courts may allow the individual to sue on the ground of fraud or other illegal conduct associated with the merger.

Valuation of Shares Valuation of shares is often a point of contention between a dissenting shareholder and the corporation. RMBCA 13.01 provides that the "fair value of shares" normally is the value on the day prior to the date on which the vote was taken. The corporation must make a written offer to purchase a dissenting shareholder's stock; the offer should be accompanied by a current balance sheet and income statement for the corporation. If the shareholder and the corporation do not agree on the fair value, a court will determine it.

Purchase of Assets

ON THE WEB A searchable database of court cases dealing with corporate litigation, including lawsuits stemming from purchases of corporate assets, is available at

http://corporate.law.widener.edu.

When a corporation acquires all or substantially all of the assets of another corporation by direct purchase, the purchasing, or *acquiring*, corporation simply extends its ownership and control over more physical assets. Because no change in the legal entity occurs, the acquiring corporation is not required to obtain shareholder approval for the purchase.[4] The U.S. Department of Justice and the Federal Trade Commission, however, significantly constrain and often prohibit mergers that could result from a purchase of assets, including takeover bids (see Chapter 32).

Note that the corporation that is selling all its assets is substantially changing its business position and perhaps its ability to carry out its corporate purposes. For that reason, the corporation whose assets are being sold must obtain the approval of both the board of directors and the shareholders. In most states and under RMBCA 13.02, a dissenting shareholder of the selling corporation can demand appraisal rights. (Occasionally, disputes arise over whether particular property or property rights were included in "all of the assets" being sold. For an example of one such dispute, see this chapter's *Business Law in the Online World* feature on page 763.)

Generally, a corporation that purchases the assets of another corporation is not responsible for the liabilities of the selling corporation. Exceptions to this rule are made in certain circumstances, however. In any of the situations listed below, the acquiring corporation will be held to have assumed *both* the assets and the liabilities of the selling corporation.

RECALL In a merger or consolidation, the surviving corporation inherits the disappearing corporation's rights *and* obligations.

1. When the purchasing corporation impliedly or expressly assumes the seller's liabilities.
2. When the sale amounts to what is in fact a merger or consolidation.
3. When the purchaser continues the seller's business and retains the same personnel (same shareholders, directors, and officers).
4. When the sale is fraudulently executed to escape liability.

In the following case, the court was asked to determine whether a transfer of assets between two corporations was for the fraudulent purpose of escaping liability.

4. If the acquiring corporation plans to pay for the assets with its own corporate stock and not enough authorized unissued shares are available, the shareholders must vote to approve the issuance of additional shares by amendment of the corporate articles. Additionally, acquiring corporations whose stock is traded in a national stock exchange can be required to obtain their own shareholders' approval if they plan to issue a significant number of shares, such as a number equal to 20 percent or more of the outstanding shares.

CASE 28.2 Eagle Pacific Insurance Co. v. Christensen Motor Yacht Corp.

Supreme Court of Washington, 1998.
135 Wash.2d 894,
959 P.2d 1052.

HISTORICAL AND SOCIAL SETTING *When one corporation sells all of its assets to another, common ownership of the two corporations may arouse suspicion that the transaction is fraudulent, and liability may be imposed for any obligations that might otherwise be avoided. As early as 1933, the Washington Supreme Court said, "Undoubtedly, it is the general rule that mere common ownership of the capital stock or interlocking directorates, or like evidences of close association, will not justify the courts in disregarding corporate identities, but where * * * the identities are so confused and intermingled as to result in probable fraud upon third persons dealing with the corporations or either of them, whether fraud be actually intended or not, then the * * * rule will apply."*[a]

FACTS Christensen Motor Yacht Corporation (CMYC) was organized to build yachts. Eagle Pacific Insurance Company issued workers' compensation policies to CMYC but canceled the policies when CMYC failed to pay the premiums. CMYC had several contracts with buyers, but the yachts had not been completed. CMYC thus lacked the ability to pay its debts. David Christensen, the chief executive officer and sole shareholder of CMYC, created a new corporation, Christensen Shipyards, Limited (CSL), to complete the boats. CMYC transferred its employees, facilities, and contracts to CSL. Meanwhile, claims had been filed against the Eagle policies, and Eagle filed a suit in a Washington state court against CMYC to collect the unpaid premiums. The court awarded Eagle $268,443. Because CMYC was insolvent, Eagle sought to recover the debt from others, including CSL as a successor corporation to CMYC. Christensen testified that he had effected the transfer between CMYC and CSL to avoid creditors and "save the business." The court ruled that CSL was liable for CMYC's debt to Eagle as a successor corporation. A state intermediate appellate court upheld the ruling. CSL appealed to the Washington Supreme Court.

a. *Associated Oil Co. v. Seiberling Rubber Co.,* 172 Wash. 204, 19 P.2d 940 (1933).

ISSUE Is CSL liable for CMYC's debt to Eagle as a successor corporation?

DECISION Yes. The Washington Supreme Court affirmed the lower court's judgment. The state supreme court held that "the transfer of assets from CMYC to CSL fits the definition of a fraudulent transfer."

REASON The court emphasized that Christensen admitted the yacht contracts were transferred to CSL to enable the construction to continue and to avoid paying creditors' bills. Because the assets were transferred to CSL to avoid the reach of the creditors, the transaction was fraudulent. "The fact that the transaction was designed to 'save the business' does not defeat imposition of successor liability."

FOR CRITICAL ANALYSIS—Ethical Consideration *If, after completing the boats, Christensen had paid all of the creditors of both corporations, would the transfer of assets from CMYC to CSL have been more acceptable?*

Purchase of Stock

TARGET CORPORATION
The corporation to be acquired in a corporate takeover; a corporation to whose shareholders a tender offer is submitted.

An alternative to the purchase of another corporation's assets is the purchase of a substantial number of the voting shares of its stock. This enables the acquiring corporation to control the **target corporation** (the corporation being acquired). The acquiring corporation deals directly with the target company's shareholders in seeking to purchase the shares they hold. It does this by making a *tender offer* to all of the shareholders of the target corporation. The tender offer is publicly advertised and addressed to all shareholders of the target company. The price of the stock in the tender offer is generally higher than the market price of the target stock prior to the announcement of the

BUSINESS LAW: //in the Online World

Who Owns the Web Site?

Most contracts to purchase the assets of another corporation are performed with little difficulty. At times, however, a dispute may arise over some matter connected with the transaction. In one case, for example, the dispute had to do with ownership rights in a Web site. The case arose after 1-800-Postcards, Inc. (1-800), purchased the assets of Popsmear, Inc., which owned and operated a Web site postcard-advertising business. The Web site address for Popsmear's business was **http://www.1800Postcards.com**. According to the purchase agreement, Popsmear's trademark rights were included in "all of the assets" being sold by Popsmear to 1-800.

The Problem with the Web Site

Problems arose when the sole owner and shareholder of Popsmear, James Morel, changed the password to the Web site. This meant that 1-800 was unable to make any administrative changes to the Web site or to create and change its e-mail boxes. When 1-800 objected to Morel's action, Morel contended that he personally, and not Popsmear, was the registered owner of the domain name and, as such, had a right to change the password. 1-800 then sued Morel for fraud and breach of contract and asked the court for a preliminary injunction against Morel's changing of the password. After all, argued 1-800, by making it impossible for 1-800 to control the Web site, Morel, in effect, had been "selling nothing" when it sold 1-800 its "trademark rights."

Did the Assets Being Sold Include the Domain Name Rights?

In determining whether to grant the preliminary injunction, the court had to decide whether the sale of assets included the domain name rights. The question was complicated by the fact that Morel was the registered owner of the domain name. The court, however, held that this "nuance" was of little significance because both Morel and Popsmear were parties to the purchase agreement. The court also emphasized that the parties "quite likely understood that the domain name registration for the Web site was among the 'assets of the business' irrespective of whether record title was in [Popsmear] or its sole shareholder, Morel." Concluding that 1-800 would likely succeed in its case against Morel and Popsmear, the court granted 1-800's request for a preliminary injunction.[a]

FOR CRITICAL ANALYSIS

Would the court have reached the same conclusion if Morel had not been a party to the purchase agreement? Why or why not?

a. *1-800-Postcards, Inc. v. Morel,* 153 F.Supp.2d 359 (S.D.N.Y. 2001).

tender offer. The higher price induces shareholders to tender their shares to the acquiring firm. The tender offer can be conditioned on the receipt of a specified number of outstanding shares by a specified date. The offering corporation can make an *exchange tender offer* in which it offers target stockholders its own securities in exchange for their target stock. In a *cash tender offer,* the offering corporation offers the target stockholders cash in exchange for their target stock.

Federal securities laws strictly control the terms, duration, and circumstances under which most tender offers are made. In addition, a majority of states have passed takeover statutes that impose additional regulations on tender offers.

A firm may respond to a tender offer in numerous ways. Sometimes, a target firm's board of directors will see a tender offer as favorable and will recommend to the shareholders that they accept it. To resist a takeover, a target company may make a *self-tender,* which is an offer to acquire stock from its own shareholders and thereby retain corporate control. Alternatively, a target corporation might resort to one of several other tactics to resist a takeover (see Exhibit 28–3 on page 764). In one commonly used tactic, known as a "poison pill," a target company gives its shareholders rights to

EXHIBIT 28–3 THE TERMINOLOGY OF TAKEOVER DEFENSES

TERM	DEFINITION
Crown Jewel	When threatened with a takeover, management makes the company less attractive to the raider by selling to a third party the company's most valuable asset (hence the term *crown jewel*).
Golden Parachute	When a takeover is successful, top management is usually changed. With this in mind, a company may establish special termination or retirement benefits that must be paid to top management if they are "retired." In other words, a departing high-level manager's parachute will be "golden" when he or she is forced to "bail out" of the company.
Greenmail	To regain control, a target company may pay a higher-than-market price to repurchase the stock that the acquiring corporation bought. When a takeover is attempted through a gradual accumulation of target stock rather than a tender offer, the intent may be to get the target company to buy back the accumulated shares at a premium price—a concept similar to blackmail.
Lobster Trap	Lobster traps are designed to catch large lobsters but to allow small lobsters to escape. In the "lobster trap" defense, holders of convertible securities (corporate bonds or stock that is convertible into common shares) are prohibited from converting the securities into common shares if the holders already own, or would own after conversion, 10 percent or more of the voting shares of stock.
Pac-Man	Named after the Atari video game, this is an aggressive defense by which the target corporation attempts its own takeover of the acquiring corporation.
Poison Pill	The target corporation gives its stockholders the right to purchase additional shares at low prices when there is a takeover attempt. This makes the takeover undesirably or even prohibitively expensive for the acquiring corporation.
Scorched Earth	The target corporation sells off assets or divisions or takes out loans that it agrees to repay in the event of a takeover, thus making itself less financially attractive to the acquiring corporation.
Shark Repellent	To make a takeover more difficult, a target company may change its articles of incorporation or bylaws. For example, the bylaws may be amended to require that a large number of shareholders approve the firm's combination. This tactic casts the acquiring corporation in the role of a shark that must be repelled.
White Knight	The target corporation solicits a merger with a third party, which then makes a better (often simply a higher) tender offer to the target's shareholders. The third party that "rescues" the target is the "white knight."

purchase additional shares at low prices when there is a takeover attempt. The use of poison pills prevents takeovers by making takeovers prohibitively expensive.

DISSOLUTION
The formal disbanding of a partnership or a corporation. Dissolution of a corporation can take place by (1) an act of the state legislature, (2) agreement of the shareholders and the board of directors, (3) the expiration of a time period stated in the certificate of incorporation, or (4) court order.

LIQUIDATION
In regard to corporations, the process by which corporate assets are converted into cash and distributed among creditors and shareholders according to specific rules of preference.

Termination

The termination of a corporation's existence has two phases. **Dissolution** is the legal death of the artificial "person" of the corporation. **Liquidation** is the process by which corporate assets are converted into cash and distributed among creditors and shareholders according to specific rules of preference (see Chapter 26).

DISSOLUTION

Dissolution of a corporation can be brought about in any of the following ways:

① An act of a legislature in the state of incorporation.

A store advertises a liquidation sale. When a corporate liquidation is voluntary, who acts as the trustee of the corporate assets? Who acts as the trustee if the corporate liquidation is involuntary?

② Expiration of the time provided in the certificate of incorporation.

③ Voluntary approval of the shareholders and the board of directors.

④ Unanimous action by all shareholders.[5]

⑤ A court decree brought about by the attorney general of the state of incorporation for any of the following reasons: (a) the failure to comply with administrative requirements (for example, failure to pay annual franchise taxes, to submit an annual report, or to have a designated registered agent), (b) the procurement of a corporate charter through fraud or misrepresentation on the state, (c) the abuse of corporate powers (*ultra vires* acts), (d) the violation of the state criminal code after the demand to discontinue has been made by the secretary of state, (e) the failure to commence business operations, or (f) the abandonment of operations before starting up [RMBCA 14.20].

"Lots of folks confuse bad management with destiny."
KIN (F. MCKINNEY) HUBBARD, 1868–1930
(American humorist and journalist)

As discussed in Chapter 27, sometimes a shareholder or a group of shareholders petitions a court for corporate dissolution. For example, the board of directors may be deadlocked. Courts hesitate to order involuntary dissolution in such circumstances unless there is specific statutory authorization to do so. If the shareholders cannot resolve the deadlock and if it will irreparably injure the corporation, however, the court will proceed with an involuntary dissolution. Courts can also dissolve a corporation in other circumstances, such as when the controlling shareholders or directors are committing fraudulent or oppressive acts or when management is misapplying or wasting corporate assets [RMBCA 14.30].

In the following case, a shareholder sued to have a corporation dissolved because he and the other shareholders could not suspend their disputes long enough to elect directors or even to choose a neutral third party to, in effect, arbitrate and select directors for them.

5. This is permitted under Delaware law—see Delaware Code Section 275(c)—but not under the RMBCA.

CASE 28.3 Chance v. Norwalk Fast Oil, Inc.

Appellate Court of Connecticut, 1999.
55 Conn.App. 272,
739 A.2d 1275.

FACTS Norwalk Fast Oil, Inc., was incorporated in Connecticut. Albert Chance owned 40 percent of the stock, and Richard Kosminoff also held 40 percent of the stock. Seymour and Morris Epstein each owned 10 percent of the stock but gave their voting rights to Chance and Kosminoff in equal shares. Thus, Chance and Kosminoff each held 50 percent of the voting rights. A shareholders' agreement provided that "in the event that a stalemate is reached after tallying the votes on any substantive issue affecting the Corporation, then it is hereby agreed that the stalemate shall be broken by Chance and Kosminoff each selecting the same third person to whom the proposed question shall be submitted, and his decision on the matter shall be binding upon the Corporation and all of its shareholders." In 1990, disputes arose between the shareholders, and they stopped holding annual meetings. In 1997, Chance called a special shareholders' meeting to elect directors. Chance and Kosminoff could not agree on whom to elect, nor could they agree on a third party to whom they should submit the issue under the stalemate provision. When they were no longer on speaking terms, Chance filed a suit in a Connecticut state court against Norwalk, Kosminoff, and the Epsteins, asking for the dissolution of Norwalk. The defendants filed a motion to dismiss on the basis of the stalemate provision. The court ordered Norwalk dissolved. The defendants appealed to a state intermediate appellate court.

ISSUE Did the trial court err in ordering that Norwalk be dissolved?

DECISION No. The state intermediate appellate court affirmed the judgment of the lower court.

REASON The appellate court concluded that Norwalk could not function with control equally divided between shareholders who could not agree on a board of directors, could not hold annual shareholders' meetings, were involved in litigation against each other, and were not on speaking terms. The court explained, "It is fundamental to the concept of a corporation that its affairs are to be controlled by a board of directors elected by a majority of the stockholders * * * . In the instant case, there is no such board and no such board can be elected. Consequently, there has not been and cannot be any deliberative control of the company by a board of directors. The corporation is a mere shell inhabited by a business. * * * The trial court, therefore, properly concluded that there is no more chance of breaking the deadlock between the parties in the future than there has been in the past."

FOR CRITICAL ANALYSIS—Social Consideration *Generally, courts are reluctant to order the dissolution of a corporation (except in extreme circumstances, such as in this case). Why is this?*

LIQUIDATION

CONTRAST Except during liquidation, directors do not act as trustees of the corporate assets. Although they are in positions of control over the corporation, they do not hold title to its property.

When dissolution takes place by voluntary action, the members of the board of directors act as trustees of the corporate assets. As trustees, they are responsible for winding up the affairs of the corporation for the benefit of corporate creditors and shareholders. This makes the board members personally liable for any breach of their fiduciary trustee duties.

Liquidation can be accomplished without court supervision unless the members of the board do not wish to act as trustees of the corporate assets, or unless shareholders or creditors can show cause to the court why the board should not be permitted to assume the trustee function. In either situation, the court will appoint a receiver to wind up the corporate affairs and liquidate corporate assets. A receiver is always appointed by the court if the dissolution is involuntary.

Key Terms

Chapter Summary Corporate Merger, Consolidation, and Termination

Merger and Consolidation (See pages 756–761.)	1. *Merger*—The legal combination of two or more corporations, the result of which is that the surviving corporation acquires all the assets and obligations of the other corporation, which then ceases to exist. 2. *Consolidation*—The legal combination of two or more corporations, the result of which is that each corporation ceases to exist and a new one emerges. The new corporation assumes all the assets and obligations of the former corporations. 3. *Procedure*—Determined by state statutes. Basic requirements are the following: a. The board of directors of each corporation involved must approve the merger or consolidation plan. b. The shareholders of each corporation must approve the merger or consolidation plan at a shareholders' meeting. c. Articles of merger or consolidation (the plan) must be filed, usually with the secretary of state. d. The state issues a certificate of merger (or consolidation) to the surviving (or newly consolidated) corporation. 4. *Short-form merger (parent-subsidiary merger)*—Possible when the parent corporation owns at least 90 percent of the outstanding shares of each class of stock of the subsidiary corporation. a. Shareholder approval is not required. b. The merger must be approved only by the board of directors of the parent corporation. c. A copy of the merger plan must be sent to each shareholder of record. d. The merger plan must be filed with the state. 5. *Appraisal rights*—Rights of dissenting shareholders (given by state statute) to receive the *fair value* for their shares when a merger or consolidation takes place. If the shareholder and the corporation do not agree on the fair value, a court will determine it.
Purchase of Assets (See pages 761–762.)	A purchase of assets occurs when one corporation acquires all or substantially all of the assets of another corporation. 1. *Acquiring corporation*—The acquiring (purchasing) corporation is not required to obtain shareholder approval; the corporation is merely increasing its assets, and no fundamental business change occurs. 2. *Acquired corporation*—The acquired (purchased) corporation is required to obtain the approval of both its directors and its shareholders for the sale of its assets, because this creates a substantial change in the corporation's business position.

(continued)

Chapter Summary Corporate Merger, Consolidation, and Termination—continued

Purchase of Stock (See pages 762–764.)	A purchase of stock occurs when one corporation acquires a substantial number of the voting shares of the stock of another (target) corporation. 1. *Tender offer*—A public offer to all shareholders of the target corporation to purchase its stock at a price that is generally higher than the market price of the target stock prior to the announcement of the tender offer. Federal and state securities laws strictly control the terms, duration, and circumstances under which most tender offers are made. 2. *Target responses*—Ways in which target corporations respond to takeover bids. These include self-tender (the target firm's offer to acquire its own shareholders' stock), poison pills, and other strategies—see Exhibit 28–3.
Termination (See pages 764–766.)	The termination of a corporation involves the following two phases: 1. *Dissolution*—The legal death of the artificial "person" of the corporation. Dissolution can be brought about in any of the following ways: a. An act of a legislature in the state of incorporation. b. Expiration of the time provided in the certificate of incorporation (corporate charter). c. Voluntary approval of the shareholders and the board of directors. d. Unanimous action by all shareholders. e. Court decree. 2. *Liquidation*—The process by which corporate assets are converted into cash and distributed to creditors and shareholders according to specified rules of preference. May be supervised by members of the board of directors (when dissolution is voluntary) or by a receiver appointed by the court to wind up corporate affairs.

For Review

① What is the difference between a corporate merger and a corporate consolidation?

② What are the four steps of the merger or consolidation procedure?

③ Under what circumstances is a corporation that purchases the assets of another corporation responsible for the liabilities of the selling corporation?

④ What actions might a target corporation take to resist a takeover attempt?

⑤ What are the two ways in which a corporation can be voluntarily dissolved? Under what circumstances might a corporation be involuntarily dissolved by state action?

Questions and Case Problems

28–1. Consolidations. Determine which of the following situations describes a consolidation:

(a) Arkon Corp. purchases all of the assets of Botrek Co.
(b) Arkon Corp. and Botrek Co. combine their firms, with Arkon Corp. as the surviving corporation.
(c) Arkon Corp. and Botrek Co. agree to combine their assets, dissolve their old corporations, and form a new corporation under a new name.
(d) Arkon Corp. agrees to sell all its accounts receivable to Botrek Co.

28–2. Corporate Combinations. Jolson is chairman of the board of directors of Artel, Inc., and Douglas is chairman of the board of directors of Fox Express, Inc. Artel is a manufacturing corporation, and Fox Express is a transportation corporation. Jolson and Douglas meet to consider the possibility of combining their corporations and activities into a single corporate entity. They consider two alternative courses of action: Artel could acquire all of the stock and assets of Fox Express, or the corporations could combine to form a new corporation, called A&F Enterprises, Inc. Both chairmen are concerned about the necessity of a formal transfer of property, liability for existing debts, and the problem of amending the articles of incorporation. Discuss what the two proposed combinations are called and the legal effect each has on the transfer of property, the liabilities of the combined corporations, and the need to amend the articles of incorporation.

28–3. Mergers. Tally Ho Co. was merged into Perfecto Corp., with Perfecto being the surviving corporation in the merger. Hanjo, a creditor of Tally Ho, brought suit against Perfecto Corp. for payment of the debt. The directors of Perfecto refused to pay, stating that Tally Ho no longer existed and that Perfecto had never agreed to assume any of Tally Ho's liabilities. Discuss fully whether Hanjo will be able to recover from Perfecto.

28–4. Purchase of Assets. Fuju Enterprises, Inc., purchased all the assets of Grosmont Corp. The directors of both corporations approved the sale, and 80 percent of Grosmont's shareholders approved. The shareholders of Fuju Enterprises, however, were never consulted. Some of these shareholders claimed that the purchase was invalid. Are they correct?

28–5. Purchase of Assets. MRS Manufacturing, Inc., manufactured tractors, which it sold to Glades Equipment, Inc. Glades Equipment sold one of the tractors to the U.S. Sugar Corp. Later, Glade and Grove Supply, Inc., bought the Glades Equipment dealership under a contract that stated the sale covered only such property "as [Glades Equipment] has on hand at the time of the . . . sale." Daniel Brown, an employee of the U.S. Sugar Corp., was operating an MRS tractor when it rolled over and killed him. His wife, Patricia, filed a product liability suit against, among others, Glade and Grove. What factors will the court consider in determining whether Glade and Grove is liable? [*Brown v. Glade and Grove Supply, Inc.*, 647 So.2d 1033 (Fla.App. 1994)]

28–6. Appraisal Rights. Travelers Corp. announced that it would merge with Primerica Corp. At a special shareholders' meeting, a vote of the Travelers shareholders revealed that 95 percent approved of the merger. Robert Brandt and other shareholders who did not approve of the merger sued Travelers and others, complaining that the defendants had not obtained "the highest possible price for shareholders." Travelers asked the court to dismiss the suit, contending that Brandt and the others had, as a remedy for their complaint, their statutory appraisal rights. On what basis might the court dismiss the suit? Discuss. [*Brandt v. Travelers Corp.*, 44 Conn.Supp. 12, 665 A.2d 616 (1995)]

28–7. Corporate Dissolution. Jerry Yarmouth incorporated J&R Interiors, Inc., and was its president, secretary, and sole shareholder. J&R failed to file annual reports and pay annual fees, however, and was involuntarily dissolved by the state. More than a year later, Yarmouth bought a workbench in J&R's name from Equipto Division of Aurora Equipment Co. When the bill was not paid, Equipto filed a suit in a Washington state court against Yarmouth, claiming that he was personally liable for payment. Yarmouth argued that he was not personally liable because he had acted as an agent for J&R. Does a corporation continue to exist after it is dissolved? If so, can it continue to conduct business? In whose favor should the court rule in this case, and why? [*Equipto Division Aurora Equipment Co. v. Yarmouth*, 83 Wash.App. 817, 924 P.2d 405 (1996)]

28–8. Purchase of Assets. Ernie Gross and his brother started Sealomatic Electronics Corp. in the 1940s, later changing the name to Solidyne Corp. Sealomatic became a division of Solidyne, which continued to make heat-sealing machines under the brand name Sealomatic. Gross bought other heat-sealing equipment makers, including Thermex and Thermatron, which became other divisions of Solidyne. After the brothers died in 1981, Solidyne was sold, and its heat-sealing equipment divisions were consolidated into a single division, Thermex-Thermatron. The new division, with its assets and liabilities, was resold to TTI Acquisitions, which merged to become Thermex-Thermatron, Inc. Thermex-Thermatron continued to use Solidyne customer lists. The names of former Solidyne divisions were on the window of Thermex-Thermatron's public sales office. Listings in phone directories maintained and paid for by Thermex-Thermatron continued to use the names of Solidyne and its former divisions. Meanwhile, Solidyne was completely dissolved. Juanita Rosales, an employee of Perfect Plastics Products, was using a Solidyne Sealomatic machine made in 1969 when it collapsed on her hand. She was seriously injured. She filed a suit in a California state court against Thermex-Thermatron and others. Is Thermex-Thermatron liable for her injury? If so, on what basis? If not, why not? How should the court rule? Explain. [*Rosales v. Thermex-Thermatron, Inc.*, 67 Cal.App.4th 187, 78 Cal.Rptr.2d 861 (1998)]

28–9. Dissolution. In 1988, Farad Mohammed and Syed Parveen formed Hina Pharmacy, Health & Beauty Aids, Inc., to operate a pharmacy in New York. Syed, an experienced pharmacist, contributed his expertise and $7,000. Farad contributed $120,000. Each took 50 percent of the Hina stock. Farad assigned his shares to his brother Azam, and Syed assigned his to his wife Aisha. A dispute soon arose over the disparity in capital contributions. The parties held only one shareholders' meeting, and they never attempted to elect directors. Syed later claimed that Azam, who exercised sole control over the daily management of Hina, kept 80 percent of the profits. Azam argued that Syed had agreed to work for 20 percent of the profits plus a salary. Syed stopped working at the pharmacy in 1994. Aisha filed a petition in a New York state court to dissolve Hina. Should the court grant the petition? If so, on what basis? If not, why not? [*In re Parveen*, 259 A.D.2d 389, 687 N.Y.S.2d 90 (1 Dept. 1999)]

TEST YOUR KNOWLEDGE—ANSWER ON THE WEB

28–10. In 1996, Robert McClellan, a licensed contractor doing business as McClellan Design and Construction, entered into a contract with Peppertree North Condominium Association, Inc., to do earthquake repair work on

Peppertree's seventy-six–unit condominium complex in Northridge, California. McClellan completed the work, but Peppertree failed to pay. In an arbitration proceeding against Peppertree to collect the amount due, McClellan was awarded $141,000, plus 10 percent interest, attorneys' fees, and costs. McClellan filed a suit in a California state court against Peppertree to confirm the award. Meanwhile, the Peppertree board of directors filed articles of incorporation for Northridge Park Townhome Owners Association, Inc., and immediately transferred Peppertree's authority, responsibilities, and assets to the new association. Two weeks later, the court issued a judgment against Peppertree. When McClellan learned about the new association, he filed a motion asking the court to add Northridge as a debtor to the judgment. Should the court grant the motion? Why or why not? [*McClellan v. Northridge Park Townhome Owners Association, Inc.*, 89 Cal.App.4th 746, 107 Cal.Rptr.2d 702 (2 Dist. 2001)]

A QUESTION OF ETHICS AND SOCIAL RESPONSIBILITY

28–11. In a corporate merger, Diamond Shamrock retained its corporate identity, and Natomas Corp. was absorbed into Diamond's corporate hierarchy. Five inside directors (directors who are also officers of the corporation) of Natomas had "golden parachutes," which were incorporated into the merger agreement. (*Golden parachutes* are special benefits provided to a corporation's top managers in the event that the company is taken over and they are forced to leave.) The terms of the parachute agreements provided that each of the five individuals would receive a payment equal to three years' compensation in the event that they left their positions at Natomas at any time for any reason other than termination for just cause. Three of the five voluntarily left their positions after three years. Under the terms of their parachute agreements, they collected over $10 million. A suit challenging the golden parachutes was brought by Gaillard, a Natomas shareholder. A trial court granted the defendants' motion for summary judgment; the court sustained the golden parachutes on the ground that the directors were protected by the business judgment rule in effecting the agreement. The appellate court held that the business judgment rule does not apply in a review of the conduct of inside directors and remanded the case for trial. [*Gaillard v. Natomas*, 208 Cal.App.3d 1250, 256 Cal.Rptr. 702 (1989)]

1. Regardless of the legal issues, are golden parachutes ethical in a general sense? Discuss.
2. What practical considerations would lead a corporation to grant its top management such seemingly one-sided agreements?
3. In the *Gaillard* case, how would your views be affected by evidence showing that the golden parachutes had been developed and presented to the board by the very individuals who were the beneficiaries of the agreements—that is, by the five inside directors?

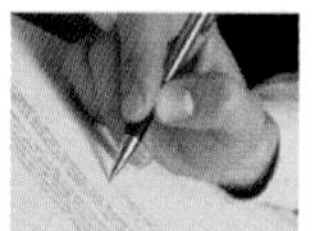

FOR CRITICAL ANALYSIS

28–12. A corporation that purchases the assets of another corporation generally is not liable for the obligations and duties of the predecessor corporation. Exceptions to this rule are made in certain circumstances, such as when the purchasing corporation assumes the liabilities, fraud is involved, or the transaction is actually a merger or merely a change of name. Why are these exceptions made?

Internet Exercises

Go to the *Business Law Today* home page at **http://blt.westbuslaw.com**. Select "Interactive Study Center" and then click on "Chapter 28." There you will find the following Internet research exercise that you can perform to learn more about mergers:

Activity 28–1: Mergers

Before the Test

Go to the *Business Law Today* home page at **http://blt.westbuslaw.com**. Click on "Interactive Quizzes." You will find at least twenty interactive questions relating to this chapter.

CHAPTER 29

Investor Protection and Online Securities Offerings

"It shall be unlawful for any person in the offer or sale of any security . . . to engage in any transaction, practice, or course of business which operates or would operate as a fraud or deceit upon the purchaser."

Securities Act of 1933, Section 17

CHAPTER CONTENTS

LEARNING OBJECTIVES

After reading this chapter, you should be able to answer the following questions:

① What is meant by the term *securities*?

② What are the two major statutes regulating the securities industry? When was the Securities and Exchange Commission created, and what are its major purposes and functions?

③ What is insider trading? Why is it prohibited?

④ What are some of the features of state securities laws?

⑤ How are securities laws being applied in the online environment?

After the stock market crash of 1929, many members of Congress argued in favor of regulating securities markets. Basically, legislation for such regulation was enacted to provide investors with more information to help them make buying and selling decisions about **securities**—generally defined as any documents evidencing corporate ownership (stock) or debts (bonds)—and to prohibit deceptive, unfair, and manipulative practices. Today, the sale and transfer of securities are heavily regulated by federal and state statutes and by government agencies.

The online world has brought some dramatic changes to securities offerings and regulation. Certain businesses can now raise funds via the Internet. Others allow their shares to be traded via chat rooms. Offering materials can be transmitted on the Web and by using CD-ROMs. The use of the Internet to purchase and sell securities has raised numerous questions: Should the

SECURITY
Generally, a stock certificate, bond, note, debenture, warrant, or other document given as evidence of an ownership interest in a corporation or as a promise of repayment by a corporation.

LANDMARK IN THE LAW
The Securities and Exchange Commission

In 1931, the Senate passed a resolution calling for an extensive investigation of securities trading. The investigation led, ultimately, to the passage by Congress of the Securities Act of 1933, which is also known as the *truth-in-securities* bill. In the following year, Congress passed the Securities Exchange Act. This 1934 act created the Securities and Exchange Commission (SEC).

Major Responsibilities of the SEC The SEC was created as an independent regulatory agency whose function was to administer the 1933 and 1934 acts. Its major responsibilities in this respect are as follows:

1. Requiring disclosure of facts concerning offerings of securities listed on national securities exchanges and of certain securities traded over the counter (OTC).
2. Regulating the trade in securities on the thirteen national and regional securities exchanges and in the over-the-counter markets.
3. Investigating securities fraud.
4. Regulating the activities of securities brokers, dealers, and investment advisers and requiring their registration.
5. Supervising the activities of mutual funds.
6. Recommending administrative sanctions, injunctive remedies, and criminal prosecution against those who violate securities laws. (The SEC can bring enforcement actions for civil violations of federal securities laws. The Fraud Section of the Criminal Division of the Department of Justice prosecutes criminal violations.)

The SEC's Expanding Regulatory Powers Since its creation, the SEC's regulatory functions have gradually been increased by legislation granting it authority in different areas. For example, to further curb securities fraud, the Securities Enforcement

rules about disclosure be applied to company-created Web sites? Can the Securities and Exchange Commission (SEC) regulate offshore offerings made via the Web? Finally, can the SEC effectively "patrol" cyberspace to curb securities fraud? The SEC enforcement mechanism for online fraudulent activities has just begun to develop, and so, too, has the law with respect to it.

NOTE Congress intended the federal securities laws to protect the public from unethical business practices.

In this chapter, we discuss the major laws governing securities offerings and trading. We then look at how these laws are being adapted to the online environment. First, though, it is necessary to understand the paramount role played by the SEC in the regulation of federal securities laws. Because of its importance in this area, we examine the origin and functions of the SEC in this chapter's *Landmark in the Law* feature.

LANDMARK IN THE LAW—Continued

Remedies and Penny Stock Reform Act of 1990[a] amended existing securities laws to allow SEC administrative law judges to hear many more types of securities violation cases; the SEC's enforcement options were also greatly expanded. The act also provides that courts can bar persons who have engaged in securities fraud from serving as officers and directors of publicly held corporations. The Securities Acts Amendments of 1990 authorized the SEC to seek sanctions against those who violate foreign securities laws.[b] Under the Market Reform Act of 1990, the SEC can suspend trading in securities in the event that prices rise and fall excessively in a short period of time.[c]

The National Securities Markets Improvement Act of 1996 expanded the power of the SEC to exempt persons, securities, and transactions from the requirements of the securities laws.[d] (This part of the act is also known as the Capital Markets Efficiency Act.) The act also limited the authority of the states to regulate certain securities transactions, as well as particular investment advisory firms.[e]

APPLICATION TO TODAY'S WORLD

Congress and the SEC are now attempting to streamline the regulatory process to make it more efficient and more relevant to today's securities trading practices, including those occurring in the online environment. As the number and types of online securities frauds increase, the SEC is trying to keep pace by expanding its online fraud division. It has created an automated surveillance system for online stock fraud. This system, which is constantly being updated, scans the Internet for words and phrases commonly used by fraud perpetrators, such as "get rich quick!" The SEC has been criticized for privacy violations, but it continues to pursue its efforts through its Office of Internet Enforcement, the so-called Cyberforce. Several hundred employees work in this division.

a. 15 U.S.C. Section 77g.
b. 15 U.S.C. Section 78a.
c. 15 U.S.C. Section 78i(h).
d. 15 U.S.C. Sections 77z-3, 78mm.
e. 15 U.S.C. Section 80b-3a.

ON THE WEB The SEC's Electronic Data Gathering Analysis and Retrieval system (EDGAR) contains information about the SEC's operations, the statutes it implements, its proposed and final rules, and its enforcement actions, as well as corporate financial information. Go to **http://www.sec.gov/edgar.shtml**.

Securities Act of 1933

The Securities Act of 1933[1] was designed to prohibit various forms of fraud and to stabilize the securities industry by requiring that all relevant information concerning the issuance of securities be made available to the investing public. Essentially, the purpose of this act is to require disclosure.

WHAT IS A SECURITY?

Section 2(1) of the Securities Act states that securities include the following:

> [A]ny note, stock, treasury stock, bond, debenture, evidence of indebtedness, certificate of interest or participation in any profit-sharing agreement, collateral-trust certificate,

1. 15 U.S.C. Sections 77–77aa.

"I refuse to believe that trading recipes is silly. Tunafish casserole is at least as real as corporate stock."

BARBARA GRIZZUTI HARRISON,
1934–
(American author)

preorganization certificate or subscription, transferable share, investment contract, voting-trust certificate, certificate of deposit for a security, fractional undivided interest in oil, gas, or other mineral rights, or, in general, any interest or instrument commonly known as a "security," or any certificate of interest or participation in, temporary or interim certificate for, receipt for, guarantee of, or warrant or right to subscribe to or purchase, any of the foregoing.[2]

Generally, the courts have interpreted the Securities Act's definition of what constitutes a security[3] to mean that a security exists in any transaction in which a person (1) invests (2) in a common enterprise (3) reasonably expecting profits (4) derived *primarily* or *substantially* from others' managerial or entrepreneurial efforts.[4]

For our purposes, it is probably convenient to think of securities in their most common forms—stocks and bonds issued by corporations. Bear in mind, however, that securities can take many forms and have been held to include whiskey, cosmetics, worms, beavers, boats, vacuum cleaners, muskrats, and cemetery lots, as well as investment contracts in condominiums, franchises, limited partnerships, oil or gas or other mineral rights, and farm animals accompanied by care agreements.

REGISTRATION STATEMENT

Section 5 of the Securities Act of 1933 broadly provides that if a security does not qualify for an exemption, that security must be *registered* before it is offered to the public either through the mails or through any facility of interstate commerce, including securities exchanges. Issuing corporations must file a *registration statement* with the SEC. Investors must be provided with a prospectus that describes the security being sold, the issuing corporation, and the investment or risk attaching to the security. In principle, the registration statement and the prospectus supply sufficient information to enable unsophisticated investors to evaluate the financial risk involved.

A registration statement discusses a security that is being offered to the public. What are the major contents of a registration statement?

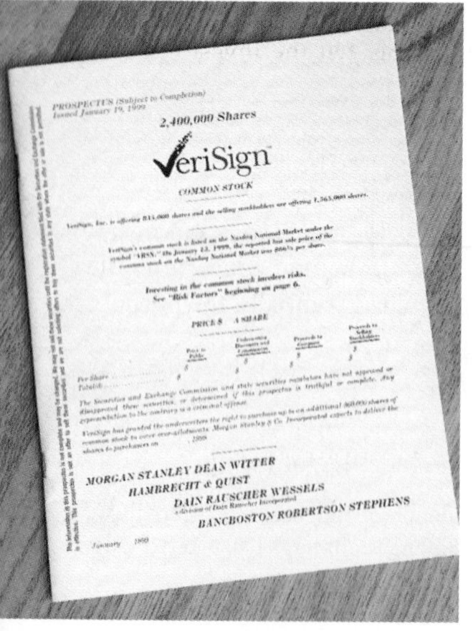

Contents of the Registration Statement The registration statement must include the following:

① A description of the significant provisions of the security offered for sale, including the relationship between that security and the other capital securities of the registrant. Also, the corporation must disclose how it intends to use the proceeds of the sale.

② A description of the registrant's properties and business.

③ A description of the management of the registrant and its security holdings; remuneration; and other benefits, including pensions and stock options. Any interests of directors or officers in any material transactions with the corporation must be disclosed.

④ A financial statement certified by an independent public accounting firm.

⑤ A description of pending lawsuits.

Those who register securities offerings with the SEC should realize that as of 1998, the SEC requires certain documents, or portions of documents, to be written in "plain English." See this chapter's *Letter of the Law* feature for more information on this topic.

2. 15 U.S.C. Section 77b(1). Amendments in 1982 added stock options.
3. See 15 U.S.C. Section 77b(a)(1).
4. *SEC v. W. J. Howey Co.*, 328 U.S. 293, 66 S.Ct. 1100, 90 L.Ed. 1244 (1946).

LETTER OF THE LAW

Securities Offerings in Plain English

The letter of the law with respect to securities offerings is becoming clearer, thanks to a "plain-English" rule adopted by the SEC in 1998.[a] The rule requires companies to use plain English in their securities offerings documents. For example, in any prospectus that a company files with the SEC, the company must utilize plain-English principles in the language and the design of the cover page, summary, and risk-factor sections of the prospectus. Agency officials have indicated that they do not act as "grammar police," but they do evaluate certain documents filed with the SEC to determine the clarity of communication.

The SEC has also taken steps to get rid of the "gobbledegook" in its existing and new rules. At one point, it even held a contest among its employees to see who could do the best job of translating either an SEC document or a document submitted to the agency into plain English.[b]

THE BOTTOM LINE

The SEC considers informing investors in "plain English" about the nature of, and the risks involved in, securities investments to be consistent with the disclosure goals of both the 1933 Securities Act and the 1934 Securities Exchange Act.

a. You can access the SEC's "Plain English Handbook" (in pdf format only) at **http://www.sec.gov/pdf/plaine.pdf**.

b. *BNA's Corporate Counsel Weekly*, Vol. 13, No. 4 (January 28, 1998), p. 1.

DON'T FORGET The purpose of the Securities Act of 1933 is disclosure—the SEC does not consider whether a security is worth the investment price.

RED HERRING
A preliminary prospectus that can be distributed to potential investors after the registration statement (for a securities offering) has been filed with the Securities and Exchange Commission. The name derives from the red legend printed across the prospectus stating that the registration has been filed but has not become effective.

TOMBSTONE AD
An advertisement, historically in a format resembling a tombstone, of a securities offering. The ad informs potential investors of where and how they may obtain a prospectus.

Other Requirements Before filing the registration statement and the prospectus with the SEC, the corporation is allowed to obtain an *underwriter*—a company that agrees to purchase the new issue of securities for resale to the public. There is a twenty-day waiting period (which can be accelerated by the SEC) after registration before the securities can be sold. During this period, oral offers between interested investors and the issuing corporation concerning the purchase and sale of the proposed securities may take place, and very limited written advertising is allowed. At this time, the so-called **red herring** prospectus may be distributed. It gets its name from the red legend printed across it stating that the registration has been filed but has not become effective.

After the waiting period, the registered securities can be legally bought and sold. Written advertising is allowed in the form of a **tombstone ad**, so named because historically the format resembled a tombstone. Such ads simply tell the investor where and how to obtain a prospectus. Normally, any other type of advertising is prohibited.

EXEMPT SECURITIES

A number of specific securities are exempt from the registration requirements of the Securities Act of 1933. These securities—which can also generally be resold without being registered—include the following:[5]

① All bank securities sold prior to July 27, 1933.

② Commercial paper (such as negotiable instruments), if the maturity date does not exceed nine months.

③ Securities of charitable organizations.

④ Securities resulting from a corporate reorganization issued for exchange with the issuer's existing security holders and certificates issued by trustees, receivers, or

5. 15 U.S.C. Section 77c.

ON THE WEB The Center for Corporate Law at the University of Cincinnati College of Law examines all of the acts discussed in this chapter. Go to **http://www.law.uc.edu/CCL.**

debtors in possession under the bankruptcy laws (bankruptcy laws were discussed in Chapter 23).

5. Securities issued exclusively for exchange with the issuer's existing security holders, provided no commission is paid (for example, stock dividends and stock splits).
6. Securities issued to finance the acquisition of railroad equipment.
7. Any insurance, endowment, or annuity contract issued by a state-regulated insurance company.
8. Government-issued securities.
9. Securities issued by banks, savings and loan associations, farmers' cooperatives, and similar institutions subject to supervision by governmental authorities.
10. In consideration of the "small amount involved,"[6] an issuer's offer of up to $5 million in securities in any twelve-month period.

For the last exemption, under Regulation A,[7] the issuer must file with the SEC a notice of the issue and an offering circular, which must also be provided to investors before the sale. This is a much simpler and less expensive process than the procedures associated with full registration. Companies are allowed to "test the waters" for potential interest before preparing the offering circular. To test the waters means to determine potential interest without actually selling any securities or requiring any commitment on the part of those who are interested. Small-business issuers (companies with less than $25 million in annual revenues and less than $25 million in outstanding voting stock) can also use an integrated registration and reporting system that uses simpler forms than the full registration system.

BE AWARE The issuer of an exempt security does not have to disclose the same information that other issuers do.

Exhibit 29–1 summarizes the securities and transactions (discussed next) that are exempt from the registration requirements under the Securities Act of 1933 and SEC regulations.

Exempt Transactions

An issuer of securities that are not exempt under one of the ten categories listed in the previous subsection can avoid the high cost and complicated procedures associated with registration by taking advantage of certain transaction exemptions. An offering may qualify for more than one exemption. These exemptions are very broad, and thus many sales occur without registration. Because there is some overlap in the coverage of the exemptions, an offering may qualify for more than one.

Small Offerings—Regulation D The SEC's Regulation D contains four separate exemptions from registration requirements for limited offers (offers that either involve a small amount of money or are made in a limited manner). Regulation D provides that any of these offerings made during any twelve-month period are exempt from the registration requirements.

Rule 504. Noninvestment company offerings up to $1 million in any one year are exempt. In contrast to investment companies (discussed later in this chapter), noninvestment companies are firms that are not engaged primarily in the business of investing or trading in securities.

6. 15 U.S.C. Section 77c(b).
7. 17 C.F.R. Sections 230.251–230.263.

EXHIBIT 29–1 EXEMPTIONS UNDER THE 1933 SECURITIES ACT

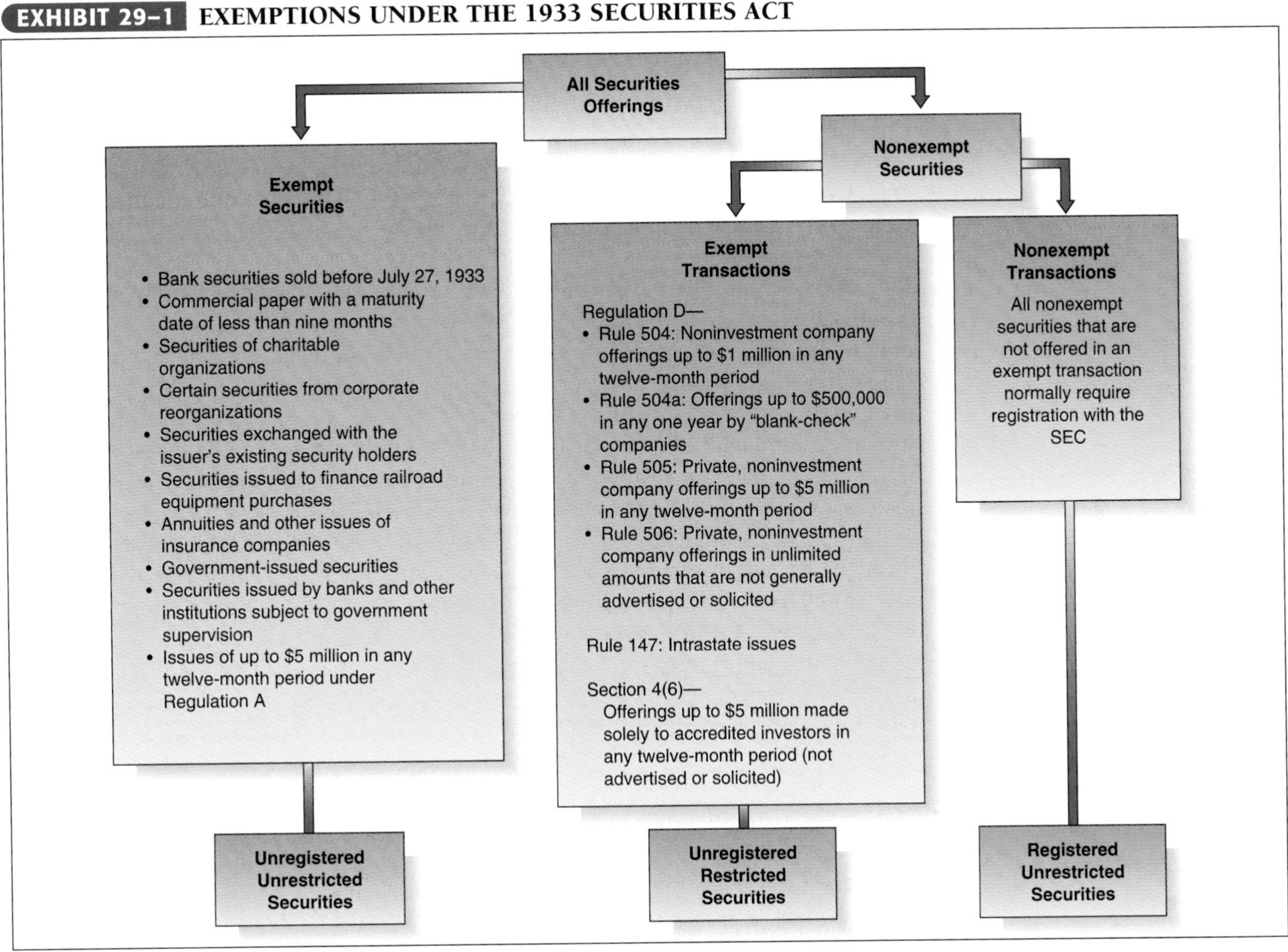

Rule 504a. Offerings up to $500,000 in any one year by so-called blank-check companies—companies with no specific business plans except to locate and acquire currently unknown businesses or opportunities—are exempt if no general solicitation or advertising is used; the SEC is notified of the sales; and precaution is taken against nonexempt, unregistered resales.[8] The limits on advertising and unregistered resales do not apply if the offering is made solely in states that provide for registration and disclosure and the securities are sold in compliance with those provisions.[9]

ACCREDITED INVESTORS
In the context of securities offerings, "sophisticated" investors, such as banks, insurance companies, investment companies, the issuer's executive officers and directors, and persons whose income or net worth exceeds certain limits.

Rule 505. Private, noninvestment company offerings up to $5 million in any twelve-month period are exempt, regardless of the number of **accredited investors** (banks, insurance companies, investment companies, the issuer's executive officers and directors, and persons whose income or net worth exceeds certain limits), so long as there

8. Precautions to be taken against nonexempt, unregistered resales include asking the investor whether he or she is buying the securities for others; before the sale, disclosing to each purchaser in writing that the securities are unregistered and thus cannot be resold, except in an exempt transaction, without first being registered; and indicating on the certificates that the securities are unregistered and restricted.
9. 17 C.F.R. Section 230.504a.

are no more than thirty-five unaccredited investors; no general solicitation or advertising is used; the SEC is notified of the sales; and precaution is taken against nonexempt, unregistered resales. If the sale involves *any* unaccredited investors, *all* investors must be given material information about the offering company, its business, and the securities before the sale. Unlike Rule 506 (discussed next), Rule 505 includes no requirement that the issuer believe each unaccredited investor "has such knowledge and experience in financial and business matters that he is capable of evaluating the merits and the risks of the prospective investment."[10]

Rule 506. Private offerings in unlimited amounts that are not generally solicited or advertised are exempt if the SEC is notified of the sales; precaution is taken against nonexempt, unregistered resales; and the issuer believes that each unaccredited investor has sufficient knowledge or experience in financial matters to be capable of evaluating the investment's merits and risks. There may be no more than thirty-five unaccredited investors, although there may be an unlimited number of accredited investors. If there are *any* unaccredited investors, the issuer must provide to *all* purchasers material information about itself, its business, and the securities before the sale.[11]

KEEP IN MIND An investor can be "sophisticated" by virtue of his or her education and experience or by investing through a knowledgeable, experienced representative.

This exemption is perhaps most important to those firms that want to raise funds through the sale of securities without registering them. It is often referred to as the *private placement* exemption because it exempts "transactions not involving any public offering."[12] This provision applies to private offerings to a limited number of persons who are sufficiently sophisticated and in a sufficiently strong bargaining position to be able to assume the risk of the investment (and who thus have no need for federal registration protection), as well as to private offerings to similarly situated institutional investors.

Small Offerings—Section 4(6) Under Section 4(6) of the Securities Act of 1933, an offer made *solely* to accredited investors is exempt if its amount is not more than $5 million. Any number of accredited investors may participate, but no unaccredited investors may do so. No general solicitation or advertising may be used; the SEC must be notified of all sales; and precaution must be taken against nonexempt, unregistered resales. Precaution is necessary because these are *restricted* securities and may be resold only by registration or in an exempt transaction.[13] (The securities purchased and sold by most people who deal in stock are called, in contrast, *unrestricted* securities.)

Intrastate Issues—Rule 147 Also exempt are intrastate transactions involving purely local offerings.[14] This exemption applies to most offerings that are restricted to residents of the state in which the issuing company is organized and doing business. For nine months after the last sale, virtually no resales may be made to nonresidents, and precautions must be taken against this possibility. These offerings remain subject to applicable laws in the state of issue.

Resales Most securities can be resold without registration (although some resales may be subject to restrictions, as discussed above in connection with specific exemptions). The Securities Act of 1933 provides exemptions for resales by most persons other than

10. 17 C.F.R. Section 230.505.
11. 17 C.F.R. Section 230.506.
12. 15 U.S.C. Section 77d(2).
13. 15 U.S.C. Section 77d(6).
14. 15 U.S.C. Section 77c(a)(11); 17 C.F.R. Section 230.147.

issuers or underwriters. The average investor who sells shares of stock does not have to file a registration statement with the SEC. Resales of restricted securities acquired under Rule 504a, Rule 505, Rule 506, or Section 4(6), however, trigger the registration requirements unless the party selling them complies with Rule 144 or Rule 144A. These rules are sometimes referred to as "safe harbors."

Rule 144. Rule 144 exempts restricted securities from registration on resale if there is adequate current public information about the issuer, the person selling the securities has owned them for at least one year, they are sold in certain limited amounts in unsolicited brokers' transactions, and the SEC is given notice of the resale.[15] "Adequate current public information" consists of the reports that certain companies are required to file under the Securities Exchange Act of 1934. A person who has owned the securities for at least three years is subject to none of these requirements, unless the person is an affiliate. An *affiliate* is one who controls, is controlled by, or is in common control with the issuer. Sales of *nonrestricted* securities by an affiliate are also subject to the requirements for an exemption under Rule 144 (except that the affiliate need not have owned the securities for at least two years).

CONTRAST Securities do not have to be held for two years to be exempt from registration on a resale under Rule 144A, as they do under Rule 144.

Rule 144A. Securities that at the time of issue are not of the same class as securities listed on a national securities exchange or quoted in a U.S. automated interdealer quotation system may be resold under Rule 144A.[16] They may be sold only to a qualified institutional buyer (an institution, such as an insurance company, an investment company, or a bank, that owns and invests at least $100 million in securities). The seller must take reasonable steps to ensure that the buyer knows that the seller is relying on the exemption under Rule 144A. A sample restricted stock certificate is shown in Exhibit 29–2 on the next page.

VIOLATIONS OF THE 1933 ACT

As mentioned, the SEC has the power to investigate and bring civil enforcement actions against companies that violate federal securities laws, including the Securities Act of 1933. Criminal violations are prosecuted by the Department of Justice. Violators may be penalized by fines up to $10,000, imprisonment for up to five years, or both. Private parties may also bring suits against those who violate federal securities laws. Those who purchase securities and suffer harm as a result of false or omitted statements, or other violations, may bring a suit in a federal court to recover their losses and other damages.

*E*Trade displays its home page. Online trading through a firm such as E*Trade does not involve personal contact with a broker. Does this mean that online trading is unregulated?*

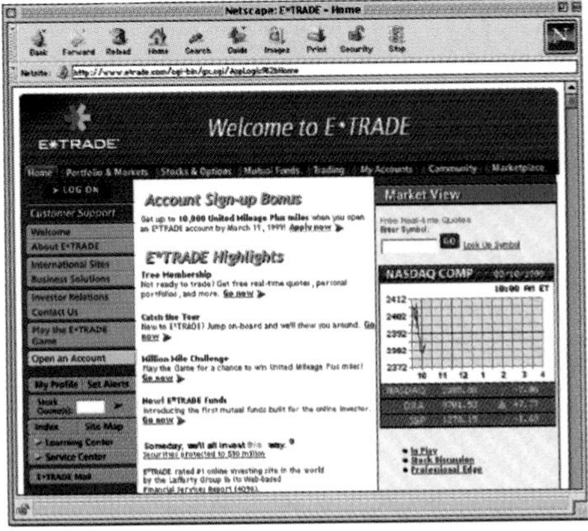

Securities Exchange Act of 1934

The Securities Exchange Act of 1934 provides for the regulation and registration of securities exchanges; brokers; dealers; and national securities associations, such as the National Association of Securities Dealers (NASD). The SEC regulates the markets in which securities are traded by maintaining a continuous disclosure system for all corporations with securities on the securities exchanges and for those companies that have assets in excess of $10 million and five hundred or more shareholders. These

15. 17 C.F.R. Section 230.144.
16. 17 C.F.R. Section 230.144A.

EXHIBIT 29–2 A SAMPLE RESTRICTED STOCK CERTIFICATE

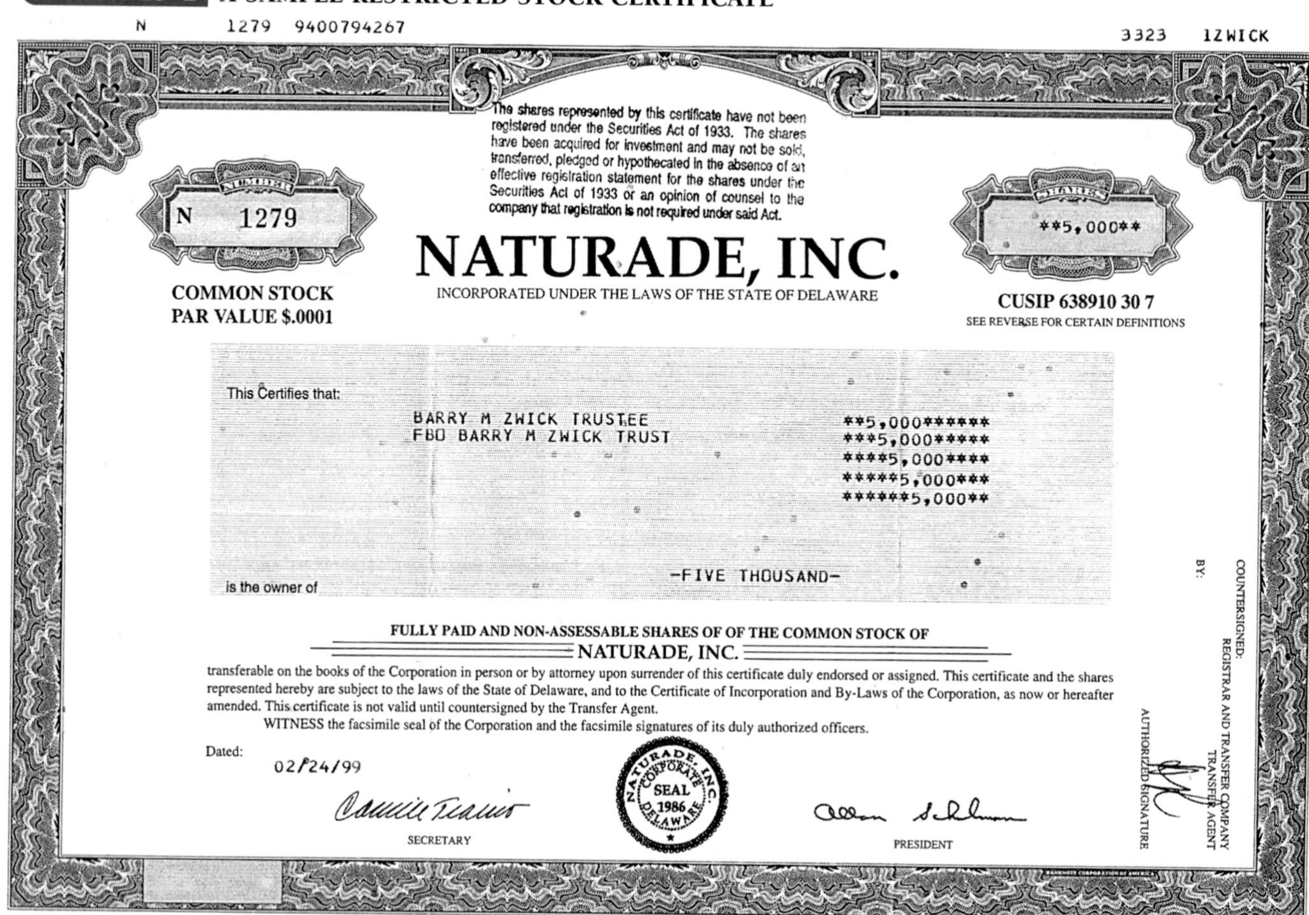

N 1279 9400794267 3323 IZWICK

The shares represented by this certificate have not been registered under the Securities Act of 1933. The shares have been acquired for investment and may not be sold, transferred, pledged or hypothecated in the absence of an effective registration statement for the shares under the Securities Act of 1933 or an opinion of counsel to the company that registration is not required under said Act.

NUMBER N 1279

SHARES **5,000**

NATURADE, INC.

INCORPORATED UNDER THE LAWS OF THE STATE OF DELAWARE

COMMON STOCK
PAR VALUE $.0001

CUSIP 638910 30 7
SEE REVERSE FOR CERTAIN DEFINITIONS

This Certifies that:
BARRY M ZWICK TRUSTEE
FBO BARRY M ZWICK TRUST

5,000****
5,000**
****5,000****
*****5,000***
******5,000**

is the owner of -FIVE THOUSAND-

FULLY PAID AND NON-ASSESSABLE SHARES OF OF THE COMMON STOCK OF
NATURADE, INC.

transferable on the books of the Corporation in person or by attorney upon surrender of this certificate duly endorsed or assigned. This certificate and the shares represented hereby are subject to the laws of the State of Delaware, and to the Certificate of Incorporation and By-Laws of the Corporation, as now or hereafter amended. This certificate is not valid until countersigned by the Transfer Agent.

WITNESS the facsimile seal of the Corporation and the facsimile signatures of its duly authorized officers.

Dated: 02/24/99

NATURADE, INC. CORPORATE SEAL 1986 DELAWARE

SECRETARY PRESIDENT

COUNTERSIGNED:
REGISTRAR AND TRANSFER COMPANY
TRANSFER AGENT
BY:
AUTHORIZED SIGNATURE

corporations are referred to as Section 12 companies because they are required to register their securities under Section 12 of the 1934 act.

The act regulates proxy solicitation for voting (discussed in Chapter 27) and allows the SEC to engage in market surveillance to regulate undesirable market practices such as fraud, market manipulation, and misrepresentation.

Section 10(b), SEC Rule 10b-5, and Insider Trading

SEC RULE 10b-5
A rule of the Securities and Exchange Commission that makes it unlawful, in connection with the purchase or sale of any security, to make any untrue statement of a material fact or to omit a material fact if such omission causes the statement to be misleading.

INSIDER TRADING
The purchase or sale of securities on the basis of information that has not been made available to the public.

Section 10(b) is one of the most important sections of the Securities Exchange Act of 1934. This section proscribes the use of "any manipulative or deceptive device or contrivance in contravention of such rules and regulations as the [SEC] may prescribe." Among the rules that the SEC has promulgated pursuant to the 1934 act is **SEC Rule 10b-5**, which prohibits the commission of fraud in connection with the purchase or sale of any security.

One of the major goals of Section 10(b) and SEC Rule 10b-5 is to prevent so-called **insider trading.** Because of their positions, corporate directors and officers often obtain advance inside information that can affect the future market value of the corporate stock. Obviously, their positions give them a trading advantage over the general public and shareholders. The 1934 Securities Exchange Act defines inside information and extends liability to officers and directors for taking advantage of such information in their personal transactions when they know that it is unavailable to the persons with whom they are dealing.

Section 10(b) of the 1934 act and SEC Rule 10b-5 cover not only corporate officers, directors, and majority shareholders but also any persons having access to or receiving information of a nonpublic nature on which trading is based.

ETHICAL ISSUE 29.1

Should liability under SEC Rule 10b-5 arise from the mere possession of inside information when trading in securities?

Suppose that an investor has a plan to trade certain stocks but then, before the trade is actually carried out, comes into the possession of inside information relating to that stock. If the investor goes ahead and implements the trading strategy, should he or she be held liable for violating SEC Rule 10b-5? After all, the investor did not intend to defraud or deceive anyone; he or she simply intended to implement a preexisting financial strategy. For some time, the courts differed in their approach to this question, which clearly has both ethical and legal implications. Some courts concluded that for liability under SEC Rule 10b-5 to arise, an investor had to "use" the inside information in his or her possession.[17] Other courts held that the mere "possession" of inside information about certain stocks, while trading in those stocks, was enough to establish liability under SEC Rule 10b-5.[18] To clarify this issue, the SEC recently adopted a new rule, Rule 10b5-1.[19] Generally, the rule allows corporate insiders to engage in prearranged or certain other securities transactions without being subject to liability under SEC Rule 10b-5. In other words, a corporate insider is now permitted to buy or sell stock without having to worry about liability if she or he, *after* deciding to buy or sell a stock, learns inside information relating to that stock.

ON THE WEB For information on investor protection, including answers to frequently asked questions on the topic of securities fraud, go to **http://www.securitieslaw.com**.

Disclosure under SEC Rule 10b-5 Any material omission or misrepresentation of material facts in connection with the purchase or sale of a security may violate not only Section 11 of the Securities Act of 1933 but also the antifraud provisions of Section 10(b) and SEC Rule 10b-5 of the 1934 act. The key to liability (which can be civil or criminal) under Section 10(b) and SEC Rule 10b-5 is whether the insider's information is *material*. The following are some examples of material facts calling for a disclosure under the rule:

1. A new ore discovery.
2. Fraudulent trading in the company stock by a broker-dealer.
3. A dividend change (whether up or down).
4. A contract for the sale of corporate assets.
5. A new discovery (process or product).
6. A significant change in the firm's financial condition.

17. See, for example, *United States v. Smith,* 155 F.3d 1051 (9th Cir. 1998).
18. See, for example, *United States v. Teicher,* 987 F.2d 112 (2d Cir. 1993).
19. 65 F.R. 51716 (August 24, 2000). The SEC's adopting release is available at **http://www.sec.gov/rules/final/33-7881.htm**.

"Anyone who says businessmen deal only in facts, not fiction, has never read old five-year projections."

MALCOLM FORBES, 1919–1990 (American publisher)

Ironically, one of the effects of SEC Rule 10b-5 was to deter the disclosure of material information. • **EXAMPLE 29.1** A company announces that its projected earnings in a certain time period will be X amount. It turns out that the forecast is wrong. The earnings are in fact much lower, and the price of the company's stock is affected—negatively. The shareholders then bring a class-action suit against the company, alleging that the directors violated SEC Rule 10b-5 by disclosing misleading financial information. •

In an attempt to rectify this problem and promote disclosure, Congress passed the Private Securities Litigation Reform Act of 1995. Among other things, the act provides a "safe harbor" for publicly held companies that make forward-looking statements, such as financial forecasts. Those who make such statements are protected against liability for securities fraud as long as the statements are accompanied by "meaningful cautionary statements identifying important factors that could cause actual results to differ materially from those in the forward-looking statement."[20]

The following is one of the landmark cases interpreting SEC Rule 10b-5. The SEC sued Texas Gulf Sulphur Company for issuing a misleading press release. The release underestimated the magnitude and the value of a mineral discovery. The SEC also sued several of Texas Gulf Sulphur's directors, officers, and employees under SEC Rule 10b-5 for purchasing large amounts of the corporate stock prior to the announcement of the corporation's rich ore discovery.

20. 15 U.S.C. Sections 77z-2, 78u-5.

Landmark and Classic Cases

CASE 29.1 SEC v. Texas Gulf Sulphur Co.

United States Court of Appeals, Second Circuit, 1968.
401 F.2d 833.

HISTORICAL AND ENVIRONMENTAL SETTING *No court has ever held that every buyer or seller is entitled to all of the information relating to all of the circumstances in every stock transaction. By the mid-1950s, however, significant understatement of the value of the assets of a company had been held to be materially misleading.*[a] *In 1957, the Texas Gulf Sulphur Company (TGS) began exploring for minerals in eastern Canada. In March 1959, aerial geophysical surveys were conducted over more than fifteen thousand square miles of the area. The operations revealed numerous and extraordinary variations in the conductivity of the rock, which indicated a remarkable concentration of commercially exploitable minerals. One site of such variations was near Timmins, Ontario. On October 29 and 30, 1963, a ground survey of the site near Timmins indicated a need to drill for further evaluation.*

a. *Speed v. Transamerica Corp.*, 99 F.Supp. 808 (D.Del. 1951).

FACTS The Texas Gulf Sulphur Company drilled a hole on November 12, 1963, that appeared to yield a core with an exceedingly high mineral content. TGS kept secret the results of the core sample. Officers and employees of the company made substantial purchases of TGS's stock or accepted stock options after learning of the ore discovery, even though further drilling was necessary to establish whether there was enough ore to be mined commercially. On April 11, 1964, an unauthorized report of the mineral find appeared in the newspapers. On the following day, April 12, TGS issued a press release that played down the discovery and stated that it was too early to tell whether the ore finding would be a significant one. Later on, TGS announced a strike of at least twenty-five million tons of ore, substantially driving up the price of TGS stock. The SEC brought suit in a federal district court against the officers and employees of TGS for violating the insider-trading prohibition of SEC Rule 10b-5. The officers and employees argued that the prohibition did not apply. They reasoned that the information on which they had traded was not material, as the mine had not been commercially proved. The court held that

CASE 29.1—Continued

most of the defendants had not violated SEC Rule 10b-5, and the SEC appealed.

ISSUE Had the officers and employees of TGS violated SEC Rule 10b-5 by purchasing the stock, even though they did not know the full extent and profit potential of the mine at the time they purchased the stock?

DECISION Yes. The federal appellate court reversed the lower court's decision and remanded the case to the trial court, holding that the employees and officers violated SEC Rule 10b-5's prohibition against insider trading.

REASON For SEC Rule 10b-5 purposes, the test of materiality is whether the information would affect the judgment of reasonable investors. Reasonable investors include speculative as well as conservative investors. "[A] major factor in determining whether the * * * discovery [of the ore] was a material fact is the importance attached to the drilling results by those who knew about it. * * * [T]he timing by those who knew of it of their stock purchases and their purchases of short-term calls [rights to buy shares at a specified price within a specified time period]—purchases in some cases by individuals who had never before purchased calls or even TGS stock—virtually compels the inference that the insiders were influenced by the drilling results. * * * We hold, therefore, that all transactions in TGS stock or calls by individuals apprised of the drilling results * * * were made in violation of Rule 10b-5."

COMMENT *This landmark case affirmed the principle that the test of whether information is "material," for SEC Rule 10b-5 purposes, is whether it would affect the judgment of reasonable investors. The corporate insiders' purchases of stock and stock options (rights to purchase stock) indicated that they were influenced by the drilling results and that the information about the drilling results was material. The courts continue to cite this case when applying SEC Rule 10b-5 to cases of alleged insider trading.*

Applicability of SEC Rule 10b-5 SEC Rule 10b-5 applies in virtually all cases concerning the trading of securities, whether on organized exchanges, in over-the-counter markets, or in private transactions. The rule covers, among other things, notes, bonds, agreements to form a corporation, and joint-venture agreements. Generally, it covers just about any form of security. It is immaterial whether a firm has securities registered under the 1933 act for the 1934 act to apply.

Although SEC Rule 10b-5 is applicable only when the requisites of federal jurisdiction—such as the use of the mails, of stock exchange facilities, or of any instrumentality of interstate commerce—are present, virtually no commercial transaction can be completed without such contact. In addition, the states have corporate securities laws, many of which include provisions similar to SEC Rule 10b-5.

ETHICAL ISSUE 29.2

Should insider trading be legal?

SEC Rule 10b-5 has broad applicability. As will be discussed shortly, the rule covers not only corporate insiders but even "outsiders"—those who receive and trade on tips received from insiders. Investigating and prosecuting violations of SEC Rule 10b-5 is costly, both for the government and for those accused of insider trading. Some people doubt that such extensive regulation is necessary and even contend that insider trading should be legal. Would there be any benefit from the legalization of insider trading? To evaluate this question, review the facts in *SEC v. Texas Gulf Sulphur Co.* (Case 29.1 in this chapter). If insider trading were legal, the discovery of the ore sample would probably have caused many more company insiders to purchase stock. Consequently, the price of Texas Gulf's stock would have increased fairly quickly. These increases presumably would have attracted the attention of outside investors, who would have learned sooner that something positive had happened to the company and would thus have had the opportunity to purchase the stock. The higher demand for the stock would have more quickly translated into higher prices for the stock and hence, perhaps, a more efficient capital market.

Outsiders and SEC Rule 10b-5 The traditional insider-trading case involves true insiders—corporate officers, directors, and majority shareholders who have access to (and trade on) inside information. Increasingly, liability under Section 10(b) of the 1934 act and SEC Rule 10b-5 has been extended to include certain "outsiders"—those persons who trade on inside information acquired indirectly. Two theories have been developed under which outsiders may be held liable for insider trading: the *tipper/tippee theory* and the *misappropriation theory.*

TIPPEE
A person who receives inside information.

Tipper/Tippee Theory. Anyone who acquires inside information as a result of a corporate insider's breach of his or her fiduciary duty can be liable under SEC Rule 10b-5. This liability extends to **tippees** (those who receive "tips" from insiders) and even remote tippees (tippees of tippees).

The key to liability under this theory is that the inside information must be obtained as a result of someone's breach of a fiduciary duty to the corporation whose shares are involved in the trading. Unless there was a breach of a duty not to disclose inside information, the disclosure was in exchange for personal benefit, and the tippee knew of this breach (or should have known of it) and benefited from it, there is no liability under this theory.[21] Is the offering of a tip as a gift of profits to someone with whom the insider has a close relationship enough to infer that the insider realized a personal benefit? That was an issue in the following case.

21. See, for example, *Chiarella v. United States,* 445 U.S. 222, 100 S.Ct. 1108, 63 L.Ed.2d 348 (1980); and *Dirks v. SEC,* 463 U.S. 646, 103 S.Ct. 3255, 77 L.Ed.2d 911 (1983).

CASE 29.2 SEC v. Warde

United States Court of Appeals,
Second Circuit, 1998.
151 F.3d 42.
http://www.tourolaw.edu/2ndcircuit/July98[a]

FACTS Edward Downe was a close friend of Fred Sullivan, chairman of Kidde, Inc. At Sullivan's request, Downe became a director of Kidde. Thomas Warde was a good friend of Downe. In June 1987, Sullivan learned that Kidde was the target of a takeover attempt by Hanson Trust PLC, a British firm. After negotiations, the Kidde board announced in August that it would merge with Hanson. The price of Kidde stock increased, and warrants for the shares, which had been priced at $1 in June, went to $26.50.[b] Between learning about the takeover attempt in June and the merger in August, Downe and Warde bought and sold warrants several times, earning very large profits. The SEC filed a suit in a federal district court against Warde and others, alleging insider trading in violation, in part, of Section 10(b). Warde contended that his purchases were based on market savvy, rumor, and public information. The jury found him liable. The court

a. This page provides access to opinions of the U.S. Court of Appeals for the Second Circuit decided in July 1998. Scroll down the list of cases to the *Warde* case and click on the link to access the opinion.

b. A *warrant* allows its owner to buy stock at a certain price before a certain date. If, before the warrant is exercised, the price goes up, the buyer profits. If the price never exceeds the level in the warrant, the warrant is worthless.

CASE 29.2—Continued

ordered him to pay more than $3 million in penalties and interest. Warde appealed to the U.S. Court of Appeals for the Second Circuit.

ISSUE Many of the issues on appeal concerned whether there was enough evidence to prove the elements of an insider-trading violation. In particular, was there proof that Downe realized a personal benefit from tipping Warde?

DECISION Yes. The U.S. Court of Appeals for the Second Circuit affirmed the lower court's decision, concluding that the SEC presented sufficient evidence to support every element necessary to hold Warde liable.

REASON The federal appellate court acknowledged that to find Warde liable as a tippee, there had to be proof that Downe realized a benefit from giving insider tips to Warde. The court explained that the benefit did not need to be "specific or tangible," however. It was enough if the tipper intended to benefit the recipient or made "a gift of confidential information" to the person. Their friendship indicated that Downe intended to benefit Warde, and Warde did benefit, just as if Downe had made the trades himself and given the profits to Warde.

FOR CRITICAL ANALYSIS—Social Consideration *How does the decision in this case make it easier for the SEC to win in other insider-trading cases?*

Misappropriation Theory. Liability for insider trading may also be established under the misappropriation theory. This theory holds that if an individual wrongfully obtains (misappropriates) inside information and trades on it for her or his personal gain, then the individual should be held liable because, in essence, the individual stole information rightfully belonging to another.

The misappropriation theory has been controversial because it significantly extends the reach of SEC Rule 10b-5 to outsiders who would not ordinarily be deemed fiduciaries of the corporations in whose stock they trade. The United States Supreme Court, however, has held that liability under SEC Rule 10b-5 can be based on the misappropriation theory.[22]

INSIDER REPORTING AND TRADING—SECTION 16(b)

Officers, directors, and certain large stockholders[23] of Section 12 corporations (corporations that are required to register their securities under Section 12 of the 1934 act) must file reports with the SEC concerning their ownership and trading of the corporations' securities.[24] To discourage such insiders from using nonpublic information about their companies for their personal benefit in the stock market, Section 16(b) of the 1934 act provides for the recapture by the corporation of all profits realized by an insider on any purchase and sale or sale and purchase of the corporation's stock within any six-month period.[25] It is irrelevant whether the insider actually uses inside information; all such short-swing profits must be returned to the corporation.

Section 16(b) applies not only to stock but to warrants, options, and securities convertible into stock. In addition, the courts have fashioned complex rules for determining profits. Corporate insiders are wise to seek specialized counsel prior to trading in the corporation's stock. Exhibit 29–3 on the following page compares the effects of SEC Rule 10b-5 and Section 16(b).

22. *United States v. O'Hagan,* 521 U.S. 642, 117 S.Ct. 2199, 138 L.Ed.2d 724 (1997).

23. Those stockholders owning 10 percent of the class of equity securities registered under Section 12 of the 1934 act.

24. 15 U.S.C. Section 78*l*.

25. When a decline is predicted in the market for a particular stock, one can realize profits by "selling short"—selling at a high price and repurchasing later at a lower price to cover the "short sale."

EXHIBIT 29–3 COMPARISON OF COVERAGE, APPLICATION, AND LIABILITIES UNDER SEC RULE 10b-5 AND SECTION 16(b)

AREA OF COMPARISON	SEC RULE 10b-5	SECTION 16(b)
What is the subject matter of the transaction?	Any security (does not have to be registered).	Any security (does not have to be registered).
What transactions are covered?	Purchase or sale.	Short-swing purchase and sale or short-swing sale and purchase.
Who is subject to liability?	Virtually anyone with inside information under a duty to disclose—including officers, directors, controlling stockholders, and tippees.	Officers, directors, and certain 10 percent stockholders.
Is omission or misrepresentation necessary for liability?	Yes.	No.
Are there any exempt transactions?	No.	Yes, there are a variety of exemptions.
Is direct dealing with the party necessary?	No.	No.
Who may bring an action?	A person transacting with an insider, the SEC, or a purchaser or seller damaged by a wrongful act.	A corporation or a shareholder by derivative action.

PROXY STATEMENTS

Section 14(a) of the Securities Exchange Act of 1934 regulates the solicitation of proxies from shareholders of Section 12 companies. The SEC regulates the content of proxy statements. As discussed in Chapter 27, a proxy statement is a statement that is sent to shareholders by corporate officials who are requesting authority to vote on behalf of the shareholders in a particular election on specified issues. Whoever solicits a proxy must fully and accurately disclose in the proxy statement all of the facts that are pertinent to the matter on which the shareholders are to vote. SEC Rule 14a-9 is similar to the antifraud provisions of SEC Rule 10b-5. Remedies for violations are extensive; they range from injunctions that prevent a vote from being taken to monetary damages.

VIOLATIONS OF THE 1934 ACT

Violations of Section 10(b) of the Securities Exchange Act of 1934 and SEC Rule 10b-5 include insider trading. This is a criminal offense, with criminal penalties. Violators of these laws may also be subject to civil liability. For any sanctions to be imposed, however, there must be *scienter*—the violator must have had an intent to defraud or knowledge of his or her misconduct (see Chapter 11). *Scienter* can be proved by showing that a defendant made false statements or wrongfully failed to disclose material facts.

Violations of Section 16(b) include the sale by insiders of stock acquired less than six months before the sale. These violations are subject to civil sanctions. Liability under Section 16(b) is strict liability. *Scienter* is not required.

In the following case, investors charged a corporation with violating Section 10(b) and SEC Rule 10b-5. The question before the court was whether the investors alleged sufficient facts to indicate *scienter.*

CASE 29.3 In re MCI Worldcom, Inc., Securities Litigation

United States District Court,
Eastern District of New York, 2000.
93 F.Supp.2d 276.

FACTS In early 1999, MCI Worldcom, Inc., began negotiating to buy SkyTel Communications, Inc., then a leading provider of wireless messaging services. When investors heard rumors of the deal, the price of SkyTel stock rose 12 percent. On the morning of May 25, an Internet news service, the Company Sleuth, reported that MCI had registered "skytelworldcom.com" as an Internet domain name.[a] SkyTel's stock price rose 16 percent before noon. At noon, Barbara Gibson, an MCI spokesperson and senior manager of corporate communication, told the media that the name registration was done by an employee acting alone and "is not an indication of official company intention." Immediately following Gibson's statement, SkyTel's stock price fell to less than the previous day's price. On May 28, MCI announced that it would buy all of SkyTel's stock for $1.3 billion. Paul Curnin and other investors who sold the stock between May 25 and 28 filed a suit in a federal district court against MCI, alleging violations of Section 10(b) and SEC Rule 10b-5. MCI filed a motion to dismiss.

ISSUE Did the shareholders properly allege *scienter*?

a. It is common for business firms to register domain names before their actual use to protect them from cybersquatters—see Chapter 5.

DECISION Yes. The court denied the motion to dismiss. The investors successfully alleged *scienter* through motive and opportunity, as well as facts from which an inference of conscious misbehavior or recklessness could be drawn.

REASON The court explained that a "plaintiff can plead [*scienter*] in one of two ways: (1) by identifying circumstances indicating conscious or reckless behavior by the defendant, or (2) by alleging facts showing a motive to commit fraud and a clear opportunity to do so." Here, the plaintiffs "assert that MCI was motivated to artificially deflate the price of SkyTel stock in order to help ensure that the acquisition price would not have to be increased. * * * [B]eing able to acquire a company for a significantly reduced price is a sufficient economic benefit to satisfy the motive requirement for *scienter*." The court added, "Plaintiffs have also alleged facts that constitute strong circumstantial evidence of conscious misbehavior or recklessness by MCI." This included MCI's denial of the domain name registration. "The [investors] understood the denial to mean there would be no takeover, as evidenced by the drop in SkyTel's price," but it "was MCI itself that registered the domain name, and not, as Ms. Gibson suggested, an MCI employee acting alone."

FOR CRITICAL ANALYSIS—Technological Consideration *What effect has the Internet had on the opportunity to commit violations of the securities laws, as well as to avoid such violations?*

Criminal Penalties For violations of Section 10(b) and Rule 10b-5, an individual may be fined up to $1 million, imprisoned for up to ten years, or both. A partnership or a corporation may be fined up to $2.5 million.

Civil Sanctions The Insider Trading Sanctions Act of 1984 permits the SEC to bring suit in a federal district court against anyone violating or aiding in a violation of the 1934 act or SEC rules by purchasing or selling a security while in the possession of material nonpublic information.[26] The violation must occur on or through the facilities of a national securities exchange or from or through a broker or dealer. Transactions pursuant to a public offering by an issuer of securities are excepted. The court may assess as a penalty as much as triple the profits gained or the loss avoided by the guilty party. Profit or loss is defined as "the difference between the purchase or sale price of the security and the value of that security as measured by the trading price

26. 15 U.S.C. Section 78u(d)(2)(A).

of the security at a reasonable period of time after public dissemination of the nonpublic information."[27]

The Insider Trading and Securities Fraud Enforcement Act of 1988 enlarged the class of persons who may be subject to civil liability for insider-trading violations. This act also gave the SEC authority to award **bounty payments** (rewards given by government officials for acts beneficial to the state) to persons providing information leading to the prosecution of insider-trading violations.[28]

BOUNTY PAYMENT
A reward (payment) given to a person or persons who perform a certain service—such as informing legal authorities of illegal actions.

Private parties may also sue violators of Section 10(b) and Rule 10b-5. A private party may obtain rescission of a contract to buy securities or damages to the extent of the violator's illegal profits. Those found liable have a right to seek contribution from those who share responsibility for the violations, including accountants, attorneys, and corporations.[29] For violations of Section 16(b), a corporation can bring an action to recover the short-swing profits.

The Regulation of Investment Companies

Investment companies, and mutual funds in particular, grew rapidly after World War II. **Investment companies** act on behalf of many smaller shareholders by buying a large portfolio of securities and professionally managing that portfolio. A **mutual fund** is a specific type of investment company that continually buys or sells to investors shares of ownership in a portfolio. Such companies are regulated by the Investment Company Act of 1940,[30] which provides for SEC regulation of their activities. The act was expanded by the 1970 amendments to the Investment Company Act. Further minor changes were made in the Securities Act Amendments of 1975 and in later years.

INVESTMENT COMPANY
A company that acts on behalf of many smaller shareholders/owners by buying a large portfolio of securities and professionally managing that portfolio.

MUTUAL FUND
A specific type of investment company that continually buys or sells to investors shares of ownership in a portfolio.

The 1940 act requires that every investment company register with the SEC and imposes restrictions on the activities of these companies and persons connected with them. For the purposes of the act, an investment company is defined as any entity that (1) is engaged primarily "in the business of investing, reinvesting, or trading in securities" or (2) is engaged in such business and has more than 40 percent of its assets in investment securities. Excluded from coverage by the act are banks, insurance companies, savings and loan associations, finance companies, oil and gas drilling firms, charitable foundations, tax-exempt pension funds, and other special types of institutions, such as closely held corporations.

All investment companies must register with the SEC by filing a notification of registration. Each year, registered investment companies must file reports with the SEC. To safeguard company assets, all securities must be held in the custody of a bank or stock exchange member, and that bank or stock exchange member must follow strict procedures established by the SEC.

No dividends may be paid from any source other than accumulated, undistributed net income. Furthermore, there are some restrictions on investment activities. For example, investment companies are not allowed to purchase securities on the margin (pay only part of the total price, borrowing the rest), sell short (sell shares not yet owned), or participate in joint trading accounts.

27. 15 U.S.C. Section 78u(d)(2)(C).
28. 15 U.S.C. Section 78u-1.
29. Note that a private cause of action under Section 10(b) and SEC Rule 10b-5 cannot be brought against accountants, attorneys, and others who "aid and abet" violations of the act. Only the SEC can bring actions against so-called aiders and abettors. See *SEC v. Fehn,* 97 F.3d 1276 (9th Cir. 1996).
30. 15 U.S.C. Sections 80a-1 to 64.

BE AWARE Federal securities laws do not take priority over state securities laws.

State Securities Laws

Today, all states have their own corporate securities laws, or "blue sky laws," that regulate the offer and sale of securities within individual state borders. (As mentioned in Chapter 10, the phrase *blue sky laws* dates to a 1917 decision by the United States Supreme Court in which the Court declared that the purpose of such laws was to prevent "speculative schemes which have no more basis than so many feet of 'blue sky.' ")[31] Article 8 of the Uniform Commercial Code, which has been adopted by all of the states, also imposes various requirements relating to the purchase and sale of securities. State securities laws apply only to intrastate transactions. Since the adoption of the 1933 and 1934 federal securities acts, the state and federal governments have regulated securities concurrently. Issuers must comply with both federal and state securities laws, and exemptions from federal law are not exemptions from state laws.

There are differences in philosophy among state statutes, but certain features are common to all state blue sky laws. Typically, state laws have disclosure requirements and antifraud provisions, many of which are patterned after Section 10(b) of the Securities Exchange Act of 1934 and SEC Rule 10b-5. State laws also provide for the registration or qualification of securities offered or issued for sale within the state and impose disclosure requirements. Unless an applicable exemption from registration is found, issuers must register or qualify their stock with the appropriate state official, often called a *corporations commissioner.* Additionally, most state securities laws regulate securities brokers and dealers. The Uniform Securities Act, which has been adopted in part by several states, was drafted to be acceptable to states with differing regulatory philosophies.

Online Securities Offerings and Disclosures

The Spring Street Brewing Company, headquartered in New York, made history when it became the first company to attempt to sell securities via the Internet. Through its online initial public offering (IPO), which ended in early 1996, Spring Street raised about $1.6 million. No commissions were paid to any brokers or any underwriters. The offering was made pursuant to Regulation A, which, as mentioned earlier in this chapter, allows small-business issuers to use a simplified registration procedure.

Any company wishing to make a traditional IPO has to comply with filing requirements dictated by federal and state law. Because such filings are costly and time consuming, online IPOs are particularly attractive to small companies and start-up ventures that may find it difficult to raise capital from institutional investors or through underwriters.

Regulations Governing Online Securities Offerings

One of the early questions posed by online offerings was whether the delivery of securities *information* via the Internet met the requirements of the Securities Act, which traditionally were applied to the delivery of paper documents. The SEC addressed this issue in its October 1995 interpretive release titled *Use of Electronic Media for Delivery Purposes.*[32] In this release, the SEC stated that "[t]he use of electronic media should be

31. *Hall v. Geiger-Jones Co.,* 242 U.S. 539, 37 S.Ct. 217, 61 L.Ed. 480 (1917).

32. Securities Act Release No. 33-7233 (October 6, 1995). The rules governing the use of electronic transmissions for delivery purposes were subsequently confirmed in Securities Act Release No. 33-7289 (May 9, 1996) and expanded in Securities Act Release No. 33-7856 (April 28, 2000).

at least an equal alternative to the use of paper-based media" and that anything that can be delivered in paper form under the current securities laws might also be delivered in electronic form.

A law firm specializing in securities regulation then asked the SEC to comment on whether a prospectus in downloadable form would meet SEC requirements. In essence, the SEC concluded that it did. There was no change in the substantive law of disclosure; only the delivery vehicle has changed.

Basically, then, when the Internet is used for delivery of a prospectus, the same rules apply as for the delivery of a paper prospectus. These rules are as follows:

① *Timely and adequate notice of the delivery of information is required.* Hosting a prospectus on a Web site does not constitute adequate notice, but separate e-mails or even postcards will satisfy the SEC's notice requirements.

② *The online communication system must be easily accessible.* This is very simple to do today because virtually anyone interested in purchasing securities has access to the Web.

③ *Some evidence of delivery must be created.* This requirement is relatively easy to satisfy. Those making online offerings can require an e-mail return receipt verification of any materials sent electronically.

Once these three requirements have been satisfied, the prospectus has been successfully delivered.

POTENTIAL LIABILITY CREATED BY ONLINE OFFERING MATERIALS

All printed prospectuses indicate that only the information given in the prospectuses can be used in conjunction with making an investment decision in the securities offered. The same wording, of course, appears on Web-based offerings. Those who create such Web-based offerings may be tempted, however, to go one step further. They may include hyperlinks to other sites that have analyzed the future prospects of the company, the products and services sold by the company, or the offering itself. To avoid potential liability, however, online offerors (the entities making the offerings) need to exercise caution when including such hyperlinks.

• **EXAMPLE 29.2** Suppose that a hyperlink goes to an analyst's Web page where the company making the offering is heavily touted. Further suppose that after the IPO, the stock price falls. By including the hyperlink on its Web site, the offering company is impliedly supporting the information presented on the linked page. In such a situation, the company may be liable under federal securities laws.[33] •

Remember also that for Regulation D offerings, only accredited investors may participate in such private placements. If the offeror places the offering circular on its Web site for general consumption by anybody on the Internet, potential problems may occur. General solicitation is restricted, obviously, because Regulation D offerings are private placements. If anyone can have access to the offering circular on the Web, the Regulation D exemption may be disqualified.

ONLINE SECURITIES OFFERINGS BY FOREIGN COMPANIES

Another question raised by Internet transactions has to do with securities offerings by foreign companies. Traditionally, foreign companies have not been able to offer new

33. See, for example, *In re Syntec Corp.*, 95 F.3d. 92 (9th Cir. 1996).

shares to the U.S. public without first registering them with the SEC. Today, however, anybody in the world can offer shares of stock worldwide via the Web.

The SEC asks that foreign issuers on the Internet implement measures to warn U.S. investors. For example, a foreign company offering shares of stock on the Internet must add a disclaimer on its Web site stating that it has not gone through the registration procedure in the United States. If the SEC believes that a Web site's offering of foreign securities has been targeted at U.S. residents, it will pursue that company in an attempt to require it to register in the United States.[34]

Online Securities Fraud

A major problem facing the SEC today is how to enforce the antifraud provisions of the securities laws in the online environment. An ongoing concern is how to curb online investment scams. One fraudulent investment scheme involved twenty thousand investors, who lost, in all, more than $3 million. Some cases have involved false claims about the earnings potential of home business programs, such as the claim that one could "earn $4,000 or more each month." Others have concerned claims of "guaranteed credit repair."

Here we look at some other significant Internet-related issues concerning securities fraud, including the use and abuse of Internet chat rooms to praise or criticize certain securities. Today, there are tens of thousands of online chat rooms devoted to the buying and selling of securities. None of these is an official site of any company, securities dealer, or other professional group. The abuse of these online chat forums for private gain in securities trading has become almost rampant, yet what can the SEC do to curb such speech? Clearly, the chat rooms cannot be shut down. After all, the First Amendment to the U.S. Constitution guarantees freedom of speech. Yet where does one draw the line between free speech and statements made to manipulate stock prices? Other issues relate to fictitious press releases and illegal offerings of securities.

Using Chat Rooms to Manipulate Stock Prices

"Pumping and dumping" occurs when a person who has purchased a particular stock heavily promotes ("pumps up") that stock—thereby creating a great demand for it and driving up its price—and then sells ("dumps") it. The practice of pumping up a stock and then dumping it is quite old. In the online world, however, the process can occur much more quickly and efficiently.

• **Example 29.3** The most famous case in this area involved Jonathan Lebed, a fifteen-year-old stock trader and Internet user from New Jersey. Lebed was the first minor ever charged with securities fraud by the SEC, but it is unlikely that he will be the last. The SEC charged that Lebed bought thinly traded stocks. After purchasing a stock, he would flood stock-related chat rooms, particularly at Yahoo!'s finance boards, with messages touting the stock's virtues. He used numerous false names so that no one would know that a single person was posting the messages. He would say that the stock was the most "undervalued stock in history" and that its price would jump by 1,000 percent "very soon." When other investors would then buy the stock, the price would go up quickly, and Lebed would sell out. The SEC forced the teenager to repay almost $300,000 in gains plus interest. He was allowed, however, to keep about $500,000 of the profits he made trading small-company stocks that he also touted on the Internet. •

34. International Series Release No. 1125 (March 23, 1998).

The SEC has been bringing an increasing number of cases against those who manipulate stock prices in this way. Consider that in 1995, such fraud resulted in only six SEC cases. By 2001, the SEC had brought an estimated one hundred actions against online perpetrators of fraudulent stock-price manipulation. (Stock prices may also be affected by negative statements about a company and its officers—see, for example, the case discussed in this chapter's *Business Law in the Online World* feature.)

BUSINESS LAW: //in the Online World

Fact versus Opinion

The SEC typically claims that fraud occurs when a false statement of fact is made. Many statements about stock, however, such as "this stock is headed for $20," are simply opinions. Opinions can never be labeled true or false at the time they are made; otherwise, they would not be opinions. As long as a person has a "genuine belief" that such an opinion is true, then, presumably, no fraud is involved. Thus, a defense that is often raised in cases involving allegedly untrue statements made via the Internet is that the statements were simply statements of opinion, not statements of fact.

In determining whether a statement is one of fact or opinion, a court will normally consider a number of factors. By way of illustration, consider a case brought by Global Telemedia International, Inc. (GTMI), against a number of "John Does" who had posted messages in online chat rooms.

The Problem Facing GTMI

In March 2000, GTMI's stock was trading at $4.70 per share. That month, persons using various aliases began to post messages in the GTMI chat room on the Raging Bull Web site. (Raging Bull is a financial service Web site that organizes chat rooms dedicated to publicly traded companies.) The messages were critical of GTMI and its officers. Over the next six months, GTMI's stock price decreased significantly—by October, the stock was closing at $0.25 a share. GTMI and its officers sued those who posted the messages, most of whom were listed as "John Does" in the suit. In the suit, GTMI alleged, among other things, defamation (see Chapter 4).

Distinguishing between Fact and Opinion

The court noted that defamation of a publicly traded company requires a "false statement of fact made with malice that caused damage." The defendants (those who posted the messages) asserted that their online statements were not actionable because they were statements of opinion, not statements of fact. Ultimately, the court agreed with the defendants. In making its decision, the court looked at the "totality of the circumstances," including the context and format of the statements, as well as the expectations of the audience in that particular situation.

Here, said the court, the context and format strongly suggested that the postings constituted opinion, not fact. "The statements were posted anonymously in the general cacophony of an Internet chat room in which about 1,000 messages a week are posted about GTMI. . . . They were part of an ongoing, freewheeling and highly animated exchange about GTMI and its turbulent history. At least several participants in addition to Defendants were repeat posters, indicating that the posters were just random individual investors interested in exchanging their views with other investors." The court went on to stress that the postings were "full of hyperbole, invective, shorthand phrases and language not generally found in fact-based documents, such as corporate press releases or SEC filings." In sum, concluded the court, the statements were not statements of fact, but statements of opinion. As such, they were not defamatory.[a]

FOR CRITICAL ANALYSIS

Why didn't GTMI sue the Web site operator, Raging Bull, instead of—or in addition to—the "John Does"?

a. *Global Telemedia International, Inc. v. Does,* 132 F.Supp.2d 1261 (C.D.Cal. 2001).

ILLEGAL SECURITIES OFFERINGS

In 1999, in the first cases involving illegal online securities offerings, the SEC filed suit against three individuals for illegally offering securities on an Internet auction site.[35] In essence, all three indicated that their companies would go public soon and attempted to sell unregistered securities via the Web auction site. All of these actions were in violation of Sections 5, 17(a)(1), and 17(a)(3) of the 1933 Securities Act.

In 2001, the SEC brought a variety of Internet-related fraud cases, many of them related to the initial three cases filed in 1999. For example, in March 2001, the SEC filed twelve separate actions in cases involving solicitations to invest in private companies that purportedly were going to go public (through an IPO).

35. *In re Davis,* SEC Administrative File No. 3-10080 (October 20, 1999); *In re Haas,* SEC Administrative File No. 3-10081 (October 20, 1999); *In re Sitaras,* SEC Administrative File No. 3-10082 (October 20, 1999).

Key Terms

accredited investor 777
bounty payment 788
insider trading 780
investment company 788
mutual fund 788
red herring 775
SEC Rule 10b-5 780
security 771
tippee 784
tombstone ad 775

Chapter Summary Investor Protection and Online Securities Offerings

Securities Act of 1933 (See pages 773–779.)	Prohibits fraud and stabilizes the securities industry by requiring disclosure of all essential information relating to the issuance of stocks to the investing public. 1. *Registration requirements*—Securities, unless exempt, must be registered with the SEC before being offered to the public through the mails or any facility of interstate commerce (including securities exchanges). The *registration statement* must include detailed financial information about the issuing corporation; the intended use of the proceeds of the securities being issued; and certain disclosures, such as interests of directors or officers and pending lawsuits. 2. *Prospectus*—A *prospectus* must be provided to investors, describing the security being sold, the issuing corporation, and the risk attaching to the security. 3. *Exemptions*—The SEC has exempted certain offerings from the requirements of the Securities Act of 1933. Exemptions may be determined on the basis of the size of the issue, whether the offering is private or public, and whether advertising is involved. Exemptions are summarized in Exhibit 29–1.

(continued)

Chapter Summary Investor Protection and Online Securities Offerings—continued

Securities Exchange Act of 1934 (See pages 779–788.)	Provides for the regulation and registration of securities exchanges, brokers, dealers, and national securities associations (such as the NASD). Maintains a continuous disclosure system for all corporations with securities on the securities exchanges and for those companies that have assets in excess of $5 million and five hundred or more shareholders (Section 12 companies). 1. *SEC Rule 10b-5 [under Section 10(b) of the 1934 act]*— a. Applies to insider trading by corporate officers, directors, majority shareholders, and any persons receiving information not available to the public who base their trading on this information. b. Liability for violation can be civil or criminal. c. May be violated by failing to disclose "material facts" that must be disclosed under this rule. d. Applies in virtually all cases concerning the trading of securities—a firm does not have to have its securities registered under the 1933 act for the 1934 act to apply. e. Liability may be based on the tipper/tippee or the misappropriation theory. f. Applies only when the requisites of federal jurisdiction (such as use of the mails, stock exchange facilities, or any facility of interstate commerce) are present. 2. *Insider trading [under Section 16(b) of the 1934 act]*—To prevent corporate officers and directors from taking advantage of inside information (information not available to the investing public), the 1934 act requires officers, directors, and shareholders owning 10 percent or more of the issued stock of a corporation to turn over to the corporation all short-term profits (called short-swing profits) realized from the purchase and sale or sale and purchase of corporate stock within any six-month period. 3. *Proxies [under Section 14(a) of the 1934 act]*—The SEC regulates the content of proxy statements sent to shareholders by corporate managers of Section 12 companies who are requesting authority to vote on behalf of the shareholders in a particular election on specified issues. Section 14(a) is essentially a disclosure law, with provisions similar to the antifraud provisions of SEC Rule 10b-5.
The Regulation of Investment Companies (See page 788.)	The Investment Company Act of 1940 provides for SEC regulation of investment company activities. It was altered and expanded by the amendments of 1970 and 1975.
State Securities Laws (See page 789.)	All states have corporate securities laws *(blue sky laws)* that regulate the offer and sale of securities within state borders; these laws are designed to prevent "speculative schemes which have no more basis than so many feet of 'blue sky.' " States regulate securities concurrently with the federal government.
Online Securities Offerings and Disclosures (See pages 789–791.)	In 1995, the SEC announced that anything that can be delivered in paper forms under current securities laws may also be delivered in electronic form. Generally, when the Internet is used for the delivery of a prospectus, the same rules apply as for the delivery of a paper prospectus. When securities offerings are made online, the offerors should be careful that any hyperlinked materials do not mislead investors. Caution should also be used when making Regulation D offerings (private placements), because general solicitation is restricted with these offerings.
Online Securities Fraud (See pages 791–792.)	A major problem facing the SEC today is how to enforce the antifraud provisions of the securities laws in the online environment. Internet-related forms of securities fraud include the manipulation of stock prices in online chat rooms and illegal securities offerings.

For Review

① What is meant by the term *securities*?
② What are the two major statutes regulating the securities industry? When was the Securities and Exchange Commission created, and what are its major purposes and functions?
③ What is insider trading? Why is it prohibited?
④ What are some of the features of state securities laws?
⑤ How are securities laws being applied in the online environment?

Questions and Case Problems

29–1. Registration Requirements. Langley Brothers, Inc., a corporation incorporated and doing business in Kansas, decides to sell no-par common stock worth $1 million to the public. The stock will be sold only within the state of Kansas. Joseph Langley, the chairman of the board, says the offering need not be registered with the Securities and Exchange Commission. His brother, Harry, disagrees. Who is right? Explain.

29–2. Registration Requirements. Huron Corp. has 300,000 common shares outstanding. The owners of these outstanding shares live in several different states. Huron decides to split the 300,000 shares two for one. Will Huron Corp. have to file a registration statement and prospectus on the 300,000 new shares to be issued as a result of the split? Explain.

29–3. Definition of a Security. The W. J. Howey Co. (Howey) owned large tracts of citrus acreage in Lake County, Florida. For several years, it planted about five hundred acres annually, keeping half of the groves itself and offering the other half to the public to help finance additional development. Howey-in-the-Hills Service, Inc., was a service company engaged in cultivating and developing these groves, including the harvesting and marketing of the crops. Each prospective customer was offered both a land sales contract and a service contract, after being told that it was not feasible to invest in a grove unless service arrangements were made. Of the acreage sold by Howey, 85 percent was sold with a service contract with Howey-in-the-Hills Service. Howey did not register with the Securities and Exchange Commission (SEC) or meet the other administrative requirements that issuers of securities must fulfill. The SEC sued to enjoin Howey from continuing to offer the land sales and service contracts. Howey responded that no SEC violation existed because no securities had been issued. Evaluate the definition of a security given in this chapter, and then determine which party should prevail in court, Howey or the SEC. [*SEC v. W. J. Howey Co.,* 328 U.S. 293, 66 S.Ct. 1100, 90 L.Ed. 1244 (1946)]

29–4. SEC Rule 10b-5. In early 1985, FMC Corp. made plans to buy some of its own stock as part of a restructuring of its balance statement. Unknown to FMC management, the brokerage firm FMC employed—Goldman, Sachs & Co.—disclosed information on the stock purchase that found its way to Ivan Boesky. FMC was one of the seven major corporations in whose stock Boesky allegedly traded using inside information. Boesky made purchases of FMC's stock between February 18 and February 21, 1986, and between March 12 and April 4, 1986. Boesky's purchases amounted to a substantial portion of the total volume of FMC stock traded during these periods. The price of FMC stock increased from $71.25 on February 20, 1986, to $97.00 on April 25, 1986. As a result, FMC paid substantially more for the repurchase of its own stock than anticipated. When FMC discovered Boesky's knowledge of its recapitalization plan, FMC sued Boesky for the excess price it had paid—approximately $220 million. Discuss whether FMC should recover under Section 10(b) of the Securities Exchange Act and SEC Rule 10b-5. [*In re Ivan F. Boesky Securities Litigation,* 36 F.3d 255 (2d Cir. 1994)]

29–5. SEC Rule 10b-5. Louis Ferraro was the chairman and president of Anacomp, Inc. In June 1988, Ferraro told his good friend Michael Maio that Anacomp was negotiating a tender offer for stock in Xidex Corp. Maio passed on the information to Patricia Ladavac, a friend of both Ferraro and Maio. Maio and Ladavac immediately purchased shares in Xidex stock. On the day that the tender offer was announced—an announcement that caused the price of Xidex shares to increase—Maio and Ladavac sold their Xidex stock and made substantial profits (Maio made $211,000 from the transactions, and Ladavac gained $78,750). The Securities and Exchange Commission (SEC) brought an action against the three individuals, alleging that they had violated, among other laws, SEC Rule 10b-5. Maio and Ladavac claimed that they had done nothing illegal. They argued that they had no fiduciary duty either to Anacomp or to Xidex, and therefore they had no duty to disclose or abstain from trading in the stock of those corporations. Had Maio and Ladavac violated SEC Rule 10b-5? Discuss fully. [*SEC v. Maio,* 51 F.3d 623 (7th Cir. 1995)]

29–6. Definition of a Security. Life Partners, Inc. (LPI), facilitates the sale of life insurance policies that are owned by persons suffering from AIDS (acquired immune deficiency syndrome) to investors at a discount. The investors pay LPI, and LPI pays the policyholder. Typically, the policyholder, in turn, assigns the policy to LPI, which also obtains the right to make LPI's president the beneficiary of the policy. On the policyholder's death, LPI receives the proceeds of the policy and pays the investor. In this way, the terminally ill sellers secure much-needed income in the final years of life, when employment is unlikely and medical bills are often staggering. The Securities and Exchange Commission (SEC) sought to enjoin (prevent) LPI from engaging in further transactions on the ground that the investment contracts were securities, which LPI had failed to register with the SEC in violation of securities laws. Do the investment contracts meet the definition of a security discussed in this chapter? Discuss fully. [*SEC v. Life Partners, Inc.*, 87 F.3d 536 (D.C.Cir. 1996)]

29–7. Section 10(b). Joseph Jett worked for Kidder, Peabody & Co., a financial services firm owned by General Electric Co. (GE). Over a three-year period, Jett allegedly engaged in a scheme to generate false profits at Kidder, Peabody to increase his performance-based bonuses. When the scheme was discovered, Daniel Chill and other GE shareholders who had bought stock in the previous year filed a suit in a federal district court against GE. The shareholders alleged that GE had engaged in securities fraud in violation of Section 10(b). They claimed that GE's interest in justifying its investment in Kidder, Peabody gave GE "a motive to willfully blind itself to facts casting doubt on Kidder's purported profitability." On what basis might the court dismiss the shareholders' complaint? Discuss fully. [*Chill v. General Electric Co.*, 101 F.3d 263 (2d Cir. 1996)]

29–8. SEC Rule 10b-5. Grand Metropolitan PLC (Grand Met) planned to make a tender offer as part of an attempted takeover of the Pillsbury Co. Grand Met hired Robert Falbo, an independent contractor, to complete electrical work as part of security renovations to its offices to prevent leaks of information concerning the planned tender offer. Falbo was given a master key to access the executive offices. When an executive secretary told Falbo that a takeover was brewing, he used his key to access the offices and eavesdrop on conversations; in this way, he learned that Pillsbury was the target. Falbo bought thousands of shares of Pillsbury stock for less than $40 per share. Within two months, Grand Met made an offer for all outstanding Pillsbury stock at $60 per share and ultimately paid up to $66 per share. Falbo made over $165,000 in profit. The Securities and Exchange Commission (SEC) filed a suit in a federal district court against Falbo and others for alleged violations of, among other things, SEC Rule 10b-5. Under what theory might Falbo be liable? Do the circumstances of this case meet all of the requirements for liability under that theory? Explain. [*SEC v. Falbo*, 14 F.Supp.2d 508 (S.D.N.Y. 1998)]

29–9. Definition of a Security. In 1997, Scott and Sabrina Levine formed Friendly Power Co. (FPC) and Friendly Power Franchise Co. (FPC-Franchise). FPC obtained a license to operate as a utility company in California. FPC granted FPC-Franchise the right to pay commissions to "operators" who converted residential customers to FPC. Each operator paid for a "franchise"—a geographic area, determined by such factors as the number of households and competition from other utilities. In exchange for 50 percent of FPC's net profits on sales to residential customers in its territory, each franchise was required to maintain a 5 percent market share of power customers in that territory. Franchises were sold to telemarketing firms, which solicited customers. The telemarketers sold interests in each franchise to between fifty and ninety-four "partners," each of whom invested money. FPC began supplying electricity to its customers in May 1998. Less than three months later, the Securities and Exchange Commission (SEC) filed a suit in a federal district court against the Levines and others, alleging that the "franchises" were unregistered securities offered for sale to the public in violation of the Securities Act of 1933. What is the definition of a security? Should the court rule in favor of the SEC? Why or why not? [*SEC v. Friendly Power Co., LLC*, 49 F.Supp.2d 1363 (S.D.Fla. 1999)]

TEST YOUR KNOWLEDGE—ANSWER ON THE WEB

29–10. 2TheMart.com, Inc., was conceived in January 1999 to launch an auction Web site to compete with eBay, Inc. On January 19, 2TheMart announced that its Web site was in its "final development" stages and expected to be active by the end of July as a "preeminent" auction site, and that the company had "retained the services of leading Web site design and architecture consultants to design and construct" the site. Based on the announcement, investors rushed to buy 2TheMart's stock, causing a rapid increase in the price. On February 3, 2TheMart entered into an agreement with IBM to take preliminary steps to plan the site. Three weeks later, 2TheMart announced that the site was "currently in final development." On June 1, 2TheMart signed a contract with IBM to design, build, and test the site, with a target delivery date of October 8. When 2TheMart's site did not debut as announced, Mary Harrington and others who had bought the stock filed a suit in a federal district court against the firm's officers, alleging violations of the Securities Exchange Act of 1934. The defendants responded, in part, that any alleged misrepresentations were not material and asked the court to dismiss the suit. How should the court rule, and why? [*In re 2TheMart.com, Inc. Securities Litigation*, 114 F.Supp.2d 955 (C.D.Ca. 2000)]

A QUESTION OF ETHICS AND SOCIAL RESPONSIBILITY

29–11. Susan Waldbaum was a niece of the president and controlling shareholder of Waldbaum, Inc. Susan's mother (the president's sister) told Susan that the company was going to be sold at a favorable price and that a tender offer was soon to be made. She told Susan not to tell anyone except her husband, Keith Loeb, about the sale. (Loeb did not work for the company and was never brought into the family's inner circle, in which family members discussed confidential business information.) The next day, Susan told her husband of the sale and cautioned him not to tell anyone because "it could possibly ruin the sale." The day after he learned of the sale, Loeb told Robert Chestman, his broker, about the sale, and Chestman purchased shares of the company for both Loeb and himself. Chestman was later convicted by a jury of, among other things, trading on misappropriated inside information in violation of SEC Rule 10b-5. [*United States v. Chestman*, 947 F.2d 551 (2d Cir. 1991)]

1. On appeal, the central question was whether Chestman had acquired the inside information about the tender offer as a

result of an insider's breach of a fiduciary duty. Could Loeb—the "tipper" in this case—be considered an insider?
2. If Loeb was not an insider, did he owe any fiduciary (legal) duty to his wife or his wife's family to keep the information confidential? Would it be fair of the court to impose such a legal duty on Loeb?

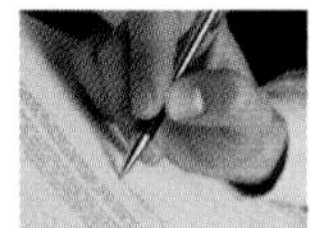

FOR CRITICAL ANALYSIS

29–12. Do you think that the tipper/tippee and misappropriation theories extend liability under SEC Rule 10b-5 too far? Why or why not?

Internet Exercises

Go to the *Business Law Today* home page at **http://blt.westbuslaw.com**. Select "Interactive Study Center" and then click on "Chapter 29." There you will find the following Internet research exercise that you can perform to learn more about the role of the SEC in securities regulation:

Activity 29–1: The SEC's Role

Before the Test

Go to the *Business Law Today* home page at **http://blt.westbuslaw.com**. Click on "Interactive Quizzes." You will find at least twenty interactive questions relating to this chapter.

CHAPTER 30

Limited Liability Companies and Partnerships

"All gains . . . are the fruit of venturing."

Herodotus, fifth century B.C.E.
(Greek historian)

CHAPTER CONTENTS

LEARNING OBJECTIVES

After reading this chapter, you should be able to answer the following questions:

① What advantages do limited liability companies and partnerships offer to businesspersons that are not offered by general partnerships or the corporate form of business?

② How are limited liability companies formed, and who decides how they will be managed and operated?

③ What is the difference between limited liability companies and limited liability partnerships?

④ What is a family limited liability partnership?

⑤ What are the key differences between the rights and liabilities of general partners and limited partners?

The two most common forms of business organization selected by two or more persons entering into business together are the partnership and the corporation. As explained in previous chapters, each form has distinct advantages and disadvantages. For partnerships, the advantage is that partnership income is taxed only once (all income is "passed through" the partnership entity to the partners themselves, who are taxed only as individuals); the disadvantage is the personal liability of the partners. For corporations, the advantage is the limited liability of shareholders; the disadvantage is the double taxation of corporate income. For many entrepreneurs and investors, the ideal business form would combine the tax advantages of the partnership with the limited liability of the corporate enterprise.

LIMITED LIABILITY COMPANY (LLC)
A hybrid form of business enterprise that offers the limited liability of a corporation and the tax advantages of a partnership.

A relatively new form of business organization, the **limited liability company (LLC)**, is a hybrid that meets these needs by offering the limited liability of a corporation and the tax advantages of a partnership. Increasingly, LLCs are becoming an organizational form of choice among businesspersons, a trend encouraged by state statutes permitting their use. As the chapter-opening quotation indicates, all gains are the "fruit of venturing," and LLCs—to the extent that they encourage business ventures—contribute to those gains.

In this chapter, we begin by examining the LLC, the origins and evolution of which are discussed in this chapter's *Landmark in the Law* feature on pages 800 and 801. We then look at a similar type of entity that is also relatively new—the limited liability partnership (LLP). The chapter concludes with a discussion of the limited partnership, a special type of partnership in which some of the partners have limited liability, and the limited liability limited partnership (LLLP).

Limited Liability Companies

ON THE WEB
You can find information on how to form an LLC, including the fees charged in each state for filing LLC articles of organization, at the Web site of BIZCORP International, Inc. Go to **http://www.bizcorp.com**.

LLCs are governed by state LLC statutes. These laws vary, of course, from state to state. In an attempt to create more uniformity among the states in this respect, in 1995 the National Conference of Commissioners on Uniform State Laws issued the Uniform Limited Liability Company Act (ULLCA), excerpts from which are included at the end of this text in Appendix F. To date, less than one-fourth of the states have adopted the ULLCA, and thus the law governing LLCs remains far from uniform. Some provisions are common to most state statutes, however, and we base our discussion of LLCs in this section on these common elements.

The Nature of the LLC

MEMBER
The term used to designate a person who has an ownership interest in a limited liability company.

LLCs share many characteristics with corporations. Like corporations, LLCs are creatures of the state. In other words, they must be formed and operated in compliance with state law. Also like corporations, LLCs are legal entities apart from their owners, who are called **members**. As a legal person, the LLC can sue or be sued, enter into contracts, and hold title to property [ULLCA 201]. Similar to shareholders in a corporation, members of an LLC enjoy limited liability [ULLCA 303]. Members of an LLC can also bring derivative actions on behalf of the LLC [ULLCA 101]. As with the corporate shareholder's derivative suit, any damages recovered go to the LLC, not to the members personally. (See, for example, the case discussed in this chapter's *Business Law in the Online World* feature on page 802.)

The terminology used to describe LLCs formed in other states or nations is also similar to the terminology used in corporate law. For example, an LLC formed in one state but doing business in another state is referred to in the second state as a *foreign LLC*.

LLC Formation

ARTICLES OF ORGANIZATION
The document filed with a designated state official by which a limited liability company is formed.

To form an LLC, **articles of organization** must be filed with a central state agency—usually the secretary of state's office [ULLCA 202]. Typically, the articles are required to include such information as the name of the business, its principal address, the name and address of a registered agent, the names of the members, and information on how the LLC will be managed [ULLCA 203]. The business's name must include the words "Limited Liability Company" or the initials "LLC" [ULLCA 105(a)].

LANDMARK IN THE LAW
Limited Liability Company (LLC) Statutes

In 1977, Wyoming became the first state to pass legislation authorizing the creation of a limited liability company (LLC). Although LLCs emerged in the United States only in 1977, they have been in existence for over a century in other areas, including several European and South American nations. The South American *limitada,* for example, is a form of business organization that operates more or less as a partnership but provides limited liability for the owners.

Taxation of LLCs In the United States, after Wyoming's adoption of an LLC statute, it still was not known how the Internal Revenue Service (IRS) would treat the LLC for tax purposes. In 1988, however, the IRS ruled that Wyoming LLCs would be taxed as partnerships instead of as corporations, providing that certain requirements were met. Prior to this ruling, only one other state—Florida, in 1982—had authorized LLCs. The 1988 ruling encouraged other states to enact LLC statutes, and in less than a decade, all states had done so.

New IRS rules that went into effect on January 1, 1997, encouraged even more widespread use of LLCs in the business world. These rules provide that any unincorporated business will automatically be taxed as a partnership unless it indicates

In addition to filing the articles of organization, a few states require that a notice of the intention to form an LLC be published in a local newspaper. About one-fourth of the states specifically require LLCs to have at least two owners, or members. The rest of the states usually permit one-member LLCs, although some LLC statutes are silent on this issue.

The following case illustrates some of the problems that can arise during the first years of a newly formed enterprise.

CASE 30.1 Skywizard.com, LLC v. Computer Personalities Systems, Inc.

United States District Court,
District of Maine, 2000.
__ F.Supp.2d __.

FACTS Gary Cubeta and Gail Ejdys founded Skywizard.com, LLC, as an Internet service provider (ISP). In May 1999, they entered into an agreement with Computer Personalities Systems, Inc. (CPSI), a retailer of computer hardware and software whose principal, George Cappell, markets products through infomercials on cable television. CPSI agreed that, among other things, beginning September 1 it would run, one weekend per month, a "special promotion," according to which a customer who bought a specified computer would receive a year's Internet service through Skywizard.com to start whenever the customer wanted. For each computer sold under this promotion, CPSI agreed to pay Skywizard.com $79. Despite this fee, the ISP incurred a loss of about $44 per year for each "special promotion" subscriber. By March 2000, most of the ISP's subscribers were people who had bought computers through CPSI, including about a third of those who bought the "special promotion" computers. CPSI had failed to run the promotion on September 1, however, and partly for this reason Skywizard.com filed

LANDMARK IN THE LAW—Continued

otherwise on the tax form. The exceptions involve publicly traded companies, companies formed under a state incorporation statute, and certain foreign-owned companies. If a business chooses to be taxed as a corporation, it can indicate this choice by checking a box on the IRS form.

Foreign Entities May Be LLC Members Part of the impetus behind the creation of LLCs in this country is that foreign investors are allowed to become LLC members. Generally, in an era increasingly characterized by global business efforts and investments, the LLC offers U.S. firms and potential investors from other countries flexibility and opportunities greater than those available through partnerships or corporations.

APPLICATION TO TODAY'S WORLD

Once it became clear that LLCs could be taxed as partnerships, the LLC form of business organization was widely adopted. Members could avoid the personal liability associated with the partnership form of business as well as the "double taxation" of the corporate form of business. Today, LLCs, which only a few years ago were largely unknown in this country, are a widely used form of business organization.

CASE 30.1—Continued

a suit in a federal district court against CPSI, alleging breach of contract. Skywizard.com estimated that 1,500 units would have been shipped if the September promotion had run and that one-third of the buyers would have subscribed to Skywizard.com, representing lost profits of $67,500.

ISSUE Is Skywizard.com entitled to damages for CPSI's breach of contract?

DECISION Yes. The court held that CPSI breached the contract to run the September promotion. The court also decided, however, that damages could not be determined because the life of Skywizard.com had been too short, and entered a judgment in favor of Skywizard.com for $100 in nominal damages.

REASON The court stated that "[r]egardless of the number of computers that CPSI may have shipped to customers had a September 1999 Special Promotion aired, the evidence is insufficient to substantiate the amount of Skywizard's damages based on loss of the $79 fee with reasonable probability. * * * [W]ere all of CPSI's Special Promotion customers to take advantage of the offer of one year's free Internet service (as they theoretically could), the $79 per customer fee would be more than offset by the cost to Skywizard to service all of the new subscribers. * * * [I]n view of the newness of the Skywizard enterprise, the fact that Skywizard imposed no deadline within which customers were obliged to accept the offer of one year's free Internet service and the fact that Skywizard's evidence at most amounted to a snapshot of its customer base as of one point in time," the court concluded that "the record is barren of sufficient historic company data from which a reliable projection of the composition of the customer base can be made. In view of the clear breach of contract, an award of nominal damages nonetheless is appropriate."

FOR CRITICAL ANALYSIS—Economic Consideration *How long should a company's "track record" be to enable it to recover lost profits for a breach of contract?*

BUSINESS LAW: //in the Online World

LLC Derivative Actions

Recall from Chapter 27 that under corporate law, a shareholder's derivative suit may be brought against third parties, or even against corporate directors and officers, to enforce a corporate cause of action or recover damages for harm caused to the corporate enterprise. The ULLCA and most state LLC statutes similarly permit LLC members to bring derivative actions for these purposes. Yet, as with a corporate shareholder's suit against a director or officer of a small, closely held corporation, it is sometimes not clear whether an LLC member should be able to bring a suit personally to recover for harms caused by LLC managers or whether the member must bring a derivative action on behalf of the LLC. Consider a case decided by a California court, which focused on just this issue.

The Fraudulent Transfer of Assets

The case was brought by three members of an eight-member LLC that had been formed to do business as an Internet service provider (ISP). The name of the LLC was PacLink Communications, LLC (PacLink-1). According to the three members (the plaintiffs), the assets of PacLink-1 were transferred to a new company, called PacLink Communications International, LLC (PacLink-2), which had been organized by four members of PacLink-1. Subsequently, the assets were again transferred, this time to PacLink Communications International, Inc. (PacLink-3), a California company organized by eHongKong.Com, Inc.

When the plaintiffs learned of these events, they sued the four business entities and the nine individuals who owned and operated them. In their suit, the plaintiffs alleged that PacLink-1's assets were transferred without their knowledge or consent. They also claimed that the companies receiving the assets paid several hundred thousand dollars to other members of PacLink-1 for the assets but that none of the money was ever distributed to the plaintiffs. The plaintiffs further contended that the "fraudulent transfers" rendered PacLink-1 insolvent and prevented the plaintiffs from being paid for their ownership interests in PacLink-1. The plaintiffs claimed that their combined ownership interests amounted to $284,000.

Personal Suit or Derivative Action?

The defendants argued that the plaintiffs lacked standing to bring a personal suit against them because, as individuals, the plaintiffs had suffered no direct injury or loss. Rather, because the plaintiffs' claim was that the value of PacLink-1, and thus their ownership interests, had been diminished, they were only entitled to sue derivatively, on behalf of PacLink-1. The trial court disagreed with the defendants and ruled that the plaintiffs could sue as individuals.

On appeal, however, the appellate court reversed the trial court's decision. The appellate court held that the plaintiffs' suit could only be brought as a derivative action on behalf of the LLC. The court reasoned that the "essence of plaintiffs' claim was that the assets of the company were fraudulently transferred without any compensation being paid to the company. This constituted an injury to the company itself. Since members of the company held no direct ownership interest in the company's assets, they could not be directly injured when the company was improperly deprived of those assets."[a]

FOR CRITICAL ANALYSIS

Why did the plaintiffs sue as individuals, rather than bring a derivative action, in the first place? Was there any benefit to suing as individuals instead of suing derivatively, on behalf of PacLink-1?

a. *PacLink Communications International, Inc. v. Superior Court,* 90 Cal.App.4th 958, 109 Cal.Rptr.2d 436 (2001).

JURISDICTIONAL REQUIREMENTS

One of the significant differences between LLCs and corporations has to do with federal jurisdictional requirements. The federal jurisdiction statute provides that a corporation is deemed to be a citizen of the state where it is incorporated and maintains its principal place of business. The statute does not mention the citizenship of partnerships, LLCs, and other unincorporated associations, but the courts have tended to regard these entities as citizens of every state in which their members are citizens.

The citizenship of LLCs may come into play when a party sues an LLC based on diversity of citizenship. Remember from Chapter 3 that in some circumstances, such as when parties to a lawsuit are from different states, a federal court can exercise diversity jurisdiction in cases in which the amount in controversy exceeds $75,000. *Total* diversity of citizenship must exist, however. • **EXAMPLE 30.1** A citizen of New York will not be able to bring a suit in federal court—on the basis of diversity jurisdiction—against multiple defendants if one of the defendants is also a citizen of New York. •

ADVANTAGES AND DISADVANTAGES OF THE LLC

Although the LLC offers many advantages to businesspersons, there are also some disadvantages attending this form of business organization. We look now at some of the advantages and disadvantages of the LLC.

Advantages of the LLC A key advantage of the LLC is that the liability of members is limited to the amount of their investments. Another advantage is the flexibility of the LLC in regard to both taxation and management.

Another advantage is that an LLC with two or more members can choose to be taxed either as a partnership or as a corporation. An LLC that wants to distribute profits to the members may prefer to be taxed as a partnership to avoid the "double taxation" characteristic of the corporate entity. Remember that a corporation as an entity pays income taxes on its profits, and the shareholders pay personal income taxes on profits distributed as dividends. Unless an LLC indicates that it wishes to be taxed as a corporation, it is automatically taxed as a partnership by the IRS. This means that the LLC as an entity pays no taxes; rather, as in a partnership, profits are "passed through" the LLC to the members who then personally pay taxes on the profits. If LLC members want to reinvest profits in the business, however, rather than distribute the profits to members, they may prefer to be taxed as a corporation if corporate income tax rates are lower than personal tax rates. Part of the attractiveness of the LLC is this flexibility with respect to taxation.

For federal income tax purposes, one-member LLCs are automatically taxed as sole proprietorships unless they indicate that they wish to be taxed as corporations. With respect to state taxes, most states follow the IRS rules. Still another advantage of the LLC for businesspersons is the flexibility it offers in terms of business operations and management—as will be discussed shortly.

REMEMBER A uniform law is a "model" law. It does not become the law of any state until the state legislature adopts it, either in part or in its entirety.

Disadvantages of the LLC The disadvantages of the LLC are relatively few. Although initially there was uncertainty over how LLCs would be taxed, that disadvantage no longer exists. One remaining disadvantage is that state LCC statutes are not yet uniform. Until all of the states have adopted the ULLCA, an LLC in one state will have to check the rules in the other states in which the firm does business to ensure that it retains its limited liability. Generally, though, most—if not all—states apply to a foreign LLC (an LLC formed in another state) the law of the state where the LLC was formed.

Still another disadvantage is the lack of case law dealing with LLCs. How the courts interpret statutes provides important guidelines for businesses. Given the relative newness of the LLC as a business form in the United States, there is not, as yet, a substantial body of case law to provide this kind of guidance.

The LLC Operating Agreement

OPERATING AGREEMENT
In a limited liability company, an agreement in which the members set forth the details of how the business will be managed and operated. State statutes typically give the members wide latitude in deciding for themselves the rules that will govern their organization.

In an LCC, the members themselves can decide how to operate the various aspects of the business by forming an **operating agreement** [ULLCA 103(a)]. Operating agreements typically contain provisions relating to management, how profits will be divided, the transfer of membership interests, whether the LLC will be dissolved on the death or departure of a member, and other important issues.

An operating agreement need not be in writing and indeed need not even be formed for an LLC to exist. Generally, though, LLC members should protect their interests by forming a written operating agreement. As with any business arrangement, disputes may arise over any number of issues. If there is no agreement covering the topic under dispute, such as how profits will be divided, the state LLC statute will govern the outcome. For example, most LLC statutes provide that if the members have not specified how profits will be divided, they will be divided equally among the members.

Generally, when an issue is not covered by an operating agreement or by an LLC statute, the principles of partnership law are applied. At issue in the following case was whether partnership law should apply to a dispute between LLC members as to how business receipts were to be divided on the firm's dissolution.

CASE 30.2 Hurwitz v. Padden

Court of Appeals of Minnesota, 1998.
581 N.W.2d 359.
http://www.lawlibrary.state.mn.us/archive/capgi.html[a]

HISTORICAL AND SOCIAL SETTING *The law has long recognized that a partnership is based on mutual trust and confidence.*[b] *In their dealings with one another, partners are subject to the highest standards of good faith and integrity. This is also true of the officers and shareholders of close corporations.*[c] *In fact, reasoning that many close corporations are partnerships under a different name, some courts have even applied partnership principles to enforce the fiduciary duty among the shareholders of close corporations.*[d]

FACTS Thomas Hurwitz and Michael Padden formed a two-person law firm as a partnership without a written agreement. They shared all proceeds on a fifty-fifty basis and reported all income as partnership income. Less than eighteen months later, Hurwitz filed articles of organization with the state of Minnesota to establish the firm as an LLC. More than three years later, Padden told Hurwitz that he wanted to dissolve their professional relationship. They resolved all business issues between them, except for a division of fees from several of the firm's cases. Hurwitz filed a suit in a Minnesota state court against Padden, seeking, among other things, a distribution of the fees on a fifty-fifty basis. The court applied the principles of partnership law, ruled that the fees should be divided equally, and entered a judgment in favor of Hurwitz for $101,750. Padden appealed, arguing in part that these principles of partnership law should not apply to an LLC.

ISSUE Do partnership principles apply to the dissolution, the winding up, and the distribution of business receipts of an LLC?

DECISION Yes. The state intermediate appellate court affirmed the decision of the lower court. The appellate court concluded that the disputed fees should be divided equally, as the receipts were divided before the dissolution.

REASON The court pointed out that the state LLC act specifically incorporated the definition and use of the term *dissolution* from the Uniform Partnership Act (UPA).

a. This page includes a partial list of Minnesota Court of Appeals opinions available in the Minnesota State Law Library online database. The last name of the parties in these cases begins with the letter G, H, or I. Scroll down the list to the *Hurwitz* name and click on the link to read the case.

b. *Prince v. Sonnesyn,* 222 Minn. 528, 25 N.W.2d 468 (1946).

c. *Evans v. Blesi,* 345 N.W.2d 775 (Minn.App. 1984), review denied (Minn. 1984).

d. See, for example, *Harris v. Mardan Business Systems, Inc.,* 421 N.W.2d 350 (Minn.App. 1988).

CASE 30.2—Continued

Under both statutes, a business entity is not terminated on dissolution but continues until all business is taken care of. The court listed the facts that influenced its application of this law to the circumstances in this case. The court noted in particular that the firm had no written agreement regarding the division of receipts before or on dissolution, the disputed fees related to work acquired before the dissolution, and before the dissolution the firm divided receipts equally between the parties.

FOR CRITICAL ANALYSIS—Social Consideration *Should the principles of partnership law apply to other forms of business entities?*

MANAGEMENT OF AN LLC

"One cannot manage too many affairs: Like pumpkins in the water, one pops up while you try to hold down the other."

CHINESE PROVERB

Basically, there are two options for managing an LLC. The members may decide in their operating agreement to be either a "member-managed" LLC or a "manager-managed" LLC. Most LLC statutes and the ULLCA provide that unless the articles of organization specify otherwise, an LLC is assumed to be member managed [ULLCA 203(a)(6)]. In a *member-managed* LLC, all of the members participate in management, and decisions are made by majority vote [ULLCA 404(a)]. In a *manager-managed* LLC, the members designate a group of persons to manage the firm. The management group may consist of only members, both members and nonmembers, or only nonmembers. Managers in a manager-managed LLC owe fiduciary duties to the LLC and its members, including the duty of loyalty and the duty of care [ULLCA 409(a) and 409(h)], just as corporate directors and officers owe fiduciary duties to the corporation and its shareholders.

The members of an LLC can also set forth in their operating agreement provisions governing decision-making procedures. For example, the agreement can include procedures for choosing or removing managers, an issue on which most LLC statutes are silent, although the ULLCA provides that members may choose and remove managers by majority vote [ULLCA 404(b)(3)]. The members are also free to include in the agreement provisions designating when and for what purposes formal members' meetings will be held. In contrast to state laws governing corporations, most state LLC statutes have no provisions regarding members' meetings. Members may also specify in their agreement how voting rights will be apportioned. If they do not, LLC statutes in most states provide that voting rights are apportioned according to each member's capital contributions. Some states provide that, in the absence of an agreement to the contrary, each member has one vote.

Limited Liability Partnerships

LIMITED LIABILITY PARTNERSHIP (LLP)
A business organizational form that is similar to the LCC but that is designed more for professionals who normally do business as partners in a partnership. The LLP is a pass-through entity for tax purposes, like the general partnership, but it limits the personal liability of the partners.

The **limited liability partnership (LLP)** is similar to the LLC but is designed more for professionals who normally do business as partners in a partnership. The major advantage of the LLP is that it allows a partnership to continue as a pass-through entity for tax purposes but limits the personal liability of the partners.

In 1991, Texas became the first state to enact an LLP statute. Other states quickly followed suit, and by 1997, virtually all of the states had enacted LLP statutes. Like LLCs, LLPs must be formed and operated in compliance with state statutes. The appropriate form must be filed with a central state agency, usually the secretary of state's office, and the business's name must include either "Limited Liability Partnership" or "LLP."

In most states, it is relatively easy to convert a traditional partnership into an LLP because the firm's basic organizational structure remains the same. Additionally, all of the statutory and common law rules governing partnerships still apply (apart from

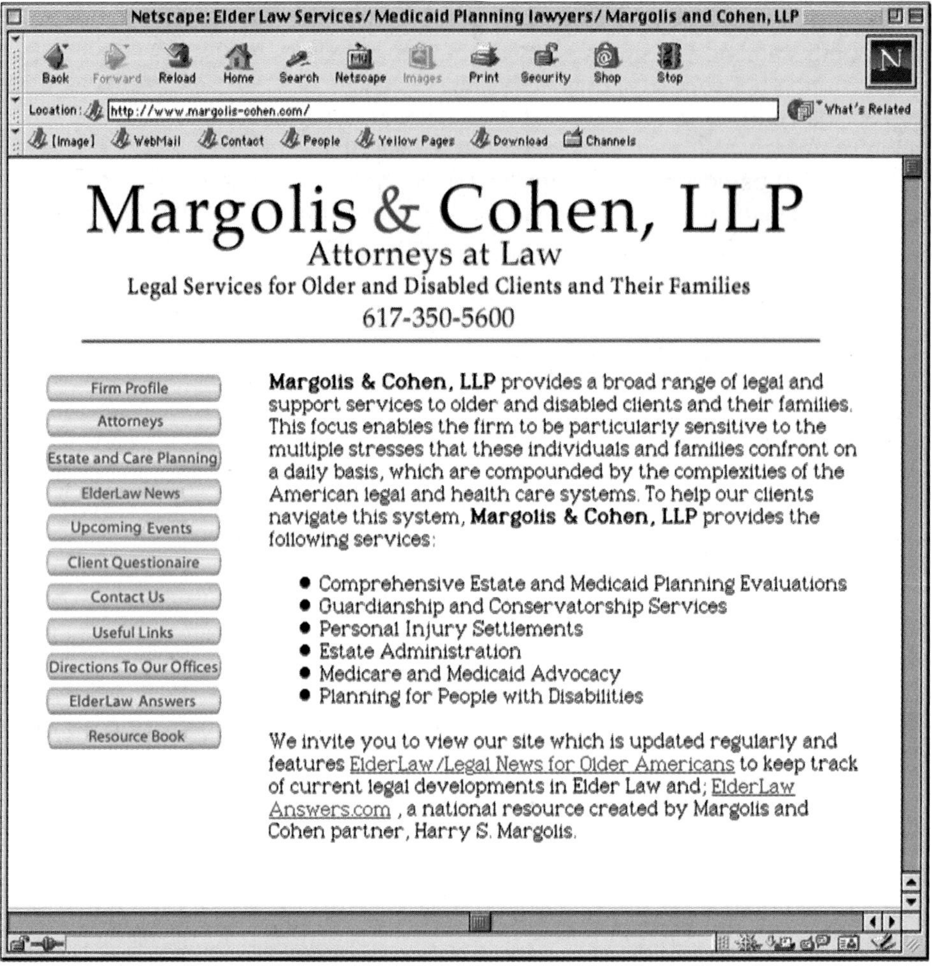

Attorneys advertise their affiliation as a limited liability partnership (LLP). What advantages do the partners in an LLP have over the participants in other forms of business organization? Are there any disadvantages to organizing a firm as an LLP?

those modified by the LLP statute). Normally, LLP statutes are simply amendments to a state's already existing partnership law.

The LLP is especially attractive for two categories of businesses: professional services and family businesses. Professional service firms include law firms and accounting firms. Family limited liability partnerships are basically business organizations in which all of the partners are related.

LIABILITY IN AN LLP

Many professionals, such as attorneys and accountants, work together using the business form of the partnership. Remember from Chapter 25 that a major disadvantage of the partnership is the unlimited personal liability of its owner-partners. Partners are also subject to joint and several (individual) liability for partnership obligations. • **EXAMPLE 30.2** A group of lawyers is operating as a partnership. A client sues one of the attorneys for malpractice and wins a large judgment, and the firm's malpractice insurance is insufficient to cover the obligation. When the attorney's personal assets are exhausted, the personal assets of the other, innocent partners can be used to satisfy the judgment.•

The LLP allows professionals to avoid personal liability for the malpractice of other partners. Although LLP statutes vary from state to state, generally each state statute limits the liability of partners in some way. For example, Delaware law protects each innocent partner from the "debts and obligations of the partnership arising from negligence, wrongful acts, or misconduct." In North Carolina, Texas, and Washington, D.C., the statutes protect innocent partners from obligations arising from "errors, omissions, negligence, incompetence, or malfeasance." Although the language of these statutes may seem to apply specifically to attorneys, virtually any group of professionals can use the LLP.

Questions remain, however, concerning the exact limits of this exemption from liability. One question is whether limits on liability apply outside the state in which the LLP was formed. Another question involves whether liability should be imposed to some extent on a negligent partner's supervising partner.

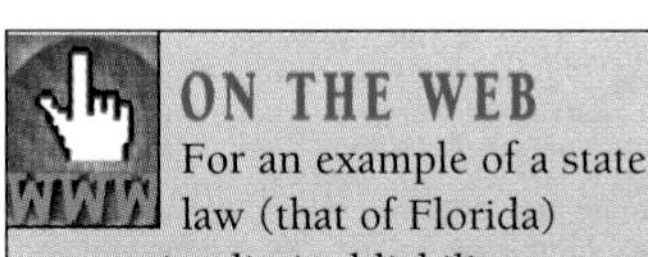

ON THE WEB For an example of a state law (that of Florida) governing limited liability partnerships, go to the Internet Legal Resource Guide's Web page at

www.ilrg.com/whatsnews/statute.html

and scroll down the page to "Registered Limited Liability Partnerships."

Liability outside the State of Formation Because state LLP statutes are not uniform, a question arises when an LLP formed in one state does business in another state. If the LLP statutes in the two states provide different liability protection, which law applies? Most states apply the law of the state in which the LLP was formed, even when the firm does business in another state. Some states, though, do not expressly recognize foreign LLPs (that is, LLPs formed in another state), and others do not require foreign LLPs to register before doing business.[1]

Supervising Partner's Liability A partner who commits a wrongful act, such as negligence, is liable for the results of the act. Also liable is the partner who supervises the party who commits a wrongful act. This is generally true for all types of partners and partnerships, including LLPs.

When the partners are members of an LLP and more than one member is negligent, there is a question as to how liability is to be shared. Is each partner jointly and severally liable for the entire result, as a general partner would be in most states? Some states provide for proportionate liability—that is, for separate determinations of the negligence of the partners.[2] The American Institute of Certified Public Accountants supports the enactment of proportionate liability statutes.[3]

• **EXAMPLE 30.3** Imagine that accountants Don and Jane are partners in an LLP, with Don supervising Jane. Jane negligently fails to file tax returns for their client, Centaur Tools. Centaur files a suit against Don and Jane. In a state that does not allow for proportionate liability, Don can be held liable for the entire loss. Under a proportionate liability statute, Don will be liable for no more than his portion of the responsibility for the missed tax deadline. (Even if Jane settles the case quickly, Don will still be liable for his portion.) •

FAMILY LIMITED LIABILITY PARTNERSHIPS

FAMILY LIMITED LIABILITY PARTNERSHIP (FLLP)
A type of limited liability partnership owned by family members or fiduciaries of family members.

A **family limited liability partnership** (FLLP) is a limited liability partnership in which the majority of the partners are persons related to each other, essentially as spouses, parents, grandparents, siblings, cousins, nephews, or nieces. A person acting in a fiduciary capacity for persons so related can also be a partner. All of the partners must be natural persons or persons acting in a fiduciary capacity for the benefit of natural persons.

Probably the most significant use of the FLLP form of business organization is in agriculture. Family-owned farms sometimes find this form to their benefit. The FLLP offers the same advantages as other LLPs with some additional advantages, such as, in Iowa, an exemption from real estate transfer taxes when partnership real estate is transferred among partners.[4]

1. See, for example, 6 Delaware Code Section 15-1101.
2. See, for example, Colorado Revised Statutes Annotated Section 13-21-111.5(1) and Utah Code Annotated Section 78-27-39.
3. Public Oversight Board of the SEC Practice Section, AICPA, *In the Public Interest: Issues Confronting the Accounting Profession* (New York: AICPA, March 5, 1993), Recommendation I-1.
4. Iowa Statutes Section 428A.2.

Limited Partnerships

LIMITED PARTNERSHIP
A partnership consisting of one or more general partners (who manage the business and are liable to the full extent of their personal assets for debts of the partnership) and one or more limited partners (who contribute only assets and are liable only up to the extent of their contributions).

GENERAL PARTNER
In a limited partnership, a partner who assumes responsibility for the management of the partnership and liability for all partnership debts.

LIMITED PARTNER
In a limited partnership, a partner who contributes capital to the partnership but who has no right to participate in the management and operation of the business. The limited partner assumes no liability for partnership debts beyond the capital contributed.

To this point, we have been discussing relatively new forms of limited liability business organizations. We now look at an older business organizational form that limits the liability of some of its owners—the **limited partnership**. Limited partnerships originated in medieval Europe and have been existence in the United States since the early 1800s. In many ways, limited partnerships are like the general partnerships discussed in Chapter 25, but they differ from general partnerships in several ways. Because of this, they are sometimes referred to as *special partnerships*.

A limited partnership consists of at least one **general partner** and one or more **limited partners**. A general partner assumes management responsibility for the partnership and so has full responsibility for the partnership and for all debts of the partnership. A limited partner contributes cash or other property and owns an interest in the firm but does not undertake any management responsibilities and is not personally liable for partnership debts beyond the amount of his or her investment. A limited partner can forfeit limited liability by taking part in the management of the business. Exhibit 30–1 on page 810 compares characteristics of general and limited partnerships.[5]

Until 1976, the law governing limited partnerships in all states except Louisiana was the Uniform Limited Partnership Act (ULPA). Since 1976, most states and the District of Columbia have adopted the revised version of the ULPA, known as the Revised Uniform Limited Partnership Act (RULPA). Because the RULPA is the dominant law governing limited partnerships in the United States, we will refer to the RULPA in the following discussion of limited partnerships.

Formation of the Limited Partnership

CERTIFICATE OF LIMITED PARTNERSHIP
The basic document filed with a designated state official by which a limited partnership is formed.

In contrast to the informal, private, and voluntary agreement that usually suffices for a general partnership, the formation of a limited partnership is a public and formal proceeding that must follow statutory requirements. A limited partnership must have at least one general partner and one limited partner, as mentioned previously. Additionally, the partners must sign a **certificate of limited partnership**, which requires information similar to that found in a corporate charter (see Chapter 26). The certificate must be filed with the designated state official—under the RULPA, the secretary of state. The certificate is usually open to public inspection.

The following case illustrates the importance of complying carefully with the formal statutory requirements imposed on limited partnerships.

5. Under the RUPA, a general partnership can be converted into a limited partnership and vice versa [RUPA 902, 903]. The RUPA also provides for the merger of a general partnership with one or more general or limited partnerships under rules that are similar to those governing corporate mergers [RUPA 905].

CASE 30.3 Miller v. Department of Revenue, State of Oregon

Supreme Court of Oregon, 1998.
327 Or. 129,
958 P.2d 833.
http://www.ejsimmons.com/advanced.html[a]

a. This page provides access to opinions of the Oregon Supreme Court decided between July 1997 and December 3, 1998. In the "Query" box, type "Loverin" and click on "Submit Query." When the results appear, click on the "full" link to access the opinion. This site is maintained by attorney E. J. Simmons.

HISTORICAL AND ECONOMIC SETTING *Oregon statutes provide that "[i]t is the intent of the [Oregon] Legislative Assembly * * * to make the Oregon personal income tax law identical in effect to the provisions of the federal Internal Revenue Code relating to the measurement of taxable income of individuals." Oregon applies federal tax laws and federal court interpretations of those laws in resolving the issues raised by taxpayers.*

CASE 30.3—Continued

*Under federal law, taxes are to be based on the "objective economic realities of a transaction rather than * * * the particular form [that] the parties employed."*[b] *Under state law, a taxpayer has the burden of proving by a preponderance of the evidence that a claimed deduction is allowable.*[c]

FACTS Robert Loverin and Paul Miller bought a low-income housing project and retained Rockwood Development Corporation to manage it. For the project, Loverin and Miller formed a limited partnership. The certificate and articles of limited partnership identified Loverin and Miller as general partners and Rockwood as the only limited partner. It allocated 2 percent of the profits and losses to the general partners and 98 percent to the limited partner. Eventually, twenty-one investors became limited partners, but none of them signed the articles or the certificate. When American Properties Corporation (APC) replaced Rockwood as a limited partner, Loverin, Miller, and the president of APC signed a document that purported to amend the articles. The document provided in part that the partners could reallocate profits and losses as they "may agree." On their income tax returns, Loverin and Miller allocated 99.9 percent of the losses to themselves. The Oregon Department of Revenue reallocated the losses according to the provisions in the original articles—2 percent to general partners and 98 percent to limited partners. Miller and others appealed to the Oregon state tax court. The court upheld the assessment, and the plaintiffs appealed to the Oregon Supreme Court.

b. *Frank Lyon Co. v. United States,* 435 U.S. 561, 98 S.Ct. 1291, 55 L.Ed.2d 550 (1978).
c. *Reed v. Department of Revenue,* 310 Or. 260, 798 P.2d 235 (1990).

ISSUE Did the fact that none of the investing limited partners signed the amended certificate or articles render the amendments invalid?

DECISION Yes. The Oregon Supreme Court affirmed the lower court's decision, concluding that Loverin and Miller were not entitled to allocate 99.9 percent of the losses to themselves.

REASON The Oregon Supreme Court explained that under state statutes, when two or more persons form a limited partnership they are required to sign a certificate of limited partnership and file it with the state. The same procedure is required to amend the certificate. The court acknowledged that Loverin, Miller, and Rockwood followed this procedure with the original articles. The court pointed out, however, that "[t]he only evidence regarding the amended articles that taxpayers submitted to the Tax Court was a document signed by taxpayers and the president of APC. There is no evidence in this record that the amended articles were signed by the 21 [other] limited partners." Without those signatures, the amended articles were not effective, and Loverin and Miller could not rely on them to allocate profits and losses.

FOR CRITICAL ANALYSIS—Economic Consideration *How might a power of attorney have been used to avoid the outcome in this case?*

RIGHTS AND LIABILITIES OF PARTNERS

General partners, unlike limited partners, are personally liable to the partnership's creditors; thus, at least one general partner is necessary in a limited partnership so that someone has personal liability. This policy can be circumvented in states that allow a corporation to be the general partner in a partnership. Because the corporation has limited liability by virtue of corporate laws, if a corporation is the general partner, no one in the limited partnership has personal liability.

Rights of Limited Partners Subject to the limitations that will be discussed here, limited partners have essentially the same rights as general partners, including the right of access to partnership books and the right to other information regarding partnership business. On dissolution, limited partners are entitled to a return of their contributions in accordance with the partnership certificate [RULPA 201(a)(10)]. They can also assign their interests subject to the certificate [RULPA 702, 704].

EXHIBIT 30–1 A COMPARISON OF GENERAL PARTNERSHIPS AND LIMITED PARTNERSHIPS

CHARACTERISTIC	GENERAL PARTNERSHIIP (UPA)	LIMITED PARTNERSHIP (RULPA)
Creation	By agreement of two or more persons to carry on a business as co-owners for profit.	By agreement of two or more persons to carry on a business as co-owners for profit. Must include one or more general partners and one or more limited partners. Filing of a certificate with the secretary of state is required.
Sharing of Profits and Losses	By agreement; or, in the absence of agreement, profits are shared equally by the partners, and losses are shared in the same ratio as profits.	Profits are shared as required in the certificate agreement, and losses are shared likewise, up to the amount of the limited partners' capital contributions. In the absence of a provision in the certificate agreement, profits and losses are shared on the basis of percentages of capital contributions.
Liability	Unlimited personal liability of all partners.	Unlimited personal liability of all general partners; limited partners liable only to the extent of their capital contributions.
Capital Contribution	No minimum or mandatory amount; set by agreement.	Set by agreement.
Management	By agreement, or in the absence of agreement, all partners have an equal voice.	General partners by agreement, or else each has an equal voice. Limited partners have no voice or else are subject to liability as general partners (but *only* if a third party has reason to believe that the limited partner is a general partner). A limited partner may act as an agent or employee of the partnership and vote on amending the certificate or on the sale or dissolution of the partnership.
Duration	By agreement, or can be dissolved by action of the partners (withdrawal), operation of law (death or bankruptcy), or court decree.	By agreement in the certificate or by withdrawal, death, or mental incompetence of a general partner in the absence of the right of the other general partners to continue the partnership. Death of a limited partner, unless he or she is the only remaining limited partner, does not terminate the partnership.
Distribution of Assets on Liquidation–Order of Priorities	1. Outside creditors. 2. Partner creditors. 3. Partners, according to capital contributions. 4. Partners, according to profits.	1. Outside creditors and partner creditors. 2. Partners and former partners entitled to distributions before withdrawal under the agreement or the RULPA. 3. Partners, according to capital contributions. 4. Partners, according to profits.

The RULPA provides a limited partner with the right to sue an outside party on behalf of the firm if the general partners with authority to do so have refused to file suit [RULPA 1001]. In addition, investor protection legislation, such as securities laws (discussed in Chapter 29), may give some protection to limited partners.

ETHICAL ISSUE 30.1

Should a limited partner be able to sue a third party whose negligence caused the partnership to fail?

As just mentioned, limited partners in a limited partnership have a number of rights. Yet, at the same time, these rights are limited. For example, a limited partner may not sue a third party with whom a limited partnership has contracted for causing the limited partnership to fail. Generally, the limited partnership itself must bring the suit—the limited partners have no standing to sue for losses that result in the failure of the enterprise. For example, in one case a limited partner invested $16 billion in BCH Energy L.P. in reliance on BCH's representations that it would build and manage plants that convert waste products into energy. BCH hired Metric Constructors to construct an energy-generating project. Serious problems caused the project to lose all funds invested. The limited partner sued Metric Constructors, contending that Metric was negligent in its construction. The court, however, held that the limited partner did not have standing to sue the contractor (Metric). The court held that any complaint brought against the contractor had to be brought by the partnership, not by its limited partner or partners.[6] While this ruling may seem unfair to the limited partner, it is consistent with the principle that limited partners should not have a say in the management of limited partnerships (as will be discussed shortly).

NOTE A limited partner is also liable to the extent of any contribution that she or he made to the partnership but later took back from the firm.

Liabilities of Limited Partners In contrast to the personal liability of general partners, the liability of a limited partner is limited to the capital that she or he contributes or agrees to contribute to the partnership [RULPA 502].

A limited partnership is formed by good faith compliance with the requirements for signing and filing the certificate, even if it is incomplete or defective. When a limited partner discovers a defect in the formation of the limited partnership, she or he can avoid future liability by causing an appropriate amendment or certificate to be filed or

6. *Energy Investors Fund, L.P. v. Metric Constructors, Inc.*, 351 N.C. 331, 525 S.E.2d 441 (2000).

INTERNATIONAL PERSPECTIVE

Liability of Limited Partners in Argentina

In the United States, the limited partnership has long been used as a business form. In large part, this is because it allows investors to enjoy the limited personal liability of limited partners.

Many other nations also permit businesspersons to establish limited partnerships. In Argentina, the limited partnership is called a *sociedad en comandita* and is closely regulated by the government. Limited partners, known as "sleeping partners," have limited liability so long as they do not participate in management. Argentinian law, however, does permit limited partners to inspect the books, express their views to managers, and offer advice at partnership meetings.

FOR CRITICAL ANALYSIS
What might happen if a limited partner in the United States offered advice to the general partners at partnership meetings?

by renouncing an interest in the profits of the partnership [RULPA 304]. If the limited partner takes neither of these actions on discovering the defect, however, the partner can be held personally liable by the firm's creditors. Liability for false statements in a partnership certificate runs in favor of persons relying on the false statements and against members who know of the falsity but still sign the certificate [RULPA 207].

Limited Partners and Management Limited partners enjoy limited liability so long as they do not participate in management [RULPA 303]. A limited partner who participates in management will be just as liable as a general partner to any creditor who transacts business with the limited partnership and believes, based on a limited partner's conduct, that the limited partner is a general partner [RULPA 303]. How much actual review and advisement a limited partner can engage in before being exposed to liability is an unsettled question.[7] A limited partner who knowingly permits his or her name to be used in the name of the limited partnership is liable to creditors who extend credit to the limited partnership without knowledge that the limited partner is not a general partner [RULPA 102, 303(d)].

Although limited partners cannot participate in management, this does not mean that the general partners are totally free of restrictions in running the business. The general partners in a limited partnership have fiduciary obligations to the partnership and to the limited partners, as the following case illustrates.

7. It is an unsettled question partly because different states have different laws. Factors to be considered under the RULPA are listed in RULPA 303(b), (c).

CASE 30.4 BT-I v. Equitable Life Assurance Society of the United States

California Court of Appeal,
Fourth District, 1999.
75 Cal.App.4th 1406,
76 Cal.App.4th 684E,
89 Cal.Rptr.2d 811.

FACTS BT-I, a general partnership, entered into a general partnership with Equitable Life Assurance Society of the United States to develop and operate an office building and retail complex in California. Banque Paribas lent the firm $62.5 million for the project. Six years later, BT-I and Equitable dissolved their general partnership and entered into a limited partnership, with Equitable as general partner and BT-I as limited partner. Equitable was given title to the retail complex and the sole right to manage the partnership. Paragraph 5.1(c) of the limited partnership agreement gave Equitable broad powers, "provided, however, . . . that in no event shall the General Partner be required to take any action . . . to prevent Banque Paribas or any other lender from exercising any remedies in connection with any loan made to the Partnership." Later, when Banque Paribas solicited bids to "sell" its loan, Equitable (in its capacity as a corporate entity) bought it for $38.5 million. On the due date, Equitable demanded full payment from the partnership, but none was made. A month later, Equitable offered to sell the loan to the partnership, but the offer was not accepted. Equitable scheduled a foreclosure sale. Three days before the sale, BT-I offered $39 million for the project, but Equitable turned it down. At the sale, Equitable bought the partnership's office building. BT-I filed a suit in a California state court against Equitable, alleging in part breach of fiduciary duty. Equitable argued that the partnership agreement allowed it to buy the loans and foreclose the same as any other lender. The court entered a judgment in Equitable's favor. BT-I appealed to a state intermediate appellate court.

ISSUE Did Equitable breach a fiduciary duty to BT-I?

DECISION Yes. The state intermediate appellate court reversed the judgment of the lower court.

REASON The appellate court held that "[a] general partner of a limited partnership is subject to the same restrictions, and has the same liabilities to the partnership and other partners, as in a general partnership." As for Equitable's argument concerning the partnership agreement, the court stated that "[e]ven if the language were broad enough to justify such an interpretation, we hold a partnership agreement cannot relieve a general partner of its fiduciary duties to a limited partner and the partnership where the purchase and foreclosure of partnership debt is involved." According to the court, Equitable's conduct in

CASE 30.4—Continued

buying and foreclosing the loans went "far beyond" what was permitted under the partnership agreement." Also, "the fact that the [Revised Uniform Limited Partnership Act] allows the parties to structure many aspects of their relationship is not a license to freely engage in self-dealing * * *. Equitable was still a fiduciary, and its conduct must be measured by fiduciary standards."

FOR CRITICAL ANALYSIS—Ethical Consideration *Generally, why does the law impose fiduciary obligations on general partners?*

DISSOLUTION

A limited partnership is dissolved in much the same way as an ordinary partnership. The retirement, death, or mental incompetence of a general partner can dissolve the partnership, but not if the business can be continued by one or more of the other general partners in accordance with their certificate or by the consent of all of the members [RULPA 801]. The death or assignment of interest of a limited partner does not dissolve the limited partnership [RULPA 702, 704, 705]. A limited partnership can be dissolved by court decree [RULPA 802].

Bankruptcy or the withdrawal of a general partner dissolves a limited partnership. Bankruptcy of a limited partner, however, does not dissolve the partnership unless it causes the bankruptcy of the limited partnership. The retirement of a general partner causes a dissolution unless the members consent to a continuation by the remaining general partners or unless this contingency is provided for in the certificate.

On dissolution, creditors' rights, including those of partners who are creditors, take first priority. Then partners and former partners receive unpaid distributions of partnership assets and, except as otherwise agreed, amounts representing returns on their contributions and amounts proportionate to their shares of the distributions [RULPA 804].

Limited Liability Limited Partnerships

LIMITED LIABILITY LIMITED PARTNERSHIP (LLLP)
A type of limited partnership in which the liability of all of the partners, including general partners, is limited to the amount of their investments.

A **limited liability limited partnership** (LLLP) is a type of limited partnership. An LLLP differs from a limited partnership in that a general partner in an LLLP has the same liability as a limited partner. That is, the liability of all partners is limited to the amount of their investments in the firm.

A few states provide expressly for LLLPs.[8] In states that do not provide for LLLPs but do allow for limited partnerships and limited liability partnerships, a limited partnership should probably still be able to register with the state as an LLLP.

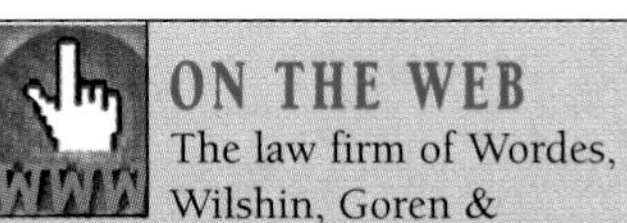

ON THE WEB
The law firm of Wordes, Wilshin, Goren & Conner offers a comparison of the advantages and disadvantages of major business forms with respect to various factors, including ease of formation, management, and ability to raise capital, at its Web site. Go to **http://www.wwgc.com/wwgc-be1.htm**.

Major Business Forms Compared

As mentioned in Chapter 25, when deciding which form of business organization would be most appropriate, businesspersons normally consider several factors, including ease of creation, the liability of the owners, tax considerations, and the need for capital. Each major form of business organization offers distinct advantages and disadvantages with respect to these and other factors. Exhibit 30–2 on pages 814 and 815 summarizes the essential advantages and disadvantages of each of the forms of business organization discussed in Chapters 25 through 29, as well as in this chapter.

8. See, for example, Colorado Revised Statutes Annotated Section 7-62-109. Other states that provide expressly for limited liability limited partnerships include Delaware, Florida, Missouri, Pennsylvania, Texas, and Virginia.

EXHIBIT 30–2 MAJOR FORMS OF BUSINESS COMPARED

CHARACTERISTIC	SOLE PROPRIETORSHIP	PARTNERSHIP	CORPORATION
Method of Creation	Created at will by owner.	Created by agreement of the parties.	Charter issued by state—created by statutory authorization.
Legal Position	Not a separate entity; owner is the business.	Not a separate legal entity in many states.	Always a legal entity separate and distinct from its owners—a legal fiction for the purposes of owning property and being a party to litigation.
Liability	Unlimited liability.	Unlimited liability.	Limited liability of shareholders—shareholders are not liable for the debts of the corporation.
Duration	Determined by owner; automatically dissolved on owner's death.	Terminated by agreement of the partners, by the death of one or more of the partners, by withdrawal of a partner, by bankruptcy, and so on.	Can have perpetual existence.
Transferability of Interest	Interest can be transferred, but individual's proprietorship then ends.	Although partnership interest can be assigned, assignee does not have full rights of a partner.	Shares of stock can be transferred.
Management	Completely at owner's discretion.	Each general partner has a direct and equal voice in management unless expressly agreed otherwise in the partnership agreement.	Shareholders elect directors, who set policy and appoint officers.
Taxation	Owner pays personal taxes on business income.	Each partner pays pro rata share of income taxes on net profits, whether or not they are distributed.	Double taxation—corporation pays income tax on net profits, with no deduction for dividends, and shareholders pay income tax on disbursed dividends they receive.
Organizational Fees, Annual License Fees, and Annual Reports	None.	None.	All required.
Transaction of Business in Other States	Generally no limitation.	Generally no limitation.[a]	Normally must qualify to do business and obtain certificate of authority.

a. A few states have enacted statutes requiring that foreign partnerships qualify to do business there.

EXHIBIT 30–2 MAJOR FORMS OF BUSINESS COMPARED—CONTINUED

CHARACTERISTIC	LIMITED PARTNERSHIP	LIMITED LIABILITY COMPANY	LIMITED LIABILITY PARTNERSHIP
Method of Creation	Created by agreement to carry on a business for a profit. At least one party must be a general partner and the other(s) limited partner(s). Certificate of limited partnership is filed. Charter must be issued by the state.	Created by an agreement of the owner-members of the company. Articles of organization are filed. Charter must be issued by the state.	Created by agreement of the partners. Certificate of a limited liability partnership is filed. Charter must be issued by state.
Legal Position	Treated as a legal entity.	Treated as a legal entity.	Generally, treated same as a general partnership.
Liability	Unlimited liability of all general partners; limited partners are liable only to the extent of capital contributions.	Member-owners' liability is limited to the amount of capital contributions or investment.	Varies from state to state but usually limits liability of a partner for certain acts committed by other partners.
Duration	By agreement in certificate, or by termination of the last general partner (withdrawal, death, and so on) or last limited partner.	Unless a single-member LLC, can have perpetual existence (same as a corporation).	Terminated by agreement of partners, by death or withdrawal of a partner, or by law (such as bankruptcy).
Transferability of Interest	Interest can be assigned (same as general partnership), but if assignee becomes a member with consent of other partners, certificate must be amended.	Member interests are freely transferable.	Interest can be assigned same as in a general partnership.
Management	General partners have equal voice or by agreement. Limited partners may not retain limited liability if they actively participate in management.	Member-owners can fully participate in management, or management is selected by owner-members who manage on behalf of the members.	Same as a general partnership.
Taxation	Generally taxed as a partnership.	LLC is not taxed, and members are taxed personally on profits "passed through" the LCC.	Same as a general partnership.
Organizational Fees, Annual License Fees, and Annual Reports	Organizational fee required; usually not others.	Organizational fee required; others vary with states.	Organizational fee required (such as a set amount per partner); usually not others.
Transaction of Business in Other States	Generally, no limitations.	Generally, no limitation but may vary depending on state.	Generally, no limitation, but state laws vary as to formation and limitation of liability.

APPLICATION Law and the Businessperson . . .

Choosing a Limited Liability Business Form*

One of the most important decisions that an entrepreneur makes is the selection of the form in which to do business. To make the best decision, a businessperson should understand all of the aspects of the variety of forms, including the legal, tax, licensing, and business considerations. It is also important that all of the participants in the business understand their actual relationship, regardless of the organizational structure.

Number of Participants

During the last decade or so, new forms of business organizations, including limited liability partnerships (LLPs) and limited liability companies (LLCs), have been added to the options for business entities. An initial consideration in choosing between these forms is the number of participants. An LLP must have two or more partners, but in many states, an LLC can have a single member (owner).

Liability Considerations

The members of an LLC are not liable for the obligations of the organization. The liability of the partners in an LLP varies from state to state. About half of the states exempt the partners from liability for any obligation of the firm. In some states, the partners are individually liable for the contractual obligations of the firm but are not liable for obligations arising from the torts of others. In either situation, each partner may be on his or her own with respect to liability unless the other partners decide to help.

Distributions from the Firm

Members and partners are generally paid by allowing them to withdraw funds from the firm against their share of the profits. In many states, a member of an LLC must repay so-called wrongful distributions even if she or he did not know that the distributions were wrongful. Under most LLP statutes, by contrast, the partners must repay only distributions that were fraudulent.

Management Structure

Both LLPs and LLCs can set up whatever management structure the participants desire to have. Also, all unincorporated business organizations, including LLPs and LLCs, are treated as partnerships for federal income tax purposes (unless an LLC elects to be treated as a corporation[a]). This means that the entities are not taxed at the firm level. Their income is passed through to the partners or members who must report it on their individual income tax returns. Some states impose additional taxes on LLCs.

The Nature of the Business

The business in which a firm engages is another factor to consider in choosing a business form. For example, with a few exceptions, professionals—accountants, attorneys, physicians, and so on—may organize as either an LLP or an LLC in any state. In many states, however, the ownership of an entity that engages in a certain profession and the liability of the owners are prescribed by state law.

Financial and Personal Relationships

Despite their importance, the legal consequences of choosing a business form are often secondary considerations to the financial and personal relationships

*This *Application* is not meant to substitute for the services of an attorney who is licensed to practice law in your state.

a. The chief benefits of electing corporate status for tax purposes are that the members generally are not subject to self-employment taxes, and fringe benefits may be provided to employee-members on a tax-reduced basis. The tax laws are complicated, however, and a professional should be consulted about the details.

APPLICATION Law and the Businessperson . . .

Choosing a Limited Liability Business Form—continued

among the participants. Work effort, motivation, ability, and other personal attributes can be significant factors, as may be fundamental business concerns such as the expenses and debts of the firm. Other practical factors to consider include the willingness of others to do business with an LLP or an LLC. A supplier, for example, may not be willing to extend credit to a firm whose partners or members will not accept personal liability for the debt.

Checklist for Choosing a Limited Liability Business Form

1. Determine the number of participants, which forms a state allows, and what limits on liability the state provides for the participants.
2. Evaluate the tax considerations.
3. Consider the business in which the firm engages, or will engage, and any restrictions that exist on that type of business.
4. Weigh such practical concerns as the financial and personal relationships among the participants, and among the participants and those with whom the firm will deal.

Key Terms

articles of organization 799
certificate of limited partnership 808
family limited liability partnership (FLLP) 807
general partner 808
limited liability company (LLC) 799
limited liability limited partnership (LLLP) 813
limited liability partnership (LLP) 805
limited partner 808
limited partnership 808
member 799
operating agreement 804

Chapter Summary Limited Liability Companies and Partnerships

Limited Liability Companies (LLCs) (See pages 799–805.)	1. *Formation*—Articles of organization must be filed with the appropriate state office—usually the office of the secretary of state—setting forth the name of the business, its principal address, the names of the owners (called *members*), and other relevant information. 2. *Advantages and disadvantages of the LLC*—Advantages of the LLC include limited liability, the option to be taxed as a partnership or as a corporation, and flexibility in deciding how the business will be managed and operated. Disadvantages relate mainly to the absence of uniformity in state LLC statutes and the lack of case law dealing with LLCs.

(continued)

Chapter Summary Limited Liability Companies and Partnerships—continued

Limited Liability Companies (LLCs)—continued	3. *Operating agreement*—When an LLC is formed, the members decide, in an operating agreement, how the business will be managed and what rules will apply to the organization. 4. *Management*—An LLC may be managed by members only, by some members and some nonmembers, or by nonmembers only.
Limited Liability Partnerships (LLPs) (See pages 805–807.)	1. *Formation*—Articles must be filed with the appropriate state agency, usually the secretary of state's office. Typically, an LLP is formed by professionals who work together as partners in a partnership. Under most state LLP statutes, it is relatively easy to convert a traditional partnership into an LLP. 2. *Liability of partners*—LLP statutes vary, but generally they allow professionals to avoid personal liability for the malpractice of other partners. The extent to which partners' limited liability will be recognized when the partnership does business in another state depends on the other state's laws. Partners in an LLP continue to be liable for their own wrongful acts and for the wrongful acts of those whom they supervise. 3. *Family limited liability partnership (FLLP)*—A form of LLP in which all of the partners are family members or fiduciaries of family members; the most significant use of the FLLP is by families engaged in agricultural enterprises.
Limited Partnerships (See pages 807–813.)	1. *Formation*—A certificate of limited partnership must be filed with the secretary of state's office or other designated state official. The certificate must include information about the business, similar to the information included in a corporate charter. The partnership consists of one or more general partners and one or more limited partners. 2. *Rights and liabilities of partners*—With some exceptions, the rights of partners are the same as the rights of partners in a general partnership. General partners have unlimited liability for partnership obligations; limited partners are liable only to the extent of their contributions. 3. *Limited partners and management*—Only general partners can participate in management. Limited partners have no voice in management; if they do participate in management activities, they risk having general-partner liability. 4. *Dissolution*—Generally, a limited partnership can be dissolved in much the same way as an ordinary partnership. The death or assignment of interest of a limited partner does not dissolve the partnership; bankruptcy of a limited partner will also not dissolve the partnership unless it causes the bankruptcy of the firm.
Limited Liability Limited Partnerships (LLLPs) (See page 813.)	A special type of limited partnership in which the liability of all partners, including general partners, is limited to the amount of their investments.

For Review

① What advantages do limited liability companies and partnerships offer to businesspersons that are not offered by general partnerships or the corporate form of business?

② How are limited liability companies formed, and who decides how they will be managed and operated?

③ What is the difference between limited liability companies and limited liability partnerships?

④ What is a family limited liability partnership?

⑤ What are the key differences between the rights and liabilities of general partners and limited partners?

Questions and Case Problems

30–1. Limited Liability Companies. John, Lesa, and Trevor form an LLC. John contributes 60 percent of the capital, and Lesa and Trevor each contribute 20 percent. Nothing is decided about how profits will be divided. John assumes that he will be entitled to 60 percent of the profits, in accordance with his contribution. Lesa and Trevor, however, assume that the profits will be divided equally. A dispute over the profits arises, and ultimately a court has to decide the issue. What law will the court apply? In most states, what will result? How could this dispute have been avoided in the first place? Discuss fully.

30–2. Liability of Limited Partners. Asher and Breem form a limited partnership with Asher as the general partner and Breem as the limited partner. Breem puts up $15,000, and Asher contributes some office equipment that he owns. A certificate of limited partnership is properly filed, and business is begun. One month later, Asher becomes ill. Instead of hiring someone to manage the business, Breem takes over complete management himself. While Breem is in control, he makes a contract with Thaler involving a large sum of money. Asher returns to work. Because of other commitments, Asher and Breem breach the Thaler contract. Thaler contends that Asher and Breem will be personally liable for damages caused by the breach if the damages cannot be satisfied out of the assets of the limited partnership. Discuss this contention.

30–3. Limited Partnerships. Dorinda, Lois, and Elizabeth form a limited partnership. Dorinda is a general partner, and Lois and Elizabeth are limited partners. Consider each of the separate events below, and discuss fully which event or events constitute a dissolution of the limited partnership.

(a) Lois assigns her partnership interest to Ashley.
(b) Elizabeth is petitioned into involuntary bankruptcy.
(c) Dorinda dies.

30–4. Liability of Limited Partners. Combat Associates was formed as a limited partnership to promote an exhibition boxing match between Lyle Alzado (a professional football player) and Muhammad Ali. Alzado and others had formed Combat Promotions; this organization was to be the general partner and Blinder, Robinson & Co. (Blinder), the limited partner in Combat Associates. The general partner's contribution consisted of assigning all contracts pertaining to the match, and the limited partner's contribution was a $250,000 letter of credit to ensure Ali's compensation. Alzado personally guaranteed to repay Blinder for any amount of loss if the proceeds of the match were less than $250,000. In preparation for the match, at Alzado's request, Blinder's president participated in interviews and a promotional rally, and the company sponsored parties and allowed its local office to be used as a ticket sales outlet. The proceeds of the match were insufficient, and Blinder sued Alzado on his guaranty. Alzado counterclaimed by asserting that Blinder had taken an active role in the control and management of Combat Associates and should be held liable as a general partner. How did the court rule on Alzado's counterclaim? Discuss. [*Blinder, Robinson & Co. v. Alzado,* 713 P.2d 1314 (Colo.App. 1985)]

30–5. Liability of General Partners. Pat McGowan, Val Somers, and Brent Roberson were general partners in Vermont Place, a limited partnership formed to construct duplexes on a tract of land in Fort Smith, Arkansas. In 1984, the partnership mortgaged the property so that it could build there. McGowan owned a separate company, Advance Development Corp., which was hired by the partnership to develop the project. On September 3, 1984, Somers and Roberson discovered that McGowan had not been paying the suppliers to the project, including National Lumber Co., and had not been making the mortgage payments. The suppliers and the bank sued the partnership and the general partners individually. Discuss whether Somers and Roberson could be held individually liable for the debts incurred by McGowan. [*National Lumber Co. v. Advance Development Corp.,* 293 Ark. 1, 732 S.W.2d 840 (1987)]

30–6. Limited Partners. Caton Avenue Associates was a limited partnership that owned rental property. Caton paid Theodore Dalmazio, one of the general partners, a management fee to manage the property. Dalmazio paid his employees with Caton's money. Dalmazio billed Caton for services that are normally performed by property management firms at no cost and also billed Caton at an hourly rate for work that is normally billed per rental unit. Alfred Friedman and the other limited partners filed a suit on Caton's behalf in a New York state court against Dalmazio and the other general partner to recover damages. On what basis might the court rule in favor of the limited partners? Explain. [*Friedman v. Dalmazio,* 644 N.Y.S.2d 548 (App.Div. 1996)]

30–7. Foreign Limited Liability Companies. Page, Scrantom, Sprouse, Tucker & Ford, a Georgia law firm, entered into a lease of office equipment in Georgia. The lessor assigned the lease to Danka Funding Company (DFC), a New York limited liability company (LLC) with its principal place of business in New Jersey. DFC was registered as a foreign LLC in New Jersey for almost two years before the registration lapsed or was withdrawn. Under the applicable statute, a foreign LLC "may not maintain any action . . . in this State until it has registered." When Page defaulted on the lease, DFC filed a complaint in a New Jersey state court against Page for more than $100,000. In its response, Page pointed out that DFC was not registered as a foreign LLC. DFC reregistered. Asserting that DFC had not been registered when it filed its suit, Page asked a federal district court to dismiss the suit. Should the court grant this request? Why or why not? [*Danka Funding, L.L.C. v. Page, Scrantom, Sprouse, Tucker & Ford, P.C.,* 21 F.Supp.2d 465 (D.N.J. 1998)]

30–8. Limited Liability Partnerships. Mudge Rose Guthrie Alexander & Ferdon, a law firm, was organized as a general partnership but converted into a limited liability partnership (LLP). Mudge's principal place of business was New York, where it was organized, but some of its members were citizens of Maryland. The firm filed a suit in a federal district court to recover unpaid legal fees from Robert Pickett and other citizens of Maryland. The defendants filed a motion to dismiss on the ground that there was not complete diversity of citizenship because some of the LLC members were Maryland citizens also. Mudge argued that an LLP was like a corporation, and therefore the citizenship of the firm's members was irrelevant. How should the court rule? Explain. [*Mudge Rose Guthrie Alexander & Ferdon v. Pickett,* 11 F.Supp.2d 449 (S.D.N.Y. 1998)]

30–9. Limited Liability Companies. Gloria Duchin, a Rhode Island resident, was the sole shareholder and chief executive officer of Gloria Duchin, Inc. (Duchin, Inc.), which manufactured metallic Christmas ornaments and other novelty items. The firm was incorporated in Rhode Island. Duchin Realty, Inc., also incorporated in Rhode Island, leased real estate to Duchin, Inc. The Duchin entities hired Gottesman Co. to sell Duchin, Inc., and to sign with the buyer a consulting agreement for Gloria Duchin and a lease for Duchin Realty's property. Gottesman negotiated a sale, a consulting agreement, and a lease with Somerset Capital Corp. James Mitchell, a resident of Massachusetts, was the chairman and president of Somerset, and Mary Mitchell, also a resident of Massachusetts, was the senior vice president. The parties agreed that to buy Duchin, Inc., Somerset would create a new limited liability company, JMTR Enterprises, LLC, in Rhode Island, with the Mitchells as its members. When the deal fell apart, JMTR filed a suit in a Massachusetts state court against the Duchin entities, alleging, among other things, breach of contract. When the defendants tried to remove the case to a federal district court, JMTR argued that the court did not have jurisdiction because there was no diversity of citizenship between the parties: all of the plaintiffs and defendants were citizens of Rhode Island. Is JMTR correct? Why or why not? [*JMTR Enterprises, LLC v. Duchin,* 42 F.Supp.2d 87 (D.Mass. 1999)]

TEST YOUR KNOWLEDGE—ANSWER ON THE WEB

30–10. Walter Matjasich and Cary Hanson organized Capital Care, LLC, in Utah. Capital Care operated, and Matjasich and Hanson managed, Heartland Care Center in Topeka, Kansas. LTC Properties, Inc., held a mortgage on the Heartland facilities. When Heartland failed as a business, its residents were transferred to other facilities. Heartland employees who provided care to the residents for five days during the transfers were not paid wages. The employees filed claims with the Kansas Department of Human Resources for the unpaid wages. Kansas state law provides that a *corporate* officer or manager may be liable for a firm's unpaid wages, but protects LLC members from personal liability generally and states that an LLC cannot be construed as a corporation. Under Utah state law, the members of an LLC can be personally liable for wages due the LLC's employees. Should Matjasich and Hanson be held personally liable for the unpaid wages? Explain. [*Matjasich v. State, Department of Human Resources,* 21 P.3d 985 (Kan. 2001)]

A QUESTION OF ETHICS AND SOCIAL RESPONSIBILITY

30–11. Mt. Hood Meadows Oregon, Ltd., was a limited partnership established to carry on the business of constructing and operating a winter sports development in the Hood River area of Oregon. Elizabeth Brooke and two of the other limited partners were dissatisfied because, for all the years in which profits were earned after 1974, the general partner distributed only 50 percent of the limited partners' taxable profits. The remaining profits were retained and reinvested in the business. Each of the limited partners was taxed on his or her distributable share of the profits, however, regardless of whether the cash was actually distributed. Brooke and the others brought an action to compel the general partner to distribute all of the limited partnership's profits. The court held that, in the absence of a limited partnership agreement concerning the distribution of profits, the decision to reinvest profits was strictly a managerial one. Unless the limited partners could prove that the general partner's conduct was inappropriate or violated a fiduciary duty, the decision of the general partner was binding on the limited partners. [*Brooke v. Mt. Hood Meadows Oregon, Ltd.,* 81 Ore.App. 387, 725 P.2d 925 (1986)]

1. The major attraction of limited partnerships is that the investors, as limited partners, are not liable for partnership obligations beyond the amount that they have invested. The "price" paid for this limited liability, however, is that limited partners have no say in management—as is well illustrated by the case described here. What ethical considerations are expressed in the rule that limited partners cannot participate in management? Do you think such a rule is fair?
2. This case also illustrates how relatively helpless the limited partners are when faced with a general partner whose actions do not correspond to the limited partners' wishes. Apart from selling their partnership shares to others (and at times, buyers are hard to find) or participating in management (and losing their limited liability as a result), limited partners have little recourse against the decisions of general partners so long as the general partners have not violated their fiduciary duties or the partnership agreement. Do you think that, because limited partners cannot participate in management, general partners have ethical duties to limited partners that go beyond those prescribed by law? If not, why not? If so, how would you describe or define such duties?

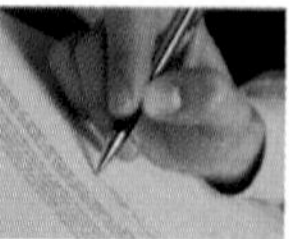

FOR CRITICAL ANALYSIS

30–12. Although a limited liability entity may be the best organizational form for most businesses, a significant number of firms may be better off as a corporation or some other form of organization. How does the fact that most of the limited liability entities are new forms for doing business affect the reasons for choosing another form of organization in which to do business? Explain.

Internet Exercises

Go to the *Business Law Today* home page at **http://blt.westbuslaw.com**. Select "Interactive Study Center" and then click on "Chapter 30." There you will find the following Internet research exercise that you can perform to learn more about limited liability companies:

Activity 30–1: Limited Liability Companies

Before the Test

Go to the *Business Law Today* home page at **http://blt.westbuslaw.com**. Click on "Interactive Quizzes." You will find at least twenty interactive questions relating to this chapter.

CHAPTER 31

Special Business Forms and Private Franchises

"Nothing contributes so much to the prosperity and happiness of a country as high profits."

David Ricardo, 1772–1823
(English economist)

CHAPTER CONTENTS

LEARNING OBJECTIVES

After reading this chapter, you should be able to answer the following questions:

① What are the essential characteristics of each of the following business forms: joint ventures, joint stock companies, syndicates, business trusts, and cooperatives?

② What is a franchise? What are the most common types of franchises?

③ What laws govern a franchising relationship?

④ What terms and conditions are typically included in a franchise contract?

⑤ When might franchisors be liable under agency laws?

Few would argue with David Ricardo's statement that high profits contribute to the "prosperity and happiness of a country." Certainly, this assumption is the basis for this country's public policy of encouraging trade and commerce. To promote commerce and profit-making activities, our government, among other things, allows entrepreneurs to choose from a variety of business organizational forms when undertaking their business ventures.

In the preceding chapters, we have examined some of the most significant business forms—including sole proprietorships, partnerships, corporations, and limited liability companies and partnerships. In this chapter, after first describing a number of forms that can be used for special types of business ventures, we look in detail at private franchises. Although the franchise is not really a business organizational form, the franchising arrangement has become widely used by those seeking to make profits.

Special Business Forms

Besides the business forms discussed in previous chapters, several other forms can be used to organize a business. For the most part, these other business forms are hybrid organizations—that is, they have characteristics similar to those of partnerships or corporations or combine features of both. These forms include joint ventures, syndicates, joint stock companies, business trusts, and cooperatives.

JOINT VENTURES

JOINT VENTURE
A joint undertaking of a specific commercial enterprise by an association of persons. A joint venture normally is not a legal entity and is treated like a partnership for federal income tax purposes.

A **joint venture** is an enterprise in which two or more persons or business entities combine their efforts or their property for a single transaction or project, or a related series of transactions or projects. For example, when several contractors combine their resources to build and sell houses in a single development, their relationship is a joint venture. The joint venture is treated much like a partnership, but it differs in that it is created in contemplation of a limited activity or a single transaction. Joint ventures are taxed like partnerships, and, unless otherwise agreed, joint venturers share profits and losses equally.

CONTRAST A partnership involves a continuing relationship of the partners. A joint venture is often a one-time association.

Members of a joint venture usually have limited powers to bind their co-venturers. A joint venture normally is not a legal entity and therefore cannot be sued as such, but its members can be sued individually. Joint ventures range in size from very small activities to huge, multimillion-dollar joint actions engaged in by some of the world's largest corporations.

SYNDICATES

SYNDICATE
An investment group of persons or firms brought together for the purpose of financing a project that they would not or could not undertake independently.

A group of individuals getting together to finance a particular project, such as the building of a shopping center or the purchase of a professional basketball franchise, is called a **syndicate** or an *investment group*. The form of such groups varies considerably. A syndicate may exist as a corporation or as a general or limited partnership. In some cases, the members merely purchase and own property jointly but have no legally recognized business arrangement.

A housing development publicizes that it offers new houses for sale. If the housing development is organized as a joint venture, what will happen to the joint venture after the last house is sold?

Joint Stock Companies

JOINT STOCK COMPANY
A hybrid form of business organization that combines characteristics of a corporation and a partnership. Usually, the joint stock company is regarded as a partnership for tax and other legally related purposes.

A **joint stock company** is a true hybrid of a partnership and a corporation. It has many characteristics of a corporation in that (1) its ownership is represented by transferable shares of stock, (2) it is usually managed by directors and officers of the company or association, and (3) it can have a perpetual existence. Most of its other features, however, are more characteristic of a partnership, and it is usually treated like a partnership. As with a partnership, a joint stock company is formed by agreement (not statute), property is usually held in the names of the members, shareholders have personal liability, and the company generally is not treated as a legal entity for purposes of a lawsuit. In a joint stock company, however, shareholders are not considered to be agents of each other, as would be the case if the company were a true partnership (see Chapter 25).

Business Trusts

BUSINESS TRUST
A form of business organization in which investors (trust beneficiaries) transfer cash or property to trustees in exchange for trust certificates that represent their investment shares. The certificate holders share in the trust's profits but have limited liability.

A **business trust** is created by a written trust agreement that sets forth the interests of the beneficiaries and the obligations and powers of the trustees. With a business trust, legal ownership and management of the property of the business stay with one or more of the trustees, and the profits are distributed to the beneficiaries.

The business trust was started in Massachusetts in an attempt to obtain the limited liability advantage of corporate status while avoiding certain restrictions on a corporation's ownership and development of real property. The business trust resembles a corporation in many respects. Beneficiaries of the trust, for example, are not personally responsible for the debts or obligations of the business trust. In fact, in a number of states, business trusts must pay corporate taxes.

Cooperatives

COOPERATIVE
An association, which may or may not be incorporated, that is organized to provide an economic service to its members. Unincorporated cooperatives are often treated like partnerships for tax and other legally related purposes. Examples of cooperatives are consumer purchasing cooperatives, credit cooperatives, and farmers' cooperatives.

A **cooperative** is an association, which may or may not be incorporated, that is organized to provide an economic service to its members (or shareholders). Most cooperatives are incorporated under either state statutes for cooperatives, general business incorporation statutes, or limited liability company (LLC) statutes. Generally, an incorporated cooperative will distribute dividends, or profits, to its owners on the basis of their transactions with the cooperative rather than on the basis of the amount of capital they contributed. Members of incorporated cooperatives have limited liability, as do shareholders of corporations or members of LLCs. Cooperatives that are unincorporated are often treated like partnerships. The members have joint liability for the cooperative's acts.

This form of business is generally adopted by groups of individuals who wish to pool their resources to gain some advantage in the marketplace. Consumer purchasing co-ops are formed to obtain lower prices through quantity discounts. Seller marketing co-ops are formed to control the market and thereby obtain higher sales prices from consumers. Co-ops range in size from small, local, consumer cooperatives to national businesses such as Ace Hardware and Land 'O Lakes, the well-known producer of dairy products.

Private Franchises

FRANCHISE
Any arrangement in which the owner of a trademark, trade name, or copyright licenses another to use that trademark, trade name, or copyright in the selling of goods and services.

Many entrepreneurs, instead of setting up a business form through which to market their own products or services, opt to purchase a franchise. A **franchise** is defined as

FRANCHISEE One receiving a license to use another's (the franchisor's) trademark, trade name, or copyright in the sale of goods and services.

FRANCHISOR One licensing another (the franchisee) to use the owner's trademark, trade name, or copyright in the sale of goods or services.

any arrangement in which the owner of a trademark, a trade name, or a copyright licenses others to use the trademark, trade name, or copyright in the selling of goods or services. A **franchisee** (a purchaser of a franchise) is generally legally independent of the **franchisor** (the seller of the franchise). At the same time, the franchisee is economically dependent on the franchisor's integrated business system. In other words, a franchisee can operate as an independent businessperson but still obtain the advantages of a regional or national organization.

The franchising boom was launched by Ray Kroc, the late founder of McDonald's, nearly fifty years ago. Today, over a third of all retail transactions and an increasing percentage of the total annual national output of the United States are generated by private franchises. Well-known franchises include McDonald's, KFC, and Burger King.

TYPES OF FRANCHISES

Because the franchising industry is so extensive and so many different types of businesses sell franchises, it is difficult to summarize the many types of franchises that now exist. Generally, though, the majority of franchises fall into one of the following three classifications: distributorships, chain-style business operations, or manufacturing or processing-plant arrangements. We briefly describe these types of franchises here.

KEEP IN MIND Because a franchise involves the licensing of a trademark, a trade name, or a copyright, the law governing intellectual property may apply in some cases.

Distributorship A *distributorship* arises when a manufacturer concern (franchisor) licenses a dealer (franchisee) to sell its product. Often, a distributorship covers an exclusive territory. An example of this type of franchise is an automobile dealership.

Chain-Style Business Operation In a *chain-style business operation*, a franchise operates under a franchisor's trade name and is identified as a member of a select group of dealers that engage in the franchisor's business. Often, the franchisor requires that the franchisee maintain certain standards of operation. In addition, sometimes the franchisee is obligated to obtain materials and supplies exclusively from the franchisor. Examples of this type of franchise are McDonald's and most other fast-food chains.

Manufacturing or Processing-Plant Arrangement In a *manufacturing or processing-plant arrangement*, the franchisor transmits to the franchisee the essential ingredients or formula to make a particular product. The franchisee then markets the product either at wholesale or at retail in accordance with the franchisor's standards. Examples of this type of franchise are Coca-Cola and other soft-drink bottling companies.

LAWS GOVERNING FRANCHISING

ON THE WEB You can find information on various types of franchising and franchise opportunities by simply keying the word "franchise" into a Web search engine, such as Yahoo.

Because a franchise relationship is primarily a contractual relationship, it is governed by contract law. If the franchise exists primarily for the sale of products manufactured by the franchisor, the law governing sales contracts as expressed in Article 2 of the Uniform Commercial Code applies (see Chapters 14 through 18). Additionally, the federal government and most states have enacted laws governing certain aspects of franchising. Generally, these laws are designed to protect prospective franchisees from dishonest franchisors and to prohibit franchisors from terminating franchises without good cause.

Federal Regulation of Franchising Automobile dealership franchisees are protected from automobile manufacturers' bad faith termination of their franchises by the

Familiar franchises compete for business. What laws govern the relationship between franchisors and franchisees?

Automobile Dealers' Franchise Act[1]—also known as the Automobile Dealers' Day in Court Act—of 1965. If a manufacturer-franchisor terminates a franchise because of a dealer-franchisee's failure to comply with unreasonable demands (for example, failure to attain an unrealistically high sales quota), the manufacturer may be liable for damages.

Another federal statute, the Petroleum Marketing Practices Act (PMPA)[2] of 1979, prescribes the grounds and conditions under which a franchisor may terminate or decline to renew a gasoline station franchise. Federal antitrust laws (discussed in Chapter 32), which prohibit certain types of anticompetitive agreements, may also apply in certain circumstances.

Additionally, the Franchise Rule of the Federal Trade Commission (FTC) requires franchisors to disclose material facts that a prospective franchisee needs to make an informed decision concerning the purchase of a franchise. The rule was designed to enable potential franchisees to weigh the risks and benefits of an investment. The rule requires written disclosures, plus a personal meeting between the franchisor and the prospective franchisee at least ten business days before the franchise agreement is signed or any payment is made in connection with the purchase of the franchise.

ETHICAL ISSUE 31.1

Should traditional franchising rules apply to the Internet?

When the FTC issued its Franchise Rule in 1978, most people had not even heard of the Internet. Today, adapting the rule to the online environment has proved difficult. For example, suppose that a franchisor has a Web site with downloadable information for prospective franchisees. Is this the equivalent of an offer that requires compliance with the FTC's Franchise Rule? Further, does the franchisor have to comply with every different state's franchise regulations? Generally, how can the interests of franchisees be protected in the cyber environment? In view of these problems, the FTC has proposed several changes to its Franchise Rule. One proposed change would require that the franchisor provide a prospective franchisee with a proper disclosure document at least fourteen days before the signing of any franchise agreement or any payment to the franchisor. In addition, to give the franchisee more time to consider the franchise contract, the franchisor would have to provide the franchisee with a copy of the contract five calendar days before the agreement is to be signed. Another proposed rule would require online franchisors to state very clearly that franchisees would not be entitled to exclusive territorial rights (these rights will be discussed shortly). Notwithstanding these changes, however, one problem would remain: given the speed with which online franchises can be created, it may be difficult—if not impossible—for the FTC to effectively regulate these relationships.

ON THE WEB For information about the FTC regulations on franchising, as well as state laws regulating franchising, go to **http://www.ftc.gov/bcp/franchise/netfran.htm**.

State Regulation of Franchising State legislation tends to be similar to federal statutes and the FTC's regulations. To protect franchisees, a state law might require the disclosure of information that is material to making an informed decision regarding the purchase of a franchise. This could include such information as the actual costs of operation, recurring expenses, and profits earned, along with data substantiating these figures. To protect franchisees against arbitrary or bad faith terminations, the law may also require that cer-

1. 15 U.S.C. Sections 1221 *et seq.*
2. 15 U.S.C. Sections 2801 *et seq.*

tain procedures be followed in terminating a franchising relationship. State deceptive trade practices acts may also prohibit certain types of actions on the part of franchisors.

In response to the need for a uniform franchise law, the National Conference of Commissioners on Uniform State Laws drafted a model law that standardizes the various state franchise regulations. Because the uniform law represents a compromise of so many diverse interests, it has met with little success in being adopted as law by the various states.

ON THE WEB A good source for information on the purchase and sale of franchises is Franchising.org, which is online at **http://www.franchising.org.**

THE FRANCHISE CONTRACT

The franchise relationship is defined by a contract between the franchisor and the franchisee. The franchise contract specifies the terms and conditions of the franchise and spells out the rights and duties of the franchisor and the franchisee. If either party fails to perform the contractual duties, that party may be subject to a lawsuit for breach of contract. Generally, statutes and case law governing franchising tend to emphasize the importance of good faith and fair dealing in franchise relationships.

Because each type of franchise relationship has its own characteristics, it is difficult to describe the broad range of details a franchising contract may include. In the remaining pages of this chapter, we look at some of the major issues that typically are addressed in a franchise contract.

Payment for the Franchise The franchisee ordinarily pays an initial fee or lump-sum price for the franchise license (the privilege of being granted a franchise). This fee is separate from the various products that the franchisee purchases from or through the

LETTER OF THE LAW
Independent Contractor or Franchisee?

When Janet Isbell, a sales representative for Mary Kay cosmetics, lost her job, she sued Mary Kay, Inc., claiming that she was a franchisee and, as such, was entitled to the protections of the state franchising law. Among other things, this law provided that a franchisor could only terminate a franchising relationship for cause and required that the franchisee be given ninety days' notice. Mary Kay responded that Isbell was not a franchisee but an independent contractor. The case eventually reached the Arkansas Supreme Court, and in deciding the issue, the court looked to the Arkansas Franchise Practices Act. The letter of the law, as spelled out in that act, was at first not too helpful. The act's definition of a franchise, for example, did not shed any light on the case at hand. The court did find one provision in the act, though, that could guide its decision. According to that provision, the act applied only to a franchise that contemplated or required the franchisee "to establish or maintain a place of business in the state." Although Isbell had rented storefront space in a Little Rock mall to use as a training center for Mary Kay representatives and hold meetings, Isbell's contract with Mary Kay did not require her to do so. Therefore, under Arkansas law, she was not a franchisee but an independent contractor.[a]

a. *Mary Kay, Inc. v. Isbell*, 338 Ark. 556, 999 S.W.2d 669 (1999).

THE BOTTOM LINE

Businesspersons should realize that the law, and not an agreement between private parties, ultimately determines whether a franchising relationship exists. In some cases, courts have held that even though parties have signed a franchising agreement, the franchisees are in fact employees because of the degree of control exercised over them by the franchisors. In other cases, courts have held that a franchising relationship exists even in the absence of a franchising contract.

franchisor. In some industries, the franchisor relies heavily on the initial sale of the franchise for realizing a profit. In other industries, the continued dealing between the parties brings profit to both. In most situations, the franchisor will receive a stated percentage of the annual sales or annual volume of business done by the franchisee. The franchise agreement may also require the franchisee to pay a percentage of advertising costs and certain administrative expenses.

Business Premises The franchise agreement may specify whether the premises for the business must be leased or purchased outright. In some cases, a building must be constructed to meet the terms of the agreement. The agreement usually will specify whether the franchisor supplies equipment and furnishings for the premises or whether this is the responsibility of the franchisee.

Location of the Franchise Typically, the franchisor will determine the territory to be served. Some franchise contracts give the franchisee exclusive rights, or "territorial rights," to a certain geographic area. Other franchise contracts, though they define the territory allotted to a particular franchise, either specifically state that the franchise is nonexclusive or are silent on the issue of territorial rights.

Many franchise cases involve disputes over territorial rights, and this is one area of franchising in which the implied covenant of good faith and fair dealing often comes into play. For example, suppose that a franchisee is not given exclusive territorial rights in the franchise contract, or the contract is silent on the issue. If the franchisor allows a competing franchise to be established nearby, the franchisee may suffer a significant loss in profits. In this situation, a court may hold that the franchisor's actions breached an implied covenant of good faith and fair dealing.

A particular problem facing franchisees in today's online world is that franchisors may attempt to sell their own products via their Web sites. See, for example, the case discussed in this chapter's *Business Law in the Online World* feature.

In the following case, the franchisee did not have any exclusive territorial rights under the franchise contract. When the franchisor built a competing operation nearby, the franchisee sued the franchisor. At issue in the case was whether the franchisor had breached an implied covenant of good faith and fair dealing.

CASE 31.1 Camp Creek Hospitality Inns, Inc. v. Sheraton Franchise Corp.

United States Court of Appeals,
Eleventh Circuit, 1998.
139 F.3d 1396.
http://www.findlaw.com/casecode/courts/11th.html[a]

FACTS In 1990, Camp Creek Hospitality Inns, Inc., entered into a contract with Sheraton Franchise Corporation (a subsidiary of ITT Sheraton Corporation) to operate a Sheraton Inn franchise west of the Atlanta airport. Because another franchisee, the Sheraton Hotel Atlanta Airport, already served that market, Sheraton named Camp Creek's facility "Sheraton Inn Hartsfield-West, Atlanta Airport." Three years later, ITT Sheraton bought a Hyatt hotel in the vicinity of the Atlanta airport and gave it the name "Sheraton Gateway Hotel, Atlanta Airport." The presence of three Sheraton properties in the same market caused some customer confusion. Also, the Inn and the Gateway competed for the same customers, which caused the Inn to suffer a decrease in the growth of its business. Camp Creek filed a suit in a federal district court against Sheraton and others, alleging in part that by establishing the Gateway, ITT Sheraton denied Camp Creek the fruits of its contract in breach of the implied covenant of good faith and fair dealing. The court issued a summary judgment in favor of the defendants. Camp Creek appealed to the U.S. Court of Appeals for the Eleventh Circuit.

a. This page contains links to recent opinions of the U.S. Court of Appeals for the Eleventh Circuit. In the "1998" row, click on the "April" link. When the results appear, click on the *Camp Creek* case name to access the opinion. This Web site is maintained by FindLaw.

CASE 31.1—Continued

ISSUE Does a franchisor violate the implied covenant of good faith and fair dealing if it competes against one of its franchisees in the same geographic market?

DECISION Yes. The U.S. Court of Appeals for the Eleventh Circuit reversed the judgment of the lower court and remanded the case for trial.

REASON The U.S. Court of Appeals for the Eleventh Circuit acknowledged that the contract was silent as to whether, and where, Sheraton could authorize a franchise to compete with Camp Creek's Sheraton Inn. Thus, Camp Creek had no contractual right to expect Sheraton to refrain from licensing additional franchises beyond the site of the Inn. The court emphasized, however, that the Gateway was not a Sheraton franchise, but a hotel that Sheraton bought and operated itself. If this "additional intra-brand competition associated with the Gateway's entry to the market" was proved harmful to the Inn, it could constitute a breach of the implied covenant of good faith and fair dealing.

FOR CRITICAL ANALYSIS—Economic Consideration *Why would a franchisor compete directly with its franchisee?*

BUSINESS LAW: //in the Online World

What Happens to Exclusive Territorial Rights in the Online Environment?

With the growth of inexpensive and easy online marketing, it was inevitable that cyberturf conflicts would eventually arise between franchisors and franchisees. Suppose, for example, that a franchise contract grants to the franchisee exclusive rights to sell the franchised product within a certain territory. What happens if the franchisor then begins to sell the product from its Web site to anyone anywhere in the world, including in the franchisee's territory? Does this constitute a breach of the franchise contract?

Drug Emporium's "Electronic Encroachment"

This issue recently came before a panel of arbitrators in an American Arbitration Association (AAA) proceeding. As you learned in Chapter 3, the AAA is a leading provider of arbitration services. The proceeding involved franchise contracts between the Drug Emporium, Inc., and several of its franchisees. The contracts provided that each franchisee had the exclusive right to conduct business in a specific geographic area. The franchisees claimed that the Drug Emporium breached its contractual obligation to honor their territories by using its Web site to sell directly to customers within the franchisees' territories.

What, Exactly, Is a "Virtual Drugstore"?

One of the first questions the arbitrating panel had to decide was whether a "virtual drugstore" is a drugstore for purposes of a franchise agreement. The panel had little difficulty in answering the question, stating that "[i]t is not for this panel to divine whether a virtual reality is real or whether it is a phantom." The panel simply noted that the company marketed the site as "the full service online drugstore," that it called the site a "drugstore" in filings with the Securities and Exchange Commission, and that it advertised the site as "your neighborhood pharmacy."

Ultimately, in what is believed to be the first ruling by a court or arbitrating panel on the issue of electronic encroachment, the arbitrating panel decided in favor of the franchisees. The panel ordered the Drug Emporium to cease marketing its goods from its Web site to potential customers who were physically located within the franchisees' territories.[a]

FOR CRITICAL ANALYSIS

Conflicts such as the one involved in this case can occur not only between franchisors and franchisees but also among competing franchisees. Can franchisees do anything to protect themselves against electronic encroachment by their franchisors or other franchisees?

a. *Emporium Drug Mart, Inc. of Shreveport v. Drug Emporium, Inc.*, No. 71-114-0012600 (American Arbitration Association, September 2, 2000).

Business Organization of the Franchisee The business organization of the franchisee is of great concern to the franchisor. Depending on the terms of the franchise agreement, the franchisor may specify particular requirements for the form and capital structure of the business. The franchise agreement may also provide that standards of operation—relating to such aspects of the business as sales quotas, quality, and record keeping—be met by the franchisee. Furthermore, a franchisor may wish to retain stringent control over the training of personnel involved in the operation and over administrative aspects of the business.

Quality Control by the Franchisor Although the day-to-day operation of the franchise business is normally left up to the franchisee, the franchise agreement may provide for the amount of supervision and control agreed on by the parties. When the franchise is a service operation, such as a motel, the contract often provides that the franchisor will establish certain standards for the facility. Typically, the contract will provide that the franchisor is permitted to make periodic inspections to ensure that the standards are being maintained so as to protect the franchise's name and reputation.

As a general rule, the validity of a provision permitting the franchisor to establish and enforce certain quality standards is unquestioned. Because the franchisor has a legitimate interest in maintaining the quality of the product or service to protect its name and reputation, it can exercise greater control in this area than would otherwise be tolerated. Increasingly, however, franchisors are finding that if they exercise too much control over the operations of their franchisees, they may incur liability under agency theory for the acts of their franchisees' employees—as the following case illustrates.

RECALL Under the doctrine of *respondeat superior*, an employer may be liable for the torts of employees if they occur within the scope of employment, without regard to the personal fault of the employer.

CASE 31.2 Miller v. D. F. Zee's, Inc.

United States District Court,
District of Oregon, 1998.
31 F.Supp.2d 792.

COMPANY PROFILE *Based in South Carolina, Flagstar Corporation franchised or owned Denny's restaurants, as well as the Carrows, Coco's, El Pollo Loco, Hardee's, and Quincy's Family Steakhouse chains. In the early 1990s, Denny's was the defendant in two civil rights class-action suits brought by African American customers who claimed that some restaurants refused to seat or serve them. Denny's paid more than $54 million to settle those suits and responded "quickly, decisively, and sincerely" to, among other things, hire and promote more minorities.*[a] *In the mid-1990s, Flagstar declared bankruptcy, sold the Hardee's and Quincy's chains, and renamed itself Advantica Restaurant Group, Inc. By the late 1990s, Advantica's annual sales approached $3 billion, with about 2 percent annual growth.*

a. Anne Faircloth, "Guess Who's Coming to Denny's," *Fortune*, August 3, 1998.

FACTS D. F. Zee's, Inc., owns a Denny's restaurant in Tualatin, Oregon. Under the franchise agreement, Zee's agreed to train and supervise employees in accordance with Denny's Operations and Food Service Standards Manuals. Denny's regularly sent inspectors to assess compliance and reserved the right to terminate the franchise for noncompliance. The Denny's logo was displayed throughout the restaurant and there was no indication that its owners were other than "Denny's." Christine Miller worked as a server at the restaurant. After several incidents of sexually inappropriate comments and conduct by her co-workers, Miller complained to Stanley Templeton, the manager. When her complaints were not acted on, Miller contacted the manager of another Denny's restaurant, who referred her to the district franchise manager for Denny's, who referred the complaint to Zee's. In the meantime, the harassment continued. Finally, Miller and three other employees filed a suit in a federal district court against Zee's, Denny's, and others. Denny's filed a motion for summary judgment, contending in part that a franchisor cannot be held liable for harassment by franchise employees.

CASE 31.2—Continued

ISSUE If a franchisee's employees act with the apparent authority of the franchisor, can the franchisor be held liable for the employees' wrongful acts?

DECISION Yes. The court denied Denny's motion for summary judgment. The court held that a franchisor may be held vicariously liable under an agency theory for the intentional acts of discrimination by the employees of a franchisee.

REASON The court concluded that Denny's was responsible for the acts of harassment by the employees at the Tualatin restaurant, because the employees were the agents of Denny's. The court explained that an agency relationship could be implied from "the circumstances and conduct of the parties." In this case, the franchise agreement required adherence to the "comprehensive, detailed" Franchise Operations and Food Service Standards Manuals. Denny's enforced this requirement by conducting regular inspections of the restaurant and by retaining the power to cancel the agreement for noncompliance. In particular, the manuals gave Denny's the right of control "in the precise parts of the franchisee's business that allegedly resulted in plaintiffs' injuries—training and discipline of employees."

FOR CRITICAL ANALYSIS—Ethical Consideration *Should a franchisor be allowed to control the operation of its franchisee without liability for the franchisee's conduct?*

Pricing Arrangements Franchises provide the franchisor with an outlet for the firm's goods and services. Depending on the nature of the business, the franchisor may require the franchisee to purchase certain supplies from the franchisor at an established price.[3] A franchisor that sets the prices at which the franchisee will resell the goods may violate state or federal antitrust laws, or both, however.

Termination of the Franchise The duration of the franchise is a matter to be determined between the parties. Generally, a franchise will start out for a short period, such as a year, so that the franchisee and the franchisor can determine whether they want to stay in business with one another. Usually, the franchise agreement will specify that termination must be "for cause," such as death or disability of the franchisee, insolvency of the franchisee, breach of the franchise agreement, or failure to meet specified sales quotas. Most franchise contracts provide that notice of termination must be given. If no set time for termination is specified, then a reasonable time, with notice, will be implied. A franchisee must be given reasonable time to wind up the business—that is, to do the accounting and return the copyright or trademark or any other property of the franchisor.

Because a franchisor's termination of a franchise often has adverse consequences for the franchisee, much franchise litigation involves claims of wrongful termination. Generally, the termination provisions of contracts are more favorable to the franchisor. This means that the franchisee, who normally invests a substantial amount of time and funds to make the franchise operation successful, may receive little or nothing for the business on termination. The franchisor owns the trademark and hence the business.

It is in this area that statutory and case law become important. The federal and state laws discussed earlier attempt, among other things, to protect franchisees from the arbitrary or unfair termination of their franchises by the franchisors. Generally, both statutory and case law emphasize the importance of good faith and fair dealing in terminating a franchise relationship.

---

3. Although a franchisor can require franchisees to purchase supplies from it, requiring a franchisee to purchase exclusively from the franchisor may violate federal antitrust laws (see Chapter 32). For two landmark cases in these areas, see *United States v. Arnold, Schwinn & Co.*, 388 U.S. 365, 87 S.Ct. 1856, 18 L.Ed.2d 1249 (1967), and *Fortner Enterprises, Inc. v. U.S. Steel Corp.*, 394 U.S. 495, 89 S.Ct. 1252, 22 L.Ed.2d 495 (1969).

In determining whether a franchisor has acted in good faith when terminating a franchise agreement, the courts generally try to balance the rights of both parties. If a court perceives that a franchisor has arbitrarily or unfairly terminated a franchise, the franchisee will be provided with a remedy for wrongful termination. If a franchisor's decision to terminate a franchise was made in the normal course of the franchisor's business operations, however, and reasonable notice of termination was given to the franchisee, normally a court would not consider such a termination wrongful. At issue in the following case was whether General Motors Corporation, Chrysler Corporation, and Toyota Motor Sales, U.S.A., Inc., acted wrongfully in terminating their franchises with a motor vehicle dealer in Ohio.

CASE 31.3 General Motors Corp. v. Monte Zinn Chevrolet Co.

Ohio Court of Appeals, Tenth District, 2000. 136 Ohio App.3d 157, 736 N.E.2d 62.

FACTS Monte Zinn operated Ohio motor vehicle dealerships, as Monte Zinn Chevrolet Company and Monte Zinn Motor Company, under separate franchise agreements with General Motors Corporation (GMC), Chrysler Corporation, and Toyota Motor Sales, U.S.A., Inc. Each agreement permitted the franchisor to terminate the dealership if the dealer was convicted of a felony. In 1995, Zinn pleaded guilty to committing a felony by violating federal statutes proscribing fraud and conspiracy to commit fraud in relation to his dealerships. He was sentenced to two years' probation and ordered to pay a fine and a special assessment. Each franchisor terminated its Zinn companies' franchise. The Zinn companies protested to the Ohio Motor Vehicle Dealers Board, a state agency that oversees motor vehicle franchises in Ohio. The board ruled in favor of the Zinn companies. The franchisors filed a suit in an Ohio state court against the Zinn companies, and the court reversed the board's order. The Zinn companies appealed to a state intermediate appellate court.

ISSUE Did the franchisors have good cause to terminate the Zinn companies' franchises?

DECISION Yes. The state intermediate appellate court affirmed the lower court's decision, citing Zinn's felony conviction and other circumstances that supported the franchisors' action.

REASON The state intermediate appellate court explained that the facts "all weigh in favor of finding good cause to terminate the franchise[s]." A "felony conviction for fraud committed by a dealer/operator undermines the trust between the manufacturer and the dealer, and between the public and the dealer." Discussing the GMC franchise, the court noted that between 1991 and 1995, the Zinn companies' "overall sales effectiveness had been in the bottom half of Chevrolet dealers in their service area and consistently ranked in the bottom twenty percent of all dealers in customer service and satisfaction." As for the Chrysler franchise, the Zinn companies "had made few investments into the dealership" and had been seriously "undercapitalized every year from 1991." Between 1992 and 1996, "their new vehicle sales volume increased at less than half the rate" of other dealers "and actually decreased between 1995 and 1996." The Zinn companies also had "performed poorly in service-related areas" and their "scores on owner loyalty" were below average. Finally, concerning the Toyota franchise, the court pointed out that Toyota "uniformly terminated dealerships following felony convictions."

FOR CRITICAL ANALYSIS—Social Consideration *Should franchisors conduct background checks on prospective franchisees, and, if so, would it have helped in this case?*

APPLICATION **Law and the Businessperson . . .**

Law and the Franchisee*

A franchise arrangement appeals to many prospective businesspersons for several reasons. Entrepreneurs who purchase franchises can operate independently and without the risks associated with products that have never been marketed before. Additionally, the franchisee can usually rely on the assistance and guidance of a management network that is regional or national in scope and has been in place for some time. Franchisees do face potential problems, however. Generally, to avoid possibly significant economic and legal problems, it is imperative that you obtain all relevant details about the business and that you have an attorney evaluate the franchise contract for possible pitfalls.

THE FRANCHISE FEE

Virtually all franchise contracts require a franchise fee payable up front or in installments. This fee often ranges between $10,000 and $50,000. For nationally known franchises, such as McDonald's, the fee may be $500,000 or more. The true cost of the franchise, however, must also include fees that are paid once the franchisee opens for business. For example, as a franchisee, you would probably pay royalties to the franchisor (for the use of the franchisor's trademark, for example) of anywhere from 2 to 8 percent of your gross sales. Another 1 to 2 percent of gross sales might go to the franchisor to cover advertising costs. Although your business would benefit from the advertising, the cost of that advertising might exceed the benefits you would realize.

ELECTRONIC ENCROACHMENT AND TERMINATION PROVISIONS

Another problem that many franchisees do not anticipate is the adverse effects on their businesses of so-called electronic encroachment. For example, suppose that a franchise contract gives the franchisee exclusive rights to operate a franchise in a certain territory. Nothing in the contract, though, indicates what will happen if the franchisor sells its products to customers located within the franchisee's territory via telemarketing, mail-order catalogues, or online services over the Internet. As a prospective franchisee, you should make sure that your franchise contract covers such contingencies and protects you against any losses you might incur if you face these types of competition in your area.

A major economic consequence, usually of a negative nature, will occur if the franchisor terminates your franchise agreement. Before you sign a franchise contract, make sure that the contract provisions regarding termination are reasonable and clearly specified.

*This *Application* is not meant to substitute for the services of an attorney who is licensed to practice law in your state.

CHECKLIST FOR THE FRANCHISEE

1. Find out all you can about the franchisor: How long has the franchisor been in business? How profitable is the business? Is there a healthy market for the product?
2. Obtain the most recent financial statement from the franchisor and a complete description of the business.
3. Obtain a clear and complete statement of all fees that you will be required to pay.
4. Will the franchisor help you in training management and employees? With promotion and advertising? By supplying capital or credit? In finding a good location for your business?
5. Visit other franchisees in the same business. Ask them about their experiences with the product, the market, and the franchisor.
6. Evaluate your training and experience in the business on which you are about to embark. Are they sufficient to ensure success as a franchisee?
7. Carefully examine the franchise contract provisions relating to termination of the franchise agreement. Are they specific enough to allow you to sue for breach of contract in the event the franchisor wrongfully terminates the contract? Find out how many franchises have been terminated in the past several years.
8. Will you have an exclusive geographic territory and, if so, for how many years? What plans does the franchisor have in regard to telemarketing, electronic marketing, and mail-order sales to customers within the territory?
9. Finally, the most important way to protect yourself is to have an attorney familiar with franchise law examine the contract before you sign it.

Key Terms

business trust 824
cooperative 824
franchise 824
franchisee 825
franchisor 825
joint stock company 824
joint venture 823
syndicate 823

Chapter Summary Special Business Forms and Private Franchises

Special Business Forms (See pages 823–824.)	1. *Joint venture*—An organization created by two or more persons in contemplation of a limited activity or a single transaction; otherwise, similar to a partnership. 2. *Syndicate*—An investment group that undertakes to finance a particular project; may exist as a corporation or as a general or limited partnership. 3. *Joint stock company*—A business form similar to a corporation in some respects (transferable shares of stock, management by directors and officers, perpetual existence) but otherwise resembling a partnership. 4. *Business trust*—Created by a written trust agreement that sets forth the interests of the beneficiaries and the obligations and powers of the trustee(s). Similar to a corporation in many respects. Beneficiaries are not personally liable for the debts or obligations of the business trust. 5. *Cooperative*—An association organized to provide an economic service, without profit, to its members. May take the form of a corporation or a partnership.
Private Franchises (See pages 824–833.)	1. *Types of franchises*— a. Distributorship (for example, automobile dealerships). b. Chain-style operation (for example, fast-food chains). c. Manufacturing/processing-plant arrangement (for example, soft-drink bottling companies, such as Coca-Cola). 2. *Laws governing franchising*— a. Franchises are governed by contract law. b. Franchises are also governed by federal and state statutory and regulatory laws, as well as agency law. 3. *The franchise contract*— a. Ordinarily requires the franchisee (purchaser) to pay a price for the franchise license. b. Specifies the territory to be served by the franchisee's firm. c. May require the franchisee to purchase certain supplies from the franchisor at an established price. d. May require the franchisee to abide by certain standards of quality relating to the product or service offered but cannot set retail resale prices. e. Usually provides for the date and/or conditions of termination of the franchise arrangement. Both federal and state statutes attempt to protect certain franchisees from franchisors who unfairly or arbitrarily terminate franchises.

For Review

① What are the essential characteristics of each of the following business forms: joint ventures, joint stock companies, syndicates, business trusts, and cooperatives?
② What is a franchise? What are the most common types of franchises?
③ What laws govern a franchising relationship?
④ What terms and conditions are typically included in a franchise contract?
⑤ When might franchisors be liable under agency laws?

Questions and Case Problems

31–1. Business Forms and Liability. Assume that Faraway Corp. is considering entering into two contracts, one with a joint stock company that distributes home products east of the Mississippi River and the other with a business trust formed by a number of sole proprietors who are sellers of home products on the West Coast. Both contracts involve large capital outlays for Faraway, which will supply each business with soft-drink dispensers. In both business organizations, at least two shareholders or beneficiaries are personally wealthy, but each organization has limited financial resources. The owner-managers of Faraway are not familiar with either form of business organization. Because each form resembles a corporation, they are concerned about whether they will be able to collect payments from the wealthy members of the business organizations in the event that either organization breaches the contract by failing to make the payments. Discuss fully Faraway's concern.

31–2. Business Organizations. Alan, Jane, and Kyle organize a nonprofit business—AJK Markets, Inc.—to buy groceries from wholesalers and sell them to consumers who buy a membership in AJK. Because the firm is a nonprofit entity, it is able to sell the groceries for less than a commercial grocer could. What form of business organization is AJK Markets? Is it significant that AJK is incorporated?

31–3. Private Franchises. May, Paul, and Vicky are recent college graduates who would like to go into business for themselves. They are considering the idea of purchasing a franchise. If they enter into a franchising arrangement, they would have the support of a larger company that could answer any questions they might have. Also, a firm that has been in business for many years would have experience with some of the problems that novice businesspersons would encounter. These and other attributes of franchises can lessen some of the risks of the marketplace. What other aspects of franchising—positive and negative—might May, Paul, and Vicky want to consider before committing themselves to a particular franchise?

31–4. Control of a Franchise. National Foods, Inc., sells franchises to its fast-food restaurants, known as Chicky-D's. Under the franchise agreement, franchisees agree to hire and train employees strictly according to Chicky-D's standards. Chicky-D's regional supervisors are required to approve all job candidates before they are hired and all general policies affecting those employees. Chicky-D's reserves the right to terminate a franchise for violating the franchisor's rules. In practice, however, Chicky-D's regional supervisors routinely approve new employees and individual franchisees' policies. After several incidents of racist comments and conduct by Tim, a recently hired assistant manager at a Chicky-D's, Sharon, a counterperson at the restaurant, resigns. Sharon files a suit in a federal district court against National. National files a motion for summary judgment, arguing that it is not liable for harassment by franchise employees. Will the court grant National's motion? Why or why not?

31–5. Private Franchises. Omega Computers, Inc., is a franchisor that grants exclusive physical territories to its franchisees with retail locations, including Pete's Digital Products. Omega sells over two hundred of the franchises before establishing an interactive Web site. On the site, a customer can order Omega's products directly from the franchisor. When Pete's sets up a Web site through which a customer can also order Omega's products, Omega and Pete's file suits against each other, alleging that each is in violation of the franchise relationship. To decide this issue, what factors should the court consider? How might these parties have avoided this conflict? Discuss.

31–6. Good Faith in Franchising Relationships. Barn-Chestnut, Inc. (BCI), entered into a franchise agreement with Grocers Development Corp. (GDC) for a Convenient Food Mart "for as long as [BCI] . . . shall have a good and valid lease" to the property. GDC sold its interest in the franchise and the property to CFM Development Corp. When the lease was about to expire, CFM offered to enter into a new lease and franchise agreement with BCI at a significantly higher price. BCI refused. When CFM refused to make another deal, BCI filed a suit against CFM in a West Virginia state court on the ground that CFM had to offer BCI a lease because the franchise was contingent on a lease. The court did not agree. BCI then argued that the implied obligation of good faith required CFM to offer to renew the lease. Essentially, the question on appeal was whether a franchisor had an obligation to renew a franchise even though there was no clause in the contract requiring that the lease/franchise be renewed. Is BCI correct in contending that the franchisor does have such an obligation? Explain. [*Barn-Chestnut, Inc. v. CFM Development Corp.*, 193 W.Va. 565, 457 S.E.2d 502 (1995)]

31–7. The Franchise Contract. Kubis & Perszyk Associates, Inc., was in business as Entre Computer. As a franchise, Entre sold, among other products, computer systems marketed by Sun Microsystems, Inc. Entre's agreement with Sun included a forum-selection clause that provided that any suit between the parties had to be filed in a California court. When Sun terminated its relationship with Entre, Entre filed a suit in a New Jersey state court. Sun asked the court to dismiss the suit on the basis of the forum-selection clause. Entre argued that the clause violated state franchise law, which invalidated such clauses in auto dealership franchises. On what basis might the court extend this law to cover Entre's franchise? Discuss. [*Kubis & Perszyk Associates, Inc. v. Sun Microsystems, Inc.*, 146 N.J. 176, 680 A.2d 618 (1996)]

31–8. Franchise Termination. C. B. Management Co. operated McDonald's restaurants in Cleveland, Ohio, under a franchise agreement with McDonald's Corp. The agreement required C. B. to make monthly payments of, among other things, certain percentages of the gross sales to McDonald's. If any payment was more than thirty days late, McDonald's had the right to terminate the franchise. The agreement stated, "No waiver by [McDonald's] of any breach . . . shall constitute a waiver of any subsequent breach." McDonald's sometimes accepted C. B.'s late payments, but when C. B. defaulted on the payments in July 1997, McDonald's gave notice of thirty days to comply or surrender possession of the restaurants. C. B. missed the deadline. McDonald's demanded that C. B. vacate the restaurants. C. B. refused. McDonald's filed a suit in a federal district court against C. B., alleging violations of the franchise agreement. C. B. counterclaimed in part that McDonald's had breached the implied covenant of good faith and fair dealing. McDonald's filed a motion to dismiss C. B.'s counterclaim. On what did C. B. base its claim? Will the court agree? Why or why not? [*McDonald's Corp. v. C. B. Management Co.*, 13 F.Supp.2d 705 (N.D.Ill. 1998)]

31–9. Franchise Termination. Heating & Air Specialists, Inc., doing business as A/C Service Co., marketed heating and air conditioning products. A/C contracted with Lennox Industries, Inc., to be a franchised dealer of Lennox products. The parties signed a standard franchise contract drafted by Lennox. The contract provided that either party could terminate the agreement with or without cause on thirty days' notice and that the agreement would terminate immediately if A/C opened another facility at a different location. At the time, A/C operated only one location in Arkansas. A few months later, A/C opened a second location in Tulsa, Oklahoma. Lennox's district sales manager gave A/C oral authorization to sell Lennox products in Tulsa, at least on a temporary basis, but nothing was put in writing. Several of Lennox's other dealers in Tulsa complained to Lennox about A/C's presence. Lennox gave A/C notice that it was terminating A/C's Tulsa franchise. Meanwhile, A/C had failed to keep its Lennox account current and owed the franchisor more than $200,000. Citing this delinquency, Lennox notified A/C that unless it paid its account within ten days, Lennox would terminate both franchises. A/C did not pay. Lennox terminated the franchises. A/C filed a suit in a federal district court against Lennox, alleging in part breach of the franchise agreement for terminating the Tulsa franchise. Is A/C correct? Explain. [*Heating & Air Specialists, Inc. v. Jones*, 180 F.3d 923 (8th Cir. 1999)]

TEST YOUR KNOWLEDGE—ANSWER ON THE WEB

31–10. In 1985, Bruce Byrne, with his sons Scott and Gordon, opened Lone Star R.V. Sales, Inc., a motor home dealership in Houston, Texas. In 1994, Lone Star became a franchised dealer for Winnebago Industries, Inc., a manufacturer of recreational vehicles. The parties renewed the franchise in 1995, but during the next year, their relationship began to deteriorate. Lone Star did not maintain a current inventory, its sales did not meet goals agreed to between the parties, and Lone Star disparaged Winnebago products to consumers and otherwise failed to actively promote them. Several times, the Byrnes subjected Winnebago employees to verbal abuse. During one phone conversation, Bruce threatened to throw a certain Winnebago sales manager off Lone Star's lot if he appeared at the dealership. Bruce was physically incapable of carrying out the threat, however. In 1998, Winnebago terminated the franchise, claiming, among many other things, that it was concerned for the safety of its employees. Lone Star filed a protest with the Texas Motor Vehicle Board. Did Winnebago have good cause to terminate Lone Star's franchise? Discuss. [*Lone Star R.V. Sales, Inc. v. Motor Vehicle Board of the Texas Department of Transportation*, 49 S.W.3d 492 (Tex.App.—Austin, 2001)]

A QUESTION OF ETHICS AND SOCIAL RESPONSIBILITY

31–11. Graham Oil Co. (Graham) had been a distributor of ARCO gasoline in Coos Bay, Oregon, for nearly forty years under successive distributorship agreements. ARCO notified Graham that it intended to terminate the franchise because Graham had not been purchasing the minimum amount of gasoline required under their most recent agreement. Graham sought a preliminary injunction against ARCO, arguing that ARCO had violated the Petroleum Marketing Practices Act (PMPA) by deliberately raising its prices so that Graham would be unable to meet the minimum gasoline requirements; thus, ARCO should not be allowed to terminate the agreement. The court ordered Graham to submit the claim to arbitration, in accordance with an arbitration clause in the distributorship agreement. Graham refused to do so, and the court granted summary judgment for ARCO. On appeal, Graham claimed that the arbitration clause was invalid because it forced him to forfeit rights given to franchisees under the PMPA, including the right to punitive damages and attorneys' fees. The appellate court agreed with Graham and remanded the case for trial. In view of these facts, answer the following questions. [*Graham Oil Co. v. Arco Products Co., A Division of Atlantic Richfield Co.*, 43 F.3d 1244 (9th Cir. 1994)]

1. Do you agree with Graham and the appellate court that statutory rights cannot be forfeited contractually, through an arbitration clause?
2. Review the discussion of arbitration in Chapter 3. Does the decision in the above case conflict with any established public policy concerning arbitration? Is the court's decision in the

case consistent with other court decisions on arbitration discussed in Chapter 3, including decisions of the United States Supreme Court?

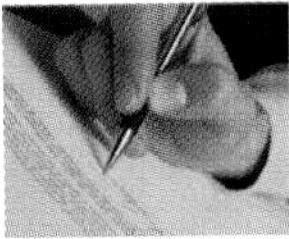

FOR CRITICAL ANALYSIS

31–12. The law permits individuals to organize their business enterprises in many different forms. What policy interests are served by granting entrepreneurs so many options? Would it be better if the law required all businesspersons to organize their businesses in the same form? Discuss.

Internet Exercises

Go to the *Business Law Today* home page at **http://blt.westbuslaw.com**. Select "Interactive Study Center" and then click on "Chapter 31." There you will find the following Internet research exercise that you can perform to learn more about franchises:

Activity 31–1: Franchises

Before the Test

Go to the *Business Law Today* home page at **http://blt.westbuslaw.com**. Click on "Interactive Quizzes." You will find at least twenty interactive questions relating to this chapter.

UNIT SIX Cumulative Business Hypothetical

John leases an office and buys computer equipment. Initially, to pay for the lease and the equipment, he goes into the business of designing Web pages. He also has an idea for a new software product that he hopes will be more profitable than designing Web pages. Whenever he has time, he works on the software.

① After six months, Mary and Paul come to work in the office to help develop John's idea. John continues to pay the rent and other expenses, including salaries for Mary and Paul. John does not expect to make a profit until the software is developed, which could take months; even then, there may be very little profit if the product is not marketed successfully. John believes that if the product is successful, however, the firm will be able to follow up with other products. In choosing a form of business organization for this firm, what are the important considerations? What are the advantages and disadvantages of each basic option?

② It is decided that an organizational form for this firm should include limited liability for its owners. The owners will include John, Mary, Paul, and some members of their respective families. One of the features of the corporate form is limited liability. Ordinarily, however, corporate income is taxed at the corporate level and at the shareholder level. Which corporate form could the firm use to avoid this double taxation? Which other forms of business organization feature limited liability? What factors, other than liability and taxation, influence a firm's choice among these forms?

③ The firm is incorporated as Digital Software, Inc. (DSI). The software is developed and marketed successfully, and DSI prospers. John, Mary, and Paul become directors of DSI. At a board meeting, Paul proposes a marketing strategy for DSI's next product, and John and Mary approve it. Implementing the strategy causes DSI's profits to drop. If the shareholders accuse Paul of breaching his fiduciary duty to DSI, what is Paul's most likely defense? If the shareholders accuse John and Mary of the same breach, what is their best defense? In either case, if the shareholders file a suit, how is a court likely to rule?

④ International Investments, Inc., makes a public offer to buy the stock of DSI. The price of the offer is higher than the market price of the stock, but DSI's board believes that the offer should not be accepted and that International's attempt to take over DSI should be resisted. What steps can DSI take to resist the takeover?

⑤ Mary and Paul withdraw from DSI to set up their own firm. To obtain operating capital, they solicit investors who agree to become "general partners." Mary and Paul designate themselves "managing partners." The investors are spread over a wide area geographically and do not know anything about Mary and Paul's business until they are contacted. Are Mary and Paul truly soliciting partners, or are they selling securities? What are the criteria for determining whether an investment is a security? What are the advantages and disadvantages of selling securities compared to soliciting partners?

UNIT SIX **Extended Case Study**

Tschetter v. Berven

The elements of the definition of a security, in the context of the securities laws, are listed in Chapter 29. The ownership of a limited liability company (LLC) is reviewed in Chapter 30. In this extended case study, we examine Tschetter v. Breven,[1] *a decision that considers whether an "investment unit" in an LLC falls within the definition of a security.*

CASE BACKGROUND

In 1994, Venerts Investment, Inc., entered into an agreement with Country Hospitality Corporation to build and run several Country Kitchen restaurants. Venerts formed Huron Kitchen LLC, a limited liability company, to construct and own one of the restaurants in Huron, South Dakota. An operating agreement was entered into in April 1995. In July, Venerts entered into a fifteen-year management contract with Country Kitchen International (CKI), which agreed to run Huron LLC's restaurant.

Venerts contacted Marvie, Kim, Clarence, and Goldie Tschetter, who bought "investment units" in Huron LLC in September. The restaurant opened that fall. Within months, financial problems led the Tschetters, and others, to personally guarantee bank loans to Huron LLC. After the restaurant closed in November 1996, the bank filed a suit in a South Dakota state court against the guarantors to recover the amount of the loans.

The Tschetters filed claims with the court against Venerts' owners, including James Berven. The Tschetters filed a motion for summary judgment, asserting in part that the Huron units were "securities" and that Venerts' owners had breached South Dakota securities law by failing to advise the Tschetters of the risks attending their investments. The court denied the motion and dismissed the Tschetters' claims. The Tschetters appealed to the South Dakota Supreme Court.

1. 2001 SD 11, 621 N.W.2d 372 (2001). This opinion may be accessed online at **http://www.state.sd.us/state/judicial.** On that page, click on "Court Opinions." On the resulting page, click on "2001 Opinions." In the "January Opinions" section, click on number "11" to access the opinion in this case. The South Dakota Unified Judicial System maintains this Web site.

MAJORITY OPINION

SABERS, Justice.

* * * *

* * * [A]n "investment contract" is a "security" when a person 1.) invests money 2.) in a common enterprise and 3.) is led to expect profits solely from the efforts of the promotor or a third party.

The critical inquiry is the third prong of the * * * test—whether Tschetters were led to expect profits solely from the efforts of the promotor or a third party. * * * [T]he use of the term "solely" is not to be taken literally. Rather, the third prong is satisfied if the efforts made by those other than the investor are the undeniably significant ones, those essential managerial efforts which effect the failure or success of the enterprise. * * * *[T]he definition of a security embodies a flexible rather than a static principle, one that is capable of adaptation to meet the countless and variable schemes devised by those who seek the use of the money of others in the promise of profits.* * * * [T]hree factors * * * aid in this determination: [Emphasis added.]

① an agreement among the parties leaves so little power in the hands of the partner or venturer that the arrangement in fact distributes power as would a limited partnership; or

② the partner or venturer is so inexperienced and unknowledgeable in business affairs that he is incapable of intelligently exercising his partnership or venture powers; or

③ the partner or venturer is so dependent on some unique entrepreneurial or managerial ability of the promoter or manager that he cannot replace the manager or the enterprise or otherwise exercise meaningful partnership or venture powers.

* * *

* * * Tschetters had substantial rights and powers. South Dakota law vests the members of an LLC with management powers in proportion to their contribution of capital. The members have the power to elect the managers of the LLC and set their responsibilities.

In addition, the Operating Agreement vested management powers of the Huron LLC in its members, which included Tschetters. These members were given notice of meetings and any member could call a meeting. The day-to-day decisions were made by two managers who were required to be members of the Huron LLC, and selected by the other members. The Huron LLC maintained and provided access to all records of actions taken by its members. Members could authorize loans on behalf of the company by agreement. The members had the authority to select an attorney to review the legal affairs of the

Huron LLC. The members had the right to receive profits and distributions when warranted. The members could authorize incidental expenses within an aggregate of $12,500. The members were empowered to make any other routine actions incidental to the day-to-day activity of Huron LLC. The members were allowed to select officers for the Huron LLC and could remove the accountant with or without cause.

* * * The minutes kept by the Huron LLC show that Tschetters were informed and active in this entity. Tschetters' actions on behalf of Huron LLC after the restaurant began to fail shows they were aware of and capable of exercising the powers which they held as members.

* * * *

We hold that the third prong of the * * * test * * * has not been met. * * *

* * * These "units" were not "securities" under this law * * *.

* * * *

We conclude that the trial court correctly granted summary judgment in favor of Venerts.

DISSENTING OPINION

GILBERTSON, Justice (dissenting * * *).

I respectfully dissent * * *. I would hold there is a question of fact as to whether the investment made by the Tschetters constituted a security * * *. I would reverse and remand for trial on this cause of action.

* * * *

The timeline of the events involved in this case is critical when examining the rights held by Tschetters in Huron LLC. * * * By the time the Tschetters received their interests in Huron LLC, their hands had effectively been tied by Venerts through the management agreement with CKI. * * *

* * * While the terms of the LLC agreement on paper would indicate that Tschetters, as members, were given an opportunity to participate in management decisions, in reality, they were already locked out by the previously signed 15-year management agreement with CKI at the time of their investment. * * *

Furthermore, the applicable test is whether the efforts made by those other than the investor are the undeniably significant ones, those essential managerial efforts which affect the failure or success of the enterprise. Under the terms of the management contract, Tschetters were precluded from exercising any managerial efforts over the enterprise, namely the restaurant.

When the owners of a limited liability company are not expected to exercise control over the day-to-day business operations * * * interests in limited liability companies should be classified as investment contracts, except in those instances in which the investor will be playing a substantial role in the management of the business.

QUESTIONS FOR ANALYSIS

① **Law.** From a reading of the opinions, what was the plaintiffs' likely argument regarding control of the LLC? What did the majority conclude on this issue, and why?

② **Law.** What was the dissent's major point concerning the control issue? What was the dissent's reasoning on this point?

③ **Social Consideration.** On what basis might the investors have maintained an action against CKI?

④ **Political Dimensions.** If investors in a limited liability entity have the power to control the enterprise but choose to remain passive, should their liability be affected?

⑤ **Implications for the Investor.** Does the holding in this case indicate legal steps that an investor might take when considering a particular investment?

Government Regulation

UNIT 7

UNIT CONTENTS

CHAPTER 32

Antitrust Law

"Free competition is worth more to society than it costs."

Oliver Wendell Holmes, Jr., 1841–1935
(Associate justice of the United States Supreme Court, 1902–1932)

CHAPTER CONTENTS

LEARNING OBJECTIVES

After reading this chapter, you should be able to answer the following questions:

① What is a monopoly? What is market power? How do these concepts relate to each other?

② What type of activity is prohibited by Section 1 of the Sherman Act? What type of activity is prohibited by Section 2 of the Sherman Act?

③ What are the four major provisions of the Clayton Act, and what types of activities do these provisions prohibit?

④ What agencies of the federal government enforce the federal antitrust laws?

⑤ What are four activities that are exempt from the antitrust laws?

Today's antitrust laws are the direct descendants of common law actions intended to limit *restraints on trade* (agreements between firms that have the effect of reducing competition in the marketplace). Such actions date to the fifteenth century in England. In America, concern over monopolistic practices arose following the Civil War with the growth of large corporate enterprises and their attempts to reduce or eliminate competition. In an attempt to thwart competition, they legally tied themselves together in business trusts. As discussed in Chapter 31, business trusts are forms of business organization in which trustees hold title to property for the benefit of others. The most powerful of these trusts, the Standard Oil trust, is examined in this chapter's *Landmark in the Law* on page 844.

Many states attempted to control such monopolistic behavior by enacting statutes outlawing the use of trusts. That is why all of the laws that regulate

ANTITRUST LAWS
Laws protecting commerce from unlawful restraints.

ON THE WEB
The Web site of Cornell University's Legal Information Institute contains the text of federal statutes relating to commerce and trade, including the Sherman Antitrust Act, at **http://www4.law.cornell.edu/uscode/15/1.html**.

economic competition today are referred to as **antitrust laws.** At the national level, Congress passed the Sherman Antitrust Act in 1890. In 1914, Congress passed the Clayton Act and the Federal Trade Commission Act to further curb anticompetitive or unfair business practices. Since their passage, the 1914 acts have been amended by Congress to broaden and strengthen their coverage.

This chapter examines these major antitrust statutes, focusing particularly on the Sherman Act and the Clayton Act, as amended, and the types of activities prohibited by those acts. Remember in reading this chapter that the basis of antitrust legislation is the desire to foster competition. Antitrust legislation was initially created—and continues to be enforced—because of our belief that competition leads to lower prices, generates more product information, and results in a better distribution of wealth between consumers and producers. As Oliver Wendell Holmes, Jr., indicated in the opening quotation, free competition is worth more to our society than the cost we pay for it. The cost is, of course, government regulation of business behavior.

The Sherman Antitrust Act

In 1890, Congress passed "An Act to Protect Trade and Commerce against Unlawful Restraints and Monopolies"—commonly known as the Sherman Antitrust Act or, more simply, as the Sherman Act. The Sherman Act was and remains one of the government's most powerful weapons in the struggle to maintain a competitive economy. Because of the act's significance, we examine its passage more closely in this chapter's *Landmark in the Law* on the following page.

MAJOR PROVISIONS OF THE SHERMAN ACT

Sections 1 and 2 contain the main provisions of the Sherman Act:

> 1: Every contract, combination in the form of trust or otherwise, or conspiracy, in restraint of trade or commerce among the several States, or with foreign nations, is hereby declared to be illegal [and is a felony punishable by fine and/or imprisonment].
>
> 2: Every person who shall monopolize, or attempt to monopolize, or combine or conspire with any other person or persons, to monopolize any part of the trade or commerce among the several States, or with foreign nations, shall be deemed guilty of a felony [and is similarly punishable].

"As a charter of freedom, the [Sherman] Act has a generality and adaptability comparable to that found to be desirable in constitutional provisions."
CHARLES EVANS HUGHES,
1862–1948
(Chief justice of the United States Supreme Court, 1930–1941)

These two sections of the Sherman Act are quite different. Violation of Section 1 requires two or more persons, as a person cannot contract or combine or conspire alone. Thus, the essence of the illegal activity is *the act of joining together.* Section 2 applies both to several people who have joined together and to individual persons because it specifies "[e]very person who . . . ." Thus, unilateral conduct can result in a violation of Section 2.

The cases brought to court under Section 1 of the Sherman Act differ from those brought under Section 2. Section 1 cases are often concerned with finding an agreement (written or oral) that leads to a restraint of trade. Section 2 cases deal with the structure of a monopoly that already exists in the marketplace. The term **monopoly** is generally used to describe a market in which there is a single or a limited number of sellers. Whereas Section 1 focuses on agreements that are restrictive—that is, agreements that have a wrongful purpose—Section 2 looks at the so-called misuse of **monopoly power** in the marketplace. Monopoly power exists when a firm has an

MONOPOLY
A term generally used to describe a market in which there is a single seller or a limited number of sellers.

MONOPOLY POWER
The ability of a monopoly to dictate what takes place in a given market.

LANDMARK IN THE LAW
The Sherman Antitrust Act of 1890

The author of the Sherman Antitrust Act of 1890, Senator John Sherman, was the brother of the famed Civil War general William Tecumseh Sherman and a recognized financial authority. Sherman had been concerned for years with the diminishing competition within American industry and the emergence of monopolies, such as the Standard Oil trust.

The Standard Oil Trust By 1890, the Standard Oil trust had become the foremost petroleum refining and marketing combination in the United States. Streamlined, integrated, and centrally and efficiently controlled, its monopoly over the industry could not be disputed. Standard Oil controlled 90 percent of the U.S. market for refined petroleum products, and small manufacturers were incapable of competing with such an industrial leviathan.

The increasing consolidation occurring in American industry, and particularly the Standard Oil trust, did not escape the attention of the American public. In March 1881, Henry Demarest Lloyd, a young journalist from Chicago, published an article in the *Atlantic Monthly* entitled "The Story of a Great Monopoly," which discussed the success of the Standard Oil Company. The article brought to the public's attention for the first time the fact that the petroleum industry in America was dominated by one firm—Standard Oil. Lloyd's article, which was so popular that the issue was reprinted six times, marked the beginning of the American public's growing awareness of, and concern over, the growth of monopolies.

The Passage of the Sherman Antitrust Act The common law regarding trade regulation was not always consistent. Certainly, it was not very familiar to the legislators of the Fifty-first Congress of the United States. The public concern over large business integrations and trusts was familiar, however. In 1888, 1889, and again in 1890, Senator Sherman introduced in Congress bills designed to destroy the large combinations of capital that were, he felt, creating a lack of balance within the nation's economy. Sherman told Congress that the Sherman Act "does not announce a new principle of law, but applies old and well-recognized principles of the common law."[a] In 1890, the bill was enacted into law.

In the pages that follow, we look closely at the major provisions of this act. Generally, the act prohibits business combinations and conspiracies that restrain trade and commerce, as well as certain monopolistic practices.

APPLICATION TO TODAY'S WORLD

The Sherman Antitrust Act remains very relevant to today's world. The widely publicized monopolization case brought by the U.S. Department of Justice and a number of state attorneys general against Microsoft Corporation is just one example of the relevance of the Sherman Act to modern business developments and practices. (This case is presented later in this chapter as Case 32.3.)

a. 21 Congressional Record 2456 (1890).

MARKET POWER
The power of a firm to control the market price of its product. A monopoly has the greatest degree of market power.

extremely great amount of **market power**—the power to affect the market price of its product. We return to a discussion of these two sections of the Sherman Act after we look at the act's jurisdictional requirements.

JURISDICTIONAL REQUIREMENTS

Because Congress can regulate only interstate commerce, the Sherman Act applies solely to restraints that affect interstate commerce. As discussed in Chapter 2, courts have construed the meaning of *interstate commerce* broadly, bringing even local activities within the regulatory power of the national government. In regard to the Sherman Act, courts have generally held that any activity that substantially affects interstate commerce is covered by the act. The Sherman Act also extends to nationals abroad who are engaged in activities that have an effect on U.S. foreign commerce. (The extraterritorial application of U.S. antitrust laws will be discussed in this chapter's *International Perspective* on page 859 as well as in Chapter 39.)

Section 1 of the Sherman Act

The underlying assumption of Section 1 of the Sherman Act is that society's welfare is harmed if rival firms are permitted to join in an agreement that consolidates their market power or otherwise restrains competition. The types of trade restraints that Section 1 of the Sherman Act prohibits generally fall into two broad categories: *horizontal restraints* and *vertical restraints*.

PER SE VIOLATIONS VERSUS THE RULE OF REASON

PER SE VIOLATION
A type of anticompetitive agreement—such as a horizontal price-fixing agreement—that is considered to be so injurious to the public that there is no need to determine whether it actually injures market competition; rather, it is in itself (*per se*) a violation of the Sherman Act.

RULE OF REASON
A test by which a court balances the positive effects (such as economic efficiency) of an agreement against its potentially anticompetitive effects. In antitrust litigation, many practices are analyzed under the rule of reason.

Some restraints are so blatantly and substantially anticompetitive that they are deemed ***per se* violations**—illegal *per se* (on their face, or inherently)—under Section 1. Other agreements, however, even though they result in enhanced market power, do not *unreasonably* restrain trade. Under what is called the **rule of reason**, anticompetitive agreements that allegedly violate Section 1 of the Sherman Act are analyzed with the view that they may, in fact, constitute reasonable restraints on trade.

The need for a rule-of-reason analysis of some agreements in restraint of trade is obvious—if the rule of reason had not been developed, virtually any business agreement could conceivably be held to violate the Sherman Act. Justice Louis Brandeis effectively phrased this sentiment in *Chicago Board of Trade v. United States*, a case decided in 1918:

> Every agreement concerning trade, every regulation of trade, restrains. To bind, to restrain, is of their very essence. The true test of legality is whether the restraint imposed is such as merely regulates and perhaps thereby promotes competition or whether it is such as may suppress or even destroy competition.[1]

ON THE WEB You can find a discussion of the *per se* rule and the rule of reason, as well as an extensive summary of antitrust laws, at **http://profs.lp.findlaw.com/antitrust/antitrust_2.html**.

When analyzing an alleged Section 1 violation under the rule of reason, a court will consider several factors. These factors include the purpose of the agreement, the parties' power to implement the agreement to achieve that purpose, and the effect or potential effect of the agreement on competition. Yet another factor that a court might consider is whether the parties could have relied on less restrictive means to achieve their purpose.

1. 246 U.S. 231, 38 S.Ct. 242, 62 L.Ed. 683 (1918).

SECTION 1—HORIZONTAL RESTRAINTS

HORIZONTAL RESTRAINT
Any agreement that in some way restrains competition between rival firms competing in the same market.

The term **horizontal restraint** is encountered frequently in antitrust law. A horizontal restraint is any agreement that in some way restrains competition between rival firms competing in the same market. In the following subsections, we look at several types of horizontal restraints.

PRICE-FIXING AGREEMENT
An agreement between competitors to fix the prices of products or services at a certain level.

Price Fixing Any agreement among competitors to fix prices constitutes a *per se* violation of Section 1. Perhaps the definitive case regarding **price-fixing agreements** remains the 1940 case of *United States v. Socony-Vacuum Oil Co.*[2] In that case, a group of independent oil producers in Texas and Louisiana were caught between falling demand due to the Great Depression of the 1930s and increasing supply from newly discovered oil fields in the region. In response to these conditions, a group of major refining companies agreed to buy "distress" gasoline (excess supplies) from the independents so as to dispose of it in an "orderly manner." Although there was no explicit agreement as to price, it was clear that the purpose of the agreement was to limit the supply of gasoline on the market and thereby raise prices.

The United States Supreme Court recognized the dangerous effects that such an agreement could have on open and free competition. The Court held that the asserted reasonableness of a price-fixing agreement is never a defense; any agreement that restricts output or artificially fixes price is a *per se* violation of Section 1. The rationale of the *per se* rule was best stated in what is now the most famous portion of the Court's opinion—footnote 59. In that footnote, Justice William O. Douglas compared a freely functioning price system to a body's central nervous system, condemning price-fixing agreements as threats to "the central nervous system of the economy."

GROUP BOYCOTT
The refusal to deal with a particular person or firm by a group of competitors; prohibited by the Sherman Act.

Group Boycotts A **group boycott** is an agreement by two or more competitors to boycott, or refuse to deal with, a particular person or firm. Such group boycotts have been held to constitute *per se* violations of Section 1 of the Sherman Act. Section 1 has been violated if it can be demonstrated that the boycott or joint refusal to deal was undertaken with the intention of eliminating competition or preventing entry into a given market. Some boycotts, such as group boycotts against a supplier for political reasons, may be protected under the First Amendment right to freedom of expression, however.

The issue in the following case was whether a *single* buyer's decision to buy from one supplier rather than another should be considered a group boycott.

2. 310 U.S. 150, 60 S.Ct. 811, 84 L.Ed.2d 1129 (1940).

CASE 32.1 NYNEX Corp. v. Discon, Inc.

Supreme Court of the United States, 1998.
525 U.S. 128,
119 S.Ct. 493,
142 L.Ed.2d 510.
http://supct.law.cornell.edu:8080/supct.supct1990ff.htm[a]

a. In the left column, in the "Decisions by party name: 1990–present" section, in the "1998" row, click on "1st party." On the page that opens, scroll to the case name and click on it. When that page opens, choose the format in which you want to view the opinion and click on its link to access it. This database is part of a site maintained by the Legal Information Institute at Cornell Law School.

FACTS NYNEX Corporation owns New York Telephone Company (NYTel), which provides telephone service to most of New York. NYTel has a monopoly on phone service in the areas that it serves. NYNEX also owns NYNEX Material Enterprises. Material Enterprises obtains removal services for NYTel. These services consist of salvaging and disposing of obsolete equipment. Material Enterprises, which had been using the services of Discon, Inc., switched its business to AT&T Technologies, Inc., which supplied the removal services at inflated prices. Material

CASE 32.1—Continued

Enterprises charged the inflated prices to NYTel, which passed the charges on to its customers. Material Enterprises later received secret rebates of the excessive charges from AT&T. (Essentially, Material Enterprises and NYNEX used NYTel's monopoly to obtain increased revenues.) When the scheme was uncovered, NYTel agreed to refund over $35 million to its customers. Discon, Inc., filed a suit in a federal district court against NYNEX and others, alleging, among other things, that as part of their scheme, the defendants had conspired to eliminate Discon from the market in favor of AT&T, because Discon had refused to participate in the rebate scheme. Discon contended that this was an illegal group boycott. The defendants filed a motion to dismiss, which the court granted. Discon appealed to the U.S. Court of Appeals for the Second Circuit, which reversed the lower court's judgment and held that the treatment of Discon could be an illegal group boycott. The defendants appealed to the United States Supreme Court.

ISSUE Is a *single* buyer's decision to buy from one supplier rather than another a group boycott?

DECISION No. The Supreme Court vacated the decision of the U.S. Court of Appeals for the Second Circuit and remanded the case for further proceedings.

REASON The Supreme Court held that the choice by a single buyer to buy from one supplier rather than another is not subject to the *per se* group boycott rule, even if there is no legitimate business reason for that buyer's purchasing decision. The Court explained that, according to precedent, "the *per se* rule in the boycott context" applies only "to cases involving horizontal agreements among direct competitors." This case "concerns only a vertical agreement and a vertical restraint, a restraint that takes the form of depriving a supplier of a potential customer." "To apply the *per se* rule here—where the buyer's decision, though not made for competitive reasons, composes part of a regulatory fraud—would transform cases involving business behavior that is improper for various reasons, say, cases involving nepotism [showing favoritism to relatives or close friends] or personal pique [annoyance or vexation], into treble-damages antitrust cases. And that *per se* rule would discourage firms from changing suppliers—even where the competitive process itself does not suffer harm. The freedom to switch suppliers lies close to the heart of the competitive process that the antitrust laws seek to encourage."

FOR CRITICAL ANALYSIS—Social Consideration *Could Discon have succeeded in a suit against NYNEX and the others under any other legal theory? Explain.*

Horizontal Market Division It is a *per se* violation of Section 1 of the Sherman Act for competitors to divide up territories or customers. • **EXAMPLE 32.1** Manufacturers A, B, and C compete against each other in the states of Kansas, Nebraska, and Iowa. By agreement, A sells products only in Kansas; B sells only in Nebraska; and C sells only in Iowa. This concerted action not only reduces marketing costs but also allows all three (assuming there is no other competition) to raise the price of the goods sold in their respective states. The same violation would take place if A, B, and C simply agreed that A would sell only to institutional purchasers (such as school districts, universities, state agencies and departments, and municipalities) in all three states, B only to wholesalers, and C only to retailers. •

Trade Associations Businesses in the same general industry or profession frequently organize trade associations to pursue common interests. A trade association's activities may include facilitating exchanges of information, representing members' business interests before governmental bodies, conducting advertising campaigns, and setting regulatory standards to govern the industry or profession.

Generally, the rule of reason is applied to many of these horizontal actions. If a court finds that a trade association practice or agreement that restrains trade is sufficiently beneficial both to the association and to the public, it may deem the restraint reasonable. Other trade association agreements may have such substantially anticompetitive effects that the court will consider them to be in violation of Section 1 of the Sherman Act.

• **EXAMPLE 32.2** In *National Society of Professional Engineers v. United States,*[3] it was held that the society's code of ethics—which prohibited members from discussing prices with a potential customer until after the customer had chosen an engineer—was a Section 1 violation. The United States Supreme Court found that this ban on competitive bidding was "nothing less than a frontal assault on the basic policy of the Sherman Act." •

Joint Ventures Joint ventures undertaken by competitors are also subject to antitrust laws. As discussed in Chapter 31, a *joint venture* is an undertaking by two or more individuals or firms for a specific purpose. If a joint venture does not involve price fixing or market divisions, the agreement will be analyzed under the rule of reason. Whether the venture will then be upheld under Section 1 depends on an overall assessment of the purposes of the venture, a strict analysis of the potential benefits relative to the likely harms, and—in some cases—an assessment of whether there are less restrictive alternatives for achieving the same goals.[4]

SECTION 1—VERTICAL RESTRAINTS

VERTICAL RESTRAINT
Any restraint on trade created by agreements between firms at different levels in the manufacturing and distribution process.

A **vertical restraint** of trade results from an agreement between firms at different levels in the manufacturing and distribution process. In contrast to horizontal relationships, which occur at the same level of operation, vertical relationships encompass the entire chain of production: the purchase of inventory, basic manufacturing, distribution to wholesalers, and eventual sale of a product at the retail level. For some products, these distinct phases may be carried out by different firms. If a single firm carries out two or more of the different functional phases involved in bringing a product to the final consumer, the firm is considered to be a **vertically integrated firm.**

VERTICALLY INTEGRATED FIRM
A firm that carries out two or more functional phases (manufacture, distribution, retailing, and so on) of a product.

Even though firms operating at different functional levels are not in direct competition with one another, they are in competition with other firms. Thus, agreements between firms standing in a vertical relationship do significantly affect competition.

Territorial or Customer Restrictions In arranging for the distribution of its product, a manufacturing firm often wishes to insulate dealers from direct competition with other dealers selling the product. To this end, it may institute territorial restrictions, or it may attempt to prohibit wholesalers or retailers from reselling the product to certain classes of buyers, such as competing retailers. There may be legitimate, procompetitive reasons for imposing such territorial or customer restrictions. • **EXAMPLE 32.3** A computer manufacturer may wish to prevent a dealer from cutting costs and undercutting rivals by providing computers without promotion or customer service, while relying on nearby dealers to provide these services. •

Vertical territorial and customer restrictions are judged under a rule of reason. In *United States v. Arnold, Schwinn & Co.,*[5] a case decided in 1967, the Supreme Court had held that vertical territorial and customer restrictions were *per se* violations of Section 1 of the Sherman Act. Ten years later, however, in *Continental T.V., Inc. v. GTE Sylvania, Inc.,*[6] the Court overturned the *Schwinn* decision and held that such vertical restrictions should be judged under the rule of reason. The *Continental* case marked a definite shift from rigid characterization of these kinds of vertical restraints to a more flexible, economic analysis of the restraints under the rule of reason.

ON THE WEB
The Federal Trade Commission (FTC) offers an abundance of information on antitrust law, including "A Plain English Guide to Antitrust Laws," at its Web site. Go to **http://www.ftc.gov/ftc/antitrust.htm.**

3. 453 U.S. 679, 98 S.Ct. 1355, 55 L.Ed.2d 637 (1978).
4. See, for example, *United States v. Morgan,* 118 F.Supp. 621 (S.D.N.Y. 1953). This case is often cited as a classic example of how to judge joint ventures under the rule of reason.
5. 388 U.S. 365, 87 S.Ct. 1856, 18 L.Ed.2d 1249 (1967).
6. 433 U.S. 36, 97 S.Ct. 2549, 53 L.Ed.2d 568 (1977).

A retail store displays a well-known designer's clothing. Is an agreement between the manufacturer and an independent retailer to sell the clothing at a certain price considered a violation of the Sherman Act?

RESALE PRICE MAINTENANCE AGREEMENT An agreement between a manufacturer and a retailer in which the manufacturer specifies what the retail price of its products must be.

Resale Price Maintenance Agreements An agreement between a manufacturer and a distributor or retailer in which the manufacturer specifies what the retail prices of its products must be is referred to as a **resale price maintenance agreement**. This type of agreement may violate Section 1 of the Sherman Act.

In a 1968 case, *Albrecht v. Herald Co.*,[7] the United States Supreme Court held that these vertical price-fixing agreements constituted *per se* violations of Section 1 of the Sherman Act. In the following case, which involved an agreement that set a maximum price for the resale of products supplied by a wholesaler to a dealer, the Supreme Court reevaluated its approach in *Albrecht*. At issue was whether such price-fixing arrangements should continue to be deemed *per se* violations of Section 1 of the Sherman Act or whether the rule of reason should be applied.

7. 390 U.S. 145, 88 S.Ct. 869, 19 L.Ed.2d 998 (1968).

CASE 32.2 State Oil Co. v. Khan

Supreme Court of the United States, 1997.
522 U.S. 3,
118 S.Ct. 275,
139 L.Ed.2d 199.
http://www.findlaw.com/casecode/supreme.html[a]

FACTS Barkat Khan leased a gas station under a contract with State Oil Company, which also agreed to supply gas to Khan for resale. Under the contract, State Oil would set a suggested retail price and sell gas to Khan for 3.25 cents per gallon less than that price. Khan could sell the gas at a higher price, but he would then be required to pay State Oil the difference (which would equal the entire profit Khan realized from raising the price). Khan failed to pay some of the rent due under the lease, and State Oil terminated the contract. Khan filed a suit in a federal district court against State Oil, alleging, among other things, price fixing in violation of the Sherman Act. The trial court granted summary judgment

(continued)

a. This page, which is part of a Web site maintained by FindLaw, contains links to opinions of the United States Supreme Court. In the "Party Name Search" box, type "Khan" and click on "Search." When the results appear, click on the case name to access the opinion.

CASE 32.2—Continued

for State Oil. Khan appealed. The U.S. Court of Appeals for the Seventh Circuit reversed this judgment, and State Oil appealed to the United States Supreme Court.

ISSUE Does an agreement that sets a maximum price for the resale of products supplied by a supplier to a distributor constitute price fixing in violation of Section 1 of the Sherman Act?

DECISION No. The United States Supreme Court vacated the decision of the appellate court and remanded the case. The Supreme Court held that vertical price fixing is not a *per se* violation of the Sherman Act but should be evaluated under the rule of reason.

REASON The Court explained that the primary purpose of antitrust law, including the Sherman Act, "is to protect interbrand competition," which can result in lower prices for consumers. When a practice that results in lower prices to consumers is "condemn[ed]," higher prices can result and competition could be harmed. For this reason, categorizing a vertical maximum price-fixing agreement as a *per se* violation of antitrust law is difficult to justify. Such agreements should, "like the majority of commercial arrangements subject to the antitrust laws," be evaluated under the rule of reason.

FOR CRITICAL ANALYSIS—Economic Consideration *Should all "commercial arrangements subject to the antitrust laws" be evaluated under the rule of reason?*

ON THE WEB The American Antitrust Institute maintains a Web site that is devoted entirely to the topic of antitrust law. The site includes news, articles, and a very detailed archive on antitrust topics. To access this site, go to **http://www.antitrustinstitute.org**.

Refusals to Deal As discussed previously, joint refusals to deal (group boycotts) are subject to close scrutiny under Section 1 of the Sherman Act. A single manufacturer acting unilaterally, however, is generally free to deal, or not to deal, with whomever it wishes. In vertical arrangements, even though a manufacturer cannot set retail prices for its products, it can refuse to deal with retailers or dealers that cut prices to levels substantially below the manufacturer's suggested retail prices. In *United States v. Colgate & Co.*,[8] for example, the United States Supreme Court held that a manufacturer's advance announcement that it would not sell to price cutters was not a violation of the Sherman Act.

In some instances, however, a unilateral refusal to deal will violate antitrust laws. These instances involve offenses proscribed under Section 2 of the Sherman Act and occur only if (1) the firm refusing to deal has—or is likely to acquire—monopoly power and (2) the refusal is likely to have an anticompetitive effect on a particular market.

Section 2 of the Sherman Act

Section 1 of the Sherman Act proscribes certain concerted, or joint, activities that restrain trade. In contrast, Section 2 condemns "every person who shall monopolize, or attempt to monopolize." Two distinct types of behavior are subject to sanction under Section 2: *monopolization* and *attempts to monopolize*. A tactic that may be involved in either offense is **predatory pricing**. Predatory pricing involves an attempt by one firm to drive its competitors from the market by selling its product at prices substantially *below* the normal costs of production; once the competitors are eliminated, the firm will attempt to recapture its losses and go on to earn higher profits by driving prices up far above their competitive levels.

PREDATORY PRICING The pricing of a product below cost with the intent to drive competitors out of the market.

8. 250 U.S. 300, 39 S.Ct. 465, 63 L.Ed. 992 (1919).

MONOPOLIZATION

MONOPOLIZATION The possession of monopoly power in the relevant market and the willful acquisition or maintenance of the power, as distinguished from growth or development as a consequence of a superior product, business acumen, or historic accident.

In *United States v. Grinnell Corp.*,[9] the United States Supreme Court defined the offense of **monopolization** as involving the following two elements: "(1) the possession of monopoly power in the relevant market and (2) the willful acquisition or maintenance of the power as distinguished from growth or development as a consequence of a superior product, business acumen, or historic accident." A violation of Section 2 requires that both these elements—monopoly power and an intent to monopolize—be established.

> **"A rule of such a nature as to bring all trade or traffic into the hands of one company, or one person, and to exclude all others, is illegal."**
>
> SIR EDWARD COKE, 1552–1634 (English jurist and legal scholar)

Monopoly Power The Sherman Act does not define *monopoly*. In economic parlance, monopoly refers to control by a single entity. It is well established in antitrust law, however, that a firm may be a monopolist even though it is not the sole seller in a market. Additionally, size alone does not determine whether a firm is a monopoly. For example, a "mom and pop" grocery located in an isolated desert town is a monopolist if it is the only grocery serving that particular market. Size in relation to the market is what matters because monopoly involves the power to affect prices and output. *Monopoly power*, as mentioned earlier in this chapter, exists when a firm has an extremely great amount of market power. If a firm has sufficient market power to control prices and exclude competition, that firm has monopoly power.

MARKET-SHARE TEST The primary measure of monopoly power. A firm's market share is the percentage of a market that the firm controls.

As difficult as it is to define market power precisely, it is even more difficult to measure it. Courts often use the so-called **market-share test**[10]—a firm's percentage share of the "relevant market"—in determining the extent of the firm's market power. A firm may be considered to have monopoly power if its share of the relevant market is 70 percent or more. This is merely a rule of thumb, however; it is not a binding principle of law. In some cases, a smaller share may be held to constitute monopoly power.[11]

The relevant market consists of two elements: (1) a relevant product market and (2) a relevant geographic market. What should the relevant product market include? No doubt, it must include all products that, although produced by different firms, have identical attributes, such as sugar. Products that are not identical, however, may sometimes be substituted for one another. Coffee may be substituted for tea, for example. In defining the relevant product market, the key issue is the degree of interchangeability between products. If one product is a sufficient substitute for another, the two products are considered to be part of the same product market. (For a case discussing the "relevant market" for domain names, see this chapter's *Business Law in the Online World* feature on the next page.)

The second component of the relevant market is the geographic boundaries of the market. For products that are sold nationwide, the geographic boundaries of the market encompass the entire United States. If a producer and its competitors sell in only a limited area (one in which customers have no access to other sources of the product), the geographic market is limited to that area. A national firm may thus compete in several distinct areas and have monopoly power in one area but not in another.

KEEP IN MIND Section 2 of the Sherman Act essentially condemns the act of monopolizing, not the possession of monopoly power.

The Intent Requirement Monopoly power, in and of itself, does not constitute the offense of monopolization under Section 2 of the Sherman Act. The offense also requires an *intent* to monopolize. A dominant market share may be the result of

9. 384 U.S. 563, 86 S.Ct. 1698, 16 L.Ed.2d 778 (1966).
10. Other measures of market power have been devised, but the market-share test is the most widely used.
11. This standard was first articulated by Judge Learned Hand in *United States v. Aluminum Co. of America*, 148 F.2d 416 (2d Cir. 1945). A 90 percent share was held to be clear evidence of monopoly power. Anything less than 64 percent, said Judge Hand, made monopoly power doubtful, and anything less than 30 percent was clearly not monopoly power.

BUSINESS LAW: //in the Online World

What Is the Relevant Product Market for Domain Names?

Most attempts to measure monopoly power involve quantifying the degree of concentration in a relevant market and/or the extent of a particular firm's ability to control that market. Accordingly, defining the relevant market is a necessary step in any monopolization case brought under Section 2 of the Sherman Act. Thus, when Stan Smith brought a monopolization case against Network Solutions, Inc. (NSI), a domain name registrar (see Chapter 5), for not allowing Smith and others to register for expired domain names, a threshold question before the court was the following: What is the relevant product market for domain names?

The Registry

At one time, NSI was the only registrar for domain names in this country. In 1998, however, the federal government opened domain name registration to competition and set up a nonprofit corporation, the Internet Corporation for Assigned Names and Numbers (ICANN), to oversee the distribution of domain names. At that time, NSI's domain name registration service was divided into two separate units: a registrar and a registry (the Registry).[a]

The registrar unit continues to register domain names. The Registry, in contrast, is the only entity of its kind. It maintains a centralized "WHOIS" database of all domain names using the ".com," ".org," and ".net" top-level domains, regardless of whether the names have been registered by NSI or one of the other eighty or so accredited registrars now in operation. The Registry's WHOIS database allows all registrars to determine almost instantaneously which domain names are already registered and therefore unavailable to others. The public can also access the Registry's WHOIS database.

At the time Smith brought his suit, the WHOIS database included approximately 163,000 expired domain names—names that had been registered but belonged to registrants who failed to pay the required registration renewal fees. NSI's policy was to give registrants a "grace period" of two to three months in which they could renew their expired registration. In the meantime, the names remained on the WHOIS database and were unavailable for others.

What Is the Relevant Product Market?

Smith claimed that by failing to make expired domain names available to himself and others, NSI had intentionally maintained an unlawful monopoly over expired domain names in violation of Section 2 of the Sherman Act. The court, however, concluded that the relevant product market was not expired domain names but all domain names—and NSI did not have monopoly power over all domain names. The court reasoned that "the relevant market includes those commodities or services that are reasonably interchangeable." Because of the "virtually limitless" supply of domain names, said the court, "there will always be reasonable substitute names available for any given name kept out of circulation."[b]

FOR CRITICAL ANALYSIS

Do you agree with the court that domain names are "reasonably interchangeable"? Why or why not?

a. In 2000, NSI became a wholly owned subsidiary of VeriSign, Inc., and the Registry was subsequently renamed VeriSign Global Registry Services. Both NSI and VeriSign were defendants in this case.

b. *Smith v. Network Solutions, Inc.*, 135 F.Supp.2d 1159 (N.D.Ala. 2001).

business acumen or the development of a superior product. It may simply be the result of historic accident. In these situations, the acquisition of monopoly power is not an antitrust violation. Indeed, it would be contrary to society's interest to condemn every firm that acquired a position of power because it was well managed, was efficient, and marketed a product desired by consumers.

If, however, a firm possesses market power as a result of carrying out some purposeful act to acquire or maintain that power through anticompetitive means, it is in violation of Section 2. In most monopolization cases, intent may be inferred from evidence that the firm had monopoly power and engaged in anticompetitive behavior.

The following case included an allegation of a violation of Section 2 of the Sherman Act.

CASE 32.3 United States v. Microsoft Corp.

United States Court of Appeals,
District of Columbia Circuit, 2001.
253 F.3d 34.
http://www.cadc.uscourts.gov[a]

HISTORICAL AND TECHNOLOGICAL SETTING *In 1981, Microsoft Corporation released the first version of its Microsoft Disk Operating System (MS-DOS). When International Business Machines Corporation (IBM) selected MS-DOS for preinstallation on its first generation of personal computers (PCs), Microsoft's product became the dominant operating system for Intel-compatible PCs.*[b] *In 1985, Microsoft began shipping a software package called Windows. Although originally a user-interface on top of MS-DOS, Windows took on more operating-system functionality over time. Throughout the 1990s, Microsoft's share of the market for Intel-compatible operating systems was more than 90 percent.*

FACTS In 1994, Netscape Communications Corporation began marketing Navigator, the first popular graphical Internet browser. Navigator worked with Java, a technology developed by Sun Microsystems, Inc. Java technology enabled applications to run on a variety of platforms, which meant that users did not need Windows. Microsoft perceived a threat to its dominance of the operating-system market and developed a competing browser, Internet Explorer (Explorer). Microsoft then began to require computer makers who wanted to install Windows to also install Explorer and exclude Navigator. Meanwhile, Microsoft commingled browser code and other code in Windows so that deleting files containing Explorer would cripple the operating system. Microsoft offered to promote and pay Internet service providers to distribute Explorer and exclude Navigator. Microsoft also developed its own Java code and deceived many independent software sellers into believing that this code would help in designing cross-platform applications when, in fact, it would run only on Windows. The U.S. Department of Justice and a number of state attorneys general filed a suit in a federal district court against Microsoft, alleging, in part, monopolization in violation of Section 2 of the Sherman Act. The court ruled against Microsoft.[c] Microsoft appealed to the U.S. Court of Appeals for the District of Columbia Circuit.

ISSUE Did Microsoft possess and maintain monopoly power in the market for Intel-compatible operating systems?

DECISION Yes. The U.S. Court of Appeals for the District of Columbia Circuit affirmed this part of the lower court's opinion. The appellate court reversed other holdings of the lower court, however, and remanded the case for a reconsideration of the appropriate remedy.

REASON The U.S. Court of Appeals for the District of Columbia Circuit rejected Microsoft's arguments, which included that in the "uniquely dynamic" software market, intent should not be inferred but rather must be proved. The court responded, "Microsoft's pattern of exclusionary conduct could only be rational if the firm knew that it possessed monopoly power." This conduct included Microsoft's restrictions on the computer makers' Windows licenses. "Microsoft's efforts to gain market share in one market (browsers) served to meet the threat to Microsoft's monopoly in another market (operating systems) by keeping rival browsers from gaining the critical mass of users necessary to attract developer attention away from Windows as the platform for software development." This also included Microsoft's other actions welding Explorer to Windows. In part, the court reasoned that the commingling of the browsing and other code deters computer makers "from pre-installing rival browsers, thereby reducing the rivals' usage share

a. On this page, in the left column, click on "Opinions." In the section headed "Please select from the following menu to find opinions by date of issue," choose "June" from the "Month" menu, select "2001" from the "Year" menu, and click on "Go!" From the result, scroll to the name of the case and click on the docket number to access the opinion. The U.S. Court of Appeals for the District of Columbia Circuit maintains this Web site.

b. An *Intel-compatible PC* is designed to function with Intel Corporation's 80×86/Pentium families of microprocessors or with compatible microprocessors.

c. The district court ordered, among other things, a structural reorganization of Microsoft, including a separation of its operating-system and applications businesses. See *United States v. Microsoft,* 97 F.Supp.2d 59 (D.D.C. 2000).

(continued)

CASE 32.3—Continued

and, hence, developers' interest in rivals' [operating systems]." The court also concluded that Microsoft's agreements with the Internet service providers were "exclusionary devices" and that Microsoft's dealings with the independent software sellers constituted "exclusionary conduct."

FOR CRITICAL ANALYSIS—Technological Consideration *What effect does the passage of time between certain conduct and the outcome of litigation have on judicial rulings that apply to technological product markets?*

COMMENT The appellate court also concluded that the trial court judge's remarks (to members of the press and others during the trial) "would give a reasonable, informed observer cause to question his impartiality in ordering the company split in two." The appellate court cited this bias as its reason for reversing the order to break up Microsoft and remanding the case to a different trial court judge to reconsider what penalty would be appropriate. Microsoft appealed to the United States Supreme Court, but the Court declined to hear the case. Essentially, the appellate court opened the door to a much lighter penalty for Microsoft. Since then, the Department of Justice and several of the state attorneys general who brought the suit agreed with Microsoft to settle the case. As of this writing, the terms of the settlement had not yet been finalized. A number of other state attorneys general did not agree to settle the case, however, and they may continue the litigation against Microsoft.

ATTEMPTS TO MONOPOLIZE

ATTEMPTED MONOPOLIZATION Any actions by a firm to eliminate competition and gain monopoly power.

Section 2 also prohibits **attempted monopolization** of a market. Any action challenged as an attempt to monopolize must have been specifically intended to exclude competitors and garner monopoly power. In addition, the attempt must have had a "dangerous" probability of success—only serious threats of monopolization are condemned as violations. The probability cannot be dangerous unless the alleged offender possesses some degree of market power.

ETHICAL ISSUE 32.1

Are we destined for more monopolies in the future?

Knowledge and information form the building blocks of the so-called new economy. Some observers believe that the nature of this new economy means that we will see an increasing number of monopolies similar to Microsoft. Consider that the basis for all antitrust law is that monopoly leads to restricted output and hence higher prices for consumers. That is how a monopolist maximizes profits relative to a competitive firm. In the knowledge-based sector, however, firms face *economies of scale* (defined as decreases in long-run average costs resulting from increases in output), so they will do the exact opposite—increase output and reduce prices. That is exactly what Microsoft has done over the years—the prices of its operating system and applications have fallen, particularly when corrected for inflation.

This may mean that antitrust authorities will have to have a greater tolerance for knowledge-based monopolies to allow them to benefit from the full economies of scale. After all, the ultimate beneficiary of such economies of scale is the consumer. In the early 1900s, economist Joseph Schumpeter argued in favor of allowing monopolies. According to his theory of "creative destruction," monopolies stimulate innovation and economic growth because firms that capture monopoly profits have a greater incentive to innovate. Those that do not survive—the firms that are "destroyed"—leave room for more efficient firms, ones that will survive.

The Clayton Act

"The commerce of the world is conducted by the strong, and usually it operates against the weak."

HENRY WARD BEECHER, 1813–1887 (American abolitionist leader)

In 1914, Congress attempted to strengthen federal antitrust laws by enacting the Clayton Act. The Clayton Act was aimed at specific anticompetitive or monopolistic practices that the Sherman Act did not cover. The substantive provisions of the act deal with four distinct forms of business behavior, which are declared illegal but not criminal. With regard to each of the four provisions, the act's prohibitions are qualified by the general condition that the behavior is illegal only if it substantially tends to lessen competition or tends to create monopoly power. The major offenses under the Clayton Act are set out in Sections 2, 3, 7, and 8 of the act.

SECTION 2—PRICE DISCRIMINATION

PRICE DISCRIMINATION
Setting prices in such a way that two competing buyers pay two different prices for an identical product or service.

Section 2 of the Clayton Act prohibits **price discrimination**, which occurs when a seller charges different prices to competitive buyers for identical goods. Because businesses frequently circumvented Section 2 of the act, Congress strengthened this section by amending it with the passage of the Robinson-Patman Act in 1936.

As amended, Section 2 prohibits price discrimination that cannot be justified by differences in production costs, transportation costs, or cost differences due to other reasons. To violate Section 2, the seller must be engaged in interstate commerce, and the effect of the price discrimination must be to substantially lessen competition or create a competitive injury. Under Section 2, as amended, a seller is prohibited from reducing a price to one buyer below the price charged to that buyer's competitor. Even offering goods to different customers at the same price but with different delivery arrangements may violate Section 2 in some circumstances.[12]

An exception is made if the seller can justify the price reduction by demonstrating that the lower price was charged temporarily and in good faith to meet another seller's equally low price to the buyer's competitor. To be predatory, a seller's pricing policies must also include a reasonable prospect that the seller will recoup its losses.[13]

SECTION 3—EXCLUSIONARY PRACTICES

Under Section 3 of the Clayton Act, sellers or lessors cannot sell or lease goods "on the condition, agreement or understanding that the . . . purchaser or lessee thereof shall not use or deal in the goods . . . of a competitor or competitors of the seller." In effect, this section prohibits two types of vertical agreements involving exclusionary practices—exclusive-dealing contracts and tying arrangements.

EXCLUSIVE-DEALING CONTRACT
An agreement under which a seller forbids a buyer to purchase products from the seller's competitors.

Exclusive-Dealing Contracts A contract under which a seller forbids a buyer to purchase products from the seller's competitors is called an **exclusive-dealing contract**. A seller is prohibited from making an exclusive-dealing contract under Section 3 if the effect of the contract is "to substantially lessen competition or tend to create a monopoly."

● **EXAMPLE 32.4** In *Standard Oil Co. of California v. United States,*[14] a leading case decided by the United States Supreme Court in 1949, the then-largest gasoline seller in the nation made exclusive-dealing contracts with independent stations in seven

12. *Bell v. Fur Breeders Agricultural Cooperative,* 3 F.Supp.2d 1241 (D.Utah 1998).
13. See, for example, *Brooke Group, Ltd. v. Brown & Williamson Tobacco Corp.,* 509 U.S. 209, 113 S.Ct. 2578, 125 L.Ed.2d 168 (1993), in which the Supreme Court held that a seller's price-cutting policies could not be predatory "[g]iven the market's realities"—the size of the seller's market share, the expanding output by other sellers, plus additional factors.
14. 37 U.S. 293, 69 S.Ct. 1051, 93 L.Ed. 1371 (1949).

western states. The contracts involved 16 percent of all retail outlets, whose sales were approximately 7 percent of all retail sales in that market. The Court noted that the market was substantially concentrated because the seven largest gasoline suppliers all used exclusive-dealing contracts with their independent retailers and together controlled 65 percent of the market. Looking at market conditions after the arrangements were instituted, the Court found that market shares were extremely stable, and entry into the market was apparently restricted. Thus, the Court held that Section 3 of the Clayton Act had been violated because competition was "foreclosed in a substantial share" of the relevant market. ●

TYING ARRANGEMENT
An agreement between a buyer and a seller in which the buyer of a specific product or service becomes obligated to purchase additional products or services from the seller.

Tying Arrangements When a seller conditions the sale of a product (the tying product) on the buyer's agreement to purchase another product (the tied product) produced or distributed by the same seller, a **tying arrangement**, or *tie-in sales agreement,* results. The legality of a tie-in agreement depends on many factors, particularly the purpose of the agreement and the agreement's likely effect on competition in the relevant markets (the market for the tying product and the market for the tied product).

● **EXAMPLE 32.5** In 1936, the United States Supreme Court held that International Business Machines and Remington Rand had violated Section 3 of the Clayton Act by requiring the purchase of their own machine cards (the tied product) as a condition to the leasing of their tabulation machines (the tying product). Because only these two firms sold completely automated tabulation machines, the Court concluded that each possessed market power sufficient to "substantially lessen competition" through the tying arrangements.[15] ●

Section 3 of the Clayton Act has been held to apply only to commodities, not to services. Tying arrangements, however, can also be considered agreements that restrain trade in violation of Section 1 of the Sherman Act. Thus, those cases involving tying arrangements of services have been brought under Section 1 of the Sherman Act. Traditionally, the courts have held tying arrangements challenged under the Sherman Act to be illegal *per se.* In recent years, however, courts have shown a willingness to look at factors that are important in a rule-of-reason analysis.

SECTION 7—MERGERS

"Combinations are no less unlawful because they have not as yet resulted in restraint."

HUGO L. BLACK, 1886–1971 (Associate justice of the United States Supreme Court, 1937–1971)

Under Section 7 of the Clayton Act, a person or business organization cannot hold stock and/or assets in another entity "where the effect . . . may be to substantially lessen competition." Section 7 is the statutory authority for preventing mergers or acquisitions that could result in monopoly power or a substantial lessening of competition in the marketplace. Section 7 applies to three specific types of mergers: horizontal mergers, vertical mergers, and conglomerate mergers. We discuss each type of merger in the following subsections.

MARKET CONCENTRATION
The percentage of a particular firm's market sales in a relevant market area.

A crucial consideration in most merger cases is the **market concentration** of a product or business. Determining market concentration involves allocating percentage market shares among the various companies in the relevant market. When a small number of companies share a large part of the market, the market is concentrated. For example, if the four largest grocery stores in Chicago accounted for 80 percent of all retail food sales, the market clearly would be concentrated in those four firms. Competition, however, is not necessarily diminished solely as a result of market concentration, and other factors will be considered in determining whether a merger will violate Section 7. One factor of particular importance in evaluating the effects of a merger is whether

15. *International Business Machines Corp. v. United States,* 298 U.S. 131, 56 S.Ct. 701, 80 L.Ed. 1085 (1936).

the merger will make it more difficult for potential competitors to enter the relevant market.

HORIZONTAL MERGER
A merger between two firms that are competing in the same marketplace.

Horizontal Mergers Mergers between firms that compete with each other in the same market are called **horizontal mergers.** If a horizontal merger creates an entity with anything other than a small percentage market share, the merger will be presumed illegal. This is because the United States Supreme Court has held that Congress, in amending Section 7 of the Clayton Act in 1950, intended to prevent mergers that increase market concentration.[16] When analyzing the legality of a horizontal merger, the courts also consider three other factors: overall concentration of the relevant product market, the relevant market's history of tending toward concentration, and whether the apparent design of the merger is to establish market power or to restrict competition.

The Federal Trade Commission and the U.S. Department of Justice have established guidelines indicating which mergers will be challenged. Under the guidelines, the first factor to be considered is the degree of concentration in the relevant market. Other factors to be considered include the ease of entry into the relevant market, economic efficiency, the financial condition of the merging firms, the nature and price of the product or products involved, and so on. If a firm is a leading one—having at least a 35 percent share and twice that of the next leading firm—any merger with a firm having as little as a 1 percent share will probably be challenged.

VERTICAL MERGER
The acquisition by a company at one level in a marketing chain of a company at a higher or lower level in the chain (such as a company merging with one of its suppliers or retailers).

Vertical Mergers A **vertical merger** occurs when a company at one stage of production acquires a company at a higher or lower stage of production. An example of a vertical merger is a company merging with one of its suppliers or retailers. Courts in the past have focused almost exclusively on "foreclosure" in assessing vertical mergers. Foreclosure occurs because competitors of the merging firms lose opportunities to sell or buy products from the merging firms.

• **EXAMPLE 32.6** In *United States v. E. I. du Pont de Nemours & Co.*,[17] du Pont was challenged for acquiring a considerable amount of General Motors (GM) stock. In holding that the transaction was illegal, the United States Supreme Court noted that the stock acquisition would enable du Pont to prevent other sellers of fabrics and finishes from selling to GM, which then accounted for 50 percent of all auto fabric and finishes purchases. •

Today, whether a vertical merger will be deemed illegal generally depends on several factors, including market concentration, barriers to entry into the market, and the apparent intent of the merging parties. Mergers that do not prevent competitors of either merging firm from competing in a segment of the market will not be condemned as "foreclosing" competition and are legal.

CONGLOMERATE MERGER
A merger between firms that do not compete with each other because they are in different markets (as opposed to horizontal and vertical mergers).

Conglomerate Mergers There are three general types of **conglomerate mergers**: market-extension, product-extension, and diversification mergers. A market-extension merger occurs when a firm seeks to sell its product in a new market by merging with a firm already established in that market. A product-extension merger occurs when a firm seeks to add a closely related product to its existing line by merging with a firm already producing that product. For example, a manufacturer might seek to extend its line of household products to include floor wax by acquiring a leading manufacturer of floor wax. Diversification occurs when a firm merges with another firm that offers a product

16. *Brown Shoe v. United States,* 370 U.S. 294, 82 S.Ct. 1502, 8 L.Ed.2d 510 (1962).
17. 353 U.S. 586, 77 S.Ct. 872, 1 L.Ed.2d 1057 (1957).

or service wholly unrelated to the first firm's existing activities. An example of a diversification merger is an automobile manufacturer's acquisition of a motel chain.

Although in a conglomerate merger no firm is removed from the marketplace, conglomerate mergers can be challenged under Section 7 of the Clayton Act. In deciding whether the act has been violated, the courts usually evaluate (1) whether the merger will allow the acquiring firm to shift assets and revenue to the acquired firm to potentially drive out businesses that compete with the acquired firm, and (2) whether the merger creates a barrier, keeping other firms from entering the relevant market.

SECTION 8—INTERLOCKING DIRECTORATES

Section 8 of the Clayton Act deals with *interlocking directorates*—that is, the practice of having individuals serve as directors on the boards of two or more competing companies simultaneously. Specifically, no person may be a director in two or more competing corporations at the same time if either of the corporations has capital, surplus, or undivided profits aggregating more than $18,142,000 or competitive sales of $1,814,200 or more. The threshold amounts are adjusted each year by the Federal Trade Commission (FTC). (The amounts given here are those announced by the FTC in 2001.)

The Federal Trade Commission Act

CONTRAST Section 5 of the Federal Trade Commission Act is broader than the other antitrust laws. It covers virtually all anticompetitive behavior, including conduct that does not violate either the Sherman Act or the Clayton Act.

The Federal Trade Commission Act was enacted in 1914, the same year the Clayton Act was written into law. Section 5 is the sole substantive provision of the act. It provides, in part, as follows: "Unfair methods of competition in or affecting commerce, and unfair or deceptive acts or practices in or affecting commerce are hereby declared illegal." Section 5 condemns all forms of anticompetitive behavior that are not covered under other federal antitrust laws. The act also created the Federal Trade Commission to implement the act's provisions.

Enforcement of Antitrust Laws

DIVESTITURE
The act of selling one or more of a company's parts, such as a subsidiary or plant; often mandated by the courts in merger or monopolization cases.

The federal agencies that enforce the federal antitrust laws are the U.S. Department of Justice (DOJ) and the Federal Trade Commission (FTC). The DOJ can prosecute violations of the Sherman Act as either criminal or civil violations. Violations of the Clayton Act are not crimes, and the DOJ can enforce that statute only through civil proceedings. The various remedies that the DOJ has asked the courts to impose include **divestiture** (making a company give up one or more of its operating functions) and dissolution. The DOJ might force a group of meat packers, for example, to divest itself of control or ownership of butcher shops.

The FTC also enforces the Clayton Act (but not the Sherman Act) and has sole authority to enforce violations of Section 5 of the Federal Trade Commission Act. FTC actions are effected through administrative orders, but if a firm violates an FTC order, the FTC can seek court sanctions for the violation.

A private party can sue for treble (triple) damages and attorneys' fees under Section 4 of the Clayton Act if the party is injured as a result of a violation of any of the federal antitrust laws, except Section 5 of the Federal Trade Commission Act. In some

INTERNATIONAL PERSPECTIVE

The Extraterritorial Application of Antitrust Laws

As mentioned earlier in this chapter, the reach of U.S. antitrust laws extends beyond the territorial borders of the United States. The U.S. government (the DOJ or the FTC) and private parties may bring an action against a foreign party that has violated Section 1 of the Sherman Act. The Federal Trade Commission Act may also be applied to foreign trade. Foreign mergers, if Section 7 of the Clayton Act applies, may also be brought within the jurisdiction of U.S. courts. Before U.S. courts will exercise jurisdiction and apply antitrust laws to actions occurring in other countries, however, normally it must be shown that the alleged violation had a substantial effect on U.S. commerce. (See Chapter 39 for a further discussion of the extraterritorial application of U.S. antitrust laws.)

In the past, companies usually had to be concerned only with U.S. antitrust laws. Today, however, many countries have adopted antitrust laws. The European Union has antitrust provisions that are broadly analogous to Sections 1 and 2 of the Sherman Act, as well as laws governing mergers. Japanese antitrust laws prohibit unfair trade practices, monopolization, and restrictions that unreasonably restrain trade. Several nations in Southeast Asia, including Vietnam, Indonesia, and Malaysia, have either enacted statutes protecting competition or are considering them for adoption. Argentina, Peru, Brazil, Chile, and several other Latin American countries have adopted modern antitrust laws as well. Most of the antitrust laws apply extraterritorially, as U.S. antitrust laws do. This means that a U.S. company may be subject to another nation's antitrust laws if the company's conduct has a substantial effect on that nation's commerce.

FOR CRITICAL ANALYSIS
Do antitrust laws place too great a burden on commerce in the global marketplace?

ON THE WEB
You can find links to the home pages for federal government agencies, including the Department of Justice and the Federal Trade Commission, at **http://www.firstgov.gov**.

instances, private parties may also seek injunctive relief to prevent antitrust violations. The courts have determined that the ability to sue depends on the directness of the injury suffered by the would-be plaintiff. Thus, a person wishing to sue under the Sherman Act must prove (1) that the antitrust violation either caused or was a substantial factor in causing the injury that was suffered and (2) that the unlawful actions of the accused party affected business activities of the plaintiff that were protected by the antitrust laws.

In recent years, more than 90 percent of all antitrust actions have been brought by private plaintiffs. One reason for this is, of course, that successful plaintiffs may recover three times the damages that they have suffered as a result of the violation. Such recoveries by private plaintiffs for antitrust violations have been rationalized as encouraging people to act as "private attorneys general" who will vigorously pursue antitrust violators on their own initiative.

Exemptions from Antitrust Laws

There are many legislative and constitutional limitations on antitrust enforcement. Most statutory and judicially created exemptions to the antitrust laws apply to the following areas or activities:

① *Labor.* Section 6 of the Clayton Act generally permits labor unions to organize and bargain without violating antitrust laws. Section 20 of the Clayton Act specifies that strikes and other labor activities are not violations of any law of the United States. A union can lose its exemption, however, if it combines with a nonlabor group rather than acting simply in its own self-interest.

② *Agricultural associations and fisheries.* Section 6 of the Clayton Act (along with the Capper-Volstead Act of 1922) exempts agricultural cooperatives from the antitrust laws. The Fisheries Cooperative Marketing Act of 1976 exempts from antitrust legislation individuals in the fishing industry who collectively catch, produce, and prepare for market their products. Both exemptions allow members of such co-ops to combine and set prices for a particular product, but do not allow them to engage in exclusionary practices or restraints of trade directed at competitors.

③ *Insurance.* The McCarran-Ferguson Act of 1945 exempts the insurance business from the antitrust laws whenever state regulation exists. This exemption does not cover boycotts, coercion, or intimidation on the part of insurance companies.

④ *Foreign trade.* Under the provisions of the 1918 Webb-Pomerene Act, American exporters may engage in cooperative activity to compete with similar foreign associations. This type of cooperative activity may not, however, restrain trade within the United States or injure other American exporters. The Export Trading Company Act of 1982 broadened the Webb-Pomerene Act by permitting the Department of Justice to certify properly qualified export trading companies. Any activity within the scope described by the certificate is exempt from public prosecution under the antitrust laws.

⑤ *Professional baseball.* In 1922, the United States Supreme Court held that professional baseball was not within the reach of federal antitrust laws because it did not involve "interstate commerce."[18] Some of the effects of this decision, however, were modified by the Curt Flood Act of 1998. (See *Ethical Issue 32.2* for a further discussion of the baseball exemption.)

⑥ *Oil marketing.* The 1935 Interstate Oil Compact allows states to determine quotas on oil that will be marketed in interstate commerce.

⑦ *Cooperative research and production.* Cooperative research among small-business firms is exempt under the Small Business Act of 1958, as amended. Research or production of a product, process, or service by joint ventures consisting of competitors is exempt under special federal legislation, including the National Cooperative Research Act of 1984 and the National Cooperative Production Amendments of 1993.

⑧ *Joint efforts by businesspersons to obtain legislative or executive action.* This is often referred to as the *Noerr-Pennington* doctrine.[19] For example, video producers may

---

18. *Federal Baseball Club of Baltimore, Inc. v. National League of Professional Baseball Clubs,* 259 U.S. 200, 42 S.Ct. 465, 66 L.Ed. 898 (1922).

19. See *United Mine Workers of America v. Pennington,* 381 U.S. 657, 89 S.Ct. 1585, 14 L.Ed.2d 626 (1965); and *Eastern Railroad Presidents Conference v. Noerr Motor Freight, Inc.,* 365 U.S. 127, 81 S.Ct. 523, 5 L.Ed.2d 464 (1961).

jointly lobby Congress to change the copyright laws, or a video-rental company may sue another video-rental firm, without being held liable for attempting to restrain trade. Though selfish rather than purely public-minded conduct is permitted, there is an exception: an action will not be protected if it is clear that the action is "objectively baseless in the sense that no reasonable [person] could reasonably expect success on the merits" and it is an attempt to make anticompetitive use of government processes.[20]

NOTE State actions include the regulation of public utilities, whose rates may be set by the states in which they do business.

⑨ *Other exemptions.* Other activities exempt from antitrust laws include activities approved by the president in furtherance of the defense of our nation (under the Defense Production Act of 1950, as amended); state actions, when the state policy is clearly articulated and the policy is actively supervised by the state;[21] and activities of regulated industries (such as the communication and banking industries) when federal commissions, boards, or agencies (such as the Federal Communications Commission and the Federal Maritime Commission) have primary regulatory authority.

ETHICAL ISSUE 32.2

Should the baseball exemption from antitrust laws be completely abolished?

The fact that, until relatively recently, baseball remained totally exempt from antitrust laws not only seemed unfair to many but also defied logic: Why was an exemption made for baseball but not for other professional sports? The answer to this perfectly reasonable question has always been the same: baseball was exempt because the United States Supreme Court, in 1922, said that it was. The Court held that baseball was a sport played only locally by local players. Because the activity purportedly did not involve interstate commerce, it did not meet the requirement for federal jurisdiction. The exemption was challenged in the early 1970s, but the Supreme Court ruled that it was up to Congress, not the Court, to overturn the exemption. In 1998, Congress did address the issue and passed the Curt Flood Act—named for the St. Louis Cardinals' star outfielder who challenged the exemption in the early 1970s. The act, however, did not overturn the 1922 Supreme Court decision but only limited some of the effects of baseball's exempt status. Essentially, the act allows players the option of suing team owners for anticompetitive practices if, for example, the owners collude to "blacklist" players, hold down players' salaries, or force players to play for specific teams. Baseball is still not subject to antitrust laws to the extent that football, basketball, and other professional sports are. Critics of the exemption continue to claim that it should be completely abolished because it simply makes no sense to continue to treat an enterprise worth $2 billion a year as a "local" activity.

20. *Professional Real Estate Investors, Inc. v. Columbia Pictures Industries, Inc.,* 508 U.S. 49, 113 S.Ct. 1920, 123 L.Ed.2d 611 (1993).

21. See *Parker v. Brown,* 347 U.S. 341, 63 S.Ct. 307, 87 L.Ed. 315 (1943).

APPLICATION Law and the Businessperson . . .

Avoiding Antitrust Problems*

Business managers need to be aware of how antitrust legislation may affect their activities. In addition to federal antitrust laws covered in this chapter, numerous state antitrust laws also exist. States also now have the power to bring civil suits to enforce federal antitrust laws. Additionally, antitrust law is subject to various interpretations by the courts. Unless a businessperson exercises caution, a court may decide that his or her actions are in violation of a federal or state statute.

If you are a business manager or owner, you should thus be careful when communicating with a direct competitor that offers products or services that are similar to those of your own company. If you know that such communications might cause problems in your line of business, you should probably arrange for the appropriate employees to attend a seminar given by legal professionals who will let your employees know what is legal and what is not in dealing with competitors. Generally, any businessperson who is worried about potential antitrust violations should seek counsel from a competent attorney specializing in antitrust law.

* This *Application* is not meant to substitute for the services of an attorney who is licensed to practice law in your state.

Checklist for Avoiding Antitrust Problems

1. Exercise caution when communicating and dealing with competitors.
2. Seek the advice of an attorney specializing in antitrust law to assure that your business practices and agreements do not violate antitrust laws.
3. If you conduct business ventures in other countries, you should obtain the advice of an attorney who is familiar with the antitrust laws of those nations.

Key Terms

antitrust law 843
attempted monopolization 854
conglomerate merger 857
divestiture 858
exclusive-dealing contract 855
group boycott 846
horizontal merger 857
horizontal restraint 846
market concentration 856
market power 845
market-share test 851
monopolization 851
monopoly 843
monopoly power 843
per se violation 845
predatory pricing 850
price discrimination 855
price-fixing agreement 846
resale price maintenance agreement 849
rule of reason 845
tying arrangement 856
vertical merger 857
vertical restraint 848
vertically integrated firm 848

Chapter Summary Antitrust Law

Sherman Antitrust Act (1890) (See pages 843–854.)	1. *Major provisions—* a. Section 1—Prohibits contracts, combinations, and conspiracies in restraint of trade. (1) Horizontal restraints subject to Section 1 include price-fixing agreements, group boycotts (joint refusals to deal), horizontal market division, trade association agreements, and joint ventures.

Chapter Summary Antitrust Law—continued

Sherman Antitrust Act (1890)—continued	(2) Vertical restraints subject to Section 1 include territorial or customer restrictions, resale price maintenance agreements, and refusals to deal. b. Section 2—Prohibits monopolies and attempts to monopolize. 2. *Jurisdictional requirements*—The Sherman Act applies only to activities that have a significant impact on interstate commerce. 3. *Interpretative rules*— a. *Per se* rule—Applied to restraints on trade that are so inherently anticompetitive that they cannot be justified and are deemed illegal as a matter of law. b. Rule of reason—Applied when an anticompetitive agreement may be justified by legitimate benefits. Under the rule of reason, the lawfulness of a trade restraint will be determined by the purpose and effects of the restraint.
Clayton Act (1914) (See pages 855–858.)	The major provisions are as follows: 1. *Section 2*—As amended in 1936 by the Robinson-Patman Act, prohibits price discrimination that substantially lessens competition and prohibits a seller engaged in interstate commerce from selling to two or more buyers goods of similar grade and quality at different prices when the result is a substantial lessening of competition or the creation of a competitive injury. 2. *Section 3*—Prohibits exclusionary practices, such as exclusive-dealing contracts and tying arrangements, when the effect may be to substantially lessen competition. 3. *Section 7*—Prohibits mergers when the effect may be to substantially lessen competition or to tend to create a monopoly. a. Horizontal mergers—The acquisition by merger or consolidation of a competing firm engaged in the same relevant market. Will be unlawful only if a merger results in the merging firms' holding a disproportionate share of the market, resulting in a substantial lessening of competition, and if the merger does not enhance consumer welfare by increasing efficiency of production or marketing. b. Vertical mergers—The acquisition by a seller of one of its buyers or vice versa. Will be unlawful if the merger prevents competitors of either merging firm from competing in a segment of the market that otherwise would be open to them, resulting in a substantial lessening of competition. c. Conglomerate mergers—The acquisition of a noncompeting business. 4. *Section 8*—Prohibits interlocking directorates.
Federal Trade Commission Act (1914) (See page 858.)	Prohibits unfair methods of competition; established and defined the powers of the Federal Trade Commission.
Enforcement of Antitrust Laws (See pages 858–859.)	Antitrust laws are enforced by the Department of Justice, by the Federal Trade Commission, and in some cases by private parties, who may be awarded treble damages and attorneys' fees.
Exemptions from Antitrust Laws (See pages 859–862.)	1. Labor unions (under Section 6 of the Clayton Act of 1914). 2. Agricultural associations and fisheries (under Section 6 of the Clayton Act of 1914, the Capper-Volstead Act of 1922, and the Fisheries Cooperative Marketing Act of 1976). 3. Insurance—when state regulation exists (under the McCarran-Ferguson Act of 1945).

(continued)

Chapter Summary Antitrust Law—continued

Exemptions from Antitrust Laws—continued	4. Export trading companies (under the Webb-Pomerene Act of 1918 and the Export Trading Company Act of 1982). 5. Professional baseball (by a 1922 judicial decision), although modified by a 1998 federal statute. 6. Oil marketing (under the Interstate Oil Compact of 1935). 7. Cooperative research and production (under various acts, including the Small Business Administration Act of 1958, as amended, the National Cooperative Research Act of 1984, and the National Cooperative Production Amendments of 1993). 8. Joint efforts by businesspersons to obtain legislative or executive action (under the *Noerr-Pennington* doctrine). 9. Other activities, including certain national defense actions, state actions, and actions of certain regulated industries.

For Review

① What is a monopoly? What is market power? How do these concepts relate to each other?
② What type of activity is prohibited by Section 1 of the Sherman Act? What type of activity is prohibited by Section 2 of the Sherman Act?
③ What are the four major provisions of the Clayton Act, and what types of activities do these provisions prohibit?
④ What agencies of the federal government enforce the federal antitrust laws?
⑤ What are four activities that are exempt from the antitrust laws?

Questions and Case Problems

32–1. Sherman Act. An agreement that is blatantly and substantially anticompetitive is deemed a *per se* violation of Section 1 of the Sherman Act. Under what rule is an agreement analyzed if it appears to be anticompetitive but is not a *per se* violation? In making this analysis, what factors will a court consider?

32–2. Antitrust Laws. Allitron, Inc., and Donovan, Ltd., are interstate competitors selling similar appliances, principally in the states of Indiana, Kentucky, Illinois, and Ohio. Allitron and Donovan agree that Allitron will no longer sell in Ohio and Indiana and that Donovan will no longer sell in Kentucky and Illinois. Have Allitron and Donovan violated any antitrust laws? If so, which law? Explain.

32–3. Antitrust Laws. The partnership of Alvaredo and Parish is engaged in the oil-wellhead service industry in the states of New Mexico and Colorado. The firm currently has about 40 percent of the market for this service. Webb Corp. competes with the Alvaredo-Parish partnership in the same state area. Webb has approximately 35 percent of the market. Alvaredo and Parish acquire the stock and assets of Webb Corp. Do the antitrust laws prohibit the type of action undertaken by Alvaredo and Parish? Discuss fully.

32–4. Horizontal Restraints. Jorge's Appliance Corp. was a new retail seller of appliances in Sunrise City. Because of its innovative sales techniques and financing, Jorge's caused the appliance department of No-Glow Department Store, a large chain store with a great deal of buying power, to lose a substantial amount of sales. No-Glow told a number of appliance manufacturers that if they continued to sell to Jorge's, No-Glow would discontinue its large volume of purchases from them. The manufacturers immediately stopped selling appliances to Jorge's. Jorge's filed suit against No-Glow and the manufacturers, claiming that their actions constituted an antitrust violation. No-Glow and the manufacturers were able to prove that Jorge's was a small retailer with a small portion of the market. They claimed that because the relevant market was not substantially affected, they were not guilty of restraint of trade. Discuss fully whether there was an antitrust violation.

32–5. Exclusionary Practices. Instant Foto Corp. is a manufacturer of photography film. At the present time, Instant Foto has approximately 50 percent of the market. Instant Foto advertises that the purchase price for its film includes photo processing by Instant Foto Corp. Instant Foto claims that its film processing is specially designed to improve the quality of photos taken with Instant Foto film. Is Instant Foto's combination of film purchase and film processing an antitrust violation? Explain.

32–6. Clayton Act, Section 2. Stelwagon Manufacturing Co. agreed with Tarmac Roofing Systems, Inc., to promote and develop a market for Tarmac's products in the Philadelphia area. In return, Tarmac promised not to sell its products to other area distributors. In 1991, Stelwagon learned that Tarmac had been selling its products to Stelwagon's competitors—the Standard Roofing Co. and the Celotex Corp.—at substantially lower prices. Stelwagon filed a suit against Tarmac in a federal district court. What is the principal factor in determining whether Tarmac violated Section 2 of the Clayton Act, as amended? Did Tarmac violate the act? [*Stelwagon Manufacturing Co. v. Tarmac Roofing Systems, Inc.*, 63 F.3d 1267 (3d Cir. 1995)]

32–7. Antitrust Laws. Great Western Directories, Inc. (GW), is an independent publisher of telephone directory Yellow Pages. GW buys information for its listings from Southwestern Bell Telephone Co. (SBT). Southwestern Bell Corp. owns SBT and Southwestern Bell Yellow Pages (SBYP), which publishes a directory in competition with GW. In June 1988, in some markets, SBT raised the price for its listing information, and SBYP lowered the price for advertising in its Yellow Pages. GW feared that these companies would do the same thing in other local markets, making it too expensive for GW to compete in those markets. Because of this fear, GW left one market and declined to compete in another. Consequently, SBYP had a monopoly in those markets. GW and another independent publisher filed a suit in a federal district court against Southwestern Bell Corp. What antitrust law, if any, did Southwestern Bell Corp. violate? Should the independent companies be entitled to damages? [*Great Western Directories, Inc. v. Southwestern Bell Telephone Co.*, 74 F.3d 613 (5th Cir. 1996)]

32–8. Restraint of Trade. The National Collegiate Athletic Association (NCAA) coordinates the intercollegiate athletic programs of its members by issuing rules and setting standards governing, among other things, the coaching staffs. The NCAA set up a "Cost Reduction Committee" to consider ways to cut the costs of intercollegiate athletics while maintaining competition. The committee included financial aid personnel, intercollegiate athletic administrators, college presidents, university faculty members, and a university chancellor. It was felt that "only a collaborative effort could reduce costs while maintaining a level playing field." The committee proposed a rule to restrict the annual compensation of certain coaches to $16,000. The NCAA adopted the rule. Basketball coaches affected by the rule filed a suit in a federal district court against the NCAA, alleging a violation of Section 1 of the Sherman Antitrust Act. Is the rule a *per se* violation of the Sherman Act, or should it be evaluated under the rule of reason? If it is subject to the rule of reason, is it an illegal restraint of trade? Discuss fully. [*Law v. National Collegiate Athletic Association*, 134 F.3d 1010 (10th Cir. 1998)]

32–9. Tying Arrangement. Public Interest Corp. (PIC) owned and operated the television station WTMV-TV in Lakeland, Florida. MCA Television, Ltd., owns and licenses syndicated television programs. The parties entered into a licensing contract with respect to several television shows. MCA conditioned the license on PIC's agreeing to take another show, *Harry and the Hendersons*. PIC agreed to this arrangement, although it would not have chosen to license *Harry* if it had not had to do so to secure the licenses for the other shows. More than two years into the contract, a dispute arose over PIC's payments, and negotiations failed to resolve the dispute. In a letter, MCA suspended PIC's broadcast rights for all of its shows and stated that "[a]ny telecasts of MCA programming by WTMV-TV . . . will be deemed unauthorized and shall constitute an infringement of MCA's copyrights." PIC nonetheless continued broadcasting MCA's programs, with the exception of *Harry*. MCA filed a suit in a federal district court against PIC, alleging breach of contract and copyright infringement. PIC filed a counterclaim, contending in part that MCA's deal was an illegal tying arrangement. Is PIC correct? Explain. [*MCA Television, Ltd. v. Public Interest Corp.*, 171 F.3d 1265 (11th Cir. 1999)]

TEST YOUR KNOWLEDGE—ANSWER ON THE WEB

32–10. In 1995, to make personal computers (PCs) easier to use, Intel Corp. and other companies developed a standard, called the Universal Serial Bus (USB) specification, to enable the easy attachment of peripherals (printers and other hardware) to PCs. Intel and others formed the Universal Serial Bus Implementers Forum (USB-IF) to promote USB technology and products. Intel, however, makes relatively few USB products and does not make any USB interconnect devices. Multivideo Labs, Inc. (MVL), designed and distributed Active Extension Cables (AECs) to connect peripheral devices to each other or to a PC. The AECs were not USB compliant, a fact that Intel employees told other USB-IF members. Asserting that this caused a "general cooling of the market" for AECs, MVL filed a suit in a federal district court against Intel, claiming in part attempted monopolization in violation of the Sherman Act. Intel filed a motion for summary judgment. How should the court rule, and why? [*Multivideo Labs, Inc. v. Intel Corp.*, __ F.Supp.2d __ (S.D.N.Y. 2000)]

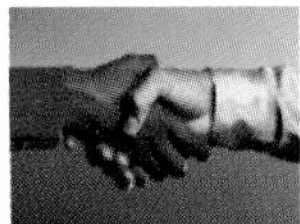

A QUESTION OF ETHICS AND SOCIAL RESPONSIBILITY

32–11. A group of lawyers in the District of Columbia regularly acted as court-appointed attorneys for indigent defendants in District of Columbia criminal cases. At a meeting of the Superior Court Trial Lawyers Association (SCTLA), the attorneys agreed to stop providing this representation until the district increased their compensation. Their subsequent boycott had a severe impact on the district's criminal justice system, and the District of Columbia gave in to the lawyers' demands for higher pay. After the lawyers had returned to work, the Federal Trade Commission filed a complaint against the SCTLA and four of its officers and, after an investigation, ruled that the SCTLA's activities constituted an illegal group boycott in violation of antitrust laws. [*Federal Trade Commission v. Superior Court Trial Lawyers Association*, 493 U.S. 411, 110 S.Ct. 768, 107 L.Ed.2d 851 (1990)]

1. The SCTLA obviously was aware of the negative impact its decision would have on the district's criminal justice system. Given this fact, do you think the lawyers behaved ethically?
2. On appeal, the SCTLA claimed that its boycott was undertaken to publicize the fact that the attorneys were underpaid and that the boycott thus constituted an expression protected by the First Amendment. Do you agree with this argument?
3. Labor unions have the right to strike when negotiations between labor and management fail to result in agreement. Is it fair to prohibit members of the SCTLA from "striking" against their employer, the District of Columbia, simply because the SCTLA is a professional organization and not a labor union?

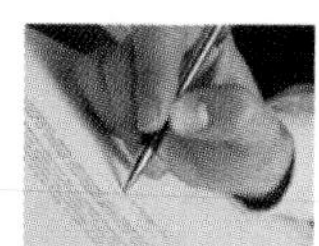

FOR CRITICAL ANALYSIS

32–12. Critics of antitrust law claim that in the long run, competitive market forces will eliminate private monopolies unless they are fostered by government regulation. Do you agree with these critics? Why or why not?

Internet Exercises

Go to the *Business Law Today* home page at **http://blt.westbuslaw.com**. Select "Interactive Study Center" and then click on "Chapter 32." There you will find the following Internet research exercise that you can perform to learn more about vertical restraints and the rule of reason:

Activity 32–1: Vertical Restraints and the Rule of Reason

Before the Test

Go to the *Business Law Today* home page at **http://blt.westbuslaw.com**. Click on "Interactive Quizzes." You will find at least twenty interactive questions relating to this chapter.

CHAPTER 33

Consumer and Environmental Law

"Subject to specific constitutional limitations, when the legislature has spoken, the public interest has been declared in terms well nigh conclusive."

William O. Douglas, 1898–1980
(Associate justice of the United States Supreme Court, 1939–1975)

CHAPTER CONTENTS

LEARNING OBJECTIVES

After reading this chapter, you should be able to answer the following questions:

1. When will advertising be deemed deceptive?
2. How does the Federal Food, Drug and Cosmetic Act protect consumers? What are the major federal statutes providing for consumer protection in credit transactions?
3. Under what common law theories may polluters be held liable?
4. What is an environmental impact statement, and who must file one? What does the Environmental Protection Agency do?
5. What major federal statutes regulate air and water pollution? What is Superfund? To what categories of persons does liability under Superfund extend?

The "public interest" referred to by Justice William O. Douglas in the opening quotation was evident during the 1960s and 1970s in what has come to be known as the consumer movement. Some have labeled the 1960s and 1970s "the age of the consumer" because so much legislation was passed to protect consumers against purportedly unsafe products and unfair practices of sellers. Since the 1980s, the impetus driving the consumer movement has lessened, to a great extent because so many of its goals have been achieved. *Consumer law* consists of all of the statutes, administrative agency rules, and judicial decisions that serve to protect the interests of consumers.

In the first part of this chapter, we examine some of the sources and some of the major issues of consumer protection. We then turn to a discussion of *environmental law,* which consists of all of the laws and regulations designed to protect and preserve our environmental resources.

Consumer Law

Sources of consumer protection exist at all levels of government. At the federal level, a number of laws have been passed to define the duties of sellers and the rights of consumers. Exhibit 33–1 indicates the areas of consumer law that are regulated by statutes. Federal administrative agencies, such as the Federal Trade Commission (FTC), also provide an important source of consumer protection. Nearly every agency and department of the federal government has an office of consumer affairs, and most states have one or more such offices, including the offices of state attorneys general, to assist consumers.

Because of the wide variation among state consumer protection laws, our primary focus here will be on federal legislation—specifically, on legislation governing deceptive advertising, telemarketing and electronic advertising, labeling and packaging, sales, health protection, product safety, and credit protection. Realize, though, that state laws often provide more sweeping and significant protections for the consumer than do federal laws. State consumer protection laws will be discussed later in this section.

Deceptive Advertising

One of the earliest—and still one of the most important—federal consumer protection laws is the Federal Trade Commission Act of 1914 (discussed in Chapter 32). The act created the FTC to carry out the broadly stated goal of preventing unfair and deceptive trade practices, including deceptive advertising, within the meaning of Section 5 of the act.

EXHIBIT 33–1 AREAS OF CONSUMER LAW REGULATED BY STATUTES

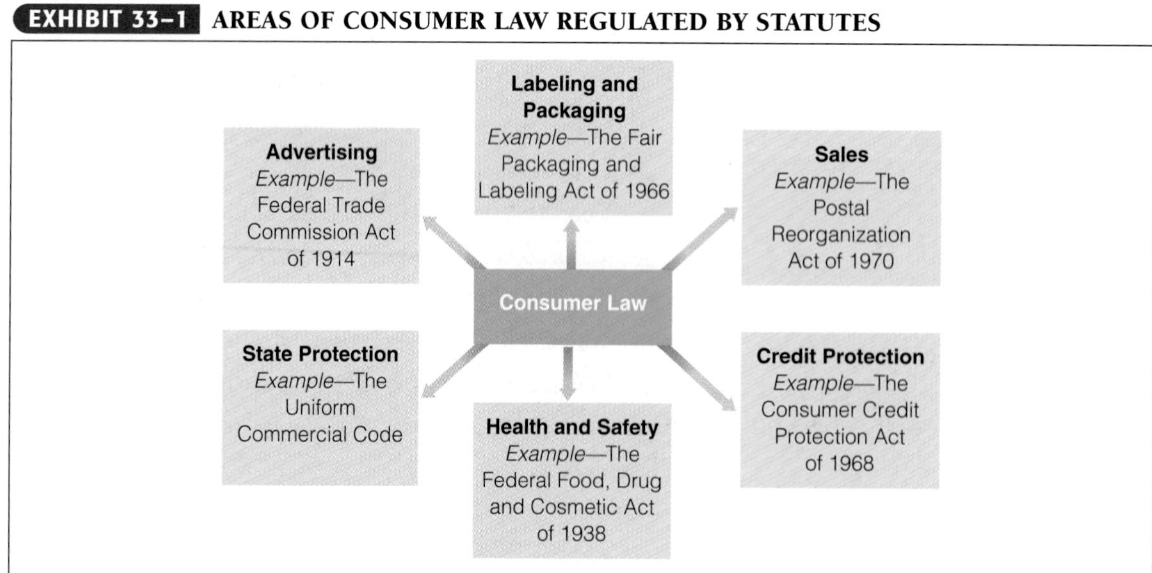

DECEPTIVE ADVERTISING
Advertising that misleads consumers, either by unjustified claims concerning a product's performance or by the omission of a material fact concerning the product's composition or performance.

Defining Deceptive Advertising Generally, **deceptive advertising** occurs if a reasonable consumer would be misled by the advertising claim. Vague generalities and obvious exaggerations are permissible. These claims are known as *puffing*. Recall from Chapter 18 that puffing, or puffery, consists of statements about a product that a reasonable person would not believe to be true. When a claim takes on the appearance of literal authenticity, however, it may create problems. Advertising that would *appear* to be based on factual evidence but that in fact is scientifically untrue will be deemed deceptive. A classic example is provided by a 1944 case in which the claim that a skin cream would restore youthful qualities to aged skin was deemed deceptive.[1]

Some advertisements contain "half-truths," meaning that the presented information is true but incomplete, and it leads consumers to a false conclusion. ● **EXAMPLE 33.1** The makers of Campbell's soups advertised that "most" Campbell's soups were low in fat and cholesterol and thus were helpful in fighting heart disease. What the ad did not say was that Campbell's soups are high in sodium, and high-sodium diets may increase the risk of heart disease. The FTC ruled that Campbell's claims were thus deceptive.● Advertising that contains an endorsement by a celebrity may be deemed deceptive if the celebrity actually makes no use of the product.

BAIT-AND-SWITCH ADVERTISING
Advertising a product at a very attractive price (the "bait") and then, once the consumer is in the store, saying that the advertised product is either not available or is of poor quality; the customer is then urged to purchase ("switched" to) a more expensive item.

Bait-and-Switch Advertising The FTC has promulgated rules to govern specific forms of advertising. One of the more important rules is contained in the FTC's "Guides on Bait Advertising."[2] The rule is designed to prohibit what is referred to as **bait-and-switch advertising**—that is, advertising a very low price for a particular item that will likely be unavailable to the consumer, who will then be encouraged to purchase a more expensive item. The low price is the "bait" to lure the consumer into the store. The salesperson is instructed to "switch" the consumer to a different item. According to the FTC guidelines, bait-and-switch advertising occurs if the seller refuses to show the advertised item, fails to have reasonable quantities of it available, fails to promise to deliver the advertised item within a reasonable time, or discourages employees from selling the item.

ON THE WEB
A government-sponsored Web site that contains reports on consumer issues, including issues relating to online deceptive advertising and other forms of online fraud, can be accessed at
http://www.consumer.gov.

Online Deceptive Advertising Deceptive advertising may occur in the online environment as well. For several years, the FTC has been quite active in monitoring online advertising and has identified hundreds of Web sites that have made false or deceptive advertising claims concerning products ranging from medical treatments for various diseases to exercise equipment and weight loss products.

In September 2000, the FTC issued new guidelines to help online businesses comply with existing laws prohibiting deceptive advertising.[3] The guidelines do not set forth new rules but rather describe how existing laws apply to online advertising. Generally, the rules emphasize that any ads—online or offline—must be truthful and not misleading and that any claims made in any ads must be substantiated. Additionally, ads cannot be unfair, defined in the guidelines as "caus[ing] or . . . likely to cause substantial consumer injury that consumers could not reasonably avoid and that is not outweighed by the benefit to consumers or competition." The guidelines also call for "clear and conspicuous" disclosure of any qualifying or limiting information. The FTC suggests that advertisers should assume that consumers will not read an entire Web page. Therefore, to satisfy the "clear and conspicuous" requirement,

1. *Charles of the Ritz Distributing Corp. v. Federal Trade Commission,* 143 F.2d 676 (2d Cir. 1944).
2. 16 C.F.R. Section 288.
3. *Advertising and Marketing on the Internet: Rules of the Road,* September 2000.

advertisers should place the disclosure as close as possible to the claim being qualified or include the disclosure within the claim itself. If such placement is not feasible, the next-best placement would be on a section of the page to which a consumer could easily scroll. Generally, hyperlinks to a disclosure are recommended only for lengthy disclosures or for disclosures that must be repeated in a variety of locations on the Web page.

FTC Actions against Deceptive Advertising The FTC receives complaints from many sources, including competitors of alleged violators, consumers, consumer organizations, trade associations, Better Business Bureaus, government organizations, and state and local officials. If enough consumers complain and the complaints are widespread, the FTC will investigate the problem and perhaps take action. If, after its investigations, the FTC believes that a given advertisement is unfair or deceptive, it drafts a formal complaint, which it sends to the alleged offender. The company may agree to settle the complaint without further proceedings.

If the company does not agree to settle a complaint, the FTC can conduct a hearing—which is similar to a trial—in which the company can present its defense. The hearing is held before an administrative law judge (ALJ) instead of a federal district court judge (see the discussion of administrative law in Chapter 1). If the FTC succeeds in proving that an advertisement is unfair or deceptive, it usually issues a **cease-and-desist order** requiring that the challenged advertising be stopped. It might also impose a sanction known as **counteradvertising** by requiring the company to advertise anew—in print, on radio, and on television—to inform the public about the earlier misinformation.

CEASE-AND-DESIST ORDER
An administrative or judicial order prohibiting a person or business firm from conducting activities that an agency or court has deemed illegal.

COUNTERADVERTISING
New advertising that is undertaken pursuant to a Federal Trade Commission order for the purpose of correcting earlier false claims that were made about a product.

When an ALJ rules against a company, the company can appeal to the full commission. The FTC commissioners listen to the parties' arguments and may uphold, modify, or reverse the ALJ's decision. If the commission rules against a company, the company can appeal the FTC's order through judicial channels, but a reviewing court generally accords great weight to the FTC's judgment. This is because the court recognizes that the FTC, as the administrative agency that deals continually with such claims, is often in a better position than the courts to determine when a practice is deceptive within the meaning of the Federal Trade Commission Act.

Telemarketing and Electronic Advertising

REMEMBER Changes in technology often require changes in the law.

The pervasive use of the telephone to market goods and services to homes and businesses led to the passage in 1991 of the Telephone Consumer Protection Act (TCPA).[4] The act prohibits telephone solicitation using an automatic telephone dialing system or a prerecorded voice. Most states also have laws regulating telephone solicitation. The TCPA also makes it illegal to transmit ads via fax without first obtaining the recipient's permission. (Similar issues have arisen with respect to junk e-mail, called "spam"—see Chapter 4.)

The act is enforced by the Federal Communications Commission and also provides for a private right of action. Consumers can recover any actual monetary loss resulting from a violation of the act or receive $500 in damages for each violation, whichever is greater. If a court finds that a defendant willfully or knowingly violated the act, the court has the discretion to treble the damages awarded.

4. 47 U.S.C. Sections 227 *et seq.*

The Telemarketing and Consumer Fraud and Abuse Prevention Act[5] of 1994 directed the FTC to establish rules governing telemarketing and to bring actions against fraudulent telemarketers. The FTC's Telemarketing Sales Rule[6] of 1995 requires a telemarketer, before making a sales pitch, to inform the recipient that the call is a sales call and to identify the seller's name and the product being sold. The rule makes it illegal for telemarketers to misrepresent information (including facts about their goods or services, earnings potential, profitability, the risk attending an investment, or the nature of a prize). Additionally, telemarketers must inform the people they call of the total cost of the goods being sold, any restrictions on obtaining or using the goods, and whether a sale will be considered final and nonrefundable. A telemarketer must also remove a consumer's name from its list of potential contacts if the customer so requests.

The following case involved telemarketers engaged in allegedly deceptive advertising.

5. 15 U.S.C. Sections 6101–6108.

6. 16 C.F.R. Sections 310.1–310.8.

CASE 33.1 Federal Trade Commission v. Growth Plus International Marketing, Inc.

United States District Court,
Northern District of Illinois, 2001.
__F.Supp.3d __.

FACTS A group of Canadian corporations and individuals engaged in a telemarketing enterprise to sell Canadian lottery packages to consumers in the United States. What the telemarketers did not tell the consumers is that the sales were illegal. In fact, the sellers affirmatively misrepresented that they were authorized to make the sales. They also misrepresented the buyers' chances of winning and used high-pressure sales tactics. The corporations included Growth Plus International Marketing, Inc. The Federal Trade Commission (FTC) filed a suit in a federal district court against Growth and the others, alleging deceptive advertising. The FTC asked the court for, among other things, a preliminary injunction.

ISSUE Do telemarketers who misrepresent their authority to sell lottery tickets and the odds of winning a lottery engage in deceptive advertising?

DECISION Yes. The court granted the FTC's request for a preliminary injunction. The court concluded that the FTC made a strong case against the defendants, whose misrepresentations misled consumers.

REASON The court explained that in this case, "the defendants were guilty of numerous misrepresentations or omissions." The "information that was misrepresented or concealed plainly was material to the consumers' decisions to purchase the tickets: The knowledge that the sale of the tickets was illegal under federal law and that the 'good chance' of winning was in fact a 1 in 14 million shot certainly are the types of information that would likely affect the decision of whether to participate in the lottery." The court also concluded that it was likely "defendants have violated the Telemarketing Sales Rule, which prohibits sellers and telemarketers from making false or misleading statements to induce persons to acquire goods or services." As for granting the injunction, "[t]here is a strong public interest in an immediate halt to illegal sale of lottery tickets accomplished through the use of misleading devices."

FOR CRITICAL ANALYSIS—Technological Consideration *Would the result in this case likely have been different if the defendants had offered the Canadian lottery tickets for sale only on the Internet?*

Labeling and Packaging

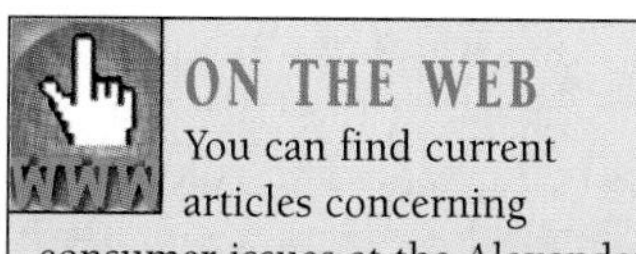

ON THE WEB You can find current articles concerning consumer issues at the Alexander Law Firm's "Consumer Law Page." Go to **http://consumerlawpage.com/intro.html**.

In addition to broadly restricting advertising, a number of federal and state laws deal specifically with the information given on labels and packages. The restrictions are designed to provide accurate information about the product and to warn about possible dangers from its use or misuse. In general, labels must be accurate. That is, they must use words that are understood by the ordinary consumer. For example, a box of cereal cannot be labeled "giant" if it would exaggerate the amount of cereal contained in the box. In some instances, labels must specify the raw materials used in the product, such as the percentage of cotton, nylon, or other fibers used in a garment. In other instances, the products must carry a warning. Cigarette packages and advertising, for example, must include one of several warnings about the health hazards associated with smoking.[7]

Federal laws regulating the labeling and packaging of products include the Fair Packaging and Labeling Act of 1966,[8] which requires that products possess labels that identify (1) the product; (2) the net quantity of the contents, as well as the quantity of servings, if the number of servings is stated; (3) the manufacturer; and (4) the packager or distributor. The act also provides that requirements may be added concerning descriptions on packages, savings claims, ingredients in nonfood products, and standards for the partial filling of packages. Food products must bear labels detailing nutrition, including fat content and type. These restrictions are enforced by the Department of Health and Human Services, as well as the FTC. The Nutrition Labeling and Education Act of 1990 requires standard nutrition facts (including fat content) on food labels; regulates the use of such terms as *fresh* and *low fat;* and, subject to the federal Food and Drug Administration's approval, authorizes certain health claims.

The Comprehensive Smokeless Tobacco Health Education Act of 1986[9] requires that producers, packagers, and importers of smokeless tobacco label their product with one of several warnings about the health hazards associated with the use of smokeless tobacco; the warnings are similar to those contained on cigarette packages. Other federal laws regulating the labeling of products include the Wool Products Labeling Act of 1939,[10] the Fur Products Labeling Act of 1951,[11] and the Flammable Fabrics Act of 1953.[12]

7. 15 U.S.C. Sections 1331 *et seq.*
8. 15 U.S.C. Sections 4401–4408.
9. 15 U.S.C. Sections 1451 *et seq.*
10. 15 U.S.C. Section 68.
11. 15 U.S.C. Section 69.
12. 15 U.S.C. Section 1191.

A warning appears on a package of cigarettes, as required by federal law. Why is Congress concerned with protecting consumers against purportedly unsafe products?

SALES

A number of statutes that protect the consumer in sales transactions concern the disclosure of certain terms in sales and provide rules governing home or door-to-door sales, mail-order transactions, referral sales, and unsolicited merchandise. The Federal Reserve Board of Governors, for example, has issued **Regulation Z**, which governs credit provisions associated with sales contracts, and numerous states have passed laws governing the remedies available to consumers in home sales. Furthermore, states have provided a number of consumer protection measures, such as implied warranties, through the adoption of the Uniform Commercial Code. In some states, the Uniform Consumer Credit Code's requirements, including disclosure requirements, also protect consumers in credit transactions.

DON'T FORGET A seller's puffery—his or her opinion about the goods—is not a legally binding warranty or promise, nor is it a deceptive advertisement.

REGULATION Z
A set of rules promulgated by the Federal Reserve Board to implement the provisions of the Truth-in-Lending Act.

Door-to-Door Sales The laws of most states single out door-to-door sales for special treatment in part because of the nature of the sales transaction. Repeat purchases are less likely than in stores, so the seller has less incentive to cultivate the goodwill of the purchaser. Furthermore, the seller is unlikely to present alternative products and their prices. Thus, a number of states have passed **"cooling-off" laws** that permit the buyers of goods sold door-to-door to cancel their contracts within a specified period of time, usually two to three days after the sale.

"COOLING-OFF" LAWS
Laws that allow buyers a period of time, such as three days, in which to cancel door-to-door sales contracts.

An FTC regulation also requires sellers to give consumers three days to cancel any door-to-door sale. Because this rule applies in addition to the relevant state statutes, consumers are given the most favorable benefits of the FTC rule and their own state statutes. In addition, the FTC rule requires that consumers be notified in Spanish of this right if the oral negotiations for the sale were in that language.

ON THE WEB To learn more about the FTC's Cooling-Off Rule, go to **http://www.ftc.gov/bcp/conline/pubs/buying/cooling.htm**.

Telephone and Mail-Order Sales Sales made by telephone or mail order are the greatest source of complaints to the nation's Better Business Bureaus. Many mail-order houses are far removed from the buyers who order from them, thus making it more difficult for a consumer to bring a complaint against a seller. To a certain extent, consumers are protected under federal laws prohibiting mail fraud, which were discussed in Chapter 6, and under state consumer protection laws that parallel and supplement the federal laws.

The FTC "Mail or Telephone Order Merchandise Rule" of 1993, which amended the FTC "Mail Order Rule" of 1975,[13] provides specific protections for consumers who purchase goods via phone lines or through the mails. The 1993 rule, which became effective in March 1994, extended the 1975 rule to include sales in which orders are transmitted using computers, fax machines, or some similar means involving telephone lines. Among other things, the rule requires mail-order merchants to ship orders within the time promised in their catalogues or advertisements, to notify consumers when orders cannot be shipped on time, and to issue a refund within a specified period of time when a consumer cancels an order.

In addition, the Postal Reorganization Act of 1970[14] provides that unsolicited merchandise sent by U.S. mail may be retained, used, discarded, or disposed of in any manner the recipient deems appropriate, without the recipient's incurring any obligation to the sender.

Online Sales In recent years, the Internet has become a vehicle for a wide variety of business-to-consumer (B2C) sales transactions. Most mail-order houses now have a

13. 16 C.F.R. Sections 435.1–435.2.
14. 39 U.S.C. Section 3009.

Web presence, and consumers can purchase from other Web sites an increasing array of goods, ranging from airline tickets to books to xylophones. Protecting consumers from fraudulent and deceptive sales practices conducted via the Internet has proved to be a challenging task. Nonetheless, the FTC and other federal agencies have brought a number of enforcement actions against those who perpetrate online fraud. Additionally, the laws mentioned earlier, such as the federal statute prohibiting wire fraud, apply to online transactions.

Some states have amended their consumer protection statutes to cover Internet transactions as well. For example, the California legislature revised its Business and Professional Code to include transactions conducted over the Internet or by "any other electronic means of communication." Previously, that code covered only telephone, mail-order catalogue, radio, and television sales. Now any entity selling over the Internet in California must explicitly create an on-screen notice indicating its refund and return policies, where its business is physically located, its legal name, and a number of other details. Various states are also setting up information sites to help consumers protect themselves.

Health and Safety Protection

Laws discussed earlier regarding the labeling and packaging of products go a long way toward promoting consumer health and safety. There is a significant distinction, however, between regulating the information dispensed about a product and regulating the content of the actual product. The classic example is tobacco products. Producers of tobacco products are required to warn consumers about the hazards associated with the use of their products. Yet the sale of tobacco products has not yet been subject to significant restrictions or banned outright despite their obvious hazards. (For a discussion of a recent attempt to regulate nicotine as a drug, see this chapter's *Letter of the Law* feature.) We now examine various laws that regulate the actual products made available to consumers.

Food and Drugs The first federal legislation regulating food and drugs was enacted in 1906 as the Pure Food and Drugs Act.[15] That law, as amended in 1938, exists now as the Federal Food, Drug and Cosmetic Act (FFDCA).[16] The act protects consumers against adulterated and misbranded foods and drugs. More recent amendments to the act added other substantive and procedural requirements. In its present form, the act establishes food standards, specifies safe levels of potentially hazardous food additives, and sets classifications of food and food advertising.

BE AWARE The Food and Drug Administration is authorized to obtain, among other things, orders for the recall and seizure of certain products.

Most of these statutory requirements are monitored and enforced by the Food and Drug Administration (FDA). Under an extensive set of procedures established by the FDA, drugs must be shown to be effective as well as safe before they may be marketed to the public, and the use of some food additives suspected of being carcinogenic is prohibited. A 1975 amendment to the FFDCA[17] authorizes the FDA to regulate medical devices, such as pacemakers and other health devices or equipment, and to withdraw from the market any such device that is mislabeled.

Consumer Product Safety Consumer product safety legislation began in 1953 with the enactment of the Flammable Fabrics Act, which prohibits the sale of highly flam-

15. 21 U.S.C. Sections 1–5, 7–15.
16. 21 U.S.C. Section 301.
17. 21 U.S.C. Sections 360(c) *et seq.*

LETTER OF THE LAW

So . . . Nicotine Cannot Be Regulated as a Drug?

In recent years, nicotine's addictive qualities have been extensively documented. Nonetheless, Congress has yet to take serious action against the tobacco companies. According to many critics, the large amount of campaign financing congressional candidates receive from those companies is to blame for the lack of action. In any event, in 1996 the FDA decided to regulate nicotine as a drug and issued a rule that, among other things, called for restrictions on the marketing and sale of tobacco products to youths. The tobacco companies sued the FDA, claiming that the agency had exceeded its authority under the Federal Food, Drug and Cosmetic Act of 1938 by attempting to regulate nicotine as a drug. Ultimately, the United States Supreme Court ruled in favor of the tobacco companies. In making its decision, the Court looked to the letter of the law, as set forth in the 1938 act. That act states specifically that the FDA shall regulate "articles intended for use in the diagnoses, cure, medication, treatment, or prevention of disease in man or other animals." The Court concluded that because tobacco products are never sold as medicine, Congress, when passing the 1938 act, could not have intended that cigarettes be included under this rubric.[a]

THE BOTTOM LINE

Nicotine is clearly a drug. Indeed, it is one of the most addictive drugs, and Americans have long known of its addictive qualities and harmful effects. Nonetheless, until Congress takes action, it is clear that the FDA does not have the authority to regulate tobacco products.

a. *Food and Drug Administration v. Brown & Williamson Tobacco Corp.*, 529 U.S. 120, 120 S.Ct. 1291, 146 L.Ed.2d 121 (2000).

mable clothing or materials. Over the next two decades, Congress enacted legislation regarding the design or composition of specific classes of products. Then, in 1972, Congress, by enacting the Consumer Product Safety Act,[18] created a comprehensive scheme of regulation over matters concerning consumer safety. The act also established far-reaching authority over consumer safety by creating the Consumer Product Safety Commission (CPSC).

The CPSC conducts research on the safety of individual products, and it maintains a clearinghouse on the risks associated with different consumer products. The Consumer Product Safety Act authorizes the CPSC to set standards for consumer products and to ban the manufacture and sale of any product that the commission deems to be potentially hazardous to consumers. The CPSC also has authority to remove from the market any products it believes to be imminently hazardous and to require manufacturers to report on any products already sold or intended for sale if the products have proved to be hazardous. Additionally, the CPSC administers other product safety legislation, such as the Child Protection and Toy Safety Act of 1969,[19] the Federal Hazardous Substances Act of 1960,[20] and the Flammable Fabrics Act.

The CPSC's authority is sufficiently broad to allow it to ban any product that the commission believes poses merely an "unreasonable risk" to the consumer. Products banned by the CPSC include various types of fireworks, cribs, and toys, as well as many products containing asbestos or vinyl chloride.

18. 15 U.S.C. Section 2051.
19. 15 U.S.C. Section 1262(e).
20. 15 U.S.C. Sections 1261–1273.

CREDIT PROTECTION

Because of the extensive use of credit by American consumers, credit protection is one of the most important areas regulated by consumer protection legislation. One of the most significant statutes regulating the credit and credit-card industry is the Truth-in-Lending Act (TILA), the name commonly given to Title 1 of the Consumer Credit Protection Act (CCPA),[21] which was passed by Congress in 1968.

Truth in Lending The TILA is basically a *disclosure law.* It is administered by the Federal Reserve Board and requires sellers and lenders to disclose credit terms or loan terms so that individuals can shop around for the best financing arrangements. TILA requirements apply only to persons who, in the ordinary course of business, lend funds, sell on credit, or arrange for the extension of credit. Thus, sales or loans made between two consumers do not come under the protection of the act. Additionally, only debtors who are natural persons (as opposed to the artificial "person" of a corporation) are protected by this law; other legal entities are not.

NOTE The Federal Reserve Board is part of the Federal Reserve System, which influences the lending and investing activities of commercial banks and the cost and availability of credit.

The disclosure requirements are found in Regulation Z, which, as mentioned earlier in this chapter, was promulgated by the Federal Reserve Board. If the contracting parties are subject to the TILA, the requirements of Regulation Z apply to any transaction involving an installment sales contract in which payment is to be made in more than four installments. Transactions subject to Regulation Z typically include installment loans, retail and installment sales, car loans, home-improvement loans, and certain real estate loans if the amount of financing is less than $25,000.

Under the provisions of the TILA, all of the terms of a credit instrument must be clearly and conspicuously disclosed. The TILA provides for contract rescission (cancellation) if a creditor fails to follow exactly the procedures required by the act.[22]

ETHICAL ISSUE 33.1

Should consumer protection laws be strictly enforced when consumers abuse these laws?

Generally, the courts strictly enforce the TILA, as well as other consumer laws. This is true even in cases in which consumers have obviously taken unfair advantage of the TILA's requirements to avoid genuine obligations that they voluntarily assumed. For example, under the TILA, borrowers are allowed three business days to rescind, without penalty, a consumer loan that uses their principal dwelling as security. The lender must state specifically the last day on which the borrower can rescind the agreement. If the lender inadvertently fails to do so, the borrower can rescind the loan within three years after it was made. Yet suppose that, on this basis alone, a consumer decides to rescind the loan within the three-year period. Is this fair to the lender? Perhaps not. Yet the courts reason that, overall, consumers will benefit from strict compliance requirements, even though some consumers may abuse the act. In essence, the TILA is a "strict liability" statute, as are most consumer protection laws. In other words, intention normally is irrelevant in determining whether a consumer protection statute has been violated.

21. 15 U.S.C. Sections 1601–1693r. The act was amended in 1980 by the Truth-in-Lending Simplification and Reform Act.

22. Note, however, that amendments to the TILA enacted in 1995 prevent borrowers from rescinding loans for minor clerical errors in closing documents [15 U.S.C. Sections 1605, 1631, 1635, 1640, and 1641].

Equal Credit Opportunity. In 1974, Congress enacted, as an amendment to the TILA, the Equal Credit Opportunity Act (ECOA).[23] The ECOA prohibits the denial of credit solely on the basis of race, religion, national origin, color, gender, marital status, or age. The act also prohibits credit discrimination on the basis of whether an individual receives certain forms of income, such as public-assistance benefits.

Under the ECOA, a creditor may not require the signature of an applicant's spouse, other than a joint applicant, on a credit instrument if the applicant qualifies under the creditor's standards of creditworthiness for the amount and terms of the credit request. Creditors are permitted to request any information from a credit applicant except information that would be used for the type of discrimination covered in the act or its amendments.

Credit-Card Rules. The TILA also contains provisions regarding credit cards. One provision limits the liability of a cardholder to $50 per card for unauthorized charges made before the creditor is notified that the card has been lost. Another provision prohibits a credit-card company from billing a consumer for any unauthorized charges if the credit card was improperly issued by the company. • **EXAMPLE 33.2** Suppose that a consumer receives an unsolicited credit card in the mail and the card is later stolen and used by the thief to make purchases. In this situation, the consumer to whom the card was sent will not be liable for the unauthorized charges.•

Further provisions of the act concern billing disputes related to credit-card purchases. If a debtor thinks that an error has occurred in billing or wishes to withhold payment for a faulty product purchased by credit card, the act outlines specific procedures for both the consumer and the credit-card company in settling the dispute.

Consumer Leases. The Consumer Leasing Act (CLA) of 1988[24] amended the TILA to provide protection for consumers who lease automobiles and other goods. The CLA applies to those who lease or arrange to lease consumer goods in the ordinary course of their business. The act applies only if the goods are priced at $25,000 or less and if the lease term exceeds four months. The CLA and its implementing regulation, Regulation M,[25] require lessors to disclose in writing all of the material terms of the lease.

Fair Credit Reporting In 1970, to protect consumers against inaccurate credit reporting, Congress enacted the Fair Credit Reporting Act (FCRA).[26] The act provides that consumer credit reporting agencies may issue credit reports to users only for specified purposes, including the extension of credit, the issuance of insurance policies, compliance with a court order, and compliance with a consumer's request for a copy of his or her own credit report. The act further provides that any time a consumer is denied credit or insurance on the basis of the consumer's credit report, or is charged more than others ordinarily would be for credit or insurance, the consumer must be notified of that fact and of the name and address of the credit reporting agency that issued the credit report.

Under the act, consumers may request the source of any information being given out by a credit agency, as well as the identity of anyone who has received an agency's report. Consumers are also permitted to have access to the information contained about them in a credit reporting agency's files. If a consumer discovers that a credit reporting

23. 15 U.S.C. Section 1643.
24. 15 U.S.C. Sections 1667–1667e.
25. 12 C.F.R. Part 213.
26. 15 U.S.C. Sections 1681 *et seq.*

agency's files contain inaccurate information about the consumer's credit standing, the agency, on the consumer's written request, must investigate the matter and delete any unverifiable or erroneous information within a reasonable period of time.

Fair Debt-Collection Practices In 1977, Congress enacted the Fair Debt Collection Practices Act (FDCPA)[27] in an attempt to curb what were perceived to be abuses by collection agencies. The act applies only to specialized debt-collection agencies that, usually for a percentage of the amount owed, regularly attempt to collect debts on behalf of someone else. Creditors who attempt to collect debts are not covered by the act unless, by misrepresenting themselves to debtors, they cause the debtors to believe they are collection agencies. The act explicitly prohibits a collection agency from using any of the following tactics:

① Contacting the debtor at the debtor's place of employment if the debtor's employer objects.

② Contacting the debtor during inconvenient or unusual times (for example, calling the debtor at three o'clock in the morning) or at any time if the debtor is being represented by an attorney.

③ Contacting third parties other than the debtor's parents, spouse, or financial adviser about payment of a debt unless a court authorizes such action.

④ Using harassment or intimidation (for example, using abusive language or threatening violence) or employing false and misleading information (for example, posing as a police officer).

⑤ Communicating with the debtor at any time after receiving notice that the debtor is refusing to pay the debt, except to advise the debtor of further action to be taken by the collection agency.

The FDCPA also requires collection agencies to include a "validation notice" whenever they initially contact a debtor for payment of a debt or within five days of that initial contact. The notice must state that the debtor has thirty days within which to dispute the debt and to request a written verification of the debt from the collection agency. The debtor's request for debt validation must be in writing. The FDCPA provides that a debt collector who fails to comply with the act is liable for actual damages, plus additional damages not to exceed $1,000[28] and attorneys' fees.

Cases brought under the FDCPA often raise questions as to who qualifies as a debt collector or debt-collecting agency subject to the act. For example, for several years it was not clear whether attorneys who attempted to collect debts owed to their clients were subject to the FDCPA's provisions. In 1995, the United States Supreme Court addressed this issue to resolve conflicting opinions in the lower courts. The Court held that an attorney who regularly tries to obtain payment of consumer debts through legal proceedings meets the FDCPA's definition of "debt collector."[29]

Another question that sometimes arises in FDCPA litigation is what, exactly, constitutes a "debt." In the following case, the court considered whether a dishonored check constituted a "debt" within the meaning of the FDCPA.

27. 15 U.S.C. Section 1692.

28. According to the U.S. Court of Appeals for the Sixth Circuit, the $1,000 limit on damages applies to each lawsuit, not to each violation. See *Wright v. Finance Service of Norwalk, Inc.,* 22 F.3d 647 (6th Cir. 1994).

29. *Heintz v. Jenkins,* 514 U.S. 291, 115 S.Ct. 1489, 131 L.Ed.2d 395 (1995).

CASE 33.2 Snow v. Jesse L. Riddle, P.C.

United States Court of Appeals,
Tenth Circuit, 1998.
143 F.3d 1350.
http://www.kscourts.org/ca10/[a]

FACTS At a Circle-K store, Alan Snow paid for merchandise with his personal check in the amount of $23.12. Circle-K deposited the check at its bank, but the check was dishonored because of insufficient funds. Circle-K sent the returned check to its attorney, Jesse L. Riddle, P.C., for collection. In a letter to Snow, Riddle wrote that "the check amount, along with a service fee of $15, must be paid within seven (7) days of this notice. If it is not paid, * * * [a] suit [will] be filed." Snow paid the check and then filed a suit in a federal district court against Riddle. Snow alleged in part that Riddle's letter violated the FDCPA because it did not contain a "validation notice." Riddle filed a motion to dismiss on the ground that the FDCPA does not cover a dishonored check because it is not an "offer or extension of credit." The court granted the motion, and Snow appealed to the U.S. Court of Appeals for the Tenth Circuit.

a. This page contains links to opinions of the U.S. Court of Appeals for the Tenth Circuit. Scroll down the list of cases and click on the *Snow* case name to access the opinion. This Web site is maintained by the Washburn University School of Law.

ISSUE Does the FDCPA cover dishonored checks?

DECISION Yes. The U.S. Court of Appeals for the Tenth Circuit reversed the decision of the lower court and remanded the case. The appellate court held that a dishonored check constitutes a debt within the meaning of the FDCPA.

REASON The court noted that the FDCPA states that "[a]busive debt collection practices contribute to the number of personal bankruptcies, to marital instability, to the loss of jobs, and to invasions of individual privacy." The purpose of the FDCPA was "to eliminate abusive debt collection practices by debt collectors." The court cited recent decisions by other courts that held that a dishonored check constituted a "debt" within the meaning of the FDCPA and stated that it was following those decisions. "Under the 'plain meaning' test, it would seem to us that a 'debt' is created where one obtains goods and gives a dishonored check in return."

FOR CRITICAL ANALYSIS—Political Consideration *Should those who write bad checks to pay for consumer goods or services be protected by the FDCPA?*

STATE CONSUMER PROTECTION LAWS

Thus far, our primary focus has been on federal legislation. State laws, however, often provide more extensive protections for consumers than do federal laws. The warranty and unconscionability provisions of the Uniform Commercial Code (discussed in Chapters 14 through 18) offer important protections for consumers against unfair practices on the part of sellers. Far less widely adopted than the UCC is the Uniform Consumer Credit Code, which has provisions concerning truth in lending, maximum credit ceilings, door-to-door sales, fine-print clauses, and other practices affecting consumer transactions.

Virtually all states have specific consumer protection acts, often titled "deceptive trade practices acts." Although state consumer protection statutes vary widely in their provisions, a common thread runs through most of them. Typically, these laws are directed at sellers' deceptive practices, such as providing false or misleading information to consumers. An example of the broad protection such legislation may provide is the Texas Deceptive Trade Practices Act of 1973, which forbids a seller from selling to a buyer anything that the buyer does not need or cannot afford. (For another example, see this chapter's *Business Law in the Online World* feature on the next page.)

BUSINESS LAW: //in the Online World

Is an Internet Ad a "Writing"?

Many statutes that require a statement or agreement to be in writing do not define specifically what *in writing* means. Traditionally, this has not posed many problems. In the online environment, however, unique questions arise. For example, among the twenty-one practices that "constitute unfair methods of competition and unfair or deceptive acts or practices" under Pennsylvania's Unfair Trade Practices and Consumer Protection Law (UTPCPL) is a "breach of written warranty." Yet what if a warranty is made via the Internet. Is this a "written warranty"?

The Claims against the Quigley Corporation

This question arose in a case brought by a class of plaintiffs who had purchased Cold-Eeze zinc lozenges. The manufacturer of the lozenges, the Quigley Corporation, had stated in ads transmitted via radio, television, and the Internet that Cold-Eeze contained a "patented formula clinically proven to reduce the severity and duration of common cold symptoms." In their suit against Quigley, the plaintiffs claimed that the company had engaged in deceptive advertising because the lozenges did not lessen the severity or duration of the common cold. In all, the plaintiffs alleged that Quigley had engaged in five practices that violated the UTPCPL: deceptive marketing of goods, marketing of altered goods, "bait" advertising, breach of written warranty, and fraud.

Quigley contended that there could be no "breach of written warranty" because the ads were not in writing. The Pennsylvania state court hearing the case agreed that the radio and TV ads were not in writing, but what about the Internet ads?

Were the Internet Ads in Writing?

In making its decision, the court considered the purpose of the UTPCPL as well as definitions of the term *writing* given in various dictionaries. The court concluded that a seller gives a buyer "a written guarantee or warranty under [the UTPCPL] if the seller intentionally sets forth the guarantee or warranty in letters, words, or the equivalent on a physical medium and gives the guarantee to the buyer in that form." The court further concluded that a "physical medium" was one that was "visible." Applying this definition to the facts of the case, the court decided that the Internet ad was in writing because "[t]he defendant intentionally set forth its Internet ad in letters and words on a visible medium—buyers' computer screens linked to the Internet."[a]

FOR CRITICAL ANALYSIS

Was Quigley's statement about Cold-Eeze an express warranty or an implied warranty?

a. *Tesauro v. The Quigley Corporation,* No. 00080111 (Pennsylvania Court of Common Pleas for Philadelphia County, April 9, 2001). For a summary of this unpublished opinion, see "Pennsylvania Court Defines 'Writing' for Consumer Fraud Purposes," *The Internet Newsletter,* May 2001, p. 9.

Environmental Law

"Man, however much he may like to pretend the contrary, is part of nature."

RACHEL CARSON,
1907–1964
(American writer and conservationist)

To this point, this chapter has dealt with government regulation of business in the interest of protecting consumers. We now turn to a discussion of the various ways in which businesses are regulated by the government in the interest of protecting the environment. Concern over the degradation of the environment has increased over time in response to the environmental effects of population growth, urbanization, and industrialization. Environmental protection is not without a price, however. For many businesses, the costs of complying with environmental regulations are high, and for some they are too high. A constant tension exists between the desirability of increasing profits and productivity and the need to protect the environment.

To a great extent, environmental law consists of statutes passed by federal, state, or local governments and regulations issued by administrative agencies. Before examining statutory and regulatory environmental laws, however, we look at the remedies available under the common law against environmental pollution.

COMMON LAW ACTIONS

Common law remedies against environmental pollution originated centuries ago in England. Those responsible for operations that created dirt, smoke, noxious odors, noise, or toxic substances were sometimes held liable under common law theories of nuisance or negligence. Today, injured individuals continue to rely on the common law to obtain damages and injunctions against business polluters.

NUISANCE
A common law doctrine under which persons may be held liable for using their property in a manner that unreasonably interferes with others' rights to use or enjoy their own property.

Nuisance Under the common law doctrine of **nuisance**, persons may be held liable if they use their property in a manner that unreasonably interferes with others' rights to use or enjoy their own property. In these situations, the courts commonly balance the equities between the harm caused by the pollution and the costs of stopping it.

Courts have often denied injunctive relief on the ground that the hardships that would be imposed on the polluter and on the community are relatively greater than the hardships suffered by the plaintiff. • **EXAMPLE 33.3** A factory that causes neighboring landowners to suffer from smoke, dirt, and vibrations may be left in operation if it is the core of a local economy. The injured parties may be awarded only their money damages. These damages may include compensation for the decrease in the value of the neighbors' property that results from the factory's operation. •

"A nuisance may be merely a right thing in the wrong place, like a pig in the parlor instead of the barnyard."

GEORGE SUTHERLAND, 1862–1942
(Associate justice of the United States Supreme Court, 1922–1938)

Property owners may be given relief from pollution in situations in which they can identify a distinct harm separate from that affecting the general public. This is referred to as a "private" nuisance. Under the common law, citizens were denied standing (access to the courts—see Chapter 3) unless they suffered a harm distinct from the harm suffered by the public at large. Some states still require this. Therefore, a group of citizens who wished to stop a new development that would cause significant water pollution was denied access to the courts on the ground that the harm to them did not differ from the harm to the general public.[30] A public authority (such as a state's attorney general) can sue to abate a "public" nuisance.

Negligence and Strict Liability An injured party may sue a business polluter in tort under the negligence and strict liability theories discussed in Chapter 4. The basis for a negligence action is the business's alleged failure to use reasonable care toward the party whose injury was foreseeable and, of course, caused by the lack of reasonable care. For example, employees might sue an employer whose failure to use proper pollution controls contaminated the air and caused the employees to suffer respiratory illnesses. A developing area of tort law involves *toxic torts*—actions against toxic polluters.

Businesses that engage in ultrahazardous activities—such as the transportation of radioactive materials—are strictly liable for whatever injuries the activities cause. In a strict liability action, the injured party does not need to prove that the business failed to exercise reasonable care.

STATE AND LOCAL REGULATION

Many states regulate the degree to which the environment may be polluted. Thus, for example, even when state zoning laws permit a business's proposed development, the

30. *Save the Bay Committee, Inc. v. Mayor of City of Savannah*, 227 Ga. 436, 181 S.E.2d 351 (1971).

proposal may have to be altered to change the development's impact on the environment. State laws may restrict a business's discharge of chemicals into the air or water or regulate its disposal of toxic wastes. States may also regulate the disposal or recycling of other wastes, including glass, metal, and plastic containers and paper. Additionally, states may restrict the emissions from motor vehicles.

City, county, and other local governments control some aspects of the environment. For instance, local zoning laws control some land use. These laws may be designed to inhibit or direct the growth of cities and suburbs or to protect the natural environment. Other aspects of the environment may be subject to local regulation for other reasons. Methods of waste and garbage removal and disposal, for example, can have a substantial impact on a community. The appearance of buildings and other structures, including advertising signs and billboards, may affect traffic safety, property values, or local aesthetics. Noise generated by a business or its customers may be annoying, disruptive, or damaging to neighbors. The location and condition of parks, streets, and other publicly used land subject to local control affect the environment and can also affect business.

In recent years, several state and local governments have passed what are referred to as *brownfields redevelopment laws*. These laws are designed to provide incentives to buyers to purchase and clean up contaminated land ("brownfields") or older buildings containing asbestos. Incentives may be in the form of tax credits, government grants, or other assistance. Currently, Congress is considering a bill that would provide such incentives to communities throughout the nation.

A factory releases effluents into the atmosphere. On what basis might affected residents file a suit to obtain relief from any damages caused by pollution?

Federal Regulation

Congress has enacted a number of statutes to control the impact of human activities on the environment. Some of these have been passed to improve the quality of air and water. Some of them specifically regulate toxic chemicals, including pesticides, herbicides, and hazardous wastes.

Environmental Regulatory Agencies Much of the body of federal law governing business activities consists of the regulations issued and enforced by administrative agencies. The most well known of the agencies regulating environmental law is, of course, the Environmental Protection Agency (EPA), which was created in 1970 to coordinate federal environmental responsibilities. Other federal agencies with authority to regulate specific environmental matters include the Department of the Interior, the Department of Defense, the Department of Labor, the Food and Drug Administration, and the Nuclear Regulatory Commission. These regulatory agencies—and all other agencies of the federal government—must take environmental factors into consideration when making significant decisions.

Most federal environmental laws provide that citizens can sue to enforce environmental regulations if government agencies fail to do so—or if agencies go too far in their enforcement actions. Typically, a threshold hurdle in such suits is meeting the requirements for standing to sue.

Assessing the Environmental Impact of Agency Actions The National Environmental Policy Act (NEPA) of 1969[31] requires that for every major federal action that

31. 42 U.S.C. Sections 4321–4370d.

ENVIRONMENTAL IMPACT STATEMENT (EIS)
A statement required by the National Environmental Policy Act for any major federal action that will significantly affect the quality of the environment. The statement must analyze the action's impact on the environment and explore alternative actions that might be taken.

significantly affects the quality of the environment, an **environmental impact statement** (EIS) must be prepared. An action qualifies as "major" if it involves a substantial commitment of resources (monetary or otherwise). An action is "federal" if a federal agency has the power to control it. Construction by a private developer of a ski resort on federal land, for example, may require an EIS.[32] Building or operating a nuclear plant, which requires a federal permit,[33] or constructing a dam as part of a federal project would require an EIS.[34] If an agency decides that an EIS is unnecessary, it must issue a statement supporting this conclusion.

An EIS must analyze (1) the impact on the environment that the action will have, (2) any adverse effects on the environment and alternative actions that might be taken, and (3) irreversible effects the action might generate. EISs have become instruments for private citizens, consumer interest groups, businesses, and others to challenge federal agency actions on the basis that the actions improperly threaten the environment.

AIR POLLUTION

Federal involvement with air pollution goes back to the 1950s, when Congress authorized funds for air-pollution research. In 1963, the federal government passed the Clean Air Act,[35] which focused on multistate air pollution and provided assistance to states. Various amendments, particularly in 1970, 1977, and 1990, strengthened the government's authority to regulate the quality of air.

Mobile Sources of Pollution Regulations governing air pollution from automobiles and other mobile sources specify pollution standards and establish time schedules for meeting the standards. For example, under the 1990 amendments to the Clean Air Act, automobile manufacturers were required to cut new automobiles' exhaust emissions of nitrogen oxide by 60 percent and of other pollutants by 35 percent by 1998. Regulations that will go into effect beginning with 2004 model cars call for nitrogen oxide tailpipe emissions to be cut by nearly 10 percent by 2007. For the first time, sport utility vehicles and light trucks are required to meet the same standards as automobiles.

Service stations are also subject to environmental regulations. The 1990 amendments required service stations to sell gasoline with a higher oxygen content in forty-one cities that experienced carbon monoxide pollution in the winter. Service stations in the most polluted urban areas, including Los Angeles and eight other cities, were required to sell even cleaner burning gasoline.

The EPA attempts to update pollution-control standards when new scientific information becomes available. In light of evidence that very small particles (2.5 microns, or millionths of a meter) of soot affect our health as significantly as larger particles, the EPA issued new particulate standards for motor vehicle exhaust systems and other sources of pollution. The EPA also instituted a more rigorous standard for ozone, which is formed when sunlight combines with pollutants from cars and other sources. Ozone is the basic ingredient of smog.

32. *Robertson v. Methow Valley Citizens' Council,* 490 U.S. 332, 109 S.Ct. 1835, 104 L.Ed.2d 351 (1989).
33. *Calvert Cliffs Coordinating Committee v. Atomic Energy Commission,* 449 F.2d 1109 (D.C. Cir. 1971).
34. *Marsh v. Oregon Natural Resources Council,* 490 U.S. 360, 109 S.Ct. 1851, 104 L.Ed.2d 377 (1989).
35. 42 U.S.C. Sections 7401 *et seq.*

ETHICAL ISSUE 33.2

Should the costs of EPA regulations be weighed against their prospective benefits?

In setting standards governing air quality, traditionally the EPA has not been required to take costs into account. Rather, the emphasis is on the benefits. For example, when the EPA issued its new rules on particulate matter and ozone, the head of the EPA claimed that the new standards would save 15,000 lives a year. Given that the EPA values a human life at $5 million, the agency calculated that the lives saved and medical expenses avoided by the strict standards would amount to $100 billion a year in benefits. Nothing was said about the costs of implementing these rules, however. Environmental groups tend to downplay these costs and to value potential lives saved very highly. In contrast, business groups, particularly those that are affected adversely by strict air standards, think that the EPA should factor in these costs. In 2000, the debate over this issue was resolved by the United States Supreme Court. In the case, a number of business groups had challenged the EPA's stricter air-quality standards, claiming that the EPA had exceeded its authority under the Clean Air Act by issuing the regulations. The groups also claimed that the EPA had to take economic costs into account when developing new regulations. The Court, however, held that the EPA had not exceeded its authority under the Clean Air Act and confirmed that the EPA did not have to take economic costs into account when creating new rules.[36]

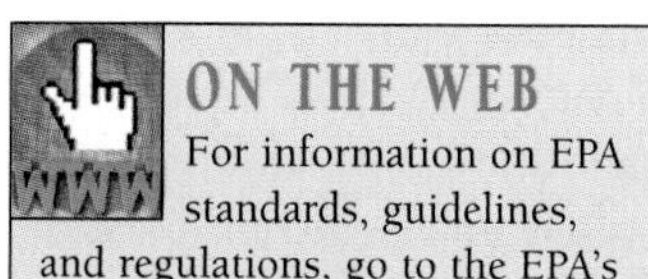

ON THE WEB For information on EPA standards, guidelines, and regulations, go to the EPA's Web site at **http://www.epa.gov**.

Stationary Sources of Pollution The Clean Air Act authorizes the EPA to establish air-quality standards for stationary sources (such as manufacturing plants) but recognizes that the primary responsibility for preventing and controlling air pollution rests with state and local governments. The EPA sets primary and secondary levels of ambient standards—that is, the maximum levels of certain pollutants—and the states formulate plans to achieve those standards. The plans are to provide for the attainment of primary standards within three years and secondary standards within a reasonable time. For economic, political, and technological reasons, however, the deadlines are often subject to change.

Different standards apply to sources of pollution in clean areas and sources in polluted areas. Different standards also apply to existing sources of pollution and major new sources. Major new sources include existing sources modified by a change in a method of operation that increases emissions. Performance standards for major sources require use of the *maximum achievable control technology,* or MACT, to reduce emissions from the combustion of fossil fuels (coal and oil). The EPA issues guidelines as to what equipment meets this standard.

Under the 1990 amendments to the Clean Air Act, 110 of the oldest coal-burning power plants in the United States had to cut their emissions by 40 percent by the year 2001 to reduce acid rain. Utilities were granted "credits" to emit certain amounts of sulfur dioxide, and those that emit less than the allowed amounts can sell their credits to other polluters. Controls on other factories and businesses are intended to reduce ground-level ozone pollution in ninety-six cities to healthful levels by 2005 (except Los Angeles, which has until 2010). The amendments also required an end to the

36. *Whitman v. American Trucking Associations,* 531 U.S. 457, 121 S.Ct. 903, 149 L.Ed.2d 1 (2000).

production of chlorofluorocarbons, carbon tetrachloride, and methyl chloroform—used in air conditioning, refrigeration, and insulation and linked to depletion of the ozone layer—by 2002.

Hazardous Air Pollutants Hazardous air pollutants are those likely to cause death or serious irreversible or incapacitating illness. In all, there are 189 of these pollutants, including asbestos, benzene, beryllium, cadmium, mercury, and vinyl chloride. These pollutants may cause cancer as well as neurological and reproductive damage. They are emitted from stationary sources by a variety of business activities, including smelting, dry cleaning, house painting, and commercial baking. Instead of establishing specific emissions standards for each hazardous air pollutant, the 1990 amendments to the Clean Air Act require industry to use pollution-control equipment that represents the maximum achievable control technology.

In 1996, the EPA issued a rule to regulate hazardous air pollutants emitted by landfills. The rule requires landfills constructed after May 30, 1991, that emit more than a specified amount of pollutants to install landfill gas collection and control systems. The rule also requires the states to impose the same requirements on landfills constructed before May 30, 1991, if they accepted waste after November 8, 1987.[37]

Violations of the Clean Air Act For violations of emission limits under the Clean Air Act, the EPA can assess civil penalties of up to $25,000 per day. Additional fines of up to $5,000 per day can be assessed for other violations, such as failing to maintain the required records. To penalize those who find it more cost effective to violate the act than to comply with it, the EPA is authorized to obtain a penalty equal to the violator's economic benefits from noncompliance. Persons who provide information about violators may be paid up to $10,000. Private citizens can also sue violators.

Those who knowingly violate the act may be subject to criminal penalties, including fines of up to $1 million and imprisonment for up to two years (for false statements or failures to report violations). Corporate officers are among those who may be subject to these penalties.

Water Pollution

"Among the treasures of our land is water—fast becoming our most valuable, most prized, most critical resource."

DWIGHT D. EISENHOWER, 1890–1969
(Thirty-fourth president of the United States, 1953–1961)

Water pollution stems mostly from industrial, municipal, and agricultural sources. Pollutants entering streams, lakes, and oceans include organic wastes, heated water, sediments from soil runoff, nutrients (including detergents, fertilizers, and human and animal wastes), and toxic chemicals and other hazardous substances. We look here at laws and regulations governing water pollution.

Navigable Waters Federal regulations governing the pollution of water can be traced back to the Rivers and Harbors Appropriations Act of 1899.[38] These regulations required a permit for discharging or depositing refuse in navigable waterways. In 1948, Congress passed the Federal Water Pollution Control Act (FWPCA),[39] but its regulatory system and enforcement powers proved to be inadequate.

In 1972, amendments to the FWPCA—known as the Clean Water Act—established the following goals: (1) make waters safe for swimming, (2) protect fish and wildlife, and (3) eliminate the discharge of pollutants into the water. The amendments set

37. 40 C.F.R. Sections 60.750–759.
38. 33 U.S.C. Sections 401–418.
39. 33 U.S.C. Sections 1251–1387.

specific time schedules, which were extended by amendment in 1977 and by the Water Quality Act of 1987.[40] Under these schedules, the EPA establishes limits on discharges of types of pollutants based on the technology available for controlling them. The 1972 amendments also required municipal and industrial polluters to apply for permits before discharging wastes into navigable waters.

Under the act, violators are subject to a variety of civil and criminal penalties. Civil penalties for each violation range from $10,000 per day to as much as $25,000 per day or per violation. Criminal penalties range from a fine of $2,500 per day and imprisonment of up to one year to a fine of $1 million and fifteen years' imprisonment. Injunctive relief and damages can also be imposed. The polluting party can be required to clean up the pollution or pay for the cost of doing so.

WETLANDS
Water-saturated areas of land that are designated by government agencies (such as the Army Corps of Engineers or the Environmental Protection Agency) as protected areas that support wildlife and therefore cannot be filled in or dredged by private contractors or parties without a permit.

Wetlands The Clean Water Act prohibits the filling or dredging of **wetlands** unless a permit is obtained from the Army Corps of Engineers. The EPA defines *wetlands* as "those areas that are inundated or saturated by surface or ground water at a frequency and duration sufficient to support, and that under normal circumstances do support, a prevalence of vegetation typically adapted for life in saturated soil conditions." In recent years, the broad interpretation of what constitutes a wetland subject to the regulatory authority of the federal government has generated substantial controversy.

● **EXAMPLE 33.4** Perhaps one of the most controversial regulations was the "migratory-bird rule" issued by the Army Corps of Engineers. Under this rule, any bodies of water that could affect interstate commerce, including seasonal ponds or waters "used or suitable for use by migratory birds" that fly over state borders, were "navigable waters" subject to federal regulation under the Clean Water Act as wetlands. In 2001, after years of controversy, the United States Supreme Court struck down the rule. The case involved a group of communities in the Chicago suburbs that wanted to build a landfill in a tract of land northwest of Chicago that had once been used as a strip mine. Over time, areas that were once pits in the mine became ponds used by a variety of migratory birds. State and local agencies approved the project, but the Army Corps of Engineers, claiming that the shallow ponds formed a habitat for migratory birds, refused to grant a permit for the landfill. A lawsuit followed, and when the case reached the Supreme Court, the Court held that the Army Corps of Engineers had exceeded its authority under the Clean Water Act. The Court stated that it was not prepared to hold that isolated and seasonable ponds, puddles, and "prairie potholes" become "navigable waters of the United States" simply because they serve as a habitat for migratory birds.[41] ●

Drinking Water Another statute governing water pollution is the Safe Drinking Water Act of 1974.[42] This act requires the EPA to set maximum levels for pollutants in public water systems. Public water system operators must come as close as possible to meeting the EPA's standards by using the best available technology that is economically and technologically feasible. The EPA is particularly concerned about contamination from underground sources. Pesticides and wastes leaked from landfills or disposed of in underground injection wells are among the more than two hundred pollutants known to exist in groundwater used for drinking in at least thirty-four states. The act was amended in 1996 to give the EPA more flexibility in setting regulatory standards.

40. This act amended 33 U.S.C. Section 1251.
41. *Solid Waste Agency of Northern Cook County v. U.S. Army Corps of Engineers,* 531 U.S. 159, 121 S.Ct. 675, 148 L.Ed.2d 576 (2001).
42. 42 U.S.C. Sections 300f to 300j-25.

Ocean Dumping The Marine Protection, Research, and Sanctuaries Act of 1972[43] (popularly known as the Ocean Dumping Act), as amended in 1983, regulates the transporting and dumping of material into ocean waters. It prohibits entirely the ocean dumping of radiological, chemical, and biological-warfare agents and high-level radioactive waste. A violation of any provision may result in a civil penalty of $50,000, and a knowing violation is a criminal offense that may result in a $50,000 fine, imprisonment for not more than a year, or both.

Oil Spills In 1989, the supertanker *Exxon Valdez* caused the worst oil spill in North American history in the waters of Alaska's Prince William Sound. A quarter of a million barrels of crude oil—more than ten million gallons—leaked out of the ship's broken hull. In response to the *Exxon Valdez* disaster, Congress passed the Oil Pollution Act of 1990.[44] Any onshore or offshore oil facility, oil shipper, vessel owner, or vessel operator that discharges oil into navigable waters or onto an adjoining shore may be liable for clean-up costs, as well as damages.

The act provides for civil penalties of $1,000 per barrel spilled or $25,000 for each day of the violation. The party held responsible for the clean-up costs can bring a civil suit, however, for contribution from other potentially liable parties. The act also created a $1 billion oil clean-up and economic compensation fund and decreed that by the year 2011, oil tankers using U.S. ports must be double hulled to limit the severity of accidental spills.

NOISE POLLUTION

Regulations concerning noise pollution include the Noise Control Act of 1972.[45] This act directed the EPA to establish noise-emission standards—for example, for railroad noise emissions. The standards must be achievable by the best available technology, and they must be economically within reason. Violations of provisions of the Noise Control Act can result in penalties of not more than $50,000 per day and imprisonment for not more than two years.

TOXIC CHEMICALS

"All property in this country is held under the implied obligation that the owner's use of it shall not be injurious to the community."

JOHN HARLAN,
1899–1971
(Associate justice of the United States Supreme Court, 1955–1971)

Originally, most environmental clean-up efforts were directed toward reducing smog and making water safe for fishing and swimming. Over time, some scientists argued that chemicals released into the environment in relatively small amounts could also pose a threat to human life and health. Control of these toxic chemicals has become an important part of environmental law.

Pesticides and Herbicides The federal statute regulating pesticides and herbicides is the Federal Insecticide, Fungicide, and Rodenticide Act (FIFRA) of 1947.[46] Under FIFRA, pesticides and herbicides must be (1) registered before they can be sold, (2) certified and used only for approved applications, and (3) used in limited quantities when applied to food crops. If a substance is identified as harmful, the EPA can cancel its registration after a hearing. If the harm is imminent, the EPA can suspend registration pending the hearing. The EPA, or state officers or employees, may also inspect factories in which these chemicals are manufactured.

43. 16 U.S.C. Sections 1401–1445.
44. 33 U.S.C. Sections 2701–2761.
45. 42 U.S.C. Sections 4901–4918.
46. 7 U.S.C. Sections 135–136y.

Under 1996 amendments to FIFRA, for a pesticide to remain on the market, there must be a "reasonable certainty of no harm" to people from exposure to the pesticide.[47] This means that there must be no more than a one-in-a-million risk to people of developing cancer from exposure in any way, including eating food that contains residues from the pesticide. Pesticide residues are in nearly all fruits and vegetables and processed foods. Under the 1996 amendments, the EPA must distribute to grocery stores brochures on high-risk pesticides that are in food, and the stores must display these brochures for consumers.

It is a violation of FIFRA to sell a pesticide or herbicide that is unregistered, a pesticide or herbicide with a registration that has been canceled or suspended, or a pesticide or herbicide with a false or misleading label. For example, it is an offense to sell a substance that is adulterated (that has a chemical strength different from the concentration declared on the label). It is also an offense to destroy or deface any labeling required under the act. The act's labeling requirements include directions for the use of the pesticide or herbicide, warnings to protect human health and the environment, a statement of treatment in the case of poisoning, and a list of the ingredients.

A commercial dealer who violates FIFRA may be imprisoned for up to one year and fined up to $25,000. Farmers and other private users of pesticides or herbicides who violate the act are subject to a $1,000 fine and incarceration for up to thirty days.

Toxic Substances The first comprehensive law covering toxic substances was the Toxic Substances Control Act of 1976.[48] The act was passed to regulate chemicals and chemical compounds that are known to be toxic—such as asbestos and polychlorinated biphenyls, popularly known as PCBs—and to institute investigation of any possible harmful effects from new chemical compounds. The regulations authorize the EPA to require that manufacturers, processors, and other organizations planning to use chemicals first determine their effects on human health and the environment. The EPA can regulate substances that potentially pose an imminent hazard or an unreasonable risk of injury to health or the environment. The EPA may require special labeling, limit the use of a substance, set production quotas, or prohibit the use of a substance altogether.

Hazardous Waste Disposal

Some industrial, agricultural, and household wastes pose more serious threats than others. If not properly disposed of, these toxic chemicals may present a substantial danger to human health and the environment. If released into the environment, they may contaminate public drinking water resources.

Resource Conservation and Recovery Act In 1976, Congress passed the Resource Conservation and Recovery Act (RCRA)[49] in reaction to an ever-increasing concern over the effects of hazardous waste materials on the environment. The RCRA required the EPA to establish regulations to monitor and control hazardous waste disposal and to determine which forms of solid waste should be considered hazardous and thus subject to regulation. The EPA has promulgated various technical requirements for limited types of facilities for storage and treatment of hazardous waste. The act also requires all producers of hazardous waste materials to label and package properly any hazardous waste to be transported.

47. 21 U.S.C. Section 346a.

48. 15 U.S.C. Sections 2601–2692.

49. 42 U.S.C. Sections 6901 *et seq.*

ON THE WEB
To learn about the RCRA's "buy-recycled" requirements and other steps the federal government has taken toward "greening the environment," go to **http://www.epa.gov/cpg**.

The RCRA was amended in 1984 and 1986 to add several new regulatory requirements to those already monitored and enforced by the EPA. The basic aims of the amendments were to decrease the use of land containment in the disposal of hazardous waste and to require compliance with the act by some generators of hazardous waste—such as those generating less than 1,000 kilograms (2,200 pounds) a month—that had previously been excluded from regulation under the RCRA.

Under the RCRA, a company may be assessed a civil penalty based on the seriousness of the violation, the probability of harm, and the extent to which the violation deviates from RCRA requirements. The assessment may be up to $25,000 for each violation.[50] Criminal penalties include fines up to $50,000 for each day of violation, imprisonment for up to two years (in most instances), or both.[51] Criminal fines and the time of imprisonment can be doubled for certain repeat offenders.

Superfund In 1980, Congress passed the Comprehensive Environmental Response, Compensation, and Liability Act (CERCLA),[52] commonly known as Superfund, to regulate the clean-up of leaking hazardous waste-disposal sites. A special federal fund was created for that purpose. Because of its impact on the business community, the act is presented here as this chapter's *Landmark in the Law.*

50. 42 U.S.C. Section 6929(g).
51. 42 U.S.C. Section 6929(d).
52. 42 U.S.C. Sections 9601–9675.

LANDMARK IN THE LAW
Superfund

The origins of the Comprehensive Environmental Response, Compensation, and Liability Act (CERCLA) of 1980, which is commonly referred to as Superfund, can be traced to drafts that the Environmental Protection Agency (EPA) started to circulate in 1978.

Dump Sites Are "Ticking Time Bombs" EPA officials emphasized the political necessity of new legislation by pointing to what they thought were "ticking time bombs"—dump sites around the country that were ready to explode and injure the public with toxic fumes.

The popular press was also running prominent stories about hazardous waste dump sites at the time. The New York Love Canal disaster first made headlines in 1978 when residents in the area complained about health problems, contaminated sludge oozing into their basements, and chemical "volcanoes" erupting in their yards as a result of the approximately 21,000 tons of chemicals that Hooker Chemical had dumped into the canal from 1942 to 1953. By the middle of May 1980, the Love Canal situation was making the national news virtually every day and remained in the headlines for a month.

CERCLA—Its Purpose and Primary Elements The basic purpose of CERCLA, which was amended in 1986 by the Superfund Amendments and Reauthorization Act, is to regulate the clean-up of leaking hazardous waste disposal sites. The act has four primary elements:

(continued)

LANDMARK IN THE LAW—Continued

- It established an information-gathering and analysis system that allows federal and state governments to characterize chemical dump sites and to develop priorities for appropriate action.
- It authorized the EPA to respond to hazardous substance emergencies and to clean up a leaking site directly through contractors or through cooperative agreements with the states if the persons responsible for the problem fail to clean up the site.
- It created a Hazardous Substance Response Trust Fund (Superfund) to pay for the clean-up of hazardous sites. Monies for the fund are obtained through taxes on certain businesses, including those processing or producing petroleum and chemical feedstock.
- It allowed the government to recover the cost of clean-up from the persons who were (even remotely) responsible for hazardous substance releases.

APPLICATION TO TODAY'S WORLD

The provisions of CERCLA profoundly affect today's businesses and business decision making. Virtually any business decision relating to the purchase and sale of property, for example, requires an analysis of previous activities on the property to determine whether those activities resulted in contamination. Additionally, to avoid violating CERCLA, owners and mangers of manufacturing plants must be extremely cautious in arranging for the removal and disposal of any hazardous waste materials. Unless Congress significantly changes CERCLA and the way that it is implemented, businesses will continue to face potentially extensive liability for violations under this act.

Potentially Responsible Parties under Superfund. Superfund provides that when a release or a threatened release of hazardous chemicals from a site occurs, the EPA can clean up the site and recover the cost of the clean-up from the following persons: (1) the person who generated the wastes disposed of at the site, (2) the person who transported the wastes to the site, (3) the person who owned or operated the site at the time of the disposal, or (4) the current owner or operator. A person falling within one of these categories is referred to as a **potentially responsible party (PRP)**.

POTENTIALLY RESPONSIBLE PARTY (PRP) A party liable for the costs of cleaning up a hazardous waste-disposal site under the Comprehensive Environmental Response, Compensation, and Liability Act (CERCLA). Any person who generated the hazardous waste, transported it, owned or operated the waste site at the time of disposal, or currently owns or operates the site may be responsible for some or all of the clean-up costs.

Joint and Several Liability under Superfund. Liability under Superfund is usually joint and several—that is, a person who generated *only a fraction of the hazardous waste* disposed of at the site may nevertheless be liable for *all* of the clean-up costs. CERCLA authorizes a party who has incurred clean-up costs to bring a "contribution action" against any other person who is liable or potentially liable for a percentage of the costs. The following case involved a challenge to a court's allocation of clean-up costs among PRPs.

CASE 33.3 Browning-Ferris Industries of Illinois, Inc. v. Ter Maat

United States Court of Appeals,
Seventh Circuit, 1999.
195 F.3d 953.
http://www.ca7.uscourts.gov[a]

FACTS In 1971, the owners of a landfill leased it to a company that later became Browning-Ferris Industries of Illinois, Inc., which operated it until the fall of 1975. During that time, the operator illegally dumped at the site a large quantity of particularly toxic wastes from an auto plant run by Chrysler Corporation. Between the fall of 1975 and 1988, M.I.G. Investments, Inc., and AAA Disposal Systems, Inc., operated the landfill. Richard Ter Maat was the president and principal shareholder of M.I.G. and AAA. In June 1988, after AAA was sold and Ter Maat moved to Florida, M.I.G. abandoned the landfill without covering it properly. Two years later, the EPA ordered that the site be cleaned up. Browning-Ferris and other companies that shared responsibility for the pollution at the site agreed to clean it up. Browning-Ferris and the others then filed a suit in a federal district court against Ter Maat, M.I.G., and AAA under CERCLA to recover the costs. The court ruled, among other things, that 45 percent of the costs was allocable to the owners of the landfill and the generators of the toxic wastes dumped in it, 22 percent was the responsibility of Browning-Ferris, and the other 33 percent was the responsibility of M.I.G. and AAA. The plaintiffs appealed to the U.S. Court of Appeals for the Seventh Circuit. Browning-Ferris claimed in part that too much of the liability for the pollution at the site had been allocated to it relative to M.I.G. and AAA. Browning-Ferris argued that the costs should be allocated according to the volume of wastes for which each party was responsible.

a. In the left-hand column, click on "Judicial Opinions." On that page, in the "Last Name or Corporation" section, click on "Begins," enter "Browning-Ferris" in the box, and click on "Search for Person." When the result appears, click on the docket number for the case to access the opinion.

ISSUE Had too much of the liability for the pollution at the site been allocated to Browning-Ferris?

DECISION No. The U.S. Court of Appeals for the Seventh Circuit held that the allocation of 22 percent of the clean-up costs to Browning-Ferris had been fair.

REASON The appellate court reasoned that there were a number of factors to consider, and the lower court had not abused its discretion in deciding that those factors warranted this allocation. The court remanded the case for the determination of other issues. "Browning-Ferris's pollution was serious enough * * * to require that the site be cleaned up, but the other pollution at the site was also enough. If Browning-Ferris's conduct was thus a sufficient though not a necessary condition of the clean up, it is not inequitable to make it contribute substantially to the cost. * * * [N]o principle of law, logic, or common sense required the court to allocate [the] total costs among the polluters on the basis of the volume of wastes alone. Not only do wastes differ in their toxicity, harm to the environment, and costs of cleaning up, and so relative volume is not a reliable guide to the marginal costs imposed by each polluter; but polluters differ in the blameworthiness of the decisions or omissions that led to the pollution, and blameworthiness is relevant to an equitable allocation of joint costs."

FOR CRITICAL ANALYSIS—Ethical Consideration *According to the court in this case, "wastes differ in their toxicity, harm to the environment, and costs of cleaning up." Does this mean that it is impossible to apportion clean-up costs for hazardous waste sites in a way that would be fair to the responsible parties? Generally, should considerations of fairness enter into the decision as to who should be responsible for cleaning up hazardous wastes?*

APPLICATION **Law and the Businessperson . . .**

Keeping Abreast of Environmental Laws*

Businesspersons today increasingly face the threat of severe civil or criminal penalties if they violate environmental laws and regulations. It therefore is necessary that every person in the business world be aware of what those laws and regulations are and how to monitor changes in them. At a minimum, knowledge of the changing and complex nature of environmental law will help a businessperson to know when to contact an attorney during the normal course of business. Consider some areas of concern that affect businesses.

Factors to Consider When Purchasing Business Property

Businesspersons often purchase business property. When engaging in such purchases, you must keep in mind the environmental problems that may arise. Realize that it is up to you as a purchaser of the property to raise environmental issues—sellers, title insurance companies, and real estate brokers will rarely pursue such matters. (A bank financing the property may worry about the potential environmental hazards of the property, however.)

As a purchaser of business property, you should learn whether there are any restrictions regarding the use of the land, such as whether the land can be cleared of trees for construction purposes. The most prominent environmental concern, however, is whether the property has been contaminated by hazardous wastes created by the previous owners.

Investigate Land-Use History

Purchasers of property can be held liable in a seemingly unending number of ways under the Comprehensive Environmental Response, Compensation, and Liability Act (CERCLA) of 1980 for the clean-up of hazardous wastes dumped by previous property owners. Although current property owners who are sued under CERCLA for clean-up costs can sue the previous owners, such litigation is uncertain and usually costly. Clearly, a more prudent course when purchasing property is to investigate the history of the use of the land. If you purchase business property, you would be well advised to hire a private environmental site inspector to determine, at a minimum, whether the land has any obvious signs of former contamination.

Investigate and Correct Environmental Violations

Today's companies have an incentive to discover their own environmental wrongdoings. As mentioned in Chapter 6, the federal sentencing guidelines encourage companies to promptly detect, disclose, and correct wrongdoing, including environmental crimes. Companies that do so are subject to lighter penalties for violations of environmental laws. Under the guidelines, a company that regularly conducts comprehensive audits of its compliance with environmental requirements, immediately reports a violation to the government, disciplines the responsible people within the corporation, and provides their names to the government should qualify for leniency.

Small businesses will find it particularly advantageous to investigate and correct environmental violations. Under current EPA guidelines, the EPA will waive all fines if a company corrects environmental violations within 180 days after being notified of the violations (or 360 days if pollution-prevention techniques are involved). The EPA's policy applies to companies with one hundred or fewer employees. The policy does not apply to criminal violations of environmental laws or to actions that pose a significant threat to public health, safety, or the environment.

*This *Application* is not meant to substitute for the services of an attorney who is licensed to practice law in your state.

APPLICATION Law and the Businessperson . . .

Keeping Abreast of Environmental Laws—continued

Checklist for the Businessperson

1. If you are in business or plan to open a business that is going to purchase real estate, use land, or engage in activities that might cause environmental damage, check with your attorney immediately.
2. If you want to avoid liability for violating environmental regulations or statutes, conduct environmental compliance audits on a regular basis. To learn whether you are doing so appropriately, check with your attorney.
3. If you are ever charged with violating an environmental regulation or law, you must check with your attorney.
4. In general, environmental law is sufficiently complex that you should never attempt to deal with it without the help of an attorney.

Key Terms

bait-and-switch advertising 869
cease-and-desist order 870
"cooling-off" laws 873
counteradvertising 870
deceptive advertising 869
environmental impact statement (EIS) 883
nuisance 881
potentially responsible party (PRP) 890
Regulation Z 873
wetlands 886

Chapter Summary Consumer and Environmental Law

CONSUMER LAW	
Deceptive Advertising (See pages 868–870.)	1. *Definition of deceptive advertising*—Generally, an advertising claim will be deemed deceptive if it would mislead a reasonable consumer. 2. *Bait-and-switch advertising*—Advertising a lower-priced product (the "bait") when the intention is not to sell the advertised product but to lure consumers into the store and convince them to buy a higher-priced product (the "switch") is prohibited by the FTC. 3. *Online deceptive advertising*—The FTC has issued guidelines to help online businesses comply with existing laws prohibiting deceptive advertising. The guidelines do not set forth new rules but rather describe how existing laws apply to online advertising. 4. *FTC actions against deceptive advertising*— a. Cease-and-desist orders—Requiring the advertiser to stop the challenged advertising. b. Counteradvertising—Requiring the advertiser to advertise to correct the earlier misinformation.

(continued)

Chapter Summary Consumer and Environmental Law—continued

Telemarketing and Electronic Advertising (See pages 870–871.)	The Telephone Consumer Protection Act of 1991 prohibits telephone solicitation using an automatic telephone dialing system or a prerecorded voice, as well as the transmission of advertising materials via fax without first obtaining the recipient's permission to do so.
Labeling and Packaging (See page 872.)	Manufacturers must comply with labeling or packaging requirements for their specific products. In general, all labels must be accurate and not misleading.
Sales (See pages 873–874.)	1. *Door-to-door sales*—The FTC requires all door-to-door sellers to give consumers three days (a "cooling-off" period) to cancel any sale. States also provide for similar protection. 2. *Telephone and mail-order sales*—Federal and state statutes and regulations govern certain practices of sellers who solicit over the telephone or through the mails and prohibit the use of the mails to defraud individuals. 3. *Online sales*—Increasingly, the Internet is being used to conduct business-to-consumer (B2C) transactions. Consumers are protected to some extent under both state and federal laws against fraudulent and deceptive online sales practices.
Health and Safety Protection (See pages 874–875.)	1. *Food and drugs*—The Federal Food, Drug and Cosmetic Act of 1938, as amended, protects consumers against adulterated and misbranded foods and drugs. The act establishes food standards, specifies safe levels of potentially hazardous food additives, and sets classifications of food and food advertising. 2. *Consumer product safety*—The Consumer Product Safety Act of 1972 seeks to protect consumers from risk of injury from hazardous products. The Consumer Product Safety Commission has the power to remove products that are deemed imminently hazardous from the market and to ban the manufacture and sale of hazardous products.
Credit Protection (See pages 875–879.)	1. *Consumer Credit Protection Act, Title I (Truth-in-Lending Act, or TILA)*—A disclosure law that requires sellers and lenders to disclose credit terms or loan terms in certain transactions, including retail and installment sales and loans, car loans, home-improvement loans, and certain real estate loans. Additionally, the TILA provides for the following: a. Equal credit opportunity—Creditors are prohibited from discriminating on the basis of race, religion, marital status, gender, and so on. b. Credit-card protection—Credit-card users may withhold payment for a faulty product sold, or for an error in billing, until the dispute is resolved; liability of cardholders for unauthorized charges is limited to $50, providing notice requirements are met; consumers are not liable for unauthorized charges made on unsolicited credit cards. c. Consumer leases—The Consumer Leasing Act (CLA) of 1988 protects consumers who lease automobiles and other goods priced at $25,000 or less if the lease term exceeds four months. 2. *Fair Credit Reporting Act*—Entitles consumers to request verification of the accuracy of a credit report and to have unverified or false information removed from their files. 3. *Fair Debt Collection Practices Act*—Prohibits debt collectors from using unfair debt-collection practices, such as contacting the debtor at his or her place of employment if the employer objects or at unreasonable times, contacting third parties about the debt, harassing the debtor, and so on.
State Consumer Protection Laws (See pages 879–880.)	State laws often provide for greater consumer protection against deceptive trade practices than do federal laws. In addition, the warranty and unconscionability provisions of the Uniform Commercial Code protect consumers against sellers' deceptive practices. The Uniform Consumer Credit Code, which has not been widely adopted by the states, provides credit protection for consumers.

Chapter Summary Consumer and Environmental Law—continued

ENVIRONMENTAL LAW	
Common Law Actions (See page 880.)	1. *Nuisance*—A common law doctrine under which actions against pollution-causing activities may be brought. An action is permissible only if an individual suffers a harm separate and distinct from that of the general public. 2. *Negligence and strict liability*—Parties may recover damages for injuries sustained as a result of a firm's pollution-causing activities if it can be demonstrated that the harm was a foreseeable result of the firm's failure to exercise reasonable care (negligence); businesses engaging in ultrahazardous activities are liable for whatever injuries the activities cause, regardless of whether the firms exercise reasonable care.
State and Local Regulation (See pages 881–882.)	Activities affecting the environment are controlled at the local and state levels through regulations relating to land use, the disposal and recycling of garbage and waste, and pollution-causing activities in general.
Federal Regulation (See pages 882–891.)	1. *Environmental protection agencies*—The most well known of the agencies regulating environmental law is the federal Environmental Protection Agency (EPA), which was created in 1970 to coordinate federal environmental programs. The EPA administers most federal environmental policies and statutes. 2. *Assessing environmental impact*—The National Environmental Policy Act of 1969 imposes environmental responsibilities on all federal agencies and requires the preparation of an environmental impact statement (EIS) for every major federal action. An EIS must analyze the action's impact on the environment, its adverse effects and possible alternatives, and its irreversible effects on environmental quality. 3. *Important areas regulated by the federal government*—Important areas regulated by the federal government include the following: a. Air pollution—Regulated under the authority of the Clean Air Act of 1963 and its amendments, particularly those of 1970, 1977, and 1990. b. Water pollution—Regulated under the authority of the Rivers and Harbors Appropriation Act of 1899, as amended, and the Federal Water Pollution Control Act of 1948, as amended by the Clean Water Act of 1972. c. Noise pollution—Regulated by the Noise Control Act of 1972. d. Toxic chemicals and hazardous waste—Pesticides and herbicides, toxic substances, and hazardous waste are regulated under the authority of the Federal Insecticide, Fungicide, and Rodenticide Act of 1947, the Toxic Substances Control Act of 1976, and the Resource Conservation and Recovery Act of 1976, respectively. The Comprehensive Environmental Response, Compensation, and Liability Act (CERCLA) of 1980, as amended, regulates the clean-up of hazardous waste disposal sites.

For Review

① When will advertising be deemed deceptive?

② How does the Federal Food, Drug and Cosmetic Act protect consumers? What are the major federal statutes providing for consumer protection in credit transactions?

③ Under what common law theories may polluters be held liable?

④ What is an environmental impact statement, and who must file one? What does the Environmental Protection Agency do?

⑤ What major federal statutes regulate air and water pollution? What is Superfund? To what categories of persons does liability under Superfund extend?

Questions and Case Problems

33–1. Clean Air Act. Current scientific knowledge indicates that there is no safe level of exposure to a cancer-causing agent. In theory, even one molecule of such a substance has the potential for causing cancer. Section 112 of the Clean Air Act requires that all cancer-causing substances be regulated to ensure a margin of safety. Some environmental groups have argued that all emissions of such substances must be eliminated if a margin of safety is to be reached. Such a total elimination would likely shut down many major U.S. industries. Should the Environmental Protection Agency totally eliminate all emissions of cancer-causing chemicals? Discuss.

33–2. Environmental Laws. Fruitade, Inc., is a processor of a soft drink called Freshen Up. Fruitade uses returnable bottles and employs a special acid to clean its bottles for further beverage processing. The acid is diluted with water and then allowed to pass into a navigable stream. Fruitade crushes its broken bottles and also throws the crushed glass into the stream. Discuss fully any environmental laws that Fruitade has violated.

33–3. Sales. On June 28, a sales representative for Renowned Books called on the Guevaras at their home. After listening to a very persuasive sales pitch, the Guevaras agreed in writing to purchase a twenty-volume set of historical encyclopedias from Renowned Books for a total price of $299. An initial down payment of $35 was required, with the remainder of the price to be paid in monthly payments over a one-year period. Two days later, the Guevaras, having second thoughts about the purchase, contacted the book company and stated that they had decided to rescind the contract. Renowned Books said this would be impossible. Has Renowned Books violated any consumer law by not allowing the Guevaras to rescind their contract? Explain.

33–4. Credit Protection. Maria Ochoa receives two new credit cards on May 1. She had solicited one of them from Midtown Department Store, and the other arrived unsolicited from High-Flying Airlines. During the month of May, Ochoa makes numerous credit-card purchases from Midtown Department Store, but she does not use the High-Flying Airlines card. On May 31, a burglar breaks into Ochoa's home and steals both credit cards, along with other items. Ochoa notifies the Midtown Department Store of the theft on June 2, but she fails to notify High-Flying Airlines. Using the Midtown credit card, the burglar makes a $500 purchase on June 1 and a $200 purchase on June 3. The burglar then charges a vacation flight on the High-Flying Airlines card for $1,000 on June 5. Ochoa receives the bills for these charges and refuses to pay them. Discuss Ochoa's liability in these situations.

33–5. Deceptive Advertising. Thompson Medical Co. marketed a new cream, called Aspercreme, which was supposed to help people with arthritis and others suffering from minor aches. Aspercreme contained no aspirin. Thompson's television advertisements stated that the product provided "the strong relief of aspirin right where you hurt" and showed the announcer holding up aspirin tablets, as well as a tube of Aspercreme. The Federal Trade Commission held that the advertisements were misleading because they led consumers to believe that Aspercreme contained aspirin. Thompson Medical Co. appealed this decision and argued that the advertisements never actually stated that its product contained aspirin. How should the court rule? Discuss. [*Thompson Medical Co. v. Federal Trade Commission,* 791 F.2d 189 (D.C. Cir. 1986)]

33–6. Equal Credit Opportunity. The Riggs National Bank of Washington, D.C., loaned more than $11 million to Samuel Linch and Albert Randolph. To obtain the loan, Linch and Randolph provided personal financial statements. Linch's statement included substantial assets that he owned jointly with his wife, Marcia. As a condition of the loan, Riggs required that Marcia, as well as Samuel and Albert, sign a personal guaranty for repayment. When the borrowers defaulted, Riggs filed a suit in a federal district court to recover its funds, based on the personal guaranties. The court ruled against the borrowers, who appealed. On what basis might the borrowers argue that Riggs violated the Equal Credit Opportunity Act? [*Riggs National Bank of Washington, D.C. v. Linch,* 36 F.3d 370 (4th Cir. 1994)]

33–7. Debt Collection. Equifax A.R.S., a debt-collection agency, sent Donna Russell a notice about one of her debts. The front of the notice stated that "[i]f you do not dispute this claim (see reverse side) and wish to pay it within the next 10 days we will not post this collection to your file." The reverse side set out Russell's rights under the Fair Debt Collection Practices Act (FDCPA), including that she had thirty days to decide whether to contest the claim. Russell filed a suit in a federal district court against Equifax. The court ruled against Russell, who appealed. On what basis might Russell argue that Equifax violated the FDCPA? [*Russell v. Equifax A.R.S.,* 74 F.3d 30 (2d Cir. 1996)]

33–8. Debt Collection. Rancho Santa Margarita Recreation and Landscape Corp., a condominium association, attempted unsuccessfully to collect an assessment fee from Andrew Ladick. The association referred the matter to the Law Offices of Gerald J. Van Gemert. Van Gemert sent Ladick a letter demanding payment of the fee. The letter did not include a Fair Debt Collection Practices Act (FDCPA) "validation notice," nor did it disclose that Van Gemert was attempting to collect a debt and that any information obtained would be used for that purpose. Ladick filed a suit in a federal district court against Van Gemert and his office, alleging violations of the FDCPA. Van Gemert filed a motion for summary judgment on the ground that the assessment was not a "debt," as defined by the FDCPA; he argued, in part, that there was no "transaction," as required by the FDCPA definition, out of which Ladick's obligation arose. Will the court agree with Van Gemert? Why or why not? [*Ladick v. Van Gemert,* 146 F.3d 1205 (10th Cir. 1998)]

33–9. Fair Debt Collection. Gloria Mahon incurred a bill of $279.70 for medical services rendered by Dr. Larry Bowen. For more than two years, Bowen sent monthly billing statements to the Mahons at their home address (where they had lived for forty-five years). Getting no response, Bowen assigned the collection of the account to Credit Bureau of Placer County, Inc. Credit Bureau uses computerized collection tracking and filing software, known as Columbia Ultimate Business Systems (CUBS). CUBS automatically generates standardized collection notices and acts as an electronic filing system for each account, recording all collection activities, including which notices are sent to whom and on what date. Credit Bureau employees monitor the activity, routinely noting whether an envelope is returned undelivered. Credit Bureau mailed three CUBS–generated notices to the Mahons. According to Credit Bureau's records, the notices were not returned, and the Mahons did not respond. Credit Bureau reported the Mahons' account as delinquent. The Mahons filed a suit in a federal district court against Credit Bureau, alleging in part that the agency had failed to send a validation notice, as required by the Fair Debt Collection Practices Act. Credit Bureau filed a motion for summary judgment. Should a notice be considered sent only if a debtor acknowledges its receipt? Why or why not? [*Mahon v. Credit Bureau of Placer County, Inc.*, 171 F.3d 1197 (9th Cir. 1999)]

TEST YOUR KNOWLEDGE—ANSWER ON THE WEB

33–10. CrossCheck, Inc., provides check authorization services to retail merchants. When a customer presents a check, the merchant contacts CrossCheck, which estimates the probability that the check will clear the bank. If the check is within an acceptable statistical range, CrossCheck notifies the merchant. If the check is dishonored, the merchant sends it to CrossCheck, which pays it. CrossCheck then attempts to redeposit it. If this fails, CrossCheck takes further steps to collect the amount. CrossCheck attempts to collect on more than two thousand checks per year and spends $2 million on these efforts, which involve about 7 percent of its employees and 6 percent of its total expenses. William Winterstein took his truck to C&P Auto Service Center, Inc., for a tune-up and paid for the service with a check. C&P contacted CrossCheck and, on its recommendation, accepted the check. When the check was dishonored, C&P mailed it to CrossCheck, which reimbursed C&P and sent a letter to Winterstein, requesting payment. Winterstein filed a suit in a federal district court against CrossCheck, asserting that the letter violated the Fair Debt Collection Practices Act. CrossCheck filed a motion for summary judgment. On what ground might the court grant the motion? Explain. [*Winterstein v. CrossCheck, Inc.*, 149 F.Supp.2d 466 (N.D.Ill. 2001)]

A QUESTION OF ETHICS AND SOCIAL RESPONSIBILITY

33–11. The Endangered Species Act of 1973 makes it unlawful for any person to "take" endangered or threatened species. The act defines *take* to mean to "harass, harm, pursue," "wound," or "kill." The secretary of the interior (Bruce Babbitt) issued a regulation that further defined *harm* to include "significant habitat modification or degradation where it actually kills or injures wildlife." A group of businesses and individuals involved in the timber industry brought an action against the secretary of the interior and others. The group complained that the application of the "harm" regulation to the red-cockaded woodpecker and the northern spotted owl had injured the group economically because it prevented logging operations (habitat modification) in Pacific Northwest forests containing these species. The group challenged the regulation's validity, contending that Congress did not intend the word *take* to include habitat modification. The case ultimately reached the United States Supreme Court, which held that the secretary reasonably construed Congress's intent when he defined *harm* to include habitat modification. [*Babbitt v. Sweet Home Chapter of Communities for a Great Oregon*, 515 U.S. 687, 115 S.Ct. 2407, 132 L.Ed.2d 597 (1995)]

1. Traditionally, the term *take* has been used to refer to the capture or killing of wildlife, usually for private gain. Is the secretary's regulation prohibiting habitat modification consistent with this definition?
2. One of the issues in this case was whether Congress intended to protect existing generations of species or future generations. How do the terms *take* and *habitat modification* relate to this issue?
3. Three dissenting Supreme Court justices contended that construing the act as prohibiting habitat modification "imposes unfairness to the point of financial ruin—not just upon the rich, but upon the simplest farmer who finds his land conscripted to national zoological use." Should private parties be required to bear the burden of preserving habitats for wildlife?
4. Generally, should the economic welfare of private parties be taken into consideration when creating and applying environmental statutes and regulations?

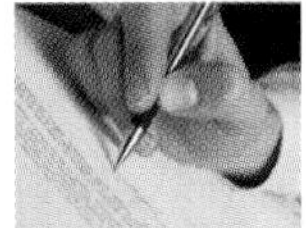

FOR CRITICAL ANALYSIS

33–12. It has been estimated that for every dollar spent cleaning up hazardous waste sites, administrative agencies spend seven dollars in overhead. Can you think of any way to trim the administrative costs associated with the clean-up of contaminated sites?

Internet Activities

Go to the Business Law Today home page at **http://blt.westbuslaw.com**. Select "Interactive Study Center" and then click on "Chapter 33." There you will find the following Internet research exercises that you can perform to learn more about consumer law and nuisance law:

Activity 33–1: Consumer Law
Activity 33–2: Nuisance Law

Before the Test

Go to the *Business Law Today* home page at **http://blt.westbuslaw.com**. Click on "Interactive Quizzes." You will find at least twenty interactive questions relating to this chapter.

CHAPTER 34

Labor and Employment Law

"Show me the country in which there are no strikes, and I'll show you the country in which there is no liberty."

Samuel Gompers, 1850–1924
(American labor leader)

CHAPTER CONTENTS

LEARNING OBJECTIVES

After reading this chapter, you should be able to answer the following questions:

1. What is the employment-at-will doctrine? When and why are exceptions to this doctrine made?
2. What federal statute governs working hours and wages? What federal statutes govern labor unions and collective bargaining?
3. What federal act was enacted to protect the health and safety of employees? What are workers' compensation laws?
4. Under the Family and Medical Leave Act of 1993, under what circumstances may an employee take family or medical leave?
5. Does electronic performance monitoring violate employees' privacy rights? What other types of activities undertaken by employers might violate the privacy rights of employees?

Until the early 1900s, most employer-employee relationships were governed by the common law. Under the common law doctrine of **employment at will**, either party may terminate the employment relationship at any time and for any reason—provided, of course, that the employment termination does not violate the provisions of an employment contract or a statute. Other common law concepts governing employment relationships include contract, agency, and tort law. Today, the workplace is extensively regulated by statutes and administrative agency regulations, thus narrowing the applicability of common law doctrines to employment relationships.

EMPLOYMENT AT WILL
A common law doctrine under which either party may terminate an employment relationship at any time for any reason, unless a contract specifies otherwise.

In the 1930s, during the Great Depression, both state and federal governments began to regulate employment relationships. Legislation during the 1930s and subsequent decades established the right of employees to form labor unions. At the heart of labor rights is the right to unionize and bargain with management for improved working conditions, salaries, and benefits. The ultimate weapon of labor is, of course, the strike. As noted in the opening quotation, the labor leader Samuel Gompers concluded that without the right to strike, there could be no liberty. A succession of other laws during and since the 1930s provided further protection for employees. Today's employers must comply with a myriad of laws and regulations to ensure that employee rights are protected.

In this chapter, we look at the most significant laws regulating employment relationships. We deal with other important laws regulating the workplace—those that prohibit employment discrimination—in the next chapter.

Wage-Hour Laws

In the 1930s, Congress enacted several laws regulating the wages and working hours of employees. In 1931, Congress passed the Davis-Bacon Act,[1] which requires contractors and subcontractors working on government construction projects to pay "prevailing wages" to their employees. In 1936, the Walsh-Healey Act[2] was passed. This act requires that employees of manufacturers or suppliers entering into contracts with agencies of the federal government be paid a minimum wage, as well as overtime pay of time and a half.

In 1938, Congress passed the Fair Labor Standards Act[3] (FLSA). This act extended wage-hour requirements to cover all employers engaged in interstate commerce or engaged in the production of goods for interstate commerce, plus selected types of businesses. We examine here the FLSA's provisions in regard to child labor, maximum hours, and minimum wages.

Children take a break from their work in a coal mine in the early twentieth century. What restrictions do employers face in employing children today?

Child Labor

The FLSA prohibits oppressive child labor. Children under fourteen years of age are allowed to do certain types of work, such as deliver newspapers, work for their parents, and work in the entertainment and (with some exceptions) agricultural areas. Children who are fourteen or fifteen years of age are allowed to work, but not in hazardous occupations. Most states require persons under sixteen years of age to obtain work permits. There are also numerous restrictions on how many hours per day and per week they can work. • **Example 34.1** Children under the age of sixteen cannot work during school hours, for more than three hours on a school day (or eight hours on a nonschool day), for more than eighteen hours during a school week (or forty hours during a nonschool week), or before 7 A.M. or after 7 P.M. (9 P.M. during the summer). •

Persons between the ages of sixteen and eighteen do not face such restrictions on working times and hours, but they cannot be employed in hazardous jobs or in jobs detrimental to their health and well-being. Persons over the age of eighteen are not affected by any of these restrictions.

1. 40 U.S.C. Sections 276a–276a-5.
2. 41 U.S.C. Sections 35–45.
3. 29 U.S.C. Sections 201–260.

HOURS AND WAGES

Under the FLSA, any employee who agrees to work more than forty hours per week must be paid no less than one and a half times his or her regular pay for all hours over forty. Note that the FLSA overtime provisions apply only after an employee has worked more than forty hours per *week*. Thus, employees who work for ten hours a day, four days per week, are not entitled to overtime pay because they do not work more than forty hours a week.

Certain employees are exempt from the overtime provisions of the act. Exempt employees fall into four categories: executives, administrative employees such as supervisors, professional employees, and outside salespersons. Generally, to fall into one of these categories, an employee must earn more than a specified amount of income per week and devote a certain percentage of work time to the performance of specific types of duties, as determined by the FLSA. To qualify as an outside salesperson, the employee must regularly engage in sales work away from the office and spend no more than 20 percent of work time per week performing duties other than sales.

MINIMUM WAGE
The lowest wage, either by government regulation or union contract, that an employer may pay an hourly worker.

The FLSA provides that a **minimum wage** of a specified amount (currently, $5.15 per hour) must be paid to employees in covered industries. Congress periodically revises this minimum wage.[4] Under the FLSA, the term *wages* includes the reasonable cost of the employer in furnishing employees with board, lodging, and other facilities if they are customarily furnished by that employer.

Labor Unions

In the 1930s, in addition to wage-hour laws, the government also enacted the first of several labor laws. These laws protect employees' rights to join labor unions, to bargain with management over the terms and conditions of employment, and to conduct strikes.

FEDERAL LABOR LAWS

Federal labor laws governing union-employer relations have developed considerably since the first law was enacted in 1932. Initially, the laws were concerned with protecting the rights and interests of workers. Subsequent legislation placed some restraints on unions and granted rights to employers. We look here at four major federal statutes regulating union-employer relations.

Norris-LaGuardia Act In 1932, Congress protected peaceful strikes, picketing, and boycotts in the Norris-LaGuardia Act.[5] The statute restricted the power of federal courts to issue injunctions against unions engaged in peaceful strikes. In effect, this act established a national policy permitting employees to organize.

National Labor Relations Act One of the foremost statutes regulating labor is the National Labor Relations Act (NLRA) of 1935.[6] This act established the rights of employees to engage in collective bargaining and to strike. The act also specifically defined a number of employer practices as unfair to labor:

4. Note that many state and local governments also have minimum-wage laws; these laws provide for higher minimum-wage rates than that required by the federal government.
5. 29 U.S.C. Sections 101–110, 113–115.
6. 20 U.S.C. Section 151.

① Interference with the efforts of employees to form, join, or assist labor organizations or interference with the efforts of employees to engage in concerted activities for their mutual aid or protection.

② An employer's domination of a labor organization or contribution of financial or other support to it.

③ Discrimination based on union affiliation in the hiring or awarding of tenure to employees.

④ Discrimination against employees for filing charges under the act or giving testimony under the act.

⑤ Refusal to bargain collectively with the duly designated representative of the employees.

The act also created the National Labor Relations Board (NLRB) to oversee union elections and to prevent employers from engaging in unfair and illegal union activities and unfair labor practices. The NLRB has the authority to investigate employees' charges of unfair labor practices and to serve complaints against employers in response to these charges. The NLRB may also issue cease-and-desist orders—orders compelling employers to cease engaging in the unfair practices—when violations are found. Cease-and-desist orders can be enforced by a circuit court of appeals if necessary. Arguments over alleged unfair labor practices are first decided by the NLRB and may then be appealed to a federal court.

To be protected under the NLRA, an individual must be an "employee," as that term is defined in the statute. Courts have long held that job applicants fall within the definition (otherwise, the NLRA's ban on discrimination in hiring would mean nothing).

Labor-Management Relations Act The Labor-Management Relations Act (LMRA) of 1947[7] was passed to proscribe certain unfair union practices, such as the *closed shop*. A **closed shop** requires union membership by its workers as a condition of employment. Although the act made the closed shop illegal, it preserved the legality of the union shop. A **union shop** does not require membership as a prerequisite for employment but can, and usually does, require that workers join the union after a specified amount of time on the job.

CLOSED SHOP
A firm that requires union membership by its workers as a condition of employment. The closed shop was made illegal by the Labor-Management Relations Act of 1947.

UNION SHOP
A place of employment where all workers, once employed, must become union members within a specified period of time as a condition of their continued employment.

RIGHT-TO-WORK LAW
A state law providing that employees may not be required to join a union as a condition of retaining employment.

The LMRA also prohibited unions from refusing to bargain with employers, engaging in certain types of picketing, and *featherbedding*—causing employers to hire more employees than necessary. The act also allowed individual states to pass their own **right-to-work laws**—laws making it illegal for union membership to be required for *continued* employment in any establishment. Thus, union shops are technically illegal in states with right-to-work laws.

Labor-Management Reporting and Disclosure Act In 1959, Congress enacted the Labor-Management Reporting and Disclosure Act (LMRDA).[8] The act established an employee bill of rights and reporting requirements for union activities. The act strictly regulates unions' internal business procedures. Union elections, for example, are regulated by the LMRDA, which requires that regularly scheduled elections of officers be held and that secret ballots be used. Ex-convicts and Communists are prohibited from holding union office. Moreover, union officials are accountable for union property and funds. Members have the right to attend and to participate in union meetings, to nominate officers, and to vote in most union proceedings.

7. 29 U.S.C. Sections 141 *et seq.*
8. 29 U.S.C. Sections 401 *et seq.*

SECONDARY BOYCOTT
A union's refusal to work for, purchase from, or handle the products of a secondary employer, with whom the union has no dispute, in order to force that employer to stop doing business with the primary employer, with whom the union has a labor dispute.

HOT-CARGO AGREEMENT
An agreement in which employers voluntarily agree with unions not to handle, use, or deal in other employers' goods that were not produced by union employees; a type of secondary boycott explicitly prohibited by the Labor-Management Reporting and Disclosure Act of 1959.

The act also made all secondary boycotts illegal. In a **secondary boycott**, a union refuses to work for, purchase from, or handle the products of a secondary employer, with whom the union has no dispute, in an attempt to force that employer to stop doing business with the primary employer, with whom the union has a labor dispute. The act also outlawed **hot-cargo agreements**, in which employers voluntarily agree with unions not to handle, use, or deal in other employers' goods that were not produced by union employees.

UNION ORGANIZATION

Suppose that the workers of a particular firm want to join a union. How is a union formed? Typically, the first step in the process is to have the workers sign authorization cards. An authorization card usually states that the worker desires to have a certain union, such as the American Federation of Labor and Congress of Industrial Organizations (AFL-CIO), represent the work force. If those in favor of the union can obtain authorization cards from a majority of the workers, they may present the cards to the employer and ask the employer to recognize the union formally. If the employer refuses to do so, the union organizers (unionizers) can petition the NLRB for an election.

Union Elections For an election to be held, the unionizers must demonstrate that at least 30 percent of the workers to be represented support a union or an election on unionization. The NLRB supervises the election and ensures secret voting and voter eligibility. If the election is a fair one and if the proposed union receives majority support, the NLRB certifies the union as the bargaining representative for the employees.

Union Election Campaigns Many labor-management disputes arise during union election campaigns. Generally, the employer has control over unionizing activities that take place on company property and during working hours. Employers may thus limit the campaign activities of union supporters. For example, an employer may prohibit all solicitations and pamphlets on company property as long as the employer has a legitimate business reason for doing so. An owner of a department store, for instance, can prohibit all solicitation in areas of the store open to the public because union campaign activities in these circumstances could seriously interfere with the store's business. The employer may not, however, discriminate in its prohibition against solicitation in the workplace. For example, the employer could not prohibit union solicitation but allow solicitation for charitable causes. Additionally, companies may not prevent union-related solicitation in work areas as long as the activity is conducted outside working hours—during lunch hours or coffee breaks, for example.

ETHICAL ISSUE 34.1

Is an employer's e-mail system a "work area"?

An emerging issue has to do with whether employers, if they allow employees to use company-owned e-mail systems for nonbusiness purposes, must permit employees to use e-mail to exchange messages related to unionization or union activities. In the few cases involving this issue, the NLRB has ruled that, in these circumstances, employees may use e-mail for communicating union-related messages. Suppose, however, that a company's policy prohibits employees from using e-mail for nonbusiness purposes. Given that employees are permitted to engage in union-related solicitation in work areas as long as they are on a break from work, should they also be able to use their employer's e-mail system while on a break? Is an e-mail system a "work area"?

To date, the NLRB has not ruled on this question, which clearly involves issues of fairness—for both employers and employees. Even if the NLRB were to decide that an employer's e-mail system is a work area, questions would remain. For example, what if an employee sends a union-related e-mail message while on a break, but the employee receiving it, without knowing its contents, opens it during working hours? Can anything be done to prevent this kind of situation from occurring?

An employer may also campaign among its workers against the union, but the NLRB carefully monitors and regulates campaign tactics by management. Otherwise, management might use its economic power to coerce the workers into voting against unionization. For example, an employer might tell its workers, "If the union wins, you'll all be fired." The NLRB prohibits employers from making such threats. If the employer issues threats or engages in other unfair labor practices, the NLRB may certify the union even though it lost the election. Alternatively, the NLRB may ask a court to order a new election.

Collective Bargaining

If a fair election is held and the union wins, the NLRB will certify the union as the *exclusive bargaining representative* of the workers. The central legal right of a union is to engage in collective bargaining on the members' behalf. **Collective bargaining** can be defined as the process by which labor and management negotiate the terms and conditions of employment, including wages, benefits, working conditions, and other matters. Collective bargaining allows union representatives to be elected by union members and to speak on behalf of the members at the bargaining table.

COLLECTIVE BARGAINING
The process by which labor and management negotiate the terms and conditions of employment, including working hours and workplace conditions.

When a union is officially recognized, it may make a demand to bargain with the employer and negotiate new terms or conditions of employment. In collective bargaining, as in most other business negotiations, each side uses its economic power to pressure or persuade the other side to grant concessions.

Bargaining is a somewhat vague term. Bargaining does not mean that one side must give in to the other or that compromises must be made. It does mean that a demand to bargain with the employer must be taken seriously and that both sides must bargain in "good faith." Good faith bargaining means that management, for example, must be willing to meet with union representatives and consider the union's wishes when negotiating a contract. Examples of bad faith bargaining on the part of management include engaging in a campaign among workers to undermine the union, constantly shifting positions on disputed contract terms, and sending bargainers who lack authority to commit the company to a contract. If an employer (or a union) refuses to bargain in good faith without justification, it has committed an unfair labor practice, and the other party may petition the NLRB for an order requiring good faith bargaining.

Strikes

Even when labor and management have bargained in good faith, they may be unable to reach a final agreement. When extensive collective bargaining has been conducted and an impasse results, the union may call a strike against the employer to pressure it into making concessions. A **strike** occurs when the unionized workers leave their jobs and refuse to work. The workers also typically picket the plant, standing outside the facility with signs that complain of management's unfairness.

STRIKE
An action undertaken by unionized workers when collective bargaining fails; the workers leave their jobs, refuse to work, and (typically) picket the employer's workplace.

A strike is an extreme action. Striking workers lose their rights to be paid, and management loses production and may lose customers, whose orders cannot be filled.

Striking workers picket to publicize their labor dispute. Why is the right to strike important to unions?

Labor law regulates the circumstances and conduct of strikes. Most strikes take the form of "economic strikes," which are initiated because the union wants a better contract. A union may also strike when the employer has engaged in unfair labor practices.

The right to strike is guaranteed by the NLRA, within limits, and strike activities, such as picketing, are protected by the free speech guarantee of the First Amendment to the Constitution. Nonworkers have a right to participate in picketing an employer. The NLRA also gives workers the right to refuse to cross a picket line of fellow workers who are engaged in a lawful strike. Employers are permitted to hire replacement workers to substitute for the workers who are on strike.

An important issue concerns the rights of strikers after a strike ends. In a typical economic strike over working conditions, the strikers have no right to return to their jobs. If satisfactory replacement workers are found, the strikers may find themselves out of work. The law does prohibit the employer from discriminating against former strikers, however. Employers must give former strikers preferential rights to any new vacancies that arise and must also retain their seniority rights. Different rules apply when a union strikes because the employer has engaged in unfair labor practices. In this situation, the employer may still hire replacements but must give the strikers back their jobs once the strike is over.

Worker Health and Safety

Under the common law, employees injured on the job had to rely on tort law or contract law theories in suits they brought against their employers. Additionally, workers had some recourse under the common law governing agency relationships (discussed in Chapter 24), which imposes a duty on a principal-employer to provide a safe workplace for an agent-employee. Today, numerous state and federal statutes protect employees and their families from the risk of accidental injury, death, or disease resulting from their employment. This section discusses the primary federal statute governing health and safety in the workplace, along with state workers' compensation acts.

THE OCCUPATIONAL SAFETY AND HEALTH ACT

At the federal level, the primary legislation for employee health and safety protection is the Occupational Safety and Health Act of 1970.[9] Congress passed this act in an attempt to ensure safe and healthful working conditions for practically every employee in the country. The act provides for specific standards that employers must meet, plus a general duty to keep workplaces safe.

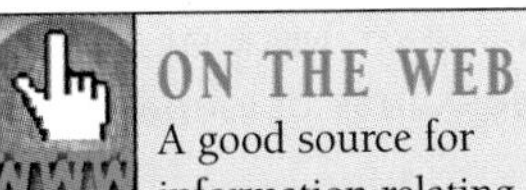

ON THE WEB

A good source for information relating to workplace health and safety is OSHA's Web site, which includes, among other things, the text of the Occupational Safety and Health Act of 1970, OSHA's regulatory standards and regulations, and instructions on how to file OSHA complaints. Go to

http://www.osha.gov.

Enforcement Agencies Three federal agencies develop and enforce the standards set by the Occupational Safety and Health Act. The Occupational Safety and Health Administration (OSHA) is part of the Department of Labor and has the authority to promulgate standards, make inspections, and enforce the act. OSHA has developed safety standards governing many workplace details, such as the structural stability of ladders and the requirements for railings. OSHA also establishes standards that protect employees against exposure to substances that may be harmful to their health.

The National Institute for Occupational Safety and Health is part of the Department of Health and Human Services. Its main duty is to conduct research on safety and

9. 29 U.S.C. Sections 553, 651–678.

health problems and to recommend standards for OSHA to adopt. Finally, the Occupational Safety and Health Review Commission is an independent agency set up to handle appeals from actions taken by OSHA administrators.

BE AWARE To check for compliance with safety standards without being cited for violations, an employer can often obtain advice from an insurer, a trade association, or a state agency.

Procedures and Violations OSHA compliance officers may enter and inspect facilities of any establishment covered by the Occupational Safety and Health Act.[10] Employees may also file complaints of violations. Under the act, an employer cannot discharge an employee who files a complaint or who, in good faith, refuses to work in a high-risk area if bodily harm or death might result.

Employers with eleven or more employees are required to keep occupational injury and illness records for each employee. Each record must be made available for inspection when requested by an OSHA inspector. Whenever a work-related injury or disease occurs, employers must make reports directly to OSHA. Whenever an employee is killed in a work-related accident or when five or more employees are hospitalized in one accident, the employer must notify the Department of Labor within forty-eight hours. If the company fails to do so, it will be fined. Following the accident, a complete inspection of the premises is mandatory.

Criminal penalties for willful violation of the Occupational Safety and Health Act are limited. Employers may be prosecuted under state laws, however. In other words, the act does not preempt state and local criminal laws.[11]

Workers' Compensation

WORKERS' COMPENSATION LAWS State statutes establishing an administrative procedure for compensating workers' injuries that arise out of—or in the course of—their employment, regardless of fault.

State **workers' compensation laws** establish an administrative procedure for compensating workers injured on the job. Instead of suing, an injured worker files a claim with the administrative agency or board that administers local workers' compensation claims.

Most workers' compensation statutes are similar. No state covers all employees. Typically excluded are domestic workers, agricultural workers, temporary employees, and employees of common carriers (companies that provide transportation services to the public). Typically, the statutes cover minors. Usually, the statutes allow employers to purchase insurance from a private insurer or a state fund to pay workers' compensation benefits in the event of a claim. Most states also allow employers to be self-insured—that is, employers who show an ability to pay claims do not need to buy insurance.

In general, the right to recover benefits is predicated wholly on the existence of an employment relationship and the fact that the injury was *accidental* and *occurred on the job or in the course of employment,* regardless of fault. Intentionally inflicted self-injury, for example, would not be considered accidental and hence would not be covered. If an injury occurred while an employee was commuting to or from work, it usually would not be considered to have occurred on the job or in the course of employment and hence would not be covered.

An employee must notify her or his employer promptly (usually within thirty days) of an injury. Generally, an employee must also file a workers' compensation claim with the appropriate state agency or board within a certain period (sixty days to two years) from the time the injury is first noticed, rather than from the time of the accident.

10. In the past, warrantless inspections were conducted. In 1978, however, the United States Supreme Court held that warrantless inspections violated the warrant clause of the Fourth Amendment to the Constitution. See *Marshall v. Barlow's, Inc.,* 436 U.S. 307, 98 S.Ct. 1816, 56 L.Ed.2d 305 (1978).

11. *Pedraza v. Shell Oil Co.,* 942 F.2d 48 (1st Cir. 1991), *cert.* denied, *Shell Oil Co. v. Pedraza,* 502 U.S. 1082, 112 S.Ct. 993, 117 L.Ed.2d 154 (1992).

An employee's acceptance of workers' compensation benefits bars the employee from suing for injuries caused by the employer's negligence. By barring lawsuits for negligence, workers' compensation laws also bar employers from raising common law defenses to negligence, such as contributory negligence, assumption of risk, or injury caused by a "fellow servant" (another employee). A worker may sue an employer who *intentionally* injures the worker, however.

The court in the following case considered whether an employee's injury in an automobile accident arose out of and in the course of employment for purposes of workers' compensation.

CASE 34.1 Rogers v. Pacesetter Corp.

Missouri Court of Appeals,
Eastern District,
Division 4, 1998.
972 S.W.2d 540.
http://www.osca.state.mo.us/courts/pubopinions.nsf [a]

COMPANY PROFILE *Pacesetter Corporation, which has been in the home-improvement business since 1962, calls itself "America's Leading Home Improvement Company!" Pacesetter sells a range of building supplies, including cabinet refacing, doors, siding, windows, and patio awnings and covers. The company designs, manufactures, finances the purchase of, installs, guarantees, and services its products, which are advertised as durable and energy efficient.*

FACTS Sean Rogers was a manager for Pacesetter Corporation. He worked at the Pacesetter offices from 9:00 A.M. to 9:00 P.M. Mondays through Fridays and 10:00 A.M. to 4:00 P.M. Saturdays. He also worked at home, drafting ads and conducting performance reviews, because he did not have enough time to do all of his work at the office. At the invitation of Rogers's supervisor, Rogers and the supervisor met at the River Port Club, a bar, to discuss a promotion. They met on a Monday, when Rogers normally conducted performance reviews at home, which he planned to do after leaving the bar. While driving home, Rogers was injured in an automobile accident. He filed a claim for workers' compensation with the Missouri Division of Workers' Compensation. After a hearing, the administrative law judge awarded Rogers temporary compensation for a permanent partial disability. Pacesetter appealed to the Missouri Labor and Industrial Relations Commission, which reversed the award. Rogers appealed to a Missouri state court.

a. This page contains links to some of the opinions of the Missouri state courts. Click on "Eastern Appellate District." When that page opens, click on "Search Opinions." In the "Search for the following word(s)" box, type "Pacesetter." From the results, click on the *Rogers* case name to access the opinion. This Web site is maintained by the Missouri Office of State Courts Administrator.

ISSUE Did Rogers's injury arise out of and in the course of employment for purposes of workers' compensation?

DECISION Yes. The court reversed the decision of the commission and remanded the case for the entry of an award of compensation.

REASON The court explained that compensation for an injury that occurs while an employee is traveling home is appropriate "when it can genuinely * * * be said that the home has become part of the employment premises." The court pointed out that Rogers regularly worked at home because he did not have sufficient time to do the work at his employer's offices and that Rogers typically conducted the performance reviews on Monday nights at home. The court stated that the work done by Rogers at home "was an integral part of the conduct of his employer's business." Pacesetter received a benefit by Rogers's working at home. The court concluded that the demands of Rogers's employment "created the expectation that work needed to be done at home for the benefit of his employer."

FOR CRITICAL ANALYSIS—Social Consideration *Should workers' compensation be denied to a worker who is injured off the employer's premises, regardless of the reason the worker is off the premises?*

Income Security

Federal and state governments participate in insurance programs designed to protect employees and their families by covering the financial impact of retirement, disability, death, hospitalization, and unemployment. The key federal law on this subject is the Social Security Act of 1935.[12]

SOCIAL SECURITY AND MEDICARE

The Social Security Act provides for old-age (retirement), survivors, and disability insurance. The act is therefore often referred to as OASDI. Both employers and employees must "contribute" under the Federal Insurance Contributions Act (FICA)[13] to help pay for the employees' loss of income on retirement. The basis for the employee's and the employer's contribution is the employee's annual wage base—the maximum amount of the employee's wages that are subject to the tax. The employer withholds the employee's FICA contribution from the employee's wages and then matches this contribution. (In 2002, employers were required to withhold 6.2 percent of each employee's wages, up to a maximum wage base of $84,900, and to match this contribution.)

BE AWARE Social Security currently covers almost all jobs in the United States. Nine out of ten workers contribute to this protection for themselves and their families.

Retired workers are then eligible to receive monthly payments from the Social Security Administration, which administers the Social Security Act. Social Security benefits are fixed by statute but increase automatically with increases in the cost of living.

Medicare, a health-insurance program, is administered by the Social Security Administration for people sixty-five years of age and older and for some under the age of sixty-five who are disabled. It has two parts, one pertaining to hospital costs and the other to nonhospital medical costs, such as visits to doctors' offices. People who have Medicare hospital insurance can also obtain additional federal medical insurance if they pay small monthly premiums, which increase as the cost of medical care increases. As with Social Security contributions, both the employer and the employee contribute to Medicare. Currently, 2.9 percent of the amount of *all* wages and salaries paid to employees goes toward financing Medicare. Unlike Social Security contributions, there is no cap on the amount of wages subject to the Medicare tax.

One issue that has arisen under FICA and the Federal Unemployment Tax Act (FUTA) (discussed later in this chapter) is whether wages should be taxed according to the rates in effect when the wages are owed or the rates in effect when the wages are actually paid. The amounts in dispute can be large, as the following case illustrates.

12. 42 U.S.C. Sections 301–1397e.
13. 26 U.S.C. Sections 3101–3125.

CASE 34.2 United States v. Cleveland Indians Baseball Co.

Supreme Court of the United States, 2001.
532 U.S. 200,
121 S.Ct. 1433,
149 L.Ed.2d 401.
http://supct.law.cornell.edu/supct/cases/historic.htm[a]

a. In the "Search" box, type "Cleveland Indians," select "Current decisions only," and click on "submit." In the result, scroll to the name of the case and click on it to access the opinion. The Legal Information Institute of Cornell Law School in Ithaca, New York, maintains this Web site.

HISTORICAL AND ECONOMIC SETTING *In any given year, the amount of FICA and FUTA tax owed depends on two factors: the tax rate and the ceiling on taxable wages (also called the wage base), which limits the amount of wages subject to tax. The rates and the ceilings increase over time. For example, in 1986, the FICA tax on employees and employers was 5.7 percent on wages up to $42,000; in 1987, it was 5.7 percent on wages up to $43,800; and in 1994, 6.2 percent on*

CASE 34.2—Continued

wages up to $60,600. The Medicare tax on employees and employers remained constant at 1.45 percent each from 1986 to 1994, but the wage base rose from $42,000 in 1986 to $43,800 in 1987, and by 1994, Congress had abolished the ceiling, subjecting all wages to the Medicare tax. In 1986 and 1987, the FUTA tax was 6.0 percent on wages up to $7,000; in 1994, it was 6.2 percent on wages up to $7,000.

FACTS In 1994, the Major League Baseball Players Association settled a grievance with twenty-six major league baseball teams for conspiring to stop the steep escalation of salaries for free agent players. Several teams agreed to pay a total of $280 million to the players. Under the agreement, the Cleveland Indians Baseball Company owed eight players a total of $610,000 in salary for 1986, and fourteen players a total of $1,457,848 for 1987. The company paid the amounts in 1994. The company also paid taxes on the amounts according to the 1994 rates and ceilings and then applied for a refund of more than $100,000, claiming that the taxes should have been computed according to the 1986 and 1987 rates and ceilings.[b] The Internal Revenue Service (IRS) denied the claim, and the company filed a suit in a federal district court against the federal government. The court ordered a refund of the FICA and FUTA taxes. The government appealed to the U.S. Court of Appeals for the Sixth Circuit, which affirmed the lower court's order. The government appealed to the United States Supreme Court.

b. All but one of the players had collected wages from the company exceeding the ceilings in 1986 and 1987. Because those players, and the company, paid the maximum amount of employment taxes in 1986 and 1987, allocating the 1994 payments back to those years would mean that they would not owe taxes on the amounts. Treating the back wages as taxable in 1994, however, would incur significant tax liability, partly because the company did not pay any of the players any other wages in 1994.

ISSUE Should wages be taxed by reference to the year that they are actually paid?

DECISION Yes. The United States Supreme Court held that taxes on wages should be computed using the rates and ceilings that apply in the year when the wages are actually paid, not those in effect in the year when the wages should have been paid. The Court reversed the decision of the lower court.

REASON The United States Supreme Court deferred to the IRS's long-standing, "steady" interpretation of the FICA and FUTA tax provisions and the IRS's own regulations. The regulations specify that the applicable employer tax is determined at the time the wages are paid by the employer, not when they were earned. In other words, the tax "is computed by applying to the wages paid by the employer the rate in effect at the time such wages are paid." The regulations do not specifically mention back wages, but the Court pointed out that the IRS "has consistently interpreted them to require taxation of back wages according to the year the wages are actually paid, regardless of when those wages were earned or should have been paid."

FOR CRITICAL ANALYSIS—Political Consideration *In this case the rule applied by the Court disadvantaged the taxpayer; in other cases, it has disadvantaged the government. With that in mind, what was Congress's likely intent regarding the FICA and FUTA tax provisions?*

PRIVATE PENSION PLANS

Significant legislation has been enacted to regulate employee retirement plans set up by employers to supplement Social Security benefits. The major federal act covering these retirement plans is the Employee Retirement Income Security Act (ERISA) of 1974.[14] This act empowers the Labor Management Services Administration of the Department of Labor to enforce its provisions governing employers who have private pension funds for their employees. ERISA does not require an employer to establish a pension plan. When a plan exists, however, ERISA establishes standards for its management.

VESTING
The creation of an absolute or unconditional right or power.

A key provision of ERISA concerns vesting. **Vesting** gives an employee a legal right to receive pension benefits at some future date when he or she stops working. Before ERISA was enacted, some employees who had worked for companies for as long as

14. 29 U.S.C. Sections 1001 *et seq.*

thirty years received no pension benefits when their employment terminated, because those benefits had not vested. ERISA establishes complex vesting rules. Generally, however, all employee contributions to pension plans vest immediately, and employee rights to employer contributions to a plan vest after five years of employment.

In an attempt to prevent mismanagement of pension funds, ERISA has established rules on how they must be invested. Pension managers must be cautious in their investments and refrain from investing more than 10 percent of the fund in securities of the employer. ERISA also contains detailed record-keeping and reporting requirements.

UNEMPLOYMENT INSURANCE

WATCH OUT A state government can place a lien on the property of an employer that does not pay unemployment taxes.

The United States has a system of unemployment insurance in which employers pay into a fund, the proceeds of which are paid out to qualified unemployed workers. The Federal Unemployment Tax Act (FUTA) of 1935[15] created a state-administered system that provides unemployment compensation to eligible individuals. The FUTA and state laws require employers that fall under the provisions of the act to pay unemployment taxes at regular intervals.

To be eligible for unemployment compensation, a worker must be willing and able to work and be actively seeking employment. Workers who have been fired for misconduct or who have voluntarily left their jobs are not eligible for benefits. Workers who can prove that they have been wrongfully discharged (wrongful discharge will be discussed later in this chapter), however, may be able to collect unemployment compensation.

COBRA

Federal legislation also addresses the issue of health insurance for workers whose jobs have been terminated—and who are thus no longer eligible for group health-insurance plans. The Consolidated Omnibus Budget Reconciliation Act (COBRA) of 1985[16] prohibits the elimination of a worker's medical, optical, or dental insurance coverage on the voluntary or involuntary termination of the worker's employment. Employers, with some exceptions, must comply with COBRA if they employ twenty or more workers and provide a benefit plan to those workers. An employer must inform employees of COBRA's provisions when a group health plan is established and must also inform a worker of the provisions if he or she faces termination or a reduction of hours that would affect his or her eligibility for coverage under the plan.

The worker has sixty days (beginning with the date that the group coverage would stop) to decide whether to continue with the employer's group insurance plan. If the worker chooses to discontinue the coverage, the employer has no further obligation. If the worker chooses to continue coverage, however, the employer is obligated to keep the policy active for up to eighteen months. If the worker is disabled, the employer must extend coverage up to twenty-nine months. The coverage provided must be the same as that enjoyed by the worker prior to the termination or reduction of work. If family members were originally included, for example, COBRA would prohibit their exclusion. The worker does not receive a free ride, however. To receive continued benefits, she or he may be required to pay all of the premium, as well as a 2 percent administrative charge.

15. 26 U.S.C. Sections 3301–3310.
16. 29 U.S.C. Sections 1161–1169.

The employer is relieved of the responsibility to provide benefit coverage if it completely eliminates its group benefit plan. An employer is also relieved of responsibility when the worker becomes eligible for Medicare, becomes covered under a spouse's health plan, becomes insured under a different plan (with a new employer, for example), or fails to pay the premium. An employer that does not comply with COBRA risks substantial penalties, such as a tax of up to 10 percent of the annual cost of the group plan or $500,000, whichever is less.

Family and Medical Leave

"It is the job of the legislature to follow the spirit of the nation, provided it is not contrary to the principles of government."

CHARLES-LOUIS DE SECONDAT, Baron de Montesquieu, 1689–1755 (French philosopher and jurist)

In 1993, Congress passed the Family and Medical Leave Act (FMLA)[17] to allow employees to take time off work for family or medical reasons. A majority of the states also have legislation allowing for a leave from employment for family or medical reasons, and many employers maintain private family-leave plans for their workers.

COVERAGE AND APPLICABILITY OF THE FMLA

The FMLA requires employers who have fifty or more employees to provide employees with up to twelve weeks of unpaid family or medical leave during any twelve-month period. During the employee's leave, the employer must continue the worker's health-care coverage and guarantee employment in the same position or a comparable position when the employee returns to work. An important exception to the FMLA, however, allows the employer to avoid reinstating of a *key employee*—defined as an employee whose pay falls within the top 10 percent of the firm's work force. Additionally, the act does not apply to employees who have worked less than one year or less than twenty-five hours a week during the previous twelve months.

Generally, an employee may take family leave to care for a newborn baby, an adopted child, or a foster child.[18] An employee may take medical leave when the employee or the employee's spouse, child, or parent has a "serious health condition" requiring care. For most absences, the employee must demonstrate that the health condition requires continued treatment by a health-care provider and includes a period of incapacity of more than three days.

Under regulations issued by the Department of Labor in 1995, employees suffering from certain chronic health conditions may take FMLA leave for their own incapacities that require absences of less than three days. For example, an employee who has asthma or diabetes may have periodic episodes of illness, rather than episodes continuing over an extended period of time. Similarly, pregnancy may involve periodic visits to a health-care provider and episodes of morning sickness. According to the regulations, employees with such conditions are covered by the FMLA.

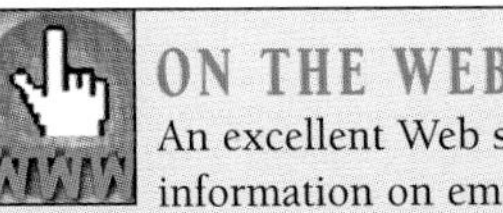

ON THE WEB
An excellent Web site for information on employee benefits—including the full text of relevant statutes, such as the FMLA or COBRA, as well as case law and current articles—is BenefitsLink. Go to **http://www.benefitslink.com/index.shtml**.

VIOLATIONS OF THE FMLA

An employer who violates the FMLA may be held liable for damages to compensate an employee for unpaid wages (or salary), lost benefits, denied compensation, and actual monetary losses (such as the cost of providing for care) up to an amount equivalent to the employee's wages for twelve weeks. The employer may also be required to reinstate an employee in her or his job or grant a promotion that had been denied. A successful

17. 29 U.S.C. Sections 2601, 2611–2619, 2651–2654.
18. The foster care must be state sanctioned before such an arrangement falls within the coverage of the FMLA.

plaintiff is also entitled to court costs; attorneys' fees; and, in cases involving bad faith on the part of the employer, double damages.

The FMLA defines an "employer" as "any person who acts, directly or indirectly, in the interest of an employer to any of the employees of such employer." Because of this broad definition, supervisors may be subject to personal liability, as employers, for violations of the act.[19]

Employee Privacy Rights

"We are rapidly entering the age of no privacy, where everyone is open to surveillance at all times; where there are no secrets."

WILLIAM O. DOUGLAS, 1898–1980 (Associate justice of the United States Supreme Court, 1939–1975)

In the last two decades, concerns about the privacy rights of employees have arisen in response to the sometimes invasive tactics used by employers to monitor and screen workers. Perhaps the greatest privacy concern in today's employment arena has to do with electronic performance monitoring. Clearly, employers need to protect themselves from liability for their employees' online activities. They also have a legitimate interest in monitoring the productivity of their workers. At the same time, employees expect to have a certain zone of privacy in the workplace. Indeed, many lawsuits have involved allegations that employers' intrusive monitoring practices violate employees' privacy rights.

ELECTRONIC MONITORING IN THE WORKPLACE

According to a recent survey by the American Management Association, more than two-thirds of employers engage in some form of surveillance of their employees.[20] The types of surveillance used are listed in Exhibit 34–1.

A variety of specially designed software products have made it easier for an employer to track employees' Internet use. For example, software is now available that allows an employer to track virtually every move made using the Internet, including the specific Web sites visited and the time spent surfing the Web. Often, employer security measures involve the use of filtering software as well. As discussed in Chapter 2, this software prevents access to specified Web sites, such as sites containing pornographic or sexually explicit images. Other filtering software may be used to screen incoming e-mail and block mail that consists of spam or that may contain a virus.

19. See, for example, *Rupnow v. TRC, Inc.*, 999 F.Supp. 1046 (N.D.Ohio 1998).

20. For a discussion of this survey and its results, see Allison R. Michael and Scott M. Lidman, "Monitoring of Employees Still Growing," *The National Law Journal*, January 29, 2001, p. B9.

EXHIBIT 34–1 ELECTRONIC MONITORING IN THE WORKPLACE

TYPE OF MONITORING	PERCENTAGE OF EMPLOYERS USING EACH TYPE
Storage and review of e-mail	27%
Storage and review of computer files	21%
Video recording of employee job performance	16%
Recording and review of telephone conversations	11%
Storage and review of voice mail messages	6%

Source: American Management Association, 2000.

The use of filtering software by public employers (government agencies) has led to charges that blocking access to Web sites violates employees' rights to free speech, which are guaranteed by the First Amendment to the Constitution. Although the use of filtering software by government institutions has been controversial, this issue does not arise in private businesses because the First Amendment's protection of free speech applies only to *government* restraints on speech, not restraints imposed in the private sector.

> **ON THE WEB**
> The American Civil Liberties Union (ACLU) has a page on its Web site devoted to employee privacy rights with respect to electronic monitoring. Go to **http://www.aclu.org/library/pbr2.html**.

Laws Protecting Employee Privacy Rights Recall from Chapter 2 that the U.S. Constitution does not contain a provision that explicitly guarantees a right to privacy. A personal right to privacy, however, has been inferred from other constitutional guarantees provided by the First, Third, Fourth, Fifth, and Ninth Amendments to the Constitution. Tort law (see Chapter 4), state constitutions, and a number of state and federal statutes also provide for privacy rights.

The major statute with which employers must comply is the Electronic Communications Privacy Act (ECPA) of 1986.[21] This act amended existing federal wiretapping law to cover electronic forms of communications, such as communications via cellular telephones or e-mail. The ECPA prohibits the intentional interception of any wire or electronic communication or the intentional disclosure or use of the information obtained by the interception. Excluded from coverage, however, are any electronic communications through devices that are "furnished to the subscriber or user by a provider of wire or electronic communication service" and that are being used by the subscriber or user, or by the provider of the service, "in the ordinary course of its business."

This "business-extension exception" to the ECPA permits employers to monitor employee electronic communications in the ordinary course of their businesses. It does not, however, permit employers to monitor employees' personal communications. Under another exception to the ECPA, however, an employer may avoid liability under the act if the employees consent to having their electronic communications intercepted by the employer. Thus, an employer may be able to avoid liability under the ECPA by simply requiring employees to sign forms indicating that they consent to such monitoring.

Clearly, the law allows employers to engage in electronic monitoring in the workplace. In fact, cases in which courts have held that an employer's monitoring of electronic communications in the workplace violated employees' privacy rights are few and far between. Yet there are some limits on how far an employer can go in monitoring employee communications—see, for example, the case discussed in this chapter's *Business Law in the Online World* feature on the following page.

Factors Considered by the Courts in Employee Privacy Cases When determining whether an employer should be held liable for violating an employee's privacy rights, the courts generally weigh the employer's interests against the employee's reasonable expectation of privacy. Generally, if employees are informed that their communications are being monitored, they cannot reasonably expect those communications to be private. If employees are not informed that certain communications are being monitored, however, the employer may be held liable for invading their privacy.

● **EXAMPLE 34.2** In one case, an employer secretly recorded conversations among his four employees by placing a tape recorder in their common office. The conversations were of a highly personal nature and included harsh criticisms of the employer. The employer immediately fired two of the employees, informing them that their termination

21. 18 U.S.C. Sections 2510–2521.

BUSINESS LAW: //in the Online World

Cybergriping in Offsite Web Forums

Not too many years ago, employees would often gather around the office water cooler to exchange news and small talk. Their conversations might touch on anything from criticisms of management policies to the latest sports statistics to gossip about office employees. For the most part, employers were rarely concerned about these personal exchanges among employees. Today, employees are increasingly gathering around what one writer has termed "virtual water coolers"[a]—chat forums or bulletin boards on private Web sites devoted to e-gossip.

A growing concern for many companies is how to deal with cybergriping in these forums that damages a company's reputation. Employers can, of course, access these sites to learn about the concerns of their employees, providing that access is open to the public. Yet what if an employer uses a false identity to access an employee's *private* Web site? Is this legal? This question was at issue in *Konop v. Hawaiian Airlines, Inc.*,[b] a case that came before the Court of Appeals for the Ninth Circuit in 2001.

Konop's Web Site

Robert Konop, a pilot for Hawaiian Airlines, Inc., maintained a Web site on which he posted bulletins critical of his employer and others. Konop controlled access to the site by requiring visitors to log in with a user name and password. Konop provided user names to certain Hawaiian employees, but not to managers or union representatives. To obtain a password, an eligible employee had to register and consent to an agreement not to disclose the site's contents.

Hawaiian vice president James Davis, concerned about what the employees were saying about management on Konop's Web site, obtained a password by using the name of Hawaiian pilot Gene Wong, with Wong's permission. Wong had never logged into the site and had never agreed to Konop's term of nondisclosure. After Konop learned what Davis had done, he sued Hawaiian, claiming, among other things, that Davis's unauthorized viewing violated the federal Wiretap Act and the Stored Communications Act. Both of these acts had been amended by the Electronic Communications Privacy Act (ECPA) to prohibit unauthorized interception of electronic communications. The trial court granted summary judgment in favor of Hawaiian, and Konop appealed.

A Close Look at the Word *Interception*

Whether Davis had violated the acts depended on how the court interpreted the word *interception.* Does interception occur only if it takes place while information is being transmitted, as the trial court concluded? Or can interception occur after the information has been transmitted and while it is in storage on a Web server? The appellate court decided that an "electronic communication in storage is no more or less private than an electronic communication in transmission." To distinguish between the two for purposes of protection from interception, said the court, "is irrational and an insupportable result given Congress's emphasis on individual privacy rights during the passage of the ECPA."

In sum, the appellate court held that the contents of private Web sites such as Konop's are "electronic communications" in intermediate storage. As such, they are protected from unauthorized interception under the Wiretap Act and unauthorized access under the Stored Communications Act. The court reversed the trial court's decision to grant summary judgment in Hawaiian's favor and remanded the case for trial.

FOR CRITICAL ANALYSIS

Does this case mean that an unlawful interception might occur when someone views a Web page?

a. Adam Cohen, "Click Here for a Hot Rumor about Your Boss," *Time,* September 11, 2000, p. 48.
b. 236 F.3d 1035 (9th Cir. 2001).

was due to their comments on the tape. In the ensuing suit, one of the issues was whether the employees, in these circumstances, had a reasonable expectation of privacy. The court held that they did and granted summary judgment in their favor. The employees clearly would not have criticized their boss if they had not assumed their conversations were private. Furthermore, the office was small, and the employees were careful that no third parties ever overheard their comments.[22] ●

22. *Dorris v. Abscher,* 179 F.3d 420 (6th Cir. 1999).

Privacy Expectations and E-Mail Systems In cases brought by employees alleging that their privacy has been invaded by e-mail monitoring, the courts have tended to hold for the employers. This is true even when employees were not informed that their e-mail would be monitored.

• **EXAMPLE 34.3** In a leading case on this issue, the Pillsbury Company promised its employees that it would not read their e-mail or terminate or discipline them based on the content of their e-mail. Despite this promise, Pillsbury intercepted employee Michael Smyth's e-mail, decided that it was unprofessional and inappropriate, and fired him. In Pennsylvania, where the discharge occurred, it is against public policy for an employer to fire an employee based on a violation of the employee's right to privacy. In Smyth's suit against the company, he claimed that his termination was a violation of this policy. The court, however, found no "reasonable expectation of privacy in e-mail communications voluntarily made by an employee to his supervisor over the company e-mail system."[23] •

ETHICAL ISSUE 34.2

Should employees have a reasonable expectation of privacy when their e-mail is password protected?

Sometimes, when their e-mail is password protected, employees may believe that their e-mail messages are private property and that the employer has no right to intrude into this private area. Nonetheless, courts are reluctant to hold that the employees' privacy interests have been violated if employers access these materials.

In one case, for example, a Texas state court refused to recognize an invasion of privacy based on Microsoft Corporation's review and release of e-mail stored in an employee's office computer. Microsoft had suspended the employee pending an investigation into accusations of sexual harassment and other misconduct. During the suspension, Microsoft read his e-mail. After the employee was fired, he sued the employer, claiming that the e-mail, which was in "personal folders" and protected by a password, was his personal property. The court reasoned that the computer was given to the employee to enable him to do his job, and therefore the e-mail on his computer was "merely an inherent part of the office environment." While some people believe that court rulings such as this are unfair to employees, others think that to rule otherwise might be equally unfair to employers. After all, as the court noted in this case, the employer provided the employee not only with the computer but also with the network connection and the e-mail application. Additionally, argues this group, given that all e-mail is transmitted over a network and thus accessible to third parties, employees should not reasonably expect that their e-mail will be totally private.[24]

OTHER TYPES OF MONITORING

In addition to monitoring their employees' online activities, employers also engage in other types of employee screening and monitoring practices. These practices, which have included lie-detector tests, drug tests, AIDS tests, and employment screening, have often been subject to challenge as violations of employee privacy rights.

---

23. *Smyth v. Pillsbury Co.*, 914 F.Supp. 97 (E.D.Pa. 1996).
24. *McLaren v. Microsoft Corp.*, 1999 WL 339015 (Tex.App.—Dallas 1999).

A man takes a polygraph test. Why are the majority of employers prohibited, in most circumstances, from requiring their employees to take polygraph tests?

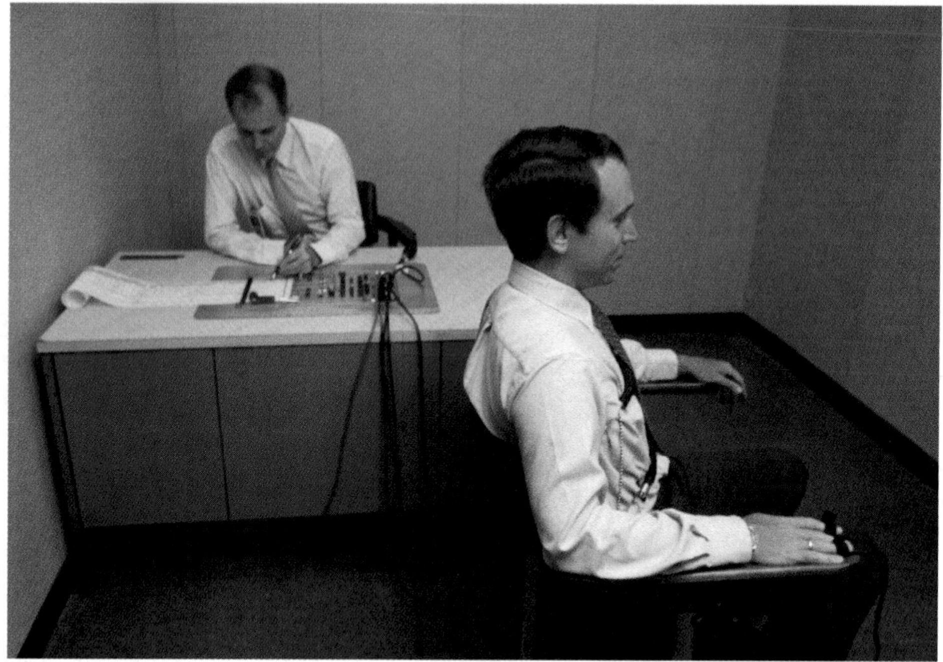

Lie-Detector Tests At one time, many employers required employees or job applicants to take polygraph examinations (lie-detector tests) in connection with their employment. To protect the privacy interests of employees and job applicants, in 1988 Congress passed the Employee Polygraph Protection Act.[25] The act prohibits employers from (1) requiring or causing employees or job applicants to take lie-detector tests or suggesting or requesting that they do so; (2) using, accepting, referring to, or asking about the results of lie-detector tests taken by employees or applicants; and (3) taking or threatening negative employment-related action against employees or applicants based on results of lie-detector tests or on their refusal to take the tests.

Employers excepted from these prohibitions include federal, state, and local government employers; certain security service firms; and companies manufacturing and distributing controlled substances. Other employers may use polygraph tests when investigating losses attributable to theft, including embezzlement and the theft of trade secrets.

Drug Testing In the interests of public safety and to reduce unnecessary costs, many employers, including the government, require their employees to submit to drug testing. State laws relating to the privacy rights of private-sector employees vary from state to state. Some state constitutions may prohibit private employers from testing for drugs, and state statutes may restrict drug testing by private employers in any number of ways. A collective bargaining agreement may also provide protection against drug testing. In some instances, employees have brought an action against the employer for the tort of invasion of privacy (discussed in Chapter 4).

Constitutional limitations apply to the testing of government employees. The Fourth Amendment provides that individuals have the right to be "secure in their persons" against "unreasonable searches and seizures" conducted by government agents.

25. 29 U.S.C. Sections 2001 *et seq.*

Drug tests have been held constitutional, however, when there was a reasonable basis for suspecting government employees of using drugs. Additionally, when drug use in a particular government job could threaten public safety, testing has been upheld. For example, a Department of Transportation rule that requires employees engaged in oil and gas pipeline operations to submit to random drug testing was upheld, even though the rule did not require that before being tested the individual must have been suspected of drug use.[26] The court held that the government's interest in promoting public safety in the pipeline industry outweighed the employees' privacy interests.

AIDS Testing A number of employers test their workers for acquired immune deficiency syndrome (AIDS). Some state laws restrict AIDS testing, and federal statutes offer some protection to employees or job applicants who have AIDS or have tested positive for the AIDS virus. The federal Americans with Disabilities Act of 1990[27] (discussed in Chapter 35), for example, prohibits discrimination against persons with disabilities, and the term *disability* has been broadly defined to include those individuals with diseases such as AIDS. The law also requires employers to reasonably accommodate the needs of persons with disabilities. As a rule, although the law may not prohibit AIDS testing, it may prohibit the discharge of employees based on the results of those tests.

KEEP IN MIND An employer may act on the basis of any professionally developed test, provided the test relates to the employment and does not violate the law.

Screening Procedures Preemployment screening procedures are another area of concern to potential employees. What kinds of questions are permissible on an employment application or a preemployment test? What kinds of questions go too far in invading the potential employee's privacy? Is it an invasion of privacy, for example, to ask questions about the potential employee's sexual orientation or religious convictions? Although an employer may believe that such information is relevant to the job for which the individual has applied, the applicant may feel differently about the matter. Generally, questions on an employment application must have a reasonable nexus, or connection, with the job for which an applicant is applying.[28]

Employment-Related Immigration Laws

The most important immigration laws governing employer-employee relationships are the Immigration Reform and Control Act (IRCA) of 1986[29] and the Immigration Act of 1990.[30] The IRCA, which is administered by the U.S. Immigration and Naturalization Service (INS), prohibits employers from hiring illegal immigrants. Employers must complete a special form—called INS Form I-9—for each employee and indicate on it that the employer has verified that the employee is either a U.S. citizen or is otherwise entitled to work in this country.

The Immigration Act of 1990 limits the number of legal immigrants entering the United States by capping the number of visas (entry permits) that are issued each year. Under the act, employers recruiting workers from other countries must complete a certification process and satisfy the Department of Labor that there is a shortage of qualified U.S. workers capable of performing the work. The employer must also establish

26. *Electrical Workers Local 1245 v. Skinner*, 913 F.2d 1454 (9th Cir. 1990).
27. 42 U.S.C. Sections 12102–12118.
28. See, for example, *Soroka v. Dayton Hudson Corp.*, 7 Cal.App.4th 203, 1 Cal.Rptr.2d 77 (1991).
29. 29 U.S.C. Section 1802.
30. This act amended various provisions of the Immigration and Nationality Act of 1952, 8 U.S.C. Sections 1101 *et seq.*

that bringing immigrants into this country will not adversely affect the existing labor market in that particular area. In this way, the act attempts to serve two purposes: encouraging skilled workers to enter this country and at the same time restricting competition for American jobs.

Wrongful Discharge

WRONGFUL DISCHARGE An employer's termination of an employee's employment in violation of the law.

Whenever an employer discharges an employee in violation of the law, the employee may bring an action for **wrongful discharge.** An employee who is protected by a statute, such as one prohibiting employment discrimination (see Chapter 35), may bring a cause of action under that statute. If an employer's actions do not violate any statute, then the question is whether the employer has violated an employment contract or a common law doctrine.

As mentioned, under the employment-at-will doctrine, an employer may hire and fire employees at will (regardless of the employees' performance) without liability, unless the decision violates the terms of an employment contract or statutory law. Because of the harsh effects of the employment-at-will doctrine for employees, courts have carved out various exceptions to the doctrine. These exceptions are based on contract theory, tort theory, and public policy.

Exceptions Based on Contract Theory

REMEMBER An implied contract may exist if a party furnishes a service expecting to be paid, and the other party, who knows (or should know) of this expectation, has a chance to reject the service and does not.

Some courts have held that an *implied* employment contract exists between an employer and an employee. If an employee is fired outside the terms of the implied contract, he or she may succeed in an action for breach of contract even though no written employment contract exists. • **Example 34.4** An employer's manual or personnel bulletin may state that, as a matter of policy, workers will be dismissed only for good cause. If the employee is aware of this policy and continues to work for the employer, a court may find that there is an implied contract based on the terms stated in the manual or bulletin.[31] •

Promises that an employer makes to employees regarding discharge policy may also be considered part of an implied contract. If the employer fires a worker in a manner contrary to the manner promised, a court may hold that the employer has violated the implied contract and is liable for damages. A few states have gone further and held that all employment contracts contain an implied covenant of good faith. This means that both sides promise to abide by the contract in good faith. If an employer fires an employee for an arbitrary or unjustified reason, the employee can claim that the covenant of good faith was breached and the contract violated.

Generally, the key consideration in determining whether an employment manual creates an implied contractual obligation is the employee's reasonable expectations.[32] For this reason, today's employers often include disclaimers in their employment manuals. Such disclaimers usually state, clearly and conspicuously, that the manual does not modify the employer's employment-at-will policy in any way and does not provide the employee with any kind of contractual rights.

Exceptions Based on Tort Theory

In a few cases, the discharge of an employee may give rise to an action for wrongful discharge under tort theories. Abusive discharge procedures may result in intentional infliction of emotional distress or defamation. • **Example 34.5** In one case, a restaurant

31. See, for example, *Pepe v. Rival Co.,* 85 F.Supp.2d 349 (D.N.J. 1999).
32. See, for example, *Doll v. Port Authority Trans-Hudson Corp.,* 92 F.Supp.2d 416 (D.N.J. 2000).

had suffered some thefts of supplies, and the manager announced that he would start firing waitresses alphabetically until the thief was identified. The first waitress fired said that she suffered great emotional distress as a result. The state's highest court upheld her claim as stating a valid cause of action.[33] ●

EXCEPTIONS BASED ON PUBLIC POLICY

The most widespread common law exception to the employment-at-will doctrine is an exception made on the basis of public policy. Courts may apply this exception when an employer fires a worker for reasons that violate a fundamental public policy of the jurisdiction. For example, a court may prevent an employer from firing a worker who serves on a jury and therefore cannot work during her or his normally scheduled working hours.

Sometimes, an employer will direct an employee to do something that violates the law. If the employee refuses to perform the illegal act, the employer might decide to fire the worker. Similarly, employees who "blow the whistle" on the wrongdoing of their employers often find themselves disciplined or even out of a job. **Whistleblowing** occurs when an employee tells a government official, upper-management authorities, or the press that his or her employer is engaged in some unsafe or illegal activity. Whistleblowers on occasion have been protected from wrongful discharge for reasons of public policy. For example, a bank was held to have wrongfully discharged an employee who pressured the employer to comply with state and federal consumer credit laws.[34]

WHISTLEBLOWING
An employee's disclosure to a government official, upper-management authorities, or the press that the employer is engaged in unsafe or illegal activities.

The following case involved an employee who was discharged for refusing to perform an illegal act. The employee sued the company, alleging that her discharge violated public policy.

33. *Agis v. Howard Johnson Co.*, 371 Mass. 140, 355 N.E.2d 315 (1976).
34. *Harless v. First National Bank in Fairmont*, 162 W.Va. 116, 246 S.E.2d 270 (1978).

CASE 34.3 Lins v. Children's Discovery Centers of America, Inc.

Court of Appeals of Washington,
Division 2, 1999.
95 Wash.App. 486,
976 P.2d 168.
http://www.findlaw.com/11stategov/wa/waca.html[a]

FACTS Children's Discovery Centers of America, Inc. (CDC), operates child-care centers. Diane Lins was a regional director in charge of six centers in the Pacific Northwest, including the state of Washington. During her tenure, CDC promoted her and gave her good performance ratings. In March 1995, Pam French was hired to be CDC's West Coast operations director, Lins's supervisor. Less than ten days later, Lins and five of her subordinates were injured in an auto accident that occurred within the course and scope of their employment. Each employee filed a workers' compensation claim. Within two weeks of the accident, French ordered Lins to fire the other five employees. French had heard that two of them were consulting attorneys and she "didn't trust either of them not to sue the company, and she was not going to allow that to happen." She harbored similar feelings about the remaining three, even though they had not seen attorneys. A Washington state statute provides that "no employer may discharge or in any manner discriminate against any employee because such employee has filed or communicated to the employer an intent to file a claim for compensation or exercise any [related] rights." Realizing that she could not lawfully perform French's order, Lins refused to do so. On May 5, French gave Lins a poor performance rating and put her on probation. On June 22, French fired Lins for "Neglect of Duties/Poor Performance." Lins filed a suit in a Washington state court against CDC, alleging that she had been wrongfully discharged in violation of the state's public policy. CDC filed a motion for summary judgment, which the court granted. Lins appealed to a state intermediate appellate court.

a. In the "Court of Appeals: Published" section, click on "1999." When the list appears, in the group of decisions released on "May 07, 1999," find the case name (it begins "IIDiane Lins") and click on the docket number ("22424-1") to access the opinion.

(continued)

CASE 34.3—Continued

ISSUE Had Lins been wrongfully discharged in violation of the state's public policy?

DECISION Yes. The Court of Appeals of Washington reversed the decision of the lower court and remanded the case for trial.

REASON The state intermediate appellate court concluded that Lins's refusal to carry out French's order was conduct protected by public policy and thus French's retaliation was unlawful. "Public policy * * * prohibits an employer from considering certain activities when deciding whether to discharge an employee. * * * [I]t is unlawful for an employer to retaliate against an employee for protected activity." To determine what is protected, a court considers "(1) whether a clear public policy exists; (2) whether that policy will be jeopardized unless the activity in issue is protected; (3) whether employers in general have overriding justification for wanting to use the activity in issue as a factor affecting the decision to discharge; and (4) whether the particular employee's activity in the case at bar was a substantial factor in (i.e., a cause of) the particular employer's decision to discharge." The court determined that in this case, all of the factors were in Lins's favor. In particular, said the court, "employers do not have any overriding justification for wanting to consider an employee's refusal to perform an unlawful order when deciding whether to fire the employee."

FOR CRITICAL ANALYSIS—Ethical Consideration *If the courts did not create public-policy exceptions to the employment-at-will doctrine, would plaintiffs such as Lins have any legal recourse against their employers?*

Whistleblower Statutes

To encourage workers to report employer wrongdoing, such as fraud, most states have enacted so-called whistleblower statutes. These statutes protect whistleblowers from subsequent retaliation on the part of employers. On the federal level, the Whistleblower Protection Act of 1989[35] protects federal employees who blow the whistle on their employers from their employers' retaliatory actions. Whistleblower statutes may also provide an incentive to disclose information by providing the whistleblower with a monetary reward. For example, the federal False Claims Reform Act of 1986[36] requires that a whistleblower who has disclosed information relating to a fraud perpetrated against the U.S. government receive between 15 and 25 percent of the proceeds if the government brings suit against the wrongdoer.

35. 5 U.S.C. Section 1201.
36. 31 U.S.C. Sections 3729–3733. This act amended the False Claims Act of 1863.

INTERNATIONAL PERSPECTIVE

Protection for British Whistleblowers

The United Kingdom also provides legal protection for whistleblowers to some extent. The British Parliament has passed legislation protecting workers who report health and safety violations by their employers. In one case, a company dismissed a worker who reported unsafe levels of a chemical, lindane, and called in a health and safety inspector. After the company fired the worker, the worker sued the employer for violating the law protecting whistleblowers and recovered approximately $12,000 in damages.

FOR CRITICAL ANALYSIS
Why might a government be reluctant to come to the aid of all whistleblowers at all times?

APPLICATION Law and the Employer. . .

Developing an Internet Policy*

Employers that make electronic communications systems (such as access to the Internet and e-mail) available to their employees face some obvious risks. One risk is that e-mail could be used to harass other employees. Another risk is that employees could subject the employer to liability by reproducing, without authorization, copyright-protected materials on the Internet. Still another risk is that confidential information contained in e-mail messages transmitted via the Internet could be intercepted by an outside party. Finally, an employer that monitors employees' Internet use in an attempt to avoid these risks faces yet another risk: the risk of being held liable for violating the employees' privacy rights. If you are an employer and find it prudent to monitor employees' Internet use, you should take certain precautions.

Remember, just one successful lawsuit against a small company can bankrupt that firm. Even if your small company wins the suit, the legal fees incurred by defending against the claim could be devastating for your firm's profits.

Inform Your Employees of the Monitoring and Obtain Their Consent

First of all, you should notify your employees that you will be monitoring their Internet communications, including their e-mail. Second, you should ask your employees to consent, in writing, to such actions. Generally, as discussed earlier in this chapter, if employees consent to employer monitoring, they cannot claim that their privacy rights have been invaded by such practices. You will find it easier to obtain employees' consent to monitoring activities if you explain why monitoring is necessary or desirable and let them know what methods will be used to monitor Internet communications. As a rule, when employees are told the reasons for monitoring and clearly understand their rights and duties with respect to the company's communications system, they are less offended by the surveillance.

Spell Out Permissible and Impermissible Internet Uses

Employees should be told which uses of the firm's communications system are permissible and which uses are prohibited. To clarify Internet policy standards, develop a comprehensive policy setting forth your standards of Internet use and illustrate through specific examples what kind of communications activities will constitute misuses and violate the policy. It is also important to let employees know what will happen if they violate the policy. The policy might state, for example, that any employee who violates the policy will be subject to disciplinary actions, including termination.

*This *Application* is not meant to substitute for the services of an attorney who is licensed to practice law in your state.

Checklist for the Employer

1. Inform employees that their Internet communications will be monitored, why monitoring is necessary or desirable, and how it will be conducted.
2. Obtain employees' written consent to having their electronic communications monitored.
3. Develop a comprehensive policy statement indicating how Internet communications should and should not be used and the consequences of misusing the firm's communications system.

Key Terms

closed shop 902
collective bargaining 904
employment at will 899
hot-cargo agreement 903
minimum wage 901
right-to-work law 902

Chapter Summary Labor and Employment Law

Wage-Hour Laws (See pages 900–901.)	1. *Davis-Bacon Act (1931)*—Requires contractors and subcontractors working on federal government construction projects to pay their employees "prevailing wages." 2. *Walsh-Healey Act (1936)*—Requires that employees of firms that contract with federal agencies be paid a minimum wage and overtime pay. 3. *Fair Labor Standards Act (1938)*—Extended wage-hour requirements to cover all employers whose activities affect interstate commerce plus certain businesses. The act has specific requirements in regard to child labor, maximum hours, and minimum wages.
Labor Unions (See pages 901–905.)	1. *Federal labor laws*— a. Norris-LaGuardia Act (1932)—Protects peaceful strikes, picketing, and primary boycotts. b. National Labor Relations Act (1935)—Established the rights of employees to engage in collective bargaining and to strike; also defined specific employer practices as unfair to labor. The National Labor Relations Board (NLRB) was created to administer and enforce the act. c. Labor-Management Relations Act (1947)—Proscribes certain unfair union practices, such as the closed shop. d. Labor-Management Reporting and Disclosure Act (1959)—Established an employee bill of rights and reporting requirements for union activities. 2. *Union organization*—Union campaign activities and elections must comply with the requirements established by federal labor laws and the NLRB. 3. *Collective bargaining*—The process by which labor and management negotiate the terms and conditions of employment (wages, benefits, working conditions, and so on). The central legal right of a labor union is to engage in collective bargaining on the members' behalf. 4. *Strikes*—When collective bargaining reaches an impasse, union members may use their ultimate weapon in labor-management struggles—the strike. A strike occurs when unionized workers leave their jobs and refuse to work.
Worker Health and Safety (See pages 905–907.)	1. The Occupational Safety and Health Act of 1970 requires employers to meet specific safety and health standards that are established and enforced by the Occupational Safety and Health Administration (OSHA). 2. State workers' compensation laws establish an administrative procedure for compensating workers who are injured in accidents that occur on the job, regardless of fault.
Income Security (See pages 907–910.)	1. *Social Security and Medicare*—The Social Security Act of 1935 provides for old-age (retirement), survivors, and disability insurance. Both employers and employees must make contributions under the Federal Insurance Contributions Act (FICA) to help pay for the employees' loss of income on retirement. The Social Security Administration administers Medicare, a health-insurance program for older or disabled persons. 2. *Private pension plans*—The federal Employee Retirement Income Security Act (ERISA) of 1974 establishes standards for the management of employer-provided pension plans. 3. *Unemployment insurance*—The Federal Unemployment Tax Act of 1935 created a system that provides unemployment compensation to eligible individuals. Covered employers are taxed to help defray the costs of unemployment compensation.

Chapter Summary Labor and Employment Law—continued

COBRA (See pages 910–911.)	The Consolidated Omnibus Budget Reconciliation Act (COBRA) of 1985 requires employers to give employees, on termination of employment, the option of continuing their medical, optical, or dental insurance coverage for a certain period.
Family and Medical Leave (See pages 911–912.)	The Family and Medical Leave Act (FMLA) of 1993 requires employers with fifty or more employees to provide their employees (except for key employees) with up to twelve weeks of unpaid family or medical leave during any twelve-month period for the following reasons: 1. *Family leave*—May be taken to care for a newborn baby, an adopted child, or a foster child. 2. *Medical leave*—May be taken when the employee or the employee's spouse, child, or parent has a serious health condition requiring care.
Employee Privacy Rights (See pages 912–917.)	A right to privacy has been inferred from guarantees provided by the First, Third, Fourth, Fifth, and Ninth Amendments to the U.S. Constitution. State laws may also provide for privacy rights. Employer practices that are often challenged by employees as invasive of their privacy rights include electronic performance monitoring, lie-detector tests, drug testing, AIDS testing, and screening procedures.
Employment-Related Immigration Laws (See pages 917–918.)	1. *Immigration Reform and Control Act (1986)*—Prohibits employers from hiring illegal immigrants; administered by the U.S. Immigration and Naturalization Service. 2. *Immigration Act (1990)*—Limits the number of legal immigrants entering the United States by capping the number of visas (entry permits) that are issued each year.
Wrongful Discharge (See pages 918–920.)	Wrongful discharge occurs whenever an employer discharges an employee in violation of the law or of an employment contract. To protect employees from some of the harsh results of the common law employment-at-will doctrine (under which employers may hire or fire employees "at will" unless a contract indicates to the contrary), courts have made exceptions to the doctrine on the basis of contract theory, tort theory, and public policy.
Whistleblower Statutes (See page 920.)	Most states have passed whistleblower statutes specifically to protect employees who "blow the whistle" on their employers from subsequent retaliation by those employers. The federal Whistleblower Protection Act of 1989 protects federal employees who report their employers' wrongdoing. The federal False Claims Reform Act of 1986 provides monetary rewards for whistleblowers who disclose information relating to fraud perpetrated against the U.S. government.

For Review

① What is the employment-at-will doctrine? When and why are exceptions to this doctrine made?

② What federal statute governs working hours and wages? What federal statutes govern labor unions and collective bargaining?

③ What federal act was enacted to protect the health and safety of employees? What are workers' compensation laws?

④ Under the Family and Medical Leave Act of 1993, under what circumstances may an employee take family or medical leave?

⑤ Does electronic performance monitoring violate employees' privacy rights? What other types of activities undertaken by employers might violate the privacy rights of employees?

Questions and Case Problems

34–1. Labor Laws. Calzoni Boating Co. is an interstate business engaged in manufacturing and selling boats. The company has five hundred nonunion employees. Representatives of these employees are requesting a four-day, ten-hours-per-day workweek, and

Calzoni is concerned that this would require paying time and a half after eight hours per day. Which federal act is Calzoni thinking of that might require this? Will the act in fact require paying time and a half for all hours worked over eight hours per day if the employees' proposal is accepted? Explain.

34–2. Health and Safety Regulations. Denton and Carlo were employed at an appliance plant. Their job required them to do occasional maintenance work while standing on a wire mesh twenty feet above the plant floor. Other employees had fallen through the mesh, one of whom was killed by the fall. When Denton and Carlo were asked by their supervisor to do work that would likely require them to walk on the mesh, they refused due to their fear of bodily harm or death. Because of their refusal to do the requested work, the two employees were fired from their jobs. Was their discharge wrongful? If so, under what federal employment law? To what federal agency or department should they turn for assistance?

34–3. Unfair Labor Practices. Suppose that Consolidated Stores is undergoing a unionization campaign. Prior to the union election, management says that the union is unnecessary to protect workers. Management also provides bonuses and wage increases to the workers during this period. The employees reject the union. Union organizers protest that the wage increases during the election campaign unfairly prejudiced the vote. Should these wage increases be regarded as an unfair labor practice? Discuss.

34–4. Workers' Compensation. Galvin Strang worked for a tractor company in one of its factories. Near his work station was a conveyor belt that ran through a large industrial oven. Sometimes, the workers would use the oven to heat their meals. Thirty-inch-high flasks containing molds were fixed at regular intervals on the conveyor and were transported into the oven. Strang had to walk between the flasks to get to his work station. One day, the conveyor was not moving, and Strang used the oven to cook a frozen pot pie. As he was removing the pot pie from the oven, the conveyor came on. One of the flasks struck Strang and seriously injured him. Strang sought recovery under the state workers' compensation law. Should he recover? Why or why not?

34–5. Privacy Rights. The city of Los Angeles requires a polygraph examination for police officers who ask to be promoted or transferred into a few specialized divisions where the work is unusually sensitive and requires a high level of integrity. Generally, those who fail the test are not promoted or transferred, but neither are they demoted or otherwise penalized. The Los Angeles Protective League filed a suit against the city in a California state court, asking the court, among other things, to order the city to stop the testing. On what basis might the court grant the league's request? On what basis might it refuse to do so? [*Los Angeles Protective League v. City of Los Angeles,* 35 Cal.App.4th 1535, 42 Cal.Rptr.2d 23 (1995)]

34–6. Whistleblowing. Barbara Kraus was vice president of nursing at the New Rochelle Hospital Medical Center. She learned that a certain doctor had written on the charts of some patients that he had performed procedures for them that he had not performed, and in fact, he had not obtained consent forms from the patients to perform those procedures. She reported this to the doctor's superiors, who took little action against the doctor. Some time later, Kraus was terminated. She filed a suit in a New York state court against the hospital to recover damages for wrongful termination. What is required for the court to rule in Kraus's favor? [*Kraus v. New Rochelle Hospital Medical Center,* 628 N.Y.S.2d 360 (1995)]

34–7. Performance Monitoring. The Communications Operations Division (COD) of the Milwaukee Police Department (MPD) received incoming emergency calls and coordinated the dispatch of officers. All incoming emergency calls were taped. The taping system was in a glass case in the middle of the COD work area. Also, the employees knew that their supervisors might monitor their calls for evaluation and training purposes. Cynthia Griffin, a COD telecommunicator, filed a suit in a federal district court against the MPD and her supervisors, alleging that they had illegally monitored her personal calls. For what reasons might the court rule in favor of the defendants? [*Griffin v. City of Milwaukee,* 74 F.3d 824 (7th Cir. 1996)]

34–8. Wrongful Discharge. Stephen Fredrick, a pilot for Simmons Airlines Corp., criticized the safety of the aircraft that Simmons used on many of its flights and warned the airline about the possible safety problems. Simmons took no action. After one of the planes crashed, Fredrick appeared on the television program *Good Morning America* to discuss his safety concerns. The same day, Fredrick refused to allow employees of Simmons to search his personal bags before a flight that he was scheduled to work. Claiming insubordination, the airline terminated Fredrick. Fredrick filed a suit in a federal district court against Simmons, claiming, among other things, that he had been discharged in retaliation for his public criticism of the safety of Simmons's aircraft and that this discharge violated the public policy of providing for safe air travel. Simmons responded that an employee who "goes public" with his or her concerns should not be protected by the law. Will the court agree with Simmons? Explain. [*Fredrick v. Simmons Airlines Corp.,* 144 F.3d 500 (7th Cir. 1998)]

34–9. Hours and Wages. Richard Ackerman was an advance sales representative and account manager for Coca-Cola Enterprises, Inc. His primary responsibility was to sell Coca-Cola products to grocery stores, convenience stores, and other sales outlets. Coca-Cola also employed merchandisers, who did not sell Coca-Cola products but performed tasks associated with their distribution and promotion, including restocking shelves, filling vending machines, and setting up displays. The account managers, who serviced the smaller accounts themselves, regularly worked between fifty-five and seventy-two hours each week. Coca-Cola paid them a salary, bonuses, and commissions, but it did not pay them—unlike the merchandisers—additional compensation for the overtime. Ackerman and the other account managers filed a suit in a federal district court against Coca-Cola, alleging that they were entitled to overtime compensation. Coca-Cola responded that because of an exemption under the Fair Labor Standards Act, it was not required to pay them overtime. Is Coca-Cola correct? Explain. [*Ackerman v. Coca-Cola Enterprises, Inc.,* 179 F.3d 1260 (10th Cir. 1999)]

TEST YOUR KNOWLEDGE—ANSWER ON THE WEB

34–10. Patience Oyoyo worked as a claims analyst in the claims management department of Baylor Healthcare Network, Inc. When questions arose about Oyoyo's performance on several occasions, department manager Debbie Outlaw met with Oyoyo to discuss, among other things, Oyoyo's personal use of a business phone. Outlaw reminded Oyoyo that company policy prohibited excessive personal calls and that these would result in the termination of her employment. Outlaw began to monitor Oyoyo's phone usage, noting lengthy outgoing calls on several occasions, including some long-distance calls. Eventually, Outlaw terminated Oyoyo's employment, and Oyoyo filed a suit in a federal district court against Baylor. Oyoyo asserted in part that in monitoring her phone calls, the employer had invaded her privacy. Baylor asked the court to dismiss this claim. In whose favor should the court rule, and why? [*Oyoyo v. Baylor Healthcare Network, Inc.*, __ F.Supp.2d __ (N.D.Tex. 2000)]

A QUESTION OF ETHICS AND SOCIAL RESPONSIBILITY

34–11. Keith Cline worked for Wal-Mart Stores, Inc., as a night maintenance supervisor. When he suffered a recurrence of a brain tumor, he took a leave from work, which was covered by the Family and Medical Leave Act (FMLA) of 1993 and authorized by his employer. When he returned to work, his employer refused to allow him to continue his supervisory job and demoted him to the status of a regular maintenance worker. A few weeks later, the company fired him, ostensibly because he "stole" company time by clocking in thirteen minutes early for a company meeting. Cline sued Wal-Mart, alleging, among other things, that Wal-Mart had violated the FMLA by refusing to return him to his prior position when he returned to work. In view of these facts, answer the following questions. [*Cline v. Wal-Mart Stores, Inc.*, 144 F.3d 294 (4th Cir. 1998)]

1. Did Wal-Mart violate the FMLA by refusing to return Cline to his prior position when he returned to work?
2. From an ethical perspective, the FMLA has been viewed as a choice on the part of society to shift to the employer family burdens caused by changing economic and social needs. What "changing" needs does the act meet? In other words, why did Congress feel that workers should have the right to family and medical leave in 1993, but not in 1983, or 1973, or earlier?
3. "Congress should amend the FMLA, which currently applies to employers with fifty or more employees, so that it applies to employers with twenty-five or more employees." Do you agree with this statement? Why or why not?

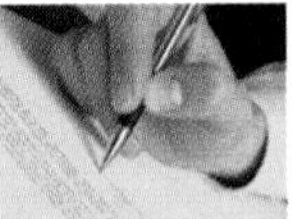

FOR CRITICAL ANALYSIS

34–12. Employees have a right to privacy, but employers also have a right to create and maintain an efficient and safe workplace. Do you think that existing laws strike an appropriate balance between employers' rights and employees' rights?

Internet Exercises

Go to the *Business Law Today* home page at **http://blt.westbuslaw.com**. Select "Interactive Study Center" and then click on "Chapter 34." There you will find the following Internet research exercises that you can perform to learn more about workers' compensation and workplace monitoring:

Activity 34–1: **Workers' Compensation**
Activity 34–2: **Workplace Monitoring and Surveillance**

Before the Test

Go to the *Business Law Today* home page at **http://blt.westbuslaw.com**. Click on "Interactive Quizzes." You will find at least twenty interactive questions relating to this chapter.

CHAPTER 35

Employment Discrimination

"Nor shall any State . . . deny to any person within its jurisdiction the equal protection of the laws."

The Fourteenth Amendment to the U.S. Constitution

CHAPTER CONTENTS

LEARNING OBJECTIVES

After reading this chapter, you should be able to answer the following questions:

① Generally, what kind of conduct is prohibited by Title VII of the Civil Rights Act of 1964, as amended?

② What is the difference between disparate-treatment discrimination and disparate-impact discrimination?

③ What remedies are available under Title VII of the 1964 Civil Rights Act, as amended?

④ What federal acts prohibit discrimination based on age and discrimination based on disability?

⑤ What are three defenses to claims of employment discrimination?

During the early 1960s we, as a nation, focused our attention on the civil rights of all Americans, including our rights under the Fourteenth Amendment to the equal protection of the laws. Out of this movement to end racial and other forms of discrimination grew a body of law protecting workers against discrimination in the workplace. This protective legislation further eroded the employment-at-will doctrine, which was discussed in the previous chapter. In the past several decades, judicial decisions, administrative agency actions, and legislation have restricted the ability of employers, and unions as well, to discriminate against workers on the basis of race, color, religion, national origin, gender, age, or disability. A class of persons defined by one or more of these criteria is known as a **protected class.**

PROTECTED CLASS

A group of persons protected by specific laws because of the group's defining characteristics. Under laws prohibiting employment discrimination, these characteristics include race, color, religion, national origin, gender, age, and disability.

Several federal statutes prohibit discrimination in the employment context against members of protected classes. The most important statute is Title VII of the Civil Rights Act of 1964.[1] Title VII prohibits discrimination on the basis of race, color, religion, national origin, and gender at any stage of employment. The Age Discrimination in Employment Act of 1967[2] and the Americans with Disabilities Act of 1990[3] prohibit discrimination on the basis of age and disability, respectively.

The focus of this chapter is on the kinds of discrimination prohibited by these federal statutes. Note, however, that discrimination against employees on the basis of any of these criteria may also violate state human rights statutes or other state laws or public policies prohibiting discrimination.

Title VII of the Civil Rights Act of 1964

EMPLOYMENT DISCRIMINATION
Treating employees or job applicants unequally on the basis of race, color, national origin, religion, gender, age, or disability; prohibited by federal statutes.

Title VII of the Civil Rights Act of 1964 and its amendments prohibit **employment discrimination** against employees, job applicants, and union members on the basis of race, color, national origin, religion, and gender at any stage of employment. Title VII applies to employers with fifteen or more employees, labor unions with fifteen or more members, labor unions that operate hiring halls (to which members go regularly to be rationed jobs as they become available), employment agencies, and state and local governing units or agencies. A special section of the act prohibits discrimination in most federal government employment.

THE EQUAL EMPLOYMENT OPPORTUNITY COMMISSION

ON THE WEB
You can find the complete text of Title VII and information about the activities of the EEOC at that agency's Web site. Go to **http://www.eeoc.gov**.

Compliance with Title VII is monitored by the Equal Employment Opportunity Commission (EEOC). A victim of alleged discrimination, before bringing a suit against the employer, must first file a claim with the EEOC. The EEOC may investigate the dispute and attempt to obtain the parties' voluntary consent to an out-of-court settlement. If voluntary agreement cannot be reached, the EEOC may then file a suit against the employer on the employee's behalf. If the EEOC decides not to investigate the claim, the victim may bring her or his own lawsuit against the employer.

The EEOC does not investigate every claim of employment discrimination, regardless of the merits of the claim. Generally, it investigates only "priority cases," such as cases involving retaliatory discharge (firing an employee in retaliation for submitting a claim to the EEOC) and cases involving types of discrimination that are of particular concern to the EEOC.

TYPES OF DISCRIMINATION

DISPARATE-TREATMENT DISCRIMINATION
A form of employment discrimination that results when an employer intentionally discriminates against employees who are members of protected classes.

Title VII prohibits both intentional and unintentional discrimination. Intentional discrimination by an employer against an employee is known as **disparate-treatment discrimination**. Because intent may sometimes be difficult to prove, courts have established certain procedures for resolving disparate-treatment cases. Suppose that a woman applies for employment with a construction firm and is rejected. If she sues on the basis of disparate-treatment discrimination in hiring, she must show that

1. 42 U.S.C. Sections 2000e–2000e-17.
2. 29 U.S.C. Sections 621–634.
3. 42 U.S.C. Sections 12102–12118.

(1) she is a member of a protected class, (2) she applied and was qualified for the job in question, (3) she was rejected by the employer, and (4) the employer continued to seek applicants for the position or filled the position with a person not in a protected class.

***PRIMA FACIE* CASE**
A case in which the plaintiff has produced sufficient evidence of his or her conclusion that the case can go to a jury; a case in which the evidence compels the plaintiff's conclusion if the defendant produces no affirmative defense or evidence to disprove it.

If the woman can meet these relatively easy requirements, she makes out a ***prima facie* case** of illegal discrimination. Making out a *prima facie* case of discrimination means that the plaintiff has met her initial burden of proof and will win in the absence of a legally acceptable employer defense (defenses to claims of employment discrimination will be discussed later in this chapter). The burden then shifts to the employer-defendant, who must articulate a legal reason for not hiring the plaintiff. To prevail, the plaintiff must then show that the employer's reason is a *pretext* (not the true reason) and that discriminatory intent actually motivated the employer's decision.

DISPARATE-IMPACT DISCRIMINATION
A form of employment discrimination that results from certain employer practices or procedures that, although not discriminatory on their face, have a discriminatory effect.

Employers often find it necessary to use interviews and testing procedures to choose from among a large number of applicants for job openings. Minimum educational requirements are also common. Employer practices, such as those involving educational requirements, may have an unintended discriminatory impact on a protected class. **Disparate-impact discrimination** occurs when, as a result of educational or other job requirements or hiring procedures, an employer's work force does not reflect the percentage of nonwhites, women, or members of other protected classes that characterizes qualified individuals in the local labor market. If a person challenging an employment practice having a discriminatory effect can show a connection between the practice and the disparity, he or she makes out a *prima facie* case, and no evidence of discriminatory intent needs to be shown. Disparate-impact discrimination can also occur when an educational or other job requirement or hiring procedure excludes members of a protected class from an employer's work force at a substantially higher rate than nonmembers, regardless of the racial balance in the employer's work force.

DISCRIMINATION BASED ON RACE, COLOR, AND NATIONAL ORIGIN

If a company's standards or policies for selecting or promoting employees have the effect of discriminating against employees or job applicants on the basis of race, color, or national origin, they are illegal—unless (except for race) they have a substantial, demonstrable relationship to realistic qualifications for the job in question. Discrimination against these protected classes in regard to employment conditions and benefits is also illegal.

• **EXAMPLE 35.1** In one case, Cynthia McCullough, an African American woman with a college degree, worked at a deli in a grocery store. More than a year later, the owner of the store promoted a white woman as "deli manager." The white woman had worked in the deli for only three months, had only a sixth-grade education, and could not calculate prices or read recipes. Although the owner gave various reasons for promoting the white woman instead of McCullough, a federal appellate court held that these reasons were likely just excuses and that the real reason was discriminatory intent.[4] •

4. *McCullough v. Real Foods, Inc.*, 140 F.3d 1123 (8th Cir. 1998). The federal district court had granted summary judgment for the employer in this case. The Eighth Circuit Court of Appeals reversed the district court's decision and remanded the case for trial.

ETHICAL ISSUE 35.1

Are English-only policies in the workplace a form of national-origin discrimination?

As the U.S. population becomes more multilingual, so does the work force. In response to this development, many employers have instituted English-only policies in their workplaces, particularly in states with large immigrant populations, such as Texas and California. Are English-only policies fair to workers who do not speak English? Do they violate Title VII's prohibition against discrimination on the basis of race or national origin, as workers in a number of lawsuits have alleged? Generally, the courts have shown a fair degree of tolerance with respect to English-only rules, especially when an employer can show that there is a legitimate business reason for the rules, such as improved communication among employees or worker safety. Yet the courts tend to regard with suspicion "blanket" English-only policies—policies that require that only English be spoken not only during work time but also on breaks, lunch hours, and the like. For example, a federal district court held that a Texas firm had engaged in disparate-treatment discrimination based on national origin by requiring that English be spoken exclusively in the workplace, including during breaks, except when employees were communicating with customers who could not speak English.[5]

DISCRIMINATION BASED ON RELIGION

Title VII of the Civil Rights Act of 1964 also prohibits government employers, private employers, and unions from discriminating against persons because of their religion. An employer must "reasonably accommodate" the religious practices of its employees, unless to do so would cause undue hardship to the employer's business. For example, if an employee's religion prohibits him or her from working on a certain day of the week or at a certain type of job, the employer must make a reasonable attempt to accommodate these religious requirements. Employers must reasonably accommodate an employee's religious belief even if the belief is not based on the tenets or dogma of a particular church, sect, or denomination. The only requirement is that the belief be sincerely held by the employee.[6]

DISCRIMINATION BASED ON GENDER

"A sign that says 'men only' looks very different on a bathroom door than a courthouse door."

THURGOOD MARSHALL, 1908–1993
(Associate justice of the United States Supreme Court, 1967–1991)

Under Title VII, as well as other federal acts, employers are forbidden to discriminate against employees on the basis of gender. Employers are prohibited from classifying jobs as male or female and from advertising in help-wanted columns that are designated male or female unless the employer can prove that the gender of the applicant is essential to the job. Furthermore, employers cannot have separate male and female seniority lists.

Generally, to succeed in a suit for gender discrimination, a plaintiff must demonstrate that gender was a determining factor in the employer's decision to hire, fire, or promote her or him. Typically, this involves looking at all of the surrounding circumstances.

5. *EEOC v. Premier Operator Services, Inc.*, 113 F.Supp.2d 1066 (N.D.Tex. 2000).

6. *Frazee v. Illinois Department of Employment Security*, 489 U.S. 829, 109 S.Ct. 1514, 103 L.Ed.2d 914 (1989).

The Pregnancy Discrimination Act of 1978,[7] which amended Title VII, expanded the definition of gender discrimination to include discrimination based on pregnancy. Women affected by pregnancy, childbirth, or related medical conditions must be treated—for all employment-related purposes, including the receipt of benefits under employee benefit programs—the same as other persons not so affected but similar in ability to work.

In the following case, the plaintiff charged the defendant with gender discrimination. The plaintiff made out a *prima facie* case, and the defendant presented a nondiscriminatory reason as a defense. Was the defendant's reason a pretext covering a discriminatory motive? That was the question before the court.

7. 42 U.S.C. Section 2000e(k).

CASE 35.1 Carey v. Mount Desert Island Hospital

United States Court of Appeals, First Circuit, 1998.
156 F.3d 31.
http://www.law.emory.edu/1circuit/aug98[a]

COMPANY PROFILE *Mount Desert Island Hospital (MDI) is a forty-nine–bed facility in Bar Harbor, Maine, with a medical staff that specializes in family practice, general surgery, internal medicine, ophthalmology, pathology, and radiology. A consulting staff includes practitioners of other medical specialties. MDI also operates an occupational health service, community health education, and affiliated health centers: Community Health Center in Southwest Harbor; Family Health Center, Women's Health Center, Breast Center, and High Street Health Center in Bar Harbor; and Northeast Harbor Clinic, open seasonally in Northeast Harbor. MDI is licensed by the state of Maine and fully accredited by the Joint Commission on Accreditation of Healthcare Organizations.*

FACTS Michael Carey was a vice president in charge of the finance department for Mount Desert Island Hospital (MDI). When the position of chief executive officer (CEO) opened up, Carey applied, and his application was endorsed by Dan Hobbs, the acting CEO. At the time, an audit of the finance department revealed some deficiencies, but the auditor concluded that the department was "already attacking the problem." MDI's board offered the CEO post to Leslie Hawkins, a woman, who accepted. Less than a year later, Hawkins terminated Carey, giving as reasons the problems cited in the audit and "lack of confidence" in Carey. Carey filed a suit in a federal district court against MDI for gender discrimination in violation of Title VII and other laws. Evidence introduced during the trial included a statement by one female executive that "we have different standards for men and women," with regard to discipline and termination; and a statement by another female executive that "it's about time that we get a woman for this [CEO] position." The court awarded Carey more than $300,000 in damages. MDI appealed to the U.S. Court of Appeals for the First Circuit.

a. This page contains links to opinions of the U.S. Court of Appeals for the First Circuit decided in August 1998. Click on the *Carey* case name to access the opinion. This Web site is maintained by Emory University School of Law in Atlanta, Georgia.

ISSUE Was there enough evidence for a jury to find that MDI's board had discriminated against Carey on the basis of gender?

DECISION Yes. The U.S. Court of Appeals for the First Circuit affirmed the lower court's judgment. The court held that that there was sufficient evidence to support a finding that the reason for Carey's discharge was gender discrimination.

REASON The U.S. Court of Appeals for the First Circuit recognized initially that this case "involv[ed] the always difficult question of probing the wellsprings of human motivation." The court acknowledged that it expected the evidence would consist of "bits and pieces" and that "occasional stray remarks" by employees would not be enough. Statements that suggest a "discriminatory atmosphere" at MDI could support a jury's finding, however. The court pointed to the statements by female executives at MDI and concluded that there was enough evidence

CASE 35.1—Continued
"to support a finding that deficiencies in Carey's handling of financial controls were not the real reason for his discharge."

FOR CRITICAL ANALYSIS—Cultural Consideration *Is it possible for jurors and judges to overcome their own prejudices in deciding cases in which gender plays a key role?*

SEXUAL HARASSMENT

SEXUAL HARASSMENT
In the employment context, the granting of job promotions or other benefits in return for sexual favors, or language or conduct that is so sexually offensive that it creates a hostile working environment.

Title VII also protects employees against **sexual harassment** in the workplace. Sexual harassment has often been classified as either *quid pro quo* harassment or hostile-environment harassment. *Quid pro quo* is a Latin phrase that is often translated to mean "something in exchange for something else." *Quid pro quo* harassment occurs when job opportunities, promotions, salary increases, and so on are given in return for sexual favors. According to the United States Supreme Court, hostile-environment harassment occurs when "the workplace is permeated with discriminatory intimidation, ridicule, and insult, that is sufficiently severe or pervasive to alter the conditions of the victim's employment and create an abusive working environment."[8]

"Justice is better than chivalry if we cannot have both."
ALICE STONE BLACKWELL,
1857–1950
(American suffragist and editor)

Generally, the courts apply this Supreme Court guideline on a case-by-case basis. Some courts have held that just one incident of sexually offensive conduct—such as a sexist remark by a co-worker or a photo on an employer's desk of his bikini-clad wife—can create a hostile environment.[9] At least one court has held that a worker may recover damages under Title VII because *other* persons were sexually harassed in the workplace.[10] According to some employment specialists, employers should assume that hostile-environment harassment has occurred if an employee claims that it has. (For either type of harassment to be *sexual* harassment, it must involve gender-based discrimination—see this chapter's *Letter of the Law* feature on page 932.)

Harassment by Supervisors What if an employee is harassed by a manager or supervisor of a large firm, and the firm itself (the "employer") is not aware of the harassment? Should the employer be held liable for the harassment nonetheless? For some time, the courts were in disagreement on this issue. Typically, employers were held liable for Title VII violations by the firm's managerial or supervisory personnel in *quid pro quo* harassment cases regardless of whether the employer knew about the harassment. In hostile-environment cases, the majority of courts tended to hold employers liable only if the employer knew or should have known of the harassment and failed to take prompt remedial action.

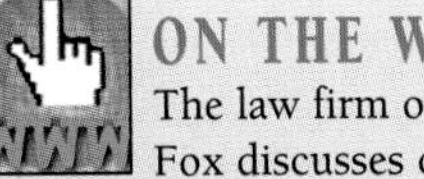

ON THE WEB
The law firm of Arent Fox discusses current issues in the area of employment law, including sexual harassment, at its Web site. Go to
http://www.arentfox.com
and, on the pull-down menu under "Business Lines," click on "Employment."

In 1998, in two separate cases, the United States Supreme Court issued some significant guidelines relating to the liability of employers for their supervisors' harassment of employees in the workplace. In *Faragher v. City of Boca Raton*,[11] the Court held that an employer (a city) could be held liable for a supervisor's harassment of employees even though the employer was unaware of the behavior. The Court reached this conclusion primarily because, although the city had a written policy against sexual harassment, the policy had not been distributed to city employees. Additionally, the city had not established any procedures that could be followed by employees who felt that they

8. *Harris v. Forklift Systems*, 510 U.S. 17, 114 S.Ct. 367, 126 L.Ed.2d 295 (1993).
9. For other examples, see *Radtke v. Everett*, 442 Mich. 368, 501 N.W.2d 155 (1993); and *Nadeau v. Rainbow Rugs, Inc.*, 675 A.2d 973 (Me. 1996).
10. *Leibovitz v. New York City Transit Authority*, 4 F.Supp.2d 144 (E.D.N.Y. 1998).
11. 524 U.S. 725, 118 S.Ct. 2275, 141 L.Ed.2d 662 (1998).

LETTER OF THE LAW

"Equal Opportunity" Harassment

The prohibition against sexual harassment in the workplace is an extension of Title VII's prohibition against gender-based discrimination. This means that there can be no sexual harassment if there is no gender-based discrimination involved. It also means, among other things, that Title VII does not protect employees from "equal opportunity" harassers—those who harass both sexes equally—because such persons are not discriminating on the basis of sex.

This point was made clear to Steven and Karen Holman, a married couple who worked for the Indiana Department of Transportation, when they sued their employer for sexual harassment. The Holmans alleged that their supervisor had sexually harassed each of them individually on separate occasions and that the supervisor retaliated against them—by denying them certain privileges and pay—when they rejected his advances. In evaluating their claim, the court looked at the letter of Title VII, which states, "It shall be an unlawful employment practice for an employer to . . . discriminate against any individual with respect to compensation, terms, conditions, or privileges of employment, because of such individual's . . . sex." The court observed that in the Holmans' case, there was no discrimination "because of . . . sex" because the supervisor harassed both of them. Thus, concluded the court, the Holmans could not maintain a Title VII action against their employer.[a]

THE BOTTOM LINE

Harassment in the workplace takes many forms, including harassment based on gender, race, national origin, religion, age, and disability. In cases alleging sexual harassment, however, the harassment must be on the basis of sex (gender), or Title VII will not apply.

a. *Holman v. Indiana,* 211 F.3d 399 (7th Cir. 2000).

were victims of sexual harassment. In *Burlington Industries, Inc. v. Ellerth,*[12] the Court ruled that a company could be held liable for the harassment of an employee by one of its vice presidents even though the employee suffered no adverse job consequences.

The guidelines set forth in these two cases have been helpful to employers and employees alike. On the one hand, employees benefit by the ruling that employers may be held liable for their supervisors' harassment even though the employers were unaware of the actions and even though the employees suffered no adverse job consequences. On the other hand, the Court made it clear in both decisions that employers have an affirmative defense against liability for their supervisors' harassment of employees if the employers can show that (1) they have taken "reasonable care to prevent and correct promptly any sexually harassing behavior" (by establishing effective harassment policies and complaint procedures, for example), and (2) the employees suing for harassment failed to follow these policies and procedures.

Harassment by Co-Workers Often, employees alleging harassment complain that the actions of co-workers, not supervisors, are responsible for creating a hostile working environment. In such cases, the employee still has a cause of action against the employer. Normally, though, the employer will be held liable only if it knew, or should have known, about the harassment and failed to take immediate remedial action.

Harassment by Nonemployees Employers may also be liable for harassment by *nonemployees* in certain circumstances. • **EXAMPLE 35.2** If a restaurant owner or manager

12. 524 U.S. 742, 118 S.Ct. 2257, 141 L.Ed.2d 633 (1998).

knows that a certain customer repeatedly harasses a waitress and permits the harassment to continue, the restaurant owner may be liable under Title VII even though the customer is not an employee of the restaurant. The issue turns on the control that the employer exerts over a nonemployee. In one case, an owner of a Pizza Hut franchise was held liable for the harassment of a waitress by two male customers because no steps were taken to prevent the harassment.[13] •

Same-Gender Harassment The courts have also had to address the issue of whether men who are harassed by other men, or women who are harassed by other women, are also protected by laws that prohibit gender-based discrimination in the workplace. For example, what if the male president of a firm demands sexual favors from a male employee? Does this action qualify as sexual harassment? For some time, the courts were widely split on this issue. In 1998, in *Oncale v. Sundowner Offshore Services, Inc.*,[14] the Supreme Court resolved the issue by holding that Title VII protection extends to situations in which individuals are harassed by members of the same gender.

Online Harassment

Employees' online activities can create a hostile working environment in many ways. Racial jokes, ethnic slurs, or other comments contained in e-mail may become the basis for a claim of hostile-environment harassment or other forms of discrimination. A worker who sees sexually explicit images on a co-worker's computer screen may find the images offensive and claim that they create a hostile working environment.

13. *Lockard v. Pizza Hut, Inc.*, 162 F.3d 1062 (10th Cir. 1998).
14. 523 U.S. 75, 118 S.Ct. 998, 140 L.Ed.2d 207 (1998).

INTERNATIONAL PERSPECTIVE

Sexual Harassment in Other Nations

The problem of sexual harassment in the workplace is not confined to the United States. Indeed, it is a worldwide problem for female workers. In Egypt, Turkey, Argentina, Brazil, and many other countries, there is no legal protection against any form of employment discrimination. Even in those countries that do have laws prohibiting discriminatory employment practices, including gender-based discrimination, those laws often do not specifically include sexual harassment as a discriminatory practice. Several countries have attempted to remedy this omission by passing new laws or amending others to specifically prohibit sexual harassment in the workplace. Japan, for example, has amended its Equal Employment Opportunity Law to include a provision making sexual harassment illegal. The revised law went into effect in 1999. In 1998, Thailand passed its first sexual-harassment law. The European Union, which some years ago outlawed gender-based discrimination, is considering a proposal that would specifically identify sexual harassment as a form of discrimination. In the meantime, old traditions die hard. Women's support groups throughout Europe contend that corporations in European countries tend to view sexual harassment with "quiet tolerance." They contrast this attitude with that of most U.S. corporations, which have implemented specific procedures to deal with harassment claims.

FOR CRITICAL ANALYSIS
Why do you think U.S. corporations are more aggressive than European companies in taking steps to prevent sexual harassment in the workplace?

Generally, employers may be able to avoid liability for online harassment if they take prompt remedial action.

• **EXAMPLE 35.3** In *Daniels v. WorldCom, Inc.*,[15] Angela Daniels, an employee of Robert Half International under contract to WorldCom, Inc., received racially harassing e-mailed jokes from another employee. After receiving the jokes, Daniels complained to WorldCom managers. Shortly afterward, the company issued a warning to the offending employee about the proper use of the e-mail system and held two meetings to discuss company policy on the use of the system. In Daniels's suit against WorldCom for racial discrimination, a federal district court concluded that the employer was not liable for its employee's racially harassing e-mails because the employer took prompt remedial action. •

Generally, employers who want to avoid online harassment in the workplace seem to be caught between the proverbial "rock and a hard place." On the one hand, if they do not take effective steps to curb such harassment, they may face liability for violating Title VII. On the other hand, if they monitor their employees' communications, they may face liability under other laws—for invading their employees' privacy, for example. Additionally, an employee who is fired for misusing the employer's computer system to, say, e-mail pornographic images to co-workers or others may claim that he or she was wrongfully discharged (see, for example, the case discussed in this chapter's *Business Law in the Online World* feature). Finally, there are constitutional rights to be considered. In one case, a court held that religious speech that unintentionally creates a hostile environment is constitutionally protected.[16]

15. 1998 WL 91261 (N.D.Tex. 1998).
16. *Meltebeke v. B.O.L.I.*, 903 P.2d 351 (Or. 1995).

BUSINESS LAW: //in the Online World

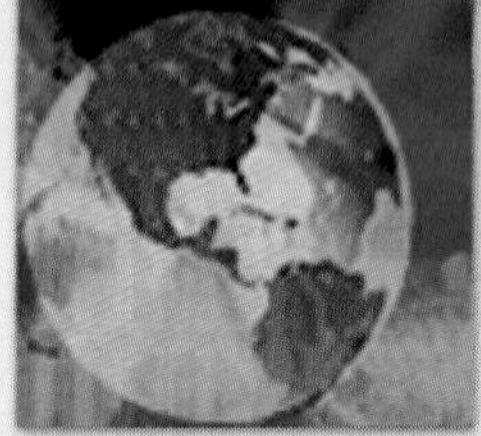

E-Mail in the Workplace and "Universal Standards of Behavior"

As mentioned in Chapter 34, many employers today establish and implement policies that specify permissible and impermissible uses of the Internet in the workplace. Yet what if employees who violate such a policy claim that they did not "knowingly" do so? In this situation, if the employer discharges the employees for violating the policy, can the employees successfully claim that they were discharged without "just cause," thus entitling them to unemployment compensation? This question recently came before a Utah appellate court in *Autoliv ASP, Inc. v. Department of Workforce Services.*[a]

Autoliv's Harassment and E-Mail Policies

Autoliv ASP, Inc., a supplier of auto-safety products, gives each of its over six thousand employees an employee handbook. Among other things, the handbook states that Autoliv will not "tolerate or permit illegal harassment or retaliation of any nature within our workforce." The handbook also states that the use of e-mail "for reasons other than transmittal of business-related information" is prohibited and that violations of company policies can result in any of several disciplinary actions, including termination.

In 1999, Autoliv learned that an employee had received offensive and sexually harassing e-mail from other Autoliv employees. The company immediately investigated and learned that two employees had, on numerous occasions, sent messages containing jokes, photos, and short videos that were sexually explicit and clearly offensive in nature. Shortly thereafter, Autoliv terminated the two employees for "improper and unauthorized use of company e-mail." When the employees applied for unemployment benefits, a threshold question was whether they had been fired with just cause. If so, they *would not* be entitled to unemployment benefits. If not, they *would* be entitled to the benefits—and Autoliv would ultimately have to pay higher unemployment taxes as a result.

a. 29 P.3d 7 (Utah Ct. App. 2001).

REMEDIES UNDER TITLE VII

Employer liability under Title VII may be extensive. If the plaintiff successfully proves that unlawful discrimination occurred, he or she may be awarded reinstatement, back pay, retroactive promotions, and damages. Compensatory damages are available only in cases of intentional discrimination. Punitive damages may be recovered against a private employer only if the employer acted with malice or reckless indifference to an individual's rights. The sum of the amount of compensatory and punitive damages is limited by the statute to specific amounts against specific employers—ranging from $50,000 against employers with one hundred or fewer employees to $300,000 against employers with more than five hundred employees.

Equal Pay Act of 1963

The Equal Pay Act of 1963 was enacted as an amendment to the Fair Labor Standards Act of 1938. Basically, the act prohibits gender-based discrimination in the wages paid for equal work on jobs when their performance requires equal skill, effort, and responsibility under similar conditions. It is job content rather than job description that controls in all cases. To determine whether the Equal Pay Act has been violated, a court will thus look to the primary duties of the two jobs. The jobs of a barber and a beautician, for example, are considered essentially "equal." So, too, are those of a tailor and a seamstress. For the act's equal pay requirements to apply, the male and female employees must work at the same establishment.

BUSINESS LAW: //in the Online World

E-Mail in the Workplace and "Universal Standards of Behavior"—Continued

Were the Employees Fired for "Just Cause"?

Under the relevant state statute, to be fired for "just cause," employees had to have "knowledge of the conduct which the employer expected." The two employees testified that they had not "knowingly" engaged in misconduct. Further, if Autoliv concluded that they were engaging in misconduct, Autoliv should have warned them and allowed them to change their conduct. The agency agreed, noting that because abuse of the company's e-mail system was common among Autoliv employees, Autoliv should have notified the employees that their misconduct would not be tolerated before firing them. Because Autoliv had not done so, the termination was without "just cause."

Autoliv appealed the agency's decision to a state appellate court, asserting on appeal that it was "incomprehensible" for the agency to hold that a worker could be unaware of the dangers of sending sexually offensive materials to co-workers through a company's computer network. The court agreed with Autoliv, stating that "[s]uch materials in the workplace could have subjected the employer to sexual harassment and sex discrimination lawsuits." The court reversed the agency's decision, concluding that "in today's workplace, the e-mail transmission of sexually explicit and offensive jokes, pictures, and videos constitutes a flagrant violation of a universal standard of behavior."

FOR CRITICAL ANALYSIS

The focus of this case was on whether the two discharged employees were entitled to unemployment benefits. Suppose, though, that the employees had sued Autoliv for wrongful discharge on the ground that their discharge constituted a violation of an implied employment contract (see Chapter 34). Could they have succeeded in such a suit? Why or why not?

A wage differential for equal work is justified if it is shown to be based on (1) seniority, (2) a merit system, (3) a system that pays according to quality or quantity of production, or (4) any factor other than gender. Small differences in job content, however, do not justify higher pay for one gender. The Equal Pay Act is administered by the EEOC.

ETHICAL ISSUE 35.2

Should market forces be considered a "factor other than sex" in compensation-discrimination cases?

Traditionally, one of the defenses employers have raised in discrimination cases brought under the Equal Pay Act has been that their pay determinations were based on the market forces of supply and demand. In other words, if, say, more women than men were available for a particular job at a lower pay rate, the employer could argue that this characteristic of the marketplace was a "factor other than sex." Employers have not always succeeded in this defense, and new guidelines on compensation discrimination issued by the Equal Employment Opportunity Commission (EEOC) in 2000 may make it even more difficult to do so. Among other things, the guidelines state that "payment of lower wages to women based on an assumption that women are available . . . at lower compensation rates does not qualify as a factor other than sex." The guidelines then state that an employer may cite market factors as a reason for compensation discrimination "only if the employer proves that any compensation disparity is not based on sex." Critics of the guidelines point out that the EEOC's somewhat circular reasoning will make it extremely difficult for employers to cite market factors as a defense at all. Although EEOC compliance guidelines are not legal requirements in themselves, they will no doubt influence case outcomes because the courts normally give deference to the EEOC's interpretations of the law.[17]

Discrimination Based on Age

Age discrimination is potentially the most widespread form of discrimination, because anyone—regardless of race, color, national origin, or gender—could be a victim at some point in life. The Age Discrimination in Employment Act (ADEA) of 1967, as amended, prohibits employment discrimination on the basis of age against individuals forty years of age or older. An amendment to the act prohibits mandatory retirement for nonmanagerial workers. For the act to apply, an employer must have twenty or more employees, and the employer's business activities must affect interstate commerce.

PROCEDURES UNDER THE ADEA

REMEMBER The Fourteenth Amendment prohibits any state from denying any person "the equal protection of the laws." This prohibition applies to the *federal* government through the due process clause of the Fifth Amendment.

The burden-shifting procedure under the ADEA is similar to that under Title VII. If a plaintiff can establish that she or he (1) was a member of the protected age group, (2) was qualified for the position from which she or he was discharged, and (3) was discharged under circumstances that give rise to an inference of discrimination, the

17. You can access the section of the EEOC's Compliance Manual that contains these guidelines at the EEOC's Web site at **http://www.eeoc.gov**. The Web site also contains an "Equal Pay" page that includes information on compensation-discrimination laws, as well as descriptions of recent EEOC equal-pay cases.

plaintiff has established a *prima facie* case of unlawful age discrimination. The burden then shifts to the employer, who must articulate a legitimate reason for the discrimination. If the plaintiff can prove that the employer's reason is only a pretext and that the plaintiff's age was a determining factor in the employer's decision, the employer will be held liable under the ADEA.

Numerous cases of alleged age discrimination have been brought against employers who, to cut costs, replaced older, higher-salaried employees with younger, lower-salaried workers. Whether a firing is discriminatory or simply part of a rational business decision to prune the company's ranks is not always clear. Companies generally defend a decision to discharge a worker by asserting that the worker could no longer perform his or her duties or that the worker's skills were no longer needed. The employee must prove that the discharge was motivated, at least in part, by age bias. Proof that qualified older employees are generally discharged before younger employees or that co-workers continually made unflattering age-related comments about the discharged worker may be enough. The plaintiff need not prove that he or she was replaced by a person outside the protected class—that is, by a person under the age of forty years.[18] Rather, the issue in all ADEA cases turns on whether age discrimination has, in fact, occurred, regardless of the age of the replacement worker.

STATE EMPLOYEES AND THE ADEA

Under the Eleventh Amendment to the Constitution, as that amendment has been interpreted by the United States Supreme Court, states are immune from lawsuits brought by private individuals in federal court, unless a state consents to the suit. In a number of cases brought in the late 1990s, state agencies that were sued by state employees for age discrimination sought to have the suits dismissed on this ground.

• **EXAMPLE 35.4** In two Florida cases, professors and librarians contended that their employers—two Florida state universities—denied them salary increases and other benefits because they were getting old and their successors could be hired at lower cost. The universities claimed that as agencies of a sovereign state, they could not be sued in federal court without the state's consent. Because the courts were rendering conflicting opinions in these cases, the United States Supreme Court agreed to address the issue. In *Kimel v. Florida Board of Regents*,[19] decided in early 2000, the Court held that the sovereign immunity granted the states by the Eleventh Amendment precluded suits against them by private parties alleging violations of the ADEA. According to the Court, Congress had exceeded its constitutional authority when it included in the ADEA a provision stating that "all employers," including state employers, were subject to the act. •

Discrimination Based on Disability

The Americans with Disabilities Act (ADA) of 1990 is designed to eliminate discriminatory employment practices that prevent otherwise qualified workers with disabilities from fully participating in the national labor force. Prior to 1990, the major federal law providing protection to those with disabilities was the Rehabilitation Act of 1973. That act covered only federal government employees and those employed under federally funded programs. Basically, the ADA requires that employers "reasonably accommodate"

18. *O'Connor v. Consolidated Coin Caterers Corp.*, 517 U.S. 308, 116 S.Ct. 1307, 134 L.Ed.2d 433 (1996).
19. 528 U.S. 62, 120 S.Ct. 631, 145 L.Ed.2d 522 (2000).

Co-workers discuss business matters. Which workers with disabilities are protected from employment discrimination by the Americans with Disabilities Act?

the needs of persons with disabilities unless to do so would cause the employer to suffer an "undue hardship." The ADA extends federal protection against disability-based discrimination to all workplaces with fifteen or more workers. Note, though, that the United States Supreme Court has held, as it did with respect to the ADEA, that lawsuits under the ADA cannot be brought against state government employers.[20]

To prevail on a claim under the ADA, a plaintiff must show that he or she (1) has a disability, (2) is otherwise qualified for the employment in question, and (3) was excluded from the employment solely because of the disability. As in Title VII cases, a claim alleging violation of the ADA may be commenced only after the plaintiff has pursued the claim through the EEOC. Plaintiffs may sue for many of the same remedies available under Title VII. They may seek reinstatement, back pay, a limited amount of compensatory and punitive damages (for intentional discrimination), and certain other forms of relief. Repeat violators may be ordered to pay fines of up to $100,000.

What Is a Disability?

The ADA is broadly drafted to define persons with disabilities as persons with a physical or mental impairment that "substantially limits" their everyday activities. More specifically, the ADA defines *disability* as "(1) a physical or mental impairment that substantially limits one or more of the major life activities of such individuals; (2) a record of such impairment; or (3) being regarded as having such an impairment."

Health conditions that have been considered disabilities under federal law include blindness, alcoholism, heart disease, cancer, muscular dystrophy, cerebral palsy, paraplegia, diabetes, acquired immune deficiency syndrome (AIDS) and the human immunodeficiency virus (HIV), and morbid obesity (defined as existing when an individual's weight is two times that of the normal person).[21] The ADA excludes from coverage certain conditions, such as kleptomania. For some time, the courts were divided on the issue of whether carpal tunnel syndrome (or other repetitive-stress injury) constituted a disability under the ADA. In 2002, in a case involving this issue, the Supreme Court unanimously held that it did not. Although an employee with carpal tunnel syndrome could not perform the manual tasks associated with her job, the injury did not "substantially limit the major life activity of performing manual tasks."[22]

A question that frequently arises in ADA cases is whether a person whose disability is controlled by medication still qualifies for protection under the ADA. That issue arose in the following case.

20. *Board of Trustees of the University of Alabama v. Garrett,* 531 U.S. 356, 121 S.Ct. 955, 148 L.Ed.2d 866 (2001).
21. *Cook v. Rhode Island Department of Mental Health,* 10 F.3d 17 (1st Cir. 1993).
22. *Toyota Motor Manufacturing, Kentucky, Inc. v. Williams,* __U.S.__, __S.Ct.__, __L.Ed.2d__ (2002).

CASE 35.2 Sutton v. United Airlines, Inc.

Supreme Court of the United States, 1999.
527 U.S. 471,
119 S.Ct. 2139,
144 L.Ed.2d 450.
http://supct.law.cornell.edu/supct/supct.1999a.html[a]

a. This page includes an alphabetical list of the 1999 decisions of the United States Supreme Court. Scroll down the list of cases to the *Sutton* case, and click on the name to access the opinion.

FACTS Karen and Kimberly Sutton are twin sisters, both of whom have severe myopia. Each woman's uncorrected visual acuity is 20/200 or worse in her right eye and 20/400 or worse in her left eye, but with the use of corrective lenses, such as glasses or contact lenses, each has vision that is 20/20 or better. In other words, without corrective lenses, neither individual can see well enough to do such things as drive a vehicle, watch television, or

CASE 35.2—Continued

shop, but with corrective measures, each functions identically to individuals without a similar impairment. In 1992, the Suttons applied to United Airlines, Inc. (UA), for employment as commercial airline pilots. They met UA's age, education, experience, and Federal Aviation Administration certification qualifications and were invited to flight simulator tests and interviews. Because the Suttons did not meet UA's minimum vision requirement, which was uncorrected visual acuity of 20/100 or better, the interviews were terminated, and neither pilot was offered a position. The Suttons filed a suit in a federal district court against UA, alleging discrimination under the Americans with Disabilities Act (ADA). The Suttons asserted in part that due to their severe myopia, they have a substantially limiting impairment and are thus disabled. The court disagreed and dismissed their complaint, and the U.S. Court of Appeals for the Tenth Circuit affirmed this judgment. The Suttons appealed to the United States Supreme Court.

ISSUE Is a condition that can be corrected with medication or a corrective device considered a disability for purposes of the ADA?

DECISION No. The United States Supreme Court affirmed the decision of the lower court.

REASON The Supreme Court held that a person is not disabled (substantially limited in any major life activity) under the ADA if he or she has a condition that can be corrected with medication or one, such as poor vision, that can be corrected with corrective devices, such as glasses. The Court stated, "A 'disability' exists only where an impairment 'substantially limits' a major life activity, not where it 'might,' 'could,' or 'would' be substantially limiting if mitigating measures were not taken. * * * To be sure, a person whose physical or mental impairment is corrected by mitigating measures still has an impairment, but if the impairment is corrected it does not 'substantially limi[t]' a major life activity."

FOR CRITICAL ANALYSIS—Political Consideration *Some claim that the courts have, in effect, "written" the ADA to some extent because it has been left to the courts to decide a number of questions that the act left open–such as the question addressed in this case. Should Congress pay more attention to details when it drafts legislation? Is it appropriate for the courts to assume such "lawmaking" responsibilities?*

Reasonable Accommodation

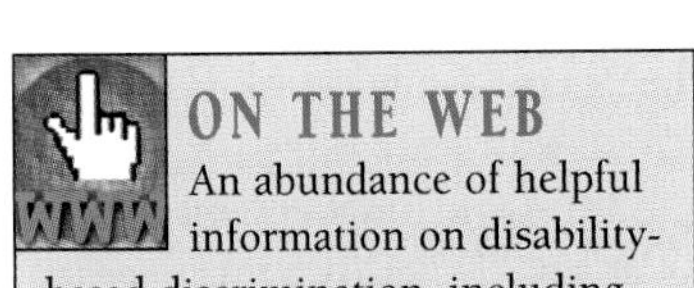

ON THE WEB An abundance of helpful information on disability-based discrimination, including the text of the ADA, can be found online at **http://janweb.icdi.wvu.edu/kinder**.

The ADA does not require that *unqualified* applicants with disabilities be hired or retained. Therefore, employers are not obligated to accommodate the needs of job applicants or employees with disabilities who are not otherwise qualified for the work. If a job applicant or an employee with a disability, with reasonable accommodation, can perform essential job functions, however, the employer must make the accommodation. Required modifications may include installing ramps for a wheelchair, establishing more flexible working hours, creating or modifying job assignments, and creating or improving training materials and procedures.

Generally, employers should give primary consideration to employees' preferences in deciding what accommodations should be made. What happens if a job applicant or employee does not indicate to the employer how her or his disability can be accommodated so that the employee can perform essential job functions? In this situation, the employer may avoid liability for failing to hire or retain the individual on the ground that the applicant or employee has failed to meet the "otherwise qualified" requirement.[23]

Employers who do not accommodate the needs of persons with disabilities must demonstrate that the accommodations will cause "undue hardship." Generally, the law offers no uniform standards for identifying what is an undue hardship other than the imposition of a "significant difficulty or expense" on the employer.

23. See, for example, *Beck v. University of Wisconsin Board of Regents,* 75 F.3d 1130 (7th Cir. 1996); and *White v. York International Corp.,* 45 F.3d 357 (10th Cir. 1995).

Usually, the courts decide whether an accommodation constitutes an undue hardship on a case-by-case basis. In one case, the court decided that paying for a parking space near the office for an employee with a disability was not an undue hardship.[24] In another case, the court held that accommodating the request of an employee with diabetes for indefinite leave until his disease was under control would create an undue hardship for the employer because the employer would not know when the employee was returning to work. The court stated that reasonable accommodation under the ADA means accommodation so that the employee can perform the job now or "in the immediate future" rather than at some unspecified distant time.[25]

We now look at some specific requirements of the ADA concerning the extent to which employers must reasonably accommodate the needs of employees with disabilities.

DON'T FORGET Preemployment screening procedures must be applied carefully in regard to all job applicants.

Job Applications and Preemployment Physical Exams Employers must modify their job-application process so that those with disabilities can compete for jobs with those who do not have disabilities. • **EXAMPLE 35.5** A job announcement that includes only a phone number would discriminate against potential job applicants with hearing impairments. Thus, the job announcement must also provide an address.•

Employers are restricted in the kinds of questions they may ask on job-application forms and during preemployment interviews (see the *Application* at the end of this chapter for guidelines on this topic). Furthermore, they cannot require persons with disabilities to submit to preemployment physicals unless such exams are required of all other applicants. Employers can condition an offer of employment on the employee's successfully passing a medical examination, but disqualifications must result from the discovery of problems that render the applicant unable to perform the job for which he or she is to be hired.

Dangerous Workers Employers are not required to hire or retain workers who, because of their disabilities, pose a "direct threat to the health or safety" of their co-workers or the public. This danger must be substantial and immediate; it cannot be speculative. In the wake of the AIDS epidemic, many employers have been concerned about hiring or continuing to employ a worker who has AIDS under the assumption that the worker might pose a direct threat to the health or safety of others in the workplace. Courts have generally held, however, that AIDS is not so contagious as to disqualify employees in most jobs. Therefore, employers must reasonably accommodate job applicants or employees who have AIDS or who test positive for HIV, the virus that causes AIDS.

Health-Insurance Plans Workers with disabilities must be given equal access to any health insurance provided to other employees. Employers can exclude from coverage preexisting health conditions and certain types of diagnostic or surgical procedures, however. An employer can also put a limit, or cap, on health-care payments under its particular group health policy—as long as such caps are "applied equally to all insured employees" and do not "discriminate on the basis of disability." Whenever a group health-care plan makes a disability-based distinction in its benefits, the plan violates the ADA. The employer must then be able to justify the distinction by proving one of the following:

① That limiting coverage of certain ailments is required to keep the plan financially sound.

24. See *Lyons v. Legal Aid Society,* 68 F.3d 1512 (2d Cir. 1995).
25. *Myers v. Hase,* 50 F.3d 278 (4th Cir. 1995).

A discussion occurs at a meeting of Alcoholics Anonymous. Should employers be allowed to discriminate against persons suffering from alcoholism?

② That coverage of certain ailments would cause such a significant increase in premium payments or their equivalent that the plan would be unappealing to a significant number of workers.

③ That the disparate treatment is justified by the risks and costs associated with a particular disability.

The ADA and Substance Abusers Drug addiction is a disability under the ADA because drug addiction is a substantially limiting impairment. Those who are currently using illegal drugs are not protected by the act. The ADA protects only persons with *former* drug addictions—those who have completed a supervised drug-rehabilitation program or are currently in a supervised rehabilitation program. Individuals who have used drugs casually in the past are not protected under the act. They are not considered addicts and therefore do not have a disability (addiction).

People recovering from alcoholism are protected by the ADA. Employers cannot legally discriminate against employees simply because they are suffering from alcoholism and must treat them in the same way they treat other employees. In other words, an employee suffering from alcoholism cannot be disciplined any differently than anyone else simply because she or he was drinking the night before and came to work late. Of course, employers have the right to prohibit the use of alcohol in the workplace and can require that employees not be under the influence of alcohol while working. Employers can also fire or refuse to hire a person suffering from alcoholism if he or she poses a substantial risk of harm to either himself or herself or to others and the risk cannot be reduced by reasonable accommodation.

HOSTILE-ENVIRONMENT CLAIMS UNDER THE ADA

As discussed earlier in this chapter, under Title VII of the Civil Rights Act of 1964, an employee may base certain types of employment-discrimination causes of action on a hostile-environment theory. Using this theory, a worker may successfully sue her or his employer, even if the worker was not fired or otherwise discriminated against.

Can a worker file a suit founded on a hostile-environment claim under the ADA? The ADA does not expressly provide for such suits, but some courts have allowed them. Others have assumed that the claim was possible without deciding whether the ADA allowed it.[26] Acts that might form the basis for such a claim would likely consist of conduct that a reasonable person would find so offensive that it would change the conditions of the person's employment.

Whether a disabled worker who was harassed by her co-workers could successfully sue her employer for a hostile environment was the issue in the following case.

26. See, for example, *Steele v. Thiokol Corp.*, 241 F.3d 1248 (10th Cir. 2001).

CASE 35.3 Flowers v. Southern Regional Physician Services, Inc.

United States Court of Appeals
Fifth Circuit 2001.
247 F.3d 229.
http://www.ca5.uscourts.gov/oparchdt.cfm[a]

a. This is the "Opinions Archive by Date Released" page within the Web site of the U.S. Court of Appeals for the Fifth Circuit. Click on "2001." When the link opens, click on "May." When that link opens, click on "May 4." From the list that appears, click on the docket number next to the name of the case to access the opinion.

(continued)

CASE 35.3—Continued

FACTS From September 1993, Sandra Flowers worked for Southern Regional Physician Services, Inc., as a medical assistant to Dr. James Osterberger. In March 1995, Margaret Hallmark, Flowers's immediate supervisor, discovered that Flowers was infected with the human immunodeficiency virus (HIV). Suddenly, Flowers, who had received only excellent performance reviews, was the subject of several negative disciplinary reports. Also, in one week, she was required to take four drug tests. Previously, she had been asked to take only one. Hallmark stopped socializing with Flowers, her co-workers began avoiding her, and the president of the hospital refused to shake her hand. In November 1995, after being put on probation twice, Flowers was fired. She filed a suit in a federal district court against Southern Regional under the ADA, arguing in part that she had been subjected to a hostile environment on the basis of her disability. The court entered a judgment in her favor and awarded her $100,000. Southern Regional appealed to the U.S. Court of Appeals for the Fifth Circuit.

ISSUE Can a hostile-environment claim be brought under the ADA?

DECISION Yes. The U.S. Court of Appeals for the Fifth Circuit held that the right to bring a hostile-environment claim can be inferred because the ADA is similar in language, purpose, and "remedial structure" to Title VII. The court added that Flowers was entitled only to nominal damages, however, because she did not prove that she actually suffered emotional injury.

REASON The court explained that "the Supreme Court interpreted Title VII, which contains language similar to that in the ADA, to provide a cause of action for harassment which is sufficiently severe or pervasive to alter the conditions of the victim's employment and create an abusive working environment." Although, unlike Title VII, the ADA does not expressly provide for a hostile-environment claim, "[w]e conclude the language of Title VII and the ADA dictates a consistent reading of the two statutes. * * * Not only are Title VII and the ADA similar in their language, they are also alike in their purposes and remedial structures. Both Title VII and the ADA are aimed at the same evil—employment discrimination against individuals of certain classes. * * * Accordingly, because Title VII has been extended to hostile work environment claims, we follow the growing consensus that [case law concerning harassment claims] be extended to claims of disability-based harassment."

FOR CRITICAL ANALYSIS—Political Consideration *What might an employer do to avoid hostile-environment claims under the ADA?*

Defenses to Employment Discrimination

The first line of defense for an employer charged with employment discrimination is, of course, to assert that the plaintiff has failed to meet his or her initial burden of proving that discrimination in fact occurred. As noted, plaintiffs bringing cases under the ADA sometimes find it difficult to meet this initial burden because they must prove that their alleged disabilities are disabilities covered by the ADA. Furthermore, plaintiffs in ADA cases must prove that they were otherwise qualified for the job and that their disabilities were the sole reason they were not hired or were fired.

Once a plaintiff succeeds in proving that discrimination occurred, the burden shifts to the employer to justify the discriminatory practice. Often, employers attempt to justify the discrimination by claiming that it was a result of a business necessity, a bona fide occupational qualification, or a seniority system. In some cases, as noted earlier, an effective antiharassment policy and prompt remedial action when harassment occurs may shield employers from liability under Title VII for sexual harassment.

BUSINESS NECESSITY
A defense to allegations of employment discrimination in which the employer demonstrates that an employment practice that discriminates against members of a protected class is related to job performance.

Business Necessity

An employer may defend against a claim of discrimination by asserting that a practice that has a discriminatory effect is a **business necessity.** • **Example 35.6** If requiring a high school diploma is shown to have a discriminatory effect, an employer might argue that a high school education is necessary for workers to perform the job at a required level of competence. If the employer can demonstrate to the court's satisfaction that there is a definite connection between a high school education and job performance, the employer will succeed in this business necessity defense. •

BONA FIDE OCCUPATIONAL QUALIFICATION

BONA FIDE OCCUPATIONAL QUALIFICATION (BFOQ) Identifiable characteristics reasonably necessary to the normal operation of a particular business. These characteristics can include gender, national origin, and religion, but not race.

Another defense applies when discrimination against a protected class is essential to a job—that is, when a particular trait is a **bona fide occupational qualification** (BFOQ). For example, a men's fashion magazine might legitimately hire only male models. Similarly, the Federal Aviation Administration can legitimately impose age limits for airline pilots. Race, however, can never be a BFOQ. Generally, courts have restricted the BFOQ defense to instances in which the employee's gender is essential to the job. In 1991, the United States Supreme Court held that even a fetal protection policy that was adopted to protect the unborn children of female employees from the harmful effects of exposure to lead was an unacceptable BFOQ.[27]

SENIORITY SYSTEMS

SENIORITY SYSTEM In regard to employment relationships, a system in which those who have worked longest for the company are first in line for promotions, salary increases, and other benefits; they are also the last to be laid off if the work force must be reduced.

An employer with a history of discrimination may have no members of protected classes in upper-level positions. Even if the employer now seeks to be unbiased, it may face a lawsuit in which the plaintiff asks a court to order that minorities be promoted ahead of schedule to compensate for past discrimination. If no present intent to discriminate is shown, and promotions or other job benefits are distributed according to a fair **seniority system** (in which workers with more years of service are promoted first, or laid off last), however, the employer has a good defense against the suit.

AFTER-ACQUIRED EVIDENCE IS NO DEFENSE

In some situations, employers have attempted to avoid liability for employment discrimination on the basis of "after-acquired evidence" of an employee's misconduct—that is, evidence of an employee's prior misconduct that is acquired after a lawsuit is under way. • **EXAMPLE 35.7** Suppose that an employer fires a worker, and the employee sues the employer for employment discrimination. During pretrial investigation, the employer learns that the employee made material misrepresentations on his or her employment application—misrepresentations that, had the employer known about them, would have served as a ground to fire the individual. •

According to the United States Supreme Court, after-acquired evidence of wrongdoing cannot be used to shield an employer entirely from liability for employment discrimination. It may, however, be used to limit the amount of damages for which the employer is liable.[28]

Affirmative Action

AFFIRMATIVE ACTION Job-hiring policies that give special consideration to members of protected classes in an effort to overcome present effects of past discrimination.

Federal statutes and regulations providing for equal opportunity in the workplace were designed to reduce or eliminate discriminatory practices with respect to hiring, retaining, and promoting employees. **Affirmative action** programs go a step further and

27. *United Auto Workers v. Johnson Controls, Inc.*, 113 U.S. 158, 111 S.Ct. 1196, 113 L.Ed.2d 158 (1991).
28. *McKennon v. Nashville Banner Publishing Co.*, 513 U.S. 352, 115 S.Ct. 879, 130 L.Ed.2d 852 (1995).

attempt to "make up" for past patterns of discrimination by giving members of protected classes preferential treatment in hiring or promotion.

Affirmative action programs have caused much controversy, particularly when they result in what is frequently called "reverse discrimination"—discrimination against "majority" workers, such as white males (or discrimination against other minority groups that may not be given preferential treatment under a particular affirmative action program). At issue is whether affirmative action programs, because of their inherently discriminatory nature, violate the equal protection clause of the Fourteenth Amendment to the Constitution.

THE *BAKKE* CASE

An early case addressing this issue, *Regents of the University of California v. Bakke,*[29] involved an affirmative action program implemented by the University of California at Davis. Allan Bakke, who had been turned down for medical school at the Davis campus, sued the university for reverse discrimination after he discovered that his academic record was better than those of some of the minority applicants who had been admitted to the program.

The United States Supreme Court held that affirmative action programs were subject to "intermediate scrutiny." Recall from the discussion of the equal protection clause in Chapter 2 that any law or action evaluated under a standard of intermediate scrutiny, to be constitutionally valid, must be substantially related to important government objectives. Applying this standard, the Court held that the university could give favorable weight to minority applicants as part of a plan to increase minority enrollment so as to achieve a more culturally diverse student body. The Court stated, however, that the use of a quota system, which explicitly reserved a certain number of places for minority applicants, violated the equal protection clause of the Fourteenth Amendment.

THE *ADARAND* CASE AND SUBSEQUENT DEVELOPMENTS

Although the *Bakke* case and later court decisions alleviated the harshness of the quota system, today's courts are going even further in questioning the constitutional validity of affirmative action programs. In 1995, in its landmark decision in *Adarand Constructors, Inc. v. Peña,*[30] the United States Supreme Court held that any federal, state, or local affirmative action program that uses racial or ethnic classifications as the basis for making decisions is subject to strict scrutiny by the courts.

In effect, the Court's opinion in *Adarand* means that an affirmative action program is constitutional only if it attempts to remedy past discrimination and does not make use of quotas or preferences. Furthermore, once such a program has succeeded in the goal of remedying past discrimination, it must be changed or dropped. Since then, other federal courts have followed the Supreme Court's lead by declaring affirmative action programs invalid unless they attempt to remedy specific practices of past or current discrimination.[31]

Some courts have gone even further. For example, the Court of Appeals for the Fifth Circuit, in its 1996 decision in *Hopwood v. State of Texas,*[32] held that an affirmative action program at the University of Texas School of Law in Austin violated the equal

29. 438 U.S. 265, 98 S.Ct. 2733, 57 L.Ed.2d 750 (1978).

30. 575 U.S. 200, 115 S.Ct. 2097, 132 L.Ed.2d 158 (1995).

31. See, for example, *Taxman v. Board of Education of the Township of Piscataway,* 91 F.3d 1547 (3d Cir. 1996); and *Schurr v. Resorts International Hotel, Inc.,* 196 F.3d 486 (3d Cir. 1999).

32. 84 F.3d 720 (5th Cir. 1996).

protection clause because it discriminated in favor of minority applicants. In its opinion, the court directly challenged the *Bakke* decision by stating that the use of race even as a means of achieving diversity on college campuses "undercuts the Fourteenth Amendment." The United States Supreme Court declined to hear the case, thus letting the lower court's decision stand. More recent decisions by the federal courts show that the courts are divided on the issue.[33] Until the Supreme Court rules definitively on the issue, affirmative action will be illegal in some areas of the country, such as the states included in the Fifth Circuit, and legal in other areas.

In the meantime, state and local governments have been taking action. California and Washington, by voter initiatives in 1996 and 1998, respectively, ended state-sponsored affirmative action in those states. Similar movements are currently under way in other state and local areas as well.

State Statutes

Although the focus of this chapter has been on federal legislation, most states also have statutes that prohibit employment discrimination. Generally, the kinds of discrimination prohibited under federal legislation are also prohibited by state laws. In addition, state statutes often provide protection for certain individuals who are not protected under federal laws. For example, a New Jersey appellate court has held that anyone over the age of eighteen is entitled to sue for age discrimination under the state law, which specifies no threshold age limit.[34]

Furthermore, as mentioned in Chapter 34, state laws prohibiting discrimination may apply to firms with fewer employees than the threshold number required under federal statutes, thus offering protection to a broader number of workers. Finally, state laws may provide additional damages, such as damages for emotional distress, that are not provided for under federal statutes.

---

33. See, for example, *Johnson v. Board of Regents of the University of Georgia,* 106 F.Supp.2d 1362 (S.D.Ga. 2000); and *Smith v. University of Washington School of Law,* 233 F.3d 1188 (9th Cir. 2000).
34. *Bergen Commercial Bank v. Sisler,* 307 N.J.Super. 333, 704 A.2d 1017 (1998).

APPLICATION Law and the Employer. . .

Interviewing Workers with Disabilities*

Many employers have been held liable under the Americans with Disabilities Act (ADA) of 1990 simply because they asked the wrong questions when interviewing job applicants with disabilities. If you are an employer, you can do several things to avoid violating the ADA.

*This *Application* is not meant to substitute for the services of an attorney who is licensed to practice law in your state.

Become Familiar with the EEOC Guidelines

As a preliminary matter, you should become familiar with the guidelines on job interviews issued by the Equal Employment Opportunity Commission (EEOC). These guidelines indicate the kinds of questions that employers may—and may not—ask job applicants with

(continued)

APPLICATION Law and the Employer. . .

Interviewing Workers with Disabilities—continued

disabilities. Often, the line between permissible and impermissible questions is a fine one. Consider these examples:

- *Ability to perform the job:* As an employer, you may ask a job applicant, "Can you do the job?" You may also ask whether the applicant can perform specific tasks related to the job. You may not ask the candidate, "How would you do the job?"—*unless* the disability is obvious, the applicant brings up the subject during the interview, or you ask the question of all applicants.
- *Absenteeism:* You may ask, "Can you meet our attendance requirements?" or "How many days were you absent last year?" You may not ask, "How many days were you sick last year?"
- *Drug use:* Generally, employers may ask about the current or past use of illegal drugs but not about drug addiction. Therefore, as an employer, you may ask, "Have you ever used illegal drugs?" or "Have you done so in the last six months?" You may not ask, "How often did you use illegal drugs?" or "Have you been treated for drug abuse?"
- *Alcohol use:* Generally, employers may ask about a candidate's drinking habits but not about alcoholism. Therefore, you may ask, "Do you drink alcohol?" or "Have you been arrested for driving while intoxicated?" but you may not ask, "How often do you drink?"
- *History of job-related injuries:* Employers may not ask a job candidate with a disability any questions about the applicant's previous job-related injuries or about workers' compensation claims submitted in the past.

Once you have made a job offer, however, you may ask the applicant questions concerning his or her disability, including questions about previous workers' compensation claims or about the extent of a drinking problem. You may also ask for medical documents verifying the nature of the applicant's disability. Generally, though, you should ask such questions only if you ask them of all applicants or if they are follow-up questions concerning the applicant's disability that she or he already disclosed during a job interview.

Obtain Legal Assistance and Instruct Staff Members

To avoid liability under the ADA, the wisest thing you can do is consult with an attorney. You should inform the attorney of the kinds of questions you typically ask job applicants during interviews or following employment offers. Then, you should work with the attorney in modifying these questions so that they are consistent with the EEOC's guidelines on permissible and impermissible questions. Finally, you should make sure that anyone on your staff who interviews job applicants receives thorough instructions on what questions may and may not be asked of candidates with disabilities. You might also remind your staff that under the ADA, the words and phraseology the interviewer uses may result in a violation of the ADA regardless of the interviewer's intentions.

Checklist for the Employer

1. Familiarize yourself with the EEOC's guidelines indicating what questions are and are not permissible when interviewing job applicants with disabilities.
2. Work with an attorney to create a list of particular types of questions that are or are not permissible under the EEOC's guidelines with respect to job candidates with disabilities.
3. Make sure that all persons in your firm who interview job applicants are thoroughly instructed as to the types of questions that they may and may not ask when interviewing job applicants with disabilities.

Key Terms

affirmative action 943
bona fide occupational qualification (BFOQ) 943
business necessity 942
disparate-impact discrimination 928
disparate-treatment discrimination 927
employment discrimination 927
prima facie case 928
protected class 926
seniority system 943
sexual harassment 931

Chapter Summary Employment Discrimination

Title VII of the Civil Rights Act of 1964 (See pages 927–935.)	Title VII prohibits employment discrimination based on race, color, national origin, religion, or gender. 1. *Procedures*—Employees must file a claim with the Equal Employment Opportunity Commission (EEOC). The EEOC may sue the employer on the employee's behalf; if not, the employee may sue the employer directly. 2. *Types of discrimination*—Title VII prohibits both intentional (disparate-treatment) and unintentional (disparate-impact) discrimination. Disparate-impact discrimination occurs when an employer's practice, such as hiring only persons with a certain level of education, has the effect of discriminating against a class of persons protected by Title VII. Title VII also extends to discriminatory practices, such as various forms of harassment, in the online environment. 3. *Remedies for discrimination under Title VII*—If a plaintiff proves that unlawful discrimination occurred, he or she may be awarded reinstatement, back pay, and retroactive promotions. Damages (both compensatory and punitive) may be awarded for intentional discrimination.
Equal Pay Act of 1963 (See pages 935–936.)	The Equal Pay Act of 1963 prohibits gender-based discrimination in the wages paid for equal work on jobs when their performance requires equal skill, effort, and responsibility under similar conditions.
Discrimination Based on Age (See pages 936–937.)	The Age Discrimination in Employment Act (ADEA) of 1967 prohibits employment discrimination on the basis of age against individuals forty years of age or older. Procedures for bringing a case under the ADEA are similar to those for bringing a case under Title VII.
Discrimination Based on Disability (See pages 937–942.)	The Americans with Disabilities Act (ADA) of 1990 prohibits employment discrimination against persons with disabilities who are otherwise qualified to perform the essential functions of the jobs for which they apply. 1. *Procedures and remedies*—To prevail on a claim under the ADA, the plaintiff must show that she or he has a disability, is otherwise qualified for the employment in question, and was excluded from the employment solely because of the disability. Procedures under the ADA are similar to those required in Title VII cases; remedies are also similar to those under Title VII. 2. *Definition of disability*—The ADA defines the term *disability* as a physical or mental impairment that substantially limits one or more major life activities; a record of such impairment; or being regarded as having such an impairment.

(continued)

Chapter Summary Employment Discrimination—continued

Discrimination Based on Disability—continued	3. *Reasonable accommodation*—Employers are required to reasonably accommodate the needs of persons with disabilities. Reasonable accommodations may include altering job-application procedures, modifying the physical work environment, and permitting more flexible work schedules. Employers are not required to accommodate the needs of all workers with disabilities. For example, employers need not accommodate workers who pose a definite threat to health and safety in the workplace or those who are not otherwise qualified for their jobs.
Defenses to Employment Discrimination (See pages 942–943.)	If a plaintiff proves that employment discrimination occurred, employers may avoid liability by successfully asserting certain defenses. Employers may assert that the discrimination was required for reasons of business necessity, to meet a bona fide occupational qualification, or to maintain a legitimate seniority system. Evidence of prior employee misconduct acquired after the employee has been fired is not a defense to discrimination.
Affirmative Action (See pages 943–945.)	Affirmative action programs attempt to "make up" for past patterns of discrimination by giving members of protected classes preferential treatment in hiring or promotion. Increasingly, such programs are being strictly scrutinized by the courts, and state-sponsored affirmative action has been banned in California and Washington.
State Statutes (See page 945.)	Generally, the kinds of discrimination prohibited by federal statutes are also prohibited by state laws. State laws may provide for more extensive protection and remedies than federal laws.

For Review

① Generally, what kind of conduct is prohibited by Title VII of the Civil Rights Act of 1964, as amended?

② What is the difference between disparate-treatment discrimination and disparate-impact discrimination?

③ What remedies are available under Title VII of the 1964 Civil Rights Act, as amended?

④ What federal acts prohibit discrimination based on age and discrimination based on disability?

⑤ What are three defenses to claims of employment discrimination?

Questions and Case Problems

35–1. Title VII Violations. Discuss fully whether any of the following actions would constitute a violation of Title VII of the 1964 Civil Rights Act, as amended:

(a) Tennington, Inc., is a consulting firm and has ten employees. These employees travel on consulting jobs in seven states. Tennington has an employment record of hiring only white males.

(b) Novo Films, Inc., is making a film about Africa and needs to employ approximately one hundred extras for this picture. Novo advertises in all major newspapers in southern California for the hiring of these extras. The ad states that only African Americans need apply.

35–2. Discrimination Based on Age. Tavo Jones had worked since 1974 for Westshore Resort, where he maintained golf carts. During the first decade, he received positive job evaluations and numerous merit pay raises. He was promoted to the position of supervisor of golf-cart maintenance at three courses. Then a new employee, Ben Olery, was placed in charge of the golf courses. He demoted Jones, who was over the age of forty, to running only one of the three cart facilities, and he froze Jones's salary indefinitely. Olery also demoted five other men over the age of forty. Another cart facility was placed under the supervision of Blake Blair. Later, the cart facilities for the three courses were again consolidated, but Blair—not Jones—was put in charge. At the time, Jones was still in his forties, and Blair was in his twenties. Jones overheard Blair say that "we are going to have to do away with these . . . old and senile" men. Jones quit and sued Westshore for employment discrimination. Should he prevail? Explain.

35–3. Disparate-Impact Discrimination. Chinawa, a major processor of cheese sold throughout the United States, employs one hundred workers at its principal processing plant. The plant is located in Heartland Corners, which has a population that is 50 percent white and 25 percent African American, with the balance Hispanic American, Asian American, and others. Chinawa requires a high school diploma as a condition of employment for its cleaning crew. Three-fourths of the white population complete high school, compared with only one-fourth of those in the minority groups. Chinawa has an all-white cleaning crew. Has Chinawa violated Title VII of the Civil Rights Act of 1964? Explain.

35–4. Defenses to Employment Discrimination. Dorothea O'Driscoll had worked as a quality control inspector for Hercules, Inc., for six years when her employment was terminated in 1986. O'Driscoll, who was over forty years of age, sued Hercules for age discrimination in violation of the Age Discrimination in Employment Act of 1967. While preparing for trial, Hercules learned that O'Driscoll had made several misrepresentations when she applied for the job. Among other things, she misrepresented her age, did not disclose a previous employer, falsely represented that she had never applied for work with Hercules before, and falsely stated that she had completed two quarters of study at a technical college. Additionally, on her application for group insurance coverage, she misrepresented the age of her son, who would otherwise have been ineligible for coverage as her dependent. Hercules defended against O'Driscoll's claim of age discrimination by stating that had it known of this misconduct, it would have terminated her employment anyway. What should the court decide? Discuss fully. [*O'Driscoll v. Hercules, Inc.*, 12 F.3d 176 (10th Cir. 1994)]

35–5. Disparate-Impact Discrimination. Local 1066 of the Steamship Clerks Union accepted only new members who were sponsored by existing members. All of the existing members were white. During a six-year period, the local admitted thirty new members, all of whom were relatives of present members and also white. The Equal Employment Opportunity Commission filed a suit in a federal district court against the union, alleging that this practice constituted disparate-impact discrimination under Title VII. The union argued that it was only continuing a family tradition. What does each party have to prove to win its case? Should the union be required to change its practice? [*EEOC v. Steamship Clerks Union, Local 1066*, 48 F.3d 594 (1st Cir. 1995)]

35–6. Discrimination Based on Disability. When the University of Maryland Medical System Corp. learned that one of its surgeons was HIV positive, the university offered him transfers to positions that did not involve surgery. The surgeon refused, and the university terminated him. The surgeon filed a suit in a federal district court against the university, alleging in part a violation of the Americans with Disabilities Act. The surgeon claimed that he was "otherwise qualified" for his former position. What does he have to prove to win his case? Should he be reinstated? [*Doe v. University of Maryland Medical System Corp.*, 50 F.3d 1261 (4th Cir. 1995)]

35–7. Discrimination Based on Race. Theodore Rosenblatt, a white attorney, worked for the law firm of Bivona & Cohen, P.C. When Bivona & Cohen terminated Rosenblatt's employment, he filed a suit in a federal district court against the firm. Rosenblatt claimed that he had been discharged because he was married to an African American and that a discharge for such a reason violated Title VII and other laws. The firm filed a motion for summary judgment, arguing that he was alleging discrimination against his wife, not himself, and thus did not have standing to sue under Title VII for racial discrimination. Should the court grant or deny the motion? Explain. [*Rosenblatt v. Bivona & Cohen, P.C.*, 946 F.Supp. 298 (S.D.N.Y. 1996)]

35–8. Religious Discrimination. Mary Tiano, a devout Roman Catholic, worked for Dillard Department Stores, Inc. (Dillard's), in Phoenix, Arizona. Dillard's considered Tiano a productive employee because her sales exceeded $200,000 a year. At the time, the store gave its managers the discretion to grant unpaid leave to employees but prohibited vacations or leave during the holiday season—October through December. Tiano felt that she had a "calling" to go on a "pilgrimage" in October 1988 to Medjugorje, Yugoslavia, where some persons claimed to have had visions of the Virgin Mary. The Catholic Church had not designated the site an official pilgrimage site, the visions were not expected to be stronger in October, and tours were available at other times. The store managers denied Tiano's request for leave, but she had a nonrefundable ticket and left anyway. Dillard's terminated her employment. For a year, Tiano searched for a new job and did not attain the level of her Dillard's salary for four years. She filed a suit in a federal district court against Dillard's, alleging religious discrimination in violation of Title VII. Can Tiano establish a *prima facie* case of religious discrimination? Explain. [*Tiano v. Dillard Department Stores, Inc.*, 139 F.3d 679 (9th Cir. 1998)]

35–9. Discrimination Based on Disability. Vaughn Murphy was first diagnosed with hypertension (high blood pressure) when he was ten years old. Unmedicated, his blood pressure is approximately 250/160. With medication, however, he can function normally and engage in the same activities as anyone else. In 1994, United Parcel Service, Inc. (UPS), hired Murphy to be a mechanic, a position that required him to drive commercial motor vehicles. To get the job, Murphy had to meet a U.S. Department of Transportation (DOT) regulation that a driver have "no current clinical diagnosis of high blood pressure likely to interfere with his/her ability to operate a commercial vehicle safely." At the time, Murphy's blood pressure was measured at 186/124, but he was erroneously certified and started work. Within a month, the error was discovered and he was fired. Murphy obtained another mechanic's job—one that did not require DOT certification—and filed a suit in a federal district court against UPS, claiming discrimination under the Americans with Disabilities Act. UPS filed a motion for summary judgment. Should the court grant UPS's motion? Explain. [*Murphy v. United Parcel Service, Inc.*, 527 U.S. 516, 119 S.Ct. 2133, 144 L.Ed.2d 484 (1999)]

TEST YOUR KNOWLEDGE—ANSWER ON THE WEB

35–10. PGA Tour, Inc., sponsors professional golf tournaments. A player may enter in several ways, but the most common method is to successfully compete in a three-stage qualifying tournament known as the "Q-School." Anyone may enter the Q-School by submitting two letters of recommendation and paying $3,000 to cover greens fees and the cost of a golf cart, which is permitted during the first two stages, but is prohibited during the third stage. The rules governing the events include the "Rules of Golf," which apply at all levels of amateur and professional golf and do not prohibit the use of golf carts, and the "hard card," which applies specifically to the PGA tour and requires the players to walk the course during most of a tournament. Casey Martin is a talented golfer with a degenerative circulatory disorder that prevents him from walking golf courses. Martin entered the Q-School and asked for permission to use a cart during the third stage. PGA refused. Martin filed a suit in a federal district court against PGA, alleging a violation of the Americans with Disabilities Act. Is a golf cart in these circumstances a "reasonable accommodation" under the ADA? Why or why not? [*PGA Tour, Inc. v. Martin,* 531 U.S. 1049, 121 S.Ct. 1879, 149 L.Ed.2d 904 (2001)]

A QUESTION OF ETHICS AND SOCIAL RESPONSIBILITY

35–11. Luz Long and three other Hispanic employees (the plaintiffs) worked as bank tellers for the Culmore branch of the First Union Corp. of Virginia. The plaintiffs often conversed with one another in Spanish, their native language. In 1992, the Culmore branch manager adopted an "English-only" policy, which required all employees to speak English during working hours unless they had to speak another language to assist customers. The plaintiffs refused to cooperate with the new policy and were eventually fired. In a suit against the bank, the plaintiffs alleged that the English-only policy discriminated against them on the basis of their national origin. The court granted the bank's motion for summary judgment, concluding that "[t]here is nothing in Title VII which . . . provides that an employee has a right to speak his or her native tongue while on the job." [*Long v. First Union Corp. of Virginia,* 894 F.Supp. 933 (E.D.Va. 1995)]

1. The bank argued that the policy was implemented in response to complaints made by fellow employees that the Spanish-speaking employees were creating a hostile environment by speaking Spanish among themselves in the presence of other employees. From an ethical perspective, is this a sufficient reason to institute an English-only policy?
2. Is it ever ethically justifiable for employers to deny bilingual employees the opportunity to speak their native language while on the job?
3. Might there be situations in which English-only policies are necessary to promote worker health and safety?
4. Generally, what are the pros and cons of English-only policies in the workplace?

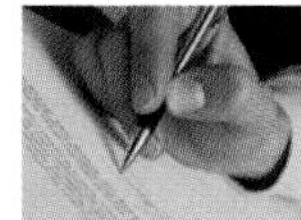

FOR CRITICAL ANALYSIS

35–12. Why has the federal government limited the application of the statutes discussed in this chapter only to firms with a specified number of employees, such as fifteen or twenty? Should these laws apply to all employers, regardless of size?

Internet Exercises

Go to the *Business Law Today* home page at **http://blt.westbuslaw.com**. Select "Interactive Study Center" and then click on "Chapter 35." There you will find the following Internet research exercises that you can perform to learn more about laws prohibiting employment discrimination:

Activity 35–1: Americans with Disabilities
Activity 35–2: Equal Employment Opportunity

Before the Test

Go to the *Business Law Today* home page at **http//blt.westbuslaw.com**. Click on "Interactive Quizzes." You will find at least twenty interactive questions relating to this chapter.

UNIT SEVEN Cumulative Business Hypothetical

Alpha Software, Inc., and Beta Products Corporation—both small firms—are competitors in the business of software research, development, and production.

① Alpha and Beta form a joint venture to research, develop, and produce new software for a particular line of computers. Does this business combination violate the antitrust laws? If so, is it a *per se* violation, or is it subject to the rule of reason? Alpha and Beta decide to merge. After the merger, Beta is the surviving firm. What aspect of this firm's presence in the market will be assessed to decide whether this merger is in violation of any antitrust laws?

② To market its products profitably, Beta considers a number of advertising and labeling proposals. One proposal is that Beta suggest in its advertising that one of its software products has a certain function without specifying on the packaging that the product does not actually have that capability. Another suggestion is that Beta sell half of a certain program in packaging that misleads the buyer into believing the entire program is included. To obtain the entire program, customers would need to buy a second product. Can Beta implement these suggestions or otherwise market its products any way it likes? If not, why not?

③ Beta generates hazardous waste from the production part of its operations. Gamma Transport Company transports the waste to Omega Waste Corporation, which owns and operates a hazardous waste-disposal site. At the site, some containers leak hazardous waste, and the Environmental Protection Agency (EPA) cleans it up. From whom can the EPA recover the cost of the clean-up?

④ Beta provides health insurance for its two hundred employees, including Dan. For personal medical reasons, Dan takes twelve weeks' leave. During this period, can Dan continue his coverage under Beta's health-insurance plan? If so, at whose expense? After Dan returns to work, Beta closes Dan's division and terminates the employees, including Dan. Can Dan continue his coverage under Beta's health-insurance plan? If so, at whose expense?

⑤ Beta has a policy against sexual harassment that includes specific procedures for reporting, investigating, and resolving incidents of alleged harassment. Kay, a Beta employee, believes that she has been the object of her supervisor's sexual comments on the job and she perceives these comments as offensive. She reports the incident, and Beta follows up with an investigation but decides that there is no basis for disciplining the supervisor. Kay subsequently quits her job and eventually files a suit against Beta. What must Kay prove to win her case? What is Beta's best defense?

National Labor Relations Board v. Kentucky River Community Care, Inc.

The National Labor Relations Act (NLRA) of 1935 is discussed in Chapter 34. The NLRA protects employees from employers' unfair labor practices. Workers are not protected, however, if they are deemed to be supervisors*—employees who exercise "independent judgment" in "responsibly . . . direct[ing]" other employees "in the interest of the employer."*[1] *In this extended case study, we examine* National Labor Relations Board v. Kentucky River Community Care, Inc.,[2] *a decision that applied this definition to a group of nurses.*

CASE BACKGROUND

In Pippa Passes, Kentucky, Kentucky River Community Care, Inc., operates the Caney Creek Developmental Complex, a care facility for residents who suffer from mental retardation and mental illness. Caney Creek employs approximately 110 professional and nonprofessional employees and a dozen managers and supervisors. In 1997, the Kentucky State District Council of Carpenters (a labor union) petitioned the National Labor Relations Board (NLRB) to represent as a single unit all 110 employees at Caney Creek.

Kentucky River objected to the inclusion of Caney Creek's six registered nurses in the bargaining unit, arguing that they were supervisors. The nurses directed some of the patient care done by the nurses' aides and, on some shifts, were responsible for maintaining adequate staffing levels. They could only ask—not force—employees to work, however. The NLRB included the nurses, directed an election, and certified the winning union as the employees' representative.

Kentucky River refused to bargain with the union. On an unfair labor practice complaint, the NLRB issued a bargaining order against the employer, who appealed to the U.S. Court of Appeals for the Sixth Circuit. The court refused to enforce the order. The NLRB appealed to the United States Supreme Court.

1. 29 U.S.C. Section 152(11).
2. 532 U.S. 706, 121 S.Ct. 1861, 149 L.Ed.2d 939 (2001). This opinion may be accessed online at **http://supct.law.cornell.edu/supct/cases/name.htm**. In the "Search" box, type "Kentucky River," select "Current decisions only," and click on "submit." In the result, scroll to the name of the case and click on it to access the opinion.

MAJORITY OPINION

Justice *SCALIA* delivered the opinion of the Court.

* * * *

* * * The only basis asserted by the Board [NLRB] * * * for rejecting respondent's [Kentucky River's] proof of [the nurses'] supervisory status * * * was the Board's interpretation * * * that employees do not use "independent judgment" when they exercise "ordinary professional or technical judgment in directing less-skilled employees to deliver services in accordance with employer-specified standards." * * *

Two aspects of the Board's interpretation are reasonable * * * . First, it is certainly true that the statutory term "independent judgment" is ambiguous with respect to the *degree* of discretion required for supervisory status. Many nominally supervisory functions may be performed without the exercise of such a degree of * * * judgment or discretion * * * as would warrant a finding of supervisory status under the Act [NLRA]. It falls clearly within the Board's discretion to determine, within reason, what scope of discretion qualifies. Second, * * * it is also undoubtedly true that the degree of judgment that might ordinarily be required to conduct a particular task may be reduced below the statutory threshold by detailed orders and regulations issued by the employer. * * *

The Board, however, argues further that the judgment even of employees who are permitted by their employer to exercise a sufficient degree of discretion is not "independent judgment" if it is a particular *kind* of judgment, namely, "ordinary professional or technical judgment in directing less-skilled employees to deliver services." The first five words of this interpretation insert a startling categorical exclusion into statutory text that does not suggest its existence. * * * [T]he Board's categorical exclusion turns on factors that have nothing to do with the degree of discretion an employee exercises. Let the judgment be significant and only loosely constrained by the employer; if it is "professional or technical" it will nonetheless not be independent. * * *

* * * [T]he Board limits its categorical exclusion with a qualifier: Only professional judgment that is applied "in directing less-skilled employees to deliver services" is excluded from the statutory category of "independent judgment." This second rule is no less striking than the first, and is directly contrary to the text of the statute. *Every* supervisory function listed by the Act is accompanied by the statutory requirement that its exercise requires the use of independent judgment before supervisory status will obtain, but the Board would apply its restriction upon "independent judgment" to just 1 of the 12 listed functions: "responsibly to direct." There is no apparent * * * justification for this * * * limitation, and the Board has offered none. Surely no conceptual justification can be found in the proposition that supervisors exercise professional, technical, or experienced judgment only when they direct other employees. Decisions to hire, * * * suspend, lay off, recall, promote, discharge, * * * or discipline other employees, must often depend upon that same judgment * * *.

* * * *

* * * [T]he Board contends that its interpretation is necessary to preserve the inclusion of "professional employees" within the coverage of the Act. * * *

What is at issue is the Board's contention that the policy of covering professional employees under the Act justifies the categorical exclusion of professional judgments from a term, "independent judgment," that naturally includes them. And further, that it justifies limiting this categorical exclusion to the supervisory function of responsibly directing other employees. These contentions contradict both the text and structure of the statute * * *.

* * * *

* * * The judgment of the Court of Appeals is affirmed.

It is so ordered.

DISSENTING OPINION

Justice *STEVENS,* * * * dissenting * * *.

* * * *

The question before us is whether the Board's interpretation [of the term "independent judgment"] is both rational and consistent with the Act. To my mind, the Board's test is both fully rational and entirely consistent with the Act.

The term "independent judgment" is indisputably ambiguous, and it is settled law that the NLRB's interpretation of ambiguous language in the National Labor Relations Act is entitled to deference. Such deference is particularly appropriate when the statutory ambiguity is compounded by the use of one ambiguous term—"independent judgment"—to modify another, equally ambiguous term—namely, "responsibly to direct."

Moreover, since Congress has expressly provided that professional employees are entitled to the protection of the Act, there is good reason to resolve the ambiguities consistently with the Board's interpretation. At the same time that Congress acted to exclude supervisors from the NLRA's protection, it explicitly extended those same protections to professionals, who, by definition, engage in work that involves "the consistent exercise of discretion and judgment in its performance." * * * [I]f the term "supervisor" is construed too broadly, without regard for the statutory context, then Congress' inclusion of professionals within the Act's protections is effectively nullified. In my opinion, the Court's approach does precisely what it accuses the Board of doing—namely, reading one part of the statute to the exclusion of the other.

QUESTIONS FOR ANALYSIS

① **Law.** What did the majority conclude on the central issue in this case, and what support did it provide for that conclusion?

② **Law.** In cases such as this one, who should have the burden of proving that an employee is, or is not, a supervisor, and why?

③ **Economic Consideration.** Which employees are affected by this decision, and what is one of the ultimate results of that decision?

④ **Political Dimensions.** As highlighted by a reading of the opinions in this case, what is the source of the opposing parties' contentions?

⑤ **Implications for the Employer.** Does the holding in this case indicate what an employer might do to exempt certain employees from the protection of federal labor laws?

Property and Its Protection

UNIT 8

UNIT CONTENTS

CHAPTER 36

Personal Property and Bailments

"The great . . . end . . . of men united into commonwealths, and putting themselves under government, is the preservation of their property."

John Locke, 1632–1704
(English political philosopher)

CHAPTER CONTENTS

LEARNING OBJECTIVES

After reading this chapter, you should be able to answer the following questions:

① What is real property? What is personal property?

② What does it mean to own property in fee simple? What is the difference between a joint tenancy and a tenancy in common?

③ What are the three elements necessary for an effective gift? How else can property be acquired?

④ What are the three elements of a bailment?

⑤ What are the basic rights and duties of the bailee? What are the rights and duties of the bailor?

PROPERTY
Legally protected rights and interests in anything with an ascertainable value that is subject to ownership.

REAL PROPERTY
Land and everything attached to it, such as trees and buildings.

PERSONAL PROPERTY
Property that is movable; any property that is not real property.

CHATTEL
All forms of personal property.

Property consists of the legally protected rights and interests a person has in anything with an ascertainable value that is subject to ownership. Property would have little value (and the word would have little meaning) if the law did not define the right to use it, to sell or dispose of it, and to prevent trespass on it. Indeed, John Locke, as indicated in the opening quotation, considered the preservation of property to be the primary reason for the establishment of government.

Property is divided into real property and personal property. **Real property** (sometimes called *realty* or *real estate*) means the land and everything permanently attached to it. Everything else is **personal property**, or *personalty*. Attorneys sometimes refer to personal property as **chattel**, a term used under the common law to denote all forms of personal property. Personal property can be tangible or intangible. *Tangible* personal property, such as a TV set or a car, has physical substance. *Intangible* personal property represents some set

"Private property began the minute somebody had a mind of his own."

E. E. CUMMINGS
1894–1962
(American poet)

of rights and interests but has no real physical existence. Stocks and bonds, patents, and copyrights are examples of intangible personal property.

In the first part of this chapter, we look at the ways in which title to property is held; the methods of acquiring ownership of personal property; and issues relating to mislaid, lost, and abandoned personal property. In the second part of the chapter, we examine bailment relationships. A *bailment* is created when personal property is temporarily delivered into the care of another without a transfer of title. This is the distinguishing characteristic of a bailment compared with a sale or a gift—there is no passage of title and no intent to transfer title.

Property Ownership

Property ownership[1] can be viewed as a bundle of rights, including the right to possess property and to dispose of it—by sale, gift, lease, or other means.

Fee Simple

FEE SIMPLE
An absolute form of property ownership entitling the property owner to use, possess, or dispose of the property as he or she chooses during his or her lifetime. On death, the interest in the property descends to the owner's heirs.

A person who holds the entire bundle of rights to property is said to be the owner in **fee simple**. The owner in fee simple is entitled to use, possess, or dispose of the property as he or she chooses during his or her lifetime, and on this owner's death, the interests in the property descend to his or her heirs. We will return to this form of property ownership in Chapter 37, in the context of ownership rights in real property. (Whether a domain name is property that can be garnished to satisfy a debt is a question explored in this chapter's *Business Law in the Online World* feature on page 958.)

Concurrent Ownership

Persons who share ownership rights simultaneously in a particular piece of property are said to be *concurrent* owners. There are two principal types of concurrent ownership: tenancy in common and joint tenancy. Other types of concurrent ownership include tenancy by the entirety and community property.

TENANCY IN COMMON
Co-ownership of property in which each party owns an undivided interest that passes to her or his heirs at death.

Tenancy in Common The term **tenancy in common** refers to a form of co-ownership in which each of two or more persons owns an *undivided* interest in the property. The interest is undivided because each tenant has rights in the *whole* property. • **EXAMPLE 36.1** Rosa and Chad together own a collection of rare stamps as tenants in common. This does not mean that Rosa owns some particular stamps and Chad others. Rather, it means that Rosa and Chad each have rights in the *entire* collection. (If Rosa owned some of the stamps and Chad owned others, then the interest would be *divided.*)•

On the death of a tenant in common, that tenant's interest in the property passes to her or his heirs. • **EXAMPLE 36.2** Should Rosa die before Chad, a one-half interest in the stamp collection would become the property of Rosa's heirs. If Rosa sold her interest to Fred before she died, Fred and Chad would be co-owners as tenants in common. If Fred died, his interest in the personal property would pass to his heirs, and they in turn would own the property with Chad as tenants in common.•

JOINT TENANCY
The joint ownership of property by two or more co-owners in which each co-owner owns an undivided portion of the property. On the death of one of the joint tenants, his or her interest automatically passes to the surviving joint tenant(s).

Joint Tenancy In a **joint tenancy**, each of two or more persons owns an undivided interest in the property, and a deceased joint tenant's interest passes to the surviving joint

1. The principles discussed in this section apply equally to real property ownership, discussed in Chapter 37.

BUSINESS LAW: //in the Online World

Is a Domain Name Property?

Recall from Chapter 23 that garnishment occurs when a creditor is permitted, by court order, to collect a debt by seizing property of the debtor that is being held by a third party. Typically, garnishment involves obtaining from the debtor's employer a portion of the debtor's wages or obtaining from the debtor's bank the funds in the debtor's bank account. In this context, consider a question that recently came before a Virginia state court: Can a debtor's domain names be garnished and sold to the highest bidder to collect a court judgment? Are domain names "property" subject to garnishment?

The question arose after a federal district court had awarded Umbro International, Inc., nearly $24,000 to cover its attorneys' fees and expenses in a lawsuit concerning a dispute over rights to the domain name *umbro.com.* Because the defendants in the suit, James Tombas and his Canadian corporation, had no assets in the United States to satisfy the judgment, Umbro instituted a garnishment proceeding in a Virginia state court against Network Solutions, Inc. (NSI), with which Tombas had registered more than twenty other domain names. Umbro sought to force a judicial sale of those names. NSI objected to the garnishment summons, arguing that domain names cannot function on the Internet in the absence of the services provided by a domain name registrar such as NSI. Thus, domain name registration agreements are essentially contracts for services, which are not subject to garnishment.

A Case of First Impression— The Trial Court's Decision

In this case of first impression (a case involving an issue never before decided by Virginia courts), the Virginia trial court determined that the judgment debtor's (Tombas's) domain name registrations were a new and "valuable form of intangible property subject to garnishment." In return for registering the names and paying the appropriate fees, the debtor obtained the exclusive right to use the names for a specified period of time. The court thus held that the debtor had a "possessory interest"—a form of property interest—in the domain names registered with NSI and that this property interest was subject to garnishment. Accordingly, the court ordered NSI to deposit control over all of the judgment debtor's Internet domain name registrations into the registry of the court for sale by the sheriff's office to the highest bidders.

The Virginia Supreme Court Reverses

NSI appealed the case to the Virginia Supreme Court, which reversed the trial court's decision and entered a judgment in NSI's favor. NSI argued that although a domain name registrant acquires the contractual right to the exclusive use of a unique domain name for a specified time period, that right is inextricably bound to the domain name services that NSI provides. The court agreed, stating that "whatever contractual rights the judgment debtor has in the domain names at issue in this appeal, those rights do not exist separate and apart from NSI's services that make the domain names operational Internet addresses."

The court pointed out that in garnishment cases, usually the question is whether the garnishee is liable to the judgment debtor and, if so, the amount due. In this case, said the court, "the only liability on the part of NSI is the provision of its Internet domain name services to the judgment debtor. Although, as Umbro points out, domain names are being bought and sold in today's marketplace, we are not willing to sanction the garnishment of NSI's services under the terms of our present garnishment statutes. Even though the Internet is a 'new avenue of commerce,' we cannot extend established legal principles beyond their statutory parameters."[a]

FOR CRITICAL ANALYSIS

Analyze the reasoning of the lower court and the state supreme court, respectively. Which argument do you find more convincing? Explain.

a. *Network Solutions, Inc. v. Umbro International, Inc.,* 259 Va. 759, 529 S.E.2d 80 (2000).

tenant or tenants. The rights of a surviving joint tenant to inherit a deceased joint tenant's ownership interest, which are referred to as *survivorship rights,* distinguish the joint tenancy from the tenancy in common. A joint tenancy can be terminated before a joint tenant's death by gift or by sale; in this situation, the person who receives the property as a gift or who purchases the property becomes a tenant in common, not a joint tenant.

• **EXAMPLE 36.3** If, in the preceding example, Rosa and Chad held their stamp collection in a joint tenancy and if Rosa died before Chad, the entire collection would become the property of Chad; Rosa's heirs would receive absolutely no interest in the collection. If Rosa, while living, sold her interest to Fred, however, the sale would terminate the joint tenancy, and Fred and Chad would become owners as tenants in common. •

FOR CRITICAL ANALYSIS
What policy considerations might motivate a government to restrict the transfer of property to legally designated heirs (such as spouses, children, and so on)?

INTERNATIONAL PERSPECTIVE

Islamic Law and Concurrent Ownership

In the United States, joint tenancy is a common form of concurrent ownership. Married couples, for example, often hold title to property, such as their homes or cars, as joint tenants with survivorship rights. In contrast, Islamic law, which is followed in Muslim countries, makes no provision for joint tenancy with rights of survivorship. Instead, concurrent owners of property are normally regarded as tenants in common. In regard to survivorship rights, Islamic law provides that an owner can transfer no more than one-third of an estate by will. The rest of the estate must be inherited by those who are designated as legal heirs under Islamic law.

TENANCY BY THE ENTIRETY
The joint ownership of property by a husband and wife. Neither party can transfer his or her interest in the property without the consent of the other.

COMMUNITY PROPERTY
A form of concurrent ownership of property in which each spouse technically owns an undivided one-half interest in property acquired during the marriage. This form of joint ownership occurs in only ten states and Puerto Rico.

Tenancy by the Entirety Concurrent ownership of property can also take the form of a **tenancy by the entirety**—a form of co-ownership between a husband and wife that is similar to a joint tenancy, except that a spouse cannot transfer his or her interest during his or her lifetime without the consent of the other spouse.

Community Property When property is held as **community property**, each spouse technically owns an undivided one-half interest in property acquired during the marriage. The community property form of ownership occurs in only ten states and Puerto Rico.

Acquiring Ownership of Personal Property

The most common way of acquiring personal property is by purchasing it. We have already discussed the purchase and sale of personal property (goods) in Chapters 14 through 18. Often, property is acquired by will or inheritance, a topic we cover in Chapter 38. Here we look at additional ways in which ownership of personal property can be acquired, including acquisition by possession, production, gift, accession, and confusion.

"In no country in the world is the love of property more active and more anxious than in the United States."

ALEXIS DE TOCQUEVILLE
1805–1859
(French historian and statesman)

POSSESSION

One example of acquiring ownership by possession is the capture of wild animals. Wild animals belong to no one in their natural state, and the first person to take possession of a wild animal normally owns it. The killing of a wild animal amounts to assuming ownership of it. Merely being in hot pursuit does not give title, however. There are two exceptions to this basic rule. First, any wild animals captured by a trespasser are the property of the landowner, not the trespasser. Second, if wild animals are captured or killed in violation of wild-game statutes, the capturer does not obtain title to the animals; rather, the state does. (Sometimes, a question arises as to what is a wild animal—see this chapter's *Letter of the Law* feature.)

Those who find lost or abandoned property also can acquire ownership rights through mere possession of the property, as will be discussed later in the chapter. (Ownership rights in real property can also be acquired through possession, such as adverse possession—see Chapter 37.)

PRODUCTION

Production—the fruits of labor—is another means of acquiring ownership of personal property. For example, writers, inventors, and manufacturers all produce personal property and thereby acquire title to it. (In some situations, though, as when a researcher is hired to invent a new product or technique, the researcher-producer may not own what is produced—see Chapter 24.)

GIFTS

GIFT
Any voluntary transfer of property made without consideration, past or present.

A **gift** is another fairly common means of acquiring and transferring ownership of real and personal property. A gift is essentially a voluntary transfer of property ownership for which no consideration is given. As discussed in Chapter 9, the presence of consideration is what distinguishes a contract from a gift. Certain conditions must exist, however, before a gift will be deemed effective in the eyes of the law. The donor (the one making the gift) must intend to make the gift, the gift must be delivered to the donee (the recipient of the gift), and the donee must accept the gift. We examine each of these requirements here, as well as the requirements of a gift made in contemplation of imminent death.

LETTER OF THE LAW

Are Clams "Wild Animals"?

Timothy Longshore was arrested and convicted for stealing clams from a private beach near Puget Sound, Washington. On appeal to the Supreme Court of Washington, Longshore argued that he had not committed theft because the landowner did not own the clams. He asserted that because clams were wild animals, or *ferae naturae,* they were not owned by anyone until someone took possession of them. The court, however, viewed the matter differently. The court emphasized that clams "ordinarily live in the soil under the waters" and belong with the land. "When taken, they must be wrenched from their beds, made well down in the soil itself." Therefore, said the court, it must follow that a private landowner "has the right to exercise dominion [control] and ownership over what is upon the land, and especially over things so closely related to the soil as clams." The court also had the letter of Washington law on its side: the Washington legislature had enacted a statute that, among other things, stated that the term *wildlife* "does not include . . . fish, shellfish, and marine invertebrates classified as food fish or shellfish."[a]

THE BOTTOM LINE

In the state of Washington, an individual who privately owns tidelands also owns any naturally occurring clams embedded in the soil.

a. *State v. Longshore,* 141 Wash.2d 414, 5 P.3d 1256 (2000).

ETHICAL ISSUE 36.1

Who owns the engagement ring?

Often, when a couple decides to marry, one party gives the other an engagement ring. What if the engagement is called off? Etiquette authorities routinely counsel that if the woman breaks the engagement, she should return the ring, but if the man calls the wedding off, the woman is entitled to keep the ring. Interestingly, the courts are coming up with a different approach. Courts in New York, Ohio, Kansas, Michigan, and a number of other states have held that an engagement ring is not a real gift. Rather, it is a "conditional gift" that becomes final only if the marriage occurs. If the marriage does not occur, the ring is returned to the donor regardless of who broke the engagement.[2] This so-called modern trend among the courts is actually similar to the law of ancient Rome, which mandated that when an engagement was broken, the woman had to return the ring, as a penalty, regardless of who was at fault. Some judges, however, disagree with the conditional-gift theory and contend that an engagement ring is a gift, and, as such, it belongs to the donee, even if the engagement is broken. As one judge stated, "Those jurisdictions that rely on the analysis that an engagement ring is a conditional gift ignore general gift law, which holds that a gift is complete if there is intent, delivery, and acceptance."[3]

ON THE WEB Who owns a gift received by a married person—the spouse who received the gift or the husband and wife jointly? To learn the answer to this question, go to Scott Law Firm's Web page at **http://www.scottlawfirm.com/property.htm**.

Donative Intent When a gift is challenged in court, the court will determine whether donative intent exists by looking at the surrounding circumstances. • **EXAMPLE 36.4** A court may look at the relationship between the parties and the size of the gift in relation to the donor's other assets. A gift to a mortal enemy is viewed with suspicion. Similarly, when a gift represents a large portion of a person's assets, the court will scrutinize the transaction closely to determine the mental capacity of the donor and ascertain whether any element of fraud or duress is present. •

Delivery The gift must be delivered to the donee. An effective delivery requires giving up complete control and **dominion** (ownership rights) over the subject matter of the gift. When a gift cannot be physically delivered, a symbolic, or *constructive,* delivery will be sufficient. **Constructive delivery** is an act that the law holds to be equivalent to an act of actual delivery. • **EXAMPLE 36.5** Suppose that you want to make a gift of various old rare coins that you have stored in a safe-deposit box. You certainly cannot deliver the box itself to the donee, and you do not want to take the coins out of the bank. In this situation, the delivery of the key to the safe-deposit box (along with appropriate instructions to the bank) constitutes a constructive delivery of the contents of the box. •

DOMINION
Ownership rights in property, including the right to possess and control the property.

CONSTRUCTIVE DELIVERY
An act equivalent to the actual, physical delivery of property that cannot be physically delivered because of difficulty or impossibility; for example, the transfer of a key to a safe constructively delivers the contents of the safe.

The delivery of intangible property—such as stocks, bonds, insurance policies, contracts, and so on—is always accomplished by symbolic, or constructive, delivery. This is because the documents represent rights and are not, in themselves, the true property.

Delivery may be accomplished by means of a third party. If the third party is the agent of the donor, the delivery is effective when the agent delivers the gift to the donee. If the third party is the agent of the donee, the gift is effectively delivered when the donor delivers the property to the donee's agent.[4] Naturally, no delivery is necessary if the gift is already in the hands of the donee.

2. See, for example, *Meyer v. Mitnick,* 244 Mich.App. 697, 625 N.W.2d 136 (2001).
3. See the dissenting opinion in *Heiman v. Parrish,* 262 Kan. 926, 942 P.2d 631 (1997).
4. *Bickford v. Mattocks,* 95 Me. 547, 50 A. 894 (1901).

In the following case, the court focused on the requirement that a donor must give up complete control and dominion over property given to the donee before a gift can be effectively delivered.

Landmark and Classic Cases

CASE 36.1 In re Estate of Piper

Missouri Court of Appeals, 1984.
676 S.W.2d 897.

FACTS Gladys Piper died intestate (without a will) in 1982. At her death, she owned miscellaneous personal property worth $5,000 and had in her purse $200 in cash and two diamond rings, known as the Andy Piper rings. The contents of her purse were taken by her niece Wanda Brown, allegedly to preserve them for the estate. Clara Kaufmann, a friend of Piper's, filed a claim against the estate for $4,800. From October 1974 until Piper's death, Kaufmann had taken Piper to the doctor, beauty shop, and grocery store; had written her checks to pay her bills; and had helped her care for her home. Kaufmann maintained that Piper had promised to pay her for these services and had given her the diamond rings as a gift. A Missouri state trial court denied her request for payment; the court found that her services had been voluntary. Kaufmann then filed a petition for delivery of personal property, the rings, which was granted by the trial court. Brown, other heirs, and the administrator of Piper's estate appealed.

ISSUE Had Gladys Piper made an effective gift of the rings to Clara Kaufmann?

DECISION No. The state appellate court reversed the judgment of the trial court on the ground that Piper had never delivered the rings to Kaufmann.

REASON Kaufmann claimed that the rings belonged to her by reason of a "consummated gift long prior to the death of Gladys Piper." Two witnesses testified for Kaufmann at the trial that Piper had told them the rings belonged to Kaufmann but that she was going to wear them until she died. The appellate court found "no evidence of any actual delivery." The court held that the essentials of a gift are (1) a present intention to make a gift on the part of the donor, (2) a delivery of the property by the donor to the donee, and (3) an acceptance by the donee. The evidence in the case showed only an intent to make a gift. Because there was no delivery—either actual or constructive—a valid gift was not made. For Piper to have made a gift, her intention would have to have been executed by the complete and unconditional delivery of the property or the delivery of a proper written instrument evidencing the gift. As this did not occur, the court found that there had been no gift.

COMMENT *Although this case is relatively recent in the long span of the law governing gifts, we present it here as a classic case because it so clearly illustrates the delivery requirement when making a gift. Assuming that Piper did, indeed, intend for Kaufmann to have the rings, it was unfortunate that Kaufmann had no right to receive them after Piper's death. Yet the alternative could lead to perhaps even more unfairness. The policy behind the delivery requirement is to protect alleged donors and their heirs from fraudulent claims based solely on parol evidence. If not for this policy, an alleged donee could easily claim that a gift was made when, in fact, it was not.*

GIFT *INTER VIVOS*
A gift made during one's lifetime and not in contemplation of imminent death, in contrast to a gift *causa mortis*.

GIFT *CAUSA MORTIS*
A gift made in contemplation of death. If the donor does not die of that ailment, the gift is revoked.

Acceptance The final requirement of a valid gift is acceptance by the donee. This rarely presents any problem, as most donees readily accept their gifts. The courts generally assume acceptance unless shown otherwise.

Gifts *Causa Mortis* A gift made during one's lifetime is termed a **gift *inter vivos*.** **Gifts *causa mortis*** (so-called *deathbed gifts*), in contrast, are made in contemplation of imminent death. A gift *causa mortis* does not become absolute until the donor dies from the contemplated illness, and it is automatically revoked if the donor recovers from the illness. Moreover, the donee must survive to take the gift. To be effective, a gift *causa mortis* must also meet the three requirements discussed earlier—donative intent, delivery, and acceptance by the donee.

● **EXAMPLE 36.6** Suppose that Young is to be operated on for a cancerous tumor. Before the operation, he delivers an envelope to a close business associate. The envelope contains a letter saying, "I realize my days are numbered, and I want to give you this check for $1 million in the event of my death from this operation." The business associate cashes the check. The surgeon performs the operation and removes the tumor. Young recovers fully. Several months later, Young dies from a heart attack that is totally unrelated to the operation. If Young's personal representative (the party charged with administering Young's estate) tries to recover the $1 million, normally she will succeed. The gift *causa mortis* is automatically revoked if the donor recovers. The *specific event* that was contemplated in making the gift was death from a particular operation. Because Young's death was not the result of this event, the gift is revoked, and the $1 million passes to Young's estate.●

ACCESSION

ACCESSION
Occurs when an individual adds value to personal property by either labor or materials. In some situations, a person may acquire ownership rights in another's property through accession.

Accession, which means "adding on" to something, occurs when someone adds value to an item of personal property by either labor or materials. When accession is accomplished with the permission of the owner, generally there is no dispute about who owns the property after the accession occurred. When accession occurs without the permission of the owner, the courts will tend to favor the owner over the improver—the one who improves the property—provided that the accession was wrongful and undertaken in bad faith. In addition, many courts will deny the improver any compensation for the value added; for example, a car thief who puts new tires on the stolen car will obviously not be compensated for the value of the new tires when the rightful owner recovers the car.

If the accession is performed in good faith, however, even without the owner's consent, ownership of the improved item most often depends on whether the accession has increased the value of the property or changed its identity. The greater the increase in value, the more likely it is that ownership will pass to the improver. If ownership so passes, the improver obviously must compensate the original owner for the value of the property prior to the accession. If the increase in value is not sufficient for ownership to pass to the improver, most courts will require the owner to compensate the improver for the value added.

CONFUSION

CONFUSION
The mixing together of goods belonging to two or more owners so that the separately owned goods cannot be identified.

Confusion is defined as the commingling (mixing together) of goods so that one person's personal property cannot be distinguished from another's. Confusion frequently occurs when the goods are *fungible*, meaning that each particle is identical to every other particle, as with grain and oil, and the goods are owned by two or more parties as tenants in common. For example, if two farmers put their Number 2–grade winter wheat into the same storage bin, confusion would occur.

If confusion of goods is caused by a person who wrongfully and willfully mixes the goods for the purpose of rendering them indistinguishable, the innocent party acquires title to the whole. If confusion occurs as a result of agreement, an honest mistake, or the act of some third party, the owners share ownership as tenants in common and will share any loss in proportion to their shares of ownership of the property.

Mislaid, Lost, and Abandoned Property

As already mentioned, one of the methods of acquiring ownership of property is to possess it. Simply finding something and holding on to it, however, does not necessarily give the finder any legal rights in the property. Different rules apply, depending on whether the property was mislaid, lost, or abandoned.

MISLAID PROPERTY

MISLAID PROPERTY
Property with which the owner has voluntarily parted and then cannot find or recover.

Property that has been placed somewhere by the owner voluntarily and then inadvertently forgotten is **mislaid property.** • **EXAMPLE 36.7** Suppose that you go to the theater. You leave your gloves on the concession stand and then forget about them. The gloves are mislaid property, and the theater owner is entrusted with the duty of reasonable care for them. • When mislaid property is found, the finder does not obtain title to the goods. Instead, the owner of the place where the property was mislaid becomes the caretaker of the property, because it is highly likely that the true owner will return.[5]

LOST PROPERTY

LOST PROPERTY
Property with which the owner has involuntarily parted and then cannot find or recover.

Property that is involuntarily left and forgotten is **lost property.** A finder of the property can claim title to the property against the whole world, *except the true owner.*[6] If the true owner demands that the lost property be returned, the finder must return it. If a third party takes possession of lost property from a finder, however, the third party cannot assert a better title than the finder. When a finder knows who the true owner of the property is and fails to return it to that person, the finder is guilty of the tort of *conversion* (the wrongful taking of another's property—see Chapter 4). Finally, many states require the finder to make a reasonably diligent search to locate the true owner of lost property.

ON THE WEB Some states and government agencies now post online a list of unclaimed property. For an example of the various types of property that may go unclaimed, go to the following Web page, which is part of the state of Delaware's Web site:

http://www.state.de.us/revenue/escheat/escheat.htm.

• **EXAMPLE 36.8** Suppose that Kormian works in a large library at night. In the courtyard on her way home, she finds a piece of gold jewelry set with stones that look like precious stones to her. She takes it to a jeweler to have it appraised. While pretending to weigh the jewelry, an employee of the jeweler removes several of the stones. If Kormian brings an action to recover the stones from the jeweler, she normally will win because she found lost property and holds valid title against everyone *except the true owner.* Because the property was lost, rather than mislaid, the finder is not the caretaker of the jewelry. Instead, the finder acquires title good against the whole world (except the true owner). •

ESTRAY STATUTE
A statute defining finders' rights in property when the true owners are unknown.

Many states have laws that encourage and facilitate the return of property to its true owner and then reward a finder for honesty if the property remains unclaimed. These laws, called **estray statutes,** provide an incentive for finders to report their discoveries by making it possible for them, after the passage of a specified period of time, to acquire legal title to the property they have found. The statute usually requires the county clerk to advertise the property in an attempt to enhance the opportunity of the owner to recover what has been lost. Some preliminary questions must always be resolved before the estray statute can be employed. The item must be lost property, not merely mislaid property. When the circumstances indicate that the property was probably lost and not mislaid or abandoned, loss is presumed as a matter of public policy, and the estray statute applies.

The law that finders of lost property may obtain good title to the property has a long history. The cases discussed in the following *Landmark in the Law* feature on the origin

5. The finder of mislaid property is an involuntary bailee (to be discussed later in this chapter).
6. See *Armory v. Delamirie,* discussed in this chapter's *Landmark in the Law* feature.

of the law of finders illustrate the doctrine of *relativity of title*. Under this doctrine, if two contestants are before the court, neither of whom can claim absolute title to the property, the one who can claim prior possession will likely have established sufficient rights to the property to win the case.

LANDMARK IN THE LAW
The Law of Finders

The well-known children's adage, "Finders keepers, losers weepers," is actually written into law—provided that the loser (the rightful owner) cannot be found. A finder of lost property may acquire good title to found personal property *against everyone except the true owner.* A number of landmark cases have made this principle clear. An early English case, *Armory v. Delamirie*,[a] is considered a landmark in Anglo-American jurisprudence concerning finders' rights in property.

Finder's Rights The plaintiff in the case was Armory, a chimney sweep who found a jewel in its setting during the course of his work. He took the jewel to a goldsmith to have it appraised. The goldsmith refused to return the jewel to Armory, claiming that Armory was not the rightful owner of the property. The court held that the finder, as prior possessor of the item, had rights to the jewel superior to those of all others except the rightful owner. The court stated, "The finder of a jewel, though he does not by such finding acquire an absolute property or ownership, yet . . . has such a property as will enable him to keep it against all but the rightful owner."

BE AWARE A finder who appropriates the personal property of another, knowing who the true owner is, can be guilty of conversion.

Who Has Rights to Wrongfully Obtained Goods? A curious situation arises when goods wrongfully obtained by one person are in turn wrongfully obtained by another, and the two parties contest each other's rights to possession. In such a situation, does the *Armory* rule still apply—that is, does the first (illegal) possessor have more rights in the property than the second (illegal) possessor? In a case that came before the Minnesota Supreme Court in 1892, *Anderson v. Gouldberg*,[b] the court said yes.

In the *Anderson* case, the plaintiffs had trespassed on another's land and wrongfully cut timber. The defendants later took the logs from the mill site, allegedly in the name of the owner of the property on which the timber had been cut. The evidence at trial indicated that both parties had illegally acquired the property. The court instructed the jury that even if the plaintiffs were trespassers when they cut the logs, they were entitled to recover them from later possessors—except the true owner or an agent of the true owner. The jury found for the plaintiffs, a decision affirmed later by the Minnesota Supreme Court. The latter court held that the plaintiffs' possession, "though wrongfully obtained," justified an action to repossess the property from another who took it from them.

APPLICATION TO TODAY'S WORLD

Although the Armory *case was decided close to three hundred years ago, the principle enunciated by the court in that case remains applicable today. Finders of lost property continue to acquire good title to the property against all but the true owner.*

a. 93 Eng.Rep. 664 (K.B. [King's Bench] 1722).
b. 51 Minn. 294, 53 N.W. 636 (1892).

ABANDONED PROPERTY

ABANDONED PROPERTY Property with which the owner has voluntarily parted, with no intention of recovering it.

Property that has been discarded by the true owner, who has no intention of reclaiming title to it, is **abandoned property**. Someone who finds abandoned property acquires title to it, and such title is good against the whole world, *including the original owner.* The owner of lost property who eventually gives up any further attempt to find it is frequently held to have abandoned the property. If a person finds abandoned property while trespassing on the property of another, title vests not in the finder but in the owner of the land.

The following case involved a find of sunken vessels embedded in the "submerged lands" off the coast of Virginia.

CASE 36.2 Sea Hunt, Inc. v. Unidentified Shipwrecked Vessel or Vessels

United States Court of Appeals,
Fourth Circuit, 2000.
221 F.3d 634.
http://www.law.emory.edu/4circuit[a]

HISTORICAL AND POLITICAL SETTING *The 1902 Treaty of Friendship and General Relations between the United States and Spain protects U.S. and Spanish shipwrecks and military grave sites. Under the terms of the treaty, Spanish vessels, like those belonging to the United States, may only be abandoned by express acts. This principle reflects the long-standing admiralty rule that when articles are lost at sea, the owner retains title to them. An inference of abandonment is permitted, but only when no owner appears.*[b]

FACTS Sailing from Cuba to Spain at the end of August 1750, *La Galga* ("The Greyhound"), a fifty-gun frigate in the Spanish Navy, sank in a hurricane off the coast of Virginia. *Juno,* a thirty-four-gun frigate, bound from Mexico for Spain, sank in a storm off the Virginia coast in January 1802. The Virginia Marine Resources Commission granted Sea Hunt, Inc., a maritime salvage company, permits to explore for shipwrecks off the Virginia coast and conduct salvage operations. Sea Hunt found the remains of *La Galga* and *Juno.* Virginia asserted ownership over the ships under the Abandoned Shipwreck Act of 1987 (ASA).[c]

a. On this page, click on "2000 Decisions." In the open menu, click on "July." In the result, click on the case name to access the opinion. Emory University School of Law in Atlanta maintains this Web site for the U.S. Court of Appeals for the Fourth Circuit.

b. See *Columbus-America Discovery Group v. Atlantic Mutual Insurance Co.,* 974 F.2d 450 (4th Cir. 1992).

c. 43 U.S.C. Sections 2101–2106. The ASA gives a state such as Virginia title to shipwrecks that are abandoned and embedded in the state's submerged lands.

Sea Hunt filed a suit in a federal district court, seeking payment for salvaging the vessels or a declaratory judgment that Virginia owned them (which would mean that items salvaged by Sea Hunt would belong to Sea Hunt under its permit). Spain opposed Sea Hunt's request, arguing that the ships belonged to Spain. The court held that Spain had abandoned *La Galga,* but had not abandoned *Juno,* and denied the salvage award. Sea Hunt and Spain appealed to the U.S. Court of Appeals for the Fourth Circuit.

ISSUE Is a nation required to expressly abandon its shipwrecks before another party can acquire title to them?

DECISION Yes. The U.S. Court of Appeals for the Fourth Circuit reversed the judgment of the lower court with regard to *La Galga* and affirmed the judgment concerning *Juno* and the denial of the salvage award.

REASON The U.S. Court of Appeals for the Fourth Circuit acknowledged that the wrecks were embedded within Virginia's submerged lands. "That, however, is not enough." The court explained that "for Virginia to acquire title to the shipwrecks and to issue salvage permits to Sea Hunt, these vessels must have been abandoned by Spain. * * * Because Spain has asserted an ownership claim to the shipwrecks, * * * express abandonment is the governing standard. To adopt a lesser standard would not only go beyond what the ASA requires. It would also abrogate America's obligations to Spain under the 1902 Treaty of Friendship and General Relations." The ASA states that "abandoned shipwrecks" are those "to which the owner has relinquished ownership rights with no

CASE 36.2—Continued

retention." The court pointed out that "[w]hen an owner comes before the court to assert his rights, relinquishment would be hard, if not impossible, to show. Requiring express abandonment where an owner makes a claim thus accords with the statutory text." The court added that abandonment may be implied, "as by an owner never asserting any control over or otherwise indicating his claim of possession." The court concluded, however, that "[a]n owner who comes forward has definitely indicated his claim of possession, and in such a case abandonment cannot be implied."

FOR CRITICAL ANALYSIS—Political Consideration *Considering the decision in the* Sea Hunt *case, what might the salvage industry do to further its interest in the commercial recovery of sunken ships?*

Bailments

BAILMENT
A situation in which the personal property of one person (a bailor) is entrusted to another (a bailee), who is obligated to return the bailed property to the bailor or dispose of it as directed.

BAILOR
One who entrusts goods to a bailee.

BAILEE
One to whom goods are entrusted by a bailor.

A **bailment** is formed by the delivery of personal property, without transfer of title, by one person, called a **bailor**, to another, called a **bailee**, usually under an agreement for a particular purpose (for example, for storage, repair, or transportation). On completion of the purpose, the bailee is obligated to return the bailed property to the bailor or to a third person or to dispose of it as directed.

Bailments usually are created by agreement but not necessarily by contract, because in many bailments not all of the elements of a contract (such as mutual assent and consideration) are present. For example, if you lend your bicycle to a friend, a bailment is created, but not by contract, because there is no consideration. Many commercial bailments, such as the delivery of clothing to the cleaners for dry cleaning, are based on contract, however.

Virtually every individual or business is affected by the law of bailments at one time or another (and sometimes even on a daily basis). When individuals deal with bailments, whether they realize it or not, they are subject to the obligations and duties that arise from the bailment relationship. The number, scope, and importance of bailments created daily in the business community and in everyday life make it desirable for every person to understand the elements necessary for the creation of a bailment and to know what rights, duties, and liabilities flow from bailments.

Elements of a Bailment

ON THE WEB
For a discussion of the origins of the term *bailment* and how bailment relationships have been defined, go to
http://www.lectlaw.com/def/b005.htm.

Not all transactions involving the delivery of property from one person to another create a bailment. For such a transfer to become a bailment, three conditions must be met. We look here at each of these conditions.

Personal Property Bailment involves only personal property; there can be no bailment of persons. Although a bailment of your luggage is created when it is transported by an airline, as a passenger you are not the subject of a bailment. Additionally, you cannot bail realty; thus, leasing your house to a tenant does not create a bailment.

Delivery of Possession In a voluntary bailment, possession of the property must be transferred to the bailee in such a way that (1) the bailee is given exclusive possession and control over the property and (2) the bailee *knowingly* accepts the personal property. If either of these conditions for effective delivery of possession is lacking, there is no bailment relationship. ● **EXAMPLE 36.9** Suppose that you take a friend out to dinner at an expensive restaurant. When you enter the restaurant, your friend checks her coat.

In the pocket of the coat is a $20,000 diamond necklace. The bailee, by accepting the coat, does not knowingly also accept the necklace; thus, a bailment of the coat exists—because the restaurant has exclusive possession and control over the coat and knowingly accepted it—but a bailment of the necklace does not exist. ●

Two types of delivery—*physical* and *constructive*—will result in the bailee's exclusive possession of and control over the property. As discussed earlier, in the context of gifts, constructive delivery is a substitute, or symbolic, delivery. What is delivered to the bailee is not the actual property bailed (such as a car) but something so related to the property (such as the car keys) that the requirement of delivery is satisfied.

In certain unique situations, a bailment is found despite the apparent lack of the requisite elements of control and knowledge. In particular, the rental of a safe-deposit box is usually held to create a bailor-bailee relationship between the customer and the bank, despite the bank's lack of knowledge of the contents and its inability to have exclusive control of the property.[7] Another example of such a situation occurs when the bailee acquires the property accidentally or by mistake—as in finding someone else's lost or mislaid property. A bailment is created even though the bailor did not voluntarily deliver the property to the bailee. Such bailments are called *constructive* or *involuntary* bailments.

Bailment Agreement A bailment agreement, or contract, can be express or implied. Although a written agreement is not required for bailments of less than one year (that is, the Statute of Frauds does not apply—see Chapter 11), it is a good idea to have one, especially when valuable property is involved.

The bailment agreement expressly or impliedly provides for the return of the bailed property to the bailor or to a third person, or it provides for disposal by the bailee. The agreement presupposes that the bailee will return the identical goods originally given by the bailor. In certain types of bailments, however, such as bailments of fungible goods, the property returned need only be equivalent property.

● **EXAMPLE 36.10** If Holman stores his grain (fungible goods) in Joe's Warehouse, a bailment is created. At the end of the storage period, however, the warehouse is not obligated to return to Holman exactly the same grain that he stored. As long as the warehouse returns goods of the same *type, grade,* and *quantity,* the warehouse—the bailee—has performed its obligation. ●

ORDINARY BAILMENTS

Bailments are either *ordinary* or *special (extraordinary)*. There are three types of ordinary bailments. The distinguishing feature among them is *which party receives a benefit from the bailment.* Ultimately, the courts may use this factor to determine the standard of care required of the bailee in possession of the personal property, and this factor will dictate the rights and liabilities of the parties. The three types of ordinary bailments are as follows:

① *Bailment for the sole benefit of the bailor.* This is a gratuitous bailment (a bailment without consideration) for the convenience and benefit of the bailor. For example, if Allen asks his friend, Sumi, to store Allen's car in her garage, and Sumi agrees to do so, the bailment of the car is for the sole benefit of the bailor (Allen).

② *Bailment for the sole benefit of the bailee.* This type of bailment typically occurs when one person lends an item to another person (the bailee) solely for the bailee's con-

7. By statute or by express contract, the rental of a safe-deposit box may be regarded as a lease of space or a license (a revocable right to use the space, for a fee—see Chapter 37) instead of a bailment.

venience and benefit. For example, Allen asks to borrow his friend Sumi's boat so that Allen can go sailing over the weekend. The bailment of the boat is for Allen's (the bailee's) sole benefit.

③ *Bailment for the mutual benefit of the bailee and the bailor.* This is the most common kind of bailment and involves some form of compensation for storing items or holding property while it is being serviced. It is a contractual bailment and is often referred to as a bailment for hire. For example, leaving your car at a service station for an oil change is a mutual-benefit bailment.

Rights of the Bailee Certain rights are implicit in the bailment agreement. A hallmark of the bailment agreement is that the bailee acquires the *right to control and possess the property temporarily.* The bailee's right of possession permits the bailee to recover damages from any third person for damage or loss of the property. If the property is stolen, the bailee has a legal right to regain possession of it or to obtain damages from any third person who has wrongfully interfered with the bailee's possessory rights. The bailee's right to regain possession of the property or to obtain damages is important because, as you will read shortly, a bailee is liable to the bailor for any loss or damage to bailed property resulting from the bailee's negligence.

Depending on the type of bailment and the terms of the bailment agreement, a bailee may also have a *right to use the bailed property.* • **EXAMPLE 36.11** If you borrow a friend's car to drive to the airport, you, as the bailee, would obviously be expected to use the car. In a bailment involving the long-term storage of a car, however, the bailee is not expected to use the car because the ordinary purpose of a storage bailment does not include use of the property.•

Except in a gratuitous bailment, a bailee has a *right to be compensated* as provided for in the bailment agreement, a right to be reimbursed for costs and services rendered in the keeping of the bailed property, or both. Even in a gratuitous bailment, a bailee has a right to be reimbursed or compensated for costs incurred in the keeping of the bailed property. • **EXAMPLE 36.12** Margo loses her pet dog, and Judith finds it. Judith takes the dog to her home and feeds it. Even though she takes good care of the dog, it becomes ill, and she calls a veterinarian. Judith pays the bill for the veterinarian's services and the medicine. Judith normally will be entitled to be reimbursed by Margo for all reasonable costs incurred in the keeping of Margo's dog.•

To enforce the right of compensation, the bailee has a right to place a *possessory lien* (which entitles a creditor to retain possession of the debtor's goods until a debt is paid) on the specific bailed property until he or she has been fully compensated. This type of lien, sometimes referred to as an artisan's lien or a *bailee's lien,* was discussed in Chapter 23.

Ordinary bailees have the *right to limit their liability* as long as the limitations are called to the attention of the bailor and are not against public policy. It is essential that the bailor in some way know of the limitation. Even if the bailor has notice, certain types of disclaimers of liability have been considered to be against public policy and therefore illegal. For example, certain exculpatory clauses limiting a person's liability for her or his own wrongful acts are often scrutinized by the courts and, in the case of bailments, are routinely held to be illegal. This is particularly true in bailments for the mutual benefit of the bailor and the bailee.

Duties of the Bailee The bailee has two basic responsibilities: (1) to take proper care of the property and (2) to surrender the property to the bailor or dispose of it in accordance with the bailor's instructions at the end of the bailment. The bailee must exercise reasonable care in preserving the bailed property. What constitutes reasonable care in a bailment situation normally depends on the nature and specific circumstances of the bailment. Traditionally, courts have determined the appropriate standard of care on the basis of the type of bailment involved. In a bailment for the sole benefit of the bailor, for example, the bailee need exercise only a slight degree of care. In a bailment for the sole benefit of the bailee, however, the bailee must exercise great care. In a mutual-benefit bailment, courts normally impose a reasonable standard of care—that is, the bailee must exercise the degree of care that a reasonable and prudent person would exercise in the same circumstances. Exhibit 36–1 illustrates these concepts.

ETHICAL ISSUE 36.2

Why do different standards of care apply to bailed goods?

The standard of care expected of a bailee clearly illustrates how the law reflects ethical principles. For example, suppose that a friend asks to borrow your business law text for the weekend. You agree to lend your friend the book. In this situation, which is a bailment for the sole benefit of the bailee (your friend), most people would agree that your friend has an ethical obligation to take great care of your book. After all, if your friend lost your book, you would incur damages. You would have to purchase another one, and if you could not, you might find it difficult to do well in your homework assignments, examinations, and so on. The situation would be different if you had loaned your book to your friend totally for your own benefit. For example, suppose that you are leaving town for the summer, and your friend offers to store several boxes of books for you until you return in the fall. In this situation, the bailment is for the sole benefit of the bailor (you). If your books are destroyed while in the bailee's (your friend's) possession and you sue the bailee for damages, a court will likely take into consideration the fact that the bailee was essentially doing you a favor by storing the books. Although bailees generally have a duty to exercise reasonable care over bailed property, what constitutes reasonable care in a specific situation normally depends on the surrounding circumstances—including the reason for the bailment and who stood to benefit from the arrangement.

A bailee's failure to exercise appropriate care in handling the bailor's property results in tort liability. The duty to relinquish the property at the end of the bailment is grounded in both contract and tort law principles. Failure to return the property con-

EXHIBIT 36–1 DEGREE OF CARE REQUIRED OF A BAILEE

Bailment for the Sole Benefit of the Bailor	Mutual-Benefit Bailment	Bailment for the Sole Benefit of the Bailee
DEGREE OF CARE →		
SLIGHT	REASONABLE	GREAT

stitutes a breach of contract or the tort of conversion, and with one exception, the bailee is liable for damages. The exception is when the obligation is excused because the goods or chattels have been destroyed, lost, or stolen through no fault of the bailee (or claimed by a third party with a superior claim).

Under the law of bailments, a bailor's proof that damage or loss to the property has occurred will, in and of itself, raise a presumption that the bailee is guilty of negligence or conversion. In other words, whenever a bailee fails to return bailed property, the bailee's negligence will be presumed by the court.

The court in the following case weighed the duty of a bailee to return bailed property to the bailor against charges that giving car keys to an intoxicated person was negligent entrustment, regardless of any bailment.

CASE 36.3 Umble v. Sandy McKie & Sons, Inc.

Appellate Court of Illinois,
Second District, 1998.
294 Ill.App.3d 449,
690 N.E.2d 157,
228 Ill.Dec. 848.

HISTORICAL AND SOCIAL SETTING *Sometimes, the question arises as to whether individuals have a duty to prevent an intoxicated driver from driving his or her vehicle. Consider an example. Edward Hoag went to the beach with several friends, including Ronald Niemeyer. After Hoag became intoxicated, Niemeyer drove Hoag's car to Niemeyer's house. Hoag then attempted to drive home but was involved in an accident in which Keith Lombardo was injured. Lombardo sued Hoag, and one of the questions in the suit was whether Niemeyer had a duty to prevent Hoag from driving Hoag's car while intoxicated. The court refused to impose such a duty on Niemeyer. The court explained that "[o]ne problem with * * * that particular form of a duty is that the standard is so broad that it would conceivably apply to gas station attendants, toll booth collectors, parking lot attendants, repair services, and onlookers who may have observed the participants get into a vehicle driven by an intoxicated person."*[a] *Most courts would agree.*

FACTS Jerome Butzen brought his car to Sandy McKie & Sons, Inc., to have a leaking tire fixed and a burned-out headlight replaced. Butzen was intoxicated, which was apparent to the McKie employees. The car was repaired, Butzen paid for the repairs, and McKie returned the car. Shortly afterwards, Butzen's car collided with one driven by Phillip Umble, who died in the collision. Mary Ellen Umble filed a suit in an Illinois state court against McKie, alleging in part that McKie was negligent in giving car keys to an obviously intoxicated driver. The court dismissed the suit, and Umble appealed.

ISSUE Did McKie, the bailee, have a duty to return the car to Butzen, the bailor, once the repairs were completed and paid for, regardless of Butzen's obvious intoxication?

DECISION Yes. The state intermediate appellate court affirmed the lower court's judgment.

REASON The state intermediate appellate court explained that negligent entrustment occurs when one entrusts something to another knowing that the other will use the thing to create an unreasonable risk of harm to a third party. The court pointed out that to be held liable, the alleged tortfeasor must have a superior right to control the property. Here, however, McKie did not have such a right. After Butzen paid for the repairs, if McKie had not returned the car, it would have been liable for the tort of conversion (see Chapter 4). "Because Butzen already owned the car, [McKie] cannot be liable for negligently 'entrusting' it to him."

FOR CRITICAL ANALYSIS—Cultural Consideration *What would be McKie's liability if Butzen had not paid for the repairs and McKie had not returned the car? Why?*

a. *Lombardo v. Hoag,* 269 N.J.Super. 36, 634 A.2d 550 (1993).

Duties of the Bailor It goes without saying that the rights of a bailor are essentially the same as the duties of a bailee. The major duty of the bailor is to provide the bailee with goods or chattels that are free from known defects that could cause injury to the bailee. In the case of a mutual-benefit bailment, the bailor must also notify the bailee of any hidden defects that the bailor could have discovered with reasonable diligence and proper inspection.

The bailor's duty to reveal defects is based on a negligence theory of tort law. A bailor who fails to give the appropriate notice is liable to the bailee and to any other person who might reasonably be expected to come into contact with the defective article. For example, if an equipment rental firm leases equipment with a *discoverable* defect, and the lessee (bailee) is not notified of such a defect and is harmed because of it, the rental firm is liable for negligence under tort law.

An exception to this rule exists if the bailment is created for the sole benefit of the bailee. Thus, if you lend your car to a friend as a favor to your friend and not for any direct return benefit to yourself, you are required to notify your friend of any *known* defect of the automobile that could cause injury but not of a defect of which you are unaware (even if it is a *discoverable* defect). If your friend is injured in an accident as a result of a defect unknown to you, you normally will not be liable.

A bailor can also incur *warranty liability* based on contract law (see Chapter 18) for injuries resulting from the bailment of defective articles. Property leased by a bailor must be *fit for the intended purpose of the bailment.* Warranties of fitness arise by law in sales contracts and leases and by judicial interpretation in the case of bailments for hire. Article 2A of the Uniform Commercial Code (UCC) extends implied warranties of merchantability and fitness for a particular purpose to bailments whenever the bailments include rights to use the bailed goods.[8]

Special Types of Bailments

Up to this point, our discussion of bailments has been concerned with ordinary bailments—bailments in which bailees are expected to exercise ordinary care in the handling of bailed property. Some bailment transactions warrant special consideration. These include bailments in which the bailee's duty of care is *extraordinary*—that is, the bailee's liability for loss or damage to the property is absolute—as is generally true in cases involving common carriers and innkeepers. Warehouse companies have the same duty of care as ordinary bailees; but, like carriers, they are subject to extensive regulation under federal and state laws, including Article 7 of the UCC.

COMMON CARRIER
An owner of a truck, railroad, airline, ship, or other vehicle that is licensed to offer transportation services to the public, generally in return for compensation or a payment.

Common Carriers Transportation providers that are publicly licensed to provide transportation services to the general public are referred to as **common carriers.** Common carriers are distinguished from private carriers, which operate transportation facilities for a select clientele. Whereas a private carrier is not bound to provide service to every person or company making a request, a common carrier must arrange carriage for all who apply, within certain limitations.[9]

The delivery of goods to a common carrier creates a bailment relationship between the shipper (bailor) and the common carrier (bailee). Unlike ordinary bailees, the common carrier is held to a standard of care based on *strict liability,* rather than reasonable

8. UCC 2A–212, 2A–213.

9. A common carrier is not required to take any and all property anywhere in all instances. Public regulatory agencies govern common carriers, and carriers can be restricted to geographic areas. They can also be limited to carrying certain kinds of goods or to providing only special types of transportation equipment.

A truck travels a highway. Why are common carriers, such as most trucking companies, subject to strict liability while ordinary bailees must exercise only "reasonable care"?

care, in protecting the bailed personal property. This means that the common carrier is absolutely liable, regardless of due care, for all loss or damage to goods except damage caused by one of the following common law exceptions: (1) an act of God, (2) an act of a public enemy, (3) an order of a public authority, (4) an act of the shipper, or (5) the inherent nature of the goods.

Common carriers cannot contract away their liability for damaged goods. Subject to government regulations, however, they are permitted to limit their dollar liability to an amount stated on the shipment contract or rate filing.[10]

Warehouse Companies *Warehousing* is the business of providing storage of property for compensation.[11] A warehouse company is a professional bailee whose responsibility differs from an ordinary bailee's in two important aspects. First, a warehouse company is empowered to issue documents of title—in particular, warehouse receipts.[12] Second, warehouse companies are subject to an extraordinary network of state and federal statutes, including Article 7 of the UCC.

A warehouse company accepts goods for storage and issues a warehouse receipt describing the property and the terms of the bailment contract. The warehouse receipt can be negotiable or nonnegotiable, depending on how it is written. It is negotiable if its terms provide that the warehouse company will deliver the goods "to the bearer" of the receipt or "to the order of" a person named on the receipt.[13]

The warehouse receipt serves multiple functions. It is a receipt for the goods stored; it is a contract of bailment; and it also represents the goods (that is, it indicates

10. Federal laws require common carriers to offer shippers the opportunity to obtain higher dollar limits for loss by paying a higher fee for the transport.

11. UCC 7–102(h) defines the person engaged in the storing of goods for hire as a "warehouseman."

12. A *document of title* is defined in UCC 1–201(15) as any "document which in the regular course of business or financing is treated as adequately evidencing that the person in possession of it is entitled to receive, hold, and dispose of the document and the goods it covers. To be a document of title, a document must purport to be issued by or addressed to a bailee and purport to cover goods in the bailee's possession."

13. UCC 7–104.

title) and hence has value and utility in financing commercial transactions. • **EXAMPLE 36.13** Ossip, a processor and canner of corn, delivers 6,500 cases of corn to Shaneyfelt, the owner of a warehouse. Shaneyfelt issues a negotiable warehouse receipt payable "to bearer" and gives it to Ossip. Ossip sells and delivers the warehouse receipt to a large supermarket chain, Better Foods, Inc. Better Foods is now the owner of the corn and has the right to obtain the cases from Shaneyfelt. It will present the warehouse receipt to Shaneyfelt, who in return will release the cases of corn to the grocery chain. •

Like ordinary bailees, a warehouse company is liable for loss or damage to property resulting from *negligence* (and therefore does not have the same liability as a common carrier). As a professional bailee, however, it is expected to exercise a high degree of care to protect and preserve the goods. A warehouse company can limit the dollar amount of its liability, but the bailor must be given the option of paying an increased storage rate for an increase in the liability limit.

"All saints can do miracles, but few of them can keep a hotel."
SAMUEL CLEMENS (MARK TWAIN)
1835–1910
(American author and humorist)

Innkeepers At common law, innkeepers, hotel owners, and similar operators were held to the same strict liability as common carriers with respect to property brought into the rooms by guests. Today, only those who provide lodging to the public for compensation as a *regular* business are covered under this rule of strict liability. Moreover, the rule applies only to those who are guests, as opposed to lodgers. A lodger is a permanent resident of the hotel or inn, whereas a guest is a transient traveler.

In many states, innkeepers can avoid strict liability for loss of guests' valuables and funds by providing a safe in which to keep them. Each guest must be clearly notified of the availability of such a safe. Statutes often limit the liability of innkeepers with regard to articles that are not kept in the safe or are of such a nature that they normally are not kept in a safe. These statutes may limit the amount of monetary damages or even provide for no liability in the absence of innkeeper negligence.

Suppose that Joyce stays for a night at the Harbor Hotel. When she returns from eating breakfast in the hotel restaurant, she discovers that the people in the room next door have forced the lock on the door between the two rooms and stolen her suitcase. Joyce claims that the hotel is liable for her loss. The hotel maintains that because it was not negligent, it is not liable. At common law, the hotel would have been liable because innkeepers were actually insurers of the property of their guests. Today, however, state statutes limit strict liability by limiting the amount of monetary damages for which the innkeeper is liable or providing that the innkeeper has no liability in the absence of negligence. Most statutes require these limitations to be posted or the guest to be notified. Such postings, or notices, are frequently found on the doors of the rooms in the motel or hotel.

Normally, the innkeeper (a motel keeper, for example) assumes no responsibility for the safety of a guest's automobile because the guest usually retains possession and control over it. If, however, the innkeeper provides parking facilities and the guest's car is entrusted to the innkeeper or to an employee, the innkeeper will be liable under the rules that pertain to parking-lot bailments (which are ordinary bailments).

APPLICATION Law and the Businessperson . . .

What to Do with Lost Property*

If you are walking down a street in New York City and come across a valuable diamond ring lying next to the gutter, what should you do with the ring? The tempting thing would be to keep it or sell it and enjoy the proceeds. That would be unethical, however; it would also be illegal under many states' laws.

An Example—New York Laws

New York law defines *lost property* to include lost property, mislaid property, abandoned property, "waifs [goods to which all ownership rights have been waived, such as goods that are found but unclaimed] and treasure trove, and other property which is found." Property includes "money, goods, chattels and tangible personal property," with some exceptions. Generally, the finder of property worth $20 or more must deposit it with police authorities (or with the owner of the premises on which the property was found) within ten days. Failure to do so is a misdemeanor, subject to a fine of up to $100 and imprisonment for not more than six months.

Other States' Lost-Property Laws

Many states have enacted lost-property statutes. The statutes differ significantly from state to state, but typically, they eliminate the distinction among lost property, mislaid property, abandoned property, and treasure trove, as the New York statute does. Many statutes also require the finder to deposit found property with local authorities, although the penalty imposed for failure to do so may not be as severe as under New York's statute (in Illinois, for example, a finder who fails to comply with the requirements of that state's lost-property statute may be fined $10). Lost-property statutes also typically require the police to attempt to find the true owner, such as by calling the owner or person in charge of the premises on which the property was found. Sometimes, the finder must advertise, at the county court, the property and its discovery.

Generally, if the true owner cannot be located within a certain period of time, which varies depending on the value of the property and whether the property is perishable, the finder gets the property. If the finder does not appear after the period of time has lapsed, the property may be sold and the proceeds disposed of as specified by the statute. In California, for instance, the proceeds from such a sale go into a state abandoned-property fund (if the state police had custody of the lost property) or become the property of the city, county, town, or village (if other police had custody).

Every statute has exceptions, of course. In some situations, an employer may have rights to property found by an employee. Property found in a safe-deposit area in a bank may also be subject to different rules.

*This *Application* is not meant to substitute for the services of an attorney who is licensed to practice law in your state.

Checklist for the Finder of Lost Property

1. To maximize your chances of legally keeping lost property, take the found property to the nearest police station.

Key Terms

abandoned property 966
accession 963
bailee 967
bailment 967
bailor 967
chattel 956
common carrier 972
community property 959
confusion 963

Chapter Summary Personal Property and Bailments

PERSONAL PROPERTY	
Definition of Personal Property (See pages 956–957.)	Personal property (personalty) is considered to include all property not classified as real property (realty). Personal property can be tangible (such as a TV set or a car) or intangible (such as stocks or bonds). Personal property may be referred to legally as *chattel*—a term used under the common law to denote all forms of personal property.
Property Ownership (See pages 957–959.)	1. *Fee simple*—Exists when individuals have the right to use, possess, or dispose of the property as they choose during their lifetimes and to pass on the property to their heirs at death. 2. *Concurrent ownership*— a. Tenancy in common—Co-ownership in which two or more persons own an undivided interest in the property; on one tenant's death, the property interest passes to his or her heirs. b. Joint tenancy—Exists when two or more persons own an undivided interest in property; on the death of a joint tenant, the property interest transfers to the remaining tenant(s), not to the heirs of the deceased. c. Tenancy by the entirety—A form of co-ownership between a husband and wife that is similar to a joint tenancy, except that a spouse cannot transfer separately his or her interest during his or her lifetime without the consent of the other spouse. d. Community property—A form of co-ownership in which each spouse technically owns an undivided one-half interest in property acquired during the marriage. This type of ownership occurs in only a few states.
Acquiring Ownership of Personal Property (See pages 959–963.)	The most common means of acquiring ownership in personal property is by purchasing it (see Chapters 14 through 18). Another way in which personal property is often acquired is by will or inheritance (see Chapter 38). The following are additional methods of acquiring personal property: 1. *Possession*—Ownership may be acquired by possession if no other person has ownership title (for example, capturing wild animals or finding abandoned property). 2. *Production*—Any product or item produced by an individual (with minor exceptions) becomes the property of that individual. 3. *Gift*—An effective gift exists when the following conditions exist: a. There is evidence of *intent* to make a gift of the property in question. b. The gift is *delivered* (physically or constructively) to the donee or the donee's agent. c. The gift is *accepted* by the donee or the donee's agent. 4. *Accession*—When someone adds value to an item of personal property by labor or materials, the added value generally becomes the property of the owner of the original property (includes accessions made in bad faith or wrongfully). Good faith accessions that substantially increase the property's value or change the identity of the property may cause title to pass to the improver.

Chapter Summary Personal Property and Bailments—continued

Acquiring Ownership of Personal Property—continued	5. *Confusion*—In the case of fungible goods, if a person wrongfully and willfully commingles goods with those of another in order to render them indistinguishable, the innocent party acquires title to the whole. Otherwise, the owners become tenants in common of the commingled goods.
Mislaid, Lost, and Abandoned Property (See pages 963–967.)	1. *Mislaid property*—Property that is placed somewhere voluntarily by the owner and then inadvertently forgotten. A finder of mislaid property will not acquire title to the goods, and the owner of the place where the property was mislaid becomes a caretaker of the mislaid property. 2. *Lost property*—Property that is involuntarily left and forgotten. A finder of lost property can claim title to the property against the whole world *except the true owner.* 3. *Abandoned property*—Property that has been discarded by the true owner, who has no intention of claiming title to the property in the future. A finder of abandoned property can claim title to it against the whole world, *including the original owner.*
	BAILMENTS
Elements of a Bailment (See pages 967–968.)	1. *Personal property*—Bailments involve only personal property. 2. *Delivery of possession*—For an effective bailment to exist, the bailee (the one receiving the property) must be given exclusive possession and control over the property, and in a voluntary bailment, the bailee must knowingly accept the personal property. 3. *The bailment agreement*—Expressly or impliedly provides for the return of the bailed property to the bailor or a third party, or for the disposal of the bailed property by the bailee.
Ordinary Bailments (See pages 968–972.)	1. *Types of bailments*— a. Bailment for the sole benefit of the bailor—A gratuitous bailment undertaken for the sole benefit of the bailor (for example, as a favor to the bailor). b. Bailment for the sole benefit of the bailee—A gratuitous loan of an article to a person (the bailee) solely for the bailee's benefit. c. Mutual-benefit (contractual) bailment—The most common kind of bailment; involves compensation between the bailee and bailor for the service provided. 2. *Rights of a bailee (duties of a bailor)*— a. The right of possession—Allows actions against third persons who damage or convert the bailed property and allows actions against the bailor for wrongful breach of the bailment. b. The right to be compensated and reimbursed for expenses—In the event of nonpayment, the bailee has the right to place a possessory (bailee's) lien on the bailed property. c. The right to limit liability—An ordinary bailee can limit his or her liability for loss or damage, provided proper notice is given and the limitation is not against public policy. In special bailments, limitations on liability for negligence or on types of losses usually are not allowed, but limitations on the monetary amount of liability are permitted. 3. *Duties of a bailee (rights of a bailor)*— a. A bailee must exercise appropriate care over property entrusted to her or him. What constitutes appropriate care normally depends on the nature and circumstances of the bailment.

(continued)

Chapter Summary Personal Property and Bailments—continued

Ordinary Bailments—continued	b. Bailed goods in a bailee's possession must be either returned to the bailor or disposed of according to the bailor's directions. A bailee's failure to return the bailed property creates a presumption of negligence and constitutes a breach of contract or the tort of conversion of goods.
Special Types of Bailments (See pages 972–974.)	1. *Common carriers*—Carriers that are publicly licensed to provide transportation services to the general public. The common carrier is held to a standard of care based on *strict liability* unless the bailed property is lost or destroyed due to (a) an act of God, (b) an act of a public enemy, (c) an order of a public authority, (d) an act of the shipper, or (e) the inherent nature of the goods. 2. *Warehouse companies*—Professional bailees that differ from ordinary bailees because they (a) can issue documents of title (warehouse receipts) and (b) are subject to state and federal statutes, including Article 7 of the UCC (as are common carriers). They must exercise a high degree of care over the bailed property and are liable for loss of or damage to property if they fail to do so. 3. *Innkeepers (hotel operators)*—Those who provide lodging to the public for compensation as a *regular* business. The common law strict liability standard to which innkeepers were once held is limited today by state statutes, which vary from state to state.

For Review

① What is real property? What is personal property?

② What does it mean to own property in fee simple? What is the difference between a joint tenancy and a tenancy in common?

③ What are the three elements necessary for an effective gift? How else can property be acquired?

④ What are the three elements of a bailment?

⑤ What are the basic rights and duties of the bailee? What are the rights and duties of the bailor?

Questions and Case Problems

36–1. Duties of the Bailee. Discuss the standard of care traditionally required of the bailee for the bailed property in each of the following situations, and determine whether the bailee breached that duty.

(a) Ricardo borrows Steve's lawn mower because his own lawn mower needs repair. Ricardo mows his front yard. To mow the back yard, he needs to move some hoses and lawn furniture. He leaves the mower in front of his house while doing so. When he returns to the front yard, he discovers that the mower has been stolen.

(b) Alicia owns a valuable speedboat. She is going on vacation and asks her neighbor, Maureen, to store the boat in one stall of Maureen's double garage. Maureen consents, and the boat is moved into the garage. Maureen needs some grocery items for dinner and drives to the store. She leaves the garage door open while she is gone, as is her custom, and the speedboat is stolen during that time.

36–2. Gifts. Reineken, very old and ill, wanted to make a gift to his nephew, Gerald. He had a friend obtain $2,500 in cash for him from his bank account, placed this cash in an envelope, and wrote on the envelope, "This is for my nephew, Gerald." Reineken then placed the envelope in his dresser drawer. When Reineken died a month later, his family found the envelope, and Gerald got word of the intended gift. Gerald then demanded that Reineken's daughter, the executor of Reineken's estate (the person who was appointed by Reineken to handle his affairs after his death), turn over the gift to him. The daughter refused to do so. Discuss fully whether Gerald can successfully claim ownership rights to the $2,500.

36–3. Gifts. In 1968, Armando was about to be shipped to Vietnam for active duty with the U.S. Marines. Shortly before he left, he gave an expensive stereo set and other personal belongings to his girlfriend, Sara, saying, "I'll probably not return from this war, so I'm giving these to you." Armando returned eighteen months later and requested that Sara return the property. Sara said that because Armando had given her these items to keep, she was not required to return them. Was a gift made in this instance, and can Armando recover his property? Discuss fully.

36–4. Requirements of a Bailment. Calvin is an executive on a business trip to the West Coast. He has driven his car on this trip and checks into the Hotel Ritz. The hotel has a guarded underground parking lot. Calvin gives his car keys to the parking-lot attendant but fails to notify the attendant that his wife's $10,000 diamond necklace is in a box in the trunk. The next day, on checking out, he discovers that his car has been stolen. Calvin wants to hold the hotel liable for both the car and the necklace. Discuss the probable success of his claim.

36–5. Gifts. William Yee and S. Hing Woo had been lovers for nearly twenty years. They held themselves out as husband and wife, and Woo wore a wedding band. Two days before his death, Yee told Woo that he felt "terribly bad" and believed he would die. He gave Woo three checks, for $42,700, $80,000, and $1,900, and told her that if he died, he wanted her "to be taken care of." After Yee's death, Woo cashed the $42,700 check and the $1,900 check. She never cashed the $80,000 check. The administrator of Yee's estate petitioned a Virginia state court to declare that Woo was not entitled to the funds represented by the checks. What will the court decide, and why? [*Woo v. Smart,* 247 Va. 365, 442 S.E.2d 690 (1994)]

36–6. Bailments. Jole Liddle, a high school student in Salem School District No. 600, played varsity basketball. A letter from Monmouth College of West Long Branch, New Jersey, addressed to Liddle in care of the coach, was delivered to Liddle's school a few days after it was mailed on July 18, 1990. The letter notified Liddle that he was being recruited for a basketball scholarship. The school, which had a policy of promptly delivering any mail sent to students in care of the school, did not deliver the letter to Liddle until seven months later. Because Monmouth College had not heard from Liddle, the college discontinued its efforts to recruit him. Liddle sued the school district, alleging that the coach was negligent in his duties as a bailee of the letter. The school district filed a motion to dismiss the case, arguing that the letter was not bailable property. Was the letter bailable property? Discuss fully. [*Liddle v. Salem School District No. 600,* 249 Ill.App.3d 768, 619 N.E.2d 530, 188 Ill.Dec. 905 (1993)]

36–7. Gratuitous Bailments. Raul Covarrubias, David Haro, and Javier Aguirre immigrated to the United States from Colima, Mexico, to find jobs and help their families. When they learned that Francisco Alcaraz-Garcia planned to travel to Colima, they asked him to deliver various sums, totaling more than $25,000, to their families. During customs inspections at the border, Alcaraz told officers of the U.S. Customs Service that he was not carrying more than $10,000. In fact, he carried more than $35,000. He was charged with—and convicted of—criminal currency and customs violations, and the government seized most of the cash. Covarrubias, Haro, and Aguirre filed a petition for the return of their money, arguing that Alcaraz was a gratuitous bailee and that they still had title to the money. Are they right? Explain fully. [*United States v. Alcaraz-Garcia,* 79 F.3d 769 (9th Cir. 1996)]

36–8. Gifts. Hugh Chalmers issued a promissory note to his father in the amount of $50,000, plus interest. The note was secured by a deed of trust on certain real estate and was payable on demand or within sixty days of the father's death. More than seventeen years later, the father assigned the deed of trust to his wife, Nina. The existence of the note was mentioned in the assignment, which was recorded in the appropriate state office with the deed of trust. After the father died, Nina found the note in a safe-deposit box. On the back of the note, the father had indorsed the note to Nina. When Chalmers refused to pay the amount due, Nina filed a lawsuit in an Arkansas state court against him. Chalmers argued that the note had not been effectively delivered. What should the court hold? Discuss. [*Chalmers v. Chalmers,* 937 S.W.2d 171 (Ark. 1997)]

36–9. Gift *Inter Vivos*. Thomas Stafford owned four promissory notes. Payments on the notes were deposited into a bank account in the names of Stafford and his daughter, June Zink, "as joint tenants with right of survivorship." Stafford kept control of the notes and would not allow Zink to spend any of the proceeds. He also kept the interest on the account. On one note, Stafford indorsed "Pay to the order of Thomas J. Stafford or June S. Zink, or the survivor." The payee on each of the other notes was "Thomas J. Stafford and June S. Zink, or the survivor." When Stafford died, Zink took possession of the notes, claiming that she had been a joint tenant of the notes with her father. Stafford's son, also Thomas, filed a suit in a Virginia state court against Zink, claiming that the notes were partly his. The son argued that their father had not made a valid gift *inter vivos* of the notes to Zink. In whose favor will the court rule? Why? [*Zink v. Stafford,* 509 S.E.2d 833 (Va. 1999)]

TEST YOUR KNOWLEDGE—ANSWER ON THE WEB

36–10. A. D. Lock owned Lock Hospitality, Inc., which in turn owned the Best Western motel in Conway, Arkansas. Joe Terry and David Stocks were preparing the motel for renovation. As they were removing the ceiling tiles in room 118, with Lock present in the room, a dusty cardboard box was noticed near the heating and air supply vent where it had apparently been concealed. Terry climbed a ladder to reach the box, opened it, and handed it to Stocks. The box was filled with more than $38,000 in old currency. Lock took possession of the box and its contents. Terry and Stocks filed a suit in an Arkansas state court against Lock and his corporation to obtain the money. Should the money be characterized as lost, mislaid, or abandoned property? To whom should the court award it? Explain. [*Terry v. Lock,* 37 S.W.3d 202 (Ark. 2001)]

A QUESTION OF ETHICS AND SOCIAL RESPONSIBILITY

36–11. George Cook stayed at a Day's Inn Motel in Nashville, Tennessee, while attending a trade show. At the trade show, Cook received orders for 225 cases of his firm's product, representing $17,336.25 in profits to the company. On the third day of his stay, Cook's room was burglarized while he was gone from the room. The burglar took Cook's order lists, as well as $174 in cash and medicine worth about $10. Cook sued the owner of the motel, Columbia Sussex Corp., alleging negligence. The motel defended by stating that it had posted a notice on the door of Cook's room informing guests of the fact that the motel would not be liable for any valuable property not placed in the motel safe for safekeeping. Given these circumstances, evaluate and answer the following questions. [*Cook v. Columbia Sussex Corp.*, 807 S.W.2d 567 (Tenn.App. 1990)]

1. The relevant state statute governing the liability of innkeepers allowed motels to disclaim their liability by posting a notice such as the one posted by Day's Inn, but the statute also required that the notice be posted "in a conspicuous manner." The notice posted by Day's Inn on the inside of the door to Cook's room was six-by-three inches in size. In your opinion, is the notice sufficiently conspicuous? If you were the guest, would you notice the disclaimer? Is it fair to guests to assume that they will notice such disclaimers? Discuss fully.
2. Should hotels or motels ever be allowed to disclaim liability by posting such notices? From a policy point of view, evaluate the implications of your answer.

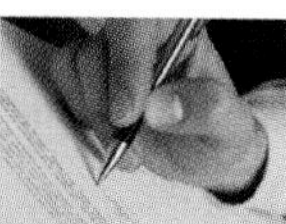

FOR CRITICAL ANALYSIS

36–12. Suppose that a certificate of deposit (CD) owned by two joint tenants (with the right of survivorship) is given by one of the joint tenants as security for a loan (without the other joint tenant's knowledge). Further suppose that the joint tenant dies after defaulting on the loan. Who has superior rights in the CD, the creditor or the other surviving joint tenant?

Internet Exercises

Go to the *Business Law Today* home page at **http://blt.westbuslaw.com**. Select "Interactive Study Center" and then click on "Chapter 36." There you will find the following Internet research exercise that you can perform to learn more about the law of bailments:

Activity 36–1: Bailments

Before the Test

Go to the *Business Law Today* home page at **http://blt.westbuslaw.com**. Click on "Interactive Quizzes." You will find at least twenty interactive questions relating to this chapter.

CHAPTER 37

Real Property

"The right of property is the most sacred of all the rights of citizenship."

Jean-Jacques Rousseau, 1712–1778
(French writer and philosopher)

CHAPTER CONTENTS

LEARNING OBJECTIVES

After reading this chapter, you should be able to answer the following questions:

① What can a person who holds property in fee simple absolute do with the property? Can a person who holds property as a life estate do the same?

② What are the requirements for acquiring property by adverse possession?

③ What limitations may be imposed on the rights of property owners?

④ What is a leasehold estate? What types of leasehold estates, or tenancies, can be created when real property is leased?

⑤ What are the respective duties of the landlord and tenant concerning the use and maintenance of leased property? Is the tenant responsible for all damages that he or she causes?

From earliest times, property has provided a means for survival. Primitive peoples lived off the fruits of the land, eating the vegetation and wildlife. Later, as the wildlife was domesticated and the vegetation cultivated, property provided pasturage and farmland. In the twelfth and thirteenth centuries in Europe, the power of feudal lords was determined by the amount of land that they held; the more land they held, the more powerful they were. After the age of feudalism passed, property continued to be an indicator of family wealth and social position. In the Western world, the protection of an individual's right to his or her property has become, in the words of Jean-Jacques Rousseau, one of the "most sacred of all the rights of citizenship."

In this chapter, we first examine closely the nature of real property. We then look at the various ways in which real property can be owned and at how ownership rights in real property are transferred from one person to another. We conclude the chapter with a discussion of leased property and landlord-tenant relationships.

The Nature of Real Property

Real property consists of land and the buildings, plants, and trees that it contains. Real property also includes subsurface and air rights, as well as personal property that has become permanently attached to real property. Whereas personal property is movable, real property—also called *real estate* or *realty*—is immovable.

LAND

ON THE WEB For links to numerous online legal sources relating to real property, go to **http://www.findlaw.com/01topics/index.html** and click on "Property Law & Real Estate."

Land includes the soil on the surface of the earth and the natural or artificial structures that are attached to it. It further includes all the waters contained on or under the surface and much, but not necessarily all, of the airspace above it. The exterior boundaries of land extend down to the center of the earth and up to the farthest reaches of the atmosphere (subject to certain qualifications).

AIR AND SUBSURFACE RIGHTS

The owner of real property has rights to the airspace above the land, as well as to the soil and minerals underneath it.

Air Rights Early cases involving air rights dealt with such matters as the right to run a telephone wire across a person's property when the wire did not touch any of the property[1] and whether a bullet shot over a person's land constituted trespass.[2] Today,

1. *Butler v. Frontier Telephone Co.,* 186 N.Y. 486, 79 N.E. 716 (1906).
2. *Herrin v. Sutherland,* 74 Mont. 587, 241 P. 328 (1925). Shooting over a person's land constitutes trespass.

A plane flies low over a residential area. Are the property owners' rights violated by such a low-flying plane?

disputes concerning air rights may involve the right of commercial and private planes to fly over property and the right of individuals and governments to seed clouds and produce rain artificially. Flights over private land normally do not violate the property owners' rights unless the flights are low and frequent enough to cause a direct interference with the enjoyment and use of the land.[3] Leaning walls or buildings and projecting eave spouts or roofs may also violate the air rights of an adjoining property owner.

"The meek shall inherit the earth, but not the mineral rights."

J. PAUL GETTY, 1892–1976 (American entrepreneur and industrialist)

Subsurface Rights In many states, the owner of the surface of a piece of land is not the owner of the subsurface, and hence the land ownership may be separated. Subsurface rights can be extremely valuable, as these rights include the ownership of minerals and, in most states, oil and natural gas. Water rights are also extremely valuable, especially in the West. When the ownership is separated into surface and subsurface rights, each owner can pass title to what she or he owns without the consent of the other owner. Each owner has the right to use the land owned, and sometimes a conflict arises between a surface owner's use and the subsurface owner's need to extract minerals, oil, or natural gas. When this occurs, one party's interest may become subservient to the other party's interest, either by statute or case decision.

Significant limitations on either air rights or subsurface rights normally have to be indicated on the deed transferring title at the time of purchase. (Deeds and the types of warranties they contain are discussed later in this chapter.)

PLANT LIFE AND VEGETATION

Plant life, both natural and cultivated, is also considered to be real property. In many instances, the natural vegetation, such as trees, adds greatly to the value of the realty. When a parcel of land is sold and the land has growing crops on it, the sale includes the crops, unless otherwise specified in the sales contract. When crops are sold by themselves, however, they are considered to be personal property or goods. Consequently, the sale of crops is a sale of goods, and therefore it is governed by the Uniform Commercial Code rather than by real property law.[4]

FIXTURES

FIXTURE
A thing that was once personal property but has become attached to real property in such a way that it takes on the characteristics of real property and becomes part of that real property.

Certain personal property can become so closely associated with the real property to which it is attached that the law views it as real property. Such property is known as a **fixture**—a thing *affixed* to realty, meaning it is attached to the real property by roots; embedded in it; permanently situated on it; or permanently attached by means of cement, plaster, bolts, nails, or screws. The fixture can be physically attached to real property, be attached to another fixture, or even be without any actual physical attachment to the land (such as a statue). As long as the owner intends the property to be a fixture, normally it will be a fixture.

Fixtures are included in the sale of land if the sales contract does not provide otherwise. The sale of a house includes the land and the house and the garage on the land, as well as the cabinets, plumbing, and windows. Because these are permanently affixed to the property, they are considered to be a part of it. Unless otherwise agreed, however, the curtains and throw rugs are not included. Items such as drapes and window-unit air conditioners are difficult to classify. Thus, a contract for the sale of a house or commercial realty should indicate which items of this sort are included in the sale.

---

3. *United States v. Causby,* 328 U.S. 256, 66 S.Ct. 1062, 90 L.Ed. 1206 (1946).

4. See UCC 2–107(2).

At issue in the following case was whether an agricultural irrigation system qualified as a fixture.

CASE 37.1 In re Sand & Sage Farm & Ranch, Inc.

United States Bankruptcy Court,
District of Kansas, 2001.
266 Bankr. 507.

FACTS In 1988, Randolf and Sandra Ardery bought an eighty-acre tract in Edwards County, Kansas. On the land was an eight-tower center-pivot irrigation system. The system consisted of an underground well and pump connected to a pipe that ran to the pivot where the water line was attached to a further system of pipes and sprinklers suspended from the towers, extending over the land in a circular fashion. The system's engine and gearhead were bolted to a concrete slab above the pump and well and were attached to the pipe. To secure a loan to buy the land, the Arderys granted to Farmers State Bank a mortgage that covered "all buildings, improvements, and fixtures." In 1996, the Arderys, and their firm Sand & Sage Farm & Ranch, Inc., granted Ag Services of America a security interest in the farm's "equipment." Nothing in the security agreement or financing statement referred to fixtures.[a] In 2000, the Arderys and Sand & Sage filed for bankruptcy in a federal bankruptcy court and asked for permission to sell the land, with the irrigation system, to Bohn Enterprises, Limited Partnership. Ag Services claimed that it had priority to the proceeds covering the value of the irrigation system. The bank responded that it had priority because the system was a "fixture."

a. Security agreements and financing statements were discussed in Chapter 22.

ISSUE Was this irrigation system a "fixture"?

DECISION Yes. The court concluded that the system was a fixture. The bank was entitled to the proceeds from its sale.

REASON The court explained that whether personal property attached to land is a fixture depends on "(i) how firmly the goods are attached or the ease of their removal (annexation); (ii) the relationship of the parties involved (intent); and (iii) how operation of the goods is related to the use of the land (adaptation). Of the three factors, intent is the controlling factor and is deduced largely from the property-owner's acts and the surrounding circumstances." Here, the irrigation system "is firmly attached to the realty. * * * [D]isassembly and removal * * * would be time-consuming and * * * expensive." As for intent, in each transaction all of the parties—except Ag Services, whose security agreement and financing statement did not refer to the irrigation system—"share[d] the intent that the system in question should pass with the land." Furthermore, the system "is suitably adapted to the land. There can be little dispute concerning the need for pivot irrigation in the semi-arid conditions of southwestern Kansas. * * * This alone demonstrates the relation between the operation of the goods and use of the land."

FOR CRITICAL ANALYSIS—Social Consideration *How can a court objectively determine whether someone did, or did not, intend an item to be a fixture?*

Ownership of Real Property

Ownership of property is an abstract concept that cannot exist independently of the legal system. No one can actually possess or *hold* a piece of land, the air above it, the earth below it, and all the water contained on it. The legal system therefore recognizes certain rights and duties that constitute ownership interests in real property.

Recall from Chapter 36 that property ownership is often viewed as a bundle of rights. One who possesses the entire bundle of rights is said to hold the property in *fee simple*, which is the most complete form of ownership. When only some of the rights in the bundle are transferred to another person, the effect is to limit the ownership rights of both the transferor of the rights and the recipient.

OWNERSHIP IN FEE SIMPLE

FEE SIMPLE ABSOLUTE
An ownership interest in land in which the owner has the greatest possible aggregation of rights, privileges, and power. Ownership in fee simple absolute is limited absolutely to a person and his or her heirs.

The most common type of property ownership today is the fee simple. Generally, the term *fee simple* is used to designate a **fee simple absolute**, in which the owner has the greatest possible aggregation of rights, privileges, and power. The fee simple is limited absolutely to a person and his or her heirs and is assigned forever without limitation or condition. Furthermore, the owner has the rights of *exclusive* possession and use of the property. A fee simple is potentially infinite in duration and can be disposed of by deed or by will (by selling or giving away). When there is no will, the fee simple passes to the owner's legal heirs.

The rights that accompany a fee simple include the right to use the land for whatever purpose the owner sees fit. Of course, certain uses of the property may be prohibited by applicable laws, including zoning laws, environmental regulations, and laws that prevent the owner from unreasonably interfering with another person's land. Another limitation on the absolute rights of owners in fee simple is the government's power of eminent domain, as you will read later in this chapter.

CONVEYANCE
The transfer of a title to land from one person to another by deed; a document (such as a deed) by which an interest in land is transferred from one person to another.

FEE SIMPLE DEFEASIBLE
An ownership interest in real property that can be taken away (by the prior grantor) on the occurrence or nonoccurrence of a specified event.

Ownership in fee simple may also become limited whenever a **conveyance**, or transfer of real property, is made to another party *conditionally*. When this occurs, the fee simple is known as a **fee simple defeasible** (the word *defeasible* means capable of being terminated or annulled). • **EXAMPLE 37.1** A conveyance "to A and his heirs as long as the land is used for charitable purposes" creates a fee simple defeasible because ownership of the property is conditioned on the land's being used for charitable purposes. The original owner retains a *partial* ownership interest because if the specified condition does not occur (if the land ceases to be used for charitable purposes), the land reverts, or returns, to the original owner. If the original owner is not living at the time, the land passes to her or his heirs. •

LIFE ESTATES

LIFE ESTATE
An interest in land that exists only for the duration of the life of some person, usually the holder of the estate.

A **life estate** is an estate that lasts for the life of some specified individual. A conveyance "to A for his life" creates a life estate.[5] In a life estate, the life tenant has fewer rights of ownership than the holder of a fee simple defeasible because the rights necessarily cease to exist on the life tenant's death.

The life tenant has the right to use the land, provided that he or she commits no waste (injury to the land). In other words, the life tenant cannot injure the land in a manner that would adversely affect its value. The life tenant can use the land to harvest crops or, if mines and oil wells are already on the land, can extract minerals and oil from it, but the life tenant cannot exploit the land by creating new wells or mines. The life tenant is entitled to any rents or royalties generated by the realty and has the right to mortgage the life estate and create liens, easements, and leases; but none can extend beyond the life of the tenant. In addition, with few exceptions, the owner of a life estate has an exclusive right to possession during his or her life.

"Few . . . men own their property. The property owns them."
ROBERT G. INGERSOLL
1833–1899
(American politician and lecturer)

Along with these rights, the life tenant also has some duties—to keep the property in repair and to pay property taxes. In short, the owner of the life estate has the same rights as a fee simple owner except that the life tenant must maintain the value of the

5. A less common type of life estate is created by the conveyance "to A for the life of B." This is known as an estate *pur autre vie*, or an estate for the duration of the life of another.

property during her or his tenancy, less the decrease in value resulting from the normal use of the property allowed by the life tenancy.

FUTURE INTERESTS

When an owner in fee simple absolute conveys the estate conditionally to another (such as with a fee simple defeasible) or for a limited period of time (such as with a life estate), the original owner still retains an interest in the land. The owner retains the right to repossess ownership of the land if the conditions of the fee simple defeasible are not met or when the life of the life-estate holder ends. The interest in the property that the owner retains (or transfers to another) is called a **future interest** because if it arises, it will only arise in the future.

FUTURE INTEREST
An interest in real property in which the person who holds the interest does not currently possess the property but may possess it in the future.

REVERSIONARY INTEREST
A future interest in property retained by the original owner.

REMAINDER
A future interest in property held by a person other than the original owner.

EXECUTORY INTEREST
A future interest, held by a person other than the grantor, that begins after the termination of the preceding estate.

If the owner retains ownership of the future interest, the future interest is described as a **reversionary interest** because the property will revert to the original owner if the condition specified in a fee simple defeasible fails or when a life tenant dies. If, however, the owner of the future interest transfers ownership rights in that future interest to another, the future interest is described as a **remainder.** For example, a conveyance "to A for life, then to B" creates a life estate for A and a remainder (future interest) for B. An **executory interest** is a type of future interest very similar to a remainder, the difference being that an executory interest does not take effect immediately on the expiration of another interest, such as a life estate. For example, a conveyance "to A and his heirs, as long as the premises are used for charitable purposes, and if not so used for charitable purposes, then to B" creates an executory interest in the property for B.

NONPOSSESSORY INTERESTS

In contrast to the types of property interests just described, some interests in land do not include any rights to possess the property. These interests are thus known as *nonpossessory interests*. Three forms of nonpossessory interests are easements, profits, and licenses.

EASEMENT
A nonpossessory right to use another's property in a manner established by either express or implied agreement.

PROFIT
In real property law, the right to enter upon and remove things from the property of another (for example, the right to enter onto a person's land and remove sand and gravel therefrom).

An **easement** is the right of a person to make limited use of another person's real property without taking anything from the property. An easement, for example, can be the right to travel over another's property. In contrast, a **profit**[6] is the right to go onto land in possession of another and take away some part of the land itself or some product of the land. If Akmed, the owner of Sandy View, gives Carmen the right to go there and remove all the sand and gravel that she needs for her cement business, Carmen has a profit. Easements and profits can be classified as either *appurtenant* or *in gross*. Because easements and profits are similar and the same rules apply to both, they are discussed together.

Easement or Profit Appurtenant An easement or profit appurtenant arises when the owner of one piece of land has a right to go onto (or to remove things from) an *adjacent* piece of land owned by another. • **EXAMPLE 37.2** Suppose that Acosta, the owner of Juniper Hills, has a right to drive his car across Green's land, Greenacres, which is adjacent to Juniper Hills. This right-of-way over Green's property is an easement appurtenant to Juniper Hills and can be used only by the owner of Juniper Hills. Acosta can convey the easement when he conveys Juniper Hills. Now suppose that the highway is

6. The term *profit,* as used here, does not refer to the "profits" made by a business firm. Rather, it means a gain or an advantage.

on the other side of Bancroft's property, which is on the other side of Green's property. To reach the highway, Acosta has easements across both Green's and Bancroft's properties. Juniper Hills and Bancroft's property are not adjacent, but Green's and Bancroft's properties are, so Acosta has an easement appurtenant. ●

CONTRAST An easement appurtenant requires two adjacent pieces of land owned by two different persons, but an easement in gross needs only one piece of land owned by someone other than the owner of the easement.

Easement or Profit in Gross An easement or profit in gross exists when one's right to use or take things from another's land does not depend on one's owning an adjacent tract of land. ● **EXAMPLE 37.3** Suppose that Avery owns a parcel of land with a marble quarry. Avery conveys to XYZ Corporation, which owns no land, the right to come onto his land and remove up to five hundred pounds of marble per day. XYZ Corporation owns a profit in gross. ● When a utility company is granted an easement to run its power lines across another's property, it obtains an easement in gross.

Effect of a Sale of Property When a parcel of land that is *benefited* by an easement or profit appurtenant is sold, the property carries the easement or profit along with it. Thus, in Example 37.2, if Acosta sells Juniper Hills to Thomas and includes the appurtenant right-of-way across Green's property in the deed to Thomas, Thomas will own both the property and the easement that benefits it.

When a parcel of land that has the *burden* of an easement or profit appurtenant is sold, the new owner must recognize its existence only if he or she knew or should have known of it or if it was recorded in the appropriate office of the county. Thus, if Acosta records his easement across Green's property in the appropriate county office before Green conveys the land, the new owner of Green's property will have to allow Acosta, or any subsequent owner of Juniper Hills, to continue to use the path across Green's property.

Creation of an Easement or Profit Easements and profits can be created by deed; by will; or by implication, necessity, or prescription. Two parties can create a contract in which they agree that one party has the right to an easement or profit on a portion of the other party's land. Creation by *deed* or *will* simply involves the delivery of a deed or a disposition in a will by the owner of an easement stating that the grantee (the person receiving the easement or profit) is granted the owner's rights in the easement or profit.

An easement or profit may be created by *implication* when the circumstances surrounding the division of a parcel of property imply its creation. If Barrow divides a parcel of land that has only one well for drinking water and conveys the half without a well to Jarad, a profit by implication arises because Jarad needs drinking water.

An easement may also be created by *necessity.* An easement by necessity does not require division of property for its existence. A person who rents an apartment, for example, has an easement by necessity in the private road leading up to it.

Easements and profits by *prescription* are created in much the same way as title to property is obtained by *adverse possession* (discussed later in this chapter). An easement arises by prescription when one person exercises an easement, such as a right-of-way, on another person's land without the landowner's consent, and the use is apparent and continues for a period of time equal to the applicable statute of limitations.

Termination of an Easement or Profit An easement or profit can be terminated or extinguished in several ways. The simplest way is to deed it back to the owner of the land that is burdened by it. Another way is to abandon it and create evidence of intent to relinquish the right to use it. Mere nonuse will not extinguish an easement or profit *unless the nonuse is accompanied by an intent to abandon.* If the easement or profit is created merely by contract, the termination of the contract terminates the easement or profit. Finally, when the owner of an easement or profit becomes the owner of the property burdened by it, it is merged into the property.

LICENSE
A revocable right or privilege of a person to come on another person's land.

License A **license** is the revocable right of a person to come onto another person's land. It is a personal privilege that arises from the consent of the owner of the land and that can be revoked by the owner. A ticket to attend a movie at a theater is an example of a license. • **EXAMPLE 37.4** Assume that a Broadway theater owner issues to Carla a ticket to see a play. If Carla is refused entry into the theater because she is improperly dressed, she has no right to force her way into the theater. The ticket is only a revocable license, not a conveyance of an interest in property. •

Transfer of Ownership

DEED
A document by which title to property (usually real property) is passed.

Ownership of real property can pass from one person to another in a number of ways. Commonly, ownership interests in land are transferred by sale, and the terms of the transfer are specified in a real estate sales contract. When real property is sold or transferred as a gift, title to the property is conveyed by means of a **deed**—the instrument of conveyance of real property. We look here at transfers of real property by deed, as well as some other ways in which ownership rights in real property can be transferred.

DEEDS

A valid deed must contain the following elements:

① The names of the buyer (grantee) and seller (grantor).

② Words evidencing an intent to convey the property (for example, "I hereby bargain, sell, grant, or give").

③ A legally sufficient description of the land.

④ The grantor's (and, sometimes, the spouse's) signature.

Additionally, to be valid, a deed must be delivered to the person to whom the property is being conveyed or to his or her agent.

WARRANTY DEED
A deed in which the grantor assures (warrants to) the grantee that the grantor has title to the property conveyed in the deed, that there are no encumbrances on the property other than what the grantor has represented, and that the grantee will enjoy quiet possession of the property; a deed that provides the greatest amount of protection for the grantee.

Warranty Deeds Different types of deeds provide different degrees of protection against defects of title. A **warranty deed** warrants the greatest number of things and thus provides the greatest protection for the buyer, or grantee. In most states, special language is required to make a deed a general warranty deed; normally, the deed must include a written promise to protect the buyer against all claims of ownership of the property. A sample warranty deed is shown in Exhibit 37–1. Warranty deeds commonly include a number of *covenants,* or promises, that the grantor makes to the grantee.

A *covenant of seisin*[7] and a *covenant of the right to convey* warrant that the seller has title to the estate that the deed describes and the power to convey the estate, respectively. The covenant of seisin specifically assures the buyer that the grantor has the property in the purported quantity and quality.

A *covenant against encumbrances* is a covenant that the property being sold or conveyed is not subject to any outstanding rights or interests that will diminish the value of the land, except as explicitly stated. Examples of common encumbrances include mortgages, liens, profits, easements, and private deed restrictions on the use of the

7. Pronounced *see*-zuhn.

EXHIBIT 37–1 A SAMPLE WARRANTY DEED

Date: May 31, 2003

Grantor: GAYLORD A. JENTZ AND WIFE, JOANN H. JENTZ

Grantor's Mailing Address (including county):
4106 North Loop Drive
Austin, Travis County, Texas

Grantee: DAVID F. FRIEND AND WIFE, JOAN E. FRIEND AS JOINT TENANTS WITH RIGHT OF SURVIVORSHIP

Grantee's Mailing Address (including county):
5929 Fuller Drive
Austin, Travis County, Texas

Consideration:
For and in consideration of the sum of Ten and No/100 Dollars ($10.00) and other valuable consideration to the undersigned paid by the grantees herein named, the receipt of which is hereby acknowledged, and for which no lien is retained, either express or implied.

Property (including any improvements):
Lot 23, Block "A", Northwest Hills, Green Acres Addition, Phase 4, Travis County, Texas, according to the map or plat of record in volume 22, pages 331-336 of the Plat Records of Travis County, Texas.

Reservations from and Exceptions to Conveyance and Warranty:

This conveyance with its warranty is expressly made subject to the following:

Easements and restrictions of record in Volume 7863, Page 53, Volume 8430, Page 35, Volume 8133, Page 152 of the Real Property Record of Travis County, Texas; Volume 22, Pages 335-339, of the Plat Records of Travis County, Texas; and to any other restrictions and easements affecting said property which are of record in Travis County, Texas.

Grantor, for the consideration and subject to the reservations from and exceptions to conveyance and warranty, grants, sells, and conveys to Grantee the property, together with all and singular the rights and appurtenances thereto in any wise belonging, to have and hold it to Grantee, Grantee's heirs, executors, administrators, successors, or assigns forever. Grantor binds Grantor and Grantor's heirs, executors, administrators, and successors to warrant and forever defend all and singular the property to Grantee and Grantee's heirs, executors, administrators, successors, and assigns against every person whomsoever lawfully claiming or to claim the same or any part thereof, except as to the reservations from and exceptions to conveyance and warranty.

When the context requires, singular nouns and pronouns include the plural.

BY: *Gaylord A. Jentz*
Gaylord A. Jentz

BY: *JoAnn H. Jentz*
JoAnn H. Jentz

(Acknowledgment)

STATE OF TEXAS
COUNTY OF TRAVIS

This instrument was acknowledged before me on the 31st day of May, 2003
by Gaylord A. and JoAnn H. Jentz

Rosemary Potter
Notary Public, State of Texas
Notary's name (printed): *Rosemary Potter*

Notary Seal

Notary's commission expires: 1/31/2006

land. (For an example of how an owner's use of the land might be restricted, see this chapter's *Letter of the Law* feature.)

A *covenant of quiet enjoyment* guarantees that the buyer will not be disturbed in her or his possession of the land by the seller or any third persons. • **EXAMPLE 37.5** Assume that Julio sells a two-acre lot and office building by warranty deed. Subsequently, a third person shows better title than Julio had and proceeds to evict the buyer. Here, the covenant of quiet enjoyment has been breached, and the buyer can sue to recover the purchase price of the land plus any other damages incurred as a result of the eviction. •

QUITCLAIM DEED
A deed intended to pass any title, interest, or claim that the grantor may have in the property but not warranting that such title is valid. A quitclaim deed offers the least amount of protection against defects in the title.

RECORDING STATUTES
Statutes that allow deeds, mortgages, and other real property transactions to be recorded so as to provide notice to future purchasers or creditors of an existing claim on the property.

Quitclaim Deeds A **quitclaim deed** offers the least amount of protection against defects in the title. Basically, a quitclaim deed conveys to the grantee whatever interest the grantor had; so if the grantor had no interest, then the grantee receives no interest. Quitclaim deeds are often used when the seller, or grantor, is uncertain as to the extent of his or her rights in the property.

Recording Statutes Every jurisdiction has **recording statutes**, which allow deeds to be recorded. Recording a deed gives notice to the public that a certain person is now the owner of a particular parcel of real estate. Thus, prospective buyers can check the public records to see whether there have been earlier transactions creating interests or rights in specific parcels of real property. Placing everyone on notice as to the identity of the true owner is intended to prevent the previous owners from fraudulently conveying the land to other purchasers. Deeds are recorded in the county where the property is located. Many state statutes require that the grantor sign the deed in the presence of two witnesses before it can be recorded.

LETTER OF THE LAW
A Shed Is One Thing, a Garage Quite Another

Shortly after Richard and Laura Dufrane purchased a home with an attached garage in a subdivision in Greenfield, Wisconsin, they began constructing a detached garage on the edge of their property. Their neighbor, Mary Pietrowski, told the Dufranes "multiple times" that the garage violated a restrictive covenant that prevented property owners in the subdivision from erecting any buildings other than one house and one garage on their land. After the garage had been built, Pietrowski asked a court to issue an order that the garage be razed.

The Dufranes argued that Pietrowski herself had violated the covenant because she had built a shed on her property. Thus, by violating the covenant herself, she had waived her equitable right to enforce it. After all, a fundamental principle of equity is that a person seeking equitable relief must come to the court with clean hands. Further, claimed the Dufranes, enforcing the covenant would lead to unjust results because Pietrowski would be allowed to maintain a violation of the restrictions on her property while enforcing the restrictions on her neighbors. The Dufranes' arguments were in vain, however. The court interpreted the letter of the law in this case to mean that building a shed constituted only a "minor violation" of the covenant, whereas building a garage was a "major violation" and materially breached the covenant. According to the court, "enforcement against a major violation of the restrictive covenant by a party who committed a minor violation does not result in an injustice." The court ordered that the garage be razed.[a]

THE BOTTOM LINE

Those who purchase real estate should check carefully to determine what restrictive covenants, if any, apply to the property.

a. *Pietrowski v. Dufrane*, 634 N.W.2d 109 (Wis.App. 2001).

Will or Inheritance

Property that is transferred on an owner's death is passed either by will or by state inheritance laws. If the owner of land dies with a will, the land passes in accordance with the terms of the will. If the owner dies without a will, state inheritance statutes prescribe how and to whom the property will pass. Transfers of property by will or inheritance are examined in detail in Chapter 38.

Adverse Possession

ADVERSE POSSESSION
The acquisition of title to real property by occupying it openly, without the consent of the owner, for a period of time specified by a state statute. The occupation must be actual, open, notorious, exclusive, and in opposition to all others, including the owner.

Adverse possession is a means of obtaining title to land without delivery of a deed. Essentially, when one person possesses the property of another for a certain statutory period of time (three to thirty years, with ten years being most common), that person, called the *adverse possessor,* acquires title to the land and cannot be removed from it by the original owner. The adverse possessor is vested with a perfect title just as if there had been a conveyance by deed.

For property to be held adversely, four elements must be satisfied:

① Possession must be actual and exclusive; that is, the possessor must take sole physical occupancy of the property.

② The possession must be open, visible, and notorious, not secret or clandestine. The possessor must occupy the land for all the world to see.

③ Possession must be continuous and peaceable for the required period of time. This requirement means that the possessor must not be interrupted in the occupancy by the true owner or by the courts.

④ Possession must be hostile and adverse. In other words, the possessor must claim the property as against the whole world. He or she cannot be living on the property with the permission of the owner.

ETHICAL ISSUE 37.1

What public policies underlie the doctrine of adverse possession?

There are a number of public-policy reasons for the adverse possession doctrine. One reason is that it furthers society's interest in resolving boundary disputes in as fair a manner as possible. For example, suppose that a couple mistakenly assumes that they own a certain strip of land by their driveway. They plant grass and shrubs in the area and maintain the property over the years. The shrubs contribute to the beauty of their lot and to the value of the property. Some thirty years later, their neighbors have a survey taken, and the results show that the strip of property actually belongs to them. In this situation, the couple could claim that they owned the property by adverse possession, and a court would likely agree.[8] The doctrine of adverse possession thus helps to determine ownership rights when title to property is in question. The doctrine also furthers the policies of rewarding possessors for putting land to productive use, keeping land in the stream of commerce, and not rewarding owners who sit on their rights too long without exercising them.

8. In a case with similar facts, a Pennsylvania court held that the party that had maintained the strip of land for over thirty years acquired title to the land by adverse possession. See *Klos v. Molenda,* 355 Pa.Super. 399, 513 A.2d 490 (1986).

EMINENT DOMAIN

EMINENT DOMAIN The power of a government to take land for public use from private citizens for just compensation.

TAKING The taking of private property by the government for public use. Under the Fifth Amendment to the Constitution, the government may not take private property for public use without "just compensation."

Even ownership in real property in fee simple absolute is limited by a superior ownership. Just as in medieval England the king was the ultimate landowner, so in the United States the government has an ultimate ownership right in all land. This right is known as **eminent domain**, and it is sometimes referred to as the condemnation power of the government to take land for public use. It gives the government a right to acquire possession of real property in the manner directed by the Constitution and the laws of the state whenever the public interest requires it. Property may be taken only for public use.

When the government takes land owned by a private party for public use, it is referred to as a **taking**, and the government must compensate the private party. Under the so-called *takings clause* of the Fifth Amendment, the government may not take private property for public use without "just compensation."

The power of eminent domain is generally invoked through condemnation proceedings. For example, when a new public highway is to be built, the government must decide where to build it and how much land to condemn. After the government determines that a particular parcel of land is necessary for public use, it brings a judicial proceeding to obtain title to the land. Then, in another proceeding, the court determines the *fair value* of the land, which is usually approximately equal to its market value.

ETHICAL ISSUE 37.2

Should eminent domain be used to promote private developments?

Issues of fairness often arise when the government takes private property for public use. One issue has to do with whether property taken by eminent domain should then be conveyed to private developers. For example, a city government may decide that it is in the public interest to have a larger parking lot for a local, privately owned sports stadium or to have a manufacturing plant locate in the city to create more jobs. In such cases, the government may condemn certain tracts of existing housing or business property and then, later, convey the land to the privately owned stadium or to the owner of the manufacturing plant. The increasingly widespread use of eminent domain for

Undeveloped seashore stretches into the distance. Should the government be permitted to take such property from private citizens for public use without compensation?

such purposes has generated substantial controversy in recent years. Government officials claim that this use of eminent domain helps bring in private developers and businesses that will provide jobs and increase tax revenues, thus revitalizing communities. Critics, however, contend that when eminent domain is used in this way, essentially one group of private owners is replaced by another group of private owners. In other words, the land is not being taken for "public" use, as required by the Fifth Amendment to the U.S. Constitution. Although the courts, by and large, have supported the government agencies in cases challenging such takings of private property, the tide may be turning. Recently, some courts have held for the landowners in these cases.[9]

Leasehold Estates

LEASE
In real property law, a contract by which the owner of real property (the landlord, or lessor) grants to a person (the tenant, or lessee) an exclusive right to use and possess the property, usually for a specified period of time, in return for rent or some other form of payment.

LEASEHOLD ESTATE
An estate in realty held by a tenant under a lease. In every leasehold estate, the tenant has a qualified right to possess and/or use the land.

TENANCY FOR YEARS
A type of tenancy under which property is leased for a specified period of time, such as a month, a year, or a period of years.

Often, real property is used by those who do not own it. A **lease** is a contract by which the owner of real property (the landlord, or lessor) grants to a person (the tenant, or lessee) an exclusive right to use and possess the property, usually for a specified period of time, in return for rent or some other form of payment. Property in the possession of a tenant is referred to as a **leasehold estate.**

The respective rights and duties of the landlord and tenant that arise under a lease agreement will be discussed shortly. Here we look at the types of leasehold estates, or tenancies, that can be created when real property is leased.

Tenancy for Years

A **tenancy for years** is created by an express contract by which property is leased for a specified period of time, such as a day, a month, a year, or a period of years. For example, signing a one-year lease to occupy an apartment creates a tenancy for years. At the end of the period specified in the lease, the lease ends (without notice), and possession of the apartment returns to the lessor. If the tenant dies during the period of the lease, the lease interest passes to the tenant's heirs as personal property. Often, leases include renewal or extension provisions.

Periodic Tenancy

PERIODIC TENANCY
A lease interest in land for an indefinite period involving payment of rent at fixed intervals, such as week to week, month to month, or year to year.

A **periodic tenancy** is created by a lease that does not specify how long it is to last but does specify that rent is to be paid at certain intervals. This type of tenancy is automatically renewed for another rental period unless properly terminated. For example, a periodic tenancy is created by a lease that states, "Rent is due on the tenth day of every month." This provision creates a tenancy from month to month. This type of tenancy can also extend from week to week or from year to year.

Under the common law, to terminate a periodic tenancy, the landlord or tenant must give at least one period's notice to the other party. If the tenancy extends from month to month, for example, one month's notice must be given prior to the last month's rent payment. State statutes may require a different period for notice of termination in a periodic tenancy, however.

9. See, for example, *In re Condemnation of 110 Washington St.,* 767 A.2d 1154 (Pa. Cmwlth. 2001); and *99 Cents Only Stores v. Lancaster Redevelopment Agency,* ___ F.Supp.2d ___ (C.D.Cal. 2001).

TENANCY AT WILL

TENANCY AT WILL A type of tenancy under which either party can terminate the tenancy without notice; usually arises when a tenant who has been under a tenancy for years retains possession, with the landlord's consent, after the tenancy for years has terminated.

Suppose that a landlord rents an apartment to a tenant "for as long as both agree." In such a situation, the tenant receives a leasehold estate known as a **tenancy at will.** Under the common law, either party can terminate the tenancy without notice (that is, "at will"). This type of estate usually arises when a tenant who has been under a tenancy for years retains possession after the termination date of that tenancy with the landlord's consent. Before the tenancy has been converted into a periodic tenancy (by the periodic payment of rent), it is a tenancy at will, terminable by either party without notice. Once the tenancy is treated as a periodic tenancy, termination notice must conform to the one already discussed for that type of tenancy. The death of either party or the voluntary commission of waste by the tenant will terminate a tenancy at will.

TENANCY AT SUFFERANCE

TENANCY AT SUFFERANCE A type of tenancy under which a tenant who, after rightfully being in possession of leased premises, continues (wrongfully) to occupy the property after the lease has been terminated. The tenant has no rights to possess the property and occupies it only because the person entitled to evict the tenant has not done so.

The mere possession of land without right is called a **tenancy at sufferance.** It is not a true tenancy. A tenancy at sufferance is not an estate because it is created when a tenant *wrongfully* retains possession of property. Whenever a tenancy for years, periodic tenancy, or tenancy at will ends and the tenant continues to retain possession of the premises without the owner's permission, a tenancy at sufferance is created. When a tenancy at sufferance arises, the owner can immediately evict the tenant.

Landlord-Tenant Relationships

ON THE WEB You can find online links to most uniform laws, including the URLTA, at **http://www.lawsource.com.**

In the past several decades, landlord-tenant relationships have become much more complex, as has the law governing them. Generally, the law has come to apply contract doctrines, such as those providing for implied warranties and unconscionability, to the landlord-tenant relationship. Increasingly, landlord-tenant relationships have become subject to specific state and local statutes and ordinances as well. In 1972, in an effort to create more uniformity in the law governing landlord-tenant relationships, the National Conference of Commissioners on Uniform State Laws issued the Uniform Residential Landlord and Tenant Act (URLTA). We look now at how a landlord-tenant relationship is created and at the respective rights and duties of landlords and tenants.

CREATING THE LANDLORD-TENANT RELATIONSHIP

A landlord-tenant relationship is established by a lease contract. As mentioned, a lease contract arises when a property owner (landlord) agrees to give another party (the tenant) the exclusive right to possess the property—usually for a price and for a specified term.

NOTE Sound business practice dictates that a lease for commercial property should be written carefully and should clearly define the parties' rights and obligations.

Form of the Lease A lease contract may be oral or written. Under the common law, an oral lease is valid. As with most oral contracts, however, a party who seeks to enforce an oral lease may have difficulty proving its existence. In most states, statutes mandate that leases be in writing for some tenancies (such as those exceeding one year). To ensure the validity of a lease agreement, it should therefore be in writing and do the following:

① Express an intent to establish the relationship.

② Provide for the transfer of the property's possession to the tenant at the beginning of the term.

③ Provide for the landlord's reversionary interest, which entitles the property owner to retake possession at the end of the term.

④ Describe the property—for example, give its street address.

⑤ Indicate the length of the term, the amount of the rent, and how and when it is to be paid.

Legal Requirements State or local law often dictates permissible lease terms. For example, a statute or ordinance might prohibit the leasing of a structure that is in a certain physical condition or is not in compliance with local building codes. Similarly, a statute may prohibit the leasing of property for a particular purpose. For instance, a state law might prohibit gambling houses. Thus, if a landlord and tenant intend that the leased premises be used only to house an illegal betting operation, their lease is unenforceable.

A property owner cannot legally discriminate against prospective tenants on the basis of race, color, national origin, religion, gender, or disability. Similarly, a tenant cannot legally promise to do something counter to laws prohibiting discrimination. A tenant, for example, cannot legally promise to do business only with members of a particular race. The public policy underlying these prohibitions is to treat all people equally. In the following case, a rental housing applicant claimed that her rental application had been denied because of her live-in boyfriend's race.

CASE 37.2 Osborn v. Kellogg

Court of Appeals of Nebraska, 1996.
4 Neb.App. 594,
547 N.W.2d 504.

FACTS Kristi Kellogg, her daughter Mindy, and her boyfriend James Greene attempted to lease half of a house. The house was owned by Keith Osborn and Pam Lyman, and managed, as rental property, by Keith's mother, Barbara Osborn. Kellogg was white. Greene was African American. The owners refused to rent to them, claiming, among other things, that three people were too many, Greene's income was too low, and Greene had not provided credit references. They later rented half of the house to the Li family, which had five members, and the other half to the Suggett family, which numbered three. Both the Li family and the Suggett family had less income than Kellogg and Greene. Kellogg had provided extensive credit references, but the Lis and the Suggetts had provided none. Kellogg filed a complaint with the Nebraska Equal Opportunity Commission (NEOC) against the Osborns and Lyman. The NEOC concluded that the defendants had discriminated against Kellogg in violation of state fair housing laws. A Nebraska state trial court adopted the NEOC's conclusion. The defendants appealed to an intermediate state appellate court.

ISSUE Had the defendants discriminated against Kellogg in violation of state fair housing laws?

DECISION Yes. The intermediate state appellate court affirmed the judgment of the lower court.

REASON The appellate court reasoned that "[w]hile Kellogg is not a member of a racial minority [but Greene was], we note that she qualifies as * * * a person who claims to have been injured by a discriminatory housing practice." The court stated, "The NEOC hearing examiner found that Kellogg proved by a preponderance of the evidence that the Osborns' seemingly legitimate reasons for rejecting Kellogg were, in fact, a pretext for intentional discrimination. * * * [W]e conclude that competent evidence supports the NEOC hearing examiner's factual findings."

(continued)

CASE 37.2—Continued

FOR CRITICAL ANALYSIS—Ethical Consideration *What if the Osborns and Lyman discriminated against Kellogg not because her boyfriend was African American but because they disapproved of cohabitation by unmarried couples? Should this form of discrimination be permissible?*

RIGHTS AND DUTIES

The rights and duties of landlords and tenants generally pertain to four broad areas of concern—the possession, use, and maintenance of leased property and, of course, rent.

ON THE WEB Many Web sites now provide information on laws and other information relating to landlord-tenant relationships. One of them is TenantNet™ at **http://www.tenant.net**.

Possession Possession involves both the obligation of the landlord to deliver possession to the tenant at the beginning of the lease term and the right of the tenant to obtain possession and retain it until the lease expires.

The covenant of quiet enjoyment mentioned previously also applies to leased premises. Under this covenant, the landlord promises that during the lease term, neither the landlord nor anyone having a superior title to the property will disturb the tenant's use and enjoyment of the property. This covenant forms the essence of the landlord-tenant relationship, and if it is breached, the tenant can terminate the lease and sue for damages.

If the landlord deprives the tenant of possession of the leased property or interferes with the tenant's use or enjoyment of it, an **eviction** occurs. An eviction occurs, for example, when the landlord changes the lock and refuses to give the tenant a new key. A **constructive eviction** occurs when the landlord wrongfully performs or fails to perform any of the undertakings the lease requires, thereby making the tenant's further use and enjoyment of the property exceedingly difficult or impossible. Examples of constructive eviction include a landlord's failure to provide heat in the winter, light, or other essential utilities.

EVICTION
A landlord's act of depriving a tenant of possession of the leased premises.

CONSTRUCTIVE EVICTION
A form of eviction that occurs when a landlord fails to perform adequately any of the undertakings (such as providing heat in the winter) required by the lease, thereby making the tenant's further use and enjoyment of the property exceedingly difficult or impossible.

Use and Maintenance of the Premises If the parties do not limit by agreement the uses to which the property may be put, the tenant may make any use of it, as long as the use is legal and reasonably relates to the purpose for which the property is adapted or ordinarily used and does not injure the landlord's interest.

The tenant is responsible for any damages to the premises that he or she causes, intentionally or negligently, and the tenant may be held liable for the cost of returning the property to the physical condition it was in at the lease's inception. Unless the parties have agreed otherwise, the tenant is not responsible for ordinary wear and tear and the property's consequent depreciation in value.

Usually, the landlord must comply with state statutes and city ordinances that delineate specific standards for the construction and maintenance of buildings. Typically, these codes contain structural requirements common to the construction, wiring, and plumbing of residential and commercial buildings. In some jurisdictions, landlords of residential property are required by statute to maintain the premises in good repair.

IMPLIED WARRANTY OF HABITABILITY
An implied promise by a landlord that rented residential premises are fit for human habitation—that is, in a condition that is safe and suitable for people to live in.

Implied Warranty of Habitability The **implied warranty of habitability** requires a landlord who leases residential property to deliver the premises to the tenant in a habitable condition—that is, in a condition that is safe and suitable for people to live in—at the beginning of a lease term and to maintain them in that condition for the lease's duration. Some state legislatures have enacted this warranty into law. In other jurisdictions, courts have based the warranty on the existence of a landlord's statutory duty to keep leased premises in good repair, or they have simply applied it as a matter of public policy.

Generally, this warranty applies to major, or *substantial*, physical defects that the landlord knows or should know about and has had a reasonable time to repair—for example, a large hole in the roof. An unattractive or annoying feature, such as a crack in the wall, may be unpleasant, but unless the crack is a structural defect or affects the residence's heating capabilities, it is probably not sufficiently substantial to make the place uninhabitable.

At issue in the following case was whether the lack of a smoke detector constituted a violation of a statutory requirement that rental property be "in reasonable repair and fit for human habitation."

CASE 37.3 Schiernbeck v. Davis

United States Court of Appeals,
Eighth Circuit, 1998.
143 F.3d 434.
http://laws.findlaw.com/8th[a]

FACTS Linda Schiernbeck rented a house from Clark and Rosa Davis. A month after moving into the house, Schiernbeck noticed a discolored circular area where, she determined, a smoke detector had previously been attached to the wall. Schiernbeck later claimed that she told Clark Davis about the missing detector. Davis did not remember the conversation. He admitted, however, that he gave Schiernbeck a detector, which she denied. At any rate, when a fire in the house severely injured Schiernbeck, she filed a suit in a federal district court against the Davises, alleging negligence and breach of contract for failing to provide a detector. The Davises filed a motion for summary judgment, arguing that they had no duty to install a detector in a rental house. The court ruled in the Davises' favor, and Schiernbeck appealed to the U.S. Court of Appeals for the Eighth Circuit.

a. This page provides access to some of the opinions of the U.S. Court of Appeals for the Eighth Circuit. In the "Search" box, type "97-3431" and click on "Search" to access the *Schiernbeck* opinion. This Web site is maintained by FindLaw.

ISSUE Does a landlord's statutory duty to keep rental premises "in reasonable repair and fit for human habitation" include installing a smoke detector?

DECISION No. The U.S. Court of Appeals for the Eighth Circuit affirmed the lower court's judgment.

REASON The U.S. Court of Appeals for the Eighth Circuit recognized that South Dakota Codified Laws, Section 43-32-8, requires a landlord to maintain leased premises "in reasonable repair and fit for human habitation." The question was whether the installation of a smoke detector fell within the language of the statute. Schiernbeck cited part of a dictionary definition of "repair" ("to supply * * * that which is lost or destroyed") and argued that this included replacing a missing smoke detector. The court disagreed, concluding that "when reading the entire definition, the term 'repair' does not encompass replacing a missing smoke detector." As for the "fit for human habitation" requirement, the court stated that a lack of running water, heat, or electricity made a place unfit, while a lack of smoke detectors, fire extinguishers, and so on, did not.

FOR CRITICAL ANALYSIS—Ethical Consideration *What is a landlord's ethical duty with respect to keeping rental premises "fit for human habitation"?*

Rent *Rent* is the tenant's payment to the landlord for the tenant's occupancy or use of the landlord's real property. Generally, the tenant must pay the rent even if she or he refuses to occupy the property or moves out, as long as the refusal or the move is unjustifiable and the lease is in force.

Under the common law, destruction by fire or flood of a building leased by a tenant did not relieve the tenant of the obligation to pay rent and did not permit the termination of the lease. Today, however, state statutes have altered the common law rule. If the building burns down, apartment dwellers in most states are not continuously liable to the landlord for the payment of rent.

NOTE Options that may be available to a tenant on a landlord's breach of the implied warranty of habitability include repairing the defect and deducting the amount from the rent, canceling the lease, and suing for damages.

In some situations, such as when a landlord breaches the implied warranty of habitability, a tenant is allowed to withhold rent as a remedy. When rent withholding is authorized under a statute (sometimes referred to as a "rent-strike" statute), the tenant must usually put the amount withheld into an *escrow account*. This account is held in the name of the depositor (in this case, the tenant) and an *escrow agent* (in this case, usually the court or a government agency), and the funds are returnable to the depositor if the third person (in this case, the landlord) fails to fulfill the escrow condition. Generally, the tenant may withhold an amount equal to the amount by which the defect rendering the premises unlivable reduces the property's rental value. How much that is may be determined in different ways, and the tenant who withholds more than is legally permissible is liable to the landlord for the excessive amount withheld.

INTERNATIONAL PERSPECTIVE

Landlord-Tenant Law in England

Unlike the law in the United States governing landlord-tenant relationships, much of which evolved under the common law, British landlord-tenant law has been created, to a great extent, by statute. English law traditionally adhered to the principle of *caveat tenant* ("let the tenant beware"). In other words, tenants had little recourse against landlords who refused to keep the leased premises in good repair.

In 1985, however, this situation began to change. In that year, the British Parliament enacted the Landlord and Tenant Act. The act sets forth details related to the landlord's obligations to maintain and repair leased premises. The act also requires that leased premises be fit for human habitation, a concept similar to the implied warranty of habitability in some U.S. jurisdictions.

FOR CRITICAL ANALYSIS
Given that tenants in the United States have traditionally had rights under the common law, why has it been necessary to enact statutes regulating landlord-tenant relationships in the United States?

TRANSFERRING RIGHTS TO LEASED PROPERTY

Either the landlord or the tenant may wish to transfer her or his rights to the leased property during the term of the lease.

Transferring the Landlord's Interest Just as any other real property owner can sell, give away, or otherwise transfer her or his property, so can a landlord—who is, of course, the leased property's owner. If complete title to the leased property is transferred, the tenant becomes the tenant of the new owner. The new owner may collect subsequent rent but must abide by the terms of the existing lease agreement.

Transferring the Tenant's Interest The tenant's transfer of his or her entire interest in the leased property to a third person is an *assignment of the lease.* A lease assignment is an agreement to transfer all rights, title, and interest in the lease to the assignee. It is a complete transfer. Many leases require that the assignment have the landlord's written consent, and an assignment that lacks consent can be avoided (nullified) by the landlord. A landlord who knowingly accepts rent from the assignee, however, will be held to have waived the requirement. An assignment does not terminate a tenant's liabilities under a lease agreement, however, because the tenant may assign rights but not duties. Thus, even though the assignee of the lease is required to pay rent, the original tenant is not released from the contractual obligation to pay the rent if the assignee fails to do so.

SUBLEASE
A lease executed by the lessee of real estate to a third person, conveying the same interest that the lessee enjoys but for a shorter term than that held by the lessee.

The tenant's transfer of all or part of the premises for a period shorter than the lease term is a **sublease.** The same restrictions that apply to an assignment of the tenant's interest in leased property apply to a sublease. • **EXAMPLE 37.6** Derek, a student, leases an apartment for a two-year period. Although Derek had planned on attending summer school, he is offered a job in Europe for the summer months and accepts. Because he does not wish to pay three months' rent for an unoccupied apartment, Derek subleases the apartment to Singleton, who becomes a sublessee. (Derek may have to obtain his landlord's consent for this sublease if the lease requires it.) Singleton is bound by the same terms of the lease as Derek, but as in a lease assignment, Derek remains liable for the obligations under the lease if Singleton fails to fulfill them.•

APPLICATION Law and the Entrepreneur . . .

How to Negotiate a Favorable Lease*

Generally, an entrepreneur starting a business is well advised to lease rather than buy property because the future success of the business is uncertain. By leasing instead of purchasing property, persons just starting out in business allow themselves some time to determine whether business profits will warrant the outright purchase of property.

FACTORS TO CONSIDER

One thing to keep in mind when leasing property is that lease contracts are usually form contracts that favor the landowner. That means that, as a prospective tenant, you need to think about negotiating terms more favorable to you. Before negotiating the terms of the lease, do some comparison shopping to see what the rent for other similar properties in the area is. Usually, rental prices for business property are stated as so many dollars per square foot (per month or per year). In commercial leases to retail stores, part or all of the rent commonly consists of a percentage of the tenant's sales made on the premises during the term of the lease. Bear in mind, too, that the nature of your business should determine, to a great extent, the location of the leased premises. If you are involved in a mail-order business, for example, you need not pay the extra price for a prime location that might be required for a restaurant business.

NEGOTIATING LEASE TERMS

When negotiating a lease, you must also determine who will pay property taxes and insurance on the property and who will be responsible for repairs of the property and utility payments. These terms are generally

*This *Application* is not meant to substitute for the services of an attorney who is licensed to practice law in your state.

(continued)

APPLICATION Law and the Entrepreneur . . .

How to Negotiate a Favorable Lease—continued

negotiable, and depending on who takes responsibility, the rent payment may be adjusted accordingly. Generally, your success in negotiating favorable lease terms will depend on the market. If the rental market is "good" (that is, if you have numerous other rental options at favorable rates), you may be able to convince the landlord that he or she should be responsible for taxes, insurance, maintenance, and the like, and possibly for improvements to the property necessary for your business. Therefore, it is important to investigate the status of the market before you begin negotiations with a potential landlord.

Checklist for the Lessee of Business Property

1. When you are starting a business, leasing rather than buying property can be advantageous, because it reduces your liability in the event that your business is unsuccessful.
2. Realize that although lease contracts normally favor the landlord, you usually can negotiate advantageous terms for your lease of the premises.
3. Make sure that the lease contract clearly indicates whether the landlord or tenant is to be responsible for taxes on the property, costs relating to necessary maintenance and repairs, and utility costs. By comparison shopping, you should be able to judge which lease terms are favorable and which are not.
4. To protect yourself in the event your business is unsuccessful, start with a short-term initial lease, perhaps with an option to renew the lease in the future.

Key Terms

Chapter Summary Real Property

The Nature of Real Property (See pages 982–984.)	Real property (also called real estate or realty) is immovable. It includes land, subsurface and air rights, plant life and vegetation, and fixtures.

Chapter Summary Real Property—continued

Ownership of Real Property (See pages 984–988.)	1. *Fee simple absolute*—The most complete form of ownership. 2. *Fee simple defeasible*—Ownership in fee simple that can end if a specified event or condition occurs. 3. *Life estate*—An estate that lasts for the life of a specified individual during which time the individual is entitled to possess, use, and benefit from the estate; ownership rights in a life estate are subject to the rights of the future-interest holder. 4. *Future interest*—A residuary interest not granted by the grantor in conveying an estate to another for life, for a specified period of time, or on the condition that a specific event does or does not occur. The grantor may retain the residuary interest (which is then called a *reversionary interest*) or transfer ownership rights in the future interest to another (the interest is then referred to as a *remainder*). 5. *Nonpossessory interest*—An interest that involves the right to use real property but not to possess it. Easements, profits, and licenses are nonpossessory interests.
Transfer of Ownership (See pages 988–993.)	1. *By deed*—When real property is sold or transferred as a gift, title to the property is conveyed by means of a deed. A deed must meet specific legal requirements. A *warranty deed* warrants the most extensive protection against defects of title. A *quitclaim deed* conveys to the grantee only whatever interest the grantor had in the property. A deed may be recorded in the manner prescribed by *recording statutes* in the appropriate jurisdiction to give third parties notice of the owner's interest. 2. *By will or inheritance*—If the owner dies after having made a valid will, the land passes as specified in the will. If the owner dies without having made a will, the heirs inherit according to state inheritance statutes. 3. *By adverse possession*—When a person possesses the property of another for a statutory period of time (three to thirty years, with ten years being the most common), that person acquires title to the property, provided the possession is actual and exclusive, open and visible, continuous and peaceable, and hostile and adverse (without the permission of the owner). 4. *By eminent domain*—The government can take land for public use, with just compensation, when the public interest requires the taking.
Leasehold Estates (See pages 993–994.)	A leasehold estate is an interest in real property that is held for only a limited period of time, as specified in the lease agreement. Types of tenancies relating to leased property include the following: 1. *Tenancy for years*—Tenancy for a period of time stated by express contract. 2. *Periodic tenancy*—Tenancy for a period determined by the frequency of rent payments; automatically renewed unless proper notice is given. 3. *Tenancy at will*—Tenancy for as long as both parties agree; no notice of termination is required. 4. *Tenancy at sufferance*—Possession of land without legal right.
Landlord-Tenant Relationships (See pages 994–999.)	1. *Lease agreement*—The landlord-tenant relationship is created by a lease agreement. State or local laws may dictate whether the lease must be in writing and what lease terms are permissible. 2. *Rights and duties*—The rights and duties that arise under a lease agreement generally pertain to the following areas:

(continued)

Chapter Summary Real Property—continued

Landlord-Tenant Relationships—continued	a. Possession—The tenant has an exclusive right to possess the leased premises, which must be available to the tenant at the agreed-on time. Under the covenant of quiet enjoyment, the landlord promises that during the lease term neither the landlord nor anyone having superior title to the property will disturb the tenant's use and enjoyment of the property. b. Use and maintenance of the premises—Unless the parties agree otherwise, the tenant may make any legal use of the property. The tenant is responsible for any damage that he or she causes. The landlord must comply with laws that set specific standards for the maintenance of real property. The implied warranty of habitability requires that a landlord furnish and maintain residential premises in a habitable condition (that is, in a condition safe and suitable for human life). c. Rent—The tenant must pay the rent as long as the lease is in force, unless the tenant justifiably refuses to occupy the property or withholds the rent because of the landlord's failure to maintain the premises properly. 3. *Transferring rights to leased property—* a. If the landlord transfers complete title to the leased property, the tenant becomes the tenant of the new owner. The new owner may then collect the rent but must abide by the existing lease. b. Generally, in the absence of an agreement to the contrary, tenants may assign their rights (but not their duties) under a lease contract to a third person. Tenants may also sublease leased property to a third person, but the original tenant is not relieved of any obligations to the landlord under the lease. In either case, the landlord's consent may be required.

For Review

① What can a person who holds property in fee simple absolute do with the property? Can a person who holds property as a life estate do the same?

② What are the requirements for acquiring property by adverse possession?

③ What limitations may be imposed on the rights of property owners?

④ What is a leasehold estate? What types of leasehold estates, or tenancies, can be created when real property is leased?

⑤ What are the respective duties of the landlord and tenant concerning the use and maintenance of leased property? Is the tenant responsible for all damages that he or she causes?

Questions and Case Problems

37–1. Tenant's Rights and Responsibilities. You are a student in college and plan to attend classes for nine months. You sign a twelve-month lease for an apartment. Discuss fully each of the following situations:

(a) You have a summer job in another town and wish to assign the balance of your lease (three months) to a fellow student who will be attending summer school. Can you do so?

(b) You are graduating in May. The lease will have three months remaining. Can you terminate the lease without liability by giving a thirty-day notice to the landlord?

37–2. Property Ownership. Antonio is the owner of a lakeside house and lot. He deeds the house and lot "to my wife, Angela, for life, then to my son, Charles." Given these facts, answer the following questions:

(a) Does Antonio have any ownership interest in the lakeside house after making these transfers? Explain.
(b) What is Angela's interest called? Is there any limitation on her rights to use the property as she wishes?
(c) What is Charles's interest called? Why?

37–3. Property Ownership. Lorenz was a wanderer twenty-two years ago. At that time, he decided to settle down on an unoccupied, three-acre parcel of land that he did not own. People in the area indicated to him that they had no idea who owned the property. Lorenz built a house on the land, got married, and raised three children while living there. He fenced in the land, installed a gate with a sign above it that read "Lorenz's Homestead," and had trespassers removed. Lorenz is now confronted by Joe Reese, who has a deed in his name as owner of the property. Reese, claiming ownership of the land, orders Lorenz and his family off the property. Discuss who has the better "title" to the property.

37–4. Deeds. Wiley and Gemma are neighbors. Wiley's lot is extremely large, and his present and future use of it will not involve the entire area. Gemma wants to build a single-car garage and driveway along the present lot boundary. Because of ordinances requiring buildings to be set back fifteen feet from an adjoining property line, and because of the placement of her existing structures, Gemma cannot build the garage. Gemma contracts to purchase ten feet of Wiley's property along their boundary line for $3,000. Wiley is willing to sell but will give Gemma only a quitclaim deed, whereas Gemma wants a warranty deed. Discuss the differences between these deeds as they would affect the rights of the parties if the title to this ten feet of land later proved to be defective.

37–5. Easements. Merton Peterson owned a golf course, a supper club, and the parking lot between them. Both golfers and club patrons always parked in the lot. Peterson sold the club and the lot to the American Legion, which sold them to VBC, Inc. (owned by Richard Beck and others). When VBC demanded rent from Peterson for use of the lot by the golf course users, Peterson filed a suit in a South Dakota state court to determine title. On what basis might the court hold that Peterson has an easement for the use of the lot? Does Peterson have an easement? [*Peterson v. Beck*, 537 N.W.2d 375 (S.Dak. 1995)]

37–6. Warranty of Habitability. James and Bernadine Winn rented a house from Rick and Cynthia McGeehan. Each month, the rent was either late or underpaid. When the McGeehans told the Winns that no further late payments would be accepted, the Winns complained of a number of habitability problems. The McGeehans made repairs. The Winns again failed to pay the rent on time. The McGeehans filed a suit in an Oregon state court to regain possession of the house. While the suit was pending, the Winns paid the rent to the court. The court held that the McGeehans were entitled to possession. The Winns appealed, claiming that they were entitled to possession. Who should have possession of the house, and why? [*Winn v. McGeehan*, 142 Or.App. 390, 921 P.2d 1337 (1996)]

37–7. Taking. Richard and Jaquelyn Jackson owned property in a residential subdivision near an airport operated by the Metropolitan Knoxville Airport Authority in Blount County, Tennessee. The Airport Authority considered extending a runway near the subdivision and undertook a study that found that the noise, vibration, and pollution from aircraft using the extension would render the Jacksons' property incompatible with residential use. The airport built the extension, bringing about the predicted results, and the Jacksons filed a suit against the Airport Authority, alleging a taking of their property. The Airport Authority responded that there was no taking because there were no direct flights over the Jacksons' property. In whose favor will the court rule, and why? [*Jackson v. Metropolitan Knoxville Airport Authority*, 922 S.W.2d 860 (Tenn. 1996)]

37–8. Warranty of Habitability. Three-year-old Nkenge Lynch fell from the window of her third-floor apartment and suffered serious and permanent injuries. There were no window stops or guards on the window. The use of window stops, even if installed, is optional with the tenant. Stanley James owned the apartment building. Zsa Zsa Kinsey, Nkenge's mother, filed a suit on Nkenge's behalf in a Massachusetts state court against James, alleging in part a breach of an implied warranty of habitability. The plaintiff did not argue that the absence of stops or guards made the apartment unfit for human habitation but that their absence "endangered and materially impaired her health and safety," and therefore the failure to install them was a breach of warranty. Should the court rule that the absence of window stops breached a warranty of habitability? Should the court mandate that landlords provide window guards? Why or why not? [*Lynch v. James*, 44 Mass.App.Ct. 448, 692 N.E.2d 81 (1998)]

37–9. Adverse Possession. In 1972, Ted Pafundi bought a quarry in West Pawlet, Vermont, from his neighbor, Marguerite Scott. The deed vaguely described the eastern boundary of the quarry as "the westerly boundary of the lands of" the neighboring property owners. Pafundi quarried green slate from the west wall until his death in 1979, when his son Gary began to work the east wall until *his* death in 1989. Gary's daughter Connie then took over operations. All of the Pafundis used the floor of the quarry as their base of operations. In 1992, N.A.S. Holdings, Inc., bought the neighboring property. A survey revealed that virtually the entire quarry was within the boundaries of N.A.S.'s property and that twenty years earlier, Ted had actually bought only a small strip of land on the west side. When N.A.S. attempted to begin quarrying, Connie blocked the access. N.A.S. filed a suit in a Vermont state court against Connie, seeking to establish title. Connie argued that she had title to the quarry through adverse possession under a state statute with a possessory period of fifteen years. What are the elements to acquire title by adverse possession? Are they satisfied in this case? In whose favor should the court rule, and why? [*N.A.S. Holdings, Inc. v. Pafundi*, 736 A.2d 280 (Vt. 1999)]

TEST YOUR KNOWLEDGE—ANSWER ON THE WEB

37–10. Jennifer Tribble leased an apartment from Spring Isle II, a limited partnership. The written lease agreement provided that if Tribble was forced to move because of a job transfer or because she accepted a new job, she could vacate on sixty days' notice and owe only an extra two months' rent plus no more than a $650 rerenting fee. The initial term was for one year, and the parties renewed the lease for a second one-year term. The security deposit was $900. State law allowed a landlord to withhold a security deposit for the nonpayment of rent but required timely notice stating valid reasons for the withholding or the tenant would be entitled to twice the amount of the deposit as damages. One month into the second term, Tribble notified Spring Isle in writing that she had accepted a new job and would move out within a week. She paid the extra rent required by the lease, but not the rerental fee, and vacated the apartment. Spring Isle wrote her a letter, stating that it was keeping the entire security deposit until the apartment was rerented or the lease term ended, whichever came first. Spring Isle later filed a suit in a Wisconsin state court against Tribble, claiming that she owed, among other things, the rest of the rent until the apartment had been rerented and the costs of rerenting. Tribble responded that withholding the security deposit was improper, and she was entitled to "any penalties." Does Tribble owe Spring Isle anything? Does Spring Isle owe Tribble anything? Explain. [*Spring Isle II v. Tribble,* 610 N.W.2d 229 (Wis.App. 2000)]

A QUESTION OF ETHICS AND SOCIAL RESPONSIBILITY

37–11. John and Terry Hoffius own property in Jackson, Michigan, which they rent. Kristal McCready and Keith Kerr responded to the Hoffiuses' ad about the property. The Hoffiuses refused to rent to McCready and Kerr, however, when they learned that the two were single and intended to live together. John Hoffius told all prospective tenants that unmarried cohabitation violated his religious beliefs. McCready and others filed a suit in a Michigan state court against the Hoffiuses. They alleged in part that the Hoffiuses' actions violated the plaintiffs' civil rights under a state law that prohibits discrimination on the basis of "marital status." The Hoffiuses responded in part that forcing them to rent to unmarried couples in violation of the Hoffiuses' religious beliefs would be unconstitutional. [*McCready v. Hoffius,* 586 N.W.2d 723 (Mich. 1998)]

1. Did the defendants violate the plaintiffs' civil rights? Explain.
2. Should a court, in the interest of preventing discrimination in housing, compel a landlord to violate his or her conscience? In other words, whose rights should prevail in this case? Why?
3. Is there an objective rule that determines when civil rights or religious freedom, or any two similarly important principles, should prevail? If so, what is it? If not, should there be?

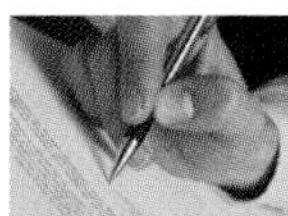

FOR CRITICAL ANALYSIS

37–12. Real property law dates back hundreds of years. What changes have occurred in society, including business and technological changes, that have affected the development and application of real property law? (Hint: Was airspace an issue three hundred years ago?)

Internet Exercises

Go to the *Business Law Today* home page at **http://blt.westbuslaw.com**. Select "Interactive Study Center" and then click on "Chapter 37." There you will find the following Internet research exercises that you can perform to learn more about the law governing real property and landlord-tenant relationships:

Activity 37–1: Real Estate Law
Activity 37–2: Fair Housing
Activity 37–3: The Rights of Tenants

Before the Test

Go to the *Business Law Today* home page at **http://blt.westbuslaw.com**. Click on "Interactive Quizzes." You will find at least twenty interactive questions relating to this chapter.

CHAPTER 38

Insurance, Wills, and Trusts

"Insurance is part charity and part business, but all common sense."

Calvin Coolidge, 1872–1933
(Thirtieth president of the United States, 1923–1929)

CHAPTER CONTENTS

LEARNING OBJECTIVES

After reading this chapter, you should be able to answer the following questions:

① What is an insurable interest? When must an insurable interest exist—at the time the insurance policy is obtained, at the time the loss occurs, or both?

② Is an insurance broker the agent of the insurance applicant or the agent of the insurer?

③ What are the basic requirements for executing a will? How may a will be revoked?

④ What is the difference between a *per stirpes* and a *per capita* distribution of an estate to the grandchildren of the deceased?

⑤ What are the four essential elements of a trust? What is the difference between an express trust and an implied trust?

Most individuals insure both real and personal property (as well as their lives). As Calvin Coolidge asserted in the opening quotation above, insurance is "all common sense"—by insuring our property, we protect ourselves against damage and loss.

The first part of this chapter focuses on insurance, which is a foremost concern of all property owners. We then examine how property is transferred on the death of its owner. Certainly, the laws of succession of property are a necessary corollary to the concept of private ownership of property. Our laws require that on death, title to the property of a decedent (one who has recently died) must be delivered in full somewhere. In this chapter, we see that this can be done by will, through trusts, or through state laws prescribing distribution of property among heirs or next of kin.

Insurance

INSURANCE
A contract in which, for a stipulated consideration, one party agrees to compensate the other for loss on a specific subject by a specified peril.

RISK
A prediction concerning potential loss based on known and unknown factors.

RISK MANAGEMENT
Planning that is undertaken to protect one's interest should some event threaten to undermine its security. In the context of insurance, risk management involves transferring certain risks from the insured to the insurance company.

Insurance is a contract by which the insurance company (the insurer) promises to pay a sum of money or give something of value to another (either the insured or the beneficiary) in the event that the insured is injured, dies, or sustains damage to her or his property as a result of particular, stated contingencies. Basically, insurance is an arrangement for *transferring and allocating risk*. In many cases, **risk** can be described as a prediction concerning potential loss based on known and unknown factors. Insurance, however, involves much more than a game of chance.

Many precautions may be taken to protect against the hazards of life. For example, an individual may wear a seat belt to protect against injuries from automobile accidents or install smoke detectors to guard against injury from fire. Of course, no one can predict whether an accident or a fire will ever occur, but individuals and businesses must establish plans to protect their personal and financial interests should some event threaten to undermine their security. This concept is known as **risk management**. The most common method of risk management is the transfer of certain risks from the individual to the insurance company.

Risk is transferred to an insurance company by a contractual agreement. The insurance contract and its provisions will be examined shortly. First, however, we look at the different types of insurance that can be obtained, insurance terminology, and the concept of insurable interest.

CLASSIFICATIONS OF INSURANCE

Insurance is classified according to the nature of the risk involved. For example, fire insurance, casualty insurance, life insurance, and title insurance apply to different types of risk. Furthermore, policies of these types differ in the persons and interests that they protect. This is reasonable because the types of losses that are expected and the types that are foreseeable or unforeseeable vary with the nature of the activity. Exhibit 38–1 presents a list of insurance classifications. (For a discussion of insurance policies designed to cover the special kinds of risks faced by online businesses, see the *Application* feature at the end of this chapter.)

EXHIBIT 38–1 INSURANCE CLASSIFICATIONS

TYPE OF INSURANCE	COVERAGE
Accident	Covers expenses, losses, and suffering incurred by the insured because of accidents causing physical injury and any consequent disability; sometimes includes a specified payment to heirs of the insured if death results from an accident.
All-risk	Covers all losses that the insured may incur except those resulting from fraud on the part of the insured.
Automobile	May cover damage to automobiles resulting from specified hazards or occurrences (such as fire, vandalism, theft, or collision); normally provides protection against liability for personal injuries and property damage resulting from the operation of the vehicle.

EXHIBIT 38–1 INSURANCE CLASSIFICATIONS—CONTINUED

TYPE OF INSURANCE	COVERAGE
Casualty	Protects against losses that may be incurred by the insured as a result of being held liable for personal injuries or property damage sustained by others.
Credit	Pays to a creditor the balance of a debt on the disability, death, insolvency, or bankruptcy of the debtor; often offered by lending institutions.
Decreasing-term life	Provides life insurance; requires uniform payments over the life (term) of the policy, but with a decreasing face value (amount of coverage).
Employer's liability	Insures employers against liability for injuries or losses sustained by employees during the course of their employment; covers claims not covered under workers' compensation insurance.
Fidelity or guaranty	Provides indemnity against losses in trade or losses caused by the dishonesty of employees, the insolvency of debtors, or breaches of contract.
Fire	Covers losses caused to the insured as a result of fire.
Floater	Covers movable property, as long as the property is within the territorial boundaries specified in the contract.
Group	Provides individual life, medical, or disability insurance coverage but is obtainable through a group of persons, usually employees; the policy premium is paid either entirely by the employer or partially by the employer and partially by the employee.
Health	Covers expenses incurred by the insured resulting from physical injury or illness and other expenses relating to health and life maintenance.
Homeowners'	Protects homeowners against some or all risks of loss to their residences and the residences' contents or liability arising from the use of the property.
Key-person	Protects a business in the event of the death or disability of a key employee.
Liability	Protects against liability imposed on the insured resulting from injuries to the person or property of another.
Life	Covers the death of the policyholder. On the death of the insured, an amount specified in the policy is paid by the insurer to the insured's beneficiary.
Major medical	Protects the insured against major hospital, medical, or surgical expenses.
Malpractice	Protects professionals (doctors, lawyers, and others) against malpractice claims brought against them by their patients or clients; a form of liability insurance.
Marine	Covers movable property (including ships, freight, and cargo) against certain perils or navigation risks during a specific voyage or time period.
Mortgage	Covers a mortgage loan; the insurer pays the balance of the mortgage to the creditor on the death or disability of the debtor.
No-fault auto	Covers personal injury and (sometimes) property damage resulting from automobile accidents. The insured submits his or her claims to his or her own insurance company, regardless of who was at fault. A person may sue the party at fault or that party's insurer only in cases involving serious medical injury and consequent high medical costs. Governed by state "no-fault" statutes.
Term life	Provides life insurance for a specified period of time (term) with no cash surrender value; usually renewable.
Title	Protects against any defects in title to real property and any losses incurred as a result of existing claims against or liens on the property at the time of purchase.

INSURANCE TERMINOLOGY

POLICY
In insurance law, a contract between the insurer and the insured in which, for a stipulated consideration, the insurer agrees to compensate the insured for loss on a specific subject by a specified peril.

PREMIUM
In insurance law, the price paid by the insured for insurance protection for a specified period of time.

UNDERWRITER
In insurance law, the insurer, or the one assuming a risk in return for the payment of a premium.

An insurance contract is called a **policy**; the consideration paid to the insurer is called a **premium**; and the insurance company is sometimes called an **underwriter.**

The parties to an insurance policy are the *insurer* (the insurance company) and the *insured* (the person covered by the insurer's provisions or the holder of the policy). Insurance contracts are usually obtained through an *agent,* who ordinarily works for the insurance company, or through a *broker,* who is ordinarily an *independent contractor.* When a broker deals with an applicant for insurance, the broker is, in effect, the applicant's agent. In contrast, an insurance agent is an agent of the insurance company, not of the applicant. As a general rule, the insurance company is bound by the acts of its agents when they act within the agency relationship (discussed in Chapter 24). A broker, however, normally has no relationship with the insurance company and is an agent of the insurance applicant. In most situations, state law determines the status of all parties writing or obtaining insurance.

ETHICAL ISSUE 38.1

Does an insurance agent have a duty to advise insurance applicants about coverage?

When a person applies for insurance coverage through an insurance company's agent, is the agent obligated to advise that person as to what coverage he or she should obtain? If the agent does not advise a client about certain types of coverage, has the agent breached a duty to the applicant? For example, suppose that a couple applies for auto insurance, and the insurance agent does not advise the couple that they should sign up for uninsured motorist coverage. Later, the couple is involved in an accident with an uninsured motorist, and the insurance company refuses to compensate them for their injuries and losses. The couple claims that the insurance agent was negligent in not advising them to sign up for uninsured motorist coverage. Was the agent negligent? No. As mentioned earlier, an insurance agent is an agent of the insurer, not the insured. As such, the agent owes fiduciary duties to the insurer (the insurance company), but not to the insured. The agent's only duties to the insured are contractual in nature. While some may think that this rule is unfair to insurance applicants, who may know less about the need for certain types of insurance coverage than the agent does, a contrary rule might create even more unfairness. As one court emphasized, a contrary rule could result in an insurance agent being held liable for failure to advise a client "of every possible insurance option" and would "remove any burden from the insured to take care of his or her own financial needs and expectations."[1]

INSURABLE INTEREST

INSURABLE INTEREST
An interest either in a person's life or well-being or in property that is sufficiently substantial that insuring against injury to (or the death of) the person or against damage to the property does not amount to a mere wagering (betting) contract.

A person can insure anything in which he or she has an **insurable interest.** Without this insurable interest, there is no enforceable contract, and a transaction to insure would have to be treated as a wager. In regard to real and personal property, an insurable interest exists when the insured derives a pecuniary benefit (a benefit consisting of or relating to money) from the preservation and continued existence of the property. Put another way, one has an insurable interest in property when one would sustain a pecuniary loss

1. *Harts v. Farmers Insurance Exchange,* 461 Mich. 1, 597 N.W.2d 47 (Mich. 1999).

from its destruction. In regard to life insurance, a person must have a reasonable expectation of benefit from the continued life of another in order to have an insurable interest in that person's life. The benefit may be pecuniary (as with so-called *key-person insurance,* which insures the lives of important employees, usually in small companies), or it may be founded on the relationship between the parties (by blood or affinity).

For property insurance, the insurable interest must exist at the time the loss occurs but need not exist when the policy is purchased. In contrast, for life insurance, the insurable interest must exist at the time the policy is obtained. The existence of an insurable interest is a primary concern in determining liability under an insurance policy.

THE INSURANCE CONTRACT

NOTE The federal government has the power to regulate the insurance industry under the commerce clause of the U.S. Constitution. Instead of exercising this power itself, Congress allows the states to regulate insurance.

An insurance contract is governed by the general principles of contract law, although the insurance industry is heavily regulated by each state. Several aspects of the insurance contract will be treated here, including the application for insurance, when the contract takes effect, important contract provisions, cancellation of the policy, and defenses that can be raised by insurance companies against payment on a policy.

Application The filled-in application form for insurance is usually attached to the policy and made a part of the insurance contract. Thus, an insurance applicant is bound by any false statements that appear in the application (subject to certain exceptions). Because the insurance company evaluates the risk factors based on the information included in the insurance application, misstatements or misrepresentations can void a policy, especially if the insurance company can show that it would not have extended insurance if it had known the true facts.

Effective Date The effective date of an insurance contract is important. In some instances, the insurance applicant is not protected until a formal written policy is issued. In other situations, the applicant is protected between the time the application is received and the time the insurance company either accepts or rejects it. Four facts should be kept in mind:

① A broker is merely the agent of an applicant. Therefore, until the broker obtains a policy, the applicant normally is not insured.

② A person who seeks insurance from an insurance company's agent will usually be protected from the moment the application is made, provided that some form of premium has been paid. Between the time the application is received and either rejected or accepted, the applicant is covered (possibly subject to medical examination). Usually, the agent will write a memorandum, or **binder**, indicating that a policy is pending and stating its essential terms.

BINDER
A written, temporary insurance policy.

③ If the parties agree that the policy will be issued and delivered at a later time, the contract is not effective until the policy is issued and delivered or sent to the applicant, depending on the agreement. Thus, any loss sustained between the time of application and the delivery of the policy is not covered.

④ Parties may agree that a life insurance policy will be binding at the time the insured pays the first premium, or the policy may be expressly contingent on the applicant's passing a physical examination. In the latter situation, if the applicant pays the premium and passes the examination, the policy coverage is in effect. If the applicant pays the premium but dies before having the physical examination, then to collect, the applicant's estate must show that the applicant *would have passed* the examination had he or she not died.

In the following case, the court had to decide whether a policy that required an applicant to be "still insurable" on the effective date of the policy should prevent the beneficiary from recovering.

CASE 38.1 Life Insurance Co. of North America v. Cichowlas

District Court of Appeal of Florida, Fourth District, 1995.
659 So.2d 1333.

FACTS Waldemar Cichowlas applied to the Life Insurance Company of North America (LINA) for insurance, naming his wife Ewa as beneficiary. The application asked if he had been hospitalized during the past five years and if he had ever been treated for lung disease. A yes answer would have affected his insurability. Waldemar truthfully answered no. The policy required that an applicant be "still insurable" on the effective date of the policy. Three weeks before the policy took effect, Waldemar was hospitalized with a lung disease. He did not tell LINA. When he died of other causes, LINA refused to pay Ewa. She filed a suit in a Florida state court against the insurer. The court ordered LINA to pay. The insurer appealed.

ISSUE Did the requirement that Waldemar be "still insurable" on the effective date of the policy prevent Ewa from recovering?

DECISION Yes. The District Court of Appeal of Florida reversed the judgment of the lower court and remanded the case.

REASON The state intermediate appellate court explained that "[c]lauses requiring that an applicant remain insurable between the filing of the application and the delivery of the policy have traditionally been approved by Florida courts." The court noted that "Mr. Cichowlas was not insurable on the effective date of the policy." Thus, "the 'still insurable' clause precluded recovery for" Ewa.

FOR CRITICAL ANALYSIS—Ethical Consideration *How might the outcome of this case have been affected if the court had held that LINA had a continuing duty to ask about the health of its applicants?*

Coinsurance Clauses Often, when taking out fire insurance policies, property owners insure their property for less than full value. Part of the reason for this is that most fires do not result in a total loss. To encourage owners to insure their property for an amount as close to full value as possible, fire insurance policies commonly include a coinsurance clause. Typically, a *coinsurance clause* provides that if the owner insures the property up to a specified percentage—usually 80 percent—of its value, she or he will recover any loss up to the face amount of the policy. If the insurance is for less than the fixed percentage, the owner is responsible for a proportionate share of the loss.

Coinsurance applies only in instances of partial loss. • **EXAMPLE 38.1** If the owner of property valued at \$100,000 takes out a policy in the amount of \$40,000 and suffers a loss of \$30,000, the recovery will be \$15,000. The formula for calculating the recovery amount is as follows:

$$\frac{\text{amount of insurance (\$40,000)}}{\text{coinsurance percentage (80\%)} \times \text{property value (\$100,000)}} = \text{recovery percentage (50\%)}$$

$$\text{recovery percentage (50\%)} \times \text{amount of loss (\$30,000)} = \text{recovery amount (\$15,000)}$$

If the owner had taken out a policy in the amount of $80,000, then, according to the same formula, the full loss would have been recovered up to the face value of the policy. ●

Other Provisions and Clauses Some other important provisions and clauses contained in insurance contracts are listed and defined in Exhibit 38–2. The courts are aware that most people do not have the special training necessary to understand the intricate terminology used in insurance policies. Thus, the words used in an insurance contract have their ordinary meanings. They are interpreted by the courts in light of the nature of the coverage involved—see, for example, this chapter's *Business Law in the Online World* feature on the next page.

When there is an ambiguity in the policy, the provision generally is interpreted against the insurance company. When the written policy has not been delivered and it is unclear whether an insurance contract actually exists, the uncertainty normally will be resolved against the insurance company. The court will presume that the policy is in effect unless the company can show otherwise. Similarly, an insurer must make sure that the insured is adequately notified of any change in coverage under an existing policy.

Cancellation The insured can cancel a policy at any time, and the insurer can cancel under certain circumstances. When an insurance company can cancel its insurance contract, the policy or a state statute usually requires that the insurer give advance written notice of the cancellation to the insured.

The insurer may cancel an insurance policy for various reasons, depending on the type of insurance. For example, automobile insurance can be canceled for nonpayment of premiums or suspension of the insured's driver's license. Property insurance can be canceled for nonpayment of premiums or for other reasons, including the insured's fraud or misrepresentation, conviction for a crime that increases the hazard insured against, or gross negligence that increases the hazard insured against. Life and health

EXHIBIT 38–2 INSURANCE CONTRACT PROVISIONS AND CLAUSES

Incontestability clause	An incontestability clause provides that after a policy has been in force for a specified length of time—usually two or three years—the insurer cannot contest statements made in the application.
Appraisal clause	Insurance policies frequently provide that if the parties cannot agree on the amount of a loss covered under the policy or the value of the property lost, an appraisal, or estimate, by an impartial and qualified third party can be demanded.
Arbitration clause	Many insurance policies include clauses that call for arbitration of disputes that may arise between the insurer and the insured concerning the settlement of claims.
Antilapse clause	An antilapse clause provides that the policy will not automatically lapse if no payment is made on the date due. Ordinarily, under such a provision, the insured has a *grace period* of thirty or thirty-one days within which to pay an overdue premium before the policy is canceled.
Cancellation	An insurance policy can be canceled for various reasons, depending on the type of insurance. When an insurance company can cancel its insurance contract, the policy or a state statute usually requires that the insurer give advance written notice of the cancellation. An insurer cannot cancel—or refuse to renew—a policy because of the national origin or race of an applicant or because the insured has appeared as a witness in a case against the company.

BUSINESS LAW: //in the Online World

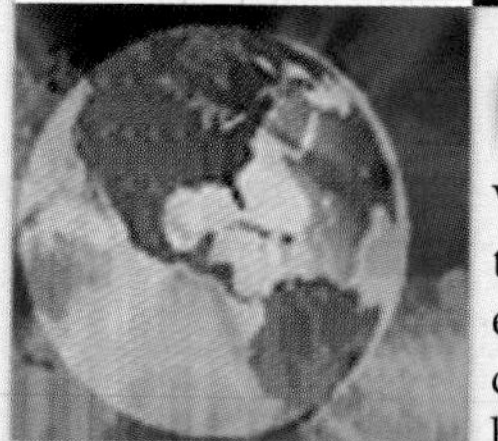

Recovering for Computer "Downtime"

When a business's computer system fails, often the damage is extensive. Customer service may come to a standstill, and data may be lost; if so, it could take hours to put the data back into the computer system. Yet traditional business insurance policies usually do not specifically cover the risks associated with computer "downtime." Thus, in a number of cases, insurers have defended against payment by claiming that these kinds of losses are not covered.

The Situation Facing Ingram Micro, Inc.

Ingram Micro, Inc., a wholesale distributor of microcomputer products, faced this situation when it experienced a half-hour power outage that caused its computers to lose all of their programming information, which Ingram employees had to reload. Due to the problems caused by the power outage, Ingram's computer network was not restored to full operation for nearly eight hours. Ingram had earlier obtained an insurance policy with American Guarantee & Liability Insurance Company to insure Ingram's "property, business income, and operations." The policy insured against all risks of "direct physical loss or damage from any cause." When Ingram submitted a claim to its insurer for the costs associated with the downtime, however, the insurer refused to pay.

The insurer argued that the computer system was not "physically damaged" by the power outage. The insurer noted that the power outage "did not adversely affect the equipment's inherent ability to accept and process data and configuration settings when they were subsequently reentered into the computer system." Ingram contended that the fact that the computers retained the ability to accept the restored information and eventually operate as before did not mean that they did not undergo "physical damage." According to Ingram, "physical damage" included loss of use and functionality.

What Does "Physical Damage" Encompass?

The question before the court was thus whether the term *physical damage* in the insurance policy included the kinds of problems encountered by Ingram after the power outage. The court held that it did. Said the court: "At a time when computer technology dominates our professional as well as our personal lives, the Court must side with Ingram's broader definition of 'physical damage.' The Court finds that 'physical damage' is not restricted to the physical destruction or harm of computer circuitry but includes loss of access, loss of use, and loss of functionality."[a]

FOR CRITICAL ANALYSIS

Why would an insurer attempt to avoid paying a property damage claim for the loss of access, use, or functionality of a computer?

a. *American Guarantee & Liability Insurance Co. v. Ingram Micro, Inc.,* ___ F.Supp.2d ___ (D.Ariz. 2000).

policies can be canceled because of false statements made by the insured in the application. An insurer cannot cancel—or refuse to renew—a policy for discriminatory reasons or other reasons that violate public policy, or because the insured has appeared as a witness in a case against the company.

State laws normally require that an insured be notified in writing of an insurance policy cancellation.[2] The same requirement applies when only part of a policy is canceled.

Defenses against Payment In attempting to avoid payment on a policy claim, an insurance company can raise any of the defenses that would be valid in any ordinary

2. At issue in one case was whether a notification of cancellation included on a diskette sent to the insured constituted "written notice" of cancellation. The court held that the computerized document, which could be printed out as "hard copy," constituted written notice. See *Clyburn v. Allstate Insurance Co.,* 826 F.Supp. 955 (D.S.C. 1993).

action on a contract, as well as some defenses that do not apply in ordinary contract actions. If the insurance company can show that the policy was procured by fraud, misrepresentation, or violation of warranties, it may have a valid defense for not paying on a claim. Improper actions, such as those that are against public policy or that are otherwise illegal, can also give the insurance company a defense against the payment of a claim or allow it to rescind the contract.

An insurance company can be prevented from asserting some defenses that are normally available, however. For example, if a company tells an insured that information requested on a form is optional, and the insured provides it anyway, the company cannot use the information to avoid its contractual obligation under the insurance contract. Similarly, incorrect statements as to the age of the insured normally do not allow the insurer to avoid payment on the death of the insured.

In the following case, an insurance company attempted to avoid payment under a policy for life and disability insurance by claiming that the policy owner did not have an insurable interest, thus rendering the policy void from the outset.

CASE 38.2 Paul Revere Life Insurance Co. v. Fima

United States Court of Appeals,
Ninth Circuit, 1997.
105 F.3d 490.
http://www.ca9.uscourts.gov[a]

COMPANY PROFILE *Disability insurance can replace part of the income that an individual loses after suffering a disabling accident or illness. The coverage may be offered by an insurance company through an employer or may be obtained from an insurer by an individual. Provident Companies, Inc., which calls itself "North America's leader in personal income protection," offers disability insurance, as well as other types of insurance, to employers and individuals. Based in Chattanooga, Tennessee, Provident traces its beginnings to 1887. Provident is the parent company of six insurance subsidiary companies, including Paul Revere Life Insurance Company.*

FACTS Raoul Fima applied to Paul Revere Life Insurance Company for a disability policy. On the application, Fima stated his income as $105,000 for the previous year and $85,000 for the current year. His actual income for those years was $21,603 and $6,320, respectively. The policy included the following incontestability clause: "After your policy has been in force for two years, . . . we cannot contest the statements in the application." Three years later, when Fima filed a claim under the policy, Revere discovered the truth regarding his income. Revere filed a suit in a federal district court against Fima, seeking to have the policy declared void *ab initio* (from the beginning) on the ground that he lacked an insurable interest. The court denied the request. Revere appealed.

ISSUE Did Fima have an insurable interest at the time he obtained the insurance policy?

DECISION Yes. The U.S. Court of Appeals for the Ninth Circuit affirmed the judgment of the lower court.

REASON The appellate court reasoned that "[e]very person has an insurable interest in his or her own life and health." Therefore, the policy was not void *ab initio.* Also, the court pointed out that "because the period for contesting the policy has passed under the incontestability clause, Revere may not now challenge the terms of the policy or the extent of Fima's insurable interest."

FOR CRITICAL ANALYSIS—Ethical Consideration *What is the underlying rationale for including incontestability clauses in insurance contracts?*

a. This page lists decisions of the U.S. Court of Appeals for the Ninth Circuit. In the left-hand column, select "Opinions." Locate the "1997" link, and click on it. Then select "January." Scroll down the list to the *Fima* case and click on the link to access the opinion.

Wills

Private ownership of property leads logically to both the protection of that property by insurance coverage while the owner is alive and the transfer of that property on the death of the owner to those designated in the owner's will. A **will** is the final declaration of how a person desires to have his or her property disposed of after death. A will, because it is a person's "last will and testament," is referred to as a *testamentary disposition* of property. It is a formal instrument that must follow exactly the requirements of state law to be effective. The reasoning behind such a strict requirement is obvious. A will becomes effective only after death. No attempts to modify it after the death of the maker are allowed because the court cannot ask the maker to confirm the attempted modifications. (Sometimes, however, the wording of the will must be "interpreted" by the courts.)

WILL
An instrument directing what is to be done with the testator's property on his or her death, made by the testator and revocable during his or her lifetime. No interests in the testator's property pass until the testator dies.

A will can serve other purposes besides the distribution of property. It can appoint a guardian for minor children or incapacitated adults. It can also appoint a personal representative to settle the affairs of the deceased. Exhibit 38–3 presents a copy of John Lennon's will. Lennon was a member of the Beatles, a popular rock group in the 1960s and 1970s.

A person who dies without having created a valid will is said to have died **intestate.** In this situation, state **intestacy laws** prescribe the distribution of the property among heirs or next of kin. If no heirs or kin can be found, title to the property will be transferred to the state.

INTESTATE
As a noun, one who has died without having created a valid will; as an adjective, the state of having died without a will.

INTESTACY LAWS
State statutes that specify how property will be distributed when a person dies intestate (without a valid will); also called statutes of descent and distribution.

Terminology of Wills

A person who makes out a will is known as a **testator** (from the Latin *testari,* "to make a will"). The court responsible for administering any legal problems surrounding a will is called a *probate court,* as mentioned in Chapter 3. When a person dies, a personal representative administers the estate and settles finally all of the decedent's (deceased person's) affairs. An **executor** is a personal representative named in the will; an **administrator** is a personal representative appointed by the court for a decedent who dies without a will, who fails to name an executor in the will, who names an executor lacking the capacity to serve, or who writes a will that the court refuses to admit to probate.

A gift of real estate by will is generally called a **devise**, and a gift of personal property by will is called a **bequest**, or **legacy.** The recipient of a gift by will is a **devisee** or **legatee**, depending on whether the gift was a devise or a legacy.

TESTATOR
One who makes and executes a will.

EXECUTOR
A person appointed by a testator in a will to see that her or his will is administered appropriately.

ADMINISTRATOR
One who is appointed by a court to handle the probate (disposition) of a person's estate if that person dies intestate (without a valid will) or if the executor named in the will cannot serve.

DEVISE
To make a gift of real property by will.

BEQUEST
A gift by will of personal property (from the verb *to bequeath*).

LEGACY
A gift of personal property under a will.

DEVISEE
One designated in a will to receive a gift of real property.

LEGATEE
One designated in a will to receive a gift of personal property.

Types of Gifts

Gifts by will can be specific, general, or residuary. A *specific* devise or bequest (legacy) describes particular property (such as "Eastwood Estate" or "my gold pocket watch") that can be distinguished from all the rest of the testator's property. A *general* devise or bequest (legacy) uses less restrictive terminology. For example, "I devise all my lands" is a general devise. A general bequest often specifies a sum of money instead of a particular item of property, such as a watch or an automobile. For example, "I give to my nephew, Carleton, $30,000" is a general bequest.

If the assets of an estate are insufficient to pay in full all general bequests provided for in the will, an *abatement,* by which the legatees receive reduced benefits, takes place. If a legatee dies prior to the death of the testator or before the legacy is payable, a *lapsed legacy* results. At common law, the legacy failed. Today, the legacy may not lapse if the legatee is in a certain blood relationship to the testator (such as a child, grandchild, brother, or sister) and has left a child or other surviving descendant.

EXHIBIT 38–3 A SAMPLE WILL

LAST WILL AND TESTAMENT
OF
JOHN WINSTON ONO LENNON

I, JOHN WINSTON ONO LENNON, a resident of the County of New York, State of New York, which I declare to be my domicile do hereby make, publish and declare this to be my Last Will and Testament, hereby revoking all other Wills, Codicils and Testamentary dispositions by me at any time heretofore made.

FIRST: The expenses of my funeral and the administration of my estate, and all inheritance, estate or succession taxes, including interest and penalties, payable by reason of my death shall be paid out of and charged generally against the principal of my residuary estate without apportionment or proration. My Executor shall not seek contribution or reimbursement for any such payments.

SECOND: Should my wife survive me, I give, devise and bequeath to her absolutely, an amount equal to that portion of my residuary estate, the numerator and denominator of which shall be determined as follows:

1. The numerator shall be an amount equal to one-half (½) of my adjusted gross estate less the value of all other property included in my gross estate for Federal Estate Tax purposes and which pass or shall have passed to my wife either under any other provision of this Will or in any manner outside of this Will in such manner as to qualify for and be allowed as a marital deduction. The words "pass," "have passed," "marital deduction" and "adjusted gross estate" shall have the same meaning as said words have under those provisions of the United States Internal Revenue Code applicable to my estate.

2. The denominator shall be an amount representing the value of my residuary estate.

THIRD: I give, devise and bequeath all the rest, residue and remainder of my estate, wheresoever situated, to the Trustees under a Trust Agreement dated November 12, 1979, which I signed with my wife YOKO ONO, and ELI GARBER as Trustees, to be added to the trust property and held and distributed in accordance with the terms of that agreement and any amendments made pursuant to its terms before my death.

FOURTH: In the event that my wife and I die under such circumstances that there is not sufficient evidence to determine which of us has predeceased the other, I hereby declare it to be my will that it shall be deemed that I shall have predeceased her and that this, my Will, and any and all of its provisions shall be construed based upon that assumption.

FIFTH: I hereby nominate, constitute and appoint my beloved wife, YOKO ONO, to act as the Executor of this my Last Will and Testament. In the event that my beloved wife YOKO ONO shall predecease me or chooses not to act for any reason, I nominate and appoint ELI GARBER, DAVID WARMFLASH and CHARLES PETTIT, in the order named, to act in her place and stead.

SIXTH: I nominate, constitute and appoint my wife YOKO ONO, as the Guardian of the person and property of any children of the marriage who may survive me. In the event that she predeceases me, or for any reason she chooses not to act in that capacity, I nominate, constitute and appoint SAM GREEN to act in her place and stead.

SEVENTH: No person named herein to serve in any fiduciary capacity shall be required to file or post any bond for the faithful performance of his or her duties, in that capacity in this or in any other jurisdiction, any law to the contrary notwithstanding.

EIGHTH: If any legatee or beneficiary under this will or the trust agreement between myself as Grantor and YOKO ONO LENNON and ELI GARBER as Trustees, dated November 12, 1979 shall interpose objections to the probate of this Will, or institute or prosecute or be in any way interested or instrumental in the institution or prosecution of any action or proceeding for the purpose of setting aside or invalidating this Will, then and in each such case, I direct that such legatee or beneficiary shall receive nothing whatsoever under this Will or the aforementioned Trust.

IN WITNESS WHEREOF, I have subscribed and sealed and do publish and declare these presents as and for my Last Will and Testament, this 12th day of November, 1979.

/s/
John Winston Ono Lennon

THE FOREGOING INSTRUMENT consisting of four (4) typewritten pages, including this page, was on the 12th day of November, 1979, signed, sealed, published and declared by JOHN WINSTON ONO LENNON, the Testator therein named as and for his Last Will and Testament, in the presence of us, who at his request, and in his presence, and in the presence of each other, have hereunto set our names as witnesses.

(The names of the three witnesses are illegible.)

Sometimes, a will provides that the *residuum*—any assets remaining after the estate's debts have been paid and specific gifts have been made—is to be distributed through a *residuary clause*. A residuary clause is used when the exact amount to be distributed cannot be determined until all of the other gifts and payouts have been made. A residuary clause can pose problems, however, when the will does not specifically name the beneficiaries to receive the residuum. In such a situation, if the court cannot determine the testator's intent, the residuum passes according to state laws of intestacy.

PROBATE PROCEDURES

"If you want to see a man's true character, watch him divide an estate."

BENJAMIN FRANKLIN
1706–1790
(American diplomat, author, and scientist)

Laws governing wills come into play when a will is probated. To *probate* a will means to establish its validity and to carry the administration of the estate through a court process. Probate laws vary from state to state. In 1969, however, the American Bar Association and the National Conference of Commissioners on Uniform State Laws approved the Uniform Probate Code (UPC). The UPC codifies general principles and procedures for the resolution of conflicts in settling estates and relaxes some of the requirements for a valid will contained in earlier state laws. Nearly all of the states have adopted some part of the UPC. Because succession and inheritance laws vary widely among states, one should always check the particular laws of the state involved.[3] Typically, probate procedures vary, depending on the size of the decedent's estate.

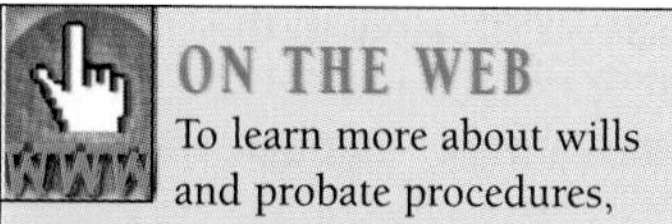

ON THE WEB To learn more about wills and probate procedures, you can access the Uniform Probate Code online at **http://www.law.cornell.edu/uniform/probate.html**.

Informal Probate For smaller estates, most state statutes provide for the distribution of assets without formal probate proceedings. Faster and less expensive methods are then used. For example, property can be transferred by affidavit (a written statement taken before a person who has authority to affirm it), and problems or questions can be handled during an administrative hearing. In addition, some state statutes provide that title to cars, savings and checking accounts, and certain other property can be passed merely by filling out forms.

A majority of states also provide for *family settlement agreements*, which are private agreements among the beneficiaries. Once a will is admitted to probate, the family members can agree to settle among themselves the distribution of the decedent's assets. Although a family settlement agreement speeds the settlement process, a court order is still needed to protect the estate from future creditors and to clear title to the assets involved. The use of these and other types of summary procedures in estate administration can save time and dollars.

Formal Probate For larger estates, formal probate proceedings normally are undertaken, and the probate court supervises every aspect of the settlement of the decedent's estate. Additionally, in some situations—such as when a guardian for minor children or for an incompetent person must be appointed, and a trust has been created to protect the minor or the incompetent person—more formal probate procedures cannot be avoided. Formal probate proceedings may take several months to complete, and as a result, a sizable portion of the decedent's assets (up to perhaps 10 percent or more) may go toward payment of court costs and fees charged by attorneys and personal representatives.

Property Transfers outside the Probate Process In the ordinary situation, a person can employ various will substitutes to avoid the cost of probate—for example, *inter vivos* trusts (discussed later in this chapter), life insurance policies or Individual Retirement Accounts (IRAs) with named beneficiaries, or joint-tenancy arrangements.

3. For example, California law differs substantially from the UPC.

ON THE WEB Estate planning—preparing for the transfer of assets to others on one's death—involves a number of tools, including wills and trusts. These and other devices that can be used in estate planning are described by the American Academy of Estate Planning Attorneys on its Web site at **http://estateplanforyou.com**.

Not all methods are suitable for every estate, but there are alternatives to complete probate administration.

REQUIREMENTS FOR A VALID WILL

A will must comply with statutory formalities designed to ensure that the testator understood his or her actions at the time the will was made. These formalities are intended to help prevent fraud. Unless they are followed, the will is declared void, and the decedent's property is distributed according to the laws of intestacy of that state. The requirements are not uniform among the jurisdictions. Most states, however, uphold certain basic requirements for executing a will. We now look at these requirements.

RECALL In most states, the age of majority for contractual purposes is also eighteen years.

Testamentary Capacity and Intent For a will to be valid, the testator must have testamentary capacity—that is, the testator must be of legal age and sound mind *at the time the will is made*. The legal age for executing a will varies, but in most states and under the UPC, the minimum age is eighteen years [UPC 2–501]. Thus, the will of a twenty-one-year-old decedent written when the person was sixteen is invalid if, under state law, the legal age for executing a will is eighteen.

The concept of "being of sound mind" refers to the testator's ability to formulate and to comprehend a personal plan for the disposition of property. Generally, a testator must (1) intend the document to be his or her last will and testament, (2) comprehend the kind and character of the property being distributed, and (3) comprehend and remember the "natural objects of his or her bounty" (usually, family members and persons for whom the testator has affection).

DON'T FORGET Undue influence can also occur in the making of a contract. The essential feature in all situations is that the party of whom advantage is taken does not exercise free will.

A valid will is one that represents the maker's intention to transfer and distribute her or his property. When it can be shown that the decedent's plan of distribution was the result of fraud or of undue influence, the will is declared invalid. Undue influence may be inferred by the court if the testator ignored blood relatives and named as beneficiary a nonrelative who was in constant close contact with the testator and in a position to influence the making of the will. For example, if a nurse or friend caring for the testator at the time of death was named as beneficiary to the exclusion of all family members, the validity of the will might well be challenged on the basis of undue influence.

In the following case, the issue before the court was whether the testator intended his estate to be distributed to his relatives and friends in sixteen equal shares or in fourteen equal shares. The court looked first at the words used by the testator in his will to determine his intent.

CASE 38.3 Estate of Klauzer

Supreme Court of South Dakota, 2000.
604 N.W.2d 474.
http://www.sdbar.org/opinions/sdindex.htm[a]

FACTS John Klauzer executed a will in 1990 and passed away in 1996. His estate was valued at $1.4 million. The will appointed his brother Frank as personal representative of the estate. The will disposed of the majority of his estate in a residuary clause:

> I hereby give, devise and bequeath unto my brother, Thomas Klauzer, my sister, Agnes Blake, my sister, Anna Malenovsky Baker, my brother, Raymond Klauzer, my niece, Jenny Culver, my niece, Judy Klauzer, my niece, Bernice Cunningham, my nephew, Wade Klauzer, my nephew, Jim Klauzer, my niece,

a. This Web site is maintained by the State Bar of South Dakota. In the left column, click on "2000 Opinions." On that page, scroll down the list to the case and click on the name to access the opinion.

(continued)

CASE 38.3—Continued

> Debra Klauzer, friends, Douglas Olson and Fern Olson, and my friends, William Hollister and Shirley Hollister, my brother, Frank Klauzer, and my sister-in-law, Patricia Klauzer, all of my property of every kind and character and wheresoever situated, in equal shares, share and share alike. That should any of the individuals above named predecease me, then their share of my estate shall go to their [descendants] surviving.

Klauzer's nephew Wade asked a South Dakota state court to supervise the administration of the estate. The court ordered in part that, under the residuary clause, the estate should be distributed in sixteen equal shares. Frank objected and appealed to the South Dakota Supreme Court. Frank argued that the twelve Klauzer relatives named in the clause should take one share each while friends, Doug and Fern Olson and William and Shirley Hollister, should receive one share per couple, resulting in a division of the estate into fourteen equal shares.

ISSUE Should the property be divided into sixteen equal shares or fourteen equal shares?

DECISION Sixteen equal shares. The South Dakota Supreme Court affirmed the decision of the lower court. The language of the will evidenced the testator's intent that his property be distributed in sixteen equal shares.

REASON The court pointed out that "[a]ll the words and provisions appearing in a will must be given effect as far as possible, and none should be cast aside as meaningless." In the will in this case, the court reasoned, "First, John refers to his friends as individuals. Second, he requests that they receive his property 'in equal shares, share and share alike.' Third, he states that if one individual predeceases him, his or her share 'shall go to their [descendants] surviving.' * * * We determine that the testator's intent is clearly expressed within the four corners of the document. We are bound by the unambiguous language of the will."

FOR CRITICAL ANALYSIS—Social Consideration *What if the court had found that the terms of the will were ambiguous? How would the estate have been distributed in that situation?*

Writing Requirements Generally, a will must be in writing. The writing itself can be informal as long as it substantially complies with the statutory requirements. In some states, a will can be handwritten in crayon or ink. It can be written on a sheet or scrap of paper, on a paper bag, or on a piece of cloth. A will that is completely in the handwriting of the testator is called a **holographic will** (sometimes referred to as an *olographic will*).

HOLOGRAPHIC WILL
A will written entirely in the signer's handwriting and usually not witnessed.

NUNCUPATIVE WILL
An oral will (often called a deathbed will) made before witnesses; usually limited to transfers of personal property.

In some cases, oral wills are found valid. A **nuncupative will** is an oral will made before witnesses. Nuncupative wills are not permitted in most states. Where authorized by statute, such wills are generally valid only if made during the last illness of the testator and are therefore sometimes referred to as *deathbed wills*. Normally, only personal property can be transferred by a nuncupative will. Statutes frequently permit soldiers and sailors to make nuncupative wills when on active duty.

Signature Requirements It is a fundamental requirement that the testator's signature appear, generally at the end of the will. Each jurisdiction dictates by statute and court decision what constitutes a signature. Initials, an X or other mark, and words such as "Mom" have all been upheld as valid when it was shown that the testators *intended* them to be signatures.

ON THE WEB
To find the wills of more than one hundred famous people from 1493 to the present, go to
http://www.ca-probate.com/wills.htm.

Witness Requirements Unless a will is a holographic will, it must be attested (sworn to) by two, and sometimes three, witnesses. The number of witnesses, their qualifications, and the manner in which the witnessing must be done are generally set out in a statute. A witness can be required to be disinterested—that is, not a beneficiary under the will. The UPC, however, provides that a will is valid even if it is attested by an interested witness [UPC 2–505]. There are no age requirements for witnesses, but they must be mentally competent.

The purpose of witnesses is to verify that the testator actually executed (signed) the will and had the requisite intent and capacity at the time. A witness does not have to

"You cannot live without the lawyers, and certainly you cannot die without them."

JOSEPH H. CHOATE
1832–1917
(American lawyer and diplomat)

read the contents of the will. Usually, the testator and all witnesses must sign in the sight or the presence of one another, but the UPC deems it sufficient if the testator acknowledges her or his signature to the witnesses [UPC 2–502]. The UPC does not require all parties to sign in the presence of one another.

Publication Requirements A will is *published* by an oral declaration by the maker to the witnesses that the document they are about to sign is his or her "last will and testament." Publication is becoming an unnecessary formality in most states, and it is not required under the UPC.

REVOCATION OF WILLS

An executed will is revocable by the maker at any time during the maker's lifetime. The maker may revoke a will by a physical act, such as tearing up the will, or by a subsequent writing. Wills can also be revoked by operation of law. Revocation can be partial or complete, and it must follow certain strict formalities.

Revocation by a Physical Act of the Maker A testator may revoke a will by intentionally burning, tearing, canceling, obliterating, or otherwise destroying it, or by having someone else do so in the presence of the maker and at the maker's direction.[4] In some states, partial revocation by physical act of the maker is recognized. Thus, those portions of a will lined out or torn away are dropped, and the remaining parts of the will are valid. In no circumstances, however, can a provision be crossed out and an additional or substitute provision written in. Such altered portions require reexecution (re-signing) and reattestation (rewitnessing).

To revoke a will by physical act, it is necessary to follow the mandates of a state statute exactly. When a state statute prescribes the specific methods for revoking a will by physical act, those are the only methods that will revoke the will.

CODICIL
A written supplement or modification to a will. A codicil must be executed with the same formalities as a will.

Revocation by a Subsequent Writing A will may also be wholly or partially revoked by a **codicil**, a written instrument separate from the will that amends or revokes provisions in the will. A codicil eliminates the necessity of redrafting an entire will merely to add to it or amend it. A codicil can also be used to revoke an entire will. The codicil must be executed with the same formalities required for a will, and it must refer expressly to the will. In effect, it updates a will because the will is "incorporated by reference" into the codicil.

A new will (second will) can be executed that may or may not revoke the first or a prior will, depending on the language used. To revoke a prior will, the second will must use language specifically revoking other wills, such as, "This will hereby revokes all prior wills." If the second will is otherwise valid and properly executed, it will revoke all prior wills. If the express *declaration of revocation* is missing, then both wills are read together. If any of the dispositions made in the second will are inconsistent with the prior will, the second will controls.

Revocation by Operation of Law Revocation by *operation of law* occurs when marriage, divorce or annulment, or the birth of a child takes place after a will has been executed. In most states, when a testator marries after executing a will that does not include the new spouse, on the testator's death the spouse can still receive the amount he or she would have taken had the testator died intestate (how an intestate's property

4. The destruction cannot be inadvertent. The maker's intent to revoke must be shown. Consequently, when a will has been burned or torn accidentally, it is normally recommended that the maker have a new document created so that it will not falsely appear that the maker intended to revoke the will.

is distributed under state laws will be discussed shortly). In effect, the will is revoked to the point of providing the spouse with an intestate share. The rest of the estate is passed under the will [UPC 2–301, 2–508]. If, however, the new spouse is otherwise provided for in the will (or by transfer of property outside the will), the new spouse will not be given an intestate amount.

At common law and under the UPC, divorce does not necessarily revoke the entire will. A divorce or an annulment occurring after a will has been executed will revoke those dispositions of property made under the will to the former spouse [UPC 2–508].

If a child is born after a will has been executed and if it appears that the deceased parent would have made a provision for the child, the child is entitled to receive whatever portion of the estate she or he is allowed under state laws providing for the distribution of an intestate's property. Most state laws allow a child to receive some portion of a parent's estate if no provision is made in the parent's will, unless it appears from the terms of the will that the testator intended to disinherit the child. Under the UPC, the rule is the same.

Intestacy Laws

"Land was never lost for want of an heir."

ENGLISH PROVERB

As mentioned, state intestacy laws determine how property will be distributed when a person dies intestate (without a valid will). These statutes are more formally known as *statutes of descent and distribution.* Intestacy laws attempt to carry out the likely intent and wishes of the decedent. These laws assume that deceased persons would have intended that their natural heirs (spouses, children, grandchildren, or other family members) inherit their property. Therefore, intestacy statutes set out rules and priorities under which these heirs inherit the property. If no heirs exist, the state will assume ownership of the property. The rules of descent vary widely from state to state.

Surviving Spouse and Children Usually, state statutes provide that first the debts of the decedent must be satisfied out of the estate; then the remaining assets pass to the surviving spouse and to the children. A surviving spouse usually receives only a share of the estate—one-half if there is also a surviving child and one-third if there are two or more children. Only if no children or grandchildren survive the decedent will a surviving spouse succeed to the entire estate.

• **Example 38.2** Assume that Allen dies intestate and is survived by his wife, Della, and his children, Duane and Tara. Allen's property passes according to intestacy laws. After Allen's outstanding debts are paid, Della will receive the homestead (either in fee simple or as a life estate) and ordinarily a one-third interest in all other property. The remaining real and personal property will pass to Duane and Tara in equal portions. • Under most state intestacy laws and under the UPC, in-laws do not share in an estate. If a child dies before his or her parents, the child's spouse will not receive an inheritance on the parents' death. For example, if Duane died before his father (Allen), Duane's spouse would not inherit Duane's share of Allen's estate.

When there is no surviving spouse or child, the order of inheritance is grandchildren, then brothers and sisters, and, in some states, parents of the decedent. These relatives are usually called *lineal descendants.* If there are no lineal descendants, then *collateral heirs*—nieces, nephews, aunts, and uncles of the decedent—make up the next group to share. If there are no survivors in any of these groups, most statutes provide for the property to be distributed among the next of kin of the collateral heirs.

Stepchildren, Adopted Children, and Illegitimate Children Under intestacy laws, stepchildren are not considered kin. Legally adopted children, however, are recognized as lawful heirs of their adoptive parents. Statutes vary from state to state in regard to the inheritance rights of illegitimate children. Generally, an illegitimate child is treated as the child of the mother and can inherit from her and her relatives. The child is usually not regarded as the legal child of the father with the right of inheritance unless paternity is established through some legal proceeding prior to the father's death. This chapter's *Landmark in the Law* feature discusses a leading case in regard to the rights of illegitimate children.

LANDMARK IN THE LAW
Trimble v. Gordon (1977)

At common law, the illegitimate child was regarded as a *filius nullius* (Latin for "child of no one") and had no right to inherit. Over time, this attitude changed. In 1977, the United States Supreme Court decided a landmark case establishing the rights of illegitimate children in the United States. In *Trimble v. Gordon*,[a] an illegitimate child sought to inherit property from her deceased natural father on the ground that an Illinois statute prohibiting inheritance by illegitimate children in the absence of a will was unconstitutional.

The Illinois Law The child was Deta Mona Trimble, daughter of Jessie Trimble and Sherman Gordon. The paternity of the father had been established before a Cook County, Illinois, circuit court in 1973. Gordon died intestate in 1974. The mother filed a petition on behalf of the child in the probate division of the county circuit court; the court denied the petition on the basis of an Illinois law disallowing the child's inheritance because she was illegitimate. Had she been legitimate, she would have been her father's sole heir. In 1975, the Illinois Supreme Court affirmed the petition's dismissal.

The Supreme Court Invalidates the Illinois Law When the case came before the United States Supreme Court in 1977, the Court acknowledged that the "judicial task here is the difficult one of vindicating constitutional rights without interfering unduly with the State's primary responsibility in this area . . . [a]nd the need for the States to draw 'arbitrary lines . . . to facilitate potentially difficult problems of proof.'" The Court held that the section of the Illinois Probate Act that prohibited Deta Mona Trimble from inheriting her father's property was unconstitutional because it "cannot be squared with the command of the Equal Protection Clause of the Fourteenth Amendment." The Court "expressly considered and rejected the argument that a State may attempt to influence the actions of men and women by imposing sanctions on the children born of their illegitimate relationships."

APPLICATION TO TODAY'S WORLD

This is a landmark case in the law because it represents a significant step toward equal rights for children. By declaring the Illinois statute unconstitutional, the Court invalidated similar laws in several other states. That does not mean, however, that all illegitimate children now have inheritance rights identical to those of legitimate children. Those state statutes that discriminate between the two classes for legitimate state purposes have thus far been allowed to stand, in the interest of recognizing each state's need to create an appropriate legal framework for the disposition of property at death.[b]

a. 430 U.S. 762, 97 S.Ct. 1459, 52 L.Ed.2d 31 (1977).
b. UPC 2-109; *White v. Randolph*, 59 Ohio St.2d 6, 391 N.E.2d 333 (1979).

Distribution to Grandchildren When an intestate is survived by descendants of deceased children, a question arises as to what share these descendants (that is, grandchildren of the intestate) will receive. One method of dividing an intestate's estate is ***per stirpes.*** Under this method, within a class or group of distributees (for example, grandchildren), the children of any one descendant take the share that their deceased parent *would have been* entitled to inherit.

PER STIRPES
A Latin term meaning "by the roots." In the law governing estate distribution, a method of distributing an intestate's estate in which each heir in a certain class (such as grandchildren) takes the share to which her or his deceased ancestor (such as a mother or father) would have been entitled.

● **EXAMPLE 38.3** Assume that Michael, a widower, has two children, Scott and Jonathan. Scott has two children (Becky and Holly), and Jonathan has one child (Paul). Scott and Jonathan die before their father, and then Michael dies. If Michael's estate is distributed *per stirpes,* Becky and Holly will each receive one-fourth of the estate (dividing Scott's one-half share). Paul will receive one-half of the estate (taking Jonathan's one-half share). Exhibit 38–4 illustrates the *per stirpes* method of distribution. ●

An estate may also be distributed on a ***per capita*** basis, which means that each person in a class or group takes an equal share of the estate. If Michael's estate is distributed *per capita,* Becky, Holly, and Paul will each receive a one-third share. Exhibit 38–5 illustrates the *per capita* method of distribution.

PER CAPITA
A Latin term meaning "per person." In the law governing estate distribution, a method of distributing the property of an intestate's estate in which each heir in a certain class (such as grandchildren) receives an equal share.

Trusts

A **trust** is any arrangement through which property is transferred from one person to a trustee to be administered for the transferor's or another party's benefit. It can also be defined as a right of property, real or personal, held by one party for the benefit of another. A trust can be created for any purpose that is not illegal or against public policy. Its essential elements are as follows:

TRUST
An arrangement in which title to property is held by one person (a trustee) for the benefit of another (a beneficiary).

① A designated beneficiary.

② A designated trustee.

EXHIBIT 38–4 ***PER STIRPES* DISTRIBUTION**

Under this method of distribution, an heir takes the share that his or her deceased parent would have been entitled to inherit, had the parent lived. This may mean that a class of distributees—the grandchildren in this example—will not inherit in equal portions. Note that Becky and Holly receive only one-fourth of Michael's estate while Paul inherits one-half.

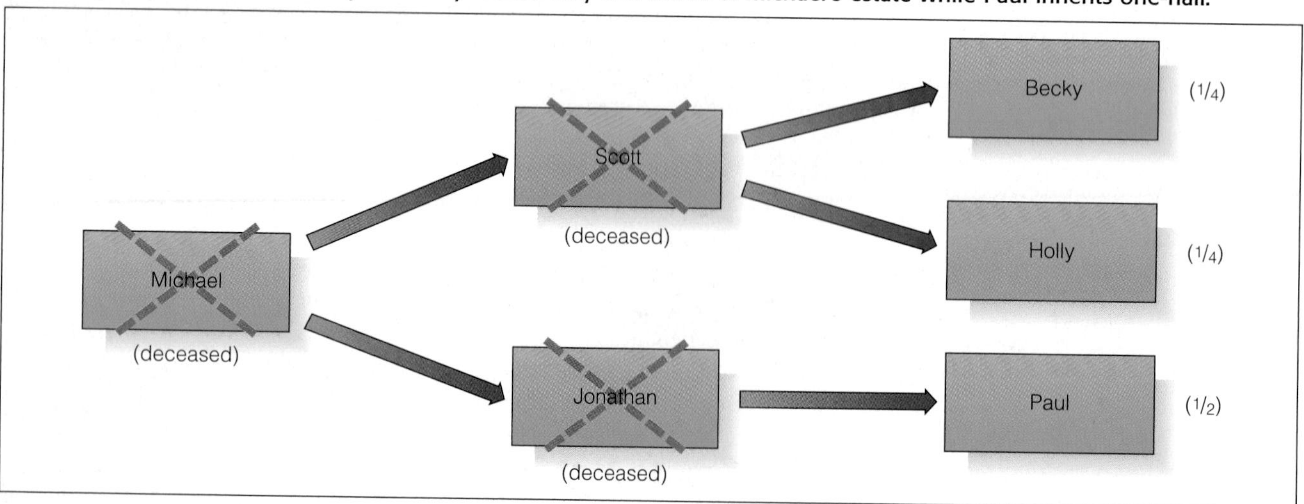

EXHIBIT 38–5 *PER CAPITA* **DISTRIBUTION**

Under this method of distribution, all heirs in a certain class—in this case, the grandchildren—inherit equally. Note that Becky and Holly in this situation each inherit one-third, as does Paul.

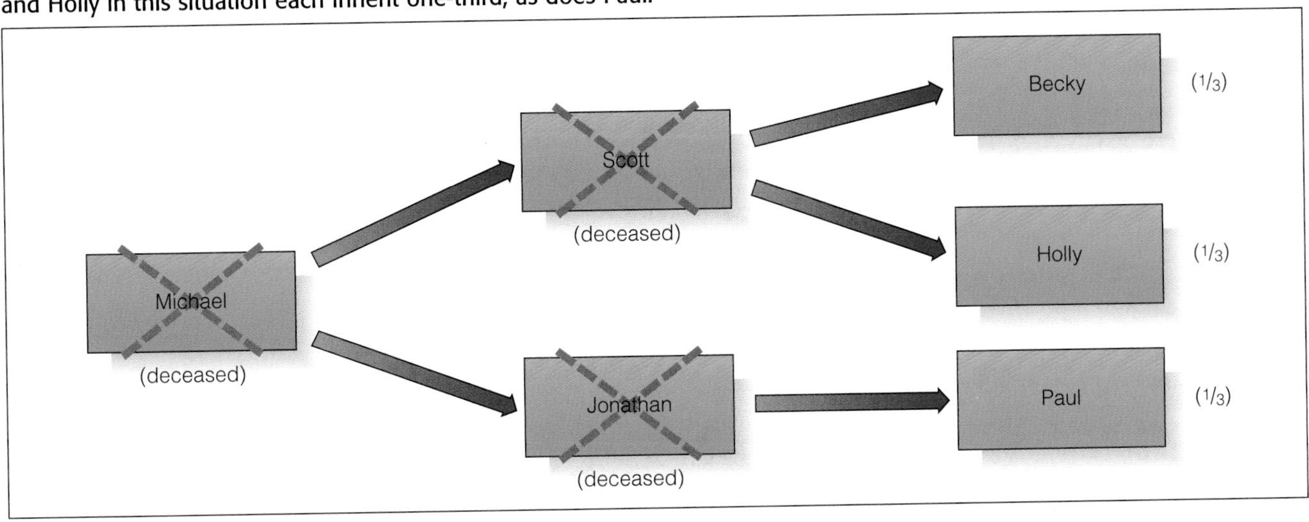

"Put not your trust in money, but put your money in trust."

OLIVER WENDELL HOLMES, JR.
1841–1935
(Associate justice of the United States Supreme Court, 1902–1932)

③ A fund sufficiently identified to enable title to pass to the trustee.

④ Actual delivery by the settlor or grantor (the person creating the trust) to the trustee with the intention of passing title.

● **EXAMPLE 38.4** If James conveys his farm to the First Bank of Minnesota to be held for the benefit of his daughters, he has created a trust. James is the settlor, the First Bank of Minnesota is the trustee, and James's daughters are the beneficiaries. This arrangement is illustrated in Exhibit 38–6.● Numerous types of trusts can be established. In this section, we look at some of the major types of trusts and their characteristics.

EXHIBIT 38–6 **TRUST ARRANGEMENT**

In a trust, there is a separation of interests in the trust property. The trustee takes *legal* title, which is the complete ownership and possession but which does not include the right to receive any benefits from the property. The beneficiary takes *equitable* title, which is the right to receive benefits from the property.

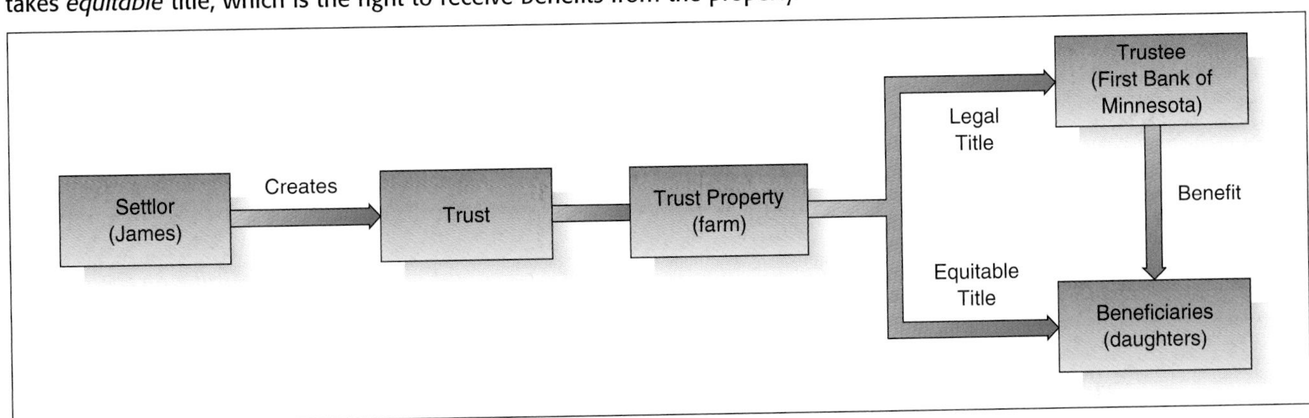

EXPRESS TRUSTS

An *express trust* is one created or declared in explicit terms, usually in writing. Express trusts fall into two categories: *inter vivos* (living) trusts and testamentary trusts (trusts provided for in a last will and testament).

***INTER VIVOS* TRUST** A trust created by the grantor (settlor) and effective during the grantor's lifetime; a trust not established by a will.

An ***inter vivos* trust** is a trust executed by a grantor during her or his lifetime. The grantor (settlor) executes a *trust deed,* and legal title to the trust property passes to the named trustee. The trustee has a duty to administer the property as directed by the grantor for the benefit and in the interest of the beneficiaries. The trustee must preserve the trust property, make it productive, and, if required by the terms of the trust agreement, pay income to the beneficiaries, all in accordance with the terms of the trust. Once the *inter vivos* trust is created, the grantor has, in effect, given over the property for the benefit of the beneficiaries. Often, setting up this type of trust offers tax-related benefits.

TESTAMENTARY TRUST A trust that is created by will and therefore does not take effect until the death of the testator.

A **testamentary trust** is a trust created by a will to come into existence on the settlor's death. Although a testamentary trust has a trustee who maintains legal title to the trust property, the trustee's actions are subject to judicial approval. This trustee can be named in the will or be appointed by the court. Thus, a testamentary trust does not fail because a trustee has not been named in the will. The legal responsibilities of the trustee are the same as in an *inter vivos* trust. If the will setting up a testamentary trust is invalid, the trust will also be invalid. The property that was supposed to be in the trust will then pass according to intestacy laws, not according to the terms of the trust.

IMPLIED TRUSTS

Sometimes, a trust will be imposed (implied) by law, even in the absence of an express trust. Implied trusts include resulting trusts and constructive trusts.

RESULTING TRUST An implied trust arising from the conduct of the parties. A trust in which a party holds the actual legal title to another's property but only for that person's benefit.

A **resulting trust** arises from the conduct of the parties. Here, the trust results, or is created, when circumstances raise an inference that the party holding legal title to the property does so for the benefit of another. • **EXAMPLE 38.5** Suppose that Garrison wants to put one acre of land she owns on the market for sale. Because she is going out of the country for two years and would not be able to deed the property to a buyer during that period, Garrison conveys the property to her good friend Oswald. Oswald will attempt to sell the property while Garrison is gone. Because the intent of the transaction in which Garrison conveyed the property to Oswald is neither a sale nor a gift, the property will be held in trust (a resulting trust) by Oswald for the benefit of Garrison. Therefore, on Garrison's return, Oswald will be required either to deed back the property to Garrison or, if the property has been sold, to turn over the proceeds (held in trust) to her. Here, the trust arises *(results from)* the *apparent intention* of the parties. •

CONSTRUCTIVE TRUST An equitable trust that is imposed in the interests of fairness and justice when someone wrongfully holds legal title to property. A court may require the owner to hold the property in trust for the person or persons who rightfully should own the property.

A **constructive trust** is an equitable trust imposed in the interests of fairness and justice. If someone wrongfully holds legal title to property—for example, if the property was obtained through fraud or in breach of a legal duty—a court may require that owner to hold the property in trust for the person or persons who rightfully should own the property. • **EXAMPLE 38.6** Suppose that Kraft is a partner in a partnership that purchases and develops real estate. Kraft learns in a partners' meeting that the partnership is considering the purchase of a vacant lot that will soon come on the market. Kraft secretly purchases the property in his own name, thus violating his fiduciary duty of loyalty to the partnership. If the partnership discovers what Kraft has done and brings a legal action against him, a court may impose a constructive trust, thus requiring Kraft to hold the property in trust for the partnership. •

SPECIAL TYPES OF TRUSTS

CHARITABLE TRUST
A trust in which the property held by the trustee must be used for a charitable purpose, such as the advancement of health, education, or religion.

SPENDTHRIFT TRUST
A trust created to protect the beneficiary from spending all the funds to which she or he is entitled. Only a certain portion of the total amount is given to the beneficiary at any one time, and most states prohibit creditors from attaching assets of the trust.

TOTTEN TRUST
A trust created by the deposit of a person's own funds in his or her own name as a trustee for another. It is a tentative trust, revocable at will until the depositor dies or completes the gift in his or her lifetime by some unequivocal act or declaration.

Certain trusts are created for special purposes. Three of these trusts that warrant discussion are charitable, spendthrift, and Totten trusts. A **charitable trust** is designed for the benefit of a segment of the public or of the public in general. Usually, to be deemed a charitable trust, a trust must be created for charitable, educational, religious, or scientific purposes.

A **spendthrift trust** is created to provide for the maintenance of a beneficiary by preventing his or her improvidence with the bestowed funds. Essentially, the beneficiary is permitted to draw only a certain portion of the total amount to which he or she is entitled at any one time. The majority of states allow spendthrift trust provisions that prohibit creditors from attaching such trusts.

A **Totten trust**[5] is created when one person deposits funds in her or his own name as a trustee for another. This trust is tentative in that it is revocable at will until the depositor dies or completes the gift in her or his lifetime by some unequivocal act or declaration (for example, delivery of the funds to the intended beneficiary). If the depositor should die before the beneficiary dies and if the depositor has not revoked the trust expressly or impliedly, the beneficiary obtains property rights to the balance on hand.

5. This type of trust derives its unusual name from *In the Matter of Totten,* 179 N.Y. 112, 71 N.E. 748 (1904).

APPLICATION Law and the Businessperson . . .

Risk Management in Cyberspace*

As mentioned elsewhere, companies doing business online face many risks that are not covered by traditional types of insurance (see Exhibit 38–1). Not surprisingly, a growing number of companies are now offering policies designed to cover Web-related risks.

INSURANCE COVERAGE FOR WEB-RELATED RISKS

For example, consider the types of coverage offered by Net Secure, a venture undertaken by IBM, several insurance companies, and a New York broker. Net Secure provides insurance protection against losses resulting from programming errors; network and Web site disruptions; the theft of electronic data and assets, including intellectual property; Web-related defamation, copyright infringement, and false advertising; and the violation of users' privacy rights.

InsureTrust.com, an insurer affiliated with three leading insurance companies—American International Group, Lloyd's of London, and Reliance National—offers similar coverage. Existing insurers, such as Lloyd's of London, Hartford Insurance, and the Chubb Group of Insurance Companies, are also adding insurance for Web-related perils to their offerings. Clearly, the market for these new types of insurance coverage is rapidly evolving, and new policies will continue to appear.

CUSTOMIZED POLICIES

Unlike traditional insurance policies, which are generally drafted by insurance companies and presented to

*This *Application* is not meant to substitute for the services of an attorney who is licensed to practice law in your state.

(continued)

APPLICATION Law and the Entrepreneur . . .

Risk Management in Cyberspace—continued

insurance applicants on a "take-it-or-leave-it" basis, Internet-particular policies are usually customized to provide protection against specific risks faced by a particular type of business. For example, an Internet service provider will face different risks than an online merchant, and a banking institution will face different risks than a law firm. The specific business-related risks are taken into consideration when determining the policy premium.

Checklist for the Businessperson

1. Determine the types of risks to which you are exposed in your Web business and try to obtain an insurance policy that specifically protects you against those risks.
2. As when procuring any type of insurance coverage, read the policy carefully, including any exclusions that may be contained in the fine print, before committing to it.
3. Do not be "penny wise and pound foolish" when it comes to insurance protection. Though insurance coverage may seem expensive, it may be much less costly than defending against a lawsuit. Often, the cost of coverage can be reduced by purchasing a policy with a high deductible.

Key Terms

administrator 1014
bequest 1014
binder 1009
charitable trust 1025
codicil 1019
constructive trust 1024
devise 1014
devisee 1014
executor 1014
holographic will 1018
insurable interest 1008
insurance 1006
inter vivos trust 1024
intestacy laws 1014
intestate 1014
legacy 1014
legatee 1014
nuncupative will 1018
per capita 1022
per stirpes 1022
policy 1008
premium 1008
resulting trust 1024
risk 1006
risk management 1006
spendthrift trust 1025
testamentary trust 1024
testator 1014
Totten trust 1025
trust 1022
underwriter 1008
will 1014

Chapter Summary Insurance, Wills, and Trusts

INSURANCE	
Classifications (See pages 1006–1007.)	See Exhibit 38–1.
Terminology (See page 1008.)	1. *Policy*—The insurance contract. 2. *Premium*—The consideration paid to the insurer for a policy.

Chapter Summary Insurance, Wills, and Trusts—continued

Terminology—continued	3. *Underwriter*—The insurance company. 4. *Parties*—Include the insurer (the insurance company), the insured (the person covered by insurance), an agent (a representative of the insurance company) or a broker (ordinarily an independent contractor), and a beneficiary (a person to receive proceeds under the policy).
Insurable Interest (See pages 1008–1009.)	An insurable interest exists whenever an individual or entity benefits from the preservation of the health or life of the insured or the property to be insured. For life insurance, an insurable interest must exist at the time the policy is issued. For property insurance, an insurable interest must exist at the time of the loss.
The Insurance Contract (See pages 1009–1013.)	1. *Laws governing*—The general principles of contract law are applied; the insurance industry is also heavily regulated by the states. 2. *Application*—An insurance applicant is bound by any false statements that appear in the application (subject to certain exceptions), which is part of the insurance contract. Misstatements or misrepresentations may be grounds for voiding the policy. 3. *Effective date*—Coverage on an insurance policy can begin when the *binder* (a written memorandum indicating that a formal policy is pending and stating its essential terms) is written; when the policy is issued; at the time of contract formation; or, depending on the terms of the contract, when certain conditions are met. 4. *Provisions and clauses*—See Exhibit 38–2. Words will be given their ordinary meanings, and any ambiguity in the policy will be interpreted against the insurance company. When the written policy has not been delivered and it is unclear whether an insurance contract actually exists, the uncertainty will be determined against the insurance company. The court will presume that the policy is in effect unless the company can show otherwise. 5. *Defenses against payment to the insured*—Defenses include misrepresentation, fraud, or violation of warranties by the applicant.
	WILLS
Terminology (See pages 1014–1016.)	1. *Intestate*—One who dies without a valid will. 2. *Testator*—A person who makes out a will. 3. *Personal representative*—A person appointed in a will or by a court to settle the affairs of a decedent. A personal representative named in the will is an *executor;* a personal representative appointed by the court for an intestate decedent is an *administrator.* 4. *Devise*—A gift of real estate by will; may be general or specific. The recipient of a devise is a *devisee.* 5. *Bequest, or legacy*—A gift of personal property by will; may be general or specific. The recipient of a bequest (legacy) is a *legatee.*
Probate Procedures (See pages 1016–1017.)	To probate a will means to establish its validity and to carry the administration of the estate through a court process. Probate laws vary from state to state. Probate procedures may be informal or formal, depending on the size of the estate and other factors, such as whether a guardian for minor children must be appointed.
Requirements for a Valid Will (See pages 1017–1019.)	1. The testator must have testamentary capacity (be of legal age and sound mind at the time the will is made). 2. A will must be in writing (except for nuncupative wills). A holographic will is completely in the handwriting of the testator.

(continued)

Chapter Summary Insurance, Wills, and Trusts—continued

Requirements for a Valid Will—continued	3. A will must be signed by the testator; what constitutes a signature varies from jurisdiction to jurisdiction. 4. A nonholographic will (an attested will) must be witnessed in the manner prescribed by state statute. 5. A will may have to be *published*—that is, the testator may be required to announce to witnesses that this is his or her "last will and testament"; not required under the UPC.
Revocation of Wills (See pages 1019–1020.)	1. *By physical act of the maker*—Tearing up, canceling, obliterating, or deliberately destroying part or all of a will. 2. *By subsequent writing*— a. Codicil—A formal, separate document to amend or revoke an existing will. b. Second will or new will—A new, properly executed will expressly revoking the existing will. 3. *By operation of law*— a. Marriage—Generally revokes part of a will written before the marriage. b. Divorce or annulment—Revokes dispositions of property made under a will to a former spouse. c. Subsequently born child—It is *implied* that the child is entitled to receive the portion of the estate granted under intestacy distribution laws.
Intestacy Laws (See pages 1020–1022.)	1. Intestacy laws vary widely from state to state. Usually, the law provides that the surviving spouse and children inherit the property of the decedent (after the decedent's debts are paid). The spouse usually will inherit the entire estate if there are no children, one-half of the estate if there is one child, and one-third of the estate if there are two or more children. 2. If there is no surviving spouse or child, then, in order, lineal descendants (grandchildren, brothers and sisters, and—in some states—parents of the decedent) inherit. If there are no lineal descendants, then collateral heirs (nieces, nephews, aunts, and uncles of the decedent) inherit.
	TRUSTS
Definition (See pages 1022–1023.)	A trust is any arrangement through which property is transferred from one person to a trustee to be administered for another party's benefit. The essential elements of a trust are (1) a designated beneficiary, (2) a designated trustee, (3) a fund sufficiently identified to enable title to pass to the trustee, and (4) actual delivery to the trustee with the intention of passing title.
Express Trusts (See page 1024.)	Express trusts are created by expressed terms, usually in writing, and fall into two categories: 1. Inter vivos *trust*—A trust executed by a grantor during his or her lifetime. 2. *Testamentary trust*—A trust created by will and coming into existence on the death of the grantor.
Implied Trusts (See page 1024.)	Implied trusts, which are imposed by law in the interests of fairness and justice, include the following: 1. *Resulting trust*—Arises from the conduct of the parties when an *apparent intention* to create a trust is present. 2. *Constructive trust*—Arises by operation of law whenever a transaction takes place in which the person who takes title to property is in equity not entitled to enjoy the beneficial interest therein.

Chapter Summary Insurance, Wills, and Trusts—continued

Special Types of Trusts (See page 1025.)	1. *Charitable trust*—A trust designed for the benefit of a public group or the public in general. 2. *Spendthrift trust*—A trust created to provide for the maintenance of a beneficiary by allowing only a certain portion of the total amount to be received by the beneficiary at any one time. 3. *Totten trust*—A trust created when one person deposits funds in his or her own name as a trustee for another.

For Review

① What is an insurable interest? When must an insurable interest exist—at the time the insurance policy is obtained, at the time the loss occurs, or both?

② Is an insurance broker the agent of the insurance applicant or the agent of the insurer?

③ What are the basic requirements for executing a will? How may a will be revoked?

④ What is the difference between a *per stirpes* and a *per capita* distribution of an estate to the grandchildren of the deceased?

⑤ What are the four essential elements of a trust? What is the difference between an express trust and an implied trust?

Questions and Case Problems

38–1. Timing of Insurance Coverage. On October 10, Joleen Vora applied for a $50,000 life insurance policy with Magnum Life Insurance Co.; she named her husband, Jay, as the beneficiary. Joleen paid the insurance company the first year's policy premium on making the application. Two days later, before she had a chance to take the physical examination required by the insurance company and before the policy was issued, Joleen was killed in an automobile accident. Jay submitted a claim to the insurance company for the $50,000. Can Jay collect? Explain.

38–2. Validity of Wills. Merlin Winters had three sons. Merlin and his youngest son, Abraham, had a falling out in 1998 and never spoke to each other again. Merlin made a formal will in 2000, leaving all his property to the two older sons and deliberately excluding Abraham. Merlin's health began to deteriorate, and by 2001 he was under the full-time care of a nurse, Julia. In 2002, he made a new will expressly revoking the 2000 will and leaving all his property to Julia. On Merlin's death, the two older sons contested the 2002 will, claiming that Julia had exercised undue influence over their father. Abraham claimed that both wills were invalid. He contended that the first one had been revoked by the second will and that the second will was invalid on the ground of undue influence. Is Abraham's contention correct? Explain.

38–3. Wills. Gary Mendel drew up a will in which he left his favorite car, a 1966 red Ferrari, to his daughter, Roberta. A year prior to his death, Mendel sold the 1966 Ferrari and purchased a 1969 Ferrari. Discuss whether Roberta will inherit the 1969 Ferrari under the terms of her father's will.

38–4. Estate Distribution. Benjamin is a widower who has two married children, Edward and Patricia. Patricia has two children, Perry and Paul. Edward has no children. Benjamin dies, and his typewritten will leaves all his property equally to his children, Edward and Patricia, and provides that should a child predecease him, the grandchildren are to take *per stirpes*. The will was witnessed by Patricia and by Benjamin's lawyer and was signed by Benjamin in their presence. Patricia has predeceased Benjamin. Edward claims the will is invalid.

(a) Discuss whether the will is valid.
(b) Discuss the distribution of Benjamin's estate if the will is invalid.
(c) Discuss the distribution of Benjamin's estate if the will is valid.

38–5. Validity of Wills. In the last fourteen years of Evelyn Maheras's life, William Cook, a Baptist pastor, became her spiritual adviser and close personal friend. Cook—and no one else—actively participated in helping Maheras draft her will. He gave Maheras a church-sponsored booklet on will drafting, recommended an attorney (a church member) to do the drafting, and reviewed the terms of the will with Maheras. When Maheras died, she left most of her estate to Cook's church. Cook personally received nothing under the will. Maheras's nephew and only heir, Richard Suagee, filed a suit against Cook in an Oklahoma state court to contest the will, arguing that Cook unduly influenced Maheras. Can a party who receives nothing under a will be regarded as having exercised undue influence over the testator?

What should the court in Maheras's case do? [*Estate of Maheras,* 897 P.2d 268 (Okla. 1995)]

38–6. Interpretation of an Insurance Contract's Terms. RLI Insurance Co. issued an insurance policy to Richard Brown to cover his aircraft. One provision of the policy excluded coverage for a "resident spouse." A different provision included coverage for "any passenger." Richard was piloting the aircraft with his wife, Janet, as a passenger when the aircraft crashed. Richard was killed, and Janet was injured. At the time, Janet and Richard had been living together. Janet filed a suit in a federal district court to collect under the policy for her injuries. RLI claimed that the policy clearly excluded Janet. Janet argued that the policy was ambiguous. What will the court decide? Why? [*RLI Insurance Co. v. Drollinger,* 97 F.3d 230 (8th Cir. 1996)]

38–7. Adopted Children. Gail MacCallum was the daughter of Anita Seymour. After the death of Gail's father, Anita married Richard Seymour, who adopted Gail the next year, when she was seven years old. The same year, Janet Seymour was born to Richard and Anita. Almost forty years later, when Richard's brother Philip died, both Gail and Janet sought to share in the estate. A Vermont state court concluded that Gail could not share in the estate because a state statute prohibited "inheritance between the person adopted . . . and collateral kin of the person or persons making the adoption." Gail appealed, arguing that the statute was unconstitutional. Will the court agree? Discuss fully. [*MacCallum v. Seymour,* 686 A.2d 935 (Vt. 1996)]

38–8. Revocation. William Laneer urged his son, also William, to join the family business. The son, who was made partner, became suspicious of the handling of the business's finances. He filed a suit against the business and reported it to the Internal Revenue Service. The elder Laneer then executed a will that disinherited his son, giving him one dollar and leaving the balance of the estate equally to his four daughters, including Bellinda Barrera. Until his death more than twenty years later, Laneer harbored ill feelings toward his son. After Laneer's death, his original copy of the will could not be found. A photocopy was found in his safe-deposit box, however, and his lawyer's original copy was entered for probate in an Arkansas state court. Barrera, who wanted her brother William to share an equal portion of the inheritance, filed a petition to contest the will. Barrera claimed, among other things, that Laneer had revoked the will, and that was why his original copy of the will could not be found. Was the will revoked? If so, to whom would the estate be distributed? [*Barrera v. Vanpelt,* 332 Ark. 482, 965 S.W.2d 780 (1998)]

38–9. Insurer's Defenses. The City of Worcester, Massachusetts, adopted an ordinance in 1990 that required rooming houses to be equipped with automatic sprinkler systems no later than September 25, 1995. In Worcester, James and Mark Duffy owned a forty-eight–room lodging house with two retail stores on the first floor. In 1994, the Duffys applied with General Star Indemnity Co. for an insurance policy to cover the premises. The application indicated that the premises had a sprinkler system. General issued a policy that required, among other safety features, a sprinkler system. Within a month, the premises were inspected on behalf of General. On the inspection form forwarded to the insurer, in the list of safety systems, next to the word "sprinkler" the inspector had inserted only a hyphen. In July 1995, when the premises sustained over $100,000 in fire damage, General learned that there was no sprinkler system. The insurer filed a suit in a federal district court against the Duffys to rescind the policy, alleging misrepresentation in their insurance application about the presence of sprinklers. How should the court rule, and why? [*General Star Indemnity Co. v. Duffy,* 191 F.3d 55 (1st Cir. 1999)]

TEST YOUR KNOWLEDGE—ANSWER ON THE WEB

38–10. Valley Furniture & Interiors, Inc., bought an insurance policy from Transportation Insurance Co. (TIC). The policy provided coverage of $50,000 for each occurrence of property loss caused by employee dishonesty. An "occurrence" was defined as "a single act or series of related acts." Valley allowed its employees to take pay advances and to buy discounted merchandise, with the advances and the cost of the merchandise deducted from their paychecks. The payroll manager was to notify the payroll company to make the deductions. Over a period of six years, without notifying the payroll company, the payroll manager issued advances to other employees and herself and bought merchandise for herself, in amounts totaling more than $200,000. Valley filed claims with TIC for three "occurrences" of employee theft. TIC considered the acts a "series of related acts" and paid only $50,000. Valley filed a suit in a Washington state court against TIC, alleging, in part, breach of contract. What is the standard for interpreting an insurance clause? How should this court define "series of related acts"? Why? [*Valley Furniture & Interiors, Inc. v. Transportation Insurance Co.,* 107 Wash.App. 104, 26 P.3d 952 (Div. 1 2001)]

A QUESTION OF ETHICS AND SOCIAL RESPONSIBILITY

38–11. Heber Burke and his wife Evelyn had been married for fifty-three years. Evelyn died, and about five months later, Heber married Lexie Damron, a widow who attended his church. Seven days after the marriage, Heber executed a will, which was drawn up by Lexie's attorney, in which he left all of his property to Lexie. Heber died three weeks later. Heber's children, Donald Burke and Beatrice Bates, contested the will, alleging that Heber lacked testamentary capacity and that Heber's will resulted from Lexie's undue influence over him. Friends and relatives of Heber testified that they had never known Heber to drink and that, although he seemed saddened by his first wife's death, he was not incapacitated by it. According to the children's witnesses, however, after Evelyn's death, Heber drank heavily and constantly, had frequent crying spells, repeatedly visited his wife's grave, tried to dig her up so that he could talk to her, and had hallucinations. The jury found the will to be invalid on the ground of undue influence, and Lexie appealed. [*Burke v. Burke,* 801 S.W.2d 691 (Ken.App. 1990)]

1. The appellate court had to weigh two conflicting policies in deciding this issue. What are these two policies, and what criteria should be used in resolving the issue?
2. Given the circumstances described above, would you infer undue influence on the part of Lexie if you were the judge? Would you conclude that Heber lacked testamentary capacity? What would be the fairest solution, in your opinion?
3. Heber's first wife, Evelyn, contributed substantially to the acquisition of the property subject to Heber's will. A natural assumption would be that Evelyn would want their children to inherit the jointly acquired property. If Heber were found to be of sound mind and not the victim of any undue influence, however, the court would allow him to disregard the children totally, if he wished, in his will. Is this fair to Evelyn's presumed intentions? To the children? Is there any solution to the possible unfairness that can result from giving people the right to disregard natural heirs in their wills?

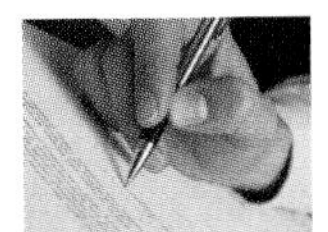

FOR CRITICAL ANALYSIS

38–12. Statistics show that the extent of risk assumed by insurance companies varies depending on the gender of the insured. Many people contend that laws prohibiting gender-based insurance rates are thus fundamentally unfair. Do you agree with this contention? Why or why not?

Internet Exercises

Go to the *Business Law Today* home page at **http://blt.westbuslaw.com**. Select "Interactive Study Center" and then click on "Chapter 38." There you will find the following Internet research exercises that you can perform to learn more about insurance, wills, and trusts, as well as elder law generally:

Activity 38–1: Disappearing Decisions
Activity 38–2: Wills and Trusts
Activity 38–3: Elder Law

Before the Test

Go to the *Business Law Today* home page at **http://blt.westbuslaw.com**. Click on "Interactive Quizzes." You will find at least twenty interactive questions relating to this chapter.

UNIT EIGHT Cumulative Business Hypothetical

Dave graduates from State University with an engineering degree and goes into business as a self-employed computer programmer.

① To advertise his services on the Internet, Dave creates and produces a short digital video. Hollywood Films, Inc., sees the video and hires Dave to program the special effects for a short sequence in a Hollywood movie. Their contract states that all rights to the sequence belong to Hollywood. Does the digital video, the movie sequence, both, or neither, belong to Dave?

② Dave leases an office in Carl's Riverside Plaza office building for a two-year term. What is Dave's obligation for the rent if he moves out before the end of the term? If Dave dies during the term, who is entitled to the possession of the office? What is Dave's obligation for the rent if Carl sells the building to Commercial Investments, Inc., before Dave's lease is up?

③ At the end of the term, Dave buys the office building from Carl, who gives Dave a warranty deed. Commercial Investments later challenges Dave's ownership of the building with its own allegedly valid deed. What will it mean if Dave is held to own the building in fee simple? If Commercial Investments is successful, can Dave recover anything from Carl?

④ Dave's programming business expands, and he hires Mary as an employee. Mary becomes invaluable to the business, and Dave obtains a key-person insurance policy on her life. She dies six years later. If it is discovered that Dave understated Mary's age when applying for the policy (which includes an incontestability clause), can the insurer legitimately refuse payment? If, one year before Mary died, she resigned to start her own programming firm, can Dave collect payment under the policy?

⑤ Over time, Dave acquires other commercial property, which eventually becomes the most lucrative part of his business. Dave wants his adult children, Frank and Terry, to get the benefit of this property when he dies. Dave does not think that Frank and Terry can manage the property, however, because they are involved in their own lives in other locations. How can Dave provide for them to get the benefit of the property under someone else's management? In his will, Dave designates Hal, his attorney, as executor. What does an executor do?

UNIT EIGHT **Extended Case Study**

Stewart v. Johnson

Chapter 37 discussed the types of leasehold estates and the law governing landlord-tenant relationships. One type of tenancy is a periodic tenancy. Termination of a periodic tenancy requires that either the landlord or the tenant give at least one period's notice to the other party. Without this notice, an attempt to terminate the relationship may be construed as a wrongful eviction. In this extended case study, we examine Stewart v. Johnson,[1] *a decision that involved these principles.*

CASE BACKGROUND

In October 1998, in Huntington, West Virginia, Ron and Vera Stewart entered into an oral agreement with Dennis Johnson. Ron Stewart agreed to perform maintenance work on Johnson's properties, which included more than $3 million in rental real estate. Johnson agreed to let the Stewarts live in one of his apartments without directly paying rent. Johnson also agreed to pay Stewart if the labor cost of his work, according to a specific hourly wage, exceeded $350 in a single month.

Stewart worked for Johnson from seven to twelve hours a day, seven days a week. Despite Stewart's repeated requests, however, Johnson never paid him. In December and January, needing food, Stewart pawned two of Johnson's tools. He retrieved and returned one, but Johnson was upset when he learned what had happened.

On February 3, Stewart finished remodeling work on Johnson's own home. Returning home the next evening, the Stewarts found on their door a note: "I got a warrant for your arrest for selling & pawning my tools. You need to vacate my premises no later than tomorrow."[2] Their apartment had been ransacked and scattered with pawn tickets. A TV set was missing. The next morning, Johnson's associate, Lou Porter, told the Stewarts to leave by noon. The Stewarts left the apartment to get a truck to move their belongings. When they returned, everything, including their pets, was gone.

The Stewarts filed a suit in a West Virginia state court against Johnson, seeking damages for wrongful eviction. The court granted judgment as a matter of law to Johnson. The Stewarts appealed to the West Virginia Supreme Court of Appeals (West Virginia's highest court).

1. 209 W.Va. 476, 549 S.E.2d 670 (2001). This opinion may be accessed online at **http://www.state.wv.us/wvsca/opinions.htm**. At the bottom of the page, in the pull-down menu, select "Spring 2001," and click on "Go." In the result, scroll to the name of the case and click on the link to access the appropriate part of the opinion.

2. Although there was not yet a warrant for Stewart's arrest, he later pled guilty to a misdemeanor charge involving stolen property.

MAJORITY OPINION

PER CURIAM.

* * * *

The Stewarts presented evidence at trial to show that they had a month-to-month tenancy with Mr. Johnson and that he failed to provide to them proper notice before terminating the tenancy. Granting judgment as a matter of law, the [trial] court ruled that the statute of frauds precluded the action; that the tenancy agreement between the parties was not in writing; and that it was indefinite in duration. In making these findings, the circuit court relied upon our general statute of frauds and the statute of frauds concerning the sale or lease of land.[3] * * *

Based upon the evidence developed at trial, it was error for the trial court to hold, as a matter of law, that such evidence established a violation of the statute of frauds concerning the sale or lease of land. The evidence presented by the Stewarts clearly established a *prima facie* case that a month-to-month tenancy existed between the parties. *The statute of frauds concerning the sale or lease of land, however, does not require that month-to-month tenancy agreements be reduced to writing.* [Emphasis added.]

Where, as here, there exists a month-to-month tenancy, West Virginia Code Section 37-6-5 requires a landlord provide notice equal to a full period of the tenancy. Through the testimony of the Stewarts and Mr. Johnson, it was shown that the oral tenancy agreement between the parties was indefinite in duration. * * * [T]he length of a tenancy indefinite in duration may be determined by the terms of the rent payment. The evidence presented by the Stewarts established that they paid Mr. Johnson $350 a month for rent, through work performed by Mr. Stewart for Mr. Johnson. It was further shown that Mr. Johnson did not provide the Stewarts with notice equal to a full period of the tenancy (one month) before evicting them. To the extent that the Stewarts presented evidence showing that

3. The Statute of Frauds requires that certain contracts, including contracts relating to interests in land, be in writing to be enforceable. This statute and its exceptions are explained fully in Chapter 11.

a month-to-month tenancy existed with Mr. Johnson, and that Mr. Johnson evicted them without providing notice equal to a full period of the tenancy, it was incumbent upon Mr. Johnson to put on evidence to refute the Stewarts' contentions. * * *

In [this] case, the trial court halted further proceedings at the close of the Stewarts' case * * *. This was error. Only when the plaintiff's evidence, considered in the light most favorable to him, fails to establish a *prima facie* right to recovery, should the trial court * * * grant judgment as a matter of law in favor of the defendant. In this regard, every reasonable and legitimate inference fairly arising from the testimony, when considered in its entirety, must be indulged in favorably to plaintiff; and the court must assume as true those facts which the jury may properly find under the evidence. The trial court failed to apply the above standards in this matter. Therefore, we must reverse and remand the case for further proceedings.

* * * *

For the foregoing reasons, the trial court's award of judgment as a matter of law to Mr. Johnson is reversed, and this case remanded for further proceedings consistent with this opinion.

Reversed and Remanded.

DISSENTING OPINION

MAYNARD, Justice, dissenting.

I dissent because I believe that the majority opinion creates a gross injustice.

At the outset, I admit that the majority, in its opinion, followed the strict confines of our landlord and tenant law. But, while the majority says that it does not condone Mr. Stewart's thievery, that is precisely the result of this decision. In West Virginia, a person can now live in a landlord's apartment, pay no rent whatsoever, steal and then pawn the landlord's property without his consent, plead guilty to a misdemeanor charge involving stolen property, and then sue the landlord for damages and collect. [Leo] Tolstoy [a Russian author] was correct when he wrote "where there is law there is injustice."

Decisions like the instant one make a mockery of the justice system by rewarding blatant dishonesty and criminal misconduct while punishing a reasonable (under these circumstances) deviation from the harsh technicalities of landlord and tenant law. Mr. Stewart's suit against his landlord is simply another example of flagrant abuse. Such abuses cause people to lose confidence in the system which is a dangerous thing in a democratic society. Unfortunately, the majority validates Mr. Stewart's abuse by ensuring that his lawsuit can go forward.

Upon remand, I hope that the landlord will counterclaim for the tort of conversion [see Chapter 4] or, at the least, receive an offset for any damages awarded to the Stewarts.

For the reasons stated above, I respectfully dissent.

QUESTIONS FOR ANALYSIS

① **Law.** Should the majority have taken the opportunity presented by this appeal to rule on the evidence?

② **Law.** In cases involving oral leases, who has the burden of proving its terms? Is this fair?

③ **Economic Consideration.** Considering that the plaintiffs did not have much income, what is noteworthy about this case?

④ **Social Dimension.** If Johnson sues the party who pawned the tool from Stewart, what would be the likely result?

⑤ **Implications for the Landlord.** Besides the eviction attempted in this case, what might a landlord do in similar circumstances to obtain relief from an employee?

The International Legal Environment

UNIT 9

UNIT CONTENTS

CHAPTER 39

International Law in a Global Economy

"Our interests are those of the open door—a door of friendship and mutual advantage. This is the only door we care to enter."

Woodrow Wilson, 1856–1924
(Twenty-eighth president of the United States, 1913–1921)

CHAPTER CONTENTS

LEARNING OBJECTIVES

After reading this chapter, you should be able to answer the following questions:

① What is the principle of comity, and why do courts deciding disputes involving a foreign law or judicial decree apply this principle?

② What is the act of state doctrine? In what circumstances is this doctrine applied?

③ Under the Foreign Sovereign Immunities Act of 1976, on what bases might a foreign state be considered subject to the jurisdiction of U.S. courts?

④ In what circumstances will U.S. antitrust laws be applied extraterritorially?

⑤ Do U.S. laws prohibiting employment discrimination apply in all circumstances to U.S. employees working for U.S. employers abroad?

Since ancient times, independent peoples and nations have traded their goods and wares with one another. In other words, international business transactions are not unique to the modern world—people have always found that they can benefit from exchanging goods with others, as suggested by President Woodrow Wilson's statement in the opening quotation. What is new in our time is that, particularly since World War II, business has become increasingly global in scope. It is not uncommon, for example, for a U.S. corporation to have investments or manufacturing plants in a foreign country, or for a foreign corporation to have operations in the United States.

Transacting business on an international level is considerably different from transacting business within the boundaries of just one nation. Buyers and sellers face far greater risks in the international marketplace than they do in a domestic context because the laws governing these transactions are more complex and uncertain. For example, the Uniform Commercial Code will govern many disputes that arise between U.S. buyers and sellers of goods unless they have provided otherwise in their contracts. What happens, however, if a U.S. buyer breaches a contract formed with a British seller? What law will govern the dispute—British or American? What if an investor owns substantial assets in a developing nation and the government of that nation decides to nationalize—assert its ownership over—the property? What recourse does the investor have against the actions of a foreign government? Questions such as these, which normally do not arise in a domestic context, can become critical in international business dealings.

Because the exchange of goods, services, and ideas on a global level is now a common activity, the student of business law should be familiar with the laws pertaining to international business transactions. In this chapter, we first examine the legal context of international business transactions. We then look at some selected areas relating to business activities in a global context, including international sales contracts, civil dispute resolution, letters of credit, and investment protection. We conclude the chapter with a discussion of the application of certain U.S. laws in a transnational setting.

International Principles and Doctrines

Recall from our discussion in Chapter 1 that *international law* is a body of written and unwritten laws that are observed by otherwise independent nations and that govern the acts of individuals as well as states. We also discussed in that chapter the major sources of international law, including international customs, treaties among nations, and international organizations and conferences. Here, we look at some other legal principles and doctrines that have evolved over time and that the courts of various nations have employed—to a greater or lesser extent—to resolve or reduce conflicts that involve a foreign element. The three important legal principles and doctrines discussed in the following sections are based primarily on courtesy and respect and are applied in the interests of maintaining harmonious relations among nations.

The Principle of Comity

COMITY
The principle by which one nation defers and gives effect to the laws and judicial decrees of another nation. This recognition is based primarily on respect.

Under what is known as the principle of **comity**, one nation will defer and give effect to the laws and judicial decrees of another country, as long as those laws and judicial decrees are consistent with the law and public policy of the accommodating nation. This recognition is based primarily on courtesy and respect.

• **Example 39.1** Assume that a Swedish seller and an American buyer have formed a contract, which the buyer breaches. The seller sues the buyer in a Swedish court, which awards damages. The buyer's assets, however, are in the United States and cannot be reached unless the judgment is enforced by a U.S. court of law. In this situation, if it is determined that the procedures and laws applied in the Swedish court were consistent with U.S. national law and policy, a court in the United States will likely defer to (and enforce) the foreign court's judgment.•

The Act of State Doctrine

ACT OF STATE DOCTRINE
A doctrine that provides that the judicial branch of one country will not examine the validity of public acts committed by a recognized foreign government within its own territory.

The **act of state doctrine** is a judicially created doctrine that provides that the judicial branch of one country will not examine the validity of public acts committed by a recognized foreign government within its own territory. This doctrine is premised on the theory that the judicial branch should not "pass upon the validity of foreign acts when to do so would vex the harmony of our international relations with that foreign nation."[1]

The act of state doctrine can have important consequences for individuals and firms doing business with, and investing in, other countries. For example, this doctrine is frequently employed in cases involving expropriation or confiscation. **Expropriation** occurs when a government seizes a privately owned business or privately owned goods for a proper public purpose and awards just compensation. When a government seizes private property for an illegal purpose or without just compensation, the taking is referred to as a **confiscation.** The line between these two forms of taking is sometimes blurred because of differing interpretations of what is illegal and what constitutes just compensation.

EXPROPRIATION
The seizure by a government of a privately owned business or personal property for a proper public purpose and with just compensation.

CONFISCATION
A government's taking of a privately owned business or personal property without a proper public purpose or an award of just compensation.

• **EXAMPLE 39.2** Tim Flaherty, an American businessperson, owns a mine in Brazil. The government of Brazil seizes the mine for public use and claims that the profits that Tim has realized from the mine in preceding years constitute just compensation. Tim disagrees, but the act of state doctrine may prevent Tim's recovery in a U.S. court. •

When applicable, both the act of state doctrine and the doctrine of sovereign immunity (to be discussed next) tend to immunize foreign governments from the jurisdiction of U.S. courts. This means that firms or individuals who own property overseas often have little legal protection against government actions in the countries in which they operate.

THE DOCTRINE OF SOVEREIGN IMMUNITY

SOVEREIGN IMMUNITY
A doctrine that immunizes foreign nations from the jurisdiction of U.S. courts when certain conditions are satisfied.

Under certain conditions, the doctrine of **sovereign immunity** immunizes (protects) foreign nations from the jurisdiction of U.S. courts. In 1976, Congress codified this rule in the Foreign Sovereign Immunities Act (FSIA). The FSIA exclusively governs the circumstances in which an action may be brought in the United States against a foreign nation, including attempts to attach a foreign nation's property.

Section 1605 of the FSIA sets forth the major exceptions to the jurisdictional immunity of a foreign state or country. A foreign state is not immune from the jurisdiction of U.S. courts when the state has "waived its immunity either explicitly or by implication" or when the action is "based upon a commercial activity carried on in the United States by the foreign state."[2]

ON THE WEB FindLaw's Web site includes an extensive array of links to international doctrines, treaties, and other nations' laws. Go to **http://www.findlaw.com** and select "International Law."

The question frequently arises as to whether an entity falls within the category of a foreign state. The question of what is a commercial activity has also been the subject of dispute. Under Section 1603 of the FSIA, a *foreign state* is defined to include both a political subdivision of a foreign state and an instrumentality of a foreign state. A *commercial activity* is broadly defined under Section 1603 to mean a commercial activity that is carried out by a foreign state within the United States. The act, however, does not define the particulars of what constitutes a commercial activity. Rather, it is left up to the courts to decide whether a particular activity is governmental or commercial in nature.

Doing Business Internationally

A U.S. domestic firm can engage in international business transactions in a number of ways. The simplest way is to seek out foreign markets for domestically produced prod-

1. *Libra Bank, Ltd. v. Banco Nacional de Costa Rica, S.A.,* 570 F.Supp. 870 (S.D.N.Y. 1983).
2. 28 U.S.C. Section 1605(a)(1), (2).

EXPORT
To sell products to buyers located in other countries.

ucts or services. In other words, U.S. firms can look abroad for **export** markets for their goods and services.

Alternatively, a U.S. firm can establish foreign production facilities so as to be closer to the foreign market or markets in which its products are sold. The advantages may include lower labor costs, fewer government regulations, and lower taxes and trade barriers. A domestic firm can obtain revenues by licensing its technology to an existing foreign company. Yet another way to expand abroad is by selling franchises to overseas entities. The presence of McDonald's, Burger King, and KFC franchises throughout the world attests to the popularity of franchising.

ON THE WEB
If you are interested in learning more details on what is involved in exporting goods to other countries, go to the state of New Mexico's Web page on "How to Export" at **http://www.edd.state.nm.us/TRADE/HOWTO/howto.htm**.

EXPORTING

Most U.S. companies make their initial foray into international business through exporting. Exporting can take two forms: direct exporting and indirect exporting. In *direct exporting,* a U.S. company signs a sales contract with a foreign purchaser that provides for the conditions of shipment and payment for the goods. (How payments are made in international transactions is discussed later in this chapter.) If sufficient business develops in a foreign country, a U.S. corporation may set up a specialized marketing organization that, for example, sells directly to consumers in that country. Such *indirect exporting* can be undertaken by appointing a foreign agent or a foreign distributor.

Foreign Agent When a U.S. firm desires a limited involvement in an international market, it will typically establish an *agency relationship* with a foreign firm. In an agency relationship (discussed in Chapter 24), one person (the agent) agrees to act on behalf of another (the principal). The foreign agent is thereby empowered to enter into contracts in the agent's country on behalf of the U.S. principal.

Foreign Distributor When a substantial market exists in a foreign country, a U.S. firm may wish to appoint a distributor located in that country. The U.S. firm and the distributor enter into a **distribution agreement**, which is a contract between the seller and the distributor setting out the terms and conditions of the distributorship—for example, price, currency of payment, availability of supplies, and method of payment. The terms and conditions primarily involve contract law. Disputes concerning distribution agreements may involve jurisdictional or other issues (discussed in detail later in this chapter). In addition, some **exclusive distributorships**—in which distributors agree to distribute only the sellers' goods—have raised antitrust problems.

DISTRIBUTION AGREEMENT
A contract between a seller and a distributor of the seller's products setting out the terms and conditions of the distributorship.

EXCLUSIVE DISTRIBUTORSHIP
A distributorship in which the seller and the distributor of the seller's products agree that the distributor has the exclusive right to distribute the seller's products in a certain geographic area.

MANUFACTURING ABROAD

An alternative to direct or indirect exporting is the establishment of foreign manufacturing facilities. Typically, U.S. firms establish manufacturing plants abroad if they believe that by doing so they will reduce costs—particularly for labor, shipping, and raw materials—and thereby be able to compete more effectively in foreign markets. Apple Computer, IBM, General Motors, and Ford are some of the many U.S. companies that have established manufacturing facilities abroad. Foreign firms have done the same in the United States. Sony, Nissan, and other Japanese manufacturers have established U.S. plants to avoid import duties that the U.S. Congress may impose on Japanese products entering this country.

An American firm can manufacture goods in other countries in several ways. They include licensing and franchising, as well as investing in a wholly owned subsidiary or a joint venture.

TECHNOLOGY LICENSING
Allowing another to use and profit from intellectual property (patents, copyrights, trademarks, innovative products or processes, and so on) for consideration. In the context of international business transactions, technology licensing is sometimes an attractive alternative to the establishment of foreign production facilities.

Licensing It is possible for U.S. firms to license their technologies to foreign manufacturers. **Technology licensing** may involve a process innovation that lowers the cost of production or a product innovation that generates a superior product. Technology licensing may be an attractive alternative to establishing foreign production facilities, particularly if the process or product innovation has been patented, because the patent protects—at least to some extent—against the possibility that the innovation might be pirated. Like any licensing agreement, a licensing agreement with a foreign-based firm calls for a payment of royalties on some basis—such as so many cents per unit produced or a certain percentage of profits from units sold in a particular geographic territory.

In some circumstances, even in the absence of a patent, a firm may be able to license the "know-how" associated with a particular manufacturing process—for example, a plant design or a secret formula. The foreign firm that agrees to sign the licensing agreement further agrees to keep the know-how confidential and to pay royalties. For example, the Coca-Cola Bottling Company licenses firms worldwide to use (and keep confidential) its secret formula for the syrup used in that soft drink in return for a percentage of the income gained from the sale of Coca-Cola by those firms.

Technology licensing benefits all parties to the transaction. Those who receive the license can take advantage of an established reputation for quality, and the firm that grants the license receives income from the foreign sales of the firm's products, as well as establishing a global reputation. Additionally, once a firm's trademark is known worldwide, the demand for other products manufactured or sold by that firm may increase—obviously an important consideration.

ON THE WEB For information on the legal requirements of doing business in other nations, a good source is the Internet Law Library's collection of laws of other nations. Go to **http://www.lawguru.com/ilawlib/index.html**.

Franchising Franchising is a well-known form of licensing. Recall from Chapter 31 that a franchise is an arrangement in which the owner of a trademark, trade name, or copyright (the franchisor) licenses another (the franchisee) to use the trademark, trade name, or copyright—under certain conditions or limitations—in the selling of goods or services in exchange for a fee, usually based on a percentage of gross or net sales. Examples of international franchises include McDonald's, the Coca-Cola Bottling Company, Holiday Inn, Avis, and Hertz.

Investing in a Wholly Owned Subsidiary or a Joint Venture Another way to expand into a foreign market is to establish a wholly owned subsidiary firm in a foreign country. A European subsidiary would likely take the form of a *société anonyme* (S.A.), which is similar to a U.S. corporation. In German-speaking nations, it would be called an *Aktiengesellschaft* (A.G.). When a wholly owned subsidiary is established, the parent company, which remains in the United States, retains complete ownership of all the facilities in the foreign country, as well as complete authority and control over all phases of the operation.

A U.S. firm can also expand into international markets through a joint venture. In a joint venture, the U.S. company owns only part of the operation; the rest is owned either by local owners in the foreign country or by another foreign entity. In a joint venture, all of the firms involved share responsibilities, as well as profits and liabilities.

"Commerce is the great equalizer. We exchange ideas when we exchange fabrics."
R. G. INGERSOLL, 1833–1899
(American lawyer and orator)

Commercial Contracts in an International Setting

Like all commercial contracts, an international contract should be in writing. For an example of an actual international sales contract, refer back to the fold-out contract in Chapter 14.

RECALL The interpretation of the words in a contract can be a matter of dispute even when both parties communicate in the same language.

Language and legal differences among nations can create special problems for parties to international contracts when disputes arise. It is possible to avoid these problems by including in a contract special provisions designating the official language of the contract, the legal forum (court or place) in which disputes under the contract will be settled, and the substantive law that will be applied in settling any disputes. Parties to international contracts should also indicate in their contracts what acts or events will excuse the parties from performance under the contract and whether disputes under the contract will be arbitrated or litigated.

Choice of Language

CHOICE-OF-LANGUAGE CLAUSE
A clause in a contract designating the official language by which the contract will be interpreted in the event of a future disagreement over the contract's terms.

A deal struck between a U.S. company and a company in another country normally involves two languages. Typically, many phrases in one language are not readily translatable into another. Consequently, the complex contractual terms involved may not be understood by one party in the other party's language. To make sure that no disputes arise out of this language problem, an international sales contract should have a **choice-of-language clause** designating the official language by which the contract will be interpreted in the event of disagreement.

FOR CRITICAL ANALYSIS
How might language differences affect the meaning of certain terms or phrases in an international contract?

INTERNATIONAL PERSPECTIVE

Language Requirements in France

In 1995, France implemented a law making the use of the French language mandatory in certain legal documents. Documents relating to securities offerings, such as prospectuses, for example, must be written in French. So must instruction manuals and warranties for goods and services offered for sale in France. Additionally, all agreements entered into with French state or local authorities, with entities controlled by state or local authorities, and with private entities carrying out a public service (such as providing electricity or other utilities) must be written in French. The law has posed problems for some businesspersons because certain legal terms or phrases in documents governed by, say, U.S. or English law have no equivalent terms or phrases in the French legal system.

Choice of Forum

FORUM-SELECTION CLAUSE
A provision in a contract designating the court, jurisdiction, or tribunal that will decide any disputes arising under the contract.

When several countries are involved, litigation may be pursued in courts in different nations. There are no universally accepted rules as to which court has jurisdiction over particular subject matter or parties to a dispute. Consequently, parties to an international transaction should always include in the contract a **forum-selection clause** indicating what court, jurisdiction, or tribunal will decide any disputes arising under the contract. It is especially important to indicate the specific court that will have jurisdiction. The forum does not necessarily have to be within the geographic boundaries of the home nation of either party. The following case involved a question about the application of a forum-selection clause.

CASE 39.1 Garware Polyester, Ltd. v. Intermax Trading Corp.

United States District Court,
Southern District of New York, 2001.
__ F.Supp.2d __.

FACTS Garware Polyester, Ltd., based in Mumbai, India, develops and makes plastics and high-tech polyester film. In 1987, Intermax Trading Corporation, based in New York, became Garware's North American sales agent. Over the next decade, the parties executed four written agreements, collectively referred to as the "Agency Agreements." Each agreement provided, "The courts at Bombay [India] alone will have jurisdiction to try out suits in respect of any claim or dispute arising out of or under this agreement or in any way relating to the same." Intermax sold Garware products on a commission basis. In some transactions, Intermax arranged for customers to order products directly from Garware. In other transactions, Intermax sold Garware products through warehouse sales by which Intermax bought products from Garware, warehoused them in the United States, and resold them. When Intermax fell behind in its payments, Garware filed a suit in a U.S. federal district court to collect on the unpaid invoices. Garware argued that the forum-selection clause did not apply to the invoices in dispute because they involved the warehouse sales, which, Garware claimed, were not part of, and did not relate to, the Agency Agreements.

ISSUE Did the forum-selection clause require the dismissal of this suit?

DECISION Yes. The court held that each of the Agency Agreements contained a valid and enforceable forum-selection clause, which applied to this suit. The court dismissed the case for improper venue.

REASON The court recognized that forum-selection clauses "eliminate uncertainty in international commerce and insure that the parties are not unexpectedly subjected to hostile forums and laws. Moreover, international comity dictates that American courts enforce these sorts of clauses out of respect for the integrity and respect of foreign tribunals." The court stated that a forum-selection clause applies when "claims grow out of the contractual relationship, or if the gist of those claims is a breach of that relationship." Here, "the 'gist' of Garware's claim is a breach of the Agency Agreements. The warehouse sales in question were made by Intermax for the purpose of selling Garware products in the contractually defined territory. The Agency Agreements specifically relate to Intermax's role as Garware's 'selling agent * * * in the United States of America * * *.' Thus, if these sales are not squarely within the scope of the Agency Agreements, they are, at the very least, related to the Agreements. Further, the parties' course of dealing supports the conclusion that the parties themselves believed the Agency Agreements included warehouse sales: as required by the Agreements, Garware paid commissions to Intermax on these sales."

FOR CRITICAL ANALYSIS—Social Consideration *Could the parties in this case have expressly waived the application of the forum-selection clause?*

CHOICE OF LAW

CHOICE-OF-LAW CLAUSE
A clause in a contract designating the law (such as the law of a particular state or nation) that will govern the contract.

A contractual provision designating the applicable law—such as the law of Germany or England or California—is called a **choice-of-law clause**. Every international contract typically includes a choice-of-law clause. At common law (and in European civil law systems), parties are allowed to choose the law that will govern their contractual relationship provided that the law chosen is the law of a jurisdiction that has a substantial relationship to the parties and to the international business transaction.

Under Section 1–105 of the Uniform Commercial Code, parties may choose the law that will govern the contract as long as the choice is "reasonable." Article 6 of the United Nations Convention on Contracts for the International Sale of Goods (discussed in Chapter 14), however, imposes no limitation on the parties' choice of what law will govern the contract. The 1986 Hague Convention on the Law Applicable to Contracts for the International Sale of Goods—often referred to as the Choice-of-Law Convention—allows unlimited autonomy in the choice of law. The Hague Convention indicates that whenever a choice of law is not specified in a contract, the governing law is that of the country in which the seller's place of business is located.

FORCE MAJEURE CLAUSE

***FORCE MAJEURE* CLAUSE**
A provision in a contract stipulating that certain unforeseen events–such as war, political upheavals, acts of God, or other events–will excuse a party from liability for nonperformance of contractual obligations.

Every contract, particularly those involving international transactions, should have a ***force majeure* clause.** *Force majeure* is a French term meaning "impossible or irresistible force"—sometimes loosely identified as "an act of God." In international business contracts, *force majeure* clauses commonly stipulate that in addition to acts of God, a number of other eventualities (such as governmental orders or regulations, embargoes, or shortages of materials) may excuse a party from liability for nonperformance.

CIVIL DISPUTE RESOLUTION

International contracts frequently include arbitration clauses. By means of such clauses, the parties agree in advance to be bound by the decision of a specified third party in the event of a dispute, as discussed in Chapter 3. The third party may be a neutral entity (such as the International Chamber of Commerce), a panel of individuals representing both parties' interests, or some other group or organization. (For an example of an arbitration clause in an international contract, refer to the fold-out exhibit in Chapter 14.) The United Nations Convention on the Recognition and Enforcement of Foreign Arbitral Awards (often referred to as the New York Convention) assists in the enforcement of arbitration clauses, as do provisions in specific treaties among nations. The New York Convention has been implemented in nearly one hundred countries, including the United States.

If a sales contract does not include an arbitration clause, litigation may occur. If the contract contains forum-selection and choice-of-law clauses, the lawsuit will be heard by a court in the forum specified and decided according to that forum's law. If no forum and choice of law have been specified, however, legal proceedings will be more complex and attended by much more uncertainty. For example, litigation may take place in two or more countries, with each country applying its own choice-of-law rules to determine which substantive law will be applied to the particular transactions.

Even if a plaintiff wins a favorable judgment in a lawsuit litigated in the plaintiff's country, there is no way to predict whether the court's judgment will be enforced by judicial bodies in the defendant's country. As discussed earlier in this chapter, under the principle of comity, the judgment may be enforced in the defendant's country, particularly if the defendant's country is the United States and the foreign court's decision is consistent with U.S. national law and policy. Other nations, however, may not be as accommodating as the United States in this respect.

Making Payment on International Transactions

Currency differences between nations and the geographic distance between parties to international sales contracts add a degree of complexity to international sales that does not exist in the domestic market. Because international contracts involve greater financial risks, special care should be taken in drafting these contracts to specify both the currency in which payment is to be made and the method of payment.

INTERNATIONAL PERSPECTIVE

Arbitration versus Litigation

One of the reasons many businesspersons find it advantageous to include arbitration clauses in their international contracts is that arbitration awards are usually easier to enforce than court judgments. As mentioned, the New York Convention provides for the enforcement of arbitration awards in those countries that have signed the convention. In contrast, the enforcement of court judgments normally depends on the principle of comity and bilateral agreements providing for such enforcement. How the principle of comity is applied varies from one nation to another, and many countries have not signed bilateral agreements agreeing to enforce judgments rendered in U.S. courts. Furthermore, even a U.S. court may not enforce a foreign court's judgment if it conflicts with U.S. laws or policies. For example, a U.S. federal appellate court refused to enforce the judgment of a British court in a libel case. The court pointed out that the judgment was contrary to the public policy of the United States generally, which "favors a much broader and more protective freedom of the press than [has] ever been provided for under English law."[a]

a. *Telnikoff v. Matusevitch,* 159 F.3d 636 (D.C. Cir. 1998).

FOR CRITICAL ANALYSIS
What might be some other advantages of arbitrating disputes involving international transactions? Are there any disadvantages?

MONETARY SYSTEMS

Although our national currency, the U.S. dollar, is one of the primary forms of international currency, any U.S. firm undertaking business transactions abroad must be prepared to deal with one or more other currencies. After all, just as a U.S. firm wants to be paid in U.S. dollars for goods and services sold abroad, so, too, does a Japanese firm want to be paid in Japanese yen for goods and services sold outside Japan. Both firms therefore must rely on the convertibility of currencies.

FOREIGN EXCHANGE MARKET
A worldwide system in which foreign currencies are bought and sold.

Foreign Exchange Markets Currencies are convertible when they can be freely exchanged one for the other at some specified market rate in a **foreign exchange market.** Foreign exchange markets comprise a worldwide system for the buying and selling of foreign currencies. At any point in time, the foreign exchange rate is set by the forces of supply and demand in unrestricted foreign exchange markets. The foreign exchange rate is simply the price of a unit of one country's currency in terms of another country's currency. For example, if today's exchange rate is one hundred Japanese yen for one dollar, that means that anybody with one hundred yen can obtain one dollar, and vice versa.

CORRESPONDENT BANK
A bank in which another bank has an account (and vice versa) for the purpose of facilitating fund transfers.

Correspondent Banking Frequently, a U.S. company can deal directly with its domestic bank, which will take care of the international funds-transfer problem. Commercial banks sometimes have **correspondent banks** in other countries. Correspondent banking is a major means of transferring funds internationally.

• **EXAMPLE 39.3** Suppose that a customer of Citibank wishes to pay a bill in euros to a company in Paris. Citibank can draw a bank check payable in euros on its account in Crédit Lyonnais, a Paris correspondent bank, and then send the check to the French company to which its customer owes the funds. Alternatively, Citibank's customer can request a wire transfer of the funds to the French company. Citibank instructs Crédit Lyonnais by wire to pay the necessary amount in euros.•

The Clearinghouse Interbank Payment System (CHIPS) handles about 90 percent of both national and international interbank transfers of U.S. funds. In addition, the Society for Worldwide International Financial Telecommunications (SWIFT) is a communication system that provides banks with messages concerning transactions.

Letters of Credit

Because buyers and sellers engaged in international business transactions are frequently separated by thousands of miles, special precautions are often taken to ensure performance under the contract. Sellers want to avoid delivering goods for which they might not be paid. Buyers desire the assurance that sellers will not be paid until there is evidence that the goods have been shipped. Thus, **letters of credit** are frequently used to facilitate international business transactions.

LETTER OF CREDIT
A written instrument, usually issued by a bank on behalf of a customer or other person, in which the issuer promises to honor drafts or other demands for payment by third persons in accordance with the terms of the instrument.

In a simple letter-of-credit transaction, the issuer (a bank) agrees to issue a letter of credit and to ascertain whether the *beneficiary* (seller) performs certain acts. In return, the *account party* (buyer) promises to reimburse the issuer for the amount paid to the beneficiary. The transaction may also involve an *advising bank* that transmits information and a *paying bank* that expedites payment under the letter of credit. Exhibit 39–1 summarizes the "life cycle" of a letter of credit.

Under a letter of credit, the issuer is bound to pay the beneficiary (seller) when the beneficiary has complied with the terms and conditions of the letter of credit. The beneficiary looks to the issuer, not to the account party (buyer), when it presents the documents required by the letter of credit. Typically, the letter of credit will require that the beneficiary deliver to the issuing bank a *bill of lading* to prove that shipment has been made. Letters of credit assure beneficiaries (sellers) of payment while at the same time assuring account parties (buyers) that payment will not be made until the beneficiaries have complied with the terms and conditions of the letter of credit.

EXHIBIT 39–1 THE "LIFE CYCLE" OF A LETTER OF CREDIT

Although the letter of credit appears quite complex at first, it is not difficult to understand. This cycle merely involves the exchange of documents (and money) through intermediaries. The following steps depict the letter-of-credit procurement cycle.

Step 1: The buyer and seller agree on the terms of sale. The sales contract dictates that a letter of credit is to be used to finance the transaction.

Step 2: The buyer completes an application for a letter of credit and forwards it to his or her bank, which will issue the letter of credit.

Step 3: The issuing (buyer s) bank then forwards the letter of credit to a correspondent bank in the seller s country.

Step 4: The correspondent s bank relays the letter of credit to the seller.

Step 5: Having received assurance of payment, the seller makes the necessary shipping arrangements.

Step 6: The seller prepares the documents required under the letter of credit and delivers them to the correspondent bank.

Step 7: The correspondent bank examines the documents. If it finds them in order, it sends them to the issuing bank and pays the seller in accordance with the terms of the letter of credit.

Step 8: The issuing bank, having received the documents, examines them. If they are in order, the issuing bank will charge the buyer s account and send the documents on to the buyer or his or her customs broker. The issuing bank also will reimburse the correspondent bank.

Step 9: The buyer or broker receives the documents and picks up the merchandise from the shipper (carrier).

Source: National Association of Purchasing Management.

DON'T FORGET A letter of credit is independent of the underlying contract between the buyer and the seller.

The Value of a Letter of Credit The basic principle behind letters of credit is that payment is made against the documents presented by the beneficiary and not against the facts that the documents purport to reflect. Thus, in a letter-of-credit transaction, the issuer does not police the underlying contract; a letter of credit is independent of the underlying contract between the buyer and the seller. Eliminating the need for banks (issuers) to inquire into whether or not actual conditions have been satisfied greatly reduces the costs of letters of credit. Moreover, the use of a letter of credit protects both buyers and sellers.

Compliance with a Letter of Credit A letter-of-credit transaction generally involves at least three separate and distinct contracts: the contract between the account party (buyer) and the beneficiary (seller); the contract between the issuer (bank) and the account party (buyer); and, finally, the letter of credit itself, which involves the issuer (bank) and the beneficiary (seller). These contracts are separate and distinct, and the issuer's obligations under the letter of credit do not concern the underlying contract between the buyer and the seller. Rather, it is the issuer's duty to ascertain whether the documents presented by the beneficiary (seller) comply with the terms of the letter of credit.

If the documents presented by the beneficiary comply with the terms of the letter of credit, the issuer (bank) must honor the letter of credit. Sometimes, however, it is difficult to determine exactly what a letter of credit requires. Moreover, the courts are divided as to whether *strict* or *substantial* compliance with the terms of a letter of credit is required. Traditionally, courts required strict compliance with the terms of a letter of credit, but in recent years, some courts have moved to a standard of *reasonable* compliance.

If the issuing bank refuses to pay the seller (beneficiary) even though the seller has complied with all the requirements of the letter of credit, the seller can bring an action to enforce payment.

Regulation of Specific Business Activities

Doing business abroad can affect the economies, foreign policy, domestic politics, and other national interests of the countries involved. For this reason, nations impose laws to restrict or facilitate international business. Controls may also be imposed by international agreement. We discuss here how different types of international activities are regulated.

INVESTING

Investing in foreign nations involves a risk that the foreign government may take possession of the investment property. Expropriation, as already mentioned, occurs when property is taken and the owner is paid just compensation for what is taken. Expropriation does not violate generally observed principles of international law. In contrast, international legal principles are violated when property is confiscated. Confiscation occurs when property is taken and no (or inadequate) compensation is paid. Few remedies are available for confiscation of property by a foreign government. Claims are often resolved by lump-sum settlements after negotiations between the United States and the taking nation.

To counter the deterrent effect that the possibility of confiscation may have on potential investors, many countries guarantee that foreign investors will be compensated if their property is taken. A guaranty can take the form of national constitutional or statutory laws or provisions in international treaties. As further protection for foreign investments, some countries provide insurance for their citizens' investments abroad.

EXPORT RESTRICTIONS AND INCENTIVES

NOTE Most countries restrict exports for the same reasons: to protect national security, to further foreign policy objectives, to prevent the spread of nuclear weapons, and to preserve scarce commodities.

The U.S. Constitution provides in Article I, Section 9, that "No Tax or Duty shall be laid on Articles exported from any State." Thus, Congress cannot impose any export taxes. Congress can, however, use a variety of other devices to control exports. Congress may set export quotas on various items, such as grain being sold abroad. Under the Export Administration Act of 1979,[3] restrictions can be imposed on the flow of technologically advanced products and technical data.

Devices to stimulate exports and thereby aid domestic businesses include export incentives and subsidies. The Revenue Act of 1971,[4] for example, gave tax benefits to firms marketing their products overseas through certain foreign sales corporations; income produced by the exports was exempt from tax. Under the Export Trading Company Act of 1982,[5] U.S. banks are encouraged to invest in export trading companies, which are formed when exporting firms join together to export a line of goods. The Export-Import Bank of the United States provides financial assistance, consisting primarily of credit guaranties given to commercial banks that in turn lend funds to U.S. exporting companies.

IMPORT RESTRICTIONS

"The notion dies hard that in some sort of way exports are patriotic but imports are immoral."

LORD HARLECH (DAVID ORMSLEY GORE), 1918–1985 (English writer)

All nations have restrictions on imports, and the United States is no exception. Restrictions include strict prohibitions, quotas, and tariffs. Under the Trading with the Enemy Act of 1917,[6] for example, no goods may be imported from nations that have been designated enemies of the United States. Other laws prohibit the importation of illegal drugs, books that urge insurrection against the United States, and agricultural products that pose dangers to domestic crops or animals.

Quotas and Tariffs Quotas are limits on the amounts of goods that can be imported. Tariffs are taxes on imports. A tariff is usually a percentage of the value of the import, but it can be a flat rate per unit (for example, per barrel of oil). Tariffs raise the prices of goods, which causes some consumers to purchase less expensive, domestically manufactured goods.

In the following case, the United States Supreme Court considered a challenge to tariff classifications imposed on clothing assembled from U.S. components and then "permapressed" in Mexico.

3. 50 U.S.C. Sections 2401–2420.
4. 26 U.S.C. Sections 991–994.
5. 15 U.S.C. Sections 4001, 4003.
6. 12 U.S.C. Section 95a.

CASE 39.2 United States v. Haggar Apparel Co.

Supreme Court of the United States, 1999.
526 U.S. 380,
119 S.Ct. 1392,
143 L.Ed.2d 480.
http://supct.law.cornell.edu/supct/supct1990ff.htm[a]

a. In the left column, in the "Decisions by party name" section, in the "1999" row, click on "2nd party." Scroll down the list of cases to "Haggar Apparel Co., United States v." and click on it to access a syllabus of the case. On that page, click on the appropriate link to read the full opinion.

COMPANY PROFILE Haggar Apparel Company (**http://www.haggar.com**) *is a leading maker of men's clothing. Haggar's products, including its "wrinkle-free" pants, are sold in more than seven thousand stores in the United States. These stores include seventy Haggar outlet stores. Haggar also makes lower-priced brands,*

(continued)

CASE 39.2—Continued

private-label clothing, and women's wear, through Jerell, Inc., its Selena and Stonebridge brands, and Haggar Canada. Haggar's products are sold all over the world. The company has wholly owned subsidiaries in Canada, Great Britain, and Japan and maintains plants in the United States, the Dominican Republic, and Mexico.

FACTS Haggar Apparel Company buys fabric in the United States, has it treated it with a chemical resin, has it cut, and then has it shipped to Mexico with thread, buttons, and zippers to make pants. The trousers are then sewn, permapressed, and shipped back to the United States. Permapressing is designed to maintain a garment's crease in the desired place and to avoid other creases or wrinkles that detract from its appearance. Permapressing is a baking process that activates the chemical resin to impart the permapress quality. To obtain that quality, extra steps would be needed if the baking were delayed until the garments were shipped back to the United States. Under a federal agency regulation, goods with U.S. components that are assembled abroad and reshipped to the United States are exempt from a duty that is charged against other incoming goods. The U.S. Customs Service levied a duty on Haggar's pants, however, under a regulation that deems all permapressing operations to be an additional step in manufacture, not part of or incidental to the assembly process. Haggar filed a suit in the U.S. Court of International Trade against the federal government, seeking a refund of the duty. Haggar argued that its permapressing was part of the assembly process. The court ruled in Haggar's favor, and the U.S. Court of Appeals for the Federal Circuit affirmed this ruling. The government appealed to the United States Supreme Court.

ISSUE Should the regulation issued by the U.S. Customs Service be enforced?

DECISION Yes. The United States Supreme Court vacated the judgment of the lower courts and remanded the case for further proceedings.

REASON The Supreme Court acknowledged that Congress authorized the U.S. Treasury Department and the Customs Service to administer the tariff regulations, which were the product of notice-and-comment rulemaking.[b] The Court held that without language to the contrary in the enabling statutes or the regulations, the tariff classifications were entitled to "judicial deference."

FOR CRITICAL ANALYSIS—Political Consideration *Why do the courts give deference to (respect or submit to) administrative agency rules?*

b. Administrative agency rulemaking was discussed in Chapter 1.

DUMPING
The selling of goods in a foreign country at a price below the price charged for the same goods in the domestic market.

Dumping The United States has specific laws directed at what it sees as unfair international trade practices. **Dumping**, for example, is the sale of imported goods at "less than fair value." "Fair value" is usually determined by the price of those goods in the exporting country. Foreign firms that engage in dumping in the United States hope to undersell U.S. businesses to obtain a larger share of the U.S. market. To prevent this, an extra tariff—known as an antidumping duty—may be assessed on the imports.

MOST-FAVORED-NATION STATUS
A status granted in an international treaty by a provision stating that the citizens of the contracting nations may enjoy the privileges accorded by either party to citizens of the most favored nations. Generally, most-favored-nation clauses are designed to establish equality of international treatment.

Minimizing Trade Barriers Restrictions on imports are also known as *trade barriers*. The elimination of trade barriers is sometimes seen as essential to the world's economic well-being. Most of the world's leading trade nations are members of the World Trade Organization (WTO), which was established in 1995. To minimize trade barriers among nations, each member country of the WTO is required to grant **most-favored-nation status** to other member countries. This means each member is obligated to treat other members at least as well as it treats the country that receives its most favorable treatment with regard to imports or exports.

Various regional trade agreements and associations also help to minimize trade barriers between nations. The European Union (EU), for example, attempts to minimize or remove barriers to trade among European member countries. The EU is the result of negotiations undertaken by European nations since the 1950s. Currently, the EU is a single integrated European trading unit made up of fifteen European nations. Another important regional trade agreement is the North American Free Trade Agreement (NAFTA). NAFTA, which became effective on January 1, 1994, created a regional trading unit consisting of Mexico, the United States, and Canada. The primary goal of NAFTA is to eliminate tariffs among these three countries on substantially all goods over a period of fifteen to twenty years.

BRIBING FOREIGN OFFICIALS

Giving cash or in-kind benefits to foreign government officials to obtain business contracts and other favors is often considered normal practice. To reduce such bribery by representatives of U.S. corporations, Congress enacted the Foreign Corrupt Practices Act in 1977.[7] This act and its implications for American businesspersons engaged in international business transactions were discussed in detail in the *Landmark in the Law* feature in Chapter 7.

U.S. Laws in a Global Context

The internationalization of business raises questions of the extraterritorial effect of a nation's laws—that is, the effect of the country's laws outside its boundaries. To what extent do U.S. domestic laws affect other nations' businesses? To what extent are U.S. businesses affected by domestic laws when doing business abroad? The following subsections discuss these questions in the context of U.S. antitrust law. We also look at the extraterritorial application of U.S. laws prohibiting employment discrimination.

U.S. ANTITRUST LAWS

U.S. antitrust laws (discussed in Chapter 32) have a wide application. They may *subject* persons in foreign nations to their provisions, as well as *protect* foreign consumers and competitors from violations committed by U.S. citizens. Consequently, *foreign persons*, a term that by definition includes foreign governments, may sue under U.S. antitrust laws in U.S. courts.

Section 1 of the Sherman Act provides for the extraterritorial effect of the U.S. antitrust laws. The United States is a major proponent of free competition in the global economy, and thus any conspiracy that has a *substantial effect* on U.S. commerce is within the reach of the Sherman Act. The violation may even occur outside the United States, and foreign governments as well as persons can be sued for violations of U.S. antitrust laws.

Before U.S. courts will exercise jurisdiction and apply antitrust laws, it must be shown that the alleged violation had a substantial effect on U.S. commerce. U.S. jurisdiction is automatically invoked, however, when a *per se* violation occurs.[8] An example of a *per se* violation is a price-fixing contract. • **EXAMPLE 39.4** If a domestic firm joins a foreign cartel to control the production, price, or distribution of goods, and this cartel has a *substantial restraining effect* on U.S. commerce, a *per se* violation may exist. Hence, both the domestic firm and the foreign cartel may be sued for violation of the U.S. antitrust laws. Likewise, if foreign firms doing business in the United States enter

7. 15 U.S.C. Sections 78m–78ff.

8. Certain types of restrictive contracts, such as price-fixing agreements, are deemed inherently anticompetitive and thus in restraint of trade as a matter of law. When such a restrictive contract is entered into, there is said to be a *per se* violation of the antitrust laws. See Chapter 32.

into a price-fixing or other anticompetitive agreement to control a portion of U.S. markets, a *per se* violation may exist. ●

In the following case, the court considered whether a criminal prosecution under the Sherman Act could be based on price-fixing activities that took place entirely outside the United States but had a substantial effect in this country.

CASE 39.3 United States v. Nippon Paper Industries Co.

United States Court of Appeals,
First Circuit, 1997.
109 F.3d 1.

COMPANY PROFILE *In 1993, two Japanese paper companies merged to form Nippon Paper Industries Company. Nippon makes paper and paper products, operating tree plantations and lumber mills in Australia and Chile. In thirteen other countries, Nippon engages in import and export activities in the chemicals, cosmetics, food, and pharmaceuticals industries. Paper production, however, accounts for about three-quarters of the company's sales. In the late 1980s and early 1990s, one of Nippon's predecessors sold thermal fax paper for use in fax machines and medical printing equipment. In 1990, North American thermal fax paper sales by Japanese firms accounted for $120 million, of which $6 million went to Nippon's predecessor.*

FACTS A federal grand jury issued a criminal indictment against Nippon Paper Industries Company (NPI) and others, charging the defendants with agreeing to fix the price of thermal fax paper throughout North America. The indictment alleged that the meetings to reach the agreement had occurred entirely in Japan but that the defendants had sold the paper through subsidiaries in the United States at above-normal prices. The indictment stated that these activities had had a substantial adverse effect on commerce in the United States and had unreasonably restrained trade in violation of Section 1 of the Sherman Act. NPI filed a motion to dismiss the indictment. The court granted the motion, declaring that a criminal antitrust prosecution could not be based on wholly extraterritorial conduct. The government appealed.

ISSUE May a criminal antitrust prosecution in the United States be based on wholly extraterritorial conduct?

DECISION Yes. The U.S. Court of Appeals for the First Circuit reversed the decision of the lower court.

REASON The appellate court stated that the criminal indictment under the Sherman Act should not be dismissed simply because the actions on which it was based occurred outside the United States. The court reasoned that "in both criminal and civil cases, the claim that Section One applies extraterritorially is based on the same language in the same section of the same statute." The court noted that "civil antitrust actions predicated on wholly foreign conduct which has an intended and substantial effect in the United States come within Section One's jurisdictional reach." The court concluded that because "the text under consideration is not merely a duplicate appearing somewhere else in the statute, but is the original phrase in the original setting," Section 1 applies.

FOR CRITICAL ANALYSIS—Economic Consideration *Why should the United States apply its antitrust laws to business firms owned by citizens or the government of another nation?*

DISCRIMINATION LAWS

As explained in Chapter 35, federal laws in the United States prohibit discrimination on the basis of race, color, national origin, religion, gender, age, and disability. These laws, as they affect employment relationships, generally apply extraterritorially. Since 1984, for example, the Age Discrimination in Employment Act of 1967 has covered U.S. employees working abroad for U.S. employers. The Americans with Disabilities

Act of 1990, which requires employers to accommodate the needs of workers with disabilities, also applies to U.S. nationals working abroad for U.S. firms.

For some time, it was uncertain whether the major U.S. law regulating discriminatory practices in the workplace, Title VII of the Civil Rights Act of 1964, applied extraterritorially. The Civil Rights Act of 1991 addressed this issue. The act provides that Title VII applies extraterritorially to all U.S. employees working for U.S. employers abroad. Generally, U.S. employers must abide by U.S. discrimination laws unless to do so would violate the laws of the country where their workplaces are located. This "foreign laws exception" allows employers to avoid being subjected to conflicting laws.

Key Terms

act of state doctrine 1037
choice-of-language clause 1041
choice-of-law clause 1042
comity 1037
confiscation 1038
correspondent bank 1044
distribution agreement 1039
dumping 1048
exclusive distributorship 1039
export 1039
expropriation 1038
force majeure clause 1043
foreign exchange market 1044
forum-selection clause 1041
letter of credit 1045
most-favored-nation status 1048
sovereign immunity 1038
technology licensing 1040

Chapter Summary International Law in a Global Economy

International Principles and Doctrines (See pages 1037–1038.)	1. *The principle of comity*—Under this principle, nations give effect to the laws and judicial decrees of other nations for reasons of courtesy and international harmony. 2. *The act of state doctrine*—A doctrine under which American courts avoid passing judgment on the validity of public acts committed by a recognized foreign government within its own territory. 3. *The doctrine of sovereign immunity*—When certain conditions are satisfied, foreign nations are immune from U.S. jurisdiction under the Foreign Sovereign Immunities Act of 1976. Exceptions are made (a) when a foreign state has "waived its immunity either explicitly or by implication" or (b) when the action is "based upon a commercial activity carried on in the United States by the foreign state."
Doing Business Internationally (See pages 1038–1040.)	Ways in which U.S. domestic firms engage in international business transactions include (a) exporting, which may involve foreign agents or distributors, and (b) manufacturing abroad through licensing arrangements, franchising operations, wholly owned subsidiaries, or joint ventures.
Commercial Contracts in an International Setting (See pages 1040–1043.)	International business contracts often include choice-of-language, forum-selection, and choice-of-law clauses to reduce the uncertainties associated with interpreting the language of the agreement and dealing with legal differences. Most domestic and international contracts include *force majeure* clauses. They commonly stipulate that certain events, such as floods, fire, accidents, labor strikes, and shortages, may excuse a party from liability for nonperformance of the contract. Arbitration clauses are also frequently found in international contracts.

(continued)

Chapter Summary International Law in a Global Economy—continued

Making Payment on International Transactions (See pages 1043–1046.)	1. *Currency conversion*—Because nations have different monetary systems, payment on international contracts requires currency conversion at a rate specified in a foreign exchange market. 2. *Correspondent banking*—Correspondent banks facilitate the transfer of funds from a buyer in one country to a seller in another. 3. *Letters of credit*—Letters of credit facilitate international transactions by ensuring payment to sellers and assuring buyers that payment will not be made until the sellers have complied with the terms of the letters of credit. Typically, compliance occurs when a bill of lading is delivered to the issuing bank.
Regulation of Specific Business Activities (See pages 1046–1049.)	In the interests of their economies, foreign policies, domestic policies, or other national priorities, nations impose laws that restrict or facilitate international business. Such laws regulate foreign investments; exporting and importing activities; and, in the United States, the bribery of foreign officials to obtain favorable contracts. The World Trade Organization attempts to minimize trade barriers among nations, as do regional trade agreements and associations, including the European Union and the North American Free Trade Agreement.
U.S. Laws in a Global Context (See pages 1049–1051.)	1. Antitrust laws—U.S. antitrust laws may be applied beyond the borders of the United States. Any conspiracy that has a substantial effect on commerce within the United States may be subject to the Sherman Act, even if the violation occurs outside the United States. 2. *Discrimination laws*—The major U.S. laws prohibiting employment discrimination, including Title VII of the Civil Rights Act of 1964, the Age Discrimination in Employment Act of 1967, and the Americans with Disabilities Act of 1990, cover U.S. employees working abroad for U.S. firms—*unless* to apply the U.S. laws would violate the laws of the host country.

For Review

① What is the principle of comity, and why do courts deciding disputes involving a foreign law or judicial decree apply this principle?

② What is the act of state doctrine? In what circumstances is this doctrine applied?

③ Under the Foreign Sovereign Immunities Act of 1976, on what bases might a foreign state be considered subject to the jurisdiction of U.S. courts?

④ In what circumstances will U.S. antitrust laws be applied extraterritorially?

⑤ Do U.S. laws prohibiting employment discrimination apply in all circumstances to U.S. employees working for U.S. employers abroad?

Questions and Case Problems

39–1. Letters of Credit. James Reynolds entered into an agreement to purchase dental supplies from Tooth-Tech, Inc. Reynolds also secured a letter of credit from Central Bank to pay for the supplies. Tooth-Tech placed sixty crates of dental supplies on board a freighter and received in return the invoices required under the letter of credit. The purchaser, Reynolds, subsequently learned that Tooth-Tech, Inc., had filled the sixty crates with rubbish, not dental supplies. Given that an issuer's obligation under a letter of credit is independent of the underlying contract between the buyer and the seller, would the issuer be required to pay the seller in this situation? Explain.

39–2. Letters of Credit. The Swiss Credit Bank issued a letter of credit in favor of Antex Industries to cover the sale of 92,000 electronic integrated circuits manufactured by Electronic Arrays. The letter of credit specified that the chips would be transported to Tokyo by ship. Antex shipped the circuits by air. Payment on the letter of credit was dishonored because the shipment by air did not fulfill the precise terms of the letter of credit. Should a court compel payment? Explain. [*Board of Trade of San Francisco v. Swiss Credit Bank*, 728 F.2d 1241 (9th Cir. 1984)]

39–3. Antitrust Claims. Billy Lamb and Carmon Willis (the plaintiffs) were tobacco growers in Kentucky. Phillip Morris, Inc., and B.A.T. Industries, PLC, routinely purchased tobacco not only from Kentucky but also from producers in several foreign countries. In 1982, subsidiaries of Phillip Morris and B.A.T. (the defendants) entered into an agreement with La Fundacion Del Niño (the Children's Foundation) of Caracas, Venezuela, headed by the wife of the president of Venezuela. The agreement provided that the two subsidiaries would donate a total of approximately $12.5 million to the Children's Foundation, and in exchange, the subsidiaries would obtain price controls on Venezuelan tobacco, elimination of controls on retail cigarette prices in Venezuela, tax deductions for the donations, and assurances that existing tax rates applicable to tobacco companies would not be increased. The plaintiffs brought an action, alleging that the Venezuelan arrangement was an inducement designed to restrain trade in violation of U.S. antitrust laws. Such an arrangement, the plaintiffs contended, would result in the artificial depression of tobacco prices to the detriment of domestic tobacco growers, while ensuring lucrative retail prices for tobacco products sold abroad. The trial court held that the plaintiffs' claim was barred by the act of state doctrine. What will result on appeal? Discuss. [*Lamb v. Phillip Morris, Inc.*, 915 F.2d 1024 (6th Cir. 1990)]

39–4. Sovereign Immunity. The Bank of Jamaica, which is wholly owned by the government of Jamaica, contracted with Chisholm & Co. in January 1981 for Chisholm to arrange for lines of credit from various U.S. banks and to obtain $50 million in credit insurance from the Export-Import Bank of the United States. This Chisholm successfully did, but subsequently the Bank of Jamaica refused the deals arranged by Chisholm; the bank then refused to pay Chisholm for its services. Chisholm sued the bank in a federal district court for breach of an implied contract. The bank moved to dismiss the case, claiming, among other things, that it was immune from the jurisdiction of U.S. courts under the doctrine of sovereign immunity. What factors will the court consider in deciding this issue? Will the court agree? Discuss fully. [*Chisholm & Co. v. Bank of Jamaica*, 643 F.Supp. 1393 (S.D.Fla. 1986)]

39–5. Forum-Selection Clauses. Royal Bed and Spring Co., a Puerto Rican distributor of furniture products, entered into an exclusive distributorship agreement with Famossul Industria e Comercio de Moveis Ltda., a Brazilian manufacturer of furniture products. Under the terms of the contract, Royal Bed was to distribute in Puerto Rico the furniture products manufactured by Famossul in Brazil. The contract contained choice-of-forum and choice-of-law clauses, which designated the judicial district of Curitiba, State of Paraná, Brazil, as the judicial forum and the Brazilian Civil Code as the law to be applied in the event of any dispute. Famossul terminated the exclusive distributorship and suspended the shipment of goods without just cause. Under Puerto Rican law, forum-selection clauses providing for foreign venues are not enforced as a matter of public policy. In what jurisdiction should Royal Bed bring suit? Discuss fully. [*Royal Bed and Spring Co. v. Famossul Industria e Comercio de Moveis Ltda.*, 906 F.2d 45 (5th Cir. 1990)]

39–6. Discrimination Claims. Radio Free Europe and Radio Liberty (RFE/RL), a U.S. corporation doing business in Germany, employs more than three hundred U.S. citizens at its principal place of business in Munich, Germany. The concept of mandatory retirement is deeply embedded in German labor policy, and a contract formed in 1982 between RFE/RL and a German labor union contained a clause that required workers to be retired when they reach the age of sixty-five. When William Mahoney and other American employees (the plaintiffs) reached the age of sixty-five, RFE/RL terminated their employment as required under its contract with the labor union. The plaintiffs sued RFE/RL for discriminating against them on the basis of age, in violation of the Age Discrimination in Employment Act of 1967. Will the plaintiffs succeed in their suit? Discuss fully. [*Mahoney v. RFE/RL, Inc.*, 47 F.3d 447 (D.C. Cir. 1995)]

39–7. Sovereign Immunity. Reed International Trading Corp., a New York corporation, agreed to sell down jackets to Alink, a Russian business. Alink referred Reed to the Bank for Foreign and Economic Affairs of the Russian Federation for payment and gave Reed a letter of credit payable in New York. When Reed tried to collect, the bank refused to pay. Reed (and others) filed a suit in a federal district court against the bank (and others). The bank qualified as a "sovereign" under the Foreign Sovereign Immunities Act and thus claimed in part that it was immune from suit in U.S. courts. On what basis might the court hold that the bank was not immune? Explain. [*Reed International Trading Corp. v. Donau Bank, A.G.*, 866 F.Supp. 750 (S.D.N.Y. 1994)]

39–8. Sovereign Immunity. Nuovo Pignone, Inc., is an Italian company that designs and manufactures turbine systems. Nuovo sold a turbine system to Cabinda Gulf Oil Co. (CABGOC). The system was manufactured, tested, and inspected in Italy, then sent to Louisiana for mounting on a platform by CABGOC's contractor. Nuovo sent a representative to consult on the mounting. The platform went to a CABGOC site off the coast of West Africa. Marcus Pere, an instrument technician at the site, was killed when a turbine within the system exploded. Pere's widow filed a suit in a U.S. federal district court against Nuovo and others. Nuovo claimed sovereign immunity on the ground that its majority shareholder at the time of the explosion was Ente Nazionale Idrocaburi, which was created by the government of Italy to lead its oil and gas exploration and development. Is Nuovo exempt from suit under the doctrine of sovereign immunity? Is it subject to suit under the "commercial activity" exception? Why or why not? [*Pere v. Nuovo Pignone, Inc.*, 150 F.3d 477 (5th Cir. 1998)]

39–9. Dumping. In response to a petition filed on behalf of the U.S. pineapple industry, the U.S. Commerce Department initiated an investigation of canned pineapple imported from Thailand. The investigation concerned Thai producers of the canned fruit, including The Thai Pineapple Public Co. The Thai producers also turned out products, such as pineapple juice and juice concentrate, outside the scope of the investigation. These products use separate parts of the same fresh pineapple, so they share raw material costs. To determine fair value and antidumping duties, the Commerce Department had to calculate the Thai producers' cost of production and, in so doing, had to allocate a portion of the shared fruit costs to the canned fruit. These allocations were based on the producers' own financial records, which were consistent with Thai generally accepted accounting principles. The result was a determination that more than 90 percent of the canned fruit sales were below the cost of production. The producers filed a suit in the U.S. Court of International Trade against the federal government, challenging this allocation. The producers argued that their records did not reflect actual production costs, which instead should be based on the weight of fresh fruit used to make the products. Did the Commerce Department act reasonably in determining the cost of production? Why or why not? [*The Thai Pineapple Public Co. v. United States*, 187 F.3d 1362 (Fed.Cir. 1999)]

TEST YOUR KNOWLEDGE—ANSWER ON THE WEB

39–10. Tonoga, Ltd., doing business as Taconic Plastics, Ltd., is a manufacturer incorporated in Ireland with its principal place of business in New York. In 1997, Taconic entered into a contract with a German construction company to supply special material for a tent project designed to shelter religious pilgrims visiting holy sites in Saudi Arabia. Most of the material was made in, and shipped from, New York. The company did not pay Taconic and eventually filed for bankruptcy. Another German firm, Werner Voss Architects and Engineers, acting as an agent for the government of Saudi Arabia, guaranteed the payments due Taconic to induce it to complete the project. When Taconic received all but the final payment, the firm filed a suit in a federal district court against the government of Saudi Arabia, claiming a breach of the guarantee and seeking to collect, in part, about $3 million. The defendant filed a motion to dismiss based, in part, on the doctrine of sovereign immunity. Under what circumstances does this doctrine apply? What are its exceptions? Should this suit be dismissed under the "commercial activity" exception? Explain. [*Tonoga, Ltd. v. Ministry of Public Works and Housing of Kingdom of Saudi Arabia*, 135 F.Supp.2d 350 (N.D.N.Y. 2001)]

A QUESTION OF ETHICS AND SOCIAL RESPONSIBILITY

39–11. Ronald Riley, an American citizen, and Council of Lloyd's, a British insurance corporation with its principal place of business in London, entered into an agreement in 1980 that allowed Riley to underwrite insurance through Lloyd's. The agreement provided that if any dispute arose between Lloyd's and Riley, the courts of England would have exclusive jurisdiction, and the laws of England would apply. Over the next decade, some of the parties insured under policies that Riley underwrote experienced large losses, for which they filed claims. Instead of paying his share of the claims, Riley filed a lawsuit in a U.S. district court against Lloyd's and its managers and directors (all British citizens or entities), seeking, among other things, rescission of the 1980 agreement. Riley alleged that the defendants had violated the Securities Act of 1933, the Securities Exchange Act of 1934, and Rule 10b-5. The defendants asked the court to enforce the forum-selection clause in the agreement. Riley argued that if the clause was enforced, he would be deprived of his rights under the U.S. securities laws. The court held that the parties were to resolve their dispute in England. [*Riley v. Kingsley Underwriting Agencies, Ltd.*, 969 F.2d 953 (10th Cir. 1992)]

1. Did the court's decision fairly balance the rights of the parties? How would you argue in support of the court's decision in this case? How would you argue against it?
2. Should the fact that an international transaction may be subject to laws and remedies different from or less favorable than those of the United States be a valid basis for denying enforcement of forum-selection and choice-of-law clauses?
3. All parties to this litigation other than Riley were British. Should this fact be considered by the court in deciding this case?

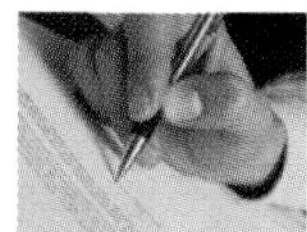

FOR CRITICAL ANALYSIS

39–12. Business cartels and monopolies that are legal in some countries may engage in practices that violate U.S. antitrust laws. In view of this fact, what are some of the implications of applying U.S. antitrust laws extraterritorially?

Internet Exercises

Go to the *Business Law Today* home page at **http://blt.westbuslaw.com**. Select "Interactive Study Center" and then click on "Chapter 39." There you will find the following Internet research exercises that you can perform to learn more about international law and engaging in overseas business operations:

Activity 39–1: The World Trade Organization
Activity 39–2: Overseas Business Opportunities

Before the Test

Go to the *Business Law Today* home page at **http://blt.westbuslaw.com**. Click on "Interactive Quizzes." You will find at least twenty interactive questions relating to this chapter.

UNIT NINE Cumulative Business Hypothetical

Macrotech, Inc., has developed an innovative computer chip and obtained a patent on it. The firm markets the chip under the trademarked brand name "Flash."

① Macrotech wants to sell the Flash chip to Nitron, Ltd., in Pacifica, a foreign country. Macrotech is concerned, however, that after an initial purchase, Nitron will duplicate the chip, pirate it, and sell the pirated version to computer manufacturers in Pacifica. To avoid this situation, Macrotech could establish its own manufacturing facility in Pacifica, but it does not want to do this. How can Macrotech, without establishing a manufacturing facility in Pacifica, protect against Flash being pirated by Nitron?

② A representative of Pixel, S.A., in Raretania, a foreign country, contacts Macrotech, says that Pixel may be interested in buying a quantity of the Flash chips, and asks for a demonstration and a list of prices. Before Pixel makes a buy, Macrotech learns that there is a proposal in Congress to tax certain exports, including products such as Flash. Macrotech also learns of a proposal to impose restrictions on the export of Flash and similar products. Which of these proposals is more likely to be implemented, and why? If Congress wanted to stimulate, rather than restrict, the export of Flash, what steps might it take?

③ Quaro Corp. and Selecta Corp., which are manufacturers in Techuan, a foreign country, make products that compete with the Flash chip. When Quaro and Selecta products seem to flood the U.S. market at low prices, Macrotech believes that its competitors have conspired to fix their prices. Can Macrotech file a suit against Quaro and Selecta in a U.S. court? If Quaro thought Macrotech was conspiring with other firms against it, could Quaro file a suit against Macrotech in a U.S. court? What could the U.S. government do if it found that Quaro and Selecta were selling their products in U.S. markets at "less than fair value"?

United States v. Hitt

Chapter 39 mentions the Export Administration Act of 1979, under which restrictions are imposed on the export of technologically advanced products. The United States can charge violators of this act with criminal offenses, including conspiracy. As noted in Chapter 6, however, an indictment must be issued within a certain period—in this case, five years—under the applicable statute of limitations. In this extended case study, we examine United States v. Hitt,[1] *a decision that involved these principles.*

CASE BACKGROUND

In the early 1990s, McDonnell Douglas Corporation closed a manufacturing plant in Columbus, Ohio, that had produced military aircraft for the United States. McDonnell Douglas and Douglas Aircraft Company (jointly, MDC) entered into an agreement with China National Aero-Technology Import and Export Corporation (CATIC) for the sale of equipment from the plant. This included sophisticated machine tools that were subject to export controls under the Export Administration Act (EAA) of 1979 and required export licenses from the U.S. Department of Commerce. In the applications for licenses to export the equipment, MDC represented that the end user was CATIC Machining Company in Beijing and that the machine tools would be used only to manufacture commercial aircraft.

In September 1994, the U.S. Department of Commerce granted the licenses, which required MDC to verify the equipment's location and usage through quarterly inspections of the CATIC facility. The equipment was shipped to China in March 1995. After the first inspection, MDC reported that the machine tools had been diverted to four different locations, including a factory in Nanchang involved in the manufacture of military equipment.

In October 1999, Robert Hitt, an executive with Douglas Aircraft, and others were charged in a federal district court with conspiring to violate the EAA. Hitt filed a motion to dismiss the charge against him, arguing that the conspiracy related only to the issuance of the licenses in September 1994 and was therefore barred by a five-year statute of limitations. The government argued that the conspiracy continued until the equipment was shipped in March 1995. The court dismissed the indictment against Hitt. The government appealed to the U.S. Court of Appeals for the District of Columbia Circuit.

1. 249 F.3d 1010 (D.C. Cir. 2001). This court opinion may be accessed online at **http://www.cadc.uscourts.gov/opinions/opinions.asp**. In the left-hand column, click on "Opinions." On that page, in the "Please select from the following menu to find opinions by date of issue" section, choose "May" and "2001" from the pull-down menus, and click on "Go!" In the result, scroll to the name of the case and click on the docket number to access the opinion. The U.S. Court of Appeals for the District of Columbia Circuit maintains this Web site.

MAJORITY OPINION

ROGERS, Circuit Judge.

* * * *

For the indictment to be timely with respect to Hitt, it must show that no more than five years prior to the filing of the indictment (i.e., at a point no earlier than October 19, 1994) (1) the conspiracy, as contemplated by the agreement, still existed, and (2) at least one overt act in furtherance of the conspiracy occurred. In examining whether these conditions are fulfilled, the crucial question * * * is the scope of the conspiratorial agreement, for it is that which determines both the duration of the conspiracy, and whether the act relied on as an overt act may properly be regarded as in furtherance of the conspiracy. Key to determining the scope of the conspiracy * * * is the extent to which there was a "meeting of minds" concerning the object of the conspiracy. * * *

* * * *

* * * Paragraph 43 [of the indictment] describes "THE CONSPIRACY" * * *:

> From in or about February, 1993 * * * the defendants * * * did unlawfully, willfully and knowingly combine, conspire, confederate and agree together to commit offenses against the United States, that is:
>
> * * *
>
> b. to willfully and knowingly make false and misleading statements and to conceal material facts from the United States Departments of Commerce and Defense in the course of obtaining export licenses * * *;
>
> * * *
>
> e. to buy and sell, before on or about August 20, 1994, machine tools to be exported from the United States subject to the [EAA] with knowledge or reason to know that a violation of the [EAA] is intended to occur * * *.

Paragraph 44 states the "Goal" of the conspiracy:

> A goal of the conspiracy was to obtain export licenses allowing the sale and exportation of machine tools to [China]. [The

CATIC defendants'] purpose, among others, was to obtain the Columbus plant machine tools for unrestricted use at undisclosed facilities within [China] * * * . [MDC] and Robert Hitt's purposes, among others, were: (a) to maintain the ongoing commercial relationship between [MDC] and CATIC and to promote the prospects for existing and future business contracts between the parties; and (b) to obtain swift approval from the United States Department of Commerce of export license applications by presenting seemingly credible and non-controversial justification and end-user information in the license applications, even if such information was not truthful * * *.

* * * *

From the plain language * * * of [the indictment], it would follow that "The Conspiracy" envisioned by the Grand Jury was confined to the defendants' false statements and concealment of information from Commerce Department officials while applying for the export licenses. The "Goal" of the conspiracy, as described in Paragraph 44, did not encompass any event occurring after the export licenses' issuance on September 14, 1994. Because [the indictment] did not allege that MDC and Hitt shared the separate purpose of the CATIC defendants to divert the machine tools in violation of the export licenses, the conspiracy was * * * completed once the export licenses were issued.

* * * *

Accordingly, we affirm the order of the district court * * *.

DISSENTING OPINION

STEPHEN F. WILLIAMS, Circuit Judge, dissenting.

* * * I would reverse the district court's dismissal of [the charge against Hitt].

* * * *

Our specific task is to determine whether the alleged actions within five years of the indictment promoted the object of the alleged conspiracy. * * *

A natural starting place is the language [in the indictment] explicitly addressing the goal of the conspiracy—"to obtain export licenses allowing the sale and exportation of machine tools to [China]." * * * The remainder of the indictment * * * shows that the grand jury was asserting that the parties' jointly intended to get the tools to China. * * *

* * * *

The indictment says that the CATIC defendants—unsurprisingly—cared about shipment: They wanted to get the equipment for "unrestricted use at undisclosed facilities within [China] * * * ." And McDonnell Douglas and Hitt are explicitly said to have purposes that would extend beyond the issuance of the licenses: They wanted to "maintain the ongoing commercial relationship between McDonnell Douglas and CATIC and to promote the prospects for existing and future business contacts between the parties." Obviously McDonnell Douglas's purpose of maintaining a favorable commercial relationship with CATIC would have been thwarted if the licenses were obtained but never used; thus McDonnell Douglas's alleged purpose fits the broader meaning, and only the broader meaning, of the stated goal.

QUESTIONS FOR ANALYSIS

① **Law.** Considering the opinions of the majority and the dissent, what is the basis for the difference in their interpretations of the indictment?

② **Law.** If the contract between MDC and CATIC concerned only obtaining export licenses, how could Hitt and the others be charged with a crime that arguably exceeded this purpose?

③ **Economic Dimension.** Why did MDC and Hitt allegedly participate in a fraudulent scheme to obtain export licenses?

④ **Ethical Consideration.** What ethical duty might support the purposes and actions of MDC in this case?

⑤ **Implications for the Businessperson.** How might a person who does business internationally avoid committing the crime alleged in the *Hitt* case just presented?

APPENDIX A

HOW TO BRIEF CASES AND ANALYZE CASE PROBLEMS

How to Brief Cases

To fully understand the law with respect to business, you need to be able to read and understand court decisions. To make this task easier, you can use a method of case analysis that is called *briefing*. There is a fairly standard procedure that you can follow when you "brief" any court case. You must first read the case opinion carefully. When you feel you understand the case, you can prepare a brief of it.

Although the format of a case brief may vary, typically it will present the essentials of the case under headings such as those listed below. This is basically the format followed by the authors when briefing the cases that have been included in this text.

1. **Citation.** Give the full citation for the case, including the name of the case, the date it was decided, and the court that decided it.
2. **Facts.** Briefly indicate (a) the reasons for the lawsuit; (b) the identity and arguments of the plaintiff(s) and defendant(s), respectively; and (c) the lower court's decision—if appropriate.
3. **Issue.** Concisely phrase, in the form of a question, the essential issue before the court. (If more than one issue is involved, you may have two—or even more—questions here.)
4. **Decision.** Indicate here—with a "yes" or "no," if possible—the court's answer to the question (or questions) in the *Issue* section above.
5. **Reason.** Summarize as briefly as possible the reasons given by the court for its decision (or decisions) and the case or statutory law relied on by the court in arriving at its decision.

For a case-specific example of what should be included under each of the above headings when briefing a case, see the review of the sample court case presented in the appendix to Chapter 1 of this text.

How to Analyze Case Problems

In addition to learning how to brief cases, students of business law also find it helpful to know how to analyze case problems. Part of the study of business law usually involves analyzing case problems, such as those included in this text at the end of each chapter.

For each case problem in this book, we provide the relevant background and facts of the lawsuit and the issue before the court. When you are assigned one of these problems, your job will be to determine how the court should decide the issue and why. In other words, you will need to engage in legal analysis and reasoning. Here we offer some suggestions on how to make this task less daunting. We begin by presenting a sample problem:

> While Janet Lawson, a famous pianist, was shopping in Quality Market, she slipped and fell on a wet floor in one of the aisles. The floor had recently been mopped by one of the store's employees, but there were no signs warning customers that the floor in that area was wet. As a result of the fall, Lawson injured her right arm and was unable to perform piano concerts for the next six months. Had she been able to perform the scheduled concerts, should would have earned approximately $60,000 over that period of time. Lawson sued Quality Market for this amount, plus another $10,000 in medical expenses. She claimed that the store's failure to warn customers of the wet floor constituted negligence and therefore the market was liable for her injuries. Will the court agree with Lawson? Discuss.

UNDERSTAND THE FACTS

This may sound obvious, but before you can analyze or apply the relevant law to a specific set of facts, you must clearly understand those facts. In other words, you should read through the case problem carefully and more than once, if necessary, to make sure you understand the identity of the plaintiff(s) and defendant(s) in the case and the progression of events that led to the lawsuit.

In the sample case just given, the identity of the parties is fairly obvious. Janet Lawson is the one bringing the suit; therefore, she is the plaintiff. Quality Market, against whom she is bringing the suit, is the defendant. Some of the case problems you may work on have multiple plaintiffs or defendants. Often, it is helpful to use abbreviations for the parties. To indicate a reference to a plaintiff, for example, the pi symbol—π—is often used, and a defendant is denoted by a delta—Δ—a triangle.

The events leading to the lawsuit are also fairly straightforward. Lawson slipped and fell on a wet floor, and she contends that Quality Market should be liable for her injuries because it was negligent in not posting a sign warning customers of the wet floor.

When you are working on case problems, realize that the facts should be accepted as they are given. For example, in our sample problem, it should be accepted that the floor was wet and that there was no sign. In other words, avoid making conjectures, such as "Maybe the floor wasn't too wet," or "Maybe an employee was getting a sign to put up," or "Maybe someone stole the sign." Questioning the facts as they are presented only adds confusion to your analysis.

LEGAL ANALYSIS AND REASONING

Once you understand the facts given in the case problem, you can begin to analyze the case. The **IRAC method** is a helpful tool to use in the legal analysis and reasoning process. IRAC is an acronym for *I*ssue, *R*ule, *A*pplication, *C*onclusion. Applying this method to our sample problem would involve the following steps:

1. First, you need to decide what legal **issue** is involved in the case. In our sample case, the basic issue is whether Quality Market's failure to warn customers of the wet floor constituted negligence. As discussed in Chapter 4, negligence is a *tort*—a civil wrong. In a tort lawsuit, the plaintiff seeks to be compensated for another's wrongful act. A defendant will be deemed negligent if he or she breached a duty of care owed to the plaintiff and the breach of that duty caused the plaintiff to suffer harm.
2. Once you have identified the issue, the next step is to determine what **rule of law** applies to the issue. To make this determination, you will want to review carefully the text of the chapter in which the problem appears to find the relevant rule of law. Our sample case involves the tort of negligence, covered in Chapter 4. The applicable rule of law is the tort law principle that business owners owe a duty to exercise reasonable care to protect their customers ("business invitees"). Reasonable care, in this context, includes either removing—or warning customers of—*foreseeable* risks about which the owner *knew* or *should have known*. Business owners need not warn customers of "open and obvious" risks, however. If a business owner breaches this duty of care (fails to exercise the appropriate degree of care toward customers), and the breach of duty causes a customer to be injured, the business owner will be liable to the customer for the customer's injuries.
3. The next—and usually the most difficult—step in analyzing case problems is the **application** of the relevant rule of law to the specific facts of the case you are studying. In our sample problem, applying the tort law principle just discussed presents few difficulties. An employee of the store had mopped the floor in the aisle where Lawson slipped and fell, but no sign was present indicating that the floor was wet. That a customer might fall on a wet floor is clearly a foreseeable risk. Therefore, the failure to warn customers about the wet floor was a breach of the duty of care owed by the business owner to the store's customers.
4. Once you have completed step 3 in the IRAC method, you should be ready to draw your **conclusion.** In our sample case, Quality Market is liable to Lawson for her injuries, because the market's breach of its duty of care caused Lawson's injuries.

The fact patterns in the case problems presented in this text are not always as simple as those presented in our sample problem. Often, for example, there may be more than one plaintiff or defendant. There also may be more than one issue involved in a case and more than one applicable rule of law. Furthermore, in some case problems the facts may indicate that the general rule of law should not apply. For example, suppose a store employee advised Lawson not to walk on the floor in the aisle because it was wet, but Lawson decided to walk on it anyway. This fact could alter the outcome of the case because the store could then raise the defense of assumption of risk (see Chapter 4). Nonetheless, a careful review of the chapter should always provide you with the knowledge you need to analyze the problem thoroughly and arrive at accurate conclusions.

APPENDIX B

THE CONSTITUTION OF THE UNITED STATES

PREAMBLE

We the People of the United States, in Order to form a more perfect Union, establish Justice, insure domestic Tranquility, provide for the common defence, promote the general Welfare, and secure the Blessings of Liberty to ourselves and our Posterity, do ordain and establish this Constitution for the United States of America.

ARTICLE I

Section 1. All legislative Powers herein granted shall be vested in a Congress of the United States, which shall consist of a Senate and House of Representatives.

Section 2. The House of Representatives shall be composed of Members chosen every second Year by the People of the several States, and the Electors in each State shall have the Qualifications requisite for Electors of the most numerous Branch of the State Legislature.

No Person shall be a Representative who shall not have attained to the Age of twenty five Years, and been seven Years a Citizen of the United States, and who shall not, when elected, be an Inhabitant of that State in which he shall be chosen.

Representatives and direct Taxes shall be apportioned among the several States which may be included within this Union, according to their respective Numbers, which shall be determined by adding to the whole Number of free Persons, including those bound to Service for a Term of Years, and excluding Indians not taxed, three fifths of all other Persons. The actual Enumeration shall be made within three Years after the first Meeting of the Congress of the United States, and within every subsequent Term of ten Years, in such Manner as they shall by Law direct. The Number of Representatives shall not exceed one for every thirty Thousand, but each State shall have at Least one Representative; and until such enumeration shall be made, the State of New Hampshire shall be entitled to chuse three, Massachusetts eight, Rhode Island and Providence Plantations one, Connecticut five, New York six, New Jersey four, Pennsylvania eight, Delaware one, Maryland six, Virginia ten, North Carolina five, South Carolina five, and Georgia three.

When vacancies happen in the Representation from any State, the Executive Authority thereof shall issue Writs of Election to fill such Vacancies.

The House of Representatives shall chuse their Speaker and other Officers; and shall have the sole Power of Impeachment.

Section 3. The Senate of the United States shall be composed of two Senators from each State, chosen by the Legislature thereof, for six Years; and each Senator shall have one Vote.

Immediately after they shall be assembled in Consequence of the first Election, they shall be divided as equally as may be into three Classes. The Seats of the Senators of the first Class shall be vacated at the Expiration of the second Year, of the second Class at the Expiration of the fourth Year, and of the third Class at the Expiration of the sixth Year, so that one third may be chosen every second Year; and if Vacancies happen by Resignation, or otherwise, during the Recess of the Legislature of any State, the Executive thereof may make temporary Appointments until the next Meeting of the Legislature, which shall then fill such Vacancies.

No Person shall be a Senator who shall not have attained to the Age of thirty Years, and been nine Years a Citizen of the United States, and who shall not, when elected, be an Inhabitant of that State for which he shall be chosen.

The Vice President of the United States shall be President of the Senate, but shall have no Vote, unless they be equally divided.

The Senate shall chuse their other Officers, and also a President pro tempore, in the Absence of the Vice President, or when he shall exercise the Office of President of the United States.

The Senate shall have the sole Power to try all Impeachments. When sitting for that Purpose, they shall be on Oath or Affirmation. When the President of the United States is tried, the Chief Justice shall preside: And no Person shall be convicted without the Concurrence of two thirds of the Members present.

Judgment in Cases of Impeachment shall not extend further than to removal from Office, and disqualification to hold and enjoy any Office of honor, Trust, or Profit under the United States: but the Party convicted shall nevertheless be liable and subject to Indictment, Trial, Judgment, and Punishment, according to Law.

Section 4. The Times, Places and Manner of holding Elections for Senators and Representatives, shall be prescribed in each State by the Legislature thereof; but the Congress may at any time by Law make or alter such Regulations, except as to the Places of chusing Senators.

The Congress shall assemble at least once in every Year, and such Meeting shall be on the first Monday in December, unless they shall by Law appoint a different Day.

Section 5. Each House shall be the Judge of the Elections, Returns, and Qualifications of its own Members, and a Majority of each shall constitute a Quorum to do Business; but a smaller Number may adjourn from day to day, and may be authorized to compel the Attendance of absent Members, in such Manner, and under such Penalties as each House may provide.

Each House may determine the Rules of its Proceedings, punish its Members for disorderly Behavior, and, with the Concurrence of two thirds, expel a Member.

Each House shall keep a Journal of its Proceedings, and from time to time publish the same, excepting such Parts as may in their Judgment require Secrecy; and the Yeas and Nays of the Members of either House on any question shall, at the Desire of one fifth of those Present, be entered on the Journal.

Neither House, during the Session of Congress, shall, without the Consent of the other, adjourn for more than three days, nor to any other Place than that in which the two Houses shall be sitting.

Section 6. The Senators and Representatives shall receive a Compensation for their Services, to be ascertained by Law, and paid out of the Treasury of the United States. They shall in all Cases, except Treason, Felony and Breach of the Peace, be privileged from Arrest during their Attendance at the Session of their respective Houses, and in going to and returning from the same; and for any Speech or Debate in either House, they shall not be questioned in any other Place.

No Senator or Representative shall, during the Time for which he was elected, be appointed to any civil Office under the Authority of the United States, which shall have been created, or the Emoluments whereof shall have been increased during such time; and no Person holding any Office under the United States, shall be a Member of either House during his Continuance in Office.

Section 7. All Bills for raising Revenue shall originate in the House of Representatives; but the Senate may propose or concur with Amendments as on other Bills.

Every Bill which shall have passed the House of Representatives and the Senate, shall, before it become a Law, be presented to the President of the United States; If he approve he shall sign it, but if not he shall return it, with his Objections to the House in which it shall have originated, who shall enter the Objections at large on their Journal, and proceed to reconsider it. If after such Reconsideration two thirds of that House shall agree to pass the Bill, it shall be sent together with the Objections, to the other House, by which it shall likewise be reconsidered, and if approved by two thirds of that House, it shall become a Law. But in all such Cases the Votes of both Houses shall be determined by Yeas and Nays, and the Names of the Persons voting for and against the Bill shall be entered on the Journal of each House respectively. If any Bill shall not be returned by the President within ten Days (Sundays excepted) after it shall have been presented to him, the Same shall be a Law, in like Manner as if he had signed it, unless the Congress by their Adjournment prevent its Return in which Case it shall not be a Law.

Every Order, Resolution, or Vote, to which the Concurrence of the Senate and House of Representatives may be necessary (except on a question of Adjournment) shall be presented to the President of the United States; and before the Same shall take Effect, shall be approved by him, or being disapproved by him, shall be repassed by two thirds of the Senate and House of Representatives, according to the Rules and Limitations prescribed in the Case of a Bill.

Section 8. The Congress shall have Power To lay and collect Taxes, Duties, Imposts and Excises, to pay the Debts and provide for the common Defence and general Welfare of the United States; but all Duties, Imposts and Excises shall be uniform throughout the United States;

To borrow Money on the credit of the United States;

To regulate Commerce with foreign Nations, and among the several States, and with the Indian Tribes;

To establish an uniform Rule of Naturalization, and uniform Laws on the subject of Bankruptcies throughout the United States;

To coin Money, regulate the Value thereof, and of foreign Coin, and fix the Standard of Weights and Measures;

To provide for the Punishment of counterfeiting the Securities and current Coin of the United States;

To establish Post Offices and post Roads;

To promote the Progress of Science and useful Arts, by securing for limited Times to Authors and Inventors the exclusive Right to their respective Writings and Discoveries;

To constitute Tribunals inferior to the supreme Court;

To define and punish Piracies and Felonies committed on the high Seas, and Offenses against the Law of Nations;

To declare War, grant Letters of Marque and Reprisal, and make Rules concerning Captures on Land and Water;

To raise and support Armies, but no Appropriation of Money to that Use shall be for a longer Term than two Years;

To provide and maintain a Navy;

To make Rules for the Government and Regulation of the land and naval Forces;

To provide for calling forth the Militia to execute the Laws of the Union, suppress Insurrections and repel Invasions;

To provide for organizing, arming, and disciplining, the Militia, and for governing such Part of them as may be employed in the Service of the United States, reserving to the States respectively, the Appointment of the Officers, and the Authority of training the Militia according to the discipline prescribed by Congress;

To exercise exclusive Legislation in all Cases whatsoever, over such District (not exceeding ten Miles square) as may, by Cession of particular States, and the Acceptance of Congress, become the Seat of the Government of the United States, and to exercise like Authority over all Places purchased by the Consent of the Legislature of the State in which the Same shall be, for the Erection of Forts, Magazines, Arsenals, dock-Yards, and other needful Buildings;—And

To make all Laws which shall be necessary and proper for carrying into Execution the foregoing Powers, and all other Powers vested by this Constitution in the Government of the United States, or in any Department or Officer thereof.

Section 9. The Migration or Importation of such Persons as any of the States now existing shall think proper to admit, shall not be prohibited by the Congress prior to the Year one thousand eight hundred and eight, but a Tax or duty may be imposed on such Importation, not exceeding ten dollars for each Person.

The privilege of the Writ of Habeas Corpus shall not be suspended, unless when in Cases of Rebellion or Invasion the public Safety may require it.

No Bill of Attainder or ex post facto Law shall be passed.

No Capitation, or other direct, Tax shall be laid, unless in Proportion to the Census or Enumeration herein before directed to be taken.

No Tax or Duty shall be laid on Articles exported from any State.

No Preference shall be given by any Regulation of Commerce or Revenue to the Ports of one State over those of another: nor shall Vessels bound to, or from, one State be obliged to enter, clear, or pay Duties in another.

No Money shall be drawn from the Treasury, but in Consequence of Appropriations made by Law; and a regular Statement and Account of the Receipts and Expenditures of all public Money shall be published from time to time.

No Title of Nobility shall be granted by the United States: And no Person holding any Office of Profit or Trust under them, shall, without the Consent of the Congress, accept of any present, Emolument, Office, or Title, of any kind whatever, from any King, Prince, or foreign State.

Section 10. No State shall enter into any Treaty, Alliance, or Confederation; grant Letters of Marque and Reprisal; coin Money; emit Bills of Credit; make any Thing but gold and silver Coin a Tender in Payment of Debts; pass any Bill of Attainder, ex post facto Law, or Law impairing the Obligation of Contracts, or grant any Title of Nobility.

No State shall, without the Consent of the Congress, lay any Imposts or Duties on Imports or Exports, except what may be absolutely necessary for executing its inspection Laws: and the net Produce of all Duties and Imposts, laid by any State on Imports or Exports, shall be for the Use of the Treasury of the United States; and all such Laws shall be subject to the Revision and Controul of the Congress.

No State shall, without the Consent of Congress, lay any Duty of Tonnage, keep Troops, or Ships of War in time of Peace, enter into any Agreement or Compact with another State, or with a foreign Power, or engage in War, unless actually invaded, or in such imminent Danger as will not admit of delay.

Article II

Section 1. The executive Power shall be vested in a President of the United States of America. He shall hold his Office during the Term of four Years, and, together with the Vice President, chosen for the same Term, be elected, as follows:

Each State shall appoint, in such Manner as the Legislature thereof may direct, a Number of Electors, equal to the whole Number of Senators and Representatives to which the State may be entitled in the Congress; but no Senator or Representative, or Person holding an Office of Trust or Profit under the United States, shall be appointed an Elector.

The Electors shall meet in their respective States, and vote by Ballot for two Persons, of whom one at least shall not be an Inhabitant of the same State with themselves. And they shall make a List of all the Persons voted for, and of the Number of Votes for each; which List they shall sign and certify, and transmit sealed to the Seat of the Government of the United States, directed to the President of the Senate. The President of the Senate shall, in the Presence of the Senate and House of Representatives, open all the Certificates, and the Votes shall then be counted. The Person having the greatest Number of Votes shall be the President, if such Number be a Majority of the whole Number of Electors appointed; and if there be more than one who have such Majority, and have an equal Number of Votes, then the House of Representatives shall immediately chuse by Ballot one of them for President; and if no Person have a Majority, then from the five highest on the List the said House shall in like Manner chuse the President. But in chusing the President, the Votes shall be taken by States, the Representation from each State having one Vote; A quorum for this Purpose shall consist of a Member or Members from two thirds of the States, and a Majority of all the States shall be necessary to a Choice. In every Case, after the Choice of the President, the Person having the greater Number of Votes of the Electors shall be the Vice President. But if there should remain two or more who have equal Votes, the Senate shall chuse from them by Ballot the Vice President.

The Congress may determine the Time of chusing the Electors, and the Day on which they shall give their Votes; which Day shall be the same throughout the United States.

No person except a natural born Citizen, or a Citizen of the United States, at the time of the Adoption of this Constitution, shall be eligible to the Office of President; neither shall any Person be eligible to that Office who shall not have attained to the Age of thirty five Years, and been fourteen Years a Resident within the United States.

In Case of the Removal of the President from Office, or of his Death, Resignation or Inability to discharge the Powers and Duties of the said Office, the same shall devolve on the Vice President, and the Congress may by Law provide for the Case of Removal, Death, Resignation or Inability, both of the President and Vice President, declaring what Officer shall then act as President, and such Officer shall act accordingly, until the Disability be removed, or a President shall be elected.

The President shall, at stated Times, receive for his Services, a Compensation, which shall neither be increased nor diminished during the Period for which he shall have been elected, and he shall not receive within that Period any other Emolument from the United States, or any of them.

Before he enter on the Execution of his Office, he shall take the following Oath or Affirmation: "I do solemnly swear (or affirm) that I will faithfully execute the Office of President of the United States, and will to the best of my Ability, preserve, protect and defend the Constitution of the United States."

Section 2. The President shall be Commander in Chief of the Army and Navy of the United States, and of the Militia of the several States, when called into the actual Service of the United States; he may require the Opinion, in writing, of the principal Officer in each of the executive Departments, upon any Subject relating to the Duties of their respective Offices, and he shall have Power to grant Reprieves and Pardons for Offenses against the United States, except in Cases of Impeachment.

He shall have Power, by and with the Advice and Consent of the Senate to make Treaties, provided two thirds of the Senators present concur; and he shall nominate, and by and with the Advice and Consent of the Senate, shall appoint Ambassadors, other public Ministers and Consuls, Judges of the supreme Court, and all other Officers of the United States, whose Appointments are not herein otherwise provided for, and which shall be established by Law; but the Congress may by Law vest the Appointment of such inferior Officers, as they think proper, in the President alone, in the Courts of Law, or in the Heads of Departments.

The President shall have Power to fill up all Vacancies that may happen during the Recess of the Senate, by granting Commissions which shall expire at the End of their next Session.

Section 3. He shall from time to time give to the Congress Information of the State of the Union, and recommend to their Consideration such Measures as he shall judge necessary and expedient; he may, on extraordinary Occasions, convene both Houses, or either of them, and in Case of Disagreement between them, with Respect to the Time of Adjournment, he may adjourn them to such Time as he shall think proper; he shall receive Ambassadors and other public Ministers; he shall take Care that the Laws be faithfully executed, and shall Commission all the Officers of the United States.

Section 4. The President, Vice President and all civil Officers of the United States, shall be removed from Office on Impeachment for, and Conviction of, Treason, Bribery, or other high Crimes and Misdemeanors.

Article III

Section 1. The judicial Power of the United States, shall be vested in one supreme Court, and in such inferior Courts as the Congress may from time to time ordain and establish. The Judges, both of the supreme and inferior Courts, shall hold their Offices during good Behaviour, and shall, at stated Times, receive for their Services a Compensation, which shall not be diminished during their Continuance in Office.

Section 2. The judicial Power shall extend to all Cases, in Law and Equity, arising under this Constitution, the Laws of the United States, and Treaties made, or which shall be made, under their Authority;—to all Cases affecting Ambassadors, other public Ministers and Consuls;—to all Cases of admiralty and maritime Jurisdiction;—to Controversies to which the United States shall be a Party;—to Controversies between two or more States;—between a State and Citizens of another State;—between Citizens of different States;—between Citizens of the same State claiming Lands under Grants of different States, and between a State, or the Citizens thereof, and foreign States, Citizens or Subjects.

In all Cases affecting Ambassadors, other public Ministers and Consuls, and those in which a State shall be a Party, the supreme Court shall have original Jurisdiction. In all the other Cases before mentioned, the supreme Court shall have appellate Jurisdiction, both as to Law and Fact, with such Exceptions, and under such Regulations as the Congress shall make.

The Trial of all Crimes, except in Cases of Impeachment, shall be by Jury; and such Trial shall be held in the State where the said Crimes shall have been committed; but when not committed within any State, the Trial shall be at such Place or Places as the Congress may by Law have directed.

Section 3. Treason against the United States, shall consist only in levying War against them, or, in adhering to their Enemies, giving them Aid and Comfort. No Person shall be convicted of Treason unless on the Testimony of two Witnesses to the same overt Act, or on Confession in open Court.

The Congress shall have Power to declare the Punishment of Treason, but no Attainder of Treason shall work Corruption of Blood, or Forfeiture except during the Life of the Person attainted.

Article IV

Section 1. Full Faith and Credit shall be given in each State to the public Acts, Records, and judicial Proceedings of every other State. And the Congress may by general Laws prescribe the Manner in which such Acts, Records and Proceedings shall be proved, and the Effect thereof.

Section 2. The Citizens of each State shall be entitled to all Privileges and Immunities of Citizens in the several States.

A Person charged in any State with Treason, Felony, or other Crime, who shall flee from Justice, and be found in another State, shall on Demand of the executive Authority of the State from which he fled, be delivered up, to be removed to the State having Jurisdiction of the Crime.

No Person held to Service or Labour in one State, under the Laws thereof, escaping into another, shall, in Consequence of any Law or Regulation therein, be discharged from such Service or Labour, but shall be delivered up on Claim of the Party to whom such Service or Labour may be due.

Section 3. New States may be admitted by the Congress into this Union; but no new State shall be formed or erected within the

Jurisdiction of any other State; nor any State be formed by the Junction of two or more States, or Parts of States, without the Consent of the Legislatures of the States concerned as well as of the Congress.

The Congress shall have Power to dispose of and make all needful Rules and Regulations respecting the Territory or other Property belonging to the United States; and nothing in this Constitution shall be so construed as to Prejudice any Claims of the United States, or of any particular State.

Section 4. The United States shall guarantee to every State in this Union a Republican Form of Government, and shall protect each of them against Invasion; and on Application of the Legislature, or of the Executive (when the Legislature cannot be convened) against domestic Violence.

Article V

The Congress, whenever two thirds of both Houses shall deem it necessary, shall propose Amendments to this Constitution, or, on the Application of the Legislatures of two thirds of the several States, shall call a Convention for proposing Amendments, which, in either Case, shall be valid to all Intents and Purposes, as part of this Constitution, when ratified by the Legislatures of three fourths of the several States, or by Conventions in three fourths thereof, as the one or the other Mode of Ratification may be proposed by the Congress; Provided that no Amendment which may be made prior to the Year One thousand eight hundred and eight shall in any Manner affect the first and fourth Clauses in the Ninth Section of the first Article; and that no State, without its Consent, shall be deprived of its equal Suffrage in the Senate.

Article VI

All Debts contracted and Engagements entered into, before the Adoption of this Constitution shall be as valid against the United States under this Constitution, as under the Confederation.

This Constitution, and the Laws of the United States which shall be made in Pursuance thereof; and all Treaties made, or which shall be made, under the Authority of the United States, shall be the supreme Law of the Land; and the Judges in every State shall be bound thereby, any Thing in the Constitution or Laws of any State to the Contrary notwithstanding.

The Senators and Representatives before mentioned, and the Members of the several State Legislatures, and all executive and judicial Officers, both of the United States and of the several States, shall be bound by Oath or Affirmation, to support this Constitution; but no religious Test shall ever be required as a Qualification to any Office or public Trust under the United States.

Article VII

The Ratification of the Conventions of nine States shall be sufficient for the Establishment of this Constitution between the States so ratifying the Same.

Amendment I [1791]

Congress shall make no law respecting an establishment of religion, or prohibiting the free exercise thereof; or abridging the freedom of speech, or of the press; or the right of the people peaceably to assembly, and to petition the Government for a redress of grievances.

Amendment II [1791]

A well regulated Militia, being necessary to the security of a free State, the right of the people to keep and bear Arms, shall not be infringed.

Amendment III [1791]

No Soldier shall, in time of peace be quartered in any house, without the consent of the Owner, nor in time of war, but in a manner to be prescribed by law.

Amendment IV [1791]

The right of the people to be secure in their persons, houses, papers, and effects, against unreasonable searches and seizures, shall not be violated, and no Warrants shall issue, but upon probable cause, supported by Oath or affirmation, and particularly describing the place to be searched, and the persons or things to be seized.

Amendment V [1791]

No person shall be held to answer for a capital, or otherwise infamous crime, unless on a presentment or indictment of a Grand Jury, except in cases arising in the land or naval forces, or in the Militia, when in actual service in time of War or public danger; nor shall any person be subject for the same offence to be twice put in jeopardy of life or limb; nor shall be compelled in any criminal case to be a witness against himself, nor be deprived of life, liberty, or property, without due process of law; nor shall private property be taken for public use, without just compensation.

Amendment VI [1791]

In all criminal prosecutions, the accused shall enjoy the right to a speedy and public trial, by an impartial jury of the State and district wherein the crime shall have been committed, which district shall have been previously ascertained by law, and to be informed of the nature and cause of the accusation; to be confronted with the witnesses against him; to have compulsory process for obtaining witnesses in his favor, and to have the Assistance of Counsel for his defence.

Amendment VII [1791]

In Suits at common law, where the value in controversy shall exceed twenty dollars, the right of trial by jury shall be preserved, and no fact tried by jury, shall be otherwise re-examined in any Court of the United States, than according to the rules of the common law.

Amendment VIII [1791]

Excessive bail shall not be required, nor excessive fines imposed, nor cruel and unusual punishments inflicted.

Amendment IX [1791]

The enumeration in the Constitution, of certain rights, shall not be construed to deny or disparage others retained by the people.

Amendment X [1791]

The powers not delegated to the United States by the Constitution, nor prohibited by it to the States, are reserved to the States respectively, or to the people.

Amendment XI [1798]

The Judicial power of the United States shall not be construed to extend to any suit in law or equity, commenced or prosecuted against one of the United States by Citizens of another State, or by Citizens or Subjects of any Foreign State.

Amendment XII [1804]

The Electors shall meet in their respective states, and vote by ballot for President and Vice-President, one of whom, at least, shall not be an inhabitant of the same state with themselves; they shall name in their ballots the person voted for as President, and in distinct ballots the person voted for as Vice-President, and they shall make distinct lists of all persons voted for as President, and of all persons voted for as Vice-President, and of the number of votes for each, which lists they shall sign and certify, and transmit sealed to the seat of the government of the United States, directed to the President of the Senate;—The President of the Senate shall, in the presence of the Senate and House of Representatives, open all the certificates and the votes shall then be counted;—The person having the greatest number of votes for President, shall be the President, if such number be a majority of the whole number of Electors appointed; and if no person have such majority, then from the persons having the highest numbers not exceeding three on the list of those voted for as President, the House of Representatives shall choose immediately, by ballot, the President. But in choosing the President, the votes shall be taken by states, the representation from each state having one vote; a quorum for this purpose shall consist of a member or members from two-thirds of the states, and a majority of all states shall be necessary to a choice. And if the House of Representatives shall not choose a President whenever the right of choice shall devolve upon them, before the fourth day of March next following, then the Vice-President shall act as President, as in the case of the death or other constitutional disability of the President.—The person having the greatest number of votes as Vice-President, shall be the Vice-President, if such number be a majority of the whole number of Electors appointed, and if no person have a majority, then from the two highest numbers on the list, the Senate shall choose the Vice-President; a quorum for the purpose shall consist of two-thirds of the whole number of Senators, and a majority of the whole number shall be necessary to a choice. But no person constitutionally ineligible to the office of President shall be eligible to that of Vice-President of the United States.

Amendment XIII [1865]

Section 1. Neither slavery nor involuntary servitude, except as a punishment for crime whereof the party shall have been duly convicted, shall exist within the United States, or any place subject to their jurisdiction.

Section 2. Congress shall have power to enforce this article by appropriate legislation.

Amendment XIV [1868]

Section 1. All persons born or naturalized in the United States, and subject to the jurisdiction thereof, are citizens of the United States and of the State wherein they reside. No State shall make or enforce any law which shall abridge the privileges or immunities of citizens of the United States; nor shall any State deprive any person of life, liberty, or property, without due process of law; nor deny to any person within its jurisdiction the equal protection of the laws.

Section 2. Representatives shall be apportioned among the several States according to their respective numbers, counting the whole number of persons in each State, excluding Indians not taxed. But when the right to vote at any election for the choice of electors for President and Vice President of the United States, Representatives in Congress, the Executive and Judicial officers of a State, or the members of the Legislature thereof, is denied to any of the male inhabitants of such State, being twenty-one years of age, and citizens of the United States, or in any way abridged, except for participation in rebellion, or other crime, the basis of representation therein shall be reduced in the proportion which the number of such male citizens shall bear to the whole number of male citizens twenty-one years of age in such State.

Section 3. No person shall be a Senator or Representative in Congress, or elector of President and Vice President, or hold any office, civil or military, under the United States, or under any State, who having previously taken an oath, as a member of Congress, or as an officer of the United States, or as a member of any State legislature, or as an executive or judicial officer of any State, to support the Constitution of the United States, shall have engaged in insurrection or rebellion against the same, or given aid or comfort to the enemies thereof. But Congress may by a vote of two-thirds of each House, remove such disability.

Section 4. The validity of the public debt of the United States, authorized by law, including debts incurred for payment of pensions and bounties for services in suppressing insurrection or rebellion, shall not be questioned. But neither the United States nor any State shall assume or pay any debt or obligation incurred in aid of insurrection or rebellion against the United States, or any claim for the loss or emancipation of any slave; but all such debts, obligations and claims shall be held illegal and void.

Section 5. The Congress shall have power to enforce, by appropriate legislation, the provisions of this article.

Amendment XV [1870]

Section 1. The right of citizens of the United States to vote shall not be denied or abridged by the United States or by any State on account of race, color, or previous condition of servitude.

Section 2. The Congress shall have power to enforce this article by appropriate legislation.

Amendment XVI [1913]

The Congress shall have power to lay and collect taxes on incomes, from whatever source derived, without apportionment among the several States, and without regard to any census or enumeration.

Amendment XVII [1913]

Section 1. The Senate of the United States shall be composed of two Senators from each State, elected by the people thereof, for six years; and each Senator shall have one vote. The electors in each State shall have the qualifications requisite for electors of the most numerous branch of the State legislatures.

Section 2. When vacancies happen in the representation of any State in the Senate, the executive authority of such State shall issue writs of election to fill such vacancies: *Provided*, That the legislature of any State may empower the executive thereof to make temporary appointments until the people fill the vacancies by election as the legislature may direct.

Section 3. This amendment shall not be so construed as to affect the election or term of any Senator chosen before it becomes valid as part of the Constitution.

Amendment XVIII [1919]

Section 1. After one year from the ratification of this article the manufacture, sale, or transportation of intoxicating liquors within, the importation thereof into, or the exportation thereof from the United States and all territory subject to the jurisdiction thereof for beverage purposes is hereby prohibited.

Section 2. The Congress and the several States shall have concurrent power to enforce this article by appropriate legislation.

Section 3. This article shall be inoperative unless it shall have been ratified as an amendment to the Constitution by the legislatures of the several States, as provided in the Constitution, within seven years from the date of the submission hereof to the States by the Congress.

Amendment XIX [1920]

Section 1. The right of citizens of the United States to vote shall not be denied or abridged by the United States or by any State on account of sex.

Section 2. Congress shall have power to enforce this article by appropriate legislation.

Amendment XX [1933]

Section 1. The terms of the President and Vice President shall end at noon on the 20th day of January, and the terms of Senators and Representatives at noon on the 3d day of January, of the years in which such terms would have ended if this article had not been ratified; and the terms of their successors shall then begin.

Section 2. The Congress shall assemble at least once in every year, and such meeting shall begin at noon on the 3d day of January, unless they shall by law appoint a different day.

Section 3. If, at the time fixed for the beginning of the term of the President, the President elect shall have died, the Vice President elect shall become President. If the President shall not have been chosen before the time fixed for the beginning of his term, or if the President elect shall have failed to qualify, then the Vice President elect shall act as President until a President shall have qualified; and the Congress may by law provide for the case wherein neither a President elect nor a Vice President elect shall have qualified, declaring who shall then act as President, or the manner in which one who is to act shall be selected, and such person shall act accordingly until a President or Vice President shall have qualified.

Section 4. The Congress may by law provide for the case of the death of any of the persons from whom the House of Representatives may choose a President whenever the right of choice shall have devolved upon them, and for the case of the death of any of the persons from whom the Senate may choose a Vice President whenever the right of choice shall have devolved upon them.

Section 5. Sections 1 and 2 shall take effect on the 15th day of October following the ratification of this article.

Section 6. This article shall be inoperative unless it shall have been ratified as an amendment to the Constitution by the legislatures of three-fourths of the several States within seven years from the date of its submission.

Amendment XXI [1933]

Section 1. The eighteenth article of amendment to the Constitution of the United States is hereby repealed.

Section 2. The transportation or importation into any State, Territory, or possession of the United States for delivery or use therein of intoxicating liquors, in violation of the laws thereof, is hereby prohibited.

Section 3. This article shall be inoperative unless it shall have been ratified as an amendment to the Constitution by conventions in the several States, as provided in the Constitution, within seven years from the date of the submission hereof to the States by the Congress.

Amendment XXII [1951]

Section 1. No person shall be elected to the office of the President more than twice, and no person who has held the office of President, or acted as President, for more than two years of a term to which some other person was elected President shall be elected to the office of President more than once. But this Article shall not apply to any person holding the office of President when this Article was proposed by the Congress, and shall not prevent any person who may be holding the office of President, or acting as President, during the term within which this Article becomes operative from holding the office of President or acting as President during the remainder of such term.

Section 2. This article shall be inoperative unless it shall have been ratified as an amendment to the Constitution by the legislatures of three-fourths of the several States within seven years from the date of its submission to the States by the Congress.

Amendment XXIII [1961]

Section 1. The District constituting the seat of Government of the United States shall appoint in such manner as the Congress may direct:

A number of electors of President and Vice President equal to the whole number of Senators and Representatives in Congress to which the District would be entitled if it were a State, but in no event more than the least populous state; they shall be in addition to those appointed by the states, but they shall be considered, for the purposes of the election of President and Vice President, to be electors appointed by a state; and they shall meet in the District and perform such duties as provided by the twelfth article of amendment.

Section 2. The Congress shall have power to enforce this article by appropriate legislation.

Amendment XXIV [1964]

Section 1. The right of citizens of the United States to vote in any primary or other election for President or Vice President, for electors for President or Vice President, or for Senator or Representative in Congress, shall not be denied or abridged by the United States, or any State by reason of failure to pay any poll tax or other tax.

Section 2. The Congress shall have power to enforce this article by appropriate legislation.

Amendment XXV [1967]

Section 1. In case of the removal of the President from office or of his death or resignation, the Vice President shall become President.

Section 2. Whenever there is a vacancy in the office of the Vice President, the President shall nominate a Vice President who shall take office upon confirmation by a majority vote of both Houses of Congress.

Section 3. Whenever the President transmits to the President pro tempore of the Senate and the Speaker of the House of Representatives his written declaration that he is unable to discharge the powers and duties of his office, and until he transmits to them a written declaration to the contrary, such powers and duties shall be discharged by the Vice President as Acting President.

Section 4. Whenever the Vice President and a majority of either the principal officers of the executive departments or of such other body as Congress may by law provide, transmit to the President pro tempore of the Senate and the Speaker of the House of Representatives their written declaration that the President is unable to discharge the powers and duties of his office, the Vice President shall immediately assume the powers and duties of the office as Acting President.

Thereafter, when the President transmits to the President pro tempore of the Senate and the Speaker of the House of Representatives his written declaration that no inability exists, he shall resume the powers and duties of his office unless the Vice President and a majority of either the principal officers of the executive department or of such other body as Congress may by law provide, transmit within four days to the President pro tempore of the Senate and the Speaker of the House of Representatives their written declaration that the President is unable to discharge the powers and duties of his office. Thereupon Congress shall decide the issue, assembling within forty-eight hours for that purpose if not in session. If the Congress, within twenty-one days after receipt of the latter written declaration, or, if Congress is not in session, within twenty-one days after Congress is required to assemble, determines by two-thirds vote of both Houses that the President is unable to discharge the powers and duties of his office, the Vice President shall continue to discharge the same as Acting President; otherwise, the President shall resume the powers and duties of his office.

Amendment XXVI [1971]

Section 1. The right of citizens of the United States, who are eighteen years of age or older, to vote shall not be denied or abridged by the United States or by any State on account of age.

Section 2. The Congress shall have power to enforce this article by appropriate legislation.

Amendment XXVII [1992]

No law, varying the compensation for the services of the Senators and Representatives, shall take effect, until an election of Representatives shall have intervened.

APPENDIX C

THE UNIFORM COMMERCIAL CODE

(Adopted in fifty-two jurisdictions; all fifty States, although Louisiana has adopted only Articles 1, 3, 4, 7, 8, and 9; the District of Columbia; and the Virgin Islands.)

The Code consists of the following articles:

Art.

1. General Provisions
2. Sales

2A. Leases

3. Commercial Paper
4. Bank Deposits and Collections

4A. Funds Transfers

5. Letters of Credit
6. Bulk Transfers (including Alternative B)
7. Warehouse Receipts, Bills of Lading and Other Documents of Title
8. Investment Securities
9. Secured Transactions: Sales of Accounts and Chattel Paper
10. Effective Date and Repealer
11. Effective Date and Transition Provisions

Article 1
GENERAL PROVISIONS

Part 1 Short Title, Construction, Application and Subject Matter of the Act

§ 1—101. Short Title.

This Act shall be known and may be cited as Uniform Commercial Code.

§ 1—102. Purposes; Rules of Construction; Variation by Agreement.

(1) This Act shall be liberally construed and applied to promote its underlying purposes and policies.

(2) Underlying purposes and policies of this Act are

(a) to simplify, clarify and modernize the law governing commercial transactions;

(b) to permit the continued expansion of commercial practices through custom, usage and agreement of the parties;

(c) to make uniform the law among the various jurisdictions.

(3) The effect of provisions of this Act may be varied by agreement, except as otherwise provided in this Act and except that the obligations of good faith, diligence, reasonableness and care prescribed by this Act may not be disclaimed by agreement but the parties may by agreement determine the standards by which the performance of such obligations is to be measured if such standards are not manifestly unreasonable.

(4) The presence in certain provisions of this Act of the words "unless otherwise agreed" or words of similar import does not imply that the effect of other provisions may not be varied by agreement under subsection (3).

(5) In this Act unless the context otherwise requires

(a) words in the singular number include the plural, and in the plural include the singular;

(b) words of the masculine gender include the feminine and the neuter, and when the sense so indicates words of the neuter gender may refer to any gender.

§ 1—103. Supplementary General Principles of Law Applicable.

Unless displaced by the particular provisions of this Act, the principles of law and equity, including the law merchant and the law relative to capacity to contract, principal and agent, estoppel, fraud, misrepresentation, duress, coercion, mistake, bankruptcy, or other validating or invalidating cause shall supplement its provisions.

§ 1—104. Construction Against Implicit Repeal.

This Act being a general act intended as a unified coverage of its subject matter, no part of it shall be deemed to be impliedly repealed by subsequent legislation if such construction can reasonably be avoided.

§ 1—105. Territorial Application of the Act; Parties' Power to Choose Applicable Law.

(1) Except as provided hereafter in this section, when a transaction bears a reasonable relation to this state and also to another state or nation the parties may agree that the law either of this state or of such other state or nation shall govern their rights and duties. Failing such agreement this Act applies to transactions bearing an appropriate relation to this state.

(2) Where one of the following provisions of this Act specifies the applicable law, that provision governs and a contrary agreement is effective only to the extent permitted by the law (including the conflict of laws rules) so specified:

Rights of creditors against sold goods. Section 2—402.

Applicability of the Article on Leases. Sections 2A—105 and 2A—106.

Applicability of the Article on Bank Deposits and Collections. Section 4—102.

Governing law in the Article on Funds Transfers. Section 4A—507.

Letters of Credit, Section 5—116.

Bulk sales subject to the Article on Bulk Sales. Section 6—103.

Applicability of the Article on Investment Securities. Section 8—106.

Perfection provisions of the Article on Secured Transactions. Section 9—103.

§ 1—106. Remedies to Be Liberally Administered.

(1) The remedies provided by this Act shall be liberally administered to the end that the aggrieved party may be put in as good a position as if the other party had fully performed but neither consequential or special nor penal damages may be had except as specifically provided in this Act or by other rule of law.

(2) Any right or obligation declared by this Act is enforceable by action unless the provision declaring it specifies a different and limited effect.

§ 1—107. Waiver or Renunciation of Claim or Right After Breach.

Any claim or right arising out of an alleged breach can be discharged in whole or in part without consideration by a written waiver or renunciation signed and delivered by the aggrieved party.

§ 1—108. Severability.

If any provision or clause of this Act or application thereof to any person or circumstances is held invalid, such invalidity shall not affect other provisions or applications of the Act which can be given effect without the invalid provision or application, and to this end the provisions of this Act are declared to be severable.

§ 1—109. Section Captions.

Section captions are parts of this Act.

Part 2 General Definitions and Principles of Interpretation

§ 1—201. General Definitions.

Subject to additional definitions contained in the subsequent Articles of this Act which are applicable to specific Articles or Parts thereof, and unless the context otherwise requires, in this Act:

(1) "Action" in the sense of a judicial proceeding includes recoupment, counterclaim, set-off, suit in equity and any other proceedings in which rights are determined.

(2) "Aggrieved party" means a party entitled to resort to a remedy.

(3) "Agreement" means the bargain of the parties in fact as found in their language or by implication from other circumstances including course of dealing or usage of trade or course of performance as provided in this Act (Sections 1—205 and 2—208). Whether an agreement has legal consequences is determined by the provisions of this Act, if applicable; otherwise by the law of contracts (Section 1—103). (Compare "Contract".)

(4) "Bank" means any person engaged in the business of banking.

(5) "Bearer" means the person in possession of an instrument, document of title, or certificated security payable to bearer or indorsed in blank.

(6) "Bill of lading" means a document evidencing the receipt of goods for shipment issued by a person engaged in the business of transporting or forwarding goods, and includes an airbill. "Airbill" means a document serving for air transportation as a bill of lading does for marine or rail transportation, and includes an air consignment note or air waybill.

(7) "Branch" includes a separately incorporated foreign branch of a bank.

(8) "Burden of establishing" a fact means the burden of persuading the triers of fact that the existence of the fact is more probable than its non-existence.

(9) "Buyer in ordinary course of business" means a person who in good faith and without knowledge that the sale to him is in violation of the ownership rights or security interest of a third party in the goods buys in ordinary course from a person in the business of selling goods of that kind but does not include a pawnbroker. All persons who sell minerals or the like (including oil and gas) at wellhead or minehead shall be deemed to be persons in the business of selling goods of that kind. "Buying" may be for cash or by exchange of other property or on secured or unsecured credit and includes receiving goods or documents of title under a pre-existing contract for sale but does not include a transfer in bulk or as security for or in total or partial satisfaction of a money debt.

(10) "Conspicuous": A term or clause is conspicuous when it is so written that a reasonable person against whom it is to operate ought to have noticed it. A printed heading in capitals (as: NON-NEGOTIABLE BILL OF LADING) is conspicuous. Language in the body of a form is "conspicuous" if it is in larger or other contrasting type or color. But in a telegram any stated term is "conspicuous". Whether a term or clause is "conspicuous" or not is for decision by the court.

(11) "Contract" means the total legal obligation which results from the parties' agreement as affected by this Act and any other applicable rules of law. (Compare "Agreement".)

(12) "Creditor" includes a general creditor, a secured creditor, a lien creditor and any representative of creditors, including an assignee for the benefit of creditors, a trustee in bankruptcy, a receiver in equity and an executor or administrator of an insolvent debtor's or assignor's estate.

(13) "Defendant" includes a person in the position of defendant in a cross-action or counterclaim.

(14) "Delivery" with respect to instruments, documents of title, chattel paper, or certificated securities means voluntary transfer of possession.

(15) "Document of title" includes bill of lading, dock warrant, dock receipt, warehouse receipt or order for the delivery of goods, and also any other document which in the regular course of business or financing is treated as adequately evidencing that the person in possession of it is entitled to receive, hold and dispose of the document and the goods it covers. To be a document of title a document must purport to be issued by or addressed to a bailee and purport to cover goods in the bailee's possession which are either identified or are fungible portions of an identified mass.

(16) "Fault" means wrongful act, omission or breach.

(17) "Fungible" with respect to goods or securities means goods or securities of which any unit is, by nature or usage of trade, the equivalent of any other like unit. Goods which are not fungible shall be deemed fungible for the purposes of this Act to the extent that under a particular agreement or document unlike units are treated as equivalents.

(18) "Genuine" means free of forgery or counterfeiting.

(19) "Good faith" means honesty in fact in the conduct or transaction concerned.

(20) "Holder" with respect to a negotiable instrument, means the person in possession if the instrument is payable to bearer or, in the cases of an instrument payable to an identified person, if the identified person is in possession. "Holder" with respect to a document of title means the person in possession if the goods are deliverable to bearer or to the order of the person in possession.

(21) To "honor" is to pay or to accept and pay, or where a credit so engages to purchase or discount a draft complying with the terms of the credit.

(22) "Insolvency proceedings" includes any assignment for the benefit of creditors or other proceedings intended to liquidate or rehabilitate the estate of the person involved.

(23) A person is "insolvent" who either has ceased to pay his debts in the ordinary course of business or cannot pay his debts as they become due or is insolvent within the meaning of the federal bankruptcy law.

(24) "Money" means a medium of exchange authorized or adopted by a domestic or foreign government and includes a monetary unit of account established by an intergovernmental organization or by agreement between two or more nations.

(25) A person has "notice" of a fact when

(a) he has actual knowledge of it; or

(b) he has received a notice or notification of it; or

(c) from all the facts and circumstances known to him at the time in question he has reason to know that it exists.

A person "knows" or has "knowledge" of a fact when he has actual knowledge of it. "Discover" or "learn" or a word or phrase of similar import refers to knowledge rather than to reason to know. The time and circumstances under which a notice or notification may cease to be effective are not determined by this Act.

(26) A person "notifies" or "gives" a notice or notification to another by taking such steps as may be reasonably required to inform the other in ordinary course whether or not such other actually comes to know of it. A person "receives" a notice or notification when

(a) it comes to his attention; or

(b) it is duly delivered at the place of business through which the contract was made or at any other place held out by him as the place for receipt of such communications.

(27) Notice, knowledge or a notice or notification received by an organization is effective for a particular transaction from the time when it is brought to the attention of the individual conducting that transaction, and in any event from the time when it would have been brought to his attention if the organization had exercised due diligence. An organization exercises due diligence if it maintains reasonable routines for communicating significant information to the person conducting the transaction and there is reasonable compliance with the routines. Due diligence does not require an individual acting for the organization to communicate information unless such communication is part of his regular duties or unless he has reason to know of the transaction

and that the transaction would be materially affected by the information.

(28) "Organization" includes a corporation, government or governmental subdivision or agency, business trust, estate, trust, partnership or association, two or more persons having a joint or common interest, or any other legal or commercial entity.

(29) "Party", as distinct from "third party", means a person who has engaged in a transaction or made an agreement within this Act.

(30) "Person" includes an individual or an organization (See Section 1—102).

(31) "Presumption" or "presumed" means that the trier of fact must find the existence of the fact presumed unless and until evidence is introduced which would support a finding of its non-existence.

(32) "Purchase" includes taking by sale, discount, negotiation, mortgage, pledge, lien, issue or re-issue, gift or any other voluntary transaction creating an interest in property.

(33) "Purchaser" means a person who takes by purchase.

(34) "Remedy" means any remedial right to which an aggrieved party is entitled with or without resort to a tribunal.

(35) "Representative" includes an agent, an officer of a corporation or association, and a trustee, executor or administrator of an estate, or any other person empowered to act for another.

(36) "Rights" includes remedies.

(37) "Security interest" means an interest in personal property or fixtures which secures payment or performance of an obligation. The retention or reservation of title by a seller of goods notwithstanding shipment or delivery to the buyer (Section 2—401) is limited in effect to a reservation of a "security interest". The term also includes any interest of a buyer of accounts or chattel paper which is subject to Article 9. The special property interest of a buyer of goods on identification of those goods to a contract for sale under Section 2—401 is not a "security interest", but a buyer may also acquire a "security interest" by complying with Article 9. Unless a consignment is intended as security, reservation of title thereunder is not a "security interest," but a consignment is in any event subject to the provisions on consignment sales (Section 2—326).

Whether a transaction creates a lease or security interest is determined by the facts of each case; however, a transaction creates a security interest if the consideration the lessee is to pay the lessor for the right to possession and use of the goods is an obligation for the term of the lease not subject to termination by the lessee, and

(a) the original term of the lease is equal to or greater than the remaining economic life of the goods,

(b) the lessee is bound to renew the lease for the remaining economic life of the goods or is bound to become the owner of the goods,

(c) the lessee has an option to renew the lease for the remaining economic life of the goods for no additional consideration or nominal additional consideration upon compliance with the lease agreement, or

(d) the lessee has an option to become the owner of the goods for no additional consideration or nominal additional consideration upon compliance with the lease agreement.

A transaction does not create a security interest merely because it provides that

(a) the present value of the consideration the lessee is obligated to pay the lessor for the right to possession and use of the goods is substantially equal to or is greater than the fair market value of the goods at the time the lease is entered into,

(b) the lessee assumes risk of loss of the goods, or agrees to pay taxes, insurance, filing, recording, or registration fees, or service or maintenance costs with respect to the goods,

(c) the lessee has an option to renew the lease or to become the owner of the goods,

(d) the lessee has an option to renew the lease for a fixed rent that is equal to or greater than the reasonably predictable fair market rent for the use of the goods for the term of the renewal at the time the option is to be performed, or

(e) the lessee has an option to become the owner of the goods for a fixed price that is equal to or greater than the reasonably predictable fair market value of the goods at the time the option is to be performed.

For purposes of this subsection (37):

(x) Additional consideration is not nominal if (i) when the option to renew the lease is granted to the lessee the rent is stated to be the fair market rent for the use of the goods for the term of the renewal determined at the time the option is to be performed, or (ii) when the option to become the owner of the goods is granted to the lessee the price is stated to be the fair market value of the goods determined at the time the option is to be performed. Additional consideration is nominal if it is less than the lessee's reasonably predictable cost of performing under the lease agreement if the option is not exercised;

(y) "Reasonably predictable" and "remaining economic life of the goods" are to be determined with reference to the facts and circumstances at the time the transaction is entered into; and

(z) "Present value" means the amount as of a date certain of one or more sums payable in the future, discounted to the date certain. The discount is determined by the interest rate specified by the parties if the rate is not manifestly unreasonable at the time the transaction is entered into; otherwise, the discount is determined by a commercially reasonable rate that takes into account the facts and circumstances of each case at the time the transaction was entered into.

(38) "Send" in connection with any writing or notice means to deposit in the mail or deliver for transmission by any other usual means of communication with postage or cost of transmission provided for and properly addressed and in the case of an instrument to an address specified thereon or otherwise agreed, or if there be none to any address reasonable under the circumstances. The

receipt of any writing or notice within the time at which it would have arrived if properly sent has the effect of a proper sending.

(39) "Signed" includes any symbol executed or adopted by a party with present intention to authenticate a writing.

(40) "Surety" includes guarantor.

(41) "Telegram" includes a message transmitted by radio, teletype, cable, any mechanical method of transmission, or the like.

(42) "Term" means that portion of an agreement which relates to a particular matter.

(43) "Unauthorized" signature means one made without actual, implied or apparent authority and includes a forgery.

(44) "Value". Except as otherwise provided with respect to negotiable instruments and bank collections (Sections 3—303, 4—210 and 4—211) a person gives "value" for rights if he acquires them

(a) in return for a binding commitment to extend credit or for the extension of immediately available credit whether or not drawn upon and whether or not a chargeback is provided for in the event of difficulties in collection; or

(b) as security for or in total or partial satisfaction of a pre-existing claim; or

(c) by accepting delivery pursuant to a preexisting contract for purchase; or

(d) generally, in return for any consideration sufficient to support a simple contract.

(45) "Warehouse receipt" means a receipt issued by a person engaged in the business of storing goods for hire.

(46) "Written" or "writing" includes printing, typewriting or any other intentional reduction to tangible form.

§1—202. Prima Facie Evidence by Third Party Documents.

A document in due form purporting to be a bill of lading, policy or certificate of insurance, official weigher's or inspector's certificate, consular invoice, or any other document authorized or required by the contract to be issued by a third party shall be prima facie evidence of its own authenticity and genuineness and of the facts stated in the document by the third party.

§ 1—203. Obligation of Good Faith.

Every contract or duty within this Act imposes an obligation of good faith in its performance or enforcement.

§ 1—204. Time; Reasonable Time; "Seasonably".

(1) Whenever this Act requires any action to be taken within a reasonable time, any time which is not manifestly unreasonable may be fixed by agreement.

(2) What is a reasonable time for taking any action depends on the nature, purpose and circumstances of such action.

(3) An action is taken "seasonably" when it is taken at or within the time agreed or if no time is agreed at or within a reasonable time.

§ 1—205. Course of Dealing and Usage of Trade.

(1) A course of dealing is a sequence of previous conduct between the parties to a particular transaction which is fairly to be regarded as establishing a common basis of understanding for interpreting their expressions and other conduct.

(2) A usage of trade is any practice or method of dealing having such regularity of observance in a place, vocation or trade as to justify an expectation that it will be observed with respect to the transaction in question. The existence and scope of such a usage are to be proved as facts. If it is established that such a usage is embodied in a written trade code or similar writing the interpretation of the writing is for the court.

(3) A course of dealing between parties and any usage of trade in the vocation or trade in which they are engaged or of which they are or should be aware give particular meaning to and supplement or qualify terms of an agreement.

(4) The express terms of an agreement and an applicable course of dealing or usage of trade shall be construed wherever reasonable as consistent with each other; but when such construction is unreasonable express terms control both course of dealing and usage of trade and course of dealing controls usage trade.

(5) An applicable usage of trade in the place where any part of performance is to occur shall be used in interpreting the agreement as to that part of the performance.

(6) Evidence of a relevant usage of trade offered by one party is not admissible unless and until he has given the other party such notice as the court finds sufficient to prevent unfair surprise to the latter.

§ 1—206. Statute of Frauds for Kinds of Personal Property Not Otherwise Covered.

(1) Except in the cases described in subsection (2) of this section a contract for the sale of personal property is not enforceable by way of action or defense beyond five thousand dollars in amount or value of remedy unless there is some writing which indicates that a contract for sale has been made between the parties at a defined or stated price, reasonably identifies the subject matter, and is signed by the party against whom enforcement is sought or by his authorized agent.

(2) Subsection (1) of this section does not apply to contracts for the sale of goods (Section 2—201) nor of securities (Section 8—113) nor to security agreements (Section 9—203).

§ 1—207. Performance or Acceptance Under Reservation of Rights.

(1) A party who with explicit reservation of rights performs or promises performance or assents to performance in a manner demanded or offered by the other party does not thereby prejudice the rights reserved. Such words as "without prejudice", "under protest" or the like are sufficient.

(2) Subsection (1) does not apply to an accord and satisfaction.

§ 1—208. Option to Accelerate at Will.

A term providing that one party or his successor in interest may accelerate payment or performance or require collateral or additional collateral "at will" or "when he deems himself insecure" or in words of similar import shall be construed to mean that he shall have power to do so only if he in good faith believes that the prospect of payment or performance is impaired. The burden of establishing lack of good faith is on the party against whom the power has been exercised.

§ 1—209. Subordinated Obligations.

An obligation may be issued as subordinated to payment of another obligation of the person obligated, or a creditor may subordinate his right to payment of an obligation by agreement with either the person obligated or another creditor of the person obligated. Such a subordination does not create a security interest as against either the common debtor or a subordinated creditor. This section shall be construed as declaring the law as it existed prior to the enactment of this section and not as modifying it. Added 1966.

Note: *This new section is proposed as an optional provision to make it clear that a subordination agreement does not create a security interest unless so intended.*

Article 2
SALES

Part 1 Short Title, General Construction and Subject Matter

§ 2—101. Short Title.

This Article shall be known and may be cited as Uniform Commercial Code—Sales.

§ 2—102. Scope; Certain Security and Other Transactions Excluded From This Article.

Unless the context otherwise requires, this Article applies to transactions in goods; it does not apply to any transaction which although in the form of an unconditional contract to sell or present sale is intended to operate only as a security transaction nor does this Article impair or repeal any statute regulating sales to consumers, farmers or other specified classes of buyers.

§ 2—103. Definitions and Index of Definitions.

(1) In this Article unless the context otherwise requires

(a) "Buyer" means a person who buys or contracts to buy goods.

(b) "Good faith" in the case of a merchant means honesty in fact and the observance of reasonable commercial standards of fair dealing in the trade.

(c) "Receipt" of goods means taking physical possession of them.

(d) "Seller" means a person who sells or contracts to sell goods.

(2) Other definitions applying to this Article or to specified Parts thereof, and the sections in which they appear are:

"Acceptance". Section 2—606.
"Banker's credit". Section 2—325.
"Between merchants". Section 2—104.
"Cancellation". Section 2—106(4).
"Commercial unit". Section 2—105.
"Confirmed credit". Section 2—325.
"Conforming to contract". Section 2—106.
"Contract for sale". Section 2—106.
"Cover". Section 2—712.
"Entrusting". Section 2—403.
"Financing agency". Section 2—104.
"Future goods". Section 2—105.
"Goods". Section 2—105.
"Identification". Section 2—501.
"Installment contract". Section 2—612.
"Letter of Credit". Section 2—325.
"Lot". Section 2—105.
"Merchant". Section 2—104.
"Overseas". Section 2—323.
"Person in position of seller". Section 2—707.
"Present sale". Section 2—106.
"Sale". Section 2—106.
"Sale on approval". Section 2—326.
"Sale or return". Section 2—326.
"Termination". Section 2—106.

(3) The following definitions in other Articles apply to this Article:

"Check". Section 3—104.
"Consignee". Section 7—102.
"Consignor". Section 7—102.
"Consumer goods". Section 9—109.
"Dishonor". Section 3—507.
"Draft". Section 3—104.

(4) In addition Article 1 contains general definitions and principles of construction and interpretation applicable throughout this Article.

§ 2—104. Definitions: "Merchant"; "Between Merchants"; "Financing Agency".

(1) "Merchant" means a person who deals in goods of the kind or otherwise by his occupation holds himself out as having knowledge or skill peculiar to the practices or goods involved in the transaction or to whom such knowledge or skill may be attributed by his employment of an agent or broker or other intermediary who by his occupation holds himself out as having such knowledge or skill.

(2) "Financing agency" means a bank, finance company or other person who in the ordinary course of business makes advances against goods or documents of title or who by arrangement with either the seller or the buyer intervenes in ordinary course to make or collect payment due or claimed under the contract for

sale, as by purchasing or paying the seller's draft or making advances against it or by merely taking it for collection whether or not documents of title accompany the draft. "Financing agency" includes also a bank or other person who similarly intervenes between persons who are in the position of seller and buyer in respect to the goods (Section 2—707).

(3) "Between merchants" means in any transaction with respect to which both parties are chargeable with the knowledge or skill of merchants.

§ 2—105. Definitions: Transferability; "Goods"; "Future" Goods; "Lot"; "Commercial Unit".

(1) "Goods" means all things (including specially manufactured goods) which are movable at the time of identification to the contract for sale other than the money in which the price is to be paid, investment securities (Article 8) and things in action. "Goods" also includes the unborn young of animals and growing crops and other identified things attached to realty as described in the section on goods to be severed from realty (Section 2—107).

(2) Goods must be both existing and identified before any interest in them can pass. Goods which are not both existing and identified are "future" goods. A purported present sale of future goods or of any interest therein operates as a contract to sell.

(3) There may be a sale of a part interest in existing identified goods.

(4) An undivided share in an identified bulk of fungible goods is sufficiently identified to be sold although the quantity of the bulk is not determined. Any agreed proportion of such a bulk or any quantity thereof agreed upon by number, weight or other measure may to the extent of the seller's interest in the bulk be sold to the buyer who then becomes an owner in common.

(5) "Lot" means a parcel or a single article which is the subject matter of a separate sale or delivery, whether or not it is sufficient to perform the contract.

(6) "Commercial unit" means such a unit of goods as by commercial usage is a single whole for purposes of sale and division of which materially impairs its character or value on the market or in use. A commercial unit may be a single article (as a machine) or a set of articles (as a suite of furniture or an assortment of sizes) or a quantity (as a bale, gross, or carload) or any other unit treated in use or in the relevant market as a single whole.

§ 2—106. Definitions: "Contract"; "Agreement"; "Contract for Sale"; "Sale"; "Present Sale"; "Conforming" to Contract; "Termination"; "Cancellation".

(1) In this Article unless the context otherwise requires "contract" and "agreement" are limited to those relating to the present or future sale of goods. "Contract for sale" includes both a present sale of goods and a contract to sell goods at a future time. A "sale" consists in the passing of title from the seller to the buyer for a price (Section 2—401). A "present sale" means a sale which is accomplished by the making of the contract.

(2) Goods or conduct including any part of a performance are "conforming" or conform to the contract when they are in accordance with the obligations under the contract.

(3) "Termination" occurs when either party pursuant to a power created by agreement or law puts an end to the contract otherwise than for its breach. On "termination" all obligations which are still executory on both sides are discharged but any right based on prior breach or performance survives.

(4) "Cancellation" occurs when either party puts an end to the contract for breach by the other and its effect is the same as that of "termination" except that the cancelling party also retains any remedy for breach of the whole contract or any unperformed balance.

§ 2—107. Goods to Be Severed From Realty: Recording.

(1) A contract for the sale of minerals or the like (including oil and gas) or a structure or its materials to be removed from realty is a contract for the sale of goods within this Article if they are to be severed by the seller but until severance a purported present sale thereof which is not effective as a transfer of an interest in land is effective only as a contract to sell.

(2) A contract for the sale apart from the land of growing crops or other things attached to realty and capable of severance without material harm thereto but not described in subsection (1) or of timber to be cut is a contract for the sale of goods within this Article whether the subject matter is to be severed by the buyer or by the seller even though it forms part of the realty at the time of contracting, and the parties can by identification effect a present sale before severance.

(3) The provisions of this section are subject to any third party rights provided by the law relating to realty records, and the contract for sale may be executed and recorded as a document transferring an interest in land and shall then constitute notice to third parties of the buyer's rights under the contract for sale.

Part 2 Form, Formation and Readjustment of Contract

§ 2—201. Formal Requirements; Statute of Frauds.

(1) Except as otherwise provided in this section a contract for the sale of goods for the price of $500 or more is not enforceable by way of action or defense unless there is some writing sufficient to indicate that a contract for sale has been made between the parties and signed by the party against whom enforcement is sought or by his authorized agent or broker. A writing is not insufficient because it omits or incorrectly states a term agreed upon but the contract is not enforceable under this paragraph beyond the quantity of goods shown in such writing.

(2) Between merchants if within a reasonable time a writing in confirmation of the contract and sufficient against the sender is received and the party receiving it has reason to know its contents, its satisfies the requirements of subsection (1) against such party unless written notice of objection to its contents is given within ten days after it is received.

(3) A contract which does not satisfy the requirements of subsection (1) but which is valid in other respects is enforceable

(a) if the goods are to be specially manufactured for the buyer and are not suitable for sale to others in the ordinary course of the seller's business and the seller, before notice of repudiation is received and under circumstances which reasonably indicate that the goods are for the buyer, has made either a substantial beginning of their manufacture or commitments for their procurement; or

(b) if the party against whom enforcement is sought admits in his pleading, testimony or otherwise in court that a contract for sale was made, but the contract is not enforceable under this provision beyond the quantity of goods admitted; or

(c) with respect to goods for which payment has been made and accepted or which have been received and accepted (Sec. 2—606).

§ 2—202. Final Written Expression: Parol or Extrinsic Evidence.

Terms with respect to which the confirmatory memoranda of the parties agree or which are otherwise set forth in a writing intended by the parties as a final expression of their agreement with respect to such terms as are included therein may not be contradicted by evidence of any prior agreement or of a contemporaneous oral agreement but may be explained or supplemented

(a) by course of dealing or usage of trade (Section 1—205) or by course of performance (Section 2—208); and

(b) by evidence of consistent additional terms unless the court finds the writing to have been intended also as a complete and exclusive statement of the terms of the agreement.

§ 2—203. Seals Inoperative.

The affixing of a seal to a writing evidencing a contract for sale or an offer to buy or sell goods does not constitute the writing a sealed instrument and the law with respect to sealed instruments does not apply to such a contract or offer.

§ 2—204. Formation in General.

(1) A contract for sale of goods may be made in any manner sufficient to show agreement, including conduct by both parties which recognizes the existence of such a contract.

(2) An agreement sufficient to constitute a contract for sale may be found even though the moment of its making is undetermined.

(3) Even though one or more terms are left open a contract for sale does not fail for indefiniteness if the parties have intended to make a contract and there is a reasonably certain basis for giving an appropriate remedy.

§ 2—205. Firm Offers.

An offer by a merchant to buy or sell goods in a signed writing which by its terms gives assurance that it will be held open is not revocable, for lack of consideration, during the time stated or if no time is stated for a reasonable time, but in no event may such period of irrevocability exceed three months; but any such term of assurance on a form supplied by the offeree must be separately signed by the offeror.

§ 2—206. Offer and Acceptance in Formation of Contract.

(1) Unless other unambiguously indicated by the language or circumstances

(a) an offer to make a contract shall be construed as inviting acceptance in any manner and by any medium reasonable in the circumstances;

(b) an order or other offer to buy goods for prompt or current shipment shall be construed as inviting acceptance either by a prompt promise to ship or by the prompt or current shipment of conforming or nonconforming goods, but such a shipment of non-conforming goods does not constitute an acceptance if the seller seasonably notifies the buyer that the shipment is offered only as an accommodation to the buyer.

(2) Where the beginning of a requested performance is a reasonable mode of acceptance an offeror who is not notified of acceptance within a reasonable time may treat the offer as having lapsed before acceptance.

§ 2—207. Additional Terms in Acceptance or Confirmation.

(1) A definite and seasonable expression of acceptance or a written confirmation which is sent within a reasonable time operates as an acceptance even though it states terms additional to or different from those offered or agreed upon, unless acceptance is expressly made conditional on assent to the additional or different terms.

(2) The additional terms are to be construed as proposals for addition to the contract. Between merchants such terms become part of the contract unless:

(a) the offer expressly limits acceptance to the terms of the offer;

(b) they materially alter it; or

(c) notification of objection to them has already been given or is given within a reasonable time after notice of them is received.

(3) Conduct by both parties which recognizes the existence of a contract is sufficient to establish a contract for sale although the writings of the parties do not otherwise establish a contract. In such case the terms of the particular contract consist of those terms on which the writings of the parties agree, together with any supplementary terms incorporated under any other provisions of this Act.

§ 2—208. Course of Performance or Practical Construction.

(1) Where the contract for sale involves repeated occasions for performance by either party with knowledge of the nature of the performance and opportunity for objection to it by the other, any course of performance accepted or acquiesced in without objection shall be relevant to determine the meaning of the agreement.

(2) The express terms of the agreement and any such course of performance, as well as any course of dealing and usage of trade, shall be construed whenever reasonable as consistent with each other; but when such construction is unreasonable, express terms

shall control course of performance and course of performance shall control both course of dealing and usage of trade (Section 1—205).

(3) Subject to the provisions of the next section on modification and waiver, such course of performance shall be relevant to show a waiver or modification of any term inconsistent with such course of performance.

§ 2—209. Modification, Rescission and Waiver.

(1) An agreement modifying a contract within this Article needs no consideration to be binding.

(2) A signed agreement which excludes modification or rescission except by a signed writing cannot be otherwise modified or rescinded, but except as between merchants such a requirement on a form supplied by the merchant must be separately signed by the other party.

(3) The requirements of the statute of frauds section of this Article (Section 2—201) must be satisfied if the contract as modified is within its provisions.

(4) Although an attempt at modification or rescission does not satisfy the requirements of subsection (2) or (3) it can operate as a waiver.

(5) A party who has made a waiver affecting an executory portion of the contract may retract the waiver by reasonable notification received by the other party that strict performance will be required of any term waived, unless the retraction would be unjust in view of a material change of position in reliance on the waiver.

§ 2—210. Delegation of Performance; Assignment of Rights.

(1) A party may perform his duty through a delegate unless otherwise agreed or unless the other party has a substantial interest in having his original promisor perform or control the acts required by the contract. No delegation of performance relieves the party delegating of any duty to perform or any liability for breach.

(2) Unless otherwise agreed all rights of either seller or buyer can be assigned except where the assignment would materially change the duty of the other party, or increase materially the burden or risk imposed on him by his contract, or impair materially his chance of obtaining return performance. A right to damages for breach of the whole contract or a right arising out of the assignor's due performance of his entire obligation can be assigned despite agreement otherwise.

(3) Unless the circumstances indicate the contrary a prohibition of assignment of "the contract" is to be construed as barring only the delegation to the assignee of the assignor's performance.

(4) An assignment of "the contract" or of "all my rights under the contract" or an assignment in similar general terms is an assignment of rights and unless the language or the circumstances (as in an assignment for security) indicate the contrary, it is a delegation of performance of the duties of the assignor and its acceptance by the assignee constitutes a promise by him to perform those duties. This promise is enforceable by either the assignor or the other party to the original contract.

(5) The other party may treat any assignment which delegates performance as creating reasonable grounds for insecurity and may without prejudice to his rights against the assignor demand assurances from the assignee (Section 2—609).

Part 3 General Obligation and Construction of Contract

§ 2—301. General Obligations of Parties.

The obligation of the seller is to transfer and deliver and that of the buyer is to accept and pay in accordance with the contract.

§ 2—302. Unconscionable Contract or Clause.

(1) If the court as a matter of law finds the contract or any clause of the contract to have been unconscionable at the time it was made the court may refuse to enforce the contract, or it may enforce the remainder of the contract without the unconscionable clause, or it may so limit the application of any unconscionable clause as to avoid any unconscionable result.

(2) When it is claimed or appears to the court that the contract or any clause thereof may be unconscionable the parties shall be afforded a reasonable opportunity to present evidence as to its commercial setting, purpose and effect to aid the court in making the determination.

§ 2—303. Allocations or Division of Risks.

Where this Article allocates a risk or a burden as between the parties "unless otherwise agreed", the agreement may not only shift the allocation but may also divide the risk or burden.

§ 2—304. Price Payable in Money, Goods, Realty, or Otherwise.

(1) The price can be made payable in money or otherwise. If it is payable in whole or in part in goods each party is a seller of the goods which he is to transfer.

(2) Even though all or part of the price is payable in an interest in realty the transfer of the goods and the seller's obligations with reference to them are subject to this Article, but not the transfer of the interest in realty or the transferor's obligations in connection therewith.

§ 2—305. Open Price Term.

(1) The parties if they so intend can conclude a contract for sale even though the price is not settled. In such a case the price is a reasonable price at the time for delivery if

(a) nothing is said as to price; or

(b) the price is left to be agreed by the parties and they fail to agree; or

(c) the price is to be fixed in terms of some agreed market or other standard as set or recorded by a third person or agency and it is not so set or recorded.

(2) A price to be fixed by the seller or by the buyer means a price for him to fix in good faith.

(3) When a price left to be fixed otherwise than by agreement of the parties fails to be fixed through fault of one party the other

may at his option treat the contract as cancelled or himself fix a reasonable price.

(4) Where, however, the parties intend not to be bound unless the price be fixed or agreed and it is not fixed or agreed there is no contract. In such a case the buyer must return any goods already received or if unable so to do must pay their reasonable value at the time of delivery and the seller must return any portion of the price paid on account.

§ 2—306. Output, Requirements and Exclusive Dealings.

(1) A term which measures the quantity by the output of the seller or the requirements of the buyer means such actual output or requirements as may occur in good faith, except that no quantity unreasonably disproportionate to any stated estimate or in the absence of a stated estimate to any normal or otherwise comparable prior output or requirements may be tendered or demanded.

(2) A lawful agreement by either the seller or the buyer for exclusive dealing in the kind of goods concerned imposes unless otherwise agreed an obligation by the seller to use best efforts to supply the goods and by the buyer to use best efforts to promote their sale.

§ 2—307. Delivery in Single Lot or Several Lots.

Unless otherwise agreed all goods called for by a contract for sale must be tendered in a single delivery and payment is due only on such tender but where the circumstances give either party the right to make or demand delivery in lots the price if it can be apportioned may be demanded for each lot.

§ 2—308. Absence of Specified Place for Delivery.

Unless otherwise agreed

(a) the place for delivery of goods is the seller's place of business or if he has none his residence; but

(b) in a contract for sale of identified goods which to the knowledge of the parties at the time of contracting are in some other place, that place is the place for their delivery; and

(c) documents of title may be delivered through customary banking channels.

§ 2—309. Absence of Specific Time Provisions; Notice of Termination.

(1) The time for shipment or delivery or any other action under a contract if not provided in this Article or agreed upon shall be a reasonable time.

(2) Where the contract provides for successive performances but is indefinite in duration it is valid for a reasonable time but unless otherwise agreed may be terminated at any time by either party.

(3) Termination of a contract by one party except on the happening of an agreed event requires that reasonable notification be received by the other party and an agreement dispensing with notification is invalid if its operation would be unconscionable.

§ 2—310. Open Time for Payment or Running of Credit; Authority to Ship Under Reservation.

Unless otherwise agreed

(a) payment is due at the time and place at which the buyer is to receive the goods even though the place of shipment is the place of delivery; and

(b) if the seller is authorized to send the goods he may ship them under reservation, and may tender the documents of title, but the buyer may inspect the goods after their arrival before payment is due unless such inspection is inconsistent with the terms of the contract (Section 2—513); and

(c) if delivery is authorized and made by way of documents of title otherwise than by subsection (b) then payment is due at the time and place at which the buyer is to receive the documents regardless of where the goods are to be received; and

(d) where the seller is required or authorized to ship the goods on credit the credit period runs from the time of shipment but post-dating the invoice or delaying its dispatch will correspondingly delay the starting of the credit period.

§ 2—311. Options and Cooperation Respecting Performance.

(1) An agreement for sale which is otherwise sufficiently definite (subsection (3) of Section 2—204) to be a contract is not made invalid by the fact that it leaves particulars of performance to be specified by one of the parties. Any such specification must be made in good faith and within limits set by commercial reasonableness.

(2) Unless otherwise agreed specifications relating to assortment of the goods are at the buyer's option and except as otherwise provided in subsections (1)(c) and (3) of Section 2—319 specifications or arrangements relating to shipment are at the seller's option.

(3) Where such specification would materially affect the other party's performance but is not seasonably made or where one party's cooperation is necessary to the agreed performance of the other but is not seasonably forthcoming, the other party in addition to all other remedies

(a) is excused for any resulting delay in his own performance; and

(b) may also either proceed to perform in any reasonable manner or after the time for a material part of his own performance treat the failure to specify or to cooperate as a breach by failure to deliver or accept the goods.

§ 2—312. Warranty of Title and Against Infringement; Buyer's Obligation Against Infringement.

(1) Subject to subsection (2) there is in a contract for sale a warranty by the seller that

(a) the title conveyed shall be good, and its transfer rightful; and

(b) the goods shall be delivered free from any security interest or other lien or encumbrance of which the buyer at the time of contracting has no knowledge.

(2) A warranty under subsection (1) will be excluded or modified only by specific language or by circumstances which give the buyer reason to know that the person selling does not claim title in himself or that he is purporting to sell only such right or title as he or a third person may have.

(3) Unless otherwise agreed a seller who is a merchant regularly dealing in goods of the kind warrants that the goods shall be delivered free of the rightful claim of any third person by way of infringement or the like but a buyer who furnishes specifications to the seller must hold the seller harmless against any such claim which arises out of compliance with the specifications.

§ 2—313. Express Warranties by Affirmation, Promise, Description, Sample.

(1) Express warranties by the seller are created as follows:

(a) Any affirmation of fact or promise made by the seller to the buyer which relates to the goods and becomes part of the basis of the bargain creates an express warranty that the goods shall conform to the affirmation or promise.

(b) Any description of the goods which is made part of the basis of the bargain creates an express warranty that the goods shall conform to the description.

(c) Any sample or model which is made part of the basis of the bargain creates an express warranty that the whole of the goods shall conform to the sample or model.

(2) It is not necessary to the creation of an express warranty that the seller use formal words such as "warrant" or "guarantee" or that he have a specific intention to make a warranty, but an affirmation merely of the value of the goods or a statement purporting to be merely the seller's opinion or commendation of the goods does not create a warranty.

§ 2—314. Implied Warranty: Merchantability; Usage of Trade.

(1) Unless excluded or modified (Section 2—316), a warranty that the goods shall be merchantable is implied in a contract for their sale if the seller is a merchant with respect to goods of that kind. Under this section the serving for value of food or drink to be consumed either on the premises or elsewhere is a sale.

(2) Goods to be merchantable must be at least such as

(a) pass without objection in the trade under the contract description; and

(b) in the case of fungible goods, are of fair average quality within the description; and

(c) are fit for the ordinary purposes for which such goods are used; and

(d) run, within the variations permitted by the agreement, of even kind, quality and quantity within each unit and among all units involved; and

(e) are adequately contained, packaged, and labeled as the agreement may require; and

(f) conform to the promises or affirmations of fact made on the container or label if any.

(3) Unless excluded or modified (Section 2—316) other implied warranties may arise from course of dealing or usage of trade.

§ 2—315. Implied Warranty: Fitness for Particular Purpose.

Where the seller at the time of contracting has reason to know any particular purpose for which the goods are required and that the buyer is relying on the seller's skill or judgment to select or furnish suitable goods, there is unless excluded or modified under the next section an implied warranty that the goods shall be fit for such purpose.

§ 2—316. Exclusion or Modification of Warranties.

(1) Words or conduct relevant to the creation of an express warranty and words or conduct tending to negate or limit warranty shall be construed wherever reasonable as consistent with each other; but subject to the provisions of this Article on parol or extrinsic evidence (Section 2—202) negation or limitation is inoperative to the extent that such construction is unreasonable.

(2) Subject to subsection (3), to exclude or modify the implied warranty of merchantability or any part of it the language must mention merchantability and in case of a writing must be conspicuous, and to exclude or modify any implied warranty of fitness the exclusion must be by a writing and conspicuous. Language to exclude all implied warranties of fitness is sufficient if it states, for example, that "There are no warranties which extend beyond the description on the face hereof."

(3) Notwithstanding subsection (2)

(a) unless the circumstances indicate otherwise, all implied warranties are excluded by expressions like "as is", "with all faults" or other language which in common understanding calls the buyer's attention to the exclusion of warranties and makes plain that there is no implied warranty; and

(b) when the buyer before entering into the contract has examined the goods or the sample or model as fully as he desired or has refused to examine the goods there is no implied warranty with regard to defects which an examination ought in the circumstances to have revealed to him; and

(c) an implied warranty can also be excluded or modified by course of dealing or course of performance or usage of trade.

(4) Remedies for breach of warranty can be limited in accordance with the provisions of this Article on liquidation or limitation of damages and on contractual modification of remedy (Sections 2—718 and 2—719).

§ 2—317. Cumulation and Conflict of Warranties Express or Implied.

Warranties whether express or implied shall be construed as consistent with each other and as cumulative, but if such construction is unreasonable the intention of the parties shall determine which warranty is dominant. In ascertaining that intention the following rules apply:

(a) Exact or technical specifications displace an inconsistent sample or model or general language of description.

(b) A sample from an existing bulk displaces inconsistent general language of description.

(c) Express warranties displace inconsistent implied warranties other than an implied warranty of fitness for a particular purpose.

§ 2—318. Third Party Beneficiaries of Warranties Express or Implied.

Note: If this Act is introduced in the Congress of the United States this section should be omitted. (States to select one alternative.)

Alternative A

A seller's warranty whether express or implied extends to any natural person who is in the family or household of his buyer or who is a guest in his home if it is reasonable to expect that such person may use, consume or be affected by the goods and who is injured in person by breach of the warranty. A seller may not exclude or limit the operation of this section.

Alternative B

A seller's warranty whether express or implied extends to any natural person who may reasonably be expected to use, consume or be affected by the goods and who is injured in person by breach of the warranty. A seller may not exclude or limit the operation of this section.

Alternative C

A seller's warranty whether express or implied extends to any person who may reasonably be expected to use, consume or be affected by the goods and who is injured by breach of the warranty. A seller may not exclude or limit the operation of this section with respect to injury to the person of an individual to whom the warranty extends. As amended 1966.

§ 2—319. F.O.B. and F.A.S. Terms.

(1) Unless otherwise agreed the term F.O.B. (which means "free on board") at a named place, even though used only in connection with the stated price, is a delivery term under which

(a) when the term is F.O.B. the place of shipment, the seller must at that place ship the goods in the manner provided in this Article (Section 2—504) and bear the expense and risk of putting them into the possession of the carrier; or

(b) when the term is F.O.B. the place of destination, the seller must at his own expense and risk transport the goods to that place and there tender delivery of them in the manner provided in this Article (Section 2—503);

(c) when under either (a) or (b) the term is also F.O.B. vessel, car or other vehicle, the seller must in addition at his own expense and risk load the goods on board. If the term is F.O.B. vessel the buyer must name the vessel and in an appropriate case the seller must comply with the provisions of this Article on the form of bill of lading (Section 2—323).

(2) Unless otherwise agreed the term F.A.S. vessel (which means "free alongside") at a named port, even though used only in connection with the stated price, is a delivery term under which the seller must

(a) at his own expense and risk deliver the goods alongside the vessel in the manner usual in that port or on a dock designated and provided by the buyer; and

(b) obtain and tender a receipt for the goods in exchange for which the carrier is under a duty to issue a bill of lading.

(3) Unless otherwise agreed in any case falling within subsection (1)(a) or (c) or subsection (2) the buyer must seasonably give any needed instructions for making delivery, including when the term is F.A.S. or F.O.B. the loading berth of the vessel and in an appropriate case its name and sailing date. The seller may treat the failure of needed instructions as a failure of cooperation under this Article (Section 2—311). He may also at his option move the goods in any reasonable manner preparatory to delivery or shipment.

(4) Under the term F.O.B. vessel or F.A.S. unless otherwise agreed the buyer must make payment against tender of the required documents and the seller may not tender nor the buyer demand delivery of the goods in substitution for the documents.

§ 2—320. C.I.F. and C. & F. Terms.

(1) The term C.I.F. means that the price includes in a lump sum the cost of the goods and the insurance and freight to the named destination. The term C. & F. or C.F. means that the price so includes cost and freight to the named destination.

(2) Unless otherwise agreed and even though used only in connection with the stated price and destination, the term C.I.F. destination or its equivalent requires the seller at his own expense and risk to

(a) put the goods into the possession of a carrier at the port for shipment and obtain a negotiable bill or bills of lading covering the entire transportation to the named destination; and

(b) load the goods and obtain a receipt from the carrier (which may be contained in the bill of lading) showing that the freight has been paid or provided for; and

(c) obtain a policy or certificate of insurance, including any war risk insurance, of a kind and on terms then current at the port of shipment in the usual amount, in the currency of the contract, shown to cover the same goods covered by the bill of lading and providing for payment of loss to the order of the buyer or for the account of whom it may concern; but the seller may add to the price the amount of the premium for any such war risk insurance; and

(d) prepare an invoice of the goods and procure any other documents required to effect shipment or to comply with the contract; and

(e) forward and tender with commercial promptness all the documents in due form and with any indorsement necessary to perfect the buyer's rights.

(3) Unless otherwise agreed the term C. & F. or its equivalent has the same effect and imposes upon the seller the same obligations and risks as a C.I.F. term except the obligation as to insurance.

(4) Under the term C.I.F. or C. & F. unless otherwise agreed the buyer must make payment against tender of the required documents and the seller may not tender nor the buyer demand delivery of the goods in substitution for the documents.

§ 2—321. C.I.F. or C. & F.: "Net Landed Weights"; "Payment on Arrival"; Warranty of Condition on Arrival.

Under a contract containing a term C.I.F. or C. & F.

(1) Where the price is based on or is to be adjusted according to "net landed weights", "delivered weights", "out turn" quantity or quality or the like, unless otherwise agreed the seller must reasonably estimate the price. The payment due on tender of the documents called for by the contract is the amount so estimated, but after final adjustment of the price a settlement must be made with commercial promptness.

(2) An agreement described in subsection (1) or any warranty of quality or condition of the goods on arrival places upon the seller the risk of ordinary deterioration, shrinkage and the like in transportation but has no effect on the place or time of identification to the contract for sale or delivery or on the passing of the risk of loss.

(3) Unless otherwise agreed where the contract provides for payment on or after arrival of the goods the seller must before payment allow such preliminary inspection as is feasible; but if the goods are lost delivery of the documents and payment are due when the goods should have arrived.

§ 2—322. Delivery "Ex-Ship".

(1) Unless otherwise agreed a term for delivery of goods "ex-ship" (which means from the carrying vessel) or in equivalent language is not restricted to a particular ship and requires delivery from a ship which has reached a place at the named port of destination where goods of the kind are usually discharged.

(2) Under such a term unless otherwise agreed

(a) the seller must discharge all liens arising out of the carriage and furnish the buyer with a direction which puts the carrier under a duty to deliver the goods; and

(b) the risk of loss does not pass to the buyer until the goods leave the ship's tackle or are otherwise properly unloaded.

§ 2—323. Form of Bill of Lading Required in Overseas Shipment; "Overseas".

(1) Where the contract contemplates overseas shipment and contains a term C.I.F. or C. & F. or F.O.B. vessel, the seller unless otherwise agreed must obtain a negotiable bill of lading stating that the goods have been loaded on board or, in the case of a term C.I.F. or C. & F., received for shipment.

(2) Where in a case within subsection (1) a bill of lading has been issued in a set of parts, unless otherwise agreed if the documents are not to be sent from abroad the buyer may demand tender of the full set; otherwise only one part of the bill of lading need be tendered. Even if the agreement expressly requires a full set

(a) due tender of a single part is acceptable within the provisions of this Article on cure of improper delivery (subsection (1) of Section 2—508); and

(b) even though the full set is demanded, if the documents are sent from abroad the person tendering an incomplete set may nevertheless require payment upon furnishing an indemnity which the buyer in good faith deems adequate.

(3) A shipment by water or by air or a contract contemplating such shipment is "overseas" insofar as by usage of trade or agreement it is subject to the commercial, financing or shipping practices characteristic of international deep water commerce.

§ 2—324. "No Arrival, No Sale" Term.

Under a term "no arrival, no sale" or terms of like meaning, unless otherwise agreed,

(a) the seller must properly ship conforming goods and if they arrive by any means he must tender them on arrival but he assumes no obligation that the goods will arrive unless he has caused the non-arrival; and

(b) where without fault of the seller the goods are in part lost or have so deteriorated as no longer to conform to the contract or arrive after the contract time, the buyer may proceed as if there had been casualty to identified goods (Section 2—613).

§ 2—325. "Letter of Credit" Term; "Confirmed Credit".

(1) Failure of the buyer seasonably to furnish an agreed letter of credit is a breach of the contract for sale.

(2) The delivery to seller of a proper letter of credit suspends the buyer's obligation to pay. If the letter of credit is dishonored, the seller may on seasonable notification to the buyer require payment directly from him.

(3) Unless otherwise agreed the term "letter of credit" or "banker's credit" in a contract for sale means an irrevocable credit issued by a financing agency of good repute and, where the shipment is overseas, of good international repute. The term "confirmed credit" means that the credit must also carry the direct obligation of such an agency which does business in the seller's financial market.

§ 2—326. Sale on Approval and Sale or Return; Consignment Sales and Rights of Creditors.

(1) Unless otherwise agreed, if delivered goods may be returned by the buyer even though they conform to the contract, the transaction is

(a) a "sale on approval" if the goods are delivered primarily for use, and

(b) a "sale or return" if the goods are delivered primarily for resale.

(2) Except as provided in subsection (3), goods held on approval are not subject to the claims of the buyer's creditors until accep-

tance; goods held on sale or return are subject to such claims while in the buyer's possession.

(3) Where goods are delivered to a person for sale and such person maintains a place of business at which he deals in goods of the kind involved, under a name other than the name of the person making delivery, then with respect to claims of creditors of the person conducting the business the goods are deemed to be on sale or return. The provisions of this subsection are applicable even though an agreement purports to reserve title to the person making delivery until payment or resale or uses such words as "on consignment" or "on memorandum". However, this subsection is not applicable if the person making delivery

(a) complies with an applicable law providing for a consignor's interest or the like to be evidenced by a sign, or

(b) establishes that the person conducting the business is generally known by his creditors to be substantially engaged in selling the goods of others, or

(c) complies with the filing provisions of the Article on Secured Transactions (Article 9).

(4) Any "or return" term of a contract for sale is to be treated as a separate contract for sale within the statute of frauds section of this Article (Section 2—201) and as contradicting the sale aspect of the contract within the provisions of this Article on parol or extrinsic evidence (Section 2—202).

§ 2—327. Special Incidents of Sale on Approval and Sale or Return.

(1) Under a sale on approval unless otherwise agreed

(a) although the goods are identified to the contract the risk of loss and the title do not pass to the buyer until acceptance; and

(b) use of the goods consistent with the purpose of trial is not acceptance but failure seasonably to notify the seller of election to return the goods is acceptance, and if the goods conform to the contract acceptance of any part is acceptance of the whole; and

(c) after due notification of election to return, the return is at the seller's risk and expense but a merchant buyer must follow any reasonable instructions.

(2) Under a sale or return unless otherwise agreed

(a) the option to return extends to the whole or any commercial unit of the goods while in substantially their original condition, but must be exercised seasonably; and

(b) the return is at the buyer's risk and expense.

§ 2—328. Sale by Auction.

(1) In a sale by auction if goods are put up in lots each lot is the subject of a separate sale.

(2) A sale by auction is complete when the auctioneer so announces by the fall of the hammer or in other customary manner. Where a bid is made while the hammer is falling in acceptance of a prior bid the auctioneer may in his discretion reopen the bidding or declare the goods sold under the bid on which the hammer was falling.

(3) Such a sale is with reserve unless the goods are in explicit terms put up without reserve. In an auction with reserve the auctioneer may withdraw the goods at any time until he announces completion of the sale. In an auction without reserve, after the auctioneer calls for bids on an article or lot, that article or lot cannot be withdrawn unless no bid is made within a reasonable time. In either case a bidder may retract his bid until the auctioneer's announcement of completion of the sale, but a bidder's retraction does not revive any previous bid.

(4) If the auctioneer knowingly receives a bid on the seller's behalf or the seller makes or procures such as bid, and notice has not been given that liberty for such bidding is reserved, the buyer may at his option avoid the sale or take the goods at the price of the last good faith bid prior to the completion of the sale. This subsection shall not apply to any bid at a forced sale.

Part 4 Title, Creditors and Good Faith Purchasers

§ 2—401. Passing of Title; Reservation for Security; Limited Application of This Section.

Each provision of this Article with regard to the rights, obligations and remedies of the seller, the buyer, purchasers or other third parties applies irrespective of title to the goods except where the provision refers to such title. Insofar as situations are not covered by the other provisions of this Article and matters concerning title became material the following rules apply:

(1) Title to goods cannot pass under a contract for sale prior to their identification to the contract (Section 2—501), and unless otherwise explicitly agreed the buyer acquires by their identification a special property as limited by this Act. Any retention or reservation by the seller of the title (property) in goods shipped or delivered to the buyer is limited in effect to a reservation of a security interest. Subject to these provisions and to the provisions of the Article on Secured Transactions (Article 9), title to goods passes from the seller to the buyer in any manner and on any conditions explicitly agreed on by the parties.

(2) Unless otherwise explicitly agreed title passes to the buyer at the time and place at which the seller completes his performance with reference to the physical delivery of the goods, despite any reservation of a security interest and even though a document of title is to be delivered at a different time or place; and in particular and despite any reservation of a security interest by the bill of lading

(a) if the contract requires or authorizes the seller to send the goods to the buyer but does not require him to deliver them at destination, title passes to the buyer at the time and place of shipment; but

(b) if the contract requires delivery at destination, title passes on tender there.

(3) Unless otherwise explicitly agreed where delivery is to be made without moving the goods,

(a) if the seller is to deliver a document of title, title passes at the time when and the place where he delivers such documents; or

(b) if the goods are at the time of contracting already identified and no documents are to be delivered, title passes at the time and place of contracting.

(4) A rejection or other refusal by the buyer to receive or retain the goods, whether or not justified, or a justified revocation of acceptance revests title to the goods in the seller. Such revesting occurs by operation of law and is not a "sale".

§ 2—402. Rights of Seller's Creditors Against Sold Goods.

(1) Except as provided in subsections (2) and (3), rights of unsecured creditors of the seller with respect to goods which have been identified to a contract for sale are subject to the buyer's rights to recover the goods under this Article (Sections 2—502 and 2—716).

(2) A creditor of the seller may treat a sale or an identification of goods to a contract for sale as void if as against him a retention of possession by the seller is fraudulent under any rule of law of the state where the goods are situated, except that retention of possession in good faith and current course of trade by a merchant-seller for a commercially reasonable time after a sale or identification is not fraudulent.

(3) Nothing in this Article shall be deemed to impair the rights of creditors of the seller

(a) under the provisions of the Article on Secured Transactions (Article 9); or

(b) where identification to the contract or delivery is made not in current course of trade but in satisfaction of or as security for a pre-existing claim for money, security or the like and is made under circumstances which under any rule of law of the state where the goods are situated would apart from this Article constitute the transaction a fraudulent transfer or voidable preference.

§ 2—403. Power to Transfer; Good Faith Purchase of Goods; "Entrusting".

(1) A purchaser of goods acquires all title which his transferor had or had power to transfer except that a purchaser of a limited interest acquires rights only to the extent of the interest purchased. A person with voidable title has power to transfer a good title to a good faith purchaser for value. When goods have been delivered under a transaction of purchase the purchaser has such power even though

(a) the transferor was deceived as to the identity of the purchaser, or

(b) the delivery was in exchange for a check which is later dishonored, or

(c) it was agreed that the transaction was to be a "cash sale", or

(d) the delivery was procured through fraud punishable as larcenous under the criminal law.

(2) Any entrusting of possession of goods to a merchant who deals in goods of that kind gives him power to transfer all rights of the entruster to a buyer in ordinary course of business.

(3) "Entrusting" includes any delivery and any acquiescence in retention of possession regardless of any condition expressed between the parties to the delivery or acquiescence and regardless of whether the procurement of the entrusting or the possessor's disposition of the goods have been such as to be larcenous under the criminal law.

(4) The rights of other purchasers of goods and of lien creditors are governed by the Articles on Secured Transactions (Article 9), Bulk Transfers (Article 6) and Documents of Title (Article 7).

Part 5 Performance

§ 2—501. Insurable Interest in Goods; Manner of Identification of Goods.

(1) The buyer obtains a special property and an insurable interest in goods by identification of existing goods as goods to which the contract refers even though the goods so identified are non-conforming and he has an option to return or reject them. Such identification can be made at any time and in any manner explicitly agreed to by the parties. In the absence of explicit agreement identification occurs

(a) when the contract is made if it is for the sale of goods already existing and identified;

(b) if the contract is for the sale of future goods other than those described in paragraph (c), when goods are shipped, marked or otherwise designated by the seller as goods to which the contract refers;

(c) when the crops are planted or otherwise become growing crops or the young are conceived if the contract is for the sale of unborn young to be born within twelve months after contracting or for the sale of crops to be harvested within twelve months or the next normal harvest season after contracting whichever is longer.

(2) The seller retains an insurable interest in goods so long as title to or any security interest in the goods remains in him and where the identification is by the seller alone he may until default or insolvency or notification to the buyer that the identification is final substitute other goods for those identified.

(3) Nothing in this section impairs any insurable interest recognized under any other statute or rule of law.

§ 2—502. Buyer's Right to Goods on Seller's Insolvency.

(1) Subject to subsection (2) and even though the goods have not been shipped a buyer who has paid a part or all of the price of goods in which he has a special property under the provisions of the immediately preceding section may on making and keeping good a tender of any unpaid portion of their price recover them from the seller if the seller becomes insolvent within ten days after receipt of the first installment on their price.

(2) If the identification creating his special property has been made by the buyer he acquires the right to recover the goods only if they conform to the contract for sale.

§ 2—503. Manner of Seller's Tender of Delivery.

(1) Tender of delivery requires that the seller put and hold conforming goods at the buyer's disposition and give the buyer any notification reasonably necessary to enable him to take delivery. The manner, time and place for tender are determined by the agreement and this Article, and in particular

(a) tender must be at a reasonable hour, and if it is of goods they must be kept available for the period reasonably necessary to enable the buyer to take possession; but

(b) unless otherwise agreed the buyer must furnish facilities reasonably suited to the receipt of the goods.

(2) Where the case is within the next section respecting shipment tender requires that the seller comply with its provisions.

(3) Where the seller is required to deliver at a particular destination tender requires that he comply with subsection (1) and also in any appropriate case tender documents as described in subsections (4) and (5) of this section.

(4) Where goods are in the possession of a bailee and are to be delivered without being moved

(a) tender requires that the seller either tender a negotiable document of title covering such goods or procure acknowledgment by the bailee of the buyer's right to possession of the goods; but

(b) tender to the buyer of a non-negotiable document of title or of a written direction to the bailee to deliver is sufficient tender unless the buyer seasonably objects, and receipt by the bailee of notification of the buyer's rights fixes those rights as against the bailee and all third persons; but risk of loss of the goods and of any failure by the bailee to honor the non-negotiable document of title or to obey the direction remains on the seller until the buyer has had a reasonable time to present the document or direction, and a refusal by the bailee to honor the document or to obey the direction defeats the tender.

(5) Where the contract requires the seller to deliver documents

(a) he must tender all such documents in correct form, except as provided in this Article with respect to bills of lading in a set (subsection (2) of Section 2—323); and

(b) tender through customary banking channels is sufficient and dishonor of a draft accompanying the documents constitutes non-acceptance or rejection.

§ 2—504. Shipment by Seller.

Where the seller is required or authorized to send the goods to the buyer and the contract does not require him to deliver them at a particular destination, then unless otherwise agreed he must

(a) put the goods in the possession of such a carrier and make such a contract for their transportation as may be reasonable having regard to the nature of the goods and other circumstances of the case; and

(b) obtain and promptly deliver or tender in due form any document necessary to enable the buyer to obtain possession of the goods or otherwise required by the agreement or by usage of trade; and

(c) promptly notify the buyer of the shipment.

Failure to notify the buyer under paragraph (c) or to make a proper contract under paragraph (a) is a ground for rejection only if material delay or loss ensues.

§ 2—505. Seller's Shipment under Reservation.

(1) Where the seller has identified goods to the contract by or before shipment:

(a) his procurement of a negotiable bill of lading to his own order or otherwise reserves in him a security interest in the goods. His procurement of the bill to the order of a financing agency or of the buyer indicates in addition only the seller's expectation of transferring that interest to the person named.

(b) a non-negotiable bill of lading to himself or his nominee reserves possession of the goods as security but except in a case of conditional delivery (subsection (2) of Section 2—507) a non-negotiable bill of lading naming the buyer as consignee reserves no security interest even though the seller retains possession of the bill of lading.

(2) When shipment by the seller with reservation of a security interest is in violation of the contract for sale it constitutes an improper contract for transportation within the preceding section but impairs neither the rights given to the buyer by shipment and identification of the goods to the contract nor the seller's powers as a holder of a negotiable document.

§ 2—506. Rights of Financing Agency.

(1) A financing agency by paying or purchasing for value a draft which relates to a shipment of goods acquires to the extent of the payment or purchase and in addition to its own rights under the draft and any document of title securing it any rights of the shipper in the goods including the right to stop delivery and the shipper's right to have the draft honored by the buyer.

(2) The right to reimbursement of a financing agency which has in good faith honored or purchased the draft under commitment to or authority from the buyer is not impaired by subsequent discovery of defects with reference to any relevant document which was apparently regular on its face.

§ 2—507. Effect of Seller's Tender; Delivery on Condition.

(1) Tender of delivery is a condition to the buyer's duty to accept the goods and, unless otherwise agreed, to his duty to pay for them. Tender entitles the seller to acceptance of the goods and to payment according to the contract.

(2) Where payment is due and demanded on the delivery to the buyer of goods or documents of title, his right as against the seller to retain or dispose of them is conditional upon his making the payment due.

§ 2—508. Cure by Seller of Improper Tender or Delivery; Replacement.

(1) Where any tender or delivery by the seller is rejected because non-conforming and the time for performance has not yet expired, the seller may seasonably notify the buyer of his intention to cure and may then within the contract time make a conforming delivery.

(2) Where the buyer rejects a non-conforming tender which the seller had reasonable grounds to believe would be acceptable with or without money allowance the seller may if he seasonably notifies the buyer have a further reasonable time to substitute a conforming tender.

§ 2—509. Risk of Loss in the Absence of Breach.

(1) Where the contract requires or authorizes the seller to ship the goods by carrier

(a) if it does not require him to deliver them at a particular destination, the risk of loss passes to the buyer when the goods are duly delivered to the carrier even though the shipment is under reservation (Section 2—505); but

(b) if it does require him to deliver them at a particular destination and the goods are there duly tendered while in the possession of the carrier, the risk of loss passes to the buyer when the goods are there duly so tendered as to enable the buyer to take delivery.

(2) Where the goods are held by a bailee to be delivered without being moved, the risk of loss passes to the buyer

(a) on his receipt of a negotiable document of title covering the goods; or

(b) on acknowledgment by the bailee of the buyer's right to possession of the goods; or

(c) after his receipt of a non-negotiable document of title or other written direction to deliver, as provided in subsection (4)(b) of Section 2—503.

(3) In any case not within subsection (1) or (2), the risk of loss passes to the buyer on his receipt of the goods if the seller is a merchant; otherwise the risk passes to the buyer on tender of delivery.

(4) The provisions of this section are subject to contrary agreement of the parties and to the provisions of this Article on sale on approval (Section 2—327) and on effect of breach on risk of loss (Section 2—510).

§ 2—510. Effect of Breach on Risk of Loss.

(1) Where a tender or delivery of goods so fails to conform to the contract as to give a right of rejection the risk of their loss remains on the seller until cure or acceptance.

(2) Where the buyer rightfully revokes acceptance he may to the extent of any deficiency in his effective insurance coverage treat the risk of loss as having rested on the seller from the beginning.

(3) Where the buyer as to conforming goods already identified to the contract for sale repudiates or is otherwise in breach before risk of their loss has passed to him, the seller may to the extent of any deficiency in his effective insurance coverage treat the risk of loss as resting on the buyer for a commercially reasonable time.

§ 2—511. Tender of Payment by Buyer; Payment by Check.

(1) Unless otherwise agreed tender of payment is a condition to the seller's duty to tender and complete any delivery.

(2) Tender of payment is sufficient when made by any means or in any manner current in the ordinary course of business unless the seller demands payment in legal tender and gives any extension of time reasonably necessary to procure it.

(3) Subject to the provisions of this Act on the effect of an instrument on an obligation (Section 3—310), payment by check is conditional and is defeated as between the parties by dishonor of the check on due presentment.

§ 2—512. Payment by Buyer Before Inspection.

(1) Where the contract requires payment before inspection non-conformity of the goods does not excuse the buyer from so making payment unless

(a) the non-conformity appears without inspection; or

(b) despite tender of the required documents the circumstances would justify injunction against honor under the provisions of this Act (Section 5—114).

(2) Payment pursuant to subsection (1) does not constitute an acceptance of goods or impair the buyer's right to inspect or any of his remedies.

§ 2—513. Buyer's Right to Inspection of Goods.

(1) Unless otherwise agreed and subject to subsection (3), where goods are tendered or delivered or identified to the contract for sale, the buyer has a right before payment or acceptance to inspect them at any reasonable place and time and in any reasonable manner. When the seller is required or authorized to send the goods to the buyer, the inspection may be after their arrival.

(2) Expenses of inspection must be borne by the buyer but may be recovered from the seller if the goods do not conform and are rejected.

(3) Unless otherwise agreed and subject to the provisions of this Article on C.I.F. contracts (subsection (3) of Section 2—321), the buyer is not entitled to inspect the goods before payment of the price when the contract provides

(a) for delivery "C.O.D." or on other like terms; or

(b) for payment against documents of title, except where such payment is due only after the goods are to become available for inspection.

(4) A place or method of inspection fixed by the parties is presumed to be exclusive but unless otherwise expressly agreed it does not postpone identification or shift the place for delivery or for passing the risk of loss. If compliance becomes impossible, inspection shall be as provided in this section unless the place or

method fixed was clearly intended as an indispensable condition failure of which avoids the contract.

§ 2—514. When Documents Deliverable on Acceptance; When on Payment.

Unless otherwise agreed documents against which a draft is drawn are to be delivered to the drawee on acceptance of the draft if it is payable more than three days after presentment; otherwise, only on payment.

§ 2—515. Preserving Evidence of Goods in Dispute.

In furtherance of the adjustment of any claim or dispute

(a) either party on reasonable notification to the other and for the purpose of ascertaining the facts and preserving evidence has the right to inspect, test and sample the goods including such of them as may be in the possession or control of the other; and

(b) the parties may agree to a third party inspection or survey to determine the conformity or condition of the goods and may agree that the findings shall be binding upon them in any subsequent litigation or adjustment.

Part 6 Breach, Repudiation and Excuse

§ 2—601. Buyer's Rights on Improper Delivery.

Subject to the provisions of this Article on breach in installment contracts (Section 2—612) and unless otherwise agreed under the sections on contractual limitations of remedy (Sections 2—718 and 2—719), if the goods or the tender of delivery fail in any respect to conform to the contract, the buyer may

(a) reject the whole; or

(b) accept the whole; or

(c) accept any commercial unit or units and reject the rest.

§ 2—602. Manner and Effect of Rightful Rejection.

(1) Rejection of goods must be within a reasonable time after their delivery or tender. It is ineffective unless the buyer seasonably notifies the seller.

(2) Subject to the provisions of the two following sections on rejected goods (Sections 2—603 and 2—604),

(a) after rejection any exercise of ownership by the buyer with respect to any commercial unit is wrongful as against the seller; and

(b) if the buyer has before rejection taken physical possession of goods in which he does not have a security interest under the provisions of this Article (subsection (3) of Section 2—711), he is under a duty after rejection to hold them with reasonable care at the seller's disposition for a time sufficient to permit the seller to remove them; but

(c) the buyer has no further obligations with regard to goods rightfully rejected.

(3) The seller's rights with respect to goods wrongfully rejected are governed by the provisions of this Article on Seller's remedies in general (Section 2—703).

§ 2—603. Merchant Buyer's Duties as to Rightfully Rejected Goods.

(1) Subject to any security interest in the buyer (subsection (3) of Section 2—711), when the seller has no agent or place of business at the market of rejection a merchant buyer is under a duty after rejection of goods in his possession or control to follow any reasonable instructions received from the seller with respect to the goods and in the absence of such instructions to make reasonable efforts to sell them for the seller's account if they are perishable or threaten to decline in value speedily. Instructions are not reasonable if on demand indemnity for expenses is not forthcoming.

(2) When the buyer sells goods under subsection (1), he is entitled to reimbursement from the seller or out of the proceeds for reasonable expenses of caring for and selling them, and if the expenses include no selling commission then to such commission as is usual in the trade or if there is none to a reasonable sum not exceeding ten per cent on the gross proceeds.

(3) In complying with this section the buyer is held only to good faith and good faith conduct hereunder is neither acceptance nor conversion nor the basis of an action for damages.

§ 2—604. Buyer's Options as to Salvage of Rightfully Rejected Goods.

Subject to the provisions of the immediately preceding section on perishables if the seller gives no instructions within a reasonable time after notification of rejection the buyer may store the rejected goods for the seller's account or reship them to him or resell them for the seller's account with reimbursement as provided in the preceding section. Such action is not acceptance or conversion.

§ 2—605. Waiver of Buyer's Objections by Failure to Particularize.

(1) The buyer's failure to state in connection with rejection a particular defect which is ascertainable by reasonable inspection precludes him from relying on the unstated defect to justify rejection or to establish breach

(a) where the seller could have cured it if stated seasonably; or

(b) between merchants when the seller has after rejection made a request in writing for a full and final written statement of all defects on which the buyer proposes to rely.

(2) Payment against documents made without reservation of rights precludes recovery of the payment for defects apparent on the face of the documents.

§ 2—606. What Constitutes Acceptance of Goods.

(1) Acceptance of goods occurs when the buyer

(a) after a reasonable opportunity to inspect the goods signifies to the seller that the goods are conforming or that he will take or retain them in spite of their nonconformity; or

(b) fails to make an effective rejection (subsection (1) of Section 2—602), but such acceptance does not occur until the buyer has had a reasonable opportunity to inspect them; or

(c) does any act inconsistent with the seller's ownership; but if such act is wrongful as against the seller it is an acceptance only if ratified by him.

(2) Acceptance of a part of any commercial unit is acceptance of that entire unit.

§ 2—607. Effect of Acceptance; Notice of Breach; Burden of Establishing Breach After Acceptance; Notice of Claim or Litigation to Person Answerable Over.

(1) The buyer must pay at the contract rate for any goods accepted.

(2) Acceptance of goods by the buyer precludes rejection of the goods accepted and if made with knowledge of a non-conformity cannot be revoked because of it unless the acceptance was on the reasonable assumption that the non-conformity would be seasonably cured but acceptance does not of itself impair any other remedy provided by this Article for non-conformity.

(3) Where a tender has been accepted

(a) the buyer must within a reasonable time after he discovers or should have discovered any breach notify the seller of breach or be barred from any remedy; and

(b) if the claim is one for infringement or the like (subsection (3) of Section 2—312) and the buyer is sued as a result of such a breach he must so notify the seller within a reasonable time after he receives notice of the litigation or be barred from any remedy over for liability established by the litigation.

(4) The burden is on the buyer to establish any breach with respect to the goods accepted.

(5) Where the buyer is sued for breach of a warranty or other obligation for which his seller is answerable over

(a) he may give his seller written notice of the litigation. If the notice states that the seller may come in and defend and that if the seller does not do so he will be bound in any action against him by his buyer by any determination of fact common to the two litigations, then unless the seller after seasonable receipt of the notice does come in and defend he is so bound.

(b) if the claim is one for infringement or the like (subsection (3) of Section 2—312) the original seller may demand in writing that his buyer turn over to him control of the litigation including settlement or else be barred from any remedy over and if he also agrees to bear all expense and to satisfy any adverse judgment, then unless the buyer after seasonable receipt of the demand does turn over control the buyer is so barred.

(6) The provisions of subsections (3), (4) and (5) apply to any obligation of a buyer to hold the seller harmless against infringement or the like (subsection (3) of Section 2—312).

§ 2—608. Revocation of Acceptance in Whole or in Part.

(1) The buyer may revoke his acceptance of a lot or commercial unit whose non-conformity substantially impairs its value to him if he has accepted it

(a) on the reasonable assumption that its nonconformity would be cured and it has not been seasonably cured; or

(b) without discovery of such non-conformity if his acceptance was reasonably induced either by the difficulty of discovery before acceptance or by the seller's assurances.

(2) Revocation of acceptance must occur within a reasonable time after the buyer discovers or should have discovered the ground for it and before any substantial change in condition of the goods which is not caused by their own defects. It is not effective until the buyer notifies the seller of it.

(3) A buyer who so revokes has the same rights and duties with regard to the goods involved as if he had rejected them.

§ 2—609. Right to Adequate Assurance of Performance.

(1) A contract for sale imposes an obligation on each party that the other's expectation of receiving due performance will not be impaired. When reasonable grounds for insecurity arise with respect to the performance of either party the other may in writing demand adequate assurance of due performance and until he receives such assurance may if commercially reasonable suspend any performance for which he has not already received the agreed return.

(2) Between merchants the reasonableness of grounds for insecurity and the adequacy of any assurance offered shall be determined according to commercial standards.

(3) Acceptance of any improper delivery or payment does not prejudice the party's right to demand adequate assurance of future performance.

(4) After receipt of a justified demand failure to provide within a reasonable time not exceeding thirty days such assurance of due performance as is adequate under the circumstances of the particular case is a repudiation of the contract.

§ 2—610. Anticipatory Repudiation.

When either party repudiates the contract with respect to a performance not yet due the loss of which will substantially impair the value of the contract to the other, the aggrieved party may

(a) for a commercially reasonable time await performance by the repudiating party; or

(b) resort to any remedy for breach (Section 2—703 or Section 2—711), even though he has notified the repudiating party that he would await the latter's performance and has urged retraction; and

(c) in either case suspend his own performance or proceed in accordance with the provisions of this Article on the seller's right to identify goods to the contract notwithstanding breach or to salvage unfinished goods (Section 2—704).

§ 2—611. Retraction of Anticipatory Repudiation.

(1) Until the repudiating party's next performance is due he can retract his repudiation unless the aggrieved party has since the repudiation cancelled or materially changed his position or otherwise indicated that he considers the repudiation final.

(2) Retraction may be by any method which clearly indicates to the aggrieved party that the repudiating party intends to perform, but must include any assurance justifiably demanded under the provisions of this Article (Section 2—609).

(3) Retraction reinstates the repudiating party's rights under the contract with due excuse and allowance to the aggrieved party for any delay occasioned by the repudiation.

§ 2—612. "Installment Contract"; Breach.

(1) An "installment contract" is one which requires or authorizes the delivery of goods in separate lots to be separately accepted, even though the contract contains a clause "each delivery is a separate contract" or its equivalent.

(2) The buyer may reject any installment which is non-conforming if the non-conformity substantially impairs the value of that installment and cannot be cured or if the non-conformity is a defect in the required documents; but if the non-conformity does not fall within subsection (3) and the seller gives adequate assurance of its cure the buyer must accept that installment.

(3) Whenever non-conformity or default with respect to one or more installments substantially impairs the value of the whole contract there is a breach of the whole. But the aggrieved party reinstates the contract if he accepts a non-conforming installment without seasonably notifying of cancellation or if he brings an action with respect only to past installments or demands performance as to future installments.

§ 2—613. Casualty to Identified Goods.

Where the contract requires for its performance goods identified when the contract is made, and the goods suffer casualty without fault of either party before the risk of loss passes to the buyer, or in a proper case under a "no arrival, no sale" term (Section 2—324) then

(a) if the loss is total the contract is avoided; and

(b) if the loss is partial or the goods have so deteriorated as no longer to conform to the contract the buyer may nevertheless demand inspection and at his option either treat the contract as voided or accept the goods with due allowance from the contract price for the deterioration or the deficiency in quantity but without further right against the seller.

§ 2—614. Substituted Performance.

(1) Where without fault of either party the agreed berthing, loading, or unloading facilities fail or an agreed type of carrier becomes unavailable or the agreed manner of delivery otherwise becomes commercially impracticable but a commercially reasonable substitute is available, such substitute performance must be tendered and accepted.

(2) If the agreed means or manner of payment fails because of domestic or foreign governmental regulation, the seller may withhold or stop delivery unless the buyer provides a means or manner of payment which is commercially a substantial equivalent. If delivery has already been taken, payment by the means or in the manner provided by the regulation discharges the buyer's obligation unless the regulation is discriminatory, oppressive or predatory.

§ 2—615. Excuse by Failure of Presupposed Conditions.

Except so far as a seller may have assumed a greater obligation and subject to the preceding section on substituted performance:

(a) Delay in delivery or non-delivery in whole or in part by a seller who complies with paragraphs (b) and (c) is not a breach of his duty under a contract for sale if performance as agreed has been made impracticable by the occurrence of a contingency the nonoccurrence of which was a basic assumption on which the contract was made or by compliance in good faith with any applicable foreign or domestic governmental regulation or order whether or not it later proves to be invalid.

(b) Where the causes mentioned in paragraph (a) affect only a part of the seller's capacity to perform, he must allocate production and deliveries among his customers but may at his option include regular customers not then under contract as well as his own requirements for further manufacture. He may so allocate in any manner which is fair and reasonable.

(c) The seller must notify the buyer seasonably that there will be delay or non-delivery and, when allocation is required under paragraph (b), of the estimated quota thus made available for the buyer.

§ 2—616. Procedure on Notice Claiming Excuse.

(1) Where the buyer receives notification of a material or indefinite delay or an allocation justified under the preceding section he may by written notification to the seller as to any delivery concerned, and where the prospective deficiency substantially impairs the value of the whole contract under the provisions of this Article relating to breach of installment contracts (Section 2—612), then also as to the whole,

(a) terminate and thereby discharge any unexecuted portion of the contract; or

(b) modify the contract by agreeing to take his available quota in substitution.

(2) If after receipt of such notification from the seller the buyer fails so to modify the contract within a reasonable time not exceeding thirty days the contract lapses with respect to any deliveries affected.

(3) The provisions of this section may not be negated by agreement except in so far as the seller has assumed a greater obligation under the preceding section.

Part 7 Remedies

§ 2—701. Remedies for Breach of Collateral Contracts Not Impaired.

Remedies for breach of any obligation or promise collateral or ancillary to a contract for sale are not impaired by the provisions of this Article.

§ 2—702. Seller's Remedies on Discovery of Buyer's Insolvency.

(1) Where the seller discovers the buyer to be insolvent he may refuse delivery except for cash including payment for all goods theretofore delivered under the contract, and stop delivery under this Article (Section 2—705).

(2) Where the seller discovers that the buyer has received goods on credit while insolvent he may reclaim the goods upon demand made within ten days after the receipt, but if misrepresentation of solvency has been made to the particular seller in writing within three months before delivery the ten day limitation does not apply. Except as provided in this subsection the seller may not base a right to reclaim goods on the buyer's fraudulent or innocent misrepresentation of solvency or of intent to pay.

(3) The seller's right to reclaim under subsection (2) is subject to the rights of a buyer in ordinary course or other good faith purchaser under this Article (Section 2—403). Successful reclamation of goods excludes all other remedies with respect to them.

§ 2—703. Seller's Remedies in General.

Where the buyer wrongfully rejects or revokes acceptance of goods or fails to make a payment due on or before delivery or repudiates with respect to a part or the whole, then with respect to any goods directly affected and, if the breach is of the whole contract (Section 2—612), then also with respect to the whole undelivered balance, the aggrieved seller may

(a) withhold delivery of such goods;

(b) stop delivery by any bailee as hereafter provided (Section 2—705);

(c) proceed under the next section respecting goods still unidentified to the contract;

(d) resell and recover damages as hereafter provided (Section 2—706);

(e) recover damages for non-acceptance (Section 2—708) or in a proper case the price (Section 2—709);

(f) cancel.

§ 2—704. Seller's Right to Identify Goods to the Contract Notwithstanding Breach or to Salvage Unfinished Goods.

(1) An aggrieved seller under the preceding section may

(a) identify to the contract conforming goods not already identified if at the time he learned of the breach they are in his possession or control;

(b) treat as the subject of resale goods which have demonstrably been intended for the particular contract even though those goods are unfinished.

(2) Where the goods are unfinished an aggrieved seller may in the exercise of reasonable commercial judgment for the purposes of avoiding loss and of effective realization either complete the manufacture and wholly identify the goods to the contract or cease manufacture and resell for scrap or salvage value or proceed in any other reasonable manner.

§ 2—705. Seller's Stoppage of Delivery in Transit or Otherwise.

(1) The seller may stop delivery of goods in the possession of a carrier or other bailee when he discovers the buyer to be insolvent (Section 2—702) and may stop delivery of carload, truckload, planeload or larger shipments of express or freight when the buyer repudiates or fails to make a payment due before delivery or if for any other reason the seller has a right to withhold or reclaim the goods.

(2) As against such buyer the seller may stop delivery until

(a) receipt of the goods by the buyer; or

(b) acknowledgment to the buyer by any bailee of the goods except a carrier that the bailee holds the goods for the buyer; or

(c) such acknowledgment to the buyer by a carrier by reshipment or as warehouseman; or

(d) negotiation to the buyer of any negotiable document of title covering the goods.

(3) (a) To stop delivery the seller must so notify as to enable the bailee by reasonable diligence to prevent delivery of the goods.

(b) After such notification the bailee must hold and deliver the goods according to the directions of the seller but the seller is liable to the bailee for any ensuing charges or damages.

(c) If a negotiable document of title has been issued for goods the bailee is not obliged to obey a notification to stop until surrender of the document.

(d) A carrier who has issued a non-negotiable bill of lading is not obliged to obey a notification to stop received from a person other than the consignor.

§ 2—706. Seller's Resale Including Contract for Resale.

(1) Under the conditions stated in Section 2—703 on seller's remedies, the seller may resell the goods concerned or the undelivered balance thereof. Where the resale is made in good faith and in a commercially reasonable manner the seller may recover the difference between the resale price and the contract price together with any incidental damages allowed under the provisions of this Article (Section 2—710), but less expenses saved in consequence of the buyer's breach.

(2) Except as otherwise provided in subsection (3) or unless otherwise agreed resale may be at public or private sale including sale by way of one or more contracts to sell or of identification to an

existing contract of the seller. Sale may be as a unit or in parcels and at any time and place and on any terms but every aspect of the sale including the method, manner, time, place and terms must be commercially reasonable. The resale must be reasonably identified as referring to the broken contract, but it is not necessary that the goods be in existence or that any or all of them have been identified to the contract before the breach.

(3) Where the resale is at private sale the seller must give the buyer reasonable notification of his intention to resell.

(4) Where the resale is at public sale

(a) only identified goods can be sold except where there is a recognized market for a public sale of futures in goods of the kind; and

(b) it must be made at a usual place or market for public sale if one is reasonably available and except in the case of goods which are perishable or threaten to decline in value speedily the seller must give the buyer reasonable notice of the time and place of the resale; and

(c) if the goods are not to be within the view of those attending the sale the notification of sale must state the place where the goods are located and provide for their reasonable inspection by prospective bidders; and

(d) the seller may buy.

(5) A purchaser who buys in good faith at a resale takes the goods free of any rights of the original buyer even though the seller fails to comply with one or more of the requirements of this section.

(6) The seller is not accountable to the buyer for any profit made on any resale. A person in the position of a seller (Section 2—707) or a buyer who has rightfully rejected or justifiably revoked acceptance must account for any excess over the amount of his security interest, as hereinafter defined (subsection (3) of Section 2—711).

§ 2—707. "Person in the Position of a Seller".

(1) A "person in the position of a seller" includes as against a principal an agent who has paid or become responsible for the price of goods on behalf of his principal or anyone who otherwise holds a security interest or other right in goods similar to that of a seller.

(2) A person in the position of a seller may as provided in this Article withhold or stop delivery (Section 2—705) and resell (Section 2—706) and recover incidental damages (Section 2—710).

§ 2—708. Seller's Damages for Non-Acceptance or Repudiation.

(1) Subject to subsection (2) and to the provisions of this Article with respect to proof of market price (Section 2—723), the measure of damages for non-acceptance or repudiation by the buyer is the difference between the market price at the time and place for tender and the unpaid contract price together with any incidental damages provided in this Article (Section 2—710), but less expenses saved in consequence of the buyer's breach.

(2) If the measure of damages provided in subsection (1) is inadequate to put the seller in as good a position as performance would have done then the measure of damages is the profit (including reasonable overhead) which the seller would have made from full performance by the buyer, together with any incidental damages provided in this Article (Section 2—710), due allowance for costs reasonably incurred and due credit for payments or proceeds of resale.

§ 2—709. Action for the Price.

(1) When the buyer fails to pay the price as it becomes due the seller may recover, together with any incidental damages under the next section, the price

(a) of goods accepted or of conforming goods lost or damaged within a commercially reasonable time after risk of their loss has passed to the buyer; and

(b) of goods identified to the contract if the seller is unable after reasonable effort to resell them at a reasonable price or the circumstances reasonably indicate that such effort will be unavailing.

(2) Where the seller sues for the price he must hold for the buyer any goods which have been identified to the contract and are still in his control except that if resale becomes possible he may resell them at any time prior to the collection of the judgment. The net proceeds of any such resale must be credited to the buyer and payment of the judgment entitles him to any goods not resold.

(3) After the buyer has wrongfully rejected or revoked acceptance of the goods or has failed to make a payment due or has repudiated (Section 2—610), a seller who is held not entitled to the price under this section shall nevertheless be awarded damages for non-acceptance under the preceding section.

§ 2—710. Seller's Incidental Damages.

Incidental damages to an aggrieved seller include any commercially reasonable charges, expenses or commissions incurred in stopping delivery, in the transportation, care and custody of goods after the buyer's breach, in connection with return or resale of the goods or otherwise resulting from the breach.

§ 2—711. Buyer's Remedies in General; Buyer's Security Interest in Rejected Goods.

(1) Where the seller fails to make delivery or repudiates or the buyer rightfully rejects or justifiably revokes acceptance then with respect to any goods involved, and with respect to the whole if the breach goes to the whole contract (Section 2—612), the buyer may cancel and whether or not he has done so may in addition to recovering so much of the price as has been paid

(a) "cover" and have damages under the next section as to all the goods affected whether or not they have been identified to the contract; or

(b) recover damages for non-delivery as provided in this Article (Section 2—713).

(2) Where the seller fails to deliver or repudiates the buyer may also

(a) if the goods have been identified recover them as provided in this Article (Section 2—502); or

(b) in a proper case obtain specific performance or replevy the goods as provided in this Article (Section 2—716).

(3) On rightful rejection or justifiable revocation of acceptance a buyer has a security interest in goods in his possession or control for any payments made on their price and any expenses reasonably incurred in their inspection, receipt, transportation, care and custody and may hold such goods and resell them in like manner as an aggrieved seller (Section 2—706).

§ 2—712. "Cover"; Buyer's Procurement of Substitute Goods.

(1) After a breach within the preceding section the buyer may "cover" by making in good faith and without unreasonable delay any reasonable purchase of or contract to purchase goods in substitution for those due from the seller.

(2) The buyer may recover from the seller as damages the difference between the cost of cover and the contract price together with any incidental or consequential damages as hereinafter defined (Section 2—715), but less expenses saved in consequence of the seller's breach.

(3) Failure of the buyer to effect cover within this section does not bar him from any other remedy.

§ 2—713. Buyer's Damages for Non-Delivery or Repudiation.

(1) Subject to the provisions of this Article with respect to proof of market price (Section 2—723), the measure of damages for non-delivery or repudiation by the seller is the difference between the market price at the time when the buyer learned of the breach and the contract price together with any incidental and consequential damages provided in this Article (Section 2—715), but less expenses saved in consequence of the seller's breach.

(2) Market price is to be determined as of the place for tender or, in cases of rejection after arrival or revocation of acceptance, as of the place of arrival.

§ 2—714. Buyer's Damages for Breach in Regard to Accepted Goods.

(1) Where the buyer has accepted goods and given notification (subsection (3) of Section 2—607) he may recover as damages for any non-conformity of tender the loss resulting in the ordinary course of events from the seller's breach as determined in any manner which is reasonable.

(2) The measure of damages for breach of warranty is the difference at the time and place of acceptance between the value of the goods accepted and the value they would have had if they had been as warranted, unless special circumstances show proximate damages of a different amount.

(3) In a proper case any incidental and consequential damages under the next section may also be recovered.

§ 2—715. Buyer's Incidental and Consequential Damages.

(1) Incidental damages resulting from the seller's breach include expenses reasonably incurred in inspection, receipt, transportation and care and custody of goods rightfully rejected, any commercially reasonable charges, expenses or commissions in connection with effecting cover and any other reasonable expense incident to the delay or other breach.

(2) Consequential damages resulting from the seller's breach include

(a) any loss resulting from general or particular requirements and needs of which the seller at the time of contracting had reason to know and which could not reasonably be prevented by cover or otherwise; and

(b) injury to person or property proximately resulting from any breach of warranty.

§ 2—716. Buyer's Right to Specific Performance or Replevin.

(1) Specific performance may be decreed where the goods are unique or in other proper circumstances.

(2) The decree for specific performance may include such terms and conditions as to payment of the price, damages, or other relief as the court may deem just.

(3) The buyer has a right of replevin for goods identified to the contract if after reasonable effort he is unable to effect cover for such goods or the circumstances reasonably indicate that such effort will be unavailing or if the goods have been shipped under reservation and satisfaction of the security interest in them has been made or tendered.

§ 2—717. Deduction of Damages From the Price.

The buyer on notifying the seller of his intention to do so may deduct all or any part of the damages resulting from any breach of the contract from any part of the price still due under the same contract.

§ 2—718. Liquidation or Limitation of Damages; Deposits.

(1) Damages for breach by either party may be liquidated in the agreement but only at an amount which is reasonable in the light of the anticipated or actual harm caused by the breach, the difficulties of proof of loss, and the inconvenience or nonfeasibility of otherwise obtaining an adequate remedy. A term fixing unreasonably large liquidated damages is void as a penalty.

(2) Where the seller justifiably withholds delivery of goods because of the buyer's breach, the buyer is entitled to restitution of any amount by which the sum of his payments exceeds

(a) the amount to which the seller is entitled by virtue of terms liquidating the seller's damages in accordance with subsection (1), or

(b) in the absence of such terms, twenty per cent of the value of the total performance for which the buyer is obligated under the contract or $500, whichever is smaller.

(3) The buyer's right to restitution under subsection (2) is subject to offset to the extent that the seller establishes

(a) a right to recover damages under the provisions of this Article other than subsection (1), and

(b) the amount or value of any benefits received by the buyer directly or indirectly by reason of the contract.

(4) Where a seller has received payment in goods their reasonable value or the proceeds of their resale shall be treated as payments for the purposes of subsection (2); but if the seller has notice of the buyer's breach before reselling goods received in part performance, his resale is subject to the conditions laid down in this Article on resale by an aggrieved seller (Section 2—706).

§ 2—719. Contractual Modification or Limitation of Remedy.

(1) Subject to the provisions of subsections (2) and (3) of this section and of the preceding section on liquidation and limitation of damages,

(a) the agreement may provide for remedies in addition to or in substitution for those provided in this Article and may limit or alter the measure of damages recoverable under this Article, as by limiting the buyer's remedies to return of the goods and repayment of the price or to repair and replacement of nonconforming goods or parts; and

(b) resort to a remedy as provided is optional unless the remedy is expressly agreed to be exclusive, in which case it is the sole remedy.

(2) Where circumstances cause an exclusive or limited remedy to fail of its essential purpose, remedy may be had as provided in this Act.

(3) Consequential damages may be limited or excluded unless the limitation or exclusion is unconscionable. Limitation of consequential damages for injury to the person in the case of consumer goods is prima facie unconscionable but limitation of damages where the loss is commercial is not.

§ 2—720. Effect of "Cancellation" or "Rescission" on Claims for Antecedent Breach.

Unless the contrary intention clearly appears, expressions of "cancellation" or "rescission" of the contract or the like shall not be construed as a renunciation or discharge of any claim in damages for an antecedent breach.

§ 2—721. Remedies for Fraud.

Remedies for material misrepresentation or fraud include all remedies available under this Article for non-fraudulent breach. Neither rescission or a claim for rescission of the contract for sale nor rejection or return of the goods shall bar or be deemed inconsistent with a claim for damages or other remedy.

§ 2—722. Who Can Sue Third Parties for Injury to Goods.

Where a third party so deals with goods which have been identified to a contract for sale as to cause actionable injury to a party to that contract

(a) a right of action against the third party is in either party to the contract for sale who has title to or a security interest or a special property or an insurable interest in the goods; and if the goods have been destroyed or converted a right of action is also in the party who either bore the risk of loss under the contract for sale or has since the injury assumed that risk as against the other;

(b) if at the time of the injury the party plaintiff did not bear the risk of loss as against the other party to the contract for sale and there is no arrangement between them for disposition of the recovery, his suit or settlement is, subject to his own interest, as a fiduciary for the other party to the contract;

(c) either party may with the consent of the other sue for the benefit of whom it may concern.

§ 2—723. Proof of Market Price: Time and Place.

(1) If an action based on anticipatory repudiation comes to trial before the time for performance with respect to some or all of the goods, any damages based on market price (Section 2—708 or Section 2—713) shall be determined according to the price of such goods prevailing at the time when the aggrieved party learned of the repudiation.

(2) If evidence of a price prevailing at the times or places described in this Article is not readily available the price prevailing within any reasonable time before or after the time described or at any other place which in commercial judgment or under usage of trade would serve as a reasonable substitute for the one described may be used, making any proper allowance for the cost of transporting the goods to or from such other place.

(3) Evidence of a relevant price prevailing at a time or place other than the one described in this Article offered by one party is not admissible unless and until he has given the other party such notice as the court finds sufficient to prevent unfair surprise.

§ 2—724. Admissibility of Market Quotations.

Whenever the prevailing price or value of any goods regularly bought and sold in any established commodity market is in issue, reports in official publications or trade journals or in newspapers or periodicals of general circulation published as the reports of such market shall be admissible in evidence. The circumstances of the preparation of such a report may be shown to affect its weight but not its admissibility.

§ 2—725. Statute of Limitations in Contracts for Sale.

(1) An action for breach of any contract for sale must be commenced within four years after the cause of action has accrued. By the original agreement the parties may reduce the period of limitation to not less than one year but may not extend it.

(2) A cause of action accrues when the breach occurs, regardless of the aggrieved party's lack of knowledge of the breach. A breach of warranty occurs when tender of delivery is made, except that where a warranty explicitly extends to future performance of the goods and discovery of the breach must await the time of such performance the cause of action accrues when the breach is or should have been discovered.

(3) Where an action commenced within the time limited by subsection (1) is so terminated as to leave available a remedy by another action for the same breach such other action may be commenced after the expiration of the time limited and within six

months after the termination of the first action unless the termination resulted from voluntary discontinuance or from dismissal for failure or neglect to prosecute.

(4) This section does not alter the law on tolling of the statute of limitations nor does it apply to causes of action which have accrued before this Act becomes effective.

Article 2A
LEASES

Part 1 General Provisions

§ 2A—101. Short Title.

This Article shall be known and may be cited as the Uniform Commercial Code—Leases.

§ 2A—102. Scope.

This Article applies to any transaction, regardless of form, that creates a lease.

§ 2A—103. Definitions and Index of Definitions.

(1) In this Article unless the context otherwise requires:

(a) "Buyer in ordinary course of business" means a person who in good faith and without knowledge that the sale to him [or her] is in violation of the ownership rights or security interest or leasehold interest of a third party in the goods buys in ordinary course from a person in the business of selling goods of that kind but does not include a pawnbroker. "Buying" may be for cash or by exchange of other property or on secured or unsecured credit and includes receiving goods or documents of title under a pre-existing contract for sale but does not include a transfer in bulk or as security for or in total or partial satisfaction of a money debt.

(b) "Cancellation" occurs when either party puts an end to the lease contract for default by the other party.

(c) "Commercial unit" means such a unit of goods as by commercial usage is a single whole for purposes of lease and division of which materially impairs its character or value on the market or in use. A commercial unit may be a single article, as a machine, or a set of articles, as a suite of furniture or a line of machinery, or a quantity, as a gross or carload, or any other unit treated in use or in the relevant market as a single whole.

(d) "Conforming" goods or performance under a lease contract means goods or performance that are in accordance with the obligations under the lease contract.

(e) "Consumer lease" means a lease that a lessor regularly engaged in the business of leasing or selling makes to a lessee who is an individual and who takes under the lease primarily for a personal, family, or household "purpose [, if" the total payments to be made under the lease contract, excluding payments for options to renew or buy, do not exceed. . . .

(f) "Fault" means wrongful act, omission, breach, or default.

(g) "Finance lease" means a lease with respect to which:

(i) the lessor does not select, manufacture or supply the goods;

(ii) the lessor acquires the goods or the right to possession and use of the goods in connection with the lease; and

(iii) one of the following occurs:

(A) the lessee receives a copy of the contract by which the lessor acquired the goods or the right to possession and use of the goods before signing the lease contract;

(B) the lessee's approval of the contract by which the lessor acquired the goods or the right to possession and use of the goods is a condition to effectiveness of the lease contract;

(C) the lessee, before signing the lease contract, receives an accurate and complete statement designating the promises and warranties, and any disclaimers of warranties, limitations or modifications of remedies, or liquidated damages, including those of a third party, such as the manufacturer of the goods, provided to the lessor by the person supplying the goods in connection with or as part of the contract by which the lessor acquired the goods or the right to possession and use of the goods; or

(D) if the lease is not a consumer lease, the lessor, before the lessee signs the lease contract, informs the lessee in writing (a) of the identity of the person supplying the goods to the lessor, unless the lessee has selected that person and directed the lessor to acquire the goods or the right to possession and use of the goods from that person, (b) that the lessee is entitled under this Article to any promises and warranties, including those of any third party, provided to the lessor by the person supplying the goods in connection with or as part of the contract by which the lessor acquired the goods or the right to possession and use of the goods, and (c) that the lessee may communicate with the person supplying the goods to the lessor and receive an accurate and complete statement of those promises and warranties, including any disclaimers and limitations of them or of remedies.

(h) "Goods" means all things that are movable at the time of identification to the lease contract, or are fixtures (Section 2A—309), but the term does not include money, documents, instruments, accounts, chattel paper, general intangibles, or minerals or the like, including oil and gas, before extraction. The term also includes the unborn young of animals.

(i) "Installment lease contract" means a lease contract that authorizes or requires the delivery of goods in separate lots to be separately accepted, even though the lease contract contains a clause "each delivery is a separate lease" or its equivalent.

(j) "Lease" means a transfer of the right to possession and use of goods for a term in return for consideration, but a sale, including a sale on approval or a sale or return, or retention or creation of a security interest is not a lease. Unless the context clearly indicates otherwise, the term includes a sublease.

(k) "Lease agreement" means the bargain, with respect to the lease, of the lessor and the lessee in fact as found in their language or by implication from other circumstances including course of dealing or usage of trade or course of performance as provided in this Article. Unless the context clearly indicates otherwise, the term includes a sublease agreement.

(l) "Lease contract" means the total legal obligation that results from the lease agreement as affected by this Article and any other applicable rules of law. Unless the context clearly indicates otherwise, the term includes a sublease contract.

(m) "Leasehold interest" means the interest of the lessor or the lessee under a lease contract.

(n) "Lessee" means a person who acquires the right to possession and use of goods under a lease. Unless the context clearly indicates otherwise, the term includes a sublessee.

(o) "Lessee in ordinary course of business" means a person who in good faith and without knowledge that the lease to him [or her] is in violation of the ownership rights or security interest or leasehold interest of a third party in the goods, leases in ordinary course from a person in the business of selling or leasing goods of that kind but does not include a pawnbroker. "Leasing" may be for cash or by exchange of other property or on secured or unsecured credit and includes receiving goods or documents of title under a pre-existing lease contract but does not include a transfer in bulk or as security for or in total or partial satisfaction of a money debt.

(p) "Lessor" means a person who transfers the right to possession and use of goods under a lease. Unless the context clearly indicates otherwise, the term includes a sublessor.

(q) "Lessor's residual interest" means the lessor's interest in the goods after expiration, termination, or cancellation of the lease contract.

(r) "Lien" means a charge against or interest in goods to secure payment of a debt or performance of an obligation, but the term does not include a security interest.

(s) "Lot" means a parcel or a single article that is the subject matter of a separate lease or delivery, whether or not it is sufficient to perform the lease contract.

(t) "Merchant lessee" means a lessee that is a merchant with respect to goods of the kind subject to the lease.

(u) "Present value" means the amount as of a date certain of one or more sums payable in the future, discounted to the date certain. The discount is determined by the interest rate specified by the parties if the rate was not manifestly unreasonable at the time the transaction was entered into; otherwise, the discount is determined by a commercially reasonable rate that takes into account the facts and circumstances of each case at the time the transaction was entered into.

(v) "Purchase" includes taking by sale, lease, mortgage, security interest, pledge, gift, or any other voluntary transaction creating an interest in goods.

(w) "Sublease" means a lease of goods the right to possession and use of which was acquired by the lessor as a lessee under an existing lease.

(x) "Supplier" means a person from whom a lessor buys or leases goods to be leased under a finance lease.

(y) "Supply contract" means a contract under which a lessor buys or leases goods to be leased.

(z) "Termination" occurs when either party pursuant to a power created by agreement or law puts an end to the lease contract otherwise than for default.

(2) Other definitions applying to this Article and the sections in which they appear are:

"Accessions". Section 2A—310(1).
"Construction mortgage". Section 2A—309(1)(d).
"Encumbrance". Section 2A—309(1)(e).
"Fixtures". Section 2A—309(1)(a).
"Fixture filing". Section 2A—309(1)(b).
"Purchase money lease". Section 2A—309(1)(c).

(3) The following definitions in other Articles apply to this Article:

"Accounts". Section 9—106.
"Between merchants". Section 2—104(3).
"Buyer". Section 2—103(1)(a).
"Chattel paper". Section 9—105(1)(b).
"Consumer goods". Section 9—109(1).
"Document". Section 9—105(1)(f).
"Entrusting". Section 2—403(3).
"General intangibles". Section 9—106.
"Good faith". Section 2—103(1)(b).
"Instrument". Section 9—105(1)(i).
"Merchant". Section 2—104(1).
"Mortgage". Section 9—105(1)(j).
"Pursuant to commitment". Section 9—105(1)(k).
"Receipt". Section 2—103(1)(c).
"Sale". Section 2—106(1).
"Sale on approval". Section 2—326.
"Sale or return". Section 2—326.
"Seller". Section 2—103(1)(d).

(4) In addition Article 1 contains general definitions and principles of construction and interpretation applicable throughout this Article.

As amended in 1990.

§ 2A—104. Leases Subject to Other Law.

(1) A lease, although subject to this Article, is also subject to any applicable:

(a) certificate of title statute of this State: (list any certificate of title statutes covering automobiles, trailers, mobile homes, boats, farm tractors, and the like);

(b) certificate of title statute of another jurisdiction (Section 2A—105); or

(c) consumer protection statute of this State, or final consumer protection decision of a court of this State existing on the effective date of this Article.

(2) In case of conflict between this Article, other than Sections 2A—105, 2A—304(3), and 2A—305(3), and a statute or decision referred to in subsection (1), the statute or decision controls.

(3) Failure to comply with an applicable law has only the effect specified therein.

As amended in 1990.

§ 2A—105. Territorial Application of Article to Goods Covered by Certificate of Title.

Subject to the provisions of Sections 2A—304(3) and 2A—305(3), with respect to goods covered by a certificate of title issued under a statute of this State or of another jurisdiction, compliance and the effect of compliance or noncompliance with a certificate of title statute are governed by the law (including the conflict of laws rules) of the jurisdiction issuing the certificate until the earlier of (a) surrender of the certificate, or (b) four months after the goods are removed from that jurisdiction and thereafter until a new certificate of title is issued by another jurisdiction.

§ 2A—106. Limitation on Power of Parties to Consumer Lease to Choose Applicable Law and Judicial Forum.

(1) If the law chosen by the parties to a consumer lease is that of a jurisdiction other than a jurisdiction in which the lessee resides at the time the lease agreement becomes enforceable or within 30 days thereafter or in which the goods are to be used, the choice is not enforceable.

(2) If the judicial forum chosen by the parties to a consumer lease is a forum that would not otherwise have jurisdiction over the lessee, the choice is not enforceable.

§ 2A—107. Waiver or Renunciation of Claim or Right After Default.

Any claim or right arising out of an alleged default or breach of warranty may be discharged in whole or in part without consideration by a written waiver or renunciation signed and delivered by the aggrieved party.

§ 2A—108. Unconscionability.

(1) If the court as a matter of law finds a lease contract or any clause of a lease contract to have been unconscionable at the time it was made the court may refuse to enforce the lease contract, or it may enforce the remainder of the lease contract without the unconscionable clause, or it may so limit the application of any unconscionable clause as to avoid any unconscionable result.

(2) With respect to a consumer lease, if the court as a matter of law finds that a lease contract or any clause of a lease contract has been induced by unconscionable conduct or that unconscionable conduct has occurred in the collection of a claim arising from a lease contract, the court may grant appropriate relief.

(3) Before making a finding of unconscionability under subsection (1) or (2), the court, on its own motion or that of a party, shall afford the parties a reasonable opportunity to present evidence as to the setting, purpose, and effect of the lease contract or clause thereof, or of the conduct.

(4) In an action in which the lessee claims unconscionability with respect to a consumer lease:

(a) If the court finds unconscionability under subsection (1) or (2), the court shall award reasonable attorney's fees to the lessee.

(b) If the court does not find unconscionability and the lessee claiming unconscionability has brought or maintained an action he [or she] knew to be groundless, the court shall award reasonable attorney's fees to the party against whom the claim is made.

(c) In determining attorney's fees, the amount of the recovery on behalf of the claimant under subsections (1) and (2) is not controlling.

§ 2A—109. Option to Accelerate at Will.

(1) A term providing that one party or his [or her] successor in interest may accelerate payment or performance or require collateral or additional collateral "at will" or "when he [or she] deems himself [or herself] insecure" or in words of similar import must be construed to mean that he [or she] has power to do so only if he [or she] in good faith believes that the prospect of payment or performance is impaired.

(2) With respect to a consumer lease, the burden of establishing good faith under subsection (1) is on the party who exercised the power; otherwise the burden of establishing lack of good faith is on the party against whom the power has been exercised.

Part 2 Formation and Construction of Lease Contract

§ 2A—201. Statute of Frauds.

(1) A lease contract is not enforceable by way of action or defense unless:

(a) the total payments to be made under the lease contract, excluding payments for options to renew or buy, are less than $1,000; or

(b) there is a writing, signed by the party against whom enforcement is sought or by that party's authorized agent, sufficient to indicate that a lease contract has been made between the parties and to describe the goods leased and the lease term.

(2) Any description of leased goods or of the lease term is sufficient and satisfies subsection (1)(b), whether or not it is specific, if it reasonably identifies what is described.

(3) A writing is not insufficient because it omits or incorrectly states a term agreed upon, but the lease contract is not enforceable under subsection (1)(b) beyond the lease term and the quantity of goods shown in the writing.

(4) A lease contract that does not satisfy the requirements of subsection (1), but which is valid in other respects, is enforceable:

(a) if the goods are to be specially manufactured or obtained for the lessee and are not suitable for lease or sale to others in the ordinary course of the lessor's business, and the lessor, before notice of repudiation is received and under circumstances that reasonably indicate that the goods are for the lessee, has made either a substantial beginning of their manufacture or commitments for their procurement;

(b) if the party against whom enforcement is sought admits in that party's pleading, testimony or otherwise in court that a lease contract was made, but the lease contract is not enforceable under this provision beyond the quantity of goods admitted; or

(c) with respect to goods that have been received and accepted by the lessee.

(5) The lease term under a lease contract referred to in subsection (4) is:

(a) if there is a writing signed by the party against whom enforcement is sought or by that party's authorized agent specifying the lease term, the term so specified;

(b) if the party against whom enforcement is sought admits in that party's pleading, testimony, or otherwise in court a lease term, the term so admitted; or

(c) a reasonable lease term.

§ 2A—202. Final Written Expression: Parol or Extrinsic Evidence.

Terms with respect to which the confirmatory memoranda of the parties agree or which are otherwise set forth in a writing intended by the parties as a final expression of their agreement with respect to such terms as are included therein may not be contradicted by evidence of any prior agreement or of a contemporaneous oral agreement but may be explained or supplemented:

(a) by course of dealing or usage of trade or by course of performance; and

(b) by evidence of consistent additional terms unless the court finds the writing to have been intended also as a complete and exclusive statement of the terms of the agreement.

§ 2A—203. Seals Inoperative.

The affixing of a seal to a writing evidencing a lease contract or an offer to enter into a lease contract does not render the writing a sealed instrument and the law with respect to sealed instruments does not apply to the lease contract or offer.

§ 2A—204. Formation in General.

(1) A lease contract may be made in any manner sufficient to show agreement, including conduct by both parties which recognizes the existence of a lease contract.

(2) An agreement sufficient to constitute a lease contract may be found although the moment of its making is undetermined.

(3) Although one or more terms are left open, a lease contract does not fail for indefiniteness if the parties have intended to make a lease contract and there is a reasonably certain basis for giving an appropriate remedy.

§ 2A—205. Firm Offers.

An offer by a merchant to lease goods to or from another person in a signed writing that by its terms gives assurance it will be held open is not revocable, for lack of consideration, during the time stated or, if no time is stated, for a reasonable time, but in no event may the period of irrevocability exceed 3 months. Any such term of assurance on a form supplied by the offeree must be separately signed by the offeror.

§ 2A—206. Offer and Acceptance in Formation of Lease Contract.

(1) Unless otherwise unambiguously indicated by the language or circumstances, an offer to make a lease contract must be construed as inviting acceptance in any manner and by any medium reasonable in the circumstances.

(2) If the beginning of a requested performance is a reasonable mode of acceptance, an offeror who is not notified of acceptance within a reasonable time may treat the offer as having lapsed before acceptance.

§ 2A—207. Course of Performance or Practical Construction.

(1) If a lease contract involves repeated occasions for performance by either party with knowledge of the nature of the performance and opportunity for objection to it by the other, any course of performance accepted or acquiesced in without objection is relevant to determine the meaning of the lease agreement.

(2) The express terms of a lease agreement and any course of performance, as well as any course of dealing and usage of trade, must be construed whenever reasonable as consistent with each other; but if that construction is unreasonable, express terms control course of performance, course of performance controls both course of dealing and usage of trade, and course of dealing controls usage of trade.

(3) Subject to the provisions of Section 2A—208 on modification and waiver, course of performance is relevant to show a waiver or modification of any term inconsistent with the course of performance.

§ 2A—208. Modification, Rescission and Waiver.

(1) An agreement modifying a lease contract needs no consideration to be binding.

(2) A signed lease agreement that excludes modification or rescission except by a signed writing may not be otherwise modified or rescinded, but, except as between merchants, such a requirement on a form supplied by a merchant must be separately signed by the other party.

(3) Although an attempt at modification or rescission does not satisfy the requirements of subsection (2), it may operate as a waiver.

(4) A party who has made a waiver affecting an executory portion of a lease contract may retract the waiver by reasonable notification received by the other party that strict performance will be required of any term waived, unless the retraction would be unjust in view of a material change of position in reliance on the waiver.

§ 2A—209. Lessee under Finance Lease as Beneficiary of Supply Contract.

(1) The benefit of the supplier's promises to the lessor under the supply contract and of all warranties, whether express or implied, including those of any third party provided in connection with or as part of the supply contract, extends to the lessee to the extent of the lessee's leasehold interest under a finance lease related to the supply contract, but is subject to the terms warranty and of the supply contract and all defenses or claims arising therefrom.

(2) The extension of the benefit of supplier's promises and of warranties to the lessee (Section 2A–209(1)) does not: (i) modify the rights and obligations of the parties to the supply contract, whether arising therefrom or otherwise, or (ii) impose any duty or liability under the supply contract on the lessee.

(3) Any modification or rescission of the supply contract by the supplier and the lessor is effective between the supplier and the lessee unless, before the modification or rescission, the supplier has received notice that the lessee has entered into a finance lease related to the supply contract. If the modification or rescission is effective between the supplier and the lessee, the lessor is deemed to have assumed, in addition to the obligations of the lessor to the lessee under the lease contract, promises of the supplier to the lessor and warranties that were so modified or rescinded as they existed and were available to the lessee before modification or rescission.

(4) In addition to the extension of the benefit of the supplier's promises and of warranties to the lessee under subsection (1), the lessee retains all rights that the lessee may have against the supplier which arise from an agreement between the lessee and the supplier or under other law.

As amended in 1990.

§ 2A—210. Express Warranties.

(1) Express warranties by the lessor are created as follows:

(a) Any affirmation of fact or promise made by the lessor to the lessee which relates to the goods and becomes part of the basis of the bargain creates an express warranty that the goods will conform to the affirmation or promise.

(b) Any description of the goods which is made part of the basis of the bargain creates an express warranty that the goods will conform to the description.

(c) Any sample or model that is made part of the basis of the bargain creates an express warranty that the whole of the goods will conform to the sample or model.

(2) It is not necessary to the creation of an express warranty that the lessor use formal words, such as "warrant" or "guarantee," or that the lessor have a specific intention to make a warranty, but an affirmation merely of the value of the goods or a statement purporting to be merely the lessor's opinion or commendation of the goods does not create a warranty.

§ 2A—211. Warranties Against Interference and Against Infringement; Lessee's Obligation Against Infringement.

(1) There is in a lease contract a warranty that for the lease term no person holds a claim to or interest in the goods that arose from an act or omission of the lessor, other than a claim by way of infringement or the like, which will interfere with the lessee's enjoyment of its leasehold interest.

(2) Except in a finance lease there is in a lease contract by a lessor who is a merchant regularly dealing in goods of the kind a warranty that the goods are delivered free of the rightful claim of any person by way of infringement or the like.

(3) A lessee who furnishes specifications to a lessor or a supplier shall hold the lessor and the supplier harmless against any claim by way of infringement or the like that arises out of compliance with the specifications.

§ 2A—212. Implied Warranty of Merchantability.

(1) Except in a finance lease, a warranty that the goods will be merchantable is implied in a lease contract if the lessor is a merchant with respect to goods of that kind.

(2) Goods to be merchantable must be at least such as

(a) pass without objection in the trade under the description in the lease agreement;

(b) in the case of fungible goods, are of fair average quality within the description;

(c) are fit for the ordinary purposes for which goods of that type are used;

(d) run, within the variation permitted by the lease agreement, of even kind, quality, and quantity within each unit and among all units involved;

(e) are adequately contained, packaged, and labeled as the lease agreement may require; and

(f) conform to any promises or affirmations of fact made on the container or label.

(3) Other implied warranties may arise from course of dealing or usage of trade.

§ 2A—213. Implied Warranty of Fitness for Particular Purpose.

Except in a finance of lease, if the lessor at the time the lease contract is made has reason to know of any particular purpose for which the goods are required and that the lessee is relying on the lessor's skill or judgment to select or furnish suitable goods, there is in the lease contract an implied warranty that the goods will be fit for that purpose.

§ 2A—214. Exclusion or Modification of Warranties.

(1) Words or conduct relevant to the creation of an express warranty and words or conduct tending to negate or limit a warranty must be construed wherever reasonable as consistent with each other; but, subject to the provisions of Section 2A—202 on parol or extrinsic evidence, negation or limitation is inoperative to the extent that the construction is unreasonable.

(2) Subject to subsection (3), to exclude or modify the implied warranty of merchantability or any part of it the language must mention "merchantability", be by a writing, and be conspicuous. Subject to subsection (3), to exclude or modify any implied warranty of fitness the exclusion must be by a writing and be conspicuous. Language to exclude all implied warranties of fitness is sufficient if it is in writing, is conspicuous and states, for example, "There is no warranty that the goods will be fit for a particular purpose".

(3) Notwithstanding subsection (2), but subject to subsection (4),

(a) unless the circumstances indicate otherwise, all implied warranties are excluded by expressions like "as is" or "with all faults" or by other language that in common understanding calls the lessee's attention to the exclusion of warranties and makes plain that there is no implied warranty, if in writing and conspicuous;

(b) if the lessee before entering into the lease contract has examined the goods or the sample or model as fully as desired or has refused to examine the goods, there is no implied warranty with regard to defects that an examination ought in the circumstances to have revealed; and

(c) an implied warranty may also be excluded or modified by course of dealing, course of performance, or usage of trade.

(4) To exclude or modify a warranty against interference or against infringement (Section 2A—211) or any part of it, the language must be specific, be by a writing, and be conspicuous, unless the circumstances, including course of performance, course of dealing, or usage of trade, give the lessee reason to know that the goods are being leased subject to a claim or interest of any person.

§ 2A—215. Cumulation and Conflict of Warranties Express or Implied.

Warranties, whether express or implied, must be construed as consistent with each other and as cumulative, but if that construction is unreasonable, the intention of the parties determines which warranty is dominant. In ascertaining that intention the following rules apply:

(a) Exact or technical specifications displace an inconsistent sample or model or general language of description.

(b) A sample from an existing bulk displaces inconsistent general language of description.

(c) Express warranties displace inconsistent implied warranties other than an implied warranty of fitness for a particular purpose.

§ 2A—216. Third-Party Beneficiaries of Express and Implied Warranties.

Alternative A

A warranty to or for the benefit of a lessee under this Article, whether express or implied, extends to any natural person who is in the family or household of the lessee or who is a guest in the lessee's home if it is reasonable to expect that such person may use, consume, or be affected by the goods and who is injured in person by breach of the warranty. This section does not displace principles of law and equity that extend a warranty to or for the benefit of a lessee to other persons. The operation of this section may not be excluded, modified, or limited, but an exclusion, modification, or limitation of the warranty, including any with respect to rights and remedies, effective against the lessee is also effective against any beneficiary designated under this section.

Alternative B

A warranty to or for the benefit of a lessee under this Article, whether express or implied, extends to any natural person who may reasonably be expected to use, consume, or be affected by the goods and who is injured in person by breach of the warranty. This section does not displace principles of law and equity that extend a warranty to or for the benefit of a lessee to other persons. The operation of this section may not be excluded, modified, or limited, but an exclusion, modification, or limitation of the warranty, including any with respect to rights and remedies, effective against the lessee is also effective against the beneficiary designated under this section.

Alternative C

A warranty to or for the benefit of a lessee under this Article, whether express or implied, extends to any person who may reasonably be expected to use, consume, or be affected by the goods and who is injured by breach of the warranty. The operation of this section may not be excluded, modified, or limited with respect to injury to the person of an individual to whom the warranty extends, but an exclusion, modification, or limitation of the warranty, including any with respect to rights and remedies, effective against the lessee is also effective against the beneficiary designated under this section.

§ 2A—217. Identification.

Identification of goods as goods to which a lease contract refers may be made at any time and in any manner explicitly agreed to by the parties. In the absence of explicit agreement, identification occurs:

(a) when the lease contract is made if the lease contract is for a lease of goods that are existing and identified;

(b) when the goods are shipped, marked, or otherwise designated by the lessor as goods to which the lease contract refers, if the lease contract is for a lease of goods that are not existing and identified; or

(c) when the young are conceived, if the lease contract is for a lease of unborn young of animals.

§ 2A—218. Insurance and Proceeds.

(1) A lessee obtains an insurable interest when existing goods are identified to the lease contract even though the goods identified are nonconforming and the lessee has an option to reject them.

(2) If a lessee has an insurable interest only by reason of the lessor's identification of the goods, the lessor, until default or insolvency or notification to the lessee that identification is final, may substitute other goods for those identified.

(3) Notwithstanding a lessee's insurable interest under subsections (1) and (2), the lessor retains an insurable interest until an option to buy has been exercised by the lessee and risk of loss has passed to the lessee.

(4) Nothing in this section impairs any insurable interest recognized under any other statute or rule of law.

(5) The parties by agreement may determine that one or more parties have an obligation to obtain and pay for insurance covering the goods and by agreement may determine the beneficiary of the proceeds of the insurance.

§ 2A—219. Risk of Loss.

(1) Except in the case of a finance lease, risk of loss is retained by the lessor and does not pass to the lessee. In the case of a finance lease, risk of loss passes to the lessee.

(2) Subject to the provisions of this Article on the effect of default on risk of loss (Section 2A—220), if risk of loss is to pass to the lessee and the time of passage is not stated, the following rules apply:

(a) If the lease contract requires or authorizes the goods to be shipped by carrier

(i) and it does not require delivery at a particular destination, the risk of loss passes to the lessee when the goods are duly delivered to the carrier; but

(ii) if it does require delivery at a particular destination and the goods are there duly tendered while in the possession of the carrier, the risk of loss passes to the lessee when the goods are there duly so tendered as to enable the lessee to take delivery.

(b) If the goods are held by a bailee to be delivered without being moved, the risk of loss passes to the lessee on acknowledgment by the bailee of the lessee's right to possession of the goods.

(c) In any case not within subsection (a) or (b), the risk of loss passes to the lessee on the lessee's receipt of the goods if the lessor, or, in the case of a finance lease, the supplier, is a merchant; otherwise the risk passes to the lessee on tender of delivery.

§ 2A—220. Effect of Default on Risk of Loss.

(1) Where risk of loss is to pass to the lessee and the time of passage is not stated:

(a) If a tender or delivery of goods so fails to conform to the lease contract as to give a right of rejection, the risk of their loss remains with the lessor, or, in the case of a finance lease, the supplier, until cure or acceptance.

(b) If the lessee rightfully revokes acceptance, he [or she], to the extent of any deficiency in his [or her] effective insurance coverage, may treat the risk of loss as having remained with the lessor from the beginning.

(2) Whether or not risk of loss is to pass to the lessee, if the lessee as to conforming goods already identified to a lease contract repudiates or is otherwise in default under the lease contract, the lessor, or, in the case of a finance lease, the supplier, to the extent of any deficiency in his [or her] effective insurance coverage may treat the risk of loss as resting on the lessee for a commercially reasonable time.

§ 2A—221. Casualty to Identified Goods.

If a lease contract requires goods identified when the lease contract is made, and the goods suffer casualty without fault of the lessee, the lessor or the supplier before delivery, or the goods suffer casualty before risk of loss passes to the lessee pursuant to the lease agreement or Section 2A—219, then:

(a) if the loss is total, the lease contract is avoided; and

(b) if the loss is partial or the goods have so deteriorated as to no longer conform to the lease contract, the lessee may nevertheless demand inspection and at his [or her] option either treat the lease contract as avoided or, except in a finance lease that is not a consumer lease, accept the goods with due allowance from the rent payable for the balance of the lease term for the deterioration or the deficiency in quantity but without further right against the lessor.

Part 3 Effect of Lease Contract

§ 2A—301. Enforceability of Lease Contract.

Except as otherwise provided in this Article, a lease contract is effective and enforceable according to its terms between the parties, against purchasers of the goods and against creditors of the parties.

§ 2A—302. Title to and Possession of Goods.

Except as otherwise provided in this Article, each provision of this Article applies whether the lessor or a third party has title to the goods, and whether the lessor, the lessee, or a third party has possession of the goods, notwithstanding any statute or rule of law that possession or the absence of possession is fraudulent.

§ 2A—303. Alienability of Party's Interest Under Lease Contract or of Lessor's Residual Interest in Goods; Delegation of Performance; Transfer of Rights.

(1) As used in this section, "creation of a security interest" includes the sale of a lease contract that is subject to Article 9, Secured Transactions, by reason of Section 9—102(1)(b).

(2) Except as provided in subsections (3) and (4), a provision in a lease agreement which (i) prohibits the voluntary or involuntary

transfer, including a transfer by sale, sublease, creation or enforcement of a security interest, or attachment, levy, or other judicial process, of an interest of a party under the lease contract or of the lessor's residual interest in the goods, or (ii) makes such a transfer an event of default, gives rise to the rights and remedies provided in subsection (5), but a transfer that is prohibited or is an event of default under the lease agreement is otherwise effective.

(3) A provision in a lease agreement which (i) prohibits the creation or enforcement of a security interest in an interest of a party under the lease contract or in the lessor's residual interest in the goods, or (ii) makes such a transfer an event of default, is not enforceable unless, and then only to the extent that, there is an actual transfer by the lessee of the lessee's right of possession or use of the goods in violation of the provision or an actual delegation of a material performance of either party to the lease contract in violation of the provision. Neither the granting nor the enforcement of a security interest in (i) the lessor's interest under the lease contract or (ii) the lessor's residual interest in the goods is a transfer that materially impairs the prospect of obtaining return performance by, materially changes the duty of, or materially increases the burden or risk imposed on, the lessee within the purview of subsection (5) unless, and then only to the extent that, there is an actual delegation of a material performance of the lessor.

(4) A provision in a lease agreement which (i) prohibits a transfer of a right to damages for default with respect to the whole lease contract or of a right to payment arising out of the transferor's due performance of the transferor's entire obligation, or (ii) makes such a transfer an event of default, is not enforceable, and such a transfer is not a transfer that materially impairs the prospect of obtaining return performance by, materially changes the duty of, or materially increases the burden or risk imposed on, the other party to the lease contract within the purview of subsection (5).

(5) Subject to subsections (3) and (4):

(a) if a transfer is made which is made an event of default under a lease agreement, the party to the lease contract not making the transfer, unless that party waives the default or otherwise agrees, has the rights and remedies described in Section 2A—501(2);

(b) if paragraph (a) is not applicable and if a transfer is made that (i) is prohibited under a lease agreement or (ii) materially impairs the prospect of obtaining return performance by, materially changes the duty of, or materially increases the burden or risk imposed on, the other party to the lease contract, unless the party not making the transfer agrees at any time to the transfer in the lease contract or otherwise, then, except as limited by contract, (i) the transferor is liable to the party not making the transfer for damages caused by the transfer to the extent that the damages could not reasonably be prevented by the party not making the transfer and (ii) a court having jurisdiction may grant other appropriate relief, including cancellation of the lease contract or an injunction against the transfer.

(6) A transfer of "the lease" or of "all my rights under the lease," or a transfer in similar general terms, is a transfer of rights and, unless the language or the circumstances, as in a transfer for security, indicate the contrary, the transfer is a delegation of duties by the transferor to the transferee. Acceptance by the transferee constitutes a promise by the transferee to perform those duties. The promise is enforceable by either the transferor or the other party to the lease contract.

(7) Unless otherwise agreed by the lessor and the lessee, a delegation of performance does not relieve the transferor as against the other party of any duty to perform or of any liability for default.

(8) In a consumer lease, to prohibit the transfer of an interest of a party under the lease contract or to make a transfer an event of default, the language must be specific, by a writing, and conspicuous.

As amended in 1990.

§ 2A—304. Subsequent Lease of Goods by Lessor.

(1) Subject to Section 2A—303, a subsequent lessee from a lessor of goods under an existing lease contract obtains, to the extent of the leasehold interest transferred, the leasehold interest in the goods that the lessor had or had power to transfer, and except as provided in subsection (2) and Section 2A—527(4), takes subject to the existing lease contract. A lessor with voidable title has power to transfer a good leasehold interest to a good faith subsequent lessee for value, but only to the extent set forth in the preceding sentence. If goods have been delivered under a transaction of purchase the lessor has that power even though:

(a) the lessor's transferor was deceived as to the identity of the lessor;

(b) the delivery was in exchange for a check which is later dishonored;

(c) it was agreed that the transaction was to be a "cash sale"; or

(d) the delivery was procured through fraud punishable as larcenous under the criminal law.

(2) A subsequent lessee in the ordinary course of business from a lessor who is a merchant dealing in goods of that kind to whom the goods were entrusted by the existing lessee of that lessor before the interest of the subsequent lessee became enforceable against that lessor obtains, to the extent of the leasehold interest transferred, all of that lessor's and the existing lessee's rights to the goods, and takes free of the existing lease contract.

(3) A subsequent lessee from the lessor of goods that are subject to an existing lease contract and are covered by a certificate of title issued under a statute of this State or of another jurisdiction takes no greater rights than those provided both by this section and by the certificate of title statute.

As amended in 1990.

§ 2A—305. Sale or Sublease of Goods by Lessee.

(1) Subject to the provisions of Section 2A—303, a buyer or sublessee from the lessee of goods under an existing lease contract

obtains, to the extent of the interest transferred, the leasehold interest in the goods that the lessee had or had power to transfer, and except as provided in subsection (2) and Section 2A—511(4), takes subject to the existing lease contract. A lessee with a voidable leasehold interest has power to transfer a good leasehold interest to a good faith buyer for value or a good faith sublessee for value, but only to the extent set forth in the preceding sentence. When goods have been delivered under a transaction of lease the lessee has that power even though:

(a) the lessor was deceived as to the identity of the lessee;

(b) the delivery was in exchange for a check which is later dishonored; or

(c) the delivery was procured through fraud punishable as larcenous under the criminal law.

(2) A buyer in the ordinary course of business or a sublessee in the ordinary course of business from a lessee who is a merchant dealing in goods of that kind to whom the goods were entrusted by the lessor obtains, to the extent of the interest transferred, all of the lessor's and lessee's rights to the goods, and takes free of the existing lease contract.

(3) A buyer or sublessee from the lessee of goods that are subject to an existing lease contract and are covered by a certificate of title issued under a statute of this State or of another jurisdiction takes no greater rights than those provided both by this section and by the certificate of title statute.

§ 2A—306. Priority of Certain Liens Arising by Operation of Law.

If a person in the ordinary course of his [or her] business furnishes services or materials with respect to goods subject to a lease contract, a lien upon those goods in the possession of that person given by statute or rule of law for those materials or services takes priority over any interest of the lessor or lessee under the lease contract or this Article unless the lien is created by statute and the statute provides otherwise or unless the lien is created by rule of law and the rule of law provides otherwise.

§ 2A—307. Priority of Liens Arising by Attachment or Levy on, Security Interests in, and Other Claims to Goods.

(1) Except as otherwise provided in Section 2A—306, a creditor of a lessee takes subject to the lease contract.

(2) Except as otherwise provided in subsections (3) and (4) and in Sections 2A—306 and 2A—308, a creditor of a lessor takes subject to the lease contract unless:

(a) the creditor holds a lien that attached to the goods before the lease contract became enforceable,

(b) the creditor holds a security interest in the goods and the lessee did not give value and receive delivery of the goods without knowledge of the security interest; or

(c) the creditor holds a security interest in the goods which was perfected (Section 9—303) before the lease contract became enforceable.

(3) A lessee in the ordinary course of business takes the leasehold interest free of a security interest in the goods created by the lessor even though the security interest is perfected (Section 9—303) and the lessee knows of its existence.

(4) A lessee other than a lessee in the ordinary course of business takes the leasehold interest free of a security interest to the extent that it secures future advances made after the secured party acquires knowledge of the lease or more than 45 days after the lease contract becomes enforceable, whichever first occurs, unless the future advances are made pursuant to a commitment entered into without knowledge of the lease and before the expiration of the 45-day period.

§ 2A—308. Special Rights of Creditors.

(1) A creditor of a lessor in possession of goods subject to a lease contract may treat the lease contract as void if as against the creditor retention of possession by the lessor is fraudulent under any statute or rule of law, but retention of possession in good faith and current course of trade by the lessor for a commercially reasonable time after the lease contract becomes enforceable is not fraudulent.

(2) Nothing in this Article impairs the rights of creditors of a lessor if the lease contract (a) becomes enforceable, not in current course of trade but in satisfaction of or as security for a pre-existing claim for money, security, or the like, and (b) is made under circumstances which under any statute or rule of law apart from this Article would constitute the transaction a fraudulent transfer or voidable preference.

(3) A creditor of a seller may treat a sale or an identification of goods to a contract for sale as void if as against the creditor retention of possession by the seller is fraudulent under any statute or rule of law, but retention of possession of the goods pursuant to a lease contract entered into by the seller as lessee and the buyer as lessor in connection with the sale or identification of the goods is not fraudulent if the buyer bought for value and in good faith.

§ 2A—309. Lessor's and Lessee's Rights When Goods Become Fixtures.

(1) In this section:

(a) goods are "fixtures" when they become so related to particular real estate that an interest in them arises under real estate law;

(b) a "fixture filing" is the filing, in the office where a mortgage on the real estate would be filed or recorded, of a financing statement covering goods that are or are to become fixtures and conforming to the requirements of Section 9—402(5);

(c) a lease is a "purchase money lease" unless the lessee has possession or use of the goods or the right to possession or use of the goods before the lease agreement is enforceable;

(d) a mortgage is a "construction mortgage" to the extent it secures an obligation incurred for the construction of an improvement on land including the acquisition cost of the land, if the recorded writing so indicates; and

(e) "encumbrance" includes real estate mortgages and other liens on real estate and all other rights in real estate that are not ownership interests.

(2) Under this Article a lease may be of goods that are fixtures or may continue in goods that become fixtures, but no lease exists under this Article of ordinary building materials incorporated into an improvement on land.

(3) This Article does not prevent creation of a lease of fixtures pursuant to real estate law.

(4) The perfected interest of a lessor of fixtures has priority over a conflicting interest of an encumbrancer or owner of the real estate if:

(a) the lease is a purchase money lease, the conflicting interest of the encumbrancer or owner arises before the goods become fixtures, the interest of the lessor is perfected by a fixture filing before the goods become fixtures or within ten days thereafter, and the lessee has an interest of record in the real estate or is in possession of the real estate; or

(b) the interest of the lessor is perfected by a fixture filing before the interest of the encumbrancer or owner is of record, the lessor's interest has priority over any conflicting interest of a predecessor in title of the encumbrancer or owner, and the lessee has an interest of record in the real estate or is in possession of the real estate.

(5) The interest of a lessor of fixtures, whether or not perfected, has priority over the conflicting interest of an encumbrancer or owner of the real estate if:

(a) the fixtures are readily removable factory or office machines, readily removable equipment that is not primarily used or leased for use in the operation of the real estate, or readily removable replacements of domestic appliances that are goods subject to a consumer lease, and before the goods become fixtures the lease contract is enforceable; or

(b) the conflicting interest is a lien on the real estate obtained by legal or equitable proceedings after the lease contract is enforceable; or

(c) the encumbrancer or owner has consented in writing to the lease or has disclaimed an interest in the goods as fixtures; or

(d) the lessee has a right to remove the goods as against the encumbrancer or owner. If the lessee's right to remove terminates, the priority of the interest of the lessor continues for a reasonable time.

(6) Notwithstanding paragraph (4)(a) but otherwise subject to subsections (4) and (5), the interest of a lessor of fixtures, including the lessor's residual interest, is subordinate to the conflicting interest of an encumbrancer of the real estate under a construction mortgage recorded before the goods become fixtures if the goods become fixtures before the completion of the construction. To the extent given to refinance a construction mortgage, the conflicting interest of an encumbrancer of the real estate under a mortgage has this priority to the same extent as the encumbrancer of the real estate under the construction mortgage.

(7) In cases not within the preceding subsections, priority between the interest of a lessor of fixtures, including the lessor's residual interest, and the conflicting interest of an encumbrancer or owner of the real estate who is not the lessee is determined by the priority rules governing conflicting interests in real estate.

(8) If the interest of a lessor of fixtures, including the lessor's residual interest, has priority over all conflicting interests of all owners and encumbrancers of the real estate, the lessor or the lessee may (i) on default, expiration, termination, or cancellation of the lease agreement but subject to the agreement and this Article, or (ii) if necessary to enforce other rights and remedies of the lessor or lessee under this Article, remove the goods from the real estate, free and clear of all conflicting interests of all owners and encumbrancers of the real estate, but the lessor or lessee must reimburse any encumbrancer or owner of the real estate who is not the lessee and who has not otherwise agreed for the cost of repair of any physical injury, but not for any diminution in value of the real estate caused by the absence of the goods removed or by any necessity of replacing them. A person entitled to reimbursement may refuse permission to remove until the party seeking removal gives adequate security for the performance of this obligation.

(9) Even though the lease agreement does not create a security interest, the interest of a lessor of fixtures, including the lessor's residual interest, is perfected by filing a financing statement as a fixture filing for leased goods that are or are to become fixtures in accordance with the relevant provisions of the Article on Secured Transactions (Article 9).

As amended in 1990.

§ 2A—310. Lessor's and Lessee's Rights When Goods Become Accessions.

(1) Goods are "accessions" when they are installed in or affixed to other goods.

(2) The interest of a lessor or a lessee under a lease contract entered into before the goods became accessions is superior to all interests in the whole except as stated in subsection (4).

(3) The interest of a lessor or a lessee under a lease contract entered into at the time or after the goods became accessions is superior to all subsequently acquired interests in the whole except as stated in subsection (4) but is subordinate to interests in the whole existing at the time the lease contract was made unless the holders of such interests in the whole have in writing consented to the lease or disclaimed an interest in the goods as part of the whole.

(4) The interest of a lessor or a lessee under a lease contract described in subsection (2) or (3) is subordinate to the interest of

(a) a buyer in the ordinary course of business or a lessee in the ordinary course of business of any interest in the whole acquired after the goods became accessions; or

(b) a creditor with a security interest in the whole perfected before the lease contract was made to the extent that the creditor makes subsequent advances without knowledge of the lease contract.

(5) When under subsections (2) or (3) and (4) a lessor or a lessee of accessions holds an interest that is superior to all interests in the whole, the lessor or the lessee may (a) on default, expiration, termination, or cancellation of the lease contract by the other party but subject to the provisions of the lease contract and this Article, or (b) if necessary to enforce his [or her] other rights and remedies under this Article, remove the goods from the whole, free and clear of all interests in the whole, but he [or she] must reimburse any holder of an interest in the whole who is not the lessee and who has not otherwise agreed for the cost of repair of any physical injury but not for any diminution in value of the whole caused by the absence of the goods removed or by any necessity for replacing them. A person entitled to reimbursement may refuse permission to remove until the party seeking removal gives adequate security for the performance of this obligation.

§ 2A—311. Priority Subject to Subordination.

Nothing in this Article prevents subordination by agreement by any person entitled to priority.

As added in 1990.

Part 4 Performance Of Lease Contract: Repudiated, Substituted And Excused

§ 2A—401. Insecurity: Adequate Assurance of Performance.

(1) A lease contract imposes an obligation on each party that the other's expectation of receiving due performance will not be impaired.

(2) If reasonable grounds for insecurity arise with respect to the performance of either party, the insecure party may demand in writing adequate assurance of due performance. Until the insecure party receives that assurance, if commercially reasonable the insecure party may suspend any performance for which he [or she] has not already received the agreed return.

(3) A repudiation of the lease contract occurs if assurance of due performance adequate under the circumstances of the particular case is not provided to the insecure party within a reasonable time, not to exceed 30 days after receipt of a demand by the other party.

(4) Between merchants, the reasonableness of grounds for insecurity and the adequacy of any assurance offered must be determined according to commercial standards.

(5) Acceptance of any nonconforming delivery or payment does not prejudice the aggrieved party's right to demand adequate assurance of future performance.

§ 2A—402. Anticipatory Repudiation.

If either party repudiates a lease contract with respect to a performance not yet due under the lease contract, the loss of which performance will substantially impair the value of the lease contract to the other, the aggrieved party may:

(a) for a commercially reasonable time, await retraction of repudiation and performance by the repudiating party;

(b) make demand pursuant to Section 2A—401 and await assurance of future performance adequate under the circumstances of the particular case; or

(c) resort to any right or remedy upon default under the lease contract or this Article, even though the aggrieved party has notified the repudiating party that the aggrieved party would await the repudiating party's performance and assurance and has urged retraction. In addition, whether or not the aggrieved party is pursuing one of the foregoing remedies, the aggrieved party may suspend performance or, if the aggrieved party is the lessor, proceed in accordance with the provisions of this Article on the lessor's right to identify goods to the lease contract notwithstanding default or to salvage unfinished goods (Section 2A—524).

§ 2A—403. Retraction of Anticipatory Repudiation.

(1) Until the repudiating party's next performance is due, the repudiating party can retract the repudiation unless, since the repudiation, the aggrieved party has cancelled the lease contract or materially changed the aggrieved party's position or otherwise indicated that the aggrieved party considers the repudiation final.

(2) Retraction may be by any method that clearly indicates to the aggrieved party that the repudiating party intends to perform under the lease contract and includes any assurance demanded under Section 2A—401.

(3) Retraction reinstates a repudiating party's rights under a lease contract with due excuse and allowance to the aggrieved party for any delay occasioned by the repudiation.

§ 2A—404. Substituted Performance.

(1) If without fault of the lessee, the lessor and the supplier, the agreed berthing, loading, or unloading facilities fail or the agreed type of carrier becomes unavailable or the agreed manner of delivery otherwise becomes commercially impracticable, but a commercially reasonable substitute is available, the substitute performance must be tendered and accepted.

(2) If the agreed means or manner of payment fails because of domestic or foreign governmental regulation:

(a) the lessor may withhold or stop delivery or cause the supplier to withhold or stop delivery unless the lessee provides a means or manner of payment that is commercially a substantial equivalent; and

(b) if delivery has already been taken, payment by the means or in the manner provided by the regulation discharges the lessee's obligation unless the regulation is discriminatory, oppressive, or predatory.

§ 2A—405. Excused Performance.

Subject to Section 2A—404 on substituted performance, the following rules apply:

(a) Delay in delivery or nondelivery in whole or in part by a lessor or a supplier who complies with paragraphs (b) and (c) is not a default under the lease contract if performance as agreed has been made impracticable by the occurrence of a contingency the nonoccurrence of which was a basic assumption on which the lease contract was made or by compliance in good faith with any applicable foreign or domestic governmental regulation or order, whether or not the regulation or order later proves to be invalid.

(b) If the causes mentioned in paragraph (a) affect only part of the lessor's or the supplier's capacity to perform, he [or she] shall allocate production and deliveries among his [or her] customers but at his [or her] option may include regular customers not then under contract for sale or lease as well as his [or her] own requirements for further manufacture. He [or she] may so allocate in any manner that is fair and reasonable.

(c) The lessor seasonably shall notify the lessee and in the case of a finance lease the supplier seasonably shall notify the lessor and the lessee, if known, that there will be delay or nondelivery and, if allocation is required under paragraph (b), of the estimated quota thus made available for the lessee.

§ 2A—406. Procedure on Excused Performance.

(1) If the lessee receives notification of a material or indefinite delay or an allocation justified under Section 2A—405, the lessee may by written notification to the lessor as to any goods involved, and with respect to all of the goods if under an installment lease contract the value of the whole lease contract is substantially impaired (Section 2A—510):

(a) terminate the lease contract (Section 2A—505(2)); or

(b) except in a finance lease that is not a consumer lease, modify the lease contract by accepting the available quota in substitution, with due allowance from the rent payable for the balance of the lease term for the deficiency but without further right against the lessor.

(2) If, after receipt of a notification from the lessor under Section 2A—405, the lessee fails so to modify the lease agreement within a reasonable time not exceeding 30 days, the lease contract lapses with respect to any deliveries affected.

§ 2A—407. Irrevocable Promises: Finance Leases.

(1) In the case of a finance lease that is not a consumer lease the lessee's promises under the lease contract become irrevocable and independent upon the lessee's acceptance of the goods.

(2) A promise that has become irrevocable and independent under subsection (1):

(a) is effective and enforceable between the parties, and by or against third parties including assignees of the parties, and

(b) is not subject to cancellation, termination, modification, repudiation, excuse, or substitution without the consent of the party to whom the promise runs.

(3) This section does not affect the validity under any other law of a covenant in any lease contract making the lessee's promises irrevocable and independent upon the lessee's acceptance of the goods.

As amended in 1990.

Part 5 Default

A. In General

§ 2A—501. Default: Procedure.

(1) Whether the lessor or the lessee is in default under a lease contract is determined by the lease agreement and this Article.

(2) If the lessor or the lessee is in default under the lease contract, the party seeking enforcement has rights and remedies as provided in this Article and, except as limited by this Article, as provided in the lease agreement.

(3) If the lessor or the lessee is in default under the lease contract, the party seeking enforcement may reduce the party's claim to judgment, or otherwise enforce the lease contract by self-help or any available judicial procedure or nonjudicial procedure, including administrative proceeding, arbitration, or the like, in accordance with this Article.

(4) Except as otherwise provided in Section 1–106(1) or this Article or the lease agreement, the rights and remedies referred to in subsections (2) and (3) are cumulative.

(5) If the lease agreement covers both real property and goods, the party seeking enforcement may proceed under this Part as to the goods, or under other applicable law as to both the real property and the goods in accordance with that party's rights and remedies in respect of the real property, in which case this Part does not apply.

As amended in 1990.

§ 2A—502. Notice After Default.

Except as otherwise provided in this Article or the lease agreement, the lessor or lessee in default under the lease contract is not entitled to notice of default or notice of enforcement from the other party to the lease agreement.

§ 2A—503. Modification or Impairment of Rights and Remedies.

(1) Except as otherwise provided in this Article, the lease agreement may include rights and remedies for default in addition to or in substitution for those provided in this Article and may limit or alter the measure of damages recoverable under this Article.

(2) Resort to a remedy provided under this Article or in the lease agreement is optional unless the remedy is expressly agreed to be exclusive. If circumstances cause an exclusive or limited remedy to fail of its essential purpose, or provision for an exclusive remedy is unconscionable, remedy may be had as provided in this Article.

(3) Consequential damages may be liquidated under Section 2A—504, or may otherwise be limited, altered, or excluded unless the limitation, alteration, or exclusion is unconscionable. Limitation, alteration, or exclusion of consequential damages for injury to the person in the case of consumer goods is prima facie unconscionable but limitation, alteration, or

exclusion of damages where the loss is commercial is not prima facie unconscionable.

(4) Rights and remedies on default by the lessor or the lessee with respect to any obligation or promise collateral or ancillary to the lease contract are not impaired by this Article.

As amended in 1990.

§ 2A—504. Liquidation of Damages.

(1) Damages payable by either party for default, or any other act or omission, including indemnity for loss or diminution of anticipated tax benefits or loss or damage to lessor's residual interest, may be liquidated in the lease agreement but only at an amount or by a formula that is reasonable in light of the then anticipated harm caused by the default or other act or omission.

(2) If the lease agreement provides for liquidation of damages, and such provision does not comply with subsection (1), or such provision is an exclusive or limited remedy that circumstances cause to fail of its essential purpose, remedy may be had as provided in this Article.

(3) If the lessor justifiably withholds or stops delivery of goods because of the lessee's default or insolvency (Section 2A—525 or 2A—526), the lessee is entitled to restitution of any amount by which the sum of his [or her] payments exceeds:

(a) the amount to which the lessor is entitled by virtue of terms liquidating the lessor's damages in accordance with subsection (1); or

(b) in the absence of those terms, 20 percent of the then present value of the total rent the lessee was obligated to pay for the balance of the lease term, or, in the case of a consumer lease, the lesser of such amount or $500.

(4) A lessee's right to restitution under subsection (3) is subject to offset to the extent the lessor establishes:

(a) a right to recover damages under the provisions of this Article other than subsection (1); and

(b) the amount or value of any benefits received by the lessee directly or indirectly by reason of the lease contract.

§ 2A—505. Cancellation and Termination and Effect of Cancellation, Termination, Rescission, or Fraud on Rights and Remedies.

(1) On cancellation of the lease contract, all obligations that are still executory on both sides are discharged, but any right based on prior default or performance survives, and the cancelling party also retains any remedy for default of the whole lease contract or any unperformed balance.

(2) On termination of the lease contract, all obligations that are still executory on both sides are discharged but any right based on prior default or performance survives.

(3) Unless the contrary intention clearly appears, expressions of "cancellation," "rescission," or the like of the lease contract may not be construed as a renunciation or discharge of any claim in damages for an antecedent default.

(4) Rights and remedies for material misrepresentation or fraud include all rights and remedies available under this Article for default.

(5) Neither rescission nor a claim for rescission of the lease contract nor rejection or return of the goods may bar or be deemed inconsistent with a claim for damages or other right or remedy.

§ 2A—506. Statute of Limitations.

(1) An action for default under a lease contract, including breach of warranty or indemnity, must be commenced within 4 years after the cause of action accrued. By the original lease contract the parties may reduce the period of limitation to not less than one year.

(2) A cause of action for default accrues when the act or omission on which the default or breach of warranty is based is or should have been discovered by the aggrieved party, or when the default occurs, whichever is later. A cause of action for indemnity accrues when the act or omission on which the claim for indemnity is based is or should have been discovered by the indemnified party, whichever is later.

(3) If an action commenced within the time limited by subsection (1) is so terminated as to leave available a remedy by another action for the same default or breach of warranty or indemnity, the other action may be commenced after the expiration of the time limited and within 6 months after the termination of the first action unless the termination resulted from voluntary discontinuance or from dismissal for failure or neglect to prosecute.

(4) This section does not alter the law on tolling of the statute of limitations nor does it apply to causes of action that have accrued before this Article becomes effective.

§ 2A—507. Proof of Market Rent: Time and Place.

(1) Damages based on market rent (Section 2A—519 or 2A—528) are determined according to the rent for the use of the goods concerned for a lease term identical to the remaining lease term of the original lease agreement and prevailing at the times specified in Sections 2A–519 and 2A–528.

(2) If evidence of rent for the use of the goods concerned for a lease term identical to the remaining lease term of the original lease agreement and prevailing at the times or places described in this Article is not readily available, the rent prevailing within any reasonable time before or after the time described or at any other place or for a different lease term which in commercial judgment or under usage of trade would serve as a reasonable substitute for the one described may be used, making any proper allowance for the difference, including the cost of transporting the goods to or from the other place.

(3) Evidence of a relevant rent prevailing at a time or place or for a lease term other than the one described in this Article offered by one party is not admissible unless and until he [or she] has given the other party notice the court finds sufficient to prevent unfair surprise.

(4) If the prevailing rent or value of any goods regularly leased in any established market is in issue, reports in official publications

or trade journals or in newspapers or periodicals of general circulation published as the reports of that market are admissible in evidence. The circumstances of the preparation of the report may be shown to affect its weight but not its admissibility.

As amended in 1990.

B. Default by Lessor

§ 2A—508. Lessee's Remedies.

(1) If a lessor fails to deliver the goods in conformity to the lease contract (Section 2A—509) or repudiates the lease contract (Section 2A—402), or a lessee rightfully rejects the goods (Section 2A—509) or justifiably revokes acceptance of the goods (Section 2A—517), then with respect to any goods involved, and with respect to all of the goods if under an installment lease contract the value of the whole lease contract is substantially impaired (Section 2A—510), the lessor is in default under the lease contract and the lessee may:

(a) cancel the lease contract (Section 2A—505(1));

(b) recover so much of the rent and security as has been paid and is just under the circumstances;

(c) cover and recover damages as to all goods affected whether or not they have been identified to the lease contract (Sections 2A—518 and 2A—520), or recover damages for nondelivery (Sections 2A—519 and 2A—520);

(d) exercise any other rights or pursue any other remedies provided in the lease contract..

(2) If a lessor fails to deliver the goods in conformity to the lease contract or repudiates the lease contract, the lessee may also:

(a) if the goods have been identified, recover them (Section 2A—522); or

(b) in a proper case, obtain specific performance or replevy the goods (Section 2A—521).

(3) If a lessor is otherwise in default under a lease contract, the lessee may exercise the rights and pursue the remedies provided in the lease contract, which may include a right to cancel the lease, and in Section 2A–519(3).

(4) If a lessor has breached a warranty, whether express or implied, the lessee may recover damages (Section 2A—519(4)).

(5) On rightful rejection or justifiable revocation of acceptance, a lessee has a security interest in goods in the lessee's possession or control for any rent and security that has been paid and any expenses reasonably incurred in their inspection, receipt, transportation, and care and custody and may hold those goods and dispose of them in good faith and in a commercially reasonable manner, subject to Section 2A—527(5).

(6) Subject to the provisions of Section 2A—407, a lessee, on notifying the lessor of the lessee's intention to do so, may deduct all or any part of the damages resulting from any default under the lease contract from any part of the rent still due under the same lease contract.

As amended in 1990.

§ 2A—509. Lessee's Rights on Improper Delivery; Rightful Rejection.

(1) Subject to the provisions of Section 2A—510 on default in installment lease contracts, if the goods or the tender or delivery fail in any respect to conform to the lease contract, the lessee may reject or accept the goods or accept any commercial unit or units and reject the rest of the goods.

(2) Rejection of goods is ineffective unless it is within a reasonable time after tender or delivery of the goods and the lessee seasonably notifies the lessor.

§ 2A—510. Installment Lease Contracts: Rejection and Default.

(1) Under an installment lease contract a lessee may reject any delivery that is nonconforming if the nonconformity substantially impairs the value of that delivery and cannot be cured or the nonconformity is a defect in the required documents; but if the nonconformity does not fall within subsection (2) and the lessor or the supplier gives adequate assurance of its cure, the lessee must accept that delivery.

(2) Whenever nonconformity or default with respect to one or more deliveries substantially impairs the value of the installment lease contract as a whole there is a default with respect to the whole. But, the aggrieved party reinstates the installment lease contract as a whole if the aggrieved party accepts a nonconforming delivery without seasonably notifying of cancellation or brings an action with respect only to past deliveries or demands performance as to future deliveries.

§ 2A—511. Merchant Lessee's Duties as to Rightfully Rejected Goods.

(1) Subject to any security interest of a lessee (Section 2A—508(5)), if a lessor or a supplier has no agent or place of business at the market of rejection, a merchant lessee, after rejection of goods in his [or her] possession or control, shall follow any reasonable instructions received from the lessor or the supplier with respect to the goods. In the absence of those instructions, a merchant lessee shall make reasonable efforts to sell, lease, or otherwise dispose of the goods for the lessor's account if they threaten to decline in value speedily. Instructions are not reasonable if on demand indemnity for expenses is not forthcoming.

(2) If a merchant lessee (subsection (1)) or any other lessee (Section 2A—512) disposes of goods, he [or she] is entitled to reimbursement either from the lessor or the supplier or out of the proceeds for reasonable expenses of caring for and disposing of the goods and, if the expenses include no disposition commission, to such commission as is usual in the trade, or if there is none, to a reasonable sum not exceeding 10 percent of the gross proceeds.

(3) In complying with this section or Section 2A—512, the lessee is held only to good faith. Good faith conduct hereunder is neither acceptance or conversion nor the basis of an action for damages.

(4) A purchaser who purchases in good faith from a lessee pursuant to this section or Section 2A—512 takes the goods free of any rights of the lessor and the supplier even though the lessee fails to comply with one or more of the requirements of this Article.

§ 2A—512. Lessee's Duties as to Rightfully Rejected Goods.

(1) Except as otherwise provided with respect to goods that threaten to decline in value speedily (Section 2A—511) and subject to any security interest of a lessee (Section 2A—508(5)):

(a) the lessee, after rejection of goods in the lessee's possession, shall hold them with reasonable care at the lessor's or the supplier's disposition for a reasonable time after the lessee's seasonable notification of rejection;

(b) if the lessor or the supplier gives no instructions within a reasonable time after notification of rejection, the lessee may store the rejected goods for the lessor's or the supplier's account or ship them to the lessor or the supplier or dispose of them for the lessor's or the supplier's account with reimbursement in the manner provided in Section 2A—511; but

(c) the lessee has no further obligations with regard to goods rightfully rejected.

(2) Action by the lessee pursuant to subsection (1) is not acceptance or conversion.

§ 2A—513. Cure by Lessor of Improper Tender or Delivery; Replacement.

(1) If any tender or delivery by the lessor or the supplier is rejected because nonconforming and the time for performance has not yet expired, the lessor or the supplier may seasonably notify the lessee of the lessor's or the supplier's intention to cure and may then make a conforming delivery within the time provided in the lease contract.

(2) If the lessee rejects a nonconforming tender that the lessor or the supplier had reasonable grounds to believe would be acceptable with or without money allowance, the lessor or the supplier may have a further reasonable time to substitute a conforming tender if he [or she] seasonably notifies the lessee.

§ 2A—514. Waiver of Lessee's Objections.

(1) In rejecting goods, a lessee's failure to state a particular defect that is ascertainable by reasonable inspection precludes the lessee from relying on the defect to justify rejection or to establish default:

(a) if, stated seasonably, the lessor or the supplier could have cured it (Section 2A—513); or

(b) between merchants if the lessor or the supplier after rejection has made a request in writing for a full and final written statement of all defects on which the lessee proposes to rely.

(2) A lessee's failure to reserve rights when paying rent or other consideration against documents precludes recovery of the payment for defects apparent on the face of the documents.

§ 2A—515. Acceptance of Goods.

(1) Acceptance of goods occurs after the lessee has had a reasonable opportunity to inspect the goods and

(a) the lessee signifies or acts with respect to the goods in a manner that signifies to the lessor or the supplier that the goods are conforming or that the lessee will take or retain them in spite of their nonconformity; or

(b) the lessee fails to make an effective rejection of the goods (Section 2A—509(2)).

(2) Acceptance of a part of any commercial unit is acceptance of that entire unit.

§ 2A—516. Effect of Acceptance of Goods; Notice of Default; Burden of Establishing Default after Acceptance; Notice of Claim or Litigation to Person Answerable Over.

(1) A lessee must pay rent for any goods accepted in accordance with the lease contract, with due allowance for goods rightfully rejected or not delivered.

(2) A lessee's acceptance of goods precludes rejection of the goods accepted. In the case of a finance lease, if made with knowledge of a nonconformity, acceptance cannot be revoked because of it. In any other case, if made with knowledge of a nonconformity, acceptance cannot be revoked because of it unless the acceptance was on the reasonable assumption that the nonconformity would be seasonably cured. Acceptance does not of itself impair any other remedy provided by this Article or the lease agreement for nonconformity.

(3) If a tender has been accepted:

(a) within a reasonable time after the lessee discovers or should have discovered any default, the lessee shall notify the lessor and the supplier, if any, or be barred from any remedy against the party notified;

(b) except in the case of a consumer lease, within a reasonable time after the lessee receives notice of litigation for infringement or the like (Section 2A—211) the lessee shall notify the lessor or be barred from any remedy over for liability established by the litigation; and

(c) the burden is on the lessee to establish any default.

(4) If a lessee is sued for breach of a warranty or other obligation for which a lessor or a supplier is answerable over the following apply:

(a) The lessee may give the lessor or the supplier, or both, written notice of the litigation. If the notice states that the person notified may come in and defend and that if the person notified does not do so that person will be bound in any action against that person by the lessee by any determination of fact common to the two litigations, then unless the person notified after seasonable receipt of the notice does come in and defend that person is so bound.

(b) The lessor or the supplier may demand in writing that the lessee turn over control of the litigation including settlement if the claim is one for infringement or the like (Section 2A—

211) or else be barred from any remedy over. If the demand states that the lessor or the supplier agrees to bear all expense and to satisfy any adverse judgment, then unless the lessee after seasonable receipt of the demand does turn over control the lessee is so barred.

(5) Subsections (3) and (4) apply to any obligation of a lessee to hold the lessor or the supplier harmless against infringement or the like (Section 2A—211).

As amended in 1990.

§ 2A—517. Revocation of Acceptance of Goods.

(1) A lessee may revoke acceptance of a lot or commercial unit whose nonconformity substantially impairs its value to the lessee if the lessee has accepted it:

(a) except in the case of a finance lease, on the reasonable assumption that its nonconformity would be cured and it has not been seasonably cured; or

(b) without discovery of the nonconformity if the lessee's acceptance was reasonably induced either by the lessor's assurances or, except in the case of a finance lease, by the difficulty of discovery before acceptance.

(2) Except in the case of a finance lease that is not a consumer lease, a lessee may revoke acceptance of a lot or commercial unit if the lessor defaults under the lease contract and the default substantially impairs the value of that lot or commercial unit to the lessee.

(3) If the lease agreement so provides, the lessee may revoke acceptance of a lot or commercial unit because of other defaults by the lessor.

(4) Revocation of acceptance must occur within a reasonable time after the lessee discovers or should have discovered the ground for it and before any substantial change in condition of the goods which is not caused by the nonconformity. Revocation is not effective until the lessee notifies the lessor.

(5) A lessee who so revokes has the same rights and duties with regard to the goods involved as if the lessee had rejected them.

As amended in 1990.

§ 2A—518. Cover; Substitute Goods.

(1) After a default by a lessor under the lease contract of the type described in Section 2A—508(1), or, if agreed, after other default by the lessor, the lessee may cover by making any purchase or lease of or contract to purchase or lease goods in substitution for those due from the lessor.

(2) Except as otherwise provided with respect to damages liquidated in the lease agreement (Section 2A—504) or otherwise determined pursuant to agreement of the parties (Sections 1—102(3) and 2A—503), if a lessee's cover is by lease agreement substantially similar to the original lease agreement and the new lease agreement is made in good faith and in a commercially reasonable manner, the lessee may recover from the lessor as damages (i) the present value, as of the date of the commencement of the term of the new lease agreement, of the rent under the new lease agreement applicable to that period of the new lease term which is comparable to the then remaining term of the original lease agreement minus the present value as of the same date of the total rent for the then remaining lease term of the original lease agreement, and (ii) any incidental or consequential damages, less expenses saved in consequence of the lessor's default.

(3) If a lessee's cover is by lease agreement that for any reason does not qualify for treatment under subsection (2), or is by purchase or otherwise, the lessee may recover from the lessor as if the lessee had elected not to cover and Section 2A—519 governs.

As amended in 1990.

§ 2A—519. Lessee's Damages for Non-Delivery, Repudiation, Default, and Breach of Warranty in Regard to Accepted Goods.

(1) Except as otherwise provided with respect to damages liquidated in the lease agreement (Section 2A—504) or otherwise determined pursuant to agreement of the parties (Sections 1—102(3) and 2A—503), if a lessee elects not to cover or a lessee elects to cover and the cover is by lease agreement that for any reason does not qualify for treatment under Section 2A—518(2), or is by purchase or otherwise, the measure of damages for non-delivery or repudiation by the lessor or for rejection or revocation of acceptance by the lessee is the present value, as of the date of the default, of the then market rent minus the present value as of the same date of the original rent, computed for the remaining lease term of the original lease agreement, together with incidental and consequential damages, less expenses saved in consequence of the lessor's default.

(2) Market rent is to be determined as of the place for tender or, in cases of rejection after arrival or revocation of acceptance, as of the place of arrival.

(3) Except as otherwise agreed, if the lessee has accepted goods and given notification (Section 2A—516(3)), the measure of damages for non-conforming tender or delivery or other default by a lessor is the loss resulting in the ordinary course of events from the lessor's default as determined in any manner that is reasonable together with incidental and consequential damages, less expenses saved in consequence of the lessor's default.

(4) Except as otherwise agreed, the measure of damages for breach of warranty is the present value at the time and place of acceptance of the difference between the value of the use of the goods accepted and the value if they had been as warranted for the lease term, unless special circumstances show proximate damages of a different amount, together with incidental and consequential damages, less expenses saved in consequence of the lessor's default or breach of warranty.

As amended in 1990.

§ 2A—520. Lessee's Incidental and Consequential Damages.

(1) Incidental damages resulting from a lessor's default include expenses reasonably incurred in inspection, receipt, transportation, and care and custody of goods rightfully rejected or goods the acceptance of which is justifiably revoked, any commercially

reasonable charges, expenses or commissions in connection with effecting cover, and any other reasonable expense incident to the default.

(2) Consequential damages resulting from a lessor's default include:

(a) any loss resulting from general or particular requirements and needs of which the lessor at the time of contracting had reason to know and which could not reasonably be prevented by cover or otherwise; and

(b) injury to person or property proximately resulting from any breach of warranty.

§ 2A—521. Lessee's Right to Specific Performance or Replevin.

(1) Specific performance may be decreed if the goods are unique or in other proper circumstances.

(2) A decree for specific performance may include any terms and conditions as to payment of the rent, damages, or other relief that the court deems just.

(3) A lessee has a right of replevin, detinue, sequestration, claim and delivery, or the like for goods identified to the lease contract if after reasonable effort the lessee is unable to effect cover for those goods or the circumstances reasonably indicate that the effort will be unavailing.

§ 2A—522. Lessee's Right to Goods on Lessor's Insolvency.

(1) Subject to subsection (2) and even though the goods have not been shipped, a lessee who has paid a part or all of the rent and security for goods identified to a lease contract (Section 2A—217) on making and keeping good a tender of any unpaid portion of the rent and security due under the lease contract may recover the goods identified from the lessor if the lessor becomes insolvent within 10 days after receipt of the first installment of rent and security.

(2) A lessee acquires the right to recover goods identified to a lease contract only if they conform to the lease contract.

C. Default by Lessee

§ 2A—523. Lessor's Remedies.

(1) If a lessee wrongfully rejects or revokes acceptance of goods or fails to make a payment when due or repudiates with respect to a part or the whole, then, with respect to any goods involved, and with respect to all of the goods if under an installment lease contract the value of the whole lease contract is substantially impaired (Section 2A—510), the lessee is in default under the lease contract and the lessor may:

(a) cancel the lease contract (Section 2A—505(1));

(b) proceed respecting goods not identified to the lease contract (Section 2A—524);

(c) withhold delivery of the goods and take possession of goods previously delivered (Section 2A—525);

(d) stop delivery of the goods by any bailee (Section 2A—526);

(e) dispose of the goods and recover damages (Section 2A—527), or retain the goods and recover damages (Section 2A—528), or in a proper case recover rent (Section 2A—529)

(f) exercise any other rights or pursue any other remedies provided in the lease contract.

(2) If a lessor does not fully exercise a right or obtain a remedy to which the lessor is entitled under subsection (1), the lessor may recover the loss resulting in the ordinary course of events from the lessee's default as determined in any reasonable manner, together with incidental damages, less expenses saved in consequence of the lessee's default.

(3) If a lessee is otherwise in default under a lease contract, the lessor may exercise the rights and pursue the remedies provided in the lease contract, which may include a right to cancel the lease. In addition, unless otherwise provided in the lease contract:

(a) if the default substantially impairs the value of the lease contract to the lessor, the lessor may exercise the rights and pursue the remedies provided in subsections (1) or (2); or

(b) if the default does not substantially impair the value of the lease contract to the lessor, the lessor may recover as provided in subsection (2).

As amended in 1990.

§ 2A—524. Lessor's Right to Identify Goods to Lease Contract.

(1) After default by the lessee under the lease contract of the type described in Section 2A—523(1) or 2A—523(3)(a) or, if agreed, after other default by the lessee, the lessor may:

(a) identify to the lease contract conforming goods not already identified if at the time the lessor learned of the default they were in the lessor's or the supplier's possession or control; and

(b) dispose of goods (Section 2A—527(1)) that demonstrably have been intended for the particular lease contract even though those goods are unfinished.

(2) If the goods are unfinished, in the exercise of reasonable commercial judgment for the purposes of avoiding loss and of effective realization, an aggrieved lessor or the supplier may either complete manufacture and wholly identify the goods to the lease contract or cease manufacture and lease, sell, or otherwise dispose of the goods for scrap or salvage value or proceed in any other reasonable manner.

As amended in 1990.

§ 2A—525. Lessor's Right to Possession of Goods.

(1) If a lessor discovers the lessee to be insolvent, the lessor may refuse to deliver the goods.

(2) After a default by the lessee under the lease contract of the type described in Section 2A—523(1) or 2A—523(3)(a) or, if agreed, after other default by the lessee, the lessor has the right to take possession of the goods. If the lease contract so provides, the lessor may require the lessee to assemble the goods and make them available to the lessor at a place to be designated by the lessor which is

reasonably convenient to both parties. Without removal, the lessor may render unusable any goods employed in trade or business, and may dispose of goods on the lessee's premises (Section 2A—527).

(3) The lessor may proceed under subsection (2) without judicial process if that can be done without breach of the peace or the lessor may proceed by action.

As amended in 1990.

§ 2A—526. Lessor's Stoppage of Delivery in Transit or Otherwise.

(1) A lessor may stop delivery of goods in the possession of a carrier or other bailee if the lessor discovers the lessee to be insolvent and may stop delivery of carload, truckload, planeload, or larger shipments of express or freight if the lessee repudiates or fails to make a payment due before delivery, whether for rent, security or otherwise under the lease contract, or for any other reason the lessor has a right to withhold or take possession of the goods.

(2) In pursuing its remedies under subsection (1), the lessor may stop delivery until

(a) receipt of the goods by the lessee;

(b) acknowledgment to the lessee by any bailee of the goods, except a carrier, that the bailee holds the goods for the lessee; or

(c) such an acknowledgment to the lessee by a carrier via reshipment or as warehouseman.

(3) (a) To stop delivery, a lessor shall so notify as to enable the bailee by reasonable diligence to prevent delivery of the goods.

(b) After notification, the bailee shall hold and deliver the goods according to the directions of the lessor, but the lessor is liable to the bailee for any ensuing charges or damages.

(c) A carrier who has issued a nonnegotiable bill of lading is not obliged to obey a notification to stop received from a person other than the consignor.

§ 2A—527. Lessor's Rights to Dispose of Goods.

(1) After a default by a lessee under the lease contract of the type described in Section 2A—523(1) or 2A–523(3)(a) or after the lessor refuses to deliver or takes possession of goods (Section 2A—525 or 2A—526), or, if agreed, after other default by a lessee, the lessor may dispose of the goods concerned or the undelivered balance thereof by lease, sale, or otherwise.

(2) Except as otherwise provided with respect to damages liquidated in the lease agreement (Section 2A—504) or otherwise determined pursuant to agreement of the parties (Sections 1—102(3) and 2A—503), if the disposition is by lease agreement substantially similar to the original lease agreement and the new lease agreement is made in good faith and in a commercially reasonable manner, the lessor may recover from the lessee as damages (i) accrued and unpaid rent as of the date of the commencement of the term of the new lease agreement, (ii) the present value, as of the same date, of the total rent for the then remaining lease term of the original lease agreement minus the present value, as of the same date, of the rent under the new lease agreement applicable to that period of the new lease term which is comparable to the then remaining term of the original lease agreement, and (iii) any incidental damages allowed under Section 2A—530, less expenses saved in consequence of the lessee's default.

(3) If the lessor's disposition is by lease agreement that for any reason does not qualify for treatment under subsection (2), or is by sale or otherwise, the lessor may recover from the lessee as if the lessor had elected not to dispose of the goods and Section 2A—528 governs.

(4) A subsequent buyer or lessee who buys or leases from the lessor in good faith for value as a result of a disposition under this section takes the goods free of the original lease contract and any rights of the original lessee even though the lessor fails to comply with one or more of the requirements of this Article.

(5) The lessor is not accountable to the lessee for any profit made on any disposition. A lessee who has rightfully rejected or justifiably revoked acceptance shall account to the lessor for any excess over the amount of the lessee's security interest (Section 2A—508(5)).

As amended in 1990.

§ 2A—528. Lessor's Damages for Non-acceptance, Failure to Pay, Repudiation, or Other Default.

(1) Except as otherwise provided with respect to damages liquidated in the lease agreement (Section 2A—504) or otherwise determined pursuant to agreement of the parties (Section 1—102(3) and 2A—503), if a lessor elects to retain the goods or a lessor elects to dispose of the goods and the disposition is by lease agreement that for any reason does not qualify for treatment under Section 2A—527(2), or is by sale or otherwise, the lessor may recover from the lessee as damages for a default of the type described in Section 2A—523(1) or 2A—523(3)(a), or if agreed, for other default of the lessee, (i) accrued and unpaid rent as of the date of the default if the lessee has never taken possession of the goods, or, if the lessee has taken possession of the goods, as of the date the lessor repossesses the goods or an earlier date on which the lessee makes a tender of the goods to the lessor, (ii) the present value as of the date determined under clause (i) of the total rent for the then remaining lease term of the original lease agreement minus the present value as of the same date of the market rent as the place where the goods are located computed for the same lease term, and (iii) any incidental damages allowed under Section 2A—530, less expenses saved in consequence of the lessee's default.

(2) If the measure of damages provided in subsection (1) is inadequate to put a lessor in as good a position as performance would have, the measure of damages is the present value of the profit, including reasonable overhead, the lessor would have made from full performance by the lessee, together with any incidental damages allowed under Section 2A—530, due allowance for costs reasonably incurred and due credit for payments or proceeds of disposition.

As amended in 1990.

§ 2A—529. Lessor's Action for the Rent.

(1) After default by the lessee under the lease contract of the type described in Section 2A—523(1) or 2A—523(3)(a) or, if agreed, after other default by the lessee, if the lessor complies with subsection (2), the lessor may recover from the lessee as damages:

(a) for goods accepted by the lessee and not repossessed by or tendered to the lessor, and for conforming goods lost or damaged within a commercially reasonable time after risk of loss passes to the lessee (Section 2A—219), (i) accrued and unpaid rent as of the date of entry of judgment in favor of the lessor (ii) the present value as of the same date of the rent for the then remaining lease term of the lease agreement, and (iii) any incidental damages allowed under Section 2A—530, less expenses saved in consequence of the lessee's default; and

(b) for goods identified to the lease contract if the lessor is unable after reasonable effort to dispose of them at a reasonable price or the circumstances reasonably indicate that effort will be unavailing, (i) accrued and unpaid rent as of the date of entry of judgment in favor of the lessor, (ii) the present value as of the same date of the rent for the then remaining lease term of the lease agreement, and (iii) any incidental damages allowed under Section 2A—530, less expenses saved in consequence of the lessee's default.

(2) Except as provided in subsection (3), the lessor shall hold for the lessee for the remaining lease term of the lease agreement any goods that have been identified to the lease contract and are in the lessor's control.

(3) The lessor may dispose of the goods at any time before collection of the judgment for damages obtained pursuant to subsection (1). If the disposition is before the end of the remaining lease term of the lease agreement, the lessor's recovery against the lessee for damages is governed by Section 2A—527 or Section 2A—528, and the lessor will cause an appropriate credit to be provided against a judgment for damages to the extent that the amount of the judgment exceeds the recovery available pursuant to Section 2A—527 or 2A—528.

(4) Payment of the judgment for damages obtained pursuant to subsection (1) entitles the lessee to the use and possession of the goods not then disposed of for the remaining lease term of and in accordance with the lease agreement.

(5) After default by the lessee under the lease contract of the type described in Section 2A—523(1) or Section 2A—523(3)(a) or, if agreed, after other default by the lessee, a lessor who is held not entitled to rent under this section must nevertheless be awarded damages for non-acceptance under Sections 2A—527 and 2A—528.

As amended in 1990.

§ 2A—530. Lessor's Incidental Damages.

Incidental damages to an aggrieved lessor include any commercially reasonable charges, expenses, or commissions incurred in stopping delivery, in the transportation, care and custody of goods after the lessee's default, in connection with return or disposition of the goods, or otherwise resulting from the default.

§ 2A—531. Standing to Sue Third Parties for Injury to Goods.

(1) If a third party so deals with goods that have been identified to a lease contract as to cause actionable injury to a party to the lease contract (a) the lessor has a right of action against the third party, and (b) the lessee also has a right of action against the third party if the lessee:

(i) has a security interest in the goods;

(ii) has an insurable interest in the goods; or

(iii) bears the risk of loss under the lease contract or has since the injury assumed that risk as against the lessor and the goods have been converted or destroyed.

(2) If at the time of the injury the party plaintiff did not bear the risk of loss as against the other party to the lease contract and there is no arrangement between them for disposition of the recovery, his [or her] suit or settlement, subject to his [or her] own interest, is as a fiduciary for the other party to the lease contract.

(3) Either party with the consent of the other may sue for the benefit of whom it may concern.

§ 2A—532. Lessor's Rights to Residual Interest.

In addition to any other recovery permitted by this Article or other law, the lessor may recover from the lessee an amount that will fully compensate the lessor for any loss of or damage to the lessor's residual interest in the goods caused by the default of the lessee.

As added in 1990.

Revised Article 3
NEGOTIABLE INSTRUMENTS

Part 1 General Provisions and Definitions

§ 3—101. Short Title.

This Article may be cited as Uniform Commercial Code—Negotiable Instruments.

§ 3—102. Subject Matter.

(a) This Article applies to negotiable instruments. It does not apply to money, to payment orders governed by Article 4A, or to securities governed by Article 8.

(b) If there is conflict between this Article and Article 4 or 9, Articles 4 and 9 govern.

(c) Regulations of the Board of Governors of the Federal Reserve System and operating circulars of the Federal Reserve Banks supersede any inconsistent provision of this Article to the extent of the inconsistency.

§ 3—103. Definitions.

(a) In this Article:

(1) "Acceptor" means a drawee who has accepted a draft.

(2) "Drawee" means a person ordered in a draft to make payment.

(3) "Drawer" means a person who signs or is identified in a draft as a person ordering payment.

(4) "Good faith" means honesty in fact and the observance of reasonable commercial standards of fair dealing.

(5) "Maker" means a person who signs or is identified in a note as a person undertaking to pay.

(6) "Order" means a written instruction to pay money signed by the person giving the instruction. The instruction may be addressed to any person, including the person giving the instruction, or to one or more persons jointly or in the alternative but not in succession. An authorization to pay is not an order unless the person authorized to pay is also instructed to pay.

(7) "Ordinary care" in the case of a person engaged in business means observance of reasonable commercial standards, prevailing in the area in which the person is located, with respect to the business in which the person is engaged. In the case of a bank that takes an instrument for processing for collection or payment by automated means, reasonable commercial standards do not require the bank to examine the instrument if the failure to examine does not violate the bank's prescribed procedures and the bank's procedures do not vary unreasonably from general banking usage not disapproved by this Article or Article 4.

(8) "Party" means a party to an instrument.

(9) "Promise" means a written undertaking to pay money signed by the person undertaking to pay. An acknowledgment of an obligation by the obligor is not a promise unless the obligor also undertakes to pay the obligation.

(10) "Prove" with respect to a fact means to meet the burden of establishing the fact (Section 1—201(8)).

(11) "Remitter" means a person who purchases an instrument from its issuer if the instrument is payable to an identified person other than the purchaser.

(b);(c) [Other definitions' section references deleted.]

(d) In addition, Article 1 contains general definitions and principles of construction and interpretation applicable throughout this Article.

§ 3—104. Negotiable Instrument.

(a) Except as provided in subsections (c) and (d), "negotiable instrument" means an unconditional promise or order to pay a fixed amount of money, with or without interest or other charges described in the promise or order, if it:

(1) is payable to bearer or to order at the time it is issued or first comes into possession of a holder;

(2) is payable on demand or at a definite time; and

(3) does not state any other undertaking or instruction by the person promising or ordering payment to do any act in addition to the payment of money, but the promise or order may contain (i) an undertaking or power to give, maintain, or protect collateral to secure payment, (ii) an authorization or power to the holder to confess judgment or realize on or dispose of collateral, or (iii) a waiver of the benefit of any law intended for the advantage or protection of an obligor.

(b) "Instrument" means a negotiable instrument.

(c) An order that meets all of the requirements of subsection (a), except paragraph (1), and otherwise falls within the definition of "check" in subsection (f) is a negotiable instrument and a check.

(d) A promise or order other than a check is not an instrument if, at the time it is issued or first comes into possession of a holder, it contains a conspicuous statement, however expressed, to the effect that the promise or order is not negotiable or is not an instrument governed by this Article.

(e) An instrument is a "note" if it is a promise and is a "draft" if it is an order. If an instrument falls within the definition of both "note" and "draft," a person entitled to enforce the instrument may treat it as either.

(f) "Check" means (i) a draft, other than a documentary draft, payable on demand and drawn on a bank or (ii) a cashier's check or teller's check. An instrument may be a check even though it is described on its face by another term, such as "money order."

(g) "Cashier's check" means a draft with respect to which the drawer and drawee are the same bank or branches of the same bank.

(h) "Teller's check" means a draft drawn by a bank (i) on another bank, or (ii) payable at or through a bank.

(i) "Traveler's check" means an instrument that (i) is payable on demand, (ii) is drawn on or payable at or through a bank, (iii) is designated by the term "traveler's check" or by a substantially similar term, and (iv) requires, as a condition to payment, a countersignature by a person whose specimen signature appears on the instrument.

(j) "Certificate of deposit" means an instrument containing an acknowledgment by a bank that a sum of money has been received by the bank and a promise by the bank to repay the sum of money. A certificate of deposit is a note of the bank.

§ 3—105. Issue of Instrument.

(a) "Issue" means the first delivery of an instrument by the maker or drawer, whether to a holder or nonholder, for the purpose of giving rights on the instrument to any person.

(b) An unissued instrument, or an unissued incomplete instrument that is completed, is binding on the maker or drawer, but nonissuance is a defense. An instrument that is conditionally issued or is issued for a special purpose is binding on the maker or drawer, but failure of the condition or special purpose to be fulfilled is a defense.

(c) "Issuer" applies to issued and unissued instruments and means a maker or drawer of an instrument.

§ 3—106. Unconditional Promise or Order.

(a) Except as provided in this section, for the purposes of Section 3—104(a), a promise or order is unconditional unless it states (i) an express condition to payment, (ii) that the promise or order is subject to or governed by another writing, or (iii) that rights or obligations with respect to the promise or order are stated in another writing. A reference to another writing does not of itself make the promise or order conditional.

(b) A promise or order is not made conditional (i) by a reference to another writing for a statement of rights with respect to collateral, prepayment, or acceleration, or (ii) because payment is limited to resort to a particular fund or source.

(c) If a promise or order requires, as a condition to payment, a countersignature by a person whose specimen signature appears on the promise or order, the condition does not make the promise or order conditional for the purposes of Section 3—104(a). If the person whose specimen signature appears on an instrument fails to countersign the instrument, the failure to countersign is a defense to the obligation of the issuer, but the failure does not prevent a transferee of the instrument from becoming a holder of the instrument.

(d) If a promise or order at the time it is issued or first comes into possession of a holder contains a statement, required by applicable statutory or administrative law, to the effect that the rights of a holder or transferee are subject to claims or defenses that the issuer could assert against the original payee, the promise or order is not thereby made conditional for the purposes of Section 3—104(a); but if the promise or order is an instrument, there cannot be a holder in due course of the instrument.

§ 3—107. Instrument Payable in Foreign Money.

Unless the instrument otherwise provides, an instrument that states the amount payable in foreign money may be paid in the foreign money or in an equivalent amount in dollars calculated by using the current bank-offered spot rate at the place of payment for the purchase of dollars on the day on which the instrument is paid.

§ 3—108. Payable on Demand or at Definite Time.

(a) A promise or order is "payable on demand" if it (i) states that it is payable on demand or at sight, or otherwise indicates that it is payable at the will of the holder, or (ii) does not state any time of payment.

(b) A promise or order is "payable at a definite time" if it is payable on elapse of a definite period of time after sight or acceptance or at a fixed date or dates or at a time or times readily ascertainable at the time the promise or order is issued, subject to rights of (i) prepayment, (ii) acceleration, (iii) extension at the option of the holder, or (iv) extension to a further definite time at the option of the maker or acceptor or automatically upon or after a specified act or event.

(c) If an instrument, payable at a fixed date, is also payable upon demand made before the fixed date, the instrument is payable on demand until the fixed date and, if demand for payment is not made before that date, becomes payable at a definite time on the fixed date.

§ 3—109. Payable to Bearer or to Order.

(a) A promise or order is payable to bearer if it:

(1) states that it is payable to bearer or to the order of bearer or otherwise indicates that the person in possession of the promise or order is entitled to payment;

(2) does not state a payee; or

(3) states that it is payable to or to the order of cash or otherwise indicates that it is not payable to an identified person.

(b) A promise or order that is not payable to bearer is payable to order if it is payable (i) to the order of an identified person or (ii) to an identified person or order. A promise or order that is payable to order is payable to the identified person.

(c) An instrument payable to bearer may become payable to an identified person if it is specially indorsed pursuant to Section 3—205(a). An instrument payable to an identified person may become payable to bearer if it is indorsed in blank pursuant to Section 3—205(b).

§ 3—110. Identification of Person to Whom Instrument Is Payable.

(a) The person to whom an instrument is initially payable is determined by the intent of the person, whether or not authorized, signing as, or in the name or behalf of, the issuer of the instrument. The instrument is payable to the person intended by the signer even if that person is identified in the instrument by a name or other identification that is not that of the intended person. If more than one person signs in the name or behalf of the issuer of an instrument and all the signers do not intend the same person as payee, the instrument is payable to any person intended by one or more of the signers.

(b) If the signature of the issuer of an instrument is made by automated means, such as a check-writing machine, the payee of the instrument is determined by the intent of the person who supplied the name or identification of the payee, whether or not authorized to do so.

(c) A person to whom an instrument is payable may be identified in any way, including by name, identifying number, office, or account number. For the purpose of determining the holder of an instrument, the following rules apply:

(1) If an instrument is payable to an account and the account is identified only by number, the instrument is payable to the person to whom the account is payable. If an instrument is payable to an account identified by number and by the name of a person, the instrument is payable to the named person, whether or not that person is the owner of the account identified by number.

(2) If an instrument is payable to:

(i) a trust, an estate, or a person described as trustee or representative of a trust or estate, the instrument is payable to the trustee, the representative, or a successor of either, whether or not the beneficiary or estate is also named;

(ii) a person described as agent or similar representative of a named or identified person, the instrument is payable to the represented person, the representative, or a successor of the representative;

(iii) a fund or organization that is not a legal entity, the instrument is payable to a representative of the members of the fund or organization; or

(iv) an office or to a person described as holding an office, the instrument is payable to the named person, the incumbent of the office, or a successor to the incumbent.

(d) If an instrument is payable to two or more persons alternatively, it is payable to any of them and may be negotiated, discharged, or enforced by any or all of them in possession of the instrument. If an instrument is payable to two or more persons not alternatively, it is payable to all of them and may be negotiated, discharged, or enforced only by all of them. If an instrument payable to two or more persons is ambiguous as to whether it is payable to the persons alternatively, the instrument is payable to the persons alternatively.

§ 3—111. Place of Payment.

Except as otherwise provided for items in Article 4, an instrument is payable at the place of payment stated in the instrument. If no place of payment is stated, an instrument is payable at the address of the drawee or maker stated in the instrument. If no address is stated, the place of payment is the place of business of the drawee or maker. If a drawee or maker has more than one place of business, the place of payment is any place of business of the drawee or maker chosen by the person entitled to enforce the instrument. If the drawee or maker has no place of business, the place of payment is the residence of the drawee or maker.

§ 3—112. Interest.

(a) Unless otherwise provided in the instrument, (i) an instrument is not payable with interest, and (ii) interest on an interest-bearing instrument is payable from the date of the instrument.

(b) Interest may be stated in an instrument as a fixed or variable amount of money or it may be expressed as a fixed or variable rate or rates. The amount or rate of interest may be stated or described in the instrument in any manner and may require reference to information not contained in the instrument. If an instrument provides for interest, but the amount of interest payable cannot be ascertained from the description, interest is payable at the judgment rate in effect at the place of payment of the instrument and at the time interest first accrues.

§ 3—113. Date of Instrument.

(a) An instrument may be antedated or postdated. The date stated determines the time of payment if the instrument is payable at a fixed period after date. Except as provided in Section 4—401(c), an instrument payable on demand is not payable before the date of the instrument.

(b) If an instrument is undated, its date is the date of its issue or, in the case of an unissued instrument, the date it first comes into possession of a holder.

§ 3—114. Contradictory Terms of Instrument.

If an instrument contains contradictory terms, typewritten terms prevail over printed terms, handwritten terms prevail over both, and words prevail over numbers.

§ 3—115. Incomplete Instrument.

(a) "Incomplete instrument" means a signed writing, whether or not issued by the signer, the contents of which show at the time of signing that it is incomplete but that the signer intended it to be completed by the addition of words or numbers.

(b) Subject to subsection (c), if an incomplete instrument is an instrument under Section 3—104, it may be enforced according to its terms if it is not completed, or according to its terms as augmented by completion. If an incomplete instrument is not an instrument under Section 3—104, but, after completion, the requirements of Section 3—104 are met, the instrument may be enforced according to its terms as augmented by completion.

(c) If words or numbers are added to an incomplete instrument without authority of the signer, there is an alteration of the incomplete instrument under Section 3—407.

(d) The burden of establishing that words or numbers were added to an incomplete instrument without authority of the signer is on the person asserting the lack of authority.

§ 3—116. Joint and Several Liability; Contribution.

(a) Except as otherwise provided in the instrument, two or more persons who have the same liability on an instrument as makers, drawers, acceptors, indorsers who indorse as joint payees, or anomalous indorsers are jointly and severally liable in the capacity in which they sign.

(b) Except as provided in Section 3—419(e) or by agreement of the affected parties, a party having joint and several liability who pays the instrument is entitled to receive from any party having the same joint and several liability contribution in accordance with applicable law.

(c) Discharge of one party having joint and several liability by a person entitled to enforce the instrument does not affect the right under subsection (b) of a party having the same joint and several liability to receive contribution from the party discharged.

§ 3—117. Other Agreements Affecting Instrument.

Subject to applicable law regarding exclusion of proof of contemporaneous or previous agreements, the obligation of a party to an instrument to pay the instrument may be modified, supplemented, or nullified by a separate agreement of the obligor and a person entitled to enforce the instrument, if the instrument is issued or the obligation is incurred in reliance on the agreement or as part of the same transaction giving rise to the agreement. To the extent an obligation is modified, supplemented, or nullified by an agreement under this section, the agreement is a defense to the obligation.

§ 3—118. Statute of Limitations.

(a) Except as provided in subsection (e), an action to enforce the obligation of a party to pay a note payable at a definite time must be commenced within six years after the due date or dates stated in the note or, if a due date is accelerated, within six years after the accelerated due date.

(b) Except as provided in subsection (d) or (e), if demand for payment is made to the maker of a note payable on demand, an action to enforce the obligation of a party to pay the note must be commenced within six years after the demand. If no demand for payment is made to the maker, an action to enforce the note is barred if neither principal nor interest on the note has been paid for a continuous period of 10 years.

(c) Except as provided in subsection (d), an action to enforce the obligation of a party to an unaccepted draft to pay the draft must be commenced within three years after dishonor of the draft or 10 years after the date of the draft, whichever period expires first.

(d) An action to enforce the obligation of the acceptor of a certified check or the issuer of a teller's check, cashier's check, or traveler's check must be commenced within three years after demand for payment is made to the acceptor or issuer, as the case may be.

(e) An action to enforce the obligation of a party to a certificate of deposit to pay the instrument must be commenced within six years after demand for payment is made to the maker, but if the instrument states a due date and the maker is not required to pay before that date, the six-year period begins when a demand for payment is in effect and the due date has passed.

(f) An action to enforce the obligation of a party to pay an accepted draft, other than a certified check, must be commenced (i) within six years after the due date or dates stated in the draft or acceptance if the obligation of the acceptor is payable at a definite time, or (ii) within six years after the date of the acceptance if the obligation of the acceptor is payable on demand.

(g) Unless governed by other law regarding claims for indemnity or contribution, an action (i) for conversion of an instrument, for money had and received, or like action based on conversion, (ii) for breach of warranty, or (iii) to enforce an obligation, duty, or right arising under this Article and not governed by this section must be commenced within three years after the [cause of action] accrues.

§ 3—119. Notice of Right to Defend Action.

In an action for breach of an obligation for which a third person is answerable over pursuant to this Article or Article 4, the defendant may give the third person written notice of the litigation, and the person notified may then give similar notice to any other person who is answerable over. If the notice states (i) that the person notified may come in and defend and (ii) that failure to do so will bind the person notified in an action later brought by the person giving the notice as to any determination of fact common to the two litigations, the person notified is so bound unless after seasonable receipt of the notice the person notified does come in and defend.

Part 2 Negotiation, Transfer, and Indorsement

§ 3—201. Negotiation.

(a) "Negotiation" means a transfer of possession, whether voluntary or involuntary, of an instrument by a person other than the issuer to a person who thereby becomes its holder.

(b) Except for negotiation by a remitter, if an instrument is payable to an identified person, negotiation requires transfer of possession of the instrument and its indorsement by the holder. If an instrument is payable to bearer, it may be negotiated by transfer of possession alone.

§ 3—202. Negotiation Subject to Rescission.

(a) Negotiation is effective even if obtained (i) from an infant, a corporation exceeding its powers, or a person without capacity, (ii) by fraud, duress, or mistake, or (iii) in breach of duty or as part of an illegal transaction.

(b) To the extent permitted by other law, negotiation may be rescinded or may be subject to other remedies, but those remedies may not be asserted against a subsequent holder in due course or a person paying the instrument in good faith and without knowledge of facts that are a basis for rescission or other remedy.

§ 3—203. Transfer of Instrument; Rights Acquired by Transfer.

(a) An instrument is transferred when it is delivered by a person other than its issuer for the purpose of giving to the person receiving delivery the right to enforce the instrument.

(b) Transfer of an instrument, whether or not the transfer is a negotiation, vests in the transferee any right of the transferor to enforce the instrument, including any right as a holder in due course, but the transferee cannot acquire rights of a holder in due course by a transfer, directly or indirectly, from a holder in due course if the transferee engaged in fraud or illegality affecting the instrument.

(c) Unless otherwise agreed, if an instrument is transferred for value and the transferee does not become a holder because of lack of indorsement by the transferor, the transferee has a specifically enforceable right to the unqualified indorsement of the transferor, but negotiation of the instrument does not occur until the indorsement is made.

(d) If a transferor purports to transfer less than the entire instrument, negotiation of the instrument does not occur. The transferee obtains no rights under this Article and has only the rights of a partial assignee.

§ 3—204. Indorsement.

(a) "Indorsement" means a signature, other than that of a signer as maker, drawer, or acceptor, that alone or accompanied by other words is made on an instrument for the purpose of (i) negotiating the instrument, (ii) restricting payment of the instrument, or (iii) incurring indorser's liability on the instrument, but regardless of the intent of the signer, a signature and its accompanying words is an indorsement unless the accompanying words, terms of the instrument, place of the signature, or other circumstances unambiguously indicate that the signature was made for a purpose other than indorsement. For the purpose of determining whether a signature is made on an instrument, a paper affixed to the instrument is a part of the instrument.

(b) "Indorser" means a person who makes an indorsement.

(c) For the purpose of determining whether the transferee of an instrument is a holder, an indorsement that transfers a security interest in the instrument is effective as an unqualified indorsement of the instrument.

(d) If an instrument is payable to a holder under a name that is not the name of the holder, indorsement may be made by the holder in the name stated in the instrument or in the holder's name or both, but signature in both names may be required by a person paying or taking the instrument for value or collection.

§ 3—205. Special Indorsement; Blank Indorsement; Anomalous Indorsement.

(a) If an indorsement is made by the holder of an instrument, whether payable to an identified person or payable to bearer, and the indorsement identifies a person to whom it makes the instrument payable, it is a "special indorsement." When specially indorsed, an instrument becomes payable to the identified person and may be negotiated only by the indorsement of that person. The principles stated in Section 3—110 apply to special indorsements.

(b) If an indorsement is made by the holder of an instrument and it is not a special indorsement, it is a "blank indorsement." When indorsed in blank, an instrument becomes payable to bearer and may be negotiated by transfer of possession alone until specially indorsed.

(c) The holder may convert a blank indorsement that consists only of a signature into a special indorsement by writing, above the signature of the indorser, words identifying the person to whom the instrument is made payable.

(d) "Anomalous indorsement" means an indorsement made by a person who is not the holder of the instrument. An anomalous indorsement does not affect the manner in which the instrument may be negotiated.

§ 3—206. Restrictive Indorsement.

(a) An indorsement limiting payment to a particular person or otherwise prohibiting further transfer or negotiation of the instrument is not effective to prevent further transfer or negotiation of the instrument.

(b) An indorsement stating a condition to the right of the indorsee to receive payment does not affect the right of the indorsee to enforce the instrument. A person paying the instrument or taking it for value or collection may disregard the condition, and the rights and liabilities of that person are not affected by whether the condition has been fulfilled.

(c) If an instrument bears an indorsement (i) described in Section 4—201(b), or (ii) in blank or to a particular bank using the words "for deposit," "for collection," or other words indicating a purpose of having the instrument collected by a bank for the indorser or for a particular account, the following rules apply:

(1) A person, other than a bank, who purchases the instrument when so indorsed converts the instrument unless the amount paid for the instrument is received by the indorser or applied consistently with the indorsement.

(2) A depositary bank that purchases the instrument or takes it for collection when so indorsed converts the instrument unless the amount paid by the bank with respect to the instrument is received by the indorser or applied consistently with the indorsement.

(3) A payor bank that is also the depositary bank or that takes the instrument for immediate payment over the counter from a person other than a collecting bank converts the instrument unless the proceeds of the instrument are received by the indorser or applied consistently with the indorsement.

(4) Except as otherwise provided in paragraph (3), a payor bank or intermediary bank may disregard the indorsement and is not liable if the proceeds of the instrument are not received by the indorser or applied consistently with the indorsement.

(d) Except for an indorsement covered by subsection (c), if an instrument bears an indorsement using words to the effect that payment is to be made to the indorsee as agent, trustee, or other fiduciary for the benefit of the indorser or another person, the following rules apply:

(1) Unless there is notice of breach of fiduciary duty as provided in Section 3—307, a person who purchases the instrument from the indorsee or takes the instrument from the indorsee for collection or payment may pay the proceeds of payment or the value given for the instrument to the indorsee without regard to whether the indorsee violates a fiduciary duty to the indorser.

(2) A subsequent transferee of the instrument or person who pays the instrument is neither given notice nor otherwise affected by the restriction in the indorsement unless the transferee or payor knows that the fiduciary dealt with the instrument or its proceeds in breach of fiduciary duty.

(e) The presence on an instrument of an indorsement to which this section applies does not prevent a purchaser of the instrument from becoming a holder in due course of the instrument unless the purchaser is a converter under subsection (c) or has notice or knowledge of breach of fiduciary duty as stated in subsection (d).

(f) In an action to enforce the obligation of a party to pay the instrument, the obligor has a defense if payment would violate an indorsement to which this section applies and the payment is not permitted by this section.

§ 3—207. Reacquisition.

Reacquisition of an instrument occurs if it is transferred to a former holder, by negotiation or otherwise. A former holder who reacquires the instrument may cancel indorsements made after the reacquirer first became a holder of the instrument. If the cancellation causes the instrument to be payable to the reacquirer or to bearer, the reacquirer may negotiate the instrument. An indorser whose indorsement is canceled is discharged, and the discharge is effective against any subsequent holder.

Part 3 Enforcement of Instruments

§ 3—301. Person Entitled to Enforce Instrument.

"Person entitled to enforce" an instrument means (i) the holder of the instrument, (ii) a nonholder in possession of the instrument who has the rights of a holder, or (iii) a person not in possession of the instrument who is entitled to enforce the instrument pursuant to Section 3—309 or 3—418(d). A person may be a person entitled to enforce the instrument even though the person is not the owner of the instrument or is in wrongful possession of the instrument.

§ 3—302. Holder in Due Course.

(a) Subject to subsection (c) and Section 3—106(d), "holder in due course" means the holder of an instrument if:

(1) the instrument when issued or negotiated to the holder does not bear such apparent evidence of forgery or alteration or is not otherwise so irregular or incomplete as to call into question its authenticity; and

(2) the holder took the instrument (i) for value, (ii) in good faith, (iii) without notice that the instrument is overdue or has been dishonored or that there is an uncured default with respect to payment of another instrument issued as part of the same series, (iv) without notice that the instrument contains an unauthorized signature or has been altered, (v) without notice of any claim to the instrument described in Section 3—306, and (vi) without notice that any party has a defense or claim in recoupment described in Section 3—305(a).

(b) Notice of discharge of a party, other than discharge in an insolvency proceeding, is not notice of a defense under subsection (a), but discharge is effective against a person who became a holder in due course with notice of the discharge. Public filing or recording of a document does not of itself constitute notice of a defense, claim in recoupment, or claim to the instrument.

(c) Except to the extent a transferor or predecessor in interest has rights as a holder in due course, a person does not acquire rights of a holder in due course of an instrument taken (i) by legal process or by purchase in an execution, bankruptcy, or creditor's sale or similar proceeding, (ii) by purchase as part of a bulk transaction not in ordinary course of business of the transferor, or (iii) as the successor in interest to an estate or other organization.

(d) If, under Section 3—303(a)(1), the promise of performance that is the consideration for an instrument has been partially performed, the holder may assert rights as a holder in due course of the instrument only to the fraction of the amount payable under the instrument equal to the value of the partial performance divided by the value of the promised performance.

(e) If (i) the person entitled to enforce an instrument has only a security interest in the instrument and (ii) the person obliged to pay the instrument has a defense, claim in recoupment, or claim to the instrument that may be asserted against the person who granted the security interest, the person entitled to enforce the instrument may assert rights as a holder in due course only to an amount payable under the instrument which, at the time of enforcement of the instrument, does not exceed the amount of the unpaid obligation secured.

(f) To be effective, notice must be received at a time and in a manner that gives a reasonable opportunity to act on it.

(g) This section is subject to any law limiting status as a holder in due course in particular classes of transactions.

§ 3—303. Value and Consideration.

(a) An instrument is issued or transferred for value if:

(1) the instrument is issued or transferred for a promise of performance, to the extent the promise has been performed;

(2) the transferee acquires a security interest or other lien in the instrument other than a lien obtained by judicial proceeding;

(3) the instrument is issued or transferred as payment of, or as security for, an antecedent claim against any person, whether or not the claim is due;

(4) the instrument is issued or transferred in exchange for a negotiable instrument; or

(5) the instrument is issued or transferred in exchange for the incurring of an irrevocable obligation to a third party by the person taking the instrument.

(b) "Consideration" means any consideration sufficient to support a simple contract. The drawer or maker of an instrument has a defense if the instrument is issued without consideration. If an instrument is issued for a promise of performance, the issuer has a defense to the extent performance of the promise is due and the promise has not been performed. If an instrument is issued for value as stated in subsection (a), the instrument is also issued for consideration.

§ 3—304. Overdue Instrument.

(a) An instrument payable on demand becomes overdue at the earliest of the following times:

(1) on the day after the day demand for payment is duly made;

(2) if the instrument is a check, 90 days after its date; or

(3) if the instrument is not a check, when the instrument has been outstanding for a period of time after its date which is unreasonably long under the circumstances of the particular

case in light of the nature of the instrument and usage of the trade.

(b) With respect to an instrument payable at a definite time the following rules apply:

(1) If the principal is payable in installments and a due date has not been accelerated, the instrument becomes overdue upon default under the instrument for nonpayment of an installment, and the instrument remains overdue until the default is cured.

(2) If the principal is not payable in installments and the due date has not been accelerated, the instrument becomes overdue on the day after the due date.

(3) If a due date with respect to principal has been accelerated, the instrument becomes overdue on the day after the accelerated due date.

(c) Unless the due date of principal has been accelerated, an instrument does not become overdue if there is default in payment of interest but no default in payment of principal.

§ 3—305. Defenses and Claims in Recoupment.

(a) Except as stated in subsection (b), the right to enforce the obligation of a party to pay an instrument is subject to the following:

(1) a defense of the obligor based on (i) infancy of the obligor to the extent it is a defense to a simple contract, (ii) duress, lack of legal capacity, or illegality of the transaction which, under other law, nullifies the obligation of the obligor, (iii) fraud that induced the obligor to sign the instrument with neither knowledge nor reasonable opportunity to learn of its character or its essential terms, or (iv) discharge of the obligor in insolvency proceedings;

(2) a defense of the obligor stated in another section of this Article or a defense of the obligor that would be available if the person entitled to enforce the instrument were enforcing a right to payment under a simple contract; and

(3) a claim in recoupment of the obligor against the original payee of the instrument if the claim arose from the transaction that gave rise to the instrument; but the claim of the obligor may be asserted against a transferee of the instrument only to reduce the amount owing on the instrument at the time the action is brought.

(b) The right of a holder in due course to enforce the obligation of a party to pay the instrument is subject to defenses of the obligor stated in subsection (a)(1), but is not subject to defenses of the obligor stated in subsection (a)(2) or claims in recoupment stated in subsection (a)(3) against a person other than the holder.

(c) Except as stated in subsection (d), in an action to enforce the obligation of a party to pay the instrument, the obligor may not assert against the person entitled to enforce the instrument a defense, claim in recoupment, or claim to the instrument (Section 3—306) of another person, but the other person's claim to the instrument may be asserted by the obligor if the other person is joined in the action and personally asserts the claim against the person entitled to enforce the instrument. An obligor is not obliged to pay the instrument if the person seeking enforcement of the instrument does not have rights of a holder in due course and the obligor proves that the instrument is a lost or stolen instrument.

(d) In an action to enforce the obligation of an accommodation party to pay an instrument, the accommodation party may assert against the person entitled to enforce the instrument any defense or claim in recoupment under subsection (a) that the accommodated party could assert against the person entitled to enforce the instrument, except the defenses of discharge in insolvency proceedings, infancy, and lack of legal capacity.

§ 3—306. Claims to an Instrument.

A person taking an instrument, other than a person having rights of a holder in due course, is subject to a claim of a property or possessory right in the instrument or its proceeds, including a claim to rescind a negotiation and to recover the instrument or its proceeds. A person having rights of a holder in due course takes free of the claim to the instrument.

§ 3—307. Notice of Breach of Fiduciary Duty.

(a) In this section:

(1) "Fiduciary" means an agent, trustee, partner, corporate officer or director, or other representative owing a fiduciary duty with respect to an instrument.

(2) "Represented person" means the principal, beneficiary, partnership, corporation, or other person to whom the duty stated in paragraph (1) is owed.

(b) If (i) an instrument is taken from a fiduciary for payment or collection or for value, (ii) the taker has knowledge of the fiduciary status of the fiduciary, and (iii) the represented person makes a claim to the instrument or its proceeds on the basis that the transaction of the fiduciary is a breach of fiduciary duty, the following rules apply:

(1) Notice of breach of fiduciary duty by the fiduciary is notice of the claim of the represented person.

(2) In the case of an instrument payable to the represented person or the fiduciary as such, the taker has notice of the breach of fiduciary duty if the instrument is (i) taken in payment of or as security for a debt known by the taker to be the personal debt of the fiduciary, (ii) taken in a transaction known by the taker to be for the personal benefit of the fiduciary, or (iii) deposited to an account other than an account of the fiduciary, as such, or an account of the represented person.

(3) If an instrument is issued by the represented person or the fiduciary as such, and made payable to the fiduciary personally, the taker does not have notice of the breach of fiduciary duty unless the taker knows of the breach of fiduciary duty.

(4) If an instrument is issued by the represented person or the fiduciary as such, to the taker as payee, the taker has notice of the breach of fiduciary duty if the instrument is (i) taken in payment of or as security for a debt known by the

taker to be the personal debt of the fiduciary, (ii) taken in a transaction known by the taker to be for the personal benefit of the fiduciary, or (iii) deposited to an account other than an account of the fiduciary, as such, or an account of the represented person.

§ 3—308. Proof of Signatures and Status as Holder in Due Course.

(a) In an action with respect to an instrument, the authenticity of, and authority to make, each signature on the instrument is admitted unless specifically denied in the pleadings. If the validity of a signature is denied in the pleadings, the burden of establishing validity is on the person claiming validity, but the signature is presumed to be authentic and authorized unless the action is to enforce the liability of the purported signer and the signer is dead or incompetent at the time of trial of the issue of validity of the signature. If an action to enforce the instrument is brought against a person as the undisclosed principal of a person who signed the instrument as a party to the instrument, the plaintiff has the burden of establishing that the defendant is liable on the instrument as a represented person under Section 3—402(a).

(b) If the validity of signatures is admitted or proved and there is compliance with subsection (a), a plaintiff producing the instrument is entitled to payment if the plaintiff proves entitlement to enforce the instrument under Section 3—301, unless the defendant proves a defense or claim in recoupment. If a defense or claim in recoupment is proved, the right to payment of the plaintiff is subject to the defense or claim, except to the extent the plaintiff proves that the plaintiff has rights of a holder in due course which are not subject to the defense or claim.

§ 3—309. Enforcement of Lost, Destroyed, or Stolen Instrument.

(a) A person not in possession of an instrument is entitled to enforce the instrument if (i) the person was in possession of the instrument and entitled to enforce it when loss of possession occurred, (ii) the loss of possession was not the result of a transfer by the person or a lawful seizure, and (iii) the person cannot reasonably obtain possession of the instrument because the instrument was destroyed, its whereabouts cannot be determined, or it is in the wrongful possession of an unknown person or a person that cannot be found or is not amenable to service of process.

(b) A person seeking enforcement of an instrument under subsection (a) must prove the terms of the instrument and the person's right to enforce the instrument. If that proof is made, Section 3—308 applies to the case as if the person seeking enforcement had produced the instrument. The court may not enter judgment in favor of the person seeking enforcement unless it finds that the person required to pay the instrument is adequately protected against loss that might occur by reason of a claim by another person to enforce the instrument. Adequate protection may be provided by any reasonable means.

§ 3—310. Effect of Instrument on Obligation for Which Taken.

(a) Unless otherwise agreed, if a certified check, cashier's check, or teller's check is taken for an obligation, the obligation is discharged to the same extent discharge would result if an amount of money equal to the amount of the instrument were taken in payment of the obligation. Discharge of the obligation does not affect any liability that the obligor may have as an indorser of the instrument.

(b) Unless otherwise agreed and except as provided in subsection (a), if a note or an uncertified check is taken for an obligation, the obligation is suspended to the same extent the obligation would be discharged if an amount of money equal to the amount of the instrument were taken, and the following rules apply:

(1) In the case of an uncertified check, suspension of the obligation continues until dishonor of the check or until it is paid or certified. Payment or certification of the check results in discharge of the obligation to the extent of the amount of the check.

(2) In the case of a note, suspension of the obligation continues until dishonor of the note or until it is paid. Payment of the note results in discharge of the obligation to the extent of the payment.

(3) Except as provided in paragraph (4), if the check or note is dishonored and the obligee of the obligation for which the instrument was taken is the person entitled to enforce the instrument, the obligee may enforce either the instrument or the obligation. In the case of an instrument of a third person which is negotiated to the obligee by the obligor, discharge of the obligor on the instrument also discharges the obligation.

(4) If the person entitled to enforce the instrument taken for an obligation is a person other than the obligee, the obligee may not enforce the obligation to the extent the obligation is suspended. If the obligee is the person entitled to enforce the instrument but no longer has possession of it because it was lost, stolen, or destroyed, the obligation may not be enforced to the extent of the amount payable on the instrument, and to that extent the obligee's rights against the obligor are limited to enforcement of the instrument.

(c) If an instrument other than one described in subsection (a) or (b) is taken for an obligation, the effect is (i) that stated in subsection (a) if the instrument is one on which a bank is liable as maker or acceptor, or (ii) that stated in subsection (b) in any other case.

§ 3—311. Accord and Satisfaction by Use of Instrument.

(a) If a person against whom a claim is asserted proves that (i) that person in good faith tendered an instrument to the claimant as full satisfaction of the claim, (ii) the amount of the claim was unliquidated or subject to a bona fide dispute, and (iii) the claimant obtained payment of the instrument, the following subsections apply.

(b) Unless subsection (c) applies, the claim is discharged if the person against whom the claim is asserted proves that the instrument or an accompanying written communication contained a conspicuous statement to the effect that the instrument was tendered as full satisfaction of the claim.

(c) Subject to subsection (d), a claim is not discharged under subsection (b) if either of the following applies:

(1) The claimant, if an organization, proves that (i) within a reasonable time before the tender, the claimant sent a conspicuous statement to the person against whom the claim is asserted that communications concerning disputed debts, including an instrument tendered as full satisfaction of a debt, are to be sent to a designated person, office, or place, and (ii) the instrument or accompanying communication was not received by that designated person, office, or place.

(2) The claimant, whether or not an organization, proves that within 90 days after payment of the instrument, the claimant tendered repayment of the amount of the instrument to the person against whom the claim is asserted. This paragraph does not apply if the claimant is an organization that sent a statement complying with paragraph (1)(i).

(d) A claim is discharged if the person against whom the claim is asserted proves that within a reasonable time before collection of the instrument was initiated, the claimant, or an agent of the claimant having direct responsibility with respect to the disputed obligation, knew that the instrument was tendered in full satisfaction of the claim.

§ 3—312. Lost, Destroyed, or Stolen Cashier's Check, Teller's Check, or Certified Check.

(a) In this section:

(1) "Check" means a cashier's check, teller's check, or certified check.

(2) "Claimant" means a person who claims the right to receive the amount of a cashier's check, teller's check, or certified check that was lost, destroyed, or stolen.

(3) "Declaration of loss" means a written statement, made under penalty of perjury, to the effect that (i) the declarer lost possession of a check, (ii) the declarer is the drawer or payee of the check, in the case of a certified check, or the remitter or payee of the check, in the case of a cashier's check or teller's check, (iii) the loss of possession was not the result of a transfer by the declarer or a lawful seizure, and (iv) the declarer cannot reasonably obtain possession of the check because the check was destroyed, its whereabouts cannot be determined, or it is in the wrongful possession of an unknown person or a person that cannot be found or is not amenable to service of process.

(4) "Obligated bank" means the issuer of a cashier's check or teller's check or the acceptor of a certified check.

(b) A claimant may assert a claim to the amount of a check by a communication to the obligated bank describing the check with reasonable certainty and requesting payment of the amount of the check, if (i) the claimant is the drawer or payee of a certified check or the remitter or payee of a cashier's check or teller's check, (ii) the communication contains or is accompanied by a declaration of loss of the claimant with respect to the check, (iii) the communication is received at a time and in a manner affording the bank a reasonable time to act on it before the check is paid, and (iv) the claimant provides reasonable identification if requested by the obligated bank. Delivery of a declaration of loss is a warranty of the truth of the statements made in the declaration. If a claim is asserted in compliance with this subsection, the following rules apply:

(1) The claim becomes enforceable at the later of (i) the time the claim is asserted, or (ii) the 90th day following the date of the check, in the case of a cashier's check or teller's check, or the 90th day following the date of the acceptance, in the case of a certified check.

(2) Until the claim becomes enforceable, it has no legal effect and the obligated bank may pay the check or, in the case of a teller's check, may permit the drawee to pay the check. Payment to a person entitled to enforce the check discharges all liability of the obligated bank with respect to the check.

(3) If the claim becomes enforceable before the check is presented for payment, the obligated bank is not obliged to pay the check.

(4) When the claim becomes enforceable, the obligated bank becomes obliged to pay the amount of the check to the claimant if payment of the check has not been made to a person entitled to enforce the check. Subject to Section 4—302(a)(1), payment to the claimant discharges all liability of the obligated bank with respect to the check.

(c) If the obligated bank pays the amount of a check to a claimant under subsection (b)(4) and the check is presented for payment by a person having rights of a holder in due course, the claimant is obliged to (i) refund the payment to the obligated bank if the check is paid, or (ii) pay the amount of the check to the person having rights of a holder in due course if the check is dishonored.

(d) If a claimant has the right to assert a claim under subsection (b) and is also a person entitled to enforce a cashier's check, teller's check, or certified check which is lost, destroyed, or stolen, the claimant may assert rights with respect to the check either under this section or Section 3—309.

Part 4 Liability of Parties

§ 3—401. Signature.

(a) A person is not liable on an instrument unless (i) the person signed the instrument, or (ii) the person is represented by an agent or representative who signed the instrument and the signature is binding on the represented person under Section 3—402.

(b) A signature may be made (i) manually or by means of a device or machine, and (ii) by the use of any name, including a trade or assumed name, or by a word, mark, or symbol executed or adopted by a person with present intention to authenticate a writing.

§ 3—402. Signature by Representative.

(a) If a person acting, or purporting to act, as a representative signs an instrument by signing either the name of the represented person or the name of the signer, the represented person is bound by the signature to the same extent the represented person would be bound if the signature were on a simple contract. If the represented person is bound, the signature of the representative is the "authorized signature of the represented person" and the represented person is liable on the instrument, whether or not identified in the instrument.

(b) If a representative signs the name of the representative to an instrument and the signature is an authorized signature of the represented person, the following rules apply:

(1) If the form of the signature shows unambiguously that the signature is made on behalf of the represented person who is identified in the instrument, the representative is not liable on the instrument.

(2) Subject to subsection (c), if (i) the form of the signature does not show unambiguously that the signature is made in a representative capacity or (ii) the represented person is not identified in the instrument, the representative is liable on the instrument to a holder in due course that took the instrument without notice that the representative was not intended to be liable on the instrument. With respect to any other person, the representative is liable on the instrument unless the representative proves that the original parties did not intend the representative to be liable on the instrument.

(c) If a representative signs the name of the representative as drawer of a check without indication of the representative status and the check is payable from an account of the represented person who is identified on the check, the signer is not liable on the check if the signature is an authorized signature of the represented person.

§ 3—403. Unauthorized Signature.

(a) Unless otherwise provided in this Article or Article 4, an unauthorized signature is ineffective except as the signature of the unauthorized signer in favor of a person who in good faith pays the instrument or takes it for value. An unauthorized signature may be ratified for all purposes of this Article.

(b) If the signature of more than one person is required to constitute the authorized signature of an organization, the signature of the organization is unauthorized if one of the required signatures is lacking.

(c) The civil or criminal liability of a person who makes an unauthorized signature is not affected by any provision of this Article which makes the unauthorized signature effective for the purposes of this Article.

§ 3—404. Impostors; Fictitious Payees.

(a) If an impostor, by use of the mails or otherwise, induces the issuer of an instrument to issue the instrument to the impostor, or to a person acting in concert with the impostor, by impersonating the payee of the instrument or a person authorized to act for the payee, an indorsement of the instrument by any person in the name of the payee is effective as the indorsement of the payee in favor of a person who, in good faith, pays the instrument or takes it for value or for collection.

(b) If (i) a person whose intent determines to whom an instrument is payable (Section 3—110(a) or (b)) does not intend the person identified as payee to have any interest in the instrument, or (ii) the person identified as payee of an instrument is a fictitious person, the following rules apply until the instrument is negotiated by special indorsement:

(1) Any person in possession of the instrument is its holder.

(2) An indorsement by any person in the name of the payee stated in the instrument is effective as the indorsement of the payee in favor of a person who, in good faith, pays the instrument or takes it for value or for collection.

(c) Under subsection (a) or (b), an indorsement is made in the name of a payee if (i) it is made in a name substantially similar to that of the payee or (ii) the instrument, whether or not indorsed, is deposited in a depositary bank to an account in a name substantially similar to that of the payee.

(d) With respect to an instrument to which subsection (a) or (b) applies, if a person paying the instrument or taking it for value or for collection fails to exercise ordinary care in paying or taking the instrument and that failure substantially contributes to loss resulting from payment of the instrument, the person bearing the loss may recover from the person failing to exercise ordinary care to the extent the failure to exercise ordinary care contributed to the loss.

§ 3—405. Employer's Responsibility for Fraudulent Indorsement by Employee.

(a) In this section:

(1) "Employee" includes an independent contractor and employee of an independent contractor retained by the employer.

(2) "Fraudulent indorsement" means (i) in the case of an instrument payable to the employer, a forged indorsement purporting to be that of the employer, or (ii) in the case of an instrument with respect to which the employer is the issuer, a forged indorsement purporting to be that of the person identified as payee.

(3) "Responsibility" with respect to instruments means authority (i) to sign or indorse instruments on behalf of the employer, (ii) to process instruments received by the employer for bookkeeping purposes, for deposit to an account, or for other disposition, (iii) to prepare or process instruments for issue in the name of the employer, (iv) to supply information determining the names or addresses of payees of instruments to be issued in the name of the employer, (v) to control the disposition of instruments to be issued in the name of the employer, or (vi) to act otherwise with respect to instruments in a responsible capacity. "Responsibility" does not include authority that merely allows an employee to have access to instruments or blank or incomplete instrument forms that are being stored or transported or are part of incoming or outgoing mail, or similar access.

(b) For the purpose of determining the rights and liabilities of a person who, in good faith, pays an instrument or takes it for value or for collection, if an employer entrusted an employee with responsibility with respect to the instrument and the employee or a person acting in concert with the employee makes a fraudulent indorsement of the instrument, the indorsement is effective as the indorsement of the person to whom the instrument is payable if it is made in the name of that person. If the person paying the instrument or taking it for value or for collection fails to exercise ordinary care in paying or taking the instrument and that failure substantially contributes to loss resulting from the fraud, the person bearing the loss may recover from the person failing to exercise ordinary care to the extent the failure to exercise ordinary care contributed to the loss.

(c) Under subsection (b), an indorsement is made in the name of the person to whom an instrument is payable if (i) it is made in a name substantially similar to the name of that person or (ii) the instrument, whether or not indorsed, is deposited in a depositary bank to an account in a name substantially similar to the name of that person.

§ 3—406. Negligence Contributing to Forged Signature or Alteration of Instrument.

(a) A person whose failure to exercise ordinary care substantially contributes to an alteration of an instrument or to the making of a forged signature on an instrument is precluded from asserting the alteration or the forgery against a person who, in good faith, pays the instrument or takes it for value or for collection.

(b) Under subsection (a), if the person asserting the preclusion fails to exercise ordinary care in paying or taking the instrument and that failure substantially contributes to loss, the loss is allocated between the person precluded and the person asserting the preclusion according to the extent to which the failure of each to exercise ordinary care contributed to the loss.

(c) Under subsection (a), the burden of proving failure to exercise ordinary care is on the person asserting the preclusion. Under subsection (b), the burden of proving failure to exercise ordinary care is on the person precluded.

§ 3—407. Alteration.

(a) "Alteration" means (i) an unauthorized change in an instrument that purports to modify in any respect the obligation of a party, or (ii) an unauthorized addition of words or numbers or other change to an incomplete instrument relating to the obligation of a party.

(b) Except as provided in subsection (c), an alteration fraudulently made discharges a party whose obligation is affected by the alteration unless that party assents or is precluded from asserting the alteration. No other alteration discharges a party, and the instrument may be enforced according to its original terms.

(c) A payor bank or drawee paying a fraudulently altered instrument or a person taking it for value, in good faith and without notice of the alteration, may enforce rights with respect to the instrument (i) according to its original terms, or (ii) in the case of an incomplete instrument altered by unauthorized completion, according to its terms as completed.

§ 3—408. Drawee Not Liable on Unaccepted Draft.

A check or other draft does not of itself operate as an assignment of funds in the hands of the drawee available for its payment, and the drawee is not liable on the instrument until the drawee accepts it.

§ 3—409. Acceptance of Draft; Certified Check.

(a) "Acceptance" means the drawee's signed agreement to pay a draft as presented. It must be written on the draft and may consist of the drawee's signature alone. Acceptance may be made at any time and becomes effective when notification pursuant to instructions is given or the accepted draft is delivered for the purpose of giving rights on the acceptance to any person.

(b) A draft may be accepted although it has not been signed by the drawer, is otherwise incomplete, is overdue, or has been dishonored.

(c) If a draft is payable at a fixed period after sight and the acceptor fails to date the acceptance, the holder may complete the acceptance by supplying a date in good faith.

(d) "Certified check" means a check accepted by the bank on which it is drawn. Acceptance may be made as stated in subsection (a) or by a writing on the check which indicates that the check is certified. The drawee of a check has no obligation to certify the check, and refusal to certify is not dishonor of the check.

§ 3—410. Acceptance Varying Draft.

(a) If the terms of a drawee's acceptance vary from the terms of the draft as presented, the holder may refuse the acceptance and treat the draft as dishonored. In that case, the drawee may cancel the acceptance.

(b) The terms of a draft are not varied by an acceptance to pay at a particular bank or place in the United States, unless the acceptance states that the draft is to be paid only at that bank or place.

(c) If the holder assents to an acceptance varying the terms of a draft, the obligation of each drawer and indorser that does not expressly assent to the acceptance is discharged.

§ 3—411. Refusal to Pay Cashier's Checks, Teller's Checks, and Certified Checks.

(a) In this section, "obligated bank" means the acceptor of a certified check or the issuer of a cashier's check or teller's check bought from the issuer.

(b) If the obligated bank wrongfully (i) refuses to pay a cashier's check or certified check, (ii) stops payment of a teller's check, or (iii) refuses to pay a dishonored teller's check, the person asserting the right to enforce the check is entitled to compensation for expenses and loss of interest resulting from the nonpayment and may recover consequential damages if the obligated bank refuses to pay after receiving notice of particular circumstances giving rise to the damages.

(c) Expenses or consequential damages under subsection (b) are not recoverable if the refusal of the obligated bank to pay occurs because (i) the bank suspends payments, (ii) the obligated bank asserts a claim or defense of the bank that it has reasonable grounds to believe is available against the person entitled to enforce the instrument, (iii) the obligated bank has a reasonable doubt whether the person demanding payment is the person entitled to enforce the instrument, or (iv) payment is prohibited by law.

§ 3—412. Obligation of Issuer of Note or Cashier's Check.

The issuer of a note or cashier's check or other draft drawn on the drawer is obliged to pay the instrument (i) according to its terms at the time it was issued or, if not issued, at the time it first came into possession of a holder, or (ii) if the issuer signed an incomplete instrument, according to its terms when completed, to the extent stated in Sections 3—115 and 3—407. The obligation is owed to a person entitled to enforce the instrument or to an indorser who paid the instrument under Section 3—415.

§ 3—413. Obligation of Acceptor.

(a) The acceptor of a draft is obliged to pay the draft (i) according to its terms at the time it was accepted, even though the acceptance states that the draft is payable "as originally drawn" or equivalent terms, (ii) if the acceptance varies the terms of the draft, according to the terms of the draft as varied, or (iii) if the acceptance is of a draft that is an incomplete instrument, according to its terms when completed, to the extent stated in Sections 3—115 and 3—407. The obligation is owed to a person entitled to enforce the draft or to the drawer or an indorser who paid the draft under Section 3—414 or 3—415.

(b) If the certification of a check or other acceptance of a draft states the amount certified or accepted, the obligation of the acceptor is that amount. If (i) the certification or acceptance does not state an amount, (ii) the amount of the instrument is subsequently raised, and (iii) the instrument is then negotiated to a holder in due course, the obligation of the acceptor is the amount of the instrument at the time it was taken by the holder in due course.

§ 3—414. Obligation of Drawer.

(a) This section does not apply to cashier's checks or other drafts drawn on the drawer.

(b) If an unaccepted draft is dishonored, the drawer is obliged to pay the draft (i) according to its terms at the time it was issued or, if not issued, at the time it first came into possession of a holder, or (ii) if the drawer signed an incomplete instrument, according to its terms when completed, to the extent stated in Sections 3—115 and 3—407. The obligation is owed to a person entitled to enforce the draft or to an indorser who paid the draft under Section 3—415.

(c) If a draft is accepted by a bank, the drawer is discharged, regardless of when or by whom acceptance was obtained.

(d) If a draft is accepted and the acceptor is not a bank, the obligation of the drawer to pay the draft if the draft is dishonored by the acceptor is the same as the obligation of an indorser under Section 3—415(a) and (c).

(e) If a draft states that it is drawn "without recourse" or otherwise disclaims liability of the drawer to pay the draft, the drawer is not liable under subsection (b) to pay the draft if the draft is not a check. A disclaimer of the liability stated in subsection (b) is not effective if the draft is a check.

(f) If (i) a check is not presented for payment or given to a depositary bank for collection within 30 days after its date, (ii) the drawee suspends payments after expiration of the 30-day period without paying the check, and (iii) because of the suspension of payments, the drawer is deprived of funds maintained with the drawee to cover payment of the check, the drawer to the extent deprived of funds may discharge its obligation to pay the check by assigning to the person entitled to enforce the check the rights of the drawer against the drawee with respect to the funds.

§ 3—415. Obligation of Indorser.

(a) Subject to subsections (b), (c), and (d) and to Section 3—419(d), if an instrument is dishonored, an indorser is obliged to pay the amount due on the instrument (i) according to the terms of the instrument at the time it was indorsed, or (ii) if the indorser indorsed an incomplete instrument, according to its terms when completed, to the extent stated in Sections 3—115 and 3—407. The obligation of the indorser is owed to a person entitled to enforce the instrument or to a subsequent indorser who paid the instrument under this section.

(b) If an indorsement states that it is made "without recourse" or otherwise disclaims liability of the indorser, the indorser is not liable under subsection (a) to pay the instrument.

(c) If notice of dishonor of an instrument is required by Section 3—503 and notice of dishonor complying with that section is not given to an indorser, the liability of the indorser under subsection (a) is discharged.

(d) If a draft is accepted by a bank after an indorsement is made, the liability of the indorser under subsection (a) is discharged.

(e) If an indorser of a check is liable under subsection (a) and the check is not presented for payment, or given to a depositary bank for collection, within 30 days after the day the indorsement was made, the liability of the indorser under subsection (a) is discharged.

§ 3—416. Transfer Warranties.

(a) A person who transfers an instrument for consideration warrants to the transferee and, if the transfer is by indorsement, to any subsequent transferee that:

(1) the warrantor is a person entitled to enforce the instrument;

(2) all signatures on the instrument are authentic and authorized;

(3) the instrument has not been altered;

(4) the instrument is not subject to a defense or claim in recoupment of any party which can be asserted against the warrantor; and

(5) the warrantor has no knowledge of any insolvency proceeding commenced with respect to the maker or acceptor or, in the case of an unaccepted draft, the drawer.

(b) A person to whom the warranties under subsection (a) are made and who took the instrument in good faith may recover from the warrantor as damages for breach of warranty an amount equal to the loss suffered as a result of the breach, but not more than the amount of the instrument plus expenses and loss of interest incurred as a result of the breach.

(c) The warranties stated in subsection (a) cannot be disclaimed with respect to checks. Unless notice of a claim for breach of warranty is given to the warrantor within 30 days after the claimant has reason to know of the breach and the identity of the warrantor, the liability of the warrantor under subsection (b) is discharged to the extent of any loss caused by the delay in giving notice of the claim.

(d) A [cause of action] for breach of warranty under this section accrues when the claimant has reason to know of the breach.

§ 3—417. Presentment Warranties.

(a) If an unaccepted draft is presented to the drawee for payment or acceptance and the drawee pays or accepts the draft, (i) the person obtaining payment or acceptance, at the time of presentment, and (ii) a previous transferor of the draft, at the time of transfer, warrant to the drawee making payment or accepting the draft in good faith that:

(1) the warrantor is, or was, at the time the warrantor transferred the draft, a person entitled to enforce the draft or authorized to obtain payment or acceptance of the draft on behalf of a person entitled to enforce the draft;

(2) the draft has not been altered; and

(3) the warrantor has no knowledge that the signature of the drawer of the draft is unauthorized.

(b) A drawee making payment may recover from any warrantor damages for breach of warranty equal to the amount paid by the drawee less the amount the drawee received or is entitled to receive from the drawer because of the payment. In addition, the drawee is entitled to compensation for expenses and loss of interest resulting from the breach. The right of the drawee to recover damages under this subsection is not affected by any failure of the drawee to exercise ordinary care in making payment. If the drawee accepts the draft, breach of warranty is a defense to the obligation of the acceptor. If the acceptor makes payment with respect to the draft, the acceptor is entitled to recover from any warrantor for breach of warranty the amounts stated in this subsection.

(c) If a drawee asserts a claim for breach of warranty under subsection (a) based on an unauthorized indorsement of the draft or an alteration of the draft, the warrantor may defend by proving that the indorsement is effective under Section 3—404 or 3—405 or the drawer is precluded under Section 3—406 or 4—406 from asserting against the drawee the unauthorized indorsement or alteration.

(d) If (i) a dishonored draft is presented for payment to the drawer or an indorser or (ii) any other instrument is presented for payment to a party obliged to pay the instrument, and (iii) payment is received, the following rules apply:

(1) The person obtaining payment and a prior transferor of the instrument warrant to the person making payment in good faith that the warrantor is, or was, at the time the warrantor transferred the instrument, a person entitled to enforce the instrument or authorized to obtain payment on behalf of a person entitled to enforce the instrument.

(2) The person making payment may recover from any warrantor for breach of warranty an amount equal to the amount paid plus expenses and loss of interest resulting from the breach.

(e) The warranties stated in subsections (a) and (d) cannot be disclaimed with respect to checks. Unless notice of a claim for breach of warranty is given to the warrantor within 30 days after the claimant has reason to know of the breach and the identity of the warrantor, the liability of the warrantor under subsection (b) or (d) is discharged to the extent of any loss caused by the delay in giving notice of the claim.

(f) A [cause of action] for breach of warranty under this section accrues when the claimant has reason to know of the breach.

§ 3—418. Payment or Acceptance by Mistake.

(a) Except as provided in subsection (c), if the drawee of a draft pays or accepts the draft and the drawee acted on the mistaken belief that (i) payment of the draft had not been stopped pursuant to Section 4—403 or (ii) the signature of the drawer of the draft was authorized, the drawee may recover the amount of the draft from the person to whom or for whose benefit payment was made or, in the case of acceptance, may revoke the acceptance. Rights of the drawee under this subsection are not affected by failure of the drawee to exercise ordinary care in paying or accepting the draft.

(b) Except as provided in subsection (c), if an instrument has been paid or accepted by mistake and the case is not covered by subsection (a), the person paying or accepting may, to the extent permitted by the law governing mistake and restitution, (i) recover the payment from the person to whom or for whose benefit payment was made or (ii) in the case of acceptance, may revoke the acceptance.

(c) The remedies provided by subsection (a) or (b) may not be asserted against a person who took the instrument in good faith and for value or who in good faith changed position in reliance on the payment or acceptance. This subsection does not limit remedies provided by Section 3—417 or 4—407.

(d) Notwithstanding Section 4—215, if an instrument is paid or accepted by mistake and the payor or acceptor recovers payment or revokes acceptance under subsection (a) or (b), the instrument is deemed not to have been paid or accepted and is treated as dishonored, and the person from whom payment is recovered has rights as a person entitled to enforce the dishonored instrument.

§ 3—419. Instruments Signed for Accommodation.

(a) If an instrument is issued for value given for the benefit of a party to the instrument ("accommodated party") and another party to the instrument ("accommodation party") signs the instrument for the purpose of incurring liability on the instrument without being a direct beneficiary of the value given for the instrument, the instrument is signed by the accommodation party "for accommodation."

(b) An accommodation party may sign the instrument as maker, drawer, acceptor, or indorser and, subject to subsection (d), is obliged to pay the instrument in the capacity in which the accommodation party signs. The obligation of an accommodation party may be enforced notwithstanding any statute of frauds and whether or not the accommodation party receives consideration for the accommodation.

(c) A person signing an instrument is presumed to be an accommodation party and there is notice that the instrument is signed for accommodation if the signature is an anomalous indorsement or is accompanied by words indicating that the signer is acting as surety or guarantor with respect to the obligation of another party to the instrument. Except as provided in Section 3—605, the obligation of an accommodation party to pay the instrument is not affected by the fact that the person enforcing the obligation had notice when the instrument was taken by that person that the accommodation party signed the instrument for accommodation.

(d) If the signature of a party to an instrument is accompanied by words indicating unambiguously that the party is guaranteeing collection rather than payment of the obligation of another party to the instrument, the signer is obliged to pay the amount due on the instrument to a person entitled to enforce the instrument only if (i) execution of judgment against the other party has been returned unsatisfied, (ii) the other party is insolvent or in an insolvency proceeding, (iii) the other party cannot be served with process, or (iv) it is otherwise apparent that payment cannot be obtained from the other party.

(e) An accommodation party who pays the instrument is entitled to reimbursement from the accommodated party and is entitled to enforce the instrument against the accommodated party. An accommodated party who pays the instrument has no right of recourse against, and is not entitled to contribution from, an accommodation party.

§ 3—420. Conversion of Instrument.

(a) The law applicable to conversion of personal property applies to instruments. An instrument is also converted if it is taken by transfer, other than a negotiation, from a person not entitled to enforce the instrument or a bank makes or obtains payment with respect to the instrument for a person not entitled to enforce the instrument or receive payment. An action for conversion of an instrument may not be brought by (i) the issuer or acceptor of the instrument or (ii) a payee or indorsee who did not receive delivery of the instrument either directly or through delivery to an agent or a co-payee.

(b) In an action under subsection (a), the measure of liability is presumed to be the amount payable on the instrument, but recovery may not exceed the amount of the plaintiff's interest in the instrument.

(c) A representative, other than a depositary bank, who has in good faith dealt with an instrument or its proceeds on behalf of one who was not the person entitled to enforce the instrument is not liable in conversion to that person beyond the amount of any proceeds that it has not paid out.

Part 5 Dishonor

§ 3—501. Presentment.

(a) "Presentment" means a demand made by or on behalf of a person entitled to enforce an instrument (i) to pay the instrument made to the drawee or a party obliged to pay the instrument or, in the case of a note or accepted draft payable at a bank, to the bank, or (ii) to accept a draft made to the drawee.

(b) The following rules are subject to Article 4, agreement of the parties, and clearing-house rules and the like:

(1) Presentment may be made at the place of payment of the instrument and must be made at the place of payment if the instrument is payable at a bank in the United States; may be made by any commercially reasonable means, including an oral, written, or electronic communication; is effective when the demand for payment or acceptance is received by the person to whom presentment is made; and is effective if made to any one of two or more makers, acceptors, drawees, or other payors.

(2) Upon demand of the person to whom presentment is made, the person making presentment must (i) exhibit the instrument, (ii) give reasonable identification and, if presentment is made on behalf of another person, reasonable evidence of authority to do so, and (. . .) sign a receipt on the instrument for any payment made or surrender the instrument if full payment is made.

(3) Without dishonoring the instrument, the party to whom presentment is made may (i) return the instrument for lack of a necessary indorsement, or (ii) refuse payment or acceptance for failure of the presentment to comply with the terms of the instrument, an agreement of the parties, or other applicable law or rule.

(4) The party to whom presentment is made may treat presentment as occurring on the next business day after the day of presentment if the party to whom presentment is made has established a cut-off hour not earlier than 2 P.M. for the receipt and processing of instruments presented for payment or acceptance and presentment is made after the cut-off hour.

§ 3—502. Dishonor.

(a) Dishonor of a note is governed by the following rules:

(1) If the note is payable on demand, the note is dishonored if presentment is duly made to the maker and the note is not paid on the day of presentment.

(2) If the note is not payable on demand and is payable at or through a bank or the terms of the note require presentment,

the note is dishonored if presentment is duly made and the note is not paid on the day it becomes payable or the day of presentment, whichever is later.

(3) If the note is not payable on demand and paragraph (2) does not apply, the note is dishonored if it is not paid on the day it becomes payable.

(b) Dishonor of an unaccepted draft other than a documentary draft is governed by the following rules:

(1) If a check is duly presented for payment to the payor bank otherwise than for immediate payment over the counter, the check is dishonored if the payor bank makes timely return of the check or sends timely notice of dishonor or nonpayment under Section 4—301 or 4—302, or becomes accountable for the amount of the check under Section 4—302.

(2) If a draft is payable on demand and paragraph (1) does not apply, the draft is dishonored if presentment for payment is duly made to the drawee and the draft is not paid on the day of presentment.

(3) If a draft is payable on a date stated in the draft, the draft is dishonored if (i) presentment for payment is duly made to the drawee and payment is not made on the day the draft becomes payable or the day of presentment, whichever is later, or (ii) presentment for acceptance is duly made before the day the draft becomes payable and the draft is not accepted on the day of presentment.

(4) If a draft is payable on elapse of a period of time after sight or acceptance, the draft is dishonored if presentment for acceptance is duly made and the draft is not accepted on the day of presentment.

(c) Dishonor of an unaccepted documentary draft occurs according to the rules stated in subsection (b)(2), (3), and (4), except that payment or acceptance may be delayed without dishonor until no later than the close of the third business day of the drawee following the day on which payment or acceptance is required by those paragraphs.

(d) Dishonor of an accepted draft is governed by the following rules:

(1) If the draft is payable on demand, the draft is dishonored if presentment for payment is duly made to the acceptor and the draft is not paid on the day of presentment.

(2) If the draft is not payable on demand, the draft is dishonored if presentment for payment is duly made to the acceptor and payment is not made on the day it becomes payable or the day of presentment, whichever is later.

(e) In any case in which presentment is otherwise required for dishonor under this section and presentment is excused under Section 3—504, dishonor occurs without presentment if the instrument is not duly accepted or paid.

(f) If a draft is dishonored because timely acceptance of the draft was not made and the person entitled to demand acceptance consents to a late acceptance, from the time of acceptance the draft is treated as never having been dishonored.

§ 3—503. Notice of Dishonor.

(a) The obligation of an indorser stated in Section 3—415(a) and the obligation of a drawer stated in Section 3—414(d) may not be enforced unless (i) the indorser or drawer is given notice of dishonor of the instrument complying with this section or (ii) notice of dishonor is excused under Section 3—504(b).

(b) Notice of dishonor may be given by any person; may be given by any commercially reasonable means, including an oral, written, or electronic communication; and is sufficient if it reasonably identifies the instrument and indicates that the instrument has been dishonored or has not been paid or accepted. Return of an instrument given to a bank for collection is sufficient notice of dishonor.

(c) Subject to Section 3—504(c), with respect to an instrument taken for collection by a collecting bank, notice of dishonor must be given (i) by the bank before midnight of the next banking day following the banking day on which the bank receives notice of dishonor of the instrument, or (ii) by any other person within 30 days following the day on which the person receives notice of dishonor. With respect to any other instrument, notice of dishonor must be given within 30 days following the day on which dishonor occurs.

§ 3—504. Excused Presentment and Notice of Dishonor.

(a) Presentment for payment or acceptance of an instrument is excused if (i) the person entitled to present the instrument cannot with reasonable diligence make presentment, (ii) the maker or acceptor has repudiated an obligation to pay the instrument or is dead or in insolvency proceedings, (iii) by the terms of the instrument presentment is not necessary to enforce the obligation of indorsers or the drawer, (iv) the drawer or indorser whose obligation is being enforced has waived presentment or otherwise has no reason to expect or right to require that the instrument be paid or accepted, or (v) the drawer instructed the drawee not to pay or accept the draft or the drawee was not obligated to the drawer to pay the draft.

(b) Notice of dishonor is excused if (i) by the terms of the instrument notice of dishonor is not necessary to enforce the obligation of a party to pay the instrument, or (ii) the party whose obligation is being enforced waived notice of dishonor. A waiver of presentment is also a waiver of notice of dishonor.

(c) Delay in giving notice of dishonor is excused if the delay was caused by circumstances beyond the control of the person giving the notice and the person giving the notice exercised reasonable diligence after the cause of the delay ceased to operate.

§ 3—505. Evidence of Dishonor.

(a) The following are admissible as evidence and create a presumption of dishonor and of any notice of dishonor stated:

(1) a document regular in form as provided in subsection (b) which purports to be a protest;

(2) a purported stamp or writing of the drawee, payor bank, or presenting bank on or accompanying the instrument

stating that acceptance or payment has been refused unless reasons for the refusal are stated and the reasons are not consistent with dishonor;

(3) a book or record of the drawee, payor bank, or collecting bank, kept in the usual course of business which shows dishonor, even if there is no evidence of who made the entry.

(b) A protest is a certificate of dishonor made by a United States consul or vice consul, or a notary public or other person authorized to administer oaths by the law of the place where dishonor occurs. It may be made upon information satisfactory to that person. The protest must identify the instrument and certify either that presentment has been made or, if not made, the reason why it was not made, and that the instrument has been dishonored by nonacceptance or nonpayment. The protest may also certify that notice of dishonor has been given to some or all parties.

Part 6 Discharge and Payment

§ 3—601. Discharge and Effect of Discharge.

(a) The obligation of a party to pay the instrument is discharged as stated in this Article or by an act or agreement with the party which would discharge an obligation to pay money under a simple contract.

(b) Discharge of the obligation of a party is not effective against a person acquiring rights of a holder in due course of the instrument without notice of the discharge.

§ 3—602. Payment.

(a) Subject to subsection (b), an instrument is paid to the extent payment is made (i) by or on behalf of a party obliged to pay the instrument, and (ii) to a person entitled to enforce the instrument. To the extent of the payment, the obligation of the party obliged to pay the instrument is discharged even though payment is made with knowledge of a claim to the instrument under Section 3—306 by another person.

(b) The obligation of a party to pay the instrument is not discharged under subsection (a) if:

(1) a claim to the instrument under Section 3—306 is enforceable against the party receiving payment and (i) payment is made with knowledge by the payor that payment is prohibited by injunction or similar process of a court of competent jurisdiction, or (ii) in the case of an instrument other than a cashier's check, teller's check, or certified check, the party making payment accepted, from the person having a claim to the instrument, indemnity against loss resulting from refusal to pay the person entitled to enforce the instrument; or

(2) the person making payment knows that the instrument is a stolen instrument and pays a person it knows is in wrongful possession of the instrument.

§ 3—603. Tender of Payment.

(a) If tender of payment of an obligation to pay an instrument is made to a person entitled to enforce the instrument, the effect of tender is governed by principles of law applicable to tender of payment under a simple contract.

(b) If tender of payment of an obligation to pay an instrument is made to a person entitled to enforce the instrument and the tender is refused, there is discharge, to the extent of the amount of the tender, of the obligation of an indorser or accommodation party having a right of recourse with respect to the obligation to which the tender relates.

(c) If tender of payment of an amount due on an instrument is made to a person entitled to enforce the instrument, the obligation of the obligor to pay interest after the due date on the amount tendered is discharged. If presentment is required with respect to an instrument and the obligor is able and ready to pay on the due date at every place of payment stated in the instrument, the obligor is deemed to have made tender of payment on the due date to the person entitled to enforce the instrument.

§ 3—604. Discharge by Cancellation or Renunciation.

(a) A person entitled to enforce an instrument, with or without consideration, may discharge the obligation of a party to pay the instrument (i) by an intentional voluntary act, such as surrender of the instrument to the party, destruction, mutilation, or cancellation of the instrument, cancellation or striking out of the party's signature, or the addition of words to the instrument indicating discharge, or (ii) by agreeing not to sue or otherwise renouncing rights against the party by a signed writing.

(b) Cancellation or striking out of an indorsement pursuant to subsection (a) does not affect the status and rights of a party derived from the indorsement.

§ 3—605. Discharge of Indorsers and Accommodation Parties.

(a) In this section, the term "indorser" includes a drawer having the obligation described in Section 3—414(d).

(b) Discharge, under Section 3—604, of the obligation of a party to pay an instrument does not discharge the obligation of an indorser or accommodation party having a right of recourse against the discharged party.

(c) If a person entitled to enforce an instrument agrees, with or without consideration, to an extension of the due date of the obligation of a party to pay the instrument, the extension discharges an indorser or accommodation party having a right of recourse against the party whose obligation is extended to the extent the indorser or accommodation party proves that the extension caused loss to the indorser or accommodation party with respect to the right of recourse.

(d) If a person entitled to enforce an instrument agrees, with or without consideration, to a material modification of the obligation of a party other than an extension of the due date, the modification discharges the obligation of an indorser or accommodation party having a right of recourse against the person whose obligation is modified to the extent the modification causes loss to the indorser or accommodation party with respect to the right of recourse. The loss suffered by the indorser or accommodation party as a result of the modification is equal to the amount of the right of recourse unless the person enforcing the instrument proves that no loss was caused by the modification or that the loss caused by the modification was an amount less than the amount of the right of recourse.

(e) If the obligation of a party to pay an instrument is secured by an interest in collateral and a person entitled to enforce the instrument impairs the value of the interest in collateral, the obligation of an indorser or accommodation party having a right of recourse against the obligor is discharged to the extent of the impairment. The value of an interest in collateral is impaired to the extent (i) the value of the interest is reduced to an amount less than the amount of the right of recourse of the party asserting discharge, or (ii) the reduction in value of the interest causes an increase in the amount by which the amount of the right of recourse exceeds the value of the interest. The burden of proving impairment is on the party asserting discharge.

(f) If the obligation of a party is secured by an interest in collateral not provided by an accommodation party and a person entitled to enforce the instrument impairs the value of the interest in collateral, the obligation of any party who is jointly and severally liable with respect to the secured obligation is discharged to the extent the impairment causes the party asserting discharge to pay more than that party would have been obliged to pay, taking into account rights of contribution, if impairment had not occurred. If the party asserting discharge is an accommodation party not entitled to discharge under subsection (e), the party is deemed to have a right to contribution based on joint and several liability rather than a right to reimbursement. The burden of proving impairment is on the party asserting discharge.

(g) Under subsection (e) or (f), impairing value of an interest in collateral includes (i) failure to obtain or maintain perfection or recordation of the interest in collateral, (ii) release of collateral without substitution of collateral of equal value, (iii) failure to perform a duty to preserve the value of collateral owed, under Article 9 or other law, to a debtor or surety or other person secondarily liable, or (iv) failure to comply with applicable law in disposing of collateral.

(h) An accommodation party is not discharged under subsection (c), (d), or (e) unless the person entitled to enforce the instrument knows of the accommodation or has notice under Section 3—419(c) that the instrument was signed for accommodation.

(i) A party is not discharged under this section if (i) the party asserting discharge consents to the event or conduct that is the basis of the discharge, or (ii) the instrument or a separate agreement of the party provides for waiver of discharge under this section either specifically or by general language indicating that parties waive defenses based on suretyship or impairment of collateral.

ADDENDUM TO REVISED ARTICLE 3

Notes to Legislative Counsel

1. If revised Article 3 is adopted in your state, the reference in Section 2—511 to Section 3—802 should be changed to Section 3—310.

2. If revised Article 3 is adopted in your state and the Uniform Fiduciaries Act is also in effect in your state, you may want to consider amending Uniform Fiduciaries Act § 9 to conform to Section 3—307(b)(2)(iii) and (4)(iii). See Official Comment 3 to Section 3—307.

Revised Article 4
BANK DEPOSITS AND COLLECTIONS

Part 1 General Provisions and Definitions

§ 4—101. Short Title.

This Article may be cited as Uniform Commercial Code—Bank Deposits and Collections.

§ 4—102. Applicability.

(a) To the extent that items within this Article are also within Articles 3 and 8, they are subject to those Articles. If there is conflict, this Article governs Article 3, but Article 8 governs this Article.

(b) The liability of a bank for action or non-action with respect to an item handled by it for purposes of presentment, payment, or collection is governed by the law of the place where the bank is located. In the case of action or non-action by or at a branch or separate office of a bank, its liability is governed by the law of the place where the branch or separate office is located.

§ 4—103. Variation by Agreement; Measure of Damages; Action Constituting Ordinary Care.

(a) The effect of the provisions of this Article may be varied by agreement, but the parties to the agreement cannot disclaim a bank's responsibility for its lack of good faith or failure to exercise ordinary care or limit the measure of damages for the lack or failure. However, the parties may determine by agreement the standards by which the bank's responsibility is to be measured if those standards are not manifestly unreasonable.

(b) Federal Reserve regulations and operating circulars, clearing-house rules, and the like have the effect of agreements under subsection (a), whether or not specifically assented to by all parties interested in items handled.

(c) Action or non-action approved by this Article or pursuant to Federal Reserve regulations or operating circulars is the exercise of ordinary care and, in the absence of special instructions, action or non-action consistent with clearing-house rules and the like or with a general banking usage not disapproved by this Article, is prima facie the exercise of ordinary care.

(d) The specification or approval of certain procedures by this Article is not disapproval of other procedures that may be reasonable under the circumstances.

(e) The measure of damages for failure to exercise ordinary care in handling an item is the amount of the item reduced by an amount that could not have been realized by the exercise of ordinary care. If there is also bad faith it includes any other damages the party suffered as a proximate consequence.

§ 4—104. Definitions and Index of Definitions.

(a) In this Article, unless the context otherwise requires:

(1) "Account" means any deposit or credit account with a bank, including a demand, time, savings, passbook, share draft, or like account, other than an account evidenced by a certificate of deposit;

(2) "Afternoon" means the period of a day between noon and midnight;

(3) "Banking day" means the part of a day on which a bank is open to the public for carrying on substantially all of its banking functions;

(4) "Clearing house" means an association of banks or other payors regularly clearing items;

(5) "Customer" means a person having an account with a bank or for whom a bank has agreed to collect items, including a bank that maintains an account at another bank;

(6) "Documentary draft" means a draft to be presented for acceptance or payment if specified documents, certificated securities (Section 8—102) or instructions for uncertificated securities (Section 8—102), or other certificates, statements, or the like are to be received by the drawee or other payor before acceptance or payment of the draft;

(7) "Draft" means a draft as defined in Section 3—104 or an item, other than an instrument, that is an order;

(8) "Drawee" means a person ordered in a draft to make payment;

(9) "Item" means an instrument or a promise or order to pay money handled by a bank for collection or payment. The term does not include a payment order governed by Article 4A or a credit or debit card slip;

(10) "Midnight deadline" with respect to a bank is midnight on its next banking day following the banking day on which it receives the relevant item or notice or from which the time for taking action commences to run, whichever is later;

(11) "Settle" means to pay in cash, by clearing-house settlement, in a charge or credit or by remittance, or otherwise as agreed. A settlement may be either provisional or final;

(12) "Suspends payments" with respect to a bank means that it has been closed by order of the supervisory authorities, that a public officer has been appointed to take it over, or that it ceases or refuses to make payments in the ordinary course of business.

(b);(c) [Other definitions' section references deleted.]

(d) In addition, Article 1 contains general definitions and principles of construction and interpretation applicable throughout this Article.

§ 4—105. "Bank"; "Depositary Bank"; "Payor Bank"; "Intermediary Bank"; "Collecting Bank"; "Presenting Bank".

In this Article:

(1) "Bank" means a person engaged in the business of banking, including a savings bank, savings and loan association, credit union, or trust company;

(2) "Depositary bank" means the first bank to take an item even though it is also the payor bank, unless the item is presented for immediate payment over the counter;

(3) "Payor bank" means a bank that is the drawee of a draft;

(4) "Intermediary bank" means a bank to which an item is transferred in course of collection except the depositary or payor bank;

(5) "Collecting bank" means a bank handling an item for collection except the payor bank;

(6) "Presenting bank" means a bank presenting an item except a payor bank.

§ 4—106. Payable Through or Payable at Bank: Collecting Bank.

(a) If an item states that it is "payable through" a bank identified in the item, (i) the item designates the bank as a collecting bank and does not by itself authorize the bank to pay the item, and (ii) the item may be presented for payment only by or through the bank.

Alternative A

(b) If an item states that it is "payable at" a bank identified in the item, the item is equivalent to a draft drawn on the bank.

Alternative B

(b) If an item states that it is "payable at" a bank identified in the item, (i) the item designates the bank as a collecting bank and does not by itself authorize the bank to pay the item, and (ii) the item may be presented for payment only by or through the bank.

(c) If a draft names a nonbank drawee and it is unclear whether a bank named in the draft is a co-drawee or a collecting bank, the bank is a collecting bank.

§ 4—107. Separate Office of Bank.

A branch or separate office of a bank is a separate bank for the purpose of computing the time within which and determining the place at or to which action may be taken or notices or orders shall be given under this Article and under Article 3.

§ 4—108. Time of Receipt of Items.

(a) For the purpose of allowing time to process items, prove balances, and make the necessary entries on its books to determine its position for the day, a bank may fix an afternoon hour of 2 P.M. or later as a cutoff hour for the handling of money and items and the making of entries on its books.

(b) An item or deposit of money received on any day after a cutoff hour so fixed or after the close of the banking day may be treated as being received at the opening of the next banking day.

§ 4—109. Delays.

(a) Unless otherwise instructed, a collecting bank in a good faith effort to secure payment of a specific item drawn on a payor other than a bank, and with or without the approval of any person involved, may waive, modify, or extend time limits imposed or permitted by this [act] for a period not exceeding two additional banking days without discharge of drawers or indorsers or liability to its transferor or a prior party.

(b) Delay by a collecting bank or payor bank beyond time limits prescribed or permitted by this [act] or by instructions is excused if (i) the delay is caused by interruption of communication or computer facilities, suspension of payments by another bank, war, emergency conditions, failure of equipment, or other circumstances beyond the control of the bank, and (ii) the bank exercises such diligence as the circumstances require.

§ 4—110. Electronic Presentment.

(a) "Agreement for electronic presentment" means an agreement, clearing-house rule, or Federal Reserve regulation or operating circular, providing that presentment of an item may be made by transmission of an image of an item or information describing the item ("presentment notice") rather than delivery of the item itself. The agreement may provide for procedures governing retention, presentment, payment, dishonor, and other matters concerning items subject to the agreement.

(b) Presentment of an item pursuant to an agreement for presentment is made when the presentment notice is received.

(c) If presentment is made by presentment notice, a reference to "item" or "check" in this Article means the presentment notice unless the context otherwise indicates.

§ 4—111. Statute of Limitations.

An action to enforce an obligation, duty, or right arising under this Article must be commenced within three years after the [cause of action] accrues.

Part 2 Collection of Items: Depositary and Collecting Banks

§ 4—201. Status of Collecting Bank As Agent and Provisional Status of Credits; Applicability of Article; Item Indorsed "Pay Any Bank".

(a) Unless a contrary intent clearly appears and before the time that a settlement given by a collecting bank for an item is or becomes final, the bank, with respect to an item, is an agent or sub-agent of the owner of the item and any settlement given for the item is provisional. This provision applies regardless of the form of indorsement or lack of indorsement and even though credit given for the item is subject to immediate withdrawal as of right or is in fact withdrawn; but the continuance of ownership of an item by its owner and any rights of the owner to proceeds of the item are subject to rights of a collecting bank, such as those resulting from outstanding advances on the item and rights of recoupment or setoff. If an item is handled by banks for purposes of presentment, payment, collection, or return, the relevant provisions of this Article apply even though action of the parties clearly establishes that a particular bank has purchased the item and is the owner of it.

(b) After an item has been indorsed with the words "pay any bank" or the like, only a bank may acquire the rights of a holder until the item has been:

(1) returned to the customer initiating collection; or

(2) specially indorsed by a bank to a person who is not a bank.

§ 4—202. Responsibility for Collection or Return; When Action Timely.

(a) A collecting bank must exercise ordinary care in:

(1) presenting an item or sending it for presentment;

(2) sending notice of dishonor or nonpayment or returning an item other than a documentary draft to the bank's transferor after learning that the item has not been paid or accepted, as the case may be;

(3) settling for an item when the bank receives final settlement; and

(4) notifying its transferor of any loss or delay in transit within a reasonable time after discovery thereof.

(b) A collecting bank exercises ordinary care under subsection (a) by taking proper action before its midnight deadline following receipt of an item, notice, or settlement. Taking proper action within a reasonably longer time may constitute the exercise of ordinary care, but the bank has the burden of establishing timeliness.

(c) Subject to subsection (a)(1), a bank is not liable for the insolvency, neglect, misconduct, mistake, or default of another bank or person or for loss or destruction of an item in the possession of others or in transit.

§ 4—203. Effect of Instructions.

Subject to Article 3 concerning conversion of instruments (Section 3—420) and restrictive indorsements (Section 3—206), only a collecting bank's transferor can give instructions that affect the bank or constitute notice to it, and a collecting bank is not liable to prior parties for any action taken pursuant to the instructions or in accordance with any agreement with its transferor.

§ 4—204. Methods of Sending and Presenting; Sending Directly to Payor Bank.

(a) A collecting bank shall send items by a reasonably prompt method, taking into consideration relevant instructions, the nature of the item, the number of those items on hand, the cost of collection involved, and the method generally used by it or others to present those items.

(b) A collecting bank may send:

(1) an item directly to the payor bank;

(2) an item to a nonbank payor if authorized by its transferor; and

(3) an item other than documentary drafts to a nonbank payor, if authorized by Federal Reserve regulation or operating circular, clearing-house rule, or the like.

(c) Presentment may be made by a presenting bank at a place where the payor bank or other payor has requested that presentment be made.

§ 4—205. Depositary Bank Holder of Unindorsed Item.

If a customer delivers an item to a depositary bank for collection:

(1) the depositary bank becomes a holder of the item at the time it receives the item for collection if the customer at the time of delivery was a holder of the item, whether or not the customer indorses the item, and, if the bank satisfies the other requirements of Section 3—302, it is a holder in due course; and

(2) the depositary bank warrants to collecting banks, the payor bank or other payor, and the drawer that the amount of the item was paid to the customer or deposited to the customer's account.

§ 4—206. Transfer Between Banks.

Any agreed method that identifies the transferor bank is sufficient for the item's further transfer to another bank.

§ 4—207. Transfer Warranties.

(a) A customer or collecting bank that transfers an item and receives a settlement or other consideration warrants to the transferee and to any subsequent collecting bank that:

(1) the warrantor is a person entitled to enforce the item;

(2) all signatures on the item are authentic and authorized;

(3) the item has not been altered;

(4) the item is not subject to a defense or claim in recoupment (Section 3—305(a)) of any party that can be asserted against the warrantor; and

(5) the warrantor has no knowledge of any insolvency proceeding commenced with respect to the maker or acceptor or, in the case of an unaccepted draft, the drawer.

(b) If an item is dishonored, a customer or collecting bank transferring the item and receiving settlement or other consideration is obliged to pay the amount due on the item (i) according to the terms of the item at the time it was transferred, or (ii) if the transfer was of an incomplete item, according to its terms when completed as stated in Sections 3—115 and 3—407. The obligation of a transferor is owed to the transferee and to any subsequent collecting bank that takes the item in good faith. A transferor cannot disclaim its obligation under this subsection by an indorsement stating that it is made "without recourse" or otherwise disclaiming liability.

(c) A person to whom the warranties under subsection (a) are made and who took the item in good faith may recover from the warrantor as damages for breach of warranty an amount equal to the loss suffered as a result of the breach, but not more than the amount of the item plus expenses and loss of interest incurred as a result of the breach.

(d) The warranties stated in subsection (a) cannot be disclaimed with respect to checks. Unless notice of a claim for breach of warranty is given to the warrantor within 30 days after the claimant has reason to know of the breach and the identity of the warrantor, the warrantor is discharged to the extent of any loss caused by the delay in giving notice of the claim.

(e) A cause of action for breach of warranty under this section accrues when the claimant has reason to know of the breach.

§ 4—208. Presentment Warranties.

(a) If an unaccepted draft is presented to the drawee for payment or acceptance and the drawee pays or accepts the draft, (i) the person obtaining payment or acceptance, at the time of presentment, and (ii) a previous transferor of the draft, at the time of transfer, warrant to the drawee that pays or accepts the draft in good faith that:

(1) the warrantor is, or was, at the time the warrantor transferred the draft, a person entitled to enforce the draft or authorized to obtain payment or acceptance of the draft on behalf of a person entitled to enforce the draft;

(2) the draft has not been altered; and

(3) the warrantor has no knowledge that the signature of the purported drawer of the draft is unauthorized.

(b) A drawee making payment may recover from a warrantor damages for breach of warranty equal to the amount paid by the drawee less the amount the drawee received or is entitled to receive from the drawer because of the payment. In addition, the drawee is entitled to compensation for expenses and loss of interest resulting from the breach. The right of the drawee to recover damages under this subsection is not affected by any failure of the drawee to exercise ordinary care in making payment. If the drawee accepts the draft (i) breach of warranty is a defense to the obligation of the acceptor, and (ii) if the acceptor makes payment with respect to the draft, the acceptor is entitled to recover from a warrantor for breach of warranty the amounts stated in this subsection.

(c) If a drawee asserts a claim for breach of warranty under subsection (a) based on an unauthorized indorsement of the draft or an alteration of the draft, the warrantor may defend by proving that the indorsement is effective under Section 3—404 or 3—405 or the drawer is precluded under Section 3—406 or 4—406 from asserting against the drawee the unauthorized indorsement or alteration.

(d) If (i) a dishonored draft is presented for payment to the drawer or an indorser or (ii) any other item is presented for payment to a party obliged to pay the item, and the item is paid, the person obtaining payment and a prior transferor of the item warrant to the person making payment in good faith that the warrantor is, or was, at the time the warrantor transferred the item, a person entitled to enforce the item or authorized to obtain payment on behalf of a person entitled to enforce the item. The person making payment may recover from any warrantor for breach of warranty an amount equal to the amount paid plus expenses and loss of interest resulting from the breach.

(e) The warranties stated in subsections (a) and (d) cannot be disclaimed with respect to checks. Unless notice of a claim for breach of warranty is given to the warrantor within 30 days after the claimant has reason to know of the breach and the identity of the warrantor, the warrantor is discharged to the extent of any loss caused by the delay in giving notice of the claim.

(f) A cause of action for breach of warranty under this section accrues when the claimant has reason to know of the breach.

§ 4—209. Encoding and Retention Warranties.

(a) A person who encodes information on or with respect to an item after issue warrants to any subsequent collecting bank and to the payor bank or other payor that the information is correctly encoded. If the customer of a depositary bank encodes, that bank also makes the warranty.

(b) A person who undertakes to retain an item pursuant to an agreement for electronic presentment warrants to any subsequent collecting bank and to the payor bank or other payor that retention and presentment of the item comply with the agreement. If a customer of a depositary bank undertakes to retain an item, that bank also makes this warranty.

(c) A person to whom warranties are made under this section and who took the item in good faith may recover from the warrantor as damages for breach of warranty an amount equal to the loss suffered as a result of the breach, plus expenses and loss of interest incurred as a result of the breach.

§ 4—210. Security Interest of Collecting Bank in Items, Accompanying Documents and Proceeds.

(a) A collecting bank has a security interest in an item and any accompanying documents or the proceeds of either:

(1) in case of an item deposited in an account, to the extent to which credit given for the item has been withdrawn or applied;

(2) in case of an item for which it has given credit available for withdrawal as of right, to the extent of the credit given, whether or not the credit is drawn upon or there is a right of charge-back; or

(3) if it makes an advance on or against the item.

(b) If credit given for several items received at one time or pursuant to a single agreement is withdrawn or applied in part, the security interest remains upon all the items, any accompanying documents or the proceeds of either. For the purpose of this section, credits first given are first withdrawn.

(c) Receipt by a collecting bank of a final settlement for an item is a realization on its security interest in the item, accompanying documents, and proceeds. So long as the bank does not receive final settlement for the item or give up possession of the item or accompanying documents for purposes other than collection, the security interest continues to that extent and is subject to Article 9, but:

(1) no security agreement is necessary to make the security interest enforceable (Section 9—203(1)(a));

(2) no filing is required to perfect the security interest; and

(3) the security interest has priority over conflicting perfected security interests in the item, accompanying documents, or proceeds.

§ 4—211. When Bank Gives Value for Purposes of Holder in Due Course.

For purposes of determining its status as a holder in due course, a bank has given value to the extent it has a security interest in an item, if the bank otherwise complies with the requirements of Section 3—302 on what constitutes a holder in due course.

§ 4—212. Presentment by Notice of Item Not Payable by, Through, or at Bank; Liability of Drawer or Indorser.

(a) Unless otherwise instructed, a collecting bank may present an item not payable by, through, or at a bank by sending to the party to accept or pay a written notice that the bank holds the item for acceptance or payment. The notice must be sent in time to be received on or before the day when presentment is due and the bank must meet any requirement of the party to accept or pay under Section 3—501 by the close of the bank's next banking day after it knows of the requirement.

(b) If presentment is made by notice and payment, acceptance, or request for compliance with a requirement under Section 3—501 is not received by the close of business on the day after maturity or, in the case of demand items, by the close of business on the third banking day after notice was sent, the presenting bank may treat the item as dishonored and charge any drawer or indorser by sending it notice of the facts.

§ 4—213. Medium and Time of Settlement by Bank.

(a) With respect to settlement by a bank, the medium and time of settlement may be prescribed by Federal Reserve regulations or circulars, clearing-house rules, and the like, or agreement. In the absence of such prescription:

(1) the medium of settlement is cash or credit to an account in a Federal Reserve bank of or specified by the person to receive settlement; and

(2) the time of settlement is:

(i) with respect to tender of settlement by cash, a cashier's check, or teller's check, when the cash or check is sent or delivered;

(ii) with respect to tender of settlement by credit in an account in a Federal Reserve Bank, when the credit is made;

(iii) with respect to tender of settlement by a credit or debit to an account in a bank, when the credit or debit is made or, in the case of tender of settlement by authority to charge an account, when the authority is sent or delivered; or

(iv) with respect to tender of settlement by a funds transfer, when payment is made pursuant to Section 4A—406(a) to the person receiving settlement.

(b) If the tender of settlement is not by a medium authorized by subsection (a) or the time of settlement is not fixed by subsection (a), no settlement occurs until the tender of settlement is accepted by the person receiving settlement.

(c) If settlement for an item is made by cashier's check or teller's check and the person receiving settlement, before its midnight deadline:

(1) presents or forwards the check for collection, settlement is final when the check is finally paid; or

(2) fails to present or forward the check for collection, settlement is final at the midnight deadline of the person receiving settlement.

(d) If settlement for an item is made by giving authority to charge the account of the bank giving settlement in the bank receiving settlement, settlement is final when the charge is made by the bank receiving settlement if there are funds available in the account for the amount of the item.

§ 4—214. Right of Charge-Back or Refund; Liability of Collecting Bank: Return of Item.

(a) If a collecting bank has made provisional settlement with its customer for an item and fails by reason of dishonor, suspension of payments by a bank, or otherwise to receive settlement for the item which is or becomes final, the bank may revoke the settlement given by it, charge back the amount of any credit given for the item to its customer's account, or obtain refund from its customer, whether or not it is able to return the item, if by its midnight deadline or within a longer reasonable time after it learns the facts it returns the item or sends notification of the facts. If the return or notice is delayed beyond the bank's midnight deadline or a longer reasonable time after it learns the facts, the bank may revoke the settlement, charge back the credit, or obtain refund from its customer, but it is liable for any loss resulting from the delay. These rights to revoke, charge back, and obtain refund terminate if and when a settlement for the item received by the bank is or becomes final.

(b) A collecting bank returns an item when it is sent or delivered to the bank's customer or transferor or pursuant to its instructions.

(c) A depositary bank that is also the payor may charge back the amount of an item to its customer's account or obtain refund in accordance with the section governing return of an item received by a payor bank for credit on its books (Section 4—301).

(d) The right to charge back is not affected by:

(1) previous use of a credit given for the item; or

(2) failure by any bank to exercise ordinary care with respect to the item, but a bank so failing remains liable.

(e) A failure to charge back or claim refund does not affect other rights of the bank against the customer or any other party.

(f) If credit is given in dollars as the equivalent of the value of an item payable in foreign money, the dollar amount of any charge-back or refund must be calculated on the basis of the bank-offered spot rate for the foreign money prevailing on the day when the person entitled to the charge-back or refund learns that it will not receive payment in ordinary course.

§ 4—215. Final Payment of Item by Payor Bank; When Provisional Debits and Credits Become Final; When Certain Credits Become Available for Withdrawal.

(a) An item is finally paid by a payor bank when the bank has first done any of the following:

(1) paid the item in cash;

(2) settled for the item without having a right to revoke the settlement under statute, clearing-house rule, or agreement; or

(3) made a provisional settlement for the item and failed to revoke the settlement in the time and manner permitted by statute, clearing-house rule, or agreement.

(b) If provisional settlement for an item does not become final, the item is not finally paid.

(c) If provisional settlement for an item between the presenting and payor banks is made through a clearing house or by debits or credits in an account between them, then to the extent that provisional debits or credits for the item are entered in accounts between the presenting and payor banks or between the presenting and successive prior collecting banks seriatim, they become final upon final payment of the item by the payor bank.

(d) If a collecting bank receives a settlement for an item which is or becomes final, the bank is accountable to its customer for the amount of the item and any provisional credit given for the item in an account with its customer becomes final.

(e) Subject to (i) applicable law stating a time for availability of funds and (ii) any right of the bank to apply the credit to an obligation of the customer, credit given by a bank for an item in a customer's account becomes available for withdrawal as of right:

(1) if the bank has received a provisional settlement for the item, when the settlement becomes final and the bank has had a reasonable time to receive return of the item and the item has not been received within that time;

(2) if the bank is both the depositary bank and the payor bank, and the item is finally paid, at the opening of the bank's second banking day following receipt of the item.

(f) Subject to applicable law stating a time for availability of funds and any right of a bank to apply a deposit to an obligation of the depositor, a deposit of money becomes available for withdrawal as of right at the opening of the bank's next banking day after receipt of the deposit.

§ 4— 216. Insolvency and Preference.

(a) If an item is in or comes into the possession of a payor or collecting bank that suspends payment and the item has not been finally paid, the item must be returned by the receiver, trustee, or agent in charge of the closed bank to the presenting bank or the closed bank's customer.

(b) If a payor bank finally pays an item and suspends payments without making a settlement for the item with its customer or the presenting bank which settlement is or becomes final, the owner of the item has a preferred claim against the payor bank.

(c) If a payor bank gives or a collecting bank gives or receives a provisional settlement for an item and thereafter suspends payments, the suspension does not prevent or interfere with the settlement's becoming final if the finality occurs automatically upon the lapse of certain time or the happening of certain events.

(d) If a collecting bank receives from subsequent parties settlement for an item, which settlement is or becomes final and the bank suspends payments without making a settlement for the item with its customer which settlement is or becomes final, the owner of the item has a preferred claim against the collecting bank.

Part 3 Collection of Items: Payor Banks

§ 4—301. Deferred Posting; Recovery of Payment by Return of Items; Time of Dishonor; Return of Items by Payor Bank.

(a) If a payor bank settles for a demand item other than a documentary draft presented otherwise than for immediate payment over the counter before midnight of the banking day of receipt, the payor bank may revoke the settlement and recover the settlement if, before it has made final payment and before its midnight deadline, it

(1) returns the item; or

(2) sends written notice of dishonor or nonpayment if the item is unavailable for return.

(b) If a demand item is received by a payor bank for credit on its books, it may return the item or send notice of dishonor and may revoke any credit given or recover the amount thereof withdrawn by its customer, if it acts within the time limit and in the manner specified in subsection (a).

(c) Unless previous notice of dishonor has been sent, an item is dishonored at the time when for purposes of dishonor it is returned or notice sent in accordance with this section.

(d) An item is returned:

(1) as to an item presented through a clearing house, when it is delivered to the presenting or last collecting bank or to the clearing house or is sent or delivered in accordance with clearing-house rules; or

(2) in all other cases, when it is sent or delivered to the bank's customer or transferor or pursuant to instructions.

§ 4—302. Payor Bank's Responsibility for Late Return of Item.

(a) If an item is presented to and received by a payor bank, the bank is accountable for the amount of:

(1) a demand item, other than a documentary draft, whether properly payable or not, if the bank, in any case in which it is not also the depositary bank, retains the item beyond midnight of the banking day of receipt without settling for it or, whether or not it is also the depositary bank, does not pay or return the item or send notice of dishonor until after its midnight deadline; or

(2) any other properly payable item unless, within the time allowed for acceptance or payment of that item, the bank either accepts or pays the item or returns it and accompanying documents.

(b) The liability of a payor bank to pay an item pursuant to subsection (a) is subject to defenses based on breach of a presentment warranty (Section 4—208) or proof that the person seeking enforcement of the liability presented or transferred the item for the purpose of defrauding the payor bank.

§ 4—303. When Items Subject to Notice, Stop-Payment Order, Legal Process, or Setoff; Order in Which Items May Be Charged or Certified.

(a) Any knowledge, notice, or stop-payment order received by, legal process served upon, or setoff exercised by a payor bank comes too late to terminate, suspend, or modify the bank's right or duty to pay an item or to charge its customer's account for the item if the knowledge, notice, stop-payment order, or legal process is received or served and a reasonable time for the bank to act thereon expires or the setoff is exercised after the earliest of the following:

(1) the bank accepts or certifies the item;

(2) the bank pays the item in cash;

(3) the bank settles for the item without having a right to revoke the settlement under statute, clearing-house rule, or agreement;

(4) the bank becomes accountable for the amount of the item under Section 4—302 dealing with the payor bank's responsibility for late return of items; or

(5) with respect to checks, a cutoff hour no earlier than one hour after the opening of the next banking day after the banking day on which the bank received the check and no later than the close of that next banking day or, if no cutoff hour is fixed, the close of the next banking day after the banking day on which the bank received the check.

(b) Subject to subsection (a), items may be accepted, paid, certified, or charged to the indicated account of its customer in any order.

Part 4 Relationship Between Payor Bank and its Customer

§ 4—401. When Bank May Charge Customer's Account.

(a) A bank may charge against the account of a customer an item that is properly payable from the account even though the charge creates an overdraft. An item is properly payable if it is authorized by the customer and is in accordance with any agreement between the customer and bank.

(b) A customer is not liable for the amount of an overdraft if the customer neither signed the item nor benefited from the proceeds of the item.

(c) A bank may charge against the account of a customer a check that is otherwise properly payable from the account, even though payment was made before the date of the check, unless the customer has given notice to the bank of the postdating describing the check with reasonable certainty. The notice is effective for the period stated in Section 4—403(b) for stop-payment orders, and must be received at such time and in such manner as to afford the bank a reasonable opportunity to act on it before the bank takes any action with respect to the check described in Section 4—303. If a bank charges against the account of a customer a check before the date stated in the notice of postdating, the bank is liable for damages for the loss resulting from its act. The loss may include damages for dishonor of subsequent items under Section 4—402.

(d) A bank that in good faith makes payment to a holder may charge the indicated account of its customer according to:

(1) the original terms of the altered item; or

(2) the terms of the completed item, even though the bank knows the item has been completed unless the bank has notice that the completion was improper.

§ 4—402. Bank's Liability to Customer for Wrongful Dishonor; Time of Determining Insufficiency of Account.

(a) Except as otherwise provided in this Article, a payor bank wrongfully dishonors an item if it dishonors an item that is properly payable, but a bank may dishonor an item that would create an overdraft unless it has agreed to pay the overdraft.

(b) A payor bank is liable to its customer for damages proximately caused by the wrongful dishonor of an item. Liability is limited to actual damages proved and may include damages for an arrest or prosecution of the customer or other consequential damages. Whether any consequential damages are proximately caused by the wrongful dishonor is a question of fact to be determined in each case.

(c) A payor bank's determination of the customer's account balance on which a decision to dishonor for insufficiency of available funds is based may be made at any time between the time the item is received by the payor bank and the time that the payor bank returns the item or gives notice in lieu of return, and no more than one determination need be made. If, at the election of the payor bank, a subsequent balance determination is made for the purpose of reevaluating the bank's decision to dishonor the item, the account balance at that time is determinative of whether a dishonor for insufficiency of available funds is wrongful.

§ 4—403. Customer's Right to Stop Payment; Burden of Proof of Loss.

(a) A customer or any person authorized to draw on the account if there is more than one person may stop payment of any item drawn on the customer's account or close the account by an order to the bank describing the item or account with reasonable certainty received at a time and in a manner that affords the bank a reasonable opportunity to act on it before any action by the bank with respect to the item described in Section 4—303. If the signature of more than one person is required to draw on an account, any of these persons may stop payment or close the account.

(b) A stop-payment order is effective for six months, but it lapses after 14 calendar days if the original order was oral and was not confirmed in writing within that period. A stop-payment order may be renewed for additional six-month periods by a writing given to the bank within a period during which the stop-payment order is effective.

(c) The burden of establishing the fact and amount of loss resulting from the payment of an item contrary to a stop-payment order or order to close an account is on the customer. The loss from payment of an item contrary to a stop-payment order may include damages for dishonor of subsequent items under Section 4—402.

§ 4—404. Bank Not Obliged to Pay Check More Than Six Months Old.

A bank is under no obligation to a customer having a checking account to pay a check, other than a certified check, which is presented more than six months after its date, but it may charge its customer's account for a payment made thereafter in good faith.

§ 4—405. Death or Incompetence of Customer.

(a) A payor or collecting bank's authority to accept, pay, or collect an item or to account for proceeds of its collection, if otherwise effective, is not rendered ineffective by incompetence of a customer of either bank existing at the time the item is issued or its collection is undertaken if the bank does not know of an adjudication of incompetence. Neither death nor incompetence of a customer revokes the authority to accept, pay, collect, or account until the bank knows of the fact of death or of an adjudication of incompetence and has reasonable opportunity to act on it.

(b) Even with knowledge, a bank may for 10 days after the date of death pay or certify checks drawn on or before the date unless ordered to stop payment by a person claiming an interest in the account.

§ 4—406. Customer's Duty to Discover and Report Unauthorized Signature or Alteration.

(a) A bank that sends or makes available to a customer a statement of account showing payment of items for the account shall either return or make available to the customer the items paid or provide information in the statement of account sufficient to allow the customer reasonably to identify the items paid. The statement of account provides sufficient information if the item is described by item number, amount, and date of payment.

(b) If the items are not returned to the customer, the person retaining the items shall either retain the items or, if the items are destroyed, maintain the capacity to furnish legible copies of the items until the expiration of seven years after receipt of the items. A customer may request an item from the bank that paid the item, and that bank must provide in a reasonable time either the item or, if the item has been destroyed or is not otherwise obtainable, a legible copy of the item.

(c) If a bank sends or makes available a statement of account or items pursuant to subsection (a), the customer must exercise reasonable promptness in examining the statement or the items to determine whether any payment was not authorized because of an alteration of an item or because a purported signature by or on behalf of the customer was not authorized. If, based on the statement or items provided, the customer should reasonably have discovered the unauthorized payment, the customer must promptly notify the bank of the relevant facts.

(d) If the bank proves that the customer failed, with respect to an item, to comply with the duties imposed on the customer by subsection (c), the customer is precluded from asserting against the bank:

(1) the customer's unauthorized signature or any alteration on the item, if the bank also proves that it suffered a loss by reason of the failure; and

(2) the customer's unauthorized signature or alteration by the same wrongdoer on any other item paid in good faith by the bank if the payment was made before the bank received notice from the customer of the unauthorized signature or alteration and after the customer had been afforded a reasonable period of time, not exceeding 30 days, in which to examine the item or statement of account and notify the bank.

(e) If subsection (d) applies and the customer proves that the bank failed to exercise ordinary care in paying the item and that the failure substantially contributed to loss, the loss is allocated between the customer precluded and the bank asserting the preclusion according to the extent to which the failure of the customer to comply with subsection (c) and the failure of the bank to exercise ordinary care contributed to the loss. If the customer proves that the bank did not pay the item in good faith, the preclusion under subsection (d) does not apply.

(f) Without regard to care or lack of care of either the customer or the bank, a customer who does not within one year after the statement or items are made available to the customer (subsection (a)) discover and report the customer's unauthorized signature on or any alteration on the item is precluded from asserting against the bank the unauthorized signature or alteration. If there is a preclusion under this subsection, the payor bank may not recover for breach or warranty under Section 4—208 with respect to the unauthorized signature or alteration to which the preclusion applies.

§ 4—407. Payor Bank's Right to Subrogation on Improper Payment.

If a payor has paid an item over the order of the drawer or maker to stop payment, or after an account has been closed, or otherwise under circumstances giving a basis for objection by the drawer or maker, to prevent unjust enrichment and only to the extent necessary to prevent loss to the bank by reason of its payment of the item, the payor bank is subrogated to the rights

(1) of any holder in due course on the item against the drawer or maker;

(2) of the payee or any other holder of the item against the drawer or maker either on the item or under the transaction out of which the item arose; and

(3) of the drawer or maker against the payee or any other holder of the item with respect to the transaction out of which the item arose.

Part 5 Collection of Documentary Drafts

§ 4—501. Handling of Documentary Drafts; Duty to Send for Presentment and to Notify Customer of Dishonor.

A bank that takes a documentary draft for collection shall present or send the draft and accompanying documents for presentment and, upon learning that the draft has not been paid or accepted in due course, shall seasonably notify its customer of the fact even though it may have discounted or bought the draft or extended credit available for withdrawal as of right.

§ 4—502. Presentment of "On Arrival" Drafts.

If a draft or the relevant instructions require presentment "on arrival", "when goods arrive" or the like, the collecting bank need not present until in its judgment a reasonable time for arrival of the goods has expired. Refusal to pay or accept because the goods have not arrived is not dishonor; the bank must notify its transferor of the refusal but need not present the draft again until it is instructed to do so or learns of the arrival of the goods.

§ 4—503. Responsibility of Presenting Bank for Documents and Goods; Report of Reasons for Dishonor; Referee in Case of Need.

Unless otherwise instructed and except as provided in Article 5, a bank presenting a documentary draft:

(1) must deliver the documents to the drawee on acceptance of the draft if it is payable more than three days after presentment, otherwise, only on payment; and

(2) upon dishonor, either in the case of presentment for acceptance or presentment for payment, may seek and follow instructions from any referee in case of need designated in the draft or, if the presenting bank does not choose to utilize the referee's services, it must use diligence and good faith to ascertain the reason for dishonor, must notify its transferor of the dishonor and of the results of its effort to ascertain the reasons therefor, and must request instructions.

However, the presenting bank is under no obligation with respect to goods represented by the documents except to follow any reasonable instructions seasonably received; it has a right to reimbursement for any expense incurred in following instructions and to prepayment of or indemnity for those expenses.

§ 4—504. Privilege of Presenting Bank to Deal With Goods; Security Interest for Expenses.

(a) A presenting bank that, following the dishonor of a documentary draft, has seasonably requested instructions but does not receive them within a reasonable time may store, sell, or otherwise deal with the goods in any reasonable manner.

(b) For its reasonable expenses incurred by action under subsection (a) the presenting bank has a lien upon the goods or their proceeds, which may be foreclosed in the same manner as an unpaid seller's lien.

Article 4A
FUNDS TRANSFERS

Part 1 Subject Matter and Definitions

§ 4A—101. Short Title.

This Article may be cited as Uniform Commercial Code—Funds Transfers.

§ 4A—102. Subject Matter.

Except as otherwise provided in Section 4A—108, this Article applies to funds transfers defined in Section 4A—104.

§ 4A—103. Payment Order—Definitions.

(a) In this Article:

(1) "Payment order" means an instruction of a sender to a receiving bank, transmitted orally, electronically, or in writing, to pay, or to cause another bank to pay, a fixed or determinable amount of money to a beneficiary if:

(i) the instruction does not state a condition to payment to the beneficiary other than time of payment,

(ii) the receiving bank is to be reimbursed by debiting an account of, or otherwise receiving payment from, the sender, and

(iii) the instruction is transmitted by the sender directly to the receiving bank or to an agent, funds-transfer system, or communication system for transmittal to the receiving bank.

(2) "Beneficiary" means the person to be paid by the beneficiary's bank.

(3) "Beneficiary's bank" means the bank identified in a payment order in which an account of the beneficiary is to be credited pursuant to the order or which otherwise is to make payment to the beneficiary if the order does not provide for payment to an account.

(4) "Receiving bank" means the bank to which the sender's instruction is addressed.

(5) "Sender" means the person giving the instruction to the receiving bank.

(b) If an instruction complying with subsection (a)(1) is to make more than one payment to a beneficiary, the instruction is a separate payment order with respect to each payment.

(c) A payment order is issued when it is sent to the receiving bank.

§ 4A—104. Funds Transfer—Definitions.

In this Article:

(a) "Funds transfer" means the series of transactions, beginning with the originator's payment order, made for the purpose of making payment to the beneficiary of the order. The term includes any payment order issued by the originator's bank or an intermediary bank intended to carry out the originator's payment order. A funds transfer is completed by acceptance by the beneficiary's bank of a payment order for the benefit of the beneficiary of the originator's payment order.

(b) "Intermediary bank" means a receiving bank other than the originator's bank or the beneficiary's bank.

(c) "Originator" means the sender of the first payment order in a funds transfer.

(d) "Originator's bank" means (i) the receiving bank to which the payment order of the originator is issued if the originator is not a bank, or (ii) the originator if the originator is a bank.

§ 4A—105. Other Definitions.

(a) In this Article:

(1) "Authorized account" means a deposit account of a customer in a bank designated by the customer as a source of payment of payment orders issued by the customer to the bank. If a customer does not so designate an account, any account of the customer is an authorized account if payment of a payment order from that account is not inconsistent with a restriction on the use of that account.

(2) "Bank" means a person engaged in the business of banking and includes a savings bank, savings and loan association, credit union, and trust company. A branch or separate office of a bank is a separate bank for purposes of this Article.

(3) "Customer" means a person, including a bank, having an account with a bank or from whom a bank has agreed to receive payment orders.

(4) "Funds-transfer business day" of a receiving bank means the part of a day during which the receiving bank is open for the receipt, processing, and transmittal of payment orders and cancellations and amendments of payment orders.

(5) "Funds-transfer system" means a wire transfer network, automated clearing house, or other communication system of a clearing house or other association of banks through which a payment order by a bank may be transmitted to the bank to which the order is addressed.

(6) "Good faith" means honesty in fact and the observance of reasonable commercial standards of fair dealing.

(7) "Prove" with respect to a fact means to meet the burden of establishing the fact (Section 1—201(8)).

(b) Other definitions applying to this Article and the sections in which they appear are:

"Acceptance"	Section 4A—209
"Beneficiary"	Section 4A—103
"Beneficiary's bank"	Section 4A—103
"Executed"	Section 4A—301
"Execution date"	Section 4A—301
"Funds transfer"	Section 4A—104
"Funds-transfer system rule"	Section 4A—501
"Intermediary bank"	Section 4A—104
"Originator"	Section 4A—104
"Originator's bank"	Section 4A—104
"Payment by beneficiary's bank to beneficiary"	Section 4A—405
"Payment by originator to beneficiary"	Section 4A—406
"Payment by sender to receiving bank"	Section 4A—403
"Payment date"	Section 4A—401
"Payment order"	Section 4A—103
"Receiving bank"	Section 4A—103
"Security procedure"	Section 4A—201
"Sender"	Section 4A—103

(c) The following definitions in Article 4 apply to this Article:

"Clearing house"	Section 4—104
"Item"	Section 4—104
"Suspends payments"	Section 4—104

(d) In addition, Article 1 contains general definitions and principles of construction and interpretation applicable throughout this Article.

§ 4A—106. Time Payment Order Is Received.

(a) The time of receipt of a payment order or communication cancelling or amending a payment order is determined by the rules applicable to receipt of a notice stated in Section 1—201(27). A receiving bank may fix a cut-off time or times on a funds-transfer business day for the receipt and processing of payment orders and communications cancelling or amending payment orders. Different cut-off times may apply to payment orders, cancellations, or amendments, or to different categories of payment orders, cancellations, or amendments. A cut-off time may apply to senders generally or different cut-off times may apply to different senders or categories of payment orders. If a payment order or communication cancelling or amending a payment order is received after the close of a funds-transfer business day or after the appropriate cut-off time on a funds-transfer business day, the receiving bank may treat the payment order or communication as received at the opening of the next funds-transfer business day.

(b) If this Article refers to an execution date or payment date or states a day on which a receiving bank is required to take action, and the date or day does not fall on a funds-transfer business day, the next day that is a funds-transfer business day is treated as the date or day stated, unless the contrary is stated in this Article.

§ 4A—107. Federal Reserve Regulations and Operating Circulars.

Regulations of the Board of Governors of the Federal Reserve System and operating circulars of the Federal Reserve Banks supersede any inconsistent provision of this Article to the extent of the inconsistency.

§ 4A—108. Exclusion of Consumer Transactions Governed by Federal Law.

This Article does not apply to a funds transfer any part of which is governed by the Electronic Fund Transfer Act of 1978 (Title XX, Public Law 95—630, 92 Stat. 3728, 15 U.S.C. § 1693 et seq.) as amended from time to time.

Part 2 Issue and Acceptance of Payment Order

§ 4A—201. Security Procedure.

"Security procedure" means a procedure established by agreement of a customer and a receiving bank for the purpose of (i) verifying that a payment order or communication amending or cancelling a payment order is that of the customer, or (ii) detecting error in the transmission or the content of the payment order or communication. A security procedure may require the use of algorithms or other codes, identifying words or numbers, encryption, callback procedures, or similar security devices. Comparison of a signature on a payment order or communication with an authorized specimen signature of the customer is not by itself a security procedure.

§ 4A—202. Authorized and Verified Payment Orders.

(a) A payment order received by the receiving bank is the authorized order of the person identified as sender if that person authorized the order or is otherwise bound by it under the law of agency.

(b) If a bank and its customer have agreed that the authenticity of payment orders issued to the bank in the name of the customer as sender will be verified pursuant to a security procedure, a payment order received by the receiving bank is effective as the order of the customer, whether or not authorized, if (i) the security procedure is a commercially reasonable method of providing security against unauthorized payment orders, and (ii) the bank proves that it accepted the payment order in good faith and in compliance with the security procedure and any written agreement or instruction of the customer restricting acceptance of payment orders issued in the name of the customer. The bank is not required to follow an instruction that violates a written agreement with the customer or notice of which is not received at a time and in a manner affording the bank a reasonable opportunity to act on it before the payment order is accepted.

(c) Commercial reasonableness of a security procedure is a question of law to be determined by considering the wishes of the customer expressed to the bank, the circumstances of the customer known to the bank, including the size, type, and frequency of payment orders normally issued by the customer to the bank, alternative security procedures offered to the customer, and security procedures in general use by customers and receiving banks similarly situated. A security procedure is deemed to be commercially reasonable if (i) the security procedure was chosen by the customer after the bank offered, and the customer refused, a security procedure that was commercially reasonable for that customer, and (ii) the customer expressly agreed in writing to be bound by any payment order, whether or not authorized, issued in its name and accepted by the bank in compliance with the security procedure chosen by the customer.

(d) The term "sender" in this Article includes the customer in whose name a payment order is issued if the order is the authorized order of the customer under subsection (a), or it is effective as the order of the customer under subsection (b).

(e) This section applies to amendments and cancellations of payment orders to the same extent it applies to payment orders.

(f) Except as provided in this section and in Section 4A—203(a)(1), rights and obligations arising under this section or Section 4A—203 may not be varied by agreement.

§ 4A—203. Unenforceability of Certain Verified Payment Orders.

(a) If an accepted payment order is not, under Section 4A—202(a), an authorized order of a customer identified as sender, but is effective as an order of the customer pursuant to Section 4A—202(b), the following rules apply:

(1) By express written agreement, the receiving bank may limit the extent to which it is entitled to enforce or retain payment of the payment order.

(2) The receiving bank is not entitled to enforce or retain payment of the payment order if the customer proves that the order was not caused, directly or indirectly, by a person (i) entrusted at any time with duties to act for the customer with respect to payment orders or the security procedure, or (ii) who obtained access to transmitting facilities of the customer or who obtained, from a source controlled by the customer and without authority of the receiving bank, information facilitating breach of the security procedure, regardless of how the information was obtained or whether the customer was at fault. Information includes any access device, computer software, or the like.

(b) This section applies to amendments of payment orders to the same extent it applies to payment orders.

§ 4A—204. Refund of Payment and Duty of Customer to Report with Respect to Unauthorized Payment Order.

(a) If a receiving bank accepts a payment order issued in the name of its customer as sender which is (i) not authorized and not effective as the order of the customer under Section 4A—202, or (ii) not enforceable, in whole or in part, against the customer under Section 4A—203, the bank shall refund any payment of the payment order received from the customer to the extent the bank is not entitled to enforce payment and shall pay interest on the refundable amount calculated from the date the bank received payment to the date of the refund. However, the customer is not entitled to interest from the bank on the amount to be refunded if the customer fails to exercise ordinary care to determine that the order was not authorized by the customer and to notify the bank of the relevant facts within a reasonable time not exceeding 90 days after the date the customer received notification from the bank that the order was accepted or that the customer's account was debited with respect to the order. The bank is not entitled to any recovery from the customer on account of a failure by the customer to give notification as stated in this section.

(b) Reasonable time under subsection (a) may be fixed by agreement as stated in Section 1—204(1), but the obligation of a receiving bank to refund payment as stated in subsection (a) may not otherwise be varied by agreement.

§ 4A—205. Erroneous Payment Orders.

(a) If an accepted payment order was transmitted pursuant to a security procedure for the detection of error and the payment order (i) erroneously instructed payment to a beneficiary not intended by the sender, (ii) erroneously instructed payment in an amount greater than the amount intended by the sender, or (iii) was an erroneously transmitted duplicate of a payment order previously sent by the sender, the following rules apply:

(1) If the sender proves that the sender or a person acting on behalf of the sender pursuant to Section 4A—206 complied with the security procedure and that the error would have been detected if the receiving bank had also complied, the sender is not obliged to pay the order to the extent stated in paragraphs (2) and (3).

(2) If the funds transfer is completed on the basis of an erroneous payment order described in clause (i) or (iii) of subsection (a), the sender is not obliged to pay the order and the receiving bank is entitled to recover from the beneficiary any amount paid to the beneficiary to the extent allowed by the law governing mistake and restitution.

(3) If the funds transfer is completed on the basis of a payment order described in clause (ii) of subsection (a), the sender is not obliged to pay the order to the extent the amount received by the beneficiary is greater than the amount intended by the sender. In that case, the receiving bank is entitled to recover from the beneficiary the excess amount received to the extent allowed by the law governing mistake and restitution.

(b) If (i) the sender of an erroneous payment order described in subsection (a) is not obliged to pay all or part of the order, and (ii) the sender receives notification from the receiving bank that the order was accepted by the bank or that the sender's account was debited with respect to the order, the sender has a duty to exercise ordinary care, on the basis of information available to the sender, to discover the error with respect to the order and to advise the bank of the relevant facts within a reasonable time, not exceeding 90 days, after the bank's notification was received by the sender. If the bank proves that the sender failed to perform that duty, the sender is liable to the bank for the loss the bank proves it incurred as a result of the failure, but the liability of the sender may not exceed the amount of the sender's order.

(c) This section applies to amendments to payment orders to the same extent it applies to payment orders.

§ 4A—206. Transmission of Payment Order through Funds-Transfer or Other Communication System.

(a) If a payment order addressed to a receiving bank is transmitted to a funds-transfer system or other third party communication system for transmittal to the bank, the system is deemed to be an agent of the sender for the purpose of transmitting the payment order to the bank. If there is a discrepancy between the terms of the payment order transmitted to the system and the terms of the payment order transmitted by the system to the bank, the terms of the payment order of the sender are those transmitted by the system. This section does not apply to a funds-transfer system of the Federal Reserve Banks.

(b) This section applies to cancellations and amendments to payment orders to the same extent it applies to payment orders.

§ 4A—207. Misdescription of Beneficiary.

(a) Subject to subsection (b), if, in a payment order received by the beneficiary's bank, the name, bank account number, or other identification of the beneficiary refers to a nonexistent or unidentifiable person or account, no person has rights as a beneficiary of the order and acceptance of the order cannot occur.

(b) If a payment order received by the beneficiary's bank identifies the beneficiary both by name and by an identifying or bank account number and the name and number identify different persons, the following rules apply:

(1) Except as otherwise provided in subsection (c), if the beneficiary's bank does not know that the name and number refer to different persons, it may rely on the number as the proper identification of the beneficiary of the order. The beneficiary's bank need not determine whether the name and number refer to the same person.

(2) If the beneficiary's bank pays the person identified by name or knows that the name and number identify different persons, no person has rights as beneficiary except the person paid by the beneficiary's bank if that person was entitled to receive payment from the originator of the funds transfer. If no person has rights as beneficiary, acceptance of the order cannot occur.

(c) If (i) a payment order described in subsection (b) is accepted, (ii) the originator's payment order described the beneficiary inconsistently by name and number, and (iii) the beneficiary's bank pays the person identified by number as permitted by subsection (b)(1), the following rules apply:

(1) If the originator is a bank, the originator is obliged to pay its order.

(2) If the originator is not a bank and proves that the person identified by number was not entitled to receive payment from the originator, the originator is not obliged to pay its order unless the originator's bank proves that the originator, before acceptance of the originator's order, had notice that payment of a payment order issued by the originator might be made by the beneficiary's bank on the basis of an identifying or bank account number even if it identifies a person different from the named beneficiary. Proof of notice may be made by any admissible evidence. The originator's bank satisfies the burden of proof if it proves that the originator, before the payment order was accepted, signed a writing stating the information to which the notice relates.

(d) In a case governed by subsection (b)(1), if the beneficiary's bank rightfully pays the person identified by number and that person was not entitled to receive payment from the originator, the amount paid may be recovered from that person to the extent allowed by the law governing mistake and restitution as follows:

(1) If the originator is obliged to pay its payment order as stated in subsection (c), the originator has the right to recover.

(2) If the originator is not a bank and is not obliged to pay its payment order, the originator's bank has the right to recover.

§ 4A—208. Misdescription of Intermediary Bank or Beneficiary's Bank.

(a) This subsection applies to a payment order identifying an intermediary bank or the beneficiary's bank only by an identifying number.

(1) The receiving bank may rely on the number as the proper identification of the intermediary or beneficiary's bank and need not determine whether the number identifies a bank.

(2) The sender is obliged to compensate the receiving bank for any loss and expenses incurred by the receiving bank as a result of its reliance on the number in executing or attempting to execute the order.

(b) This subsection applies to a payment order identifying an intermediary bank or the beneficiary's bank both by name and an identifying number if the name and number identify different persons.

(1) If the sender is a bank, the receiving bank may rely on the number as the proper identification of the intermediary or beneficiary's bank if the receiving bank, when it executes the sender's order, does not know that the name and number identify different persons. The receiving bank need not determine whether the name and number refer to the same person or whether the number refers to a bank. The sender is obliged to compensate the receiving bank for any loss and expenses incurred by the receiving bank as a result of its reliance on the number in executing or attempting to execute the order.

(2) If the sender is not a bank and the receiving bank proves that the sender, before the payment order was accepted, had notice that the receiving bank might rely on the number as the proper identification of the intermediary or beneficiary's bank even if it identifies a person different from the bank identified by name, the rights and obligations of the sender

and the receiving bank are governed by subsection (b)(1), as though the sender were a bank. Proof of notice may be made by any admissible evidence. The receiving bank satisfies the burden of proof if it proves that the sender, before the payment order was accepted, signed a writing stating the information to which the notice relates.

(3) Regardless of whether the sender is a bank, the receiving bank may rely on the name as the proper identification of the intermediary or beneficiary's bank if the receiving bank, at the time it executes the sender's order, does not know that the name and number identify different persons. The receiving bank need not determine whether the name and number refer to the same person.

(4) If the receiving bank knows that the name and number identify different persons, reliance on either the name or the number in executing the sender's payment order is a breach of the obligation stated in Section 4A—302(a)(1).

§ 4A—209. Acceptance of Payment Order.

(a) Subject to subsection (d), a receiving bank other than the beneficiary's bank accepts a payment order when it executes the order.

(b) Subject to subsections (c) and (d), a beneficiary's bank accepts a payment order at the earliest of the following times:

(1) When the bank (i) pays the beneficiary as stated in Section 4A—405(a) or 4A—405(b), or (ii) notifies the beneficiary of receipt of the order or that the account of the beneficiary has been credited with respect to the order unless the notice indicates that the bank is rejecting the order or that funds with respect to the order may not be withdrawn or used until receipt of payment from the sender of the order;

(2) When the bank receives payment of the entire amount of the sender's order pursuant to Section 4A—403(a)(1) or 4A—403(a)(2); or

(3) The opening of the next funds-transfer business day of the bank following the payment date of the order if, at that time, the amount of the sender's order is fully covered by a withdrawable credit balance in an authorized account of the sender or the bank has otherwise received full payment from the sender, unless the order was rejected before that time or is rejected within (i) one hour after that time, or (ii) one hour after the opening of the next business day of the sender following the payment date if that time is later. If notice of rejection is received by the sender after the payment date and the authorized account of the sender does not bear interest, the bank is obliged to pay interest to the sender on the amount of the order for the number of days elapsing after the payment date to the day the sender receives notice or learns that the order was not accepted, counting that day as an elapsed day. If the withdrawable credit balance during that period falls below the amount of the order, the amount of interest payable is reduced accordingly.

(c) Acceptance of a payment order cannot occur before the order is received by the receiving bank. Acceptance does not occur under subsection (b)(2) or (b)(3) if the beneficiary of the payment order does not have an account with the receiving bank, the account has been closed, or the receiving bank is not permitted by law to receive credits for the beneficiary's account.

(d) A payment order issued to the originator's bank cannot be accepted until the payment date if the bank is the beneficiary's bank, or the execution date if the bank is not the beneficiary's bank. If the originator's bank executes the originator's payment order before the execution date or pays the beneficiary of the originator's payment order before the payment date and the payment order is subsequently cancelled pursuant to Section 4A—211(b), the bank may recover from the beneficiary any payment received to the extent allowed by the law governing mistake and restitution.

§ 4A—210. Rejection of Payment Order.

(a) A payment order is rejected by the receiving bank by a notice of rejection transmitted to the sender orally, electronically, or in writing. A notice of rejection need not use any particular words and is sufficient if it indicates that the receiving bank is rejecting the order or will not execute or pay the order. Rejection is effective when the notice is given if transmission is by a means that is reasonable in the circumstances. If notice of rejection is given by a means that is not reasonable, rejection is effective when the notice is received. If an agreement of the sender and receiving bank establishes the means to be used to reject a payment order, (i) any means complying with the agreement is reasonable and (ii) any means not complying is not reasonable unless no significant delay in receipt of the notice resulted from the use of the noncomplying means.

(b) This subsection applies if a receiving bank other than the beneficiary's bank fails to execute a payment order despite the existence on the execution date of a withdrawable credit balance in an authorized account of the sender sufficient to cover the order. If the sender does not receive notice of rejection of the order on the execution date and the authorized account of the sender does not bear interest, the bank is obliged to pay interest to the sender on the amount of the order for the number of days elapsing after the execution date to the earlier of the day the order is cancelled pursuant to Section 4A—211(d) or the day the sender receives notice or learns that the order was not executed, counting the final day of the period as an elapsed day. If the withdrawable credit balance during that period falls below the amount of the order, the amount of interest is reduced accordingly.

(c) If a receiving bank suspends payments, all unaccepted payment orders issued to it are are deemed rejected at the time the bank suspends payments.

(d) Acceptance of a payment order precludes a later rejection of the order. Rejection of a payment order precludes a later acceptance of the order.

§ 4A—211. Cancellation and Amendment of Payment Order.

(a) A communication of the sender of a payment order cancelling or amending the order may be transmitted to the receiving bank orally, electronically, or in writing. If a security procedure is in effect between the sender and the receiving bank, the communication is not effective to cancel or amend the order unless the communication is verified pursuant to the security procedure or the bank agrees to the cancellation or amendment.

(b) Subject to subsection (a), a communication by the sender cancelling or amending a payment order is effective to cancel or amend the order if notice of the communication is received at a time and in a manner affording the receiving bank a reasonable opportunity to act on the communication before the bank accepts the payment order.

(c) After a payment order has been accepted, cancellation or amendment of the order is not effective unless the receiving bank agrees or a funds-transfer system rule allows cancellation or amendment without agreement of the bank.

(1) With respect to a payment order accepted by a receiving bank other than the beneficiary's bank, cancellation or amendment is not effective unless a conforming cancellation or amendment of the payment order issued by the receiving bank is also made.

(2) With respect to a payment order accepted by the beneficiary's bank, cancellation or amendment is not effective unless the order was issued in execution of an unauthorized payment order, or because of a mistake by a sender in the funds transfer which resulted in the issuance of a payment order (i) that is a duplicate of a payment order previously issued by the sender, (ii) that orders payment to a beneficiary not entitled to receive payment from the originator, or (iii) that orders payment in an amount greater than the amount the beneficiary was entitled to receive from the originator. If the payment order is cancelled or amended, the beneficiary's bank is entitled to recover from the beneficiary any amount paid to the beneficiary to the extent allowed by the law governing mistake and restitution.

(d) An unaccepted payment order is cancelled by operation of law at the close of the fifth funds-transfer business day of the receiving bank after the execution date or payment date of the order.

(e) A cancelled payment order cannot be accepted. If an accepted payment order is cancelled, the acceptance is nullified and no person has any right or obligation based on the acceptance. Amendment of a payment order is deemed to be cancellation of the original order at the time of amendment and issue of a new payment order in the amended form at the same time.

(f) Unless otherwise provided in an agreement of the parties or in a funds-transfer system rule, if the receiving bank, after accepting a payment order, agrees to cancellation or amendment of the order by the sender or is bound by a funds-transfer system rule allowing cancellation or amendment without the bank's agreement, the sender, whether or not cancellation or amendment is effective, is liable to the bank for any loss and expenses, including reasonable attorney's fees, incurred by the bank as a result of the cancellation or amendment or attempted cancellation or amendment.

(g) A payment order is not revoked by the death or legal incapacity of the sender unless the receiving bank knows of the death or of an adjudication of incapacity by a court of competent jurisdiction and has reasonable opportunity to act before acceptance of the order.

(h) A funds-transfer system rule is not effective to the extent it conflicts with subsection (c)(2).

§ 4A—212. Liability and Duty of Receiving Bank Regarding Unaccepted Payment Order.

If a receiving bank fails to accept a payment order that it is obliged by express agreement to accept, the bank is liable for breach of the agreement to the extent provided in the agreement or in this Article, but does not otherwise have any duty to accept a payment order or, before acceptance, to take any action, or refrain from taking action, with respect to the order except as provided in this Article or by express agreement. Liability based on acceptance arises only when acceptance occurs as stated in Section 4A—209, and liability is limited to that provided in this Article. A receiving bank is not the agent of the sender or beneficiary of the payment order it accepts, or of any other party to the funds transfer, and the bank owes no duty to any party to the funds transfer except as provided in this Article or by express agreement.

Part 3 Execution of Sender's Payment Order by Receiving Bank

§ 4A—301. Execution and Execution Date.

(a) A payment order is "executed" by the receiving bank when it issues a payment order intended to carry out the payment order received by the bank. A payment order received by the beneficiary's bank can be accepted but cannot be executed.

(b) "Execution date" of a payment order means the day on which the receiving bank may properly issue a payment order in execution of the sender's order. The execution date may be determined by instruction of the sender but cannot be earlier than the day the order is received and, unless otherwise determined, is the day the order is received. If the sender's instruction states a payment date, the execution date is the payment date or an earlier date on which execution is reasonably necessary to allow payment to the beneficiary on the payment date.

§ 4A—302. Obligations of Receiving Bank in Execution of Payment Order.

(a) Except as provided in subsections (b) through (d), if the receiving bank accepts a payment order pursuant to Section 4A—209(a), the bank has the following obligations in executing the order:

(1) The receiving bank is obliged to issue, on the execution date, a payment order complying with the sender's order and to follow the sender's instructions concerning (i) any intermediary bank or funds-transfer system to be used in carrying out the funds transfer, or (ii) the means by which payment

orders are to be transmitted in the funds transfer. If the originator's bank issues a payment order to an intermediary bank, the originator's bank is obliged to instruct the intermediary bank according to the instruction of the originator. An intermediary bank in the funds transfer is similarly bound by an instruction given to it by the sender of the payment order it accepts.

(2) If the sender's instruction states that the funds transfer is to be carried out telephonically or by wire transfer or otherwise indicates that the funds transfer is to be carried out by the most expeditious means, the receiving bank is obliged to transmit its payment order by the most expeditious available means, and to instruct any intermediary bank accordingly. If a sender's instruction states a payment date, the receiving bank is obliged to transmit its payment order at a time and by means reasonably necessary to allow payment to the beneficiary on the payment date or as soon thereafter as is feasible.

(b) Unless otherwise instructed, a receiving bank executing a payment order may (i) use any funds-transfer system if use of that system is reasonable in the circumstances, and (ii) issue a payment order to the beneficiary's bank or to an intermediary bank through which a payment order conforming to the sender's order can expeditiously be issued to the beneficiary's bank if the receiving bank exercises ordinary care in the selection of the intermediary bank. A receiving bank is not required to follow an instruction of the sender designating a funds-transfer system to be used in carrying out the funds transfer if the receiving bank, in good faith, determines that it is not feasible to follow the instruction or that following the instruction would unduly delay completion of the funds transfer.

(c) Unless subsection (a)(2) applies or the receiving bank is otherwise instructed, the bank may execute a payment order by transmitting its payment order by first class mail or by any means reasonable in the circumstances. If the receiving bank is instructed to execute the sender's order by transmitting its payment order by a particular means, the receiving bank may issue its payment order by the means stated or by any means as expeditious as the means stated.

(d) Unless instructed by the sender, (i) the receiving bank may not obtain payment of its charges for services and expenses in connection with the execution of the sender's order by issuing a payment order in an amount equal to the amount of the sender's order less the amount of the charges, and (ii) may not instruct a subsequent receiving bank to obtain payment of its charges in the same manner.

§ 4A—303. Erroneous Execution of Payment Order.

(a) A receiving bank that (i) executes the payment order of the sender by issuing a payment order in an amount greater than the amount of the sender's order, or (ii) issues a payment order in execution of the sender's order and then issues a duplicate order, is entitled to payment of the amount of the sender's order under Section 4A—402(c) if that subsection is otherwise satisfied. The bank is entitled to recover from the beneficiary of the erroneous order the excess payment received to the extent allowed by the law governing mistake and restitution.

(b) A receiving bank that executes the payment order of the sender by issuing a payment order in an amount less than the amount of the sender's order is entitled to payment of the amount of the sender's order under Section 4A—402(c) if (i) that subsection is otherwise satisfied and (ii) the bank corrects its mistake by issuing an additional payment order for the benefit of the beneficiary of the sender's order. If the error is not corrected, the issuer of the erroneous order is entitled to receive or retain payment from the sender of the order it accepted only to the extent of the amount of the erroneous order. This subsection does not apply if the receiving bank executes the sender's payment order by issuing a payment order in an amount less than the amount of the sender's order for the purpose of obtaining payment of its charges for services and expenses pursuant to instruction of the sender.

(c) If a receiving bank executes the payment order of the sender by issuing a payment order to a beneficiary different from the beneficiary of the sender's order and the funds transfer is completed on the basis of that error, the sender of the payment order that was erroneously executed and all previous senders in the funds transfer are not obliged to pay the payment orders they issued. The issuer of the erroneous order is entitled to recover from the beneficiary of the order the payment received to the extent allowed by the law governing mistake and restitution.

§ 4A—304. Duty of Sender to Report Erroneously Executed Payment Order.

If the sender of a payment order that is erroneously executed as stated in Section 4A—303 receives notification from the receiving bank that the order was executed or that the sender's account was debited with respect to the order, the sender has a duty to exercise ordinary care to determine, on the basis of information available to the sender, that the order was erroneously executed and to notify the bank of the relevant facts within a reasonable time not exceeding 90 days after the notification from the bank was received by the sender. If the sender fails to perform that duty, the bank is not obliged to pay interest on any amount refundable to the sender under Section 4A—402(d) for the period before the bank learns of the execution error. The bank is not entitled to any recovery from the sender on account of a failure by the sender to perform the duty stated in this section.

§ 4A—305. Liability for Late or Improper Execution or Failure to Execute Payment Order.

(a) If a funds transfer is completed but execution of a payment order by the receiving bank in breach of Section 4A—302 results in delay in payment to the beneficiary, the bank is obliged to pay interest to either the originator or the beneficiary of the funds transfer for the period of delay caused by the improper execution. Except as provided in subsection (c), additional damages are not recoverable.

(b) If execution of a payment order by a receiving bank in breach of Section 4A—302 results in (i) noncompletion of the funds transfer, (ii) failure to use an intermediary bank designated by the originator, or (iii) issuance of a payment order that does not comply with the terms of the payment order of the originator, the bank is liable to the originator for its expenses in the funds transfer and for incidental expenses and interest losses, to the extent not covered by subsection (a), resulting from the improper execution. Except as provided in subsection (c), additional damages are not recoverable.

(c) In addition to the amounts payable under subsections (a) and (b), damages, including consequential damages, are recoverable to the extent provided in an express written agreement of the receiving bank.

(d) If a receiving bank fails to execute a payment order it was obliged by express agreement to execute, the receiving bank is liable to the sender for its expenses in the transaction and for incidental expenses and interest losses resulting from the failure to execute. Additional damages, including consequential damages, are recoverable to the extent provided in an express written agreement of the receiving bank, but are not otherwise recoverable.

(e) Reasonable attorney's fees are recoverable if demand for compensation under subsection (a) or (b) is made and refused before an action is brought on the claim. If a claim is made for breach of an agreement under subsection (d) and the agreement does not provide for damages, reasonable attorney's fees are recoverable if demand for compensation under subsection (d) is made and refused before an action is brought on the claim.

(f) Except as stated in this section, the liability of a receiving bank under subsections (a) and (b) may not be varied by agreement.

Part 4 Payment

§ 4A—401. Payment Date.

"Payment date" of a payment order means the day on which the amount of the order is payable to the beneficiary by the beneficiary's bank. The payment date may be determined by instruction of the sender but cannot be earlier than the day the order is received by the beneficiary's bank and, unless otherwise determined, is the day the order is received by the beneficiary's bank.

§ 4A—402. Obligation of Sender to Pay Receiving Bank.

(a) This section is subject to Sections 4A—205 and 4A—207.

(b) With respect to a payment order issued to the beneficiary's bank, acceptance of the order by the bank obliges the sender to pay the bank the amount of the order, but payment is not due until the payment date of the order.

(c) This subsection is subject to subsection (e) and to Section 4A—303. With respect to a payment order issued to a receiving bank other than the beneficiary's bank, acceptance of the order by the receiving bank obliges the sender to pay the bank the amount of the sender's order. Payment by the sender is not due until the execution date of the sender's order. The obligation of that sender to pay its payment order is excused if the funds transfer is not completed by acceptance by the beneficiary's bank of a payment order instructing payment to the beneficiary of that sender's payment order.

(d) If the sender of a payment order pays the order and was not obliged to pay all or part of the amount paid, the bank receiving payment is obliged to refund payment to the extent the sender was not obliged to pay. Except as provided in Sections 4A—204 and 4A—304, interest is payable on the refundable amount from the date of payment.

(e) If a funds transfer is not completed as stated in subsection (c) and an intermediary bank is obliged to refund payment as stated in subsection (d) but is unable to do so because not permitted by applicable law or because the bank suspends payments, a sender in the funds transfer that executed a payment order in compliance with an instruction, as stated in Section 4A—302(a)(1), to route the funds transfer through that intermediary bank is entitled to receive or retain payment from the sender of the payment order that it accepted. The first sender in the funds transfer that issued an instruction requiring routing through that intermediary bank is subrogated to the right of the bank that paid the intermediary bank to refund as stated in subsection (d).

(f) The right of the sender of a payment order to be excused from the obligation to pay the order as stated in subsection (c) or to receive refund under subsection (d) may not be varied by agreement.

§ 4A—403. Payment by Sender to Receiving Bank.

(a) Payment of the sender's obligation under Section 4A—402 to pay the receiving bank occurs as follows:

(1) If the sender is a bank, payment occurs when the receiving bank receives final settlement of the obligation through a Federal Reserve Bank or through a funds-transfer system.

(2) If the sender is a bank and the sender (i) credited an account of the receiving bank with the sender, or (ii) caused an account of the receiving bank in another bank to be credited, payment occurs when the credit is withdrawn or, if not withdrawn, at midnight of the day on which the credit is withdrawable and the receiving bank learns of that fact.

(3) If the receiving bank debits an account of the sender with the receiving bank, payment occurs when the debit is made to the extent the debit is covered by a withdrawable credit balance in the account.

(b) If the sender and receiving bank are members of a funds-transfer system that nets obligations multilaterally among participants, the receiving bank receives final settlement when settlement is complete in accordance with the rules of the system. The obligation of the sender to pay the amount of a payment order transmitted through the funds-transfer system may be satisfied, to the extent permitted by the rules of the system, by setting off and applying against the sender's obligation the right of the sender to receive payment from the receiving bank of the amount of any other payment order transmitted to the sender by the receiving bank through the funds-transfer system. The aggregate balance of obligations owed by each sender to each receiving bank in the funds-transfer system may be satisfied, to the extent permitted by the rules of the system, by setting off and applying against that balance the aggregate balance of obligations owed to the sender by other members of the system. The aggregate balance is determined after the right of setoff stated in the second sentence of this subsection has been exercised.

(c) If two banks transmit payment orders to each other under an agreement that settlement of the obligations of each bank to the other under Section 4A—402 will be made at the end of the day or other period, the total amount owed with respect to all orders transmitted by one bank shall be set off against the total amount owed with respect to all orders transmitted by the other bank. To the extent of the setoff, each bank has made payment to the other.

(d) In a case not covered by subsection (a), the time when payment of the sender's obligation under Section 4A—402(b) or 4A—402(c) occurs is governed by applicable principles of law that determine when an obligation is satisfied.

§ 4A—404. Obligation of Beneficiary's Bank to Pay and Give Notice to Beneficiary.

(a) Subject to Sections 4A—211(e), 4A—405(d), and 4A—405(e), if a beneficiary's bank accepts a payment order, the bank is obliged to pay the amount of the order to the beneficiary of the order. Payment is due on the payment date of the order, but if acceptance occurs on the payment date after the close of the funds-transfer business day of the bank, payment is due on the next funds-transfer business day. If the bank refuses to pay after demand by the beneficiary and receipt of notice of particular circumstances that will give rise to consequential damages as a result of nonpayment, the beneficiary may recover damages resulting from the refusal to pay to the extent the bank had notice of the damages, unless the bank proves that it did not pay because of a reasonable doubt concerning the right of the beneficiary to payment.

(b) If a payment order accepted by the beneficiary's bank instructs payment to an account of the beneficiary, the bank is obliged to notify the beneficiary of receipt of the order before midnight of the next funds-transfer business day following the payment date. If the payment order does not instruct payment to an account of the beneficiary, the bank is required to notify the beneficiary only if notice is required by the order. Notice may be given by first class mail or any other means reasonable in the circumstances. If the bank fails to give the required notice, the bank is obliged to pay interest to the beneficiary on the amount of the payment order from the day notice should have been given until the day the beneficiary learned of receipt of the payment order by the bank. No other damages are recoverable. Reasonable attorney's fees are also recoverable if demand for interest is made and refused before an action is brought on the claim.

(c) The right of a beneficiary to receive payment and damages as stated in subsection (a) may not be varied by agreement or a funds-transfer system rule. The right of a beneficiary to be notified as stated in subsection (b) may be varied by agreement of the beneficiary or by a funds-transfer system rule if the beneficiary is notified of the rule before initiation of the funds transfer.

§ 4A—405. Payment by Beneficiary's Bank to Beneficiary.

(a) If the beneficiary's bank credits an account of the beneficiary of a payment order, payment of the bank's obligation under Section 4A—404(a) occurs when and to the extent (i) the beneficiary is notified of the right to withdraw the credit, (ii) the bank lawfully applies the credit to a debt of the beneficiary, or (iii) funds with respect to the order are otherwise made available to the beneficiary by the bank.

(b) If the beneficiary's bank does not credit an account of the beneficiary of a payment order, the time when payment of the bank's obligation under Section 4A—404(a) occurs is governed by principles of law that determine when an obligation is satisfied.

(c) Except as stated in subsections (d) and (e), if the beneficiary's bank pays the beneficiary of a payment order under a condition to payment or agreement of the beneficiary giving the bank the right to recover payment from the beneficiary if the bank does not receive payment of the order, the condition to payment or agreement is not enforceable.

(d) A funds-transfer system rule may provide that payments made to beneficiaries of funds transfers made through the system are provisional until receipt of payment by the beneficiary's bank of the payment order it accepted. A beneficiary's bank that makes a payment that is provisional under the rule is entitled to refund from the beneficiary if (i) the rule requires that both the beneficiary and the originator be given notice of the provisional nature of the payment before the funds transfer is initiated, (ii) the beneficiary, the beneficiary's bank, and the originator's bank agreed to be bound by the rule, and (iii) the beneficiary's bank did not receive payment of the payment order that it accepted. If the beneficiary is obliged to refund payment to the beneficiary's bank, acceptance of the payment order by the beneficiary's bank is nullified and no payment by the originator of the funds transfer to the beneficiary occurs under Section 4A—406.

(e) This subsection applies to a funds transfer that includes a payment order transmitted over a funds-transfer system that (i) nets obligations multilaterally among participants, and (ii) has in effect a loss-sharing agreement among participants for the purpose of providing funds necessary to complete settlement of the obligations of one or more participants that do not meet their settlement obligations. If the beneficiary's bank in the funds transfer accepts a payment order and the system fails to complete settlement pursuant to its rules with respect to any payment order in the funds transfer, (i) the acceptance by the beneficiary's bank is nullified and no person has any right or obligation based on the acceptance, (ii) the beneficiary's bank is entitled to recover payment from the beneficiary, (iii) no payment by the originator to the beneficiary occurs under Section 4A—406, and (iv) subject to Section 4A—402(e), each sender in the funds transfer is excused from its obligation to pay its payment order under Section 4A—402(c) because the funds transfer has not been completed.

§ 4A—406. Payment by Originator to Beneficiary; Discharge of Underlying Obligation.

(a) Subject to Sections 4A—211(e), 4A—405(d), and 4A—405(e), the originator of a funds transfer pays the beneficiary of the originator's payment order (i) at the time a payment order for the benefit of the beneficiary is accepted by the beneficiary's bank in the funds transfer and (ii) in an amount equal to the amount of the order accepted by the beneficiary's bank, but not more than the amount of the originator's order.

(b) If payment under subsection (a) is made to satisfy an obligation, the obligation is discharged to the same extent discharge would result from payment to the beneficiary of the same amount in money, unless (i) the payment under subsection (a) was made by a means prohibited by the contract of the beneficiary with respect to the obligation, (ii) the beneficiary, within a reasonable time after receiving notice of receipt of the order by the beneficiary's bank, notified the originator of the beneficiary's refusal of the payment, (iii) funds with respect to the order were not withdrawn by the beneficiary or applied to a debt of the beneficiary, and (iv) the beneficiary would suffer a loss that could reasonably have been avoided if payment had been made by a means complying with the contract. If payment by the originator does not result in discharge under this section, the originator is subrogated to the rights of the beneficiary to receive payment from the beneficiary's bank under Section 4A—404(a).

(c) For the purpose of determining whether discharge of an obligation occurs under subsection (b), if the beneficiary's bank accepts a payment order in an amount equal to the amount of the originator's payment order less charges of one or more receiving banks in the funds transfer, payment to the beneficiary is deemed to be in the amount of the originator's order unless upon demand by the beneficiary the originator does not pay the beneficiary the amount of the deducted charges.

(d) Rights of the originator or of the beneficiary of a funds transfer under this section may be varied only by agreement of the originator and the beneficiary.

Part 5 Miscellaneous Provisions

§ 4A—501. Variation by Agreement and Effect of Funds-Transfer System Rule.

(a) Except as otherwise provided in this Article, the rights and obligations of a party to a funds transfer may be varied by agreement of the affected party.

(b) "Funds-transfer system rule" means a rule of an association of banks (i) governing transmission of payment orders by means of a funds-transfer system of the association or rights and obligations with respect to those orders, or (ii) to the extent the rule governs rights and obligations between banks that are parties to a funds transfer in which a Federal Reserve Bank, acting as an intermediary bank, sends a payment order to the beneficiary's bank. Except as otherwise provided in this Article, a funds-transfer system rule governing rights and obligations between participating banks using the system may be effective even if the rule conflicts with this Article and indirectly affects another party to the funds transfer who does not consent to the rule. A funds-transfer system rule may also govern rights and obligations of parties other than participating banks using the system to the extent stated in Sections 4A—404(c), 4A—405(d), and 4A—507(c).

§ 4A—502. Creditor Process Served on Receiving Bank; Setoff by Beneficiary's Bank.

(a) As used in this section, "creditor process" means levy, attachment, garnishment, notice of lien, sequestration, or similar process issued by or on behalf of a creditor or other claimant with respect to an account.

(b) This subsection applies to creditor process with respect to an authorized account of the sender of a payment order if the creditor process is served on the receiving bank. For the purpose of determining rights with respect to the creditor process, if the receiving bank accepts the payment order the balance in the authorized account is deemed to be reduced by the amount of the payment order to the extent the bank did not otherwise receive payment of the order, unless the creditor process is served at a time and in a manner affording the bank a reasonable opportunity to act on it before the bank accepts the payment order.

(c) If a beneficiary's bank has received a payment order for payment to the beneficiary's account in the bank, the following rules apply:

(1) The bank may credit the beneficiary's account. The amount credited may be set off against an obligation owed by the beneficiary to the bank or may be applied to satisfy creditor process served on the bank with respect to the account.

(2) The bank may credit the beneficiary's account and allow withdrawal of the amount credited unless creditor process with respect to the account is served at a time and in a manner affording the bank a reasonable opportunity to act to prevent withdrawal.

(3) If creditor process with respect to the beneficiary's account has been served and the bank has had a reasonable opportunity to act on it, the bank may not reject the payment order except for a reason unrelated to the service of process.

(d) Creditor process with respect to a payment by the originator to the beneficiary pursuant to a funds transfer may be served only on the beneficiary's bank with respect to the debt owed by that bank to the beneficiary. Any other bank served with the creditor process is not obliged to act with respect to the process.

§ 4A—503. Injunction or Restraining Order with Respect to Funds Transfer.

For proper cause and in compliance with applicable law, a court may restrain (i) a person from issuing a payment order to initiate a funds transfer, (ii) an originator's bank from executing the payment order of the originator, or (iii) the beneficiary's bank from releasing funds to the beneficiary or the beneficiary from withdrawing the funds. A court may not otherwise restrain a person from issuing a payment order, paying or receiving payment of a payment order, or otherwise acting with respect to a funds transfer.

§ 4A—504. Order in Which Items and Payment Orders May Be Charged to Account; Order of Withdrawals from Account.

(a) If a receiving bank has received more than one payment order of the sender or one or more payment orders and other items that are payable from the sender's account, the bank may charge the sender's account with respect to the various orders and items in any sequence.

(b) In determining whether a credit to an account has been withdrawn by the holder of the account or applied to a debt of the holder of the account, credits first made to the account are first withdrawn or applied.

§ 4A—505. Preclusion of Objection to Debit of Customer's Account.

If a receiving bank has received payment from its customer with respect to a payment order issued in the name of the customer as sender and accepted by the bank, and the customer received notification reasonably identifying the order, the customer is precluded from asserting that the bank is not entitled to retain the payment unless the customer notifies the bank of the customer's objection to the payment within one year after the notification was received by the customer.

§ 4A—506. Rate of Interest.

(a) If, under this Article, a receiving bank is obliged to pay interest with respect to a payment order issued to the bank, the amount payable may be determined (i) by agreement of the sender and receiving bank, or (ii) by a funds-transfer system rule if the payment order is transmitted through a funds-transfer system.

(b) If the amount of interest is not determined by an agreement or rule as stated in subsection (a), the amount is calculated by multiplying the applicable Federal Funds rate by the amount on which interest is payable, and then multiplying the product by the number of days for which interest is payable. The applicable Federal Funds rate is the average of the Federal Funds rates published by the Federal Reserve Bank of New York for each of the days for which interest is payable divided by 360. The Federal Funds rate for any day on which a published rate is not available is the same as the published rate for the next preceding day for which there is a published rate. If a receiving bank that accepted a payment order is required to refund payment to the sender of the order because the funds transfer was not completed, but the failure to complete was not due to any fault by the bank, the interest payable is reduced by a percentage equal to the reserve requirement on deposits of the receiving bank.

§ 4A—507. Choice of Law.

(a) The following rules apply unless the affected parties otherwise agree or subsection (c) applies:

(1) The rights and obligations between the sender of a payment order and the receiving bank are governed by the law of the jurisdiction in which the receiving bank is located.

(2) The rights and obligations between the beneficiary's bank and the beneficiary are governed by the law of the jurisdiction in which the beneficiary's bank is located.

(3) The issue of when payment is made pursuant to a funds transfer by the originator to the beneficiary is governed by the law of the jurisdiction in which the beneficiary's bank is located.

(b) If the parties described in each paragraph of subsection (a) have made an agreement selecting the law of a particular jurisdiction to govern rights and obligations between each other, the law of that jurisdiction governs those rights and obligations, whether or not the payment order or the funds transfer bears a reasonable relation to that jurisdiction.

(c) A funds-transfer system rule may select the law of a particular jurisdiction to govern (i) rights and obligations between participating banks with respect to payment orders transmitted or processed through the system, or (ii) the rights and obligations of some or all parties to a funds transfer any part of which is carried out by means of the system. A choice of law made pursuant to clause (i) is binding on participating banks. A choice of law made pursuant to clause (ii) is binding on the originator, other sender, or a receiving bank having notice that the funds-transfer system might be used in the funds transfer and of the choice of law by the system when the originator, other sender, or receiving bank issued or accepted a payment order. The beneficiary of a funds transfer is bound by the choice of law if, when the funds transfer is initiated, the beneficiary has notice that the funds-transfer system might be used in the funds transfer and of the choice of law by the system. The law of a jurisdiction selected pursuant to this subsection may govern, whether or not that law bears a reasonable relation to the matter in issue.

(d) In the event of inconsistency between an agreement under subsection (b) and a choice-of-law rule under subsection (c), the agreement under subsection (b) prevails.

(e) If a funds transfer is made by use of more than one funds-transfer system and there is inconsistency between choice-of-law rules of the systems, the matter in issue is governed by the law of the selected jurisdiction that has the most significant relationship to the matter in issue.

Revised (1995) Article 5
LETTERS OF CREDIT

§ 5—101. Short Title.

This article may be cited as Uniform Commercial Code—Letters of Credit.

§ 5—102. Definitions.

(a) In this article:

(1) "Adviser" means a person who, at the request of the issuer, a confirmer, or another adviser, notifies or requests another adviser to notify the beneficiary that a letter of credit has been issued, confirmed, or amended.

(2) "Applicant" means a person at whose request or for whose account a letter of credit is issued. The term includes a person who requests an issuer to issue a letter of credit on behalf of another if the person making the request undertakes an obligation to reimburse the issuer.

(3) "Beneficiary" means a person who under the terms of a letter of credit is entitled to have its complying presentation honored. The term includes a person to whom drawing rights have been transferred under a transferable letter of credit.

(4) "Confirmer" means a nominated person who undertakes, at the request or with the consent of the issuer, to honor a presentation under a letter of credit issued by another.

(5) "Dishonor" of a letter of credit means failure timely to honor or to take an interim action, such as acceptance of a draft, that may be required by the letter of credit.

(6) "Document" means a draft or other demand, document of title, investment security, certificate, invoice, or other record, statement, or representation of fact, law, right, or opinion (i) which is presented in a written or other medium permitted by the letter of credit or, unless prohibited by the letter of credit, by the standard practice referred to in Section 5—108(e) and (ii) which is capable of being examined for compliance with the terms and conditions of the letter of credit. A document may not be oral.

(7) "Good faith" means honesty in fact in the conduct or transaction concerned.

(8) "Honor" of a letter of credit means performance of the issuer's undertaking in the letter of credit to pay or deliver an item of value. Unless the letter of credit otherwise provides, "honor" occurs

(i) upon payment,

(ii) if the letter of credit provides for acceptance, upon acceptance of a draft and, at maturity, its payment, or

(iii) if the letter of credit provides for incurring a deferred obligation, upon incurring the obligation and, at maturity, its performance.

(9) "Issuer" means a bank or other person that issues a letter of credit, but does not include an individual who makes an engagement for personal, family, or household purposes.

(10) "Letter of credit" means a definite undertaking that satisfies the requirements of Section 5—104 by an issuer to a beneficiary at the request or for the account of an applicant or, in the case of a financial institution, to itself or for its own account, to honor a documentary presentation by payment or delivery of an item of value.

(11) "Nominated person" means a person whom the issuer (i) designates or authorizes to pay, accept, negotiate, or otherwise give value under a letter of credit and (ii) undertakes by agreement or custom and practice to reimburse.

(12) "Presentation" means delivery of a document to an issuer or nominated person for honor or giving of value under a letter of credit.

(13) "Presenter" means a person making a presentation as or on behalf of a beneficiary or nominated person.

(14) "Record" means information that is inscribed on a tangible medium, or that is stored in an electronic or other medium and is retrievable in perceivable form.

(15) "Successor of a beneficiary" means a person who succeeds to substantially all of the rights of a beneficiary by operation of law, including a corporation with or into which the beneficiary has been merged or consolidated, an administrator, executor, personal representative, trustee in bankruptcy, debtor in possession, liquidator, and receiver.

(b) Definitions in other Articles applying to this article and the sections in which they appear are:

"Accept" or "Acceptance" Section 3—409

"Value" Sections 3—303, 4—211

(c) Article 1 contains certain additional general definitions and principles of construction and interpretation applicable throughout this article.

§ 5—103. Scope.

(a) This article applies to letters of credit and to certain rights and obligations arising out of transactions involving letters of credit.

(b) The statement of a rule in this article does not by itself require, imply, or negate application of the same or a different rule to a situation not provided for, or to a person not specified, in this article.

(c) With the exception of this subsection, subsections (a) and (d), Sections 5—102(a)(9) and (10), 5—106(d), and 5—114(d), and except to the extent prohibited in Sections 1—102(3) and 5—117(d), the effect of this article may be varied by agreement or by a provision stated or incorporated by reference in an undertaking. A term in an agreement or undertaking generally excusing liability or generally limiting remedies for failure to perform obligations is not sufficient to vary obligations prescribed by this article.

(d) Rights and obligations of an issuer to a beneficiary or a nominated person under a letter of credit are independent of the existence, performance, or nonperformance of a contract or arrangement out of which the letter of credit arises or which underlies it, including contracts or arrangements between the issuer and the applicant and between the applicant and the beneficiary.

§ 5—104. Formal Requirements.

A letter of credit, confirmation, advice, transfer, amendment, or cancellation may be issued in any form that is a record and is authenticated (i) by a signature or (ii) in accordance with the agreement of the parties or the standard practice referred to in Section 5—108(e).

§ 5—105. Consideration.

Consideration is not required to issue, amend, transfer, or cancel a letter of credit, advice, or confirmation.

§ 5—106. Issuance, Amendment, Cancellation, and Duration.

(a) A letter of credit is issued and becomes enforceable according to its terms against the issuer when the issuer sends or otherwise transmits it to the person requested to advise or to the beneficiary. A letter of credit is revocable only if it so provides.

(b) After a letter of credit is issued, rights and obligations of a beneficiary, applicant, confirmer, and issuer are not affected by an amendment or cancellation to which that person has not consented except to the extent the letter of credit provides that it is revocable or that the issuer may amend or cancel the letter of credit without that consent.

(c) If there is no stated expiration date or other provision that determines its duration, a letter of credit expires one year after its stated date of issuance or, if none is stated, after the date on which it is issued.

(d) A letter of credit that states that it is perpetual expires five years after its stated date of issuance, or if none is stated, after the date on which it is issued.

§ 5—107. Confirmer, Nominated Person, and Adviser.

(a) A confirmer is directly obligated on a letter of credit and has the rights and obligations of an issuer to the extent of its confirmation. The confirmer also has rights against and obligations to the issuer as if the issuer were an applicant and the confirmer had issued the letter of credit at the request and for the account of the issuer.

(b) A nominated person who is not a confirmer is not obligated to honor or otherwise give value for a presentation.

(c) A person requested to advise may decline to act as an adviser. An adviser that is not a confirmer is not obligated to honor or give value for a presentation. An adviser undertakes to the issuer and to the beneficiary accurately to advise the terms of the letter of credit, confirmation, amendment, or advice received by that person and undertakes to the beneficiary to check the apparent authenticity of the request to advise. Even if the advice is inaccurate, the letter of credit, confirmation, or amendment is enforceable as issued.

(d) A person who notifies a transferee beneficiary of the terms of a letter of credit, confirmation, amendment, or advice has the rights and obligations of an adviser under subsection (c). The terms in the notice to the transferee beneficiary may differ from the terms in any notice to the transferor beneficiary to the extent permitted by the letter of credit, confirmation, amendment, or advice received by the person who so notifies.

§ 5—108. Issuer's Rights and Obligations.

(a) Except as otherwise provided in Section 5—109, an issuer shall honor a presentation that, as determined by the standard practice referred to in subsection (e), appears on its face strictly to comply with the terms and conditions of the letter of credit. Except as otherwise provided in Section 5—113 and unless otherwise agreed with the applicant, an issuer shall dishonor a presentation that does not appear so to comply.

(b) An issuer has a reasonable time after presentation, but not beyond the end of the seventh business day of the issuer after the day of its receipt of documents:

(1) to honor,

(2) if the letter of credit provides for honor to be completed more than seven business days after presentation, to accept a draft or incur a deferred obligation, or

(3) to give notice to the presenter of discrepancies in the presentation.

(c) Except as otherwise provided in subsection (d), an issuer is precluded from asserting as a basis for dishonor any discrepancy if timely notice is not given, or any discrepancy not stated in the notice if timely notice is given.

(d) Failure to give the notice specified in subsection (b) or to mention fraud, forgery, or expiration in the notice does not preclude the issuer from asserting as a basis for dishonor fraud or forgery as described in Section 5—109(a) or expiration of the letter of credit before presentation.

(e) An issuer shall observe standard practice of financial institutions that regularly issue letters of credit. Determination of the issuer's observance of the standard practice is a matter of interpretation for the court. The court shall offer the parties a reasonable opportunity to present evidence of the standard practice.

(f) An issuer is not responsible for:

(1) the performance or nonperformance of the underlying contract, arrangement, or transaction,

(2) an act or omission of others, or

(3) observance or knowledge of the usage of a particular trade other than the standard practice referred to in subsection (e).

(g) If an undertaking constituting a letter of credit under Section 5—102(a)(10) contains nondocumentary conditions, an issuer shall disregard the nondocumentary conditions and treat them as if they were not stated.

(h) An issuer that has dishonored a presentation shall return the documents or hold them at the disposal of, and send advice to that effect to, the presenter.

(i) An issuer that has honored a presentation as permitted or required by this article:

(1) is entitled to be reimbursed by the applicant in immediately available funds not later than the date of its payment of funds;

(2) takes the documents free of claims of the beneficiary or presenter;

(3) is precluded from asserting a right of recourse on a draft under Sections 3—414 and 3—415;

(4) except as otherwise provided in Sections 5—110 and 5—117, is precluded from restitution of money paid or other value given by mistake to the extent the mistake concerns discrepancies in the documents or tender which are apparent on the face of the presentation; and

(5) is discharged to the extent of its performance under the letter of credit unless the issuer honored a presentation in which a required signature of a beneficiary was forged.

§ 5—109. Fraud and Forgery.

(a) If a presentation is made that appears on its face strictly to comply with the terms and conditions of the letter of credit, but a required document is forged or materially fraudulent, or honor of the presentation would facilitate a material fraud by the beneficiary on the issuer or applicant:

(1) the issuer shall honor the presentation, if honor is demanded by (i) a nominated person who has given value in good faith and without notice of forgery or material fraud, (ii) a confirmer who has honored its confirmation in good faith, (iii) a holder in due course of a draft drawn under the letter of credit which was taken after acceptance by the issuer or nominated person, or (iv) an assignee of the issuer's or nominated person's deferred obligation that was taken for value and without notice of forgery or material fraud after the obligation was incurred by the issuer or nominated person; and

(2) the issuer, acting in good faith, may honor or dishonor the presentation in any other case.

(b) If an applicant claims that a required document is forged or materially fraudulent or that honor of the presentation would facilitate a material fraud by the beneficiary on the issuer or applicant, a court of competent jurisdiction may temporarily or permanently enjoin the issuer from honoring a presentation or grant similar relief against the issuer or other persons only if the court finds that:

(1) the relief is not prohibited under the law applicable to an accepted draft or deferred obligation incurred by the issuer;

(2) a beneficiary, issuer, or nominated person who may be adversely affected is adequately protected against loss that it may suffer because the relief is granted;

(3) all of the conditions to entitle a person to the relief under the law of this State have been met; and

(4) on the basis of the information submitted to the court, the applicant is more likely than not to succeed under its claim of forgery or material fraud and the person demanding honor does not qualify for protection under subsection (a)(1).

§ 5—110. Warranties.

(a) If its presentation is honored, the beneficiary warrants:

(1) to the issuer, any other person to whom presentation is made, and the applicant that there is no fraud or forgery of the kind described in Section 5—109(a); and

(2) to the applicant that the drawing does not violate any agreement between the applicant and beneficiary or any other agreement intended by them to be augmented by the letter of credit.

(b) The warranties in subsection (a) are in addition to warranties arising under Article 3, 4, 7, and 8 because of the presentation or transfer of documents covered by any of those articles.

§ 5—111. Remedies.

(a) If an issuer wrongfully dishonors or repudiates its obligation to pay money under a letter of credit before presentation, the beneficiary, successor, or nominated person presenting on its own behalf may recover from the issuer the amount that is the subject of the dishonor or repudiation. If the issuer's obligation under the letter of credit is not for the payment of money, the claimant may obtain specific performance or, at the claimant's election, recover an amount equal to the value of performance from the issuer. In either case, the claimant may also recover incidental but not consequential damages. The claimant is not obligated to take action to avoid damages that might be due from the issuer under this subsection. If, although not obligated to do so, the claimant avoids damages, the claimant's recovery from the issuer must be reduced by the amount of damages avoided. The issuer has the burden of proving the amount of damages avoided. In the case of repudiation the claimant need not present any document.

(b) If an issuer wrongfully dishonors a draft or demand presented under a letter of credit or honors a draft or demand in breach of its obligation to the applicant, the applicant may recover damages resulting from the breach, including incidental but not consequential damages, less any amount saved as a result of the breach.

(c) If an adviser or nominated person other than a confirmer breaches an obligation under this article or an issuer breaches an obligation not covered in subsection (a) or (b), a person to whom the obligation is owed may recover damages resulting from the breach, including incidental but not consequential damages, less any amount saved as a result of the breach. To the extent of the confirmation, a confirmer has the liability of an issuer specified in this subsection and subsections (a) and (b).

(d) An issuer, nominated person, or adviser who is found liable under subsection (a), (b), or (c) shall pay interest on the amount owed thereunder from the date of wrongful dishonor or other appropriate date.

(e) Reasonable attorney's fees and other expenses of litigation must be awarded to the prevailing party in an action in which a remedy is sought under this article.

(f) Damages that would otherwise be payable by a party for breach of an obligation under this article may be liquidated by agreement or undertaking, but only in an amount or by a formula that is reasonable in light of the harm anticipated.

§ 5—112. Transfer of Letter of Credit.

(a) Except as otherwise provided in Section 5–113, unless a letter of credit provides that it is transferable, the right of a beneficiary to draw or otherwise demand performance under a letter of credit may not be transferred.

(b) Even if a letter of credit provides that it is transferable, the issuer may refuse to recognize or carry out a transfer if:

(1) the transfer would violate applicable law; or

(2) the transferor or transferee has failed to comply with any requirement stated in the letter of credit or any other

requirement relating to transfer imposed by the issuer which is within the standard practice referred to in Section 5–108(e) or is otherwise reasonable under the circumstances.

§ 5—113. Transfer by Operation of Law.

(a) A successor of a beneficiary may consent to amendments, sign and present documents, and receive payment or other items of value in the name of the beneficiary without disclosing its status as a successor.

(b) A successor of a beneficiary may consent to amendments, sign and present documents, and receive payment or other items of value in its own name as the disclosed successor of the beneficiary. Except as otherwise provided in subsection (e), an issuer shall recognize a disclosed successor of a beneficiary as beneficiary in full substitution for its predecessor upon compliance with the requirements for recognition by the issuer of a transfer of drawing rights by operation of law under the standard practice referred to in Section 5—108(e) or, in the absence of such a practice, compliance with other reasonable procedures sufficient to protect the issuer.

(c) An issuer is not obliged to determine whether a purported successor is a successor of a beneficiary or whether the signature of a purported successor is genuine or authorized.

(d) Honor of a purported successor's apparently complying presentation under subsection (a) or (b) has the consequences specified in Section 5—108(i) even if the purported successor is not the successor of a beneficiary. Documents signed in the name of the beneficiary or of a disclosed successor by a person who is neither the beneficiary nor the successor of the beneficiary are forged documents for the purposes of Section 5—109.

(e) An issuer whose rights of reimbursement are not covered by subsection (d) or substantially similar law and any confirmer or nominated person may decline to recognize a presentation under subsection (b).

(f) A beneficiary whose name is changed after the issuance of a letter of credit has the same rights and obligations as a successor of a beneficiary under this section.

§ 5—114. Assignment of Proceeds.

(a) In this section, "proceeds of a letter of credit" means the cash, check, accepted draft, or other item of value paid or delivered upon honor or giving of value by the issuer or any nominated person under the letter of credit. The term does not include a beneficiary's drawing rights or documents presented by the beneficiary.

(b) A beneficiary may assign its right to part or all of the proceeds of a letter of credit. The beneficiary may do so before presentation as a present assignment of its right to receive proceeds contingent upon its compliance with the terms and conditions of the letter of credit.

(c) An issuer or nominated person need not recognize an assignment of proceeds of a letter of credit until it consents to the assignment.

(d) An issuer or nominated person has no obligation to give or withhold its consent to an assignment of proceeds of a letter of credit, but consent may not be unreasonably withheld if the assignee possesses and exhibits the letter of credit and presentation of the letter of credit is a condition to honor.

(e) Rights of a transferee beneficiary or nominated person are independent of the beneficiary's assignment of the proceeds of a letter of credit and are superior to the assignee's right to the proceeds.

(f) Neither the rights recognized by this section between an assignee and an issuer, transferee beneficiary, or nominated person nor the issuer's or nominated person's payment of proceeds to an assignee or a third person affect the rights between the assignee and any person other than the issuer, transferee beneficiary, or nominated person. The mode of creating and perfecting a security interest in or granting an assignment of a beneficiary's rights to proceeds is governed by Article 9 or other law. Against persons other than the issuer, transferee beneficiary, or nominated person, the rights and obligations arising upon the creation of a security interest or other assignment of a beneficiary's right to proceeds and its perfection are governed by Article 9 or other law.

§ 5—115. Statute of Limitations.

An action to enforce a right or obligation arising under this article must be commenced within one year after the expiration date of the relevant letter of credit or one year after the [claim for relief] [cause of action] accrues, whichever occurs later. A [claim for relief] [cause of action] accrues when the breach occurs, regardless of the aggrieved party's lack of knowledge of the breach.

§ 5—116. Choice of Law and Forum.

(a) The liability of an issuer, nominated person, or adviser for action or omission is governed by the law of the jurisdiction chosen by an agreement in the form of a record signed or otherwise authenticated by the affected parties in the manner provided in Section 5—104 or by a provision in the person's letter of credit, confirmation, or other undertaking. The jurisdiction whose law is chosen need not bear any relation to the transaction.

(b) Unless subsection (a) applies, the liability of an issuer, nominated person, or adviser for action or omission is governed by the law of the jurisdiction in which the person is located. The person is considered to be located at the address indicated in the person's undertaking. If more than one address is indicated, the person is considered to be located at the address from which the person's undertaking was issued. For the purpose of jurisdiction, choice of law, and recognition of interbranch letters of credit, but not enforcement of a judgment, all branches of a bank are considered separate juridical entities and a bank is considered to be located at the place where its relevant branch is considered to be located under this subsection.

(c) Except as otherwise provided in this subsection, the liability of an issuer, nominated person, or adviser is governed by any rules of custom or practice, such as the Uniform Customs and Practice for Documentary Credits, to which the letter of credit, confirmation, or other undertaking is expressly made subject. If (i) this article would govern the liability of an issuer, nominated person, or adviser under subsection (a) or (b), (ii) the relevant undertaking incorporates rules of custom or practice, and (iii) there is conflict between this article and those rules as applied to that undertaking, those rules govern except to the extent of any conflict with the nonvariable provisions specified in Section 5—103(c).

(d) If there is conflict between this article and Article 3, 4, 4A, or 9, this article governs.

(e) The forum for settling disputes arising out of an undertaking within this article may be chosen in the manner and with the binding effect that governing law may be chosen in accordance with subsection (a).

§ 5—117. Subrogation of Issuer, Applicant, and Nominated Person.

(a) An issuer that honors a beneficiary's presentation is subrogated to the rights of the beneficiary to the same extent as if the issuer were a secondary obligor of the underlying obligation owed to the beneficiary and of the applicant to the same extent as if the issuer were the secondary obligor of the underlying obligation owed to the applicant.

(b) An applicant that reimburses an issuer is subrogated to the rights of the issuer against any beneficiary, presenter, or nominated person to the same extent as if the applicant were the secondary obligor of the obligations owed to the issuer and has the rights of subrogation of the issuer to the rights of the beneficiary stated in subsection (a).

(c) A nominated person who pays or gives value against a draft or demand presented under a letter of credit is subrogated to the rights of:

(1) the issuer against the applicant to the same extent as if the nominated person were a secondary obligor of the obligation owed to the issuer by the applicant;

(2) the beneficiary to the same extent as if the nominated person were a secondary obligor of the underlying obligation owed to the beneficiary; and

(3) the applicant to same extent as if the nominated person were a secondary obligor of the underlying obligation owed to the applicant.

(d) Notwithstanding any agreement or term to the contrary, the rights of subrogation stated in subsections (a) and (b) do not arise until the issuer honors the letter of credit or otherwise pays and the rights in subsection (c) do not arise until the nominated person pays or otherwise gives value. Until then, the issuer, nominated person, and the applicant do not derive under this section present or prospective rights forming the basis of a claim, defense, or excuse.

Transition Provisions

§ [ ]. Effective Date.

This [Act] shall become effective on _______, 199__.

§ [ ]. Repeal.

This [Act] [repeals] [amends] [insert citation to existing Article 5].

§ [ ]. Applicability.

This [Act] applies to a letter of credit that is issued on or after the effective date of this [Act]. This [Act] does not apply to a transaction, event, obligation, or duty arising out of or associated with a letter of credit that was issued before the effective date of this [Act].

§ [ ]. Savings Clause.

A transaction arising out of or associated with a letter of credit that was issued before the effective date of this [Act] and the rights, obligations, and interests flowing from that transaction are governed by any statute or other law amended or repealed by this [Act] as if repeal or amendment had not occurred and may be terminated, completed, consummated, or enforced under that statute or other law.

Article 6
BULK TRANSFERS

§ 6—101. Short Title.

This Article shall be known and may be cited as Uniform Commercial Code—Bulk Transfers.

§ 6—102. "Bulk Transfers"; Transfers of Equipment; Enterprises Subject to This Article; Bulk Transfers Subject to This Article.

(1) A "bulk transfer" is any transfer in bulk and not in the ordinary course of the transferor's business of a major part of the materials, supplies, merchandise or other inventory (Section 9—109) of an enterprise subject to this Article.

(2) A transfer of a substantial part of the equipment (Section 9—109) of such an enterprise is a bulk transfer if it is made in connection with a bulk transfer of inventory, but not otherwise.

(3) The enterprises subject to this Article are all those whose principal business is the sale of merchandise from stock, including those who manufacture what they sell.

(4) Except as limited by the following section all bulk transfers of goods located within this state are subject to this Article.

§ 6—103. Transfers Excepted From This Article.

The following transfers are not subject to this Article:

(1) Those made to give security for the performance of an obligation;

(2) General assignments for the benefit of all the creditors of the transferor, and subsequent transfers by the assignee thereunder;

(3) Transfers in settlement or realization of a lien or other security interests;

(4) Sales by executors, administrators, receivers, trustees in bankruptcy, or any public officer under judicial process;

(5) Sales made in the course of judicial or administrative proceedings for the dissolution or reorganization of a corporation and of which notice is sent to the creditors of the corporation pursuant to order of the court or administrative agency;

(6) Transfers to a person maintaining a known place of business in this State who becomes bound to pay the debts of the transferor in full and gives public notice of that fact, and who is solvent after becoming so bound;

(7) A transfer to a new business enterprise organized to take over and continue the business, if public notice of the transaction is given and the new enterprise assumes the debts of the transferor and he receives nothing from the transaction except an interest in the new enterprise junior to the claims of creditors;

(8) Transfers of property which is exempt from execution.

Public notice under subsection (6) or subsection (7) may be given by publishing once a week for two consecutive weeks in a newspaper of general circulation where the transferor had its principal place of business in this state an advertisement including the names and addresses of the transferor and transferee and the effective date of the transfer.

§ 6—104. Schedule of Property, List of Creditors.

(1) Except as provided with respect to auction sales (Section 6—108), a bulk transfer subject to this Article is ineffective against any creditor of the transferor unless:

(a) The transferee requires the transferor to furnish a list of his existing creditors prepared as stated in this section; and

(b) The parties prepare a schedule of the property transferred sufficient to identify it; and

(c) The transferee preserves the list and schedule for six months next following the transfer and permits inspection of either or both and copying therefrom at all reasonable hours by any creditor of the transferor, or files the list and schedule in (a public office to be here identified).

(2) The list of creditors must be signed and sworn to or affirmed by the transferor or his agent. It must contain the names and business addresses of all creditors of the transferor, with the amounts when known, and also the names of all persons who are known to the transferor to assert claims against him even though such claims are disputed. If the transferor is the obligor of an outstanding issue of bonds, debentures or the like as to which there is an indenture trustee, the list of creditors need include only the name and address of the indenture trustee and the aggregate outstanding principal amount of the issue.

(3) Responsibility for the completeness and accuracy of the list of creditors rests on the transferor, and the transfer is not rendered ineffective by errors or omissions therein unless the transferee is shown to have had knowledge.

§ 6—105. Notice to Creditors.

In addition to the requirements of the preceding section, any bulk transfer subject to this Article except one made by auction sale (Section 6—108) is ineffective against any creditor of the transferor unless at least ten days before he takes possession of the goods or pays for them, whichever happens first, the transferee gives notice of the transfer in the manner and to the persons hereafter provided (Section 6—107).

§ 6—106. Application of the Proceeds.

In addition to the requirements of the two preceding sections:

(1) Upon every bulk transfer subject to this Article for which new consideration becomes payable except those made by sale at auction it is the duty of the transferee to assure that such consideration is applied so far as necessary to pay those debts of the transferor which are either shown on the list furnished by the transferor (Section 6—104) or filed in writing in the place stated in the notice (Section 6—107) within thirty days after the mailing of such notice. This duty of the transferee runs to all the holders of such debts, and may be enforced by any of them for the benefit of all.

(2) If any of said debts are in dispute the necessary sum may be withheld from distribution until the dispute is settled or adjudicated.

[(3) If the consideration payable is not enough to pay all of the said debts in full distribution shall be made pro rata.]

Note: *This section is bracketed to indicate division of opinion as to whether or not it is a wise provision, and to suggest that this is a point on which State enactments may differ without serious damage to the principle of uniformity. In any State where this section is omitted, the following parts of sections, also bracketed in the text, should also be omitted, namely:*
Section 6—107(2)(e).
6—108(3)(c).
6—109(2).

In any State where this section is enacted, these other provisions should be also.

Optional Subsection (4)

[(4) The transferee may within ten days after he takes possession of the goods pay the consideration into the (specify court) in the county where the transferor had its principal place of business in this state and thereafter may discharge his duty under this section by giving notice by registered or certified mail to all the persons to whom the duty runs that the consideration has been paid into that court and that they should file their claims there. On motion of any interested party, the court may order the distribution of the consideration to the persons entitled to it.]

Note: *Optional subsection (4) is recommended for those states which do not have a general statute providing for payment of money into court.*

§ 6—107. The Notice.

(1) The notice to creditors (Section 6—105) shall state:

(a) that a bulk transfer is about to be made; and

(b) the names and business addresses of the transferor and transferee, and all other business names and addresses used by the transferor within three years last past so far as known to the transferee; and

(c) whether or not all the debts of the transferor are to be paid in full as they fall due as a result of the transaction, and if so, the address to which creditors should send their bills.

(2) If the debts of the transferor are not to be paid in full as they fall due or if the transferee is in doubt on that point then the notice shall state further:

(a) the location and general description of the property to be transferred and the estimated total of the transferor's debts;

(b) the address where the schedule of property and list of creditors (Section 6—104) may be inspected;

(c) whether the transfer is to pay existing debts and if so the amount of such debts and to whom owing;

(d) whether the transfer is for new consideration and if so the amount of such consideration and the time and place of payment; [and]

[(e) if for new consideration the time and place where creditors of the transferor are to file their claims.]

(3) The notice in any case shall be delivered personally or sent by registered or certified mail to all the persons shown on the list of creditors furnished by the transferor (Section 6—104) and to all other persons who are known to the transferee to hold or assert claims against the transferor.

§ 6—108. Auction Sales; "Auctioneer".

(1) A bulk transfer is subject to this Article even though it is by sale at auction, but only in the manner and with the results stated in this section.

(2) The transferor shall furnish a list of his creditors and assist in the preparation of a schedule of the property to be sold, both prepared as before stated (Section 6—104).

(3) The person or persons other than the transferor who direct, control or are responsible for the auction are collectively called the "auctioneer". The auctioneer shall:

(a) receive and retain the list of creditors and prepare and retain the schedule of property for the period stated in this Article (Section 6—104);

(b) give notice of the auction personally or by registered or certified mail at least ten days before it occurs to all persons shown on the list of creditors and to all other persons who are known to him to hold or assert claims against the transferor; [and]

[(c) assure that the net proceeds of the auction are applied as provided in this Article (Section 6—106).]

(4) Failure of the auctioneer to perform any of these duties does not affect the validity of the sale or the title of the purchasers, but if the auctioneer knows that the auction constitutes a bulk transfer such failure renders the auctioneer liable to the creditors of the transferor as a class for the sums owing to them from the transferor up to but not exceeding the net proceeds of the auction. If the auctioneer consists of several persons their liability is joint and several.

§ 6—109. What Creditors Protected; [Credit for Payment to Particular Creditors].

(1) The creditors of the transferor mentioned in this Article are those holding claims based on transactions or events occurring before the bulk transfer, but creditors who become such after notice to creditors is given (Sections 6—105 and 6—107) are not entitled to notice.

[(2) Against the aggregate obligation imposed by the provisions of this Article concerning the application of the proceeds (Section 6—106 and subsection (3)(c) of 6—108) the transferee or auctioneer is entitled to credit for sums paid to particular creditors of the transferor, not exceeding the sums believed in good faith at the time of the payment to be properly payable to such creditors.]

§ 6—110. Subsequent Transfers.

When the title of a transferee to property is subject to a defect by reason of his noncompliance with the requirements of this Article, then:

(1) a purchaser of any of such property from such transferee who pays no value or who takes with notice of such noncompliance takes subject to such defect, but

(2) a purchaser for value in good faith and without such notice takes free of such defect.

§ 6—111. Limitation of Actions and Levies.

No action under this Article shall be brought nor levy made more than six months after the date on which the transferee took possession of the goods unless the transfer has been concealed. If the transfer has been concealed, actions may be brought or levies made within six months after its discovery.

Article 6 Alternative B*

§ 6—101. Short Title.

This Article shall be known and may be cited as Uniform Commercial Code—Bulk Sales.

§ 6—102. Definitions and Index of Definitions.

(1) In this Article, unless the context otherwise requires:

* Approved in substance by the National Conference of Commissioners on Uniform State Laws and The American Law Institute. States have the choice of adopting this alternative to the existing Article 6 or repealing Article 6 entirely (Alternative A).

(a) "Assets" means the inventory that is the subject of a bulk sale and any tangible and intangible personal property used or held for use primarily in, or arising from, the seller's business and sold in connection with that inventory, but the term does not include:

(i) fixtures (Section 9—313(1)(a)) other than readily removable factory and office machines;

(ii) the lessee's interest in a lease of real property; or

(iii) property to the extent it is generally exempt from creditor process under nonbankruptcy law.

(b) "Auctioneer" means a person whom the seller engages to direct, conduct, control, or be responsible for a sale by auction.

(c) "Bulk sale" means:

(i) in the case of a sale by auction or a sale or series of sales conducted by a liquidator on the seller's behalf, a sale or series of sales not in the ordinary course of the seller's business of more than half of the seller's inventory, as measured by value on the date of the bulk-sale agreement, if on that date the auctioneer or liquidator has notice, or after reasonable inquiry would have had notice, that the seller will not continue to operate the same or a similar kind of business after the sale or series of sales; and

(ii) in all other cases, a sale not in the ordinary course of the seller's business of more than half the seller's inventory, as measured by value on the date of the bulk-sale agreement, if on that date the buyer has notice, or after reasonable inquiry would have had notice, that the seller will not continue to operate the same or a similar kind of business after the sale.

(d) "Claim" means a right to payment from the seller, whether or not the right is reduced to judgment, liquidated, fixed, matured, disputed, secured, legal, or equitable. The term includes costs of collection and attorney's fees only to the extent that the laws of this state permit the holder of the claim to recover them in an action against the obligor.

(e) "Claimant" means a person holding a claim incurred in the seller's business other than:

(i) an unsecured and unmatured claim for employment compensation and benefits, including commissions and vacation, severance, and sick-leave pay;

(ii) a claim for injury to an individual or to property, or for breach of warranty, unless:

(A) a right of action for the claim has accrued;

(B) the claim has been asserted against the seller; and

(C) the seller knows the identity of the person asserting the claim and the basis upon which the person has asserted it; and

(States to Select One Alternative)

Alternative A

[(iii) a claim for taxes owing to a governmental unit.]

Alternative B

[(iii) a claim for taxes owing to a governmental unit, if:

(A) a statute governing the enforcement of the claim permits or requires notice of the bulk sale to be given to the governmental unit in a manner other than by compliance with the requirements of this Article; and

(B) notice is given in accordance with the statute.]

(f) "Creditor" means a claimant or other person holding a claim.

(g)(i) "Date of the bulk sale" means:

(A) if the sale is by auction or is conducted by a liquidator on the seller's behalf, the date on which more than ten percent of the net proceeds is paid to or for the benefit of the seller; and

(B) in all other cases, the later of the date on which:

(I) more than ten percent of the net contract price is paid to or for the benefit of the seller; or

(II) more than ten percent of the assets, as measured by value, are transferred to the buyer.

(ii) For purposes of this subsection:

(A) delivery of a negotiable instrument (Section 3—104(1)) to or for the benefit of the seller in exchange for assets constitutes payment of the contract price pro tanto;

(B) to the extent that the contract price is deposited in an escrow, the contract price is paid to or for the benefit of the seller when the seller acquires the unconditional right to receive the deposit or when the deposit is delivered to the seller or for the benefit of the seller, whichever is earlier; and

(C) an asset is transferred when a person holding an unsecured claim can no longer obtain through judicial proceedings rights to the asset that are superior to those of the buyer arising as a result of the bulk sale. A person holding an unsecured claim can obtain those superior rights to a tangible asset at least until the buyer has an unconditional right, under the bulk-sale agreement, to possess the asset, and a person holding an unsecured claim can obtain those superior rights to an intangible asset at least until the buyer has an unconditional right, under the bulk-sale agreement, to use the asset.

(h) "Date of the bulk-sale agreement" means:

(i) in the case of a sale by auction or conducted by a liquidator (subsection (c)(i)), the date on which the seller engages the auctioneer or liquidator; and

(ii) in all other cases, the date on which a bulk-sale agreement becomes enforceable between the buyer and the seller.

(i) "Debt" means liability on a claim.

(j) "Liquidator" means a person who is regularly engaged in the business of disposing of assets for businesses contemplating liquidation or dissolution.

(k) "Net contract price" means the new consideration the buyer is obligated to pay for the assets less:

(i) the amount of any proceeds of the sale of an asset, to the extent the proceeds are applied in partial or total satisfaction of a debt secured by the asset; and

(ii) the amount of any debt to the extent it is secured by a security interest or lien that is enforceable against the asset before and after it has been sold to a buyer. If a debt is secured by an asset and other property of the seller, the amount of the debt secured by a security interest or lien that is enforceable against the asset is determined by multiplying the debt by a fraction, the numerator of which is the value of the new consideration for the asset on the date of the bulk sale and the denominator of which is the value of all property securing the debt on the date of the bulk sale.

(l) "Net proceeds" means the new consideration received for assets sold at a sale by auction or a sale conducted by a liquidator on the seller's behalf less:

(i) commissions and reasonable expenses of the sale;

(ii) the amount of any proceeds of the sale of an asset, to the extent the proceeds are applied in partial or total satisfaction of a debt secured by the asset; and

(iii) the amount of any debt to the extent it is secured by a security interest or lien that is enforceable against the asset before and after it has been sold to a buyer. If a debt is secured by an asset and other property of the seller, the amount of the debt secured by a security interest or lien that is enforceable against the asset is determined by multiplying the debt by a fraction, the numerator of which is the value of the new consideration for the asset on the date of the bulk sale and the denominator of which is the value of all property securing the debt on the date of the bulk sale.

(m) A sale is "in the ordinary course of the seller's business" if the sale comports with usual or customary practices in the kind of business in which the seller is engaged or with the seller's own usual or customary practices.

(n) "United States" includes its territories and possessions and the Commonwealth of Puerto Rico.

(o) "Value" means fair market value.

(p) "Verified" means signed and sworn to or affirmed.

(2) The following definitions in other Articles apply to this Article:

(a) "Buyer."	Section 2—103(1)(a).
(b) "Equipment."	Section 9—109(2).
(c) "Inventory."	Section 9—109(4).
(d) "Sale."	Section 2—106(1).
(e) "Seller."	Section 2—103(1)(d).

(3) In addition, Article 1 contains general definitions and principles of construction and interpretation applicable throughout this Article.

§ 6—103. Applicability of Article.

(1) Except as otherwise provided in subsection (3), this Article applies to a bulk sale if:

(a) the seller's principal business is the sale of inventory from stock; and

(b) on the date of the bulk-sale agreement the seller is located in this state or, if the seller is located in a jurisdiction that is not a part of the United States, the seller's major executive office in the United States is in this state.

(2) A seller is deemed to be located at his [or her] place of business. If a seller has more than one place of business, the seller is deemed located at his [or her] chief executive office.

(3) This Article does not apply to:

(a) a transfer made to secure payment or performance of an obligation;

(b) a transfer of collateral to a secured party pursuant to Section 9—503;

(c) a sale of collateral pursuant to Section 9—504;

(d) retention of collateral pursuant to Section 9—505;

(e) a sale of an asset encumbered by a security interest or lien if (i) all the proceeds of the sale are applied in partial or total satisfaction of the debt secured by the security interest or lien or (ii) the security interest or lien is enforceable against the asset after it has been sold to the buyer and the net contract price is zero;

(f) a general assignment for the benefit of creditors or to a subsequent transfer by the assignee;

(g) a sale by an executor, administrator, receiver, trustee in bankruptcy, or any public officer under judicial process;

(h) a sale made in the course of judicial or administrative proceedings for the dissolution or reorganization of an organization;

(i) a sale to a buyer whose principal place of business is in the United States and who:

(i) not earlier than 21 days before the date of the bulk sale, (A) obtains from the seller a verified and dated list of claimants of whom the seller has notice three days before the seller sends or delivers the list to the buyer or (B) conducts a reasonable inquiry to discover the claimants;

(ii) assumes in full the debts owed to claimants of whom the buyer has knowledge on the date the buyer receives the list of claimants from the seller or on the date the buyer completes the reasonable inquiry, as the case may be;

(iii) is not insolvent after the assumption; and

(iv) gives written notice of the assumption not later than 30 days after the date of the bulk sale by sending or delivering a notice to the claimants identified in subparagraph (ii) or by filing a notice in the office of the [Secretary of State];

(j) a sale to a buyer whose principal place of business is in the United States and who:

(i) assumes in full the debts that were incurred in the seller's business before the date of the bulk sale;

(ii) is not insolvent after the assumption; and

(iii) gives written notice of the assumption not later than 30 days after the date of the bulk sale by sending or delivering a notice to each creditor whose debt is assumed or by filing a notice in the office of the [Secretary of State];

(k) a sale to a new organization that is organized to take over and continue the business of the seller and that has its principal place of business in the United States if:

(i) the buyer assumes in full the debts that were incurred in the seller's business before the date of the bulk sale;

(ii) the seller receives nothing from the sale except an interest in the new organization that is subordinate to the claims against the organization arising from the assumption; and

(iii) the buyer gives written notice of the assumption not later than 30 days after the date of the bulk sale by sending or delivering a notice to each creditor whose debt is assumed or by filing a notice in the office of the [Secretary of State];

(l) a sale of assets having:

(i) a value, net of liens and security interests, of less than $10,000. If a debt is secured by assets and other property of the seller, the net value of the assets is determined by subtracting from their value an amount equal to the product of the debt multiplied by a fraction, the numerator of which is the value of the assets on the date of the bulk sale and the denominator of which is the value of all property securing the debt on the date of the bulk sale; or

(ii) a value of more than $25,000,000 on the date of the bulk-sale agreement; or

(m) a sale required by, and made pursuant to, statute.

(4) The notice under subsection (3)(i)(iv) must state: (i) that a sale that may constitute a bulk sale has been or will be made; (ii) the date or prospective date of the bulk sale; (iii) the individual, partnership, or corporate names and the addresses of the seller and buyer; (iv) the address to which inquiries about the sale may be made, if different from the seller's address; and (v) that the buyer has assumed or will assume in full the debts owed to claimants of whom the buyer has knowledge on the date the buyer receives the list of claimants from the seller or completes a reasonable inquiry to discover the claimants.

(5) The notice under subsections (3)(j)(iii) and (3)(k)(iii) must state: (i) that a sale that may constitute a bulk sale has been or will be made; (ii) the date or prospective date of the bulk sale; (iii) the individual, partnership, or corporate names and the addresses of the seller and buyer; (iv) the address to which inquiries about the sale may be made, if different from the seller's address; and (v) that the buyer has assumed or will assume the debts that were incurred in the seller's business before the date of the bulk sale.

(6) For purposes of subsection (3)(l), the value of assets is presumed to be equal to the price the buyer agrees to pay for the assets. However, in a sale by auction or a sale conducted by a liquidator on the seller's behalf, the value of assets is presumed to be the amount the auctioneer or liquidator reasonably estimates the assets will bring at auction or upon liquidation.

§ 6—104. Obligations of Buyer.

(1) In a bulk sale as defined in Section 6—102(1)(c)(ii) the buyer shall:

(a) obtain from the seller a list of all business names and addresses used by the seller within three years before the date the list is sent or delivered to the buyer;

(b) unless excused under subsection (2), obtain from the seller a verified and dated list of claimants of whom the seller has notice three days before the seller sends or delivers the list to the buyer and including, to the extent known by the seller, the address of and the amount claimed by each claimant;

(c) obtain from the seller or prepare a schedule of distribution (Section 6—106(1));

(d) give notice of the bulk sale in accordance with Section 6—105;

(e) unless excused under Section 6—106(4), distribute the net contract price in accordance with the undertakings of the buyer in the schedule of distribution; and

(f) unless excused under subsection (2), make available the list of claimants (subsection (1)(b)) by:

(i) promptly sending or delivering a copy of the list without charge to any claimant whose written request is received by the buyer no later than six months after the date of the bulk sale;

(ii) permitting any claimant to inspect and copy the list at any reasonable hour upon request received by the buyer no later than six months after the date of the bulk sale; or

(iii) filing a copy of the list in the office of the [Secretary of State] no later than the time for giving a notice of the bulk sale (Section 6—105(5)). A list filed in accordance with this subparagraph must state the individual, partnership, or corporate name and a mailing address of the seller.

(2) A buyer who gives notice in accordance with Section 6—105(2) is excused from complying with the requirements of subsections (1)(b) and (1)(f).

§ 6—105. Notice to Claimants.

(1) Except as otherwise provided in subsection (2), to comply with Section 6—104(1)(d) the buyer shall send or deliver a written notice of the bulk sale to each claimant on the list of claimants

(Section 6—104(1)(b)) and to any other claimant of which the buyer has knowledge at the time the notice of the bulk sale is sent or delivered.

(2) A buyer may comply with Section 6—104(1)(d) by filing a written notice of the bulk sale in the office of the [Secretary of State] if:

(a) on the date of the bulk-sale agreement the seller has 200 or more claimants, exclusive of claimants holding secured or matured claims for employment compensation and benefits, including commissions and vacation, severance, and sick-leave pay; or

(b) the buyer has received a verified statement from the seller stating that, as of the date of the bulk-sale agreement, the number of claimants, exclusive of claimants holding secured or matured claims for employment compensation and benefits, including commissions and vacation, severance, and sick-leave pay, is 200 or more.

(3) The written notice of the bulk sale must be accompanied by a copy of the schedule of distribution (Section 6—106(1)) and state at least:

(a) that the seller and buyer have entered into an agreement for a sale that may constitute a bulk sale under the laws of the State of ________ ;

(b) the date of the agreement;

(c) the date on or after which more than ten percent of the assets were or will be transferred;

(d) the date on or after which more than ten percent of the net contract price was or will be paid, if the date is not stated in the schedule of distribution;

(e) the name and a mailing address of the seller;

(f) any other business name and address listed by the seller pursuant to Section 6—104(1)(a);

(g) the name of the buyer and an address of the buyer from which information concerning the sale can be obtained;

(h) a statement indicating the type of assets or describing the assets item by item;

(i) the manner in which the buyer will make available the list of claimants (Section 6—104(1)(f)), if applicable; and

(j) if the sale is in total or partial satisfaction of an antecedent debt owed by the seller, the amount of the debt to be satisfied and the name of the person to whom it is owed.

(4) For purposes of subsections (3)(e) and (3)(g), the name of a person is the person's individual, partnership, or corporate name.

(5) The buyer shall give notice of the bulk sale not less than 45 days before the date of the bulk sale and, if the buyer gives notice in accordance with subsection (1), not more than 30 days after obtaining the list of claimants.

(6) A written notice substantially complying with the requirements of subsection (3) is effective even though it contains minor errors that are not seriously misleading.

(7) A form substantially as follows is sufficient to comply with subsection (3):

Notice of Sale

(1) ________ , whose address is ________ , is described in this notice as the "seller."

(2) ________ , whose address is ________ , is described in this notice as the "buyer."

(3) The seller has disclosed to the buyer that within the past three years the seller has used other business names, operated at other addresses, or both, as follows: ____ .

(4) The seller and the buyer have entered into an agreement dated ________ , for a sale that may constitute a bulk sale under the laws of the State of ______.

(5) The date on or after which more than ten percent of the assets that are the subject of the sale were or will be transferred is ________ , and [if not stated in the schedule of distribution] the date on or after which more than ten percent of the net contract price was or will be paid is ________ .

(6) The following assets are the subject of the sale: ____ .

(7) [If applicable] The buyer will make available to claimants of the seller a list of the seller's claimants in the following manner: ________________________ .

(8) [If applicable] The sale is to satisfy $ ________ of an antecedent debt owed by the seller to ________ .

(9) A copy of the schedule of distribution of the net contract price accompanies this notice.

[End of Notice]

§ 6—106. Schedule of Distribution.

(1) The seller and buyer shall agree on how the net contract price is to be distributed and set forth their agreement in a written schedule of distribution.

(2) The schedule of distribution may provide for distribution to any person at any time, including distribution of the entire net contract price to the seller.

(3) The buyer's undertakings in the schedule of distribution run only to the seller. However, a buyer who fails to distribute the net contract price in accordance with the buyer's undertakings in the schedule of distribution is liable to a creditor only as provided in Section 6—107(1).

(4) If the buyer undertakes in the schedule of distribution to distribute any part of the net contract price to a person other than the seller, and, after the buyer has given notice in accordance with Section 6—105, some or all of the anticipated net contract price is or becomes unavailable for distribution as a consequence of the buyer's or seller's having complied with an order of court, legal process, statute, or rule of law, the buyer is excused from any obligation arising under this Article or under any contract with the seller to distribute the net contract price in accordance with the buyer's undertakings in the schedule if the buyer:

(a) distributes the net contract price remaining available in accordance with any priorities for payment stated in the schedule of distribution and, to the extent that the price is insufficient to pay all the debts having a given priority, distributes the price pro rata among those debts shown in the schedule as having the same priority;

(b) distributes the net contract price remaining available in accordance with an order of court;

(c) commences a proceeding for interpleader in a court of competent jurisdiction and is discharged from the proceeding; or

(d) reaches a new agreement with the seller for the distribution of the net contract price remaining available, sets forth the new agreement in an amended schedule of distribution, gives notice of the amended schedule, and distributes the net contract price remaining available in accordance with the buyer's undertakings in the amended schedule.

(5) The notice under subsection (4)(d) must identify the buyer and the seller, state the filing number, if any, of the original notice, set forth the amended schedule, and be given in accordance with subsection (1) or (2) of Section 6—105, whichever is applicable, at least 14 days before the buyer distributes any part of the net contract price remaining available.

(6) If the seller undertakes in the schedule of distribution to distribute any part of the net contract price, and, after the buyer has given notice in accordance with Section 6—105, some or all of the anticipated net contract price is or becomes unavailable for distribution as a consequence of the buyer's or seller's having complied with an order of court, legal process, statute, or rule of law, the seller and any person in control of the seller are excused from any obligation arising under this Article or under any agreement with the buyer to distribute the net contract price in accordance with the seller's undertakings in the schedule if the seller:

(a) distributes the net contract price remaining available in accordance with any priorities for payment stated in the schedule of distribution and, to the extent that the price is insufficient to pay all the debts having a given priority, distributes the price pro rata among those debts shown in the schedule as having the same priority;

(b) distributes the net contract price remaining available in accordance with an order of court;

(c) commences a proceeding for interpleader in a court of competent jurisdiction and is discharged from the proceeding; or

(d) prepares a written amended schedule of distribution of the net contract price remaining available for distribution, gives notice of the amended schedule, and distributes the net contract price remaining available in accordance with the amended schedule.

(7) The notice under subsection (6)(d) must identify the buyer and the seller, state the filing number, if any, of the original notice, set forth the amended schedule, and be given in accordance with subsection (1) or (2) of Section 6—105, whichever is applicable, at least 14 days before the seller distributes any part of the net contract price remaining available.

§ 6—107. Liability for Noncompliance.

(1) Except as provided in subsection (3), and subject to the limitation in subsection (4):

(a) a buyer who fails to comply with the requirements of Section 6—104(1)(e) with respect to a creditor is liable to the creditor for damages in the amount of the claim, reduced by any amount that the creditor would not have realized if the buyer had complied; and

(b) a buyer who fails to comply with the requirements of any other subsection of Section 6—104 with respect to a claimant is liable to the claimant for damages in the amount of the claim, reduced by any amount that the claimant would not have realized if the buyer had complied.

(2) In an action under subsection (1), the creditor has the burden of establishing the validity and amount of the claim, and the buyer has the burden of establishing the amount that the creditor would not have realized if the buyer had complied.

(3) A buyer who:

(a) made a good faith and commercially reasonable effort to comply with the requirements of Section 6—104(1) or to exclude the sale from the application of this Article under Section 6—103(3); or

(b) on or after the date of the bulk-sale agreement, but before the date of the bulk sale, held a good faith and commercially reasonable belief that this Article does not apply to the particular sale

is not liable to creditors for failure to comply with the requirements of Section 6—104. The buyer has the burden of establishing the good faith and commercial reasonableness of the effort or belief.

(4) In a single bulk sale the cumulative liability of the buyer for failure to comply with the requirements of Section 6—104(1) may not exceed an amount equal to:

(a) if the assets consist only of inventory and equipment, twice the net contract price, less the amount of any part of the net contract price paid to or applied for the benefit of the seller or a creditor; or

(b) if the assets include property other than inventory and equipment, twice the net value of the inventory and equipment less the amount of the portion of any part of the net contract price paid to or applied for the benefit of the seller or a creditor which is allocable to the inventory and equipment.

(5) For the purposes of subsection (4)(b), the "net value" of an asset is the value of the asset less (i) the amount of any proceeds of the sale of an asset, to the extent the proceeds are applied in partial or total satisfaction of a debt secured by the asset and (ii) the amount of any debt to the extent it is secured by a security interest or lien that is enforceable against the asset before and after it has been sold to a buyer. If a debt is secured by an asset and other property of the seller, the amount of the debt secured by a security interest or lien that is enforceable against the asset is determined by multiplying the debt by a fraction, the numerator

of which is the value of the asset on the date of the bulk sale and the denominator of which is the value of all property securing the debt on the date of the bulk sale. The portion of a part of the net contract price paid to or applied for the benefit of the seller or a creditor that is "allocable to the inventory and equipment" is the portion that bears the same ratio to that part of the net contract price as the net value of the inventory and equipment bears to the net value of all of the assets.

(6) A payment made by the buyer to a person to whom the buyer is, or believes he [or she] is, liable under subsection (1) reduces pro tanto the buyer's cumulative liability under subsection (4).

(7) No action may be brought under subsection (1)(b) by or on behalf of a claimant whose claim is unliquidated or contingent.

(8) A buyer's failure to comply with the requirements of Section 6—104(1) does not (i) impair the buyer's rights in or title to the assets, (ii) render the sale ineffective, void, or voidable, (iii) entitle a creditor to more than a single satisfaction of his [or her] claim, or (iv) create liability other than as provided in this Article.

(9) Payment of the buyer's liability under subsection (1) discharges pro tanto the seller's debt to the creditor.

(10) Unless otherwise agreed, a buyer has an immediate right of reimbursement from the seller for any amount paid to a creditor in partial or total satisfaction of the buyer's liability under subsection (1).

(11) If the seller is an organization, a person who is in direct or indirect control of the seller, and who knowingly, intentionally, and without legal justification fails, or causes the seller to fail, to distribute the net contract price in accordance with the schedule of distribution is liable to any creditor to whom the seller undertook to make payment under the schedule for damages caused by the failure.

§ 6—108. Bulk Sales by Auction; Bulk Sales Conducted by Liquidator.

(1) Sections 6—104, 6—105, 6—106, and 6—107 apply to a bulk sale by auction and a bulk sale conducted by a liquidator on the seller's behalf with the following modifications:

(a) "buyer" refers to auctioneer or liquidator, as the case may be;

(b) "net contract price" refers to net proceeds of the auction or net proceeds of the sale, as the case may be;

(c) the written notice required under Section 6—105(3) must be accompanied by a copy of the schedule of distribution (Section 6—106(1)) and state at least:

(i) that the seller and the auctioneer or liquidator have entered into an agreement for auction or liquidation services that may constitute an agreement to make a bulk sale under the laws of the State of ________ ;

(ii) the date of the agreement;

(iii) the date on or after which the auction began or will begin or the date on or after which the liquidator began or will begin to sell assets on the seller's behalf;

(iv) the date on or after which more than ten percent of the net proceeds of the sale were or will be paid, if the date is not stated in the schedule of distribution;

(v) the name and a mailing address of the seller;

(vi) any other business name and address listed by the seller pursuant to Section 6—104(1)(a);

(vii) the name of the auctioneer or liquidator and an address of the auctioneer or liquidator from which information concerning the sale can be obtained;

(viii) a statement indicating the type of assets or describing the assets item by item;

(ix) the manner in which the auctioneer or liquidator will make available the list of claimants (Section 6—104(1)(f)), if applicable; and

(x) if the sale is in total or partial satisfaction of an antecedent debt owed by the seller, the amount of the debt to be satisfied and the name of the person to whom it is owed; and

(d) in a single bulk sale the cumulative liability of the auctioneer or liquidator for failure to comply with the requirements of this section may not exceed the amount of the net proceeds of the sale allocable to inventory and equipment sold less the amount of the portion of any part of the net proceeds paid to or applied for the benefit of a creditor which is allocable to the inventory and equipment.

(2) A payment made by the auctioneer or liquidator to a person to whom the auctioneer or liquidator is, or believes he [or she] is, liable under this section reduces pro tanto the auctioneer's or liquidator's cumulative liability under subsection (1)(d).

(3) A form substantially as follows is sufficient to comply with subsection (1)(c):

Notice of Sale

(1) ________ , whose address is ________ , is described in this notice as the "seller."

(2) ______ , whose address is ______ , is described in this notice as the "auctioneer" or "liquidator."

(3) The seller has disclosed to the auctioneer or liquidator that within the past three years the seller has used other business names, operated at other addresses, or both, as follows: ________________ .

(4) The seller and the auctioneer or liquidator have entered into an agreement dated ________ for auction or liquidation services that may constitute an agreement to make a bulk sale under the laws of the State of __________ .

(5) The date on or after which the auction began or will begin or the date on or after which the liquidator began or will begin to sell assets on the seller's behalf is ________ , and [if not stated in the schedule of distribution] the date on or after which more than ten percent of the net proceeds of the sale were or will be paid is ________ .

(6) The following assets are the subject of the sale: ________________________________ .

(7) [If applicable] The auctioneer or liquidator will make available to claimants of the seller a list of the seller's claimants in the following manner: ________ .

(8) [If applicable] The sale is to satisfy $ ________ of an antecedent debt owed by the seller to ________ .

(9) A copy of the schedule of distribution of the net proceeds accompanies this notice.

[End of Notice]

(4) A person who buys at a bulk sale by auction or conducted by a liquidator need not comply with the requirements of Section 6—104(1) and is not liable for the failure of an auctioneer or liquidator to comply with the requirements of this section.

§ 6—109. What Constitutes Filing; Duties of Filing Officer; Information from Filing Officer.

(1) Presentation of a notice or list of claimants for filing and tender of the filing fee or acceptance of the notice or list by the filing officer constitutes filing under this Article.

(2) The filing officer shall:

(a) mark each notice or list with a file number and with the date and hour of filing;

(b) hold the notice or list or a copy for public inspection;

(c) index the notice or list according to each name given for the seller and for the buyer; and

(d) note in the index the file number and the addresses of the seller and buyer given in the notice or list.

(3) If the person filing a notice or list furnishes the filing officer with a copy, the filing officer upon request shall note upon the copy the file number and date and hour of the filing of the original and send or deliver the copy to the person.

(4) The fee for filing and indexing and for stamping a copy furnished by the person filing to show the date and place of filing is $ ______ for the first page and $ ______ for each additional page. The fee for indexing each name beyond the first two is $ ________ .

(5) Upon request of any person, the filing officer shall issue a certificate showing whether any notice or list with respect to a particular seller or buyer is on file on the date and hour stated in the certificate. If a notice or list is on file, the certificate must give the date and hour of filing of each notice or list and the name and address of each seller, buyer, auctioneer, or liquidator. The fee for the certificate is $ ________ if the request for the certificate is in the standard form prescribed by the [Secretary of State] and otherwise is $ ________ . Upon request of any person, the filing officer shall furnish a copy of any filed notice or list for a fee of $ ________ .

(6) The filing officer shall keep each notice or list for two years after it is filed.

§ 6—110. Limitation of Actions.

(1) Except as provided in subsection (2), an action under this Article against a buyer, auctioneer, or liquidator must be commenced within one year after the date of the bulk sale.

(2) If the buyer, auctioneer, or liquidator conceals the fact that the sale has occurred, the limitation is tolled and an action under this Article may be commenced within the earlier of (i) one year after the person bringing the action discovers that the sale has occurred or (ii) one year after the person bringing the action should have discovered that the sale has occurred, but no later than two years after the date of the bulk sale. Complete noncompliance with the requirements of this Article does not of itself constitute concealment.

(3) An action under Section 6—107(11) must be commenced within one year after the alleged violation occurs.

Article 7
Warehouse Receipts, Bills of Lading and Other Documents of Title

Part 1 General

§ 7—101. Short Title.

This Article shall be known and may be cited as Uniform Commercial Code—Documents of Title.

§ 7—102. Definitions and Index of Definitions.

(1) In this Article, unless the context otherwise requires:

(a) "Bailee" means the person who by a warehouse receipt, bill of lading or other document of title acknowledges possession of goods and contracts to deliver them.

(b) "Consignee" means the person named in a bill to whom or to whose order the bill promises delivery.

(c) "Consignor" means the person named in a bill as the person from whom the goods have been received for shipment.

(d) "Delivery order" means a written order to deliver goods directed to a warehouseman, carrier or other person who in the ordinary course of business issues warehouse receipts or bills of lading.

(e) "Document" means document of title as defined in the general definitions in Article 1 (Section 1—201).

(f) "Goods" means all things which are treated as movable for the purposes of a contract of storage or transportation.

(g) "Issuer" means a bailee who issues a document except that in relation to an unaccepted delivery order it means the person who orders the possessor of goods to deliver. Issuer includes any person for whom an agent or employee purports to act in issuing a document if the agent or employee has real or apparent authority to issue documents, notwithstanding that the issuer received no goods or that the goods were misdescribed or that in any other respect the agent or employee violated his instructions.

(h) "Warehouseman" is a person engaged in the business of storing goods for hire.

(2) Other definitions applying to this Article or to specified Parts thereof, and the sections in which they appear are:

"Duly negotiate". Section 7—501.

"Person entitled under the document". Section 7—403(4).

(3) Definitions in other Articles applying to this Article and the sections in which they appear are:

"Contract for sale". Section 2—106.

"Overseas". Section 2—323.

"Receipt" of goods. Section 2—103.

(4) In addition Article 1 contains general definitions and principles of construction and interpretation applicable throughout this Article.

§ 7—103. Relation of Article to Treaty, Statute, Tariff, Classification or Regulation.

To the extent that any treaty or statute of the United States, regulatory statute of this State or tariff, classification or regulation filed or issued pursuant thereto is applicable, the provisions of this Article are subject thereto.

§ 7—104. Negotiable and Nonnegotiable Warehouse Receipt, Bill of Lading or Other Document of Title.

(1) A warehouse receipt, bill of lading or other document of title is negotiable

(a) if by its terms the goods are to be delivered to bearer or to the order of a named person; or

(b) where recognized in overseas trade, if it runs to a named person or assigns.

(2) Any other document is nonnegotiable. A bill of lading in which it is stated that the goods are consigned to a named person is not made negotiable by a provision that the goods are to be delivered only against a written order signed by the same or another named person.

§ 7—105. Construction Against Negative Implication.

The omission from either Part 2 or Part 3 of this Article of a provision corresponding to a provision made in the other Part does not imply that a corresponding rule of law is not applicable.

Part 2 Warehouse Receipts: Special Provisions

§ 7—201. Who May Issue a Warehouse Receipt; Storage Under Government Bond.

(1) A warehouse receipt may be issued by any warehouseman.

(2) Where goods including distilled spirits and agricultural commodities are stored under a statute requiring a bond against withdrawal or a license for the issuance of receipts in the nature of warehouse receipts, a receipt issued for the goods has like effect as a warehouse receipt even though issued by a person who is the owner of the goods and is not a warehouseman.

§ 7—202. Form of Warehouse Receipt; Essential Terms; Optional Terms.

(1) A warehouse receipt need not be in any particular form.

(2) Unless a warehouse receipt embodies within its written or printed terms each of the following, the warehouseman is liable for damages caused by the omission to a person injured thereby:

(a) the location of the warehouse where the goods are stored;

(b) the date of issue of the receipt;

(c) the consecutive number of the receipt;

(d) a statement whether the goods received will be delivered to the bearer, to a specified person, or to a specified person or his order;

(e) the rate of storage and handling charges, except that where goods are stored under a field warehousing arrangement a statement of that fact is sufficient on a nonnegotiable receipt;

(f) a description of the goods or of the packages containing them;

(g) the signature of the warehouseman, which may be made by his authorized agent;

(h) if the receipt is issued for goods of which the warehouseman is owner, either solely or jointly or in common with others, the fact of such ownership; and

(i) a statement of the amount of advances made and of liabilities incurred for which the warehouseman claims a lien or security interest (Section 7—209). If the precise amount of such advances made or of such liabilities incurred is, at the time of the issue of the receipt, unknown to the warehouseman or to his agent who issues it, a statement of the fact that advances have been made or liabilities incurred and the purpose thereof is sufficient.

(3) A warehouseman may insert in his receipt any other terms which are not contrary to the provisions of this Act and do not impair his obligation of delivery (Section 7—403) or his duty of care (Section 7—204). Any contrary provisions shall be ineffective.

§ 7—203. Liability for Nonreceipt or Misdescription.

A party to or purchaser for value in good faith of a document of title other than a bill of lading relying in either case upon the description therein of the goods may recover from the issuer damages caused by the nonreceipt or misdescription of the goods, except to the extent that the document conspicuously indicates that the issuer does not know whether any part or all of the goods in fact were received or conform to the description, as where the description is in terms of marks or labels or kind, quantity or condition, or the receipt or description is qualified by "contents, condition and quality unknown", "said to contain" or the like, if such indication be true, or the party or purchaser otherwise has notice.

§ 7—204. Duty of Care; Contractual Limitation of Warehouseman's Liability.

(1) A warehouseman is liable for damages for loss of or injury to the goods caused by his failure to exercise such care in regard to them as a reasonably careful man would exercise under like circumstances but unless otherwise agreed he is not liable for

damages which could not have been avoided by the exercise of such care.

(2) Damages may be limited by a term in the warehouse receipt or storage agreement limiting the amount of liability in case of loss or damage, and setting forth a specific liability per article or item, or value per unit of weight, beyond which the warehouseman shall not be liable; provided, however, that such liability may on written request of the bailor at the time of signing such storage agreement or within a reasonable time after receipt of the warehouse receipt be increased on part or all of the goods thereunder, in which event increased rates may be charged based on such increased valuation, but that no such increase shall be permitted contrary to a lawful limitation of liability contained in the warehouseman's tariff, if any. No such limitation is effective with respect to the warehouseman's liability for conversion to his own use.

(3) Reasonable provisions as to the time and manner of presenting claims and instituting actions based on the bailment may be included in the warehouse receipt or tariff.

(4) This section does not impair or repeal . . .

Note: *Insert in subsection (4) a reference to any statute which imposes a higher responsibility upon the warehouseman or invalidates contractual limitations which would be permissible under this Article.*

§ 7—205. Title Under Warehouse Receipt Defeated in Certain Cases.

A buyer in the ordinary course of business of fungible goods sold and delivered by a warehouseman who is also in the business of buying and selling such goods takes free of any claim under a warehouse receipt even though it has been duly negotiated.

§ 7—206. Termination of Storage at Warehouseman's Option.

(1) A warehouseman may on notifying the person on whose account the goods are held and any other person known to claim an interest in the goods require payment of any charges and removal of the goods from the warehouse at the termination of the period of storage fixed by the document, or, if no period is fixed, within a stated period not less than thirty days after the notification. If the goods are not removed before the date specified in the notification, the warehouseman may sell them in accordance with the provisions of the section on enforcement of a warehouseman's lien (Section 7—210).

(2) If a warehouseman in good faith believes that the goods are about to deteriorate or decline in value to less than the amount of his lien within the time prescribed in subsection (1) for notification, advertisement and sale, the warehouseman may specify in the notification any reasonable shorter time for removal of the goods and in case the goods are not removed, may sell them at public sale held not less than one week after a single advertisement or posting.

(3) If as a result of a quality or condition of the goods of which the warehouseman had no notice at the time of deposit the goods are a hazard to other property or to the warehouse or to persons, the warehouseman may sell the goods at public or private sale without advertisement on reasonable notification to all persons known to claim an interest in the goods. If the warehouseman after a reasonable effort is unable to sell the goods he may dispose of them in any lawful manner and shall incur no liability by reason of such disposition.

(4) The warehouseman must deliver the goods to any person entitled to them under this Article upon due demand made at any time prior to sale or other disposition under this section.

(5) The warehouseman may satisfy his lien from the proceeds of any sale or disposition under this section but must hold the balance for delivery on the demand of any person to whom he would have been bound to deliver the goods.

§ 7—207. Goods Must Be Kept Separate; Fungible Goods.

(1) Unless the warehouse receipt otherwise provides, a warehouseman must keep separate the goods covered by each receipt so as to permit at all times identification and delivery of those goods except that different lots of fungible goods may be commingled.

(2) Fungible goods so commingled are owned in common by the persons entitled thereto and the warehouseman is severally liable to each owner for that owner's share. Where because of overissue a mass of fungible goods is insufficient to meet all the receipts which the warehouseman has issued against it, the persons entitled include all holders to whom overissued receipts have been duly negotiated.

§ 7—208. Altered Warehouse Receipts.

Where a blank in a negotiable warehouse receipt has been filled in without authority, a purchaser for value and without notice of the want of authority may treat the insertion as authorized. Any other unauthorized alteration leaves any receipt enforceable against the issuer according to its original tenor.

§ 7—209. Lien of Warehouseman.

(1) A warehouseman has a lien against the bailor on the goods covered by a warehouse receipt or on the proceeds thereof in his possession for charges for storage or transportation (including demurrage and terminal charges), insurance, labor, or charges present or future in relation to the goods, and for expenses necessary for preservation of the goods or reasonably incurred in their sale pursuant to law. If the person on whose account the goods are held is liable for like charges or expenses in relation to other goods whenever deposited and it is stated in the receipt that a lien is claimed for charges and expenses in relation to other goods, the warehouseman also has a lien against him for such charges and expenses whether or not the other goods have been delivered by the warehouseman. But against a person to whom a negotiable warehouse receipt is duly negotiated a warehouseman's lien is limited to charges in an amount or at a rate specified on the receipt or if no charges are so specified then to a reasonable charge for storage of the goods covered by the receipt subsequent to the date of the receipt.

(2) The warehouseman may also reserve a security interest against the bailor for a maximum amount specified on the receipt for charges other than those specified in subsection (1), such as for money advanced and interest. Such a security interest is gov-

erned by the Article on Secured Transactions (Article 9).

(3)(a) A warehouseman's lien for charges and expenses under subsection (1) or a security interest under subsection (2) is also effective against any person who so entrusted the bailor with possession of the goods that a pledge of them by him to a good faith purchaser for value would have been valid but is not effective against a person as to whom the document confers no right in the goods covered by it under Section 7—503.

(b) A warehouseman's lien on household goods for charges and expenses in relation to the goods under subsection (1) is also effective against all persons if the depositor was the legal possessor of the goods at the time of deposit. "Household goods" means furniture, furnishings and personal effects used by the depositor in a dwelling.

(4) A warehouseman loses his lien on any goods which he voluntarily delivers or which he unjustifiably refuses to deliver.

§ 7—210. Enforcement of Warehouseman's Lien.

(1) Except as provided in subsection (2), a warehouseman's lien may be enforced by public or private sale of the goods in bloc or in parcels, at any time or place and on any terms which are commercially reasonable, after notifying all persons known to claim an interest in the goods. Such notification must include a statement of the amount due, the nature of the proposed sale and the time and place of any public sale. The fact that a better price could have been obtained by a sale at a different time or in a different method from that selected by the warehouseman is not of itself sufficient to establish that the sale was not made in a commercially reasonable manner. If the warehouseman either sells the goods in the usual manner in any recognized market therefor, or if he sells at the price current in such market at the time of his sale, or if he has otherwise sold in conformity with commercially reasonable practices among dealers in the type of goods sold, he has sold in a commercially reasonable manner. A sale of more goods than apparently necessary to be offered to ensure satisfaction of the obligation is not commercially reasonable except in cases covered by the preceding sentence.

(2) A warehouseman's lien on goods other than goods stored by a merchant in the course of his business may be enforced only as follows:

(a) All persons known to claim an interest in the goods must be notified.

(b) The notification must be delivered in person or sent by registered or certified letter to the last known address of any person to be notified.

(c) The notification must include an itemized statement of the claim, a description of the goods subject to the lien, a demand for payment within a specified time not less than ten days after receipt of the notification, and a conspicuous statement that unless the claim is paid within the time the goods will be advertised for sale and sold by auction at a specified time and place.

(d) The sale must conform to the terms of the notification.

(e) The sale must be held at the nearest suitable place to that where the goods are held or stored.

(f) After the expiration of the time given in the notification, an advertisement of the sale must be published once a week for two weeks consecutively in a newspaper of general circulation where the sale is to be held. The advertisement must include a description of the goods, the name of the person on whose account they are being held, and the time and place of the sale. The sale must take place at least fifteen days after the first publication. If there is no newspaper of general circulation where the sale is to be held, the advertisement must be posted at least ten days before the sale in not less than six conspicuous places in the neighborhood of the proposed sale.

(3) Before any sale pursuant to this section any person claiming a right in the goods may pay the amount necessary to satisfy the lien and the reasonable expenses incurred under this section. In that event the goods must not be sold, but must be retained by the warehouseman subject to the terms of the receipt and this Article.

(4) The warehouseman may buy at any public sale pursuant to this section.

(5) A purchaser in good faith of goods sold to enforce a warehouseman's lien takes the goods free of any rights of persons against whom the lien was valid, despite noncompliance by the warehouseman with the requirements of this section.

(6) The warehouseman may satisfy his lien from the proceeds of any sale pursuant to this section but must hold the balance, if any, for delivery on demand to any person to whom he would have been bound to deliver the goods.

(7) The rights provided by this section shall be in addition to all other rights allowed by law to a creditor against his debtor.

(8) Where a lien is on goods stored by a merchant in the course of his business the lien may be enforced in accordance with either subsection (1) or (2).

(9) The warehouseman is liable for damages caused by failure to comply with the requirements for sale under this section and in case of willful violation is liable for conversion.

Part 3 Bills of Lading: Special Provisions

§ 7—301. Liability for Nonreceipt or Misdescription; "Said to Contain"; "Shipper's Load and Count"; Improper Handling.

(1) A consignee of a nonnegotiable bill who has given value in good faith or a holder to whom a negotiable bill has been duly negotiated relying in either case upon the description therein of the goods, or upon the date therein shown, may recover from the issuer damages caused by the misdating of the bill or the nonreceipt or misdescription of the goods, except to the extent that the document indicates that the issuer does not know whether any part of all of the goods in fact were received or conform to the description, as where the description is in terms of marks or

labels or kind, quantity, or condition or the receipt or description is qualified by "contents or condition of contents of packages unknown", "said to contain", "shipper's weight, load and count" or the like, if such indication be true.

(2) When goods are loaded by an issuer who is a common carrier, the issuer must count the packages of goods if package freight and ascertain the kind and quantity if bulk freight. In such cases "shipper's weight, load and count" or other words indicating that the description was made by the shipper are ineffective except as to freight concealed by packages.

(3) When bulk freight is loaded by a shipper who makes available to the issuer adequate facilities for weighing such freight, an issuer who is a common carrier must ascertain the kind and quantity within a reasonable time after receiving the written request of the shipper to do so. In such cases "shipper's weight" or other words of like purport are ineffective.

(4) The issuer may by inserting in the bill the words "shipper's weight, load and count" or other words of like purport indicate that the goods were loaded by the shipper; and if such statement be true the issuer shall not be liable for damages caused by the improper loading. But their omission does not imply liability for such damages.

(5) The shipper shall be deemed to have guaranteed to the issuer the accuracy at the time of shipment of the description, marks, labels, number, kind, quantity, condition and weight, as furnished by him; and the shipper shall indemnify the issuer against damage caused by inaccuracies in such particulars. The right of the issuer to such indemnity shall in no way limit his responsibility and liability under the contract of carriage to any person other than the shipper.

§ 7—302. Through Bills of Lading and Similar Documents.

(1) The issuer of a through bill of lading or other document embodying an undertaking to be performed in part by persons acting as its agents or by connecting carriers is liable to anyone entitled to recover on the document for any breach by such other persons or by a connecting carrier of its obligation under the document but to the extent that the bill covers an undertaking to be performed overseas or in territory not contiguous to the continental United States or an undertaking including matters other than transportation this liability may be varied by agreement of the parties.

(2) Where goods covered by a through bill of lading or other document embodying an undertaking to be performed in part by persons other than the issuer are received by any such person, he is subject with respect to his own performance while the goods are in his possession to the obligation of the issuer. His obligation is discharged by delivery of the goods to another such person pursuant to the document, and does not include liability for breach by any other such persons or by the issuer.

(3) The issuer of such through bill of lading or other document shall be entitled to recover from the connecting carrier or such other person in possession of the goods when the breach of the obligation under the document occurred, the amount it may be required to pay to anyone entitled to recover on the document therefor, as may be evidenced by any receipt, judgment, or transcript thereof, and the amount of any expense reasonably incurred by it in defending any action brought by anyone entitled to recover on the document therefor.

§ 7—303. Diversion; Reconsignment; Change of Instructions.

(1) Unless the bill of lading otherwise provides, the carrier may deliver the goods to a person or destination other than that stated in the bill or may otherwise dispose of the goods on instructions from

(a) the holder of a negotiable bill; or

(b) the consignor on a nonnegotiable bill notwithstanding contrary instructions from the consignee; or

(c) the consignee on a nonnegotiable bill in the absence of contrary instructions from the consignor, if the goods have arrived at the billed destination or if the consignee is in possession of the bill; or

(d) the consignee on a nonnegotiable bill if he is entitled as against the consignor to dispose of them.

(2) Unless such instructions are noted on a negotiable bill of lading, a person to whom the bill is duly negotiated can hold the bailee according to the original terms.

§ 7—304. Bills of Lading in a Set.

(1) Except where customary in overseas transportation, a bill of lading must not be issued in a set of parts. The issuer is liable for damages caused by violation of this subsection.

(2) Where a bill of lading is lawfully drawn in a set of parts, each of which is numbered and expressed to be valid only if the goods have not been delivered against any other part, the whole of the parts constitute one bill.

(3) Where a bill of lading is lawfully issued in a set of parts and different parts are negotiated to different persons, the title of the holder to whom the first due negotiation is made prevails as to both the document and the goods even though any later holder may have received the goods from the carrier in good faith and discharged the carrier's obligation by surrender of his part.

(4) Any person who negotiates or transfers a single part of a bill of lading drawn in a set is liable to holders of that part as if it were the whole set.

(5) The bailee is obliged to deliver in accordance with Part 4 of this Article against the first presented part of a bill of lading lawfully drawn in a set. Such delivery discharges the bailee's obligation on the whole bill.

§ 7—305. Destination Bills.

(1) Instead of issuing a bill of lading to the consignor at the place of shipment a carrier may at the request of the consignor procure the bill to be issued at destination or at any other place designated in the request.

(2) Upon request of anyone entitled as against the carrier to control the goods while in transit and on surrender of any outstanding bill of lading or other receipt covering such goods, the issuer

may procure a substitute bill to be issued at any place designated in the request.

§ 7—306. Altered Bills of Lading.

An unauthorized alteration or filling in of a blank in a bill of lading leaves the bill enforceable according to its original tenor.

§ 7—307. Lien of Carrier.

(1) A carrier has a lien on the goods covered by a bill of lading for charges subsequent to the date of its receipt of the goods for storage or transportation (including demurrage and terminal charges) and for expenses necessary for preservation of the goods incident to their transportation or reasonably incurred in their sale pursuant to law. But against a purchaser for value of a negotiable bill of lading a carrier's lien is limited to charges stated in the bill or the applicable tariffs, or if no charges are stated then to a reasonable charge.

(2) A lien for charges and expenses under subsection (1) on goods which the carrier was required by law to receive for transportation is effective against the consignor or any person entitled to the goods unless the carrier had notice that the consignor lacked authority to subject the goods to such charges and expenses. Any other lien under subsection (1) is effective against the consignor and any person who permitted the bailor to have control or possession of the goods unless the carrier had notice that the bailor lacked such authority.

(3) A carrier loses his lien on any goods which he voluntarily delivers or which he unjustifiably refuses to deliver.

§ 7—308. Enforcement of Carrier's Lien.

(1) A carrier's lien may be enforced by public or private sale of the goods, in bloc or in parcels, at any time or place and on any terms which are commercially reasonable, after notifying all persons known to claim an interest in the goods. Such notification must include a statement of the amount due, the nature of the proposed sale and the time and place of any public sale. The fact that a better price could have been obtained by a sale at a different time or in a different method from that selected by the carrier is not of itself sufficient to establish that the sale was not made in a commercially reasonable manner. If the carrier either sells the goods in the usual manner in any recognized market therefor or if he sells at the price current in such market at the time of his sale or if he has otherwise sold in conformity with commercially reasonable practices among dealers in the type of goods sold he has sold in a commercially reasonable manner. A sale of more goods than apparently necessary to be offered to ensure satisfaction of the obligation is not commercially reasonable except in cases covered by the preceding sentence.

(2) Before any sale pursuant to this section any person claiming a right in the goods may pay the amount necessary to satisfy the lien and the reasonable expenses incurred under this section. In that event the goods must not be sold, but must be retained by the carrier subject to the terms of the bill and this Article.

(3) The carrier may buy at any public sale pursuant to this section.

(4) A purchaser in good faith of goods sold to enforce a carrier's lien takes the goods free of any rights of persons against whom the lien was valid, despite noncompliance by the carrier with the requirements of this section.

(5) The carrier may satisfy his lien from the proceeds of any sale pursuant to this section but must hold the balance, if any, for delivery on demand to any person to whom he would have been bound to deliver the goods.

(6) The rights provided by this section shall be in addition to all other rights allowed by law to a creditor against his debtor.

(7) A carrier's lien may be enforced in accordance with either subsection (1) or the procedure set forth in subsection (2) of Section 7—210.

(8) The carrier is liable for damages caused by failure to comply with the requirements for sale under this section and in case of willful violation is liable for conversion.

§ 7—309. Duty of Care; Contractual Limitation of Carrier's Liability.

(1) A carrier who issues a bill of lading whether negotiable or nonnegotiable must exercise the degree of care in relation to the goods which a reasonably careful man would exercise under like circumstances. This subsection does not repeal or change any law or rule of law which imposes liability upon a common carrier for damages not caused by its negligence.

(2) Damages may be limited by a provision that the carrier's liability shall not exceed a value stated in the document if the carrier's rates are dependent upon value and the consignor by the carrier's tariff is afforded an opportunity to declare a higher value or a value as lawfully provided in the tariff, or where no tariff is filed he is otherwise advised of such opportunity; but no such limitation is effective with respect to the carrier's liability for conversion to its own use.

(3) Reasonable provisions as to the time and manner of presenting claims and instituting actions based on the shipment may be included in a bill of lading or tariff.

Part 4 Warehouse Receipts and Bills of Lading: General Obligations

§ 7—401. Irregularities in Issue of Receipt or Bill or Conduct of Issuer.

The obligations imposed by this Article on an issuer apply to a document of title regardless of the fact that

(a) the document may not comply with the requirements of this Article or of any other law or regulation regarding its issue, form or content; or

(b) the issuer may have violated laws regulating the conduct of his business; or

(c) the goods covered by the document were owned by the bailee at the time the document was issued; or

(d) the person issuing the document does not come within the definition of warehouseman if it purports to be a warehouse receipt.

§ 7—402. Duplicate Receipt or Bill; Overissue.

Neither a duplicate nor any other document of title purporting to cover goods already represented by an outstanding document of the same issuer confers any right in the goods, except as provided in the case of bills in a set, overissue of documents for fungible goods and substitutes for lost, stolen or destroyed documents. But the issuer is liable for damages caused by his overissue or failure to identify a duplicate document as such by conspicuous notation on its face.

§ 7—403. Obligation of Warehouseman or Carrier to Deliver; Excuse.

(1) The bailee must deliver the goods to a person entitled under the document who complies with subsections (2) and (3), unless and to the extent that the bailee establishes any of the following:

(a) delivery of the goods to a person whose receipt was rightful as against the claimant;

(b) damage to or delay, loss or destruction of the goods for which the bailee is not liable [, but the burden of establishing negligence in such cases is on the person entitled under the document];

Note: *The brackets in (1)(b) indicate that State enactments may differ on this point without serious damage to the principle of uniformity.*

(c) previous sale or other disposition of the goods in lawful enforcement of a lien or on warehouseman's lawful termination of storage;

(d) the exercise by a seller of his right to stop delivery pursuant to the provisions of the Article on Sales (Section 2—705);

(e) a diversion, reconsignment or other disposition pursuant to the provisions of this Article (Section 7—303) or tariff regulating such right;

(f) release, satisfaction or any other fact affording a personal defense against the claimant;

(g) any other lawful excuse.

(2) A person claiming goods covered by a document of title must satisfy the bailee's lien where the bailee so requests or where the bailee is prohibited by law from delivering the goods until the charges are paid.

(3) Unless the person claiming is one against whom the document confers no right under Sec. 7—503(1), he must surrender for cancellation or notation of partial deliveries any outstanding negotiable document covering the goods, and the bailee must cancel the document or conspicuously note the partial delivery thereon or be liable to any person to whom the document is duly negotiated.

(4) "Person entitled under the document" means holder in the case of a negotiable document, or the person to whom delivery is to be made by the terms of or pursuant to written instructions under a nonnegotiable document.

§ 7—404. No Liability for Good Faith Delivery Pursuant to Receipt or Bill.

A bailee who in good faith including observance of reasonable commercial standards has received goods and delivered or otherwise disposed of them according to the terms of the document of title or pursuant to this Article is not liable therefor. This rule applies even though the person from whom he received the goods had no authority to procure the document or to dispose of the goods and even though the person to whom he delivered the goods had no authority to receive them.

Part 5 Warehouse Receipts and Bills of Lading: Negotiation and Transfer

§ 7—501. Form of Negotiation and Requirements of "Due Negotiation".

(1) A negotiable document of title running to the order of a named person is negotiated by his indorsement and delivery. After his indorsement in blank or to bearer any person can negotiate it by delivery alone.

(2)(a) A negotiable document of title is also negotiated by delivery alone when by its original terms it runs to bearer.

(b) When a document running to the order of a named person is delivered to him the effect is the same as if the document had been negotiated.

(3) Negotiation of a negotiable document of title after it has been indorsed to a specified person requires indorsement by the special indorsee as well as delivery.

(4) A negotiable document of title is "duly negotiated" when it is negotiated in the manner stated in this section to a holder who purchases it in good faith without notice of any defense against or claim to it on the part of any person and for value, unless it is established that the negotiation is not in the regular course of business or financing or involves receiving the document in settlement or payment of a money obligation.

(5) Indorsement of a nonnegotiable document neither makes it negotiable nor adds to the transferee's rights.

(6) The naming in a negotiable bill of a person to be notified of the arrival of the goods does not limit the negotiability of the bill nor constitute notice to a purchaser thereof of any interest of such person in the goods.

§ 7—502. Rights Acquired by Due Negotiation.

(1) Subject to the following section and to the provisions of Section 7—205 on fungible goods, a holder to whom a negotiable document of title has been duly negotiated acquires thereby:

(a) title to the document;

(b) title to the goods;

(c) all rights accruing under the law of agency or estoppel, including rights to goods delivered to the bailee after the document was issued; and

(d) the direct obligation of the issuer to hold or deliver the goods according to the terms of the document free of any defense or claim by him except those arising under the terms of the document or under this Article. In the case of a delivery order the bailee's obligation accrues only upon acceptance and the obligation acquired by the holder is that the issuer and any indorser will procure the acceptance of the bailee.

(2) Subject to the following section, title and rights so acquired are not defeated by any stoppage of the goods represented by the document or by surrender of such goods by the bailee, and are not impaired even though the negotiation or any prior negotiation constituted a breach of duty or even though any person has been deprived of possession of the document by misrepresentation, fraud, accident, mistake, duress, loss, theft or conversion, or even though a previous sale or other transfer of the goods or document has been made to a third person.

§ 7—503. Document of Title to Goods Defeated in Certain Cases.

(1) A document of title confers no right in goods against a person who before issuance of the document had a legal interest or a perfected security interest in them and who neither

(a) delivered or entrusted them or any document of title covering them to the bailor or his nominee with actual or apparent authority to ship, store or sell or with power to obtain delivery under this Article (Section 7—403) or with power of disposition under this Act (Sections 2—403 and 9—307) or other statute or rule of law; nor

(b) acquiesced in the procurement by the bailor or his nominee of any document of title.

(2) Title to goods based upon an unaccepted delivery order is subject to the rights of anyone to whom a negotiable warehouse receipt or bill of lading covering the goods has been duly negotiated. Such a title may be defeated under the next section to the same extent as the rights of the issuer or a transferee from the issuer.

(3) Title to goods based upon a bill of lading issued to a freight forwarder is subject to the rights of anyone to whom a bill issued by the freight forwarder is duly negotiated; but delivery by the carrier in accordance with Part 4 of this Article pursuant to its own bill of lading discharges the carrier's obligation to deliver.

§ 7—504. Rights Acquired in the Absence of Due Negotiation; Effect of Diversion; Seller's Stoppage of Delivery.

(1) A transferee of a document, whether negotiable or nonnegotiable, to whom the document has been delivered but not duly negotiated, acquires the title and rights which his transferor had or had actual authority to convey.

(2) In the case of a nonnegotiable document, until but not after the bailee receives notification of the transfer, the rights of the transferee may be defeated

(a) by those creditors of the transferor who could treat the sale as void under Section 2—402; or

(b) by a buyer from the transferor in ordinary course of business if the bailee has delivered the goods to the buyer or received notification of his rights; or

(c) as against the bailee by good faith dealings of the bailee with the transferor.

(3) A diversion or other change of shipping instructions by the consignor in a nonnegotiable bill of lading which causes the bailee not to deliver to the consignee defeats the consignee's title to the goods if they have been delivered to a buyer in ordinary course of business and in any event defeats the consignee's rights against the bailee.

(4) Delivery pursuant to a nonnegotiable document may be stopped by a seller under Section 2—705, and subject to the requirement of due notification there provided. A bailee honoring the seller's instructions is entitled to be indemnified by the seller against any resulting loss or expense.

§ 7—505. Indorser Not a Guarantor for Other Parties.

The indorsement of a document of title issued by a bailee does not make the indorser liable for any default by the bailee or by previous indorsers.

§ 7—506. Delivery Without Indorsement: Right to Compel Indorsement.

The transferee of a negotiable document of title has a specifically enforceable right to have his transferor supply any necessary indorsement but the transfer becomes a negotiation only as of the time the indorsement is supplied.

§ 7—507. Warranties on Negotiation or Transfer of Receipt or Bill.

Where a person negotiates or transfers a document of title for value otherwise than as a mere intermediary under the next following section, then unless otherwise agreed he warrants to his immediate purchaser only in addition to any warranty made in selling the goods

(a) that the document is genuine; and

(b) that he has no knowledge of any fact which would impair its validity or worth; and

(c) that his negotiation or transfer is rightful and fully effective with respect to the title to the document and the goods it represents.

§ 7—508. Warranties of Collecting Bank as to Documents.

A collecting bank or other intermediary known to be entrusted with documents on behalf of another or with collection of a draft or other claim against delivery of documents warrants by such delivery of the documents only its own good faith and authority. This rule applies even though the intermediary has purchased or made advances against the claim or draft to be collected.

§ 7—509. Receipt or Bill: When Adequate Compliance With Commercial Contract.

The question whether a document is adequate to fulfill the obligations of a contract for sale or the conditions of a credit is governed by the Articles on Sales (Article 2) and on Letters of Credit (Article 5).

Part 6 Warehouse Receipts and Bills of Lading: Miscellaneous Provisions

§ 7—601. Lost and Missing Documents.

(1) If a document has been lost, stolen or destroyed, a court may order delivery of the goods or issuance of a substitute document and the bailee may without liability to any person comply with such order. If the document was negotiable the claimant must post security approved by the court to indemnify any person who may suffer loss as a result of non-surrender of the document. If the document was not negotiable, such security may be required at the discretion of the court. The court may also in its discretion order payment of the bailee's reasonable costs and counsel fees.

(2) A bailee who without court order delivers goods to a person claiming under a missing negotiable document is liable to any person injured thereby, and if the delivery is not in good faith becomes liable for conversion. Delivery in good faith is not conversion if made in accordance with a filed classification or tariff or, where no classification or tariff is filed, if the claimant posts security with the bailee in an amount at least double the value of the goods at the time of posting to indemnify any person injured by the delivery who files a notice of claim within one year after the delivery.

§ 7—602. Attachment of Goods Covered by a Negotiable Document.

Except where the document was originally issued upon delivery of the goods by a person who had no power to dispose of them, no lien attaches by virtue of any judicial process to goods in the possession of a bailee for which a negotiable document of title is outstanding unless the document be first surrendered to the bailee or its negotiation enjoined, and the bailee shall not be compelled to deliver the goods pursuant to process until the document is surrendered to him or impounded by the court. One who purchases the document for value without notice of the process or injunction takes free of the lien imposed by judicial process.

§ 7—603. Conflicting Claims; Interpleader.

If more than one person claims title or possession of the goods, the bailee is excused from delivery until he has had a reasonable time to ascertain the validity of the adverse claims or to bring an action to compel all claimants to interplead and may compel such interpleader, either in defending an action for nondelivery of the goods, or by original action, whichever is appropriate.

Revised (1994) Article 8 INVESTMENT SECURITIES

Part 1 Short Title and General Matters

§ 8—101. Short Title.

This Article may be cited as Uniform Commercial Code—Investment Securities.

§ 8—102. Definitions.

(a) In this Article:

(1) "Adverse claim" means a claim that a claimant has a property interest in a financial asset and that it is a violation of the rights of the claimant for another person to hold, transfer, or deal with the financial asset.

(2) "Bearer form," as applied to a certificated security, means a form in which the security is payable to the bearer of the security certificate according to its terms but not by reason of an indorsement.

(3) "Broker" means a person defined as a broker or dealer under the federal securities laws, but without excluding a bank acting in that capacity.

(4) "Certificated security" means a security that is represented by a certificate.

(5) "Clearing corporation" means:

(i) a person that is registered as a "clearing agency" under the federal securities laws;

(ii) a federal reserve bank; or

(iii) any other person that provides clearance or settlement services with respect to financial assets that would require it to register as a clearing agency under the federal securities laws but for an exclusion or exemption from the registration requirement, if its activities as a clearing corporation, including promulgation of rules, are subject to regulation by a federal or state governmental authority.

(6) "Communicate" means to:

(i) send a signed writing; or

(ii) transmit information by any mechanism agreed upon by the persons transmitting and receiving the information.

(7) "Entitlement holder" means a person identified in the records of a securities intermediary as the person having a security entitlement against the securities intermediary. If a person acquires a security entitlement by virtue of Section 8—501(b)(2) or (3), that person is the entitlement holder.

(8) "Entitlement order" means a notification communicated to a securities intermediary directing transfer or redemption of a financial asset to which the entitlement holder has a security entitlement.

(9) "Financial asset," except as otherwise provided in Section 8—103, means:

(i) a security;

(ii) an obligation of a person or a share, participation, or other interest in a person or in property or an enterprise of a person, which is, or is of a type, dealt in or traded on financial markets, or which is recognized in any area in which it is issued or dealt in as a medium for investment; or

(iii) any property that is held by a securities intermediary for another person in a securities account if the securities intermediary has expressly agreed with the other person that the property is to be treated as a financial asset under this Article.

As context requires, the term means either the interest itself or the means by which a person's claim to it is evidenced, including a certificated or uncertificated security, a security certificate, or a security entitlement.

(10) "Good faith," for purposes of the obligation of good faith in the performance or enforcement of contracts or duties within this Article, means honesty in fact and the observance of reasonable commercial standards of fair dealing.

(11) "Indorsement" means a signature that alone or accompanied by other words is made on a security certificate in registered form or on a separate document for the purpose of assigning, transferring, or redeeming the security or granting a power to assign, transfer, or redeem it.

(12) "Instruction" means a notification communicated to the issuer of an uncertificated security which directs that the transfer of the security be registered or that the security be redeemed.

(13) "Registered form," as applied to a certificated security, means a form in which:

(i) the security certificate specifies a person entitled to the security; and

(ii) a transfer of the security may be registered upon books maintained for that purpose by or on behalf of the issuer, or the security certificate so states.

(14) "Securities intermediary" means:

(i) a clearing corporation; or

(ii) a person, including a bank or broker, that in the ordinary course of its business maintains securities accounts for others and is acting in that capacity.

(15) "Security," except as otherwise provided in Section 8—103, means an obligation of an issuer or a share, participation, or other interest in an issuer or in property or an enterprise of an issuer:

(i) which is represented by a security certificate in bearer or registered form, or the transfer of which may be registered upon books maintained for that purpose by or on behalf of the issuer;

(ii) which is one of a class or series or by its terms is divisible into a class or series of shares, participations, interests, or obligations; and

(iii) which:

(A) is, or is of a type, dealt in or traded on securities exchanges or securities markets; or

(B) is a medium for investment and by its terms expressly provides that it is a security governed by this Article.

(16) "Security certificate" means a certificate representing a security.

(17) "Security entitlement" means the rights and property interest of an entitlement holder with respect to a financial asset specified in Part 5.

(18) "Uncertificated security" means a security that is not represented by a certificate.

(b) Other definitions applying to this Article and the sections in which they appear are:

Appropriate person	Section 8—107
Control	Section 8—106
Delivery	Section 8—301
Investment company security	Section 8—103
Issuer	Section 8—201
Overissue	Section 8—210
Protected purchaser	Section 8—303
Securities account	Section 8—501

(c) In addition, Article 1 contains general definitions and principles of construction and interpretation applicable throughout this Article.

(d) The characterization of a person, business, or transaction for purposes of this Article does not determine the characterization of the person, business, or transaction for purposes of any other law, regulation, or rule.

§ 8—103. Rules for Determining Whether Certain Obligations and Interests Are Securities or Financial Assets.

(a) A share or similar equity interest issued by a corporation, business trust, joint stock company, or similar entity is a security.

(b) An "investment company security" is a security. "Investment company security" means a share or similar equity interest issued by an entity that is registered as an investment company under the federal investment company laws, an interest in a unit investment trust that is so registered, or a face-amount certificate issued by a face-amount certificate company that is so registered. Investment company security does not include an insurance policy or endowment policy or annuity contract issued by an insurance company.

(c) An interest in a partnership or limited liability company is not a security unless it is dealt in or traded on securities exchanges or in securities markets, its terms expressly provide that it is a security governed by this Article, or it is an investment company security. However, an interest in a partnership or limited liability company is a financial asset if it is held in a securities account.

(d) A writing that is a security certificate is governed by this Article and not by Article 3, even though it also meets the requirements of that Article. However, a negotiable instrument governed by Article 3 is a financial asset if it is held in a securities account.

(e) An option or similar obligation issued by a clearing corporation to its participants is not a security, but is a financial asset.

(f) A commodity contract, as defined in Section 9—115, is not a security or a financial asset.

§ 8—104. Acquisition of Security or Financial Asset or Interest Therein.

(a) A person acquires a security or an interest therein, under this Article, if:

(1) the person is a purchaser to whom a security is delivered pursuant to Section 8—301; or

(2) the person acquires a security entitlement to the security pursuant to Section 8—501.

(b) A person acquires a financial asset, other than a security, or an interest therein, under this Article, if the person acquires a security entitlement to the financial asset.

(c) A person who acquires a security entitlement to a security or other financial asset has the rights specified in Part 5, but is a purchaser of any security, security entitlement, or other financial asset held by the securities intermediary only to the extent provided in Section 8—503.

(d) Unless the context shows that a different meaning is intended, a person who is required by other law, regulation, rule, or agreement to transfer, deliver, present, surrender, exchange, or otherwise put in the possession of another person a security or financial asset satisfies that requirement by causing the other person to acquire an interest in the security or financial asset pursuant to subsection (a) or (b).

§ 8—105. Notice of Adverse Claim.

(a) A person has notice of an adverse claim if:

(1) the person knows of the adverse claim;

(2) the person is aware of facts sufficient to indicate that there is a significant probability that the adverse claim exists and deliberately avoids information that would establish the existence of the adverse claim; or

(3) the person has a duty, imposed by statute or regulation, to investigate whether an adverse claim exists, and the investigation so required would establish the existence of the adverse claim.

(b) Having knowledge that a financial asset or interest therein is or has been transferred by a representative imposes no duty of inquiry into the rightfulness of a transaction and is not notice of an adverse claim. However, a person who knows that a representative has transferred a financial asset or interest therein in a transaction that is, or whose proceeds are being used, for the individual benefit of the representative or otherwise in breach of duty has notice of an adverse claim.

(c) An act or event that creates a right to immediate performance of the principal obligation represented by a security certificate or sets a date on or after which the certificate is to be presented or surrendered for redemption or exchange does not itself constitute notice of an adverse claim except in the case of a transfer more than:

(1) one year after a date set for presentment or surrender for redemption or exchange; or

(2) six months after a date set for payment of money against presentation or surrender of the certificate, if money was available for payment on that date.

(d) A purchaser of a certificated security has notice of an adverse claim if the security certificate:

(1) whether in bearer or registered form, has been indorsed "for collection" or "for surrender" or for some other purpose not involving transfer; or

(2) is in bearer form and has on it an unambiguous statement that it is the property of a person other than the transferor, but the mere writing of a name on the certificate is not such a statement.

(e) Filing of a financing statement under Article 9 is not notice of an adverse claim to a financial asset.

§ 8—106. Control.

(a) A purchaser has "control" of a certificated security in bearer form if the certificated security is delivered to the purchaser.

(b) A purchaser has "control" of a certificated security in registered form if the certificated security is delivered to the purchaser, and:

(1) the certificate is indorsed to the purchaser or in blank by an effective indorsement; or

(2) the certificate is registered in the name of the purchaser, upon original issue or registration of transfer by the issuer.

(c) A purchaser has "control" of an uncertificated security if:

(1) the uncertificated security is delivered to the purchaser; or

(2) the issuer has agreed that it will comply with instructions originated by the purchaser without further consent by the registered owner.

(d) A purchaser has "control" of a security entitlement if:

(1) the purchaser becomes the entitlement holder; or

(2) the securities intermediary has agreed that it will comply with entitlement orders originated by the purchaser without further consent by the entitlement holder.

(e) If an interest in a security entitlement is granted by the entitlement holder to the entitlement holder's own securities intermediary, the securities intermediary has control.

(f) A purchaser who has satisfied the requirements of subsection (c)(2) or (d)(2) has control even if the registered owner in the case of subsection (c)(2) or the entitlement holder in the case of subsection (d)(2) retains the right to make substitutions for the uncertificated security or security entitlement, to originate instructions or entitlement orders to the issuer or securities intermediary, or otherwise to deal with the uncertificated security or security entitlement.

(g) An issuer or a securities intermediary may not enter into an agreement of the kind described in subsection (c)(2) or (d)(2) without the consent of the registered owner or entitlement holder, but an issuer or a securities intermediary is not required to enter into such an agreement even though the registered owner or entitlement holder so directs. An issuer or securities intermediary that has entered into such an agreement is not required to confirm the existence of the agreement to another party unless requested to do so by the registered owner or entitlement holder.

§ 8—107. **Whether Indorsement, Instruction, or Entitlement Order Is Effective.**

(a) "Appropriate person" means:

(1) with respect to an indorsement, the person specified by a security certificate or by an effective special indorsement to be entitled to the security;

(2) with respect to an instruction, the registered owner of an uncertificated security;

(3) with respect to an entitlement order, the entitlement holder;

(4) if the person designated in paragraph (1), (2), or (3) is deceased, the designated person's successor taking under other law or the designated person's personal representative acting for the estate of the decedent; or

(5) if the person designated in paragraph (1), (2), or (3) lacks capacity, the designated person's guardian, conservator, or other similar representative who has power under other law to transfer the security or financial asset.

(b) An indorsement, instruction, or entitlement order is effective if:

(1) it is made by the appropriate person;

(2) it is made by a person who has power under the law of agency to transfer the security or financial asset on behalf of the appropriate person, including, in the case of an instruction or entitlement order, a person who has control under Section 8—106(c)(2) or (d)(2); or

(3) the appropriate person has ratified it or is otherwise precluded from asserting its ineffectiveness.

(c) An indorsement, instruction, or entitlement order made by a representative is effective even if:

(1) the representative has failed to comply with a controlling instrument or with the law of the State having jurisdiction of the representative relationship, including any law requiring the representative to obtain court approval of the transaction; or

(2) the representative's action in making the indorsement, instruction, or entitlement order or using the proceeds of the transaction is otherwise a breach of duty.

(d) If a security is registered in the name of or specially indorsed to a person described as a representative, or if a securities account is maintained in the name of a person described as a representative, an indorsement, instruction, or entitlement order made by the person is effective even though the person is no longer serving in the described capacity.

(e) Effectiveness of an indorsement, instruction, or entitlement order is determined as of the date the indorsement, instruction, or entitlement order is made, and an indorsement, instruction, or entitlement order does not become ineffective by reason of any later change of circumstances.

§ 8—108. **Warranties in Direct Holding.**

(a) A person who transfers a certificated security to a purchaser for value warrants to the purchaser, and an indorser, if the transfer is by indorsement, warrants to any subsequent purchaser, that:

(1) the certificate is genuine and has not been materially altered;

(2) the transferor or indorser does not know of any fact that might impair the validity of the security;

(3) there is no adverse claim to the security;

(4) the transfer does not violate any restriction on transfer;

(5) if the transfer is by indorsement, the indorsement is made by an appropriate person, or if the indorsement is by an agent, the agent has actual authority to act on behalf of the appropriate person; and

(6) the transfer is otherwise effective and rightful.

(b) A person who originates an instruction for registration of transfer of an uncertificated security to a purchaser for value warrants to the purchaser that:

(1) the instruction is made by an appropriate person, or if the instruction is by an agent, the agent has actual authority to act on behalf of the appropriate person;

(2) the security is valid;

(3) there is no adverse claim to the security; and

(4) at the time the instruction is presented to the issuer:

(i) the purchaser will be entitled to the registration of transfer;

(ii) the transfer will be registered by the issuer free from all liens, security interests, restrictions, and claims other than those specified in the instruction;

(iii) the transfer will not violate any restriction on transfer; and

(iv) the requested transfer will otherwise be effective and rightful.

(c) A person who transfers an uncertificated security to a purchaser for value and does not originate an instruction in connection with the transfer warrants that:

(1) the uncertificated security is valid;

(2) there is no adverse claim to the security;

(3) the transfer does not violate any restriction on transfer; and

(4) the transfer is otherwise effective and rightful.

(d) A person who indorses a security certificate warrants to the issuer that:

(1) there is no adverse claim to the security; and

(2) the indorsement is effective.

(e) A person who originates an instruction for registration of transfer of an uncertificated security warrants to the issuer that:

(1) the instruction is effective; and

(2) at the time the instruction is presented to the issuer the purchaser will be entitled to the registration of transfer.

(f) A person who presents a certificated security for registration of transfer or for payment or exchange warrants to the issuer that the person is entitled to the registration, payment, or exchange, but a purchaser for value and without notice of adverse claims to whom transfer is registered warrants only that the person has no knowledge of any unauthorized signature in a necessary indorsement.

(g) If a person acts as agent of another in delivering a certificated security to a purchaser, the identity of the principal was known to the person to whom the certificate was delivered, and the certificate delivered by the agent was received by the agent from the principal or received by the agent from another person at the direction of the principal, the person delivering the security certificate warrants only that the delivering person has authority to act for the principal and does not know of any adverse claim to the certificated security.

(h) A secured party who redelivers a security certificate received, or after payment and on order of the debtor delivers the security certificate to another person, makes only the warranties of an agent under subsection (g).

(i) Except as otherwise provided in subsection (g), a broker acting for a customer makes to the issuer and a purchaser the warranties provided in subsections (a) through (f). A broker that delivers a security certificate to its customer, or causes its customer to be registered as the owner of an uncertificated security, makes to the customer the warranties provided in subsection (a) or (b), and has the rights and privileges of a purchaser under this section. The warranties of and in favor of the broker acting as an agent are in addition to applicable warranties given by and in favor of the customer.

§ 8—109. Warranties in Indirect Holding.

(a) A person who originates an entitlement order to a securities intermediary warrants to the securities intermediary that:

(1) the entitlement order is made by an appropriate person, or if the entitlement order is by an agent, the agent has actual authority to act on behalf of the appropriate person; and

(2) there is no adverse claim to the security entitlement.

(b) A person who delivers a security certificate to a securities intermediary for credit to a securities account or originates an instruction with respect to an uncertificated security directing that the uncertificated security be credited to a securities account makes to the securities intermediary the warranties specified in Section 8—108(a) or (b).

(c) If a securities intermediary delivers a security certificate to its entitlement holder or causes its entitlement holder to be registered as the owner of an uncertificated security, the securities intermediary makes to the entitlement holder the warranties specified in Section 8—108(a) or (b).

§ 8—110. Applicability; Choice of Law.

(a) The local law of the issuer's jurisdiction, as specified in subsection (d), governs:

(1) the validity of a security;

(2) the rights and duties of the issuer with respect to registration of transfer;

(3) the effectiveness of registration of transfer by the issuer;

(4) whether the issuer owes any duties to an adverse claimant to a security; and

(5) whether an adverse claim can be asserted against a person to whom transfer of a certificated or uncertificated security is registered or a person who obtains control of an uncertificated security.

(b) The local law of the securities intermediary's jurisdiction, as specified in subsection (e), governs:

(1) acquisition of a security entitlement from the securities intermediary;

(2) the rights and duties of the securities intermediary and entitlement holder arising out of a security entitlement;

(3) whether the securities intermediary owes any duties to an adverse claimant to a security entitlement; and

(4) whether an adverse claim can be asserted against a person who acquires a security entitlement from the securities intermediary or a person who purchases a security entitlement or interest therein from an entitlement holder.

(c) The local law of the jurisdiction in which a security certificate is located at the time of delivery governs whether an adverse claim can be asserted against a person to whom the security certificate is delivered.

(d) "Issuer's jurisdiction" means the jurisdiction under which the issuer of the security is organized or, if permitted by the law of that jurisdiction, the law of another jurisdiction specified by the issuer. An issuer organized under the law of this State may specify the law of another jurisdiction as the law governing the matters specified in subsection (a)(2) through (5).

(e) The following rules determine a "securities intermediary's jurisdiction" for purposes of this section:

(1) If an agreement between the securities intermediary and its entitlement holder specifies that it is governed by the law of a particular jurisdiction, that jurisdiction is the securities intermediary's jurisdiction.

(2) If an agreement between the securities intermediary and its entitlement holder does not specify the governing law as provided in paragraph (1), but expressly specifies that the securities account is maintained at an office in a particular jurisdiction, that jurisdiction is the securities intermediary's jurisdiction.

(3) If an agreement between the securities intermediary and its entitlement holder does not specify a jurisdiction as provided in paragraph (1) or (2), the securities intermediary's jurisdiction is the jurisdiction in which is located the office identified in an account statement as the office serving the entitlement holder's account.

(4) If an agreement between the securities intermediary and its entitlement holder does not specify a jurisdiction as provided in paragraph (1) or (2) and an account statement does not identify an office serving the entitlement holder's account as provided in paragraph (3), the securities intermediary's jurisdiction is the jurisdiction in which is located the chief executive office of the securities intermediary.

(f) A securities intermediary's jurisdiction is not determined by the physical location of certificates representing financial assets, or by the jurisdiction in which is organized the issuer of the financial asset with respect to which an entitlement holder has a security entitlement, or by the location of facilities for data processing or other record keeping concerning the account.

§ 8—111. Clearing Corporation Rules.

A rule adopted by a clearing corporation governing rights and obligations among the clearing corporation and its participants in the clearing corporation is effective even if the rule conflicts with this [Act] and affects another party who does not consent to the rule.

§ 8—112. Creditor's Legal Process.

(a) The interest of a debtor in a certificated security may be reached by a creditor only by actual seizure of the security certificate by the officer making the attachment or levy, except as otherwise provided in subsection (d). However, a certificated security for which the certificate has been surrendered to the issuer may be reached by a creditor by legal process upon the issuer.

(b) The interest of a debtor in an uncertificated security may be reached by a creditor only by legal process upon the issuer at its chief executive office in the United States, except as otherwise provided in subsection (d).

(c) The interest of a debtor in a security entitlement may be reached by a creditor only by legal process upon the securities intermediary with whom the debtor's securities account is maintained, except as otherwise provided in subsection (d).

(d) The interest of a debtor in a certificated security for which the certificate is in the possession of a secured party, or in an uncertificated security registered in the name of a secured party, or a security entitlement maintained in the name of a secured party, may be reached by a creditor by legal process upon the secured party.

(e) A creditor whose debtor is the owner of a certificated security, uncertificated security, or security entitlement is entitled to aid from a court of competent jurisdiction, by injunction or otherwise, in reaching the certificated security, uncertificated security, or security entitlement or in satisfying the claim by means allowed at law or in equity in regard to property that cannot readily be reached by other legal process.

§ 8—113. Statute of Frauds Inapplicable.

A contract or modification of a contract for the sale or purchase of a security is enforceable whether or not there is a writing signed or record authenticated by a party against whom enforcement is sought, even if the contract or modification is not capable of performance within one year of its making.

§ 8—114. Evidentiary Rules Concerning Certificated Securities.

The following rules apply in an action on a certificated security against the issuer:

(1) Unless specifically denied in the pleadings, each signature on a security certificate or in a necessary indorsement is admitted.

(2) If the effectiveness of a signature is put in issue, the burden of establishing effectiveness is on the party claiming under the signature, but the signature is presumed to be genuine or authorized.

(3) If signatures on a security certificate are admitted or established, production of the certificate entitles a holder to recover on it unless the defendant establishes a defense or a defect going to the validity of the security.

(4) If it is shown that a defense or defect exists, the plaintiff has the burden of establishing that the plaintiff or some person under whom the plaintiff claims is a person against whom the defense or defect cannot be asserted.

§ 8—115. Securities Intermediary and Others Not Liable to Adverse Claimant.

A securities intermediary that has transferred a financial asset pursuant to an effective entitlement order, or a broker or other agent or bailee that has dealt with a financial asset at the direction of its customer or principal, is not liable to a person having an adverse claim to the financial asset, unless the securities intermediary, or broker or other agent or bailee:

(1) took the action after it had been served with an injunction, restraining order, or other legal process enjoining it from doing so, issued by a court of competent jurisdiction, and had a reasonable opportunity to act on the injunction, restraining order, or other legal process; or

(2) acted in collusion with the wrongdoer in violating the rights of the adverse claimant; or

(3) in the case of a security certificate that has been stolen, acted with notice of the adverse claim.

§ 8—116. Securities Intermediary as Purchaser for Value.

A securities intermediary that receives a financial asset and establishes a security entitlement to the financial asset in favor of an entitlement holder is a purchaser for value of the financial asset. A securities intermediary that acquires a security entitlement to a financial asset from another securities intermediary acquires the security entitlement for value if the securities intermediary acquiring the security entitlement establishes a security entitlement to the financial asset in favor of an entitlement holder.

Part 2 Issue and Issuer

§ 8—201. Issuer.

(a) With respect to an obligation on or a defense to a security, an "issuer" includes a person that:

(1) places or authorizes the placing of its name on a security certificate, other than as authenticating trustee, registrar, transfer agent, or the like, to evidence a share, participation, or other interest in its property or in an enterprise, or to evidence its duty to perform an obligation represented by the certificate;

(2) creates a share, participation, or other interest in its property or in an enterprise, or undertakes an obligation, that is an uncertificated security;

(3) directly or indirectly creates a fractional interest in its rights or property, if the fractional interest is represented by a security certificate; or

(4) becomes responsible for, or in place of, another person described as an issuer in this section.

(b) With respect to an obligation on or defense to a security, a guarantor is an issuer to the extent of its guaranty, whether or not its obligation is noted on a security certificate.

(c) With respect to a registration of a transfer, issuer means a person on whose behalf transfer books are maintained.

§ 8—202. Issuer's Responsibility and Defenses; Notice of Defect or Defense.

(a) Even against a purchaser for value and without notice, the terms of a certificated security include terms stated on the certificate and terms made part of the security by reference on the certificate to another instrument, indenture, or document or to a constitution, statute, ordinance, rule, regulation, order, or the like, to the extent the terms referred to do not conflict with terms stated on the certificate. A reference under this subsection does not of itself charge a purchaser for value with notice of a defect going to the validity of the security, even if the certificate expressly states that a person accepting it admits notice. The terms of an uncertificated security include those stated in any instrument, indenture, or document or in a constitution, statute, ordinance, rule, regulation, order, or the like, pursuant to which the security is issued.

(b) The following rules apply if an issuer asserts that a security is not valid:

(1) A security other than one issued by a government or governmental subdivision, agency, or instrumentality, even though issued with a defect going to its validity, is valid in the hands of a purchaser for value and without notice of the particular defect unless the defect involves a violation of a constitutional provision. In that case, the security is valid in the hands of a purchaser for value and without notice of the defect, other than one who takes by original issue.

(2) Paragraph (1) applies to an issuer that is a government or governmental subdivision, agency, or instrumentality only if there has been substantial compliance with the legal requirements governing the issue or the issuer has received a substantial consideration for the issue as a whole or for the particular security and a stated purpose of the issue is one for which the issuer has power to borrow money or issue the security.

(c) Except as otherwise provided in Section 8—205, lack of genuineness of a certificated security is a complete defense, even against a purchaser for value and without notice.

(d) All other defenses of the issuer of a security, including nondelivery and conditional delivery of a certificated security, are ineffective against a purchaser for value who has taken the certificated security without notice of the particular defense.

(e) This section does not affect the right of a party to cancel a contract for a security "when, as and if issued" or "when distributed" in the event of a material change in the character of the security that is the subject of the contract or in the plan or arrangement pursuant to which the security is to be issued or distributed.

(f) If a security is held by a securities intermediary against whom an entitlement holder has a security entitlement with respect to the security, the issuer may not assert any defense that the issuer could not assert if the entitlement holder held the security directly.

§ 8—203. Staleness as Notice of Defect or Defense.

After an act or event, other than a call that has been revoked, creating a right to immediate performance of the principal obligation represented by a certificated security or setting a date on or after which the security is to be presented or surrendered for redemption or exchange, a purchaser is charged with notice of any defect in its issue or defense of the issuer, if the act or event:

(1) requires the payment of money, the delivery of a certificated security, the registration of transfer of an uncertificated security, or any of them on presentation or surrender of the security certificate, the money or security is available on the date set for payment or exchange, and the purchaser takes the security more than one year after that date; or

(2) is not covered by paragraph (1) and the purchaser takes the security more than two years after the date set for surrender or presentation or the date on which performance became due.

§ 8—204. Effect of Issuer's Restriction on Transfer.

A restriction on transfer of a security imposed by the issuer, even if otherwise lawful, is ineffective against a person without knowledge of the restriction unless:

(1) the security is certificated and the restriction is noted conspicuously on the security certificate; or

(2) the security is uncertificated and the registered owner has been notified of the restriction.

§ 8—205. Effect of Unauthorized Signature on Security Certificate.

An unauthorized signature placed on a security certificate before or in the course of issue is ineffective, but the signature is effective in favor of a purchaser for value of the certificated security if the purchaser is without notice of the lack of authority and the signing has been done by:

(1) an authenticating trustee, registrar, transfer agent, or other person entrusted by the issuer with the signing of the security certificate or of similar security certificates, or the immediate preparation for signing of any of them; or

(2) an employee of the issuer, or of any of the persons listed in paragraph (1), entrusted with responsible handling of the security certificate.

§ 8—206. Completion of Alteration of Security Certificate.

(a) If a security certificate contains the signatures necessary to its issue or transfer but is incomplete in any other respect:

(1) any person may complete it by filling in the blanks as authorized; and

(2) even if the blanks are incorrectly filled in, the security certificate as completed is enforceable by a purchaser who took it for value and without notice of the incorrectness.

(b) A complete security certificate that has been improperly altered, even if fraudulently, remains enforceable, but only according to its original terms.

§ 8—207. Rights and Duties of Issuer with Respect to Registered Owners.

(a) Before due presentment for registration of transfer of a certificated security in registered form or of an instruction requesting registration of transfer of an uncertificated security, the issuer or indenture trustee may treat the registered owner as the person exclusively entitled to vote, receive notifications, and otherwise exercise all the rights and powers of an owner.

(b) This Article does not affect the liability of the registered owner of a security for a call, assessment, or the like.

§ 8—208. Effect of Signature of Authenticating Trustee, Registrar, or Transfer Agent.

(a) A person signing a security certificate as authenticating trustee, registrar, transfer agent, or the like, warrants to a purchaser for value of the certificated security, if the purchaser is without notice of a particular defect, that:

(1) the certificate is genuine;

(2) the person's own participation in the issue of the security is within the person's capacity and within the scope of the authority received by the person from the issuer; and

(3) the person has reasonable grounds to believe that the certificated security is in the form and within the amount the issuer is authorized to issue.

(b) Unless otherwise agreed, a person signing under subsection (a) does not assume responsibility for the validity of the security in other respects.

§ 8—209. Issuer's Lien.

A lien in favor of an issuer upon a certificated security is valid against a purchaser only if the right of the issuer to the lien is noted conspicuously on the security certificate.

§ 8—210. Overissue.

(a) In this section, "overissue" means the issue of securities in excess of the amount the issuer has corporate power to issue, but an overissue does not occur if appropriate action has cured the overissue.

(b) Except as otherwise provided in subsections (c) and (d), the provisions of this Article which validate a security or compel its issue or reissue do not apply to the extent that validation, issue, or reissue would result in overissue.

(c) If an identical security not constituting an overissue is reasonably available for purchase, a person entitled to issue or validation may compel the issuer to purchase the security and deliver it if certificated or register its transfer if uncertificated, against surrender of any security certificate the person holds.

(d) If a security is not reasonably available for purchase, a person entitled to issue or validation may recover from the issuer the price the person or the last purchaser for value paid for it with interest from the date of the person's demand.

Part 3 Transfer of Certificated and Uncertificated Securities

§ 8—301. Delivery.

(a) Delivery of a certificated security to a purchaser occurs when:

(1) the purchaser acquires possession of the security certificate;

(2) another person, other than a securities intermediary, either acquires possession of the security certificate on behalf of the purchaser or, having previously acquired possession of the certificate, acknowledges that it holds for the purchaser; or

(3) a securities intermediary acting on behalf of the purchaser acquires possession of the security certificate, only if the certificate is in registered form and has been specially indorsed to the purchaser by an effective indorsement.

(b) Delivery of an uncertificated security to a purchaser occurs when:

(1) the issuer registers the purchaser as the registered owner, upon original issue or registration of transfer; or

(2) another person, other than a securities intermediary, either becomes the registered owner of the uncertificated security on behalf of the purchaser or, having previously become the registered owner, acknowledges that it holds for the purchaser.

§ 8—302. **Rights of Purchaser.**

(a) Except as otherwise provided in subsections (b) and (c), upon delivery of a certificated or uncertificated security to a purchaser, the purchaser acquires all rights in the security that the transferor had or had power to transfer.

(b) A purchaser of a limited interest acquires rights only to the extent of the interest purchased.

(c) A purchaser of a certificated security who as a previous holder had notice of an adverse claim does not improve its position by taking from a protected purchaser.

§ 8—303. **Protected Purchaser.**

(a) "Protected purchaser" means a purchaser of a certificated or uncertificated security, or of an interest therein, who:

(1) gives value;

(2) does not have notice of any adverse claim to the security; and

(3) obtains control of the certificated or uncertificated security.

(b) In addition to acquiring the rights of a purchaser, a protected purchaser also acquires its interest in the security free of any adverse claim.

§ 8—304. **Indorsement.**

(a) An indorsement may be in blank or special. An indorsement in blank includes an indorsement to bearer. A special indorsement specifies to whom a security is to be transferred or who has power to transfer it. A holder may convert a blank indorsement to a special indorsement.

(b) An indorsement purporting to be only of part of a security certificate representing units intended by the issuer to be separately transferable is effective to the extent of the indorsement.

(c) An indorsement, whether special or in blank, does not constitute a transfer until delivery of the certificate on which it appears or, if the indorsement is on a separate document, until delivery of both the document and the certificate.

(d) If a security certificate in registered form has been delivered to a purchaser without a necessary indorsement, the purchaser may become a protected purchaser only when the indorsement is supplied. However, against a transferor, a transfer is complete upon delivery and the purchaser has a specifically enforceable right to have any necessary indorsement supplied.

(e) An indorsement of a security certificate in bearer form may give notice of an adverse claim to the certificate, but it does not otherwise affect a right to registration that the holder possesses.

(f) Unless otherwise agreed, a person making an indorsement assumes only the obligations provided in Section 8—108 and not an obligation that the security will be honored by the issuer.

§ 8—305. **Instruction.**

(a) If an instruction has been originated by an appropriate person but is incomplete in any other respect, any person may complete it as authorized and the issuer may rely on it as completed, even though it has been completed incorrectly.

(b) Unless otherwise agreed, a person initiating an instruction assumes only the obligations imposed by Section 8—108 and not an obligation that the security will be honored by the issuer.

§ 8—306. **Effect of Guaranteeing Signature, Indorsement, or Instruction.**

(a) A person who guarantees a signature of an indorser of a security certificate warrants that at the time of signing:

(1) the signature was genuine;

(2) the signer was an appropriate person to indorse, or if the signature is by an agent, the agent had actual authority to act on behalf of the appropriate person; and

(3) the signer had legal capacity to sign.

(b) A person who guarantees a signature of the originator of an instruction warrants that at the time of signing:

(1) the signature was genuine;

(2) the signer was an appropriate person to originate the instruction, or if the signature is by an agent, the agent had actual authority to act on behalf of the appropriate person, if the person specified in the instruction as the registered owner was, in fact, the registered owner, as to which fact the signature guarantor does not make a warranty; and

(3) the signer had legal capacity to sign.

(c) A person who specially guarantees the signature of an originator of an instruction makes the warranties of a signature guarantor under subsection (b) and also warrants that at the time the instruction is presented to the issuer:

(1) the person specified in the instruction as the registered owner of the uncertificated security will be the registered owner; and

(2) the transfer of the uncertificated security requested in the instruction will be registered by the issuer free from all liens, security interests, restrictions, and claims other than those specified in the instruction.

(d) A guarantor under subsections (a) and (b) or a special guarantor under subsection (c) does not otherwise warrant the rightfulness of the transfer.

(e) A person who guarantees an indorsement of a security certificate makes the warranties of a signature guarantor under subsection (a) and also warrants the rightfulness of the transfer in all respects.

(f) A person who guarantees an instruction requesting the transfer of an uncertificated security makes the warranties of a special signature guarantor under subsection (c) and also warrants the rightfulness of the transfer in all respects.

(g) An issuer may not require a special guaranty of signature, a guaranty of indorsement, or a guaranty of instruction as a condition to registration of transfer.

(h) The warranties under this section are made to a person taking or dealing with the security in reliance on the guaranty, and the guarantor is liable to the person for loss resulting from their breach. An indorser or originator of an instruction whose signature, indorsement, or instruction has been guaranteed is liable to a guarantor for any loss suffered by the guarantor as a result of breach of the warranties of the guarantor.

§ 8—307. Purchaser's Right to Requisites for Registration of Transfer.

Unless otherwise agreed, the transferor of a security on due demand shall supply the purchaser with proof of authority to transfer or with any other requisite necessary to obtain registration of the transfer of the security, but if the transfer is not for value, a transferor need not comply unless the purchaser pays the necessary expenses. If the transferor fails within a reasonable time to comply with the demand, the purchaser may reject or rescind the transfer.

Part 4 Registration

§ 8—401. Duty of Issuer to Register Transfer.

(a) If a certificated security in registered form is presented to an issuer with a request to register transfer or an instruction is presented to an issuer with a request to register transfer of an uncertificated security, the issuer shall register the transfer as requested if:

(1) under the terms of the security the person seeking registration of transfer is eligible to have the security registered in its name;

(2) the indorsement or instruction is made by the appropriate person or by an agent who has actual authority to act on behalf of the appropriate person;

(3) reasonable assurance is given that the indorsement or instruction is genuine and authorized (Section 8—402);

(4) any applicable law relating to the collection of taxes has been complied with;

(5) the transfer does not violate any restriction on transfer imposed by the issuer in accordance with Section 8—204;

(6) a demand that the issuer not register transfer has not become effective under Section 8—403, or the issuer has complied with Section 8—403(b) but no legal process or indemnity bond is obtained as provided in Section 8—403(d); and

(7) the transfer is in fact rightful or is to a protected purchaser.

(b) If an issuer is under a duty to register a transfer of a security, the issuer is liable to a person presenting a certificated security or an instruction for registration or to the person's principal for loss resulting from unreasonable delay in registration or failure or refusal to register the transfer.

§ 8—402. Assurance That Indorsement or Instruction Is Effective.

(a) An issuer may require the following assurance that each necessary indorsement or each instruction is genuine and authorized:

(1) in all cases, a guaranty of the signature of the person making an indorsement or originating an instruction including, in the case of an instruction, reasonable assurance of identity;

(2) if the indorsement is made or the instruction is originated by an agent, appropriate assurance of actual authority to sign;

(3) if the indorsement is made or the instruction is originated by a fiduciary pursuant to Section 8—107(a)(4) or (a)(5), appropriate evidence of appointment or incumbency;

(4) if there is more than one fiduciary, reasonable assurance that all who are required to sign have done so; and

(5) if the indorsement is made or the instruction is originated by a person not covered by another provision of this subsection, assurance appropriate to the case corresponding as nearly as may be to the provisions of this subsection.

(b) An issuer may elect to require reasonable assurance beyond that specified in this section.

(c) In this section:

(1) "Guaranty of the signature" means a guaranty signed by or on behalf of a person reasonably believed by the issuer to be responsible. An issuer may adopt standards with respect to responsibility if they are not manifestly unreasonable.

(2) "Appropriate evidence of appointment or incumbency" means:

(i) in the case of a fiduciary appointed or qualified by a court, a certificate issued by or under the direction or supervision of the court or an officer thereof and dated within 60 days before the date of presentation for transfer; or

(ii) in any other case, a copy of a document showing the appointment or a certificate issued by or on behalf of a person reasonably believed by an issuer to be responsible or, in the absence of that document or certificate, other evidence the issuer reasonably considers appropriate.

§ 8—403. Demand That Issuer Not Register Transfer.

(a) A person who is an appropriate person to make an indorsement or originate an instruction may demand that the issuer not register transfer of a security by communicating to the issuer a notification that identifies the registered owner and the issue of which the security is a part and provides an address for communications directed to the person making the demand. The demand is effective only if it is received by the issuer at a time and in a manner affording the issuer reasonable opportunity to act on it.

(b) If a certificated security in registered form is presented to an issuer with a request to register transfer or an instruction is presented to an issuer with a request to register transfer of an uncertificated security after a demand that the issuer not register transfer has become effective, the issuer shall promptly communicate to (i) the person who initiated the demand at the address provided in the demand and (ii) the person who presented the security for registration of transfer or initiated the instruction requesting registration of transfer a notification stating that:

(1) the certificated security has been presented for registration of transfer or the instruction for registration of transfer of the uncertificated security has been received;

(2) a demand that the issuer not register transfer had previously been received; and

(3) the issuer will withhold registration of transfer for a period of time stated in the notification in order to provide the person who initiated the demand an opportunity to obtain legal process or an indemnity bond.

(c) The period described in subsection (b)(3) may not exceed 30 days after the date of communication of the notification. A shorter period may be specified by the issuer if it is not manifestly unreasonable.

(d) An issuer is not liable to a person who initiated a demand that the issuer not register transfer for any loss the person suffers as a result of registration of a transfer pursuant to an effective indorsement or instruction if the person who initiated the demand does not, within the time stated in the issuer's communication, either:

(1) obtain an appropriate restraining order, injunction, or other process from a court of competent jurisdiction enjoining the issuer from registering the transfer; or

(2) file with the issuer an indemnity bond, sufficient in the issuer's judgment to protect the issuer and any transfer agent, registrar, or other agent of the issuer involved from any loss it or they may suffer by refusing to register the transfer.

(e) This section does not relieve an issuer from liability for registering transfer pursuant to an indorsement or instruction that was not effective.

§ 8—404. **Wrongful Registration.**

(a) Except as otherwise provided in Section 8—406, an issuer is liable for wrongful registration of transfer if the issuer has registered a transfer of a security to a person not entitled to it, and the transfer was registered:

(1) pursuant to an ineffective indorsement or instruction;

(2) after a demand that the issuer not register transfer became effective under Section 8—403(a) and the issuer did not comply with Section 8—403(b);

(3) after the issuer had been served with an injunction, restraining order, or other legal process enjoining it from registering the transfer, issued by a court of competent jurisdiction, and the issuer had a reasonable opportunity to act on the injunction, restraining order, or other legal process; or

(4) by an issuer acting in collusion with the wrongdoer.

(b) An issuer that is liable for wrongful registration of transfer under subsection (a) on demand shall provide the person entitled to the security with a like certificated or uncertificated security, and any payments or distributions that the person did not receive as a result of the wrongful registration. If an overissue would result, the issuer's liability to provide the person with a like security is governed by Section 8—210.

(c) Except as otherwise provided in subsection (a) or in a law relating to the collection of taxes, an issuer is not liable to an owner or other person suffering loss as a result of the registration of a transfer of a security if registration was made pursuant to an effective indorsement or instruction.

§ 8—405. **Replacement of Lost, Destroyed, or Wrongfully Taken Security Certificate.**

(a) If an owner of a certificated security, whether in registered or bearer form, claims that the certificate has been lost, destroyed, or wrongfully taken, the issuer shall issue a new certificate if the owner:

(1) so requests before the issuer has notice that the certificate has been acquired by a protected purchaser;

(2) files with the issuer a sufficient indemnity bond; and

(3) satisfies other reasonable requirements imposed by the issuer.

(b) If, after the issue of a new security certificate, a protected purchaser of the original certificate presents it for registration of transfer, the issuer shall register the transfer unless an overissue would result. In that case, the issuer's liability is governed by Section 8—210. In addition to any rights on the indemnity bond, an issuer may recover the new certificate from a person to whom it was issued or any person taking under that person, except a protected purchaser.

§ 8—406. **Obligation to Notify Issuer of Lost, Destroyed, or Wrongfully Taken Security Certificate.**

If a security certificate has been lost, apparently destroyed, or wrongfully taken, and the owner fails to notify the issuer of that fact within a reasonable time after the owner has notice of it and the issuer registers a transfer of the security before receiving notification, the owner may not assert against the issuer a claim for registering the transfer under Section 8–404 or a claim to a new security certificate under Section 8–405.

§ 8—407. Authenticating Trustee, Transfer Agent, and Registrar.

A person acting as authenticating trustee, transfer agent, registrar, or other agent for an issuer in the registration of a transfer of its securities, in the issue of new security certificates or uncertificated securities, or in the cancellation of surrendered security certificates has the same obligation to the holder or owner of a certificated or uncertificated security with regard to the particular functions performed as the issuer has in regard to those functions.

Part 5 Security Entitlements

§ 8—501. Securities Account; Acquisition of Security Entitlement from Securities Intermediary.

(a) "Securities account" means an account to which a financial asset is or may be credited in accordance with an agreement under which the person maintaining the account undertakes to treat the person for whom the account is maintained as entitled to exercise the rights that comprise the financial asset.

(b) Except as otherwise provided in subsections (d) and (e), a person acquires a security entitlement if a securities intermediary:

(1) indicates by book entry that a financial asset has been credited to the person's securities account;

(2) receives a financial asset from the person or acquires a financial asset for the person and, in either case, accepts it for credit to the person's securities account; or

(3) becomes obligated under other law, regulation, or rule to credit a financial asset to the person's securities account.

(c) If a condition of subsection (b) has been met, a person has a security entitlement even though the securities intermediary does not itself hold the financial asset.

(d) If a securities intermediary holds a financial asset for another person, and the financial asset is registered in the name of, payable to the order of, or specially indorsed to the other person, and has not been indorsed to the securities intermediary or in blank, the other person is treated as holding the financial asset directly rather than as having a security entitlement with respect to the financial asset.

(e) Issuance of a security is not establishment of a security entitlement.

§ 8—502. Assertion of Adverse Claim against Entitlement Holder.

An action based on an adverse claim to a financial asset, whether framed in conversion, replevin, constructive trust, equitable lien, or other theory, may not be asserted against a person who acquires a security entitlement under Section 8—501 for value and without notice of the adverse claim.

§ 8—503. Property Interest of Entitlement Holder in Financial Asset Held by Securities Intermediary.

(a) To the extent necessary for a securities intermediary to satisfy all security entitlements with respect to a particular financial asset, all interests in that financial asset held by the securities intermediary are held by the securities intermediary for the entitlement holders, are not property of the securities intermediary, and are not subject to claims of creditors of the securities intermediary, except as otherwise provided in Section 8—511.

(b) An entitlement holder's property interest with respect to a particular financial asset under subsection (a) is a pro rata property interest in all interests in that financial asset held by the securities intermediary, without regard to the time the entitlement holder acquired the security entitlement or the time the securities intermediary acquired the interest in that financial asset.

(c) An entitlement holder's property interest with respect to a particular financial asset under subsection (a) may be enforced against the securities intermediary only by exercise of the entitlement holder's rights under Sections 8—505 through 8—508.

(d) An entitlement holder's property interest with respect to a particular financial asset under subsection (a) may be enforced against a purchaser of the financial asset or interest therein only if:

(1) insolvency proceedings have been initiated by or against the securities intermediary;

(2) the securities intermediary does not have sufficient interests in the financial asset to satisfy the security entitlements of all of its entitlement holders to that financial asset;

(3) the securities intermediary violated its obligations under Section 8—504 by transferring the financial asset or interest therein to the purchaser; and

(4) the purchaser is not protected under subsection (e).

The trustee or other liquidator, acting on behalf of all entitlement holders having security entitlements with respect to a particular financial asset, may recover the financial asset, or interest therein, from the purchaser. If the trustee or other liquidator elects not to pursue that right, an entitlement holder whose security entitlement remains unsatisfied has the right to recover its interest in the financial asset from the purchaser.

(e) An action based on the entitlement holder's property interest with respect to a particular financial asset under subsection (a), whether framed in conversion, replevin, constructive trust, equitable lien, or other theory, may not be asserted against any purchaser of a financial asset or interest therein who gives value, obtains control, and does not act in collusion with the securities intermediary in violating the securities intermediary's obligations under Section 8—504.

§ 8—504. Duty of Securities Intermediary to Maintain Financial Asset.

(a) A securities intermediary shall promptly obtain and thereafter maintain a financial asset in a quantity corresponding to the aggregate of all security entitlements it has established in favor of its entitlement holders with respect to that financial asset. The securities intermediary may maintain those financial assets directly or through one or more other securities intermediaries.

(b) Except to the extent otherwise agreed by its entitlement holder, a securities intermediary may not grant any security interests in a financial asset it is obligated to maintain pursuant to subsection (a).

(c) A securities intermediary satisfies the duty in subsection (a) if:

(1) the securities intermediary acts with respect to the duty as agreed upon by the entitlement holder and the securities intermediary; or

(2) in the absence of agreement, the securities intermediary exercises due care in accordance with reasonable commercial standards to obtain and maintain the financial asset.

(d) This section does not apply to a clearing corporation that is itself the obligor of an option or similar obligation to which its entitlement holders have security entitlements.

§ 8—505. Duty of Securities Intermediary with Respect to Payments and Distributions.

(a) A securities intermediary shall take action to obtain a payment or distribution made by the issuer of a financial asset. A securities intermediary satisfies the duty if:

(1) the securities intermediary acts with respect to the duty as agreed upon by the entitlement holder and the securities intermediary; or

(2) in the absence of agreement, the securities intermediary exercises due care in accordance with reasonable commercial standards to attempt to obtain the payment or distribution.

(b) A securities intermediary is obligated to its entitlement holder for a payment or distribution made by the issuer of a financial asset if the payment or distribution is received by the securities intermediary.

§ 8—506. Duty of Securities Intermediary to Exercise Rights as Directed by Entitlement Holder.

A securities intermediary shall exercise rights with respect to a financial asset if directed to do so by an entitlement holder. A securities intermediary satisfies the duty if:

(1) the securities intermediary acts with respect to the duty as agreed upon by the entitlement holder and the securities intermediary; or

(2) in the absence of agreement, the securities intermediary either places the entitlement holder in a position to exercise the rights directly or exercises due care in accordance with reasonable commercial standards to follow the direction of the entitlement holder.

§ 8—507. Duty of Securities Intermediary to Comply with Entitlement Order.

(a) A securities intermediary shall comply with an entitlement order if the entitlement order is originated by the appropriate person, the securities intermediary has had reasonable opportunity to assure itself that the entitlement order is genuine and authorized, and the securities intermediary has had reasonable opportunity to comply with the entitlement order. A securities intermediary satisfies the duty if:

(1) the securities intermediary acts with respect to the duty as agreed upon by the entitlement holder and the securities intermediary; or

(2) in the absence of agreement, the securities intermediary exercises due care in accordance with reasonable commercial standards to comply with the entitlement order.

(b) If a securities intermediary transfers a financial asset pursuant to an ineffective entitlement order, the securities intermediary shall reestablish a security entitlement in favor of the person entitled to it, and pay or credit any payments or distributions that the person did not receive as a result of the wrongful transfer. If the securities intermediary does not reestablish a security entitlement, the securities intermediary is liable to the entitlement holder for damages.

§ 8—508. Duty of Securities Intermediary to Change Entitlement Holder's Position to Other Form of Security Holding.

A securities intermediary shall act at the direction of an entitlement holder to change a security entitlement into another available form of holding for which the entitlement holder is eligible, or to cause the financial asset to be transferred to a securities account of the entitlement holder with another securities intermediary. A securities intermediary satisfies the duty if:

(1) the securities intermediary acts as agreed upon by the entitlement holder and the securities intermediary; or

(2) in the absence of agreement, the securities intermediary exercises due care in accordance with reasonable commercial standards to follow the direction of the entitlement holder.

§ 8—509. Specification of Duties of Securities Intermediary by Other Statute or Regulation; Manner of Performance of Duties of Securities Intermediary and Exercise of Rights of Entitlement Holder.

(a) If the substance of a duty imposed upon a securities intermediary by Sections 8—504 through 8—508 is the subject of other statute, regulation, or rule, compliance with that statute, regulation, or rule satisfies the duty.

(b) To the extent that specific standards for the performance of the duties of a securities intermediary or the exercise of the rights of an entitlement holder are not specified by other statute, regulation, or rule or by agreement between the securities intermediary and entitlement holder, the securities intermediary shall perform its duties and the entitlement holder shall exercise its rights in a commercially reasonable manner.

(c) The obligation of a securities intermediary to perform the duties imposed by Sections 8—504 through 8—508 is subject to:

(1) rights of the securities intermediary arising out of a security interest under a security agreement with the entitlement holder or otherwise; and

(2) rights of the securities intermediary under other law, regulation, rule, or agreement to withhold performance of its

duties as a result of unfulfilled obligations of the entitlement holder to the securities intermediary.

(d) Sections 8—504 through 8—508 do not require a securities intermediary to take any action that is prohibited by other statute, regulation, or rule.

§ 8—510. Rights of Purchaser of Security Entitlement from Entitlement Holder.

(a) An action based on an adverse claim to a financial asset or security entitlement, whether framed in conversion, replevin, constructive trust, equitable lien, or other theory, may not be asserted against a person who purchases a security entitlement, or an interest therein, from an entitlement holder if the purchaser gives value, does not have notice of the adverse claim, and obtains control.

(b) If an adverse claim could not have been asserted against an entitlement holder under Section 8—502, the adverse claim cannot be asserted against a person who purchases a security entitlement, or an interest therein, from the entitlement holder.

(c) In a case not covered by the priority rules in Article 9, a purchaser for value of a security entitlement, or an interest therein, who obtains control has priority over a purchaser of a security entitlement, or an interest therein, who does not obtain control. Purchasers who have control rank equally, except that a securities intermediary as purchaser has priority over a conflicting purchaser who has control unless otherwise agreed by the securities intermediary.

§ 8—511. Priority among Security Interests and Entitlement Holders.

(a) Except as otherwise provided in subsections (b) and (c), if a securities intermediary does not have sufficient interests in a particular financial asset to satisfy both its obligations to entitlement holders who have security entitlements to that financial asset and its obligation to a creditor of the securities intermediary who has a security interest in that financial asset, the claims of entitlement holders, other than the creditor, have priority over the claim of the creditor.

(b) A claim of a creditor of a securities intermediary who has a security interest in a financial asset held by a securities intermediary has priority over claims of the securities intermediary's entitlement holders who have security entitlements with respect to that financial asset if the creditor has control over the financial asset.

(c) If a clearing corporation does not have sufficient financial assets to satisfy both its obligations to entitlement holders who have security entitlements with respect to a financial asset and its obligation to a creditor of the clearing corporation who has a security interest in that financial asset, the claim of the creditor has priority over the claims of entitlement holders.

Part 6 Transition Provisions for Revised Article 8

§ 8—601. Effective Date.

This [Act] takes effect....

§ 8—602. Repeals.

This [Act] repeals....

§ 8—603. Savings Clause.

(a) This [Act] does not affect an action or proceeding commenced before this [Act] takes effect.

(b) If a security interest in a security is perfected at the date this [Act] takes effect, and the action by which the security interest was perfected would suffice to perfect a security interest under this [Act], no further action is required to continue perfection. If a security interest in a security is perfected at the date this [Act] takes effect but the action by which the security interest was perfected would not suffice to perfect a security interest under this [Act], the security interest remains perfected for a period of four months after the effective date and continues perfected thereafter if appropriate action to perfect under this [Act] is taken within that period. If a security interest is perfected at the date this [Act] takes effect and the security interest can be perfected by filing under this [Act], a financing statement signed by the secured party instead of the debtor may be filed within that period to continue perfection or thereafter to perfect.

Revised (1999) Article 9 SECURED TRANSACTIONS

Part 1 General Provisions

[Subpart 1. Short Title, Definitions, and General Concepts]

§ 9—101. Short Title.

This article may be cited as Uniform Commercial Code—Secured Transactions.

§ 9—102. Definitions and Index of Definitions.

(a) In this article:

(1) "Accession" means goods that are physically united with other goods in such a manner that the identity of the original goods is not lost.

(2) "Account", except as used in "account for", means a right to payment of a monetary obligation, whether or not earned by performance, (i) for property that has been or is to be sold, leased, licensed, assigned, or otherwise disposed of, (ii) for services rendered or to be rendered, (iii) for a policy of insurance issued or to be issued, (iv) for a secondary obligation incurred or to be incurred, (v) for energy provided or to be provided, (vi) for the use or hire of a vessel under a charter or other contract, (vii) arising out of the use of a credit or charge card or information contained on or for use with the card, or (viii) as winnings in a lottery or other game of chance operated or sponsored by a State, governmental unit of a State, or person licensed or authorized to operate the game by a State or governmental unit of a State. The term includes health-care insurance receivables. The term does not include (i) rights to

payment evidenced by chattel paper or an instrument, (ii) commercial tort claims, (iii) deposit accounts, (iv) investment property, (v) letter-of-credit rights or letters of credit, or (vi) rights to payment for money or funds advanced or sold, other than rights arising out of the use of a credit or charge card or information contained on or for use with the card.

(3) "Account debtor" means a person obligated on an account, chattel paper, or general intangible. The term does not include persons obligated to pay a negotiable instrument, even if the instrument constitutes part of chattel paper.

(4) "Accounting", except as used in "accounting for", means a record:

(A) authenticated by a secured party;

(B) indicating the aggregate unpaid secured obligations as of a date not more than 35 days earlier or 35 days later than the date of the record; and

(C) identifying the components of the obligations in reasonable detail.

(5) "Agricultural lien" means an interest, other than a security interest, in farm products:

(A) which secures payment or performance of an obligation for:

(i) goods or services furnished in connection with a debtor's farming operation; or

(ii) rent on real property leased by a debtor in connection with its farming operation;

(B) which is created by statute in favor of a person that:

(i) in the ordinary course of its business furnished goods or services to a debtor in connection with a debtor's farming operation; or

(ii) leased real property to a debtor in connection with the debtor's farming operation; and

(C) whose effectiveness does not depend on the person's possession of the personal property.

(6) "As-extracted collateral" means:

(A) oil, gas, or other minerals that are subject to a security interest that:

(i) is created by a debtor having an interest in the minerals before extraction; and

(ii) attaches to the minerals as extracted; or

(B) accounts arising out of the sale at the wellhead or minehead of oil, gas, or other minerals in which the debtor had an interest before extraction.

(7) "Authenticate" means:

(A) to sign; or

(B) to execute or otherwise adopt a symbol, or encrypt or similarly process a record in whole or in part, with the present intent of the authenticating person to identify the person and adopt or accept a record.

(8) "Bank" means an organization that is engaged in the business of banking. The term includes savings banks, savings and loan associations, credit unions, and trust companies.

(9) "Cash proceeds" means proceeds that are money, checks, deposit accounts, or the like.

(10) "Certificate of title" means a certificate of title with respect to which a statute provides for the security interest in question to be indicated on the certificate as a condition or result of the security interest's obtaining priority over the rights of a lien creditor with respect to the collateral.

(11) "Chattel paper" means a record or records that evidence both a monetary obligation and a security interest in specific goods, a security interest in specific goods and software used in the goods, a security interest in specific goods and license of software used in the goods, a lease of specific goods, or a lease of specific goods and license of software used in the goods. In this paragraph, "monetary obligation" means a monetary obligation secured by the goods or owed under a lease of the goods and includes a monetary obligation with respect to software used in the goods. The term does not include (i) charters or other contracts involving the use or hire of a vessel or (ii) records that evidence a right to payment arising out of the use of a credit or charge card or information contained on or for use with the card. If a transaction is evidenced by records that include an instrument or series of instruments, the group of records taken together constitutes chattel paper.

(12) "Collateral" means the property subject to a security interest or agricultural lien. The term includes:

(A) proceeds to which a security interest attaches;

(B) accounts, chattel paper, payment intangibles, and promissory notes that have been sold; and

(C) goods that are the subject of a consignment.

(13) "Commercial tort claim" means a claim arising in tort with respect to which:

(A) the claimant is an organization; or

(B) the claimant is an individual and the claim:

(i) arose in the course of the claimant's business or profession; and

(ii) does not include damages arising out of personal injury to or the death of an individual.

(14) "Commodity account" means an account maintained by a commodity intermediary in which a commodity contract is carried for a commodity customer.

(15) "Commodity contract" means a commodity futures contract, an option on a commodity futures contract, a commodity option, or another contract if the contract or option is:

(A) traded on or subject to the rules of a board of trade that has been designated as a contract market for such a contract pursuant to federal commodities laws; or

(B) traded on a foreign commodity board of trade, exchange, or market, and is carried on the books of a commodity intermediary for a commodity customer.

(16) "Commodity customer" means a person for which a commodity intermediary carries a commodity contract on its books.

(17) "Commodity intermediary" means a person that:

(A) is registered as a futures commission merchant under federal commodities law; or

(B) in the ordinary course of its business provides clearance or settlement services for a board of trade that has been designated as a contract market pursuant to federal commodities law.

(18) "Communicate" means:

(A) to send a written or other tangible record;

(B) to transmit a record by any means agreed upon by the persons sending and receiving the record; or

(C) in the case of transmission of a record to or by a filing office, to transmit a record by any means prescribed by filing-office rule.

(19) "Consignee" means a merchant to which goods are delivered in a consignment.

(20) "Consignment" means a transaction, regardless of its form, in which a person delivers goods to a merchant for the purpose of sale and:

(A) the merchant:

(i) deals in goods of that kind under a name other than the name of the person making delivery;

(ii) is not an auctioneer; and

(iii) is not generally known by its creditors to be substantially engaged in selling the goods of others;

(B) with respect to each delivery, the aggregate value of the goods is $1,000 or more at the time of delivery;

(C) the goods are not consumer goods immediately before delivery; and

(D) the transaction does not create a security interest that secures an obligation.

(21) "Consignor" means a person that delivers goods to a consignee in a consignment.

(22) "Consumer debtor" means a debtor in a consumer transaction.

(23) "Consumer goods" means goods that are used or bought for use primarily for personal, family, or household purposes.

(24) "Consumer-goods transaction" means a consumer transaction in which:

(A) an individual incurs an obligation primarily for personal, family, or household purposes; and

(B) a security interest in consumer goods secures the obligation.

(25) "Consumer obligor" means an obligor who is an individual and who incurred the obligation as part of a transaction entered into primarily for personal, family, or household purposes.

(26) "Consumer transaction" means a transaction in which (i) an individual incurs an obligation primarily for personal, family, or household purposes, (ii) a security interest secures the obligation, and (iii) the collateral is held or acquired primarily for personal, family, or household purposes. The term includes consumer-goods transactions.

(27) "Continuation statement" means an amendment of a financing statement which:

(A) identifies, by its file number, the initial financing statement to which it relates; and

(B) indicates that it is a continuation statement for, or that it is filed to continue the effectiveness of, the identified financing statement.

(28) "Debtor" means:

(A) a person having an interest, other than a security interest or other lien, in the collateral, whether or not the person is an obligor;

(B) a seller of accounts, chattel paper, payment intangibles, or promissory notes; or

(C) a consignee.

(29) "Deposit account" means a demand, time, savings, passbook, or similar account maintained with a bank. The term does not include investment property or accounts evidenced by an instrument.

(30) "Document" means a document of title or a receipt of the type described in Section 7—201(2).

(31) "Electronic chattel paper" means chattel paper evidenced by a record or records consisting of information stored in an electronic medium.

(32) "Encumbrance" means a right, other than an ownership interest, in real property. The term includes mortgages and other liens on real property.

(33) "Equipment" means goods other than inventory, farm products, or consumer goods.

(34) "Farm products" means goods, other than standing timber, with respect to which the debtor is engaged in a farming operation and which are:

(A) crops grown, growing, or to be grown, including:

(i) crops produced on trees, vines, and bushes; and

(ii) aquatic goods produced in aquacultural operations;

(B) livestock, born or unborn, including aquatic goods produced in aquacultural operations;

(C) supplies used or produced in a farming operation; or

(D) products of crops or livestock in their unmanufactured states.

(35) "Farming operation" means raising, cultivating, propagating, fattening, grazing, or any other farming, livestock, or aquacultural operation.

(36) "File number" means the number assigned to an initial financing statement pursuant to Section 9—519(a).

(37) "Filing office" means an office designated in Section 9—501 as the place to file a financing statement.

(38) "Filing-office rule" means a rule adopted pursuant to Section 9—526.

(39) "Financing statement" means a record or records composed of an initial financing statement and any filed record relating to the initial financing statement.

(40) "Fixture filing" means the filing of a financing statement covering goods that are or are to become fixtures and satisfying Section 9—502(a) and (b). The term includes the filing of a financing statement covering goods of a transmitting utility which are or are to become fixtures.

(41) "Fixtures" means goods that have become so related to particular real property that an interest in them arises under real property law.

(42) "General intangible" means any personal property, including things in action, other than accounts, chattel paper, commercial tort claims, deposit accounts, documents, goods, instruments, investment property, letter-of-credit rights, letters of credit, money, and oil, gas, or other minerals before extraction. The term includes payment intangibles and software.

(43) "Good faith" means honesty in fact and the observance of reasonable commercial standards of fair dealing.

(44) "Goods" means all things that are movable when a security interest attaches. The term includes (i) fixtures, (ii) standing timber that is to be cut and removed under a conveyance or contract for sale, (iii) the unborn young of animals, (iv) crops grown, growing, or to be grown, even if the crops are produced on trees, vines, or bushes, and (v) manufactured homes. The term also includes a computer program embedded in goods and any supporting information provided in connection with a transaction relating to the program if (i) the program is associated with the goods in such a manner that it customarily is considered part of the goods, or (ii) by becoming the owner of the goods, a person acquires a right to use the program in connection with the goods. The term does not include a computer program embedded in goods that consist solely of the medium in which the program is embedded. The term also does not include accounts, chattel paper, commercial tort claims, deposit accounts, documents, general intangibles, instruments, investment property, letter-of-credit rights, letters of credit, money, or oil, gas, or other minerals before extraction.

(45) "Governmental unit" means a subdivision, agency, department, county, parish, municipality, or other unit of the government of the United States, a State, or a foreign country. The term includes an organization having a separate corporate existence if the organization is eligible to issue debt on which interest is exempt from income taxation under the laws of the United States.

(46) "Health-care-insurance receivable" means an interest in or claim under a policy of insurance which is a right to payment of a monetary obligation for health-care goods or services provided.

(47) "Instrument" means a negotiable instrument or any other writing that evidences a right to the payment of a monetary obligation, is not itself a security agreement or lease, and is of a type that in ordinary course of business is transferred by delivery with any necessary indorsement or assignment. The term does not include (i) investment property, (ii) letters of credit, or (iii) writings that evidence a right to payment arising out of the use of a credit or charge card or information contained on or for use with the card.

(48) "Inventory" means goods, other than farm products, which:

(A) are leased by a person as lessor;

(B) are held by a person for sale or lease or to be furnished under a contract of service;

(C) are furnished by a person under a contract of service; or

(D) consist of raw materials, work in process, or materials used or consumed in a business.

(49) "Investment property" means a security, whether certificated or uncertificated, security entitlement, securities account, commodity contract, or commodity account.

(50) "Jurisdiction of organization", with respect to a registered organization, means the jurisdiction under whose law the organization is organized.

(51) "Letter-of-credit right" means a right to payment or performance under a letter of credit, whether or not the beneficiary has demanded or is at the time entitled to demand payment or performance. The term does not include the right of a beneficiary to demand payment or performance under a letter of credit.

(52) "Lien creditor" means:

(A) a creditor that has acquired a lien on the property involved by attachment, levy, or the like;

(B) an assignee for benefit of creditors from the time of assignment;

(C) a trustee in bankruptcy from the date of the filing of the petition; or

(D) a receiver in equity from the time of appointment.

(53) "Manufactured home" means a structure, transportable in one or more sections, which, in the traveling mode, is eight body feet or more in width or 40 body feet or more in length, or, when erected on site, is 320 or more square feet, and which is built on a permanent chassis and designed to be used as a dwelling with or without a permanent foundation when connected to the required utilities, and includes the plumb-

ing, heating, air-conditioning, and electrical systems contained therein. The term includes any structure that meets all of the requirements of this paragraph except the size requirements and with respect to which the manufacturer voluntarily files a certification required by the United States Secretary of Housing and Urban Development and complies with the standards established under Title 42 of the United States Code.

(54) "Manufactured-home transaction" means a secured transaction:

(A) that creates a purchase-money security interest in a manufactured home, other than a manufactured home held as inventory; or

(B) in which a manufactured home, other than a manufactured home held as inventory, is the primary collateral.

(55) "Mortgage" means a consensual interest in real property, including fixtures, which secures payment or performance of an obligation.

(56) "New debtor" means a person that becomes bound as debtor under Section 9—203(d) by a security agreement previously entered into by another person.

(57) "New value" means (i) money, (ii) money's worth in property, services, or new credit, or (iii) release by a transferee of an interest in property previously transferred to the transferee. The term does not include an obligation substituted for another obligation.

(58) "Noncash proceeds" means proceeds other than cash proceeds.

(59) "Obligor" means a person that, with respect to an obligation secured by a security interest in or an agricultural lien on the collateral, (i) owes payment or other performance of the obligation, (ii) has provided property other than the collateral to secure payment or other performance of the obligation, or (iii) is otherwise accountable in whole or in part for payment or other performance of the obligation. The term does not include issuers or nominated persons under a letter of credit.

(60) "Original debtor", except as used in Section 9—310(c), means a person that, as debtor, entered into a security agreement to which a new debtor has become bound under Section 9—203(d).

(61) "Payment intangible" means a general intangible under which the account debtor's principal obligation is a monetary obligation.

(62) "Person related to", with respect to an individual, means:

(A) the spouse of the individual;

(B) a brother, brother-in-law, sister, or sister-in-law of the individual;

(C) an ancestor or lineal descendant of the individual or the individual's spouse; or

(D) any other relative, by blood or marriage, of the individual or the individual's spouse who shares the same home with the individual.

(63) "Person related to", with respect to an organization, means:

(A) a person directly or indirectly controlling, controlled by, or under common control with the organization;

(B) an officer or director of, or a person performing similar functions with respect to, the organization;

(C) an officer or director of, or a person performing similar functions with respect to, a person described in subparagraph (A);

(D) the spouse of an individual described in subparagraph (A), (B), or (C); or

(E) an individual who is related by blood or marriage to an individual described in subparagraph (A), (B), (C), or (D) and shares the same home with the individual.

(64) "Proceeds", except as used in Section 9—609(b), means the following property:

(A) whatever is acquired upon the sale, lease, license, exchange, or other disposition of collateral;

(B) whatever is collected on, or distributed on account of, collateral;

(C) rights arising out of collateral;

(D) to the extent of the value of collateral, claims arising out of the loss, nonconformity, or interference with the use of, defects or infringement of rights in, or damage to, the collateral; or

(E) to the extent of the value of collateral and to the extent payable to the debtor or the secured party, insurance payable by reason of the loss or nonconformity of, defects or infringement of rights in, or damage to, the collateral.

(65) "Promissory note" means an instrument that evidences a promise to pay a monetary obligation, does not evidence an order to pay, and does not contain an acknowledgment by a bank that the bank has received for deposit a sum of money or funds.

(66) "Proposal" means a record authenticated by a secured party which includes the terms on which the secured party is willing to accept collateral in full or partial satisfaction of the obligation it secures pursuant to Sections 9—620, 9—621, and 9—622.

(67) "Public-finance transaction" means a secured transaction in connection with which:

(A) debt securities are issued;

(B) all or a portion of the securities issued have an initial stated maturity of at least 20 years; and

(C) the debtor, obligor, secured party, account debtor or other person obligated on collateral, assignor or assignee of a secured obligation, or assignor or assignee of a security interest is a State or a governmental unit of a State.

(68) "Pursuant to commitment", with respect to an advance made or other value given by a secured party, means pursuant

to the secured party's obligation, whether or not a subsequent event of default or other event not within the secured party's control has relieved or may relieve the secured party from its obligation.

(69) "Record", except as used in "for record", "of record", "record or legal title", and "record owner", means information that is inscribed on a tangible medium or which is stored in an electronic or other medium and is retrievable in perceivable form.

(70) "Registered organization" means an organization organized solely under the law of a single State or the United States and as to which the State or the United States must maintain a public record showing the organization to have been organized.

(71) "Secondary obligor" means an obligor to the extent that:

(A) the obligor's obligation is secondary; or

(B) the obligor has a right of recourse with respect to an obligation secured by collateral against the debtor, another obligor, or property of either.

(72) "Secured party" means:

(A) a person in whose favor a security interest is created or provided for under a security agreement, whether or not any obligation to be secured is outstanding;

(B) a person that holds an agricultural lien;

(C) a consignor;

(D) a person to which accounts, chattel paper, payment intangibles, or promissory notes have been sold;

(E) a trustee, indenture trustee, agent, collateral agent, or other representative in whose favor a security interest or agricultural lien is created or provided for; or

(F) a person that holds a security interest arising under Section 2—401, 2—505, 2—711(3), 2A—508(5), 4—210, or 5—118.

(73) "Security agreement" means an agreement that creates or provides for a security interest.

(74) "Send", in connection with a record or notification, means:

(A) to deposit in the mail, deliver for transmission, or transmit by any other usual means of communication, with postage or cost of transmission provided for, addressed to any address reasonable under the circumstances; or

(B) to cause the record or notification to be received within the time that it would have been received if properly sent under subparagraph (A).

(75) "Software" means a computer program and any supporting information provided in connection with a transaction relating to the program. The term does not include a computer program that is included in the definition of goods.

(76) "State" means a State of the United States, the District of Columbia, Puerto Rico, the United States Virgin Islands, or any territory or insular possession subject to the jurisdiction of the United States.

(77) "Supporting obligation" means a letter-of-credit right or secondary obligation that supports the payment or performance of an account, chattel paper, a document, a general intangible, an instrument, or investment property.

(78) "Tangible chattel paper" means chattel paper evidenced by a record or records consisting of information that is inscribed on a tangible medium.

(79) "Termination statement" means an amendment of a financing statement which:

(A) identifies, by its file number, the initial financing statement to which it relates; and

(B) indicates either that it is a termination statement or that the identified financing statement is no longer effective.

(80) "Transmitting utility" means a person primarily engaged in the business of:

(A) operating a railroad, subway, street railway, or trolley bus;

(B) transmitting communications electrically, electromagnetically, or by light;

(C) transmitting goods by pipeline or sewer; or

(D) transmitting or producing and transmitting electricity, steam, gas, or water.

(b) The following definitions in other articles apply to this article:

"Applicant"	Section 5—102
"Beneficiary"	Section 5—102
"Broker"	Section 8—102
"Certificated security"	Section 8—102
"Check"	Section 3—104
"Clearing corporation"	Section 8—102
"Contract for sale"	Section 2—106
"Customer"	Section 4—104
"Entitlement holder"	Section 8—102
"Financial asset"	Section 8—102
"Holder in due course"	Section 3—302
"Issuer" (with respect to a letter of credit or letter-of-credit right)	Section 5—102
"Issuer" (with respect to a security)	Section 8—201
"Lease"	Section 2A—103
"Lease agreement"	Section 2A—103
"Lease contract"	Section 2A—103
"Leasehold interest"	Section 2A—103
"Lessee"	Section 2A—103

"Lessee in ordinary course of business"	Section 2A—103
"Lessor"	Section 2A—103
"Lessor's residual interest"	Section 2A—103
"Letter of credit"	Section 5—102
"Merchant"	Section 2—104
"Negotiable instrument"	Section 3—104
"Nominated person"	Section 5—102
"Note"	Section 3—104
"Proceeds of a letter of credit"	Section 5—114
"Prove"	Section 3—103
"Sale"	Section 2—106
"Securities account"	Section 8—501
"Securities intermediary"	Section 8—102
"Security"	Section 8—102
"Security certificate"	Section 8—102
"Security entitlement"	Section 8—102
"Uncertificated security"	Section 8—102

(c) Article 1 contains general definitions and principles of construction and interpretation applicable throughout this article.

§ 9—103. Purchase-Money Security Interest; Application of Payments; Burden of Establishing.

(a) In this section:

(1) "purchase-money collateral" means goods or software that secures a purchase-money obligation incurred with respect to that collateral; and

(2) "purchase-money obligation" means an obligation of an obligor incurred as all or part of the price of the collateral or for value given to enable the debtor to acquire rights in or the use of the collateral if the value is in fact so used.

(b) A security interest in goods is a purchase-money security interest:

(1) to the extent that the goods are purchase-money collateral with respect to that security interest;

(2) if the security interest is in inventory that is or was purchase-money collateral, also to the extent that the security interest secures a purchase-money obligation incurred with respect to other inventory in which the secured party holds or held a purchase-money security interest; and

(3) also to the extent that the security interest secures a purchase-money obligation incurred with respect to software in which the secured party holds or held a purchase-money security interest.

(c) A security interest in software is a purchase-money security interest to the extent that the security interest also secures a purchase-money obligation incurred with respect to goods in which the secured party holds or held a purchase-money security interest if:

(1) the debtor acquired its interest in the software in an integrated transaction in which it acquired an interest in the goods; and

(2) the debtor acquired its interest in the software for the principal purpose of using the software in the goods.

(d) The security interest of a consignor in goods that are the subject of a consignment is a purchase-money security interest in inventory.

(e) In a transaction other than a consumer-goods transaction, if the extent to which a security interest is a purchase-money security interest depends on the application of a payment to a particular obligation, the payment must be applied:

(1) in accordance with any reasonable method of application to which the parties agree;

(2) in the absence of the parties' agreement to a reasonable method, in accordance with any intention of the obligor manifested at or before the time of payment; or

(3) in the absence of an agreement to a reasonable method and a timely manifestation of the obligor's intention, in the following order:

(A) to obligations that are not secured; and

(B) if more than one obligation is secured, to obligations secured by purchase-money security interests in the order in which those obligations were incurred.

(f) In a transaction other than a consumer-goods transaction, a purchase-money security interest does not lose its status as such, even if:

(1) the purchase-money collateral also secures an obligation that is not a purchase-money obligation;

(2) collateral that is not purchase-money collateral also secures the purchase-money obligation; or

(3) the purchase-money obligation has been renewed, refinanced, consolidated, or restructured.

(g) In a transaction other than a consumer-goods transaction, a secured party claiming a purchase-money security interest has the burden of establishing the extent to which the security interest is a purchase-money security interest.

(h) The limitation of the rules in subsections (e), (f), and (g) to transactions other than consumer-goods transactions is intended to leave to the court the determination of the proper rules in consumer-goods transactions. The court may not infer from that limitation the nature of the proper rule in consumer-goods transactions and may continue to apply established approaches.

§ 9—104. Control of Deposit Account.

(a) A secured party has control of a deposit account if:

(1) the secured party is the bank with which the deposit account is maintained;

(2) the debtor, secured party, and bank have agreed in an authenticated record that the bank will comply with

instructions originated by the secured party directing disposition of the funds in the deposit account without further consent by the debtor; or

(3) the secured party becomes the bank's customer with respect to the deposit account.

(b) A secured party that has satisfied subsection (a) has control, even if the debtor retains the right to direct the disposition of funds from the deposit account.

§ 9—105. **Control of Electronic Chattel Paper.**

A secured party has control of electronic chattel paper if the record or records comprising the chattel paper are created, stored, and assigned in such a manner that:

(1) a single authoritative copy of the record or records exists which is unique, identifiable and, except as otherwise provided in paragraphs (4), (5), and (6), unalterable;

(2) the authoritative copy identifies the secured party as the assignee of the record or records;

(3) the authoritative copy is communicated to and maintained by the secured party or its designated custodian;

(4) copies or revisions that add or change an identified assignee of the authoritative copy can be made only with the participation of the secured party;

(5) each copy of the authoritative copy and any copy of a copy is readily identifiable as a copy that is not the authoritative copy; and

(6) any revision of the authoritative copy is readily identifiable as an authorized or unauthorized revision.

§ 9—106. **Control of Investment Property.**

(a) A person has control of a certificated security, uncertificated security, or security entitlement as provided in Section 8—106.

(b) A secured party has control of a commodity contract if:

(1) the secured party is the commodity intermediary with which the commodity contract is carried; or

(2) the commodity customer, secured party, and commodity intermediary have agreed that the commodity intermediary will apply any value distributed on account of the commodity contract as directed by the secured party without further consent by the commodity customer.

(c) A secured party having control of all security entitlements or commodity contracts carried in a securities account or commodity account has control over the securities account or commodity account.

§ 9—107. **Control of Letter-of-Credit Right.**

A secured party has control of a letter-of-credit right to the extent of any right to payment or performance by the issuer or any nominated person if the issuer or nominated person has consented to an assignment of proceeds of the letter of credit under Section 5—114(c) or otherwise applicable law or practice.

§ 9—108. **Sufficiency of Description.**

(a) Except as otherwise provided in subsections (c), (d), and (e), a description of personal or real property is sufficient, whether or not it is specific, if it reasonably identifies what is described.

(b) Except as otherwise provided in subsection (d), a description of collateral reasonably identifies the collateral if it identifies the collateral by:

(1) specific listing;

(2) category;

(3) except as otherwise provided in subsection (e), a type of collateral defined in [the Uniform Commercial Code];

(4) quantity;

(5) computational or allocational formula or procedure; or

(6) except as otherwise provided in subsection (c), any other method, if the identity of the collateral is objectively determinable.

(c) A description of collateral as "all the debtor's assets" or "all the debtor's personal property" or using words of similar import does not reasonably identify the collateral.

(d) Except as otherwise provided in subsection (e), a description of a security entitlement, securities account, or commodity account is sufficient if it describes:

(1) the collateral by those terms or as investment property; or

(2) the underlying financial asset or commodity contract.

(e) A description only by type of collateral defined in [the Uniform Commercial Code] is an insufficient description of:

(1) a commercial tort claim; or

(2) in a consumer transaction, consumer goods, a security entitlement, a securities account, or a commodity account.

[Subpart 2. Applicability of Article]

§ 9—109. **Scope.**

(a) Except as otherwise provided in subsections (c) and (d), this article applies to:

(1) a transaction, regardless of its form, that creates a security interest in personal property or fixtures by contract;

(2) an agricultural lien;

(3) a sale of accounts, chattel paper, payment intangibles, or promissory notes;

(4) a consignment;

(5) a security interest arising under Section 2—401, 2—505, 2—711(3), or 2A—508(5), as provided in Section 9—110; and

(6) a security interest arising under Section 4—210 or 5—118.

(b) The application of this article to a security interest in a secured obligation is not affected by the fact that the obligation is itself secured by a transaction or interest to which this article does not apply.

(c) This article does not apply to the extent that:

(1) a statute, regulation, or treaty of the United States preempts this article;

(2) another statute of this State expressly governs the creation, perfection, priority, or enforcement of a security interest created by this State or a governmental unit of this State;

(3) a statute of another State, a foreign country, or a governmental unit of another State or a foreign country, other than a statute generally applicable to security interests, expressly governs creation, perfection, priority, or enforcement of a security interest created by the State, country, or governmental unit; or

(4) the rights of a transferee beneficiary or nominated person under a letter of credit are independent and superior under Section 5—114.

(d) This article does not apply to:

(1) a landlord's lien, other than an agricultural lien;

(2) a lien, other than an agricultural lien, given by statute or other rule of law for services or materials, but Section 9—333 applies with respect to priority of the lien;

(3) an assignment of a claim for wages, salary, or other compensation of an employee;

(4) a sale of accounts, chattel paper, payment intangibles, or promissory notes as part of a sale of the business out of which they arose;

(5) an assignment of accounts, chattel paper, payment intangibles, or promissory notes which is for the purpose of collection only;

(6) an assignment of a right to payment under a contract to an assignee that is also obligated to perform under the contract;

(7) an assignment of a single account, payment intangible, or promissory note to an assignee in full or partial satisfaction of a preexisting indebtedness;

(8) a transfer of an interest in or an assignment of a claim under a policy of insurance, other than an assignment by or to a health-care provider of a health-care-insurance receivable and any subsequent assignment of the right to payment, but Sections 9—315 and 9—322 apply with respect to proceeds and priorities in proceeds;

(9) an assignment of a right represented by a judgment, other than a judgment taken on a right to payment that was collateral;

(10) a right of recoupment or set-off, but:

(A) Section 9—340 applies with respect to the effectiveness of rights of recoupment or set-off against deposit accounts; and

(B) Section 9—404 applies with respect to defenses or claims of an account debtor;

(11) the creation or transfer of an interest in or lien on real property, including a lease or rents thereunder, except to the extent that provision is made for:

(A) liens on real property in Sections 9—203 and 9—308;

(B) fixtures in Section 9—334;

(C) fixture filings in Sections 9—501, 9—502, 9—512, 9—516, and 9—519; and

(D) security agreements covering personal and real property in Section 9—604;

(12) an assignment of a claim arising in tort, other than a commercial tort claim, but Sections 9—315 and 9—322 apply with respect to proceeds and priorities in proceeds; or

(13) an assignment of a deposit account in a consumer transaction, but Sections 9—315 and 9—322 apply with respect to proceeds and priorities in proceeds.

§ 9—110. Security Interests Arising under Article 2 or 2A.

A security interest arising under Section 2—401, 2—505, 2—711(3), or 2A—508(5) is subject to this article. However, until the debtor obtains possession of the goods:

(1) the security interest is enforceable, even if Section 9—203(b)(3) has not been satisfied;

(2) filing is not required to perfect the security interest;

(3) the rights of the secured party after default by the debtor are governed by Article 2 or 2A; and

(4) the security interest has priority over a conflicting security interest created by the debtor.

Part 2 Effectiveness of Security Agreement; Attachment of Security Interest; Rights of Parties to Security Agreement

[Subpart 1. Effectiveness and Attachment]

§ 9—201. General Effectiveness of Security Agreement.

(a) Except as otherwise provided in [the Uniform Commercial Code], a security agreement is effective according to its terms between the parties, against purchasers of the collateral, and against creditors.

(b) A transaction subject to this article is subject to any applicable rule of law which establishes a different rule for consumers and [insert reference to (i) any other statute or regulation that regulates the rates, charges, agreements, and practices for loans, credit sales, or other extensions of credit and (ii) any consumer-protection statute or regulation].

(c) In case of conflict between this article and a rule of law, statute, or regulation described in subsection (b), the rule of law, statute, or regulation controls. Failure to comply with a statute or regulation described in subsection (b) has only the effect the statute or regulation specifies.

(d) This article does not:

(1) validate any rate, charge, agreement, or practice that violates a rule of law, statute, or regulation described in subsection (b); or

(2) extend the application of the rule of law, statute, or regulation to a transaction not otherwise subject to it.

§ 9—202. Title to Collateral Immaterial.

Except as otherwise provided with respect to consignments or sales of accounts, chattel paper, payment intangibles, or promissory notes, the provisions of this article with regard to rights and obligations apply whether title to collateral is in the secured party or the debtor.

§ 9—203. Attachment and Enforceability of Security Interest; Proceeds; Supporting Obligations; Formal Requisites.

(a) A security interest attaches to collateral when it becomes enforceable against the debtor with respect to the collateral, unless an agreement expressly postpones the time of attachment.

(b) Except as otherwise provided in subsections (c) through (i), a security interest is enforceable against the debtor and third parties with respect to the collateral only if:

(1) value has been given;

(2) the debtor has rights in the collateral or the power to transfer rights in the collateral to a secured party; and

(3) one of the following conditions is met:

(A) the debtor has authenticated a security agreement that provides a description of the collateral and, if the security interest covers timber to be cut, a description of the land concerned;

(B) the collateral is not a certificated security and is in the possession of the secured party under Section 9—313 pursuant to the debtor's security agreement;

(C) the collateral is a certificated security in registered form and the security certificate has been delivered to the secured party under Section 8—301 pursuant to the debtor's security agreement; or

(D) the collateral is deposit accounts, electronic chattel paper, investment property, or letter-of-credit rights, and the secured party has control under Section 9—104, 9—105, 9—106, or 9—107 pursuant to the debtor's security agreement.

(c) Subsection (b) is subject to Section 4—210 on the security interest of a collecting bank, Section 5—118 on the security interest of a letter-of-credit issuer or nominated person, Section 9—110 on a security interest arising under Article 2 or 2A, and Section 9—206 on security interests in investment property.

(d) A person becomes bound as debtor by a security agreement entered into by another person if, by operation of law other than this article or by contract:

(1) the security agreement becomes effective to create a security interest in the person's property; or

(2) the person becomes generally obligated for the obligations of the other person, including the obligation secured under the security agreement, and acquires or succeeds to all or substantially all of the assets of the other person.

(e) If a new debtor becomes bound as debtor by a security agreement entered into by another person:

(1) the agreement satisfies subsection (b)(3) with respect to existing or after-acquired property of the new debtor to the extent the property is described in the agreement; and

(2) another agreement is not necessary to make a security interest in the property enforceable.

(f) The attachment of a security interest in collateral gives the secured party the rights to proceeds provided by Section 9—315 and is also attachment of a security interest in a supporting obligation for the collateral.

(g) The attachment of a security interest in a right to payment or performance secured by a security interest or other lien on personal or real property is also attachment of a security interest in the security interest, mortgage, or other lien.

(h) The attachment of a security interest in a securities account is also attachment of a security interest in the security entitlements carried in the securities account.

(i) The attachment of a security interest in a commodity account is also attachment of a security interest in the commodity contracts carried in the commodity account.

§ 9—204. After-Acquired Property; Future Advances.

(a) Except as otherwise provided in subsection (b), a security agreement may create or provide for a security interest in after-acquired collateral.

(b) A security interest does not attach under a term constituting an after-acquired property clause to:

(1) consumer goods, other than an accession when given as additional security, unless the debtor acquires rights in them within 10 days after the secured party gives value; or

(2) a commercial tort claim.

(c) A security agreement may provide that collateral secures, or that accounts, chattel paper, payment intangibles, or promissory notes are sold in connection with, future advances or other value, whether or not the advances or value are given pursuant to commitment.

§ 9—205. Use or Disposition of Collateral Permissible.

(a) A security interest is not invalid or fraudulent against creditors solely because:

(1) the debtor has the right or ability to:

(A) use, commingle, or dispose of all or part of the collateral, including returned or repossessed goods;

(B) collect, compromise, enforce, or otherwise deal with collateral;

(C) accept the return of collateral or make repossessions; or

(D) use, commingle, or dispose of proceeds; or

(2) the secured party fails to require the debtor to account for proceeds or replace collateral.

(b) This section does not relax the requirements of possession if attachment, perfection, or enforcement of a security interest depends upon possession of the collateral by the secured party.

§ 9—206. Security Interest Arising in Purchase or Delivery of Financial Asset.

(a) A security interest in favor of a securities intermediary attaches to a person's security entitlement if:

(1) the person buys a financial asset through the securities intermediary in a transaction in which the person is obligated to pay the purchase price to the securities intermediary at the time of the purchase; and

(2) the securities intermediary credits the financial asset to the buyer's securities account before the buyer pays the securities intermediary.

(b) The security interest described in subsection (a) secures the person's obligation to pay for the financial asset.

(c) A security interest in favor of a person that delivers a certificated security or other financial asset represented by a writing attaches to the security or other financial asset if:

(1) the security or other financial asset:

(A) in the ordinary course of business is transferred by delivery with any necessary indorsement or assignment; and

(B) is delivered under an agreement between persons in the business of dealing with such securities or financial assets; and

(2) the agreement calls for delivery against payment.

(d) The security interest described in subsection (c) secures the obligation to make payment for the delivery.

[Subpart 2. Rights and Duties]

§ 9—207. Rights and Duties of Secured Party Having Possession or Control of Collateral.

(a) Except as otherwise provided in subsection (d), a secured party shall use reasonable care in the custody and preservation of collateral in the secured party's possession. In the case of chattel paper or an instrument, reasonable care includes taking necessary steps to preserve rights against prior parties unless otherwise agreed.

(b) Except as otherwise provided in subsection (d), if a secured party has possession of collateral:

(1) reasonable expenses, including the cost of insurance and payment of taxes or other charges, incurred in the custody, preservation, use, or operation of the collateral are chargeable to the debtor and are secured by the collateral;

(2) the risk of accidental loss or damage is on the debtor to the extent of a deficiency in any effective insurance coverage;

(3) the secured party shall keep the collateral identifiable, but fungible collateral may be commingled; and

(4) the secured party may use or operate the collateral:

(A) for the purpose of preserving the collateral or its value;

(B) as permitted by an order of a court having competent jurisdiction; or

(C) except in the case of consumer goods, in the manner and to the extent agreed by the debtor.

(c) Except as otherwise provided in subsection (d), a secured party having possession of collateral or control of collateral under Section 9—104, 9—105, 9—106, or 9—107:

(1) may hold as additional security any proceeds, except money or funds, received from the collateral;

(2) shall apply money or funds received from the collateral to reduce the secured obligation, unless remitted to the debtor; and

(3) may create a security interest in the collateral.

(d) If the secured party is a buyer of accounts, chattel paper, payment intangibles, or promissory notes or a consignor:

(1) subsection (a) does not apply unless the secured party is entitled under an agreement:

(A) to charge back uncollected collateral; or

(B) otherwise to full or limited recourse against the debtor or a secondary obligor based on the nonpayment or other default of an account debtor or other obligor on the collateral; and

(2) subsections (b) and (c) do not apply.

§ 9—208. Additional Duties of Secured Party Having Control of Collateral.

(a) This section applies to cases in which there is no outstanding secured obligation and the secured party is not committed to make advances, incur obligations, or otherwise give value.

(b) Within 10 days after receiving an authenticated demand by the debtor:

(1) a secured party having control of a deposit account under Section 9—104(a)(2) shall send to the bank with which the deposit account is maintained an authenticated statement that releases the bank from any further obligation to comply with instructions originated by the secured party;

(2) a secured party having control of a deposit account under Section 9—104(a)(3) shall:

(A) pay the debtor the balance on deposit in the deposit account; or

(B) transfer the balance on deposit into a deposit account in the debtor's name;

(3) a secured party, other than a buyer, having control of electronic chattel paper under Section 9—105 shall:

(A) communicate the authoritative copy of the electronic chattel paper to the debtor or its designated custodian;

(B) if the debtor designates a custodian that is the designated custodian with which the authoritative copy of the electronic chattel paper is maintained for the secured party, communicate to the custodian an authenticated record releasing the designated custodian from any further obligation to comply with instructions originated by the secured party and instructing the custodian to comply with instructions originated by the debtor; and

(C) take appropriate action to enable the debtor or its designated custodian to make copies of or revisions to the authoritative copy which add or change an identified assignee of the authoritative copy without the consent of the secured party;

(4) a secured party having control of investment property under Section 8—106(d)(2) or 9—106(b) shall send to the securities intermediary or commodity intermediary with which the security entitlement or commodity contract is maintained an authenticated record that releases the securities intermediary or commodity intermediary from any further obligation to comply with entitlement orders or directions originated by the secured party; and

(5) a secured party having control of a letter-of-credit right under Section 9—107 shall send to each person having an unfulfilled obligation to pay or deliver proceeds of the letter of credit to the secured party an authenticated release from any further obligation to pay or deliver proceeds of the letter of credit to the secured party.

§ 9—209. Duties of Secured Party If Account Debtor Has Been Notified of Assignment.

(a) Except as otherwise provided in subsection (c), this section applies if:

(1) there is no outstanding secured obligation; and

(2) the secured party is not committed to make advances, incur obligations, or otherwise give value.

(b) Within 10 days after receiving an authenticated demand by the debtor, a secured party shall send to an account debtor that has received notification of an assignment to the secured party as assignee under Section 9—406(a) an authenticated record that releases the account debtor from any further obligation to the secured party.

(c) This section does not apply to an assignment constituting the sale of an account, chattel paper, or payment intangible.

§ 9—210. Request for Accounting; Request Regarding List of Collateral or Statement of Account.

(a) In this section:

(1) "Request" means a record of a type described in paragraph (2), (3), or (4).

(2) "Request for an accounting" means a record authenticated by a debtor requesting that the recipient provide an accounting of the unpaid obligations secured by collateral and reasonably identifying the transaction or relationship that is the subject of the request.

(3) "Request regarding a list of collateral" means a record authenticated by a debtor requesting that the recipient approve or correct a list of what the debtor believes to be the collateral securing an obligation and reasonably identifying the transaction or relationship that is the subject of the request.

(4) "Request regarding a statement of account" means a record authenticated by a debtor requesting that the recipient approve or correct a statement indicating what the debtor believes to be the aggregate amount of unpaid obligations secured by collateral as of a specified date and reasonably identifying the transaction or relationship that is the subject of the request.

(b) Subject to subsections (c), (d), (e), and (f), a secured party, other than a buyer of accounts, chattel paper, payment intangibles, or promissory notes or a consignor, shall comply with a request within 14 days after receipt:

(1) in the case of a request for an accounting, by authenticating and sending to the debtor an accounting; and

(2) in the case of a request regarding a list of collateral or a request regarding a statement of account, by authenticating and sending to the debtor an approval or correction.

(c) A secured party that claims a security interest in all of a particular type of collateral owned by the debtor may comply with a request regarding a list of collateral by sending to the debtor an authenticated record including a statement to that effect within 14 days after receipt.

(d) A person that receives a request regarding a list of collateral, claims no interest in the collateral when it receives the request, and claimed an interest in the collateral at an earlier time shall comply with the request within 14 days after receipt by sending to the debtor an authenticated record:

(1) disclaiming any interest in the collateral; and

(2) if known to the recipient, providing the name and mailing address of any assignee of or successor to the recipient's interest in the collateral.

(e) A person that receives a request for an accounting or a request regarding a statement of account, claims no interest in the obligations when it receives the request, and claimed an interest in the obligations at an earlier time shall comply with the request within 14 days after receipt by sending to the debtor an authenticated record:

(1) disclaiming any interest in the obligations; and

(2) if known to the recipient, providing the name and mailing address of any assignee of or successor to the recipient's interest in the obligations.

(f) A debtor is entitled without charge to one response to a request under this section during any six-month period. The secured party may require payment of a charge not exceeding $25 for each additional response.

Part 3 Perfection and Priority

[Subpart 1. Law Governing Perfection and Priority]

§ 9—301. Law Governing Perfection and Priority of Security Interests.

Except as otherwise provided in Sections 9—303 through 9—306, the following rules determine the law governing perfection, the effect of perfection or nonperfection, and the priority of a security interest in collateral:

(1) Except as otherwise provided in this section, while a debtor is located in a jurisdiction, the local law of that jurisdiction governs perfection, the effect of perfection or nonperfection, and the priority of a security interest in collateral.

(2) While collateral is located in a jurisdiction, the local law of that jurisdiction governs perfection, the effect of perfection or nonperfection, and the priority of a possessory security interest in that collateral.

(3) Except as otherwise provided in paragraph (4), while negotiable documents, goods, instruments, money, or tangible chattel paper is located in a jurisdiction, the local law of that jurisdiction governs:

(A) perfection of a security interest in the goods by filing a fixture filing;

(B) perfection of a security interest in timber to be cut; and

(C) the effect of perfection or nonperfection and the priority of a nonpossessory security interest in the collateral.

(4) The local law of the jurisdiction in which the wellhead or minehead is located governs perfection, the effect of perfection or nonperfection, and the priority of a security interest in as-extracted collateral.

§ 9—302. Law Governing Perfection and Priority of Agricultural Liens.

While farm products are located in a jurisdiction, the local law of that jurisdiction governs perfection, the effect of perfection or nonperfection, and the priority of an agricultural lien on the farm products.

§ 9—303. Law Governing Perfection and Priority of Security Interests in Goods Covered by a Certificate of Title.

(a) This section applies to goods covered by a certificate of title, even if there is no other relationship between the jurisdiction under whose certificate of title the goods are covered and the goods or the debtor.

(b) Goods become covered by a certificate of title when a valid application for the certificate of title and the applicable fee are delivered to the appropriate authority. Goods cease to be covered by a certificate of title at the earlier of the time the certificate of title ceases to be effective under the law of the issuing jurisdiction or the time the goods become covered subsequently by a certificate of title issued by another jurisdiction.

(c) The local law of the jurisdiction under whose certificate of title the goods are covered governs perfection, the effect of perfection or nonperfection, and the priority of a security interest in goods covered by a certificate of title from the time the goods become covered by the certificate of title until the goods cease to be covered by the certificate of title.

§ 9—304. Law Governing Perfection and Priority of Security Interests in Deposit Accounts.

(a) The local law of a bank's jurisdiction governs perfection, the effect of perfection or nonperfection, and the priority of a security interest in a deposit account maintained with that bank.

(b) The following rules determine a bank's jurisdiction for purposes of this part:

(1) If an agreement between the bank and the debtor governing the deposit account expressly provides that a particular jurisdiction is the bank's jurisdiction for purposes of this part, this article, or [the Uniform Commercial Code], that jurisdiction is the bank's jurisdiction.

(2) If paragraph (1) does not apply and an agreement between the bank and its customer governing the deposit account expressly provides that the agreement is governed by the law of a particular jurisdiction, that jurisdiction is the bank's jurisdiction.

(3) If neither paragraph (1) nor paragraph (2) applies and an agreement between the bank and its customer governing the deposit account expressly provides that the deposit account is maintained at an office in a particular jurisdiction, that jurisdiction is the bank's jurisdiction.

(4) If none of the preceding paragraphs applies, the bank's jurisdiction is the jurisdiction in which the office identified in an account statement as the office serving the customer's account is located.

(5) If none of the preceding paragraphs applies, the bank's jurisdiction is the jurisdiction in which the chief executive office of the bank is located.

§ 9—305. Law Governing Perfection and Priority of Security Interests in Investment Property.

(a) Except as otherwise provided in subsection (c), the following rules apply:

(1) While a security certificate is located in a jurisdiction, the local law of that jurisdiction governs perfection, the effect of perfection or nonperfection, and the priority of a security interest in the certificated security represented thereby.

(2) The local law of the issuer's jurisdiction as specified in Section 8—110(d) governs perfection, the effect of perfection or nonperfection, and the priority of a security interest in an uncertificated security.

(3) The local law of the securities intermediary's jurisdiction as specified in Section 8—110(e) governs perfection, the effect of perfection or nonperfection, and the priority of a security interest in a security entitlement or securities account.

(4) The local law of the commodity intermediary's jurisdiction governs perfection, the effect of perfection or nonperfection,

and the priority of a security interest in a commodity contract or commodity account.

(b) The following rules determine a commodity intermediary's jurisdiction for purposes of this part:

(1) If an agreement between the commodity intermediary and commodity customer governing the commodity account expressly provides that a particular jurisdiction is the commodity intermediary's jurisdiction for purposes of this part, this article, or [the Uniform Commercial Code], that jurisdiction is the commodity intermediary's jurisdiction.

(2) If paragraph (1) does not apply and an agreement between the commodity intermediary and commodity customer governing the commodity account expressly provides that the agreement is governed by the law of a particular jurisdiction, that jurisdiction is the commodity intermediary's jurisdiction.

(3) If neither paragraph (1) nor paragraph (2) applies and an agreement between the commodity intermediary and commodity customer governing the commodity account expressly provides that the commodity account is maintained at an office in a particular jurisdiction, that jurisdiction is the commodity intermediary's jurisdiction.

(4) If none of the preceding paragraphs applies, the commodity intermediary's jurisdiction is the jurisdiction in which the office identified in an account statement as the office serving the commodity customer's account is located.

(5) If none of the preceding paragraphs applies, the commodity intermediary's jurisdiction is the jurisdiction in which the chief executive office of the commodity intermediary is located.

(c) The local law of the jurisdiction in which the debtor is located governs:

(1) perfection of a security interest in investment property by filing;

(2) automatic perfection of a security interest in investment property created by a broker or securities intermediary; and

(3) automatic perfection of a security interest in a commodity contract or commodity account created by a commodity intermediary.

§ 9—306. Law Governing Perfection and Priority of Security Interests in Letter-of-Credit Rights.

(a) Subject to subsection (c), the local law of the issuer's jurisdiction or a nominated person's jurisdiction governs perfection, the effect of perfection or nonperfection, and the priority of a security interest in a letter-of-credit right if the issuer's jurisdiction or nominated person's jurisdiction is a State.

(b) For purposes of this part, an issuer's jurisdiction or nominated person's jurisdiction is the jurisdiction whose law governs the liability of the issuer or nominated person with respect to the letter-of-credit right as provided in Section 5—116.

(c) This section does not apply to a security interest that is perfected only under Section 9—308(d).

§ 9—307. Location of Debtor.

(a) In this section, "place of business" means a place where a debtor conducts its affairs.

(b) Except as otherwise provided in this section, the following rules determine a debtor's location:

(1) A debtor who is an individual is located at the individual's principal residence.

(2) A debtor that is an organization and has only one place of business is located at its place of business.

(3) A debtor that is an organization and has more than one place of business is located at its chief executive office.

(c) Subsection (b) applies only if a debtor's residence, place of business, or chief executive office, as applicable, is located in a jurisdiction whose law generally requires information concerning the existence of a nonpossessory security interest to be made generally available in a filing, recording, or registration system as a condition or result of the security interest's obtaining priority over the rights of a lien creditor with respect to the collateral. If subsection (b) does not apply, the debtor is located in the District of Columbia.

(d) A person that ceases to exist, have a residence, or have a place of business continues to be located in the jurisdiction specified by subsections (b) and (c).

(e) A registered organization that is organized under the law of a State is located in that State.

(f) Except as otherwise provided in subsection (i), a registered organization that is organized under the law of the United States and a branch or agency of a bank that is not organized under the law of the United States or a State are located:

(1) in the State that the law of the United States designates, if the law designates a State of location;

(2) in the State that the registered organization, branch, or agency designates, if the law of the United States authorizes the registered organization, branch, or agency to designate its State of location; or

(3) in the District of Columbia, if neither paragraph (1) nor paragraph (2) applies.

(g) A registered organization continues to be located in the jurisdiction specified by subsection (e) or (f) notwithstanding:

(1) the suspension, revocation, forfeiture, or lapse of the registered organization's status as such in its jurisdiction of organization; or

(2) the dissolution, winding up, or cancellation of the existence of the registered organization.

(h) The United States is located in the District of Columbia.

(i) A branch or agency of a bank that is not organized under the law of the United States or a State is located in the State in which the branch or agency is licensed, if all branches and agencies of the bank are licensed in only one State.

(j) A foreign air carrier under the Federal Aviation Act of 1958, as amended, is located at the designated office of the agent upon which service of process may be made on behalf of the carrier.

(k) This section applies only for purposes of this part.

[Subpart 2. Perfection]

§ 9—308. When Security Interest or Agricultural Lien Is Perfected; Continuity of Perfection.

(a) Except as otherwise provided in this section and Section 9—309, a security interest is perfected if it has attached and all of the applicable requirements for perfection in Sections 9—310 through 9—316 have been satisfied. A security interest is perfected when it attaches if the applicable requirements are satisfied before the security interest attaches.

(b) An agricultural lien is perfected if it has become effective and all of the applicable requirements for perfection in Section 9—310 have been satisfied. An agricultural lien is perfected when it becomes effective if the applicable requirements are satisfied before the agricultural lien becomes effective.

(c) A security interest or agricultural lien is perfected continuously if it is originally perfected by one method under this article and is later perfected by another method under this article, without an intermediate period when it was unperfected.

(d) Perfection of a security interest in collateral also perfects a security interest in a supporting obligation for the collateral.

(e) Perfection of a security interest in a right to payment or performance also perfects a security interest in a security interest, mortgage, or other lien on personal or real property securing the right.

(f) Perfection of a security interest in a securities account also perfects a security interest in the security entitlements carried in the securities account.

(g) Perfection of a security interest in a commodity account also perfects a security interest in the commodity contracts carried in the commodity account.

Legislative Note: Any statute conflicting with subsection (e) must be made expressly subject to that subsection.

§ 9—309. Security Interest Perfected upon Attachment.

The following security interests are perfected when they attach:

(1) a purchase-money security interest in consumer goods, except as otherwise provided in Section 9—311(b) with respect to consumer goods that are subject to a statute or treaty described in Section 9—311(a);

(2) an assignment of accounts or payment intangibles which does not by itself or in conjunction with other assignments to the same assignee transfer a significant part of the assignor's outstanding accounts or payment intangibles;

(3) a sale of a payment intangible;

(4) a sale of a promissory note;

(5) a security interest created by the assignment of a health-care-insurance receivable to the provider of the health-care goods or services;

(6) a security interest arising under Section 2—401, 2—505, 2—711(3), or 2A—508(5), until the debtor obtains possession of the collateral;

(7) a security interest of a collecting bank arising under Section 4—210;

(8) a security interest of an issuer or nominated person arising under Section 5—118;

(9) a security interest arising in the delivery of a financial asset under Section 9—206(c);

(10) a security interest in investment property created by a broker or securities intermediary;

(11) a security interest in a commodity contract or a commodity account created by a commodity intermediary;

(12) an assignment for the benefit of all creditors of the transferor and subsequent transfers by the assignee thereunder; and

(13) a security interest created by an assignment of a beneficial interest in a decedent's estate.

§ 9—310. When Filing Required to Perfect Security Interest or Agricultural Lien; Security Interests and Agricultural Liens to Which Filing Provisions Do Not Apply.

(a) Except as otherwise provided in subsection (b) and Section 9—312(b), a financing statement must be filed to perfect all security interests and agricultural liens.

(b) The filing of a financing statement is not necessary to perfect a security interest:

(1) that is perfected under Section 9—308(d), (e), (f), or (g);

(2) that is perfected under Section 9—309 when it attaches;

(3) in property subject to a statute, regulation, or treaty described in Section 9—311(a);

(4) in goods in possession of a bailee which is perfected under Section 9—312(d)(1) or (2);

(5) in certificated securities, documents, goods, or instruments which is perfected without filing or possession under Section 9—312(e), (f), or (g);

(6) in collateral in the secured party's possession under Section 9—313;

(7) in a certificated security which is perfected by delivery of the security certificate to the secured party under Section 9—313;

(8) in deposit accounts, electronic chattel paper, investment property, or letter-of-credit rights which is perfected by control under Section 9—314;

(9) in proceeds which is perfected under Section 9—315; or

(10) that is perfected under Section 9—316.

(c) If a secured party assigns a perfected security interest or agricultural lien, a filing under this article is not required to continue the perfected status of the security interest against creditors of and transferees from the original debtor.

§ 9—311. Perfection of Security Interests in Property Subject to Certain Statutes, Regulations, and Treaties.

(a) Except as otherwise provided in subsection (d), the filing of a financing statement is not necessary or effective to perfect a security interest in property subject to:

(1) a statute, regulation, or treaty of the United States whose requirements for a security interest's obtaining priority over the rights of a lien creditor with respect to the property preempt Section 9—310(a);

(2) [list any certificate-of-title statute covering automobiles, trailers, mobile homes, boats, farm tractors, or the like, which provides for a security interest to be indicated on the certificate as a condition or result of perfection, and any non-Uniform Commercial Code central filing statute]; or

(3) a certificate-of-title statute of another jurisdiction which provides for a security interest to be indicated on the certificate as a condition or result of the security interest's obtaining priority over the rights of a lien creditor with respect to the property.

(b) Compliance with the requirements of a statute, regulation, or treaty described in subsection (a) for obtaining priority over the rights of a lien creditor is equivalent to the filing of a financing statement under this article. Except as otherwise provided in subsection (d) and Sections 9—313 and 9—316(d) and (e) for goods covered by a certificate of title, a security interest in property subject to a statute, regulation, or treaty described in subsection (a) may be perfected only by compliance with those requirements, and a security interest so perfected remains perfected notwithstanding a change in the use or transfer of possession of the collateral.

(c) Except as otherwise provided in subsection (d) and Section 9—316(d) and (e), duration and renewal of perfection of a security interest perfected by compliance with the requirements prescribed by a statute, regulation, or treaty described in subsection (a) are governed by the statute, regulation, or treaty. In other respects, the security interest is subject to this article.

(d) During any period in which collateral subject to a statute specified in subsection (a)(2) is inventory held for sale or lease by a person or leased by that person as lessor and that person is in the business of selling goods of that kind, this section does not apply to a security interest in that collateral created by that person.

Legislative Note: This Article contemplates that perfection of a security interest in goods covered by a certificate of title occurs upon receipt by appropriate State officials of a properly tendered application for a certificate of title on which the security interest is to be indicated, without a relation back to an earlier time. States whose certificate-of-title statutes provide for perfection at a different time or contain a relation-back provision should amend the statutes accordingly.

§ 9—312. Perfection of Security Interests in Chattel Paper, Deposit Accounts, Documents, Goods Covered by Documents, Instruments, Investment Property, Letter-of-Credit Rights, and Money; Perfection by Permissive Filing; Temporary Perfection without Filing or Transfer of Possession.

(a) A security interest in chattel paper, negotiable documents, instruments, or investment property may be perfected by filing.

(b) Except as otherwise provided in Section 9—315(c) and (d) for proceeds:

(1) a security interest in a deposit account may be perfected only by control under Section 9—314;

(2) and except as otherwise provided in Section 9—308(d), a security interest in a letter-of-credit right may be perfected only by control under Section 9—314; and

(3) a security interest in money may be perfected only by the secured party's taking possession under Section 9—313.

(c) While goods are in the possession of a bailee that has issued a negotiable document covering the goods:

(1) a security interest in the goods may be perfected by perfecting a security interest in the document; and

(2) a security interest perfected in the document has priority over any security interest that becomes perfected in the goods by another method during that time.

(d) While goods are in the possession of a bailee that has issued a nonnegotiable document covering the goods, a security interest in the goods may be perfected by:

(1) issuance of a document in the name of the secured party;

(2) the bailee's receipt of notification of the secured party's interest; or

(3) filing as to the goods.

(e) A security interest in certificated securities, negotiable documents, or instruments is perfected without filing or the taking of possession for a period of 20 days from the time it attaches to the extent that it arises for new value given under an authenticated security agreement.

(f) A perfected security interest in a negotiable document or goods in possession of a bailee, other than one that has issued a negotiable document for the goods, remains perfected for 20 days without filing if the secured party makes available to the debtor the goods or documents representing the goods for the purpose of:

(1) ultimate sale or exchange; or

(2) loading, unloading, storing, shipping, transshipping, manufacturing, processing, or otherwise dealing with them in a manner preliminary to their sale or exchange.

(g) A perfected security interest in a certificated security or instrument remains perfected for 20 days without filing if the secured party delivers the security certificate or instrument to the debtor for the purpose of:

(1) ultimate sale or exchange; or

(2) presentation, collection, enforcement, renewal, or registration of transfer.

(h) After the 20-day period specified in subsection (e), (f), or (g) expires, perfection depends upon compliance with this article.

§ 9—313. When Possession by or Delivery to Secured Party Perfects Security Interest without Filing.

(a) Except as otherwise provided in subsection (b), a secured party may perfect a security interest in negotiable documents, goods, instruments, money, or tangible chattel paper by taking possession of the collateral. A secured party may perfect a security interest in certificated securities by taking delivery of the certificated securities under Section 8—301.

(b) With respect to goods covered by a certificate of title issued by this State, a secured party may perfect a security interest in the goods by taking possession of the goods only in the circumstances described in Section 9—316(d).

(c) With respect to collateral other than certificated securities and goods covered by a document, a secured party takes possession of collateral in the possession of a person other than the debtor, the secured party, or a lessee of the collateral from the debtor in the ordinary course of the debtor's business, when:

(1) the person in possession authenticates a record acknowledging that it holds possession of the collateral for the secured party's benefit; or

(2) the person takes possession of the collateral after having authenticated a record acknowledging that it will hold possession of collateral for the secured party's benefit.

(d) If perfection of a security interest depends upon possession of the collateral by a secured party, perfection occurs no earlier than the time the secured party takes possession and continues only while the secured party retains possession.

(e) A security interest in a certificated security in registered form is perfected by delivery when delivery of the certificated security occurs under Section 8—301 and remains perfected by delivery until the debtor obtains possession of the security certificate.

(f) A person in possession of collateral is not required to acknowledge that it holds possession for a secured party's benefit.

(g) If a person acknowledges that it holds possession for the secured party's benefit:

(1) the acknowledgment is effective under subsection (c) or Section 8—301(a), even if the acknowledgment violates the rights of a debtor; and

(2) unless the person otherwise agrees or law other than this article otherwise provides, the person does not owe any duty to the secured party and is not required to confirm the acknowledgment to another person.

(h) A secured party having possession of collateral does not relinquish possession by delivering the collateral to a person other than the debtor or a lessee of the collateral from the debtor in the ordinary course of the debtor's business if the person was instructed before the delivery or is instructed contemporaneously with the delivery:

(1) to hold possession of the collateral for the secured party's benefit; or

(2) to redeliver the collateral to the secured party.

(i) A secured party does not relinquish possession, even if a delivery under subsection (h) violates the rights of a debtor. A person to which collateral is delivered under subsection (h) does not owe any duty to the secured party and is not required to confirm the delivery to another person unless the person otherwise agrees or law other than this article otherwise provides.

§ 9—314. Perfection by Control.

(a) A security interest in investment property, deposit accounts, letter-of-credit rights, or electronic chattel paper may be perfected by control of the collateral under Section 9—104, 9—105, 9—106, or 9—107.

(b) A security interest in deposit accounts, electronic chattel paper, or letter-of-credit rights is perfected by control under Section 9—104, 9—105, or 9—107 when the secured party obtains control and remains perfected by control only while the secured party retains control.

(c) A security interest in investment property is perfected by control under Section 9—106 from the time the secured party obtains control and remains perfected by control until:

(1) the secured party does not have control; and

(2) one of the following occurs:

(A) if the collateral is a certificated security, the debtor has or acquires possession of the security certificate;

(B) if the collateral is an uncertificated security, the issuer has registered or registers the debtor as the registered owner; or

(C) if the collateral is a security entitlement, the debtor is or becomes the entitlement holder.

§ 9—315. Secured Party's Rights on Disposition of Collateral and in Proceeds.

(a) Except as otherwise provided in this article and in Section 2—403(2):

(1) a security interest or agricultural lien continues in collateral notwithstanding sale, lease, license, exchange, or other disposition thereof unless the secured party authorized the disposition free of the security interest or agricultural lien; and

(2) a security interest attaches to any identifiable proceeds of collateral.

(b) Proceeds that are commingled with other property are identifiable proceeds:

(1) if the proceeds are goods, to the extent provided by Section 9—336; and

(2) if the proceeds are not goods, to the extent that the secured party identifies the proceeds by a method of tracing, including application of equitable principles, that is permitted under law other than this article with respect to commingled property of the type involved.

(c) A security interest in proceeds is a perfected security interest if the security interest in the original collateral was perfected.

(d) A perfected security interest in proceeds becomes unperfected on the 21st day after the security interest attaches to the proceeds unless:

(1) the following conditions are satisfied:

(A) a filed financing statement covers the original collateral;

(B) the proceeds are collateral in which a security interest may be perfected by filing in the office in which the financing statement has been filed; and

(C) the proceeds are not acquired with cash proceeds;

(2) the proceeds are identifiable cash proceeds; or

(3) the security interest in the proceeds is perfected other than under subsection (c) when the security interest attaches to the proceeds or within 20 days thereafter.

(e) If a filed financing statement covers the original collateral, a security interest in proceeds which remains perfected under subsection (d)(1) becomes unperfected at the later of:

(1) when the effectiveness of the filed financing statement lapses under Section 9—515 or is terminated under Section 9—513; or

(2) the 21st day after the security interest attaches to the proceeds.

§ 9—316. Continued Perfection of Security Interest Following Change in Governing Law.

(a) A security interest perfected pursuant to the law of the jurisdiction designated in Section 9—301(1) or 9—305(c) remains perfected until the earliest of:

(1) the time perfection would have ceased under the law of that jurisdiction;

(2) the expiration of four months after a change of the debtor's location to another jurisdiction; or

(3) the expiration of one year after a transfer of collateral to a person that thereby becomes a debtor and is located in another jurisdiction.

(b) If a security interest described in subsection (a) becomes perfected under the law of the other jurisdiction before the earliest time or event described in that subsection, it remains perfected thereafter. If the security interest does not become perfected under the law of the other jurisdiction before the earliest time or event, it becomes unperfected and is deemed never to have been perfected as against a purchaser of the collateral for value.

(c) A possessory security interest in collateral, other than goods covered by a certificate of title and as-extracted collateral consisting of goods, remains continuously perfected if:

(1) the collateral is located in one jurisdiction and subject to a security interest perfected under the law of that jurisdiction;

(2) thereafter the collateral is brought into another jurisdiction; and

(3) upon entry into the other jurisdiction, the security interest is perfected under the law of the other jurisdiction.

(d) Except as otherwise provided in subsection (e), a security interest in goods covered by a certificate of title which is perfected by any method under the law of another jurisdiction when the goods become covered by a certificate of title from this State remains perfected until the security interest would have become unperfected under the law of the other jurisdiction had the goods not become so covered.

(e) A security interest described in subsection (d) becomes unperfected as against a purchaser of the goods for value and is deemed never to have been perfected as against a purchaser of the goods for value if the applicable requirements for perfection under Section 9—311(b) or 9—313 are not satisfied before the earlier of:

(1) the time the security interest would have become unperfected under the law of the other jurisdiction had the goods not become covered by a certificate of title from this State; or

(2) the expiration of four months after the goods had become so covered.

(f) A security interest in deposit accounts, letter-of-credit rights, or investment property which is perfected under the law of the bank's jurisdiction, the issuer's jurisdiction, a nominated person's jurisdiction, the securities intermediary's jurisdiction, or the commodity intermediary's jurisdiction, as applicable, remains perfected until the earlier of:

(1) the time the security interest would have become unperfected under the law of that jurisdiction; or

(2) the expiration of four months after a change of the applicable jurisdiction to another jurisdiction.

(g) If a security interest described in subsection (f) becomes perfected under the law of the other jurisdiction before the earlier of the time or the end of the period described in that subsection, it remains perfected thereafter. If the security interest does not become perfected under the law of the other jurisdiction before the earlier of that time or the end of that period, it becomes unperfected and is deemed never to have been perfected as against a purchaser of the collateral for value.

[Subpart 3. Priority]

§ 9—317. Interests That Take Priority over or Take Free of Security Interest or Agricultural Lien.

(a) A security interest or agricultural lien is subordinate to the rights of:

(1) a person entitled to priority under Section 9—322; and

(2) except as otherwise provided in subsection (e), a person that becomes a lien creditor before the earlier of the time:

(A) the security interest or agricultural lien is perfected; or

(B) one of the conditions specified in Section 9—203(b)(3) is met and a financing statement covering the collateral is filed.

(b) Except as otherwise provided in subsection (e), a buyer, other than a secured party, of tangible chattel paper, documents, goods, instruments, or a security certificate takes free of a security interest or agricultural lien if the buyer gives value and receives delivery of the collateral without knowledge of the security interest or agricultural lien and before it is perfected.

(c) Except as otherwise provided in subsection (e), a lessee of goods takes free of a security interest or agricultural lien if the lessee gives value and receives delivery of the collateral without knowledge of the security interest or agricultural lien and before it is perfected.

(d) A licensee of a general intangible or a buyer, other than a secured party, of accounts, electronic chattel paper, general intangibles, or investment property other than a certificated security takes free of a security interest if the licensee or buyer gives value without knowledge of the security interest and before it is perfected.

(e) Except as otherwise provided in Sections 9—320 and 9—321, if a person files a financing statement with respect to a purchase-money security interest before or within 20 days after the debtor receives delivery of the collateral, the security interest takes priority over the rights of a buyer, lessee, or lien creditor which arise between the time the security interest attaches and the time of filing.

§ 9—318. No Interest Retained in Right to Payment That Is Sold; Rights and Title of Seller of Account or Chattel Paper with Respect to Creditors and Purchasers.

(a) A debtor that has sold an account, chattel paper, payment intangible, or promissory note does not retain a legal or equitable interest in the collateral sold.

(b) For purposes of determining the rights of creditors of, and purchasers for value of an account or chattel paper from, a debtor that has sold an account or chattel paper, while the buyer's security interest is unperfected, the debtor is deemed to have rights and title to the account or chattel paper identical to those the debtor sold.

§ 9—319. Rights and Title of Consignee with Respect to Creditors and Purchasers.

(a) Except as otherwise provided in subsection (b), for purposes of determining the rights of creditors of, and purchasers for value of goods from, a consignee, while the goods are in the possession of the consignee, the consignee is deemed to have rights and title to the goods identical to those the consignor had or had power to transfer.

(b) For purposes of determining the rights of a creditor of a consignee, law other than this article determines the rights and title of a consignee while goods are in the consignee's possession if, under this part, a perfected security interest held by the consignor would have priority over the rights of the creditor.

§ 9—320. Buyer of Goods.

(a) Except as otherwise provided in subsection (e), a buyer in ordinary course of business, other than a person buying farm products from a person engaged in farming operations, takes free of a security interest created by the buyer's seller, even if the security interest is perfected and the buyer knows of its existence.

(b) Except as otherwise provided in subsection (e), a buyer of goods from a person who used or bought the goods for use primarily for personal, family, or household purposes takes free of a security interest, even if perfected, if the buyer buys:

(1) without knowledge of the security interest;

(2) for value;

(3) primarily for the buyer's personal, family, or household purposes; and

(4) before the filing of a financing statement covering the goods.

(c) To the extent that it affects the priority of a security interest over a buyer of goods under subsection (b), the period of effectiveness of a filing made in the jurisdiction in which the seller is located is governed by Section 9—316(a) and (b).

(d) A buyer in ordinary course of business buying oil, gas, or other minerals at the wellhead or minehead or after extraction takes free of an interest arising out of an encumbrance.

(e) Subsections (a) and (b) do not affect a security interest in goods in the possession of the secured party under Section 9—313.

§ 9—321. Licensee of General Intangible and Lessee of Goods in Ordinary Course of Business.

(a) In this section, "licensee in ordinary course of business" means a person that becomes a licensee of a general intangible in good faith, without knowledge that the license violates the rights of another person in the general intangible, and in the ordinary course from a person in the business of licensing general intangibles of that kind. A person becomes a licensee in the ordinary course if the license to the person comports with the usual or customary practices in the kind of business in which the licensor is engaged or with the licensor's own usual or customary practices.

(b) A licensee in ordinary course of business takes its rights under a nonexclusive license free of a security interest in the general intangible created by the licensor, even if the security interest is perfected and the licensee knows of its existence.

(c) A lessee in ordinary course of business takes its leasehold interest free of a security interest in the goods created by the lessor, even if the security interest is perfected and the lessee knows of its existence.

§ 9—322. Priorities among Conflicting Security Interests in and Agricultural Liens on Same Collateral.

(a) Except as otherwise provided in this section, priority among conflicting security interests and agricultural liens in the same collateral is determined according to the following rules:

(1) Conflicting perfected security interests and agricultural liens rank according to priority in time of filing or perfection.

Priority dates from the earlier of the time a filing covering the collateral is first made or the security interest or agricultural lien is first perfected, if there is no period thereafter when there is neither filing nor perfection.

(2) A perfected security interest or agricultural lien has priority over a conflicting unperfected security interest or agricultural lien.

(3) The first security interest or agricultural lien to attach or become effective has priority if conflicting security interests and agricultural liens are unperfected.

(b) For the purposes of subsection (a)(1):

(1) the time of filing or perfection as to a security interest in collateral is also the time of filing or perfection as to a security interest in proceeds; and

(2) the time of filing or perfection as to a security interest in collateral supported by a supporting obligation is also the time of filing or perfection as to a security interest in the supporting obligation.

(c) Except as otherwise provided in subsection (f), a security interest in collateral which qualifies for priority over a conflicting security interest under Section 9—327, 9—328, 9—329, 9—330, or 9—331 also has priority over a conflicting security interest in:

(1) any supporting obligation for the collateral; and

(2) proceeds of the collateral if:

(A) the security interest in proceeds is perfected;

(B) the proceeds are cash proceeds or of the same type as the collateral; and

(C) in the case of proceeds that are proceeds of proceeds, all intervening proceeds are cash proceeds, proceeds of the same type as the collateral, or an account relating to the collateral.

(d) Subject to subsection (e) and except as otherwise provided in subsection (f), if a security interest in chattel paper, deposit accounts, negotiable documents, instruments, investment property, or letter-of-credit rights is perfected by a method other than filing, conflicting perfected security interests in proceeds of the collateral rank according to priority in time of filing.

(e) Subsection (d) applies only if the proceeds of the collateral are not cash proceeds, chattel paper, negotiable documents, instruments, investment property, or letter-of-credit rights.

(f) Subsections (a) through (e) are subject to:

(1) subsection (g) and the other provisions of this part;

(2) Section 4—210 with respect to a security interest of a collecting bank;

(3) Section 5—118 with respect to a security interest of an issuer or nominated person; and

(4) Section 9—110 with respect to a security interest arising under Article 2 or 2A.

(g) A perfected agricultural lien on collateral has priority over a conflicting security interest in or agricultural lien on the same collateral if the statute creating the agricultural lien so provides.

§ 9—323. Future Advances.

(a) Except as otherwise provided in subsection (c), for purposes of determining the priority of a perfected security interest under Section 9—322(a)(1), perfection of the security interest dates from the time an advance is made to the extent that the security interest secures an advance that:

(1) is made while the security interest is perfected only:

(A) under Section 9—309 when it attaches; or

(B) temporarily under Section 9—312(e), (f), or (g); and

(2) is not made pursuant to a commitment entered into before or while the security interest is perfected by a method other than under Section 9—309 or 9—312(e), (f), or (g).

(b) Except as otherwise provided in subsection (c), a security interest is subordinate to the rights of a person that becomes a lien creditor to the extent that the security interest secures an advance made more than 45 days after the person becomes a lien creditor unless the advance is made:

(1) without knowledge of the lien; or

(2) pursuant to a commitment entered into without knowledge of the lien.

(c) Subsections (a) and (b) do not apply to a security interest held by a secured party that is a buyer of accounts, chattel paper, payment intangibles, or promissory notes or a consignor.

(d) Except as otherwise provided in subsection (e), a buyer of goods other than a buyer in ordinary course of business takes free of a security interest to the extent that it secures advances made after the earlier of:

(1) the time the secured party acquires knowledge of the buyer's purchase; or

(2) 45 days after the purchase.

(e) Subsection (d) does not apply if the advance is made pursuant to a commitment entered into without knowledge of the buyer's purchase and before the expiration of the 45-day period.

(f) Except as otherwise provided in subsection (g), a lessee of goods, other than a lessee in ordinary course of business, takes the leasehold interest free of a security interest to the extent that it secures advances made after the earlier of:

(1) the time the secured party acquires knowledge of the lease; or

(2) 45 days after the lease contract becomes enforceable.

(g) Subsection (f) does not apply if the advance is made pursuant to a commitment entered into without knowledge of the lease and before the expiration of the 45-day period.

§ 9—324. Priority of Purchase-Money Security Interests.

(a) Except as otherwise provided in subsection (g), a perfected purchase-money security interest in goods other than inventory or livestock has priority over a conflicting security interest in the same goods, and, except as otherwise provided in Section 9—327, a perfected security interest in its identifiable proceeds also has priority, if the purchase-money security interest is perfected when the debtor receives possession of the collateral or within 20 days thereafter.

(b) Subject to subsection (c) and except as otherwise provided in subsection (g), a perfected purchase-money security interest in inventory has priority over a conflicting security interest in the same inventory, has priority over a conflicting security interest in chattel paper or an instrument constituting proceeds of the inventory and in proceeds of the chattel paper, if so provided in Section 9—330, and, except as otherwise provided in Section 9—327, also has priority in identifiable cash proceeds of the inventory to the extent the identifiable cash proceeds are received on or before the delivery of the inventory to a buyer, if:

(1) the purchase-money security interest is perfected when the debtor receives possession of the inventory;

(2) the purchase-money secured party sends an authenticated notification to the holder of the conflicting security interest;

(3) the holder of the conflicting security interest receives the notification within five years before the debtor receives possession of the inventory; and

(4) the notification states that the person sending the notification has or expects to acquire a purchase-money security interest in inventory of the debtor and describes the inventory.

(c) Subsections (b)(2) through (4) apply only if the holder of the conflicting security interest had filed a financing statement covering the same types of inventory:

(1) if the purchase-money security interest is perfected by filing, before the date of the filing; or

(2) if the purchase-money security interest is temporarily perfected without filing or possession under Section 9—312(f), before the beginning of the 20-day period thereunder.

(d) Subject to subsection (e) and except as otherwise provided in subsection (g), a perfected purchase-money security interest in livestock that are farm products has priority over a conflicting security interest in the same livestock, and, except as otherwise provided in Section 9—327, a perfected security interest in their identifiable proceeds and identifiable products in their unmanufactured states also has priority, if:

(1) the purchase-money security interest is perfected when the debtor receives possession of the livestock;

(2) the purchase-money secured party sends an authenticated notification to the holder of the conflicting security interest;

(3) the holder of the conflicting security interest receives the notification within six months before the debtor receives possession of the livestock; and

(4) the notification states that the person sending the notification has or expects to acquire a purchase-money security interest in livestock of the debtor and describes the livestock.

(e) Subsections (d)(2) through (4) apply only if the holder of the conflicting security interest had filed a financing statement covering the same types of livestock:

(1) if the purchase-money security interest is perfected by filing, before the date of the filing; or

(2) if the purchase-money security interest is temporarily perfected without filing or possession under Section 9—312(f), before the beginning of the 20-day period thereunder.

(f) Except as otherwise provided in subsection (g), a perfected purchase-money security interest in software has priority over a conflicting security interest in the same collateral, and, except as otherwise provided in Section 9—327, a perfected security interest in its identifiable proceeds also has priority, to the extent that the purchase-money security interest in the goods in which the software was acquired for use has priority in the goods and proceeds of the goods under this section.

(g) If more than one security interest qualifies for priority in the same collateral under subsection (a), (b), (d), or (f):

(1) a security interest securing an obligation incurred as all or part of the price of the collateral has priority over a security interest securing an obligation incurred for value given to enable the debtor to acquire rights in or the use of collateral; and

(2) in all other cases, Section 9—322(a) applies to the qualifying security interests.

§ 9—325. Priority of Security Interests in Transferred Collateral.

(a) Except as otherwise provided in subsection (b), a security interest created by a debtor is subordinate to a security interest in the same collateral created by another person if:

(1) the debtor acquired the collateral subject to the security interest created by the other person;

(2) the security interest created by the other person was perfected when the debtor acquired the collateral; and

(3) there is no period thereafter when the security interest is unperfected.

(b) Subsection (a) subordinates a security interest only if the security interest:

(1) otherwise would have priority solely under Section 9—322(a) or 9—324; or

(2) arose solely under Section 2—711(3) or 2A—508(5).

§ 9—326. Priority of Security Interests Created by New Debtor.

(a) Subject to subsection (b), a security interest created by a new debtor which is perfected by a filed financing statement that is effective solely under Section 9—508 in collateral in which a new debtor has or acquires rights is subordinate to a security interest in the same collateral which is perfected other than by a filed financing statement that is effective solely under Section 9—508.

(b) The other provisions of this part determine the priority among conflicting security interests in the same collateral perfected by filed financing statements that are effective solely under Section 9—508. However, if the security agreements to which a new debtor became bound as debtor were not entered into by the same original debtor, the conflicting security interests rank according to priority in time of the new debtor's having become bound.

§ 9—327. Priority of Security Interests in Deposit Account.

The following rules govern priority among conflicting security interests in the same deposit account:

(1) A security interest held by a secured party having control of the deposit account under Section 9—104 has priority over a conflicting security interest held by a secured party that does not have control.

(2) Except as otherwise provided in paragraphs (3) and (4), security interests perfected by control under Section 9—314 rank according to priority in time of obtaining control.

(3) Except as otherwise provided in paragraph (4), a security interest held by the bank with which the deposit account is maintained has priority over a conflicting security interest held by another secured party.

(4) A security interest perfected by control under Section 9—104(a)(3) has priority over a security interest held by the bank with which the deposit account is maintained.

§ 9—328. Priority of Security Interests in Investment Property.

The following rules govern priority among conflicting security interests in the same investment property:

(1) A security interest held by a secured party having control of investment property under Section 9—106 has priority over a security interest held by a secured party that does not have control of the investment property.

(2) Except as otherwise provided in paragraphs (3) and (4), conflicting security interests held by secured parties each of which has control under Section 9—106 rank according to priority in time of:

(A) if the collateral is a security, obtaining control;

(B) if the collateral is a security entitlement carried in a securities account and:

(i) if the secured party obtained control under Section 8—106(d)(1), the secured party's becoming the person for which the securities account is maintained;

(ii) if the secured party obtained control under Section 8—106(d)(2), the securities intermediary's agreement to comply with the secured party's entitlement orders with respect to security entitlements carried or to be carried in the securities account; or

(iii) if the secured party obtained control through another person under Section 8—106(d)(3), the time on which priority would be based under this paragraph if the other person were the secured party; or

(C) if the collateral is a commodity contract carried with a commodity intermediary, the satisfaction of the requirement for control specified in Section 9—106(b)(2) with respect to commodity contracts carried or to be carried with the commodity intermediary.

(3) A security interest held by a securities intermediary in a security entitlement or a securities account maintained with the securities intermediary has priority over a conflicting security interest held by another secured party.

(4) A security interest held by a commodity intermediary in a commodity contract or a commodity account maintained with the commodity intermediary has priority over a conflicting security interest held by another secured party.

(5) A security interest in a certificated security in registered form which is perfected by taking delivery under Section 9—313(a) and not by control under Section 9—314 has priority over a conflicting security interest perfected by a method other than control.

(6) Conflicting security interests created by a broker, securities intermediary, or commodity intermediary which are perfected without control under Section 9—106 rank equally.

(7) In all other cases, priority among conflicting security interests in investment property is governed by Sections 9—322 and 9—323.

§ 9—329. Priority of Security Interests in Letter-of-Credit Right.

The following rules govern priority among conflicting security interests in the same letter-of-credit right:

(1) A security interest held by a secured party having control of the letter-of-credit right under Section 9—107 has priority to the extent of its control over a conflicting security interest held by a secured party that does not have control.

(2) Security interests perfected by control under Section 9—314 rank according to priority in time of obtaining control.

§ 9—330. Priority of Purchaser of Chattel Paper or Instrument.

(a) A purchaser of chattel paper has priority over a security interest in the chattel paper which is claimed merely as proceeds of inventory subject to a security interest if:

(1) in good faith and in the ordinary course of the purchaser's business, the purchaser gives new value and takes possession of the chattel paper or obtains control of the chattel paper under Section 9—105; and

(2) the chattel paper does not indicate that it has been assigned to an identified assignee other than the purchaser.

(b) A purchaser of chattel paper has priority over a security interest in the chattel paper which is claimed other than merely as proceeds of inventory subject to a security interest if the purchaser gives new value and takes possession of the chattel paper or obtains control of the chattel paper under Section 9—105 in good faith, in the ordinary course of the purchaser's business, and without knowledge that the purchase violates the rights of the secured party.

(c) Except as otherwise provided in Section 9—327, a purchaser having priority in chattel paper under subsection (a) or (b) also has priority in proceeds of the chattel paper to the extent that:

(1) Section 9—322 provides for priority in the proceeds; or

(2) the proceeds consist of the specific goods covered by the chattel paper or cash proceeds of the specific goods, even if the purchaser's security interest in the proceeds is unperfected.

(d) Except as otherwise provided in Section 9—331(a), a purchaser of an instrument has priority over a security interest in the instrument perfected by a method other than possession if the purchaser gives value and takes possession of the instrument in good faith and without knowledge that the purchase violates the rights of the secured party.

(e) For purposes of subsections (a) and (b), the holder of a purchase-money security interest in inventory gives new value for chattel paper constituting proceeds of the inventory.

(f) For purposes of subsections (b) and (d), if chattel paper or an instrument indicates that it has been assigned to an identified secured party other than the purchaser, a purchaser of the chattel paper or instrument has knowledge that the purchase violates the rights of the secured party.

§ 9—331. Priority of Rights of Purchasers of Instruments, Documents, and Securities under Other Articles; Priority of Interests in Financial Assets and Security Entitlements under Article 8.

(a) This article does not limit the rights of a holder in due course of a negotiable instrument, a holder to which a negotiable document of title has been duly negotiated, or a protected purchaser of a security. These holders or purchasers take priority over an earlier security interest, even if perfected, to the extent provided in Articles 3, 7, and 8.

(b) This article does not limit the rights of or impose liability on a person to the extent that the person is protected against the assertion of a claim under Article 8.

(c) Filing under this article does not constitute notice of a claim or defense to the holders, or purchasers, or persons described in subsections (a) and (b).

§ 9—332. Transfer of Money; Transfer of Funds from Deposit Account.

(a) A transferee of money takes the money free of a security interest unless the transferee acts in collusion with the debtor in violating the rights of the secured party.

(b) A transferee of funds from a deposit account takes the funds free of a security interest in the deposit account unless the transferee acts in collusion with the debtor in violating the rights of the secured party.

§ 9—333. Priority of Certain Liens Arising by Operation of Law.

(a) In this section, "possessory lien" means an interest, other than a security interest or an agricultural lien:

(1) which secures payment or performance of an obligation for services or materials furnished with respect to goods by a person in the ordinary course of the person's business;

(2) which is created by statute or rule of law in favor of the person; and

(3) whose effectiveness depends on the person's possession of the goods.

(b) A possessory lien on goods has priority over a security interest in the goods unless the lien is created by a statute that expressly provides otherwise.

§ 9—334. Priority of Security Interests in Fixtures and Crops.

(a) A security interest under this article may be created in goods that are fixtures or may continue in goods that become fixtures. A security interest does not exist under this article in ordinary building materials incorporated into an improvement on land.

(b) This article does not prevent creation of an encumbrance upon fixtures under real property law.

(c) In cases not governed by subsections (d) through (h), a security interest in fixtures is subordinate to a conflicting interest of an encumbrancer or owner of the related real property other than the debtor.

(d) Except as otherwise provided in subsection (h), a perfected security interest in fixtures has priority over a conflicting interest of an encumbrancer or owner of the real property if the debtor has an interest of record in or is in possession of the real property and:

(1) the security interest is a purchase-money security interest;

(2) the interest of the encumbrancer or owner arises before the goods become fixtures; and

(3) the security interest is perfected by a fixture filing before the goods become fixtures or within 20 days thereafter.

(e) A perfected security interest in fixtures has priority over a conflicting interest of an encumbrancer or owner of the real property if:

(1) the debtor has an interest of record in the real property or is in possession of the real property and the security interest:

(A) is perfected by a fixture filing before the interest of the encumbrancer or owner is of record; and

(B) has priority over any conflicting interest of a predecessor in title of the encumbrancer or owner;

(2) before the goods become fixtures, the security interest is perfected by any method permitted by this article and the fixtures are readily removable:

(A) factory or office machines;

(B) equipment that is not primarily used or leased for use in the operation of the real property; or

(C) replacements of domestic appliances that are consumer goods;

(3) the conflicting interest is a lien on the real property obtained by legal or equitable proceedings after the security interest was perfected by any method permitted by this article; or

(4) the security interest is:

(A) created in a manufactured home in a manufactured-home transaction; and

(B) perfected pursuant to a statute described in Section 9—311(a)(2).

(f) A security interest in fixtures, whether or not perfected, has priority over a conflicting interest of an encumbrancer or owner of the real property if:

(1) the encumbrancer or owner has, in an authenticated record, consented to the security interest or disclaimed an interest in the goods as fixtures; or

(2) the debtor has a right to remove the goods as against the encumbrancer or owner.

(g) The priority of the security interest under paragraph (f)(2) continues for a reasonable time if the debtor's right to remove the goods as against the encumbrancer or owner terminates.

(h) A mortgage is a construction mortgage to the extent that it secures an obligation incurred for the construction of an improvement on land, including the acquisition cost of the land, if a recorded record of the mortgage so indicates. Except as otherwise provided in subsections (e) and (f), a security interest in fixtures is subordinate to a construction mortgage if a record of the mortgage is recorded before the goods become fixtures and the goods become fixtures before the completion of the construction. A mortgage has this priority to the same extent as a construction mortgage to the extent that it is given to refinance a construction mortgage.

(i) A perfected security interest in crops growing on real property has priority over a conflicting interest of an encumbrancer or owner of the real property if the debtor has an interest of record in or is in possession of the real property.

(j) Subsection (i) prevails over any inconsistent provisions of the following statutes:

[List here any statutes containing provisions inconsistent with subsection (i).]

Legislative Note: States that amend statutes to remove provisions inconsistent with subsection (i) need not enact subsection (j).

§ 9—335. Accessions.

(a) A security interest may be created in an accession and continues in collateral that becomes an accession.

(b) If a security interest is perfected when the collateral becomes an accession, the security interest remains perfected in the collateral.

(c) Except as otherwise provided in subsection (d), the other provisions of this part determine the priority of a security interest in an accession.

(d) A security interest in an accession is subordinate to a security interest in the whole which is perfected by compliance with the requirements of a certificate-of-title statute under Section 9—311(b).

(e) After default, subject to Part 6, a secured party may remove an accession from other goods if the security interest in the accession has priority over the claims of every person having an interest in the whole.

(f) A secured party that removes an accession from other goods under subsection (e) shall promptly reimburse any holder of a security interest or other lien on, or owner of, the whole or of the other goods, other than the debtor, for the cost of repair of any physical injury to the whole or the other goods. The secured party need not reimburse the holder or owner for any diminution in value of the whole or the other goods caused by the absence of the accession removed or by any necessity for replacing it. A person entitled to reimbursement may refuse permission to remove until the secured party gives adequate assurance for the performance of the obligation to reimburse.

§ 9—336. Commingled Goods.

(a) In this section, "commingled goods" means goods that are physically united with other goods in such a manner that their identity is lost in a product or mass.

(b) A security interest does not exist in commingled goods as such. However, a security interest may attach to a product or mass that results when goods become commingled goods.

(c) If collateral becomes commingled goods, a security interest attaches to the product or mass.

(d) If a security interest in collateral is perfected before the collateral becomes commingled goods, the security interest that attaches to the product or mass under subsection (c) is perfected.

(e) Except as otherwise provided in subsection (f), the other provisions of this part determine the priority of a security interest that attaches to the product or mass under subsection (c).

(f) If more than one security interest attaches to the product or mass under subsection (c), the following rules determine priority:

(1) A security interest that is perfected under subsection (d) has priority over a security interest that is unperfected at the time the collateral becomes commingled goods.

(2) If more than one security interest is perfected under subsection (d), the security interests rank equally in proportion to the value of the collateral at the time it became commingled goods.

§ 9—337. Priority of Security Interests in Goods Covered by Certificate of Title.

If, while a security interest in goods is perfected by any method under the law of another jurisdiction, this State issues a certificate of title that does not show that the goods are subject to the security interest or contain a statement that they may be subject to security interests not shown on the certificate:

(1) a buyer of the goods, other than a person in the business of selling goods of that kind, takes free of the security interest if the buyer gives value and receives delivery of the goods after issuance of the certificate and without knowledge of the security interest; and

(2) the security interest is subordinate to a conflicting security interest in the goods that attaches, and is perfected under Section 9—311(b), after issuance of the certificate and without the conflicting secured party's knowledge of the security interest.

§ 9—338. Priority of Security Interest or Agricultural Lien Perfected by Filed Financing Statement Providing Certain Incorrect Information.

If a security interest or agricultural lien is perfected by a filed financing statement providing information described in Section 9—516(b)(5) which is incorrect at the time the financing statement is filed:

(1) the security interest or agricultural lien is subordinate to a conflicting perfected security interest in the collateral to the extent that the holder of the conflicting security interest gives value in reasonable reliance upon the incorrect information; and

(2) a purchaser, other than a secured party, of the collateral takes free of the security interest or agricultural lien to the extent that, in reasonable reliance upon the incorrect information, the purchaser gives value and, in the case of chattel paper, documents, goods, instruments, or a security certificate, receives delivery of the collateral.

§ 9—339 Priority Subject to Subordination.

This article does not preclude subordination by agreement by a person entitled to priority.

[Subpart 4. Rights of Bank]

§ 9—340. Effectiveness of Right of Recoupment or Set-Off against Deposit Account.

(a) Except as otherwise provided in subsection (c), a bank with which a deposit account is maintained may exercise any right of recoupment or set-off against a secured party that holds a security interest in the deposit account.

(b) Except as otherwise provided in subsection (c), the application of this article to a security interest in a deposit account does not affect a right of recoupment or set-off of the secured party as to a deposit account maintained with the secured party.

(c) The exercise by a bank of a set-off against a deposit account is ineffective against a secured party that holds a security interest in the deposit account which is perfected by control under Section 9—104(a)(3), if the set-off is based on a claim against the debtor.

§ 9—341. Bank's Rights and Duties with Respect to Deposit Account.

Except as otherwise provided in Section 9—340(c), and unless the bank otherwise agrees in an authenticated record, a bank's rights and duties with respect to a deposit account maintained with the bank are not terminated, suspended, or modified by:

(1) the creation, attachment, or perfection of a security interest in the deposit account;

(2) the bank's knowledge of the security interest; or

(3) the bank's receipt of instructions from the secured party.

§ 9—342. Bank's Right to Refuse to Enter into or Disclose Existence of Control Agreement.

This article does not require a bank to enter into an agreement of the kind described in Section 9—104(a)(2), even if its customer so requests or directs. A bank that has entered into such an agreement is not required to confirm the existence of the agreement to another person unless requested to do so by its customer.

Part 4 Rights of Third Parties

§ 9—401. Alienability of Debtor's Rights.

(a) as otherwise provided in subsection (b) and Sections 9—406, 9—407, 9—408, and 9—409, whether a debtor's rights in collateral may be voluntarily or involuntarily transferred is governed by law other than this article.

(b) An agreement between the debtor and secured party which prohibits a transfer of the debtor's rights in collateral or makes the transfer a default does not prevent the transfer from taking effect.

§ 9—402. Secured Party Not Obligated on Contract of Debtor or in Tort.

The existence of a security interest, agricultural lien, or authority given to a debtor to dispose of or use collateral, without more, does not subject a secured party to liability in contract or tort for the debtor's acts or omissions.

§ 9—403. Agreement Not to Assert Defenses against Assignee.

(a) In this section, "value" has the meaning provided in Section 3—303(a).

(b) Except as otherwise provided in this section, an agreement between an account debtor and an assignor not to assert against an assignee any claim or defense that the account debtor may have against the assignor is enforceable by an assignee that takes an assignment:

(1) for value;

(2) in good faith;

(3) without notice of a claim of a property or possessory right to the property assigned; and

(4) without notice of a defense or claim in recoupment of the type that may be asserted against a person entitled to enforce a negotiable instrument under Section 3—305(a).

(c) Subsection (b) does not apply to defenses of a type that may be asserted against a holder in due course of a negotiable instrument under Section 3—305(b).

(d) In a consumer transaction, if a record evidences the account debtor's obligation, law other than this article requires that the record include a statement to the effect that the rights of an assignee are subject to claims or defenses that the account debtor could assert against the original obligee, and the record does not include such a statement:

(1) the record has the same effect as if the record included such a statement; and

(2) the account debtor may assert against an assignee those claims and defenses that would have been available if the record included such a statement.

(e) This section is subject to law other than this article which establishes a different rule for an account debtor who is an individual and who incurred the obligation primarily for personal, family, or household purposes.

(f) Except as otherwise provided in subsection (d), this section does not displace law other than this article which gives effect to an agreement by an account debtor not to assert a claim or defense against an assignee.

§ 9—404. Rights Acquired by Assignee; Claims and Defenses against Assignee.

(a) Unless an account debtor has made an enforceable agreement not to assert defenses or claims, and subject to subsections (b) through (e), the rights of an assignee are subject to:

(1) all terms of the agreement between the account debtor and assignor and any defense or claim in recoupment arising from the transaction that gave rise to the contract; and

(2) any other defense or claim of the account debtor against the assignor which accrues before the account debtor receives a notification of the assignment authenticated by the assignor or the assignee.

(b) Subject to subsection (c) and except as otherwise provided in subsection (d), the claim of an account debtor against an assignor may be asserted against an assignee under subsection (a) only to reduce the amount the account debtor owes.

(c) This section is subject to law other than this article which establishes a different rule for an account debtor who is an individual and who incurred the obligation primarily for personal, family, or household purposes.

(d) In a consumer transaction, if a record evidences the account debtor's obligation, law other than this article requires that the record include a statement to the effect that the account debtor's recovery against an assignee with respect to claims and defenses against the assignor may not exceed amounts paid by the account debtor under the record, and the record does not include such a statement, the extent to which a claim of an account debtor against the assignor may be asserted against an assignee is determined as if the record included such a statement.

(e) This section does not apply to an assignment of a health-care-insurance receivable.

§ 9—405. Modification of Assigned Contract.

(a) A modification of or substitution for an assigned contract is effective against an assignee if made in good faith. The assignee acquires corresponding rights under the modified or substituted contract. The assignment may provide that the modification or substitution is a breach of contract by the assignor. This subsection is subject to subsections (b) through (d).

(b) Subsection (a) applies to the extent that:

(1) the right to payment or a part thereof under an assigned contract has not been fully earned by performance; or

(2) the right to payment or a part thereof has been fully earned by performance and the account debtor has not received notification of the assignment under Section 9—406(a).

(c) This section is subject to law other than this article which establishes a different rule for an account debtor who is an individual and who incurred the obligation primarily for personal, family, or household purposes.

(d) This section does not apply to an assignment of a health-care-insurance receivable.

§ 9—406. Discharge of Account Debtor; Notification of Assignment; Identification and Proof of Assignment; Restrictions on Assignment of Accounts, Chattel Paper, Payment Intangibles, and Promissory Notes Ineffective.

(a) Subject to subsections (b) through (i), an account debtor on an account, chattel paper, or a payment intangible may discharge its obligation by paying the assignor until, but not after, the account debtor receives a notification, authenticated by the assignor or the assignee, that the amount due or to become due has been assigned and that payment is to be made to the assignee. After receipt of the notification, the account debtor may discharge its obligation by paying the assignee and may not discharge the obligation by paying the assignor.

(b) Subject to subsection (h), notification is ineffective under subsection (a):

(1) if it does not reasonably identify the rights assigned;

(2) to the extent that an agreement between an account debtor and a seller of a payment intangible limits the account debtor's duty to pay a person other than the seller and the limitation is effective under law other than this article; or

(3) at the option of an account debtor, if the notification notifies the account debtor to make less than the full amount of any installment or other periodic payment to the assignee, even if:

(A) only a portion of the account, chattel paper, or payment intangible has been assigned to that assignee;

(B) a portion has been assigned to another assignee; or

(C) the account debtor knows that the assignment to that assignee is limited.

(c) Subject to subsection (h), if requested by the account debtor, an assignee shall seasonably furnish reasonable proof that the assignment has been made. Unless the assignee complies, the account debtor may discharge its obligation by paying the assignor, even if the account debtor has received a notification under subsection (a).

(d) Except as otherwise provided in subsection (e) and Sections 2A—303 and 9—407, and subject to subsection (h), a term in an agreement between an account debtor and an assignor or in a promissory note is ineffective to the extent that it:

(1) prohibits, restricts, or requires the consent of the account debtor or person obligated on the promissory note to the assignment or transfer of, or the creation, attachment, perfection, or enforcement of a security interest in, the account, chattel paper, payment intangible, or promissory note; or

(2) provides that the assignment or transfer or the creation, attachment, perfection, or enforcement of the security interest may give rise to a default, breach, right of recoupment, claim, defense, termination, right of termination, or remedy under the account, chattel paper, payment intangible, or promissory note.

(e) Subsection (d) does not apply to the sale of a payment intangible or promissory note.

(f) Except as otherwise provided in Sections 2A—303 and 9—407 and subject to subsections (h) and (i), a rule of law, statute, or regulation that prohibits, restricts, or requires the consent of a government, governmental body or official, or account debtor to the assignment or transfer of, or creation of a security interest in, an account or chattel paper is ineffective to the extent that the rule of law, statute, or regulation:

(1) prohibits, restricts, or requires the consent of the government, governmental body or official, or account debtor to the assignment or transfer of, or the creation, attachment, perfection, or enforcement of a security interest in the account or chattel paper; or

(2) provides that the assignment or transfer or the creation, attachment, perfection, or enforcement of the security interest may give rise to a default, breach, right of recoupment, claim, defense, termination, right of termination, or remedy under the account or chattel paper.

(g) Subject to subsection (h), an account debtor may not waive or vary its option under subsection (b)(3).

(h) This section is subject to law other than this article which establishes a different rule for an account debtor who is an individual and who incurred the obligation primarily for personal, family, or household purposes.

(i) This section does not apply to an assignment of a health-care-insurance receivable.

(j) This section prevails over any inconsistent provisions of the following statutes, rules, and regulations:

[List here any statutes, rules, and regulations containing provisions inconsistent with this section.]

Legislative Note: States that amend statutes, rules, and regulations to remove provisions inconsistent with this section need not enact subsection (j).

§ 9—407. Restrictions on Creation or Enforcement of Security Interest in Leasehold Interest or in Lessor's Residual Interest.

(a) Except as otherwise provided in subsection (b), a term in a lease agreement is ineffective to the extent that it:

(1) prohibits, restricts, or requires the consent of a party to the lease to the assignment or transfer of, or the creation, attachment, perfection, or enforcement of a security interest in an interest of a party under the lease contract or in the lessor's residual interest in the goods; or

(2) provides that the assignment or transfer or the creation, attachment, perfection, or enforcement of the security interest may give rise to a default, breach, right of recoupment, claim, defense, termination, right of termination, or remedy under the lease.

(b) Except as otherwise provided in Section 2A—303(7), a term described in subsection (a)(2) is effective to the extent that there is:

(1) a transfer by the lessee of the lessee's right of possession or use of the goods in violation of the term; or

(2) a delegation of a material performance of either party to the lease contract in violation of the term.

(c) The creation, attachment, perfection, or enforcement of a security interest in the lessor's interest under the lease contract or the lessor's residual interest in the goods is not a transfer that materially impairs the lessee's prospect of obtaining return performance or materially changes the duty of or materially increases the burden or risk imposed on the lessee within the purview of Section 2A—303(4) unless, and then only to the extent that, enforcement actually results in a delegation of material performance of the lessor.

§ 9—408. Restrictions on Assignment of Promissory Notes, Health-Care-Insurance Receivables, and Certain General Intangibles Ineffective.

(a) Except as otherwise provided in subsection (b), a term in a promissory note or in an agreement between an account debtor and a debtor which relates to a health-care-insurance receivable or a general intangible, including a contract, permit, license, or franchise, and which term prohibits, restricts, or requires the consent of the person obligated on the promissory note or the account debtor to, the assignment or transfer of, or creation, attachment, or perfection of a security interest in, the promissory note, health-care-insurance receivable, or general intangible, is ineffective to the extent that the term:

(1) would impair the creation, attachment, or perfection of a security interest; or

(2) provides that the assignment or transfer or the creation, attachment, or perfection of the security interest may give rise to a default, breach, right of recoupment, claim, defense, termination, right of termination, or remedy under the promissory note, health-care-insurance receivable, or general intangible.

(b) Subsection (a) applies to a security interest in a payment intangible or promissory note only if the security interest arises out of a sale of the payment intangible or promissory note.

(c) A rule of law, statute, or regulation that prohibits, restricts, or requires the consent of a government, governmental body or official, person obligated on a promissory note, or account debtor to the assignment or transfer of, or creation of a security interest in, a promissory note, health-care-insurance receivable, or general intangible, including a contract, permit, license, or franchise between an account debtor and a debtor, is ineffective to the extent that the rule of law, statute, or regulation:

(1) would impair the creation, attachment, or perfection of a security interest; or

(2) provides that the assignment or transfer or the creation, attachment, or perfection of the security interest may give rise to a default, breach, right of recoupment, claim, defense, termination, right of termination, or remedy under the promissory note, health-care-insurance receivable, or general intangible.

(d) To the extent that a term in a promissory note or in an agreement between an account debtor and a debtor which relates to a health-care-insurance receivable or general intangible or a rule of law, statute, or regulation described in subsection (c) would be effective under law other than this article but is ineffective under subsection (a) or (c), the creation, attachment, or perfection of a security interest in the promissory note, health-care-insurance receivable, or general intangible:

(1) is not enforceable against the person obligated on the promissory note or the account debtor;

(2) does not impose a duty or obligation on the person obligated on the promissory note or the account debtor;

(3) does not require the person obligated on the promissory note or the account debtor to recognize the security interest, pay or render performance to the secured party, or accept payment or performance from the secured party;

(4) does not entitle the secured party to use or assign the debtor's rights under the promissory note, health-care-insurance receivable, or general intangible, including any related information or materials furnished to the debtor in the transaction giving rise to the promissory note, health-care-insurance receivable, or general intangible;

(5) does not entitle the secured party to use, assign, possess, or have access to any trade secrets or confidential information of the person obligated on the promissory note or the account debtor; and

(6) does not entitle the secured party to enforce the security interest in the promissory note, health-care-insurance receivable, or general intangible.

(e) This section prevails over any inconsistent provisions of the following statutes, rules, and regulations:

[List here any statutes, rules, and regulations containing provisions inconsistent with this section.]

Legislative Note: States that amend statutes, rules, and regulations to remove provisions inconsistent with this section need not enact subsection (e).

§ 9—409. Restrictions on Assignment of Letter-of-Credit Rights Ineffective.

(a) A term in a letter of credit or a rule of law, statute, regulation, custom, or practice applicable to the letter of credit which prohibits, restricts, or requires the consent of an applicant, issuer, or nominated person to a beneficiary's assignment of or creation of a security interest in a letter-of-credit right is ineffective to the extent that the term or rule of law, statute, regulation, custom, or practice:

(1) would impair the creation, attachment, or perfection of a security interest in the letter-of-credit right; or

(2) provides that the assignment or the creation, attachment, or perfection of the security interest may give rise to a default, breach, right of recoupment, claim, defense, termination, right of termination, or remedy under the letter-of-credit right.

(b) To the extent that a term in a letter of credit is ineffective under subsection (a) but would be effective under law other than this article or a custom or practice applicable to the letter of credit, to the transfer of a right to draw or otherwise demand performance under the letter of credit, or to the assignment of a right to proceeds of the letter of credit, the creation, attachment, or perfection of a security interest in the letter-of-credit right:

(1) is not enforceable against the applicant, issuer, nominated person, or transferee beneficiary;

(2) imposes no duties or obligations on the applicant, issuer, nominated person, or transferee beneficiary; and

(3) does not require the applicant, issuer, nominated person, or transferee beneficiary to recognize the security interest, pay or render performance to the secured party, or accept payment or other performance from the secured party.

Part 5 Filing

[Subpart 1. Filing Office; Contents and Effectiveness of Financing Statement]

§ 9—501. Filing Office.

(a) Except as otherwise provided in subsection (b), if the local law of this State governs perfection of a security interest or agricultural lien, the office in which to file a financing statement to perfect the security interest or agricultural lien is:

(1) the office designated for the filing or recording of a record of a mortgage on the related real property, if:

(A) the collateral is as-extracted collateral or timber to be cut; or

(B) the financing statement is filed as a fixture filing and the collateral is goods that are or are to become fixtures; or

(2) the office of [ ] [or any office duly authorized by [ ]], in all other cases, including a case in which the collateral is goods that are or are to become fixtures and the financing statement is not filed as a fixture filing.

(b) The office in which to file a financing statement to perfect a security interest in collateral, including fixtures, of a transmitting utility is the office of [ ]. The financing statement also constitutes a fixture filing as to the collateral indicated in the financing statement which is or is to become fixtures.

Legislative Note: The State should designate the filing office where the brackets appear. The filing office may be that of a governmental official (e.g., the Secretary of State) or a private party that maintains the State's filing system.

§ 9—502 Contents of Financing Statement; Record of Mortgage as Financing Statement; Time of Filing Financing Statement.

(a) Subject to subsection (b), a financing statement is sufficient only if it:

(1) provides the name of the debtor;

(2) provides the name of the secured party or a representative of the secured party; and

(3) indicates the collateral covered by the financing statement.

(b) Except as otherwise provided in Section 9—501(b), to be sufficient, a financing statement that covers as-extracted collateral or timber to be cut, or which is filed as a fixture filing and covers goods that are or are to become fixtures, must satisfy subsection (a) and also:

(1) indicate that it covers this type of collateral;

(2) indicate that it is to be filed [for record] in the real property records;

(3) provide a description of the real property to which the collateral is related [sufficient to give constructive notice of a mortgage under the law of this State if the description were contained in a record of the mortgage of the real property]; and

(4) if the debtor does not have an interest of record in the real property, provide the name of a record owner.

(c) A record of a mortgage is effective, from the date of recording, as a financing statement filed as a fixture filing or as a financing statement covering as-extracted collateral or timber to be cut only if:

(1) the record indicates the goods or accounts that it covers;

(2) the goods are or are to become fixtures related to the real property described in the record or the collateral is related to the real property described in the record and is as-extracted collateral or timber to be cut;

(3) the record satisfies the requirements for a financing statement in this section other than an indication that it is to be filed in the real property records; and

(4) the record is [duly] recorded.

(d) A financing statement may be filed before a security agreement is made or a security interest otherwise attaches.

Legislative Note: Language in brackets is optional. Where the State has any special recording system for real property other than the usual grantor-grantee index (as, for instance, a tract system or a title registration or Torrens system) local adaptations of subsection (b) and Section 9—519(d) and (e) may be necessary. See, e.g., Mass. Gen. Laws Chapter 106, Section 9—410.

§ 9—503. Name of Debtor and Secured Party.

(a) A financing statement sufficiently provides the name of the debtor:

(1) if the debtor is a registered organization, only if the financing statement provides the name of the debtor indicated on the public record of the debtor's jurisdiction of organization which shows the debtor to have been organized;

(2) if the debtor is a decedent's estate, only if the financing statement provides the name of the decedent and indicates that the debtor is an estate;

(3) if the debtor is a trust or a trustee acting with respect to property held in trust, only if the financing statement:

(A) provides the name specified for the trust in its organic documents or, if no name is specified, provides the name of the settlor and additional information sufficient to distinguish the debtor from other trusts having one or more of the same settlors; and

(B) indicates, in the debtor's name or otherwise, that the debtor is a trust or is a trustee acting with respect to property held in trust; and

(4) in other cases:

(A) if the debtor has a name, only if it provides the individual or organizational name of the debtor; and

(B) if the debtor does not have a name, only if it provides the names of the partners, members, associates, or other persons comprising the debtor.

(b) A financing statement that provides the name of the debtor in accordance with subsection (a) is not rendered ineffective by the absence of:

(1) a trade name or other name of the debtor; or

(2) unless required under subsection (a)(4)(B), names of partners, members, associates, or other persons comprising the debtor.

(c) A financing statement that provides only the debtor's trade name does not sufficiently provide the name of the debtor.

(d) Failure to indicate the representative capacity of a secured party or representative of a secured party does not affect the sufficiency of a financing statement.

(e) A financing statement may provide the name of more than one debtor and the name of more than one secured party.

§ 9—504. Indication of Collateral.

A financing statement sufficiently indicates the collateral that it covers if the financing statement provides:

(1) a description of the collateral pursuant to Section 9—108; or

(2) an indication that the financing statement covers all assets or all personal property.

§ 9—505. Filing and Compliance with Other Statutes and Treaties for Consignments, Leases, Other Bailments, and Other Transactions.

(a) A consignor, lessor, or other bailor of goods, a licensor, or a buyer of a payment intangible or promissory note may file a financing statement, or may comply with a statute or treaty described in Section 9—311(a), using the terms "consignor", "consignee", "lessor", "lessee", "bailor", "bailee", "licensor", "licensee", "owner", "registered owner", "buyer", "seller", or words of similar import, instead of the terms "secured party" and "debtor".

(b) This part applies to the filing of a financing statement under subsection (a) and, as appropriate, to compliance that is equivalent to filing a financing statement under Section 9—311(b), but the filing or compliance is not of itself a factor in determining whether the collateral secures an obligation. If it is determined for another reason that the collateral secures an obligation, a security interest held by the consignor, lessor, bailor, licensor, owner, or buyer which attaches to the collateral is perfected by the filing or compliance.

§ 9—506. Effect of Errors or Omissions.

(a) A financing statement substantially satisfying the requirements of this part is effective, even if it has minor errors or omissions, unless the errors or omissions make the financing statement seriously misleading.

(b) Except as otherwise provided in subsection (c), a financing statement that fails sufficiently to provide the name of the debtor in accordance with Section 9—503(a) is seriously misleading.

(c) If a search of the records of the filing office under the debtor's correct name, using the filing office's standard search logic, if any, would disclose a financing statement that fails sufficiently to provide the name of the debtor in accordance with Section 9—503(a), the name provided does not make the financing statement seriously misleading.

(d) For purposes of Section 9—508(b), the "debtor's correct name" in subsection (c) means the correct name of the new debtor.

§ 9—507. Effect of Certain Events on Effectiveness of Financing Statement.

(a) A filed financing statement remains effective with respect to collateral that is sold, exchanged, leased, licensed, or otherwise disposed of and in which a security interest or agricultural lien continues, even if the secured party knows of or consents to the disposition.

(b) Except as otherwise provided in subsection (c) and Section 9—508, a financing statement is not rendered ineffective if, after the financing statement is filed, the information provided in the financing statement becomes seriously misleading under Section 9—506.

(c) If a debtor so changes its name that a filed financing statement becomes seriously misleading under Section 9—506:

(1) the financing statement is effective to perfect a security interest in collateral acquired by the debtor before, or within four months after, the change; and

(2) the financing statement is not effective to perfect a security interest in collateral acquired by the debtor more than four months after the change, unless an amendment to the financing statement which renders the financing statement not seriously misleading is filed within four months after the change.

§ 9—508. Effectiveness of Financing Statement If New Debtor Becomes Bound by Security Agreement.

(a) Except as otherwise provided in this section, a filed financing statement naming an original debtor is effective to perfect a security interest in collateral in which a new debtor has or acquires rights to the extent that the financing statement would have been effective had the original debtor acquired rights in the collateral.

(b) If the difference between the name of the original debtor and that of the new debtor causes a filed financing statement that is effective under subsection (a) to be seriously misleading under Section 9—506:

(1) the financing statement is effective to perfect a security interest in collateral acquired by the new debtor before, and within four months after, the new debtor becomes bound under Section 9B—203(d); and

(2) the financing statement is not effective to perfect a security interest in collateral acquired by the new debtor more than four months after the new debtor becomes bound under Section 9—203(d) unless an initial financing statement providing the name of the new debtor is filed before the expiration of that time.

(c) This section does not apply to collateral as to which a filed financing statement remains effective against the new debtor under Section 9—507(a).

§ 9—509. Persons Entitled to File a Record.

(a) A person may file an initial financing statement, amendment that adds collateral covered by a financing statement, or amendment that adds a debtor to a financing statement only if:

(1) the debtor authorizes the filing in an authenticated record or pursuant to subsection (b) or (c); or

(2) the person holds an agricultural lien that has become effective at the time of filing and the financing statement covers only collateral in which the person holds an agricultural lien.

(b) By authenticating or becoming bound as debtor by a security agreement, a debtor or new debtor authorizes the filing of an initial financing statement, and an amendment, covering:

(1) the collateral described in the security agreement; and

(2) property that becomes collateral under Section 9—315(a)(2), whether or not the security agreement expressly covers proceeds.

(c) By acquiring collateral in which a security interest or agricultural lien continues under Section 9—315(a)(1), a debtor authorizes the filing of an initial financing statement, and an amendment, covering the collateral and property that becomes collateral under Section 9—315(a)(2).

(d) A person may file an amendment other than an amendment that adds collateral covered by a financing statement or an amendment that adds a debtor to a financing statement only if:

(1) the secured party of record authorizes the filing; or

(2) the amendment is a termination statement for a financing statement as to which the secured party of record has failed to file or send a termination statement as required by Section 9—513(a) or (c), the debtor authorizes the filing, and the termination statement indicates that the debtor authorized it to be filed.

(e) If there is more than one secured party of record for a financing statement, each secured party of record may authorize the filing of an amendment under subsection (d).

§ 9—510. Effectiveness of Filed Record.

(a) A filed record is effective only to the extent that it was filed by a person that may file it under Section 9—509.

(b) A record authorized by one secured party of record does not affect the financing statement with respect to another secured party of record.

(c) A continuation statement that is not filed within the six-month period prescribed by Section 9—515(d) is ineffective.

§ 9—511. Secured Party of Record.

(a) A secured party of record with respect to a financing statement is a person whose name is provided as the name of the secured party or a representative of the secured party in an initial financing statement that has been filed. If an initial financing statement is filed under Section 9—514(a), the assignee named in the initial financing statement is the secured party of record with respect to the financing statement.

(b) If an amendment of a financing statement which provides the name of a person as a secured party or a representative of a secured party is filed, the person named in the amendment is a secured party of record. If an amendment is filed under Section 9—514(b), the assignee named in the amendment is a secured party of record.

(c) A person remains a secured party of record until the filing of an amendment of the financing statement which deletes the person.

§ 9—512. Amendment of Financing Statement.

[Alternative A]

(a) Subject to Section 9—509, a person may add or delete collateral covered by, continue or terminate the effectiveness of, or, subject to subsection (e), otherwise amend the information provided in, a financing statement by filing an amendment that:

(1) identifies, by its file number, the initial financing statement to which the amendment relates; and

(2) if the amendment relates to an initial financing statement filed [or recorded] in a filing office described in Section 9—501(a)(1), provides the information specified in Section 9—502(b).

[Alternative B]

(a) Subject to Section 9—509, a person may add or delete collateral covered by, continue or terminate the effectiveness of, or, subject to subsection (e), otherwise amend the information provided in, a financing statement by filing an amendment that:

(1) identifies, by its file number, the initial financing statement to which the amendment relates; and

(2) if the amendment relates to an initial financing statement filed [or recorded] in a filing office described in Section 9—501(a)(1), provides the date [and time] that the initial financing statement was filed [or recorded] and the information specified in Section 9—502(b).

[End of Alternatives]

(b) Except as otherwise provided in Section 9—515, the filing of an amendment does not extend the period of effectiveness of the financing statement.

(c) A financing statement that is amended by an amendment that adds collateral is effective as to the added collateral only from the date of the filing of the amendment.

(d) A financing statement that is amended by an amendment that adds a debtor is effective as to the added debtor only from the date of the filing of the amendment.

(e) An amendment is ineffective to the extent it:

(1) purports to delete all debtors and fails to provide the name of a debtor to be covered by the financing statement; or

(2) purports to delete all secured parties of record and fails to provide the name of a new secured party of record.

Legislative Note: States whose real-estate filing offices require additional information in amendments and cannot search their records by both the name of the debtor and the file number should enact Alternative B to Sections 9—512(a), 9—518(b), 9—519(f), and 9—522(a).

§ 9—513. Termination Statement.

(a) A secured party shall cause the secured party of record for a financing statement to file a termination statement for the financing statement if the financing statement covers consumer goods and:

(1) there is no obligation secured by the collateral covered by the financing statement and no commitment to make an advance, incur an obligation, or otherwise give value; or

(2) the debtor did not authorize the filing of the initial financing statement.

(b) To comply with subsection (a), a secured party shall cause the secured party of record to file the termination statement:

(1) within one month after there is no obligation secured by the collateral covered by the financing statement and no commitment to make an advance, incur an obligation, or otherwise give value; or

(2) if earlier, within 20 days after the secured party receives an authenticated demand from a debtor.

(c) In cases not governed by subsection (a), within 20 days after a secured party receives an authenticated demand from a debtor, the secured party shall cause the secured party of record for a financing statement to send to the debtor a termination statement for the financing statement or file the termination statement in the filing office if:

(1) except in the case of a financing statement covering accounts or chattel paper that has been sold or goods that are the subject of a consignment, there is no obligation secured by the collateral covered by the financing statement and no commitment to make an advance, incur an obligation, or otherwise give value;

(2) the financing statement covers accounts or chattel paper that has been sold but as to which the account debtor or other person obligated has discharged its obligation;

(3) the financing statement covers goods that were the subject of a consignment to the debtor but are not in the debtor's possession; or

(4) the debtor did not authorize the filing of the initial financing statement.

(d) Except as otherwise provided in Section 9—510, upon the filing of a termination statement with the filing office, the financing statement to which the termination statement relates ceases to be effective. Except as otherwise provided in Section 9—510, for purposes of Sections 9—519(g), 9—522(a), and 9—523(c), the filing with the filing office of a termination statement relating to a financing statement that indicates that the debtor is a transmitting utility also causes the effectiveness of the financing statement to lapse.

§ 9—514. **Assignment of Powers of Secured Party of Record.**

(a) Except as otherwise provided in subsection (c), an initial financing statement may reflect an assignment of all of the secured party's power to authorize an amendment to the financing statement by providing the name and mailing address of the assignee as the name and address of the secured party.

(b) Except as otherwise provided in subsection (c), a secured party of record may assign of record all or part of its power to authorize an amendment to a financing statement by filing in the filing office an amendment of the financing statement which:

(1) identifies, by its file number, the initial financing statement to which it relates;

(2) provides the name of the assignor; and

(3) provides the name and mailing address of the assignee.

(c) An assignment of record of a security interest in a fixture covered by a record of a mortgage which is effective as a financing statement filed as a fixture filing under Section 9—502(c) may be made only by an assignment of record of the mortgage in the manner provided by law of this State other than [the Uniform Commercial Code].

§ 9—515. **Duration and Effectiveness of Financing Statement; Effect of Lapsed Financing Statement.**

(a) Except as otherwise provided in subsections (b), (e), (f), and (g), a filed financing statement is effective for a period of five years after the date of filing.

(b) Except as otherwise provided in subsections (e), (f), and (g), an initial financing statement filed in connection with a public-finance transaction or manufactured-home transaction is effective for a period of 30 years after the date of filing if it indicates that it is filed in connection with a public-finance transaction or manufactured-home transaction.

(c) The effectiveness of a filed financing statement lapses on the expiration of the period of its effectiveness unless before the lapse a continuation statement is filed pursuant to subsection (d). Upon lapse, a financing statement ceases to be effective and any security interest or agricultural lien that was perfected by the financing statement becomes unperfected, unless the security interest is perfected otherwise. If the security interest or agricultural lien becomes unperfected upon lapse, it is deemed never to have been perfected as against a purchaser of the collateral for value.

(d) A continuation statement may be filed only within six months before the expiration of the five-year period specified in subsection (a) or the 30-year period specified in subsection (b), whichever is applicable.

(e) Except as otherwise provided in Section 9—510, upon timely filing of a continuation statement, the effectiveness of the initial financing statement continues for a period of five years commencing on the day on which the financing statement would have become ineffective in the absence of the filing. Upon the expiration of the five-year period, the financing statement lapses in the same manner as provided in subsection (c), unless, before the lapse, another continuation statement is filed pursuant to subsection (d). Succeeding continuation statements may be filed in the same manner to continue the effectiveness of the initial financing statement.

(f) If a debtor is a transmitting utility and a filed financing statement so indicates, the financing statement is effective until a termination statement is filed.

(g) A record of a mortgage that is effective as a financing statement filed as a fixture filing under Section 9—502(c) remains effective as a financing statement filed as a fixture filing until the mortgage is released or satisfied of record or its effectiveness otherwise terminates as to the real property.

§ 9—516. **What Constitutes Filing; Effectiveness of Filing.**

(a) Except as otherwise provided in subsection (b), communication of a record to a filing office and tender of the filing fee or acceptance of the record by the filing office constitutes filing.

(b) Filing does not occur with respect to a record that a filing office refuses to accept because:

(1) the record is not communicated by a method or medium of communication authorized by the filing office;

(2) an amount equal to or greater than the applicable filing fee is not tendered;

(3) the filing office is unable to index the record because:

(A) in the case of an initial financing statement, the record does not provide a name for the debtor;

(B) in the case of an amendment or correction statement, the record:

(i) does not identify the initial financing statement as required by Section 9—512 or 9—518, as applicable; or

(ii) identifies an initial financing statement whose effectiveness has lapsed under Section 9—515;

(C) in the case of an initial financing statement that provides the name of a debtor identified as an individual or an amendment that provides a name of a debtor identified as an individual which was not previously provided in the financing statement to which the record relates, the record does not identify the debtor's last name; or

(D) in the case of a record filed [or recorded] in the filing office described in Section 9—501(a)(1), the record does not provide a sufficient description of the real property to which it relates;

(4) in the case of an initial financing statement or an amendment that adds a secured party of record, the record does not provide a name and mailing address for the secured party of record;

(5) in the case of an initial financing statement or an amendment that provides a name of a debtor which was not previously provided in the financing statement to which the amendment relates, the record does not:

(A) provide a mailing address for the debtor;

(B) indicate whether the debtor is an individual or an organization; or

(C) if the financing statement indicates that the debtor is an organization, provide:

(i) a type of organization for the debtor;

(ii) a jurisdiction of organization for the debtor; or

(iii) an organizational identification number for the debtor or indicate that the debtor has none;

(6) in the case of an assignment reflected in an initial financing statement under Section 9—514(a) or an amendment filed under Section 9—514(b), the record does not provide a name and mailing address for the assignee; or

(7) in the case of a continuation statement, the record is not filed within the six-month period prescribed by Section 9—515(d).

(c) For purposes of subsection (b):

(1) a record does not provide information if the filing office is unable to read or decipher the information; and

(2) a record that does not indicate that it is an amendment or identify an initial financing statement to which it relates, as required by Section 9—512, 9—514, or 9—518, is an initial financing statement.

(d) A record that is communicated to the filing office with tender of the filing fee, but which the filing office refuses to accept for a reason other than one set forth in subsection (b), is effective as a filed record except as against a purchaser of the collateral which gives value in reasonable reliance upon the absence of the record from the files.

§ 9—517. Effect of Indexing Errors.

The failure of the filing office to index a record correctly does not affect the effectiveness of the filed record.

§ 9—518. Claim Concerning Inaccurate or Wrongfully Filed Record.

(a) A person may file in the filing office a correction statement with respect to a record indexed there under the person's name if the person believes that the record is inaccurate or was wrongfully filed.

[Alternative A]

(b) A correction statement must:

(1) identify the record to which it relates by the file number assigned to the initial financing statement to which the record relates;

(2) indicate that it is a correction statement; and

(3) provide the basis for the person's belief that the record is inaccurate and indicate the manner in which the person believes the record should be amended to cure any inaccuracy or provide the basis for the person's belief that the record was wrongfully filed.

[Alternative B]

(b) A correction statement must:

(1) identify the record to which it relates by:

(A) the file number assigned to the initial financing statement to which the record relates; and

(B) if the correction statement relates to a record filed [or recorded] in a filing office described in Section 9—501(a)(1), the date [and time] that the initial financing statement was filed [or recorded] and the information specified in Section 9—502(b);

(2) indicate that it is a correction statement; and

(3) provide the basis for the person's belief that the record is inaccurate and indicate the manner in which the person believes the record should be amended to cure any inaccuracy or provide the basis for the person's belief that the record was wrongfully filed.

[End of Alternatives]

(c) The filing of a correction statement does not affect the effectiveness of an initial financing statement or other filed record.

Legislative Note: States whose real-estate filing offices require additional information in amendments and cannot search their records by both the name of the debtor and the file number should enact Alternative B to Sections 9–512(a), 9—518(b), 9—519(f), and 9—522(a).

[Subpart 2. Duties and Operation of Filing Office]

§ 9—519. Numbering, Maintaining, and Indexing Records; Communicating Information Provided in Records.

(a) For each record filed in a filing office, the filing office shall:

(1) assign a unique number to the filed record;

(2) create a record that bears the number assigned to the filed record and the date and time of filing;

(3) maintain the filed record for public inspection; and

(4) index the filed record in accordance with subsections (c), (d), and (e).

(b) A file number [assigned after January 1, 2002,] must include a digit that:

(1) is mathematically derived from or related to the other digits of the file number; and

(2) aids the filing office in determining whether a number communicated as the file number includes a single-digit or transpositional error.

(c) Except as otherwise provided in subsections (d) and (e), the filing office shall:

(1) index an initial financing statement according to the name of the debtor and index all filed records relating to the initial financing statement in a manner that associates with one another an initial financing statement and all filed records relating to the initial financing statement; and

(2) index a record that provides a name of a debtor which was not previously provided in the financing statement to which the record relates also according to the name that was not previously provided.

(d) If a financing statement is filed as a fixture filing or covers as-extracted collateral or timber to be cut, [it must be filed for record and] the filing office shall index it:

(1) under the names of the debtor and of each owner of record shown on the financing statement as if they were the mortgagors under a mortgage of the real property described; and

(2) to the extent that the law of this State provides for indexing of records of mortgages under the name of the mortgagee, under the name of the secured party as if the secured party were the mortgagee thereunder, or, if indexing is by description, as if the financing statement were a record of a mortgage of the real property described.

(e) If a financing statement is filed as a fixture filing or covers as-extracted collateral or timber to be cut, the filing office shall index an assignment filed under Section 9—514(a) or an amendment filed under Section 9—514(b):

(1) under the name of the assignor as grantor; and

(2) to the extent that the law of this State provides for indexing a record of the assignment of a mortgage under the name of the assignee, under the name of the assignee.

[Alternative A]

(f) The filing office shall maintain a capability:

(1) to retrieve a record by the name of the debtor and by the file number assigned to the initial financing statement to which the record relates; and

(2) to associate and retrieve with one another an initial financing statement and each filed record relating to the initial financing statement.

[Alternative B]

(f) The filing office shall maintain a capability:

(1) to retrieve a record by the name of the debtor and:

(A) if the filing office is described in Section 9—501(a)(1), by the file number assigned to the initial financing statement to which the record relates and the date [and time] that the record was filed [or recorded]; or

(B) if the filing office is described in Section 9—501(a)(2), by the file number assigned to the initial financing statement to which the record relates; and

(2) to associate and retrieve with one another an initial financing statement and each filed record relating to the initial financing statement.

[End of Alternatives]

(g) The filing office may not remove a debtor's name from the index until one year after the effectiveness of a financing statement naming the debtor lapses under Section 9—515 with respect to all secured parties of record.

(h) The filing office shall perform the acts required by subsections (a) through (e) at the time and in the manner prescribed by filing-office rule, but not later than two business days after the filing office receives the record in question.

[(i) Subsection[s] [(b)] [and] [(h)] do[es] not apply to a filing office described in Section 9—501(a)(1).]

Legislative Notes:

1. States whose filing offices currently assign file numbers that include a verification number, commonly known as a "check digit," or can implement this requirement before the effective date of this Article should omit the bracketed language in subsection (b).

2. In States in which writings will not appear in the real property records and indices unless actually recorded the bracketed language in subsection (d) should be used.

3. States whose real-estate filing offices require additional information in amendments and cannot search their records by both the name of the debtor and the file number should enact Alternative B to Sections 9—512(a), 9—518(b), 9—519(f), and 9—522(a).

4. A State that elects not to require real-estate filing offices to comply with either or both of subsections (b) and (h) may adopt an applicable variation of subsection (i) and add "Except as otherwise provided in subsection (i)," to the appropriate subsection or subsections.

§ 9—520. Acceptance and Refusal to Accept Record.

(a) filing office shall refuse to accept a record for filing for a reason set forth in Section 9—516(b) and may refuse to accept a record for filing only for a reason set forth in Section 9—516(b).

(b) If a filing office refuses to accept a record for filing, it shall communicate to the person that presented the record the fact of and reason for the refusal and the date and time the record would have been filed had the filing office accepted it. The communication must be made at the time and in the manner prescribed by filing-office rule but [, in the case of a filing office described in Section 9—501(a)(2),] in no event more than two business days after the filing office receives the record.

(c) A filed financing statement satisfying Section 9–502(a) and (b) is effective, even if the filing office is required to refuse to accept it for filing under subsection (a). However, Section 9—338 applies to a filed financing statement providing information described in Section 9—516(b)(5) which is incorrect at the time the financing statement is filed.

(d) If a record communicated to a filing office provides information that relates to more than one debtor, this part applies as to each debtor separately.

Legislative Note: A State that elects not to require real-property filing offices to comply with subsection (b) should include the bracketed language.

§ 9—521. Uniform Form of Written Financing Statement and Amendment.

(a) A filing office that accepts written records may not refuse to accept a written initial financing statement in the following form and format except for a reason set forth in Section 9—516(b):

[NATIONAL UCC FINANCING STATEMENT (FORM UCC)(REV. 7/29/98)]

[NATIONAL UCC FINANCING STATEMENT ADDENDUM (FORM UCC 1Ad)(REV. 07/29/98)]

(b) A filing office that accepts written records may not refuse to accept a written record in the following form and format except for a reason set forth in Section 9—516(b):

[NATIONAL UCC FINANCING STATEMENT AMENDMENT (FORM UCC)(REV. 07/29/98)]

[NATIONAL UCC FINANCING STATEMENT AMENDMENT ADDENDUM (FORM UCC3Ad)(REV. 07/29/98)]

§ 9—522. Maintenance and Destruction of Records.

[Alternative A]

(a) The filing office shall maintain a record of the information provided in a filed financing statement for at least one year after the effectiveness of the financing statement has lapsed under Section 9—515 with respect to all secured parties of record. The record must be retrievable by using the name of the debtor and by using the file number assigned to the initial financing statement to which the record relates.

[Alternative B]

(a) The filing office shall maintain a record of the information provided in a filed financing statement for at least one year after the effectiveness of the financing statement has lapsed under Section 9—515 with respect to all secured parties of record. The record must be retrievable by using the name of the debtor and:

(1) if the record was filed [or recorded] in the filing office described in Section 9—501(a)(1), by using the file number assigned to the initial financing statement to which the record relates and the date [and time] that the record was filed [or recorded]; or

(2) if the record was filed in the filing office described in Section 9—501(a)(2), by using the file number assigned to the initial financing statement to which the record relates.

[End of Alternatives]

(b) Except to the extent that a statute governing disposition of public records provides otherwise, the filing office immediately may destroy any written record evidencing a financing statement. However, if the filing office destroys a written record, it shall maintain another record of the financing statement which complies with subsection (a).

Legislative Note: States whose real-estate filing offices require additional information in amendments and cannot search their records by both the name of the debtor and the file number should enact Alternative B to Sections 9—512(a), 9—518(b), 9—519(f), and 9—522(a).

§ 9—523. Information from Filing Office; Sale or License of Records.

(a) If a person that files a written record requests an acknowledgment of the filing, the filing office shall send to the person an image of the record showing the number assigned to the record pursuant to Section 9—519(a)(1) and the date and time of the filing of the record. However, if the person furnishes a copy of the record to the filing office, the filing office may instead:

(1) note upon the copy the number assigned to the record pursuant to Section 9—519(a)(1) and the date and time of the filing of the record; and

(2) send the copy to the person.

(b) If a person files a record other than a written record, the filing office shall communicate to the person an acknowledgment that provides:

(1) the information in the record;

(2) the number assigned to the record pursuant to Section 9—519(a)(1); and

(3) the date and time of the filing of the record.

(c) The filing office shall communicate or otherwise make available in a record the following information to any person that requests it:

(1) whether there is on file on a date and time specified by the filing office, but not a date earlier than three business days before the filing office receives the request, any financing statement that:

(A) designates a particular debtor [or, if the request so states, designates a particular debtor at the address specified in the request];

(B) has not lapsed under Section 9—515 with respect to all secured parties of record; and

(C) if the request so states, has lapsed under Section 9—515 and a record of which is maintained by the filing office under Section 9—522(a);

(2) the date and time of filing of each financing statement; and

(3) the information provided in each financing statement.

(d) In complying with its duty under subsection (c), the filing office may communicate information in any medium. However, if requested, the filing office shall communicate information by issuing [its written certificate] [a record that can be admitted into evidence in the courts of this State without extrinsic evidence of its authenticity].

(e) The filing office shall perform the acts required by subsections (a) through (d) at the time and in the manner prescribed by filing-office rule, but not later than two business days after the filing office receives the request.

(f) At least weekly, the [insert appropriate official or governmental agency] [filing office] shall offer to sell or license to the public on a nonexclusive basis, in bulk, copies of all records filed in it under this part, in every medium from time to time available to the filing office.

Legislative Notes:

1. States whose filing office does not offer the additional service of responding to search requests limited to a particular address should omit the bracketed language in subsection (c)(1)(A).

2. A State that elects not to require real-estate filing offices to comply with either or both of subsections (e) and (f) should specify in the appropriate subsection(s) only the filing office described in Section 9—501(a)(2).

§ 9—524. Delay by Filing Office.

Delay by the filing office beyond a time limit prescribed by this part is excused if:

(1) the delay is caused by interruption of communication or computer facilities, war, emergency conditions, failure of equipment, or other circumstances beyond control of the filing office; and

(2) the filing office exercises reasonable diligence under the circumstances.

§ 9—525. Fees.

(a) Except as otherwise provided in subsection (e), the fee for filing and indexing a record under this part, other than an initial financing statement of the kind described in subsection (b), is [the amount specified in subsection (c), if applicable, plus]:

(1) $[X] if the record is communicated in writing and consists of one or two pages;

(2) $[2X] if the record is communicated in writing and consists of more than two pages; and

(3) $[½X] if the record is communicated by another medium authorized by filing-office rule.

(b) Except as otherwise provided in subsection (e), the fee for filing and indexing an initial financing statement of the following kind is [the amount specified in subsection (c), if applicable, plus]:

(1) $______ if the financing statement indicates that it is filed in connection with a public-finance transaction;

(2) $______ if the financing statement indicates that it is filed in connection with a manufactured-home transaction.

[Alternative A]

(c) The number of names required to be indexed does not affect the amount of the fee in subsections (a) and (b).

[Alternative B]

(c) Except as otherwise provided in subsection (e), if a record is communicated in writing, the fee for each name more than two required to be indexed is $______.

[End of Alternatives]

(d) The fee for responding to a request for information from the filing office, including for [issuing a certificate showing] [communicating] whether there is on file any financing statement naming a particular debtor, is:

(1) $______ if the request is communicated in writing; and

(2) $______ if the request is communicated by another medium authorized by filing-office rule.

(e) This section does not require a fee with respect to a record of a mortgage which is effective as a financing statement filed as a fixture filing or as a financing statement covering as-extracted collateral or timber to be cut under Section 9—502(c). However, the recording and satisfaction fees that otherwise would be applicable to the record of the mortgage apply.

Legislative Notes:

1. To preserve uniformity, a State that places the provisions of this section together with statutes setting fees for other services should do so without modification.

2. A State should enact subsection (c), Alternative A, and omit the bracketed language in subsections (a) and (b) unless its indexing system entails a substantial additional cost when indexing additional names.

§ 9—526. Filing-Office Rules.

(a) The [insert appropriate governmental official or agency] shall adopt and publish rules to implement this article. The filing-office rules must be:

(1)] consistent with this article[; and

(2) adopted and published in accordance with the [insert any applicable state administrative procedure act]].

(b) To keep the filing-office rules and practices of the filing office in harmony with the rules and practices of filing offices in other jurisdictions that enact substantially this part, and to keep the technology used by the filing office compatible with the technology used by filing offices in other jurisdictions that enact substantially this part, the [insert appropriate governmental official or agency], so far as is consistent with the purposes, policies, and provisions of this article, in adopting, amending, and repealing filing-office rules, shall:

(1) consult with filing offices in other jurisdictions that enact substantially this part; and

(2) consult the most recent version of the Model Rules promulgated by the International Association of Corporate Administrators or any successor organization; and

(3) take into consideration the rules and practices of, and the technology used by, filing offices in other jurisdictions that enact substantially this part.

§ 9—527. Duty to Report.

The [insert appropriate governmental official or agency] shall report [annually on or before ________] to the [Governor and Legislature] on the operation of the filing office. The report must contain a statement of the extent to which:

(1) the filing-office rules are not in harmony with the rules of filing offices in other jurisdictions that enact substantially this part and the reasons for these variations; and

(2) the filing-office rules are not in harmony with the most recent version of the Model Rules promulgated by the International Association of Corporate Administrators, or any successor organization, and the reasons for these variations.

Part 6 Default

[Subpart 1. Default and Enforcement of Security Interest]

§ 9—601. Rights after Default; Judicial Enforcement; Consignor or Buyer of Accounts, Chattel Paper, Payment Intangibles, or Promissory Notes.

(a) After default, a secured party has the rights provided in this part and, except as otherwise provided in Section 9—602, those provided by agreement of the parties. A secured party:

(1) may reduce a claim to judgment, foreclose, or otherwise enforce the claim, security interest, or agricultural lien by any available judicial procedure; and

(2) if the collateral is documents, may proceed either as to the documents or as to the goods they cover.

(b) A secured party in possession of collateral or control of collateral under Section 9—104, 9—105, 9—106, or 9—107 has the rights and duties provided in Section 9—207.

(c) The rights under subsections (a) and (b) are cumulative and may be exercised simultaneously.

(d) Except as otherwise provided in subsection (g) and Section 9—605, after default, a debtor and an obligor have the rights provided in this part and by agreement of the parties.

(e) If a secured party has reduced its claim to judgment, the lien of any levy that may be made upon the collateral by virtue of an execution based upon the judgment relates back to the earliest of:

(1) the date of perfection of the security interest or agricultural lien in the collateral;

(2) the date of filing a financing statement covering the collateral; or

(3) any date specified in a statute under which the agricultural lien was created.

(f) A sale pursuant to an execution is a foreclosure of the security interest or agricultural lien by judicial procedure within the meaning of this section. A secured party may purchase at the sale and thereafter hold the collateral free of any other requirements of this article.

(g) Except as otherwise provided in Section 9—607(c), this part imposes no duties upon a secured party that is a consignor or is a buyer of accounts, chattel paper, payment intangibles, or promissory notes.

§ 9–602. Waiver and Variance of Rights and Duties.

Except as otherwise provided in Section 9—624, to the extent that they give rights to a debtor or obligor and impose duties on a secured party, the debtor or obligor may not waive or vary the rules stated in the following listed sections:

(1) Section 9—207(b)(4)(C), which deals with use and operation of the collateral by the secured party;

(2) Section 9—210, which deals with requests for an accounting and requests concerning a list of collateral and statement of account;

(3) Section 9—607(c), which deals with collection and enforcement of collateral;

(4) Sections 9—608(a) and 9—615(c) to the extent that they deal with application or payment of noncash proceeds of collection, enforcement, or disposition;

(5) Sections 9—608(a) and 9—615(d) to the extent that they require accounting for or payment of surplus proceeds of collateral;

(6) Section 9–609 to the extent that it imposes upon a secured party that takes possession of collateral without judicial process the duty to do so without breach of the peace;

(7) Sections 9—610(b), 9—611, 9—613, and 9—614, which deal with disposition of collateral;

(8) Section 9—615(f), which deals with calculation of a deficiency or surplus when a disposition is made to the secured party, a person related to the secured party, or a secondary obligor;

(9) Section 9—616, which deals with explanation of the calculation of a surplus or deficiency;

(10) Sections 9—620, 9—621, and 9—622, which deal with acceptance of collateral in satisfaction of obligation;

(11) Section 9—623, which deals with redemption of collateral;

(12) Section 9—624, which deals with permissible waivers; and

(13) Sections 9—625 and 9—626, which deal with the secured party's liability for failure to comply with this article.

§ 9—603. Agreement on Standards Concerning Rights and Duties.

(a) The parties may determine by agreement the standards measuring the fulfillment of the rights of a debtor or obligor and the duties of a secured party under a rule stated in Section 9—602 if the standards are not manifestly unreasonable.

(b) Subsection (a) does not apply to the duty under Section 9—609 to refrain from breaching the peace.

§ 9—604. Procedure If Security Agreement Covers Real Property or Fixtures.

(a) If a security agreement covers both personal and real property, a secured party may proceed:

(1) under this part as to the personal property without prejudicing any rights with respect to the real property; or

(2) as to both the personal property and the real property in accordance with the rights with respect to the real property, in which case the other provisions of this part do not apply.

(b) Subject to subsection (c), if a security agreement covers goods that are or become fixtures, a secured party may proceed:

(1) under this part; or

(2) in accordance with the rights with respect to real property, in which case the other provisions of this part do not apply.

(c) Subject to the other provisions of this part, if a secured party holding a security interest in fixtures has priority over all owners and encumbrancers of the real property, the secured party, after default, may remove the collateral from the real property.

(d) A secured party that removes collateral shall promptly reimburse any encumbrancer or owner of the real property, other than the debtor, for the cost of repair of any physical injury caused by the removal. The secured party need not reimburse the encumbrancer or owner for any diminution in value of the real property caused by the absence of the goods removed or by any necessity of replacing them. A person entitled to reimbursement may refuse permission to remove until the secured party gives adequate assurance for the performance of the obligation to reimburse.

§ 9—605. Unknown Debtor or Secondary Obligor.

A secured party does not owe a duty based on its status as secured party:

(1) to a person that is a debtor or obligor, unless the secured party knows:

(A) that the person is a debtor or obligor;

(B) the identity of the person; and

(C) how to communicate with the person; or

(2) to a secured party or lienholder that has filed a financing statement against a person, unless the secured party knows:

(A) that the person is a debtor; and

(B) the identity of the person.

§ 9—606. Time of Default for Agricultural Lien.

For purposes of this part, a default occurs in connection with an agricultural lien at the time the secured party becomes entitled to enforce the lien in accordance with the statute under which it was created.

§ 9—607. Collection and Enforcement by Secured Party.

(a) If so agreed, and in any event after default, a secured party:

(1) may notify an account debtor or other person obligated on collateral to make payment or otherwise render performance to or for the benefit of the secured party;

(2) may take any proceeds to which the secured party is entitled under Section 9—315;

(3) may enforce the obligations of an account debtor or other person obligated on collateral and exercise the rights of the debtor with respect to the obligation of the account debtor or other person obligated on collateral to make payment or otherwise render performance to the debtor, and with respect to any property that secures the obligations of the account debtor or other person obligated on the collateral;

(4) if it holds a security interest in a deposit account perfected by control under Section 9—104(a)(1), may apply the balance of the deposit account to the obligation secured by the deposit account; and

(5) if it holds a security interest in a deposit account perfected by control under Section 9—104(a)(2) or (3), may instruct the bank to pay the balance of the deposit account to or for the benefit of the secured party.

(b) If necessary to enable a secured party to exercise under subsection (a)(3) the right of a debtor to enforce a mortgage nonjudicially, the secured party may record in the office in which a record of the mortgage is recorded:

(1) a copy of the security agreement that creates or provides for a security interest in the obligation secured by the mortgage; and

(2) the secured party's sworn affidavit in recordable form stating that:

(A) a default has occurred; and

(B) the secured party is entitled to enforce the mortgage nonjudicially.

(c) A secured party shall proceed in a commercially reasonable manner if the secured party:

(1) undertakes to collect from or enforce an obligation of an account debtor or other person obligated on collateral; and

(2) is entitled to charge back uncollected collateral or otherwise to full or limited recourse against the debtor or a secondary obligor.

(d) A secured party may deduct from the collections made pursuant to subsection (c) reasonable expenses of collection and enforcement, including reasonable attorney's fees and legal expenses incurred by the secured party.

(e) This section does not determine whether an account debtor, bank, or other person obligated on collateral owes a duty to a secured party.

§ 9—608. Application of Proceeds of Collection or Enforcement; Liability for Deficiency and Right to Surplus.

(a) If a security interest or agricultural lien secures payment or performance of an obligation, the following rules apply:

(1) A secured party shall apply or pay over for application the cash proceeds of collection or enforcement under Section 9—607 in the following order to:

(A) the reasonable expenses of collection and enforcement and, to the extent provided for by agreement and not prohibited by law, reasonable attorney's fees and legal expenses incurred by the secured party;

(B) the satisfaction of obligations secured by the security interest or agricultural lien under which the collection or enforcement is made; and

(C) the satisfaction of obligations secured by any subordinate security interest in or other lien on the collateral subject to the security interest or agricultural lien under which the collection or enforcement is made if the secured party receives an authenticated demand for proceeds before distribution of the proceeds is completed.

(2) If requested by a secured party, a holder of a subordinate security interest or other lien shall furnish reasonable proof of the interest or lien within a reasonable time. Unless the holder complies, the secured party need not comply with the holder's demand under paragraph (1)(C).

(3) A secured party need not apply or pay over for application noncash proceeds of collection and enforcement under Section 9—607 unless the failure to do so would be commercially unreasonable. A secured party that applies or pays over for application noncash proceeds shall do so in a commercially reasonable manner.

(4) A secured party shall account to and pay a debtor for any surplus, and the obligor is liable for any deficiency.

(b) If the underlying transaction is a sale of accounts, chattel paper, payment intangibles, or promissory notes, the debtor is not entitled to any surplus, and the obligor is not liable for any deficiency.

§ 9—609. Secured Party's Right to Take Possession after Default.

(a) After default, a secured party:

(1) may take possession of the collateral; and

(2) without removal, may render equipment unusable and dispose of collateral on a debtor's premises under Section 9—610.

(b) A secured party may proceed under subsection (a):

(1) pursuant to judicial process; or

(2) without judicial process, if it proceeds without breach of the peace.

(c) If so agreed, and in any event after default, a secured party may require the debtor to assemble the collateral and make it available to the secured party at a place to be designated by the secured party which is reasonably convenient to both parties.

§ 9—610. Disposition of Collateral after Default.

(a) After default, a secured party may sell, lease, license, or otherwise dispose of any or all of the collateral in its present condition or following any commercially reasonable preparation or processing.

(b) Every aspect of a disposition of collateral, including the method, manner, time, place, and other terms, must be commercially reasonable. If commercially reasonable, a secured party may dispose of collateral by public or private proceedings, by one or more contracts, as a unit or in parcels, and at any time and place and on any terms.

(c) A secured party may purchase collateral:

(1) at a public disposition; or

(2) at a private disposition only if the collateral is of a kind that is customarily sold on a recognized market or the subject of widely distributed standard price quotations.

(d) A contract for sale, lease, license, or other disposition includes the warranties relating to title, possession, quiet enjoyment, and the like which by operation of law accompany a voluntary disposition of property of the kind subject to the contract.

(e) A secured party may disclaim or modify warranties under subsection (d):

(1) in a manner that would be effective to disclaim or modify the warranties in a voluntary disposition of property of the kind subject to the contract of disposition; or

(2) by communicating to the purchaser a record evidencing the contract for disposition and including an express disclaimer or modification of the warranties.

(f) A record is sufficient to disclaim warranties under subsection (e) if it indicates "There is no warranty relating to title, possession, quiet enjoyment, or the like in this disposition" or uses words of similar import.

§ 9—611. Notification before Disposition of Collateral.

(a) In this section, "notification date" means the earlier of the date on which:

(1) a secured party sends to the debtor and any secondary obligor an authenticated notification of disposition; or

(2) the debtor and any secondary obligor waive the right to notification.

(b) Except as otherwise provided in subsection (d), a secured party that disposes of collateral under Section 9—610 shall send to the persons specified in subsection (c) a reasonable authenticated notification of disposition.

(c) To comply with subsection (b), the secured party shall send an authenticated notification of disposition to:

(1) the debtor;

(2) any secondary obligor; and

(3) if the collateral is other than consumer goods:

(A) any other person from which the secured party has received, before the notification date, an authenticated notification of a claim of an interest in the collateral;

(B) any other secured party or lienholder that, 10 days before the notification date, held a security interest in or other lien on the collateral perfected by the filing of a financing statement that:

(i) identified the collateral;

(ii) was indexed under the debtor's name as of that date; and

(iii) was filed in the office in which to file a financing statement against the debtor covering the collateral as of that date; and

(C) any other secured party that, 10 days before the notification date, held a security interest in the collateral perfected by compliance with a statute, regulation, or treaty described in Section 9—311(a).

(d) Subsection (b) does not apply if the collateral is perishable or threatens to decline speedily in value or is of a type customarily sold on a recognized market.

(e) A secured party complies with the requirement for notification prescribed by subsection (c)(3)(B) if:

(1) not later than 20 days or earlier than 30 days before the notification date, the secured party requests, in a commercially reasonable manner, information concerning financing statements indexed under the debtor's name in the office indicated in subsection (c)(3)(B); and

(2) before the notification date, the secured party:

(A) did not receive a response to the request for information; or

(B) received a response to the request for information and sent an authenticated notification of disposition to each secured party or other lienholder named in that response whose financing statement covered the collateral.

§ 9—612. Timeliness of Notification before Disposition of Collateral.

(a) Except as otherwise provided in subsection (b), whether a notification is sent within a reasonable time is a question of fact.

(b) In a transaction other than a consumer transaction, a notification of disposition sent after default and 10 days or more before the earliest time of disposition set forth in the notification is sent within a reasonable time before the disposition.

§ 9—613. Contents and Form of Notification before Disposition of Collateral: General.

Except in a consumer-goods transaction, the following rules apply:

(1) The contents of a notification of disposition are sufficient if the notification:

(A) describes the debtor and the secured party;

(B) describes the collateral that is the subject of the intended disposition;

(C) states the method of intended disposition;

(D) states that the debtor is entitled to an accounting of the unpaid indebtedness and states the charge, if any, for an accounting; and

(E) states the time and place of a public disposition or the time after which any other disposition is to be made.

(2) Whether the contents of a notification that lacks any of the information specified in paragraph (1) are nevertheless sufficient is a question of fact.

(3) The contents of a notification providing substantially the information specified in paragraph (1) are sufficient, even if the notification includes:

(A) information not specified by that paragraph; or

(B) minor errors that are not seriously misleading.

(4) A particular phrasing of the notification is not required.

(5) The following form of notification and the form appearing in Section 9—614(3), when completed, each provides sufficient information:

NOTIFICATION OF DISPOSITION
OF COLLATERAL

To: [Name of debtor, obligor, or other person to which the notification is sent]

From: [Name, address, and telephone number of secured party]

Name of Debtor(s): [Include only if debtor(s) are not an addressee]

[For a public disposition:]

We will sell [or lease or license, as applicable] the [describe collateral] [to the highest qualified bidder] in public as follows:

Day and Date: _______

Time: _______

Place: _______

[For a private disposition:]

We will sell [or lease or license, as applicable] the [describe collateral] privately sometime after [day and date].

You are entitled to an accounting of the unpaid indebtedness secured by the property that we intend to sell [or lease or license, as applicable] [for a charge of $_______]. You may request an accounting by calling us at [telephone number].

[End of Form]

§ 9—614. Contents and Form of Notification before Disposition of Collateral: Consumer-Goods Transaction.

In a consumer-goods transaction, the following rules apply:

(1) A notification of disposition must provide the following information:

(A) the information specified in Section 9—613(1);

(B) a description of any liability for a deficiency of the person to which the notification is sent;

(C) a telephone number from which the amount that must be paid to the secured party to redeem the collateral under Section 9—623 is available; and

(D) a telephone number or mailing address from which additional information concerning the disposition and the obligation secured is available.

(2) A particular phrasing of the notification is not required.

(3) The following form of notification, when completed, provides sufficient information:

[Name and address of secured party]

[Date]

NOTICE OF OUR PLAN TO SELL PROPERTY

[Name and address of any obligor who is also a debtor]

Subject: [Identification of Transaction]

We have your [describe collateral], because you broke promises in our agreement.

[For a public disposition:]

We will sell [describe collateral] at public sale. A sale could include a lease or license. The sale will be held as follows:

Date: _______

Time: _______

Place: _______

You may attend the sale and bring bidders if you want.

[For a private disposition:]

We will sell [describe collateral] at private sale sometime after [date]. A sale could include a lease or license.

The money that we get from the sale (after paying our costs) will reduce the amount you owe. If we get less money than you owe, you [will or will not, as applicable] still owe us the difference. If we get more money than you owe, you will get the extra money, unless we must pay it to someone else.

You can get the property back at any time before we sell it by paying us the full amount you owe (not just the past due payments), including our expenses. To learn the exact amount you must pay, call us at [telephone number].

If you want us to explain to you in writing how we have figured the amount that you owe us, you may call us at [telephone number] [or write us at [secured party's address]] and request a written explanation. [We will charge you $_______ for the explanation if we sent you another written explanation of the amount you owe us within the last six months.]

If you need more information about the sale call us at [telephone number] [or write us at [secured party's address]].

We are sending this notice to the following other people who have an interest in [describe collateral] or who owe money under your agreement:

[Names of all other debtors and obligors, if any]

[End of Form]

(4) A notification in the form of paragraph (3) is sufficient, even if additional information appears at the end of the form.

(5) A notification in the form of paragraph (3) is sufficient, even if it includes errors in information not required by paragraph (1), unless the error is misleading with respect to rights arising under this article.

(6) If a notification under this section is not in the form of paragraph (3), law other than this article determines the effect of including information not required by paragraph (1).

§ 9—615. Application of Proceeds of Disposition; Liability for Deficiency and Right to Surplus.

(a) A secured party shall apply or pay over for application the cash proceeds of disposition under Section 9—610 in the following order to:

(1) the reasonable expenses of retaking, holding, preparing for disposition, processing, and disposing, and, to the extent provided for by agreement and not prohibited by law, reasonable attorney's fees and legal expenses incurred by the secured party;

(2) the satisfaction of obligations secured by the security interest or agricultural lien under which the disposition is made;

(3) the satisfaction of obligations secured by any subordinate security interest in or other subordinate lien on the collateral if:

(A) the secured party receives from the holder of the subordinate security interest or other lien an authenticated demand for proceeds before distribution of the proceeds is completed; and

(B) in a case in which a consignor has an interest in the collateral, the subordinate security interest or other lien is senior to the interest of the consignor; and

(4) a secured party that is a consignor of the collateral if the secured party receives from the consignor an authenticated demand for proceeds before distribution of the proceeds is completed.

(b) If requested by a secured party, a holder of a subordinate security interest or other lien shall furnish reasonable proof of the interest or lien within a reasonable time. Unless the holder does so, the secured party need not comply with the holder's demand under subsection (a)(3).

(c) A secured party need not apply or pay over for application noncash proceeds of disposition under Section 9—610 unless the failure to do so would be commercially unreasonable. A secured party that applies or pays over for application noncash proceeds shall do so in a commercially reasonable manner.

(d) If the security interest under which a disposition is made secures payment or performance of an obligation, after making the payments and applications required by subsection (a) and permitted by subsection (c):

(1) unless subsection (a)(4) requires the secured party to apply or pay over cash proceeds to a consignor, the secured party shall account to and pay a debtor for any surplus; and

(2) the obligor is liable for any deficiency.

(e) If the underlying transaction is a sale of accounts, chattel paper, payment intangibles, or promissory notes:

(1) the debtor is not entitled to any surplus; and

(2) the obligor is not liable for any deficiency.

(f) The surplus or deficiency following a disposition is calculated based on the amount of proceeds that would have been realized in a disposition complying with this part to a transferee other than the secured party, a person related to the secured party, or a secondary obligor if:

(1) the transferee in the disposition is the secured party, a person related to the secured party, or a secondary obligor; and

(2) the amount of proceeds of the disposition is significantly below the range of proceeds that a complying disposition to a person other than the secured party, a person related to the secured party, or a secondary obligor would have brought.

(g) A secured party that receives cash proceeds of a disposition in good faith and without knowledge that the receipt violates the rights of the holder of a security interest or other lien that is not subordinate to the security interest or agricultural lien under which the disposition is made:

(1) takes the cash proceeds free of the security interest or other lien;

(2) is not obligated to apply the proceeds of the disposition to the satisfaction of obligations secured by the security interest or other lien; and

(3) is not obligated to account to or pay the holder of the security interest or other lien for any surplus.

§ 9—616. Explanation of Calculation of Surplus or Deficiency.

(a) In this section:

(1) "Explanation" means a writing that:

(A) states the amount of the surplus or deficiency;

(B) provides an explanation in accordance with subsection (c) of how the secured party calculated the surplus or deficiency;

(C) states, if applicable, that future debits, credits, charges, including additional credit service charges or interest, rebates, and expenses may affect the amount of the surplus or deficiency; and

(D) provides a telephone number or mailing address from which additional information concerning the transaction is available.

(2) "Request" means a record:

(A) authenticated by a debtor or consumer obligor;

(B) requesting that the recipient provide an explanation; and

(C) sent after disposition of the collateral under Section 9—610.

(b) In a consumer-goods transaction in which the debtor is entitled to a surplus or a consumer obligor is liable for a deficiency under Section 9—615, the secured party shall:

(1) send an explanation to the debtor or consumer obligor, as applicable, after the disposition and:

(A) before or when the secured party accounts to the debtor and pays any surplus or first makes written demand on the consumer obligor after the disposition for payment of the deficiency; and

(B) within 14 days after receipt of a request; or

(2) in the case of a consumer obligor who is liable for a deficiency, within 14 days after receipt of a request, send to the consumer obligor a record waiving the secured party's right to a deficiency.

(c) To comply with subsection (a)(1)(B), a writing must provide the following information in the following order:

(1) the aggregate amount of obligations secured by the security interest under which the disposition was made, and, if the amount reflects a rebate of unearned interest or credit service charge, an indication of that fact, calculated as of a specified date:

(A) if the secured party takes or receives possession of the collateral after default, not more than 35 days before the secured party takes or receives possession; or

(B) if the secured party takes or receives possession of the collateral before default or does not take possession of the collateral, not more than 35 days before the disposition;

(2) the amount of proceeds of the disposition;

(3) the aggregate amount of the obligations after deducting the amount of proceeds;

(4) the amount, in the aggregate or by type, and types of expenses, including expenses of retaking, holding, preparing for disposition, processing, and disposing of the collateral, and attorney's fees secured by the collateral which are known to the secured party and relate to the current disposition;

(5) the amount, in the aggregate or by type, and types of credits, including rebates of interest or credit service charges, to which the obligor is known to be entitled and which are not reflected in the amount in paragraph (1); and

(6) the amount of the surplus or deficiency.

(d) A particular phrasing of the explanation is not required. An explanation complying substantially with the requirements of subsection (a) is sufficient, even if it includes minor errors that are not seriously misleading.

(e) A debtor or consumer obligor is entitled without charge to one response to a request under this section during any six-month period in which the secured party did not send to the debtor or consumer obligor an explanation pursuant to subsection (b)(1). The secured party may require payment of a charge not exceeding $25 for each additional response.

§ 9—617. Rights of Transferee of Collateral.

(a) A secured party's disposition of collateral after default:

(1) transfers to a transferee for value all of the debtor's rights in the collateral;

(2) discharges the security interest under which the disposition is made; and

(3) discharges any subordinate security interest or other subordinate lien [other than liens created under [cite acts or statutes providing for liens, if any, that are not to be discharged]].

(b) A transferee that acts in good faith takes free of the rights and interests described in subsection (a), even if the secured party fails to comply with this article or the requirements of any judicial proceeding.

(c) If a transferee does not take free of the rights and interests described in subsection (a), the transferee takes the collateral subject to:

(1) the debtor's rights in the collateral;

(2) the security interest or agricultural lien under which the disposition is made; and

(3) any other security interest or other lien.

§ 9—618. Rights and Duties of Certain Secondary Obligors.

(a) A secondary obligor acquires the rights and becomes obligated to perform the duties of the secured party after the secondary obligor:

(1) receives an assignment of a secured obligation from the secured party;

(2) receives a transfer of collateral from the secured party and agrees to accept the rights and assume the duties of the secured party; or

(3) is subrogated to the rights of a secured party with respect to collateral.

(b) An assignment, transfer, or subrogation described in subsection (a):

(1) is not a disposition of collateral under Section 9—610; and

(2) relieves the secured party of further duties under this article.

§ 9—619. Transfer of Record or Legal Title.

(a) In this section, "transfer statement" means a record authenticated by a secured party stating:

(1) that the debtor has defaulted in connection with an obligation secured by specified collateral;

(2) that the secured party has exercised its post-default remedies with respect to the collateral;

(3) that, by reason of the exercise, a transferee has acquired the rights of the debtor in the collateral; and

(4) the name and mailing address of the secured party, debtor, and transferee.

(b) A transfer statement entitles the transferee to the transfer of record of all rights of the debtor in the collateral specified in the statement in any official filing, recording, registration, or certificate-of-title system covering the collateral. If a transfer statement is presented with the applicable fee and request form to the official or office responsible for maintaining the system, the official or office shall:

(1) accept the transfer statement;

(2) promptly amend its records to reflect the transfer; and

(3) if applicable, issue a new appropriate certificate of title in the name of the transferee.

(c) A transfer of the record or legal title to collateral to a secured party under subsection (b) or otherwise is not of itself a disposition of collateral under this article and does not of itself relieve the secured party of its duties under this article.

§ 9—620. Acceptance of Collateral in Full or Partial Satisfaction of Obligation; Compulsory Disposition of Collateral.

(a) Except as otherwise provided in subsection (g), a secured party may accept collateral in full or partial satisfaction of the obligation it secures only if:

(1) the debtor consents to the acceptance under subsection (c);

(2) the secured party does not receive, within the time set forth in subsection (d), a notification of objection to the proposal authenticated by:

(A) a person to which the secured party was required to send a proposal under Section 9—621; or

(B) any other person, other than the debtor, holding an interest in the collateral subordinate to the security interest that is the subject of the proposal;

(3) if the collateral is consumer goods, the collateral is not in the possession of the debtor when the debtor consents to the acceptance; and

(4) subsection (e) does not require the secured party to dispose of the collateral or the debtor waives the requirement pursuant to Section 9—624.

(b) A purported or apparent acceptance of collateral under this section is ineffective unless:

(1) the secured party consents to the acceptance in an authenticated record or sends a proposal to the debtor; and

(2) the conditions of subsection (a) are met.

(c) For purposes of this section:

(1) a debtor consents to an acceptance of collateral in partial satisfaction of the obligation it secures only if the debtor agrees to the terms of the acceptance in a record authenticated after default; and

(2) a debtor consents to an acceptance of collateral in full satisfaction of the obligation it secures only if the debtor agrees to the terms of the acceptance in a record authenticated after default or the secured party:

(A) sends to the debtor after default a proposal that is unconditional or subject only to a condition that collateral not in the possession of the secured party be preserved or maintained;

(B) in the proposal, proposes to accept collateral in full satisfaction of the obligation it secures; and

(C) does not receive a notification of objection authenticated by the debtor within 20 days after the proposal is sent.

(d) To be effective under subsection (a)(2), a notification of objection must be received by the secured party:

(1) in the case of a person to which the proposal was sent pursuant to Section 9—621, within 20 days after notification was sent to that person; and

(2) in other cases:

(A) within 20 days after the last notification was sent pursuant to Section 9—621; or

(B) if a notification was not sent, before the debtor consents to the acceptance under subsection (c).

(e) A secured party that has taken possession of collateral shall dispose of the collateral pursuant to Section 9—610 within the time specified in subsection (f) if:

(1) 60 percent of the cash price has been paid in the case of a purchase-money security interest in consumer goods; or

(2) 60 percent of the principal amount of the obligation secured has been paid in the case of a non-purchase-money security interest in consumer goods.

(f) To comply with subsection (e), the secured party shall dispose of the collateral:

(1) within 90 days after taking possession; or

(2) within any longer period to which the debtor and all secondary obligors have agreed in an agreement to that effect entered into and authenticated after default.

(g) In a consumer transaction, a secured party may not accept collateral in partial satisfaction of the obligation it secures.

§ 9—621. Notification of Proposal to Accept Collateral.

(a) A secured party that desires to accept collateral in full or partial satisfaction of the obligation it secures shall send its proposal to:

(1) any person from which the secured party has received, before the debtor consented to the acceptance, an authenticated notification of a claim of an interest in the collateral;

(2) any other secured party or lienholder that, 10 days before the debtor consented to the acceptance, held a security interest in or other lien on the collateral perfected by the filing of a financing statement that:

(A) identified the collateral;

(B) was indexed under the debtor's name as of that date; and

(C) was filed in the office or offices in which to file a financing statement against the debtor covering the collateral as of that date; and

(3) any other secured party that, 10 days before the debtor consented to the acceptance, held a security interest in the collateral perfected by compliance with a statute, regulation, or treaty described in Section 9—311(a).

(b) A secured party that desires to accept collateral in partial satisfaction of the obligation it secures shall send its proposal to any secondary obligor in addition to the persons described in subsection (a).

§ 9—622. Effect of Acceptance of Collateral.

(a) A secured party's acceptance of collateral in full or partial satisfaction of the obligation it secures:

(1) discharges the obligation to the extent consented to by the debtor;

(2) transfers to the secured party all of a debtor's rights in the collateral;

(3) discharges the security interest or agricultural lien that is the subject of the debtor's consent and any subordinate security interest or other subordinate lien; and

(4) terminates any other subordinate interest.

(b) A subordinate interest is discharged or terminated under subsection (a), even if the secured party fails to comply with this article.

§ 9—623. Right to Redeem Collateral.

(a) A debtor, any secondary obligor, or any other secured party or lienholder may redeem collateral.

(b) To redeem collateral, a person shall tender:

(1) fulfillment of all obligations secured by the collateral; and

(2) the reasonable expenses and attorney's fees described in Section 9—615(a)(1).

(c) A redemption may occur at any time before a secured party:

(1) has collected collateral under Section 9—607;

(2) has disposed of collateral or entered into a contract for its disposition under Section 9—610; or

(3) has accepted collateral in full or partial satisfaction of the obligation it secures under Section 9—622.

§ 9—624. Waiver.

(a) A debtor or secondary obligor may waive the right to notification of disposition of collateral under Section 9—611 only by an agreement to that effect entered into and authenticated after default.

(b) A debtor may waive the right to require disposition of collateral under Section 9—620(e) only by an agreement to that effect entered into and authenticated after default.

(c) Except in a consumer-goods transaction, a debtor or secondary obligor may waive the right to redeem collateral under Section 9—623 only by an agreement to that effect entered into and authenticated after default.

[Subpart 2. Noncompliance with Article]

§ 9—625. Remedies for Secured Party's Failure to Comply with Article.

(a) If it is established that a secured party is not proceeding in accordance with this article, a court may order or restrain collection, enforcement, or disposition of collateral on appropriate terms and conditions.

(b) Subject to subsections (c), (d), and (f), a person is liable for damages in the amount of any loss caused by a failure to comply with this article. Loss caused by a failure to comply may include loss resulting from the debtor's inability to obtain, or increased costs of, alternative financing.

(c) Except as otherwise provided in Section 9—628:

(1) a person that, at the time of the failure, was a debtor, was an obligor, or held a security interest in or other lien on the collateral may recover damages under subsection (b) for its loss; and

(2) if the collateral is consumer goods, a person that was a debtor or a secondary obligor at the time a secured party failed to comply with this part may recover for that failure in any event an amount not less than the credit service charge plus 10 percent of the principal amount of the obligation or the time-price differential plus 10 percent of the cash price.

(d) A debtor whose deficiency is eliminated under Section 9—626 may recover damages for the loss of any surplus. However, a debtor or secondary obligor whose deficiency is eliminated or reduced under Section 9—626 may not otherwise recover under subsection (b) for noncompliance with the provisions of this part relating to collection, enforcement, disposition, or acceptance.

(e) In addition to any damages recoverable under subsection (b), the debtor, consumer obligor, or person named as a debtor in a filed record, as applicable, may recover $500 in each case from a person that:

(1) fails to comply with Section 9—208;

(2) fails to comply with Section 9—209;

(3) files a record that the person is not entitled to file under Section 9—509(a);

(4) fails to cause the secured party of record to file or send a termination statement as required by Section 9—513(a) or (c);

(5) fails to comply with Section 9—616(b)(1) and whose failure is part of a pattern, or consistent with a practice, of noncompliance; or

(6) fails to comply with Section 9—616(b)(2).

(f) A debtor or consumer obligor may recover damages under subsection (b) and, in addition, $500 in each case from a person that, without reasonable cause, fails to comply with a request under Section 9—210. A recipient of a request under Section 9—210 which never claimed an interest in the collateral or obligations that are the subject of a request under that section has a reasonable excuse for failure to comply with the request within the meaning of this subsection.

(g) If a secured party fails to comply with a request regarding a list of collateral or a statement of account under Section 9—210, the secured party may claim a security interest only as shown in the list or statement included in the request as against a person that is reasonably misled by the failure.

§ 9—626. Action in Which Deficiency or Surplus Is in Issue.

(a) In an action arising from a transaction, other than a consumer transaction, in which the amount of a deficiency or surplus is in issue, the following rules apply:

(1) A secured party need not prove compliance with the provisions of this part relating to collection, enforcement, disposition, or acceptance unless the debtor or a secondary obligor places the secured party's compliance in issue.

(2) If the secured party's compliance is placed in issue, the secured party has the burden of establishing that the collection, enforcement, disposition, or acceptance was conducted in accordance with this part.

(3) Except as otherwise provided in Section 9—628, if a secured party fails to prove that the collection, enforcement, disposition, or acceptance was conducted in accordance with the provisions of this part relating to collection, enforcement, disposition, or acceptance, the liability of a debtor or a secondary obligor for a deficiency is limited to an amount by which the sum of the secured obligation, expenses, and attorney's fees exceeds the greater of:

(A) the proceeds of the collection, enforcement, disposition, or acceptance; or

(B) the amount of proceeds that would have been realized had the noncomplying secured party proceeded in accordance with the provisions of this part relating to collection, enforcement, disposition, or acceptance.

(4) For purposes of paragraph (3)(B), the amount of proceeds that would have been realized is equal to the sum of the secured obligation, expenses, and attorney's fees unless the secured party proves that the amount is less than that sum.

(5) If a deficiency or surplus is calculated under Section 9—615(f), the debtor or obligor has the burden of establishing that the amount of proceeds of the disposition is significantly below the range of prices that a complying disposition to a

person other than the secured party, a person related to the secured party, or a secondary obligor would have brought.

(b) The limitation of the rules in subsection (a) to transactions other than consumer transactions is intended to leave to the court the determination of the proper rules in consumer transactions. The court may not infer from that limitation the nature of the proper rule in consumer transactions and may continue to apply established approaches.

§ 9—627. Determination of Whether Conduct Was Commercially Reasonable.

(a) The fact that a greater amount could have been obtained by a collection, enforcement, disposition, or acceptance at a different time or in a different method from that selected by the secured party is not of itself sufficient to preclude the secured party from establishing that the collection, enforcement, disposition, or acceptance was made in a commercially reasonable manner.

(b) A disposition of collateral is made in a commercially reasonable manner if the disposition is made:

(1) in the usual manner on any recognized market;

(2) at the price current in any recognized market at the time of the disposition; or

(3) otherwise in conformity with reasonable commercial practices among dealers in the type of property that was the subject of the disposition.

(c) A collection, enforcement, disposition, or acceptance is commercially reasonable if it has been approved:

(1) in a judicial proceeding;

(2) by a bona fide creditors' committee;

(3) by a representative of creditors; or

(4) by an assignee for the benefit of creditors.

(d) Approval under subsection (c) need not be obtained, and lack of approval does not mean that the collection, enforcement, disposition, or acceptance is not commercially reasonable.

§ 9—628. Nonliability and Limitation on Liability of Secured Party; Liability of Secondary Obligor.

(a) Unless a secured party knows that a person is a debtor or obligor, knows the identity of the person, and knows how to communicate with the person:

(1) the secured party is not liable to the person, or to a secured party or lienholder that has filed a financing statement against the person, for failure to comply with this article; and

(2) the secured party's failure to comply with this article does not affect the liability of the person for a deficiency.

(b) A secured party is not liable because of its status as secured party:

(1) to a person that is a debtor or obligor, unless the secured party knows:

(A) that the person is a debtor or obligor;

(B) the identity of the person; and

(C) how to communicate with the person; or

(2) to a secured party or lienholder that has filed a financing statement against a person, unless the secured party knows:

(A) that the person is a debtor; and

(B) the identity of the person.

(c) A secured party is not liable to any person, and a person's liability for a deficiency is not affected, because of any act or omission arising out of the secured party's reasonable belief that a transaction is not a consumer-goods transaction or a consumer transaction or that goods are not consumer goods, if the secured party's belief is based on its reasonable reliance on:

(1) a debtor's representation concerning the purpose for which collateral was to be used, acquired, or held; or

(2) an obligor's representation concerning the purpose for which a secured obligation was incurred.

(d) A secured party is not liable to any person under Section 9—625(c)(2) for its failure to comply with Section 9—616.

(e) A secured party is not liable under Section 9—625(c)(2) more than once with respect to any one secured obligation.

Part 7 Transition

§ 9—701. Effective Date.

This [Act] takes effect on July 1, 2001.

§ 9—702. Savings Clause.

(a) Except as otherwise provided in this part, this [Act] applies to a transaction or lien within its scope, even if the transaction or lien was entered into or created before this [Act] takes effect.

(b) Except as otherwise provided in subsection (c) and Sections 9—703 through 9—709:

(1) transactions and liens that were not governed by [former Article 9], were validly entered into or created before this [Act] takes effect, and would be subject to this [Act] if they had been entered into or created after this [Act] takes effect, and the rights, duties, and interests flowing from those transactions and liens remain valid after this [Act] takes effect; and

(2) the transactions and liens may be terminated, completed, consummated, and enforced as required or permitted by this [Act] or by the law that otherwise would apply if this [Act] had not taken effect.

(c) This [Act] does not affect an action, case, or proceeding commenced before this [Act] takes effect.

§ 9—703. Security Interest Perfected before Effective Date.

(a) A security interest that is enforceable immediately before this [Act] takes effect and would have priority over the rights of a person that becomes a lien creditor at that time is a perfected security interest under this [Act] if, when this [Act] takes effect, the applicable requirements for enforceability and perfection under this [Act] are satisfied without further action.

(b) Except as otherwise provided in Section 9—705, if, immediately before this [Act] takes effect, a security interest is enforceable and would have priority over the rights of a person that becomes a lien creditor at that time, but the applicable requirements for enforceability or perfection under this [Act] are not satisfied when this [Act] takes effect, the security interest:

(1) is a perfected security interest for one year after this [Act] takes effect;

(2) remains enforceable thereafter only if the security interest becomes enforceable under Section 9—203 before the year expires; and

(3) remains perfected thereafter only if the applicable requirements for perfection under this [Act] are satisfied before the year expires.

§ 9—704. **Security Interest Unperfected before Effective Date.**

A security interest that is enforceable immediately before this [Act] takes effect but which would be subordinate to the rights of a person that becomes a lien creditor at that time:

(1) remains an enforceable security interest for one year after this [Act] takes effect;

(2) remains enforceable thereafter if the security interest becomes enforceable under Section 9—203 when this [Act] takes effect or within one year thereafter; and

(3) becomes perfected:

(A) without further action, when this [Act] takes effect if the applicable requirements for perfection under this [Act] are satisfied before or at that time; or

(B) when the applicable requirements for perfection are satisfied if the requirements are satisfied after that time.

§ 9—705. **Effectiveness of Action Taken before Effective Date.**

(a) If action, other than the filing of a financing statement, is taken before this [Act] takes effect and the action would have resulted in priority of a security interest over the rights of a person that becomes a lien creditor had the security interest become enforceable before this [Act] takes effect, the action is effective to perfect a security interest that attaches under this [Act] within one year after this [Act] takes effect. An attached security interest becomes unperfected one year after this [Act] takes effect unless the security interest becomes a perfected security interest under this [Act] before the expiration of that period.

(b) The filing of a financing statement before this [Act] takes effect is effective to perfect a security interest to the extent the filing would satisfy the applicable requirements for perfection under this [Act].

(c) This [Act] does not render ineffective an effective financing statement that, before this [Act] takes effect, is filed and satisfies the applicable requirements for perfection under the law of the jurisdiction governing perfection as provided in [former Section 9—103]. However, except as otherwise provided in subsections (d) and (e) and Section 9—706, the financing statement ceases to be effective at the earlier of:

(1) the time the financing statement would have ceased to be effective under the law of the jurisdiction in which it is filed; or

(2) June 30, 2006.

(d) The filing of a continuation statement after this [Act] takes effect does not continue the effectiveness of the financing statement filed before this [Act] takes effect. However, upon the timely filing of a continuation statement after this [Act] takes effect and in accordance with the law of the jurisdiction governing perfection as provided in Part 3, the effectiveness of a financing statement filed in the same office in that jurisdiction before this [Act] takes effect continues for the period provided by the law of that jurisdiction.

(e) Subsection (c)(2) applies to a financing statement that, before this [Act] takes effect, is filed against a transmitting utility and satisfies the applicable requirements for perfection under the law of the jurisdiction governing perfection as provided in [former Section 9—103] only to the extent that Part 3 provides that the law of a jurisdiction other than the jurisdiction in which the financing statement is filed governs perfection of a security interest in collateral covered by the financing statement.

(f) A financing statement that includes a financing statement filed before this [Act] takes effect and a continuation statement filed after this [Act] takes effect is effective only to the extent that it satisfies the requirements of Part 5 for an initial financing statement.

§ 9—706. **When Initial Financing Statement Suffices to Continue Effectiveness of Financing Statement.**

(a) The filing of an initial financing statement in the office specified in Section 9—501 continues the effectiveness of a financing statement filed before this [Act] takes effect if:

(1) the filing of an initial financing statement in that office would be effective to perfect a security interest under this [Act];

(2) the pre-effective-date financing statement was filed in an office in another State or another office in this State; and

(3) the initial financing statement satisfies subsection (c).

(b) The filing of an initial financing statement under subsection (a) continues the effectiveness of the pre-effective-date financing statement:

(1) if the initial financing statement is filed before this [Act] takes effect, for the period provided in [former Section 9—403] with respect to a financing statement; and

(2) if the initial financing statement is filed after this [Act] takes effect, for the period provided in Section 9—515 with respect to an initial financing statement.

(c) To be effective for purposes of subsection (a), an initial financing statement must:

(1) satisfy the requirements of Part 5 for an initial financing statement;

(2) identify the pre-effective-date financing statement by indicating the office in which the financing statement was filed and providing the dates of filing and file numbers, if any, of the financing statement and of the most recent continuation statement filed with respect to the financing statement; and

(3) indicate that the pre-effective-date financing statement remains effective.

§ 9—707. Amendment of Pre-Effective-Date Financing Statement.

(a) In this section, "Pre-effective-date financing statement" means a financing statement filed before this [Act] takes effect.

(b) After this [Act] takes effect, a person may add or delete collateral covered by, continue or terminate the effectiveness of, or otherwise amend the information provided in, a pre-effective-date financing statement only in accordance with the law of the jurisdiction governing perfection as provided in Part 3. However, the effectiveness of a pre-effective-date financing statement also may be terminated in accordance with the law of the jurisdiction in which the financing statement is filed.

(c) Except as otherwise provided in subsection (d), if the law of this State governs perfection of a security interest, the information in a pre-effective-date financing statement may be amended after this [Act] takes effect only if:

(1) the pre-effective-date financing statement and an amendment are filed in the office specified in Section 9—501;

(2) an amendment is filed in the office specified in Section 9—501 concurrently with, or after the filing in that office of, an initial financing statement that satisfies Section 9—706(c); or

(3) an initial financing statement that provides the information as amended and satisfies Section 9—706(c) is filed in the office specified in Section 9—501.

(d) If the law of this State governs perfection of a security interest, the effectiveness of a pre-effective-date financing statement may be continued only under Section 9—705(d) and (f) or 9—706.

(e) Whether or not the law of this State governs perfection of a security interest, the effectiveness of a pre-effective-date financing statement filed in this State may be terminated after this [Act] takes effect by filing a termination statement in the office in which the pre-effective-date financing statement is filed, unless an initial financing statement that satisfies Section 9—706(c) has been filed in the office specified by the law of the jurisdiction governing perfection as provided in Part 3 as the office in which to file a financing statement.

§ 9—708. Persons Entitled to File Initial Financing Statement or Continuation Statement.

A person may file an initial financing statement or a continuation statement under this part if:

(1) the secured party of record authorizes the filing; and

(2) the filing is necessary under this part:

(A) to continue the effectiveness of a financing statement filed before this [Act] takes effect; or

(B) to perfect or continue the perfection of a security interest.

§ 9—709. Priority.

(a) This [Act] determines the priority of conflicting claims to collateral. However, if the relative priorities of the claims were established before this [Act] takes effect, [former Article 9] determines priority.

(b) For purposes of Section 9—322(a), the priority of a security interest that becomes enforceable under Section 9—203 of this [Act] dates from the time this [Act] takes effect if the security interest is perfected under this [Act] by the filing of a financing statement before this [Act] takes effect which would not have been effective to perfect the security interest under [former Article 9]. This subsection does not apply to conflicting security interests each of which is perfected by the filing of such a financing statement.

APPENDIX D

THE UNIFORM PARTNERSHIP ACT

(Adopted in forty-nine states [all of the states except Louisiana], the District of Columbia, the Virgin Islands, and Guam. The adoptions by Alabama and Nebraska do not follow the official text in every respect, but they are substantially similar, with local variations.)

The Act consists of 7 Parts as follows:

I. Preliminary Provisions

II. Nature of Partnership

III. Relations of Partners to Persons Dealing with the Partnership

IV. Relations of Partners to One Another

V. Property Rights of a Partner

VI. Dissolution and Winding Up

VII. Miscellaneous Provisions

An Act to make uniform the Law of Partnerships

Be it enacted, etc.:

Part I Preliminary Provisions

Sec. 1. Name of Act

This act may be cited as Uniform Partnership Act.

Sec. 2. Definition of Terms

In this act, "Court" includes every court and judge having jurisdiction in the case.

"Business" includes every trade, occupation, or profession.

"Person" includes individuals, partnerships, corporations, and other associations.

"Bankrupt" includes bankrupt under the Federal Bankruptcy Act or insolvent under any state insolvent act.

"Conveyance" includes every assignment, lease, mortgage, or encumbrance.

"Real property" includes land and any interest or estate in land.

Sec. 3. Interpretation of Knowledge and Notice

(1) A person has "knowledge" of a fact within the meaning of this act not only when he has actual knowledge thereof, but also when he has knowledge of such other facts as in the circumstances shows bad faith.

(2) A person has "notice" of a fact within the meaning of this act when the person who claims the benefit of the notice:

(a) States the fact to such person, or

(b) Delivers through the mail, or by other means of communication, a written statement of the fact to such person or to a proper person at his place of business or residence.

Sec. 4. Rules of Construction

(1) The rule that statutes in derogation of the common law are to be strictly construed shall have no application to this act.

(2) The law of estoppel shall apply under this act.

(3) The law of agency shall apply under this act.

(4) This act shall be so interpreted and construed as to effect its general purpose to make uniform the law of those states which enact it.

(5) This act shall not be construed so as to impair the obligations of any contract existing when the act goes into effect, nor to affect any action or proceedings begun or right accrued before this act takes effect.

Sec. 5. Rules for Cases Not Provided for in This Act.

In any case not provided for in this act the rules of law and equity, including the law merchant, shall govern.

Part II Nature of Partnership

Sec. 6. Partnership Defined

(1) A partnership is an association of two or more persons to carry on as co-owners a business for profit.

(2) But any association formed under any other statute of this state, or any statute adopted by authority, other than the authority of this state, is not a partnership under this act, unless such association would have been a partnership in this state prior to the adoption of this act; but this act shall apply to limited partnerships except in so far as the statutes relating to such partnerships are inconsistent herewith.

Sec. 7. Rules for Determining the Existence of a Partnership

In determining whether a partnership exists, these rules shall apply:

(1) Except as provided by Section 16 persons who are not partners as to each other are not partners as to third persons.

(2) Joint tenancy, tenancy in common, tenancy by the entireties, joint property, common property, or part ownership does not of itself establish a partnership, whether such co-owners do or do not share any profits made by the use of the property.

(3) The sharing of gross returns does not of itself establish a partnership, whether or not the persons sharing them have a joint or common right or interest in any property from which the returns are derived.

(4) The receipt by a person of a share of the profits of a business is prima facie evidence that he is a partner in the business, but no such inference shall be drawn if such profits were received in payment:

(a) As a debt by installments or otherwise,

(b) As wages of an employee or rent to a landlord,

(c) As an annuity to a widow or representative of a deceased partner,

(d) As interest on a loan, though the amount of payment vary with the profits of the business,

(e) As the consideration for the sale of a good-will of a business or other property by installments or otherwise.

Sec. 8. Partnership Property

(1) All property originally brought into the partnership stock or subsequently acquired by purchase or otherwise, on account of the partnership, is partnership property.

(2) Unless the contrary intention appears, property acquired with partnership funds is partnership property.

(3) Any estate in real property may be acquired in the partnership name. Title so acquired can be conveyed only in the partnership name.

(4) A conveyance to a partnership in the partnership name, though without words of inheritance, passes the entire estate of the grantor unless a contrary intent appears.

Part III Relations of Partners to Persons Dealing with the Partnership

Sec. 9. Partner Agent of Partnership as to Partnership Business

(1) Every partner is an agent of the partnership for the purpose of its business, and the act of every partner, including the execution in the partnership name of any instrument, for apparently carrying on in the usual way the business of the partnership of which he is a member binds the partnership, unless the partner so acting has in fact no authority to act for the partnership in the particular matter, and the person with whom he is dealing has knowledge of the fact that he has no such authority.

(2) An act of a partner which is not apparently for the carrying on of the business of the partnership in the usual way does not bind the partnership unless authorized by the other partners.

(3) Unless authorized by the other partners or unless they have abandoned the business, one or more but less than all the partners have no authority to:

(a) Assign the partnership property in trust for creditors or on the assignee's promise to pay the debts of the partnership,

(b) Dispose of the good-will of the business,

(c) Do any other act which would make it impossible to carry on the ordinary business of a partnership,

(d) Confess a judgment,

(e) Submit a partnership claim or liability to arbitration or reference.

(4) No act of a partner in contravention of a restriction on authority shall bind the partnership to persons having knowledge of the restriction.

Sec. 10. Conveyance of Real Property of the Partnership

(1) Where title to real property is in the partnership name, any partner may convey title to such property by a conveyance executed in the partnership name; but the partnership may recover such property unless the partner's act binds the partnership under the provisions of paragraph (1) of section 9, or unless such property has been conveyed by the grantee or a person claiming through such grantee to a holder for value without knowledge that the partner, in making the conveyance, has exceeded his authority.

(2) Where title to real property is in the name of the partnership, a conveyance executed by a partner, in his own name, passes the equitable interest of the partnership, provided the act is one within the authority of the partner under the provisions of paragraph (1) of section 9.

(3) Where title to real property is in the name of one or more but not all the partners, and the record does not disclose the right of the partnership, the partners in whose name the title stands may convey title to such property, but the partnership may recover such property if the partners' act does not bind the partnership under the provisions of paragraph (1) of section 9, unless the purchaser or his assignee, is a holder for value, without knowledge.

(4) Where the title to real property is in the name of one or more or all the partners, or in a third person in trust for the partnership, a conveyance executed by a partner in the partnership name, or in his own name, passes the equitable interest of the partnership, provided the act is one within the authority of the partner under the provisions of paragraph (1) of section 9.

(5) Where the title to real property is in the names of all the partners a conveyance executed by all the partners passes all their rights in such property.

Sec. 11. Partnership Bound by Admission of Partner

An admission or representation made by any partner concerning partnership affairs within the scope of his authority as conferred by this act is evidence against the partnership.

Sec. 12. Partnership Charged with Knowledge of or Notice to Partner

Notice to any partner of any matter relating to partnership affairs, and the knowledge of the partner acting in the particular matter, acquired while a partner or then present to his mind, and the knowledge of any other partner who reasonably could and should have communicated it to the acting partner, operate as notice to or knowledge of the partnership, except in the case of a fraud on the partnership committed by or with the consent of that partner.

Sec. 13. Partnership Bound by Partner's Wrongful Act

Where, by any wrongful act or omission of any partner acting in the ordinary course of the business of the partnership or with the authority of his co-partners, loss or injury is caused to any person, not being a partner in the partnership, or any penalty is incurred, the partnership is liable therefor to the same extent as the partner so acting or omitting to act.

Sec. 14. Partnership Bound by Partner's Breach of Trust

The partnership is bound to make good the loss:

(a) Where one partner acting within the scope of his apparent authority receives money or property of a third person and misapplies it; and

(b) Where the partnership in the course of its business receives money or property of a third person and the money or property so received is misapplied by any partner while it is in the custody of the partnership.

Sec. 15. Nature of Partner's Liability

All partners are liable

(a) Jointly and severally for everything chargeable to the partnership under sections 13 and 14.

(b) Jointly for all other debts and obligations of the partnership; but any partner may enter into a separate obligation to perform a partnership contract.

Sec. 16. Partner by Estoppel

(1) When a person, by words spoken or written or by conduct, represents himself, or consents to another representing him to any one, as a partner in an existing partnership or with one or more persons not actual partners, he is liable to any such person to whom such representation has been made, who has, on the faith of such representation, given credit to the actual or apparent partnership, and if he has made such representation or consented to its being made in a public manner he is liable to such person, whether the representation has or has not been made or communicated to such person so giving credit by or with the knowledge of the apparent partner making the representation or consenting to its being made.

(a) When a partnership liability results, he is liable as though he were an actual member of the partnership.

(b) When no partnership liability results, he is liable jointly with the other persons, if any, so consenting to the contract or representation as to incur liability, otherwise separately.

(2) When a person has been thus represented to be a partner in an existing partnership, or with one or more persons not actual partners, he is an agent of the persons consenting to such representation to bind them to the same extent and in the same manner as though he were a partner in fact, with respect to persons who rely upon the representation. Where all the members of the existing partnership consent to the representation, a partnership act or obligation results; but in all other cases it is the joint act or obligation of the person acting and the persons consenting to the representation.

Sec. 17. Liability of Incoming Partner

A person admitted as a partner into an existing partnership is liable for all the obligations of the partnership arising before his admission as though he had been a partner when such obligations were incurred, except that this liability shall be satisfied only out of partnership property.

Part IV Relations of Partners to One Another

Sec. 18. Rules Determining Rights and Duties of Partners

The rights and duties of the partners in relation to the partnership shall be determined, subject to any agreement between them, by the following rules:

(a) Each partner shall be repaid his contributions, whether by way of capital or advances to the partnership property and share equally in the profits and surplus remaining after all liabilities, including those to partners, are satisfied; and must contribute towards the losses, whether of capital or otherwise, sustained by the partnership according to his share in the profits.

(b) The partnership must indemnify every partner in respect of payments made and personal liabilities reasonably incurred by him in the ordinary and proper conduct of its business, or for the preservation of its business or property.

(c) A partner, who in aid of the partnership makes any payment or advance beyond the amount of capital which he agreed to contribute, shall be paid interest from the date of the payment or advance.

(d) A partner shall receive interest on the capital contributed by him only from the date when repayment should be made.

(e) All partners have equal rights in the management and conduct of the partnership business.

(f) No partner is entitled to remuneration for acting in the partnership business, except that a surviving partner is entitled to reasonable compensation for his services in winding up the partnership affairs.

(g) No person can become a member of a partnership without the consent of all the partners.

(h) Any difference arising as to ordinary matters connected with the partnership business may be decided by a majority of the partners; but no act in contravention of any agreement between the partners may be done rightfully without the consent of all the partners.

Sec. 19. Partnership Books

The partnership books shall be kept, subject to any agreement between the partners, at the principal place of business of the partnership, and every partner shall at all times have access to and may inspect and copy any of them.

Sec. 20. Duty of Partners to Render Information

Partners shall render on demand true and full information of all things affecting the partnership to any partner or the legal representative of any deceased partner or partner under legal disability.

Sec. 21. Partner Accountable as a Fiduciary

(1) Every partner must account to the partnership for any benefit, and hold as trustee for it any profits derived by him without the consent of the other partners from any transaction connected with the formation, conduct, or liquidation of the partnership or from any use by him of its property.

(2) This section applies also to the representatives of a deceased partner engaged in the liquidation of the affairs of the partnership as the personal representatives of the last surviving partner.

Sec. 22. Right to an Account

Any partner shall have the right to a formal account as to partnership affairs:

(a) If he is wrongfully excluded from the partnership business or possession of its property by his co-partners,

(b) If the right exists under the terms of any agreement,

(c) As provided by section 21,

(d) Whenever other circumstances render it just and reasonable.

Sec. 23. Continuation of Partnership beyond Fixed Term

(1) When a partnership for a fixed term or particular undertaking is continued after the termination of such term or particular undertaking without any express agreement, the rights and duties of the partners remain the same as they were at such termination, so far as is consistent with a partnership at will.

(2) A continuation of the business by the partners or such of them as habitually acted therein during the term, without any settlement or liquidation of the partnership affairs, is prima facie evidence of a continuation of the partnership.

Part V Property Rights of a Partner

Sec. 24. Extent of Property Rights of a Partner

The property rights of a partner are (1) his rights in specific partnership property, (2) his interest in the partnership, and (3) his right to participate in the management.

Sec. 25. Nature of a Partner's Right in Specific Partnership Property

(1) A partner is co-owner with his partners of specific partnership property holding as a tenant in partnership.

(2) The incidents of this tenancy are such that:

(a) A partner, subject to the provisions of this act and to any agreement between the partners, has an equal right with his partners to possess specific partnership property for partnership purposes; but he has no right to possess such property for any other purpose without the consent of his partners.

(b) A partner's right in specific partnership property is not assignable except in connection with the assignment of rights of all the partners in the same property.

(c) A partner's right in specific partnership property is not subject to attachment or execution, except on a claim against the partnership. When partnership property is attached for a partnership debt the partners, or any of them, or the representatives of a deceased partner, cannot claim any right under the homestead or exemption laws.

(d) On the death of a partner his right in specific partnership property vests in the surviving partner or partners, except where the deceased was the last surviving partner, when his right in such property vests in his legal representative. Such surviving partner or partners, or the legal representative of the last surviving partner, has no right to possess the partnership property for any but a partnership purpose.

(e) A partner's right in specific partnership property is not subject to dower, curtesy, or allowances to widows, heirs, or next of kin.

Sec. 26. Nature of Partner's Interest in the Partnership

A partner's interest in the partnership is his share of the profits and surplus, and the same is personal property.

Sec. 27. Assignment of Partner's Interest

(1) A conveyance by a partner of his interest in the partnership does not of itself dissolve the partnership, nor, as against the other partners in the absence of agreement, entitle the assignee, during the continuance of the partnership, to interfere in the management or administration of the partnership business or affairs, or to require any information or account of partnership transactions, or to inspect the partnership books; but it merely entitles the assignee to receive in accordance with his contract the profits to which the assigning partner would otherwise be entitled.

(2) In case of a dissolution of the partnership, the assignee is entitled to receive his assignor's interest and may require an account from the date only of the last account agreed to by all the partners.

Sec. 28. Partner's Interest Subject to Charging Order

(1) On due application to a competent court by any judgment creditor of a partner, the court which entered the judgment, order, or decree, or any other court, may charge the interest of the debtor partner with payment of the unsatisfied amount of such judgment debt with interest thereon; and may then or later appoint a receiver of his share of the profits, and of any other money due or to fall due to him in respect of the partnership, and make all other orders, directions, accounts and inquiries which the debtor partner might have made, or which the circumstances of the case may require.

(2) The interest charged may be redeemed at any time before foreclosure, or in case of a sale being directed by the court may be purchased without thereby causing a dissolution:

(a) With separate property, by any one or more of the partners, or

(b) With partnership property, by any one or more of the partners with the consent of all the partners whose interests are not so charged or sold.

(3) Nothing in this act shall be held to deprive a partner of his right, if any, under the exemption laws, as regards his interest in the partnership.

Part VI Dissolution and Winding up

Sec. 29. Dissolution Defined

The dissolution of a partnership is the change in the relation of the partners caused by any partner ceasing to be associated in the carrying on as distinguished from the winding up of the business.

Sec. 30. Partnership not Terminated by Dissolution

On dissolution the partnership is not terminated, but continues until the winding up of partnership affairs is completed.

Sec. 31. Causes of Dissolution

Dissolution is caused:

(1) Without violation of the agreement between the partners,

(a) By the termination of the definite term or particular undertaking specified in the agreement,

(b) By the express will of any partner when no definite term or particular undertaking is specified,

(c) By the express will of all the partners who have not assigned their interests or suffered them to be charged for their separate debts, either before or after the termination of any specified term or particular undertaking,

(d) By the expulsion of any partner from the business bona fide in accordance with such a power conferred by the agreement between the partners;

(2) In contravention of the agreement between the partners, where the circumstances do not permit a dissolution under any other provision of this section, by the express will of any partner at any time;

(3) By any event which makes it unlawful for the business of the partnership to be carried on or for the members to carry it on in partnership;

(4) By the death of any partner;

(5) By the bankruptcy of any partner or the partnership;

(6) By decree of court under section 32.

Sec. 32. Dissolution by Decree of Court

(1) On application by or for a partner the court shall decree a dissolution whenever:

(a) A partner has been declared a lunatic in any judicial proceeding or is shown to be of unsound mind,

(b) A partner becomes in any other way incapable of performing his part of the partnership contract,

(c) A partner has been guilty of such conduct as tends to affect prejudicially the carrying on of the business,

(d) A partner wilfully or persistently commits a breach of the partnership agreement, or otherwise so conducts himself in matters relating to the partnership business that it is not reasonably practicable to carry on the business in partnership with him,

(e) The business of the partnership can only be carried on at a loss,

(f) Other circumstances render a dissolution equitable.

(2) On the application of the purchaser of a partner's interest under sections 28 or 29 [should read 27 or 28];

(a) After the termination of the specified term or particular undertaking,

(b) At any time if the partnership was a partnership at will when the interest was assigned or when the charging order was issued.

Sec. 33. General Effect of Dissolution on Authority of Partner

Except so far as may be necessary to wind up partnership affairs or to complete transactions begun but not then finished, dissolution terminates all authority of any partner to act for the partnership,

(1) With respect to the partners,

(a) When the dissolution is not by the act, bankruptcy or death of a partner; or

(b) When the dissolution is by such act, bankruptcy or death of a partner, in cases where section 34 so requires.

(2) With respect to persons not partners, as declared in section 35.

Sec. 34. Rights of Partner to Contribution from Copartners after Dissolution

Where the dissolution is caused by the act, death or bankruptcy of a partner, each partner is liable to his copartners for his share of any liability created by any partner acting for the partnership as if the partnership had not been dissolved unless

(a) The dissolution being by act of any partner, the partner acting for the partnership had knowledge of the dissolution, or

(b) The dissolution being by the death or bankruptcy of a partner, the partner acting for the partnership had knowledge or notice of the death or bankruptcy.

Sec. 35. Power of Partner to Bind Partnership to Third Persons after Dissolution

(1) After dissolution a partner can bind the partnership except as provided in Paragraph (3).

(a) By any act appropriate for winding up partnership affairs or completing transactions unfinished at dissolution;

(b) By any transaction which would bind the partnership if dissolution had not taken place, provided the other party to the transaction

(I) Had extended credit to the partnership prior to dissolution and had no knowledge or notice of the dissolution; or

(II) Though he had not so extended credit, had nevertheless known of the partnership prior to dissolution, and, having no knowledge or notice of dissolution, the fact of dissolution had not been advertised in a newspaper of general circulation in the place (or in each place if more than one) at which the partnership business was regularly carried on.

(2) The liability of a partner under paragraph (1b) shall be satisfied out of partnership assets alone when such partner had been prior to dissolution

(a) Unknown as a partner to the person with whom the contract is made; and

(b) So far unknown and inactive in partnership affairs that the business reputation of the partnership could not be said to have been in any degree due to his connection with it.

(3) The partnership is in no case bound by any act of a partner after dissolution

(a) Where the partnership is dissolved because it is unlawful to carry on the business, unless the act is appropriate for winding up partnership affairs; or

(b) Where the partner has become bankrupt; or

(c) Where the partner has no authority to wind up partnership affairs; except by a transaction with one who

(I) Had extended credit to the partnership prior to dissolution and had no knowledge or notice of his want of authority; or

(II) Had not extended credit to the partnership prior to dissolution, and, having no knowledge or notice of his want of authority, the fact of his want of authority has not been advertised in the manner provided for advertising the fact of dissolution in paragraph (1bII).

(4) Nothing in this section shall affect the liability under Section 16 of any person who after dissolution represents himself or consents to another representing him as a partner in a partnership engaged in carrying on business.

Sec. 36. Effect of Dissolution on Partner's Existing Liability

(1) The dissolution of the partnership does not of itself discharge the existing liability of any partner.

(2) A partner is discharged from any existing liability upon dissolution of the partnership by an agreement to that effect between himself, the partnership creditor and the person or partnership continuing the business; and such agreement may be inferred from the course of dealing between the creditor having knowledge of the dissolution and the person or partnership continuing the business.

(3) Where a person agrees to assume the existing obligations of a dissolved partnership, the partners whose obligations have been assumed shall be discharged from any liability to any creditor of the partnership who, knowing of the agreement, consents to a material alteration in the nature or time of payment of such obligations.

(4) The individual property of a deceased partner shall be liable for all obligations of the partnership incurred while he was a partner but subject to the prior payment of his separate debts.

Sec. 37. Right to Wind Up

Unless otherwise agreed the partners who have not wrongfully dissolved the partnership or the legal representative of the last surviving partner, not bankrupt, has the right to wind up the partnership affairs; provided, however, that any partner, his legal representative or his assignee, upon cause shown, may obtain winding up by the court.

Sec. 38. Rights of Partners to Application of Partnership Property

(1) When dissolution is caused in any way, except in contravention of the partnership agreement, each partner, as against his copartners and all persons claiming through them in respect of their interests in the partnership, unless otherwise agreed, may have the partnership property applied to discharge its liabilities, and the surplus applied to pay in cash the net amount owing to the respective partners. But if dissolution is caused by expulsion of a partner, bona fide under the partnership agreement and if the expelled partner is

discharged from all partnership liabilities, either by payment or agreement under section 36(2), he shall receive in cash only the net amount due him from the partnership.

(2) When dissolution is caused in contravention of the partnership agreement the rights of the partners shall be as follows:

(a) Each partner who has not caused dissolution wrongfully shall have,

(I) All the rights specified in paragraph (1) of this section, and

(II) The right, as against each partner who has caused the dissolution wrongfully, to damages for breach of the agreement.

(b) The partners who have not caused the dissolution wrongfully, if they all desire to continue the business in the same name, either by themselves or jointly with others, may do so, during the agreed term for the partnership and for that purpose may possess the partnership property, provided they secure the payment by bond approved by the court, or pay to any partner who has caused the dissolution wrongfully, the value of his interest in the partnership at the dissolution, less any damages recoverable under clause (2a II) of the section, and in like manner indemnify him against all present or future partnership liabilities.

(c) A partner who has caused the dissolution wrongfully shall have:

(I) If the business is not continued under the provisions of paragraph (2b) all the rights of a partner under paragraph (1), subject to clause (2a II), of this section,

(II) If the business is continued under paragraph (2b) of this section the right as against his co-partners and all claiming through them in respect of their interests in the partnership, to have the value of his interest in the partnership, less any damages caused to his co-partners by the dissolution, ascertained and paid to him in cash, or the payment secured by bond approved by the court, and to be released from all existing liabilities of the partnership; but in ascertaining the value of the partner's interest the value of the good-will of the business shall not be considered.

Sec. 39. Rights Where Partnership Is Dissolved for Fraud or Misrepresentation

Where a partnership contract is rescinded on the ground of the fraud or misrepresentation of one of the parties thereto, the party entitled to rescind is, without prejudice to any other right, entitled,

(a) To a lien on, or right of retention of, the surplus of the partnership property after satisfying the partnership liabilities to third persons for any sum of money paid by him for the purchase of an interest in the partnership and for any capital or advances contributed by him; and

(b) To stand, after all liabilities to third persons have been satisfied, in the place of the creditors of the partnership for any payments made by him in respect of the partnership liabilities; and

(c) To be indemnified by the person guilty of the fraud or making the representation against all debts and liabilities of the partnership.

Sec. 40. Rules for Distribution

In settling accounts between the partners after dissolution, the following rules shall be observed, subject to any agreement to the contrary:

(a) The assets of the partnership are:

(I) The partnership property,

(II) The contributions of the partners necessary for the payment of all the liabilities specified in clause (b) of this paragraph.

(b) The liabilities of the partnership shall rank in order of payment, as follows:

(I) Those owing to creditors other than partners,

(II) Those owing to partners other than for capital and profits,

(III) Those owing to partners in respect of capital,

(IV) Those owing to partners in respect of profits.

(c) The assets shall be applied in the order of their declaration in clause (a) of this paragraph to the satisfaction of the liabilities.

(d) The partners shall contribute, as provided by section 18(a) the amount necessary to satisfy the liabilities; but if any, but not all, of the partners are insolvent, or, not being subject to process, refuse to contribute, the other partners shall contribute their share of the liabilities, and, in the relative proportions in which they share the profits, the additional amount necessary to pay the liabilities.

(e) An assignee for the benefit of creditors or any person appointed by the court shall have the right to enforce the contributions specified in clause (d) of this paragraph.

(f) Any partner or his legal representative shall have the right to enforce the contributions specified in clause (d) of this paragraph, to the extent of the amount which he has paid in excess of his share of the liability.

(g) The individual property of a deceased partner shall be liable for the contributions specified in clause (d) of this paragraph.

(h) When partnership property and the individual properties of the partners are in possession of a court for distribution, partnership creditors shall have priority on partnership property and separate creditors on individual property, saving the rights of lien or secured creditors as heretofore.

(i) Where a partner has become bankrupt or his estate is insolvent the claims against his separate property shall rank in the following order:

(I) Those owing to separate creditors,

(II) Those owing to partnership creditors,

(III) Those owing to partners by way of contribution.

Sec. 41. Liability of Persons Continuing the Business in Certain Cases

(1) When any new partner is admitted into an existing partnership, or when any partner retires and assigns (or the representative

of the deceased partner assigns) his rights in partnership property to two or more of the partners, or to one or more of the partners and one or more third persons, if the business is continued without liquidation of the partnership affairs, creditors of the first or dissolved partnership are also creditors of the partnership so continuing the business.

(2) When all but one partner retire and assign (or the representative of a deceased partner assigns) their rights in partnership property to the remaining partner, who continues the business without liquidation of partnership affairs, either alone or with others, creditors of the dissolved partnership are also creditors of the person or partnership so continuing the business.

(3) When any partner retires or dies and the business of the dissolved partnership is continued as set forth in paragraphs (1) and (2) of this section, with the consent of the retired partners or the representative of the deceased partner, but without any assignment of his right in partnership property, rights of creditors of the dissolved partnership and of the creditors of the person or partnership continuing the business shall be as if such assignment had been made.

(4) When all the partners or their representatives assign their rights in partnership property to one or more third persons who promise to pay the debts and who continue the business of the dissolved partnership, creditors of the dissolved partnership are also creditors of the person or partnership continuing the business.

(5) When any partner wrongfully causes a dissolution and the remaining partners continue the business under the provisions of section 38(2b), either alone or with others, and without liquidation of the partnership affairs, creditors of the dissolved partnership are also creditors of the person or partnership continuing the business.

(6) When a partner is expelled and the remaining partners continue the business either alone or with others, without liquidation of the partnership affairs, creditors of the dissolved partnership are also creditors of the person or partnership continuing the business.

(7) The liability of a third person becoming a partner in the partnership continuing the business, under this section, to the creditors of the dissolved partnership shall be satisfied out of partnership property only.

(8) When the business of a partnership after dissolution is continued under any conditions set forth in this section the creditors of the dissolved partnership, as against the separate creditors of the retiring or deceased partner or the representative of the deceased partner, have a prior right to any claim of the retired partner or the representative of the deceased partner against the person or partnership continuing the business, on account of the retired or deceased partner's interest in the dissolved partnership or on account of any consideration promised for such interest or for his right in partnership property.

(9) Nothing in this section shall be held to modify any right of creditors to set aside any assignment on the ground of fraud.

(10) The use by the person or partnership continuing the business of the partnership name, or the name of a deceased partner as part thereof, shall not of itself make the individual property of the deceased partner liable for any debts contracted by such person or partnership.

Sec. 42. Rights of Retiring or Estate of Deceased Partner When the Business Is Continued

When any partner retires or dies, and the business is continued under any of the conditions set forth in section 41 (1, 2, 3, 5, 6), or section 38(2b) without any settlement of accounts as between him or his estate and the person or partnership continuing the business, unless otherwise agreed, he or his legal representative as against such persons or partnership may have the value of his interest at the date of dissolution ascertained, and shall receive as an ordinary creditor an amount equal to the value of his interest in the dissolved partnership with interest, or, at his option or at the option of his legal representative, in lieu of interest, the profits attributable to the use of his right in the property of the dissolved partnership; provided that the creditors of the dissolved partnership as against the separate creditors, or the representative of the retired or deceased partner, shall have priority on any claim arising under this section, as provided by section 41(8) of this act.

Sec. 43. Accrual of Actions

The right to an account of his interest shall accrue to any partner, or his legal representative, as against the winding up partners or the surviving partners or the person or partnership continuing the business, at the date of dissolution, in the absence of any agreement to the contrary.

Part VII Miscellaneous Provisions

Sec. 44. When Act Takes Effect

This act shall take effect on the ___ day of ___ one thousand nine hundred and ___.

Sec. 45. Legislation Repealed

All acts or parts of acts inconsistent with this act are hereby repealed.

APPENDIX E

THE REVISED MODEL BUSINESS CORPORATION ACT (EXCERPTS)

Chapter 2. INCORPORATION

§ 2.01 Incorporators

One or more persons may act as the incorporator or incorporators of a corporation by delivering articles of incorporation to the secretary of state for filing.

§ 2.02 Articles of Incorporation

(a) The articles of incorporation must set forth:

(1) a corporate name * * * ;

(2) the number of shares the corporation is authorized to issue;

(3) the street address of the corporation's initial registered office and the name of its initial registered agent at that office; and

(4) the name and address of each incorporator.

(b) The articles of incorporation may set forth:

(1) the names and addresses of the individuals who are to serve as the initial directors;

(2) provisions not inconsistent with law regarding:

(i) the purpose or purposes for which the corporation is organized;

(ii) managing the business and regulating the affairs of the corporation;

(iii) defining, limiting, and regulating the powers of the corporation, its board of directors, and shareholders;

(iv) a par value for authorized shares or classes of shares;

(v) the imposition of personal liability on shareholders for the debts of the corporation to a specified extent and upon specified conditions;

(3) any provision that under this Act is required or permitted to be set forth in the bylaws; and

(4) a provision eliminating or limiting the liability of a director to the corporation or its shareholders for money damages for any action taken, or any failure to take any action, as a director, except liability for (A) the amount of a financial benefit received by a director to which he is not entitled; (B) an intentional infliction of harm on the corporation or the shareholders; (C) [unlawful distributions]; or (D) an intentional violation of criminal law.

(c) The articles of incorporation need not set forth any of the corporate powers enumerated in this Act.

§ 2.03 Incorporation

(a) Unless a delayed effective date is specified, the corporate existence begins when the articles of incorporation are filed.

(b) The secretary of state's filing of the articles of incorporation is conclusive proof that the incorporators satisfied all conditions precedent to incorporation except in a proceeding by the state to cancel or revoke the incorporation or involuntarily dissolve the corporation.

§ 2.04 Liability for Preincorporation Transactions

All persons purporting to act as or on behalf of a corporation, knowing there was no incorporation under this Act, are jointly and severally liable for all liabilities created while so acting.

§ 2.05 Organization of Corporation

(a) After incorporation:

(1) if initial directors are named in the articles of incorporation, the initial directors shall hold an organizational meeting, at the call of a majority of the directors, to complete the organization of the corporation by appointing officers, adopting bylaws, and carrying on any other business brought before the meeting;

(2) if initial directors are not named in the articles, the incorporator or incorporators shall hold an organizational meeting at the call of a majority of the incorporators:

(i) to elect directors and complete the organization of the corporation; or

(ii) to elect a board of directors who shall complete the organization of the corporation.

(b) Action required or permitted by this Act to be taken by incorporators at an organizational meeting may be taken without a meeting if the action taken is evidenced by one or more written consents describing the action taken and signed by each incorporator.

(c) An organizational meeting may be held in or out of this state.

* * * *

Chapter 3. PURPOSES AND POWERS

§ 3.01 Purposes

(a) Every corporation incorporated under this Act has the purpose of engaging in any lawful business unless a more limited purpose is set forth in the articles of incorporation.

(b) A corporation engaging in a business that is subject to regulation under another statute of this state may incorporate under this Act only if permitted by, and subject to all limitations of, the other statute.

§ 3.02 General Powers

Unless its articles of incorporation provide otherwise, every corporation has perpetual duration and succession in its corporate name and has the same powers as an individual to do all things necessary or convenient to carry out its business and affairs, including without limitation power:

(1) to sue and be sued, complain and defend in its corporate name;

(2) to have a corporate seal, which may be altered at will, and to use it, or a facsimile of it, by impressing or affixing it or in any other manner reproducing it;

(3) to make and amend bylaws, not inconsistent with its articles of incorporation or with the laws of this state, for managing the business and regulating the affairs of the corporation;

(4) to purchase, receive, lease, or otherwise acquire, and own, hold, improve, use, and otherwise deal with, real or personal property, or any legal or equitable interest in property, wherever located;

(5) to sell, convey, mortgage, pledge, lease, exchange, and otherwise dispose of all or any part of its property;

(6) to purchase, receive, subscribe for, or otherwise acquire; own, hold, vote, use, sell, mortgage, lend, pledge, or otherwise dispose of; and deal in and with shares or other interests in, or obligations of, any other entity;

(7) to make contracts and guarantees, incur liabilities, borrow money, issue its notes, bonds, and other obligations (which may be convertible into or include the option to purchase other securities of the corporation), and secure any of its obligations by mortgage or pledge of any of its property, franchises, or income;

(8) to lend money, invest and reinvest its funds, and receive and hold real and personal property as security for repayment;

(9) to be a promoter, partner, member, associate, or manager of any partnership, joint venture, trust, or other entity;

(10) to conduct its business, locate offices, and exercise the powers granted by this Act within or without this state;

(11) to elect directors and appoint officers, employees, and agents of the corporation, define their duties, fix their compensation, and lend them money and credit;

(12) to pay pensions and establish pension plans, pension trusts, profit sharing plans, share bonus plans, share option plans, and benefit or incentive plans for any or all of its current or former directors, officers, employees, and agents;

(13) to make donations for the public welfare or for charitable, scientific, or educational purposes;

(14) to transact any lawful business that will aid governmental policy;

(15) to make payments or donations, or do any other act, not inconsistent with law, that furthers the business and affairs of the corporation.

* * * *

Chapter 5. OFFICE AND AGENT

§ 5.01 Registered Office and Registered Agent

Each corporation must continuously maintain in this state:

(1) a registered office that may be the same as any of its places of business; and

(2) a registered agent, who may be:

(i) an individual who resides in this state and whose business office is identical with the registered office;

(ii) a domestic corporation or not-for-profit domestic corporation whose business office is identical with the registered office; or

(iii) a foreign corporation or not-for-profit foreign corporation authorized to transact business in this state whose business office is identical with the registered office.

* * * *

§ 5.04 Service on Corporation

(a) A corporation's registered agent is the corporation's agent for service of process, notice, or demand required or permitted by law to be served on the corporation.

(b) If a corporation has no registered agent, or the agent cannot with reasonable diligence be served, the corporation may be served by registered or certified mail, return receipt requested, addressed to the secretary of the corporation at its principal office. Service is perfected under this subsection at the earliest of:

(1) the date the corporation receives the mail;

(2) the date shown on the return receipt, if signed on behalf of the corporation; or

(3) five days after its deposit in the United States Mail, if mailed postpaid and correctly addressed.

(c) This section does not prescribe the only means, or necessarily the required means, of serving a corporation.

Chapter 6. SHARES AND DISTRIBUTIONS

* * * *

Subchapter B. Issuance of Shares

* * * *

§ 6.21 Issuance of Shares

(a) The powers granted in this section to the board of directors may be reserved to the shareholders by the articles of incorporation.

(b) The board of directors may authorize shares to be issued for consideration consisting of any tangible or intangible property or benefit to the corporation, including cash, promissory notes, services performed, contracts for services to be performed, or other securities of the corporation.

(c) Before the corporation issues shares, the board of directors must determine that the consideration received or to be received for shares to be issued is adequate. That determination by the board of directors is conclusive insofar as the adequacy of consideration for the issuance of shares relates to whether the shares are validly issued, fully paid, and nonassessable.

(d) When the corporation receives the consideration for which the board of directors authorized the issuance of shares, the shares issued therefor are fully paid and nonassessable.

(e) The corporation may place in escrow shares issued for a contract for future services or benefits or a promissory note, or make other arrangements to restrict the transfer of the shares, and may credit distributions in respect of the shares against their purchase price, until the services are performed, the note is paid, or the benefits received. If the services are not performed, the note is not paid, or the benefits are not received, the shares escrowed or restricted and the distributions credited may be cancelled in whole or part.

* * * *

§ 6.27 Restriction on Transfer or Registration of Shares and Other Securities

(a) The articles of incorporation, bylaws, an agreement among shareholders, or an agreement between shareholders and the corporation may impose restrictions on the transfer or registration of transfer of shares of the corporation. A restriction does not affect shares issued before the restriction was adopted unless the holders of the shares are parties to the restriction agreement or voted in favor of the restriction.

(b) A restriction on the transfer or registration of transfer of shares is valid and enforceable against the holder or a transferee of the holder if the restriction is authorized by this section and its existence is noted conspicuously on the front or back of the certificate or is contained in the information statement [sent to the shareholder]. Unless so noted, a restriction is not enforceable against a person without knowledge of the restriction.

(c) A restriction on the transfer or registration of transfer of shares is authorized:

(1) to maintain the corporation's status when it is dependent on the number or identity of its shareholders;

(2) to preserve exemptions under federal or state securities law;

(3) for any other reasonable purpose.

(d) A restriction on the transfer or registration of transfer of shares may:

(1) obligate the shareholder first to offer the corporation or other persons (separately, consecutively, or simultaneously) an opportunity to acquire the restricted shares;

(2) obligate the corporate or other persons (separately, consecutively, or simultaneously) to acquire the restricted shares;

(3) require the corporation, the holders of any class of its shares, or another person to approve the transfer of the restricted shares, if the requirement is not manifestly unreasonable;

(4) prohibit the transfer of the restricted shares to designated persons or classes of persons, if the prohibition is not manifestly unreasonable.

(e) For purposes of this section, "shares" includes a security convertible into or carrying a right to subscribe for or acquire shares.

* * * *

Chapter 7. SHAREHOLDERS

Subchapter A. Meetings

§ 7.01 Annual Meeting

(a) A corporation shall hold annually at a time stated in or fixed in accordance with the bylaws a meeting of shareholders.

(b) Annual shareholders' meetings may be held in or out of this state at the place stated in or fixed in accordance with the bylaws.

If no place is stated in or fixed in accordance with the bylaws, annual meetings shall be held at the corporation's principal office.

(c) The failure to hold an annual meeting at the time stated in or fixed in accordance with a corporation's bylaws does not affect the validity of any corporate action.

* * * *

§ 7.05 Notice of Meeting

(a) A corporation shall notify shareholders of the date, time, and place of each annual and special shareholders' meeting no fewer than 10 nor more than 60 days before the meeting date. Unless this Act or the articles of incorporation require otherwise, the corporation is required to give notice only to shareholders entitled to vote at the meeting.

(b) Unless this Act or the articles of incorporation require otherwise, notice of an annual meeting need not include a description of the purpose or purposes for which the meeting is called.

(c) Notice of a special meeting must include a description of the purpose or purposes for which the meeting is called.

(d) If not otherwise fixed * * *, the record date for determining shareholders entitled to notice of and to vote at an annual or special shareholders' meeting is the day before the first notice is delivered to shareholders.

(e) Unless the bylaws require otherwise, if an annual or special shareholders' meeting is adjourned to a different date, time, or place, notice need not be given of the new date, time, or place if the new date, time, or place is announced at the meeting before adjournment. * * *

* * * *

§ 7.07 Record Date

(a) The bylaws may fix or provide the manner of fixing the record date for one or more voting groups in order to determine the shareholders entitled to notice of a shareholders' meeting, to demand a special meeting, to vote, or to take any other action. If the bylaws do not fix or provide for fixing a record date, the board of directors of the corporation may fix a future date as the record date.

(b) A record date fixed under this section may not be more than 70 days before the meeting or action requiring a determination of shareholders.

(c) A determination of shareholders entitled to notice of or to vote at a shareholders' meeting is effective for any adjournment of the meeting unless the board of directors fixes a new record date, which it must do if the meeting is adjourned to a date more than 120 days after the date fixed for the original meeting.

(d) If a court orders a meeting adjourned to a date more than 120 days after the date fixed for the original meeting, it may provide that the original record date continues in effect or it may fix a new record date.

Subchapter B. Voting

§ 7.20 Shareholders' List for Meeting

(a) After fixing a record date for a meeting, a corporation shall prepare an alphabetical list of the names of all its shareholders who are entitled to notice of a shareholders' meeting. The list must be arranged by voting group (and within each voting group by class or series of shares) and show the address of and number of shares held by each shareholder.

(b) The shareholders' list must be available for inspection by any shareholder, beginning two business days after notice of the meeting is given for which the list was prepared and continuing through the meeting, at the corporation's principal office or at a place identified in the meeting notice in the city where the meeting will be held. A shareholder, his agent, or attorney is entitled on written demand to inspect and, subject to the requirements of section 16.02(c), to copy the list, during regular business hours and at his expense, during the period it is available for inspection.

(c) The corporation shall make the shareholders' list available at the meeting, and any shareholder, his agent, or attorney is entitled to inspect the list at any time during the meeting or any adjournment.

(d) If the corporation refuses to allow a shareholder, his agent, or attorney to inspect the shareholders' list before or at the meeting (or copy the list as permitted by subsection (b)), the [name or describe] court of the county where a corporation's principal office (or, if none in this state, its registered office) is located, on application of the shareholder, may summarily order the inspection or copying at the corporation's expense and may postpone the meeting for which the list was prepared until the inspection or copying is complete.

(e) Refusal or failure to prepare or make available the shareholders' list does not affect the validity of action taken at the meeting.

* * * *

§ 7.22 Proxies

(a) A shareholder may vote his shares in person or by proxy.

(b) A shareholder may appoint a proxy to vote or otherwise act for him by signing an appointment form, either personally or by his attorney-in-fact.

(c) An appointment of a proxy is effective when received by the secretary or other officer or agent authorized to tabulate votes. An appointment is valid for 11 months unless a longer period is expressly provided in the appointment form.

* * * *

§ 7.28 Voting for Directors; Cumulative Voting

(a) Unless otherwise provided in the articles of incorporation, directors are elected by a plurality of the votes cast by the shares entitled to vote in the election at a meeting at which a quorum is present.

(b) Shareholders do not have a right to cumulate their votes for directors unless the articles of incorporation so provide.

(c) A statement included in the articles of incorporation that "[all] [a designated voting group of] shareholders are entitled to cumulate their votes for directors" (or words of similar import) means that the shareholders designated are entitled to multiply the number of votes they are entitled to cast by the number of directors for whom they are entitled to vote and cast the product for a single candidate or distribute the product among two or more candidates.

(d) Shares otherwise entitled to vote cumulatively may not be voted cumulatively at a particular meeting unless:

(1) the meeting notice or proxy statement accompanying the notice states conspicuously that cumulative voting is authorized; or

(2) a shareholder who has the right to cumulate his votes gives notice to the corporation not less than 48 hours before the time set for the meeting of his intent to cumulate his votes during the meeting, and if one shareholder gives this notice all other shareholders in the same voting group participating in the election are entitled to cumulate their votes without giving further notice.

* * * *

Subchapter D. Derivative Proceedings

* * * *

§ 7.41 Standing

A shareholder may not commence or maintain a derivative proceeding unless the shareholder:

(1) was a shareholder of the corporation at the time of the act or omission complained of or became a shareholder through transfer by operation of law from one who was a shareholder at that time; and

(2) fairly and adequately represents the interests of the corporation in enforcing the right of the corporation.

§ 7.42 Demand

No shareholder may commence a derivative proceeding until:

(1) a written demand has been made upon the corporation to take suitable action; and

(2) 90 days have expired from the date the demand was made unless the shareholder has earlier been notified that the demand has been rejected by the corporation or unless irreparable injury to the corporation would result by waiting for the expiration of the 90 day period.

* * * *

Chapter 8. DIRECTORS AND OFFICERS

Subchapter A. Board of Directors

* * * *

§ 8.02 Qualifications of Directors

The articles of incorporation or bylaws may prescribe qualifications for directors. A director need not be a resident of this state or a shareholder of the corporation unless the articles of incorporation or bylaws so prescribe.

§ 8.03 Number and Election of Directors

(a) A board of directors must consist of one or more individuals, with the number specified in or fixed in accordance with the articles of incorporation or bylaws.

(b) If a board of directors has power to fix or change the number of directors, the board may increase or decrease by 30 percent or less the number of directors last approved by the shareholders, but only the shareholders may increase or decrease by more than 30 percent the number of directors last approved by the shareholders.

(c) The articles of incorporation or bylaws may establish a variable range for the size of the board of directors by fixing a minimum and maximum number of directors. If a variable range is established, the number of directors may be fixed or changed from time to time, within the minimum and maximum, by the shareholders or the board of directors. After shares are issued, only the shareholders may change the range for the size of the board or change from a fixed to a variable-range size board or vice versa.

(d) Directors are elected at the first annual shareholders' meeting and at each annual meeting thereafter unless their terms are staggered under section 8.06.

* * * *

§ 8.08 Removal of Directors by Shareholders

(a) The shareholders may remove one or more directors with or without cause unless the articles of incorporation provide that directors may be removed only for cause.

(b) If a director is elected by a voting group of shareholders, only the shareholders of that voting group may participate in the vote to remove him.

(c) If cumulative voting is authorized, a director may not be removed if the number of votes sufficient to elect him under cumulative voting is voted against his removal. If cumulative voting is not authorized, a director may be removed only if the number of votes cast to remove him exceeds the number of votes cast not to remove him.

(d) A director may be removed by the shareholders only at a meeting called for the purpose of removing him and the meeting notice must state that the purpose, or one of the purposes, of the meeting is removal of the director.

* * * *

Subchapter B. Meetings and Action of the Board

§ 8.20 Meetings

(a) The board of directors may hold regular or special meetings in or out of this state.

(b) Unless the articles of incorporation or bylaws provide otherwise, the board of directors may permit any or all directors to participate in a regular or special meeting by, or conduct the meeting through the use of, any means of communication by which all directors participating may simultaneously hear each other during the meeting. A director participating in a meeting by this means is deemed to be present in person at the meeting.

* * * *

§ 8.22 Notice of Meeting

(a) Unless the articles of incorporation or bylaws provide otherwise, regular meetings of the board of directors may be held without notice of the date, time, place, or purpose of the meeting.

(b) Unless the articles of incorporation or bylaws provide for a longer or shorter period, special meetings of the board of directors must be preceded by at least two days' notice of the date, time, and place of the meeting. The notice need not describe the purpose of the special meeting unless required by the articles of incorporation or bylaws.

* * * *

§ 8.24 Quorum and Voting

(a) Unless the articles of incorporation or bylaws require a greater number, a quorum of a board of directors consists of:

(1) a majority of the fixed number of directors if the corporation has a fixed board size; or

(2) a majority of the number of directors prescribed, or if no number is prescribed the number in office immediately before the meeting begins, if the corporation has a variable-range size board.

(b) The articles of incorporation or bylaws may authorize a quorum of a board of directors to consist of no fewer than one-third of the fixed or prescribed number of directors determined under subsection (a).

(c) If a quorum is present when a vote is taken, the affirmative vote of a majority of directors present is the act of the board of directors unless the articles of incorporation or bylaws require the vote of a greater number of directors.

(d) A director who is present at a meeting of the board of directors or a committee of the board of directors when corporate action is taken is deemed to have assented to the action taken unless: (1) he objects at the beginning of the meeting (or promptly upon his arrival) to holding it or transacting business at the meeting; (2) his dissent or abstention from the action taken is entered in the minutes of the meeting; or (3) he delivers written notice of his dissent or abstention to the presiding officer of the meeting before its adjournment or to the corporation immediately after adjournment of the meeting. The right of dissent or abstention is not available to a director who votes in favor of the action taken.

* * * *

Subchapter C. Standards of Conduct

§ 8.30 General Standards for Directors

(a) A director shall discharge his duties as a director, including his duties as a member of a committee:

(1) in good faith;

(2) with the care an ordinarily prudent person in a like position would exercise under similar circumstances; and

(3) in a manner he reasonably believes to be in the best interests of the corporation.

(b) In discharging his duties a director is entitled to rely on information, opinions, reports, or statements, including financial statements and other financial data, if prepared or presented by:

(1) one or more officers or employees of the corporation whom the director reasonably believes to be reliable and competent in the matters presented;

(2) legal counsel, public accountants, or other persons as to matters the director reasonably believes are within the person's professional or expert competence; or

(3) a committee of the board of directors of which he is not a member if the director reasonably believes the committee merits confidence.

(c) A director is not acting in good faith if he has knowledge concerning the matter in question that makes reliance otherwise permitted by subsection (b) unwarranted.

(d) A director is not liable for any action taken as a director, or any failure to take any action, if he performed the duties of his office in compliance with this section.

* * * *

Subchapter D. Officers

* * * *

§ 8.41 Duties of Officers

Each officer has the authority and shall perform the duties set forth in the bylaws or, to the extent consistent with the bylaws, the duties prescribed by the board of directors or by direction of an officer authorized by the board of directors to prescribe the duties of other officers.

§ 8.42 Standards of Conduct for Officers

(a) An officer with discretionary authority shall discharge his duties under that authority:

(1) in good faith;

(2) with the care an ordinarily prudent person in a like position would exercise under similar circumstances; and

(3) in a manner he reasonably believes to be in the best interests of the corporation.

(b) In discharging his duties an officer is entitled to rely on information, opinions, reports, or statements, including financial statements and other financial data, if prepared or presented by:

(1) one or more officers or employees of the corporation whom the officer reasonably believes to be reliable and competent in the matters presented; or

(2) legal counsel, public accountants, or other persons as to matters the officer reasonably believes are within the person's professional or expert competence.

(c) An officer is not acting in good faith if he has knowledge concerning the matter in question that makes reliance otherwise permitted by subsection (b) unwarranted.

(d) An officer is not liable for any action taken as an officer, or any failure to take any action, if he performed the duties of his office in compliance with this section.

* * * *

Chapter 11. MERGER AND SHARE EXCHANGE

§ 11.01 Merger

(a) One or more corporations may merge into another corporation if the board of directors of each corporation adopts and its shareholders (if required * * *) approve a plan of merger.

(b) The plan of merger must set forth:

(1) the name of each corporation planning to merge and the name of the surviving corporation into which each other corporation plans to merge;

(2) the terms and conditions of the merger; and

(3) the manner and basis of converting the shares of each corporation into shares, obligations, or other securities of the surviving or any other corporation or into cash or other property in whole or part.

(c) The plan of merger may set forth:

(1) amendments to the articles of incorporation of the surviving corporation; and

(2) other provisions relating to the merger.

* * * *

§ 11.04 Merger of Subsidiary

(a) A parent corporation owning at least 90 percent of the outstanding shares of each class of a subsidiary corporation may merge the subsidiary into itself without approval of the shareholders of the parent or subsidiary.

(b) The board of directors of the parent shall adopt a plan of merger that sets forth:

(1) the names of the parent and subsidiary; and

(2) the manner and basis of converting the shares of the subsidiary into shares, obligations, or other securities of the parent or any other corporation or into cash or other property in whole or part.

(c) The parent shall mail a copy or summary of the plan of merger to each shareholder of the subsidiary who does not waive the mailing requirement in writing.

(d) The parent may not deliver articles of merger to the secretary of state for filing until at least 30 days after the date it mailed a copy of the plan of merger to each shareholder of the subsidiary who did not waive the mailing requirement.

(e) Articles of merger under this section may not contain amendments to the articles of incorporation of the parent corporation (except for amendments enumerated in section 10.02).

* * * *

§ 11.06 Effect of Merger or Share Exchange

(a) When a merger takes effect:

(1) every other corporation party to the merger merges into the surviving corporation and the separate existence of every corporation except the surviving corporation ceases;

(2) the title to all real estate and other property owned by each corporation party to the merger is vested in the surviving corporation without reversion or impairment;

(3) the surviving corporation has all liabilities of each corporation party to the merger;

(4) a proceeding pending against any corporation party to the merger may be continued as if the merger did not occur or the surviving corporation may be substituted in the proceeding for the corporation whose existence ceased;

(5) the articles of incorporation of the surviving corporation are amended to the extent provided in the plan of merger; and

(6) the shares of each corporation party to the merger that are to be converted into shares, obligations, or other securities of the surviving or any other corporation or into cash or other property are converted and the former holders of the shares are entitled only to the rights provided in the articles of merger or to their rights under chapter 13.

(b) When a share exchange takes effect, the shares of each acquired corporation are exchanged as provided in the plan, and the former holders of the shares are entitled only to the exchange rights provided in the articles of share exchange or to their rights under chapter 13.

* * * *

Chapter 13. DISSENTERS' RIGHTS

Subchapter A. Right to Dissent and Obtain Payment for Shares

* * * *

§ 13.02 Right to Dissent

(a) A shareholder is entitled to dissent from, and obtain payment of the fair value of his shares in the event of, any of the following corporate actions:

(1) consummation of a plan of merger to which the corporation is a party (i) if shareholder approval is required for the merger by [statute] or the articles of incorporation and the shareholder is entitled to vote on the merger or (ii) if the corporation is a subsidiary that is merged with its parent under section 11.04;

(2) consummation of a plan of share exchange to which the corporation is a party as the corporation whose shares will be acquired, if the shareholder is entitled to vote on the plan;

(3) consummation of a sale or exchange of all, or substantially all, of the property of the corporation other than in the usual and regular course of business, if the shareholder is entitled to vote on the sale or exchange, including a sale in dissolution, but not including a sale pursuant to court order

or a sale for cash pursuant to a plan by which all or substantially all of the net proceeds of the sale will be distributed to the shareholders within one year after the date of sale;

(4) an amendment of the articles of incorporation that materially and adversely affects rights in respect of a dissenter's shares because it:

(i) alters or abolishes a preferential right of the shares;

(ii) creates, alters, or abolishes a right in respect of redemption, including a provision respecting a sinking fund for the redemption or repurchase, of the shares;

(iii) alters or abolishes a preemptive right of the holder of the shares to acquire shares or other securities;

(iv) excludes or limits the right of the shares to vote on any matter, or to cumulate votes, other than a limitation by dilution through issuance of shares or other securities with similar voting rights; or

(v) reduces the number of shares owned by the shareholder to a fraction of a share if the fractional share so created is to be acquired for cash * * *; or

(5) any corporate action taken pursuant to a shareholder vote to the extent the articles of incorporation, bylaws, or a resolution of the board of directors provides that voting or nonvoting shareholders are entitled to dissent and obtain payment for their shares.

(b) A shareholder entitled to dissent and obtain payment for his shares under this chapter may not challenge the corporate action creating his entitlement unless the action is unlawful or fraudulent with respect to the shareholder or the corporation.

* * * *

Subchapter B. Procedure for Exercise of Dissenters' Rights

* * * *

§ 13.21 Notice of Intent to Demand Payment

(a) If proposed corporate action creating dissenters' rights under section 13.02 is submitted to a vote at a shareholders' meeting, a shareholder who wishes to assert dissenters' rights (1) must deliver to the corporation before the vote is taken written notice of his intent to demand payment for his shares if the proposed action is effectuated and (2) must not vote his shares in favor of the proposed action.

(b) A shareholder who does not satisfy the requirements of subsection (a) is not entitled to payment for his shares under this chapter.

* * * *

§ 13.25 Payment

(a) * * * [A]s soon as the proposed corporate action is taken, or upon receipt of a payment demand, the corporation shall pay each dissenter * * * the amount the corporation estimates to be the fair value of his shares, plus accrued interest.

* * * *

§ 13.28 Procedure If Shareholder Dissatisfied with Payment or Offer

(a) A dissenter may notify the corporation in writing of his own estimate of the fair value of his shares and amount of interest due, and demand payment of his estimate (less any payment under section 13.25) * * * if:

(1) the dissenter believes that the amount paid under section 13.25 * * * is less than the fair value of his shares or that the interest due is incorrectly calculated;

(2) the corporation fails to make payment under section 13.25 within 60 days after the date set for demanding payment; or

(3) the corporation, having failed to take the proposed action, does not return the deposited certificates or release the transfer restrictions imposed on uncertificated shares within 60 days after the date set for demanding payment.

(b) A dissenter waives his right to demand payment under this section unless he notifies the corporation of his demand in writing under subsection (a) within 30 days after the corporation made or offered payment for his shares.

* * * *

Chapter 14. DISSOLUTION

Subchapter A. Voluntary Dissolution

* * * *

§ 14.02 Dissolution by Board of Directors and Shareholders

(a) A corporation's board of directors may propose dissolution for submission to the shareholders.

(b) For a proposal to dissolve to be adopted:

(1) the board of directors must recommend dissolution to the shareholders unless the board of directors determines that because of conflict of interest or other special circumstances it should make no recommendation and communicates the basis for its determination to the shareholders; and

(2) the shareholders entitled to vote must approve the proposal to dissolve as provided in subsection (e).

(c) The board of directors may condition its submission of the proposal for dissolution on any basis.

(d) The corporation shall notify each shareholder, whether or not entitled to vote, of the proposed shareholders' meeting in accordance with section 7.05. The notice must also state that the purpose, or one of the purposes, of the meeting is to consider dissolving the corporation.

(e) Unless the articles of incorporation or the board of directors (acting pursuant to subsection (c)) require a greater vote or a vote by voting groups, the proposal to dissolve to be adopted must be approved by a majority of all the votes entitled to be cast on that proposal.

* * * *

§ 14.05 Effect of Dissolution

(a) A dissolved corporation continues its corporate existence but may not carry on any business except that appropriate to wind up and liquidate its business and affairs, including:

(1) collecting its assets;

(2) disposing of its properties that will not be distributed in kind to its shareholders;

(3) discharging or making provision for discharging its liabilities;

(4) distributing its remaining property among its shareholders according to their interests; and

(5) doing every other act necessary to wind up and liquidate its business and affairs.

(b) Dissolution of a corporation does not:

(1) transfer title to the corporation's property;

(2) prevent transfer of its shares or securities, although the authorization to dissolve may provide for closing the corporation's share transfer records;

(3) subject its directors or officers to standards of conduct different from those prescribed in chapter 8;

(4) change quorum or voting requirements for its board of directors or shareholders; change provisions for selection, resignation, or removal of its directors or officers or both; or change provisions for amending its bylaws;

(5) prevent commencement of a proceeding by or against the corporation in its corporate name;

(6) abate or suspend a proceeding pending by or against the corporation on the effective date of dissolution; or

(7) terminate the authority of the registered agent of the corporation.

* * * *

Subchapter C. Judicial Dissolution

§ 14.30 Grounds for Judicial Dissolution

The [name or describe court or courts] may dissolve a corporation:

(1) in a proceeding by the attorney general if it is established that:

(i) the corporation obtained its articles of incorporation through fraud; or

(ii) the corporation has continued to exceed or abuse the authority conferred upon it by law;

(2) in a proceeding by a shareholder if it is established that:

(i) the directors are deadlocked in the management of the corporate affairs, the shareholders are unable to break the deadlock, and irreparable injury to the corporation is threatened or being suffered, or the business and affairs of the corporation can no longer be conducted to the advantage of the shareholders generally, because of the deadlock;

(ii) the directors or those in control of the corporation have acted, are acting, or will act in a manner that is illegal, oppressive, or fraudulent;

(iii) the shareholders are deadlocked in voting power and have failed, for a period that includes at least two consecutive annual meeting dates, to elect successors to directors whose terms have expired; or

(iv) the corporate assets are being misapplied or wasted;

(3) in a proceeding by a creditor if it is established that:

(i) the creditor's claim has been reduced to judgment, the execution on the judgment returned unsatisfied, and the corporation is insolvent; or

(ii) the corporation has admitted in writing that the creditor's claim is due and owing and the corporation is insolvent; or

(4) in a proceeding by the corporation to have its voluntary dissolution continued under court supervision.

* * * *

Chapter 16. RECORDS AND REPORTS

Subchapter A. Records

§ 16.01 Corporate Records

(a) A corporation shall keep as permanent records minutes of all meetings of its shareholders and board of directors, a record of all actions taken by the shareholders or board of directors without a meeting, and a record of all actions taken by a committee of the board of directors in place of the board of directors on behalf of the corporation.

(b) A corporation shall maintain appropriate accounting records.

(c) A corporation or its agent shall maintain a record of its shareholders, in a form that permits preparation of a list of the names and addresses of all shareholders, in alphabetical order by class of shares showing the number and class of shares held by each.

(d) A corporation shall maintain its records in written form or in another form capable of conversion into written form within a reasonable time.

(e) A corporation shall keep a copy of the following records at its principal office:

(1) its articles or restated articles of incorporation and all amendments to them currently in effect;

(2) its bylaws or restated bylaws and all amendments to them currently in effect;

(3) resolutions adopted by its board of directors creating one or more classes or series of shares, and fixing their relative

rights, preferences, and limitations, if shares issued pursuant to those resolutions are outstanding;

(4) the minutes of all shareholders' meetings, and records of all action taken by shareholders without a meeting, for the past three years;

(5) all written communications to shareholders generally within the past three years, including the financial statements furnished for the past three years * * *;

(6) a list of the names and business addresses of its current directors and officers; and

(7) its most recent annual report delivered to the secretary of state * * *.

§ 16.02 Inspection of Records by Shareholders

(a) Subject to section 16.03(c), a shareholder of a corporation is entitled to inspect and copy, during regular business hours at the corporation's principal office, any of the records of the corporation described in section 16.01(e) if he gives the corporation written notice of his demand at least five business days before the date on which he wishes to inspect and copy.

(b) A shareholder of a corporation is entitled to inspect and copy, during regular business hours at a reasonable location specified by the corporation, any of the following records of the corporation if the shareholder meets the requirements of subsection (c) and gives the corporation written notice of his demand at least five business days before the date on which he wishes to inspect and copy:

(1) excerpts from minutes of any meeting of the board of directors, records of any action of a committee of the board of directors while acting in place of the board of directors on behalf of the corporation, minutes of any meeting of the shareholders, and records of action taken by the shareholders or board of directors without a meeting, to the extent not subject to inspection under section 16.02(a);

(2) accounting records of the corporation; and

(3) the record of shareholders.

(c) A shareholder may inspect and copy the records identified in subsection (b) only if:

(1) his demand is made in good faith and for a proper purpose;

(2) he describes with reasonable particularity his purpose and the records he desires to inspect; and

(3) the records are directly connected with his purpose.

(d) The right of inspection granted by this section may not be abolished or limited by a corporation's articles of incorporation or bylaws.

(e) This section does not affect:

(1) the right of a shareholder to inspect records under section 7.20 or, if the shareholder is in litigation with the corporation, to the same extent as any other litigant;

(2) the power of a court, independently of this Act, to compel the production of corporate records for examination.

(f) For purposes of this section, "shareholder" includes a beneficial owner whose shares are held in a voting trust or by a nominee on his behalf.

APPENDIX F

THE UNIFORM LIMITED LIABILITY COMPANY ACT (EXCERPTS)

[ARTICLE] 2. ORGANIZATION

Section 201. Limited liability company as legal entity.

A limited liability company is a legal entity distinct from its members.

Section 202. Organization.

(a) One or more persons may organize a limited liability company, consisting of one or more members, by delivering articles of organization to the office of the [Secretary of State] for filing.

(b) Unless a delayed effective date is specified, the existence of a limited liability company begins when the articles of organization are filed.

(c) The filing of the articles of organization by the [Secretary of State] is conclusive proof that the organizers satisfied all conditions precedent to the creation of a limited liability company.

Section 203. Articles of organization.

(a) Articles of organization of a limited liability company must set forth:

(1) the name of the company;

(2) the address of the initial designated office;

(3) the name and street address of the initial agent for service of process;

(4) the name and address of each organizer;

(5) whether the company is to be a term company and, if so, the term specified;

(6) whether the company is to be manager-managed, and, if so, the name and address of each initial manager; and

(7) whether one or more of the members of the company are to be liable for its debts and obligations under Section 303(c).

(b) Articles of organization of a limited liability company may set forth:

(1) provisions permitted to be set forth in an operating agreement; or

(2) other matters not inconsistent with law.

(c) Articles of organization of a limited liability company may not vary the nonwaivable provisions of Section 103(b). As to all other matters, if any provision of an operating agreement is inconsistent with the articles of organization:

(1) the operating agreement controls as to managers, members, and members' transferees; and

(2) the articles of organization control as to persons, other than managers, members and their transferees, who reasonably rely on the articles to their detriment.

* * * *

Section 208. Certificate of existence or authorization.

(a) A person may request the [Secretary of State] to furnish a certificate of existence for a limited liability company or a certificate of authorization for a foreign limited liability company.

(b) A certificate of existence for a limited liability company must set forth:

(1) the company's name;

(2) that it is duly organized under the laws of this State, the date of organization, whether its duration is at-will or for a specified term, and, if the latter, the period specified;

(3) if payment is reflected in the records of the [Secretary of State] and if nonpayment affects the existence of the

company, that all fees, taxes, and penalties owed to this State have been paid;

(4) whether its most recent annual report required by Section 211 has been filed with the [Secretary of State];

(5) that articles of termination have not been filed; and

(6) other facts of record in the office of the [Secretary of State] which may be requested by the applicant.

(c) A certificate of authorization for a foreign limited liability company must set forth:

(1) the company's name used in this State;

(2) that it is authorized to transact business in this State;

(3) if payment is reflected in the records of the [Secretary of State] and if nonpayment affects the authorization of the company, that all fees, taxes, and penalties owed to this State have been paid;

(4) whether its most recent annual report required by Section 211 has been filed with the [Secretary of State];

(5) that a certificate of cancellation has not been filed; and

(6) other facts of record in the office of the [Secretary of State] which may be requested by the applicant.

(d) Subject to any qualification stated in the certificate, a certificate of existence or authorization issued by the [Secretary of State] may be relied upon as conclusive evidence that the domestic or foreign limited liability company is in existence or is authorized to transact business in this State.

* * * *

[ARTICLE] 3.

RELATIONS OF MEMBERS AND MANAGERS TO PERSONS DEALING WITH LIMITED LIABILITY COMPANY

* * * *

Section 303. Liability of members and managers.

(a) Except as otherwise provided in subsection (c), the debts, obligations, and liabilities of a limited liability company, whether arising in contract, tort, or otherwise, are solely the debts, obligations, and liabilities of the company. A member or manager is not personally liable for a debt, obligation, or liability of the company solely by reason of being or acting as a member or manager.

(b) The failure of a limited liability company to observe the usual company formalities or requirements relating to the exercise of its company powers or management of its business is not a ground for imposing personal liability on the members or managers for liabilities of the company.

(c) All or specified members of a limited liability company are liable in their capacity as members for all or specified debts, obligations, or liabilities of the company if:

(1) a provision to that effect is contained in the articles of organization; and

(2) a member so liable has consented in writing to the adoption of the provision or to be bound by the provision.

* * * *

[ARTICLE] 4.

RELATIONS OF MEMBERS TO EACH OTHER AND TO LIMITED LIABILITY COMPANY

* * * *

Section 404. Management of limited liability company.

(a) In a member-managed company:

(1) each member has equal rights in the management and conduct of the company's business; and

(2) except as otherwise provided in subsection (c) or in Section 801(b)(3)(i), any matter relating to the business of the company may be decided by a majority of the members.

(b) In a manager-managed company:

(1) each manager has equal rights in the management and conduct of the company's business;

(2) except as otherwise provided in subsection (c) or in Section 801(b)(3)(i), any matter relating to the business of the company may be exclusively decided by the manager or, if there is more than one manager, by a majority of the managers; and

(3) a manager:

(i) must be designated, appointed, elected, removed, or replaced by a vote, approval, or consent of a majority of the members; and

(ii) holds office until a successor has been elected and qualified, unless the manager sooner resigns or is removed.

(c) The only matters of a member or manager-managed company's business requiring the consent of all of the members are:

(1) the amendment of the operating agreement under Section 103;

(2) the authorization or ratification of acts or transactions under Section 103(b)(2)(ii) which would otherwise violate the duty of loyalty;

(3) an amendment to the articles of organization under Section 204;

(4) the compromise of an obligation to make a contribution under Section 402(b);

(5) the compromise, as among members, of an obligation of a member to make a contribution or return money or other property paid or distributed in violation of this [Act];

(6) the making of interim distributions under Section 405(a), including the redemption of an interest;

(7) the admission of a new member;

(8) the use of the company's property to redeem an interest subject to a charging order;

(9) the consent to dissolve the company under Section 801(b)(2);

(10) a waiver of the right to have the company's business wound up and the company terminated under Section 802(b);

(11) the consent of members to merge with another entity under Section 904(c)(1); and

(12) the sale, lease, exchange, or other disposal of all, or substantially all, of the company's property with or without goodwill.

(d) Action requiring the consent of members or managers under this [Act] may be taken without a meeting.

(e) A member or manager may appoint a proxy to vote or otherwise act for the member or manager by signing an appointment instrument, either personally or by the member's or manager's attorney-in-fact.

* * * *

APPENDIX G

RESTATEMENT (SECOND) OF TORTS (EXCERPTS)

Section 402 A. Special liability of seller of product for physical harm to user or consumer.

(1) One who sells any product in a defective condition unreasonably dangerous to the consumer or to his property is subject to liability for physical harm thereby caused to the ultimate user or consumer, or to his property, if

(a) the seller is engaged in the business of selling such a product, and

(b) it is expected to and does reach the user or consumer without substantial change in the condition in which it is sold.

(2) The rule stated in Subsection (1) applies although

(a) the seller has exercised all possible care in the preparation and sale of his product, and

(b) the user or consumer has not bought the product from or entered into any contractual relation with the seller.

Section 402 B. Misrepresentation by seller of chattels to consumer.

One engaged in the business of selling chattels who, by advertising, labels, or otherwise, makes to the public a misrepresentation of a material fact concerning the character or quality of a chattel sold by him is subject to liability for physical harm to a consumer of the chattel caused by justifiable reliance upon the misrepresentation, even though

(a) it is not made fraudulently or negligently, and

(b) the consumer has not bought the chattel from or entered into any contractual relations with the seller.

APPENDIX H

RESTATEMENT (THIRD) OF TORTS (EXCERPTS)

Section 2. CATEGORIES OF PRODUCT DEFECT

A product is defective when, at the time of sale or distribution, it contains a manufacturing defect, is defective in design, or is defective because of inadequate instructions or warnings. A product:
(a) contains a manufacturing defect when the product departs from its intended design even though all possible care was exercised in the preparation and marketing of the product;

(b) is defective in design when the foreseeable risks of harm posed by the product could have been reduced or avoided by the adoption of a reasonable alternative design by the seller or other distributor, or a predecessor in the commercial chain of distribution, and the omission of the alternative design renders the product not reasonably safe;

(c) is defective because of inadequate instructions or warnings when the foreseeable risks of harm posed by the product could have been reduced or avoided by the provision of reasonable instructions or warnings by the seller or other distributor, or a predecessor in the commercial chain of distribution, and the omission of the instructions or warnings renders the product not reasonably safe.

* * * *

Section 10. LIABILITY OF COMMERCIAL PRODUCT SELLER OR DISTRIBUTOR FOR HARM CAUSED BY POST-SALE FAILURE TO WARN

(a) One engaged in the business of selling or otherwise distributing products is subject to liability for harm to persons or property caused by the seller's failure to provide a warning after the time of sale or distribution of a product if a reasonable person in the seller's position would provide such a warning.

(b) A reasonable person in the seller's position would provide a warning after the time of sale if:

(1) the seller knows or reasonably should know that the product poses a substantial risk of harm to persons or property; and
(2) those to whom a warning might be provided can be identified and can reasonably be assumed to be unaware of the risk of harm; and
(3) a warning can be effectively communicated to and acted on by those to whom a warning might be provided; and
(4) the risk of harm is sufficiently great to justify the burden of providing a warning.

* * * *

Section 17. APPORTIONMENT OF RESPONSIBILITY BETWEEN OR AMONG PLAINTIFF, SELLERS AND DISTRIBUTORS OF DEFECTIVE PRODUCTS, AND OTHERS

(a) A plaintiff's recovery of damages for harm caused by a product defect may be reduced if the conduct of the plaintiff combines with the product defect to cause the harm and the plaintiff's conduct fails to conform to generally applicable rules establishing appropriate standards of care.

(b) The manner and extent of the reduction under Subsection (a) and the apportionment of plaintiff's recovery among multiple defendants are governed by generally applicable rules apportioning responsibility.

APPENDIX I

SHERMAN ANTITRUST ACT OF 1890 (EXCERPTS)

Section. 1 Every contract, combination in the form of trust or otherwise, or conspiracy, in restraint of trade or commerce among the several States, or with foreign nations, is hereby declared to be illegal. Every person who shall make any such contract or engage in any such combination or conspiracy shall be deemed guilty of a felony, and, on conviction thereof, shall be punished by fine not exceeding one million dollars if a corporation, or, if any other person, one hundred thousand dollars or by imprisonment not exceeding three years, or by both said punishments in the discretion of the court.

Section 2. Every person who shall monopolize, or attempt to monopolize, or conspire with any other person or persons, to monopolize any part of the trade or commerce among the several States, or with foreign nations, shall be deemed guilty of a felony, and, on conviction thereof, shall be punished by fine not exceeding one million dollars if a corporation, or, if any other person, one hundred thousand dollars or by imprisonment not exceeding three years, or by both said punishments, in the discretion of the court.

APPENDIX J

SECURITIES ACT OF 1933 (EXCERPTS)

Definitions

Section 2. When used in this title, unless the context requires—

(1) The term "security" means any note, stock, treasury stock, bond, debenture, evidence of indebtedness, certificate of interest or participation in any profit-sharing agreement, collateral-trust certificate, preorganization certificate or subscription, transferable share, investment contract, voting-trust certificate, certificate of deposit for a security, fractional undivided interest in oil, gas, or other mineral rights, any put, call, straddle, option, or privilege on any security, certificate of deposit, or group or index of securities (including any interest therein or based on the value thereof), or any put, call, straddle, option, or privilege entered into on a national securities exchange relating to foreign currency, or, in general, any interest or participation in, temporary or interim certificate for, receipt for, guarantee of, or warrant or right to subscribe to or purchase, any of the foregoing.

Exempted Securities

Section 3. (a) Except as hereinafter expressly provided the provisions of this title shall not apply to any of the following classes of securities:

* * * *

(2) Any security issued or guaranteed by the United States or any territory thereof, or by the District of Columbia, or by any State of the United States, or by any political subdivision of a State or Territory, or by any public instrumentality of one or more States or Territories, or by any person controlled or supervised by and acting as an instrumentality of the Government of the United States pursuant to authority granted by the Congress of the United States; or any certificate of deposit for any of the foregoing; or any security issued or guaranteed by any bank; or any security issued by or representing an interest in or a direct obligation of a Federal Reserve Bank. * * *

(3) Any note, draft, bill of exchange, or banker's acceptance which arises out of a current transaction or the proceeds of which have been or are to be used for current transactions, and which has a maturity at the time of issuance of not exceeding nine months, exclusive of days of grace, or any renewal thereof the maturity of which is likewise limited;

(4) Any security issued by a person organized and operated exclusively for religious, educational, benevolent, fraternal, charitable, or reformatory purposes and not for pecuniary profit, and no part of the net earnings of which inures to the benefit of any person, private stockholder, or individual;

* * * *

(11) Any security which is a part of an issue offered and sold only to persons resident within a single State or Territory, where the issuer of such security is a person resident and doing business within, or, if a corporation, incorporated by and doing business within, such State or Territory.

(b) The Commission may from time to time by its rules and regulations and subject to such terms and conditions as may be described therein, add any class of securities to the securities exempted as provided in this section, if it finds that the enforcement of this title with respect to such securities is not necessary in the public interest and for the protection of investors by reason of the small amount involved or the limited character of the public offering; but no issue of securities shall be exempted under this subsection where the aggregate amount at which such issue is offered to the public exceeds $5,000,000.

Exempted Transactions

Section 4. The provisions of section 5 shall not apply to—

(1) transactions by any person other than an issuer, underwriter, or dealer.

(2) transactions by an issuer not involving any public offering.

(3) transactions by a dealer (including an underwriter no longer acting as an underwriter in respect of the security involved in such transactions), except—

(A) transactions taking place prior to the expiration of forty days after the first date upon which the security was bona fide offered to the public by the issuer or by or through an underwriter.

(B) transactions in a security as to which a registration statement has been filed taking place prior to the expiration of forty days after the effective date of such registration statement or prior to the expiration of forty days after the first date upon which the security was bona fide offered to the public by the issuer or by or through an underwriter after such effective date, whichever is later (excluding in the computation of such forty days any time during which a stop order issued under section 8 is in effect as to the security), or such shorter period as the Commission may specify by rules and regulations or order, and

(C) transactions as to the securities constituting the whole or a part of an unsold allotment to or subscription by such dealer as a participant in the distribution of such securities by the issuer or by or through an underwriter.

With respect to transactions referred to in clause (B), if securities of the issuer have not previously been sold pursuant to an earlier effective registration statement the applicable period, instead of forty days, shall be ninety days, or such shorter period as the Commission may specify by rules and regulations or order.

(4) brokers' transactions, executed upon customers' orders on any exchange or in the over-the-counter market but not the solicitation of such orders.

* * * *

(6) transactions involving offers or sales by an issuer solely to one or more accredited investors, if the aggregate offering price of an issue of securities offered in reliance on this paragraph does not exceed the amount allowed under Section 3(b) of this title, if there is no advertising or public solicitation in connection with the transaction by the issuer or anyone acting on the issuer's behalf, and if the issuer files such notice with the Commission as the Commission shall prescribe.

Prohibitions Relating to Interstate Commerce and the Mails

Section 5. (a) Unless a registration statement is in effect as to a security, it shall be unlawful for any person, directly or indirectly—

(1) to make use of any means or instruments of transportation or communication in interstate commerce or of the mails to sell such security through the use or medium of any prospectus or otherwise; or

(2) to carry or cause to be carried through the mails or in interstate commerce, by any means or instruments of transportation, any such security for the purpose of sale or for delivery after sale.

(b) It shall be unlawful for any person, directly or indirectly—

(1) to make use of any means or instruments of transportation or communication in interstate commerce or of the mails to carry or transmit any prospectus relating to any security with respect to which a registration statement has been filed under this title, unless such prospectus meets the requirements of section 10, or

(2) to carry or to cause to be carried through the mails or in interstate commerce any such security for the purpose of sale or for delivery after sale, unless accompanied or preceded by a prospectus that meets the requirements of subsection (a) of section 10.

(c) It shall be unlawful for any person, directly, or indirectly, to make use of any means or instruments of transportation or communication in interstate commerce or of the mails to offer to sell or offer to buy through the use or medium of any prospectus or otherwise any security, unless a registration statement has been filed as to such security, or while the registration statement is the subject of a refusal order or stop order or (prior to the effective date of the registration statement) any public proceeding of examination under section 8.

APPENDIX K

SECURITIES EXCHANGE ACT OF 1934 (EXCERPTS)

Definitions and Application of Title

Section 3. (a) When used in this title, unless the context otherwise requires—

* * * *

(4) The term "broker" means any person engaged in the business of effecting transactions in securities for the account of others, but does not include a bank.

(5) The term "dealer" means any person engaged in the business of buying and selling securities for his own account, through a broker or otherwise, but does not include a bank, or any person insofar as he buys or sells securities for his own account, either individually or in some fiduciary capacity, but not as part of a regular business.

* * * *

(7) The term "director" means any director of a corporation or any person performing similar functions with respect to any organization, whether incorporated or unincorporated.

(8) The term "issuer" means any person who issues or proposes to issue any security; except that with respect to certificates of deposit for securities, voting-trust certificates, or collateral-trust certificates, or with respect to certificates of interest or shares in an unincorporated investment trust not having a board of directors or the fixed, restricted management, or unit type, the term "issuer" means the person or persons performing the acts and assuming the duties of depositor or manager pursuant to the provisions of the trust or other agreement or instrument under which such securities are issued; and except that with respect to equipment-trust certificates or like securities, the term "issuer" means the person by whom the equipment or property is, or is to be, used.

(9) The term "person" means a natural person, company, government, or political subdivision, agency, or instrumentality of a government.

Regulation of the Use of Manipulative and Deceptive Devices

Section 10. It shall be unlawful for any person, directly or indirectly, by the use of any means or instrumentality of interstate commerce or of the mails, or of any facility of any national securities exchange—

(a) To effect a short sale, or to use or employ any stop-loss order in connection with the purchase or sale, of any security registered on a national securities exchange, in contravention of such rules and regulations as the Commission may prescribe as necessary or appropriate in the public interest or for the protection of investors.

(b) To use or employ, in connection with the purchase or sale of any security registered on a national securities exchange or any security not so registered, any manipulative or deceptive device or contrivance in contravention of such rules and regulations as the Commission may prescribe as necessary or appropriate in the public interest or for the protection of investors.

APPENDIX L

AMERICANS WITH DISABILITIES ACT OF 1990 (EXCERPTS)

Title I—EMPLOYMENT

Sec. 101. Definitions.

As used in this title: * * *

(8) **Qualified individual with a disability.**—The term "qualified individual with a disability" means an individual with a disability who, with or without reasonable accommodation, can perform the essential functions of the employment position that such individual holds or desires. For the purposes of this title, consideration shall be given to the employer's judgment as to what functions of a job are essential, and if an employer has prepared a written description before advertising or interviewing applicants for the job, this description shall be considered evidence of the essential functions of the job.

(9) **Reasonable accommodation.**—The term "reasonable accommodation" may include—

(A) making existing facilities used by employees readily accessible to and usable by individuals with disabilities; and

(B) job restructuring, part-time or modified work schedules, reassignment to a vacant position, acquisition or modification of equipment or devices, appropriate adjustment or modifications of examinations, training materials or policies, the provision of qualified readers or interpreters, and other similar accommodations for individuals with disabilities.

(10) **Undue Hardship.**—

(A) **In general.**—The term "undue hardship" means an action requiring significant difficulty or expense, when considered in light of the factors set forth in subparagraph (B).

(B) **Factors to be considered.**—In determining whether an accommodation would impose an undue hardship on a covered entity, factors to be considered include—

(i) the nature and cost of accommodation needed under this Act;

(ii) the overall financial resources of the facility or facilities involved in the provision of the reasonable accommodation; the number of persons employed at such facility; the effect on expenses and resources, or the impact otherwise of such accommodation upon the operation of the facility;

(iii) the overall financial resources of the covered entity; the overall size of the business of a covered entity with respect to the number of its employees; the number, type, and location of its facilities; and

(iv) the type of operation or operations of the covered entity, including the composition, structure, and functions of the workforce of such entity; the geographic separateness, administrative, or fiscal relationship of the facility or facilities in question to the covered entity.

Sec. 102. Discrimination.

(a) **General Rule.**—No covered entity shall discriminate against a qualified individual with a disability because of the disability of such individual in regard to job application procedures, the hiring, advancement, or discharge of employees, employee compensation, job training, and other terms, conditions, and privileges of employment.

(b) **Construction.**—As used in subsection (a), the term "discriminate" includes—

(1) limiting, segregating, or classifying a job applicant or employee in a way that adversely affects the opportunities or status of such applicant or employee because of the disability of such applicant or employee;

(2) participating in a contractual or other arrangement or relationship that has the effect of subjecting a covered entity's qualified applicant or employee with a disability to the discrimination prohibited by this title (such relationship includes a relationship with an employment or referral agency, labor union, an organization providing fringe benefits to an employee of the covered entity, or an organization providing training and apprenticeship programs);

(3) utilizing standards, criteria, or methods of administration—

(A) that have the effect of discrimination on the basis of disability; or

(B) that perpetuate the discrimination of others who are subject to common administrative control;

(4) excluding or otherwise denying equal jobs or benefits to a qualified individual because of the known disability of an individual with whom the qualified individual is known to have a relationship or association;

(5)

(A) not making reasonable accommodations to the known physical or mental limitations of an otherwise qualified individual with a disability who is an applicant or employee, unless such covered entity can demonstrate that the accommodation would impose an undue hardship on the operation of the business of such covered entity; or

(B) denying employment opportunities to a job applicant or employee who is an otherwise qualified individual with a disability, if such denial is based on the need of such covered entity to make reasonable accommodation to the physical or mental impairments of the employee or applicant;

(6) using qualification standards, employment tests or other selection criteria that screen out or tend to screen out an individual with a disability or a class of individuals with disabilities unless the standard, test or other selection criteria, as used by the covered entity, is shown to be job-related for the position in question and is consistent with business necessity; and

(7) failing to select and administer tests concerning employment in the most effective manner to ensure that, when such test is administered to a job applicant or employee who has a disability that impairs sensory, manual, or speaking skills, such test results accurately reflect the skills, aptitude, or whatever other factor of such applicant or employee that such test purports to measure, rather than reflecting the impaired sensory, manual, or speaking skills of such employee or applicant (except where such skills are the factors that the test purports to measure). * * *

Sec. 104. Illegal Use of Drugs and Alcohol. * * *

(b) **Rules of Construction.**—Nothing in subsection (a) shall be construed to exclude as a qualified individual with a disability an individual who—

(1) has successfully completed a supervised drug rehabilitation program and is no longer engaging in the illegal use of drugs, or has otherwise been rehabilitated successfully and is no longer engaging in such use;

(2) is participating in a supervised rehabilitation program and is no longer engaging in such use; or

(3) is erroneously regarded as engaging in such use, but is not engaging in such use; except that it shall not be a violation of this Act for a covered entity to adopt or administer reasonable policies or procedures, including but not limited to drug testing, designed to ensure that an individual described in paragraph (1) or (2) is no longer engaging in the illegal use of drugs. * * *

Sec. 107. Enforcement.

(a) **Powers, Remedies, and Procedures.**—The powers, remedies, and procedures set forth in sections 705, 706, 707, 709, and 710 of the Civil Rights Act of 1964 (42 U.S.C. 2000e-4, 2000e-5, 2000e-6, 2000e-8, and 2000e-9) shall be the powers, remedies, and procedures this title provides to the Commission, to the Attorney General, or to any person alleging discrimination on the basis of disability in violation of any provision of this Act, or regulations promulgated under section 106, concerning employment.

(b) **Coordination.**—The agencies with enforcement authority for actions which allege employment discrimination under this title and under the Rehabilitation Act of 1973 shall develop procedures to ensure that administrative complaints filed under this title and under the Rehabilitation Act of 1973 are dealt with in a manner that avoids duplication of effort and prevents imposition of inconsistent or conflicting standards for the same requirements under this title and the Rehabilitation Act of 1973. The Commission, the Attorney General, and the Office of Federal Contract Compliance Programs shall establish such coordinating mechanisms (similar to provisions contained in the joint regulations promulgated by the Commission and the Attorney General at part 42 of title 28 and part 1691 of title 29, Code of Federal Regulations, and the Memorandum of Understanding between the Commission and the Office of Federal Contract Compliance Programs dated January 16, 1981 (46 Fed. Reg. 7435, January 23, 1981)) in regulations implementing this title and Rehabilitation Act of 1973 not later than 18 months after the date of enactment of this Act.

Sec. 108. Effective Date.

This title shall become effective 24 months after the date of enactment.

APPENDIX M

UNITED NATIONS CONVENTION ON CONTRACTS FOR THE INTERNATIONAL SALE OF GOODS (EXCERPTS)

Part I. SPHERE OF APPLICATION AND GENERAL PROVISIONS

* * * *

Chapter II—General Provisions

* * * *

Article 8

(1) For the purposes of this Convention statements made by and other conduct of a party are to be interpreted according to his intent where the other party knew or could not have been unaware what that intent was.

(2) If the preceding paragraph is not applicable, statements made by and other conduct of a party are to be interpreted according to the understanding that a reasonable person of the same kind as the other party would have had in the same circumstances.

(3) In determining the intent of a party or the understanding a reasonable person would have had, due consideration is to be given to all relevant circumstances of the case including the negotiations, any practices which the parties have established between themselves, usages and any subsequent conduct of the parties.

Article 9

(1) The parties are bound by any usage to which they have agreed and by any practices which they have established between themselves.

(2) The parties are considered, unless otherwise agreed, to have impliedly made applicable to their contract or its formation a usage of which the parties knew or ought to have known and which in international trade is widely known to, and regularly observed by, parties to contracts of the type involved in the particular trade concerned.

* * * *

Article 11

A contract of sale need not be concluded in or evidenced by writing and is not subject to any other requirement as to form. It may be proved by any means, including witnesses.

* * * *

Part II. FORMATION OF THE CONTRACT

Article 14

(1) A proposal for concluding a contract addressed to one or more specific persons constitutes an offer if it is sufficiently definite and indicates the intention of the offeror to be bound in case of acceptance. A proposal is sufficiently definite if it indicates the goods and expressly or implicitly fixes or makes provision for determining the quantity and the price.

(2) A proposal other than one addressed to one or more specific persons is to be considered merely as an invitation to make offers, unless the contrary is clearly indicated by the person making the proposal.

Article 15

(1) An offer becomes effective when it reaches the offeree.

(2) An offer, even if it is irrevocable, may be withdrawn if the withdrawal reaches the offeree before or at the same time as the offer.

Article 16

(1) Until a contract is concluded an offer may be revoked if the revocation reaches the offeree before he has dispatched an acceptance.

(2) However, an offer cannot be revoked:

(a) If it indicates, whether by stating a fixed time for acceptance or otherwise, that it is irrevocable; or

(b) If it was reasonable for the offeree to rely on the offer as being irrevocable and the offeree has acted in reliance on the offer.

Article 17

An offer, even if it is irrevocable, is terminated when a rejection reaches the offeror.

Article 18

(1) A statement made by or other conduct of the offeree indicating assent to an offer is an acceptance. Silence or inactivity does not in itself amount to acceptance.

(2) An acceptance of an offer becomes effective at the moment the indication of assent reaches the offeror. An acceptance is not effective if the indication of assent does not reach the offeror within the time he has fixed or, if no time is fixed, within a reasonable time, due account being taken of the circumstances of the transaction, including the rapidity of the means of communication employed by the offeror. An oral offer must be accepted immediately unless the circumstances indicate otherwise.

(3) However, if, by virtue of the offer or as a result of practices which the parties have established between themselves or of usage, the offeree may indicate assent by performing an act, such as one relating to the dispatch of the goods or payment of the price, without notice to the offeror, the acceptance is effective at the moment the act is performed, provided that the act is performed within the period of time laid down in the preceding paragraph.

Article 19

(1) A reply to an offer which purports to be an acceptance but contains additions, limitations or other modifications is a rejection of the offer and constitutes a counter-offer.

(2) However, a reply to an offer which purports to be an acceptance but contains additional or different terms which do not materially alter the terms of the offer constitutes an acceptance, unless the offeror, without undue delay, objects orally to the discrepancy or dispatches a notice to that effect. If he does not so object, the terms of the contract are the terms of the offer with the modifications contained in the acceptance.

(3) Additional or different terms relating, among other things, to the price, payment, quality and quantity of the goods, place and time of delivery, extent of one party's liability to the other or the settlement of disputes are considered to alter the terms of the offer materially.

* * * *

Article 22

An acceptance may be withdrawn if the withdrawal reaches the offeror before or at the same time as the acceptance would have become effective.

* * * *

Part III. SALE OF GOODS

Chapter I—General Provisions

Article 25

A breach of contract committed by one of the parties is fundamental if it results in such detriment to the other party as substantially to deprive him of what he is entitled to expect under the contract, unless the party in breach did not foresee and a reasonable person of the same kind in the same circumstances would not have foreseen such a result.

* * * *

Article 28

If, in accordance with the provisions of this Convention, one party is entitled to require performance of any obligation by the other party, a court is not bound to enter a judgment for specific performance unless the court would do so under its own law in respect of similar contracts of sale not governed by this Convention.

Article 29

(1) A contract may be modified or terminated by the mere agreement of the parties.

(2) A contract in writing which contains a provision requiring any modification or termination by agreement to be in writing may not be otherwise modified or terminated by agreement. However, a party may be precluded by his conduct from asserting such a provision to the extent that the other party has relied on that conduct.

* * * *

Chapter II—Obligations of the Seller

* * * *

Section II. Conformity of the Goods and Third Party Claims

Article 35

(1) The seller must deliver goods which are of the quantity, quality and description required by the contract and which are contained or packaged in the manner required by the contract.

(2) Except where the parties have agreed otherwise, the goods do not conform with the contract unless they:

(a) Are fit for the purposes for which goods of the same description would ordinarily be used;

(b) Are fit for any particular purpose expressly or impliedly made known to the seller at the time of the conclusion of the contract, except where the circumstances show that the buyer did not rely, or that it was unreasonable for him to rely, on the seller's skill and judgment;

(c) Possess the qualities of goods which the seller has held out to the buyer as a sample or model;

(d) Are contained or packaged in the manner usual for such goods or, where there is no such manner, in a manner adequate to preserve and protect the goods.

(3) The seller is not liable under subparagraphs (a) to (d) of the preceding paragraph for any lack of conformity of the goods if at the time of the conclusion of the contract the buyer knew or could not have been unaware of such lack of conformity.

* * * *

Article 64

(1) The seller may declare the contract avoided:

(a) If the failure by the buyer to perform any of his obligations under the contract or this Convention amounts to a fundamental breach of contract; or

(b) If the buyer does not, within the additional period of time fixed by the seller in accordance with paragraph (1) of article 63, perform his obligation to pay the price or take delivery of the goods, or if he declares that he will not do so within the period so fixed.

(2) However, in cases where the buyer has paid the price, the seller loses the right to declare the contract avoided unless he does so:

(a) In respect of late performance by the buyer, before the seller has become aware that performance has been rendered; or

(b) In respect of any breach other than late performance by the buyer, within a reasonable time:

(i) After the seller knew or ought to have known of the breach; or

(ii) After the expiration of any additional period of time fixed by the seller in accordance with paragraph (1) of article 63, or after the buyer has declared that he will not perform his obligations within such an additional period.

* * * *

Chapter IV—Passing of Risk

* * * *

Article 67

(1) If the contract of sale involves carriage of the goods and the seller is not bound to hand them over at a particular place, the risk passes to the buyer when the goods are handed over to the first carrier for transmission to the buyer in accordance with the contract of sale. If the seller is bound to hand the goods over to a carrier at a particular place, the risk does not pass to the buyer until the goods are handed over to the carrier at that place. The fact that the seller is authorized to retain documents controlling the disposition of the goods does not affect the passage of the risk.

(2) Nevertheless, the risk does not pass to the buyer until the goods are clearly identified to the contract, whether by markings on the goods, by shipping documents, by notice given to the buyer or otherwise.

* * * *

Chapter V—Provisions Common to the Obligations of the Seller and of the Buyer

Section I. Anticipatory Breach and Instalment Contracts

Article 71

(1) A party may suspend the performance of his obligations if, after the conclusion of the contract, it becomes apparent that the other party will not perform a substantial part of his obligations as a result of:

(a) A serious deficiency in his ability to perform or in his creditworthiness; or

(b) His conduct in preparing to perform or in performing the contract.

(2) If the seller has already dispatched the goods before the grounds described in the preceding paragraph become evident, he may prevent the handing over of the goods to the buyer even though the buyer holds a document which entitles him to obtain them. The present paragraph relates only to the rights in the goods as between the buyer and the seller.

(3) A party suspending performance, whether before or after dispatch of the goods, must immediately give notice of the suspension to the other party and must continue with performance if the other party provides adequate assurance of his performance.

Article 72

(1) If prior to the date for performance of the contract it is clear that one of the parties will commit a fundamental breach of contract, the other party may declare the contract avoided.

(2) If time allows, the party intending to declare the contract avoided must give reasonable notice to the other party in order to permit him to provide adequate assurance of his performance.

(3) The requirements of the preceding paragraph do not apply if the other party has declared that he will not perform his obligations.

Article 73

(1) In the case of a contract for delivery of goods by instalments, if the failure of one party to perform any of his obligations in respect of any instalment constitutes a fundamental breach of contract with respect to that instalment, the other party may declare the contract avoided with respect to that instalment.

(2) If one party's failure to perform any of his obligations in respect of any instalment gives the other party good grounds to conclude that a fundamental breach of contract will occur with respect to future instalments, he may declare the contract avoided for the future, provided that he does so within a reasonable time.

(3) A buyer who declares the contract avoided in respect of any delivery may, at the same time, declare it avoided in respect of deliveries already made or of future deliveries if, by reason of their interdependence, those deliveries could not be used for the purpose contemplated by the parties at the time of the conclusion of the contract.

Section II. Damages

Article 74

Damages for breach of contract by one party consist of a sum equal to the loss, including loss of profit, suffered by the other party as a consequence of the breach. Such damages may not exceed the loss which the party in breach foresaw or ought to have foreseen at the time of the conclusion of the contract, in the light of the facts and matters of which he then knew or ought to have known, as a possible consequence of the breach of contract.

Article 75

If the contract is avoided and if, in a reasonable manner and within a reasonable time after avoidance, the buyer has bought goods in replacement or the seller has resold the goods, the party claiming damages may recover the difference between the contract price and the price in the substitute transaction as well as any further damages recoverable under article 74.

Article 76

(1) If the contract is avoided and there is a current price for the goods, the party claiming damages may, if he has not made a purchase or resale under article 75, recover the difference between the price fixed by the contract and the current price at the time of avoidance as well as any further damages recoverable under article 74. If, however, the party claiming damages has avoided the contract after taking over the goods, the current price at the time of such taking over shall be applied instead of the current price at the time of avoidance.

(2) For the purposes of the preceding paragraph, the current price is the price prevailing at the place where delivery of the goods should have been made or, if there is no current price at that place, the price at such other place as serves as a reasonable substitute, making due allowance for differences in the cost of transporting the goods.

Article 77

A party who relies on a breach of contract must take such measures as are reasonable in the circumstances to mitigate the loss, including loss of profit, resulting from the breach. If he fails to take such measures, the party in breach may claim a reduction in the damages in the amount by which the loss should have been mitigated.

APPENDIX N

DIGITAL MILLENNIUM COPYRIGHT ACT OF 1998 (EXCERPTS)

Sec. 1201. Circumvention of copyright protection systems

(a) VIOLATIONS REGARDING CIRCUMVENTION OF TECHNOLOGICAL MEASURES—(1)(A) No person shall circumvent a technological measure that effectively controls access to a work protected under this title. * * *

* * * *

(b) ADDITIONAL VIOLATIONS—(1) No person shall manufacture, import, offer to the public, provide, or otherwise traffic in any technology, product, service, device, component, or part thereof, that—

(A) is primarily designed or produced for the purpose of circumventing protection afforded by a technological measure that effectively protects a right of a copyright owner under this title in a work or a portion thereof;

(B) has only limited commercially significant purpose or use other than to circumvent protection afforded by a technological measure that effectively protects a right of a copyright owner under this title in a work or a portion thereof; or

(C) is marketed by that person or another acting in concert with that person with that person's knowledge for use in circumventing protection afforded by a technological measure that effectively protects a right of a copyright owner under this title in a work or a portion thereof.

* * * *

Sec. 1202. Integrity of copyright management information

(a) FALSE COPYRIGHT MANAGEMENT INFORMATION—No person shall knowingly and with the intent to induce, enable, facilitate, or conceal infringement—

(1) provide copyright management information that is false, or

(2) distribute or import for distribution copyright management information that is false.

(b) REMOVAL OR ALTERATION OF COPYRIGHT MANAGEMENT INFORMATION—No person shall, without the authority of the copyright owner or the law—

(1) intentionally remove or alter any copyright management information,

(2) distribute or import for distribution copyright management information knowing that the copyright management information has been removed or altered without authority of the copyright owner or the law, or

(3) distribute, import for distribution, or publicly perform works, copies of works, or phonorecords, knowing that copyright management information has been removed or altered without authority of the copyright owner or the law, knowing, or, with respect to civil remedies under section 1203, having reasonable grounds to know, that it will induce, enable, facilitate, or conceal an infringement of any right under this title.

(c) DEFINITION—As used in this section, the term "copyright management information" means any of the following information conveyed in connection with copies or phonorecords of a work or performances or displays of a work, including in digital form, except that such term does not include any personally identifying information about a user of a work or of a copy, phonorecord, performance, or display of a work:

(1) The title and other information identifying the work, including the information set forth on a notice of copyright.

(2) The name of, and other identifying information about, the author of a work.

(3) The name of, and other identifying information about, the copyright owner of the work, including the information set forth in a notice of copyright.

(4) With the exception of public performances of works by radio and television broadcast stations, the name of, and other identifying information about, a performer whose performance is fixed in a work other than an audiovisual work.

(5) With the exception of public performances of works by radio and television broadcast stations, in the case of an audiovisual work, the name of, and other identifying information about, a writer, performer, or director who is credited in the audiovisual work.

(6) Terms and conditions for use of the work.

(7) Identifying numbers or symbols referring to such information or links to such information.

(8) Such other information as the Register of Copyrights may prescribe by regulation, except that the Register of Copyrights may not require the provision of any information concerning the user of a copyrighted work.

* * * *

Sec. 512. Limitations on liability relating to material online

(a) TRANSITORY DIGITAL NETWORK COMMUNICATIONS—A service provider shall not be liable for monetary relief, or, except as provided in subsection (j), for injunctive or other equitable relief, for infringement of copyright by reason of the provider's transmitting, routing, or providing connections for, material through a system or network controlled or operated by or for the service provider, or by reason of the intermediate and transient storage of that material in the course of such transmitting, routing, or providing connections, if—

(1) the transmission of the material was initiated by or at the direction of a person other than the service provider;

(2) the transmission, routing, provision of connections, or storage is carried out through an automatic technical process without selection of the material by the service provider;

(3) the service provider does not select the recipients of the material except as an automatic response to the request of another person;

(4) no copy of the material made by the service provider in the course of such intermediate or transient storage is maintained on the system or network in a manner ordinarily accessible to anyone other than anticipated recipients, and no such copy is maintained on the system or network in a manner ordinarily accessible to such anticipated recipients for a longer period than is reasonably necessary for the transmission, routing, or provision of connections; and

(5) the material is transmitted through the system or network without modification of its content.

APPENDIX O

UNIFORM ELECTRONIC TRANSACTIONS ACT (EXCERPTS)

* * * *

Section 5. USE OF ELECTRONIC RECORDS AND ELECTRONIC SIGNATURES; VARIATION BY AGREEMENT.

(a) This [Act] does not require a record or signature to be created, generated, sent, communicated, received, stored, or otherwise processed or used by electronic means or in electronic form.

(b) This [Act] applies only to transactions between parties each of which has agreed to conduct transactions by electronic means. Whether the parties agree to conduct a transaction by electronic means is determined from the context and surrounding circumstances, including the parties' conduct.

(c) A party that agrees to conduct a transaction by electronic means may refuse to conduct other transactions by electronic means. The right granted by this subsection may not be waived by agreement.

(d) Except as otherwise provided in this [Act], the effect of any of its provisions may be varied by agreement. The presence in certain provisions of this [Act] of the words "unless otherwise agreed," or words of similar import, does not imply that the effect of other provisions may not be varied by agreement.

(e) Whether an electronic record or electronic signature has legal consequences is determined by this [Act] and other applicable law.

Section 6. CONSTRUCTION AND APPLICATION. This [Act] must be construed and applied:

(1) to facilitate electronic transactions consistent with other applicable law;

(2) to be consistent with reasonable practices concerning electronic transactions and with the continued expansion of those practices; and

(3) to effectuate its general purpose to make uniform the law with respect to the subject of this [Act] among States enacting it.

Section 7. LEGAL RECOGNITION OF ELECTRONIC RECORDS, ELECTRONIC SIGNATURES, AND ELECTRONIC CONTRACTS.

(a) A record or signature may not be denied legal effect or enforceability solely because it is in electronic form.

(b) A contract may not be denied legal effect or enforceability solely because an electronic record was used in its formation.

(c) If a law requires a record to be in writing, an electronic record satisfies the law.

(d) If a law requires a signature, an electronic signature satisfies the law.

* * * *

Section 10. EFFECT OF CHANGE OR ERROR. If a change or error in an electronic record occurs in a transmission between parties to a transaction, the following rules apply:

(1) If the parties have agreed to use a security procedure to detect changes or errors and one party has conformed to the procedure, but the other party has not, and the nonconforming party would have detected the change or error had that party also conformed, the conforming party may avoid the effect of the changed or erroneous electronic record.

(2) In an automated transaction involving an individual, the individual may avoid the effect of an electronic record that resulted from an error made by the individual in dealing with the electronic agent of another person if the electronic agent did not provide an opportunity for the prevention or

correction of the error and, at the time the individual learns of the error, the individual:

(A) promptly notifies the other person of the error and that the individual did not intend to be bound by the electronic record received by the other person;

(B) takes reasonable steps, including steps that conform to the other person's reasonable instructions, to return to the other person or, if instructed by the other person, to destroy the consideration received, if any, as a result of the erroneous electronic record; and

(C) has not used or received any benefit or value from the consideration, if any, received from the other person.

(3) If neither paragraph (1) nor paragraph (2) applies, the change or error has the effect provided by other law, including the law of mistake, and the parties' contract, if any.

(4) Paragraphs (2) and (3) may not be varied by agreement.

APPENDIX P

UNIFORM COMPUTER INFORMATION TRANSACTIONS ACT (EXCERPTS)

Section 104. MIXED TRANSACTIONS: AGREEMENT TO OPT-IN OR OPT-OUT. The parties may agree that this [Act], including contract-formation rules, governs the transaction, in whole or part, or that other law governs the transaction and this [Act] does not apply, if a material part of the subject matter to which the agreement applies is computer information or informational rights in it that are within the scope of this [Act], or is subject matter within this [Act] under Section 103(b), or is subject matter excluded by Section 103(d)(1) or (2). However, any agreement to do so is subject to the following rules:

(1) An agreement that this [Act] governs a transaction does not alter the applicability of any rule or procedure that may not be varied by agreement of the parties or that may be varied only in a manner specified by the rule or procedure, including a consumer protection statute [or administrative rule]. In addition, in a mass-market transaction, the agreement does not alter the applicability of a law applicable to a copy of information in printed form.

(2) An agreement that this [Act] does not govern a transaction:

  (A) does not alter the applicability of Section 214 or 816; and

  (B) in a mass-market transaction, does not alter the applicability under [this Act] of the doctrine of unconscionability or fundamental public policy or the obligation of good faith.

(3) In a mass-market transaction, any term under this section which changes the extent to which this [Act] governs the transaction must be conspicuous.

(4) A copy of a computer program contained in and sold or leased as part of goods and which is excluded from this [Act] by Section 103(b)(1) cannot provide the basis for an agreement under this section that this [Act] governs the transaction.

* * * *

Section 107. LEGAL RECOGNITION OF ELECTRONIC RECORD AND AUTHENTICATION; USE OF ELECTRONIC AGENTS.

(a) A record or authentication may not be denied legal effect or enforceability solely because it is in electronic form.

(b) This [Act] does not require that a record or authentication be generated, stored, sent, received, or otherwise processed by electronic means or in electronic form.

(c) In any transaction, a person may establish requirements regarding the type of authentication or record acceptable to it.

(d) A person that uses an electronic agent that it has selected for making an authentication, performance, or agreement, including manifestation of assent, is bound by the operations of the electronic agent, even if no individual was aware of or reviewed the agent's operations or the results of the operations.

* * * *

Section 202. FORMATION IN GENERAL.

(a) A contract may be formed in any manner sufficient to show agreement, including offer and acceptance or conduct of both parties or operations of electronic agents which recognize the existence of a contract.

(b) If the parties so intend, an agreement sufficient to constitute a contract may be found even if the time of its making is undetermined, one or more terms are left open or to be agreed on, the records of the parties do not otherwise establish a contract, or one party reserves the right to modify terms.

(c) Even if one or more terms are left open or to be agreed upon, a contract does not fail for indefiniteness if the parties intended to make a contract and there is a reasonably certain basis for giving an appropriate remedy.

(d) In the absence of conduct or performance by both parties to the contrary, a contract is not formed if there is a material disagreement about a material term, including a term concerning scope.

(e) If a term is to be adopted by later agreement and the parties intend not to be bound unless the term is so adopted, a contract is not formed if the parties do not agree to the term. In that case, each party shall deliver to the other party, or with the consent of the other party destroy, all copies of information, access materials, and other materials received or made, and each party is entitled to a return with respect to any contract fee paid for which performance has not been received, has not been accepted, or has been redelivered without any benefit being retained. The parties remain bound by any restriction in a contractual use term with respect to information or copies received or made from copies received pursuant to the agreement, but the contractual use term does not apply to information or copies properly received or obtained from another source.

Section 203. OFFER AND ACCEPTANCE IN GENERAL. Unless otherwise unambiguously indicated by the language or the circumstances:

(1) An offer to make a contract invites acceptance in any manner and by any medium reasonable under the circumstances.

(2) An order or other offer to acquire a copy for prompt or current delivery invites acceptance by either a prompt promise to ship or a prompt or current shipment of a conforming or nonconforming copy. However, a shipment of a nonconforming copy is not an acceptance if the licensor seasonably notifies the licensee that the shipment is offered only as an accommodation to the licensee.

(3) If the beginning of a requested performance is a reasonable mode of acceptance, an offeror that is not notified of acceptance or performance within a reasonable time may treat the offer as having lapsed before acceptance.

(4) If an offer in an electronic message evokes an electronic message accepting the offer, a contract is formed:

(A) when an electronic acceptance is received; or

(B) if the response consists of beginning performance, full performance, or giving access to information, when the performance is received or the access is enabled and necessary access materials are received.

* * * *

Section 209. MASS-MARKET LICENSE.

(a) A party adopts the terms of a mass-market license for purposes of Section 208 only if the party agrees to the license, such as by manifesting assent, before or during the party's initial performance or use of or access to the information. A term is not part of the license if:

(1) the term is unconscionable or is unenforceable under Section 105(a) or (b); or

(2) subject to Section 301, the term conflicts with a term to which the parties to the license have expressly agreed.

(b) If a mass-market license or a copy of the license is not available in a manner permitting an opportunity to review by the licensee before the licensee becomes obligated to pay and the licensee does not agree, such as by manifesting assent, to the license after having an opportunity to review, the licensee is entitled to a return under Section 112 and, in addition, to:

(1) reimbursement of any reasonable expenses incurred in complying with the licensor's instructions for returning or destroying the computer information or, in the absence of instructions, expenses incurred for return postage or similar reasonable expense in returning the computer information; and

(2) compensation for any reasonable and foreseeable costs of restoring the licensee's information processing system to reverse changes in the system caused by the installation, if:

(A) the installation occurs because information must be installed to enable review of the license; and

(B) the installation alters the system or information in it but does not restore the system or information after removal of the installed information because the licensee rejected the license.

(c) In a mass-market transaction, if the licensor does not have an opportunity to review a record containing proposed terms from the licensee before the licensor delivers or becomes obligated to deliver the information, and if the licensor does not agree, such as by manifesting assent, to those terms after having that opportunity, the licensor is entitled to a return.

* * * *

Section 211. PRETRANSACTION DISCLOSURES IN INTERNET-TYPE TRANSACTIONS. This section applies to a licensor that makes its computer information available to a licensee by electronic means from its Internet or similar electronic site. In such a case, the licensor affords an opportunity to review the terms of a standard form license which opportunity satisfies Section 112(e) with respect to a licensee that acquires the information from that site, if the licensor:

(1) makes the standard terms of the license readily available for review by the licensee before the information is delivered or the licensee becomes obligated to pay, whichever occurs first, by:

(A) displaying prominently and in close proximity to a description of the computer information, or to instructions or steps for acquiring it, the standard terms or a reference to an electronic location from which they can be readily obtained; or

(B) disclosing the availability of the standard terms in a prominent place on the site from which the computer information is offered and promptly furnishing a copy of the standard terms on request before the transfer of the computer information; and

(2) does not take affirmative acts to prevent printing or storage of the standard terms for archival or review purposes by the licensee.

APPENDIX Q

ELECTRONIC SIGNATURES IN GLOBAL AND NATIONAL COMMERCE ACT OF 2000 (EXCERPTS)

SEC. 101. GENERAL RULE OF VALIDITY.

(a) IN GENERAL—Notwithstanding any statute, regulation, or other rule of law (other than this title and title II), with respect to any transaction in or affecting interstate or foreign commerce—

(1) a signature, contract, or other record relating to such transaction may not be denied legal effect, validity, or enforceability solely because it is in electronic form; and

(2) a contract relating to such transaction may not be denied legal effect, validity, or enforceability solely because an electronic signature or electronic record was used in its formation.

* * * *

(d) RETENTION OF CONTRACTS AND RECORDS—

(1) ACCURACY AND ACCESSIBILITY—If a statute, regulation, or other rule of law requires that a contract or other record relating to a transaction in or affecting interstate or foreign commerce be retained, that requirement is met by retaining an electronic record of the information in the contract or other record that—

(A) accurately reflects the information set forth in the contract or other record; and

(B) remains accessible to all persons who are entitled to access by statute, regulation, or rule of law, for the period required by such statute, regulation, or rule of law, in a form that is capable of being accurately reproduced for later reference, whether by transmission, printing, or otherwise.

(2) EXCEPTION—A requirement to retain a contract or other record in accordance with paragraph (1) does not apply to any information whose sole purpose is to enable the contract or other record to be sent, communicated, or received.

(3) ORIGINALS—If a statute, regulation, or other rule of law requires a contract or other record relating to a transaction in or affecting interstate or foreign commerce to be provided, available, or retained in its original form, or provides consequences if the contract or other record is not provided, available, or retained in its original form, that statute, regulation, or rule of law is satisfied by an electronic record that complies with paragraph (1).

(4) CHECKS—If a statute, regulation, or other rule of law requires the retention of a check, that requirement is satisfied by retention of an electronic record of the information on the front and back of the check in accordance with paragraph (1).

* * * *

(g) NOTARIZATION AND ACKNOWLEDGMENT—If a statute, regulation, or other rule of law requires a signature or record relating to a transaction in or affecting interstate or foreign commerce to be notarized, acknowledged, verified, or made under oath, that requirement is satisfied if the electronic signature of the person authorized to perform those acts, together with all other information required to be included by other applicable statute, regulation, or rule of law, is attached to or logically associated with the signature or record.

(h) ELECTRONIC AGENTS—A contract or other record relating to a transaction in or affecting interstate or foreign commerce may not be denied legal effect, validity, or enforceability solely because its formation, creation, or delivery involved the action of one or more electronic agents so long as the action of any such electronic agent is legally attributable to the person to be bound.

(i) INSURANCE—It is the specific intent of the Congress that this title and title II apply to the business of insurance.

(j) INSURANCE AGENTS AND BROKERS—An insurance agent or broker acting under the direction of a party that enters into a contract by means of an electronic record or electronic signature may not be held liable for any deficiency in the electronic procedures agreed to by the parties under that contract if—

(1) the agent or broker has not engaged in negligent, reckless, or intentional tortious conduct;
(2) the agent or broker was not involved in the development or establishment of such electronic procedures; and
(3) the agent or broker did not deviate from such procedures.

* * * *

SEC. 103. SPECIFIC EXCEPTIONS.

(a) EXCEPTED REQUIREMENTS—The provisions of section 101 shall not apply to a contract or other record to the extent it is governed by—

(1) a statute, regulation, or other rule of law governing the creation and execution of wills, codicils, or testamentary trusts;
(2) a State statute, regulation, or other rule of law governing adoption, divorce, or other matters of family law; or
(3) the Uniform Commercial Code, as in effect in any State, other than sections 1–107 and 1–206 and Articles 2 and 2A.

(b) ADDITIONAL EXCEPTIONS—The provisions of section 101 shall not apply to—

(1) court orders or notices, or official court documents (including briefs, pleadings, and other writings) required to be executed in connection with court proceedings;
(2) any notice of—
    (A) the cancellation or termination of utility services (including water, heat, and power);
    (B) default, acceleration, repossession, foreclosure, or eviction, or the right to cure, under a credit agreement secured by, or a rental agreement for, a primary residence of an individual;
    (C) the cancellation or termination of health insurance or benefits or life insurance benefits (excluding annuities); or
    (D) recall of a product, or material failure of a product, that risks endangering health or safety; or
(3) any document required to accompany any transportation or handling of hazardous materials, pesticides, or other toxic or dangerous materials.

APPENDIX R

SPANISH EQUIVALENTS FOR IMPORTANT LEGAL TERMS IN ENGLISH

Abandoned property: bienes abandonados
Acceptance: aceptación; consentimiento; acuerdo
Acceptor: aceptante
Accession: toma de posesión; aumento; accesión
Accommodation indorser: avalista de favor
Accommodation party: firmante de favor
Accord: acuerdo; convenio; arregio
Accord and satisfaction: transacción ejecutada
Act of state doctrine: doctrina de acto de gobierno
Administrative law: derecho administrativo
Administrative process: procedimiento o metódo administrativo
Administrator: administrador (-a)
Adverse possession: posesión de hecho susceptible de proscripción adquisitiva
Affirmative action: acción afirmativa
Affirmative defense: defensa afirmativa
After-acquired property: bienes adquiridos con posterioridad a un hecho dado
Agency: mandato; agencia
Agent: mandatorio; agente; representante
Agreement: convenio; acuerdo; contrato
Alien corporation: empresa extranjera
Allonge: hojas adicionales de endosos
Answer: contestación de la demande; alegato
Anticipatory repudiation: anuncio previo de las partes de su imposibilidad de cumplir con el contrato
Appeal: apelación; recurso de apelación
Appellate jurisdiction: jurisdicción de apelaciones
Appraisal right: derecho de valuación
Arbitration: arbitraje
Arson: incendio intencional
Articles of partnership: contrato social
Artisan's lien: derecho de retención que ejerce al artesano
Assault: asalto; ataque; agresión
Assignment of rights: transmisión; transferencia; cesión
Assumption of risk: no resarcimiento por exposición voluntaria al peligro
Attachment: auto judicial que autoriza el embargo; embargo

Bailee: depositario
Bailment: depósito; constitución en depósito
Bailor: depositante
Bankruptcy trustee: síndico de la quiebra
Battery: agresión; física
Bearer: portador; tenedor
Bearer instrument: documento al portador
Bequest or legacy: legado (de bienes muebles)
Bilateral contract: contrato bilateral
Bill of lading: conocimiento de embarque; carta de porte
Bill of Rights: declaración de derechos
Binder: póliza de seguro provisoria; recibo de pago a cuenta del precio
Blank indorsement: endoso en blanco
Blue sky laws: leyes reguladoras del comercio bursátil
Bond: título de crédito; garantía; caución
Bond indenture: contrato de emisión de bonos; contrato del ampréstito
Breach of contract: incumplimiento de contrato
Brief: escrito; resumen; informe
Burglary: violación de domicilio
Business judgment rule: regla de juicio comercial
Business tort: agravio comercial

Case law: ley de casos; derecho casuístico

Cashier's check: cheque de caja
Causation in fact: causalidad en realidad
Cease-and-desist order: orden para cesar y desistir
Certificate of deposit: certificado de depósito
Certified check: cheque certificado
Charitable trust: fideicomiso para fines benéficos
Chattel: bien mueble
Check: cheque
Chose in action: derecho inmaterial; derecho de acción
Civil law: derecho civil
Close corporation: sociedad de un solo accionista o de un grupo restringido de accionistas
Closed shop: taller agremiado (emplea solamente a miembros de un gremio)
Closing argument: argumento al final
Codicil: codicilo
Collateral: guarantía; bien objeto de la guarantía real
Comity: cortesía; cortesía entre naciones
Commercial paper: instrumentos negociables; documentos a valores commerciales
Common law: derecho consuetudinario; derecho común; ley común
Common stock: acción ordinaria
Comparative negligence: negligencia comparada
Compensatory damages: daños y perjuicios reales o compensatorios
Concurrent conditions: condiciones concurrentes
Concurrent jurisdiction: competencia concurrente de varios tribunales para entender en una misma causa
Concurring opinion: opinión concurrente
Condition: condición
Condition precedent: condición suspensiva
Condition subsequent: condición resolutoria
Confiscation: confiscación
Confusion: confusión; fusión
Conglomerate merger: fusión de firmas que operan en distintos mercados
Consent decree: acuerdo entre las partes aprobado por un tribunal
Consequential damages: daños y perjuicios indirectos
Consideration: consideración; motivo; contraprestación
Consolidation: consolidación
Constructive delivery: entrega simbólica
Constructive trust: fideicomiso creado por aplicación de la ley
Consumer protection law: ley para proteger el consumidor
Contract: contrato
Contract under seal: contrato formal o sellado
Contributory negligence: negligencia de la parte actora
Conversion: usurpación; conversión de valores
Copyright: derecho de autor
Corporation: sociedad anómina; corporación; persona juridica
Co-sureties: cogarantes
Counterclaim: reconvención; contrademanda
Counteroffer: contraoferta
Course of dealing: curso de transacciones
Course of performance: curso de cumplimiento
Covenant: pacto; garantía; contrato
Covenant not to sue: pacto or contrato a no demandar
Covenant of quiet enjoyment: garantía del uso y goce pacífico del inmueble
Creditors' composition agreement: concordato preventivo
Crime: crimen; delito; contravención
Criminal law: derecho penal
Cross-examination: contrainterrogatorio
Cure: cura; cuidado; derecho de remediar un vicio contractual
Customs receipts: recibos de derechos aduaneros

Damages: daños; indemnización por daños y perjuicios
Debit card: tarjeta de dé bito
Debtor: deudor
Debt securities: seguridades de deuda
Deceptive advertising: publicidad engañosa
Deed: escritura; título; acta translativa de domino
Defamation: difamación
Delegation of duties: delegación de obligaciones
Demand deposit: depósito a la vista
Depositions: declaración de un testigo fuera del tribunal
Devise: legado; deposición testamentaria (bienes inmuebles)
Directed verdict: veredicto según orden del juez y sin participación activa del jurado
Direct examination: interrogatorio directo; primer interrogatorio
Disaffirmance: repudiación; renuncia; anulación
Discharge: descargo; liberación; cumplimiento
Disclosed principal: mandante revelado
Discovery: descubrimiento; producción de la prueba
Dissenting opinion: opinión disidente
Dissolution: disolución; terminación
Diversity of citizenship: competencia de los tribunales federales para entender en causas cuyas partes intervinientes son cuidadanos de distintos estados
Divestiture: extinción premature de derechos reales
Dividend: dividendo
Docket: orden del día; lista de causas pendientes
Domestic corporation: sociedad local
Draft: orden de pago; letrade cambio
Drawee: girado; beneficiario
Drawer: librador
Duress: coacción; violencia

Easement: servidumbre
Embezzlement: desfalco; malversación
Eminent domain: poder de expropiación
Employment discrimination: discriminación en el empleo
Entrepreneur: empresario
Environmental law: ley ambiental
Equal dignity rule: regla de dignidad egual
Equity security: tipo de participación en una sociedad
Estate: propiedad; patrimonio; derecho
Estop: impedir; prevenir
Ethical issue: cuestión ética
Exclusive jurisdiction: competencia exclusiva

Exculpatory clause: cláusula eximente
Executed contract: contrato ejecutado
Execution: ejecución; cumplimiento
Executor: albacea
Executory contract: contrato aún no completamente consumado
Executory interest: derecho futuro
Express contract: contrato expreso
Expropriation: expropriación

Federal question: caso federal
Fee simple: pleno dominio; dominio absoluto
Fee simple absolute: dominio absoluto
Fee simple defeasible: dominio sujeta a una condición resolutoria
Felony: crimen; delito grave
Fictitious payee: beneficiario ficticio
Fiduciary: fiduciaro
Firm offer: oferta en firme
Fixture: inmueble por destino, incorporación a anexación
Floating lien: gravamen continuado
Foreign corporation: sociedad extranjera; U.S. sociedad constituída en otro estado
Forgery: falso; falsificación
Formal contract: contrato formal
Franchise: privilegio; franquicia; concesión
Franchisee: persona que recibe una concesión
Franchisor: persona que vende una concesión
Fraud: fraude; dolo; engaño
Future interest: bien futuro

Garnishment: embargo de derechos
General partner: socio comanditario
General warranty deed: escritura translativa de domino con garantía de título
Gift: donación
Gift *causa mortis*: donación por causa de muerte
Gift *inter vivos*: donación entre vivos
Good faith: buena fe
Good faith purchaser: comprador de buena fe

Holder: tenedor por contraprestación
Holder in due course: tenedor legítimo
Holographic will: testamento olográfico
Homestead exemption laws: leyes que exceptúan las casas de familia de ejecución por duedas generales
Horizontal merger: fusión horizontal

Identification: identificación
Implied-in-fact contract: contrato implícito en realidad
Implied warranty: guarantía implícita
Implied warranty of merchantability: garantía implícita de vendibilidad
Impossibility of performance: imposibilidad de cumplir un contrato
Imposter: imposter
Incidental beneficiary: beneficiario incidental; beneficiario secundario
Incidental damages: daños incidentales
Indictment: auto de acusación; acusación
Indorsee: endorsatario
Indorsement: endoso
Indorser: endosante
Informal contract: contrato no formal; contrato verbal
Information: acusación hecha por el ministerio público
Injunction: mandamiento; orden de no innovar
Innkeeper's lien: derecho de retención que ejerce el posadero
Installment contract: contrato de pago en cuotas
Insurable interest: interés asegurable
Intended beneficiary: beneficiario destinado
Intentional tort: agravio; cuasi-delito intencíonal
International law: derecho internaciónal
Interrogatories: preguntas escritas sometidas por una parte a la otra o a un testigo
***Inter vivos* trust:** fideicomiso entre vivos
Intestacy laws: leyes de la condición de morir intestado
Intestate: intestado
Investment company: compañia de inversiones
Issue: emisión

Joint tenancy: derechos conjuntos en un bien inmueble en favor del beneficiario sobreviviente
Judgment *n.o.v.*: juicio no obstante veredicto
Judgment rate of interest: interés de juicio
Judicial process: acto de procedimiento; proceso jurídico
Judicial review: revisión judicial
Jurisdiction: jurisdicción

Larceny: robo; hurto
Law: derecho; ley; jurisprudencia
Lease: contrato de locación; contrato de alquiler
Leasehold estate: bienes forales
Legal rate of interest: interés legal
Legatee: legatario
Letter of credit: carta de crédito
Levy: embargo; comiso
Libel: libelo; difamación escrita
Life estate: usufructo
Limited partner: comanditario
Limited partnership: sociedad en comandita
Liquidation: liquidación; realización
Lost property: objetos perdidos

Majority opinion: opinión de la mayoría
Maker: persona que realiza u ordena; librador
Mechanic's lien: gravamen de constructor
Mediation: mediación; intervención
Merger: fusión
Mirror image rule: fallo de reflejo
Misdemeanor: infracción; contravención
Mislaid property: bienes extraviados
Mitigation of damages: reducción de daños
Mortgage: hypoteca
Motion to dismiss: excepción parentoria
Mutual fund: fondo mutual

Negotiable instrument: instrumento negociable
Negotiation: negociación
Nominal damages: daños y perjuicios nominales
Novation: novación
Nuncupative will: testamento nuncupativo

Objective theory of contracts: teoria objetiva de contratos
Offer: oferta

Offeree: persona que recibe una oferta
Offeror: oferente
Order instrument: instrumento o documento a la orden
Original jurisdiction: jurisdicción de primera instancia
Output contract: contrato de producción

Parol evidence rule: regla relativa a la prueba oral
Partially disclosed principal: mandante revelado en parte
Partnership: sociedad colectiva; asociación; asociación de participación
Past consideration: causa o contraprestación anterior
Patent: patente; privilegio
Pattern or practice: muestra o práctica
Payee: beneficiario de un pago
Penalty: pena; penalidad
Per capita: por cabeza
Perfection: perfeción
Performance: cumplimiento; ejecución
Personal defenses: excepciones personales
Personal property: bienes muebles
Per stirpes: por estirpe
Plea bargaining: regateo por un alegato
Pleadings: alegatos
Pledge: prenda
Police powers: poders de policia y de prevención del crimen
Policy: póliza
Positive law: derecho positivo; ley positiva
Possibility of reverter: posibilidad de reversión
Precedent: precedente
Preemptive right: derecho de prelación
Preferred stock: acciones preferidas
Premium: recompensa; prima
Presentment warranty: garantía de presentación
Price discrimination: discriminación en los precios
Principal: mandante; principal
Privity: nexo jurídico
Privity of contract: relación contractual
Probable cause: causa probable
Probate: verificación; verificación del testamento
Probate court: tribunal de sucesiones y tutelas
Proceeds: resultados; ingresos
Profit: beneficio; utilidad; lucro
Promise: promesa
Promisee: beneficiario de una promesa
Promisor: promtente
Promissory estoppel: impedimento promisorio
Promissory note: pagaré; nota de pago
Promoter: promotor; fundador
Proximate cause: causa inmediata o próxima
Proxy: apoderado; poder
Punitive, or exemplary, damages: daños y perjuicios punitivos o ejemplares

Qualified indorsement: endoso con reservas
Quasi contract: contrato tácito o implícito
Quitclaim deed: acto de transferencia de una propiedad por finiquito, pero sin ninguna garantía sobre la validez del título transferido

Ratification: ratificación
Real property: bienes inmuebles
Reasonable doubt: duda razonable
Rebuttal: refutación
Recognizance: promesa; compromiso; reconocimiento
Recording statutes: leyes estatales sobre registros oficiales
Redress: reporacíon
Reformation: rectificación; reforma; corrección
Rejoinder: dúplica; contrarréplica
Release: liberación; renuncia a un derecho
Remainder: substitución; reversión
Remedy: recurso; remedio; reparación
Replevin: acción reivindicatoria; reivindicación
Reply: réplica
Requirements contract: contrato de suministro
Rescission: rescisión
Res judicata: cosa juzgada; res judicata
Respondeat superior: responsabilidad del mandante o del maestro
Restitution: restitución
Restrictive indorsement: endoso restrictivo
Resulting trust: fideicomiso implícito
Reversion: reversión; sustitución
Revocation: revocación; derogación
Right of contribution: derecho de contribución
Right of reimbursement: derecho de reembolso
Right of subrogation: derecho de subrogación
Right-to-work law: ley de libertad de trabajo
Robbery: robo
Rule 10b-5: Regla 10b-5

Sale: venta; contrato de compreventa
Sale on approval: venta a ensayo; venta sujeta a la aprobación del comprador
Sale or return: venta con derecho de devolución
Sales contract: contrato de compraventa; boleto de compraventa
Satisfaction: satisfacción; pago
Scienter: a sabiendas
S corporation: S corporación
Secured party: acreedor garantizado
Secured transaction: transacción garantizada
Securities: volares; titulos; seguridades
Security agreement: convenio de seguridad
Security interest: interés en un bien dado en garantía que permite a quien lo detenta venderlo en caso de incumplimiento
Service mark: marca de identificación de servicios
Shareholder's derivative suit: acción judicial entablada por un accionista en nombre de la sociedad
Signature: firma; rúbrica
Slander: difamación oral; calumnia
Sovereign immunity: immunidad soberana
Special indorsement: endoso especial; endoso a la orden de una person en particular
Specific performance: ejecución precisa, según los términos del contrato
Spendthrift trust: fideicomiso para pródigos
Stale check: cheque vencido
Stare decisis: acatar las decisiones, observar los precedentes
Statutory law: derecho estatutario; derecho legislado; derecho escrito
Stock: acciones

Stock warrant: certificado para la compra de acciones
Stop-payment order: orden de suspensión del pago de un cheque dada por el librador del mismo
Strict liability: responsabilidad uncondicional
Summary judgment: fallo sumario

Tangible property: bienes corpóreos
Tenancy at will: inguilino por tiempo indeterminado (según la voluntad del propietario)
Tenancy by sufferance: posesión por tolerancia
Tenancy by the entirety: locación conyugal conjunta
Tenancy for years: inguilino por un término fijo
Tenancy in common: specie de copropiedad indivisa
Tender: oferta de pago; oferta de ejecución
Testamentary trust: fideicomiso testamentario
Testator: testador (-a)
Third party beneficiary contract: contrato para el beneficio del tercero-beneficiario
Tort: agravio; cuasi-delito
Totten trust: fideicomiso creado por un depósito bancario
Trade acceptance: letra de cambio aceptada
Trademark: marca registrada
Trade name: nombre comercial; razón social
Traveler's check: cheque del viajero
Trespass to land: ingreso no authorizado a las tierras de otro
Trespass to personal property: violación de los derechos posesorios de un tercero con respecto a bienes muebles
Trust: fideicomiso; trust

Ultra vires: ultra vires; fuera de la facultad (de una sociedad anónima)
Unanimous opinion: opinión unámine
Unconscionable contract or clause: contrato leonino; cláusula leonino
Underwriter: subscriptor; asegurador
Unenforceable contract: contrato que no se puede hacer cumplir
Unilateral contract: contrato unilateral
Union shop: taller agremiado; empresa en la que todos los empleados son miembros del gremio o sindicato
Universal defenses: defensas legitimas o legales
Usage of trade: uso comercial
Usury: usura

Valid contract: contrato válido
Venue: lugar; sede del proceso
Vertical merger: fusión vertical de empresas
Voidable contract: contrato anulable
Void contract: contrato nulo; contrato inválido, sin fuerza legal
Voir dire: examen preliminar de un testigo a jurado por el tribunal para determinar su competencia
Voting trust: fideicomiso para ejercer el derecho de voto

Waiver: renuncia; abandono
Warranty of habitability: garantía de habitabilidad
Watered stock: acciones diluídos; capital inflado
White-collar crime: crimen administrativo
Writ of attachment: mandamiento de ejecución; mandamiento de embargo
Writ of *certiorari*: auto de avocación; auto de certiorari
Writ of execution: auto ejecutivo; mandamiento de ejecutión
Writ of mandamus: auto de mandamus; mandamiento; orden judicial

GLOSSARY

A

Abandoned Property Property with which the owner has voluntarily parted, with no intention of recovering it.

Acceleration Clause A clause that allows a payee or other holder of a time instrument to demand payment of the entire amount due, with interest, if a certain event occurs, such as a default in the payment of an installment when due.

Acceptance A voluntary act by the offeree that shows assent, or agreement, to the terms of an offer; may consist of words or conduct.

Acceptor A drawee that is legally obligated to pay an instrument when the instrument is presented later for payment.

Access Contract A contract formed for the purpose of obtaining, by electronic means, access to another's database or information processing system.

Accession Occurs when an individual adds value to personal property by either labor or materials. In some situations, a person may acquire ownership rights in another's property through accession.

Accommodation Party A person who signs an instrument for the purpose of lending his or her name as credit to another party on the instrument.

Accord and Satisfaction A common means of settling a disputed claim, in which a debtor offers to pay a lesser amount than the creditor purports to be owed. The creditor's acceptance of the offer creates an accord (agreement), and when the accord is executed, satisfaction occurs.

Accredited Investors In the context of securities offerings, "sophisticated" investors, such as banks, insurance companies, investment companies, the issuer's executive officers and directors, and persons whose income or net worth exceeds certain limits.

Act of State Doctrine A doctrine that provides that the judicial branch of one country will not examine the validity of public acts committed by a recognized foreign government within its own territory.

Actionable Capable of serving as the basis of a lawsuit. An actionable claim can be pursued in a lawsuit or other court action.

Actual Malice Real and demonstrable evil intent. In a defamation suit, a statement made about a public figure normally must be made with actual malice (with either knowledge of its falsity or a reckless disregard of the truth) for liability to be incurred.

Adhesion Contract A "standard-form" contract, such as that between a large retailer and a consumer, in which the stronger party dictates the terms.

Adjudicate To render a judicial decision. In the administrative process, the proceeding in which an administrative law judge hears and decides on issues that arise when an administrative agency charges a person or a firm with violating a law or regulation enforced by the agency.

Administrative Agency A federal or state government agency established to perform a specific function. Administrative agencies are authorized by legislative acts to make and enforce rules to administer and enforce the acts.

Administrative Law The body of law created by administrative agencies (in the form of rules, regulations, orders, and decisions) in order to carry out their duties and responsibilities.

Administrative Law Judge (ALJ) One who presides over an administrative agency hearing and has the power to administer oaths, take testimony, rule on questions of evidence, and make determinations of fact.

Administrative Process The procedure used by administrative agencies in the administration of law.

Administrator One who is appointed by a court to handle the probate (disposition) of a person's estate if that person dies intestate (without a valid will) or if the executor named in the will cannot serve.

Adverse Possession The acquisition of title to real property by occupying it openly, without the consent of the owner, for a period of time specified by a state statute. The occupation must be actual, open, notorious, exclusive, and in opposition to all others, including the owner.

Affirmative Action Job-hiring policies that give special consideration to members of protected classes in an effort to overcome present effects of past discrimination.

After-Acquired Property Property that is acquired by the debtor after the execution of a security agreement.

Agency A relationship between two parties in which one party (the agent) agrees to represent or act for the other (the principal).

Agent A person who agrees to represent or act for another, called the principal.

Agreement A meeting of two or more minds in regard to the terms of a contract; usually broken down into two events—an offer by one party to form a contract, and an acceptance of the offer by the person to whom the offer is made.

Alien Corporation A designation in the United States for a corporation formed in another country but doing business in the United States.

Alienation The process of transferring land out of one's possession (thus "alienating" the land from oneself).

Allonge A piece of paper firmly attached to a negotiable instrument, on which transferees can make indorsements if there is no room left on the instrument itself.

Alternative Dispute Resolution (ADR) The resolution of disputes in ways other than those involved in the traditional judicial process. Negotiation, mediation, and arbitration are examples of ADR methods.

Answer Procedurally, a defendant's response to the plaintiff's complaint.

Anticipatory Repudiation An assertion or action by a party indicating that he or she will not perform an obligation that the party is contractually obligated to perform at a future time.

Antitrust Laws Laws protecting commerce from unlawful restraints.

Appraisal Right The right of a dissenting shareholder, who objects to an extraordinary transaction of the corporation (such as a merger or a consolidation), to have his or her shares appraised and to be paid the fair value of those shares by the corporation.

Appropriation In tort law, the use by one person of another person's name, likeness, or other identifying characteristic without permission and for the benefit of the user.

Arbitration The settling of a dispute by submitting it to a disinterested third party (other than a court), who renders a decision that is (most often) legally binding.

Arbitration Clause A clause in a contract that provides that, in case of a dispute, the parties will submit the dispute to arbitration rather than litigate the dispute in court.

Arson The intentional burning of another's dwelling. Some statutes have expanded this to include any real property regardless of ownership and the destruction of property by other means—for example, by explosion.

Articles of Incorporation The document filed with the appropriate governmental agency, usually the secretary of state, when a business is incorporated. State statutes usually prescribe what kind of information must be contained in the articles of incorporation.

Articles of Organization The document filed with a designated state official by which a limited liability company is formed.

Articles of Partnership A written agreement that sets forth each partner's rights and obligations with respect to the partnership.

Artisan's Lien A possessory lien given to a person who has made improvements and added value to another person's personal property as security for payment for services performed.

Assault Any word or action intended to make another person fearful of immediate physical harm; a reasonably believable threat.

Assignee A party to whom the rights under a contract are transferred, or assigned.

Assignment The act of transferring to another all or part of one's rights arising under a contract.

Assignor A party who transfers (assigns) his or her rights under a contract to another party (called the assignee).

Assumption of Risk A doctrine whereby a plaintiff may not recover for injuries or damages suffered from risks he or she knows of and has voluntarily assumed. A defense against negligence that can be used when the plaintiff has knowledge of and appreciates a danger and voluntarily exposes himself or herself to the danger.

Attachment In a secured transaction, the process by which a secured creditor's interest "attaches" to the property of another (collateral) and the creditor's security interest becomes enforceable. In the context of judicial liens, a court-ordered seizure and taking into custody of property prior to the securing of a judgment for a past-due debt.

Attempted Monopolization Any actions by a firm to eliminate competition and gain monopoly power.

Authenticate To sign a record, or with the intent to sign a record, to execute or to adopt an electronic sound, symbol, or the like to link with the record. A record is retrievable information inscribed on a tangible medium or stored in an electronic or other medium.

Automated Clearinghouse (ACH) An electronic banking system used to transfer payments and settle accounts.

Automatic Stay In bankruptcy proceedings, the suspension of virtually all litigation and other action by creditors against the debtor or the debtor's property. The stay is effective the moment the debtor files a petition in bankruptcy.

Award The amount of money awarded to a plaintiff in a civil lawsuit as damages.

B

B2B Transaction A business-to-business transaction conducted via the Internet; an online sale or lease of goods or services from one business party to another.

B2C Transaction A business-to-consumer transaction conducted via the Internet; an online sale or lease of goods or services from a business party to a consumer.

Bailee One to whom goods are entrusted by a bailor. Under the UCC, a party who, by a bill of lading, warehouse receipt, or other document of title, acknowledges possession of goods and/or contracts to deliver them.

Bailment A situation in which the personal property of one person (a bailor) is entrusted to another (a bailee), who is obligated to return the bailed property to the bailor or dispose of it as directed.

Bailor One who entrusts goods to a bailee.

Bait-and-Switch Advertising Advertising a product at a very attractive price (the "bait") and then, once the consumer is in the store, saying that the advertised product is either not available or is of poor quality; the customer is then urged to purchase ("switched" to) a more expensive item.

Bankruptcy Court A federal court of limited jurisdiction that handles only bankruptcy proceedings. Bankruptcy proceedings are governed by federal bankruptcy law.

Battery The unprivileged, intentional touching of another.

Bearer A person in the possession of an instrument payable to bearer or indorsed in blank.

Bearer Instrument Any instrument that is not payable to a specific person, including instruments payable to the bearer or to "cash."

Bequest A gift by will of personal property (from the verb to bequeath).

Beyond a Reasonable Doubt The standard of proof used in criminal cases. If there is any reasonable doubt that a criminal defendant did not commit the crime with which she or he has been charged, then the verdict must be "not guilty."

Bilateral Contract A type of contract that arises when a promise is given in exchange for a return promise.

Bill of Rights The first ten amendments to the U.S. Constitution.

Binder A written, temporary insurance policy.

Binding Authority Any source of law that a court must follow when deciding a case. Binding authorities include constitutions, statutes, and regulations that govern the issue being decided, as well as court decisions that are controlling precedents within the jurisdiction.

Blank Indorsement An indorsement that specifies no particular indorsee and that can consist of a mere signature. An order instrument that is indorsed in blank becomes a bearer instrument.

Blue Laws State or local laws that prohibit the performance of certain types of commercial activities on Sunday.

Blue Sky Laws State laws that regulate the offer and sale of securities.

Bona Fide Occupational Qualification (BFOQ) Identifiable characteristics reasonably necessary to the normal operation of a particular business. These characteristics can include gender, national origin, and religion, but not race.

Bond A certificate that evidences a corporate (or government) debt. It is a security that involves no ownership interest in the issuing entity.

Bond Indenture A contract between the issuer of a bond and the bondholder.

Bounty Payment A reward (payment) given to a person or persons who perform a certain service—such as informing legal authorities of illegal actions.

Breach of Contract The failure, without legal excuse, of a promisor to perform the obligations of a contract.

Brief A formal legal document submitted by the attorney for the appellant or the appellee (in answer to the appellant's brief) to an appellate court when a case is appealed. The appellant's brief outlines the facts and issues of the case, the judge's rulings or jury's findings that should be reversed or modified, the applicable law, and the arguments on the client's behalf.

Browse-Wrap Terms Terms and conditions of use that are presented to an Internet user at the time certain products, such as software, are being downloaded but that need not be agreed to (by clicking "I agree," for example) before being able to install or use the product.

Burglary The unlawful entry or breaking into a building with the intent to commit a felony. (Some state statutes expand this to include the intent to commit any crime.)

Business Ethics Ethics in a business context; a consensus of what constitutes right or wrong behavior in the world of business and the application of moral principles to situations that arise in a business setting.

Business Invitee A person, such as a customer or a client, who is invited onto business premises by the owner of those premises for business purposes.

Business Judgment Rule A rule that immunizes corporate management from liability for actions that result in corporate losses or damages if the actions are undertaken in good faith and are within both the power of the corporation and the authority of management to make.

Business Necessity A defense to allegations of employment discrimination in which the employer demonstrates that an employment practice that discriminates against members of a protected class is related to job performance.

Business Tort The wrongful interference with another's business rights.

Business Trust A form of business organization in which investors (trust beneficiaries) transfer cash or property to trustees in exchange for trust certificates that represent their investment shares. The certificate holders share in the trust's profits but have limited liability.

Bylaws A set of governing rules adopted by a corporation or other association.

C

Case Law The rules of law announced in court decisions. Case law includes the aggregate of reported cases that interpret judicial precedents, statutes, regulations, and constitutional provisions.

Cashier's Check A check drawn by a bank on itself.

Categorical Imperative A concept developed by the philosopher Immanuel Kant as an ethical guideline for behavior. In deciding whether an action is right or wrong, or desirable or undesirable, a person should evaluate the action in terms of what would happen if everybody else in the same situation, or category, acted the same way.

Causation in Fact An act or omission without which an event would not have occurred.

Cease-and-Desist Order An administrative or judicial order prohibiting a person or business firm from conducting activities that an agency or court has deemed illegal.

Certificate of Deposit (CD) A note of a bank in which the bank acknowledges a receipt of money from a party and promises to repay the money, with interest, to the party on a certain date.

Certificate of Incorporation The primary document that evidences corporate existence (often referred to as the *corporate charter*).

Certificate of Limited Partnership The basic document filed with a designated state official by which a limited partnership is formed.

Certified Check A check that has been accepted in writing by the bank on which it is drawn. Essentially, the bank, by certifying (accepting) the check, promises to pay the check at the time the check is presented.

Charging Order In partnership law, an order granted by a court to a judgment creditor that entitles the creditor to attach profits or assets of a partner on the dissolution of the partnership.

Charitable Trust A trust in which the property held by the trustee must be used for a charitable purpose, such as the advancement of health, education, or religion.

Chattel All forms of personal property.

Check A draft drawn by a drawer ordering the drawee bank or financial institution to pay a certain amount of money to the holder on demand.

Checks and Balances The national government is composed of three separate branches: the executive, the legislative, and the judicial branches. Each branch of the government exercises a check on the actions of the others.

Choice-of-Language Clause A clause in a contract designating the official language by which the contract will be interpreted in the event of a future disagreement over the contract's terms.

Choice-of-Law Clause A clause in a contract designating the law (such as the law of a particular state or nation) that will govern the contract.

Chose in Action A right that can be enforced in court to recover a debt or to obtain damages.

Citation A reference to a publication in which a legal authority—such as a statute or a court decision—or other source can be found.

Civil Law The branch of law dealing with the definition and enforcement of all private or public rights, as opposed to criminal matters.

Civil Law System A system of law derived from that of the Roman Empire and based on a code rather than case law; the predominant system of law in the nations of continental Europe and the nations that were once their colonies. In the United States, Louisiana, because of its historical ties to France, has in part a civil law system.

Clearinghouse A system or place where banks exchange checks and drafts drawn on each other and settle daily balances.

Click-on Agreement An agreement that arises when a buyer, engaging in a transaction on a computer, indicates his or her assent to be bound by the terms of an offer by clicking on a button that says, for example, "I agree"; sometimes referred to as a *click-on license* or a *click-wrap agreement*.

Close Corporation A corporation whose shareholders are limited to a small group of persons, often including only family members. The rights of shareholders of a close corporation usually are restricted regarding the transfer of shares to others.

Closed Shop A firm that requires union membership by its workers as a condition of employment. The closed shop was made illegal by the Labor-Management Relations Act of 1947.

Co-Surety A joint surety; a person who assumes liability jointly with another surety for the payment of an obligation.

Codicil A written supplement or modification to a will. A codicil must be executed with the same formalities as a will.

Collateral Under Article 9 of the UCC, the property subject to a security interest, including accounts and chattel paper that have been sold.

Collateral Promise A secondary promise that is ancillary (subsidiary) to a principal transaction or primary contractual relationship, such as a promise made by one person to pay the debts of another if the latter fails to perform. A collateral promise normally must be in writing to be enforceable.

Collecting Bank Any bank handling an item for collection, except the payor bank.

Collective Bargaining The process by which labor and management negotiate the terms and conditions of employment, including working hours and workplace conditions.

Comity The principle by which one nation defers and gives effect to the laws and judicial decrees of another nation. This recognition is based primarily on respect.

Commerce Clause The provision in Article I, Section 8, of the U.S. Constitution that gives Congress the power to regulate interstate commerce.

Commingle To mix together. To put funds or goods together into one mass so that the funds or goods are so mixed that they no longer have separate identities. In corporate law, if personal and corporate interests are commingled to the extent that the corporation has no separate identity, a court may "pierce the corporate veil" and expose the shareholders to personal liability.

Common Carrier An owner of a truck, railroad, airline, ship, or other vehicle that is licensed to offer transportation services to the public, generally in return for compensation or a payment.

Common Law That body of law developed from custom or judicial decisions in English and U.S. courts, not attributable to a legislature.

Common Stock Shares of ownership in a corporation that give the owner of the stock a proportionate interest in the corporation with regard to control, earnings, and net assets. Shares of common stock are lowest in priority with respect to payment of dividends and distribution of the corporation's assets on dissolution.

Community Property A form of concurrent ownership of property in which each spouse technically owns an undivided one-half interest in property acquired during the marriage. This form of joint ownership occurs in only ten states and Puerto Rico.

Comparative Negligence A theory in tort law under which the liability for injuries resulting from negligent acts is shared by all persons who were guilty of negligence (including the injured party), on the basis of each person's proportionate carelessness.

Compensatory Damages A money award equivalent to the actual value of injuries or damages sustained by the aggrieved party.

Complaint The pleading made by a plaintiff alleging wrongdoing on the part of the defendant; the document that, when filed with a court, initiates a lawsuit.

Computer Crime Any act that is directed against computers and computer parts, that uses computers as instruments of crime, or that involves computers and constitutes abuse.

Computer Information As defined by the Uniform Computer Information Transactions Act, "information in an electronic form obtained from or through use of a computer, or that is in digital or an equivalent form capable of being processed by a computer."

Concurrent Conditions Conditions that must occur or be performed at the same time; they are mutually dependent. No obligations arise until these conditions are simultaneously performed.

Concurrent Jurisdiction Jurisdiction that exists when two different courts have the power to hear a case. For example, some cases can be heard in a federal or a state court.

Condition A qualification, provision, or clause in a contractual agreement, the occurrence or nonoccurrence of which creates, suspends, or terminates the obligations of the contracting parties.

Condition Precedent In a contractual agreement, a condition that must be met before a party's promise becomes absolute.

Condition Subsequent A condition in a contract that, if not fulfilled, operates to terminate a party's absolute promise to perform.

Confession of Judgment The act or agreement of a debtor in permitting a judgment to be entered against him or her by a creditor, for an agreed sum, without the institution of legal proceedings.

Confiscation A government's taking of a privately owned business or personal property without a proper public purpose or an award of just compensation.

Confusion The mixing together of goods belonging to two or more owners so that the separately owned goods cannot be identified.

Conglomerate Merger A merger between firms that do not compete with each other because they are in different markets (as opposed to horizontal and vertical mergers).

Consent The voluntary agreement to a proposition or an act of another; a concurrence of wills.

Consequential Damages Special damages that compensate for a loss that does not directly or immediately result from the breach (for example, lost profits). For the plaintiff to collect special damages, they must have been reasonably foreseeable at the time the breach or injury occurred.

Consideration Generally, the value given in return for a promise. The consideration must result in a detriment to the promisee (something of legally sufficient value and bargained for) or a benefit to the promisor.

Consignment A transaction in which an owner of goods (the consignor) delivers the goods to another (the consignee) for the consignee to sell. The consignee pays the consignor only for the goods that are sold by the consignee.

Consolidation A contractual and statutory process in which two or more corporations join to become a completely new corporation. The original corporations cease to exist, and the new corporation acquires all their assets and liabilities.

Constitutional Law Law based on the U.S. Constitution and the constitutions of the various states.

Constructive Delivery An act equivalent to the actual, physical delivery of property that cannot be physically delivered because of difficulty or impossibility; for example, the transfer of a key to a safe constructively delivers the contents of the safe.

Constructive Eviction A form of eviction that occurs when a landlord fails to perform adequately any of the undertakings (such as providing heat in the winter) required by the lease, thereby making the tenant's further use and enjoyment of the property exceedingly difficult or impossible.

Constructive Trust An equitable trust that is imposed in the interests of fairness and justice when someone wrongfully holds legal title to property. A court may require the owner to hold the property in trust for the person or persons who rightfully should own the property.

Consumer-Debtor An individual whose debts are primarily consumer debts (debts for purchases made primarily for personal or household use).

Continuation Statement A statement that, if filed within six months prior to the expiration date of the original financing statement, continues the perfection of the original security interest for another five years. The perfection of a security interest can be continued in the same manner indefinitely.

Contract An agreement that can be enforced in court; formed by two or more competent parties who agree, for consideration, to perform or to refrain from performing some legal act now or in the future.

Contractual Capacity The threshold mental capacity required by law for a party who enters into a contract to be bound by that contract.

Contributory Negligence A theory in tort law under which a complaining party's own negligence contributed to or caused his or her injuries. Contributory negligence is an absolute bar to recovery in a minority of jurisdictions.

Conversion The wrongful taking or retaining possession of a person's personal property and placing it in the service of another.

Conveyance The transfer of a title to land from one person to another by deed; a document (such as a deed) by which an interest in land is transferred from one person to another.

"Cooling-Off" Laws Laws that allow buyers a period of time, such as three days, in which to cancel door-to-door sales contracts.

Cooperative An association, which may or may not be incorporated, that is organized to provide an economic service to its members. Unincorporated cooperatives are often treated like partnerships for tax and other legally related purposes. Examples of cooperatives are consumer purchasing cooperatives, credit cooperatives, and farmers' cooperatives.

Copyright The exclusive right of "authors" to publish, print, or sell an intellectual production for a statutory period of time. A copyright has the same monopolistic nature as a patent or trademark, but it differs in that it applies exclusively to works of art, literature, and other works of authorship (including computer programs).

Corporate Charter The document issued by a state agency or authority (usually the secretary of state) that grants a corporation legal existence and the right to function.

Corporate Social Responsibility The concept that corporations can and should act ethically and be accountable to society for their actions.

Corporation A legal entity formed in compliance with statutory requirements. The entity is distinct from its shareholder-owners.

Correspondent Bank A bank in which another bank has an account (and vice versa) for the purpose of facilitating fund transfers.

Cost-Benefit Analysis A decision-making technique that involves weighing the costs of a given action against the benefits of that action.

Counteradvertising New advertising that is undertaken pursuant to a Federal Trade Commission order for the purpose of correcting earlier false claims that were made about a product.

Counterclaim A claim made by a defendant in a civil lawsuit against the plaintiff. In effect, the defendant is suing the plaintiff.

Counteroffer An offeree's response to an offer in which the offeree rejects the original offer and at the same time makes a new offer.

Course of Dealing Prior conduct between parties to a contract that establishes a common basis for their understanding.

Course of Performance The conduct that occurs under the terms of a particular agreement; such conduct indicates what the parties to an agreement intended it to mean.

Covenant Not to Sue An agreement to substitute a contractual obligation for some other type of legal action based on a valid claim.

Cover Under the UCC, a remedy that allows the buyer or lessee, on the seller's or lessor's breach, to purchase the goods, in good faith and within a reasonable time, from another seller or lessor and substitute them for the goods due under the contract. If the cost of cover exceeds the cost of the contract goods, the breaching seller or lessor will be liable to the buyer or lessee for the difference, plus incidental and consequential damages.

Cram-Down Provision A provision of the Bankruptcy Code that allows a court to confirm a debtor's Chapter 11 reorganization plan even though only one class of creditors has accepted it. To exercise the court's right under this provision, the court must demonstrate that the plan does not discriminate unfairly against any creditors and is fair and equitable.

Creditors' Composition Agreement An agreement formed between a debtor and his or her creditors in which the creditors agree to accept a lesser sum than that owed by the debtor in full satisfaction of the debt.

Crime A wrong against society proclaimed in a statute and, if committed, punishable by society through fines, removal from public office, and/or imprisonment—and, in some cases, death.

Criminal Law Law that defines and governs actions that constitute crimes. Generally, criminal law has to do with wrongful actions committed against society for which society demands redress.

Cure The right of a party who tenders nonconforming performance to correct that performance within the contract period [UCC 2–508(1)].

Cyber Crime A crime that occurs online, in the virtual community of the Internet, as opposed to the physical world.

Cyber Mark A trademark in cyberspace.

Cyber Stalker A person who commits the crime of stalking in cyberspace. Generally, stalking consists of harassing a person and putting that person in reasonable fear for his or her safety or the safety of the person's immediate family.

Cyber Terrorist A hacker whose purpose is to exploit a target computer for a serious impact, such as corrupting a program to sabotage a business.
Cyber Tort A tort committed in cyberspace.
Cyberlaw An informal term used to refer to all laws governing electronic communications and transactions, particularly those conducted via the Internet.
Cybernotary A legally recognized authority that can certify the validity of digital signatures.
Cybersquatting An act that occurs when a person registers a domain name that is the same as, or confusingly similar to, the trademark of another and offers to sell the domain name back to the trademark owner.

D

Damages Money sought as a remedy for a breach of contract or a tortious action.
Debit Card A plastic card that allows the bearer to transfer funds to a merchant's account, provided that the bearer authorizes the transfer by providing personal identification.
Debtor Under Article 9 of the UCC, a debtor is any party who owes payment or performance of a secured obligation, whether or not the party actually owns or has rights in the collateral.
Debtor in Possession (DIP) In Chapter 11 bankruptcy proceedings, a debtor who is allowed to continue in possession of the estate in property (the business) and to continue business operations.
Deceptive Advertising Advertising that misleads consumers, either by unjustified claims concerning a product's performance or by the omission of a material fact concerning the product's composition or performance.
Deed A document by which title to property (usually real property) is passed.
Defamation Anything published or publicly spoken that causes injury to another's good name, reputation, or character.
Default The failure to observe a promise or discharge an obligation. The term is commonly used to mean the failure to pay a debt when it is due.
Default Judgment A judgment entered by a court against a defendant who has failed to appear in court to answer or defend against the plaintiff's claim.
Default Rules Rules that apply under the Uniform Computer Information Transactions Act only in the absence of an agreement between contracting parties indicating otherwise.
Defendant One against whom a lawsuit is brought; the accused person in a criminal proceeding.
Defense That which a defendant offers and alleges in an action or suit as a reason why the plaintiff should not recover or establish what she or he seeks.
Deficiency Judgment A judgment against a debtor for the amount of a debt remaining unpaid after collateral has been repossessed and sold.
Delegatee A party to whom contractual obligations are transferred, or delegated.
Delegation of Duties The act of transferring to another all or part of one's duties arising under a contract.
Delegator A party who transfers (delegates) her or his obligations under a contract to another party (called the delegatee).
Depositary Bank The first bank to receive a check for payment.
Deposition The testimony of a party to a lawsuit or a witness taken under oath before a trial.
Destination Contract A contract for the sale of goods in which the seller is required or authorized to ship the goods by carrier and tender delivery of the goods at a particular destination. The seller assumes liability for any losses or damage to the goods until they are tendered at the destination specified in the contract.
Devise To make a gift of real property by will.
Devisee One designated in a will to receive a gift of real property.
Digital Cash Funds contained on computer software, in the form of secure programs stored on microchips and other computer devices.
Disaffirmance The legal avoidance, or setting aside, of a contractual obligation.
Discharge The termination of an obligation. In contract law, discharge occurs when the parties have fully performed their contractual obligations or when events, conduct of the parties, or operation of the law releases the parties from performance. In bankruptcy proceedings, discharge occurs when the debtor's dischargeable debts are extinguished.
Disclosed Principal A principal whose identity is known to a third party at the time the agent makes a contract with the third party.
Discovery A phase in the litigation process during which the opposing parties may obtain information from each other and from third parties prior to trial.
Disparagement of Property An economically injurious falsehood made about another's product or property. A general term for torts that are more specifically referred to as slander of quality or slander of title.
Disparate-Impact Discrimination A form of employment discrimination that results from certain employer practices or procedures that, although not discriminatory on their face, have a discriminatory effect.
Disparate-Treatment Discrimination A form of employment discrimination that results when an employer intentionally discriminates against employees who are members of protected classes.
Dissolution The formal disbanding of a partnership or a corporation. It can take place by (1) acts of the partners or, in a corporation, of the shareholders and board of directors; (2) the death of a partner; (3) the expiration of a time period stated in a partnership agreement or a certificate of incorporation; or (4) judicial decree.
Distributed Network A network that can be used by persons located (distributed) around the country or the globe to share computer files.
Distribution Agreement A contract between a seller and a distributor of the seller's products setting out the terms and conditions of the distributorship.
Diversity of Citizenship Under Article III, Section 2, of the Constitution, a basis for federal district court jurisdiction over a lawsuit between (1) citizens of different states, (2) a foreign country and citizens of a state or of different states, or (3) citizens of a state and citizens or subjects of a foreign country. The amount in controversy must be more than $75,000 before a federal district court can take jurisdiction in such cases.
Divestiture The act of selling one or more of a company's parts, such as a subsidiary or plant; often mandated by the courts in merger or monopolization cases.
Dividend A distribution to corporate shareholders of corporate profits or income, disbursed in proportion to the number of shares held.
Docket The list of cases entered on a court's calendar and thus scheduled to be heard by the court.
Document of Title Paper exchanged in the regular course of business that evidences the right to possession of goods (for example, a bill of lading or a warehouse receipt).

Domain Name The last part of an Internet address, such as "westlaw.com." The top level (the part of the name to the right of the period) represents the type of entity that operates the site ("com" is an abbreviation for "commercial"). The second level (the part of the name to the left of the period) is chosen by the entity.
Domestic Corporation In a given state, a corporation that does business in, and is organized under the law of, that state.
Dominion Ownership rights in property, including the right to possess and control the property.
Double Jeopardy A situation occurring when a person is tried twice for the same criminal offense; prohibited by the Fifth Amendment to the Constitution.
Draft Any instrument drawn on a drawee that orders the drawee to pay a certain sum of money, usually to a third party (the payee), on demand or at a definite future time.
Dram Shop Act A state statute that imposes liability on the owners of bars and taverns, as well as those who serve alcoholic drinks to the public, for injuries resulting from accidents caused by intoxicated persons when the sellers or servers of alcoholic drinks contributed to the intoxication.
Drawee The party that is ordered to pay a draft or check. With a check, a bank or a financial institution is always the drawee.
Drawer The party that initiates a draft (such as a check), thereby ordering the drawee to pay.
Due Process Clause The provisions of the Fifth and Fourteenth Amendments to the Constitution that guarantee that no person shall be deprived of life, liberty, or property without due process of law. Similar clauses are found in most state constitutions.
Dumping The selling of goods in a foreign country at a price below the price charged for the same goods in the domestic market.
Duress Unlawful pressure brought to bear on a person, causing the person to perform an act that she or he would not otherwise perform.
Duty of Care The duty of all persons, as established by tort law, to exercise a reasonable amount of care in their dealings with others. Failure to exercise due care, which is normally determined by the "reasonable person standard," constitutes the tort of negligence.

E

E-Agent According to the Uniform Computer Information Transactions Act, "a computer program, electronic or other automated means used to independently initiate an action or to respond to electronic messages or performances without review by an individual."
E-Contract A contract that is formed electronically.
E-Money Prepaid funds recorded on a computer or a card (such as a smart card or a stored-value card).
E-Signature As defined by the Uniform Electronic Transactions Act, "an electronic sound, symbol, or process attached to or logically associated with a record and executed or adopted by a person with the intent to sign the record."
Early Neutral Case Evaluation A form of alternative dispute resolution in which a neutral third party evaluates the strengths and weaknesses of the disputing parties' positions; the evaluator's opinion forms the basis for negotiating a settlement.
Easement A nonpossessory right to use another's property in a manner established by either express or implied agreement.
Electronic Fund Transfer (EFT) A transfer of funds with the use of an electronic terminal, a telephone, a computer, or magnetic tape.
Emancipation In regard to minors, the act of being freed from parental control; occurs when a child's parent or legal guardian relinquishes the legal right to exercise control over the child. Normally, a minor who leaves home to support himself or herself is considered emancipated.
Embezzlement The fraudulent appropriation of funds or other property by a person to whom the funds or property has been entrusted.
Eminent Domain The power of a government to take land for public use from private citizens for just compensation.
Employment at Will A common law doctrine under which either party may terminate an employment relationship at any time for any reason, unless a contract specifies otherwise.
Employment Discrimination Treating employees or job applicants unequally on the basis of race, color, national origin, religion, gender, age, or disability; prohibited by federal statutes.
Enabling Legislation A statute enacted by Congress that authorizes the creation of an administrative agency and specifies the name, composition, purpose, and powers of the agency being created.
Entrapment In criminal law, a defense in which the defendant claims that he or she was induced by a public official—usually an undercover agent or police officer—to commit a crime that he or she would otherwise not have committed.
Environmental Impact Statement (EIS) A statement required by the National Environmental Policy Act for any major federal action that will significantly affect the quality of the environment. The statement must analyze the action's impact on the environment and explore alternative actions that might be taken.
Equal Dignity Rule In most states, a rule stating that express authority given to an agent must be in writing if the contract to be made on behalf of the principal is required to be in writing.
Equal Protection Clause The provision in the Fourteenth Amendment to the Constitution that guarantees that no state will "deny to any person within its jurisdiction the equal protection of the laws." This clause mandates that the state governments treat similarly situated individuals in a similar manner.
Equitable Principles and Maxims General propositions or principles of law that have to do with fairness (equity).
Establishment Clause The provision in the First Amendment to the Constitution that prohibits Congress from creating any law "respecting an establishment of religion."
Estate in Property In bankruptcy proceedings, all of the debtor's legal and equitable interests in property currently held, wherever located, together with certain jointly owned property, property transferred in transactions voidable by the trustee, proceeds and profits from the property of the estate, and certain property interests to which the debtor becomes entitled within 180 days after filing for bankruptcy.
Estopped Barred, impeded, or precluded.
Estray Statute A statute defining finders' rights in property when the true owners are unknown.
Ethics Moral principles and values applied to social behavior.
Eviction A landlord's act of depriving a tenant of possession of the leased premises.
Exclusionary Rule In criminal procedure, a rule under which any evidence that is obtained in violation of the accused's constitutional rights guaranteed by the Fourth, Fifth, and Sixth Amendments, as well as any evidence derived from illegally obtained evidence, will not be admissible in court.

Exclusive-Dealing Contract An agreement under which a seller forbids a buyer to purchase products from the seller's competitors.
Exclusive Distributorship A distributorship in which the seller and the distributor of the seller's products agree that the distributor has the exclusive right to distribute the seller's products in a certain geographic area.
Exclusive Jurisdiction Jurisdiction that exists when a case can be heard only in a particular court or type of court.
Exculpatory Clause A clause that releases a contractual party from liability in the event of monetary or physical injury, no matter who is at fault.
Executed Contract A contract that has been completely performed by both parties.
Execution An action to carry into effect the directions in a court decree or judgment.
Executive Agency An administrative agency within the executive branch of government. At the federal level, executive agencies are those within the cabinet departments.
Executor A person appointed by a testator in a will to see that her or his will is administered appropriately.
Executory Contract A contract that has not as yet been fully performed.
Executory Interest A future interest, held by a person other than the grantor, that begins after the termination of the preceding estate.
Export To sell products to buyers located in other countries.
Express Contract A contract in which the terms of the agreement are stated in words, oral or written.
Express Warranty A seller's or lessor's oral or written promise or affirmation of fact ancillary to an underlying sales or lease agreement, as to the quality, description, or performance of the goods being sold or leased.
Expropriation The seizure by a government of a privately owned business or personal property for a proper public purpose and with just compensation.
Extension Clause A clause in a time instrument that allows the instrument's date of maturity to be extended into the future.

F

Family Limited Liability Partnership (FLLP) A type of limited liability partnership owned by family members or fiduciaries of family members.
Federal Form of Government A system of government in which the states form a union and the sovereign power is divided between a central government and the member states.
Federal Question A question that pertains to the U.S. Constitution, acts of Congress, or treaties. A federal question provides a basis for federal jurisdiction.
Federal Reserve System A network of twelve district banks and related branches located around the country and headed by the Federal Reserve Board of Governors. Most banks in the United States have Federal Reserve accounts.
Fee Simple An absolute form of property ownership entitling the property owner to use, possess, or dispose of the property as he or she chooses during his or her lifetime. On death, the interest in the property descends to the owner's heirs.
Fee Simple Absolute An ownership interest in land in which the owner has the greatest possible aggregation of rights, privileges, and power. Ownership in fee simple absolute is limited absolutely to a person and his or her heirs.
Fee Simple Defeasible An ownership interest in real property that can be taken away (by the prior grantor) on the occurrence or nonoccurrence of a specified event.
Felony A crime—such as arson, murder, rape, or robbery—that carries the most severe sanctions, which range from one year in a state or federal prison to the death penalty.
Fictitious Payee A payee on a negotiable instrument whom the maker or drawer does not intend to have an interest in the instrument. Indorsements by fictitious payees are treated as authorized indorsements under Article 3 of the UCC.
Fiduciary As a noun, a person having a duty created by his or her undertaking to act primarily for another's benefit in matters connected with the undertaking. As an adjective, a relationship founded on trust and confidence.
Filtering Software A computer program that includes a pattern through which data are passed. When designed to block access to certain Web sites, the pattern blocks the retrieval of a site whose URL or key words are on a list within the program.
Financing Statement A document prepared by a secured creditor, and filed with the appropriate state or local official, to give notice to the public that the creditor has a security interest in collateral belonging to the debtor named in the statement. The financing statement must contain the names and addresses of both the debtor and the secured party, and describe the collateral by type or item.
Firm Offer An offer (by a merchant) that is irrevocable without consideration for a stated period of time or, if no definite period is stated, for a reasonable time (neither period to exceed three months). A firm offer by a merchant must be in writing and must be signed by the offeror.
Fixture A thing that was once personal property but has become attached to real property in such a way that it takes on the characteristics of real property and becomes part of that real property.
Floating Lien A security interest in proceeds, after-acquired property, or collateral subject to future advances by the secured party (or all three); a security interest in collateral that is retained even when the collateral changes in character, classification, or location.
***Force Majeure* Clause** A provision in a contract stipulating that certain unforeseen events—such as war, political upheavals, acts of God, or other events—will excuse a party from liability for nonperformance of contractual obligations.
Foreign Corporation In a given state, a corporation that does business in the state without being incorporated therein.
Foreign Exchange Market A worldwide system in which foreign currencies are bought and sold.
Forgery The fraudulent making or altering of any writing in a way that changes the legal rights and liabilities of another.
Formal Contract A contract that by law requires a specific form, such as being executed under seal, for its validity.
Forum-Selection Clause A provision in a contract designating the court, jurisdiction, or tribunal that will decide any disputes arising under the contract.
Franchise Any arrangement in which the owner of a trademark, trade name, or copyright licenses another to use that trademark, trade name, or copyright in the selling of goods and services.
Franchisee One receiving a license to use another's (the franchisor's) trademark, trade name, or copyright in the sale of goods and services.
Franchisor One licensing another (the franchisee) to use the owner's trademark, trade name, or copyright in the sale of goods or services.

Fraudulent Misrepresentation Any misrepresentation, either by misstatement or omission of a material fact, knowingly made with the intention of deceiving another and on which a reasonable person would and does rely to his or her detriment.
Free Exercise Clause The provision in the First Amendment to the Constitution that prohibits Congress from making any law "prohibiting the free exercise" of religion.
Fungible Goods Goods that are alike by physical nature, by agreement, or by trade usage. Examples of fungible goods are wheat, oil, and wine that are identical in type and quality. When owners of fungible goods hold the goods as tenants in common, title and risk can pass without actually separating the goods being sold from the mass of fungible goods.
Future Interest An interest in real property in which the person who holds the interest does not currently possess the property but may possess it in the future.

G

Garnishment A legal process used by a creditor to collect a debt by seizing property of the debtor (such as wages) that is being held by a third party (such as the debtor's employer).
General Partner In a limited partnership, a partner who assumes responsibility for the management of the partnership and liability for all partnership debts.
Gift Any voluntary transfer of property made without consideration, past or present.
Gift *Causa Mortis* A gift made in contemplation of death. If the donor does not die of that ailment, the gift is revoked.
Gift *Inter Vivos* A gift made during one's lifetime and not in contemplation of imminent death, in contrast to a gift *causa mortis*.
Good Faith Purchaser A purchaser who buys without notice of any circumstance that would put a person of ordinary prudence on inquiry as to whether the seller has valid title to the goods being sold.
Good Samaritan Statute A state statute stipulating that persons who provide emergency services to, or rescue, others in peril—unless they do so recklessly, thus causing further harm—cannot be sued for negligence.
Grand Jury A group of citizens called to decide, after hearing the state's evidence, whether a reasonable basis (probable cause) exists for believing that a crime has been committed and whether a trial ought to be held.
Group Boycott The refusal to deal with a particular person or firm by a group of competitors; prohibited by the Sherman Act.
Guarantor A person who agrees to satisfy the debt of another (the debtor) only after the principal debtor defaults; a guarantor's liability is thus secondary.

H

Hacker A person who uses one computer to break into another. Professional computer programmers refer to such persons as "crackers."
Historical School A school of legal thought that emphasizes the evolutionary process of law and that looks to the past to discover what the principles of contemporary law should be.
Holder Any person in the possession of an instrument drawn, issued, or indorsed to him or her, to his or her order, to bearer, or in blank.
Holder in Due Course (HDC) A holder who acquires a negotiable instrument for value; in good faith; and without notice that the instrument is overdue, that it has been dishonored, that any person has a defense against it or a claim to it, or that the instrument contains unauthorized signatures, has been altered, or is so irregular or incomplete as to call into question its authenticity.
Holographic Will A will written entirely in the signer's handwriting and usually not witnessed.
Homestead Exemption A law permitting a debtor to retain the family home, either in its entirety or up to a specified dollar amount, free from the claims of unsecured creditors or trustees in bankruptcy.
Horizontal Merger A merger between two firms that are competing in the same marketplace.
Horizontal Restraint Any agreement that in some way restrains competition between rival firms competing in the same market.
Hot-Cargo Agreement An agreement in which employers voluntarily agree with unions not to handle, use, or deal in other employers' goods that were not produced by union employees; a type of secondary boycott explicitly prohibited by the Labor-Management Reporting and Disclosure Act of 1959.

I

Identification In a sale of goods, the express designation of the goods provided for in the contract.
Identity Theft Occurs when a person steals another's identifying information—such as a name, date of birth, or Social Security number—and uses the information to access the victim's financial resources.
Implied Warranty A warranty that arises by law by implication or inference from the nature of the transaction or the relative situation or circumstances of the parties.
Implied Warranty of Fitness for a Particular Purpose A warranty that goods sold or leased are fit for a particular purpose. The warranty arises when any seller or lessor knows the particular purpose for which a buyer or lessee will use the goods and knows that the buyer or lessee is relying on the skill and judgment of the seller or lessor to select suitable goods.
Implied Warranty of Habitability An implied promise by a landlord that rented residential premises are fit for human habitation—that is, in a condition that is safe and suitable for people to live in.
Implied Warranty of Merchantability A warranty that goods being sold or leased are reasonably fit for the general purpose for which they are sold or leased, are properly packaged and labeled, and are of proper quality. The warranty automatically arises in every sale or lease of goods made by a merchant who deals in goods of the kind sold or leased.
Implied-in-Fact Contract A contract formed in whole or in part from the conduct of the parties (as opposed to an express contract).
Impossibility of Performance A doctrine under which a party to a contract is relieved of his or her duty to perform when performance becomes objectively impossible or totally impracticable (through no fault of either party).
Imposter One who, by use of the mails, telephone, or personal appearance, induces a maker or drawer to issue an instrument in the name of an impersonated payee. Indorsements by imposters are treated as authorized indorsements under Article 3 of the UCC.
Incidental Beneficiary A third party who incidentally benefits from a contract but whose benefit was not the reason the contract was formed; an incidental beneficiary has no rights in a contract and cannot sue to have the contract enforced.

Incidental Damages All costs resulting from a breach of contract, including all reasonable expenses incurred because of the breach.
Independent Contractor One who works for, and receives payment from, an employer but whose working conditions and methods are not controlled by the employer. An independent contractor is not an employee but may be an agent.
Independent Regulatory Agency An administrative agency that is not considered part of the government's executive branch and is not subject to the authority of the president. Independent agency officials cannot be removed without cause.
Indictment A charge by a grand jury that a named person has committed a crime.
Indorsee The person to whom a negotiable instrument is transferred by indorsement.
Indorsement A signature placed on an instrument for the purpose of transferring one's ownership rights in the instrument.
Indorser A person who transfers an instrument by signing (indorsing) it and delivering it to another person.
Informal Contract A contract that does not require a specified form or formality to be valid.
Information A formal accusation or complaint (without an indictment) issued in certain types of actions (usually criminal actions involving lesser crimes) by a law officer, such as a magistrate.
Innkeeper's Lien A possessory lien placed on the luggage of hotel guests for hotel charges that remain unpaid.
Insider Trading The purchase or sale of securities on the basis of "inside information" (information that has not been made available to the public).
Insolvent Under the UCC, a term describing a person who ceases to pay "his debts in the ordinary course of business or cannot pay his debts as they become due or is insolvent within the meaning of federal bankruptcy law" [UCC 1–201(23)].
Installment Contract Under the UCC, a contract that requires or authorizes delivery in two or more separate lots to be accepted and paid for separately.
Insurable Interest An interest either in a person's life or well-being or in property that is sufficiently substantial that insuring against injury to (or the death of) the person or against damage to the property does not amount to a mere wagering (betting) contract.
Insurance A contract in which, for a stipulated consideration, one party agrees to compensate the other for loss on a specific subject by a specified peril.
Integrated Contract A written contract that constitutes the final expression of the parties' agreement. If a contract is integrated, evidence extraneous to the contract that contradicts or alters the meaning of the contract in any way is inadmissible.
Intellectual Property Property resulting from intellectual, creative processes.
Intended Beneficiary A third party for whose benefit a contract is formed; an intended beneficiary can sue the promisor if such a contract is breached.
Intentional Tort A wrongful act knowingly committed.
***Inter Vivos* Trust** A trust created by the grantor (settlor) and effective during the grantor's lifetime; a trust not established by a will.
Intermediary Bank Any bank to which an item is transferred in the course of collection, except the depositary or payor bank.
International Law The law that governs relations among nations. National laws, customs, treaties, and international conferences and organizations are generally considered to be the most important sources of international law.
Interrogatories A series of written questions for which written answers are prepared, usually with the assistance of the party's attorney, and then signed under oath by a party to a lawsuit.
Intestacy Laws State statutes that specify how property will be distributed when a person dies intestate (without a valid will); also called statutes of descent and distribution.
Intestate As a noun, one who has died without having created a valid will; as an adjective, the state of having died without a will.
Investment Company A company that acts on behalf of many smaller shareholders/owners by buying a large portfolio of securities and professionally managing that portfolio.

J

Joint and Several Liability In partnership law, a doctrine under which a plaintiff may sue, and collect a judgment from, one or more of the partners separately (severally, or individually) or all of the partners together (jointly). This is true even if one of the partners sued did not participate in, ratify, or know about whatever it was that gave rise to the cause of action.
Joint Liability Shared liability. In partnership law, partners incur joint liability for partnership obligations and debts. For example, if a third party sues a partner on a partnership debt, the partner has the right to insist that the other partners be sued with him or her.
Joint Stock Company A hybrid form of business organization that combines characteristics of a corporation and a partnership. Usually, the joint stock company is regarded as a partnership for tax and other legally related purposes.
Joint Tenancy The joint ownership of property by two or more co-owners in which each co-owner owns an undivided portion of the property. On the death of one of the joint tenants, his or her interest automatically passes to the surviving joint tenant(s).
Joint Venture A joint undertaking of a specific commercial enterprise by an association of persons. A joint venture normally is not a legal entity and is treated like a partnership for federal income tax purposes.
Judicial Review The process by which a court decides on the constitutionality of legislative enactments and actions of the executive branch.
Jurisdiction The authority of a court to hear and decide a specific action.
Jurisprudence The science or philosophy of law.
Justiciable Controversy A controversy that is not hypothetical or academic but real and substantial; a requirement that must be satisfied before a court will hear a case.

L

Larceny The wrongful taking and carrying away of another person's personal property with the intent to permanently deprive the owner of the property. Some states classify larceny as either grand or petit, depending on the property's value.
Law A body of enforceable rules governing relationships among individuals and between individuals and their society.
Lease In real property law, a contract by which the owner of real property (the landlord, or lessor) grants to a person (the tenant, or lessee) an exclusive right to use and possess the property, usually for a specified period of time, in return for rent or some other form of payment.
Lease Agreement In regard to the lease of goods, an agreement in which one person (the lessor) agrees to transfer the right to the pos-

session and use of property to another person (the lessee) in exchange for rental payments.

Leasehold Estate An estate in realty held by a tenant under a lease. In every leasehold estate, the tenant has a qualified right to possess and/or use the land.

Legacy A gift of personal property under a will.

Legal Positivism A school of legal thought centered on the assumption that there is no law higher than the laws created by the government. Laws must be obeyed, even if they are unjust, to prevent anarchy.

Legal Realism A school of legal thought of the 1920s and 1930s that generally advocated a less abstract and more realistic approach to the law, an approach that takes into account customary practices and the circumstances in which transactions take place. The school left a lasting imprint on American jurisprudence.

Legatee One designated in a will to receive a gift of personal property.

Lessee A person who acquires the right to the possession and use of another's goods in exchange for rental payments.

Lessor A person who sells the right to the possession and use of goods to another in exchange for rental payments.

Letter of Credit A written instrument, usually issued by a bank on behalf of a customer or other person, in which the issuer promises to honor drafts or other demands for payment by third persons in accordance with the terms of the instrument.

Levy The obtaining of money by legal process through the seizure and sale of property, usually done after a writ of execution has been issued.

Libel Defamation in writing or other form (such as in a videotape) having the quality of permanence.

License A revocable right or privilege of a person to come on another person's land.

Lien An encumbrance on a property to satisfy a debt or protect a claim for payment of a debt.

Life Estate An interest in land that exists only for the duration of the life of some person, usually the holder of the estate.

Limited Liability Company (LLC) A hybrid form of business enterprise that offers the limited liability of a corporation and the tax advantages of a partnership.

Limited Liability Limited Partnership (LLLP) A type of limited partnership in which the liability of all of the partners, including general partners, is limited to the amount of their investments.

Limited Liability Partnership (LLP) A business organizational form that is similar to the LCC but that is designed more for professionals who normally do business as partners in a partnership. The LLP is a pass-through entity for tax purposes, like the general partnership, but it limits the personal liability of the partners.

Limited Partner In a limited partnership, a partner who contributes capital to the partnership but who has no right to participate in the management and operation of the business. The limited partner assumes no liability for partnership debts beyond the capital contributed.

Limited Partnership A partnership consisting of one or more general partners (who manage the business and are liable to the full extent of their personal assets for debts of the partnership) and one or more limited partners (who contribute only assets and are liable only up to the extent of their contributions).

Liquidated Damages An amount, stipulated in the contract, that the parties to a contract believe to be a reasonable estimation of the damages that will occur in the event of a breach.

Liquidation In bankruptcy proceedings, the sale of all of the nonexempt assets of a debtor and the distribution of the proceeds to the debtor's creditors; Chapter 7 of the Bankruptcy Code provides for liquidation bankruptcy proceedings. In regard to corporations, the process by which corporate assets are converted into cash and distributed among creditors and shareholders according to specific rules of preference.

Litigation The process of resolving a dispute through the court system.

Long Arm Statute A state statute that permits a state to obtain personal jurisdiction over nonresident defendants. A defendant must have certain "minimum contacts" with that state for the statute to apply.

Lost Property Property with which the owner has involuntarily parted and then cannot find or recover.

M

Mailbox Rule A rule providing that an acceptance of an offer becomes effective on dispatch (on being placed in an official mailbox), if mail is, expressly or impliedly, an authorized means of communication of acceptance to the offeror.

Maker One who promises to pay a fixed amount of money to the holder of a promissory note or a certificate of deposit (CD).

Malpractice Professional misconduct or the lack of the requisite degree of skill as a professional. Negligence—the failure to exercise due care—on the part of a professional, such as a physician, is commonly referred to as malpractice.

Market Concentration The percentage of a particular firm's market sales in a relevant market area.

Market Power The power of a firm to control the market price of its product. A monopoly has the greatest degree of market power.

Market-Share Test The primary measure of monopoly power. A firm's market share is the percentage of a market that the firm controls.

Mass-Market License An e-contract that is presented with a package of computer information in the form of a *click-on license* or a *shrink-wrap license*.

Mechanic's Lien A statutory lien on the real property of another, created to ensure payment for work performed and materials furnished in the repair or improvement of real property, such as a building.

Mediation A method of settling disputes outside of court by using the services of a neutral third party, who acts as a communicating agent between the parties and assists them in negotiating a settlement.

Member The term used to designate a person who has an ownership interest in a limited liability company.

Merchant A person who is engaged in the purchase and sale of goods. Under the UCC, a person who deals in goods of the kind involved in the sales contract or who holds himself or herself out as having skill or knowledge peculiar to the practices or use of the goods being purchased or sold. For definitions, see UCC 2–104.

Merger A contractual and statutory process in which one corporation (the surviving corporation) acquires all of the assets and liabilities of another corporation (the merged corporation). The shareholders of the merged corporation either are paid for their shares or receive shares in the surviving corporation.

Meta Tag A key word in a document that can serve as an index reference to the document. On the Web, search engines return results based, in part, on the tags in Web documents.

Mini-Trial A private proceeding in which each party to a dispute argues its position before the other side and vice versa. A neutral third party may be present as an adviser and may render an opinion if the parties fail to reach an agreement.
Minimum Wage The lowest wage, either by government regulation or union contract, that an employer may pay an hourly worker.
Mirror Image Rule A common law rule that requires that the terms of the offeree's acceptance adhere exactly to the terms of the offeror's offer for a valid contract to be formed.
Misdemeanor A lesser crime than a felony, punishable by a fine or incarceration in jail for up to one year.
Mislaid Property Property with which the owner has voluntarily parted and then cannot find or recover.
Mitigation of Damages A rule requiring a plaintiff to have done whatever was reasonable to minimize the damages caused by the defendant.
Money Laundering Falsely reporting income that has been obtained through criminal activity as income obtained through a legitimate business enterprise—in effect, "laundering" the "dirty money."
Monopolization The possession of monopoly power in the relevant market and the willful acquisition or maintenance of the power, as distinguished from growth or development as a consequence of a superior product, business acumen, or historic accident.
Monopoly A term generally used to describe a market in which there is a single seller or a limited number of sellers.
Monopoly Power The ability of a monopoly to dictate what takes place in a given market.
Moral Minimum The minimum degree of ethical behavior expected of a business firm, which is usually defined as compliance with the law.
Mortgagee Under a mortgage agreement, the creditor who takes a security interest in the debtor's property.
Mortgagor Under a mortgage agreement, the debtor who gives the creditor a security interest in the debtor's property in return for a mortgage loan.
Most-Favored-Nation Status A status granted in an international treaty by a provision stating that the citizens of the contracting nations may enjoy the privileges accorded by either party to citizens of the most favored nations. Generally, most-favored-nation clauses are designed to establish equality of international treatment.
Motion for a Directed Verdict In a jury trial, a motion for the judge to take the decision out of the hands of the jury and direct a verdict for the party who filed the motion on the ground that the other party has not produced sufficient evidence to support her or his claim.
Motion for a New Trial A motion asserting that the trial was so fundamentally flawed (because of error, newly discovered evidence, prejudice, or other reason) that a new trial is necessary to prevent a miscarriage of justice.
Motion for Judgment *N.O.V.* A motion requesting the court to grant judgment in favor of the party making the motion on the ground that the jury verdict against him or her was unreasonable and erroneous.
Motion for Judgment on the Pleadings A motion by either party to a lawsuit at the close of the pleadings requesting the court to decide the issue solely on the pleadings without proceeding to trial. The motion will be granted only if no facts are in dispute.
Motion for Summary Judgment A motion requesting the court to enter a judgment without proceeding to trial. The motion can be based on evidence outside the pleadings and will be granted only if no facts are in dispute.
Motion to Dismiss A pleading in which a defendant asserts that the plaintiff's claim fails to state a cause of action (that is, has no basis in law) or that there are other grounds on which a suit should be dismissed.
Mutual Fund A specific type of investment company that continually buys or sells to investors shares of ownership in a portfolio.

N

National Law Law that pertains to a particular nation (as opposed to international law).
Natural Law The belief that government and the legal system should reflect universal moral and ethical principles that are inherent in human nature. The natural law school is the oldest and one of the most significant schools of legal thought.
Necessaries Necessities required for life, such as food, shelter, clothing, and medical attention; may include whatever is believed to be necessary to maintain a person's standard of living or financial and social status.
Negligence The failure to exercise the standard of care that a reasonable person would exercise in similar circumstances.
Negligence *Per Se* An action or failure to act in violation of a statutory requirement.
Negotiable Instrument A signed writing that contains an unconditional promise or order to pay an exact sum of money on demand or at an exact future time to a specific person or order, or to bearer.
Negotiation With respect to dispute settlement, a process in which parties attempt to settle their dispute informally, with or without attorneys to represent them. With respect to negotiable instruments, the transfer of an instrument in such form that the transferee (the person to whom the instrument is transferred) becomes a holder.
No-Par Shares Corporate shares that have no face value—that is, no specific dollar amount is printed on their face.
Nominal Damages A small monetary award (often one dollar) granted to a plaintiff when no actual damage was suffered.
Notary Public A public official authorized to attest to the authenticity of signatures.
Novation The substitution, by agreement, of a new contract for an old one, with the rights under the old one being terminated. Typically, novation involves the substitution of a new person who is responsible for the contract and the removal of the original party's rights and duties under the contract.
Nuisance A common law doctrine under which persons may be held liable for using their property in a manner that unreasonably interferes with others' rights to use or enjoy their own property.
Nuncupative Will An oral will (often called a deathbed will) made before witnesses; usually limited to transfers of personal property.

O

Objective Theory of Contracts A theory under which the intent to form a contract will be judged by outward, objective facts (what the party said when entering into the contract, how the party acted or appeared, and the circumstances surrounding the transaction) as interpreted by a reasonable person, rather than by the party's own secret, subjective intentions.
Offer A promise or commitment to perform or refrain from performing some specified act in the future.
Offeree A person to whom an offer is made.
Offeror A person who makes an offer.

Online Dispute Resolution (ODR) The resolution of disputes with the assistance of organizations that offer dispute-resolution services via the Internet.
Operating Agreement In a limited liability company, an agreement in which the members set forth the details of how the business will be managed and operated. State statutes typically give the members wide latitude in deciding for themselves the rules that will govern their organization.
Optimum Profits The amount of profits that a business can make and still act ethically, as opposed to maximum profits, defined as the amount of profits a firm can make if it is willing to disregard ethical concerns.
Option Contract A contract under which the offeror cannot revoke his or her offer for a stipulated time period, and the offeree can accept or reject the offer during this period without fear that the offer will be made to another person. The offeree must give consideration for the option (the irrevocable offer) to be enforceable.
Order for Relief A court's grant of assistance to a complainant. In bankruptcy proceedings, the order relieves the debtor of the immediate obligation to pay the debts listed in the bankruptcy petition.
Order Instrument A negotiable instrument that is payable "to the order of an identified person" or "to an identified person or order."
Output Contract An agreement in which a seller agrees to sell and a buyer agrees to buy all or up to a stated amount of what the seller produces.
Overdraft A check that is written on a checking account in which there are insufficient funds to cover the check and that is paid by the bank.

P

Par-Value Shares Corporate shares that have a specific face value, or formal cash-in value, written on them, such as one dollar.
Parol Evidence Rule A substantive rule of contracts, as well as a procedural rule of evidence, under which a court will not receive into evidence the parties' prior negotiations, prior agreements, or contemporaneous oral agreements if that evidence contradicts or varies the terms of the parties' written contract.
Partially Disclosed Principal A principal whose identity is unknown by a third person, but the third person knows that the agent is or may be acting for a principal at the time the agent and the third person form a contract.
Partnering Agreement An agreement between a seller and a buyer who frequently do business with each other on the terms and conditions that will apply to all subsequently formed electronic contracts.
Partnership An agreement by two or more persons to carry on, as co-owners, a business for profit.
Past Consideration An act done before the contract is made, which ordinarily, by itself, cannot be consideration for a later promise to pay for the act.
Patent A government grant that gives an inventor the exclusive right or privilege to make, use, or sell his or her invention for a limited time period.
Payee A person to whom an instrument is made payable.
Payor Bank The bank on which a check is drawn (the drawee bank).
Peer-to-Peer (P2P) Networking A technology that allows Internet users to access files on other users' computers.
Penalty A contractual clause that states that a certain amount of money damages will be paid in the event of a future default or breach of contract. The damages are not a measure of compensation for the contract's breach but rather a punishment for a default. The agreement as to the amount will not be enforced, and recovery will be limited to actual damages.
Per Capita A Latin term meaning "per person." In the law governing estate distribution, a method of distributing the property of an intestate's estate in which each heir in a certain class (such as grandchildren) receives an equal share.
***Per Se* Violation** A type of anticompetitive agreement—such as a horizontal price-fixing agreement—that is considered to be so injurious to the public that there is no need to determine whether it actually injures market competition; rather, it is in itself (*per se*) a violation of the Sherman Act.
Per Stirpes A Latin term meaning "by the roots." In the law governing estate distribution, a method of distributing an intestate's estate in which each heir in a certain class (such as grandchildren) takes the share to which her or his deceased ancestor (such as a mother or father) would have been entitled.
Perfection The legal process by which secured parties protect themselves against the claims of third parties who may wish to have their debts satisfied out of the same collateral; usually accomplished by filing a financing statement with the appropriate government official.
Performance In contract law, the fulfillment of one's duties arising under a contract with another; the normal way of discharging one's contractual obligations.
Periodic Tenancy A lease interest in land for an indefinite period involving payment of rent at fixed intervals, such as week to week, month to month, or year to year.
Personal Defenses Defenses that can be used to avoid payment to an ordinary holder of a negotiable instrument but not a holder in due course (HDC) or a holder with the rights of an HDC.
Personal Property Property that is movable; any property that is not real property.
Persuasive Authority Any legal authority or source of law that a court may look to for guidance but on which it need not rely in making its decision. Persuasive authorities include cases from other jurisdictions and secondary sources of law.
Petition In Bankruptcy The document that is filed with a bankruptcy court to initiate bankruptcy proceedings. The official forms required for a petition in bankruptcy must be completed accurately, sworn to under oath, and signed by the debtor.
Petty Offense In criminal law, the least serious kind of criminal offense, such as a traffic or building-code violation.
Piercing the Corporate Veil An action in which a court disregards the corporate entity and holds the shareholders personally liable for corporate debts and obligations.
Plaintiff One who initiates a lawsuit.
Plea Bargaining The process by which a criminal defendant and the prosecutor in a criminal case work out a mutually satisfactory disposition of the case, subject to court approval; usually involves the defendant's pleading guilty to a lesser offense in return for a lighter sentence.
Pleadings Statements made by the plaintiff and the defendant in a lawsuit that detail the facts, charges, and defenses involved in the litigation; the complaint and answer are part of the pleadings.
Pledge A common law security device (retained in Article 9 of the UCC) in which possession of personal property is turned over to the

creditor as security for the payment of a debt and retained by the creditor until the debt is paid.

Police Powers Powers possessed by states as part of their inherent sovereignty. These powers may be exercised to protect or promote the public order, health, safety, morals, and general welfare.

Policy In insurance law, a contract between the insurer and the insured in which, for a stipulated consideration, the insurer agrees to compensate the insured for loss on a specific subject by a specified peril.

Positive Law The body of conventional, or written, law of a particular society at a particular point in time.

Potentially Responsible Party (PRP) A party liable for the costs of cleaning up a hazardous waste-disposal site under the Comprehensive Environmental Response, Compensation, and Liability Act (CERCLA). Any person who generated the hazardous waste, transported it, owned or operated the waste site at the time of disposal, or currently owns or operates the site may be responsible for some or all of the clean-up costs.

Power of Attorney A written document, which is usually notarized, authorizing another to act as one's agent; can be special (permitting the agent to do specified acts only) or general (permitting the agent to transact all business for the principal).

Precedent A court decision that furnishes an example or authority for deciding subsequent cases involving identical or similar facts.

Predatory Behavior Business behavior that is undertaken with the intention of unlawfully driving competitors out of the market.

Predatory Pricing The pricing of a product below cost with the intent to drive competitors out of the market.

Preemption A doctrine under which certain federal laws preempt, or take precedence over, conflicting state or local laws.

Preemptive Rights Rights held by shareholders that entitle them to purchase newly issued shares of a corporation's stock, equal in percentage to shares currently held, before the stock is offered to any outside buyers. Preemptive rights enable shareholders to maintain their proportionate ownership and voice in the corporation.

Preference In bankruptcy proceedings, property transfers or payments made by the debtor that favor (give preference to) one creditor over others. The bankruptcy trustee is allowed to recover payments made both voluntarily and involuntarily to one creditor in preference over another.

Preferred Stock Classes of stock that have priority over common stock as to both payment of dividends and distribution of assets on the corporation's dissolution.

Premium In insurance law, the price paid by the insured for insurance protection for a specified period of time.

Prenuptial Agreement An agreement made before marriage that defines each partner's ownership rights in the other partner's property. Prenuptial agreements must be in writing to be enforceable.

Presentment The act of presenting an instrument to the party liable on the instrument to collect payment; presentment also occurs when a person presents an instrument to a drawee for a required acceptance.

Presentment Warranties Implied warranties, made by any person who presents an instrument for payment or acceptance, that (1) the person obtaining payment or acceptance is entitled to enforce the instrument or is authorized to obtain payment or acceptance on behalf of a person who is entitled to enforce the instrument, (2) the instrument has not been altered, and (3) the person obtaining payment or acceptance has no knowledge that the signature of the drawer of the instrument is unauthorized.

Price Discrimination Setting prices in such a way that two competing buyers pay two different prices for an identical product or service.

Price-Fixing Agreement An agreement between competitors to fix the prices of products or services at a certain level.

***Prima Facie* Case** A case in which the plaintiff has produced sufficient evidence of his or her conclusion that the case can go to a jury; a case in which the evidence compels the plaintiff's conclusion if the defendant produces no affirmative defense or evidence to disprove it.

Primary Source of Law A document that establishes the law on a particular issue, such as a constitution, a statute, an administrative rule, or a court decision.

Principal In agency law, a person who agrees to have another, called the agent, act on her or his behalf.

Principle of Rights The principle that human beings have certain fundamental rights (to life, freedom, and the pursuit of happiness, for example). Those who adhere to this "rights theory" believe that a key factor in determining whether a business decision is ethical is how that decision affects the rights of various groups. These groups include the firm's owners, its employees, the consumers of its products or services, its suppliers, the community in which it does business, and society as a whole.

Privilege In tort law, the ability to act contrary to another person's right without that person's having legal redress for such acts. Privilege may be raised as a defense to defamation.

Privity of Contract The relationship that exists between the promisor and the promisee of a contract.

Probable Cause Reasonable grounds for believing that a person should be arrested or searched.

Probate Court A state court of limited jurisdiction that conducts proceedings relating to the settlement of a deceased person's estate.

Procedural Law Law that establishes the methods of enforcing the rights established by substantive law.

Proceeds Under Article 9 of the UCC, whatever is received when the collateral is sold or otherwise disposed of, such as by exchange.

Product Liability The legal liability of manufacturers, sellers, and lessors of goods to consumers, users, and bystanders for injuries or damages that are caused by the goods.

Profit In real property law, the right to enter upon and remove things from the property of another (for example, the right to enter onto a person's land and remove sand and gravel therefrom).

Promise A declaration that something either will or will not happen in the future.

Promisee A person to whom a promise is made.

Promisor A person who makes a promise.

Promissory Estoppel A doctrine that applies when a promisor makes a clear and definite promise on which the promisee justifiably relies; such a promise is binding if justice will be better served by the enforcement of the promise.

Promissory Note A written promise made by one person (the maker) to pay a fixed amount of money to another person (the payee or a subsequent holder) on demand or on a specified date.

Promoter A person who takes the preliminary steps in organizing a corporation, including (usually) issuing a prospectus, procuring stock subscriptions, making contract purchases, securing a corporate charter, and the like.

Property Legally protected rights and interests in anything with an ascertainable value that is subject to ownership.

Prospectus A document required by federal or state securities laws that describes the financial operations of the corporation, thus allowing investors to make informed decisions.
Protected Class A group of persons protected by specific laws because of the group's defining characteristics. Under laws prohibiting employment discrimination, these characteristics include race, color, religion, national origin, gender, age, and disability.
Proximate Cause Legal cause; exists when the connection between an act and an injury is strong enough to justify imposing liability.
Proxy In corporation law, a written agreement between a stockholder and another under which the stockholder authorizes the other to vote the stockholder's shares in a certain manner.
Puffery A salesperson's often exaggerated claims concerning the quality of property offered for sale. Such claims involve opinions rather than facts and are not considered to be legally binding promises or warranties.
Punitive Damages Money damages that may be awarded to a plaintiff to punish the defendant and deter future similar conduct.
Purchase-Money Security Interest (PMSI) A security interest that arises when a seller or lender extends credit for part or all of the purchase price of goods purchased by a buyer.

Q

Qualified Indorsement An indorsement on a negotiable instrument in which the indorser disclaims any contract liability on the instrument; the notation "without recourse" is commonly used to create a qualified indorsement.
Quasi Contract A fictional contract imposed on parties by a court in the interests of fairness and justice; usually imposed to avoid the unjust enrichment of one party at the expense of another.
Quitclaim Deed A deed intended to pass any title, interest, or claim that the grantor may have in the property but not warranting that such title is valid. A quitclaim deed offers the least amount of protection against defects in the title.
Quorum The number of members of a decision-making body that must be present before business may be transacted.

R

Ratification The act of accepting and giving legal force to an obligation that previously was not enforceable.
Real Property Land and everything attached to it, such as trees and buildings.
Reasonable Person Standard The standard of behavior expected of a hypothetical "reasonable person." The standard against which negligence is measured and that must be observed to avoid liability for negligence.
Receiver In a corporate dissolution, a court-appointed person who winds up corporate affairs and liquidates corporate assets.
Record According to the Uniform Electronic Transactions Act, information that is either inscribed on a tangible medium or stored in an electronic or other medium and that is retrievable. The Uniform Computer Information Transactions Act uses the term *record* instead of *writing*.
Recording Statutes Statutes that allow deeds, mortgages, and other real property transactions to be recorded so as to provide notice to future purchasers or creditors of an existing claim on the property.
Red Herring A preliminary prospectus that can be distributed to potential investors after the registration statement (for a securities offering) has been filed with the Securities and Exchange Commission. The name derives from the red legend printed across the prospectus stating that the registration has been filed but has not become effective.
Reformation A court-ordered correction of a written contract so that it reflects the true intentions of the parties.
Regulation E A set of rules issued by the Federal Reserve System's Board of Governors to protect users of elecronic fund transfer systems.
Regulation Z A set of rules promulgated by the Federal Reserve Board to implement the provisions of the Truth-in-Lending Act.
Release A contract in which one party forfeits the right to pursue a legal claim against the other party.
Remainder A future interest in property held by a person other than the original owner.
Remedy The relief given to an innocent party to enforce a right or compensate for the violation of a right.
Replevin An action to recover identified goods in the hands of a party who is wrongfully withholding them from the other party. Under the UCC, this remedy is usually available only if the buyer or lessee is unable to cover.
Reply Procedurally, a plaintiff's response to a defendant's answer.
Requirements Contract An agreement in which a buyer agrees to purchase and the seller agrees to sell all or up to a stated amount of what the buyer needs or requires.
Res Ipsa Loquitur A doctrine under which negligence may be inferred simply because an event occurred, if it is the type of event that would not occur in the absence of negligence. Literally, the term means "the facts speak for themselves."
Resale Price Maintenance Agreement An agreement between a manufacturer and a retailer in which the manufacturer specifies what the retail price of its products must be.
Rescission A remedy whereby a contract is canceled and the parties are returned to the positions they occupied before the contract was made; may be effected through the mutual consent of the parties, by their conduct, or by court decree.
Respondeat Superior In Latin, "Let the master respond." A doctrine under which a principal or an employer is held liable for the wrongful acts committed by agents or employees while acting within the course and scope of their agency or employment.
Restitution An equitable remedy under which a person is restored to his or her original position prior to loss or injury, or placed in the position he or she would have been in had the breach not occurred.
Restrictive Indorsement Any indorsement on a negotiable instrument that requires the indorsee to comply with certain instructions regarding the funds involved. A restrictive indorsement does not prohibit the further negotiation of the instrument.
Resulting Trust An implied trust arising from the conduct of the parties. A trust in which a party holds the actual legal title to another's property but only for that person's benefit.
Retained Earnings The portion of a corporation's profits that has not been paid out as dividends to shareholders.
Reversionary Interest A future interest in property retained by the original owner.
Revocation In contract law, the withdrawal of an offer by an offeror; unless the offer is irrevocable, it can be revoked at any time prior to acceptance without liability.
Right of Contribution The right of a co-surety who pays more than his or her proportionate share on a debtor's default to recover the excess paid from other co-sureties.

Right of First Refusal The right to purchase personal or real property—such as corporate shares or real estate—before the property is offered for sale to others.

Right of Reimbursement The legal right of a person to be restored, repaid, or indemnified for costs, expenses, or losses incurred or expended on behalf of another.

Right of Subrogation The right of a person to stand in the place of (be substituted for) another, giving the substituted party the same legal rights that the original party had.

Right-to-Work Law A state law providing that employees may not be required to join a union as a condition of retaining employment.

Risk A prediction concerning potential loss based on known and unknown factors.

Risk Management Planning that is undertaken to protect one's interest should some event threaten to undermine its security. In the context of insurance, risk management involves transferring certain risks from the insured to the insurance company.

Robbery The act of forcefully and unlawfully taking personal property of any value from another; force or intimidation is usually necessary for an act of theft to be considered a robbery.

Rule of Four A rule of the United States Supreme Court under which the Court will not issue a writ of *certiorari* unless at least four justices approve of the decision to issue the writ.

Rule of Reason A test by which a court balances the positive effects (such as economic efficiency) of an agreement against its potentially anticompetitive effects. In antitrust litigation, many practices are analyzed under the rule of reason.

Rulemaking The process undertaken by an administrative agency when formally adopting a new regulation or amending an old one. Rulemaking involves notifying the public of a proposed rule or change and receiving and considering the public's comments.

S

S Corporation A close business corporation that has met certain requirements as set out by the Internal Revenue Code and thus qualifies for special income tax treatment. Essentially, an S corporation is taxed the same as a partnership, but its owners enjoy the privilege of limited liability.

Sale The passing of title to property from the seller to the buyer for a price.

Sale on Approval A type of conditional sale in which the buyer may take the goods on a trial basis. The sale becomes absolute only when the buyer approves of (or is satisfied with) the goods being sold.

Sale or Return A type of conditional sale in which title and possession pass from the seller to the buyer; however, the buyer retains the option to return the goods during a specified period even though the goods conform to the contract.

Sales Contract A contract for the sale of goods under which the ownership of goods is transferred from a seller to a buyer for a price.

Scienter Knowledge by the misrepresenting party that material facts have been falsely represented or omitted with an intent to deceive.

Search Warrant An order granted by a public authority, such as a judge, that authorizes law enforcement personnel to search particular premises or property.

Seasonably Within a specified time period, or, if no period is specified, within a reasonable time.

SEC Rule 10b-5 A rule of the Securities and Exchange Commission that makes it unlawful, in connection with the purchase or sale of any security, to make any untrue statement of a material fact or to omit a material fact if such omission causes the statement to be misleading.

Secondary Boycott A union's refusal to work for, purchase from, or handle the products of a secondary employer, with whom the union has no dispute, in order to force that employer to stop doing business with the primary employer, with whom the union has a labor dispute.

Secondary Source of Law A publication that summarizes or interprets the law, such as a legal encyclopedia, a legal treatise, or an article in a law review.

Secured Party A lender, seller, or any other person in whose favor there is a security interest, including a person to whom accounts or chattel paper has been sold.

Secured Transaction Any transaction in which the payment of a debt is guaranteed, or secured by personal property owned by the debtor or in which the debtor has a legal interest.

Security Generally, a stock certificate, bond, note, debenture, warrant, or other document given as evidence of an ownership interest in a corporation or as a promise of repayment by a corporation.

Security Agreement An agreement that creates or provides for a security interest between the debtor and a secured party.

Security Interest Any interest "in personal property or fixtures which secures payment or performance of an obligation" [UCC 1–201(37)].

Self-Defense The legally recognized privilege to protect oneself or one's property against injury by another. The privilege of self-defense protects only acts that are reasonably necessary to protect oneself, one's property, or another person.

Self-Incrimination The giving of testimony that may subject the testifier to criminal prosecution. The Fifth Amendment to the Constitution protects against self-incrimination by providing that no person "shall be compelled in any criminal case to be a witness against himself."

Seniority System In regard to employment relationships, a system in which those who have worked longest for the company are first in line for promotions, salary increases, and other benefits; they are also the last to be laid off if the work force must be reduced.

Service Mark A mark used in the sale or the advertising of services to distinguish the services of one person from those of others. Titles, character names, and other distinctive features of radio and television programs may be registered as service marks.

Sexual Harassment In the employment context, the granting of job promotions or other benefits in return for sexual favors, or language or conduct that is so sexually offensive that it creates a hostile working environment.

Shareholder's Derivative Suit A suit brought by a shareholder to enforce a corporate cause of action against a third person.

Shelter Principle The principle that the holder of a negotiable instrument who cannot qualify as a holder in due course (HDC), but who derives his or her title through an HDC, acquires the rights of an HDC.

Shipment Contract A contract for the sale of goods in which the seller is required or authorized to ship the goods by carrier. The seller assumes liability for any losses or damage to the goods until they are delivered to the carrier.

Short-Form Merger A merger between a subsidiary corporation and a parent corporation that owns at least 90 percent of the outstanding shares of each class of stock issued by the subsidiary corporation. Short-form mergers can be accomplished without the approval of the shareholders of either corporation.

Shrink-Wrap Agreement An agreement whose terms are expressed in a document located inside a box in which goods (usually software) are packaged; sometimes called a *shrink-wrap license*.
Signature Under the UCC, "any symbol executed or adopted by a party with a present intention to authenticate a writing."
Slander Defamation in oral form.
Slander of Quality (Trade Libel) The publication of false information about another's product, alleging that it is not what its seller claims.
Slander of Title The publication of a statement that denies or casts doubt on another's legal ownership of any property, causing financial loss to that property's owner.
Small Claims Court A special court in which parties may litigate small claims (such as $5,000 or less). Attorneys are not required in small claims courts and, in some states, are not allowed to represent the parties.
Smart Card A card containing a microprocessor that permits storage of funds via security programming, can communicate with other computers, and does not require online authorization for fund transfers.
Sociological School A school of legal thought that views the law as a tool for promoting justice in society.
Sole Proprietorship The simplest form of business, in which the owner is the business. The owner reports business income on his or her personal income tax return and is legally responsible for all debts and obligations incurred by the business.
Sovereign Immunity A doctrine that immunizes foreign nations from the jurisdiction of U.S. courts when certain conditions are satisfied.
Spam Bulk, unsolicited ("junk") e-mail.
Special Indorsement An indorsement on an instrument that indicates the specific person to whom the indorser intends to make the instrument payable; that is, it names the indorsee.
Specific Performance An equitable remedy requiring exactly the performance that was specified in a contract; usually granted only when money damages would be an inadequate remedy and the subject matter of the contract is unique (for example, real property).
Spendthrift Trust A trust created to protect the beneficiary from spending all the funds to which she or he is entitled. Only a certain portion of the total amount is given to the beneficiary at any one time, and most states prohibit creditors from attaching assets of the trust.
Stale Check A check, other than a certified check, that is presented for payment more than six months after its date.
Standing to Sue The requirement that an individual must have a sufficient stake in a controversy before he or she can bring a lawsuit. The plaintiff must demonstrate that he or she either has been injured or threatened with injury.
Stare Decisis A common law doctrine under which judges are obligated to follow the precedents established in prior decisions.
Statute of Frauds A state statute under which certain types of contracts must be in writing to be enforceable.
Statute of Limitations A federal or state statute setting the maximum time period during which a certain action can be brought or certain rights enforced.
Statutory Law The body of law enacted by legislative bodies (as opposed to constitutional law, administrative law, or case law).
Stock An equity (ownership) interest in a corporation, measured in units of shares.
Stock Certificate A certificate issued by a corporation evidencing the ownership of a specified number of shares in the corporation.
Stock Warrant A certificate that grants the owner the option to buy a given number of shares of stock, usually within a set time period.
Stop-Payment Order An order by a bank customer to his or her bank not to pay or certify a certain check.
Stored-Value Card A card bearing magnetic stripes that hold magnetically encoded data, providing access to stored funds.
Strict Liability Liability regardless of fault. In tort law, strict liability is imposed on a merchant who introduces into commerce a good that is unreasonably dangerous when in a defective condition.
Strike An action undertaken by unionized workers when collective bargaining fails; the workers leave their jobs, refuse to work, and (typically) picket the employer's workplace.
Sublease A lease executed by the lessee of real estate to a third person, conveying the same interest that the lessee enjoys but for a shorter term than that held by the lessee.
Substantive Law Law that defines, describes, regulates, and creates legal rights and obligations.
Summary Jury Trial (SJT) A method of settling disputes, used in many federal courts, in which a trial is held, but the jury's verdict is not binding. The verdict acts only as a guide to both sides in reaching an agreement during the mandatory negotiations that immediately follow the summary jury trial.
Summons A document informing a defendant that a legal action has been commenced against him or her and that the defendant must appear in court on a certain date to answer the plaintiff's complaint. The document is delivered by a sheriff or any other person so authorized.
Supremacy Clause The provision in Article VI of the Constitution that provides that the Constitution, laws, and treaties of the United States are "the supreme Law of the Land." Under this clause, state and local laws that directly conflict with federal law will be rendered invalid.
Surety A person, such as a cosigner on a note, who agrees to be primarily responsible for the debt of another.
Suretyship An express contract in which a third party to a debtor-creditor relationship (the surety) promises to be primarily responsible for the debtor's obligation.
Symbolic Speech Nonverbal expressions of beliefs. Symbolic speech, which includes gestures, movements, and articles of clothing, is given substantial protection by the courts.
Syndicate An investment group of persons or firms brought together for the purpose of financing a project that they would not or could not undertake independently.

T

Taking The taking of private property by the government for public use. Under the Fifth Amendment to the Constitution, the government may not take private property for public use without "just compensation."
Tangible Property Property that has physical existence and can be distinguished by the senses of touch, sight, and so on. A car is tangible property; a patent right is intangible property.
Target Corporation The corporation to be acquired in a corporate takeover; a corporation to whose shareholders a tender offer is submitted.
Technology Licensing Allowing another to use and profit from intellectual property (patents, copyrights, trademarks, innovative products or processes, and so on) for consideration. In the context of international business transactions, technology licensing is sometimes an

attractive alternative to the establishment of foreign production facilities.

Tenancy at Sufferance A type of tenancy under which a tenant who, after rightfully being in possession of leased premises, continues (wrongfully) to occupy the property after the lease has been terminated. The tenant has no rights to possess the property and occupies it only because the person entitled to evict the tenant has not done so.

Tenancy at Will A type of tenancy under which either party can terminate the tenancy without notice; usually arises when a tenant who has been under a tenancy for years retains possession, with the landlord's consent, after the tenancy for years has terminated.

Tenancy by the Entirety The joint ownership of property by a husband and wife. Neither party can transfer his or her interest in the property without the consent of the other.

Tenancy for Years A type of tenancy under which property is leased for a specified period of time, such as a month, a year, or a period of years.

Tenancy in Common Co-ownership of property in which each party owns an undivided interest that passes to her or his heirs at death.

Tender An unconditional offer to perform an obligation by a person who is ready, willing, and able to do so.

Tender Offer An offer to purchase shares made by one company directly to the shareholders of another (target) company; often referred to as a "takeover bid."

Testamentary Trust A trust that is created by will and therefore does not take effect until the death of the testator.

Testator One who makes and executes a will.

Third Party Beneficiary One for whose benefit a promise is made in a contract but who is not a party to the contract.

Tippee A person who receives inside information.

Tombstone Ad An advertisement, historically in a format resembling a tombstone, of a securities offering. The ad informs potential investors of where and how they may obtain a prospectus.

Tort A civil wrong not arising from a breach of contract. A breach of a legal duty that proximately causes harm or injury to another.

Tortfeasor One who commits a tort.

Totten Trust A trust created by the deposit of a person's own funds in his or her own name as a trustee for another. It is a tentative trust, revocable at will until the depositor dies or completes the gift in his or her lifetime by some unequivocal act or declaration.

Trade Acceptance A draft that is drawn by a seller of goods ordering the buyer to pay a specified sum of money to the seller, usually at a stated time in the future. The buyer accepts the draft by signing the face of the draft, thus creating an enforceable obligation to pay the draft when it comes due. On a trade acceptance, the seller is both the drawer and the payee.

Trade Dress The image and overall appearance of a product—for example, the distinctive decor, menu, layout, and style of service of a particular restaurant. Basically, trade dress is subject to the same protection as trademarks.

Trade Name A term that is used to indicate part or all of a business's name and that is directly related to the business's reputation and goodwill. Trade names are protected under the common law (and under trademark law, if the name is the same as the firm's trademarked property).

Trade Secrets Information or processes that give a business an advantage over competitors who do not know the information or processes.

Trademark A distinctive mark, motto, device, or emblem that a manufacturer stamps, prints, or otherwise affixes to the goods it produces so that they may be identified on the market and their origins made known. Once a trademark is established (under the common law or through registration), the owner is entitled to its exclusive use.

Transfer Warranties Implied warranties, made by any person who transfers an instrument for consideration to subsequent transferees and holders who take the instrument in good faith, that (1) the transferor is entitled to enforce the instrument, (2) all signatures are authentic and authorized, (3) the instrument has not been altered, (4) the instrument is not subject to a defense or claim of any party that can be asserted against the transferor, and (5) the transferor has no knowledge of any insolvency proceedings against the maker, the acceptor, or the drawer of the instrument.

Traveler's Check A check that is payable on demand, drawn on or payable through a financial institution (bank), and designated as a traveler's check.

Trespass to Land The entry onto, above, or below the surface of land owned by another without the owner's permission or legal authorization.

Trespass to Personal Property The unlawful taking or harming of another's personal property; interference with another's right to the exclusive possession of his or her personal property.

Trust An arrangement in which title to property is held by one person (a trustee) for the benefit of another (a beneficiary).

Trust Indorsement An indorsement for the benefit of the indorser or a third person; also known as an agency indorsement. The indorsement results in legal title vesting in the original indorsee.

Tying Arrangement An agreement between a buyer and a seller in which the buyer of a specific product or service becomes obligated to purchase additional products or services from the seller.

U

Ultra Vires A Latin term meaning "beyond the powers"; in corporate law, acts of a corporation that are beyond its express and implied powers to undertake.

Unconscionable Contract or Clause A contract or clause that is void on the basis of public policy because one party, as a result of disproportionate bargaining power, is forced to accept terms that are unfairly burdensome and that unfairly benefit the dominating party.

Underwriter In insurance law, the insurer, or the one assuming a risk in return for the payment of a premium.

Undisclosed Principal A principal whose identity is unknown by a third person, and the third person has no knowledge that the agent is acting for a principal at the time the agent and the third person form a contract.

Unenforceable Contract A valid contract rendered unenforceable by some statute or law.

Unilateral Contract A contract that results when an offer can be accepted only by the offeree's performance.

Union Shop A place of employment where all workers, once employed, must become union members within a specified period of time as a condition of their continued employment.

Universal Defenses Defenses that are valid against all holders of a negotiable instrument, including holders in due course (HDCs) and holders with the rights of HDCs.

Unreasonably Dangerous Product In product liability, a product that is defective to the point of threatening a consumer's health and safety. A product will be considered unreasonably dangerous if it is dangerous beyond the expectation of the ordinary consumer or if a less dangerous alternative was economically feasible for the manufacturer, but the manufacturer failed to produce it.

Usage of Trade Any practice or method of dealing having such regularity of observance in a place, vocation, or trade as to justify an expectation that it will be observed with respect to the transaction in question.

U.S. Trustee A government official who performs certain administrative tasks that a bankruptcy judge would otherwise have to perform.

Usury Charging an illegal rate of interest.

Utilitarianism An approach to ethical reasoning that evaluates behavior not on the basis of any absolute ethical or moral values but on the consequences of that behavior for those who will be affected by it. In utilitarian reasoning, a "good" decision is one that results in the greatest good for the greatest number of people affected by the decision.

V

Valid Contract A contract that results when the elements necessary for contract formation (agreement, consideration, legal purpose, and contractual capacity) are present.

Venue The geographic district in which an action is tried and from which the jury is selected.

Vertical Merger The acquisition by a company at one level in a marketing chain of a company at a higher or lower level in the chain (such as a company merging with one of its suppliers or retailers).

Vertical Restraint Any restraint on trade created by agreements between firms at different levels in the manufacturing and distribution process.

Vertically Integrated Firm A firm that carries out two or more functional phases (manufacture, distribution, retailing, and so on) of a product.

Vesting The creation of an absolute or unconditional right or power.

Void Contract A contract having no legal force or binding effect.

Voidable Contract A contract that may be legally avoided (canceled, or annulled) at the option of one or both of the parties.

Voir Dire French verbs that mean, literally, "to see" and "to speak." In jury trials, the phrase refers to the process in which the attorneys question prospective jurors to determine whether they are biased or have any connection with a party to the action or with a prospective witness.

Voting Trust An agreement (trust contract) under which legal title to shares of corporate stock is transferred to a trustee who is authorized by the shareholders to vote the shares on their behalf.

W

Warranty Deed A deed in which the grantor assures (warrants to) the grantee that the grantor has title to the property conveyed in the deed, that there are no encumbrances on the property other than what the grantor has represented, and that the grantee will enjoy quiet possession of the property; a deed that provides the greatest amount of protection for the grantee.

Watered Stock Shares of stock issued by a corporation for which the corporation receives, as payment, less than the stated value of the shares.

Wetlands Water-saturated areas of land that are designated by government agencies (such as the Army Corps of Engineers or the Environmental Protection Agency) as protected areas that support wildlife and therefore cannot be filled in or dredged by private contractors or parties without a permit.

Whistleblowing An employee's disclosure to a government official, upper-management authorities, or the press that the employer is engaged in unsafe or illegal activities.

White-Collar Crime Nonviolent crime committed by individuals or corporations to obtain a personal or business advantage.

Will An instrument directing what is to be done with the testator's property on his or her death, made by the testator and revocable during his or her lifetime. No interests in the testator's property pass until the testator dies.

Winding Up The second of two stages in the termination of a partnership or corporation. Once the firm is dissolved, it continues to exist legally until the process of winding up all business affairs (collecting and distributing the firm's assets) is complete.

Workers' Compensation Laws State statutes establishing an administrative procedure for compensating workers' injuries that arise out of—or in the course of—their employment, regardless of fault.

Workout An out-of-court agreement between a debtor and his or her creditors in which the parties work out a payment plan or schedule under which the debtor's debts can be discharged.

Writ of *Certiorari* A writ from a higher court asking the lower court for the record of a case.

Writ of Attachment A court's order, prior to a trial to collect a debt, directing the sheriff or other officer to seize nonexempt property of the debtor. If the creditor prevails at trial, the seized property can be sold to satisfy the judgment.

Writ of Execution A court's order, after a judgment has been entered against the debtor, directing the sheriff to seize (levy) and sell any of the debtor's nonexempt real or personal property. The proceeds of the sale are used to pay off the judgment, accrued interest, and costs of the sale; any surplus is paid to the debtor.

Wrongful Discharge An employer's termination of an employee's employment in violation of the law.

TABLE OF CASES

INDEX

C

E

N

O

P

PHOTO CREDITS

All chapter and unit opener montages are comprised of PhotoDisc images. 5 From the painting by Benjamin Ferrers in National Portrait Gallery, Photo: Corbis-Bettmann; 10 © Michael Evans, Corbis Sygma; 12 AP/Wide World Photos; 31 PhotoDisc; 40 AP/Wide World Photos; 44 © Chris Brown, Stock Boston; 46 © Amy C. Etra, PhotoEdit; 65 Corbis-Bettmann; 76 AP/Wide World Photos; 78 Photo by Richard Strauss, Smithsonian Institution, Collection of the Supreme Court of the United States; 110 © Frederick D. Bodin, Stock Boston; 119 © Steve Myerson, International Stock; 135 © Mike Mazzaschi, Stock Boston; 136 AP/Wide World Photos; 137 Photo in the Public Domain; 169 Marta Lavandier, AP/Wide World Photos; 170 Steve Ueckert, Pool, AP/Wide World Photos; 175 © Michael Newman, PhotoEdit; 181 Reprinted with permission of the Daily Breeze © 1995; 183 NYPD, AP/Wide World Photos; 197 © Ted Horowitz, Getty Images; 205 © Barbara Alper, Stock Boston; 223 © Ron Chapple, Getty Images; 226 © Billy E. Barnes, PhotoEdit; 242 © Steve Benbow, Stock Boston; 243 © Bob Daemmrich, Stock Boston; 248 © Michael Newman, PhotoEdit; 267 © Michael Newman, PhotoEdit; 271 © M. Borchi/Photo Researchers; 291 © Mark Mellett, Stock Boston; 296 © Ewing Galloway, Inc.; 313 © David Young-Wolff, PhotoEdit; 323 © Joseph Nettis, Stock Boston; 324 © Tony Freeman, PhotoEdit; 329 © Dick Luria, Getty Images; 342 © Elizabeth Simpson, Getty Images; 362 Telegraph Colour Library, Getty Images; 377 AP Wide World Photos; 380 © Andy Sacks, Getty Images; 388 © Wayne Eastep, Getty Images; 389 Toby Talbot, AP/Wide World Photos; 410 © Tony Freeman, PhotoEdit; 412 Yakima Herlad-Republic, Gordon King, AP/Wide World Photos; 418 AP/Wide World Photos; 471 © Steve Leonard, Black Star; 523 Index Stock Photography, Inc.; 551 © Bob Daemmrich, Stock Boston; 559 © Myrleen Ferguson, PhotoEdit; 610 © Myrleen Ferguson, PhotoEdit; 617 © Tony Freeman, PhotoEdit; 622 © Tony Freeman, PhotoEdit; 653 Comstock; 654 © Amy C. Etra, PhotoEdit; 661 © Michael Newman, PhotoEdit; 677 © Phil Borden, PhotoEdit; 687 © Jose L. Palaez, Getty Images, 707 © McIntyre, Photo Researchers; 734 © John Terence Turner, Getty Images; 739 © Tom Carroll, International Stock; 742 © Amy C. Etra, PhotoEdit; 765 © Robert Brenner, PhotoEdit; 774 © David Young-Wolff, PhotoEdit; 823 © Michael Newman, PhotoEdit; 826 © Day Williams, Photo Researchers; 849 © John Coletti, Stock Boston; 872 PhotoEdit; 882 PhotoDisc; 900 The Library of Congress; 905 © Jonathan Nourak, PhotoEdit; 916 © Conklin, PhotoEdit; 938 © Johnny Stockshooter, International Stock; 941 © John Boykin, PhotoEdit; 973 © Peter Vadnai, Getty Images; 982 © Jonathan Nourok, PhotoEdit. 992 © Vic Bider/PhotoEdit.

List of Selected Abbreviations

A.	*Atlantic Reporter*
A.2d	*Atlantic Reporter, Second Series*
AAA	American Arbitration Association
ABA	American Bar Association
ADA	Americans with Disabilities Act
ADEA	Age Discrimination in Employment Act
ADR	alternative dispute resolution
aff'd	affirmed
A.G.	*Aktiengesellschaft* (a German corporation)
AICPA	American Institute of Certified Public Accountants
ALI	American Law Institute
ALJ	administrative law judge
APA	Administrative Procedure Act
ATM	automated teller machine
Bankr.	*Bankruptcy Reporter*
BFOQ	bona fide occupational qualification
C.&F.	cost and freight
Cal.Rptr.	*California Reporter*
CD	certificate of deposit
CERCLA	Comprehensive Environmental Response, Compensation and Liability Act (Superfund)
cert.	*certiorari*
cert. den.	*certiorari* denied
C.F.R.	*Code of Federal Regulations*
C.I.F.	cost, insurance, and freight
CISG	United Nations Convention on Contracts for the International Sale of Goods
C.O.D.	cash on delivery
CPSC	Consumer Product Safety Commission
Ct.	Court
Ct.App.	Court of Appeals
DIP	debtor in possession
ECOA	Equal Credit Opportunity Act
EEOC	Equal Employment Opportunity Commission
EFS	effective financing statement
EFT	electronic fund transfer
EFTA	Electronic Fund Transfer Act
EIS	environmental impact statement
EPA	Environmental Protection Agency
ERISA	Employee Retirement Income Security Act
EU	European Union
F.	*Federal Reporter*
F.2d	*Federal Reporter, Second Series*
F.3d	*Federal Reporter, Third Series*
F.A.S.	free alongside (ship)
FASB	Financial Accounting Standards Board
FCC	Federal Communications Commission
FCPA	Foreign Corrupt Practices Act
FDA	Food and Drug Administration
Fed	Federal Reserve Board of Governors
F.O.B.	free on board
F.Supp.	*Federal Supplement*
FTC	Federal Trade Commission
GAAP	generally accepted accounting principles
GAAS	generally accepted auditing standards
GATT	General Agreement on Tariffs and Trade
GmbH	*Gesellschaft mit beschränkter Haftung*
HDC	holder in due course
LBO	leveraged buyout
L.Ed.	*Lawyers' Edition of the Supreme Court Reports*
LLC	limited liability company
LLP	limited liability partnership
Ltd.	Limited
MBCA	Model Business Corporation Act
N.A.	National Association
NAFTA	North American Free Trade Agreement
NASD	National Association of Securities Dealers
NCC	National Conference of Commissioners (on Uniform State Laws)
N.E.	*North Eastern Reporter*
N.E.2d	*North Eastern Reporter, Second Series*
NEPA	National Environmental Policy Act
NLRA	National Labor Relations Act
NLRB	National Labor Relations Board
NRC	Nuclear Regulatory Commission
N.T. & S.A.	National Trust & Savings Association
N.W.	*North Western Reporter*
N.W.2d	*North Western Reporter, Second Series*
N.Y.S.	*New York Supplement*
OASDI	Old Age, Survivors, and Disability Insurance
OSHA	Occupational Safety and Health Administration
OTC	over the counter
P.	*Pacific Reporter*
P.2d	*Pacific Reporter, Second Series*
P.A.	Professional Association
P.C.	Professional Corporation
PIN	personal identification number
PRP	potentially responsible party
RICO	Racketeer Influenced and Corrupt Organizations Act
RMBCA	Revised Model Business Corporation Act
RULPA	Revised Uniform Limited Partnership Act
RUPA	Revised Uniform Partnership Act
S.A.	Savings Association; *Société Anonyme* (French corporation); *Sociedad Anónima* (Latin American corporation)
S.C.	Service Corporation
S.Ct.	*Supreme Court Reporter*
S.E.2d	*South Eastern Reporter, Second Series*
SEC	Securities and Exchange Commission
S.W.2d	*South Western Reporter, Second Series*
So.	*Southern Reporter*
So.2d	*Southern Reporter, Second Series*
TILA	Truth-in-Lending Act
UCC	Uniform Commercial Code
UCCC	Uniform Consumer Credit Code
ULPA	Uniform Limited Partnership Act
UPA	Uniform Partnership Act
UPAA	Uniform Prenuptial Agreements Act
UPC	Uniform Probate Code
U.S.	*United States Reports*
U.S.C.	*United States Code*
U.S.C.A.	*United States Code Annotated*
WTO	World Trade Organization